W9-ABI-349

The
CHELSEA HOUSE LIBRARY
of LITERARY CRITICISM

The

CHELSEA HOUSE LIBRARY
of LITERARY CRITICISM

The

MAJOR AUTHORS EDITION
of the
NEW MOULTON'S LIBRARY *of* LITERARY CRITICISM

Volume 5

Victorian

General Editor

HAROLD BLOOM

1988
CHELSEA HOUSE PUBLISHERS
NEW YORK
NEW HAVEN   PHILADELPHIA

EDITOR
S. T. Joshi

ASSOCIATE EDITOR
Jack Bishop

EDITORIAL COORDINATOR
Karyn Gullen Browne

COPY CHIEF
Richard Fumosa

EDITORIAL STAFF
Marie Claire Cebrian
Jacques L. Denis
Stephen L. Mudd

PICTURE RESEARCH
Justine Blau

DESIGN
Susan Lusk

Printed and bound in the United States of America.

3 5 7 9 8 6 4 2

Library of Congress Cataloging in Publication Data

The Major authors edition of the New Moulton's library of literary criticism.
   (The Chelsea House library of literary criticism)
   Bibliography: v. 1, pp. 665–667.
   Contents: v. 1. Medieval—Late Renaissance—[etc.]—v. 5. Victorian.
   1. English literature—History and criticism—Collected works. 2. American literature—History and criticism—Collected works. I. Bloom, Harold. II. Title: New Moulton's library of literary criticism. III. Series.
PR85.M33 1985   820′.9   84-27426
ISBN 0-87754-815-3 (v. 1)
       0-87754-819-6 (v. 5)

CONTENTS

William Makepeace Thackeray. 2545
Nathaniel Hawthorne 2577
Charles Dickens. 2613
George Eliot (Mary Ann Evans) 2649
Thomas Carlyle. 2683
Ralph Waldo Emerson 2723
Henry Wadsworth Longfellow 2771
Anthony Trollope. 2805
Emily Dickinson 2837
Matthew Arnold. 2855
Robert Browning 2893
Herman Melville 2935
Alfred, Lord Tennyson 2961
Walt Whitman. 3009
Walter Pater 3049
Robert Louis Stevenson. 3075
John Ruskin 3105
Oscar Wilde 3137
Stephen Crane. 3169

Additional Reading. 3191

The Index to this series, *The Major Authors Edition*, appears in Volume 6.

WILLIAM MAKEPEACE THACKERAY

WILLIAM MAKEPEACE THACKERAY

1811–1863

William Makepeace Thackeray was born on July 18, 1811, in Calcutta, where his father worked as a collector for the East India Company. In 1817, after his father's death, he was sent to school in England, where his mother and her new husband joined him in 1819. Thackeray attended the Charterhouse School, where he was not happy, and in 1829 entered Trinity College, Cambridge, where he formed a close friendship with Edward FitzGerald. In 1830 he left Cambridge without a degree and traveled in Germany, where he met the aging Goethe. After returning to London in 1831, Thackeray briefly studied law at the Middle Temple, and in 1834 purchased the *National Standard*, a weekly paper which ceased publication a year later. Thackeray next became an art student, first in London, then in Paris (1834–35). By this time he had lost almost his entire inheritance, probably because of the collapse of the Indian agency-houses, and between 1834 and 1837, while living in Paris, he supported himself by working as a journalist.

In 1836 Thackeray published *Flore et Zephyr*, his first book. In that same year he married Isabella Shawe, who gave birth to a daughter, Anne, after they had returned to London in 1837. Once in London Thackeray began to write for *Fraser's Magazine* and other journals, including the *Morning Chronicle*, the *New Monthly Magazine*, and the *Times*. To *Fraser's* he contributed *The Yellowplush Correspondence* (1837–38), with which he first gained a large readership; *Catherine* (1839–40); *A Shabby Genteel Story* (1840); *The Great Hoggarty Diamond* (1841); and *The Luck of Barry Lyndon* (1844). His first full-length volume, *The Paris Sketch Book*, appeared in 1840.

In 1840, after having given birth to a second and third daughter, Thackeray's wife suffered a mental breakdown and became permanently insane. Thackeray first placed her in the care of a French doctor, then in a private home in England, and sent his children to his mother's home in Paris, where they remained until 1846. In 1842 Thackeray began contributing to *Punch*, which published not only his essays and humorous sketches, but also his caricatures. *The Irish Sketch Book* (1843), with a preface signed for the first time with Thackeray's name, rather than with one of several humorous pseudonyms he had previously used, was followed by *The Snobs of England* (later republished as *The Book of Snobs*), which had appeared in *Punch* in 1846–47.

Thackeray's first important novel, *Vanity Fair*, appeared in monthly installments in 1847–48, with illustrations by the author. It was followed by *Punch's Prize Novelists* (1847), a collection of parodies of leading contemporary authors, and by several other important novels: *The History of Pendennis* (1848–50), *The History of Henry Esmond* (1852), and *The Newcomes* (1853–55). In 1852–53, and again in 1855–56, Thackeray went on lecture tours of the United States, where his novel *The Virginians* (1857–59) is partly set. His lectures on the *English Humourists of the Eighteenth Century*, first delivered in 1851, were published in 1853, while those on the *Four Georges*, first delivered in 1854–55, appeared in print in 1861.

In 1859 Thackeray became the first editor of the *Cornhill Magazine*, for which he wrote *Lovel the Widower* (1860), a story; the *Roundabout Papers* (1860–63), a series of essays; *The Adventures of Philip* (1861–62), his last complete novel; and *Denis Duval* (1864), an unfinished novel published after his sudden death on Christmas Eve of 1863. Thackeray's daughter, Anne Thackeray Ritchie, published *Chapters from Some Memoirs* in 1894. Thackeray's *Letters and Private Papers*, edited by Gordon Ray, were published in 1945–46.

Personal

Thackeray has very rarely come athwart me since his return: he is a big fellow, soul and body; of many gifts and qualities (particularly in the Hogarth line, with a dash of Sterne superadded), of enormous *appetite* withal, and very uncertain and chaotic in all points except his *outer breeding*, which is fixed enough, and *perfect* according to the modern English style. I rather dread explosions in his history. A *big*, fierce, weeping, hungry man; not a strong one. Ay de mi! —THOMAS CARLYLE, Letter to Ralph Waldo Emerson (Sept. 9, 1853)

I breakfasted this morning with Fowler of Lincoln to meet Thackeray (the author) who delivered his lecture on George III in Oxford last night. I was much pleased with what I saw of him—his manner is simple and unaffected: he shows no anxiety to shine in conversation though full of fun and anecdote when drawn out. He seemed delighted with the reception he had met with last night: the undergraduates seem to have behaved with most unusual moderation.—LEWIS CARROLL, *Diary*, May 9, 1857

My conviction was, that beneath an occasional affectation of cynicism, there was a tenderness of heart which he was more eager to repress than to exhibit; that he was no idolater of rank in the sense in which Moore was said dearly to love a lord, but had his best pleasures in the society of those of his own social position—men of letters and artists; and that, however fond of "the full flow of London talk," his own home was the centre of his affections. He was a sensitive man, as I have seen on more than one occasion.—CHARLES KNIGHT, *Passages of a Working Life*, 1863, Pt. 3, Ch. 2

I saw him first, nearly twenty-eight years ago, when he proposed to become the illustrator of my earliest book. I saw him last, shortly before Christmas, at the Athenæum Club, when he told me that he had been in bed three days—that, after these attacks, he was troubled with cold shiverings, "which quite took the power of work out of him"—and that he had it in his mind to try a new remedy which he laughingly described. He was very cheerful, and looked very bright. In the night of that day week, he died.

The long interval between those two periods is marked in my remembrance of him by many occasions when he was supremely humourous, when he was irresistibly extravagant, when he was softened and serious, when he was charming with children. But, by none do I recall him more tenderly than by two or three that start out of the crowd, when he unexpectedly presented himself in my room, announcing how that some passage in a certain book had made him cry yesterday, and how that he had come to dinner, "because he couldn't help it," and must talk such passage over. No one can ever have seen him more genial, natural, cordial, fresh, and honestly impulsive, than I have seen him at those times. No one can be surer than I, of the greatness and the goodness of the heart that then disclosed itself.—CHARLES DICKENS, "In Memoriam," *Cornhill Magazine*, Feb. 1864, p. 129

General

There is a man in our own days whose words are not framed to tickle delicate ears: who, to my thinking, comes before the great ones of society, much as the son of Imlah came before the throned Kings of Judah and Israel; and who speaks truth as deep, with a power as prophet-like and as vital—a mien as dauntless and as daring. Is the satirist of *Vanity Fair* admired in high places? I cannot tell; but I think if some of those amongst whom he hurls the Greek fire of his sarcasm, and over whom he flashes the levin-brand of his denunciation, were to take his warnings in time—they or their seed might yet escape a fatal Ramoth-Gilead.

Why have I alluded to this man? I have alluded to him, Reader, because I think I see in him an intellect profounder and more unique than his contemporaries have yet recognized; because I regard him as the first social regenerator of the day— as the very master of that working corps who would restore to rectitude the warped system of things; because I think no commentator on his writings has yet found the comparison that suits him, the terms which rightly characterise his talent. They say he is like Fielding: they talk of his wit, humour, comic powers. He resembles Fielding as an eagle does a vulture: Fielding could stoop on carrion, but Thackeray never does. His wit is bright, his humour attractive, but both bear the same relation to his serious genius, that the mere lambent sheet-lightning playing under the edge of the summer-cloud, does to the electric death-spark hid in its womb. Finally; I have alluded to Mr. Thackeray, because to him—if he will accept the tribute of a total stranger—I have dedicated this second edition of *Jane Eyre*.—CHARLOTTE BRONTË, "Preface" to *Jane Eyre*, 1847

In Dickens, the lower part of "the World" is brought into the Police Court, as it were, and there, after cross-examination, discharged or committed, as the case may be. The characters are real and low, but they are facts. That is one way. Thackeray's is another and better. One of his books is like a Dionysius ear, through which you hear the World talking, entirely unconscious of being overheard.—JAMES RUSSELL LOWELL, Letter to C. F. Briggs (Feb. 15, 1854)

Thackeray finds that God has made no allowance for the poor thing in his universe;—more's the pity, he thinks;—but 'tis not for us to be wiser: we must renounce ideals, and accept

London.—RALPH WALDO EMERSON, "Literature," *English Traits*, 1856

Mr. Thackeray is, as a novelist, so pointed and unmistakable a contrast to Mr. Dickens, that it is interesting to find them writing at the same time. Thackeray is as little of an idealizer as it seems possible to be, if you write novels at all. He cuts into conventionalism so daringly, that you fear sometimes, as when he gives you a novel without a hero, that he goes too far, and puts in peril the essence of his Art. If he does idealize, it is not in the manner of Dickens, but in one strikingly different. He selects characters as Dickens selects characteristics. But he depends for success not on the power of his personages to evoke sympathy, negative or positive, but on their strict correspondence with fact. It cannot, perhaps, be said that he, any more than Mr. Dickens, reaches the Shakspearian substratum of character. His eye is that of an artist. It has been trained to take in the whole aspect of the outer man, not only in the minutiæ of his dress, but in the whole monotonous circumstance of his every day life. His popularity is the most powerful evidence to which one could easily point, of the capacity residing in the exhibition of bare, or even repulsive fact, to interest mankind. It is said that Thackeray abandoned the career of an artist, because, according to his own avowal, he could only caricature. He felt the absence of the higher idealizing power. His novels exhibit the radical qualities which would have distinguished his pictures. It is not emotionally that we regard them. They call forth no glow of admiration, no warm, loving sympathy, no wonder, no reverence. He makes his appeal to sterner, colder powers, to reflection, to the cynic's philosophy, to contempt. It may be better, higher, more noble and self-denying, in him, to do so; but the fact is patent. And its inevitable consequence has been and will be, a popularity not so wide, a command over the heart not so great, as those of men who permit fancy to lay on color, and imagination to heighten life. ⟨. . .⟩

If it were asked what one aspect of life Mr. Thackeray has distinctively exhibited, the answer could be given in one word,—the trivial aspect. The characters he draws are neither the best of men nor the worst. But the atmosphere of triviality which envelopes them all was never before so plainly perceivable. He paints the world as a great Vanity Fair, and none has done that so well.

The realism of Thackeray can hardly fail to have a good effect in fictitious literature. It represents the extreme point of reaction against the false idealism of the Minerva Press. It is a pre-raphaelite school of novel writing. And as pre-raphaelitism is not to be valued in itself, so much as in being the passage to a new and nobler ideal, the stern realism of Thackeray may lead the way to something better than itself.—PETER BAYNE, "The Modern Novel: Dickens—Bulwer—Thackeray," *Essays in Biography and Criticism*, 1857, pp. 389–92

It is Thackeray's aim to represent life as it is actually and historically—men and women, as they are, in those situations in which they are usually placed, with that mixture of good and evil and of strength and foible which is to be found in their characters, and liable only to those incidents which are of ordinary occurrence. He will have no faultless characters, no demigods—nothing but men and brethren. And from this it results that, when once he has conceived a character, he works downwards and inwards in its treatment of it, making it firm and clear at all points in its relations to hard fact, and cutting down, where necessary, to the very foundations. ⟨. . .⟩ Mr. Thackeray, I believe, is as perfect a master in his kind of art as is to be found in the whole series of British prose writers; a man in whom strength of understanding, acquired knowledge of men, subtlety of perception, deep philosophic humour, and exquisiteness of literary taste, are combined in a degree and after a manner not seen in any known precedent.—DAVID MASSON, *British Novelists and Their Styles*, 1859, pp. 248–49

Thackeray's range is limited. His genius is not opulent, but it is profuse. He does not create many types, but he endlessly illustrates what he does create. In this he reminds a traveler of Ruysdael and Wouvermann, the old painters. There are plenty of their pictures in the German galleries, and there is no mistaking them. This is a Ruysdael, how rich and tranquil! this is a Wouvermann, how open and smiling! are the instinctive words with which you greet them. The scope, the method, almost the figures and the composition are the same in each Ruysdael, in each Wouvermann, but you are not troubled. Ruysdael's heavy tree, Wouvermann's white horse, are not less agreeable in Dresden than in Berlin, or Munich, or Vienna. And shall we not be as tolerant in literature as in painting? Why should we expect simple pastoral nature in Victor Hugo, or electrical bursts of passion in Scott, or the "ideal" in Thackeray?—GEORGE WILLIAM CURTIS, "The Easy Chair," *Harper's New Monthly Magazine*, Aug. 1862, p. 423

Thackeray, like Sterne, looked at every thing—at nature, at life, at art—from a *sensitive* aspect. His mind was, to some considerable extent, like a woman's mind. It could comprehend abstractions when they were unrolled and explained before it but it never naturally created them; never of itself, and without external obligation, devoted itself to them. The visible scene of life—the streets, the servants, the clubs, the gossip, the West End—fastened on his brain. These were to him reality. They burnt in upon his brain; they pained his nerves; their influence reached him through many avenues which ordinary men do not feel much, or to which they are altogether impervious. He had distinct and rather painful sensations where most men have but confused and blurred ones. Most men have felt the *instructive* headache, during which they are more acutely conscious than usual of all which goes on around them,—during which every thing seems to pain them, and in which they understand it because it pains them, and they cannot get their imagination away from it. Thackeray had a nerve-ache of this sort always. He acutely felt every possible passing fact, every trivial interlude in society. Hazlitt used to say of himself, and used to say truly, that he could not enjoy the society in a drawing-room for thinking of the opinion which the footman formed of his odd appearance as he went upstairs. Thackeray had too healthy and stable a nature to be thrown so wholly off his balance; but the footman's view of life was never out of his head. The obvious facts which suggest it to the footman poured it in upon him; he could not exempt himself from them. As most men say that the earth *may* go round the sun, but in fact, when we look at the sun, we cannot help believing it goes round the earth,—just so this most impressible, susceptible genius could not help half accepting, half believing the common ordinary sensitive view of life, although he perfectly knew in his inner mind and deeper nature that this apparent and superficial view of life was misleading, inadequate, and deceptive. He could not help seeing everything, and what he saw made so near and keen an impression upon him that he could not again exclude it from his understanding; it stayed there, and disturbed his thoughts.

If, he often says, 'people could write about that of which they are really thinking, how interesting books would be!' More than most writers of fiction, he felt the difficulty of abstracting his thoughts and imagination from near facts which *would*

make themselves felt. The sick wife in the next room, the unpaid baker's bill, the lodging-house keeper who doubts your solvency; these, and such as these,—the usual accompaniments of an early literary life,—are constantly alluded to in his writings. Perhaps he could never take a grand enough view of literature, or accept the truth of 'high art,' because of his natural tendency to this stern and humble realism. He knew that he was writing a tale which would appear in a green magazine (with others) on the 1st of March, and would be paid for perhaps on the 11th, by which time, probably, 'Mr. Smith' would have to 'make up a sum,' and would again present his *little account*. There are many minds besides his who feel an interest in these realities, though they yawn over 'high art' and elaborate judgments.

A painfulness certainly clings like an atmosphere round Mr. Thackeray's writings, in consequence of his inseparable and ever-present realism. We hardly know where it is, yet we are all conscious of it less or more. A free and bold writer, Sir Walter Scott, throws himself far away into fictitious worlds, and soars there without effort, without pain, and with unceasing enjoyment. You see, as it were, between the lines of Mr. Thackeray's writing, that his thoughts were never long away from the close proximate scene. His writings might be better if it had been otherwise; but they would have been less peculiar, less individual; they would have wanted their character, their flavour, if he had been able, while writing them, to forget for many moments the ever-attending, the ever-painful sense of himself.

Hence have arisen most of the censures upon him, both as he seemed to be in society and as he was in his writings. He was certainly uneasy in the common and general world, and it was natural that he should be so. The world poured in upon him, and *inflicted* upon his delicate sensibility a number of petty pains and impressions which others do not feel at all, or which they feel but very indistinctly. As he sat he seemed to read off the passing thoughts—the base, common, ordinary impressions—of every one else. Could such a man be at ease? Could even a quick intellect be asked to set in order with such velocity so many data? Could any temper, however excellent, be asked to bear the contemporaneous influx of innumerable minute annoyances? Men of ordinary nerves, who feel a little of the pains of society, who perceive what really passes, who are not absorbed in the petty pleasures of sociability, could well observe how keen was Thackeray's *sensation* of common events, could easily understand how difficult it must have been for him to keep mind and temper undisturbed by a miscellaneous tide at once so incessant and so forcible.

He could not emancipate himself from such impressions even in a case where most men hardly feel them. Many people have—it is not difficult to have—some vague sensitive perception of what is passing in the minds of the guests, of the ideas of such as sit at meat; but who remembers that there are also nervous apprehensions, also a latent mental life among those who 'stand and wait'—among the floating figures which pass and carve? But there was no impression to which Mr. Thackeray was more constantly alive, or which he was more apt in his writings to express.—WALTER BAGEHOT, "Sterne and Thackeray" (1864), *Collected Works*, ed. Norman St. John-Stevas, 1965, Vol. 2, pp. 304–6

Let me see—have we exchanged a word about Thackeray since his Death? I am quite surprised to see how I sit moping about him: to be sure, I keep reading his Books. Oh, the *Newcomes* are fine! And now I have got hold of *Pendennis*, and seem to like that much more than when I first read it. I keep hearing him say so much of it; and really think I shall hear his Step up the Stairs to this Lodging as in old Charlotte St. thirty years ago. Really, a great Figure has sunk under Earth.—EDWARD FITZGERALD, Letter to George Crabbe (Jan. 12, 1864)

Now, the great merit of Thackeray I take to be, that he *has* reflected—with lucid beauty, with admirable sense, and taste, and impartiality—the whole range of the characteristic English society of his age. He is not a fashionable novelist, though he introduces persons of fashion; nor a military or clerical novelist, though he introduces soldiers and clergymen. His roll of books, like the Bayeux tapestry, gives us the whole generation—men of wit, business, war, art; women beautiful and plain, loving and hateful, clever and stupid. There are types and occupations, no doubt, which he has not meddled with. But such abundant material exists in his books to show what kind of man is an English gentleman of the nineteenth century, that his omissions are of little importance. By the reality with which he painted, he has taught us to divine for ourselves what he did not paint.

Let it be remarked, too, that this admirable fidelity to nature, enlivened with a humour never grotesque, and tinged with a sentiment never maudlin, is wholly Thackeray's own. Many have imitated him, but he imitated nobody. None of the thousand moods or fashions of our modes of our schools of thinking are repeated in his books—even in the earliest of them. He deals neither in Wertherism, Byronism, nor Carlyleism; the French "literature of despair" rolled harmlessly as passing thunder over his head. He worshipped no side of life or thought exclusively; *Ivanhoe* did not fascinate him with chivalry, nor *Wilhelm Meister* with art; nor did the modern realism of fiction destroy his sympathy with romance. His strong intellect kept its independence from the beginning; his strong moral nature did justice from the beginning. Faithfully, and regardless of all sentimental whimpering, he laid bare the selfishness, meanness, and servility of the age. But with equal truth, he brought on the stage noble and kindly characters like Colonel Newcome, Ethel Newcome, and Henry Esmond. Severe upon society as society, he had the strongest faith in human nature; and his own great heart beat responsive to all that was generous in history, or fiction, or the world of his time.

The independence and originality of Thackeray's character as a writer makes it difficult to indicate the sources of the culture by which his genius was formed. The writers of his own age who got the start of him in popularity taught him nothing; but in his youth the genius of Sir Walter Scott towered over Europe, and it is certain that he was deeply influenced by Sir Walter. They had a good deal in common, especially a sound worldly shrewdness tempered by kindness of a homely character, and by humour of that robust sort which finds food for itself in the daily incidents of life. They both had a strong respect for society even while laughing at its prejudices, and never allowed the literature to which their lives were devoted to usurp superiority over other interest. The resemblance between them, however, was rather moral than intellectual. Sir Walter had a general influence over Thackeray, no doubt, as himself the real father of the truthful and natural novel of the nineteenth century; but he had no special influence, and the character of his genius was very different. Thackeray was without Scott's feudal sympathies, and had far less romance and historical feeling; neither was his imagination so various as that of Scott—which created such diverse characters as Rebecca and Jeannie Deans—nor his vein of poetry so rich. In one point the late writer had an advantage—he wrote a better

style. The prose of Scott is cumbrous, and apt to be verbose; whereas Thackeray's English is one of his greatest merits. It is pure, clear, simple in its power, and harmonious; clean, sinewy, fine and yet strong, like the legs of a racehorse. Style is a gift born with a man, but its character is greatly modified by his education and experience. One sees very distinctly in Thackeray's style, as in his way of thinking and feeling about things, the English public-school and university man—the tone of one born and bred in the condition of a gentleman. The facts of his birth and education coloured his thought and his style, just as Scott's was coloured, even more decidedly, by the family traditions of his ancient border-race. He was never zealous for the classics; but the classics form a man who has been nourished on them, whether he is conscious of it or not. We none of us remember taking in our mother's milk, but we know what it has done for us for all that. Thackeray was saturated with Horace, especially the lyrical part of the Venusian; he was also very fond of Montaigne, and intimate with him. In fact, Latin writers, French writers, and the English writers of the eighteenth century, seem to have constituted his favourite reading. Yet he was always more a man of the world than a man of books; and if we allow much influence over the formation of his style to the sources just indicated, we may also see in it a certain conversational ease and grace, which is not a result only of reading, and which is the direct opposite of the detestable style, formed upon newspapers, of so many inferior men. To hit the right mean between a bookishness which is too stiff and a colloquialism which is too loose, is one of the rarest achievements in literature, and one that more than any other secures to an author the position of a classic. No English novelist approached this standard in Thackeray's time so nearly as he, and perhaps no previous novelist except the incomparable Fielding.—JAMES HANNAY, *Studies on Thackeray*, 1864, pp. 8–14

When the great master of English prose left us suddenly in the maturity of his powers, with his enduring position in literature fairly won and recognized, his death saddened us rather through the sense of our own loss than from the tragic regret which is associated with an unaccomplished destiny. More fortunate than Fielding, he was allowed to take the measure of his permanent fame. The niche wherein he shall henceforth stand was chiselled while he lived. One by one the doubters confessed their reluctant faith, unfriendly critics dropped their blunted steel, and no man dared to deny him the place which was his, and his only, by right of genius.

In one sense, however, he was misunderstood by the world, and he has died before that profounder recognition which he craved had time to mature. All the breadth and certainty of his fame failed to compensate him for the lack of this; the man's heart coveted that justice which was accorded only to the author's brain.—BAYARD TAYLOR, "William Makepeace Thackeray" (1864), *Critical Essays and Literary Notes*, 1880, p. 134

Thackeray was a *master* in every sense, having as it were, in himself, a double quantity of being. Robust humor and lofty sentiment alternated so strangely in him, that sometimes he seemed like the natural son of Rabelais, and at others he rose up a very twin brother of the Stratford Seer. There was nothing in him amorphous and unconsidered. Whatever he chose to do was always perfectly done. There was a genuine Thackeray flavor in everything he was willing to say or to write. He detected with unfailing skill the good or the vile wherever it existed. He had an unerring eye, a firm understanding, and abounding truth.—JAMES T. FIELDS, "Thackeray," *Yesterdays with Authors*, 1871, p. 35

Of course I took the greatest delight in Thackeray's lectures, though not always disposed to assent to his critical judgment of the English humorists, but, with the entranced audience, yielded myself to the charm of his unaffected and spirited manner of delivery, to his close analysis of character, to his humane and generous sentiments, to his pathetic turns of thought, and, with profound relish, to his clear, sweet, and simple English, in the use of which I can scarcely think he has had his equal. It was all so different in style and matter, to my taste, from the writings of another noted novelist of the day, whose popular readings of his own stories I attended once or twice, with little comparative interest. Indeed, I feel about Dickens's novels pretty much as the exiled French king did about the merry exhibition, in the anecdote already related—that they are all very well for once, with no little power of momentarily affecting our sympathies, though with some mental reservation, but feeling no more desire to see them again than I should wish to renew my fictitious tears, when taken unawares, over the exaggerated pictures of *Uncle Tom's Cabin*. On the other hand, I experience an ever new delight in reading again and again whatever Thackeray has written. Nor do I believe that Thackeray himself regarded Dickens as in any sense a rival, though he would naturally refrain from giving expression to any dissent from the overwhelming popular estimate of his contemporary's writings. But time has already settled, in part at least, the question between the novels of these famous authors. It may be doubted whether any grave English judge would now think of taking a story of Dickens to the bench with him for perusal in the intermission of business; while Thackeray's are books to recur to in the study and in moments of languor when nothing else seems fitted to furnish the longed-for entertainment. He has sometimes been severely commented upon by very loyal English critics for his ridicule and unsparing denunciation in his lectures upon the *Four Georges*. But see how later history takes his part.—GEORGE LAMB, "Recollections of Thackeray," *Harper's New Monthly Magazine*, Jan. 1877, pp. 259–60

About Mr. Thackeray I had no clear notion in any way, except that he seemed cynical; and my first real interest in him arose from reading M. A. Titmarsh in Ireland, during my Tynemouth illness. I confess to being unable to read *Vanity Fair*, from the moral disgust it occasions; and this was my immediate association with the writer's name when I next met him, during the visit to London in 1851. I could not follow his lead into the subject of the Bullers, (then all dead) so strong was my doubt of his real feeling. I was, I fear, rather rough and hard when we talked of *Vanity Fair*; but a sudden and most genuine change of tone,—of voice, face and feeling,—that occurred on my alluding to Dobbin's admirable turning of the tables on Amelia, won my trust and regard more than any thing he had said yet. *Pendennis* much increased my respect and admiration; and *Esmond* appears to me *the* book of the century, in its department. I have read it three times; and each time with new wonder at its rich ripe wisdom, and at the singular charm of Esmond's own character. The power that astonishes me the most in Thackeray is his fertility, shown in the way in which he opens glimpses into a multitudinous world as he proceeds. The chief moral charm is in the paternal vigilance and sympathy which constitute the spirit of his narration. The first drawback in his books, as in his manners, is the impression conveyed by both that he never can have known a good and sensible woman. I do not believe he has any idea whatever of such women as abound among the matronage of England,—women of excellent capacity and cultivation applied to the natural business of life. It is perhaps not changing the subject to say next what the other drawback is. Mr. Thackeray has said more, and more effectually, about snobs and snobbism than any other man; and yet his frittered life, and his obedience to the call of the great are the observed of all observers. As it is so, so it must be; but "O! the pity of it! the pity of it!" Great and unusual allowance is to be made in his case, I am aware; but this does not lessen the concern occasioned by the spectacle of one after another of the aristocracy of nature making the ko-tow to the aristocracy of accident. If society does not owe all it would be thankful to owe to Mr. Thackeray, yet it is under deep and large obligations to him; and if he should even yet be seen to be as wise and happy in his life and temper as he might be any day, he may do much that would far transcend all his great and rising achievements thus far; and I who shall not see it would fain persuade myself that I foresee it. He who stands before the world as a sage *de jure* must surely have impulses to be a sage *de facto*.—HARRIET MARTINEAU, *Autobiography*, ed. Maria Weston Chapman, 1877, Vol. 2, pp. 60–61

His knowledge of human nature was supreme, and his characters stand out as human beings, with a force and a truth which has not, I think, been within the reach of any other English novelist in any period. I know no character in fiction, unless it be Don Quixote, with whom the reader becomes so intimately acquainted as with Colonel Newcombe. How great a thing it is to be a gentleman at all parts! How we admire the man of whom so much may be said with truth! Is there any one of whom we feel more sure in this respect than of Colonel Newcombe? It is not because Colonel Newcombe is a perfect gentleman that we think Thackeray's work to have been so excellent, but because he has had the power to describe him as such, and to force us to love him, a weak and silly old man, on account of this grace of character.

It is evident from all Thackeray's best work that he lived with the characters he was creating. He had always a story to tell until quite late in life; and he shows us that this was so, not by the interest which he had in his own plots,—for I doubt whether his plots did occupy much of his mind,—but by convincing us that his characters were alive to himself. With Becky Sharpe, with Lady Castlewood and her daughter, and with Esmond, with Warrington, Pendennis, and the Major, with Colonel Newcombe, and with Barry Lyndon, he must have lived in perpetual intercourse. Therefore he has made these personages real to us.

Among all our novelists his style is the purest, as to my ear it is also the most harmonious. Sometimes it is disfigured by a slight touch of affectation, by little conceits which smell of the oil;—but the language is always lucid. The reader, without labour, knows what he means, and knows all that he means. As well as I can remember, he deals with no episodes. I think that any critic, examining his work minutely, would find that every scene, and every part of every scene, adds something to the clearness with which the story is told. Among all his stories there is not one which does not leave on the mind a feeling of distress that women should ever be immodest or men dishonest,—and of joy that women should be so devoted and men so honest. How we hate the idle selfishness of Pendennis, the worldliness of Beatrix, the craft of Becky Sharpe!—how we love the honesty of Colonel Newcombe, the nobility of Esmond, and the devoted affection of Mrs. Pendennis! The hatred of evil and love of good can hardly have come upon so many readers without doing much good.

Late in Thackeray's life,—he never was an old man, but towards the end of his career,—he failed in his power of charming, because he allowed his mind to become idle. In the plots which he conceived, and in the language which he used, I do not know that there is any perceptible change; but in *The Virginians* and in *Philip* the reader is introduced to no character with which he makes a close and undying acquaintance. And this, I have no doubt, is so because Thackeray himself had no such intimacy. His mind had come to be weary of that fictitious life which is always demanding the labour of new creation, and he troubled himself with his two Virginians and his Philip only when he was seated at his desk.—ANTHONY TROLLOPE, *An Autobiography*, 1883, Ch. 13

Thackeray had a quarrel with himself and a quarrel with society; but his was not a temper to push things to extremes. He could not acquiesce in the ways of the world, its shabbiness, its shams, its snobbery, its knavery; he could not acquiesce, and yet it is only for born prophets to break with the world and go forth into the wilderness crying, "Repent!" Why affect to be a prophet, and wear camels' hair and eat locusts and wild honey, adding one more sham to the many, when after all the club is a pleasant lounge, and anthropology is a most attractive study? Better patch up a truce with the world, which will not let one be a hero, but is not wholly evil; the great criminals are few; men in general are rather weak than wicked; vain and selfish, but not malignant. It is infinitely diverting to watch the ways of the petty human animal. One can always preserve a certain independence by that unheroic form of warfare suitable to an unheroic age—satire; one can even in a certain sense stand above one's own pettiness by virtue of irony; and there is always the chance of discovering some angel wandering unrecognised among the snobs and the flunkeys in the form of a brave, simple-hearted man or pure-souled, tender woman. Whether right or wrong, this compromise with the world is only for a few days. Heigh-ho! everything hastens to the common end—*vanitas vanitatum.* ⟨. . .⟩

Thackeray had not the austerity and lonely strength needful for a prophet; he would not be a pseudo-prophet; therefore he chose his part—to remain in the world, to tolerate the worldlings, and yet to be their adversary and circumventer, or at least a thorn in their sides.—EDWARD DOWDEN, "Victorian Literature," *Transcripts and Studies*, 1888, pp. 168–71

Personally, he scarce appeals to us as the ideal gentleman; if there were nothing else, perpetual nosing after snobbery at least suggests the snob; but about the men he made, there can be no such question of reserve. And whether because he was himself a gentleman in a very high degree, or because his methods were in a very high degree suited to this class of work, or from the common operation of both causes, a gentleman came from his pen by the gift of nature. He could draw him as a character part, full of pettiness, tainted with vulgarity, and yet still a gentleman, in the inimitable Major Pendennis. He could draw him as the full-blown hero in Colonel Esmond. He could draw him—the next thing to the work of God—human and true and noble and frail, in Colonel Newcome. If the art of being a gentleman were forgotten, like the art of staining glass, it might be learned anew from that one character.—ROBERT LOUIS STEVENSON, "Some Gentlemen in Fiction," 1888

It is precisely because Thackeray, discerning so well the abundant misery and hollowness in life, discerns also all that is not miserable and hollow, that he is so great. He has neither the somewhat bestial pessimism of M. Zola, nor the fatuous gaiety of M. Ohnet. Like any classic, he stands the test of experience, of psychology. We have mentioned together Swift, Addison, and Steele; we might take Lucretius, Virgil, and Horace. Each has left a picture of patrician life, glittering and tedious. Lucretius, contrasting the splendour without and the gloom within; Virgil, the restlessness and haste with the placid peace of the country; Horace, content to let it all go by, neither envying nor despising. Something of each, again, is in Thackeray: an English classic not less true and real than the classic Romans.

Most of the disputes about Thackeray's art, in the strict sense of art, are occupied with the personal note in his novels: with the intrusion, as some call it, of his personality. Art, we are told, is impersonal; and we believe it. But if that imply that no novel should reflect its author's spirit, then no artistic novel has yet been written. It is a question of words: each writer has his manner of work and habit of mind; let him follow those faithfully, and the result will be good, if he be an artist. Who wishes away Fielding's enchanting chapters between the books of *Tom Jones*? Or who wishes to find essays by Flaubert between the chapters of *Madame Bovary*? Each follows his own way, and there are many ways in art. Thackeray's reflections and discussions do not spoil his story, because they are not mere moralising, which the reader might do for himself. Whenever a reader stops, and says to himself, that the writer might have credited his readers with wits enough to see such and such a thing, without being shown it, then the writer has been superfluous. A sentence instead of a word, a chapter instead of a page, are unpardonable sins: but who can say, that he could have done Thackeray's reflections for himself? And they do not occur in the course of actual narration: Rawdon Crawley confronts Lord Steyne, Lady Castlewood welcomes Esmond at Winchester, without any dissertation from Thackeray. At least, let us call these passages of personal meditation a wrong thing done exquisitely; beyond that we refuse to go.—LIONEL JOHNSON, *Academy*, March 7, 1891, p. 227

Another great name here somewhat wofully misrepresented is that of Thackeray; whose "White Squall" is now and then rather too provocative of such emotions as nature's might provoke in the digestive economy of a bad sailor. To make the gorge rise at it is hardly the sign or the property of elegance in verse: and if indecency, which means nothing more than unseemliness, is very properly considered as a reason for excluding from elegant society the most brilliant examples of the most illustrious writers ever touched by so much as a passing shade of it, the rule should be applied equally to every variety of the repulsive and the unbecoming—not by any means only to matters of sexual indecorum and erotic indelicacy. To none of the other selections from the lighter work of the same illustrious hand is any such objection or suggestion applicable: but not one of them shows Thackeray at his very best as a comic poet.—ALGERNON CHARLES SWINBURNE, "Social Verse" (1891), *Studies in Prose and Poetry*, 1894, pp. 106–7

It is true that Thackeray did not entirely escape the fate which seems to fall on every satirist of being carried too far in his onslaught upon hypocrisy and attacking some things which are in no way deserving of censure. His detestation of humbug was so intense that he seems to forget that there is some of it which we could scarcely do without. Indeed, were all descriptions of humbug to be swept off the face of the earth at once, the very best Christians would be at each other's throats in half an hour. He blamed the writers of the day for being too mealy-mouthed in their descriptions of character. "Since the author of *Tom Jones* was buried, no writer of fiction among us has been permitted to depict to his utmost power a *Man*." We do not know whether Thackeray had temporarily forgotten that it pleased Fielding to put his hero, in an episode of which Colonel Newcome afterwards spoke with just severity, into a position so disgraceful that no subsequent writer to our knowledge had ventured to reproduce it, until M. Octave Mirabeau presented a still more repulsive picture in his extremely powerful and intensely disagreeable novel, *Le Calvaire*. Thackeray himself did not venture to go so far into the life of his man, but only set himself to lop off all possible heroic attributes. Indeed Pendennis, who was to be the real Man without any unnatural decoration, is in reality a very innocent person, with plenty of faults no doubt, but these chiefly of the kind that arise from weakness of character. We are not, indeed, sure that Thackeray's philosophy might not be reduced to a belief that feebleness is the distinguishing characteristic of the male of the human species: but this is by no means a striking view, especially when it is the central figure of a book, ordinarily distinguished as the hero, who is chiefly marked by the peculiar instability which distinguishes him from the stronger figures around him. If Pendennis is the natural man, to what class does George Warrington or Captain Strong belong? or even Major Pendennis, all of whom have at least sufficient strength and individuality to follow out their own objects as seems good in their eyes? Why should we see anything more characteristic of the real man in the wavering figure to which our attention is chiefly directed?

However, Thackeray's desire to represent an unvarnished picture of man as he really is, did not prevent him, as we have already seen, from giving to his next work a central figure which does not fall below the heroic level. Henry Esmond, with all his virtues, is quite as real as Arthur Pendennis. We will not, however, add to what we have already said about this noble figure save as the centre of a very wonderful production. *Esmond* is beyond doubt the first of Thackeray's novels as a work of art. There is something in the exquisite finish and harmony of this book which we can only express by the epithet, artistic; it is a pure combination of perfect taste and perfect workmanship which puts it in a separate class, in which many of the greatest literary works have no claim to rank. The genuine literary artist is not common; Balzac might be cited as a specimen, and George Eliot in her early works: and perhaps, without going quite so high, we might say that we have at present a literary artist of high excellence in Mr. R. L. Stevenson. As a composition *Esmond* is almost without a flaw. The details of the execution are all worked out in the same masterly manner, and the language is perfect. We may take as one instance of the exquisite finish of the minor points the little explanation of Esmond's prejudice against Marlborough. He is, of course, a man with views of his own concerning his contemporaries whom he judges according to the light in which they present themselves to him, and, as it happens, he is the opponent of the great general and a merciless critic of his conduct. This is natural enough, but there is a yet further light of reality communicated by the revelation in the footnote added by Esmond's daughter, which tells us how Marlborough had spoken of him as having "the hang-dog look of his rogue of a father." Esmond, himself, did not know that this was the origin of his prejudice and that these few words which he had possibly forgotten, had an influence on his whole life. It is like some of the stray touches in Shakespeare,—when Stephano wonders how Caliban came to speak his language, or Sir Toby prays that "the spirit of humours intimate reading aloud" to Malvolio,—mere by-strokes of the pencil, which a less perfect workman would have utterly neglected, but which have a wonderful effect in realising the scene in the minds of both author and spectator.—MARGARET OLIPHANT, *The Victorian Age of English Literature*, 1892, Vol. 1, pp. 290–93

Thackeray's readers were and are limited by the limitations of his subjects, by nothing else. He did much that Scott did not attempt and that Dickens could not have conceived; but for every million that can understand Scott and Dickens there are probably only a thousand that can understand Thackeray. His minute observation of the upper classes of his day is lost on persons to whom those classes are not familiar, partly because such persons do not recognize what he is dealing with, and partly because they are not interested in the questions with which he is most preoccupied. Indeed, of all great novelists Thackeray is the narrowest, not because the range of his vision is confined to the upper classes, for these viewed comprehensively form a complete microcosm and in many ways exhibit the problems and possibilities of life better than any other class; but because, accepting the upper classes as the world, he views them from one position only, and his view of them is extremely partial. Only a few of his characters he knows from the inside; all the rest he knows from the outside only. Men who were clients of the world or its victims, who were struggling with it or hostile to it—these men Thackeray knew from the inside. But the world itself, which for him meant the aristocratic class as a body—he was familiar with its aspect, but he never understood its spirit. Major Pendennis and his nephew, Rawdon Crawley, George Osborne, and Colonel Newcome—he knew these as if each of them were himself. Lord Steyne, Lord Bareacres, and Sir Pitt Crawley he knew merely as a vigilant witness. Hence the narrowness of his view as compared to Scott and Dickens. Hence he seems such a dwarf when placed beside them. And his narrowness of view finds another expression of itself in the fewness of his types of character. It has been well said, for instance, that he could draw but two women—the bad and the good, Becky Sharp being the prototype of the one and Amelia Sedley of the other.

All this, however, is mentioned merely to show why Thackeray's appeal to the world must have always been comparatively limited, and limited not only *to* the upper classes, but *among* them. Whether in process of time the number of his readers is diminishing, I repeat I am unable to say. A more important question is whether the interest with which he is read now is as fresh and vital as that with which he was read originally. I should say it was not; and I should say so for this reason, that as compared with Scott and Dickens he lacked the qualities by which the vitality of his work could be perpetuated. He lacked their extraordinary breadth and their extraordinary variety; he lacked the qualities that made them so peculiarly and so comprehensively national. They each gave us a nation—a nation which still lives; Thackeray gave us a fragment of a generation, which already is almost past.—W. H. MALLOCK, "Are Scott, Dickens, and Thackeray Obsolete?," *Forum*, Dec. 1892, pp. 512–13

The charge of cynicism which it was at one time usual to bring against Thackeray has been again and again repelled by those who knew him best, who gladdened in his sunny humour and loved him for his ardent friendship and unobtrusive generosity. That he was the truest of friends, and the brightest and most genial of talkers in a small circle of intimate companions, is incontestable. But, on the other hand, certain of his admirers have misrepresented him almost as thoroughly as have his detractors. They have spoken of him as if he had been some tender sentimentalist with meekness ever in his heart and honey ever on his tongue. He was not only a bitter satirist in his writings; his scorn of humbug, or of what he deemed humbug, repeatedly broke out in fierce or taunting speech and in speech which was not always justified. The letter which he wrote to Mr. Edmund Yates, in the course of the quarrel in which Dickens was involved, would alone prove how roughly, not to say brutally, he could assert himself against anyone who crossed his path. To talk of him as a "gentle censor" is to talk twaddle. His heart was worthy of his intellect; when he loved, he loved with exquisite tenderness; but he regarded the mass of mankind with a half-laughing, half-pitiful sense of their wickedness and weakness, and at times with impatient contempt. That is the prevailing impression left by his novels, despite occasional passages, sometimes beautiful and touching, sometimes verging on the mawkish, in which the words are the words of the optimist.

There are, no doubt, some who have otherwise shown themselves to be sound judges of literature, who regard Thackeray's view of life as somewhat narrow, and his moralising as often cheap and tedious. They hold that his genius was in a measure misapplied to the study of things paltry and sordid; that he was a great master of words, rather than a great imaginative writer; that as a satirist he was repetitive to weariness, and brooded persistently over follies and foibles which it had been wiser to pass by with a smile. They say, with truth, that he lacked the charm of the born storyteller, and too often sank the artist in the preacher. None the less, he remains a master in some ways unexcelled.

It is the veriest truism to repeat that in all the range of fiction there are no men and women more keenly studied, more vividly portrayed, more consistently developed, than Thackeray's greatest creations. Becky Sharp and Major Pendennis and Beatrix Esmond seem wellnigh as secure of immortality as Falstaff and Rosalind. No novelist has treated the story of a youthful, ill-starred love with more delicate insight and touching sympathy than this so-called cynic. And no novelist since Fielding has written such admirable English. Of Thackeray, far more justly than of Macaulay, it might have been said, "Where did he get that style?" There is none more original, as there is none more attractive, in the kingdom of English prose. It has the ease of the happiest talk, and the grace, the finish, the verbal sparkle and glow of perfect literary art. His so-called ballads have the charm that belongs to the wholly or half-playful exercises, the recreations in rhyme, of a supreme literary craftsman. They are not verses of society; they are either too richly humorous, or too sharply satiric, or too deeply coloured by feeling. Through them, as all through his prose, mirth glides by the easiest transitions into sadness, mockery trembles into tenderness, to the strain of boon good-fellowship succeeds the irrepressible reminder that all below is vanity. Carelessly as they seem to have been penned, they abound in happy rhymes and turns of phrase, they show the hand of the writer born to work in metre no less than in prose. "The White Squall" is a really wonderful *tour de force* of vivid, rattling description and novel, dexterous rhyming; there is the true martial note in the rough swinging verses of *The Chronicle of the Drum*; and as for the Irish Ballads, they seem bound to amuse till the drying up of the fountain of laughter. Since Burns wrote the "Ordination," no more telling, mirth-provoking bit of satire has been done in rhyme than the immortal "Battle of Limerick"; and where could there be found a more delicious revel of vocables, all honeyed by the Milesian usage, than in Mr. Moloney's account of the ball that was given to the Nepaulese ambassador? As for the serious pieces, we should think little of the head or heart of the man who ever read the ballad of "Bouillabaisse" unmoved by its exquisite

tenderness, unstirred by its brave good-feeling. "Piscator and Piscatrix," slight as it is, shows how charmingly, with what a delicate interplay of sympathy with humour, Thackeray could, had he chosen, have cast a love idyl into verse. And the "Age of Wisdom" would of itself prove that he could give words the true singing flight, would of itself make us wish that this great master of prose had taken his lyric gift more seriously. —WALTER WHYTE, "William Makepeace Thackeray," *The Poets and the Poetry of the Century*, ed. Alfred H. Miles, 1894, Vol. 10, pp. 319–22

I am distinctly conscious of being indebted to Thackeray for having led me out of the "moon-illumined magic night" of German romanticism (in which I once revelled) and accustomed me, by degrees, to a wholesomer, though less poetic, light. Vividly do I remember the distaste, the resentment, with which as a youth of twenty I flung away *The Virginians* at the chapter where Harry's calf-love for Maria is satirized. Like a sting to the quick was to me the remark about his pressing "the wilted vegetable" with rapture to his lips, or was it his heart? The delicious, good-natured ridicule with which the infatuation of Pen for Miss Fotheringay is treated in *Pendennis* hurt and disgusted me. I felt as if the author were personally abusing me. For I was then at the age when Pen's madness seemed to verge more nearly on sublimity than on foolishness. Accordingly I had a low opinion of Thackeray in those days.

But for all that, I could not help reading him; and, truth to tell, I owe him a debt of gratitude which it would be difficult to over-estimate. He saved me from no end of dangerous follies by kindling in me a spark of sobering self-criticism, which enabled me to catch little side-glimpses of myself, when I was on the verge of committing a *bêtise*. He aroused in me a salutary scepticism as to the worth of much which the world has stamped with its approval. He blew away a good deal of that romantic haze which hid reality from me and prevented me from appraising men and things at their proper value. Though no crude Sunday-school moral is appended to *Pendennis*, *The Newcomes* or *Vanity Fair*, he must be duller than an ox to the subtler sense who does not feel in the pervasive atmosphere of these books a wholesome moral tonic. And who can make the acquaintance of Colonel Newcome without having the character of the man stamped on his very soul and feeling a glow of enthusiasm for his nobleness, uprightness and lofty sense of honor? It is because he is so touchingly human, so pathetically true, that he makes so deep an impression. And as for Clive and Rose and the Campaigner, their fates have an educational worth beyond a hundred sermons. Though Thackeray does not often scold his bad and questionable characters (as does, for instance, Dickens), and though he permits an occasional smile to lurk between the lines at Becky Sharp's reprehensible cleverness, there is nowhere any confusion of moral values; and the voice that speaks has a half paternal cadence of genial wisdom and resignation.—HJALMAR HJORTH BOYESEN, "The Great Realists and the Empty Story-Tellers," *Forum*, Feb. 1895, p. 727

It was of the organ-builder that I had Thackeray's books first. He knew their literary quality, and their rank in the literary world; but I believe he was surprised at the passion I instantly conceived for them. He could not understand it; he deplored it almost as a moral defect in me; though he honored it as a proof of my critical taste. In a certain measure he was right.

What flatters the worldly pride in a young man is what fascinates him with Thackeray. With his air of looking down on the highest, and confidentially inviting you to be of his company in the seat of the scorner he is irresistible; his very confession that he is a snob, too, is balm and solace to the reader who secretly admires the splendors he affects to despise. His sentimentality is also dear to the heart of youth, and the boy who is dazzled by his satire is melted by his easy pathos. Then, if the boy has read a good many other books, he is taken with that abundance of literary turn and allusion in Thackeray; there is hardly a sentence but reminds him that he is in the society of a great literary swell, who has read everything, and can mock or burlesque life right and left from the literature always at his command. At the same time he feels his mastery, and is abjectly grateful to him in his own simple love of the good for his patronage of the unassuming virtues. It is so pleasing to one's vanity, and so safe, to be of the master's side when he assails those vices and foibles which are inherent in the system of things, and which one can contemn with vast applause so long as one does not attempt to undo the conditions they spring from.

I exulted to have Thackeray attack the aristocrats, and expose their wicked pride and meanness, and I never noticed that he did not propose to do away with aristocracy, which is and must always be just what it has been, and which cannot be changed while it exists at all. He appeared to me one of the noblest creatures that ever was when he derided the shams of society; and I was far from seeing that society, as we have it, was necessarily a sham; when he made a mock of snobbishness I did not know but snobbishness was something that might be reached and cured by ridicule. Now I know that so long as we have social inequality we shall have snobs; we shall have men who bully and truckle, and women who snub and crawl. I know that it is futile to spurn them, or lash them for trying to get on in the world, and that the world is what it must be from the selfish motives which underlie our economic life. But I did not know these things then, nor for long afterwards, and so I gave my heart to Thackeray, who seemed to promise me in his contempt of the world a refuge from the shame I felt for my own want of figure in it. He had the effect of taking me into the great world, and making me a party to his splendid indifference to titles, and even to royalties; and I could not see that sham for sham he was unwittingly the greatest sham of all.

I think it was *Pendennis* I began with, and I lived in the book to the very last line of it, and made its alien circumstance mine to the smallest detail. I am still not sure but it is the author's greatest book, and I speak from a thorough acquaintance with every line he has written, except the *Virginians*, which I have never been able to read quite through; most of his work I have read twice, and some of it twenty times.

After reading *Pendennis* I went to *Vanity Fair*, which I now think the poorest of Thackeray's novels—crude, heavy-handed, caricatured. About the same time I revelled in the romanticism of *Henry Esmond*, with its pseudo-eighteenth-century sentiment, and its appeals to an overwrought ideal of gentlemanhood and honor. It was long before I was duly revolted by Esmond's transfer of his passion from the daughter to the mother whom he is successively enamoured of. I believe this unpleasant and preposterous affair is thought one of the fine things in the story; I do not mind owning that I thought it so myself when I was seventeen; and if I could have found a Beatrix to be in love with, and a Lady Castlewood to be in love with me, I should have asked nothing finer of fortune. The glamour of *Henry Esmond* was all the deeper because I was reading the *Spectator* then, and was constantly in the company of Addison, and Steele, and Swift, and Pope, and all the wits at Will's, who are presented evanescently in the romance. The intensely literary keeping, as well as quality, of the story I suppose is what formed its highest fascination for me; but that effect of great world which it imparts to the reader, making him citizen, and, if he will, leading citizen of it, was what helped turn my head.

This is the toxic property of all Thackeray's writing. He is himself forever dominated in imagination by the world, and even while he tells you it is not worth while he makes you feel that it is worth while. It is not the honest man, but the man of honor, who shines in his page; his meek folk are proudly meek, and there is a touch of superiority, a glint of mundane splendor, in his lowliest. He rails at the order of things, but he imagines nothing different, even when he shows that its baseness, and cruelty, and hypocrisy are wellnigh inevitable, and, for most of those who wish to get on in it, quite inevitable. He has a good word for the virtues, he patronizes the Christian graces, he pats humble merit on the head; he has even explosions of indignation against the insolence and pride of birth, and purse-pride. But, after all, he is of the world, worldly, and the highest hope he holds out is that you may be in the world and despise its ambitions while you compass its ends.

I should be far from blaming him for all this. He was of his time; but since his time men have thought beyond him, and seen life with a vision which makes his seem rather purblind. He must have been immensely in advance of most of the thinking and feeling of his day, for people then used to accuse his sentimental pessimism of cynical qualities which we could hardly find in it now. It was the age of intense individualism, when you were to do right because it was becoming to you, say, as a gentleman, and you were to have an eye single to the effect upon your character, if not your reputation; you were not to do a mean thing because it was wrong, but because it was mean. It was romanticism carried into the region of morals. But I had very little concern then as to that sort of error.

I was on a very high æsthetic horse, which I could not have conveniently stooped from if I had wished; it was quite enough for me that Thackeray's novels were prodigious works of art, and I acquired merit, at least with myself, for appreciating them so keenly, for liking them so much. It must be, I felt with far less consciousness than my formulation of the feeling expresses, that I was of some finer sort myself to be able to enjoy such a fine sort. No doubt I should have been a coxcomb of some kind, if not that kind, and I shall not be very strenuous in censuring Thackeray for his effect upon me in this way. No doubt the effect was already in me, and he did not so much produce it as find it.—WILLIAM DEAN HOWELLS, "Thackeray," *My Literary Passions*, 1895

And now to come to Thackeray. Assuredly he is very far inferior to Balzac in genius. Nor has he Balzac's talent. He has not that grasp of principles, that faculty of co-ordination, that power of generalization, which Balzac possessed in such ample measure. But he had naturally a great deal in common with Balzac: originality of intellect, perspicuity of observation, a warm and potent instinct—if I may so speak—of practical life, of all its conditions, and of all its contrasts. Like Balzac, too, he possessed a certain divinatory power, a sort of gift of moral second sight. Mrs. Ritchie, in her fascinating book, which all the world has just been reading, *Chapters from Some Memoirs*, tells us that, "he sometimes spoke of a curious uncomfortable feeling he had about some people, as if uncomfortable facts in their history were actually revealed to him," a feeling which was afterwards, not unfrequently, justified. It is a curious gift and a note of the highest genius.—WILLIAM SAMUEL LILLY,

"The Humourist as Philosopher—Thackeray," *Four English Humourists of the Nineteenth Century*, 1895, p. 51

I admire Thackeray's style, and the pathetic quality in his writings; in this he never faltered. I like his sardonic melancholy. Thackeray, in a passing mood, might quite well have said: 'Who breathes must suffer, and who thinks must mourn, and he alone is blest who ne'er was born.'

He shows knowledge of human nature and much acquaintance with life—not a wide acquaintance, but complete within its limits. The vernacular of his Fokers and his Fred Bayhams is classical, and so is their slang.—FREDERICK LOCKER-LAMPSON, *My Confidences*, 1895, p. 302

But there are two ends, according to the proverb, to some if not all subjects; and it is not seldom asked whether there was not a decline as well as a growth of Thackeray's powers, and whether anything but *Vanity Fair, Pendennis, The Newcomes*, and *Esmond* can be considered to present that power at its height. It is impossible not to observe, in passing, what a genius that must be as to which it is matter of dispute whether anything has to be *added* to such a literary baggage as that of the four books just enumerated. The least of them would be a passport to and a provision for eternity; and we are inquiring whether the gentleman has any more titles and any more luggage than all four. Let me only say that I am more and more convinced that he has: that he has others even besides *The Four Georges, The English Humourists*, and the *Roundabout Papers*, which even his most grudging critics would in the same good-natured manner allow. I have never quite understood the common depreciation of *The Virginians*, which contains things equal, if not superior, to the very finest of its author's other work, and includes the very ripest expression of his philosophy of life. For though indeed I do not approve a novel more because it contains the expression of a philosophy of life, others do. So, too, the irregularity and formlessness of plot which characterised most of Thackeray's work undoubtedly appear in it; but then, according to the views of our briskest and most modern critics, plot is a very subordinate requisite in a novel, and may be very well dispensed with. Here again I do not agree, and I should say that Thackeray's greatest fault was his extreme inattention to construction, which is all the more remarkable inasmuch as he was by no means a very rapid or an extremely prolific writer. But if both these faults were infinitely greater than they are, I should say that the perfect command of character and the extraordinary criticisms of life which *The Virginians* contains save it, and not merely save it, but place it far above almost everything outside its writer's own work. —GEORGE SAINTSBURY, "Thackeray," *Corrected Impressions*, 1895

Barry Lyndon (1840) should have been enough, alone, to prove that an author of the first class had arisen, who was prepared to offer to the sickly taste of the age, to its false optimism, its superficiality, the alterative of a caustic drollery and a scrupulous study of nature. But the fact was that Thackeray had not, in any of those early sketches to which we now turn back with so much delight, mastered the technical art of story-telling. The study of Fielding appeared to reveal to him the sort of evolution, the constructive pertinacity, which had hitherto been lacking. He read *Jonathan Wild* and wrote *Barry Lyndon*; by a still severer act of self-command, he studied *Tom Jones* and composed *Vanity Fair*. The lesson was now learned. Thackeray was a finished novelist; but, alas! he was nearly forty years of age, and he was to die at fifty-two. The brief remainder of his existence was crowded with splendid work; but Thackeray

is unquestionably one of those writers who give us the impression of having more in them than accident ever permitted them to produce.

Fielding had escorted the genius of Thackeray to the doors of success, and it became convenient to use the name in contrasting the new novelist with Dickens, who was obviously of the tribe of Smollett. But Thackeray was no consistent disciple of Fielding, and when we reach his masterpieces— *Esmond*, for instance—the resemblance between the two writers has become purely superficial. Thackeray is more difficult to describe in a few words than perhaps any other author of his merit. He is a bundle of contradictions—slipshod in style, and yet exquisitely mannered; a student of reality in conduct, and yet carried away by every romantic mirage of sentiment and prejudice; a cynic with a tear in his eye, a pessimist that believes the best of everybody. The fame of Thackeray largely depends on his palpitating and almost pathetic vitality; he suffers, laughs, reflects, sentimentalises, and meanwhile we run beside the giant figure, and, looking up at the gleam of the great spectacles, we share his emotion. His extraordinary power of entering into the life of the eighteenth century, and reconstructing it before us, is the most definite of his purely intellectual claims to our regard. But it is the character of the man himself—plaintive, affectionate, protean in its moods, like April weather in its changes—that, fused with unusual completeness into his works, preserves for us the human intensity which is Thackeray's perennial charm as a writer.—EDMUND GOSSE, *A Short History of Modern English Literature*, 1897, pp. 352–54

A writer is as great as his finest work—Thackeray takes his place in Literature as the author of *Esmond, Vanity Fair, Pendennis, Barry Lyndon, The Newcomes, Rebecca and Rowena*, and *The Roundabout Papers*—and I believe his name will stand to future ages as that of the most representative Englishman of Letters of our age, and as that of the greatest master of fiction since Henry Fielding.—LEWIS MELVILLE, *The Life of William Makepeace Thackeray*, 1899, Vol. 2, p. 250

Thackeray took no print from the romantic generation; he passed it over, and went back to Addison, Fielding, Goldsmith, Swift. His masters were the English humourists of the eighteenth century. He planned a literary history of that century, a design which was carried out on other lines by his son-in-law, Leslie Stephen. If he wrote historical novels, their period was that of the Georges, and not of Richard the Lion Heart. It will not do, of course, to lay too much stress on Thackeray, whose profession was satire and whose temper purely anti-romantic.—HENRY A. BEERS, *A History of English Romanticism in the Nineteenth Century*, 1901, pp. 397–98

If, then, we find that in all great walks of life—in the Church, in war, in commerce, and in diplomacy—Mr. Thackeray has nothing but abuse and sneers for success; if we find that he loves to portray the ludicrous and the discreditable only, is it unfair to say that he is the Apostle of Mediocrity? Mediocre ways of life, mediocre thoughts, mediocre inclinations (miscalled passions), mediocre achievements—these, if not positively enjoined, as they sometimes are, are in effect all that is left to one who takes Mr. Thackeray for his guide. For the rest, never had a mean gospel so doughty an Apostle.—WALTER FREWEN LORD, "The Apostle of Mediocrity," *Nineteenth Century*, March 1902, p. 410

Thackeray possessed in a greater measure than any other English writer the *style coulant*, which Baudelaire ascribed in dispraise to George Sand. His words flow like snow-water upon the mountainside. He could no more restrain the current of his prose than a gentle slope could turn a rivulet back upon its course. His sentences dash one over the other in an often aimless succession, as though impelled by a force independent of their author. The style, as employed by Thackeray, has its obvious qualities and defects. It is so easy that it may be followed by the idlest reader, who willingly applies to literature the test of conversation. The thread of argument or of character is so loosely held that it need not elude a half-awakened attention. On the other hand, the style must needs be at times inaccurate and undistinguished. The solecisms of which he is guilty, and they are not few, may readily be forgiven. It is more difficult to pardon the frequent lack of distinction, especially as in *Esmond* Thackeray proved that he could write, if he would, with perfect artistry. But the method of his more familiar books seems the result less of artifice than of temperament. He seldom gives you the impression that he has studied to produce a certain effect. An effect is there, of course, facile and various, but beyond his management. He is so little conscious of his craft, that he rarely arrives at the right phrase, thus presenting an obvious contrast to Disraeli, who, often careless in composition, yet sowed his pages with pearls of speech which time cannot dim. But how little do we take away from the most of Thackeray beyond a general impression of gentlemanly ease!

From this it follows that he possessed no economy of speech. He never used one word, if a page and a half could adequately express the meaning, and at all save his high moments you miss a controlling hand, a settled purpose. Nor is this remarkable, when you recall the shifts and starts in which he did his work. He was of those who write better anywhere than in their own house. He would carry his unfinished manuscript to Greenwich with him, and write a chapter after dinner, or he would go off to Paris, and compose as he went. "I should never be at home," he told Elwin, "if I could help it. . . . I write less at home than anywhere. I did not write ten pages of *The Newcomes* in that house at Brompton. . . . This"—meaning a hotel—"is the best place to work in."

While Thackeray left the words to look after themselves, he confesses himself the humble slave of his own characters. "Once created," said he, "they lead me, and I follow where they direct." He devised his actors as by instinct, and without realising the full meaning of the drama in which they played their part. "I have no idea where it all comes from," he told Elwin. "I have never seen the people I describe, nor heard the conversations I put down. I am often astonished myself to read it when I have got it on paper." It is not strange, therefore, that he regarded the personages in his own dramas as quite outside himself. "I have been surprised," says he, "at the observations made by some of my characters. It seems as if an occult power was moving the pen." And it was precisely this externality which linked Thackeray and his characters in the bonds of acquaintance. Had they been the deliberate and conscious creations of his brain, they would have been at once more and less familiar to him. He would have remembered precisely where the strings lay which pulled the figures; but he could not have said, "I know the people utterly—I know the sound of their voices." He would not have seen Philip Firmin in a chance visitor; he would not have recognised the drunken swagger of Captain Costigan, when he met him, years after his creation, in a tavern. We may be quite sure that he never encountered Sir Francis or Beatrix Esmond, for these he made himself; but the majority of his characters grew without his knowledge, and even against his will. "That turning back to the old pages," he murmurs in a passage of genuine lament,

"produces anything but elation of mind. Would you not pay a pretty fine to be able to cancel some of them? Ah, the sad old pages, the dull old pages!"

It was this fatality, this frank obedience to his own puppets and his own pen, which explains the frequent formlessness of Thackeray's work. But though he permitted most of his books to write themselves, it must not be thought that his style was uniformly hazardous. Despite its occasional inaccuracy, despite its loose texture, it has many shining qualities. It is graphic, various, and at times eloquent. It is easy to recall a hundred passages which would entitle Thackeray to a high place among the writers of English. The Waterloo chapters of *Vanity Fair*, much of *Esmond*, Harry Warrington's first visit to England, Denis Duval's journey to London,—these, to name but a few, are touched by the hand of a master, who need fear comparison with none. Even where Thackeray's prose is least under control, it inspires no more than his own regret that he did not write "a completely good book." For it is always the prose of a man of letters.

Now, in Thackeray's time scholarship was not fashionable. Neither Dickens nor Bulwer (save in his last novels) give you a sense of literary allusion. But Thackeray, in his most careless mood, suggests the classics or hints at the eighteenth century. As he wrote rather as an essayist than as a novelist, as his style was a sincere, untrammelled expression of his mind, he reveals his literary preferences by a thousand light touches. His reading, if not wide, was deep. He was perfectly familiar with both the Augustan ages. Horace he knew best of all, and quoted most constantly. Nothing pleases him better than to allude in a phrase to his favourite poet. "Nuper—in former days—I too have militated," thus he writes in *The Roundabout Papers*, "the years slip away fugacius;" and again, "to-morrow the diffugient snows will give place to Spring." Above all, he loved the Augustan doctrine of an easy life. The contemner of Swift naturally found Juvenal a "truculent brute," but he felt a natural sympathy for the satirist of Venusia, who timidly avoided unpleasant themes, and who, had he lived in the nineteenth century, would have been a man about town, and have haunted the very clubs to which Thackeray himself belonged. And when he chose to express himself in verse, he echoed with skill and fidelity both the manner and the philosophy of Horace.—CHARLES WHIBLEY, *William Makepeace Thackeray*, 1903, pp. 234–38

Works

VANITY FAIR

I brought away the last four numbers of *Vanity Fair*, and read one of them in bed, during the night. Very good, indeed, beats Dickens out of the world.—JANE WELSH CARLYLE, Letter to Thomas Carlyle (Sept. 16, 1847)

In forming our general estimate of this writer, we wish to be understood as referring principally, if not exclusively, to *Vanity Fair* (a novel in monthly parts), though still unfinished; so immeasurably superior, in our opinion, is this to every other known production of his pen. The great charm of this work is its entire freedom from mannerism and affectation both in style and sentiment,—the confiding frankness with which the reader is addressed,—the thoroughbred carelessness with which the author permits the thoughts and feelings suggested by the situations to flow in their natural channel, as if conscious that nothing mean or unworthy, nothing requiring to be shaded, gilded, or dressed up in company attire, could fall from him. In a word, the book is the work of a gentleman, which is one great merit; and not the work of a fine (or would-be fine) gentleman, which is another. Then, again, he never exhausts, elaborates, or insists too much upon anything; he drops his finest remarks and happiest illustrations as Buckingham dropped his pearls, and leaves them to be picked up and appreciated as chance may bring a discriminating observer to the spot. His effects are uniformly the effects of sound wholesome legitimate art; and we need hardly add that we are never harrowed up with physical horrors of the Eugène Sue school in his writings, or that there are no melodramatic villains to be found in them. One touch of nature makes the whole world kin, and here are touches of nature by the dozen. His pathos (though not so deep as Mr. Dickens') is exquisite; the more so, perhaps, because he seems to struggle against it, and to be half ashamed of being caught in the melting mood: but the attempt to be caustic, satirical, ironical, or philosophical, on such occasions, is uniformly vain; and again and again have we found reason to admire how an originally fine and kind nature remains essentially free from worldliness, and, in the highest pride of intellect, pays homage to the heart.

Vanity Fair was certainly meant for a satire: the follies, foibles and weaknesses (if not vices) of the world we live in, were to be shown up in it, and we can hardly be expected to learn philanthropy from the contemplation of them. —ABRAHAM HAYWARD, "Thackeray's Writings," *Edinburgh Review*, Jan. 1848, p. 50

You mention Thackeray and the last number of *Vanity Fair*. The more I read Thackeray's works the more certain I am that he stands alone—alone in his sagacity, alone in his truth, alone in his feeling (his feeling, though he makes no noise about it, is about the most genuine that ever lived on a printed page), alone in his power, alone in his simplicity, alone in his self-control. Thackeray is a Titan, so strong that he can afford to perform with calm the most herculean feats; there is the charm and majesty of repose in his greatest efforts; *he* borrows nothing from fever, his is never the energy of delirium—his energy is sane energy, deliberate energy, thoughtful energy. The last number of *Vanity Fair* proves this peculiarly. Forcible, exciting in its force, still more impressive than exciting, carrying on the interest of the narrative in a flow, deep, full resistless, it is still quiet—as quiet as reflection, as quiet as memory; and to me there are parts of it that sound as solemn as an oracle. Thackeray is never borne away by his own ardour—he has it under control. His genius obeys him—it is his servant, it works no fantastic changes at its own wild will, it must still achieve the task which reason and sense assign it, and none other. Thackeray is unique. I *can* say no more, I *will* say no less.—CHARLOTTE BRONTË, Letter to W. S. Williams (March 29, 1848)

Vanity Fair, by W. M. Thackeray, one of the most brilliant of English magazine-writers, is an attempt, somewhat after the manner of Fielding, to represent the world as it is, especially the selfish, heartless, and cunning portion of it. The author has Fielding's cosy manner of talking to his readers in the pauses of his narrative, and, like Fielding, takes his personages mostly from ordinary life. The novel, though it touches often upon topics which have been worn threadbare, and reproduces many commonplace types of character, is still, on the whole, a fresh and vigorous transcript of English life, and has numerous profound touches of humanity and humor. Sir Pitt Crawley, a sort of combination of Sir John Brute, Sir Tunbelly Clumsy, and Squire Western, is a very striking piece of caricature; but though exceedingly ludicrous, is hardly natural. George Osborne, Dobbin, and Amelia are characters almost literally

true to nature, and are developed with consummate skill and fidelity. Mr. Osborne, we fear, is too fair a representative of the English man of business of the middle class,—selfish, arrogant, purse-proud, cringing to superiors, and ferocious to inferiors, rejoicing in a most profound ignorance of his own meanness and cruelty, and ever disposed to rise on the ruin of his neighbours. That disposition in English society, of every class, to trample on the one immediately beneath it, and to fawn on the one immediately above it, Thackeray felicitously represents in this portrait and in other characters. Nothing can be more edifying than Mr. Osborne's conversations with his son George, on his intimacy with men of rank who fleece him at cards, and on his duty to break off a match with Amelia after her father has become bankrupt. But the finest character in the whole novel is Miss Rebecca Sharp, an original personage, worthy to be called the author's own, and as true to life as hypocrisy, ability, and cunning can make her. She is altogether the most important person in the work, being the very impersonation of talent, tact, and worldliness, and one who works her way with a graceful and effective impudence unparalleled among managing women.

Of all the novels on our list, *Vanity Fair* is the only one in which the author is content to represent actual life. His page swarms with personages whom we recognize at once as genuine. It is also noticeable, that Thackeray alone preserves himself from the illusions of misanthropy or sentimentality, and though dealing with a host of selfish and malicious characters, his book leaves no impression that the world is past praying for, or that the profligate have it. His novel, as a representation of life, is altogether more comprehensive and satisfying than either of the others. Each may excel him in some particular department of character and passion, but each is confined to a narrow space, and discolors or shuts out the other portions of existence. Thackeray looks at the world from no exclusive position, and his view accordingly includes a superficial, if not a substantial whole; and it is creditable to the healthiness of his mind, that he could make so wide a survey without contracting either of the opposite diseases of misanthropy or worldliness.—EDWIN P. WHIPPLE, "Novels of the Season," *North American Review*, Oct. 1848, pp. 368–69

In this book the artist—and he was an eminently great artist— seemed to have endeavored to drive mankind to their own unaided struggles, taking away from them all good examples and leaving them to conclude that nothing is real but folly and perfidy. ⟨. . .⟩

In the literature of fiction there is not to be found a picture drawn more artistically than Rebecca Sharp. She was of the sort upon whom it suited the author to exert his consummate powers. He painted her to the life, with pretended reluctance to evil, suspected, yet not fully known to be persuasible to consent, demanding risk, high pay, so that the pursuit, of which, if easy, a bold lover would weary, acquired the eagerness which must not be allowed to abate. No woman could better understand the trick, as sung by the shepherd in Virgil, of casting her apple and then fleeing to the covert of willows:

> Malo me Galatea petit lasciva puella;
> Et fugit ad salices; et se cupit ante videri.

It is a sad commentary on the powerlessness and the hopelessness of a poor young woman without other gift than mere virtue to obtain success that appears to attend upon insidiousness and fraud. It would have been a good sight to see the lifting of such a one, even though slowly and through difficulties, where so many thousands of poor girls do rise through toil and patient waiting. In default of this the next best would have been to drive her to the frustration of every dishonorable purpose that had tempted her from the path of rectitude. Better than both of these, for the highest purposes of instruction, would have been pictures of young women who endured temptation and outrage without expecting and without receiving reward except such as came from the testimony of a good conscience and of suffering for the sake of Him who ennobled suffering and put it above successes, victories, and triumphs. For had there not lived in such a career Agnes and Afra, Rose and Eulalia, Lucy and Blandina? If such as these be outside of the art of the novelist, then surely he may hold up to our view young girls such as Richardson presented with generous sympathy to the public of his day. Alas! the eyes of that public were yet moist with tears when the profligate Fielding made them laugh both at them over whom they had wept and at themselves. It was such a joke to imagine it possible for as poor a girl as Pamela to marry a rich, hardened bachelor and reform him after marriage, or for another like Clarissa to endure such trials and yet continue spotless in her virtue! No, no; Rebecca Sharp must be what she was, have a better time than even Amelia Sedley, and thus be made to exhibit that virtue is worth not even as much as a semblance that is suspected and almost known to be false. Satire, indeed! Satire upon the men in highest society, for of the two from this class whom he exhibited one was a heartless profligate, the other a loathsome brute; satire even upon marriage, for the couple who were truest to each other were the O'Dowds, whose rudeness was sufficient to make all of both sexes feel like keeping away from marriage altogether, if this is to be considered a fair illustration of its most honorable estate.—RICHARD MALCOLM JOHNSTON, "The Extremity of Satire," *Catholic World*, Feb. 1886, pp. 688–90

ESMOND

Thackeray I saw for ten minutes: he was just in the agony of finishing a Novel: which has arisen out of the Reading necessary for his Lectures, and relates to those Times—of Queen Anne, I mean. He will get £1000 for his Novel. He was wanting to finish it, and rush off to the Continent, I think, to shake off the fumes of it.—EDWARD FITZGERALD, Letter to Frederick Tennyson (June 8, 1852)

Of our late Editor's works, the best known, and most widely appreciated are, no doubt, *Vanity Fair*, *Pendennis*, *The Newcomes*, and *Esmond*. The first on the list has been the most widely popular with the world at large. *Pendennis* has been the best loved by those who have felt and tasted the delicacy of Thackeray's tenderness. *The Newcomes* stands conspicuous for the character of the Colonel, who as an English gentleman has no equal in English fiction. *Esmond*, of all his works, has most completely satisfied the critical tastes of those who profess themselves to read critically. For myself, I own that I regard *Esmond* as the first and finest novel in the English language. Taken as a whole, I think that it is without a peer. There is in it a completeness of historical plot, and an absence of that taint of unnatural life which blemishes, perhaps, all our other historical novels, which places it above its brethren. And, beyond this, it is replete with a tenderness which is almost divine,—a tenderness which no poetry has surpassed. Let those who doubt this go back and study again the life of Lady Castlewood. In *Esmond*, above all his works, Thackeray achieves the great triumph of touching the innermost core of his subject, without ever wounding the taste. We catch all the aroma, but the palpable body of the thing never stays with us

till it palls us. Who ever wrote of love with more delicacy than Thackeray has written in *Esmond?* May I quote one passage of three or four lines? Who is there that does not remember the meeting between Lady Castlewood and Harry Esmond after Esmond's return. "'Do you know what day it is?' she continued. 'It is the 29th December; it is your birthday! But last year we did not drink it;—no, no! My lord was cold, and my Harry was like to die; and my brain was in a fever; and we had no wine. But now,—now you are come again, bringing your sheaves with you, my dear.' She burst into a wild flood of weeping as she spoke; she laughed and sobbed on the young man's heart, crying out wildly,—'bringing your sheaves with you,—your sheaves with you!'"

But if *Esmond* be, as a whole, our best English novel, Colonel Newcome is the finest single character in English fiction. That it has been surpassed by Cervantes, in *Don Quixote*, we may, perhaps, allow, though *Don Quixote* has the advantage of that hundred years which is necessary to the perfect mellowing of any great work. When Colonel Newcome shall have lived his hundred years, and the lesser works of Thackeray and his compeers shall have died away, then, and not till then, will the proper rank of this creation in literature be appreciated.—ANTHONY TROLLOPE, "W. M. Thackeray," *Cornhill Magazine*, Feb. 1864, pp. 136–37

If I could possess only *one* of his works, I think I should choose *Henry Esmond*. To my thinking, it is a marvel in literature, and I have read it oftener than any of the other works.—JAMES T. FIELDS, "Thackeray," *Yesterdays with Authors*, 1871, p. 16

Of Thackeray's works certainly the most remarkable and perhaps the best is *Esmond*. Many novelists following in the wake of Scott have attempted to reproduce for us past manners, scenes, and characters; but in *Esmond* Thackeray not only does this—he reproduces for us the style in which men wrote and talked in the days of Queen Anne. To reproduce the forgotten phraseology, to remember always not how his age would express an idea, but how Steele, or Swift, or Addison would have expressed it, might have been pronounced impossible of accomplishment. Yet in *Esmond* Thackeray did accomplish it, and with perfect success. The colouring throughout is exquisite and harmonious, never by a single false note is the melody broken. Of his writings in general perhaps the most noticeable characteristic is the hatred they express for all sorts of false pretences, sham sentiment, and unreal professions. He is never wearied of directing his scathing satire against whited sepulchres of all descriptions. "Call things by their right names; do not gloss over the villany of Lord Steyne because he is a lord; do not condone George Osborne's selfishness because he is handsome; don't pretend to be what you are not, and do not let false shame make you conceal what you are," is the burden of his message. To his scorn and hatred of vice and meanness he added sincere love and admiration of all that is true, and good, and honourable. A large-hearted, thoughtful man, the temptations and trials and sorrows of humanity affected him deeply. His pathos is as touching and sincere as his humour is subtle and delicate. His numerous "asides" to the reader are full of "that sad wisdom which experience brings," in striking contrast to those of Dickens, who, when he leaves his story to indulge in moralising, is generally trite and feeble. In a characteristic passage Thackeray apologises for the frequency of his casual reflections. "Perhaps of all novel-spinners now extant," he says, "the present writer is the most addicted to preaching. Does he not stop perpetually in his story and begin to preach to you? . . . I say *peccavi* loudly and heartily," he adds, but there was no need of this expression of repentance, whether sincere or not, for none ever wished Thackeray's "asides" fewer or shorter. Thackeray's fame as a novelist has caused his poems, of which he wrote a good many, generally in a half-serious, half-comic vein, to be frequently less noticed than they deserve. His admirable mock-heroic ballads and society verses attain a degree of excellence very rarely reached by such performances.

Was Thackeray a cynic? The question has been often asked and variously answered. If we use "cynic" in the proper sense of the word as defined by Johnson, "a philosopher of the snarling or currish sort; a follower of Diogenes; a rude man; a snarler; a misanthrope," most assuredly it cannot with any propriety be applied to him. But in ordinary *parlance* we use "cynic" in a sense different from any of these, meaning by it a man who is apt to look on life with a glance half sad, half humorous, who is prone to be distrustful of fine appearances and professions, who sees keenly the grains of dust mingled in the gold of the finest character, and who is fully aware of the latent meanness and selfish ambition which often lurk under actions professing to be noble and generous. In this sense of the word, Thackeray was a cynic. *Vanitas vanitatum*: all is vanity, is his often-repeated cry; none knew better than he with what richly gilded coverings we are apt to clothe the evil passions and desires of our nature.—HENRY J. NICOLL, *Landmarks of Literature*, 1882, pp. 389–91

THE NEWCOMES

Mr. S—— is a friend of Thackeray, and, speaking of the last number of *The Newcomes*,—so touching that nobody can read it aloud without breaking down,—he mentioned that Thackeray himself had read it to James Russell Lowell and William Story in a cider-cellar! I read all the preceding numbers of *The Newcomes* to my wife, but happened not to have an opportunity to read this last, and was glad of it,—knowing that my eyes would fill, and my voice quiver —NATHANIEL HAWTHORNE, *The English Note-Books*, 1855

This is Mr. Thackeray's masterpiece, as it is undoubtedly one of the masterpieces of English fiction, if fiction is the proper term to apply to the most minute and faithful transcript of actual life which is anywhere to be found. The ordinary resource of novelists is to describe characters under exceptional circumstances, to show them influenced by passions which seldom operate in their excess with each individual, and to make them actors in adventures which in their aggregate happen to few or none. It is the picked passages of existence which they represent, and these again are often magnified and coloured beyond the measure of nature. Mr. Thackeray looks at life under its ordinary aspects, and copies it with a fidelity and artistic skill which are surprising. Men, women, and children talk, act, and think in his pages exactly as they are talking, acting, and thinking at every hour of every day. The same thorns, the majority of them self-planted, are festering in myriads of bosoms; the same false ambition and crooked devices are fermenting in a thousand hearts; the same malice, lying, and slandering in all their grades, petty and great, are issuing from legions of mouths, and the same mixture of kindness and generosity are checking and tempering the evil. You find yourself in the saloon where upon gala days you are a guest; in the house you frequent as a familiar friend; in the club of which you are a member; you meet there your acquaintances, you hear again the conversation which you have often heard before, and it is by no means unlikely that among the assembled company you may be startled by coming upon the very image of yourself. Truth is never sacrificed to

piquancy. The characters in the *Newcomes* are not more witty, wise, or farcical than their prototypes; the dull, the insipid, and the foolish, speak according to their own fashion and not with the tongue of the author; the events which befall them are nowhere made exciting at the expense of probability. Just as the stream of life runs on through these volumes, so may it be seen to flow in the world itself by whoever takes up the same position on the bank. ⟨. . .⟩

Mr. Thackeray is a humourist, as every writer of fiction must be who takes an extended view of human nature. There are few persons who do not deviate in some particular from common forms or common sense; who are not guilty of some vanity, affectation, whim, or inconsistency, which, however far, perchance, from promoting mirth among those who have to bear with them, are comic in the description. The simple Colonel Newcome, when he fancies himself an adept in the wiles of the world, though, 'if he had lived to be as old as Jahaleel, a boy could still have cheated him;' Mrs. Hobson worshipping rank, and pretending to despise the society she cannot obtain; the airs and cowardice of Barnes; the self-importance and primness of Miss Honeyman, who, instead of feeling ashamed at being a gentlewoman reduced to let lodgings, is proud to be a lodging-house keeper who was once a gentle-woman; the clerical impostures of her bland brother, the French-English of Paul de Florac, and his efforts to personate John Bull; Mr. Gandish insisting upon the indifference to 'igh art' as shown in the neglect of his monster pictures, and talking of the heroic in his vulgar language, afford a hundred examples of the ridiculous. Most of the actors in the *Newcomes* are tinged with it, but the quality is always in subjection to truth. There is none of the farcical extravagance which calls forth peals of laughter, always easy to be provoked by absurdity and caricature. In Frederick Bayham there is a two-fold source of merriment, for besides the smiles produced by unconscious infirmities, there is a fertile vein of fun in his expedients and vivacity. It is a peculiar charm of the light and pleasant wit which sparkles through the narrative that it never has the air of being studied. It shines forth in a name, an epithet, a parenthesis, in numberless undefinable ways, and always as if it sprung out of the subject, and had not been introduced for the sake of being facetious.

The execution of the work is not below the conception. Mr. Thackeray is deeply imbued with all our best literature. Numerous phrases and fragments of sentences attest his familiarity with the classic authors of his country—a familiarity which is not less surely shown by the perennial flow of his easy and graceful language. There is no appearance of effort, no studied artifice of composition, but neither is there any approach to baldness in the simplicity of his phraseology, or to carelessness in the freedom of his style. The narrative runs on in a rich abundance of strong, idiomatic, sterling English, often applied in a novel and felicitous manner, and sufficiently adorned by occasional metaphors of the same masculine stamp. He even manages to give additional raciness by the not unfrequent use of colloquial vulgarisms, which if they were introduced with less skill would debase his style. It is with reluctance we confess that he has turned language to good account which in all other hands has hitherto revolted every person of cultivated mind, for we fear the evil effects of his example, and are sorry the black patches should heighten the beauty.—WHITWELL ELWIN, "*The Newcomes*," *Quarterly Review*, Sept. 1855, pp. 350–58

This is by far the best of Thackeray's stories. In his earlier works, the scornful has taken precedence of the humane element. His aim has been to satirize pretension, folly, and fashionable vice rather than to present aught that could challenge admiration or deserve imitation. Here the prominent personages command our entire sympathy, and the leading character our profound reverence; while the baser traits of secondary actors are softened and relieved by the admixture of good which is seldom wanting in actual life. Only this was needed to give Thackeray, as a novelist, the vantage-ground over Dickens; for there can be no difference of opinion as to his superiority in the command of language and in artistical resources and skill.—ANDREW PRESTON PEABODY, *North American Review*, Jan. 1856, p. 284

The *Newcomes* was written in the years that came between my father's first and second journey to America. He began the preface at Baden on the 7th of July 1853, he finished his book at Paris on the 28th of June 1855, and in the autumn of that year he returned to America. The story had been in his mind for a long time. While still writing *Esmond* he speaks of a new novel "opening with something like Fareham and the old people there," and of "a hero who will be born in India, and have a half-brother and sister." And there is also the description to be read of the little wood near to Berne, in Switzerland, into which he strayed one day, and where, as he tells us, "the story was actually revealed to him."—ANNE THACKERAY RITCHIE, "Introduction" to *The Newcomes*, 1898–99, p. xxii

ENGLISH HUMOURISTS AND FOUR GEORGES

Went to Thackeray's lecture on the Humorists at Willis's Rooms. It was a very large assembly, including Mrs. Carlyle, Dickens, Leslie, and innumerable noteworthy people. Thackeray is a much older-looking man than I had expected; a square, powerful face, and most acute and sparkling eyes, grayish hair and eyebrows. He reads in a definite, rather dry manner, but makes you understand thoroughly what he is about. The lecture was full of point, but the subject was not a very interesting one, and he tried to fix our sympathy on his good-natured, volatile, and frivolous hero rather more than was meet. "Poor Dick Steele!" one ends with, as one began; and I cannot see, more than I did before, the element of greatness in him.—CAROLINE FOX, *Journal* (June 12, 1851), *Memories of Old Friends*, ed. Horace N. Pym, 1882, p. 292

⟨. . .⟩ that, as a readable book, this ⟨*English Humourists of the Eighteenth Century*⟩ has seldom been surpassed. Whatever quantity of summer-salmon, *hotch-potch*, veal pie, and asparagus you may have been discussing, and however dreary you may feel after your dinner, Thackeray's amusing anecdotes and conversational style will keep you awake. Next to Macaulay and Hazlitt, he is the most entertaining of critics. You read his lectures with quite as much gusto as you do *Pendennis*, and with infinitely more than you do such dull mimicry of the past as is to be found in *Esmond*. Clever, too, of course, sagacious often, and sometimes powerful, are his criticisms, and a geniality not frequent in his fictions is often here. Sympathy with his subject is also a quality he possesses and parades; indeed, he appears as one born out of his proper time, and seems, occasionally, to sigh for the age of big-wigs, bagnios, and sponging-houses. Such are, we think, the main merits of this very popular volume.—GEORGE GILFILLAN, "Thackeray," *A Third Gallery of Portraits*, 1854, pp. 261–62

I have heard Thackeray's four lectures on the four Georges, truculent enough in their general satire,—though not much beyond the last half-volume of *Harry Esmond* about Queen Anne,—but full of generous passages about individuals. The sketches of the German princes of the seventeenth century, and down to the middle of the eighteenth, with which he opened, amused me more than anything else. They were capital. The passage most applauded was a beautiful tribute of loyalty to Queen Victoria, and the tone and manners of her Court. It was given, on his part, with much feeling, and brought down the house—always crowded—very fervently.—GEORGE TICKNOR, Letter to Sir Edmund Head (Dec. 23, 1855), *Life, Letters, and Journals of George Ticknor*, ed. Anna Ticknor, 1876, Vol. 2, p. 294

He was a complete success. He was as delightful as his own literary personages are, and so "like his writings" that every one spoke of it. His allusions, his voice, his looks, were all just what we had expected. Never did a long-hoped-for hero fill the bill so thoroughly. His loving and life-giving genius spoke in every word. Wonderful examples of excellence those papers on *The Four Georges*, and delivered in a clear, fine, rich voice. Their simplicity was matchless, and the fun in him came out as he described the fourth George, and then stopped, not smiling himself, while we all laughed. He silently stood, his head tipped back, and then calmly wiped his spectacles and went on. He had a charm as a speaker which no one has since caught: it defies analysis, as does his genius. It was Thackerayian. —M. E. W. SHERWOOD, *An Epistle to Posterity*, 1897, p. 79

JOHN FOSTER KIRK
From "Thackeray, as a Novelist"
North American Review, July 1853, pp. 212–19

If men are unable to penetrate the important secrets of the sex, women are no less unwilling to reveal them. It is only one who has herself overleaped the bounds of tyrannical custom, who ever ventures to depict that struggle which, at some period of life, a proud and ardent woman can hardly fail to pass through. And when such a picture is presented by a Dudevant or a Hahn-Hahn, the sex itself is always foremost to cry out against it, as unfeminine and monstrous. It is in fact a betrayal—a revelation of internal weakness to the common foe. To suffer with a smiling face, is the supreme duty of womanhood. The *femme incomprise*, who whimpers and complains, is an object of scorn to her sisters; just as the Indians repudiate one of their own tribe, who, captured and tormented by the enemy, is unable to repress his groans. Ambition,—aspirations for self—by which the angels fell, is also the deadliest sin of our terrestrial angels; while in man, it is a virtue that leads to honor and reward. Hence women are divided by a strong barrier into two classes; women who submit, and women who rebel; women who are tender, loving, devoted, who sacrifice self, and think only of their husbands and their children; and women who are ambitious, independent, indignant at their trammels, who seek for a career, who cannot sink their own aspirations in those of another, and who think and strive only for themselves; women whom society smiles upon and approves, and women whom society suspects, and in extreme cases disowns. Whether all the restrictions from which this great breach originates, are necessary and natural, or whether the victims only are to blame, it is not our province to inquire. Thackeray, who paints the world as he finds it, reproduces again and again these two contrasted classes of women. His Becky and Amelia, his Beatrix and Lady Castlewood, are the magnetic poles of repulsion and attraction. If the former class display intellect superior to that of the latter, this we think is entirely natural. It is the active and original mind that is most likely to stray beyond the limits which a law, not altogether free from an arbitrary character, has assigned to it; and the experience that it thus gains, sharpens powers which might have rusted from want of exercise. After all, the qualities of Becky Sharp are just those by which men commonly attain success in life, especially in political life; her maxim was the same as that which every obscure man adopts who looks forward to fame; "she had her own way to make in the world; there was no one to take care of her." And if she sometimes makes use of methods not quite legitimate, consider the difficulties of one who had no beaten track to walk on, but was forced to make the ladder by which she was to climb. Had she been placed in a position which afforded free play to her talents, mankind would have applauded the very character which it now condemns. There is no great queen whose actions are recorded by history, who, if she had developed in a private sphere those qualities by which she acquired glory on a throne, would not have been put under the ban of society; while a Mary Tudor is made infamous for having done what all the good women—the Amelias and Lady Castlewoods—would have done, had they been in her place, sacrificed her own better feelings to the obligations imposed on her by the superior sex.

The picture, therefore, which Thackeray gives us of the female mind, is a correct, but, as we have already said, not a complete picture. The struggle that ends in resignation, the impatience that at length folds its wings in despair—the mind, in short, of which we obtain a glimpse in *Jane Eyre* and *Villette*, that, with intellect and imagination chafing beneath their trammels, is yet curbed by the pious consciousness that abnegation is the highest act of the free will—Thackeray does not attempt to exhibit. On one side, is the woman who triumphs over the prejudice of education, because she has never known the restraint of principle; and on the other, the willing slave who never questions the righteousness of her destiny, whose heart may sometimes beat a little against the bars, but whose intellect is always quiescent. But the world cries out against this representation, and finds these fond mothers and devoted wives weak and foolish. Yet this we think one of Thackeray's highest merits, that he has not, as most writers have done, put into one category the folly that springs from love, and the folly that has its source in selfish blindness; that he has shown how love and self-sacrifice are holy and beautiful things, even when they are but instincts, and receive no light from the intellect. Besides, Thackeray's aim is not to cultivate our taste for what is rare, but to quicken our appreciation of what is common; and we cannot but think that the ordinary effect of the existing constitution of society, is to divorce the intellect from the affections. Where there is no weakness there will be no submission; where there is no folly, there will be no blindness; where there is no blindness there will be precious little love. Amelia is a fool, you say, to make an idol of Osborne, and bring her daily offering to his selfish shrine; a fool to let that boy who succeeds to his father's place in her heart, grasp its tender fibres with the same rude and heedless hand, and thus prodigally to sow where she could reap no harvest but bitter tears. We grant the folly. But ask your own heart what is its sweetest yet most painful memory. Do you never dream that you are back again in those old years, when thoughtless love was thus squandered upon you? Do you never wake with a remorseful pang, sharper than any that the ambiguous deeds of the hardened present can inflict, and think what a blessed thing it would be if you could stanch the wounds which your barbed arrow made, and expiate that ignorance and self-engrossment by watchful, tender care? And if this be so, can you now criticize the extravagant love which you abused,

and sneer at it as folly, and blame the indulgence which spoilt you, and made you selfish, and tell how you would have been a wiser and a better man, if you had been more wisely trained? But you have had no such experience—you never suffered from such indiscreet affection, or you were thoughtful and grateful, and have no need to look penitently at the past? You are fortunate. But others are less so; and among these is Thackeray. For it is not the voice of a mere observer that we recognize in this reiterated tale of the fond desperation of a loving nature torn by the jagged rock to which it clings, but the trembling tones of one who speaks from the emotions of his own heart. Here, if anywhere, we get an insight into the man himself, and catch the echo of his own experience, his sufferings, and his errors,—

> Was er irrte, was er strebte,
> Was er litt, und was er lebte.

However different the persons and the scene, this tale interweaves itself more or less with the action. Osborne, Pendennis, Esmond, Barry Lyndon, contrasted as they are in character and fate,—this experience is common to them all; or rather it is the author himself whose hand, at the slightest suggestion, strikes involuntarily the mournful chords of vain regret and self-reproach.

In truth, with all his great powers of observation, Thackeray is in a remarkable degree *subjective*. And this is the source of the great artistic defects from which none of his works are free. He sees deep into the characters he conceives, but he never loses his own individuality in theirs, never allows them to move freely along, and pass the thread of the story from hand to hand. He is a spectator, as we have said, but a noisy one, who continually interrupts the performance by his commentaries. The persons of his drama never soliloquize, never make such reflections as the scene would naturally provoke from them. Soliloquy and reflection abound, but it all falls to the share of the author, or of his fictitious representative. Hence the failure, to a certain extent, when he adopts the autobiographical form of relation. Esmond, Barry Lyndon, even Yellowplush, talk always in the Thackerayan vein,—utter statements peculiar to him, and seldom very appropriate in them. The story does not flow with a steady current, like Fielding's; there is no succession of scenes, connected only by sufficient explanatory remarks, as in Miss Austen. Scene, narration, and remark are presented to us in bits, and so intermixed with one another as to form a *quartum quid*. The Aristotelian rule, that there should in every work be a beginning, a middle, and an end, was never so sinned against as by Thackeray. Except by the number of pages, you have seldom any clue by which to conjecture how far you have advanced, or when you are to expect the *dénouement*. Two thirds of *Pendennis* seems more like the prelude than the actual story; all the important action is crowded into the rapid and masterly scenes at the close. *Esmond* is still more tantalizing. The story is never fairly set agoing throughout the three volumes. We make several successive starts, under the guidance of a train of incidents, and in company with certain personages; but before we have got far the steam is let off, the passengers all leave, and we are obliged to take a new conveyance, with precisely the same results. If the style be the purest, the plot is the weakest, of any novel in the English language. It may be said that, as the work assumes the form of an autobiography, the features to which we object maintain the verisimilitude. But want of connection and broken threads in a narrative are endurable only when they are unavoidable; and a novelist gains no more by adopting the restrictions of biography, than a dramatist by preserving the arbitrary unities of time and place. Yet some of the scenes in *Esmond* are the most perfect which Thackeray has given us. The author, in the person of his hero—himself prematurely wise and observant—comes forward on the stage; and his remarks, made thus *vivâ voce*, as it were, are appropriate to the occasion. But these scenes are few; the principal persons in them are not always those in whom we are most interested; and the action assigned to each character is too meagre to give vitality and strong interest to the book.

We have called these peculiarities of Thackeray defects. But the tendency from which they arise is among the inherent qualities of his mind, and the source, in no small degree, of his originality and power. It is not in his nature to content himself with the contemplation of men's actions, or with the exhibition of their characters;—to be absorbed in art, and to think only of the most effective mode in which to embody his conceptions. He cannot hold up a corrupt heart or a brainless head, and call it—in anatomical phrase—"a beautiful specimen." He cannot, like Fielding, hunt Human Nature for the mere sport of the thing; nor hide his own feelings in impenetrable reserve, or leave them to be inferred by the reader, as Miss Austen does. He copies faithfully the image painted by any object upon the retina of his imagination; but he transcribes not less minutely the emotions of his own heart. Every incident which he relates leads to some utterance of his feelings. His tone changes with the theme. His irony often reminds us of Fielding's, but it is never, like Fielding's, sustained throughout the work. From playful banter, he falls into a strain of melancholy reflection, or rises to stormy invective, and withering scorn. His works make us as well acquainted with his opinions and character as if each were a chapter of his autobiography. Hence it is that the critics have had so much to say about Thackeray's "views of life;" hence their wise admonitions that he should alter those views, that he should see the world's affairs in a more cheerful light,—in other words, that he should dance when he is inclined to weep, and, in short, be a different man from what Nature and the Fates have made him.

In *range* of observation, Thackeray is certainly unrivalled by any other novelist. Miss Austen's sphere, as we have already said, is an extremely limited one. Fielding is a literary vagrant, who meets indeed in his rambles with a great variety of characters, but seldom stays long enough amongst any respectable or stationary portion of society to become thoroughly acquainted with its usages. But Thackeray is familiar with the customs of every class. *Vanity Fair* is not a "fashionable novel," and yet in what other work shall we find so truthful a picture of what is called "high life"? As for *Pendennis*, the book should have been entitled *London*. It should be read with a map of the great metropolis spread out upon the table. The out-door and in-door life of the West-End, of the Inns of Court, and of Paternoster Row, are all represented with wonderful spirit and accuracy. In the *Book of Snobs*, Thackeray traces the vein of vulgarity and meanness through all the strata of English society. Never was satire so keen and unflinching. It is the boldest book ever written by a man who had no personal pique to gratify. We are not surprised that the author of it should have been blackballed at the clubs; the wonder rather is, that the doors of private mansions do not "grate harsh thunder" when he stands before them, and that "Jeames" does not positively refuse to take up his name. That private hospitality should have been so freely extended to him during his visit to this country, is a matter of less surprise; for it is a peculiarity of the American people, arising doubtless from the strength of its patriotic feelings, that, while we cannot bear even the softest touch upon any sore spot in our national character, we are so

far from any desire to conceal our individual foibles, that we thrust them, as it were, with artless unconcern, into the face of every observer. As long as Thackeray was pledged, therefore, not to write a book upon the country, he was at liberty to enrich his experience by an ample survey of our domestic manners. Yet there is much in his appearance and in his character to disarm the fears of even a sensitive mind. We forget the keenness of his mental eye, when we perceive that his bodily vision is imperfect without the aid of spectacles. His wisdom seems no longer premature or alarming, when we observe the venerable complexion of his hair. His language may be stern and severe, but his voice, soft and pleasant, is incapable of giving due expression to any but kindly sentiments. And in revenge of an intellect so powerful and scrutinizing, Nature has given him a warm and generous heart, that will not suffer him, like other satirists, to poison the arrows which he sends with such unerring aim.

MARGARET OLIPHANT
From "Mr. Thackeray and His Novels"

Blackwood's Edinburgh Magazine, January 1855, pp. 88–96

Future generations will speak of Dickens and Thackeray as we speak of Pepys and Evelyn, and they are quite as dissimilar; but if aught of evil should befall the regnant sovereign of this realm of fancy, we will have a civil war forthwith to decide which of these pretenders shall mount the vacant throne. In the mean time, it is premature to agitate the question; there is no just ground of comparison between these two whose names are so commonly pronounced together. Perhaps there are no two men among their host of readers who are further apart from each other than Mr Dickens and Mr Thackeray; but instead of unnecessarily enlarging upon the difference, we count it better wisdom to take up this pretty pink volume, patiently waiting the conclusion of a rambling preamble, to remind us, that it has nothing to do with Mr Dickens, but in every page of it is solely Mr Thackeray's own.

And the *Rose and the Ring* is not a political satire, though one of its princes is of Crim Tartary; and we are afraid that those who look for one of Mr Thackeray's wicked and witty comments upon the world in general, will be disappointed in this book. He is not in the vein of teaching either; his Christmas carol does not treat of a magical dream and a wonderful transformation, like some other Christmas carols of our acquaintance. Thanks to Mr Thackeray, this fairy tale is a pure flash of mirth and laughter, and knows no moral. The little children and the great children may venture for once to enjoy their sport in peace, without being called upon to square up into a row with humility and receive their lesson at the end. There are two princes, and two princesses, and two fairy gifts, endowing the fortunate possessors with unlimited beauty and loveableness; and, like a skilful artist, after a few complications, Mr Thackeray contrives to bestow those fairy tokens upon the two poor souls who require to be attracted to one another, and leaves the true lovers to the inalienable glamour of their love. If Angelica loses her rose, or Bulbo his ring, the domestic happiness of this royal pair is not greatly to be calculated upon; and the public peace of the realms of Paflagonia and Crim Tartary may very possibly be disturbed once more; but magnanimous Giglio deprives *his* queen of the enchanted jewel with his own hand, and finds her quite as lovely without its magical influence;—and so Mr Thackeray, who is by no means apt to rhapsodise on this subject, makes a very seemly obeisance to True Love, the oldest of all the witchcrafts. We will not do our readers the injustice to tell them at second-hand how poor little Betsinda danced before their majesties in her one shoe—or how, by means of this little slipper, the persecuted Rosalba attained to her throne—or of Prince Giglio's infatuation with the grim old Countess Gruffanuff—or the magical bag which supplied him with everything he wanted, from blacking for his boots to armour for his battle;—but we have no doubt that everybody who has not read the *Rose and the Ring*, will be satisfied to know that Mr Thackeray dispenses poetic justice with an unfaltering hand—that the exile has his own again—and that the usurpers are sent upon their travels. We will not pause to point out the catastrophe of Gruffanuff, and the lesson it impresses upon the brethren of that unfortunate servitor; but we will promise the fireside circle, which has the *Rose and the Ring* read aloud for its general edification, one hearty laugh at the great and unlooked-for discomfiture of the Countess Gruffanuff.

We are bound to say, that while Mr Thackeray has been disporting himself among the family of Newcomes, Mr Michael Angelo Titmarsh, in his episodical existence, has made great use of his time since his last appearance before the Christmas-keeping public. Mr Titmarsh may rest assured that no thunder will sour the beer which has so little acid in it by nature. The fairy Blackstick is a much more agreeable presiding genius than Lady Kicklebury; and Mr Titmarsh has never before produced so pleasant a picture-book, nor one whose pictures were so worthy of the text. These illustrations are greatly superior to all their predecessors by the same hand; they are so good that the artist is fairly entitled to rank with the author in this pleasant production; and altogether, amidst our wars and our troubles, in this Christmas which is darkened and shadowed over to so many households, and at a time when common tribulation and anxiety put us in charity with all our neighbours, we are glad that we have to thank Mr Thackeray for the honest laugh which is not at any one's expense.

Mr Thackeray, in his own proper person, has not made less progress in kindness and good humour than has his *alter ego*, if we trace his course from *Vanity Fair* to the *Newcomes*. Everybody praises Becky Sharp, and the history in which she fills so important a place. Does everybody like that clever, unbelieving, disagreeable book? But there is nothing to be said on the subject of *Vanity Fair*, which has not been said already—that all its rogues are clever and amusing, and all its good characters fools—that Amelia is a greater libel upon womankind than Becky herself, and that there is a heated crowded atmosphere in the story which has scarcely any relief, seeing that the good people are by no means a match for the bad, and cannot even pretend to balance the heavy scale of evil. There is no one in the book who has the remotest claim to our affection but Dobbin—good Dobbin, with his faithful heart and his splay feet. Why should the Major have splay feet, Mr Thackeray? Must the man who is not distinguished by moral obliquity have some physical misfortune to make amends? But the splay feet carry their owner into the heart of our regard, despite their unloveliness. The warmest admirer of Miss Rebecca Sharp is not moved to bestow his affection upon that amiable young lady; and though poor, little, silly Amelia may chance to touch a heart for a moment as she watches in Russell Square for a glimpse of her boy, she is quite too insignificant a person to insure any regard for herself. Mr Thackeray made a very clever book; and Mr Thackeray's book made a great sensation and success. There are many admirable things in it—a great sparkle of sayings and happy turns of expression; and the scenes are cut sharp and clear in their

outline, and dullness is not within these pages. Nevertheless, we carry but one personage with us in real kindness when we close the volume. Of all its men and women, only Major Dobbin is worth the least morsel of love.

In Mr Thackeray's second grand exposition of his own principles, and of the human panorama of which he is a spectator and historian—in *Pendennis*—we find a little more to commend. There is Warrington, who has no splay feet; there is sweet Mrs Pendennis, whom we consent to accept as an angel. It is a sad thing to think of Warrington, such a man as he is, spending his life in those chambers in Lamb Court, with nothing to do but to write articles, the fate of which he cares nothing for, only the Haunt to solace that great heart of his when the day's work is done, and no particular motive for living except the custom and habit of it. Few can paint a wasted life, and great powers wearing down with the continual dropping of every day, better than Mr Thackeray; but we are glad to think that he has still the means of rescue for this character in the exhaustless resources of fiction. Will not Mr Thackeray take into his gracious consideration ways and means for disposing of the graceless unknown Mrs Warrington, and leave Bluebeard free to make his fortune once more? We will answer for the entire satisfaction of the general population of these British Islands with any proceeding of the kind; and we do not doubt that Mr Warrington, when he is a free man, will find some one more faithful than Laura, and will not be forsaken a second time for such a coxcomb as Pen. Pendennis himself, though he is good-looking and fashionable, and writes a successful novel, is but a very poor fellow after all—not only falling far short of an ideal hero, but not much to brag of for a very ordinary man. Mr Thackeray avowedly scorns the loftiness of common romance, and will not have an exalted personage for the principal figure on his canvass; but Mr Arthur Pendennis does not possess a single feature of the heroic. Unfortunately, when we ought to admire, we are a great deal more likely to despise; and this, though it may be original, is neither true art nor noble; it is not original either; but Mr Pen is a meaner sinner than Tom Jones.

Leaving Pen—and leaving Laura, who is a very doubtful person, and whom we do not profess to make much of—if Pen is not the best husband in the world, popular opinion, we are afraid, will pronounce that popular sentence, "Served her right!"—there is much more satisfaction in meeting with Harry Foker, who is Mr Thackeray's special property, the type of a class which our novelist has brought out of the shadows into the clearest and kindliest illumination. Good Harry Foker, who has no great share of brains—who does not spell very well, perhaps—whose habits are not what they ought to be, but who is the soul of honour, of unpretending simple courage and kind-heartedness. Some score of Harry Fokers, doing, with simple straightforwardness, what their commander ordered, have ridden with open eyes, and without a moment's faltering, right into the open-mouthed destruction, and made heroes of themselves upon the wintry heights of Sebastopol. Not a refined gentleman by any means, it is only genius that can commend this brave good-hearted simpleton to all our affections. A lesser artist might have been afraid of a character so little intellectual, and felt its defective points a reproach to his invention; but Mr Thackeray has been able to seize upon the genuine sparkle of this uncut jewel, upon the reverence for goodness, the humble self-estimation, the tender-heartedness, and the unsuspected pathos which lie in its depths. It is strange, when he has proved himself so capable of its exercise, that Mr Thackeray should so much overlook this true alchemy of genius. Is it best to drag the veil of decorum from a hidden evil, or to disclose a vein of native excellence—a secret even to its owner? Mr Thackeray, who scares his innocent readers with vague intimation of pitfalls round about them, and shocks mamma with terrific hints of the unmentionable ill-doing familiar to the thoughts of her pretty boy at school, does better service when Harry Foker, and Jack Belsize, and even Rawdon Crawley, show their honest hearts to us, than when he produces Mr Pendennis, with all his gifts, as a specimen of modern education, and the civilisation of the nineteenth century. What a simple noble gentleman is Lord Kew, who rises just above the strata of the Belsize formation! Such a hero as he is would leave us little to desire.

Only in one respect does *Pendennis* sin more grossly than *Vanity Fair*. Blanche Amory is more detestable, because she is less clever than Becky. How much does Mr Thackeray owe to the world of womankind, by way of reparation for foisting into their ranks such a creation as this! Nothing less than a Desdemona can atone for such an insult. Can Mr Thackeray make a Desdemona? He has added some few pleasant people to our acquaintance in his day—Warrington may make amends for Pen, but who is to make amends for Blanche?

And here we touch upon our author's greatest imperfection. Mr Thackeray does not seem acquainted with anything feminine between a nursery-maid and a fine lady—an indiscriminate idolater of little children, and an angler for a rich husband. The "perfect woman, nobly planned," has no place in the sphere of Mr Thackeray's fancy. Perhaps the secret of this may be, that Mr Thackeray's world is a conventional world; and that even while he attacks its weak points, "society," the sphere with which he is best acquainted, represents this many-sided globe in our historian's eyes. The mother and the cousin in the little country-house, weeping and adoring as they read the hero's letters, telling each other of his childhood, those blessed days when Pen was in petticoats, seeing in all this heaven and earth only the bit of consecrated soil under his shadow and the sky over his head, and furious at every other pretender for his gracious favour—that is one side of the picture. On the other is Miss Amory, with that bad leer in her eyes, which we are rejoiced to see has disappeared from the sketches of Mr Michael Angelo Titmarsh, calculating her chances of a husband, amusing Mr Pen into that last resource of idleness—falling in love; weeping "Mes Larmes" in public, and in private cuffing her little brother; and Blanche is the other side of the golden shield, the obverse of the coin, the completion of Mr Thackeray's circle of female character. It is not a flattering estimate of Englishwomen which will be formed from the pages of this author, whom, of all others, we should fancy our neighbours over the Channel most likely to form their judgment from. Though Blanche has expanded into Beatrice, and Beatrice progressed to Ethel, the character is still far from satisfactory. And we must once more assure Mr Thackeray, that he owes his countrywomen an Isabella or a Desdemona to make amends.

In the one other creation of *Pendennis*, Mr Thackeray puts forth all his power. The Major rescues *his* class still more clearly out of the shadows than Harry Foker does; henceforward, instead of wordy descriptions of this old gentleman of the clubs, it will be quite enough to say that he is like Major Pendennis. This impersonation is so broad and clear that there is no mistaking it or its identity. There are certain portraits which convince us that they are admirable likenesses, though we are perfectly unacquainted with the original; and even those to whom "society" is an unknown country, must recognise, as an unmistakable individual, this specimen of the aborigines of "the world." Getting on in "society" is the chief end of man to

Major Pendennis—it is the grand vocation and duty of life. You must be moderately good, moderately brave and honourable, because the want of these qualities is apt to endanger your success in life; and with all the perseverance and ardour which wins battles or makes fortunes, the Major devotes himself to securing an invitation to Gaunt House, or a gracious recognition from the Marquis of Steyn. It would be a pure waste of sympathy, in author or readers, to condole with the loveless, joyless condition of this old man of fashion. Loves and joys are out of the Major's way—they would simply embarrass and annoy him, these troublesome emotions; the Major has his pleasures instead; and his place in society, which he fills in a manner perfectly becoming the high end he has in view.

When we leave *Pendennis*, we find that Mr Thackeray takes a great leap out of his ordinary domain. It is no longer the English of the present day, careless and easy, just touched with the slang for which our author has a special gift, but it is English of the Augustan age, English which is balanced with antithesis, and polished into epigram, the English of those dainty people who wore bag-wigs and ruffles, patches and powder. Though we have serious fault to find with the story of Esmond, we are constrained to admit, at the outset, that the execution of this story is exquisite. In comparison with this, almost every other historical work we are acquainted with, except the romances of Scott, is a mere piece of masquerade. The age is not a great age, we confess, in spite of its Blenheim and its Ramilies, its Steele and its Addison; but such as it is, we have it here, a picture which is not merely paint, but is about the best example of absolute reproduction which our literature possesses. Nothing can be more real or touching—more like a veritable page of biography, if biographers were usually endowed with such a style as Mr Thackeray confers upon Harry Esmond—than the story of the solitary boy at Castlewood, his patrons and his teachers. The picture is perfect in its truth to nature, which is universal, and to manners, which are limited and transitory. Harry Esmond is not a boy of Queen Victoria's time, in the little cavalier's suit proper to Queen Anne's—he is not in advance of his age, nor has any consciousness of Waterloo dimming the glory of Blenheim. We never find ourselves deceived in him through all his history—the mask does not slip aside for a moment to show a modern face underneath. This book is a marvellous historical picture; in this point of view it is an unrivalled performance, and worthy of all the plaudits which a work, attended by so many difficulties, has a right to claim.

Nevertheless, with so much in its favour, this admirable production carries failure in it as a story, as a piece of human life represented for the sympathy of all humanity—our most sacred sentiments are outraged, and our best prejudices shocked by the leading feature of this tale. It is not only that Lady Castlewood is the confidant of the hero's passionate love for her daughter, yet compensates his disappointment in that quarter with her own hand—but it is the intolerable idea that this woman, who is pure as an angel, and as severe in her judgment of the backsliding as a pure woman may be—a wife—and, still more, a mother, defended by the spotless love of little children—nevertheless cherishes for years a secret attachment to the boy to whom she gives the protection of her roof! This error is monstrous and unredeemable. If we do not count it among the affronts which Mr Thackeray puts upon his countrywomen, it is because it is too gross an error to look like truth; but it is not less disagreeable on this score. Mr Thackeray has spent all his pains to make this character a loveable and womanly one, and Rachel, Lady Castlewood, is a very "sweet" person we confess, and would be worthy the idolatry of her historian but for this unaccountable blunder. The Love of the poets is young for a necessity. If it is fashionable to have a hero of discreet years, it requires nothing less than a long, constant, single attachment to make a heroine of middle age in any respect tolerable. A woman who loves two men must always condescend to a little derogation from her primal dignity—and the woman who contracts two marriages must be excused, in romance, by either a forced match, in the first instance, or the saddest and completest disappointment. In any way it is degradation to the heroine of our fancy—but Mr Thackeray must thrust *his* lady still further down. What had Lady Castlewood done that she should be compelled to fall in love with Harry Esmond, her daughter's adorer, her husband's faithful attendant, her own devoted and respectful son?

The hero himself is a hero in the proper acceptation of the word. It is not the faulty modern young gentleman any longer, but the antique ideal which Mr Thackeray has resorted to, in consent, perhaps reluctant, but certainly complete, to the old canons of his art. Harry Esmond has all the generosity, all the unselfishness, all the unrewarded and unappreciated virtues of genuine romance. When your hero is an ordinary sinner, it is possible to make him a more distinct personage than your ideal excellence can be—so that Esmond does not always stand quite clear from his background, and has not perhaps such a crisp sharp outline as Mr Arthur Pendennis. To make up for this, there is rather more distinctness than is desirable in the character of Beatrice. This bold, unscrupulous, and daring beauty, in whom the passion for admiration and the delight of conquest seem to possess the full power of passions more gross in their nature, is another of Mr Thackeray's special belongings. Her triumph in her own dazzling charms, and the mischief they make everywhere—the impetus with which her magnificent vanity carries her on—the trickery to which she stoops, and the intrigues into which she enters—never because her own heart is interested, but solely from an insatiable longing to madden every one about her—are combined with a singular power. This splendid creature not only obeys her natural impulse to destroy, but glories in the havoc she makes, and goes forth to new conquests in exulting power over the graves of her victims. For the good of humanity, we may venture to hope that, except within the pages of *Esmond*, the world knows few Beatrices; but it is impossible to deny the power and strength with which this cruel syren is drawn.

And what shall we say to Ethel Newcome? Ethel is not Beatrice, yet she is little better than a proper nineteenth century development of that all-conquering beauty. For our own part, we confess to being in the most perfect bewilderment as to the conclusion of the loves of these cousins, whose fate Mr Thackeray has yet to seal. Though the Bumbelcund bank confers a fortune on Clive, will it confer upon Ethel suitable dispositions to make the young gentleman happy? or is it consistent with the dignity of Mr Clive Newcome to be accepted as a *pis aller*? or must Clive marry Rosey after all, and sink down into humdrum domestic happiness, and leave the brilliant star for which he sighed to sparkle into a still brighter firmament, or to shoot and fall into the unfathomable darkness which swallowed Beatrice? We flatter ourselves that, in twenty years' experience of novel-reading, we have attained to as clear a prescience of a *denouement* as most people; but Mr Thackeray, with his tantalising interviews, and all his hints of the future, puzzles and outwits our ordinary penetration. While the conclusion is not as yet, and everything is possible, we do not even find ourselves in a position to advise Mr Thackeray; we can but assure him honestly, that we see no outlet for him, though we expect he is to make himself a

brilliant one. If Clive marries Ethel, how shall we vindicate the dignity of these young people, who cannot marry each other without a mutual sacrifice of pride and propriety; and if Clive marries Rosey, alas for Clive! Solemnly assuring Mr Thackeray of this dilemma, we leave him to make the best of it, only warning him of a storm of universal dissatisfaction if Clive marries no one at all—a miserable expedient, to which, we fear, *we* should be driven were the conclusion of the *Newcomes* left to our inventive powers.

There is no book of Mr Thackeray which is so worthy of a great reputation as this uncompleted story. As full of character as its predecessors, it redeems their errors gallantly; and we could almost fancy that, in the scorn of genius for that accusation which pronounced him unable to manage the ideal, Mr Thackeray has showered a glory of manliness and goodness upon the inhabitants of this little world. There has never been a nobler sketch than that of the Colonel. The innocent heart and simple honour of this old man, and his horror of all falsehood and impurity, are enough to cover a multitude of Mr Thackeray's sins. We can understand how every individual worth caring for in the story or out of it rejoices to gain the acquaintance of Thomas Newcome. We are grateful to Lady Anne, and like her ever after, for her true apprehension of our Colonel's courtly manners, and old-fashioned chivalrous politeness. We are as ready to adopt him into our heart as Mr Pendennis and Mr Warrington can be; and Ethel herself gains an additional attraction when we see her beautiful eyes shining with pride for her noble old uncle. The key-note of the story is struck high and sweet in this character, which is at once so lofty and so childlike; and we cannot pass it by without once more admiring Mr Thackeray's skill in the retrospective story—the record of Thomas Newcome's misfortunes and troubles in his boyhood, which is almost as well done as the corresponding period in the history of Henry Esmond.

It is not easy to thread at a glance the lively maze of Mr Thackeray's story—to tell how pretty Ethel is engaged to Lord Kew by family arrangement, and how the young lady filches a green ticket from the Suffolk Street Gallery, with Sold upon it, and comes down to dinner wearing this label, like a wilful and rebellious young lady as she is; nor how good Colonel Newcome, whose great ambition it was to marry Clive to Ethel, and be a happy man in his old age, is balked by this engagement, and goes away sadly to India, to grow rich, if he can, for his dear boy's sake; how Clive is a painter, and varies between ostentation of his art and the least morsel of shame for being engaged in it; how he makes a brave effort, and tears himself away from Ethel, and has almost got the better of his passion; how, of a sudden, the spirit of his dream is changed by hearing that Lord Kew and Ethel have broken off their engagement, at the first intimation of which poor young Clive finds out that he has not forgotten her, and comes home post-haste to try his hopeless chance once more; how there is a most noble Marquis of Ferintosh in the field before him; how the hero and the heroine have little sparring-matches of courtship, but never come any nearer a conclusion; and how last month brings us to the climax of a farewell, which we, for our own part, have no faith in. Ethel Newcome, like Beatrice, is sometimes intoxicated with her own beauty, and the applauses it brings—sometimes carried off her balance with the *afflatus* of conquest and victory; but Ethel, we are glad to say, is much improved from her forerunner, and is a much less hopeless character than the beautiful tormentor of Harry Esmond. Is Ethel to consume what remnants are left to her of that fresh girl's heart she had when we first knew her—when she first fell in love with her good uncle—and be a great lady, and blaze her youthful days away in barren splendour? She likes being a great lady, you perceive—such a being was not born for love in a cottage, or for Clive's five hundred a-year, and odd position. Has Mr Thackeray prepared this beautiful victim for Moloch, or is there hope for Ethel still? The oracle preserves inexorable silence, and smiles upon our queries. We are quite as curious as you are, young lady; but we venture to predict that Miss Ethel Newcome, even though Mr Thackeray may have compunctions on her behalf, can never "settle down" to romantic happiness. She will have to fulfil her destiny, and marry a most noble marquis. She is surely not for Clive the painter, whether he is to be made a Crœsus or a beggar, by means of the Bumbelcund Bank.

Clive himself, the handsome, dashing open-hearted young fellow, is an admirable hero. He is not called upon for feats of extraordinary generosity or self-sacrifice. His circumstances do not require Clive to take upon himself other people's burdens, or other people's penalties. He has only to enjoy himself, to paint when he pleases, and when he does not please, to draw his father's remittances, and look handsome, and be as happy as he can. There is no great demand made upon Clive's goodness throughout the story; yet we are quite content with him, and willing to believe that he will be equal to an emergency when it comes. We cannot refrain from making one quotation to illustrate the character of Clive, and the quality which, of all other qualities, Mr Thackeray expounds best. Clive is talking to his father:—

"At Newcome, when they go on about the Newcomes, and that great ass, Barnes Newcome, gives himself his airs, I am ready to die of laughing. That time I went down to Newcome, I went to see old Aunt Sarah, and she told me everything, and showed me the room where my grandfather—you know; and do you know, I was a little hurt at first, for I thought we were swells till then. And when I came back to school, where, perhaps, I had been giving myself airs, and bragging about Newcome, why, you know, I thought it was right to tell the fellows."

"That's a man," said the Colonel with delight; though, had he said, "That's a boy," he had spoken more correctly.

This is a very delicate touch, and shows the hand of a master. Mr Thackeray's young hero, who is so honest and truthful in his boyish days, does not degenerate as he grows a man.

Lord Kew, too, simple, noble, and manful, is a further example of Mr Thackeray's most felicitous vein. These young men, who have no great intellectual elevation, and whose rank only makes them perfectly humble, unpretending, and free of all temptations to exaggerate themselves, seem characters on whom our author dwells *con amore*. Then there is the Vicomte de Florac, with his amusing French English, and his middle-aged princess, and that witch and malignant fairy, old Lady Kew, and Barnes Newcome the disagreeable, and the various family circles of this most respectable kindred, with all their nicely-touched gradations of character. There is no mist in this book; every one is an individual, pleasant or otherwise, and detaches himself or herself clearly from the background. The story is not in very good order, broken up as it is by retrospections and anticipations; and it is not good taste of Mr Pendennis to appear so frequently before the curtain, and remind us unpleasantly that it is fiction we are attending to, and not reality; but we think the great mass of his readers will bear us out in our opinion, that the *Newcomes* is not only the

most agreeable story, but the cleverest book which Mr Thackeray has yet contributed for the amusement and edification of the admiring public.

When all this is said, there still remains a great deal to say which is less complimentary to our novelist. It is not, perhaps, the most agreeable information in the world to understand that our innocent schoolboys must plunge into a very equivocal abyss of "pleasure," before they can come forth purged and renovated like Lord Kew. We are not very glad to hear that somebody could make revelations to us of our brothers and sons and fathers, such as the Duchesse d'Ivry did to Miss Ethel Newcome. We cannot acknowledge that between the innocence of youth and the goodness of matured life, there lies a land of darkness through which every man must pass; nor do we perceive the advantage of convincing Mr Thackeray's youthful audience that this is a necessity. The religious circles of our community have of late very much devoted themselves to that class of "young men" for whom so many lectures, and sermons, and "means of improvement," are provided. We are not quite sure of the wisdom of thus making into a class the exuberant young life, which is, in fact, the world. When boys have ceased to be boys, they become human creatures of the highest order of existence. It is no compliment to their discernment to prepare for them mental food which is not suitable for their fathers or their teachers. They are men, with a larger inheritance of hope than their seniors; but their pride is not to be piqued into rebellion, by thrusting them into a half-way position between the man and the boy. But Mr Thackeray has a natural vocation in respect to his youthful countrymen. If he should happen, in fact, to be a grandfather, in disposition he is a young man continually—it is the life and pursuits of young men in which he is most skilled. Manliness, truthfulness, honour, and courage, are the qualities which he celebrates; and though Mr Thackeray is a favourite in countless households, it is not to be disputed that his stronghold is among those whose portraits he draws so truthfully, and whose life he describes with so much zest. Now here is scope and verge enough for any amount of genius; but surely it is not advisable that our teacher should lead his pupils to great harm on the way to great good. Is not that the loftiest purity which does not find it needful to fall?

We are afraid Mr Thackeray is beyond the reach of advice in respect to his female characters. Ethel is very attractive, very brilliant; but we would rather not have our daughters resemble this young lady, it must be confessed; and poor pretty Rosey, with all her goodness, is nobody, and Mr Thackeray intends that she should be so. If this is not good morals, it is still less good art. Providence has exempted woman from the grosser temptations, and romance has gifted her with a more ethereal life. If we do not bid Mr Thackeray create a woman of the highest order, or if we are doubtful of his capacity for this delicate formation, we may still beg him to add a little common-sense to his feminine goodness. When these tender pretty fools are rational creatures, the world of Mr Thackeray's imagination will have a better atmosphere; for besides marrying, and contriving opportunities to give in marriage, besides the nursery and its necessities, there are certain uses for womankind in this world of ours, and we are not so rich in good influences as to forfeit any of them. A coronet is certainly not an idol the worship of which gives much elevation to the spirits of its adorers; but when Lord Kew is so little ostentatious of his decoration, why should Ethel, and her friends for her, compass heaven and earth to obtain such another? Does not Mr Thackeray think this is too hackneyed a subject for his fresh and unexhausted invention? Might not the next Ethel do something better by way of novelty, and leave this field to Mrs Gore and Mrs Trollope, and the host of lesser ladies who devote their talents to the noble art of making matches?

We are not sure how far the English language will be benefited by the dialogues of Mr Thackeray; they are very clever, very entertaining, and their slang is admirable; but it is very doubtful if it will be an advantage to make these Islands no better than a broad margin for the witticisms and the dialect of Cockaigne. Our light literature begins to have a great savour of the Cockney in it. Our noble ally on the other side of the Channel does not seem so much the better of making Paris France, that we should repeat the experiment. London is the greatest town in existence, but it is not England, though the dialect of its many vagabonds seems in a fair way for becoming the classic English of our generation. Mr Thackeray's narrative is so pure and vigorous in its language, and his colloquial freedoms are so lively and entertaining, that there are no real exceptions to be taken to him; but every Thackeray and every Dickens has a host of imitators, and it is not an agreeable prospect to contemplate the English of Shakespeare and Bacon overwhelmed with a flood of Cockneyisms—a consummation which seems to approach more nearly every day.

Mr Thackeray is no poet; for one of the highest of the poet's vocations, and perhaps the noblest work of which genius is capable, is to embody the purest ideal soul in the most life-like human garments; and this is an effort which our author has not yet attempted. Perhaps the title which Mr Thackeray would rather choose for himself would be that of an historian of human nature. In his sphere he is so eminently. Human nature in its company dress, and with all its foibles on, is the subject he delights to treat of; but Mr Thackeray is not great in home scenes, where the conventional dress is off, and the good that is in a man expands under the cheerful glow of the domestic fire. Mr Thackeray does not drape his hero in the purple, or make pictures of him as he walks loftily among suffering men; but takes him to pieces with wicked mirth, calling upon all men to laugh with him at the idol's demolition. We are no advocates for idol or for hero worship; but when we remember that there was once in this world a Man who was at once divine and human, whom we are all encouraged to make our example, and following whose wonderful footsteps some have attained to a life grander than that of common humanity, we feel that the highest ideal of the poets is but a fit and seemly acknowledgment of the excellence which has been made possible to our favoured race; and that the circle of life and manners is not complete, till we have admitted into it the loftiest as well as the lowest example of human existence—the saint no less than the sinner.

DAVID MASSON
From "Thackeray"
Macmillan's Magazine, February 1864, pp. 363–68

Thackeray's special place in British literature is that of a star of the first magnitude, but of a colour and mode of brilliancy peculiarly its own, in the composite cluster known as our Novelists, our Humourists, our Imaginative Prose-writers. As this is, however, a very numerous cluster, including writers of all degrees of importance, from the smallest up to some so great that we rank them among the chiefs of our total literature, and are not afraid to cite them as our British equivalents to such names of a larger world as Cervantes, Rabelais, and Jean Paul, so there are many ways in which, on our examining the cluster, it will resolve itself into groups. More especially, there is one way of looking at this large order of writers, according to which they shall seem to part, not so much into groups as into two great divisions, each including names of all degrees of magnitude. Now, although, if we view the cluster entire, without seeking to resolve it at all, Thackeray will strike us simply by his superior magnitude, and although, on the other hand, however minutely we may analyse the cluster, we shall find none precisely like Thackeray, and he will continue to strike us still by his intense peculiarity of hue, yet, if we do persuade ourselves to attend to such a general subdivision of the cluster into two main classes as has been hinted at, Thackeray will then, on the whole, seem to range himself rather with one of the classes than with the other.

While all writers of fiction make it their business to invent stories, and by the presentation of imaginary scenes, imaginary actions, and imaginary characters, to impart to the minds of their fellows a more prompt, rousing, and impassioned kind of pleasure than attends the reading either of speculative disquisitions or of laborious reproductions of real history, and while most of them, in doing so, strew a thousand incidental opinions and fancies by the way, and deviate into delightful and humorous whimsies, a considerable number of such writers are found to differ from the rest in respect of the constant presence in their fictions of a certain heart of doctrine, the constant ruling of their imaginations by a personal philosophy or mode of thinking. It is not always in the fictions of those novelists respecting whom we may know independently that they were themselves men of substantial and distinct moral configuration, of decided ways of thinking and acting, that we find this characteristic. Scott is an instance. He was a man of very solid and distinct personality; and yet, at the outset of his fictions, we see him always, as it were, putting on a dreaming-cap, which transports him away into realms far removed from his own personal position and experience, and from the direct operation of his own moralities. And so with others. When they begin to invent, they put on the dreaming-cap; and many cases might be cited in which this extraordinary power of the dreaming-cap might appear to have been all that the writers possessed—in which, apart from it, they might seem to have had no substantial personality at all. Whether Shakespeare, the greatest genius of the dreaming-cap that ever lived, had any coequal personality himself, of the features of which a glimpse is now recoverable, is, as all know, one of the vexed questions of literary history. We have an opinion of our own on this matter. In every case, we hold, there is an unseverable relation between the personality and the poetic genius, between what a man is and what he can imagine. Dreams themselves are fantastic constructions out of the *débris* of all the sensations, thoughts, feelings, and experiences, remembered or not remembered, of the waking-life; all that any power of the dreaming-cap, however extraordinary, can do, is to remove one into remoter wastes of the great plain of forgetfulness whereon this *débris* lies shimmering, and to release one more and more from the rule of the waking will or the waking reason in the fantasies that rise from it, and flit and melt into each other. Yet, just as some dreams are closer in their resemblance to waking tissues of thought, and more regulated by the logic of waking reason, than others, so, though in all cases the imaginations of a writer, the creations of his literary genius, are related by absolute necessity to his personal individuality, there are many cases in which the relation is so much more subtle and occult than in others, that we find it convenient in these cases to suppose it non-existing, and to think of the imagination as a kind of special white-winged faculty that can float off at any moment from its poise on the personality, move to any distance whithersoever it listeth, and return again at its own sweet will. Hence, for example, among our writers of prose-fiction, we distinguish such a writer as Scott from such a writer as Swift. The connexion, in Swift's case, between his fictions and his personal philosophy and mode of thought is direct and obvious. In his inventions and fancies he does not move away from himself; he remains where he is, in his fixed and awful habit of mind—expressing that habit or its successive moods in constructions fantastic in form, but of regulated and calculated meaning, and capable at once of exact interpretation. Even his Islands of Lilliput and Brobdingnag, his Laputa, and his country of the Houynhmns and Yahoos, are not so much visions into which he has been carried by any power of the dreaming-cap, as fell Swiftian allegories of the stationary intellect. And, though Swift is almost unique among British writers in respect of the degree to which he thus made imagination a kind of architect-contractor for fixed moods of the reason, he may yet stand as, in this respect, an exaggerated exemplar of a whole class of our writers of fiction. In other words, as has been already said, there is a class of our writers of prose-fiction, including writers of as great total power as are to be found in the class that arrive at their fancies by means of the dreaming-cap, but differing from that class by the presence in their fictions of a more constant element of doctrine, a more distinct vein of personal philosophy.

Thackeray was, on the whole, of the latter class. That he may be considered as belonging to it is one reason the more for maintaining its co-ordinate importance with the other class, and for not giving that other class, as has sometimes been proposed, a theoretical superiority as being more entitled, in virtue of their power with the dreaming-cap, to the high designation of creative or imaginative writers. One reason the more, we say—for might it not have been recollected that even Goethe, whose range of dream was as wide as that of most men, made his imagination but a kind of architect-contractor for his reason in his great prose-novel, and that, if we rank among our highest British artists a Sir Joshua Reynolds, we do not put our Hogarth beneath him? A creative writer! Who shall say that Thackeray did not give us creations? What reader of these pages, at all events, will say it, after his memory has been refreshed by our contributor with those recollections of a few of the wondrous creations that took flight from the single novel of *Vanity Fair* into that vast population of ideal beings of diverse characters and physiognomies with which the genius of imaginative writers has filled the ether of the real world? Nay, on the question whether Thackeray *should* be so decidedly attached to the class of writers of fiction with which at first sight we associate him, there may be some preliminary hesitation. In his smaller pieces, for example—some of his odd whims and absurdities in prose and verse—did he not break away into a riot of humour, a lawlessness of sheer zanyism, as exquisitely suggestive of genius making faces at its keeper as anything we have seen since Shakespeare's clowns walked the earth and sang those jumbled shreds of sense and nonsense which we love now as so keenly Shakespearian, and would not lose for the world? The dreaming-cap!—why, here we have the dreaming-cap, and bells attached to it. He moves to any distance out of sight, and still, by the tinkle, we can follow him and hear "the fool i' the forest." We are not sure but that in some of these small grotesques of Thackeray we have relics of a wilder variety of pure genius than in his more elaborate fictions. But, again, even in some of these larger and more continuous constructions of his genius in fiction, we have examples of a power which he possessed of going out of

himself, and away from the habits and humours of his own time and circumstances, into tracts where the mere act of producing facsimiles or verisimilitudes of what he had directly seen and known was not sufficient, and he had to move with the stealthy step of a necromancer, recalling visions of a vanished life. When we think, for instance, of his *Esmond*, and of passages in his other novels where he gives play to his imagination in the historic, and assumes so easily a certain quaintness of conception and of phraseology to correspond, we seem even to catch a glimpse of what that marvellous dreaming-power of the so-called creative writers may after all in part consist in—to wit, a wide range of really historic interest in their own waking persons, and a habit of following out their trains of historic speculation and enthusiasm, rather than their passing observations and experiences, in their dreams. Thackeray, at all events, had a remarkable historic faculty within a certain range of time, which it was perhaps owing to the more paying nature of fiction than of history in these days that he did not more expressly use and develop. The Life of Talleyrand, which he once had in contemplation, before the days of his universal celebrity as a novelist, would have been, if done as Thackeray could have done it, a masterpiece of peculiar eighteenth-nineteenth-century biography. Nor is the story, jocularly spread by himself some years ago, that he meant to continue Macaulay's unfinished *History of England*, taking it up at the reign of Queen Anne, without a certain significance. One of the many distinctions among men is as to the portion of the past by which their imaginations are most fondly fascinated and with which they feel themselves most competent to deal in recollection. Macaulay's real and native historic range began where he began his History—in the interval between the Civil Wars and the Revolution of 1688. Thackeray's began a little later—at the date of Queen Anne's accession, and the opening of the eighteenth century. And, as within this range he would have been a good and shrewd historian, so within this range his imagination moves easily and gracefully in fiction. A man of the era of the later Georges by his birth and youth, and wholly of the Victorian era by his maturity and literary activity, he can go as far back as to Queen Anne's reign by that kind of imaginative second-sight which depends on delight in transmitted reminiscence.

As a Victorian, however, taking for the matter of most of his fictions life as he saw it around him, or as he could recollect it during his own much-experienced and variously-travelled career from his childhood upwards, Thackeray *was* one of those novelists whose writings are distinguished by a constant heart of doctrine, a permanent vein of personal philosophy. Our long and now hackneyed talk about him as a Realist, and our habit of contrasting him perpetually with Dickens, as more a novelist of the Fantastic or Romantic School, are recognitions of this. It would ill become us here and now to resort again to the full pedantry of this contrast; but, in a certain sense, as none knew better than Thackeray himself, there *was* a kind of polar opposition between his method and Dickens's in their art as humourists and writers of fiction. With extraordinary keenness of perception, with the eye of a lynx for the facts, physiognomies, and humours of real life, and taking the suggestions of real life with marvellous aptness for his hints, Dickens does move away with these suggestions into a kind of vacant ground of pure fancy, where the relations and the mode of exhibition may be ideal, and there shapes such tales of wonder and drollery, and holds such masques and revels of imaginary beings, as (witness how we use them, and how our talk and our current literature are enriched by references to them) no genius but his has produced in our day. In him we do see, after a fashion entirely his own, that particular kind of power which we have called the power of the dreaming-cap, and which is oftenest named ideality. Thackeray, on the other hand, is sternly, ruthlessly real. Men and women as they are, and the relations of life as he has actually seen and known them, or in as near approach to facsimile of reality as the conditions of invention of stories for general reading will permit—these are what Thackeray insists on giving us. Fortunate age to have had two such representatives of styles of art the co-existence of which—let us not call it mutual opposition—is everlastingly possible and everlastingly desirable! Fortunate still in having the one master-artist left; unfortunate now, as we all feel—and that artist more than most of us—in having lost the other! For in Thackeray we have lost not only our great master of reality in the matter of prose-fiction, but also the spokesman of a strong personal philosophy, a bracing personal mode of thought, which pervaded all he wrote. Thackeray, it has been well said, is best thought of, in some respects, as a sage, a man of experienced wisdom, and a conclusive grasp of the world and its worth, expressing himself, partly by accident, through the particular modes of story-writing and humorous extravaganza. And what was his philosophy? To tell that wholly, to throw into systematic phrase one tithe even of the characteristic and recurring trains of thought that passed through that grave brain, is what no man can hope to do. But the essential philosophy of any mind is often a thing of few and simple words, repeating a form of thought that it requires no elaborate array of propositions to express, and that may have been as familiar to an ancient Chaldæan making his camel's neck his pillow in the desert as it is to a sage in modern London. It is that elementary mode of thought which comes and goes oftenest, and into which one always sinks when one is meditative and alone. And so may we not recognise Thackeray's habitual philosophy in a peculiar variation of these words of the Laureate, which he makes to be spoken by the hero of his "Maud"?—

> We are puppets, Man in his pride, and Beauty fair in
> her flower:
> Do we move ourselves, or are moved by an unseen
> hand at a game
> That pushes us off the board, and others ever
> succeed?
> Ah yet, we cannot be kind to each other here for an
> hour;
> We whisper, and hint, and chuckle, and grin at a
> brother's shame;
> However we brave it out, we men are a little breed.
>
> A monstrous eft was of old the Lord and Master of
> Earth;
> For him did his high sun flame, and his river
> billowing ran,
> And he felt himself in his force to be Nature's
> crowning race.
> As nine months go to the shaping an infant ripe for
> his birth,
> So many a million of ages have gone to the making
> of man:
> He now is the first, but is he the last? is he not too
> base?
>
> The man of science himself is fonder of glory, and
> vain,
> An eye well-practised in nature, a spirit bounded and
> poor;

> The passionate heart of the poet is whirled into folly
> and vice.
> I would not marvel at either, but keep a temperate
> brain;
> For not to desire or admire, if a man could learn it
> were more
> Than to walk all day like the sultan of old in a garden
> of spice.

Such, in some form, though not, perhaps, precisely in this high-rolled and semi-geologic form, was Thackeray's philosophy, breathed through his writings. That we are a little breed—poets, philosophers, and all of us—that is what he told us. Nature's crowning race?—Oh no; too base for that! Many stages beyond the Eft, certainly; but far yet from even the ideal of our own talk and our pretensions to each other. And so he lashed us, and dissected us, and tore off our disguises. He did it in great matters and he did it in small matters; and, that he might draw a distinction between the great matters and the small matters, he generalised the smaller kinds of baseness and littleness of our time, against which he most persistently directed his satires, under the mock-heroic title of Snobbism. Anti-Snobbism was his doctrine as applied to many particulars of our own and of recent times—Victorian or Georgian. But he took a wider range than that, and laid bare the deeper blacknesses and hypocrisies of our fairly-seeming lives. And we called him a cynic in revenge. A cynic! No more will that word be heard about Thackeray. How, in these few weeks since he was laid in Kensal Green, have his secret deeds of goodness, the instances of his incessant benevolence and kindheartedness to all around him, leapt into regretful light. A cynic! We might have known, while we used it, that the word was false. Had he not an eye for the piety and the magnanimity of real human life, its actually attained and incalculable superiorities over the Eft; and did he not exult, to the verge of the sentimental, in reproductions of these in the midst of his descriptions of meannesses? And did he not always, at least, include himself for better or for worse in that breed of men of which the judgment must be so mixed? Not to desire or admire, but to walk all day like a sultan in his garden, was a dignity of isolation to which he had never attained. He did not hold himself aloof. Ah! how he came among us here in London, simply, quietly, grandly, the large-framed, massive-headed, and grey-haired sage that he was—comporting himself as one of us, though he was weightier than all of us; listening to our many-voiced clamour, and dropping in his wise occasional word; nay, not forbidding, but rather joining with a smile, if, in hilarity, we raised his own song of evening festivity:—

> Here let us sport,
> Boys as we sit,
> Laughter and wit
> Flashing so free:
> Life is but short;
> When we are gone,
> Let them sing on
> Round the old tree.

Ah! the old tree remains, and the surviving company still sits round it, and they will raise the song in the coming evenings as in the evenings gone by. But the chair of the sage is vacant. It will be long before London, or the nation, or our literature, shall see a substitute for the noble Thackeray.

W. E. HENLEY
"Thackeray"
Views and Reviews
1890, pp. 10–22

It is odd to note how opinions differ as to the greatness of Thackeray and the value of his books. Some regard him as the greatest novelist of his age and country and as one of the greatest of any country and any age. These hold him to be not less sound a moralist than excellent as a writer, not less magnificently creative than usefully and delightfully cynical, not less powerful and complete a painter of manners than infallible as a social philosopher and incomparable as a lecturer on the human heart. They accept Amelia Sedley for a very woman; they believe in Colonel Newcome—'by *Don Quixote* out of *Little Nell*'—as in something venerable and heroic; they regard William Dobbin and 'Stunning' Warrington as finished and subtle portraitures; they think Becky Sharp an improvement upon Mme. Marneffe and Wenham better work than Rigby; they are in love with Laura Bell, and refuse to see either cruelty or caricature in their poet's presentment of Alcide de Mirobolant. Thackeray's fun, Thackeray's wisdom, Thackeray's knowledge of men and women, Thackeray's morality, Thackeray's view of life, 'his wit and humour, his pathos, and his umbrella,' are all articles of belief with them. Of Dickens they will not hear; Balzac they incline to despise; if they make any comparison between Thackeray and Fielding, or Thackeray and Richardson, or Thackeray and Sir Walter, or Thackeray and Disraeli, it is to the disadvantage of Disraeli and Scott and Richardson and Fielding. All these were well enough in their way and day; but they are not to be classed with Thackeray. It is said, no doubt, that Thackeray could neither make stories nor tell them; but he liked stories for all that, and by the hour could babble charmingly of *Ivanhoe* and the *Mousquetaires*. It is possible that he was afraid of passion, and had no manner of interest in crime. But then, how hard he bore upon snobs, and how vigorously he lashed the smaller vices and the meaner faults! It may be beyond dispute that he was seldom good at romance, and saw most things—art and nature included—rather prosaically and ill-naturedly, as he might see them who has been for many years a failure, and is naturally a little resentful of other men's successes; but then, how brilliant are his studies of club humanity and club manners! how thoroughly he understands the feelings of them that go down into the west in broughams! If he writes by preference for people with a thousand a year, is it not the duty of everybody with a particle of self-respect to have that income? Is it possible that any one who has it not can have either wit or sentiment, humour or understanding? Thackeray writes *of* gentlemen *for* gentlemen; therefore he is alone among artists; therefore he is 'the greatest novelist of his age.' That is the faith of the true believer: that the state of mind of him that reveres less wisely than thoroughly, and would rather be damned with Thackeray than saved with any one else.

The position of them that wear their rue with a difference, and do not agree that all literature is contained in *The Book of Snobs* and *Vanity Fair*, is more easily defended. They like and admire their Thackeray in many ways, but they think him rather a writer of genius who was innately and irredeemably a Philistine than a supreme artist or a great man. To them there is something artificial in the man and something insincere in the artist: something which makes it seem natural that his best work should smack of the literary *tour de force*, and that he

should never have appeared to such advantage as when, in *Esmond* and in *Barry Lyndon*, he was writing up to a standard and upon a model not wholly of his own contrivance. They admit his claim to eminence as an adventurer in 'the discovery of the Ugly'; but they contend that even there he did his work more shrewishly and more pettily than he might; and in this connection they go so far as to reflect that a snob is not only 'one who meanly admires mean things,' as his own definition declares, but one who meanly detests mean things as well. They agree with Walter Bagehot that to be perpetually haunted by the plush behind your chair is hardly a sign of lofty literary and moral genius; and they consider him narrow and vulgar in his view of humanity, limited in his outlook upon life, inclined to be envious, inclined to be tedious and pedantic, prone to repetitions, and apt in bidding for applause to appeal to the baser qualities of his readers and to catch their sympathy by making them feel themselves spitefully superior to their fellow-men. They look at his favourite heroines—at Laura and Ethel and Amelia; and they can but think him stupid who could ever have believed them interesting or admirable or attractive or true. They listen while he regrets it is impossible for him to attempt the picture of a man; and, with Barry Lyndon in their mind's-eye and the knowledge that Casanova and Andrew Bowes suggested no more than that, they wonder if the impossibility was not a piece of luck for him. They hear him heaping contumely upon the murders and adulteries, the excesses in emotion, that pleased the men of 1830 as they had pleased the Elizabethans before them; and they see him turning with terror and loathing from these—which after all are effects of vigorous passion—to busy himself with the elaborate and careful narrative of how Barnes Newcome beat his wife, and Mrs. Mackenzie scolded Colonel Newcome to death, and old Twysden bragged and cringed himself into good society and an interest in the life and well-being of a little cad like Captain Woolcomb; and it is not amazing if they think his morality more dubious in some ways than the morality he is so firmly fixed to ridicule and to condemn. They reflect that he sees in Beatrix no more than the makings of a Bernstein; and they are puzzled, when they come to mark the contrast between the two portraitures and the difference between the part assigned to Mrs. Esmond and the part assigned to the Baroness, to decide if he were short-sighted or ungenerous, if he were inapprehensive or only cruel. They weary easily of his dogged and unremitting pursuit of the merely conventional man and the merely conventional woman; they cannot always bring themselves to be interested in the cupboard drama, the tea-cup tragedies and cheque-book and bandbox comedies, which he regards as the stuff of human action and the web of human life; and from their theory of existence they positively refuse to eliminate the heroic qualities of romance and mystery and passion, which are—as they have only to open their newspapers to see—essentials of human achievement and integral elements of human character. They hold that his books contain some of the finest stuff in fiction: as, for instance, Rawdon Crawley's discovery of his wife and Lord Steyne, and Henry Esmond's return from the wars, and those immortal chapters in which the Colonel and Frank Castlewood pursue and run down their kinswoman and the Prince. But they hold, too, that their influence is dubious, and that few have risen from them one bit the better or one jot the happier.

Genius apart, Thackeray's morality is that of a highly respectable British cynic; his intelligence is largely one of trifles; he is wise over trivial and trumpery things. He delights in reminding us—with an air!—that everybody is a humbug; that we are all rank snobs; that to misuse your aspirates is to be ridiculous and incapable of real merit; that Miss Blank has just slipped out to post a letter to Captain Jones; that Miss Dash wears false teeth and a wig; that General Tufto is almost as tightly laced as the beautiful Miss Hopper; that there's a bum-bailiff in the kitchen at Number Thirteen; that the dinner we ate t'other day at Timmins's is still to pay; that all is vanity; that there's a skeleton in every house; that passion, enthusiasm, excess of any sort, is unwise, abominable, a little absurd; and so forth. And side by side with these assurances are admirable sketches of character and still more admirable sketches of habit and of manners—are the Pontos and Costigan, Gandish and Talbot Twysden and the unsurpassable Major, Sir Pitt and Brand Firmin, the heroic De la Pluche and the engaging Farintosh and the versatile Honeyman, a crowd of vivid and diverting portraitures besides; but they are not different—in kind at least—from the reflections suggested by the story of their several careers and the development of their several individualities. Esmond apart, there is scarce a man or a woman in Thackeray whom it is possible to love unreservedly or respect thoroughly. That gives the measure of the man, and determines the quality of his influence. He was the average clubman *plus* genius and a style. And, if there is any truth in the theory that it is the function of art not to degrade but to ennoble—not to dishearten but to encourage—not to deal with things ugly and paltry and mean but with great things and beautiful and lofty—then, it is argued, his example is one to depreciate and to condemn.

Thus the two sects: the sect of them that are with Thackeray and the sect of them that are against him. Where both agree is in the fact of Thackeray's pre-eminence as a writer of English and the master of one of the finest prose styles in literature. His manner is the perfection of conversational writing. Graceful yet vigorous; adorably artificial yet incomparably sound; touched with modishness yet informed with distinction; easily and happily rhythmical yet full of colour and quick with malice and with meaning; instinct with urbanity and instinct with charm—it is a type of high-bred English, a climax of literary art. He may not have been a great man but assuredly he was a great writer; he may have been a faulty novelist but assuredly he was a rare artist in words. Setting aside Cardinal Newman's, the style he wrote is certainly less open to criticism than that of any other modern Englishman. He was neither super-eloquent like Mr. Ruskin nor a Germanised Jeremy like Carlyle; he was not marmoreally emphatic as Landor was, nor was he slovenly and inexpressive as was the great Sir Walter; he neither dallied with antithesis like Macaulay nor rioted in verbal vulgarisms with Dickens; he abstained from technology and what may be called Lord Burleighism as carefully as George Eliot indulged in them, and he avoided conceits as sedulously as Mr. George Meredith goes out of his way to hunt for them. He is a better writer than any one of these, in that he is always a master of speech and of himself, and that he is always careful yet natural and choice yet seemingly spontaneous. He wrote as a very prince among talkers, and he interfused and interpenetrated English with the elegant and cultured fashion of the men of Queen Anne and with something of the warmth, the glow, the personal and romantic ambition, peculiar to the century of Byron and Keats, of Landor and Dickens, of Ruskin and Tennyson and Carlyle. Unlike his only rival, he had learnt his art before he began to practise it. Of the early work of the greater artist a good half is that of a man in the throes of education: the ideas, the thoughts, the passion, the poetry, the humour, are of the best, but the expression is self-conscious, strained, ignorant. Thackeray had no such blemish. He wrote dispassionately, and

he was a born writer. In him there is no hesitation, no fumbling, no uncertainty. The style of *Barry Lyndon* is better and stronger and more virile than the style of *Philip*; and unlike the other man's, whose latest writing is his best, their author's evolution was towards decay.

He is so superior a person that to catch him tripping is a peculiar pleasure. It is a satisfaction apart, for instance, to reflect that he has (it must be owned) a certain gentility of mind. Like the M.P. in *Martin Chuzzlewit*, he represents the Gentlemanly Interest. That is his mission in literature, and he fulfils it thoroughly. He appears sometimes as Mr. Yellow-plush, sometimes as Mr. Fitzboodle, sometimes as Michael Angelo Titmarsh, but always in the Gentlemanly Interest. In his youth (as ever) he is found applauding the well-bred Charles de Bernard, and remarking of Balzac and Dumas that the one is 'not fit for the *salon*,' and the other 'about as genteel as a courier.' Balzac and Dumas are only men of genius and great artists: the real thing is to be 'genteel' and write—as *Gerfeuil (sic)* is written—'in a gentleman-like style.' A few pages further on in the same pronouncement (a review of *Jérôme Paturot*), I find him quoting with entire approval Reybaud's sketch of 'a great character, in whom the *habitué* of Paris will perhaps recognise a certain likeness to a certain celebrity of the present day, by name Monsieur Hector Berlioz, the musician and critic.' The description is too long to quote. It sparkles with all the *fadaises* of anti-Berliozian criticism, and the point is that the hero, after conducting at a private party (which Berlioz never did) his own 'hymn of the creation that has been lost since the days of the deluge,' 'called for his cloak and his clogs, and walked home, where he wrote a critique for the newspapers of the music which he had composed and directed.' In the Gentlemanly Interest Mr. Titmarsh translates this sorry little libel with the utmost innocence of approval. It is *The Paris Sketch-Book* over again. That Monsieur Hector Berlioz may possibly have known something of his trade and been withal as honest a man and artist as himself seems never to have occurred to him. He knows nothing of Monsieur Hector except that he is a 'hairy romantic,' and that whatever he wrote it was not *Batti, batti*; but that nothing is enough. 'Whether this little picture is a likeness or not,' he is ingenuous enough to add, 'who shall say?' But,—and here speaks the bold but superior Briton—'it is a good caricature of a race in France, where geniuses *poussent* as they do nowhere else; where poets are prophets, where romances have revelations.' As he goes on to qualify *Jérôme Paturot* as a 'masterpiece,' and as 'three volumes of satire in which there is not a particle of bad blood,' it seems fair to conclude that in the Gentlemanly Interest all is considered fair, and that to accuse a man of writing criticisms on his own works is to be 'witty and entertaining,' and likewise 'careless, familiar, and sparkling' to the genteelest purpose possible in this genteelest of all possible worlds.

HENRY D. SEDGWICK, JR.
From "Some Aspects of Thackeray"
Atlantic, November 1898, pp. 707–19

I

Twenty years ago, at Harvard College, in the rooms of all students of certain social pretensions who affected books, you were sure to see on the most conspicuous shelf, in green and gold or in half calf, the works of William Makepeace Thackeray. The name, boldly printed, greeted you as you entered the door, and served, together with sundry red-sealed certificates and beribboned silver medals, to inform you of the general respectability and gentility of your host. Of a Sunday morning, this student was likely to be discovered complacent over the *Book of Snobs* or serious over *Vanity Fair.*

Public opinion went that Thackeray was the novelist of gentlemen and for gentlemen; that Dickens was undoubtedly strong, but he had not had the privilege of knowing and of delineating the things which were adapted to interest the most select of Harvard undergraduates. In every fold there are some to lower the general standard of critical excellence; there were some partisans of Dickens. They were judged, as minorities are, found guilty of running counter to accepted opinions, and outlawed from further literary criticism.

These Harvard critics did not make for themselves this opinion of Thackeray; they brought it with them from home.

We suppose that parents, what time their son started in the world on the first path which diverged from theirs, deemed that they were equipping him with the best master to teach him concerning the ways of that world. Theirs was the old lack of faith, so common to the fearful; they sought to guard their son from the world by pointing out to him its vanity, its folly, its emptiness. "Oh, if he shall only know what the world is," they thought, "he will escape its evils to come." So they gave him Thackeray, and wrote him long letters on idleness and vice. His bookshelves and his inner pockets thus encumbered, the youth found Harvard College a miniature of the world of which he had been warned. There were materials enough for such a conclusion. A seeker will find what he goes forth to seek. The youth learned his Thackeray well, spent four years enjoying his little *Vanity Fair,* and then departed from Cambridge to help build up the larger world of Vanity which shows so fine in America to-day.

There is no phenomenon so interesting as the unconscious labor of boys and men over the task of shaping, hewing, whittling, and moulding the world into accord with their anticipations. All lend helping hands to the great master implement, public expectation. A young fellow goes to college, and joins a group of a dozen others. Brown, the rake, thinks, "Here's a Lothario who will sup at Dame Quickly's with me;" Smith, the boxer, says, "A quick eye,—I'll make a boxer of him;" Jones, who translates Homer for the group, sees rhythm and Theocritus in the newcomer's curly hair; Robinson, the philosopher, feels a fellow Hegelian. These rival expectations leap out to meet the stranger; they struggle among themselves. Of the students, some agree with Brown, some with Smith, others with Robinson or Jones. The sturdiest of these expectations chokes out the others and survives. After a short time— our young fellow yet entirely undiscovered—a strong current of unanimous expectation has decided that he shall be a boxer. All obstacles to the execution of this judgment are taken away, and moral earthworks are quickly thrown up, guarding him from Brown, Jones, and Robinson. Expectation seats him beside Smith; expectation turns the conversation upon champions of the ring; expectation draws the gloves upon his fists; it offers him no Eastcheap, no Theocritus, no Hegel. The youth takes boxing lessons; soon he learns the language of the fraternity; he walks, runs, avoids mince pies, eschews books, and with a single eye looks forward to a bout in Hemenway Gymnasium. Thus the tricksy spirit expectation shapes the destinies of common humankind. Thus do parents begin to expect that their son will see the world with their own and Thackeray's beam-troubled eyes; they insist that he shall, and in due time he does.

Once convince a young man that Thackeray's world is the real world, that vulgarity, meanness, trickery, and fraud abound, and you put him in a yoke from which he shall never free himself. This is the yoke of base expectation. This is what is known in Scripture as "the world;" it is the habit of screwing up the eyes and squinting in order to see unworthiness, baseness, vice, and wickedness; it is a creeping blindness to nobler things. The weapon against the world is, as of old, to use a word of great associations, faith. Faith is nothing but noble expectation, and all education should be to supplant base expectation by noble expectation. What is the human world in which we live but a mighty mass of sensitive matter, highly susceptible to the great force of human expectation, which flows about it like an ever shifting Gulf Stream, now warming and prospering noble people, and then wantonly comforting the unworthy?

Feeble folk that we are, we have in this power of creation an element of divinity in us. Our expectations hover about like life-giving agencies. We are conscious that our hopes and our fears are at work all the time helping the oncoming of that which we hope or fear. The future is like a newborn babe stretching out its arms to the stronger. It may be that this power in us is weak, intermittent, often pitiably feeble; but now and again comes a man with a larger measure of divine life, and his great expectations pass into deeds. Before every Trafalgar first comes an expectation that duty will be done.

Thackeray has no faith; he does not entertain high expectations. His characters do shameless things, and Thackeray says to the reader, "Be not surprised, injured-seeming friend; you would have done the like under the like temptation." At first you contradict, you resent; but little by little Thackeray's opinion of you inoculates you; the virus takes; you lose your conviction that you would have acted differently; you concede that such conduct was not impossible, even for you,—no, nor improbable,— and, on the whole, after reflection, that the conduct was excusable, was good enough, was justified, was inevitable, was right, was scrupulously right, and only a Don Quixote would have acted otherwise.

Nothing sickens and dies so quickly as noble expectation. Luxury, comfort, custom, the ennui of hourly exertion, the dint of disappointment, assail it unceasingly: if a man of ten talents, like Thackeray, joins the assailants, is it not just that admiration of him should be confined to those who are willing to admire talents, irrespective of the use to which they are put?

II

⟨. . .⟩ Thackeray was bred when Englishmen were forsaking "swords for ledgers," and deserting "the student's bower for gold." His father died when he was very young. His mother married for her second husband an Indian officer, and Thackeray was sent to school in England.

In a new biographical edition of Thackeray's works which Messrs. Harper & Brothers are publishing, Mrs. Ritchie has written brief memories of her father at the beginning of each volume, with special relation to its contents. These memories are done with filial affection. Thackeray's kindness, his tenderness, his sympathetic nature, are written large on every page. He has many virtues. He dislikes vice, drunkenness, betrayal of women, pettifogging, huckstering, lying, cheating, knavery, the annoyance and tomfoolery of social distinctions. He would like to leave the world better than he found it, but he cannot see. Pettiness, the vulgarity of money, the admiration of mean things, hang before him like a curtain at the theatre. Romeo may be on fire, Hotspur leap for the moon, Othello stab Iago, Lear die in Cordelia's lap; but the sixteenth of an inch of frieze and fustian keeps it all from him.

At nineteen Thackeray spent a winter at Weimar. He soon

writes to his mother of Goethe as "the great lion of Weimar." He is not eager to possess the great measures of life. He is not sensitive to Goethe, but to the court of Pumpernickel. He wishes he were a cornet in Sir John Kennaway's yeomanry, that he might wear the yeoman's dress. "A yeomanry dress is always a handsome and respectable one."

In 1838, when in Paris, he writes: "I have just come from seeing *Marion Delorme*, the tragedy of Victor Hugo, and am so sickened and disgusted with the horrid piece that I have hardly heart to write." He did not look through pain and extravagance into the noble passion of the play. He lived in a moral Pumpernickel where the ideal is kept outside the town gates.

Pumpernickel was his home, and he has depicted it in *Vanity Fair*. This book reflects Thackeray's intellectual image in his prime; it is his first great novel, and is filled with the most vivid and enduring of his beliefs and convictions. There are in it a vigor, an independence, and a sense of power that come when a man faces his best opportunity. Into it Thackeray has put what he deemed the truest experiences of his life. He has also written two long sequels to it. *The Newcomes* is the story of his stepfather, Major Carmichael-Smyth in *Vanity Fair*; *Pendennis*, that of Thackeray himself and his mother wandering in its outskirts. There is this one family of nice people, gathered into an ark as it were, floating over the muddy waters. Thackeray was able to see that his immediate family were not rogues; he was also able to draw a most noble gentleman, Henry Esmond, by the help of the idealizing lens of a hundred odd years; but the world he thought he saw about him is the world of *Vanity Fair*.

Thackeray had so many fine qualities that one cannot but feel badly to see him in such a place. Had his virtues—his kindness, his tenderness, his charm, his capacity for affection—been energetic enough to dominate his entire character, he would have lived among far different scenes; his readers would have beheld him potting flowers by some vinecovered house in a village where neighbors were simple, honest, and true,—where round the corner stood a Mermaid Tavern, to which poets and far-voyaging sailors would come, full of stories about a glorious world. Who would not have liked to sit by Thackeray's hearth in such a home, a fire warming his kindly feet, his good cheroot gayly burning, a mug at his elbow, and he reading his last manuscript? Was it Thackeray's fault that this was not to be? Or did he suffer the incidental misfortunes which large causes bring to individuals as they follow their own regardless paths?

III

Thackeray is the poet of respectability. His working time stretches from the Reform Act almost to the death of Lord Palmerston. He chronicles the contemporary life of a rich, money-getting generation of merchants and manufacturers, lifted into sudden importance in the national life by steamboats and railroads, by machinery for spinning, weaving, mining, by Arkwright, Watt, Davy, and Stephenson. His is a positive, matter-of-fact world, of which Peel is the statesman and Macaulay the man of letters. Macaulay, in his essay on Bacon, has given us the measure of its spiritual elevation: "We have sometimes thought that an amusing fiction might be written, in which a disciple of Epictetus and a disciple of Bacon should be introduced as fellow travelers. They come to a village where the smallpox has just begun to rage, and find houses shut-up, intercourse suspended, the sick abandoned, mothers weeping in terror over their children. The Stoic assures the dismayed population that there is nothing bad in the smallpox; and that,

to a wise man, disease, deformity, death, the loss of friends, are not evils. The Baconian takes out a lancet and begins to vaccinate. They find a body of miners in great dismay. An explosion of noisome vapors has just killed many of those who were at work; and the survivors are afraid to venture into the cavern. The Stoic assures them that such an accident is nothing but a mere ἀποπροήγμενον. The Baconian, who has no such fine word at his command, contents himself with devising a safety-lamp. They find a shipwrecked merchant wringing his hands on the shore. His vessel, with an inestimable cargo, has just gone down, and he is reduced in a moment from opulence to beggary. The Stoic exhorts him not to seek happiness in things which lie without himself; the Baconian constructs a diving-bell. It would be easy to multiply illustrations of the difference between the philosophy of thorns and the philosophy of fruit, the philosophy of words and the philosophy of works." This is the very nobility of machinery. As we read, we listen to the buzz and whir of wheels, the drip of oil-cans, the creaking and straining of muscle and steel. Such things serve, no doubt, in default of other agencies, to create a great empire, but the England of Thackeray's day was a *nouveau riche*, self-made, proud of its lack of occupation other than money-getting. Thackeray was fallen upon evil times. He was born into this moral estate of Pumpernickel, and he has described it with the vividness and vigor of complete comprehension. He has immense cleverness. He knows whereof he talks. Never has a period had so accomplished an historian. The *bourgeoisie* have their epic in *Vanity Fair*.

During the formative period of Thackeray's life the English nation was passing under the influence of machinery. There was the opportunity of a great man of letters, such as Thackeray, to look to it that literature should respond to the stimulus of added power, and grow so potent that it would determine what direction the national life should take. At such a time of national expansion, literature should have seen England in the flush of coming greatness; it should have roused itself to re-create her in nobler imagination, and have spent itself in making her accept this estimate and expectation, and become an England dominating material advantages and leading the world.

The interest in life is this potentiality and malleability. The alloted task of men and women is to take this potentiality and shape it. Men who have strong intelligence and quick perceptions, like Thackeray, accomplish a great deal in the way of giving a definite form to the material with which life furnishes us. What Michelangelo says of marble is true of life:—

Non ha l'ottimo artista alcun concetto
Ch'un marmo solo in se non circoscriva
Col suo soverchio.

The problem of life is to uncover the figures hiding in this material: shall it be Caliban, Circe, Philip Sidney, Jeanne d'Arc? Thackeray, with what Mrs. Ritchie calls "his great deal of common sense," saw Major Pendennis and Becky Sharp; and he gave more effective cuttings and chiselings and form to the potential life of England than any other man of his time.

The common apology for such a novelist is that he describes what he sees. This is the worst with which we charge him. We charge Thackeray with seeing what he describes; and what justification has a man, in a world like this, to spend his time looking at Barnes Newcome and Sir Pitt Crawley? Thackeray takes the motes and beams floating in his mind's eye for men and women, writes about them, and calls his tale a history.

Thackeray wrote, on finishing *Vanity Fair*, that all the characters were odious except Dobbin. Poor Thackeray, what a world to see all about him, with his tender, affectionate nature! Even Colonel Newcome is so crowded round by a mob of rascally fellows that it is hard to do justice to Thackeray's noblest attempt to be a poet. But why see a world, and train children to see a world, where

The great man is a vulgar clown?

A world with such an unreal standard must be an unreal world. In the real world vulgar clowns are not great men. Thackeray sees a world all topsy-turvy, and it does not occur to him that he, and not the world, is at fault. This is the curse of faithlessness. He himself says, "The world is a looking-glass, and gives back to every man the reflection of his own face."

Thackeray has been praised as a master of reality. As reality is beyond our ken, the phrase is unfortunate; but the significance of it is that if a man will portray to the mob the world with which the mob is familiar, they will huzza themselves hoarse. Has not the Parisian mob shouted for Zola? Do not the Madrileños cheer Valdés? Do not Ouida and the pale youth of Rome and Paris holla, "d'Annunzio! d'Annunzio!" There is no glory here. The poet, not in fine frenzy, but in sober simplicity, tells the mob, not what they see, but what they cannot of themselves perceive, with such a tone of authority that they stand gaping and likewise see.

Thackeray's love of reality was merely an embodiment of the popular feeling which proposed to be direct, business-like, and not to tolerate any nonsense. People felt that a money-getting country must take itself seriously. The Reform Act had brought political control to the bourgeoisie, men of common sense; no ranters, no will-o'-the-wisp chasers, but "burgomasters and great oneyers,"—men who thought very highly of circumstances under which they were prosperous, and asked for no more beautiful sight than their own virtues. Influenced by the sympathetic touch of this atmosphere, novel-readers found their former favorites old-fashioned. Disraeli, Samuel Warren, Bulwer Lytton, G. P. R. James, seemed false, theatrical, and sentimental. Thackeray was of this opinion, and he studied the art of caricature as the surest means of saving himself from any such fantastic nonsense. He approached life as a city man,—one who was convinced that the factories of London, not the theories of the philosopher, were the real motive force underneath all the busy flow of outward life. He found his talents exactly suited to this point of view. His memory was an enormous wallet, into which his hundred-handed observation was day and night tossing scraps and bits of daily experience. He saw the meetings of men as he passed: lords, merchants, tinsmiths, guardsmen, tailors, cooks, valets, nurses, policemen, boys, applewomen,—everybody whom you meet of a morning between your house and your office in the city. He remarked the gestures, he heard the words, he guessed what had gone before, he divined what would happen thereafter: and each sight, sound, guess, and divination was safely stowed away in his marvelous wallet. England of the forties, as Thackeray saw it, is in *Vanity Fair, Pendennis*, and *The Newcomes*. "I ask you to believe," he says in the preface to *Pendennis*, "that this person writing strives to tell the truth."

Where lies the truth? Are men merely outward parts of machinery, exposed to view, while down below in the engine-room steam and electricity determine their movements? Or do men live and carry on their daily routine under the influence of some great thought of which they are half unconscious, but by which they are shaped, moulded, and moved? A French poet says:—

Le vrai Dieu, le Dieu fort, est le Dieu des idées.

But Macaulay says that the philosophy of Plato began with words and ended with words; that an acre in Middlesex is better than a principality in Utopia. The British public applauded Macaulay, and young Thackeray took the hint.

IV

Nobody can question Thackeray's style. His fame is proof of its excellence. Even if a man will flatter the mob by saying that he sees what they see, he cannot succeed without skill of expression. Readers are slow to understand. They need grace, pithy sentences, witty turns of phrase, calculated sweep of periods and paragraphs. They must have no labor of attention; the right adjective alone will catch their eyes; they require their pages plain, clear, perspicuous. In all these qualities Thackeray is very nearly perfect. Hardly anybody would say that there is a novel better written than *Vanity Fair*. The story runs as easily as the hours. Chapter after chapter in the best prose carries the reader comfortably on. Probably this excellence is due to Thackeray's great powers of observation. His eyes saw everything, saving for the blindness of his inward eye, and his memory held it. He was exceedingly sensitive. Page after page is filled with the vividness of well-chosen detail. He cultivated the art of writing most assiduously. From 1830 to 1847, when *Vanity Fair*, the first of his great novels, was published, he was writing all the time, and for almost all of that time as a humorist, drawing caricatures,—a kind of writing perhaps better adapted than any other to cultivate the power of portraying scenes. The caricaturist is restricted to a few lines; his task does not allow him to fill in, to amplify; he must say his say in little. The success of wit is the arrangement of a dozen words. This training for sixteen continuous years taught Thackeray a style which, for his subjects, has no equal in English literature.

To-day we greatly admire Stevenson and Kipling. We applaud Stevenson's style for its cultivation and its charm; we heap praises upon Kipling's for its dash, vigor, and accuracy of detail. All these praises are deserved; but when we take up Thackeray again, we find pages and pages written in a style more cultivated than Stevenson's and equally charming, and with a dash, vigor, and nicety of detail that Kipling might envy. Descriptions that would constitute the bulk of an essay for the one, or of a story for the other, do hasty service as prologues to Thackeray's chapters. Conversations of a happy theatrical turn, with enough exaggeration to appear wholly natural, which Stevenson and Kipling never rivaled, come crowding together in his long novels.

There are two famous scenes which are good examples of Thackeray's power,—one of his sentiment, one of his humor. The first is Colonel Newcome's death in the Charterhouse. The second is the first scene between Pendennis and the Fotheringay. "Pen tried to engage her in conversation about poetry and about her profession. He asked her what she thought of Ophelia's madness, and whether she was in love with Hamlet or not. 'In love with such a little ojus wretch as that stunted manager of a Bingley?' She bristled with indignation at the thought. Pen explained it was not of her he spoke, but of Ophelia of the play. 'Oh, indeed; if no offense was meant, none was taken: but as for Bingley, indeed, she did not value him,—not that glass of punch.' Pen next tried her on Kotzebue. 'Kotzebue? Who was he?' 'The author of the play in which she had been performing so admirably.' 'She did not know that—the man's name at the beginning of the book was Thompson,' she said. Pen laughed at her adorable simplicity. He told her of the melancholy fate of the author of the play, and how Sand had killed him. . . . 'How beautiful she is!' thought Pen, cantering homewards. 'How simple and how tender! How charming it is to see a woman of her genius busying herself with the humble offices of domestic life, cooking dishes to make her old father comfortable, and brewing him drink! How rude it was of me to begin to talk about professional matters, and how well she turned the conversation! . . . Pendennis, Pendennis,—how she spoke the word! Emily, Emily! how good, how noble, how beautiful, how perfect, she is!'"

This scene is very close upon farce, and it is in that borderland that Thackeray's extraordinary skill shows itself most conspicuous. Difficult, however, as it must be to be a master there,—and the fact that Thackeray has no rival in this respect proves it,—it is easy work compared to drawing a scene of real love, of passion. Perhaps some actions of Lady Castlewood are Thackeray's only attempt thereat. The world of passion is not his world. His ear is not attuned to

> Das tiefe, schmerzenvolle Glück
> Des Hasses Kraft, die Macht der Liebe.

Charlotte Brontë, Tourgenef, Hawthorne, Hugo, Balzac, all excel him. Thackeray hears the click of custom against custom, the throb of habit, the tick-tick of vulgar life, all the sounds of English social machinery. The different degrees of social efficiency and inefficiency rivet his attention. What interests him is the relation that Henry Foker or Blanche Amory bears to the standard of social excellence accepted by commercial England in the forties. He is never—at least as an artist—disturbed by any scheme of metaphysics. His English common sense is never lured afield by any speculations about the value of a human being uncolored by the shadows of time and space. He is never troubled by doubts of standards, by skepticism as to uses, ends, purposes; he has a hard-and-fast British standard. He draws Colonel Newcome as an object of pity; he surrounds him with tenderness and sympathy. Here is Thackeray at his highest. But he never suggests to the reader that Colonel Newcome is not a man to be pitied, but to be envied; not a failure, but a success; not unhappy, but most fortunate. The great poets of the world have turned the malefactor's cross into the symbol of holiness. Thackeray never departs from the British middle class conceptions of triumph and failure. In all his numerous dissertations and asides to the reader, he wrote like the stalwart Briton he was, good, generous, moral, domestic, stern, and tender. You never forget his Puritan ancestry, you can rely upon his honesty; but he is not pure-minded or humble. He dislikes wrong, but he never has a high enough conception of right to hate wrong. His view is that it is a matter to be cured by policemen, propriety, and satire.

Satire is the weapon of the man at odds with the world and at ease with himself. The dissatisfied man—a Juvenal, a Swift, a youthful Thackeray—belabors the world with vociferous indignation; like the wind on the traveler's back, the beating makes him hug his cloaking sins the tighter. Wrong runs no danger from such chastisement. The fight against wrong is made by the man discontented with himself and careless of the world. Satire is harmless as a moral weapon. It is an old-fashioned fowling piece, fit for a man of wit, intelligence, and a certain limited imagination. It runs no risk of having no quarry; the world to it is one vast covert of lawful game. It goes a-traveling with wit, because both are in search of the unworthy. It is well suited to a brilliant style. It is also a conventional department in literature, and as such is demanded by publishers and accepted by the public.

Thackeray was born with dexterity of observation, nimbleness of wit, and a quick sense of the incongruous and the grotesque. He lost his fortune when a young man. He wrote for a livelihood, and naturally turned to that branch of literature which was best suited to his talents. It was his misfortune that satire is bad for a man's moral development. It intensified his natural disbelief in the worth of humanity, but gave him the schooling that enabled him to use his powers so brilliantly.

Thackeray was often hampered by this habit of looking at the grotesque side of things. It continually dragged him into farce, causing feebleness of effect where there should have been power. Sir Pitt Crawley, Jos Sedley, the struggle over Miss Crawley, Harry Foker, the Chevalier de Florac, Aunt Hoggerty, are all in the realm of farce. This is due partly to Thackeray's training, and partly to his attitude toward life. If life consists of money, clothes, and a bundle of social relations, our daily gravity, determination, and vigor are farcical, because they are so out of place; they are as incongruous as a fish in trousers. But Thackeray forgets that there is something disagreeable in this farce, as there would be in looking into Circe's sty and seeing men groveling over broken meats. To be sure, Thackeray makes believe that he finds it comic to see creatures of great pretensions busy themselves so continually with the pettiest things. But it too often seems as if the comic element consisted in our human pretensions, and as if Thackeray merely kept bringing them to the reader's notice for the sake of heightening the contrast between men and their doings.

V

Thackeray is not an innovator; he follows the traditions of English literature. He is in direct descent from the men of the *Spectator*, Addison, Steele, and their friends, and from Fielding. He has far greater powers of observation, wit, humor, sentiment, and description than the Spectator group. He excels Fielding in everything except as a story-teller, and in a kind of intellectual power that is more easily discerned in Fielding than described,—a kind of imperious understanding that breaks down a path before it, whereas Thackeray's intelligence looks in at a window or peeps through the keyhole. Fielding is the bigger, coarser man of the two; Thackeray is the cleverer. Each is thoroughly English. Fielding embodies the England of George I.; Thackeray, that same England refined by the revolutionary ideas of 1789, trained by long wars, then materialized by machinery, by a successful bourgeoisie and the quick accession of wealth. Each is a good fellow,—quick in receiving ideas, but slow to learn a new point of view. Fielding is inferior to Thackeray in education, in experience of many men, and in foreign travel. Tom Jones is the begetter of Arthur Pendennis, Jonathan Wild of Barry Lyndon. Some of Fielding's heroines, wandering out of *Tom Jones* and *Amelia*, have strayed into *Pendennis*, *Vanity Fair*, and *The Newcomes*. The fair émigrées change their names, but keep their thoughts and behavior.

It is said that a lady once asked Thackeray why he made all his women fools or knaves. "Madam, I know no others." It may be that living in Paris in his youth hurt his insight into women; it may be that the great sorrow of his wife's insanity instinctively turned his thoughts from the higher types of women; perhaps his life in Bohemia and in clubs limited his knowledge during the years when novel-writing was his chief occupation. The truth seems to be that Thackeray, like Fielding, was a man's man,—he understood one cross-section of a common man, his hopes, aims, fears, wishes, habits, and manners; but he was very ignorant of women. He says:

"Desdemona was not angry with Cassio, though there is very little doubt she saw the lieutenant's partiality for her (and I, for my part, believe that many more things took place in that sad affair than the worthy Moorish officer ever knew of); why, Miranda was even very kind to Caliban, and we may be pretty sure for the same reason. Not that she would encourage him in the least, the poor uncouth monster,—of course not." Shakespeare and Thackeray looked differently at women.

Thackeray lacked the poet's eye; he could not see and was not troubled.

> Ahi quanto nella mente mi commossi,
> Quando mi volsi per veder Beatrice,
> Per non poter vedere, ben ch'io fossi
> Presso di lei, e nel mondo felice!

But poor Thackeray was never near the ideal, and never in paradise. Some critic has said of him that because he had Eden in his mind's eye, this world appeared a Vanity Fair. No criticism could be more perverted; he had Vanity Fair in his mind's eye, and therefore could not see paradise.

This treatment of women is half from sheer ignorance, and half from Thackeray's habit of dealing in caricature with subjects of which he is ignorant. He behaves toward foreign countries very much as he does toward women. France, Germany, Italy, appear like geography in an opera bouffe. They are places for English blackguards to go to, and very fit places for them, tenanted as they are by natives clad in outlandish trousers, and bearded and moustachioed like pards. His delineations of Germany, and those pen-and-ink sketches by Richard Doyle in his delightful Brown, Jones and Robinson, made so strong an impression upon an ignorant portion of the public, of which we were, that it was frightened to death in 1871, when it thought of the French armies trampling down poor little Germany. Thackeray looked on Germany, as he did upon the world, with the greedy eye of the caricaturist, and he could not refrain from his grotesque sketches. Of the French he says: "In their aptitude to swallow, to utter, to enact humbugs, these French people, from Majesty downwards, beat all the other nations of this earth. In looking at these men, their manners, dresses, opinions, politics, actions, history, it is impossible to preserve a grave countenance; instead of having Carlyle to write a *History of the French Revolution*, I often think it should be handed over to Dickens or Theodore Hook. . . . I can hardly bring my mind to fancy that anything is serious in France,—it seems to be all rant, tinsel, and stage-play." His attitude toward French literature is distorted by lack of sympathy to an astonishing degree.

Thackeray's fault was not merely a certain narrowness of mind, but also that he allowed himself to see only the grotesque and disagreeable, until habit and nature combined to blind him to other things.

VI

Thackeray is not a democrat. Democracy, like many another great and vague social conception, is based upon a fundamental truth, of which truth adherents to the conception are often ignorant, although they brush against it in the dark and unwittingly draw in strength for their belief. The fundamental truth of democracy is that the real pleasures of life are increased by sharing them,—that exclusiveness renders pleasure insipid. One reason why democracy has prevailed so greatly is that everywhere, patent to everybody, in the simplest family life, there is proof of this truth. A man amuses himself skipping stones: the occupation has a pleasure hardly to be detected; with a wife it is interesting, with children it becomes exciting. Every new sharer adds to the father's stock of delight, so that at last he lies awake on winter nights thinking of the summer's pleasure. With a slight application of logic, democrats have struggled, and continually do struggle, to break down all the bastions, walls, fences, and demilunes that time, prejudice, and ignorance have erected between men. They wish to have a ready channel from man to man, through which the emotional floods of life can pour;

> For they, at least,
> Have dream'd that human hearts might blend
> In one, and were through faith released
> From isolation without end.

What is the meaning of patriotism? Does the patriot think his country wiser, better, more gifted, more generous, than another? Perhaps, and in this he is almost certainly wrong; but the power of patriotism to disregard truth lies in the fact that it is one of the most powerful conductors of human emotion ever discovered. It is part of the old human cry, "Self is so small; make me part of something large." *Esprit de corps*, which makes people unreasonable and troubles the calculations of the bloodless man, is a like conductor of the emotions in lesser matters; and the fact is familiar that the larger the body, the greater is the emotion generated.

Humanity has had a hard task in civilizing itself; in periods of ignorance, ill humor, and hunger it has built up a most elaborate system, which has been a great factor in material prosperity. This system is the specialization of labor, which serves to double the necessary differences among men, and to make every specialty and every difference a hindrance to the joys that should be in commonalty spread. The age of machinery increased specialization, specialization increased wealth, wealth was popularly supposed to be the panacea for human ills; and the bars and barriers between men were repaired and strengthened. Specialization in Thackeray's time was in the very air; everything was specialized,—trade was specialized, society was specialized, money was specialized; there was money made, money inherited from father, money inherited from grandfather,—money, like blood, growing purer and richer the further back it could be traced. Every act of specialization produced a new batch of social relations.

Thackeray is very sensitive, especially to this elaborate system of specialization, and to its dividing properties, strengthened and repaired by the commercial Briton. Thackeray has no gift for abstraction; he does not take a man and grow absorbed in him as a spiritual being, as a creature in relations with some Absolute; he sees men shut off and shut up in all sorts of little coops. He is all attentive to the coops. The world to him is one vast zoölogical garden, this Vanity Fair of his. He does not care that the creatures are living, growing, eating, sun-needing animals; he is interested in the feathers, the curl of the tail, the divided toe, the pink eye, the different occupations, clothes, habits, which separate them into different groups. A democrat does not care for such classification; on the contrary, he wishes to efface it as much as possible. He wishes to abstract man from his conditions and surroundings, and contemplate him as a certain quantity of human essence. He looks upon the distinctions of rank, of occupation, of customs and habits, as so many barricades upon the great avenues of human emotions; Napoleon-like, he would sweep them away. He regards man as a serious reality, and these accidents of social relations as mere shadows passing over. This is the Christian position. This is the attitude of Victor Hugo, George Eliot, George Sand, Hawthorne, Tourgenef, Tolstoi, Charlotte Brontë.

NATHANIEL HAWTHORNE

NATHANIEL HAWTHORNE

1804–1864

Nathaniel Hawthorne was born in Salem, Massachusetts, on July 4, 1804; he was descended on both sides from prominent New England Puritans. In 1809, after the death of his father, Hawthorne began living, along with his mother and two sisters, at the home of his maternal grandparents. After studying at Samuel Archer's School (1819), Hawthorne attended Bowdoin College in Brunswick, Maine (1821–25), where his classmates included Henry Wadsworth Longfellow. In 1825 Hawthorne returned to Salem to live with his mother.

Rather than entering a trade or profession as was expected of him, Hawthorne spent the next dozen years or so in relative isolation, concentrating on reading and writing. In 1828 he published a novel, *Fanshawe*, which drew heavily on his experiences at Bowdoin. Published anonymously and at his own expense, this book was later withdrawn by Hawthorne, who destroyed every copy he could find. Between 1830 and 1837 Hawthorne wrote tales and sketches for various periodicals (notably S. G. Goodrich's annual *The Token*), and in 1837 a collection was published as *Twice-Told Tales*; an expanded edition appeared in 1842. After becoming engaged to Sophia Peabody in 1839, Hawthorne took a job as a measurer in the Boston custom house (1839–40), and in 1841 he joined the Brook Farm Community in West Roxbury, Massachusetts, from which he withdrew after several months. In 1842 Hawthorne and Sophia were married; they settled in Concord, where Hawthorne became a friend of Emerson, Thoreau, Margaret Fuller, and A. Bronson Alcott.

In 1846, the year in which his son Julian was born, Hawthorne published *Mosses from an Old Manse*, a collection of sketches and tales reprinted from a variety of periodicals, including the *Democratic Review*. Between 1846 and 1849 he worked as a surveyor in the Salem custom house, and in 1850 he published *The Scarlet Letter*, which won him considerable fame. In this novel set in seventeenth-century New England, Hawthorne sought to explore the Puritan conscience through a drama of adultery and revenge. During 1850 and 1851 Hawthorne lived in Lenox, Massachusetts, where he became friendly with Herman Melville. In 1851, the year in which his daughter Rose was born, Hawthorne published his second novel, *The House of the Seven Gables*, a story of ancestral guilt partially based on his own family history. Also in that year appeared a third collection of shorter pieces, *The Snow-Image and Other Twice-Told Tales*. *The Blithedale Romance*, based in large part on Hawthorne's experiences at Brook Farm, appeared in 1852, and was followed by two works for children, *A Wonder-Book for Girls and Boys* (1852) and *Tanglewood Tales* (1853), both based on Greek mythology.

In 1853 Hawthorne was appointed by President Franklin Pierce to serve as United States consul at Liverpool, a position he filled until 1857. He then spent the years 1857 to 1859 living in Rome and Florence, an experience that inspired his third novel, *The Marble Faun* (1860; retitled *Transformation* in England); this was to be his last completed work of fiction. In 1860 Hawthorne returned to Concord, where he spent the rest of his life, and in 1863 published *Our Old Home*, a series of essays on England and Anglo-American relations. In 1864 Hawthorne traveled to New Hampshire in an attempt to improve his failing health. On May 19 of that year he died at Plymouth, leaving unfinished four works; *Dr. Grimshawe's Secret* (first published in 1883), *Septimius Felton; or, The Elixir of Life* (1872), *The Ancestral Footstep* (1883), and *The Dolliver Romance* (1876). After his death Sophia Hawthorne edited his English, American, and European notebooks, and there have also been several collected editions of his letters. A landmark critical edition of his work is being published by Ohio State University Press.

Personal

I have not yet concluded what profession I shall have. The being a minister is of course out of the question. I should not think that even you could desire me to choose so dull a way of life. Oh, no, mother, I was not born to vegetate forever in one place, and to live and die as calm and tranquil as—a puddle of water. As to lawyers, there are so many of them already that one half of them (upon a moderate calculation) are in a state of actual starvation. A physician, then, seems to be "Hobson's choice;" but yet I should not like to live by the diseases and infirmities of my fellow-creatures. And it would weigh very heavily on my conscience, in the course of my practice, if I should chance to send any unlucky patient "ad inferum," which being interpreted is, "to the realms below." Oh that I

was rich enough to live without a profession! What do you think of my becoming an author, and relying for support upon my pen? Indeed, I think the illegibility of my handwriting is very author-like. How proud you would feel to see my works praised by the reviewers, as equal to the proudest productions of the scribbling sons of John Bull. But authors are always poor devils, and therefore Satan may take them. I am in the same predicament as the honest gentleman in *Espriella's Letters*.

I am an Englishman, and naked I stand here,
    A-musing in my mind what garment I shall wear.

But as the mail closes soon, I must stop the career of my pen. I will only inform you that I now write no poetry, or anything else.—NATHANIEL HAWTHORNE, Letter to His

Mother (March 13, 1821), cited in Julian Hawthorne, *Nathaniel Hawthorne and His Wife*, 1884, Vol. 1, pp. 107–8

Hawthorne ⟨. . .⟩ was of a rather sturdy form, his hair dark and bushy, his eye steel-gray, his brow thick, his mouth sarcastic, his complexion stony, his whole aspect cold, moody, distrustful. He stood aloof, and surveyed the world from shy and sheltered positions.—S. G. GOODRICH, *Recollections of a Lifetime*, 1856, Vol. 2, pp. 269–70

I sent my letter at once; from all that I had heard of Mr. Hawthorne's shyness, I thought it doubtful if he would call, and I was therefore very much pleased when his card was sent in this morning. Mr. Hawthorne was more chatty than I had expected, but not any more diffident. He remained about five minutes, during which time he took his hat from the table and put it back once a minute, brushing it each time. The engravings in the books are much like him. He is not handsome, but looks as the author of his books should look; a little strange and odd, as if not of this earth. He has large, bluish-gray eyes; his hair stands out on each side, so much so that one's thoughts naturally turn to combs and hair-brushes and toilet ceremonies as one looks at him.—MARIA MITCHELL, *Journal* (Aug. 5, 1857), *Life, Letters, and Journals of Maria Mitchell*, ed. Phebe Mitchell Kendall, 1896, p. 89

You will have seen, with profound sorrow, the announcement of the death of the dearest and most cherished among our early friends.

You will wish to know something more of Hawthorne's last days than the articles in the newspapers furnish. ⟨. . .⟩

We arrived at Plymouth about six o'clock. After taking a little tea and toast in his room, and sleeping for nearly an hour upon the sofa, he retired. A door opened from my room to his, and our beds were not more than five or six feet apart. I remained up an hour or two after he fell asleep. He was apparently less restless than the night before. The light was left burning in my room—the door open—and I could see him without moving from my bed. I went, however, between one and two o'clock to his bedside, and supposed him to be in a profound slumber. His eyes were closed, his position and face perfectly natural. His face was towards my bed. I awoke again between three and four o'clock, and was surprised—as he had generally been restless—to notice that his position was unchanged—exactly the same that it was two hours before. I went to his bedside, placed my hand upon his forehead and temple, and found that he was dead. He evidently had passed from natural sleep to that sleep from which there is no waking, without suffering, and without the slightest movement. ⟨. . .⟩

The funeral is to take place at Concord, Monday, at one o'clock. I wish you could be there. I go to Lowell this afternoon, and shall drive across the country to C. to-morrow evening. I need not tell you how lonely I am, and how full of sorrow.—FRANKLIN PIERCE, Letter to Horatio Bridge (May 21, 1864), cited in Horatio Bridge, *Personal Recollections of Nathaniel Hawthorne*, 1893, pp. 176–79

How beautiful it was, that one bright day
    In the long week of rain!
Though all its splendour could not chase away
    The omnipresent pain.

The lovely town was white with apple-blooms,
    And the great elms o'erhead
Dark shadows wove on their aerial looms
    Shot through with golden thread.

Across the meadows, by the gray old manse,
    The historic river flowed:

I was as one who wanders in a trance,
    Unconscious of his road.

The faces of familiar friends seemed strange;
    Their voices I could hear,
And yet the words they uttered seemed to change
    Their meaning to my ear.

For the one face I looked for was not there,
    The one low voice was mute;
Only an unseen presence filled the air,
    And baffled my pursuit.

Now I look back, and meadow, manse, and stream
    Dimly my thought defines;
I only see—a dream within a dream—
    The hill-top hearsed with pines.

I only hear above his place of rest
    Their tender undertone,
The infinite longings of a troubled breast,
    The voice so like his own.

There in seclusion and remote from men
    The wizard hand lies cold,
Which at its topmost speed let fall the pen,
    And left the tale half told.

Ah! who shall lift that wand of magic power,
    And the lost clew regain?
The unfinished window in Aladdin's tower
    Unfinished must remain!
        —HENRY WADSWORTH LONGFELLOW, "Hawthorne," 1864

Hawthorne was of the darker temperament and tendencies. His sensitiveness and sadness were native, and he cultivated them apparently alike by solitude, the pursuits and studies in which he indulged, till he became almost fated to know gayer hours only by stealth. By disposition friendly, he seemed the victim of his temperament, as if he sought distance, if not his pen, to put himself in communication, and possible sympathy with others,—with his nearest friends, even. His reserve and imprisonment were more distant and close, while the desire for conversation was livelier, than any one I have known. There was something of strangeness even in his cherished intimacies, as if he set himself afar from all and from himself with the rest; the most diffident of men, as coy as a maiden, he could only be won by some cunning artifice, his reserve was so habitual, his isolation so entire, the solitude so vast. How distant people were from him, the world they lived in, how he came to know so much about them, by what stratagem he got into his own house or left it, was a marvel. Fancy fixed, he was not to be jostled from himself for a moment, his mood was so persistent. There he was in the twilight, there he stayed. Was he some damsel imprisoned in that manly form pleading alway for release, sighing for the freedom and companionships denied her? Or was he some Assyrian ill at ease afar from the olives and the East? Had he strayed over with William the Conqueror, and true to his Norman nature, was the baron still in republican America, secure in his castle, secure in his tower, whence he could defy all invasion of curious eyes? What neighbor of his ever caught him on the highway, or ventured to approach his threshold?

His bolted Castle gates, what man should ope,
    Unless the Lord did will
    To prove his skill,
And tempt the fates hid in his horoscope?

Yet if by chance admitted, welcome in a voice that a woman might own for its hesitancy and tenderness; his eyes telling the rest.

For such the noble language of his eye,
That when of words his lips were destitute,
Kind eyebeams spake while yet his tongue was mute.

Your intrusion was worth the courage it cost; it emboldened to future assaults to carry this fort of bashfulness. During all the time he lived near me, our estates being separated only by a gate and shaded avenue, I seldom caught sight of him; and when I did it was but to lose it the moment he suspected he was visible; oftenest seen on his hill-top screened behind the shrubbery and disappearing like a hare into the bush when surprised. I remember of his being in my house but twice, and then he was so ill at ease that he found excuse for leaving politely forthwith,—"the stove was so hot," "the clock ticked so loud." Yet he once complained to me of his wish to meet oftener, and dwelt on the delights of fellowship, regretting he had so little. ⟨. . .⟩

He strove by disposition to be sunny and genial, traits not native to him. Constitutionally shy, recluse, melancholy, only by shafts of wit and flow of humor could he deliver himself. There was a soft sadness in his smile, a reserve in his glance, telling how isolate he was. Was he ever one of his company while in it? There was an aloofness, a *besides*, that refused to affiliate himself with himself, even. His readers must feel this, while unable to account for it, perhaps, or express it adequately. A believer in transmitted traits needs but read his pedigree to find the genesis of what characterized him distinctly, and made him and his writings their inevitable sequel. Everywhere you will find persons of his type and complexion similar in cast of character and opinions.—A. BRONSON ALCOTT, "Hawthorne" (July 1869), *Concord Days*, 1872, pp. 193–97

In him opposite qualities met, and were happily and harmoniously blended; and this was true of him physically as well as intellectually. He was tall and strongly built, with broad shoulders, deep chest, a massive head, black hair, and large dark eyes. Wherever he was he attracted attention by his imposing presence. He looked like a man who might have held the stroke-oar in a university boat. And his genius, as all the world knows, was of masculine force and sweep.

But, on the other hand, no man had more of the feminine element than he. He was feminine in his quick perceptions, his fine insight, his sensibility to beauty, his delicate reserve, his purity of feeling. No man comprehended woman more perfectly; none has painted woman with a more exquisite and ethereal pencil. And his face was as mobile and rapid in its changes of expression as is the face of a young girl. His lip and cheek heralded the word before it was spoken. His eyes would darken visibly under the touch of a passing emotion, like the waters of a fountain ruffled by the breeze of summer. So, too, he was the shyest of men. The claims and courtesies of social life were terrible to him. The thought of making a call would keep him awake in his bed. At breakfast, he could not lay a piece of butter upon a lady's plate without a little trembling of the hand: this is a fact, and not a phrase. He was so shy that in the presence of two intimate friends he would be less easy and free-spoken than in that of only one.

And yet the presence of his kind was cordial, and in some sense necessary to him. If his shyness held him back, his sympathies drew him out with a force nearly as strong. And, unlike most men who are at once intellectual and shy, he was not a lover, or a student, of books. He read books as they came in his way, or for a particular purpose, but he made no claim to the honors of learning or scholarship. A great library had no charms for him. He rarely bought a book, and the larger part of his small collection had come to him by gift. His mind did not feed upon the printed page. It will be noticed that in his writings he very seldom introduces a quotation or makes any allusion to the writings of others. The raptures of the bibliomaniac, fondling his tall copies, his wide margins, his unique specimens, his vellum pages, were as strange to him as are the movements of a violin-player's arm to the deaf man's eye.—GEORGE S. HILLARD, "The English Note-Books of Nathaniel Hawthorne," *Atlantic*, Sept. 1870, pp. 258–59

That most lovable of writers was also—to those who knew him intimately—one of the most lovable of men. My acquaintance with him was slight; but it has left on my mind a vivid impression of his painful shyness in general society, and the retiring—nay, morbid delicacy—with which he shrank from notice.—S. C. HALL, *Retrospect of a Long Life*, 1883, p. 420

The door was opened to my ring by a tall handsome boy whom I suppose to have been Mr. Julian Hawthorne; and the next moment I found myself in the presence of the romancer, who entered from some room beyond. He advanced carrying his head with a heavy forward droop, and with a pace for which I decided that the word would be *pondering*. It was the pace of a bulky man of fifty, and his head was that beautiful head we all know from the many pictures of it. But Hawthorne's *look* was different from that of any picture of him that I have seen. It was sombre and brooding, as the look of such a poet should have been; it was the look of a man who had dealt faithfully and therefore sorrowfully with that problem of evil which forever attracted, forever evaded Hawthorne. It was by no means troubled; it was full of a dark repose. Others who knew him better and saw him oftener were familiar with other aspects, and I remember that one night at Longfellow's table, when one of the guests happened to speak of the photograph of Hawthorne which hung in a corner of the room, Lowell said, after a glance at it, "Yes, it's good; but it hasn't his fine *accipitral* look."

In the face that confronted me, however, there was nothing of keen alertness; but only a sort of quiet, patient intelligence, for which I seek the right word in vain. It was a very regular face, with beautiful eyes; the mustache, still entirely dark, was dense over the fine mouth. Hawthorne was dressed in black, and he had a certain effect which I remember, of seeming to have on a black cravat with no visible collar. He was such a man that if I had ignorantly met him anywhere I should have instantly felt him to be a personage.—WILLIAM DEAN HOWELLS, "My First Visit to New England" (1894), *Literary Friends and Acquaintance*, 1900

General

His style is classical and pure, his imagination exceedingly delicate and fanciful, and through all his writings there runs a vein of sweetest poetry.

Perhaps we have no writer so deeply imbued with the early literature of America; or who can so well portray the times and manners of the Puritans.

Hitherto Mr. Hawthorne has published no work of magnitude; but it is to be hoped that one who has shown such unequivocal evidence of talent will soon give to the world some production which shall place him in a higher rank than can be obtained by one whose efforts are confined to the sphere of magazines and annuals.—HORATIO BRIDGE (1836), *Personal Recollections of Nathaniel Hawthorne*, 1893, p. 71

He is peculiar and *not* original—unless in those detailed fancies and detached thoughts which his want of general originality will deprive of the appreciation due to them, in preventing them forever reaching the *public* eye. He is infinitely too fond of allegory, and can never hope for popularity so long as he persists in it. This he will not do, for allegory is at war with the whole tone of his nature, which disports itself never so well as when escaping from the mysticism of his Goodman Browns and White Old Maids into the hearty, genial, but still Indian-summer sunshine of his Wakefields and Little Annie's Rambles. Indeed, *his* spirit of "metaphor run-mad" is clearly imbibed from the phalanx and phalanstery atmosphere in which he has been so long struggling for breath. He has not half the material for the exclusiveness of authorship that he possesses for its universality. He has the purest style, the finest taste, the most available scholarship, the most delicate humor, the most touching pathos, the most radiant imagination, the most consummate ingenuity; and with these varied good qualities he has done *well* as a mystic. But is there any one of these qualities which should prevent his doing doubly as well in a career of honest, upright, sensible, prehensible and comprehensible things? Let him mend his pen, get a bottle of visible ink, come out from the Old Manse, cut Mr. Alcott, hang (if possible) the editor of *The Dial*, and throw out of the window to the pigs all his odd numbers of *The North American Review*.—EDGAR ALLAN POE, "Nathaniel Hawthorne" (1847), *Essays and Reviews*, ed. G. R. Thompson, 1984, pp. 587–88

There is Hawthorne, with genius so shrinking and rare
That you hardly at first see the strength that is there;
A frame so robust, with a nature so sweet,
So earnest, so graceful, so solid, so fleet,
Is worth a descent from Olympus to meet;
'T is as if a rough oak that for ages had stood,
With his gnarled bony branches like ribs of the wood,
Should bloom, after cycles of struggle and scathe,
With a single anemone trembly and rathe;
His strength is so tender, his wildness so meek,
That a suitable parallel sets one to seek,—
He's a John Bunyan Fouqué, a Puritan Tieck;
When Nature was shaping him, clay was not granted
For making so full-sized a man as she wanted,
So, to fill out her model, a little she spared
From some finer-grained stuff for a woman prepared,
And she could not have hit a more excellent plan
For making him fully and perfectly man.
The success of her scheme gave her so much delight,
That she tried it again, shortly after, in Dwight;
Only, while she was kneading and shaping the clay,
She sang to her work in her sweet childish way,
And found, when she'd put the last touch to his soul,
That the music had somehow got mixed with the whole.
          —JAMES RUSSELL LOWELL, A *Fable for Critics*,
          1848

⟨. . .⟩ decidedly the greatest living literary man in this country, greatest, in romance, now writing the English language. —RUFUS W. GRISWOLD, Letter to James T. Fields (Jan. 24, 1850), *Passages from the Correspondence and Other Papers of Rufus W. Griswold*, ed. W. M. Griswold, 1898, p. 258

I think we have no romancer but yourself, nor have had any for this long time. I had become so set in this feeling, that but for your last two stories I should have given up hoping, and believed that all we were to look for in the way of spontaneous growth were such languid, lifeless, sexless creations as in the view of certain people constitute the chief triumphs of a sister art as manifested among us.

But there is rich red blood in Hester, and the flavor of the sweet-fern and the bayberry are not truer to the soil than the native sweetness of our little Phœbe! The Yankee mind has for the most part budded and flowered in pots of English earth, but you have fairly raised yours as a seedling in the natural soil. My criticism has to stop here; the moment a fresh mind takes in the elements of the common life about us and transfigures them, I am contented to enjoy and admire, and let others analyze. Otherwise I should be tempted to display my appreciating sagacity in pointing out a hundred touches, transcriptions of nature, of character, of sentiment, true as the daguerreotype, free as crayon sketching, which arrested me even in the midst of the palpitating story. Only one word, then this: that the solid reality and homely truthfulness of the actual and present part of the story are blended with its weird and ghostly shadows with consummate skill and effect; this was perhaps the special difficulty of the story.—OLIVER WENDELL HOLMES, Letter to Nathaniel Hawthorne (April 9, 1851), cited in George Parsons Lathrop, A *Study of Hawthorne*, 1876, p. 232

Hawthorne is a grand favourite of mine, and I shall be sorry if he do not go on surpassing himself.—GEORGE ELIOT, Letter to Mrs. Taylor (Aug. 19, 1852)

First, then, on this special shelf stands Nathaniel Hawthorne's *Twice-Told Tales*. It is difficult to explain why I like these short sketches and essays, written in the author's early youth, better than his later, more finished, and better-known novels and romances. The world sets greater store by *The Scarlet Letter* and *Transformation* than by this little book—and, in such matters of liking against the judgment of the world, there is no appeal. I think the reason of my liking consists in this—that the novels were written for the world, while the tales seem written for the author; in these he is actor and audience in one. Consequently, one gets nearer him, just as one gets nearer an artist in his first sketch than in his finished picture. And after all, one takes the greatest pleasure in those books in which a peculiar personality is most clearly revealed. A thought may be very commendable *as* a thought, but I value it chiefly as a window through which I can obtain insight on the thinker; and Mr Hawthorne's personality is peculiar, and specially peculiar in a new country like America. He is quiet, fanciful, quaint, and his humour is shaded by a certain meditativeness of spirit. Although a Yankee, he partakes of none of the characteristics of a Yankee. His thinking and his style have an antique air. His roots strike down through the visible mould of the present, and draw sustenance from the generations under ground. The ghosts that haunt the chamber of his mind are the ghosts of dead men and women. He has a strong smack of the Puritan; he wears around him, in the New-England town, something of the darkness and mystery of the aboriginal forest. He is a shy, silent, sensitive, much-ruminating man, with no special overflow of animal spirits. He loves solitude and the things which age has made reverent. There is nothing modern about him. Emerson's writing has a cold cheerless glitter, like the new furniture in a warehouse, which will come of use by and by; Hawthorne's, the rich, subdued colour of furniture in a Tudor mansion-house—which has winked to long-extinguished fires, which has been toned by the usage of departed generations. In many of the *Twice-Told Tales* this peculiar personality is charmingly exhibited. He writes of the street or the sea-shore, his eye takes in every object, however trifling, and on these he hangs comments melancholy and humorous. He does not require to go far for a subject; he will stare on the puddles in the street of a New-England village, and immediately it becomes a Mediterranean Sea with empires lying on its muddy shores. If the sermon be written out fully in your heart, almost any text will be suitable—if you have to find your sermon *in* your text, you may search the Testament, New and Old, and be as poor at the close of Revelation as when you started at the first book of Genesis. Several of the papers which I like best are monologues, fanciful, humorous, or melancholy; and of these, my chief favourites are—"Sunday at Home," "Night Sketches," "Footprints on the Sea-shore," and the "Seven Vagabonds." This last seems to me almost the most exquisite thing which has flowed from its author's pen—a perfect little drama, the place a showman's waggon, the time the falling of a summer shower, full of subtle suggestions, which, if followed, will lead the reader away out of the story altogether; and illuminated by a grave, wistful kind of humour, which plays in turns upon the author's companions, and upon the author himself. Of all Mr Hawthorne's gifts, this gift of humour—which would light up the skull and cross-bones of a village churchyard, which would be silent at a dinner-table—is to me the most delightful.

Then this writer has a strangely weird power. He loves ruins like the ivy, he skims the twilight like the bat, he makes himself a familiar of the phantoms of the heart and brain. He believes in ghosts; perhaps he has seen one burst on him from the impalpable air. He is fascinated by the jarred brain and the ruined heart. Other men collect china, books, pictures, jewels, this writer collects singular human experiences, ancient wrongs and agonies, murders done on unfrequented roads, crimes that seem to have no motive, and all the dreary mysteries of the world of will. To his chamber of horrors Madame Tussaud's is nothing. With proud, prosperous, healthy men, Mr Hawthorne has little sympathy; he prefers a cracked piano to a new one, he likes cobwebs in the corner of his rooms. All this peculiar taste comes out strongly in the little book in whose praise I am writing. I read "The Minister's Black Veil," and find it the first sketch of the *Scarlet Letter*. In "Wakefield"—the story of the man who left his wife, remaining away twenty years, but who yet looked upon her every day to appease his burning curiosity as to her manner of enduring his absence—I find the keenest analysis of an almost incomprehensible act. And then Mr Hawthorne has a skill in constructing allegories which no one of his contemporaries, either English or American, possesses. These allegorical papers may be read with pleasure, for their ingenuity, their grace, their poetical feeling; but just as, gazing on the surface of a stream, admiring the ripples and eddies, and the widening rings made by the butterfly falling into it, you begin to be conscious that there is something at the bottom, and gradually a dead face wavers upwards from the oozy weeds, becoming every moment more clearly defined, so through Mr Hawthorne's graceful sentences, if read attentively, begins to flash the hidden meaning, a meaning, perhaps, the writer did not care to express formally and in set terms, and which he merely suggests and leaves the reader to make out for himself. If you have the book I am writing about, turn up "David Swan," "The Great Carbuncle," "The Fancy Show-box," and after you have read these, you will understand what I mean.—ALEXANDER SMITH, "A Shelf in My Bookcase," *Dreamthorp*, 1863, pp. 190–94

Hawthorne was a genius. As a master of prose, he will come in the first class of all who have written the English language. He had not the grand style, but who has had a delicacy of touch superior to his?—CHARLES SUMNER, Letter to Henry Wadsworth Longfellow (May 21, 1864), cited in Edward L. Pierce, *Memoir and Letters of Charles Sumner*, 1893, Vol. 4, p. 202

In a patch of sunlight, flecked by the shade of tall, murmuring pines, at the summit of a gently swelling mound where the wild-flowers had climbed to find the light and the stirring of fresh breezes, the tired poet was laid beneath the green turf. Poet let us call him, though his chants were not modulated in the rhythm of verse. The element of poetry is air: we know the poet by his atmospheric effects, by the blue of his distances, by the softening of every hard outline he touches, by the silvery mist in which he veils deformity and clothes what is common so that it changes to awe-inspiring mystery, by the clouds of gold and purple which are the drapery of his dreams. And surely we have had but one prose-writer who could be compared with him in aërial perspective, if we may use the painter's term. If Irving is the Claude of our unrhymed poetry, Hawthorne is its Poussin.—OLIVER WENDELL HOLMES, "Hawthorne," *Atlantic*, July 1864, pp. 100–101

The death of Nathaniel Hawthorne is a national event. In original creative genius no name in our literature is superior to his; and while everybody was asking whether it were impossible to write an American novel, he wrote romances that were hardly possible elsewhere, because they were so purely American. There was never, certainly, an author more utterly independent than Hawthorne of the circumstances that surrounded him. In his style, even, which, for a rich, idiomatic raciness, is unsurpassed, there was no touch of any of the schools of his time. It was as clear and simple as Thackeray's, and as felicitous; but there was a flush of color in it, sometimes, of which Thackeray has no trace. But of the literary influences of his time, and even of his personal association, there is no sign in his writings. The form in which his world was revealed, like that world itself, was entirely his own.

Nor was there any foreign flavor whatever in his genius. It was not a growth of the English, or the German, or the French; nor was it eclectic. It was American. It was almost New England, except for that universality which belongs to such genius, and which made the *Marble Faun* no less a characteristic work of Hawthorne's than the *Scarlet Letter*. Yet in both there is the same general quality, although one is a story of old Puritan days in Boston, and the other of modern life in Rome.

It is remarkable that Hawthorne was an author, and a copious one, long before he was generally recognized. His delight, in former days, was to insist that no writer was so obscure as he; and it is one evidence of the vitality of his power that he still wrote on. He piped, and the world would not sing; he played, and it would not dance. But he was sent to be a piper, and so he piped until the world paused, charmed by the rare melody, and acknowledged the master. His place in our literature he took at once when the *Scarlet Letter* was published, and in that place he was never disturbed, and will always remain. ⟨. . .⟩

The charm of his writings is imperishable. The fresh glow of genius which pervades them, apart from the essential interest of the stories, is indescribable. They have an individual pungency which does not always mark the works of our authors of an equal fame. The sparkle of humor which glitters every where upon his page, often weird but never dull, and a certain steadiness and self-possession of tone, equally free from rhetoric or baldness, certify a manly vigor and character which does not necessarily distinguish so subtle and poetic a nature. —GEORGE WILLIAM CURTIS, "Editor's Easy Chair," *Harper's New Monthly Magazine*, Aug. 1864, p. 405

The Puritanism of the past found its unwilling poet in Hawthorne, the rarest creative imagination of the century, the rarest in some ideal respects since Shakespeare.—JAMES RUSSELL LOWELL, "Thoreau" (1865), *Works*, Riverside ed., Vol. 1, p. 365

The devotee of Hawthorne is unrelenting in certain moody prejudices, Epicurean in his tastes and aspirations, and dreamy and uncertain in his theory of this life and the next.—NOAH PORTER, *Books and Reading*, 1870, p. 230

Hawthorne seems to me the most of a Man of Genius America has produced in the way of Imagination: yet I have never found an Appetite for his Books.—EDWARD FITZGERALD, Letter to W. F. Pollock (Nov. 1872)

Hawthorne, it is true, expanded so constantly, that however many works he might have produced, it seems unlikely that any one of them would have failed to record some large movement in his growth; and therefore it is perhaps to be regretted that his life could not have been made to solely serve his genius, so that we might have had the whole sweep of his imagination clearly exposed. As it is, he has not given us a large variety of characters; and Hester, Zenobia, and Miriam bear a certain general likeness one to another. Phœbe, however, is quite at the opposite pole of womanhood; Hilda is as unlike any of them as it is easy to conceive of her being; and Priscilla, again, is a feminine nature of unique calibre, as weird but not so warm as Goethe's Mignon, and at the same time a distinctly American type, in her nervous yet captivating fragility. In Priscilla and Phœbe are embodied two widely opposed classes of New England women. The male characters, with the exception of Donatello and Hollingsworth, are not so remarkable as the feminine ones: Coverdale and Kenyon come very close together, both being artistic and both reflectors for the persons that surround them; and Dimmesdale is to some extent the same character,—with the artistic escape closed upon his passions, so that they turn within and ravage his heart,—arrested and altered by Puritan influences. Chillingworth is perhaps too devilish a shape of revenge to be discussed as a human individual. Septimius, again, is distinct; and the characterization of Westervelt, in *Blithedale*, slight as it is, is very stimulating. Perhaps, after all, what leads us to pronounce upon the whole fictitious company a stricture of homogeneity is the fact that the author, though presenting us each time with a set of persons sufficiently separate from his previous ones, does not emphasize their differences with the same amount of external description that we habitually depend upon from a novelist. The similarity is more in the author's mode of presentation than in the creations themselves.

This monotone in which all the personages of his dramas share is nearly related with some special distinctions of his genius. He is so fastidious in his desire for perfection, that he can scarcely permit his actors to speak loosely or ungrammatically: though retaining their essential individuality, they are endowed with the author's own delightful power of expression. This outward phasis of his work separates it at once from that of the simple novelist, and leads us to consider the special applicability to it of the term "romance." He had not the realistic tendency, as we usually understand that, but he possessed the power to create a new species of fiction. For the kind of romance that he has left us differs from all compositions previously so called. It is not romance in the sense of D'Urfé's or Scudéri's; it is very far from coming within the scope of Fielding's "romances"; and it is entirely unconnected with the tales of the German Romantic school. It is not the romance of sentiment; nor that of incident, adventure, and character viewed under a worldly coloring: it has not the mystic

and melodramatic bent belonging to Tieck and Novalis and Fouqué. There are two things which radically isolate it from all these. The first is its quality of revived belief. Hawthorne, as has been urged already, is a great believer, a man who has faith; his belief goes out toward what is most beautiful, and this he finds only in moral truth. With him, poetry and moral insight are sacredly and indivisibly wedded, and their progeny is perfect beauty. This unsparingly conscientious pursuit of the highest truth, this metaphysical instinct, found in conjunction with a varied and tender appreciation of all forms of human or other life, is what makes him so decidedly the representative of a wholly new order of novelists. Belief, however, is not what he has usually been credited with, so much as incredulity. But the appearance of doubt is superficial, and arises from his fondness for illuminating fine but only half-perceptible traces of truth with the torch of superstition. Speaking of the supernatural, he says in his English journal: "It is remarkable that Scott should have felt interested in such subjects, being such a worldly and earthly man as he was; but then, indeed, almost all forms of popular superstition do clothe the ethereal with earthly attributes, and so make it grossly perceptible." This observation has a still greater value when applied to Hawthorne himself. And out of this questioning belief and transmutation of superstition into truth—for such is more exactly his method—proceeds also that quality of value and rarity and awe-enriched significance, with which he irradiates real life until it is sublimed to a delicate cloud-image of the eternal verities.

If these things are limitations, they are also foundations of a vast originality. Every greatness must have an outline. So that, although he is removed from the list of novelists proper, although his spiritual inspiration scares away a large class of sympathies, and although his strictly New England atmosphere seems to chill and restrain his dramatic fervor, sometimes to his disadvantage, these facts, on the other hand, are so many trenches dug around him, fortifying his fair eminence. Isolation and a certain degree of limitation, in some such sense as this, belong peculiarly to American originality. But Hawthorne is the embodiment of the youth of this country; and though he will doubtless furnish inspiration to a long line of poets and novelists, it must be hoped that they, likewise, will stand for other phases of its development, to be illustrated in other ways. No tribute to Hawthorne is less in accord with the biddings of his genius than that which would merely make a school of followers.

It is too early to say what position Hawthorne will take in the literature of the world; but as his influence gains the ascendant in America, by prompting new and *un*-Hawthornesque originalities, it is likely also that it will be made manifest in England, according to some unspecifiable ratio. Not that any period is to be distinctly colored by the peculiar dye in which his own pages are dipped; but the renewed tradition of a highly organized yet simple style, and still more the masculine tenderness and delicacy of thought and the fine adjustment of æsthetic and ethical obligations, the omnipresent truthfulness which he carries with him, may be expected to become a constituent part of very many minds widely opposed among themselves. I believe there is no fictionist who penetrates so far into individual consciences as Hawthorne; that many persons will be found who derive a profoundly religious aid from his unobtrusive but commanding sympathy. In the same way, his sway over the literary mind is destined to be one of no secondary degree. "Deeds are the offspring of words," says Heine; "Goethe's pretty words are childless." Not so with Hawthorne's. Hawthorne's repose is the acme of motion; and though turning on an axis of conservatism, the radicalism of his mind is irresistible; he is one of the most powerful because most unsuspected revolutionists of the world. Therefore, not only is he an incalculable factor in private character, but in addition his unnoticed leverage for the thought of the age is prodigious. These great abilities, subsisting with a temper so modest and unaffected, and never unhumanized by the abstract enthusiasm for art, place him on a plane between Shakespere and Goethe. With the universality of the first only just budding within his mind, he has not so clear a response to all the varying tones of lusty human life, and the individuality in his utterance amounts, at particular instants, to constraint. With less erudition than Goethe, but also less of the freezing pride of art, he is infinitely more humane, sympathetic, holy. His creations are statuesquely moulded like Goethe's, but they have the same quick music of heart-throbs that Shakespere's have. Hawthorne is at the same moment ancient and modern, plastic and picturesque.—GEORGE PARSONS LATHROP, A *Study of Hawthorne*, 1876, pp. 326–31

> But he whose quickened eye
> Saw through New England's life her inmost spirit,—
> Her heart, and all the stays on which it leant,—
> Returns not, since he laid the pencil by
> Whose mystic touch none other shall inherit!
> —EDMUND CLARENCE STEDMAN, "Hawthorne," 1877

Hawthorne appalls—entices.—EMILY DICKINSON, Letter to Thomas Wentworth Higginson (1879)

One of the most characteristic of Hawthorne's literary methods is his habitual use of guarded under-statements and veiled hints. It is not a sign of weakness, but of conscious strength, when he surrounds each delineation with a sort of penumbra, takes you into his counsels, offers hypotheses, as, "May it not have been?" or, "Shall we not rather say?" and sometimes, like a conjurer, urges particularly upon you the card he does not intend you to accept. He seems not quite to know whether Arthur Dimmesdale really had a fiery scar on his breast, or what finally became of Miriam and her lover. He will gladly share with you any information he possesses, and, indeed, has several valuable hints to offer; but that is all. The result is, that you place yourself by his side to look with him at his characters, and gradually share with him the conviction that they must be real. Then, when he has you thus in possession, he calls your attention to the profound ethics involved in the tale, and yet does it so gently that you never think of the moral as being obtrusive.

All this involved a trait which was always supreme in him,—a marvellous self-control. He had by nature that gift which the musical composer Jomelli went to a teacher to seek,—"the art of not being embarrassed by his own ideas." Mrs. Hawthorne told me that her husband grappled alone all winter with *The Scarlet Letter*, and came daily from his study with a knot in his forehead; and yet his self-mastery was so complete that every sentence would seem to have crystallized in an atmosphere of perfect calm. We see the value of this element in his literary execution, when we turn from it to that of an author so great as Lowell, for instance, and see him often entangled and weighed down by his own rich thoughts, his style being overcrowded by the very wealth it bears. Hawthorne never needed Italic letters to distribute his emphasis, never a footnote for assistance. There was no conception so daring that he shrank from attempting it; and none that he could not so master as to state it, if he pleased, in terms of monosyllables. —THOMAS WENTWORTH HIGGINSON, "Hawthorne," *Short Studies of American Authors*, 1880, pp. 8–9

In Hawthorne, whose faculty was developed among scholars and with the finest additaments of scholarship, we have our first true artist in literary expression, as well as the most completely equipped genius of romance. His subtle insight into the elements of character was marvelous. He was original and purely American,—Puritan, even, in his cast of thought and in all the internal and external conditions of his creation. But art is of no country. All ages temper the steel of the fine workman; all literatures whet the edge of his tools. In his sense of the controlling influence of powers beyond the individual's grasp, Hawthorne was Grecian. *The Scarlet Letter* and *The Blithedale Romance* are as fierce, unrelenting tragedy—controlling not only the actors but the writer—as anything in Æschylus. But Hawthorne's Fate came in the more modern form of "heredity." There were no angry gods; the "Sisters Three" had their origin in the ancestral stock a few generations back. His sense of their power, however, was intense, and was deeply based in the constitution of his own mind. He was too sane a man, of course, to yield credence to the Puritan suspicion of demonic influences, yet he was too much of a seer not to have discovered that, whether demons exist in nature or not, there are demons which are the projections of our own minds; and the struggle of his art was so to materialize these projections as to give them, not the reality which Cotton Mather insisted upon, but a spiritualized reality equally potent over the actions of men. Mr. Henry James, Jr., has pointed out—very justly, it would seem—a use made of the "scarlet letter" wherein Hawthorne overreached himself,—where the spiritual projection becomes labored and artificial. As far as Hawthorne attempts to make this image a potent force in Arthur Dimmesdale's mind, his instinct is unerring; but when he tries to make it visible to little Pearl and Roger Chillingworth, he passes from art into artifice. There is, perhaps, no natural person in *The Scarlet Letter*, just as there is no natural Hamlet in life; but we must accept Arthur Dimmesdale as a marvelous embodiment of the Puritan conscience acting upon the finest human clay,—a clay made sensitive to every emotion, quickened by every intellectual force.

The artistic evolution of the plot is as perfect as that of the *Œdipus Tyrannus*. So, too, in *The House of Seven Gables*, Judge Pyncheon is equally an embodiment of the granitic forces of the Puritan temperament, inheriting, not its finer conscience, but its untempered rigidity as acted upon by the forces of life. The man breaks at last, but he never bends. In the same way each character in Hawthorne's small list is a finished study, at once local in its surroundings and general in its psychological elements. It is a study of man in his special environment,—more scientific than the science of to-day, because it does what science fails to do; it tries to settle the spiritual element in its true place as a factor in man's life. Others have surpassed Hawthorne in the management of external conduct, of dialogue, of home life, of local scenery; but none have reached the depth to which he penetrated in the study of the human heart as the creature of its own creation. In every higher qualification of the artist, he easily excels. His style is masterly in ease, grace, clearness,—the winning, absorbing, entrancing quality. His skill in hinting in ideal and spiritual elements is the most perfect in our day. His mastery of light and shade—the power of deepening gloom by sunshine and intensifying sunshine by means of darkness—is of the finest order, at once the gift of original perception and the result of most assiduous practice. Probably few writers ever made so many successes that were failures, or so many failures that were successes; that is, few ever did so much that was to others artistically perfect in order that they might do something artistically perfect to themselves. Mr. James marvels at the existence of the *Note-Books*; yet their publication has thrown a flood of light not only upon the workings of Hawthorne's mind but on the sources of his artistic effects. They supplement with a sunny external quality the gloom of his psychology. They show us in his own nature a capacity for beauty and sweetness, where his own generation saw only a capacity for morbid analysis; that is, they furnish the biography of the sympathetic side of his mind, while the novels represent what was equally real to his emotional nature. No doubt, while his actual life was simple and pure-minded, capable of absorbing beauty and interest, he had, in imagination, lived through the tortures of the damned. He had given to Hester and Dimmesdale no exaltation or despair of which he was not himself capable, and probably none which he had not, by sheer force of imagination, without any adequate external cause, passed through. Others have been capable of such moods—the moods of "angels and ministers of grace" as well as of demons—without being either sinners or angels; but few have obtained the power of expressing them as he did. He spiritualized everything he touched, with a quality which is felt but cannot be analyzed,— which eludes every attempt to fix it. Little Pearl, standing in front of Governor Bellingham's mansion, looking at the "bright wonder of a house, began to caper and dance, and imperatively required that the whole breadth of sunshine should be stripped off its front and given her to play with." It was no harder to strip off that sunshine for little Pearl than it is to detach and handle the spiritual quality of these romances.

We had never reached such insight, or such grace of style, before Hawthorne, and we have never reached it since. As a writer, he was long in obscurity and had little influence on other authors. Emerging into something like local note when the first series of *Twice-Told Tales* was published, in 1837, he dawned upon a wider field, in 1842, with the addition of the *Second Series*. The intensity of his gloom was lightened in the *Mosses from an Old Manse* in 1846, and he then reached a larger circle of readers. In 1850, '51, and '52, he became national in fame, and soon reached the height.—JAMES HERBERT MORSE, "The Native Element in American Fiction," *Century Magazine*, July 1883, pp. 293–94

Simpler, clearer, more elegant English has never—even by Swift, Addison, or Goldsmith—been made the vehicle of thought and emotion equally profound, delicate, variant, and tortuous. Singularly choice and appropriate in diction; flowing and placid in movement, always sweet and pellucid, giving to objects a subtle ethereal aspect. His pen is a magician's wand, 'creating the semblance of a world out of airy matter, with the impalpable beauty of a soap-bubble.' We have all been exhorted to give days and nights to Addison. Rather, let us give days and nights to Macaulay, Carlyle and Hawthorne.

Standing aloof from common interests, looking at the present with shaded eyes, into the past with a half-wistful gaze, attracted by the remote, strange, and unusual, with a style admirably adapted to produce the effect of weird-like mystery,—Hawthorne is not a novelist. His fictions, in conception and performance, are always and essentially romances. Yet have they a character of fundamental trueness to spiritual laws, of harmony with time, place, and circumstance,—of realism existing in an ideal atmosphere, or invested with the halo of a poetic medium. We have not the worn-out paraphernalia of abbeys, castles, courts, gentry, aristocracy, and sovereigns; but we have types, mental conditions,—beyond the sphere of habitual experience, indeed, yet belonging profoundly to spirit and to man. No civilization has produced a romantic genius at

all comparable in power to his. Other writers have been more learned, more dramatic, more versatile, more comprehensive. His stories are generally deficient in converging unity. His personages seldom reveal themselves; but, as in the *Marble Faun*, we are told what they are, in page upon page of description, keen, minute, finished,—marvellous workmanship. No one ever depended so little upon plot or incident. Facts are subordinated to the influences with which they are charged. He is not a portrait-painter who sets forth a complete individuality. His forte is not in adventure, not in movement; but in the depicture of the rare and the occult, in the operation and results of involved and conflicting motives, feelings, and tendencies. He is here a solitary original in English letters. It may be questioned whether the *Scarlet Letter*, as an example of imaginative writing, has its parallel in any literature.—ALFRED H. WELSH, *Development of English Literature and Language*, 1883, Vol. 2, pp. 512–13

⟨. . .⟩ In New England, the history with which we are most familiar is that according to Nathaniel Hawthorne. Now dark and sombre, now warm and full of sunlight, always picturesque and imaginative, the story of the past, disconnected and uncertain, but yet vivid and real, has been woven by the hand of the enchanter to charm and fascinate all who listen. In Hawthorne's pages the ancient Puritan society, austere and rigid, and the later colonial aristocracy, laced and powdered, live and move, a delight to the present generation. But over all alike, over grave and gay, over the forbidding and the attractive, the delicate and morbid genius of the novelist has cast an air of mystery. In these stories we live in an atmosphere of half-told secrets, which are withal so real that we cannot help believing that somewhere, in some musty records or in letters yellow with time, we shall find answers to the questionings with which they fill our minds. Surely there must have been some one who had peeped beneath the black veil, who had known Maule and the Pynchons, who had seen the prophetic pictures, who could tell us what the little world of Boston said about Hester Prynne and little Pearl, about Arthur Dimmesdale and Roger Chillingworth. One cannot help looking on every page of New England history for the characters of Hawthorne, and for an explanation of their lives. Disappointment always ensues, but hope is revived with each old manuscript that finds its way into print.—HENRY CABOT LODGE, *Studies in History*, 1884, pp. 21–22

He was a great writer—the greatest writer in prose fiction whom America has produced.—ANDREW LANG, "To Edgar Allan Poe," *Letters to Dead Authors*, 1886, p. 149

The people are gaining upon Nathaniel Hawthorne's works. A century hence, when the most popular authors of to-day are forgotten, he will probably be more widely read than ever. —EDWARD P. ROE, "The Element of Life in Fiction," *Forum*, April 1888, p. 229

It is hardly necessary to add that success, such as Hawthorne's, implies the happiest expression. Not to dwell on Hawthorne's style, simple mention may be made of his power of condensation, his exquisite application of the law of contrast, his repose, his judgment or taste; and, over and above all, his poet's skill in suggestiveness and in the creation of atmosphere, his primal power of pure, bold, sustained imagination— imagination which, for purity and subtilty has been equalled in English literature perhaps not more than once before since the robe fell from the shoulders of the unapproachable Elizabethan.—JOHN VANCE CHENEY, "Hawthorne," *The Golden Guess: Essays on Poetry and the Poets*, 1891, pp. 291–92

The Scarlet Letter is beyond doubt the foremost story yet written on this continent, and the fact that it holds the third place in this long list is both suggestive and encouraging. *The Marble Faun* follows close upon its greater companion; for, however fascinating the later book in its subtle psychologic insight and however beautiful its art, it remains true that the earlier story surpasses it in closeness of construction and in depth and intensity of human interest. That a book of such quality finds so wide a reading shows that the finest art does not fail to charm when it allies itself with the deepest life. —HAMILTON W. MABIE, "The Most Popular Novels in America," *Forum*, Dec. 1893, p. 512

I suppose there are few English readers of fiction, having a taste for better things than the merely sensational novel, who are not acquainted with *The Scarlet Letter, The House of the Seven Gables*, and other works of Nathaniel Hawthorne, though I am afraid they are now less read—and, may I add, appreciated—than they were thirty years ago. Perhaps there is a reason for this; Hawthorne's works remind us of the laborious, patient, and delicate art of the fine gem-cutter, and to "taste" them thoroughly every detail has to be noticed and dwelt upon, and its suggestiveness remembered. A writer who produces this sort of work cannot be extremely voluminous, and, nowadays, for an author to retain his popularity he must be constantly producing some new thing—constantly, as it were, keeping himself "in evidence."—CAMILLA TOULMIN CROSLAND, *Landmarks of a Literary Life*, 1893, pp. 210–11

To men of our time, beyond doubt, his work seems generally not fantastic but imaginative, and surely not meretricious but in its own way beautiful. Nor is this the whole story: almost alone among our writers, we may say, Hawthorne has a lasting native significance. For this there are surely two good reasons. In the first place, he is almost the solitary American artist who has phrased his meaning in words of which the beauty seems sure to grow with the years. In the second place, what marks him as most impregnably American is this: when we look close to see what his meaning really was, we find it a thing that in the old days, at last finally dead and gone, had been the great motive power of his race. What Hawthorne really voices is that strange, morbid, haunting sense of other things that we see or hear, which underlay the intense idealism of the emigrant Puritans, and which remains perhaps the most inalienable emotional heritage of their children. It is Hawthorne, in brief, who finally phrases the meaning of such a life as Theophilus Eaton lived and Cotton Mather recorded.—BARRETT WENDELL, "American Literature," *Stelligeri and Other Essays concerning America*, 1893, p. 139

Hawthorne was no transcendentalist. He dwelt much in a world of ideas, and he sometimes doubted whether the tree on the bank or its image in the stream were the more real. But this had little in common with the philosophical idealism of his neighbors. He reverenced Emerson, and he held kindly intercourse—albeit a silent man and easily bored—with Thoreau and Ellery Channing, and even with Margaret Fuller. But his sharp eyes saw whatever was whimsical or weak in the apostles of the new faith. He had little enthusiasm for causes or reforms, and among so many abolitionists he remained a Democrat, and even wrote a campaign life of his friend Pierce.—HENRY A. BEERS, *Initial Studies in American Letters*, 1895, p. 123

Of the moderns, Hawthorne possesses in a remarkable degree the power of impressing unity on his creations. His hand is firm. He never wavers in style, stand-point, aim, or subject by a hair's-breadth. His plots are simple, his motives more so; in fact, no people ever were dominated by so few impulses as are the characters in Hawthorne's romances. There is something Greek in their simplicity, although they are as unlike a Greek conception of humanity as are Caliban or Ariel. But they never waver. Such as the author conceived them in the first chapter, they remain to the end. There is no growth or development of character. This gives his tales an atmosphere which is never blown away by any nineteenth-century wind, and a unity which insures them a place in the literature which endures. There is a certain sameness about his style which might become monotonous in spite of its wonderful charm, and a limited experience of life which might become uninteresting, and an impress of a poverty-stricken and repellent external world which might become disheartening, but the unity is so thoroughly artistic that the pleasure received far outweighs the annoyance which is caused by the depressing and fatalistic atmosphere which envelops some of his romances.—CHARLES F. JOHNSON, *Elements of Literary Criticism*, 1898, pp. 34–35

Nearly all the Gothic machinery of Walpole, Mrs. Radcliffe, and Godwin is to be found in this Puritan: high winds, slamming doors, moonlight and starlight, magic and witchcraft, mysterious portraits, transformations, malignant beings, the elixir of life, the skeleton, the funeral, and the corpse in its shroud. To these sources of excitement were added, as time went on, mesmerism and clairvoyance. The novelty of Hawthorne's work is in his treatment. Like Shakespeare, he offers only a partial explanation of his unusual phemonena or none at all. Most unconventional is his use of witchcraft, as was pointed out by Poe, in 'The Hollow of Three Hills,' where to the imagination of the woman of sin, as she lays her head upon the witch's knees beneath the magic cloak, distant scenes of sorrow for which she is responsible are conveyed, not by viewing them in a magic mirror, but by the subtle sense of sound. And almost equally novel is the use made of the fountain of youth in 'Dr. Heidegger's Experiment.' The persecuting demon of romance, when he appears in Hawthorne's pages under the name of Roger Chillingworth, or the Spectre of the Catacomb, is a personification of the mistakes, misfortunes, and sins of our past life, which will not out of our imagination. The transformations—Pearl from a capricious, elfish being into a sober woman, and Donatello from a thoughtless, voluptuous animal into a man who feels the sad weight of humanity—have their analogies in real life. The supernatural world was with Hawthorne but the inner world of the conscience.

The ethical import of his narrative is always conveyed by means of a fanciful symbolism. The embroidered A that is hung about Hester Prynne's neck, the red stigma over Arthur Dimmesdale's heart, and Pearl in scarlet dress, are obviously symbolical. The black veil with which a Puritan minister conceals his face is the shadow of a dark deed. Donatello's hair-tipped ears are suggestions of his animalism. Moreover, Hawthorne was inclined to interpret figuratively events, nature, and art. Little Pearl runs from her mother and cannot be coaxed to return; that is typical of a moral gulf separating them. The sunless wood in which Hester stands alone images a moral solitude. Light streaming through the painted windows of a Gothic church is a foretaste of the 'glories of the better world.' As Hawthorne views a half-finished bust, and sees the human face struggling to get out of the marble, he remarks: 'As this bust in the block of marble, so does our individual fate exist in the limestone of time.' It has been said that Poe was a myth maker; Hawthorne likewise built up his own myths, and then he allegorized them like Bacon, turning them into apologues. Even the allegorical interpretation sometimes given to *The Marble Faun* is not to be ridiculed, for the allegory is there. Whatever may have been the origin of language, it has now become, in its common use, a direct representation of things, ideas, and feelings. Hawthorne did not always so treat it, but rather conceived of it as a system of hieroglyphics; a secret he does not call a secret, 'it is a wild venomous thing' imprisoned in the heart. This is the way of Spenser.

The story of Hawthorne is only half told when we say he refined Gothic art and fashioned it to high ethical purposes. As in the case of Poe, one of his great charms is his workmanship in structure and style. In the technique of the short tale, Poe was at least his equal; in the longer tale, where Poe left many loose ends, Hawthorne succeeded twice—in *The Scarlet Letter* (1850) and *The House of the Seven Gables* (1851). Poe modelled his style on Defoe and De Quincey, now suggesting the one and now the other. Hawthorne by laborious practice acquired a more individual style; the good taste of Addison and Irving are visible in it, and the brooding and dreamy fancy of Tieck, disguised however in the fusion.—WILBUR L. CROSS, *The Development of the English Novel*, 1899, pp. 163–66

Hawthorne's work you may read from end to end without the temptation to transfer so much as a line to the commonplace book. The road has taken you through many interesting scenes, and past many a beautiful landscape; you may have felt much and learned much; you might be glad to turn back straightway and travel the course over again; but you will have picked up no coin or jewel to put away in a cabinet. This characteristic of Hawthorne is the more noteworthy because of the moral quality of his work. A mere story-teller may naturally keep his narrative on the go, as we say,—that is one of the chief secrets of his art; but Hawthorne was not a mere story-teller. He was a moralist,—Emerson himself hardly more so; yet he has never a moral sentence. The fact is, he did not make sentences; he made books. The story, not the sentence, nor even the paragraph or the chapter, was the unit. The general truth—the moral—informed the work. Not only was it not affixed as a label; it was not given anywhere a direct and separable verbal expression. If the story does not convey it to you, you will never get it. Hawthorne, in short, was what, for lack of a better word, we may call a literary artist.—BRADFORD TORREY, "Writers That Are Quotable," *Atlantic*, March 1899, p. 407

Works

TWICE-TOLD TALES

When a new star rises in the heavens, people gaze after it for a season with the naked eye, and with such telescopes as they may find. In the stream of thought, which flows so peacefully deep and clear, through the pages of this book, we see the bright reflection of a spiritual star, after which men will be fain to gaze "with the naked eye and with the spy-glasses of criticism." This star is but newly risen; and ere long the observations of numerous star-gazers, perched up on armchairs and editors' tables, will inform the world of its magnitude and its place in the heaven of poetry, whether it be in the paw of the Great Bear, or on the forehead of Pegasus, or on the strings of the Lyre, or in the wing of the Eagle. Our own observations are as follows. To this little work we would say, "Live ever, sweet, sweet book." It comes from the hand of a man of genius. Everything about it has the freshness of morning and of May. These flowers and green leaves of poetry have not the dust of the highway upon them. They have been gathered fresh from the secret places of a peaceful and gentle heart. There flow deep waters, silent, calm, and cool; and the green trees look into them, and "God's blue heaven." The book, though in prose, is written nevertheless by a poet. He looks upon all things in the spirit of love, and with lively sympathies; for to him external form is but the representation of internal being, all things having a life, an end and aim. ⟨. . .⟩

Another characteristic of this writer is the exceeding beauty of his style. It is as clear as running waters are. Indeed he uses words as mere stepping-stones, upon which, with a free and youthful bound, his spirit crosses and recrosses the bright and rushing stream of thought. Some writers of the present day have introduced a kind of Gothic architecture into their style. All is fantastic, vast, and wondrous in the outward form, and within is mysterious twilight, and the swelling sound of an organ, and a voice chanting hymns in Latin, which need a translation for many of the crowd. To this we do not object. Let the priest chant in what language he will, so long as he understands his own mass-book. But if he wishes the world to listen and be edified, he will do well to choose a language that is generally understood.—HENRY WADSWORTH LONGFELLOW, "Hawthorne's *Twice-Told Tales*," *North American Review*, July 1837, pp. 59, 63

Mr. Hawthorne's volumes appear to us misnamed in two respects. In the first place they should not have been called *Twice-Told Tales*—for this is a title which will not bear *repetition*. If in the first collected edition they were twice-told, of course now they are thrice-told.—May we live to hear them told a hundred times! In the second place, these compositions are by no means *all* "Tales." The most of them are essays properly so called. It would have been wise in their author to have modified his title, so as to have had reference to all included. This point could have been easily arranged.

But under whatever titular blunders we receive this book, it is most cordially welcome. We have seen no prose composition by any American which can compare with *some* of these articles in the higher merits, or indeed in the lower; while there is not a single piece which would do dishonor to the best of the British essayists.

"The Rill from the Town Pump" which, through the *ad captandum* nature of its title, has attracted more of public notice than any one other of Mr. Hawthorne's compositions, is perhaps, the *least* meritorious. Among his best, we may briefly mention "The Hollow of the Three Hills;" "The Minister's Black Veil;" "Wakefield;" "Mr. Higginbotham's Catastrophe;" "Fancy's Show-Box;" "Dr. Heidegger's Experiment;" "David Swan;" "The Wedding Knell;" and "The White Old Maid." It is remarkable that all these, with one exception, are from the first volume.

The style of Mr. Hawthorne is purity itself. His *tone* is singularly effective—wild, plaintive, thoughtful, and in full accordance with his themes. We have only to object that there is insufficient diversity in these themes themselves, or rather in their character. His *originality* both of incident and of reflection is very remarkable; and this trait alone would ensure him at least *our* warmest regard and commendation. We speak here chiefly of the tales; the essays are not so markedly novel. Upon the whole we look upon him as one of the few men of indisputable genius to whom our country has as yet given birth.—EDGAR ALLAN POE, "Nathaniel Hawthorne" (1842), *Essays and Reviews*, ed. G. R. Thompson, 1984, pp. 568–69

From the press of Munroe & Co., Boston, in the year 1837, appeared *Twice-Told Tales*. Though not widely successful in their day and generation, they had the effect of making me known in my own immediate vicinity; insomuch that, however reluctantly, I was compelled to come out of my owl's nest and lionize in a small way. Thus I was gradually drawn somewhat into the world, and became pretty much like other people. My long seclusion had not made me melancholy or misanthropic, nor wholly unfitted me for the bustle of life; and perhaps it was the kind of discipline which my idiosyncrasy demanded, and chance and my own instincts, operating together, had caused me to do what was fittest.—NATHANIEL HAWTHORNE, Letter to Richard Henry Stoddard (1853), cited in Julian Hawthorne, *Nathaniel Hawthorne and His Wife*, 1884, Vol. 1, p. 98

THE SCARLET LETTER

We shall entirely mislead our reader if we give him to suppose that *The Scarlet Letter* is coarse in its details, or indecent in its phraseology. This very article of our own, is far less suited to ears polite, than any page of the romance before us; and the reason is, we call things by their right names, while the romance never hints the shocking words that belong to its things, but, like Mephistophiles, insinuates that the arch-fiend himself is a very tolerable sort of person, if nobody would call him Mr. Devil. We have heard of persons who could not bear the reading of some Old Testament Lessons in the service of the Church: such persons would be delighted with our author's story; and damsels who shrink at the reading of the Decalogue, would probably luxuriate in bathing their imagination in the crystal of its delicate sensuality. The langauge of our author, like patent blacking, "would not soil the whitest linen," and yet the composition itself, would suffice, if well laid on, to Ethiopize the snowiest conscience that ever sat like a swan upon that mirror of heaven, a Christian maiden's imagination. We are not sure we speak quite strong enough, when we say, that we would much rather listen to the coarsest scene of Goldsmith's *Vicar*, read aloud by a sister or daughter, than to hear from such lips, the perfectly chaste language of a scene in *The Scarlet Letter*, in which a married wife and her reverend paramour, with their unfortunate offspring, are introduced as the actors, and in which the whole tendency of the conversation is to suggest a sympathy for their sin, and an anxiety that they may be able to accomplish a successful escape beyond the seas, to some country where their shameful commerce may be perpetuated. Now, in Goldsmith's story there are very coarse words, but we do not remember anything that saps the foundations of the moral sense, or that goes to create unavoidable sympathy with unrepenting sorrow, and deliberate, premeditated sin. The *Vicar of Wakefield* is sometimes coarsely virtuous, but *The Scarlet Letter* is delicately immoral. —ARTHUR CLEVELAND COXE, "The Writings of Hawthorne," *Church Review*, Jan. 1851, p. 507

I was reading (rather re-reading) the other evening the introductory chapter to the *Scarlet Letter*. It is admirably written. Not having any great sympathy with a custom-house—nor, indeed, with Salem, except that it seems to be Hawthorne's birth-place—all my attention was concentrated on the *style*, which seems to me excellent.—BRYAN WALLER PROCTER, Letter to James T. Fields (Feb. 1853), cited in James T. Fields, "'Barry Cornwall' and Some of His Friends," *Harper's New Monthly Magazine*, Dec. 1875, pp. 59–60

Speaking of Thackeray, I cannot but wonder at his coolness in respect to his own pathos, and compare it with my emotions, when I read the last scene of *The Scarlet Letter* to my wife, just after writing it,—tried to read it rather, for my voice swelled and heaved, as if I were tossed up and down on an ocean as it

subsides after a storm. But I was in a very nervous state then, having gone through a great diversity of emotion, while writing it, for many months. I think I have never overcome my own adamant in any other instance.—NATHANIEL HAWTHORNE, *The English Note-Books*, 1855

I believe and am sure that *The Scarlet Letter* will endure as long as the language in which it is written; and should that language become dead, the wonderful work will be translated. Mr. S. C. Hall says I am to tell you that your works will live when marble crumbles into dust. I can well understand that even genius stands breathless in silence, watching events; still, master, you must send us forth some fresh enchantment ere-long, though you have done so much.—BERKELEY AIKIN, Letter to Nathaniel Hawthorne (1862), cited in Julian Hawthorne, *Nathaniel Hawthorne and His Wife*, 1884, Vol. 2, p. 305

It is conflict that we have in *Jane Eyre*, an assertion of individual will, a fine capacity of individual emotion, and all this in conflict with the world opposing. But it is struggle, not conflict, the inner, not the outer, warfare, that we have in Hester Prynne. It is the stir and the struggle of the soul afflicted, punished, but growing into larger development, into riper life, through this stress and struggle and affliction. And if I seemed to indicate that the novel was in process of development when I wrote that the vitality of the assertion of life was the essence of individuality, and that because of this vitality *Jane Eyre* was an indication of an advance in the art of fiction beyond the spirit and the method of Jane Austen's day, then I may further claim now that the completed picture of the soul of Hester Prynne is indicative of a step in advance as great as, if less marked than, the step from Jane Austen to Charlotte Brontë. It is a step in advance because the picture of Hester Prynne portrays a human soul not merely as a strong, demanding individuality, but as under stress of such relation to verdict of law and to the rights of fellow-mortals as to compel its development into a completed personality. The novel of the *Scarlet Letter* is one of the links in the development of the novel from a means of portraying single phases of emotion to a vehicle of highest expressional power. It was written by a psychological student of the problems which harass the human soul.

⟨. . .⟩ It is a tragedy—a tragedy sombre, intense, unrelieved. It is almost a fatalistic tragedy; almost as stern as if it had been written by Æschylus. It is not a love story; it is not a story of youth; it is not a story of contemporaneous life; it is not a story of eager hope. Hester Prynne having sinned is doomed for punishment to wear the scarlet letter as the symbol of the seared soul forever on her bosom; made an outcast from social joy forever. And the story is the record of the growth of the thoughtless soul of the girl, Hester Prynne, into the sad, strong soul of a mature woman. As accessories to this record of growth, we have scenery of circumstance and scenery of characters. To get perspective, atmosphere, verisimilitude, Hawthorne goes back to a recognizable era of past history. He paints with steadiness the outward aspects, and makes credible the inner motive, of the Puritan Colony in the Boston of 1658. Yet the book is in no sense an historical novel. To give vividness, concreteness, objectivity, to this story of the inner life, to this record of the growth of the conscience, of the growth of responsibility, of the growth of religion, within the breast of Hester Prynne, Hawthorne uses the symbolism which is the picture language of the infancy of awakening fancy. In the story he carries on the crude symbolism of the Puritan court of justice decreeing a visible A as an objective reminder of the branded heart—carries on this crude symbolism into the most delicate and refined suggestions. The unseen forces, the unseen monitors, the unseen avengers, float before our eyes, are painted on the clouds, are burned upon the flesh, in mystic symbols. These mystic symbols are like the weird sisters in *Macbeth*; they are the objectification of mystery. The revelation of the working of the spirit of regeneration upon the soul of Hester Prynne is embodied for us in the weird child, Pearl. She is a living symbol, at once the incarnation of sin, the personification of the Scarlet Letter, the emblem of hope, and the prophecy of pardon. All this is the poetry of mysticism. Yet the *Scarlet Letter* is no more a mystical romance than it is an historical novel.

But if we have mediæval mysticism in the symbolism of the work, we have something very like Greek simplicity and Greek directness in the development. The novel is a Greek tragedy. Like the Greek, it is synthetic and creative rather than analytic. Like the Greek tragedy, the novel of the *Scarlet Letter* has a single story, few principal characters, largeness, unity of treatment, directness, sternness, relentlessness. As in the Greek tragedy, also, the story begins after the guilt has been incurred, and the motive of the story is the relation of the soul of man to Nemesis and justice. There is Greek suggestion even in the minor detail; Pearl is as a chorus to voice for us the comment of the unseen powers. There is Greek atmosphere. All the characters seem to be being rather than acting. Yet the novel is no more a Greek tragedy than it is an historical tale; it is no more a Greek tragedy than it is a mediæval romance. It is, in one, a Greek tragedy, a mediæval romance, a modern historical tale. It is a master work, limited to no age, belonging to all experiences, to all time.—FRANCIS HOVEY STODDARD, *The Evolution of the English Novel*, 1900, pp. 75–80

THE HOUSE OF THE SEVEN GABLES

The House of the Seven Gables was finished yesterday. Mr. Hawthorne read me the close, last evening. There is unspeakable grace and beauty in the conclusion, throwing back upon the sterner tragedy of the commencement an ethereal light, and a dear home-loveliness and satisfaction. How you will enjoy the book,—its depth of wisdom, its high tone, the flowers of Paradise scattered over all the dark places, the sweet wall-flower scent of Phœbe's character, the wonderful pathos and charm of old Uncle Venner. I only wish you could have heard the Poet sing his own song, as I did; but yet the book needs no adventitious aid,—it makes its own music, for I read it all over again to myself yesterday, except the last three chapters.—SOPHIA HAWTHORNE, Letter (Jan. 27, 1851), cited in Julian Hawthorne, *Nathaniel Hawthorne and His Wife*, 1884, Vol. 1, p. 383

The *House of the Seven Gables*, in my opinion, is better than *The Scarlet Letter*; but I should not wonder if I had refined upon the principal character a little too much for popular appreciation; nor if the romance of the book should be found somewhat at odds with the humble and familiar scenery in which I invest it. But I feel that portions of it are as good as anything I can hope to write, and the publisher speaks encouragingly of its success.—NATHANIEL HAWTHORNE, Letter to Horatio Bridge (March 15, 1851), cited in Horatio Bridge, *Personal Recollections of Nathaniel Hawthorne*, 1893, p. 125

I have been so delighted with *The House of the Seven Gables* that I cannot help sitting down to tell you so. I thought I could not forgive you if you wrote anything better than *The Scarlet Letter*; but I cannot help believing it a great triumph that you should have been able to deepen and widen the impression

made by such a book as that. It seems to me that the "House" is the most valuable contribution to New England history that has been made. It is with the highest art that you have typified (in the revived likeness of Judge Pyncheon to his ancestor the Colonel) that intimate relationship between the Present and the Past in the way of ancestry and descent, which historians so carefully overlook. Yesterday is commonly looked upon and written about as of no kin to To-day, though the one is legitimate child of the other, and has its veins filled with the same blood. And the chapter about Alice and the Carpenter,—Salem, which would not even allow you so much as Scotland gave Burns, will build you a monument yet for having shown that she did not hang her witches for nothing. I suppose the true office of the historian is to reconcile the present with the past.—JAMES RUSSELL LOWELL, Letter to Nathaniel Hawthorne (April 24, 1851), cited in Julian Hawthorne, *Nathaniel Hawthorne and His Wife*, 1884, Vol. 1, pp. 390–91

The contents of this book do not belie its clustering romantic title. With great enjoyment we spent almost an hour in each separate gable. This book is like a fine old chamber, abundantly but still judiciously furnished with precisely that sort of furniture best fitted to furnish it. There are rich hangings, whereon are braided scenes from tragedies. There is old china with rare devices, set about on the carved beaufet; there are long and indolent lounges to throw yourself upon; there is an admirable sideboard, plentifully stored with good viands; there is a smell of old wine in the pantry; and finally, in one corner, there is a dark little black-letter volume in golden clasps, entitled *Hawthorne: A Problem*. . . .

We think the book for pleasantness of running interest surpasses the other work of the author. The curtains are now drawn; the sun comes in more; genialities peep out more. Were we to particularize what has most struck us in the deeper passages, we should point out the scene where Clifford, for a minute, would fain throw himself from the window, to join the procession; or the scene where the Judge is left seated in his ancestral chair.

Clifford is full of an awful truth throughout. He is conceived in the finest, truest spirit. He is no caricature. He is Clifford. And here we would say, that did the circumstances permit, we should like nothing better than to devote an elaborate and careful paper to the full consideration and analysis of the purpose and significance of what so strongly characterizes all of this author's writing. There is a certain tragic phase of humanity, which, in our opinion, was never more powerfully embodied than by Hawthorne: we mean the tragicalness of human thought in its own unbiased, native, and profound workings. We think that into no recorded mind has the intense feeling of the whole truth ever entered more deeply than into this man's. By whole truth, we mean the apprehension of the absolute condition of present things as they strike the eye of the man who fears them not, though they do their worst to him.—HERMAN MELVILLE, Letter to Nathaniel Hawthorne (1851), cited in George Parsons Lathrop, *A Study of Hawthorne*, 1876, pp. 230–31

Accept my most cordial thanks for the little volume you have had the kindness to send me. I prize it as the right hand of fellowship extended to me by one whose friendship I am proud and happy to make, and whose writings I have regarded with admiration as among the very best that have ever issued from the American press.—WASHINGTON IRVING, Letter to Nathaniel Hawthorne (1852), cited in Julian Hawthorne, *Nathaniel Hawthorne and His Wife*, 1884, Vol. 1, p. 440

THE BLITHEDALE ROMANCE

It is enough for me that you have put another rose into your chaplet, and I will not ask whether it outblooms or outswells its sister flowers. Zenobia is a splendid creature, and I wish there were more such rich and ripe women about. I wish, too, you could have wound up your story without killing her, or that at least you had given her a drier and handsomer death. Priscilla is an exquisite sketch. I don't know whether you have quite explained Hollingsworth's power over two such diverse natures. Your views about reform and reformers and spiritual rappings are such as I heartily approve. Reformers need the enchantment of distance. Your sketches of things visible, detached observations, and style generally, are exquisite as ever. May you live a thousand years, and write a book every year! —GEORGE S. HILLARD, Letter to Nathaniel Hawthorne (July 27, 1852), cited in Julian Hawthorne, *Nathaniel Hawthorne and His Wife*, 1884, Vol. 1, p. 448

The Blithedale Romance is no bundle of biographies: it has been more properly described as "a humanitarian ballet danced by four figures, who quarrel and dance out of tune." The central idea is, in this case, almost too obvious: the proposition to be proved is that the exaggeration of right may turn to wrong—*Summum jus, summa injuria*. It is *Measure for Measure* without the treason in Angelo's blood, though Hollingsworth is, in the result, as cruel as Angelo meant to be. Much of the work is a comment on the melancholy truth that "half the work of the wise is to counteract the mischief done by the good;" but the only wise man on the stage is Coverdale, and he is not strong enough: all he has to tell us in the end is, by his own confession, "Nothing, nothing, nothing!" Silas Foster interrupting the regenerators of society with the question, "Which man among you is the best judge of swine?" and the discovery, soon made by the masquerading Arcadians, that "intellectual activity is incompatible with any large amount of bodily exercise," point to the foregone conclusion. The descriptive skill displayed in the book is beyond praise. Nowhere has the author more successfully availed himself of his favourite trick of antithesis. The man whose life is ruined by too much, and the man whose life is an emptiness from too little, purpose; the magnificent Zenobia,—the most Titian-like figure on Hawthorne's canvas,—pulsing in every vein with passionate life, and the veiled lady, the pale "anemone," whose appearance in the drama is like the sigh of a flute in a rich orchestra;—these are not more strikingly contrasted than old Moodie, the frail shadow of Fauntleroy, and Westervelt, charlatan and "salamander"—people who seem to have walked entire out of some unwritten novel of Balzac. The variety in the scenery is similarly enhanced by juxtaposition, as of the Hermitage and the Hotel, Elliot's Pulpit and the Boarding-house; just as the healthy atmosphere of the fields is set off by the miasmas of Mesmerism and Spiritualism, which, in this instance, represent the inevitable element of superstition. *The Blithedale Romance* has attracted an unusual amount of attention from French critics, owing to the interest taken by their countrymen in the social problem—a problem which it, however, suggests and sets aside rather than discusses, the references to Fourierism, etc., being mere interpolations cut short by Hollingsworth's dogmatism. The only point made plain is the baleful and blighting effect of the philanthropy that overrides private personal claims. The book is the tragedy of which Dickens' Mrs. Jellaby is the comedy; and it is the most dismal ever written by the author, the only rays of light being the rustic scenes, and the impressive emancipation of Priscilla in the village hall. The finding of Zenobia's body is, perhaps, the most ghastly description in literature: it is aggravated to a climax by the horrible cynicism of Coverdale's remark, that had she foreseen "how ill it would become her, she would no more have committed the dreadful act than have exhibited herself in public in a badly-fitting garment." Time passes, and the impartial torturer meets the philanthropic bird of prey with the question, "Up to this moment, how many criminals have you reformed?" "No one," said Hollingsworth, with his eyes still fixed on the ground. "Ever since we parted, I have been busy with a single murderer." It is a fit close to the wreck of idealisms and the holocaust of aspirations, that leaves us with a deeper sense of the mockery of life, of more utter hopelessness than any other English work of fiction, excepting perhaps *Middlemarch*.—JOHN NICHOL, *American Literature*, 1882, pp. 345–47

THE MARBLE FAUN

⟨. . .⟩ I have said a dozen times that nobody can write English but you. With regard to the story, which has been somewhat criticised, I can only say that to me it is quite satisfactory. I like those shadowy, weird, fantastic, Hawthornesque shapes flitting through the golden gloom, which is the atmosphere of the book. I like the misty way in which the story is indicated rather than revealed; the outlines are quite definite enough from the beginning to the end to those who have imagination enough to follow you in your airy flights; and to those who complain, I suppose that nothing less than an illustrated edition, with a large gallows on the last page, with Donatello in the most pensile of attitudes,—his ears revealed through a white night-cap,—would be satisfactory. I beg your pardon for such profanation, but it really moves my spleen that people should wish to bring down the volatile figures of your romance to the level of an every-day romance. . . . The way in which the two victims dance through the Carnival on the last day is very striking. It is like a Greek tragedy in its effect, without being in the least Greek.—JOHN LOTHROP MOTLEY, Letter to Nathaniel Hawthorne (March 29, 1860), cited in George Parsons Lathrop, *A Study of Hawthorne*, 1876, pp. 262–63

I've finished *the* book, and am, I think, more angry at your tantalizing cruelty than either *Athenæum* or *Saturday Review*. I want to know a hundred things you do not tell me,—who Miriam was, what was the crime in which she was concerned and of which all Europe knew, what was in the packet, what became of Hilda, whether Miriam married Donatello, whether Donatello got his head cut off, etc. Of course you'll say I ought to *guess*; well, if I do guess, it is but a guess, and I want to *know*. Yesterday I wrote a review of you in the *Examiner*, and in spite of my natural indignation, I hope you will not altogether dislike what I have said. In other respects I admire *Monte Beni* more than I can tell you; and I suppose no one now will visit Rome without a copy of it in his hand. Nowhere are descriptions to be found so beautiful, so true, and so pathetic. And there are little bits of *you* in the book which are best of all,—half moralizing, half thinking aloud. There is a bit about *women sewing* which Harriet raves about. There are bits about Catholicism and love and sin, which are marvellously thought and gloriously written. HENRY BRIGHT, Letter to Nathaniel Hawthorne (1860), cited in Julian Hawthorne, *Nathaniel Hawthorne and His Wife*, 1884, Vol. 2, p. 240

Smith and Elder certainly do take strange liberties with the titles of books. I wanted to call it *The Marble Faun*, but they insisted upon *Transformation*, which will lead the reader to anticipate a sort of pantomime. They wrote me some days ago that the edition was nearly all sold, and that they are going to print another; to which I mean to append a few pages, in the shape of a conversation between Kenyon, Hilda, and the author, throwing some further light on matters which seem to have been left too much in the dark. For my own part, however, I should prefer the book as it now stands. —NATHANIEL HAWTHORNE, Letter to Henry Bright (1860), cited in Julian Hawthorne, *Nathaniel Hawthorne and His Wife*, 1884, Vol. 2, p. 241

I was greatly pleased with the success of your last book, *The Marble Faun*. It seemed to me at first, until I got well a-going, a little difficult to seize the thread; but when I once found it, I went rapidly forward unto the end. I always consider the rapidity with which I can read a story the test of its merit, at least for me. Many others have spoken to me of its effect on them. I greatly enjoyed the Italian criticism. As a matter of art, there is possibly always a certain danger in combining didactic and dramatic situations; but if any field is open to this, it should be Italy. "Corinne," I think, deals in character rather than criticism. I should be ashamed to tell you how often I have read *The Marble Faun*.—WILLIAM ELLERY CHANNING, Letter to Nathaniel Hawthorne (Sept. 3, 1860), cited in Julian Hawthorne, *Nathaniel Hawthorne and His Wife*, 1884, Vol. 2, p. 265

Marble Faun, whether consciously or not, illustrates that invasion of the æsthetic by the moral which has confused art by dividing its allegiance, and dethroned the old dynasty without as yet firmly establishing the new in an acknowledged legitimacy.—JAMES RUSSELL LOWELL, "Swinburne's Tragedies" (1866), *Works*, Riverside ed., Vol. 2, pp. 125–26

In all we may find our way to some mystic monument of eternal law, or pluck garlands from some new-budded bough of moral truth. The romance is like a portal of ebony inlaid with ivory,—another gate of dreams,—swinging softly open into regions of illimitable wisdom. But some pause on the threshold, unused to such large liberty; and these cry out, in the words of a well-known critic, "It begins in mystery, and ends in mist."

   Though the book was very successful, few readers grasped the profounder portions. It is a vast exemplar of the author's consummate charm as a simple storyteller, however, that he exercised a brilliant fascination over all readers, notwithstanding the heavy burden of uncomprehended truths which they were obliged to carry with them. Some critics complain of the extent to which Roman scenery and the artistic life in Rome have been introduced; but, to my mind, there is scarcely a word wasted in the two volumes. The "vague sense of ponderous remembrances" pressing down and crowding out the present moment till "our individual affairs are but half as real here as elsewhere," is essential to the perspective of the whole; and nothing but this rich picturesqueness and variety could avail to balance the depth of tragedy which has to be encountered; so that the nicety of art is unquestionable. It is strange, indeed, that this great modern religious romance should thus have become also the ideal representative of ruined Rome—the home of ruined religions—in its æsthetic aspects.—GEORGE PARSONS LATHROP, *A Study of Hawthorne*, 1876, pp. 260–61

The shadow of a Miriam's guilt dims the purity of a Hilda's innocence. But in painting life as it is, it is always possible to paint it as it ought to be. When it is said that Hawthorne makes us familiar with sin and suffering, it must be remembered that there is a familiarity which degrades and another which ennobles. Out of this sombre background Hawthorne evokes the greatness of human nature. The radiance of a spiritual sky falls upon his darkest picture. From the standpoint of the philosopher or the theologian, every writer will always be subject to criticism, for the reason that the standpoints are many. An early critic complained that Hawthorne was morbid because he evinced "so little conception of the remedial system which God has provided for the sins and sorrows of mankind." Granting the fact set forth in this narrow arraignment, it remains true that without avowing distinctly any ethical purpose Hawthorne is ever revealing the sublimity of life, the grandeur of human nature. The fire of his crucible is a purifying flame. However realistic the woes or littlenesses he portrays, they neither crush nor disgust. His vision was too all-embracing, his purpose too deep for this. He is the thinker interpreting to us the world of reality, not the mirror reflecting it. Even as the realist he reflected the sky above our heads as well as the mud under our feet. ⟨. . .⟩

   I may mention one delicious quality in the melancholy of Hawthorne for which we are always grateful—its impersonality. His eye looks outward. There is analysis, but not self-analysis, no introspection. He shows us suffering humanity, not the suffering Hawthorne. His is no Byronic literature of personal griefs, with its littlenesses, self-infatuations, and idolatry. There is, of course, the melancholy of the temperament, the constitutional tendency of the individual, but no autobiography of a bitter personal experience. He is summing up greater than individual issues. It is infinitely refreshing to be free from this oppressive sense of subjective suffering, the single accidental experience, so insignificant when compared with the general law and so fatal to dispassionate analysis.

   I may mention one impression derived from a last re-reading of *The Marble Faun* which is perhaps wholly personal, but which has lessened its first effect as a work of art. The local color and descriptive passages of Hawthorne's earlier works impart the information necessary to the setting of the story, and no more. What may be called the decorative elements are so intimately associated with the constructive plan that each heightens the effect of the other. I cannot recall a writer more successful in this union of ornamental detail and organic structure. It is like the pediment end of the Doric order, whose beauty is not applied but wrought in. Whenever this is true, a style, whether in literature or architecture, painting or sculpture, gains immensely in dignity and unity. I do not say that it is not true of *The Marble Faun*, nor that its local color is less natural than that of Hawthorne's New England novels; but that mingled with what is strictly necessary to the scenic effect is a great deal of information which belongs to the guide-book rather than the work of art. Hawthorne's analysis of a painting or interpretation of a statue is often vital to the story, and has a value apart from its relation to it; but there is much of description and history which belongs rather to a work like Irving's *Alhambra* than to a romance.

   For this very reason, however, the illustration of *The Marble Faun* is withdrawn from the realm of imagination. We would have no other Donatello than that of Praxiteles, desire no Hilda's Tower but that of the Via Portoghese. The present edition, glorious in red and gold, yet exquisitely tasteful, with its fifty photogravures, is a gem in bookmaking. Remembering that this work was received with so little favor that Hawthorne used to say of it, "The thing is a failure," it makes one wish he might see this last effort to array it in the beauty it deserves. —ARTHUR SHERBURNE HARDY, "Hawthorne's Italian Romance," *Book Buyer*, Nov. 1889, pp. 427–28

In *The Marble Faun* his pure and tranquil grace of style is at its best. The economy of incident is not so strict as in the statuesque simplicity of the *Scarlet Letter* groupings, nor is the dramatic intensity so keen; but there is Hawthorne's own rich, subdued, autumnal coloring, with the first soft shadows deepening into sable. Emerson, whom Hawthorne's Concord journal once noted as coming to call "with a sunbeam in his face," unwittingly returned the compliment by saying that Hawthorne "rides well his horse of the night." Gloom has its own enchantment, and so has mystery, but the issues of this romance were left in an uncertainty that its readers found hard to bear. Hawthorne would not help them. He was fertile in misleading suggestions and tricksy hypotheses, but perhaps he hardly knew the actual fate of Miriam and Donatello. Such a "cloudy veil" as he found stretched over "the abyss" of his own nature may have been interposed between himself and the innermost secrets of his characters. Supernatural forces, too, entered in, as in life, amid the personages of his tales and played their inscrutable parts beside them. Among the baffling questions is one suggested by Hawthorne's younger daughter, who, with her husband, George Parsons Lathrop, poet and novelist, has embraced the Roman faith. Mrs. Lathrop claims that *The Marble Faun*, if closely studied, shows in the treatment of sin and atonement a significant divergence from the Puritan romances.—KATHARINE LEE BATES, *American Literature*, 1897, pp. 314–15

ANDREW PRESTON PEABODY
From "Nathaniel Hawthorne"

North American Review, January 1853, pp. 227–33

It is difficult to refer Hawthorne to any recognized class of writers. So far as our cognizance extends, he is the only individual of his class. In the popular sense of the word, he writes no poetry. We infer his incapacity of rhyme and metre, from his having adopted prose for his Carriers' Addresses, and other similar productions, which are usually cast in metrical forms. Nor yet is his language distinguished by euphony. It never flows spontaneously in numbers, as do so many of the descriptive and pathetic passages in Dickens's stories. On the other hand, it is often crisp and harsh, betraying little sensitiveness to musical accords and cadences; and we should despair of finding a paragraph of his, in which the sound could, by the most skilful reading, be made to enhance the impression of the sense. Yet more, we cannot remember a single poetical quotation in all his writings; and, though books are occasionally referred to, mention is never, or almost never, made of a poet or a poem. His own favorite reading does not, we therefore conclude, lie in this direction, nor yet, as we apprehend, in any direction in which his fancy could borrow forms or colors, or could find nourishment homogeneous with its creations. Indeed, if we may judge from such hints as he furnishes of his own literary habits, the books with which he is chiefly familiar are the dryest of chronicles, which furnish the raw material for many of his stories.

Yet with so much that must be alleged to the discredit of his poetical affinities, Hawthorne is preëminently a poet. It belongs to his genius not merely to narrate or describe, not merely to invent characters and incidents of the same constituent elements with those in history or in real life; but to create out of nothing—to place before the imagination objects and personages which derive their verisimilitude not from their resemblance to the actual, but from their self-coherency. Plain story-telling, whether true or fictitious, is entirely beyond, or rather beneath, his capacity. He undertook, a few years ago, to

write historical sketches of New England, in the Peter Parley style, for the behoof of children. He succeeded so admirably that people of mature and venerable age became children for the nonce, that they might read the legends of *Grandfather's Chair*; but it was not history; it was the offspring of Hawthorne's own brain, draped in Puritan costumes, and baptized with ancestral names. A year or two ago, he conceived the plan of reëditing some of the fables of the classic mythology; but the result was a Pantheon all his own, rigidly true, indeed, to the letter of antiquity, and thus vindicating his title to genuine scholarship, while yet gods and heroes, Gorgons and Chimeræ, Atlas and Pegasus, all bore as close kindred to him as Minerva to Jupiter. In fine, his golden touch is as unfailing as was that of Midas, and transmutes whatever he lays hand upon. Even brutes, and homely household implements, and the motley livery of the pauper, yield to his alchemy, and are no longer coarse and sordid, yet without losing their place or their nature. In like manner, he so transforms incidents and transactions of the most trivial character, as to render them grand, pathetic, or grotesque. We may, perhaps, define more accurately this element of his power, by pressing still farther the metaphors already employed. His golden touch, we would then say, imposes no superficial glitter, but brings out upon the surface, and concentrates in luminous points, the interior gilding, which is attached to the meanest objects and the lowliest scenes by their contact with the realm of sentiment, emotion, and spiritual life. He literally transforms, draws the hidden soul of whatever he describes to the light of day, and often veils exterior phenomena from clear view by the very tissue of motives, loves, antipathies, mental and moral idiosyncrasies, which they are wont to conceal. He thus, often, when least successful in the development of a plot, gives us portraitures of character as vivid as if they were wrought in flame-colors, and transcripts of inward experience so graphic that to read them is to live them over.

But with Hawthorne's close fidelity as a painter of man's interior nature and life, there is, after all, a subtle coloring and shading derived from no model, and so characteristic as to defy imitation. His heroes, while true in thought and speech to the parts which they are made to personate, always assume a tone of discourse or sentiment which we can imagine in him and in no other, under the supposed circumstances. His stories are, in fact, like Miss Kemble's dramatic readings, in which something of the same personality must betray itself in Caliban and Juliet, in Falstaff and Hamlet, in Coriolanus and King Lear. It is this which gives a prominent, and perhaps the chief, charm of his writings. They are, in the truest sense of the word, autobiographical; and, with repeated opportunities for cultivating his acquaintance by direct intercourse, we have learned from his books immeasurably more of his mental history, tastes, tendencies, sympathies, and opinions, than we should have known had we enjoyed his daily converse for a lifetime. Diffident and reserved as to the habitudes of the outer man, yet singularly communicative and social in disposition and desire, he takes his public for his confidant, and betrays to thousands of eyes likes and dislikes, whims and reveries, veins of mirthful and of serious reflection, moods of feeling both healthful and morbid, which it would be beyond his power to disclose through the ear, even to the most intimate of friends or the dearest of kindred.

As a writer of stories, whether in the form of tales, novels, or romances, Hawthorne will not bear comparison with his contemporaries in the same department, or measurement by any conventional rule. The most paltry tale-maker for magazines and newspapers can easily excel him in what we might term the mechanical portion of his art. His plots are seldom well devised or skilfully developed. They are either too simple to excite curiosity and attract interest, or too much involved for him to clear them up to the reader's satisfaction. His conversations, too, are not such as seem natural, in the sense of being probable or possible, but natural only because they are more rigidly true to fact and feeling than speech ever is. There is also, not infrequently, an incompleteness in his choicest productions, not as if he had been careless or hurried in their execution, but as if they had been too intimately a portion of his own being for separate existence,—as if they had been too deeply rooted in their native soil to bear transplanting. But, if he lacks skill in the management of his plot, he is independent of it. Were he to eliminate every thing of a narrative character from the best of his stories, we doubt whether their currency or his reputation would suffer detriment. Indeed, he is often most successful, where he does not even attempt narration, but selects some single scene, object, or incident, as the nucleus for a cluster of fancies and musings, melancholy, grave, humorous, or gay, either by itself, each in turn, or all blending and mutually interpretating, as in actual life, in which grief has its comic, and laughter its tragic, side. Thus, of his earlier series, none impress us as more truly worthy of his genius than "The Sister Years," a sketch of the midnight interview of the worn and jaded Old Year with her blooming and sanguine successor, the New Year; "Snow Flakes," a mere series of winter fireside fantasies; and "Night Sketches beneath an Umbrella," a description of what might be seen by any eye that looked beneath the surface on a short walk in Salem on a rainy evening.

Hawthorne has written nothing more likely to survive his times than several simply, yet gorgeously, wrought and highly suggestive allegories, among which "The Celestial Railroad" holds the first place, and deserves an immortality coeval with that of the great prose-epic which furnished its theme. He represents the railroad as built, in conformity with the spirit of the times, on a route intersecting at intervals the path of Bunyan's Pilgrim, which it is designed to supersede. The old enemies of the foot-travellers have been bought over by offices on the new road, and Apollyon is engineer. Onward the cars rattle over the Slough of Despond, on a shaky causeway built of books of German rationalism and Transcendental divinity. They pass unchallenged within sight of the wicket-gate. The easy-cushioned passengers can hardly find gibes pungent enough for two determined pilgrims, whom they see trudging over the now grass-grown path, and Apollyon helps the sport by squirting steam at them. At Vanity-Fair is the chief station-house, at which they make a protracted pause for refreshment and amusement. Then, when they have satiated themselves with its gayeties, they hurry through the residue of the way, though with a dim sense of insecurity, and beset by sights and sounds of the direst omen. Arrived at the terminus, they find the black River of Death rolling angrily at their feet. No means of crossing have been provided by the projectors of the new road, or are vouchsafed to its passengers by the lord of the old way. And, as they despair of breasting the current unguided and unaided, and see its depths yawning for their utter perdition, they lift their eyes, and the despised pilgrims, who had not been ashamed of the ancient Christ-marked path, have already crossed the River, angels are leading them up the shining banks, up the crystal hills, the golden gates are opened for them, and the harps of heaven ring their welcome.

After this manner, Hawthorne's stories are generally written to illustrate some idea or sentiment, to which, and not to the personages or incidents, the author manifestly solicits his

reader's heed. He is a philosopher, with a strong dash of the humorist in his composition; human life and society constitute his field of speculation; and his queries and conclusions tend, through his poetic instincts, to concrete rather than abstract forms. With him, a tale takes the place of an apophthegm; an allegory, of a homily; a romance, of an ethical treatise. He seems incapable, not from penury, but from wealth of mind, of presenting a naked thought. The outward passage of every creation of his intellect lies through the inexhaustible vestry of an imagination swarming with textures and tints strange, fantastic, sometimes sombre, sometimes radiant, always beautiful. There is thus in his writings a philosophical completeness and unity, even when, in an artistical point of view, (as is often the case,) they are fragmentary or desultory. But, while a single thought gives its pervading hue and tone to a story or a volume, and that thought is always a brilliant of faultless lustre, he abounds in lesser gems of kindred perfectness. We know of no living or recent writer, from whom it would be possible to select so many sentences that might stand alone, as conveying ideas clearly defined and vividly expressed by imagery which at once astonishes by its novelty, charms by its aptness, and dazzles by its beauty. And there are numerous single metaphors of his comprised in a word or two, that, once read, recur perpetually to the memory, and supplant ever after their more literal, yet immeasurably less significant, synonymes.

The early history of New England, more largely than any other source, has supplied Hawthorne with names, events, and incidents, for his creations. The manners, customs, beliefs, superstitions of the Puritans, and their immediate descendants, seem to have taken the strongest hold upon his fancy. Their times are his heroic age, and he has made it mythological. As illustrative of history, his stories are eminently untrustworthy; for, where he runs parallel with recorded fact in his narrative of events, the spirit that animates and pervades them is of his own creation. Thus, in the *Scarlet Letter*, he has at once depicted the exterior of early New England life with a fidelity that might shame the most accurate chronicler, and defaced it by passions too fierce and wild to have been stimulated to their desolating energy under colder skies than of Spain or Italy. At the same time, he has unwittingly defamed the fathers of New England, by locating his pictures of gross impurity and sacrilegious vice where no shadow of reproach, and no breath but of immaculate fame, had ever rested before. He thus has violated one of the most sacred canons of literary creation. A writer, who borrows nothing from history, may allow himself an unlimited range in the painting of character; but he who selects a well-known place and epoch for his fiction, is bound to adjust his fiction to the analogy of fact, and especially to refrain from outraging the memory of the dead for the entertainment of the living.

RICHARD HOLT HUTTON
From "Nathaniel Hawthorne"
Literary Essays
1871, pp. 437–58

Hawthorne has been called a mystic, which he was not,— and a psychological dreamer, which he was in very slight degree. He was really the ghost of New England,—I do not mean the "spirit," nor the "phantom," but the ghost in the older sense in which that term is used, the thin, rarefied essence which is supposed to be found somewhere behind the physical organisation: embodied, indeed, and not at all in a shadowy or diminutive earthly tabernacle, but yet only half embodied in it, endowed with a certain painful sense of the gulf between his nature and its organisation, always recognising the gulf, always trying to bridge it over, and always more or less unsuccessful in the attempt. His writings are not exactly spiritual writings, for there is no dominating spirit in them. They are ghostly writings. Hawthorne was, to my mind, a sort of sign to New England of the divorce that has been going on there (and not less perhaps in old England) between its people's spiritual and earthly nature, and of the difficulty which they will soon feel, if they are to be absorbed more and more in that shrewd hard common sense which is one of their most striking characteristics, in even *communicating* with their former self. Hawthorne, with all his shyness, and tenderness, and literary reticence, shows very distinct traces also of understanding well the cold, inquisitive, and shrewd spirit which besets the Yankees even more than other commercial peoples. His heroes have usually not a little of this hardness in them. Coverdale, for instance, in *The Blithedale Romance*, and Holgrave, in *The House of the Seven Gables*, are of this class of shrewd, cold inquisitive heroes. Indeed there are few of his tales without a character of this type. But though Hawthorne had a deep sympathy with the practical as well as the literary genius of New England, it was always in a ghostly kind of way, as though he were stricken by some spell which half-paralysed him, and so prevented him from communicating with the life around him, as though he saw it only by a reflected light. His spirit haunted rather than ruled his body; his body hampered his spirit.

Yet his external career was not only not romantic, but identified with all the dullest routine of commercial duties. That a man who consciously *telegraphed*, as it were, with the world, transmitting meagre messages through his material organisation, should have been first a custom-house officer in Massachusetts, and then the consul in Liverpool, brings out into the strongest possible relief the curiously representative character in which he stood to New England as its literary or intellectual ghost. There is nothing more ghostly in his writings than his account of the consulship in Liverpool,—how he began by trying to communicate frankly with his fellow-countrymen, how he found the task more and more difficult, and gradually drew back into the twilight of his reserve, how he shrewdly and somewhat coldly watched "the dim shadows as they go and come," speculated idly on their fate, and all the time discharged the regular routine of consular business, witnessing the usual depositions, giving captains to captainless crews, affording meagrely doled-out advice or assistance to Yankees when in need of a friend, listening to them when they were only anxious to offer, not ask, assistance, and generally observing them from that distant and speculative outpost of the universe whence all common things looked strange.

Hawthorne, who was a delicate critic of himself, was well aware of the shadowy character of his own genius, though hardly aware that precisely here lay its curious and thrilling power. In the preface to *Twice-told Tales* he tells us frankly, "The book, if you would see anything in it, requires to be read in the clear brown twilight atmosphere in which it was written; if opened in the sunshine, it is apt to look exceedingly like a volume of blank pages."

It is one of his favourite theories that there must be a vague, remote, and shadowy element in the subject-matter of any narrative with which his own imagination can successfully deal. Sometimes he apologises for this idealistic limitation to his artistic aims. "It was a folly," he says in his preface to *The Scarlet Letter*, "with the materiality of this daily life pressing so intrusively upon me, to attempt to fling myself back into another age, or to insist on creating the semblance of a world out of airy matter, when at every moment the impalpable beauty of my soap-bubble was broken by the rude contact of some actual circumstance. The wiser effort would have been to diffuse thought and imagination through the opaque substance of to-day, and thus to make it a bright transparency; to spiritualise the burden that began to weigh so heavily; to seek resolutely the true and indestructible value that lay hidden in the petty and wearisome incidents and ordinary characters with which I was now conversant. The fault was mine. The page of life that was spread out before me was so dull and common-place only because I had not fathomed its deeper import. A better book than I shall ever write was there; leaf after leaf presenting itself to me just as it was written out by the reality of the flitting hour, and vanishing as fast as written, only because my brain wanted the insight and my hand the cunning to transcribe it. At some future day, it may be, I shall remember a few scattered fragments and broken paragraphs and write them down, and find the letters turn to gold upon the page."

And yet that dissatisfaction with his own idealism which Hawthorne here expresses never actually sufficed to divert his efforts into the channel indicated. In *The Blithedale Romance* he tells us that he chose the external scenery of the Socialist community at Brook Farm "merely to establish a theatre, a little removed from the highway of ordinary travel, where the creatures of his brain may play their phantasmagorical antics without exposing them to too close a comparison with the actual events of real lives. In the old countries with which fiction has long been conversant, a certain conventional privilege seems to be awarded to the romancer; his work is not put exactly side by side with nature; and he is allowed a license with regard to every-day probability, in view of the improved effects which he is bound to produce thereby. Among ourselves, on the contrary, there is as yet no such Fairy Land so like the real world that, in a suitable remoteness, one cannot well tell the difference, but with an atmosphere of strange enchantment, beheld through which the inhabitants have a propriety of their own. This atmosphere is what the American romancer wants. In its absence, the beings of imagination are compelled to show themselves in the same category as actually living mortals,—a necessity that generally renders the paint and pasteboard of their composition but too painfully discernible." And once more, in the preface to his last novel, *Transformation*, he reiterates as his excuse for laying the scene in Italy, that "no author without a trial can conceive of the difficulty of writing a romance about a country where there is no shadow, no antiquity, no mystery, no picturesque and gloomy wrong, nor anything but a commonplace prosperity in broad and simple daylight, as is happily the case with my dear native land. It will be very long, I trust, before romance writers may find congenial and easily-handled themes either in the annals of our stalwart republic, or in any characteristic and probable event of our individual lives. Romance and poetry, ivy, lichens, and wall-flowers, need ruin to make them grow." These passages throw much light on the secret affinities of Hawthorne's genius. But it would be a mistake to conclude from them, as he himself would apparently have us, that he is a mere romantic idealist, in the sense in which these words are commonly used,—that he is one all whose dramatic conceptions are but the unreal kaleidoscopic combinations of fancies in his own brain.

I may, perhaps, accept a phrase of which Hawthorne himself was fond,—"the moonlight of romance,"—and compel it to explain something of the secret of his characteristic genius. There are writers—chiefly poets, but also occasionally writers of fanciful romances like Longfellow's *Hyperion*—whose productions are purely ideal, are not only seen by the light of their own imagination but constituted out of it,—made of moonshine,—and rendered vivid and beautiful, so far as they are vivid and beautiful, with the vividness and beauty merely of the poet's own mind. In these cases there is no distinction between the delineating power and the delineated object; the dream is indistinguishable from the mind of the dreamer, and varies wholly with its laws. Again, at the opposite extreme, there is a kind of creative imagination which has its origin in a deep sympathy with, and knowledge of, the real world. That which it deals with is actual life as it has existed, or still exists, in forms so innumerable that it is scarcely possible to assert that its range is more limited than life itself. Of course the only adequate example of such an imagination is Shakespeare's, and this kind of imaginative power resembles sunlight, not only in its brilliancy, but especially in this, that it casts a light so full and equable over the universe it reveals, that we never think of its source at all. We forget altogether, as we do by common daylight, that the light by which we see is not part and parcel of the world which it presents to us. The sunlight is so efficient that we forget the sun. We find so rich and various a world before us, dressed in its own proper colours, that no one is reminded that the medium by which those proper colours are seen is uniform and from a single source. We merge the delineative magic by which the scene is illuminated, in the details of the scene itself.

Between these two kinds of creative imagination there is another, which also shows a real world, but shows it so dimly in comparison with the last as to keep constantly before our minds the unique character of the light by which we see. The ideal light itself becomes a more prominent element in the picture than even the objects on which it shines; and yet is made so chiefly by the very fact of shining on those objects which we are accustomed to think of as they are seen in their own familiar details in full daylight. If the objects illuminated were not real and familiar, the light would not seem so mysterious; it is the pale uniform tint, the loss of colour and detail, and yet the vivid familiar outline and the strong shadow, which produce what Hawthorne calls the "moonlight of romance." "Moonlight in a familiar room," he says, in his preface to *The Scarlet Letter*, "falling so white upon the carpet, and showing all its figures so distinctly, making every object so minutely visible, yet so unlike a morning or noontide visibility,—is a medium the most suitable for a romance writer to get acquainted with his illusive guests. There is the little domestic scenery of the well-known apartment; the chairs, with each its separate individuality; the centre table, sustaining a work-basket, a volume or two, and an extinguished lamp; the sofa, the bookcase, the picture on the wall;—all these details, so completely seen, are so spiritualised by the unusual light, that they seem to lose their actual substance and become things of intellect. Nothing is too small or too trifling to undergo this change and acquire dignity thereby. A child's shoe, the doll seated in her little wicker carriage, the hobby-horse,—whatever, in a word, has been used or played with during the day, is now invested with a quality of strangeness and remoteness, though still almost as vividly present as by daylight. Thus, therefore, the floor of our familiar room has become a neutral territory, somewhere between the real world and fairyland, where the Actual and the Imaginary may meet, and each imbue itself with the nature of the other." Sir Walter Scott's delineative power partakes both of this moonlight imagination

and of the other more powerful, brilliant, and realistic kind. Often it is a wide genial sunshine, of which we quite forget the source in the vividness of the common life which it irradiates. At other times, again, when Scott is in his Black Douglas mood, as I may call it, it has all the uniformity of tint and the exciting pallor of what Hawthorne terms the moonlight of romance.

At all events, there is no writer to whose creations the phrase applies more closely than to Hawthorne's own. His characters are by no means such unreal webs of moonshine as the idealists proper constitute into the figures of their romance. They are real and definitely outlined, but they are all seen in a single light,—the contemplative light of the particular idea which has floated before him in each of his stories,—and they are seen, not fully and in their integrity, as things are seen by daylight, but like things touched by moonlight,—only so far as they are lighted up by the idea of the story. The thread of unity which connects his tales is always some pervading thought of his own; they are not written mainly to display character, still less for the mere narrative interest, but for the illustration they cast on some idea or conviction of their author's. Amongst English writers of fiction, we have many besides Shakespeare whose stories are merely appropriate instruments for the portraiture of character, and who therefore never conceive themselves bound to confine themselves scrupulously to the one aspect most naturally developed by the tale. Once introduced, their characters are given in full,—both that side of them which is, so to say, turned *towards* the story, and others which are not. Other writers, again, make the characters quite subsidiary to the epical interest of the plot, using them only to heighten the colouring of the action it describes. Hawthorne's tales belong to neither of these classes. Their unity is ideal. His characters are often real and distinct, but they are illuminated only from one centre of thought. So strictly is this true of them that he has barely *room* for a novel in the ordinary sense of the word. If he were to take his characters through as many phases of life as are ordinarily comprised in a novel, he could not keep the ideal unity of his tales unbroken; he would be obliged to delineate them from many different points of view. Accordingly his novels are not novels in the ordinary sense; they are ideal situations, expanded by minute study and trains of clear, pale thought into the dimensions of novels. A very small group of figures is presented to the reader in some marked ideal relation; or if it be in consequence of some critical event, then it must be some event which has struck the author as rich in ideal or spiritual suggestion. But it is not usually in his way—though his last complete novel gives us one remarkable exception to this observation—to seize any glowing crisis of action where the passion is lit or the blow is struck that gives a new mould to life, for his delineation; he prefers to assume the crisis past, and to delineate as fully as he can the ideal situation to which it has given rise; when it is beginning to assume a fainter and more chronic character. ⟨. . .⟩

His power over his readers always arises from much the same cause as that of his own fanciful creation,—the minister who wore the black veil as a symbol of the veil which is on all hearts, and who startled men less because he was hidden from their view than because he made them aware of their own solitude. "Why do you tremble at *me alone?*" says the mild old man on his deathbed, from beneath his black veil, and with the glimmering smile on his half-hidden lips; "tremble also at each other! Have men avoided me, and women shown no pity, and children screamed and fled only from my black veil? What but the mystery which it obscurely typifies has made this piece of crape so awful? When the friend shows his inmost heart to his friend, the lover to his best beloved, when man does not vainly shrink from the eye of his Creator, loathsomely treasuring up the secret of his sin, then deem me a monster for the symbol beneath which I have lived and died! I look around me, and lo! on every visage a black veil?" Hawthorne, with the pale melancholy smile that seems to be always on his lips, speaks from a somewhat similar solitude. Indeed I suspect the story was a kind of parable of his own experience.

But, though Hawthorne's imagination was a solitary and twilight one, there was nothing allegorical about his genius. If we want to find his power at the very highest, we must look to his instinctive knowledge of what we may call the laws, not exactly of *discordant* emotions, but of emotions which *ought* to be mutually exclusive, and which combine with the thrill and the shudder of disease. This is almost the antithesis of Allegory. And he makes his delineation of such "unblest unions" the more striking, because it stands out from a background of healthy life, of genial scenes and simple beauties, which renders the contrast the more thrilling. I have often heard the term "cobweby" applied to his romances; and their most marking passages certainly cause the same sense of unwelcome shrinking to the spirit which a line of unexpected cobweb suddenly drawn across the face causes physically when one enters a deserted but familiar room. Edgar Poe, indeed, is much fuller of uncanny terrors; but then there is nothing in his writings of the healthy, simple, and natural background which gives sin and disease all its horror. It is the pure and severe New England simplicity which Hawthorne paints so delicately that brings out in full relief the adulterous mixture of emotions on which he spends his main strength. I might almost say that he has carried into human affairs the old Calvinistic type of imagination. The same strange combination of clear simplicity, high faith, and reverential realism, with a reluctant, but for that very reason intense and devouring, conviction of the large comprehensiveness of the Divine Damnation which that grim creed taught its most honest believers to consider as the true trust in God's providence, Hawthorne copies into his pictures of human life. He presents us with a scene of pale severe beauty, full of truthful goodness, and then he uncovers in some one point of it a plague-spot, that, half-concealed as he keeps it, yet runs away with the imagination till one is scarcely conscious of anything else. Just as Calvinism, with all its noble features, can never keep its eyes off that one fact, as it thinks it, of God's calm foreknowledge of a widespread damnation; and this gradually encroaches on the attention till the mind is utterly absorbed in the fascinating terror of the problem how to combine the clashing emotions of love and horror which its image of Him inspires;—so Hawthorne's finest tales, with all the simplicity of their general outline, never detain you long from some uneasy mixture of emotions which only disease can combine in the same subject, until at last you ask for nothing but the brushing clean away of the infected web.

SIR LESLIE STEPHEN
From "Nathaniel Hawthorne" (1875)
Hours in a Library (1874–79)
1904, Volume 1, pp. 244–70

The story which perhaps generally passes for his masterpiece is *Transformation*, for most readers assume that a writer's longest book must necessarily be his best. In the present case, I think that this method, which has its conveniences, has

not led to a perfectly just conclusion. In *Transformation*, Hawthorne has for once the advantage of placing his characters in a land where "a sort of poetic or fairy precinct," as he calls it, is naturally provided for them. The very stones of the streets are full of romance, and he cannot mention a name that has not a musical ring. Hawthorne, moreover, shows his usual tact in confining his aims to the possible. He does not attempt to paint Italian life and manners; his actors belong by birth, or by a kind of naturalisation, to the colony of the American artists in Rome; and he therefore does not labour under the difficulty of being in imperfect sympathy with his creatures. Rome is a mere background, and surely a most felicitous background, to the little group of persons who are effectually detached from all such vulgarising associations with the mechanism of daily life in less poetical countries. The centre of the group, too, who embodies one of Hawthorne's most delicate fancies, could have breathed no atmosphere less richly perfumed with old romance. In New York he would certainly have been in danger of a Barnum's museum, beside Washington's nurse and the woolly horse. It is a triumph of art that a being whose nature trembles on the very verge of the grotesque should walk through Hawthorne's pages with such undeviating grace. In the Roman dreamland he is in little danger of such prying curiosity, though even there he can only be kept out of harm's way by the admirable skill of his creator. Perhaps it may be thought by some severe critics that, with all his merits, Donatello stands on the very outside verge of the province permitted to the romancer. But without cavilling at what is indisputably charming, and without dwelling upon certain defects of construction which slightly mar the general beauty of the story, it has another weakness which it is impossible quite to overlook. Hawthorne himself remarks that he was surprised, in re-writing his story, to see the extent to which he had introduced descriptions of various Italian objects. "Yet these things," he adds, "fill the mind everywhere in Italy, and especially in Rome, and cannot be kept from flowing out upon the page when one writes freely and with self-enjoyment." The associations which they called up in England were so pleasant that he could not find it in his heart to cancel. Doubtless that is the precise truth, and yet it is equally true that they are artistically out of place. There are passages which recall the guide-book. To take one instance—and, certainly, it is about the worst—the whole party is going to the Coliseum, where a very striking scene takes place. On the way they pass a baker's shop.

> "The baker is drawing his loaves out of the oven," remarked Kenyon. "Do you smell how sour they are? I should fancy that Minerva (in revenge for the desecration of her temples) had slyly poured vinegar into the batch, if I did not know that the modern Romans prefer their bread in the acetous fermentation."

The instance is trivial, but it is characteristic. Hawthorne had doubtless remarked the smell of the sour bread, and to him it called up a vivid recollection of some stroll in Rome; for, of all our senses, the smell is notoriously the most powerful in awakening associations. But then what do we who read him care about the Roman taste for bread "in acetous fermentation"? When the high-spirited girl is on the way to meet her tormenter, and to receive the provocation which leads to his murder, why should we be worried by a gratuitous remark up about Roman baking? It somehow jars upon our taste, and we are certain that, in describing a New England village, Hawthorne would never have admitted a touch which has no conceivable bearing upon the situation. There is almost a superabundance of minute local colour in his American Romances, as, for example, in the *House of the Seven Gables;* but still, every touch, however minute, is steeped in the sentiment and contributes to the general effect. In Rome the smell of a loaf is sacred to his imagination, and intrudes itself upon its own merits, and, so far as we can discover, without reference to the central purpose. If a baker's shop impresses him unduly because it is Roman, the influence of ancient ruins and glorious works of art is of course still more distracting. The mysterious Donatello, and the strange psychological problem which he is destined to illustrate, are put aside for an interval, whilst we are called upon to listen to descriptions and meditations, always graceful, and often of great beauty in themselves, but yet, in a strict sense, irrelevant. Hawthorne's want of familiarity with the scenery is of course responsible for part of this failing. Had he been a native Roman, he would not have been so preoccupied with the wonders of Rome. But it seems that for a romance bearing upon a spiritual problem, the scenery, however tempting, is not really so serviceable as the less prepossessing surroundings of America. The objects have too great an intrinsic interest. A counter-attraction distorts the symmetry of the system. In the shadow of the Coliseum and St. Peter's you cannot pay much attention to the troubles of a young lady whose existence is painfully ephemeral. Those mighty objects will not be relegated to the background, and condescend to act as mere scenery. They are, in fact, too romantic for a romance. The fountain of Trevi, with all its allegorical marbles, may be a very picturesque object to describe, but for Hawthorne's purposes it is really not equal to the town-pump at Salem; and Hilda's poetical tower, with the perpetual light before the Virgin's image, and the doves floating up to her from the street, and the column of Antoninus looking at her from the heart of the city, somehow appeals less to our sympathies than the quaint garret in the House of the Seven Gables, from which Phœbe Pyncheon watched the singular idiosyncrasies of the superannuated breed of fowls in the garden. The garret and the pump are designed in strict subordination to the human figures: the tower and the fountain have a distinctive purpose of their own. Hawthorne, at any rate, seems to have been mastered by his too powerful auxiliaries. A human soul, even in America, is more interesting to us than all the churches and picture-galleries in the world; and, therefore, it is as well that Hawthorne should not be tempted to the too easy method of putting fine description in place of sentiment.

But how was the task to be performed? How was the imaginative glow to be shed over the American scenery, so provokingly raw and deficient in harmony? A similar problem was successfully solved by a writer whose development, in proportion to her means of cultivation, is about the most remarkable of recent literary phenomena. Miss Brontë's bleak Yorkshire moors, with their uncompromising stone walls, and the valleys invaded by factories, are at first sight as little suited to romance as New England itself, to which, indeed, both the inhabitants and the country have a decided family resemblance. Now that she has discovered for us the fountains of poetic interest, we can all see that the region is not a mere stony wilderness; but it is well worth while to make a pilgrimage to Haworth, if only to discover how little the country corresponds to our preconceived impressions, or, in other words, how much depends upon the eye which sees it, and how little upon its intrinsic merits. Miss Brontë's marvellous effects are obtained by the process which enables an "intense and glowing mind" to see everything through its own atmosphere. The

ugliest and most trivial objects seem, like objects heated by the sun, to radiate back the glow of passion with which she has regarded them. Perhaps this singular power is still more conspicuous in *Villette*, where she had even less of the raw material of poetry. An odd parallel may be found between one of the most striking passages in *Villette* and one in *Transformation*. Lucy Snowe in one novel, and Hilda in the other, are left to pass a summer vacation, the one in Brussels and the other in pestiferous Rome. Miss Snowe has no external cause of suffering but the natural effect of solitude upon a homeless and helpless governess. Hilda has to bear about with her the weight of a terrible secret, affecting, it may be, even the life of her dearest friend. Each of them wanders into a Roman Catholic church, and each, though they have both been brought up in a Protestant home, seeks relief at the confessional. So far the cases are alike, though Hilda, one might have fancied, has by far the strongest cause for emotion. And yet, after reading the two descriptions—both excellent in their way—one might fancy that the two young ladies had exchanged burdens. Lucy Snowe is as tragic as the innocent confidante of a murderess; Hilda's feelings never seem to rise above that weary sense of melancholy isolation which besieges us in a deserted city. It is needless to ask which is the best bit of work artistically considered. Hawthorne's style is more graceful and flexible; his descriptions of the Roman Catholic ceremonial and its influence upon an imaginative mind in distress are far more sympathetic, and imply wider range of intellect. But Hilda scarcely moves us like Lucy. There is too much delicate artistic description of picture-galleries and of the glories of St. Peter's to allow the poor little American girl to come prominently to the surface. We have been indulging with her in some sad but charming speculations, and not witnessing the tragedy of a deserted soul. Lucy Snowe has very inferior materials at her command; but somehow we are moved by a sympathetic thrill: we taste the bitterness of the awful cup of despair which, as she tells us, is forced to her lips in the night-watches; and are not startled when so prosaic an object as the row of beds in the dormitory of a French school suggests to her images worthy of rather stately tombs in the aisles of a vast cathedral, and recalls dead dreams of an elder world and a mightier race long frozen in death. Comparisons of this kind are almost inevitably unfair; but the difference between the two illustrates one characteristic—we need not regard it as a defect—of Hawthorne. His idealism does not consist in conferring grandeur upon vulgar objects by tinging them with the reflection of deep emotion. He rather shrinks than otherwise from describing the strongest passions, or shows their working by indirect touches and under a side-light. An excellent example of his peculiar method occurs in what is in some respects the most perfect of his works, the *Scarlet Letter*. There, again, we have the spectacle of a man tortured by a life-long repentance. The Puritan Clergyman, reverenced as a saint by all his flock, conscious of a sin which, once revealed, will crush him to the earth, watched with a malignant purpose by the husband whom he has injured, unable to summon up the moral courage to tear off the veil, and make the only atonement in his power, is a singularly striking figure, powerfully conceived and most delicately described. He yields under terrible pressure to the temptation of escaping from the scene of his prolonged torture with the partner of his guilt. And then, as he is returning homewards after yielding a reluctant consent to the flight, we are invited to contemplate the agony of his soul. The form which it takes is curiously characteristic. No vehement pangs of remorse, or desperate hopes of escape overpower his faculties in any simple and straightforward fashion. The poor minister is seized with a strange hallucination. He meets a venerable deacon, and can scarcely restrain himself from uttering blasphemies about the Communion-supper. Next appears an aged widow, and he longs to assail her with what appears to him to be an unanswerable argument against the immortality of the soul. Then follows an impulse to whisper impure suggestions to a fair young maiden, whom he has recently converted. And, finally, he longs to greet a rough sailor with a "volley of good, round, solid, satisfactory, and heaven-defying oaths." The minister, in short, is in that state of mind which gives birth in its victim to a belief in diabolical possession; and the meaning is pointed by an encounter with an old lady, who, in the popular belief, was one of Satan's miserable slaves and dupes, the witches, and is said—for Hawthorne never introduces the supernatural without toning it down by a supposed legendary transmission—to have invited him to meet her at the blasphemous Sabbath in the forest. The sin of endeavouring to escape from the punishment of his sins had brought him into sympathy with wicked mortals and perverted spirits.

This mode of setting forth the agony of a pure mind tainted by one irremovable blot, is undoubtedly impressive to the imagination in a high degree; far more impressive, we may safely say, than any quantity of such rant as very inferior writers could have poured out with the utmost facility on such an occasion. Yet it might possibly be mentioned that a poet of the highest order would have produced the effect by more direct means. Remorse overpowering and absorbing does not embody itself in these recondite and, one may almost say, over-ingenious fancies. Hawthorne does not give us so much the pure passion as some of its collateral effects. He is still more interested in the curious psychological problem than moved by sympathy with the torture of the soul. We pity poor Mr. Dimmesdale profoundly, but we are also interested in him as the subject of an experiment in analytical psychology. We do not care so much for his emotions as for the strange phantoms which are raised in his intellect by the disturbance of his natural functions. The man is placed upon the rack, but our compassion is aroused, not by feeling our own nerves and sinews twitching in sympathy, but by remarking the strange confusion of ideas produced in his mind, the singularly distorted aspect of things in general introduced by such an experience, and hence, if we please, inferring the keenest of the pangs which have produced them. This turn of thought explains the real meaning of Hawthorne's antipathy to poor John Bull. That worthy gentleman, we will admit, is in a sense more gross and beefy than his American cousin. His nerves are stronger, for we need not decide whether they should be called coarser or less morbid. He is not, in the proper sense of the word, less imaginative, for a vigorous grasp of realities is rather a proof of a powerful than a defective imagination. But he is less accessible to those delicate impulses which are to the ordinary passions as electricity to heat. His imagination is more intense and less mobile. The devils which haunt the two races partake of the national characteristics. John Bunyan, Dimmesdale's contemporary, suffered under the pangs of a remorse equally acute, though with apparently far less cause. The devils who tormented him whispered blasphemies in his ears; they pulled at his clothes; they persuaded him that he had committed the unpardonable sin. They caused the very stones in the streets and tiles on the houses, as he says, to band themselves together against him. But they had not the refined and humorous ingenuity of the American fiends. They tempted him, as their fellows tempted Dimmesdale, to sell his soul; but they were too much in earnest to insist upon queer breaches of

decorum. They did not indulge in that quaint play of fancy which tempts us to believe that the devils in New England had seduced the "tricksy spirit," Ariel, to indulge in practical jokes at the expense of a nobler victim than Stephano or Caliban. They were too terribly diabolical to care whether Bunyan blasphemed in solitude or in the presence of human respectabilities. Bunyan's sufferings were as poetical, but less conducive to refined speculation. His were the fiends that haunt the valley of the shadow of death; whereas Hawthorne's are to be encountered in the dim regions of twilight, where realities blend inextricably with mere phantoms, and the mind confers only a kind of provisional existence upon the "airy nothings" of its creation. Apollyon does not appear armed to the teeth and throwing fiery darts, but comes as an unsubstantial shadow threatening vague and undefined dangers, and only half-detaching himself from the background of darkness. He is as intangible as Milton's Death, not the vivid reality which presented itself to mediæval imaginations.

This special attitude of mind is probably easier to the American than to the English imagination. The craving for something substantial, whether in cookery or in poetry, was that which induced Hawthorne to keep John Bull rather at arm's length. We may trace the working of similar tendencies in other American peculiarities. Spiritualism and its attendant superstitions are the gross and vulgar form of the same phase of thought as it occurs in men of highly-strung nerves but defective cultivation. Hawthorne always speaks of these modern goblins with the contempt they deserve, for they shocked his imagination as much as his reason; but he likes to play with fancies which are not altogether dissimilar, though his refined taste warns him that they become disgusting when grossly translated into tangible symbols. Mesmerism, for example, plays an important part in the *Blithedale Romance* and the *House of the Seven Gables*, though judiciously softened and kept in the background. An example of the danger of such tendencies may be found in those works of Edgar Poe, in which he seems to have had recourse to strong stimulants to rouse a flagging imagination. What is exquisitely fanciful and airy in Hawthorne is too often replaced in his rival by an attempt to overpower us by dabblings in the charnel-house and prurient appeals to our fears of the horribly revolting. After reading some of Poe's stories one feels a kind of shock to one's modesty. We require some kind of spiritual ablution to cleanse our minds of his disgusting images; whereas Hawthorne's pure and delightful fancies, though at times they may have led us too far from the healthy contact of everyday interests, never leave a stain upon the imagination, and generally succeed in throwing a harmonious colouring upon some objects in which we had previously failed to recognise the beautiful. To perform that duty effectually is perhaps the highest of artistic merits; and though we may complain of Hawthorne's colouring as too evanescent, its charm grows upon us the more we study it.

Hawthorne seems to have been slow in discovering the secret of his own power. The *Twice-Told Tales*, he tells us, are only a fragmentary selection from a great number which had an ephemeral existence in long-forgotten magazines, and were sentenced to extinction by their author. Though many of the survivors are very striking, no wise reader will regret that sentence. It could be wished that other authors were as ready to bury their innocents, and that injudicious admirers might always abstain from acting as resurrection-men. The fragments, which remain with all their merits, are chiefly interesting as illustrating the intellectual development of their author. Hawthorne, in his preface to the collected edition (all Hawthorne's prefaces are remarkably instructive) tells us what to think of them. The book, he says, "requires to be read in the clear brown twilight atmosphere in which it was written; if opened in the sunshine it is apt to look exceedingly like a volume of blank pages." The remark, with deductions on the score of modesty, is more or less applicable to all his writings. But he explains, and with perfect truth, that though written in solitude, the book has not the abstruse tone which marks the written communications of a solitary mind with itself. The reason is that the sketches "are not the talk of a secluded man with his own mind and heart, but his attempts . . . to open an intercourse with the world." They may, in fact, be compared to Brümmel's failures; and, though they do not display the perfect grace and fitness which would justify him in presenting himself to society, they were well worth taking up to illustrate the skill of the master's manipulation. We see him trying various experiments to hit off that delicate mean between the fanciful and the prosaic, which shall satisfy his taste and be intelligible to the outside world. Sometimes he gives us a fragment of historical romance, as in the story of the stern old regicide who suddenly appears from the woods to head the colonists of Massachusetts in a critical emergency; then he tries his hand at a bit of allegory, and describes the search for the mythical carbuncle which blazes by its inherent splendour on the face of a mysterious cliff in the depths of the untrodden wilderness, and lures old and young, the worldly and the romantic, to waste their lives in the vain effort to discover it—for the carbuncle is the ideal which mocks our pursuit, and may be our curse or our blessing. Then perhaps we have a domestic piece—a quiet description of a New England country scene, touched with a grace which reminds us of the creators of Sir Roger de Coverley or the Vicar of Wakefield. Occasionally there is a fragment of pure *diablerie*, as in the story of the lady who consults the witch in the hollow of the three hills; and more frequently he tries to work out one of those strange psychological problems which he afterwards treated with more fulness of power. The minister who, for an unexplained reason, puts on a black veil one morning in his youth, and wears it until he is laid with it in his grave—a kind of symbolic prophecy of Dimmesdale; the eccentric Wakefield (whose original, if I remember rightly, is to be found in *King's Anecdotes*), who leaves his house one morning for no particular reason, and though living in the next street, does not reveal his existence to his wife for twenty years; and the hero of the "Wedding Knell" the elderly bridegroom whose early love has jilted him, but agrees to marry him when she is an elderly widow and he an old bachelor, and who appals the marriage party by coming to the church in his shroud, with the bell tolling as for a funeral—all these bear the unmistakable stamp of Hawthorne's mint, and each is a study of his favourite subject, the borderland between reason and insanity. In many of these stories appears the element of interest, to which Hawthorne clung the more closely both from early associations and because it is the one undeniable poetical element in the American character. Shallow-minded people fancy Puritanism to be prosaic, because the laces and ruffles of the Cavaliers are a more picturesque costume at a masked ball than the dress of the Roundheads. The Puritan has become a grim and ugly scarecrow, on whom every buffoon may break his jest. But the genuine old Puritan spirit ceases to be picturesque only because of its sublimity: its poetry is sublimed into religion. The great poet of the Puritans fails, as far as he fails, when he tries to transcend the limits of mortal imagination—

> The living throne, the sapphire blaze,
> Where angels tremble as they gaze,

He saw: but blasted with excess of light,
Closed his eyes in endless night.

To represent the Puritan from within was not, indeed, a task suitable to Hawthorne's powers. Carlyle has done that for us with more congenial sentiment than could have been well felt by the gentle romancer. Hawthorne fancies the grey shadow of a stern old forefather wondering at his degenerate son. "A writer of story-books! What kind of business in life, what mode of glorifying God, or being serviceable to mankind in his day and generation, may that be? Why, the degenerate fellow might as well have been a fiddler!" And yet the old strain remains, though strangely modified by time and circumstance. In Hawthorne it would seem that the peddling element of the old Puritans had been reduced to its lowest point; the more spiritual element had been refined till it is probable enough that the ancestral shadow would have refused to recognise the connection. The old dogmatical framework to which he attached such vast importance had dropped out of his descendant's mind, and had been replaced by dreamy speculation, obeying no laws save those imposed by its own sense of artistic propriety. But we may often recognise, even where we cannot express in words, the strange family likeness which exists in characteristics which are superficially antagonistic. The man of action may be bound by subtilities to the speculative metaphysician; and Hawthorne's mind, amidst the most obvious differences, had still an affinity to his remote forefathers. Their bugbears had become his playthings; but the witches, though they have no reality, have still a fascination for him. The interest which he feels in them, even in their now shadowy state, is a proof that he would have believed in them in good earnest a century and a half earlier. The imagination, working in a different intellectual atmosphere, is unable to project its images upon the external world; but it still forms them in the old shape. His solitary musings necessarily employ a modern dialect, but they often turn on the same topics which occurred to Jonathan Edwards in the woods of Connecticut. Instead of the old Puritan speculations about predestination and free-will, he dwells upon the transmission by natural laws of an hereditary curse, and upon the strange blending of good and evil, which may cause sin to be an awakening impulse in a human soul. The change which takes place in Donatello in consequence of his crime is a modern symbol of the fall of man and the eating the fruit of the knowledge of good and evil. As an artist he gives concrete images instead of abstract theories; but his thoughts evidently delight to dwell in the same regions where the daring speculations of his theological ancestors took their origin. Septimius, the rather disagreeable hero of his last romance, is a peculiar example of a similar change. Brought up under the strict discipline of New England, he has retained the love of musing on insoluble mysteries, though he has abandoned the old dogmatic guide-posts. When such a man finds that the orthodox scheme of the universe provided by his official pastors has somehow broken down with him, he forms some audacious theory of his own, and is perhaps plunged into an unhallowed revolt against the divine order. Septimius, under such circumstances, develops into a kind of morbid and sullen Hawthorne. He considers—as other people have done—that death is a disagreeable fact, but refuses to admit that it is inevitable. The romance tends to show that such a state of mind is unhealthy and dangerous, and Septimius is contrasted unfavourably with the vigorous natures who preserve their moral balance by plunging into the stream of practical life. Yet Hawthorne necessarily sympathises with the abnormal being whom he creates. Septimius illustrates the dangers of the musing temperament, but the dangers are produced by a combination of an essentially selfish nature with the meditative tendency. Hawthorne, like his hero, sought refuge from the hard facts of commonplace life by retiring into a visionary world. He delights in propounding much the same questions as those which tormented poor Septimius, though for obvious reasons, he did not try to compound an elixir of life by means of a recipe handed down from Indian ancestors. The strange mysteries in which the world and our nature are shrouded are always present to his imagination; he catches dim glimpses of the laws which bring out strange harmonies, but, on the whole, tend rather to deepen than to clear the mysteries. He loves the marvellous, not in the vulgar sense of the word, but as a symbol of perplexity which encounters every thoughtful man in his journey through life. Similar tenants at an earlier period might, with almost equal probability, have led him to the stake as a dabbler in forbidden sciences, or have caused him to be revered as one to whom a deep spiritual instinct had been granted.

Meanwhile, as it was his calling to tell stories to readers of the English language in the nineteenth century, his power is exercised in a different sphere. No modern writer has the same skill in so using the marvellous as to interest without unduly exciting our incredulity. He makes, indeed, no positive demands on our credulity. The strange influences which are suggested rather than obtruded upon us are kept in the background, so as not to invite, nor indeed to render possible, the application of scientific tests. We may compare him once more to Miss Brontë, who introduces, in *Villette*, a haunted garden. She shows us a ghost who is for a moment a very terrible spectre indeed, and then, very much to our annoyance, rationalises him into a flesh-and-blood lover. Hawthorne would neither have allowed the ghost to intrude so forcibly, nor have expelled him so decisively. The garden in his hands would have been haunted by a shadowy terror of which we could render no precise account to ourselves. It would have refrained from actual contact with professors and governesses; and as it would never have taken bodily form, it would never have been quite dispelled. His ghosts are confined to their proper sphere, the twilight of the mind, and never venture into the broad glare of daylight. We can see them so long as we do not gaze directly at them; when we turn to examine them they are gone, and we are left in doubt whether they were realities or an ocular delusion generated in our fancy by some accidental collocation of half-seen objects. So in the *House of the Seven Gables* we may hold what opinion we please as to the reality of the curse which hangs over the Pyncheons and the strange connection between them and their hereditary antagonists; in the *Scarlet Letter* we may, if we like, hold that there was really more truth in the witch legends which colour the imaginations of the actors than we are apt to dream of in our philosophy; and in *Transformation* we are left finally in doubt as to the great question of Donatello's ears, and the mysterious influence which he retains over the animal world so long as he is unstained by bloodshed. In *Septimius* alone, it seems to me that the supernatural is left in rather too obtrusive a shape in spite of the final explanations; though it might possibly have been toned down had the story received the last touches of the author. The artifice, if so it may be called, by which this is effected—and the romance is just sufficiently dipped in the shadow of the marvellous to be heightened without becoming offensive—sounds, like other things, tolerably easy when it is explained; and yet the difficulty is enormous, as may appear on reflection as well as from the extreme rarity of any satisfactory work in the same style by other artists. With the exception of a

touch or two in Scott's stories, such as the impressive Bodach Glas, in *Waverley*, and the apparition in the exquisite *Bride of Lammermoor*, it would be difficult to discover any parallel.

In fact Hawthorne was able to tread in that magic circle only by an exquisite refinement of taste, and by a delicate sense of humour, which is the best preservative against all extravagance. Both qualities combine in that tender delineation of character which is, after all, one of his greatest charms. His Puritan blood shows itself in sympathy, not with the stern side of the ancestral creed, but with the feebler characters upon whom it weighed as an oppressive terror. He resembles, in some degree, poor Clifford Pynchcon, whose love of the beautiful makes him suffer under the stronger will of his relatives and the prim stiffness of their home. He exhibits the suffering of such a character all the more effectively because, with his kindly compassion there is mixed a delicate flavour of irony. The more tragic scenes affect us, perhaps, with less sense of power; the playful, though melancholy, fancy seems to be less at home when the more powerful emotions are to be excited; and yet once, at least, he draws one of those pictures which engrave themselves instantaneously on the memory. The grimmest or most passionate of writers could hardly have improved the scene where the body of the magnificent Zenobia is discovered in the river. Every touch goes straight to the mark. The narrator of the story, accompanied by the man whose coolness has caused the suicide, and the shrewd, unimaginative Yankee farmer, who interprets into coarse, downright language the suspicions which they fear to confess to themselves, are sounding the depths of the river by night in a leaky punt with a long pole. Silas Foster represents the brutal, commonplace comments of the outside world, which jar so terribly on the more sensitive and closely intersected actors in the tragedy.

> Heigho! [he soliloquises, with offensive loudness], life and death together make sad work for us all. Then I was a boy, bobbing for fish; and now I'm getting to be an old fellow, and here I be, groping for a dead body! I tell you what lads, if I thought anything had really happened to Zenobia, I should feel kind o' sorrowful.

That is the discordant chorus of the gravediggers in *Hamlet*. At length the body is found, and poor Zenobia is brought to the shore with her knees still bent in the attitude of prayer, and her hands clenched in immitigable defiance. Foster tries in vain to straighten the dead limbs. As the teller of the story gazes at her, the grimly ludicrous reflection occurs to him that if Zenobia had foreseen all "the ugly circumstances of death—how ill it would become her, the altogether unseemly aspect which she must put on, and especially old Silas Foster's efforts to improve the matter—she would no more have committed the dreadful act than have exhibited herself to a public assembly in a badly-fitting garment."

HENRY JAMES
From *Hawthorne*
1879, pp. 106–17

If Hawthorne was in a sombre mood, and if his future was painfully vague, *The Scarlet Letter* contains little enough of gaiety or of hopefulness. It is densely dark, with a single spot of vivid colour in it; and it will probably long remain the most consistently gloomy of English novels of the first order. But I just now called it the author's masterpiece, and I imagine it will continue to be, for other generations than ours, his most substantial title to fame. The subject had probably lain a long time in his mind, as his subjects were apt to do; so that he appears completely to possess it, to know it and feel it. It is simpler and more complete than his other novels; it achieves more perfectly what it attempts, and it has about it that charm, very hard to express, which we find in an artist's work the first time he has touched his highest mark—a sort of straightness and naturalness of execution, an unconsciousness of his public, and freshness of interest in his theme. It was a great success, and he immediately found himself famous. The writer of these lines, who was a child at the time, remembers dimly the sensation the book produced, and the little shudder with which people alluded to it, as if a peculiar horror were mixed with its attractions. He was too young to read it himself; but its title, upon which he fixed his eyes as the book lay upon the table, had a mysterious charm. He had a vague belief, indeed, that the "letter" in question was one of the documents that come by the post, and it was a source of perpetual wonderment to him that it should be of such an unaccustomed hue. Of course it was difficult to explain to a child the significance of poor Hester Prynne's blood-coloured A. But the mystery was at last partly dispelled by his being taken to see a collection of pictures (the annual exhibition of the National Academy), where he encountered a representation of a pale, handsome woman, in a quaint black dress and a white coif, holding between her knees an elfish-looking little girl, fantastically dressed, and crowned with flowers. Embroidered on the woman's breast was a great crimson A, over which the child's fingers, as she glanced strangely out of the picture, were maliciously playing. I was told that this was Hester Prynne and little Pearl, and that when I grew older I might read their interesting history. But the picture remained vividly imprinted on my mind; I had been vaguely frightened and made uneasy by it; and when, years afterwards, I first read the novel, I seemed to myself to have read it before, and to be familiar with its two strange heroines. I mention this incident simply as an indication of the degree to which the success of *The Scarlet Letter* had made the book what is called an actuality. Hawthorne himself was very modest about it; he wrote to his publisher, when there was a question of his undertaking another novel, that what had given the history of Hester Prynne its "vogue" was simply the introductory chapter. In fact, the publication of *The Scarlet Letter* was in the United States a literary event of the first importance. The book was the finest piece of imaginative writing yet put forth in the country. There was a consciousness of this in the welcome that was given it— a satisfaction in the idea of America having produced a novel that belonged to literature, and to the forefront of it. Something might at last be sent to Europe as exquisite in quality as anything that had been received, and the best of it was that the thing was absolutely American; it belonged to the soil, to the air; it came out of the very heart of New England.

It is beautiful, admirable, extraordinary; it has in the highest degree that merit which I have spoken of as the mark of Hawthorne's best things—an indefinable purity and lightness of conception, a quality which in a work of art affects one in the same way as the absence of grossness does in a human being. His fancy, as I just now said, had evidently brooded over the subject for a long time; the situation to be represented had disclosed itself to him in all its phases. When I say in all its phases, the sentence demands modification; for it is to be remembered that if Hawthorne laid his hand upon the well-worn theme, upon the familiar combination of the wife, the

lover, and the husband, it was, after all, but to one period of the history of these three persons that he attached himself. The situation is the situation after the woman's fault has been committed, and the current of expiation and repentance has set in. In spite of the relation between Hester Prynne and Arthur Dimmesdale, no story of love was surely ever less of a "love-story." To Hawthorne's imagination the fact that these two persons had loved each other too well was of an interest comparatively vulgar; what appealed to him was the idea of their moral situation in the long years that were to follow. The story, indeed, is in a secondary degree that of Hester Prynne; she becomes, really, after the first scene, an accessory figure; it is not upon her the *dénoûment* depends. It is upon her guilty lover that the author projects most frequently the cold, thin rays of his fitfully-moving lantern, which makes here and there a little luminous circle, on the edge of which hovers the livid and sinister figure of the injured and retributive husband. The story goes on, for the most part, between the lover and the husband—the tormented young Puritan minister, who carries the secret of his own lapse from pastoral purity locked up beneath an exterior that commends itself to the reverence of his flock, while he sees the softer partner of his guilt standing in the full glare of exposure and humbling herself to the misery of atonement—between this more wretched and pitiable culprit, to whom dishonour would come as a comfort and the pillory as a relief, and the older, keener, wiser man, who, to obtain satisfaction for the wrong he has suffered, devises the infernally ingenious plan of conjoining himself with his wronger, living with him, living upon him; and while he pretends to minister to his hidden ailment and to sympathise with his pain, revels in his unsuspected knowledge of these things, and stimulates them by malignant arts. The attitude of Roger Chillingworth, and the means he takes to compensate himself—these are the highly original elements in the situation that Hawthorne so ingeniously treats. None of his works are so impregnated with that after-sense of the old Puritan consciousness of life to which allusion has so often been made. If, as M. Montégut says, the qualities of his ancestors *filtered* down through generations into his composition, *The Scarlet Letter* was, as it were, the vessel that gathered up the last of the precious drops. And I say this not because the story happens to be of so-called historical cast, to be told of the early days of Massachusetts, and of people in steeple-crowned hats and sad-coloured garments. The historical colouring is rather weak than otherwise; there is little elaboration of detail, of the modern realism of research; and the author has made no great point of causing his figures to speak the English of their period. Nevertheless, the book is full of the moral presence of the race that invented Hester's penance—diluted and complicated with other things, but still perfectly recognisable. Puritanism, in a word, is there, not only objectively, as Hawthorne tried to place it there, but subjectively as well. Not, I mean, in his judgment of his characters in any harshness of prejudice, or in the obtrusion of a moral lesson; but in the very quality of his own vision, in the tone of the picture, in a certain coldness and exclusiveness of treatment.

The faults of the book are, to my sense, a want of reality and an abuse of the fanciful element—of a certain superficial symbolism. The people strike me not as characters, but as representatives, very picturesquely arranged, of a single state of mind; and the interest of the story lies, not in them, but in the situation, which is insistently kept before us, with little progression, though with a great deal, as I have said, of a certain stable variation; and to which they, out of their reality, contribute little that helps it to live and move. I was made to feel this want of reality, this over-ingenuity, of *The Scarlet Letter*, by chancing not long since upon a novel which was read fifty years ago much more than to-day, but which is still worth reading—the story of *Adam Blair*, by John Gibson Lockhart. This interesting and powerful little tale has a great deal of analogy with Hawthorne's novel—quite enough, at least, to suggest a comparison between them; and the comparison is a very interesting one to make, for it speedily leads us to larger considerations than simple resemblances and divergences of plot.

Adam Blair, like Arthur Dimmesdale, is a Calvinistic minister who becomes the lover of a married woman, is overwhelmed with remorse at his misdeed, and makes a public confession of it; then expiates it by resigning his pastoral office and becoming a humble tiller of the soil, as his father had been. The two stories are of about the same length, and each is the masterpiece (putting aside, of course, as far as Lockhart is concerned, the *Life of Scott*) of the author. They deal alike with the manners of a rigidly theological society, and even in certain details they correspond. In each of them, between the guilty pair, there is a charming little girl; though I hasten to say that Sarah Blair (who is not the daughter of the heroine, but the legitimate offspring of the hero, a widower) is far from being as brilliant and graceful an apparition as the admirable little Pearl of *The Scarlet Letter*. The main difference between the two tales is the fact that in the American story the husband plays an all-important part, and in the Scottish plays almost none at all. *Adam Blair* is the history of the passion, and *The Scarlet Letter* the history of its sequel; but nevertheless, if one has read the two books at a short interval, it is impossible to avoid confronting them. I confess that a large portion of the interest of *Adam Blair*, to my mind, when once I had perceived that it would repeat in a great measure the situation of *The Scarlet Letter*, lay in noting its difference of tone. It threw into relief the passionless quality of Hawthorne's novel, its element of cold and ingenious fantasy, its elaborate imaginative delicacy. These things do not precisely constitute a weakness in *The Scarlet Letter*; indeed, in a certain way they constitute a great strength; but the absence of a certain something warm and straightforward, a trifle more grossly human and vulgarly natural, which one finds in *Adam Blair*, will always make Hawthorne's tale less touching to a large number of even very intelligent readers, than a love-story told with the robust, synthetic pathos which served Lockhart so well. His novel is not of the first rank (I should call it an excellent second-rate one), but it borrows a charm from the fact that his vigorous, but not strongly imaginative, mind was impregnated with the reality of his subject. He did not always succeed in rendering this reality; the expression is sometimes awkward and poor. But the reader feels that his vision was clear, and his feeling about the matter very strong and rich. Hawthorne's imagination, on the other hand, plays with the theme so incessantly, leads it such a dance through the moon-lighted air of his intellect, that the thing cools off, as it were, hardens and stiffens, and, producing effects much more exquisite, leaves the reader with a sense of having handled a splendid piece of silversmith's work. Lockhart, by means much more vulgar, produces at moments a greater illusion, and satisfies our inevitable desire for something, in the people in whom it is sought to interest us, that shall be of the same pitch and the same continuity with ourselves. Above all, it is interesting to see how the same subject appears to two men of a thoroughly different cast of mind and of a different race. Lockhart was struck with the warmth of the subject that offered itself to him, and Hawthorne with its coldness; the one with its glow, its sentimental interest—the other with its shadow, its moral interest. Lockhart's story is as decent, as severely draped, as *The Scarlet Letter*; but the author has a more vivid sense than appears to have imposed itself upon Hawthorne, of some of the incidents of the situation he describes; his tempted man and tempting woman are more actual and personal; his heroine in especial, though not in the least a delicate or a subtle conception, has a sort of credible, visible, palpable property, a vulgar roundness and relief, which are lacking to the dim and chastened image of Hester Prynne. But I am going too far; I am comparing simplicity with subtlety, the usual with the refined. Each man wrote as his turn of mind impelled him, but each expressed something more than himself. Lockhart was a dense, substantial Briton, with a taste for the concrete, and Hawthorne was a thin New Englander, with a miasmatic conscience.

In *The Scarlet Letter* there is a great deal of symbolism; there is, I think, too much. It is overdone at times, and becomes mechanical; it ceases to be impressive, and grazes triviality. The idea of the mystic A which the young minister finds imprinted upon his breast and eating into his flesh, in sympathy with the embroidered badge that Hester is condemned to wear, appears to me to be a case in point. This suggestion should, I think, have been just made and dropped; to insist upon it and return to it, is to exaggerate the weak side of the subject. Hawthorne returns to it constantly, plays with it, and seems charmed by it; until at last the reader feels tempted to declare that his enjoyment of it is puerile. In the admirable scene, so superbly conceived and beautifully executed, in which Mr. Dimmesdale, in the stillness of the night, in the middle of the sleeping town, feels impelled to go and stand upon the scaffold where his mistress had formerly enacted her dreadful penance, and then, seeing Hester pass along the street, from watching at a sick-bed, with little Pearl at her side, calls them both to come and stand there beside him—in this masterly episode the effect is almost spoiled by the introduction of one of these superficial conceits. What leads up to it is very fine—so fine that I cannot do better than quote it as a specimen of one of the striking pages of the book.

> But before Mr. Dimmesdale had done speaking, a light gleamed far and wide over all the muffled sky. It was doubtless caused by one of those meteors which the nightwatcher may so often observe burning out to waste in the vacant regions of the atmosphere. So powerful was its radiance that it thoroughly illuminated the dense medium of cloud betwixt the sky and earth. The great vault brightened, like the dome of an immense lamp. It showed the familiar scene of the street with the distinctness of mid-day, but also with the awfulness that is always imparted to familiar objects by an unaccustomed light. The wooden houses, with their jutting stories and quaint gable-peaks; the doorsteps and thresholds, with the early grass springing up about them; the garden-plots, black with freshly-turned earth; the wheel-track, little worn, and, even in the market-place, margined with green on either side;—all were visible, but with a singularity of aspect that seemed to give another moral interpretation to the things of this world than they had ever borne before. And there stood the minister, with his hand over his heart; and Hester Prynne, with the embroidered letter glimmering on her bosom; and little Pearl, herself a symbol, and the connecting link between these two. They stood in the noon of that strange and solemn splendour, as if it were the light that is

to reveal all secrets, and the daybreak that shall unite all that belong to one another.

That is imaginative, impressive, poetic; but when, almost immediately afterwards, the author goes on to say that "the minister looking upward to the zenith, beheld there the appearance of an immense letter—the letter A—marked out in lines of dull red light," we feel that he goes too far, and is in danger of crossing the line that separates the sublime from its intimate neighbour. We are tempted to say that this is not moral tragedy, but physical comedy. In the same way, too much is made of the intimation that Hester's badge had a scorching property, and that if one touched it one would immediately withdraw one's hand. Hawthorne is perpetually looking for images which shall place themselves in picturesque correspondence with the spiritual facts with which he is concerned, and of course the search is of the very essence of poetry. But in such a process discretion is everything, and when the image becomes importunate it is in danger of seeming to stand for nothing more serious than itself. When Hester meets the minister by appointment in the forest, and sits talking with him while little Pearl wanders away and plays by the edge of the brook, the child is represented as at last making her way over to the other side of the woodland stream, and disporting herself there in a manner which makes her mother feel herself, "in some indistinct and tantalising manner, estranged from Pearl; as if the child, in her lonely ramble through the forest, had strayed out of the sphere in which she and her mother dwelt together, and was now vainly seeking to return to it." And Hawthorne devotes a chapter to this idea of the child's having, by putting the brook between Hester and herself, established a kind of spiritual gulf, on the verge of which her little fantastic person innocently mocks at her mother's sense of bereavement. This conception belongs, one would say, quite to the lighter order of a story-teller's devices, and the reader hardly goes with Hawthorne in the large development he gives to it. He hardly goes with him either, I think, in his extreme predilection for a small number of vague ideas which are represented by such terms as "sphere" and "sympathies." Hawthorne makes too liberal a use of these two substantives; it is the solitary defect of his style; and it counts as a defect partly because the words in question are a sort of specialty with certain writers immeasurably inferior to himself.

I had not meant, however, to expatiate upon his defects, which are of the slenderest and most venial kind. *The Scarlet Letter* has the beauty and harmony of all original and complete conceptions, and its weaker spots, whatever they are, are not of its essence; they are mere light flaws and inequalities of surface. One can often return to it; it supports familiarity, and has the inexhaustible charm and mystery of great works of art. It is admirably written. Hawthorne afterwards polished his style to a still higher degree; but in his later productions—it is almost always the case in a writer's later productions—there is a touch of mannerism. In *The Scarlet Letter* there is a high degree of polish, and at the same time a charming freshness; his phrase is less conscious of itself.

ANTHONY TROLLOPE
From "The Genius of Nathaniel Hawthorne"
North American Review, September 1879, pp. 204–22

There never surely was a powerful, active, continually effective mind less round, more lop-sided, than that of Nathaniel Hawthorne. ⟨. . .⟩

I have been specially driven to think of this by the strong divergence between Hawthorne and myself. It has always been my object to draw my little pictures as like to life as possible, so that my readers should feel that they were dealing with people whom they might probably have known, but so to do it that the every-day good to be found among them should allure, and the every-day evil repel; and this I have attempted, believing that such ordinary good and ordinary evil would be more powerful in repelling or alluring than great and glowing incidents which, though they might interest, would not come home to the minds of readers. Hawthorne, on the other hand, has dealt with persons and incidents which were often but barely within the bounds of possibility,—which were sometimes altogether without those bounds,—and has determined that his readers should be carried out of their own little mundane ways, and brought into a world of imagination in which their intelligence might be raised, if only for a time, to something higher than the common needs of common life.

⟨. . .⟩ Hawthorne is severe, but his severity is never of a nature to form laws for life. His is a mixture of romance and austerity, quite as far removed from the realities of Puritanism as it is from the sentimentalism of poetry. He creates a melancholy which amounts almost to remorse in the minds of his readers. There falls upon them a conviction of some unutterable woe which is not altogether dispelled till other books and other incidents have had their effects. The woe is of course fictitious, and therefore endurable,—and therefore alluring. And woe itself has its charm. It is a fact that the really miserable will pity the comfortable insignificance of those who are not unhappy, and that they are apt even to boast of their own sufferings. There is a sublimity in mental and even in corporal torment which will sometimes make the position of Lucifer almost enviable. "All is not lost" with him! Prometheus chained, with the bird at his liver, had wherewithal to console himself in the magnificence of his thoughts. And so in the world of melancholy romance, of agony more realistic than melancholy, to which Hawthorne brings his readers, there is compensation to the reader in the feeling that, in having submitted himself to such sublime affliction, he has proved himself capable of sublimity. The bird that feeds upon your vitals would not have gorged himself with common flesh. You are beyond measure depressed by the weird tale that is told to you, but you become conscious of a certain grandness of nature in being susceptible to such suffering. When you hear what Hawthorne has done to others, you long to search his volumes. When he has operated upon you, you would not for the world have foregone it. You have been ennobled by that familiarity with sorrow. You have been, as it were, sent through the fire and purged of so much of your dross. For a time, at least, you have been free from the mundane touch of that beef and ale with which novelists of a meaner school will certainly bring you in contact. No one will feel himself ennobled at once by having read one of my novels. But Hawthorne, when you have studied him, will be very precious to you. He will have plunged you into melancholy, he will have overshadowed you with black forebodings, he will almost have crushed you with imaginary sorrows; but he will have enabled you to feel yourself an inch taller during the process. Something of the sublimity of the transcendent, something of the mystery of the unfathomable, something of the brightness of the celestial, will have attached itself to you, and you will all but think that you too might live to be sublime, and revel in mingled light and mystery.

The creations of American literature generally are no doubt more given to the speculative,—less given to the realistic,—than are those of English literature. On our side of the water we deal more with beef and ale, and less with dreams. Even with the broad humor of Bret Harte, even with the broader humor of Artemus Ward and Mark Twain, there is generally present an undercurrent of melancholy, in which pathos and satire are intermingled. There was a touch of it even with the simple-going Cooper and the kindly Washington Irving. Melancholy and pathos, without the humor, are the springs on which all Longfellow's lines are set moving. But in no American writer is to be found the same predominance of weird imagination as in Hawthorne. There was something of it in M. G. Lewis—our Monk Lewis as he came to be called, from the name of a tale which he wrote; but with him, as with many others, we feel that they have been weird because they have desired to be so. They have struggled to achieve the tone with which their works are pervaded. With Hawthorne we are made to think that he could not have been anything else if he would. It is as though he could certainly have been nothing else in his own inner life. We know that such was not actually the case. Though a man singularly reticent,—what we generally call shy,—he could, when things went well with him, be argumentative, social, and cheery. I have seen him very happy over canvas-back ducks, and have heard him discuss, almost with violence, the superiority of American vegetables. Indeed, he once withered me with a scorn which was anything but mystic or melancholy because I expressed a patriotic preference for English peas. And yet his imagination was such that the creations of his brain could not have been other than such as I have described. Oliver Wendell Holmes has written a well-known story, weird and witch-like also, and has displayed much genius in the picture which he has given us of Elsie Venner. But the reader is at once aware that Holmes compelled himself to the construction of *Elsie Venner*, and feels equally sure that Hawthorne wrote "The Marble Faun" because he could not help himself.

I will take a few of his novels,—those which I believe to be the best known,—and will endeavor to illustrate my idea of his genius by describing the manner in which his stories have been told.

The Scarlet Letter is, on the English side of the water, perhaps the best known. It is so terrible in its pictures of diseased human nature as to produce most questionable delight. The reader's interest never flags for a moment. There is nothing of episode or digression. The author is always telling his one story with a concentration of energy which, as we can understand, must have made it impossible for him to deviate. The reader will certainly go on with it to the end very quickly, entranced, excited, shuddering, and at times almost wretched. His consolation will be that he too has been able to see into these black deeps of the human heart. The story is one of jealousy,—of love and jealousy,—in which love is allowed but little scope, but full play is given to the hatred that can spring from injured love. A woman has been taken in adultery,—among the Puritans of Boston some two centuries since,—and is brought upon the stage that she may be punished by a public stigma. She was beautiful and young, and had been married to an old husband who had wandered away from her for a time. Then she has sinned, and the partner of her sin, though not of her punishment, is the young minister of the church to which she is attached. It is her doom to wear the Scarlet Letter, the letter A, always worked on her dress,—always there on her bosom, to be seen by all men. The first hour of her punishment has to be endured, in the middle of the town, on the public scaffold, under the gaze of all men. As she stands there, her husband comes by chance into the town and sees her, and

she sees him, and they know each other. But no one else in Boston knows that they are man and wife. Then they meet, and she refuses to tell him who has been her fellow sinner. She makes no excuse for herself. She will bear her doom and acknowledge its justice, but to no one will she tell the name of him who is the father of her baby. For her disgrace has borne its fruit, and she has a child. The injured husband is at once aware that he need deal no further with the woman who has been false to him. Her punishment is sure. But it is necessary for his revenge that the man too shall be punished,—and to punish him he must know him. He goes to work to find him out, and he finds him out. Then he does punish him with a vengeance and brings him to death,—does it by the very stress of mental misery. After a while the woman turns and rebels against the atrocity of fate,—not on her own account, but for the sake of that man the sight of whose sufferings she can not bear. They meet once again, the two sinful lovers, and a hope of escape comes upon them,—and another gleam of love. But fate in the shape of the old man is too strong for them. He finds them out, and, not stopping to hinder their flight, merely declares his purpose of accompanying them! Then the lover succumbs and dies, and the woman is left to her solitude. That is the story.

The personages in it with whom the reader will interest himself are four,—the husband, the minister who has been the sinful lover, the woman, and the child. The reader is expected to sympathize only with the woman,—and will sympathize only with her. The husband, an old man who has knowingly married a young woman who did not love him, is a personification of that feeling of injury which is supposed to fall upon a man when his honor has been stained by the falseness of a wife. He has left her and has wandered away, not even telling her of his whereabout. He comes back to her without a sign. The author tells us that he had looked to find his happiness in her solicitude and care for him. The reader, however, gives him credit for no love. But the woman was his wife, and he comes back and finds that she had gone astray. Her he despises, and is content to leave to the ascetic cruelty of the town magistrates; but to find the man out and bring the man to his grave by slow torture is enough of employment for what is left to him of life and energy.

With the man, the minister, the lover, the reader finds that he can have nothing in common, though he is compelled to pity his sufferings. The woman has held her peace when she was discovered and reviled and exposed. She will never whisper his name, never call on him for any comfort or support in her misery; but he, though the very shame is eating into his soul, lives through the seven years of the story, a witness of her misery and solitude, while he himself is surrounded by the very glory of sanctity. Of the two, indeed, he is the greater sufferer. While shame only deals with her, conscience is at work with him. But there can be no sympathy, because he looks on and holds his peace. Her child says to him,—her child, not knowing that he is her father, not knowing what she says, but in answer to him when he would fain take her little hand in his during the darkness of night,—"Wilt thou stand here with mother and me to-morrow noontide"? He can not bring himself to do that, though he struggles hard to do it, and therefore we despise him. He can not do it till the hand of death is upon him, and then the time is too late for reparation in the reader's judgment. Could we have sympathized with a pair of lovers, the human element would have prevailed too strongly for the author's purpose.

He seems hardly to have wished that we should sympathize even with her; or, at any rate, he has not bid us in so many words to do so, as is common with authors. Of course, he has wished it. He has intended that the reader's heart should run over with ruth for the undeserved fate of that wretched woman. And it does. She is pure as undriven snow. We know that at some time far back she loved and sinned, but it was done when we did not know her. We are not told so, but come to understand, by the wonderful power of the writer in conveying that which he never tells, that there has been no taint of foulness in her love, though there has been deep sin. He never even tells us why that letter A has been used, though the abominable word is burning in our ears from first to last. We merely see her with her child, bearing her lot with patience, seeking no comfort, doing what good she can in her humble solitude by the work of her hands, pointed at from all by the finger of scorn, but the purest, the cleanest, the fairest also among women. She never dreams of supposing that she ought not to be regarded as vile, while the reader's heart glows with a longing to take her soft hand and lead her into some pleasant place where the world shall be pleasant and honest and kind to her. I can fancy a reader so loving the image of Hester Prynne as to find himself on the verge of treachery to the real Hester of flesh and blood who may have a claim upon him. Sympathy can not go beyond that; and yet the author deals with her in a spirit of assumed hardness, almost as though he assented to the judgment and the manner in which it was carried out. In this, however, there is a streak of that satire with which Hawthorne always speaks of the peculiar institutions of his own country. The worthy magistrates of Massachusetts are under his lash throughout the story, and so is the virtue of her citizens and the chastity of her matrons, which can take delight in the open shame of a woman whose sin has been discovered. Indeed, there is never a page written by Hawthorne not tinged by satire.

The fourth character is that of the child, Pearl. Here the author has, I think, given way to a temptation, and in doing so has not increased the power of his story. The temptation was, that Pearl should add a picturesque element by being an elf and also a charming child. Elf she is, but, being so, is incongruous with all else in the story, in which, unhuman as it is, there is nothing of the ghost-like, nothing of the unnatural. The old man becomes a fiend, so to say, during the process of the tale; but he is a man-fiend. And Hester becomes sublimated almost to divine purity; but she is still simply a woman. The minister is tortured beyond the power of human endurance; but neither do his sufferings nor his failure of strength adequate to support them come to him from any miraculous agency. But Pearl is miraculous,—speaking, acting, and thinking like an elf,—and is therefore, I think, a drawback rather than an aid. The desolation of the woman, too, would have been more perfect without the child. It seems as though the author's heart had not been hard enough to make her live alone;—as sometimes when you punish a child you can not drive from your face that gleam of love which shoots across your frown and mars its salutary effect.

Hatred, fear, and shame are the passions which revel through the book. To show how a man may so hate as to be content to sacrifice everything to his hatred; how another may fear so that, even though it be for the rescue of his soul, he can not bring himself to face the reproaches of the world; how a woman may bear her load of infamy openly before the eyes of all men,—this has been Hawthorne's object. And surely no author was ever more successful. The relentless purpose of the man, in which is exhibited no passion, in which there is hardly a touch of anger, is as fixed as the hand of Fate. No one in the town knew that the woman was his wife. She had never loved him. He had left her alone in the world. But she was his wife;

and, as the injury had been done to him, the punishment should follow from his hands! When he finds out who the sinner was, he does not proclaim him and hold him up to disgrace; he does not crush the almost adored minister of the gospel by declaring the sinner's trespass. He simply lives with his enemy in the same house, attacking not the man's body,—to which, indeed, he acts as a wise physician,—but his conscience, till we see the wretch writhing beneath the treatment.

Hester sees it too, and her strength, which suffices for the bearing of her own misery, fails her almost to fainting as she understands the condition of the man she has loved. Then there is a scene, the one graceful and pretty scene in the book, in which the two meet,—the two who were lovers,—and dare for a moment to think that they can escape. They come together in a wood, and she flings away, but for a moment, the badge of her shame, and lets down the long hair which has been hidden under her cap, and shines out before the reader for once,—just for that once,—as a lovely woman. She counsels him to fly, to go back across the waters to the old home whence he had come, and seek for rest away from the cruelty of his tyrant. When he pleads that he has no strength left to him for such action, then she declares that she will go with him and protect him and minister to him and watch over him with her strength. Yes; this woman proposes that she will then elope with the partner of her former sin. But no idea comes across the reader's mind of sinful love. The poor wretch can not live without service, and she will serve him. Were it herself that was concerned, she would remain there in her solitude, with the brand of her shame still open upon her bosom. But he can not go alone, and she too will therefore go.

As I have said before, the old man discovers the plot, and crushes their hopes simply by declaring that he will also be their companion. Whether there should have been this gleam of sunshine in the story the critic will doubt. The parent who would be altogether like Solomon should not soften the sternness of his frown by any glimmer of parental softness. The extreme pain of the chronicle is mitigated for a moment. The reader almost fears that he is again about to enjoy the satisfaction of a happy ending. When the blackness and the rumbling thunder-claps and the beating hailstones of a mountain storm have burst with all their fearful glories on the wanderer among the Alps, though he trembles and is awestruck and crouches with the cold, he is disappointed rather than gratified when a little space of blue sky shows itself for a moment through the clouds. But soon a blacker mantle covers the gap, louder and nearer comes the crash, heavier fall the big drops till they seem to strike him to the bone. The storm is awful, majestic, beautiful;—but is it not too pitiless? So it is with the storm which bursts over that minister's head when the little space of blue has vanished from the sky.

But through all this intensity of suffering, through this blackness of narrative, there is ever running a vein of drollery. As Hawthorne himself says, "a lively sense of the humorous again stole in among the solemn phantoms of her thought." He is always laughing at something with his weird, mocking spirit. The very children when they see Hester in the streets are supposed to speak of her in this wise: "Behold, verily, there is the woman of the scarlet letter. Come, therefore, and let us fling mud at her." Of some religious book he says, "It must have been a work of vast ability in the somniferous school of literature." "We must not always talk in the market-place of what happens to us in the forest," says even the sad mother to her child. Through it all there is a touch of burlesque,—not as to the suffering of the sufferers, but as to the great question whether it signifies much in what way we suffer, whether by crushing sorrows or little stings. Who would not sooner be Prometheus than a yesterday's tipsy man with this morning's sick-headache? In this way Hawthorne seems to ridicule the very woes which he expends himself in depicting.

As a novel *The House of the Seven Gables* is very inferior to *The Scarlet Letter*. The cause of this inferiority would, I think, be plain to any one who had himself been concerned in the writing of novels. When Hawthorne proposed to himself to write *The Scarlet Letter*, the plot of his story was clear to his mind. He wrote the book because he had the story strongly, lucidly manifest to his own imagination. In composing the other he was driven to search for a plot, and to make a story. *The Scarlet Letter* was written because he had it to write, and the other because he had to write it. The novelist will often find himself in the latter position. He has characters to draw, lessons to teach, philosophy perhaps which he wishes to expose, satire to express, humor to scatter abroad. These he can employ gracefully and easily if he have a story to tell. If he have none, he must concoct something of a story laboriously, when his lesson, his characters, his philosophy, his satire, and his humor will be less graceful and less easy. All the good things I have named are there in *The House of the Seven Gables*; but they are brought in with less artistic skill, because the author has labored over his plot, and never had it clear to his own mind.

There is a mystery attached to the house. That is a matter of course. A rich man obtained the ground on which it was built by fraud from a poor man, and the poor man's curse falls on the rich man's descendants, and the rich man with his rich descendants are abnormally bad, though very respectable. They not only cheat but murder. The original poor man was hung for witchcraft,—only because he had endeavored to hold his own against the original rich man. The rich men in consequence die when they come to advanced age, without any apparent cause of death, sitting probably upright in their chairs, to the great astonishment of the world at large, and with awful signs of blood about their mouths and shirt-fronts. And each man as he dies is in the act of perpetrating some terrible enormity against some poor member of his own family. The respectable rich man with whom we become personally acquainted in the story,—for as to some of the important characters we hear of them only by the records which are given of past times,—begins by getting a cousin convicted of a murder of which he knew that his kinsman was not guilty, and is preparing to have the same kinsman fraudulently and unnecessarily put into a lunatic asylum, when he succumbs to the fate of his family and dies in his chair, all covered with blood. The unraveling of these mysteries is vague, and, as I think, inartistic. The reader is not carried on by any intense interest in the story itself, and comes at last not much to care whether he does or does not understand the unraveling. He finds that his interest in the book lies elsewhere,—that he must seek it in the characters, lessons, philosophy, satire, and humor, and not in the plot. With *The Scarlet Letter* the plot comes first, and the others follow as accessories.

Two or three of the characters here drawn are very good. The wicked and respectable gentleman who dees the doom of his family, and dies in his chair all covered with blood, is one Judge Pyncheon. The persistent, unbending, cruel villainy of this man,—whose heart is as hard as a millstone, who knows not the meaning of conscience, to whom money and respectability are everything,—was dear to Hawthorne's heart. He likes to revel in an excess of impossible wickedness, and has done so with the Judge. Though we do not care much for the mysteries of the Judge's family, we like the Judge himself, and we like to feel that the author is pouring out his scorn on the padded respectables of his New England world. No man had a stronger belief than Hawthorne in the superiority of his own country; no man could be more sarcastic as to the deficiencies of another,—as I had reason to discover in that affair of the peas; but, nevertheless, he is always throwing out some satire as to the assumed virtues of his own immediate countrymen. It comes from him in little touches as to every incident he handles. In truth, he can not write without satire; and, as in these novels he writes of his own country, his shafts fall necessarily on that.

But the personage we like best in the book is certainly Miss Hepzibah Pyncheon. She is a cousin of the Judge, and has become, by some family arrangement, the life-possessor of the house with seven gables. She is sister also of the man who had been wrongly convicted of murder, and who, when released after a thirty-years' term of imprisonment, comes also to live at the house. Miss Hepzibah, under a peculiarly ill-grained exterior, possesses an affectionate heart and high principles. Driven by poverty, she keeps a shop,—a cent-shop, a term which is no doubt familiar enough in New England, and by which it would be presumed that all her articles were to be bought for a cent each, did it not appear by the story that she dealt also in goods of greater value. She is a lady by birth, and can not keep her cent-shop without some feeling of degradation; but that is preferable to the receiving of charity from that odious cousin the Judge. Her timidity, her affection, her true appreciation of herself, her ugliness, her hopelessness, and general incapacity for everything,—cent-shop-keeping included,—are wonderfully drawn. There are characters in novels who walk about on their feet, who stand upright and move, so that readers can look behind them, as one seems to be able to do in looking at a well-painted figure on the canvas. There are others, again, so wooden that no reader expects to find in them any appearance of movement. They are blocks roughly hewed into some more or less imperfect forms of humanity, which are put into their places and which there lie. Miss Hepzibah is one of the former. The reader sees all round her, and is sure that she is alive,—though she is so incapable.

Then there is her brother Clifford, who was supposed to have committed the murder, and who, in the course of the chronicle, comes home to live with his sister. There are morsels in his story, bits of telling in the description of him, which are charming, but he is not so good as his sister, being less intelligible. Hawthorne himself had not realized the half-fatuous, dreamy, ill-used brother, as he had the sister. In painting a figure it is essential that the artist should himself know the figure he means to paint.

There is yet another Pyncheon,—Phœbe Pyncheon, who comes from a distance, Heaven knows why, to live with her far-away cousin. She is intended as a ray of sunlight,—as was Pearl in *The Scarlet Letter*,—and is more successful. As the old maid Pyncheon is capable of nothing, so is the young maid Pyncheon capable of everything. She is, however, hardly wanted in the story, unless it be that the ray of sunlight was necessary. And there is a young "daguerreotypist,"—as the photographer of the day used to be called,—who falls in love with the ray of sunlight, and marries her at the end; and who is indeed the lineal descendant of the original ill-used poor man who was hung as a witch. There is just one love-scene in the novel, most ghastly in its details; for the young man offers his love, and the girl accepts it, while they are aware that the wicked, respectable old Judge is sitting, all smeared with blood, and dead, in the next room to them. The love-scene, and the hurrying up of the marriage, and all the dollars which they inherit from the wicked Judge, and the "handsome dark-green barouche" prepared for their departure, which is altogether unfitted to the ideas which the reader has formed respecting them, are quite unlike Hawthorne, and would seem almost to have been added by some every-day, beef-and-ale, realistic novelist, into whose hands the unfinished story had unfortunately fallen.

But no one should read *The House of the Seven Gables* for the sake of the story, or neglect to read it because of such faults as I have described. It is for the humor, the satire, and what I may perhaps call the philosophy which permeates it, that its pages should be turned. Its pages may be turned on any day, and under any circumstances. To *The Scarlet Letter* you have got to adhere till you have done with it; but you may take this volume by bits, here and there, now and again, just as you like it. There is a description of a few poultry, melancholy, unproductive birds, running over four or five pages, and written as no one but Hawthorne could have written it. There are a dozen pages or more in which the author pretends to ask why the busy Judge does not move from his chair,—the Judge the while having dree'd his doom and died as he sat. There is a ghastly spirit of drollery about this which would put the reader into full communion with Hawthorne if he had not read a page before, and did not intend to read a page after. To those who can make literary food of such passages as these, *The House of the Seven Gables* may be recommended. To others it will be caviare.

Mosses from an Old Manse will be caviare to many. By this I intend no slight to the intelligence of the many readers who may not find themselves charmed by such narratives. In the true enjoyment of Hawthorne's work there is required a peculiar mood of mind. The reader should take a delight in looking round corners, and in seeing how places and things may be approached by other than the direct and obvious route. No writer impresses himself more strongly on the reader who will submit to him; but the reader must consent to put himself altogether under his author's guidance, and to travel by queer passages, the direction of which he will not perceive till, perhaps, he has got quite to the end of them. In *The Scarlet Letter*, though there are many side paths, there is a direct road, so open that the obstinately straightforward traveler will find his way, though he will not, perhaps, see all that there is to be seen. In *The House of the Seven Gables* a kind of thoroughfare does at last make itself visible, though covered over with many tangles. In the volume of which I am now speaking there is no pathway at all. The reader must go where the writer may choose to take him, and must consent to change not only his ground, but the nature of his ground, every minute. This, as the name implies, is a collection of short stories,—and of course no thread or general plot is expected in such a compilation. But here the short narratives are altogether various in their style, no one of them giving any clew as to what may be expected to follow. They are, rather than tales, the jottings down of the author's own fancies, on matters which have subjected themselves to his brain, one after the other, in that promiscuous disorder in which his manner of thinking permitted him to indulge. He conceives a lovely woman, who has on her cheek a "birth-mark," so trifling as to be no flaw to her beauty. But her husband sees it, and, seeing it, can not rid himself of the remembrance of it. He is a man of science, concerned with the secrets of chemistry, and goes to work to concoct some ichor by which the mark may be eradicated. Just as success is being accomplished, the lady dies under the experiment. "You have aimed loftily," she says to her husband,

at her last gasp; "you have done nobly. Do not repent." Whether the husband does repent we are not told; but the idea left is that, seeking something more than mortal perfection, he had thrown away the happiness which, as a mortal, he might have enjoyed. This is transcendental enough; but it is followed, a few pages on, by the record of Mrs. Bullfrog, who had got herself married to Mr. Bullfrog, as the natural possessor of all feminine loveliness, and then turns out to be a hideous virago, with false hair and false teeth, but who is at last accepted graciously by Bullfrog, because her money is real. The satire is intelligible, and is Hawthornean, but why Hawthorne should have brought himself to surround himself with objects so disagreeable the reader does not understand.

"The Select Party" is pleasant enough. It is held in a castle in the air, made magnificent with all architectural details, and there the Man of Fancy, who is its owner, entertains the Oldest Inhabitant, Nobody, M. Ondit, the Clerk of the Weather, Mother Carey, the Master Genius of his Age,—a young American, of course,—and sundry others, who among them have a good deal to say which is worth hearing. The student of Hawthorne will understand what quips and quirks will come from this mottled company.

Then there is an Italian, one Rappacini, and his daughter, weird, ghostlike, and I must own very unintelligible. The young lady, however, has learned under the teaching of her father, who is part doctor, part gardener, and part conjurer, to exist on the essence of a flower which is fatal to everybody else. She becomes very detrimental to her lover, who has no such gifts, and the story ends as a tragedy. There is a very pretty prose pastoral called "Buds and Bird-Voices," which is simply the indulgence of a poetic voice in the expression of its love of nature. "The Hall of Fantasy" is a mansion in which some unfortunates make their whole abode and business, and "contract habits which unfit them for all the real employments of life. Others,—but these are few,—possess the faculty, in their occasional visits, of discovering a purer truth than the world can impart." The reader can imagine to himself those who, under Hawthorne's guidance, would succeed and those who would fail by wandering into this hall. "The Procession of Life" is perhaps the strongest piece in the book,—the one most suggestive and most satisfactory. Hawthorne imagines that, by the blowing of some trumpet such as has never yet been heard, the inhabitants of the world shall be brought together under other circumstances than those which at present combine them. The poor now associate with the poor, the rich with the rich, the learned with the learned, the idle with the idle, the orthodox with the orthodox, and so on. By this new amalgamation the sick shall associate with the sick, the strong-bodied with the strong, the weak-bodied with the weak, the gifted with the gifted, the sorrowful with the sorrowful, the wicked with the wicked, and the good with the good. Here is a specimen of Hawthorne's manner in bringing the wicked together: "The hideous appeal has swept round the globe. Come all ye guilty ones, and rank yourselves in accordance with the brotherhood of crime. This, indeed, is an awful summons. I almost tremble to look at the strange partnerships that begin to be formed, reluctantly, but by the invincible necessity of like to like, in this part of the procession. A forger from the State prison seizes the arm of a distinguished financier. . . . Here comes a murderer with his clanking chain, and pairs himself,—horrible to tell!—with as pure and upright a man, in all observable respects, as ever partook of the consecrated bread and wine. . . . Why do that pair of flaunting girls, with the pert, affected laugh, and the sly leer at the bystander, intrude themselves into the same rank with yonder decorous matron and that somewhat prudish maiden?" The scope for irony and satire which Hawthorne could get from such a marshaling as this was unbounded.

There is a droll story, with a half-hidden meaning, called "Drowne's Wooden Image," in which Copley the painter is brought upon the scene, so that I am led to suppose that there was a Drowne who carved head-pieces for ships in Boston, and who, by some masterpiece in his trade, and by the help of Hawthorne, has achieved a sort of immortality. Here the man, by dint of special energy on this special job,—he is supposed to be making a figure-head for a ship,—hews out of the wood a female Frankenstein, all alone, but lovely as was the other one hideous. The old idea, too, is conveyed that, as within every block of marble, so within every log of wood, there is a perfection of symmetry and beauty, to be reached by any one who may have the gift of properly stripping off the outlying matter.

"P.'s Correspondence" is the last I will mention. P. is a madman, who, in writing to his friend in Boston from his madhouse chamber, imagines himself to have met in London Byron, Burns, Scott, and a score of other literary worthies, still alive as he supposes, but who by the stress of years have been changed in all their peculiarities, as men are changed when they live long. Byron becomes very religious, and professes excessive high-church tendencies,—as certain excellent and over-liberal friends of mine have in their old age become more timid and more conservative than they who were to the manner born. Hawthorne adds to this the joke that all his own American literary contemporaries,—men whom he knew to be alive, and with whom he probably was intimate,—are, alas! dead and gone. The madman weeps over Bryant, Whittier, and Longfellow, while he has been associating with Keats, Canning, and John Kemble.

Such is the nature of the Mosses from the old Manse each morsel of moss damp, tawny, and soft, as it ought to be, but each with enough of virus to give a sting to the tender hand that touches it.

I have space to mention but one other of our author's works; *The Marble Faun*, as it is called in America, and published in England under the name of *Transformation; or, The Romance of Monte Beni*. The double name, which has given rise to some confusion, was, I think, adopted with the view of avoiding the injustice to which American and English authors are subjected by the want of international copyright. Whether the object was attained, or was in any degree attainable by such means, I do not know.

In speaking of *The Marble Faun*, as I will call the story, I hardly know whether, as a just critic, to speak first of its faults or of its virtues. As one always likes to keep the sweetest bits for the end of the banquet, I will give priority of place to my caviling. The great fault of the book lies in the absence of arranged plot. The author, in giving the form of a novel to the beautiful pictures and images which his fancy has enabled him to draw, and in describing Rome and Italian scenes as few others have described them, has in fact been too idle to carry out his own purpose of constructing a tale. We will grant that a novelist may be natural or supernatural. Let us grant, for the occasion, that the latter manner, if well handled, is the better and the more efficacious. And we must grant also that he who soars into the supernatural need not bind himself by any of the ordinary trammels of life. His men may fly, his birds may speak. His women may make angelic music without instruments. His cherubs may sit at the piano. This wide latitude, while its adequate management is much too difficult for ordinary hands, gives facility for the working of a plot. But

there must be some plot, some arrangement of circumstances, with an intelligible conclusion, or the reader will not be satisfied. If, then, a ghost, who,—or shall I say which?—is made on all occasions to act as a *Deus ex machina*, and to create and to solve every interest, we should know something of the ghost's antecedents, something of the causes which have induced him, or it, to meddle in the matter under discussion. The ghost of Hamlet's father had a manifest object, and the ghost of Banquo a recognized cause. In *The Marble Faun* there is no ghost, but the heroine of the story is driven to connive at murder, and the hero to commit murder, by the disagreeable intrusion of a personage whose *raison d'être* is left altogether in the dark. "The gentle reader," says our author as he ends his narrative, "would not thank us for one of those minute elucidations which are so tedious and after all so unsatisfactory in clearing up the romantic mysteries of a story." There our author is, I think, in error. His readers will hardly be so gentle as not to require from him some explanation of the causes which have produced the romantic details to which they have given their attention, and will be inclined to say that it should have been the author's business to give an explanation neither tedious nor unsatisfactory. The critic is disposed to think that Hawthorne, as he continued his narrative, postponed his plot till it was too late, and then escaped from his difficulty by the ingenious excuse above given. As a writer of novels, I am bound to say that the excuse can not be altogether accepted.

But the fault, when once admitted, may be well pardoned on account of the beauty of the narrative. There are four persons,—or five, including the mysterious intruder who is only, I think, seen and never heard, but who is thrown down the Tarpeian rock and murdered. Three of them are artists,— a lady named Miriam, who is haunted by the mysterious one and is an assenting party to his murder; another lady named Hilda, an American from New England, who lives alone in a tower surrounded by doves; and a sculptor, one Kenyon, also from the States, who is in love with Hilda. The fourth person is the Faun, as to whom the reader is left in doubt whether he be man or Satyr,—human, or half god half animal. As to this doubt the critic makes no complaint. The author was within his right in creating a creature partaking of these different attributes, and it has to be acknowledged on his behalf that the mystery which he has thrown over this offspring of his brain has been handled by him, a writer of prose, not only with profound skill but with true poetic feeling. This faun, who is Count of Monte Beni,—be he most god, or man, or beast; let him have come from the hills and the woods and the brooks like a Satyr of old, or as any other count from his noble ancestors and ancestral towers,—attaches himself to Miriam, as a dog does to a man, not with an expressed human love in which there is a longing for kisses and a hope for marriage, but with a devotion half doglike as I have said, but in its other half godlike and heavenly pure. He scampers round her in his joy, and is made happy simply by her presence, her influence, and her breath. He is happy, except when the intruder intrudes, and then his jealousy is that as of a dog against an intruding hound. There comes a moment in which the intrusion of the intruder is unbearable. Then he looks into Miriam's eyes, and, obtaining the assent for which he seeks, he hurls the intruder down the Tarpeian rock into eternity. After that the light-hearted creature, overwhelmed by the weight of his sin, becomes miserable, despondent, and unable to bear the presence of her who had so lately been all the world to him. In the end light-hearted joy returns to him; but the reason for this second change is not so apparent.

The lives of Kenyon and Hilda are more commonplace,

but, though they are commonplace between man and woman, the manner in which they are told is very beautiful. She is intended to represent perfect innocence, and he manly honesty. The two characters are well conceived and admirably expressed.

In *The Marble Faun*, as in all Hawthorne's tales written after *The Scarlet Letter*, the reader must look rather for a series of pictures than for a novel. It would, perhaps, almost be well that a fastidious reader should cease to read when he comes within that border, toward the end, in which it might be natural to expect that the strings of a story should be gathered together and tied into an intelligible knot. This would be peculiarly desirable in regard to *The Marble Faun*, in which the delight of that fastidious reader, as derived from pictures of character and scenery, will be so extreme that it should not be marred by a sense of failure in other respects.

In speaking of this work in conjunction with Hawthorne's former tales, I should be wrong not to mention the wonderful change which he effected in his own manner of writing when he had traveled out from Massachusetts into Italy. As every word in his earlier volumes savors of New England, so in *The Marble Faun* is the flavor entirely that of Rome and of Italian scenery. His receptive imagination took an impress from what was around him, and then gave it forth again with that wonderful power of expression which belonged to him. Many modern writers have sought to give an interest to their writings by what is called local coloring; but it will too often happen that the reader is made to see the laying on of the colors. In Hawthorne's Roman chronicle the tone of the telling is just as natural,—seems to belong as peculiarly to the author,—as it does with *The Scarlet Letter* or *The House of the Seven Gables*.

GEORGE E. WOODBERRY
From *Nathaniel Hawthorne*
1902, pp. 189–202

The Scarlet Letter is a great and unique romance, standing apart by itself in fiction; there is nothing else quite like it. Of all Hawthorne's works it is most identified with his genius in popular regard, and it has the peculiar power that is apt to invest the first work of an author in which his originality finds complete artistic expression. It is seldom that one can observe so plainly the different elements that are primary in a writer's endowment coalesce in the fully developed work of genius; yet in this romance there is nothing either in method or perception which is not to be found in the earlier tales; what distinguishes it is the union of art and intuition as they had grown up in Hawthorne's practice and had developed a power to penetrate more deeply into life. Obviously at the start there is the physical object in which his imagination habitually found its spring, the fantastically embroidered scarlet letter on a woman's bosom which he had seen in the Puritan group described in "Endicott and the Red Cross." It had been in his mind for years, and his thoughts had centred on it and wandered out from it, tracking its mystery. It has in itself that decorative quality, which he sought in the physical object,— the brilliant and rich effect, startling to the eye and yet more to the imagination as it blazes forth with a secret symbolism and almost intelligence of its own. It multiplies itself, as the tale unfolds, with greater intensity and mysterious significance and dread suggestion, as if in mirrors set round about it,—in the slowly disclosed and fearful stigma on the minister's hidden heart over which he ever holds his hand, where it has become

flesh of his flesh; in the growing elf-like figure of the child, who, with her eyes always fastened on the open shame of the letter on her mother's bosom or the hidden secret of the hand on her father's breast, has become herself the symbol, half revealed and half concealed, is dressed in it, as every reader remembers, and fantastically embodies it as if the thing had taken life in her; and, as if this were not enough, the scarlet letter, at a climax of the dark story, lightens forth over the whole heavens as a symbol of what cannot be hid even in the intensest blackness of night. The continual presence of the letter seems to have burnt into Hawthorne's own mind, till at the end of the narrative he says he would gladly erase its deep print from the brain where long meditation had fixed it. In no other work is the physical symbol so absorbingly present, so reduplicated, so much alive in itself. It is the brand of sin on life. Its concrete vividness leads the author also by a natural compulsion as well as an artistic instinct to display his story in that succession of high-wrought scenes, tableaux, in fact, which was his characteristic method of narrative, picturesque, pictorial, almost to be described as theatrical in spectacle. The background, also, as in the early tales, is of the slightest, no more than will suffice for the acting of the drama as a stage setting sympathetic with the central scene,—a town, with a prison, a meeting-house, a pillory, a governor's house, other habitations on a street, a lonely cottage by the shore, the forest round about all; and for occasion and accessories, only a woman's sentence, the incidental death of Winthrop unmarked in itself, a buccaneering ship in the harbor, Indians, Spanish sailors, rough matrons, clergy; this will serve, for such was Hawthorne's fine economy, knowing that this story was one in which every materialistic element must be used at its lowest tone. Though the scene lay in this world, it was but transitory scaffolding; the drama was one of the eternal life.

The characteristic markings of Hawthorne's genius are also to be found in other points. He does not present the scene of life, the crowd of the world with its rich and varied fullness of interest, complexity of condition and movement, and its interwoven texture of character, event, and fate, such as the great novelists use; he has only a few individual figures, and these are simplified by being exhibited, not in their complete lives, but only in that single aspect of their experience which was absorbing to themselves and constituted the life they lived in the soul itself. There are three characters, Hester, the minister, and the physician; and a fourth, the child, who fulfills the function of the chorus in the old drama, in part a living comment, in part a spectator and medium of sympathy with the main actors. In all four of these that trait of profound isolation in life, so often used before in the earlier tales, is strongly brought out; about each is struck a circle which separates not only one from another, but from all the world, and in the midst of it, as in a separate orb, each lives an unshared life. It is inherent, too, in such a situation that the mystery that had fascinated Hawthorne in so many forms, the secrecy of men's bosoms, should be a main theme in the treatment. He has also had recourse to that method of violent contrast which has been previously illustrated; on the one hand the publicity of detected wrongdoing, on the other the hidden and unsuspected fact; here the open shame and there the secret sin, whose sameness in a double life is expressed by the identity of the embroidered letter and the flesh-wrought stigma. But it is superfluous to illustrate further the genesis of this romance out of Hawthorne's art and matter in his earlier work, showing how naturally it rose by a concentration of his powers on a single theme that afforded them scope, intensity, and harmony at once. The new thing here is the power of his genius to penetrate, as was said above, deep into life.

The romance begins where common tales end. The crime has been committed; in it, in its motives, circumstances, explanation, its course of passion and human tide of life, Hawthorne takes no interest. All that is past, and, whatever it was, now exists only as sin; it has passed from the region of earthly fact into that of the soul, out of all that was temporal into the world where eternal things only are. Not crime, not passion, not the temptation and the fall, but only sin now staining the soul in consequence is the theme; and the course of the story concerns man's dealing with sin, in his own breast or the breasts of others. It is a study of punishment, of vengeance if one will; this is the secret of its gloom, for the idea of salvation, of healing, is but little present and is not felt; there is no forgiveness in the end, in any sense to dispel the darkness of evil or promise the dawn of new life in any one of these tortured souls. The sin of the lovers is not the centre of the story, but only its initial source; that sin breeds sin is the real principle of its being; the minister is not punished as a lover, but as the hypocrite that he becomes, and the physician is punished as the revenger that he becomes. Hester's punishment is visibly from the law, and illustrates the law's brutality, the coarse hand of man for justice, the mere physical blow meant to hurt and crush; it is man's social way of dealing with sin, and fails because it makes no connection with the soul; the victim rises above it, is emancipated from its ideas, transforms the symbol of disgrace into a message of mercy to all who suffer, and annuls the gross sentence by her own higher soul-power. The minister's punishment, also, is visibly from the physician, who illustrates man's individual way of dealing with sin in another; but it is not the minister's suffering under the hand of revenge working subtly in secret that arrests our attention; it is the physician's own degeneracy into a devil of hate through enjoyment of the sight and presence of this punishment, that stamps him into the reader's mind as a type of the failure of such a revenge. "Vengeance is mine, saith the Lord" is the text here blazed forth. In the sphere of the soul human law and private revenge have no place. It is in that sphere that Hester is seen suffering in the touch of the child, being unable to adjust the broken harmonies of life; her incapacity to do that is the ever-present problem that keeps her wound open, not to be stanched, but rather breaking with a more intimate pain with the unfolding of little Pearl's wide-eyed soul. In that sphere, too, the minister is seen suffering—not for the original sin, for that is overlaid, whelmed, forgotten, by the second and heavier transgression of hypocrisy, cowardice, desertion,—but merely from self-knowledge, the knowledge that he is a living lie. The characters, so treated, become hardly more than types, humanly outlined in figure, costume, and event, symbolic pictures of states of the soul, so simplified, so intense, so elementary as to belong to a phantasmagoric rather than a realistic world, to that mirror of the soul which is not found in nature but in spiritual self-consciousness, where the soul is given back to itself in its nakedness, as in a secret place.

Yet it is in the sense of reality that this romance is most intense. It is a truthful story, above all; and only its truth could make it tolerable to the imagination and heart, if indeed it be tolerable to the heart at all. A part of this reality is due to the fact that there is a story here that lies outside of the moral scheme in which Hawthorne's conscious thought would confine it; the human element in it threatens from time to time to break the mould of thought and escape from bondage, because, simple as the moral scheme is, human life is too complex to be solved by it even in this small world of the three guilty ones and the child. This weakness of the moral scheme, this rude strength of human nature, this sense of a larger solution, are most felt when Hawthorne approaches the love element, and throughout in the character of Hester, in whom alone human nature retains a self-assertive power. The same thing is felt vaguely, but certainly, in the lack of sympathy between Hawthorne and the Puritan environment he depicts. He presents the community itself, its common people, its magistrates and clergy, its customs, temper, and atmosphere, as forbidding, and he has no good word for it; harshness characterizes it, and that trait discredits its ideals, its judgments, and its entire interpretation of life. Hester, outcast from it, is represented as thereby enfranchised from its narrowness, enlightened, escaped into a world of larger truth:—

"The world's law was no law for her mind. It was an age in which the human intellect, newly emancipated, had taken a more active and a wider range than for many centuries before. Men of the sword had overthrown nobles and kings. Men bolder than these had overthrown and rearranged—not actually, but within the sphere of theory, which was their most real abode—the whole system of ancient prejudice, wherewith was linked much of ancient principle. Hester Prynne imbibed this spirit. She assumed a freedom of speculation, then common enough on the other side of the Atlantic, but which our forefathers, had they known it, would have held to be a deadlier crime than that stigmatized by the scarlet letter. In her lonesome cottage, by the sea-shore, thoughts visited her, such as dared to enter no other dwelling in New England; shadowy guests, that would have been as perilous as demons to their entertainer, could they have been seen so much as knocking at her door."

This is the foregleam of the next age, felt in her mind, the coming of a larger day. Hawthorne does not develop this or justify it; he only states it as a fact of life. And in the motive of the story, the love of Hester and Arthur, much is left dim; but what is discerned threatens to be unmanageable within the limits of the scheme. Did Hester love her lover, and he love her, through those seven years in silence? Did either of them ever repent their passion for its own sake? And when Hester's womanhood came back in its bloom and her hair fell shining in the forest sunlight, and she took her lover, hand and head and form, in all his broken suffering to her affectionate care and caress, and planned the bold step that they go out together across the seas and live in each other's lives like lovers in truth and reality,—was this only the resurrection of a moment or the firm vital force of a seven years' silent passion? Had either of them ever repented, though one was a coward and the other a condemned and public criminal before the law, and both had suffered? Was not the true sin, as is suggested, the source of all this error, the act of the physician who had first violated Hester's womanhood in a loveless marriage as he had now in Arthur's breast "violated in cold blood the sanctity of a human heart"? "Thou and I," says Arthur, "never did so." The strange words follow, strange for Hawthorne to have written, but better attesting his truth to human nature than all his morality:—

"Never, never!" whispered she. "What we did had a consecration of its own. We felt it so! We said so to each other! Hast thou forgotten it?"

"Hush, Hester!" said Arthur Dimmesdale, rising from the ground. "No; I have not forgotten!"

That confession is the stroke of genius in the romance that humanizes it with a thrill that is felt through every page of the stubborn, dark, harsh narrative of misery. It was not a sin against love that had been committed; it was a sin against the soul; and the sin against the soul lay in the lack of confession, which becomes the cardinal situation of the romance solved in the minister's dying acknowledgment. But the love problem is never solved, both Hester and Roger Chillingworth, one with her mystery of enduring love, the other with his mystery of insatiable hatred, are left with the issue, the meaning of their lives inexplicable, untold. Yet it is from the presence of these elements in the story that something of its intense reality comes.

It remains true, however, that the essential reality lies in the vivid sense of sin, and its experience in conscience. Hawthorne has not given a historical view of New England life; such a village, with such a tragedy, never existed, in that environing forest of the lone seacoast; but he has symbolized historical New England by an environment that he created round a tragedy that he read in the human heart, and in this tragedy itself he was able also to symbolize New England life in its internal features. One thing stood plainly out in our home Puritanism,—spirituality; the transcendent sense of the reality of the soul's life with God, its conscience, its perils, and its eternal issue. Spirituality remained the inheritance of the New England blood; and Hawthorne, who was no Puritan in doctrine or sympathy even, was Puritan in temperament, and hence to him, too, spirituality in life was its main element. He took that sin of passion which has ever been held typical of sin against the purity of the soul's nature, and transformed it into the symbol of all sin, and in its manifestation revolved the aspects of sin as a presence in the soul after the act,—the broken law disturbing life's external harmonies but working a worse havoc within, mining all with corruption there, while it infects with disease whatever approaches it from without. It is by its moral universality that the romance takes hold of the imagination; the scarlet letter becomes only a pictorial incident, but while conscience, repentance, confession, the modes of punishment, and the modes of absolution remain instant and permanent facts, in the life of the soul, many a human heart will read in this book as in a manual of its own intimate hours.

The romance is thus essentially a parable of the soul's life in sin; in its narrower scope it is the work of the moral intellect allegorizing its view of life; and where creative genius enters into it, in the Shakespearean sense of life in its own right, it tends to be a larger and truer story breaking the bonds of its religious scheme. It has its roots in Puritanism, but it is only incidentally a New England tale; its substance is the most universal experience of human nature in religious life, taking its forms only, its local habitation and name, from the Puritan colony in America, and these in a merely allegorical, not historical manner. Certain traits, however, ally it more closely to New England Puritanism. It is a relentless tale; the characters are singularly free from self-pity, and accept their fate as righteous; they never forgave themselves, they show no sign of having forgiven one another; even God's forgiveness is left under a shadow in futurity. They have sinned against the soul, and something implacable in evil remains. The minister's dying words drop a dark curtain over all.

"Hush, Hester, hush!" said he, with tremulous solemnity. "The law we broke!—the sin here so awfully revealed!—let these alone be in thy thoughts! I fear! I fear! It may be that, when we forgot our God,—when we violated our reverence each for the other's soul,—it was thenceforth vain to hope that we could meet hereafter, in an everlasting and pure reunion."

Mercy is but a hope. There is also a singular absence of prayer in the book. Evil is presented as a thing without remedy, that cannot change its nature. The child, even, being the fruit of sin, can bring, Hester and Arthur doubt, no good for others or herself. In the scheme of Puritan thought, however, the atonement of Christ is the perpetual miracle whereby salvation comes, not only hereafter but in the holier life led here by grace. There is no Christ in this book. Absolution, so far as it is hinted at, lies in the direction of public confession, the efficacy of which is directly stated, but lamely nevertheless; it restores truth, but it does not heal the past. Leave the dead past to bury its dead, says Hawthorne, and go on to what may remain; but life once ruined is ruined past recall. So Hester, desirous of serving in her place the larger truth she has come to know, is stayed, says Hawthorne, because she "recognized the impossibility that any mission of divine and mysterious truth should be confided to a woman stained with sin, bowed down with shame, or even burdened with a life-long sorrow." That was never the Christian gospel nor the Puritan faith. Indeed, Hawthorne here and elsewhere anticipates those ethical views which are the burden of George Eliot's moral genius, and contain scientific pessimism. This stoicism, which was in Hawthorne, is a primary element in his moral nature, in him as well as in his work; it is visited with few touches of tenderness and pity; the pity one feels is not in him, it is in the pitiful thing, which he presents objectively, sternly, unrelentingly. It must be confessed that as an artist he appears unsympathetic with his characters; he is a moral dissector of their souls, minute, unflinching, thorough, a vivisector here; and he is cold because he has passed sentence on them, condemned them. There is no sympathy with human nature in the book; it is a fallen and ruined thing suffering just pain in its dying struggle. The romance is steeped in gloom. Is it too much to suggest that in ignoring prayer, the atonement of Christ, and the work of the Spirit in men's hearts, the better part of Puritanism has been left out, and the whole life of the soul distorted? Sin in the soul, the scarlet flower from the dark soil, we see; but, intent on that, has not the eye, and the heart, too, forgotten the large heavens that ensphere all—even this evil flower—and the infinite horizons that reach off to the eternal distance from every soul as from their centre? This romance is the record of a prison-cell, unvisited by any ray of light save that earthly one which gives both prisoners to public ignominy; they are seen, but they do not see. These traits of the book, here only suggested, have kinship with the repelling aspects of Puritanism, both as it was and as Hawthorne inherited it in his blood and breeding; so, in its transcendent spirituality, and in that democracy which is the twin-brother of spirituality in all lands and cultures, by virtue of which Hawthorne here humiliates and strips the minister who is the type of the spiritual aristocrat in the community, there is the essence of New England; but, for all that, the romance is a partial story, an imperfect fragment of the old life, distorting, not so much the Puritan ideal—which were a little matter—but the spiritual life itself. Its truth, intense, fascinating, terrible as it is, is a half-truth, and the darker half; it is the shadow of which the other half is light; it is the wrath of which the other half is love. A book from which light and love are absent may hold us by its truth to what is dark in life; but, in the highest sense, it is a false book. It is a chapter in the literature of moral despair, and is perhaps most tolerated as a condemnation of the creed which, through imperfect comprehension, it travesties.

CHARLES DICKENS

CHARLES DICKENS

1812–1870

Charles John Huffam Dickens was born in Landport, Portsmouth, on February 7, 1812. The family moved to London in 1814, to Chatham in 1817, and then back to London in 1822. By 1824 increasing financial difficulties led Dickens's parents to put him to work at a shoe-blacking warehouse; later that same year his father was briefly imprisoned for debt. Memories of this painful period in his life were to affect much of Dickens's later writing, in particular the early chapters of *David Copperfield*.

After studying at the Wellington House Academy in London (1824–27), Dickens worked as a solicitor's clerk (1827–28), and then became a reporter for the *Morning Chronicle* (1834–36). In 1836–37 a collection of articles contributed to various periodicals appeared in two volumes as *Sketches by "Boz," Illustrative of Every-Day Life and Every-Day People.* This was followed by the enormously popular *Posthumous Papers of the Pickwick Club,* published in twenty monthly numbers (beginning in April 1836) and appearing in book form, as a loosely constructed novel, in 1837. Also in 1836 Dickens married Catherine Hogarth, by whom he had ten children before their separation in 1858.

Between 1837 and 1839 Dickens published a second novel, *Oliver Twist,* in monthly numbers in *Bentley's Miscellany,* a new periodical of which Dickens was the first editor. This was followed in 1838–39 by *Nicholas Nickelby,* another novel that appeared in monthly installments. In 1840 Dickens founded his own weekly, *Master Humphrey's Clock* (1840–41), in which appeared his novels *The Old Curiosity Shop* (1840–41) and *Barnaby Rudge* (1841). In 1842 he and his wife visited the United States and Canada, and after returning Dickens published *American Notes* (1842), two volumes of impressions which caused much offense in the U.S. He then wrote *Martin Chuzzlewit,* a novel set partly in America, which appeared in monthly installments between 1843 and 1844.

In 1843 Dickens published *A Christmas Carol,* the first in a series of Christmas books, the others being *The Chimes* (1844), *The Cricket on the Hearth* (1845), *The Battle of Life* (1846), and *The Haunted Man* (1848). In 1846 he founded the Radical *Daily News,* which he briefly edited himself, and to which he contributed "Pictures of Italy," after visiting Italy in 1844 and again in 1845. During a visit to Switzerland in 1846 Dickens wrote his novel *Dombey and Son,* which appeared in monthly parts between 1846 and 1848. In 1850 he started the periodical *Household Words*; in 1859 it was incorporated into *All the Year Round,* which Dickens continued to edit until his death. Much of his later work was published in these two periodicals, including *David Copperfield* (1849–50), *Bleak House* (1852–53), *Hard Times* (1854), *Little Dorrit* (1855–57), *A Tale of Two Cities* (1859), *Great Expectations* (1860–61), and *Our Mutual Friend* (1864–65).

During these years of intense productivity Dickens also found time to direct amateur theatrical productions, sometimes of his own plays. He also became involved in a variety of philanthropical activities, gave public readings, and in 1867–68 visited America for a second time. Dickens died suddenly in 1870 on June 9, leaving unfinished his last novel, *The Mystery of Edwin Drood,* which was first published later that same year. Several editions of his collected letters have been published. Despite Dickens's tremendous popularity during and after his own life, it was not until the twentieth century that serious critical studies began to appear. Modern critical opinion has tended to favor the later works, which are more somber and complex, over the earlier ones, which are characterized by boisterous humor and broad caricature.

Personal

He is a fine little fellow, Boz, as I think; clear blue intelligent eyes, eyebrows that he arches amazingly, large protrusive rather loose mouth,—a face of the most extreme *mobility,* which he shuttles about, eyebrows, eyes, mouth and all, in a very singular manner while speaking; surmount this with a loose coil of common-coloured hair, and set it on a small compact figure, very small, and dressed rather *à la d'Orsay* than well: this is Pickwick; for the rest a quiet shrewd-looking little fellow, who seems to guess pretty well what he is, and what others are.—THOMAS CARLYLE, Letter to John A. Carlyle (March 17, 1840)

Arrival of Charles Dickens. Among the passengers in the *Britannia* is Mr. Charles Dickens and his wife. This gentleman is the celebrated "Boz," whose name "rings through the world with loud applause"; the fascinating writer whose fertile imagination and ready pen conceived and sketched the immortal Pickwick, his prince of valets and his bodyguard of choice cronies, who has made us laugh with "Mantalini," and cry with "poor little Nell," caused us to shrink with horror from the effects of lynch law, as administered by the misguided Lord George Gordon, and to listen with unmitigated delight to the ticking of "Master Humphrey's Clock." The visit of this popular writer has been heralded in advance. He was expected by this packet, and I signed three or four days ago, with a number of other persons, a letter to be presented to him on his arrival in this city, giving him a hearty welcome and inviting him to a public dinner, which, from the spirit which appears to prevail on the subject, will be no common affair.—PHILIP HONE, *Diary*, Jan. 24, 1842

Called on Dickens at 10.30 A.M. by appointment, as he leaves at one. He was at breakfast. Sat down with him. He was very agreeable and full of life. He is the *cleverest* man I ever met. I mean he impresses you more with the alertness of his various powers. His forces are all light infantry and light cavalry, and always in marching order. There are not many heavy pieces, but few *sappers and miners*, the scientific corps is deficient, and I fear there is no chaplain in the garrison.—RICHARD HENRY DANA, *Journal* (Feb. 5, 1842), cited in Charles Francis Adams, *Richard Henry Dana: A Biography*, 1890, Vol. 1, p. 33

I admire and love the man exceedingly, for he has a deep warm heart, a noble sympathy with and respect for human nature, and great intellectual gifts wherewith to make these fine moral ones fruitful for the delight and consolation and improvement of his fellow-beings.—FRANCES ANN KEMBLE, Letter (April 22, 1842), *Records of a Later Life*, 1882, p. 318

At a dinner-party at Mr. Holland's last evening, a gentleman, in instance of Charles Dickens's unweariability, said that during some theatrical performances in Liverpool he acted in play and farce, spent the rest of the night making speeches, feasting, and drinking at table, and ended at seven o'clock in the morning by jumping leap-frog over the backs of the whole company.—NATHANIEL HAWTHORNE, *The English Note-Books*, Oct. 22, 1853

Dickens is forty-five years old, cheerful, amiable, noble, and good. However highly I may place him as an author, I must prize him just as highly as an actor in tragedy, as well as in comedy.—HANS CHRISTIAN ANDERSEN, Letter to the Grand Duke of Weimar (Aug. 9, 1857)

Of his attractive points in society and conversation I have particularised little, because in truth they were himself. Such as they were, they were never absent from him. His acute sense of enjoyment gave such relish to his social qualities that probably no man, not a great wit or a professed talker, ever left, in leaving any social gathering, a blank so impossible to fill up. In quick and varied sympathy, in ready adaptation to every whim or humour, in help to any mirth or game, he stood for a dozen men. If one may say such a thing, he seemed to be always the more himself for being somebody else, for continually putting off his personality. His versatility made him unique.—JOHN FORSTER, *The Life of Charles Dickens*, 1872–74, Bk. 11, Ch. 3

In publishing the more private letters, we do so with the view of showing him in his homely, domestic life—of showing how in the midst of his own constant and arduous work, no household matter was considered too trivial to claim his care and attention. He would take as much pains about the hanging of a picture, the choosing of furniture, the superintending any little improvement in the house, as he would about the more serious business of his life; thus carrying out to the very letter his favourite motto of "What is worth doing at all is worth doing well."—MAMIE DICKENS, GEORGINA HOGARTH, "Preface" to *The Letters of Charles Dickens*, 1882, Vol. 1, p. viii

His extraordinary charm of manner, never capriciously changed, the smile and laugh always ready—that sympathy, too, which rises before me, and was really unique—I can call no one to mind that possessed it or possesses it now in the same degree.—PERCY FITZGERALD, "Charles Dickens as an Editor," *Recreations of a Literary Man*, 1882, pp. 31–32

Dickens was only thirty-three when I first saw him, being just two years my junior. I have said what he appeared to me then. As I knew him afterwards, and to the end of his days, he was a strikingly manly man, not only in appearance but in bearing. The lustrous brilliancy of his eyes was very striking. And I do not think that I have ever seen it noticed, that those wonderful eyes which saw so much and so keenly, were appreciably, though to a very slight degree, near sighted eyes. Very few persons, even among those who knew him well, were aware of this, for Dickens never used a glass. But he continually exercised his vision by looking at distant objects, and making them out as well as he could without any artificial assistance. It was an instance of that force of will in him, which compelled a naturally somewhat delicate frame to comport itself like that of an athlete. Mr. Forster somewhere says of him, 'Dickens's habits were robust, but his health was not.' This is entirely true as far as my observation extends.

Of the general charm of his manner I despair of giving any idea to those who have not seen or known him. This was a charm by no means dependent on his genius. He might have been the great writer he was and yet not have warmed the social atmosphere wherever he appeared with that summer glow which seemed to attend him. His laugh was brimful of enjoyment. There was a peculiar humorous protest in it when recounting or hearing anything specially absurd, as who should say ''Pon my soul this is *too* ridiculous! This passes all bounds!' and bursting out afresh as though the sense of the ridiculous overwhelmed him like a tide, which carried all hearers away with it, and which I well remember. His enthusiasm was boundless. It entered into everything he said or did. It belonged doubtless to that amazing fertility and wealth of ideas and feeling that distinguished his genius.—THOMAS ADOLPHUS TROLLOPE, *What I Remember*, 1888

General

His more obvious excellences are of the kind which are easily understood by all classes—by the stable-boy as well as the statesman. His intimate knowledge of character, his familiarity with the language and experience of low life, his genuine humor, his narrative power, and the cheerfulness of his philosophy, are traits that impress themselves on minds of every description. But, besides these, he has many characteristics to interest the higher orders of mind. They are such as to recommend him peculiarly to Americans. His sympathies seek out that class with which American institutions and laws sympathize most strongly. He has found subjects of thrilling interest in the passions, sufferings, and virtues of the mass. As Dr. Channing has said, "he shows that life in its rudest form may wear a tragic grandeur, that, amid follies or excesses provoking laughter or scorn, the moral feelings do not wholly die, and that the haunts of the blackest crime are sometimes lighted up by the presence and influence of the noblest souls." Here we have the secret of the attentions that have been showered upon Mr. Dickens. That they may have been carried too far is possible; yet we are disposed to regard them, even in their excess, with favor. We have so long been accustomed to seeing the homage of the multitude paid to men of mere titles, or military chieftains, that we have grown tired of it. We are glad to see the mind asserting its supremacy, to find its rights more generally recognized. We rejoice that a young man, without birth, wealth, title, or a sword, whose only claims to distinction are in his intellect and heart, is received with a feeling that was formerly rendered only to kings and conquerors. The author, by his genius, has contributed happy moments to the lives of thousands, and it is right that the thousands should recompense him for the gift.—WILLIAM CULLEN BRYANT, *New York Evening Post* (Feb. 18, 1842), cited in Parke Godwin, A *Biography of William Cullen Bryant*, 1883, Vol. 1, pp. 396–97

Do you know that the royal Boz lives close to us, three doors from Mr. Kenyon in Harley Place? The new numbers appear to me admirable, and full of life and blood—whatever we may say to the thick rouging and extravagance of gesture. There is a beauty, a tenderness, too, in the organ scene, which is worthy of the gilliflowers. But my admiration for 'Boz' fell from its 'sticking place,' I confess, a good furlong, when I read Victor Hugo; and my creed is, that, *not* in his tenderness, which is as much his own as his humour, but in his serious powerful Jew-trial scenes, he has followed Hugo closely, and never scarcely looked away from *Les Trois jours d'un condamné*.
—ELIZABETH BARRETT BROWNING, Letter to James Martin (Feb. 6, 1843)

The immediate and almost unprecedented popularity he attained was owing not more to his own genius than to the general contempt for the school he supplanted. After ten years of conventional frippery and foppery, it was a relief to have once more a view of the earth and firmament,—to feel once more one of those touches of nature "which make the whole world kin." Here was a man, at last, with none of the daintiness of genteel society in his manner, belonging to no clique or sect, with sympathies embracing widely varying conditions of humanity, and whose warm heart and observant eye had been collecting from boyhood those impressions of man and nature which afterwards gushed out in exquisite descriptions of natural scenery, or took shape in his Pickwicks, Wellers, Vardens, Pecksniffs, and their innumerable brotherhood.

Dickens, as a novelist and prose poet, is to be classed in the front rank of the noble company to which he belongs. He has revived the novel of genuine practical life, as it existed in the works of Fielding, Smollett, and Goldsmith, but at the same time has given to his materials an individual coloring and expression peculiarly his own. His characters, like those of his great exemplars, constitute a world of their own, whose truth to nature every reader instinctively recognized in connection with their truth to Dickens. Fielding delineates with more exquisite art, standing more as the spectator of his personages, and commenting on their actions with an ironical humor, and a seeming innocence of insight, which pierces not only into but through their very nature, laying bare their inmost unconscious springs of action, and in every instance indicating that he understands them better than they understand themselves. It is this perfection of knowledge and insight which gives to his novels their naturalness, their freedom of movement, and their value as lessons in human nature as well as consummate representations of actual life. Dickens's eye for the forms of things is as accurate as Fielding's, and his range of vision more extended; but he does not probe so profoundly into the heart of what he sees, and he is more led away from the simplicity of truth by a tricksy spirit of fantastic exaggeration. Mentally he is indisputably below Fielding; but in tenderness, in pathos, in sweetness and purity of feeling, in that comprehensiveness of sympathy which springs from a sense of brotherhood with mankind, he is as indisputably above him.

The tendency of Dickens's genius, both in delineating the actual and the imaginary, is to personify, to individualize. This makes his page all alive with character. Not only does he never treat of man in the abstract, but he gives personality to the rudest shows of nature, everything he touches becoming

symbolic of human sympathies or antipathies. There is no writer more deficient in generalization. His comprehensiveness is altogether of the heart, but that heart, like the intelligence of Bacon's cosmopolite, is not "an island cut off from other men's lands, but a continent which joins to them." His observation of life thus beginning and ending with individuals, it seems strange that those highly sensitive and patriotic Americans who paid him the compliment of flying into a passion with his peevish remarks on our institutions, should have overlooked the fact that his mind was altogether destitute of the generalizing qualities of a statesman, and that an angry humorist might have made equally ludicrous pictures of any existing society. When his work on America was quoted in the French Chamber of Deputies, M. de Tocqueville ridiculed the notion that any opinions of Mr. Dickens should be referred to in that place as authoritative. There is a great difference between the criticism of a statesman and the laughter of a tourist, especially when the tourist laughs not from his heart, but his bile. The statesman passes over individual peculiarities to seize on general principles, while the whole force of the other lies in the description of individual peculiarities. Dickens, detecting with the nicest tact the foibles of men, and capable of setting forth our Bevans, Colonel Tompkinses, and Jefferson Bricks, in all the comic splendor of humorous exaggeration, is still unqualified to abstract a general idea of national character from his observation of persons. A man immeasurably inferior to him in creative genius might easily excel him in that operation of the mind. Indeed, were Dickens's understanding as comprehensive as his heart, and as vigorous as his fancy, he would come near realizing the ideal of a novelist; but, as it is, it is as ridiculous to be angry with any generalizations of his on American institutions and politics, as it would be to inveigh against him for any heresies he might blunder into about innate ideas, the freedom of the will, or original sin. Besides, as Americans, we have a decided advantage over our transatlantic friends, even in the matter of being caricatured by the novelist whom both are rivals in admiring; for certainly, if there be any character in which Dickens has seized on a national trait, that character is Pecksniff, and that national trait is English.

The whole originality and power of Dickens lies in this instinctive insight into individual character, to which we have already referred. He has gleaned all his facts from observation and sympathy, in a diligent scrutiny of actual life, and no contemporary author is less indebted to books. His style is all his own, its quaint texture of fancy and humor being spun altogether from his own mind, with hardly a verbal felicity which bears the mark of being stolen. In painting character he is troubled by no uneasy sense of himself. When he is busy with Sam Weller or Mrs. Nickleby, he forgets Charles Dickens. Not taking his own character as the test of character, but entering with genial warmth into the peculiarities of others, and making their joys and sorrows his own, his perceptions are not bounded by his personality, but continually apprehend and interpret new forms of individual being; and thus his mind, by the readiness with which it genially assimilates other minds, and the constancy with which it is fixed on objects external to itself, grows with every exercise of its powers. By this felicity of nature, the man who began his literary life with a condemned farce, a mediocre opera, and some slight sketches of character, written in a style which but feebly indicated the germs of genius, produced before the expiration of eight years, *The Pickwick Papers, Oliver Twist, Nicholas Nickleby, The Old Curiosity Shop*, and *Martin Chuzzlewit*, in a continually ascending scale of intellectual excellence, and achieved a fame not only gladly recognized wherever the English tongue was spoken, but which extended into France, Germany, Italy, and Holland, and caused the translation of his works into languages of which he hardly understood a word. Had he been an egotist, devoured by a ravenous vanity for personal display, and eager to print the image of himself on the popular imagination, his talents would hardly have made him known beyond the street in which he lived, and his mind by self-admiration would soon have been self-consumed. His fellow-feeling with his race is his genius.—EDWIN P. WHIPPLE, "Novels and Novelists: Charles Dickens" (1844), *Literature and Life*, 1849, pp. 58–63

> As when a friend (himself in music's list)
> Stands by some rare, full-handed organist,
> And glorying as he sees the master roll
> The surging sweets through all their depths of soul,
> Cannot, encouraged by his smile, forbear
> With his own hand to join them here and there;
> And so, if little, yet add something more
> To the sound's volume and the golden roar;
> So I, dear friend, Charles Dickens, though thy hand
> Needs but itself, to charm from land to land,
> Make bold to join in summoning men's ears
> To this thy new-found music of our spheres,
> In hopes that by thy Household Words and thee
> The world may haste to days of harmony.
>   —LEIGH HUNT, "To Charles Dickens," 1849

The English novels of these days seem to me the more detestable the one than the other—Dickens all cant (Liberal cant, the worst sort) and caricature.—MARY RUSSELL MITFORD, Letter to Mr. Starkey (Jan. 31, 1853)

We have one great novelist who is gifted with the utmost power of rendering the external traits of our town population; and if he could give us their psychological character—their conceptions of life, and their emotions—with the same truth as their idiom and manners, his books would be the greatest contribution Art has ever made to the awakening of social sympathies. But while he can copy Mrs. Plornish's colloquial style with the delicate accuracy of a sun-picture, while there is the same startling inspiration in his description of the gestures and phrases of "Boots," as in the speeches of Shakespeare's mobs or numskulls, he scarcely ever passes from the humorous and external to the emotional and tragic, without becoming as transcendent in his unreality as he was a moment before in his artistic truthfulness. But for the precious salt of his humour, which compels him to reproduce external traits that serve, in some degree, as a corrective to his frequently false psychology, his preternaturally virtuous poor children and artisans, his melodramatic boatmen and courtesans, would be as noxious as Eugène Sue's idealized proletaires in encouraging the miserable fallacy that high morality and refined sentiment can grow out of harsh social relations, ignorance, and want; or that the working classes are in a condition to enter at once into a millennial state of *altruism*, wherein every one is caring for every one else, and no one for himself.—GEORGE ELIOT, "Natural History of German Life: Riehl," 1856

Dickens, with preternatural apprehension of the language of manners and the varieties of street life; with pathos and laughter, with patriotic and still enlarging generosity, writes London tracts. He is a painter of English details, like Hogarth; local and temporary in his tints and style, and local in his aims.—RALPH WALDO EMERSON, "Literature," *English Traits*, 1856

⟨. . .⟩ if we glance over the wit and satire of the popular writers of the day, we shall find that the *manner* of it, so far as it is distinctive, is always owing to Dickens; and that out of his first exquisite ironies branched innumerable other forms of wit, varying with the disposition of the writers; original in the matter and substance of them, yet never to have been expressed as they now are, but for Dickens.—JOHN RUSKIN, *Modern Painters*, 1856, Vol. 3, Pt. 4, App. 3

And his genius is worthy of honor. No writer could be named on whom the indefinable gift has been more manifestly conferred. His early works are all aglow with genius. The supreme potency with which he commands it, is shown in the total absence of effort, in the classic chasteness and limpid flow, of thought, fancy, and diction. You are in a meadow just after dawn; the flowers are fresh as if they had awakened from slumber, and the dew is on them all. A word, an idea, a glimpse of beauty, is always at hand; the writer never tarries a moment; yet there is no display, no profusion, of opulence. You do not see him waving the wand; the tear of the smile is on your cheek before you are aware.

The distinctive power of Dickens lies, we think, in a sympathy of extraordinary range, exquisite delicacy, and marvellous truth. He does not so much look, with steady, unparticipating gaze, until he knows and remembers the exact features of life: he feels. With all human sorrow he could weep; with all human mirth he could laugh; and when he came to write, every emotion he aimed at exciting was made sure, by being first experienced in his own breast. It was not with the individual man, in the wholeness of his life, in the depths of his identity, that he naturally concerned himself. It was kindness, rather than the one kind man, that he saw. It was mirth, rather than the whole character which is modified by humor. Qualities, capacities, characteristics, rather than complete men, glassed themselves in the mirror of his clear and open soul. With all his accuracy in detailed portraiture, it is a superficial perception of the order of his genius, which does not see that its power rested naturally less on realism, than on a peculiar, delicate and most captivating idealization. Pickwick, at least in the whole earlier part of his history, is an impossible personage. He belongs to broad farce. But we laugh at his impossible conversation with the cabman. We laugh at his impossible credulity as he listens to Jingle. We laugh at his impossible simplicity at the review. The far-famed Sam Weller, too, corresponds to no reality. The Londoner born and bred is apt to be the driest and most uninteresting of beings. All things lost for him the gloss of novelty when he was fifteen years old. He would suit the museum of a *nil admirari* philosopher, as a specimen, shrivelled and adust, of the ultimate result of his principle. But Dickens collected more jokes than all the cabmen in London would utter in a year, and bestowed the whole treasure upon Sam. His eye was far too acute for the comical to let it rest on any one funny man. In the case of those of his characters whom we are simply to admire and love, the same distinctive mode of treatment is exhibited. Rose Maylie and Esther Summerson are breathing epitomes of the tendernesses, the sweetnesses, the beauties, of life. Oliver Twist concentrates the single good qualities of a hundred children. The kind-hearted man, Dickens's stock character, be his name Pickwick, Jarndyce, or Clennam, seems always radically the same, and corresponds well enough with our theory. Perhaps it is essential deficiency in the highest power of individualization, which drives Mr. Dickens, it may be unconsciously, to affix, by way of labels, to the personages of his story, those insignificant peculiarities which all can perceive.

Amid the tumult and distracting blaze of his fame, one is by no means safe from the blunder of overlooking the kernel of genuine and precious humanity, of honest kindliness, of tender yet expansive benignity, which is in the centre of Dickens's being. His nature must originally have been most sweetly tuned. He must from the first have abounded in those qualities, which are so beautiful and winning when combined with manly character and vigorous powers; a cheerful gentleness, a loving hopefulness, a willingness to take all things and men for the best, an eye for the loveable; such a disposition as one finds in Goldsmith, a passionate admiration of happy human faces, a delight in the sports and laughter of children.—PETER BAYNE, "The Modern Novel: Dickens—Bulwer—Thackeray," *Essays in Biography and Criticism: First Series*, 1857, pp. 384–86

The true objection to Dickens is, that his idealism tends too much to extravagance and caricature. It would be possible for an ill-natured critic to go through all his works, and to draw out in one long column a list of their chief characters, annexing in a parallel column the phrases or labels by which these characters are distinguished, and of which they are generalizations—the "There's some credit in being jolly here" of Mark Tapley; the "It isn't of the slightest consequence" of Toots; the "Something will turn up" of Mr. Micawber, &c., &c. Even this, however, is a mode of art legitimate, I believe, in principle, as it is certainly most effective in fact. There never was a Mr. Micawber in nature, exactly as he appears in the pages of Dickens; but Micawberism pervades nature through and through; and to have extracted this quality from nature, embodying the full essence of a thousand instances of it in one ideal monstrosity, is a feat of invention. From the incessant repetition by Mr. Dickens of this inventive process openly and without variation, except in the results, the public have caught what is called his mannerism or trick; and hence a certain recoil from his later writings among the cultivated and fastidious. But let any one observe our current table-talk or our current literature, and, despite this profession of dissatisfaction, and in the very circles where it most abounds, let him note how gladly Dickens is used, and how frequently his phrases, his fancies, and the names of his characters come in, as illustration, embellishment, proverb, and seasoning. Take any periodical in which there is a severe criticism of Dickens's last publication; and, ten to one, in the same periodical, and perhaps by the same hand, there will be a leading article, setting out with a quotation from Dickens that flashes on the mind of the reader the thought which the whole article is meant to convey, or containing some allusion to one of Dickens's characters which enriches the text in the middle and floods it an inch round with colour and humour.—DAVID MASSON, *British Novelists and Their Styles*, 1859, pp. 251–52

> You ask me what I see in Dickens . . .
> A game-cock among bantam chickens.
> —WALTER SAVAGE LANDOR, "Dickens," 1863

If Mr. Dickens's characters were gathered together, they would constitute a town populous enough to send a representative to Parliament. Let us enter. The style of architecture is unparalleled. There is an individuality about the buildings. In some obscure way they remind one of human faces. There are houses sly-looking, houses wicked-looking, houses pompous-looking. Heaven bless us! what a rakish pump! what a self-important town-hall! what a hard-hearted prison! The dead walls are covered with advertisements of Mr. Sleary's circus. Newman Noggs comes shambling along. Mr. and the Misses Pecksniff come sailing down the sunny side of the street. Miss Mercy's parasol is gay; papa's neckcloth is white, and terribly starched. Dick Swiveller leans against a wall, his hands in his pockets, a primrose held between his teeth, contemplating the opera of Punch and Judy, which is being conducted under the management of Messrs. Codlings and Short. You turn a corner and you meet the coffin of little Paul Dombey borne along. Who would have thought of encountering a funeral in this place? In the afternoon you hear the rich tones of the organ from Miss La Creevy's first floor, for Tom Pinch has gone to live there now; and as you know all the people as you know your own brothers and sisters, and consequently require no letters of introduction, you go up and talk with the dear old fellow about all his friends and your friends, and towards evening he takes your arm, and you walk out to see poor Nelly's grave—a place which he visits often, and which he dresses with flowers with his own hands.—ALEXANDER SMITH, "On Vagabonds," *Dreamthorp*, 1863, pp. 287–88

To give so much pleasure, to add so much to the happiness of the world, by his writings, as Mr. Dickens has succeeded in doing, is a felicity that has never been attained in such full measure by any other author. For the space of a generation he has done his beneficent work, and there are few English-speaking men or women who do not feel themselves under peculiar obligation to the great novelist, and bound to him, not by any mere cold literary tie, but by the warm and vital cords of personal sympathy. The critic gladly lays down his pen in presence of a genius which has won for itself such a recognition, and willingly adopts the words of Ben Jonson in addressing one of his great contemporaries:—

> I yield, I yield. The matter of your praise
> Flows in upon me, and I cannot raise
> A bank against it: nothing but the round,
> Large clasp of Nature such a wit can bound.

If we reflect what contemporary literature would be without Dickens's works,—how much enjoyment would be taken out of our lives,—how much knowledge of human nature and feeling for it, how much genial humor, how much quickening of sympathy, how much heartiness, would be lost, had this long series of books never appeared, we can better appreciate what we owe to their writer. ⟨. . .⟩

No one thinks first of Mr. Dickens as a writer. He is at once, through his books, a friend. He belongs among the intimates of every pleasant-tempered and large-hearted person. He is not so much the guest as the inmate of our homes. He keeps holidays with us, he helps us to celebrate Christmas with heartier cheer, he shares at every New Year in our good wishes: for, indeed, it is not in his purely literary character that he has done most for us, it is as a man of the largest humanity, who has simply used literature as the means by which to bring himself into relation with his fellow-men, and to inspire them with something of his own sweetness, kindness, charity, and good-will.

He is the great magician of our time. His wand is a book, but his power is in his own heart. It is a rare piece of good fortune for us that we are the contemporaries of this benevolent genius, and that he comes among us in bodily presence, bringing in his company such old and valued friends as Mr. Pickwick, and Sam Weller, and Nicholas Nickleby, and David Copperfield, and Boots at the Swan, and Dr. Marigold.—CHARLES ELIOT NORTON, "Charles Dickens," *North American Review*, April 1868, pp. 671–72

But Mr. Dickens's peculiar gift, and his best gift, was not the accumulation and delineation of such items as paint a past period—costume, antiquarian lexicography, archæology generally. These are transitory, and are already dead. There have been great masters in the art of grouping and painting them, no doubt. But the art of this master was in painting the qualities of humanity, not of its costume—the feelings, sentiments, and passions that are everlasting as man. It might therefore have been expected that this part of the work would usurp upon the other in the composition of historical fiction; and so it was accordingly.—F. B. PERKINS, *Charles Dickens: A Sketch of His Life and Works*, 1870, p. 63

I have been sunning myself in Dickens—even in his later and very inferior *Mutual Friend*, and *Great Expectations*—Very inferior to his best: but with things better than any one else's best, caricature as they may be. I really must go and worship at Gadshill, as I have worshipped at Abbotsford, though with less Reverence, to be sure. But I must look on Dickens as a mighty Benefactor to Mankind.—EDWARD FITZGERALD, Letter to Fanny Kemble (Aug. 24, 1874)

Of Mr. Dickens I have seen but little in face-to-face intercourse; but I am glad to have enjoyed that little. There may be, and I believe there are, many who go beyond me in admiration of his works,—high and strong as is my delight in some of them. Many can more keenly enjoy his peculiar humour,—delightful as it is to me; and few seem to miss as I do the pure plain daylight in the atmosphere of his scenery. So many fine painters have been mannerists as to atmosphere and colour that it may be unreasonable to object to one more: but the very excellence and diversity of Mr. Dickens's powers makes one long that they should exercise their full force under the broad open sky of nature, instead of in the most brilliant palace of art. While he tells us a world of things that are natural and even true, his personages are generally, as I suppose is undeniable, profoundly unreal. It is a curious speculation what effect his universally read works will have on the foreign conception of English character. Washington Irving came here expecting to find the English life of Queen Anne's days, as his *Sketch-Book* shows: and very unlike his preconception was the England he found. And thus it must be with Germans, Americans and French who take Mr. Dickens's books to be pictures of our real life.—Another vexation is his vigorous erroneousness about matters of science, as shown in *Oliver Twist* about the new poor-law (which he confounds with the abrogated old one) and in *Hard Times*, about the controversies of employers. Nobody wants to make Mr. Dickens a Political Economist; but there are many who wish that he would abstain from a set of difficult subjects, on which all true sentiment must be underlain by a sort of knowledge which he has not. The more fervent and inexhaustible his kindliness, (and it is fervent and inexhaustible,) the more important it is that it should be well-informed and well-directed, that no errors of his may mislead his readers on the one hand, nor lessen his own genial influence on the other.

The finest thing in Mr. Dickens's case is that he, from time to time, proves himself capable of progress,—however vast his preceding achievements had been. In humour, he will hardly surpass *Pickwick*, simply because *Pickwick* is scarcely surpassable in humour: but in several crises, as it were, of his fame, when every body was disappointed, and his faults seemed running his graces down, there has appeared something so prodigiously fine as to make us all joyfully exclaim that Dickens can never permanently fail. It was so with *Copperfield*: and I hope it may be so again with the new work which my survivors will soon have in their hands.—Meantime, every indication seems to show that the man himself is rising. He is a virtuous and happy family man, in the first place. His glowing and generous heart is kept steady by the best domestic influences: and we may fairly hope now that he will fulfil the natural purpose of his life, and stand by literature to the last; and again, that he will be an honour to the high vocation by prudence as well as by power: so that the graces of genius and generosity may rest on the finest basis of probity and prudence; and that his old age may be honoured as heartily as his youth and manhood have been admired.—Nothing could exceed the frank kindness and consideration shown by him in the correspondence and personal intercourse we have had; and my cordial regard has grown with my knowledge of him. —HARRIET MARTINEAU, *Autobiography*, ed. Maria Weston Chapman, 1877, Vol. 2, pp. 61–63

Dickens had little or no knowledge of human character, and evidently cared very little about the study. His stories are fairy tales made credible by the masterly realism with which he described all the surroundings and accessories, the costumes and the ways of his men and women. While we are reading of a man whose odd peculiarities strike us with a sense of reality as if we had observed them for ourselves many a time, while we see him surrounded by streets and houses which seem to us rather more real and a hundred times more interesting than those through which we pass every day, we are not likely to observe very quickly, or to take much heed of the fact when we do observe it, that the man acts on various important occasions of his life as only people in fairy stories ever do act.—JUSTIN MCCARTHY, *A History of Our Own Times*, 1879–80, Ch. 29

Chief in thy generation born of men
   Whom English praise acclaimed as English-born,
   With eyes that matched the worldwide eyes of morn
For gleam of tears or laughter, tenderest then
When thoughts of children warmed their light, or when
   Reverence of age with love and labour worn,
   Or godlike pity fired with godlike scorn,
Shot through them flame that winged thy swift live pen:
Where stars and suns that we behold not burn,
   Higher even than here, though highest was here thy place,
   Love sees thy spirit laugh and speak and shine
With Shakespeare and the soft bright soul of Sterne
   And Fielding's kindliest might and Goldsmith's grace;
   Scarce one more loved or worthier love than thine.
      —ALGERNON CHARLES SWINBURNE, "Dickens," 1882

Dickens was not—and to whom in these latter ages of literature could such a term be applied?—a self-made writer, in the sense that he owed nothing to those who had gone before him. He was most assuredly no classical scholar,—how could he have been? But I should hesitate to call him an ill-read man, though he certainly was neither a great nor a catholic reader, and though he could not help thinking about *Nicholas Nickleby* while he was reading the *Curse of Kehama*. In his own branch of literature his judgment was sound and sure-footed. It was of course a happy accident, that as a boy he imbibed that taste for good fiction which is a thing inconceivable to the illiterate. Sneers have been directed against the poverty of his bookshelves in his earlier days of authorship; but I fancy there were not many popular novelists in 1839 who would have taken down with them into the country for a summer sojourn, as Dickens did to Petersham, not only a couple of Scott's novels, but Goldsmith, Swift, Fielding, Smollett, and the British Essayists; nor is there one of these national classics—unless it be Swift—with whom Dickens' books or letters fail to show him to have been familiar. Of Goldsmith's books, he told Forster, in a letter which the biographer of Goldsmith modestly suppressed, he "had no indifferent perception—to the best of his remembrance—when little more than a child." He discusses with understanding the relative literary merits of the serious and humorous papers in *The Spectator*; and, with regard to another work of unique significance in the history of English fiction, *Robinson Crusoe*, he acutely observed that "one of the most popular books on earth has nothing in it to make anyone laugh or cry." "It is a book," he added, which he "read very much." It may be noted, by the way, that he was an attentive and judicious student of Hogarth; and that thus his criticisms of humorous pictorial art rested upon as broad a basis of comparison as did his judgment of his great predecessors in English humorous fiction.

Among these predecessors it has become usual to assert that Smollett exercised the greatest influence upon Dickens. It is no doubt true that in David Copperfield's library Smollett's books are mentioned first, and in the greatest number, that a vision of Roderick Random and Strap haunted the very wicket-gate at Blunderstone, that the poor little hero's first thought on entering the King's Bench prison was the strange company whom Roderick met in the Marshalsea; and that the references to Smollett and his books are frequent in Dickens' other books and in his letters. Leghorn seemed to him "made illustrious" by Smollett's grave, and in a late period of his life he criticises his chief fictions with admirable justice. "Humphry Clinker," he writes, "is certainly Smollett's best. I am rather divided between *Peregrine Pickle* and *Roderick Random*, both extraordinarily good in their way, which is a way without tenderness; but you will have to read them both, and I send the first volume of *Peregrine* as the richer of the two." An odd volume of *Peregrine* was one of the books with which the waiter at the *Holly Tree Inn* endeavoured to beguile the lonely Christmas of the snowed-up traveller, but the latter "knew every word of it already." In the *Lazy Tour*, "Thomas, now just able to grope his way along, in a doubled-up condition, was no bad embodiment of Commodore Trunnion." I have noted, moreover, coincidences of detail which bear witness to Dickens' familiarity with Smollett's works. To Lieutenant Bowling and Commodore Trunnion, as to Captain Cuttle, every man was a "brother," and to the Commodore, as to Mr. Smallweed, the most abusive substantive addressed to a woman admitted of intensification by the epithet "brimstone." I think Dickens had not forgotten the opening of the *Adventures of an Atom* when he wrote a passage in the opening of his own *Christmas Carol*; and that the characters of Tom Pinch and Tommy Traddles—the former more especially—were not conceived without some thought of honest Strap. Furthermore, it was Smollett's example that probably suggested to Dickens the attractive jingle in the title of his *Nicholas Nickleby*. But these are for the most part mere details. The manner of Dickens as a whole resembles Fielding's more strikingly than Smollett's, as it was only natural that it should. The irony of Smollett is drier than was reconcileable with Dickens' nature; it is only in the occasional extravagances of his humour that the former anticipates anything in the latter, and it is only the coarsest scenes of Dickens earlier books—such as that between Noah, Charlotte, and Mrs. Sowerberry in *Oliver Twist*—which recall the whole manner of his predecessor. They resemble one another in their descriptive accuracy, and in the accumulation of detail by which they produce instead of obscuring vividness of impression; but it was impossible that Dickens should prefer the general method of the novel of adventure pure and simple, such as Smollett produced after the example of *Gil Blas*, to the less crude form adopted by Fielding, who adhered to earlier and nobler models. With

Fielding's, moreover, Dickens' whole nature was congenial; they both had that tenderness which Smollett lacked; and the circumstance that of all English writers of the past, Fielding's name alone was given by Dickens to one of his sons, shows how, like so many of Fielding's readers, he had learnt to love him with an almost personal affection. The very spirit of the author of *Tom Jones*—that gaiety which, to borrow the saying of a recent historian concerning Cervantes, renders even brutality agreeable, and that charm of sympathetic feeling which makes us love those of his characters which he loves himself—seem astir in some of the most delightful passages of Dickens' most delightful books.—ADOLPHUS WILLIAM WARD, *Dickens*, 1882, pp. 197–200

There can be no doubt that the most popular novelist of my time—probably the most popular English novelist of any time—has been Charles Dickens. He has now been dead nearly six years, and the sale of his books goes on as it did during his life. The certainty with which his novels are found in every house—the familiarity of his name in all English-speaking countries—the popularity of such characters as Mrs. Gamp, Micawber, and Pecksniff, and many others whose names have entered into the English language and become well-known words—the grief of the country at his death, and the honours paid to him at his funeral,—all testify to his popularity. Since the last book he wrote himself, I doubt whether any book has been so popular as his biography by John Forster. There is no withstanding such testimony as this. Such evidence of popular appreciation should go for very much, almost for everything, in criticism on the work of a novelist. The primary object of a novelist is to please; and this man's novels have been found more pleasant than those of any other writer. It might of course be objected to this, that though the books have pleased they have been injurious, that their tendency has been immoral and their teaching vicious; but it is almost needless to say that no such charge has ever been made against Dickens. His teaching has ever been good. From all which, there arises to the critic a question whether, with such evidence against him as to the excellence of this writer, he should not subordinate his own opinion to the collected opinion of the world of readers. To me it almost seems that I must be wrong to place Dickens after Thackeray and George Eliot, knowing as I do that so great a majority put him above those authors.

My own peculiar idiosyncrasy in the matter forbids me to do so: I do acknowledge that Mrs. Gamp, Micawber, Pecksniff, and others have become household words in every house, as though they were human beings; but to my judgment they are not human beings, nor are any of the characters human which Dickens has portrayed. It has been the peculiarity and the marvel of this man's power, that he has invested his puppets with a charm that has enabled him to dispense with human nature. There is a drollery about them, in my estimation, very much below the humour of Thackeray, but which has reached the intellect of all; while Thackeray's humour has escaped the intellect of many. Nor is the pathos of Dickens human. It is stagey and melodramatic. But it is so expressed that it touches every heart a little. There is no real life in Smike. His misery, his idiotcy, his devotion for Nicholas, his love for Kate, are all overdone and incompatible with each other. But still the reader sheds a tear. Every reader can find a tear for Smike. Dickens's novels are like Boucicault's plays. He has known how to draw his lines broadly, so that all should see the colour.

He, too, in his best days, always lived with his characters;—and he, too, as he gradually ceased to have the power of doing so, ceased to charm. Though they are not human beings, we all remember Mrs. Gamp and Pickwick. The Boffins and Veneerings do not, I think, dwell in the minds of so many.

Of Dickens's style it is impossible to speak in praise. It is jerky, ungrammatical, and created by himself in defiance of rules—almost as completely as that created by Carlyle. To readers who have taught themselves to regard language, it must therefore be unpleasant. But the critic is driven to feel the weakness of his criticism, when he acknowledges to himself—as he is compelled in all honesty to do—that with the language, such as it is, the writer has satisfied the great mass of the readers of his country. Both these great writers have satisfied the readers of their own pages; but both have done infinite harm by creating a school of imitators. No young novelist should ever dare to imitate the style of Dickens. If such a one wants a model for his language, let him take Thackeray.—ANTHONY TROLLOPE, *An Autobiography*, 1883, Ch. 13

Dickens must not only have had exceptional powers of observation and imagination, but *extra*-ordinary intensity of sympathy with *ordinary* feelings and beliefs. His genius in characterization tends to the grotesque and extravagant; his personages, in their names as in their qualities, produce on us the effect of strangeness; the plots of the novels in which they appear would with any other characters seem grossly improbable, and yet his mind is unmistakably rooted in common sense and common humanity. He thus succeeds in giving his readers all the pleasure which comes from contemplating what is strange, odd, and eccentric, without disquieting them by any paradoxes in morals or shocking them by any perversions of homely natural sentiment. The *Christmas Carol*, for example, is as wild in grotesque fancy as a dream of Hoffmann, yet in feeling as solid and sweet and humane as a sermon of Channing. It impresses us somewhat as we are impressed by the sight of the Bible as illustrated by Gustave Doré. Thus held fast to common, homely truths and feelings by his sentiments, he can safely give reins to his imagination in his creations. The keenest of observers, both of things and persons, all that he observes is still taken up and transformed by his imagination—becomes *Dickensized*, in fact—so that, whether he describes a landscape, or a boot-jack, or a building, or a man, we see the object, not as it is in itself, but as it is deliciously bewitched by his method of looking at it. Everything is suggested by his outward experience, but modified by his inward experience. The result is that we do not have in him an exact transcript of life, but an individualized ideal of life from his point of view. He has, in short, discovered and colonized one of the waste districts of Imagination, which we may call Dickens-land or Dickens-ville; from his own brain he has peopled it with some fourteen hundred persons, and it agrees with the settlements made there by Shakespeare and Scott in being better known than such geographical countries as Canada and Australia, and it agrees with them equally in confirming us in the belief of the *reality* of a population which has no *actual* existence. It is distinguished from all other colonies in Brainland by the ineffaceable peculiarities of its colonizer; its inhabitants don't die like other people, but, alas! they also now can't increase; but whithersoever any of them may wander they are recognized at once, by an unmistakable birthmark, as belonging to the race of Dickens. A man who has done this is not merely one of a thousand, but one of a thousand millions; for he has created an ideal population which is more interesting to human beings than the great body of their own actual friends and neigh-

bors.—EDWIN P. WHIPPLE, "In Dickens-Land," *Scribner's Magazine*, Dec. 1887, pp. 744–45

Here was a man and an artist, the most strenuous, one of the most endowed; and for how many years he laboured in vain to create a gentleman! With all his watchfulness of men and manners, with all his fiery industry, with his exquisite native gift of characterisation, with his clear knowledge of what he meant to do, there was yet something lacking. In part after part, novel after novel, a whole menagerie of characters, the good, the bad, the droll, and the tragic, came at his beck like slaves about an Oriental despot; there was only one who stayed away: the gentleman. If this ill fortune had persisted it might have shaken man's belief in art and industry. But years were given and courage was continued to the indefatigable artist; and at length, after so many and such lamentable failures, success began to attend upon his arms. David Copperfield scrambled through on hands and knees; it was at least a negative success; and Dickens, keenly alive to all he did, must have heaved a sigh of infinite relief. Then came the evil days, the days of *Dombey* and *Dorrit*, from which the lover of Dickens willingly averts his eyes; and when that temporary blight had passed away, and the artist began with a more resolute arm to reap the aftermath of his genius, we find him able to create a Carton, a Wrayburn, a Twemlow. No mistake about these three; they are all gentlemen: the sottish Carton, the effete Twemlow, the insolent Wrayburn, all have doubled the cape.

There were never in any book three perfect sentences on end; there was never a character in any volume but it somewhere tripped. We are like dancing dogs and preaching women: the wonder is not that we should do it well, but that we should do it at all. And Wrayburn, I am free to admit, comes on one occasion to the dust. I mean, of course, the scene with the old Jew. I will make you a present of the Jew for a card-board figure; but that is neither here nor there: the ineffectuality of the one presentment does not mitigate the grossness, the baseness, the inhumanity of the other. In this scene, and in one other (if I remember aright) where it is echoed, Wrayburn combines the wit of the omnibus-cad with the good feeling of the Andaman Islander: in all the remainder of the book, throughout a thousand perils, playing (you would say) with difficulty, the author swimmingly steers his hero on the true course. The error stands by itself, and it is striking to observe the moment of its introduction. It follows immediately upon one of the most dramatic passages in fiction, that in which Bradley Headstone barks his knuckles on the churchyard wall. To handle Bradley (one of Dickens's superlative achievements) were a thing impossible to almost any man but his creator; and even to him, we may be sure, the effort was exhausting. Dickens was a weary man when he had barked the schoolmaster's knuckles, a weary man and an excited; but the tale of bricks had to be finished, the monthly number waited; and under the false inspiration of irritated nerves, the scene of Wrayburn and the Jew was written and sent forth; and there it is, a blot upon the book and a buffet to the reader.

I make no more account of his passage than of that other in *Hamlet*: a scene that has broken down, the judicious reader cancels for himself. And the general tenor of Wrayburn, and the whole of Carton and Twemlow, are beyond exception. Here, then, we have a man who found it for years an enterprise beyond his art to draw a gentleman, and who in the end succeeded. Is it because Dickens was not a gentleman himself that he so often failed? and if so, then how did he succeed at last? Is it because he was a gentleman that he succeeded? and if so, what made him fail? I feel inclined to stop this paper here, after the manner of conundrums, and offer a moderate reward for a solution. But the true answer lies probably deeper than did ever plummet sound. And mine (such as it is) will hardly appear to the reader to disturb the surface.

These verbal puppets (so to call them once again) are things of a divided parentage: the breath of life may be an emanation from their maker, but they themselves are only strings of words and parts of books; they dwell in, they belong to, literature; convention, technical artifice, technical gusto, the mechanical necessities of the art, these are the flesh and blood with which they are invested. If we look only at Carton and Wrayburn, both leading parts, it must strike us at once that both are most ambitiously attempted; that Dickens was not content to draw a hero and a gentleman plainly and quietly; that after all his ill-success, he must still handicap himself upon these fresh adventures, and make Carton a sot, and sometimes a cantankerous sot, and Wrayburn insolent to the verge, and sometimes beyond the verge, of what is pardonable. A moment's thought will show us this was in the nature of his genius, and a part of his literary method. His fierce intensity of design was not to be slaked with any academic portraiture; not all the arts of individualisation could perfectly content him; he must still seek something more definite and more express than nature. All artists, it may be properly argued, do the like; it is their method to discard the middling and the insignificant, to disengage the charactered and the precise. But it is only a class of artists that pursue so singly the note of personality; and is it not possible that such a preoccupation may disable men from representing gentlefolk? The gentleman passes in the stream of the day's manners, inconspicuous. The lover of the individual may find him scarce worth drawing. And even if he draw him, on what will his attention centre but just upon those points in which his model exceeds or falls short of his subdued ideal— but just upon those points in which the gentleman is not genteel? Dickens, in an hour of irritated nerves, and under the pressure of the monthly number, defaced his Wrayburn. Observe what he sacrifices. The ruling passion strong in his hour of weakness, he sacrifices dignity, decency, the essential human beauties of his hero; he still preserves the dialect, the shrill note of personality, the mark of identification. Thackeray, under the strain of the same villainous system, would have fallen upon the other side; his gentleman would still have been a gentleman, he would have only ceased to be an individual figure.

There are incompatible ambitions. You cannot paint a Vandyke and keep it a Franz Hals.—ROBERT LOUIS STEVENSON, "Some Gentlemen in Fiction," 1888

Dickens's imagination was diligent from the outset; with him conception was not less deliberate and careful than development; and so much he confesses when he describes himself as 'in the first stage of a new book, which consists in going round and round the idea, as you see a bird in his cage go about and about his sugar before he touches it.' 'I have no means,' he writes to a person wanting advice, 'of knowing whether you are patient in the pursuit of this art; but I am inclined to think that you are not, and that you do not discipline yourself enough. When one is impelled to write this or that, one has still to consider: "How much of this will tell for what I mean? How much of it is my own wild emotion and superfluous energy— how much remains that is truly belonging to this ideal character and these ideal circumstances?" It is in the laborious struggle to make this distinction, and in the determination to try for it, that the road to the correction of faults lies. [Perhaps I may remark, in support of the sincerity with which I write

this, that I am an impatient and impulsive person myself, but that it has been for many years the constant effort of my life to practise at my desk what I preach to you.]' Such golden words could only have come from one enamoured of his art, and holding the utmost endeavour in its behalf of which his heart and mind were capable for a matter of simple duty. They are a proof that Dickens—in intention at least, and if in intention then surely, the fact of his genius being admitted, to some extent in fact as well—was an artist in the best sense of the term.

In the beginning he often wrote exceeding ill, especially when he was doing his best to write seriously. He developed into an artist in words as he developed into an artist in the construction and the evolution of a story. But his development was his own work, and it is a fact that should redound eternally to his honour that he began in newspaper English, and by the production of an imitation of the *novela picaresca*—a string of adventures as broken and disconnected as the adventures of Lazarillo de Tormes or Peregrine Pickle, and went on to become an exemplar. A man self-made and self-taught, if he knew anything at all about the 'art for art' theory—which is doubtful—he may well have held it cheap enough. But he practised Millet's dogma—*Dans l'art il faut sa peau*—as resolutely as Millet himself, and that, too, under conditions that might have proved utterly demoralising had he been less robust and less sincere. He began as a serious novelist with Ralph Nickleby and Lord Frederick Verisopht; he went on to produce such masterpieces as Jonas Chuzzlewit and Doubledick, and Eugene Wrayburn and the immortal Mrs. Gamp, and Fagin and Sikes and Sydney Carton, and many another. The advance is one from positive weakness to positive strength, from ignorance to knowledge, from incapacity to mastery, from the manufacture of lay figures to the creation of human beings.

His faults were many and grave. He wrote some nonsense; he sinned repeatedly against taste; he could be both noisy and vulgar; he was apt to be a caricaturist where he should have been a painter; he was often mawkish and often extravagant; and he was sometimes more inept than a great writer has ever been. But his work, whether bad or good, has in full measure the quality of sincerity. He meant what he did; and he meant it with his whole heart. He looked upon himself as representative and national—as indeed he was; he regarded his work as a universal possession; and he determined to do nothing that for lack of pains should prove unworthy of his function. If he sinned it was unadvisedly and unconsciously; if he failed it was because he knew no better. You feel that as you read. The freshness and fun of *Pickwick*—a comic middle-class epic, so to speak—seem mainly due to high spirits; and perhaps that immortal book should be described as a first improvisation by a young man of genius not yet sure of either expression or ambition and with only vague and momentary ideas about the duties and necessities of art. But from *Pickwick* onwards to *Edwin Drood* the effort after improvement is manifest. What are *Dombey* and *Dorrit* themselves but the failures of a great and serious artist? In truth the man's genius did but ripen with years and labour; he spent his life in developing from a popular writer into an artist. He extemporised *Pickwick*, it may be, but into *Copperfield* and *Chuzzlewit* and the *Tale of Two Cities* and *Our Mutual Friend* he put his whole might, working at them with a passion of determination not exceeded by Balzac himself. He had enchanted the public without an effort; he was the best-beloved of modern writers almost from the outset of his career. But he had in him at least as much of the French artist as of the middle-class Englishman; and if all his life he never ceased from self-education but went unswervingly in pursuit of culture, it was out of love for his art and because his conscience as an artist would not let him do otherwise. We have been told so often to train ourselves by studying the practice of workmen like Gautier and Hugo and imitating the virtues of work like *Hernani* and *Quatre-Vingt-Treize* and *L'Education sentimentale*—we have heard so much of the æsthetic impeccability of Young France and the section of Young England that affects its qualities and reproduces its fashions—that it is hard to refrain from asking if, when all is said, we should not do well to look for models nearer home? if in place of such moulds of form as *Mademoiselle de Maupin* we might not take to considering stuff like *Rizpah* and *Our Mutual Friend?*

Yes, he had many and grave faults. But so had Sir Walter and the good Dumas; so, to be candid, had Shakespeare himself—Shakespeare the king of poets. To myself he is always the man of his unrivalled and enchanting letters—is always an incarnation of generous and abounding gaiety, a type of beneficent earnestness, a great expression of intellectual vigour and emotional vivacity. I love to remember that I came into the world contemporaneously with some of his bravest work, and to reflect that even as he was the inspiration of my boyhood so is he a delight of my middle age. I love to think that while English literature endures he will be remembered as one that loved his fellow-men, and did more to make them happy and amiable than any other writer of his time.—W. E. HENLEY, "Dickens," *Views and Reviews*, 1890, pp. 3–9

The might of that great talent no one can gainsay, though in the light of the truer work which has since been done his literary principles seem almost as grotesque as his theories of political economy. In no one direction was his erring force more felt than in the creation of holiday literature as we have known it for the last half-century. Creation, of course, is the wrong word; it says too much; but in default of a better word, it may stand. He did not make something out of nothing; the material was there before him; the mood and even the need of his time contributed immensely to his success, as the volition of the subject helps on the mesmerist; but it is within bounds to say that he was the chief agency in the development of holiday literature as we have known it, as he was the chief agency in universalizing the great Christian holiday as we now have it. Other agencies wrought with him and after him; but it was he who rescued Christmas from Puritan distrust, and humanized it and consecrated it to the hearts and homes of all.—WILLIAM DEAN HOWELLS, *Criticism and Fiction*, 1891, pp. 174–75

He accepted the past; it was the present by which he was consciously fascinated; and the past had no meaning for him except as connected with it. An old building for him was not like a dead man, but like an old man—an old man making faces either grotesque or sinister. For him everything was alive with the life of his own day. Houses, crooked courts, four-post bedsteads, cabs, portmanteaus, chimney-pots, and all inanimate objects winked at him, laughed with him, and spoke to him in the vernacular of the streets, and were forever saying to him something fresh and pungent. He had all the familiarity with the life around him that could be produced by the most close acquaintance with it; and yet he was always watching it with the surprise and expectant freshness which, as a rule, belong only to those to whom it is still a novelty. And this vision of his he communicated to his readers. He made them see not what they had not seen before, but what they had not noticed before. He made them conscious of their own uncon-

scious observations. His genius acted on the surface of English life as spilt water acts on the surface of unpolished marble. It suddenly made visible all its colors and veinings; and in this way he may be said to have revealed England to itself: and he still does so.

It is true that this general statement must be made with one reservation. One part of English life was entirely beyond his grasp. He knew nothing of the highest class. He had no true knowledge even of the upper ranks of the middle class. His lords, his baronets, his majors, his ladies and gentlemen generally are not even like enough to reality to be called caricatures. But if we accept these classes and speak only of the bulk of the nation, no writer ever knew the English nation and represented the English nation so thoroughly and comprehensively as Dickens. His style is full of the faults of a man imperfectly educated. Errors of taste abound in it, and much of his sentiment is mawkish, or constrained, or false; and yet, in spite of this, not only do his writings embody the shrewdest, the truest, the widest, and the most various observations of the life around him, but they show him to be, in a certain sense, one of the greatest of English poets. In saying this I am making no allusion to any passages which sentimental admirers of him may consider poetical, or which he probably thought poetical himself. I am alluding to the manner in which, throughout his works, he not only presents what are commonly called the facts of life, but actually gives us that elusive atmosphere which in life surrounds these facts and imparts to them those changing aspects by which in life we know them; an atmosphere impregnated with wandering thoughts and sentiments and volatile associations—an element whch would seem to defy description. This Dickens has described. It penetrates his works and permeates them.

One example may be given, a single touch. He is describing some lawyer's office with dim, dusty windows, and among other details he notes this: that there was on the floor an enormous faded stain, "as if some by-gone clerk had cut his throat there and had bled ink." The whole past and present of the place is suggested in these few words, and what he felt and described in a lawyer's office he felt and described in nearly every scene he dealt with. He felt and he seized its human and, above all, its national meaning. He did this even in cases where it might be thought he would have failed to do so. I said he knew nothing of the highest upper classes; but in a certain way he understood their life as a factor in the life of the country, through certain of their surroundings. He knew the meaning and the sentiment of old English parks, of lodges, and gray gate-posts, damp and mottled with lichens. He knew the spirit which haunted the whispering avenue and hung above the twisted chimney-stacks and mullioned window of the hall; but his comprehension stopped at the front door. It was never at home inside. With this reservation, Dickens is England; and if he could not describe what the upper class see among themselves, he describes what they see whenever they go out of doors. To move out of the seclusion of polite life in England is to walk with Dickens. It is so still, as it was in his own days; and if any proof is needed in addition to those I have already mentioned, it may be found in the English language as spoken at this moment. Dickens' characters exist not in his books only. They have walked out of his books and taken their places among living people. Their looks and manners are social and not literary facts; their jokes and phrases are the common property of the nation. Of one other novelist only can this be said, and that novelist is Scott.—W. H. MALLOCK, "Are Scott, Dickens, and Thackeray Obsolete?," *Forum*, Dec. 1892, pp. 511–12

He is at his best in his earlier works, where he makes small pretence to art. In my opinion his masterpiece is *Pickwick*—"a comic middle-class epic" it has been called, perhaps not unhappily. It is irresistibly funny; inimitably fresh; incomparably fantastic; a farce, but a farce of a very high order. Dickens himself always thought slightingly of it. He was ambitious, laudably ambitious, to do greater things. And during the whole of his literary life he toiled earnestly, passionately, to attain a higher standard. I think he came nearest to that standard in *David Copperfield*. There is much—very much—there which we could wish away. In fact I, if I take the book up, give effect to my wish, and practically put aside a great deal of it. And no doubt many other readers do the same. But it is informed by a simple power, a sober veracity, a sustained interest, peculiarly its own among its author's works. Dickens's young men are, as a rule, impossible. They are well-nigh all of the same inane type. He seems to have got them out of an Adelphi melodrama. But David Copperfield, who is a transcript from his own troublous and distressed childhood and youth, is, at all events, human. His young women are as inane as his young men. His amatory scenes—good heavens let us not speak of them and their mawkish sentimentalities! What a theme for a poet had he in Steerforth and Little Em'ly! How George Sand would have treated it! How George Eliot has treated a similar theme in *Adam Bede!* But Dickens possessed no words to tell forth that idyll. And if he had possessed them he dared not to have uttered them. He stood in too much awe of Mr. Podsnap's "young person." The history of the love of Steerforth and Little Em'ly was impossible to him. He could not have narrated it if he would; and he would not if he could.

I think he never again wrote so felicitously as in *David Copperfield*. No doubt he did many fine things afterwards in the way of genre painting. We may regard him as a literary Teniers. But as years went on his manner seems to me to grow more unnatural, more stilted, more intolerable. The higher art which he tried to grasp, ever eluded him. There is an absence of composition in his work; there is no play of light and shade; there is no proportion, no perspective. His books cannot be said to be composed, they are improvised.—WILLIAM SAMUEL LILLY, "Dickens," *Four English Humourists of the Nineteenth Century*, 1895, pp. 14–15

Now, with the solitary exception of Sir Walter Scott, it is probable that no man ever inspired such a host of imitators as Charles Dickens. There is not a writer of fiction at this hour, in any land where fiction is a recognised trade or art, who is not, whether he knows it and owns it, or no, largely influenced by Dickens. His method has got into the atmosphere of fiction, as that of all really great writers must do, and we might as well swear to unmix our oxygen and hydrogen as to stand clear of his influences. To stand clear of those influences you must stand apart from all modern thought and sentiment. You must have read nothing that has been written in the last sixty years, and you must have been bred on a desert island. Dickens has a living part in the life of the whole wide world. He is on a hundred thousand magisterial benches every day. There is not a hospital patient in any country who has not at this minute a right to thank God that Dickens lived. What his blessed and bountiful hand has done for the poor and oppressed, and them that had no helper, no man knows. He made charity and good feeling a religion. Millions and millions of money have flowed from the coffers of the rich for the benefit of the poor because of his books. A great part of our daily life, and a good deal of the best of it, is of his making.

No single man ever made such opportunities for himself.

No single man was ever so widely and permanently useful. No single man ever sowed gentleness and mercy with so broad a sweep. ⟨. . .⟩

The chief fault the superficial modern critic has to find with Dickens is a sort of rumbustious boisterousness in the expression of emotion. But let one thing be pointed out, and let me point it out in my own fashion. Tom Hood, who was a true poet, and the best of our English wits, and probably as good a judge of good work as any person now alive, went home after meeting with Dickens, and in a playful enthusiasm told his wife to cut off his hand and bottle it, because it had shaken hands with Boz. Lord Jeffrey, who was cold as a critic, cried over little Nell. So did Sydney Smith, who was very far from being a blubbering sentimentalist. To judge rightly of any kind of dish you must bring an appetite to it. Here is the famous Dickens pie, when first served, pronounced inimitable, not by a class or a clique, but by all men in all lands. But you get it served hot, and you get it served cold, it is rehashed in every literary restaurant, you detect its flavour in your morning leader and your weekly review. The pie gravy finds its way into the prose and the verse of a whole young generation. It has a striking flavour, an individual flavour. It gets into everything. We are weary of the ceaseless resurrections of that once so toothsome dish. Take it away.

The original pie is no worse and no better, but thousands of cooks have had the recipe for it, and have tried to make it. Appetite may have vanished, but the pie was a good pie.

No simile runs on all fours, and this parable in a pie-dish is a poor traveller.

But this principle of judgment applies of necessity to all great work in art. It does not apply to merely good work, for that is nearly always imitative, and therefore not much provocative of imitation. It happens sometimes that an imitator, to the undiscerning reader, may even seem better than the man he mimics, because he has a modern touch. But remember, in his time the master also was a modern.

The new man says of Dickens that his sentiment rings false. This is a mistake. It rings old-fashioned. No false note ever moved a world, and the world combined to love his very name. There were tears in thousands of households when he died, and they were as sincere and as real as if they had arisen at the loss of a personal friend.

We, who in spite of fashion remain true to our allegiance to the magician of our youth, who can never worship or love another as we loved and worshipped him, are quite contented in the slight inevitable dimming of his fame.—DAVID CHRISTIE MURRAY, *My Contemporaries in Fiction*, 1897, pp. 9–14

Dickens has been called the favourite novelist of the middle classes. If the statement be true, it is creditable to their good taste and freedom from prejudice. He certainly did not flatter them. He disliked Dissenters quite as much as Matthew Arnold, whereas Thackeray gave them the Clapham Sect, to which they are not entitled. But the popularity of Dickens in his lifetime was in fact universal. Everybody read his books, because nobody could help reading them. They required no education except a knowledge of the alphabet, and they amused scholars as much as crossing-sweepers. No man ever made a more thorough conquest of his generation. Indeed he was only too successful. Imitation may be the sincerest form of flattery. It is the most dangerous form of admiration. And if ever there was an *exemplar vitiis imitabile*, it was Dickens. His influence upon literature, apart from his contributions to it, has been disastrous. The school of Dickens, for which he cannot be held responsible, is happily at last dying out. Their dreary mechanical jokes, their hideous unmeaning caricatures, their descriptions that describe nothing, their spasms of false sentiment, their tears of gin and water, have ceased to excite even amusement, and provoke only unmitigated disgust. With their disappearance from the stage, and consignment to oblivion, the reputation of the great man they injured is relieved from a temporary strain. The position of Dickens himself is unassailed and unassailable. In this or that generation he may be less read or more. He must always remain an acknowledged master of fiction and a prince of English humorists.—HERBERT PAUL, "The Apotheosis of the Novel," *Nineteenth Century*, May 1897, p. 773

The question, "Will Dickens last?" has been asked a hundred times in print since Dickens died; and many times, and in various ways, has the question been answered. All men admit that Sir Charles Grandison has become a bore, where he is known at all; that G. P. R. James's solitary horseman has ridden on, entirely out of the sight of the present-day reader; that Cooper's Indians and backwoodsmen no longer scalp the imagination of the boy of the period; that Marryat's midshipmen have been left alone and neglected at the mastheads to which he was so fond of sending them; that no one but the antiquary in literature cares now for Waverley or Rob Roy. But it is too soon yet to say how long it will be before Bleak House will become an uninhabitable ruin, or when the firm of Dombey and Son will go out of business altogether. Don Quixote is as vigorous as he was three centuries ago. Robinson Crusoe, born in 1719, still retains all the freshness of youth; who can prophesy how Mr. Samuel Pickwick, the Don Quixote of 1839, will be regarded in 1998? or how Mr. Samuel Weller, his man Friday, will be looked upon by the readers of a hundred years from to-day?

Dickens certainly wrote for his own time, and generally *of* his own time. And during his own time he achieved a popularity without parallel in the history of fiction. But the fashions of all times change; and although Dickens has been in fashion longer than most of his contemporaries, and is still the fashion among old-fashioned folk, there are acute critics who say that his day is over. The booksellers and the officials of circulating libraries tell a different story, however; and when little children, who never heard the name of Dickens, who knew nothing of his great reputation, turn from *Alice in Wonderland* and *Little Lord Fauntleroy* to the *Cricket on the Hearth*, loving the old as much as they love the new, it would seem as if the sun had not yet set upon Dickens; and that the night which is to leave him in total darkness is still far off. —LAURENCE HUTTON, "Charles Dickens," *Outlook*, Oct. 1898, p. 321

Dickens was from the very first a check to mediævalism. After he began writing, knights and ladies and tournaments became rarer. He awakened the interest of the public in the social condition of England after the Napoleonic wars. The Scott novel had come swollen with prefaces, notes, and appendixes, to show that it was true to the spirit of history; the Dickens novel came considerably enlarged with personal experiences, anecdotes, stories from friends, and statistics, to show that it was founded upon facts. Instead of the pageant of the Middle Age, we now have, in the novels of those who have learned their art from Dickens, strikes and riots, factories and granaries and barns in blaze, employee shooting employer, underground tenements, sewing-garrets, sweating-establishments, workhouses, truck-stores, the ravages of typhus, enthusiastic descriptions of model factories, model prisons, model cottages, discussions of the new poor law, of trade unions, of Chartism,

and of the relations of the rich and the poor. The new characters are operatives in factories, agricultural laborers, miners, tailors, seamstresses, and paupers. Patience, longsuffering, gentleness, in stalwart or angelic form, is oppressed by viragoes, tall and bearded and of flashing eyes, or by gentlemen of bloated red faces. Dickens never advocated in his novels any specific means of reform.—WILBUR L. CROSS, *The Development of the English Novel*, 1899, pp. 192–93

Is there any other maker of story in modern English literature—after all allowances have been made, and not forgetting that some current criticism of the man of Gadshill will have it that he is for a more careless age—who has begun to furnish such a portrait-gallery of worthies and adorable grotesques—a motley crowd whom we all know and enjoy and love? I wot not. The fact that Dickens is at times a trifle inchoate or careless in his English, or allows his exuberance to lead him into exaggeration, or fails to blend perfectly the discordant elements of comedy and tragedy, sinks into insignificance when set over against such a faculty as this.—RICHARD BURTON, "The Fundamentals of Fiction," *Forces in Fiction and Other Essays*, 1902, p. 7

Works

PICKWICK PAPERS

The popularity of this writer is one of the most remarkable literary phenomena of recent times, for it has been fairly earned without resorting to any of the means by which most other writers have succeeded in attracting the attention of their contemporaries. He has flattered no popular prejudice and profited by no passing folly: he has attempted no caricature sketches of the manners or conversation of the aristocracy; and there are very few political or personal allusions in his works. Moreover, his class of subjects are such as to expose him at the outset to the fatal objection of vulgarity; and, with the exception of occasional extracts in the newspapers, he received little or no assistance from the press. Yet, in less than six months from the appearance of the first number of the *Pickwick Papers*, the whole reading public were talking about them—the names of Winkle, Wardell, Weller, Snodgrass, Dodson and Fogg, had become familiar in our mouths as household terms; and Mr. Dickens was the grand object of interest to the whole tribe of 'Leo-hunters,' male and female, of the metropolis. Nay, Pickwick chintzes figured in linendrapers' windows, and Weller corduroys in breeches-makers' advertisements; Boz cabs might be seen rattling through the streets, and the portrait of the author of *Pelham* or *Crichton* was scraped down or pasted over to make room for that of the new popular favourite in the omnibusses. This is only to be accounted for on the supposition that a fresh vein of humour had been opened; that a new and decidedly original genius had sprung up.—JOHN WILSON CROKER, "The Pickwick Papers," *Quarterly Review*, Dec. 1837, p. 484

It has been said that *The Pickwick Papers* was its author's best book; and, in certain respects, this judgment is sound. Humor was Mr. Dickens's great distinctive trait; and for humor, pure and simple, he produced in all his life nothing quite equal to *Pickwick*—nothing so sustained, so varied, so unstrained. He afterwards became more conscious of his humor as he wrote, and showed his consciousness. He let us see the preparation of his fun; he made points like an actor who feels that the points are expected by his audience, and also feels, and shows that he feels, that by the use of certain means he can make them. The spontaneous humor of *Pickwick* was never equalled, even by its author. He afterwards gave to too many of his humorous characters certain peculiarities of person, manner, or speech, on which he rung a limited range of changes; and this degenerated into a trick, like the giving of what in stage cant is called a gag to a comic actor, which he uses deliberately to force a laugh. This was a needless device in Mr. Dickens, whose humor seemed exhaustless.—RICHARD GRANT WHITE, "The Styles of Dickens and Disraeli," *Galaxy*, Aug. 1870, p. 258

I well remember my sensations of astonishment and interest when the first number of *Pickwick* was brought me, and I looked it over. Forster was with me at the time. How, on the introduction of Sam Weller, the work took the town by storm, and its author, who, only a short time before, had been an unnoticed parliamentary reporter, reached at a bound the summit of success, and became the literary lion of the day, I need not here describe.

No man since Walter Scott has so amply and efficiently supplied in fiction the intellectual need of the age; but that great man did not do a tithe of what Dickens has done to quicken its social and moral progress.—S. C. HALL, *Retrospect of a Long Life*, 1883, p. 394

The first numbers of the book—which was issued in twenty monthly parts—at once took the public fancy, laying the foundation of a popularity which has never decreased. There is perhaps no book more widely known in the English language, nor, strangely enough, many which have been received with such favour on the Continent, though it is intensely national in character. It is, indeed, an almost perfect specimen of the strictly English quality of fun—using English in its very narrowest sense as applying only to that part of her Majesty's dominions called England—which differs as greatly from the humour of Scotland and Ireland as from French wit or American extravagance. We could quote instances of more genuinely humorous scenes than that of the trial in *Pickwick*, but we cannot think of anything so irresistibly funny. It is hardly high comedy, but neither is it merely farcical; and it has the great qualities of being always good-humoured and hardly ever grotesque.

Another secret of the success of *Pickwick*, perhaps, is that it is not in the ordinary sense of the word, a novel. There is no continuous story to speak of, only a collection of amusing scenes of high average excellence, though of course containing some that are of inferior merit. Nor do we find in *Pickwick* any real delineation of character, with the exception, perhaps, of the Wellers, who are, however, as little real as they are always amusing.—MARGARET OLIPHANT, *The Victorian Age of English Literature*, 1892, Vol. 1, pp. 251–52

BARNABY RUDGE

His opening chapters assure us that he has at length discovered the secret of his true strength, and that *Barnaby Rudge* will appeal principally to the *imagination*. Of this faculty we have many striking instances in the few numbers already issued. We see it where the belfry man in the lonely church at midnight, about to toll the "passing-bell," is struck with horror at hearing the solitary note of another, and awaits, aghast, a repetition of the sound. We recognise it more fully where this single note is discovered, in the morning, to have been that of an alarm pulled by the hand of one in the death-struggle with a murderer:—also in the expression of countenance which is so strikingly attributed to Mrs. Rudge—"the capacity for expressing terror"—something only dimly seen, but never absent for a moment—"the shadow of some look to which an instant of

intense and most unutterable horror only could have given rise." This is a conception admirably adapted to whet curiosity in respect to the character of that event which is hinted at as forming the ground-work of the novel; and so far is well suited to the purposes of a periodical story. But this observation should not fail to be made—that the anticipation must surpass the reality; that no matter how terrific be the circumstances which, in the *dénouement*, shall appear to have occasioned the expression of countenance worn habitually by Mrs. Rudge, still they will not be able to satisfy the mind of the reader. He will surely be disappointed. The skilful intimation of horror held out by the artist produces an effect which will deprive his conclusion, of all. These intimations—these dark hints of some uncertain evil—are often rhetorically praised as effective—but are only justly so praised where there is *no dénouement* whatever—where the reader's imagination is left to clear up the mystery for itself—and this, we suppose, is not the design of Mr. Dickens.

But the chief points in which the ideality of this story is apparent are the creation of the hero Barnaby Rudge, and the commingling with his character, as accessory, that of the human-looking raven. Barnaby we regard as an original idea altogether, so far as novel-writing is concerned. He is peculiar, inasmuch as he is an idiot endowed with the fantastic qualities of the madman, and has been born possessed with a maniacal horror of blood—the result of some terrible spectacle seen by his mother during pregnancy. The design of Mr. Dickens is here two-fold—first that of increasing our anticipation in regard to the deed committed—exaggerating our impression of its atrocity—and, secondly, that of causing this horror of blood on the part of the idiot, to bring about, in consistence with poetical justice, the condemnation of the murderer:—for it is a murder that has been committed. We say in accordance with poetical justice—and, in fact, it will be seen hereafter that Barnaby, the idiot, is the murderer's own son. The horror of blood which he feels is the mediate result of the atrocity, since this atrocity it was which impressed the imagination of the pregnant mother; and poetical justice will therefore be well fulfilled when this horror shall urge on the son to the conviction of the father in the perpetrator of the deed.—EDGAR ALLAN POE, "Charles Dickens" (1841), *Essays and Reviews*, ed. G. R. Thompson, 1984, pp. 218–19

OLD CURIOSITY SHOP

But if the conception of this story deserves praise, its execution is beyond all—and here the subject naturally leads us from the generalisation which is the proper province of the critic, into details among which it is scarcely fitting that he should venture. ⟨. . .⟩

When we speak in this manner of the *Old Curiosity Shop*, we speak with entire deliberation, and know quite well what it is we assert. We do not mean to say that it is perfect, as a whole—this could not well have been the case under the circumstances of its composition. But we know that, in all the higher elements which go to make up literary greatness, it is supremely excellent. We think, for instance, that the introduction of Nelly's brother (and here we address those who have read the work) is supererogatory—that the character of Quilp would have been more in keeping had he been confined to petty and grotesque acts of malice—that his death should have been made the *immediate* consequence of his attempt at revenge upon Kit; and that after matters had been put fairly in train for this poetical justice, he should not have perished by an accident inconsequential upon his villany. We think, too, that there is an air of *ultra*-accident in the finally discovered relationship between Kit's master and the bachelor of the old church—that the sneering politeness put into the mouth of Quilp, with his manner of commencing a question which he wishes answered in the affirmative, with an affirmative interrogatory, instead of the ordinary negative one—are fashions borrowed from the author's own Fagin—that he has repeated himself in many other instances—that the practical tricks and love of mischief of the dwarf's boy are too nearly consonant with the traits of the master—that so much of the propensities of Swiveller as relate to his inapposite appropriation of odds and ends of verse, is stolen from the generic loafer of our fellow-townsman, Neal—and that the writer has suffered the overflowing kindness of his own bosom to mislead him in a very important point of art, when he endows so many of his *dramatis personæ* with a warmth of feeling so very rare in reality. Above all, we acknowledge that the death of Nelly is excessively painful—that it leaves a most distressing oppression of spirit upon the reader—and should, therefore, have been avoided.

But when we come to speak of the excellences of the tale these defects appear really insignificant. It embodies more *originality* in every point, but in character especially, than any single work within our knowledge. There is the grandfather—a truly profound conception; the gentle and lovely Nelly—we have discoursed of her before; Quilp, with mouth like that of the panting dog—(a bold idea which the engraver has neglected to embody) with his hilarious antics, his cowardice, and his very petty and spoilt-child-like malevolence; Dick Swiveller, that prince of good-hearted, good-for-nothing, lazy, luxurious, poetical, brave, romantically generous, gallant, affectionate, and not over-and-above honest, "glorious Apollos;" the marchioness, his bride; Tom Codlin and his partner; Miss Sally Brass, that "fine fellow;" the pony that had an opinion of its own; the boy that stood upon his head; the sexton; the man at the forge; not forgetting the dancing dogs and baby Nubbles. There are other admirably drawn characters—but we note these for their remarkable originality, as well as for their wonderful keeping, and the glowing colors in which they are painted. We have heard some of them called caricatures—but the charge is grossly ill-founded. No critical principle is more firmly based in reason than that a certain amount of exaggeration is essential to the proper depicting of truth itself. We do not paint an object to be true, but to appear true to the beholder. Were we to copy nature with accuracy the object copied would seem unnatural. The columns of the Greek temples, which convey the idea of absolute proportion, are very considerably thicker just beneath the capital than at the base. We regret that we have not left ourselves space in which to examine this whole question as it deserves. We must content ourselves with saying that caricature seldom exists (unless in so gross a form as to disgust at once) where the component parts are *in keeping*; and that the laugh excited by it, in any case, is radically distinct from that induced by a properly artistical *incongruity*—the source of all mirth. Were these creations of Mr. Dickens' really caricatures they would not live in public estimation beyond the hour of their first survey. We regard them as *creations*—(that is to say as original combinations of character) only not all of the highest order, because the elements employed are not always of the highest. In the instances of Nelly, the grandfather, the Sexton, and the man of the furnace, the force of the creative intellect could scarcely have been engaged with nobler material, and the result is that these personages belong to the most august regions of the *Ideal*.

In truth, the great feature of the *Curiosity Shop* is its chaste, vigorous, and glorious *imagination*. This is the one charm, all potent, which alone would suffice to compensate for a world more of error than Mr. Dickens ever committed. It is not only seen in the conception, and general handling of the story, or in the invention of character; but it pervades every sentence of the book. We recognise its prodigious influence in every inspired word. It is this which induces the reader who is at all ideal, to pause frequently, to re-read the occasionally quaint phrases, to muse in uncontrollable delight over thoughts which, while he wonders he has never hit upon them before, he yet admits that he never has encountered. In fact it is the wand of the enchanter. ⟨. . .⟩

Upon the whole we think the *Curiosity Shop* very much the best of the works of Mr. Dickens. It is scarcely possible to speak of it too well. It is in all respects a tale which will secure for its author the enthusiastic admiration of every man of genius.—EDGAR ALLAN POE, "Charles Dickens" (1841), *Essays and Reviews*, ed. G. R. Thompson, 1984, pp. 213–17

Whatever may be the separate beauty of Nell's position as to character and situation in relation to her grandfather, it is dreadfully marred to me by the extravagance and caricature (as so often happens in Dickens) of the gambling insanity in the old man. Dickens, like all novelists anxious only for effect, misunderstands the true impulse in obstinate incorrigible gamesters: it is not faith, unconquerable faith, in their luck; it is the very opposite principle—a despair of their own luck—rage and hatred in consequence, as at a blind enemy working in the dark, and furious desire to affront this dark malignant power; just as in the frenzy of hopeless combat you will see a man without a chance, and knowing that he does but prolong his adversary's triumph, yet still flying again with his fists at the face which he can never reach. Without love on the old man's part to Nell, hers for him would be less interesting; and *with* love of any strength, the old fool could not *but* have paused. The risk was *instant:* it ruined Nell's hopes of a breakfast; it tended to a jail. Now Alnaschar delusions take a different flight—they settle on the future. Extravagance and want of fidelity to nature and the possibilities of life are what everywhere mar Dickens to me; and these faults are fatal, because the *modes* of life amongst which these extravagances intrude are always the absolute realities of vulgarised life as it exists in plebeian ranks amongst our countrymen at this moment. Were the mode of life one more idealised or removed from our own, I might be less sensible of the insupportable extravagances. —THOMAS DE QUINCEY, Letter to His Daughter (Sept. 19, 1847), cited in Alexander Hay Japp (as "H. A. Page"), *Thomas De Quincey: His Life and Writings*, 1877, Vol. 1, pp. 348–49

I admire Nell in the *Old Curiosity Shop* exceedingly. No doubt the whole thing is a good deal borrowed from Wilhelm Meister. But little Nell is a far purer, lovelier, more *English* conception than Mignon, treasonable as the saying would seem to some. No doubt it was suggested by Mignon.—SARA COLERIDGE, Letter to Aubrey De Vere (Oct. 2, 1849), *Memoir and Letters of Sara Coleridge*, ed. Edith Coleridge, 1874, Vol. 2, p. 407

Above the pines the moon was slowly drifting,
  The river sang below;
The dim Sierras, far beyond, uplifting
  Their minarets of snow.

The roaring camp-fire, with rude humor, painted
  The ruddy tints of health
On haggard face and form that drooped and fainted
  In the fierce race for wealth;

Till one arose, and from his pack's scant treasure
  A hoarded volume drew,

And cards were dropped from hands of listless leisure
  To hear the tale anew.
And then, while round them shadows gathered faster,
  And as the firelight fell,
He read aloud the book wherein the Master
  Had writ of "Little Nell."

Perhaps 't was boyish fancy,—for the reader
  Was youngest of them all,—
But, as he read, from clustering pine and cedar
  A silence seemed to fall;

The fir-trees, gathering closer in the shadows,
  Listened in every spray,
While the whole camp with "Nell" on English meadows
  Wandered and lost their way.

And so in mountain solitudes—o'ertaken
  As by some spell divine—
Their cares dropped from them like the needles shaken
  From out the gusty pine.

Lost is that camp and wasted all its fire;
  And he who wrought that spell?
Ah! towering pine and stately Kentish spire,
  Ye have one tale to tell!

Lost is that camp, but let its fragrant story
  Blend with the breath that thrills
With hop-vine's incense all the pensive glory
  That fills the Kentish hills.

And on that grave where English oak and holly
  And laurel wreaths entwine,
Deem it not all a too presumptuous folly,
  This spray of Western pine!
          —BRET HARTE, "Dickens in Camp," 1870

I believe that the first book—the first real, substantial book—I read through was *The Old Curiosity Shop*. At all events, it was the first volume of Dickens which I made my own. And I could not have lighted better in my choice. At ten years old, or so, one is not ready for *Pickwick*. I remember very well the day when I plunged into that sea of mirth; I can hear myself, half choked with laughter, clamoring for the attention of my elders whilst I read aloud this and that passage from the great Trial. But *The Old Curiosity Shop* makes strong appeal to a youthful imagination, and contains little that is beyond its scope. Dickens's sentiment, however it may distress the mature mind of our later day, is not unwholesome, and, at all events in this story, addresses itself naturally enough to feelings unsubdued by criticism. His quality of picturesqueness is here seen at its best, with little or nothing of that melodrama which makes the alloy of *Nicholas Nickleby* and *Oliver Twist*—to speak only of the early books. The opening scene, that dim-lighted storehouse of things old and grotesque, is the best approach to Dickens's world, where sights of every day are transfigured in the service of romance. The kindliness of the author's spirit, his overflowing sympathy with poor and humble folk, set one's mind to a sort of music which it is good to live with; and no writer of moralities ever showed triumphant virtue in so cheery a light as that which falls upon these honest people when rascality has got its deserts. Notably good, too, whether for young or old, is the atmosphere of rural peace breathed in so many pages of this book; I know that it helped to make conscious in me a love of English field and lane and village, one day to become a solacing passion. In *The Old Curiosity Shop*, town is set before you only for effect of contrast; the aspiration of the story is to the country road winding along under a pure sky. Others have pictured with a closer fidelity the scenes of English rustic life, but who succeeds better than Dickens in throwing a charm upon the wayside inn and the village church? Among his supreme merits is that of having presented in abiding form one of the best of our national ideals—rural homeliness. By the way of happiest emotions, the child reader takes this ideal into mind and heart; and perhaps it is in great part because Dickens's books are still so much read, because one sees edition after edition scattered over town and country homes, that one cannot wholly despair of this new England which tries so hard to be unlike the old.—GEORGE GISSING, "Dickens in Memory," *Critic*, Jan. 1902, pp. 48–49

AMERICAN NOTES

A thousand thanks to you for your charming book! and for all the pleasure, profit, and *relief* it has afforded me. You *have* been very tender to our sensitive friends beyond sea, and really said nothing which should give any serious offence to any moderately rational patriot among them. The *Slavers*, of course, will give you no quarter, and I suppose you did not expect they should. But I do not think you could have said less, and my whole heart goes along with every word you have written. Some people will be angry too, that you have been so strict to observe their *spitting*, and neglect of ablutions, &c. And more, that you should have spoken with so little reverence of their courts of law and state legislature, and even of their grand Congress itself. But all this latter part is done in such a spirit of good-humoured playfulness, and so mixed up with clear intimations that you have quite as little veneration for things of the same sort *at home*, that it will not be easy to represent it as the fruit of *English* insolence and envy.—FRANCIS, LORD JEFFREY, Letter to Charles Dickens (Oct. 16, 1842), cited in Lord Henry Cockburn, *Life of Lord Jeffrey*, 1852, Vol. 2, p. 294

I have read Dickens's book. It is jovial and good-natured, and at times very severe. You will read it with delight and, for the most part, approbation. He has a grand chapter on Slavery. *Spitting* and *politics at Washington* are the other topics of censure. Both you and I would censure them with equal severity, to say the least.—HENRY WADSWORTH LONGFELLOW, Letter to Charles Sumner (Oct. 16, 1842), cited in Samuel Longfellow, *Life of Henry Wadsworth Longfellow*, 1891, Vol. 1, p. 421

This morning I received Dickens's book. I have now read it. It is impossible for me to review it; nor do I think that you would wish me to do so. I can not praise it, and I will not cut it up. I can not praise it, though it contains a few lively dialogues and descriptions; for it seems to me to be, on the whole, a failure. It is written like the worst parts of *Humphrey's Clock*. What is meant to be easy and sprightly is vulgar and flippant, as in the first two pages. What is meant to be fine is a great deal too fine for me, as the description of the Fall of Niagara. A reader who wants an amusing account of the United States had better go to Mrs. Trollope, coarse and malignant as she is. A reader who wants information about American politics, manners, and literature had better go even to so poor a creature as Buckingham. In short, I pronounce the book, in spite of some gleams of genius, at once frivolous and dull.

Therefore I will not praise it. Neither will I attack it; first, because I have eaten salt with Dickens; secondly, because he is a good man, and a man of real talent; thirdly, because he hates slavery as heartily as I do; and, fourthly, because I wish to see him enrolled in our blue-and-yellow corps, where he may do excellent service as a skirmisher and sharpshooter.—THOMAS BABINGTON MACAULAY, Letter to Macvey Napier

(Oct. 19, 1842), cited in G. Otto Trevelyan, *The Life and Letters of Lord Macaulay*, 1876, Vol. 2, p. 109

Such being our opinion of Mr. Dickens's faculties and opportunities for observation, we expected from him a book, not without large defects both positive and negative, but containing some substantial and valuable addition to our stock of information with regard to this most interesting country—interesting not only for the indissoluble connexion of its interests with our own, but likewise as the quarter from which we must look for light on the great question of these times,—What is to become of *Democracy*, and how is it to be dealt with? We cannot say that our expectations are justified by the result. Though the book is said to have given great offence on the other side of the Atlantic, we cannot see any sufficient reason for it. To us it appears that Mr. Dickens deserves great praise for the care with which he has avoided all offensive topics, and abstained from amusing his readers at the expense of his entertainers; and if we had an account of the temptations in this kind which he has resisted, we do not doubt that the reserve and self-control which he has exercised would appear scarcely less than heroical. But, on the other hand, we cannot say that his book throws any new light on his subject. He has done little more than confide to the public what should have been a series of letters for the entertainment of his private friends. Very agreeable and amusing letters they would have been; and as such, had they been posthumously published, would have been read with interest and pleasure. As it is, in the middle of our amusement at the graphic sketches of life and manners, the ludicrous incidents, the wayside conversations about nothing, so happily told, and the lively remarks, with which these *Notes* abound—in the middle of our respect for the tone of good sense and good humour which runs through them—and in spite of a high appreciation of the gentlemanly feeling which has induced him to refrain from all personal allusions and criticisms, and for the modesty which has kept him silent on so many subjects, concerning which most persons in the same situation (not being reminded of the worthlessness of their opinions by the general inattention of mankind to what they say) are betrayed into the delivery of oracles—in the middle of all this we cannot help feeling that we should have respected Mr. Dickens more if he had kept his book to himself; if he had been so far dissatisfied with these *American Notes* as to shrink from the "general circulation" of them; if he had felt unwilling to stand by and see his nothings trumpeted to all corners of the earth, quoted and criticised in every newspaper, passing through edition after edition in England, and settling in clouds of sixpenny copies all over the United States. That he had nothing better to say is no reproach to him. He had much to say about international copyright, and that, we doubt not, was well worth hearing; we only wish it had been heard with more favour. But, having nothing better to say, why say anything? Or why, at least, sound a trumpet before him to call men away from their business to listen? To us it seems to imply a want of respect either for himself or for his subject, that he should be thus prompt to gratify the prurient public appetite for novelty, by bringing the fruits of his mind into the market unripe. This, however, is a matter of taste. In reputation, so easy and abundant a writer will suffer little from an occasional mistake. Though this book should only live till New Year's Day, it will have lived long enough for his fame; for on that day we observe that he is himself to come forth again in a series of monthly numbers, so that none but himself will be his extinguisher. —JAMES SPEDDING, "Dickens's *American Notes*" (1843), *Reviews and Discussions*, 1849, pp. 247–48

A CHRISTMAS CAROL

I do not mean that the *Christmas Carol* is quite as brilliant or self-evident as the sun at noonday; but it is so spread over England by this time, that no sceptic, no *Fraser's Magazine*,—no, not even the godlike and ancient *Quarterly* itself (venerable, Saturnian, bigwigged dynasty!) could review it down. ⟨. . .⟩

In fact, one might as well detail the plot of the *Merry Wives of Windsor*, or *Robinson Crusoe*, as recapitulate here the adventures of Scrooge the miser, and his Christmas conversion. I am not sure that the allegory is a very complete one, and protest, with the classics, against the use of blank verse in prose; but here all objections stop. Who can listen to objections regarding such a book as this? It seems to me a national benefit, and to every man or woman who reads it a personal kindness. The last two people I heard speak of it were women; neither knew the other, or the author, and both said, by way of criticism, "God bless him!" A Scotch philosopher, who nationally does not keep Christmas-day, on reading the book, sent out for a turkey, and asked two friends to dine—this is a fact! Many men were known to sit down after perusing it, and write off letters to their friends, not about business, but out of their fulness of heart, and to wish old acquaintances a happy Christmas. Had the book appeared a fortnight earlier, all the prize cattle would have been gobbled up in pure love and friendship, Epping denuded of sausages, and not a turkey left in Norfolk. His royal highness's fat stock would have fetched unheard-of prices, and Alderman Bannister would have been tired of slaying. But there is a Christmas for 1844, too; the book will be as early then as now, and so let speculators look out.

As for Tiny Tim, there is a certain passage in the book regarding that young gentleman, about which a man should hardly venture to speak in print or in public, any more than he would of any other affections of his private heart. There is not a reader in England but that little creature will be a bond of union between the author and him; and he will say of Charles Dickens, as the woman just now, "God Bless Him!" What a feeling is this for a writer to be able to inspire, and what a reward to reap!—WILLIAM MAKEPEACE THACKERAY, "A Box of Novels," *Fraser's Magazine*, Feb. 1844, pp. 168–69

It is easy, too, to say of Dickens that he makes us acquainted with many unsavory characters—people whom we would hardly care to associate with in real life, or to touch without gloves; and it is easy to ask why one need be so familiar with them and their disreputable haunts on paper. But what a thrill ran through the whole English-speaking race when *A Christmas Carol in Prose* announced to it that Marley was dead, to begin with—as dead as a door-nail! No carol that ever was sung so stirred the deep heart of humanity. The world laughed and cried over it, and Scrooge and Scrooge's nephew, and old Fezziwig, and Bob Cratchit, and Tiny Tim, became household words in a million homes. It was not Scrooge only that the Ghost of Christmas Past led backward over the pathway of the years, showing him the wasted opportunities, the graves of buried loves and hopes, the monuments raised to pride and hatred, the littlenesses, the meannesses, the barrenness that made "the shadows of the things that have been" so terrible. It was not to him only that the Ghost of Christmas Present revealed the things that were, the light struggling with darkness, patience and faith and hope and innocent merrymaking in lowliest homes, the love that sweetens penury, and, side by side with it, the degradation that is unutterable. And not to Scrooge alone, thank God, did Christmas Future show that the past, with all its records of sin and misery, could be blotted out, and a new page written.—JULIA C. R. DORR, "Christmas and Its Literature," *Book Buyer*, Dec. 1868, pp. 284–85

MARTIN CHUZZLEWIT

Dickens, Boz—For Shame. Dickens has just published as one of the chapters of *Martin Chuzzlewit* an account of the arrival of his hero in New York, and what he saw, and heard, and did, and suffered, in this land of pagans, brutes, and infidels. I am sorry to see it. Thinking that Mr. Dickens has been ungenerously treated by my countrymen, I have taken his part on most occasions; but he has now written an exceedingly foolish libel upon us, from which he will not obtain credit as an author, nor as a man of wit, any more than as a man of good taste, good nature, or good manners. It is difficult to believe that such unmitigated trash should have flown from the same pen that drew the portrait of the immortal *Pickwick* and his expressive gaiters, the honest locksmith and his pretty Dolly of Clerkenwell, and poor little Nell, who has caused so many tears to flow. Shame, Mr. Dickens! Considering all that we did for you, if, as some folks say, I and others made fools of ourselves to make much of you, you should not afford them the triumph of saying, "There! We told you so!" "It serves you right!" and such other consolatory phrases. If we were fools you were the cause of it, and should have stood by us. *"Et tu, Brute!"*—PHILIP HONE, *Diary*, July 29, 1843

This last work contains, besides all the fun, some very marked and available morals. I scarce know any book in which the evil and odiousness of selfishness is more forcibly brought out, or in a greater variety of exhibitions. In the midst of the merry quotations, or at least on any fair opportunity, I draw the boys' attention to these points, bid them remark how *unmanly* is the selfishness of young Martin, and I insist upon it that Tom Pinch's character, if it could really exist, would be a very beautiful one. But I doubt, as I do in regard to *Pickwick*, that so much sense, and deep, solid goodness, could coexist with such want of discernment and liability to be gulled. Tigg is very clever, and the boys roar with laughter at the "what's-his-name place whence no thingumbob ever came back;" but this is only a new edition of Jingle and Smangles; Mark Tapley, also, is a second Sam Weller. The new characters are Pecksniff, and the thrice-notable Sairey Gamp, with Betsy Prig to show her off. —SARA COLERIDGE, Letter to Mrs. H. M. Jones (Aug. 17, 1848), *Memoir and Letters of Sara Coleridge*, ed. Edith Coleridge, 1874, Vol. 2, p. 346

I liked *Martin Chuzzlewit*, ⟨. . .⟩ and the other day I read a great part of it again, and found it roughly true in the passages that referred to America, though it was surcharged in the serious moods, and caricatured in the comic. The English are always inadequate observers; they seem too full of themselves to have eyes and ears for any alien people; but as far as an Englishman could, Dickens had caught the look of our life in certain aspects. His report of it was clumsy and farcical; but in a large, loose way it was like enough; at least he had caught the note of our self-satisfied, intolerant, and hypocritical provinciality, and this was not altogether lost in his mocking horseplay.—WILLIAM DEAN HOWELLS, "Dickens," *My Literary Passions*, 1895

DAVID COPPERFIELD

I have read *David Copperfield*; it seems to me very good— admirable in some parts. You said it had affinity to *Jane Eyre*. It has, now and then—only what an advantage has Dickens in his varied knowledge of men and things!—CHARLOTTE BRONTË, Letter to W. S. Williams (Sept. 13, 1849)

⟨. . .⟩ I did not find it easy to get sufficiently far away from it, in the first sensations of having finished it, to refer to it with the composure which this formal heading would seem to require. My interest in it was so recent and strong, and my mind was so divided between pleasure and regret—pleasure in the achievement of a long design, regret in the separation from many companions—that I was in danger of wearying the reader with personal confidences and private emotions.

Besides which, all that I could have said of the Story to any purpose, I had endeavoured to say in it.

It would concern the reader little, perhaps, to know how sorrowfully the pen is laid down at the close of a two-years' imaginative task; or how an Author feels as if he were dismissing some portion of himself into the shadowy world, when a crowd of the creatures of his brain are going from him for ever. Yet, I had nothing else to tell; unless, indeed, I were to confess (which might be of less moment still), that no one can ever believe this Narrative in the reading more than I believed it in the writing.

So true are these avowals at the present day, that I can now only take the reader into one confidence more. Of all my books, I like this the best. It will be easily believed that I am a fond parent to every child of my fancy, and that no one can ever love that family as dearly as I love them. But, like many fond parents, I have in my heart of hearts a favourite child. And his name is David Copperfield.—CHARLES DICKENS, "Preface" to *David Copperfield*, 1850

Have you read *David Copperfield*, by the way? How beautiful it is—how charmingly fresh and simple! In those admirable touches of tender humour—and I should call humour, Bob, a mixture of love and wit—who can equal this great genius? There are little words and phrases in his books which are like personal benefits to the reader. What a place it is to hold in the affections of men! What an awful responsibility hanging over a writer! What man holding such a place, and knowing that his words go forth to vast congregations of mankind,—to grown folks—to their children, and perhaps to their children's children,—but must think of his calling with a solemn and humble heart! May love and truth guide such a man always! It is an awful prayer; may heaven further its fulfilment!—WILLIAM MAKEPEACE THACKERAY, "Mr. Brown the Elder Takes Mr. Brown the Younger to a Club," *Sketches and Travels in London*, 1850

As I was stepping into the house Dickens came out to meet me, with bright looks and a hearty greeting. He looked a little older than when we said good-bye ten years ago; but that was partly owing to the beard he had grown. His eyes were bright as ever; the smile on his lips was the same; his frank voice was just as friendly,—ay, and if possible, more winning still. He was now in the prime of manhood in his 45th year; full of youth and life and eloquence, and rich in a rare humour that glowed with kindliness. I know not how to describe him better than in the words of one of my first letters home: "Take the best out of all Dickens's writings, combine them into the picture of a man, and there thou hast Charles Dickens." And such as in the first hour he stood before me, the very same he remained all the time of my visit; ever genuine, and cheerful, and sympathetic.—HANS CHRISTIAN ANDERSEN, "A Visit to Charles Dickens," *Temple Bar*, Dec. 1870, p. 29

I have said that in *David Copperfield* Dickens is freer from defect than in any other of his works. It is rarely that public opinion has ratified an author's judgment so completely as it has here. As we all know, this was Dickens's favourite, and the reason we all know. It may be noted in passing how characteristic of the two men is their choice. To Dickens *David Copperfield* was, to use his own words, his favourite child, because in its pages he saw the reflection of his own youth. Thackeray, though he never spoke out on such matters, is generally believed to have looked not a little into his own heart when he wrote *Pendennis*. Yet his favourite was *Esmond*, for *Esmond* he rightly felt to be the most complete and perfect of his works; in that exquisite book his *art* touched its highest point. With *David Copperfield*, no doubt the secret of the writer's partiality is in some sense the secret of the reader's. Though none, perhaps, have been so outspoken as Hogg, every man takes pleasure in writing about himself, and we are always pleased to hear what he has to say; egotism, as Macaulay says, so unpopular in conversation, is always popular in writing. But not in the charm of autobiography alone lies the fascination which this delightful book has exercised on every class of readers. It is not only Dickens's most attractive work, but it is his best work. And it is his best for this reason, that whereas in all his others he is continually striving to realise the conception of his fancy, in this alone his business is to idealise the reality; in this alone, as it seems to me, his imagination prevails over his fancy. In this alone he is never grotesque, or for him so rarely that we hardly care to qualify the adverb. Nowhere else is his pathos so tender and so sure; nowhere else is his humour, though often more boisterous and more abundant, so easy and so fine; nowhere else is his observation so vivid and so deep; nowhere else has he held with so sure a hand the balance between the classes. If in the character of Daniel Pegotty more eloquently and more reasonably than he has ever done elsewhere, even in honest Joe Gargery, he has enlarged on his favourite abiding-place for virtue, he has also nowhere else been so ready and so glad to welcome her in those more seemly places wherein for the most part he can find no resting-place for her feet. Weak-minded as Doctor Strong is, fatuous, if the reader pleases, we are never asked to laugh at the kindly, chivalrous old scholar, as we are at Sir Leicester Dedlock; Clara Pegotty is no better woman than Agnes Wickfield. And even in smaller matters, and in the characters of second-rate importance, we may find the same sureness of touch. It has been made a reproach against him that his characters are too apt to be forgotten in the externals of their callings, that they never speak without some allusion to their occupations, and cannot be separated from them. In the extraordinary number and variety of characters that he has drawn, no doubt one can find instances of this. For so many of these characters, nearly all, indeed, of the comic ones, real as he has made them to us, are not, when we come to examine them, realities, but rather conceptions of his fancy, which he has to shape into realities by the use of certain traits and peculiarities of humanity with which his extraordinary observation has supplied him. Major Pendennis, and Costigan, and Becky Sharp *are* realities whom Thackeray idealises, makes characters of fiction out of. But Sam Weller and Mrs. Gamp are the children of fancy whom Dickens makes real, partly by the addition of sundry human attributes, but even more so by the marvellous skill and distinctness with which he brings them and keeps them before us. But in order to do this he is obliged never to lose sight, or to suffer us to lose sight, of those peculiarities, whether of speech, or manner, or condition, which make them for us the realities that they are. And in so doing it cannot but happen that he seems to thrust those peculiarities at times somewhat too persistently upon us. In *David Copperfield* this is not so, or much less so than anywhere else, except, of course, in *The Tale of Two Cities*, Dickens's only essay at the romance proper,

where the characters are subordinate to the story. We may see this, for example, by comparing Omer, the undertaker, in *David Copperfield*, with Mould, the undertaker, in *Martin Chuzzlewit*. Mould and all his family live in a perpetual atmosphere of funerals; his children are represented as solacing their young existences by "playing at buryin's down in the shop, and follerin' the order-book to its long home in the iron safe;" and Mr. Mould's own idea of fellowship is of a person "one would almost feel disposed to bury for nothing, and do it neatly, too!" On his first introduction, after old Anthony's death, he sets the seal on his personality by the remark that Jonas's liberal orders for the funeral prove "what was so forcibly observed by the lamented theatrical poet—*buried at Stratford*—that there is good in everything." That touch is very comical, but also very grotesque; it is a touch of fancy, not of nature. But when David Copperfield, as a man, recalls himself to the recollection of the good-hearted Omer, who had known him as a boy, the undertaker is revealed in a very different fashion. "To be sure," said Mr. Omer, touching my waistcoat with his forefinger; "and there was a little child too! *There was two parties. The little party was laid along with the other party.* Over at Blunderstone it was, of course. Dear me! And how have you been since?" Every one must be conscious of the difference here.—MOWBRAY MORRIS, "Charles Dickens," *Fortnightly Review*, Dec. 1882, pp. 776–77

I am trying to get rested by reading Dickens, and am over *David Copperfield* now. I had never read it, I find, though Mr. Micawber has become so proverbial that, finding his name in it, I thought I had. Dickens says in his preface that David Copperfield was his "favorite child," and I don't wonder, for it is amazingly well done so far as I have got.—JAMES RUSSELL LOWELL, Letter to Charles Eliot Norton (April 8, 1887)

WALTER BAGEHOT
From "Charles Dickens" (1858)
Collected Works, ed. Norman St. John-Stevas
1965, Volume 2, pp. 81–107

His genius is essentially irregular and unsymmetrical. Hardly any English writer perhaps is much more so. His style is an example of it. It is descriptive, racy, and flowing; it is instinct with new imagery and singular illustration; but it does not indicate that due proportion of the faculties to one another which is a beauty in itself, and which cannot help diffusing beauty over every happy word and moulded clause. ⟨. . .⟩

The truth is that Mr. Dickens wholly wants the two elements which we have spoken of as one or other requisite for a symmetrical genius. He is utterly deficient in the faculty of reasoning. 'Mamma, what shall I think about?' said the small girl. 'My dear, don't think,' was the old-fashioned reply. We do not allege that in the strict theory of education this was a correct reply; modern writers think otherwise; but we wish someone would say it to Mr. Dickens. He is often troubled with the idea that he must reflect, and his reflections are perhaps the worst reading in the world. There is a sentimental confusion about them; we never find the consecutive precision of mature theory, or the cold distinctness of clear thought. Vivid facts stand out in his imagination, and a fresh illustrative style brings them home to the imagination of his readers; but his continuous philosophy utterly fails in the attempt to harmonise them,—to educe a theory or elaborate a precept from them. Of his social thinking we shall have a few words to say in detail; his didactic humour is very unfortunate: no writer is less fitted for an excursion to the imperative mood. At present we only say what is so obvious as scarcely to need saying, that his abstract understanding is so far inferior to his picturesque imagination as to give even to his best works the sense of jar and incompleteness, and to deprive them altogether of the crystalline finish which is characteristic of the clear and cultured understanding.

Nor has Mr. Dickens the easy and various sagacity which, as has been said, gives a unity to all which it touches. He has, indeed, a quality which is near allied to it in appearance. His shrewdness in some things, especially in traits and small things, is wonderful. His works are full of acute remarks on petty doings, and well exemplify the telling power of minute circumstantiality. But the minor species of perceptive sharpness is so different from diffused sagacity, that the two scarcely ever are to be found in the same mind. There is nothing less like the great lawyer, acquainted with broad principles and applying them with distinct deduction, than the attorney's clerk who catches at small points like a dog biting at flies. 'Over-sharpness' in the student is the most unpromising symptom of the logical jurist. You must not ask a horse in blinkers for a large view of a landscape. In the same way, a detective ingenuity in microscopic detail is of all mental qualities most unlike the broad sagacity by which the great painters of human affairs have unintentionally stamped the mark of unity on their productions. They show by their treatment of each case that they understand the whole of life; the special delineator of fragments and points shows that he understands them only. In one respect the defect is more striking in Mr. Dickens than in any other novelist of the present day. The most remarkable deficiency in modern fiction is its omission of the business of life, of all those countless occupations, pursuits, and callings in which most men live and move, and by which they have their being. In most novels money *grows*. You have no idea of the toil, the patience, and the wearing anxiety by which men of action provide for the day, and lay up for the future, and support those that are given into their care. Mr. Dickens is not chargeable with this omission. He perpetually deals with the pecuniary part of life. Almost all his characters have determined occupations, of which he is apt to talk even at too much length. When he rises from the toiling to the luxurious classes, his genius in most cases deserts him. The delicate refinement and discriminating taste of the idling orders are not in his way; he knows the dry arches of London Bridge better than Belgravia. He excels in inventories of poor furniture, and is learned in pawnbrokers' tickets. But, although his creative power lives and works among the middle class and industrial section of English society, he has never painted the highest part of their daily intellectual life. He made, indeed, an attempt to paint specimens of the apt and able man of business in *Nicholas Nickleby*; but the Messrs. Cheeryble are among the stupidest of his characters. He forgot that breadth of platitude is rather different from breadth of sagacity. His delineations of middle-class life have in consequence a harshness and meanness which do not belong to that life in reality. He omits the relieving element. He describes the figs which are sold, but not the talent which sells figs well. And it is the same want of the diffused sagacity in his own nature which has made his pictures of life so odd and disjointed, and which has deprived them of symmetry and unity. ⟨. . .⟩

Mr. Dickens's humour is indeed very much a result of ⟨. . .⟩ two peculiarities ⟨. . .⟩ His power of detailed observation and his power of idealising individual traits of character— sometimes of one or other of them, sometimes of both of them

together. His similes on matters of external observation are so admirable that everybody appreciates them, and it would be absurd to quote specimens of them; nor is it the sort of excellence which best bears to be paraded for the purposes of critical example. Its off-hand air and natural connection with the adjacent circumstances are inherent parts of its peculiar merit. Every reader of Mr. Dickens's works knows well what we mean. And who is not a reader of them?

But his peculiar humour is even more indebted to his habit of vivifying external traits, than to his power of external observation. He, as we have explained, expands traits into people; and it is a source of true humour to place these, when so expanded, in circumstances in which only people—that is, complete human beings—can appropriately act. The humour of Mr. Pickwick's character is entirely of this kind. He is a kind of incarnation of simple-mindedness and what we may call obvious-mindedness. The conclusion which each occurrence or position in life most immediately presents to the unsophisticated mind is that which Mr. Pickwick is sure to accept. The proper accompaniments are given to him. He is a stout gentleman in easy circumstances, who is irritated into originality by no impulse from within, and by no stimulus from without. He is stated to have 'retired from business.' But no one can fancy what he was in business. Such guileless simplicity of heart and easy impressibility of disposition would soon have induced a painful failure amid the harsh struggles and the tempting speculations of pecuniary life. As he is represented in the narrative, however, nobody dreams of such antecedents. Mr. Pickwick moves easily over all the surface of English life from Goswell Street to Dingley Dell, from Dingley Dell to the Ipswich elections, from drinking milk-punch in a wheelbarrow to sleeping in the approximate pound, and no one ever thinks of applying to him the ordinary maxims which we should apply to any common person in life, or to any common personage in a fiction. Nobody thinks it is wrong in Mr. Pickwick to drink too much milk-punch in a wheelbarrow, to introduce worthless people of whom he knows nothing to the families of people for whom he really cares; nobody holds him responsible for the consequences; nobody thinks there is anything wrong in his taking Mr. Bob Sawyer and Mr. Benjamin Allen to visit Mr. Winkle senior, and thereby almost irretrievably offending him with his son's marriage. We do not reject moral remarks such as these, but they never occur to us. Indeed, the indistinct consciousness that such observations are possible, and that they are hovering about our minds, enhances the humour of the narrative. We are in a conventional world, where the mere maxims of common life do not apply, and yet which has all the amusing detail, and picturesque elements, and singular eccentricities of common life. Mr. Pickwick is a personified ideal; a kind of amateur in life, whose course we watch through all the circumstances of ordinary existence, and at whose follies we are amused just as really skilled people are at the mistakes of an amateur in their art. His being in the pound is not wrong; his being the victim of Messrs. Dodson is not foolish. 'Always shout with the mob,' said Mr. Pickwick. 'But suppose there are two mobs,' said Mr. Snodgrass. 'Then shout with the loudest,' said Mr. Pickwick. This is not in him weakness or time-serving or want of principle, as in most even of fictitious people it would be. It is his way. Mr. Pickwick was expected to say something, so he said 'Ah!' in a grave voice. This is not pompous as we might fancy, or clever as it might be if intentionally devised; it is simply his way. Mr. Pickwick gets late at night over the wall behind the back-door of a young-ladies' school, is found in that sequestered place by the schoolmistress and the boarders and the cook, and there is a dialogue between them. There is nothing out of possibility in this; it is his way. The humour essentially consists in treating as a moral agent a being who really is not a moral agent. We treat a vivified accident as a man, and we are surprised at the absurd results. We are reading about an acting thing, and we wonder at its scrapes, and laugh at them as if they were those of the man. There is something of this humour in every sort of farce. Everybody knows these are not real beings acting in real life, though they talk as if they were, and want us to believe that they are. Here, as in Mr. Dickens's books, we have exaggerations pretending to comport themselves as ordinary beings, caricatures acting as if they were characters.

At the same time it is essential to remember, that however great may be and is the charm of such exaggerated personifications, the best specimens of them are immensely less excellent, belong to an altogether lower range of intellectual achievements, than the real depiction of actual living men. It is amusing to read of beings *out of* the laws of morality, but it is more profoundly interesting, as well as more instructive, to read of those whose life in its moral conditions resembles our own. We see this most distinctly when both the representations are given by the genius of the same writer. Falstaff is a sort of sack-holding paunch, an exaggerated over-development which no one thinks of holding down to the commonplace rules of the ten commandments and the statute-law. We do not think of them in connection with him. They belong to a world apart. Accordingly, we are vexed when the king discards him and reproves him. Such a fate was a necessary adherence on Shakespeare's part to the historical tradition; he never probably thought of departing from it, nor would his audience have perhaps endured his doing so. But to those who look at the historical plays as pure works of imaginative art, it seems certainly an artistic misconception to have developed so marvellous an *un*moral impersonation, and then to have subjected it to an ethical and punitive judgment. Still, notwithstanding this error, which was very likely inevitable, Falstaff is probably the most remarkable specimen of caricature-representation to be found in literature. And its very excellence of execution only shows how inferior is the kind of art which creates only such representations. Who could compare the genius, marvellous as must be its fertility, which was needful to create a Falstaff, with that shown in the higher productions of the same mind in Hamlet, Ophelia, and Lear? We feel instantaneously the difference between the aggregating accident which rakes up from the externalities of life other accidents analogous to itself, and the central ideal of a real character which cannot show itself wholly in any accidents, but which exemplifies itself partially in many, which unfolds itself gradually in wide spheres of action, and yet, as with those we know best in life, leaves something hardly to be understood, and after years of familiarity is a problem and a difficulty to the last. In the same way, the embodied characteristics and grotesque exaggerations of Mr. Dickens, notwithstanding all their humour and all their marvellous abundance, can never be for a moment compared with the great works of the real painters of essential human nature.

There is one class of Mr. Dickens's pictures which may seem to form an exception to this criticism. It is the delineation of the outlaw, we might say the anti-law, world in *Oliver Twist*. In one or two instances Mr. Dickens has been so fortunate as to hit on characteristics which, by his system of idealisation and continual repetition, might really be brought to look like a character. A man's trade or profession in regular life can only exhaust a very small portion of his nature; no approach is made to the essence of humanity by the exaggeration of the traits which typify a beadle or an undertaker. With the outlaw world it is somewhat different. The bare fact of a man belonging to that world is so important to his nature, that if it is artistically developed with coherent accessories, some approximation to a distinctly natural character will be almost inevitably made. In the characters of Bill Sykes and Nancy this is so. The former is the skulking ruffian who may be seen any day at the police-courts, and whom any one may fancy he sees by walking through St. Giles's. You cannot attempt to figure to your imagination the existence of such a person without being thrown into the region of the passions, the will, and the conscience; the mere fact of his maintaining, as a condition of life and by settled profession, a struggle with regular society, necessarily brings these deep parts of his nature into prominence; great crime usually proceeds from abnormal impulses or strange effort. Accordingly, Mr. Sykes is the character most approaching to a coherent man who is to be found in Mr. Dickens's works. We do not say that even here there is not some undue heightening admixture of caricature; but this defect is scarcely thought of amid the general coherence of the picture, the painful subject, and the wonderful command of strange accessories. Miss Nancy is a still more delicate artistic effort. She is an idealisation of the girl who may also be seen at the police-courts and St. Giles's; as bad, according to occupation and common character, as a woman can be, yet retaining a tinge of womanhood, and a certain compassion for interesting suffering, which under favouring circumstances might be the germ of a regenerating influence. We need not stay to prove how much the imaginative development of such a personage must concern itself with our deeper humanity; how strongly, if excellent, it must be contrasted with everything conventional or casual or superficial. Mr. Dickens's delineation is in the highest degree excellent. It possesses not only the more obvious merits belonging to the subject, but also that of a singular delicacy of expression and idea. Nobody fancies for a moment that they are reading about anything beyond the pale of ordinary propriety. We read the account of the life which Miss Nancy leads with Bill Sykes without such an idea occurring to us: yet when we reflect upon it, few things in literary painting are more wonderful than the depiction of a professional life of sin and sorrow, so as not even to startle those to whom the deeper forms of either are but names and shadows. Other writers would have given as vivid a picture: Defoe would have poured out even a more copious measure of telling circumstantiality, but he would have narrated his story with an inhuman distinctness which, if not impure is *un*pure; French writers, whom we need not name, would have enhanced the interest of their narrative by trading on the excitement of stimulating scenes. It would be injustice to Mr. Dickens to say that he has surmounted these temptations; the unconscious evidence of innumerable details proves that, from a certain delicacy of imagination and purity of spirit, he has not even experienced them. Criticism is the more bound to dwell at length on the merits of these delineations, because no artistic merit can make *Oliver Twist* a pleasing work. The squalid detail of crime and misery oppresses us too much. If it is to be read at all, it should be read in the first hardness of the youthful imagination, which no touch can move too deeply, and which is never stirred with tremulous suffering at the 'still sad music of humanity.' The coldest critic in later life may never hope to have again the apathy of his boyhood.

It perhaps follows from what has been said of the characteristics of Mr. Dickens's genius, that he would be little skilled in planning plots for his novels. He certainly is not so skilled. He says in his preface to the *Pickwick Papers*, 'that they were designed for the introduction of diverting characters and incidents; that no ingenuity of plot was attempted, or even at that time considered very feasible by the author in connection with the desultory plan of publication adopted;' and he adds an expression of regret that 'these chapters had not been strung together on a stronger thread of more general interest.' It is extremely fortunate that no such attempt was made. In the cases in which Mr. Dickens has attempted to make a long connected story, or to develop into scenes or incidents a plan in any degree elaborate, the result has been a complete failure. A certain consistency of genius seems necessary for the construction of a consecutive plot. An irregular mind naturally shows itself in incoherency of incident and aberration of character. The method in which Mr. Dickens's mind works, if we are correct in our criticism upon it, tends naturally to these blemishes. Caricatures are necessarily isolated; they are produced by the exaggeration of certain conspicuous traits and features; each being is enlarged on its greatest side; and we laugh at the grotesque grouping and the startling contrast. But the connection between human beings on which a plot depends is rather severed than elucidated by the enhancement of their diversities. Interesting stories are founded on the intimate relations of men and women. These intimate relations are based not on their superficial traits, or common occupations, or most visible externalities, but on the inner life of heart and feeling. You simply divert attention from that secret life by enhancing the perceptible diversities of common human nature, and the strange anomalies into which it may be distorted. The original germ of *Pickwick* was a 'Club of Oddities.' The idea was professedly abandoned; but traces of it are to be found in all Mr. Dickens's books. It illustrates the professed grotesqueness of the characters as well as their slender connection.

The defect of plot is heightened by Mr. Dickens's great, we might say complete, inability to make a love-story. A pair of lovers is by custom a necessity of narrative fiction, and writers who possess a great general range of mundane knowledge, and but little knowledge of the special sentimental subject, are often in amusing difficulties. The watchful reader observes the transition from the hearty description of well-known scenes, or prosaic streets, or journeys by wood and river, to the pale colours of ill-attempted poetry, to such sights as the novelist wishes he need not try to see. But few writers exhibit the difficulty in so aggravated a form as Mr. Dickens. Most men by taking thought can make a lay figure to look not so very unlike a young gentleman, and can compose a telling schedule of ladylike charms. Mr. Dickens has no power of doing either. The heroic character—we do not mean the form of character so-called in life and action, but that which is hereditary in the heroes of novels—is not suited to his style of art. Hazlitt wrote an essay to inquire 'Why the heroes of romances are insipid;' and without going that length, it may safely be said that the character of the agreeable young gentleman who loves and is loved should not be of the most marked sort. Flirtation ought not to be an exaggerated pursuit. Young ladies and their admirers should not express themselves in the heightened and imaginative phraseology suited to Charley Bates and the Dodger. Humour is of no use, for no one makes love in jokes: a tinge of insidious satire may perhaps be permitted as a rare and occasional relief, but it will not be thought 'a pretty book' if so malicious an element be at all habitually perceptible. The broad farce in which Mr. Dickens indulges is thoroughly out of place. If you caricature a pair of lovers ever so little, by the necessity of their calling you make them ridiculous. One of Sheridan's best comedies is remarkable for having no scene in which the hero and heroine are on the stage together; and Mr.

Moore suggests that the shrewd wit distrusted his skill in the light dropping love-talk which would have been necessary. Mr. Dickens would have done well to imitate so astute a policy; but he has none of the managing shrewdness which those who look at Sheridan's career attentively will probably think not the least remarkable feature in his singular character. Mr. Dickens, on the contrary, pours out painful sentiments as if he wished the abundance should make up for the inferior quality. The excruciating writing which is expended on Miss Ruth Pinch passes belief. Mr. Dickens is not only unable to make lovers talk, but to describe heroines in mere narrative. As has been said, most men can make a jumble of blue eyes and fair hair and pearly teeth, that does very well for a young lady, at least for a good while; but Mr. Dickens will not, probably cannot, attain even to this humble measure of descriptive art. He vitiates the repose by broad humour, or disenchants the delicacy by an unctuous admiration.

This deficiency is probably nearly connected with one of Mr. Dickens's most remarkable excellencies. No one can read Mr. Thackeray's writings without feeling that he is perpetually treading as close as he dare to the border-line that separates the world which may be described in books from the world which it is prohibited so to describe. No one knows better than this accomplished artist where that line is, and how curious are its windings and turns. The charge against him is that he knows it but too well; that with an anxious care and a wistful eye he is ever approximating to its edge, and hinting with subtle art how thoroughly he is familiar with, and how interesting he could make the interdicted region on the other side. He never violates a single conventional rule; but at the same time the shadow of the immorality that is not seen is scarcely ever wanting to his delineation of the society that is seen. Everyone may perceive what is passing in his fancy. Mr. Dickens is chargeable with no such defect: he does not seem to feel the temptation. By what we may fairly call an instinctive purity of genius, he not only observes the conventional rules, but makes excursions into topics which no other novelist could safely handle, and, by a felicitous instinct, deprives them of all impropriety. No other writer could have managed the humour of Mrs. Gamp without becoming unendurable. At the same time it is difficult not to believe that this singular insensibility to the temptations to which many of the greatest novelists have succumbed is in some measure connected with his utter inaptitude for delineating the portion of life to which their art is specially inclined. He delineates neither the love-affairs which ought to be, nor those which ought not to be.

Mr. Dickens's indisposition to 'make capital' out of the most commonly tempting part of human sentiment is the more remarkable because he certainly does not show the same indisposition in other cases. He has naturally great powers of pathos; his imagination is familiar with the common sorts of human suffering; and his marvellous conversancy with the detail of existence enables him to describe sick-beds and death-beds with an excellence very rarely seen in literature. A nature far more sympathetic than that of most authors has familiarised him with such subjects. In general, a certain apathy is characteristic of book-writers, and dulls the efficacy of their pathos. Mr. Dickens is quite exempt from this defect; but, on the other hand, is exceedingly prone to a very ostentatious exhibition of the opposite excellence. He dwells on dismal scenes with a kind of fawning fondness; and he seems unwilling to leave them, long after his readers have had more than enough of them. He describes Mr. Dennis the hangman as having a professional fondness for his occupation: he has the same sort of fondness apparently for the profession of death-painter. The painful details he accumulates are a very serious drawback from the agreeableness of his writings. Dismal 'light literature' is the dismallest of reading. The reality of the police-reports is sufficiently bad, but a fictitious police-report would be the most disagreeable of conceivable compositions. Some portions of Mr. Dickens's books are liable to a good many of the same objections. They are squalid from noisome trivialities, and horrid with terrifying crime. In his earlier books this is commonly relieved at frequent intervals by a graphic and original mirth. As—we will not say age, but maturity, has passed over his powers, this counteractive element has been lessened; the humour is not so happy as it was, but the wonderful fertility in painful *minutiæ* still remains.

Mr. Dickens's political opinions have subjected him to a good deal of criticism, and to some ridicule. He has shown, on many occasions, the desire,—which we see so frequent among able and influential men,—to start as a political reformer. Mr. Spurgeon said, with an application to himself, 'If you've got the ear of the public, *of course* you must begin to tell it its faults.' Mr. Dickens has been quite disposed to make this use of his popular influence. Even in *Pickwick* there are many traces of this tendency; and the way in which it shows itself in that book and in others is very characteristic of the time at which they appeared. The most instructive political characteristic of the years from 1825 to 1845 is the growth and influence of the scheme of opinion which we call radicalism. There are several species of creeds which are comprehended under this generic name, but they all evince a marked reaction against the worship of the English constitution and the affection for the English *status quo*, which were then the established creed and sentiment. All radicals are anti-Eldonites. This is equally true of the Benthamite or philosophical radicalism of the early period, and the Manchester or 'definite-grievance' radicalism, among the last vestiges of which we are now living. Mr. Dickens represents a species different from either. His is what we may call the 'sentimental radicalism;' and if we recur to the history of the time, we shall find that there would not originally have been any opprobrium attaching to such a name. The whole course of the legislation, and still more of the administration, of the first twenty years of the nineteenth century were marked by a harsh unfeelingness which is of all faults the most contrary to any with which we are chargeable now. The world of the 'Six Acts,' of the frequent executions, of the Draconic criminal law, is so far removed from us that we cannot comprehend its having ever existed. It is more easy to understand the recoil which has followed. All the social speculation, and much of the social action of the few years succeeding the Reform Bill bear the most marked traces of the reaction. The spirit which animates Mr. Dickens's political reasonings and observations expresses it exactly. The vice of the then existing social authorities and of the then existing public had been the forgetfulness of the pain which their own acts evidently produced,—an unrealising habit which adhered to official rules and established maxims, and which would not be shocked by the evident consequences, by proximate human suffering. The sure result of this habit was the excitement of the habit precisely opposed to it. Mr. Carlyle, in his *Chartism*, we think, observes of the poor-law reform: 'It was then, above all things, necessary that outdoor relief should cease. But how? What means did great Nature take for accomplishing that most desirable end? She created a race of men who believed the cessation of outdoor relief to be the one thing needful.' In the same way, and by the same propensity to exaggerated opposition which is inherent in human nature, the unfeeling obtuseness of the early part of this century was to be corrected by an extreme, perhaps an excessive, sensibility to human suffering in the years which have followed. There was most adequate reason for the sentiment in its origin, and it had a great task to perform in ameliorating harsh customs and repealing dreadful penalties; but it has continued to repine at such evils long after they ceased to exist, and when the only facts that at all resemble them are the necessary painfulness of due punishment and the necessary rigidity of established law.

Mr. Dickens is an example both of the proper use and of the abuse of the sentiment. His earlier works have many excellent descriptions of the abuses which had descended to the present generation from others whose sympathy with pain was less tender. Nothing can be better than the description of the poor debtor's gaol in *Pickwick*, or of the old parochial authorities in *Oliver Twist*. No doubt these descriptions are caricatures, all his delineations are so; but the beneficial use of such art can hardly be better exemplified. Human nature endures the aggravation of vices and foibles in written description better than that of excellencies. We cannot bear to hear even the hero of a book for ever called 'just;' we detest the recurring praise even of beauty, much more of virtue. The moment you begin to exaggerate a character of true excellence, you spoil it; the traits are too delicate not to be injured by heightening or marred by over-emphasis. But a beadle is made for caricature. The slight measure of pomposity that humanises his unfeelingness introduces the requisite comic element; even the turnkeys of a debtors' prison may by skilful hands be similarly used. The contrast between the destitute condition of Job Trotter and Mr. Jingle and their former swindling triumph, is made comic by a rarer touch of unconscious art. Mr. Pickwick's warm heart takes so eager an interest in the misery of his old enemies, that our colder nature is tempted to smile. We endure the over-intensity, at any rate the unnecessary aggravation, of the surrounding misery; and we endure it willingly, because it brings out better than anything else could have done the half-comic intensity of a sympathetic nature.

It is painful to pass from these happy instances of well-used power to the glaring abuses of the same faculty in Mr. Dickens's later books. He began by describing really removable evils in a style which would induce all persons, however insensible, to remove them if they could; he has ended by describing the natural evils and inevitable pains of the present state of being in such a manner as must tend to excite discontent and repining. The result is aggravated, because Mr. Dickens never ceases to hint that these evils are removable, though he does not say by what means. Nothing is easier than to show the evils of anything. Mr. Dickens has not unfrequently spoken, and what is worse, he has taught a great number of parrot-like imitators to speak, in what really is, if they knew it, a tone of objection to the necessary constitution of human society. If you will only write a description of it, any form of government will seem ridiculous. What is more absurd than a despotism, even at its best? A king of ability or an able minister sits in an orderly room filled with memorials, and returns, and documents, and memoranda. These are his world; among these he of necessity lives and moves. Yet how little of the real life of the nation he governs can be represented in an official form! How much of real suffering is there that statistics can never tell! how much of obvious good is there that no memorandum to a minister will ever mention! how much deception is there in what such documents contain! how monstrous must be the ignorance of the closet statesman, after all his life of labour, of much that a ploughman could tell him of! A free government is almost worse, as it must read in a written delineation. Instead of the real attention of a laborious and anxious statesman, we have now the shifting caprices of a popular assembly—elected for one object, deciding on another; changing with the turn of debate; shifting in its very composition; one set of men coming down to vote to-day, to-morrow another and often unlike set, most of them eager for the dinner-hour, actuated by unseen influences,—by a respect for their constituents, by the dread of an attorney in a far-off borough. What people are these to control a nation's destinies, and wield the power of an empire, and regulate the happiness of millions! Either way we are at fault. Free government seems an absurdity, and despotism is so too. Again, every form of law has a distinct expression, a rigid procedure, customary rules and forms. It is administered by human beings liable to mistake, confusion, and forgetfulness, and in the long run, and on the average, is sure to be tainted with vice and fraud. Nothing can be easier than to make a case, as we may say, against any particular system, by pointing out with emphatic caricature its inevitable miscarriages, and by pointing out nothing else. Those who so address us may assume a tone of philanthropy, and for ever exult that they are not so unfeeling as other men are; but the real tendency of their exhortations is to make men dissatisfied with their inevitable condition, and what is worse, to make them fancy that its irremediable evils can be remedied, and indulge in a succession of vague strivings and restless changes. Such, however,—though in a style of expression somewhat different,—is very much the tone with which Mr. Dickens and his followers have in later years made us familiar. To the second-hand repeaters of a cry so feeble, we can have nothing to say; if silly people cry because they think the world is silly, let them cry; but the founder of the school cannot, we are persuaded, peruse without mirth the lachrymose eloquence which his disciples have perpetrated. The soft moisture of irrelevant sentiment cannot have entirely entered into his soul. A truthful genius must have forbidden it. Let us hope that this pernicious example may incite someone of equal genius to preach with equal efficiency a sterner and a wiser gospel; but there is no need just now for us to preach it without genius.

There has been much controversy about Mr. Dickens's taste. A great many cultivated people will scarcely concede that he has any taste at all; a still larger number of fervent admirers point, on the other hand, to a hundred felicitous descriptions and delineations which abound in apt expressions and skilful turns and happy images,—in which it would be impossible to alter a single word without altering for the worse; and naturally inquire whether such excellences in what is written do not indicate good taste in the writer. The truth is that Mr. Dickens has what we may call creative taste; that is to say, the habit or faculty, whichever we may choose to call it, which at the critical instant of artistic production offers to the mind the right word, and the right word only. If he is engaged on a good subject for caricature, there will be no defect of taste to preclude the caricature from being excellent. But it is only in moments of imaginative production that he has any taste at all. His works nowhere indicate that he possesses in any degree the passive taste which decides what is good in the writings of other people and what is not, and which performs the same critical duty upon a writer's own efforts when the confusing mists of productive imagination have passed away. Nor has Mr. Dickens the gentlemanly instinct which in many minds supplies the place of purely critical discernment, and which, by constant association with those who know what is best, acquires a second-hand perception of that which is best. He has no tendency to conventionalism for good or for evil; his merits are far removed from the ordinary path of writers, and it was not

probably so much effort to him as to other men to step so far out of that path: he scarcely knew how far it was. For the same reason he cannot tell how faulty his writing will often be thought, for he cannot tell what people will think.

A few pedantic critics have regretted that Mr. Dickens had not received what they call a regular education. And if we understand their meaning, we believe they mean to regret that he had not received a course of discipline which would probably have impaired his powers. A regular education should mean that ordinary system of regulation and instruction which experience has shown to fit men best for the ordinary pursuits of life. It applies the requisite discipline to each faculty in the exact proportion in which that faculty is wanted in the pursuits of life; it develops understanding, and memory, and imagination, each in accordance with the scale prescribed. To men of ordinary faculties this is nearly essential; it is the only mode in which they can be fitted for the inevitable competition of existence. To men of regular and symmetrical genius also, such a training will often be beneficial. The world knows pretty well what are the great tasks of the human mind, and has learnt in the course of ages with some accuracy what is the kind of culture likely to promote their exact performance. A man of abilities, extraordinary in degree but harmonious in proportion, will be the better for having submitted to the kind of discipline which has been ascertained to fit a man for the work to which powers in that proportion are best fitted; he will do what he has to do better and more gracefully; culture will add a touch to the finish of nature. But the case is very different with men of irregular and anomalous genius, whose excellences consist in the *aggravation* of some special faculty, or at the most of one or two. The discipline which will fit him for the production of great literary works is that which will most develop the peculiar powers in which he excels; the rest of the mind will be far less important; it will not be likely that the culture which is adapted to promote this special development will also be that which is most fitted for expanding the powers of common men in common directions. The precise problem is to develop the powers of a strange man in a strange direction. In the case of Mr. Dickens, it would have been absurd to have shut up his observant youth within the walls of a college. They would have taught him nothing about Mrs. Gamp there; Sam Weller took no degree. The kind of early life fitted to develop the power of apprehensive observation is a brooding life in stirring scenes; the idler in the streets of life knows the streets; the bystander knows the picturesque effect of life better than the player; and the meditative idler amid the hum of existence is much more likely to know its sound and to take in and comprehend its depths and meanings than the scholastic student intent on books, which if they represent any world, represent one which has long passed away, which commonly try rather to develop the reasoning understanding than the seeing observation, which are written in languages that have long been dead. You will not train by such discipline a caricaturist of obvious manners.

Perhaps, too, a regular instruction and daily experience of the searching ridicule of critical associates would have detracted from the *pluck* which Mr. Dickens shows in all his writings. It requires a great deal of courage to be a humorous writer; you are always afraid that people will laugh at you instead of with you: undoubtedly there is a certain eccentricity about it. You take up the esteemed writers, Thucydides and the *Saturday Review*; after all, they do not make you laugh. It is not the function of really artistic productions to contribute to the mirth of human beings. All sensible men are afraid of it, and it is only with an extreme effort that a printed joke attains to the perusal of the public: the chances are many to one that the anxious producer loses heart in the correction of the press, and that the world never laughs at all. Mr. Dickens is quite exempt from this weakness. He has what a Frenchman might call the courage of his faculty. The real daring which is shown in the *Pickwick Papers*, in the whole character of Mr. Weller senior, as well as in that of his son, is immense, far surpassing any which has been shown by any other contemporary writer. The brooding irregular mind is in its first stage prone to this sort of courage. It perhaps knows that its ideas are 'out of the way;' but with the infantine simplicity of youth it supposes that originality is an advantage. Persons more familiar with the ridicule of their equals in station (and this is to most men the great instructress of the college time) well know that of all qualities this one most requires to be clipped and pared and measured. Posterity, we doubt not, will be entirely perfect in every conceivable element of judgment; but the existing generation like what they have heard before—it is much easier. It required great courage in Mr. Dickens to write what his genius has compelled them to appreciate.

We have throughout spoken of Mr. Dickens as he was, rather than as he is; or, to use a less discourteous phrase, and we hope a truer, of his early works rather than of those which are more recent. We could not do otherwise consistently with the true code of criticism. A man of great genius, who has written great and enduring works, must be judged mainly by them; and not by the inferior productions which, from the necessities of personal position, a fatal facility of composition, or other cause, he may pour forth at moments less favourable to his powers. Those who are called on to review these inferior productions themselves, must speak of them in the terms they may deserve; but those who have the more pleasant task of estimating as a whole the genius of the writer, may confine their attention almost wholly to those happier efforts which illustrate that genius. We should not like to have to speak in detail of Mr. Dickens's later works, and we have not done so. There are, indeed, peculiar reasons why a genius constituted as his is (at least if we are correct in the view which we have taken of it) would not endure without injury during a long life the applause of the many, the temptations of composition, and the general excitement of existence. Even in his earlier works it was impossible not to fancy that there was a weakness of fibre unfavourable to the longevity of excellence. This was the effect of his deficiency in those masculine faculties of which we have said so much,—the reasoning understanding and firm far-seeing sagacity. It is these two component elements which stiffen the mind, and give a consistency to the creed and a coherence to its effects,—which enable it to protect itself from the rush of circumstances. If to a deficiency in these we add an extreme sensibility to circumstances,—a mobility, as Lord Byron used to call it, of emotion, which is easily impressed, and still more easily carried away by impression,—we have the idea of a character peculiarly unfitted to bear the flux of time and chance. A man of very great determination could hardly bear up against them with such slight aids from within and with such peculiar sensibility to temptation. A man of merely ordinary determination would succumb to it; and Mr. Dickens has succumbed. His position was certainly unfavourable. He has told us that the works of his later years, inferior as all good critics have deemed them, have yet been more read than those of his earlier and healthier years. The most characteristic part of his audience, the lower middle-class, were ready to receive with delight the least favourable productions of his genius. Human nature cannot endure this; it is too much to have to endure a coincident temptation both from within and from without. Mr. Dickens was too much inclined by natural disposition to lachrymose eloquence and exaggerated caricature. Such was the kind of writing which he wrote most easily. He found likewise that such was the kind of writing that was read most readily; and of course he wrote that kind. Who would have done otherwise? No critic is entitled to speak very harshly of such degeneracy, if he is not sure that he could have coped with difficulties so peculiar. If that rule is to be observed, who is there that will not be silent? No other Englishman has attained such a hold on the vast populace; it is little, therefore, to say that no other has surmounted its attendant temptations.

GEORGE HENRY LEWES
From "Dickens in Relation to Criticism"
Fortnightly Review, February 1872, pp. 143–49

There probably never was a writer of so vast a popularity whose genius was so little *appreciated* by the critics. The very splendour of his successes so deepened the shadow of his failures that to many eyes the shadows supplanted the splendour. Fastidious readers were loath to admit that a writer could be justly called great whose defects were so glaring. They admitted, because it was indisputable, that Dickens delighted thousands, that his admirers were found in all classes, and in all countries; that he stirred the sympathy of masses not easily reached through Literature, and always stirred healthy, generous emotions; that he impressed a new direction on popular writing, and modified the Literature of his age, in its spirit no less than in its form; but they nevertheless insisted on his defects as if these outweighed all positive qualities; and spoke of him either with condescending patronage, or with sneering irritation. Surely this is a fact worthy of investigation? Were the critics wrong, and if so, in what consisted their error? How are we to reconcile this immense popularity with this critical contempt? The private readers and the public critics who were eager to take up each successive number of his works as it appeared, whose very talk was seasoned with quotations from and allusions to these works, who, to my knowledge, were wont to lay aside books of which they could only speak in terms of eulogy, in order to bury themselves in the "new number" when the well-known green cover made its appearance—were nevertheless at this very time niggard in their praise, and lavish in their scorn of the popular humorist. It is not long since I heard a very distinguished man express measureless contempt for Dickens, and a few minutes afterwards, in reply to some representations on the other side, admit that Dickens had "entered into his life."

Dickens has proved his power by a popularity almost unexampled, embracing all classes. Surely it is a task for criticism to exhibit the sources of that power? If everything that has ever been alleged against the works be admitted, there still remains an immense success to be accounted for. It was not by their defects that these works were carried over Europe and America. It was not their defects which made them the delight of grey heads on the bench, and the study of youngsters in the counting-house and school-room. Other writers have been exaggerated, untrue, fantastic, and melodramatic; but they have gained so little notice that no one thinks of pointing out their defects. It is clear, therefore, that Dickens had powers which enabled him to triumph in spite of the weaknesses which clogged them; and it is worth inquiring what those powers were, and their relation to his undeniable defects.

I am not about to attempt such an inquiry, but simply to

indicate two or three general points of view. It will be enough merely to mention in passing the primary cause of his success, his overflowing fun, because even uncompromising opponents admit it. They may be ashamed of their laughter, but they laugh. A revulsion of feeling at the preposterousness or extravagance of the image may follow the burst of laughter, but the laughter is irresistible, whether rational or not, and there is no arguing away such a fact.

Great as Dickens is in fun, so great that Fielding and Smollett are small in comparison, he would have been only a passing amusement for the world had he not been gifted with an imagination of marvellous vividness, and an emotional, sympathetic nature capable of furnishing that imagination with elements of universal power. Of him it may be said with less exaggeration than of most poets, that he was of "imagination all compact;" if the other higher faculties were singularly deficient in him, this faculty was imperial. He was a seer of visions; and his visions were of objects at once familiar and potent. Psychologists will understand both the extent and the limitation of the remark, when I say that in no other perfectly sane mind (Blake, I believe, was not perfectly sane) have I observed vividness of imagination approaching so closely to hallucination. Many who are not psychologists may have had some experience in themselves, or in others, of that abnormal condition in which a man hears voices, and sees objects, with the distinctness of direct perception, although silence and darkness are without him; these *revived* impressions, revived by an internal cause, have precisely the same force and clearness which the impressions originally had when produced by an external cause. In the same degree of vividness are the images *constructed* by his mind in explanation of the voices heard or objects seen: when he imagines that the voice proceeds from a personal friend, or from Satan tempting him, the friend or Satan stands before him with the distinctness of objective reality; when he imagines that he himself has been transformed into a bear, his hands are seen by him as paws. In vain you represent to him that the voices he hears have no external existence; he will answer, as a patient pertinently answered Lélut: "You believe that I am speaking to you because you hear me, is it not so? Very well, I believe that voices are speaking to me because I hear them." There is no power of effacing such conviction by argument. You may get the patient to assent to any premises you please, he will not swerve from his conclusions. I once argued with a patient who believed he had been transformed into a bear; he was quite willing to admit that the idea of such a transformation was utterly at variance with all experience; but he always returned to his position that God being omnipotent there was no reason to doubt his power of transforming men into bears: what remained fixed in his mind was the image of himself under a bear's form.

The characteristic point in the hallucinations of the insane, that which distinguishes them from hallucinations equally vivid in the sane, is the coercion of the image in *suppressing comparison* and all control of experience. Belief always accompanies a vivid image, for a time; but in the sane this belief will not persist against rational control. If I see a stick partly under water, it is impossible for me not to have the same feeling which would be produced by a bent stick out of the water—if I see two plane images in the stereoscope, it is impossible not to have the feeling of seeing one solid object. But these beliefs are rapidly displaced by reference to experience. I know the stick is not bent, and that it will not appear bent when removed from the water. I know the seeming solid is not an object in relief, but two plane pictures. It is by similar focal adjustment of the mind that sane people know that their

hallucinations are unreal. The images may have the vividness of real objects, but they have not the properties of real objects, they do not preserve consistent relations with other facts, they appear in contradiction to other beliefs. Thus if I see a black cat on the chair opposite, yet on my approaching the chair feel no soft object, and if my terrier on the hearthrug looking in the direction of the chair shows none of the well-known agitation which the sight of a cat produces, I conclude, in spite of its distinctness, that the image is an hallucination.

Returning from this digression, let me say that I am very far indeed from wishing to imply any agreement in the common notion that "great wits to madness nearly are allied;" on the contrary, my studies have led to the conviction that nothing is less like genius than insanity, although some men of genius have had occasional attacks; and further, that I have never observed any trace of the insane temperament in Dickens's works, or life, they being indeed singularly free even from the eccentricities which often accompany exceptional powers; nevertheless, with all due limitations, it is true that there is considerable light shed upon his works by the action of the imagination in hallucination. To him also *revived* images have the vividness of sensations; to him also *created* images have the coercive force of realities, excluding all control, all contradiction. What seems preposterous, impossible to us, seemed to him simple fact of observation. When he imagined a street, a house, a room, a figure, he saw it not in the vague schematic way of ordinary imagination, but in the sharp definition of actual perception, all the salient details obtruding themselves on his attention. He, seeing it thus vividly, made us also see it; and believing in its reality however fantastic, he communicated something of his belief to us. He presented it in such relief that we ceased to think of it as a picture. So definite and insistent was the image, that even while knowing it was false we could not help, for a moment, being affected, as it were, by his hallucination.

This glorious energy of imagination is that which Dickens had in common with all great writers. It was this which made him a creator, and made his creations universally intelligible, no matter how fantastic and unreal. His types established themselves in the public mind like personal experiences. Their falsity was unnoticed in the blaze of their illumination. Every humbug seemed a Pecksniff, every nurse a Gamp, every jovial improvident a Micawber, every stinted serving-wench a Marchioness. Universal experiences became individualised in these types; an image and a name were given, and the image was so suggestive that it seemed to *express* all that it was found to *recall*, and Dickens was held to have depicted what his readers supplied. Against such power criticism was almost idle. In vain critical reflection showed these figures to be merely masks,— not characters, but personified characteristics, caricatures and distortions of human nature,—the vividness of their presentation triumphed over reflection: their creator managed to communicate to the public his own unhesitating belief. Unreal and impossible as these types were, speaking a language never heard in life, moving like pieces of simple mechanism always in one way (instead of moving with the infinite fluctuations of organisms, incalculable yet intelligible, surprising yet familiar), these unreal figures affected the uncritical reader with the force of reality; and they did so in virtue of their embodiment of some real characteristic vividly presented. The imagination of the author laid hold of some well-marked physical trait, some peculiarity of aspect, speech, or manner which every one recognised at once; and the force with which this was presented made it occupy the mind to the exclusion of all critical doubts: only reflection could detect the incongruity. Think of what this implies! Think how little the mass of men are given to reflect on their impressions, and how their minds are for the most part occupied with sensations rather than ideas, and you will see why Dickens held an undisputed sway. Give a child a wooden horse, with hair for mane and tail, and wafer spots for colouring, he will never be disturbed by the fact that this horse does not move its legs, but runs on wheels—the general suggestion suffices for his belief; and this wooden horse, which he can handle and draw, is believed in more than a pictured horse by a Wouvermanns or an Ansdell. It may be said of Dickens's human figures that they too are wooden, and run on wheels; but these are details which scarcely disturb the belief of admirers. Just as the wooden horse is brought within the range of the child's emotions, and dramatizing tendencies, when he can handle and draw it, so Dickens's figures are brought within the range of the reader's interests, and receive from these interests a sudden illumination, when they are the puppets of a drama every incident of which appeals to the sympathies. With a fine felicity of instinct he seized upon situations having an irresistible hold over the domestic affections and ordinary sympathies. He spoke in the mother-tongue of the heart, and was always sure of ready listeners. He painted the life he knew, the life every one knew; for if the scenes and manners were unlike those we were familiar with, the feelings and motives, the joys and griefs, the mistakes and efforts of the actors were universal, and therefore universally intelligible; so that even critical spectators who complained that these broadly painted pictures were artistic daubs, could not wholly resist their effective suggestiveness. He set in motion the secret springs of sympathy by touching the domestic affections. He painted nothing ideal, heroic; but all the resources of the bourgeois epic were in his grasp. The world of thought and passion lay beyond his horizon. But the joys and pains of childhood, the petty tyrannies of ignoble natures, the genial pleasantries of happy natures, the life of the poor, the struggles of the street and back parlour, the insolence of office, the sharp social contrasts, east-wind and Christmas jollity, hunger, misery, and hot punch—these he could deal with, so that we laughed and cried, were startled at the revelation of familiar facts hitherto unnoted, and felt our pulses quicken as we were hurried along with him in his fanciful flight.

Such were the sources of his power. To understand how it is that critics quite competent to recognise such power, and even so far amenable to it as to be moved and interested by the works in spite of all their drawbacks, should have forgotten this undenied power, and written or spoken of Dickens with mingled irritation and contempt, we must take into account two natural tendencies—the bias of opposition, and the bias of technical estimate.

The bias of opposition may be illustrated in a parallel case. Let us suppose a scientific book to be attracting the attention of Europe by the boldness, suggestiveness, and theoretic plausibility of its hypotheses; this work falls into the hands of a critic sufficiently grounded in the science treated to be aware that its writer, although gifted with great theoretic power and occasional insight into unexplored relations, is nevertheless pitiably ignorant of the elementary facts and principles of the science; the critic noticing the power, and the talent of lucid exposition, is yet perplexed and irritated at ignorance which is inexcusable, and a reckless twisting of known facts into impossible relations, which seems wilful; will he not pass from marvelling at this inextricable web of sense and nonsense, suggestive insight and mischievous error, so jumbled together that the combination of this sagacity with this glaring inefficiency is a paradox, and be driven by the anger of

opposition into an emphatic assertion that the belauded philosopher is a charlatan and an ignoramus? A chorus of admirers proclaims the author to be a great teacher, before whom all contemporaries must bow; and the critic observes this teacher on one page throwing out a striking hypothesis of some geometric relations in the planetary movements, and on another assuming that the hypothenuse is equal to its perpendicular and base, because the square of the hypothenuse is equal to the squares of its sides—in one chapter ridiculing the atomic theory, and in another arguing that carbonic acid is obtained from carbon and nitrogen—can this critic be expected to join in the chorus of admirers? and will he not rather be exasperated into an opposition which will lead him to undervalue the undeniable qualities in his insistance on the undeniable defects?

Something like this is the feeling produced by Dickens's works in many cultivated and critical readers. They see there human character and ordinary events pourtrayed with a mingled verisimilitude and falsity altogether unexampled. The drawing is so vivid yet so incorrect, or else is so blurred and formless, with such excess of *effort* (as of a showman beating on the drum) that the doubt arises how an observer so remarkably keen could make observations so remarkably false, and miss such very obvious facts; how the rapid glance which could swoop down on a peculiarity with hawk-like precision, could overlook all that accompanied and was organically related to that peculiarity; how the eye for characteristics could be so blind to character, and the ear for dramatic idiom be so deaf to dramatic language; finally, how the writer's exquisite susceptibility to the grotesque could be insensible to the occasional grotesqueness of his own attitude. Michael Angelo is intelligible, and Giotto is intelligible; but a critic is nonplussed at finding the invention of Angelo with the drawing of Giotto. It is indeed surprising that Dickens should have observed man, and not been impressed with the fact that man is, in the words of Montaigne, *un être ondoyant et diverse*. And the critic is distressed to observe the substitution of mechanisms for minds, puppets for characters. It is needless to dwell on such monstrous failures as Mantalini, Rosa Dartle, Lady Dedlock, Esther Summerson, Mr. Dick, Arthur Gride, Edith Dombey, Mr. Carker—needless, because if one studies the successful figures one finds even in them only touches of verisimilitude. When one thinks of Micawber always presenting himself in the same situation, moved with the same springs, and uttering the same sounds, always confident on something turning up, always crushed and rebounding, always making punch—and his wife always declaring she will never part from him, always referring to his talents and her family—when one thinks of the "catchwords" personified as characters, one is reminded of the frogs whose brains have been taken out for physiological purposes, and whose actions henceforth want the distinctive peculiarity of organic action, that of fluctuating spontaneity. Place one of these brainless frogs on his back and he will at once recover the sitting posture; draw a leg from under him, and he will draw it back again; tickle or prick him and he will push away the object, or take *one* hop out of the way; stroke his back, and he will utter *one* croak. All these things resemble the actions of the unmutilated frog, but they differ in being *isolated* actions, and *always the same:* they are as uniform and calculable as the movements of a machine. The uninjured frog may or may not croak, may or may not hop away; the result is never calculable, and is rarely a single croak or a single hop. It is this complexity of the organism which Dickens wholly fails to conceive; his characters have nothing fluctuating and incalculable in them, even when they embody true observations; and very often they are creations so fantastic that one is at a loss to understand how he could, without hallucination, believe them to be like reality. There are dialogues bearing the traces of straining effort at effect, which in their incongruity painfully resemble the absurd and eager expositions which insane patients pour into the listener's ear when detailing their wrongs, or their schemes. Dickens once declared to me that every word said by his characters was distinctly *heard* by him; I was at first not a little puzzled to account for the fact that he could hear language so utterly unlike the language of real feeling, and not be aware of its preposterousness; but the surprise vanished when I thought of the phenomena of hallucination. And here it may be needful to remark in passing that it is not because the characters are badly drawn and their language unreal, that they are to be classed among the excesses of imagination; otherwise all the bad novelists and dramatists would be credited with that which they especially want— powerful imagination. His peculiarity is not the incorrectness of the drawing, but the vividness of the imagination which while rendering that incorrectness insensible to him, also renders it potent with multitudes of his fellowmen. For although his weakness comes from excess in one direction, the force which is in excess must not be overlooked; and it is overlooked or undervalued by critics who, with what I have called the bias of opposition, insist only on the weakness.

FREDERIC HARRISON
From "Charles Dickens"
Studies in Early Victorian Literature
1895, pp. 133–44

Here lies the secret of his power over such countless millions of readers. He not only paints a vast range of ordinary humanity and suffering or wearied humanity, but he speaks for it and lives in it himself, and throws a halo of imagination over it, and brings home to the great mass of average readers a new sense of sympathy and gaiety. This humane kinship with the vulgar and the common, this magic which strikes poetry out of the dust of the streets, and discovers traces of beauty and joy in the most monotonous of lives, is, in the true and best sense of the term, Christ-like, with a message and gospel of hope. Thackeray must have had Charles Dickens in his mind when he wrote: "The humourous writer professes to awaken and direct your love, your pity, your kindness,— your scorn for untruth, pretension, imposture,—your tenderness for the weak, the poor, the oppressed, the unhappy." Charles Dickens, of all writers of our age, assuredly did this in every work of his pen, for thirty-three years of incessant production. It is his great title to honour; and a novelist can desire no higher title than this.

There is another quality in which Charles Dickens is supreme,—in purity. Here is a writer who is realistic, if ever any writer was, in the sense of having closely observed the lowest strata of city life, who has drawn the most miserable outcasts, the most abandoned men and women in the dregs of society, who has invented many dreadful scenes of passion, lust, seduction, and debauchery; and yet in forty works and more you will not find a page which a mother need withhold from her grown daughter. As Thackeray wrote of his friend: "I am grateful for the innocent laughter and the sweet and unsullied page which the author of *David Copperfield* gives to my children." We need not formulate any dogma or rule on

such a topic, nor is it essential that all books should be written *virginibus puerisque*; but it is certain that every word of Charles Dickens was so written, even when he set himself (as he sometimes did) to describe animal natures and the vilest of their sex. Dickens is a realist in that he probes the gloomiest recesses and faces the most disheartening problems of life: he is an idealist in that he never presents us the common or the vile with mere commonplace or repulsiveness, and without some ray of humane and genial charm to which ordinary eyes are blind. Dickens, then, was above all things a humourist, an inexhaustible humourist, to whom the humblest forms of daily life wore a certain sunny air of genial mirth; but the question remains if he was a humourist of the highest order: was he a poet, a creator of abiding imaginative types? Old Johnson's definition of humour as "grotesque imagery," and "grotesque" as meaning some distortion in figure, may not be adequate as a description of humour, but it well describes the essential feature of Charles Dickens. His infallible instrument is caricature,—which strictly means an "overload," as Johnson says, "an exaggerated resemblance." Caricature is a likeness having some comical exaggeration or distortion. Now, caricature is a legitimate and potent instrument of humour, which great masters have used with consummate effect. Leonardo da Vinci, Michael Angelo, Rembrandt, Hogarth, use it; but only at times, and in a subsidiary way. Rabelais, Swift, Fielding, use this weapon not unfrequently; Shakespeare very sparingly; Goldsmith and Scott, I think, almost never. Caricature, the essence of which is exaggeration of some selected feature, distortion of figure, disproportion of some part, is a potent resource, but one to which the greater masters resort rarely and with much moderation.

Now, with Charles Dickens caricature—that comical exaggeration of a particular feature, distortion of some part beyond nature—is not only the essence of his humour, but it is the universal and ever-present source of his mirth. It would not be true to say that exaggeration is the sole form of humour that he uses, but there is hardly a character of his to which it is not applied, nor a scene of which it is not the pervading "motive." Some feature, some oddity, some temperament is seized, dwelt upon, played with, and turned inside out, with incessant repetition and unwearied energy. Every character, except the walking gentleman and the walking lady, the insipid lover, or the colourless friend, have some feature thrust out of proportion, magnified beyond nature. Sam Weller never speaks without his anecdote, Uriah is always "'umble," Barkis is always "willin'," Mark Tapley is always "jolly," Dombey is always solemn, and Toots is invariably idiotic. It is no doubt natural that Barnaby's Raven should always want tea, whatever happens, for the poor bird has but a limited vocabulary. But one does not see why articulate and sane persons like Captain Cuttle, Pecksniff, and Micawber should repeat the same phrases under every condition and to all persons. This, no doubt, is the essence of farce: it may be irresistibly droll as farce, but it does not rise beyond farce. And at last even the most enthusiastic Pickwickian wearies of such monotony of iteration.

Now, the keynote of caricature being the distortion of nature, it inevitably follows that humourous exaggeration is unnatural, however droll; and, where it is the main source of the drollery, the picture as a whole ceases to be within the bounds of nature. But the great masters of the human heart invariably remain true to nature; not merely true to a selected feature, but to the natural form as a whole. Falstaff, in his wildest humour, speaks and acts as such a man really might speak and act. He has no catchphrase on which he harps, as if

THE CHELSEA HOUSE LIBRARY OF LITERARY CRITICISM

he were a talking-machine wound up to emit a dozen sounds. Parson Adams speaks and acts as such a being might do in nature. The comic characters of Goldsmith, Scott, or Thackeray do not outrun and defy nature, nor does their drollery depend on any special and abnormal feature, much less on any stock phrase which they use as a label. The illustrations of Cruikshank and Phiz are delightfully droll, and often caricatures of a high order. But being caricatures they overload and exaggerate nature, and indeed are always, in one sense, impossible in nature. The grins, the grimaces, the contortions, the dwarfs, the idiots, the monstrosities of these wonderful sketches could not be found in human beings constructed on any known anatomy. And Dickens's own characters have the same element of unnatural distortion. It is possible that these familiar caricatures have even done harm to his reputation. His creations are of a higher order of art and are more distinctly spontaneous and original. But the grotesque sketches with which he almost uniformly presented his books accentuate the element of caricature on which he relied; and often add an unnatural extravagance beyond that extravagance which was the essence of his own method.

The consequence is that everything in Dickens is "in the excess," as Aristotle would say, and not "in the mean." Whether it is Tony Weller, or "the Shepherd," or the Fat Boy, Hugh or the Raven, Toots or Traddles, Micawber or Skimpole, Gamp or Mantalini,—all are overloaded in the sense that they exceed nature, and are more or less extravagant. They are wonderful and delightful caricatures, but they are impossible in fact. The similes are hyperbolic; the names are grotesque; the incidents partake of harlequinade, and the speeches of roaring farce. It is often wildly droll, but it is rather the drollery of the stage than of the book. The characters are never possible in fact; they are not, and are not meant to be, nature; they are always and everywhere comic distortions of nature. Goldsmith's Dr. Primrose tells us that he chose his wife for the same qualities for which she chose her wedding gown. That is humour, but it is also pure, literal, exact truth to nature. David Copperfield's little wife is called a lap-dog, acts like a lap-dog, and dies like a lap-dog; the lap-dog simile is so much overdone that we are glad to get rid of her, and instead of weeping with Copperfield, we feel disposed to call him a ninny.

Nothing is more wonderful in Dickens than his exuberance of animal spirits, that inexhaustible fountain of life and gaiety, in which he equals Scott and far surpasses any other modern. The intensity of the man, his electric activity, his spasmodic nervous power, quite dazzle and stun us. But this restless gaiety too often grows fatiguing, as the rollicking fun begins to pall upon us, as the jokes ring hollow, and the wit gets stale by incessant reiteration. We know how much in real life we get to hate the joker who does not know when to stop, who repeats his jests, and forces the laugh when it does not flow freely. Something of the kind the most devoted of Dickens's readers feel when they take in too much at one time. None but the very greatest can maintain for long one incessant outpour of drollery, much less of extravagance. Aristophanes could do it; Shakespeare could do it; so could Cervantes; and so, too, Rabelais. But then, the wildest extravagance of these men is so rich, so varied, so charged with insight and thought, and in the case of Rabelais, so resplendent with learning and suggestion, that we never feel satiety and the cruel sense that the painted mask on the stage is grinning at us, whilst the actor behind it is weary and sad. When one who is not amongst the very greatest pours forth the same inextinguishable laughter in the same key, repeating the same tricks, and multiplying kindred oddities, people of cultivation enjoy it heartily once, twice, it

may be a dozen times, but at last they make way for the young bloods who can go thirty-seven times to see "Charley's Aunt."

A good deal has been said about Dickens's want of reading; and his enthusiastic biographer very fairly answers that Charles Dickens's book was the great book of life, of which he was an indefatigable student. When other men were at school and at college, he was gathering up a vast experience of the hard world, and when his brother writers were poring over big volumes in their libraries, he was pacing up and down London and its suburbs with inexhaustible energy, drinking in oddities, idiosyncrasies, and wayside incidents at every pore. It is quite true: London is a microcosm, an endless and bottomless Babylon; which, perhaps, no man has ever known so well as did Charles Dickens. This was his library: here he gathered that vast encyclopædia of human nature, which some are inclined to call "cockney," but if it be, "Cockayne" must be a very large country indeed. Still, the fact remains, that of book-learning of any kind Dickens remained, to the end of his days, perhaps more utterly innocent than any other famous English writer since Shakespeare. His biographer labours to prove that he had read Fielding and Smollett, Don Quixote and Gil Blas, The Spectator, and Robinson Crusoe. Perhaps he had, like most men who have learned to read. But, no doubt, this utter severance from books, which we feel in his tales, will ultimately tell against his immortality.

This rigid abstinence from books, which Dickens practised on system, had another reaction that we notice in his style. Not only do we feel in reading his novels that we have no reason to assume that he had ever read anything except a few popular romances, but we note that he can hardly be said to have a formed literary style of his own. Dickens had mannerisms, but hardly a style. In some ways, this is a good thing: much less can he be said to have a bad style. It is simply no style. He knows nothing of the crisp, modulated, balanced, and reserved mastery of phrase and sentence which marks Thackeray. Nor is it the easy simplicity of Robinson Crusoe and the Vicar of Wakefield. The tale spins along, and the incidents rattle on with the volubility of a good story-teller who warms up as he goes, but who never stops to think of his sentences and phrases. He often gets verbose, rings the changes on a point which he sees to have caught his hearers; he plays with a fancy out of measure, and turns his jest inside out and over and over, like a fine comic actor when the house is in a roar. His language is free, perfectly clear, often redundant, sometimes grandiloquent, and usually addressed more to the pit than to the boxes. And he is a little prone to slide, even in his own proper person, into those formal courtesies and obsolete compliments which forty years ago survived amongst the superior orders of bagmen and managing clerks.

There is an old topic of discussion whether Dickens could invent an organic and powerful plot, and carry out an elaborate scheme with perfect skill. It is certain that he has never done so, and it can hardly be said that he has ever essayed it. The serial form in parts, wherein almost all his stories were cast, requiring each number of three chapters to be "assorted," like sugar-plums, with grave and gay, so as to tell just enough but not too much, made a highly wrought scheme almost impossible. It is plain that Charles Dickens had nothing of that epical gift which gave us Tom Jones and Ivanhoe. Perhaps the persistent use of the serial form shows that he felt no interest in that supreme art of an immense drama duly unfolded to a prepared end. In Pickwick there neither was, nor could there be, any organic plot. In Oliver Twist, in Barnaby Rudge, in Dombey, in Bleak House, in the Tale of Two Cities, there are indications of his possessing this power, and in certains parts of these tales we seem to be in the presence of a great master of epical narration. But the power is not sustained; and it must be confessed that in none of these tales is there a complete and equal scheme. In most of the other books, especially in those after *Bleak House*, the plot is so artless, so *décousu*, so confused, that even practised readers of Dickens fail to keep it clear in their mind. The serial form, where a leading character wanders about to various places, and meets a succession of quaint parties, seems to be that which suited his genius and which he himself most entirely enjoyed.

In contrast with the Pickwickian method of comic rambles in search of human "curios," Dickens introduced some darker effects and persons of a more or less sensational kind. Some of these are as powerful as anything in modern fiction; and Fagin and Bill Sikes, Smike and poor Jo, the Gordon riots and the storms at sea, may stand beside some tableaux of Victor Hugo for lurid power and intense realism. But it was only at times and during the first half of his career that Dickens could keep clear of melodrama and somewhat stagey blue fire. And at times his blue fire was of a very cheap kind. Rosa Dartle and Carker, Steerforth and Blandois, Quilp and Uriah Heep, have a melancholy glitter of the footlights over them. We cannot see what the villains want, except to look villainous, and we fail to make out where is the danger to the innocent victims. We find the villain of the piece frantically struggling to get some paper, or to get hold of some boy or girl. But as the scene is in London in the nineteenth century, and not in Naples in the fifteenth century, we cannot see who is in real danger, or why, or of what. And with all this, Dickens was not incapable of bathos, or tragedy suddenly exploding in farce. The end of Krook by spontaneous combustion is such a case: but a worse case is the death of Dora, Copperfield's baby wife, along with that of the lapdog, Jip. This is one of those unforgotten, unpardonable, egregious blunders in art, in feeling, even in decency, which must finally exclude Charles Dickens from the rank of the true immortals.

But his books will long be read for his wonderful successes, and his weaker pieces will entirely be laid aside, as are the failures of so many great men, the rubbish of Fielding, of Goldsmith, of Defoe; which do nothing now to dim the glory of *Tom Jones*, *The Vicar of Wakefield*, and *Robinson Crusoe*. The glory of Charles Dickens will always be in his *Pickwick*, his first, his best, his inimitable triumph. It is true that it is a novel without a plot, without beginning, middle, or end, with much more of caricature than of character, with some extravagant tom-foolery, and plenty of vulgarity. But its originality, its irrepressible drolleries, its substantial human nature, and its intense vitality, place it quite in a class by itself. We can no more group it, or test it by any canon of criticism, than we could group or define *Pantagruel* or *Faust*. There are some works of genius which seem to transcend all criticism, of which the very extravagances and incoherences increase the charm. And *Pickwick* ought to live with *Gil Blas* and *Tristram Shandy*. In a deeper vein, the tragic scenes in *Oliver Twist* and in *Barnaby Rudge* must long hold their ground, for they can be read and reread in youth, in manhood, in old age. The story of Dotheboys Hall, the Yarmouth memories of Copperfield, little Nell, Mrs. Gamp, Micawber, Toots, Captain Cuttle, Pecksniff, and many more will long continue to delight the youth of the English-speaking races. But few writers are remembered so keenly by certain characters, certain scenes, incidental whimsies, and so little for entire novels treated strictly as works of art. There is no reason whatever for pretending that all these scores of tales are at all to be compared with the best of them, or that the invention of some inimitable scenes and characters

is enough to make a supreme and faultless artist. The young and the uncritical make too much of Charles Dickens, when they fail to distinguish between his best and his worst. Their fastidious seniors make too little of him, when they note his many shortcomings and fail to see that in certain elements of humour he has no equal and no rival. If we mean Charles Dickens to live we must fix our eye on these supreme gifts alone.

GEORGE GISSING
From "Humour and Pathos"
Charles Dickens: A Critical Study
1898, pp. 197–215

To write of Dickens at all, is to presuppose his humour. The plan of my essay has necessitated a separate consideration of the various features of his work, and at moments it may have appeared that I found fault without regard to a vast counterbalance; but it was never possible for me to lose sight of that supreme quality of his genius which must be now dwelt upon with undivided attention. It was as a humorist that Dickens made his name; and in a retrospect of his life's activity one perceives that his most earnest purposes depended for their furtherance upon this genial power, which he shares with nearly all the greatest of English writers. Holding, as he did, that the first duty of an author is to influence his reader for good, Dickens necessarily esteemed as the most precious of his gifts that by virtue of which he commanded so great an audience. Without his humour, he might have been a vigorous advocate of social reform, but as a novelist assuredly he would have failed; and as to the advocacy of far-reaching reforms by men who have only earnestness and eloquence to work with, English history tells its tale. Only because they laughed with him so heartily, did multitudes of people turn to discussing the question his page suggested. As a story-teller pure and simple, the powers that remain to him, if humour be subtracted, would never have ensured popularity. Nor, on the other hand, would they have availed him in the struggle for artistic perfection, which is a better thing. Humour is the soul of his work. Like the soul of man, it permeates a living fabric which, but for its creative breath, could never have existed.

In his earliest writing we discover only the suggestion of this quality. The *Sketches* have a touch of true humour, but (apart from the merits of acute observation and great descriptive power) there is much more of merely youthful high spirits, tending to the farcical. Such a piece as "The Tuggs's at Ramsgate" is distinct farce, and not remarkably good of its kind. This vein Dickens continued to work throughout his career, and often with great success. One must distinguish between the parts of his writing which stir to mere hilarity, and his humour in the strict sense of the word. It is none of my business to define that term, which has long ago been adequately expounded; enough that the humorist has by no means invariably a chuckle in his throat; at moments of his supreme success, he will hardly move us to more of merriment than appears in a thoughtful smile. But there is a perfectly legitimate, and tolerably wide, range for the capers of a laughing spirit, and as a writer of true farce I suppose Dickens has never been surpassed. *Pickwick* abounds in it, now quite distinct from, and now all but blending with, the higher characteristic. One can imagine that the public approval of his *Sketches* had given the author an impetus which carried him of a sudden into regions of extravagant buoyancy and mirthfulness. The first few pages are farce of the frankest. Winkle, Snodgrass, and Tupman remain throughout farcical characters, but not so Mr. Pickwick himself. Farce is the election at Eatanswill, and the quarrel of the rival Editors, and many another well-remembered passage. Only a man of genius has the privilege of being so emphatically young. "Though the merriment was rather boisterous, still it came from the heart and not from the lips; and this is the right sort of merriment after all." How could one better describe, than in these words from the book itself, that overflowing cheeriness which conquered Dickens's first public! Or take the description of old Wardle coming through the early sunshine to bid Mr. Pickwick good morning,—"out of breath with his own anticipations of pleasure". Alas! old gentlemen, however jolly, do not get breathless in this fashion; but the young may, and Dickens, a mere boy himself, was writing for the breathless boyhood of many an age to come.

The farce in his younger work always results from this exuberance of spirits; later, he introduces it deliberately; with conscious art—save perhaps at those moments when the impulse of satire is too much for him. One easily recalls his best efforts in this direction. The wild absurdity of the Muffin Company at the beginning of *Nickleby* shows him still in his boyish mood, and the first chapter of *Chuzzlewit* finds him unluckily reverting to it at the moment when he was about to produce a masterpiece of genuine humour. Mr. Mantalini is capital fun; he never quite loses his hold upon one, and to the end we shall laugh over the "demnition egg" and the "demnition bow-wows". At this stage Dickens was capable of a facetiousness of descriptive phrase which hints the peril involved in a reputation such as he had won. "Madame Mantalini wrung her hands for grief and rung the bell for her husband; which done, she fell into a chair and a fainting fit simultaneously." When he had written that passage, and allowed it to stand, his genius warned him; I remember nothing so dangerous in aftertime. Quilp, at his best, is rich entertainment; in Dick Swiveller we touch higher things. The scene between little David Copperfield and the waiter (chapter v) seems to me farce, though very good; country innkeepers were never in the habit of setting a dish-load of cutlets before a little boy who wanted dinner, and not even the shrewdest of waiters, having devoured them all, could make people believe that it was the little boy's achievement; but the comic vigour of the thing is irresistible. Better still is the forced marriage of Jack Bunsby to the great MacStinger. Here, I think, Dickens reaches his highest point. We cannot call it "screaming" farce; it appeals not only to the groundlings. Laughter holding both his sides was never more delightfully justified; gall and the megrims were never more effectually dispelled. It is the ludicrous in its purest form, tainted by no sort of unkindliness, and leaving behind it nothing but the wholesome aftertaste of self-forgetful mirth.

We may notice how Dickens makes use of farcical extravagance to soften the bitterness of truth. When Sally Brass goes down into the grimy cellar-kitchen to give the little slavey her food, we are told that she cut from the joint "two square inches of cold mutton", and bade her victim never say that she had not had meat in *that* house. This makes one laugh; who can refrain? If he had avoided exaggeration, and shown us the ragged, starving child swallowing the kind of meal which was really set before her, who could have endured it? The point is vastly important for an understanding of Dickens's genius and his popularity. That "two square inches" makes all the difference between painful realism and fiction universally acceptable; it is the secret of Dickens's power for good. Beside it may

be set another instance. Judy Smallweed, in *Bleak House*, likewise has her little slavey over whom she tyrannizes; a child, too, who has won our sympathy in a high degree, and whom we could not bear to see brutally used. She *is* brutally used; but then Judy Smallweed is a comical figure; so comical that no one takes her doings with seriousness. Harsh words and broken meats are again provocative of laughter, when in very truth we should sob. With Dickens's end in view, how wise his method! After merriment comes the thought: "But what a shame!" And henceforth the reader thinks sympathetically of poor little girls, whether ruled by vicious trollops or working under easier conditions. Omit the jest—and the story becomes too unpleasant to remember.

Between Dickens's farce and his scenes of humour the difference is obvious. In Mantalini or Jack Bunsby we have nothing illuminative; they amuse, and there the matter ends. But true humour always suggests a thought, always throws light on human nature. The humorist may not be fully conscious of his own meaning; he always, indeed, implies more than he can possibly have thought out; and therefore it is that we find the best humour inexhaustible, ever fresh when we return to it, ever, as our knowledge of life increases, more suggestive of wisdom. ⟨. . .⟩

Inseparable from the gift of humour is that of pathos. It was Dickens's misfortune that, owing to habits of his mind already sufficiently discussed, he sometimes elaborated pathetic *scenes*, in the theatrical sense of the word. I do not attribute to him the cold insincerity so common in the work of playwrights; but at times he lost self-restraint and unconsciously responded to the crude ideals of a popular audience. Emphasis and iteration, however necessary for such hearers, were out of place in pathetic narrative. Thus it comes about that he is charged with mawkishness, and we hear of some who greatly enjoy his humour rapidly turning the pages meant to draw a tear. Chiefly, I suppose, it is the death of Paul Dombey that such critics have in mind; they would point also to the death of Jo, the crossing-sweeper, and to that of little Nell. On a re-perusal of these chapters, I feel that nothing can be said in defence of Jo; on his death-bed he is an impossible creature, and here for once moral purpose has been undeniably fatal to every quality of art. Regarding the other narratives, it strikes me that they have been too hastily condemned. The one line which describes the death of Paul's mother is better, no doubt, than the hundreds through which we follow the fading of Paul himself; but these pages I cannot call mawkish, for I do not feel that they are flagrantly untrue. The tear may rise or not—that depends upon how we are constituted—but we are really standing by the bed of a gentle little child, precociously gifted and cruelly overwrought, and, if the situation is to be presented at all, it might be much worse done. Such pathos is called "cheap". I can only repeat that in Dickens's day, the lives, the happiness of children were very cheap indeed, and that he had his purpose in insisting on their claims to attention. As for the heroine of *The Old Curiosity Shop*, distaste for her as a pathetic figure seems to me unintelligent. She is a child of romance; her death is purely symbolical, signifying the premature close of any sweet, innocent, and delicate life. Heaven forbid that I should attribute to Dickens a deliberate allegory; but, having in mind those hapless children who were then being tortured in England's mines and factories, I like to see in Little Nell a type of their sufferings; she, the victim of avarice, dragged with bleeding feet along the hard roads, ever pursued by heartless self-interest, and finding her one safe refuge in the grave. Look back upon the close of that delightful novel, and who can deny its charm? Something I shall have to say presently about the literary style; but as a story of peaceful death it is beautifully imagined and touchingly told.

Of true pathos Dickens has abundance. The earliest instance I can call to mind is the death of the Chancery prisoner in *Pickwick*, described at no great length, but very powerful over the emotions. It worthily holds a place amid the scenes of humour enriching that part of the book. We feel intensely the contrast between the prisoner's life and that which was going on in the free world only a few yards away; we see in his death a pitifulness beyond words. A scene in another book,—*Bleak House*,—this, too, connected with that accursed system of imprisonment for debt, shows Dickens at his best in bringing out the pathos of child-life. The man known to Mr. Skimpole as "Coavinses" has died, and Coavinses' children, viewed askance by neighbours because of their father's calling, are living alone in a garret. They are presented as simply as possible—nothing here of stage emphasis—yet the eyes dazzle as we look. I must quote a line or two. "We were looking at one another," says Esther Summerson, "and at these two children, when there came into the room a very little girl, childish in figure but shrewd and older-looking in the face—pretty faced too—wearing a womanly sort of bonnet much too large for her, and drying her bare arms on a womanly sort of apron. Her fingers were white and wrinkled with washing, and the soap-suds were yet smoking which she wiped off her arms. But for this, she might have been a child playing at washing and imitating a poor working-woman with a quick observation of the truth." It is Charley, of course, who had found a way to support herself and the younger ones. We see how closely the true pathetic and a "quick observation" are allied. Another picture shown us in Esther's narrative, that of the baby's death in the starved labourer's cottage, moves by legitimate art. Still more of it is felt in the story of Doctor Marigold, the Cheap-Jack, whose child is dying in his arms, whilst for daily bread he plays buffoon before the crowd. This is a noble piece of work, and defies criticism. The tale is told by the man himself as simply as possible; he never insists upon the pitifulness of his position. We hear his whispers to the child, between his hoarse professional shoutings and the guffaws in front; then he finds his word of tenderness brings no response— he looks closer—he turns from the platform. A piece of work that might atone for literary sins far worse than Dickens ever committed.

Little Dorrit is strong in pathos, as in humour. Dickens's memories of childhood made his touch very sure whenever he dealt with the squalid prison-world, and life there was for him no less fertile in pathos than death. Very often it is inextricably blended with his humour; in the details of the Marshalsea picture, who shall say which element of his genius prevails? Yet, comparing it with the corresponding scenes in *Pickwick*, we perceive a subdual of tone, which comes not only of advancing years, but of riper art; and as we watch the Dorrits step forth from the prison door, it is another mood than that which accompanied the release of Mr. Pickwick. Pathos of this graver and subtler kind is the distinguishing note of *Great Expectations*, a book which Dickens meant, and rightly meant, to end in the minor key. The old convict, Magwitch, if he cannot be called a tragical personality, has feeling enough to move the reader's deeper interest, and in the very end acquires through suffering a dignity which makes him very impressive. Rightly seen, is there not much pathos in the story of Pip's foolishness? It would be more manifest if we could forget Lytton's imbecile suggestion, and restore the original close of the story.

To the majority of readers it seemed—and perhaps still seems—that Dickens achieved his best pathos in the Christmas books. Two of those stories answered their purpose admirably; the other two showed a flagging spirit; but not even in the *Carol* can we look for anything to be seriously compared with the finer features of his novels. The true value of these little books lies in their deliberate illustration of a theme which occupied Dickens's mind from first to last. Writing for the season of peace, good-will, and jollity, he sets himself to exhibit these virtues in an idealization of the English home. The type of domestic beauty he finds, as a matter of course, beneath a humble roof. And we have but to glance in memory through the many volumes of his life's work to recognize that his gentlest, brightest humour, his simplest pathos, occur in those unexciting pages which depict the everyday life of poor and homely English folk. This is Dickens's most delightful aspect, and I believe it is the most certainly enduring portion of what he has left us.

ALGERNON CHARLES SWINBURNE
From "Charles Dickens"
Quarterly Review, July 1902, pp. 20–32

It is only when such names as Shakespeare's or Hugo's rise and remain as the supreme witnesses of what was highest in any particular country at any particular time that there can be no question among any but irrational and impudent men as to the supremacy of their greatest. England, under the reign of Dickens, had other great names to boast of which may well be allowed to challenge the sovereignty of his genius. But as there certainly was no Shakespeare and no Hugo to rival and eclipse his glory, he will probably and naturally always be accepted and acclaimed as the greatest Englishman of his generation. His first works or attempts at work gave little more promise of such a future than if he had been a Coleridge or a Shelley. No one could have foreseen what all may now foresee in the *Sketches by Boz*—not only a quick and keen-eyed observer, 'a chiel amang us takin' notes' more notable than Captain Grose's, but a great creative genius. Nor could any one have foreseen it in the early chapters of *Pickwick*—which, at their best, do better the sort of thing which had been done fairly well before. Sam Weller and Charles Dickens came to life together, immortal and twin-born. In *Oliver Twist* the quality of a great tragic and comic poet or dramatist in prose fiction was for the first time combined with the already famous qualities of a great humorist and a born master in the arts of narrative and dialogue.

Like the early works of all other great writers whose critical contemporaries have failed to elude the kindly chance of beneficent oblivion, the early works of Dickens have been made use of to depreciate his later, with the same enlightened and impartial candour which on the appearance of *Othello* must doubtless have deplored the steady though gradual decline of its author's genius from the unfulfilled promise of excellence held forth by *Two Gentlemen of Verona*. There may possibly be some faint and flickering shadow of excuse for the dullards, if unmalignant, who prefer *Nicholas Nickleby* to the riper and sounder fruits of the same splendid and inexhaustible genius. Admirable as it is, full of life and sap and savour, the strength and the weakness of youth are so singularly mingled in the story and the style that readers who knew nothing of its date might naturally have assumed that it must have been the writer's first attempt at fiction. There is perhaps no question which would more thoroughly test the scholarship of the student than this:—What do you know of Jane Dibabs and Horatio Peltiogrus? At fourscore and ten it might be thought 'too late a week' for a reader to revel with insuppressible delight in a first reading of the chapters which enrol all worthy readers in the company of Mr Vincent Crummles; but I can bear witness to the fact that this effect was produced on a reader of that age who had earned honour and respect in public life, affection and veneration in private. It is not, on the other hand, less curious and significant that Sydney Smith, who had held out against Sam Weller, should have been conquered by Miss Squeers; that her letter, which of all Dickens's really good things is perhaps the most obviously imitative and suggestive of its model, should have converted so great an elder humorist to appreciation of a greater than himself; that the echo of familiar fun, an echo from the grave of Smollett, should have done what finer and more original strokes of comic genius had unaccountably failed to do. But in all criticism of such work the merely personal element of the critic, the natural atmosphere in which his mind or his insight works, and uses its faculties of appreciation, is really the first and last thing to be taken into account.

No mortal man or woman, no human boy or girl, can resist the fascination of Mr and Mrs Quilp, of Mr and Miss Brass, of Mr Swiveller and his Marchioness; but even the charm of Mrs Jarley and her surroundings, the magic which enthrals us in the presence of a Codlin and a Short, cannot mesmerise or hypnotise us into belief that the story of *The Old Curiosity Shop* is in any way a good story. But it is the first book in which the background or setting is often as impressive as the figures which can hardly be detached from it in our remembered impression of the whole design. From Quilp's Wharf to Plashwater Weir Mill Lock, the river belongs to Dickens by right of conquest or creation. The part it plays in more than a few of his books is indivisible from the parts played in them by human actors beside it or upon it. Of such actors in this book, the most famous as an example of her creator's power as a master of pathetic tragedy would thoroughly deserve her fame if she were but a thought more human and more credible. 'The child' has never a touch of childhood about her; she is an impeccable and invariable portent of devotion, without a moment's lapse into the humanity of frailty in temper or in conduct. Dickens might as well have fitted her with a pair of wings at once. A woman might possibly be as patient, as resourceful, as indefatigable in well-doing and as faultless in perception of the right thing to do; it would be difficult to make her deeply interesting, but she might be made more or less of an actual creature. But a child whom nothing can ever irritate, whom nothing can ever baffle, whom nothing can ever misguide, whom nothing can ever delude, and whom nothing can ever dismay, is a monster as inhuman as a baby with two heads.

Outside the class which excludes all but the highest masterpieces of poetry it is difficult to find or to imagine a faultless work of creation—in other words, a faultless work of fiction; but the story of *Barnaby Rudge* can hardly, in common justice, be said to fall short of this crowning praise. And in this book, even if not in any of its precursors, an appreciative reader must recognise a quality of humour which will remind him of Shakespeare, and perhaps of Aristophanes. The impetuous and irrepressible volubility of Miss Miggs, when once her eloquence breaks loose and finds vent like raging water or fire, is powerful enough to overbear for the moment any slight objection which a severe morality might suggest with respect to the rectitude and propriety of her conduct. It is impossible to be rigid in our judgment of

a toiling, moiling, constant-working, always-being-found-fault-with, never-giving-satisfactions, nor-having-no-time-to-clean-oneself, potter's wessel,' whose 'only becoming occupations is to help young flaunting pagins to brush and comb and titivate theirselves into whitening and suppulchres, and leave the young men to think that there an't a bit of padding in it nor no pinching-ins nor fillings-out nor pomatums nor deceits nor earthly wanities.

To have made malignity as delightful for an instant as simplicity, and Miss Miggs as enchanting as Mrs Quickly or Mrs Gamp, is an unsurpassable triumph of dramatic humour.

But the advance in tragic power is even more notable and memorable than this. The pathos, indeed, is too cruel; the tortures of the idiot's mother and the murderer's wife are so fearful that interest and sympathy are wellnigh superseded or overbalanced by a sense of horror rather than of pity; magnificent as is the power of dramatic invention which animates every scene in every stage of her martyrdom. Dennis is the first of those consummate and wonderful ruffians, with two vile faces under one frowsy hood, whose captain or commander-in-chief is Rogue Riderhood; more fearful by far, though not (one would hope) more natural, than Henriet Cousin, who could hardly breathe when fastening the rope round Esmeralda's neck, 'tant la chose l'apitoyait'; a divine touch of surviving humanity which would have been impossible to the more horrible hangman whose mortal agony in immediate prospect of the imminent gallows is as terribly memorable as anything in the tragedy of fiction or the poetry of prose. His fellow hangbird is a figure no less admirable throughout all his stormy and fiery career till the last moment; and then he drops into poetry. Nor is it poetry above the reach of Silas Wegg which 'invokes the curse of all its victims on that black tree, of which he is the ripened fruit.' The writer's impulse was noble; but its expression or its effusion is such as indifference may deride and sympathy must deplore. Twice only did the greatest English writer of his day make use of history as a background or a stage for fiction; the use made of it in *Barnaby Rudge* is even more admirable in the lifelike tragedy and the terrible comedy of its presentation than the use made of it in A *Tale of Two Cities*.

Dickens was doubtless right in his preference of 'David Copperfield' to all his other masterpieces; it is only among dunces that it is held improbable or impossible for a great writer to judge aright of his own work at its best, to select and to prefer the finest and the fullest example of his active genius; but, when all deductions have been made from the acknowledgment due to the counter-claim of *Martin Chuzzlewit*, the fact remains that in that unequal and irregular masterpiece his comic and his tragic genius rose now and then to the very highest pitch of all. No son of Adam and no daughter of Eve on this God's earth, as his occasional friend Mr Carlyle might have expressed it, could have imagined it possible—humanly possible—for anything in later comedy to rival the unspeakable perfection of Mrs Quickly's eloquence at its best; at such moments as when her claim to be acknowledged as Lady Falstaff was reinforced, if not by the spiritual authority of Master Dumb, by the correlative evidence of Mrs Keech; but no reader above the level of intelligence which prefers to Shakespeare the Parisian Ibsen and the Norwegian Sardou can dispute the fact that Mrs Gamp has once and again risen even to that unimaginable supremacy of triumph.

At the first interview vouchsafed to us with the adorable Sairey, we feel that no words can express our sense of the divinely altruistic and devoted nature which finds utterance in the sweetly and sublimely simple words—'If I could afford to lay all my feller creeturs out for nothink, I would gladly do it: sich is the love I bear 'em.' We think of little Tommy Harris, and the little red worsted shoe gurgling in his throat; of the previous occasion when his father sought shelter and silence in an empty dog-kennel; of that father's immortally infamous reflection on the advent of his ninth; of religious feelings, of life, and the end of all things; of Mr Gamp, his wooden leg, and their precious boy; of her calculations and her experiences with reference to birth and death; of her views as to the expediency of travel by steam, which anticipated Ruskin's and those of later dissenters from the gospel of hurry and the religion of mechanism; of the contents of Mrs Harris's pocket; of the incredible incredulity of the infidel Mrs Prig; we think of all this, and of more than all this, and acknowledge with infinite thanksgiving of inexhaustible laughter and of rapturous admiration the very greatest comic poet or creator that ever lived to make the life of other men more bright and more glad and more perfect than ever, without his beneficent influence, it possibly or imaginably could have been.

The advance in power of tragic invention, the increased strength in grasp of character and grip of situation, which distinguishes Chuzzlewit from Nickleby, may be tested by comparison of the leading villains. Ralph Nickleby might almost have walked straight off the boards on which the dramatic genius of his nephew was employed to bring into action two tubs and a pump: Jonas Chuzzlewit has his place of eminence for ever among the most memorable types of living and breathing wickedness that ever were stamped and branded with immortality by the indignant genius of a great and unrelenting master. Neither Vautrin nor Thénardier has more of evil and of deathless life in him.

It is not only by his masterpieces, it is also by his inferior works or even by his comparative failures that the greatness of a great writer may be reasonably judged and tested. We can measure in some degree the genius of Thackeray by the fact that *Pendennis*, with all its marvellous wealth of character and humour and living truth, has never been and never will be rated among his very greatest works. *Dombey and Son* cannot be held nearly so much of a success as *Pendennis*. I have known a man of the very highest genius and the most fervent enthusiasm for that of Dickens who never could get through it. There is nothing of a story, and all that nothing (to borrow a phrase from Martial) is bad. The Roman starveling had nothing to lose, and lost it all: the story of Dombey has no plot, and that a very stupid one. The struttingly offensive father and his gushingly submissive daughter are failures of the first magnitude. Little Paul is a more credible child than little Nell; he sometimes forgets that he is foredoomed by a more than Pauline or Calvinistic law of predestination to die in the odour of sentiment, and says or thinks or does something really and quaintly childlike. But we get, to say the least, a good deal of him; and how much too little do we get of Jack Bunsby! Not so very much more than of old Bill Barley; and yet those two ancient mariners are berthed for ever in the inmost shrine of our affections. Another patch of the very brightest purple sewn into the sometimes rather threadbare stuff or groundwork of the story is the scene in which the dissolution of a ruined household is so tragicomically set before us in the breaking up of the servants' hall. And when we think upon the cherished names of Toots and Nipper, Gills and Cuttle, Rob the Grinder and good Mrs Brown, we are tempted to throw conscience to the winds, and affirm that the book is a good book.

But even if we admit that here was an interlude of comparative failure, we cannot but feel moved to acclaim with all the more ardent gratitude the appearance of the next and perhaps the greatest gift bestowed on us by this magnificent and immortal benefactor. *David Copperfield*, from the first chapter to the last, is unmistakable by any eye above the level and beyond the insight of a beetle's as one of the masterpieces to which time can only add a new charm and an unimaginable value. The narrative is as coherent and harmonious as that of *Tom Jones*; and to say this is to try it by the very highest and apparently the most unattainable standard. But I must venture to reaffirm my conviction that even the glorious masterpiece of Fielding's radiant and beneficent genius, if in some points superior, is by no means superior in all. Tom is a far completer and more living type of gallant boyhood and generous young manhood than David; but even the lustre of Partridge is pallid and lunar beside the noontide glory of Micawber. Blifil is a more poisonously plausible villain than Uriah: Sophia Western remains unequalled except by her sister heroine Amelia as a perfectly credible and adorable type of young English womanhood, naturally 'like one of Shakespeare's women,' socially as fine and true a lady as Congreve's Millamant or Angelica. But even so large-minded and liberal a genius as Fielding's could never have conceived any figure like Miss Trotwood's, any group like that of the Peggottys. As easily could it have imagined and realised the magnificent setting of the story, with its homely foreground of street or wayside and its background of tragic sea.

The perfect excellence of this masterpiece has perhaps done some undeserved injury to the less impeccable works of genius which immediately succeeded it. But in *Bleak House* the daring experiment of combination or alternation which divides a story between narrative in the third person and narrative in the first is justified and vindicated by its singular and fascinating success. 'Esther's narrative' is as good as her creator's; and no enthusiasm of praise could overrate the excellence of them both. For wealth and variety of character none of the master's works can be said to surpass and few can be said to equal it. When all necessary allowance has been made for occasional unlikeliness in detail or questionable methods of exposition, the sustained interest and the terrible pathos of Lady Dedlock's tragedy will remain unaffected and unimpaired. Any reader can object that a lady visiting a slum in the disguise of a servant would not have kept jewelled rings on her fingers for the inspection of a crossing-sweeper, or that a less decorous and plausible way of acquainting her with the fact that a scandalous episode in her early life was no longer a secret for the family lawyer could hardly have been imagined than the public narrative of her story in her own drawing-room by way of an evening's entertainment for her husband and their guests. To these objections, which any Helot of culture whose brain may have been affected by habitual indulgence in the academic delirium of self-complacent superiority may advance or may suggest with the most exquisite infinity of impertinence, it may be impossible to retort an equally obvious and inconsiderable objection.

But to a far more serious charge, which even now appears to survive the confutation of all serious evidence, it is incomprehensible and inexplicable that Dickens should have returned no better an answer than he did. Harold Skimpole was said to be Leigh Hunt; a rascal after the order of Wainewright, without the poisoner's comparatively and diabolically admirable audacity of frank and fiendish self-esteem, was assumed to be meant for a portrait or a caricature of an honest man and a man of unquestionable genius. To this most serious and most disgraceful charge Dickens merely replied that he never anticipated the identification of the rascal Skimpole with the fascinating Harold—the attribution of imaginary villainy to the original model who suggested or supplied a likeness for the externally amiable and ineffectually accomplished lounger and shuffler through life. The simple and final reply should have been that indolence was the essential quality of the character and conduct and philosophy of Skimpole—'a perfectly idle man: a mere amateur,' as he describes himself to the sympathetic and approving Sir Leicester; that Leigh Hunt was one of the hardest and steadiest workers on record, throughout a long and chequered life, at the toilsome trade of letters; and therefore that to represent him as a heartless and shameless idler would have been about as rational an enterprise, as lifelike a design after the life, as it would have been to represent Shelley as a gluttonous and canting hypocrite or Byron as a loyal and unselfish friend. And no one as yet, I believe, has pretended to recognise in Mr Jarndyce a study from Byron, in Mr Chadband a libel on Shelley.

Of the two shorter novels which would suffice to preserve for ever the fame of Dickens, some readers will as probably always prefer *Hard Times* as other will prefer *A Tale of Two Cities*. The later of these is doubtless the most ingeniously and dramatically invented and constructed of all the master's works; the earlier seems to me the greater in moral and pathetic and humorous effect. The martyr workman, beautiful as is the study of his character and terrible as is the record of his tragedy, is almost too spotless a sufferer and a saint; the lifelong lapidation of this unluckier Stephen is somewhat too consistent and insistent and persistent for any record but that of a martyrology; but the obdurate and histrionic affectation which animates the brutality and stimulates the selfishness of Mr Bounderby is only too lamentably truer and nearer to the unlovely side of life. Mr Ruskin—a name never to be mentioned without reverence—thought otherwise; but in knowledge and insight into character and ethics that nobly minded man of genius was no more comparable to Dickens that in sanity of ardour and rationality of aspiration for progressive and practical reform.

As a social satirist Dickens is usually considered to have shown himself at his weakest; the curious and seemingly incorrigible ignorance which imagined that the proper title of Sir John Smith's wife was Lady John Smith, and that the same noble peer could be known to his friends and parasites alternately as Lord Jones and Lord James Jones, may naturally make us regret the absence from their society of our old Parisian friend Sir Brown, Esquire; but though such singular designations as these were never rectified or removed from the text of 'Nicholas Nickleby,' and though a Lady Kew was as far outside the range of his genius as a Madame Marneffe, his satire of social pretension and pretence was by no means always 'a swordstroke in the water' or a flourish in the air. Mrs Sparsit is as typical and immortal as any figure of Molière's; and the fact that Mr Sparsit was a Powler is one which can never be forgotten.

There is no surer way of testing the greatness of a really great writer than by consideration of his work at its weakest, and comparison of that comparative weakness with the strength of lesser men at their strongest and their best. The romantic and fanciful comedy of *Love's Labour's Lost* is hardly a perceptible jewel in the sovereign crown of Shakespeare; but a single passage in a single scene of it—the last of the fourth act—is more than sufficient to outweigh, to outshine, to eclipse and efface for ever the dramatic lucubrations or prescriptions of Dr Ibsen—Fracastoro of the drama—and his volubly grateful patients. Among the mature works of Dickens and of Thackeray, I suppose most readers would agree in the opinion

that the least satisfactory, if considered as representative of the author's incomparable powers, are *Little Dorrit* and *The Virginians*; yet no one above the intellectual level of an Ibsenite or a Zolaist will doubt or will deny that there is enough merit in either of these books for the stable foundation of an enduring fame.

The conception of *Little Dorrit* was far happier and more promising than that of *Dombey and Son*; which indeed is not much to say for it. Mr Dombey is a doll; Mr Dorrit is an everlasting figure of comedy in its most tragic aspect and tragedy in its most comic phase. Little Dorrit herself might be less untruly than unkindly described as Little Nell grown big, or, in Milton's phrase, 'writ large.' But on that very account she is a more credible and therefore a more really and rationally pathetic figure. The incomparable incoherence of the parts which pretend in vain to compose the incomposite story may be gauged by the collapse of some of them and the vehement hurry of cramped and halting invention which huddles up the close of it without an attempt at the rational and natural evolution of others. It is like a child's dissected map with some of the counties or kingdoms missing. Much, though certainly not all, of the humour is of the poorest kind possible to Dickens; and the reiterated repetition of comic catchwords and tragic illustrations of character is such as to affect the nerves no less than the intelligence of the reader with irrepressible irritation. But this, if he be wise, will be got over and kept under by his sense of admiration and of gratitude for the unsurpassable excellence of the finest passages and chapters. The day after the death of Mr Merdle is one of the most memorable dates in all the record of creative history—or, to use one word in place of two, in all the record of fiction. The fusion of humour and horror in the marvellous chapter which describes it is comparable only with the kindred work of such creators as the authors of *Les Misérables* and *King Lear*. And nothing in the work of Balzac is newer and truer and more terrible than the relentless yet not unmerciful evolution of the central figure in the story. The Father of the Marshalsea is so pitiably worthy of pity as well as of scorn that it would have seemed impossible to heighten or to deepen the contempt or the compassion of the reader; but when he falls from adversity to prosperity he succeeds in soaring down and sinking up to a more tragicomic ignominy of more aspiring degradation. And his end is magnificent.

It must always be interesting as well as curious to observe the natural attitude of mind, the inborn instinct of intelligent antipathy or sympathy, discernible or conjecturable in the greatest writer of any nation at any particular date, with regard to the characteristic merits or demerits of foreigners. Dickens was once most unjustly taxed with injustice to the French, by an evidently loyal and cordial French critic, on the ground that the one Frenchman of any mark in all his books was a murderer. The polypseudonymous ruffian who uses and wears out as many stolen names as ever did even the most cowardly and virulent of literary poisoners is doubtless an unlovely figure: but not even Mr Peggotty and his infant niece are painted with more tender and fervent sympathy than the good Corporal and little Bebelle. Hugo could not—even omnipotence has its limits—have given a more perfect and living picture of a hero and a child. I wish I could think he would have given it as the picture of an English hero and an English child. But I do think that Italian readers of *Little Dorrit* ought to appreciate and to enjoy the delightful and admirable personality of Cavalletto. Mr Baptist in Bleeding Heart Yard is as attractively memorable a figure as his excellent friend Signor Panco.

And how much more might be said—would the gods annihilate but time and space for a worthier purpose than that of making two lovers happy—of the splendid successes to be noted in the least successful book or books of this great and inexhaustible writer! And if the figure or development of the story in *Little Dorrit*, the shapeliness in parts or the proportions of the whole, may seem to have suffered from tight-lacing in this part and from padding in that, the harmony and unity of the masterpiece which followed it made ample and magnificent amends. In *A Tale of Two Cities* Dickens, for the second and last time, did history the honour to enrol it in the service of fiction. This faultless work of tragic and creative art has nothing of the rich and various exuberance which makes of *Barnaby Rudge* so marvellous an example of youthful genius in all the glowing growth of its bright and fiery April; but it has the classic and poetic symmetry of perfect execution and of perfect design. One or two of the figures in the story which immediately preceded it are unusually liable to the usually fatuous objection which dullness has not yet grown decently ashamed of bringing against the characters of Dickens: to the charge of exaggeration and unreality in the posture or the mechanism of puppets and of daubs, which found its final and supremely offensive expression in the chattering duncery and the impudent malignity of so consummate and pseudosophical a quack as George Henry Lewes. Not even such a past-master in the noble science of defamation could plausibly have dared to cite in support of his insolent and idiotic impeachment either the leading or the supplementary characters in *A Tale of Two Cities*. The pathetic and heroic figure of Sydney Carton seems rather to have cast into the shade of comparative neglect the no less living and admirable figures among and over which it stands and towers in our memory. Miss Pross and Mr Lorry, Madame Defarge and her husband, are equally and indisputably to be recognised by the sign of eternal life.

Among the highest landmarks of success ever reared for immortality by the triumphant genius of Dickens, the story of *Great Expectations* must for ever stand eminent beside that of *David Copperfield*. These are his great twin masterpieces.

Great as they are, there is nothing in them greater than the very best things in some of his other books: there is certainly no person preferable and there is possibly no person comparable to Samuel Weller or to Sarah Gamp. Of the two childish and boyish autobiographers, David is the better little fellow though not the more lifelike little friend; but of all first chapters is there any comparable for impression and for fusion of humour and terror and pity and fancy and truth to that which confronts the child with the convict on the marshes in the twilight? And the story is incomparably the finer story of the two; there can be none superior, if there be any equal to it, in the whole range of English fiction. And except in *Vanity Fair* and *The Newcomes*, if even they may claim exception, there can surely be found no equal or nearly equal number of living and everliving figures. The tragedy and the comedy, the realism and the dreamery of life, are fused or mingled together with little less than Shaksperean strength and skill of hand. To have created Abel Magwitch is to be a god indeed among the creators of deathless men. Pumblechook is actually better and droller and truer to imaginative life than Pecksniff: Joe Gargery is worthy to have been praised and loved at once by Fielding and by Sterne: Mr Jaggers and his clients, Mr Wemmick and his parent and his bride, are such figures as Shakespeare, when dropping out of poetry, might have created, if his lot had been cast in a later century. Can as much be said for the creatures of any other man or god? The ghastly tragedy of Miss Havisham could only have been made at once credible and endurable by Dickens; he alone could have reconciled the strange and sordid horror with the noble and pathetic survival of possible emotion and repentance. And he alone could have eluded condemnation for so gross an oversight as the escape from retribution of so important a criminal as the 'double murderer and monster' whose baffled or inadequate attempts are enough to make Bill Sikes seem comparatively the gentlest and Jonas Chuzzlewit the most amiable of men. I remember no such flaw in any other story I ever read. But in this story it may well have been allowed to pass unrebuked and unobserved; which yet I think it should not.

GEORGE ELIOT

GEORGE ELIOT
Mary Ann Evans
1819–1880

George Eliot was born Mary Ann (later Marian) Evans in Arbury, Warwickshire, on November 22, 1819. The daughter of an agent for an estate in Warwickshire, she attended schools in Griff, Attleborough, Nuneaton, and Coventry between 1824 and 1835. While at school she became a convert to Evangelicalism, which she later renounced under the influence of Charles Bray, a freethinking manufacturer whom she first met in 1841. Still strongly attracted by religious concepts of love and duty, in 1844 she began a translation of Strauss's *Das Leben Jesu*, which appeared anonymously in 1846 as *The Life of Jesus, Critically Examined*.

In 1849 Evans made her first trip to the Continent, accompanied by the Brays. After returning to England in 1850 she met John Chapman, who had published her translation of Strauss, and in 1851 she became a paying guest in the Chapmans' London home, where her infatuation with Chapman proved an embarrassment. In that same year Chapman purchased the *Westminster Review*, which Evans helped edit, and to which she contributed regularly. In 1854 Evans published a translation of Feuerbach's *The Essence of Christianity*. By this time she had entered into a relationship with George Henry Lewes, a married man, with whom she began living after they returned from a trip to Germany in 1854, the first of many trips to the Continent they were to make together over the next twenty years.

Having begun to write fiction only a year earlier, in 1857 Evans published "The Sad Fortunes of the Rev. Amos Barton," the first of the *Scenes of Clerical Life*. This appeared in *Blackwood's Edinburgh Magazine* under the pseudonym "George Eliot," as did two other pieces, "Mr. Gilfil's Love-Story" and "Janet's Repentance," published later that same year. These works were well received, and there was much speculation as to the identity of the author, who was widely believed to be a clergyman or a clergyman's wife. In 1859 Evans published *Adam Bede*, which immediately established her as a leading novelist. It was followed by *The Mill on the Floss* in 1860 and *Silas Marner* in 1861. In 1860 Evans visited Florence, where she conceived the idea for *Romola* (1863), a novel that began to appear in serial form in *Cornhill Magazine* in 1862. *Felix Holt* was published in 1866 and was followed in 1868 by *The Spanish Gypsy*, a dramatic poem inspired by Tintoretto. *Middlemarch* appeared in installments in 1871–72, as did *Daniel Deronda*, her last great novel, in 1874–76. *The Legend of Jubal and Other Poems* was published in 1874.

In November 1878 George Henry Lewes died of cancer. Two years later, in May 1880, Evans married John Cross, a man twenty years her junior whom she had met in Rome and who had subsequently become her financial advisor. Shortly afterwards she was taken seriously ill, and on December 22, 1880, she died, leaving incomplete the *Impressions of Theophrastus Such*. At the time of her death George Eliot was widely regarded as the greatest contemporary English novelist; but soon afterwards her reputation began somewhat to decline. At the present time she is once again held in high critical esteem. *The George Eliot Letters*, edited by Gordon S. Haight, appeared in seven volumes in 1954–55, and *The Essays of George Eliot*, edited by Thomas Pinney, were published in 1963.

Personal

Miss Evans (who wrote *Adam Bede*) was the daughter of a steward, and gained her exact knowledge of English rural life by the connection with which this origin brought her with the farmers. She was entirely self-educated, and has made herself an admirable scholar in classical as well as in modern languages. Those who knew her had always recognized her wonderful endowments, and only watched to see in what way they would develop themselves. She is a person of the simplest manners and character, amiable and unpretending.—NATHANIEL HAWTHORNE, *The French and Italian Note-Books*, Feb. 5, 1860

She is delightful in a *tête-à-tête*, and speaks in a soft soprano voice, which almost sounds like a fine falsetto, with her strong masculine face.—HALLAM TENNYSON, *Journal* (July 22, 1871), cited in Hallam Tennyson, *Alfred Lord Tennyson: A Memoir*, 1897, Vol. 2, p. 107

Mrs. Lewes is all genius and culture. Had she never written a page of fiction, nay, had she never written a line of poetry or prose, she must have been regarded with wonder and admiration by all who knew her as a woman of vast and varied knowledge; a woman who could think deeply and talk brilliantly, who could play high and severe classical music like a professional performer, and could bring forth the most delicate and tender aroma of nature and poetry lying deep in the heart of some simple, old-fashioned Scotch or English ballad. Nature, indeed, seemed to have given to this extraordinary woman all the gifts a woman could ask or have—save one. It will not, I hope, be considered a piece of gossiping personality if I allude to a fact which must, some day or other, be part of literary history. Mrs. Lewes is not beautiful. In her appearance there is nothing whatever to attract admiration.—JUSTIN MCCARTHY, "'George Eliot' and George Lewes," *Modern Leaders*, 1872, p. 137

However much I may lament the circumstance, Westminster Abbey is a Christian Church and not a Pantheon, and the Dean thereof is officially a Christian priest, and we ask him to bestow exceptional Christian honours by this burial in the Abbey. George Eliot is known not only as a great writer, but as a person whose life and opinions were in notorious antagonism to Christian practice in regard to marriage, and Christian theory in regard to dogma. How am I to tell the Dean that I think he ought to read over the body of a person who did not repent of what the Church considers moral sin, a service not one solitary proposition in which she would have accepted for truth while she was alive? How am I to urge him to do that which, if I were in his place, I should most emphatically refuse to do?

You tell me that Mrs. Cross wished for the funeral in the Abbey. While I desire to entertain the greatest respect for her wishes, I am very sorry to hear it. I do not understand the feeling which could create such a desire on any personal grounds, save those of affection, and the natural yearning to be near even in death to those whom we have loved. And on public grounds the wish is still less intelligible to me. One cannot eat one's cake and have it too. Those who elect to be free in thought and deed must not hanker after the rewards, if they are to be so called, which the world offers to those who put up with its fetters.

Thus, however I look at the proposal it seems to me to be a profound mistake, and I can have nothing to do with it. —THOMAS HENRY HUXLEY, Letter to Herbert Spencer (Dec. 27, 1880), cited in Leonard Huxley, *Life and Letters of Thomas Henry Huxley*, 1900, Vol. 2, p. 19

It is difficult for any one admitted to the great honor of friendship with either Mr. Lewes or George Eliot to speak of their home without seeming intrusive, in the same way that he would have been who, unauthorized, introduced visitors, yet something may be said to gratify a curiosity which surely is not now impertinent or ignoble. When London was full, the little drawing-room in St. John's Wood was now and then crowded to overflowing with those who were glad to give their best of conversation, of information, and sometimes of music, always to listen with eager attention to whatever their hostess might say, when all that she said was worth hearing. Without a trace of pedantry, she led the conversation to some great and lofty strain. Of herself and her works she never spoke; of the works and thoughts of others she spoke with reverence, and sometimes even too great tolerance. But those afternoons had the highest pleasure when London was empty or the day wet, and only a few friends were present, so that her conversation assumed a more sustained tone than was possible when the rooms were full of shifting groups. It was then that, without any premeditation, her sentences fell as fully formed, as wise, as weighty, as epigrammatic, as any to be found in her books. Always ready, but never rapid, her talk was not only good in itself, but it encouraged the same in others, since she was an excellent listener, and eager to hear. Yet interesting as seemed to her, as well as to those admitted to them, her afternoons in London, she was always glad to escape when summer came, either for one of the tours on the Continent in which she so delighted, or lately to the charming home she had made in Surrey. She never tired of the lovely scenery about Witley, and the great expanse of view obtainable from the tops of the many hills.—C. KEGAN PAUL, "George Eliot," *Harper's New Monthly Magazine*, May 1881, p. 921

The Life of Marian Evans had much I never knew—a Doom of Fruit without the Bloom, like the Niger Fig.

> Her Losses make our Gains ashamed—
> She bore Life's empty Pack

> As gallantly as if the East
> Were swinging at her Back.
> Life's empty Pack is heaviest,
> As every Porter knows—
> In vain to punish Honey—
> It only sweeter grows.
> —EMILY DICKINSON, Letter to Thomas Niles (April 1883)

During all her later life the central and organic idea which gave unity to her existence was a burning love for her fellow-men. I have somewhere seen that in conversation she once said to a friend: "What I look to is a time when the impulse to help our fellows shall be as immediate and as irresistible as that which I feel to grasp something firm if I am falling;" and the narrator of this speech adds that at the end of it she grasped the mantel-piece as if actually saving herself from a fall, with an intensity which made the gesture most eloquent.

You will observe that of the two commandments in which the Master summed up all duty and happiness,—namely, to love the Lord with all our heart, soul and mind and to love our neighbor as ourself, George Eliot's whole life and work were devoted to the exposition of the latter. She has been blamed for devoting so little attention to the former; as for me, I am too heartily grateful for the stimulus of human love which radiates from all her works to feel any sense of lack or regret.—SIDNEY LANIER, *The English Novel*, 1883, p. 301

I may mention here that my wife told me the reason she fixed on this name was that George was Mr. Lewes's Christian name, and Eliot was a good mouth-filling, easily pronounced word.—JOHN W. CROSS, *George Eliot's Life as Related in Her Letters and Journals*, 1884, Vol. 1, p. 310

She had long features, and would have been called plain but for her solemn, earnest eyes, which had an expression quite in keeping with her voice, which was one not easily forgotten. I never detected in her any trace of genial humour, though I doubt not that it was latent in her; and I thought her a person who had drawn her ideas far more from books and an acquaintance with certain types of humanity whom she had set herself deliberately to study—albeit with rare perception—than from an easy intuitive familiarity with all sorts and conditions of men. But she worked out *thoroughly* what she knew by the intuition of genius, though in this she was very far inferior to Scott. Thus she wrote the *Spanish Gypsy*, having only seen such gypsies two or three times. One day she told me that in order to write *Daniel Deronda*, she had read through two hundred books. I longed to tell her that she had better have learned Yiddish and talked with two hundred Jews, and been taught, as I was by my friend Solomon the Sadducee, the art of distinguishing Fräulein Löwenthal of the Ashkenazim from Senorita Aguado of the Sephardim *by the corners of their eyes!*—CHARLES GODFREY LELAND, *Memoirs*, 1893, p. 390

General

It is impossible to read *Adam Bede* without thinking of *Jane Eyre*, and yet there are no points of likeness between these two works save the mystery in which they were at first wrapped, and the sex of the authors to whom we owe them. Miss Brontë's novel has more dash, more vigor, more eloquence; and I am not sure whether there is anything to be found in Miss Evans's work equal to Jane Eyre's flight when, after leaving Rochester's house, she wanders at random, the victim of a conflict of feelings dominated by the inexorable authority of duty. But here Miss Brontë's superiority ceases. She soon betrays her want of experience. She flies to melodramatic devices; her creations have more strength than truth; and, in short, what remains of her book after a second reading is no great thing. It is quite otherwise with Miss Evans; in her novels everything is simple, mature, finished, and it is scarcely possible to re-read them without discovering fresh beauties.

Besides, after *Jane Eyre* Charlotte Brontë merely repeated herself; while her rival has as yet given no sign of exhaustion. I have mentioned the surprises which George Eliot sprang on the public, but the public had not yet come to the end of them. After recovering from the excitement caused by so great a merit and so great a success, readers (who are soon tired of admiration) said to themselves that it was their turn. "Let us wait and see," said they, "what her next work will be like." The next work was not long delayed. *The Mill on the Floss* appeared a year after *Adam Bede*, and the most fastidious criticism was obliged to acknowledge that, if there was a little less finish in the new-comer, the power and talent which it showed were not less. Yet another year—less than a year—has passed away, and *Silas Marner* comes to show in its turn that the author, among the other secrets of genius, possesses that of fecundity. —EDMOND SCHERER, "George Eliot" (1861), *Essays on English Literature*, tr. George Saintsbury, 1891, pp. 5–6

It is one of the greatest merits of the greatest living writer of fiction—of the authoress of *Adam Bede*—that she never brings you to anything without preparing you for it; she has no loose lumps of beauty; she puts in nothing at random; after her greatest scenes, too, a natural sequence of subordinate realities again tones down the mind to this sublunary world. Her logical style—the most logical, probably, which a woman ever wrote—aids in this matter her natural sense of due proportion. There is not a space of incoherency—not a gap. It is not natural to begin with the point of a story, and she does not begin with it. When some great marvel has been told, we all wish to know what came of it, and she tells us. Her natural way, as it seems to those who do not know its rarity, of telling what happened produces the consummate effect of gradual enchantment and as gradual disenchantment.—WALTER BAGEHOT, "Sterne and Thackeray" (1864), *Collected Works*, ed. Norman St. John-Stevas, 1965, Vol. 2, pp. 289–90

It is not in her conceptions nor her composition that George Eliot is strongest: it is in her *touches*. In these she is quite original. She is a good deal of a humorist, and something of a satirist; but she is neither Dickens nor Thackeray. She has over them the great advantage that she is also a good deal of a philosopher; and it is to this union of the keenest observation with the ripest reflection, that her style owes its essential force. She is a thinker,—not, perhaps, a passionate thinker, but at least a serious one; and the term can be applied with either adjective neither to Dickens nor Thackeray. The constant play of lively and vigorous thought about the objects furnished by her observation animates these latter with a surprising richness of color and a truly human interest. It gives to the author's style, moreover, that lingering, affectionate, comprehensive quality which is its chief distinction; and perhaps occasionally it makes her tedious. George Eliot is so little tedious, however, because, if, on the one hand, her reflection never flags, so, on the other, her observation never ceases to supply it with material. Her observation, I think, is decidedly of the feminine kind: it deals, in preference, with small things. This fact may be held to explain the excellence of what I have called her pictures, and the comparative feebleness of her dramatic movement.—HENRY JAMES, "The Novels of George Eliot," *Atlantic*, Oct. 1866, p. 488

There is enough easy pleasantry in George Eliot's novels to explain the constant assertion of the critics that she is a humorist. Yet is she not rather a wit? Is there not more wit than humor in the pungent sayings of Mrs. Poyser? The sense of incongruity which lies at the bottom of all fun finds most often with George Eliot, as with Mrs. Poyser, its best expression in a keen incisiveness which lays bare the truth, rather than in the soft light of drollery that illuminates it. When she says that there is in men and women a capacity for sorrow which distinguishes them from the most human chimpanzee or orang-outang, we feel the full force of a power in its natural use; but the "Florentine Joke" is one of those attempts at protracted dramatic humor in which we see the appreciation of the ludicrous that raised the conception, and yet cannot enjoy the execution. The night attack of Maurice Christian on the brains of the half-crazy, drunken Tommy does not provoke to laughter, and no one can help feeling a sympathy with the perpetrator, who yawns over it before going to bed.

But an odder thing in George Eliot than any attempts of such a kind is that she should so often have called in the assistance of Dickens. If there was one thing in the world that seemed certain, it was that she would not, could not, imitate, yet constantly she has imitated Dickens. There was a quaint form of humor that he introduced, and of which every one has now a large supply on hand, both for purposes of conversation and for writing, which enveloped familiar ideas, the more familiar the idea the better, in a suave, elaborate diction, which could give an absurd look to anything. It delighted him to pay out his thoughts with grandiose detail and meaningless circumlocution, and to feel the surprise of those who grasped the end to find that they had hold of spool cotton, instead of an electric cable. This manner has grown a little monotonous, even in his hands, and has been trodden to death by so many other's feet that there seems no reason why so cautious an analyzer as George Eliot should have fallen into it. That she should have done so is one of the highest triumphs of Dickens. It was a stern literary fate that forced a person so rich in expression into copying the peculiarities, of all others, which had been hackneyed by every crumb-eater who needed out-door relief.—ARTHUR SEDGWICK, "*Felix Holt, the Radical*," *North American Review*, Oct. 1866, pp. 562–63

Not less injurious, in its way, to dramatic perfection is the system of minute and deliberate analysis pursued by George Eliot. It makes us look to her books rather for instances of her remarkable acumen, and the terse statement of her perceptions, than for a sympathetic rendition of human nature that shall charm and soothe us, at the same time that it instructs or educates. Her writing does not soothe, because she keeps so constantly before us the stern effort she is making, not to swerve from strict analysis. The authoress presides too watchfully over the progress of our acquaintance with the imaginary beings to whom she has introduced us; and we should be more at ease, if she would omit some of the more wordy of her examinations into their mental status at each new turn of the story. There are instances of fine dramatic handling in her books, from which we may cite those culminating scenes between Stephen Guest and Maggie Tulliver, in *The Mill on the Floss*. But these superior passages only throw forward upon our notice the too frequent consciousness and restraint which disturb her work. The novelist, it is true, must observe a certain economy, holding back the more telling dramatic effects for particular passages. But the difference should be in the degree, rather than in the quality, of dramatic force; a kind of difference well exemplified in Hawthorne's *Scarlet Letter*. George Eliot's open analysis, too, has a tendency to lead her insensibly into partiality, a thing which she is by this very means strenuously trying to avoid. That tendency she has almost wholly overcome in *Middlemarch*, which is distinguished for a fine impartiality. But it is in this same crowning work that we find, perhaps more strongly exemplified than in any other of her books, the final defect of her system. In a book of this kind all that can be said about the characters *is* said; but, after all, the result is not so good as if something had been withheld, for our imaginations to reach after. Despite the vigorous bloom, the insistent life of *Middlemarch*, do we not feel that there is an overwrought completion about it? The persons of the story are elaborated almost to exhaustion; there appears to be a lack of proportion in the prominence so fully accorded to each individual in his or her turn, for minor characters are dwelt upon too much in detail; and there is little or no mystery of distance about any of the figures, at any time. We have struck bottom, with these people, beyond hope of recalling that thought of illimitably profound humanity which indicates the unknown quantity in character, and which gives Shakespeare's personages their lasting title to our love or consideration. The secret of dramatic effect is simply this, that in real life ultimate truth seldom finds a pure utterance. In drama, therefore, we have a situation presented as nearly as possible (subject to æsthetic laws) in the way in which it would present itself in the fact; the involved truths of the whole proceeding being illustrated by the partial expressions of each individual, on his own behalf or in estimating his fellows; so that the final, fleeting essence of the matter lies within the scope of inference only. And in proportion as dramatic skill is successful, it stimulates in us the disposition and ability to make such inference. But George Eliot would cut us off from this last spiritual, intangible result, by reducing everything to absolute statement, and endeavoring to fix the final issues in penetrating and permanent phrases. I would not underrate the magnificent obligations which George Eliot has laid upon the race; my admiration of her brave and noble genius is in no way lessened by the opinion that her method restricts the range and power of the novel unnecessarily. As an effort of clear intellectual penetration into life, we could hardly demand anything better than *Middlemarch*. But it is still too much an effort, and not enough an accomplished insight; it remains, as the author has called it, a study, rather than a finished dramatic representation.—GEORGE PARSONS LATHROP, "Growth of the Novel," *Atlantic*, June 1874, pp. 688–89

I set out with saying that George Eliot makes no distinctive impression for herself of sex, either in her intellectual or in her moral quality. This, when I consider her, as I undertook to do, in her books alone, still seems to me to be true. But as often as I permit myself to consider her likewise in her reputed relation to that school of philosophy which teaches the ancient doctrine of necessity, under the modern name of development, I tend somehow to experience an almost contrary feeling. There is apparently a contrast here between George Eliot and her brethren in philosophical faith. Her attitude is not altogether the same as theirs toward the creed which they unite in confessing. Her brethren believe with the head, and, so far as appears, do not doubt with the heart. George Eliot assents, perhaps unquestioningly, with her head. But her heart demurs and rebels. It is a woman's voice after all that one hears crying that monotonous passionate cry throughout George Eliot's works—a cry of helpless grief, of outraged, implacable sense of wrong, against this great, deaf, impassible universe. Not that her mind is therefore less. It is only that therefore her heart is more. And our George Eliot is still by so much greater than we found her, by how much she proves after all to be a woman.

—WILLIAM CLEAVER WILKINSON, "The Literary and Ethical Quality of George Eliot's Novels," A *Free Lance in the Field of Life and Letters*, 1874, p. 49

George Eliot's metrical work has special interest, coming from a woman acknowledged to be, in her realistic yet imaginative prose, at the head of living female writers. She has brought all her energies to bear, first upon the construction of a drama, which was only a *succès d'estime*, and recently upon a new volume containing "The Legend of Jubal" and other poems. The result shows plainly that Mrs. Lewes, though possessed of great intellect and sensibility, is not, in respect to metrical expression, a poet. Nor has she a full conception of the simple strength and melody of English verse, her polysyllabic language, noticeable in the moralizing passages of *Middlemarch*, being very ineffective in her poems. That wealth of thought which atones for all her deficiencies in prose does not seem to be at her command in poetry. *The Spanish Gypsy* reads like a second-rate production of the Byronic school. "The Legend of Jubal" and "How Lisa Loved the King" suffer by comparison with the narrative poems, in rhymed pentameter, of Morris, Longfellow, or Stoddard. A little poem in blank-verse, entitled "O may I join the choir invisible!" and setting forth her conception of the "religion of humanity," is worth all the rest of her poetry, for it is the outburst of an exalted soul, foregoing personal immortality and compensated by a vision of the growth and happiness of the human race.—EDMUND CLARENCE STEDMAN, *Victorian Poets*, 1875, p. 254

The fiction of this second period has one really great name, and one only. The author of *Adam Bede* and *The Mill on the Floss* stands on a literary level with Dickens and Thackeray and Charlotte Brontë. "George Eliot," as this author chooses to call herself, is undoubtedly a great writer, merely as a writer. Her literary career began as a translator and an essayist. Her tastes seemed then to lead her wholly into the somewhat barren fields where German metaphysics endeavor to come to the relief, or the confusion, of German theology. She became a contributor to the *Westminster Review*; then she became its assistant editor, and worked assiduously for it under the direction of Dr. John Chapman, the editor. She had mastered many sciences as well as literatures. Probably no other novel-writer, since novel-writing became a business, ever possessed anything like her scientific knowledge. Unfortunately, her scientific knowledge "o'er informed" her later novels, and made them oppressive to readers who longed for the early freshness of *Adam Bede*. George Eliot does not seem to have found out, until she had passed what is conventionally regarded as the age of romance, that she had in her, high above all other gifts, the faculty of the novelist. When an author who is not very young makes a great hit at last, we soon begin to learn that he had already made many attempts in the same direction, and his publishers find an eager demand for the stories and sketches which, when they first appeared, utterly failed to attract attention. But it does not seem that Miss Marian Evans, as she then was, ever published anything in the way of fiction previous to the series of sketches which appeared in *Blackwood's Magazine*, and were called *Scenes of Clerical Life*. These sketches attracted considerable attention, and were much admired; but not many people probably saw in them the capacity which produced *Adam Bede* and *Romola*. With the publication of *Adam Bede* came a complete triumph. The author was elevated at once and by acclamation to the highest rank among living novelists. In one of the first numbers of the *Cornhill Magazine*, Thackeray, in a gossiping paragraph about novelists of the day, whom he mentioned alphabetically and by their initials, spoke of "E" as a "star of the first magnitude just risen on the horizon." Nothing is much rarer than the union of the scientific and the literary or artistic temperaments. So rare is it that the exceptional, the almost solitary instance of Goethe comes up at once, distinct and striking to the mind. English novelists are even less likely to have anything of a scientific taste than French or German. Dickens knew nothing of science, and had, indeed, as little knowledge of any kind, save that which is derived from observation, as any respectable Englishman could well have. Thackeray was a man of varied reading, versed in the lighter literature of several languages, and strongly imbued with artistic tastes; but he had no care for science, and knew of it only what every one has to learn at school. Lord Lytton's science was a mere sham. Charlotte Brontë was genius and ignorance. George Eliot is genius and culture. Had she never written a page of fiction, she must have been regarded with admiration by all who knew her as a woman of deep thought and of a varied knowledge such as men complacently believe to be the possession only of men. It was not this, however, which made her a great novelist. Her eyes were not turned inward, or kept down in metaphysical contemplation. She studied the living world around her. She had an eye for external things keen almost as that of Dickens or Balzac. George Eliot is the only novelist who can paint such English people as the Poysers and the Tullivers just as they are. She looks into the very souls of such people. She tracks out their slow, peculiar mental processes; she reproduces them fresh and firm from very life. Mere realism, mere photographing, even from the life, is not in art a great triumph. But George Eliot can make her dullest people interesting and dramatically effective. She can paint two dull people with quite different ways of dulness—a dull man and a dull woman, for example—and the reader is astonished to find how utterly distinct the two kinds of stupidity are, and how intensely amusing both can be made. ⟨. . .⟩ George Eliot has infused into the novel some elements it never had before; and so thoroughly infused them, that they blend with all the other materials, and do not form anywhere a solid lump or mass distinguishable from the rest. There are philosophical novels—*Wilhelm Meister*, for example—which are weighed down and loaded with philosophy, and which the world only admires in spite of the philosophy. There are political novels—Lord Beaconsfield's, for instance—which are only intelligible to those who make politics and political personalities a study, and which viewed merely as stories would not be worth speaking about. There are novels with a great direct purpose in them, such as *Uncle Tom's Cabin*, or *Bleak House*, or Mr. Charles Reade's *Hard Cash*. But these, after all, are only magnificent pamphlets, splendidly illustrated diatribes. The deep philosophic thought of George Eliot's best novels quietly suffuses and illumines them everywhere. There is no sermon here, no lecture there, no solid mass interposing between this incident and that, no ponderous moral hung around the neck of this or that personage. The reader feels that he is under the spell of one who is not merely a great story-teller, but who is also a deep thinker.—JUSTIN MC-CARTHY, *A History of Our Own Times*, 1879–80, Ch. 67

> If each for each be all he can,
> A very God is man to man.

Every one of George Eliot's works might be read as a commentary on that text. In each there is a moral crisis, which depends on some strong efflux of the feeling of human fellowship—sometimes pouring forth unchecked, but with unwonted energy, and sometimes overcoming the counter impulses of egoistic pleasure or pain,—some selfish craving, some angered pride, some wounded and bleeding love. I need not recall each individual instance. Throughout the earlier novels, where there is less of visible purpose and more of mere humorous portraiture than in the later ones, this lesson nevertheless is always recurring. *Romola*, the most laboriously executed of all her works,—the book which, as she said, "she began a young woman and ended an old one,"—is almost from first to last one strain of grave insistence on the human bond. Or consider especially her poems; for these, though often failing in that instinctive melody which is the indispensable birth-gift of poets, are yet the most concentrated expression of herself which she has left behind her. The poems move through more ideal scenes, but they enforce the self-same lesson; they teach that as the mounting spirit becomes more conscious of its own being, it becomes more conscious also of the bonds which unite it to its kin; that thus the higher a man is, the closer he is drawn to the lowest, and greatness is not an exemption, but a debt the more.—F. W. H. MYERS, "George Eliot," *Modern Essays*, 1883

At the present moment George Eliot is the first of English novelists, and I am disposed to place her second of those of my time. She is best known to the literary world as a writer of prose fiction, and not improbably whatever of permanent fame she may acquire will come from her novels. But the nature of her intellect is very far removed indeed from that which is common to the tellers of stories. Her imagination is no doubt strong, but it acts in analysing rather than in creating. Everything that comes before her is pulled to pieces so that the inside of it shall be seen, and be seen if possible by her readers as clearly as by herself. This searching analysis is carried so far that, in studying her latter writings, one feels oneself to be in company with some philosopher rather than with a novelist. I doubt whether any young person can read with pleasure either *Felix Holt*, *Middlemarch*, or *Daniel Deronda*. I know that they are very difficult to many that are not young.

Her personifications of character have been singularly terse and graphic, and from them has come her great hold on the public,—though by no means the greatest effect which she has produced. The lessons which she teaches remain, though it is not for the sake of the lessons that her pages are read. Seth Bede, Adam Bede, Maggie and Tom Tulliver, old Silas Marner, and, much above all, Tito, in *Romola*, are characters which, when once known, can never be forgotten. I cannot say quite so much for any of those in her later works, because in them the philosopher so greatly overtops the portrait-painter, that, in the dissection of the mind, the outward signs seem to have been forgotten. In her, as yet, there is no symptom whatever of that weariness of mind which, when felt by the reader, induces him to declare that the author has written himself out. It is not from decadence that we do not have another Mrs. Poyser, but because the author soars to things which seem to her to be higher than Mrs. Poyser.

It is, I think, the defect of George Eliot that she struggles too hard to do work that shall be excellent. She lacks ease. Latterly the signs of this have been conspicuous in her style, which has always been and is singularly correct, but which has become occasionally obscure from her too great desire to be pungent. It is impossible not to feel the struggle, and that feeling begets a flavour of affectation. In *Daniel Deronda*, of which at this moment only a portion has been published, there are sentences which I have found myself compelled to read three times before I have been able to take home to myself all that the writer has intended. Perhaps I may be permitted here to say, that this gifted woman was among my dearest and most intimate friends.—ANTHONY TROLLOPE, *An Autobiography*, 1883, Ch. 13

Religion even to George Eliot is not an inner power of Divine mystery awakening the conscience. It is at best an intellectual exercise, or a scenic picture, or a beautiful memory. Her early Evangelicalism peeled off her like an outer garment, leaving behind only a rich vein of dramatic experience which she afterwards worked into her novels. There is no evidence of her great change having produced in her any spiritual anxiety. There is nothing indeed in autobiography more wonderful than the facility with which this remarkable woman parted first with her faith and then with the moral sanctions which do so much to consecrate life, while yet constantly idealising life in her letters, and taking such a large grasp of many of its moral realities. Her scepticism and then her eclectic Humanitarianism have a certain benignancy and elevation unlike vulgar infidelity of any kind. There are gleams of a much higher life everywhere in her thought. There is much self-distrust, but no self-abasement. There is a strange externality,—as if the Divine had never come near to her save by outward form or picture,—never pierced to any dividing asunder of soul and spirit. Amidst all her sadness—and her life upon the whole is a very sad one—there are no depths of spiritual dread (of which dramatically—as in *Romola*—she had yet a vivid conception), or even of spiritual tenderness.—JOHN TULLOCH, *Movements of Religious Thought in Britain during the Nineteenth Century*, 1885

(Charles Reade) had no stomach for the fulsome eulogy piled on George Eliot, the less so because it became an open secret that this bold advertisement was the outcome of judicious wire-pulling. As an artist he conceived it the right of every member of his craft to demand a fair field and no favor. No marvel, therefore, if when, stung by a keen sense of injustice, he delivered himself rather slightingly of the idol before whom, at the bidding of her own Nebuchadnezzar behind the scenes, the entire press of England did obeisance.—CHARLES L. READE, COMPTON READE, *Charles Reade: A Memoir*, 1887, pp. 301–2

George Eliot was, indisputably, a woman of genius, but her writings (the popular verdict to the contrary notwithstanding) include, at most, only one novel of the first rank. Her excellence is in her wise sayings. The tune she plays is trivial; the merit is in the variations.—WALTER LEWIN, "The Abuse of Fiction," *Forum*, Aug. 1889, p. 665

It remains for me to sum up in this last chapter the principal characteristics of George Eliot's art, the lines of development which it followed, and the aims which she set herself in working it out. For this purpose her poetry may be set on one side. It was always subordinate to her prose and, as has been maintained in the foregoing pages, was mainly a concentrated form of expression specially adapted to her more subtle and imaginative thoughts. To deal, then, with her novels: Which of them do we rank the highest? It would probably be difficult to get any large number of people to unite in the same conclusion. The popular vote, as shown by the publishers' account books, is, I believe, in favour of *Adam Bede*. It is not difficult to understand this. The title of the novel—the names of the first created man and of the first English writer—strikes the keynote of its character. The scene is laid in the heart of the Midlands. The story is a simple tale of a thoughtless boy and a ruined girl—simple yet full of tragic pathos. The deeper thought of the book is expressed in the forms of Puritanism, like all deeper thought in the great mass of English people. It is the wittiest of George Eliot's novels. It

is written straight out of her own life. Adam Bede was her father, Dinah was her aunt, the name Poyser seems to be compounded of the names of her mother and her stepmother. The story of Hetty was a true one, and may have lain nearer to her heart than is generally supposed. All this goes to justify the popular verdict. Like the ancient wrestler, she drew her strength from mother earth, and in no book did she touch mother earth so closely.

But although this is the popular, it is not the universal opinion. Men of letters, I believe, give the palm to *Silas Marner*. They are attracted by the exquisite workmanship of the story. The plot was constructed by George Eliot out of the merest hint. The story was written in haste, at one gush. It is a perfect gem—a pure work of art, in which the demands of art have alone to be considered. A large class of admirers would give their vote to *Romola*. It is, as I have said before, perhaps, the best historical novel ever written. Replete with learning, weighted with knowledge in every page, the finish is so rare that the joints between erudition and imagination cannot be discovered. Read it when you have never been to Florence, it will make you long to go there; read it when you have learnt to love Florence, it will make you love Florence more; read it when you have studied the Renaissance, which George Eliot had studied so deeply, and you will feel its beauties as those feel the beauties of a symphony of Beethoven who know the score by heart. There is the character of Tito, so special yet so universal, the creature of his own age and yet the creature of any age, the embodiment of weak selfishness which knows not where it goes, now and ever the most fruitful cause of human misery; and Romola herself, a saint living in the world, a prototype of Dorothea. Yet, say others, the book has great inherent faults. All historical novels are inartistic; they are bad, as historical pictures are bad, as programme music is bad. No historical picture represents the scene as it actually occurred; no music ever realized to us the sound of a storm, a nightingale, or a quail. The armour of erudition encumbers the limbs; the wise man, like the brave brothers in *Princess Ida*, throws it off when he goes into action. Again, the novel is not a true picture of Italian life. Men who have lived long in Italy, and have drunk deeply of its spirit, complain that they cannot read the book with pleasure. The life of Tuscany which it describes is to them a nightmare, a Frankenstein, an artificial monster, not living flesh and blood.

I might quote the highest authority for the superiority of *Middlemarch*, in which George Eliot returns to the Midlands. It is a great prose epic, large in size, commanding in structure, affording an ample space for a great artist to work upon. Perhaps even more than *Adam Bede* has it become part of the ordinary furniture of our minds, of the current coin of our thoughts. Casaubon, Will Ladislaw, Mr. Brooke are types which are ever present with us, like Becky Sharpe and Colonel Newcome; and if Dorothea and Lydgate are more remote, it is because they are rarer characters, not because they are less truly drawn. *Middlemarch* gives George Eliot the chiefest claim to stand by the side of Shakespeare. Both drew their inspiration from the same sources, the villages and the country houses which we know so well.

If I am asked the question with which I set out, I always reply—her last novel, *Daniel Deronda*. I know well, only too well, the criticisms which have been levelled at the book from its first appearance to the present day. I have become tired and sick of hearing that the characters are unreal, that there is not a man or woman in the story whom you can take away with you and live with. I know that Daniel is thought to be a prig, and the Jew Mordecai a bore; that Gwendolen is thought impossible, and Grandcourt a stage villain; that the language is held to be strained and uncouth, full of far-fetched tropes and metaphors drawn from unfamiliar science. It is said there is no motive power in the action, no reason for the characters behaving as they behave. What rational person can care for the return of the Jews to Palestine? Is a young man who stakes his life on such an issue worthy of five minutes' consideration? Would a handsome young Englishman, brought up as a Christian at a public school or university, be suddenly over-joyed to find that he was a Jew? No, in *Daniel Deronda* thought and learning have usurped the place of art. It belongs to the worst type of all novels, a novel with a tendency. The influence of George Lewes, which may have strengthened his wife's mind at first, has acquired in this a fatal predominance. Biological studies have ruined her fine sensibility. George Eliot has passed her prime. As in the "Transfiguration" of Raphael, we see in *Deronda* the downward movement of a great mind, a movement which, if followed, would have disastrous effect upon the national literature.

With none of this can I agree. To me *Daniel Deronda* is one step further upwards in the career of a soaring genius who was destined, if life was spared, to achieve greater heights than any to which it had yet risen. It is the result of the normal and regular growth of unrivalled powers which were ever seeking subjects more and more worthy for their exercise. It is as superior to *Adam Bede* as *Hamlet* is superior to *Much Ado about Nothing*. It is an effort to realize the highest purposes of art, to seize the strongest passions, the loftiest heights and the lowest depths of human nature. If it fails in execution it is because the task cannot yet be accomplished. But if the work is ever to be done, the way must be paved by partial failure. It is better to have tried and failed, than never to have tried at all.—OSCAR BROWNING, *Life of George Eliot*, 1890, pp. 140–44

Twenty years ago it required, if not a genuine strength of mind, at any rate a certain amount of "cussedness," not to be a George-Eliotite. All, or almost all, persons who had "got culture" admired George Eliot, and not to do so was to be at best a Kenite among the chosen people, at worst an outcast, a son of Edom and Moab and Philistia. Two very different currents met and mingled among the worshippers who flocked in the flesh to St. John's Wood, or read the books in ecstasy elsewhere. There was the rising tide of the æsthetic, revering the creator of Tito. There was the agnostic herd, faithful to the translator of Strauss and the irregular partner of Mr. G. H. Lewes. I have always found myself most unfortunately indis-posed to follow any fashion, and I never remember having read a single book of George Eliot's with genuine and whole-hearted admiration. Yet an experience which I once went through enables me, I think, to speak about her at least without ignorance. When *Daniel Deronda* appeared, my friend, the late Dr. Appleton, asked me to review it for the *Academy*. My hands were the reverse of full at the time, and as there were some books of the author's which I had not read, and others which I had not read for some time, I thought it might be worth while to get an entire set and read it through in chronological order, and so "get the atmosphere" before attacking that Ebrew Jew. I have spent many days with less pleasure and less profit than those which I spent on this task. And when I had finished it, I came to an opinion which I have since seen little reason to change.

Something of what has been already said about Charlotte Brontë will apply also to this very different contemporary and craftsfellow of hers. Neither of them seems to have had in any great degree the male faculties of creation and judgment. Both,

and Miss Evans especially, had in no ordinary degree the female faculty of receiving, assimilating, and reproducing. During a long and studious youth she received and assimilated impressions of persons, of scenes, of books. At a rather belated crisis of feeling she experienced what I suppose must be called Love, and at the same time was exposed to a fresh current of thought, such as it was. She travelled and enriched her store; she frequented persons of distinction and was influenced by them. And then it came out in novels, at first pretty simple, and really powerful; then less simple, but ingeniously repro-ductive of certain phases of thought and sentiment which were current; last of all reflective of hardly anything (save in scattered and separate scenes where she always excelled) except strange crotchets of will-worship, which she had taken up to replace the faith that she had cast out, but that was evidently more or less neccessary to her.

She began with those *Scenes of Clerical Life*, which some very fervent worshippers of hers, I believe, put at the head of all her work in merit as in time, but which I should rank decidedly below the best parts of *Adam Bede* and the wonderful opening of *Silas Marner*. Then came the great triumph, *Adam Bede*, itself. Of course it is extremely clever; but no one who calls himself a critic can afford to forget the circumstances in which it appeared. Dickens's best work was done, and his mannerism was already disgusting some readers. Thackeray, though at his very best, had not reached full popularity, and was entirely different in style and subject. Charlotte Brontë was dead or dying,—I forget which; there was nobody else who could even pretend to the first class. How could *Adam Bede* fail?

The Mill on the Floss was not likely, the circumstances being still the same, to diminish the author's vogue, and I suppose it is her best book, though it may not contain her best scenes. The objection which is often made and still oftener felt to the repulsiveness of Maggie's worship of a counter-jumping cad like Stephen, is somewhat uncritical. I suspect that most women resent it, because they feel the imputation to be true: and most men out of a not wholly dissimilar feeling which acts a little differently. *Silas Marner* again has qualities of great-ness, though the narrative and characters are slight for a book. But between these earlier novels and the later batch a great gulf is fixed. Hardly after *Silas* do we find anything, except in patches and episodes, that is really "genial" in George Eliot's work. *Felix Holt* and *Middlemarch* are elaborate studies of what seemed to the author to be modern characters and society,—studies of immense effort and erudition not unenlightened by humour, but on the whole dead. *Romola* is an attempt—still more Herculean, and still more against the grain—to resusci-tate the past. As for *Daniel Deronda*, it is a kind of night-mare,—a parochial and grotesque idea having thoroughly mastered the writer and only allowed her now and then to get free in the character of Grandcourt and (less often) in that of Gwendolen. I think *Theophrastus Such* has met with rather undeserved contempt, due to the fact that *Deronda* had already begun to sap the foundations of its author's popularity. The poems are laboured and thoroughly unpoetical expositions of crotchet and theory. The essays are neither better nor worse than a vast number of essays by quite second-rate authors. —GEORGE SAINTSBURY, "Three Mid-Century Novelists," *Corrected Impressions*, 1895

The time has scarcely yet arrived when an estimate can be formed of the permanent position of George Eliot in literature. Perhaps during her lifetime there was a tendency to rate her genius too high; but it may be equally true that the reaction has been too strong, and that her fame has in recent years suffered from undue disparagement. This at least seems indisputable, that early in her literary career she attained to an excellence of work which she never surpassed, and from which her later works present a distinct retrogression. The recognition of this fact need not imply any desire to derogate from her genius; but it is undoubtedly a misfortune for her as an author that she should have so far wandered from the sphere in which her special genius did its best work, and should have entered upon other regions in which that genius worked with less freedom. This is not the place to discuss her literary work, except in relation to its qualities of style; but the same process which, in the judgment of many, injuriously affected her work on the whole, did exercise its most baneful effect in the special sphere of style.

The work of George Eliot which first arrested attention and compelled admiration were the *Scenes of Clerical Life.* There the quality most conspicious is the intensity of emotion, the concentration of tragic feeling within the sphere of commonplace life. The canvas is small; the incident is uneventful; there is no complexity of plot, and no august dramatic picture. But what impresses us most is, nevertheless, the intense depth of tragic feeling. There is none of the delicate monotone of Jane Austen's novels, with their smoothness of movement, their subtle delicacy of description, their avoidance of any touch of tragedy. But in George Eliot the depth of feeling is portrayed with restless effort and certainty of hand, and no elaboration is spared that may heighten the effect. The commonplace, the humorous, the restful picture of everyday life, is skilfully worked in; but we never for one moment are allowed to forget that all the side touches are mere contributions to one special aim—that of increasing the intensity of the tragic chord that is to be struck. The style corresponds exactly to this central aim. Not a sentence is other than elaborately framed. Each antithesis of feeling is carefully pressed home. Each incident that is to heighten the effect is told with almost painful care. Each touch of humour is so expressed as to heighten the note of tragedy and contrast. In the very narrowing of the scene, and in the concentration with which it is focussed, we have another proof of the determination with which the author's purpose is kept in view. ⟨. . .⟩

Her genius was certainly great, and her style was often eloquent, always elaborate and skilful, and, in its earlier phases, instinct with feeling and force. But as she left the simplicity of her earlier canvas, so her style lost its distinctive character, and was less closely allied to her genius. Its analytical precision wearies us; its elaboration seems to be studied in order to produce an impression upon that vague entity—the average reader; and what was at first the impulse of the eager student of human nature, seeking an outlet for emotion in delicacy and subtlety of expression, became a literary trick and an imposing pedantry. It was only the strength of her intellectual power that preserved her genius from being even more depressed by an acquired and unnatural habit.—HENRY CRAIK, "George Eliot," *English Prose*, ed. Henry Craik, 1896, Vol. 5, pp. 663–66

From the death of Dickens in 1870 to her own in 1880, she was manifestly the most prominent novelist in England. Yet it is important to realise that, like all the other Victorian novelists of eminence until we reach Mr. George Meredith, she was born in the rich second decade of the century. It was not until some years after the death of Charlotte Brontë that *Scenes of Clerical Life* revealed a talent which owed much to the bold, innovating spirit of that great woman, but which was evidently exercised by a more academic hand. The style of

these short episodes was so delicately brilliant that their hardness was scarcely apparent.

The *Scenes* certainly gave promise of a writer in the first rank. In *Adam Bede,* an elaborate romance of bygone provincial manners, this promise was repeated, although, by an attentive ear, the under-tone of the mechanism was now to be detected. In the *Mill on the Floss* and *Silas Marner* a curious phenomenon appeared—George Eliot divided into two personages. The close observer of nature, mistress of laughter and tears, exquisite in the intensity of cumulative emotion, was present still, but she receded; the mechanician, overloading her page with pretentious matter, working out her scheme as if she were building a steam-engine, came more and more to the front. In *Felix Holt* and on to *Daniel Deronda* the second personage preponderated, and our ears were deafened by the hum of the philosophical machine, the balance of scenes and sentences, the intolerable artificiality of the whole construction.

George Eliot is a very curious instance of the danger of self-cultivation. No writer was ever more anxious to improve herself and conquer an absolute mastery over her material. But she did not observe, as she entertained the laborious process, that she was losing those natural accomplishments which infinitely outshone the philosophy and science which she so painfully acquired. She was born to please, but unhappily she persuaded herself, or was persuaded, that her mission was to teach the world, to lift its moral tone, and, in consequence, an agreeable rustic writer, with a charming humour and very fine sympathetic nature, found herself gradually uplifted until, about 1875, she sat enthroned on an educational tripod, an almost ludicrous pythoness. From the very first she had been weak in that quality which more than any other is needed by a novelist, imaginative invention. So long as she was humble, and was content to reproduce, with the skilful subtlety of her art, what she had personally heard and seen, her work had delightful merit. But it was an unhappy day when she concluded that strenuous effort, references to a hundred abstruse writers, and a whole technical system of rhetoric would do the wild-wood business of native imagination. The intellectual self-sufficiency of George Eliot has suffered severe chastisement. At the present day scant justice is done to her unquestionable distinction of intellect or to the emotional intensity of much of her early work.—EDMUND GOSSE, *A Short History of Modern English Literature*, 1897, pp. 369–71

George Eliot gave prose-fiction a substance which it had never had before among any people. That her ethical system has logical inconsistencies we may admit. While intending to keep close to empiricism, she really admits transcendentalism in what she says about the inner and better self, and the command of duty, which she at least once calls a divine voice. Undoubtedly, too, the very greatest of English moralists was free from conscious systems; by deep intuition he displayed the emotions that sway men to action. But there has been only one Shakespeare. When systems become antiquated, the work that was reared upon them falls. Positivism was antiquated some years ago, and evolution has taken its place. George Eliot is, however, connected with the theories of her time more in appearance than in reality. In her ways of thinking, there is less of Comte than of Wordsworth and Thomas à Kempis, both of whom taught renunciation as a command. Between Dante and George Eliot there is a suggestive analogy. Dante expressed himself in the terms of the grotesque philosophy of the Middle Age. Thomas Aquinas is no longer read, while the fame of Dante increases more and more every day. Why? because the scholasticism of St. Thomas is only the vesture of Dante's own profound meditations, which each generation for itself may translate into its own language. So of George Eliot. Her moral discernments, often clothed in the language of positivism, are nevertheless imbedded everlastingly in the inherited thought of the ages. With a precision and a minuteness never possible before her time, she worked out the Hebrew formula, that they who sow the wind, shall reap the whirlwind; which was likewise the Greek idea, that when a wrong is done, the Eumenides, daughters of earth and darkness, will awake from their sleep and avenge it. And with the terrible earnestness of Æschylus, she reiterated the tragic corollary: 'We can conceive no retribution that does not spread beyond its mark in pulsations of unmerited pain.'—WILBUR L. CROSS, *The Development of the English Novel*, 1899, pp. 250–52

Works

ADAM BEDE

When, on October 29, I had written to the end of the love-scene at the Farm between Adam and Dinah, I sent the MS. to Blackwood, since the remainder of the third volume could not affect the judgment passed on what had gone before. He wrote back in warm admiration, and offered me, on the part of the firm, £800 for four years' copyright. I accepted the offer. The last words of the third volume were written and despatched on their way to Edinburgh, November the 16th, and now on the last day of the same month I have written this slight history of my book. I love it very much, and am deeply thankful to have written it, whatever the public may say to it—a result which is still in darkness, for I have at present had only four sheets of the proof. The book would have been published at Christmas, or rather early in December, but that Bulwer's *What Will He Do with It?* was to be published by Blackwood at that time, and it was thought that this novel might interfere with mine.—GEORGE ELIOT, *Journal* (Nov. 16, 1858), cited in *George Eliot's Life as Related in Her Letters and Journals,* ed. John W. Cross, 1884, Vol. 2, pp. 51–52

The Book was actually *Adam Bede*, and *Adam Bede* "justified my enthusiasm"; to say the least!

Oh yes! It was as good as *going into the country for one's health*, the reading of that Book was!—Like a visit to Scotland *minus* the fatigues of the long journey, and the grief of seeing friends grown old, and Places that knew me knowing me no more! I could fancy in reading it, to be seeing and hearing once again a crystal-clear, musical, Scotch stream, such as I long to lie down beside and—*cry* at (!) for gladness and sadness; after long stifling sojourn in the South; where there is no *water* but what is stagnant or muddy!

In truth, it is a beautiful most *human* Book! Every *Dog* in it, not to say every man woman and child in it, is brought home to one's 'business and bosom,' an individual fellow-creature! I found myself in charity with the whole human race when I laid it down—the *canine* race I had *always* appreciated—"not wisely but too well!"—the *human*, however,—Ach!—*that* has troubled me—as badly at times as "twenty gallons of milk on one's mind"! For the rest; why you are so good to *me* is still a *mystery*, with every appearance of remaining so! Yet have I lavished more childish conjecture on it than on anything since I *was* a child, and got mistified about.—JANE WELSH CARLYLE, Letter to Thomas Carlyle (Feb. 20, 1859)

I ought long since to have thanked you for *Adam Bede*. But I never had a moment to look at it till arriving here, and ordered by the doctors to abstain from all "work."

I owe the author much gratitude for some very pleasing hours. The book indeed is worthy of great admiration. There are touches of beauty in the conception of human character that are exquisite, and much wit and much poetry embedded in the "dialect," which nevertheless the author over-uses.

The style is remarkably good whenever it is English and not provincial—racy, original, and nervous.

I congratulate you on having found an author of such promise, and published one of the very ablest works of fiction I have read for years.—EDWARD BULWER-LYTTON, Letter to John Blackwood (April 24, 1859), cited in *George Eliot's Life as Related in Her Letters and Journals,* ed. John W. Cross, 1884, Vol. 2, pp. 74–75

Adam Bede has taken its place among the actual experiences and endurances of my life. Every high quality that was in the former book ⟨*Scenes of Clerical Life*⟩, is in that, with a World of Power added thereunto. The conception of Hetty's character is so extraordinarily subtle and true, that I laid the book down fifty times, to shut my eyes and think about it. I know nothing so skilful, determined, and uncompromising. The whole country life that the story is set in, is so real, and so droll and genuine, and yet so selected and polished by art, that I cannot praise it enough to you. And that part of the book which follows Hetty's trial (and which I have observed to be not as widely understood as the rest), affected me far more than any other, and exalted my sympathy with the writer to its utmost height. You must not suppose that I am writing this to *you*. I have been saying it over and over again, here and elsewhere, until I feel in a ludicrously apologetic state for repeating myself on this paper.—CHARLES DICKENS, Letter to George Eliot (July 10, 1859)

Of "Dinah" we scarcely can trust ourselves to speak. The character is so eminently and heartily Christian, even in the most of its finer shades, that we do not care to point out the particulars in which it betrays the want of the entirest sympathy on the part of the author. Surely it was written from the fresh remembrances of days of warm and confiding Christian faith, now perhaps under the chill of an honest, and a temporary eclipse.—NOAH PORTER, *Books and Reading*, 1870, p. 119

Whether, in Dinah Morris, George Eliot intended to represent Mrs. Evans or not, she did represent her faithfully and fully. The influence of her aunt's holy life and simple faith on the youthful but troubled mind of Mary Ann Evans was very great, as may be seen from her own words. In writing of her aunt, she says: "She was very gentle and quiet in her manners, very loving, and (what she must have been from the very first) a truly religious soul, in whom the love of God and love of man were fused together." This was written in 1859. I have had the pleasure and privilege of reading some letters from the great novelist to Mrs. Elizabeth Evans, written during the years 1839, 1840, and 1841, in which the writer regrets her inability to realize for herself the deep spiritual peace and happiness experienced by Mrs. Evans. That a great admiration and affection was felt by the writer of these letters for her aunt is evident, and when all form of religious belief was given up by George Eliot, the grief of Mrs. Evans can be better imagined than described. With such evidence before them, it is hardly to be wondered at if the public believe that Mrs. Elizabeth Evans more than "suggested" Dinah Morris. The only point at which the writer has deviated from the fact is in the marriage of Dinah and Adam. As a matter of fact the real Dinah married Seth Bede (Samuel Evans). Adam was George Eliot's father, Robert Evans.—L. BULKLEY, "Dinah Morris and Mrs. Elizabeth Evans," *Century Magazine*, Aug. 1882, p. 552

⟨. . .⟩ *Adam Bede* was a new book, and in this I had my first knowledge of that great intellect for which I had no passion, indeed, but always the deepest respect, the highest honor; and which has from time to time profoundly influenced me by its ethics.

I state these things simply and somewhat baldly; I might easily refine upon them, and study that subtle effect for good and for evil which young people are always receiving from the fiction they read; but this is not the time or place for the inquiry, and I only wish to own that so far as I understand it, the chief part of my ethical experience has been from novels. The life and character I have found portrayed there have appealed always to the consciousness of right and wrong implanted in me; and from no one has this appeal been stronger than from George Eliot. Her influence continued through many years, and I can question it now only in the undue burden she seems to throw upon the individual, and her failure to account largely enough for motive from the social environment. There her work seems to me unphilosophical.
—WILLIAM DEAN HOWELLS, "George Eliot, Hawthorne, Goethe, Heine," *My Literary Passions*, 1895

SILAS MARNER

I have read the M.S. you have sent of *Silas Marner* with the greatest admiration. The first 100 pages are very sad, almost oppressive, but relieved by the most exquisite touches of nature and natural feelings hit off in the fewest and most happily chosen words. I wish the picture had been a more cheery one and embraced higher specimens of humanity, but you paint so naturally that in your hands the veriest earthworms become most interesting perfect studies in fact.

The child found on the hearth replacing the poor weaver's lost treasure is a beautiful idea and is I hope to be the medium of restoring the unfortunate Silas to a more Christian frame of mind. How perfectly you paint the poor creature quite at sea when his simple faith was cut from under his feet.

The conclave at the Rainbow is beyond price and no one but yourself could have done Mrs. Winthrop. She is perfect. Nancy Lammeter is very good and her toilette in presence of the Miss Gunns is screaming, but Priscilla is my favourite; she promises to be a truly rich bit of character. I cannot help feeling sorry that you have done for the only one of the Cass family who had anything about him to redeem the breed.

My only objection to the story is the want of brighter lights and some characters of whom one can think with pleasure as fellow creatures, but this may come in the sequel of the story and in the meantime the touches of nature, the humour, and the power and precision are as wonderful as in anything you have ever written. Are you sure you will be able to wind up in the space you allot to yourself? I should almost doubt it.—JOHN BLACKWOOD, Letter to George Eliot (Feb. 19, 1861)

To a certain extent, I think *Silas Marner* holds a higher place than any of the author's works. It is more nearly a masterpiece; it has more of that simple, rounded, consummate aspect, that absence of loose ends and gaping issues, which marks a classical work. What was attempted in it, indeed, was within more immediate reach than the heart-trials of Adam Bede and Maggie Tulliver. A poor, dull-witted, disappointed Methodist cloth-weaver; a little golden-haired foundling child; a well-meaning, irresolute country squire, and his patient, childless

wife;—these, with a chorus of simple, beer-loving villagers, make up the *dramatis personæ*. More than any of its brother-works, "Silas Marner," I think, leaves upon the mind a deep impression of the grossly material life of agricultural England in the last days of the old *régime*,—the days of full-orbed Toryism, of Trafalgar and of Waterloo, when the invasive spirit of French domination threw England back upon a sense of her own insular solidity, and made her for the time doubly, brutally, morbidly English. Perhaps the best pages in the work are the first thirty, telling the story of poor Marner's disappointments in friendship and in love, his unmerited disgrace, and his long, lonely twilight-life at Raveloe, with the sole companionship of his loom, in which his muscles moved "with such even repetition, that their pause seemed almost as much a constraint as the holding of his breath." Here, as in all George Eliot's books, there is a middle life and a low life; and here, as usual, I prefer the low life. In *Silas Marner*, in my opinion, she has come nearest the mildly rich tints of brown and gray, the mellow lights and the undreadful corner-shadows of the Dutch masters whom she emulates.—HENRY JAMES, "The Novels of George Eliot," *Atlantic*, Oct. 1866, p. 482

I have no doubt myself that *Silas Marner* comes nearer to being a great success than any of the more elaborate books. Yet *Silas Marner* is about one-fifth part of the length of *Middlemarch*; and its plot, *mise-en-scène*, and incidents are simplicity itself. There is no science, no book-learning, and but few ethical problems in it from beginning to end; and it all goes in one small volume, for the tale concerns but the neighbours of one quiet village. Yet the quaint and idyllic charm of the piece, the perfection of tone and keeping, the harmony of the landscape, the pure, deep humanity of it, all make it a true and exquisite work of high art.

Modern English (and I am one of those who hold that the best modern English is as good as any in our literature) has few pieces of description more gem-like in its crystalline facets than the opening chapter that tells of the pale, uncanny weaver of Raveloe in his stone cottage by the deserted pit. Some of us can remember such house weavers in such lonesome cottages on the Northern moors, and have heard the unfamiliar rattle of the loom in a half-ruinous homestead. How perfect is that vignette of Raveloe—"a village where many of the old echoes lingered, undrowned by new voices"—with its "strange lingering echoes of the old demon-worship aming the grey-haired peasantry!" The entire picture of the village and its village life a hundred years ago, is finished with the musical and reserved note of poetry, such as we are taught to love in Wordsworth and Tennyson. And for quiet humour modern literature has few happier scenes than the fireside at the "Rainbow," with Macey and Winthrop, the butcher and the farrier, over their pipes and their hot potations, and the quarrel about "seeing ghos'es," about smelling them!

Within this most graceful and refined picture of rural life there is a dominant ethical motive which she herself describes as its aim, "to set in a strong light the remedial influences of pure, natural, human relations." This aim is perfectly worked out: it is a right and healthy conception, not too subtle, not too common:—to put it in simpler words than hers, it is how a lonely, crabbed, ill-used old man is humanised by the love of a faithful and affectionate child. The form is poetic: the moral is both just and noble: the characters are living, and the story is original, natural, and dramatic. The only thing, indeed, which *Silas Marner* wants to make it a really great romance is more ease, more rapidity, more "go." The melody runs so uniformly in minor keys, the sense of care, meditation, and introspection is so apparent in every line, the amount of serious thought lavished by the writer and required of the reader is so continuous, that we are not carried away, we are not excited, inspired, and thrilled as we are by *Jane Eyre* or *Esmond*. We enjoy a beautiful book with a fine moral, set in exquisite prose, with consummate literary resources, full of fine thoughts, true, ennobling thoughts, and with no weak side at all, unless it be the sense of being over-wrought, like a picture which has been stippled over in every surface.

A clever French woman said of George Eliot's conversation—*elle s'écoute quand elle parle!* Just so, as we read on we seem to see how she held up each sentence into the light as it fell from her pen, scrutinised it to see if some rarer phrase might not be compacted, some subtler thought excogitated. Of all the more important tales, *Silas Marner* is that wherein we least feel this excessive thoughtfulness. And thus it is the best. Perhaps other born romancers would have thrown into it more life, energy, jollity, or passion. Thackeray would have made the weaver a serio-comic hermit: Dickens would have made Eppie a sentimental angel; Charlotte Brontë would have curdled our blood; Trollope might have made more of Nancy's courting. But no one of them could have given us a more lofty lesson "of the remedial influences of pure, natural, human relations." The only doubt is, whether a novel is the medium for such lessons. On this, opinions are, and will remain, divided. The lesson and the art ought both to be faultless. —FREDERIC HARRISON, "George Eliot," *Studies in Early Victorian Literature*, 1895, pp. 211–13

MIDDLEMARCH

I suppose you cannot have read *Middlemarch*, as you say nothing about it. It stands quite alone. As one only just moistens one's lips with an exquisite liqueur, to keep the taste as long as possible in one's mouth, I never read more than a single chapter of *Middlemarch* in the evening, dreading to come to the last, when I must wait two months for a renewal of the pleasure. The depth of humour has certainly never been surpassed in English literature. If there is ever a shade too much learning, that is Lewes's fault.—CONNOP THIRLWALL, Letter (June 4, 1872), cited in *Letters to a Friend*, ed. Arthur Penrhyn Stanley, 1881, p. 278

In *Middlemarch* the peculiar powers of the author are exhibited in the highest and widest play of their development. None of her books is so deeply thoughtful, none commands so broad a view of the human horizon, none is so rich in personal portraiture.—ALFRED H. WELSH, *Development of English Literature and Language*, 1883, Vol. 2., p. 447

In truth, *Middlemarch* is to me as a landscape seen in the twilight; *au teint grisâtre*. It is from first to last the plaint of a lost ideal. I do not think it even a true rendering of life as it was lived in England sixty years ago. It would be easy to account for this by saying that the writer had lost "the wider hope." I prefer not to do it. Such an explanation is, indeed, so far obviously true as that in a country town the most strenuous belief, the most unflagging work, is religious. But the scepticism of *Middlemarch* also extends to things social and human.—BESSIE RAYNER BELLOC, *In a Walled Garden*, 1894, p. 12

George Eliot's style, though sometimes beautiful with a grave and dignified beauty, never rises above a certain level. She never really lets herself go. Most people would probably agree with Mr. Stephen's coldly judicious estimate of *Middlemarch*. He seems to have at the back of his mind a conviction that books ought not to be written at all, but that, as they are, one must try not to exaggerate their importance, and yet to say what one can for them. He can say for *Middlemarch* that 'it is clearly a work of extraordinary power, full of subtle and accurate observation; and gives, if a melancholy, yet an undeniably truthful portraiture of the impression made by the society of the time upon one of the keenest observers, though upon an observer looking upon the world from a certain distance, and rather too much impressed by the importance of philosophers and theorists.' This view is not quite consistent with the opinion, also held by Mr. Stephen, that the moral of *Middlemarch* is to do your work well and not to bother about ideals. But, consistent or inconsistent, if it be correct, there seems to be no particular reason why anybody should ever read *Middlemarch* again.

I must confess, though the confession may invalidate my judgment, that I cannot look at *Middlemarch* in the light of cold reason at all. I remember too well the hungry, boyish appetite with which I devoured the green paper volumes in which it successively appeared. Celia's dislike of hearing Mr. Casaubon eat his soup, and her wonder whether Locke had a mole on his forehead, were, I think, to be quite candid, a welcome relief after the faultless Dorothea's ideal aspirations. But Dorothea's unhappy marriage, and the misfortune of Lydgate coming too late, and the irresponsible Ladislaw sprawling on Rosamond's hearthrug, and Mr. Casaubon's pathetic hunt after the key to all mythologies, and Mr. Brooke's universal sciolism, which never carried him too far, and Mr. Borthrop Trumbull's pomposity, and Mrs. Cadwallader's wit were all delightful, as to me they are delightful still. And what a wonderful character is Caleb Garth! Mr. Stephen calls him a 'pale duplicate' of Adam Bede. To me he seems an entirely fresh creation, and in many ways Adam's superior. He is the type of the strong, silent, capable man, who can act but not talk, the perfection of British energy and modesty, resembling that far older class concerning whom the son of Sirach says that they are not found where parables are spoken, but they maintain the state of the world, and all their desire is in the work of their craft. In absolute contrast to him stands Mr. Brooke, who can talk but not act; 'such a leaky fool,' as Lydgate says, always ready to take up his parable at a moment's notice on any conceivable subject, with the genial preface, 'I went into that at one time, you know.' 'Wordsworth now, I knew Wordsworth.' 'Virgil?' But Mr. Brooke reflected just in time that with the Laureate of Augustus he could not claim acquaintance. He did not shine at the election meeting 'with a glass of sherry hurrying like smoke through his ideas.' On a private occasion he was never wanting; with the small change of conversation he was amply provided, and he had a subtly mysterious instinct for not being a bore. Bulstrode, the sanctimonious and fraudulent banker, is more conventional. Yet, as we are reminded, he was not one of those coarse hypocrites who consciously affect beliefs and emotions for the sake of gulling the world. He believed in himself. He had his point of view. The sixth commandment in Clough's *Latest Decalogue* exactly describes the extent to which he would go in contravening the moral law—

Thou shalt not kill, but need'st not strive
Officiously to keep alive.

His dull wife, who became heroic when her husband was in the dust, is a beautiful example of the way in which George Eliot could ennoble the sordid and the commonplace. Old Featherstone the miser is not a pleasant picture, but he is marvellously vivid, with his almost pathetic inability to go to sleep in church. His conclusion from long attendance upon divine worship was the very mundane one that God Almighty stuck to the land, making folks rich with corn and cattle. He was an ignorant and graceless old sinner, but as real as Sir Peter Crawley, and less disgusting. The courtship of Fred Vincy and Mary Garth is delightful in its simplicity, tempered by humour. Mr. Farebrother, though not quite such an attractive clergyman as Mr. Gilfil or Mr. Irwine, is admirable in his geniality, his independence, and his thirst for knowledge. Dorothea and Mr. Casaubon are comparative failures. They are supposed to have nothing in common, but they have the common element of stupidity. 'No man is the wiser for his learning,' said one of the most learned men in a learned age. But even Mr. Casaubon's learning is sham, and he could not have imposed upon a really intellectual girl. As for Dorothea, she might have been a good listener to a clever husband, but her own remarks are vapid in the extreme. *Middlemarch* contains an inordinately large number of characters, and yet every one of them is distinct, and most of them the reader feels that he must have personally known. Mr. Stephen desiderates 'a closer contact with the world of realities.' Unhappy marriages are real enough, and there are two in *Middlemarch*. He would also have 'less preoccupation with certain speculative doctrines.' The chief speculators in *Middlemarch* are Mr. Casaubon and Mr. Brooke. Both are held up to ridicule and contempt. Lydgate's researches are purely biological, and eminently suitable to his profession. If *Middlemarch* be not read, the world, even the world of realities, is the loser. —HERBERT PAUL, "George Eliot," *Nineteenth Century*, June 1902, pp. 941–43

DANIEL DERONDA

Daniel Deronda has succeeded in awaking in my somewhat worn-out mind an interest. So many stories are tramping over one's mind in every modern magazine nowadays that one is macadamized, so to speak. It takes something unusual to make a sensation. This does excite and interest me, as I wait for each number with eagerness.—HARRIET BEECHER STOWE, Letter to George Eliot (March 18, 1876), cited in Charles Edward Stowe, *Life of Harriet Beecher Stowe*, 1889, pp. 473–74

Daniel Deronda is essentially, both in conception and in form, a Romance: and George Eliot has not only never written a romance before, but is herself, by the uncompromising realism of her former works, a main cause for the disesteem into which romantic fiction has fallen—a disesteem that has even turned the tea-cup into a heroine and the tea-spoon into a hero. George Eliot should be the last to complain that the inimitable realism of *Middlemarch* has thrown a cold shade over the truth and wisdom that borrow the form of less probable fiction in *Daniel Deronda*. She is in the position of every great artist who having achieved glory in one field sets out to conquer another. The world is not prone to believe in many-sided genius: one supremacy is enough for one man.

In short, I cannot help thinking that George Eliot's new novel has caused some passing disappointment because it is not another *Adam Bede* or *Middlemarch*, and not because it is *Daniel Deronda*. The first criticism of a book is sure to be founded on a comparison with others. Fortunately, *Daniel Deronda* lies so far outside George Eliot's other works in every important respect as to make direct comparison impossible. It cannot be classed as first, or second, or third, or last—that favourite but feeble make-shift for criticism, as if any book, or picture, or song could be called worse in itself because another is better, or better because another is worse. I believe that

Daniel Deronda is absolutely good—and the whole language of criticism contains no stronger form of literary creed. Not only so, but I believe that it promises to secure for its author a more slowly growing, perhaps less universal, but deeper and higher fame than the works with which it does not enter into rivalry. In any case it marks an era in the career of the greatest English novelist of our time. It is as much a first novel, from a fresh hand and mind, as if no scene of clerical life had ever been penned. And, as such, it calls for more special criticism even than *Middlemarch*—the crown and the climax of the series that began with the sad fortunes of the Reverend Amos Barton. It is not even to be compared with *Romola*—that was no romance in the sense that the term must be applied to *Daniel Deronda* as the key to its place and nature.

However we may divide and subdivide, there are in reality only two distinct orders of fiction. Unfortunately, while we have a distinctive name for the one, we have none for the other. Perhaps the difference between the fiction which deals with ordinary or actual things and people and that which deals with extraordinary things and people is so marked and obvious that no names are wanted to express it any more than a scientific term is needed to express the difference between an eagle and a phœnix. The important point is that *Daniel Deronda* is very broadly distinguishable from all its predecessors by not dealing with types—with the ordinary people who make up the actual world, and with the circumstances, events, characteristics, and passions that are common to us all. We have all been so accustomed to see ourselves and all our relations and friends mirrored and dissected that we naturally expected to find the same familiar looking-glass or microscope in *Daniel Deronda*. It is small consolation to a plain man, who looks forward to the ever-new pleasure of examining his own photograph, to be presented with the portrait of a stranger, though the stranger may be handsomer and less common than he. Nevertheless it may well be that he will prize the picture most when he is in the mood to remember that the world does not consist wholly of types, and that the artist who ignores the existence of even improbable exceptions gives a very inadequate, nay, a very false representation of the *comédie humaine*.—R. E. FRANCILLON, "George Eliot's First Romance," *Gentleman's Magazine*, Oct. 1876, pp. 411–13

Compared with *Middlemarch*, its immediate predecessor, *Daniel Deronda* is a variation rather than an advance. It is both better and poorer than the former,—more stimulating at the opening and less satisfactory at the close. We doubt whether George Eliot will ever exceed her present reach of achievement; but we have full faith in her power of retaining it for some time to come.—BAYARD TAYLOR, "George Eliot" (1876), *Critical Essays and Literary Notes*, 1880, p. 347

I have always thought, for instance, that the figure of Daniel Deronda, whose portrait, blurred and uncertain as it is, has been drawn with the most amazing care and with endless touches and re-touches, must have become at last to George Eliot a kind of awful veiled spectre, always in her brain, always seeming about to reveal his true features and his mind, but never doing it, so that to the end she never clearly perceived what manner of man he was, nor what was his real character.—WALTER BESANT, *The Art of Fiction*, 1884, p. 21

That wise and tender Book I hope you have seen—It is full of sad (high) nourishment.—EMILY DICKINSON, Letter to Maria Whitney (Spring 1885)

HENRY JAMES

Galaxy, March 1873, pp. 424–28

Middlemarch is at once one of the strongest and one of the weakest of English novels. Its predecessors as they appeared might have been described in the same terms; *Romola*, is especially a rare masterpiece, but the least *entraînant* of masterpieces. *Romola* sins by excess of analysis; there is too much description and too little drama; too much reflection (all certainly of a highly imaginative sort) and too little creation. Movement lingers in the story, and with it attention stands still in the reader. The error in *Middlemarch* is not precisely of a similar kind, but it is equally detrimental to the total aspect of the work. We can well remember how keenly we wondered, while its earlier chapters unfolded themselves, what turn in the way of form the story would take—that of an organized, moulded, balanced composition, gratifying the reader with a sense of design and construction, or a mere chain of episodes, broken into accidental lengths and unconscious of the influence of a plan. We expected the actual result, but for the sake of English imaginative literature which, in this line is rarely in need of examples, we hoped for the other. If it had come we should have had the pleasure of reading, what certainly would have seemed to us in the immediate glow of attention, the first of English novels. But that pleasure has still to hover between prospect and retrospect. *Middlemarch* is a treasure-house of details, but it is an indifferent whole.

Our objection may seem shallow and pedantic, and may even be represented as a complaint that we have had the less given us rather than the more. Certainly the greatest minds have the defects of their qualities, and as George Eliot's mind is preëminently contemplative and analytic, nothing is more natural than that her manner should be discursive and expansive. "Concentration" would doubtless have deprived us of many of the best things in the book—of Peter Featherstone's grotesquely expectant legatees, of Lydgate's medical rivals, and of Mary Garth's delightful family. The author's purpose was to be a generous rural historian, and this very redundancy of touch, born of abundant reminiscence, is one of the greatest charms of her work. It is as if her memory was crowded with antique figures, to whom for very tenderness she must grant an appearance. Her novel is a picture—vast, swarming, deep-colored, crowded with episodes, with vivid images, with lurking master-strokes, with brilliant passages of expression; and as such we may freely accept it and enjoy it. It is not compact, doubtless; but when was a panorama compact? And yet, nominally, *Middlemarch* has a definite subject—the subject indicated in the eloquent preface. An ardent young girl was to have been the central figure, a young girl framed for a larger moral life than circumstance often affords, yearning for a motive for sustained spiritual effort and only wasting her ardor and soiling her wings against the meanness of opportunity. The author, in other words, proposed to depict the career of an obscure St. Theresa. Her success has been great, in spite of serious drawbacks. Dorothea Brooks is a genuine creation, and a most remarkable one when we consider the delicate material in which she is wrought. George Eliot's men are generally so much better than the usual trowsered offspring of the female fancy, that their merits have perhaps overshadowed those of her women. Yet her heroines have always been of an exquisite quality, and Dorothea is only that perfect flower of conception of which her predecessors were the less unfolded blossoms. An indefinable moral elevation is the sign of these admirable creatures; and of the representation of this quality in its

superior degrees the author seems to have in English fiction a monopoly. To render the expression of a soul requires a cunning hand; but we seem to look straight into the unfathomable eyes of the beautiful spirit of Dorothea Brooks. She exhales a sort of aroma of spiritual sweetness, and we believe in her as in a woman we might providentially meet some fine day when we should find ourselves doubting of the immortality of the soul. By what unerring mechanism this effect is produced—whether by fine strokes or broad ones, by description or by narration, we can hardly say; it is certainly the great achievement of the book. Dorothea's career is, however, but an episode, and though doubtless in intention, not distinctly enough in fact, the central one. The history of Lydgate's *menage*, which shares honors with it, seems rather to the reader to carry off the lion's share. This is certainly a very interesting story, but on the whole it yields in dignity to the record of Dorothea's unresonant woes. The "love-problem," as the author calls it, of Mary Garth, is placed on a rather higher level than the reader willingly grants it. To the end we care less about Fred Vincy than appears to be expected of us. In so far as the writer's design has been to reproduce the total sum of life in an English village forty years ago, this common-place young gentleman, with his somewhat meagre tribulations and his rather neutral egotism, has his proper place in the picture; but the author narrates his fortunes with a fulness of detail which the reader often finds irritating. The reader indeed is sometimes tempted to complain of a tendency which we are at loss exactly to express—a tendency to make light of the serious elements of the story and to sacrifice them to the more trivial ones. Is it an unconscious instinct or is it a deliberate plan? With its abundant and massive ingredients *Middlemarch* ought somehow to have depicted a weightier drama. Dorothea was altogether too superb a heroine to be wasted; yet she plays a narrower part than the imagination of the reader demands. She is of more consequence than the action of which she is the nominal centre. She marries enthusiastically a man whom she fancies a great thinker, and who turns out to be but an arid pedant. Here, indeed, is a disappointment with much of the dignity of tragedy; but the situation seems to us never to expand to its full capacity. It is analyzed with extraordinary penetration, but one may say of it, as of most of the situations in the book, that it is treated with too much refinement and too little breadth. It revolves too constantly on the same pivot; it abounds in fine shades, but it lacks, we think, the great dramatic *chiaroscuro*. Mr. Casaubon, Dorothea's husband (of whom more anon) embittered, on his side, by matrimonial disappointment, takes refuge in vain jealousy of his wife's relations with an interesting young cousin of his own and registers this sentiment in a codicil to his will, making the forfeiture of his property the penalty of his widow's marriage with this gentleman. Mr. Casaubon's death befalls about the middle of the story, and from this point to the close our interest in Dorothea is restricted to the question, will she or will she not marry Will Ladislaw? The question is relatively trivial and the implied struggle slightly factitious. The author has depicted the struggle with a sort of elaborate solemnity which in the interviews related in the last two books tends to become almost ludicrously excessive.

The dramatic current stagnates; it runs between hero and heroine almost a game of hair-splitting. Our dissatisfaction here is provoked in great measure by the insubstantial character of the hero. The figure of Will Ladislaw is a beautiful attempt, with many finely-completed points; but on the whole it seems to us a failure. It is the only eminent failure in the book, and its defects are therefore the more striking. It lacks sharpness of outline and depth of color; we have not found ourselves believing in Ladislaw as we believe in Dorothea, in Mary Garth, in Rosamond, in Lydgate, in Mr. Brooke and Mr. Casaubon. He is meant, indeed, to be a light creature (with a large capacity for gravity, for he finally gets into Parliament), and a light creature certainly should not be heavily drawn. The author, who is evidently very fond of him, has found for him here and there some charming and eloquent touches; but in spite of these he remains vague and impalpable to the end. He is, we may say, the one figure which a masculine intellect of the same power as George Eliot's would not have conceived with the same complacency; he is, in short, roughly speaking, a woman's man. It strikes us as an oddity in the author's scheme that she should have chosen just this figure of Ladislaw as the creature in whom Dorothea was to find her spiritual compensations. He is really, after all, not the ideal foil to Mr. Casaubon which her soul must have imperiously demanded, and if the author of the "Key to all Mythologies" sinned by lack of order, Ladislaw too has not the concentrated fervor essential in the man chosen by so nobly strenuous a heroine. The impression once given that he is a *dilettante* is never properly removed, and there is slender poetic justice in Dorothea's marrying a *dilettante*. We are doubtless less content with Ladislaw, on account of the noble, almost sculptural, relief of the neighboring figure of Lydgate, the real hero of the story. It is an illustration of the generous scale of the author's picture and of the conscious power of her imagination that she has given us a hero and heroine of broadly distinct interests—erected, as it were, two suns in her firmament, each with its independent solar system. Lydgate is so richly successful a figure that we have regretted strongly at moments, for immediate interests' sake, that the current of his fortunes should not mingle more freely with the occasionally thin-flowing stream of Dorothea's. Toward the close, these two fine characters are brought into momentary contact so effectively as to suggest a wealth of dramatic possibility between them; but if this train had been followed we should have lost Rosamond Vincy—a rare psychological study. Lydgate is a really complete portrait of a *man*, which seems to us high praise. It is striking evidence of the altogether superior quality of George Eliot's imagination that, though elaborately represented, Lydgate should be treated so little from what we may roughly (and we trust without offence) call the sexual point of view. Perception charged with feeling has constantly guided the author's hand, and yet her strokes remain as firm, her curves as free, her whole manner as serenely impersonal, as if, on a small scale, she were emulating the creative wisdom itself. Several English romancers—notably Fielding, Thackeray, and Charles Reade—have won great praise for their figures of women: but they owe it, in reversed conditions, to a meaner sort of art, it seems to us, than George Eliot has used in the case of Lydgate; to an indefinable appeal to masculine prejudice—to a sort of titillation of the masculine sense of difference. George Eliot's manner is more philosophic—more broadly intelligent, and yet her result is as concrete or, if you please, as picturesque. We have no space to dwell on Lydgate's character; we can but repeat that he is a vividly consistent, manly figure—powerful, ambitious, sagacious, with the maximum rather than the minimum of egotism, strenuous, generous, fallible, and altogether human. A work of the liberal scope of *Middlemarch* contains a multitude of artistic intentions, some of the finest of which became clear only in the meditative after-taste of perusal. This is the case with the balanced contrast between the two histories of Lydgate and Dorothea. Each is a tale of matrimonial infelicity, but the conditions in each are so different and the

circumstances so broadly opposed that the mind passes from one to the other with that supreme sense of the vastness and variety of human life, under aspects apparently similar, which it belongs only to the greatest novels to produce. The most perfectly successful passages in the book are perhaps those painful fireside scenes between Lydgate and his miserable little wife. The author's rare psychological penetration is lavished upon this veritably mulish domestic flower. There is nothing more powerfully real than these scenes in all English fiction, and nothing certainly more *intelligent*. Their impressiveness, and (as regards Lydgate) their pathos, is deepened by the constantly low key in which they are pitched. It is a tragedy based on unpaid butchers' bills, and the urgent need for small economies. The author has desired to be strictly real and to adhere to the facts of the common lot, and she has given us a powerful version of that typical human drama, the struggles of an ambitious soul with sordid disappointments and vulgar embarrassments. As to her catastrophe we hesitate to pronounce (for Lydgate's ultimate assent to his wife's worldly programme is nothing less than a catastrophe). We almost believe that some terrific explosion would have been more probable than his twenty years of smothered aspiration. Rosamond deserves almost to rank with Tito in *Romola* as a study of a gracefully vicious, or at least of a practically baleful nature. There is one point, however, of which we question the consistency. The author insists on her instincts of coquetry, which seems to us a discordant note. They would have made her better or worse—more generous or more reckless; in either case more manageable. As it is, Rosamond represents, in a measure, the fatality of British decorum.

In reading, we have marked innumerable passages for quotation and comment; but we lack space and the work is so ample that half a dozen extracts would be an ineffective illustration. There would be a great deal to say on the broad array of secondary figures, Mr. Casaubon, Mr. Brooke, Mr. Bulstrode, Mr. Farebrother, Caleb Garth, Mrs. Cadwallader, Celia Brooke. Mr. Casaubon is an excellent invention; as a dusky *repoussoir* to the luminous figure of his wife he could not have been better imagined. There is indeed something very noble in the way in which the author has apprehended his character. To depict hollow pretentiousness and mouldy egotism with so little of narrow sarcasm and so much of philosophic sympathy, is to be a rare moralist as well as a rare story-teller. The whole portrait of Mr. Casaubon has an admirably sustained greyness of tone in which the shadows are never carried to the vulgar black of coarser artists. Every stroke contributes to the unwholesome, helplessly sinister expression. Here and there perhaps (as in his habitual diction), there is a hint of exaggeration; but we confess we like fancy to be fanciful. Mr. Brooke and Mr. Garth are in their different lines supremely genial creations; they are drawn with the touch of a Dickens chastened and intellectualized. Mrs. Cadwallader is, in another walk of life, a match for Mrs. Poyser, and Celia Brooke is as pretty a fool as any of Miss Austen's. Mr. Farebrother and his delightful "womankind" belong to a large group of figures begotten of the superabundance of the author's creative instinct. At times they seem to encumber the stage and to produce a rather ponderous mass of dialogue; but they add to the reader's impression of having walked in the Middlemarch lanes and listened to the Middlemarch accent. To but one of these accessory episodes—that of Mr. Bulstrode, with its multiplex ramifications—do we take exception. It has a slightly artificial cast, a melodramatic tinge, unfriendly to the richly natural coloring of the whole. Bulstrode himself—with the history of whose troubled conscience the author has taken great pains—is, to our sense, too diffusely treated; he never grasps the reader's attention. But the touch of genius is never idle or vain. The obscure figure of Bulstrode's comely wife emerges at the needful moment, under a few light strokes, into the happiest reality.

All these people, solid and vivid in their varying degrees, are members of a deeply human little world, the full reflection of whose antique image is the great merit of these volumes. How bravely rounded a little world the author has made it—with how dense an atmosphere of interests and passions and loves and enmities and strivings and failings, and how motley a group of great folk and small, all after their kind, she has filled it, the reader must learn for himself. No writer seems to us to have drawn from a richer stock of those long-cherished memories which one's later philosophy makes doubly tender. There are few figures in the book which do not seem to have grown mellow in the author's mind. English readers may fancy they enjoy the "atmosphere" of *Middlemarch*; but we maintain that to relish its inner essence we must—for reasons too numerous to detail—be an American. The author has commissioned herself to be real, her native tendency being that of an idealist, and the intellectual result is a very fertilizing mixture. The constant presence of thought, of generalizing instinct, of *brain*, in a word, behind her observation, gives the latter its great value and her whole manner its high superiority. It denotes a mind in which imagination is illumined by faculties rarely found in fellowship with it. In this respect—in that broad reach of vision which would make the worthy historian of solemn fact as well as wanton fiction—George Eliot seems to us among English romancers to stand alone. Fielding approaches her, but to our mind, she surpasses Fielding. Fielding was didactic—the author of *Middlemarch* is really philosophic. These great qualities imply corresponding perils. The first is the loss of simplicity. George Eliot lost hers some time since: it lies buried (in a splendid mausoleum) in *Romola*. Many of the discursive portions of *Middlemarch* are, as we may say, too clever by half. The author wishes to say too many things, and to say them too well; to recommend herself to a scientific audience. Her style, rich and flexible as it is, is apt to betray her on these transcendental flights; we find, in our copy, a dozen passages marked "obscure." *Silas Marner* has a delightful tinge of Goldsmith—we may almost call it: *Middlemarch* is too often an echo of Messrs. Darwin and Huxley. In spite of these faults—which it seems graceless to indicate with this crude rapidity—it remains a very splendid performance. It sets a limit, we think, to the development of the old-fashioned English novel. Its diffuseness, on which we have touched, makes it too copious a dose of pure fiction. If we write novels so, how shall we write History? But it is nevertheless a contribution of the first importance to the rich imaginative department of our literature.

JOSEPH JACOBS
From "Mordecai: A Protest
against the Critics" (1877)
Jewish Ideals and Other Essays
1896, pp. 61–83

The critics have had their say: the recording angels of literature, more sorrowful than angry, have written down *Daniel Deronda* a failure. And there seems to be at least this much of truth in their judgment, that one of the parts of which the book is composed has failed to interest or even to reach its audience. For the least observant reader must have noticed that *Daniel Deronda* is made up of two almost unconnected parts, either of which can be read without the other. Every "book" after the first is divided into two parts, whose only claim to be included under the same covers is the common action or inaction of the eponymous hero. One set of characters and interests centres round the fate and fortunes of Gwendolen Harleth, and of this part of the book we can surely say that it has excited as much interest and bitten as deeply into men's minds as any of the author's previous studies of female character. Indeed, we would submit that George Eliot's last portrait of femal egoism is in many ways her best; her hand has become more tender, and, because more tender, more true than when she drew such narrow types as Hetty Sorrel and Rosamond Vincy, so unnaturally consistent in their selfishness. The story of Gwendolen Harleth's purification from egoism is, then, one might say, even a greater success than the former pictures of girlish struggles, and displays the author's distinguishing excellences in undiminished brilliancy. But there is another part of the book with which the English-speaking public and its literary "tasters" have failed to sympathise, and which they have mostly been tempted to omit on reperusal. The tragedy of Mordecai Cohen's missionary labours, on which the author has spent immense labour of invention and research, must be pronounced to have completely failed in reaching and exciting the interest and sympathy of the ordinary reader. Mr. Bagehot has told us that the greatest pain man can feel is the pain of a new idea, and the readers of *Daniel Deronda* have refused painfully to assimilate the new idea of the Mordecai part of the book. This idea we take to be that Judaism stands on the same level as Christianity, perhaps even on a higher level, in point of rationality and capacity to satisfy the wants of the religious consciousness, "the hitherto neglected reality," to use the author's own words (ii. 292), "that Judaism is something still throbbing in human lives, still making for them the only conceivable vesture of the world." The difficulty of accepting this new idea comes out most prominently in the jar most readers must have felt in the omission of any explanation of the easy transition of Deronda from the Christianity in which he was bred to the Judaism into which he had been born.

The present notice proposes to discuss the failure of this unsuccessful part, from the standpoint of one for whom this initial difficulty does not exist, and who has from his childhood seen the world habited in those Hebrew Old Clothes of which Mr. Carlyle and others have spoken so slightingly. And the first thing that it is natural for a Jew to say about *Daniel Deronda* is some expression of gratitude for the wonderful completeness and accuracy with which George Eliot has portrayed the Jewish nature. Hitherto the Jew in English fiction has fared unhappily, being always represented as a monstrosity, most frequently on the side of malevolence and greed, as in Marlowe's Barabas and Dickens's Fagin, or sometimes, as in Dickens's Riah, still more exasperatingly on the side of impossible benevolence. What we want is truth, not exaggeration, and truth George Eliot has given us with the large justice of the great artist. The gallery of Jewish portraits contained in *Daniel Deronda* gives in a marvellously full and accurate way all the many sides of our complex national character. The artistic element, with the proper omission of painting and sculpture, in which Jews, though eminent, have not been pre-eminent, is well represented by Klesmer, Mirah, and the Alcharisi. Ezra Cohen is a type of the commonplace Jew, the familiar figure of prosperous mercantile dealing, the best-known trait of Jews to

Englishmen; while little Jacob exhibits in a very humorous form the well-known precocity of Jewish children. The affectionate relations of Ezra Cohen and his mother, and the tender respect of Mordecai and Mirah for the memory of theirs, point to the exceptional influence of the Mother and the Home in the inner life of Jews. Then in Kalonymos, whom we feel tempted to call the Wandering Jew, we get the nomadic spirit which has worked in Israel from times long previous to the Dispersion, while all must join in the scorn the author evidently feels for Pash, the Jew who is no Jew. Yet he is the representative of what might be called the Heine side of Jewry—the wit and cynicism that reached their greatest intensity in the poet of Young Germany. The more temperate Gideon represents, it is to be feared, a large proportion of English Jews, one not ashamed of his race, yet not proud of it, and willing to see the racial and religious distinctions we have fought for so valiantly die out and perish utterly among men. Perhaps the most successful of the minor portraits is that of the black sheep Lapidoth, the Jew with no redeeming love for family, race, or country to preserve him from that sordid egoism—the new name for wickedness—into which he has sunk. His utter unconsciousness of good and evil is powerfully depicted in the masterly analysis of his state of mind before purloining Deronda's ring. To some extent the weird figure of the Alcharisi serves as a sort of companion picture of female renunciation of racial claims, but the struggle between her rebellious will and what old-fashioned folk call the Will of God (Professor Clifford would perhaps name it the Tribal Will) raises her to a tragic height which makes Deronda's mother perhaps the most imposing figure in the book. Deronda himself, by the circumstance of his education, is prevented from typifying any of the social distinctions of a Jew, yet it is not unlikely that his gravity of manner and many-sided sympathy were meant by the author to be taken as hereditary traits.

These, with Ram the bookseller, the English Jew of the pre-emancipation era, and some minor characters, give to the reader a most complete picture of Jews and Jewesses in their habits as they live, of Jews and Jewesses as members of a peculiar people in relation to the Gentile world. To point the moral of human fallibility, besides some minor slips in ceremonial details, on which it were ungrateful to dwell, [1] we cannot but think (a critic is nothing if not critical) that the author has failed to give in Mirah an adequate type of Jewish girlhood. Mirah is undoubtedly tame; and tameness, for those who know them, is the last infirmity of Jewish girls. Still, even here the sad experience of Mirah's youth may be held to have somewhat palliated any want of brightness, and the extra vivacity of Mrs. Cohen junior perhaps supplies the deficiency.

So much for the outer life of Judaism. The English reader will find here no idea so startlingly novel as to raise opposition to its admission, or to disturb his complacent feeling of superiority over Jews in all but a certain practical sagacity (he calls it sharpness or cunning), which must be postulated to explain the "differentia of success" characterising the Jewish species of commercial dealings. One new fact he may indeed profitably learn: from the large group of Jewish characters in *Daniel Deronda* he may perhaps gather that there are Jews and Jews, that they are not all Lapidoths, nor even all Ezra Cohens, as he has been accustomed to think.

But the new idea of which we have spoken is embodied in the person of Mordecai Cohen, the Jew *par excellence* of the book, the embodiment of the inner life of Judaism. The very fact of this recognition of an inner life, not to speak of the grand personality in which she has typified it, entitles George Eliot to the heart-deep gratitude of all Jews; the more so inasmuch as

she has hazarded and, at least temporarily, lost success for her most elaborated production by endeavouring to battle with the commonplace and conventional ideas about Judaism. The present article aims at striking another blow to convince the English world of the existence in the present day, and for all past time, of a spiritual life in Judaism. And we can conceive of no better point of defence for the position than the historic probability of the character of Mordecai, which critics have found so mystic, vague, and impossible.

For those who know anything of the great leaders of spiritual Judaism will recognise in Mordecai all the traits that have characterised them. Saul of Tarsus, Ibn Gebirol (Avicebron), Jehuda Halevi, Ibn Ezra, Maimonides, Abrabanel, Spinoza, Mendelssohn (not to mention other still more unfamiliar names) were all men like Mordecai—rich in inward wealth, yet content to earn a scanty livelihood by some handicraft; ardently spiritual, yet keenly alive to the claims of home affection; widely erudite, yet profoundly acquainted with human nature; mystics, yet with much method in their mysticism. The author seems even to have a bolder application of the historic continuity of the Hebraic spirit in view: she evidently wishes Mordecai to be regarded as a "survival" of the prophetic spirit, a kind of Isaiah Redivivus. Hence a somewhat unreal effect is produced by his use of a diction similar to what might be expected from a "Greater Prophet" stepping out of the pages of the Authorised Version. Still, it is to be remembered that we almost always see Mordecai in states of intense excitement, when his thought would naturally clothe itself in the forms in which all his literary efforts had been written. He speaks in a sufficiently prosaic and unbiblical style when the subject is prosaic, as to Daniel Deronda at their first meeting (ii. 336): "What are you disposed to give for it?" "I believe Mr. Ram will be satisfied with half-a-crown, sir," remarks sufficiently on the level of nineteenth-century conversation to give Mordecai some community with ordinary folk.

There is yet another quality which Mordecai shares with the sages and prophets of the past: he is a layman. The natural thing for a writer describing "a spiritual destiny embraced eagerly in youth," a representative of the religious life of a nation, would be to describe some young priest ardently striving for the spiritual enlightenment of his flock, some Mr. Tryan, some Savonarola; and it would have been right for all other religions. But in Judaism the inner development of the Spirit has been carried on almost entirely by laymen: the Jewish Summa Theologiæ, *The Guide to the Perplexed (Morê Nebouchim)* of Maimonides, was written by a physician. We shall be using more familiar illustrations when we remind the reader that Moses and, above all, the prophets were men from the lay community, not members of an organised priesthood. This may account for that spirit of Compromise (writers of the New English call it "adaptation to environment"), which is as marked a characteristic of the religious history of Jews as of the political history of Englishmen. Other religions have had churches, bureaucracies; Judaism has had a synagogue, a representative assembly.

Mordecai shares yet another gift of his predecessors: he is a poet. The fragment in chapter xxxviii. commencing—

Away from me the garment of forgetfulness,
Withering the heart,

might well be a translation from a Piut of Ibn Gebirol or a Selicha of Jehuda Halevi, and makes him a fit *dramatis persona* of that "national tragedy lasting 1500 years, in which the actors have been also the heroes and the poets."

We do not speak without knowledge of the history of Jews,

post-biblical as well as biblical, when we say that Mordecai Cohen is a lineal successor of those great leaders of spiritual Judaism who have fought in the van in that moral warfare which Judaism has waged and won against the whole world; a fitting companion of that valiant band which has guarded through the ages the ark of the Lord intrusted to Israel's keeping 4000 years ago; a noble representative of that spirit of resistance that has repulsed the most powerful disintegrating forces ever brought against a nation or a creed. A "nation of shopkeepers" has produced a Milton, a Shelley, a Newman; a "nation of pawnbrokers," if you will, has given birth to a Jehuda Halevi, a Spinoza, a Mordecai. ⟨. . .⟩

We have laid so much stress upon the artistic truth of Mordecai's character because, if this be granted, it is inexplicable that the central incident of the Jewish part of *Daniel Deronda*, the meeting on the bridge between him and Deronda, should have failed to strike readers as perhaps the most remarkable incident in English fiction. If Mordecai has artistic reality, we contend that the meeting on the bridge in chapter xl. reaches a tragic intensity which almost transcends the power of the novel, and would perhaps require the manifold emotive inlets of the Wagnerian drama to do it justice—eye, ear, brain, and heart should all be responsive. We boldly deny greater tragic intensity to any incident in Shakespeare. Nor are there wanting signs that the author herself, no contemptible critic of her own productions, sets an equal value on the incident. In the motto prefixed to chapter xxxviii., describing Mordecai's yearnings, she tells us in Brownesque English—

"There be who hold that the deeper tragedy were a Prometheus bound, not *after*, but *before*, he had well got the celestial fire into the νάρθηξ, whereby it might be conveyed to mortals. Thrust by the Kratos and Bia of instituted methods into a solitude of despised ideas, fastened in throbbing helplessness by the fatal pressure of poverty and disease—a solitude where many pass by, but none regard."

In other words, George Eliot considers the circumstances of Mordecai's fate to surpass in tragic pathos the most colossal monument of Greek dramatic art. Notice, too, the care with which she leads up to the incident. In chapter xxxvii. we have Deronda coming to the Meyricks at Chelsea to announce to Mirah the forthcoming visit of Klesmer, and the chapter finishes as he is leaving Chelsea. The next chapter (xxxviii.) is filled with a description of Mordecai's yearning for a spiritual successor, and give us *en passant* a fine picture of the scene of the meeting (iii. 137). We get here, in short, all we need to understand and sympathise with the final episode of the "book;" but lest we should come upon the fulfilment of the prophecy with too vivid a memory of the author's sublimation of the idea of prophecy, we have interposed, like a comic scene in an Elizabethan tragedy, the magnificent account of Klesmer's visit to the Meyricks in chap. xxxix., which clearly occurred *after* the events described in chapter xl., which takes up the stream of narrative from chapter xxxvii.

It seems to us clear that all this seemingly inartistic transposition of events is intended to make the incident of chapter xl. stand out more sharply into relief. We have the miracle explained away, it is true—the modern analytic spirit requires it—but the author wishes us to forget the explanation, or at least to relegate the intellectual element of chapter xxxviii. to the unconscious background, where it may be ready to assist, though not present to obstruct, emotion. All this care appears to show the importance attached by the author to the last chapter of Book v.

And in itself, apart from what the author may think of it,

what a soul-moving incident is there contained! A representative of an ancient world-important people, whose royalty of wrongs makes the aristocracies of Europe appear petty, finds himself clutched by the gripping hands of want and death before he can move the world to that vision of the Phœnix-rise of Israel which the prophetic instincts of his race have brought up clear before him. Careless of his own comfort, careless of coming death, he desires only to live anew—as the quasi-Positivist doctrine of the Cabbala bids him live—in "minds made nobler by his presence." His prophetic vision pictures to him the very lineaments of his spiritual *alter ego*, whom he pathetically thinks of as differing from himself in all externals, and, as death draws nigh, the very scene of their meeting. And in this nineteenth century, in prosaic London, this inward vision of the poor consumptive Jew is fulfilled to the letter.

Would it be too bold a suggestion if we suspected the author of having typified in the meeting of Deronda and Mordecai that

> One far-off divine event
> To which the whole creation moves,

the meeting of Israel and its Redeemer? In personal characteristics, in majestic gravity (we cannot imagine Deronda laughing), in width of sympathy and depth of tenderness, even in outward appearance, Daniel resembles the great Galilean Pharisee whom all Christendom has accepted as in very truth the Messiah that will restore Judæa to the Holy People. To say the least, the author suggests the audacity in her comparison of the two to the figures of Jesus and the Pharisee in Titian's "Tribute Money." ⟨. . .⟩

Enough has perhaps been said to show that Mordecai's views about the future of Judaism and of Jews have all history and much reason on their side, and display those powers of intellectual intuition of the future which the psychological system of Maimonides assigns to the Prophet. And we have perhaps contributed somewhat to an explanation of Deronda's acceptance of his spiritual inheritance. Like Mordecai, Deronda protests against the "blasphemy of the time," that men should stand by as spectators of life instead of living. But before he meets with Mordecai, what noble work in life has this young and cultured Englishman with his thousands a year? This age of unfaith gives no outlet for his deep, spiritual yearnings, nor for those of thousands like him. The old beliefs are gone; the world is godless, and Deronda cannot, for all the critics have said, offer to Gwendolen Grandcourt any consolation in the higher order of things instead of the vague platitudes which alone remain to be offered. Yet there comes to this young ardent soul an angel of the Lord (albeit in the shape of a poor Jew watch-mender) with a burning message, giving a mission in life as grand as the most far-reaching ideal he could have formed. Is it strange that his thirsty soul should have swallowed up the soul of Mordecai, in the Cabbalistic way which the latter often refers to? Is it strange that Deronda should not have refused the heritage of his race when offered by the hands of Mirah's brother? But is it not strange that the literary leaders of England should have failed to see aught but unsatisfactory vagueness in all the parts of *Daniel Deronda* which treat of the relations of the hero with Mordecai Cohen? Is it possible that they have failed to see the grandeur and beauty of these incidents because of the lack of that force of imagination necessary to pierce to the pathos of a contemporary tragedy, however powerful their capacity might be to see the romance of a Rebecca of York, or the pathos of a Baruch Spinoza?

One possible source of misconception for English readers

may be mentioned. Since the time of Moses Mendelssohn the home of spiritual Judaism has been in Germany, and George Eliot, whose pages are informed with the writings of German Jews like Zunz, Geiger, and Grätz, has, with true historic insight, attributed Mordecai's spiritual birth to the teachings of his German uncle. English Judaism is without signs of life: the only working of the spirit, the abortive reform agitation, was due to a similar movement in Germany. And English Jews have themselves much to blame for the neglect that English criticism has shown for Mordecai.

What we have attempted to show has been that the adverse criticism on the Mordecai part of *Daniel Deronda* has been due to lack of sympathy and want of knowledge on the part of the critics, and hence its failure is not (if we must use the word) objective. If a young lady refuses to see any pathos in Othello's fate because she dislikes dark complexions, we blame the young lady, not Shakespeare; and if the critics have refused to see the pathos of Mordecai's fate because he is a Jew of the present day, so much the worse for the critics.

Notes

1. E.g., Taliths or fringed mantles are not worn on Friday nights (ii. 292–300); the Kaddish, or prayer in honour of the dead, is only said for eleven months, not eleven years (iv. 92), and then only by a son. Mirah seems to be under the same delusion (ii. 306). Before breaking the bread (ii. 356), Cohen should have "made Kiddush," i.e., pronounced a blessing over some sacramental wine. It is doubtful whether Cohen would have paid money and written a pawn-ticket on Sabbath eve, but this may be intentional.

GEORGE WILLIS COOKE
"The Limitations of Her Thought"
George Eliot: A Critical Study of Her Life, Writings and Philosophy
1884, pp. 413–24

It must be remembered that George Eliot does not use the novel merely for the purpose of inculcating certain doctrines, and that her genius for artistic creation is of a very high order. In dealing with her as a thinker and as a moral and religious teacher, she is to be regarded, first of all, as a poet and an artist. Her ethics are subordinate to her art; her religion is subsidiary to her genius. That she always deliberately set about the task of introducing her positivism into the substance of her novels is not to be supposed. This would be to imply a forgetfulness on her part of her own methods, and a prostration of art to purposes she would have scorned to adopt. This is evidently true, however, that certain features of the positive and the evolution philosophy had so thoroughly approved themselves to her mind as to cause them to be accepted as a completely satisfactory explanation of the world, so far as any explanation is possible. So heartily were they received, so fully did they become incorporated with the substance of her thinking, that she viewed all human experiences in their light. They had ceased to be theory and speculation with her. When she thought about the world, when she observed the acts of men, the positivist explanation was at once applied, and instinctively.

That she did teach positivism is unfortunately true, so far as her literary touch and expression is concerned. That philosophy affects all her books with its subtly insinuating flavor, and it gives meaning and bias to most of them. They thus gain in definiteness of purpose, in moral vigor, in

minutely faithful study of some phases of human experience, and in a massive impression of thoughtfulness which her work creates. At the same time, they undoubtedly lose in value as studies of life; in free range of expression for her genius, her poetry and her art; and in that spiritual vision which looks forward with keen gazing eyes of hope and confident inquiry.

Her teaching, like most teaching, is a mingled good and evil. In more than one direction her ethical and religious influence was most wholesome and effective. She brought into clear light a few great facts, and made them the more conspicuous by the strong emphasis she gave them. This is, in the main, the method of all teaching and of all progress. Development seldom proceeds in a direct line, but rather, so far as man is concerned, by forcible emphasis laid on some great fact which has been previously neglected. The idealism of a previous age had shown the value of certain facts and tendencies in human nature, but it had exaggerated some faculties and capacities of man, as well as neglected others. In consequence, our own time swings to the other extreme, and cannot have too much of evolution and positivism.

Idealism is in human nature, and will give itself expression. Positivism is also a result of our experience and of our study of the universe, both material and mental; it is a result of the desire for definite knowledge. As a re-action against the excesses of idealism it is a powerful leaven, and it brings into necessary prominence those facts which are neglected by the opposite philosophy. It takes account of facts, and scorns mysticism; and it thus appeals to a deep-seated bias of the time.

George Eliot's books have an interest as an attempt at an interpretation of life from its more practical and realistic side, and not less as a re-action against the influences of very nearly all the great literary minds of the earlier half of the century in England. Under the lead of Coleridge and Wordsworth, and influenced by German thought and literature, a remarkable movement was then developed in English literature. The outcome of that movement has been surpassed only by that of the age of Shakspere. Freshness of thought, love of nature, profound humanitarian convictions, and spontaneity wedded to great largeness of ideas, characterize this period and its noble work. Such an age is almost invariably followed by an age of re-action, criticism, realism and analysis. An instinctive demand for a portrayal of the more positive side of life, and the influence of science, have developed a new literary school. For doctrine it teaches agnosticism, and in method it cares mainly for art and beauty of form. Towards the development of the new school George Eliot has been a leading influence, though her sympathies have not gone with all its tendencies and results.

If Wordsworth exaggerated the importance of the intuitive and personal, George Eliot equally exaggerated the value of the historic and hereditary. It was desirable, however, that the relations of life to the past should be brought out more distinctly by a literary development of their relations to the present, and that the influence of social heredity should be seen as affecting life on all sides. Tradition is a large and persistent element in the better life of the race, while the past certainly has a powerful influence over the present. This fact was neglected by Wordsworth, and especially is it neglected by the intuitive philosophies. They ignore the lessons of the past, and assume that a new and perfect world is to be evoked from the depths of consciousness. That to think a better world is to create a better world, they seem to take for granted, while the fact is that the truer life is the result of a painful and long-continued struggle against adverse conditions. What has been, persists in remaining, and the past, with all its narrowness and prejudices, continues to influence men more powerfully than does clear thought or regard for the truth. Emotion and sentiment cling about what has become sacred with age. Channels for thought and activity having once been made, it is very difficult to abandon them for untried paths approved even by reason.

The historic view is one of much importance, and is likely to be overlooked by the poets and novelists. It is also ignored by the radicals in morals and religion. Much which George Eliot says on this subject is of great value, and may be heeded with the utmost profit. Her words of wisdom, however, lose much of their value because they utterly ignore those spontaneous and supernatural elements of man's higher life which lift it quite out of the region of dependence on history.

There is something to be said in behalf of George Eliot's attitude towards religion, which caused her to hold it in reverence, even when rejecting the objective validity of its dogmas. Yet much more is to be said for that other attitude, which is faithful to the law of reason, and believes that reason is competent to say some truer and larger word on a subject of such vital importance and such constant interest to man. That both reason and tradition are to be listened to reverently is true, but George Eliot so zealously espoused the cause of tradition as to give it an undue prominence. Her lesson was needed, however, and we may be all the better able to profit by it because she was so much an enthusiast in proclaiming its value. The even poise of perfect truth is no more to be had from her pages than from those of others.

The emphasis she laid on feeling and sentiment was a needed one, as a counterpoise to the exaggerations of rationalism. Man does live in his feelings more than in his reason. He is a being of sentiment, a creature of impulse, his social life is one of the affections. In all the ranges of his moral, religious and social life he is guided mainly by his emotions and sentiments. It cannot be said, however, as George Eliot would have us say, that these are human born and have no higher meaning. They are the outgrowth of spiritual reality, as well as of human experience; they repeat the foregleams and foresights of a

far-off divine event,
To which the whole creation moves.

Life is enriched and flooded with light by the emotions, and feeling, true and tender and pure, is as much the symbol of humanity as reason itself. It was therefore well that some one should attempt to justify the emotional life against the aspersions of those who have done it grave injustice. It is true that man is not a being who wholly arrives at his method of life through reason, but feeling lends quite as important aid. He does not only think, but he has emotions as well; he not only weighs evidence, but he acts by impulse. He is continually led by the emotions, sentiments and impulses created for him by the life of ages past. Without emotion there could be no art, no poetry and no music. Without emotion there would be no religion and no spiritual life. Sentiment sweetens, beautifies and endears all that is human and natural

Emotion and the affections, however, seem to be shorn of their highest beauty and glory when they are restricted to a merely earthly origin and compass of power. It is altogether impossible to believe that their own impulse to look beyond the human is a delusion, and that they really have nothing to report that is valid from beyond the little round which man treads. To believe in the human beauty and glory of the feelings, and to rejoice in their power to unite us to our kind,

need imply no forgetfulness of their demand for a wider expression and a higher communion.

Her theory of the origin of feeling is not to be accepted. It means something more than an inheritance of ancestral experience. It is the result rather than the cause of reason, for reason has an influence she did not acknowledge, and an original capacity which she never saw. Her view of feeling was mainly theoretical, for she was led in her attitude towards the facts of life, not by sentiment, but by reason. Hers was a thoughtful rather than an impulsive mind, and given to logic more than to emotion.

Her enthusiasm for altruism, her zeal for humanity, lends a delightful feature to her books. It gives a glow and a consecration to her work, and makes her as great a prophet as positivism is capable of creating. And it is no idle power she awakens in her positivist faith in man. She shames those who claim a broader and better faith. Zeal for man is no mean gospel, as she gives life and meaning to it in her books. To live for others, too many are not likely to do. She made altruism beautiful, she made it a consecration and a religion. Those who cannot accept her agnosticism and her positivism may learn much from her faith in man and from her enthusiasm for humanity. No faith is worth much which does not lead to a truer and a more helpful love of man. Any faith is good in so far as it makes us more humane and sympathetic. In this regard, the radicalism of George Eliot was a great advance on much of the freethinking of our century. She desired to build, not to destroy. She was no iconoclast, no hater of what other men love and venerate. Her tendencies were all on the side of progress, good order and social growth.

Her conception of the organic social life of the race is one of great value. It led her to believe in the possibility of a social organization in the future based on science, and better capable of meeting all the wants of mankind than the more personal and competitive methods have done. This belief in the organic unity of the race is not necessarily positivist in its character, for Hegel entertained it as fully as does Herbert Spencer. The larger social life will come, however, as individuals are moved to lead the way, and not alone as the result of a general evolutionary process. On its mental side, her social theory is to be regarded with grave suspicions, for it brings all minds to the same level. No mind of commanding influence is to be found in her books. No powerful intellect gives greatness to any of her plots. Her Felix Holt is not a man of original and positive thought. We accept, but do not enthusiastically admire him. Deronda is a noble character, but he in no sense represents the largest things of which a social leader is capable. He disappoints and is weak, and he has no power to create the highest kind of leadership. In other words, he is not a great man. The world's reformers have been of another temper and mettle. He is no Mazzini, no Luther. George Eliot's social theories left no room for such men. They were superfluous in her social system. The man not to be explained by heredity and tradition had no place in her books; and no genius, no great man, can ever be explained by heredity and tradition alone.

George Eliot evidently desired to destroy individualism as a social force. The individual, according to her teaching, is to renounce himself for the sake of the race. He is to live, not as a personal being, but as a member of the social organization; to develop his altruistic nature, not to perfect his personal character. The finer flavor of personality is brushed mercilessly away by this method.

Reason needs to be justified in opposition to her excessive praise of feeling. Meanwhile, the capacity of man to live a life higher than that of his social state is to be asserted. He is indeed a member of humanity, but humanity does not absorb him to the cost of his personality. Life is strong in those ages in which the individual is able to assert his own personality, in opposition to what is imperfect and untrue in the life of his time. This failure to recognize the worth and capacity of the individual is a most serious defect in George Eliot's work, and mars it in many directions. A very competent critic has shown how serious is the limitation arising in this manner, and permeating her books with a false conception of life.

"So far as George Eliot's life is concerned," says Mr. Stopford Brooke, "she was eager in her self-development, and as eager in her sympathies. But it was a different matter in the main drift of her work. She lowered the power of individualism. Nay, she did not believe in its having any self-caused or God-caused existence. Few have individualized their characters more than she did, and of these characters we have many distinct types. But she individualized them with, I may say, almost the set purpose of showing that their individualism was to be sacrificed to the general welfare of the race. The more her characters cling to their individuality the more they fail in reaching happiness or peace. If they are noble characters, they are finally obliged, through their very nobility, to surrender all their ideals, all their personal hopes, all the individual ends they hoped to develop; and they reach peace finally only through utter surrender of personality in humanity. The characters of her books who do not do this, who cling to their individuality and maintain it, succeed in life, for the most part, if they are strong; are broken to pieces if they are weak; but in all cases, save one, are not the noble but the ignoble characters. The whole of her books is a suppressed attack on individualism, and an exaltation of self-renunciation as the only force of progress, as the only ground of morality. I leave aside here, as apart from the moral side of the subject, the view that individual power or weakness of any kind is the consequence of the past, of race, of physical causes. What a man is found to do is not affected by that, in her view. . . . No one can deny that the morality is a lofty one, and, as far as it asserts self-renunciation, entirely useful; we have with all our hearts to thank George Eliot for that part of her work. But when sacrifice of self is made, in its last effort, equivalent to the sacrifice of individuality, the doctrine of self-renunciation is driven to a vicious extreme. It is not self-sacrifice which is then demanded, it is suicide . . . Fully accepted, it would reduce the whole of the human race to hopelessness. That, indeed, is the last result. A sad and fatal hopelessness of life broods over all the nobler characters. All their early ideals are sacrificed, all their early joys depart, all the pictures they formed are blotted out. They gain peace through renunciation, after long failure; some happiness in yielding to the inevitable, and harmonizing life with it; and some blessedness in doing all they can for the progress of those who follow them, for the good of those that are with them. Their self is conquered, not through ennoblement of personality, but through annihilation of personality. And having surrendered their separate personality, they then attain the fitting end, silence forevermore. It is no wonder that no characters are so sad, that none steep the reader in such hopelessness of joy, as the noble characters of the later works of George Eliot. They want the mighty power, the enkindling hopes, the resurrection of life, the joy and rapture which deepens toward death and enables man to take up the ideals of youth again."

If too severe in some directions, this criticism is substantially sound. It does not matter what theory of personality we adopt, in a philosophical sense, if that theory upholds personal confidence and force of will. If it does not do this, the whole result is evil. This lack of faith in personality saddened all the work done by George Eliot. In theory a believer in an everbrightening future, and no pessimist, yet the outcome of her work is dark with despondency and grief.

Life is sad, hard and ascetic in her treatment of it. An ascetic tone runs through all her work, the result of her theories of renunciation. The same sternness and cheerlessness is to be seen in the poetry and painting of the pre-Raphaelites. The joy, freshness and sunniness of Raphael is not to be found in their work. Life is painful, puritanic and depressing to them. Old age seems to be upon them, or the decadence of a people that has once been great. Human nature does not need that this strain be put upon it. Life is stronger when more assertive of itself. It has a right to assert itself in defiance of mere rules, and only when it does so is it true and great. The ascetic tone is one of the worst results of a scientific view of the world as applied to literature; for it is thoroughly false both in fact and in sentiment. The strong, hopeful, youthful look at life is the one which literature demands, and because it is the nearest the heart and spirit of life itself. The dead nation produces a dead literature. The age made doubtful by an excess of science produces a literature burdened with sadness and pain. Great and truthful as it may be, it lacks in power to conquer the world. It shows, not the power of Homer, but the power of Lucretius.

Her altruism has its side of truth, but not all of the truth is in it. Any system of thought which sees nothing beyond man is not likely to find that which is most characteristic in man himself. He is to be fathomed, if fathomed at all, by some other line than that of his own experience. If he explains the universe, the universe is also necessary to explain him. Man apart from the supersensuous is as little to be understood as man apart from humanity. He belongs to a Universal Order quite as much as he belongs to the human order. Man may be explained by evolution, but evolution is not to be explained by anything in the nature of man. It requires some larger field of vision to take note of that elemental law. Not less true is it that mind does not come obediently under this method of explanation, that it demands account of how matter is transformed into thought. The law of thought needs to be solved after mind is evolved.

There is occasion for surprise that a mind so acute and logical as George Eliot's did not perceive that the evolution philosophy has failed to settle any of the greater problems suggested by Kant. The studies of Darwin and Spencer have certainly made it impossible longer to accept Locke's theory of the origin of all knowledge in individual experience, but they have not in any degree explained the process of thought or the origin of ideas. The gulf between the physiological processes in the brain and thought has not been bridged even by a rope walk. The total disparity of mind and matter resists all efforts to reduce them to one. The utmost which the evolution philosophy has so far done, is to attempt to prove that mind is a function of matter or of the physiological process. This conclusion is as far as possible from being that of unity of mind and matter.

That man is very ignorant, and that this world ought to demand the greater share of his attention and energies, are propositions every reasonable person is ready to accept. Granted their truth, all that is necessarily true in agnosticism has been arrived at. It is a persistent refusal to see what lies behind outward facts which gives agnosticism all its practical justification. Art itself is a sufficient refutation of the assertion that we know nothing of what lies behind the apparent. That we know something of causes, every person who uses his own mind may be aware. At the same time, the rejection of the doctrine of rights argues obedience to a theory, rather than humble acceptance of the facts of history. That doctrine of rights, so scorned by George Eliot, has wrought most of the great and wholesome social changes of modern times. Her theory of duties can show no historic results whatever.

To separate George Eliot's theories from her genius it seems impossible to do, but this it is necessary to do in order to give both their proper place. All praise, her work demands on its side where genius is active. It is as a thinker, as a theorizer, she is to be criticised and to be declared wanting. Her work was crippled by her philosophy, or if not crippled, then it was made less strong of limb and vigorous of body by that same philosophy. It is true of her as of Wordsworth, that she grew prosy because she tried to be philosophical. It is true of her as it is not true of him, that her work lacks in the breadth which a large view of the world gives. His was no provincial conception of nature or of man. Hers was so in a most emphatic sense. The philosophy she adopted is not and cannot become the philosophy of more than a small number of persons. In the nature of the case it is doomed to be the faith of a few students and cultured people. It can stir no common life, develop no historic movements, inaugurate no reforms, nor give to life a diviner meaning. Whether it be true or not,—and this need not here be asked,—this social and moral limitation of its power is enough to condemn it for the purposes of literature. In so far as George Eliot's work is artistic, poetic, moral and human, it is very great, and no word too strong can be said in its praise. It is not too excessive enthusiasm to call her, on the whole, the equal of any novelist. Her genius is commanding and elemental. She has originality, strength of purpose, and a profound insight into character. Yet her work is weakened by its attachment to a narrow theory of life. Her philosophy is transitory in its nature. It cannot hold its own, as developed by her, for any great length of time. It has the elements of its own destruction in itself. The curious may read her for her speculations; the many will read her for her realism, her humanity and her genius. In truth, then, it would have been better if her work had been inspired by great spiritual aims and convictions.

VIDA D. SCUDDER
From "George Eliot and the Social Conscience"
Social Ideals in English Letters
1898, pp. 180–92

These souls of the new order George Eliot was first among English novelists to recognize and describe. Probably this is because she was herself one of them. Her books express the restless and inquiring mood of the central Victorian period. It is no longer enough to picture life, as do the earlier novelists: with George Eliot, we seek to wrest from life its hidden secrets. Her attitude is that of the thinking people of her time: deeply agitated by ethical problems, trying earnestly to adjust itself to widening horizons and to contracting skies.

The interests that controlled English thought between 1830 and 1870 were chiefly religious; and the most obvious fact about George Eliot's novels is their spiritual appeal. To run over the tables of contents in the leading magazines during these years, and compute proportion of subjects, would convince any one that religious speculation dominated all other questions in the mind of the reading public. From the

beginning of the period, a yearning for the religious temper met a profound discontent with religious formulæ. The most life-communicating men of the day, John Stuart Mill, Cardinal Newman, Spencer, Harrison, Maurice, were all in one way or another of the religious type. The iconoclastic instinct, in matters spiritual, had ceased to give pleasure, and almost every leader of skeptical thought was in his own way making efforts toward construction. A fresh and mighty synthetic principle was introduced into the thought-world as years went on by the scientific theory formulated by the followers of Darwin; and as soon as it appeared and made its significance felt, earnest minds took up the attempt to correlate the religious instinct with evolutionary ethics. Of all the people engaged in this endeavor, George Eliot was the most vividly human. Every one of her books bears witness to the painstaking ardor of her attempts at readjustment, the sincerity of spirit with which she sought to replace the sanctions for high morality once found in dogma by new sanctions, equally stringent, found in natural law.

To transform morals and art by the infusion of evolutionary ideas—to find in the revelation of the forces that had shaped the visible universe a substitute for the old revelation from the Invisible on which humanity had been used to lean— might seem quest absorbing enough for one generation. But progress was breathlessly rapid during that half-century; nor can we fully account for the genesis of George Eliot's books without a new factor. Her work is as important in its social as in its religious aspect. It is profoundly significant as marking the transition between a period preoccupied with relations of life and evolution to that next period, in which we still live, quite as intensely absorbed with the relations of life and democracy. The first order of problems was her chief conscious interest, as it was that of the circle in which she moved; to the second, her books bear witness all the stronger because largely unconscious.

No one, reading her, can fail to see the close connection by which one order of thought led into the other. The tremendous contribution made by evolutionary ethics to the social ideal can hardly be overrated. George Eliot, first of imaginative writers, was alive to the solemn and formative power of heredity and environment, and their shaping force in the determination of duty. From *Romola* to *The Spanish Gypsy* and *Daniel Deronda*, her plots are constructed almost wholly to show how all personal passions and desires, however laudable, should yield if they come in contact with the great principles which carry the race onward toward expanding life. Study of these inexorable principles quickens in thought a new sense of the organic relation of each atom to the social whole. George Eliot's finer characters recognize with wonder or feel with constraining force the relation of the individual experience to that human past from which it sprang, that present which surrounds it, that future which it must help to create. Their intense social consciousness is possible only to an age which had outlived revolution in history, and was facing evolution in thought. Evolutionary ethics directly led the way to an enlarged recognition of social responsibility. This recognition was, as we have seen, entirely lacking in society as pictured by Dickens and Thackeray: George Eliot is the first novelist to show us a society in which it is at work.

Even apart from this great achievement, the social value of her books is high. With her two brilliant predecessors, she completes the social survey of the Victorian novel. She was bred in the country, close in heart and origin to the agricultural life of England; and her early books, *Adam Bede*, *Silas Marner*, and *The Mill on the Floss*, reflect this life, in all its quaint and leisurely charm. An England uninvaded by competition or spiritual unrest, where telegrams are unknown and the railroad is a distant rumor,—an England unchanged in essentials from the time of Shakespeare,—smiles on us from these fair and serene pages. All this attractive life belongs to the past. To-day, Dolly Winthrop can hardly keep the quaint *naïveté* of her theology, nor can it be easy even in quiet corners to find Mrs. Poyser superintending the butter, or Mrs. Tulliver weeping over the family linen. But George Eliot gave us a real gift in these kindly pictures of the England of her girlhood, showing the honesty and simplicity, the strong uprightness, the tranquil intelligence independent of book-learning, that lingered in the rural population before the word or thing "Proletariat" was thought of.

These early books are the most winning that George Eliot ever wrote. Perhaps this is because the best art has a way of springing from the heart of childish memories; perhaps because her subjects have great intrinsic beauty. To invest the lives of the ignorant and simple with pathos, dignity, and charm was almost a new departure for fiction when she began to create. Nothing more clearly evidences the strength of the impulse which sends our sophisticated world back to nature, than the growth since her day of the attraction which drew her. Under the guidance of Hardy, of Verga, of Tolstoi, we are coming to feel that the noblest art, because the most sincere, is that which reveals the free movement of elemental human passions in the large simplicity of the lives of the poor. George Eliot's early books take their place in a great literary group, strongly expressive of one phase in the most modern social feeling.

But her later books, if they probe less deep into primal instincts, have a more direct bearing on the problems that perplex us, and therefore a keener interest for the artificial creatures that we have become. She turned from those delightful pastorals where the idyllic, the grotesque, and the profoundly human blend in so tranquil a harmony; she described the stirrings of discontent, the seething of new forces, in the England of the central Victorian period. After *Silas Marner*, her books reflect the interests of the eager intellectual circle into which, as a mature woman, she entered in London. Thackeray and Dickens had showed us the life of the average, the majority,—of Poverty and Fashion, equally unintellectual. George Eliot, a few years later, showed the life, the mood, the questions, of the small minority of thinking people.

Never, surely, were books more wistful than those great novels, *Romola, Middlemarch, Daniel Deronda*. Their animus is wholly new: it is neither scorn nor laughter; it is sympathy. This sympathy, more than any other quality, gives to the work of George Eliot a depth of thoughtfulness unsounded by the shallow criticism on life of her predecessors.

In social significance, *Middlemarch* is probably the most important novel of the central Victorian period. It is certainly the most comprehensive. The social environment of the book, sketched with remarkable breadth and power, is really a summary of that which we have learned to know in essay and novel. Here is the gentry,—a country gentry, this time,—Mr. Brooke and the Chethams, with their mild dilettanteism, their lack of purpose or ideals. Here is the bourgeois society of the town, divided from the country by a seemingly impassable gulf: the Bulstrodes and Vincys, painfully devoid of sweetness and light. In the intrigue centring around old Featherstone, George Eliot has tried her hand at types that the offhand melodrama of Dickens would have treated more successfully. But Arnold himself never drew a better Philistine than Bulstrode, with his "double Hell, of not making money and not saving his soul," nor is any one of Thackeray's women more selfish, bewitching,

and trivially clever than Rosamund. George Eliot's studies of clergy are in all her books a new feature, unparalleled in fiction unless we return to the capital work of Miss Austen. *Middlemarch* gives none of her favorite and sympathetic pictures of dissent; but the Established Church is represented by admirable if rather depressing types, in Mr. Cadwallader, Mr. Farebrother, and Mr. Casaubon. Certainly, wherever the force for social salvation may reside, it is not in these gentlemen.

All these minor characters, whom Thackeray would have treated with contempt and Dickens with jest, George Eliot touches with unfailing pathos and redeems to human dignity; yet her obvious intention is to furnish through them a typical social background. Against this conventional society, she places in clear, warm relief two figures: Lydgate, the representative of intellectual force; Dorothea, the representative of moral force. Both rebel against convention, both in their different ways are routed by the world.

In Dorothea, that sweet and bewildered person, a new type of heroine appears upon the stage. Dickens' liking went out to fragile, emotional, and kittenish young ladies. In Louisa Bounderby of *Hard Times*, we may perhaps catch, as she visits Stephen Blackpool, her husband's "hand," a hint of wider compassion; but the hint is of the faintest. Thackeray, in Ethel Newcome, showed a restless, spirited, brilliant creature, ill at ease in the only life open to her. But Dorothea is run in another mould from these. That curious sense of the organic whole, that modern craving for untrammeled fellowship, for which the term altruism is degrading and no other term exists, gathers intensely in her person, and is the source of the warm glow that streams through the dreary book. Dorothea is the first example noted in English fiction of that new personal type which suffers with atoning pain for the sorrows of the world. Her life fails Wholly unguided, differing from the modern woman by her lack of any adequate training, or indeed of any training at all, she finds no cause for which to live, and had she found one, is too solely a creature of noble instincts to serve it effectively. Her marriage with Ladislaw can hardly be held more reassuring than that with Casaubon: for the brilliant young Bohemian—"a sort of a Shelley, you know," says Mr. Brooke—surely illustrates the frivolity of the forces of revolt, as conceived by George Eliot, against the solid background of English respectability, the Cadwalladers and Chethams and Bulstrodes and Brookes. Poor Dorothea! Her power has not yet changed from impulse to purpose. She represents only the second stage in the evolution of the modern heroine as a social force. The first is shown in the domestic and soft-hearted ladies of Thackeray and Dickens; the last, so far, appears in such characters as Besant's Valentine and Mrs. Ward's Marcella,—women strong to achieve in their activities and influence that large coöperation with the forces making for righteousness which earlier heroines never imagined nor desired, and which Dorothea only dreamed.

How George Eliot herself construed the significance of her Dorothea is evident from the Prelude to *Middlemarch*. She reminds us in a lovely passage of the great life of St. Theresa, and continues: "That Spanish woman who lived three hundred years ago was certainly not the last of her kind. Many Theresas have been born who found for themselves no epic life wherein there was a constant unfolding of far-resonant action: perhaps only a life of mistakes, the offspring of a certain spiritual grandeur ill-matched with the meanness of opportunity; perhaps a tragic failure which found no sacred poet, and sank unwept into oblivion. With dim lights and tangled circumstance, they tried to shape their thought and deed in noble agreement; but after all, to common eyes their struggle seemed mere inconsistency and formlessness: for these later-born Theresas were helped by no coherent social faith and order which could perform the function of knowledge for the ardently willing soul."

Middlemarch, to the author, was doubtless the epos of failure. It expressed her impassioned protest against modern society, with its lack of a "coherent social faith and order," its mammonism and dilettanteism, its conventional class-divisions, its utter inability to present to young, large, eager natures a cause to live and die for, an atmosphere in which they could expand. But to us, the book, with all its sadness, is full of hope. It marks the turn of the tide in modern fiction; for it shows characters in whom a new social idealism is stirring, and their very failure implies the promise of social salvation.

Once again, George Eliot wrote with infinite pains a large book of social studies. If *Middlemarch* is the novel of failure, *Daniel Deronda* was meant to be the novel of triumph. No character in *Middlemarch* escapes the invisible walls of the modern prison: *Daniel Deronda* opens for its hero a way to freedom, to achievement, to the self-surrender which is rapture and success.

We have already seen how hard put to it is the nineteenth century when a hero for its romances is required. It is of no use, as even great Sir Walter reveals, to import imitations from the past: they may swagger and fight and love and perform unlikely feats to any extent,—they will be only ghosts after all. For the real hero must not be a survival nor an accident; he must be formed, evolved, created, by the special conditions of his own age. The militant hero is an anomaly and an absurdity in a novel that draws its background from a peaceful commercial civilization. We want a hero who shall reveal exalted possibilities of action and devotion in the ordinary circumstances that surround the average man.

Now when the writers of fiction had been reduced to such straits that the "gorilla type" of Jane Eyre's Rochester became popular, things were really at a sad pass. Neither Bulwer nor Trollope nor Reade nor Wilkie Collins evolved nor discovered a hero. They made some faint experiments on bolder lines than those attempted by Dickens or Thackeray, but as a rule they vibrated, like their betters, between the hysterical and the insipid, and it is impossible even to recall the names of the young gentlemen who fill their leading rôles. The dearth of heroes by 1870 seemed hopeless.

Daniel Deronda was then a work of great audacity. For it was deliberately planned to present a new heroic type. Deronda is no reminiscence nor survival: he is a hero who could never have existed till our own day.

Many people have thought him a failure. He has been called shadowy, impossible,—worse still, priggish. And it is true that Derondas do not stand in wait for us at every street-corner, true also that the average man, if he meets them in real life, as he is more likely to do now than he was when the book was written, is pretty sure to resent them there as much as he does in fiction. Yet Deronda is not faultless; the modern mania of hesitation, which threatens at one time to control him, is no trait of an ideal character. But whether the drawing be executed well or ill, the conception of the character was as original as it was significant. Deronda's consciousness sends out its sensitive fibres through the whole human race, and realizes the mighty organism from within. The impulse to compassion and to service, helplessly astir in Dorothea, is in him both dominant and enlightened. The drama of the book consists in its gradual victory over every ordinary ambition and claim. For Deronda cannot spend his life in vague accidental

usefulness, a sentimental philanthropist at large. He craves a duty; but he has a strong dislike to inventing one. He can work freely and powerfully only where he belongs. At last a summons comes, and from the most unexpected quarter. The reputed son of an English baronet discovers that he is a Jew, and his people claim him. Daniel's decision is not doubtful. Fellowship with the British aristocracy, a career in Parliament, marriage with the fascinating Gwendolen, are open to him; from these he turns away, to ally himself with a race vulgar and despised. We leave him fearing that he is embarked in a hopeless cause,—the restoration of the Jews to Palestine,—but confident that he has found the emancipation which brings life, in the service of an ideal such as a commercial civilization sighed for in vain.

What drew George Eliot to the strange plot of this book? Partly, no doubt, her Hebrew sympathies: the appeal of the most wonderful racial romance ever known by the world. Largely also the opportunity offered by the situation for study of the interplay of two great natural forces, heredity and environment. These mighty forces, which so profoundly impressed her imagination, unite in most of her books to determine duty. Here they pull different ways; the resultant struggle is intensely dramatic, and heredity, the stronger, conquers. But it is impossible to account for Deronda entirely on lines of either romantic or scientific inspiration. The novel was George Eliot's last, and it appeared in 1876. By that time, social unrest was fervently at work, though it did not yet fully understand its own nature. Karl Marx was in London: only brief years were to pass before *The International* should be re-formed. A new conception, startling as that of evolution, was in the air, and demanded new readjustments. It was the conception of social democracy.

George Eliot's formulæ were those of the scientific era just closing, not those of the democratic era just at hand. But her spirit faced the future. *Daniel Deronda* reveals the sharp class cleavage breaking down under the influence of a great impulse, and the passivity of life is at an end. The book is tentative, transitional, inadequate; it marks the very beginning of a new spirit. Ten years earlier, Deronda could not have been conceived: he is no contemporary of Pendennis. Ten years later, one may be allowed to question whether he would have found his release from conventionality through a side-issue. He discovers that he is a Jew, and sacrifices all the world holds dear to identify himself with his race. Well and good! Yet the Hebrew is only one detail in the problem of the modern democracy. Had the book been written in 1886, we may easily imagine Deronda finding his cause in devotion to a wider social freedom, and espousing the side of the proletariat.

W. C. BROWNELL
"George Eliot"
Scribner's Magazine, December 1900, pp. 711–26

I

How long is it since George Eliot's name has been the subject of even a literary allusion? What has become of a vogue that only yesterday, it seems, was so great? Of course, every day has its own fiction—even ours, such as it is. But this does not exclude popular interest in august survival—Thackeray, Dickens, Jane Austen, Reade, Trollope, Charlotte Brontë, everyone but Bulwer and George Eliot, I should say. As to Bulwer, perhaps, speculation would be surplusage. The neglect, however, into which so little negligible a writer as

George Eliot has indubitably fallen is one of the most curious of current literary phenomena, and an interesting one to consider, since considering it involves also a consideration at the same time of the remarkable genius that is the subject of it. It is probably largely due to the fact that from a purely intellectual point of view people in books or out of them are both less interesting and less idiosyncratic than we were wont to suppose when George Eliot's fame was at its height.

The novelty of psychological fiction was a powerful source of attraction, in the first place. For any such fiction as hers, which keeps one actively thinking not only some but all of the time, the stimulus of novelty is requisite, because only under such stimulus does the mind experience the zest that alone sustains the needed alertness of appreciation. In the second place its *ex vi termini* superiority—surely no stuff of fiction could have the dignity and the significance of the human mind!—gave it an irrefutable claim on our esteem. The novelty has disappeared. We have had a surfeit of psychological fiction since George Eliot's day. Psychology, too, has entered as an element into almost every other variety of fiction. And the glamour of novelty gone, we have been able to discern the defects, once obscured by the qualities, of the purely intellectual element of fiction when it wholly overshadows all others. We now recognize that science had invaded the domain of literature—*dona ferens* and undistrusted. The current reaction, started perhaps, exemplified certainly, by Stevenson—the significance of whose work is purely "literary"—is so great as to have sacrificed seriousness along with science. But it is not necessary to exalt the puerile in order to establish the insufficiency of the pedantic. And to pedantry, however obscurely felt or unconsciously manifested, disproportionate preoccupation with the intellectual element in fiction is apt, popularly, to be ascribed.

II

George Eliot certainly stands at the head of psychological novelists, and though within far narrower limits she has here and there been equalled—by Mr. Hardy, for example; and in highly differentiated types, in the subtleties and *nuances* of the *genre* by Mr. Henry James—it is probable that the *genre* itself will decay before any of its practitioners will, either in depth or range, surpass its master spirit. As George Eliot herself remarks, "Of all forms of mistake, prophecy is the most gratuitous," but we may conjecture that the psychological novel, in its present explicit sense, will disappear before her own pre-eminence in the writing of it is successfully challenged. She is, thus, and is likely to remain, a unique figure. More than any other writer's her characters have—and for the serious readers of the future will continue to have—the specifically intellectual interest. This interest, indeed, is so marked in them that one is tempted to call it the only one they possess. What goes on in their minds is almost the sole concern of their creator. Our attention is so concentrated on what they think that we hardly know how they feel, or whether—in many cases, at least, where we nevertheless have a complete inventory of their mental furniture—they feel at all. They are themselves also prodigiously interested in their mental processes. They do a tremendous lot of thinking. In any emergency or crisis their minds fairly buzz, like a wound clock with the pendulum removed. We assist at the spectacle of a cogitation that seems to be pursued by the thinkers themselves with disinterested devotion. At all events the stars of the company not only practise but enjoy mental exercise to an extent not elsewhere to be met with. I have heard it remarked in qualification of the legitimate interest of Thackeray's characters that they "never

seem to have any fun with their minds," and it is certainly true that in the concert of powers of which the nature of Thackeray's personages is composed, the mind does not hold a notable hegemony. The personages themselves are rarely either introspective or mentally energetic for pure love of the exercise. But the drama itself of George Eliot's world is largely an intellectual affair. The soul, the temperament, the heart—in the scriptural sense—the whole nature plays a subordinate part. The plot turns on what the characters think. The characters are individualized by their mental complexions; their evolution is a mental one; they change, develop, deteriorate in consequence of seeing things differently. Their troubles are largely mental perplexities; in her agony of soul Romola goes to Savonarola and Gwendolen to Deronda for light, not heat. The prescriptions they receive are also terribly explicit—addressed quite exclusively to the reason and wholly unlike that obtained by Nicodemus "by night." The courtship of Esther and Felix Holt is mainly an interchange of "views." There are exceptions—notably Maggie Tulliver and Dorothea, the two characters which have been called, with ample reason, one may guess, autobiographic. But the exceptions accentuate the rule. As a rule the atmosphere of each novel is saturated with thought. Certainly nowhere else in fiction is there any such apotheosis of intellect both express and implied.

Yet it is the temperament, not the thinking of men and women, that is permanently and rewardingly interesting in that field of literature which fiction constitutes. Sociology rather than psychology is its auxiliary science—because, no doubt, sociology is hardly to be called a science at all. Thought is a universal and automatic process compared with feeling, than which it is far less idiosyncratic and particular. It is comparatively impersonal. It does not distinguish individuals with any very salient sharpness. Other things being equal—which, perhaps, they rarely are, but that is nothing—people think very much alike. It has been remarked of the insufficiency of argument that a legislative vote was never changed by a speech. The mind is far less recondite than is generally imagined, except in so far as it is complicated by feeling. Turgenieff legitimately complains of Zola that he tells us how Gervaise Coupeau feels, but never what she thinks. But the converse exclusiveness is a greater defect. Surely the characters of Turgenieff himself that remain in our memory are those whose feelings he has described rather than those whose minds he has exhibited to us. Who knows what Gemma, or the Russian Dido in *Spring Floods* thinks? Or, rather, we know what they *must* think without being told—their thinking being clearly a mere corollary of their feeling, which is admirably set forth. Why is Maggie Tulliver such a definite entity to us, beside Felix Holt, for example? Because she feels more and is shown to us from this point of view. Felix, even, would have had very much the same and no more interest for us if his creator had furnished him with an entirely different stock of the notions in which he is so rich. Why is Tom Tulliver not so interesting a character but, being profoundly uninteresting rather from any but a curious standpoint, so characteristic a masterpiece of George Eliot's genius? Because he is differentiated mentally, almost exclusively, with the result of nearly complete colorlessness—so wholly is color in character a matter of temperament—and because George Eliot's intellectual preoccupation is here, therefore, an advantage and not a limitation in the work of characterization. She has not made Tom interesting, but she has made his lack of interest real, and so vividly real as to be profoundly suggestive, and therefore the point of departure for interesting speculation in the reflective mind. Where the lack of temperament is not, however, the point of the character to be illustrated, her practice is less productive. Her major premise, that all people are mentally interesting, is seen to be at fault when she deals with personages the discrimination of whose intellectual peculiarities certainly needs to be supplemented by a consideration of that side of them which says, "I myself am heaven and hell." The soul is always interesting—in its traits, its potentialities, its mystery—whatever its incarnation. It is permitted us to believe—but even if theretofore the statement had been a supercilious supposition, George Eliot would have demonstrated its soundness—that there are many of our fellow-creatures whose minds hardly repay study. How many pages of *Middlemarch* that encyclopædic panorama of the provincial human mind—are there devoted to the meeting of hospital trustees to elect a chaplain? Who remembers the outcome, even if, indeed, he remembers that the contest was between a church clergyman and a dissenting minister? But who, that remembers the incident at all, does not recall how completely the mental equipment and processes of each of the mainly insignificant members of the board are exposed and documented? And with what result? Chiefly, I think, that of leading one to inquire, "Why?"

III

One consequence of this intellectual preoccupation and point of view is incontestable; whatever one's predilections one cannot gainsay that it is fatal to action. In George Eliot's world nothing ever happens, one is tempted to say; certainly less, very much less, than in the world of any other writer of fiction of the first rank. Sometimes nature intervenes, as in the flood of *The Mill on the Floss*. Sometimes there is a catastrophe of a human but impersonal order, as in *Romola*. Nothing dramatic is evolved out of the action that is a resultant of the forces of character, for of these forces the intellectual only and not the passional have been elaborately dealt with. The infanticide in *Adam Bede* is a barely concrete excuse for the structure of moral analysis erected upon it. The intensest incident inspired by love—before George Eliot certainly a not neglected element of fiction—is the kissing of Maggie's arm by Stephen Guest; though the tragedy of this book is too splendid to suffer from any limitation. Mr. Frederic Myers notes that the only love-letter in all the novels was written by Mr. Casaubon. There are whole chapters of mental analysis leading up to Dorothea's marriage, and the marriage itself takes place off the stage and is chronicled in a line. Nothing is more characteristic than the way in which the catastrophe of *Daniel Deronda* is treated. George Eliot leaves the telling of it entirely to Gwendolen. Anyone interested in the fate of Grandcourt (perhaps he is not quite "convincing" enough to be popular) would resent the abruptness of his drowning, his sudden disappearance from the face of the earth, his demise only to be described later as material for casuistry.

It is undoubtedly true that George Eliot shrank instinctively from the melodramatic. "At this stage of the world if a man wants to be taken seriously he must keep clear of melodrama," she makes Deronda observe. She certainly wanted to be taken seriously, and she certainly has been; even solemnly. But her instinctive feeling in this respect was greatly reinforced by her practice of limiting the field of her fiction as she did. The drama with which she was concerned was the interior drama, the successive mental changes whereby a person gradually attains his or her development; and to this anything like elaborateness or complication of plot, any narrative of events or record of incidents which play so important a part in fiction, even when they are merely the background that sets off the characters concerned in them, seems inappo-

site. Her themes are in general so high and her treatment so serious, the moral so inevitable, so like the moral of life itself—the life and reality of which any book of hers is the equivalent in literature—that even tragedy itself, where she employs it, seems a little artificial, a little contrived and arranged, a concession perhaps to precedent, an expedient at best, less *typical* at all events than the moral it enforces and decidedly inferior to it in reality, in convincing illusion. Indeed where her practice did not exclude it altogether, her tragedy itself comes very near the confines of melodrama, from which her instinctive repugnance does not save her and which she would probably have handled better but for her predetermined consecration to the undramatic and philosophical. One need mention in illustration only *The Spanish Gypsy*, in which melodrama abounds—though melodrama, it is true, of the mildest-mannered kind that ever flourished on the banks of the Guadalquivir or arrayed itself in Andalusian vesture. But there is a tincture of melodrama even in such a tragedy as the end of *Romola*. Imagine even Zola, who is none too scrupulous in such a situation but who "understands himself" admirably in it, resorting to the "poetic justice" of Baldasarre's final reunion with Tito in the death grapple in the Arno. The whole Baldasarre part of the book indeed is melodrama, and the least successful of the motives of the story. The Hawthornesque incident of the secret panel in *Daniel Deronda*, which when moved disclosed the dead face adumbrating the tragedy of Grandcourt's death, is melodrama, albeit of an awkwardness that shows a flagging fancy and a tired hand. In short it cannot be said that George Eliot's true theme—the constitution and development of the human mind and its effect on the conduct and character of the soul, its subject—either receives, or especially needs perhaps, the aid of action, of the dramatic element upon which nevertheless a very considerable part of the general interest in fiction depends.

IV

An analogous but more important trait is the lack of creative imagination which is implied, as the lack of action is involved, in the scientific turn of her genius. Whatever dramatic demands upon a novelist's characters one may forego, the vivid and enduring interest of the characters themselves requires an imaginative differentiation. Otherwise they lose in concrete effect very much in proportion to their abstract interest, which in George Eliot's characters is very great. And it is the concrete effect which, in any work of art, is of fundamental value. George Eliot's world is certainly less concrete than its moral inspiration, which is often as definite as a proposition. Her characters are thus, it is true, perfectly typical—in spite of the extent to which they are psychologically individualized. And this constitutes for them a family distinction of importance. The characters of no other novelist are discriminated so nicely at the same time that they have also a clear representative value. They occupy a middle ground in this respect, one may say, between the personages of Thackeray, who is accused lately of having no psychology, and those of Hawthorne which, as Mr. James points out, are never types. It is partly for this reason, perhaps, that they are so rarely our companions, our intimates, as the characters of even inferior novelists are, though I imagine it is mainly because they are mentally instead of temperamentally individualized, and because it is the sense, the volitions and the emotions rather than the intellect of people that in fiction as in life attach them to us and give them other than a quasi-scientific interest for us. And, besides, George Eliot's star characters, if types, are apt to be *rare* types and, from that fact also, depend largely on their speculative interest. "Yet surely," as she says herself (in "Janet's Repentance"), "the only true knowledge of our fellow-man is that which enables us to feel with him, which gives us a fine ear for the heart-pulses that are beating under the mere clothes of circumstance and opinion." We do not, I think, sufficiently *feel* with George Eliot's personages. They have too much a speculative, and too little an imaginative, origin and suggestion.

It is for this reason, perhaps, more than any other, that one can hardly claim for her the quality of the "born novelist," in the integral, exclusive, and felicitous sense in which Thackeray was one. Nevertheless, it is as certainly true that in the creation of character her remarkable gifts were at their best. She thought about other things, to be sure, when this was the matter in hand, and did this less well in consequence. Moreover, she did other things, and did them from their own point of view. But she did these less well still than the worst of her character-construction. Whereas, for example, the fact that she wrote *The Spanish Gypsy* at all attests the incompleteness of her native call as a novelist, its marked inferiority to her novels, in spite of its sincerity, its ambitiousness and its notable excellences, gives a certain relief to the genuineness of her true vocation. It is not perhaps to say very much to say that her characters are her own, and in a more intimate sense than that of their family likeness to which I have alluded. No one else could have created them. They have no fellows outside her world. Anyone else would have portrayed the same types, even, very differently. But this is so *eminently* true—so much truer than it is of some novelists of very high rank, of the romancers in general, very often, surely—that in itself it witnesses the harmony with which her genius expressed itself in fiction, and shows why she wrote novels better than she wrote anything else. Add to this the particular quality of her genius and its eminence, and the high rank of her fiction is deduced as the third term of a syllogism. It is indeed a body of work that not only is of the first order but that stands quite by itself.

It was doubtless in thinking mainly of George Eliot, whose aptest pupil he was, that more than a score of years ago Mr. Hardy spoke of fiction as having "taken a turn for better or worse, for analyzing rather than depicting character and emotion." It was certainly George Eliot who more than any other practitioner gave fiction this turn—a turn still followed, with whatever modifications, and illustrated in all serious examples of the art, so much so that a novel without the psychological element is almost as much of a solecism as a picture with a conventional *chiaroscuro*. Analyzing, synthetizing—the terms do not matter much; in any mental exercise of importance, both processes are involved. Nothing could be more systematically synthetic than the patient way in which, having arrived, deductively, no doubt, from the suggestions of observation, at the idea of a character, and then analytically induced the traits that belong to it, George Eliot puts these together in orderly demonstration of the validity of her original theorem. This, to be sure, relates to the mental process of the artist rather than to the technic, which is certainly analytic enough in the case of George Eliot. But it is worth while, perhaps, in accepting Mr. Hardy's expression as practically adequate enough to indicate to us the turn in fiction that he had in mind, nevertheless to remember that with George Eliot, at least, analysis has no tyrannical preponderance over other faculties of the mind, and that so far from being allowed in unchecked monopoly to unravel its material into uninteresting and unrelated shreds, it merely co-operates with these to a truly creative end. A character of George Eliot is never picked to pieces, in a word. It is perfectly coherent and original—as

original and coherent as a character of Dickens, for example, which is not analyzed at all.

It is, however, not the product of the imagination. Its conception—let us say, rather, its invention—is less irresponsible and spontaneous, than if it were; itself therefore, has on the whole, less vitality—less reality, which is the vitality of a character of fiction. It is the result of the travail of the mind, the incarnation of an idea, not the image of a vision. Such a character as Gwendolen in *Daniel Deronda* is as truly a creative, as if she were not also a critical product, but it is clear that inductively conceived she is deductively delineated—one cannot avoid seeing the machinery, so to say, of the author's mind throughout the process, and applying to it the terms of logic rather than of literature. She is an essay, with illustrations, on the egoistic girl to whom her own personality is of immense, of absorbing importance, who counts wantonly on imposing it, and who "falls on dark mountains" and comes to infinite disaster, in thus following out the uncompromising law of her development, when she comes in contact and into conflict with the crushing forces of circumstances, and finds the world quite other than her pygmy and peremptory conception of it—finds it not only not ductile, but pitilessly despotic. Nothing could be finer than such an idea, nothing more interesting than the essay, with its incarnating illustration, in which it is expressed. The defect—at least the distinction—of the character, is that the idea was born before, and conditions, its embodiment. With all her characterization, therefore—the invariable light green of her costume, for example, on which her creator leans with such evident helplessness—Gwendolen is imperfectly exteriorized. Always in exteriorization George Eliot's touch shows less zest than in examination. At times it is fatigued, often infelicitous, and now and then grotesque; Deronda's mother, with her orange dress and black lace and bare arms, is a caricature, a mere postulate of her profession of public singer. And not only is Gwendolen ineffectively presented; she is incompletely realized as an individual, in virtue of her creator's absorption in her typical significance. You are impressed by her interest in her own personality as a significant moral trait, but you are more interested in the trait than in the personality; the personality is more elusive, not quite varied enough; what else does she do, think, feel, say, besides explicitly exhibit egoism? one asks. Like every other character of her extraordinary creator she is thoroughly *in* character. She is conceived and exhibited with an absolutely informing consistency and with a strictness unusual even in psychological fiction. Mr. Hardy, for instance (such stress does he lay on the *ewig Weibliche*), makes two women, whom he takes pains to show as of the most disparate organizations, do the same thing—act in a way which if natural to one of them, would, for that very reason, be out of character in the other.

But consistency is not only not completeness, not fulness, not variety, not productive of special interest and pleasure; it is a decidedly inferior element in the production of illusion, the illusion that is a condition of vitality in a character of fiction. Beside unexpectedness it is, in this regard, of no merit whatever. The consistency of Bulstrode, Tito, Felix Holt, ends by boring us. You want a personage in a book as out of it to act in a way that you cannot everlastingly prefigure. To surprise but not shock expectant intelligence involves, however, the aid of the creative imagination. And we have only to turn from Gwendolen to Daniel Deronda himself to realize how much George Eliot's other faculties exceeded her imagination. She is for once unhampered by any scientific description to the laws of reality. She has almost with *gaîte de cœur* abandoned, in this instance, her old reliance of observation, aided by sympathetic divination. She has made Deronda out of whole cloth. She has done everything for him, and spared no pains to make him attractive and personal. He has a "grand face," though a young man; his smile is occasional and, therefore, "the reverse of the continual smile that discredits all expression." He is just what she wants to make him—her imaginative ideal. He is no more real than Charlotte Brontë's Rochester. We owe him entirely to his author's creative imagination. The result is aptly enough implied in a letter written—obviously in Scotch—by Stevenson to a reviewer friend, when the book came out. "Did you— I forget," he says, "did you have a kick at the stern works of that melancholy puppy and humbug, Daniel Deronda himself? the Prince of Prigs; the literary abomination of desolation in the way of manhood; a type which is enough to make a man forswear the love of women, if that is how it is to be gained." The whole structure and color of the book indeed (Gwendolen and her affairs apart) may be said to be George Eliot's one explicit imaginative flight and—shall we say therefore—her one colossal failure.

The irresponsible imagination has certainly much to answer for as an element of fiction and a factor in its composition. But at the present day it is plainly superfluous to dwell on the fact. The weight of current criticism is altogether against it, whatever the practice of the hour. And not only in fiction but in plastic art the errors for which it is no doubt justly held responsible have come to wear the aspect of solecisms. The application of a realistic standard is become almost instinctive. What is imaginative seems imaginary, and beauty that is not also obviously truth has lost its intimate appeal. There are signs of reaction, and no doubt the "imagemaking" faculty will again receive the recognition that for the moment more or less exclusively rewards the observation which normally—and notably in most very notable works of art—has the humbler rôle of verification and correction. And the reason is that creation is inconceivable without it. The criticism that constructs in fancy an inherent antagonism between it and truth is blind to the fact that it is through the imagination that the human mind arrives at truth as well as at error. Discovery is ideally deduced; it is the guerdon of hypothesis—without which, in the field of art, at all events, the mind rests in the suspense that has been noted as a mark of hysteria. In science, not less than in art, synthesis is an imaginative process. In a word, the truth-loving sceptic of the imagination is confuted by the inevitable procedure of the mind, and must admit the platitude that to see that a thing is so it is necessary first to see the thing. In all art worth talking about, therefore, the imagination is inevitably present. It may count as a feeble or as a powerful force. It may shine by the beauty, by the truth of the images it constructs or evokes, or be obscured by the data accumulated for its justification by diligent induction. But empirical scrutiny and sharpness of perception will never take its place. And its absence means an artistic vacuum. With George Eliot it certainly counts for proportionally less than it does in any great writer of fiction. Of course there are compensations, as I have endeavored to indicate. One need not prefer *Monte Cristo* to *Middlemarch*.

Apparently in this respect of the imagination, as in others, she did not herself sufficiently recognize the genuineness of her vocation as a novelist. At all events she did not depend on it. Yet there are characters and situations, there are in fact whole novels, among her works which show that it would have triumphantly withstood any strain she might have put on it. *The Mill on the Floss, The Scenes from Clerical Life*, show what her genius left to itself could, unaided, accomplish. But she was not content to leave it to itself. She

had other ambitions—ambitions which she could attain, which a woman with less intellect (there have been none with more) could not, which would attract less a man of equal genius, which the very circumstances of her sex—given her environment on the one hand and her powers on the other—teased her toward with fatal explicitness. "See that you hold yourself fast by the intellect," said Emerson in a famous passage, the acme of his eloquence. "It is this domineering temper of the sensual world that creates the extreme need of the priests of science; and it is the office and right of the intellect to make and not take its estimate." Never was this ideal more enthusiastically followed than by George Eliot. She illustrates it even a little literally. The result is a certain dryness, a certain mechanical effect for which unimaginative is just the epithet. She brought her mind to bear on everything and almost ceremoniously, so to say. This was clearly enough instinctive with her. There is nothing artificial in it. And this saves it from pedantry. She was intellectually very high-bred. There is not a hint, a shadow of vulgarity in any of her books. She is at home with the very best and has no inclination for anything else; she has no moments when her sense for the excellent relaxes and sags into irresponsibility. Without austerity—without much humor, too, surely, except in so far as the appreciation implies the possession of it—she is never tempted into caricature. She has no excess of high spirits thus to mislead her, but in any case her taste is a sure reliance. Her taste, indeed, is the part of her intellectual equipment which is perhaps most clearly instinctive. Æsthetically considered it is less trustworthy, but in the intellectual sphere—where taste has an important office—it shows itself a certain winnower of the worth while from the common. If at need it tolerates the commonplace, it is because the particular commonplace has its significance; and if it is a little eager in its appreciation of the significant which is also the eccentric, it is because it is easily and aristocratically at home with eccentricity itself. It is absolutely—singularly—free from display. In that sense, at all events, she was not in the least a pedant. Her pedantry, to call it so, was pedantry in the sense of literalness—and seen as such, mainly from an æsthetic view-point. Her erudite, even recondite, air, at times, is perfectly in accord with the most thorough-going simplicity. It is wholly natural. A sentence encrusted with erudition and intricate with logical involution is with her a native and unpretentious expression. Any pedantry, in other words, to be detected in her writings is apt to be a matter of form, an error from which the æsthetic sense alone (in which she was conspicuously deficient) and no amount of intellect can protect one. Even if now and then the substance is as flat as the statement is solemn, it is never tinctured by that variety of mediocrity which is of the essence of pedantry and which we know as vulgarity—there is not in all her writings a touch or a trace of it, as I have said. "All her eagerness for acquirement," she says of Dorothea, "lay within that full current of sympathetic motive in which her ideas and impulses were habitually swept along. She did not want to deck herself with knowledge—to wear it loose from the nerves and blood that fed her action." That is very nobly said, and it is doubtless autobiographic. But did ever such "eagerness for acquirement" as that of Dorothea's creator characterize any other novelist of her calibre? And erudition, however triumphantly assimilated, aside, the spontaneity that vivifies its creations is of a different order from a pure exercise of the intellect, however instinctive. And this spontaneity she may be said to have so instinctively alloyed with reflection, so transmuted by thought, that often she seems to lack it altogether.

V

One may speak of George Eliot's style as of the snakes in Iceland. She has no style. Her substance will be preserved for "the next ages" by its own pungency or not at all. No one will ever read her for the sensuous pleasure of the process. She is a notable contradiction of the common acceptance of Buffon's *"le style c'est l'homme."* Her very marked individuality expresses itself in a way which may be called a characteristic manner, but which lacks the "order and movement" that Buffon defined style to be when he was defining it instead of merely saying something about it. In itself, moreover, this is not often a felicitous manner. It is inspired by the wish to be pointed, to be complete, to give an impeccable equivalent in expression for the content of thought, to be adequately articulate. In her aim at exactness she neglects even energy. Her statements are scientific, but never even rudimentarily rhetorical, if we except the use of irony, in which she was sometimes very happy. Of modulation she never seems to have thought. Any element of periodic quality, of rhythm, of recurrence, of alternation, succession, inversion, for the sake of effect, decorating instead of merely expressing significance, she would no doubt have eschewed had any ever occurred to her, as plainly it never did. Rhetoric of any degree, in short, probably seemed to her meretricious if—which one doubts—she ever considered it at all. She was the slave of the meaning, hypnotized apparently by the sense, and deaf to the sound, of what she wrote. Her taste was noticeably good in avoiding the pretentious, but her tact was insufficient to save her from the complicated and the awkward. Her puritan predilections should have suggested simplicity to her, but simplicity is the supreme quality which she not only wholly lacks, but never even strives for; the one salient characteristic of her style—of her manner of writing, that is to say—is its complexity.

Thus there are no "passages," either "fine" or in any way sustained, in her works; at least I think of none, and if any exist I suspect they are put into the mouths of some personage with whom they are "in character"—in which case they would be sure to be very well done indeed. Every sentence stands by itself; by its sententious self, therefore. The "wit and wisdom" of the author are crystallized in phrases, not distilled in fluid diction. Their truth strikes us sharply, penetrates us swiftly; the mind tingles agreeably under the slight shock, instead of glowing in expansive accord and dilating with gradual conviction. Often these sentences have the force, the ring, of proverbs—of those of Solomon, too, rather than those of Sancho Panza. Some of them, on the other hand, have the air less of the Sibyl than of "saws," and suggest the wiseacre more than the philosophic moralist. At times they have the trenchant crispness of La Rochefoucauld; at others, even in the novels, the unravelled looseness premonitory of the appalling Theophrastus Such. The manner naturally takes on the character of the substance, and we have thus this formal sententiousness—now epigrammatic, as I say, and now otiose and obscure—because of the writer's exclusive consecration to the content which itself varies, of course, from the pithy to the commonplace. Her defective æsthetic feeling, her lack indeed of the æsthetic sense nowhere comes out more clearly than in this absorption in the significance to the neglect of the aspect of the picture she is presenting. This picture, and even the personages who people it, seem to have for her at least a disproportionate attraction in virtue of their typical to the exclusion of their individual interest—sharply individualized as her characters are in the matter of psychology alone. She seems so impressed with their universal appeal and representative

office, with the principle her facts illustrate and enforce, with the ulterior meaning and value of her "criticism of life," as to have at all events distinctly less zest in depicting than in defining her material. For fiction this indubitably means a tame style.

Lacking in æsthetic feeling as she was, she was probably more or less conscious of this. Her attempts to circumvent it are now and then deplorable. They are invariably verbiage of one kind or another. The refuge of pedantry in its endeavor to escape dulness is apt to be sportiveness, and it is perhaps when she is playful that George Eliot comes nearer pedantry than at any other time. Even in moments when her erudition seems elaborate and essentially inapposite, we are always conscious that it does not seem so to her, and that not only is there no parade about it, but also that neither is it in the least mechanical. It is the native, however awkward, expression of a kind of tempered enthusiasm. At times, certainly, the sense of humor failed her equally with the æsthetic sense, of which in a large—or strict—sense it is, of course, a subdivision; and the artist who could objectively reproduce such humor as that of *Adam Bede*, and *The Mill on the Floss* could also, when it came to self-expression, illustrate the very acme of dulness. Her facetiousness is, at its worst, as bad as Dickens's; and, at her worst, she writes as badly, without the mitigation of his extraordinary high spirits and infectious hilarity. Without, too, his bad taste, though with, as I said, the tactlessness which is the next thing to it. The moral element in taste involves self-respect. And in anything moral George Eliot is never deficient. Her intelligence saves her; it is too serious, it has too much poise, and it sees temptation as a kind of sophistry— temptation, I mean, to put up with the second rate on account of its tinsel, for example. But the tact that shows one when he is hitting and when he is missing the mark, she does not infallibly possess and often when, apparently, she seems to herself to be exhibiting the light touch, she is bravely ponderous. With a little more tact, a little more humor, a little more æsthetic sense, some of her significance might have been even more striking, and certainly some of it would not have seemed so absolutely flat.

But why discuss her style at all, one asks one's self. No one can have any doubt that, though, in general, it serves her well enough, and sometimes expresses adequately the most searching subtleties of observation and reflection, nevertheless its idiosyncrasies are defects. And of style in any large sense surely no great writer ever had so little. Her constant references in her letters to her "art" have an odd sound. Yet even here one's last word must be a recognition of the extraordinary way in which her intellect atones for sensuous deficiencies. Could two better words be found, for a slight example, to characterize the first impression Rome makes on the stranger than "stupendous fragmentariness." One of her characters, "like most tyrannous people, had that dastardly kind of self-restraint which enabled him to control his temper where it suited his convenience to do so." The adverb is felicity itself. And in her letters one can see how safely her intelligence guides her through the museum maze of plastic art for which she had so little native feeling, but in which less than many an æsthetic temperament is she either imposed upon or unappreciative. In art, as in life, she has an acute sense if not a sensitive feeling for what is distinctly worth while.

VI

No one, however, as I have intimated, would infer her personality from her style—certainly not that trait of her personality which, in spite of her apotheosis of the intellect, distinguishes her from the so-called intellectual woman, and which I take to be intimately characteristic. In books or in fact, the first impression made by the so-called intellectual woman is that of the inadequacy of the intellect. There is so much else that is worth while, one reflects in the presence of such thorough-going exclusions. The attractiveness of the susceptibility and even the will is thrown into effective relief. Intuitions seem to gain a new sanction, instinctiveness a new charm, spontaneity a new grace, irresponsibility a new excuse—qualities intimately associated with women. The limitedness of the intellect, the distant view of sympathetic relations, fancy, unexpectedness, clairvoyance, all lying without its confines, become depressingly plain. One naturally reacts under the exaggerated emphasis of importance and all-sufficiency that the intellect receives from the intellectual woman in general, whose consecration to it is so complete, so obvious, so naively unconscious of what exists beyond its pale. It is not so much that she is too intellectual. At times one finds that she might be even more so, even if less strictly so, with advantage. It is that she seems to be unaware that compared with character or even temperament the intellect itself is terribly concrete and communicable. And perhaps there is nothing that sets George Eliot off from the mass of her sex for whom the intellect is a universal talisman, so much as the circumstance that she does not make this impression. On the contrary, one's impression is of the plenary power and sufficiency of the intellect unaided and unillumined *ab extra*. So searching and fruitful are its processes as exhibited in her works; so pregnant are the discoveries of her scrutiny and reflection in the heretofore unexplored regions of human character and moral relations; so pithy are her deductions; so stimulant is her turning of her "allowance of knowledge into principles" (as she says of Dorothea), that one feels almost that other faculties are surplusage, and that the field of fiction as well as that of science belongs to the intellect, thus shown to be capable unaided of such distinguished results. Other relations, one feels, remain to be discovered, other principles to be formulated, other mysteries of thought and passion and conduct, of the real world and the correlative ideal one, to be solved by this magic divining-rod, this mighty crystallizing force. Partly this impression is produced by George Eliot's superiority. Intellect *enough* is its own sanction and imposes itself. But partly also it is due to her attitude, with which for the moment, owing to her superiority, we are perforce in accord, and which is that of the fanatical worshipper at the intellect's shrine.

How early her complete consecration to the things of the mind took place would doubtless have been difficult for herself to tell. It must, however, have been in the nature of a conversion. She was doubtless always, as she describes Dorothea, "ardent, theoretic, and intellectually consequent," but the break which she made with her early traditions and beliefs must have been in the nature of a transformation from a nature emotional and expansive because fundamentals are settled, into one in which scepticism stimulates inquiry and which, therefore, in proportion to its seriousness, is driven to aggrandize the intellect, which is the instrument of inquiry. This change, whether or no induced by her acquaintance with the sociologists and positivists whom she met when she first began literary work, antedates her work in fiction, which fact and the fact that it *was* a change can hardly fail to account for much in this fiction. It is, in a word, the work of a woman, of an extraordinarily intellectual woman, of a woman who had come to concentrate her interest and effort within purely intellectual lines *after* a spiritual experience in which the emotions probably played a predominant part. Its notable complexity is hardly surprising.

Her environment probably accounts for the evolution of her genius. Nothing could be less favorable to the harmonious development of the intellectual side of Mary Ann Evans, one would say, than the environment of Mrs. Lewes, even though she may have been converted from "orthodoxy" before going to London at all. Science, which spared Dorothea and never made the acquaintance of Maggie Tulliver, took possession of her. Metaphysic, philosophy, sociology, theology enthralled her "ardent, theoretic, and intellectually consequent" nature. Her emotional side, which one may judge not only from early accounts but from the very latest was wonderfully sensitive and refined, became forthwith subordinated instead of developed so far as regards its expression in her very objective books. She became, even in the intellectual field, almost the ideal nonconformist. Other points of view, which she appreciated wonderfully, she appreciated through comprehension rather than sympathy. She was too objective for altruism of the mind, even. Her writings are almost invariably marked by elevation, but elevation to which there is no lift. Her spirit has no wings. Her letters show her stoicism to have been severely ethical and without sentimental alloy. To do good to others, to look at the practical results of our actions and not bother about how we feel concerning them, is very much the sum of her credo. Of God, Immortality, Duty, the last only is left to us, Mr. Myers dolefully records her as asseverating. This may be true, of course, but, even so, to be preoccupied with its truth must inevitably be a handicap to a writer of imaginative fiction—God and immortality connote so much ideality. Her thinking was eclectic and shows the lack of comradeship, of harmony and accord, of those fostering influences of concert under which thought flowers in luxuriant spontaneity. "Our duty is faithful tradition where we can attain it," she makes the solemn Deronda assert. But faithful tradition is just what she did not attain—just what practically, I think, she came to have very little feeling for. She wished instead to "prove all things," for which operation she had indeed an admirable equipment, but in which she showed too exclusive a zest. Tradition at all events never dupes her. Nothing amuses her more than—in the best taste always, assuredly—to expose the insubstantiality of its pretentions on just occasion. The net result of her mature theory and practice is a noble work performed for truth, somewhat to the neglect of the beautiful and the good, except in so far as these benefit indirectly from any service done to truth. And even so far as truth itself is concerned, though we get unexpected, felicitous, and cogent glimpses of it—and what is more, a sense that its deeps are both inexhaustible and infinitely alluring—nevertheless one feels that there is an order of truth itself for which the intellect alone has not quite the test, and which is of overmastering significance, though it can only be imaginatively perceived. "Il faut avoir la foi et ne pas croire," says Claude Bernard. All dogma quite aside, it is certain that George Eliot once possessed what we know (but do not understand) as "faith," and that when she wrote her novels she had substituted for instead of adding to it the sapient scepticism unveiling illusions which is such an integral element of her fiction. She is in consequence more nearly unique; she is more isolated; but she is also less authoritative and less complete. There is therefore an atmosphere of cause and effect, of fatalism, of insistent and predetermined gloom which pervades her books and which is hostile to the variety pertinent to a report of nature that is round and full. In this way her microcosm is a little more distorted than perhaps it need have been, but for her conversion—her whole-souled conversion—to positivism.

VII

Would she have done better to have followed what I take to have been her native bent? Who would wish any great writer different? Who would take the *risk?* Yet I must say I think there would be a minimum of risk in the case of George Eliot. And for this reason. Her development seems to me to have proceeded on lines increasingly inharmonious with her native endowment. Her temperament was an ardent one, yet increasingly contained instead of exercised. Her whole nature was tremulously sensitive to impressions, and it constantly steeled itself to systematic reflection. Her faculty of observation was marvellous, and she became more and more of a recluse as time went on. She absorbed altogether the best part of her material—that of which her first books and *Middlemarch* are composed—before she began to write at all; afterward her material was necessarily so extraneously attained as to be by comparison factitious. She was, if not profoundly, at least acutely religious, and she became a positivist. Intimately emotional, avidly exigent of sympathy, having that imperious need of giving one's self which assails truly independent but affectionate souls, her expression steadily grew in impassibility and in a stoic consideration of the impersonal as the highest good; and duty to others—to the community, the world, the race indeed—became a sort of refuge for what ideality she allowed herself. When one thinks of her early years and their associations, her precocity and emotional development, and then of the immense spiritual contrast involved in her work in London, her union with Lewes, her friendship with Mr. Spencer, her emancipation, if one likes, and the subsequent seclusion which certainly had its ideal, but also inevitably its artificial side—when one follows the evolution of her genius from the earlier books through *Romola, Middlemarch,* and *Daniel Deronda* to *Theophrastus Such,* getting gradually farther away from her native substance and quality, and ending in comparative ineptitude, one comprehends her marriage and surcease from activity. She had re-entered regularity, had ceased to be exceptional and "attained tradition"—in the words I have already cited. It could not be that she should not rest in a kind of peace unattainable through conscious effort and intimately grateful after a life of intense mental activity further stimulated by an elevated and really ideal, but nevertheless peculiar position. Nothing is more touching than Mr. Cross's account—of a delicacy in itself equivalent to poetry—of her last years. She had done her work. And it had been done during a sort of prolonged excursion into the realm of science, where the native temperament and genius that might otherwise have powerfully modified the product of an extraordinary intellect, had been deflected if not repressed.

For no judgment of George Eliot can be discerning which does not consider the vital fact that she was—even in a degree really typical—a woman. She belonged to the subjective sex, and is the most objective of novelists. It is the fashion at present to neglect the distinction of sex in speaking of women, and pay them the compliment, or do them the justice, of treating them severally as individuals, discriminated merely as men are discriminated. Nevertheless until their distinction in certain fields of activity is as much a matter of course as that of men— until there are no more "Women's Buildings" at world's fairs, for example, and the propaganda in favor of the sex as an entity ceases to obscure the individual standard which naturally tends to get itself established if let alone—anything like the eminence of George Eliot's powers will be singularized because of the possessor's sex. It *is*—as yet—generally remarkable, worthy of remark, that a woman should have reached such a height of accomplishment. But that her accomplishment should have been in the field of thought rather than in that of feeling, and so splendidly successful in this field as almost to have originated a species in the domain of fiction, is specifically the notable phenomenon in George Eliot's case. Why is she so unlike George Sand and Charlotte Brontë—one may exclude Jane Austen, in thinking of precedents, as exclusively an artist. Is it because of her different and in the main superior mental quality, and the greater subordination of feeling to thought in her original makeup? Probably not. Whatever George Eliot became there can be no doubt that Mary Ann Evans was a woman in whom the idiosyncrasies of sex were particularly developed. As to the existence of such idiosyncrasies and their native, elemental, and possibly ineradicable character George Eliot herself never had any doubts. The difference between the sexes is one of the phenomena that compose her material. Her writings are full of man considered as man, and woman as woman. She has widened the sphere of woman's interest for us, but has not obscured its identity. The impartiality of her view, however, excludes the patronage which the as yet, perhaps, more susceptible sex is as yet quick to feel, and her caustic treatment of masculine foibles excuses her occasional dry compassion for what the author of "Janet's Repentance" calls "Poor women's hearts!"

"Poor women's hearts!" What became of hers? In the transition from Miss Evans to George Eliot through Mrs. Lewes, one cannot help speculating. Its interests certainly grew both more limited and less concrete—more limited in the sense involved in her isolation, her concentration of feeling within the smallest of circles and her absorption in geometrically increasing ratio in the things of the mind; less concrete as her ethics took on more and more a humanitarian color, and the good of society in general became the main concern of her speculative meditation. One has only to imagine Mr. Casaubon more human, less a pedant, more a real scholar and minus his littlenesses, to divine that Dorothea might have developed into a philosopher of moment, losing in the process the edge of those qualities which render her so sympathetic to Lydgate, to Ladislaw and to ourselves. Had she, under such circumstances, written novels, they might easily, like those of her creator, have been noteworthily objective, and have missed the personal charm of native feminine genius which is now so conspiciously characteristic of her. Had George Eliot not fallen in love with science; had not her feeling for the world of her girlhood atrophied with the loss of faith in its standards, so that she got more and more domesticated in a foreign environment, and even predisposed to exotic themes, suggested by intellectual and acquired rather than native and sentimental interests—*Romola, The Spanish Gypsy,* and *Daniel Deronda,* for instance; had she not given the rein to her curiosity and become absorbed in the world of books, of literature rather than its raw material, which she could nevertheless handle to such admirable ends; had she not, as it were, made herself over into an intelligent force from being a person with idiosyncrasies, and expressly subordinated the susceptibility in which, not only as a woman, but as an individual, she was so strong, to the more purely intellectual development which she could only share with so many masters, we should have had works of undoubtedly more charm, and, such was the native force of her genius, of equal power. We should have had, in fine, more books like *The Mill on the Floss; Middlemarch* would have been more condensed; *Felix Holt* would have been dramatic; we should have lost *Romola,* perhaps, but we should have escaped *Daniel Deronda.* It is not that, as is so often the case with writers who study significance rather than form, her early books are superior to the later because the sense of selection is more acute and exclusions more rigorous at the beginning of a career than at its apogee, when everything that occurs to the author seems to him for that reason worth saying. They are superior because, unlike the later ones, they are cast within the lines of her native capacity, because they do not call for imaginative power, for artistic synthesis and dramatic vigor, but amply illustrate her sympathetic feeling, her closeness of observation, her faculty for loading with serious significance and almost ominous suggestion the most ordinary and unpretentious data of human life by drawing out their typical quality at the same time that they are psychologically differentiated in a way to make them extraordinarily individual and real. "Depend upon it, my dear lady," she says in her first story, "you would gain unspeakably if you would learn with me to see some of the poetry and the pathos, the tragedy and the comedy, lying in the experience of the human soul that looks out through dull gray eyes and that speaks in a voice of quite ordinary tones." *That* is George Eliot's truest note, and it is a note struck by no one else; we have nowadays plenty of fiction woven around dull gray eyes and voices of ordinary tones, but the experience of the human soul is not often what these express. It is a note also which is far less prominent in the writer's later novels, the novels that help us to understand what Mr. George Moore means by saying that she "tried to write like a man." One feels like replying to Mr. Moore, incidentally suggesting emulation of this effort to him, that at least she succeeded. But anyone who agrees with me in dividing her books into two groups, those written before "Romola" and those written afterwards, will hardly find it fanciful to see in the former a native, and in the latter an acquired, point of view and manner of treatment. When one considers the potentialities of the author of *The Mill on the Floss*—a work in which passion and the tumult of the soul are not objectively analyzed but sympathetically portrayed with unsurpassed vividness and elemental power, a work which is indisputably one of the great literary epitomes of the pathos and tragedy of human existence—it is hard to reconcile one's self to the evolution in which temperament disappeared so completely in devotion to the intellect alone as to result in the jejune artificiality of *Daniel Deronda*.

It would be idle, and certainly I have no disposition, to belittle the value of the literature produced between these two books. *Romola* is unique in its way, and has hosts of admirers. There are readers to whom it introduced the Italian Renaissance, who, in its pages first read of Florence, Savonarola, the Medici. There are scholars who shared George Eliot's enthusiasm for "the City by the Arno" and "the wonderful fifteenth century," so cordially as to credit *Romola* with having successfully reproduced a moment and a milieu which they were only too grateful to have recalled. Besides, there is that masterpiece of evolution, the character of Tito Melema. *Felix Holt* contains at least the lovable Mr. Lyon, and though the wearisome wordiness of the book is a handicap from which it will always suffer, it will always remain a highly interpretive picture of a momentous epoch in English political and social history—the birth, in fact, of the modern English world engendered by the Reform Bill. *Middlemarch* anyone can praise. It is probably the "favorite novel" of most "intellectual" readers among us— at least those who are old enough to remember its serial appearance. It is, indeed, a half dozen novels in one. Its scale is cyclopædic, as I said, and it is the microcosm of a community rather than a story concerned with a unified plot and set of characters. And it is perhaps the writer's fullest expression of her philosophy of life.

VIII

It is these books and *Daniel Deronda*, rather than the earlier *Scenes from Clerical Life, Adam Bede, Silas Marner*, and *The Mill on the Floss*, however, which determine her position as so much less an artist than a moralist. She is in truth a moralist, and a moralist of the first class. I do not of course mean the sense in which Fénelon, for example, or Paley is a moralist. Expressly and in form a novelist of her rank is an artist, in whose work the moral significance is either spontaneously generated or incidentally induced. But essentially and spiritually speaking, George Eliot, whatever her superficial classification, is so far less an artist than a moralist, that it is as the latter that she is of value to us and is most likely to appeal to the future. It is as a moralist that she is a real contributor to literature, that she is at her best, that she is of the first class and that among novelists, at least, she is if not unrivalled, at all events unsurpassed. No such explicit "criticism of life" as hers exists in fiction. Thackeray, for example, is a moralist, too. He was very fond of his office of "week-day preacher." But he is a moralist not only because his picture of life is so true and vital, but in virtue of moralizing, of commenting on his story and his characters, drawing out their natural suggestions, weaving around them a web of artistic embroidery, eliciting and enforcing the lesson they contain. With George Eliot the story and characters themselves are conceived as examples and illustrations of the moral she has in mind to begin with, and a part of its systematic setting forth. The moral is her first concern. Her characters are concrete—remarkably concrete— expressions of pure abstractions, not images. Arthur Pendennis is the result of an attempt to depict the average man of his day and station. Tito Melema incarnates the idea that shrinking from the unpleasant is subtly and tragically demoralizing. There can be no doubt as to which is the creation of the more specific and unalloyed moralist. George Eliot's "moralizing" is always a sort of logical coda or corollary of the moral idea or truth which her character or incident happens to be illustrating, and is never the artistic moral suggestion of the subject. This is probably why it is tolerably dull, so often. It is apt but inferred, sound but not spontaneous. At any rate it is not in her *obiter* that her success as a moralist lies, it is in the very essence, subject, and attributes of her work.

This world was not to her the pure spectacle it is to the pure artist, nor even the profoundly moving and significant spectacle it is to the reflective and philosophic artist. Its phenomena were not *disjecta membra* to be impressionistically reproduced or combined in agreeable and interesting syntheses. They were data of an exorable moral concatenation of which it interested her to divine the secret. What chiefly she sought in them was the law of cause and effect, the law of moral fatality informing and connecting them. Since the time of the Greek drama this law has never been brought out more eloquently, more cogently, more inexorably or—may one not say, thinking of Shakespeare?—more baldly. But at the same time she makes human responsibility perfectly plain. No attentive reader can hope for an acquittal at her hands in virtue of being the plaything of destiny. She is more than mindful, also, of the futilities as well as the tragedies of existence and, indeed, gives them a tragic aspect. *Middlemarch*, for example, read in the light —the sombre light— of its preface, is a striking showing of her penetration into the recesses of the commonplace, and of the else undiscovered deeps which there reward her subtlety; with the result, too, of causing the reader to reflect on infinity, as he does after a look through the telescope or microscope—an effect only to be produced by a master. But neither in the tragic nor the trifling does she engage the freedom of the individual, and if she shows the victim in the toils of fate, she shows also with relentless clearness how optionally he got there. Her central thought is the tremendous obligation of duty. Duty is in a very special way to her "the law of human life." The impossibility of avoiding it, the idleness of juggling with it, the levity of expecting with impunity to neglect it, are so many facets of her persistent preoccupation.

⟨. . .⟩ At all events it is certain that her mature philosophy does not take account of the miracle of grace. As a moralist this is her great defect, or rather deficiency. That subtle dynamic impulse of the will which the psychologists leave the theologians to describe as "the new birth," and which, as a matter of fact, fills a tremendous rôle in the drama of cause and effect, she makes little of. It lay natively within the folds of her sympathetic mind in earlier years, as "Janet's Repentance," for example, sufficiently witnesses, and it is certainly one of the most familiar of phenomena. We may know nothing of it, empirically, ourselves, but it is certainly as common as any other moral agency, if not indeed more common than all others. Moreover, not only are its energy and its effects to be observed in others, and in all ranks of the intellectual scale, from Philip's eunuch to Saul of Tarsus, from a crowd of Moody and Sankey penitents to the last French realistic *raffiné*, but every modern consciousness which looks deeply into itself discerns therein the potentiality of it— a potentiality definite enough to be at least a demonstration of its existence elsewhere. The miracle of grace, in a word, is a common enough and prominent enough factor in the universal moral problem to reward if not exact the attention of the artist who is also a moralist, and in excluding it the modern stoic exhibits a real limitation.

Its exclusion from consideration of so eminent a novelist as George Eliot is undoubtedly due to the lack of imagination and the predominance of intellect already noted in her genius and her practice. It is itself closely allied with mysticism, no doubt; it belongs, perhaps, in the domain of mysticism. And to deal with the mystic, or even to entertain an inclination to deal with it, necessitates the possession of the imaginative faculty and its cordial, unembarrassed, spontaneous activity, undeterred by fear of error and unrestrained by backward or side glances at the quite otherwise seductive data of ascertained truth. There is no shade of mysticism in George Eliot's moral philosophy, whose tenets and whose logic proceed from the processes of the mind and have little relation with "the vision" without which, says the wise man, "the people perish." Everything is taken on the side of it that appeals to the intelligence. Gwendolen comes to grief because she does not realize that domination is impracticable—because, in a word, of intellectual blindness. Grandcourt's baseness is an intellectual perversion, not a sensuous one. The story of Tito's mere repugnance to what is unpleasant becoming at last readiness for any crime is the story of a moral decline exhibited in a succession of mental phases. Even error is a kind of alienation and sin essentially a mistake. The notion of "dying to" it nowhere appears—I do not mean *pro forma*, in which shape perhaps it belongs less to literature than to dogma, but by implication. We are still in the penumbra, one would say, of the Old Testament. The *natural* results of error, the natural and integral sanctions of morality are convincingly, refreshingly, and stimulatingly considered to the exclusion of the preternatural; but the natural content of religion is quite neglected. Here, as elsewhere, she takes the scientific, the intellectual view of the phenomena which compose her material, and with her the mind in this field excludes the soul as in the field of art it does the imagination.

But with whatever limitations, her position as a classic is doubtless assured. There are types of human character of which she has fixed the image in striking individual incarnation for all time; and her philosophy is of an ethical cogency and stimulant veracity that make her fiction one of the notablest contributions ever made to the criticism of life. It is none the less true, to be sure, that her survival will mean the surmounting of such obstacles to enduring fame as a limited imaginative faculty, a defective sense of art, and an inordinate aggrandizement of the purely intellectual element in human character, which implies an imperfect sense of the completeness of human nature and the comprehensiveness of human life. But no other novelist gives one such a poignant, sometimes such an insupportable, sense that life is immensely serious, and no other, in consequence, is surer of being read, and read indefinitely, by serious readers.

SIR LESLIE STEPHEN
From *George Eliot*
1902, pp. 200–206

I have said that George Eliot's peculiar place among the novelists of the time was in some sense determined by the philosophical tendencies which were shared by none of her contemporaries. I do not mean to imply that it was her proper function to propagate any philosophical doctrine, and have tried to point out the defects due to her inclinations in that direction. Novels should, I take it, be transfigured experience; they should be based upon the direct observation and the genuine emotions which it has inspired: when they are deliberately intended to be a symbolism of any general formula, they become unreal as representative of fact, and unsatisfactory as philosophical exposition. George Eliot's early success and the faults of her later work illustrate, I have said, the right and wrong methods. But, in conclusion, I may try to indicate what seems to me to be the quality which, in spite of inevitable shortcomings in undertaking the impossible, gives the permanent interest of her works. That, I think, appears most simply by regarding them as implicit autobiography. George Eliot gives a direct picture of the England of her early days, and, less directly, a picture of its later developments. Her picture of the old country life owes its charm to the personal memories, and may possibly have a little personal colouring. If a novelist could be thoroughly "realistic," and give the truth, the whole truth, and nothing but the truth, there would no doubt be a good deal to add to the descriptions of the life at Shepperton and Dorlcote Mill. But, then, I do not believe that any human intellect can give the whole truth about anything. What can be given truly is the impression made upon the mind of the observer; and when the observer has a mind of such reflective power, so much insight, and such tenderness and sensibility as George Eliot's, its impressions will correspond to realities, and reveal most interesting though not all-comprehensive truths. The combination of an exquisitely sympathetic and loving nature with a large and tolerant intellect is manifest throughout. George Eliot could see the absurdities, and even the brutalities, of her neighbours plainly, but understood them well enough to make them intelligible, not mere absurdities to be caricatured; she saw the charming aspects of the old order with equal clearness, but has no illusions which would convert the country into a pretty Arcadia; and her sympathy with sorrow and unsatisfied longings is too deep and reflective to allow her to stray into mere sentimentalism. Her pathos is powerful because it is always under command. The more superficial writer treats an era of misery as implying a grievance which can be summarily removed, or finds in it an opportunity of exhibiting his own sensibility. Her feeling is too deep and her perception of the complexity of its causes too thorough to admit of such treatment. We see the tender woman who has gone through much experience, always devotedly attached by the strongest ties of affection; but always reflecting, shrinking from excesses of passion or of scoffing, and trying to see men and life as parts of a wider order.

The same personal element appears in her later work in spite of the defects which I take to be undeniable. George Eliot, as we have seen, looked on the world with a certain aloofness. She read little of the ephemeral literature of the day, and apparently thought very ill of what she did read. She looked at the political warfare from a distance, and did not go into the society deeply interested in such matters. The "Priory" was frequented by a circle whose talk was of philosophy and scientific discoveries, and which was more interested in theories than in the gossip of the day. She had not therefore the experience which could enable her to describe contemporary life, with its social and political ambitions and the rough struggle for existence in which practical lawyers and men of business are mainly occupied. She thinks of the world chiefly as the surrounding element of sordid aims into which her idealists are to go forth with such hope as may be of leavening the mass. She could not, therefore, draw lifelike portraits of such characters as were the staple of the ordinary novelist. The questions, however, in which she was profoundly interested were undeniably of the highest importance. The period of her writings was one in which, as we can now see more clearly than at the time, very significant changes were taking place in English thought and life. Controversies on "evolutionism" and socialism and democracy were showing the set of the current. George Eliot's heroes and heroines are all more or less troubled by the results, whether they live ostensibly in England or in distant countries and centuries. I need say nothing more of her special view of the questions at issue. But, incidentally, as one may say, she came, in treating of her favourite theme—the idealist in search of a vocation—to exhibit her own characteristics. The long gallery of heroines, from Milly Barton to Gwendolen Harleth, have various tasks set to them, in which we may be more or less interested. But the women themselves, whatever their outward circumstances, have an interest unsurpassed by any other writer. They have, of course, a certain family likeness; and if Maggie is most like her creator, the others show an affinity to some of her characteristics. George Eliot is reported to have said that the character which she found most difficult to support was that of Rosamond Vincy, the young woman who paralyses Lydgate. One can understand the statement, for it is Rosamond's function to do exactly what is most antipathetic to her biographer. She is the embodied contradictory of her creator's morality. Yet she, too, is a vigorous portrait, and the whole series may be given triumphantly as a proof of what is called "knowledge of the human heart." I dislike the phrase, because it seems to imply that an abstract science with that subject-matter is in existence—which I should certainly deny. But if it only means that George Eliot could—without any formula—sympathise with a singularly wide range of motive and feeling, and especially with noble and tender natures, and represent the concrete embodiment with extraordinary power, then I can fully subscribe to the opinion. I think, as I have said, that one is always conscious that her women are drawn from the inside, and that her most successful men are substantially women in disguise. But the two sexes have a good deal in common; and in the setting forth some of the moral and intellectual processes which we can all understand, George Eliot shows unsurpassable skill. Here and there, no doubt, there is too much explicit "psychological analysis," and a rather ponderous enumeration of obvious aphorisms in the pomp of scientific analogy. But she is singularly powerful in describing the conflicts of emotions; the ingenious modes of self-deception in which most of us acquire considerable skill; the uncomfortable results of keeping a conscience till we have learnt to come to an understanding with it; the grotesque mixture of motives which results when we have reached a *modus vivendi*; the downright hypocrisy of the lower nature, or the comparatively pardonable and even commendable state of mind of the person who has a thoroughly consistent code of action, though he unconsciously interprets its laws in a non-natural sense to suit his convenience. George Eliot's power of watching and describing the various manœuvres by which people keep their self-respect and satisfy their feelings shows her logical subtlety, which appears again in her quaint description of the odd processes which take the place of reasoning in the uneducated intelligence.

George Eliot believed that a work of art not only may, but must, exercise also an ethical influence. I will not inquire how much influence is actually exerted by novels upon the morality of their readers; but so far as any influence is exerted, it is due, I think, in the last resort to the personality of the novelist. That is to say, that from reading George Eliot's novels we are influenced in the same way as by an intimacy with George Eliot herself. Undoubtedly, in effect, that might vary indefinitely according to the prejudices and character of the other party. But, in any case, we feel that the writer with whom we have been in contact possessed a singularly wide and reflective intellect, a union of keen sensibility with a thoroughly tolerant spirit, a desire to appreciate all the good hidden under the commonplace and narrow, a lively sympathy with all the nobler aspirations, a vivid insight into the perplexities and delusions which beset even the strongest minds, brilliant powers of wit, at once playful and pungent, and, if we must add, a rather melancholy view of life in general, a melancholy which is not nursed for purposes of display, but forced upon a fine understanding by the view of a state of things which, we must admit, does not altogether lend itself to a cheerful optimism. I have endeavoured to point out what limitations must be adopted by an honest critic. George Eliot's works, as I have read, have not, at the present day, quite so high a position as was assigned to them by contemporary enthusiasm. That is a common phenomenon enough; and, in her case, I take it to be due chiefly to the partial misdirection of her powers in the later period. But when I compare her work with that of other novelists, I cannot doubt that she had powers of mind and a richness of emotional nature rarely equalled, or that her writings—whatever their shortcomings—will have a corresponding value in the estimation of thoughtful readers.

THOMAS CARLYLE

Thomas Carlyle

1795–1881

Thomas Carlyle was born at Ecclefechan in Dumfriesshire, Scotland, on December 4, 1795. The son of a stonemason who was a devout member of a Dissenting branch of the Presbyterian church, he was educated at Annan Academy and at Edinburgh University. His first intention had been to enter the ministry, but he was soon dissuaded from this course. Upon leaving the university he first took a position as a tutor of mathematics, then decided upon a literary career. His *Life of Friedrich Schiller* was published in the *London Magazine* in 1823–24 and in book form in 1825. It was followed by translations of Goethe's *Wilhelm Meister's Apprenticeship* and *Wilhelm Meister's Travels*, which appeared in 1824 and 1827 respectively, the latter being included in his volume of selections from German authors, *German Romance: Translations from the German with Biographical and Critical Notices* (1827).

In 1826 Carlyle married Jane Baillie Welsh, a doctor's daughter who is remembered today as a literary hostess and as one of the best letter-writers in English, whose correspondents included Browning, Tennyson, and John Forster. In 1828 the Carlyles moved for economic reasons from Edinburgh to an isolated farm in Craigenputtock, Nithsdale, where they remained for six years, before settling in London.

Carlyle's *Sartor Resartus: The Life and Opinions of Herr Teufelsdröckh*, part philosophy and part veiled autobiography, appeared in *Fraser's Magazine* in 1833–34, and in book form in 1836. It was followed in 1837 by an historical work, *The French Revolution*, which first brought him to the attention of the general public. Carlyle increased his fame through a series of lectures, *On Heroes, Hero-Worship and the Heroic in History*, delivered in 1840 and published in 1841. In 1843 appeared *Past and Present*, which dealt with the problems of the industrial poor. In this and other works Carlyle expressed a deep distrust of democracy and a longing for a hierarchically ordered, authoritarian society. This strong anti-democratic sentiment is exaggeratedly expressed in his "Occasional Discourse on the Nigger Question" (1849) and *Latter-Day Pamphlets* (1850), while his admiration for Cromwell is reflected in his edition of *Oliver Cromwell's Letters and Speeches* (1845), and his admiration for Frederick the Great is displayed in his massive biography, published in six volumes between 1848 and 1865. Carlyle also wrote a *Life of John Sterling* (1851), and in 1872 began a history of the *Early Kings of Norway*.

In 1866 Carlyle's wife died, a blow from which he had difficulty recovering. In 1871 he gave her personal papers and letters to his friend, the historian James Anthony Froude, who published them in 1883, after Carlyle's death. Carlyle received the Prussian Order of Merit in 1874, and in 1875 declined a baronetcy. He died on February 5, 1881. Froude's four-volume biography, which generated much controversy because of its frankness, appeared between 1882 and 1884. Since his death, much of Carlyle's correspondence has been published, including his letters to Emerson (1883), Goethe (1887), and John Stuart Mill (1923). *The Collected Letters of Thomas and Jane Carlyle*, edited by C. R. Sanders and K. J. Fielding, is in progress.

Personal

Carlyle breakfasted with me, and I had an interesting morning with him. He is a deep-thinking German scholar, a character, and a singular compound. His voice and manner, and even the style of his conversation, are those of a religious zealot, and he keeps up that character in his declamations against the anti-religious. And yet, if not the god of his idolatry, at least he has a priest and prophet of his church in Goethe, of whose profound wisdom he speaks like an enthusiast. But for him, Carlyle says, he should not now be alive. He owes everything to him! But in strange union with such idolatry is his admiration of Buonaparte. Another object of his eulogy is—Cobbett, whom he praises for his humanity and love of the poor! Singular, and even whimsical, combinations of love and reverence these.—Henry Crabb Robinson, *Diary*, Feb. 12, 1832

Mr C. lives among some desolate hills in the parish of Dunscore 15 or 16 miles from Dumfries. He had heard of my purpose from his friend who gave me my letter & insisted on dismissing my gig which went back to Dumfries to return for me the next day in time to secure my seat in the evening coach for the south. So I spent near 24 hours with him. He lives with his wife, a most agreeable accomplished woman, in perfect solitude. There is not a person to speak to within 7 miles. He is the most simple frank amiable person—I became acquainted with him at once, we walked over several miles of hills & talked upon all the great questions that interest us most. The comfort of meeting a man of genius is that he speaks sincerely that he feels himself to be so rich that he is above the meanness of pretending to knowledge which he has not & Carlyle does not pretend to have solved the great problems but rather to be an observer of their solution as it goes forward in the world. I asked him at what religious development the concluding passage in his piece in the *Edin. Review* upon German Literature (say 5 years ago) & some passages in the piece called "Characteristics," pointed? he replied, that he was not competent to state it even to himself—he waited rather to see.—My own feeling was that I had met with men of far less power who had yet greater insight into religious truth.—He is as you might guess from his papers the most catholic of philosophers—he forgives & loves everybody & wishes each to struggle on in his own place &

arrive at his own ends, but his respect for eminent men or rather his scale of eminence is almost the reverse of the popular scale; Scott, Mackintosh,—Jeffrey;—Gibbon;—even Bacon are no heroes of his; stranger yet he hardly admires Socrates, the glory of the Greek world—but Burns & Samuel Johnson; Mirabeau he said, interested him, & I suppose whoever else has given himself with all his heart to a leading instinct & has not *calculated* too much. But I cannot think of sketching even his opinions or repeating his conversation here. I will cheerfully do it when you visit me in America. He talks finely, seems to love the broad Scotch, & i loved him very much, at once. I am afraid he finds his entire solitude tedious, but I could not help congratulating him upon his treasure in his wife & I hope they will not leave the moors. tis so much better for a man of letters to nurse himself in seclusion than to be filed down to the common level by the compliances & imitations of city society.—And you have found out the virtues of solitude I remember with much pleasure.—RALPH WALDO EMERSON, Letter to Alexander Ireland (Aug. 30, 1833)

After all, however, I found time to make a visit to Carlyle, and to hear one of his lectures. He is rather a small, spare, ugly Scotchman, with a strong accent, which I should think he takes no pains to mitigate. His manners are plain and simple, but not polished, and his conversation much of the same sort. He is now lecturing for subsistence, to about a hundred persons, who pay him, I believe, two guineas each. . . . To-day he spoke—as I think he commonly does—without notes, and therefore as nearly extempore as a man can who prepares himself carefully, as it was plain he had done. His course is on Modern Literature, and his subject to-day was that of the eighteenth century; in which he contrasted Johnson and Voltaire very well, and gave a good character of Swift. He was impressive, I think, though such lecturing could not well be very popular; and in some parts, if he were not poetical, he was picturesque. He was nowhere obscure, nor were his sentences artificially constructed, though some of them, no doubt, savored of his peculiar manner.—GEORGE TICKNOR, *Journal* (June 1, 1838), *Life, Letters, and Journals of George Ticknor*, ed. Anna Ticknor, 1876, Vol. 2, pp. 180–81

His manners and conversation are as unformed as his style; and yet, withal, equally full of genius. In conversation, he piles thought upon thought and imagining upon imagining, till the erection seems about to topple down with its weight. He lives in great retirement,—I fear almost poverty. To him, London and its mighty maze of society are nothing; neither he nor his writings are known.—CHARLES SUMNER, Letter to George S. Hillard (Dec. 4, 1838), cited in Edward L. Pierce, *Memoir and Letters of Charles Sumner*, 1877, Vol. 2, p. 22

Some one writes about 'notes for a biography' in some beggarly *Spirit of the Age* or other rubbish basket—rejected *nem. con.* What have I to do with their *Spirits of the Age?* To have my 'life' surveyed and commented on by all men even wisely is no object with me, but rather the opposite; how much less to have it done *unwisely!* The world has no business with my life; the world will never know my life, if it should write and read a hundred biographies of me. The main facts of it even are known, and are likely to be known, to myself alone of created men. The 'goose goddess' which they call 'Fame'! *Ach Gott!* —THOMAS CARLYLE, *Journal* (Oct. 10, 1843), cited in James Anthony Froude, *Thomas Carlyle: A History of His Life in London, 1834–1881*, 1884, Vol. 1, p. 1

Accustomed to the infinite wit and exuberant richness of his writings, his talk is still an amazement and a splendor scarcely

to be faced with steady eyes. He does not converse;—only harangues. It is the usual misfortune of such marked men,—happily not one invariable or inevitable,—that they cannot allow other minds room to breathe, and show themselves in their atmosphere, and thus miss the refreshment and instruction which the greatest never cease to need from the experience of the humblest. Carlyle allows no one a chance, but bears down all opposition, not only by his wit and onset of words, resistless by their sharpness as so many bayonets, but by actual physical superiority,—raising his voice, and rushing on his opponent with a torrent of sound. This is not in the least from unwillingness to allow freedom to others. On the contrary, no man would more enjoy a manly resistance to his thought. But it is the habit of a mind accustomed to follow out its own impulse, as the hawk its prey, and which knows not how to stop in the chase. Carlyle, indeed, is arrogant and overbearing; but in his arrogance there is no littleness,—no self-love. It is the heroic arrogance of some old Scandinavian conqueror;—it is his nature, and the untamable energy that has given him power to crush the dragons. You do not love him, perhaps, nor revere; and perhaps, also, he would only laugh at you if you did; but you like him heartily, and like to see him the powerful smith, the Siegfried, melting all the old iron in his furnace till it glows to a sunset red, and burns you, if you senselessly go too near. He seems, to me, quite isolated,—lonely as the desert,—yet never was a man more fitted to prize a man, could he find one to match his mood. He finds them, but only in the past. He sings, rather than talks. He pours upon you a kind of satirical, heroical, critical poem, with regular cadences, and generally, near the beginning, hits upon some singular epithet, which serves as a *refrain* when his song is full, or with which, as with a knitting needle, he catches up the stitches, if he has chanced, now and then, to let fall a row. For the higher kinds of poetry he has no sense, and his talk on that subject is delightfully and gorgeously absurd. He sometimes stops a minute to laugh at it himself, then begins anew with fresh vigor; for all the spirits he is driving before him seem to him as Fata Morgana, ugly masks, in fact, if he can but make them turn about; but he laughs that they seem to others such dainty Ariels. His talk, like his books, is full of pictures; his critical strokes masterly. Allow for his point of view, and his survey is admirable. He is a large subject. I cannot speak more or wiselier of him now, nor needs it;—his works are true, to blame and praise him,—the Siegfried of England,—great and powerful, if not quite invulnerable, and of a might rather to destroy evil, than legislate for good. —MARGARET FULLER, Letter (Dec. 1846), *Memoirs*, 1852, Vol. 2, pp. 188–90

Thomas Carlyle is really a notable monster, and to be respected for the many noble thoughts he has elaborated and for the words of wisdom which he has flung abroad to bear divine fruit among foolish-hearted men; but I can't help thinking, face to face in a small parlour he is rather terrible, and I fancy prophets are best exhibited in the pulpit, or in the wilderness. A few grand moral instincts burn so intensely in the hearts of these men that they have no room for anything else: they rush out from their smoking sanctuary with a flaming sword in their hand, and whoever follows them not and fights is accounted a heretic. Scottish and English Universities, British Houses of Parliament, orthodox theologies, railroads, and free trade, were all shaken out and sifted under the category of Sham; while Oliver Cromwell and his Ironsides, and the old Covenanters who sang psalms and handled pikes on Dunse Moor, were held up to admiration as the only heroes in this country for the last two hundred years.—JOHN STUART BLACKIE, Letter to Augusta

Wyld (1848), cited in Anna M. Stoddart, *John Stuart Blackie: A Biography*, 1895, Vol. 1, pp. 241–42

⟨. . .⟩ what shall I say of Carlyle? Perhaps it will be childish to say anything of *him* after no more acquaintance than an hour's conversation. Of my impressions accept a few words. I confess to being very much pleased and a little disappointed. Pleased that the appearance of the man was so much more *loveable*, and disappointed that it was rather less *great* than I had expected. I was prepared for a face, manner and expression less tender but more profound. Not in the vulgar sense of mystic alchemical fakir profundity, I don't mean that. If there be any truth in his theory of 'Wudtan'—if there be divinity in *movement*—then is Carlyle divine. Body, hands, eyes, lips, eyebrows—almost cheeks, for even they seem mutable—did you ever see such a personification of motion? I felt, in seeing and hearing, that I could love the man as few men can be loved; but I went away hoping and trusting less—though I never trusted much—in the *sage*. We had a long talk (he was very kind to me), and if I had been blindfold and heard it in the street I could have sworn at once to the speaker. But it made me melancholy to see how hopeless—no affectation of despair, but heartfelt black hopelessness—he is of himself and all mankind. We had a tough argument whether it were better to have learned to make shoes or to have written *Sartor Resartus.*—SYDNEY DOBELL, Letter to George Gilfillan (Dec. 12, 1849), *The Life and Letters of Sydney Dobell*, ed. Emily Jolly, 1878, Vol. 1, pp. 112–13

Here, also, I became acquainted with Thomas Carlyle, one of the kindest and best, as well as most eloquent of men; though in his zeal for what is best he sometimes thinks it incumbent on him to take not the kindest tone, and in his eloquent demands of some hearty uncompromising creed on our parts, he does not quite set the example of telling us the amount of his own. Mr. Carlyle sees that there is a good deal of rough work in the operations of nature: he seems to think himself bound to consider a good deal of it devilish, after the old Covenanter fashion, in order that he may find something angelical in giving it the proper quantity of vituperation and blows; and he calls upon us to prove our energies and our benevolence by acting the part of the wind rather than the sun, of warring rather than peace-making, of frightening and forcing rather than conciliating and persuading. Others regard this view of the one thing needful, however strikingly set forth, as an old and obsolete story, fit only to be finally done with, and not worth the repetition of the old series of reactions, even for the sake of those analogies with the physical economy of the world, which, in the impulse which nature herself gives us towards progression, we are not bound to suppose everlastingly applicable to its moral and spiritual development. If mankind are destined never to arrive at years of discretion, the admonition is equally well-founded and unnecessary; for the old strifes will be continued at all events, the admonition (at best) being a part of them. And even then, I should say that the world is still a fine, rich, strenuous, beautiful, and desirable thing, always excepting the poverty that starves, and one or two other evils which on no account must we consent to suppose irremediable. But if the case be otherwise, if the hopes which nature herself has put into our hearts be something better than incitements to hopeless action, merely for the action's sake, and this beautiful planet be destined to work itself into such a condition as we feel to be the only fit condition for that beauty, then, I say, with every possible respect for my admirable friend, who can never speak but he is worth hearing, that the tale which he condescends to tell is no better than our old nursery figment of the *Black Man and the Coal-hole*, and that the growing desire of mankind for the cessation of bitterness, and for the prevalence of the sweets of gentleness and persuasion, is an evidence that the time has arrived for dropping the thorns and husks of the old sourness and austerity, and showing ourselves worthy of "the goods the gods provide us".

Mr. Carlyle's antipathy to "shams", is highly estimable and salutary. I wish Heaven may prosper his denouncements of them, wherever they exist. But the danger of the habit of denouncing—of looking at things from the anti-pathetic instead of the sympathetic side—is, that a man gets such a love for the pleasure and exaltation of fault-finding, as tempts him, in spite of himself, to make what he finds; till at length he is himself charged with being a "sham"; that is to say, a pretender to perceptions and virtues which he does not prove, or at best a willing confounder of what differs from modes and appearances of his own, with violations of intrinsical wisdom and goodness. Upon this principle of judgment, nature herself and the universe might be found fault with; and the sun and the stars denounced for appearing no bigger than they do, or for not confining the measure of their operation to that of the taper we read by. Mr. Carlyle adoped a peculiar semi-German style, from the desire of putting thoughts on his paper instead of words, and perhaps of saving himself some trouble in the process. I feel certain that he does it from no other motive; and I am sure he has a right to help himself to every diminuition of trouble, seeing how many thoughts and feelings he undergoes. He also strikes an additional blow with the peculiarity, rouses men's attention by it, and helps his rare and powerful understanding to produce double its effect. It would be hard not to dispense with a few verbs and nominative cases, in consideration of so great a result. Yet, if we were to judge him by one of his own summary processes, and deny him the benefit of his notions of what is expedient and advisable, how could he exculpate this style, in which he denounces so many "shams", of being itself a sham? of being affected, unnecessary, and ostentatious? a jargon got up to confound pretension with performance, and reproduce endless German talk under the guise of novelty?

Thus much in behalf of us dulcet signors of philanthropy, and conceders of good intention, whom Mr. Carlyle is always girding at, and who beg leave to say that they have not confined their lives to words, any more than the utterers of words more potential, but have had their "actions" too, and their sufferings, and even their thoughts, and have seen the faces of the gods of wonder and melancholy; albeit they end with believing them to be phantoms (however useful) of bad health, and think nothing finally potential but gentleness and persuasion.

It has been well said, that love money as people may, there is generally something which they love better: some whim, or hobby-horse; some enjoyment or recreation; some personal, or political, or poetical predilection; some good opinion of this or that class of men; some club of one's fellows, or dictum of one's own; with a thousand other *somes* and probabilities. I believe that what Mr. Carlyle loves better than his fault-finding, with all its eloquence, is the face of any human creature that looks suffering, and loving, and sincere; and I believe further, that if the fellow-creature were suffering only, and neither loving nor sincere, but had come to a pass of agony in this life, which put him at the mercies of some good man for some last help and consolation towards his grave, even at the risk of loss to repute, and a sure amount of pain and vexation, that man, if the groan reached him in its forlornness, would be Thomas Carlyle.—LEIGH HUNT, *Autobiography*, 1850, Ch. 24

Are you aware that Carlyle travelled with us to Paris? He left a deep impression with me. It is difficult to conceive of a more interesting human soul, I think. All the bitterness is love with the point reversed. He seems to me to have a profound sensibility—so profound and turbulent that it unsettles his general sympathies. Do you guess what I mean the least in the world? or is it as dark as my writings are of course?—ELIZABETH BARRETT BROWNING, Letter to Mrs. Jameson (Oct. 22, 1851)

I have seen Carlyle's face under all aspects, from the deepest gloom to the most reckless or most genial mirth; and it seemed to me that each mood would make a totally different portrait. The sympathetic is by far the finest, in my eyes. His excess of sympathy has been, I believe, the master-pain of his life. He does not know what to do with it, and with its bitterness, seeing that human life is full of pain to those who look out for it: and the savageness which has come to be a main characteristic of this singular man is, in my opinion, a mere expression of his intolerable sympathy with the suffering. He cannot express his love and pity in natural acts, like other people; and it shows itself too often in unnatural speech. But to those who understand his eyes, his shy manner, his changing colour, his sigh, and the constitutional *pudeur* which renders him silent about every thing that he feels the most deeply, his wild speech and abrupt manner are perfectly intelligible. I have felt to the depths of my heart what his sympathy was in my days of success and prosperity and apparent happiness without drawback; and again in sickness, pain, and hopelessness of being ever at ease again: I have observed the same strength of feeling towards all manner of sufferers; and I am confident that Carlyle's affections are too much for him, and the real cause of the "ferocity" with which he charges himself, and astonishes others. It must be such a strong love and honour as his friends feel for him that can compensate for the pain of witnessing his suffering life. —HARRIET MARTINEAU, *Autobiography*, ed. Maria Weston Chapman, 1877, Vol. 1, pp. 287–88

I intend no disparagement of Carlyle's moral qualities, in saying that he was almost sure finally to disappoint one's admiration. I merely mean to say that he was without that breadth of humanitary sympathy which one likes to find in distinguished men; that he was deficient in spiritual as opposed to moral force. He was a man of great simplicity and sincerity in his personal manners and habits, and exhibited even an engaging sensibility to the claims of one's physical fellowship. But he was wholly impenetrable to the solicitations both of your heart and your understanding. I think he felt a helpless dread and distrust of you instantly that he found you had any positive hope in God or practical love to man. His own intellectual life consisted so much in bemoaning the vices of his race, or drew such inspiration from despair, that he could not help regarding a man with contempt the instant he found him reconciled to the course of history. Pity is the highest style of intercourse he allowed himself with his kind. He compassionated all his friends in the measure of his affection for them. "Poor John Sterling," he used always to say; "poor John Mill, poor Frederic Maurice, poor Neuberg, poor Arthur Helps, poor little Browning, poor little Lewes," and so on; as if the temple of his friendship were a hospital, and all its inmates scrofulous or paralytic. You wondered how any mere mortal got legitimately endowed with a commiseration so divine for the inferior race of man; and the explanation that forced itself upon you was that he enjoyed an inward power and beatitude so redundant as naturally to seek relief in these copious outward showers of compassionate benediction. Especially did Carlyle conceive that no one could be actively interested in the

progress of the species without being intellectually off his balance, and in need of tenderness from all his friends. His own sympathy went out freely to cases of individual suffering, and he believed that there was an immense amount of *specific* divine mercy practicable to us. That is to say, he felt keenly whatever appealed to his senses, and willingly patronized a fitful, because that is a picturesque, Providence in the earth. He sympathized with the starving Spitalfield weaver; and would have resented the inhumanity of the slave's condition as sharply as any one, if he had had visual contact with it, and were not incited, by the subtle freemasonry that unites aristocratic pretension in literature with the same pretension in politics, to falsify his human instincts. I remember the pleasure he took in the promise that Indian corn might be found able to supplant the diseased potato in Ireland; and he would doubtless have admitted ether and chloroform to be exquisitely ordained ministers of the Divine love. But as to any sympathy with human nature itself and its inexorable wants, or any belief in a breadth of the Divine mercy commensurate with those wants, I could never discern a flavor of either in him. He scoffed with hearty scorn at the contented imbecility of Church and State with respect to social problems, but his own indifference to these things, save in so far as they were available to picturesque palaver, was infinitely more indolent and contented. He would have been the last man formally to deny the Divine existence and providence; but that these truths had any human virtue, any living efficacy to redeem us out of material and spiritual penury, I do not think he ever dreamt of such a thing. That our knowledge of God was essentially expansive; that revelation contemplated its own spiritual enlargement and fulfilment in the current facts of human history, in the growth and enlargement of the human mind itself,—so that Thomas Carlyle, if only he had not been quite so stubborn and conceited, might have proved himself far better and not far worse posted in the principles of the Divine administration than even Plato was, and so have freed himself from the dismal necessity he was all his life under to ransack the graves of the dead, in order to find some spangle, still untarnished, of God's reputed presence in our nature,—all this he took every opportunity to assure you was the saddest bosh. "Poor John Mill," he exclaimed one night,—"poor John Mill is writing away there in the *Edinburgh Review* about what he calls the Philosophy of History! As if any man could ever know the road he is going, when once he gets astride of such a distracted steed as that!" —HENRY JAMES, SR., "Some Personal Recollections of Carlyle" (1881), *Literary Remains*, 1884, pp. 423–26

General

We are indeed weakest in the department of aesthetics and we can wait a long time till we strike upon a man like Carlyle. But it is very nice, that we now with the close communication between French, English and Germans, come into the condition of correcting one another. That is the great benefit which comes out in a world literature and which will always display itself more. Carlyle has written the life of Schiller and everywhere so judged him as a German will not easily judge him. On the other hand we see clear about Shakespeare and Byron and know how to value their merits better perhaps than the English themselves.—JOHANN WOLFGANG VON GOETHE (1827), cited in Johann Peter Eckermann, *Conversations with Goethe*, 1830, tr. John Oxenford

Mr. Carlyle is an independent witness, having no professional bias or interest; evidently emancipated from ecclesiastical prejudices; and deriving his inspiration, not from Chrysostom or Augustine, but from Goëthe and Richter. Let us hear what he says, and in his own words, for Mr. Carlyle's words are not the least of his peculiarities. To use his own description of the Marquis of Mirabeau—

> He has the indisputablest ideas; but then his style! In very truth it is the strangest of styles, though one of the richest; a style full of originality, picturesqueness, sunny vigour; but all cased and slated over three-fold, in metaphor and trope; distracted into tortuosities, dislocations; starting out into crotchets, cramp-turns, quaintnesses, and hidden satire, which the French herd had no ear for. Strong meat too tough for babes.

To this peculiarity of style we attribute not a little of the interest which Mr. Carlyle's writings have excited. Readers are sick of the weak, vapid slops with which the press is now inundated, when every one who can spell and write, and couple verbs with nominative cases, thinks it his duty to publish. The general correctness of style at present is a remarkable fact. At the time when Aristotle and Plato *thought*, very few of their countrymen could *write* grammatically: and Aristotle himself lays no little stress on correct syntax as a necessary but rare excellence in an orator. At present, when *no one thinks*, *every one writes* and speaks correctly. In fact, we have been so busy with writing and speaking that we have had no time to think. But Mr. Carlyle has disdained the easy-beaten track, and struck out a new taste in writing, combining, we had almost said, all possible faults, and yet not unlikely to become popular. We have no intention of relapsing into the superficial criticisms of a by-gone day, and regarding style as the most important part of composition. But Mr. Carlyle himself knows, and has taken pains to illustrate a great truth, that between the internal spirit of thought and the external form into which it is cast, there is a vital connexion, as between soul and body. If the spirit is clear, simple, unaffected, unambitious, equable, earnest, and conscious of truth and sincerity, the words which it utters, even though unpolished and illiterate, will present a similar perspicuity, simplicity, and natural eloquence. There will be few of what are called quaintnesses—no flippancies—no strange, abrupt transitions from high to low, from the solemn to the ludicrous—little that is grotesque. Such a man will not deal with words as with counters, which he may toss about and huddle together at random, merely to express his own chance conceptions;—he will use them with caution and reverence as living things, which cannot be emptied of their own power, or be thrown to the world to be the passive symbols of him who uses them, but have their own significancy, and do their own work, and enter into the minds of others to turn and bend them in a mysterious way, so that he who deals with words is dealing with things, and not only with things, but persons. His very language will be to him as a living being, as a minister of God, with which he dares not trifle; but must act towards it reverently, and send it out on its mission with a chastened and quiet heart. So men in the presence of their superiors compose their countenance and dress into order and simplicity; and just as we should judge of the character of a state-officer who, when engaged in some high duty, appeared before his sovereign with a torn or soiled dress, or some strange fanciful costume of his own invention— we judge of a writer who, when employed in conveying truth to the public mind, is neglectful of the dress in which he clothes it, or forces it into some uncouth, misshapen and tangled masquerade habit, which, if it indicates vigour and wealth, shows the one chiefly by convulsions, and the other by an ill regulated extravagance. It was Basil, we think, who

prognosticated the apostasy of Julian while he was yet a student at Athens, because he twisted about his head, and never looked stedfastly at anything. Ambrose refused to ordain one of his own officers, who afterwards lapsed into Arianism, because he walked conceitedly and irregularly; and words have also their physiognomy, and thinking men may judge by them. —WILLIAM SEWELL, "Carlyle's Works," *Quarterly Review*, Sept. 1840, pp. 451–52

Mr. Carlyle formerly wrote for the review,—a man of talents, though, in my opinion, absurdly overpraised by some of his admirers. I believe, though I do not know, that he ceased to write because the oddities of his diction and his new words compounded à la Teutonique drew such strong remonstrances from Napier.—THOMAS BABINGTON MACAULAY, Letter to Leigh Hunt (Oct. 29, 1841)

Mr. Tennyson is quaint only; he is never, as some have supposed him, obscure—except, indeed, to the uneducated, whom he does not address. Mr. Carlyle, on the other hand, is obscure only; he is seldom, as some have imagined him, quaint. So far he is right; for although quaintness, employed by a man of judgment and genius, may be made auxiliary to a *poem*, whose true thesis is beauty, and beauty alone, it is grossly, and even ridiculously, out of place in a work of prose. But in his obscurity it is scarcely necessary to say that he is wrong. Either a man intends to be understood, or he does not. If he write a book which he intends *not* to be understood, we shall be very happy indeed not to understand it; but if he write a book which he means to be understood, and, in this book, be at all possible pains to prevent us from understanding it, we can only say that he is an ass—and this, to be brief, is our private opinion of Mr. Carlyle, which we now take the liberty of making public.—EDGAR ALLAN POE, "William Ellery Channing" (1843), *Essays and Reviews*, ed. G. R. Thompson, 1984, pp. 460–61

Have you seen the review of Carlyle in the last *Christian Remembrancer?* I never read any of his books, for though divers people profess to understand and admire them, the few passages I have looked at seem always such absurd and unintelligible rant that I feel no desire to go on further. They say that his style is formed on German writers, and that an acquaintance with the language would make me appreciate them, but I do not see what is gained by that so long as the affected ass professes to talk English.—EDWARD A. FREEMAN, Letter to Eleanor Gutch (May 16, 1848), cited in W. R. W. Stephens, *The Life and Letters of Edward A. Freeman*, 1895, Vol. 1, p. 93

There are persons, mole-blind to the soul's make and style,
Who insist on a likeness 'twixt him ⟨Emerson⟩ and Carlyle;
To compare him with Plato would be vastly fairer,
Carlyle's the more burly, but E. is the rarer;
He sees fewer objects, but clearlier, truelier,
If C.'s as original, E.'s more peculiar;
That he's more of a man you might say of the one,
Of the other he's more of an Emerson;
C.'s the Titan, as shaggy of mind as of limb,—
E. the clear-eyed Olympian, rapid and slim,
The one's two thirds Norseman, the other half Greek,
Where the one's most abounding, the other's to seek;
C.'s generals require to be seen in the mass,
E.'s specialties gain if enlarged by the glass;
C. gives nature and God his own fits of the blues,
And rims common-sense things with mystical hues,—
E. sits in a mystery calm and intense,
And looks coolly around him with sharp common-sense;

C. shows you how every-day matters unite
With the dim transdiurnal recesses of night,—
While E., in a plain, preternatural way,
Makes mysteries matters of mere every day;
C. draws all his characters quite *à la* Fuseli,—
He don't sketch their bundles of muscles and thews illy,
But he paints with a brush so untamed and profuse,
They seem nothing but bundles of muscles and thews;
E. is rather like Flaxman, lines strait and severe,
And a colorless outline, but full, round, and clear;—
To the men he thinks worthy he frankly accords
The design of a white marble statue in words.
C. labors to get at the centre, and then
Take a reckoning from there of his actions and men;
E. calmly assumes the said centre as granted,
And, given himself, has whatever is wanted.
—JAMES RUSSELL LOWELL, A *Fable for Critics,*
1848

I like Carlyle better and better. His style I do not like, nor do I always concur in his opinions, nor quite fall in with his hero-worship; but there is a manly love of truth, an honest recognition and fearless vindication of intrinsic greatness, of intellectual and moral worth, considered apart from birth, rank, or wealth, which commands my sincere admiration. Carlyle would never do for a contributor to the *Quarterly.* I have not read his *French Revolution.*—CHARLOTTE BRONTË, Letter to W. S. Williams (April 16, 1849)

Carlyle's "Pantheism" is not like that of Oersted or any philosopher, and is, I fear, an unmanageable object of attack. It is so wholly unsystematic, illogical, wild, and fantastic, that thought finds nothing in it to grapple with. How can one refute the utterances of an oracle or the spleen of a satirist? His power over intellectual men appears to me not unlike that of Joe Smith the prophet over the Mormons; dependent on strength of will and massive effrontery of dogma persevered in amid a universal incertitude weakening other men. The sick and anxious always like best the physician who has most assurance; they are comforted by the presence of so much *force,*—just as poor prostrate France will believe in rifles and eagles after ceasing to believe in anything else. Carlyle's influence appears to spring much less from what he says, estimated by its own persuasiveness, than from the mere consideration that such a man as he thinks all moral and religious doctrine just so much unbelievable trash. I know not how such an influence can be met, except by a positiveness as powerful and as gifted.—JAMES MARTINEAU, Letter to R. H. Hutton (May 19, 1852), cited in James Drummond, *The Life and Letters of James Martineau,* 1902, Vol. 1, pp. 340–41

There have been times when I have accepted your judgment of Carlyle, and have added to it some bitterness of my own, arising out of the disappointment that a man who has taught *me* so much should outrage some of my strongest convictions. Last week I renewed my intercourse with him, which for various reasons, partly accidental, has been interrupted. I went to his house with much reluctance and some fear. After a long conversation with him, I came away with a strong conviction, that very much more is expressed in that oscillation of his mind between democracy and absolutism, to which the *Spectator* alluded in its criticism on his *Frederick,* than this reviewer, or than you, are willing to admit. Ever since his *Cromwell,* indeed long before, I have always been persuaded that a profound theocratic belief was really at the basis of his mind; that in the French Revolution he heard the voice of God speaking to the kings of the earth; and that losing it among the

cries of democracy, he sought for it again in the believing rulers of the seventeenth century; that not willing to suppose it utterly silent at any time, he listened for it and thought he discovered it in the stern decrees and the war with cant of the unbelieving rulers of the eighteenth. There are terrible contradictions in his thoughts, which express themselves in his wild speech. But the contradictions belong to the time: we may find them in ourselves. And they cannot be resolved, as you fancy they may, into the mere worship of might. That comes uppermost at times; often he recoils from it with the intensest horror, and affirms and feels Justice to be the one ruler in heaven and earth. The infinite wail for a real and not a nominal father, for a real and not an imaginary king, comes out in Carlyle more than in any man I know, and I am shocked at myself when I feel how I have been refusing to hear it, and only interpreting it by the devil's cry, "What have I do with thee?" which mingles in it. Irving shows the other side of Carlyle's Puritanism. He was utterly and purely a theologian; God was all in all to him. From God he must begin. And how to establish a relation between God and mankind on the Calvinistic hypothesis, which he nobly determined not to abandon for any Arminian or semi-Arminian compromises; this was the problem in trying to solve which he gave up his fame and his life. From what I have read of Mrs. Oliphant I cannot believe that she has succeeded in presenting this struggle clearly to her readers. But if she has given even a hint of it, so that people may feel him to have been the most vigorous Protestant against the religion of the newspapers and Exeter Hall that has appeared in our generation, she deserves much gratitude. I hope you will not let your dislike of Carlyle, which if you will search into it you will find to be more democratic than divine, colour your judgment of his friend, whom, in spite of enormous prejudice against him, I was forced and am now more than ever forced to reverence and love.—FREDERICK DENISON MAURICE, Letter to J. M. Ludlow (May 30, 1862), *The Life of Frederick Denison Maurice,* ed. Frederick Maurice, 1884, Vol. 2, pp. 404–5

I have already mentioned Carlyle's earlier writings as one of the channels through which I received the influences which enlarged my early narrow creed; but I do not think that those writings, by themselves, would ever have had any effect on my opinions. What truths they contained, though of the very kind which I was already receiving from other quarters, were presented in a form and vesture less suited than any other to give them access to a mind trained as mine had been. They seemed a haze of poetry and German metaphysics, in which almost the only clear thing was a strong animosity to most of the opinions which were the basis of my mode of thought; religious scepticism, utilitarianism, the doctrine of circumstances, and the attaching any importance to democracy, logic, or political economy. Instead of my having been taught anything, in the first instance, by Carlyle, it was only in proportion as I came to see the same truths through media more suited to my mental constitution, that I recognized them in his writings. Then, indeed, the wonderful power with which he put them forth made a deep impression upon me, and I was during a long period one of his most fervent admirers; but the good his writings did me, was not as philosophy to instruct, but as poetry to animate. Even at the time when our acquaintance commenced, I was not sufficiently advanced in my new modes of thought, to appreciate him fully; a proof of which is, that on his showing me the manuscript of *Sartor Resartus,* his best and greatest work, which he had just then finished, I made little of it; though when it came out about two years afterwards in

Fraser's Magazine I read it with enthusiastic admiration and the keenest delight. I did not seek and cultivate Carlyle less on account of the fundamental differences in our philosophy. He soon found out that I was not "another mystic," and when for the sake of my own integrity I wrote to him a distinct profession of all those of my opinions which I knew he most disliked, he replied that the chief difference between us was that I "was as yet consciously nothing of a mystic." I do not know at what period he gave up the expectation that I was destined to become one; but though both his and my opinions underwent in subsequent years considerable changes, we never approached much nearer to each other's modes of thought than we were in the first years of our acquaintance. I did not, however, deem myself a competent judge of Carlyle. I felt that he was a poet, and that I was not; that he was a man of intuition, which I was not; and that as such, he not only saw many things long before me, which I could only when they were pointed out to me, hobble after and prove, but that it was highly probable he could see many things which were not visible to me even after they were pointed out. I knew that I could not see round him, and could never be certain that I saw over him; and I never presumed to judge him with any definiteness, until he was interpreted to me by one greatly the superior of us both—who was more a poet than he, and more a thinker than I—whose own mind and nature included his, and infinitely more.
—JOHN STUART MILL, *Autobiography*, 1873, Ch. 5

It is not the intellect alone, or the imagination alone, which can become sensible of the highest virtue in the writings of Mr Carlyle. He is before all else a power with reference to conduct. He too cannot live without a divine presence. He finds in it the entire material universe, "the living garment of God." Teufelsdröckh among the Alps is first awakened from his stony sleep at the "Centre of Indifference" by the glory of the white mountains, the azure dome, the azure winds, the black tempest marching in anger through the distance. He finds the divine presence in the spirit of man, and in the heroic leaders of our race. But in duty,—in duty, not in happiness,—is found God's most intimate presence with the soul. "Let him who gropes painfully in darkness or uncertain light, and prays vehemently that the dawn may ripen into day, lay this . . . precept well to heart, *Do the Duty which lies nearest to thee.*" That this duty should not harden and shrivel into a mere round of mechanical observances, man must look up and admit into his heart the greatness and mystery that surround him, the Immensities, the Infinities, the Silence, the deep Eternity. Then once more he must return to the definite and the practicable. Mr Carlyle is a mystic in the service of what is nobly positive, and it is easy to see how his transcendental worship of humanity, together with his reverence for duty, might condense and materialize themselves for the needs of a generation adverse to transcendental ways of thought, into the ethical doctrines of Comte.

The mysterious awe with which Mr Carlyle regards force,—"Force, force, everywhere force; we ourselves a mysterious force in the centre of that. . . . Surely to the atheistic thinker, if such an one were possible, it must be a miracle too, this huge illimitable whirlwind of force which envelopes us here,"—this awed contemplation of force, coalescing with Mr Carlyle's veneration for man as the true Shekinah, visible revelation of God, leads directly to his hero-worship. A concentration in a human person of this force, which is divine, constitutes a hero, and becomes the highest and most definite presentation of whatever we had worshipped in the vague as immense, eternal, and infinite. Fortunately and unfortu-

nately, Mr Carlyle does not require the heroic force to be invariably of a moral kind,—fortunately, for the poet and artist might otherwise as such possess no claim to his homage; unfortunately, because where the question of morality ought to be raised, Mr Carlyle does not always put the question. Mr Carlyle is so deeply impressed by the fact that truthfulness, virtue, rectitude of a certain kind, the faithful adaptation of means to ends, are needful in order to bring anything to effect, that where ends are successfully achieved, he assumes some of the virtuous force of the world to have been present. With this falls in his sense of the sacredness of fact; to recognize fact, to accept conditions, and thereby to conquer,—such is the part of the hero who would be a victor. Add to all this, the stoical temper, a sternness in Mr Carlyle's nature, which finds expression in his scorn for mere happiness, and we shall understand how his transcendentalism makes us acquainted with strange heroes. To suppress a Jamaica riot it will contribute if women be whipped with piano-wire; to perceive this sacred fact, to apply the piano-wire faithfully and effectively, as in the sight of all the Immensities and Eternities, to suppress the riot—how heroic, how divine! Behold, there is still among us in these days of cant and shoddy, a king, a can-ning, an able-man; let us fall down before him and adore in silence!
—EDWARD DOWDEN, "The Transcendental Movement and Literature" (1877), *Studies in Literature*, 1878, pp. 74–76

However much or little he may yet do, he certainly ought to be recognised as one of the chief influences of his time. Bad as is our political morality, and grievous as are our social shortcomings, we are at least awakened to a sense of our sins: and I cannot but ascribe this awakening mainly to Carlyle. What Wordsworth did for poetry, in bringing us out of a conventional idea and method to a true and simple one, Carlyle has done for morality. He may be himself the most curious opposition to himself,—he may be the greatest mannerist of his age while denouncing conventionalism,—the greatest talker while eulogising silence,—the most woful complainer while glorifying fortitude,—the most uncertain and stormy in mood, while holding forth serenity as the greatest good within the reach of Man: but he has nevertheless infused into the mind of the English nation a sincerity, earnestness, healthfulness and courage which can be appreciated only by those who are old enough to tell what was our morbid state when Byron was the representative of our temper, the Clapham Church of our religion, and the rotten-borough system of our political morality. If I am warranted in believing that the society I am bidding farewell to is a vast improvement upon that which I was born into, I am confident that the blessed change is attributable to Carlyle more than to any single influence besides.—HARRIET MARTINEAU, *Autobiography*, ed. Maria Weston Chapman, 1877, Vol. 1, pp. 291–92

Anything I can do to help in raising a memorial to Carlyle shall be most willingly done. Few men can have dissented more strongly from his way of looking at things than I; but I should not yield to the most devoted of his followers in gratitude for the bracing wholesome influence of his writings when, as a very young man, I was essaying without rudder or compass to strike out a course for myself.—THOMAS HENRY HUXLEY, Letter to Lord Stanley (March 9, 1881), cited in Leonard Huxley, *Life and Letters of Thomas Henry Huxley*, 1900, Vol. 2, p. 34

I never much liked Carlyle. He seemed to me to be "carrying coals to Newcastle," as our proverb says; preaching earnestness to a nation which had plenty of it by nature, but was less abundantly supplied with several other useful things. —MATTHEW ARNOLD, Letter to M. Fontanès (March 25, 1881)

To sum up, if I had to characterize the moral and intellectual influence exercised by Carlyle, I should say that he seems to me to have, above all things, helped to loosen the fetters of positive creed in which thought was imprisoned among his countrymen. Carlyle was a mystic, and mysticism here, as elsewhere, discharged the function which belongs to it in the chain of systems: to wit, that of dissolving dogma under pretence of spiritualizing it, of shattering faith under pretence of enlarging it. When men heard Carlyle speak so much of divinity and eternity, of mystery and adoration, they hailed him as the preacher of a religion higher and wider than current belief. In vain did orthodoxy, more keen-sighted, point out the negations which lay hid under the writer's formulas. It is so pleasant to free oneself without appearing to break too sharply with consecrated words and institutions! Since then speculation has made much way in England. The universal mysteries of our author have been exchanged for exact research, precise definitions, rigorous ascertainments. I do not know whether Carlyle was aware of it, but he lived long enough to see his influence exhausted, his teaching out of date. It is true that, as consolation, he could take himself to witness that he had served as the transition between the past and the present, and that this is in the long run the best glory to which a thinker can pretend here below.—EDMOND SCHERER, "Thomas Carlyle" (1881), *Essays on English Literature*, tr. George Saintsbury, 1891, p. 235

As a representative author, a literary figure, no man else will bequeath to the future more significant hints of our stormy era, its fierce paradoxes, its din, and its struggling parturition periods, than Carlyle. He belongs to our own branch of the stock too; neither Latin nor Greek, but altogether Gothic. Rugged, mountainous, volcanic, he was himself more a French revolution than any of his volumes. In some respects, so far in the Nineteenth century, the best equipt, keenest mind, even from the college point of view, of all Britain; only he had an ailing body. Dyspepsia is to be traced in every page, and now and then fills the page. One may include among the lessons of his life—even though that life stretch'd to amazing length—how behind the tally of genius and morals stands the stomach, and gives a sort of casting vote.

Two conflicting agonistic elements seem to have contended in the man, sometimes pulling him different ways like wild horses. He was a cautious, conservative Scotchman, fully aware what a fœtid gas-bag much of modern radicalism is; but then his great heart demanded reform, demanded change—often terribly at odds with his scornful brain. No author ever put so much wailing and despair into his books, sometimes palpable, oftener latent. He reminds me of that passage in Young's poems where as death presses closer and closer for his prey, the soul rushes hither and thither, appealing, shrieking, berating, to escape the general doom.

Of short-comings, even positive blur-spots, from an American point of view, he had serious share.

Not for his merely literary merit, (though that was great)—not as "maker of books," but as launching into the self-complacent atmosphere of our days a rasping, questioning, dislocating agitation and shock, is Carlyle's final value. It is time the English-speaking peoples had some true idea about the verteber of genius, namely power. As if they must always have it cut and bias'd to the fashion, like a lady's cloak! What a needed service he performs! How he shakes our comfortable

reading circles with a touch of the old Hebraic anger and prophecy—and indeed it is just the same. Not Isaiah himself more scornful, more threatening: "The crown of pride, the drunkards of Ephraim, shall be trodden under feet: And the glorious beauty which is on the head of the fat valley shall be a fading flower." (The word prophecy is much misused; it seems narrow'd to prediction merely. That is not the main sense of the Hebrew word translated "prophet;" it means one whose mind bubbles up and pours forth as a fountain, from inner, divine spontaneities revealing God. Prediction is a very minor part of prophecy. The great matter is to reveal and outpour the God-like suggestions pressing for birth in the soul. This is briefly the doctrine of the Friends or Quakers.)

Then the simplicity and amid ostensible frailty the towering strength of this man—a hardy oak knot, you could never wear out—an old farmer dress'd in brown clothes, and not handsome—his very foibles fascinating. Who cares that he wrote about Dr. Francia, and "Shooting Niagara" and "the Nigger Question,"—and didn't at all admire our United States? (I doubt if he ever thought or said half as bad words about us as we deserve.) How he splashes like leviathan in the seas of modern literature and politics! Doubtless, respecting the latter, one needs first to realize, from actual observation, the squalor, vice and doggedness ingrain'd in the bulk-population of the British Islands, with the red tape, the fatuity, the flunkeyism everywhere, to understand the last meaning in his pages. Accordingly, though he was no chartist or radical, I consider Carlyle's by far the most indignant comment or protest anent the fruits of feudalism to-day in Great Britain—the increasing poverty and degradation of the homeless, landless twenty millions, while a few thousands, or rather a few hundreds, possess the entire soil, the money, and the fat berths. Trade and shipping, and clubs and culture, and prestige, and guns, and a fine select class of gentry and aristocracy, with every modern improvement, cannot begin to salve or defend such stupendous hoggishness.

The way to test how much he has left his country were to consider, or try to consider, for a moment, the array of British thought, the resultant *ensemble* of the last fifty years, as existing to-day, *but with Carlyle left out.* It would be like an army with no artillery. The show were still a gay and rich one—Byron, Scott, Tennyson, and many more—horsemen and rapid infantry, and banners flying—but the last heavy roar so dear to the ear of the train'd soldier, and that settles fate and victory, would be lacking.

For the last three years we in America have had transmitted glimpses of a thin-bodied, lonesome, wifeless, childless, very old man, lying on a sofa, kept out of bed by indomitable will, but, of late, never well enough to take the open air. I have noted this news from time to time in brief descriptions in the papers. A week ago I read such an item just before I started out for my customary evening stroll between eight and nine. In the fine cold night, unusually clear, (Feb. 5, '81,) as I walk'd some open grounds adjacent, the condition of Carlyle, and his approaching—perhaps even then actual—death, filled me with thoughts eluding statement, and curiously blending with the scene. The planet Venus, an hour high in the west, with all her volume and lustre recover'd, (she has been shorn and languid for nearly a year,) including an additional sentiment I never noticed before—not merely voluptuous, Paphian, steeping, fascinating—now with calm commanding seriousness and hauteur—the Milo Venus now. Upward to the zenith, Jupiter, Saturn, and the moon past her quarter, trailing in procession, with the Pleiades following, and the constellation Taurus, and red Aldebaran. Not a cloud in heaven. Orion strode through the southeast, with his glittering belt—and a trifle below hung the sun of the night, Sirius. Every star dilated, more vitreous, nearer than usual. Not as in some clear nights when the larger stars entirely outshine the rest. Every little star or cluster just as distinctly visible, and just as nigh. Berenice's hair showing every gem, and new ones. To the northeast and north the Sickle, the Goat and kids, Cassiopea, Castor and Pollux, and the two Dippers. While through the whole of this silent indescribable show, inclosing and bathing my whole receptivity, ran the thought of Carlyle dying. (To soothe and spiritualize, and, as far as may be, solve the mysteries of death and genius, consider them under the stars at midnight.)

And now that he has gone hence, can it be that Thomas Carlyle, soon to chemically dissolve in ashes and by winds, remains an identity still? In ways perhaps eluding all the statements, lore and speculations of ten thousand years— eluding all possible statements to mortal sense—does he yet exist, a definite, vital being, a spirit, an individual—perhaps now wafted in space among those stellar systems, which, suggestive and limitless as they are, merely edge more limitless, far more suggestive systems? I have no doubt of it. In silence, of a fine night, such questions are answer'd to the soul, the best answers that can be given. With me, too, when depress'd by some specially sad event, or tearing problem, I wait till I go out under the stars for the last voiceless satisfaction.—WALT WHITMAN, "Death of Thomas Carlyle" (1881), *Prose Works*, ed. Floyd Stovall, 1963, Vol. 1, pp. 249–53

Carlyle's defects of feeling—if such there were—could only have reference to the distribution of his sympathy, not to its amount. His pity was vast, and only his division of it between black and white could be called in question. The condition of his toiling fellow-countrymen oppressed him like a nightmare. Day and night for years he had brooded upon this subject, if haply a gleam might be discerned showing the way towards amelioration. Braver or wiser words were never addressed to the aristocracy of England than those addressed to them by Carlyle. Braver or wiser words were never addressed to the Radicalism of England than those uttered by the same strenuous spirit. He saw clearly the iniquity of the Corn Laws, and his condemnation fell upon them, like the stone of Scripture, grinding them to powder. With equal clearness he saw the vanity of expecting political wisdom from intellectual ignorance, however backed by numbers. It was like digging for diamonds in Thames mud. Hence the pressing need of public education, and hence his powerful advocacy, in advance, of what his friend Forster has, in these later days, in great part realised. He urged the necessity of an organised system of emigration, and it might have been well had his prevision been translated long ago into action. But though, as regards these and other matters, he uttered his views with a strength and clearness peculiar to himself, his aim, politically, was rather to elevate and ennoble public life generally than to enunciate special measures. His influence went far beyond the sphere of politics. No man of his day and generation threw so much of resolution and moral elevation into the hearts and lives of the young. Concerning the claims of duty and the dignity of work, never man spake like this man. A friend and I agreed some time ago to describe him as "dynamic," not "didactic"—a spiritual force, which warmed, moved, and invigorated, but which refused to be clipped into precepts. He desired truth in the inward parts. To the Sham, however highly placed and run after, his language was: "Depart hence, in the Devil's name, unworshipped by at least one man, and leave the thoroughfare clear." But his spirit leaped to recognise true merit and

manfulness in all their phases and spheres of action. Braidwood amid the flames of Tooley Street, and the riddled *Vengeur* sinking to the cry of "*Viva la République!*" found in his strong soul sympathetic admiration. He, however, prized courage less than truth; and when he found the story of the *Vengeur* to be a lie, he transfixed it, and hung it up as an historic scarecrow. The summer lightning of his humour, and the splendour of an imagination, perhaps without a parallel in literature, served only to irradiate and vivify labours marked by a thoroughness in searching, and a patience in sifting, never yet surpassed. The bias of his mind was certainly towards what might be called the military virtues; thinking, as he did, that they could not be dispensed with in the present temper of the world. But, though he bore about him the image and superscription of a great military commander, had he been a statesman, as he might well have been, he would at any fit and proper moment have joyfully accepted as the weapons of his warfare, instead of the sword and spear, the ploughshare and pruning-hook of peaceful civic life.

One point, touching Carlyle's ethics, may be referred to here. Taking all that science has done in the past, all that she has achieved in the present, and all that she is likely to compass in the future—will she at length have told us everything, rendering our knowledge of this universe rounded and complete? The answer is clear. After science has completed her mission upon earth, the finite known will still be embraced by the infinite unknown. And this "boundless contiguity of shade," by which our knowledge is hemmed in, will always tempt the exercise of belief and imagination. The human mind, in its structural and poetic capacity, can never be prevented from building its castles—on the rock or in the air, as the case may be—in this ultra-scientific region. Certainly the mind of Carlyle could not have been prevented from doing so. Out of pure Unintelligence he held that Intelligence never could have sprung, and so, at the heart of things, he placed an Intelligence—an Energy which, "to avoid circuitous periphrasis, we call God." I am here repeating his own words to myself. Every reader of his works will have recognised the burning intensity of his conviction that this universe is ruled by veracity and justice, which are sure in the end to scorch and dissipate all falsehood and wrong.

And now I come to the charge so frequently made against him, that he was the apostle of Might. He felt, perhaps more deeply than his assailants, the radical and ineffaceable difference which often subsists between might and right. But

> His faith was large in time,
> And that which shapes it to some perfect end,

His own words, which are to be found in the 8th chapter of *Chartism*, are these:—"Might and Right do differ frightfully from hour to hour; but give them centuries to try it in, and they are found in the end to be identical." Viewed in the light of this utterance, the advocacy of Might is not, in the abstract, offensive; for it meant at bottom the assertion that, in the end, that only is mighty which has the "Law of the Universe" on its side. With Carlyle, as with Empedocles, Lucretius, and Darwin, the Fit survives. His doctrine is the doctrine of science, not "touched" but saturated with religious emotion. For the operation of Force—the scientific agent—his deep and yearning soul substituted the operation of the Energy before referred to, which, to avoid periphrasis, we call God.—JOHN TYNDALL, "On Unveiling the Statue of Thomas Carlyle" (1882), *New Fragments*, 1900, pp. 393–96

Carlyle is one whose great work we have to use, not one whom we have to follow; who suggested many things to the last generation, who will leave little enough to the next. Even in history, where his true mission was, and where he has left such noble monuments, we cannot trust ourselves to him. His estimates are too often extravagant or misleading. Outrageous over-praise is to be found with no less wanton disparagement. To call good old Johnson "the last of the Romans;" poor Burns "the thunder-god;" to single out Mirabeau as the man who might have saved France in the Revolution, and Napoleon as the man who closed it, is hardly less extravagant than to pour a torrent of contempt on the philosophers, the economists, the statesmen, the movements of the Eighteenth Century and the Nineteenth—indeed, on almost all men and all women in these luckless eras, except the two or three who are saved in the Universal Deluge and are taken up in the Carlylean ark. And the memory of Carlyle is heavily weighted by all that he has said about military tyranny, slavery, and the negro. Three words, three ideas form the saving faith of our times— Evolution, the People, Humanity: and these three ideas were ever to Thomas Carlyle what a red flag is to a bull.

What then, in sooth, is the meaning of these strange contradictions! What is the riddle of a nature which seems to have poured forth its last drop only to puzzle us more? Here is a man with poetic gifts of the first rank, a born artist, yet whose art is a perpetual torment to him, having to the last something uncouth and abortive in all its creations. Here is a man with an insight that at times touches that of Tacitus, Bacon, or Goethe, yet whose gift ends in a wearisome knack of caricature. Here is one of the great masters of the English tongue, who finally settles into a tiresome mannerism. A man, one would think, of really religious nature, whose religion it is hardly possible to put into words, who with "God," "devil," "hell," and "damnation" as often on his lips as on a carter's, appears now to have denied that any of these had practical effect on human affairs in any literal sense. And so one who has written some of the most powerful books of this century, and deeply stirred the mind of the last generation, has passed away without leaving more than a chapter in the history of literature, without founding anything, leaving behind him to carry on his work two or three men who have just learned to mimic his cloudy jeremiads.

We can all see now that he really, in his heart, believed in nothing. All beliefs, demonstrations, certainties of other people he swept away. There were hundreds and thousands, he thinks, of "greater men than Newton." Everything like a system, a set of doctrines, even a few coherent principles, was all mere cant, windbags, shams, inanities. The old Hebrew belief was "Houndsditch;" the modern belief in realities was atheism. Carlyle, like Descartes, made a *tabula rasa* of all belief. He then interpreted *cogito ergo sum* to mean, "I think, therefore I am; no one else thinks, therefore all others are shams." But Carlyle, being not a philosopher, but a prose poet, could get no further. Having come out of Houndsditch himself, he hugged the rags of Houndsditch to his dying day round his brawny limbs. The Bible continued to serve him with horrible expletives and apocalyptic tropes. Calvinism had bred in him the moody, dogged, mystical temper of the Cameronian peasant. He flung off the creed, but he kept the temper. Metaphysics, of the Kantian or Hegelian kind, he rejected also, retaining, unluckily, the key to the cloudland, the *Ich* and the *Nicht-Ich*, the bare idea of absolute and transcendental. Hence Carlyle, rejecting at once all theologies, all philosophies, all syntheses alike, and bound by his very ideal to ridicule the possibility of any theology, any philosophy, any synthesis, was forced into a creed that at last got stereotyped into the simple words, "I believe in Thomas

Carlyle; which faith, unless a man keep, without doubt he shall perish everlastingly."

And so it was that a man, by nature of noble sincerity and unselfishness, of keen vision and profound yearning after goodness and truth, came, by the power of a gloomy superstition, to reach such heights of maniacal egoism, such depths of corrosive inhumanity, as he and his friends have scattered through these posthumous volumes. And with all this raving about atheists and unbelievers, Thomas Carlyle stands pilloried on the pedestal which he so laboriously framed for himself, as of all modern Englishmen the one most utterly naked of any intelligible belief. For neither he nor his biographer can get any further in any definite proposition than that this earth was tophet, and Thomas Carlyle the only wise man in it. There is not in these volumes one philosophic, religious, or social doctrine—nothing constructive, directing, or fruitful. There is railing, mockery, and imprecation of a truly Gargantuan kind; but what of real, humane, positive, or systematic? Words, words, pictures, tropes, sublimities enough to make the major and the minor prophets; but nothing to hold by, to work with, or to teach.

It comes out that this flux of talk about devil, hell, tophet, and heaven, is all allegory or image. Thomas Carlyle never believed that the devil really made the cocks to crow or spoiled his porridge, or that his good friends and neighbours would end in everlasting fire. No! nor that God specially interposed for him to enable him to finish his chapter or digest his dinner, or that all the petty trifles of his life were the peculiar work of "His unspeakable mercy." All this was cant, trick of irreverent speech, habit of bilious self-absorption, nothing else. The Immensities and Unspeakabilities come at last to this. One might as well say the Brutalities, and the Self-idolatries, and the Utter Nonsensicalities. For at the close of his long life Carlyle found out at last that God "does nothing." An otiose God, then, surveying unmoved "this dusty, fuliginous chaos," is the residuum of all this furious apostrophising.

Wreck, failure, hopelessness: these are the words which the faithful disciple inscribes on his master's grave. The greatest will and courage cannot help the man who obstinately defies his fellow-men. The grandest literary genius will enable no man to solve *de novo* by his own single insight the problems of philosophy and life. The most passionate yearning after right will not suffice to him who resolves to seek right by the light of his own unaided conscience. And thus the great brain and the fine nature of Carlyle end in an egoism that comes perilously near to mania. No "thinker" indeed he, if by thinking we mean the coherent working out of complex questions to practical results. None but a few literary dreamers even call him thinker. And it is not given to poets or to prophets to teach us philosophy, nor duty, nor truth. Nay, the sons of the prophet can do little now but show us how hopelessly their master ended, when he pretended to teach as well as to picture, to astonish, or to stimulate.

What a pitiful tale is this so-called life! A grand imagination stinging itself to death, like a scorpion, in its frenzy of self-absorption; a generous heart turned to gall because it had lost its way, lost all hope of finding a way; an "influence," a master of speech, a glorious inciter to great things; an "influence," deeper doubtless than Coleridge, higher than Johnson, but how much lower than the mighty Burke! Let us think of him sadly and kindly, lying amongst the Annandale peasants from whom he came forth and of whom he was ever one. Compare the cruel storms in the life of this lost soul with the serene humanity of those whom he nicknamed atheists. Read the autobiography of Hume, and see how a really great thinker could die, with sweetness, hope, and love in every tone. Or read the memoirs of Gibbon, or the life of Turgot, of Adam Smith, of Condorcet. Or, lastly, compare these fuliginous railings and wailings with the manly, self-possessed, simple story told by the magnanimous spirit of John Mill. They found peace; while the wild spirit who in life covered them with his mockery, went tossing down to his last rest in scorn, hate, and despair. "Wa, wa," he tells us the dying Frankish King cried, "who is this mighty power which pulls down the strongest?" "Wa, wa," wails Thomas Carlyle, recognising a power too strong to be resisted. That power is humanity, the human race, which his long life was devoted to deriding, and which now, in his death, still honours him as a brother of rare genius and mighty purpose.—FREDERIC HARRISON, "Froude's Life of Carlyle" (1885), *The Choice of Books and Other Literary Pieces*, 1886, pp. 194–99

The truth is that Carlyle was strongly individualistic in his whole tone of mind. He had, at least, no firm grasp of the organic unity or *solidarity* of human life, or of the creative powers of those social forces which arise, not from the individuals taken separately, but from the way in which they act and react upon each other in society. In his own life he stood apart from other men, confident in himself and his judgments; and though penetrating in his insight into character, yet he was quite incapable of the "give and take" of social life, or, indeed, of doing anything in regard to others, except simply to insist on his own will and his own opinions. It was in harmony with this that, in his view of history, he had his eye fixed mainly on the doings of certain leaders, and far too little on the general stream of thought and life which carried both leaders and followers along with it. In this point of view the very title of Emerson's book, *Representative Men*, is a kind of silent criticism upon Carlyle's *Heroes and Hero-Worship*. In social politics, again, Carlyle had far too high an estimate of the advantage of men being *driven* into the right road, and far too low an estimate of the difference between that method and the method of governing them through their own will.

At the same time, every one must admit that Carlyle is right in saying that the success of this, as of every system, must depend greatly on the ability of men to recognise and to reverence those who are their true guides and superiors, though such reverence need by no means imply anything like an absolute submission, either of opinion or will. But Carlyle, whom we may call the modern Elijah, was ever too apt, like the ancient Elijah, to think that he was standing alone, and above all others required to be told that there were yet seven thousand men in Israel who had not bowed the knee to Baal. And as in his picture of history he was apt to become almost a special pleader for the individual he had selected as hero, so in politics he was inclined to regard all responsibility of the rulers to the people as a hindrance to the efficient ruling of the hero when he should be found. On the other hand, our view of his political thought would not be complete without noting how much he did to banish the eighteenth-century theory of the limitations of the government to the functions of a grand policeman, and to revive the old Platonic idea that the State had a social and ethical work to perform—an idea which, it may be remarked, could scarcely be realised in modern times by any Government without a strong democratic force behind it.

With these insufficient words I must leave Carlyle's political pamphlets. Their great power lies, not in the specific proposals which they contain, or even in the truth of their analysis of the political situation, but in their constant preaching of the lesson that a moral regeneration of society is more important than any change of the machinery of government, and is indeed necessary to make any such change effective. They lift us out of the atmosphere of party, and force us to look beyond special measures to the deepest social problems; and they are full of words of reproof, of warning, and encouragement, winged with insight, humour, and imagination, which thrill through us like battle music. After everything has been said that can be said in the way of criticism, we are forced to recognise that no English writer in this century has done more to elevate and purify our ideals of life, and to make us conscious that the things of the spirit are real, and that, in the last resort, there is no other reality.—EDWARD CAIRD, "The Genius of Carlyle," *Essays on Literature and Philosophy*, 1892, Vol. 1, pp. 264–67

The general verdict on Carlyle's literary career assigns to him the first place among the authors of his time. No writer of our generation, in or out of England, has combined such abundance with such power. Regarding his rank as a writer there is little or no dispute: it is admitted that the irregularities and eccentricities of his style are bound up with its richness. In estimating the value of his thought we must distinguish between instruction and inspiration. If we ask what new truths he has taught, what problems he has definitely solved, our answers must be few. This is a perhaps inevitable result of the manner of his writing, or rather of the nature of his mind. Aside from political parties, he help to check their exaggerations by his own; seeing deeply into the under-current evils of the time, even when vague in his remedies he was of use in his protest against leaving these evils to adjust themselves—what has been called "the policy of drifting"—or of dealing with them only by catchwords. No one set a more incisive brand on the meanness that often marks the unrestrained competition of great cities; no one was more effective in his insistence that the mere accumulation of wealth may mean the ruin of true prosperity; no one has assailed with such force the mammon-worship and the frivolity of his age. Everything he writes comes home to the individual conscience: his claim to be regarded as a moral exemplar has been diminished, his hold on us as an ethical teacher remains unrelaxed. It has been justly observed that he helped to modify "the thought rather than the opinion of two generations." His message, as that of Emerson, was that "life must be pitched on a higher plane." Goethe said to Eckermann in 1827 that Carlyle was a moral force so great that he could not tell what he might produce. His influence has been, though not continuously progressive, more marked than that of any of his compeers, among whom he was, if not the greatest, certainly the most imposing personality. It had two culminations; shortly after the appearance of *The French Revolution*, and again towards the close of the seventh decade of the author's life. To the enthusiastic reception of his works in the Universities, Mr. Froude has borne eloquent testimony, and the more academically restrained Arnold admits that "the voice of Carlyle, overstrained and misused since, sounded then in Oxford fresh and comparatively sound," though, he adds, "The friends of one's youth cannot always support a return to them." In the striking article in the *St. James' Gazette* of the date of the great author's death we read: "One who had seen much of the world and knew a large proportion of the remarkable men of the last thirty years declared that Mr. Carlyle was by far the most impressive person he had ever known, the man who conveyed most forcibly to those who approached him [best on resistance principles] that general impression of genius and force of character which it is impossible either to mistake or to define." Thackeray, as well as Ruskin and Froude, acknowledged him as, beyond the range of his own *métier*, his master, and the American Lowell, penitent for past disparagement, confesses that "all modern Literature has felt his influence in the right direction"; while the Emersonian hermit Thoreau, a man of more intense though more restricted genius than the poet politician, declares— "Carlyle alone with his wide humanity has, since Coleridge, kept to us the promise of England. His wisdom provokes rather than informs. He blows down narrow walls, and struggles, in a lurid light, like the Jöthuns, to throw the old woman Time; in his work there is too much of the anvil and the forge, not enough hay-making under the sun. He makes us act rather than think: he does not say, know thyself, which is impossible, but know thy work. He has no pillars of Hercules, no clear goal, but an endless Atlantic horizon. He exaggerates. Yes; but he makes the hour great, the picture bright, the reverence and admiration strong; while mere precise fact is a coil of lead." Our leading journal on the morning after Carlyle's death wrote of him in a tone of well-tempered appreciation: "We have had no such individuality since Johnson. Whether men agreed or not, he was a touchstone to which truth and falsehood were brought to be tried. A preacher of Doric thought, always in his pulpit and audible, he denounced wealth without sympathy, equality without respect, mobs without leaders, and life without aim." To this we may add the testimony of another high authority in English letters, politically at the opposite pole: "Carlyle's influence in kindling enthusiasm for virtues worthy of it, and in stirring a sense of the reality on the one hand and the unreality on the other, of all that men can do and suffer, has not been surpassed by any teacher now living. Whatever later teachers may have done in definitely shaping opinion . . . here is the friendly fire-bearer who first conveyed the Promethean spark; here the prophet who first smote the rock." Carlyle, writes one of his oldest friends, "may be likened to a fugleman; he stood up in the front of Life's Battle and showed in word and action his notion of the proper attitude and action of men. He was, in truth, a prophet, and he has left his gospels." To those who contest that these gospels are for the most part negative, we may reply that to be taught what not to do is to be far advanced on the way to do.

In nothing is the generation after him so prone to be unjust to a fresh thinker as with regard to his originality. A physical discovery, as Newton's, remains to ninety-nine out of a hundred a mental miracle; but a great moral teacher "labours to make himself forgotten." When he begins to speak he is suspected of insanity; when he has won his way he receives a Royal Commission to appoint the judges; as a veteran he is shelved for platitude. So Horace is regarded as a mere jewelry store of the Latin, Bacon, in his *Essays*, of the English, wisdom, which they each in fact helped to create. Carlyle's paradoxes have been exaggerated, his partialities intensified in his followers; his critical readers, not his disciples, have learnt most from him; he has helped across the Slough of Despond only those who have also helped themselves. When all is said of his dogmatism, his petulance, his "evil behaviour," he remains the master spirit of his time, its Censor, as Macaulay is its Panegyrist, and Tennyson its Mirror. He has saturated his nation with a wholesome tonic, and the practice of any one of his precepts for the conduct of life is ennobling. More intense than Wordsworth, more intelligible than Browning, more fervid than Mill, he has indicated the pitfalls in our civilisation. His works have done much to mould the best thinkers in two continents, in both of which he has been the Greatheart to many pilgrims. Not a few could speak in the words of the friend whose memory he has so affectionately preserved, "Towards me it is still more true than towards England that no one has been and done like you." A champion of ancient virtue, he appeared in his own phrase applied to Fichte, as "a Cato Major among degenerate men." Carlyle had more than the shortcomings of a Cato; he had all the inconsistent vehemence of an imperfectly balanced mind; but he had a far wider range and deeper sympathies. The message of the modern preacher transcended all mere applications of the text *delenda est*. He denounced, but at the same time nobly exhorted, his age. A storm-tossed spirit, "tempest-buffeted," he was "citadel-crowned" in his unflinching purpose and the might of an invincible will.—JOHN NICHOL, *Thomas Carlyle*, 1892, pp. 241–45

Any inventory, however brief, of Carlyle's substance, would be incomplete without some reference to his quarrel with Science. To Science a large part of the best intelligence of our age has been devoted,—a sign of the breaking away of the best minds from the cretinizing quibbles of theology into fields where knowledge can be ascertained. It is a truism that Science has advanced farther in our century than in all preceding time. By what paradox, then, should Carlyle slight its splendid achievements? Was it not because he revolted from the materialistic tendency which he believed to be inseparable from Science, a tendency which predominated a generation ago more than it does to-day? Materialism Carlyle regarded as a Gorgon's head, the sight of which would inevitably petrify man's moral nature.

Moreover, Carlyle's method differed radically from that of the scientific man, who describes processes and investigates relations, but does not explain causes. Pledged to his allegiance to tangible facts, the man of science looks at things serially, pays heed to an individual as a link in an endless chain rather than as an individual, lays emphasis on averages rather than on particulars. To him this method is alone honest, and, thanks to it, a single science to-day commands more authenticated facts than all the sciences had fifty years ago. But there are facts of supreme importance which, up to the present at least, this method does not solve. The mystery of the origin of life still confronts us. Consciousness, the Sphinx, still mutely challenges the caravans which file before her. The revelations of Science seem, under one aspect, but descriptions of the habitations of life from the protoplasmic cell up to the human body. Immense though the value of such a register be, we are not deceived into imagining that it explains ultimates. How came life into protoplasm at all? Whence each infinitesimal increment of life, recognizable at last in the budding of some new organ? And when we arrive at man, whence came his personality? Each of us is not only one in a genealogical series stretching back to the unreasoning, conscienceless *amœba*, but a clearly defined individual, a little world in himself, to whom his love, his sorrow, his pain and joy and terror, transcend in vividness all the experiences of all previous men: a microcosm, having its own immediate relations—absolute relations—with the infinite macrocosm. Science, bent on establishing present laws, measures by æons, counts by millions, and has warrant for ignoring your brief span or mine; but to you and me these few decades are all in all. However it may fare with the millions, you and I have vital, pressing needs, to supply which the experience of the entire animal kingdom can give us no help. Upon these most human needs Carlyle fastened, to the exclusion of what he held to be unnecessary to the furtherance of our spiritual welfare. He busied himself with ultimates and the Absolute. Not the stages of development, but the development attained; not the pedigree of conscience, but conscience as the supreme present reality; not the species, but the individual,—were his absorbing interests.

Thus we see how Carlyle approached the great questions of life invariably as a moralist. Mere erudition, which too often tends away from the human, did not attract him. Science, which he beheld still unspiritualized, he undervalued: what boots it to know the "mileage and tonnage" of the universe, when our foremost need is to build up character? In politics, in philosophy, in religion, likewise, he set this consideration above all others: before its august presence outward reforms dwindled into insignificance.

Such was the substance of Carlyle's message. Remarkable as is its range, profound as is its import, it required for its consummation the unique powers of utterance which Carlyle possessed. Among the masters of British prose he holds a position similar to that of Michael Angelo among the masters of painting. Power, elemental, titanic, rushing forth from an inexhaustible moral nature, yet guided by art, is the quality in both which first startles our wonder. The great passages in Carlyle's works, like the Prophets and Sibyls of the Sixtine Chapel, have no peers: they form a new species, of which they are the only examples. They seem to defy the ordinary canons of criticism; but if they break the rules it is because whoever made the rules did not foresee the possibility of such works. Transcendent Power, let it take whatever shape it will,—volcano, torrent, Cæsar, Buonarotti, Carlyle,—proclaims: "Here I am,—a fact: make of me what you can! You shall not ignore me!"—WILLIAM ROSCOE THAYER, "Carlyle" (1895), *Throne-Makers*, 1899, pp. 182–85

⟨. . .⟩ in spite of all his magniloquent dreaming, Carlyle is true or means to be true to the uncompromising facts of life; he dreams only that he may the more victoriously labor; and in his Gospel of Work and his doctrine of Hero-worship he returns from the misty regions of transcendentalism and confronts the practical concerns of common life. No one is more contemptuous than Carlyle of dilettante web-spinning, or of idle playing with emotion. Byron's egoistic woe, he scorns and ridicules. One of his mandates in *Sartor Resartus* is "Close thy Byron; open thy Goethe." "What if thou wert born and predestined not to be Happy, but to be Unhappy! Art thou nothing other than a Vulture, then, that fliest through the Universe seeking after somewhat to *eat*; and shrieking dolefully because carrion enough is not given thee?" All the private, individual grieving which the Romanticists had so plangently or so delicately and picturesquely phrased for the delectation of their age Carlyle contemns. He sends the laggard euphuist back to actual life, and bids him forget himself and his fine words in some practical task. "There is endless hope in work." "'Tools and the Man,'—that, henceforth to all time, is now our Epic." "Do the Duty which lies nearest thee." In these principles and precepts, Carlyle reveals a practical, ethical interest not to be found in such purely Romantic prose-writers as Lamb, Hazlitt, and De Quincey; and by virtue of this new and decisive interest he belongs to the later or post-Romantic age. He is not primarily an imaginative artist, not a mere dreamer; he insists that dreams be realized in the hard, unmalleable stuff of life. His "Heroes" are simply the workers who thus victoriously embody their dreams in solid fact. Mahomet, Dante, Luther, Rousseau,—they all saw beyond the conventional shows of things; they were all seers or dreamers; but they were also more than dreamers and triumphantly brought their dreams to pass in some portion or other of the recalcitrant material offered them by the world-order. Carlyle's Hero is the Deformed

Romanticist transformed into a laborious worker of results. His last word to beautifully complaining visionaries is a charge that they immerse themselves in the Actual: "Yes here, in this poor, miserable, hampered, despicable Actual, wherein thou even now standest, here or nowhere is thy Ideal: work it out therefrom; and working, believe, live, be free. Fool! the Ideal is in thyself, the impediment too is in thyself: thy Condition is but the stuff thou art to shape that same Ideal out of; what matters whether such stuff be of this sort or that, so the Form thou give it be heroic, be poetic?"

On the need, then, of a synthesis between the actual and the ideal, Carlyle insists with much gorgeous rhetoric. But if he be asked for definite and close suggestions about this synthesis, his answers are apt to be vague or even impatient. "Let not any Parliament Member ask of this Editor, What is to be done? . . . Editors are not here, foremost of all, to say How. . . . An Editor's stipulated work is to apprise *thee* that it must be done. The 'way to do it,'—is to try it, knowing that thou shalt die if it be not done." This is both ungracious and tantalizingly elusive. But its vagueness is characteristic of the whole post-Romantic attitude toward conventional life. After all, the post-Romanticists were not passionately enough in love with the actual to follow out its facts and their laws with patient fidelity through all their complications and variations. They saw life and they loved life in its large contours, in its pageantry, under its more moving and more typical aspects. They lacked the microscopic eye and the ingenious instinct for detail that are characteristic of the modern artist and of the modern commentator on life. It remained for the scientific spirit with its fine loyalty to fact, and for realism with its delicate sense of the worth of the passing moment,—of the *phase*,—to carry still further the return to the regions of the actual.—LEWIS E. GATES, "English Literature of the Nineteenth Century: A Retrospect: II. The Return to Conventional Life," *Critic*, March 1900, pp. 273–75

Works

SARTOR RESARTUS

The only thing about the work, tending to prove that it is what it purports to be, a commentary on a real German treatise, is the style, which is a sort of Babylonish dialect, not destitute, it is true, of richness, vigor, and at times a sort of singular felicity of expression, but very strongly tinged throughout with the peculiar idiom of the German language. This quality in the style, however, may be a mere result of a great familiarity with German literature, and we cannot, therefore, look upon it as in itself decisive, still less as outweighing so much evidence of an opposite character.

From what has been said, our readers will gather, with sufficient assurance, that the work before us is a sort of philosophical romance in which the author undertakes to give, in the form of a review of a German treatise on dress, and a notice of the life of the writer, his own opinions upon Matters and Things in General. The hero, Professor Teufelsdroeckh, seems to be intended for a portrait of human nature as affected by the moral influences to which, in the present state of society, a cultivated mind is naturally exposed. Teufelsdroeckh is a foundling, brought up by poor but respectable parents, and educated for the legal profession. He is called to the bar, or as the phrase is in Germany, admitted as a listener (*auscultator*), and having little business and no property, finds himself rather at a loss for the means of subsistence. While lingering in this uncertain state, he forms an acquaintance with an English traveller, named Towgood, and is patronized to a certain extent by Count Zahdarm, a nobleman whose lady occasionally invites him to a sort of entertainment, which would be called here a blue-stocking party, or *Blue Congress*, but which is dignified in Germany by the more classical title of an *æsthetic tea*. At one of these "æsthetic teas," he falls in love with the Flower-Goddess Blumine ⟨. . .⟩ who seems to be a sort of *demoiselle de compagnie* to the Countess, and who, after lending for a time an apparently favorable ear to his suit, all at once changes her mind, and marries his English friend Towgood. This result increases the uneasiness under which Teufelsdroeckh was previously laboring, and he finally quits his profession and place of residence, and sets forth upon his travels, which appear to have been extensive, and are described with sufficient exactness, though in general terms. The worst thing about his case is, that in addition to want, idleness, and disappointment in love and friendship, he fell into a kind of scepticism, or rather absolute unbelief. From this, however, he is gradually restored by a series of changes in his intellectual and moral character, amounting altogether to a sort of philosophical conversion. These changes are described in successive chapters under the titles of the *Everlasting No*, the *Centre of Indifference*, and the *Everlasting Yes*, which may be said to constitute the kernel of the work. Being now in a comfortable frame of mind, the wanderer appeals to his pen as a means of obtaining subsistence, and by a diligent use of it obtains pretty soon the professorship of Things in General at the University of Nobody-knows-where. Here he flourishes in tranquil contentment, and publishes the remarkable, close-printed, close-meditated volume, which forms the subject of the present editor's learned commentary.—ALEXANDER H. EVERETT, "Thomas Carlyle," *North American Review*, Oct. 1835, pp. 459–60

Have you, dear Patty, read any of T. Carlyle's books? He is a grand favourite of mine, and I venture to recommend to you his *Sartor Resartus*. I dare say a barrister of your acquaintance has it. His soul is a shrine of the brightest and purest philanthropy, kindled by the live coal of gratitude and devotion to the Author of all things. I should observe that he is not "orthodox."—GEORGE ELIOT, Letter to Martha Jackson (Dec. 16, 1841)

There is a certain tremour in returning to a book which has been an *avatar* to one's youth, an author who has been among the authentic gods of one's dawning years. Can that early impression survive the hard light of settled judgment? How many a figure which once loomed to us colossal has shrunk to most human dimensions in that searching light! To one it is the Byron of his youth that has thus wilted away; to another the Tennyson that has revealed unsuspected limitations. However, a final judgment may resolve that the divinity, after all, was there. It is an experiment nigh as dubious as the re-reading of young love-letters. These reflections are suggested to us by turning over the elaborate new edition of *Sartor Resartus*, edited for Messrs. Black by Mr. J. A. S. Barrett. It is an excellent edition in most respects, with a quite admirable introduction; though the incessant foot-notes irritatingly insist on informing us about everything, from the situation of Downing-street to that of Otaheite. But what concerned us was apart from all editions. It was how *Sartor* would read, thus verily *Resartus*, by matured judgment, after having long lain on the shelf of reverencing memory.

On the whole, there was small need for fear. What it loses in perception of defects (and that mostly discounted by general knowledge of the Carlylean weaknesses) it gains by deeper perception of its fundamental depths. What first strikes you is the remaining evidences in it of what one might call the prehistoric Carlyle style. You had not remembered—rather, had not noticed this. At the outset of the book you find sentences of an almost flowing symmetry and orderliness, well-nigh balance, quite unlooked-for in the author of the *French Revolution*. Take the very first:

> Considering our present advanced state of culture, and how the Torch of Science has now been brandished and borne about, with more or less effect, for five thousand years and upwards; how, in these times especially, not only the torch still burns, and perhaps more fiercely than ever, but innumerable Rush-lights, and sulphur matches, kindled thereat, are also glancing in every direction, so that not the smallest cranny or dog-hole in Nature or Art can remain unilluminated—it might strike the reflective mind with some surprise that hitherto little or nothing of a fundamental character, whether in the way of philosophy or history, has been written on the subject of Clothes.

Had Carlyle never written but so, he would not have perturbed our fathers and grandfathers with such deep dismay, not to say scandal, at his revolutionary assaults on the English tongue. But as he warms to his work, he falls into that "Babylonish dialect" which we recognise for genuine Carlylese. The phrase cleaves to it not inaptly for good no less than for ill. It has a certain Babylonian spaciousness of barbaric and primæval grandeur, amazing and imposing, even while it offends a Greek sense of form and clearness. On its ill side he has himself described it with that felicitous and aloof sense of self-criticism which some of the greatest authors possess— believing in themselves far too strongly not to be capable of amused laughter at themselves.

> Of his sentences perhaps not more than nine-tenths stand straight on their legs; the remainder are in quite angular attitudes, buttressed up by props (of parentheses and dashes), and ever with this or the other tag-rag hanging from them; a few even sprawl-out helplessly on all sides, quite broken-backed and dismembered.

That is as severe and true a criticism as could be passed on the mechanics of his style. A more damaging charge is the fact that his peculiarities are so largely imported. The other day we heard a man disrelish Carlyle's style on the ground that he (the speaker) "knew German." It is to be wished that Carlyle were less Germanic: the least tolerable of mannerisms are foreign mannerisms. But under this German vesture the body of his style is, after all, racily English. His way is largely the way of a man condensing remarks in a notebook, and makes for pregnancy. With all his juggling and sword-brandishing, Carlyle's manner is essentially pregnant, hieroglyphic; his packed and gnarled sentences, no less than his constant images, are in the nature of hieroglyphs; the mechanism of his style is indeed the complement of its internal character, and both are labour-saving devices, means for putting much in a little room.

The great passages fall on the ear as splendidly and authoritatively as of yore; they have taken no rust from the inclemency of time. If here and there one finds a passage stilted, an all too deliberate effect after poetic effects in prose, the best have yet the unsought eloquence and elevation of deep personal feeling. They roll like boulders down a mountain slope, with rough, thunderous jar and concussion, yet striking out a harmony in their rugged contact beyond the reach of shaped and quarried law. Fiery and fuliginous (to use his own favoured word), with rent and streaming storm-rack of turmoiled imagery, their splendour zig-zigs against a ground of murky and jostling utterance, from which they emerge and into which they fall back. Or one might say these sudden and strongly contrasted passages of eloquence which fleck the tortured mass of his general speech are as the blue eye of the typhoon, opening a steady deep in the midst of the whirling blackness around. Such are some of those fragments in the "Everlasting Yea," or the emergence of Teufelsdrockh on the granite battlements of the Polar Sea.

But *Sartor* is nothing if not a semi-prophetic book, as prophecy goes nowadays: it is in this aspect that it appeals to or repels us; it is its gleams and rifts of truth that focus the attention. For here also Carlyle is every way the reverse of equable and self-contained, moving by stormful and uncertain energies, with sudden swirling sunward rushes, whence he swerves with baffled and beating pinions to collect himself for another upward dart. His teaching, tempestuous and fitful, abounds in cloven profundities of gloom, and luminous interpaces of height. By these, in the main, we must gauge him. Nor must we attribute to him more than he claimed for himself, or deny his limitations. To him Christianity was a dissolved or dissolving myth, the spirit of which survived, awaiting incarnation in some new and modern *mythus*. To supply that reincarnation he addressed himself; yet in the main awakened only a yearning and most justified dissatisfaction with the sordid age in which he lived, but failed to satisfy the yearning he created. "Carlyle," said Clough, "has led us all out into the wilderness and left us there." Many truths are to be found in him, in this *Sartor* above all; but Truth herself shows flittingly through shifting vapours, doubtful if she were seen at all. In an age of the grossest materiality, no smug "scientific" explanations could loosen his clutch on the perpetual Pentecostal miracle of Nature. He saw and burningly proclaimed her to be manifestly wonderful and prophetic. No rationalism could shut from him the inwardness which was latent in all outwardness; externality almost ceased for him in the miraculous light which permeated and emanated from it. For this and things like these *Sartor* is most thankworthy. The maturer one is the more one discerns and honours these penetrant glimpses which for an instant make matter translucent. Yet glimpses they are, and instantaneous, transient. Perhaps they could not be otherwise—certainly not in Carlyle. Cloud-tossed and lightning-torn because himself could never get to himself any clear account of what he knew or believed as a whole; because his burning intuitions could never combine into any diffused radiance of system. And those who despise system, be sure, are those who cannot see life whole, but only by brief intensity of levin-flashes which leave behind momentary spaces of clear vision skirted by darkness and "the collied night." Such are apt to confound true system with the iron pedantry which narrows all truth within a brick-built Babel, circumvallated by courses of "logic formulæ"—as Carlyle himself would phrase it. "How paint to the sensual eye what passes in the Holy-of-Holies of Man's Soul; in what words, known to these profane times, speak even afar off of the unspeakable?" he asks. Which is most true; yet he who confines himself wholly to such swift-dislimning adumbrations of partly glimpsed truths, however super-sensual, cannot claim to be a complete teacher, even on our mundane and imperfect plane of completeness, where Christ Himself did not teach all things, leaving that to the spirit in each man's heart. So Carlyle is a teacher "as in a glass darkly," a teacher by fits and glimpses; from whom they will learn most who least attempt the vanity of systematising him, of "giving an account" of him. So we have seen a photograph

of Vesuvius in eruption, where the tightly-defined edges of the voluming vapours were as strenuously false to the truth of nature as they were faithful to the rigid logic of the hard-eyed camera. These volcanic Carlylean shapes of truth you cannot photograph and reduce to linear definition, mingled as they are with scoriac showers of misperception and even untruth. For least of all men had this eruptive, prejudiced peasant any infallibility. An infallible Scotsman were too frightful a portent for the world or his country to endure. Often, indeed, would we fain display where Carlyle followed hot and fierce as any bloodhound the trail of truth, and where he stopped, suddenly baulked, as by that magic rock-door which shut out the lame boy who pursued the wake of the Pied Piper; but we withhold. For our business here has been a little semi-retrospective criticism, not to prophesy regarding a partial prophet. —FRANCIS THOMPSON, "*Sartor* Re-read," *Academy*, July 6, 1901, pp. 17–18

THE FRENCH REVOLUTION

This is not so much a history, as an epic poem; and notwithstanding, or even in consequence of this, the truest of histories. It is the history of the French Revolution, and the poetry of it, both in one; and on the whole no work of greater genius, either historical or poetical, has been produced in this country for many years.

It is a book on which opinion will be for some time divided; nay, what talk there is about it, while it is still fresh, will probably be oftenest of a disparaging sort; as indeed is usually the case, both with men's works and with men themselves, of distinguished originality. For a thing which is unaccustomed, must be a very small thing indeed, if mankind can at once see into it and be sure that it is good: when, therefore, a considerable thing, which is also an unaccustomed one, appears, those who will hereafter approve, sit silent for a time, making up their minds; and those only to whom the mere novelty is a sufficient reason for disapproval, speak out. We need not fear to prophesy that the suffrages of a large class of the very best qualified judges will be given, even enthusiastically, in favor of the volumes before us; but we will not affect to deny that the sentiment of another large class of readers (among whom are many entitled to the most respectful attention on other subjects) will be far different; a class comprehending all who are repelled by quaintness of manner. For a style more peculiar than that of Mr. Carlyle, more unlike the jog-trot characterless uniformity which distinguishes the English style of this age of Periodicals, does not exist. Nor indeed can this style be wholly defended even by its admirers. Some of its peculiarities are mere mannerisms, arising from some casual association of ideas, or some habit accidentally picked up; and what is worse, many sterling thoughts are so disguised in phraseology borrowed from the spiritualist school of German poets and metaphysicians, as not only to obscure the meaning, but to raise, in the minds of most English readers, a not unnatural nor inexcusable presumption of there being no meaning at all. Nevertheless, the presumption fails in this instance (as in many other instances); there is not only a meaning, but generally a true, and even a profound meaning, and, although a few dicta about the 'mystery' and the 'infinitude' which are in the universe and in man, and such like topics, are repeated in varied phrases greatly too often for our taste, this must be borne with, proceeding, as one cannot but see, from feelings the most solemn, and the most deeply rooted which can lie in the heart of a human being. These transcendentalisms, and the accidental mannerisms excepted, we pronounce the style of this book to be not only good, but of surpassing excellence; excelled, in its kind, only by the great masters of epic poetry; and a most suitable and glorious vesture of a work which is itself, as we have said, an epic poem.—JOHN STUART MILL, "The French Revolution," *London and Westminster Review*, July 1837, pp. 17–18

Carlyle *does* offend my classical taste; but the worst of it is that I have been absolutely riveted to his first volume, which I have this minute finished, and that I am hungering for the next. A very extraordinary writer certainly, and though somewhat, I must think, of a jargonist, and too wordy and full of repetition, yet sagacious, if not profound, and wonderfully candid. I think, too, that he shows an exactness and extent of knowledge of his subject which very advantageously distinguishes him from poetical historians in general.—LUCY AIKIN, Letter to William Ellery Channing (April 18, 1838), *Correspondence of William Ellery Channing and Lucy Aikin*, ed. Anna Letitia Le Breton, 1874, p. 309

I am very heavy indeed with a kind of Influenza, which has blocked up most of my senses, and put a wet blanket over my brains. This state of head has not been improved by trying to get through a new book much in fashion—Carlyle's *French Revolution*—written in a German style. An Englishman writes of French Revolutions in a German style. People say the book is very deep: but it appears to me that the meaning *seems* deep from lying under mystical language. There is no repose, nor equable movement in it: all cut up into short sentences half reflective, half narrative; so that one labours through it as vessels do through what is called a short sea—small, contrary going waves caused by shallows, and straits, and meeting tides, etc. I like to sail before the wind over the surface of an even-rolling eloquence, like that of Bacon or the Opium Eater.—EDWARD FITZGERALD, Letter to Bernard Barton (April 1838)

I commend to your notice, if it comes in your way, Carlyle on the French Revolution. A queer, tiresome, obscure, profound, and original work. The writer has not very *clear* principles and views, I fear, but they are very deep.—JOHN HENRY NEWMAN, Letter to Mrs. J. Mozley (April 23, 1839)

The great merit of Mr Carlyle as a writer, and the great pleasure which his writings give, arise from their *suggestive* character. He is always furnishing hints for thought; a slight sentence, a passing observation, often seem to open long vistas of reflection; but he rarely thinks out a subject for his reader: he never weighs, and reasons, and arrives at balanced conclusions. His brief outlines first arrest the attention, and then provoke objection: we feel tempted to debate and argue every point with him, proposition by proposition; but it is wonderful on how much more cordial terms we part with a companion of this description—angered though we may have felt at times by mutual contradiction—than with one of those formal and useful guides who fall under the general denomination of historian—to which, in plain truth, Mr Carlyle has no title whatever.—HERMAN MERIVALE, "Carlyle on the French Revolution," *Edinburgh Review*, July 1840, pp. 415–16

Carlyle's book on the French Revolution has been called the great modern epic, and so it is—an epic as true and germane to this age, as Homer's was to his. Chaos come again, and overwhelming all extant order,—the wild volcano of mad democracy bursting and consuming the accumulated rubbish and corruption of centuries,—all the paradoxes of human nature face to face, blind popular passion and starving multitudes confronting court imbecility, conventionality, nostrums

of political doctrinaires and effete diplomacy,—panic and trembling uncertainty controlled by clear-seeing determined will; and all these by great inscrutable forces together driven on to their doom. In the midst of all the tumults and confusion, some Mirabeau appearing as the cloud-compeller—the one man who, had he lived, might have guided the tremendous forces to some certain end. "Honor to the strong man in these ages who has shaken himself loose of shams, and is something. There lay verily in him sincerity, a great free earnestness; nay, call it Honesty." This is a word we have heard almost to weariness. This, though said of Mirabeau, is the refrain in all his works—the admiration of clear-seeing penetrating intelligence, backed by adamantine will. So these be present, we shall not much inquire what may be their moral purpose, or whether they have a moral purpose at all. The strong intellect and the strong will are an emanation from the central force of the universe, and as such have a right to rule.—JOHN CAMPBELL SHAIRP, "Prose Poets: Thomas Carlyle," *Aspects of Poetry* (1881), 1882, pp. 368–69

Take, for instance, *The French Revolution*. It has been to me an inexhaustible joy for twenty or thirty years past to read the excellent persons who, in English and French and German, have undertaken to "correct" Carlyle. They have demonstrated in I dare say the most sufficient and triumphant way that he sometimes represents a thing as having happened at two o'clock on Thursday when it actually happened on Tuesday at three o'clock. They have, I believe, made some serious emendations in the number of leagues travelled and the *menu* of the meals eaten by Louis the Sixteenth on his way to and from Varennes. But have they to the satisfaction of the *phronimos*, the Aristotelian intelligent person, altered or destroyed one feature in the Carlylian picture of the uprising and of the Terror? Not they. On the contrary, the greatest of them all, M. Taine, after protesting against Carlyle in his youth, came to tread in Carlyle's very steps in his age. And it could not be otherwise. The French Revolution of Carlyle is the French Revolution as it happened, as it was. The French Revolution of the others is the French Revolution dug up in lifeless fragments by excellent persons with the newest patent pickaxes. I do not know whether this extraordinary historico-biographical faculty can be in any way connected, after the fashion of cause and effect, with his other great quality, his peculiar way of treating ethics and politics, the only subjects in which he seems to have taken a thorough interest. Man to him was indeed a "political beast" in the old phrase, extending the meaning to ethics as the Greeks themselves would have done. Here again there were no doubt gaps, especially that huge one of his complete incapacity to enter into the very important division of human sentiment, which is called for shortness love. Of "the way of a man with a maid" Carlyle never showed much comprehension, nor in it much interest, which is doubtless a pity. But of the way of a man in political society he showed a very great comprehension indeed, as well as of that other way which his forefathers would have called "walking with God," that is to say, of personal conduct and attitude towards the fortunes and mysteries of life.

It is here that his gift of many-coloured and many-formed language was applied most remarkably and perhaps most profitably. As has been said, or hinted, above, it is not to Carlyle that you must go for positive precepts of any kind. But as a negative teacher he has few equals. "Don't funk; don't cant; don't gush; don't whine; don't chatter;"—these and some others like them were his commandments, and I do not know where to look for a better set of their kind. But they were elementary and trivial in reference to certain larger and vaguer precepts of the Carlylian decalogue or myriologue. The two greatest of these, as it seems to me, are, "Never mistake the amount, infinitesimal if not *minus*, of your own personal worth and importance in this world," on the one hand, and "Never care for any majority of other infinitesimals who happen to be against you," on the other. Ever since 1789 at least, the idol from which men should have prayed to be kept, and which has been growing year by year and decade by decade, is the worship of the majority; and the cream, the safest and soundest part of the Carlylian doctrine is: "Don't care one rap, or the ten-thousandth part of one rap, for the majority. You may be—you very likely are—a fool yourself; but it is as nearly as possible certain that the majority of the majority are fools, and therefore, though you need not necessarily set yourself against them, you are absolutely justified in neglecting them." "Do your duty," which he also preached, is of course a more strictly virtuous doctrine, and it is also a much older one. But it is open to the retort, "Yes, but what *is* my duty?" which is never specially easy and often extremely difficult to answer. Nor is it more specially suited for this day than for any other. But "Don't worship the majority" is the very commandment needed in the nineteenth century, and likely, it would seem, to be needed still more in the twentieth. Even if, as it rarely may be, the majority is right, the fact that it is the majority does not make it so, and when there is no reason for believing it to be right except that it is the majority, then that is reason sufficient for electing to regard it as wrong.

This anti-democratic tone and temper—enforced and fed, it may be, in his own case, by too much indulgence in the luxury of scorn, by too much contempt for his fellows, by too unsocial a view of life—was, as it seems to me, what Carlyle had to teach and did teach. His applications of it in particular may not always have been wise, but they were made always with the most astonishing *diable au corps*, and in a style which, though I should be very sorry to see it generally imitated, and though it was sometimes very nearly bad, was at its best surpassed by no style, either in English or in any other language, for pure force and intense effect,—full of lights and colours, now as fierce as those of fire, now as tender as those of fire also,—full of voices covering the whole gamut from storm to whisper. Whether the great volume of his work, the exceptions, the inequalities, the crotchets and lacks of catholicity in it, will seriously injure that work with posterity is of course very difficult to say. Work which requires, as this does, a certain initiation and novitiate, perhaps also a certain pre-established harmony of temper and taste, is always heavily weighted in competing for the attention of posterity. But I hope at least that Carlyle will continue even in the evil days to inspire some with determination *malignum spernere vulgus*; and I feel nearly sure that when the tide turns, as it must some day, and the rule of the best and fewest, not of the most and worst, again becomes the favourite, his works will supply texts for the orthodox as they now do for heretics. At any rate, I am sure that no one who ever goes to them will miss the splendours of pure literature which illuminate their rugged heights and plateaus, and that some at least will recognise and rejoice in the high air of love for noble things and contempt for things base which sweeps over and through them.—GEORGE SAINTSBURY, "Thomas Carlyle," *Corrected Impressions*, 1895

PAST AND PRESENT

FATHER SAURTEIG,—Thanks to thee for thy new *work*—a real piece of work such as even thou hadst not before given us the like of—not even in *Sartor Resartus*. I could wish thou hadst not put forth more of this at once than the two or three first books, and that the *first* had been placed last of these. Thou shouldst have begun assuredly with thy true revivification of the men of St. Edmundsburg.

Neither can I agree with my teacher in what he more than once proclaimeth as his judgment general, touching Olivier of Tyburn; nor, indeed, am I very sure that I leap as yet contentedly to any of thy distinct conclusions, save one—namely, that we are all wrong and all like to be damned (p. 158). But I thank thee for having made me conscious of life and feeling for sundry hours by thy pages, whether figurative, or narrative, or didactic. Thou hast done a book such as no other living man could do or dream of doing.

Give us more of thy pictures of the past. Bad is the present, and black exceedingly the future, and even thou canst do little for either of them, except truly that thou canst enable thy fellows now breathing to breathe more nimbly whenever it so pleaseth thee to indite a page of Carlylism.—JOHN GIBSON LOCKHART, Letter to Thomas Carlyle (April 27, 1843), cited in Andrew Lang, *The Life and Letters of John Gibson Lockhart*, 1897, Vol. 2, pp. 238–39

We are at some loss how to state what strikes us as the fault of this remarkable book, for the variety and excellence of the talent displayed in it is pretty sure to leave all special criticism in the wrong. And we may easily fail in expressing the general objection which we feel. It appears to us as a certain disproportion in the picture, caused by the obtrusion of the whims of the painter. In this work, as in his former labors, Mr. Carlyle reminds us of a sick giant. His humors, are expressed with so much force of constitution, that his fancies are more attractive and more credible than the sanity of duller men. But the habitual exaggeration of the tone wearies whilst it stimulates. It is felt to be so much deduction from the universality of the picture. It is not serene sunshine, but everything is seen in lurid stormlights. Every object attitudinizes, to the very mountains and stars almost, under the refractions of this wonderful humorist, and instead of the common earth and sky, we have a Martin's Creation or Judgment Day. A crisis has always arrived which requires a *deus ex machinâ*. One can hardly credit, whilst under the spell of this magician, that the world always had the same bankrupt look, to foregoing ages as to us,—as of a failed world just recollecting its old withered forces to begin again and try and do a little business. It was perhaps inseparable from the attempt to write a book of wit and imagination on English politics that a certain local emphasis and of effect, such as is the vice of preaching, should appear, producing on the reader a feeling of forlornness by the excess of value attributed to circumstances. But the splendor of wit cannot outdazzle the calm daylight, which always shows every individual man in balance with his age, and able to work out his own salvation from all the follies of that, and no such glaring contrasts or severalties in that or this. Each age has its own follies, as its majority is made up of foolish young people; its superstitions appear no superstitions to itself; and if you should ask the contemporary, he would tell you with pride or with regret (according as he was practical or poetic) that it had none. But after a short time, down go its follies and weakness, and the memory of them; its virtues alone remain, and its limitation assumes the poetic form of a beautiful superstition, as the dimness of our sight clothes the objects in the horizon with mist and color. The revelation of Reason is this of the unchangeableness of the fact of humanity under all its subjective aspects, that to the cowering it always cowers, to the daring it opens great avenues. The ancients are only venerable to us, because distance has destroyed what was trivial; as the sun and stars affect us only grandly, because we cannot reach to their smoke and surfaces, and say, Is that all?—RALPH WALDO EMERSON, *Dial*, July 1843, pp. 100–101

Of all those who assailed the new industrial world created by the *Wealth of Nations* and the steam-engine, Carlyle was the greatest; and *Past and Present*, the book in which he flung out his denunciations, is the most tender and pathetic picture of the Past, the most unsparing indictment of the Present that exists in modern English literature. 'England,' wrote Carlyle, 'is full of wealth, of multifarious produce, supply for human wants in every kind; yet England is dying of inanition.' Throwing impatiently aside such explanations of this contradiction as those at which I hinted a few minutes ago, Carlyle fixed his eyes on two facts which he asserted to be at the root of the nation's suffering. The first was *want of permanence*. Gazing on the ever-shifting scene of the Present; the perpetual moving to and fro of men in search of wealth; workmen breaking away from masters, and masters discarding workmen; and contrasting this with the quiet, restful Past, when men lived together in contentment whole lifetimes, and formed unbroken habits of affection; Carlyle passionately declared that, unless we could bring back permanence those habits of affection on which our whole life rests could never more be formed, and society must fall in pieces and dissolve. 'I am for permanence,' he cried, 'in all things, at the earliest possible moment and to the latest possible. Blessed is he that continueth where he is.' And only in the restoration of the old system of employment, in the substitution of the principle of permanent contract for temporary (then every day gaining ground), did he see some faint hope for the future. 'The Principle of Permanence year by year better seen into and elaborated, may enlarge itself, expand gradually on every side into a system. This once secured, the basis of all good results were laid.' The second fact which Carlyle singled out as closely connected with the first was what he called the *cash-nexus*—'man's duty to man resolving itself into handing him certain metal pieces, and then shoving him out of doors'—and the contemplation of it filled him with that same immeasurable indignation and rage which he poured out upon want of permanence. 'We call it a society,' he writes, 'and go about proposing openly the totalest separation and isolation. Our life is not a mutual helpfulness; but rather, cloaked under due laws-of-war, named fair competition and so forth, it is a mutual hostility. We have profoundly forgotten everywhere that *cash-payment* is not the sole relation of human beings; we think, nothing doubting, that *it* absolves and liquidates all engagements of man. "My starving workers?" answers the rich mill-owner. "Did I not hire them fairly in the market? Did I not pay them to the last sixpence the sum covenanted for? What have I to do with them more?"' Do with them more? Carlyle would have had him do infinitely more— would have had him cherish them as human beings and not forget them as hands; would have had him guide and protect them, help them in sickness and misfortune, and not dismiss them even when trade was bad, and profits were gone. In one word, Carlyle would have had the rich govern and protect the poor as they did in the past.

But what said the poor themselves whose cause Carlyle so eagerly pleaded? Did they accept his view? No! The poor believed that the time for government by the rich had passed; that the time had come for government by the whole people. 'Give us,' cried the Chartists, who represented the aspirations of the people, 'give us, not government by the rich, but government by the people, not protection, but political rights—give us, in one word, our Charter, and then will this dread interval of darkness and of anguish pass away; then will that dawn come for which we have watched so long, and justice, love, and plenty inhabit this land, and there abide.'

Who was right, Carlyle or the people? The people! Yes! the people were right—the people who, sick with hunger and deformed with toil, dreamed that Democracy would bring deliverance. The people were right; Democracy, so giantlike and threatening, which, with rude strength severs sacred ties and stamps out ancient landmarks, Democracy, though in ways undreamt of, did bring deliverance. For Democracy is sudden like the sea, and grows dark with storms and sweeps away many precious things; but, like the sea, it reflects the light of the wide heavens and cleanses the shores of human life. —ARNOLD TOYNBEE, *Lectures on the Industrial Revolution in the Eighteenth Century in England*, 1884, pp. 209–11

JOHN STERLING
From "Carlyle's Works"

London and Westminster Review, October 1839, pp. 8–23

The speculative seer, if of a high and genuine order, must needs, by spiritual instinct, regard the universe as a divine vision, and the reason as an inspired organ for beholding this; which is equally the implicit faith of philosopher, poet, and hero. But the sage is by nature and purpose also a dialectician, and labours to define the primal truth he sees; to pursue it into all its ramifications; and show that these afford, or indeed are, the true solution of all the facts and classes of facts, which direct observation discloses to all men, but which it cannot interpret. Now the systematic process of ratiocination is one from which Mr Carlyle turns with comparative indifference. He values the master truth of the philosopher, not as an idea to be worked upon, and minutely evolved by the understanding, but to be taken into the character and affections, to rule the will, and to shape and glorify the whole structure of the man and of his life.

Neither does he exactly resemble the poets, in whom he so much delights, and whose worth he has so keenly insisted on. These men, especially Goethe, Schiller, and Jean Paul, but also all great creative singers, having a true insight into the wondrousness and depth of things, and the harmony in which they grow together in the midst of conflicts and jarrings which are themselves essential to this harmony—do not make it their business to unfold the idea of it as an object of speculation. Neither do they directly labour to realize it more evidently in practice and fact. But stirred and enlightened by it, and filled from it with a breath of its melodious joy, they shape its images as given them from without, and new-born within their souls, into fresh and fair semblances that reproduce in partial shows of the whole, a more vocal and facile display of its true being. Their own delight in the beauty and worth of real existence pours itself into their reproduction of it. Aiming neither at teaching men as the philosopher, nor at exciting and organizing them anew on a nobler model, as the practical hero,—they do indirectly impart their own living consciousness of truth, and draw men, without exhorting them, towards the higher regions where the poet dwells rejoicing.

Such is not the case with Mr Carlyle; he does not rest at ease in the contemplation of fair pictures of life, leaving them to find their own reception, and work silently their own vague effect upon mankind. The practical problem and struggle of Man entirely possesses him. With its force he speaks, towards its aim he works. He seldom relaxes to enjoy the aspect of images, however beautiful, however familiar to his heart, unless they have a direct significance and efficiency for this end. And finding no sufficient peace in the music of sweet song, he loves the resounding lyre which builds up the walls of cities, or the blast of the trumpet which throws them down.

Not that he wants poetry any more than philosophy. But they are his wings and not his heaven. His heart and mouth are full of them, but they are not the springs of his existence. The man among the Germans, whose works at first sight his undoubtedly the most resemble, is that strange, huge mass of lambent, innocuous fire, full of gas-jets and grotesque tongues, and salamanders and flaming eyes—Jean Paul Richter. They are like, in the apparent rudeness, harshness, lawless capriciousness of style; full of meanings and images, but these looking incoherent, or at least as yet unreconciled. Both constantly use words sanctioned by no custom or even precedent, and, of course, though often expressive, sometimes not compensating for their oddness by any special felicity. In both it looks as if there were strong, nay overpowering, self-will and self-consciousness. The thought, as well as speech, often finds its sufficient explanation in the peculiarities of individual character, rather than in the demands and laws of the matter handled. In neither is there much exercise of skill in logical abstractions, and their discipline; or much clear delineation of objects, uncoloured by the particular and casual feelings of the artist. As to their views of human life they have also much in common. The ground in both appears to be furnished by a deep and fervid sense of whatever is noblest and fairest in man's active powers,—and this realized not only in the imaginative consciousness, but in the personal character of each. Alike they shrink with even fastidious and self-compacent vivacity from all the forms, blazonries, and authorities of social existence, when these happen to be insufficiently supported by the worth of the men whom Nature's habitual irony has thus dignified. A fine and genuine, nay stern and sublime, enthusiasm, a puritanic Quixotism, for the lovely, the true, the right, the everlasting,—is heightened and softened in both by the perpetual presence of a graver than Cervantean humour, which blends with and repeats the lofty feeling in a mode of kindred contrast. Both the German and the Englishman use whatever portions and aspects of the phenomenal world they advert to, neither for their simple and direct beauty, nor as facts having their meaning and purport in themselves; but as hints and whispers of a higher and unseen world, the proper abode of man. In each there is a fulness and warmth of nature, which would suffice to place them among the sacred band, the immortals of history. And in each also there is something unfashioned, excessive, tumultuous, far indeed from the vulgar chaotic fury and darkness of passions and prejudices, but still at war with the brightness and heavenly peace which are rather suggested and promised to the heart than made apparent to the eye.

With these obvious points of resemblance there are also very considerable discrepancies, partly doubtless to be explained by the difference of time, still more by that of country, and most of all by that original variety of structure which shows itself between every pair of ploughmen, nay of plough-horses, and more and more clearly comes out as the effect of a universal law the higher we rise in the class of beings we contemplate. The two men of whom we speak are of the highest that the earth produces, the genial teachers of truth, and inspired painters of symbols for the fundamental realities of our existence. The distinctions between the two are accordingly deep and extensive. In Jean Paul, much as there is of

struggle, and, in details, of unappeased contradiction, and jarring unevenness, the prevalent spirit is that of earnest, eager, childlike sympathy. This fills him most often with joy, always with satisfaction. The healthful, cordial abundance of his emotions and fancies is all he needs. Thus replete and bright with the best gifts of life, after a youth of bitter pangs and conflicts, his hearts seems to repose in its own ceaseless activity, and unweariedly creates new images of men's unaffected joys and ennobling sorrows, and unlimited powers of love and hope. But (in this a true poet) all life is for him only a storehouse of expressive, shining, startling, or burlesque images. But with Mr Carlyle the case is far otherwise: he lives to fight, breathes war-flames of disdain and zeal, and moves only to wrestle and trample forward.

The clearness of the eye to see whatever is permanent and substantial, and the fervour and strength of heart to love it as the sole good of life, are thus, in our view, Mr Carlyle's pre-eminent characteristics, as those of every man entitled to the fame of the most generous order of greatness. Not to paint the good which he sees and loves, or see it painted, and enjoy the sight; not to understand it, and exult in the knowledge of it; but to take his position upon it, and for it alone to breathe, to move, to fight, to mourn, and die—this is the destination which he has chosen for himself. His avowal of it and exhortation to do the like is the object of all his writings. And, reasonably considered, it is no mean service to which he is thus bound. For the real, the germinal truth of nature, is not a dead series of physical phenomena, into the like of which all phenomena are cunningly to be explained away. This pulseless, rigid iron frame-work, on which the soft soil of human life is placed, and above which its aërial flowers and foliage rise, does not pass with him for the essential and innermost principle of all. It is rather that which, being itself poorest,—the poorest of faculties can apprehend. As physical mechanism, it is that which is most palpable and undeniable by any, because it is that which lies nearest the nothingness whence it has been hardly rescued, and is, therefore, most akin to minds in whose meanness of structure or culture, even human existence might seem scarce better than nothingness. He knows, few in our nation so well, that of a world of mere machinery, the highest king and priest would be the neatest clock-work figure. And in such a world, a being feeling ever towards a somewhat beyond what he can weigh and measure, and looking up to find above himself that which is too high for him to understand, would be an anomaly as lawless and incredible as the wildest fabled monster, the Minotaur, the Chimera, the Titan,—the Sphynx itself,—nay a more delirious riddle than any that in dreams it proposes to us.

On the other hand, neither is for him the solid, abiding, inexhaustible, that merely which is received as such by popular acquiescence. It must needs be a truth which the spirit, cleared and strengthened by manifold knowledge and experience, and above all, by strong and steadfast endeavour, can rest in, and say: This I mean, not because it is told me, were my informants all the schools of Rabbins or a hierarchy of angels; but because I have looked into it, tried it, found it healthful and sufficient, and thus know that it will stand the stress of life. We may be right or wrong in our estimate of Mr Carlyle, but we cannot be mistaken in supposing that on this kind of anvil have all truly great men been fashioned, and of metal thus honest and enduring.

Further, it must be said, that true as is his devotion to the truth, so flaming and cordial is his hatred of the false, in whatever shapes and names delusions may show themselves. Affectations, quackeries, tricks, frauds, swindlings commercial or literary, baseless speculations, loud ear-catching rhetoric, melodramatic sentiment, moral drawlings and hyperboles, religious cant, clever political shifts, and conscious or half-conscious fallacies, all in his view, come under the same hangman's rubric,—proceed from the same offal heart. However plausible, popular and successful, however dignified by golden and purple names, they are lies against ourselves,—against whatever in us is not altogether reprobate and infernal. His great argument, theme of his song, spirit of his language, lies in this, that there is a work for man worth doing, which is to be done with the whole of his heart, not the half or any other fraction. Therefore, if any reserve be made, any corner kept for something unconnected with this true work and sincere purpose, the whole is thereby vitiated and accurst. So far as his arm reaches he is undoing whatever in nature is holy: ruining whatever is the real creation of the great worker of all. This truth of purpose is to the soul what life is to the body of man; that which unites and organizes the mass, keeping all the parts in due proportion and concord, and restraining them from sudden corruption into worthless dust.

From this turn of mind and ground-plan of conviction it follows, that to Mr Carlyle the objects of chief interest are memorable persons—men who have fought strongly the good fight. And more especially, though not exclusively, does he revere and study those living nearest to our own time and circumstances, in whom we may find monumental examples of the mode in which our difficulties are to be conquered. These men he rejoices, and eminently succeeds, in delineating; in enabling us to see what is essential and physiognomical in each, and how the facts of nature and society favoured and opposed the formation of his life into a large completeness. The hindrances such a man had to overcome, the energies by which he vanquished them, and the work, whatever it may have been, which he thus accomplished for mankind, appear in these pictures with lucid clearness, marked with a force and decision of hand and style worthy of the greatest masters.

Thus having taken anxious measure of the perplexities and dangers of human life in its higher progresses, he has learnt also to pity, with a mother's tenderness, the failings and confusions of those against whom these hostile forces have prevailed. His proudest and most heroic odes in honour of the conquerors are mingled with or followed by some strain of pity for those who have fallen and been swallowed up in the conflict. The dusky millions of human shapes that flit around us, and in history stream away, fill him with an almost passionate sorrow. Their hunger and nakedness, their mistakes, terrors, pangs, and ignorances, press upon his soul like personal calamities. Of him, more than of all other English writers, perhaps writers of any country, it is true, that not in words and fits of rhetorical sentiment, but in the foundation of his being, man, however distant and rude a shadow, is to him affecting, venerable, full of a divine strength, which, for the most part, is rather cramped and tortured than ripened to freedom in this fleshly life and world. This kind of feeling must be felt as truly distinguishing him by all who read his works. For though similar expressions to some of his have been used by many, from no one, at least in our language, have they proceeded with so resolute and grand a force of radiant clearness and adamantine conviction.

Only when the sufferers are in the foreground and his main objects, does he seem to forget that their oppressors or despisers, the tyrannous, luxurious, frivolous, empty-hearted, are also themselves victims, playing the part of destroyers: that circumstances had done wrong to them, no less than to those whom they harass and degrade: and that to be slowly poisoned with sweet baits in the flush and abundance of life, and so to sink away in sottish dreams, is not at all less horrible than to be gradually starved and worn to death, while courage, or at least dumb endurance, confronts the inevitable blow, and hope whispers in the sharpened ear, that a better destiny lies beyond. But when these base and selfish souls of lower earth—the men of pleasure, who, to all beneath them, are men of pain—come themselves before him, he well comprehends what they perhaps could least understand, that they too are to be pitied as well as blamed; although the tragedy of their lives is not that to which it is most important to call a world of spectators.

Thus loving the ideal realised in things and persons, not expounded in systematic thought; zealous as a missionary for the concrete, and towards the abstract severe as an inquisitor; this writer very naturally holds in detestation all attempts to give dialectics any important place in human life. He admits, indeed, that reflection inevitably produces thoughts which find no sufficient symbols in any single objects, but are the ideal roots of whole classes of existence, and finally pass into one great principle of life originating and organizing all that is. But the attempt to define this in any precise form of words, though it has been the aim, as he admits, of many of the greatest among men, meets with small sympathy from him. Above all does he scorn, rend, explode, and excommunicate while he despises, the endeavour to trace out the various lines and steps by which this first principle is logically arrived at, and then again from it are deduced the conceptions corresponding to the facts of the universe.

Now although in Mr Carlyle's view of this matter there be, as we believe, some, perhaps much prejudice, his judgment is mainly determined by an indubitable truth which he sees with clearest eyes; and only, as we think, regards it too exclusively. It is certain that men with whom this enterprise of logical construction and deduction has been the great task of life, have seldom been open to a sufficient course of outward and inward experience not to undervalue all but the scanty set of facts on which they base their scheme. Nay, more, inasmuch as these facts have not been looked at by the light of analogies from many others, there are sides even of them which the theory takes no account of. Thus it never can exhaust, that is, adequately interpret, even the things which it counts worthy of notice. The man, fancying his brain the sunny mirror of the universe, lives in fact in a small sham world, where there is at best a spark of light amid thick shadows that wear hardly a semblance of realities.

Further still, as he who has devoted himself exclusively or chiefly to the formation and arrangement of definitions is likely to have been led thereto by a preponderance of the merely ratiocinative faculty, and a deficiency of the nobler and more substantial powers, these, and their correlatives in objects, are not what he is apt to seek for or to acknowledge anywhere. His theory is likely to leave out whatever is deepest and most essential in the universe. Now all things being linked together and interfused, in the lowest things there must be some power or capacity corresponding to something above it, and by which it is ultimately related to the highest of all. But this is precisely what the too narrow and mechanical inquirer cannot comprehend. Therefore even the lowest and most lifeless forms of things, which correspond best to his own stiff and angular faculty of reasoning, are, as to their true meaning and most important relations, altogether beyond his ken.

As the merely logical thinker is apt to be thus defective in his views, so also in his practice is he sure to be detected as artificial and abortive. By a judicious use of the phraseology of the day, and the exercise of conjuring ingenuity in rather a higher than the manual mode, he may easily pass, while he deals only with words, for a wise, almost an all-wise, Doctor. But when he comes to deal with things as a practical worker, his ignorance of that which is essential in them necessarily baffles him, as often as he quits the vulgar empirical rules which rest merely on unsystematic experience. Success in his own department—of definition and refutation—and blindness to all beyond it, fill him with hopeless conceit and self-assurance, and failing in all that he attempts practically, he will most often be led to throw the blame upon the poor unconscious World, which, having its own affairs to attend to, obstinately and spitefully will not be what he has so demonstratively proved it is.

As Mr Carlyle now plaintively, now indignantly teaches, no less does such a man fail when he undertakes to delineate objects as an artist, than when he handles them as a practician. For this, too, it is necessary that he should in the first place know what is truly vital in each thing, or at all events in that central one to which in his new creation the others are to be related, that so he may light this with a blaze of imagination, and leave out of view only the accidental, partial, and insignificant.

There is then a true and most pregnant, nay a humane meaning in the constant flayings and extirpations to which the merely logical man is subjected by Mr Carlyle. But his treatment is so hard that any bowels of compassion, not unnaturally and dangerously indurated, must yearn towards the sufferer, thus dissected alive, while the operator, moreover, grins during the process with a disdainful glee, harder to be borne than much anatomy. Even with this alarming example before us, we may, perhaps, venture to suggest that all human beings must be more or less abstract thinkers; and that though logical thinking is much and fatally overrated when it withdraws men's attention from the premises to the mode of arguing from them, yet it is of indispensable use in giving clearness and compactness to our knowledge, and in enabling us, with light mastery, to impart it to others. It is also certain that of some of the wisest of mankind, it has been the special vocation to be dialecticians. Of the schoolmen, for instance, whom Mr Carlyle speaks of, as if they had been employed literally, not figuratively, in splitting hairs,—there can be no serious doubt that the divine promptings of their age and of their own souls impelled them to the worthiest study of the most arduous problems of man's existence. They laboured for the highest end then known among mankind, with a zeal and insight, according to the measure of what was then possible, which has seldom been equalled in later times. In the fourteenth century Luther would have been, as Wickliffe was, a pre-eminent schoolman. And Mr Carlyle, could he have been then born, would, like Dante, have been imbued with the Aristotelian method, and have been ready to encounter all opponents in arguments founded on Peter Lombard, and marshalled in all the forms of syllogistic mood and figure.

We have said that this writer's great power is in historic delineation of men and events, to which he gives extraordinary vividness and boldness; and this, not by knack or system, or a draughtsman's eye for the outwardly picturesque, but by intense feeling of the effectual and expressive everywhere, and of the relation in which all objects stand to the natural hearts of men. But there is another series of facts for which his mind is far less generously open, than for the characters and deeds of persons. These are the beliefs which each age and individual has framed for himself, or accepted. To these he does not give much heed; of course not denying, or mistaking, the certainty that all beliefs have followed each other in the history of the world

according to a fixed law, and are connected by the same with all the circumstances of each generation; and that, in obedience to this law, they emerge, unfold themselves, pass away, or are transmuted into other modes of faith. But he dwells on little else than the importance of the spirit with which the creed is held, the degree of seriousness and devotion in the believer's mind,—rather than the quality and amount of truth which his belief embodies.

Now it is no unfruitful and minute, but a spacious and teeming field of thought, which spreads before us when we begin to inquire, not so much what manner of man was Heraclitus or Plato, Athanasius, or Luther, or Leibnitz—as what was the doctrine that each of them taught; what view did it unfold of Nature, Man, and God; how was it linked with what had gone before, and what followed it; and how did the truth of the one mind become moulded by the thoughts of generations before it passed into the reason of the following sage; and how changed by him did it again go forth to create and burn within the bosoms of its next inheritors?

Assuredly Mr Carlyle would not deny this to be worth considering. But it is not a study with which, so far as we can see, he concerns himself peculiarly. And in consequence of this indifference of his, one is sometimes tempted, in reading him, to fancy that in his view, it is only a delusion, however unavoidable, by which importance is attached to the beliefs and denials of mankind; the honesty and zeal with which we believe being very slightly dependent on the object of our faith. No doubt the stupid arrogance of multitudes does lean with ridiculous weight on many theories or phrases which for them in their state of feeling might really be shuffled, and interchanged, and redistributed among the contending parties by mere chance, without any but the slightest effect upon their state of soul. And remarkable it sometimes is, when an ordinary mortal, who unwillingly pays his yearly taxes, and willingly reads his daily newspaper, professes, with full belief that he believes, some scheme of faith such as might suit a disguised archangel, such as ought to encircle the adoring head with a halo of mythological glories, and raise the feet in sovereign loftiness above the cares and perturbations of mortality, while the man shall all the while be crawling in the mire, and thinking only of his prospective mess of pottage. Yet there is some relation, most definite and certain, however indirect, between his creed and him. The fetish religion of Africa as clearly bears the marks of negro-barbarism, as the epicurism of Lucretius, and the stoicism of Marcus Aurelius, express the refinement of Rome. The philosophy of Aristotle is not accidentally, but by the necessity of the man's constitution and circumstances, distinct from the lore of Plato; the theology of Augustine from that of Fénelon; and again, the speculations of the Brahmins from those of the Rabbins. It must be worth while to understand what these distinctions are, whence they arise, and to what they tend; for the expressed belief is a standard, though not an infallible one, whereby to ascertain that real belief which is as genuine a fact of man's life as any other. No belief is ever professed by any one, which has not been at some time the real conviction of somebody. And the thoughts that a man thinks are, when we can really ascertain them, as significant of what he is as any action of his life. ⟨. . .⟩

We have now said much, too much for our readers, too little for the subject, on what seem to us the chief peculiarities of a most memorable man. But any one who should take up the writings themselves with no other preconception than that which we have attempted to give him, would doubtless be startled at the strangeness of the style which prevails more or less throughout them. They are not careless, headlong, passionate, confused; but they bear a constant look of oddity which seems at first mere wilful wantonness, and which we only afterwards find to be the discriminating stamp of original and strong feeling. This—this feeling, rooted in profound susceptibility and matured into a central vivifying power—is, we should say, the author's most extraordinary distinction. For it is not the ostentatious, impetuous sentiment, which calls, a sufficient audience being by, on heaven and earth for sympathy, and would wish for that of Tartarus too, as an additional acknowledgment of its sublime sincerity. Here, on the contrary, the feeling is not that which the man is proud of, and would fain exhibit. He shrinks from the profession, nay, from the sense of it; even painfully labours to trifle, and be at ease, that he may hide from others, and may for himself forget, the thorny fagot-load of his own emotions. Yet make them known he must; for they are not those of some private personal grief or passion, from which he may escape into literature or science, and leave his pains and longings behind him; but his sensibilities are burning with a slow, immense fire, kindled by the very theme on which he writes, and compelling him to write. The greatness and weakness, the infinite hopes and unquenchable reality of human life; the aching pressure of the body and its wants on the myriads of millions in whom celestial force sleeps and dreams of hell; the sight of follies, frauds, cruelties, and lascivious luxury in the midst of a race thus endowed and thus suffering; and the unconquerable will and thought with which the few work out the highest calling of all men; these it is, and not self-indulging distresses and theatrical aspirations of his own, which boil and storm within. Therefore does he speak with the solid strength and energy which gives so serious, and rugged an aspect to his sentences; while, perpetually checking himself, from a wise man's shame at excessive emotion, and from the knowledge that others will but half sympathize with him, he adds to his most weighty utterances a turn of irony which relieves the excessive strain.

It must also be considered that, having looked piercingly and bravely into the doings of the world, and found much thereof false, and much more only half true, he is constantly led to speak of things either held in esteem or blandly tolerated, and to convey his knowledge of their worthlessness in a tone of quiet, deliberate scorn, which couples itself in friendly dissonance with his fervid worship of many a ragged, outcast heroism;—as the answer of an Arab Sheik to the messenger of a Pasha requiring the free son of the desert to pay tribute, compared with his welcome to his tents of the naked, wandering stranger.

Add to this, that Mr Carlyle's resolution to convey his meaning at all hazards, makes him seize the most effectual and sudden words in spite of usage and fashionable taste: and that, therefore, when he can get a brighter tint, a more expressive form, by means of some strange—we must call it—Carlylism; English, Scotch, German, Greek, Latin, French, Technical, Slang, American, or Lunar, or altogether superlunar, transcendental, and drawn from the eternal Nowhere,—he uses it with a courage which might blast an academy of lexicographers into a Hades, void even of vocables.

We should infer from Mr Carlyle's style that he is not naturally fluent, or at least had not been led in very early life, when alone, perhaps, it can be done, to use with smooth dexterity a conventional mechanism of discourse on all the topics known in civilized life. Where this, which may be called the rain-spout or parish-pump faculty, has been much developed, it is very difficult, if not impossible, to gain that short, sharp, instantaneous mode of expression which says what the speaker feels to be the right thing, and no more, and so leaves

it. But if, from circumstances of any kind, whether of personal seclusion, or of silent and severe habits in those about us in childhood, this knack or gift has not been carried to any very awful perfection, such as one finds in barristers, preachers, literary journeymen, leaders of the House of Commons, auctioneers, and the like—and if, nevertheless, there is real matter crowding and glowing for utterance—a man's speech is likely to have a pith and directness otherwise extremely hard of attainment, and which recals the reason given by old Gaunt, in *Richard II*, for the hope that his own dying counsels may influence the young king:—

> Where words are scarce, they are seldom spent in
> vain:
> For they breathe truth that breathe their words in
> pain.

Furthermore, it may be observed, on the choice of words shown in this author's writings, that his clear and irresistible eye for the substantial and significant in all objects, and his carelessness of the merely abstract, show themselves in an immediateness and prominence of expression, to which we see nothing in its kind equal in modern English books. His style is not so much a figured as an embossed one. The shapes which it exhibits have not only neatness and strength, which those of a clever rhetorician often have; but a truth and life, which show them to be prompted by the writer's feeling and experience of things, and not arranged from a calculation of what will be the effect on others.

HENRY DAVID THOREAU
From "Thomas Carlyle and His Works" (1847)
Writings
1906, Volume 4, pp. 323–33

He has the English for his mother-tongue, though with a Scotch accent, or never so many accents, and thoughts also, which are the legitimate growth of native soil, to utter therewith. His style is eminently colloquial, and no wonder it is strange to meet with in a book. It is not literary or classical; it has not the music of poetry, nor the pomp of philosophy, but the rhythms and cadences of conversation endlessly repeated. It resounds with emphatic, natural, lively, stirring tones, muttering, rattling, exploding, like shells and shot, and with like execution. So far as it is a merit in composition that the written answer to the spoken word, and the spoken word to a fresh and pertinent thought in the mind, as well as to the half thoughts, the tumultuary misgivings and expectancies, this author is, perhaps, not to be matched in literature.

He is no mystic, either, more than Newton or Arkwright or Davy, and tolerates none. Not one obscure line, or half line, did he ever write. His meaning lies plain as the daylight, and he who runs may read; indeed, only he who runs *can* read, and keep up with the meaning. It has the distinctness of picture to his mind, and he tells us only what he sees printed in largest English type upon the face of things. He utters substantial English thoughts in plainest English dialects; for it must be confessed, he speaks more than one of these. All the shires of England, and all the shires of Europe, are laid under contribution to his genius; for to be English does not mean to be exclusive and narrow, and adapt one's self to the apprehension of his nearest neighbor only. And yet no writer is more thoroughly Saxon. In the translation of those fragments of Saxon poetry, we have met with the same rhythm that occurs so often in his poem on the French Revolution. And if you would know where many of those obnoxious Carlyleisms and Germanisms came from, read the best of Milton's prose, read those speeches of Cromwell which he has brought to light, or go and listen once more to your mother's tongue. So much for his German extraction.

Indeed, for fluency and skill in the use of the English tongue, he is a master unrivaled. His felicity and power of expression surpass even his special merits as historian and critic. Therein his experience has not failed him, but furnished him with such a store of winged, ay and legged words, as only a London life, perchance, could give account of. We had not understood the wealth of the language before. Nature is ransacked, and all the resorts and purlieus of humanity are taxed, to furnish the fittest symbol for his thought. He does not go to the dictionary, the word-book, but to the word-manufactory itself, and has made endless work for the lexicographers. Yes, he has that same English for his mother-tongue that you have, but with him it is no dumb, muttering, mumbling faculty, concealing the thoughts, but a keen, unwearied, resistless weapon. He has such command of it as neither you nor I have; and it would be well for any who have a lost horse to advertise, or a town-meeting warrant, or a sermon, or a letter to write, to study this universal letter-writer, for he knows more than the grammar or the dictionary.

The style is worth attending to, as one of the most important features of the man which we at this distance can discern. It is for once quite equal to the matter. It can carry all its load, and never breaks down nor staggers. His books are solid and workmanlike, as all that England does; and they are graceful and readable also. They tell of huge labor done, well done, and all the rubbish swept away, like the bright cutlery which glitters in shop windows, while the coke and ashes, the turnings, filings, dust, and borings lie far away at Birmingham, unheard of. He is a masterly clerk, scribe, reporter, writer. He can reduce to writing most things,—gestures, winks, nods, significant looks, patois, brogue, accent, pantomime, and how much that had passed for silence before does he represent by written words. The countryman who puzzled the city lawyer, requiring him to write, among other things, his call to his horses, would hardly have puzzled him; he would have found a word for it, all right and classical, that would have started his team for him. Consider the ceaseless tide of speech forever flowing in countless cellars, garrets, *parlors*; that of the French, says Carlyle, "only ebbs toward the short hours of night," and what a drop in the bucket is the printed word. Feeling, thought, speech, writing, and, we might add, poetry, inspiration,—for so the circle is completed; how they gradually dwindle at length, passing through successive colanders, into your history and classics, from the roar of the ocean, the murmur of the forest, to the squeak of a mouse; so much only parsed and spelt out, and punctuated, at last. The few who can talk like a book, they only get reported commonly. But this writer reports a new *Lieferung*.

One wonders how so much, after all, was expressed in the old way, so much here depends upon the emphasis, tone, pronunciation, style, and spirit of the reading. No writer uses so profusely all the aids to intelligibility which the printer's art affords. You wonder how others had contrived to write so many pages without emphatic or italicized words, they are so expressive, so natural, so indispensable here, as if none had ever used the demonstrative pronouns demonstratively before. In another's sentences the thought, though it may be immortal, is as it were embalmed, and does not *strike* you, but here it is so freshly living, even the body of it not having passed through the

ordeal of death, that it stirs in the very extremities, and the smallest particles and pronouns are all alive with it. It is not simple dictionary *it*, yours or mine, but IT. The words did not come at the command of grammar, but of a tyrannous, inexorable meaning; not like standing soldiers, by vote of Parliament, but any able-bodied countryman pressed into the service, for "Sire, it is not a revolt, it is a revolution."

We have never heard him speak, but we should say that Carlyle was a rare talker. He has broken the ice, and streams freely forth like a spring torrent. He does not trace back the stream of his thought, silently adventurous, up to its fountainhead, but is borne away with it, as it rushes through his brain like a torrent to overwhelm and fertilize. He holds a talk with you. His audience is such a tumultuous mob of thirty thousand as assembled at the University of Paris, before printing was invented. Philosophy, on the other hand, does not talk, but write, or, when it comes personally before an audience, lecture or read; and therefore it must be read to-morrow, or a thousand years hence. But the talker must naturally be attended to at once; he does not talk on without an audience; the winds do not long bear the sound of his voice. Think of Carlyle reading his *French Revolution* to any audience. One might say it was never written, but spoken; and thereafter reported and printed, that those not within sound of his voice might know something about it. Some men read to you something which they have written in a dead *language*, of course, but it may be in a living *letter*, in a Syriac, or Roman, or Runic character. Men must *speak* English who can *write* Sanskrit; they must speak a modern language who write, perchance, an ancient and universal one. We do not live in those days when the learned used a learned language. There is no writing of Latin with Carlyle; but as Chaucer, with all reverence to Homer, and Virgil, and Messieurs the Normans, sung his poetry in the homely Saxon tongue, and Locke has at least the merit of having done philosophy into English, so Carlyle has done a different philosophy still further into English, and thrown open the doors of literature and criticism to the populace.

Such a style,—so diversified and variegated! It is like the face of a country; it is like a New England landscape, with farmhouses and villages, and cultivated spots, and belts of forests and blueberry swamps round about, with the fragrance of shad-blossoms and violets on certain winds. And as for the reading of it, it is novel enough to the reader who has used only the diligence, and old line mail-coach. It is like traveling, sometimes on foot, sometimes in a gig tandem; sometimes in a full coach, over highways, mended and unmended, for which you will prosecute the town; on level roads, through French departments, by Simplon roads over the Alps; and now and then he hauls up for a relay, and yokes in an unbroken colt of a Pegasus for a leader, driving off by cart-paths, and across lots, by corduroy roads and gridiron bridges; and where the bridges are gone, not even a string-piece left, and the reader has to set his breast and swim. You have got an expert driver this time, who has driven ten thousand miles, and was never known to upset; can drive six in hand on the edge of a precipice, and touch the leaders anywhere with his snapper.

With wonderful art he grinds into paint for his picture all his moods and experiences, so that all his forces may be brought to the encounter. Apparently writing without a particular design or responsibility, setting down his soliloquies from time to time, taking advantage of all his humors, when at length the hour comes to declare himself, he puts down in plain English, without quotation marks, what he, Thomas Carlyle, is ready to defend in the face of the world, and fathers the rest, often quite as defensible, only more modest, or plain-spoken, or insinuating, upon "Sauerteig," or some other gentleman long employed on the subject. Rolling his subject how many ways in his mind, he meets it now face to face, wrestling with it at arm's length, and striving to get it down, or throw it over his head; and if that will not do, or whether it will do or not, tries the back stitch and side hug with it, and downs it again, scalps it, draws and quarters it, hangs it in chains, and leaves it to the winds and dogs. With his brows knit, his mind made up, his will resolved and resistless, he advances, crashing his way through the host of weak, half-formed, *dilettante* opinions, honest and dishonest ways of thinking, with their standards raised, sentimentalities and conjectures, and tramples them all into dust. See how he prevails; you don't even hear the groans of the wounded and dying. Certainly it is not so well worth the while to look through any man's eyes at history, for the time, as through his; and his way of looking at things is fastest getting adopted by his generation.

It is not in man to determine what his style shall be. He might as well determine what his thoughts shall be. We would not have had him write always as in the chapter on Burns, and the Life of Schiller, and elsewhere. No; his thoughts were ever irregular and impetuous. Perhaps as he grows older and writes more he acquires a truer expression; it is in some respects manlier, freer, struggling up to a level with its fountain-head. We think it is the richest prose style we know of.

Who cares what a man's style is, so it is intelligible,—as intelligible as his thought. Literally and really, the style is no more than the *stylus*, the pen he writes with; and it is not worth scraping and polishing, and gilding, unless it will write his thoughts the better for it. It is something for use, and not to look at. The question for us is, not whether Pope had a fine style, wrote with a peacock's feather, but whether he uttered useful thoughts. Translate a book a dozen times from one language to another, and what becomes of its style? Most books would be worn out and disappear in this ordeal. The pen which wrote it is soon destroyed, but the poem survives. We believe that Carlyle has, after all, more readers, and is better known to-day for this very originality of style, and that posterity will have reason to thank him for emancipating the language, in some measure, from the fetters which a merely conservative, aimless, and pedantic literary class had imposed upon it, and setting an example of greater freedom and naturalness. No man's thoughts are new, but the style of their expression is the never-failing novelty which cheers and refreshes men. If we were to answer the question, whether the mass of men, as we know them, talk as the standard authors and reviewers write, or rather as this man writes, we should say that he alone begins to write their language at all, and that the former is, for the most part, the mere *effigies* of a language, not the best method of concealing one's thoughts even, but frequently a method of doing without thoughts at all.

In his graphic description of Richter's style, Carlyle describes his own pretty nearly; and no doubt he first got his own tongue loosened at that fountain, and was inspired by it to equal freedom and originality. "The language," as he says of Richter, "groans with indescribable metaphors and allusions to all things, human and divine, flowing onward, not like a river, but like an inundation; circling in complex eddies, chafing and gurgling, now this way, now that;" but in Carlyle, "the proper current" never "sinks out of sight amid the boundless uproar." Again: "His very language is Titanian,—deep, strong, tumultuous, shining with a thousand hues, fused from a thousand elements, and winding in labyrinthic mazes."

In short, if it is desirable that a man be eloquent, that he talk much, and address himself to his own age mainly, then this is not a bad style of doing it. But if it is desired rather that he pioneer into unexplored regions of thought, and speak to silent centuries to come, then, indeed, we could wish that he had cultivated the style of Goethe more, that of Richter less; not that Goethe's is the kind of utterance most to be prized by mankind, but it will serve for a model of the best that can be successfully cultivated.

But for style, and fine writing, and Augustan ages, that is but a poor style, and vulgar writing, and a degenerate age, which allows us to remember these things. This man has something to communicate. Carlyle's are not, in the common sense, works of art in their origin and aim; and yet, perhaps, no living English writer evinces an equal literary talent. They are such works of art only as the plow and corn-mill and steam-engine,—not as pictures and statues. Others speak with greater emphasis to scholars, as such, but none so earnestly and effectually to all who can read. Others give their advice, he gives his sympathy also. It is no small praise that he does not take upon himself the airs, has none of the whims, none of the pride, the nice vulgarities, the starched, impoverished isolation, and cold glitter of the spoiled children of genius. He does not need to husband his pearl, but excels by a greater humanity and sincerity.

He is singularly serious and untrivial. We are everywhere impressed by the rugged, unwearied, and rich sincerity of the man. We are sure that he never sacrificed one jot of honest thought to art or whim, but to utter himself in the most direct and effectual way,—that is the endeavor. These are merits which will wear well. When time has worn deeper into the substance of these books, this grain will appear. No such sermons have come to us here out of England, in late years, as those of this preacher,—sermons to kings, and sermons to peasants, and sermons to all intermediate classes. It is in vain that John Bull, or any of his cousins, turns a deaf ear, and pretends not to hear them: nature will not soon be weary of repeating them. There are words less obviously true, more for the ages to hear, perhaps, but none so impossible for this age not to hear. What a cutting cimeter was that *Past and Present*, going through heaps of silken stuffs, and glibly through the necks of men, too, without their knowing it, leaving no trace! He has the earnestness of a prophet. In an age of pedantry and dilettantism, he has no grain of these in his composition. There is nowhere else, surely, in recent readable English, or other books, such direct and effectual teaching, reproving, encouraging, stimulating, earnestly, vehemently, almost like Mahomet, like Luther; not looking behind him to see how his *Opera Omnia* will look, but forward to other work to be done. His writings are a gospel to the young of this generation; they will hear his manly, brotherly speech with responsive joy, and press forward to older or newer gospels.

JAMES RUSSELL LOWELL
From "Carlyle" (1866)
Works, Riverside ed.
1890, Volume 2, pp. 91–109

It is certainly more agreeable to be grateful for what we owe an author, than to blame him for what he cannot give us. But it is sometimes the business of a critic to trace faults of style and of thought to their root in character and temperament, to show their necessary relation to, and dependence on, each other, and to find some more trustworthy explanation than mere wantonness of will for the moral obliquities of a man so largely moulded and gifted as Mr. Carlyle. So long as he was merely an exhorter or dehorter, we were thankful for such eloquence, such humor, such vivid or grotesque images, and such splendor of illustration as only he could give; but when he assumes to be a teacher of moral and political philosophy, when he himself takes to compounding the social panaceas he has made us laugh at so often, and advertises none as genuine but his own, we begin to inquire into his qualifications and his defects, and to ask ourselves whether his patent pill differ from others except in the larger amount of aloes, or have any better recommendation than the superior advertising powers of a mountebank of genius. Comparative criticism teaches us that moral and æsthetic defects are more nearly related than is commonly supposed. Had Mr. Carlyle been fitted out completely by nature as an artist, he would have had an ideal in his work which would have lifted his mind away from the muddier part of him, and trained him to the habit of seeking and seeing the harmony rather than the discord and contradiction of things. His innate love of the picturesque, (which is only another form of the sentimentalism he so scoffs at, perhaps as feeling it a weakness in himself,)[1] once turned in the direction of character, and finding its chief satisfaction there, led him to look for that ideal of human nature in individual men which is but fragmentarily represented in the entire race, and is rather divined from the aspiration, forever disenchanted to be forever renewed, of the immortal part in us, than found in any example of actual achievement. A wiser temper would have seen something more consoling than disheartening in the continual failure of men eminently endowed to reach the standard of this spiritual requirement, would perhaps have found in it an inspiring hint that it is mankind, and not special men, that are to be shaped at last into the image of God, and that the endless life of the generations may hope to come nearer that goal of which the short-breathed threescore years and ten fall too unhappily short.

But Mr. Carlyle has invented the Hero-cure, and all who recommend any other method, or see any hope of healing elsewhere, are either quacks and charlatans or their victims. His lively imagination conjures up the image of an impossible he, as contradictorily endowed as the chief personage in a modern sentimental novel, who, at all hazards, must not lead mankind like a shepherd, but bark, bite, and otherwise worry them toward the fold like a truculent sheep-dog. If Mr. Carlyle would only now and then recollect that men are men, and not sheep, nay, that the farther they are from being such, the more well grounded our hope of one day making something better of them! It is indeed strange that one who values Will so highly in the greatest should be blind to its infinite worth in the least of men; nay, that he should so often seem to confound it with its irritable and purposeless counterfeit, Wilfulness. The natural impatience of an imaginative temperament, which conceives so vividly the beauty and desirableness of a nobler manhood and a diviner political order, makes him fret at the slow moral processes by which the All-Wise brings about his ends, and turns the very foolishness of men to his praise and glory. Mr. Carlyle is for calling down fire from Heaven whenever he cannot readily lay his hand on the match-box. No doubt it is somewhat provoking that it should be so easy to build castles in the air, and so hard to find tenants for them. It is a singular intellectual phenomenon to see a man, who earlier in life so thoroughly appreciated the innate weakness and futile tendency of the "storm and thrust" period of German literature, constantly assimilating, as he grows older, more and more nearly to its principles and practice. It is no longer the

sagacious and moderate Goethe who is his type of what is highest in human nature, but far rather some Götz of the Iron Hand, some assertor of the divine legitimacy of *Faustrecht*. It is odd to conceive the fate of Mr. Carlyle under the sway of any of his heroes, how Cromwell would have scorned him as a babbler more long-winded than Prynne, but less clear and practical, how Friedrich would have scoffed at his tirades as *dummes Zeug* not to be compared with the romances of Crébillon *fils*, or possibly have clapped him in a marching regiment as a fit subject for the cane of the sergeant. Perhaps something of Mr. Carlyle's irritability is to be laid to the account of his early schoolmastership at Kirkcaldy. This great booby World is such a dull boy, and will not learn the lesson we have taken such pains in expounding for the fiftieth time. Well, then, if eloquence, if example, if the awful warning of other little boys who neglected their accidence and came to the gallows, if none of these avail, the birch at least is left, and we will try that. The dominie spirit has become every year more obtrusive and intolerant in Mr. Carlyle's writing, and the rod, instead of being kept in its place as a resource for desperate cases, has become the alpha and omega of all successful training, the one divinely-appointed means of human enlightenment and progress, in short, the final hope of that absurd animal who fancies himself a little lower than the angels. Have we feebly taken it for granted that the distinction of man was reason? Never was there a more fatal misconception. It is in the gift of unreason that we are unenviably distinguished from the brutes, whose nobler privilege of instinct saves them from our blunders and our crimes.

But since Mr. Carlyle has become possessed with the hallucination that he is head-master of this huge boys' school which we call the world, his pedagogic birch has grown to the taller proportions and more ominous aspect of a gallows. His article on Dr. Francia was a panegyric of the halter, in which the gratitude of mankind is invoked for the self-appointed dictator who had discovered in Paraguay a tree more beneficent than that which produced the Jesuits' bark. Mr. Carlyle seems to be in the condition of a man who uses stimulants, and must increase his dose from day to day as the senses become dulled under the spur. He began by admiring strength of character and purpose and the manly self-denial which makes a humble fortune great by steadfast loyalty to duty. He has gone on till mere strength has become such washy weakness that there is no longer any titillation in it; and nothing short of downright violence will rouse his nerves now to the needed excitement. At first he made out very well with remarkable men; then, lessening the water and increasing the spirit, he took to Heroes: and now he must have downright *in*humanity, or the draught has no savor; so he gets on at last to Kings, types of remorseless Force, who maintain the political views of Berserkers by the legal principles of Lynch. Constitutional monarchy is a failure, representative government is a gabble, democracy a birth of the bottomless pit; there is no hope for mankind except in getting themselves under a good driver who shall not spare the lash. And yet, unhappily for us, these drivers are providential births not to be contrived by any cunning of ours, and Friedrich II. is hitherto the last of them. Meanwhile the world's wheels have got fairly stalled in mire and other matter of every vilest consistency and most disgustful smell. What are we to do? Mr. Carlyle will not let us make a lever with a rail from the next fence, or call in the neighbors. That would be too commonplace and cowardly, too anarchical. No; he would have us sit down beside him in the slough and shout lustily for Hercules. If that indispensable demigod will not or cannot come, we can find a useful and instructive solace, during the intervals of shouting, in a hearty abuse of human nature, which, at the long last, is always to blame.

Since *Sartor Resartus* Mr. Carlyle has done little but repeat himself with increasing emphasis and heightened shrillness. Warning has steadily heated toward denunciation, and remonstrance soured toward scolding. The image of the Tartar prayer-mill, which he borrowed from Richter and turned to such humorous purpose, might be applied to himself. The same phrase comes round and round, only the machine, being a little crankier, rattles more, and the performer is called on for a more visible exertion. If there be not something very like cant in Mr. Carlyle's later writings, then cant is not the repetition of a creed after it has become a phrase by the cooling of that white-hot conviction which once made it both the light and warmth of the soul. I do not mean intentional and deliberate cant, but neither is that which Mr. Carlyle denounces so energetically in his fellowmen of that conscious kind. I do not mean to blame him for it, but mention it rather as an interesting phenomenon of human nature. The stock of ideas which mankind has to work with is very limited, like the alphabet, and can at best have an air of freshness given it by new arrangements and combinations, or by application to new times and circumstances. Montaigne is but Ecclesiastes writing in the sixteenth century, Voltaire but Lucian in the eighteenth. Yet both are original, and so certainly is Mr. Carlyle, whose borrowing is mainly from his own former works. But he does this so often and so openly, that we may at least be sure that he ceased growing a number of years ago, and is a remarkable example of arrested development.

The cynicism, however, which has now become the prevailing temper of his mind, has gone on expanding with unhappy vigor. In Mr. Carlyle it is not, certainly, as in Swift, the result of personal disappointment, and of the fatal eye of an accomplice for the mean qualities by which power could be attained that it might be used for purposes as mean. It seems rather the natural corruption of his exuberant humor. Humor in its first analysis is a perception of the incongruous, and in its highest development, of the incongruity between the actual and the ideal in men and life. With so keen a sense of the ludicrous contrast between what men might be, nay, wish to be, and what they are, and with a vehement nature that demands the instant realization of his vision of a world altogether heroic, it is no wonder that Mr. Carlyle, always hoping for a thing and always disappointed, should become bitter. Perhaps if he expected less he would find more. Saul seeking his father's asses found himself turned suddenly into a king; but Mr. Carlyle, on the lookout for a king, always seems to find the other sort of animal. He sees nothing on any side of him but a procession of the Lord of Misrule, in gloomier moments, a Dance of Death, where everything is either a parody of whatever is noble, or an aimless jig that stumbles at last into the annihilation of the grave, and so passes from one nothing to another. Is a world, then, which buys and reads Mr. Carlyle's works distinguished only for its "fair, large ears"? If he who has read and remembered so much would only now and then call to mind the old proverb, *Nec deus, nec lupus, sed homo!* If he would only recollect that, from the days of the first grandfather, everybody has remembered a golden age behind him! No doubt Adam depreciated the apple which the little Cain on his knee was crunching, by comparison with those he himself had tasted in Eden.

The very qualities, it seems to me, which came so near making a great poet of Mr. Carlyle, disqualify him for the office of historian. The poet's concern is with the appearances of things, with their harmony in that whole which the imagination demands for its satisfaction, and their truth to that ideal nature which is the proper object of poetry. History, unfortunately, is very far from being ideal, still farther from an exclusive interest in those heroic or typical figures which answer all the wants of the epic and the drama and fill their utmost artistic limits. Mr. Carlyle has an unequalled power and vividness in painting detached scenes, in bringing out in their full relief the oddities or peculiarities of character; but he has a far feebler sense of those gradual changes of opinion, that strange communication of sympathy from mind to mind, that subtle influence of very subordinate actors in giving a direction to policy or action, which we are wont somewhat vaguely to call the progress of events. His scheme of history is purely an epical one, where only leading figures appear by name and are in any strict sense operative. He has no conception of the people as anything else than an element of mere brute force in political problems, and would sniff scornfully at that unpicturesque common-sense of the many, which comes slowly to its conclusions, no doubt, but compels obedience even from rulers the most despotic when once its mind is made up. His history of Frederick is, of course, a Fritziad; but next to his hero, the cane of the drill-sergeant and iron ramrods appear to be the conditions which to his mind satisfactorily account for the result of the Seven Years War. It is our opinion, which subsequent events seem to justify, that, had there not been in the Prussian people a strong instinct of nationality, Protestant nationality too, and an intimate conviction of its advantages, the war might have ended quite otherwise. Frederick II. left the machine of war which he received from his father even more perfect than he found it, yet within a few years of his death it went to pieces before the shock of French armies animated by an idea. Again a few years, and the Prussian soldiery, inspired once more by the old national fervor, were victorious. After all, is it not moral forces that make the heaviest battalions, other things being tolerably equal? Were it not for the purely picturesque bias of Mr. Carlyle's genius, for the necessity which his epical treatment lays upon him of always having a protagonist, we should be astonished that an idealist like him should have so little faith in ideas and so much in matter.

Mr. Carlyle's manner is not so well suited to the historian as to the essayist. He is always great in single figures and striking episodes, but there is neither gradation nor continuity. He has extraordinary patience and conscientiousness in the gathering and sifting of his material, but is scornful of commonplace facts and characters, impatient of whatever will not serve for one of his clever sketches, or group well in a more elaborate figure-piece. He sees history, as it were, by flashes of lightning. A single scene, whether a landscape or an interior, a single figure or a wild mob of men, whatever may be snatched by the eye in that instant of intense illumination, is minutely photographed upon the memory. Every tree and stone, almost every blade of grass; every article of furniture in a room; the attitude or expression, nay, the very buttons and shoe-ties of a principle figure; the gestures of momentary passion in a wild throng,—everything leaps into vision under that sudden glare with a painful distinctness that leaves the retina quivering. The intervals are absolute darkness. Mr. Carlyle makes us acquainted with the isolated spot where we happen to be when the flash comes, as if by actual eyesight, but there is no possibility of a comprehensive view. No other writer compares with him for vividness. He is himself a witness, and makes us witnesses of whatever he describes. This is genius beyond a question, and of a very rare quality, but it is not history. He has not the cold-blooded impartiality of the historian; and while he entertains us, moves us to tears or laughter, makes us the unconscious captives of his ever-changeful mood, we find that he has taught us comparatively little. His imagination is so powerful that it makes him the contemporary of his characters, and thus his history seems to be the memoirs of a cynical humorist, with hearty likes and dislikes, with something of acridity in his partialities whether for or against, more keenly sensitive to the grotesque than to the simply natural, and who enters in his diary, even of what comes within the range of his own observation, only so much as amuses his fancy, is congenial with his humor, or feeds his prejudice. Mr. Carlyle's method is accordingly altogether pictorial, his hasty temper making narrative wearisome to him. In his *Friedrich*, for example, we get very little notion of the civil administration of Prussia; and when he comes, in the last volume, to his hero's dealings with civil reforms, he confesses candidly that it would tire him too much to tell us about it, even if he knew anything at all satisfactory himself.

Mr. Carlyle's historical compositions are wonderful prose poems, full of picture, incident, humor, and character, where we grow familiar with his conception of certain leading personages, and even of subordinate ones, if they are necessary to the scene, so that they come out living upon the stage from the dreary limbo of names; but this is no more history than the historical plays of Shakespeare. There is nothing in imaginative literature superior in its own way to the episode of Voltaire in the *Fritziad*. It is delicious in humor, masterly in minute characterization. We feel as if the principal victim (for we cannot help feeling all the while that he is so) of this mischievous genius had been put upon the theatre before us by some perfect mimic like Foote, who had studied his habitual gait, gestures, tones, turn of thought, costume, trick of feature, and rendered them with the slight dash of caricature needful to make the whole composition tell. It is in such things that Mr. Carlyle is beyond all rivalry, and that we must go back to Shakespeare for a comparison. But the mastery of Shakespeare is shown perhaps more strikingly in his treatment of the ordinary than of the exceptional. His is the gracious equality of Nature herself. Mr. Carlyle's gift is rather in the representation than in the evolution of character; and it is a necessity of his art, therefore, to exaggerate slightly his heroic, and to carica-ture in like manner his comic parts. His appreciation is less psychological than physical and external. Grimm relates that Garrick, riding once with Préville, proposed to him that they should counterfeit drunkenness. They rode through Passy accordingly, deceiving all who saw them. When beyond the town Préville asked how he had succeeded. "Excellently," said Garrick, "as to your body; but your legs were not tipsy." Mr. Carlyle would be as exact in his observation of nature as the great actor, and would make us *see* a drunken man as well; but we doubt whether he could have conceived that unmatchable scene in *Antony and Cleopatra*, where the tipsiness of Lepidus pervades the whole metaphysical no less than the physical part of the triumvir. If his sympathies bore any proportion to his instinct for catching those traits which are the expression of character, but not character itself, we might have had a great historian in him instead of a history-painter. But that which is a main element in Mr. Carlyle's talent, and does perhaps more than anything else to make it effective, is a defect of his nature. The cynicism which renders him so entertaining precludes him from any just conception of men and their motives, and from any sane estimate of the relative importance of the events which concern them. I remember a picture of Hamon's, where before a Punch's theatre are gathered the wisest of mankind in rapt attention. Socrates sits on a front bench, absorbed in the spectacle, and in the corner stands Dante making entries in his note-book. Mr. Carlyle as an historian leaves us in somewhat such a mood. The world is a puppet-show, and when we have watched the play out, we depart with a half-comic conscious-ness of the futility of all human enterprise, and the ludicrous-ness of all man's action and passion on the stage of the world. Simple, kindly, blundering Oliver Goldsmith was after all wiser, and his Vicar, ideal as Hector and not less immortal, is a demonstration of the perennial beauty and heroism of the homeliest human nature. The cynical view is congenial to certain moods, and is so little inconsistent with original nobleness of mind, that it is not seldom the acetous fermen-tation of it; but it is the view of the satirist, not of the historian, and takes in but a narrow arc in the circumference of truth. Cynicism in itself is essentially disagreeable. It is the intellec-tual analogue of the truffle; and though it may be very well in giving a relish to thought for certain palates, it cannot supply the substance of it. Mr. Carlyle's cynicism is not that highbred weariness of the outsides of life which we find in Ecclesiastes. It goes much deeper than that to the satisfactions, not of the body or the intellect, but of the very soul as well. It vaunts itself; it is noisy and aggressive. What the wise master puts into the mouth of desperate ambition, thwarted of the fruit of its crime, as the fitting expression of passionate sophistry, seems to have become an article of his creed. With him

> Life *is* a tale
> Told by an idiot, full of sound and fury,
> Signifying nothing.

He goes about with his Diogenes dark-lantern, professing to seek a man, but inwardly resolved to find a monkey. He loves to flash it suddenly on poor human nature in some ridiculous or degrading posture. He admires still, or keeps affirming that he admires, the doughty, silent, hard-working men who go honestly about their business; but when we come to his later examples, we find that it is not loyalty to duty or to an inward ideal of high-mindedness that he finds admirable in them, but a blind unquestioning vassalage to whomsoever it has pleased him to set up for a hero. He would fain replace the old feudalism with a spiritual counterpart, in which there shall be an obligation to soul-service. He who once popularized the word *flunkey* by ringing the vehement changes of his scorn upon it, is at last forced to conceive an ideal flunkeyism to squire the hectoring Don Belianises of his fancy about the world. Failing this, his latest theory of Divine government seems to be the cudgel. Poets have sung all manner of vegetable loves; Petrarch has celebrated the laurel, Chaucer the daisy, and Wordsworth the gallows-tree; it remained for the ex-pedagogue of Kirkcaldy to become the volunteer laureate of the rod and to imagine a world created and directed by a divine Dr. Busby. We cannot help thinking that Mr. Carlyle might have learned something to his advantage by living a few years in the democracy which he scoffs at as heartily *a priori* as if it were the demagogism which Aristophanes derided from expe-rience. The Hero, as Mr. Carlyle understands him, was a makeshift of the past; and the ideal of manhood is to be found hereafter in free communities, where the state shall at length sum up and exemplify in itself all those qualities which poets were forced to imagine and typify because they could not find them in the actual world.

In the earlier part of his literary career, Mr. Carlyle was the denouncer of shams, the preacher up of sincerity, manli-ness, and a living faith, instead of a droning ritual. He had intense convictions, and he made disciples. With a compass of diction unequalled by any other public performer of the time, ranging as it did from the unbookish freshness of the Scottish peasant to the most far-sought phrase of literary curiosity, with humor, pathos, and eloquence at will, it was no wonder that he found eager listeners in a world longing for a sensation, and forced to put up with the West-End gospel of *Pelham*. If not a profound thinker, he had what was next best,—he felt profoundly, and his cry came out of the depths. The stern Calvinism of his early training was rekindled by his imagination to the old fervor of Wishart and Brown, and became a new phenomenon as he reproduced it subtilized by German transcendentalism and German culture. Imagination, if it lay hold of a Scotchman, possesses him in the old demoniac sense of the word, and that hard logical nature, if the Hebrew fire once get fair headway in it, burns unquenchable as an anthracite coal-mine. But to utilize these sacred heats, to employ them, as a literary man is always tempted, to keep the domestic pot a-boiling,—is such a thing possible? Only too possible, we fear; and Mr. Carlyle is an example of it. If the languid public long for a sensation, the excitement of making one becomes also a necessity of the successful author, as the intellectual nerves grow duller and the old inspiration that came unbidden to the bare garret grows shier and shier of the comfortable parlor. As he himself said thirty years ago of Edward Irving, "Unconsciously, for the most part in deep unconsciousness, there was now the impossibility to live neglected,—to walk on the quiet paths where alone it is well with us. Singularity must henceforth succeed singularity. O foulest Circean draught, thou poison of Popular Applause! madness is in thee and death; thy end is Bedlam and the grave." Mr. Carlyle won his first successes as a kind of preacher in print. His fervor, his oddity of manner, his pugnacious paradox, drew the crowd; the truth, or, at any rate, the faith that underlay them all, brought also the fitter audience, though fewer. But the curse was upon him; he must attract, he must astonish. Thenceforth he has been forced to revamp his telling things; and the oddity, as was inevitable, has become always odder, the paradoxes more paradoxical. No very large share of truth falls to the apprehension of any one man; let him keep it sacred, and beware of repeating it till it turn to falsehood on his lips by becoming ritual. Truth always has a bewitching savor of newness in it, and novelty at the first taste recalls that original sweetness to the tongue; but alas for him who would make the one a substitute for the other! We seem to miss of late in Mr. Carlyle the old sincerity. He has become the purely literary man, less concerned about what he says than about how he shall say it to best advantage. The Muse should be the companion, not the guide, says he whom Mr. Carlyle has pronounced "the wisest of this generation." What would be a virtue in the poet is a vice of the most fatal kind in the teacher, and, alas that we should say it! the very Draco of shams, whose code contained no penalty milder than capital for the most harmless of them, has become at last something very like a sham himself. Mr. Carlyle continues to be a voice crying in the wilderness, but no longer a voice with any earnest conviction behind it, or in a wilderness where there is other than imaginary privation. Hearing him rebuke us for being humbugs and impostors, we are inclined to answer, with the ambassador of Philip II., when his master reproached him with forgetting substance in ceremony, "Your Majesty forgets that you are only a ceremony yourself." And Mr. Carlyle's teaching, moreover, if teaching we may call it, belongs to what the great German, whose disciple he is, condemned as the "literature of despair." An apostle to the gentiles might hope for some fruit of his preaching; but of what avail an apostle who shouts his message down the mouth of the pit to poor lost souls, whom he can positively assure only that it is impossible to get out? Mr.

Carlyle lights up the lanterns of his Pharos after the ship is already rolling between the tongue of the sea and the grinders of the reef. It is very brilliant, and its revolving flashes touch the crests of the breakers with an awful picturesqueness; but in so desperate a state of things, even Dr. Syntax might be pardoned for being forgetful of the picturesque. The Toryism of Scott sprang from love of the past; that of Carlyle is far more dangerously infectious, for it is logically deduced from a deep disdain of human nature.

Notes

1. Thirty years ago, when this was written, I ventured only a hint that Carlyle was essentially a sentimentalist. In what has been published since his death I find proof of what I had divined rather than definitely formulated. (1888.)

SIR LESLIE STEPHEN
"Carlyle's Ethics"
Hours in a Library (1874–79)
1904, Volume 4, pp. 232–80

I have sometimes wondered of late what would have been the reception accorded to an autobiographical sketch by St. John the Baptist. It would, one may suppose, have contained some remarks not very palatable to refined society. The scoffers indeed would have covered their delight in an opportunity for lowering a great reputation by a plausible veil of virtuous indignation. The Pharisees would have taken occasion to dwell upon the immoral contempt of the stern prophet for the maxims of humdrum respectability. The Sadducees would have aired their orthodoxy by lamenting his open denunciations of shams, which, in their opinion, were quite as serviceable as real beliefs. Both would have agreed that nothing but a mean personal motive could have prompted such an outrageous utterance of discontent. And the good, kindly, well-meaning people—for, doubtless, there were some such even at the court of Herod—would have been sincerely shocked at the discovery that the vehement denunciations to which they had listened were in good truth the utterance of a tortured and unhappy nature, which took in all sincerity a gloomy view of the prospects of their society and the intrinsic value of its idols, instead of merely getting up indignation for purposes of pulpit oratory. They—complacent optimists, as kindly people are apt to be—have made up their minds that a genuine philosopher is always a benevolent, white-haired old gentleman, overflowing with philanthropic sentiment, convinced that all is for the best, and that even the "miserable sinners" are excellent people at bottom; and are grievously shocked at the discovery that anybody can still believe in the existence of the devil as a potent agent in human affairs. If we have any difficulty in imagining such criticisms, we may easily realise them by reading certain criticisms upon the *Reminiscences* of the last prophet—for we may call him a prophet whatever we think of the sources of his inspiration—who has passed from among us. The reflection which has most frequently occurred to me is one put with characteristic force by Carlyle himself in describing the sight of Charles X. going to see the portrait of "the child of miracle."

> How tragical are men once more; how merciless withal to one another! I had not the least pity for Charles Dix's pious pilgriming to such an object; the poor mother of it, and her immense hopes and pains, I did not even think of them.

And so, the average criticism of that most tragical and pathetic monologue—in reality a soliloquy to which we have somehow been admitted—that prolonged and painful moan of remorse and desolation coming from a proud and intensely affectionate nature in its direst agony—a record which will be read with keen sympathy and interest when ninety-nine of a hundred of the best contemporary books have been abandoned to the moths—has been such as would have been appropriate for the flippant assault of some living penny-a-liner upon the celebrities of to-day. The critics have had an eye for nothing but the harshness and the gloom, and have read without a tear, without even a touch of sympathy, a confession more moving, more vividly reflecting the struggles and the anguish of a great man, than almost anything in our literature.

Enough of this: though in speaking of Carlyle at this time it is impossible to pass it over in complete silence. I intend only to say something of Carlyle's teaching, which seems to be as much misunderstood by some critics as his character. It should require little impartiality or insight at the present day to do something like justice to a teacher who belonged essentially to a past generation. When Carlyle was still preaching upon questions of the day, my juvenile sympathies—such as they were—were always on the side of his opponents. But he and his opinions have passed into the domain of history, and we can, or at least we should, judge of them as calmly as we can of Burke and of Milton. In the year 1789, you might have sympathised with Mackintosh, or with Tom Paine, rather than with the great opponent of the Revolution; and you may even now hold that they were more in the right as to the immediate issues than Burke. But it would, indeed, be a narrow mind which could not now perceive that Burke, as a philosophic writer upon politics, towers like a giant amidst pigmies above the highest of his contemporaries; and that the value of his principles is scarcely affected by the particular application. Though Carlyle touched upon more recent events, we can already make the same distinction, and we must make it if we would judge fairly in his case.

The most obvious of all remarks about Carlyle is one expressed (I think) by Sir Henry Taylor in the phrase that he was "a Calvinist who had lost his creed." Rather we should say he was a Calvinist who had dropped the dogmas out of his creed. It is no doubt a serious question what remains of a creed when thus eviscerated; or, again, how long it is likely to survive such an operation. But for the present purpose it is enough to say that what remained for Carlyle was the characteristic temper of mind and the whole mode of regarding the universe. He often declared that the Hebrew Scriptures, though he did not adhere to the orthodox view of their authority, contained the most tenable theory of the world ever propounded to mankind. Without seeking to define what was the element which he had preserved, and what it was that he had abandoned, or attempting the perilous task of drawing a line between the essence and accidents of a creed, it is in any case clear that Carlyle was as Scottish in faith as in character; that he would have taken and imposed the Covenant with the most thoroughgoing and *exanimo* assent and consent; and that the difference between him and his forefathers was one rather of particular beliefs than of essential sentiment. He had changed rather the data upon which his convictions were based than the convictions themselves. He revered what his fathers revered, but he revered the same principle in other manifestations, and to them this would naturally appear as a profanation, whilst from his point of view it was but a legitimate extension of their fundamental beliefs.

The more one reads Carlyle the further one traces the consequences of this belief. The Puritan creed, one may say, is not popular at the present day for reasons which might easily be assigned; and those who dislike it in any form are not conciliated by the omission of its external peculiarities. And, on the other hand, the omission naturally alienates many who would otherwise sympathise. When Carlyle speaks of "the Eternities" and "the Silences," he is really using a convenient periphrasis for thoughts more naturally expressed by most people in the language peculiar to Cromwell—the translation is often given side by side with the original in the comments upon Cromwell's letters and speeches—and his mode of speech is dictated by the feeling that the old dogmatic forms are too narrow and too much associated with scholastic pedantry to be appropriate in presence of such awful mysteries. He is, as Teufelsdröckh would have said, dropping the old clothes of belief only that he may more fittingly express the living reality.

To Carlyle, for example, the later developments of Irvingism, the speaking with tongues, and so forth, appeared as simply contemptible, or, when sanctioned by the friend whose memory he cherished so pathetically, as inexpressibly pitiable. It was a hopeless attempt to cling to the worn-out rags, a dropping of the substance to grasp the shadow; ending, therefore, in a mere grotesque caricature of belief which made genuine belief all the more difficult of attainment. You are seeking for outward signs and wonders when you should be impressed by the profound and all-pervading mysteries of the universe; and therefore falling into the hands of mere charlatans, and taking the morbid hysterics of over-excited women for the revelation conveyed by all nature to those who have ears to hear. Has not the word "spiritual," till now expressive of the highest emotions possible to human beings, got itself somehow stained and debased by association with the loathsome tricks practised by impostors aided by the prurient curiosity of their dupes? The perversion of the highest instincts which leads a man in his very anxiety to find a true prophet and spiritual leader to put up with some miserable Cagliostro—a quack working "miracles" by sleight of hand and phosphorus—appeared to Carlyle, and surely appeared to him most rightly, as the saddest of all conceivable aberrations of human nature; saddest because some men with a higher strain of character are amenable to such influences. But when Carlyle came to specify what was and what was not quackery of this kind, and included much that was still sacred to others, he naturally had to part company with many who would otherwise have sympathised. Miss Martineau, he tells us, was described as not only stripping herself naked, but stripping to the bone. Carlyle seems to some people to be performing this last operation, though to himself it appeared in the opposite light.

To Carlyle himself the liberation from the old clothes or external casing of belief constituted what he regarded as equivalent to the conversion of the "old Christian people." He emerged, he tells us, into a higher atmosphere, and gained a "constant inward happiness that was quite royal and supreme, in which all temporal evil was transient and insignificant:" a happiness, he adds, which he never quite lost, though in later years it suffered more frequent eclipse. For this he held himself to be "endlessly indebted" to Goethe; for Goethe had in his own fashion trod the same path and achieved the same victory. Conversion, as meaning the conscious abandonment of beliefs which have once formed an integral and important part of a man's life, is a process which indeed must be very exceptional with all men of real force of character. Carlyle, it is plain, was so far from undergoing such a process, that he retained much which would have been little in harmony with the teaching of his master. For, whilst everybody can see that Goethe reached a region of philosophic serenity, we must take Carlyle's "royal and supreme happiness" a little on trust. If his earlier writings have some gleams of the happier mood, we are certainly much more frequently in the region of murky gloom, shrouded by the Tartarean and "fuliginous" vapours of the lower earth. If his studies of Goethe and German literature opened a door of escape from the narrow prejudices which made the air of Edinburgh oppressive to him, they certainly did not help him to shake off the old Puritan sentiments which were bred in the bone, and no mere external trapping.

Critics have spoken as though Carlyle had become a disciple of some school of German metaphysics. It is, doubtless, true enough that he valued the great German thinkers as representing to his mind a victorious reaction against the scepticism of Hume, or the materialism of Hume's French successors. But he sympathised with the general tendency without caring to bewilder himself in any of the elaborate systems evolved by Kant or his followers. The reader, he says in the earlier essay on Novalis,

> would err widely who supposed that this transcendental system of metaphysics was a mere intellectual card-castle, or logical hocus-pocus . . . without any bearing on the practical interests of men. On the contrary . . . it is the most serious in its purport of all philosophies propounded in these latter ages;

and he proceeds to indicate their purport, and to hint, as one writing for uncongenial readers, his respect for German "mysticism." He thought, that is, that these mystics, transcendentalists, and so forth, were vindicating faith against scepticism, idealism against materialism, a belief in the divine order against atheistic negations; and, moreover, that their fundamental creed was inexpugnable, resting on a basis of solid reason instead of outworn dogma. As for the superstructure, the systems of this or that wonderful professor to explain the universe in general, he probably held them to be "card-castles"—mere cobwebs of the brain—at best arid, tentative gropings in the right direction. He had far too much of true Scotish shrewdness—even in the higher regions of thought—to trust body or soul to the truth of such flimsy materials. This comes out in his view of Coleridge, who so far sympathised with him as to have imbibed consolation from the same sources. No reader of the life of Sterling can forget the chapter—one of the most vivid portraits ever drawn even by Carlyle—devoted to Coleridge as the oracle of the "innumerable brave souls" still engaged in the London turmoil—a portrait which suggests incidentally how much was left unspoken in the hastier touches of the *Reminiscences*. We can see the oracle not answering your questions, nor decidedly setting out towards an answer, but accumulating

> formidable apparatus, logical swim-bladders, transcendental life-preservers, and other precautionary and vehiculatory gear for setting out; ending by losing himself in the morass and in the mazes of theosophic philosophy,

where now and then "glorious islets" would rise out of the haze, only to be lost again in the surrounding gloom. In his talk, as in him, "a ray of heavenly inspiration struggled in a tragically ineffectual degree against the weakness of flesh and blood." He had "skirted the deserts of infidelity," but "had not had the courage, in defiance of pain and terror, to press resolutely across such deserts to the new firm lands of faith beyond." Many disciples have of course seen more in Coleridge; but even his warmest admirers must admit the general truth of the picture, and confess that if Coleridge cast

a leaven of much virtue into modern English speculation, he never succeeded in working out a downright answer to the philosophical perplexities of his day, or in promulgating a distinct rule of faith or life. To Carlyle this was enough to condemn Coleridge as a teacher. Coleridge, in his view, failed because he adhered to the "old clothes;" tried desperately to breathe life into dead creeds; and, encumbered with such burdens, could not make the effort necessary to cross the "desert." He lingered fatally round the starting-point, and succeeded only in starting "strange spectral Puseyisms, monstrous illusory hybrids, and ecclesiastical chimeras which now roam the earth in a very lamentable manner."

The judgment is in many ways characteristic of Carlyle. To the genuine Puritan a creed is nothing which does not immediately embody itself in a war-cry. It must have a direct forcible application to life. It must divide light from darkness, distinguish friends from enemies,—both external and internal,—nerve your arms for the battle, and plant your feet on solid standing-ground. It must be no flickering ray in the midst of gloom, but a steady, unquenchable light—a permanent "star to every wandering bark." Coleridge would stimulate only to uncertain musings, instead of animating to strenuous endeavour. The same sentiment utters itself in Carlyle's favourite exaltation of silence above speech—a phrase paradoxical if literally taken, but in substance an emphatic assertion of the futility of the uncertain meanderings in the regions of abstract speculation which hinder a man from girding himself at once to deadly wrestle with the powers of darkness.

This is but a new version of the Puritan contempt for the vain speculations of human wisdom when he is himself conscious of an inner light guiding him infallibly through the labyrinths of the world. The Puritan contempt for æsthetic enjoyments springs from the same root, and is equally characteristic of Carlyle. He can never see much difference between fiction and lying.

> Fiction [he says] or idle falsity of any kind was never tolerable, except in a world which did itself abound in practical lies and solid shams. . . . A serious soul, can it wish, even in hours of relaxation, that you should fiddle empty nonsense to it? A serious soul would desire to be entertained either with silence or with what was truth, and had fruit in it, and was made by the Maker of us all,—

a doctrine which will clearly not commend itself to an æsthetic world. "Poetry, fiction in general, he [Carlyle the father] had universally seen treated as not only idle, but false and criminal," and the son adhered to the opinion except so far as he came to admit that fiction might in a sense be true. The ground-feeling is still that of some old Puritan, preaching, like Baxter, as "a dying man to dying men," and at most tolerant of anything not directly tending to edification. Carlyle, of course, belonged emphatically to the imaginative as distinguished from the speculative order of minds. He was a man of intuitions, not of discursive thought: who felt before he reasoned: to whom it was a mental necessity that a principle should clothe itself in concrete flesh and blood, and if possible in some definite historical hero, before he could fully believe in it. He wanted vivid images in place of abstract formulas. His indifference to the metaphysical was not simply that of the practical man who regards all such inquiries as leading to hopeless and bottomless quagmires of doubt and a paralysis of all active will; as an attempt, doomed to failure from the beginning, to get off your own shadow, and to twist and twirl till your pigtail hangs before you; though this, too, counts for much in his teaching; but it was also the antipathy of the imaginative mind to the passionless analyser who "explains" the living organism by reducing it to a dead mechanism. It is, indeed, remarkable that Carlyle had a certain comparative respect even for the materialist and utilitarian whom he so harshly denounced. Such a man was at least better than the ineffectual dilettante or dealer in small shams and phantasms. Anything thoroughgoing, even a thoroughgoing rejection of the highest elements of life, so far deserved respect as at least affording some firm starting-point. But, for the most part, the scientific frame of mind, so far as it implies a tranquil dissecting of concrete phenomena into their dead elements, jarred upon every fibre of his nature. Political economy, which treats society as a complex piece of machinery, and the logic which resolves the universe itself into a mere heap of separable atoms, seemed to him hopelessly barren, and uninteresting to the higher mind. Mill's talk and books—which specially represented this mode of thought for him—were "sawdustish;" for what is sawdust but the dead product of a living growth deprived of its organising principle and reduced to mere dry, indigestible powder? To the poetic as to the religious nature of Carlyle, such a process was to make the whole world weary, stale, flat, and unprofitable. Carlyle, therefore, must be judged as a poet, and not as a dealer in philosophic systems; as a seer or a prophet, not as a theorist or a man of calculations. And, therefore, if I were attempting any criticism of his literary merits, I should dwell upon his surpassing power in his peculiar province. Admitting that every line he wrote has the stamp of his idiosyncrasies, and consequently requires a certain congeniality of temperament in the reader, I should try to describe the strange spell which it exercises over the initiated. If you really hate the grotesque, the gloomy, the exaggerated, you are of course disqualified from enjoying Carlyle. You must take leave of what ordinarily passes even for common-sense, of all academical canons of taste, and of any weak regard for symmetry or simplicity, before you enter the charmed circle. But if you can get rid of your prejudices for the nonce, you will certainly be rewarded by seeing visions such as are evoked by no other magician. The common-sense reappears in the new shape of strange, vivid flashes of humour and insight casting undisputed gleams of light into many dark places; and dashing off graphic portraits with a single touch. And if you miss the serene atmosphere of calmer forms of art, it is something to feel at times, as no one but Carlyle can make you feel, that each instant is the "conflux of two eternities;" that our little lives, in his favourite Shakespearean phrase, are "rounded with sleep;" that history is like the short space lighted up by a flickering taper in the midst of infinite glooms and mysteries, and its greatest events brief scenes in a vast drama of conflicting forces, where the actors are passing in rapid succession—rising from and vanishing into the all-embracing darkness. And if there is something oppressive to the imagination when we stay long in this singular region, over which the same inspiration seems to be brooding which created the old Northern mythology with its grim gigantesque, semi-humorous figures, we are rewarded by the vividness of the pictures standing out against the surrounding emptiness; some little groups of human figures, who lived and moved like us in the long-past days; or of vignettes of scenery, like the Alpine sunrise in the *Sartor Resartus*, or the sight of sleeping Haddington from the high moorland in the *Reminiscences*, as bright and vivid for us as our own memories, and revealing unsuspected sensibilities in the writer. Though he scorned the word-painters and description-mongers, no one was a better landscape painter. It is perhaps idle to dwell upon characteristics which one either feels or cannot be persuaded into feeling. Those to whom he is on the whole repugnant may

admit him to be occasionally a master of the picturesque; and sometimes endeavour to put him out of court on the strength of this formula. A mere dealer, many exclaim, in oddities and grotesques, who will sacrifice anything to produce a startling effect, whose portraits are caricatures, whose style is torn to pieces by excessive straining after emphasis, and who systematically banishes all those half-tones which are necessary to faithful portraiture in the search after incessant contrasts of light and shade.

Let us first remark in regard to this that Carlyle himself peremptorily and emphatically denied that the distinction here assumed between the poet and the philosopher could be more than superficial. The philosopher only reaches his goal so far as his analysis leads to a synthesis, or as his abstract speculations can be embodied in definite concrete vision. And the poet is a mere idler, with no substantial or permanent value in him, unless he is uttering thoughts equally susceptible of philosophical exposition.

> The hero [he says] can be poet, prophet, king, priest, or what you will, according to the kind of world he finds himself born into. I confess I have no notion of a truly great man that could not be all sorts of men. The poet who could merely sit on a chair and compose stanzas could never make a stanza worth much. He could not sing the heroic warrior, unless he himself were an heroic warrior too.

To this doctrine—though with various logical distinctions and qualifications which seem incongruous with Carlyle's vehement dogmatic utterances—I, for one, would willingly subscribe; and I hold further that in strenuously asserting and enforcing it Carlyle was really laying down the fundamental doctrine of all sound criticism, whether of art or literature or life. Any teaching, that is, which attempts to separate the poet from the man as though his excellence were to be measured by a radically different set of tests is, to my mind, either erroneous or trifling and superficial. The point at which one is inclined to part company with this teaching is different. I do not condemn Carlyle for judging the poet as he judges the hero, for the substantial worth of the man whom it reveals to us; but I admit that his ideal man has a certain stamp of Puritanical narrowness. So, for example, there is something characteristic in his judgments not only of Coleridge, but of Lamb or Scott. He judges Lamb as the spoilt child of Cockney circles, as the Baptist in his garment of camel's hair might have judged some favourite courtier cracking jokes for the amusement of Herodias's daughter. And of Scott, though he strives to do justice to the pride of all Scotchmen, and admits Scott's merit in breathing life into the past, his real judgment is based upon the maxim that literature must have higher aims "than that of harmlessly amusing indolent languid men." Scott was not one who had gone through spiritual convulsions, who had "dwelt and wrestled amid dark pains and throes," but on the whole a prosperous easy-going gentleman, who found out the art of "writing impromptu novels to buy farms with;" and who can therefore by no means claim the entire devotion of the rigorous ascetic prophet to whom happiness is inconceivable except as the reward of victorious conflicts with the deadly enemies of the soul. To me it seems that the error in such judgments is one of omission; but the omission is certainly considerable. For Carlyle's tacit assumption seems to be that the conscience should be not only the supreme but the single faculty of the soul; that morality is not only a necessary, but the sole, condition of all excellence; and, therefore, that an ethical judgment is not merely implied in every æsthetic judgment, but is the sole essence and meaning of it. Our minds, according to some of his Puritan teachers, should be so exclusively set upon working out our salvation that every kind of aim not consciously directed to this ultimate end is a trifling which is closely akin to actual sin. Carlyle, accepting or unconsciously imbibing the spirit of such teaching, reserves his whole reverence for rigid and lofty natures, deserving beyond all question of reverence, but wanting in elements essential to the full development of our natures, and therefore, in the long run, to a broad morality.

This leads us to his most emphatically asserted doctrines. No one could assert more forcibly, emphatically, and frequently than Carlyle that morality or justice is the one indispensable thing; that justice means the law of God; that the sole test of the merits of any human law is its conformity to the divine law; and that, as he puts it, all history is an

> inarticulate Bible, and in a dim, intricate manner reveals the divine appearances in this lower world. For God did make this world, and does for ever govern it; the loud roaring loom of time, with all its French revolutions, Jewish revelations, "weaves the vesture thou seest Him by." There is no biography of a man, much less any history or biography of a nation, but wraps in it a message out of heaven, addressed to the hearing ear and the not-hearing.

It is needless to quote particular passages. This clearly is the special doctrine of Carlyle, embodied in all his works; preached in season and (often enough) out of season; which possesses him rather than is possessed by him; the sum and substance of the message which he had to deliver to the world, and spent his life and energy in delivering with emphasis. And yet we are constantly told that Carlyle was a cynic who believed in nothing but brute force. If such a criticism came only from those who had been repelled by his style from reading his books,—or again, only from the shallow and Pharisaical, who mistake any attack upon the arrangements to which they owe their comfort for an attack upon the eternal laws of the universe,—it might be dismissed with contempt. And this is, indeed, all that much of the average talk about Carlyle deserves. But there is a more solid ground in the objection, which brings us in face of Carlyle's most disputable teaching, and is worth considering.

We have, in fact, to consider the principle so often ascribed to him that Might makes Right; and this may be interpreted into the immoral doctrine that force is the one thing admirable, and success the sole test of merit. Cromwell was right because he cut off Charles's head, and Charles wrong because he lost his head. Frederick's political immorality is condoned because Frederick succeeded in making Prussia great; Napoleon was right so long as he was victorious, and was condemned because he ended in St. Helena. That, as some critics suppose, was Carlyle's meaning, and they very naturally denounce it as an offensive and cynical theory.

Now in one sense Carlyle's doctrine is the very reverse of this. His theory is the opposite one, that Right makes Might. He admires Cromwell, for example, and Cromwell is the hero after his own heart, expressly on the ground that Cromwell is the perfect embodiment of the Puritan principle, and that the essence of Puritanism was to

> see God's own law made good in this world. . . . Eternal justice; that God's will be done on earth as it is in heaven; corollaries enough will flow from that, if that be there: if that be not there, no corollary good for much will flow.

How does a doctrine apparently, at least, implying an unqualified belief in the absolute supremacy of right, a conviction that nothing but the rule of right can give a satisfactory basis for any human arrangement, get itself transmuted into an appearance of the opposite, of being a kind of Hobbism, deducing all morality from sheer force? Such transmutations, or apparent meetings of opposite extremes, are not uncommon, and the process might perhaps be most forcibly illustrated by a history of the old Puritans themselves. But it will be quite enough for my purpose to indicate, as briefly as may be, Carlyle's own method, which is of course guided as well by his temper as by his primary assumptions. He is predisposed in every way to take the sternest view of morality. He means by virtue, by no means an indiscriminate extension of all-comprehending benevolence, of goodwill to rogues and scoundrels, or amiable desire that everybody should have as pleasant a time of it as possible. Justice, according to him, and the most stringent and unflinching justice, is the essential basis of all morality. Love, doubtless, is the fulfilling of the law; but along with that truth you must also recognise the awful and mysterious truth, that hell itself is one product of the divine love. Love itself implies the destruction of evil and of the evil-doers. From this assumption it is not surprising if much modern philanthropy appeared to him as mere sentimentalism, a weak sympathy even for the suffering which is the divinely appointed remedy for social diseases, the mere effeminate shrinking from the surgical knife. The cardinal virtue from which all others might be inferred is not benevolence, but veracity, respect for facts and hatred of shams. This was not with Carlyle, as with some of his teachers, an abstract theorem of metaphysics, but the expression of his whole character, of that Puritanic fervour which tested all doctrine by its immediate practical influence upon the will, and which forced even his poetical imagination to spend itself not in creating images, but in realising as vividly as possible the actual facts of history.

Carlyle's application of these principles brings out a remarkable result.

> Puritanism [he says] was a genuine thing, for Nature has adopted it, and it has grown and grows. I say sometimes, that everything goes by wager of battle in this world; that *strength*, well understood, is the measure of all worth. Give a thing time; if it can succeed it is a right thing.

This is one form of Carlyle's essential principle, and is it not also the essential principle of Mr. Darwin's famous theory? It is an explicit assertion of the doctrine of the struggle for existence, though applied here to Knox and the Puritans instead of to the origin of species. And yet, as we may note in passing, the evolutionists are, as a fact, the most ready to condemn Carlyle's immorality, whilst Carlyle could never find words adequate to express his contempt for them. In that thorough carrying out of this principle, Carlyle is approaching that profound problem which in one shape or other haunts all philosophies: What kind of victory may we expect for right in this world? If Might and Right were strictly identical, it would seem here that we might start indifferently from either basis. "This succeeds; therefore it is right," would be as tenable an argument as—"This is right; therefore it will succeed." Yet one doctrine has an edifying sound, and the other seems to be the very reverse of edifying. Moralists vie with each other in proclaiming their belief in the ultimate success of good causes, and yet indignantly deny that the goodness of a cause should be inferred from its success. We agree to applaud the prophecy, cited with applause by Carlyle himself, that Napoleon's empire would fail because founded upon injustice; but we are startled by an inference from the failure to the injustice. But why should there be so vast a difference in what seem to be equivalent modes of reasoning? Carlyle's answer would follow from the words just cited. You must, he says, "give a thing time." Nobody can deny the temporary prosperity of the wicked, and certainly Carlyle could not deny that injustice may flourish long before it produces the inevitable crash. "The mills of God grind slowly, though they grind exceeding small." And, therefore, it may make all the difference whether we make the success the premiss or the conclusion. For though, in the long run, the good causes may be trusted to succeed in time, and we may see in history the proof that they have succeeded, yet at any moment the test of success may be precarious whilst that of justice is infallible. We may distinguish the wheat from the tares before the reaper has cast one aside and preserved the other. At the moment the injustice of Napoleon's empire was manifest, though the cracks and fissures which were to cause its crumbling were still hidden from any observer.

By what signs, then, other than the ultimate test of success, can we discern the just from the unjust? That, of course, is the vital point which must decide upon the character of Carlyle's morality; and it is one which, in my opinion, he cannot be said to have answered distinctly. He gives, indeed, a test satisfactory to himself, and he enforces and applies it with superabundant energy and variety of phrase. That is right, one may say briefly, which will "work." The sham is hollow, and must be crushed in the tug and wrestle of the warring world. The reality survives and gathers strength. Veracity in equivalent phrase is the condition of vitality. Truth endures; the lie perishes. But in applying this or his vast vocabulary of similar phrases, we come to a difficulty. "The largest veracity ever *done* in Parliament" was, he says, Sir Robert Peel's abolition of the Corn Laws. But how can you *do* veracity? What is a lie?—a question, as he observes, worth asking by the "practical English mind;" and to which he accordingly proceeds to give an answer. He insists, that is, very eloquently and vehemently, upon the inevitable results of all lying, and of all legislative and other action which proceeds upon the assumption of a falsity or an error which passes itself off for a truth. In all which I, for one, admit that there is not only truth, but truth nobly expressed and applied to the confutation of some most pestilent errors; and yet, as one must also admit, there is still an ambiguity. May it not, in fact, cover that exaltation of mere success which is so often objected to in him? Some tyrannical institution—slavery, for example—lives and flourishes through long ages. Is it thereby justified? Is it not a fact, and if fact and truth are the same things, is it not a truth sanctioned by the eternal veracities and so forth, and therefore entitled to our respect? This is one more form of that fundamental problem which really perplexes Carlyle's moral teaching, and which he has at least the merit of bringing into prominence, though not of answering. In fact, we may recognise in it an ancient philosophical controversy not yet set at rest; for, since the beginning of ethical theorising, thinkers of various schools have tried in one way or other to deduce virtue from truth, and to identify all vice with error. But the reference is enough to show the difference of Carlyle's method. He might respect the metaphysician who held a doctrine so far analogous to his own; but the metaphysical method appeared to him as a mere formal logic-chopping, where the essence of the teaching escaped amidst barren demonstrations of verbal identities.

The real answer is here again a new version of the old Puritan answer. The Puritan fell back upon the will of God revealed through the Bible, whose authority was manifest by the inner light. If the wicked were allowed to triumph for a time, there was no danger of being misled by their success, for they were condemned in advance by the plain fact of their renunciation of the inspired guide. For Carlyle, the "hero" takes the place of, or rather is put side by side with, the older organs of inspiration. Every hero conveys in fact a new revelation to mankind; he conveys a divine message, not, it is true, with infallible precision, or without an admixture of human error, but still the very kernel and essence of his teaching. He may come as prophet, king, poet, philosopher, and you may reject or accept his message at your peril. You may recognise it, as the Puritan recognised the authority of his Bible, by the spontaneous witness of your higher nature, and you will recognise it so long as you have not given yourself up to believe a lie. And if you demand some external proofs, you must be referred, not to some particular signs and wonders, but to what you may, if you please, call the "success" of the message; the fact, that is, that the hero has contributed some permanent element to the thoughts and lives of mankind, that he has revealed some enduring truth, created some permanent symbol of our highest feelings, or wrought some organic change in the very structure of society. There is a danger undoubtedly of confounding some temporary crystal palace or dazzling edifice of mere glass with an edifice founded on the rock and solid as the pyramids. The hero may be confounded with the sham, as, unfortunately, shams and realities are most frequently confounded in this world. But they differ for all that, and the true man recognises the difference as the religious man knows the hypocrite from the saint. The test is indifferently the truth or the soundness of the work; they must coincide; but the test can only be applied by one who really loves the truth.

It is easy to point out the dangers of this position. It rests, after all you may say, upon the individual conviction, and lends itself too easily to that kind of dogmatism in which Carlyle indulged so freely, and which consists in asserting that any doctrine or system which he dislikes is an incarnate lie, and pronouncing that it is therefore doomed to failure. And, on the other hand, it may be equally perverted in the opposite direction by claiming a sacred character for every "lie" not yet exploded. Carlyle, beyond all question, was a man of intense prejudices, and the claim to inspiration, even to the inspiration of our teachers, very easily passes into a deification of our own prejudices. No one was more liable to that error; but it is better worth our while to look at some other aspect of his teaching.

For we may surely accept without hesitation one application of the doctrine which is of the first importance with Carlyle, and which he has taught so incessantly and impressively that to him more than to any other man may be attributed the general recognition of its truth. The success of any system of thought—the permanent influence, that is, of any great man or of any great institution—must be due to the truth which it contains, or to its real value to mankind. This doctrine has become so much of a commonplace, and harmonises so fully with all modern historical methods, that we are apt to overlook the service done by Carlyle in its explicit assertion and rigorous application to facts. When he was delivering his lectures upon hero-worship, intelligent people were still in the attitude of mind represented, for example, by Gibbon's famous explanation of the success of Christianity, as due, amongst other things, to the zeal of the early believers, as if the zeal required no explanation; when, on the other side, it was thought proper to explain Mahometanism, not by the admixture of genuine truth which it contained, but as a simple imposture. Carlyle still speaks like a man advancing a disputed theory when he urges in this latter case that to explain the power of Mahomet's sword, you must explain the force which wielded the sword; and that the ingenious hypothesis of a downright cheat will by no means serve the turn. This doctrine is now generally accepted, unless by a few clever people who still cherish the wire-pulling heresy which makes history a puppet-show manipulated by ingenious scoundrels, instead of a vast co-operation of organic forces. Carlyle, however, has done more than any writer to make such barren and degrading explanations impossible for all serious thinkers. His *Cromwell* has at least exploded once for all the simple-minded "hypocrisy" theory, as the essay upon Johnson destroyed the ingenious doctrine that a man could write a good book simply because he was a fool. Whether his portraits are accurate or not, they are at least set before us as conceivable and consistent human beings. The prosaic historian and biographer takes the average verdict of commonplace observers: if he is a partisan, he is content with the contemporary caricatures of the party to which he belongs; if he wishes to be impartial, he strikes a rough average between opposite errors; and if he wishes to be dazzling, he calmly combines incompatible judgments. Macaulay's works, with all their merits, are a perfect gallery of such portraits—rhetorically excellent, but hopelessly flimsy in substance: of angelic Whigs and fiendish Tories, and of strange monsters like his Bacon and his Boswell, made by quietly heaping together meanness and wisdom, sense and folly, and inviting you to accept a string of paradoxes as a sober statement of fact. The truly imaginative writer has to go deeper than this. He begins where the rhetorician ends. A great work, as he instinctively sees, implies a great force. A man can only leave his mark upon history so far as he is animated, and therefore worthy to be animated, by a great idea. The secret of his nature is to be discovered by a sympathetic imagination acting by a kind of poetical induction. Gathering together all his recorded acts and utterances, the masses of recorded facts, preserved, often in hopeless confusion and misrepresentation, by his contemporaries, you must brood over them till at last you gain a clear vision of the underlying unity of character which manifests itself in these various ways. Then, at last, you may recognise the true hero, and discover unsuspected unity of purpose and strength of conviction, where the hasty judgments passed by contemporaries and those who set them upon isolated fragments of his career make a bewildering chaos of inconsistency. The process is admirably illustrated in the study of Cromwell, and the result has the merit of being at least a possible, if not a correct, theory of a great man.

This, again, is connected with another aspect of Carlyle's teaching—as valuable, though perhaps its value is not even now as generally recognised. For the tendency of his mind is always to substitute what is sometimes called the dynamical for the merely mechanical view of history. It is a necessity for his imagination to penetrate to the centre instead of remaining at the circumference; to unveil the actual forces which govern the working of the superficial phenomena, instead of losing himself in the external phenomena themselves. The true condition for understanding history is to gain a clear perception of the genuine beliefs, the wants, and passions which actually sway men's souls, instead of working simply at the complicated wheels and pulleys of the political machinery, or accepting the masses of idle verbiage which conceal our true thoughts from ourselves and from each other. An implicit faith in the potency of the machinery, and an equal neglect of the real driving force, was, in his view, the original sin of political theory. The constitution-mongers of the Delolme or Siéyès type, the men who fancied that government (as one of them said) was like "a

dance where everything depended on the disposition of the figures," and nothing, therefore, on the nature of the dancers, have pretty well passed away. Carlyle saw the same vital fallacies in such nostrums as the ballot or the scheme so enthusiastically advocated by Hare and Mill.

> If of ten men nine are recognisable as fools, which is a common calculation, how in the name of wonder will you get a ballot-box to grind you out a wisdom from the votes of those ten men? Never by any conceivable ballot-box, nor by all the machinery in Bromwicham or out of it, will you attain such a result.

Whether Carlyle was right or wrong in the particular application I do not presume to say. Such a change as the ballot may perhaps imply more than a mere change of machinery. But I certainly cannot doubt that he is right in the essence of his contention: that a perception of the difference between the merely mechanical details and the vital forces of a society is essential to any sound political theorising; and that half our pet schemes of reform fail just from this cause, that they expect to change the essence by modifying the surface, and are therefore equivalent to plans for obtaining mechanical results without expending energy.

To have asserted these principles so emphatically is one of Carlyle's greatest merits; and if he obtained emphasis at the cost of exaggeration, overstatement, grotesque straining of language and imagery, and much substantial error as to facts, I can only say that the service remains, and is inestimable. But there is a less pleasing qualification to be made. The objection to the ballot as a purely mechanical arrangement is combined, as we have just seen, with the objection founded upon the prevalence of fools. That stinging phrase, "mostly fools," has stuck in our throats. The prophet who tells us that we are wicked may be popular—perhaps, because our consciences are on his side; but the prophet who calls us fools is likely to provoke our wrath. I, at least, never met a man who relished that imputation, even if he admitted it to contain a grain of truth. But, palatable or not, it is clearly fundamental with Carlyle. The world is formed of "dull millions, who, as a dull flock, roll hither and thither, whithersoever they are led;" the great men are the "guides of the dull host, who follow them as by an irrevocable decree." They are the heroes to whom alone are granted real powers of vision and command; realities amongst shams, and knowers amongst vague feelers after knowledge. We need not ask how this theory was reached; whether it is the spontaneous sentiment of a proud and melancholy character, or really a fair estimate of the facts; or, again, a deduction from the "hero" doctrine. With that doctrine, at any rate, it naturally coincides. To exalt the stature of your hero, you must depress his fellows. If Gulliver is to be a giant, he must go to Lilliput. There is, however, a gap in the argument which is characteristically neglected by Carlyle. He would never have fairly accepted the doctrine—whose was it?—that, though a man may be wiser than anybody there is something wiser than he—namely, everybody. The omission is critical, and has many consequences. For one may fully admit Carlyle's estimate: one may hold the difference between a Shakespeare and an average contributor to the poet's corner of a newspaper, or between a born leader of men, a Cromwell and a Chatham, and the enormous majority of his followers, as something hardly expressible in words: one may admit that the history of thought or society reveals the more clearly, the more closely it is studied, the height to which the chosen few tower above the average; one may even diminish the percentage of the wise from a tenth to a hundredth or a thousandth and yet one may hold to the superior wisdom of the mass. No ballot-box, it is true, will make the folly of the nine equal to the wisdom of the one. Or it can tend that was only if the foolish majority have some sense of the need of superior guidance. But the ignorance and folly of mankind, their incapacity for forming any trustworthy judgment on any given point, may also be consistent with a capacity for groping after truth, and they have the advantage of trying experiments on a large scale. The fact that a creed commends itself to the instincts of many men in many ages is a better proof—Carlyle himself being the judge—that it contains some truth than the isolated judgment of the most clearsighted philosopher. The fact that an institution actually makes men happy and calls forth their loyalty is a more forcible argument in its favour than the opinion of the most experienced statesman. And, therefore, the fact that any society is chiefly made up of fools is quite consistent with the belief that it is collectively the organ through which truth gradually manifests itself and wins a wider recognition. *Securus judicat orbis* may be a true maxim if we interpret it to mean that the world decides—not as the experimenter but as the experiment. Carlyle systematically overlooks this blind, semi-conscious process of co-operation upon which the "hero" is really as dependent as the dull flock which he leads. History, as he is fond of saying, is the essence of innumerable biographies. To find the essence of the biographies, again, he goes to the essential biographies; that is, to the biographies of the men who give the impulse, not of those who passively submit to the impulse. This apotheosis of the individual is dictated by his imaginative idiosyncrasy, as much as by his theory of history. He must have the picturesque concrete fact; the living hero to be the incarnation of the idea; and, accordingly, history in his page is like a gigantic panorama in which the painter sacrifices everything to obtain the strongest contrasts, and makes his lights stand out against vast breadths of unspeakable gloom. The hero is thus made to sum up the whole effectual force, and all that is done by the Greeks is attributed to the arm of Achilles. Some awkward results follow. Frederick is a hero who has obvious moral defects, and readers are startled by Carlyle's worship of such an idol. Yet it follows from the assumptions. For Frederick, in Carlyle's theory, means the development of the German nation. That the growth of the German influence in Europe was a phenomenon which naturally and rightfully excited Carlyle's strongest enthusiasm requires no demonstration. If the credit of that, as of every other great achievement, must be given to some solitary hero, Frederick doubtless has the best claim to the honour. We may no doubt say that Frederick, in spite of this, was selfish and cynical, and may confine our praises to allowing his possession of perspicacity enough to see the capabilities of his position. A great man may do an involuntary service to mankind, because his genius inclines him to range himself on the side of the strongest forces, and therefore of what we vaguely call progress. But the hero-worshipper naturally regards him as not merely an instrument, but the conscious and efficient cause of the progress itself.

Hence, too, the apparent immorality which some people discern in Carlyle's denunciations of "red tape" formulas, and the ordinary conventions of society. Undoubtedly, such fetters must snap like packthread when opposed to the deeper forces which govern the growth of nations. No set of engagements on paper will keep a nation on its legs if it is rotten at the core, or maintain a balance of power between forces which are daily growing unequal. It is idle to suppose that any contract can bind, or otherwise preserve, the vitality of effete institutions.

And hence arise a good many puzzling questions for political casuistry. It is hard to say at what precise point it becomes necessary to snap the bonds, and when the necessity of change makes revolution, with all its mischiefs, preferable to stagnation. The hero-worshipper who regards his idol as the supreme moving force has to make him also the infallible judge in such matter. He stands above—not the ultimate rules of morality, but—the whole system of regulations and compromises by which men must govern themselves in normal times—and decides when they must be suspended in the name of the higher law. The only appeal from his decision is the appeal to facts. If the apparent hero be really self-seeking and vulgarly ambitious, he and his empire will be crushed like Napoleon's. If, on the whole, his decision be right, as inspired from above, he will lay the foundations of a new order on an unshakable basis. And, therefore, Carlyle is naturally attracted to the revolutionary periods, when the underlying forces come to the surface; when the foundations of the great deep are broken up, all conventions summarily swept aside, and the direct as well as the ultimate attention is to the great principles of its social life. Therefore he sympathises with Mirabeau, who had "swallowed all formulas," and still more with Cromwell, whose purpose, in his view, was to make the laws of England a direct application of the laws of God. Puritan and Jacobin are equally impatient for the instantaneous advent of the millennium, and so far attract equally the man who shares their hatred of compromise and temporising with the world.

Here we come to the final problem. Cromwell's Parliament, he says, failed in their attempt to realise their "noble, and surely necessary, attempt. [Nay, they] could not but fail; [they had]"

> the sluggishness, the slavish half-and-halfness, the greediness, the cowardice, and general fatuity and falsity of some ten million men against it—alas! the whole world and what we call the Devil and all his angels against it!

This is the true revolutionary doctrine. The fact that a reform would only succeed fully if men were angels is with the ordinary Conservative a reason for not reforming at all; and with your genuine fanatic a reason not for declining the impracticable, but for denouncing the facts. We have, however, to ask how it fits in with any such theory of progress as was possible for Carlyle. For some such theory must be held by any one who makes the victory of truth and justice over shams and falsehoods a corner-stone of his system. It has been asked, in fact, whether there is not a gross inconsistency here. If Cromwell's success proved him to be a hero, did not the Restoration upset the proof? The answer, frequently and emphatically given by Carlyle, as in the lecture on the hero as king, is an obvious one. Cromwell represents an intermediate stage between Luther and the French Revolution. Luther told the Pope that he was a "chimera;" and the French gave the same piece of information to other "chimeras." The whole process is a revolt against certain gigantic shams, and the success very inadequately measured by any special incident in the struggle. The French Revolution, with all its horrors, was a "return to truth," though, as it were, to a truth "clad in hellfire:" and its advent should be hailed as "shipwrecked mariners might hail the sternest rock, in a world otherwise all of baseless seas and waves." And throughout this vast revolutionary process, our hope rests upon the "certainty of heroes being sent us;" and that certainty "shines like a polestar, through murk dustclouds, and all manner of down-rushing and conflagration."

It is well that we have a "certainty" of the coming hero; for the essay seems to show the weakness of all excessive reliance upon individuals. Cromwell's life, as he tells us emphatically, was the life of the Commonwealth, and Cromwell's life was at the mercy of a "stray bullet." Where then is a certainty of progress in a world thus dependent upon solitary heroes, in a wilderness of fools, liable to be snuffed out at a moment's notice? So far as certainty means a scientific conviction resting on the observation of facts, we, of course, cannot have it. It is a certainty which follows from our belief in the overruling Power which will send heroes when there is work for heroes to do. And Carlyle can at times, especially in his earlier writings, declare his faith in such a progress with full conviction.

> The English Whig [says Herr Teufelsdröckh] has, in the second generation, become an English Radical, who, in the third, it is to be hoped, will become an English rebuilder. Find mankind where thou wilt, thou findest it in living movement, in progress faster or slower; the phœnix soars aloft, hovers with outstretched wings, filling earth with her music; or, as now, she sinks, and with spheral swansong immolates herself in flame, that she may soar the higher and sing the clearer.

And the phrase, as I think, gives the theory which in fact is more or less explicitly contained in all Carlyle's writings.

It is plain, however, that progress, so understood, is a progress consistent with long periods of the reverse of progress. It implies an alternation of periods of reconstruction and vital energy with others of decay and degeneration. And in this I do not know that Carlyle differs from other philosophers. Few people are sanguine enough to hold that every generation improves upon the preceding. But the modern believer in progress undoubtedly believes that this actual generation is better than the last, and that the next will be better still; and is very apt to impute bad motives to any one who differs from him. Here, of course, he must come into flat opposition to Carlyle. For Carlyle, to put it briefly, regarded the present state of things as analogous to that the Lower Empire; a time of dissolution of old bonds and of a general ferment which was destroying the very tissues of society. So far he agrees, of course, with many Conservatives; but he differs from them in regarding the process as necessary, and even ultimately beneficial. The disease is one which must run its course; the best hope is that it may run it quickly; the attempt to suppress the symptoms and to regain health by making time run backwards is simply chimerical. Thus he was in the painful position of one who sees a destructive process going on of which he recognises the necessity whilst all the immediate results are bad.

To the ardent believer in progress such a state of mind is, of course, repulsive. It implies misanthropy, cynicism, and disbelief in mankind. Nor can anybody deny that Carlyle's gloomy and dyspeptic constitution palpably biassed his view of his contemporaries as well as of their theories. The "mostly fools" expresses a deeply rooted feeling, and we might add "mostly bores," and to a great extent humbugs. And this, of course, implies a very low estimate of the powers of unheroic mankind, and therefore of their rights. If most men are fools, their right to do as they please is a right to knock their heads against stone walls. Carlyle perhaps overlooked the fact that even that process may be useful training for fools. But even here he asserted a doctrine wrongly applied rather than false in principle. It shocks one to find an open advocacy of slavery for black Quashee. But we must admit, and admit for the reasons given by Carlyle, that even slavery may be better than sheer

anarchy and barbarism; that, historically speaking, the system of slavery represents a necessary stage in civilisation; and therefore that the simple abolition of slavery—a recognition of unconditional "right" without reference to the possession of the instincts necessary for higher kinds of society—might be disguised cruelty. The error was in the hasty assumption that his Quashee was, in fact, in this degraded state; and the haste to accept this disheartening belief was but too characteristic. That liberty might mean barbarism was true; that it actually did mean it in certain given cases was a rash assumption too much in harmony with his ordinary aversion to the theorists of his time.

This applies to all Carlyle's preachings about contemporary politics; the weakest of his writings are those in which his rash dogmatism, coloured by his gloomy temperament, was employed upon unfamiliar topics. But the pith and essence of them all is the intense conviction that the one critical point for modern statesmen is the creation of a healthy substratum to the social structure. That the lives of the great masses are squalid, miserable, and vicious, and must be elevated by the spread of honesty, justice, and the unflinching extirpation of corrupt elements, the substitution of rigorous rulers for idle professors of official pedantry, busy about everything but the essential—that is the sum and substance of the teaching. That he attributes too much to the legislative power, and has too little belief in the capacities of the average man, may be true enough. But this one thing must be said in conclusion. The bitterness, the gloom, even the apparent brutality, is a proof of the strength of his sympathies. He is savage with the physician because he is appalled at the virulence of the disease and the inadequacy of the remedy. He may shriek "quack" too hastily, and be too ready to give over the patient as desperate. And yet I am frequently struck by a contrast. I meet a good friend who holds up his hands at Carlyle's ferocity. We talk, and I find that he holds that in politics we are all going to sheer destruction or "shooting Niagara;" that the miserable Radicals are sapping all public spirit; that faith is being undermined by malcontents and atheists; that the merchant has become a gambler, and the tradesman a common cheat; that the "British workman" is a phrase which may be used with the certainty of provoking a sneer; and, briefly, that there is not a class in the country which is not on the highroad to decay, or an institution beyond the reach of corruption. And yet my friend sits quietly down and enjoys his dinner as heartily as if he were expecting the millennium. What shall I say? That he does not believe what he says, or that his digestive apparatus is in most enviable order? I know not; but certainly Carlyle was not capable of this. He took things too terribly in earnest. When workmen scamped the alterations in his house, or the railway puffed its smoke into his face, he saw visible symbols of modern degeneracy, and thought painfully of the old honest, wholesome life in Annandale—of steady, God-fearing farmers and self-respecting workmen. All that swept away by progress and "prosperity beyond example"! That was his reflection; perhaps it was very weak, as certainly it was very unpleasant, to worry himself about what he could not help, and sprang, let us say, all from a defective digestion. And yet, though I cannot think without pity of the man of genius who felt so keenly and thought so gloomily of the evils around us, I feel infinitely more respect for his frame of mind than for that of the man who, sharing, verbally at least, this opinion, can let it calmly lie in his mind without the least danger to his personal comfort.

G. K. CHESTERTON
"Thomas Carlyle" (1902)
Varied Types
1908, pp. 109–22

There are two main moral necessities for the work of a great man: the first is that he should believe in the truth of his message; the second is that he should believe in the acceptability of his message. It was the whole tragedy of Carlyle that he had the first and not the second.

The ordinary capital, however, which is made out of Carlyle's alleged gloom is a very paltry matter. Carlyle had his faults, both as a man and as a writer, but the attempt to explain his gospel in terms of his 'liver' is merely pitiful. If indigestion invariably resulted in a *Sartor Resartus*, it would be a vastly more tolerable thing than it is. Diseases do not turn into poems; even the decadent really writes with the healthy part of his organism. If Carlyle's private faults and literary virtues ran somewhat in the same line, he is only in the situation of every man; for every one of us it is surely very difficult to say precisely where our honest opinions end and our personal predilections begin. But to attempt to denounce Carlyle as a mere savage egotist cannot arise from anything but a pure inability to grasp Carlyle's gospel. 'Ruskin', says a critic, 'did, all the same, verily believe in God; Carlyle believed only in himself.' This is certainly a distinction between the author he has understood and the author he has not understood. Carlyle believed in himself, but he could not have believed in himself more than Ruskin did; they both believed in God, because they felt that if everything else fell into wrack and ruin, themselves were permanent witnesses to God. Where they both failed was not in belief in God or in belief in themselves; they failed in belief in other people. It is not enough for a prophet to believe in his message; he must believe in its acceptability. Christ, St Francis, Bunyan, Wesley, Mr Gladstone, Walt Whitman, men of indescribable variety, were all alike in a certain faculty of treating the average man as their equal, of trusting to his reason and good feeling without fear and without condescension. It was this simplicity of confidence not only in God, but in the image of God, that was lacking in Carlyle.

But the attempts to discredit Carlyle's religious sentiment must absolutely fall to the ground. The profound security of Carlyle's sense of the unity of the Cosmos is like that of a Hebrew prophet; and it has the same expression that it had in the Hebrew prophets—humour. A man must be very full of faith to jest about his divinity. No Neo-Pagan delicately suggesting a revival of Dionysius, no vague, half-converted Theosophist groping towards a recognition of Buddha, would every think of cracking jokes on the matter. But to the Hebrew prophets their religion was so solid a thing, like a mountain or a mammoth, that the irony of its contact with trivial and fleeting matters struck them like a blow. So it was with Carlyle. His supreme contribution, both to philosophy and literature, was his sense of the sarcasm of eternity. Other writers have seen the hope or the terror of the heavens, he alone saw the humour of them. Other writers had seen that there could be something elemental and eternal in a song or statue, he alone saw that there could be something elemental and eternal in a joke. No one who ever read it will forget the passage, full of dark and agnostic gratification, in which he narrates that some Court chronicler described Louis XV as 'falling asleep in the Lord'. 'Enough for us that he did fall asleep; that, curtained in thick night, under what keeping we ask not, he at least will never,

through unending ages, insult the face of the sun any more . . . and we go on, if not to better forms of beastliness, at least to fresher ones.'

The supreme value of Carlyle to English literature was that he was the founder of modern irrationalism; a movement fully as important as modern rationalism. A great deal is said in these days about the value or valuelessness of logic. In the main, indeed, logic is not a productive tool so much as a weapon of defence. A man building up an intellectual system has to build like Nehemiah, with a sword in one hand and the trowel in the other. The imagination, the constructive quality, is the trowel, and argument is the sword. A wide experience of actual intellectual affairs will lead most people to the conclusion that logic is mainly valuable as a weapon wherewith to exterminate logicians.

But though this may be true enough in practice, it scarcely clears up the position of logic in human affairs. Logic is a machine of the mind, and if it is used honestly it ought to bring out an honest conclusion. When people say that you can prove anything by logic, they are not using words in a fair sense. What they mean is that you can prove anything by bad logic. Deep in the mystic ingratitude of the soul of man there is an extraordinary tendency to use the name for an organ, when what is meant is the abuse or decay of that organ. Thus we speak of a man suffering from 'nerves', which is about as sensible as talking about a man suffering from ten fingers. We speak of 'liver' and 'digestion' when we mean the failure of liver and the absence of digestion. And in the same manner we speak of the dangers of logic, when what we really mean is the danger of fallacy.

But the real point about the limitation of logic and the partial overthrow of logic by writers like Carlyle is deeper and somewhat different. The fault of the great mass of logicians is not that they bring out a false result, or, in other words, are not logicians at all. Their fault is that by an inevitable psychological habit they tend to forget that there are two parts of a logical process—the first the choosing of an assumption, and the second the arguing upon it; and humanity, if it devotes itself too persistently to the study of sound reasoning, has a certain tendency to lose the faculty of sound assumption. It is astonishing how constantly one may hear from rational and even rationalistic persons such a phrase as 'He did not prove the very thing with which he started', or 'The whole of his case rested upon a pure assumption', two peculiarities which may be found by the curious in the works of Euclid. It is astonishing, again, how constantly one hears rationalists arguing upon some deep topic, apparently without troubling about the deep assumption involved, having lost their sense, as it were, of the real colour and character of a man's assumption. For instance, two men will argue about whether patriotism is a good thing and never discover until the end, if at all, that the cosmopolitan is basing his whole case upon the idea that man should, if he can, become as God with equal sympathies and no prejudices, while the rationalist denies any such duty at the very start, and regards man as an animal who has preferences, as a bird has feathers.

Thus it was with Carlyle: he startled men by attacking not arguments but assumptions. He simply brushed aside all the matter which the men of the nineteenth century held to be incontrovertible, and appealed directly to the very different class of matters which they knew to be true. He induced men to study less the truth of their reasoning and more the truth of the assumption upon which they reasoned. Even where his view was not the highest truth, it was always a refreshing and beneficent heresy. He denied every one of the postulates upon which the age of reason based itself. He denied the theory of progress which assumed that we must be better off than the people of the twelfth century. Whether we were better than the people of the twelfth century according to him depended entirely upon whether we chose or deserved to be.

He denied every type and species of prop or association or support which threw the responsibility upon civilization or society, or anything but the individual conscience. He has often been called a prophet. The real ground of the truth of this phrase is often neglected. Since the last era of purely religious literature, the era of English Puritanism, there has been no writer in whose eyes the soul stood so much alone.

Carlyle was, as we have suggested, a mystic, and mysticism was with him, as with all its genuine professors, only a transcendent form of common sense. Mysticism and common sense alike consist in a sense of the dominance of certain truths and tendencies which cannot be formally demonstrated or even formally named. Mysticism and common sense are alike appeals to realities that we all know to be real, but which have no place in argument except as postulates. Carlyle's work did consist in breaking through formulae, old and new, to these old and silent and ironical sanities. Philosophers might abolish kings a hundred times over, he maintained, they could not alter the fact that every man and woman does choose a king and repudiate all the pride of citizenship for the exultation of humility. If inequality of this kind was a weakness, it was a weakness bound up with the very strength of the universe. About hero worship, indeed, few critics have done the smallest justice to Carlyle. Misled by those hasty and choleric passages in which he sometimes expressed a preference for mere violence, passages which were a great deal more connected with his temperament than with his philosophy, they have finally imbibed the notion that Carlyle's theory of hero worship was a theory of terrified submission to stern and arrogant men. As a matter of fact, Carlyle is really inhumane about some questions, but he is never inhumane about hero worship. His view is not that human nature is so vulgar and silly a thing that it must be guided and driven; it is, on the contrary, that human nature is so chivalrous and fundamentally magnanimous a thing that even the meanest have it in them to love a leader more than themselves, and to prefer loyalty to rebellion. When he speaks of this trait in human nature Carlyle's tone invariably softens. We feel that for the moment he is kindled with admiration of mankind, and almost reaches the verge of Christianity. Whatever else was acid and captious about Carlyle's utterances, his hero worship was not only humane, it was almost optimistic. He admired great men primarily, and perhaps correctly, because he thought that they were more human than other men. The evil side of the influence of Carlyle and his religion of hero worship did not consist in the emotional worship of valour and success; that was a part of him, as, indeed, it is a part of all healthy children. Where Carlyle really did harm was in the fact that he, more than any modern man, is responsible for the increase of that modern habit of what is vulgarly called 'Going the whole hog'. Often in matters of passion and conquest it is a singularly hoggish hog. This remarkable modern craze for making one's philosophy, religion, politics, and temper all of a piece, to seeking in all incidents for opportunities to assert and reassert some favourite

mental attitude, is a thing which existed comparatively little in other centuries. Solomon and Horace, Petrarch and Shakespeare were pessimists when they were melancholy, and optimists when they were happy. But the optimist of today seems obliged to prove that gout and unrequited love make him dance with joy, and the pessimist of today to prove that sunshine and a good supper convulse him with inconsolable anguish. Carlyle was strongly possessed with this mania for spiritual consistency. He wished to take the same view of the wars of the angels and of the paltriest riot at Donnybrook Fair. It was this species of insane logic which led him into his chief errors, never his natural enthusiasms. Let us take an example. Carlyle's defence of slavery is a thoroughly ridiculous thing, weak alike in argument and in moral instinct. The truth is, that he only took it up from the passion for applying everywhere his paradoxical defence of aristocracy. He blundered, of course, because he did not see that slavery has nothing in the world to do with aristocracy, that it is, indeed, almost its opposite. The defence which Carlyle and all its thoughtful defenders have made for aristocracy was that a few persons could more rapidly and firmly decide public affairs in the interests of the people. But slavery is not even supposed to be a government for the good of the governed. It is a possession of the governed avowedly for the good of the governors. Aristocracy uses the strong for the service of the weak; slavery uses the weak for the service of the strong. It is no derogation to man as a spiritual being, as Carlyle firmly believed he was, that he should be ruled and guided for his own good like a child—for a child who is always ruled and guided we regard as the very type of spiritual existence. But it is a derogation and an absolute contradiction to that human spirituality in which Carlyle believed that a man should be owned like a tool for someone else's good, as if he has no personal destiny in the Cosmos. We draw attention to this particular error of Carlyle's because we think that it is a curious example of the waste and unclean places into which that remarkable animal 'the whole hog' more than once led him.

In this respect Carlyle has had an unquestionably long and an unquestionably bad influence. The whole of that recent political ethic which conceives that if we only go far enough we may finish a thing for once and all, that being strong consists chiefly in being deliberately deaf and blind, owes a great deal of its complete sway to his example. Out of him flows most of the philosophy of Nietzsche, who is in modern times the supreme maniac of this moonstruck consistency. Though Nietzsche and Carlyle were in reality profoundly different, Carlyle being a stiff-necked peasant and Nietzsche a very fragile aristocrat, they are alike in this one quality of which we speak, the strange and pitiful audacity with which they applied their single ethical test to everything in heaven and earth. The disciple of Nietzsche, indeed, embraces immorality like an austere and difficult faith. He urges himself to lust and cruelty with the same tremendous enthusiasm with which a Christian urges himself to purity and patience; he struggles as a monk struggles with bestial visions and temptations with the ancient necessities of honour and justice and compassion. To this madhouse, it can hardly be denied, has Carlyle's intellectual courage brought many at last.

RALPH WALDO EMERSON

RALPH WALDO EMERSON

1803–1882

Ralph Waldo Emerson was born in Boston on May 25, 1803; his father, a Unitarian minister, died in 1811, leaving the family in difficult financial circumstances. Emerson attended the Boston Public Latin School (1812–17) and Harvard College (1817–1821), and in 1825, after several years of teaching, entered the Harvard Divinity School. He received a degree in divinity in 1827 and became junior pastor of Boston's Second Church in 1829, the year in which he also married Helen Tucker. In 1831 Emerson's wife died, and in the following year Emerson resigned from the Second Church, feeling unable to believe in the sacrament of the Lord's Supper. During 1832–33 he traveled in Europe, and while in England met Coleridge, Wordsworth, and Carlyle.

After returning to the U.S., Emerson became active as a lecturer, and began to evolve the new quasi-religious concept of Transcendentalism, expressed in his essay *Nature* (1836). In 1837 he delivered his influential lecture "The American Scholar," in which he called on America to assert its intellectual independence; this was followed in 1838 by the "Divinity School Address," also delivered at Harvard, which forcefully argued the principal tenet of Transcendentalism, that knowledge of reality is derived from personal intuition and not from objective experience. Meanwhile, in 1835, Emerson had married Lydia Jackson, by whom he had four children between 1836 and 1844. Also in 1835 Emerson moved to Concord, where he formed, in 1838, a close friendship with his neighbor Henry David Thoreau.

In 1840 the *Dial* began publication; this was the literary organ of the so-called Transcendental Club, which had been meeting informally at Emerson's house and elsewhere since 1836. In the *Dial*, edited first by Margaret Fuller (1840–42) and then by Emerson himself (1842–44), Emerson published a number of poems, including "The Problem" and "Wood-Notes," and also the essays "Self-Reliance," "Compensation," and "The Over-Soul," gathered in *Essays* (1841). The second volume of *Essays*, containing "The Poet," appeared in 1844, after the *Dial* had ceased publication, and was followed in 1846 by a collection of *Poems*. Throughout 1845 Emerson delivered a series of lectures on Plato, Napoleon, Swedenborg, and others, collected in 1850 as *Representative Men*.

In 1847–48 Emerson traveled in Europe for a second time, visiting France and England. His experiences in England, where he was much admired, led him to publish his portrait of the English national character, *English Traits* (1856). From 1851 Emerson began to be actively involved in campaigning against slavery, and throughout the 1850s he also continued to publish poems and prose, notably in the *Atlantic*. In 1860 he published *The Conduct of Life*, followed by *May Day and Other Pieces* (1866) and *Society and Solitude* (1870). During 1872–73 Emerson traveled in Europe and the Near East, visiting France, Italy, Egypt, Greece, and the British Isles. The decade following his return from Europe was marked by a gradual loss of mental powers, but he nonetheless managed to publish a final volume, *Letters and Social Aims* (1875), written in collaboration with Ellen and James Eliot Cabot, and also had a hand in preparing the 1876 edition of his *Selected Poems*. Emerson died at his home in Concord on April 27, 1882. His *Letters* have been edited by Ralph J. Rush (6 vols., 1939), his *Journals* by William H. Gilman et al. (16 vols., 1960–82), and his *Collected Works* by Joseph Slater et al. (1971–   ).

Personal

Our third happiness was the arrival of a certain young unknown friend, named Emerson, from Boston, in the United States, who turned aside so far from his British, French, and Italian travels to see me here! He had an introduction from Mill, and a Frenchman (Baron d'Eichthal's nephew) whom John knew at Rome. Of course we could do no other than welcome him; the rather as he seemed to be one of the most lovable creatures in himself we had ever looked on. He stayed till next day with us, and talked and heard talk to his heart's content, and left us all really sad to part with him —THOMAS CARLYLE, Letter to His Mother (Aug. 26, 1833), *The Correspondence of Thomas Carlyle and Ralph Waldo Emerson*, 1883, Vol. 1, p. 4

Proceeded to Cambridge, to hear the valedictory sermon by Mr. Emerson. In this he surpassed himself as much as he surpasses others in the general way. I shall give no abstract. So beautiful, so just, so true, and terribly sublime was his picture of the faults of the Church in its present position. My soul is roused, and this week I shall write the long-meditated sermons on the state of the Church and the duties of these times. —THEODORE PARKER, *Journal* (July 15, 1838), cited in John Weiss, *Life and Correspondence of Theodore Parker*, 1864, Vol. 1, p. 113

I occupy or *improve*, as we Yankees say, two acres only of God's earth, on which is my house, my kitchen-garden, my orchard of thirty young trees, my empty barn. My house is now a very good one for comfort, & abounding in room. Besides my house, I have, I believe, $22,000, whose income in ordinary years is 6 per cent. I have no other tithe or glebe except the income of my winter lectures which was last winter 800 dollars. Well, with this income, here at home, I am a rich man. I stay at home and go abroad at my own instance. I have food, warmth, leisure, books, friends. Go away from home,—I am rich no longer. I never have a dollar to spend on a fancy. As no wise man, I suppose ever was rich in the sense of *freedom to spend*, because of the inundation of claims, so neither am I, who am not wise. But at home I am rich,—rich enough for ten brothers. My wife Lidian is an incarnation of Christianity,—I call her Asia—& keeps my philosophy from Antinomianism. My mother—whitest, mildest, most conservative of ladies, whose only exception to her universal preference of old things is her son; my boy, a piece of love & sunshine, well worth my watching from morning to night; these & three domestic women who cook & sew & run for us, make all my household. Here I sit & read & write with very little system & as far as regards composition with the most fragmentary result: paragraphs incompressible each sentence an infinitely repellent particle. In summer with the aid of a neighbor, I manage my garden; & a week ago I set out on the west side of my house forty young pine trees to protect me or my son from the wind of January. The ornament of the place is the occasional presence of some ten or twelve persons good & wise who visit us in the course of the year.—RALPH WALDO EMERSON, Letter to Thomas Carlyle (May 10, 1838)

Ralph Waldo Emerson is one of three brothers, all quite remarkable persons, and he is the only survivor. The other two died young, but everybody hoped great things of them. Their father, I think, was a country clergyman, passing rich on little more than £30 a year. They all, however, received good educations, and were distinguished scholars in our oldest and best University—that of Cambridge. Ralph must be now about thirty-eight years old. He has studied theology, has been settled (that is the American word to express the idea) as pastor of an Unitarian congregation in Boston; was much liked in this character, but speculated too deeply even for Unitarians; pushed his beliefs and unbeliefs very far; rejected much of the Christian faith; espoused much of the Swedenborgian; was disinclined to administer the Sacrament of the Lord's Supper; and then parted from his congregation in Boston. This was about six years ago; he then retired to a little country house at Concord, about twenty miles from Boston, within sight of the spot where the first British soldier fell in the war of the Revolution. Here he has kept ever since—thinking, reading, and writing; still regarded as a Christian clergyman, but without any charge. During the winter months delivering lectures in Boston, in character not unlike Carlyle's here, and to audiences brought together in the same way, and for the double purpose of spreading knowledge and getting money. A series of biographies formed one of his courses, and he has several times treated of the true nature and uses of history, and of the way in which it should be written. I need give you no hint about his style or his writings, for you know as much of both as I do. As a speaker in delivering his lectures, sermons, or discourses he is remarkable. His voice is good, his enunciation clear and distinct; his manner his own, but very striking. He is always self-possessed, and his strange fancies fall upon the ear in the most musical cadences. His voice is now low and then again high, like an Æolian harp; but this is natural, not affected, and I think anywhere before an educated audience he would be deemed a remarkable speaker. In person he is tall and graceful. Some people think him slightly mad (one of his brothers died insane, and the other brother had been insane before his death), others think him almost inspired. Old men are not prepared to receive or listen to or read his thoughts. The young of both classes think highly of him. He has a great influence over many of the young minds of my acquaintance, who always couple him with Carlyle. I think him neither mad nor inspired, but original, thoughtful, and peculiar, with his mind tinged with some habits of speculation that are less

practical than beautiful, and with a fearless honesty that makes him speak what he thinks, counting little any worldly considerations. In other times he might have been a philosopher or a reformer, but he would always have been tolerant and gentle, and he would have gone into uncomplaining exile if the powers that were bade him. I have hastily dotted down some things about Emerson according to your wish. I hope I have not said too much. When we meet in conversation I can explain whatever is left uncertain in your mind. I should not forget to state that he has been twice married. His first wife died young—under twenty, I think. By her he had a small property, which is to him an independence, enabling him to gratify all those "small desires which ask but little room," and which fill the life of a retiring literary man in all countries, and particularly in America. Emerson had no children by his first wife. He loved her and lamented her much, and cherished her memory in the Swedenborgian way. He has since married again a person who sympathises with him. When his child was born, about two years ago, men and women were astonished, and inquired if the infant has wings. This is enough. —CHARLES SUMNER, Letter to Lord Houghton (March 2, 1839), cited in T. Wemyss Reid, *The Life, Letters, and Friendships of Richard Monckton Milnes, First Lord Houghton*, 1891, Vol. 1, pp. 237–39

It is the doom of the Christian Church to be always distracted with controversy, and where religion is most in honor, there the perversity of the human heart breeds the sharpest conflicts of the brain. The sentiment of religion is at this time, perhaps, more potent and prevailing in New England than in any other portion of the Christian world. For many years since the establishment of the theological school at Andover, the Calvinists and Unitarians have been battling with each other upon the Atonement, the Divinity of Jesus Christ, and the Trinity. This has now very much subsided; but other wandering of mind takes the place of that, and equally lets the wolf into the fold. A young man, named Ralph Waldo Emerson, a son of my once loved friend William Emerson, and a classmate of my lamented son George, after failing in the every-day avocations of a Unitarian preacher and school-master, starts a new doctrine of transcendentalism, declares all the old revelations superannuated and worn out, and announces the approach of new revelations and prophecies.—JOHN QUINCY ADAMS, *Diary*, Aug. 2, 1840

It is 8 o'clock, A.M.: and the thin gentleman in black, with a small jointed cane under his arm, his eyes deeply sunken in his head, has asked that spiritual-looking boy in blue nankeens, who seems to be about ten years old, to "touch the bell,"—it was a privilege to do this;—and there he stands! that boy— whose image, more than any other's, is still deeply stamped upon my mind, as I then saw him and loved him, I knew not why, and thought him so angelic and remarkable,—feeling toward him more than a boy's emotion, as if a new spring of brotherly affection had suddenly broken loose in my heart. There is no indication of turbulence and disquiet about *him*; but with a happy combination of energy and gentleness, how truly is he the father of the man! He has touched the bell, and while he takes his seat among his fellows, he little dreams that, in after-times, he will strike a different note, and call around him a school of the transcendental philosophy. He is RALPH WALDO EMERSON.—RUFUS DAWES, "Boyhood Memories," *Boston Miscellany*, Feb. 1843, p. 60

It was with a feeling of predetermined dislike that I had the curiosity to look at Emerson at Lord Northampton's, a fortnight ago, when, in an instant, all my dislike vanished. He has one of the most interesting countenances I ever beheld—a combination of intelligence and sweetness that quite disarmed me. I was introduced to him.—HENRY CRABB ROBINSON, Letter to Thomas Robinson (April 22, 1848)

The next topic is Emerson, whom I left yesterday on the deck of the Halifax steamer and saw pass rapidly down the Mersey on his way home. He came to Oxford just at the end of Lent Term and stayed three days. Everybody liked him, and as the orthodox mostly had never heard of him, they did not suspect him. He is the quietest, plainest, unobtrusivest man possible—will talk but will rarely *discourse* to more than a single person—and wholly declines 'roaring.' He is very Yankee to look at, lank and sallow and not quite without the twang; but his look and voice are pleasing nevertheless and give you the impression of perfect intellectual cultivation as completely as would any great scientific man in England—Faraday, or Owen for instance, more in their way perhaps than in that of Wordsworth or Carlyle. Some people thought him very like Newman. But his manner is much simpler. I told him I had sent my copy of his Poems to the Antipodes with you. Whereupon he gave me another. I have been with him a great deal, for he came over to Paris and was there a month—during which we dined together daily; and since that I have seen him often in London and finally here. I liked his Lectures (he gave six in London) better than either his conversation or his appearance. I should say, his appearance is common, in the Lectures he looked prophetic at times. They were all *read*. One thing that struck everybody is that he is much less Emersonian than his Essays. There is no dogmatism or arbitrariness or positiveness about him. However, I have perhaps talked enough about him. Your sister Mary was at the lectures and you will perhaps have her report too.—ARTHUR HUGH CLOUGH, Letter to Thomas Arnold (July 16, 1848)

Last night I heard Emerson give a lecture. I pity the reporter who attempts to give it to the world. I began to listen with a determination to remember it in order, but it was without method, or order, or system. It was like a beam of light moving in the undulatory waves, meeting with occasional meteors in its path; it was exceedingly captivating. It surprised me that there was not only no commonplace thought, but there was no commonplace expression. If he quoted, he quoted from what we had not read; if he told an anecdote, it was one that had not reached us. At the outset he was very severe upon the science of the age. He said that inventors and discoverers helped themselves very much, but they did not help the rest of the world; that a great man was felt to the centre of the Copernican system; that a botanist dried his plants, but the plants had their revenge and dried the botanist; that a naturalist bottled up reptiles, but in return the man was bottled up.

There was a pitiful truth in all this, but there are glorious exceptions. Professor Peirce is anything but a formula, though he deals in formulæ.

The lecture turned at length upon beauty, and it was evident that personal beauty had made Emerson its slave many a time, and I suppose every heart in the house admitted the truth of his words. . . .

It was evident that Mr. Emerson was not at ease, for he declared that good manners were more than beauty of face, and good expression better than good features. He mentioned that Sir Philip Sydney was not handsome, though the boast of English society; and he spoke of the astonishing beauty of the Duchess of Hamilton, to see whom hundreds collected when she took a ride. I think in these cases there is something besides beauty; there was rank in that of the Duchess, in the case of Sydney there was no need of beauty at all.—MARIA MITCHELL, *Journal* (Nov. 14, 1855), *Life, Letters, and Journals of Maria Mitchell*, ed. Phebe Mitchell Kendall, 1896, pp. 45–47

Never had I a better piece of luck befall me: a long and blessed evening with Emerson, in a way I couldn't have wish'd better or different. For nearly two hours he has been placidly sitting where I could see his face in the best light, near me. Mrs. S⟨anborn⟩'s back-parlor well fill'd with people, neighbors, many fresh and charming faces, women, mostly young, but some old. My friend A. B. Alcott and his daughter Louisa were there early. A good deal of talk, the subject Henry Thoreau—some new glints of his life and fortunes, with letters to and from him—one of the best by Margaret Fuller, others by Horace Greeley, Channing, &c.—one from Thoreau himself, most quaint and interesting. (No doubt I seem'd very stupid to the room-full of company, taking hardly any part in the conversation; but I had "my own pail to milk in," as the Swiss proverb puts it.) My seat and relative arrangement were such that, without being rude, or anything of the kind, I could just look squarely at E., which I did a good part of the two hours. On entering, he had spoken very briefly and politely to several of the company, then settled himself in his chair, a trifle push'd back, and, though a listener and apparently an alert one, remain'd silent through the whole talk and discussion. A lady friend quietly took a seat next him, to give special attention. A good color in his face, eyes clear, with the well-known expression of sweetness, and the old clear-peering aspect quite the same.

Next Day.—Several hours at E.'s house, and dinner there. An old familiar house, (he has been in it thirty-five years,) with surroundings, furnishment, roominess, and plain elegance and fullness, signifying democratic ease, sufficient opulence, and an admirable old-fashioned simplicity—modern luxury, with its mere sumptuousness and affectation, either touch'd lightly upon or ignored altogether. Dinner the same. Of course the best of the occasion (Sunday, September 18, '81) was the sight of E. himself. As just said, a healthy color in the cheeks, and good light in the eyes, cheery expression, and just the amount of talking that best suited, namely, a word or short phrase only where needed, and almost always with a smile. Besides Emerson himself, Mrs. E., with their daughter Ellen, the son Edward and his wife, with my friend F. S. and Mrs. S., and others, relatives and intimates. Mrs. Emerson, resuming the subject of the evening before, (I sat next to her,) gave me further and fuller information about Thoreau, who, years ago, during Mr. E.'s absence in Europe, had lived for some time in the family, by invitation.—WALT WHITMAN, "A Visit, at the Last, to R. W. Emerson" (1881), *Prose Works*, ed. Floyd Stovall, 1963, Vol. 1, pp. 278–80

Though I could never find in Emerson's effusions as a *Vates* so rich a vein of thought or so awakening a power as his most devoted readers were able to recognise, yet in his own personality he appeared to me almost all that is noble, lovely, and venerable; and in his critical and ethical writings, where he commented on the given matter of life, manners, and character, to rise to the very perfection of moral judgment, pure and keen without a trace of Cynicism, and with a selecting enthusiasm for all beauty and good, calm and passionless because full of faith in them as the permanency of the world.

I first heard of him in 1830, from Henry Ware and his wife, who visited me in my early married life in Dublin; and I have a faint impression that even then he was spoken of by the elder minister with a shade of reserve, as if the want of congeniality between the evangelical pastor and the independent thinker was already inwardly felt. Three years afterwards, in 1833, he sought me out in Liverpool, introduced by Henry Ware, and told me the story of his scruple about the Communion. He was then in a very indeterminate state of mind about questions on religion, and I was struck with the mixture of clear decision on the subject which had led to action, and of modest suspense on topics which he had not fully thought out. But I made up my mind that he would not be likely to return to the ministry.—JAMES MARTINEAU, Letter to Alexander Ireland (Dec. 31, 1882), cited in James Drummond, *The Life and Letters of James Martineau*, 1902, Vol. 2, pp. 312–13

As I count it the greatest honor and happiness of my life to have known Mr. Emerson, I gladly accede to a request for such recollections as may be of interest. My first remembrance is of the morning when I was sent to inquire for little Waldo, then lying very ill. His father came to me so worn with watching, and changed by sorrow, that I was startled, and could only stammer out my message.

"Child, he is dead," was his answer.

Then the door closed, and I ran home to tell the sad tidings. I was only eight years old, and that was my first glimpse of a great grief; but I never have forgotten the anguish that made a familiar face so tragical, and gave those few words more pathos than the sweet lamentation of the "Threnody."

Later, when we went to school with the little Emersons in their father's barn, I remember many happy times when the illustrious papa was our good playfellow. Often piling us into a bedecked hay-cart, he took us to berry, bathe, or picnic at Walden, making our day charming and memorable by showing us the places he loved, the wood-people Thoreau had introduced to him, or the wild-flowers whose hidden homes he had discovered. So that when years afterward we read of "the sweet Rhodora in the wood," and "the burly, dozing humblebee," or laughed over "The Mountain and the Squirrel," we recognized old friends, and thanked him for the delicate truth and beauty which made them immortal for us and others.

When the book-mania fell upon me at fifteen, I used to venture into Mr. Emerson's library, and ask what I should read, never conscious of the audacity of my demand, so genial was my welcome. His kind hand opened to me the riches of Shakespeare, Dante, Goethe, and Carlyle; and I gratefully recall the sweet patience with which he led me round the book-lined room till "the new and very interesting book" was found, or the indulgent smile he wore when I proposed something far above my comprehension.

"Wait a little for that," he said. "Meantime try this; and, if you like it, come again."

For many of these wise books I am waiting still, very patiently; because in his own I have found the truest delight, the best inspiration of my life. When these same precious volumes were tumbled out of the window, while his house was burning some years ago, as I stood guarding the scorched, wet pile, Mr. Emerson passed by, and, surveying the devastation with philosophic calmness, only said, in answer to my lamentations,—

"I see my library under a new aspect. Could you tell me where my good neighbors have flung my boots?"

In the tribulations of later life, this faithful house-friend was an earthly Providence, conferring favors so beautifully that they were no burden, and giving such sympathy, in joy and sorrow, that very tender ties were knit between this beneficent nature and the grateful hearts he made his own. Acquaintance with such a man is an education in itself, for "the essence of greatness is the perception that virtue is enough;" and, living what he wrote, his influence purified and brightened like sunshine.

Many a thoughtful young man and woman owe to Emerson the spark that kindled their highest aspirations, and showed them how to make the conduct of life a helpful lesson, not a blind struggle.

> For simple maids and noble youth
> Are welcome to the man of truth:
> Most welcome they who need him most;
> They feed the spring which they exhaust,
>   For greater need
>   Draws better deed.

He was, in truth, like his own Saadi,—a "cheerer of men's hearts."

"Friendship," "Love," "Self-Reliance," "Heroism," and "Compensation," among the essays, have become to many readers as precious as Christian's scroll; and certain poems live in the memory as sacred as hymns, so helpful and inspiring are they. No better books for earnest young people can be found. The truest words are often the simplest; and, when wisdom and virtue go hand in hand, none need fear to listen, learn, and love.

The marble walk that leads to his hospitable door has been trodden by the feet of many pilgrims from all parts of the world, drawn thither by their love and reverence for him. In that famous study, his townspeople have had the privilege of seeing many of the great and good men and women of our time, and learning of their gracious host the finest lessons of true courtesy. I have often seen him turn from distinguished guests, to say a wise or kindly word to some humble worshipper sitting modestly in a corner, content merely to look and listen, and who went away to cherish that memorable moment long and gratefully.

Here, too, in the pleasant room, with the green hills opposite, and the pines murmuring musically before the windows, Emerson wrote essays more helpful than most sermons; lectures which created the lyceum; poems full of power and sweetness; and, better than song or sermon, has lived a life so noble, true, and beautiful, that its wide-spreading influence is felt on both sides of the sea.

In all reforms he was among the foremost on the side of justice and progress. When Faneuil Hall used to be a scene of riot and danger in anti-slavery days, I remember sitting up aloft, an excited girl, among the loyal women who never failed to be there; and how they always looked for that serene face on the platform, and found fresh courage in the mere sight of the wisest man in America, standing shoulder to shoulder with the bravest. When woman's suffrage was most unpopular, his voice and pen spoke for the just cause, undaunted by the fear of ridicule which silences so many.

His own simple, abstemious habits were his best testimony in favor of temperance in all things; while, in religion, he believed that each soul must choose its own aids, and prove the vitality of its faith by high thinking and holy living.

When travelling in various countries, I found his fame had gone before; and people were eager to hear something of the Concord poet, seer, and philosopher. In a little town upon the Rhine, where our party paused for a night, unexpectedly delayed, two young Germans, reading the word Boston on the labels of our trunks as they stood in the yard of the inn, begged to come in and see the Americans; and their first question was,—

"Tell us about Emerson."

We gladly told them what they asked; and they listened as eagerly as we did to any thing we could hear concerning their great countryman, Goethe.

A letter once came to me from the Far West, in which a girl asked what she should read to build up a noble character. It was a remarkable letter; and, when I inquired what books she most desired, she answered, "All of Emerson's: he helps me most."

A prisoner just from Concord jail came to see me on his release, and proved to be an intelligent, book-loving young man, who had been led into crime by his first fit of intoxication. In talking with him, he said Emerson's books were a comfort to him, and he had spent some of the money earned in prison to buy certain volumes to take with him as guides and safeguards for the future.

In England his honored name opened many doors to us, and we felt as proud of our acquaintance with him as Englishmen feel of the medals with which their Queen decorates them; so widely was he known, so helpful was his influence, so ennobling the mere reflection of his virtue and his genius. Longfellow was beloved by children; and of Emerson it might be said, as of Plato, "He walks with his head among the stars, yet carries a blessing in his heart for every little child."

When he returned from his second visit to Europe, after his house was burned, he was welcomed by the schoolchildren, who lined his passage from the cars to the carriage, where a nosegay of blooming grandchildren awaited him; and escorted by a smiling troop of neighbors, old and young, he was conducted under green arches to his house. Here they sang "Sweet Home," gave welcoming cheers, and marched away to come again soon after to a grand house-warming in the old mansion which had been so well restored that nothing seemed changed.

Many a gay revel has been held under the pines, whole schools taking possession of the poet's premises; and many a child will gladly recall hereafter the paternal face that smiled on them, full of interest in their gambols, and of welcome for the poorest. Mrs. Emerson, from her overflowing garden, planted flowers along the roadside, and in the plot of ground before the nearest schoolhouse, to beautify the children's daily life. Sweeter and more imperishable than these will be the recollections of many kindnesses bestowed by one, who, in the truest sense of the word, was a friend to all.

As he lay dying, children stopped to ask if he were better; and all the sunshine faded out of the little faces when the sad answer came. Very willing feet roamed the woods for green garlands to decorate the old church where he would come for the last time; busy hands worked till midnight, that every house should bear some token of mourning; Spring gave him her few early flowers and budding boughs from the haunts that will know him no more; and old and young forgot, for a little while, their pride in the illustrious man, to sorrow for the beloved friend and neighbor.

Life did not sadden his cheerful philosophy; success could not spoil his exquisite simplicity; age could not dismay him, and he met death with sweet serenity.

He wrote, "Nothing can bring you peace but yourself. Nothing can bring you peace but the triumph of principles." And this well-earned peace transfigured the beautiful dead face so many eyes beheld with tender reverence, seeming to assure us that our august friend and master had passed into the larger life, for which he was ready, still to continue,—

Without hasting, without rest,
Lifting Better up to Best;

Planting seeds of knowledge pure.
Through earth to ripen, through heaven endure.
—LOUISA MAY ALCOTT, "Reminiscences of Ralph Waldo Emerson," *Some Noted Princes, Authors, and Statesmen of Our Time*, ed. James Parton, 1885, pp. 284–88

General

Mr. Emerson, to speak scientifically, is no philosopher. He is a philosopher neither in the order of his mind, nor in his method of investigation. He explains nothing, accounts for nothing, solves no intellectual problem, and affords no practical instruction. He proposes nothing of all this, and, therefore, is not to be censured for not doing it. He is to be regarded as a Seer, who rises into the regions of the Transcendental, and reports what he sees, and in the order in which he sees it. His worth can be determined, that is, the accuracy of his reports can be properly judged of, by none except those who rise to the same regions, and behold the universe from the same point of view.

Writers like Mr. Emerson are seldom to be consulted for clear, logical, systematic expositions of any subject or doctrine, never for the purpose of taking them as teachers or guides in the formation of opinions; but for the suggestions, the incentives to thought they furnish, and the life they kindle up within us. They are thought by some to be writers without any practical value for mankind; but they have, in fact, a very high practical value; only not of the every-day sort, only not that of dogmatic teachers or scientific expositors. They present new aspects of things, or at least old familiar objects in new dresses, the various subjects of thought and inquiry in new relations, break up old associations, and excite to greater and fresher mental activity. After having read them, we cannot say that we are wiser or more learned than we were before; we cannot say that we have become acquainted with any new facts in the history of man or of the universe, or that we have any new ideas in regard to the human soul or its Creator; but we feel, that somehow or other new virtue has been imparted to us, that a change has come over us, and that we are no longer what we were, but greater and better.

These are not the only writers we need; but they have their place, and one of high trust, and of no slight influence. Their influence is not sudden, noisy, obvious to all senses, but slow, silent, subtle, permanent, entering into and becoming an integrant part of the life of the age, sometimes of the ages. They live and exert a power over the souls of men, long after their names are forgotten, and their works have ceased to be read. They are never in vogue with the multitude, but they are admired in select circles, who inhale their spirit, and breathe it into other and larger circles, who in their turn breathe it into the souls of all men. Though they may seem to have no practical aim, and no reference to every-day life, they have in the end a most important practical bearing, and exert a controlling influence over even the business concerns of the world. Let no one, then, regard them as mere idle dreamers, as mere literary toys, with whose glitter we may amuse ourselves, but without significance for the world of reality. They appear always for good or evil, and their appearance usually marks an epoch.—ORESTES AUGUSTUS BROWNSON, "Emerson's *Essays*," *Boston Quarterly Review*, July 1841, p. 292

J. Sterling showed me Emerson's book (*Essays*), and drew a parallel between him and Carlyle; he was the Plato, and Carlyle the Tacitus. Emerson is the systematic thinker; Carlyle has the clearer insight, and has many deeper things than Emerson.—CAROLINE FOX, *Journal* (June 8, 1841), *Memories of Old Friends*, ed. Horace N. Pym, 1882, p. 140

To the great reading public entering Mr. Fraser's and other shops in quest of daily provender, it may be as well to state, on the very threshold, that this little Reprint of an American Book of Essays is in no wise the thing suited for them; that not the great reading public, but only the small thinking public, and perhaps only a portion of these, have any question to ask concerning it. No Editor or Reprinter can expect such a Book ever to become popular here. But, thank Heaven, the small thinking public has now also a visible existence among us, is visibly enlarging itself. At the present time it can be predicted, what some years ago it could not be, that a certain number of human creatures will be found extant in England to whom the words of a man speaking from the heart of him, in what fashion soever, under what obstructions soever, will be welcome;—welcome, perhaps, as a brother's voice, to 'wanderers in the labyrinthic Night!' For those, and not for any other class of persons, is this little Book reprinted and recommended. Let such read, and try; ascertain for themselves, whether this *is* a kind of articulate human voice speaking words, or only another of the thousand thousand ventriloquisms, mimetic echoes, hysteric shrieks, hollow laughters, and mere *in*articulate mechanical babblements, the soul-confusing din of which already fills all places? I will not anticipate their verdict; but I reckon it safe enough, and even a kind of duty in these circumstances, to invite them to *try*.

The name of Ralph Waldo Emerson is not entirely new in England: distinguished Travellers bring us tidings of such a man; fractions of his writings have found their way into the hands of the curious here; fitful hints that there is, in New England, some spiritual Notability called Emerson, glide through Reviews and Magazines. Whether these hints were true or not true, readers are now to judge for themselves a little better.

Emerson's writings and speakings amount to something:—and yet hitherto, as seems to me, this Emerson is perhaps far less notable for what he has spoken or done, than for the many things he has not spoken and has forborne to do. With uncommon interest I have learned that this, and in such a never-resting locomotive country too, is one of those rare men who have withal the invaluable talent of sitting still! That an educated man of good gifts and opportunities, after looking at the public arena, and even trying, not with ill success, what its tasks and its prizes might amount to, should retire for long years into rustic obscurity; and, amid the all-pervading jingle of dollars and loud chaffering of ambitions and promotions, should quietly, with cheerful deliberateness, sit down to spend *his* life not in Mammon-worship, or the hunt for reputation, influence, place or any outward advantage whatsoever: this, when we get notice of it, is a thing really worth noting. As Paul Louis Courrier said: *"Ce qui me distingue de tous mes contemporains c'est que je n'ai pas la prétention d'être roi."* 'All my contemporaries;'—poor contemporaries! It is as if the man said: Yes, ye contemporaries, be it known to you, or let it remain unknown, There is one man who does not need to be a king; king neither of nations, nor of parishes or cliques, nor even of *cent-per-annums*; nor indeed of anything at all save of himself only. 'Realities?' Yes, your dollars are real, your cotton and molasses are real; so are Presidentships, Senatorships, celebrations, reputations, and the wealth of Rothschild: but to me, on the whole, they are not the reality that will suffice. To me, without some other reality, they are mockery, and amount

to *zero*, nay to a negative quantity. ETERNITIES surround this god-given Life of mine: what will all the dollars in creation do for me? Dollars, dignities, senate-addresses, review-articles, gilt coaches or cavalcades, with world-wide huzzaings and parti-coloured beef-eaters never so many: O Heaven, what were all these? Behold, ye shall have all these, and I will endeavour for a thing other than these. Behold, we will entirely agree to differ in this matter; I to be in your eyes nothing, you to be something, to be much, to be all things:—wherefore, adieu in God's name; go ye that way, I go this!——Pity that a man, for such cause, should be so distinguished from *all* his contemporaries! It is a misfortune partly of these our peculiar times. Times and nations of any strength have always privately held in them many such men. Times and nations that hold none or few of such, may indeed seem to themselves strong and great, but are only bulky, loud; no heart or solidity in them;—*great*, as the blown bladder is, which by and by will collapse and become small enough!

For myself I have looked over with no common feeling to this brave Emerson, seated by his rustic hearth, on the other side of the Ocean (yet not altogether parted from me either), silently communing with his own soul, and with the God's World it finds itself alive in yonder. Pleasures of Virtue, Progress of the Species, Black Emancipation, New Tarif, Eclecticism, Locofocoism, ghost of Improved-Socinianism: these with many other ghosts and substances are squeaking, jabbering, according to their capabilities, round this man; to one man among the sixteen millions their jabber is all unmusical. The silent voices of the Stars above, and of the green Earth beneath, are profitabler to him,—tell him gradually that these others are but ghosts, which will shortly have to vanish; that the Life-Fountain these proceeded out of does not vanish! The words of such a man, what words he finds good to speak, are worth attending to. By degrees a small circle of living souls eager to hear is gathered. The silence of this man has to become speech: may this too, in its due season, prosper for him!—Emerson has gone to lecture, various times, to special audiences, in Boston, and occasionally elsewhere. Three of those Lectures, already printed, are known to some here; as is the little Pamphlet called *Nature*, of somewhat earlier date. It may be said, a great meaning lies in these pieces, which as yet finds no adequate expression for itself. A noteworthy though very unattractive work, moreover, is that new Periodical they call *The Dial*, in which he occasionally writes; which appears indeed generally to be imbued with his way of thinking, and to proceed from the circle that learns of him. This present little Volume of *Essays*, printed in Boston a few months ago, is Emerson's first Book. An unpretending little Book, composed probably, in good part, from mere Lectures which already lay written. It affords us, on several sides, in such manner as it can, a direct glimpse into the man and that spiritual world of his.

Emerson, I understand, was bred to Theology; of which primary bent his latest way of thought still bears traces. In a very enigmatic way, we hear much of the 'universal soul,' of the &c. &c.: flickering like bright bodiless Northern Streamers, notions and half-notions of a metaphysic, theosophic, theologic kind are seldom long wanting in these *Essays*. I do not advise the British Public to trouble itself much with all that; still less, to take offence at it. Whether this Emerson be 'a Pantheist,' or what kind of Theist or *Ist* he may be, can perhaps as well remain undecided. If he prove a devout-minded, veritable, original man, this for the present will suffice. *Ists* and *Isms* are rather growing a weariness. Such a man does not readily range himself under *Isms*. A man to whom the 'open secret of the universe' is no longer a closed one, what can his *speech* of it be in these days? All human speech, in the best days, all human thought that can or could articulate itself in reference to such things, what is it but the eager stammering and struggling as of a wondering infant,—in view of the Unnameable! That this little Book has no 'system,' and points or stretches far beyond all systems, is one of its merits. We will call it the soliloquy of a true soul, alone under the stars, in this day. In England as elsewhere the voice of a true soul, *any* voice of such, may be welcome to some. For in England as elsewhere old dialects and formulas are mostly lying dead: some dim suspicion, or clear knowledge, indicates on all hands that they are as good as dead;—and how can the skilfullest *galvanizing* make them any more live? For they are dead: and their galvanic motions, O Heavens, are not of a pleasant sort!—That one man more, in the most modern dialect of this year 1841, recognises the oldest everlasting truths: here is a thing worth seeing, among the others. One man more who knows, and believes of very certainty, that Man's Soul is still alive, that God's Universe is still godlike, that of all Ages of Miracles ever seen, or dreamt of, by far the most miraculous is this age in this hour; and who with all these devout beliefs has dared, like a valiant man, to bid chimeras, "*Be* chimerical; disappear, and let us have an end of you!"—is not this worth something? In a word, while so many Benthamisms, Socialisms, Fourrierisms, *professing* to have no soul, go staggering and lowing like monstrous mooncalves, the product of a heavy-laden moonstruck age; and, in this same baleful 'twelfth hour of the night,' even galvanic Puseyisms, as we say, are visible, and dancings of the sheeted dead,—shall not any voice of a living man be welcome to us, even because it is alive?

For the rest, what degree of mere literary talent lies in these utterances, is but a secondary question; which every reader may gradually answer for himself. What Emerson's talent is, we will not altogether estimate by this Book. The utterance is abrupt, fitful; the great idea not yet embodied struggles towards an embodiment. Yet everywhere there is the true heart of a man; which is the parent of all talent; which without much talent cannot exist. A breath as of the green country,—all the welcomer that it is *New*-England country, not second-hand but first-hand country,—meets us wholesomely everywhere in these *Essays*: the authentic green Earth is there, with her mountains, rivers, with her mills and farms. Sharp gleams of insight arrest us by their pure intellectuality; here and there, in heroic rusticism, a tone of modest manfulness, of mild invincibility, low-voiced but lion-strong, makes us too thrill with a noble pride. Talent? Such ideas as dwell in this man, how can they ever speak themselves with *enough* of talent? The talent is not the chief question here. The idea, that is the chief question. Of the living acorn you do not ask first, How *large* an acorn art thou? The smallest living acorn is fit to be the parent of oaktrees without end,—could clothe all New England with oaktrees by and by. You ask it, first of all: Art thou a living acorn? Certain, now, that thou art not a dead mushroom, as the most are?—

But, on the whole, our Book is short; the Preface should not grow too long. Closing these questionable parables and intimations, let me in plain English recommend this little Book as the Book of an original veridical man, worthy the acquaintance of those who delight in such; and so: Welcome to it whom it may concern!—THOMAS CARLYLE, "Preface by the English Editor" to *Essays*, 1841, pp. v–xiii

Mr. Ralph Waldo Emerson belongs to a class of gentlemen with whom we have no patience whatever—the mystics for

mysticism's sake. Quintilian mentions a pedant who taught obscurity, and who once said to a pupil "this is excellent, for I do not understand it myself." How the good man would have chuckled over Mr. E.! His present *rôle* seems to be the out-Carlyling Carlyle. *Lycophron Tenebrosus* is a fool to him. The best answer to his twaddle is *cui bono?*—a very little Latin phrase very generally mistranslated and misunderstood—*cui bono?*—to whom is it a benefit? If not to Mr. Emerson individually, then surely to no man living.

His love of the obscure does not prevent him, nevertheless, from the composition of occasional poems in which beauty is apparent *by flashes*. Several of his effusions appeared in the *Western Messenger*—more in the *Dial*, of which he is the soul—or the sun—or the shadow. We remember the "Sphynx," the "Problem," the "Snow Storm," and some fine old-fashioned verses entitled "Oh fair and stately maid whose eye."—EDGAR ALLAN POE, "A Chapter on Autography" (1842), *Complete Works*, ed. James A. Harrison, 1902, Vol. 15, p. 260

Emerson again is a critic, poet, philosopher, with talent not so conspicuous, not so adequate to his task; but his field is still higher, his task more arduous. Lives a far more intense life; seeks to realize a divine life; his affections and intellect equally developed. Has advanced farther, and a new heaven opens to him. Love and Friendship, Religion, Poetry, the Holy are familiar to him. The life of an Artist; more variegated, more observing, finer perception; not so robust, elastic; practical enough in his own field; faithful, a judge of men. There is no such general critic of men and things, no such trustworthy and faithful man. More of the divine realized in him than in any. A poetic critic, reserving the unqualified nouns for the gods. ⟨. . .⟩

Emerson has special talents unequalled. The divine in man has had no more easy, methodically distinct expression. His personal influence upon young persons greater than any man's. In his world every man would be a poet, Love would reign, Beauty would take place, Man and Nature would harmonize. ⟨. . .⟩

Emerson does not consider things in respect to their essential utility, but an important partial and relative one, as works of art perhaps. His probes pass one side of their centre of gravity. His exaggeration is of a part, not of the whole. —HENRY DAVID THOREAU, *Journal* (1845–47), *Writings*, 1906, Vol. 7, pp. 431–33

He has not written a line which is not considered in the interest of mankind. He never writes in the interest of a section, of a party, of a church, of a man, always in the interest of mankind. Hence comes the ennobling influence of his works. Most of the literary men of America, most of the men of superior education, represent the ideas and interests of some party; in all that concerns the welfare of the Human Race, they are proportionably behind the mass who have only the common culture; so while the thought of the people is democratic, putting man before the accidents of man, the literature of the nation is aristocratic, and opposed to the welfare of mankind. Emerson belongs to the exceptional literature of the times—and while his culture joins him to the history of man, his ideas and his whole life enable him to represent also the nature of man, and so to write for the future. He is one of the rare exceptions amongst our educated men, and helps redeem American literature from the reproach of imitation, conformity, meanness of aim, and hostility to the progress of mankind. No faithful man is too low for his approval and encouragement; no faithless man too high and popular for his rebuke.—THEODORE

PARKER, "The Writings of Ralph Waldo Emerson," *Massachusetts Quarterly Review*, March 1850, p. 254

How little the all-important art of making meaning pellucid is studied now! Hardly any popular writer, except myself, thinks of it. Many seem to aim at being obscure. Indeed, they may be right enough in one sense; for many readers give credit for profundity to whatever is obscure, and call all that is perspicuous, shallow. But, corragio! and think of A.D. 2850. Where will your Emersons be then? But Herodotus will still be read with delight. We must do our best to be read too.—THOMAS BABINGTON MACAULAY, *Journal* (Jan. 12, 1850), cited in G. Otto Trevelyan, *The Life and Letters of Lord Macaulay*, 1876, Vol. 2, p. 234

To abuse a man because he does not write like Joseph Addison or Samuel Johnson is absurd: they may with the same reason condemn him for being himself, instead of somebody else. It is the criticism of the fool. Emerson certainly has a style more marked than most writers, but he has likewise a greater individuality of thought to accompany it. When a teacher utters profounder thought than the untaught have been accustomed to hear, the latter accuse him of being mystical or transcendental: just as boys of the lower form grumble at Euclid, and abuse their tutor. There seems something galling to an inferior mind in the confession of ignorance. It appears to wound self-love or egotism more than any other accusation. The generality would prefer to be suspected of knavery, than of boobyism. This will account for the virulence of the blockhead: to surpass him in genius or learning is to make him your deadly enemy. A warfare is always waged by the dull against the witty; they have the worst of it, and fools though they are, *they know it*: the alpha and omega of dulness is *to this extent, no more*. They are sensible of their stupidity. We admit this to be unpleasant, but it is unavoidable, and by way of consolation we recommend the old adage of—

> What can't be cured,
> Must be endured.

So there's an end of the matter, and they had better rest in silence under the misfortune. ⟨. . .⟩

We were going to say, to any *unprejudiced* mind Emerson's writings must commend themselves; we were going to say this, when the difficulty struck us of finding *any* unprejudiced mind. We are all prejudiced, either by birth, or habit, or education, and therefore we can only hope for two classes who will appreciate Emerson—the highly cultured and the ignorant; these last, however, must be those that think for themselves. It is the middle class, the men who have a smattering of all things and know nothing entirely, to whom Emerson appears as an Atheist, a Pantheist, and an Infidel. To the first he approves himself a man—a great and worthy teacher; and to the last he is new life, new light—a spiritual sun which shines as freely, as warmly on their hearts as the sun of nature does upon their bodies. We have *felt* the truth of what we say, and therefore do not feel any diffidence in telling our experience. We belong to the lowest class; we have believed with our fathers and elders, we have doubted and thought, thought earnestly and long, and found comfort, and joy, and pleasure in the instruction Emerson has afforded us. His views have been to us a new existence, or rather have shown us the true value of the existence God has already given to us. His views have set us on our feet again, and gave us hope, and heart, and courage, when all else has proved vain, authoritative, and arbitrary. Our study of Emerson has not been exclusive; we have had time to taste of most of the poetry and

philosophy written in the English language from Chaucer downwards; and we again declare that we know of no author that is so full of suggestion, speaks so directly to the heart, and is so free from the prejudices of the time, and the fashions in which we live. Bacon, the great Lord Bacon, sinks to a mere politician alongside Emerson. But we do not, nevertheless, undervalue Bacon; he was a great man in his time, and exercised a wide influence upon his age and ages after. But he was neither so deep-seeing nor so true-spoken as Emerson; for proof take any Essay these two have written on the *same* subject—'Love,' for instance—and compare them, and see how much one excels the other. Bacon's spirit, great as it was (and it was marvellous for his age), never mounted so high, never extended so wide, never descended so low as Emerson's. There is one reason, however, that is obvious why our author should greatly eclipse these luminaries, and that is, he has had all their light, all their genius to assist his own. We can trace in his writings many thoughts he has got from Chaucer, Sidney, Herbert, Shakspeare, Bacon, the Elder Dramatists, from the Greeks, from the Romans, from the Hindoos, from the Scandinavians, from the Germans, and lastly from his own experience, on which last he himself sets most value, and justly, seeing that all *his* teachers' worth was thus obtained. Truth being universal, and not anything exclusive, to those who will receive it is as common as the air we breathe, and, like the best of all things, should be most acceptable. Emerson and his philosophy are as remarkable things in this age as are the locomotive, the electric telegraph, and the daguerreotype. They are, too, exercising as deep an influence, slowly but surely winning men to look rightly at things, and with their own eyes. He is a pioneer as brave, and as indomitable in clearing away obstructions to the growth of mind, as are those of the West in clearing the soil. Many a great work and many a noble deed will yet take its date from his words, and if they have the power to produce such fruit, and we affirm that they have to a high degree, who shall say this man is an opponent to Christianity? Who, indeed, but those who make that doctrine a business, and not a rule of life! ⟨. . .⟩

Mr. Emerson possesses so many characteristics of genius that his want of universality is the more to be regretted; the leading feature of his mind is intensity; he is deficient in heart sympathy. Full to overflowing with intellectual appreciation, he is incapable of that embracing reception of impulses which gives to Byron so large a measure of influence and fame. Emerson is elevated, but not expansive; his flight is high, but not extensive. He has a magnificent vein of the purest gold, but it is not a mine. To vary our illustration somewhat, he is not a world, but a district; a lofty and commanding eminence we admit, but only a very small portion of the true Poet's universe. What, however, he has done is permanent, and America will always in after times be proud of Ralph Waldo Emerson, and consider him one of her noblest sons.—THOMAS POWELL, "Ralph Waldo Emerson," *The Living Authors of America*, 1850, pp. 66–67, 75–77

It is a singular fact, that Mr. Emerson is the most steadily attractive lecturer in America. Into that somewhat cold-waterish region adventurers of the sensational kind come down now and then with a splash, to become disregarded King Logs before the next season. But Mr. Emerson always draws. A lecturer now for something like a third of a century, one of the pioneers of the lecturing system, the charm of his voice, his manner, and his matter has never lost its power over his earlier hearers, and continually winds new ones in its enchanting meshes. What they do not fully understand they take on trust, and listen, saying to themselves, as the old poet of Sir Philip Sidney,—

> A sweet, attractive, kind of grace,
> A full assurance given by looks,
> Continual comfort in a face,
> The lineaments of gospel books.

We call it a singular fact, because we Yankees are thought to be fond of the spread-eagle style, and nothing can be more remote from that than his. We are reckoned a practical folk, who would rather hear about a new air-tight stove than about Plato; yet our favorite teacher's practicality is not in the least of the Poor Richard variety. If he have any Buncombe constituency, it is that unrealized commonwealth of philosophers which Plotinus proposed to establish; and if he were to make an almanac, his directions to farmers would be something like this: "OCTOBER: *Indian Summer*; now is the time to get in your early Vedas." What, then, is his secret? Is it not that he out-Yankees us all? that his range includes us all? that he is equally at home with the potato-disease and original sin, with pegging shoes and the Over-soul? that, as we try all trades, so has he tried all cultures? and above all, that his mysticism gives us a counterpoise to our super-practicality?

There is no man living to whom, as a writer, so many of us feel and thankfully acknowledge so great an indebtedness for ennobling impulses,—none whom so many cannot abide. What does he mean? ask these last. Where is his system? What is the use of it all? What the deuse have we to do with Brahma? I do not propose to write an essay on Emerson at this time. I will only say that one may find grandeur and consolation in a starlit night without caring to ask what it means, save grandeur and consolation; one may like Montaigne, as some ten generations before us have done, without thinking him so systematic as some more eminently tedious (or shall we say tediously eminent?) authors; one may think roses as good in their way as cabbages, though the latter would make a better show in the witness-box, if cross-examined as to their usefulness; and as for Brahma, why, he can take care of himself, and won't bite us at any rate.

The bother with Mr. Emerson is, that, though he writes in prose, he is essentially a poet. If you undertake to paraphrase what he says, and to reduce it to words of one syllable for infant minds, you will make as sad work of it as the good monk with his analysis of Homer in the *Epistolæ Obscurorum Virorum*. We look upon him as one of the few men of genius whom our age has produced, and there needs no better proof of it than his masculine faculty of fecundating other minds. Search for his eloquence in his books and you will perchance miss it, but meanwhile you will find that it has kindled all your thoughts. For choice and pith of language he belongs to a better age than ours, and might rub shoulders with Fuller and Browne,—though he does use that abominable word *reliable*. His eye for a fine, telling phrase that will carry true is like that of a backwoodsman for a rifle; and he will dredge you up a choice word from the mud of Cotton Mather himself. A diction at once so rich and so homely as his I know not where to match in these days of writing by the page; it is like homespun cloth of gold. The many cannot miss his meaning, and only the few can find it. It is the open secret of all true genius. It is wholesome to angle in those profound pools, though one be rewarded with nothing more than the leap of a fish that flashes his freckled side in the sun and as suddenly absconds in the dark and dreamy waters again. There is keen excitement, though there be no ponderable acquisition. If we carry nothing home in our baskets, there is ample gain in dilated lungs and

stimulated blood. What does he mean, quotha? He means inspiring hints, a divining-rod to your deeper nature. No doubt, Emerson, like all original men, has his peculiar audience, and yet I know none that can hold a promiscuous crowd in pleased attention so long as he. As in all original men, there is something for every palate. "Would you know," says Goethe, "the ripest cherries? Ask the boys and the blackbirds."—JAMES RUSSELL LOWELL, "Emerson the Lecturer" (1861–68), *Works*, Riverside ed., Vol. 1, pp. 349–52

I discovered a copy of Emerson's *Society and Solitude*, republished in London by Sampson Low. The sight of it was like manna in the wilderness. I became the happy owner of it at once, and it afforded me a rich feast for the rest of the journey. Some portions of it, I think, are equal to anything that Emerson has ever written. Emerson is a great master in his way. His style has an incomparable charm. Its silvery rhythm captivates the ear. The affluence of his illustrations diffuses a flavor of oriental spicery over his pages. As he confesses in the essay on "Books," his learning is second-hand; but everything sticks which his mind can appropriate. He defends the use of translations, and I doubt whether he has ever read ten pages of his great authorities, Plato, Plutarch, Montaigne, or Goethe, in the original. He is certainly no friend of profound study, any more than of philosophical speculation. Give him a few brilliant and suggestive glimpses, and he is content. His catalogue of books is limited in the extreme, and presents few hints of practical value. Much of the work is devoted to the comparative influence of solitude and society, in addition to the chapter with that title. The subject is touched in several of the essays, especially in those on "Clubs" and "Domestic Life." Emerson is fond of conversation, but it always disappoints him. With him it is an experiment constantly repeated, but always without success. His final conclusion is that the true man has no companion. There may be times when two persons may hold genuine communion, but the presence of a third person is impertinent, and always breaks the charm. Such occasions, however, are rare, and must be numbered by moments, and not by hours. His remarks on Art show his want of philosophic culture. The principal point which he urges is that Nature is the foundation of Art, and that the great Artist is spontaneous, and not reflective; both good points, but by no means original. Take away the splendid language in which they are clothed, I find that but little valuable instruction remains. There are frequent hints of the grand Platonic theory of the True, the Beautiful, the Good, as the exponents of the Infinite in Humanity, which long since ripened in my mind, as the true "Intellectual System of the Universe;" but he does not appear to be aware of its fathomless significance.

In thus renewing my acquaintance with Emerson, I am struck with certain rare combinations which may serve to explain his position. His rejection of dogmas is cool and merciless; but he shows no sympathy with vulgar and destructive radicalism. He asserts an unlimited freedom of the individual, but maintains a moral tone, rigid almost to asceticism. With the wild havoc which he makes of popular opinion, he always respects the dignity of human nature. Emerson is essentially a poet. His intuitions are in the form of images. Few men have such positive tendencies toward the Ideal. But his sympathy with external nature is equally strong. He is a keen and accurate observer. His perceptions are true, so far as concerns the material world and the qualities of character that are universal in man. His judgment of individuals is often prejudiced. The practical shrewdness interwoven with his poetical nature is one of the secrets of his power. You attempt to follow his lofty flight among the purple clouds, almost believing that he has "hitched his wagon to a star," when he suddenly drops down to earth, and surprises you with an utterance of the homeliest wisdom. On this account, when they get over the novelty of his manner, plain men are apt to find themselves at home with him. His acquaintance with common things, all household ways and words, the processes of every-day life on the farm, in the kitchen and stable, as well as in the drawing-room and library, engages their attention, and produces a certain kindly warmth of fellowship, which would seem to be incompatible with the coldness of his nature. Emerson is not without a tincture of science. He often makes a happy use of its results, in the way of comparison and illustration. But I do not suppose that he could follow a demonstration of Euclid, or one of the fine analyses in physics of Tyndall or Huxley. Of such a writer as Herbert Spencer he has probably no more than a faint comprehension. Emerson has less wit than I have usually been inclined to believe; of humor only a slender trace. Perhaps the subtlety and refinement of his illustrations may sometimes have the appearance of wit, but not its real flavor or effect.—GEORGE RIPLEY, *Journal* (1869), cited in Octavius Brooks Frothingham, *George Ripley*, 1882, pp. 266–68

In the regions we call Nature, towering beyond all measurement, with infinite spread, infinite depth and height—in those regions, including Man, socially and historically, with his moral-emotional influences—how small a part, (it came in my mind to-day,) has literature really depicted—even summing up all of it, all ages. Seems at its best some little fleet of boats, hugging the shores of a boundless sea, and never venturing, exploring the unmapp'd—never, Columbus-like, sailing out for New Worlds, and to complete the orb's rondure. Emerson writes frequently in the atmosphere of this thought, and his books report one or two things from that very ocean and air, and more legibly address'd to our age and American polity than by any man yet. But I will begin by scarifying him—thus proving that I am not insensible to his deepest lessons. I will consider his books from a democratic and western point of view. I will specify the shadows on these sunny expanses. Somebody has said of heroic character that "wherever the tallest peaks are present, must inevitably be deep chasms and valleys." Mine be the ungracious task (for reasons) of leaving unmention'd both sunny expanses and sky-reaching heights, to dwell on the bare spots and darknesses. I have a theory that no artist or work of the very first class may be or can be without them.

First, then, these pages are perhaps too perfect, too concentrated. (How good, for instance, is good butter, good sugar. But to be eating nothing but sugar and butter all the time! even if ever so good.) And though the author has much to say of freedom and wildness and simplicity and spontaneity, no performance was ever more based on artificial scholarships and decorums at third or fourth removes, (he calls it culture,) and built up from them. It is always a *make*, never an unconscious *growth*. It is the porcelain figure or statuette of lion, or stag, or Indian hunter—and a very choice statuette too—appropriate for the rosewood or marble bracket of parlor or library; never the animal itself, or the hunter himself. Indeed, who wants the real animal or hunter? What would that do amid astral and bric-a-brac and tapestry, and ladies and gentlemen talking in subdued tones of Browning and Longfellow and art? The least suspicion of such actual bull, or Indian, or of Nature carrying out itself, would put all those good people to instant terror and flight.

Emerson, in my opinion, is not most eminent as poet or artist or teacher, though valuable in all those. He is best as critic, or diagnoser. Not passion or imagination or warp or weakness, or any pronounced cause or specialty, dominates him. Cold and bloodless intellectuality dominates him. (I know the fires, emotions, love, egotisms, glow deep, perennial, as in all New Englanders—but the façade hides them well—they give no sign.) He does not see or take one side, one presentation only or mainly, (as all the poets, or most of the fine writers anyhow)—he sees all sides. His final influence is to make his students cease to worship anything—almost cease to believe in anything, outside of themselves. These books will fill, and well fill, certain stretches of life, certain stages of development—are, (like the tenets or theology the author of them preach'd when a young man,) unspeakably serviceable and precious as a stage. But in old or nervous or solemnest or dying hours, when one needs the impalpably soothing and vitalizing influences of abysmic Nature, or its affinities in literature or human society, and the soul resents the keenest mere intellection, they will not be sought for.

For a philosopher, Emerson possesses a singularly dandified theory of manners. He seems to have no notion at all that manners are simply the signs by which the chemist or metallurgist knows his metals. To the profound scientist, all metals are profound, as they really are. The little one, like the conventional world, will make much of gold and silver only. Then to the real artist in humanity, what are called bad manners are often the most picturesque and significant of all. Suppose these books becoming absorb'd, the permanent chyle of American general and particular character—what a well-wash'd and grammatical, but bloodless and helpless, race we should turn out! No, no, dear friend; though the States want scholars, undoubtedly, and perhaps want ladies and gentlemen who use the bath frequently, and never laugh loud, or talk wrong, they don't want scholars, or ladies and gentlemen, at the expense of all the rest. They want good farmers, sailors, mechanics, clerks, citizens—perfect business and social relations—perfect fathers and mothers. If we could only have these, or their approximations, plenty of them, fine and large and sane and generous and patriotic, they might make their verbs disagree from their nominatives, and laugh like volleys of musketeers, if they should please. Of course these are not all America wants, but they are first of all to be provided on a large scale. And, with tremendous errors and escapades, this, substantially, is what the States seem to have an intuition of, and to be mainly aiming at. The plan of a select class, superfined, (demarcated from the rest,) the plan of Old World lands and literatures, is not so objectionable in itself, but because it chokes the true plan for us, and indeed is death to it. As to such special class, the United States can never produce any equal to the splendid show, (far, far beyond comparison or competition here,) of the principal European nations, both in the past and at the present day. But an immense and distinctive commonalty over our vast and varied area, west and east, south and north—in fact, for the first time in history, a great, aggregated, real PEOPLE, worthy the name, and made of develop'd heroic individuals, both sexes—is America's principal, perhaps only, reason for being. If ever accomplish'd, it will be at least as much, (I lately think, doubly as much,) the result of fitting and democratic sociologies, literatures and arts—if we ever get them—as of our democratic politics.

At times it has been doubtful to me if Emerson really knows or feels what Poetry is at its highest, as in the Bible, for instance, or Homer or Shakspere. I see he covertly or plainly likes best superb verbal polish, or something old or odd—

Waller's "Go, lovely rose," or Lovelace's lines "to Lucasta"—the quaint conceits of the old French bards, and the like. Of *power* he seems to have a gentleman's admiration—but in his inmost heart the grandest attribute of God and Poets is always subordinate to the octaves, conceits, polite kinks, and verbs.

The reminiscence that years ago I began like most youngsters to have a touch (though it came late, and was only on the surface) of Emerson-on-the-brain—that I read his writings reverently, and address'd him in print as "Master," and for a month or so thought of him as such—I retain not only with composure, but positive satisfaction. I have noticed that most young people of eager minds pass through this stage of exercise.

The best part of Emersonianism is, it breeds the giant that destroys itself. Who wants to be any man's mere follower? lurks behind every page. No teacher ever taught, that has so provided for his pupil's setting up independently—no truer evolutionist.—WALT WHITMAN, "Emerson's Books (The Shadows of Them)" (1880), *Prose Works*, ed. Floyd Stovall, 1964, Vol. 2, pp. 515–18

It may be Emerson's boast that he has no system. This restlessness under any, even nominal, *régime* is a characteristic of contemporaneous philosophy outside the church. There is liberty enough in the church; and, in fact, beyond it we see nothing but imprisonment, for nothing so practically chains the intellect of man as irresponsible freedom. It is like the liberty of the ocean enjoyed (?) by a mariner without sails or compass. A Catholic philosopher can speculate as much as he pleases. The security of the faith gives him a delightful sense of safe freedom. Like O'Connell's driving a coach and four through an act of Parliament, he may go to the outermost verge of speculation. St. Thomas moves the most outrageous fallacies, speculations, and objections, and discusses them, too, with all the boldness of intellectual freedom. It is Dr. Marshall, we think, who shows that all intellectual activity and freedom are enjoyed within the spacious bounds of Catholic truth. Even in theology there are wide differences. The Catholic intellect is supposed to be completely bridled. We once read a powerful arraignment of our Scriptural proofs for purgatory, written by an eminent Protestant theologian. He must have been surprised to learn that Catholic theologians do not attach all importance to the Scriptural argument for purgatory. The different schools of Catholic theology argue *pro* and *con.* as keenly as old Dr. Johnson himself would have desired, but without the slightest detriment to the unity of the faith. Nothing can be falser than the received Protestant notion that we are helplessly bound by a network of petty definitions and regulations. There are, however, great and immovable principles which are understood to guide and vivify the Catholic intellect. And such systemization is necessary to all knowledge. Without it a man's mind, like Emerson's, wanders comet-like, attracting attention by its vagaries, but is of no intelligible use to the universe, and gives no light, except of a nebulous and perlexing nature.

Nathaniel Hawthorne, who, of all American writers, had the true transcendental mind, ridicules it unsparingly. His doleful experience upon Brook Farm, when he attempted to milk a cow, may have had a practical awakening effect upon his dreams. In a little sketch entitled "The Celestial Railroad," in which he whimsically carries out Bunyan's *Pilgrim's Progress*, he introduces Giant Transcendentalism, who has taken the place of Giant Pope, and Giant Despair, that interrupted Christian's progress to the Delectable Mountains. Giant Transcendentalism is a huge, amorphous monster,

utterly indescribable, and speaking an unintelligible language. This language, which Emerson strives to make articulate, we read with mingled amusement and astonishment in the German writers. Emerson is not a member of the *Kulturkampf*, like Carlyle. His mind does not take in their wild rhapsodies. His essay on Goethe (in *Representative Men*) is cold and unappreciative when compared with the Scotchman's eulogies. We firmly believe that no healthy intellect can feed upon Fichte, Schelling, Hegel, or even Kant, who was the most luminous intellect of the group. Emerson has not the stolid pertinacity of Herr Teufelsdröckh. His genius is French. He delights in paradox and verbal gymnastics. Carlyle works with a sort of furious patience at such a prosaic career as Frederick the Great's. He gets up a factitious enthusiasm about German *Herzhogs* and *Erstfursts*. Emerson would look with dainty disdain upon his Cyclopean work among big, dusty, musty folios and the hammering out of shining sentences from such pig-iron.

Whence his transcendentalism? We believe that it has two elements, nature-worship and Swedenborgianism. Of nature-worship we have very little. Like Thomson, the author of the *Seasons*, who wrote the finest descriptions of scenery in bed at ten o'clock in the morning, we are frightfully indifferent to the glories of earth, sea, and sky, whilst theoretically capable of intense rapture. This tendency to adore nature, and this intense modern cultivation of the natural sciences, we take as indicative of the husks of religion given by Protestantism. Man's intellect seeks the certain, and where he cannot find it in the supernatural he will have recourse to the natural. The profound attention paid to all the mechanical and natural sciences, to the exclusion, if not denial, of supernatural religion, is the logical result of the absurdity of Protestantism. Perhaps Emerson's poetic feeling has much to do with his profound veneration for fate, nature, and necessity, which are his true god, with a very little Swedenborgianism to modify them.

And here we meet him on his philosophy of words. A word, according to St. Thomas, should be the *adæquatio rei et intellectus*, for a word is really the symbol and articulation of truth. Where words convey no clear or precise idea to the mind they are virtually false. The terminology of Emerson falls even below Carlyle's in obscurity. What does he mean by the one-soul? What by compensation? What by fate and necessity? *Explica terminos* is the command of logic and reason; yet he maunders on in vague and extravagant speech, using terms which it is very probable he himself only partly or arbitrarily understands. He is not master of his own style. His own words hurry him along. This fatal bondage to style spoils his best thoughts. He seems to aim at striking phrases and ends in paradox. His very attempt to strengthen and compress his sentences weakens and obscures his meaning. The oracular style does not carry well. He is happiest where he does not don the prophetic or poetical mantle. When we get a glimpse of his shrewd character, he is as gay as a lark and sharp as a fox. He muffles himself in transcendentalism, but fails to hide his clear sense, which he cannot entirely bury or obfuscate. It seems strange to us that such a mind could be permanently influenced by the fantasies of Swedenborg, whom he calls a mystic, but who, very probably, was a madman. The pure mysticism of the Catholic Church is not devoid of what to those who have not the light to read it may seem to wear a certain air of extravagance, which, apparently, would be no objection to Emerson; but it is kept within strict rational bounds by the doctrinal authority of the church. We do not suppose that Emerson ever thought it worth his while to study the mystic or ascetic theology of the church, though here and there in his writings he refers to the example of saints, and quotes their sayings and doings. But it must be a strange mental state that passively admits the wild speculations of Swedenborgianism with its gross ideas of heaven and its fanciful interpretations of Scripture. Besides, Emerson clearly rejects the divinity of Jesus Christ, which is extravagantly (if we may use the expression) set forth in Swedenborgianism, to the exclusion of the Father and the Holy Ghost. He is, or was, a Unitarian, and his allusions to our Blessed Lord have not even the reverence of Carlyle.

Naturalism, as used in the sense of the Vatican decrees, is the proper word to apply to the Emersonian teaching. He has the Yankee boastfulness, materialistic spirit, and general laudation of the natural powers. His transcendentalism has few of the spiritual elements of German thought. He does not believe in contemplation, but stimulates to activity. In his earlier essays he seemed pantheistic, but his last book (*Society and Solitude*) affirmed his doubt and implicit denial of immortality. He appears to be a powerful personality, for he has certainly influenced many of the finer minds of New England, and, no doubt, he leads a noble and intellectual life. His exquisite aestheticism takes away the grossness of the results to which his naturalistic philosophy leads, and it is with regret that we note in him that intellectual pride which effectually shuts his mind even to the gentlest admonitions and enlightenments of divine grace.

It is a compliment to our rather sparse American authorship and scholarship that England regards him as the typical American thinker and writer. We do not so regard him ourselves, for his genius lacks the sturdy American originality and reverent spirit. But Emerson made a very favorable impression upon Englishmen when he visited their island, and he wrote the best book on England (*English Traits*) that, perhaps, any American ever produced. The quiet dignity and native independence of the book charmed John Bull, who was tired of our snobbish eulogiums of himself and institutions. Emerson met many literary men, who afterward read his books and praised his style. He has the air of boldness and the courage of his opinions. Now and then he invents a striking phrase which sets one a-thinking. He has also in perfection the art of quoting, and his whole composition betokens the artist and scholar.

There is a high, supersensual region, imagination, fantasy, or soul-life, in which he loves to disport, and to which he gives the strangest names. One grows a little ashamed of what he deems his own unimaginativeness when he encounters our philosopher "bestriding these lazy-pacing clouds." He wonders at the "immensities, eternities, and fates" that seem to exert such wondrous powers. When Emerson gets into this strain he quickly disappears either in the clouds or in a burrow, according to the taste and judgment of different readers. There is often a fine feeling in these passages which we can understand yet not express. Sublime they are not, though obscurity may be considered one of the elements of sublimity. They are emotional. Emerson belongs rather to the sensualistic school; at least, he ascribes abounding power to the feelings, and, in fact, he is too heated and enthusiastic for the coldness and calmness exacted by philosophical speculation. Many of his essays read like violent sermons; and his worst ones are those in which he attempts to carry out a ratiocination. He is dictatorial. He announces but does not prove. He appears at times to be in a Pythonic fury, and proclaims his oracles with much excitement and contortion. It is impossible to analyze an essay, or hold on to the filmy threads by which his thoughts hang

together. It is absurd to call him a philosopher who has neither system, clearness of statement, nor accuracy of thought. —JOSEPH O'CONNOR, "Ralph Waldo Emerson," *Catholic World*, April 1878, pp. 92–95

There can be no greater misfortune for a sincere and truthful mind like Emerson's than to have to get a living by "orating." This was his predicament, however; and there can be no doubt that his mind and his writings were the worse for this necessity. His philosophy afforded him only a very narrow range of subject. In all his essays and lectures he is but ringing the changes upon three or four ideas—which are really commonplace, though his sprightly wit and imagination give them freshness; and it is impossible to read any single essay, much less several in succession, without feeling that the licence of tautology is used to its extremest limits. In a few essays—for example, "The Poet," "Character," and "Love"—the writer's heart is so much in the matter that these endless variations of one idea have the effect of music which delights us to the end with the reiteration of an exceedingly simple theme; but in many other pieces it is impossible not to detect that weariness of the task of having to coin dollars out of transcendental sentiments to which Emerson's letters and journals often bear witness. But, whether delighted with or weary of his labour, there is no progress in his thought, which resembles the spinning of a cockchafer on a pin rather than the flight of a bird on its way from one continent to another.—COVENTRY PATMORE, "Emerson," *Principle in Art*, 1889, pp. 130–31

Emerson expressed, before all things, as was extremely natural at the hour and in the place, the value and importance of the individual, the duty of making the most of one's self, of living by one's own personal light, and carrying out one's own disposition. He reflected with beautiful irony upon the exquisite impudence of those institutions which claim to have appropriated the truth and to dole it out, in proportionate morsels, in exchange for a subscription. He talked about the beauty and dignity of life, and about every one who is born into the world being born to the whole, having an interest and a stake in the whole. He said "all that is clearly due to-day is not to lie," and a great many other things which it would be still easier to present in a ridiculous light. He insisted upon sincerity and independence and spontaneity, upon acting in harmony with one's nature, and not comforming and compromising for the sake of being more comfortable. He urged that a man should await his call, his finding the thing to do which he should really believe in doing, and not be urged by the world's opinion to do simply the world's work. "If no call should come for years, for centuries, then I know that the want of the Universe is the attestation of faith by my abstinence. . . . If I cannot work, at least I need not lie." The doctrine of the supremacy of the individual to himself, of his originality, and, as regards his own character, *unique* quality, must have had a great charm for people living in a society in which introspection—thanks to the want of other entertainment—played almost the part of a social resource.—HENRY JAMES, *Nathaniel Hawthorne*, 1879, pp. 82–83

Emerson's fame will probably be independent of any single contribution to the world's literature. For his merit does not appear to consist either in his rhetoric, or his philosophy, or his poetry, but rather in the genial spirit of the man, and in the generous and wholesome influence which he diffuses around him, like some bracing and exhilarating atmosphere. In a different sense from that of the sermon or the ethical homily, it "does one good" to read him; for he braces the sinews and sets the blood coursing more freely through the veins. In this respect he stands at the opposite pole to Carlyle, who supplies the malodorous and distasteful medicine, while Emerson gives the tonic of blithe air and happy sunshine. His spirits are so unfailing, his mental attitude is so sane and manlike, that he cannot even bear that one should mention his maladies, lest he become the querulous valetudinarian. "I beseech you by all angels to hold your peace and not pollute the morning, to which all the housemates bring serene and pleasant thoughts, by corruption and groans. Come out of the azure. Love the day." The distemper known as "blue devils" did not apparently haunt Emerson. "All my hurts my garden spade can heal," he says; albeit that his son, when he saw him digging, is reported to have told him to beware lest he should "dig his leg." There remains, however, a certain desultoriness which will probably prevent Emerson's work from becoming anything more than inspiring and suggestive. Perhaps this is the inevitable accompaniment of one who embraces a transcendental creed, like the shadow which lies across the valley even of him who walks on the heights. Perhaps it is the especial drawback of the modern American mind, which seems to rejoice in impressions and effects and symphonies as though they were the same as honest and full-blooded work. So Emerson himself thought when he asserted that the true dignity of the scholar was not realised in America. "The mark of American merit in painting, in sculpture, in poetry, in fiction, in eloquence, seems to be a certain grace without grandeur, and itself not new but derivative; a vase of fair outline, but empty, which whoso sees may fill with what wit and character is in him, but which does not, like the charged cloud, overflow with terrible beauty and emit lightning on all beholders." The grace of Emerson no one can deny, though even this is inferior to the literary finish and elegance of Hawthorne; but that he was not new but derivative, let his spiritual exemplars testify, who were Plato and Coleridge, Swedenborg and Wordsworth.—W. L. COURTNEY, "Ralph Waldo Emerson," *Fortnightly Review*, Sept. 1885, p. 331

He came from a race of clergymen; doubtless much of his elevation of character and austere sense of the grandeur of the moral sentiment is his by inheritance; but after entering the ministry he soon found that even Unitarianism was a limitation of his intellectual independence to which he could not submit; and, in the homely New England phrase, "he set up on his own account," responsible *for* nobody, and not responsible *to* anybody. His radicalism penetrated to the very root of dissent, for it was founded on the idea that in all organizations, social, political, and religious, there must be an element which checks the free exercise of individual thought; and the free exercise of his individual thinking he determined should be controlled by nothing instituted and authoritative on the planet. Descartes himself did not begin his philosophizing with a more complete self-emancipation from all the opinions generally accepted by mankind. But Descartes was a reasoner; Emerson is a seer and a poet; and he was the last man to attempt to overthrow accredited systems in order to substitute for them a dogmatic system of his own. In his view of the duty of "man thinking," this course would have been to violate his fundamental principle, which was that nobody "could lay copyright on the world;" that no theory could include Nature; that the greatest thinker and discoverer could only add a few items of information to what the human mind had previously won from "the vast and formless infinite;" and that the true work of a scholar was not to inclose the field of matter and mind by a system which encircled it, but to extend our knowledge in straight

lines, leading from the vanishing points of positive knowledge into the illimitable unknown spaces beyond. Emerson's peculiar sphere was psychology. By a certain felicity of his nature he was a non-combatant; indifferent to logic, he suppressed all the processes of his thinking, and announced its results in affirmations; and none of the asperities which commonly afflict the apostles of dissent ever ruffled the serene spirit of this universal dissenter. He could never be seduced into controversy. He was assailed both as an atheist and as a pantheist; as a writer so obscure that nobody could understand what he meant, and also as a mere verbal trickster, whose only talent consisted in vivifying commonplaces, or in converting, by inversion, stale truisms into brilliant paradoxes; and all these varying charges had only the effect of lighting up his face with that queer, quizzical, inscrutable smile, that amused surprise at the misconceptions of the people who attacked him, which is noticeable in all portraits and photographs of his somewhat enigmatical countenance. His method was very simple and very hard. It consisted in growing up to a level with the spiritual objects he perceived, and his elevation of thought was thus the sign and accompaniment of a corresponding elevation of character. In his case, as in the case of Channing, there was an unconscious return to Jonathan Edwards, and to all the great divines whose "souls had sight" of eternal verities. What the orthodox saints called the Holy Ghost, he, without endowing it with personality, called the Over Soul. He believed with them that in God we live and move and have our being; that only by communicating with this Being can we have any vital individuality; and that the record of a communication with Him or It was the most valuable of all contributions to literature, whether theological or human. The noblest passages in his writings are those in which he celebrates this august and gracious communion of the Spirit of God with the soul of man; and they are the most serious, solemn, and uplifting passages which can perhaps be found in our literature. Here was a man who had earned the right to utter these noble truths by patient meditation and clear insight. Carlyle exclaimed, in a preface to an English edition of one of Emerson's later volumes: "Here comes our brave Emerson, with *news* from the empyrean!" That phrase exactly hits Emerson as a transcendental thinker. His insights were, in some sense, revelations; he could "gossip on the eternal politics;" and just at the time when science, relieved from the pressure of theology, announced materialistic hypotheses with more than the confidence with which the bigots of theological creeds had heretofore announced their dogmas, this serene American thinker had won his way into all the centres of European intelligence, and delivered his quiet protest against every hypothesis which put in peril the spiritual interests of humanity. It is curious to witness the process by which this heresiarch has ended in giving his evidence, or rather his experience, that God is not the Unknowable of Herbert Spencer, but that, however infinitely distant He may be from the human understanding, He is still intimately near to the human soul. And Emerson knows by experience what the word *soul* really means!

> Were she a body, how could she remain
>   Within the body which is less than she?
> Or how could she the world's great shape contain,
>   And in our narrow breasts contained be?
> All bodies are confined within some place,
>   But she all place within herself confines;
> All bodies have their measure and their space,
>   *But who can draw the soul's dimensive lines?*

In an unpublished speech at a celebration of Shakspeare's

birthday, he spoke of Shakspeare as proving to us that "the soul of man is deeper, wider, higher than the spaces of astronomy;" and in another connection he says that "a man of thought must feel that thought is the parent of the universe," that "the world is *saturated* with deity and with law."

It is this depth of spiritual experience and subtilty of spiritual insight which distinguish Emerson from all other American authors, and make him an elementary power as well as an elementary thinker. The singular attractiveness, however, of his writings comes from his intense perception of Beauty, both in its abstract quality as the "awful loveliness" which such poets as Shelley celebrated, and in the more concrete expression by which it fascinates ordinary minds. His imaginative faculty, both in the conception and creation of beauty, is uncorrupted by any morbid sentiment. His vision reaches to the very sources of beauty,—the beauty that cheers. The great majority even of eminent poets are "saddest when they sing." They contrast life with the beautiful possibilities of life which their imaginations suggest, and though their discontent with the actual may inspire by the energy of its utterance, it tends also to depress by emphasizing the impossibility of realizing the ideals it depicts. But the perception of beauty in nature or in human nature, whether it be the beauty of a flower or of a soul, makes Emerson joyous and glad; he exults in celebrating it, and he communicates to his readers his own ecstatic mood. He has been a diligent student of many literatures and many religions; but all his quotations from them show that he rejects everything in his manifold readings which does not tend to cheer, invigorate, and elevate, which is not nutritious food for the healthy human soul. If he is morbid in anything, it is in his comical hatred of all forms of physical, mental, and moral disease. He agrees with Dr. Johnson in declaring that "every man is a rascal as soon as he is sick." "I once asked," he says, "a clergyman in a retired town who were his companions—what men of ability he saw. He replied that he spent his time with the sick and the dying. I said he seemed to me to need quite other company, and all the more that he had this; for if people were sick and dying to any purpose, we should leave all and go to them, but, as far as I had observed, they were as frivolous as the rest, and sometimes much more frivolous." Indeed, Emerson, glorying in his own grand physical and moral health, and fundamentally brave, is impatient of all the weaknesses of humanity, especially those of men of genius. He never could be made to recognize the genius of Shelley, except in a few poems, because he was disgusted with the wail that persistently runs through Shelley's wonderfully imaginative poetry. In his taste, as in his own practice as a writer, he is a stout believer in the desirableness and efficacy of mental tonics, and a severe critic of the literature of discontent and desperation. He looks curiously on while a poet rages against destiny and his own miseries, and puts the ironical query, "Why so hot, my little man?" His ideal of manhood was originally derived from the consciousness of his own somewhat haughty individuality, and it has been fed by his study of the poetic and historic records of persons who have dared to do heroic acts and dared to utter heroic thoughts. Beauty is never absent from his celebration of these, but it is a beauty that never enfeebles, but always braces and cheers.—EDWIN P. WHIPPLE, "American Literature" (1886), *American Literature and Other Papers*, 1887, pp. 59–65

He comes to many at the moment when he ought to come, and at the very instant when they were in mortal need of new interpretations. Heroic moments are less obvious, those of abnegation have not yet returned; only daily life remains to us, and yet we cannot live without grandeur. He has given to life, which had lost its traditional horizon, an almost acceptable meaning, and perhaps he has even been able to show us that it is strange enough, profound enough, great enough, to need no other end than itself. He does not know any more of it than the others do; but he affirms with more courage, and he has confidence in the mystery. You must live, all you who travel through days and years, without activities, without thought, without light, because your life, despite everything, is incomprehensible and divine. You must live because no one has a right to subtract any commonplace weeks from their spiritual sequence. You must live because there is not an hour without intimate miracles and ineffable meanings. You must live because there is not an act, not a word, not a gesture, which is free from inexplicable claims in a world "where there are many things to do, and few things to know."

Lives are neither great nor small, and the deed of Regulus or of Leonidas has no importance when I compare it with a moment of my soul's secret existence. It might do what they have done or not; these things do not reach it; and the soul of Regulus when he returned to Carthage was probably as distracted and indifferent as that of a mechanic on his way to the factory. The soul is far apart from all our deeds. It is far away from all our thoughts. It lives alone in the depth of our being a life of which it does not speak; and of the heights where it reigns, its various modes of activity can make out nothing. We walk weighed down by the weight of the soul, and there is no proportion between it and us. It perhaps never thinks of that which we are doing, and this can be read in our countenance. If one should ask an intelligence from another world what is the typical expression of the faces of men, it would reply doubtless, after having seen them in joys, in griefs, and in restless moods: "They look as if they were thinking of something else." Be great, wise, or eloquent; the soul of the beggar who holds out his hand at the corner of the bridge will not be jealous, but yours will perhaps envy him his silence. The hero needs the approbation of the ordinary man, but the ordinary man does not demand the approbation of heroes, and he pursues his course undisquieted, like one who has all his treasures in a safe place. "When Socrates speaks," says Emerson, "Lysis and Menexenus are afflicted by no shame that they do not speak. They also are good. He likewise defers to them, loves them, whilst he speaks. Because a true and natural man contains and is the same truth which an eloquent man articulates; but in the eloquent man, because he can articulate it, it seems something the less to reside, and he turns to these, silent, beautiful, with the more inclination and respect." ['Intellect.']

Man is eager for explanations. He must have his life shown to him. He rejoices to find anywhere an exact interpretation of a petty gesture he has been making for twenty-five years; yet there is no petty gesture here, but the main attitude of the common soul. You will not find the eternal quality of the soul of a Marcus Aurelius here. But Marcus Aurelius was thought itself. Who among us, moreover, leads the life of a Marcus Aurelius? One is man here, nothing more, not magnified arbitrarily, but grown nearer through habit. Here is John who is trimming his trees, Peter who is building his house; here are you who talk to me of the harvest, and I who give you my hand; yet we are made so that we draw nigh to the gods and are astonished at what we effect. We did not know that the laws of the universe attended upon us, and we turn about and stare without saying anything, like people who have seen a miracle.

Emerson comes to affirm simply this equal and secret

greatness of life. He encompasses us with silence and wonder. He puts a shaft of light under the foot of the artisan coming out of his workshop. He shows us all the powers of heaven and earth busied in supporting the threshold where two neighbors speak of the falling rain or the rising wind; and above these two wayfarers accosting each other he makes us see the face of one god smiling upon another. He is nearer to us than any one in our every-day life, the most watchful and persistent of monitors, the most upright and scrupulous, perhaps the most human. He is the sage of commonplace days; and commonplace days are the sum and substance of our being.

The most of a year passes without passions, without virtues, without miracles. Let us learn to reverence the small hours of life. If I have been able to work this morning, in the spirit of Marcus Aurelius, do not find fault with what I have accomplished, for I know well enough that something has come of it. But if I think that I have wasted my day in worthless undertakings, and you can prove to me that I have lived as worthily as a hero, and that my soul has lost none of its prerogatives, you will have done more than if you had persuaded me to save my enemy; for you will have increased within me the sense, the grandeur, and the desire of life; and to-morrow perhaps I shall be able to live with reverence. —Maurice Maeterlinck, "Emerson," trs. Charlotte Porter, Helen A. Clarke, *Poet-Lore*, 1898, pp. 82–84

The secret of his style is his diction. It may be described as seventeenth-century diction, and is derived from his early familiarity with old English writers. It fits both the man, his profession, and the quality of his ideas. He obtains by it verbal clearness, and in the short sentence which he especially cultivated he achieves weight and point, which are both oratorical qualities. He had also in his earlier writings fluidity, not in thought but in eloquence, the flow of the orator, for comparatively brief passages; in the *Essays* this quality is almost lost, owing to the way in which these writings were composed by selection and rearrangement from more extended compositions; the method had its advantages, for condensation and brilliancy of detail, but it necessarily forfeited consecutiveness, harmony, and naturalness. The posthumous publications, made up of uncollected papers and extracts from his manuscripts, in successive editions of his complete works, add nothing to his reputation, though they afford fuller illustrations of his life and thought. In style, except in the speeches, they are inferior. He had the same defects in prose as in verse; his taste was often at fault in both word and phrase, so far as the diction is concerned, and his effort for effect in short sentences sometimes betrayed him to expressions that are grotesque and result in caricature of the thought. He was not a great writer in the sense in which Bacon, Montaigne, or Pascal are great writers; but he was a writer with greatness of mind, just as he was not a great poet, but a poet with greatness of imagination.—George Edward Woodberry, *Ralph Waldo Emerson*, 1907, pp. 186–87

Works

PROSE

The essays have ⟨. . .⟩ been obnoxious to many charges. To that of obscurity, or want of perfect articulation. Of "Euphuism," as an excess of fancy in proportion to imagination, and an inclination at times to subtlety at the expense of strength, has been styled. The human heart complains of inadequacy, either in the nature or experience of the writer, to represent its full vocation and its deeper needs. Sometimes it speaks of this

want as "underdevelopment" or a want of expansion which may yet be remedied; sometimes doubts whether "in this mansion there be either hall or portal to receive the loftier of the passions." Sometimes the soul is deified at the expense of nature, then again nature at that of man, and we are not quite sure that we can make a true harmony by balance of the statements. This writer has never written one good work, if such a work be one where the whole commands more attention than the parts, if such an one be produced only where, after an accumulation of materials, fire enough be applied to fuse the whole into one new substance. This second series is superior in this respect to the former, yet in no one essay is the main stress so obvious as to produce on the mind the harmonious effect of a noble river or tree in full leaf. Single passages and sentences engage our attention too much in proportion. These essays, it has been justly said, tire like a string of mosaics or a house built of medals. We miss what we expect in the work of the great poet or the great philosopher, the liberal air of all the zones: the glow, uniform yet various in tint, which is given to a body by free circulation of the heart's blood from the hour of birth. Here is undoubtedly the man of ideas, but we want the ideal man also; want the heart and genius of human life to interpret it, and here our satisfaction is not so perfect. We doubt this friend raised himself too early to the perpendicular and did not lie along the ground long enough to hear the secret whispers of our parent life. We could wish he might be thrown by conflicts on the lap of mother earth, to see if he would not rise again with added powers.

All this we may say, but it cannot excuse us from benefiting by the great gifts that have been given and assigning them their due place.

Some painters paint on a red ground. And this color may be supposed to represent the groundwork most immediately congenial to most men, as it is the color of blood and represents human vitality. The figures traced upon it are instinct with life in its fullness and depths.

But other painters paint on a gold ground. And a very different but no less natural, because also a celestial beauty, is given to their works who choose for their foundation the color of the sunbeam, which nature has preferred for her most precious product, and that which will best bear the test of purification, gold.

If another simile may be allowed, another no less apt is at hand. Wine is the most brilliant and intense expression of the powers of earth—it is her potable fire, her answer to the sun. It exhilarates, it inspires, but then it is liable to fever and intoxicate too the careless partaker.

Mead was the chosen drink of the northern gods. And this essence of the honey of the mountain bee was not thought unworthy to revive the souls of the valiant who had left their bodies on the fields of strife below.

Nectar should combine the virtues of the ruby wine, the golden mead, without their defects or dangers.

Two high claims our writer can vindicate on the attention of his contemporaries. One from his *sincerity*. You have his thought just as it found place in the life of his own soul. Thus, however near or relatively distant its approximation to absolute truth, its action on you cannot fail to be healthful. It is a part of the free air.

He belongs to that band of whom there may be found a few in every age, and who now in known human history may be counted by hundreds, who worship the one God only, the God of Truth. They worship not saints nor creeds nor churches nor relics nor idols in any form. The mind is kept open to truth, and life only valued as a tendency toward it. This must be illustrated by acts and words of love, purity, and intelligence. Such are the salt of the earth; let the minutest crystal of that salt be willingly by us held in solution.

The other is through that part of his life which, if sometimes obstructed or chilled by the critical intellect, is yet the prevalent and the main source of his power. It is that by which he imprisons his hearer only to free him again as a "liberating God" (to use his own words). But indeed let us use them altogether, for none other, ancient or modern, can worthily express how, making present to us the courses and destinies of nature, he invests himself with her serenity and animates us with her joy.

"Poetry was all written before time was, and whenever we are so finely organized that we can penetrate into that region where the air is music, we hear those primal warblings and attempt to write them down, but we lose ever and anon a word or a verse, and substitute something of our own, and thus mistreat the poem. The men of more delicate ear write down these cadences more faithfully, and these transcripts, though imperfect, become the songs of the nations.

"As the eyes of Lyncaeus were said to see through the earth, so the poet turns the world to glass, and shows us all things in their right series and procession. For through that better perception he stands one step nearer to things, and sees the flowing or metamorphosis; perceives that thought is multiform; that within the form of every creature is a force impelling it to ascend into a higher form; and following with his eyes the life, uses the forms which express that life, and so the speech flows with the flowing of nature."

Thus have we in a brief and unworthy manner indicated some views of these books. The only true criticism of these or any good books may be gained by making them the companions of our lives. Does every accession of knowledge or a juster sense of beauty make us prize them more? Then they are good indeed, and more immortal than mortal. Let that test be applied to these; essays which will lead to great and complete poems—somewhere.—MARGARET FULLER, "Emerson's Essays," *New York Daily Tribune*, Dec. 7, 1844

Emerson's *Essays* I read with much interest, and often with admiration, but they are of mixed gold and clay—deep and invigorating truth, dreary and depressing fallacy seem to me combined therein.—CHARLOTTE BRONTË, Letter to W. S. Williams (Feb. 4, 1849)

I have also bought Emerson's *Representative Men*, a shilling book of Bohn's; with very good scattered thoughts in it: but scarcely leaving any large impression with one, or establishing a theory. So at least it has seemed to me: but I have not read very carefully.—EDWARD FITZGERALD, Letter to John Allen (March 4, 1850)

No American, perhaps we may add no English, reader needs to be told who and what Mr. Emerson is. In poetry and in prose, by spoken discourse and by written books, he has stamped his personality too deeply to be effaced upon the literature and speculations of the age. Some things he has published will live as long as the language itself; but much of his verse, constructed upon whims rather than under the influence of the spirit of poetry, will die out among the short-lived oddities of the day. Much of his prose, too, the production of imitation, unconscious perhaps, of vicious foreign models, can scarcely be expected to survive the charm which hangs about his person and lingers in the magic tones of his voice.

Mr. Emerson is a great writer, and an honest and independent thinker, on the whole. He is not, however, what

one of the idolaters has lately called him, a Phœbus Apollo, descended from Olympus with hurtling arrows and the silver twanging bow. He is neither the god of the lyre, nor will his shafts deal death among the host of those who fail to reverence *his priest*, though Emerson, too, Phœbus-like, has often "walked in darkness like the Night." This conversion of a modern Yankee into a Pagan god is a dangerous attempt to apply the *rationalistic* principle to persons and things of the present day. Some disciple of the school of historical skepticism has been trying his hand at turning Mr. Emerson into a *myth*. We object to the proceeding altogether, not knowing where it will end, and whose turn will come next. Homer, Lycurgus, Solon, and other nebulous spots in the sky of antiquity, have already been resolved, and now Mr. Emerson is undergoing the same process. That great *realist*, Mr. Weller, Senior, hit the nail on the head and struck out the true principle for such cases. "Wot I like in that 'ere style of writing," said he, after listening to his son Sam's *valentine*, "is that there 'aint no callin' names in it,—no Wenusses, nor nothin' o' that kind; wot's the good o' callin' a young 'ooman a Wenus or a angel, Sammy?"

The present volume 〈*Representative Men*〉 is marked strongly both by the excellences and defects of Mr. Emerson's other writings. His style is often musical, clear, and brilliant; words are selected with so rare a felicity that they have the shine of diamonds, and they cut their meaning on the reader's mind as the diamond's edge leaves its trace deep and sharp on the surface of glass. But by and by, we fall upon a passage which either conveys no distinct sense, or in which some very common-place thought is made to sound with the clangor of a braying trumpet. Quaintness of thought and expression is his easily besetting sin; and here lies the secret of his sympathy with Carlyle, that highly gifted master of oddity and affectation. As a writer, Mr. Emerson is every way Carlyle's superior, would he but let the Carlylese dialect alone. He has more imagination, more refinement and subtlety of thought, more taste in style, more exquisite sense of rhythm. Perhaps his range of intellectual vision is not so broad. He has not the learning of Carlyle, nor the abundant humor, which sometimes reconciles us even to absurdity. But Mr. Emerson has a more delicate wit, a wit often quite irresistible by its unexpected turns, and the sudden introduction of effective contrasts. Carlyle has an extraordinary abundance of words, a store of epithets, good, bad, and indifferent, by which the reader is often flooded; Emerson is more temperate and artistic. And yet we catch him, every now and then, mimicking the Scotchman, as if Carlyle were the master, and Emerson the pupil. He imitates Carlyle's affectation of odd and quaint expressions; he imitates him in the structure of his sentences; he imitates him in borrowing from the Germans a transcendental coloring, and in putting on an air of indifference to all positive opinions, an assumption of even-handed impartiality towards all religious systems. The trick of grotesque illustration by common or vulgar objects, he has caught from the Platonic Socrates. But setting aside these imitations and affectations, there hovers over much of his writing a peculiar and original charm, drawn from no source but the delicate and beautiful mind of the author himself.—CHARLES ELIOT NORTON, "Emerson's *Representative Men*," *North American Review*, April 1850, pp. 520–21

What now shall be said of Emerson's prose? Was Matthew Arnold right when, as an experienced critic calmly judging the favourite author of his youth, he denied that the *Essays*, the lectures, and *English Traits* formed a body of prose of sufficient merit to entitle Emerson to be ranked as a great man of letters?

It seems as if the time had come for Emerson's countrymen frankly to accept this verdict. Because of deficiencies both of style and of substance Emerson does not belong to the small class of the great masters of prose. His style, despite the fact that *Nature* and many of the essays contain pages of eloquent prose almost equal in power and beauty to noble poetry, was nearly always that of the lecturer or preacher rather than that of the writer. He too frequently lost the note of distinction and was content if he satisfied his far from exigent audiences. In diction, to be sure, he was a conscious and consummate master, and it need scarcely be said that few writers have surpassed him in the ability to compose a pregnant sentence. But, as is generally admitted and as is shown by his practice of piecing his notes together, he was rarely able to evolve a paragraph, much more a whole essay, in a masterly or even in a workmanlike fashion. It may be granted that critics have overemphasized his lack of coherence, that there is more logical unity in his essays than appears on first reading, that *English Traits* and the later volumes are far from being mere strings of "Orphic Sayings"; but the fact seems to remain that the prose style of Emerson from first to last lacks the firmness, the compass, the precision, the flexibility, the individuality, we demand of the prose writers whom we denominate masters.

In substance also he seems to be less great than he appeared to his contemporaries. This is partly due, paradoxically enough, to his own greatness. He has so leavened the thought of America with his fine idealism, his splendid belief in the capacity and the sacred rights and duties of the individual, his fearless democratic radicalism, that the latter-day reader receives as a matter of course utterances that thrilled the bosoms of youthful Americans two generations ago. The inspired seer is often in danger of seeming to be only a charming, somewhat impractical old gentleman. This attitude is obviously unjust to Emerson, and, to be candid, is probably seldom assumed by any sound-minded, sound-hearted reader of such nobly stimulating essays as those on "Self-Reliance" and "Spiritual Laws," or of the excellent, if less lofty, papers that make up *The Conduct of Life,* or of the homely discourse on "Civilization," in which, almost without warning, we are suddenly given the injunction—"Hitch your wagon to a star." But despite the continued sale of his works, despite popular votes that place him well to the front of American authors, it may fairly be held that not a few modern readers hold somewhat aloof from him both because of their familiarity with his leading ideas and because of his defects of substance. He is a great inciter to plain living and high thinking, but he is no longer an undisputed oracle on such subjects as "History," "Art," and the like, however charmingly and suggestively he may write about them. It is impossible not to perceive the discursiveness and the rashness of generalization displayed in *English Traits.* His defective sense of literary values, his excessive use of the speaker's privilege to plunder all the provinces of human culture, his relentless exploitation of his happy talent for discovering and presenting apt and telling illustrations, his irritating unwillingness to admit a pessimistic argument within the range of his mental vision, his almost fatal bias for stating half-truths only—these limitations of his genius detract sufficiently from the substantial value of his work to make it probable, if not certain, that his place is not with the world's masters of thought. On the other hand, it is equally true to maintain that no one can better gauge books and men when he understands them, that no one can range the fields of scholarship with more grace and divine right, that no one has better comprehended or employed the art of illustration, that no one can face unpleasant facts more bravely than Emerson

when he thinks fit, or can more effectively express the scorn or reproach they deserve.—WILLIAM P. TRENT, A *History of American Literature, 1607–1865,* 1903, pp. 333–36

POETRY

As for Emerson's verse (though he has written some as exquisite as any in the language) I suppose we must give it up. That he had a sense of the higher harmonies of language no one that ever heard him lecture can doubt. The structure of his prose, as one listened to it, was as nobly metrical as the King James version of the Old Testament, and this made it all the more puzzling that he should have been absolutely insensitive to the harmony of verse. For it was there he failed—single verses are musical enough. I never shall forget the good-humoredly puzzled smile with which he once confessed to me his inability to apprehend the value of accent in verse.—JAMES RUSSELL LOWELL, Letter to James B. Thayer (Dec. 24, 1883)

Many find the poems of Emerson obscure. This obscurity results very largely from the fact of their strength. So far as the content of the poems is concerned, this consists of the thoughts and images that would present themselves to a poetic nature that had caught the fullest intellectual and spiritual impulse of his time. To the comprehension of these the poet, if he be indeed such, can furnish little help. If he utters a thought it is not simply as a thought that he utters it. As we have seen, the ideas in the poetry of Emerson rarely present themselves except as creations of the imagination. In other words, the poet deals with pictures. If one recognizes what is placed before him, well and good; if he does not, he must study it out for himself. Emerson speaks in one case of "leopard-colored rills." When I first read these poems in my youth, I remember that I was troubled with this phrase. I had never seen enough, or had never observed enough, to recognize the beauty and truth of the epithet. I could only wait till the thing recalled the words. If Emerson had supposed that any reader would not recognize the meaning he could have explained it and told how the effect was produced. He could have said that, given a bottom of reddish sand with shadows or ripples playing over it, we should have something that might suggest the skin of a leopard; but in this case we should have an approach to prose. So if Emerson had explained the spiritual imagery of his poems, he might have made them more clear, but with a like defect. It is the province of the imagination to gather up into single living forms whatever is offered to its view. The horizon will vary according to the position or the insight of the poet. If what it presents be familiar, all will recognize and comprehend; so far as it is less familiar, will there be obscurity. The question to ask in this latter case is, whether the thought of the poet be fantastic or fanciful; that is, whether it be his private thought; or, on the other hand, whether it lie in the pathway of the race. If when we reach it we find it human and normal, then it is not the fault of the poet, but to his praise, that we have found it at first obscure. It is, I repeat, because he is a poet that he appeals not directly to the understanding but to the imagination of the reader, which he assumes to be in harmony with his own. Even the essays of Emerson were at first found obscure. One writer compared the reading of them to the making one's way through a swamp. You put your foot upon some little hummock that bears its weight, and then look about you to find a resting place for the next step. Rarely now are his essays found obscure. Indeed, we can scarcely understand to-day the difficulty that beset their first reading. The difference is that at the time the style and the range of the thought were new; now, thanks largely to Emerson himself, they have become familiar.

In the poetry the difficulty is greater, partly because the thought is higher and subtler; partly because, as has just been shown, poetry appeals to the imagination rather than to the understanding. To this it must be added that because the style of Emerson is so strong and epigrammatic the thought is doubly barred. So far as the expression is concerned, we must pronounce our judgment not according to the degree of the difficulty in comprehending, but according to the fitness of the expression as felt when comprehension has been reached. It will often be found, when the meaning flashes upon the mind, that the very difficulty is the beauty of the phrase.—C. C. EVERETT, "The Poems of Emerson," *Andover Review*, March 1887, pp. 239–40

The poetry of Emerson, whatever its special manner or theme, is the poetry of acquiescence, optimism, idealism, spiritualism, individualism. It often has a didactic and magisterial tone, rather than the moralizing tone of Wordsworth or Cowper. "Do this," "shun that," it swiftly says. "Be not a fool, not a money-maker, but a poet and a lover of the beautiful and the good." Nature, rightly understood, is a fit and lovely thing, and so is the soul at its best. Poetry notes and intensely describes some of the qualities of each, or of both. It was no wonder that Emerson anticipated, in half-a-dozen poems, the later conclusions of the evolutionists. He was the singer of the upward march of nature and the onward march of man. His poetic field was too broad to be tilled thoroughly in many parts. He was too proverbial to be a great constructive artist. He gives us saws, sayings, admonitions, flashes, glimpses, few broad constructed pictures. With these we are content, and do not ask him for epics, tragedies, or "Excursions," having poems like those already named; or "Good-bye, Proud World," "The Sphinx," and the "Concord Hymn"; or lines like

> He builded better than he knew;
>
> Earth proudly wears the Parthenon
> As the best gem upon her zone;
>
> The silent organ loudest chants
> The master's requiem;
>
> And conscious law is king of kings;
>
> Or music pours on mortals
> Its beautiful disdain.

Emerson's poetic art was at times of exquisite quality, a lovely presentation of noble thought. The perfection of verbal melody exists when the reader or hearer cannot conceive of any other way of singing the thought; and not a few of Emerson's lines or poems well bear this test. When this art gives place to grim force we do not feel, as Lowell said of Whittier, that Emerson as poet is

> Both singing and striking in front of the war
> And hitting his foes with the mallet of Thor,

for Emerson's stern strength is not that of a Taillefer but rather that of a Saxon law-maker. He announces, with all his force, but does not wage war in defence of the sayings he has uttered with oracular positiveness. Emerson is one more illustration of the fact, too often forgotten, that a poet can be forcible and lyrical at the same time; rooted in cold, deep thought and giving to the warm winds the loveliest flowers of beauty. Emerson, more than any American poet, severely tests and almost defies the laws of poetics, as they have been deduced from other languages and applied to English scansion; but yet from his work may be selected many an example proving anew that English is capable of fine and deliberate metrical and melodious effects. He who recognizes Emerson's aims and methods will attempt neither to prove all his failures to be

glorious successes, which men are too blind to see; nor to declare him rugged or unmelodious or obscure,—the poet who, when he would, could sing so sweet and clear a song. —CHARLES F. RICHARDSON, *American Literature, 1607–1885,* 1887, Vol. 2, pp. 169–71

If Emerson had been frequently sustained at the heights he was capable of reaching, he would unquestionably have been one of the sovereign poets of the world. At its very best his phrase is so new and so magical, includes in its easy felicity such a wealth of fresh suggestion and flashes with such a multitude of side-lights, that we cannot suppose that it will ever be superseded or will lose its charm. He seems to me like a very daring but purblind diver, who flings himself headlong into the ocean, and comes up bearing, as a rule, nothing but sand and common shells, yet who every now and then rises grasping some wonderful and unique treasure. In his prose, of course, Emerson was far more a master of the medium than in poetry. He never became an easy versifier; there seems to have been always a difficulty to him, although an irresistible attraction, in the conduct of a piece of work confined within rhyme and rhythm. He starts with a burst of inspiration; the wind drops and his sails flap the mast before he is out of port; a fresh puff of breeze carries him round the corner; for another page, the lyrical *afflatus* wholly gone, he labours with the oar of logic; when suddenly the wind springs up again, and he dances into a harbour. We are so pleased to find the voyage successfully accomplished that we do not trouble to inquire whether or no this particular port was the goal he had before him at starting. I think there is hardly one of Emerson's octo-syllabic poems of which this will not be found to be more or less an accurate allegorical description. This is not quite the manner of Milton or Shelley, although it may possess its incidental advantages.

It cannot be in candour denied that we obtain a very strange impression by turning from what has been written about Emerson to his own poetry. All his biographers and critics unite, and it is very sagacious of them to do so, in giving us little anthologies of his best lines and stanzas, just as writers on *Hudibras* extract miscellanies of the fragmentary wit of Butler. Judged by a chain of these selected jewels, Emerson gives us the impression of high imagination and great poetical splendour. But the volume of his verse, left to produce its own effect, does not fail to weaken this effect. I have before me at this moment his first collected *Poems*, published, as he said, at "the solstice of the stars of his intellectual firmament." It holds the brilliant fragments that we know so well, but it holds them as a mass of dull quartz may sparkle with gold dust. It has odes about Contocook and Agischook and the Over-God, long nebulous addresses to no one knows whom, about no one knows what; for pages upon pages it wanders away into mere cacophonous eccentricity. It is Emerson's misfortune as a poet that his technical shortcomings are for ever being more severely reproved by his own taste and censorship than we should dare to reprove them. To the author of "The World-Soul," in shocking verses, we silently commend his own postulate in exquisite prose, that "Poetry requires that splendour of expression which carries with it the proof of great thoughts." Emerson, as a verse-writer, is so fragmentary and uncertain that we cannot place him among the great poets; and yet his best lines and stanzas seem as good as theirs. Perhaps we ought to consider him, in relation to Wordsworth and Shelley, as an asteroid among the planets.—EDMUND GOSSE, "Has America Produced a Poet?" (1889), *Questions at Issue*, 1893, pp. 86–88

It seems to me that, with Emerson, verse was not, as a general thing, so natural and congenial a form of expression that it drew him magnetically and irresistibly. I admit that marked exceptions must be made to this statement. And there are noble poems and parts of poems which seem the pure and spontaneous prompting of the Muse. Notably those where he is plainly swayed by a strong tide of emotion, or touched by some vivid fancy or natural picture—as in his 'Threnody,' the 'Rhodora,' 'The Amulet,' 'Rubies,' 'Each and All,' 'The Snow-storm' and parts of the 'Wood-Notes.' His poem, 'The Problem'—almost matchless as it is—is less an outflow of lyric expression than a brilliant mosaic of thoughts concisely and poetically expressed; a poem (in this respect, though not otherwise) like Gray's *Elegy*, where many of the couplets, as there the quatrains, might change places without seriously dislocating the whole structure.

Though perhaps never guilty of writing *invita Minerva*, he is naturally more epigrammatic than lyric. It is only in the fusion of an emotion or an ideal that he *flows*. And even then his stream is roughened and impeded by serious technical limitations. For such long elemental wave-sweeps as Milton or Byron or Shelley or Keats delighted in, he was unfit. He lacked one essential element, the sensuous—and this includes the rhythmical sense. The form is slighted—the thought or the picture only prized. But every complete poet should be an artist too, and know how to wed beautiful thoughts to beautiful forms, and in the most harmonious union. Here, I think, was Emerson's deficiency. I am sure that in all times of literature, those poems will live longest that best fulfill the demand for a perfect soul in a perfect body.

But what then? Shall we quarrel with our poet because he is not a complete rhythmical artist? Shall we not rather trust to the impression he makes by the rare thought and original diction shining through lines which are incomplete, which are halting, odd, extravagant, or obscure, but which are so much a natural way he has of expressing himself that they may be said to be full of 'an art that Nature makes'? The imperfect structure of many of his poems can never hide from us those wonderfully graphic touches wherein he is so alive to Nature—those memorable couplets or those 'skyey sentences' (a term he so felicitously applies to Shakespeare),—or those happy condensations of thoughts into phrases that have become as household words to us.

As to the question of rank of this or that poet, or of comparison of one with another, my feeling is that there can be little profit in such speculation, even in the form of professional criticism. I don't think that musicians hold many warm debates about the respective merits of Beethoven, Mendelssohn, Schubert or Schumann. When we see, hear, feel Beauty, we acknowledge and applaud it. I think we grow less and less inclined to be dogmatically critical as to the relative greatness of the plays of Shakespeare; and we don't stand debating whether the sunset of last evening was finer than that of a week ago.

Whatever the technical imperfections of Emerson's verse, it is beyond question that we are lifted by his rare though broken music into chambers of thought and mystical sentiment, to which few poets of our day have the key. If he is not a great poetic artist, he is a great seer and inspirer—and of prose-poets our first.—C. P. CRANCH, "Emerson's Limitations as a Poet," *Critic*, Feb. 27, 1892, p. 129

GEORGE GILFILLAN
"Emerson"
A Third Gallery of Portraits
1854, pp. 328–36

The fame of Emerson has had a singular cycle of history, within the last thirteen years, in Britain. His first Essays, re-published in 1841, with a preface by Carlyle, were, on the whole, coldly welcomed by the public; with the exceptions of the *Eclectic Review*, which praised their genius while condemning their opinions, and *Tait's Magazine*, the monthly and quarterly press either ignored or abused them. Their admirers, indeed, were very ardent, but they were very few, and principally young men, whose enthusiasm was slightly shaded with a sceptical tendency. Between this period and his visit to Britain, in 1848, a great revolution in his favour had taken place. The publication of a second volume of Essays, still more peculiar and daring than the first, the re-appearance of his tractate, entitled *Nature*—the most complete and polished of all his works—the deepening enthusiasm of his admirers, and the exertions of one or two of them, who had gained the ear of the public, and were determined to fill it with his fame, as well as the real merit of his writings, had amply prepared the country for his approach, when, among the last days of 1847, he set the impress of his foot upon our shores. Then his name and influence came to a culminating point, and ever since they seem to us to have declined. For this, various causes may be assigned.

In the first place, his appearance disappointed many; they did not meet the rapt, simple, dreaming enthusiast of whom they had been dreaming.

Secondly, his Lectures were chiefly *double entendres*. There were alike commissions and omissions in them, which proved this to a certainty. We have seen him scanning an audience ere he resolved which of two lectures he should give. Think of Paul on Mars Hill, balancing between two Greek variations of his immortal speech, or, on consideration, choosing another text than "Ye men of Athens, I perceive that in all things ye worship DEMONS too much." We have heard of him, too, sacrificing, to suit an audience, the principal pith, marrow, and meaning of a whole lecture; as if, in quoting the words, "thou shalt worship the Lord thy God," he had slily and *sub voce* substituted the little word "not." Nay, even when there was no such disingenuous concealment or subtraction, there was a game of "hide-and-seek" continually going on—a use of Scripture phrases in an unscriptural sense, a trimming, and turning, and terror at the prejudices of his audience, altogether unworthy of his genius. Indeed, we wonder that the tribe of expectant materialists in England and Scotland, with Holyoake, MacAll, and George Combe at their head, had not, disgusted at the doubledealing of their American champion, met at Berwick-upon-Tweed, and burned him in effigy. *They*, at least, are direct, and honest, and thoroughgoing men, we mean animals, for they are perpetually boasting of their lineal descent from brutes, and reptiles, and fishes, and slime, and everything but God, and we are not disposed to deny *their* far-come *and dearly-won honours*, or to quarrel, so far as *they* are concerned, with this mud heraldry.

Thirdly, the better portion of the age is fast becoming sick of all systems of mere negation. And what else is Emerson's? Any man who has ever thought for himself is competent to deny, and even to make his system of denial almost impregnable. A child of six or seven is quite able to trace the syllable

No. To use again the allusion of the prophet, "it is a populous city—No;" and assuredly Emerson keeps one of its principal gates. But, with the exception of a mangled Platonism, although he seldom if ever quotes the Greek of Plato, there is not a trace of system, of consistent intuition, of progressive advancement in thought, in all his writings. In one part of them he makes man's soul all; in a second, he makes nature all; and, in a third, he magnifies some shadowy abstraction which he calls the "Oversoul," a sort of sublime overhead negro-driver, compelling men to hell or heaven, as seems good in his own blind eyes. In one place he declares that society never advances, and in another he gives a chart of a Millennium in society which love is by "pushing" to produce. Contradictory intuitions, as he would call them, abound in almost every page, and the question naturally arises, which are we to believe? which of the deliverances of this Paul-Pyrrho, this oracular sceptic, this captive to the "Oversoul," are we to receive as *his*? To refute them were difficult, because, in the first place, it is not easy to see what they are; because, secondly, he often saves us the trouble, by contradicting them next page or volume himself; and because, thirdly, while it is the simplest matter in the world to rear or to dwell in the "City No," it is the most difficult matter to overturn it. It is like hunting a dream, or trampling on a shade, or fitting out an expedition to overset Aladdin's palace.

Such are some of the reasons why Emerson's influence over the young, sincere, and liberal minds of the age must rapidly go down—like an October sun, very bright, but which is too late for ripening anything, and which, after a brief meridian, and a briefer afternoon, sinks, as if in haste and confusion, below the horizon. Another reason we are reluctantly, and in deep sorrow, compelled to add—Emerson is *one of the few sceptics* who has *personally*, and by *name*, insulted the Lord Jesus Christ, and, through him, that Humanity of which Jesus is the Hope, the Glory, the Ideal, and the Crown. This extreme Carlyle has always avoided, and he has never spoken of Christ, or of the Divine Mystery implied in him, but with deep reverence. Many other of the sublimer order of doubters have been equally guarded. But Emerson, with Julian the Apostate, Voltaire, Paine, and Francis Newman, must bear the brand of using language to Christ which no man of culture would now apply to a Cæsar, a Danton, or a Napoleon. He says, "this *shoves* Jesus and Judas both aside." He speaks, again, of Christ's "tropes," as if the man who died on Calvary because he *would* not lie, was an exaggerator and a rhetorician, when he said, "I and my Father are one," or, "he that has seen me, has seen the Father."

We have heard a dog baying at the moon—we have heard of a maniac spitting foam at the stars—we have watched the writhings of crushed mediocrity as it gazed on the bright pages of genius—and we have understood, excused, pitied, and forgiven all such in their morbid or mistaken feelings. But how one calling himself a man, and reputed really a man of genius, could, in his most unhappy hour, have uttered a word against our Brother—God—the Eternal Child—the Babe in the Manger—the Boy in the Temple—the Carpenter in the Shed—the Weeper at the Grave—the Sufferer on the Cross—the Risen from the Tomb—the Exalted to the Heavens—the Friend by eminence of our fallen Family—the Expected from the Clouds—The Type and Test of whatever is holy, and charitable, and lovely, and lofty in the race of man—passes our conceptions, and has strained to its utmost *our* power of forgiveness.

Why, we must also inquire, has he said such things, and yet not said more of Jesus? "What thinkest thou of Christ?" If he was an impostor, say so. If he was a madman, say so. If he was God in human shape, say so. If he is merely the conventional ideal of human nature, say so more distinctly. If he is neither, nor all of these, then *what is he?* whence has he come? Emerson, while striking hard, and often, and openly, at the divinity of Jesus, and not sparing quiet *sotto voce* insinuations against his character and his power over the minds of men, has never yet propounded or sought to propound any probable or intelligible theory of Christ. He has simply, with muttered, or more than muttered, sneers or sighs over his unacknowledged claims, turned away, refusing to look at or to worship this "great sight."

Man seems the Christ of Emerson. And a sorry Christ he is. "Man," says Bacon, "is the god of the dog;" but were a dog fancying himself a man, it were a supposition less monstrous than the universal Immanuelism of Emerson. If man be the Christ, where are the works which prove him so? If every man has the divinity within him, why are the majority of men so corrupt and malignant? If the history of man be the history of God in human nature, why is it little else than one tissue of blood, falsehood, and low sin? We think he might far more plausibly start and defend the hypothesis that man *is* the devil; and that his history has hitherto been but a long development of diabolism. And, in proving this, he might avail himself to great advantage of Quetelet's tables, which demonstrate the significant fact, that certain works of a rather infernal character, such as murder, arson, and rape, re-appear in steady and mathematical succession, and no more than summer and winter, seed-time and harvest, are ever to cease. The presence of such an eternal law would go far to prove that man was an immutable and hopeless child of hell.

Many strange deductions seem to follow from Emerson's theory, nay, are more or less decidedly admitted by him. If man be the Christ or God incarnate, then there can be no such thing as guilt, and there ought to be no such thing as punishment. Whatever is done, is done, not by God's permission or command, but by God himself. God is at once the judge and the offender. If man be God incarnate, it follows that he is the creator of all things. This Emerson repeatedly intimates. The sun is but a splendid mote in man's eye; the moon is but his produced and prolonged smile; the earth is the shadow of his shape; the stars are lustres in the room of his soul; the universe is the bright precipitate of his thought. He is the Alpha and Omega, the beginning of the Creation of God, and its ending too. "The simplest person," he says, "who, in his integrity, worships God, *becomes* God." It follows, again, that no supernaturalism ever did or ever could exist. It was, according to Emerson, Moses, not Jehovah, who spoke on Sinai. It was Isaiah's own human soul which saw the fate of empires as distinctly as we see stars falling through the midnight. It was the mere man Christ Jesus who taught, and worked, and died in Judea. The possibility, in like manner, of any future revelation from heaven is ignored—ignored by the denial of any heaven save the mind of man. This is the dunghill-Olympus on which Emerson seats his shadowy gods. And whatever strange and aerial-seeming shapes may hereafter appear upon its summit, are to be in reality only sublimated mud—the beauty and the strength of—dirt. "Man," to use Foster's language, is to produce an "apotheosis of himself, by the hopeful process of exhausting his own corruptions," or sublimating them into a putrid holiness.

It follows, again, that, whatever he may say in particular passages, there can be no advancing or steady progress in humanity. The laws which develop it are unchangeable, the climate in which it lives is subject to very slight variations; its

"Oversoul" is a stern demon, with, perhaps, as he says, "a secret kindness in its heart," but outwardly a very Moloch of equal calm and cruelty; and under his eye, society and man must work, and bleed, and suffer on, upon this rolling earth, as on an eternal treadmill in a mist. 'Tis a gospel of despair, which in reality he teaches, of the deepest and the most fixed despair. The dungeon into which he introduces his captives is cold and low; it has no outlet: no key called Promise is to be found therein; the sky, indeed, is seen above through the dome, but it is distant—dark—with strange and melancholy stars, and but one hope, like a cup of prison-water, is handed round among the dwellers in this dreary abode—that of Death. And yet, but of late thousands of our young, rising, and gifted minds were, and many are still, forsaking the free atmosphere, the strait but onward way, and the high-hung star of hope, and Christianity, for this dismal insulated and under-ground abyss, where the very light is as darkness. It follows, again, that humility and all its cognate virtues are mere mistakes. "Trust thyself—every heart vibrates to that iron string." A greater than Emerson said, two thousand years ago, "Blessed are the poor in spirit, for theirs is the kingdom of heaven;" and another of the same school said, "When ye are weak, then are ye strong." We are not defending a false or voluntary humility. But surely, unless you can prove that all strength, and purity, and peace, are enclosed in yourself, to bow before the higher—to draw strength from the stronger—to worship the divine—is the dictate of cultured instinct, as well as of common sense. Almost all the powers and elements of nature combine in teaching man the one great simple word, "bend." "Bend," the winds say it to the tall pines, and they gain the curve of their magnificence by obeying. "Bend," gravitation says it to the earth, as she sweeps in her course round the sun; and she knows the whisper of her ruler, and stoops and bows before the skiey blaze. "Bend," the proud portals of human knowledge say it to all aspirants, and were it the brow of a Bacon or a Newton, it must in reverence bow. "Bend," the doors, the ancient doors of heaven, say it, in the music of their golden hinges, to all who would pass therein; and the Son of Man himself, although he could have prayed to his Father, and presently obtained twelve legions of angels, had to learn obedience, to suffer, to bow the head, ere as a King of Glory he entered in. "Trust thyself." No; Christianity says, "Mistrust thyself—trust God. Do thy humble duty, and call the while on the lofty help that is above thee." Even Shelley, a far more gifted mind than Emerson, tells us, borrowing the thought from Burke, to "*fear ourselves, and love all human-kind.*"

It follows, finally, that there seems no hope to us from the exclusive and idolatrous devotion to nature which Emerson has practised and recommends. He, appearing to believe that nature is his *own* work, has conned its pages with all the fondness which a young author feels for his first poems. And yet he has learned from it, or at least taught us, extremely little. If he has, as he says, met "God in the bush," why no particulars of the interview? Why no intelligible precept, no new law, from that "burning bush" of the West? Why does nature, in his hands, remain as cold, silent, enigmatic, and repulsive—we mean as a moral teacher—as ever it was? Why does its "old silence" remain silent still, or only insult us with fragments of mysticism and echoes of blasphemy? Alas! Emerson's *Essays* are another proof of what Hazlitt, from bitter experience, said long ago, "Neither poetry nor nature are sufficient for the soul of man." And although Emerson has, with more severe self-purgation, if not with a truer heart, approached the shrine, he has derived, or at least circulated, quite as little of real knowledge, or of real satisfaction and

peace, as the honest but hapless author of *The Spirit of the Age.*

The fact is (and we are grieved to announce it), this writer, with all his talk about spiritualism and idealism, seems to us, in essence, if anything at all, a mere materialist—believing not, however, in the wide matter of suns and stars, but in the sublimated matter of his proper brain. He has brought the controversy of ages to a point—the point of his own head. This he claps and clasps, and says, "Talk of God, Heaven, Jesus, Shakspere, the earth, the stars—it's *all here.*" Even as, not long ago, we heard a poor woman, in fever, declaring that there was "more sense in her head than in all the world besides!" And into what wilds have some of his followers, both in America and here, wandered, till, in search of their master, they have lost themselves. One of them will make an earth-heap among the woods, and show his companions how God *should* make a world. Others take to living on acorns and water; and one lady, of some abilities, has lately written a small volume of poems, in which, amid many other symptoms of the most rabid Emersonianism, such as sneering at the power and influence of the Bible, magnifying the soul, &c., she, in one little copy of verses, avows herself a *worshipper of the Sun*—it being the epic, we suppose, of *her* transcendent spirit!

It is high time that all such egregious nonsense should be exposed; and we only regret that our space does not permit us more fully at present to expose it. We "bide our time." And we can speak the more freely, that *we* have passed through a section of the Emersonian shadow ourselves—never into its deepest gloom, but along the outskirts of its cold and hopeless darkness. *We,* however, never lost our faith in Jesus, nor regarded Emerson's notions of Him with any other feelings but disgust and sorrow. *We* never "kissed our hands" to the sun. But we at one time regarded Emerson as a sincere man, astray on one of the by-paths from the road leading up to the "City." We have seen reason to change our mind, and to say of him, and of all such, "Beward of the Flatterer." His system, to our knowledge, has shaken belief, has injured morality, has poisoned the purest natures, has embittered the sweetest tempers, has all but maddened the strongest minds, has been for years a thick cosmical cloud between lofty souls and the God of their childhood and their fathers, has not even led to that poor, beggarly, outwardly clean life, in which he seems to believe all morality to consist (as if the plagues of the *soul* were not infinitely worse than the diseases of the body), and has led to life "without hope and without God in the world." And without laying all the blame of this—and it has been the experience of hundreds—upon Emerson himself, we do advisedly lay it upon the back of his heartless and hopeless creed.

After all this, to speak of Emerson's genius seems mere impertinence. It is little to the point, and, besides, has often been largely descanted on by us and others. It is undoubtedly of a high order. If he cannot interpret, he can paint, nature as few else can. He has watched and followed all her motions like a friendly spy. He has the deepest egotistic interest in her. He appropriates her to himself, and because he loves and clasps, imagines that he has made her. His better writings seem shaken, sifted, and cooled in the winds of the American autumn. The flush on his style is like the red hue of the Indian summer inscribed upon the leaf. One of the most inconsistent and hopelessly wrong of American thinkers, he is the greatest of American poets. We refer not to his verse—which is, in general, woven mist, involving little—but to the beautiful and abrupt utterances about nature in his prose. No finer things about the outward features, and the transient meanings of creation, have been said, since the Hebrews, than are to be found in some of his books. But he has never, like them, pierced to the grand doctrine of the Divine Personality and Fatherhood.

MATTHEW ARNOLD
From "Emerson" (1884)
Discourses in America
1885, pp. 150–207

I was reading the other day a notice of Emerson by a serious and interesting American critic. Fifty or sixty passages in Emerson's poems, says this critic,—who had doubtless himself been nourished on Emerson's writings, and held them justly dear,—fifty or sixty passages from Emerson's poems have already entered into English speech as matter of familiar and universally current quotation. Here is a specimen of that personal sort of estimate which, for my part, even in speaking of authors dear to me, I would try to avoid. What is the kind of phrase of which we may fairly say that it has entered into English speech as matter of familiar quotation? Such a phrase, surely, as the "Patience on a monument" of Shakespeare; as the "Darkness visible" of Milton; as the "Where ignorance is bliss" of Gray. Of not one single passage in Emerson's poetry can it be truly said that it has become a familiar quotation like phrases of this kind. It is not enough that it should be familiar to his admirers, familiar in New England, familiar even throughout the United States; it must be familiar to all readers and lovers of English poetry. Of not more than one or two passages in Emerson's poetry can it, I think, be truly said, that they stand ever-present in the memory of even many lovers of English poetry. A great number of passages from his poetry are no doubt perfectly familiar to the mind and lips of the critic whom I have mentioned, and perhaps of a wide circle of American readers. But this is a very different thing from being matter of universal quotation, like the phrases of the legitimate poets.

And, in truth, one of the legitimate poets, Emerson, in my opinion, is not. His poetry is interesting, it makes one think; but it is not the poetry of one of the born poets. I say it of him with reluctance, although I am sure that he would have said it of himself; but I say it with reluctance, because I dislike giving pain to his admirers, and because all my own wish, too, is to say of him what is favourable. But I regard myself, not as speaking to please Emerson's admirers, not as speaking to please myself; but rather, I repeat, as communing with Time and Nature concerning the productions of this beautiful and rare spirit, and as resigning what of him is by their unalterable decree touched with caducity, in order the better to mark and secure that in him which is immortal.

Milton says that poetry ought to be simple, sensuous, impassioned. Well, Emerson's poetry is seldom either simple, or sensuous, or impassioned. In general it lacks directness; it lacks concreteness; it lacks energy. His grammar is often embarrassed; in particular, the want of clearly-marked distinction between the subject and the object of his sentence is a frequent cause of obscurity in him. A poem which shall be a plain, forcible, inevitable whole he hardly ever produces. Such good work as the noble lines graven on the Concord Monument is the exception with him; such ineffective work as the "Fourth of July Ode" or the "Boston Hymn" is the rule. Even passages and single lines of thorough plainness and commanding force are rare in his poetry. They exist, of course; but when

we meet with them they give us a slight shock of surprise, so little has Emerson accustomed us to them. Let me have the pleasure of quoting one or two of these exceptional passages:—

> So nigh is grandeur to our dust,
>   So near is God to man,
> When Duty whispers low, *Thou must*,
>   The youth replies, *I can.*

Or again this:—

> Though love repine and reason chafe,
>   There came a voice without reply:
> "'Tis man's perdition to be safe,
>   When for the truth he ought to die."

Excellent! but how seldom do we get from him a strain blown so clearly and firmly! Take another passage where his strain has not only clearness, it has also grace and beauty:—

> And ever, when the happy child
> In May beholds the blooming wild,
> And hears in heaven the bluebird sing,
> "Onward," he cries, "your baskets bring!
> In the next field is air more mild,
> And o'er yon hazy crest is Eden's balmier spring."

In the style and cadence here there is a reminiscence, I think, of Gray; at any rate, the pureness grace and beauty of these lines are worthy even of Gray. But Gray holds his high rank as a poet, not merely by the beauty and grace of passages in his poems; not merely by a diction generally pure in an age of impure diction: he holds it, above all, by the power and skill with which the evolution of his poems is conducted. Here is his grand superiority to Collins, whose diction in his best poem, the "Ode to Evening," is purer than Gray's; but then the "Ode to Evening" is like a river which loses itself in the sand, whereas Gray's best poems have an evolution sure and satisfying. Emerson's "Mayday," from which I just now quoted, has no real evolution at all; it is a series of observations. And, in general, his poems have no evolution. Take for example his "Titmouse." Here he has an excellent subject; and his observation of Nature, moreover, is always marvellously close and fine. But compare what he makes of his meeting with his titmouse with what Cowper or Burns makes of the like kind of incident! One never quite arrives at learning what the titmouse actually did for him at all, though one feels a strong interest and desire to learn it; but one is reduced to guessing, and cannot be quite sure that after all one has guessed right. He is not plain and concrete enough,—in other words, not poet enough,—to be able to tell us. And a failure of this kind goes through almost all his verse, keeps him amid symbolism, and allusion, and the fringes of things, and in spite of his spiritual power deeply impairs his poetic value. Through the inestimable virtue of concreteness, a simple poem like "The Bridge" of Longfellow or the "School Days" of Mr. Whittier is of more poetic worth, perhaps, than all the verse of Emerson.

I do not, then, place Emerson among the great poets. But I go further, and say that I do not place him among the great writers, the great men of letters. Who are the great men of letters? They are men like Cicero, Plato, Bacon, Pascal, Swift, Voltaire,—writers with, in the first place, a genius and instinct for style; writers whose prose is by a kind of native necessity true and sound. Now the style of Emerson, like the style of his transcendentalist friends and of the *Dial* so continually,—the style of Emerson is capable of falling into a strain like this, which I take from the beginning of his "Essay on Love:" "Every soul is a celestial Venus to every other soul. The heart has its sabbaths and jubilees, in which the world appears as a hymeneal feast, and all natural sounds and the circle of the seasons are erotic odes and dances." Emerson altered this sentence in the later editions. Like Wordsworth, he was in later life fond of altering; and in general his later alterations, like those of Wordsworth, are not improvements. He softened the passage in question, however, though without really mending it. I quote it in its original and strongly-marked form. Arthur Stanley used to relate that, about the year 1840, being in conversation with some Americans in quarantine at Malta and thinking to please them he declared his warm admiration for Emerson's *Essays*, then recently published. However, the Americans shook their heads, and told him that for home taste Emerson was decidedly too *greeny*. We will hope, for their sakes, that the sort of thing they had in their heads was such writing as I have just quoted. Unsound it is indeed, and in a style almost impossible to a born man of letters.

It is a curious thing, that quality of style which marks the great writer, the born man of letters. It resides in the whole tissue of his work, and of his work regarded as a composition for literary purposes. Brilliant and powerful passages in a man's writings do not prove his possession of it; it lies in their whole tissue. Emerson has passages of noble and pathetic eloquence, such as those which I quoted at the beginning; he has passages of shrewd and felicitous wit; he has crisp epigrams; he has passages of exquisitely touched observation of nature. Yet he is not a great writer; his style has not the requisite wholeness of good tissue. Even Carlyle is not, in my judgment, a great writer. He has surpassingly powerful qualities of expression, far more powerful than Emerson's, and reminding one of the gifts of expression of the great poets,—of even Shakespeare himself. What Emerson so admirably says of Carlyle's "devouring eyes and portraying hand," "those thirsty eyes, those portrait-eating, portrait-painting eyes of thine, those fatal perceptions," is thoroughly true. What a description is Carlyle's of the first publisher of *Sartor Resartus*, "to whom the idea of a new edition of *Sartor* is frightful, or rather ludicrous, unimaginable"; of this poor Fraser, in whose "wonderful world of Tory pamphleteers, Conservative Younger-brothers, Regent Street Loungers, Crockford Gamblers, Irish Jesuits, drunken reporters, and miscellaneous unclean persons (whom nitre and much soap will not wash clean) not a soul has expressed the smallest wish that way!" What a portrait, again, of the well-beloved John Sterling! "One, and the best, of a small class extant here, who, nigh drowning in a black wreck of Infidelity (lighted up by some glare of Radicalism only, now growing *dim* too), and about to perish, saved themselves into a Coleridgian Shovel-Hattedness." What touches in the invitation of Emerson to London! "You shall see blockheads by the million; Pickwick himself shall be visible,—innocent young Dickens, reserved for a questionable fate. The great Wordsworth shall talk till you yourself pronounce him to be a bore. Southey's complexion is still healthy mahogany brown, with a fleece of white hair, and eyes that seem running at full gallop. Leigh Hunt, man of genius in the shape of a cockney, is my near neighbour, with good humour and no common-sense; old Rogers with his pale head, white, bare, and cold as snow, with those large blue eyes, cruel, sorrowful, and that sardonic shelf chin." How inimitable it all is! And finally, for one must not go on for ever, this version of a London Sunday, with the public-houses closed during the hours of divine service! "It is silent Sunday; the populace not yet admitted to their beershops, till the respectabilities conclude their rubric mummeries,—a much more audacious feat than beer." Yet even Carlyle is not, in my judgment, to be called a great writer; one cannot think of ranking him with men like Cicero and Plato and Swift and Voltaire. Emerson freely promises to Carlyle immortality for

his histories. They will not have it. Why? Because the materials furnished to him by that devouring eye of his and that portraying hand were not wrought in and subdued by him to what his work, regarded as a composition for literary purposes, required. Occurring in conversation, breaking out in familiar correspondence, they are magnificent, inimitable; nothing more is required of them; thus thrown out anyhow, they serve their turn and fulfil their function. And therefore I should not wonder if really Carlyle lived, in the long run, by such an invaluable record as that correspondence between him and Emerson, of which we owe the publication to Mr. Charles Norton,—by this and not by his works, as Johnson lives in Boswell, not by his works. For Carlyle's sallies, as the staple of a literary work, become wearisome; and as time more and more applies to Carlyle's works its stringent test, this will be felt more and more. Shakespeare, Molière, Swift,—they too had, like Carlyle, the devouring eye and the portraying hand. But they are great literary masters, they are supreme writers, because they knew how to work into a literary composition their materials, and to subdue them to the purposes of literary effect. Carlyle is too wilful for this, too turbid, too vehement.

You will think I deal in nothing but negatives. I have been saying that Emerson is not one of the great poets, the great writers. He has not their quality of style. He is, however, the propounder of a philosophy. The Platonic dialogues afford us the example of exquisite literary form and treatment given to philosophical ideas. Plato is at once a great literary man and a great philosopher. If we speak carefully, we cannot call Aristotle or Spinoza or Kant great literary men, or their productions great literary works. But their work is arranged with such constructive power that they build a philosophy and are justly called great philosophical writers. Emerson cannot, I think, be called with justice a great philosophical writer. He cannot build; his arrangement of philosophical ideas has no progress in it, no evolution; he does not construct a philosophy. Emerson himself knew the defects of his method, or rather want of method, very well; indeed, he and Carlyle criticise themselves and one another in a way which leaves little for any one else to do in the way of formulating their defects. Carlyle formulates perfectly the defects of his friend's poetic and literary production when he says of the *Dial*: "For me it is too ethereal, speculative, theoretic; I will have all things condense themselves, take shape and body, if they are to have my sympathy." And, speaking of Emerson's orations he says: "I long to see some concrete Thing, some Event, Man's Life, American Forest, or piece of Creation, which this Emerson loves and wonders at, well *Emersonised*,—depictured by Emerson, filled with the life of Emerson, and cast forth from him, then to live by itself. If these orations balk me of this, how profitable soever they may be for others, I will not love them." Emerson himself formulates perfectly the defect of his own philosophical productions when he speaks of his "formidable tendency to the lapidary style. I build my house of boulders." "Here I sit and read and write," he says again, "with very little system, and as far as regards composition, with the most fragmentary result; paragraphs incompressible, each sentence an infinitely repellent particle." Nothing can be truer; and the work of a Spinoza or Kant, of the men who stand as great philosophical writers, does not proceed in this wise.

Some people will tell you that Emerson's poetry indeed is too abstract, and his philosophy too vague, but that his best work is his *English Traits*. The *English Traits* are, beyond question, very pleasant reading. It is easy to praise them, easy to commend the author of them. But I insist on always trying Emerson's work by the highest standards. I esteem him too much to try his work by any other. Tried by the highest standards, and compared with the work of the excellent markers and recorders of the traits of human life,—of writers like Montaigne, La Bruyère, Addison,—the *English Traits* will not stand the comparison. Emerson's observation has not the disinterested quality of the observation of these masters. It is the observation of a man systematically benevolent, as Hawthorne's observation in *Our Old Home* is the work of a man chagrined. Hawthorne's literary talent is of the first order. His subjects are generally not to me subjects of the highest interest; but his literary talent is of the first order, the finest, I think, which America has yet produced,—finer, by much, than Emerson's. Yet *Our Old Home* is not a masterpiece any more than *English Traits*. In neither of them is the observer disinterested enough. The author's attitude in each of these cases can easily be understood and defended. Hawthorne was a sensitive man, so situated in England that he was perpetually in contact with the British Philistine; and the British Philistine is a trying personage. Emerson's systematic benevolence comes from what he himself calls somewhere his "persistent optimism"; and his persistent optimism is the root of his greatness and the source of his charm. But still let us keep our literary conscience true, and judge every kind of literary work by the laws really proper to it. The kind of work attempted in the *English Traits* and in *Our Old Home* is work which cannot be done perfectly with a bias such as that given by Emerson's optimism or by Hawthorne's chagrin. Consequently, neither *English Traits* nor *Our Old Home* is a work of perfection in its kind.

Not with the Miltons and Grays, not with the Platos and Spinozas, not with the Swifts and Voltaires, not with the Montaignes and Addisons, can we rank Emerson. His work of various kinds, when one compares it with the work done in a corresponding kind by these masters, fails to stand the comparison. No man could see this clearer than Emerson himself. It is hard not to feel despondency when we contemplate our failures and shortcomings: and Emerson, the least self-flattering and the most modest of men, saw so plainly what was lacking to him that he had his moments of despondency. "Alas, my friend," he writes in reply to Carlyle, who had exhorted him to creative work,—"Alas, my friend, I can do no such gay thing as you say. I do not belong to the poets, but only to a low department of literature,—the reporters; suburban men." He deprecates his friend's praise; praise "generous to a fault," he calls it; praise "generous to the shaming of me,—cold, fastidious, ebbing person that I am. Already in a former letter you had said too much good of my poor little arid book, which is as sand to my eyes. I can only say that I heartily wish the book were better; and I must try and deserve so much favour from the kind gods by a bolder and truer living in the months to come,—such as may perchance one day relax and invigorate this cramp hand of mine. When I see how much work is to be done; what room for a poet, for any spiritualist, in this great, intelligent, sensual and avaricious America,—I lament my fumbling fingers and stammering tongue." Again, as late as 1870, he writes to Carlyle: "There is no example of constancy like yours, and it always stings my stupor into temporary recovery and wonderful resolution to accept the noble challenge. But 'the strong hours conquer us;' and I am the victim of miscellany,—miscellany of designs, vast debility, and procrastination." The forlorn note belonging to the phrase "vast debility," recalls that saddest and most discouraged of writers, the author of *Obermann*, Senancour, with whom Emerson has in truth a certain kinship. He has in common with Senancour his pureness, his passion for nature, his single

eye; and here we find him confessing, like Senancour, a sense in himself of sterility and impotence.

And now I think I have cleared the ground. I have given up to envious Time as much of Emerson as Time can fairly expect ever to obtain. We have not in Emerson a great poet, a great writer, a great philosophy-maker. His relation to us is not that of one of those personages; yet it is a relation of, I think, even superior importance. His relation to us is more like that of the Roman Emperor Marcus Aurelius. Marcus Aurelius is not a great writer, a great philosophy-maker; he is the friend and aider of those who would live in the spirit. Emerson is the same. He is the friend and aider of those who would live in the spirit. All the points in thinking which are necessary for this purpose he takes; but he does not combine them into a system, or present them as a regular philosophy. Combined in a system by a man with the requisite talent for this kind of thing, they would be less useful than as Emerson gives them to us; and the man with the talent so to systematise them would be less impressive than Emerson. They do very well as they now stand;—like "boulders," as he says;—in "paragraphs incompressible, each sentence an infinitely repellent particle." In such sentences his main points recur again and again, and become fixed in the memory.

We all know them. First and foremost, character. Character is everything. "That which all things tend to educe,—which freedom, cultivation, intercourse, revolutions, go to form and deliver,—is character." Character and self-reliance. "Trust thyself! every heart vibrates to that iron string." And yet we have our being in a *not ourselves*. "There is a power above and behind us, and we are the channels of its communications." But our lives must be pitched higher. "Life must be lived on a higher plane; we must go up to a higher platform, to which we are always invited to ascend; there the whole scene changes." The good we need is for ever close to us, though we attain it not. "On the brink of the waters of life and truth, we are miserably dying." This good is close to us, moreover, in our daily life, and in the familiar, homely places. "The unremitting retention of simple and high sentiments in obscure duties,"—that is the maxim for us. "Let us be poised and wise, and our own to-day. Let us treat the men and women well,—treat them as if they were real; perhaps they are. Men live in their fancy, like drunkards whose hands are too soft and tremulous for successful labour. I settle myself ever firmer in the creed, that we should not postpone and refer and wish, but do broad justice where we are, by whomsoever we deal with; accepting our actual companions and circumstances, however humble or odious, as the mystic officials to whom the universe has delegated its whole pleasure for us." "Massachusetts, Connecticut River, and Boston Bay, you think paltry places, and the ear loves names of foreign and classic topography. But here we are; and if we will tarry a little we may come to learn that here is best. See to it only that thyself is here." Furthermore, the good is close to us *all*. "I resist the scepticism of our education and of our educated men. I do not believe that the differences of opinion and character in men are organic. I do not recognise, beside the class of the good and the wise, a permanent class of sceptics, or a class of conservatives, or of malignants, or of materialists. I do not believe in two classes." "Every man has a call of the power to do something unique." Exclusiveness is deadly. "The exclusive in social life does not see that he excludes himself from enjoyment in the attempt to appropriate it. The exclusionist in religion does not see that he shuts the door of heaven on himself in striving to shut out others. Treat men as pawns and ninepins, and you shall suffer as well as they. If you leave out their heart you shall lose your own." "The selfish man suffers more from his selfishness than he from whom that selfishness withholds some important benefit." A sound nature will be inclined to refuse ease and self-indulgence. "To live with some rigour of temperance, or some extremes of generosity, seems to be an asceticism which common good-nature would appoint to those who are at ease and in plenty, in sign that they feel a brotherhood with the great multitude of suffering men." Compensation, finally, is the great law of life; it is everywhere, it is sure, and there is no escape from it. This is that "law alive and beautiful, which works over our heads and under our feet. Pitiless, it avails itself of our success when we obey it, and of our ruin when we contravene it. Men are all secret believers in it. It rewards actions after their nature. The reward of a thing well done is to have done it." "The thief steals from himself, the swindler swindles himself. You must pay at last your own debt."

This is tonic indeed! And let no one object that it is too general; that more practical, positive direction is what we want; that Emerson's optimism, self-reliance, and indifference to favourable conditions for our life and growth, have in them something of danger. "Trust thyself;" "what attracts my attention shall have it;" "though thou shouldst walk the world over, thou shalt not be able to find a condition inopportune or ignoble;" "what we call vulgar society is that society whose poetry is not yet written, but which you shall presently make as enviable and renowned as any." With maxims like these, we surely, it may be said, run some risk of being made too well satisfied with our own actual self and state, however crude and imperfect they may be. "Trust thyself?" It may be said that the common American or Englishman is more than enough disposed already to trust himself. I often reply, when our sectarians are praised for following conscience: Our people are very good in following their conscience; where they are not so good is in ascertaining whether their conscience tells them right. "What attracts my attention shall have it?" Well, that is our people's plea when they run after the Salvation Army, and desire Messrs. Moody and Sankey. "Thou shalt not be able to find a condition inopportune or ignoble?" But think of the turn of the good people of our race for producing a life of hideousness and immense ennui; think of that specimen of your own New England life which Mr. Howells gives us in one of his charming stories which I was reading lately; think of the life of that ragged New England farm in the *Lady of the Aroostook*; think of Deacon Blood, and Aunt Maria, and the straight-backed chairs with black horse-hair seats, and Ezra Perkins with perfect self-reliance depositing his travellers in the snow! I can truly say that in the little which I have seen of the life of New England, I am more struck with what has been achieved than with the crudeness and failure. But no doubt there is still a great deal of crudeness also. Your own novelists say there is, and I suppose they say true. In the New England, as in the Old, our people have to learn, I suppose, not that their modes of life are beautiful and excellent already; they have rather to learn that they must transform them.

To adopt this line of objection to Emerson's deliverances would, however, be unjust. In the first place, Emerson's points are in themselves true, if understood in a certain high sense; they are true and fruitful. And the right work to be done, at the hour when he appeared, was to affirm them generally and absolutely. Only thus could he break through the hard and fast barrier of narrow, fixed ideas which he found confronting him, and win an entrance for new ideas. Had he attempted developments which may now strike us as expedient, he would have excited fierce antagonism, and probably effected little or nothing. The time might come for doing other work later, but the work which Emerson did was the right work to be done then.

In the second place, strong as was Emerson's optimism, and unconquerable as was his belief in a good result to emerge from all which he saw going on around him, no misanthropical satirist ever saw shortcomings and absurdities more clearly than he did, or exposed them more courageously. When he sees "the meanness," as he calls it, "of American politics," he congratulates Washington on being "long already happily dead," on being "wrapt in his shroud and for ever safe." With how firm a touch he delineates the faults of your two great political parties of forty years ago! The Democrats, he says, "have not at heart the ends which give to the name of democracy what hope and virtue are in it. The spirit of our American radicalism is destructive and aimless; it is not loving; it has no ulterior and divine ends, but is destructive only out of hatred and selfishness. On the other side, the conservative party, composed of the most moderate, able, and cultivated part of the population, is timid, and merely defensive of property. It vindicates no right, it aspires to no real good, it brands no crime, it proposes no generous policy. From neither party, when in power, has the world any benefit to expect in science, art, or humanity, at all commensurate with the resources of the nation." Then with what subtle though kindly irony he follows the gradual withdrawal in New England, in the last half century, of tender consciences from the social organisations,—the bent for experiments such as that of Brook Farm and the like,—follows it in all its "dissidence of dissent and Protestantism of the Protestant religion!" He even loves to rally the New Englander on his philanthropical activity, and to find his beneficence and its institutions a bore! "Your miscellaneous popular charities, the education at college of fools, the building of meeting-houses to the vain end to which many of these now stand, alms to sots, and the thousand-fold relief societies,—though I confess with shame that I sometimes succumb and give the dollar, yet it is a wicked dollar which by and by I shall have the manhood to withhold." "Our Sunday schools and churches and pauper societies are yokes to the neck. We pain ourselves to please nobody. There are natural ways of arriving at the same ends at which these aim but do not arrive." "Nature does not like our benevolence or our learning much better than she likes our frauds and wars. When we come out of the caucus, or the bank, or the Abolition Convention, or the Temperance meeting, or the Transcendental Club, into the fields and woods, she says to us: 'So hot, my little Sir?'"

Yes, truly, his insight is admirable; his truth is precious. Yet the secret of his effect is not even in these; it is in his temper. It is in the hopeful, serene, beautiful temper wherewith these, in Emerson, are indissolubly joined; in which they work, and have their being. He says himself: "We judge of a man's wisdom by his hope, knowing that the perception of the inexhaustibleness of nature is an immortal youth." If this be so, how wise is Emerson! for never had man such a sense of the inexhaustibleness of nature, and such hope. It was the ground of his being; it never failed him. Even when he is sadly avowing the imperfection of his literary power and resources, lamenting his fumbling fingers and stammering tongue, he adds: "Yet, as I tell you, I am very easy in my mind and never dream of suicide. My whole philosophy, which is very real, teaches acquiescence and optimism. Sure I am that the right word will be spoken though I cut out my tongue." In his old age, with friends dying and life failing, his tone of cheerful, forward-looking hope is still the same: "A multitude of young men are growing up here of high promise, and I compare gladly the social poverty of my youth with the power on which these draw." His abiding word for us, the word by which being dead he yet speaks to us, is this: "That which befits us, embosomed in beauty and wonder as we are, is cheerfulness and courage, and the endeavour to realise our aspirations. Shall not the heart, which has received so much, trust the Power by which it lives?"

One can scarcely overrate the importance of thus holding fast to happiness and hope. It gives to Emerson's work an invaluable virtue. As Wordsworth's poetry is, in my judgment, the most important work done in verse, in our language, during the present century, so Emerson's *Essays* are, I think, the most important work done in prose. His work is more important than Carlyle's. Let us be just to Carlyle, provoking though he often is. Not only has he that genius of his which makes Emerson say truly of his letters, that "they savour always of eternity." More than this may be said of him. The scope and upshot of his teaching are true; "his guiding genius," to quote Emerson again, is really "his moral sense, his perception of the sole importance of truth and justice." But consider Carlyle's temper, as we have been considering Emerson's; take his own account of it: "Perhaps London is the proper place for me after all, seeing all places are *im*proper: who knows? Meanwhile, I lead a most dyspeptic, solitary, self-shrouded life; consuming, if possible in silence, my considerable daily allotment of pain; glad when any strength is left in me for working, which is the only use I can see in myself,—too rare a case of late. The ground of my existence is black as death; too black, when all *void* too; but at times there paint themselves on it pictures of gold, and rainbow, and lightning; all the brighter for the black ground, I suppose. Withal, I am very much of a fool."—No, not a fool, but turbid and morbid, wilful and perverse. "We judge of a man's wisdom by his hope."

Carlyle's perverse attitude towards happiness cuts him off from hope. He fiercely attacks the desire for happiness; his grand point in *Sartor*, his secret in which the soul may find rest, is that one shall cease to desire happiness, that one should learn to say to oneself: "What if thou wert born and predestined not to be happy, but to be unhappy!" He is wrong; Saint Augustine is the better philosopher, who says: "Act we *must* in pursuance of what gives us most delight." Epictetus and Augustine can be severe moralists enough; but both of them know and frankly say that the desire for happiness is the root and ground of man's being. Tell him and show him that he places his happiness wrong, that he seeks for delight where delight will never be really found; then you illumine and further him. But you only confuse him by telling him to cease to desire happiness, and you will not tell him this unless you are already confused yourself.

Carlyle preached the dignity of labour, the necessity of righteousness, the love of veracity, the hatred of shams. He is said by many people to be a great teacher, a great helper for us, because he does so. But what is the due and eternal result of labour, righteousness, veracity?—Happiness. And how are we drawn to them by one who, instead of making us feel that with them is happiness, tells us that perhaps we were predestined not to be happy but to be unhappy?

You will find, in especial, many earnest preachers of our popular religion to be fervent in their praise and admiration of Carlyle. His insistence on labour, righteousness, and veracity pleases them; his contempt for happiness pleases them too. I read the other day a tract against smoking, although I do not happen to be a smoker myself. "Smoking," said the tract, "is liked because it gives agreeable sensations. Now it is a positive objection to a thing that it gives agreeable sensations. An earnest man will expressly avoid what gives agreeable sensations." Shortly afterwards I was inspecting a school, and I found the children reading a piece of poetry on the common theme that we are here to-day and gone to-morrow. I shall soon be gone, the speaker in this poem was made to say,—

> And I shall be glad to go,
> For the world at best is a weary place,
> And my pulse is getting low.

How usual a language of popular religion that is, on our side of the Atlantic at any rate! But then our popular religion, in disparaging happiness here below, knows very well what it is after. It has its eye on a happiness in a future life above the clouds, in the New Jerusalem, to be won by disliking and rejecting happiness here on earth. And so long as this ideal stands fast, it is very well. But for very many it now stands fast no longer; for Carlyle, at any rate, it had failed and vanished. Happiness in labour, righteousness and veracity,—in the life of the spirit,—here was a gospel still for Carlyle to preach, and to help others by preaching. But he baffled them and himself by preferring the paradox that we are not born for happiness at all.

Happiness in labour, righteousness and veracity; in all the life of the spirit; happiness and eternal hope;—that was Emerson's gospel. I hear it said that Emerson was too sanguine; that the actual generation in America is not turning out so well as he expected. Very likely he was too sanguine as to the near future; in this country it is difficult not to be too sanguine. Very possibly the present generation may prove unworthy of his high hopes; even several generations succeeding this may prove unworthy of them. But by his conviction that in the life of the spirit is happiness, and by his hope that this life of the spirit will come more and more to be sanely understood, and to prevail, and to work for happiness,—by this conviction and hope Emerson was great, and he will surely prove in the end to have been right in them. In this country it is difficult, as I said, not to be sanguine. Very many of your writers are over-sanguine, and on the wrong grounds. But you have two men who in what they have written show their sanguineness in a line where courage and hope are just, where they are also infinitely important, but where they are not easy. The two men are Franklin and Emerson.[1] These two are, I think, the most distinctively and honourably American of your writers; they are the most original and the most valuable. Wise men everywhere know that we must keep up our courage and hope; they know that hope is, as Wordsworth well says,—

> The paramount *duty* which Heaven lays,
> For its own honour, on man's suffering heart.

But the very word *duty* points to an effort and a struggle to maintain our hope unbroken. Franklin and Emerson maintained theirs with a convincing ease, an inspiring joy. Franklin's confidence in the happiness with which industry, honesty, and economy will crown the life of this work-day world, is such that he runs over with felicity. With a like felicity does Emerson run over, when he contemplates the happiness eternally attached to the true life in the spirit. You cannot prize him too much, nor heed him too diligently. He has lessons for both the branches of our race. I figure him to my mind as visible upon earth still, as still standing here by Boston Bay, or at his own Concord, in his habit as he lived, but of heightened stature and shining feature, with one hand stretched out towards the East, to our laden and labouring England; the other towards the ever-growing West, to his own dearly-loved America,—"great, intelligent, sensual, avaricious America." To us he shows for guidance his lucid freedom, his cheerfulness and hope; to you his dignity, delicacy, serenity, elevation.

Notes

1. I found with pleasure that this conjunction of Emerson's name with Franklin's had already occurred to an accomplished writer and delightful man, a friend of Emerson, left almost the sole survivor, alas! of the famous literary generation of Boston,—Dr. Oliver Wendell Holmes. Dr. Holmes has kindly allowed me to print here the ingenious and interesting lines, hitherto unpublished, in which he speaks of Emerson thus:—

> Where in the realm of thought, whose air is song,
> Does he, the Buddha of the West, belong?
> He seems a wingéd Franklin, sweetly wise,
> Born to unlock the secrets of the skies;
> And which the nobler calling—if 'tis fair
> Terrestrial with celestial to compare—
> To guide the storm-cloud's elemental flame,
> Or walk the chambers whence the lightning came
> Amidst the sources of its subtile fire,
> And steal their effluence for his lips and lyre?

HENRY JAMES, SR.
"Mr. Emerson"
Literary Remains
1884, pp. 293–302

At all events, if we are still to go on cherishing any such luxury as a private conscience towards God, I greatly prefer for my own part that it should be an evil conscience. Conscience was always intended as a rebuke and never as an exhilaration to the private citizen; and so let it flourish till the end of our wearisome civilization. There are many signs, however, that this end is near. My recently deceased friend Mr. Emerson, for example, was all his days an arch traitor to our existing civilized regimen, inasmuch as he unconsciously managed to set aside its fundamental principle in doing without conscience, which was the entire secret of his very exceptional interest to men's speculation. He betrayed it to be sure without being at all aware of what he was doing; but this was really all that he distinctively did to my observation. His nature had always been so innocent, so unaffectedly innocent, that when in later life he began to cultivate a club consciousness, and to sip a glass of wine or smoke a cigar, I felt very much outraged by it. I felt very much as if some renowned Boston belle had suddenly collapsed and undertaken to sell newspapers at a street corner. "Why, Emerson, is this *you* doing such things?" I exclaimed. "What profanation! Do throw the unclean things behind your back!" But, no; he was actually proud of his accomplishments! This came from his never knowing (intellectually) what he stood for in the evolution of New England life. He was lineally descended to begin with, from a half-score of comatose New England clergymen, in whose behalf probably the religious instinct had been used up. Or, what to their experience had been religion, became in that of their descendant *life*. The actual truth, at any rate, was that he never felt a movement of the life of conscience from the day of his birth till that of his death. I could never see any signs of such a life in him. I remember, to be sure, that he had a great gift of friendship, and that he was very plucky in behalf of his friends whenever they felt themselves assailed—as plucky as a woman. For instance, whenever Wendell Phillips ventilated his not untimely wit at the expense of our club-house politicians, Emerson, hearing his friends among these latter com-

plain, grew indignant, and for several days you would hear nothing from his lips but excessive eulogies of Mr. Garrison, which sounded like nothing else in the world but revilings of Mr. Phillips. But, bless your heart! there was not a bit of conscience in a bushel of such experiences, but only wounded friendship, which is a totally different and much lower thing.

The infallible mark of conscience is that it is always a subjective judgment couched in some such language as this: "God be merciful to *me* a sinner!" and never an objective judgment such as this: *God damn Wendell Phillips, or some other of my friends!* This latter judgment is always an outbreak of ungovernable temper on our part, and was never known to reach the ear of God save in this guise: *God* BLESS *W.P. or any other friend implicated!* Now Emerson was seriously incapable of a subjective judgment upon himself; he did not know the inward difference between good and evil, so far as he was himself concerned. No doubt he perfectly comprehended the outward or moral difference between these things; but I insist upon it that he never so much as dreamed of any inward or spiritual difference between them. For this difference is vitally seen only when oneself seems unchangeably evil to his own sight, and one's neighbor unchangeably good in the comparison. How could Emerson ever have known this difference? I am satisfied that he never in his life had felt a temptation *to bear false-witness* against his neighbor, *to steal*, *to commit adultery*, or *to murder*; how then should he have ever experienced what is technically called a conviction of sin?—that is, a conviction of himself as *evil* before God, and all other men as *good*. One gets a conviction of the evil that attaches to the natural selfhood in man in no other way than—as I can myself attest—by this growing acquaintance with his own moral infirmity, and the consequent gradual decline of his self-respect. For I myself had known all these temptations—in forms of course more or less modified—by the time I was fourteen or fifteen years old; so that by the time I had got to be twenty-five or thirty (which was the date of my first acquaintance with Emerson) I was saturated with a sense of spiritual evil—no man ever more so possibly, since I felt thoroughly *self-condemned* before God. Good heavens! how soothed and comforted I was by the innocent lovely look of my new acquaintance, by his tender courtesy, his generous laudatory appreciation of my crude literary ventures! and how I used to lock myself up with him in his bed-room, swearing that before the door was opened I would arrive at the secret of his immense superiority to the common herd of literary men! I might just as well have locked myself up with a handful of diamonds, so far as any capacity of self-cognizance existed in him. I found in fact, before I had been with him a week, that the immense superiority I ascribed to him was altogether personal or practical—by no means intellectual; that it came to him by birth or genius like a woman's beauty or charm of manners; that no other account was to be given of it in truth than that Emerson himself was an unsexed woman, a veritable fruit of almighty power in the sphere of our *nature*.

This after a while grew to be a great discovery to me; but I was always more or less provoked to think that Emerson himself should take no intellectual stock in it. On the whole I may say that at first I was greatly disappointed in him, because his intellect never kept the promise which his lovely face and manners held out to me. He was to my senses a literal divine presence in the house with me; and we cannot recognize literal divine presences in our houses without feeling sure that they will be able to say something of critical importance to one's intellect. It turned out that any average old dame in a horse-car would have satisfied my intellectual rapacity just as well as

Emerson. My standing intellectual embarrassment for years had been to get at the bottom of the difference between law and gospel in humanity—between the head and the heart of things—between the great God almighty, in short, and the intensely wooden and ridiculous gods of the nations. Emerson, I discovered immediately, had never been the least of an expert in this sort of knowledge; and though his immense personal fascination always kept up, he at once lost all intellectual prestige to my regard. I even thought that I had never seen a man more profoundly devoid of spiritual understanding. This prejudice grew, of course, out of my having inherited an altogether narrow ecclesiastical notion of what spiritual understanding was. I supposed it consisted unmistakably in some doctrinal lore concerning man's regeneration, to which, however, my new friend was plainly and signally incompetent. Emerson, in fact, derided this doctrine, smiling benignly whenever it was mentioned. I could make neither head nor tail of him according to men's ordinary standards—the only thing that I was sure of being that he, like Christ, was somehow divinely begotten. He seemed to me unmistakably virgin-born whenever I looked at him, and reminded me of nothing so much as of those persons dear to Christ's heart who should come after him professing no allegiance to him—having never heard his name pronounced, and yet perfectly fulfilling his will. He never seemed for a moment to antagonize the church of his own consent, but only out of condescension to his interlocutor's weakness. In fact he was to all appearance entirely ignorant of the church's existence until you recalled it to his imagination; and even then I never knew anything so implacably and uniformly mild as his judgments of it were. He had apparently lived all his life in a world where it was only subterraneously known; and, try as you would, you could never persuade him that any the least living power attached to it. The same profound incredulity characterized him in regard to the State; and it was only in his enfeebled later years that he ever lent himself to the idea of society as its destined divine form. I am not sure indeed that the lending was ever very serious. But he was always greedy, with all a Yankee's greediness, after facts, and would at least appear to listen to you with earnest respect and sympathy whenever you plead for society as the redeemed form of our nature.

In short he was, as I have said before, fundamentally treacherous to civilization, without being at all aware himself of the fact. He himself, I venture to say, was peculiarly unaware of the fact. He appeared to me utterly unconscious of himself as either good or evil. He had no conscience, in fact, and lived by perception, which is an altogether lower or less spiritual faculty. The more universalized a man is by genius or natural birth, the less is he spiritually individualized, making up in breadth of endowment what he lacks in depth. This was remarkably the case with Emerson. In his books or public capacity he was constantly electrifying you by sayings full of divine inspiration. In his talk or private capacity he was one of the least remunerative men I ever encountered. No man could look at him speaking (or when he was silent either, for that matter) without having a vision of the divinest beauty. But when you went to him to hold discourse about the wondrous phenomenon, you found him absolutely destitute of reflective power. He had apparently no private personality; and if any visitor thought he discerned traces of such a thing, you may take for granted that the visitor himself was a man of large imaginative resources. He was nothing else than a show-figure of almighty power in our nature; and that he was destitute of all the apparatus of humbuggery that goes to eke out more or less the private pretension in humanity, only completed and

confirmed the extraordinary fascination that belonged to him. He was full of living inspiration to me whenever I saw him; and yet I could find in him no trivial sign of the selfhood which I found in other men. He was like a vestal virgin, indeed, always in ministry upon the altar; but the vestal virgin had doubtless a prosaic side also, which related her to commonplace people. Now Emerson was so far *unlike* the virgin: he had no prosaic side relating him to ordinary people. Judge Hoar and Mr. John Forbes constituted his spontaneous political conscience; and his domestic one (equally spontaneous) was supplied by loving members of his own family—so that he only connected with the race at second-hand, and found all the material business of life such as voting and the payment of taxes transacted for *him* with marvellous lack of friction.

Incontestably the main thing about him, however, as I have already said, was that he unconsciously brought you face to face with the infinite in humanity. When I looked upon myself, or upon the ordinary rabble of ecclesiastics and politicians, everything in us seemed ridiculously undivine. When I looked upon Emerson, these same undivine things were what gave *him* his manifest divine charm. The reason was that in him everything seemed innocent by the transparent absence of selfhood, and in us everything seemed foul and false by its preternatural activity. The difference between us was made by innocence altogether. I never thought it was a real or spiritual difference, but only a natural or apparent one. But such as it was, it gave me my first living impression of the great God almighty who alone is at work in human affairs, avouching his awful and adorable spiritual infinitude only through the death and hell wrapped up in our finite experience. This was Emerson's incontestable virtue to every one who appreciated him, that he recognized no God outside of himself and his interlocutor, and recognized him there only as the *liaison* between the two, taking care that all their intercourse should be holy with a holiness undreamed of before by man or angel. For it is not a holiness taught by books or the example of tiresome, diseased, self-conscious saints, but simply by one's own redeemed flesh and blood. In short, the only holiness which Emerson recognized, and for which he consistently lived, was innocence. And innocence—glory be to God's spiritual incarnation in our nature!—has no other root in us than our unconscious flesh and bones. That is to say, it attaches only to what is definitively universal or natural in our experience, and hence appropriates itself to individuals only in so far as they learn to denude themselves of personality or self-consciousness; which reminds one of Christ's mystical saying: *He that findeth his life (in himself) shall lose it, and he that loseth his life for my sake shall find it.*

EDMUND CLARENCE STEDMAN
From "Ralph Waldo Emerson"
Poets of America
1885, pp. 133–79

I

The grasses had scarcely taken root on Emerson's grave among the pines when a discussion of his genius began, to which so many have contributed, that we already are asking Lowell's question concerning Shakespeare,—Can anything new be said of him? One thing, it seems to me, may be said, at least in a new way and as a clew to his work as a poet. While, of all his brotherhood, he is the radiant exemplar of his own statement, that in spirit "the true poet and the true philosopher are one," nevertheless, of all verse his own shows most clearly that the Method of the poet not only is not one with that of the philosopher, but is in fact directly opposed to it. The poet, as an artist, does not move in the direction which was Emerson's by instinct and selection. The Ideal philosophy scrutinizes every phase of Nature to find the originating sense, the universal soul, the pure identity; it follows Nature's trails to their common beginning, inverting her process of evolution, working back from infinite variety to the primal unity. This, too, is the spirit of the poet,—to find the soul of things. But in method he is an artist: his poetry is an art that imitates Nature's own habit. He works from unity to countless results and formations, from the pure thought to visible symbols, from the ideal to the concrete. As a poet, Emerson found himself in a state, not of distraction, but often of indecision, *between the methods of philosophy and art.* To bear this in mind is to account more readily for the peculiar beauties and deficiencies of his verse,—and thus to accept it as it is, and not without some understanding of its value.

Hermann Grimm recurs to the dispute whether our sage was a poet, a philosopher, or a prophet. The fact is that he was born with certain notes of song; he had the poet's eye and ear, and was a poet just so far as, being a philosopher, he accepted poetry as the expression of thought in its rare and prophetic moods, and just so far as, in exquisite moments, he had the mastery of this form of expression.

Emerson's prose is full of poetry, and his poems are light and air. But this statement, like so many of his own, gives only one side of a truth. His prose is just as full of every-day sense and wisdom; and something different from prose, however sublunary and imaginative, is needed to constitute a poem. His verse, often diamond-like in contrast with the feldspar of others, at times is ill-cut and beclouded. His prose, then, is that of a wise-man, plus a poet; and his verse, by turns, light and twilight, air and vapor. Yet we never feel, as in reading Wordsworth, that certain of his measures are wholly prosaic. He was so careless of ordinary standards, that few of his own craft have held his verse at its worth. It is said that his influence was chiefly, like that of Socrates, upon the sensitive and young, and such is the case with all fresh influences; but I take it that those who have fairly assimilated Emerson's poetry in their youth have been not so much born poets as born thinkers of a poetic cast. It is inevitable, and partakes of growth by exercise, that poets in youth should value a master's sound and color and form, rather than his priceless thought. They are drawn to the latter by the former, or not at all. Yet when poets, even in this day of refinement, have served their technical apprenticeship, the depth and frequent splendor of Emerson's verse grow upon them. They half suspect that he had the finest touch of all when he chose to apply it. It becomes a question whether his discords are those of an undeveloped artist, or the sudden craft of one who knows all art and can afford to be on easy terms with it. I think there is evidence on both sides;—that he had seasons when feeling and expression were in circuit, and others when the wires were down, and that he was as apt to attempt to send a message at one time as at the other. But he suggested the subtilty and swiftness of the soul's reach, even when he failed to sustain it.

I have said that of two poets, otherwise equal, the one who acquires the broadest knowledge will draw ahead of him who only studies his art, and the poet who thinks most broadly and deeply will draw ahead of all. There can be little doubt of Emerson as a thinker, or as a poet for thinkers satisfied with a deep but abstract and not too varied range. Yet he did not use his breadth of culture and thought to diversify the purpose, form, symbolism, of his poems. They are mostly in one key.

They teach but one lesson; that, to be sure, is the first and greatest of all, but they fail to present it, after Nature's method, in many forms of living and beautiful interest,—to exemplify it in action, and thus bring it within universal sympathy. That this should be so was, I say, inevitable from the field of Emerson's research,—that of pure rather than of applied philosophy. Thus far, however, he represents Thought in any adjustment of our poetic group, and furthermore,—his thought being independent and emancipatory,—the American conflict with superstition, with servility to inherited usage and opinion.

We shall see that he had himself a noble and comprehensive ideal of what a typical poet should be, and was aware that his own song fell short of it. Still, he called himself a poet, and the consent of the best minds has sustained him in his judgment. His prose alone, as Lowell said, showed that he was essentially a poet; another with reason declared of his spoken essays that they were "not so much lectures as grave didactic poems, theogonies," adorned with "odes" and "eclogues." Thirty years later a cool and subtile writer looks back to find them the "most poetical, the most beautiful, productions of the American mind." For once the arbiters agree, except in a question akin to the dispute whether all things consist solely of spirit or solely of matter. Common opinion justified Mr. Sanborn's fine paradox that, instead of its being settled that Emerson could not write poetry, it was settled that he could write nothing else. We know his distaste for convention, his mistrust of "tinkle" and "efficacious rhymes." But his gift lifted him above his will; even while throwing out his grapnel, clinging to prose as the firm ground of his work, he rose involuntarily and with music. And it well may be that at times he wrote verse as an avowal of his nativity, and like a noble privileged to use the language of the court. Certainly he did not restrict himself to the poet's calling with the loyalty of Tennyson and Longfellow. In verse, however careful of his phrase, he was something of a rhapsodist, not apt to gloss his revelations and exhortings with the nice perfection of those others. He must be reviewed as one whose verse and parable and prophecy alike were means to an end,—that end not art, but the enfranchisement and stimulation of his people and his time. When Longfellow, the poet of graceful art and of sympathy as tender as his voice, took his departure, there went up a cry as from a sense of fireside loss. People everywhere dwelt upon the story of his life and recalled his folk-songs. Emerson glided away almost unperceived under the shadow of the popular bereavement. But soon, and still multiplying from the highest sources, tributes to his genius began to appear,—searching, studying, expounding him,—as when a grand nature, an originating force, has ceased to labor for us. This is the best of fame: to impress the selected minds, which redistribute the effect in steadfast circles of extension. More than his associates, Emerson achieved this fame. He had the great man's intellect, which, according to Landor, "puts in motion the intellect of others." He was, besides, so rare a personage, that one who seeks to examine his writings apart from the facts and conduct of his life needs must wander off in contemplation of the man himself. Yet anything that others can write of him is poor indeed beside a collect of his own golden sayings. He felt his work to be its own and best interpreter, and of recent authors who have justly held this feeling he doubtless was the chief.

II

His writings, then, are the key to his biography—the scroll of a life which, as for essential matter, and as he said of Plato's, was chiefly "interior." To quote his own language further,

"Great geniuses have the shortest biographies." Among the external points of significance in Emerson's story are those derived from his ancestral strain, for he was of pure and even gentle English blood, "through eight generations of cultured, conscientious, and practical ministers." He himself, as we know, assumed the profession of his father and forefathers, and for a time was a Unitarian preacher in Boston; this, after the stated courses at Harvard, where he read and wrote philosophy, nor failed to cultivate the Muse—for whose art he had shown a rare aptness even in childhood. The office and honors of the Class Poet fell to him, as to Lowell in after years. In letters he had Everett, Ticknor, and Edward Channing for instructors. In theology he was deeply influenced by Channing, the divine,—the true founder, through the work of Emerson and lesser pupils, of our liberal religious structure. Emerson projected the lines of the master so far beyond their first draft that he was unable long to remain within the Unitarian limits of that day. Some one has cleverly said that his verse, "Good-bye, proud world!" came from one whose future gave no cause for epigrams like that of Madame de Sévigné on Cardinal de Retz—of whom she wrote that he pretended to retire from a world which he saw was retiring from him. The separation from the church, and the retreat to Concord, were the beginning of Emerson's long career as poet, lecturer, essayist, thinker and inspirer. The details of his social, domestic, and civic relations are all upon record. Nothing could be more seemly than his lifelong abode in the New England village of Concord, the home of his line, the birth-place of our liberties; and it became, largely through his presence, the source of our most resultful thought. Here he blended, in his speech and action, the culture of the university, nigh at hand, with the shrewd prudence of the local neighborhood, as became a poet and sage imbued with patriotism, morals, and the wisdom of practical life. Here, though crossing the ocean more than once, and inspecting other lands with the regard that sees for once and all, he otherwise exemplified during half a century his own conception of the clear spirit—that needs not to go afar upon its quests, because it vibrates boundlessly, and includes all things within reach and ken. For the rest, the life of Emerson appertained to the household, the library, the walk, the talk with all sorts and conditions of men, communion with rare natures, the proper part in local and national movement. As a lecturer, his range was the country at large, but the group that drew about him made Concord a modern Academe. Unconsciously he idealized them all with the halo of his own attributes. To him they all were of the breed so exquisitely characterized in his reference to Margaret Fuller's "Friends." "I remember," he says, "these persons as a fair, commanding troop, every one of them adorned by some splendor of beauty, of grace, of talent, or of character, and comprising in their band persons who have since disclosed sterling worth and elevated aims in the conduct of life." Thus year after year a tide, that ceases not with the death of him who mainly attracted it, has set toward Concord,—a movement of pilgrims craving spiritual exaltation and the interplay of mind with mind. The poet's moral and intellectual experiences are revealed in discourses, always beginning with the memorable sermon on the Lord's Supper, which prefigured his emancipation from dogma,[1] and the essay on Nature, wherein he applied a new vision to the world about us. These were the Alpha of his conviction and insight; his after-speech followed consistently and surely, "as the night the day." He created his own audience, whose demand for his thought grew by what it fed on, beginning in a section, and spreading not only through a country but over many lands. If it is true that "he was not the

prince of transcendentalists but the prince of idealists," the history of New England transcendentalism is no less a corollary to the problem of Emerson's life.

Our starry memories of the places and people that once knew Emerson radiate always from one centre—the presence of the sage himself. Many pupils, catching something of his own sure and precise art of delineation, have drawn his image for us, dwelling upon the sinewy bending figure, the shining and expectant face, the union of masculinity and sweetness in his bearing. His "full body tone" is recalled, "full and sweet rather than sonorous, yet flexible, and haunted by many modulations." Persuasion sat upon his lips. The epithet "sun-accustomed" is applied to Emerson's piercing eyes by one, a woman and a poet, who marked the aquiline effect of his noble profile. I, too, remember him in this wise, and as the most serene of men: one whose repose, whose tranquillity, was not the contentment of an idler housed in worldly comforts, but the token of spiritual adjustment to all the correspondences of life; as the bravest and most deferential, the proudest in self-respect, yet recognizing in deep humility the supremacy of universal law. No man so receptive, and none with so plain and absolute a reservation of his own ground. Even in the shadow and silence of his closing years, he bore the mien of one assured that

> the gods reclaim not from the seer
> Their gift, although he ceases here to sing,
> And, like the antique sage, a covering
> Draws round his head, knowing what change is near.

III

It is not my province to take part in the discussion of Emerson's philosophy, his system or lack of system. Some notion of this, however, must affect our thoughts of him as a poet, since of all moderns he most nearly fulfilled Wordsworth's inspired prediction, uttered sixty years ago, of the approaching union of the poet and the philosopher. He deemed the higher office that of the poet,—of him who quaffs the brook that flows fast by the oracles,—yet doubtless thought himself not so well endowed with melody and passion that his teaching should be subordinate to his song. But the latter was always the flowering of his philosophic thought, and it is essential to keep in view the basis of that pure reflection. He looked upon Nature as pregnant with Soul; for him the Spirit always moved upon the face of the waters. The incomprehensible plan was perfect: whatever is, is right. Thus far he knew, and was an optimist with reverent intent. It was in vain to ask him to assert what he did not know, to avow a creed founded upon his hopes. If a theist, with his intuition of an all-pervading life, he no less felt himself a portion of that life, and the sense of omnipresence was so clearly the dominant sense of its attributes, that to call him a theist rather than a pantheist is simply a dispute about terms; to pronounce him a Christian theist is to go beyond his own testimony. Such a writer must be judged by the concurrence of his books; they are his record, and the parole evidence of no associate can weigh against his written manifest for an instant. His writings assure us that he accepted all bibles and creeds for what good there was in them. One thing for him was "certain": "Religions are obsolete when lives do not proceed from them." He saw that "unlovely, nay frightful, is the solitude of the soul which is without God in the world"; but the creeds and dogmas of anthropomorphic theology were merely germinal. "Man," thus far, has "made all religions, and will yet make new and even higher faiths."

Emerson, a man of our time, while a transcendentalist, looking inward rather than to books for his wisdom, studied well the past, and earlier sages were the faculty of his school. A latter-day eclectic, he took from all literatures their best and essential. A Platonic idealist, he was not averse to the inductive method of Aristotle; he had the Alexandrian faith and ecstasy, the Epicurean zest and faculty of selection; like the Stoics, he observed morals, heroism, self-denial, and frugality. There is much in his teachings that recalls the beautiful ethics of Marcus Aurelius, and the words of Epictetus, as reported by Arrian. This spiritual leanings never stinted his regard of men and manners. He kept a sure eye on the world; he was not only a philosopher, but the paragon of gentlemen, with something more than the Oriental, the Grecian, or the Gallic, tact. He relished to the full the brave distinctions, the portraitures and tests of Plutarch, and found the best of all good company in the worldly wise, the cheery and comfortable Montaigne. One may almost say that he refined and digested what was good in all philosophies, and nothing more. He would get hold of Swedenborg, the mystic, yet not be Swedenborg exclusively, nor imitate the rhetoric of the Sophists, the pride of the Cynics. From all he learned what each confesses in the end,—the limitations of inquiry,—that the Finite cannot measure, though it may feel, the Infinite. No more would he formulate a philosophy, but within it he could recognize nature, art, taste, morals, laws, religion, and the chance of immortality. When it was said that he had no new system, he thought that he needed none, and was sceptical of classification.

It appears that he found the key to his own nature in Plato, being an idealist first of all. His intuitive faculty was so determined that ideality and mysticism gave him the surest promise of realities; his own intellect satisfied him of the power of intellect. Plainly hearing an interior voice, he had no doubt that other men were similarly monished. Plato, the guide of his youth, remained his type of philosopher and man. To Plato's works alone should Omar's saying of the Koran be applied: "Burn the libraries, for their value is in this book." Nowhere else was there such a range of speculation. "Out of Plato come all things." And thus he held to the last. "Of Plato," he said, years afterward, "I hesitate to speak, lest there should be no end. . . . Why should not young men be educated on this book? It would suffice for the tuition of the race." Yet Emerson's philosophy was a greater advance from Neo-Platonism than the Alexandrians were able to make upon the lines indicated by their elemental master. In personal life and bearing, Plotinus, with whom our poet seems to have been most in sympathy, was very closely his prototype. There is first to be noted the curious resemblance between the eclectic, investigating Alexandrian age and our present time; and secondly, it is Plotinus of whom we are told that "He lived at the same time with himself and with others, and the inward activity of his spirit ceased only during his hours of sleep. . . . His written style was close, pregnant, and richer in thought than in words, yet enthusiastic, and always pointing to the main object. He was more eloquent in his oral communications, and was said to be very clever in finding the appropriate word, even if he failed in accuracy on the whole. Besides this, the beauty of his person was increased when discoursing; his countenance was lighted up with genius." Taylor's translations of selections from the Works of Plotinus, published in 1817 and 1834, must have fallen into Emerson's hands, and I am satisfied of their impression upon his mind. As one examines the lives and writings of the two men, the likeness is still more notable, especially with respect to their views of fate, will, ethics, the "higher law," the analysis of the beautiful, and in

the ardor with which young students, and many of the elderly and wise, listened to their respective teachings. Emerson was a Plotinus reanimate after the lapse of sixteen centuries of Christianity. He has now, like the Neo-Platonist, "led back the Divine principle within" him "to the God who is all in all."

To the great thinkers of the past, the New England teacher, without fear or boasting, well might feel himself allied. The accepted great, free of the ordinary bounds of place and time, recognize one another across the vague, like stars of the prime magnitude in the open night. Emerson knew the haps and signs of genius: "Whenever we find a man higher by a whole head than any of his contemporaries, it is sure to come in doubt what are his real works." We cannot say "What is master, and what school." "As for their borrowings and adaptings, they know how to borrow. . . . A great man is one of the affinities, who takes of everything." But they are not above the law of perfect life; virtue, simplicity, absolute sincerity, these are their photosphere. "Live as on a mountain. Let men see, let them know, a real man, who lives as he was meant to live." To this Roman standard the New Englander subjoined the shrewd, kindly wisdom of his stock and region. He was eminent among those whose common sense is the most telling point to be made against Locke's negation of innate ideas,—whose judgment is so apt that, granting Locke's theory, it can be accounted for only by the modern theory of ideas prenatal and inherited. His written wisdom is more effective than Montaigne's, being less dependent on citations. He knew by instinct what our novelists learn from observation and experience; or is it that they study chiefly their own time and neighborhood, while he sat aloof and with the ages? Thus strong in equipment, sound in heart, and lofty of intellect, we find him revered by his pupils, and without a living peer in the faculty of elevating the purpose of those who listened to his buoyant words. We must confess that a differentiation between master and school, and between members of the school, after awhile became manifest. That such a process was inevitable is plain, when Emerson's transcendental and self-reliant laws of conduct are kept in mind.

One may say, in illustration, that his philosophical method bears to the inductive or empirical a relation similar to that between the poetry of self-expression and the poetry of aesthetic creation,—a relation of the subjective to the objective. The former kind of verse often is the more spontaneous, since it has its birth in the human need for utterance. It is the cry of adolescence and femininity, the resource of sensitive natures in which emotion outvies the sense of external beauty or power. It was the voice of Shakespeare's youth, nor was it ever quieted throughout the restless careers of Byron, Heine, and de Musset. But we accept as the great works of the poets their intellectual and objective creations, wherein the artist has gone beyond his own joy and pain, his narrow intro-vision, to observe, combine, transfigure, the outer world of nature and life. Such the epics, idyls, dramas, of the masters. When subjective poetry is the yield of a lofty nature, or of an ideal and rapturous womanhood like Mrs. Browning's, it is a boon and revelation to us all; but when, as too often, it is the spring-rise of a purling, commonplace streamlet, its egotism grows pitiful and repulsive. This lesson has been learned, and now our minor poets, in their fear of it, strive to give pleasure to our sense of the beautiful, and work as artists,—though somewhat too delicately,—rather than to pose as exceptional beings, "among men, but not of them."

As with the subjective poets, so with many of the transcendental acolytes. The force of Emerson lay in the depth and clearness of his intentions. He gave us the revelation and prophecy of a man among millions. Such a teacher aids the self-development of noble minds; his chief peril is that of nurturing a weaker class that cannot follow where he leads. Some of its enthusiasts will scarcely fail to set too high a value upon their personal impulses. They "still revere," but forget to "still suspect" themselves "in lowliness of heart." For the rest, the down-East instinct is advisory and homiletic; New Englanders are prone to teach, and slower to be taught. Emerson, however, grew to be their superior man, the one to whom all agreed to listen, and from whom all quote. His example, also, has somewhat advanced the art of listening, in which he was so perfect, with forward head and bright, expectant visage. His inculcations were of freedom, of the self-guidance that learns to unlearn and bears away from tradition; yet this, too, will breed false liberty of conceit in minor votaries, whose inward light may do well enough for themselves, yet not suffice for the light of the world. Hence the public, accepting Emerson, has been less tolerant of more than one Emersonian, with his *ego, et rex meus*. After all is said, we must see that our transcendentalists were a zealous, aspiring band of seekers after the true, the beautiful, and the good; what they have lacked in deference they have made up in earnestness and spirituality. There have been receptive natures among them, upon whom, as indeed upon the genius of his people far and wide, the tonic effect of Emerson's life and precept has been immeasurable. Goethe's declaration of himself that he had been "to the Germans in general, and to the young German poets in particular, their liberator," may, with perfect truth, be applied to Emerson, and to a generation that has thriven on his word. He has taught his countrymen the worth of virtue, wisdom, courage,—above all, to fashion life upon a self-reliant pattern, obeying the dictates of their own souls.

IV

Recognizing Emerson's high mood as that of a most original poet, I wish chiefly to consider his relations to poetry and the poetic art. His imaginative essays are not poems. Speech is not song; the rarest mosaic lacks the soul of the canvas swept by the brush. The credentials that he presented from time to time, and mostly in that dawn when poets sing if ever, are few and fragmentary, but they will suffice. They are the trophies, the wreaths and golden vessels, the *spolia opima*, which he set before the shrine of the goddess. They are the avowal of a rare spirit that there are things which cannot be rendered in prose; that Poetry claims a finer art, a supremer utterance, for her service, and that she alone can stamp the coins and bronzes which carry to the future the likeness of her viceroy.

In his verse, Emerson's spiritual philosophy and laws of conduct appear again, but transfigured. Always the idea of Soul, central and pervading, of which Nature's forms are but the created symbols. As in his early discourse he recognized two entities, Nature and the Soul, so to the last he believed Art to be simply the union of Nature with man's will—Thought symbolizing itself through Nature's aid. Thought, sheer ideality, was his sovereign; he was utterly trustful of its guidance. The law of poetic beauty depends on the beauty of the thought, which, perforce, assumes the fittest, and therefore most charming, mode of expression. The key to art is the eternal fitness of things; this is the sure test and solvent. Over and again he asserted his conviction: "Great thoughts insure musical expression. Every word should be the right word. . . . The Imagination wakened brings its own language, and that is always musical. . . . Whatever language the poet uses, the secret of tone is at the heart of the poem." He cites Möller, who

taught that the building which was fitted accurately to answer its end would turn out to be beautiful, though beauty had not been intended. (The enforced beauty of even the rudest sailing craft always has seemed to me the most striking illustration of this truth.) In fine, Emerson sees all forms of art symbolizing but one Reason, not one mind, but The Mind that made the world. He refers "all production at last to an aboriginal Power." It is easy to discern that from the first he recognized "the motion and the spirit," which to Wordsworth were revealed only by the discipline of years; but his song went beyond the range of landscape and peasant, touching upon the verities of life and thought. "Brahma" is of the presentation of the truth manifest to the oldest and most eastern East, and beyond which the West can never go. How strange that these quatrains could have seemed strange! They reveal the light of Asia, but no less the thought of Plato—who said that in all nations certain minds dwell on the "fundamental Unity," and "lose all being in one Being." Everywhere one stuff, under all forms, this the woven symbolism of the universal Soul, the only reality, the single and subdivided Identity that alone can "keep and pass and turn again," that is at once the doubter and the doubt, the slayer and the slain, light and shadow, the hither and the yon. Love is but the affinity of its portions, the desire for reunion, the knowledge of soul by soul, to which the eyes of lovers are but windows. Art is the handiwork of the soul, with materials created by itself, building better than it knows, the bloom of attraction and necessity.

Thus far the theory of Emerson's song. It does not follow that he composed upon a theory. At times I think him the first of our lyric poets, his turns are so wild and unexpected; and he was never commonplace, even when writing for occasions. His verse changes unawares from a certain tension and angularity that were congenital, to an ethereal, unhampered freedom, the poetic soul in full glow, the inner music loosed and set at large. Margaret Fuller wrote that his poems were "mostly philosophical, which is not the truest kind of poetry." But this depends upon the measure of its didacticism. Emerson made philosophical poetry imaginative, elevating, and thus gave new evidence that the poet's realm is unbounded. If he sought first principles, he looked within himself for them, and thus portrays himself, not only the penetrative thinker, but the living man, the citizen, the New England villager, whose symbols are drawn from the actual woods and hills of a neighborhood. Certainly he went to rural nature for his vigor, his imagery and adornments. An impassioned sense of its beauty made him the reverse of the traditional descriptive poet. Most poetry of nature justly is termed didactic; most philosophical verse the same. Miss Fuller failed to make distinctions. All feel what didacticism signifies, but let us try to formulate it.

Didacticism is the gospel of half-truths. Its senses are torpid; it fails to catch and convey the soul of truth, which is beauty. Truth shorn of its beauty is tedious and not poetical. We weary of didactic verse, therefore, not because of its truth, but because of its self-delusive falsehood. It flourishes with a dull and prosaic generation. The true poet, as Mrs. Browning saw, is your only truth-teller, because he gives the truth complete in beauty or not at all.

Emerson doubts his power to capture the very truth of nature. Its essence—its beauty—is so elusive; it flees and leaves but a corpse behind; it is the pearly glint of the shells among the bubbles of the latest wave:—

> I fetched my sea-born treasures home;
> But the poor, unsightly, noisome things
> Had left their beauty on the shore,
> With the sun, and the sand, and the wild uproar.

But such poems as the "Forerunners" show how closely he moved, after all, upon the trail of the evading sprite. He seemed, by the first intention, and with an exact precision of grace and aptness, to put in phrases what he saw and felt,—and he saw and felt so much more than others! He had the aboriginal eye, and the civilized sensibility; he caught both the external and the scientific truth of natural things, and their poetic charm withal. As he triumphed over the untruthfulness of the mere verse-maker, and the dulness of the moralist, his instant, sure, yet airy transcripts gave his poems of nature a quality with out a counterpart. Some of his measures had at least the flutter of the twig whence the bird has just flown. He did not quite fail of that music music-born,

> a melody born of melody,
> Which melts the world into a sea.
> Toil could never compass it;
> Art its height could never hit.

He infused his meditations with the sheen of Day itself,—of

> one of the charméd days
> When the genius of God doth flow;
> The wind may alter twenty ways,
> A tempest cannot blow;
> It may blow north, it still is warm;
> Or south, it still is clear;
> Or east, it smells like a clover-farm;
> Or west, no thunder fear.

He returns with delight to Nature's blending of her laws of beauty and use, perceiving that she

> beats in perfect tune,
> And rounds with rhyme her every rune,
> Whether she work in land or sea,
> Or hide underground her alchemy.
> Thou canst not wave thy staff in air,
> Or dip thy paddle in the lake,
> But it carves the box of beauty there,
> And the ripples in rhymes the oar forsake.

"Woodnotes" is full of lyrical ecstasy and lightsome turns and graces. To assimilate such a poem of nature, or "The Problem," that masterpiece of religion and art, is to feed on holy dew, and to comprehend how the neophytes who were bred upon it find the manna of noontide somewhat rank and innutritious. "May-Day" is less lyrical, more plainly descriptive of the growth and meaning of the Spring, but not in any part didactic. It is the record of the poet's training, a match to Wordsworth's portrayal of his subjective communing with Nature in youth; its spirit is the same with Lowell's woodland joyousness, one of child-like and unquestioning zest. Finally, this poet's scenic joinery is so true, so mortised with the one apt word, as where he says that the wings of Time are "*pied* with morning and with night," and the one best word or phrase is so unlooked for, that, as I say, we scarcely know whether all this comes by grace of instinct, or with search and artistic forethought. It seems "the first fine careless rapture"; the labor, which results in the truth of Tennyson's landscape and the pathos of Longfellow's, may be there, but is not to be detected, and in these touches, if not otherwise, he excelled his compeers. His generalizations pertain to the unseen world; viewing the actual, he puts its strength and fineness alike into a line or epithet. He was born with an unrivalled faculty of selection. Monadnock is the "constant giver," the Titan that "heeds his sky-affairs"; the tiny humming-bee a "voyager of light and noon," a "yellow-breeched philosopher," and again an "animated torrid zone"; the defiant titmouse, an "atom in full breath." For a snow-storm, or the ocean, he uses his broader brush, but once only and well. His minute truth and sense of values are held in honor by his pupils Whitman and Burroughs, our poetic familiars of the field, and by all to whom the seasonable marvels of the pastoral year are not unwelcome or unknown.

Thus keenly Emerson's instinct reponded to the beauty of Nature. I have hinted that her secure laws were the chief promoters of his imagination. It coursed along her hidden ways. In this he antedated Tennyson, and was less didactic than Goethe and kindred predecessors. His foresight gave spurs to the intellect of Tyndall and other investigators,—to their ideal faculty, without which no explorer moves from post to outpost of discovery. Correlatively, each wonder-breeding point attained by the experimentalists was also occupied by our eager and learned thinker from the moment of its certainty. Each certainty gave him joy; reasoning *a priori* from his sense of a spiritual Force, the seer anticipated the truths demonstrated by the inductive workers, and expected the demonstration. Even in "The Sphinx," the first poem of his first collection, the conservation of force, the evolution from the primordial atom, are made to subserve his mystical faith in a broad Identity. Here, thirty years before Tennyson made his most compact expression of the central truth,—

> Flower in the crannied wall . . .
> Little flower—but if I could understand
> What you are, root and all, and all in all,
> I should know what God and man is,

Emerson had put it in this wise:—

> Thorough a thousand voices
> Spoke the universal dame:
> "Who telleth one of my meanings,
> Is master of all I am."

The reference, in "Bacchus," to the ascent of life from form to form, still remains incomparable for terseness and poetic illumination:—

> I, drinking this,
> Shall hear far Chaos talk with me;
> Kings unborn shall walk with me;
> And the poor grass shall plot and plan
> What it will do when it is man.

And in "Woodnotes" he discoursed of

> the genesis of things,
> Of tendency through endless ages,
> Of star-dust and star-pilgrimages,
> Of rounded worlds, of space and time,
> Of the old flood's subsiding slime;

but always thinks of the universal Soul as the only reality,—of creation's process as simply the metamorphosis which

> Melts things that be to things that seem,
> And solid nature to a dream.

Even in the pathetic "Threnody" he stays his anguish with faith in the beneficence of Law. With more passion and less method than afterward gave form to *In Memoriam*, he declared that the "mysteries of Nature's heart" were "past the blasphemics of grief." He saw

> the genius of the whole,
> Ascendant in the primal soul,
> Beckon it when to go and come."

Such a poet was not like to go backward. The "Song of Nature" is his pæan to her verities, still more clearly manifest in his riper years. This superb series of quatrains, cumulative as thunder-heads and fired with lyric glory, will lend its light to whatsoever the poetry of the future has in reserve for us.

It should be noted that Emerson's vision of the sublime in scientific discovery increased his distaste for mere style, and moved him to contentment with the readiest mode of expression. It tempered his eulogy of "Art," and made him draw this contrast: "Nature transcends all moods of thought, and its secret we do not yet find. But a gallery stands at the mercy of our moods, and there is a moment when it becomes frivolous. I do not wonder that Newton, with an attention habitually engaged on the paths of planets and suns, should have wondered what the Earl of Pembroke found to admire in 'stone dolls.'"

Right here we observe (deferring matters of construction) that our seer's limitations as a poet are indicated by his dependence on out-door nature, and by his failure to utilize those higher symbols of the prime Intelligence which comprise the living, acting, suffering world of man. With a certain pride of reserve, that did not lessen his beautiful deference to individuals, he proclaimed "the advantage which the country life possesses for a powerful mind over the artificial and curtailed life of cities." He justified solitude by saying that great men, from Plato to Wordsworth, did not live in a crowd, but descended into it from time to time as benefactors. Above all he declared—"I am by nature a poet, and therefore must live in the country." But here a Goethe, or de Musset, or Browning might rejoin: "And I am a poet, and need the focal life of the town." If man be the paragon of life on this globe, his works and passions the rarest symbols of the life unseen, then the profoundest study is mankind. Emerson's theorem was a restriction of the poet's liberties. One can name great poets who would have been greater but for the trammels of their seclusion. I believe that Emerson's came from self-knowledge. He kept his range with incomparable tact and philosophy. Poets of a wider franchise—with Shakespeare at their front—have found that genius gains most from Nature during that formative period when one reads her heart, if ever, and that afterward he may safely leave her, as a child his mother, to return from time to time, but still to do his part among the ranks of men.

Emerson makes light of travel for pleasure and observation, but ever more closely would observe the ways of the inanimate world. Yet what are man's works but the works of Nature by one remove? To one poet is given the ear to comprehend the murmur of the forest, to another the sense that times the heartbeats of humanity. Few have had Emerson's inward eye, but it is well that some have not been restricted to it. He clung by attraction, no less than by circumstance, to "a society in which introspection," as Mr. James has shrewdly written, "thanks to the want of other entertainment, played almost the part of a social resource." His verse, in fact, is almost wholly void of the epic and dramatic elements which inform the world's great works of art. Action, characterization, specific sympathy, and passion are wanting in his song. His voice comes "like a falling star" from a skyey dome of pure abstraction. Once or twice, some little picture from life,—a gypsy girl, a scarcely outlined friend or loved one,—but otherwise no personage in his works except, it may be, the poet himself, the Saadi of his introspective song: even that wise and joyous bard restored in fragments, suggested rather than portrayed. Emerson would be the "best bard, because the wisest," if the wisdom of his song illustrated itself in living types. He knew the human world, none better, and generalized the sum of its attainments,—was gracious, shrewd, and calm,—but could not hold up the mirror and show us to ourselves. He was that unique songster, a poet of fire and vision, quite above the moralist, yet neither to be classed as objective or subjective; he perceived the source of all passion and wisdom, yet rendered neither the hearts of others nor his own. His love poetry is eulogized, but it wants the vital grip wherewith his "Concord Fight" and "Boston Hymn" fasten on our sense of manhood and patriotism. It chants of Love, not of the beloved; its flame is pure and general as moonlight and as high-removed. "All mankind love a lover," and it is not enough to discourse upon the philosophy of "Love," "Experience," "Power," "Friendship." Emerson's "Bacchus" must press for him

> wine, but wine which never grew
> In the belly of the grape.

His deepest yearnings are expressed in that passionate outburst,—the momentary human wail over his dead child,—and in the human sense of lost companionship when he tells us,—

> In the long sunny afternoon,
> The plain was full of ghosts.

Oftener he moves apart; his blood is ichor, not our own; his thoughts are with the firmament. We reverence his vocation, and know ourselves unfitted for it. He touches life more nearly in passages that have the acuteness, the practical wisdom of his prose works and days; but these are not his testimonials as a poet. His laying on of hands was more potent; a transmitted heat has gone abroad through the ministry of his disciples, who practise as he preached, and sometimes transcend both his preaching and his practice. All the same, the originator of a force is greater than others who add four-fold to its momentum. They are never so manifestly his pupils as when they are "scarifying" and "sounding and exploring" him, "reporting where they touch bottom and where not," on ground of their own, but with a pleasant mockery of the master's word and wont. There was a semblance between the poets Emerson and Rossetti, first, in the small amount of their lyrical work, and again in the positive influence which each exerted upon his pupils. In quality the Concord seer, and the English poet who was at once the most spiritual and sensuous of his own school, were wholly unlike. Rossetti was touched with white fire, but dreamed of souls that meet and glow when disembodied. The spirits of his beatified thrill with human passion. Our seer brought something of heaven to earth, while Rossetti yearned to carry life through death to heaven. ⟨. . .⟩

Popular instinct, recognized by those who compile our anthologies, forbids an author to be great in more than one way. These editors go to Emerson for point and wisdom, and too seldom for his truth to nature and his strictly poetic charm. Yet who excels him in quality? That Margaret Fuller had a fine ear, and an independent one, proved by her admission that "in melody, in subtilty of thought and expression," he took the highest rank. He often captures us with absolute beauty, the poetry that poets love,—the lilt and melody of Shelley (whose vagueness irked him) joined to precision of thought and outline. Poe might have envied "Uriel" his lutings of the spangled heaven; he could not have read "Woodnotes," or he would have found something kindred in the bard who said,—

> Quit thy friends as the dead in doom,
> And build to them a final tomb;
> Let the starred shade that nightly falls
> Still celebrate their funerals,
> And the bell of beetle and of bee
> Knell their melodious memory.

Emerson "listened to the undersong," but rejoiced no less in the "divine ideas below" of the Olympian bards,

> Which always find us young
> And always keep us so.

His modes of expression, like his epithets, are imaginative. The snow is "the north-wind's masonry"; feeling and thought are scarcely deeper than his speech; he puts in words the "tumultuous privacy of storm," of the "sweet varieties of chance." With what high ecstasy of pain he calls upon the deep-eyed boy, the hyacinthine boy, of his marvellous "Threnody!" Time confirms the first impression that this is the most spontaneous, the most elevating, of lyrical elegies,—that it transcends even the divine verse of Bishop King's invocation to his entombed wife. How abrupt, how exquisitely ideal, the opening phrase! Afterward, and throughout, the pure spirit of poetry rarefied by the passion of its theme: the departed child is the superangelic symbol of the beauty, the excellence, that shall be when time ripens and the harmonies of nature are revealed,—when life is no longer a dream within a dream. Read the "Threnody" anew. What grace! What Æolian music, what yearning! What prophecy and exaltation! See how emotion becomes the soul of art. Or is it that true passion cannot but express itself in verse at once simple and sensuous, thus meeting all the cardinal points of Milton's law?

One readily perceives that "Merlin" conveys Emerson's spirited conception of the art and manners of the bard. His should be no trivial harp:—

> No jingling serenader's art,
> Nor tinkle of piano strings;
> . . .
> The kingly bard
> Must smite the cords rudely and hard,
> As with hammer or with mace;
> . . .
> He shall not his brain encumber
> With the coil of rhythm and number;
> But leaving rule and pale forethought,
> He shall aye climb
> For his rhyme.

Thus fearlessly should a poet compel the Muse; and even to a broader liberty of song one, at least, of Emerson's listeners pushed with deliberate zeal. Walt Whitman was stimulated by this teaching, and by the rugged example of Carlyle, to follow resolutely the method which suited his bent and project; and Emerson's "Mithridates," we may say, is at once the key-note and best defence of Whitman's untrammelled, all-heralding philosophy. The descriptive truth, the lusty Americanism, of the democratic chanter took hold upon the master's expectant heart. A later modification of the first welcome, and the omission of the new songs from "Parnassus," had no bearing upon the question of their morals or method; Emerson was moved solely by his taste,—and New England taste has a supreme dislike of the unsavory. The world, even the Concord world, is not wholly given over to prudery. It has little dread, nowadays, of the voluptuous in art, ancient or modern. But to those of Puritan stock cleanliness is even more than godliness. There is no "fair perdition" tempting us in the "Song of Myself" and the "Children of Adam." But here are things which, whether vessels of honor or dishonor, one does not care to have before him too often or too publicly, and which were unattractive to the pure and temperate seer, whose race had so long inhabited the clean-swept keeping-rooms of the land of mountain breezes and transparent streams. The matter was one of artistic taste and of the inclinations of Emerson's nature, rather than of prudery or censorship.

As for his own style, Emerson was impressed in youth by the free-hand manner of the early dramatists, whom he read with avidity. He soon formed his characteristic measure, varying with "sixes," "sevens," and "eights," resembling Ben Jonson's lyrical style, but even more like that of Milton,

Marvell, and other worthies of the Protectorate. In spirit and imagery, in blithe dithyrambic wisdom, he gained much from his favorite Orientals—Saadi and Hafiz. One stately and various measure he rarely essayed, but showed that it was well suited to his genius. In "Musketaquid" and "Sea-Shore" we see the aptness of his ear and hand for blank verse. The little poem of "Days," imitated from the antique, is unmatched, outside of Landor, for compression and self-poise:—

> Daughters of Time, the hypocritic Days,
> Muffled and dumb like barefoot dervishes,
> And marching single in an endless file,
> Bring diadems and fagots in their hands.
> To each they offer gifts after his will,
> Bread, kingdoms, stars, and sky that holds them all.
> I, in my pleachéd garden, watched the pomp,
> Forgot my morning wishes, hastily
> Took a few herbs and apples, and the Day
> Turned and departed silent. I, too late,
> Under her solemn fillet saw the scorn.

We could wish that Emerson had written more blank verse,—a measure suited to express his highest thought and imagination. Probably, however, he said all that he had to say in verse of any kind. He was not one to add a single line for the sake of a more liberal product.

He is thought to have begun so near the top that there was little left to climb. None of his verse is more pregnant than that which came in the first glow, but the later poems are free from those grotesque sayings which illustrate the fact that humor and a lively sense of the absurd often are of slow development in the brain of an earnest thinker. There was, it must be owned, a tinge of provincial arrogance, and there were expressions little less than ludicrous, in his early defiance of usage. He was too sincere a personage to resort to the grotesque as a means of drawing attention. Of him, the leader, this at least could not be suspected. Years afterward he revised his poems, as if to avoid even the appearance of affectation. On the whole, it is as well that he left "The Sphinx" unchanged; that remarkable poem is a fair gauge of its author's traits. The opening is strongly lyrical and impressive. The close is the flower of poesy and thought. The general tone is quaint and mystical. Certain passages, however, like that beginning "The fiend that man harries," are curiously awkward, and mar the effect of an original, almost an epochal, poem. This would not be admitted by the old-fashioned Emersonian,—never, by any chance, a poet pure and simple,—who makes it a point of faith to defend the very passages where the master nods. Just so the thick-and-thin Browningite, who testifies his adoration by counting the *m*'s and *n*'s of the great dramatist's volumes, and who, also, never is a poet pure and simple, celebrates Mr. Browning's least poetic experiments as his masterpieces. I think that the weakness of "transcendental" art is as fairly manifest in Emerson's first and chief collection of verse as were its felicities,—the former belonging to the school, the latter to the seer's own genius. Poe, to whom poetry was solely an expression of beauty, was irritated to a degree not to be explained by contempt for all things East. He extolled quaintness, and justly detested obscurity. He was prejudiced against the merits of such poets as Channing and Cranch by their prophetic bearing, which he berated soundly as an effort to set up as poets "of *unusual* depth and *very* remarkable powers of mind." Admitting the grace of one, he said that it was "laughable to see that the transcendental poets, if beguiled for a minute or two into respectable English and common-sense, are always sure to remember their cue just as they get to the end of their song, and round off with a bit of doggerel." Their thought was the "cant of thought," in adopting which "the cant of phraseology is adopted at the same time." This was serviceable criticism, *et ab hoste*, though Poe's lack of moral, and keenness of artistic, sense made him too sure of the insincerity of those who place conviction above expression. And Mr. James sees that Emerson's philosophy was "drunk in by a great many fine moral appetites with a sense of intoxication." The seer himself was intoxicated at times, and spoke, like the hasheesh-eaters, with what then seemed to him music and sanity. In a more reflecting season he excluded from his select edition certain pieces from which too many had taken their cues,—for example, the "Ode" to W. H. Channing, "The World-Soul," and "Tact." The Ode begins finely with a manner caught from Ben Jonson's ode "To Himself," and we can ill spare one passage ("The God who made New Hampshire"); but was it the future compiler of "Parnassus" who preceded this with laughter-stirring rhymes, and shortly avowed that "Things are of the snake," and again that "Things are in the saddle, And ride mankind"? Well, he lived to feel that to poets, "of all men, the severest criticism is due," and that "Poetry requires that splendor of expression which carries with it the proof of great thoughts."

But the forte of bardlings is the foible of a bard. Emerson became his own censor, and did wisely and well. We have seen that his art, even now, upon its constructive side, must often seem defective,—unsatisfactory to those whose love of proportion is a moral instinct. Many poets and critics will feel it so. The student of Emerson learns that he, too, moved upon their plane, but would not be confined to it. More than other men, he found himself a vassal of the unwritten law, whether his impulse lifted him above, or sent him below, the plane of artistic expression. If he could not sustain the concert-pitch of his voice at his best, he certainly knew what is perfection, and said of art much that should be said. He was not, he did not wish to be, primarily an artist: he borrowed Art's aid for his lofty uses, and held her at her worth. His essay on Art would be pronounced sound by a Goethe or a Lessing, though such men probe less deep for the secret principle of things, and deal more featly with the exterior. Elsewhere he insists that we must "disabuse us of our superstitious associations with place and time, with number and size. . . . Where the heart is, there the muses, there to gods sojourn. . . . A great man makes his climate genial in the imagination of man, and its air the beloved element of all delicate spirits." And again (like Arnold) he speaks of the modernness of all good books: "What is well done, I feel as if I did; what is ill done, I reck not of." He revised his prose less carefully, for republication, than his verse, and doubtless felt surer of it. He himself would have been the first to declare, as to the discordant and grotesque portions of his verse or prose, that the thought was proportionately defective,—not strong and pure enough to insure the beauty of the art which was its expression. Above all he knew, he confessed, that it is the first duty of a poet to express his thoughts naturally, counting among "the traits common to all works of the highest art,—that they are universally intelligible, that they restore to us the simplest state of mind." This was his own canon. Where he failed of it, he might not surely know; where he knew, there he rebuked himself. He struck out, in his self-distrust, many things of value to those who loved his verse. We dwell with profit on the fact that he retained so little that should be stricken out.

V

It is but a foolish surmise whether Emerson's prose or verse will endure the longer, for they are of the same stuff, warp and woof, and his ideality crosses and recrosses each, so that either is cloth-of-gold. Of whichever a reader may first lay hold, he will be led to examine the whole fabric of the author's work. Few writers, any one of whose essays, met with for the first time, seems more like a revelation! It will not be, I think, until that time when all his prose has passed into a large book, such as the volume we call Montaigne, that its full strength and importance can be felt. In certain respects it dwarfs other modern writing, and places him among the great essayists. These are not the efforts of a reviewer of books or affairs, but chapters on the simplest, the greatest, the immemorial topics, those that lie at the base of life and wisdom: such as Love, Experience, Character, Manners, Fate, Power, Worship—lastly, Nature herself, and Art her ideal counterpart. If to treat great themes worthily is a mark of greatness, the chooser of such themes begins with the instinct of great design. Bacon's elementary essays excepted, there are none in English of which it can be more truly averred that there is nothing superfluous in them. Compare them with the rest in theme and method. Carlyle, outside of *Sartor Resartus* and *Hero-Worship*, usually reviews books, histories, individuals, at extreme length, and with dramatic comment and analysis. Emerson treats of the principles behind all history, and his laconic phrases are the very honey-cells of thought. There are let-downs and surplus-age even in Landor. Throughout Emerson's writings each word is of value; they are the discourse of one who has digested all the worthy books, and who gives us their results, with latter-day discoveries of his own. He is the citizen of a new world, observing other realms and eras from an unrestricted point of view.

The intent of our essayist is the highest, and by no means that of writing for the exercise or glory of authorship. "Fatal," he declares, "to the man of letters is the lust of display. . . . A mistake of the main end to which they labor is incidental to literary men, who, dealing with the organ of language . . . learn to enjoy the pride of playing with this splendid engine, but rob it of its almightiness by failing to work with it." He estimates books at their worth. They "are for nothing but to inspire. I had better never see a book than to be warped by its attraction clean out of my own orbit, and made a satellite instead of a system."

Thus the thought of Style, it may be, should enter into the mind of neither writer nor reader. Style makes itself, and Emerson's is the apothegmatic style of one bent upon uttering his immediate thoughts,—hence strong in sentences, and only by chance suited to the formation of an essay. Each sentence is an idea, an epigram, or an image, or a flash of spiritual light. His letters to Carlyle show that he was at one time caught by the manner of the author whose character, at least, seemed of the most import to him. This was but a passing trace. When he was fresh from the schools, his essays were structural and orderly, but more abstract than in latter years. During his mature and haply less spiritual period, had he cared to write a history, the English would have been pure English, the narrative racy and vigorous. Portions of the *English Traits* make this plain. Since De Foe, where have we found anything more idiomatic than his account of Wordsworth delivering a sonnet?

> This recitation was so unlooked for and surprising,—he, the old Wordsworth, standing apart, and reciting to me in a garden-walk, like a schoolboy declaiming,—that I at first was near to laugh; but recollecting myself, that I had come thus far to see a poet, and he was chanting poems to me, I saw that he

was right and I was wrong, and gladly gave myself up to hear.

Note also Emerson's account of an ocean voyage. For charm of landscape-painting, take such a passage as that, in the second essay on Nature, beginning: "There are days which occur in this climate." But terseness is the distinctive feature of his style. "Men," he said, "descend to meet." "We are all discerners of spirits." "He [a traveller] carries ruins to ruins. No one has compressed more sternly the pith of his discourse.

No poet, let us at once add, has written prose and shown more incontestably his special attribute. Emerson's whole argument is poetic, if that work is poetic which reaches its aim through the analogies of things, and whose quick similitudes have the heat, the light, the actinism, of the day-beam, and of which the language is rhythmic without degeneracy,—clearly the language of prose, always kept from weakness by the thought which it conveys. No man's writing was more truly his speech, and no man's speech so rhythmic: "There are Muses in the woods to-day, and whispers to be heard in the breezes"; and again, "Hawthorne rides well his horse of the night." As he spoke, so he wrote: "Give me health and a day, and I will make the pomp of emperors ridiculous"; "The conscious ship hears all the praise"; of young idealists, "The tough world had its revenge the moment they put the horses of the sun to plough in its furrow"; of Experience, "was it Boscovich who found out that bodies never come in contact? Well, souls never touch their objects. An innavigable sea washes with silent waves between us and the things we aim at and converse with." In the same essay,—"Dream delivers us to dream, and there is no end to illusion. Life is a train of moods like a string of beads, and as we pass through them, they prove to be many-colored lenses which paint the world their own hue."[2] And of Love's world, with the cadences of Ecclesiastes,—"When the day was not long enough, but the night, too, must be consumed. . . . When the moonlight was a pleasing fever, and the stars were letters, and the flowers ciphers, and the air was coined into song; when all business seemed impertinence, all the men and women running to and fro in the streets mere pictures." But to show the poetry of Emerson's prose is to give the whole of it; these essays are of the few which make us tolerate the conceit of "prose poems." Their persistent recourse to imagery and metaphor, their suggestions of the secret relations of things, at times have subjected them to the charge of being obscure. The fault was not in the wine:—

Hast thou a drunken soul?
Thy bane is in thy shallow skull, not in my silver
    bowl!

In mature years the essayist pays more regard to life about him, to the world as it is; he is more equatorial, less polar and remote. His insight betrays itself in every-day wisdom. He is the shrewd, the benignant, the sagacious, Emerson, writing with pleasant aptitude, like Hesiod or Virgil, of domestic routine, and again of the Conduct of Life, of Manners, Behavior, Prudence, Grace. This is in the philosophic order or progress, from the first principles to the application of them. Some of his followers, however, take him to task, unwilling that the master should venture beyond the glory of his cloud. As for his unique treatises upon Behavior, it was natural that he should be led to think upon that topic, since in gentle bearing, in his sweetness, persuasiveness, and charm of smile and voice, he was not excelled by any personage of our time, and what he said of it is of more value than the sayings of those who think such a matter beneath his regard. His views of civic duty and concerning the welfare of the Republic are the best rejoinder

to his early strictures upon Homer and Shakespeare for the temporal and local features of their master-works. As a critic he was ever expectant, on the lookout for something good and new, and sometimes found the one good thing in a man or work and valued it unduly. When he made a complete examination, as in his chapter on Margaret Fuller, he excelled as a critic and delineator. *Parnassus* is not judicial, but oddly made up of his own likings, yet the best rules of criticism are to be found in its preface. With the exception of *English Traits*, he published no long treatise upon a single theme. His general essays and lectures, however, constitute a treatise upon Man and Nature, and of themselves would serve as America's adequate contribution to the English literature of his period. We are told of an unprinted series of his essays that may be grouped as a book on the Natural History of the Intellect. Should these see the light, it would be curious to compare them with the work of some professional logician—with the standard treatise of President Porter, for instance—upon a similar theme. Something in quantity may yet be added to Emerson's literary remains. But it will not differ in quality; we have had the gist of it: for he was a writer who, though his essays were the fruit of a prolonged life, never wrote himself out. Often an author has gained repute by one or two original works, while his ordinary efforts, if not devoted to learned or scientific research, have been commonplace. The flame of Emerson's intellect never fades or flickers, and never irks us. It burns with elemental light, neither of artifice nor of occasion, serene as that of a star, and with an added power to heat the distance which receives it.

VI

In summing up the traits of Emerson one almost ceases to be critical, lest the highest praise may not be quite undue. More than when Bion died, the glades and towns lament him, for he left no heir to the Muse which he taught his pupils. In certain respects he was our most typical poet, having the finest intuition and a living faith in it,—and because there was a sure intellect behind his verse, and because his influence affected not simply the tastes and emotions, but at last the very spirit, of his countrymen. He began where many poets end, seeking at once the upper air, the region of pure thought and ideality. His speech was wisdom, and his poesy its exhalation. When he failed in either, it seemed to be through excess of divining. His triumphs were full of promise for those who dare to do their best. He was as far above Carlyle as the affairs of the soul and universe are above those of the contemporary, or even the historic, world. His problem, like that of Archimedes, was more than the taking of cities and clash of arms. The poet is unperturbed by temporal distractions; yet poets and dreamers, concerned with the ideal, share in the world's battle equally with men of action and practical life. Only, while the latter fight on the ground, the idealists, like the dauntless ghosts of the Huns and Romans, lift the contest to the air. Emerson was the freest and most ideal of them all, and what came to him by inheritance or prophetic forecast he gave like a victor. He strove not to define the creeds, but to stimulate the intellect and purpose of those who are to make the future. If poetry be that which shapes and elevates, his own was poetry indeed. To know the heart of New England you must hear the songs of his compeers; but listening to those of Emerson, the east and west have yielded to the current of its soul.

The supreme poet will be not alone a seer, but also a persistent artist of the beautiful. Of those who come before the time for such a poet is ripe, Longfellow on the whole has done the most to foster the culture of poetry among us as a liberal art.

Emerson has given us thought, the habit of thinking, the will to think for ourselves. He drained the vats of politics and philosophy, for our use, of all that was sweet and fructifying, and taught his people self-judgement, self-reliance, and to set their courses by the stars. He placed chief value upon those primitive laws which are the only sure basis of national law and letters. And as a poet, his verse was the sublimation of his rarest mood, that changed as water into cloud, catching the first beams of sunrise on its broken edges, yet not without dark and vaguely blending spots between. Emerson and Longfellow came at the parting of the ways. They are of the very few whom we now recognize as the true founders of an American literature. No successors with more original art and higher imagination can labor to more purpose. If the arrow hits its mark, the aim was at the bowstring; the river strengthens and broadens, but the sands of gold wash down from near its source.

Not a few are content with that poetry which returns again and again to its primal conceptions, yet suggests infinite pathways and always inspires,—the poetry of a hermitage whose Lar is Nature, and whose well-spring flows with clear and shining Thought. To such,—who care less for sustained flights of objective song, who can withdraw themselves from passion and dramatic life, who gladly accept isolated cadences and scattered, though exquisite, strains of melody in lieu of symphonic music "wandering on as loth to die,"—Emerson will seem the most precious of our native poets. He will not satisfy those who look for the soul incarnate in sensuous and passionate being. Such readers with Professor Dowden, find him the type of the New World transcendentalist, the creature of the drying American climate, one "whose nervous energy has been exalted," so "that he loves light better than warmth." He is not the minstrel for those who would study men in action and suffering, rather than as heirs to knowledge and the raptured mind. He is not a warrior, lover, raconteur, dramatist, but an evangelist and seer. The greatest poet must be all in one, and I have said that Emerson was among the foremost to avow it. Modern bards poorly satisfy him, being meagre of design, and failing to guide and console. Wordsworth was an exception, yet he had "written longer than he was inspired." Tennyson, with all his tune and color, "climbs no mount of vision." Even Shakespeare was too traditional, though one learns from him that "tradition supplies a better fable than any invention can." In face of the greatest he felt that "the world still wants its poet-priest, a reconciler, who shall not trifle with Shakespeare the player, nor shall grope in graves with Swedenborg the mourner; but who shall see, speak, and act with equal inspiration." Thus clearly he conceived of the poet's office, and equally was he assured that he himself was not, and could not be, the perfect musician. He chose the part of the forerunner and inspirer, and when the true poet shall come to America, it will be because such an one as Emerson has gone before him and prepared the way for his song, his vision, and his recognition.

Notes

1. Definitely set forth in his Address before the Senior Class in Divinity College, Cambridge, July 15, 1838.
2.   Life, like a dome of many-colored glass,
         Stains the white radiance of eternity.
                    (Shelley's *Adonais*.)

GEORGE SANTAYANA
"Emerson"
Interpretations of Poetry and Religion
1900, pp. 217–33

Those who knew Emerson, or who stood so near to his time and to his circle that they caught some echo of his personal influence, did not judge him merely as a poet or philosopher, nor identify his efficacy with that of his writings. His friends and neighbours, the congregations he preached to in his younger days, the audiences that afterward listened to his lectures, all agreed in a veneration for his person which had nothing to do with their understanding or acceptance of his opinions. They flocked to him and listened to his word, not so much for the sake of its absolute meaning as for the atmosphere of candour, purity, and serenity that hung about it, as about a sort of sacred music. They felt themselves in the presence of a rare and beautiful spirit, who was in communion with a higher world. More than the truth his teaching might express, they valued the sense it gave them of a truth that was inexpressible. They became aware, if we may say so, of the ultra-violet rays of his spectrum, of the inaudible highest notes of his gamut, too pure and thin for common ears.

This effect was by no means due to the possession on the part of Emerson of the secret of the universe, or even of a definite conception of ultimate truth. He was not a prophet who had once for all climbed his Sinai or his Tabor, and having there beheld the transfigured reality, descended again to make authoritative report of it to the world. Far from it. At bottom he had no doctrine at all. The deeper he went and the more he tried to grapple with fundamental conceptions, the vaguer and more elusive they became in his hands. Did he know what he meant by Spirit or the "Over-Soul"? Could he say what he understood by the terms, so constantly on his lips, Nature, Law, God, Benefit, or Beauty? He could not, and the consciousness of that incapacity was so lively within him that he never attempted to give articulation to his philosophy. His finer instinct kept him from doing that violence to his inspiration.

The source of his power lay not in his doctrine, but in his temperament, and the rare quality of his wisdom was due less to his reason than to his imagination. Reality eluded him; he had neither diligence nor constancy enough to master and possess it; but his mind was open to all philosophic influences, from whatever quarter they might blow; the lessons of science and the hints of poetry worked themselves out in him to a free and personal religion. He differed from the plodding many, not in knowing things better, but in having more ways of knowing them. His grasp was not particularly firm, he was far from being, like a Plato or an Aristotle, past master in the art and the science of life. But his mind was endowed with unusual plasticity, with unusual spontaneity and liberty of movement—it was a fairyland of thoughts and fancies. He was like a young god making experiments in creation: he blotched the work, and always began again on a new and better plan. Every day he said, "Let there be light," and every day the light was new. His sun, like that of Heraclitus, was different every morning.

What seemed, then, to the more earnest and less critical of his hearers a revelation from above was in truth rather an insurrection from beneath, a shaking loose from convention, a disintegration of the normal categories of reason in favour of various imaginative principles, on which the world might have been built, if it had been built differently. This gift of revolutionary thinking allowed new aspects, hints of wider laws, premonitions of unthought-of fundamental unities to spring constantly into view. But such visions were necessarily fleeting, because the human mind had long before settled its grammar, and discovered, after much grouping and many defeats, the general forms in which experience will allow itself to be stated. These general forms are the principles of common sense and positive science, no less imaginative in their origin than those notions which we now call transcendental, but grown prosaic, like the metaphors of common speech, by dint of repetition.

Yet authority, even of this rational kind, sat lightly upon Emerson. To reject tradition and think as one might have thought if no man had ever existed before was indeed the aspiration of the Transcendentalists, and although Emerson hardly regarded himself as a member of that school, he largely shared its tendency and passed for its spokesman. Without protesting against tradition, he smilingly eluded it in his thoughts, untamable in their quiet irresponsibility. He fled to his woods or to his "pleachèd garden," to be the creator of his own worlds in solitude and freedom. No wonder that he brought thence to the tightly conventional minds of his contemporaries a breath as if from paradise. His simplicity in novelty his profundity, his ingenuous ardour must have seemed to them something heavenly, and they may be excused if they thought they detected inspiration even in his occasional thin paradoxes and guileless whims. They were stifled with conscience and he brought them a breath of Nature; they were surfeited with shallow controversies and he gave them poetic truth.

Imagination, indeed, is his single theme. As a preacher might under every text enforce the same lessons of the gospel, so Emerson traces in every sphere the same spiritual laws of experience—compensation, continuity, the self-expression of the Soul in the forms of Nature and of society, until she finally recognizes herself in her own work and sees its beneficence and beauty. His constant refrain is the omnipotence of imaginative thought; its power first to make the world, then to understand it, and finally to rise above it. All Nature is an embodiment of our native fancy, all history a drama in which the innate possibilities of the spirit are enacted and realized. While the conflict of life and the shocks of experience seem to bring us face to face with an alien and overwhelming power, reflection can humanize and rationalize that power by conceiving its laws; and with this recognition of the rationality of all things comes the sense of their beauty and order. The destruction which Nature seems to prepare for our special hopes is thus seen to be the victory of our impersonal interests. To awaken in us this spiritual insight, an elevation of mind which is at once an act of comprehension and of worship, to substitute it for lower passions and more servile forms of intelligence—that is Emerson's constant effort. All his resources of illustration, observation, and rhetoric are used to deepen and clarify this sort of wisdom.

Such thought is essentially the same that is found in the German romantic or idealistic philosophers, with whom Emerson's affinity is remarkable, all the more as he seems to have borrowed little or nothing from their works. The critics of human nature, in the eighteenth century, had shown how much men's ideas depend on their predispositions, on the character of their senses and the habits of their intelligence. Seizing upon this thought and exaggerating it, the romantic philosophers attributed to the spirit of man the omnipotence which had belonged to God, and felt that in this way they were reasserting the supremacy of mind over matter and establishing it upon a safe and rational basis.

The Germans were great system-makers, and Emerson cannot rival them in the sustained effort of thought by which they sought to reinterpret every sphere of being according to their chosen principles. But he surpassed them in an instinctive sense of what he was doing. He never represented his poetry as science, nor countenanced the formation of a new sect that should nurse the sense of a private and mysterious illumination, and relight the fagots of passion and prejudice. He never tried to seek out and defend the universal implications of his ideas, and never wrote the book he had once planned on the law of compensation, foreseeing, we may well believe, the sophistries in which he would have been directly involved. He fortunately preferred a fresh statement on a fresh subject. A suggestion once given, the spirit once aroused to speculation, a glimpse once gained of some ideal harmony, he chose to descend again to common sense and to touch the earth for a moment before another flight. The faculty of idealization was itself what he valued. Philosophy for him was rather a moral energy flowering into sprightliness of thought than a body of serious and defensible doctrines. In practising transcendental speculation only in this poetic and sporadic fashion, Emerson retained its true value and avoided its greatest danger. He secured the freedom and fertility of his thought and did not allow one conception of law or one hint of harmony to sterilize the mind and prevent the subsequent birth within it of other ideas, no less just and imposing than their predecessors. For we are not dealing at all in such a philosophy with matters of fact or with such verifiable truths as exclude their opposites. We are dealing only with imagination, with the art of conception, and with the various forms in which reflection, like a poet, may compose and recompose human experience.

A certain disquiet mingled, however, in the minds of Emerson's contemporaries with the admiration they felt for his purity and genius. They saw that he had forsaken the doctrines of the Church; and they were not sure whether he held quite unequivocally any doctrine whatever. We may not all of us share the concern for orthodoxy which usually caused this puzzled alarm: we may understand that it was not Emerson's vocation to be definite and dogmatic in religion any more than in philosophy. Yet that disquiet will not, even for us, wholly disappear. It is produced by a defect which naturally accompanies imagination in all but the greatest minds. I mean disorganization. Emerson not only conceived things in new ways, but he seemed to think the new ways might cancel and supersede the old. His imagination was to invalidate the understanding. That inspiration which should come to fulfil seemed too often to come to destroy. If he was able so constantly to stimulate us to fresh thoughts, was it not because he demolished the labour of long ages of reflection? Was not the startling effect of much of his writing due to its contradiction to tradition and to common sense?

So long as he is a poet and in the enjoyment of his poetic license, we can blame this play of mind only by a misunderstanding. It is possible to think otherwise than as common sense thinks; there are other categories beside those of science. When we employ them we enlarge our lives. We add to the world of fact any number of worlds of the imagination in which human nature and the eternal relations of ideas may be nobly expressed. So far our imaginative fertility is only a benefit: it surrounds us with the congenial and necessary radiation of art and religion. It manifests our moral vitality in the bosom of Nature.

But sometimes imagination invades the sphere of understanding and seems to discredit its indispensable work. Common sense, we are allowed to infer, is a shallow affair: true insight changes all that. When so applied, poetic activity is not an unmixed good. It loosens our hold on fact and confuses our intelligence, so that we forget that intelligence has itself every prerogative of imagination, and has besides the sanction of practical validity. We are made to believe that since the understanding is something human and conditioned, something which might have been different, as the senses might have been different, and which we may yet, so to speak, get behind—therefore the understanding ought to be abandoned. We long for higher faculties, neglecting those we have, we yearn for intuition, closing our eyes upon experience. We become mystical.

Mysticism, as we have said, is the surrender of a category of thought because we divine its relativity. As every new category, however, must share this reproach, the mystic is obliged in the end to give them all up, the poetic and moral categories no less than the physical, so that the end of his purification is the atrophy of his whole nature, the emptying of his whole heart and mind to make room, as he thinks, for God. By attacking the authority of the understanding as the organon of knowledge, by substituting itself for it as the herald of a deeper truth, the imagination thus prepares its own destruction. For if the understanding is rejected because it cannot grasp the absolute, the imagination and all its works—art, dogma, worship—must presently be rejected for the same reason. Common sense and poetry must both go by the board, and conscience must follow after: for all these are human and relative. Mysticism will be satisfied only with the absolute, and as the absolute, by its very definition, is not representable by any specific faculty, it must be approached through the abandonment of all. The lights of life must be extinguished that the light of the absolute may shine, and the possession of everything in general must be secured by the surrender of everything in particular.

The same diffidence, however, the same constant renewal of sincerity which kept Emerson's flights of imagination near to experience, kept his mysticism also within bounds. A certain mystical tendency is pervasive with him, but there are only one or two subjects on which he dwells with enough constancy and energy of attention to make his mystical treatment of them pronounced. One of these is the question of the unity of all minds in the single soul of the universe, which is the same in all creatures; another is the question of evil and of its evaporation in the universal harmony of things. Both these ideas suggest themselves at certain turns in every man's experience, and might receive a rational formulation. But they are intricate subjects, obscured by many emotional prejudices, so that the labour, impartiality, and precision which would be needed to elucidate them are to be looked for in scholastic rather than in inspired thinkers, and in Emerson least of all. Before these problems he is alternately ingenuous and rhapsodical and in both moods equally helpless. Individuals no doubt exist, he says to himself. But, ah! Napoleon is in every schoolboy. In every squatter in the western prairies we shall find an owner—

> Of Caesar's hand and Plato's brain,
> Of Lord Christ's heart, and Shakespeare's strain.

But how? we may ask. Potentially? Is it because any mind, were it given the right body and the right experience, were it made over, in a word, into another mind, would resemble that other mind to the point of identity? Or is it that our souls are already so largely similar that we are subject to many kindred promptings and share many ideals unrealizable in our particular

circumstances? But then we should simply be saying that if what makes men different were removed, men would be indistinguishable, or that, in so far as they are now alike, they can understand one another by summoning up their respective experiences in the fancy. There would be no mysticism in that, but at the same time, alas, no eloquence, no paradox, and, if we must say the word, no nonsense.

On the question of evil, Emerson's position is of the same kind. There is evil, of course, he tells us. Experience is sad. There is a crack in everything that God has made. But, ah! the laws of the universe are sacred and beneficent. Without them nothing good could arise. All things, then, are in their right places and the universe is perfect above our querulous tears. Perfect? we may ask. But perfect from what point of view, in reference to what ideal? To its own? To that of a man who renouncing himself and all naturally dear to him, ignoring the injustice, suffering, and impotence in the world, allows his will and his conscience to be hypnotized by the spectacle of a necessary evolution, and lulled into cruelty by the pomp and music of a tragic show? In that case the evil is not explained, it is forgotten; it is not cured, but condoned. We have surrendered the category of the better and the worse, the deepest foundation of life and reason; we have become mystics on the one subject on which, above all others, we ought to be men.

Two forces may be said to have carried Emerson in this mystical direction; one, that freedom of his imagination which we have already noted, and which kept him from the fear of self-contradiction; the other the habit of worship inherited from his clerical ancestors and enforced by his religious education. The spirit of conformity, the unction, the loyalty even unto death inspired by the religion of Jehovah, were dispositions acquired by too long a discipline and rooted in too many forms of speech, of thought, and of worship for a man like Emerson, who had felt their full force, ever to be able to lose them. The evolutions of his abstract opinions left that habit unchanged. Unless we keep this circumstance in mind, we shall not be able to understand the kind of elation and sacred joy, so characteristic of his eloquence, with which he propounds laws of Nature and aspects of experience which, viewed in themselves, afford but an equivocal support to moral enthusiasm. An optimism so persistent and unclouded as his will seem at variance with the description he himself gives of human life, a description coloured by a poetic idealism, but hardly by an optimistic bias.

We must remember, therefore, that this optimism is a pious tradition, originally justified by the belief in a personal God and in a providential government of affairs for the ultimate and positive good of the elect, and that the habit of worship survived in Emerson as an instinct after those positive beliefs had faded into a recognition of "spiritual laws." We must remember that Calvinism had known how to combine an awestruck devotion to the Supreme Being with no very roseate picture of the destinies of mankind, and for more than two hundred years had been breeding in the stock from which Emerson came a willingness to be, as the phrase is, "damned for the glory of God."

What wonder, then, that when, for the former inexorable dispensation of Providence, Emerson substituted his general spiritual and natural laws, he should not have felt the spirit of worship fail within him? On the contrary, his thought moved in the presence of moral harmonies which seemed to him truer, more beautiful, and more beneficent than those of the old theology. An independent philosopher would not have seen in those harmonies an object of worship or a sufficient basis for optimism. But he was not an independent philosopher, in spite of his belief in independence. He inherited the problems and the preoccupations of the theology from which he started, being in this respect like the German idealists, who, with all their pretence of absolute metaphysics, were in reality only giving elusive and abstract forms to traditional theology. Emerson, too, was not primarily a philosopher, but a Puritan mystic with a poetic fancy and a gift for observation and epigram, and he saw in the laws of Nature, idealized by his imagination, only a more intelligible form of the divinity he had always recognized and adored. His was not a philosophy passing into a religion, but a religion expressing itself as a philosophy and veiled, as at its setting it descended the heavens, in various tints of poetry and science.

If we ask ourselves what was Emerson's relation to the scientific and religious movements of his time, and what place he may claim in the history of opinion, we must answer that he belong very little to the past, very little to the present, and almost wholly to that abstract sphere into which mystical or philosophic aspiration has carried a few men in all ages. The religious tradition in which he was reared was that of Puritanism, but of a Puritanism which, retaining its moral intensity and metaphysical abstraction, had minimized its doctrinal expression and become Unitarian. Emerson was indeed the Psyche of Puritanism, "the latest-born and fairest vision far" of all that "faded hierarchy." A Puritan whose religion was all poetry, a poet whose only pleasure was thought, he showed in his life and personality the meagreness, the constraint, the frigid and conscious consecration which belonged to his clerical ancestors, while his inmost impersonal spirit ranged abroad over the fields of history and Nature, gathering what ideas it might, and singing its little snatches of inspired song.

The traditional element was thus rather an external and unessential contribution to Emerson's mind; he had the professional tinge, the decorum, the distinction of an old-fashioned divine; he had also the habit of writing sermons, and he had the national pride and hope of a religious people that felt itself providentially chosen to establish a free and godly commonwealth in a new world. For the rest, he separated himself from the ancient creed of the community with a sense rather of relief than of regret. A literal belief in Christian doctrines repelled him as unspiritual, as manifesting no understanding of the meaning which, as allegories, those doctrines might have to a philosophic and poetical spirit. Although as a clergyman he was at first in the habit of referring to the Bible and its lessons as to a supreme authority, he had no instinctive sympathy with the inspiration of either the Old or the New Testament; in Hafiz or Plutarch, in Plato or Shakespeare, he found more congenial stuff.

While he thus preferred to withdraw, without rancour and without contempt, from the ancient fellowship of the church, he assumed an attitude hardly less cool and deprecatory toward the enthusiasms of the new era. The national ideal of democracy and freedom had his entire sympathy; he allowed himself to be drawn into the movement against slavery; he took a curious and smiling interest in the discoveries of natural science and in the material progress of the age. But he could go no farther. His contemplative nature, his religious training, his dispersed reading, made him stand aside from the life of the world, even while he studied it with benevolent attention. His heart was fixed on eternal things, and he was in no sense a prophet for his age or country. He belonged by nature to that mystical company of devout souls that recognize no particular home and are dispersed throughout history, although not without intercommunication. He felt his affinity to the Hindoos and the Persians, to the Platonists and the Stoics. Like them he remains "a friend and aider of those who would live in

the spirit." If not a star of the first magnitude, he is certainly a fixed star in the firmament of philosophy. Alone as yet among Americans, he may be said to have won a place there, if not by the originality of his thought, at least by the originality and beauty of the expression he gave to thoughts that are old and imperishable.

SIR LESLIE STEPHEN
"Emerson"
National Review, February 1901, pp. 882–98

Many years ago I had the chance of laying up an interesting reminiscence. Lowell took me to visit Emerson in his house at Concord, and, as it happened, had to leave me to perform the function of an interviewer by myself. But instead of recording an impression I have to make a confession. I was young enough at that time to believe in great authors, and to desire to offer acceptable incense. Unluckily, I had not read a word of Emerson, and on the way I had innocently confided to Lowell that I took him to be a kind of Carlyle. I did not know that Lowell had drawn an inimitably witty contrast between the two, beginning—

> There are persons mole-blind to the soul's make and
>   style,
> Who insist on a likeness 'twixt him and Carlyle.

Though he did not accuse me of "mole-blindness," Lowell managed to intimate courteously that I was somehow in the dark. The sense of my ignorance struck me dumb. The brilliant remark which was to show at once that I appreciated Emerson, and that my appreciation was worthy having, refused to present itself. What Emerson thought of the intruder I know not, but our conversation fell hopelessly flat; and I was a happy man when Lowell relieved guard. I came away, indeed, with a certain impression of my host's personal simplicity and dignity. If I had not offered homage he had not shown the least wish that I should fall upon my knees, and had received me as at least a human being—a claim upon his courtesy which he admitted like a true democrat. Still, I was left with a problem unsolved. Emerson's ablest countrymen, I found, were never tired of expressing their gratitude to him. He had pronounced their "literary Declaration of Independence." His first lectures had made an epoch. He had removed the scales from their eyes, revealed the barrenness of the intellectual wilderness in which they had been wandering, and given them a Pisgah-sight of a new land "flowing with freedom's honey and milk." The question remained: What was the secret of his power? Then and since I have tried to answer it, partly by the obvious expedient of reading his books, and partly by reading various criticisms. I hope that I have learnt something, in spite of grave disqualifications. I was not impressed at the impressible age, and do not, I fear, belong to the class which takes most freely the impression of the Emersonian stamp. Yet it may be of some interest to more congenial disciples to know how their prophet affects one of the profane vulgar. If some rays from the luminary can pierce the opaque medium of my Philistinism it will show their intrinsic brilliance.

Matthew Arnold characteristically explained to an American audience that Emerson was not a great poet, nor a great philosopher, nor even a great man of letters. For all that, he was the friend and aider "of those who would live in the spirit." Perhaps the phrase is a little vague, though it, no doubt, indicates the truth. Emerson was the founder and leader of the

American "Transcendentalists," and Transcendentalists, I suppose, were people who meant to "live in the spirit." The name is alarming, but it represents a very harmless and a very commendable phenomenon. In Emerson's youth his countrymen were in need of a sharp intellectual shock. Their understanding, in Coleridgean phrase—this faculty which is useful in clearing forests and accumulating dollars—was thoroughly wide-awake; but their reason—the faculty which cultivates poetry and "divine philosophy"—had somehow sunk into slumber. A vague craving for better things had been roused, though by no leader with authoritative credentials. There were no trained professors profoundly learned in the past history of thought to come forward and propound new solutions of the enigma of the universe. Active but superficially educated youths were ready to take for a beacon any light, ancient or modern, of which they happened to catch a glimpse. Some enthusiasts had vague impressions that there was such a thing as German philosophy, and had heard of Schelling through Cousin or Coleridge. One swore by Pythagoras; and others took up Plotinus, or found what they wanted in Swedenborg or in Jacob Behmen, or set up some mystic doctrine of their own. "Transcendentalism" took its name from Kant, but implied no familiarity with Kant's special metaphysical system. It meant a "wave of sentiment"—a vague desire for some kind of intellectual flying machine—some impulse that would lift you above the prosaic commonplace world into the charmed regions of philosophy and poetry. Emerson had no more academical training than his followers, and, in one sense, was certainly not a "great philosopher." If "philosophy" means such a logical system as was worked out by Kant or Hegel, he was not a philosopher at all. He positively disliked such philosophies. "Who," he asked, "has not looked into a metaphysical book? And what sensible man ever looked twice?" You may collate and distil all the systems, he declared, and you will get nothing by it. We have as yet nothing but "tendency and indication." Systems are merely the outside husk, worthless except as a temporary embodiment of the essential truth. Emerson, that is, is a denizen of the region where philosophy is not differentiated from poetry. "I am," he said, "in all my theory, ethics, and politics, a poet"; and he ridicules the impression that his "transcendentalism" was, as some people fancied, "a known and fixed element, like salt or meal"—a rigid and definite creed. All the argument and all the wisdom, he declares, is not in the treatise on metaphysics, "but in the sonnet or the play." Transcendentalism, indeed, had its philosophical affinities: it represented idealism as against materialism; or, as Emerson occasionally puts it, takes the side of Plato against Locke. Lockism is the influx of "decomposition and prose," while Platonism means growth. The Platonic is the poetic tendency; the "so-called scientific" is the negative and poisonous. Spenser, Burns, Byron, and Wordsworth will be Platonists; and "the dull men will be Lockists."

The average American had fallen into such "Lockism," and Emerson, when he came to England, found the fully-blown type flourishing and triumphant. The "brilliant Macaulay," he said, represented the spirit of the governing classes, and Macaulay had explicitly declared (in his essay on Bacon) that "good" meant simply solid, sensual benefits—good food and good clothes and material comfort. Emerson does not argue with men in whom the faculty of vision is non-existent or clouded by want of use. He is content simply to see. One result is indicated in the charming correspondence with Carlyle. Each most cordially appreciated the merits of the other, and Carlyle, like Emerson, called himself a "mystic," and soared above "Lockism." But the visions of the two took a

very different colouring. Emerson praises *Sartor Resartus* with a characteristic qualification. Carlyle's grim humour and daring flights of superabundant imagination cover a "simple air," he complains, with a "volley of variations." You are, he says, dispensing "that which is rarest, the simplest truths, truths which lie next to consciousness, which only the Platos and the Goethes perceive," and he hopes for the hour "when the word will be as simple and so as resistless as the thought"; for the hour, that is, when a Carlyle would be an Emerson. To find effective utterance for these "simplest truths" is, in fact, Emerson's special function. The difficulty of the task is proverbial. A simple truth is a very charming thing; but it has an uncomfortable trick of sinking into a truism. If you try to make it something more it is apt to collide with other simple truths. The function of the system-maker is to persuade the various truths to keep the peace by assigning to each its proper limits and stating it with due reserves and qualifications. But that is precisely what Emerson altogether declines to do. The most obvious peculiarity of his style corresponds. His lectures are a "mosaic" of separate sentences; each, as he put it himself, an "infinitely repellent particle." Carlyle, praising the beauty and simplicity of his sentences, complains that the paragraph is not "a beaten ingot," but "a beautiful square bag of duckshot held together by canvas." Proverbs, says Emerson, are statements of an absolute truth, and thus the sanctuary of the intuitions. They are, indeed, absolute statements of truth; and for that reason, as Sancho Panza might have pointed out, you can always quote a proverb on each side of every alternative. Solomon tells us to answer a fool and not to answer a fool according to his folly. "More haste, worse speed" is true; but it is equally true that "the early bird catches the worm." Emerson is a master of the gnomic utterances which are to the cultivated what proverbs are to the vulgar. He is well aware that they are not always reconcilable; but it is not his function to reconcile them. He cares nothing for consistency. He wishes to say what he feels to-day with "the proviso that to-morrow, perhaps, I shall contradict it all." "A foolish consistency is the hobgoblin of little minds. . . . With consistency a great soul has nothing whatever to do. . . . Speak what you think now in hard words, and to-morrow speak what to-morrow thinks in hard words again, though it contradict everything you said to-day." The peculiarity seems to have annoyed his friends with a turn for logic. Argument was for him an absurdity. He approved as a rule for a debating society (what often enough corresponds to the practice) that no one should reply to a previous speaker. You thought that you had contradicted him; he placidly accepted both your statements and his own. He is simply playing a different tune, not denying that yours may be harmonious. The region of simple truths would seem to be altogether above the sphere in which controversy is possible. You should never conform to a church or sect, or to public opinion as to your past utterances. Leave the truths to assimilate by spontaneous affinity.

One charm of Emerson is due to this affable reception of all opinions. On his first appearance in a pulpit he is described as "the most gracious of mortals, with a face all benignity," and preached with an indefinite air of simplicity and wisdom. His lectures radiate benignity and simplicity. He had no dogmas to proclaim or heretics to denounce. He is simply uttering an inspiration which has come to him. He is not a mystagogue, affecting superinducal wisdom and in possession of the only clue to the secret. If you sympathize, well and good; if you cannot, you may translate his truth into your own. The ascent into this serene region, above all the noise of controversy, has its disadvantages. Carlyle complains gently that his friend is in danger of parting from fact and soaring into perilous altitudes. He is "soliloquizing on the mountain tops." It is easy to "screw oneself up into high and ever higher altitudes of transcendentalism," to see nothing beneath one but "the everlasting snows of the Himalaya, the earth shrinking to a planet, and the indigo firmament sowing itself with stars." Come back to the earth, he exclaims; and readers of Emerson must occasionally echo the exhortation. And yet, in his own way, Emerson was closer to the everyday world than Carlyle himself; and it is the curious union of the two generally inconsistent qualities which gives a peculiar flavour to Emersonian teaching. Lowell puts it admirably in his comparison of Emerson and Carlyle:—

C. gives nature and God his own fits of the blues,
And rims common-sense things with mystical hues;
E. sits in a mystery calm and intense,
And looks coolly round him with calm common-
    sense;
C. shows you how everyday matters unite,
With the dim trans-diurnal recesses of night;
While E., in a plain preternatural way,
Makes mysteries matters of mere every day.

Emerson's curious position of equilibrium between the two worlds of mystery and broad daylight comes out in his literary tastes. His reading was wide but desultory. He was entirely free from the superstition which besets the ordinary scholar and makes him unhappy till he has read a book through and got it up as a student gets up a book for an examination. Emerson looks for inspiration, not for information. He puts a book down as soon as it bores him, and does not care a straw for its authenticity or for its place assigned to it in the orthodox literary tribunals. He is content if it "makes his top spin"—as he says—if, that is, it stimulates thought or fires the imagination. "What is best in literature," he says, "is the affirming, prophesying, spermatic words of men-making poets." Shakespeare is to be valued not because he is so much greater than yourself, but because, by your receptivity of him, you become aware of the power of your own soul. To Emerson the value of a book is measured by its dynamic effect upon himself. For some great names he cared little. The list of uninteresting writers included Shelley, Aristophanes, Cervantes, Miss Austen, and Dickens. He thought Dante a prodigy, but fitter for a museum than for a welcome to your own study. In compensation he is sometimes strangely enthusiastic about very obscure people. In speaking of literature in England, his appreciation of his friend Carlyle is checked by his dislike of the Carlylian pessimism; but he finds one consolation. There is a writer whose mind has "a long Atlantic roll not known except in the deepest water"; and who is elsewhere declared to have a "vigour of understanding and imagination comparable only to Lord Bacon's." This cheering exception to British stupidity turns out, to our surprise, to be a Mr. Wilkinson. I confess that I am not acquainted with his works, which, according to Emerson, "had thrown all contemporary philosophy in England into the shade." Wilkinson (a man of real ability, as a biographical dictionary informs me) had impressed Emerson by his exposition of Swedenborg. When Emerson made Swedenborg himself one of his representative men, Carlyle had to exclaim: "*Missed* the consummate flower and divine ultimate elixir of philosophy, say you? By heaven, in clutching at it and almost getting it he has tumbled into Bedlam!" Emerson would apparently reply not by denying the truth of the remark, but by declaring it to be irrelevant. Swedenborg, like other prophets, fell into absurdities when he became a system-monger, and Emerson could condemn some of the results sharply enough. He was not the less grateful for the inspiration,

because associated with absurdities, which might qualify the prophet for Bedlam. Swedenborg's leading thought, he says, is given in Milton's lines:—

What if earth
Be but the shadow of Heaven and things therein
Each to the other more like than on earth is thought?

Swedenborg, he thinks, was the first to give a scientific statement of the poetical doctrine of "symbolism." He had inverted the point of view of the "poisonous" kind of science. The ideal world is the reality, and the material world should be regarded as merely a kind of "picture language." Emerson wonders that when this fruitful seed of thought was once sown men did not put by all other science to work out the results. Yet people continue to take more interest in every spider, or fossil, or fungus, than in trying to discover "the meaning and upshot of the frame of things." It may be, he thinks, but centuries will be required to elaborate so profound a conception.

The impression made upon Emerson by this doctrine appears both in his own teaching and in numerous references to Swedenborg as one of the greatest leaders of thought, to be classed with the Platos and Shakespeares; and yet Emerson is equally attracted by men to whom mysticism would be another name for nonsense. From his boyhood he had studied Montaigne, another of his "Representative men," of whom he speaks with a kind of personal affection. Montaigne appears in the *Representative Men* as the typical "sceptic"; and scepticism goes rather awkwardly with mysticism and the imperative claims of direct intuition of simple truths. Yet Emerson finds scepticism congenial so far as it implies toleration. It represents contempt for the formalism and exaggeration of "bigots and blockheads"; and every superior mind must pass through this "domain of equilibration." He delights, therefore, in Montaigne's hospitable reception of every conceivable variety of opinion. Montaigne, it is true, not only begins, but ends with doubt. "*Que sçais je?*" is his last word. But then, it is his superlative merit to admit frankly that there are doubts, instead of trying to smother them. The difference seems to be that while Montaigne remains balanced between opposite opinions, Emerson seems to hold that, though opposed, they may both be true. If we can rise to a higher sphere we shall see that they are complimentary instead of contradictory. But Montaigne has evidently another charm for Emerson. His amazing frankness, his delight in laying bare all his own weaknesses, makes the essays an incomparable text-book for the student of human nature. Montaigne has no literary affectation; he talks rather than writes. "Cut his words and they would bleed; they are vascular and alive." Montaigne plays no antics; he is "stout and solid; tastes every moment of the day; likes pain because it makes him feel himself and realize things, as we pinch ourselves to know that we are awake." If Emerson could soar into mystic regions, he is equally delighted with the broad daylight, in which you can see the actual every-day play of human nature, stripped bare of every sort of conventional disguise. The man of genius, he says, must draw strength from pure reason, and his aim from common-sense. The two poles are equally necessary, if he is not to be either too mean or too vague. That, again, is one of the merits which he sees in Plato. Plato is the "balanced soul." He combines the mystical and the practical element. He can be transcendental and yet is at home in common life. He can illustrate his philosophy from the world which philosophers despise: "from mares and puppies, from pitchers and soup-ladles; from cooks and criers; the shops of potters, horse doctors, butchers, and fishmongers." It is this synthesis or equal poise between two opposite poles of thought which stamps his genius as unique. Yet Emerson can be equally impressed by men who represent only one side of the antithesis. He makes, perhaps, more references to Napoleon than to any one, except Swedenborg. Napoleon is "the man of the world"; the idol of common men," because he had the common qualities in a transcendent degree. He hated sentiment and despised "ideologists"; he had no moral scruples and no magnanimity. But his supreme practical ability, his "enormous self-trust," his power of seeing to the heart of things, his making readiness in every emergency and "two o'clock in the morning courage" commands our respect. "I find it easy," says Emerson, "to translate all his technics into all of mine." There is more philosophy in his despatches than in the sermons of the Academy. "We like everything to do its office, whether it be a milch-cow or a rattlesnake"; and Napoleon at least represents a stupendous natural force. Emerson was fond of reading books upon Napoleon. They were at any rate instructive documents in the study of character. The list of authors recommended in his lecture upon "books" is characteristic. You must, of course, read the great poets. But his special favourites are, on one side, Plotinus and the Neoplatonists; and on the other, the books which give an insight into character. Plutarch, both the *Lives* and the *Morals*, should be in the smallest library; *Confessions* and autobiographies, Augustine, Benvenuto Cellini, and Rousseau; the table-talks of Luther, or Selden, or Coleridge; and books of anecdotes are invaluable. Anybody, meanwhile, will do for history: Hume and Goldsmith, as well as Gibbon. History represents merely the background in which the great lives are set; and what you should really want is to be brought into contact with inspiring minds, not to get up dates and external facts. Emerson is weak in criticism, if the critic is to give a judicial estimate of a man's proper position in the development of poetry or philosophy; but he can say most clearly and forcibly what is the message which any great writer has delivered to him personally.

This, I think, shows how one may approach one secret of reading Emerson himself. He combines Yankee shrewdness in singular fashion with the exaltation of the mystic. The mysticism is bewildering, if not simply nonsensical, to the poor "Lockist" or the average common-sense mortal. If asked to accept it as a systematic creed, he will declare that it is mere theosophical moonshine: too vague to have any meaning, or meaning something which is palpably absurd. But, then, one may also read Emerson as Emerson read his predecessors: for stimulus or inspiration, not as a propounder of solid, substantial truths. We are not to take his philosophy for a system of truths, but for a series of vivid intuitions. His "Declaration of Independence" proclaims a truth which may be stated in many dialects. Like its political parallel, it asserts that every man has indisputable rights, to be abrogated by no human authority. But it is not aggressive or dogmatic. It does not remind us of Fourth of July celebrations, which treated George III. like a grotesque Guy Faux. The emancipation is to be effected, not by iconoclasm, but by rousing the slumbering faculties. It implies a duty to yourself, as well as a right against your rulers. The enemy to be overcome is the torpor which accepts traditions and conventions as ultimate. They benumb the soul, and make it a part of a dead mechanism, when it should be a part of the living force which moulds the world. You should be an active instead of a passive agent in that process; you must be, in his phrase, "self-reliant"; you must develop your own powers and obey your instincts, without submitting to any external rule. You then become a "ripple of the stream of tendency." "Beware," he says, "when the great God lets loose a thinker on this planet." The new thought

represents a "new influx of divinity into the mind." The doctrine is sometimes expressed in language learnt from the mystics. The beautiful state of the soul is measured by its capacity for "ecstasy." Every man is capable of divine illumination, and can be elevated by intercourse with the spiritual world. The "ecstasy" corresponds to the "inner light" of the Quakers. It recalls, as he says, "the trances of Socrates, Plotinus, Porphyry, Behmen, Fox, Bunyan, Pascal, Guion, and Swedenborg." The "rapt saint," he declares, is the only logician; not exhortation, not argument, becomes our lips, but "pæans of joy and praise." He speaks of the ecstatic state with a kind of awe in the essay on self-reliance as something which cannot be fully uttered. "The soul raised over passion beholds identity and Eternal causation, perceives the self-existence of truth and right, and calms itself with knowing that all things go well."

Certainly Emerson is on the threshold of mysticism. His peculiarity is that he stops there. He does not lose his balance. He respects common-sense, and dreads to disturb his vague aspirations by translating them into a definite system. He does not wish us to swallow mystic formulas as necessary or sufficient keys to the puzzle. He is only saying with benevolent unction what corresponds to Carlyle's fierce denunciations of cants and shams; and may even be translated into the phraseology of the humble "Lockist." The Lockist, too, is aware of the evil of dead "survivals," and the importance of encouraging new intellectual variations. The difference between his prose and Emerson's poetry is great enough; but he may sympathize with the spirit, at least, of the rapture with which Emerson sets forth the blessings of intellectual independence, and the need that an individual be true to himself. Emerson's version was congenial to his audience at the time. One can understand the nature of the stimulus, even if we don't quite appreciate the merits of the "ecstatic state."

In one of its aspects Emerson's philosophy or poetry, whichever be its proper name, has scandalized his critics. His optimism, they think, is irritating. The most hopeless of all consolations is the denial that there is any need for consolation. The latter-day philosopher prefers thorough-going pessimism, and scornfully rejects Emerson's futile attempts to ignore the dark side of the world. Undoubtedly Emerson was an unequivocal optimist. "My whole philosophy, which is very real," he said to Carlyle, "teaches acquiescence and optimism." He laments his "stammering tongue and fumbling fingers," but he is not going to commit or recommend suicide. When men degrade each other, and desponding doctrines are spread, the "scholar," he said, in one of the early epoch-making lectures, "must be a bringer of hope, and must reinforce man against himself." "Power," he says elsewhere, "dwells with cheerfulness. . . . A man should make life and nature happier to us or he had better have never been born." All the talent in the world, he declares, cannot save a Schopenhauer from being odious. I confess that I do not altogether dislike this old-fashioned creed. It suited, no doubt, the time and place. America, it has been said, is the land of hope; and in Emerson's youth some symptoms which alarm modern observers were hardly perceptible. When he came to England in 1847 he was shocked by the "tragic spectacles" of misery and degradation in the streets of the great towns; and thanked God that his children were being brought up in a land where such things were unknown. The external circumstances help to explain the difference between him and Carlyle, upon whom the English pauperism and squalor had impressed the opposite lesson. But, apart from the surroundings, optimism is clearly of the essence of Emerson's temperament and philosophy. It is the teaching of the "ecstatic state." Wordsworth's nature worship lifted him to the "blessed mood" in which the

> Burthen of the mystery
> Of all this unintelligible world
> Is lightened,

and enabled him to "see into the life of things" and the harmony of the universe. With Emerson the "blessed mood" becomes normal. The greatest teachers have seen that "all nature is the rapid efflux of goodness executing and organizing itself." He frequently, as has been said, speaks as an evolutionist before Darwin. But for him evolution is rather emanation, and it does not mean a blind struggle for existence but the regular unrolling of a divine and benevolent drama, implying steady progress to perfection. Evil, he can declare, is only privation. It has no real existence, and vanishes when you can see the whole instead of dwelling upon isolated facts. Many philosphers have used similar words, and their opponents reply that such sayings are words and nothing more. To declare that this is the best or the worst of all possible worlds, as the impartial cynic is accustomed to suggest against both sides, is in reality to declare the state of your own liver. Your universe is the other side of yourself, and to give a theory which shall be valid for everyone is to claim omniscience. Emerson, at any rate, does not profess to argue; he simply asserts, and the assertion comes to this, that it is possible to take a cheerful view of things in general. That, at least, defines the point of view from which his writing may get as an inspiring source if not as revelations of fact. The essays in which he develops these doctrines most explicitly, the "Oversoul," "Compensation," "Circles," and the like, may be futile considered as philosophical dogmas; and there is not even a pretence of proving their truth. They may still be regarded as studies of the spirit in which a man may serenely front the trials of life and find comfort from forebodings. Emerson has been often compared to the great stoic moralists, and like them, he indulges in the hyperbolic and paradoxical. Macaulay, in the essay upon Bacon, in which Emerson found the typical Lockist, suggests an "amusing fiction" illustrative of the contrast. Two travellers find a village full of small-pox. The Baconian traveller vaccinates the sufferers. The stoic assures the villagers that to the wise man disease and the loss of friends is no evil. A merchant has lost his ship. The Baconian makes a diving-bell and fishes up the cargo; while the stoic exhorts him not to seek happiness in things outside himself. That is the difference, says Macaulay, between the "philosophy of words" and the "philosophy of works." When Baconians have suppressed disease and disaster the stoic will doubtless have less call for his consolations. While such things remain with us some sort of moral discipline will have its uses; and if the stoic paradoxes when taken literally are hard of acceptance by anybody who has had the toothache, they were exaggerations of principles which have formed noble characters and even had their utility in the world. The exhortations of Epictetus and Marcus Aurelius have really encouraged men who had not yet been provided with diving-bells and vaccination. The wise man of the stoics is to become independent of chance and change by identifying himself with reason; and Emerson's disciple is to perceive that in all evils there is compensation when we look upon the world as the evolution of divine ideas. He may remind us of another philosopher whom he resembled in frugality, dignity, and cheerful acceptance of life. They coincide in one significant saying. "A free man," says Spinoza, in what has been called "one of the most weighty sayings ever uttered," "thinks of death least of all things, and his wisdom is a meditation not of

death but of life." So Emerson tells us that "a wise man in our time caused to be written on his tomb, 'think on living.'" We are not to waste life in doubts and fears; and one great mark of progress is that the old system of meditating upon death and surrounding the thought with terrors has gone out of fashion. That is Emerson's answer by anticipation to the charge that he has not spoken sufficiently of the terror of death.

That you should train youself to take evil bravely and cheerful is a maxim more likely to be condemned as commonplace than as paradoxical. The statement becomes paradoxical when we deny the existence of evil, and immoral if it be understood as advice to ignore instead of facing the inevitable. Emerson certainly accepts some rather startling positions. The first lesson of history, he says, is "the good of evil": "Good is a good doctor, but Bad is sometimes a better!" and he illustrates the point by some remarkable cases. The contrast of good and evil is expressed in art, and explains its powers. "What would painter do, or what would poet or saint do but for the crucifixions and hells?" But for death, as Mr. Weller remarked, what would become of the undertakers? Emerson admires great men of all classes—"scourges of God and failings of the human race." They are all parts of the general system:—

> If plague or earthquake break not Heaven's design,
> Why, then, a Borgia or a Catiline?

The knaves, he calmly observes, win in every political struggle and a change of government means delivering society from the hands of one to the hands of another set of criminals, and the march of civilization is "a train of felonies." Yet a "beneficent tendency" streams irresistibly through the centuries, even through evil agents. Once he knew a "burly Boniface" in a rural capital. This gentleman "introduced all the fiends into the town, and united in his own person the functions of bully, incendiary, bankrupt, and burglar! And yet he was the most public-spirited citizen. The "Boss," as he would be called in modern language, was, at the same time, "a Man of Ross." The moral is that his energy was good, and only wanted to be directed to the better objects. Such illustrations of the "good of evil" are certainly rather startling, and may explain why Emerson has even been described as without a conscience. Emerson, like his mystic guides, has a tendency to what theologians call "antinomianism." The inner world is the whole real world, and a morality which takes outer consequences for a criterion becomes merely prudential. Moral goodness for him implies the harmony of the individual soul. The man approaches perfection so far as the eyes of his spirit are always open to the inner light, and his whole nature acts spontaneously in conformity with the divine will. Obedience to the moral law is equivocal or worthless so far as it depends upon any extrinsic motive. If imposed from without it so far rather savours of evil. Virtue, to be genuine, must be the absolutely spontaneous efflux of the character, not a mere disguise for hopes of reward and fear of punishment. Emerson insists upon this aspect of the truth, till even spontaneous wickedness seems to be better than compulsory goodness. Each man, he says, should "plant himself indomitably upon his instincts." A "valued adviser" warned him against trusting his instincts against venerable traditions. Your impulses, he said, may be from below, not from above. Well, he replied, "if I am the devil's child, I will live then from the devil." No law, he adds, can be sacred to me but that of my nature. That is right which is according to my constitution, and that wrong which is against it. Emerson therefore accepts a thorough individualism. All associations impress limitation by others. Each man is "cramped and diminished" by his associates. He distrusted even the movements encouraged by transcendentalism. "Professed philanthropists, it is strange and horrible to say, are an altogether odious set of people, whom one would shun as the worst of liars and canters." Temperance and anti-slavery, and so forth, are poor things when prosecuted for themselves as an end, though appealing to generous motives. The reason is that all associations must be a product of, not dependent upon, a bond. The "union is only perfect when all the unities are isolated." When each man sees the truth for himself, all will come together. Reform, therefore, even in the case of slavery, should proceed by the gradual elevation of the human spirit, not by direct legislation and outward agitation. When you trust to external means instead of acting upon the soul you become mechanical, and take narrow and distorted views of the evil. The transcendentalists, so far so they accepted this view, were regarded as mere apostles of "culture." They were inclined to stand aside from active life, and leave things to be gradually improved by the slow infiltration of higher ideals. Emerson, says Lowell, was a truer follower of Goethe than Carlyle; his teaching tended to self-culture and the development of the individual man, till it seemed "almost Pythagorean in its voluntary seclusion from commonwealth affairs." Emerson, in his lecture upon the transcendentalists, accepts and apologizes for this tendency. They can afford to stand aside from the world where even good causes are spoilt by compromise and associated with vulgar motives. There is, he admits, a difficulty in keeping upon the higher levels of thought, in retaining the faith which reveals itself in intuition and ecstasy. Yet the world may find room for "some few persons of purer fire" to serve as "collectors of the heavenly spark, with power to convey the electricity to others." The thought which the hermit "strove to proclaim by silence" will spread till it has reorganized society.

If Emerson were to be treated as a system-maker we might suggest that he is only accentuating one aspect of a single truth. Virtue certainly is not obedience to an outward law, but the spontaneous outcome of the man's nature. It is not the less the nature which fits a man for social life. "Self-culture" does not imply retreat to a hermitage, for the most efficient culture is in the active discharge of duties. The simple truth requires to be limited by its correlatives. In any case, nothing could be really less chargeable against Emerson than an approach to ethical insensibility. It is precisely the keenness and delicacy of his moral sense which attracts us and gives point to his best sentences. He is not the man to retire to a palace of art or find in æsthetic indulgence an anodyne to dull his sympathies with human sorrow. He can indeed admire the teachers who, like Shakespeare and Montaigne, look upon morality with a certain impartiality. Shakespeare, he rather quaintly asserts, "is our city of refuge if we tire of the saints." But the critic ought to show the relation between Shakespeare and Swedenborg. Now Swedenborg's great merit is the "immolation of genius and fame at the shrine of conscience." The "atmosphere of moral sentiment opens to every wretch that has reason the doors of the universe," and "all men are commanded by the saint." If Emerson's optimism leads him to dwell upon the "good of evil," and to see the use of "scourges of God" and vulgar political scoundrels, it is because they are for him the instruments of an essentially moral force. He can condemn a vulgar exaltation over mechanical continuous railways and telegraphs; but, instead of simply denouncing them, like Ruskin, he sees their good side, and believes that in time they will become instruments of the world spirit. His "pantheism" is not belief in a power superior to or indifferent to morality, but one to which the true, the good, and the beautiful are identical. We want something beyond Shakespeare and Goethe. "We, too, must

write Bibles to unite again the heavenly and the earthly worlds." The teacher who is to come will see into the ultimate laws; "see to identity of the law of gravitation with purity of heart," and show that "duty is one thing with science, with beauty, and with joy."

This, no doubt, verges upon the poetical; it is hard of acceptance for the poor "Lockist"; and can be fully appreciated only by those who have access to the "ecstatic state." Others must be content to take a lower point of view. The title of one of Emerson's books—*The Conduct of Life*—defines one less inaccessible aspect of his teaching. If he has not penetrated the secret of the universe, he can show by example what attitude and disposition of mind can make the universe tolerable. It may be suggested to the pessimist that as he cannot understand the general system of things, and certainly cannot alter it, he may as well learn how to make the best of it. Emerson may supply useful hints for such an enterprise. "The true preacher," he says, "can be known by this, that he deals out to the people his life." The phrase may explain his own secret. He had, for one thing, to depend upon popular lecturing, a trade which, it must be granted, has its drawbacks. He had, he complained, to go about "peddling with his literary pack of notions," dropping pearls before superficial hearers who would turn them into twaddle and extravagance. Still, he took his mission simply and seriously, gave what he had, and tried to indicate "the ideal and holy life," . . . to "celebrate the spiritual powers," in contrast to the mechanical philosophy of the time, and "appeal to the great optimism self-affirmed in all bosoms." His simplicity and sincerity moved congenial hearers to aspire to regions of thought higher than those of the counting-house or the market, and impressed upon them at least the beauty and dignity of Emerson's own character. His aphorism—it has, I fear, a twang of the popular lecturer about it—"hitch your waggon to a star" sums up the moral, and the power depends as much upon the sweetness of disposition as upon the mystical doctrine. The charm appears in his best poetry, in spite of its admitted shortcomings. His characteristic want of continuity made him as incapable of evolving a central idea as of expounding an argument. As in prose, he often coins exquisite phrases, but he is abrupt and fragmentary and apt to break down both in grammar and rhythm. A true inspiration comes as it came to Blake in the midst of much incoherence and stammering utterance. Few poems are more touching than the "Dirge" and the "Threnody," in which he commemorates his brothers and the son who died in infancy. The "Threnody" recalls Wordsworth in the simplicity and in the concluding meditation where he finds soothing, if not fully consoling, thought. What orthodox critics may say of it I know not, but, at any rate, few poems bring one into so close a contact with a perfectly sweet nature, or could show how a great sorrow should be met by a man equally brave and tender. In the essay upon "Experience"—in which, it must be confessed, it is not easy to put any clear interpretation—he refers again to the loss of his son. "Grief," he says, "makes us idealists. The world becomes a dream. Life is a train of moods"; the moods "are many-coloured lenses which paint the world their own hue." And yet the dream is somehow the reality. The facts, as he has learnt from Swedenborg, are only symbols. Life wears "a visionary face." It is hard, he admits, to keep ourselves at this mystical point of view. The poet who is to show us the truth under the outside world has not yet come. The prosaic person will refuse a consolation which proposes, according to him, to drop substantial facts for dreams and shadows. Yet he may allow that the emotion is in itself beautiful. If he cannot accept the optimist view of the world, he can, perhaps, learn from the optimist how to take the inevitable cheerfully. Emerson admits in one essay that Fate is a reality and has a very ugly side to it. Yet he ends by exhorting us to "build altars to the beautiful necessity"; and, without bothering us with the metaphysical puzzles, to find comfort in the thought that "all is made of one piece," and that the Law which we dread is really "Intelligence," which vivifies nature, and somehow makes Fate identical with Freedom. This is not remarkable for lucidity, and to the prosaic reasoner may seem to amount to the statement that a man of fine moral nature may protect himself against harsh truth by cultivating pleasant illusions. Yet, it shows how, without yielding to illusions, such a man can make his life beautiful. The secret is indicated in the beautiful essays upon "Love" and "Friendship." In speaking of "Friendship" Emerson becomes a little too high-flown, because he is suspicious of even cementing friendship by actual services. The stoics held that friendship was only possible for the wise man; and Emerson thinks that it requires such "rare and costly" means that it can seldom be realized. It is the product of the spontaneous affinity of soul, which must be independent of all external circumstance or reciprocity of kind actions. In the essay where he manages to give a new charm even to the ancient topic of Love, he puts a more acceptable theory. He speaks in a prose-poem, which reminds us of Mr. Meredith's "Love in a Valley," of the recollection "of the days when happiness was not happy enough, but must be drugged with the rubbish of pain and fear; for he touched the secret of the matter who said of love—

All other pleasures are not worth its pains;

and when the day was not enough but the night, too, must be consumed in keen recollections; when the head boiled all night on the pillow with the generous deed it resolved on; when the moonlight was a pleasing fever, and the stars were letters and the flowers ciphers, and the air was carved into song; when all business seemed an impertinence, and all the men and women running to and fro in the streets mere pictures." Love may generate illusions; but it makes the strong gentle and gives the coward heart. The lover becomes a "new man, with new perceptions, new and keener purposes, and a religious solemnity of character and aims." And thus love, which is "the deification of persons, become more impersonal every day"; and the passion of Romeo for Juliet "puts us in training for a love which knows not sex nor person nor partiality, but which seeks virtue and wisdom to the end of increasing virtue and wisdom."

I do Emerson injustice in taking a few sentences out of his fine rapture; and it would be out of place to consider the cold-blooded criticism that a Romeo sometimes fails to develop in this desirable fashion. I only refer to it to indicate the process by which, as I think, the prosaic person may get some profit even from Emerson's mysticism. It may be unintelligible or false if taken as a solid philosophy. It reveals, at any rate, the man himself, the pure, simple-minded, high-feeling man, made of the finest clay of human nature; the one man who, to Carlyle, uttered a genuine human voice, and soothed the profound glooms of dyspeptic misanthropy; a little too apt, no doubt, to fall into the illusion of taking the world to be as comfortably constituted as himself; and apt also to withdraw from the ugly drama, in which the graver passions are inextricably mixed up with the heroic and the rational, to the remote mountain-tops of mystical reflection. Yet nobody could be more fitted to communicate the "electric shock" to his disciples, because of his keen perception of the noble elements of life, in superiority to all the vulgar motives and modes of thought, which were not the less attractive because he could not see his way to any harmonious or consistent system of thought.

HENRY WADSWORTH LONGFELLOW

HENRY WADSWORTH LONGFELLOW

1807–1882

Henry Wadsworth Longfellow was born in Portland, Maine, on February 27, 1807. Between 1822 and 1825 he studied at Bowdoin College, where he knew Hawthorne, and upon his graduation the college offered him a professorship of modern languages. In order to prepare for this position Longfellow spent the years 1826–29 studying in France, Spain, Italy, and Germany. Upon returning he assumed his professorship, which he held from 1829 to 1835. Longfellow married Mary Storer Potter in 1831, and in 1835 accepted an offer to become professor of Modern Languages and Belles-Lettres at Harvard. During 1835–36 he studied abroad, mostly in Scandinavia and Germany, to prepare for this position, which he assumed in 1836. Before his return, however, Longfellow suffered a terrible blow when in 1835 his wife died in Amsterdam.

Longfellow's prose romance *Hyperion* was published in 1839, as was the collection *Voices of the Night*, which included his poems "A Psalm of Life," "Footsteps of Angels," and "The Reaper and the Flowers." In 1841 appeared *Ballads and Other Poems*, which included "The Wreck of the Hesperus" and "The Village Blacksmith." In 1842 Longfellow spent several months in Germany, and while there formed a friendship with the German poet Ferdinand Freiligrath. During the return voyage he wrote his *Poems on Slavery*, published later that year. In 1843 Longfellow married Fanny Appleton, by whom he had four children.

By the time of his second marriage Longfellow was already one of the most widely read poets in America, and the following years only increased his reputation. The poems and collections that made him, after Tennyson, the most popular poet in the English-speaking world include *The Belfry of Bruges and Other Poems* (1845), *Evangeline* (1847), *The Song of Hiawatha* (1855), and *The Courtship of Miles Standish and Other Poems* (1858). In 1854 Longfellow resigned his Harvard professorship, but his retirement was marred by his wife's accidental death in 1861. In 1863 appeared the first part of *Tales of a Wayside Inn*, containing "Paul Revere's Ride," and *The Song of King Olaf*. Between 1867 and 1870 Longfellow published his three-volume translation of Dante's *Divine Comedy*, followed in 1872 by what Longfellow considered his greatest achievement, the collected *Christus* trilogy, consisting of three previously published works, *The Divine Tragedy* (1871), *The Golden Legend* (1851), and *The New England Tragedies* (1868). *Three Books of Song*, containing the second part of *Tales of a Wayside Inn*, *Judas Maccabeus*, and translations, appeared in 1872, and was followed in 1873 by *Aftermath*, containing the third part of *Tales of a Wayside Inn* and other poems. In 1875 Longfellow published *The Masque of Pandora and Other Poems*, in which are included "The Hanging of the Crane" and "Morituri Salutamus." This was followed in 1880 by *Ultima Thule*, and in 1882 by *In the Harbor*, the last work of Longfellow to be published during his lifetime.

Longfellow died in Cambridge on March 24, 1882. A long fragment of his poem *Michael Angelo* appeared posthumously in 1883, and in 1886 his brother Samuel published the two-volume *Life of Henry Wadsworth Longfellow*, to which a third volume was added in 1891. Longfellow letters have been edited by Andrew Hilen (6 vols., 1966–82).

Personal

H. W. Longfellow is a native of the State of Maine, and one of the Professors in Bowdoin College. He is now in Europe. —SAMUEL KETTELL, *Specimens of American Poetry*, 1829, Vol. 3, p. 238

I cannot forbear saying how much pleasure it gave me to see your few words about Longfellow. He cares not at all for politics or statistics, for the Syrian question, or the disasters of Afghanistan. But to him the magnificent world of literature and Nature is open; every beauty of sentiment and truth and language has for him a relish; and every heart that feels is sure of a response from him. I feel for his genius and worth the greatest reverence, as for him personally the warmest love. —CHARLES SUMNER, Letter to George Sumner (July 8, 1842), cited in Edward L. Pierce, *Memoir and Letters of Charles Sumner*, 1877, Vol. 2, p. 215

I need not praise the sweetness of his song,
   Where limpid verse to limpid verse succeeds

Smooth as our Charles, when, fearing lest he wrong
The new moon's mirrored skiff, he slides along,
   Full without noise, and whispers in his reeds.
With loving breath of all the winds, his name
   Is blown about the world; but to his friends
A sweeter secret hides behind his fame,
And Love steals shyly through the loud acclaim
   To murmur a *God bless you!* and there ends.

As I muse backward up the checkered years
   Wherein so much was given, so much was lost,
Blessings in both kinds, such as cheapen tears,—
But, hush! this is not for profaner ears:
   Let them drink molten pearls, nor dream the cost.
Some suck up poison from a sorrow's core,
   As nought but nightshade grew upon earth's ground:
Love turned all his to heart's-ease; and the more
Fate tried his bastions, she but forced a door
   Leading to sweeter manhood and more sound.

Even as a wind-waved fountain's swaying shade

Seems of mixed race, a gray wraith shot with sun,
So through his trial faith translucent rayed,
Till darkness, half disnatured so, betrayed
    A heart of sunshine that would fain o'errun.

Surely, if skill in song the shears may stay
    And of its purpose cheat the charmed abyss,
If our poor life be lengthened by a lay,
He shall not go, although his presence may,
    And the next age in praise shall double this.

Long days be his, and each as lusty-sweet
    As gracious natures find his song to be!
May Age steal on with softly-cadenced feet,
Falling in music as for him were meet
    Whose choicest verse is harsher-toned than he!
        —JAMES RUSSELL LOWELL, "To H. W. L. (On
        His Birthday, 27th February, 1867)" (1867),
        cited in Samuel Longfellow, *Life of Henry
        Wadsworth Longfellow*, 1891, Vol. 3, pp.
        84–85

I suppose you don't remember Longfellow, though he remembers you in a black velvet frock very well. He is now white-haired and white-bearded, but remarkably handsome. He still lives in his old house, where his beautiful wife was burnt to death. I dined with him the other day, and could not get the terrific scene out of my imagination. She was in a blaze in an instant, rushed into his arms with a wild cry, and never spoke afterwards.—CHARLES DICKENS, Letter to Charles Dickens, Jr. (Nov. 30, 1867)

In no other conspicuous figure in literary history are the man and the poet more indissolubly blended than in Longfellow. The poet was the man, and the man the poet. What he was to the stranger reading in distant lands, by

The long wash of Australasian seas,

that he was to the most intimate of his friends. His life and character were perfectly reflected in his books. There is no purity or grace or feeling or spotless charm in his verse which did not belong to the man. There was never an explanation to be offered for him; no allowance was necessary for the eccentricity or grotesqueness or wilfulness or humor of genius. Simple, modest, frank, manly, he was the good citizen, the self-respecting gentleman, the symmetrical man.

He lived in an interesting historic house in a venerable university town, itself the suburb of a great city; the highway running by his gate and dividing the smooth grass and modest green terraces about the house from the fields and meadows that sloped gently to the placid Charles, and the low range of distant hills that made the horizon. Through the little gate passed an endless procession of pilgrims of every degree and from every country to pay homage to their American friend. Every morning came the letters of those who could not come in person, and with infinite urbanity and sympathy and patience the master of the house received them all, and his gracious hospitality but deepened the admiration and affection of the guests. His nearer friends sometimes remonstrated at his sweet courtesy to such annoying "devastators of the day." But to an urgent complaint of his endless favor to a flagrant offender, Longfellow only answered, good-humoredly, "If I did not speak kindly to him, there is not a man in the world who would." On the day that he was taken ill, six days only before his death, three schoolboys came out from Boston on their Saturday holiday to ask his autograph. The benign lover of children welcomed them heartily, showed them a hundred interesting objects in his house, then wrote his name for them, and for the last time.

Few men had known deeper sorrow. But no man ever mounted upon his sorrow more surely to higher things. Blessed and beloved, the singer is gone, but his song remains, and its pure and imperishable melody is the song of the lark in the morning of our literature:

Type of the wise who soar but never roam,
True to the kindred points of heaven and home.
    —GEORGE WILLIAM CURTIS, "Longfellow"
    (1882), *Literary and Social Essays*, 1894, pp.
    202–4

"Not to be tuneless in old age!"
Ah! surely blest his pilgrimage,
    Who, in his winter's snow,
Still sings with note as sweet and clear
As in the morning of the year
    When the first violets blow!

Blest!—but more blest, whom summer's heat,
Whom spring's impulsive stir and beat,
    Have taught no feverish lure;
Whose Muse, benignant and serene,
Still keeps his autumn chaplet green
    Because his verse is pure!

Lie calm, O white and laureate head!
Lie calm, O Dead, that art not dead,
    Since from the voiceless grave,
Thy voice shall speak to old and young
While song yet speaks an English tongue
    By Charles' or Thamis' wave!
        —AUSTIN DOBSON, "H. W. Longfellow: In Me-
        moriam," *Athenaeum*, April 1, 1882, p. 411

If asked to describe Longfellow's appearance, I should compare him to the ideal representations of early Christian saints and prophets. There is a kind of halo of goodness about him, a benignity in his expression which one associates with St. John at Patmos saying to his followers and brethren, "Little children, love one another!" Longfellow's house has an historical interest attaching to it apart from its being the poet's dwelling, for it was here that Washington had his headquarters after the battle of Bunker's Hill, and the room which tradition says was occupied by the General was curiously enough the same which Longfellow first inhabited when, a new-fledged Professor at Cambridge, he lodged here in 1837, little expecting that this house, then let to various lodgers, would one day be his. In this historic chamber, on the second story, the earliest of his poems were written; here the translations from Old Spanish and German poems were made; and here his *Outre Mer*, the first series of the poems that made his name known throughout the world of literature, was penned. The building, which is known as Craigie House, from the name of a former proprietor, once Apothecary-General of the Northern provincial army, is not unlike in character to many an old mansion about Chiswick or Richmond of the time of Queen Anne or George I.

The grounds in which it stands are said to be beautiful, but I saw nothing of them, for our visit, being necessarily a very short one, made one not inclined when once in the poet's study to leave it, even were the gardens of Armida close at hand; but on entering and leaving Craigie House I noticed some fine old trees, venerable enough to have given shade to Washington and to have dropped their leaves at his feet more than a century ago.

The walls of the entrance hall are lined with wainscoting, and the staircase is of dark old oak. On the landing stands an ancient clock, that must, I should think, bring one of the best known of Longfellow's poems into the mind of every visitor.

Almost involuntarily on seeing it one repeats the lines on "The Old Clock on the Stairs."

The poet's study is on the right and on the ground-floor; this room also rejoices in ancient wainscoted walls. Here are no modern decorations, no modern wall-papers, or new-fangled furniture; above the chimney-piece is placed one of the circular diminishing mirrors that our grandparents liked so well; this is crowned by a golden eagle with outspread pinions; but whether the bird is emblematical of America or not I cannot tell.

The poet's study-table—the anvil on which so much precious ore has been hammered out—occupies the middle of the room. It is littered with books and papers. The latest arrival I saw from Europe was the new edition of Swinburne's *Poems and Ballads*. German and French literature are well represented, as well as English, on the well-filled shelves of the book-cases that line the walls of Longfellow's sanctum.

By the side of this table stands a statuette of an elderly man in a long frock-coat, his hands placed behind him. This is said to be the best likeness of Goethe extant. On the walls are portraits of relations and friends of the poet. Had I the power that the late Nassau Senior possessed to such an extraordinary extent of being able to remember and set down conversations, I should write a more interesting account than this one I fear is, but not having it, I must be content with merely recording that for upwards of an hour I listened to as pleasant a conversation as I ever remember to have heard between these old friends. Mr. Ward's flow of recollections and reminiscences is amazing, and Longfellow, although no great talker, proved himself to be, what is almost rarer, a capital listener.

Longfellow spoke as if his journeyings were over, as if he should not return to the Old World; his impressions of his travels in Europe, the first of which he made more than forty years ago, are pleasant ones. There are certainly few places in Europe which could be more attractive to the poet than his home in Massachusetts. Longfellow has had the rare fortune of being thoroughly appreciated in his own country and in other countries during his lifetime; how different probably would have been the career of Byron, of Keats, or of Shelley, had it been thus with them! It would be presumptuous for me, and out of place, to do more here than allude to the universal popularity of Longfellow's works wherever English is spoken; I believe it is not an exaggeration to say that his works are more popular than those of any other living poet. What child is there who has not heard of "Excelsior," or *Evangeline*, of *Miles Standish*, or of *Hiawatha*? What songs more popular than "The Bridge," and "I know a maiden fair to see"? Or who, after reading the "Psalm of Life," or the "Footsteps of Angels," does not feel a little less worldly, a little less of the earth, earthy? The world, indeed, owes a deep debt of gratitude to Henry Wadsworth Longfellow.—Lord Ronald Gower, *My Reminiscences* (1883), 1895, pp. 454–56

Here sits our Poet, Laureate, if you will.
Long has he worn the wreath, and wears it still.
Dead? Nay, not so; and yet they say his bust
Looks down on marbles covering royal dust,
Kings by the Grace of God, or Nature's grace;
Dead! No! Alive! I see him in his place,
Full-featured, with the bloom that heaven denies
Her children, pinched by cold New England skies,
Too often, while the nursery's happier few
Win from a summer cloud its roseate hue.
Kind, soft-voiced, gentle, in his eye there shines
The ray serene that filled Evangeline's.
Modest he seems, not shy; content to wait

Amid the noisy clamor of debate
The looked-for moment when a peaceful word
Smooths the rough ripples louder tongues have stirred.
In every tone I mark his tender grace
And all his poems hinted in his face:
What tranquil joy his friendly presence gives!
How could I think him dead? He lives! He lives!
—Oliver Wendell Holmes, "At the Saturday Club," 1884

Longfellow was not expansive, nor do I remember his ever becoming enthusiastic over anything or anybody. One who knew nothing of his domestic life might have fancied that he was cold, and certainly he did not possess that social magnetism which made Lowell the loadstone of so many hearts, and made the exercise of that attraction necessary to his own enjoyment of existence. Longfellow adored his wife and children; but beyond that circle, it seemed to me, he had no imperious longing to know or be known. He had likes and dislikes; but so far as I understood him, no strong antipathies or ardent friendships. He had warm friendships for Lowell, the Nortons, and Agassiz, for example, but I think he had but a mild regard for Emerson, and I remember his saying one day that Emerson used his friends like lemons,—squeezing them till they were dry, and then throwing them away. This showed that he misunderstood Emerson, but perhaps intelligibly, for Longfellow had few of those qualities which interested Emerson, and there could not have been much in common to both. Emerson liked men who gave him problems to solve,—something to learn,—while Longfellow was transparent, limpid as a clear spring reflecting the sky and showing all that was in its depths; and to Emerson he offered no problem. I never saw him angry but once, and that was at his next-door neighbor shooting at a robin in a cherry-tree that stood near the boundary between the two gardens. The small shot carried over and rattled about us where we sat on the verandah of the old Washington house, but showed the avicidal intent, and Longfellow went off at once to protest against the barbarity, not at all indignant at the personal danger, if he thought of any.

His adoration of his wife was fully justified, for rarely have I seen a woman in whom a Juno-like dignity and serenity were so wedded to personal beauty and to the fine culture of brain and heart, which commanded reverence from the most ordinary acquaintance, as in her. No one who had seen her at home could ever forget the splendid vision, and the last time I ever saw her, so far as I remember, was in summer time, when she and her two daughters, all in white muslin, like creatures of another world, evanescent, translucent, stood in the doorway to say good-by to me. In the same costume, a little later, she met death. She was making impressions in sealing-wax, to amuse her daughters, when a flaming drop fell on the inflammable stuff, and in an instant she was in flames, burned to death before help could come. It was then that they found that Longfellow was not the cold man they had generally believed him. He never recovered from the bereavement, and shortly after he became a Spiritualist, and, until he in his glad turn passed the gates of death, he lived in what he knew to be the light of her presence. And certainly if such a thing as communion across that grim threshold can be, this was the occasion which made it possible. There was something angelic about them both, even in this life,—a natural innocence and large beneficence and equanimity which, in the chance and contradiction of life, could rarely be found in wedded state.
—William James Stillman, *The Autobiography of a Journalist*, 1901, Vol. 1, pp. 233–35

General

I read your poems over and over, and over again, and continue to read them at all my leisure hours; and they grow upon me at every re-perusal. Nothing equal to some of them was ever written in this world,—this western world, I mean; and it would not hurt my conscience much to include the other hemisphere. I have not yet begun the review of the *Poems* and *Hyperion*. My heart and brain are troubled and fevered now with ten thousand other matters; but soon I will set about it. God send you many a worthier reviewer.—NATHANIEL HAWTHORNE, Letter to Henry Wadsworth Longfellow (Dec. 26, 1839), cited in Samuel Longfellow, *Life of Henry Wadsworth Longfellow*, 1891, Vol. 1, p. 349

H. W. Longfellow (Professor of Moral Philosophy at Harvard) is entitled to the first place among the poets of America— certainly to the first place among those who have put themselves prominently forth as poets. His good qualities are all of the highest order, while his sins are chiefly those of affectation and imitation—an imitation sometimes verging upon downright theft.

His manuscript is remarkably good, and is fairly exemplified in the signature. We see here plain indications of the force, vigor, and glowing richness of his literary style; the deliberate and steady *finish* of his compositions. The man who writes thus may not accomplish much, but what he does will always be thoroughly done. The main beauty, or at least one great beauty of his poetry, is that of *proportion*; another is a freedom from extraneous embellishment. He oftener runs into affectation through his endeavors at simplicity than through any other cause. Now this rigid simplicity and proportion are easily perceptible in the manuscript which, altogether, is a very excellent one.—EDGAR ALLAN POE, "A Chapter on Autography" (1841), *Complete Works*, ed. James A. Harrison, 1902, Vol. 15, pp. 191–92

Much as we admire the genius of Mr. Longfellow, we are fully sensible of his many errors of affectation and imitation. His artistical skill is great, and his ideality high. But his conception of the *aims* of poesy *is all wrong*; and this we shall prove at some future day—to our own satisfaction, at least. His didactics are all *out of place*. He has written brilliant poems—by accident; that is to say when permitting his genius to get the better of his conventional habit of thinking—a habit deduced from German study. ⟨. . .⟩

Of the pieces which constitute the present volume ⟨*Ballads and Other Poems*⟩, there are not more than one or two thoroughly fulfilling the idea above proposed; although the volume as a whole is by no means so chargeable with didacticism as Mr. Longfellow's previous book. We would mention as poems *nearly true*, "The Village Blacksmith;" "The Wreck of the Hesperus" and especially "The Skeleton in Armor." In the first-mentioned we have the *beauty* of simple-mindedness as a genuine thesis; and this thesis is inimitably handled until the concluding stanza, where the spirit of legitimate poesy is aggrieved in the pointed antithetical deduction of a *moral* from what has gone before. In "The Wreck of the Hesperus" we have the *beauty* of child-like confidence and innocence, with that of the father's stern courage and affection. But, with slight exception, those particulars of the storm here detailed are not poetic subjects. Their thrilling *horror* belongs to prose, in which it could be far more effectively discussed, as Professor Longfellow may assure himself at any moment by experiment. There *are* points of a tempest which afford the loftiest and truest poetical themes—points in which pure

beauty is found, or, better still, beauty heightened into the sublime, by terror. But when we read, among other similar things, that

> The salt sea was frozen on her breast,
> The salt tears in her eyes,

we feel, if not positive disgust, at least a chilling sense of the inappropriate. In the "Skeleton in Armor" we find a pure and perfect thesis artistically treated. We find the beauty of bold courage and self-confidence, of love and maiden devotion, of reckless adventure, and finally of life-contemning grief. Combined with all this we have numerous *points* of beauty apparently insulated, but all aiding the main effect or impression. The heart is stirred, and the mind does not lament its malinstruction. The metre is simple, sonorous, well-balanced and fully adapted to the subject. Upon the whole, there are fewer truer poems than this. It has but one defect—an important one. The prose remarks prefacing the narrative are really *necessary*. But every work of art should contain within itself all that is requisite for its own comprehension. And this remark is especially true of the ballad. In poems of magnitude the mind of the reader is not, at all times, enabled to include, in one comprehensive survey, the proportions and proper adjustment of the whole. He is pleased, if at all, with particular passages; and the sum of his pleasure is compounded of the sums of the pleasurable sentiments inspired by these individual passages in the progress of perusal. But, in pieces of less extent, the pleasure is *unique*, in the proper acceptation of this term— the understanding is employed, without difficulty, in the contemplation of the picture *as a whole*; and thus its effect will depend, in great measure, upon the perfection of its finish, upon the nice adaptation of its constituent parts, and especially, upon what is rightly termed by Schlegel *the unity or totality of interest*. But the practice of prefixing explanatory passages is utterly at variance with such unity. By the prefix, we are either put in possession of the subject of the poem; or some hint, historic fact, or suggestion, is thereby afforded, not included in the body of the piece, which, without the hint, is incomprehensible. In the latter case, while perusing the poem, the reader must revert, in mind at least, to the prefix, for the necessary explanation. In the former, the poem being a mere paraphrase of the prefix, the interest is divided between the prefix and the paraphrase. In either instance the totality of effect is destroyed.

Of the other original poems in the volume before us, there is none in which the aim of instruction, or *truth*, has not been too obviously substituted for the legitimate aim, *beauty*. In our last number, we took occasion to say that a didactic moral might be happily made the *under-current* of a poetical theme, and, in *Burton's Magazine*, some two years since, we treated this point at length, in a review of Moore's *Alciphron*; but the moral thus conveyed is invariably an ill effect when obtruding beyond the upper current of the thesis itself. Perhaps the worst specimen of this obtrusion is given us by our poet in "Blind Bartimeus" and the "Goblet of Life," where, it will be observed that the *sole* interest of the upper current of meaning depends upon its relation or reference to the under. What we read upon the surface would be *vox et preterea nihil* in default of the moral beneath. The Greek *finales* of "Blind Bartimeus" are an affectation altogether inexcusable. What the small, second-hand, Gibbon-ish pedantry of Byron introduced, is unworthy the imitation of Longfellow.

Of the translations we scarcely think it necessary to speak at all. We regret that our poet will persist in busying himself about such matters. *His* time might be better employed in original conception. Most of these versions are marked with the error upon which we have commented. This error is in fact, essentially Germanic. "The Luck of Edenhall," however, is a truly beautiful poem; and we say this with all that deference which the opinion of the *Democratic Review* demands. This composition appears to us *one of the very finest*. It has all the free, hearty, *obvious* movement of the true ballad-legend. The greatest force of language is combined in it with the richest imagination, acting in its most legitimate province. Upon the whole, we prefer it even to the "Sword-Song" of Körner. The pointed moral with which it terminates is so exceedingly natural—so perfectly fluent from the incidents—that we have hardly heart to pronounce it in ill taste. We may observe of this ballad, in conclusion, that its subject is more *physical* than is usual in Germany. Its images are rich rather in physical than in moral beauty. And this tendency, in Song, is the true one. It is chiefly, if we are not mistaken—it is chiefly amid forms of physical loveliness (we use the word *forms* in its widest sense as embracing modifications of sound and color) that the soul seeks the realization of its dreams of BEAUTY. It is to her demand in this sense especially, that the poet, who is wise, will most frequently and most earnestly respond.—EDGAR ALLAN POE, "Henry Wadsworth Longfellow" (1842), *Essays and Reviews*, ed. G. R. Thompson, 1984, pp. 682–83, 690–92

I have been looking over the collection of your poems recently published by Carey & Hart with Huntington's illustrations. They appear to me more beautiful than on former readings, much as I then admired them. The exquisite music of your verse dwells more agreeably than ever on my ear, and more than ever am I affected by their depth of feeling and their spirituality and the creative power with which they set before us passages from the great drama of life.

I have been reading aloud to my wife some of your poems that pleased me most, and she would not be content till I had written to express to you something of the admiration which I could not help manifesting as I read them. I am not one of those who believe that a true poet is insensible to the excellence of his writings, and know that you can well afford to dispense with such slight corroboration as the general judgment in your favor could derive from any opinion of mine. You must allow me, however, to add my voice to the many which make up the sum of poetic fame.—WILLIAM CULLEN BRYANT, Letter to Henry Wadsworth Longfellow (Jan. 31, 1846)

> But hey-day! What's this? Messieurs Mathews and
>   Poe,
> You must n't fling mud-balls at Longfellow so,
> Does it make a man worse that his character's such
> As to make his friends love him (as you think) too much?
> Why, there is not a bard at this moment alive
> More willing than he that his fellows should thrive;
> While you are abusing him thus, even now
> He would help either one of you out of a slough;
> You may say that he's smooth and all that till you're hoarse,
> But remember that elegance also is force;
> After polishing granite as much as you will,
> The heart keeps its tough old persistency still;
> Deduct all you can, *that* still keeps you at bay;
> Why, he'll live till men weary of Collins and Gray.
> I'm not over-fond of Greek metres in English,
> To me rhyme's a gain, so it be not too jinglish,
> And your modern hexameter verses are no more
> Like Greek ones than sleek Mr. Pope is like Homer;
> As the roar of the sea to the coo of a pigeon is,
> So, compared to your moderns, sounds old Melesigenes;
> I may be too partial, the reason, perhaps, o't is

> That I've heard the old blind man recite his own rhapsodies,
> And my ear with that music impregnate may be,
> Like the poor exiled shell with the soul of the sea,
> Or as one can't bear Strauss when his nature is cloven
> To its deeps within deeps by the stroke of Beethoven;
> But, set that aside, and 't is truth that I speak,
> Had Theocritus written in English, not Greek,
> I believe that his exquisite sense would scarce change a line
> In that rare, tender, virgin-like pastoral *Evangeline.*
> That's not ancient nor modern, its place is apart
> Where time has no sway, in the realm of pure Art,
> 'T is a shrine of retreat from Earth's hubbub and strife
> As quiet and chaste as the author's own life.
> —JAMES RUSSELL LOWELL, A *Fable for Critics*,
>   1848

The distinguishing qualities of Longfellow seem to be beauty of imagination, delicacy of taste, wide sympathy, and mild earnestness, expressing themselves sometimes in forms of quaint and fantastic fancy, but always in chaste and simple language. His imagination sympathises more with the correct, the classical, and the refined, than with that outer and sterner world, where dwell the dreary, the rude, the fierce, and the terrible shapes of things. The scenery he describes best is the storied richness of the Rhine, or the golden glories of the Indian summer, or the environs of the old Nova Scotian village, or the wide billowing prairie; and not those vast forests, where a path for the sunbeams must be hewn, nor those wildernesses of snow, where the storm and the wing of the condor divide the sovereignty. In the midst of such dreadful solitudes, his genius rather shivers and cowers, than rises and reigns. He is a spirit of the Beautiful, more than of the Sublime; he has lain on the lap of Loveliness, and not been dandled, like a lion-cub, on the knees of Terror. The magic he wields, though soft, is true and strong. If not a prophet, torn by a secret burden, and uttering it in wild, tumultuous strains, he is a genuine poet, who has sought for, and found inspiration, now in the story and scenery of his own country, and now in the lays and legends of other lands, whose native vein, in itself exquisite, has been highly cultivated and delicately cherished.

It is to us a proof of Longfellow's originality, that he bears so well and meekly his load of accomplishments and acquirements. His ornaments, unlike those of the Sabine maid, have not crushed him, nor impeded the motions of his own mind. He has transmuted a lore, gathered from many languages, into a quick and rich flame, which we feel to be the flame of Genius.

It is evident that his principal obligations are due to German literature, which over him, as over so many at the present day, exerts a certain wild witchery, and is tasted with all the sweetness of the forbidden fruit. No writer in America has more steeped his soul in the spirit of German poetry, its blended homeliness and romance, its simplicity and fantastic emphasis, than Longfellow. And if he does not often trust himself amidst the weltering chaos of its philosophies, you see him, lured by their fascination, hanging over their brink, and rapt in wonder at their strange, gigantic, and ever shifting forms. Indeed his *Hyperion* contains two or three most exquisite bits of transcendentalism.

Longfellow is rather a romantic and sentimental, than a philosophical poet. He throws into verse the feelings, moods, and fancies of the young or female mind of genius, not the mature cogitations of profound philosophy. His song is woven of moonlight, not of strong summer sunshine. To glorify abstractions, to flush clear naked truth into beauty, to "build" up poems slowly and solidly, as though he were piling pyramids, is neither his aim nor his attainment. He gathers, on the contrary, roses and lilies,—the roses of the hedge and lilies of the field, as well as those of the garden,—and wreathes them into chaplets for the brow and neck of the beautiful. His poetry is that of sentiment, rather than of thought. But the sentiment is never false, nor strained, nor mawkish. It is always mild, generally manly, and sometimes it approaches the sublime. It touches both the female part of man's mind and the masculine part of woman's. He can at one time start unwonted tears in the eyes of men, and at another kindle on the cheeks of women a glorious glow of emotion, which the term *blush* cannot adequately measure; as far superior to it as is the splendour of a sunset to the bloom of a peach.

We have been struck with the variety of Longfellow's poems. He has written hitherto no large, recondite work. His poems are all short—effusions, not efforts. He has exhibited no traces of a comic vein. His sphere is that of sentiment, moralising elegantly upon many objects. And yet within that sphere there is little mannerism, repetition, or self-imitation. His sentiment assumes a great variety of aspects. Now it is tender to tears, and now heroic to daring; now it muses, and now it dreams; now it is a reverie, and now a rapture; now it is an allegory, now a psalm, and again a song; everything, in short, save a monotony. Nor is this the many-sidedness of a mockingbird. The sentiment of the varied song, as well as the song of the varied sentiment, is ever *his own*.

One of the most pleasing characteristics of this writer's works is their intense humanity. A man's heart beats in his every line. His writings all

> Take a sober colour from the eye,
> That hath kept watch o'er man's mortality.

He loves, pities, and feels with, as well as for, his fellow "human mortal." Hence his writing is blood-warm. He is a brother, speaking to men as brothers, and as brothers are they responding to his voice. Byron addressed men as reptiles or fiends; Wordsworth and others soliloquise, careless whether their voice be listened to or not. But no poet can be loved, as well as admired, who does not speak from the broad level of humanity. If we dare apply the language, "he must be touched with a fellow-feeling of our infirmities, and have been tempted in all points as we are." He must have fallen and risen, been sick and sad, been joyful and pensive, drank of the full cup of man's lot, ere he can so write that man will take his writings to his heart, and appropriate them as part of the great general human stock. A prophet may wrap himself up in austere and mysterious solitude; a poet must come "eating and drinking." Thus came Shakspere, Dryden, Burns, Scott, Goethe; and thus have come in our day Dickens, Hood, and Longfellow. —GEORGE GILFILLAN, "Henry Wadsworth Longfellow," *A Second Gallery of Literary Portraits*, 1850, pp. 374–77

He is too apt to consult poetical precedents, instead of boldly chalking out a path for himself. His very studies have been against him. When a poet trusts to another for his thoughts he will soon lose his individuality. We do not say this has actually happened to Mr. Longfellow, but we see many evidences of a tendency to indulge in that fatal habit, which we think in his case springs more from indolence than want of power. Let him resolutely think and write for himself, retaining his force, elegance, and purity of diction, but throwing from him his undue elaboration and diffusiveness of execution: let him care less for what others have written, and more of what he ought and can write, and boldly throwing away his artificial supports, soar unaided into an element of his own: let him scorn another's balloon, and boldly take to his own wings, and then

America will have reason to consider as one of her best poets Henry Wadsworth Longfellow.—THOMAS POWELL, "Henry Wadsworth Longfellow," *The Living Authors of America*, 1850, p. 168

⟨. . .⟩ Longfellow's hexameters generally 'read themselves' easily enough, and ⟨. . .⟩ it is to be overcritical to complain of them in this respect; still, I don't think they are a good type of hexameter.—MATTHEW ARNOLD, Letter to His Mother (April 14, 1862)

Perhaps the main constituent of Longfellow as a poetical writer is intelligence. I mean "intelligence" in the current semi-technical sense wherein that word is used—as we speak of the "intelligence" of the age, or of "the intelligent classes," or "intelligent working-man." Intelligence in this sense is not to be confounded with "intellect" in a more abstract or exalted application of the term: the most "intelligent" man is not necessarily the most "intellectual"—still less, the greatest for the higher purposes of the poetic or other noble art. This intelligence is a certain openness to information of all sorts, and a readiness at turning it to practical account; a workmanlike knowledge and mastery of all kinds of mental tools; in especial, a great susceptibility to "the spirit of the age." It presupposes considerable culture co-related to its own direct objects; in the case of Longfellow, this culture is both solid and spacious. He was in a high sense a literary man; and next, a literary artist; and thirdly, a literary artist in the domain of poetry. It would not be true to say that his art is of the intensest kind or most magical potency; but it is art, and imbues whatever he performs. In so far as a literary artist in poetry is a poet, Longfellow is a poet, and should (to the silencing of all debates and demurs) be freely confessed and handsomely installed as such. How far he is a poet in a further sense than this remains to be determined.

Having thus summarily considered "the actual quality of the work" as derived from the endowments of the worker, I next proceed to "the grounds upon which the vast popularity of the poems has rested." One main and in itself all-sufficient ground has just been stated: that the sort of intelligence of which Longfellow was so conspicuous an example includes preëminently "a great susceptibility to the spirit of the age." The man who meets the spirit of the age halfway will be met halfway by that; will be adopted as a favourite child, and warmly reposited in the heart. Such has been the case with Longfellow. In sentiment, in perception, in culture, in selection, in utterance, he represents, with adequate and even influential but not overwhelming force, the tendencies and adaptabilities of the time; he is a good type of the "bettermost," not the exceptionally very best, minds of the central or later-central period of the nineteenth century; and, having the gift of persuasive speech and accomplished art, he can enlist the sympathies of readers who approach his own level of intelligence, and can dominate a numberless multitude of those who belong to lower planes but who share none the less his own general conceptions and aspirations. He is like a wide-spreading tree on the top of a gentle acclivity, to which the lines of all trees lower down point and converge, and of which the shadow rests upon them with kindly proximity and protection. This is popularity. The question whether the popularity will be prolonged into enduring fame is much the same as the question in what degree the spirit of our own age will be operative in time to come. As long as it *is* operative, the same relation between Longfellow and the public of poetic readers will subsist: when it declines, his influence will also wane, unless some other and supereminent qualities are his, appealing to that which is permanent in man, and not transitional as one generation yields its place to another.

The poetic performances of Longfellow may perhaps be distinguished into three categories. In the first of these there is a certain pretence—an inflation of mind, and over-strained *ad captandum* use of temporary catch-words or figure-heads of thought and sentiment, an audible and visible appeal to "the finest feelings of our nature"—an essentially false note, pre-destined to be found out in the long run. The finest feelings of our nature are indeed the things most deserving to be appealed to: but there is a way of appealing to them which smacks not less of the assertion, "I am myself the man who knows these feelings and can rouse them in you," than of any more modest frame of mind, or simpler phase of natural emotion; and this may strike some people as too often the way in which Longfellow apostrophizes them. "Excelsior" appears to me to be prominently one of these compositions. They will not only not be enduringly admired, but will be rejected with some degree of angry irritation. The second class includes the great bulk of his writing. It is good enough for its time and its public, and is even within limits good intrinsically; but has not any such powerful vital stamina as to survive chance and change, the perpetual flux of things: it is not of the stuff to remain a fixed quantity when so much else, in mind and matter, shall have altered. The third class includes some small compositions here and there, and in especial the two long poems, *Evangeline* and *Hiawatha*, published respectively in 1847 and 1855. These, if I am not mistaken, are works made for posterity and for permanence. *Evangeline*, whatever may be its shortcomings and blemishes, takes so powerful a hold of the feelings that the fate which would at last merge it in oblivion could only be a very hard and even a perverse one. Who that has read it has ever forgotten it? or in whose memory does it rest as other than a long-drawn sweetness and sadness that has become a portion, and a purifying portion, of the experiences of the heart? *Hiawatha* has a different claim. It is a work *sui generis*, and alone; moreover, manly, interesting, and a choice and difficult piece of execution, without strain or parade. The native American legends and aboriginal tone of thought have to be preserved in some form or other, as a matter of natural and national necessity: they are here compactly preserved in a good poem, the work of a skilled artist. Were there a better poem than *Hiawatha* forthcoming for the particular purpose, the fate of this work would be remitted to casualty. But it is the first, may be the last, of any distinguished value, and is amply fine enough to endure. I can hardly imagine it superseded, nor, until superseded, overlooked.

This leads us to consider for a moment whether Longfellow impressed himself upon the time, or qualified for posterity, as the American poet *par excellence*. I do not think he did. *Hiawatha* will live as the poem of the American native tribes, not as the poem of America; *Evangeline* will live as an idyll of the heart associated with American scenery in close-linked intercommunion, but also not as an absolutely national and typical work: and the other compositions of Longfellow having claims of the same order appear to be in full measure subject to the chances and mischances of "natural selection in the struggle for life." The real American poet is Walt Whitman—a man enormously greater than Longfellow or any other of his poetic compatriots.—WILLIAM MICHAEL ROSSETTI, "Henry Wadsworth Longfellow," *Lives of Famous Poets*, 1878, pp. 388–91

In speaking of Hawthorne in these pages, and in comparing his genius with that of others, I mentioned the purity of Longfellow, and I said that "the seraphic excellence of *Hiawatha* and *Evangeline* could have proceeded only from a mind which the world's roughness had neither toughened nor tainted." Such, to my thinking, is the peculiar nature of Longfellow's muse. But he is pure without the slightest affectation of purity. Among our own bards there are those with whom the same delicacy is their peculiar characteristic. Cowper is as pure as could be any strictest lady. But with him it amounts almost to an affectation. He rises, especially in his *Task*, to great heights of poetry;—beyond, perhaps, those which, in his simplicity, Longfellow attempts. He is, too, a complete master of the melody of versification, whereas Longfellow, in the peculiar manner and methods which he has adopted, becomes sometimes almost prosaic. But a study of Longfellow's works leaves on the reader's mind a feeling that he is pure because of his nature. Cowper, on the other hand, raises a conviction that he is pure by having overcome his nature. He seems to betray a former connection with original sin. The other is simply living the life he has ever lived, in which sin has had no part. If he be seraphic, it is because he was born and bred so, and to be seraphic has come easy to him. That Cowper must have had stirring struggles with the devil in his youth, and have conquered him, is quite certain. Cowper delights in old women, as being less wicked than old men, and is pious, mad, and inspired. Longfellow takes the people as they come, and is neither pious, nor mad, nor, to the outward sense, inspired. But he is a great poet, and his poetry is perfectly pure.

He is, I think, essentially unlike his countrymen,—so much so, that, of all the poets of his day, he is the last that I should have guessed to be an American had I come across his works in ignorance of the fact. He is never loud, far-fetched, funny, or extravagant. He is unlike Bryant, Poe, Lowell, and Bret Harte. Italian poetry, which he delights to translate,—probably from the relief which he finds in having occasionally to supply words only and not ideas,—has been his model. As he is pure, so also is he graceful. But that for which you have to look, and will most surely find in his poetry, is pathos. Now a story of love may be delightfully told, and yet not be pathetic. Look at Rosalind, where the comedy, fresh and sweet as it is, frustrates pathos; or even Juliet, where the love leaps from passion to tragedy, and never quite enters on the melancholy realm of pathos. Look at your dictionary, and you shall see that pathos is called passion. The words, indeed, from their derivation, should mean the same; but the meaning they convey to us at present is very different. No one would, I think, describe the story of Evangeline as one of strong passion, but no story more pathetic was ever written. A soft melancholy, which may rise indeed sometimes to tragic sorrow, but which never loses its softness and never ceases to be tender, is necessary to pathos. And such is the distinguishing characteristic of Longfellow in all his longer popular poems.—ANTHONY TROLLOPE, "Henry Wadsworth Longfellow," *North American Review*, April 1881, pp. 384–85

Camden, April 3, '82.—I have just return'd from an old forest haunt, where I love to go occasionally away from parlors, pavements, and the newspapers and magazines—and where, of a clear forenoon, deep in the shade of pines and cedars and a tangle of old laurel-trees and vines, the news of Longfellow's death first reach'd me. For want of anything better, let me lightly twine a sprig of the sweet ground-ivy trailing so plentifully through the dead leaves at my feet, with reflections of that half hour alone, there in the silence, and lay it as my contribution on the dead bard's grave.

Longfellow in his voluminous works seems to me not only to be eminent in the style and forms of poetical expression that mark the present age, (an idiosyncrasy, almost a sickness, of verbal melody,) but to bring what is always dearest as poetry to the general human heart and taste, and probably must be so in the nature of things. He is certainly the sort of bard and counteractant most needed for our materialistic, self-assertive, money-worshipping, Anglo-Saxon races, and especially for the present age in America—an age tyrannically regulated with reference to the manufacturer, the merchant, the financier, the politician and the day workman—for whom and among whom he comes as the poet of melody, courtesy, deference— poet of the mellow twilight of the past in Italy, Germany, Spain, and in Northern Europe—poet of all sympathetic gentleness—and universal poet of women and young people. I should have to think long if I were ask'd to name the man who has done more, and in more valuable directions, for America.

I doubt if there ever was before such a fine intuitive judge and selecter of poems. His translations of many German and Scandinavian pieces are said to be better than the vernaculars. He does not urge or lash. His influence is like good drink or air. He is not tepid either, but always vital, with flavor, motion, grace. He strikes a splendid average, and does not sing exceptional passions, or humanity's jagged escapades. He is not revolutionary, brings nothing offensive or new, does not deal hard blows. On the contrary, his songs soothe and heal, or if they excite, it is a healthy and agreeable excitement. His very anger is gentle, is at second hand, (as in the "Quadroon Girl" and the "Witnesses.")

There is no undue element of pensiveness in Longfellow's strains. Even in the early translation, the Manrique, the movement is as of strong and steady wind or tide, holding up and buoying. Death is not avoided through his many themes, but there is something almost winning in his original verses and renderings on that dread subject—as, closing "the Happiest Land" dispute,

> And then the landlord's daughter
> Up to heaven rais'd her hand,
> And said, "Ye may no more contend,
> There lies the happiest land."

To the ungracious complaint-charge of his want of racy nativity and special originality, I shall only say that America and the world may well be reverently thankful—can never be thankful enough—for any such singing-bird vouchsafed out of the centuries, without asking that the notes be different from those of other songsters; adding what I have heard Longfellow himself say, that ere the New World can be worthily original, and announce herself and her own heroes, she must be well saturated with the originality of others, and respectfully consider the heroes that lived before Agamemnon.—WALT WHITMAN, "Death of Longfellow" (1882), *Prose Works*, ed. Floyd Stovall, 1963, Vol. 1, pp. 284–86

Our poet of grace and sentiment left us in the after-glow of an almost ideal career. He had lived at the right time, and with the gift of years; and he died before the years came for him to say, I have no pleasure in them. Not all the daughters of music were brought low. He scarcely could have realized that people were calling his work elementary, that men whose originality had isolated them, like Emerson and Browning,—and even metrical experts, the inventors of new modes,—were gaining favor with a public which had somewhat outgrown him; that he was to be slighted for the very qualities which had made him beloved and famous, or that other qualities, too long needed, were to be overvalued as if partly for the need's sake.

But they are wrong who make light of Longfellow's service as an American poet. His admirers may form no longer a critical majority, yet he surely helped to quicken the New World sense of beauty, and to lead a movement which precedes the rise of a national school. I think that the poet himself, reading his own sweet songs, felt the apostolic nature of his mission,—that it was religious, in the etymological sense of the word, the binding back of America to the Old World taste and imagination. Our true rise of Poetry may be dated from Longfellow's method of exciting an interest in it, as an expression of beauty and feeling, at a time when his countrymen were ready for something more various and human than the current meditations on nature. It was inevitable that he should first set his face toward a light beyond the sea, and I have said that his youthful legend aptly was *Outre Mer*. An escape was in order from the asceticism which two centuries had both modified and confirmed. How could this be effected? Not at once by the absolute presentation of beauty. A Keats, pledged to this alone, could not have propitiated the ancestral spirit. Puritanism was opposed to beauty as a strange god, and to sentiment as an idle thing. Longfellow so adapted the beauty and sentiment of other lands to the convictions of his people, as to beguile their reason through the finer senses, and speedily to satisfy them that loveliness and righteousness may go together. His poems, like pictures seen on household walls, were a protest against barrenness and the symptoms of a new taste.

They made their way more readily, also, by their response to the inherited Anglo-Saxon instincts of his own region. His early predilections, strengthened during a stay in Germany, were chiefly for the poetry and romance of that land. He read his heart in its songs, which he so loved to translate for us. A new generation may be at a loss to conceive the effect of Longfellow's work when it first began to appear. I may convey something of this by what is at once a memory and an illustration. Take the case of a child whose Sunday outlook was restricted, in a decaying Puritan village, to a wooden meetinghouse of the old Congregational type. The interior—plain, colorless, rigid with dull white pews and dismal galleries— increased the spiritual starvation of a young nature unconsciously longing for color and variety. Many a child like this one, on a first holiday visit to the town, seeing the vine-grown walls, the roofs and arches, of a graceful Gothic church, has felt a sense of something rich and strange; and many, now no longer children, can remember that the impression upon entrance was such as the stateliest cathedral now could not renew. The columns and tinted walls, the ceiling of oak and blue, the windows of gules and azure and gold,—the service, moreover, with its chant and organ-roll,—all this enraptured and possessed them. To the one relief hitherto afforded them, that of nature's picturesqueness,—which even Calvinism endured without compunction,—was added a new joy, a glimpse of the beauty and sanctity of human art. A similar delight awaited the first readers of Longfellow's prose and verse. Here was a painter and romancer indeed, who had journeyed far and returned with gifts for all at home, and who promised often and again to

> sing a more wonderful song
> Or tell a more marvellous tale.

And thus it chanced that, well as he afterward sang of his own sea and shore, he now is said to have been the least national of our poets. His verse, it is true, was like a pulsatory cord, sustaining our new-born ideality with nourishment from the mother-land, until it grew to vigor of its own. Yet he was more widely read than his associates, and seemed to foreigners the incumbent American laureate. His native themes, like some of Tennyson's, were chosen with deliberation and as if for their availability. But from the first he was a poet of sentiment, and equally a craftsman of unerring taste. He always gave of his best; neither toil nor trouble could dismay him until art had done its perfect work. It was a kind of genius,—his sure perception of the fit and attractive. Love flows to one whose work is lovely. Besides, he was a devotee to one calling,—not a critic, journalist, lecturer, or man of affairs,—and even his prose romances were akin to poems. A long and spotless life was pledged to song, and verily he had his reward. Successors may find a weakness in his work, but who can rival him in bearing and reputation? His worldly wisdom was of the gospel kind, so gently tempered as to breed no evil. His life and works together were an edifice fairly built,—the House Beautiful, whose air is peace, where repose and calm are ministrant, and where the raven's croak, symbol of the unrest of a more perturbed genius, is never heard. Thus the clerkly singer fulfilled his office,—which was not in the least creative,—and had the tributes he most desired: love and honor during his life-time, and the assurance that no song of his took flight but to rest again and again "in the heart of a friend."—EDMUND CLARENCE STEDMAN, "Henry Wadsworth Longfellow," *Poets of America*, 1885, pp. 180–83

Longfellow had not Bryant's depth of feeling for ancient history or for external nature. The moral ether which Emerson inhaled upon the peaks of thought was too rare for Longfellow. Morality to Emerson was the very breath of existence; to Longfellow it was a sentiment. Poe's best poetic efforts are evidence of an imagination more completely self-sufficient than Longfellow's was. In the best of Whittier's poems the pulse of human sympathy beats more strongly than in any of our poet's songs. Still more unlike Longfellow's sentimentality is the universal range of Whitman's manly, outspoken kinsmanship with all living things.

We feel that in these points Longfellow comes short. How then has he outdistanced those men so easily? By virtue of his artistic eclecticism. He was not the single-minded priest of nature that Bryant was; but he took the words out of Bryant's lips, and sang them in a hundred measures. He lowered Emerson's philosophical Puritanism to the capacity of toilers in the streets; Emerson may have aimed, like Goethe, at being "humanity's high-priest"—Longfellow was content to be humanity's city missionary, so long as the common people heard him gladly. Although he was not of heroic mould, he was at least twenty times a nobler man than Poe, with a fund of miscellaneous culture, and a knowledge of human nature that in the long run more than compensated for any inferiority his imagination presented in comparison with Poe's brightest inspirations. He had not the keenness of Poe's artistic sensibility, yet it can at least be said of him that he would have scorned the atrocious, if rare, faults that so disfigure Poe's writings in verse. The same width of learning in matters of general culture, to which allusion has just been made, gave Longfellow an appeal to far larger audiences than those that Whittier can attract; and by his gracious choice of subjects, and his treatment of these in almost every form of verse dear to the people, Longfellow has of course laid himself out—and successfully—to win a hearing where Whitman, with all his boasted feeling for democracy, is looked upon as an intellectual Coriolanus, contemptuous and uncouth.

To reach purely sensuous beauty, or abstract intellectual beauty of a still more exquisite sort, is to be a Keats or a

Shelley, at least, if not to be a Shakespeare; and it is not necessary to give Longfellow equal rank as an artist with Keats or Shelley. But much as we must reverence and rejoice in the more purely artistic work of men like these, the world still needs poets of another sort to warm ordinary blood. The facts of ordinary homely life—our cradling, our childish sorrows, our youthful temptations, the struggles of maturity, the helpfulness of friends, the decay and regrets of old age, the daily deeds of Death—must we not ever have new poets to sing about these things to us, and hearten us for our work? Could Keats and Shelley have done much with these themes, had they tried? Let it be admitted that Longfellow almost totally lacked the higher imagination that is the originally creative and sustaining power in poetry: we must still give him credit for a wondrously fertile fancy. Along with this pure fancy, he possessed a curiously happy facility in selecting uncommon aspects of common themes; and furthermore, in a few of his ballads—in his *Evangeline*, in his *Hiawatha*—he laid hold of very uncommon themes. Most of these themes, common or uncommon, he embellished by his fancy with such a wealth of tender and beautiful sayings, that in every civilized land his verses have become household favourites, permeating the lives of rising generations. It is idle to say that such an achievement could be wrought by talent of a commonplace order. To how many hundreds of imitators did Longfellow set a style? Has any one of these imitators come within measurable distance of him? The answer to this question must be "No." But these imitators—with their allies who squall "Excelsior" in drawing-rooms—have done much to give the critical a distaste for Longfellow's manner of work. Popularity undoubtedly caused Longfellow to write too easily; the public have continued to accept too eagerly all that he wrote; and therefore it seems to some a merciful task for the army of accomplished pooh-poohers to step in, in the name of the higher criticism, and announce that Longfellow may have been all very well for the vulgar, but was not really a poet of any consequence. Such a judgment does not belong to enlightened criticism. He who has written verses that are committed to heart by millions for the gladdening of their lives, must have written much that is true poetry; and although he is not necessarily among the twelve greatest poets of the world, he is incontestably a great benefactor and a great man.—ERIC S. ROBERTSON, *Life of Henry Wadsworth Longfellow*, 1887, pp. 174–77

In the first place, what are we to say of Longfellow? I am very far from being one of those who reject the accomplished and delicate work of this highly-trained artist. If I may say so, no chapter of Mr. Stedman's book seems to me to surpass in skill that in which he deals with the works of Longfellow, and steers with infinite tact through the difficulties of the subject. In the face of those impatient youngsters who dare to speak of Longfellow and of Tupper in a breath, I assert that the former was, within his limitations, as true a poet as ever breathed. His skill in narrative was second only to that of Prior and of Lafontaine. His sonnets, the best of them, are among the most pleasing objective sonnets in the language. Although his early, and comparatively poor, work was exaggeratedly praised, his head was not turned, but, like a conscientious artist, he rose to better and better things, even at the risk of sacrificing his popularity. It is a pleasure to say this at the present day, when Longfellow's fame has unduly declined; but it is needless, of course, to dwell on the reverse of the medal, and disprove what nobody now advances, that he was a great or original poet. Originality and greatness were just the qualities he lacked. I have pointed out elsewhere that Longfellow was singularly

2779

under Swedish influences, and that his real place is in Swedish literature, chronologically between Tegnér and Runeberg. Doubtless he seemed at first to his own people more original than he was, through his habit of reproducing an exotic tone very exactly.—EDMUND GOSSE, "Has America Produced a Poet?" (1889), *Questions at Issue*, 1893, pp. 82–83

The ocean as confidant, a Laertes that can neither avoid his Hamlets nor bid them hold their peace, is a modern invention. Byron and Shelley discovered it; Heine took it into his confidence, and told it the story of his loves; Wordsworth made it a moral influence; Browning loved it in his way, but his way was not often the poet's; to Matthew Arnold it was the voice of destiny, and its message was a message of despair; Hugo conferred with it as with an humble friend, and uttered such lofty things over it as are rarely heard upon the lips of man. And so with living lyrists each after his kind. Lord Tennyson listens and looks until it strikes him out an undying note of passion, or yearning, or regret—

> Sunset and evening star,
> And one clear call for me;

Mr. Swinburne maddens with the wind and the sounds and the scents of it, until there passes into his verse a something of its vastness and its vehemency, the rapture of its inspiration, the palpitating, many-twinkling miracle of its light; Mr. William Morris has been taken with the manner of its melancholy; while to Whitman it has been 'the great Camerado' indeed, for it gave him that song of the brown bird bereft of his mate in whose absence the half of him had not been told to us.

But to Longfellow alone was it given to see that stately galley which Count Arnaldos saw; his only to hear the steersman singing that wild and wondrous song which none that hears it can resist, and none that has heard it may forget. Then did he learn the old monster's secret—the word of his charm, the core of his mystery, the human note in his music, the quality of his influence upon the heart and the mind of man; and then did he win himself a place apart among sea poets. With the most of them it is a case of *Ego et rex meus*: It is I and the sea, and my egoism is as valiant and as vocal as the other's. But Longfellow is the spokesman of a confraternity; what thrills him to utterance is the spirit of that strange and beautiful freemasonry established as long ago as when the first sailor steered the first keel out into the unknown, irresistible water-world, and so established the foundations of the eternal brotherhood of man with ocean. To him the sea is a place of mariners and ships. In his verse the rigging creaks, the white sail fills and crackles, there are blown smells of pine and hemp and tar; you catch the home wind on your cheeks; and old shipmen, their eyeballs white in their bronzed faces, with silver rings and gaudy handkerchiefs, come in and tell you moving stories of the immemorial, incommunicable deep. He abides in a port; he goes down to the docks, and loiters among the galiots and brigantines; he hears the melancholy song of the chanty-men; he sees the chips flying under the shipwright's adze; he smells the pitch that smokes and bubbles in the caldron. And straightway he falls to singing his variations on the ballad of Count Arnaldos; and the world listens, for its heart beats in his song.—W. E. HENLEY, "Longfellow," *Views and Reviews*, 1890, pp. 151–53

> The winds have talked with him confidingly;
> 　The trees have whispered to him; and the night
> 　Hath held him gently as a mother might,
> And taught him all sad tones of melody:
> The mountains have bowed to him; and the sea,
> 　In clamorous waves, and murmurs exquisite,

> Hath told him all her sorrow and delight—
> 　Her legends fair—her darkest mystery.
> 　His verse blooms like a flower, night and day;
> Bees cluster round his rhymes; and twitterings
> 　Of lark and swallow, in an endless May,
> Are mingling with the tender songs he sings.—
> 　Nor shall he cease to sing—in every lay
> Of Nature's voice he sings—and will alway.
> 　　—JAMES WHITCOMB RILEY, "Longfellow" (1892),
> 　　　　*Complete Works*, 1916, Vol. 6, p. 1561

The art of Longfellow is something too precious among our heritages from the past not to be valued at its full worth. It was the hardly saving grace which Hawthorne owned in the American literature of his time, and it is the art of Longfellow which takes from the American poetry of his generation the aspect of something fragmentary and fugitive. Whatever else it had from others, from Emerson, from Bryant, from Whittier, from Holmes, from Lowell, it had standing and presence and recognition among the world literatures from the art of Longfellow. We had other poets easily more American than he, but he was above all others the American poet, and he was not the less American because he accepted the sole conditions on which American poetry could then embody itself. As far as he ever came to critical consciousness in the matter he acted upon the belief, which he declared, that we could not be really American without being in the best sense European; that unless we brought to our New World life the literature of the Old World, we should not know or say ourselves aright. It seems to us, therefore, that Mr. Carpenter's speculations as to what sort of poet Longfellow might have been if he had been differently environed, or had been obliged in the West, or elsewhere, to enter more hardily into the struggle of life, are beside the question. Longfellow was what he was, and as it is probable that no man is idly or unmeaningly born of certain parents and not of certain others, so it seems reasonable to suppose there is some sort of order in a man's place and time which he can scarcely be even imagined outside of. Longfellow's place was in Cambridge among apparently smooth things, and his life was apparently tranquil and even, but these appearances cannot conceal the fact that his life included in its course all the sorrow and all the tragedy that can educate a man to sympathy with other human lives. Longfellow's time was that period which Mr. Carpenter calls sentimental, but which we should rather call ethical and emotional, and which Longfellow certainly reflected in the poetry of his early and middle manner. But beneath its surface aspects his art was instinctively seeking the meanings of its aspects. These were what the meanings of humanity are in every time, whether the time is optimistic or pessimistic, ethical or scientific: they were very simple meanings, the eternal desire of the race to orient itself aright with love and death, with sin and sorrow, with hope and despair. The soul is apparently busy with many other things, with war, money, office, letters, arts, ambitions, interests, but it is really the mind that is busy with such things; the soul, the very man, moves in the round of those elemental meanings, and it is the affair of poetic art to find them out and report them in the language of the day. Its task is a process of translation out of the old dialects of the past; and he who shows himself aptest in the new version is the greatest poet of his age. Did Tennyson add anything to the thinking and feeling of England in his day, or did he merely surprise his fellow-Englishmen with a new gloss of the thoughts and feelings which have always been in the world, but which the time required in terms more intelligible than those of the past? If Tennyson expressed the most of thinking and feeling Englishmen to themselves, in the same measure Longfellow expressed the like Americans. —WILLIAM DEAN HOWELLS, "Editor's Easy Chair," *Harper's New Monthly Magazine*, April 1902, pp. 834–35

Works

EVANGELINE

This poem has a historical foundation in the removal and dispersion of the inhabitants of the French province of Acadie, in 1755, by order of the British authorities. The event is one of the most remarkable in American history; and the story of Evangeline and her lover is of itself as poetical as the fable of the *Odyssey*, besides that it comes to the heart as a fact that has had actual place in human life. A young maiden is separated from the youth to whom she is betrothed, and conveyed to a different province; she spends her whole subsequent life in efforts to rejoin him, unavailingly, till, in old age, she finds him on his death-bed, in an almshouse. It is a theme, indeed, not to be trusted in the hands of an ordinary writer, who would bring out only its gloom and wretchedness; it required the true poet's deeper insight to present it to us, as we find it here, its pathos all illuminated with beauty,—so that the impression of the poem is nowhere dismal nor despondent, and glows with the purest sunshine where we might the least expect it, on the pauper's death-bed. We remember no such triumph as the author has here achieved, transfiguring Evangeline, now old and gray, before our eyes, and making us willingly acquiesce in all the sorrow that has befallen her, for the sake of the joy which is prophesied and realized within her.

The story is told with the utmost simplicity—with the simplicity of high and exquisite art, which causes it to flow onward as naturally as the current of a stream. Evangeline's wanderings give occasion to many pictures both of northern and southern scenery and life; but these do not appear as if brought in designedly, to adorn the tale; they seem to throw their beauty inevitably into the calm mirror of its bosom, as it flows past them. So it is with all the adornments of the poem; they seem to have come unsought. Beautiful thoughts spring up like roses, and gush forth like violets along a wood-path, but never in any entanglement or confusion; and it is chiefly because beauty is kept from jostling with beauty, that we recognize the severe intellectual toil, which must have been bestowed upon this sweet and noble poem. It was written with no hasty hand, and in no light mood. The author has done himself justice, and has regard to his well-earned fame; and, by this work of his maturity—a poem founded on American history, and embodying itself in American life and manners— he has placed himself on an eminence higher than he had yet attained, and beyond the reach of envy. Let him stand, then, at the head of our list of native poets, until some one else shall break up the rude soil of our American life, as he has done, and produce from it a lovelier and nobler flower than this poem of Evangeline!

Mr. Longfellow has made what may be considered an experiment, by casting his poem into hexameters. The first impressions of many of his readers will be adverse; but, when it is perceived how beautifully plastic this cumbrous measure becomes in his hands—how thought and emotion incorporate and identify themselves with it—how it can compass great ideas, or pick up familiar ones—how it swells and subsides with the nature and necessities of the theme—and, finally, how musical it is, whether it imitate a forest-wind or the violin of an Acadian fiddler—we fully believe that the final judgment will be in its favor. Indeed, we cannot conceive of the poem as existing in any other measure.—NATHANIEL HAWTHORNE, *Salem Advertiser*, Nov. 13, 1847

Is this natural poetry? Does the narrative *require* these "dying falls?" We answer, no; the measure jars upon us; it is as though we were reading intense prose before a slowly nodding China mandarin. The face falls at the end of every line. Where was the necessity for choosing such a form? It cannot be that the idea of its appropriateness rose up spontaneously in the author's mind on his first conceiving the piece, and that he used it because he *felt it to be the best*; at least it is to be hoped it did not. That motion which Coleridge calls the life of poetry, is here a very melancholy life indeed. It is a "body of this death." Was it because it was a new form, and the author wished to show that "some things could be done as well as others?" Then he should not have attempted it for three reasons: *first*, the motive is unworthy of a poet; *secondly*, the same thing or others very like had been tried before a hundred times, and it is evident to any student that it has never succeeded, because it does not accord with the structure of our language; and *thirdly*, no one has a right to try such novelties without being, like Collins in his "Ode to Evening," successful. Was it because the old forms were exhausted? How much richer would be an imitation, were it necessary to make such, of the melody of *Comus*, than such a monotonous tune as this! We have tried all ways of reading it, now minding accents and pauses, now reading it as prose; but it is neither one thing nor the other, and whether as prose or verse is equally cold, affected and unnatural. The whole book did not accustom us to it; and from its growing more and more tedious till the end, we do not believe another would, twice as bulky.

But it may be urged, *Evangeline* is in a walk of art to which strictness of criticism should not be applied. It is not attempted to make the characters natural, but only to make them in harmony with each other. It is raised very high into the poetic region; and the mind which approaches it must for the nonce lay aside common sense and put on spectacles which turn all things to gold. To appreciate such constancy as *Evangeline*'s, one must be very refined indeed. The whole work, in short, is so *fine* that it required these awkward inclined planes of lines, that perpetually carry the reader down—and down—and down-a—in order to make it sufficiently remote and strange. It is a painting on glass, and has laws of its own. The attempt is not to idealize, but to create.

So far as such opinions recognize the propriety of works of art in which the fancy shall give the whole a delicate and peculiar hue, their justice must be admitted, of course. We suffer ourselves to be pleased with transparencies around lamps; we see landscapes in the frost pictures on windows; there are innumerable golden regions above the sunset, and miniatures of them in the glowing coals; nay, faces of angels and devils peep out upon us even from the papered walls. Whatever the fancy permits will come into poetry. There may be good poems as literal as the *Tales of the Hall*, and others equally good, as fanciful as the *Faery Queen*. But in one, as much as in the other, the form and *motion* should be, because it must be, created by, and conform with, and belong to, and be a part of the essence of, the whole. For example, take the *Ancient Mariner*: nothing is more common than the ballad form; but that form was never so written before. The poetry of the piece takes that old measure and moulds it anew into an eloquent motion peculiar to itself, harmonizing with and heightening its general effect. The verse of the poem is as original as any element of it; but how clearly did it grow to be what it is, under the guidance of the poet of course, yet still *as of necessity*.

But in *Evangeline* there is no such concinnity. The verse stands out like an awkward declaimer, or a bashful schoolboy rehearsing young Norval, or Hohen Linden. It has no connection with the poetry; the two are in the condition of a couple divorced *a mensa et thoro*, but not *a vinculo matrimonii*; they are mingled but not combined; in mixtion, not in solution. We are not called upon to be first affected with the tale as we proceed, and left to admire at its elegance, but are asked to admire first, and to be affected secondarily. The difference is just this, that the author is affected and not we. He is determined to be fine, and consequently determinately so. "O wad some power the giftie gie us!"—and most especially in writing poetry, for there it is impossible to hide the secret purpose. When the spirit of the Muse is upon us, and we must prophecy; when the whole soul is compelled by an angel with a fiery sword; when, as Milton saith, the poet is "soaring in the high region of his fancy, with his garland and singing robes about him;" then these over-niceties do not appear, or if they do, they are at once pardoned and passed by. When the hot simoom of the IMAGINATION sweeps across the burning wastes of the soul, the birds and beasts which people it fly before the blast, and the silly young estriches of our vanity run till they fall and die; but when the strong north wind of the WILL sweeps along with only a great cloud of dust, the silly creatures stick their heads in the sand and abide its utmost fierceness!—G. W. PECK, *"Evangeline," American Review*, Feb. 1848, pp. 162–63

I did not, I am sure, make any such comparison of Longfellow's *Evangeline* with other American poems as you heard ascribed to me. What I said was, that it had given me altogether more pleasure in the reading than any poem which had lately appeared—than any poem which had been published within several years. And this is true. I have never made any attempt to analyze the sources of this pleasure. The poem interested and affected me strongly. Whatever may be said of the parts, they are all harmonized by a poetic feeling, of great sweetness and gentleness, which belongs to the author. My ear admits nay delights in the melody of the hexameter as he has managed it. I no doubt expressed my satisfaction with the poem in warm terms, but the idea of bringing its poetic merits into comparison with whatever had been written in America never entered into my head.—WILLIAM CULLEN BRYANT, Letter to Richard Henry Dana (Sept. 12, 1848)

Thank you so much for *Evangeline*, which is full of the beautiful, and is most deeply pathetic, as much so as the story of Margaret in the *Excursion*. Perhaps you will think me paradoxical (no, *you* would not, I believe, though many would), when I say that this deep pathos is not the right thing in a poem. I could not take the story and the poetry together, but was obliged to skim through it, and see how the misery went on, and how it ended, before I could *read the poem*. I think a poem ought not to have a more touching interest than Spenser's *Faerie Queen*, Ariosto, and Tasso. ⟨. . .⟩

It does not clearly appear why Gabriel should lose sight of Evangeline on leaving Acadia. Perhaps we shall be told, as we are of the story of Margaret, that it is matter of *fact*. This would not excuse it, if it *looks* improbable; and depend upon it *in the fact* there was something different, something that prevented the difficulty which suggests itself in the written tale. *Evangeline* seems to be, in some sort, an imitation of Voss's *Luise*. The opening, especially, could remind any one who had read the *Luise*, of that remarkable Idyll. It is far inferior to that, I think, both in the general conception, and in the execution. Voss's hexameters are perfect. The German lan-

guage admits of that metre, the English hardly does so. Some of Longfellow's lines are but quasi-metre, so utterly inharmonious and so prosaic in regard to the diction. I do not think there will ever be a continuous strain of good hexameters in our language, though there may be a good line here and there.—SARA COLERIDGE, Letter to Aubrey De Vere (Sept. 1848), *Memoir and Letters of Sara Coleridge*, ed. Edith Coleridge, 1873, Vol. 2, pp. 183–85

The hexameter is, comparatively, still unfamiliar in England; many people have a great dislike to it. A certain degree of unfamiliarity, a certain degree of dislike, are obstacles with which it is not wise to contend. It is difficult to say at present whether the dislike to this rhythm is so strong and so widespread that it will prevent its ever becoming thoroughly familiar. I think not, but it is too soon to decide. I am inclined to think that the dislike of it is rather among the professional critics than among the general public; I think the reception which Mr. Longfellow's *Evangeline* has met with indicates this. I think that even now, if a version of the *Iliad* in English hexameters were made by a poet who, like Mr. Longfellow, has that indefinable quality which renders him popular,—something *attractive* in his talent, which communicates itself to his verses,—it would have a great success among the general public. Yet a version of Homer in hexameters of the *Evangeline* type would not satisfy the judicious, nor is the definite establishment of this type to be desired; and one would regret that Mr. Longfellow should, even to popularise the hexameter, give the immense labour required for a translation of Homer, when one could not wish his work to stand. Rather it is to be wished that by the efforts of poets like Mr. Longfellow in original poetry, and the efforts of less distinguished poets in the task of translation, the hexameter may gradually be made familiar to the ear of the English public; at the same time that there gradually arises, out of all these efforts, an improved type of this rhythm; a type which some man of genius may sign with the final stamp, and employ in rendering Homer; a hexameter which may be as superior to Voss's as Shakspeare's blank verse is superior to Schiller's. I am inclined to believe that all this travail will actually take place, because I believe that modern poetry is actually in want of such an instrument as the hexameter.—MATTHEW ARNOLD, *On Translating Homer*, 1861

THE SONG OF HIAWATHA

Sanborn brought me your good gift of *Hiawatha*; but I have not read it without many interruptions, nor finished it till yesterday. I have always one foremost satisfaction in reading your books,—that I am safe. I am in variously skilful hands, but first of all they are safe hands. However, I find this Indian poem very wholesome; sweet and wholesome as maize; very proper and pertinent for us to read, and showing a kind of manly sense of duty in the poet to write. The dangers of the Indians are, that they are really savage, have poor, small, sterile heads,—no thoughts; and you must deal very roundly with them, and find them in brains. And I blamed your tenderness now and then, as I read, in accepting a legend or a song, when they had so little to give. I should hold you to your creative function on such occasions. But the costume and machinery, on the whole, is sweet and melancholy, and agrees with the American landscape. And you have the distinction of opening your own road. You may well call it an "Indian Edda." My boy finds it "like the story of Thor," meaning the *Hammersheimt*, which he admires. I found in the last cantos a pure gleam or two of blue sky, and learned thence to tax the rest of the poem as too abstemious.—RALPH WALDO EMERSON, Letter to Henry Wadsworth Longfellow (Nov. 25, 1855), cited in Samuel Longfellow, *Life of Henry Wadsworth Longfellow*, 1891, Vol. 2, pp. 294–95

I liked *Hiawatha* and I think it is liked here very generally, and none the worse for being Indian.—ARTHUR HUGH CLOUGH, Letter to F. J. Child (Jan. 16, 1856)

This poem, in which a series of idylls are strung together, on the thread of an idea common to Indian and Scandinavian legend, has been called an American *Odyssey*, an aboriginal *Arabian Nights' Entertainments*, the *Ancient Mariner* of Transatlantic verse—comparisons nearly as dangerous as that between Bryant and Wordsworth, too courageously instituted by injudicious friends. The merit of *Hiawatha* is rather that it is *sui generis*, a transparent allegory, a sheaf of ballads, a child's story book, and a poem full of morning breezes. Though apparently written *currente calamo*, it really yields to none of the author's works in artistic finish. The verse is indeed somewhat monotonous, and painfully open to parody; but, within the limits of the volume, it preserves, with its few notes, the freshness of a linnet's song. It has been said that the popular imagination plagiarises itself in every country: the common basis of national legend is here seen to stretch beyond the circle of the Aryan races. *Hiawatha* is, like Triptolemus or Bramah, the civiliser. His friends Kwasind and Chibiabos are respectively Hercules the monster-slayer and Apollo the singer, while some of the attributes of Hermes are divided between Iagoo and Paupakewis. But these Indian demi-gods come into closer contact with simpler forms of existence: their counsellors are beavers and sturgeons, their oracles streams and birds. Into the spirit of this primitive life Longfellow has thrown himself as completely as he has into that of Norse Paganism in the *Challenge of Thor*. He is at home among the pine groves and the prairies, and the great lakes of the Northland, and

> All the many sounds of nature,
> Borrow sweetness from his singing.

Hiawatha speaks of them with the familiarity of an inhabitant: there is no trace of the grandiose style of the tourist, and here and there, notably in the capture of Kagahgee the king of the ravens, there is a touch of genuine humour. In the best episodes of the volume—as the account of the hero's infancy, of his early associates, of his sailing forth on his mission of peace and good works, of the wooing and the death of Minnehaha, of the son of the evening star, of the weird ghosts and the ghastly famine,—the parable of human life under a guise of half-savage manners, life with its three great stages of birth and love and decay, is told in a narrative of childlike tenderness and masculine grasp, lit by an imagination like an Aurora Borealis. A New York critic ridicules the European view that *Hiawatha* is an American poem: it belongs, he insists, to the wigwam and not to the Exchange. It is true that the feverish ardour of Wall Street has no place in its pages; but in celebrating Red Indian life, it inevitably discloses some of the features of the people who have met and clashed with that life. Mr. Hepworth Dixon, in one of those observant works which have suffered partly from the prejudice of the public, partly from the haste and questionable tact of the writer, justly dwells on the extent to which the New Zealand myth about the strength of the dead man passing into his conqueror applies to the pioneers of the West. *Hiawatha* sings the dirge of a nearly vanished race in strains that recall the Briton legends on the death of Arthur; but it has also a prophetic side—from the

meeting point of two worlds of men, it looks before as well as after—

> I beheld, too, in that vision,
> All the secrets of the future,
> Of the distant days that shall be.
> I beheld the westward marches
> Of the unknown crowded nations.
> All the land was full of people,
> Restless, struggling, toiling, striving,
> Speaking many tongues, yet feeling
> But one heart beat in their bosoms.
> In the woodlands rang their axes,
> Smoked their towns in all the valleys;
> Over all the lakes and rivers,
> Rushed their great canoes of thunder.

—JOHN NICHOL, *American Literature*, 1882, pp. 202–4

TRANSLATION OF DANTE

When I received the first volume of your translation of Dante, I thought I should not acknowledge your kindness in sending it until I had received the remainder. But I will wait no longer. The second volume has come out; and not only the main principles of the great work, but the details and finish are as plain as they ever will be.

There can be, I think, no doubt that you have done something astonishing. I should not have thought it possible beforehand, and do not altogether comprehend now how you have accomplished it. I was led on, canto by canto, wondering all the time whether you would give out or stumble; but you never did, so far as I could observe, and I meant to be watchful. The movement of your verse—its cadence and rhythm, I mean—explain, perhaps, a good deal of your power, or rather conceal it; although I confess I do not, after some consideration, understand how you make us feel a sort of presence of the *terza rima*, in a measure so different. But you do; at least to me. Whether you have not encumbered yourself with heavier and more embarrassing conditions than permit the free poetical movement which an absolutely English reader covets, is a question that must be settled by the popular voice, as separate from that of scholastic lovers of Dante. On that bench of judges I can never be competent to sit; I shall always read your translation with the original ringing in my ears.

I know nothing like it; *nil simile aut secundum*. It reminds me, however, of a few lines—not above ten or twelve—translated from the *Odyssey* by Wolf, which I read half a century ago, done with the most extraordinary strictness, and at the same time with grace and fluency. But I remember thinking, as I read them, that Wolf, with all his genius and pluck, could not in the same way make a translation of Homer, if he should have a thousand years given him for the task. —GEORGE TICKNOR, Letter to Henry Wadsworth Longfellow (June 1, 1867), cited in Samuel Longfellow, *Life of Henry Wadsworth Longfellow*, 1891, Vol. 3, pp. 90–91

Mr. Longfellow has set about making a reconstructive translation, and he has succeeded in the attempt. In view of what he has done, no one can ever wish to see the old methods of Pope and Cary again resorted to. It is only where he fails to be truly realistic that he comes short of success. And ⟨. . .⟩ it is oftenest through sheer excess of *literalism* that he ceases to be realistic, and departs from the spirit of his author instead of coming nearer to it. In the *Paradiso*, Canto X. 1–6, his method leads him into awkwardness:—

Looking into His Son with all the love
Which each of them eternally breathes forth,
The primal and unutterable Power
Whate'er before the mind or eye revolves
With so much order made, there can be none
Who this beholds without enjoying Him.

This seems clumsy and halting, yet it is an extremely literal paraphrase of a graceful and flowing original:—

Guardando nel suo figlio con l' amore
Che l' uno e l' altro eternalmente spira,
Lo primo ed ineffabile Valore,
Quanto per mente o per loco si gira
Con tanto ordine fe', ch' esser non puote
Senza gustar di lui chi ciò rimira.

Now to turn a graceful and flowing sentence into one that is clumsy and halting is certainly not to reproduce it, no matter how exactly the separate words are rendered, or how closely the syntactic constructions match each other. And this consideration seems conclusive as against the adequacy of the literalist method. That method is inadequate, not because it is too *re-alistic*, but because it runs continual risk of being too *verbalistic*. It has recently been applied to the translation of Dante by Mr. Rossetti, and it has sometimes led him to write curious verses. For instance, he makes Francesca say to Dante,—

O gracious and benignant *animal!*

for

O animal grazioso e benigno!

Mr. Longfellow's good taste has prevented his doing anything like this, yet Mr. Rossetti's extravagance is due to an unswerving adherence to the very rules by which Mr. Longfellow has been guided.

Good taste and poetic genius are, however, better than the best of rules, and so, after all said and done, we can only conclude that Mr. Longfellow has given us a great and noble work not likely soon to be equalled. Leopardi somewhere, in speaking of the early Italian translators of the classics and their well-earned popularity, says, who knows but Caro will live in men's remembrance as long as Virgil? "La belle destinée," adds Sainte-Beuve, "de ne pouvoir plus mourir, sinon avec un immortel!" Apart from Mr. Longfellow's other titles to undying fame, such a destiny is surely marked out for him, and throughout the English portions of the world his name will always be associated with that of the great Florentine.—JOHN FISKE, "Longfellow's Dante" (1867), *The Unseen World and Other Essays*, 1876, pp. 263–65

His translation is the most faithful version of Dante that has ever been made. He is himself too much a poet not to feel that, in one sense, it is impossible to translate a poem; but he is also too much a poet not to feel that sympathy with his author which enables him to transfuse as much as possible of the subtile spirit of poesy into a version of which the first object was to be faithful to the author's meaning. His work is the work of a scholar who is also a poet. Desirous to give to a reader unacquainted with the Italian the means of knowing precisely *what* Dante wrote, he has followed the track of his master step by step, foot by foot, and has tried, so far as the genius of translation allowed, to show also *how* Dante wrote. The poem is still a poem in his version, and, though destitute, by necessity, of some of the most beautiful qualities of the original, it does not fail to charm with its rhythm, as well as to delight and instruct with its thought.—CHARLES ELIOT NORTON, "Longfellow's Translation of the *Divine Comedy*," *North American Review*, July 1867, pp. 133–34

The review does not change my opinion of Mr. Longfellow's translation—not as the best possible, by any means, but as the best probable. The fault I should find with the criticism is one whereof the author seems to be conscious himself—at least in some measure. It is laid out on too large a scale. His portico is as much too large as that of our Boston Court-House. It seems rather an attempt to show how much the critic knows (and I am heartily glad to find an American who knows so much) than to demonstrate the defects of the translation. (N.B. My faith in him is a little shaken by what he says of Philalethes, whose notes are excellent, but his version Dutch to the last ditch. Blanc also is a very dull fellow. His "Vocabolario," barring some etymological blunders, is valuable, though to a knower of Dante chiefly as an index, but his comment as void of insight as Bentley's on Milton.) Nobody who is intimate with the original will find any translation of the *Divine Comedy* more referashing than *cobs*. Has not Dante himself told us that no poetry can be translated? But, after all is said, I think Mr. Longfellow's the best thus far, as being the most accurate. It is to be looked on, I think, as measured prose—like our version of Job, for example, though without that mastery of measure in which our Bible translators are unmatched except by Milton. I mean where they are at their best, as in Job, the songs of Deborah and Barak, the death of Sisera, and some parts of the Psalms. Mr. Longfellow is not a scholar in the German sense of the word—that is to say, he is no pedant; but he certainly *is* a scholar in another and perhaps a higher sense; I mean in range of acquirement and the flavor that comes of it. I agree with the critic that he should not have cited prose translations of Homer and Virgil; but I should not say with the critic that the Mantuan could be rendered in Scott's measures, nor, I am sure, would Dante have heard it said without indignation. Wordsworth's "Laodamia," with its reminiscences of the sixth book, comes nearer the Maronian march.

But I am heartily glad to find so enthusiastic a student of the poet *chi sovra gli altri come aquila vola*, and have to thank him for giving me the names of two books on Dante which I do not yet possess and with which I shall hasten to supply myself. What he says of the poet as an Italian is true and striking. Yet he *was* a Ghibelline for all that—just as our Democrats are the firmest believers in the One Man power.—JAMES RUSSELL LOWELL, Letter to James B. Thayer (Oct. 1867)

It would give me great pleasure to be a guest at your dinner next week, and to testify my admiration of the writings of Mr. Longfellow, in particular of his translation of Dante, but for the occupations in which I am now engaged, and I must say, also, the habit of seclusion incident to my time of life, and gaining strength as I grow older. Allow me to plead these as my excuse for not coming to the dinner to which you have so kindly invited me. Meantime, I take this opportunity to express in words what my presence could not express more emphatically. Mr. Longfellow has translated Dante as a great poet should be translated. After this version, no other will be attempted until the present form of the English language shall have become obsolete, for, whether we regard fidelity to the sense, aptness in the form of expression, or the skilful transfusion of the poetic spirit of the original into the phrases of another language, we can look for nothing more perfect. It is fitting that Mr. Longfellow's friends should congratulate him, as I heartily do, on the successful completion of his great task.—WILLIAM CULLEN BRYANT, Letter to James T. Field (Oct. 31, 1867), cited in Parke Godwin, *A Biography of William Cullen Bryant*, 1883, Vol. 2, p. 265

———

EDWIN P. WHIPPLE
From "Poets and Poetry of America" (1844)
Essays and Reviews
1850, Volume 1, pp. 58–66

It is quite common for the critics of Longfellow's poetry to escape the trouble of analysis by offering some smooth eulogium to his taste, and some "lip-homage" to his artistical ability. Mr. Griswold satisfies his conscience by saying that "Longfellow's works are eminently picturesque, and are distinguished for nicety of epithet, and elaborate, scholarly finish. He has feeling, a rich imagination, and a cultivated taste." It seems to us that these terms are as applicable to other American poets as to Longfellow. They do not indicate the characteristics of his genius, or give a glimpse of the spirit by which it is pervaded. A person, in reading the "Psalm of Life," does not say that this poem is "distinguished for nicety of epithet, and elaborate, scholarly finish;" but rather, that this poem touches the heroic string of my nature,—breathes energy into my heart,—sustains my lagging purposes,—and fixes my thoughts on what is stable and eternal. Without questioning the artistical excellence of this poet, we still think that it is thrust forward too prominently in all notices of his writings. That which lies behind his style and mere mechanical skill should be first considered. The thought is of more importance than the manner of saying it. If the former be worthless, then the latter is not worth consideration. A poet who expresses nothing, with great "nicety of epithet," or with "elaborate, scholarly finish," is still only good for nothing. The questions which are of real moment relate to qualities which lie deeper than rhetoric.

The great characteristic of Longfellow, that of addressing the moral nature through the imagination, of linking moral truth to intellectual beauty, is a far greater excellence. His artistical ability is admirable, because it is not seen. It is rather mental than mechanical. In truth, it may be doubted if he is more distinguished as an artist than Dana or Bryant. If, by saying that a poem is artistical, we mean that its form corresponds with its spirit, that it is fashioned into the likeness of the thought or emotion it is intended to convey, then *The Buccaneer* and *Thanatopsis* are as artistical as any of the *Voices of the Night*. If mere skill in the use of multitudinous metres be meant, then Percival is more artistical than either. If mechanical ingenuity in forcing sentiment into forms to which it has no affinity be the meaning, then to be artistical is a fault or an affectation. The best artist is he who accommodates his diction to his subject, and in this sense, Longfellow is an artist. By learning "to labor and to wait," by steadily brooding over the chaos in which thought and emotion first appear to the mind, and giving shape and life to both before uttering them in words, he has obtained a singular mastery of expression. By this we do not mean that he has a large command of language. No fallacy is greater than that which confounds fluency with expression. Washerwomen, and boys at debating clubs, often display more fluency than Webster; but his words are to theirs as the roll of thunder to the patter of rain. Language generally receives its significance and power from the person who uses it. Unless permeated by the higher faculties of the mind,—unless it be, not the clothing, but the creature, of thought,—it is quite an humble power. There are some writers who repose undoubting confidence in words. If their minds be filled with the epithets of poetry, they fondly deem that they have clutched its essence. In a piece of inferior verse, we often observe expressions which have been employed with great effect by genius, but which seem to burn the fingers, and disconcert the equanimity, of the aspiring word-catcher who presses them into his service. Felicity, not fluency, of language is a merit. There is such a thing, likewise, as making a style the expression of the nature of the writer who uses it. The rhetorical arrangement of Johnson is often pedantic, but it does not appear so bad in his writings as in the monstrous masses of verbiage beneath which the thin frames of his imitators are crushed. The style of Carlyle is faulty, when judged by the general rules of taste; but we should not desire that the rough gallop of his sentences should be changed for the graceful ambling of Addison's, without a corresponding change in his psychological condition.

Longfellow has a perfect command of that expression which results from restraining rather than cultivating fluency; and his manner is adapted to his theme. He rarely, if ever, mistakes "emotions for conceptions." He selects with great delicacy and precision the exact phrase which best expresses or suggests his idea. He colors his style with the skill of a painter; and in compelling words to picture thought, he not only has the warm flush and bright tints of language at his command, but he arrests its evanescent hues. In the higher department of his art,—that of so combining his words and images that they make music to the soul as well as to the ear, and convey not only his feelings and thoughts but also the very tone and condition of the soul in which they have their being,—he has given exquisite examples in "Maidenhood" and "Endymion." In what Mr. Griswold very truly calls one of his best poems, "The Skeleton in Armor," he manages a difficult verse with great skill. There is much of the old Norse energy in this composition,—that rough, ravenous battle-spirit, which, for a time, makes the reader's blood rush and tingle in warlike sympathy. But the manner in which the passions of the savage are modified by the sentiment of the lover, and the stout, death-defying heart of the warrior yields to that gentle but irresistible power which conquers without arms and enslaves without fetters, constitutes the great charm of the poem.

> Once as I told in glee
> Tales of the stormy sea,
> Soft eyes looked love on me,
>   Burning, yet tender;
> And, as the white stars shine
> On the dark Norway pine,
> On that dark heart of mine
>   Fell their soft splendor.

It would be easy to say much of Longfellow's singular felicity in addressing the moral nature of man. It has been said of him, sometimes in derision, that all his poems have a moral. There is, doubtless, a tendency in his mind to evolve some useful meaning from his finest imaginations, and to preach when he should only sing; but we still think that the moral of his compositions is rarely thrust intrudingly forward, but rather flows naturally from the subject. There is nothing of the spirit of Joseph Surface in his genius; he does not pride himself on being a man of "noble sentiments." The morality of the "Psalm of Life" is commonplace. If versified by a poetaster, it would inspire no deep feeling, and strengthen no high purposes. But the worn axioms of didactic verse have the breath of a new life breathed into them when they are touched by genius. We are made to love and to follow what before we merely assented to with a lazy acquiescence.

> Lives of great men all remind us
> We can make our lives sublime,

And, departing, leave behind us
Footprints on the sands of time.
Footprints that perhaps another,
   Sailing o'er life's solemn main,
A forlorn and shipwrecked brother,
   Seeing, shall take heart again.

This is very different from saying, that, if we follow the example of the great and good, we shall live a noble life, and that the records of our deeds and struggles will strengthen the breasts of those who come after us to do and to suffer.

Longfellow's verse occupies a position half way between the poetry of actual life and the poetry of transcendentalism. Like all neutrals, he is liable to attack from the zealots of both parties; but it seems to us that he has hit the exact point, beyond which no poet can at present go, without being neglected or ridiculed. He idealizes real life; he elicits new meaning from many of its rough shows; he clothes subtle and delicate thoughts in familiar imagery; he embodies high moral sentiment in beautiful and ennobling forms; he inweaves the golden threads of spiritual being into the texture of common existence; he discerns and addresses some of the finest sympathies of the heart; but he rarely soars into those regions of abstract imagination, where the bodily eye cannot follow, but where that of the seer is gifted with a "pervading vision." Though he fixes a keen glance on those filmy and fleeting shades of thought and feeling which common minds overlook, or are incompetent to grasp, he has his eye open a little wider, perhaps, when its gaze is directed to the outward world, than when it is turned within. His imagination, in the sphere of its activity, is almost perfect in its power to shape in visible forms, or to suggest, by cunning verbal combinations, the feeling or thought he desires to express; but it lacks the strength and daring, the wide magnificent sweep, which characterize the imagination of such poets as Shelley. He has little of the unrest and frenzy of the bard. We know, in reading him, that he will never miss his mark; that he will risk nothing; that he will aim to do only what he feels he can do well. An air of repose, of quiet power, is around his compositions. He rarely loses sight of common interests and sympathies. He displays none of the stinging earnestness, the vehement sensibility, the gusts of passion, which distinguish poets of the impulsive class. His spiritualism is not seen in wild struggles after an ineffable Something, for which earth can afford but imperfect symbols, and of which even abstract words can suggest little knowledge. He appears perfectly satisfied with his work. Like his own "Village Blacksmith," he retires every night with the feeling that something has been attempted, and something *done.*

The intellectual tendencies of Longfellow, judging from the mystical charm which many of his poems possess, seem to be purely spiritual. But his keen sense of what is physically pleasurable keeps them in check, and gives a more sensuous property to his imagination than what simply inheres in it. Were it not that young misses have made the phrase of equivocal meaning, we would call him "a beautiful poet." He has a feeling exquisitely fine for what is generally understood by the term *beauty,*—that is, for actual, earthly beauty, idealized and refined by the imagination, embodied in graceful shapes, or beheld in that soft, dreamy light of fancy, which makes it more witching to the senses than when seen in bolder outlines. There is a slight dash of epicureanism in his conception of the quality, when his sentiment and sensations are commingled by his imagination; and a sense of luxury steals over the heart, in reading many of his apparently most spiritualized descriptions.

His sense of beauty, though uncommonly vivid, is not the highest of which the mind is capable. He has little conception of its mysterious spirit;—of that Beauty, of which all physical loveliness is but the shadow, which awes and thrills the soul into which it enters, and lifts the imagination into regions "to which the heaven of heavens is but a veil." His mind never appears oppressed, nor his sight dimmed, by its exceeding glory. He feels, and loves, and creates, what is beautiful; but he hymns no reverence, he pays no adoration, to the Spirit of Beauty. He would never exclaim with Shelley, "O awful Loveliness!"

We say this rather to make a distinction than to note a fault; to show how far the spiritual element in Longfellow's poetry is modified by the sensuous properties of his genius, than to blame him for the combination. Indeed, by a majority of critics and readers, this combination is deemed a high merit. If they found any fault with Longfellow, it would be, that he is too transcendental. It is the cant nowadays, that poetry is soaring beyond the ken of us "poor humans." A poet, who occasionally dwells in abstract imaginations, is pelted with pet epithets, and accused of lacking human sympathy. This arises, we think, from a too narrow definition of the term. It is true, that men have a quicker sense of their relations to external nature and to each other than to God: to shows rather than to substances; and their hearts are more readily kindled by what is addressed to their blood and physical temperament, than by what speaks to their spiritual nature. Still, he must be a daring and somewhat impudent person, who decides upon the whole reach of human sympathies by the range of his own, and calls that meaningless and unprofitable which his own heart echoes feebly or not at all. Lust, falsehood, and intemperance, have been so often idealized by poets, and have found so ready a response from "human sympathies," that in some minds they have become significant of the whole meaning of the phrase. If the term human weakness, or criminality, were substituted for it in many cases, there would be a gain to the science of definition. Every man has a theory of human sympathies to fit his own tastes; and his system is often so sharp a satire on his moral perceptions, that he would manifest much more prudence in its concealment than in shouting it forth in the markets and public places of criticism.

The sympathies which Longfellow addresses are fine and poetical, but not the most subtle of which the soul is capable. The kindly affections, the moral sentiments, the joys, sorrows, regrets, aspirations, loves, and wishes of the heart, he has consecrated by new ideal forms and ascriptions. He inculcates with much force that poetic stoicism which teaches us to reckon earthly evils at their true worth, and endure with patience what results inevitably from our condition,—as in the "Psalm of Life," "Excelsior," "The Light of Stars," and in passages of other poems. "The Village Blacksmith" and "God's Acre" have a rough grandeur, and "Maidenhood" and "Endymion" a soft, sweet, mystical charm, which advantageously display the range of his powers. Perhaps "Maidenhood" is the most finely poetical of all his poems. Nothing of its kind can be more exquisitely beautiful than this delicate creation. It appears like the utterance of a dream. In *The Spanish Student,* the affluence of his imagination in images of grace, grandeur, and beauty, is most strikingly manifested. The objection to it, as a play, is its lack of skill or power in the dramatic exhibition of character; but read merely as a poem cast in the form of dialogue, it is one of the most beautiful in American literature. None of his other pieces so well illustrates all his poetical qualities,—his imagination, his fancy, his sentiment, and his manner. It seems to comprehend the whole extent of his genius.

MARGARET FULLER
From "American Literature"
Papers on Literature and Art
1846

We must confess to a coolness towards Mr. Longfellow, in consequence of the exaggerated praises that have been bestowed upon him. When we see a person of moderate powers receive honors which should be reserved for the highest, we feel somewhat like assailing him and taking from him the crown which should be reserved for grander brows. And yet this is perhaps ungenerous. It may be that the management of publishers, the hyperbole of paid or undiscerning reviewers, or some accidental cause which gives a temporary interest to productions beyond what they would permanently command, have raised such a one to a place as much above his wishes as his claims, and which he would rejoice with honorable modesty to vacate at the approach of one worthier. We the more readily believe this of Mr. Longfellow, as one so sensible to the beauties of other writers and so largely indebted to them *must* know his own comparative rank better than his readers have known it for him.

And yet so much adulation is dangerous. Mr. Longfellow, so lauded on all hands—now able to collect his poems which have circulated so widely in previous editions, and been paid for so handsomely by the handsomest annuals, in this beautiful volume, illustrated by one of the most distinguished of our younger artists—has found a flatterer in that very artist. The portrait which adorns this volume is not merely flattered or idealized, but there is an attempt at adorning it by expression thrown into the eyes with just that which the original does not possess, whether in face or mind. We have often seen faces whose usually coarse and heavy lineaments were harmonized at times into beauty by the light that rises from the soul into the eyes. The intention Nature had with regard to the face and its wearer, usually eclipsed beneath bad habits or a bad education, is then disclosed, and we see what hopes death has in store for that soul. But here the enthusiasm thrown into the eyes only makes the rest of the face look more weak, and the idea suggested is the anomalous one of a dandy Pindar.

Such is not the case with Mr. Longfellow himself. He is never a Pindar, though he is sometimes a dandy even in the clean and elegantly ornamented streets and trim gardens of his verse. But he is still more a man of cultivated taste, delicate though not deep feeling, and some though not much poetic force.

Mr. Longfellow has been accused of plagiarism. We have been surprised that anyone should have been anxious to fasten special charges of this kind upon him, when we had supposed it so obvious that the greater part of his mental stores were derived from the works of others. He has no style of his own growing out of his own experiences and observations of nature. Nature with him, whether human or external, is always seen through the windows of literature. There are in his poems sweet and tender passages descriptive of his personal feelings, but very few showing him as an observer at first hand of the passions within or the landscape without.

This want of the free breath of nature, this perpetual borrowing of imagery, this excessive because superficial culture which he has derived from an acquaintance with the elegant literature of many nations and men out of proportion to the experience of life within himself, prevent Mr. Longfellow's

verses from ever being a true refreshment to ourselves. He says in one of his most graceful verses:

> From the cool cisterns of the midnight air
> My spirit drank repose;
> The fountain of perpetual peace flows there,
> From those deep cisterns flows.

Now this is just what we cannot get from Mr. Longfellow. No solitude of the mind reveals to us the deep cisterns.

Let us take, for example of what we do not like, one of his worst pieces, the "Prelude to the Voices of the Night"—

> Beneath some patriarchal tree
> I lay upon the ground;
> His hoary arms uplifted be,
> And all the broad leaves over me
> Clapped their little hands in glee
> With one continuous sound.

What an unpleasant mixture of images! Such never rose in a man's mind as he lay on the ground and looked up to the tree above him. The true poetry for this stanza would be to give us an image of what was in the writer's mind as he lay there and looked up. But this idea of the leaves clapping their little hands with glee is taken out of some book; or at any rate is a book thought and not one that came in the place, and jars entirely with what is said of the tree uplifting its hoary arms. Then take this other stanza from a man whose mind *should* have grown up in familiarity with the American *genius loci*:

> Therefore at Pentecost, which brings
> The Spring clothed like a bride,
> When nestling buds unfold their wings,
> And bishop's caps have golden rings,
> Musing upon many things,
> I sought the woodlands wide.

Musing upon many things—aye! and upon many books too, or we should have nothing of Pentecost or bishop's caps with their golden rings. For ourselves, we have not the least idea what bishop's caps are—are they flowers—or what? Truly the schoolmaster was abroad in the woodlands that day! As to the conceit of the wings of the buds, it is a false image, because one that cannot be carried out. Such will not be found in the poems of poets; with such the imagination is all compact, and their works are not dead mosaics with substance inserted merely because pretty, but living growths, homogeneous and satisfactory throughout.

Such instances could be adduced everywhere throughout the poems, depriving us of any clear pleasure from any one piece, and placing his poems beside such as those of Bryant in the same light as that of the prettiest *made* shell, beside those whose every line and hue tells a history of the action of winds and waves and the secrets of one class of organizations.

But do we therefore esteem Mr. Longfellow a willful or conscious plagiarist? By no means. It is his misfortune that other men's thoughts are so continually in his head as to overshadow his own. The order of fine development is for the mind the same as the body, to take in just so much food as will sustain it in its exercise and assimilate with its growth. If it is so assimilated—if it becomes a part of the skin, hair, and eyes of the man, it is his own, no matter whether he pick it up in the woods or borrow from the dish of a fellow-man or receive it in the form of manna direct from Heaven. "Do you ask the genius," said Goethe, "to give an account of what he has taken from others? As well demand of the hero an account of the beeves and loaves which have nourished him to such martial stature."

But Mr. Longfellow presents us not with a new product in

which all the old varieties are melted into a fresh form, but rather with a tastefully arranged museum, between whose glass cases are interspersed neatly potted rose trees, geraniums, and hyacinths, grown by himself with aid of indoor heat. Still we must acquit him of being a willing or conscious plagiarist. Some objects in the collection are his own; as to the rest, he has the merit of appreciation and a rearrangement not always judicious, but the result of feeling on his part.

Such works as Mr. Longfellow's we consider injurious only if allowed to usurp the place of better things. The reason of his being overrated here is because through his works breathes the air of other lands, with whose products the public at large is but little acquainted. He will do his office, and a desirable one, of promoting a taste for the literature of these lands before his readers are aware of it. As a translator he shows the same qualities as in his own writings; what is forcible and compact he does not render adequately; grace and sentiment he appreciates and reproduces. Twenty years hence when he stands upon his own merits, he will rank as a writer of elegant if not always accurate taste, of great imitative power, and occasional felicity in an original way where his feelings are really stirred. He has touched no subject where he has not done somewhat that is pleasing, though also his poems are much marred by ambitious failings.

⟨. . .⟩ We have not wished to depreciate these writings below their current value more than truth absolutely demands. We have not forgotten that if a man cannot himself sit at the feet of the Muse, it is much if he prizes those who may; it makes him a teacher to the people. Neither have we forgotten that Mr. Longfellow has a genuine respect for his pen, never writes carelessly, nor when he does not wish to, nor for money alone. Nor are we intolerant to those who prize hothouse bouquets beyond all the free beauty of nature; that helps the gardener and has its uses. But still let us not forget—*Excelsior!*

HENRY NORMAN
"A Study of Longfellow"
Fortnightly Review, January 1883, pp. 100–115

There will be held, in the first month of the new year, at the Lyceum Theatre, by the permission of Mr. Henry Irving, a meeting of the Longfellow Memorial Committee, when the sub-committee will present a report on the best use to be made of the large sum of money that has been already subscribed for perpetuating in some visible shape the memory of the most popular of American poets.

When George Ticknor wrote to recommend Longfellow to Dean Milman he said of him: "He is a most amiable and agreeable person, of whom we are all very fond." When Mr. Matthew Arnold has occasion to mention *Evangeline*, he speaks of it as "Mr. Longfellow's pleasing and popular poem." When Longfellow visited the Queen—he himself is authority for this statement—she actually said as he was taking his leave, "We shall not forget you. Why, all my servants read your poetry." These three quotations express the general mental attitude toward Longfellow and his poetry; in each case the words are kind enough and—with one possible exception—the speaker meant to be complimentary; but there is an undertone of depreciation, and a distant suggestion of the unpleasant significance of faint praise. In short, and in spite of the present remarkable display of public good-will in high places, there can be no doubt that the tendency of cultured English opinion has

long been to class him with the poets of mediocrity—a race unpleasing alike to gods, men, and publishers.

At the present moment it is interesting to inquire what are the special reasons that have led to this classification of Longfellow with the mediocre poets, and before his personality is lost in the "remarkable retirement of the grave," to consider him from the standpoint of a criticism midway between cultured disdain and popular eulogy. The literary notice which his works have received has been of such a superficial or one-sided character that an attempt to estimate them with some knowledge of the circumstances of their origin, and on their merits, is much to be desired. The brilliant composition of the Memorial Committee must not be allowed to conceal the fact that it, too, is a popular movement, and therefore without influence upon dispassionate criticism. The striking inequality of Longfellow's work renders the thankless task of discrimination the duty of some one who has honoured him as a man, for it is the best service towards securing the just appreciation of him as a poet.

The first of the special reasons, then, for the low rank of Longfellow's poetry is that much of it is didactic. The circumstances of his life made this tendency unavoidable: his Puritan birth and education gave him the moral fibre for which the New England character is noted, his direct ancestors being among those early pilgrims of whom Emerson has said that they were so righteous they had to hold on to the huckleberry bushes for fear of being translated. Then his Puritan temperament was fertilised by several years of residence in Germany at the time when the rabid naturalism of the *Sturm und Drang* had crystallized into a firm and enthusiastic humanism. A tender-hearted man, in comfortable and easy surroundings, following, like all the young American writers of his time, in the footsteps of Bryant, with this fertilised Puritanism, how could his verses be anything but didactic? And didactic verse, as such, was heartily welcomed; we find the delighted critics declaring that his poems "are of a nature to encourage the best and purest sentiments," that his lines "are as happy in their expression as they are correct in their moral tendency;" and as late as 1844, E. P. Whipple writing that Longfellow's great characteristic is "addressing the moral nature through the imagination, of linking moral truth to intellectual beauty." So, being applauded, he went on, perfectly conscious of what he was doing, and of the audience he was addressing,—"Maiden, who read'st this simple rhyme," for instance. His life and all his writings show that he was profoundly in earnest; he was not preaching merely because preaching was popular. His prose works, in particular, are permeated with the simple doctrines of the "Psalm of Life." "Therefore should every man wait;—should bide his time. Not in listless idleness,—not in useless pastime,—not in querulous dejection, but in constant steady, cheerful endeavours, always willing and fulfilling, and accomplishing his task." Similar sentiments furnish mottoes for two of his books, and occur again and again in their pages. Now, waiving any discussion of the theory of didactic poetry, the fact is clear that this age professes to believe in art for art's sake; the artist must not be conscious of any purpose; his function is to depict; truth "to be loved, needs only to be seen." Mr. Buchanan, for instance, is so well aware of this fact that he feels compelled to preface his latest novels, which show nothing much worse than what the Germans call a *Tendenz*, with a kind of defiant apology. So it is not to be expected that the critical public which patronises the modern school of poetry will tolerate the crudeness of such rhymed exhortation as "Be resolute and calm." Longfellow's natural bent and circumstances made him didactic, and he secured his first laurels by following this bent; we belong to an age which is horrified at what has been wittily called "the illicit conveyance of useful knowledge," and which looks upon preaching out of church as savouring of impertinence; so we have handed his poems over to that class of readers upon whose shelves they stand by the side of the Bible and the *Pilgrim's Progress*.

In the second place, Longfellow has been judged by his early poems. It was a misfortune for a man destined to a long and gradual development that his first efforts should attract so much attention, for people have continued to bear them in mind long after he has ceased to be fairly reflected in them. The poetry by which Longfellow is known to-day to the majority of his readers thus consists of verses written while he was still uncertain whether he was singing or preaching, and long before he had any conception of poetry as distinct from verse-writing. Take, for instance, the two pieces which are indissolubly connected with his name—the "Psalm of Life" and "Excelsior." The first of these is so familiar to us that we can hardly bring ourselves to consider the thought of it apart from the form.

We can escape this difficulty, however, by taking it in a foreign tongue. "La vie des grands hommes nous apprend que nous pouvons rendre nos existences sublimes." The language of the translation is at least as fine as that of the original, and how extremely commonplace—or worse—the thought is! So, too, is the whole poem when we have once escaped from the youthful and pulpit associations which cling to it. Yet the above translation is by M. Emile Montégut, in the *Revue des Deux Mondes*, and is not, as might be thought, one made for the present occasion. No wonder he declares that the *jolis détails* in Longfellow's poetry are *trop souvent noyés dans de mélancoliques puérilités*.

"Excelsior" is no better. Mr. M. W. Rossetti has aptly described it as *ad captandum* poetry, i.e. depending for its effect, like some of Mr. Aldrich's stories, upon a kind of trick—in this case the recurrence of the catch-word "Excelsior!" Making all allowance for allegory, the imagery is preposterous. It is impossible to sympathize with a young man who commits suicide by climbing an Alpine mountain at night with no other object than to keep getting higher. As some one has said, it was a foregone conclusion that he would be frozen to death. And when, in addition, he refuses all shelter and even declines advice as to the precautions to be observed by any one who wishes to get as high as possible, and carries in his hand a banner with "Excelsior"—which, by the way, is the motto of the State of New York—upon it, the poem becomes ridiculous, and even, as Mr. Rossetti suggests, irritating. We are told that it symbolizes the man of genius in his struggle to attain his ideal, ever striving to climb higher and higher, and scorning everything that might distract him. But it is hardly necessary to stop to point out that the metaphor breaks down at almost every point.

Besides early poems which are unworthy of his subsequent attainments, Longfellow is known by other early poems of considerable merit which have become wearisome by dint of constant repetition. They have been subjected to a barrel-organ treatment, and like many good sayings and stirring songs have become at last intolerable. It is only the greatest works that can be constantly repeated without palling. Thus in the fact that Longfellow is known to the majority of his readers by his early poems, and that these were either originally commonplace or have become commonplace by an unfortunate popularity, we find a further reason for the comparatively low estimate in which he is held.

In any estimate of his genius Longfellow deserves atten-

tion first for his prose, and all the more because it is probable that of five hundred persons who are fairly familiar with all his poetry, there is not more than one that has read his prose works. Without counting contributions to the *North American Review*, which are no longer of any special value, Longfellow's prose consists of three works, *Outre-Mer*, a "pilgrimage;" *Hyperion*, a "romance;" and *Kavanagh*, a "tale." The two thin octavo volumes of the original edition of *Hyperion* recall a couple of interesting incidents of Longfellow's life. The publisher, Colman, of New York, became bankrupt immediately after their appearance, and all the copies, except the few that were already sold, were seized by the creditors and kept for nearly eighteen months. This was a cruel blow for a young author, and Longfellow said, when he told me the story, "Of course I was in despair, for I supposed the book was entirely ruined," adding with a quiet chuckle, "but it managed to survive." Paul Fleming, the hero, represents Longfellow himself (he once acknowledged the portrait so far as to say, "He was what I thought I might have been"), and Mary Ashburton, the heroine, is the Miss Appleton whom the poet afterwards married, and to win whose love by a faithful picture of his own feelings before and after her refusal of him, the book was written. So, at least, the story runs, and if it is true, the romance was no less successful in private than in public.

Longfellow's prose has four distinct characteristics: clearness and originality of style, remarkable erudition, humour, and an unbounded fertility of imagination. It is sufficient to mention the first two of these, but the second two have been generally overlooked, and they throw so much light upon Longfellow's temperament and therefore upon his poetry, that they call for special notice. He has never received due credit for his humour, which has been pronounced indifferent by the critics, who were probably among the majority who have not read the poet's prose, and it will remain indifferent to people who roar over "Josh Billings" and the *Danbury News*; but if space permitted it would be easy to show that Longfellow was a humourist of much originality and merit. One example may be given: the old servant, he tells us in *Kavanagh*, was about to retire from the family, "being engaged to a travelling dentist, who, in filling her teeth with amalgam, had seized the opportunity to fill a soft place in her heart with something still more dangerous and mercurial." This is a perfectly characteristic specimen, and it would be difficult to find in the pages of professed wits anything neater and lighter. Among his friends Longfellow was famous for his wit and as a capital *raconteur*.

In one of his essays, Emerson says, "I had rather have a good symbol of my thought, or a good analogy, than the suffrage of Kant or Plato." If this is a reasonable preference, Longfellow's unbounded fertility of imagination is an important testimony to the merit of his work. I called it the fourth characteristic of his prose, but it would be more accurately described as the most prominent of his mental traits. His style is charming, his humour is "choicely good," and his scholarship is extensive; but the play of his imagination is beyond all question the greatest of his powers. It is perfectly described in the following account of one of his heroes: "Imagination was the ruling power of his mind. His thoughts were twin-born; the thought itself, and its figurative semblance in the outer world. Thus, through the quiet, still waters of his soul each image floated double, swan and shadow." This is literally true of Longfellow; almost every thought came to him clothed in some simile, it seems as if he could grasp his own ideas only through some material presentation of them; he was indeed what he called himself in his last poem,

A dreamer of dreams,
To whom what is and what seems
Are often the same.

For instance, describing the village schoolmaster, he says: "They saw him daily moiling and delving in the common path like a beetle, and little thought that underneath that hard and cold exterior lay folded delicate golden wings, wherewith, when the heat of the day was over, he soared and revelled in the evening air." A beautiful peasant-girl offered to tell him the story of the Liebenstein, "but before she began she rested a moment on her oars, and taking the crucifix which hung suspended from her neck, kissed it, and then let it sink into her bosom, as if it were an anchor she was letting down into her heart." What could be prettier? And here is an original one: The old professor "loved solitude, and silence, and candle-light, and the deep midnight. 'For,' said he, 'if the morning hours are the wings of the day, I only fold them about me to sleep more sweetly, knowing that, at its other extremity, the day, like the fowls of the air, has an epicurean morsel—a parson's nose; and on this oily midnight my spirit revels and is glad.'" It would be difficult to match this delightful and racy comparison. This double sight, however, sometimes betrayed its possessor, as in the following instance: "The passing years had drunk a portion of the light from her eyes, and left their traces on her cheeks, as birds that drink at lakes leave their footprints on the margin." This is too good, it is hardly credible that such a thought and simile "floated double" into any one's mind.

Had Longfellow written nothing but his three prose works, he would have deserved a name in American letters, as much for the literary excellence of his books as for his services in breaking the way for an American knowledge of German authors. Upon the heels of this supposition naturally comes the wish that he had given us more prose; most people would willingly exchange the *New England Tragedies* for another *Hyperion*, and would give the *Divine Tragedy* to boot. But after 1849 he never turned his pen to prose.

Longfellow's poetry is very varied in character, he has tried his wine in every kind of vessel, and, as has been said, it is very unequal in quality. Leigh Hunt said that authors must sift their own works to save posterity the trouble of choice—"posterity is so rich and idle"—but Longfellow constantly added to his volumes and never subtracted from them. The selected poems of Byron, Wordsworth, and Shelley have lately appeared, to present their authors in a fair light; but each of these was more independent of the critic's selective art than was the author of "Excelsior" and the *Saga of King Olaf*. With all deference to the great popularity of many of his poems, and after due consideration of the subtleties of American eulogy, it seems clear enough that much of Longfellow's poetry has little or no permanent value. An occasional nod may be forgiven even to Homer, but Longfellow nods too often. Versification was so easy to him, and his sympathy was so much more prompt than discriminating—as shown, for instance, in his toleration of bores and the ridiculous apology he once gave for it—"Who would be kind to them if I were not?"—that he seldom refused an invitation to write, or checked his own impulse to do so. The latest illustration of this is afforded by his action when the children of Cambridge presented him on his birthday with a chair made from the wood of the "spreading chestnut-tree." It was a pretty gift, and might have been fittingly acknowledged, one would think, in a simple letter. Longfellow, however, composed a string of verses, and caused a thousand copies to be printed and distributed to the children. It is all very well to say that he thus gave pleasure to the children of Cambridge, and that they would treasure the lines addressed to them by the great poet; but there is a good sense, as well as a bad one, in which a man may write with a view to his biographers, and even if we admit that "this splendid ebon throne" is an appropriate epithet for an ordinary black arm-chair, it is still difficult to understand how a man of Longfellow's good taste could so far forget himself as to go out of his way to demand in pompous verse "by what right divine" he could claim a thing that had just been given to him.

With epic poetry properly so called, Longfellow had, of course, nothing to do. He wrote, however, two long poems which have been termed miniature epics. These are *Evangeline* and the *Song of Hiawatha*. The first is a middle member of an interesting literary pedigree. J. H. Voss was the creator of the modern idyllic epic, his *Luise* appearing in 1795. Goethe's *Hermann und Dorothea* was published in 1797, and its relation to the preceding work may be determined from what Goethe said of Voss some time afterwards. "There are few who have had such an influence as he upon the higher German culture. One who is so permeated with his worth as I am scarcely knows how to honour his memory too much." In 1847 *Evangeline* appeared, and although I know of no direct evidence to connect it with Goethe's poem, Longfellow's extensive acquaintance with German literature, and the similarity of the two works, make the source of his inspiration reasonably certain. In 1848 the *Bothie of Tober-na-Vuolich* was published, and we have Clough's own testimony concerning its origin. He wrote to Emerson, "Will you convey to Mr. Longfellow the fact that it was a reading of his *Evangeline* aloud to my mother and sister which, coming after a reperusal of the Iliad, occasioned this outbreak of hexameters." So we have a direct line of descent, *Luise*, *Hermann und Dorothea*, *Evangeline*, *The Bothie of Tober-na-Vuolich*.

Evangeline was Longfellow's favourite of his own poems, and yet he was indebted for the story almost as it stands, to Hawthorne, with whom it was not original. Under the date of October 24th, 1838, the story is sketched out in Hawthorne's note-book, with the statement that it was given to him by "H. L. C——" (Conolly), who had it from a French Canadian. James T. Fields tells how Hawthorne made it over to Longfellow for a poem, not caring much for it himself for a story, and finding that it struck Longfellow's fancy. The groundwork of the poem Longfellow got, he once said, from a visit to the poor-house in Philadelphia. Strange to say, he was never in Nova Scotia, where the scene is laid, but drew his information about the life of the people from the Abbé Raynal, and his history from Haliburton. This work did more to establish Longfellow's reputation than any of his previous ones, and if, as has been said by one of the profoundest of critics, poems are to be judged by the state of mind in which they leave the reader, the high place which *Evangeline* occupies in popular esteem is justly awarded to it; for its chaste style and homely imagery, with its sympathetic and occasionally dramatic story, produce a refined and elevated impression, and present a beautiful and invigorating picture of "affection that hopes, and endures, and is patient," of "the beauty and strength of woman's devotion."

Longfellow's countrymen were proud of his success with *Evangeline*, but they were still more delighted when the *Song of Hiawatha* appeared, for it seemed to them to herald the advent of the long-looked-for American poet, the messiah of their national literature. At last they found themselves possessed of a poem which owed nothing to previous literature or European tradition, but sang of the prairie, the mountains, the rivers, the races, and the mythology of their own great West.

The success of the book was enormous: ten thousand copies were sold in five weeks, and fifty thousand in eighteen months. By many foreign critics, too, *Hiawatha* was enthusiastically received. M. Emile Montégut, for instance, wrote of it in the *Revue des Deux Mondes* as follows: "Puisse le succès de cette œuvre charmante persuader à M. Longfellow de marcher dans cette voie sans être tenté d'en sortir désormais!" Even Mr. Rossetti said it was "made for posterity and permanence;" Mr. Bright has recently recommended it as a remedy for sickness and loneliness; and at least two of the English reviews in their obituary notices assigned to it the highest place among Longfellow's poems. And in the memorial article in the *Atlantic Monthly*, Mr. O. B. Frothingham expresses contemporary American opinion as follows: "*Hiawatha* is, not merely as a work of art, but as a moral achievement, greatly in advance of *Evangeline*. It is, in our opinion, the poet's masterpiece, the fullest expression of his mind. Theme and treatment perfectly correspond; the former calling forth all the poet's peculiar talent; the latter taxing, yet exquisitely illustrating, his literary skill."

Now, we have here either a magnificent poetical work in *Hiawatha*, or else a vast amount of misplaced admiration. I think the latter is the case. At any rate the question will bear examination.

Longfellow believed that he had found in the writings of Schoolcraft, the historian of the Indian tribes of North America, the materials for a new epic, an American saga. It was natural that a poet with sympathetic knowledge of the previous spontaneous epics of the world, and who had just safely accomplished one long poetic flight, should seek eagerly for the legendary material to enable him to make another and longer one. But it is trite to suggest that the *Heimskringla* and the *Nibelungenlied* are as impossible to us as the Doric temple or the Gothic cathedral: both factors in their creation are gone—the spirit which could produce them and the need which they satisfied. Instead of holding, therefore, that the Iroquois tradition of Hiawatha found its voice in Longfellow as the Sagas found theirs in some unknown minstrel, or as the Hebrew word came to the prophet, I am inclined to think that Longfellow looked about him for material for a poem which should be like the old poems, and thought he had found it in the Iroquois legend, and that, therefore, Mr. Lowell throws out a true hint when he speaks of Longfellow as "driven to take refuge among the red men."

The most striking feature in this "Indian Edda," as its author called it, is the metre. This is simple enough in itself, being nothing but a trochaic dimeter, but it is remarkable as being chosen for an English poem of some five thousand six hundred lines. It is difficult to understand how any one could have thought that the machine-like monotony of over twenty thousand successive trochees would be anything but extremely wearisome; but it is much more difficult to understand how any one can read them without finding out the fact. The beautiful flexibility of Greek, and the opportunities it afforded for the building up of words and sentences delightful in themselves as music and intelligence combined, made such metres beautiful in the hands of Greek writers, but the English language is not sufficiently malleable and musical to warrant us in dropping the "ornaments of rhyme" and confining ourselves to a measure so extremely simple. The monotony of the versification of *Hiawatha* is revealed by the first lines, and is present, with a few exceptions, throughout the whole poem; and even these exceptions are passages which are beautiful, not because of the metre, but in spite of it. In reading them one does not notice the metre, and they would be equally effective

if printed as prose. A curious defence of the metre of *Hiawatha* has been made by a French critic: "La mélodie des vers, rapide et monotone, ressemble singulièrement aux voix de la nature, qui ne se fatigue jamais de répéter toujours les mêmes sons." This is ingenious, but inadequate, for the sounds of nature are not monotonous, but infinitely varied; it would be just as true to say that nature's colouring is monotonous because the forest is all green. The forest green is beautiful because of its infinite variety of tints and play of light, and the sounds of nature are entrancing because they are never constant; the noise of the waterfall changes every moment, and even the "burly, dozing humble-bee" sweeps the whole gamut as he approaches or recedes. The cuckoo, too,—an excellent illustration, as his note is not a bad trochee,—understands the rhetorical value of the pause: it is terrible to think of him crying "cuckoo" twenty thousand times.

There is, however, a much graver charge to be brought against *Hiawatha*. The poem, as a whole, is without interest. The character of Hiawatha is nothing worth mentioning, and the deeds by which he educates his brethren and frees them from oppression do not arouse our sympathy in any way; the whole story is little better than an Indian nursery tale. Longfellow has, too, drawn so freely upon the uncouth redskin dialect that he has made much of his work positively ludicrous. Pau-Puk-Keewis, Gitche-Gumee, Sheshebwug, Mudjekeewis, Baimwawa, Sah-sah-je-wun, Kah-gah-gee, the Puk-widjies, the Jeebi,—how could any one write a great poem with such *dramatis personæ* as these? The work contains, of course, occasional quaint and pretty passages, and one or two pieces of really vigorous writing—e.g., the beginning of the nineteenth canto,—but as a whole it seems an example of genuine poetic power and sympathy misapplied, and can hardly have failed, by its immense circulation, to exert a weakening influence on American literature.

Of all forms of poetry the lyric is pre-eminently the one which should rest upon what has been called the "autobiographic basis," and almost every one of Longfellow's lyrics has this characteristic. The autobiographic basis, however, is of two kinds, personal and local. The personal is seen when the lyric has its origin in some deep-rooted emotion in the poet's breast, love, disappointment, jealousy, anger; the local basis is when the lyric is the expression of the poet's emotional relationship to some merely local interest, a view, a house, or even a person. In many cases it is difficult to draw the line between the two, but when the distinction can be clearly made there is no doubt that the former is the higher and greater kind of poetic inspiration; its interest is common to all men, and not half universal and half local. A glance through the index of Longfellow's collected works shows that the autobiographic basis of the majority of his lyrics is the local one. "To the River Charles," "The Belfry of Bruges," "The Arsenal at Springfield," "The Lighthouse," "The Fire of Driftwood," "The Herons of Elmwood," "The Bridge,"—these are specimens of the subjects that attracted his pen. Some concrete interest is necessary to call forth the sympathy of the less cultivated reader, the man who is accustomed to have each of his thoughts linked to a fact, and hence the welcome which these lyrics have received from those who form the majority of our society. They exhibit no sudden transport when a poetic idea reveals itself; none of the insight of great passion; little of the suggestion of an original view. Given a man of healthy temperament, of tender heart, of much cultivation, with a genuine poetic faculty, whose life had been passed in circumstances of comfort and uneventful privacy, and these are just the lyrics that he would naturally write. This is not saying so little as might at first appear, for such a coincidence of man and circumstances is rare in our time. And though there is much of Longfellow's lyrical poetry that is commonplace enough, there is not wanting some that belongs to a high order of verse.

A poet who was the reflection and echo of our common life to such an extent as Longfellow would naturally find much of his inspiration take the corresponding poetical form, the epic-lyric. "King Witlaf's Drinking Horn" and the "Wreck of the Hesperus" are among the best, as they are the best known of his ballads. "Paul Revere's Ride" suggests and can sustain comparison with Browning's "How They Brought the Good News from Ghent." But by far his best single epic-lyric piece is the "Skeleton in Armour," a splendid and powerful piece of versification. There is nothing in English that has caught the old Norse spirit better than Longfellow's *Saga of King Olaf*, the Musician's tale at the Wayside Inn. It is the single time when Longfellow has been strong, when he has shown real passion. With great variety of style and metre he has wrought the *Heimskringla* into an animated and impulsive English poem. The best of the twenty-two divisions of the Saga are "Thora of Rimol," "The Wraith of Odin," "Thangbrand the Priest," "King Olaf's Christmas," and "King Olaf and Earl Sigvald." The *Tales of a Wayside Inn* exhibit all the marked features of Longfellow's poetical work. The following key to the persons who figure in them was given to me by the late Mr. John Owen, Longfellow's first publisher and life-long Bohemian friend: The Landlord, Lyman Howe (the scene is laid in the old Howe Tavern, near Sudbury, Massachusetts); the Student, Henry Ware Wales; the Spanish Jew, Isaac Edraeles; the Sicilian, Luigi Monti; the Musician, Ole Bull; the Poet, Thomas W. Parsons; the Theologian, Samuel Longfellow. Three of these persons are still living. It is perhaps hardly necessary to add that their meeting under such circumstances is wholly fictitious; they were not even all mutually acquainted, and their only common ground was in the poet's imagination. It is much to be doubted if most of them—possibly including the author himself—ever stopped at the Wayside Inn at all.

The sonnet was a form of poetical expression well suited to Longfellow's genius. So far as his muse bore him he was accustomed to think clearly; he had great power of imagination, and an accurate aim in literary matters. Besides these he was possessed of a characteristic which is perhaps the one most conspicuous by its absence from the school of poetry prevalent at the present day, viz. a constant self-control. A dithyramb would have been impossible to him; he never lost sight of the artistic quality of the work he had in hand, and the freest of his songs exhibits a complete subordination of the parts. Just as in the *prestissimo* each finger of the pianist falls accurately upon the proper note, so, in the most rapid utterance of which the sonnet-writer is capable, accuracy of accent, syllable, contrasted rhyme, quatrain, and octave, must be strictly secured. To this difficult end self-control is the one indispensable attribute.

As we might expect, most of Longfellow's sonnets are in the legitimate form, and in a majority of cases they preserve the due separation of the quatrains, an observance which is easily, and therefore frequently, neglected. He had, too, the power to make the sonnet sing, one of its primary attributes, and one which is utterly absent from many of the complicated sonnets of the last few years. It is, however, probable that the readers of Longfellow's sonnets will be conscious of missing something to which they are accustomed, and on reflection will find that something to be richness and luxury of imagery and language. The self-control, however, which is demanded by the sonnet gives it necessarily a certain asceticism; it is a finely-chiselled,

well-fitted work of art, and we miss a familiar luxuriance in sonnets which answer this description, only because our taste has been vitiated by constant reading of bad examples. Let any one who doubts this compare a couple of sonnets from the earlier English poets—say Ben Jonson, or Shakspere, or even Wordsworth—with any of the sonnets of D. G. Rossetti, for instance, and see if he does not find the latter by comparison cloying, burning, overladen, and tangled. Leigh Hunt's fourth rule for the sonnet was, "It must not have a speck of obscurity." One may almost say that half our contemporary sonnets have not a speck of transparency.

It is questionable whether the English language contains a series of six original sonnets equal in every point to those which are prefixed to Longfellow's translation of the *Divina Commedia*. They are perfect in form, splendid and yet moderate in language, and full of scholarly suggestion; they exhibit a distinct progression of thought, and, though they are of great virility, their singing quality never relaxes. The sonnets on "Giotto's Tower," "Night," "President Garfield," "My Books," "Possibilities," the pathetic "Victor and Vanquished," and several of his earlier ones, exhibit Longfellow's best work, and are surpassed by few modern sonnets, if by any.

If, in addition to a knowledge of many languages, a poet possesses a true gift of song, the same qualities which make him a good sonneteer will make him a good translator. The same clearness, subordination of himself to the style of his model, constant self-control in avoiding unwarranted addition or subtraction—these are the indispensables to good translation. To reproduce the total impression made by the original, with only the slightest possible departure from exact transcription—to turn literalism into realism—should be the translator's ideal. An example of such a translation is furnished by Strodtmann's rendering of Tennyson's "Bugle Song," beginning, *Es fällt der Strahl auf Burg und Thal*. Longfellow, by his extensive linguistic knowledge and skill with rhyme and metres, was exceptionally well fitted for the work of translation, and he employed his gifts to such good purpose that it is not too much to say of him that, as a translator, he had no living rival.

Every one knows that it is much more difficult to translate a folk-song well than an artistic poem, and every one who is familiar with the rollicking side of German university life remembers the never-failing *Kneiplied* of sweet *Aennchen von Tharau*, and what a really large place it holds in the hearts of the students, each of whom believes in its peculiar applicability to a certain *Aennchen* of his own, present or to come. So a few stanzas from it will serve to show Longfellow's facility. He translated it directly from the Low German of its author, Simon Dach; the following German words are Herder's translation, by which it is generally known in Germany. This will explain the few discrepancies.

> Aennchen von Tharau hat wieder ihr Herz
> Auf mich gerichtet in Lieb und in Schmerz.
>
> . . .
>
> Krankheit, Verfolgung, Betrübniss und Pein
> Soll unsrer Liebe Verknotigung sein.
> Würdest du gleich einmal von mir getrennt,
> Lebtest da, wo man die Sonne kaum kennt;
> Ich will dir folgen durch Wälder, durch Meer,
> Eisen und Kerker und feindliches Heer.
> Aennchen von Tharau, mein Licht, meine Sonn',
> Mein Leben schliesst sich um deines herum.
>
> Annie of Tharaw her heart once again,
> To me has surrendered in joy and in pain.
>
> . . .

Oppression and sickness, and sorrow and pain,
Shall be to our true love as links to the chain.
Should'st thou be torn from me to wander alone,
In a desolate land where the sun is scarce known,
Through forests I'll follow, and where the sea flows,
Through ice, and through iron, through armies of
    foes.
Annie of Tharaw, my light and my sun,
The threads of our two lives are woven in one.

Longfellow's great work as a translator, however, and perhaps the great work of his life, is his three splendid volumes of the *Divina Commedia*. His election to the position of the first President of the Dante Society at Cambridge—a position in which Mr. James Russell Lowell has succeeded him—was a fitting recognition of this work. As early as 1839, in his *Voices of the Night*, he published translations of a few of the chosen passages of the poem, but it was not until 1863, when in need of some anodyne for the shock caused by the terrible death of his wife, that he determined to attempt a version of the entire *Divine Comedy*. The people of Florence had given notice of their approaching celebration of the sixth centenary of Dante's birth, and had invited the co-operation of all lovers of the poet, so there was a special appropriateness in the time of his work. The translation of the *Inferno* was completed and sent to the printer. He then invited two of his intimate friends, Mr. Charles Eliot Norton, Professor of the History of Art, at Harvard University—the *chiarissimo signore* and *profondo cognoscitore di Dante* to whom Witte dedicated his *variorum* edition of the *Vita Nuova*—and Mr. Lowell, to assist him in the delicate work of final revision. Mr. Norton has given the following account of their meetings:—"Every Wednesday evening Mr. Lowell and I met in Mr. Longfellow's study to listen while he read a canto of his translation from the proof-sheet. We paused over every doubtful passage, discussed the various readings, considered the true meaning of obscure words and phrases, sought for the most exact equivalent of Dante's expression, objected, criticised, praised, with a freedom that was made perfect by Mr. Longfellow's absolute sweetness, simplicity, and modesty, and by the entire confidence which existed between us." Ten copies of an *édition de luxe* of the translation of the *Inferno* were printed, bearing the special dedication, *In Commemorazione del Secentesimo Anniversario della Nascita di Dante Alighieri*, and five of them were despatched to Florence as a New World contribution to the festival of May, 1865. The two remaining parts were prepared with the same care, and the three volumes of the complete translation appeared early in 1867. With what sympathy Longfellow performed his great task may be learned from the following extract from a private note which he wrote while at work on Dante:—"How different from this gossip is the divine Dante with which I begin the morning! I write a few lines every day before breakfast. It is the first thing I do—the morning prayer, the key-note of the day."

To give anything like an adequate account of this translation, and to cite passages for comparison with the original, would take up far too much space. For the same reason a number of eulogistic reviews which are before me must all be condensed into the statement that the work has received the commendation of almost every famous Dante scholar, and, with very few exceptions, of every literary authority. There can be no doubt that Longfellow's presentation of the "medieval miracle of song" is by far the best that we have, and probably the best that we shall have in English, and that it will take final rank among the greatest achievements of American letters.

To raise again here the old question of Longfellow's originality would be to depart widely from the intention of discussing only the unfamiliar aspects of his work. The best thing that has been said upon the subject, and one which contains more truth than do all the pages of literary comparisons, is the following remark of a German critic:—"Besondere Originalität wird man bei Longfellow vergeblich suchen, wenn man sie nicht in seiner bezaubernden Gemüthstiefe erblicken will." "We shall look in vain for any special originality in Longfellow, if we are not willing to perceive it in his fascinating depth of heart." This is the whole truth in the matter: Longfellow possessed an aboriginal humanity of disposition; his spirit seemed to go back from the modern complication of motives to the sources of human feeling.

Two days after Longfellow's death a friend of mine who knew him very well wrote to me as follows:—"It is surprising how the man has taken hold of the hearts of all. I have never heard him say anything very striking, or very grand or beautiful, yet his face is always associated in my mind with qualities partaking of all three. He had not a majestic presence to stir you into great feeling for himself personally, yet one could not see his face, nor see or know his daily life and ways, without being deeply inspired by the simplicity, purity, and entire unselfishness of his nature." This is an admirable statement of the common experience. The smaller acts and sayings of his life, assumedly the best indexes of a man's character, showed the "invincible sweetness" of the underlying disposition. I remember that he told me once that a Chicago lady had sent him a packet containing two hundred of her visiting-cards, with the request that he would put his autograph upon each of them, as she was about to give a reception to her friends, and wished to present them with some pleasing memento of the occasion. I expressed the hope that the lady's cards had promptly found their way to his waste-basket. "Oh, no!" he said in a tone of surprise, and almost of reproach, and added, as if it were the most natural thing in the world, "I returned them with a note, saying that the many demands upon my time made it quite impossible for me to do as she asked." Mr. William Winter has told us that when he once alluded to Poe's attacks upon Longfellow—mostly contemptible fabrications—the latter only said gravely, "My work seemed to give him much trouble, first and last; but Mr. Poe is dead, and I am alive, and still writing, and that is the end of the matter." Then he picked up a volume of Poe, and particularly commended certain pieces. And one who knew Longfellow intimately all his life has just said, "Nothing human that I ever saw exceeded the tenacity of his friendship." In the light of these anecdotes it is not surprising to learn of the universal affection that was felt for him, or to find one reviewer saying, "How like a benediction on our homes his music falls!"

All this bears testimony to the correctness of the German critic in attributing Longfellow's originality to his *Gemüthstiefe*, or depth of heart; and to those who hold with Lotze and his school that the choicest parts of our experience are those that come to us from the *Gemüth*, this originality will seem one of no mean order.

In conclusion, setting aside for the moment what it has been the special object of this study to show, namely, that, besides writing a quantity of commonplace verse, Longfellow has done really first-rate work in several fields, and that he is, therefore, entitled to a higher rank than that to which the critics have customarily assigned him; and admitting all that any one wishes about art for its own sake, we must still recognise and honour his position as a teacher of the people. It is certain that multitudes of people have received direct help from Longfellow's poetry—their lives have gained new sentiment, their sorrows have been made less dismal, they have been strengthened in their efforts to live decently.

Longfellow preserved to the end the vigorous and cheery tone of his song; not even such a subject as "Morituri Salutamus" could dampen it. While some men of genius in their worship at what one of their own number has called the "altar to the unknown god of unachieved desire," are writhing in their efforts to parade all the sensuousness of which human nature is capable, this simple man with his sweetness of life— a "sweetness as of home-made bread"—must not be allowed to pass away without our reverent recognition. His was not the gift of "song which shall spur you to soar," but we may be confident that whenever the army of true bards is mustered, the suffrage of future ages will not grudge him the fulfilment of his modest hope—"to have my place preserved among the rest."

H. E. SCUDDER
From "Longfellow's Art"
Atlantic, March 1887, pp. 399–409

It is customary to speak of Longfellow as if his Americanism was an accident, his natural disposition leading him really to an emigration in thought and sentiment to the other side of the Atlantic. In point of fact, he passed through the experience of many ingenuous American youth. He ardently desired an introduction to the Old World; he entered quickly and warmly into the spirit of the past, but instead of losing himself in this spirit, he found himself; he took his spiritual bearings, and as a result set his face more positively westward than could have been possible had he never gone through the process of orientation. It is a superficial judgment which determines the nationality of a literary artist by his choice of subjects alone. Longfellow in Europe jotting down in his diary subjects drawn from life in the Maine woods was no more essentially American than he was essentially European when he was sitting in his study in Brunswick and writing *Outre-Mer*. The residence in Europe made him eager for his American life; the return to America brought back with a rush the recollection of European scenes. In both cases the artist was employing the convenient perspective of time and space. What was remote shaped itself more definitely into picturesque relations to his mind; only to the student just returned from Europe, after three years of incessant occupation with new and suggestive forms of life and art, his own personal experience offers so rich and tumultuous a collection of themes that all else is for the time held in abeyance.

This was markedly true in Longfellow's case, because his mind by natural disposition busied itself with the secondary rather than with the primary facts of nature and society. He was born and trained until he was nineteen in a society and amidst scenes exceedingly simple, almost elemental, indeed. No one can read the chapters in his *Life* which deal with his home in Portland and his education at Bowdoin College, especially no one can have recollection of the primitive, provincial period of New England which had its culmination just before the first steamer crossed the Atlantic, without perceiving how much had been eliminated from the American variation of the English mind by the absence for two centuries of familiar contact with university, cathedral, castle, theatre, gallery, and barracks. The brick college, the wooden meeting-house, the merchant's square-built house, the singing-school, the peripatetic Greek slave, the muster,—all these marked the limits of expression, and by consequence the strength of reacting

influence. The effect upon individual minds differed according to the original constitution of those minds. Hawthorne, gathering blueberries under the pines of Brunswick with his friend Bridge, was subjected to very much the same influences as Longfellow. He went out into the world later, it is true, than his great contemporary, but the author of *The Scarlet Letter* did not need to draw his breath of inspiration from any mediæval chronicle or under the shadow of Strasburg Cathedral; an old newspaper in the Salem Custom-House was enough for him. Longfellow, on the other hand, was writing of Italian scenery and Venetian gondoliers when his visits to Italy and Venice had been only in boats with sails rigged from the leaves of books. Even when treating of distinctly American subjects, as in the poem of "The Indian Hunter," he borrowed his expression from traditions of English poetry:—

> The foot of the reaper moved slow on the lawn,
> And the sickle cut down the yellow corn;
> The mower sung loud by the meadow-side,
> Where the mists of evening were spreading wide;
> And the voice of the herdsmen came up by the lea,
> And the dance went round by the greenwood tree.

Was all that the result of observations on a Maine farm? No; it indicates a mind sensitive to poetic influences as derived not so much from direct contact with nature as from indirect acquaintance through books. It is doubtful if there is a single line in the poems written before his journey to Europe which describes an aspect of nature specifically noted by the poet, unless it be two or three lines in his poem "Autumn," where he says:—

> The purple finch,
> That on wild cherry and red cedar feeds,
> A winter bird, comes with its plaintive whistle,
> And pecks by the witch-hazel;

while there are repeated instances of entirely second-hand reflections of scenes which were impossible to his eye, as when, in his poem "To Ianthe," he says:—

> As I mark the moss-grown spring
> By the twisted holly,

and,

> Twisted close the ivy clings
> To the oak that's hoarest.

Even when dealing with a slight historic fact, as in the "Hymn of the Moravian Nuns of Bethlehem," he translates the entire incident into terms of foreign import. The dying flame of day shoots its ray through the chancel; the glimmering tapers shed faint light on the cowled head; the burning censer swings before the altar; the nuns' sweet hymn is sung low in the dim, mysterious aisle. Yet the poem, masquerading in foreign dress, has a native fire and an enthusiasm kindled by the thought of personal sacrifice in a great cause. So, too, in the "Burial of the Minnisink," where the red chief is only a mere transliteration of mediæval knight, the poetic passion flames forth in a single bold phrase at the end of the poem:—

> They buried the dark chief; they freed
> Beside the grave his battle steed;
> And swift an arrow cleaved its way
> To his stern heart! One piercing neigh
> Arose, and on the dead man's plain,
> The rider grasps his steed again.

It may be said, therefore, with some confidence that Longfellow's mental growth was accelerated, not changed, by his study in Europe; that the bent of his genius was toward the artistic use of the reflected forms of nature and of the product of human forces; that he sought instinctively for those expressions of life which had color and richness, not for those which had elemental significance; and that, failing to note such expressions in the life about him, he endowed the scenes which he depicted with qualities borrowed from an older, more complex civilization. The very sober needlewomen of the Moravian sisterhood were seen through painted glass; the squaws who sold baskets in Portland became a dark-haired virgin train, chanting the death dirge of the slain; and it is only an anthropologist, accustomed to the meagre results of an exploration among mounds, who will at first glance detect the plain truth concerning the savage, when he reads:—

> A dark cloak of the roebuck's skin
> Covered the warrior, and within
> Its heavy folds the weapons, made
> For the hard toils of war, were laid;
> The cuirass, woven of plaited reeds,
> And the broad belt of shells and beads.

A Norse viking stood in the light of an Oldtown Indian, when the poet was sketching.

It was a mind thus sensitive to rich color and complex form, and restrained from large opportunities during its adolescence, that a three years' wandering through Europe brought a fullness of experience which enlarged and strengthened it, and not merely supplied it with new objects of exercise. Why was it that, after writing verse with pleasure for two or three years, Longfellow should suddenly drop the occupation, declare his poetic career finished, and devote himself assiduously to prose? And why, to anticipate a further development, did he then return to prose deliberately but once more after another decade? From 1824 to 1826 he was writing those poems which are classed as juvenile or earlier poems. From 1831 to 1838 he wrote the bulk of his miscellaneous prose and *Outre-Mer* and *Hyperion*. In 1838 he resumed his poetic career with "Flowers" and "A Psalm of Life," and in 1848 he wrote *Kavanagh*.

I have half answered the first question already. When he went to Europe in 1826, it was ostensibly to qualify himself for the post of professor of modern languages in Bowdoin College. Immediately, to use the energetic phrase, his eyes were opened, and in seeing the rich deposit of an old civilization, where history had for centuries been building a house for the imagination, he was conscious of power, he found himself. Yet he needed time for the thorough orientation which his nature demanded. There are some poets who become naturalized in antiquity as soon as they land after their first voyage. Keats was one of these. There are others who, if they take out their papers early, do not at once exercise the rights of citizenship, and Longfellow was one of these. The period between his first emigration to Europe, in 1826, and his final settlement at Cambridge, in 1836, was one of accumulation and disposition of his treasures. The circumstances of his outer life, his successive journeys for specific purpose, his brief trial of teaching at Bowdoin, his experiments in literature, corresponded with the internal adjustment of his mind to its vocation. It was his apprentice time, and only when *Hyperion* was executed did he feel within himself that he had become a master.

His prose during this decade indicates very clearly his spiritual and artistic growth. He had come, by travel and study, into possession of a great store of material, the value of which he was ready to discern. It took him ten years, however, to make all this material really his own; he began the process by simple description, and prose was the natural vehicle. His letters show how quickly he caught the spirit of what he saw, and a comparison of *Outre-Mer* with them indicates the presence in his mind of a distinct literary sense. One may prefer the directness of the letters, but cannot help seeing that when Longfellow set up the same material in his book he was studying the form of presentation, and recognized that literature was something other than letter-writing. Along with and following *Outre-Mer* were those special studies of modern language and literature which confessed the student rather than the traveler; and then came *Hyperion*, in which the imaginative constructive power began to reassert itself, and all the aspects of life and literature which had met the eye of the traveler and student were considered by the poetic mind and the creative genius. As has been so often pointed out, the tale is a rescript, only slightly disguised, of the poet's spiritual as well as external experience; but only when one considers it as the final outcome of a period of mental reconstruction does one apprehend the entire significance of the work. It marks the completion of Longfellow's apprenticeship to literature, and, like most such critical works, it is as prophetic as it is historical.

When, shortly after the publication of *Hyperion*, Longfellow suddenly resolved to publish a volume of poems, it may be fairly assumed that he was in no sense renouncing prose, but only thinking of himself as an active *littérateur*, who was not shut up to any one form of expression. He was not yet, indeed, so conscious of his destiny that he could not outline, a few days later, a plan of literary work which embraced a history of English poetry, a novel, a series of sketches, and only one poem. His resolution to issue *Voices of the Night* undoubtedly sprang from the growing recognition of his poetic faculty, and from the fact that he had for some time past been testing his power. In truth, one of the most interesting phases of the apprenticeship to literature which Longfellow passed through was the manner in which he kept alive that spark of poetic fire which, feeble enough in his adolescence, was yet genuine. In the same letter in which he wrote to his sister, "My poetic career is finished," he attempted a translation of a lovely little Portuguese song, and as soon as he began his series of prose writings he began also that series of translations which would alone have given him the name of poet. It was necessary, in the course of his critical work, to give examples of verse, and he was thus constantly impelled to use the metrical form; then when he essayed the romance form, and cast his scenes largely in Germany, the very structure of his work called for those "flowers of song" which were the essential expression of the life which he was translating into artistic mode.

Throughout his life Longfellow found in the work of translation a gentle stimulus to his poetic faculty, and resorted to it when he wished to quicken his spirit. "I agree with you entirely," he writes to Freiligrath, November 24, 1843, "in what you say about translations. It is like running a ploughshare through the soil of one's mind; a thousand germs of thought start up (excuse this agricultural figure), which otherwise might have lain and rotted in the ground. Still, it sometimes seems to me like an excuse for being lazy,—like leaning on another man's shoulder." This is, however, but a partial explanation of the place which translation held in Longfellow's art. One must go back to the very nature of this poet to see why it is that so large a proportion of his poetical work was either direct translation or a reconstruction from foreign material. In the recent complete edition of his writings, three of the nine volumes of poetry are given to the translation of Dante, with, to be sure, the voluminous apparatus of notes and illustrations, while of another volume about two thirds of the matter consist of translations from various languages. But the longest section of *Tales of a Wayside Inn*, the Musician's Tale of the *Saga of King Olaf*, is scarcely other than a paraphrase; "The Mother's Ghost," in the same book, is openly from the Danish; and *Christus, Judas Maccabœus,* and *Michael Angelo* are largely indebted to other forms of literature for their very phrases. It would not be difficult for one, running through the entire body of poems, to find in those relating to foreign subjects a constant indirect reference to existing literary material. Not only so, but in such poems as *The Courtship of Miles Standish* and *Evangeline* the scaffolding which the poet used could easily be put up again by the historical student; of the *Tales of a Wayside Inn,* only one is in any peculiar sense the poet's invention; while *Hiawatha* is Schoolcraft translated into poetry.

It is when one enlarges the conception of the word "translation" that one perceives the value as well as the limitations of Longfellow's art. He was a consummate translator, because the vision and faculty divine which he possessed was directed toward the reflection of the facts of nature and society, rather than toward the facts themselves. He was like one who sees a landscape in a Claude Lorraine glass; by some subtle power of the mirror everything has been composed for him. Thus, when he came to use the rich material of history, of poetry, and of other arts, Longfellow saw these in forms already existing, and his art was not so much a reconstruction out of crude material as a representation, a rearrangement, in his own exquisite language, of what he found and admired. He was first of all a composer, and he saw his subjects in their relations rather than in their essence. To tell over again old tales, to reproduce in forms of delicate fitness the scenes and narratives which others had invented,—this was his delight; for in doing this he was conscious of his power and he worked with ease. Thus it is that the lyrical translations which he made in his student days are really his own poems; he rendered the foreign form in a perfect English form; his work in this regard was that of an engraver, not that of a photographer. He has himself said on the general subject of translation:—

> The great art of translating well lies in the power of rendering literally the words of a foreign author, while at the same time we preserve the spirit of the original. But how far one of these requisites of a good translation may be sacrificed to the other, how far a translator is at liberty to embellish the original before him while clothing it in a new language, is a question which has been decided differently by persons of different tastes. The sculptor, when he transfers to the inanimate marble the form and features of a living being, may be said not only to copy, but to translate. But the sculptor cannot represent in marble the beauty and expression of the human eye; and in order to remedy this defect as far as possible, he is forced to transgress the rigid truth of nature. By sinking the eye deeper, and making the brow more prominent above it, he produces a stronger light and shade, and thus gives to the statue more of the spirit and life of the original than he could have done by an exact copy. So, too, the translator.

In that which was technically translation, then, Longfellow made the foreign poems his own without sacrificing the truth of the originals; in that which was in a more general sense translation, the transfer, namely, of the spirit rather than the precise form of foreign art, he preserved the essential quality of what he took so perfectly as to lead many to underestimate the value of his own share in the result. Yet this fine sense of form, this intuitive perception of fitness, was an inestimable endowment of the artist, and is one of his passports to immortality. It is, however, most appreciable in those forms of art which are least dependent upon passion and more allied with the common experience; in dramatic art it has less significance. The use of the hexameter in *Evangeline* and the adoption of the *Kalevala* measure in *Hiawatha* are illustrations of how a great artist will choose forms perfectly fitted to his purpose, yet exceedingly dangerous in the hands of less skillful workmen. The pathway of English poetry is strewn with the bones of hexametrical beasts of burden, but Longfellow's *Evangeline* has made the journey to the present time with every prospect of carrying her rider to the gates of whatever blessed country of immunity from criticism awaits the poet. An interesting illustration of Longfellow's unerring sense of form is furnished by a trifling experiment which he made when engaged upon *Evangeline.* He records in his diary the completion of the second canto of Part II., and adds, "I tried a passage of it in the common rhymed English pentameter. It is the song of the mocking-bird:—

> Upon a spray that overhung the stream,
> The mocking-bird, awaking from his dream,
> Poured such delirious music from his throat
> That all the air seemed listening to his note.
> Plaintive at first the song began, and slow;
> It breathed of sadness, and of pain, and woe;
> Then, gathering all his notes, abroad he flung
> The multitudinous music from his tongue,—
> As, after showers, a sudden gust again
> Upon the leaves shakes down the rattling rain.

Taken by itself this verse falls agreeably on the ear, but it needs only a moment's thought to perceive that the story of Evangeline given in this measure would have been robbed of that lingering melancholy, that pathos of lengthening shadows, which resides in the hexameter as Longfellow has handled it. Something of all this may be seen even in the few lines of the poem which render the passage just given:—

> Then from a neighboring thicket the mocking-bird,
>   wildest of singers,
> Swinging aloft on a willow spray that hung o'er the
>   water,
> Shook from his little throat such floods of delirious
>   music
> That the whole air and the woods and the waves
>   seemed silent to listen.
> Plaintive at first were the tones and sad; then soaring
>   to madness
> Seemed they to follow or guide the revel of frenzied
>   Bacchantes.
> Single notes were then heard, in sorrowful, low
>   lamentation;
> Till, having gathered them all, he flung them abroad
>   in derision,
> As when, after a storm, a gust of wind through the
>   tree-tops
> Shakes down the rattling rain in a crystal shower on
>   the branches.

The limitations of the rhymed pentameter are clearly seen in a comparison of the two forms,—its limitations, and also its brief gain, for as the expression of a single moment the shorter form is more immediate in its operation. One catches the incident on the wing, instead of watching it slowly from inception to close, and I suspect that Longfellow may have been led to make this little experiment from a perception, as he wrote the hexameters, of the slight loss thereby sustained; if so, it is only another illustration of his exquisite sense of form.

The deliberate note which a poet strikes at the outset of his career may wisely be taken as indicative of his conscious judgment of his own vocation. Although, as we have seen, Longfellow grew into poetry through the exercise of translation, and by a decade of fruitful study acquired that mastery of form which fixed his place in literature as primarily an artist, it is equally true that the spirit which in youth at once chose poetry as expression was not changed, but only held in reserve through the formative period, and as soon as true maturity came broke forth once more in its native language. The "Prelude" which opens *Voices of the Night* and "L'Envoi" which closes the volume together disclose the poet's attitude toward his verse. He had gathered his recent poems, and chosen from his scattered translations and his earlier work such examples as came nearest to his more educated taste, and now proposed sending them out into the world. The very title of the volume hinted at the poet's mood. From the *Orestes* of Euripides he took his motto, and paraphrased it in the last stanza of the opening poem, "Hymn to the Night":—

> Peace! Peace! Orestes-like I breathe this prayer!
>   Descend with broad-winged flight,
> The welcome, the thrice-prayed for, the most fair,
>   The best-beloved Night!

The title *Voices of the Night* was first given to the poem "Footsteps of Angels," and all of the poems in the section, that is, all the poems which sprang from the new birth of poetry in his mind, strike a single key,—that of consolation; and so full is the poet of this sense of his poetic mission that he breaks forth at the close of his "Prelude" in these words, catching, characteristically, at a phrase of Sir Philip Sidney's:—

> Look, then, into thine heart, and write!
>   Yes, into Life's deep stream!
> All forms of sorrow and delight,
> All solemn Voices of the Night,
> That can soothe thee, or affright,
>   Be these henceforth thy theme.

There is no doubt that the poet's personal history in the period immediately preceding the appearance of "A Psalm of Life" and similar poems had much to do with this mood, and certainly this "theme" was by no means thenceforth his only one, although it reappeared frequently. It was natural, also, that his recent study of Jean Paul and other sentimental Germans should affect his choice and treatment of subjects, but there is a deeper, more fundamental account. Longfellow's nature was one of religious bent; his training had been that of the liberal school, and his interest in institutional, historical Christianity was rather æsthetic than inbred. He was also a man of deep reserve, and shrank not only from the disclosure of his intimate feeling, but generally from all revelation of sacred experience. He found in poetry a form of expression which permitted great freedom of speech without necessary reference to the personality of the author. Behind this almost transparent screen he could give full utterance to his own interior life, all the while appearing as the priest of humanity. It was not his own loss which he registered in "Resignation," although the occasion of the poem came from his own loss, but he generalized his grief, and took refuge in his office as spokesman for the crowd of sorrowful ones. Thus his personal outlook supplied the fervor of "A Psalm of Life," and infused into those lines of commonplaces a poetic spirit which makes them have the sound of a trumpet call; but the lines could not be tracked home to their author by any clue which his personal history might furnish. His home, his friends, the multitudinous experience in emotion of a sensitive nature, constantly supplied him with impulses to poetic expression, but, with very

rare exceptions, he spoke for himself and others, not for himself alone.

It was for this reason, in part, that he seized so readily upon the symbols of religion which he found in historic Christianity, and made use of them as forms in his poetic art. His delight in *The Golden Legend* was not only an artist's pleasure in rich color and form, but the pleasure of a religious nature working in material that allowed full scope to motives born of religious faith. The remark of Ruskin, often quoted, that "Longfellow, in his *Golden Legend*, has entered more closely into the temper of the monk, for good and for evil, than ever yet theological writer or historian, though they may have given their life's labor to the analysis," is in support of this view. Longfellow read the monk as he read all mediæval Christianity, from the vantage of a man sympathetic with religion in whatever sincere form it took, unembarrassed by any personal concern in the church which enshrined this particular faith, and keenly sensitive to whatever filled the imagination; while, as a poet, and especially as a poet of high order as composer, he was able to select just those noble and essential features which justify claims to reverence and admiration, and to oppose as shades those features which could be regarded as transient and accidental.

How important an element in Longfellow's art was his religious feeling appears when one considers the two works which dominated his life. I have said that the deliberate note which a poet strikes at the beginning of his career ought to be heeded for the disclosure which it makes of his consciousness of vocation; and the psalms of life which stirred Longfellow's spirit, as he once more found expression in poetry, showed him as a priest of humanity; they were indicative of a nature religious, emotional, reserved, yet eagerly desirous of translating his discovery of himself into broad, universal terms. The time from 1837 to 1841, marked in his life by the entrance upon residence at Cambridge, with its duties in teaching not yet irksome, was a period of quick poetic exercise and the trial of a variety of forms. It saw, besides the *Voices of the Night*, experiments in ballads, like "The Wreck of the Hesperus" and "The Skeleton in Armor"; a drama, *The Spanish Student*; his famous poem, "Excelsior," in which his art executed its most splendid feat in bridging the gulf between the sublime and the ridiculous; and it offers to the reader of his life a picture of spirited youth, weighted, indeed, by physical infirmity, but with the foot in the stirrup. Yet what was he thinking of? What was he planning to do? It was near the close of 1841 that he wrote in his diary:—

"This evening it has come into my mind to undertake a long and elaborate poem by the holy name of Christ, the theme of which would be the various aspects of Christendom in the Apostolic, Middle, and Modern Ages;" and he adds, characteristically using a quotation to express his own deepest thought, "And the swete smoke of the odorous incense whych came of the wholsome and fervent desyres of them that had fayth ascended up before God, out of the aungel's hande."

It was not till 1873 that the work as it now stands was published; and for those two and thirty years which represent almost the whole of his productive period the subject of the trilogy seems never to have been long absent from his mind. As I have said elsewhere, the theme, in its majesty, was a flame by night and a pillar of cloud by day, which led his mind in all its onward movement, and he esteemed the work which he had undertaken as the really great work of his life. His religious nature was profoundly moved by it, and the degree of doubt which attended every step of his progress marked the height of the endeavor which he put forth. There was nothing violent or eccentric in this sudden resolution. The entry in his journal, his biographer states, is the only one for that year, but his correspondence and the dates of his poems indicate clearly enough that the course of his mental and spiritual life was flowing in a direction which made this resolve a most natural and at the same time inspiring expression of his personality. He had been singing those psalms of life, triumphant, sympathetic, aspiring, which showed how strong a hold the ethical principle had of him; he had been steeping his soul in Dante; he had been moved by the tender ecclesiasticism of *The Children of the Lord's Supper*, and in recording a passage in the life of Christ had fancied himself a monk of the Middle Ages; while the whole tenor of his life and thought had shown how strong a personal apprehension he had of the divine in humanity.

In all that calls for delicate taste, a fine sense of fitness, and a skillful use of material already formed, this trilogy, like the other dramatic writings of Longfellow, has the poet's distinctive mark. In no part is this more clear than in *The Divine Tragedy*. A large portion of this drama is a deftly arranged mosaic of passages from the Evangelists, and the reader is at first quite as much struck with the rhythmical character of the King James version, which permits the words to fall so easily into the metrical order, as he is with the poet's skill in selection and adjustment. Probably the indifference shown by people in general to this drama is due in part to the feeling that nothing very novel was offered. In fact, Longfellow's reverence is sufficient to explain his lack of success. The desire which he had to accomplish the great work of *Christus* sprang not only from a poet's conception of the great movement involved in the subject, but from a deep sense of personal obligation. He approached this dramatic representation of the Christ somewhat as a painter might propose a Crucifixion as a votive offering, only that while the painter, in a great period of religious art, would be working in a perfectly well understood and accepted mode, this poet was artistically alone, and was not merely not helped, but actually hindered, by the prevalent religious temper. Thorwaldsen's Christ is an example of how an artist, unincumbered by too strong a personal feeling, was able to avail himself of the sympathy of his fellow-believers. The statue, repeated large and small, has become the type of Lutheran Protestant Christianity; but it has become so because its sculptor drew from Lutheranism his conception of the Christ, not so much as the Sufferer as the Friend. Longfellow, on the other hand, has added nothing to the New England conception of the Christ, because he neither met the requirements of the traditional faith which concentrated all the drama into one act, nor was able to precipitate the floating views of the liberal theology into so striking a dramatic form as to present a figure which would be recognized as the one that men were looking for. Perhaps that was too much to ask under any circumstances, and certainly, as a human hero of a drama, a more disappointing subject could not be found than the Man of Nazareth. At any rate, Longfellow was not the one to lay sacrilegious hands on the ark of his own hopes, and he could not as an artist deny himself as a reverent believer.

After all, the very presence of those qualities which we have observed in Longfellow's art seems to exclude the admission of that requisite to dramatic art,—passion. The graces which enrich the lyrical and narrative work are somewhat foreign from the drama. One needs to break bounds there, the bounds not of law, but of conventions, and the most orderly and reasonable succession of scenes can hardly put the reader into that state of forgetfulness of self which the drama should compel. There is one scene in *Judas Maccabæus*, where the

mother of the seven sons listens to the voices of her children as they undergo torments in the dungeon of the citadel, which is conceived with fine force; and yet, upon closer examination, one is obliged to concede that Longfellow was here displaying not so much dramatic conception as that admirable faculty in the adjustment and arrangement of forms already at hand to which I have several times referred.

The question was asked incidentally, on a previous page, why, after once abandoning prose at the end of a decade of work in it, Longfellow should return to prose after another decade given almost wholly to poetry. In 1838 *Hyperion* was written, and was followed at once by *Voices of the Night*. In 1848 *Kavanagh* appeared, and was the last piece of prose produced by the author. It stands in the midst also of a poetic period: *Evangeline* had just been finished, and *The Golden Legend* was begun shortly after *Kavanagh* was published, while the volume *The Seaside and the Fireside* collected a number of noticeable short poems.

It is probable that in writing *Kavanagh* Longfellow was obeying an impulse which often seizes artists, to lay at rest some ghost of a purpose that has pursued them. In his earliest plans for literary work, made on his first journey to Europe, he had outlined several sketches of American life. He made one or two essays in this direction after his return, but hid them away in annuals so carefully that only recently have they been unearthed. He was also somewhat in love with the character of a country schoolmaster, since it seemed to furnish the opportunity for combining the two elements of a recluse and a man of learning and taste. Then he could not help having his opinions about the national literature which was exercising the minds of the writers of his day, and as in *Hyperion* he had disclosed something of his personal life under the veil of a romance, so in *Kavanagh* he made a pleasing rural story the vehicle for carrying reflections and opinions which he wished once for all to be rid of. He had done with reviewing and prose work in general; whatever he did now must be in some form of art, and *Kavanagh* seems to have answered its purpose of materializing the floating forms which had been in its author's vision for many years. After this he used the economy of a wise artist, and worked in that material and in those forms which most completely satisfied the bent of his genius.

Yet *Kavanagh*, in another aspect, is interesting for its witness to a controlling principle in Longfellow's art. In ⟨a⟩ passage from *Michael Angelo* ⟨. . .⟩ the great sculptor is made to speak in his old age of

> The fever to accomplish some great work
> That will not let us sleep.

If there were any such fever in Longfellow's case, as I think the writing of *Michael Angelo* intimates, there certainly was from the beginning of his career a most healthy and normal activity of life, which stirred him to the achievement of great works, in distinction from the familiar, frequent exercise of the poetic faculty. That lovely lyric, "The Arrow and the Song," which might well stand as a prelude to Longfellow's shorter poems, is headed in the recent edition by an extract from the author's diary: "Before church wrote 'The Arrow and the Song,' which came into my mind as I stood with my back to the fire, and glanced on to the paper with arrow's speed. Literally an improvisation." The spontaneity of his art is again and again illustrated by just such lyrics as this, and no one can follow these shorter flights of song in connection with Longfellow's life without being impressed by the ease with which they sped from his bow and the directness of their aim. But to see this is to see only one side of Longfellow's artistic power. One needs also to keep in mind the seriousness with which he regarded his art, and the clear purpose always in his mind to build large and strong. It is not impossible that his several attempts at dramatic composition may have been due in part to this temper which impelled him to use all his strength, and to justify his gift of song by something more than swallow dips. *Hyperion* was necessary to his mind, though he might have broken up much of the work into independent, minor sketches. Scarcely had he been reborn to poetry before he was at work on *The Spanish Student*. He was then also projecting *Christus*, and evidently feeling the weight of the great theme. The length of time which it remained in his mind is an illustration of the large circle on which his thought sailed, and his poetic career is marked to the end by the deliberate inception, elaboration, and completion of great works.

It is not possible to reconstruct the conversation which Mr. Greene and Mr. Longfellow had in their youth upon the house-top at Naples, but the more one studies the art which has made one of these names a household word, the more one is able to see the "deep cisterns" from which the pure stream has flowed. The gift of nature which made Longfellow an artist to his finger-tips was reinforced by that broad, free study which enriched his mind with a multitude of familiar figures and forms, and behind all lay a reverent, devout character, which constantly obeyed the impulse to work, to create, to be.

GEORGE SAINTSBURY
From "Longfellow's Poems" (1907)
Prefaces and Essays
1933, pp. 324–44

Longfellow is among the least difficult authors to read, and he should be among the easiest to criticise; though, owing to some faults of his own and more of his critics', he has not always proved so. It is certainly an unfortunate thing for a poet that his most universally known and perhaps, for a long time at any rate, his most popular poem should be one of his own worst. It is still more unfortunate (for after all, a poet cannot help the bad taste of his readers) that it should be bad of and in itself. It is most unfortunate of all that its badness should exaggerate, accentuate, and caricature certain rather too frequent characteristics of his. Now all these things are true of "Excelsior". The most Rhadamanthine and the most ingenious of critics could hardly strain his severity or his ingenuity in finding fault with it. The title does not mean what it ought to mean to make any sense whatever of the piece; and does mean something quite different—a blunder which is accentuated by its being used as a refrain, and by the astoundingly unlucky description of it as in "an unknown tongue". The conduct of the ungrammatical youth is that of a mere lunatic; even Alpine Clubs, which were hardly founded when Longfellow wrote, would not defend it. That of the maiden would, in the famous French phrase, "make dragoons blush". And the theology of the conclusion matches the morality of the maiden and the Latinity and common sense of the youth, by intimating divine approval of what was, on the showing of the poet, pure suicide without a purpose or an aim—unless indeed the youth knew no other way to get to Italy to effect that improvement in his Latin of which there was such urgent need. The charges, often foolishly enough brought of late, against mid-nineteenth-century "sentiment" are here amply justified. The whole thing is sheer silliness—silliness so intense that, with the accompa-

nying want of scholarship, it would damn even an allowance of poetic expression much greater than that given here. One could but heartily wish the thing unwritten if it were not a curious literary *point de repère*, as to the way in which false taste, in poet and in readers at the same time, lashes the poet into a kind of paroxysm now and then.

But this paroxysm was never repeated. It is true, as has been said, that the worst things in it are caricatures and exaggerations of things that occur frequently in Longfellow; but these things in themselves are not despicable, and they are almost invariably accompanied by something else which redeems and transforms them. It will be, for most competent judges, something, that poets who may be called "greater", in critical slang, than he is—who are at any rate members of an extremely different school—have had a curious habit of "taking notes" from him, not in the manner which foolish people call plagiarism, but as poets take from poets. The use made by Baudelaire (not exactly an exponent of early or mid-Victorian sentiment) of "The Psalm of Life" in one of the finest of his poems, "Le Guignon", is unmistakable, and has not been mistaken. Yet "The Psalm of Life" is one of the most mixed and dangerous of Longfellow's pieces;—it has been riddled with ridicule—or rather ridicule has attempted to riddle it, and has sometimes made a hole or two. Mr. Swinburne is scarcely of the Longfellovian fellowship as that is understood by unfavourable critics; and yet some of the very finest and most characteristic verses of the Prelude to *Songs before Sunrise*—

Because man's soul is man's god still,

fall in curiously with a stanza of another of the *Voices of the Night*, "The Light of Stars" beginning—

The star of the unconquered will.

Those who like tracing parallel passages will have good game with Longfellow and his successors among the English-writing poets of the last seventy years. But is this because he has "imitated" others, or because others have "imitated" him in the silly sense which has been already blackmarked? Not at all. It is because to him, as to all true poets, the great commonplaces of life have presented themselves, and because he has known how to treat these commonplaces with the poetic treatment which makes them not common.

What may be said, not against but of Longfellow, with truth is that in treating these great commonplaces he is, as a rule, more indulgent to the common auditor than the greatest poets are, or than some who are not greater than he is; and that sometimes, as in "Excelsior" and elsewhere, this indulgence leads him astray. He is in almost all respects the opposite of his contemporary Browning, just as their other contemporary Tennyson makes up a trinity of opposites with them both. Longfellow is one of the most *automatic* of poets—to every subject that presents itself he gives, like some springs, a sort of coating of true and natural but never artificially finished poetry, varying a good deal with the quality of his subject, the fulness or slackness, concentration or dilatation of the spring itself at the moment, and other accidents. Browning is the least automatic, the most determined to submit all matters that come in his way to an apparently eccentric process of his own—a process involving sometimes (not always) a minimum of artistic expenditure, but personal and wayward to the *n*th. Tennyson, as little automatic as Browning, is the pure artist, never satisfied till he has brought everything to his own ideal of perfection in expression and form. It follows that Browning cannot translate at all—he can only *transpose* into a key of his own utterly different from the original; that Tennyson has left us but a little translation or direct imitation, but that of curious perfection; that Longfellow almost seems to prefer translation, and while more than fairly faithful, manages always to give it a flavour of his own.

If we pass from his translations to his original verse, the same or an analogous quality confronts us. Longfellow is never startlingly felicitous; nor, on the other hand, does the sense of his felicity grow on us as we perceive more and more fully the exquisiteness of the art with which, but without artificiality, it is attained. You never have to question yourself, or him, to find out what he means; and you never are tempted almost or altogether to neglect his meaning, for the sake of the poetic supremacy with which it is conveyed. But that meaning is never contemptible—it is not so even in "Excelsior", if the piece could be stripped of its absurdities of expression and ornament. It is sometimes very admirable; and it is almost invariably conveyed with less or more—not unfrequently with a very considerable "more"—of poetic treatment.

Now these are the conditions and specifications of a kind of poet who never can be too plentiful, and who, as a matter of fact, is decidedly rare. If, as some people talk with commendable gravity, poetry is a high and holy thing which ought to be cultivated like religion—that which enables the greatest number of persons to cultivate it is surely to be welcomed. If, on the other hand, as light and frivolous folk prefer to insist, poetry is one of the greatest and absolutely the most harmless of pleasures—surely again, the man who offers this in a manner that the multitude can and do appreciate, is a benefactor of his species. Nay, more, there must as surely be something not of the first-comer, something which Apollo has not given to everybody, in the man who can do this. There are so many poets who have not succeeded in giving pleasure to anybody, whether of the great vulgar or of the small, whether of the promiscuous or the fastidious feeders!

We may, however, devote a few words to this "small vulgar" itself, and beat up its quarters briefly but without much mercy. For my own part, I made up my mind long ago that the critic who pooh-poohs Longfellow's poetry is a bad critic. For one of the attributes of the critic is that he shall be, strictly by derivation and definition, a *separator*, a man who is able to discern the good from the bad, even though they be mixed like the heap of grain that Venus set Psyche to sort. A critic who must have his poetry sorted out for him, presented in its quiddity, "neat", to vary the metaphor, may pride himself upon his taste, but is in effect confessing his incompetence. In many cases, I fear, even the taste is not quite so genuine as it appears or would like to appear. The critics in question would too certainly at one time have adopted one current standard of poetic supremacy, at another another. At any rate, they may be left in the mire with this dilemma. If they cannot see the poetry in Longfellow because of the other things not quite so poetical which are there, they lack the first qualification of the critic, which is to know poetry when he sees it. If they cannot separate and judge it, they lack the second, which is to see it and treat it by itself. So, enough of them.

Adopting a different style of criticism ourselves, it may be well for us to survey the different divisions of the poet's verse, no one of which can be completely represented here, while large parts of it can only be represented at all by a sort of brick-of-the-house process. This last, however, is no such great misfortune, for Longfellow, in this not differing from most other poets, is by no means at his best in his longest poems, even the non-dramatic ones. Of the dramatic pieces, *The Spanish Student* and the little miracle-play inserted in *The Golden Legend* are by far the best. But of course it is open to anyone to say that neither is a *play* at all; the second being a

mere clever *pastiche*, while the first is partly that, and still more a loosely told but capital story which the whim of the writer has thrown into dramatic instead of narrative form. And there is a good deal in this, though for my part I should not like *The Spanish Student* so well if it were not partly in verse, and I never read it afresh without liking it better. The *New England Tragedies*, the *Divine Tragedy (Christus)*, and *Michael Angelo* are exposed to the same critical description, which, however, would have to take a more uncomplimentary colouring. The slight but ambitious *Masque of Pandora* is by no means without merit; but it wanted another man, and above all a younger man, to write it.

Very pedantic critics of form might object to the separation of *The Golden Legend* itself from this group. To my fancy, however, it occupies a middle place between the dramatic and the purely narrative pieces. It proceeds, no doubt, as the excellent old French phrase has it, "by personages"—there are names as shoulder-headings to the different paragraphs of the verse. But in reality it is nearly as pure a narrative as the original *Der Arme Heinrich* of Hartmann von der Aue, from which it was taken. The speakers (except perhaps Elsie) have no personality—we can neglect them altogether, or at least regard them as the personages of a poem with "then said So-and-so" forming part of the verse. Often, there is no reason why there should be any "So-and-so" at all. The thing is really a sort of dreamy panorama with a certain number of cinematograph effects to enliven it—a thing that poets found out ages and ages before panoramas or cinematographs were invented or thought of. And it is (to me at least) a very delightful thing. I happen to have a fairly wide acquaintance with medieval poetry in the original tongues, and a great devotion to the Middle Ages. I do not say that Longfellow has gone very deeply into medieval sentiment. It was not his way to go very deeply, or to *appear* to go very deeply (which is perhaps a different thing), into anything. He may in parts and passages be at a disadvantage with Mr. William Morris, as he certainly is in *The Wayside Inn*. But here also his "superficiality", as it seems to some folk, has a curious quality of not being so very superficial after all. His etching is not deeply bitten; his colour is but a sort of preliminary wash. But somehow or other both are right as far as they go, and both give to the spectator an effect much more trustworthy than some far more heavily treated plates and pictures. The opening *diablerie*, and that of the scene between Prince Henry and Lucifer; the "Tale of the Monk Felix" and Elsie's of the Sultan's daughter; Lucifer in the church; the Prince's picture of the cathedral; Friar Claus in the cellar; the Abbess's soliloquy; the Prince and Elsie at Genoa; the voyage; the crucial scene, and the lovers' final dialogue—are things as to which I shall respectfully ask any critic to be very sure of his criticship before he dismisses them as ordinary. We must try to make room for most of them here; and if we have to leave out any, the omission will more than justify itself should it send anyone to the original. I think I can promise that, if he has any natural taste for poetry, he will not be satisfied till he knows the whole of the poem itself. For combined variety and charm there is nothing of Longfellow's in bulk that can be compared to it.

At this point, years ago at any rate, there would have been, supposing that many people read the words which I have just written, a chorus of indignant voices, interrupting to cry, "What! do you mean to say that you prefer this second-hand medieval medley to *Evangeline?*" Certainly, I prefer it very much; and what is more, I am certain, as I by no means always am, that, whether I prefer it or not, it ought to be preferred. *Evangeline* is a pretty poem; it lends itself admirably to illustration for drawing-room-table books; it was a clever revival of an old though hopeless experiment in metre; its sentiment is not false; and it has some beautiful passages. We need not attach the slightest importance to the American criticism which says that Longfellow did not take the trouble to go west and south to get local colour for the bayous and the prairies—that he is not true to it. I think the bayous rather nice myself; and, as I am not likely ever to visit the originals, I do not care whether they are like or not. We need not attend to the grave historians who tell us (I believe quite correctly) that the Acadians, instead of being mercilessly, were rather long-sufferingly dealt with. These things do not matter to poetry at all. The poem, as it seems to me, suffers from two quite different defects, one of matter, one of form. The weakness in matter is twofold. In the first place, the characters, with hardly the slight exception of "Basil the Blacksmith", have no character at all. Longfellow is never very strong at this; but even Elsie in the *Legend* is far more of a person than Evangeline, and Prince Henry than Gabriel. Secondly, the pathetic conclusion is one of those "possible improbabilities" which, as all good critics have noticed from the dawn of criticism, are far worse than probable impossibilities. How did all those years pass? Of course, if Evangeline made a point of a "stern chase", if she insisted on always coming up with Gabriel (as an Irishman might say) just after he had gone somewhere else—there is nothing to say. But when she settled at Philadelphia it was different. The post may not have been very effective, and there may have been no newspapers to advertise in; but trappers wandered everywhere, and though, as I have said, it is possible, it is in the very last degree improbable that even three or four years could have passed, let alone the twenty or thirty required by the story, before Gabriel heard of her whereabouts. It is all very well to say that this is a prosaic criticism, like Mrs. Barbauld's when she told Coleridge that *The Ancient Mariner* was deficient in probability. Coleridge has brought it about that the *poetical* reader of *The Ancient Mariner* never thinks about probability: and Longfellow has not done this. He has not achieved the "suspension of disbelief", in Coleridge's own great words.

We ought, however, to give some special attention to the form of this, which is also the form of *The Courtship of Miles Standish*—the English hexameter. Longfellow had tried this earlier, in his translation of Tegnér's *Children of the Lord's Supper* and one or two other pieces. It was not surprising that so careful a student of the Germans—who had taken to the metre pretty far back in the eighteenth century—should attempt it; but the previous experiments of Coleridge might have influenced him even without this. I shall frankly say that for my part I believe this English hexameter to be a hopeless and impossible mistake, always and in every form, *as such*;—though it can be made a very effective measure by letting it follow its natural bent with us and become anapaestic. But this is not the place for a prosodic disquisition of the general kind. We must confine ourselves to the special faults or merits of Longfellow's hexameter. The defects of the whole, and of most individual lines, seem to me—in spite of some passable verses and a few effective and fairly sustained passages—to be undeniable. The chief of them, which in a way includes or excuses all or most of the others, is a quality for which French has one short and final word of three letters, *mou*; but which we cannot indicate at all exactly by "soft", and only piecemeal and inadequately by "flaccid" and others. The line lacks spring, coil and recoil, resilience and its corollary resonance. I myself think the not uncommon opinion that English has few spondees incorrect; but Longfellow is very unlucky with his,

though, oddly enough, he is fond of that rather dangerous thing the spondaic ending. Usually he oscillates between almost wholly dactylic lines of a very loose, fragile, and rickety construction, and spondees of such a questionable character as

> *She in turn related her love and all its disasters,*

where it is difficult to say whether "she in"—which is little more than *one* syllable, or "turn-re"—which hardly any pronunciation will get into more than a trochee, is the more incompetent representative of the double-long foot. But not to spend too much time upon technical details (which could be largely multiplied, but for which we have no room), it may be said, I think, without any injustice, that, save in a few passages, the effect of the whole is monotonously slipshod, and very inferior to that even of rhythmical prose.

The Courtship of Miles Standish itself needs little notice; none indeed as far as the vehicle is concerned. It was naturally interesting to Americans, as dealing with the rather slender and not always pleasant materials of their early history, and to the poet and his friends as embodying a family tradition. But these things of course have nothing to do with poetic merit itself. As a story it is so slight that to criticise it as such—to point out that Priscilla is rather pert for a Puritan maiden, and that John Alden is a nincompoop or something worse—would be absurd. But if people like it they may; I suppose those who do would call it "idyllic".

Not thus to be dismissed is *Hiawatha*, though a great deal of what has been said by others about *Hiawatha*, its fidelity to authorities, the trustworthiness of these authorities, and so forth, may be dismissed with alacrity and decision. It is enough to say that the effect which the poet wished to produce—the presentation of an entirely strange civilisation, or half-civilisation, with imagery, diction, metre and all, adapted in strangeness—is well and even triumphantly achieved. No matter where he got the metre, and no matter whether he mixed the local colour in more senses than one. The whole is of a piece—united and congruous in effect, without gap or jar. And this is a merit which some people put highest in poetry, and which nobody can put low. Of course, the Devil's Advocate, seeing his advantage, may go on and ask whether it is not all rather *too* complete, rather *too* much of a piece—whether the unvarying and unvaried plainsong of the trochaic dimeter does not "get on the nerves" after a time, and not so very long a time; whether the constant repetition of barbaric words with their English synonyms does not overpass the effect of strange terms in poetry, and begin to produce rather that of reading a lexicon; whether Longfellow's old defect of insufficiently marked character—though Pau-puk-Keewis and Iagoo, and even Nokomis, have some—is not unfortunately felt. Perhaps the poet's counsel will have to "confess and avoid" a little in this part of the matter. But on reading *Hiawatha* again, after a good many years' interval, I find that it bears the test much better than some things which I used to like when I liked it first, and which the outrage of time has, I fear, irreparably defaced for me. Perhaps it would stand shortening or thinning; but then it is fair to remember that it is, from one point of view, such a mere "bundle of episodes"—there is so very little connection running through it, except the unity of treatment spoken of above, and the presence of Hiawatha as a sort of "hero-when-wanted"—that there is no need to read it all at once. Read in batches, and at the right moment, it is very good reading, not merely for the exotic manners and unfamiliar imagery, not merely for the pleasant if not overdone music of the soft, strange, Indian names, but for other things more sheerly poetical. Indeed, as I look through the twenty-two cantos yet again, to determine what to give here, the whole being impossible, I find myself rather unexpectedly confronted with that other difficulty, what *not* to give, which is the selector's greatest compliment. I have given rather less than I might, with the same hope, as in the case of *The Spanish Student* and *The Golden Legend*, that the fragments will serve as baits.

Of Longfellow's *magnum opus* in a certain sense, *The Tales of a Wayside Inn*, I shall not say much. It was a little unfortunate, as I have said, in coinciding with a not wholly dissimilar attempt, Mr. William Morris's *Earthly Paradise*, which has not only much more art as a whole, but a much higher level of poetical merit in the parts. Where the contact is even closer, as in "King Robert of Sicily", the contrast is especially disastrous. But read in itself, and as a frank attempt at tale-telling in verse rather than at narrative poetry, it is good pastime enough, and sometimes something very much better. The worst thing about it is its exceeding inequality. The opening story, "Paul Revere's Ride", has the drawback that the excellent Paul does not seem to have run the slightest danger, though, if his friend in the belfry had been observed and caught (as he ought to have been), and hanged (as he might have been with much better right than André), it would have given some point. "The Ballad of Carmilhan", again, is an imitation of the worst German manner—sham "silly sooth"; its failure being intensified by the reminder which the name gives of a very different thing in German, Hauff's most powerful and gruesome prose story. Elsewhere there are excellent things—much if not all of *The Saga of King Olaf*, and many smaller ones. But the distinction which I have just drawn had better be kept in mind throughout.

And so we are left with those shorter poems which, if people would only throw away mistaken traditional theories of poetry, are the real test of a poet's gift, unless he is an altogether exceptional person as well as poet, like Dante. In a short poem, the poet has only got to attend to the poetry. He can leave the story and the characters to the persons to whom they properly belong—the novelist and the dramatist. There is nothing to prevent him being as "subjective" or as "objective" as he chooses. Instead of being more or less tied to one metre, he may try a hundred in as many different poems. He has not the slightest excuse for "padding"; and his critics have no excuse for excusing him if he does pad. The immense, the legitimate, the natural charm of variety, instead of having to be painfully sought for, presents itself unsought to him, unless he is so incompetent that *ex hypothesi* he falls out of our consideration. From the stock objections of the criticaster to digressions, episodes, purple patches, etc., he is free by the very fact of the matter.

Accordingly, all Longfellow's best work is of this kind, and there is a very great deal of it. He never lost his skill at it, from the early *Voices of the Night* to the singularly beautiful introduction of *Ultima Thule*. If he made his worst slip here in "Excelsior", he redeemed that slip by almost literally a hundred things that were not slips. As to the objections to "sentiment", "convention", "over-facility" and the like, I have hinted the lines of an impregnable fortification against them above, and it is not necessary to expand or emphasise these lines much. Sentiment, when it becomes (as it has rather a tendency to become) sentimentalism, is not the best of things; but it is at any rate better than the cheap and childish paradox, and much better than the banal brutality, which have been sometimes offered in its place. All conventions (except in pure "manners") are bad; but a clean and kindly convention is, at any rate, less bad than a dirty and ill-natured one. As for

over-facility, that opens a very difficult critical question, which I venture to think not many of the objectors are quite learned in their craft enough to handle. For this quality is very intimately connected with that other, of adapting poetry to the general capacity, which has been noted above.

For my part, I am sorry "as a Christian" (compare Rowena's observation and Wamba's comment) for those who cannot see poetry in Longfellow's lyrics; but my sorrow in any other capacity is a good deal tempered by uncharitable doubt whether they *really* see the poetry of Poe or of Whitman, of Rossetti or of Blake. I am extremely glad, as a matter of pure humanity, that there are a large number of persons who can and do see it.

It is to be seen in various forms and ways—in description, suggestion, musical accompaniment of thought. Of the two famous poetic processes, Longfellow, no doubt, oftener adopts that of adorning and exalting the familiar than that of seizing and making familiar the strange; but it would be unjust (the refusal is indeed at the root of all the injustice that has been done to him) to refuse him command of a certain middle way, a combination of the two nearer to the earth than to the ether, but not involving banishment from this latter. And this is what makes his companionship and guideship so valuable for those who are not exactly at home on the mountain-tops of poetry; who cannot (or cannot at first) breathe its more rarefied air. Some, of course, of his things, especially the "Psalm of Life" itself, are so hackneyed, so sullied by the ignoble use of cheap quotation and stale tagging of morals, that it needs the accident of fresh acquaintance, or the much rarer property of that real critical spirit which is proof against all hackneying, to enjoy them thoroughly. Others, like "The Bridge" for instance, pay the rather comic and unfair but very real penalty of being so indissolubly associated with their usual musical setting that the actual poetical music is, as it were, dinned out of hearing. But in late work as in early, in the unhackneyed things as in the hackneyed, there never fails for long together, or rather there is almost always present, this unpretentious and apparently easy gift of communicating something of poetical treatment, something of poetical effect, to everything, or almost everything, that is touched. It may be a happy epithet of description; it may be a musical phrase or rhythm; it may be a suggestion of thought or feeling just charmed into freedom from the merely prosaic and banal; it may even be a borrowed plume of reading freshly set in the poet's cap, a relish of out-of-the-way literature happily instilled; it may be a dozen other things tedious to particularise. But the poeticising—the disrealising and yet realising—touch is always in it, or in it so often as to obscure and cover the failures. Nay, these failures themselves, save in one or two cases, especially that gibbeted above, are themselves so modest and so little offending, that, even without the successes, they would almost escape notice. The entire absence of pretentiousness is here also a wonderful preservative. Longfellow may be sometimes insignificant, he may oftimes have the rather evanescent touch of the *improvisatore*, but he is never positively dull or offensive, rarely absurd.

Not often has a poet made a more definite promise than in the *Voices of the Night*, which, be it remembered, appeared in 1839 after a considerable apprenticeship both to speech and silence, but some years before the capital appearances of Tennyson in the *Poems* of 1842, and of Browning in *Bells and Pomegranates*. They are all given here as they were finally united by their author; and though no large handful, it is a handful of very pleasant delights. The Prelude—with its well-chosen combination of the metrical qualities of the Ballad quatrain and the Romance six—is really a remarkable foreshadowing of Longfellow's poetical career, and the baggage he was to take with him on it: the delight in Nature; the delight in a quiet but not vulgar fancy; the delight in literature; the sympathy with humanity; the sense—rather remarkable in a person of so equable a temper, and showing itself at a time when the "browner shades" were not even near   of the passing of time and the vanity of things. And this variety shows itself at more development in what follows—the graceful "Hymn to the Night"; the "fine confused feeling" and "extremely valuable thoughts", as Wordsworth said of his own poems, of the "Psalm of Life"; the more than pretty sentiment of "The Reaper", and the not less than fine bravery of "The Light of Stars".

For the two original ballads, "The Skeleton in Armour" and "The Wreck of the Hesperus", I shall never shirk declaring admiration. If not the strongest of meat, they are dishes of milk very well crumbled with bread for poetical babes; and the said babes, when they grow up, will be very lucky if they find no worse food even then, and may come back to them with relish from the strong meat itself. The first *Miscellaneous Poems* sustain the note well, especially "It is not always May"; and "The Goblet of Life" is, I think, better than its *Psalm*, a sentiment which may sound immoral, but which corresponds to the general experience of critical readers of poetry.

"The Belfry of Bruges" shows Longfellow in that peculiar character of his, the character of a poetical cicerone of foreign lands and the things appertaining to them, and the note is not monotonous. It is true that there are some weak things here which, accordingly, we do not give, it not being necessary, as in the case of "Excelsior", to justify unfavourable criticism, to escape the charge of *not* giving the poet's most famous things. "The Arsenal at Springfield", for instance, is a piece of mere claptrap, out of harmony with some of his own most spirited work, and merely an instance of a cant common at the time, though unhappily not unknown in many other times.

Of the *Songs and Sonnets*, "Seaweed" is peculiarly beautiful, and the famous "The Day Is Done" is one of those which I shall not throw to the sentiment-hunting wolves. The sonnet itself was not one of Longfellow's special domains; he was not quite intense enough for it in meaning on the one hand, nor quite impeccable enough in form on the other. "The Evening Star" is the best of them, "The Cross of Snow", for all its pathetic subject (his wife's death) and its not unhappy idea, being ruined by the *un*blessed word "bene*dight*".

But I am letting myself be betrayed into too much particularisation. To specify the pleasant things in *The Seaside and the Fireside* and in *Birds of Passage* would most unjustifiably curtail the room available for those good things themselves. Let me only mention "The Building of the Ship", so admirably conducted and climaxed, with its famous and justly praised political ending—one of the rare pieces of political verse which need no special prejudice in favour of their sentiments to conciliate admiration; "Chrysaor", the most Browningesque thing in Longfellow; the *almost* adequate "Secret of the Sea", and the delectable "King Witlaf's Drinking-Horn", in the first parcel: the stately and noble "Ladder of St. Augustine", and "Haunted Houses", "My Lost Youth", the once more famous "Golden Mile-stone", "Santa Filomena", "Sandalphon" (oddly suggestive and unsuggestive of a poet of the next generation who has never had his meed, Mr. O'Shaughnessy), "Weariness", and many another, in the second.

Some think this kind of sampling an impertinence, but I do not believe that either good poets or good critics agree with them. One is only performing the modest duty of an ancient apprentice, when he shouted, "What d'ye lack?" and vaunted the wares offered. If they were good wares they were none the worse, and those who were induced to buy them were the better. And these are good wares!

ANTHONY TROLLOPE

ANTHONY TROLLOPE

1815–1882

Anthony Trollope was born in Bloomsbury, London, on April 24, 1815. His father, a failed farmer and lawyer, died in 1835, by which time his mother, Frances Trollope, had already begun to support the family by publishing a series of extremely successful books, beginning in 1832 with *Domestic Manners of the Americans*. Despite the financial difficulties that colored his early life, Anthony Trollope received a thorough education at Harrow and Winchester (1822–34), and upon graduating became a junior clerk in the general Post Office in London. He was appointed Deputy Postal Surveyor for Banagher, Ireland, in 1841, and in 1844 married Rose Heseltine, by whom he had two sons, Henry (b. 1846) and Frederick (b. 1847). Trollope did not return to England permanently until 1859, and even after that frequently traveled on official business, as in 1861 when he visited the United States. By 1867, when he resigned from the Post Office, Trollope had become a successful civil servant, responsible for several important reforms, including the introduction into England of the first pillar-box for letters.

Trollope's extremely prolific literary career began in 1847 with the appearance of his novel *The Macdermots of Ballycloran*. It was followed by forty-six other novels, several travel books, various biographies, and a number of collections of short stories and sketches. His principal novels include the "Barsetshire" series, consisting of *The Warden* (1855), *Barchester Towers* (1857), *Doctor Thorne* (1858), *Framley Parsonage* (1861), *The Small House at Allington* (1864), and *The Last Chronicle of Barset* (1867), and the "Palliser" series, consisting of *Can You Forgive Her?* (1864), *Phineas Finn* (1869), *The Eustace Diamonds* (1873), *Phineas Redux* (1876), *The Prime Minister* (1876), and *The Duke's Children* (1880). In addition to these two series, which were of primary importance in introducing the convention of the novel-cycle into English fiction, Trollope's principal novels include *The Three Clerks* (1857), *The Bertrams* (1859), *Orley Farm* (1862), *The Belton Estate* (1866), *The Claverings* (1867), *He Knew He Was Right* (1869), *The Vicar of Bullhampton* (1870), *The Way We Live Now* (1875), *The American Senator* (1877), *Doctor Wortle's School* (1881), *Ayala's Angel* (1881) and *Mr. Scarborough's Family* (1883).

In 1868 Trollope stood unsuccessfully for Parliament, and from 1867 to 1870 edited *St. Paul's Magazine*. He wrote his *Autobiography* (published posthumously in 1883) in 1875–76 and died in London on December 6, 1882. His *Letters*, edited by N. John Hall, were published in two volumes in 1983.

Personal

Nobody could see anything of him without feeling that he was in the presence of an exceptionally high-minded as well as an exceptionally gifted man, a man of strong feelings as of strong sense, but a man who well knew how to keep his feelings in check, and a man whose practice as well as his theory was Christian. ⟨. . .⟩

Besides the wisdom which one could always draw upon by paying him a visit in his study after his appointed hours of work, there was an atmosphere of cheerfulness, of good humor, of light-heartedness, and of good feeling about him which could not but do one good. He loved fun; he loved laughing; he loved his kind. There was not one scrap of sentimentality about him, but there was plenty of sensibility, as well as sense.—WALTER HERRIES POLLOCK, "Anthony Trollope," *Harper's New Monthly Magazine*, May 1883, pp. 911–12

⟨He⟩ was a broad-shouldered, sturdy man of middle height, with a ruddy countenance, and snow-white, tempestuous beard and hair. He wore large, gold-rimmed spectacles, but his eyes were black and brilliant, and looked at his interlocutor with a certain genial fury of inspection. He seemed to be in a state of some excitement; he spoke volubly and almost boisterously, and his voice was full-toned and powerful, though pleasant to the ear. He turned himself, as he spoke, with a burly briskness, from one side to another, addressing himself first to this auditor and then to that, his words bursting forth from beneath his white mustache with such an impetus of hearty breath, that it seemed as if all opposing arguments must be blown quite away. Meanwhile he flourished in the air an ebony walking-stick, with much vigor of gesticulation, and narrowly missing, as it appeared, the pates of his listeners. He was clad in evening dress, though the rest of the company was, for the most part, in mufti; and he was an exceedingly fine-looking old gentleman. At the first glance, you would have taken him to be some civilized and modernized Squire Western, nourished with beef and ale, and roughly hewn out of the most robust and least refined variety of human clay. Looking at him more narrowly, however, you would have reconsidered this judgment. Though his general contour and aspect were massive and sturdy, the lines of his features were delicately cut; his complexion was remarkably pure and fine, and his face was susceptible of very subtle and sensitive changes of expression. Here was a man of abundant physical strength and vigor, no doubt, but carrying within him a nature more than commonly alert and impressible. His organization, though thoroughly healthy, was both complex and high-wrought; his character was simple and straightforward to a fault, but he was abnormally conscientious, and keenly alive to others' opinion concerning him. It might be thought that he was overburdened with self-esteem, and unduly opinionated; but, in fact, he was but over-anxious to secure the good-will and agreement of all with whom he came in contact. There was some peculiarity in him—some element or bias in his composition that made him different from other men; but, on the other hand, there was an ardent solicitude to annul or reconcile this difference, and to prove himself to be, in fact, of absolutely the same cut and quality as all the rest of the world. Hence he was in a demonstrative, expository or argumentative mood; he could not sit quiet in the face of a divergence between himself and his associates; he was incorrigibly strenuous to obliterate or harmonize the irreconcilable points between him and others; and since these points remained irreconcilable, he remained in a constant state of storm and stress on the subject.

It was impossible to help liking such a man, at first sight; and I believe that no man in London society was more generally liked than Anthony Trollope. There was something pathetic in his attitude, as above indicated; and a fresh and boyish quality always invested him. His artlessness was boyish, and so were his acuteness and his transparent but somewhat belated good sense. He was one of those rare persons who not only have no reserves, but who can afford to dispense with them. After he had shown you all he had in him, you would have seen nothing that was not gentlemanly, honest and clean. He was a quick-tempered man, and the ardor and hurry of his temperament made him seem more so than he really was; but he was never more angry than he was forgiving and generous. He was hurt by little things, and little things pleased him; he was suspicious and perverse, but in a manner that rather endeared him to you than otherwise. Altogether, to a casual acquaintance, who knew nothing of his personal history, he was something of a paradox—an entertaining contradiction. The recent publication of his autobiography has explained many things in his character that were open to speculation; and, indeed, the book is not only the most interesting and amusing that its author has ever written, but it places its subject before the reader more completely and comprehensibly than most autobiographies do. This, however, is due much less to any direct effort or intention on the writer's part, than to the unconscious self-revelation which meets the reader on every page. No narrative could be simpler, less artificial; and yet, everywhere, we read between the lines, and, so to speak, discover Anthony Trollope in spite of his efforts to discover himself to us.—JULIAN HAWTHORNE, "The Maker of Many Books," *Manhattan*, Dec. 1883, pp. 573–74

It is as pleasant to me 'to smoke my canaster and tipple my ale in the shade,' as Thackeray says, as to any man. Anthony had no such turn. Work to him was a necessity and a satisfaction. He used often to say that he envied me the capacity for being idle. Had he possessed it, poor fellow, I might not now be speaking of him in the past tense. And still less than of me could it be said of him that he was ever driven to literary work *deficiente crumenâ*. But he laboured during the whole of his manhood life with an insatiable ardour that (taking into consideration his very efficient discharge of his duties as Post Office surveyor) puts my industry into the shade.—THOMAS ADOLPHUS TROLLOPE, *What I Remember*, 1888

Filled with the enthusiasm of one who had very rarely met a popular author, I entered Strathtyrum that day. The sight of the great novelist was a blow. He was singularly unkempt, and his clothes were very wrinkled and ill-made. His manner was a further blow. We listened for the melodious accents which were due from those lips: but they did not come. Indeed, he was the only man I had heard swear in decent society for uncounted years. The swearing, which was repeated, was the most disagreeable of all: the actual asseverating, by the Holiest Name, of some trumpery statement. How could that man have written the well-remembered sentences which had charmed

one through these years?—ANDREW K. H. BOYD, *Twenty-five Years of St. Andrews*, 1892, Vol. 1, pp. 100–101

My brother was sitting in his library in New York, when, in response to his 'Come in,' the door flew open, and a stout, hairy-faced, ruddy-complexioned Englishman burst in upon his solitude like a rough shaggy Newfoundland dog about to leap upon him in the exuberance of animal spirits.

'My name is Anthony Trollope!' exclaimed the visitor in a brusque voice, 'and I've brought you a letter of introduction from a mutual friend in England.'

In physique, manner, and speech he might have been taken for a dragoon in mufti, or a sportsman fresh from an invigorating run in the fields; certainly not for a novelist whose forte lay in depicting the salient traits of English clergymen, the delicate shades of character among English maidens, and in composing those inimitable love-letters which so plentifully bestrew the pages of his life-like romances. During his visit to New York, Trollope was introduced to many of our literary men, and to such social gatherings as might interest a man of his pursuits. He wore spectacles, through which he seemed to inspect men and things with a quiet scrutiny, as if making perpetual mental memoranda for future use. In conversation he would sometimes ask a question, or make a suggestion respecting people to whom he had been introduced, which indicated a keen perception of the weak spots in their characters; but this was always said in a good-humoured way that left no sting behind it.—CHARLES K. TUCKERMAN, *Personal Recollections of Notable People*, 1895, Vol. 2, pp. 8–9

General

It is odd enough that my own individual taste is for quite another class of works than those which I myself am able to write. If I were to meet with such books as mine by another writer, I don't believe I should be able to get through them. Have you ever read the novels of Anthony Trollope? They precisely suit my taste,—solid and substantial, written on the strength of beef and through the inspiration of ale, and just as real as if some giant had hewn a great lump out of the earth and put it under a glass case, with all its inhabitants going about their daily business, and not suspecting that they were being made a show of. And these books are just as English as a beef-steak. Have they ever been tried in America? It needs an English residence to make them thoroughly comprehensible; but still I should think that human nature would give them success anywhere.—NATHANIEL HAWTHORNE, Letter to Joseph M. Field (Feb. 11, 1860), cited in Anthony Trollope, *An Autobiography*, 1883, Ch. 8

If Mr. Trollope paints—and he paints firmly, consistently, and with a quiet obstinate kind of art—all that can be found in English society, the sooner that society is changed for something of a more decided pattern the better. No one can care for the faint and obscure outlines, and the colourless sort of wool, with which Mr. Trollope weaves his human and his faded tapestry.—J. HAIN FRISWELL, "Anthony Trollope," *Modern Men of Letters Honestly Criticised*, 1870, pp. 143–44

I set my Reader last night on beginning *The Mill on the Floss*. I couldn't take to it more than to others I have tried by the Greatest Novelist of the Day: but I will go on a little further. Oh for some more brave Trollope; who I am sure conceals a much profounder observation than these Dreadful *Denners* of Romance under his lightsome and sketchy touch—as Gainsboro compared to Denner.—EDWARD FITZGERALD, Letter to W. F. Pollock (Nov. 30, 1873)

Mr. Anthony Trollope carries to its utmost limit the realism begun by Thackeray. He has none of Thackeray's genius; none of his fancy or feeling; none of his genuine creative power. He can describe with minute photographic faithfulness the ways, the talk, and sometimes even the emotions of a Belgravian family, of a nobleman's country-house, or the "womankind" of a dean in a cathedral town. He does not trouble himself with passion or deep pathos, although he has got as far as to describe very touchingly the mental pains of a pretty girl thrown over by her lover, and has suggested with some genuine power the blended emotion, half agony of sorrow, half sense of relief, experienced by an elderly clergyman on the death of a shrewish wife. It was natural that, after the public had had a long succession of Mr. Trollope's novels, there should come a ready welcome for the school of fiction which was called the sensational. Of this school Mr. Wilkie Collins headed one class and Miss Braddon the other. Miss Braddon dealt in what we may call simple, straightforward murders and bigamies, and such like material; Mr. Wilkie Collins made his crimes always of an enigmatic nature, and compelled the reader to puzzle them out as if they were morbid conundrums. Mr. Trollope, however, continued to have his *clientèle* all the time that the sensational school in its various classes or branches was flourishing and fading. Mr. Trollope's readers may have turned away for a moment to hear what became of the lady who dropped her husband down the well, or to guess at the secret of the mysterious Woman in White. But they soon turned loyally back to follow the gentle fortunes of Lily Dale, and to hear what was going on in the household of Framley Parsonage and under the stately roof of the Duke of Omnium.—JUSTIN McCARTHY, *A History of Our Own Times*, 1879–80, Ch. 67

I will not do Mr. Trollope such an ill turn as to compare him with George Eliot, the greatest, I suppose, of all writers of fiction till she took to theories and Jews. It was a wonderful feat to draw Romola; it was a wonderful feat to draw Mrs. Poyser; but for the same hand to draw Romola and Mrs. Poyser was something more than wonderful; if the fact were not certain, one would deem it impossible. Now assuredly Mr. Trollope could not have drawn Romola, and I do not think that he could have drawn Mrs. Poyser. Yet the characters of George Eliot and the characters of Mr. Trollope have something in common, something which stands in contrast with the characters, for instance, of Dickens. Those of the latter that I know, seem, to me at least, to be forced and unnatural caricatures; if they belong at all to the *genus* Man, it can only be to the species Cockney. I never came across such people, and I do not wish to come across them. But George Eliot's characters are true to the universal nature of man. We know that her English characters are real; we feel that her Florentine characters must be equally real. So, in a lower walk, it is with Mr. Trollope. If his characters have not the depth of George Eliot's, they have equal truth. We have seen people like a great many of them, and we feel that we easily might come across people like the others. Mr. Trollope had certainly gone far to write himself out; his later work is far from being so good as his earlier. But after all, his worst work is better than a great many people's best; and, considering the way in which it was done, it is wonderful that it was done at all. I myself know what fixed hours of work are and their value; but I could not undertake to write about William Rufus or Appius Claudius up to a certain moment on the clock, and to stop at that moment. I suppose it was from his habits of official business that Mr. Trollope learned to do it, and every man undoubtedly knows best how to do his own work. Still it is strange that works of imagination

did not suffer by such a way of doing. That work is now over; the intellectual wheel that has ground for us so much harmless pleasure has stopped.—EDWARD A. FREEMAN, "Anthony Trollope," *Macmillan's Magazine*, Jan. 1883, p. 240

His theory of work had much to do with his failures—using the word in the critical, not in the commercial sense—because he held consistently that literature, as a question of mere production, is subject to precisely the same laws as the production of shoes by a cordwainer, and can be turned out day by day in fixed quantities with the same even level of quality, and without the need of breaks between to let the mind recover its spring. But the unrelieved flatness of more than half of his own books (though never falling, it may be freely granted, below mediocrity) is, in truth, the confutation of his theory, much as the cognate example of Southey proves in poetry, apart from the physiological fact that this steady exercise of brain-power is possible only for those who enjoy the perfect health of Anthony Trollope, and know dyspepsia and neuralgia only by report. He shows himself fully conscious of his own small power of contriving a plot, and avows his preference for the theory of the novel which makes it chiefly a study of character; and it is certain that his own reputation will rest mainly on a small group of figures in a few of his books. His own favourite, the Duke of Omnium (Plantagenet Palliser), will perhaps not be one of these; and Archdeacon Grantley, Mrs. Proudie, and Mr. Crawley are more likely to live.—RICHARD F. LITTLEDALE, *Academy*, Oct. 27, 1883, p. 274

Hence, in the first place, a swarm of romancers, who have properly no place in literature, and who represent every variety of mediocrity, from the fussy and furious dead-level of sensationalism to the tame and timid dead-level of conventionality. Some put blood in their ink, some water, but it must be said that in these matters blood is not always thicker than water. Rise a step above this level; introduce some art in the plot and some truth in the characterization; keep as close to actual life as a photographer; be as diffuse and dogged in details as is consistent with preserving a kind of languid interest; economize material, whether of incident or emotion; realize Carlyle's sarcasm that England contains twenty millions of people, mostly bores—and you have Anthony Trollope, the most unromantic of romancers, popular in virtue of his skill in reproducing a population.—EDWIN P. WHIPPLE, "In Dickens-Land," *Scribner's Magazine*, Dec. 1887, p. 743

Anthony Trollope and Charles Reade 〈. . .〉 will always stand together in the front of the second rank of Victorian novelists, which might well be the first rank of an age less exceptionally gifted.

〈. . .〉 It was not until 1853 that the publication of *The Warden* established him at once in the position which he kept more or less till the end of his life. We do not think that in any of his after works Mr. Trollope ever surpassed this story, or produced anything so perfect in its subdued tones as the picture of the elderly and humble-minded clergyman, so true, so simple and so mild, yet invulnerable in gentle resolution when his conscience had been awakened and he had perceived his position to be untenable, according to his own high yet completely unostentatious standard of right and wrong. Mr. Harding may take his place among the best and most delicately drawn of those new men and women who have been added to our spiritual acquaintance (and their name is legion) during this age, so wealthy in fiction. He does not come up to the high standard of Colonel Newcome or Esmond, but he is, in his way, as real, and even more unconsciously and gently noble-minded than they. His mild and happy life as Warden of the picturesque old Hospital, doing good to everybody round him, sinking into the gentle languor of age among his old men whom he cherishes and loves; with his fiddle, by which he breathes forth his troubles and despondencies when they arise; his well-married, ambitious daughter, and his pretty young one, the solace of his life;—and the rising cloud that comes over him, his conflicts within and without against the renunciation which his friends think so foolish, and the sudden strength of unalterable conviction which gives the mild old man strength to stand against them all,—are so admirably done that we are made to share at once in the soft determination which is beyond all argument, and the exasperated incapacity of everybody around to perceive any reason why he should take the step which he feels so incumbent on him. The little sunny cathedral town, the gentle drowsy atmosphere, into which as yet no bustling new life has come, the old bishop and his old clergy going down the quiet path together, is perfectly rendered, and Barchester entered at once and permanently into the record of English sees, from the day when this little book, one volume and no more, was given to the world.

It was, however, more than "the Warden," it was a little world of well-known figures that came into view along with Mr. Harding. Everybody concluded, not knowing Mr. Trollope as yet, that he was at least the son of a Canon or other ecclesiastical dignitary steeped in the life of the Close, and drawing, if not individual sketches, yet pictures from a memory filled with long processions of Deans, Archdeacons and other clerical folk. It remains one of the wonders of which there are so many in literature, how a young man struggling into life, whose antecedents had been anything but those of a Cathedral, the son of an almost nomad family, and with little that was beautiful in his life and circumstances, should have been the one to introduce that serene yet sorely tried old man, with all those towers and cloisters behind him, and the characteristic atmosphere and tone of so strongly marked a community to the acquaintance of the world. But these contrasts and paradoxes are of continual occurrence in the works of real genius. From this beginning rose a series of books which in their day interested all readers as much, or nearly as much, as Thackeray or Dickens. Perhaps none of all the characters created by these masters entered into the general life and conversation more than did Mrs. Proudie, the wife of the new Bishop of Barchester, whose sway over him and the diocese was so real a thing both to Barchester and to England, and over whom, when she suddenly and unaccountably died in the height of her activity and fame, the whole country raised a wail of regret and remonstrance to earth and heaven. It is very rarely that a novelist produces such an effect as this. It was indeed more real and loud than our grief over the beautiful and touching tragedy of Colonel Newcome—for there seemed still a prospect of endless amusement in Mrs. Proudie, and no reason in the world why she should die. Her absolute reality and firm standing upon the common soil, a woman whom we all knew, perhaps had something to do with this triumph over the higher imagination.

We cannot pause upon the Archdeacon, whose creation is as distinct and masterly, nor his wife, nor the many other members of that most characteristic community—which extends into life on every side, even reaching so far as the Duke of Omnium and that remarkable young politician and statesman, his heir Mr. Plantagenet Palliser. The last *Chronicle of Barset* added a stronger note of tragedy to the varied story which began with Mr. Harding, in the person of another clergyman, Mr. Crawley, the poor, proud, learned parson with his overflowing family, and the false accusation which hung over

him for so long. Posterity, to which we all appeal, will find nowhere any better illustration of the Victorian age than in this series of admirable fiction—if it does not lose its way among the intolerable number of books which put forward a somewhat similar claim. Mr. Trollope wrote a great many more novels. He wrote indeed a great deal too many for his own reputation, not only because of the fact that in so much there could not but be considerable inequality, but also because the voluminous writer is always less likely to secure a favourable judgment than the more reticent or of slower productive power, whose claim is more easily investigated, and the best he can do or has done more clearly identified. He added to this effect in his own person by a cheerful vaunting of his mode of work, and humorous exaggeration of the just so many words a day which he bound himself to write. He has been thence represented as a man working by the most prosaic methods at a mere trade of novel writing, an exceedingly false as well as highly injurious representation. The man who could write the *Chronicles of Barchester*, may well be content to rest upon these admirable works his claim to enduring fame.—MARGARET OLIPHANT, *The Victorian Age of English Literature*, 1892, Vol. 2, pp. 281–87

You cannot be at perfect ease with a friend who does not joke, and I suppose this is what deprived me of a final satisfaction in the company of Anthony Trollope, who jokes heavily or not at all, and whom I should otherwise make bold to declare the greatest of English novelists; as it is, I must put before him Jane Austen, whose books, late in life, have been a youthful rapture with me. Even without much humor Trollope's books have been a vast pleasure to me through their simple truthfulness. Perhaps if they were more humorous they would not be so true to the British life and character present in them in the whole length and breadth of its expansive commonplaceness. It is their serious fidelity which gives them a value unique in literature, and which if it were carefully analyzed would afford a principle of the same quality in an author who was undoubtedly one of the finest of artists as well as the most Philistine of men.—WILLIAM DEAN HOWELLS, "Valdés, Galdós, Verga, Zola, Trollope, Hardy," *My Literary Passions*, 1895

I hold that the best of Trollope's stories are excellent reading. He has admirable qualities as a writer of fiction; indeed he has helped to ameliorate the asperities of our middle-class existence. He gives us enough, sometimes more than enough; but still he has a happy tact of omission. Trollope's chief excellence is in the portrayal of character; the dialogue is what people naturally use; it is even more than that—they could not well use any other. I am fond of his heroines; they are affectionate and true; one knows pretty well what they are going to do next, one always feels safe with them. His young people are not discouraged by the tedium of *la grâce* or bezique, or other equally mild amusements: they smile and dance and whisper themselves into each other's hearts, and, what is so very agreeable about them, they are generally content to remain there. Trollope's ideal of happiness has nothing in it of the unattainable. We know he had not the distinction of Thackeray, the exuberant genius of Dickens, or the vivid and vehement force of Charles Reade; but not seldom he is worthy of their company; and his tone can compare favourably with that of any of his illustrious contemporaries, from Bulwer and Disraeli to the geniuses just mentioned. Trollope has a fund of common sense and hearty good nature. It is the tone of a gentleman of the middle class, who is able to esteem and do justice to all classes. A novelist should deal with fancies and feelings that are natural without being obvious; perhaps Trollope did not sufficiently recognise this distinction; however, he did his best, and thus I hope the intention of his being was achieved.—FREDERICK LOCKER-LAMPSON, *My Confidences*, 1895, pp. 334–35

Almost immediately after Trollope's death appeared an *Autobiography* in which, with praiseworthy but rather indiscreet frankness, he detailed habits of work of a mechanical kind, the confession of which played into the hands of those who had already begun to depreciate him as a mere book-maker. It is difficult to say how many novels he wrote, persevering as he did in composition up to the very time of his death; and it is certain that the productions of his last decade were, as a rule, very inferior to his best. This best is to be found chiefly, but not entirely, in what is called the "Barsetshire" series, clustering round a county and city which are more or less exactly Hampshire and Winchester, beginning in 1855 with *The Warden*, a good but rather immature sketch, and continuing through *Barchester Towers* (perhaps his masterpiece), *Doctor Thorne, Framley Parsonage*, and *The Small House at Allington* (the two latter among the early triumphs of the *Cornhill Magazine*), to *The Last Chronicle of Barset* (1867), which runs *Barchester Towers* very hard, if it does not surpass it. Other favourite books of his were *The Three Clerks, Orley Farm, Can You Forgive Her*, and *Phineas Finn*—nor does this by any means exhaust the list even of his good books.

It has been said that Trollope is a typical novelist, and the type is of sufficient importance to receive a little attention, even in space so jealously allotted as ours must be. The novel craved by and provided for the public of this second period (it has also been said) was a novel of more or less ordinary life, ranging from the lower middle to the upper class, correctly observed, diversified by sufficient incident not of an extravagant kind, and furnished with description and conversation not too epigrammatic but natural and fairly clever. This norm Trollope hit with surprising justness, and till the demand altered a little or his own hand failed (perhaps there was something of both) he continued to hit it. His interests and experiences were fairly wide; for, besides being active in his Post Office duties at home and abroad, he was an enthusiastic fox-hunter, fairly fond of society and of club-life, ambitious enough at least to try other paths than those of fiction in his *Thackeray* (a failure), his *Cicero* (a worse failure), and other things. And everything that he saw he could turn into excellent novel-material. No one has touched him in depicting the humours of a public office, few in drawing those of cathedral cities and the hunting-field. If his stories, as stories, are not of enthralling interest or of very artfully constructed plots, their craftsmanship in this respect leaves very little to complain of. And he can sometimes, as in the Stanhope family of *Barchester Towers*, in Mrs. Proudie *passim*, in Madalina Demolines, and in others, draw characters very little removed from those who live with us for ever. It is extremely improbable that there will ever be a much better workman of his own class; and his books are certainly, at their best, far better than all but one or two that appear, not merely in any given year nowadays, but in any given lustrum. Yet the special kind of their excellence, the facts that they reflect their time without transcending it, and that in the way of merely reflective work each time prefers its own workmen and is never likely to find itself short of them, together with the great volume of Trollope's production, are certainly against him; and it is hard even for those who enjoyed him most, and who can still enjoy him, to declare positively that there is enough of the permanent and immortal in him to justify the hope of a resurrection.—GEORGE SAINTSBURY, *A History of Nineteenth Century Literature*, 1896, pp. 329–31

⟨. . .⟩ a writer who followed Thackeray in the systematic confinement of his studies to the "comfortable" classes of society, but who has nowhere displayed the faintest traces of Thackeray's subtle humour, his genuine though restrained pathos, his unrivalled insight into character, or his admirable prose style. Within certain narrow limits—those, for instance, of the cathedral close—Trollope was not without an eye for character, and he has portrayed certain naturally humorous types to be found within these limits with a fidelity which in itself assures for them a humorous effect; but speaking generally, his art, in its mechanical realism, stands related to Thackeray's as that of the cheap photographer to the masterly portrait-painter's. It is the commonplace carried to its highest power; and the fact that for so long a series of years he stood unquestioned at the head of his branch of the literary profession and commanded a public so large that the amount of his professional earnings was for his day unprecedented, affords a phenomenon almost as discouraging in itself as the reign of Mr. Tupper in another field of literature. Indeed, if it would be unjust to the novelist to treat the two instances as precisely parallel, it is only because, vast as may be the interval which divides the third-rate in prose fiction from the first-rate, the difference between the poetaster and the poet is one not in degree but in kind.—H. D. TRAILL, *Social England*, 1897, Vol. 6, p. 517

Trollope's plots, so far as he may have any, are conventional. Finding from experience that a novel would not sell without a dash of love-making, and believing that one plot was as good as another, he hit upon two situations he thought true to real life; and he employed them over and over: a young woman vacillating in her choice between two or more professed lovers, or a young man deciding after much concluding which of two girls he shall marry. Upon the novel of mystery and difficulty in which Wilkie Collins was an adept, he looked in wonder, and once dabbled with it, only to mar the beauty of his most tragic last chronicle of Barset. Dispensing for the most part with the 'wearing work' and the 'agonizing doubt' of the skilful plot manipulator, he sits down comfortably and writes about his cathedral folk; men and women come and go; he relates what they said and did, and draws full-length portraits of them. His main regret is 'that no mental method of daguerreotype or photography has yet been discovered by which the characters of men can be reduced to writing and put into grammatical language with an unerring precision of truthful description.' With his mind concentrated upon his characters, he looks them full in the face, perplexed by no ethical or philosophical medium. By virtue of this directness, he is the great chronicler of English fiction.—WILBUR L. CROSS, *The Development of the English Novel*, 1899, pp. 223–24

The later years of Anthony Trollope's working career gave a curious denial to a doctrine once laid down to me with much emphasis by a great London publisher of popular novels. The publisher declared that when once a novelist had got his public, the public never would leave him. 'The trouble,' he said, 'is to get hold of the public; but once the novelist has got it, you may take my word for it, his public never will leave him, it will last out his lifetime anyhow; he could n't shake it off even if he tried.' I was but a young beginner at the time, and knew little about the matter, and I took the words of my esteemed friend, the publisher, as gospel, and could only envy the happy lot of the novelist who had actually got his public. But I am afraid that my friend's doctrine was not always borne out by those hard facts which interfere with the universal recognition of so many doctrines. Trollope's literary fame certainly went through the three stages of slow growth, splendid maturity, and steady decline. In his later days his readers fell off to an astonishing degree, and time almost seemed to have come round, as in the case of Cassius, and where he did begin, there did he end, with a sadly limited circulation. He took his decaying popularity with as much composure as he had taken his early lack of popularity, as doggedly and uncomplainingly as he took his frequent falls in those hunting-fields which at one time he loved so well. He had made his name, however, in the meantime; and his best novels have a secure place in the literature of Queen Victoria's reign.—JUSTIN McCARTHY, *Reminiscences*, 1899, Vol. 1, pp. 374–75

Lord Beaconsfield was the Paul Veronese of English Novelists. It would be waste of time to inquire what artist's name could be bracketed with Anthony Trollope, for Mr. Trollope was not an artist, he was a photographer. It was only for the improvement of his style that he subjected himself to discipline. In this he persevered until he developed a narrative style which, for his purpose, could hardly be surpassed: it is lucid and easy, if somewhat commonplace. For the rest of an artist's work Trollope cared nothing. He did not devise new and startling plots, life as he knew it being sufficiently varied and interesting to satisfy ordinary people. He took pride in remaining an ordinary person himself, and in appealing to everyday emotion and narrating everyday experiences. What he saw he could tell better, perhaps, than anybody else, as Mr. Browning somewhat grudgingly said of Andrea del Sarto. What he did not see, did not exist for him. He had something of the angry impatience of the middle-class mind with all points of view not his own. In *Barchester Towers* he permitted himself to gibe at the recently published novel *Tancred*, and for the author as well as the work he cherished a feeling of contemptuous dislike. There could be no finer tribute to Lord Beaconsfield's genius. *Tancred* is as far beyond anything that Mr. Trollope wrote as *Orley Farm* is superior to a Chancery pleading; and we have but to lay *Alroy* on the same table with *The Prime Minister* to see where Anthony Trollope stands. ⟨. . .⟩

All Mr. Trollope's characters live under the domination of four leading ideas: the supremacy of the House of Commons in the government of this country, the authority of the Press, the grip of the Chruch on the life of the nation, and the prestige of the marriage tie.

⟨. . .⟩ his detail is as clearly cut as possible. We remember exactly how many children Archdeacon Grantly had, and how many thousands a year income. The Vicar of Bullhampton and the Dean of Brotherton were both combative men, but are no more to be confused than one intimate friend is to be confused with another intimate friend. Mr. Emilius, Mr. Groschut and Mr. Slope are all advertising clergymen; but who could mistake Slope for Emilius? John Crumb is as different as possible from Sam Brattle; Squire Amedroz a different creature altogether from Squire Dale or Squire Carbury. Lord de Courcy, Lord Brotherton and the Marquis of Auld Reekie are all invalidish gentlemen with bad tempers; and each is as different from his brother-noble as Lord Trowbridge is from all three.

To remember all this is not a question of memory: it is the result of Mr. Trollope's method. Other writers have gone deep into detail—Lord Lytton for example, and Mr. Dickens. But nobody remembers the detail of Lord Lytton's work; and the detail of Dickens's work is remembered only after long study—the result of downright affection for the man, although it is thirty years since he left us. With Mr. Trollope it is different. His detail is remembered—cannot, in fact, be forgotten—even

although it is often in appearance trivial. Every piece of detail is important and consistent with its neighbour. Even the fact that the Marquis of Mountfidgett 'bought a great many marble statues' (which was the Duke of Omnium's contemptuous way of describing a man with a cultivated taste in the fine arts) does not escape one's memory; and the Marquis of Mountfidgett is a character merely alluded to in *The Prime Minister* as a man who asked for the late Marquis's Garter and did not get it.

To say all this, if it be true, is to claim a very high place for Mr. Trollope as a master of plot and narrative; and a very high place is undoubtedly his by right. If we insist on denying that Mr. Trollope was an artist, we must at least admit that his photography was consummate; but if we are tempted to relent, and describe him as an artist, we are at once restrained by remembering the indignation with which Mr. Trollope himself repudiated the idea that he was any more of an artist than a bootmaker.—WALTER FREWEN LORD, "The Novels of Anthony Trollope," *Nineteenth Century*, May 1901, pp. 805–16

⟨. . .⟩ the conspicuous merit of Trollope's novels, in the eyes of his own countrymen, is their value as pictures of contemporary manners. Here he may claim to have been surpassed by no writer of his own generation.

⟨. . .⟩ He crowded his canvas with figures; he pursued the fortunes of three or four sets of people at the same time, caring little how the fate of the one set affected that of the others; he made his novel a sort of chronicle which you might open anywhere and close anywhere, instead of a drama animated by one idea and converging towards one centre. He neglected the art which uses incidents small in themselves to lead up to the *dénoûment* and make it more striking. He took little pains with his diction, seeming not to care how he said what he had to say. These defects strike those who turn over his pages to-day. But to those who read him in the 'fifties or 'sixties, the carelessness was redeemed by, or forgotten in, the vivacity with which the story moved, the freshness and faithfulness of its pictures of character and manners.—JAMES BRYCE, "Anthony Trollope," *Studies in Contemporary Biography*, 1903, pp. 123, 130

UNSIGNED
From *"Orley Farm"*
National Review, January 1863, pp. 36–40

M r. Trollope is incapable of conceiving a tragedy, or of doing justice to it when circumstances bring it in his way, we have well nigh exhausted the complaints that need be brought against him. It is a more agreeable task to touch upon the many excellent qualities which have concurred in recommending him to the good will of his countrymen. His pages are unsullied by a single touch of malice, unkindness, or revenge. His amusing sketch in *The Warden* of three bishops, given as a burlesque account of the three sons of the archdeacon, proves that he could, if he pleased, be personal to the greatest effect; and every author must have little spites and dislikes of his own, which only a resolute good feeling can prevent from intruding upon his canvas. Mr. Trollope never sins in this respect, and his immunity from this failing might well be accepted as an apology for a host of minor delinquencies. Another great charm is, that the author is for the most part kept well out of sight, and if he appears, shows himself thoroughly interested in the piece, and sincerely desirous that his audience should be so likewise. Mr. Thackeray's curious taste for careless, rambling, "round-about" writing, and the clever knack he has of making the most of "an infinite deal of nothing," has set the fashion to a host of imitators, who do not scruple to stop at every convenient point of their narration to indulge in a few personal confidences, and enunciate their views about their story, themselves, or the world in general. Mr. Thackeray, in particular, loses no opportunity of, so to speak, yawning in public; saying how dreadfully tiresome his novels are to him, how he falls asleep over them at the club, and strongly recommends his friends to do the same. Mr. Trollope has no touch of this affectation; he does his very best: he believes in the piece, he detests the villains, admires the heroes, and can scarcely refrain from caressing his pet heroine when she crosses his path. If he comes for a few moments on the stage, it is only to bustle about, to adjust the ropes, to hurry the scene-shifters, and to assure the beholders that no pains are being spared for their entertainment. Mr. Thackeray, on the contrary, lolls in dressed in a dressing-gown and slippers, stretches his arms, cries, "Eheu! fugaces,—monsieur, mon cher confrère;" and acknowledges that he has often done vilely before, but never so vilely as on the present occasion.

Mr. Trollope does not, however, invariably preserve the wholesome rule of impersonality. Though a thorough optimist, and believing in his heart that the world is the best of all possible worlds, he has one or two little grievances which keep us just short of absolute perfection. With characteristic carelessness and high spirits, he points out the tiny flaw which he has discovered, and adds a scarcely serious murmur to the general chorus of complaint. One of his troubles, for instance, is, that there should be such wicked people as lawyers in the world, and he grows quite sentimental over the circumstance that gentlemen should put off their consciences when they put on their wigs, and consent, for the small remuneration of one guinea, to make the worse appear the better cause. In support of his views, he has constructed an elaborate trial scene, with a proper apparatus of bullying counsel, lying attorneys, frightened witnesses, and, finally, frustrated justice. A discriminating critic, who appears to write with professional enthusiasm, has been at the pains to tear the whole thing to pieces, and to show that in every essential particular Mr. Trollope did not know what he was talking about, that no such facts as those on which he grounds his insinuation could possibly exist, and that all but a few black sheep in the profession do precisely what Mr. Trollope says that they ought. So much good labour seems to us in a large degree wasted upon a writer with whom instruction is necessarily subsidiary to amusement, and who scarcely pretends to any but the most superficial acquaintance with the evils of which he complains. Some of the details of the trial, especially the cross-examination by the counsel for the defence, are so ludicrously unlike real life, that it is evident Mr. Trollope's visits to a court of justice have been few and far between, and have left on his mind only a vague and indistinct impression, which nothing but the haze in which it is involved preserves from instant exposure. Ideas of this kind hardly admit of being definitely stated, but may be easily insinuated in the course of a story constructed for the purpose of exemplifying them. Witnesses, no doubt, are sometimes bullied into confusion and even forgetfulness; but Mr. Trollope cannot seriously mean that when a poor fool like Kenneby gets into the box to swear away another person's life or character, his capacity to remember any thing, and the degree in which he actually does remember the particular facts in question, ought not to be tested with the utmost severity. It is curious that, in the very case which Mr. Trollope frames in his own support, the performers do precisely that which justice required. Mr.

Chaffanbrass, from the Old Bailey, may have been a great rogue; but he acted quite properly, and served the general interests of society in demonstrating that Dockwrath had private motives of the very strongest kind for supporting the prosecution, just as Mr. Furnival acted quite properly in showing that Kenneby had only half his wits about him, and had no such accurate recollection of a matter which happened twenty years before as to justify a conviction for perjury. Mr. Trollope probably meant nothing more than that barristers are sometimes vulgar and unscrupulous, and judges sometimes petulant and overbearing; but he should beware of discussing as a grievance that which is really a necessity, and of grounding on imaginary and impossible facts an imputation on the honour and good faith of a profession which certainly contains in its ranks as many scrupulous and high-minded gentlemen as any other.

It would be easy to multiply instances of the same sort of unsubstantial complaint thrown in without any real conviction, as a sort of sentimental garnishing to a matter-of-fact narrative. In his last tale, for instance, the author stops in the midst of the description of a village to contrast our present ideas of rural grandeur with those of our forefathers. In old times the good squire "sat himself down close to his God and his tenants," and placed his house so as "to afford comfort, protection, and patronage" to those around him; nowadays "a solitude in the centre of a park is the only eligible site; no cottage must be seen but the cottage *orné* of the gardener; the village, if it cannot be abolished, must be got out of sight; the sound of the church-bells is not desirable," &c.; in fact, the present race of country gentlemen are a sad falling away from the traditional benevolence of their race. Does Mr. Trollope, we wonder, really believe this? What is the golden age with which the present iron epoch is contrasted? Does he look back with a loving eye upon feudal times and the "droits de seigneurie"? or are we wrong in believing that the maxim, that property has duties as well as rights, has never been more thoroughly accepted than in our day, and that the squires of England, more perhaps than any other class of proprietors in existence, are alive to the responsibilities of their position, and struggling conscientiously "to afford comfort, protection, and patronage" of the most substantial sort to their poorer neighbours?

We can afford to touch only upon one other characteristic of Mr. Trollope's writings, to which he would, we think, do well to pay attention,—their occasional broad vulgarity. He drops every now and then with suspicious ease into a society which is simply repulsive in its stupid coarseness; and as he has not the extravagant fun that Dickens pours over low life, and which has immortalised such personages as Mrs. Gamp, these parts of Mr. Trollope's writings are singularly tedious and unattractive. Some people have a genius for such descriptions: the authoress of *Adam Bede* can draw a set of countrymen drinking in a public-house so humorously that we forget every thing but the fun of the scene; but Mr. Trollope's commercial gentlemen, lodging-house keepers, and attorneys, are simply snobs, into whose proceedings one feels no wish to pry, and who might with great advantage be banished altogether from the picture. A stupid violent man like Moulder, coming home half tipsy, and proceeding to complete the process of intoxication before his wife and friends, must be very amusing indeed meanwhile, if we are to look on without disgust; in Mr. Trollope's hands he is any thing but amusing, and tries to atone for his dulness by being unnecessarily coarse. Mr. Trollope succeeds capitally in depicting nice young ladies like Madeline Staveley, and pleasant gentlemanly lads like Peregrine Orme;

and he may contentedly resign the portraiture of Moulders, Kantwises, and Kennebys, to artists whose knowledge of life is more varied than his own, or whose conceptive ability enables them, as in some rare instances is the case, to dispense with the experience from which all but the very highest sort of artists are obliged to draw.

A. V. DICEY
"Anthony Trollope"
Nation, March 12, 1874, pp. 174–75

Mr. Trollope is the most successful of literary artisans. He pursues literature as a profession, and can turn out a particular kind of work at any moment, and in any quantity he chooses. As a mere feat of intellectual energy, there is something marvellous in the rapid production of his novels. Before reviewers have criticised one, they find that another is all but finished, a second commenced, and a third advertised to appear shortly. But yesterday *Phineas Redux* was his latest book, and now Mr. Trollope is at work again pouring forth at least one new serial. Moreover, the products of his brain are always workmanlike articles. He writes for the market, and his powers of supply are limited simply by the public demand. But he never produces work made simply to sell. He fixes to himself a standard of literary excellence which he never falls greatly below; his standard is exactly that of the so-called intelligent reader. He meets the wishes of that large class of persons whose taste is too good to be satisfied with Miss Braddon, and not good enough to enjoy George Eliot. He is, therefore, deservedly the most read, though far from the greatest, of living English novelists. His deficiencies and his merits are worth examination, both because he is a very remarkable writer, and because of the light they throw on the feelings of the generation who find in him their ideal of an agreeable story-teller. The author of *Barchester Towers* has marked talents, and in some of his earlier works shows that he has in him the making of a great writer. But the most friendly critics can hardly deny that Mr. Trollope's later stories are at least as remarkable for their quantity as their quality, and that Mr. Trollope himself will never take rank in the first class of English novelists. In several of the characteristics which have distinguished the most eminent writers of fiction he is markedly deficient. He is absolutely devoid, for example, of the power to create a plot. Of this he is so fully aware, that in *Phineas Redux* he gives up at once the attempt to throw any doubt over his hero's innocence of the murder laid to his charge. He does not even possess skill enough to devise a combination of circumstances under which Phineas may plausibly be suspected of crime. The truth with which the details of the trial are painted conceals for a moment, but for a moment only, the fact that such a trial could never have taken place, since there never existed ground for plausible suspicion, to say nothing of ground for arraignment or conviction. Mr. Trollope, again, has none of the lavish fertility and originality of invention which make Dickens, with all his faults and shortcomings, one of the first among writers of fiction. The author of *Pickwick* never worked out a single coherent or absolutely natural character, but the number of original characters he has suggested is almost unlimited; and writers of a different stamp (notably Thackeray) have more than once made a reputation by working out, with a care and subtlety of which Dickens was incapable, conceptions of which his exuberant fancy has afforded the suggestion. No doubt, all the pictures of Dickens are caricatures, but his caricatures often throw more light on human nature than Trollope's most lifelike portraits. To say that Mr. Trollope has not the humor of Dickens is to say nothing; for such an assertion only means that he cannot rival a humorist who, all deductions being made, is still the greatest of the century. But a critic may go much further than this, and may point out with truth that Mr. Trollope hardly ever excites in the minds of his readers any vivid feeling of amusement. Whenever he attempts broad fun he resembles his mother, and displays a good deal of her vulgarity, without anything like her power.

Inability to construct a plot and incapacity to excite laughter are defects, but not fatal defects. A different fault, which will tell fatally against Mr. Trollope's lasting reputation, is that he has not produced any of those great and original characters which are to be found in the works of Thackeray, Miss Brontë, or George Eliot. He has drawn sketches, such as the portrait of Mrs. Proudie, which may stand as representatives of a class; but throughout the whole of his works there is not to be found a single character, such as Colonel Newcome, or Becky Sharp, or Jane Eyre, or Dorothea, which is a permanent addition to the world of English fiction. Take, for example, *Phineas Redux*. Phineas himself and Madam Max have each a certain individuality, but neither of them makes up a consistent whole. Phineas appears, when first we know him, as an amiable but decidedly hungry political adventurer. An adventurer he continues to the end of the tale; for he goes into public life prepared to play double or quits, and to make his fortune out of the public. But this man, who could never have got into the position he occupied without reckless boldness and cool nerve, appears at the end of his career as much affected by the groundless and disproved suspicion of crime as would be a timid young lady. Add to this that, after taking an eager part in the game of politics, he throws up his cards for motives which would have appeared out of place even in a political purist. Madame Max is open to similar criticism. When first introduced on the scene she is an adventuress endowed with some good qualities. As painted in *Phineas Redux*, she is a high-minded lady who sacrifices everything to the dictates of moral delicacy. This inconsistency in the development of character is a fault never to be found in the works of masters. The Beatrice who appears as a selfish young girl in *Esmond* reappears as a selfish, debonaire old woman of seventy in *The Virginians*, but the selfish old lady is simply the gay, heartless girl hardened by the experience of a long and disreputable life. This failure to develop the growth of character is connected with a far more serious defect. Mr. Trollope lacks entirely the intellectual truthfulness which compels Thackeray or Balzac to paint the most repulsive persons or the most painful scenes in all their hideous reality. Mr. Trollope might possibly have conceived to himself the picture of Sir Pitt Crawley, but he would certainly not have done more than vaguely suggest the nature of the baronet's life, and would never have drawn the revolting details of his old age. The truth is that Mr. Trollope is essentially a superficial writer and delights to deal with the outside of things. He has never successfully described the working of strong feeling. Whenever he has attempted to depict violent passion, he has always in fact described, not strong feeling, but the most obvious outward signs of feeling. Lady Laura's hopeless passion for Phineas ought to form the tragic part of *Phineas Redux*. The picture of her affection is not without a certain coarse power; but you hear far too much of the lady's throwing herself about "sprawling" (to use her brother's expression) on the floor, and far too little of the struggle between pride and affection which ought to have made the real tragedy of the situation. It is, in fact, this essential superficiality which places Mr. Trollope so far below writers who, like Miss Brontë, have not half his technical literary skill nor a quarter of his general knowledge of the world. But this delight in the outside of things, if it is Mr. Trollope's weakest point, is also in some sense the basis of his immense popular success.

This success will be found at bottom to depend upon two characteristics. The first and the best is his unrivalled power of depicting manner and all that is connected with manner. It is this power which makes him so strong in the description of the characteristic traits by which one class of men is distinguished from another. His lawyers, his clergymen, his bagmen, or his members of Parliament are not in themselves noteworthy personages, but they all possess exactly the salient traits of the class to which they belong. Mr. Chaffanbrass, for example, is not half so humorous a person as Sergeant Buzfuz; but every one must feel that Sergeant Buzfuz is an admirable piece of satire, while Mr. Chaffanbrass is simply a faithful portrait of a great *nisi-prius* advocate. Take again Bishop Proudie. There is nothing whatever remarkable about him. The chief feature of his character is (if we may be allowed a bull) that it is featureless, but he combines in himself all the petty traits of the feebler class of clergymen. The gift which makes Mr. Trollope the painter of classes makes him also the inimitable critic of manner. It is curious to observe how much of his works is taken up with disquisitions on the effect of manner. Why one man gets a predominance over his neighbors by the mere force of self-assertion; why a youth cannot compete with an older person who in all substantial qualities is by far his inferior; why a duke who never through life did anything is respected by all men, whilst his successor, who is always laboring for the public good, is thought little of and unfavorably criticised, are the enquires which Mr. Trollope delights to propound, and answers by tracing out the effect of men's manner or carriage. The maxim (taken in its most restricted sense) that "manners make the man" is not the doctrine on which a very profound observer would build up his account of human nature; but it is the dogma which exactly suits a critic like Mr. Trollope, who notes with extraordinary acuteness all the outside aspects of men, and believes in the immense effect of small causes. For in everything Mr. Trollope is acute rather than subtle or profound; and this absence of subtlety or profundity is the second characteristic which flows, like the first, from his habit of looking at the outside of things, and which secures his popularity. In nothing is this commonness of view more apparent than in the political reflections with which *Phineas Redux* is filled. All Mr. Trollope's remarks on politics are sensible. They are admirably expressed, and are of that kind which commends itself to the "constant reader" of the daily press. But they are marked by a total absence of originality. We, in fact, doubt whether Mr. Trollope has ever made a single remark which throws a ray of new light on the nature of English politics or on the motives which actuate English politicians. His one idea seems to be that the contests of party are regulated simply by the wish to get what he describes as a "slice of the cake." That politicians, like other men, look sharp after their own interests, is a truism too obvious to need or support a repetition. But to conceive that a desire for the emoluments of office is the main motive by which even the most worthless partisans are actuated, is to show not only great ignorance of English politics, but also still greater ignorance of the complexity of human nature. The desire for success, a vague idea of benefiting the public, an almost instinctive wish to defeat opponents, loyalty to party, a zeal for watchwords, which very likely the persons who employ them scarcely

understand—these and a hundred other motives, many of them too subtle to be readily summed up, are the mainspring of a politician's activity. The hunger for a "slice of the cake" is, it may be suspected, but rarely the deciding motive in the conduct of a public man. But the easy solution of the problems of political life, that every man is actuated by motives of the basest self-interest, is certain to be acceptable to the mass of readers, not because it is true, but because it is intelligible, and this characteristic of easy intelligibility pervades all Mr. Trollope's views of life. That it is a good thing to be well off, that it is well to act honorably, that it is about the best of all things to be a well-to-do English gentleman, and that it is quite the best of all things to be at once a well-to-do English gentleman and a master of fox-hounds, are the sort of maxims which Mr. Trollope directly or indirectly presents for the acceptance of his admirers. The creed he holds is in fact that the life of an English gentleman is the most satisfactory kind of life which any man can spend. It is the creed of thousands, and the teaching of the teacher who propounds it is certain to be acceptable. The source, in fact, of Mr. Trollope's success is to be found in the satisfaction which he gives to the almost universal liking for accurate sketches of everyday life, and to the equally universal admiration for the easy optimism which sees in English society, as it now exists, the best of all possible arrangements in the best of all possible worlds. The generation of whom Mr. Trollope is a prophet are no doubt a generation who hate exaggeration and stilted sentiment; but an age which worships commonplace will be found, while free from some of the vices, also to lack some of the virtues of an age like that which pardoned a good deal of false sentiment in an author who could produce a character as lovely and natural as Clarissa.

ANTHONY TROLLOPE
From Chapters 10 and 20
An Autobiography
1883

Critics, if they ever trouble themselves with these pages, will, of course, say that in what I have now said I have ignored altogether the one great evil of rapid production,— namely, that of inferior work. And of course if the work was inferior because of the too great rapidity of production, the critics would be right. Giving to the subject the best of my critical abilities, and judging of my own work as nearly as possible as I would that of another, I believe that the work which has been done quickest has been done the best. I have composed better stories—that is, have created better plots— than those of *The Small House at Allington* and *Can You Forgive Her?* and I have portrayed two or three better characters than are to be found in the pages of either of them; but taking these books all through, I do not think that I have ever done better work. Nor would these have been improved by any effort in the art of story telling, had each of these been the isolated labour of a couple of years. How short is the time devoted to the manipulation of a plot can be known only to those who have written plays and novels;—I may say also, how very little time the brain is able to devote to such wearing work. There are usually some hours of agonising doubt, almost of despair,—so at least it has been with me,—or perhaps some days. And then, with nothing settled in my brain as to the final development of events, with no capability of settling anything, but with a most distinct conception of some character or characters, I have rushed at the work as a rider rushes at a fence which he does not see. Sometimes I have encountered what, in hunting language, we call a cropper. I had such a fall in two novels of mine, of which I have already spoken—*The Bertrams* and *Castle Richmond*. I shall have to speak of other such troubles. But these failures have not arisen from over-hurried work. When my work has been quicker done,—and it has sometimes been done very quickly—the rapidity has been achieved by hot pressure, not in the conception, but in the telling of the story. Instead of writing eight pages a day, I have written sixteen; instead of working five days a week, I have worked seven. I have trebled my usual average, and have done so in circumstances which have enabled me to give up all my thoughts for the time to the book I have been writing. This has generally been done at some quiet spot among the mountains,—where there has been no society, no hunting, no whist, no ordinary household duties. And I am sure that the work so done has had in it the best truth and the highest spirit that I have been able to produce. At such times I have been able to imbue myself thoroughly with the characters I have had in hand. I have wandered alone among the rocks and woods, crying at their grief, laughing at their absurdities, and thoroughly enjoying their joy. I have been impregnated with my own creations till it has been my only excitement to sit with the pen in my hand, and drive my team before me at as quick a pace as I could make them travel.

The critics will again say that all this may be very well as to the rough work of the author's own brain, but it will be very far from well in reference to the style in which that work has been given to the public. After all, the vehicle which a writer uses for conveying his thoughts to the public should not be less important to him than the thoughts themselves. An author can hardly hope to be popular unless he can use popular language. That is quite true; but then comes the question of achieving a popular—in other words, I may say, a good and lucid style. How may an author best acquire a mode of writing which shall be agreeable and easily intelligible to the reader? He must be correct, because without correctness he can be neither agreeable nor intelligible. Readers will expect him to obey those rules which they, consciously or unconsciously, have been taught to regard as binding on language; and unless he does obey them, he will disgust. Without much labour, no writer will achieve such a style. He has very much to learn; and, when he has learned that much, he has to acquire the habit of using what he has learned with ease. But all this must be learned and acquired,—not while he is writing that which shall please, but long before. His language must come from him as music comes from the rapid touch of the great performer's fingers; as words come from the mouth of the indignant orator; as letters fly from the fingers of the trained compositor; as the syllables tinkled out by little bells form themselves to the ear of the telegraphist. A man who thinks much of his words as he writes them will generally leave behind him work that smells of oil. I speak here, of course, of prose; for in poetry we know what care is necessary, and we form our taste accordingly.

Rapid writing will no doubt give rise to inaccuracy,—chiefly because the ear, quick and true as may be its operation, will occasionally break down under pressure, and, before a sentence be closed, will forget the nature of the composition with which it was commenced. A singular nominative will be disgraced by a plural verb, because other pluralities have intervened and have tempted the ear into plural tendencies. Tautologies will occur, because the ear, in demanding fresh emphasis, has forgotten that the desired force has been already expressed. I need not multiply these causes of error, which must have been stumbling-blocks indeed when men wrote in the long sentences of Gibbon, but which Macaulay, with his multiplicity of divisions, has done so much to enable us to avoid. A rapid writer will hardly avoid these errors altogether. Speaking of myself, I am ready to declare that, with much training, I have been unable to avoid them. But the writer for the press is rarely called upon—a writer of books should never be called upon—to send his manuscript hot from his hand to the printer. It has been my practice to read everything four times at least—thrice in manuscript and once in print. Very much of my work I have read twice in print. In spite of this I know that inaccuracies have crept through,—not single spies, but in battalions. From this I gather that the supervision has been insufficient, not that the work itself has been done too fast. I am quite sure that those passages which have been written with the greatest stress of labour, and consequently with the greatest haste, have been the most effective and by no means the most inaccurate. ⟨. . .⟩

It will not, I am sure, be thought that, in making my boast as to the quantity, I have endeavoured to lay claim to any literary excellence. That, in the writing of books, quantity without quality is a vice and a misfortune, has been too manifestly settled to leave a doubt on such a matter. But I do lay claim to whatever merit should be accorded to me for persevering diligence in my profession. And I make the claim, not with a view to my own glory, but for the benefit of those who may read these pages, and when young may intend to follow the same career. *Nulla dies sine linea.* Let that be their motto. And let their work be to them as is his common work to the common labourer. No gigantic efforts will then be necessary. He need tie no wet towels round his brow, nor sit for thirty hours at his desk without moving,—as men have sat, or said that they have sat. More than nine-tenths of my literary work has been done in the last twenty years, and during twelve of those years I followed another profession. I have never been a slave to this work, giving due time, if not more than due time, to the amusements I have loved. But I have been constant,—and constancy in labour will conquer all difficulties. *Gutta cavat lapidem non vi, sed saepe cadendo.*

It may interest some if I state that during the last twenty years I have made by literature something near £70,000. As I have said before in these pages, I look upon the result as comfortable, but not splendid.

It will not, I trust, be supposed by any reader that I have intended in this so-called autobiography to give a record of my inner life. No man ever did so truly,—and no man ever will. Rousseau probably attempted it, but who doubts but that Rousseau has confessed in much the thoughts and convictions rather than the facts of his life? If the rustle of a woman's petticoat has ever stirred my blood; if a cup of wine has been a joy to me; if I have thought tobacco at midnight in pleasant company to be one of the elements of an earthly paradise; if now and again I have somewhat recklessly fluttered a £5 note over a card-table;—of what matter is that to any reader? I have betrayed no woman. Wine has brought me to no sorrow. It has been the companionship of smoking that I have loved, rather than the habit. I have never desired to win money, and I have lost none. To enjoy the excitement of pleasure, but to be free from its vices and ill effects,—to have the sweet, and leave the bitter untasted,—that has been my study. The preachers tell us that this is impossible. It seems to me that hitherto I have succeeded fairly well. I will not say that I have never scorched a finger,—but I carry no ugly wounds.

HENRY JAMES
"Anthony Trollope"
Century Magazine, July 1883, pp. 385–95

When, a few months ago, Anthony Trollope laid down his pen for the last time, it was a sign of the complete extinction of that group of admirable writers who, in England, during the preceding half-century, had done so much to elevate the art of the novelist. The author of *The Warden*, of *Barchester Towers*, of *Framley Parsonage*, does not, to our mind, stand on the very same level as Dickens, Thackeray, and George Eliot; for his talent was of a quality less fine than theirs. But he belonged to the same family—he had as much to tell us about English life; he was strong, genial, and abundant. He published too much; the writing of novels had ended by becoming, with him, a perceptibly mechanical process. Dickens was prolific; Thackeray produced with a freedom for which we are constantly grateful; but we feel that these writers had their periods of gestation. They took more time to look at their subject; relatively (for to-day there is not much leisure, at best, for those who undertake to entertain a hungry public) they were able to wait for inspiration. Trollope's fecundity was prodigious; there was no limit to the work he was ready to do. It is not unjust to say that he sacrificed quality to quantity. Abundance, certainly, is in itself a great merit; almost all the greatest writers have been abundant. But Trollope's fertility was fantastic, incredible; he himself contended, we believe, that he had given to the world a greater number of printed pages of fiction than any of his literary contemporaries. Not only did his novels follow each other without visible intermission, overlapping and treading on each other's heels, but most of these works are of extraordinary length. *Orley Farm, Can You Forgive Her?*, *He Knew He Was Right*, are exceedingly voluminous tales. *The Way We Live Now* is one of the longest of modern novels. Trollope produced, moreover, in the intervals of larger labor, a great number of short stories, many of them charming, as well as various books of travel and two or three biographies. He was the great improvvisatore of these latter years. Two distinguished story-tellers of the other sex—one in France and one in England—have shown an extraordinary facility of composition; but Trollope's pace was brisker even than that of the wonderful Madame Sand and the delightful Mrs. Oliphant. He had taught himself to keep this pace, and had reduced his admirable faculty to a habit. Every day of his life he wrote a certain number of pages of his current tale, a number sacramental and invariable, independent of mood and place. It was once the fortune of the author of these lines to cross the Atlantic in his company, and he has never forgotten the magnificent example of stiff persistence which it was in the power of the eminent novelist to give on that occasion. The season was unpropitious; the vessel overcrowded, the voyage detestable; but Trollope shut himself up in his cabin every morning for a purpose which, on the part of a distinguished writer who was also an invulnerable sailor, could only be communion with the muse. He drove his pen as steadily on the tumbling ocean as in Montague Square, and as his voyages were many it was his practice before sailing to come down to the ship and confer with the carpenter, who was instructed to rig up a rough writing-table in his small sea-chamber. Trollope has been accused of being deficient in imagination, but in the face of such a fact as that the charge will scarcely seem just. The power to shut one's eyes, one's ears (to say nothing of another sense) upon the scenery of a pitching Cunarder and open them upon the loves and sorrows of Lily Dale, or the conjugal embarrassments of Lady Glencora Palliser, is certainly a faculty which has an element of the magical. The imagination that Trollope possessed he had, at least, thoroughly at his command. I speak of all this in order to explain (in part) why it was that, with his extraordinary gift, there was always in him a certain touch of the common. He abused his gift, overworked it, rode his horse too hard. As an artist he never took himself seriously; many people will say this was why he was so delightful. The people who take themselves seriously are prigs and bores; and Trollope, with his perpetual story, which was the only thing he cared about, his strong good sense, hearty good nature, generous appreciation of life in all its varieties, responds in perfection to a certain English ideal. According to that ideal it is rather dangerous to be definitely or consciously an artist—to have a system, a doctrine, a form. Trollope, from the first, went in, as they say, for having as little form as possible; it is probably safe to affirm that he had no "views" whatever on the subject of novel-writing. His whole manner is that of a man who regards the practice as one of the more delicate industries, but has never troubled his head nor clogged his pen with theories about the nature of his business. Fortunately he was not obliged to do so, for he had an easy road to success; and his honest, familiar, deliberate way of treating his readers as if he were one of them and shared their indifference to a general view, their limitations of knowledge, their love of a comfortable ending, endeared him to many persons in England and America. It is in the name of some chosen form that, of late years, things have been made most disagreeable for the novel-reader, who has been treated by several votaries of the new experiments in fiction to unwonted and bewildering sensations. With Trollope we were always safe; there were sure to be no new experiments.

His great, his inestimable merit was a complete appreciation of reality. This gift is not rare in the annals of English fiction; it would naturally be found in a walk of literature in which the feminine mind has labored so fruitfully. Women are delicate and patient observers; they hold their noses close, as it were, to the texture of life. They feel and perceive the real (as well as the desirable), and their observations are recorded in a thousand delightful volumes. Trollope, therefore, with his eyes comfortably fixed on the familiar, the actual, was far from having invented a *genre*, as the French say; his great distinction is that, in resting there, his vision took in so much of the field. And then he *felt* all common, human things as well as saw them; felt them in a simple, direct, salubrious way, with their sadness, their gladness, their charm, their comicality, all their obvious and measurable meanings. He never wearied of the preëstablished round of English customs—never needed a respite or a change—was content to go on indefinitely watching the life that surrounded him and holding up his mirror to it. Into this mirror the public, at first especially, grew very fond of looking—for it saw itself reflected in all the most credible and supposable ways, with that curiosity that people feel to know how they look when they are represented "just as they are" by a painter who does not desire to put them into an attitude, to drape them for an effect, to arrange his light and his accessories. This exact and on the whole agreeable image, projected upon a surface without a strong intrinsic tone, constitutes mainly the entertainment that Trollope offered his readers. The striking thing to the critic was that his robust and patient mind had no particular bias, his imagination no light of its own. He saw things neither pictorially and grotesquely like Dickens; nor with that combined disposition to satire and to literary form which gives such "body," as they say of wine, to the manner of Thackeray; nor with anything of the philosophic, the transcendental cast—the desire to follow them to their remote relations—which we associate with the name of George Eliot. Trollope had his element of fancy, of satire, of irony; but these qualities were not very highly developed, and he walked mainly by the light of his good sense, his clear, direct vision of the things that lay nearest, and his great natural kindness. There is something remarkably tender and friendly in his feeling about all human perplexities; he takes the good-natured, moderate, conciliatory view—the humorous view, perhaps, for the most part, yet without a touch of mockery or cynicism. As he grew older, and had sometimes to go further afield for his subjects, he acquired a savor of bitterness and reconciled himself sturdily to treating of the disagreeable. A more copious record of disagreeable things could scarcely be imagined, for instance, than *The Way We Live Now*. But, in general, he has a wholesome mistrust of morbid analysis, an aversion to inflicting pain. He has an infinite love of detail, but his details are, for the most part, the innumerable items of the familiar. When the French are disposed to pay a compliment to the English mind, they are so good as to say that there is in it something remarkably *honnête*. If I might borrow this epithet without seeming to be patronizing, I should apply it to the genius of Anthony Trollope. He represents in an eminent degree this natural decorum of the English spirit, and represents it all the better that there is not in him a grain of the mawkish or the prudish. He writes, he feels, he judges like a man, talking plainly and frankly about many things, and is by no means destitute of a certain saving grace of coarseness. But he has kept the purity of his imagination, and held fast to old-fashioned reverences and preferences. He thinks it a suffcent objection to several topics to say simply that they are unclean. There was nothing in his theory of the storyteller's art that tended to convert the reader's or the writer's mind into a vessel for polluting things. He recognized the right of the vessel to protest, and would have regarded such a protest as conclusive. With a considerable turn for satire, though this, perhaps, is more evident in his early novels than in his later ones, he had as little as possible of the quality of irony. He never played with a subject, never juggled with the sympathies or the credulity of his reader, was never in the least paradoxical or mystifying. He sat down to his theme in a serious, business-like way, with his elbows on the table and his eye occasionally wandering to the clock.

To touch successively upon these points is to attempt a portrait, which I shall perhaps not altogether have failed to produce. The source of his success in describing the things that lay nearest to him, and describing them without any of those artistic perversions that come, as we have said, from a powerful imagination, from a cynical humor, or from a desire to look, as George Eliot expresses it, for the suppressed transitions that unite all contrasts, the essence of this love of reality was his extreme interest in character. This is the fine and admirable quality in Trollope, this is what will preserve his best things in spite of those deficiencies which keep him from standing on quite the same level as the masters. Indeed, this quality is so much one of the finest (to my mind at least) that it makes me wonder the more that the writer who had it so abundantly and so naturally should not have just that distinction which Trollope lacks and which we find in his three brilliant contemporaries. If he was in any degree a man of genius (and I hold that he was), it was in virtue of this happy, instinctive perception of character. His knowledge of human nature, his observation of the common behavior of men and women, was not reasoned, nor acquired, not even particularly studied. All

human doings deeply interested him. Human life, to his mind, was a perpetual story; but he never attempted to take the so-called scientific view, the view which has lately found ingenious advocates among the countrymen and successors of Balzac. He had no airs of being able to tell you *why* people in a given situation would conduct themselves in a particular way; it was enough for him that he felt their feelings and struck the right note, because he had, as it were, a good ear. If he was a knowing psychologist, he was so by grace; he was just and true without apparatus and without effort. He must have had a great taste for morals; he evidently believed that such things are the basis of the interest of fiction. We must be careful, of course, in attributing convictions and opinions to Trollope, who, as I have said, had as little as possible of the pedantry of his art, and whose occasional chance utterances in regard to the object of the novelist and his means of achieving it are of an almost startling simplicity. But we certainly do not go too far in saying that he gave his practical testimony in favor of the idea that the interest of a work of fiction is great in proportion as the people stand on their feet. His great effort was evidently to make them stand so; if he achieved this result by the quietest and most unpretending touches, it was nevertheless the measure of his success. If he had taken sides on the rather superficial opposition between novels of character and novels of plot, I can imagine him to have said (except that he never expressed himself in epigrams) that he preferred the former class, inasmuch as character in itself is plot, while plot is by no means character. It is more safe indeed to believe that his great good sense would have prevented him from taking an idle controversy seriously. Character, in any sense in which we can get at it, is action, and action is plot, and any plot which hangs together, even if it pretend to interest us only in the fashion of a Chinese puzzle, plays upon our emotion, our suspense, by means of personal tones. We care what happens to people only in proportion as we know what people are. Trollope's great apprehension of the real, which was what made him so interesting, came to him through his desire to satisfy us on this point—to tell us what certain people were and what they did in consequence of being so. That is the purpose of each of his tales; and if these things produce an illusion, it comes from the gradual abundance of his testimony as to the temper, the tone, the passions, the habits, the moral nature, of a certain number of contemporary Britons.

His stories, in spite of their great length, deal very little in the unusual, the unexpected, the complicated; as a general thing, he has no great story to tell. The thing is not so much a story as a picture; we hesitate to call it a picture only, because the author gives us an impression of not possessing in any appreciable degree that temperament which is known as the artistic. There is not even, as a general thing, much description, in the sense which the present votaries of realism in France attach to that word. The author lays his scene in a few deliberate, not especially pictorial strokes, and never dreams of finishing the piece for the sake of enabling the reader to hang it up. The finish, such as it is, comes later, from the slow, gradual, sometimes rather heavy accumulation of small incidents. These incidents are sometimes of the smallest; Trollope turns them out inexhaustibly, repeats them freely, unfolds them without haste and without rest. But they are all of the most homogeneous sort, and they are none the worse for that. The point to be made is that they have no great spectacular interest (we beg pardon of innumerable love-affairs that Trollope has described) like many of the incidents, say, of Walter Scott and of Alexandre Dumas: if we care to know about them (as repetitions of a familiar case), it is because the author has managed, in his solid, definite, somewhat lumbering way, to tell us that about the men and women concerned which has already excited on their behalf the impression of life. It is a marvel by what homely arts, by what plain persistence, Trollope contrives to excite this impression. Take, for example, such a work as *The Vicar of Bullhampton*. It would be difficult to give the *donnée* of this slow but excellent story, which is a capital example of interest produced by the quietest conceivable means. The principal persons in it are a lively, jovial, high-tempered country clergyman, a young woman who is in love with her cousin, and a small, rather dull squire, who is in love with the young woman. There is no connection between the affairs of the clergyman and those of the two other persons, save that these two are the Vicar's friends. The Vicar gives countenance, for Christian charity's sake, to a young countryman, who is suspected (falsely, as it appears) of murder, and also to the lad's sister, who is more than suspected of leading an immoral life. Various people are shocked at his indiscretion, but in the end he is shown to have been no worse a clergyman because he is a good fellow. A cantankerous nobleman, who has a spite against him, causes a Methodist conventicle to be erected at the gates of the vicarage; but afterward, finding that he has no title to the land used for this obnoxious purpose, causes the conventicle to be pulled down, and is reconciled with the parson, who accepts an invitation to stay at the castle. Mary Lowther, the heroine of *The Vicar of Bullhampton*, is sought in marriage by Mr. Harry Gilmore, to whose passion she is unable to respond; she accepts him, however, making him understand that she does not love him and that her affections are fixed upon her kinsman, Captain Marrable, whom she would marry (and who would marry her) if he were not too poor to support a wife. If Mr. Gilmore will take her on these terms, she will become his spouse; but she gives him all sorts of warnings. They are not superfluous; for, as Captain Marrable presently inherits a fortune, she throws over Mr. Gilmore, who retires to foreign lands, heartbroken, inconsolable. This is the substance of *The Vicar of Bullhampton*; the reader will see that it is not a very tangled skein. But if the interest is quiet, it is extreme and constant, and it comes altogether from excellent portraiture. It is essentially a moral interest. There is something masterly in the steadiness and certainty with which, in work of this kind, Trollope handles his brush. The Vicar's nature is thoroughly understood and expressed, and his monotonous friend the Squire, a man with limitations, as the phrase is, but possessed and consumed by a genuine passion, is equally near to truth.

Trollope has described again and again the ravages of love, and it is wonderful to see how well, in these delicate matters, his plain good sense and good taste serve him. His story is always primarily a love-story, and a love-story constructed on an inveterate system. There is a young lady who has two lovers, or a young man who has two sweethearts; we are treated to the innumerable forms in which this dilemma may present itself and the consequences, sometimes pathetic, sometimes grotesque, which spring from such false situations. Trollope is not what is called a colorist; still less is he a poet. He is seated on the back of heavy-footed prose. But his account of those sentiments which the poets are supposed to have made their own is apt to be as touching as demonstrations more lyrical. There is something wonderfully vivid in the state of mind of the unfortunate Harry Gilmore, of whom I have just spoken; and his history, which has no more pretensions to style than if it were cut out of yesterday's newspaper, lodges itself in the imagination in all sorts of classic company. He is not handsome, nor clever, nor rich, nor romantic, nor distinguished in

any way; he is simply a rather dull, narrow-minded, stiff, obstinate, common-place, conscientious modern Englishman, exceedingly in love and, from his own point of view, exceedingly ill-used. He is interesting because he suffers, and because we are curious to see the form that suffering will take in that particular nature. Our good fortune, with Trollope, is that the person put before us will have a certain particular nature. The author has cared enough about the character of such a person to find out exactly what it is. Another particular nature in *The Vicar of Bullhampton* is the surly, sturdy, skeptical old farmer Jacob Brattle, who doesn't want to be patronized by the parson, and in his dumb, dusky, half-brutal, half-spiritual melancholy, surrounded by domestic troubles, financial embarrassments, and a puzzling world, declines altogether to be won over to clerical optimism. Such a figure as Jacob Brattle, purely episodical though it be, is an excellent English portrait. As thoroughly English, and the most striking thing in the book, is the combination, in the nature of Frank Fenwick—the delightful Vicar—of the patronizing, conventional, clerical element, with all sorts of manliness and spontaneity; the union or, to a certain extent, the contradiction of official and personal geniality. Trollope touches these points in a way that shows that he knows his man. Delicacy is not his great sign; but when it is necessary he can be as delicate as anyone else.

I alighted, just now, at a venture, upon the history of Frank Fenwick; it is far from being a conspicuous work in the immense list of Trollope's novels. But, to choose an example, one must choose arbitrarily; for examples of almost anything that one may wish to say are numerous to embarrassment. In speaking of a writer who produced so much and produced always in the same way, there is perhaps a certain unfairness in choosing at all. As no work has higher pretensions than any other, there may be a certain unkindness in holding an individual production up to the light. "Judge me in the lump," we can imagine the author saying; "I have only undertaken to entertain the British public. I don't pretend that each of my novels is an organic whole." Trollope had no time to give his tales a classic roundness; yet there is (in spite of an extraordinary defect) something of that quality in the thing that first revealed him. *The Warden* was published in 1855. It made a great impression; and when, in 1857, *Barchester Towers* followed it, every one saw that English literature had a novelist the more. These were not the works of a young man, for Anthony Trollope had been born in 1815. It is remarkable to reflect, by the way, that his prodigious fecundity (he had published before *The Warden* three or four novels which attracted little attention) was inclosed between his fortieth and his sixty-seventh year. Trollope had lived long enough in the world to learn a good deal about it; and his maturity of feeling and evidently large knowledge of English life were for much in the impression produced by the two clerical tales. It was easy to see that he would be a novelist of weight. What he knew, to begin with, was the clergy of the Church of England, and the manners and feelings that prevail in cathedral towns. This, for a while, was his specialty, and, as always happens in such cases, the public was disposed to prescribe to him that path. He knew about bishops, archdeacons, prebendaries, precentors and about their wives and daughters; he knew what these dignitaries say to each other when they are collected together, aloof from secular ears. He even knew what sort of talk goes on between a bishop and a bishop's lady when the august couple are enshrouded in the privacy of the episcopal bedroom. This knowledge, somehow, was rare and precious. No one, as yet, had been bold enough to snatch the illuminating torch from the very summit of the altar. Trollope enlarged his field very speedily. There is, as I remember that work, as little as possible of the ecclesiastical in the tale of *The Three Clerks*, which came after *Barchester Towers*. But he always retained traces of his early observation of the clergy; he introduced them frequently, and he always did them easily and well. There is no ecclesiastical figure, however, so good as the first—no creation of this sort so happy as the admirable Mr. Harding. *The Warden* is an excellent little story, and a signal instance of Trollope's habit of offering us the spectacle of a character. A motive more delicate, more slender, as well as more charming, could scarcely be conceived. It is simply the history of an old man's conscience.

The good and gentle Mr. Harding, precentor of Barchester Cathedral, also holds the post of warden of Hiram's Hospital, an ancient charity, where twelve old paupers are maintained in comfort. The office is in the gift of the bishop, and its emoluments are as handsome as the labor of the place is small. Mr. Harding has for years drawn his salary in quiet gratitude; but his moral repose is broken by hearing it at last begun to be said that the wardenship is a sinecure, that the salary is a scandal, and that a large part, at least, of his easy income ought to go to the pensioners of the hospital. He is sadly troubled and perplexed, and when the great London newspapers take up the affair he is overwhelmed with confusion and shame. He thinks the newspapers are right—he perceives that the warden is an overpaid and a rather useless functionary. The only thing he can do is to resign the place. He has no means of his own—he is only a quiet, modest, innocent old man, with a taste, a passion, for old church music and the violoncello. But he determines to resign, and he does resign in spite of the sharp opposition of his friends. He does what he thinks right, and goes to live in lodgings over a shop in the Barchester high-street. That is all the story, and it has exceeding beauty. The question of Mr. Harding's resignation becomes a drama, and we anxiously wait for the catastrophe. Trollope never did anything happier than the picture of this sweet and serious little old gentleman, who on most of the occasions of life has shown a lamblike softness and compliance, but in this particular matter opposes a silent, impenetrable obstinacy to the urgency of the friends who insist on his keeping his sinecure—fixing his mild, detached gaze on the distance and making imaginary passes with his fiddle-bow while they demonstrate his pusillanimity. The subject of *The Warden*, exactly viewed, is the opposition of the two natures of Archdeacon Grantley and Mr. Harding, and there is nothing finer in all Trollope than the vividness with which this opposition is presented. The archdeacon is as happy a portrait as the precentor—an image of the full-fed, worldly churchman, taking his stand squarely upon his rich temporalities, and regarding the church frankly as a fat social pasturage. It required the greatest tact and temperance to make the picture of Archdeacon Grantley stop just where it does. The type, impartially considered, is detestable, but the individual may be full of amenity. Trollope allows his archdeacon all the virtues he was likely to possess, but he makes his spiritual grossness wonderfully natural. No charge of exaggeration is possible, for we are made to feel that he is conscientious as well as arrogant, and comfortable as well as hard. He is one of those figures that spring into being all at once, and solidify in the author's grasp. These two capital portraits are what we carry away from *The Warden*, which some persons profess to regard as the author's masterpiece. We remember, while it was still something of a novelty, to have heard a judicious critic say that it had much of the charm of *The Vicar of Wakefield*. Anthony Trollope would not have accepted this compliment, and would not have

wished this little tale to pass before several of its successors. He would have said, very justly, that it gives too small a measure of his knowledge of life. It has, however, a certain classic roundness, though, as we said a moment since, there is a blemish on its fair face. The chapter on Dr. Pessimist Anticant and Mr. Sentiment would be a mistake almost inconceivable, if Trollope had not in other places taken pains to show us that for certain forms of satire (the more violent, doubtless), he had absolutely no gift. Dr. Anticant is a parody of Carlyle, and Mr. Sentiment is an exposure of Dickens; and both these little *jeux d'esprit* are as infelicitous as they are misplaced. It was no less luckless an inspiration to convert Archdeacon Grantley's three sons, denominated respectively Charles James, Henry, and Samuel, into little effigies of three distinguished English bishops of that period, whose well-known peculiarities are reproduced in the description of these unnatural urchins. The whole passage, as we meet it, is a sudden disillusionment; we are transported from the mellow atmosphere of an assimilated Barchester to the air of unsuccessful allegory.

I may take occasion to remark here upon a very curious fact—the fact that there are certain precautions in the way of producing that illusion dear to the intending novelist which Trollope not only habitually scorned to take, but really, as we may say, asking pardon for the heat of the thing, delighted wantonly to violate. He took a suicidal satisfaction in reminding the reader that the story he was telling was only, after all, a make-believe. He habitually referred to the work in hand (in the course of that work) as a novel and to himself as a novelist, and was fond of letting the reader know that this novelist could direct the course of events according to his pleasure. Already, in *Barchester Towers*, he falls into this pernicious trick. In describing the wooing of Eleanor Bold by Mr. Arabin, he has occasion to say that the lady might have acted in a much more direct and natural way than the way he attributes to her. But if she had, he adds, "where would have been my novel?" The last chapter of the same story begins with the remark, "The end of a novel, like the end of a children's dinner party, must be made up of sweetmeats and sugar-plums." These little slaps at credulity (we might give many more specimens) are very discouraging, but they are even more inexplicable; for they are deliberately inartistic, even judged from the point of view of that rather vague consideration of form which is the only canon we have a right to impose upon Trollope. It is impossible to imagine what a novelist takes himself to be, unless he regard himself as an historian and his narrative as a history. It is only as an historian that he has the smallest *locus standi*. As a narrator of fictitious events, he is nowhere; to insert into his attempt a back-bone of logic, he must relate events that are assumed to be real. This assumption permeates, animates all the work of the most solid story-tellers; we need only mention (to select a single instance) the magnificent historical tone of Balzac, who would as soon have thought of admitting to the reader that he was deceiving him as Garrick or John Kemble would have thought of pulling off their disguise in front of the foot-lights. Therefore, when Trollope suddenly winks at us and reminds us that he is telling us an arbitrary thing, we are startled and shocked in quite the same way as if Macaulay or Motley were to drop the historic mask and intimate that William of Orange was a myth or the Duke of Alva an invention.

It is a part of this same ambiguity of mind as to what constitutes evidence that Trollope should sometimes endow his people with such fantastic names. Dr. Pessimist Anticant and Mr. Sentiment make, as we have seen, an awkward appearance in a modern novel; and Mr. Neversay Die, Mr. Stickatit, Mr.

Rerechild and Mr. Fillgrave (the two last the family physicians) are scarcely more felicitous. It would be better to go back to Bunyan at once. There is a person mentioned in *The Warden* under the name of Mr. Quiverful—a poor clergyman, with a dozen children, who holds the living of Puddingdale. This name is a humorous allusion to his overflowing nursery, and it matters little so long as he is not brought to the front. But in *Barchester Towers*, which carries on the history of Hiram's Hospital, Mr. Quiverful becomes, as a candidate for Mr. Harding's vacant place, an important element, and the reader is made proportionately unhappy by the primitive character of this satiric note. A Mr. Quiverful, with fourteen children (which is the number attained in *Barchester Towers*) is too difficult to believe in. We can believe in the name, and we can believe in the children; but we cannot manage the combination. It is probably not unfair to say that if Trollope derived half his inspiration from life he derived the other half from Thackeray; his earlier novels, in especial, suggest an honorable emulation of the author of *The Newcomes*. Thackeray's names were perfect; they always had a meaning, and (except in his absolutely jocose productions, where they were still admirable) we can imagine, even when they are most expressive, that they should have been borne by real people. But in this, as in other respects, Trollope's hand was heavier than his master's; though, when he is content not to be too comical, his appellations are sometimes fortunate enough. Mrs. Proudie is excellent for Mrs. Proudie, and even the Duke of Omnium and Gatherum Castle rather minister to illusion than destroy it. Indeed, the names of houses and places, throughout Trollope, are full of color.

I would speak in some detail of *Barchester Towers* if this did not seem to commit me to the prodigious task of appreciating each of Trollope's works in succession. Such an attempt as that is so far from being possible, that I must frankly confess to not having read everything that proceeded from his pen. There came a moment in his vigorous career (it was even a good many years ago) when I renounced the effort to "keep up" with him. It ceased to seem obligatory to have read his last story; it ceased soon to be very possible to know which was his last. Before that, I had been punctual, devoted; and the memories of the earlier period are delightful. It reached, if I remember correctly, to about the publication of *He Knew He Was Right*; after which, to my recollection (oddly enough, too, for that novel was good enough to encourage a continuance of past favors, as the shop-keepers say), the picture becomes dim and blurred. The author of *Orley Farm* and *The Small House at Allington* ceased to produce individual works; his activity became one huge "serial." Here and there, in the vast fluidity, a more compact mass detached itself. *The Last Chronicle of Barset*, for instance, is one of his most powerful things; it contains the sequel of the terrible history of Mr. Crawley, the starving curate—an episode full of that absolutely truthful pathos of which Trollope was so often a master, and which occasionally raised him quite to the level of his two immediate predecessors in the vivid treatment of English life—great artists whose pathetic effects were sometimes too visibly prepared. For the most part, however, he should be judged by the productions of the first half of his career; later, the strong wine was rather too copiously watered. His practice, his acquired facility, were such, that his hand went of itself, as it were, and the thing looked superficially like a fresh inspiration. But it was not fresh, it was rather stale; and though there was no appearance of effort, there was a fatal dryness of texture. It was too little of a new story and too much of an old one. Some of these ultimate compositions—*Phineas Redux* (*Phineas Finn* is much

better) *The Prime Minister, John Caldigate, The American Senator, The Duke's Children*—have the strangest mechanical movement. What stands Trollope always in good stead (in addition to the ripe habit of writing) is his various knowledge of the English world—to say nothing of his occasionally laying under contribution the American. His American portraits, by the way (they are several in number), are always friendly; they hit it off more happily than the attempt to depict American character from the European point of view is accustomed to do: though indeed, as we ourselves have not yet learned to represent our types very finely,—are not apparently even very sure what our types are,—it is perhaps not to be wondered at that transatlantic talent should miss the mark. The weakness of transatlantic talent, in this particular, is apt to be want of knowledge; but Trollope's knowledge has all the air of being excellent, though not intimate. Had he indeed striven to learn the way to the American heart? No less than twice and, possibly, even oftener has he rewarded the merit of a scion of the British aristocracy with the hand of an American girl. The American girl was destined sooner or later to make her entrance into British fiction, and Trollope's treatment of this complicated being is full of good humor and of that fatherly indulgence, that almost motherly sympathy, which characterizes his attitude throughout toward the youthful feminine. He has not mastered all the springs of her delicate organism, nor sounded all the mysteries of her conversation. Indeed, as regards these latter phenomena, he has observed a few of which he has been the sole observer. "I got to be thinking if any one of them should ask me to marry him," words attributed to Miss Boncassen, in *The Duke's Children*, have much more the note of English-American than of American-English. But, on the whole, in these matters Trollope does very well. His fund of acquaintance with his own country—and, indeed, with the world at large—was apparently inexhaustible, and it gives his novels an airy, spacious quality which we should not know where to look for elsewhere in the same degree, and which is the sign of an extraordinary difference between such an horizon as his and the limited world-outlook, as the Germans would say, of the brilliant writers who practice the art of realistic fiction on the other side of the Channel. Trollope was familiar with all sorts and orders of men, with the business of life, with affairs, with the great world of sport, with every component part of the ancient fabric of English society. He had traveled all over the globe (more than once, we believe), and for him, therefore, the background of the human drama was a very extensive scene. He had none of the pedantry of the cosmopolite; he remained a sturdy and sensible middle-class Englishman. But his work is full of implied reference to the whole arena of modern energy. He was for many years concerned in the management of the Post-office; and we can imagine no experience more fitted to impress a man with the diversity of human relations. It is possibly from this source that he derived his fondness for transcribing the letters of his love-lorn maidens and other embarrassed persons. No contemporary story-teller deals so much in letters; the modern English epistle (very happily imitated, for the most part) is his unfailing resource.

There is perhaps little reason in it, but I find myself comparing this tone of allusion to many lands and many things, and whatever it brings us of easier respiration, with that narrow vision of humanity which accompanies the strenuous, serious work lately offered us in such abundance by the votaries of art for art who sit so long at their desks on Parisian *quatrièmes*. The contrast is complete, and it would be interesting, had we space to do so here, to see how far it goes. On one side a wide, good-humored, superficial glance at a good many things; on the other a gimlet-like consideration of a few. Trollope's plan, as well as Zola's, was to describe the life that lay near him; but the two writers differ immensely as to what constitutes life and what constitutes nearness. For Trollope the emotions of a nursery-governess in Australia would take precedence of the adventures of a depraved countess in Paris or London. They both undertake to do the same thing—to depict French and English manners; but the English writer (with his unsurpassed industry) is so occasional, so accidental, so full of the echoes of voices that are not the voice of the muse. Gustave Flaubert, Émile Zola, Alphonse Daudet, on the other hand, are nothing if not concentrated and sedentary. Trollope's realism is as instinctive, as inveterate as theirs; but nothing could mark more the difference between the French and English mind than the difference in the application, on one side and the other, of this system. We say system, though on Trollope's part it is none. He has no visible, certainly no explicit care for the literary part of the business; he writes easily, comfortably, and profusely, but his style has nothing in common either with the vivid brush-work of Daudet or the calculated harmonies of Flaubert. He accepted all the common restrictions, and found that even within the barriers there was plenty of material. He attaches a preface to one of his novels—*The Vicar of Bullhampton*, before mentioned—for the express purpose of explaining why he has introduced a young woman who may, in truth, as he says, be called a "castaway"; and in relation to this episode he remarks that it is the object of the novelist's art to entertain the young people of both sexes. Writers of the French school would, of course, protest indignantly against such a formula as this, which is the only one of the kind that I remember to have encountered in Trollope's pages. It is narrow, assuredly; but Trollope's practice was really much larger than such a theory. And indeed any theory was good which enabled him to produce the works which he put forth between 1856 and 1869, or later. In spite of his want of doctrinal richness, I think he tells us, on the whole, more about life than the "naturalists" in our sister republic. I say this with the full consciousness of the opportunities an artist loses in leaving so many corners unvisited, so many topics untouched, simply because I think his perception of character was more naturally just and temperate than that of the naturalists. This has been from the beginning the good fortune of our English providers of fiction, as compared with the French. They are inferior in audacity, in neatness, in acuteness, in intellectual vivacity, in the arrangement of material, in the art of characterizing visible things. But they have been more at home in the moral world; they have put their finger on the right chord of the conscience. This is the value of much of the work done by the feminine wing of the school—work which presents itself to French taste as terribly gray and insipid. Much of it is exquisitely human, and that, after all, is a merit. As regards Trollope, one may perhaps characterize him best, in opposition to what I have ventured to call the sedentary school, by saying that he was a novelist who hunted the fox. Hunting was for years his most valued recreation, and I remember that, when I made in his company the voyage of which I have spoken, he had timed his return from the antipodes exactly to be able to avail himself of the first day on which it should be possible to ride to hounds. He "worked" the hunting-field largely. It constantly re-appears in his novels. It was excellent material.

But it would be hard to say (within the circle in which he revolved) what material he neglected. I have allowed myself to be detained so long by general considerations, that I have almost forfeited the opportunity to give examples. I have spoken of *The Warden*, not only because it made his reputation, but because, taken in conjunction with *Barchester Towers*, it is thought by many people to be his most vigorous story. *Barchester Towers* is admirable; it has an almost Thackerayan richness. Archdeacon Grantley is still more powerfully developed, and Mr. Harding is as charming as ever. Mrs. Proudie is ushered into a world in which she was to make so great an impression. Mrs. Proudie has become classical; of all Trollope's characters, she is the most often referred to. She is exceedingly good; but I do not think she is quite so good as her fame and as several figures from the same hand that have not won as much honor. She is rather too violent, too vixenish, too sour. The truly awful female bully—the completely fatal episcopal spouse—would have, I think, a more insidious form, a greater amount of superficial padding. The Stanhope family, in *Barchester Towers*, are a real *trouvaille*, and the idea of transporting the Signora Vesey-Neroni into a cathedral-town was an inspiration. There could not be a better example of Trollope's manner of attaching himself to character than the whole picture of Bertie Stanhope. Bertie is a delightful creation; and the scene in which, at the party given by Mrs. Proudie, he puts this majestic woman to rout is one of the most amusing in all the chronicles of Barset. It is perhaps permitted to wish, by the way, that this triumph had been effected by intellectual means rather than by physical; though, indeed, if Bertie had not despoiled her of her drapery we should have lost the lady's admirable "Unhand it, sir!" Mr. Arabin is charming, and the henpecked bishop has painful truth; but Mr. Slope, I think, is a little too arrant a scamp. He is rather too much what the French call *ancien jeu*; he goes too coarsely to work, and his clamminess and cant are somewhat overdone. He is an interesting illustration, however, of the author's dislike (at that period, at least) of the bareness of evangelical piety. In one respect *Barchester Towers* is (to the best of our recollection) unique, being the only one of Trollope's novels in which the interest does not center more or less upon a simple maiden in her flower. The novel does not contain the least young girl; though we know that this attractive object was to lose nothing by waiting. Eleanor Bold is a charming and natural person; but Eleanor Bold is not in her flower. After this, however, Trollope settled down steadily to the English girl; he took possession of her; he turned her inside out. He never made her a subject of heartless satire, as cynical fabulists of other lands have been known to make the sparkling daughters of those climes; he bestowed upon her the most serious, the most patient, the most tender, the most copious consideration. He is evidently always more or less in love with her, and it is a wonder how under these circumstances he should make her so objective, plant her so well on her feet. But, as I have said, if he was a lover, he was a paternal lover; as competent as a father who has had fifty daughters. He has presented the British maiden under innumerable names, in every station and in every emergency in life, and with every combination of moral and physical qualities. She is always definite and natural. She plays her part most properly. She has always health in her cheek and gratitude in her eye. She has not a touch of the morbid, and is delightfully tender, modest and fresh. Trollope's heroines have a strong family likeness, but it is a wonder how finely he discriminates between them. One feels, as one reads him, like a man with "sets" of female cousins. Such a person is inclined at first to lump each group together; but presently he finds that even in the groups there are subtle differences. Trollope's girls, for that matter, would make delightful cousins. He has scarcely drawn, that we can remember, a disagreeable damsel. Lady Alexandrina de Courcy is disagreeable, and so is Amelia Roper, and so are various provincial (and, indeed, metropolitan) spinsters, who set their caps at young clergymen and Government-clerks. Griselda Grantley was a stick; and considering that she was intended to be attractive, Alice Vavasor does not commend herself particularly to our affections. But the young women I have mentioned had ceased to belong to the tender category; they had entered the period of toughness or flatness. Not that Trollope's more mature spinsters invariably fall into these extremes. Miss Thorne of Ullathorne, Miss Dunstable, Miss Mackenzie, Rachel Ray (if she may be called mature), Miss Baker and Miss Todd, in *The Bertrams*, Lady Julia Guest, who comforts poor John Eames: these and many other amiable figures rise up to contradict the idea. A gentleman who had sojourned in many lands was once asked by a lady (neither of these persons was English) in what country he had found the women most to his taste. "Well, in England," he replied. "In England?" the lady repeated. "Oh, yes," said her interlocutor; "they are so affectionate!" The remark was fatuous; but it has the merit of describing Trollope's heroines. They are so affectionate. Mary Thorne, Lucy Robarts, Adela Gauntlet, Lily Dale, Nora Rowley, Grace Crawley, have a kind of clinging tenderness, a passive sweetness, which is quite in the old English tradition. Trollope's genius is not the genius of Shakspere, but his heroines have something of the fragrance of Imogen and Desdemona. There are two little stories, to which, I believe, his name has never been affixed, but which he is known to have written, that contain an extraordinarily touching representation of the passion of love in its most modest form. In *Linda Tressel* and *Nina Balatka* the vehicle is plodding prose, but the effect is none the less poignant. And in regard to this I may say that in a hundred places in Trollope the extremity of pathos is reached by the homeliest means. He often achieved a very eminent degree of the tragical. The long, slow process of the conjugal wreck of Louis Trevelyan and his wife (in *He Knew He Was Right*), with that rather ponderous movement which is often characteristic of Trollope, arrives at last at an impressive completeness of misery. It is the history of an accidental rupture between two stiff-necked and ungracious people,—"the little rift within the lute,"—which widens at last into a gulf of anguish. Touch is added to touch; one small, stupid, fatal aggravation to another; and as we gaze into the widening breach we wonder at the materials of which tragedy sometimes composes itself. I have always remembered the chapter called "Casalunga," toward the close of *He Knew He Was Right*, as a very powerful picture of the insanity of stiff-neckedness. Louis Trevelyan, separated from his wife, alone, haggard, suspicious, unshaven, undressed, living in a desolate villa on a hill-top near Siena, and returning doggedly to his fancied wrong, which he has nursed until it becomes an hallucination, is a picture worthy of Balzac. Here and in several other places Trollope has dared to be thoroughly logical; he has not sacrificed to conventional optimism; he has not been afraid of a misery which should be too much like life. He has had the same courage in the history of the wretched Mr. Crawley, and in that of the much to be pitied Lady Mason. In this latter episode, he found an admirable subject. A quiet, charming, tender-souled English gentlewoman, who (as I remember the story of *Orley Farm*) forges a codicil to a will in order to benefit her son, a young prig who doesn't appreciate immoral heroism, and who is suspected, accused, tried, and saved from conviction only by some turn of fortune that I forget; who is, furthermore, an object of high-bred, respectful, old-fashioned gallantry on the part of a neighboring baronet, so that she sees herself dishonored in his eyes as well as con-

demned in those of her boy: such a personage and such a situation would be sure to yield, under Trollope's handling, the last drop of their reality.

There are many more things to say about him than I am able to add to these very general observations, the limit of which I have already passed. It would be natural, for instance, for a critic who affirms that his principal merit is the portrayal of individual character, to enumerate several of the figures that he has produced. I have not done this, and I must ask the reader who is not acquainted with Trollope to take my assertion on trust; the reader who knows him will easily make a list for himself. No account of him is complete in which allusion is not made to his practice of carrying certain persons from one story to another—a practice which he may be said to have inherited from Thackeray, as Thackeray may be said to have borrowed it from Balzac. It is a great mistake, however, to speak of it as an artifice which would not naturally occur to a writer proposing to himself to make a general portrait of a society. He has to construct that society, and it adds to the illusion in any given case that certain other cases correspond with it. Trollope constructed a great many things—a clergy, an aristocracy, a *bourgeoisie*, an administrative class, a specimen of the political world. His political novels are distinctly dull, and I confess I have not been able to read them. He evidently took a good deal of pains with his aristocracy; it makes its first appearance, if I remember right, in *Doctor Thorne*, in the person of the Lady Arabella de Courcy. It is difficult for us in America to measure the success of that picture, which is probably, however, not absolutely to the life. There is in *Doctor Thorne*, and some other works, too constant a reference to the distinction of classes—as if people's consciousness of this matter were not (as one may say) chronic, but permanently acute. It is true that, if Trollope's consciousness had not been acute, he would, perhaps, not have given us Lady Lufton and Lady Glencora Palliser. Both of these noble persons are as living as possible, though I see Lady Lufton, with her terror of Lucy Robarts, the best. There is a touch of poetry in the figure of Lady Glencora; but I think there is a weak spot in her history. The actual woman would have made a fool of herself to the end with Burgo Fitzgerald; she would not have discovered the merits of Plantagenet Palliser—or if she had, she would not have cared about them. It is an illustration of the business-like way in which Trollope laid out his work, that he always provided a sort of underplot to alternate with his main story—a strain of narrative of which the scene is usually laid in a humbler walk of life. It is to his underplot that he generally relegates his vulgar people, his disagreeable young women; and I have often admired the pertinacity with which he unfolds this more depressing branch of the tale. Now and then, it may be said, as in *Ralph the Heir*, the story appears to be all underplot and all vulgar people. These, however, are details. As I have already intimated, it is difficult to specify in Trollope's work, on account of the immense quantity of it; and there is sadness in the thought that this enormous mass does not present itself in a very portable form to posterity.

Trollope did not write for posterity; he wrote for the day, the moment; but these are just the writers of whom posterity is apt to take hold. So much of the life of his time is reflected in his novels, that we must believe a part of the record will be saved; and they are full of so much that is sound and true and genial, that readers with an eye to that sort of entertainment will always be sure, in a certain proportion, to turn to them. Trollope will remain one of the most trustworthy, though not one of the most eloquent, of the writers who have helped the heart of man to know itself. The heart of man does not always desire this knowledge; it prefers sometimes to look at history in another way—to look at the manifestations, without troubling about the motives. There are two kinds of taste in the appreciation of imaginative literature: the taste for emotions of surprise, and the taste for emotions of familiarity. It is the latter that Trollope gratifies, and he gratifies it the more that the medium of his own mind, through which we see what he shows us, gives confidence to our sympathy. His natural rightness and purity are so real that the good things he projects must be real. A race is fortunate when it has a good deal of the sort of imagination—of imaginative feeling—that had fallen to the share of Anthony Trollope. Our English race, happily, has much of it.

FREDERIC HARRISON
"Anthony Trollope"
Studies in Early Victorian Literature
1895, pp. 183–204

S ome of our younger friends who read the name which heads this essay may incline to think that it ought to be very short indeed, nay, be limited to a single remark; and, like the famous chapter on the snakes in Iceland, it should simply run—that Anthony Trollope has no place at all in Victorian literature. We did not think so in England in the fifties, the sixties, and the seventies, in the heyday of Victorian romance; and I do not think we ought to pass that judgment now in this last quinquennium of our century. I shall have to put our friend Anthony in a very moderate and prosaic rank; I shall not conceal my sense of his modest claims and conspicuous faults, of his prolixity, his limited sphere, his commonplace. But in view of the enormous popularity he once enjoyed, of the space he filled for a whole generation, I cannot altogether omit him from these studies of the Victorian writers.

I have, too, a personal reason for including him in the series. I knew him well, knew his subjects, and his stage. I have seen him at work at the "Megatherium Club," chatted with him at the "Universe," dined with him at George Eliot's, and even met him in the hunting-field. I was familiar with the political personages and crises which he describes; and much of the local colouring in which his romances were framed was for years the local colouring that I daily saw around me. Most of the famous writers of whom I have been speaking in this series (with the exception of Charlotte Brontë) I have often seen and heard speak in public and in private, but I cannot be said to have known them as friends. But Anthony Trollope I knew well. I knew the world in which he lived, I saw the scenes, the characters, the life he paints, day by day in the same clubs, in the same rooms, and under the same conditions as he saw them. To re-read some of his best stories, as I have just done, is to me like looking through a photographic album of my acquaintances, companions, and familiar reminiscences of some thirty years ago. I can hear the loud voice, the honest laugh, see the keen eyes of our old friend as I turn to the admirable vignette portrait in his posthumous *Autobiography*, and I can almost hear him tell the anecdotes recounted in that pleasant book.

Does the present generation know that frank and amusing book,—one of the most brisk and manly autobiographies in our language? Of course it is garrulous, egoistical, self-complacent in a way. When a famous writer, at the close of a long career of varied activity, takes up his pen to tell us how he has lived, and how his books were written, and what he has

loved, seen, suffered, and striven for,—it is his business to be garrulous; we want him to talk about himself, and to give us such peeps into his own heart and brain as he chooses to unlock. That is what an "autobiography" means. And never did man do this in a more hearty, manly, good-tempered spirit, with more good sense, with more modest *bonhomie*, with a more genial egoism. He has been an enormous worker; he is proud of his industry. He has fought his way under cruel hardships to wealth and fame: and he is well satisfied with his success. He has had millions of readers; he has been well paid; he has had good friends; he has enjoyed life. He is happy in telling us how he did it. He does not overrate himself. He believes some of his work is good: at least it is honest, pure, sound work which has pleased millions of readers. Much of his work he knows to be poor stuff, and he says so at once. He makes no pretence to genius; he does not claim to be a hero; he has no rare qualities—or none but industry and courage—and he has met with no peculiar sufferings and no cruel and undeserved rebuffs. He has his own ideas about literary work,—you may think them commonplace, mechanical, mercenary ideas,—but that is a true picture of Anthony Trollope; of his strong, manly, pure mind, of his clear head, of his average moral sense: a good fellow, a warm friend, a brave soul, a genial companion.

With all his artless self-complacency in his own success, Trollope took a very modest estimate of his own powers. I remember a characteristic discussion about their modes of writing between Trollope and George Eliot at a little dinner party in her house.[1] "Why!" said Anthony, "I sit down every morning at 5:30 with my watch on my desk, and for three hours I regularly produce 250 words every quarter of an hour." George Eliot positively quivered with horror at the thought,— she who could write only when she felt in the vein, who wrote, re-wrote, and destroyed her manuscript two or three times, and as often as not sat at her table without writing at all, "There are days and days together," she groaned out, "when I cannot write a line." "Yes!" said Trollope, "with imaginative work like yours that is quite natural; but with my mechanical stuff it's a sheer matter of industry. It's not the head that does it,—it's the cobbler's wax on the seat and the sticking to my chair!" In his *Autobiography* he has elaborately explained this process,—how he wrote day by day, including Sundays, whatever his duties, his amusements, or the place; measuring out every page, counting the words, and exacting the given quantity hour by hour. He wrote continuously 2500 words in each day, and at times more than 25,000 words in a week. He wrote whilst engaged in severe professional drudgery, whilst hunting thrice a week, and in the whirl of London society. He wrote in railway trains, on a sea voyage, and in a town club room. Whether he was on a journey, or pressed with office reports, or visiting friends, he wrote just the same. *Dr. Thorne* was written whilst he was very sea-sick in a gale at sea, or was negotiating a treaty with Nubar Pasha; and the day after finishing *Dr. Thorne* he began *The Bertrams*. It is one of the most amazing, and one of the most comical, records of literary activity we have. No one can suppose that work of a very high class can be so produced at all. Nor does Trollope pretend that it is of a high class. He says it is honest work, the best he could do.

He takes a strange pleasure in recounting these feats of literary productiveness. He poses as the champion of the age in quantity and rapidity. This lightning novelist could produce a volume in two or three weeks; and thus he could easily turn out three novels of three volumes each in a year. He gives us an exact list of sixty works produced in about thirty-five years, and a total of about £70,000 as the earning of some twenty-four years. He insists that he never neglected his Post-Office work, but was an invaluable and energetic public servant; he insists that, much as he enjoyed his literary profits, he was never misled by the desire of money; and he insists that he could have done no better work if he had written much less, or if he had given more time to each book. In all this he does not convince us. He certainly showed transcendent force of will, of nerve, and of endurance. "It's dogged as does it!" says Giles Hoggett to Mr. Crawley, in *The Last Chronicle of Barset*; and if "dogged" could make a great novelist, Anthony Trollope was pre-eminently "dogged." But a great novelist needs other gifts. And to tell us that he would not have done better work if his whole life had been given to his work, if every book, every chapter of every book were the fruit of ample meditation and repeated revision, if he had never written with any thought of profit, never written but what he could not contain hidden within him,—this is to tell us palpable nonsense.

Trollope's sixty works no doubt exceed the product of any Englishman of our age; but they fall short of the product of Dumas, George Sand, and Scribe. And, though but a small part of the sixty works can be called good, the inferior work is not discreditable: it is free from affectation, extravagance, nastiness, or balderdash. It never sinks into such tawdry stuff as Bulwer, Disraeli, and even Dickens, could indite in their worst moods. Trollope is never bombastic, or sensational, or prurient, or grotesque. Even at his worst, he writes pure, bright, graceful English; he tells us about wholesome men and women in a manly tone, and if he becomes dull, he is neither ridiculous nor odious. He is very often dull: or rather utterly commonplace. It is the fashion with the present generation to assert that he is never anything but commonplace; but this is the judgment of a perverted taste. His besetting danger is certainly the commonplace. It is true that he is almost never dramatic, or powerful, or original. His plots are of obvious and simple construction; his characters are neither new, nor subtle, nor powerful; and his field is strictly limited to special aspects of the higher English society in town and country. But in his very best work, he has risen above commonplace and has painted certain types of English men and women with much grace and consummate truth.

One of Trollope's strong points and one source of his popularity was a command over plain English almost perfect for his own limited purpose. It is limpid, flexible, and melodious. It never rises into eloquence, poetry, or power; but it is always easy, clear, simple, and vigorous. Trollope was not capable of the sustained mastery over style that we find in *Esmond*, nor had he the wit, passion, and pathos at Thackeray's command. But of all contemporaries he comes nearest to Thackeray in easy conversations and in quiet narration of incidents and motives. Sometimes, but very rarely, Trollope is vulgar,—for good old Anthony had a coarse vein: it was in the family:—but as a rule his language is conspicuous for its ease, simplicity, and unity of tone. This was one good result of his enormous rapidity of execution. His books read from cover to cover, as if they were spoken in one sitting by an *improvisatore* in one and the same mood, who never hesitated an instant for a word, and who never failed to seize the word he wanted. This ease and mastery over speech was the fruit of prodigious practice and industry both in office work and in literary work. It is a mastery which conceals itself, and appears to the reader the easiest thing in the world. How few out of many millions have studied that subtle mechanism of ear and thought which created the melodious ripple of these fluent and pellucid words.

His work has one special quality that has not been sufficiently noticed. It has the most wonderful unity of texture and a perfect harmony of tone. From the first line to the last, there is never a sentence or a passage which strikes a discordant note; we are never worried by a spasmodic phrase, nor bored by fine writing that fails to "come off." Nor is there ever a paragraph which we need to read over again, or a phrase that looks obscure, artificial, or enigmatic. This can hardly be said of any other novelist of this century, except of Jane Austen, for even Thackeray himself is now and then artificial in *Esmond*, and the vulgarity of *Yellowplush* at last becomes fatiguing. Now Trollope reproduces for us that simplicity, unity, and ease of Jane Austen, whose facile grace flows on like the sprightly talk of a charming woman, mistress of herself and sure of her hearers. This uniform ease, of course, goes with the absence of all the greatest qualities of style; absence of any passion, poetry, mystery, or subtlety. He never rises, it is true, to the level of the great masters of language. But, for the ordinary incidents of life amongst well-bred and well-to-do men and women of the world, the form of Trollope's tales is almost as well adapted as the form of Jane Austen.

In absolute realism of spoken words Trollope has hardly any equal. His characters utter quite literally the same words, and no more, that such persons utter in actual life. The characters, it is true, are the average men and women we meet in the educated world, and the situations, motives, and feelings described are seldom above or below the ordinary incidents of modern life. But within this very limited range of incident, and for this very common average of person and character, the conversations are photographic or stenographic reproductions of actual speech. His letters, especially his young ladies' letters, are singularly real, life-like, and characteristic. We have long got rid of the artificial eloquence and the studied witticisms of the older school. Richardson, Fielding, Goldsmith, and Scott put into the mouths of their heroes and heroines elaborate speeches, poetry, eloquence, and epigrams which are no more like real speech than the allocutions of kings and queens in Shakespeare are like natural talk. That has long been discarded. Jane Austen and Thackeray make their men and women discourse as men and women do. But perhaps with Thackeray, the talk is too racy, too brilliant, too rich with wit, humour, and character, to be quite literally truthful. Now, Trollope, taking a far lower and simpler line, makes his characters talk with literal truth to nature.

This photographic realism of conversation is common enough now: but it has too often the defects of photography; it is bleared, coarse, and ill-favoured. As we all know, in the new realism a young woman and her lover talk thus: "Old gal! why so glum?" said he—"It's my luck!" says she, and flings her straw hat on the floor. That is the new photographic style, but it does not please us of an older generation. Now Trollope makes his people utter such phrases as the characters he presents to us actually use in real life,—or rather such phrases as they did use thirty years ago. And yet, although he hardly ever rises into eloquence, wit, brilliancy, or sinks into any form of talk either unnaturally tall, or unnaturally low,—still, the conversations are just sufficiently pointed, humorous, or characteristic, to amuse the reader and develop the speaker's character. Trollope in this exactly hits the happy mean. Like Mr. Woodhouse's gruel, his conversations are "thin—but not so very thin." He never attempts grandiloquence; but then he never sinks into the fashionable bathos of—"Sugar in your tea, dear?"—"Another lump, if you please,"—nor does he fall into the fashionable realism of—"Dry up, old man!" No! Trollope's characters speak with literal nature; and yet with enough of point, humour, vigour, to make it pleasant reading.

We may at once confess to his faults and limitations. They

are plain enough, constant, and quite incapable of defence. Out of his sixty works, I should be sorry to pick more than ten as being worth a second reading, or twenty which are worth a first reading. Nor amongst the good books could I count any of the last ten years. The range of characters is limited to the clergy and professional men of a cathedral city, to the county families and the respectabilities of a quiet village, to the life of clubs, public offices, and Parliament in London, and to the ways of "society" as it existed in England in the third quarter of the present century. The plots are neither new nor ingenious; the incidents are rarely more than commonplace; the characters are seldom very powerful, or original, or complex. There are very few "psychologic problems," very few dramatic situations, very few revelations of a new world and unfamiliar natures. There are some natural scenes in Ireland; now and then a cook-maid, a farmer, a labourer, or a clerk, come on the stage and play their short parts with faultless demeanour. But otherwise, the entire company appear in the frock-coats and crinolines of the period, and every scene is played in silk hats, bonnets, and regulation evening toilette.

But within this limited range of life, this uniformity of "genteel comedy," Trollope has not seldom given us pieces of inimitable truthfulness and curious delicacy of observation. The dignitaries of the cathedral close, the sporting squires, the county magnates, the country doctors, and the rectory home, are drawn with a precision, a refinement, an absolute fidelity that only Jane Austen could compass. There is no caricature, no burlesque, nothing improbable or over-wrought. The bishop, the dean, the warden, the curate, the apothecary, the duke, the master of fox-hounds, the bishop's wife, the archdeacon's lady, the vicar's daughter, the governess, the undergraduate,—all are perfectly true to nature. So, too, are the men in the clubs in London, the chiefs, subordinates, and clerks in the public offices, the ministers and members of Parliament, the leaders, and rank and file of London "society." They never utter a sentence which is not exactly what such men and women do utter; they do and they think nothing but what such men and women think and do in real life. Their habits, conversation, dress, and interests are photographically accurate, to the point of illusion. It is not high art—but it is art. The field is a narrow one; the actors are ordinary. But the skill, grace, and humour with which the scenes are caught, and the absolute illusion of truthfulness, redeem it from the commonplace.

The stage of Trollope's drama is not a wide one, but it is far wider than that of Jane Austen. His plots and incidents are sufficiently trite and ordinary, but they are dramatic and original, if contrasted with those of *Emma* or *Mansfield Park*. No one will compare little Jane's delicate palfrey with Anthony's big-boned hunter; nor would any one commit the bad taste of treating these quadrupeds as if they were entered for a race; but a narrow stage and familiar incidents are not necessarily fatal to true art. If Trollope had done nothing more than paint ordinary English society with photographic accuracy of detail, it would not be a great performance. But he has done more than this. In the Barsetshire series, at any rate, he has risen to a point of drawing characters with a very subtle insight and delicate intuition. The warden, the bishop, Mrs. Proudie, Dr. Thorne, Mary Thorne, Lily Dale, Lady Arabella, and, above all, Mr. Crawley, are characters definitely conceived, profoundly mastered, and truly portrayed. Trollope evidently judged Crawley to be his greatest creation, and the *Last Chronicle of Barset* to be his principal achievement. In this he was doubtless right. There are real characters also in the two *Phineas Finn* tales. Chiltern, Finn, Glencora Palliser,

Laura Kennedy, and Marie Goesler, are subtly conceived and truly worked out. This is enough to make a decent reputation, however flat be the interminable pot-boilers that precede and follow them.

The list of Trollope's real successes is not very long. The six tales of the Barsetshire cycle, *The Warden*, *Barchester Towers*, *Doctor Thorne*, *Framley Parsonage*, *The Small House at Allington*, *The Last Chronicle of Barset*, are unquestionably his main achievements; and of these either *Doctor Thorne* or *The Last Chronicle* is the best. The Crawley story is undoubtedly the finest thing Trollope ever did; but for myself, I enjoy the unity, completeness, and masterly scheme of *Doctor Thorne*, and I like Mary Thorne better than any of Trollope's women. If, to the six Barset tales, we add *Orley Farm*, *The Claverings*, the two *Phineas Finns*, and the *Eustace Diamonds*, we shall include, perhaps, more than posterity will ever trouble itself about, and almost exactly one-fifth of the novels he left behind. The ten or twelve of Trollope's best will continue to be read, and will, in a future generation, no doubt, regain not a little of their early vogue. This will be due, in part, to their own inherent merit as graceful, truthful, subtle observation of contemporary types, clothed in a style of transparent ease. Partly, it will be due to this: that these tales will reproduce for the future certain phases of life in the nineteenth century in England with minute fidelity and the most literal realism.

This is no doubt the cause of the revulsion of opinion by which in some English circles Trollope has suffered of late. If there are fashions, habits, and tastes which the rising generation is certain to despise, it is such as were current in the youth of their own parents about thirty or forty years before them. The collars, the bonnets, the furniture, the etiquette, the books of that age always seem to the young to be the last word of all that is awkward and "bad form," although in two or three generations these very modes regain a certain quaint charm. And for the moment poor Anthony represents to the emancipated youth of our time all that was "banal" and prosy some thirty years ago. The taste of our youth sets hard for a new heaven, or at least a new earth, and if not that, it may be a new hell. Novels or poems without conundrums, without psychologic problems, with no sexual theorems to solve, with no unique idiosyncrasies to fathom, without anything unnatural, or sickening, without hospital nastinesses,—are all, we are assured, unworthy the notice of the youth of either sex who are really up to date. In the style of the new pornographic and clinical school of art, the sayings and doings of wholesome men and women who live in drawing-rooms and regularly dress before dinner are "beastly rot," and fit for no one but children and old maids.

But we conservatives of an older school are grateful to Anthony that he produced for the last generation an immense collection of pleasant tales without a single foul spot or unclean incident. It was his boast that he had never written a line which a pure woman could not read without a blush. This is no doubt one of the grounds on which he is so often denounced as *passé*. His tales, of course, are full of love, and the love is not always discreet or virtuous. There are cases of guilty love, of mad love, of ungoverned and unreasoning passion. But there is not an impure or prurient passage in the whole library of tales. Much more than this: in the centre of almost every tale, we are taken to the heart of a spotless, loving, refined, brave English girl. In nothing does Anthony Trollope delight more than when he unveils to us the secret thoughts of a noble-hearted maiden who loves strongly but who has a spirit as strong as her love, a clear brain and a pure will. In nothing is he more successful; nowhere is he more subtle, more true, more interesting. In this fine gift, he surpasses all his contemporaries, and almost all other English novelists. Mary Thorne, Lily Dale, Lucy Roberts,—I would almost add, Martha Dunstable,—may not be heroines of romance, and are certainly not great creations. But they are pure, right-minded, delicate, brave women; and it does one good to be admitted to the sacred confessional of their hearts.

It must be admitted that they are "young ladies," nurtured in the conventional refinement of the last generation, high-bred, and trained in the jealous sensitiveness of what was thought to be "maiden modesty" thirty or forty years ago. That is their misfortune to-day; it is now rather silly to be a "young lady" at all, and the old-fashioned "maiden modesty" of their mothers and grandmothers is become positively ridiculous. Young women of the present date, we are assured in the language of our gilded youth, have to be either "jolly girls" or "crocks"; and Mary Thorne and Lily Dale are certainly not "jolly girls." Their trials and agonies are not different from those which may happen in any ordinary family, and the problems they have to solve are those which may await any girl at any time. But the subtle touches with which we are admitted to their meditations, the delicate weighing of competing counsels and motives, the living pulses of heart and brain, and the essential soundness and reality of the mental and moral crisis,—are all told with an art that may be beneath that of Jane Austen, but which certainly is akin to hers, and has the same quality of pure and simple human nature. Pure and simple human nature is, for the moment, out of fashion as the subject of modern romance. But it remains a curious problem how the boisterous, brawny, thick-skinned lump of manhood whom we knew as Anthony Trollope ever came to conceive so many delicate and sensitive country maidens, and to see so deeply and so truly into the heart of their maiden meditations.

Trollope is equally successful with some other social problems and characters of unstable equilibrium. They are none of them very profound or exalted studies in psychology; but they are truthful, natural, and ingenious; and it needed a sure and delicate hand to make them interesting and life-like. The feeble, solemn, timid, vacillating bishop, driven to distraction by some clerical scandal in his tea-cup of a diocese; the pompous ecclesiastic with wounded dignity and family quarrels; the over-sensitive priest whose conscience is more acute than his brain; the weak, generous, cowardly owner of an embarrassed estate; the honest and impulsive youth placed between love and duty; the loving girl who will not sacrifice dignity to love; the public official who is torn between conscience and self-interest; the man in a great position who does not know his own mind; the man with honest principles who is tempted above his strength by love, ambition, or ruin,—all of these live in the pages of Trollope with perfect truth to nature and reality of movement. It would be too much to say that any of them are masterly creations, unless it be Crawley and the Proudies, but they are absolutely truthful, real, living portraits. The situations are not very striking, but then they are perfectly natural. And the characters never say or do a thing which oversteps by a hair's-breadth the probable and natural conduct of such persons.

All this is now said to be commonplace, goody-goody, and Philistine. There are no female acrobats, burglers, gutter-urchins, crapulous prostitutes, no pathological anatomy of diseased bodies and carious souls, hardly a single case of adultery in all Trollope. But they who can exist without these stimulants may find pleasant reading yet in his best work. *The Last Chronicle of Barset* is a really good tale which deserves to live, and the whole Crawley episode rises to the level of fine

imaginative work. *Doctor Thorne* is a sound, pleasant, ingenious story from beginning to end. It has perhaps the best plot of all Trollope's books, and, singularly enough, it is the only plot which he admits not to be his own. I count Mary Thorne as his best woman and Doctor Thorne as one of his best men. The unity of *Doctor Thorne* is very striking and ingenious. The stage is crowded: there are nearly a score of well-marked characters and five distinct households; but the whole series works into the same plot; the scene is constantly varied, and yet there is no double plot or separate companies. Thus, though the whole story revolves round the fortunes of a single family, the interest and the movement never flag for a page. The machinery is very simple; the characters are of average strength and merit; the incidents and issues are ordinary enough. And the general effect is wholesome, manly, womanly, refined, and true to nature.

The episcopal and capitular group of ecclesiastics round the Cathedral of Barchester is Trollope's main creation, and is destined to endure for some time. It is all in its way inimitably true and subtly graduated from bishop to dean, from dean to canon, and so on through the whole chapter down to the verger and the porter. The relations of these dignitaries to each other, the relation of their womankind to each other, the relation of the clerical world to the town world and to the county world, their conventional etiquette, their jealousies, their feuds, their scandals, and their entertainments, are all marked with admirable truth and a refined touch. The relation of the village respectabilities to the county families, the relation of the county families to the great ducal magnate, are all given with curious precision and subtle discrimination. When *The Warden* appeared just forty years ago, I happened to be a pupil in the chambers of the late Sir Henry Maine, then a famous critic of the *Saturday Review*; and I well remember his interest and delight in welcoming a new writer, from whom he thought so much might be expected. The relations of London "Society" to the parliamentary and ministerial world as described in Trollope's later books are all treated with entire mastery. It is this thorough knowledge of the organism of English society which specially distinguishes Trollope. It is a quality in which Thackeray alone is his equal; and Thackeray himself has drawn no complex social organism with such consummate completeness as Trollope's Barchester Close. It is of course purely English, locally true to England only. But it is, as Nathaniel Hawthorne said, "solid and substantial," "as real as if it were a great lump out of the earth,"—"just as English as a beefsteak."

What makes all that so strange is this, that when he began to write novels, Trollope had far less experience than have most cultivated men of cathedral closes, rectories, and county families. He had never been to a college, and till past middle life he never had access to the higher grades of English society. He never at any time, and certainly not when the Barchester cycle began, had any footing whatever in clerical circles, and but little intimate acquaintance with young ladies of birth and refinement in country homes. He never was much thrown with the young bloods of the army, of the universities, or of Parliament. He rarely consorted with dukes or county magnates, and he never lived in the centre of the political world. Yet this rough, self-taught, busy Post-Office surveyor in Ireland, perpetually travelling about the country on the inspections of his duty, managed to see to the very marrow of the prelates of a cathedral, to the inner histories of the duke's castle and the squire's home, into the secret musings of the rector's daughter, and into the tangled web of parliamentary intrigue. He did all this with a perfectly sure and subtle touch, which was often, it is true, somewhat tame, and is never perhaps of any very great brilliance, but which was almost faultlessly true, never extravagant, never unreal. And, to add to the wonder, you might meet him for an hour; and, however much you might like his bluff, hearty, resonant personality, you would have said he was the last man to have any delicate sympathy with bishops, dukes, or young ladies.

His insight into parliamentary life was surprisingly accurate and deep. He had not the genius of Disraeli, but his pictures are utterly free from caricature or distortion of any kind. In his photographic portraiture of the British Parliament he surpassed all his contemporaries; and inasmuch as such studies can only have a local and sectional interest, they have probably injured his popularity and his art. His conduct of legal intricacies and the ways of lawyers is singularly correct; and the long and elaborate trial scene in *Phineas Redux* is a masterpiece of natural and faithful descriptions of an Old Bailey criminal trial in which "society" happens to be involved. Yet of courts of law, as of bishops' palaces, rectory firesides, the lobbies of Parliament, and ducal "house parties," Trollope could have known almost nothing except as an occasional and outside observer. The life of London clubs, the habits and *personnel* of a public office, the hunting-field, and the social hierarchy and ten commandments observed in a country town,—these things Trollope knew to the minutest shade, and he has described them with wonderful truth and zest.

There was a truly pathetic drollery in his violent passion for certain enjoyments,—hunting, whist, and the smoking-room of his club. I cannot forget the comical rage which he felt at Professor Freeman's attack on fox-hunting. I am not a sporting man myself; and, though I may look on fox-hunting as one of the less deadly sins involved in "sport," I know nothing about it. But it chanced that as a young man I had been charged with the duty of escorting a certain young lady to a "meet" of fox-hounds in Essex. A fox was found; but what happened I hardly remember; save this, that, in the middle of a hot burst, I found myself alongside of Anthony Trollope, who was shouting and roaring out "What!—what are you doing here?" And he was never tired of holding me up to the scorn of the "Universe" club as a deserter from the principles of Professor Freeman and John Morley. I had taken no part in the controversy, but it gave him huge delight to have detected such backsliding in one of the school he detested. Like other sporting men who imagine that their love of "sport" is a love of nature, when it is merely a pleasure in physical exercise, Trollope cared little for the poetic aspect of nature. His books, like Thackeray's, hardly contain a single fine picture of the country, of the sea, of mountains, or of rivers. Compared with Fielding, Scott, Charlotte Brontë, Dickens, George Eliot, he is a man blind to the loveliness of nature. To him, as to other fox-hunters, the country was good or bad as it promised or did not promise a good "run." Though Trollope was a great traveller, he rarely uses his experiences in a novel, whereas Scott, Thackeray, Dickens, Bulwer, George Eliot fill their pages with foreign adventures and scenes of travel. His hard riding as an overgrown heavy-weight, his systematic whist playing, his loud talk, his burly ubiquity and irrepressible energy in everything,—formed one of the marvels of the last generation. And that such a colossus of blood and bone should spend his mornings, before we were out of bed, in analysing the hypersensitive conscience of an archdeacon, the secret confidences whispered between a prudent mamma and a love-lorn young lady, or the subtle meanderings of Marie Goesler's heart,—this was a real psychologic problem.

There can be no doubt that this constitutional vehe-mence of his, this hypertrophy of blood and muscle, injured his work and dimmed his reputation. Much of his work he ought to have burnt. His classical studies are worthless, his *Life of Thackeray* and his *Travels* are mere book-making. His novels, even the best, are revised and printed with scandalous haste. He speaks of a "*toga virile*" and of "the *husband* of his bosom," for *wife*; and there are misprints in every paragraph. When, in his *Autobiography*, he let the public into the story of his method, of his mechanical writing so many words per hour, of his beginning a new tale the day after he finished the last, of his having no particular plot, and hardly thinking about a plot, and all the little trade secrets of his factory, the public felt some disgust and was almost inclined to think it had been cheated out of its £70,000.

Anthony Trollope was not a fraud, nor even a mere tradesman. His reputation may perhaps partially revive, and some of his best work may be read in the next century. His best work will of course be a mere residuum of his sixty books, as is the best of nearly all prolific writers. I am inclined to think the permanent survival may be limited to the *Barchester* cycle, with *Orley Farm* and the two *Phineas Finns*. In any case, his books will hereafter bear a certain historical interest, as the best record of actual manners in the higher English society between 1855 and 1875. That value nothing can take away, however dull, *connu*, and out of date the books may now seem to our new youth. It is a curious problem why our new youth persists in filling its stomach with the poorest trash that is "new,"—i.e. published in 1895, whilst it will not look at a book that is "old,"—i.e. published in 1865, though both are equally unknown to the young reader. If our new youth ever could bring itself to take up a book having 1865 on its title-page, it might find in the best of Anthony Trollope much subtle observation, many manly and womanly natures, unfailing purity of tone, and wholesome enjoyment.

Notes

1. This anecdote has been doubted, on the ground that such rapid composition is impossible. But Trollope in his *Autobiography* asserts this fact, exactly as he told George Eliot, except that the first half hour was occupied by re-reading the work of the previous day. The average morning's work was thus 2500 words, written in two and a half hours.

SIR LESLIE STEPHEN
From "Anthony Trollope"
National Review, September 1901, pp. 69–84

If any one is disposed to cultivate the frame of mind appropriate for Trollope he should begin by reading the *Autobiography*. That will put his mind in the proper key. Trollope indeed gives fair notice that he does not mean to give us a "record of his inner life." He is not about to turn himself inside out in the manner of Rousseau. He must, no doubt, like all of us, have had an "inner life," though one can hardly suppose that it presented any of the strange phenomena which delight the student of morbid psychology. He professes to tell us only such facts as might have been seen by an outside observer. He tells us, however, enough to suggest matter for speculation to persons interested in education. Nobody ever met the adult Trollope in the flesh without receiving one impression. Henry VIII., we are told—and it is one of the few statements which make that monarch attractive—"loved a man." If so, he would clearly have loved Trollope. In person,

Trollope resembled the ideal beefeater; square and sturdy, and as downright as a box on the ear. The simple, masculine character revealed itself in every lineament and gesture. His talk was as hearty and boisterous as a gust of a north-easter—a Kingsley north-easter that is, not blighting, but bracing and genial. The first time I met him was in a low room, where he was talking with a friend almost as square and sturdy as himself. It seemed as if the roof was in danger of being blown off by the vigour of the conversational blasts. And yet, if I remember rightly, they were not disputing, but simply competing in the utterance of a perfectly harmless sentiment in which they cordially agreed. A talker of feeble lungs might be unable to get his fair share in the discussion; but not because Trollope was intentionally overbearing, or even rough. His kindliness and cordiality were as unmistakable as his sincerity; and if he happened to impinge upon his hearers' sore points, it was from clumsiness, not malignity. He was incapable of shyness or diffidence, and would go at any subject as gallantly as he rode at a stiff fence in the hunting-field. His audacity sprang not from conceit, but from a little over-confidence in the power of downright common sense.

Here is the problem to which I referred. If we inquired how such a character had been developed, the last hypothesis which we should make would be that it was due to such surroundings as are described in the *Autobiography*. If one wished to bring up a lad to be a sneak, a cynic, and a humbug, one would deal with him as Trollope was dealt with in his childhood. Many distinguished men have preserved painful impressions of their school-days. Thackeray has sufficiently indicated what he thought of the morality of a public school in his day. Dickens felt bitterly to the end of his life the neglect from which he suffered during part of his childhood. Trollope had a more painful and prolonged experience than either. His father was a man of such oddity and perversity that it must have required all the son's filial duty in later years not to introduce him in a novel. He would have been more interesting as a model than the gentleman who stood for Micawber, though certainly without Micawber's peculiar claims to be attractive. He was a man of ability and learning, who had ruined good prospects at the bar, by a singular facility for quarrelling with his bread and butter. By way of retrieving his position, he had taken to farming, of which he was absolutely ignorant; and when he got into the inevitable difficulties, he set about compiling a gigantic *Encyclopædia Ecclesiastica*, for which he was equally incompetent, and which would have ruined a publisher had any such person been forthcoming. He was most anxious, his son assures us, to do his duty to his family, but equally misguided in his plans for their welfare. Anthony's chief recollections at least were of standing in a convenient position while his amiable parent was shaving, so that his hair might be pulled at any slip in Latin grammar, and of being knocked down for stupidity by a folio Bible. It was all meant in kindness, but only produced obstinate idleness. The child was sent as a day boy to Harrow, where the headmaster could only express his horror that so dirty a little wretch should belong to the school; and his comrades unanimously excluded him from their society. Then he was sent to a private school, where the master treated him as a degraded being, for faults committed by others, and had not the manliness to confess when he discovered his mistake. His next experience was at Winchester, where his elder brother thrashed him daily with a thick stick. Being big, awkward, ugly, ill-dressed, and dirty, he was generally despised and "suffered horribly." Then he returned to Harrow, and was at the same time employed occasionally as a labourer on his father's farm. He was universally despised, excluded from all games, and, though he "gravitated upwards" to near the top of the school, by force of seniority, represented at the age of nineteen the densest ignorance of his lessons attainable even by a boy at an English public school. The one pleasant thing that he could remember was that he once turned against an oppressor. The bully was so well thrashed that he had to be sent home for repairs.

The spirit in which Trollope took this cruelty is characteristic. Less painful experience of the life at a public school helped to convince Cowper that human nature was radically corrupt, and Shelley that the existence of a merciful Providence was doubtful, and Thackeray that there was something radically wrong in the social order. Trollope, who hated tyranny as earnestly as any one, seems only to have drawn the modest inference that the discipline at Winchester and Harrow was imperfect; and, for the time, he did not even go so far. He was always, as he says, "craving for love," even for the love of the young bullies who made his life a burthen. He was miserable in his school-days, because he "envied the popularity of popular boys." They lived in a social paradise from which he was excluded. But he apparently did not think that his exclusion was wrong. It was simply natural—part of the inevitable and providential order of nature. He accepted the code under which he suffered as if it had been the obvious embodiment of right reason. It was quite proper that poverty and clumsiness should be despised and bullied; that was implied in the essential idea of a public school, and his comrades naturally treated him as a herd of wild animals may trample upon an intruder of an inferior species. It "was their nature to," and there was no more to be said about it. It is pathetic to observe the average child accepting its misery as part of a sacred tradition; but in Trollope's case it had one advantage: he bore no malice to anybody. The brother who had thrashed him every day became, as he testifies, the best of brothers, and Trollope cherished no resentment against individuals or to the system. The toughness looked like stupidity, but, at any rate, was an admirable preservative against the temptations to which a more sensitive and reflective nature would have been liable of revolting against morality in general, or meeting tyranny by hypocrisy and trickery. ⟨. . .⟩

It seems, in the first place, that in one respect his early life had been propitious in spite of all probability. His mother had supplied the one bright influence. One of his father's most preposterous schemes had turned out well by sheer accident. He had sent his wife, Heaven knows why, to open a bazaar in Cincinnati. She was to make a fortune by selling pin-cushions and pepper-boxes to the natives of that remote region, whom he must apparently have supposed to be in the state of savages ready to barter valuables for beads. The Yankee was not quite so innocent. She of course lost all her money, but came home to describe the "domestic manners" of her customers with a sharpness which for a time set England and America by the ears. She discovered that she had a pure vein of rather vulgar satire, and worked it to such effect that, though she was over fifty when she began to write, she published 114 volumes before her death. She managed to keep her family afloat, and Trollope, in his darkest days, saw that one possible road to success lay in following her footsteps. He perceived that he had not genius to be a poet, nor the erudition necessary for a historian. But he had a certain taste for reading. He had, even in his boyhood, indulged during the intervals of bullying in occasional rambles through such literature as came in his way, and had decided that *Pride and Prejudice* was the best novel in the language. At the Post Office he had learnt French and brushed up his Latin sufficiently to enjoy Horace. Then he had been given to what he calls the "dangerous mental practice" of castle-building. He solaced his loneliness by carrying on imaginary stories of which he was himself the hero, and which he characteristically kept within the limits of possibility. He could not fancy himself handsome, or a philosopher, by any stretch of mind, but he could imagine himself to be clever and chivalrous enough to be attractive to beautiful young women. This suggested that in his mind, as in his mother's, there was a mine of literary material, and he resolved that novel writing was the one career open to him. Accordingly he set to work in a thoroughly business-like spirit, and slowly and doggedly forced himself upon publishers.

"Nobody but a fool," says the great Johnson, "ever wrote except for money." Trollope holds at least that the love of money is a perfectly honourable and sufficient reason for writing. "We know," he says, "that the more a man earns the more useful he is to his fellow-men"—a fine, sweeping maxim, which certainly has its convenience. It is true, he declares, of lawyers and doctors, and would be true of clergymen if (which is a rather large assumption) the best men were always made bishops. It is equally true of authors. Shakespeare wrote for money, and so did Byron, Scott, Tennyson, Dickens, Macaulay, and Carlyle were not above being paid. "Take away from English authors their copyrights, and you would very soon take away from England her authors." He wrote therefore, as he avows, for the very same reasons which prompt the barrister to go to the bar, or the baker to set up his oven. I have certain qualms about the theory of copyright—though I don't mention them to my publishers. It is not that I would deprive authors of their reward. In the ideal state of things, I fancy, the promising author will be infallibly recognised by the scientific critic; a parental government will then pay him a handsome salary and trust to his honour to do his best and take his time; and his works, if any, will then be circulated gratis. That scheme would avoid the objection which occurs to Trollope's theory. We can hardly assume that the author's usefulness to his fellow creatures is precisely proportioned to his earnings. On the contrary, the great evil of to-day is that an author has constantly to choose whether he will do the best, or whether he will do the most profitable work in his power. Tennyson and Carlyle, to take Trollope's examples, would never have reached their excellence had they not dared to be poor till middle age. Had they accepted Trollope's maxim, we should have had masses of newspaper articles and keepsake rhyming instead of *Sartor Resartus* and *In Memoriam*.

The temptation of the present system to sacrifice quality to quantity, and to work exhausted brains instead of accumulating thought, is too obvious to be insisted upon. When we look at Trollope's turnout, we are tempted to take him for an example of the consequences. George Eliot, as Mr. Harrison tells us—and we can well believe it—was horror-struck when she heard of Trollope's methods. When he began a new book, he allowed a fixed time for its completion, and day by day entered in a diary the number of pages written. A page meant 250 words. He had every word counted, and never failed to deliver his tale of words at the time prefixed. "Such appliances," people told him, "were beneath the notice of a man of genius." He never fancied himself, he replied, to be a man of genius, but "had I been so, I think I might well have subjected myself to these trammels." He could hardly "repress his scorn" when he was told that an imaginative writer should wait for "inspiration." The tallow candle, he declares, might as well wait "for the divine moment of melting." Nay, he recommends youthful aspirants to "avoid enthusiastic rushes with their pen." They should sit down at their desks like lawyers' clerks and work till

their tasks are done. Then they may rival Trollope, at any rate in quantity. During a period of twelve years (1859 to 1871) he did his official duties so as to leave no pretext for fault-finding; he hunted twice a week, he played whist daily, went freely into society, took his holidays, and yet turned out more work, including articles of all kinds in periodicals, than any contemporary author. He was up every morning at 5.30; spent half an hour in reading the previous day's work; and then wrote 250 words every quarter of an hour, for two hours and a half. He wrote when he was travelling on a railway, or on shipboard, and in the course of his career turned out some fifty novels, besides other work, including a Life of Cicero which showed at least his daring. He lamented, I remember, at one time that Mrs. Gore (who wrote seventy novels and 200 volumes) was still ahead of him; but perhaps, counting all his writing, he had equalled her before his death.

It would be absurd to argue gravely against Trollope's simple-minded views; to appeal to the demigods of literature who have thought, like George Eliot, that there was a difference between "tallow chandling" and bookwriting; and that, if inspiration be a daring word, some time must at least be allowed for ideas to ripen and harmonise, and that it may be well to await some overmastering mood, that will not come regularly when an old groom calls you at 5.30 A.M. It is more to the purpose to admit frankly that some great writers have been almost equally productive. Scott took almost as business-like a view as Trollope. Lockhart tells us how an idle youth was irritated by the shadow of a hand behind a window-blind; and by noting the provoking pertinacity with which it added sheet to sheet with the regularity of a copying machine, and how it afterwards appeared that the sheets were those of *Waverley*. Scott, it may be replied, was only pouring out the stores of imagery which had been accumulating for many years, when as yet he had no thought of bringing them to market. Moreover, in some twelve years of excessive production even Scott's vein was pretty nearly exhausted. What stores, one may ask, had Trollope to draw upon? The answer suggests that Trollope was not quite so black as he painted himself. When he comes to lay down rules for the art—or trade—he shows that three hours a day did not include the whole of his labours. A novelist, he declares, must write "because he has a story to tell, not because he has to tell a story." To do so, he must "live with his characters." They must be with him when he wakes and when he lies down to sleep. He must know them as he knows his best friends. Trollope says that he knew the actors in his own stories—"the tone of the voice, the colour of the hair, every flame of the eye, and the very clothes they wear." He knew precisely what each of them would say on any given occasion. He declares, in answer to the complaint of over-rapidity, that he wrote best when he wrote quickest. That, he says, when he was away from hunting and whist, in "some quiet spot among the mountains" where he could be absorbed among his characters, "I have wandered about among the rocks and woods, crying at their grief, laughing at their absurdities, and thoroughly enjoying their joy. I have been impregnated with my own creations till it has been my only excitement to sit with my pen in my hand and drive them before me at as quick a pace as I could make them travel."

This surely is sound doctrine: but Trollope is justifying one set of critics in order to answer another. He wrote best, he admits, when his mind was fullest, and freest from distraction; that is, when he had the "inspiration," a "rush of enthusiasm," against which he warns his disciples. No doubt a man may write quickly at such moments. The great Goethe—if one may introduce such an august example—tells us that he was at times so eager to get his thoughts upon paper that he could not even wait to put the sheet straight, and dashed down his verses diagonally. George Eliot—to come a bit nearer to Trollope—wrote her finest part of *Adam Bede* without a pause or a correction. That you should write quickly when you are "inspired" is natural; but that does not prove that that person's inspiration is superfluous. These unconscious admissions must qualify the statement about the 250 words every quarter of an hour. Trollope's genuine gift showed itself in that practice of "castle building" which, as he tells us, he always kept up. His ideal architecture, it is true, was of a humble and prosaic kind. He did not venture into regions of old romance; nor discover ideal excellence in Utopias of the future; or even observe that the most commonplace houses may be the background for great passions or tragedies. He always kept, as he says, to the probable. His imaginary world was conterminous with that in which he lived. As he tramped along the high road he saw wayside cottages or vicarages, or perhaps convenient hunting-boxes, and provided them with a charming girl to flirt with, and one or two good fellows for after-dinner talk; and made himself an ideal home such as might be provided by the most ordinary course of events. This meant such day-dreaming as just repeats the events of the day—only supplying the touch of simple sentimentalism. A good many men of business, I fancy, are sentimentalists in secret, and after a day of stockbroking or law conveyancing enjoy in strict privacy a little whimpering over a novel. Trollope had abundant tenderness of nature and his sentimentalism is perfectly genuine, though he did find it convenient to bring it to market. That was a main source of his popularity. There were—as the public held—such nice girls in his stories. Once, he tells us, he tried to write a novel without love. He took for his heroine an unattractive old maid in money difficulties; but he had to wind up by allowing her to make a romantic marriage. It is this quaint contrast between the burly, vigorous man of the world and the author's young ladies, who provide him with such sentiment as he can appreciate, that somehow attracts us even by force of commonplace.

Trollope claims another merit—not to the modern taste. "I have ever thought of myself," he says, "as a preacher of sermons, and my pulpit as one which I could make both salutary and agreeable to my audience." Young people, he thinks, receive a large part of their education from novels, and a good novelist should inculcate sound morality. Beatrix Esmond, for example, with her beauty and heartlessness, might seem to be a dangerous example to set before girls. But as she is so treated that every girl will pray to be unlike her, and every youth to avoid the wiles of which she was a mistress, a sermon is preached which no clergyman could rival. Let us hope so—though I must confess to a weakness both for Beatrix and Becky Sharp which may imply some injury to my morals. One point, at least, may be granted. "I do believe," says Trollope, "that no girl has risen from the reading of my pages less modest than she was before, and that some may have learnt from them that modesty is a charm worth possessing." The phrase reminds me of my favourite critic, who declared that there was not a word in Dr. Watts' sermons "which could call a blush to the cheek of modesty." Trollope certainly deserves that rather negative praise. When a novelist courts popularity by appealing to a perverted taste for the morally repulsive, I consider him to be a blackguard—even though he may be an "artist"; and, at the day of judgment, he will hardly, I suppose, be divided into two.

Trollope's moral purpose, however, led him into difficulty. The "regions of absolute will," he says, "are foul and odious";

but there is a "border-land" where flowers are mixed with weeds and where the novelist is tempted to enter. The "border-land," one would rather say, is conterminous with the world; and the novelist who will not speak of it will have to abandon any dealings with human nature. Trollope was confined within narrow limits. One of his novels was refuted by a religious periodical because it spoke of dancing without reprobation. A dignitary of the Church of England remonstrated with him because one of his heroines was tempted to leave her husband for a lover. Trollope replied forcibly enough by asking him whether he ever denounced adultery from his pulpit. If so, why should not the same denunciation be uttered from the pulpit of the novelist? The dignitary judiciously invited him to spend a week in the country and talk over the subject. The visit never came off, and, if that dignitary be now alive, we would like to know what he thinks of Trollope's successors. In one novel Trollope ventured upon a bolder step, and described the career of a female outcast. The difficulty, however, imposed limitations. If a novelist is to be a preacher, he cannot simply overlook what he ought to denounce. Trollope was, in principle, a thorough "realist," but he had to write in popular magazines and submit to their conventions. It may be a difficult question whether a "realistic" description of vice makes vice more disgusting or stimulates a morbid interest. Trollope, at any rate, was in the awkward position of a realist bound to ignore realities. He had to leave gaps in his pictures of life which have, perhaps, been filled up by his successors.

We can see plainly enough what we must renounce in order to enjoy Trollope. We must cease to bother ourselves about art. We must not ask for exquisite polish of style. We must be content with good homespun phrases which give up all their meaning on the first reading. We must not desire brilliant epigrams suggesting familiarity with æsthetic doctrines or theories of the universe. A brilliant modern novelist is not only clever, but writes for clever readers. He expects us to understand oblique references to esoteric theories, and to grasp a situation from a delicate hint. We are not to be bothered with matter-of-fact details, but to have facts sufficiently adumbrated to enable us to accept the æsthetic impression. Trollope writes like a thorough man of business or a lawyer stating a case. We must know exactly the birth, parentage, and circumstances of all the people concerned, and have a precise statement of what afterwards happens to everybody mentioned in the course of the story. We must not care for artistic unity. Trollope admits that he could never construct an intricate plot to be gradually unravelled. That, in fact, takes time and thought. He got hold of some leading incident, set his characters to work, and followed out any series of events which happened to be involved. In one of his stories, if I remember rightly, the love affairs of four different couples get mixed up, and each of them has to be followed out to a conclusion. He simply looks on, and only takes care to make his report consistent and intelligible. To accept such writing in the corresponding spirit implies, no doubt, the confession that you are a bit of a Philistine, and can put up with the plainest of bread and butter, and dispense with all the finer literary essences. I think, however, that at times one's state is the more gracious for accepting the position. There is something so friendly and simple and shrewd about one's temporary guide that one is the better for taking a stroll with him and listening to gossiping family stories, even though they be rather rambling and never scandalous. One difficulty is suggested, indeed, by Trollope's sacrifice of all other aims to the duty of fidelity. We begin to ask whether it can be worth while to read a novel which is a mere reflection of the commonplace. Would it not be better to read genuine biographies and narratives of real events? One answer might be suggested by Walpole's famous remark about history which, as he said, must be false. When we read the lives of people we have known and observe the singular transformations which take place, we are sometimes tempted to think that biography is an organised attempt to misrepresent the past. Trollope is at least conscientiously labouring to avoid that error with a zeal which few Boswells can rival. His fiction is in that respect even truer than history. Hawthorne said at an early period that Trollope's novels precisely suited his taste. They are "solid, substantial, written on the strength of beef and through the inspiration of ale, and just as real as if some giant had hewn a great lump out of the earth and put it under a glass case, with all its inhabitants going about their daily business, and not suspecting that they were being made a show of." Trollope was delighted, as he well might be, with such praise from so different a writer, and declares that this passage defined the aim of his novels "with wonderful accuracy." They represent, that is, the average English society of the time more faithfully even than memoirs of real persons, because there is no motive for colouring the motives of an imaginary person.

Is this really the case? Will our descendants get an accurate conception of England in the middle of the nineteenth century? Or if some "medium" could call us up for cross-examination, should we have to warn posterity not to trust too implicitly to the portraiture. Trollope's best achievement, I take it, was the series of Barsetshire novels. They certainly passed at the time for a marvel of fidelity. Trollope tells us that he was often asked when he had lived in a cathedral close and become intimate with archdeacons; and had been able to answer that he had never lived in a close and had never spoken to an archdeacon. He had evolved the character, he declares, "out of his moral consciousness," and is pleasantly complacent over his creation. Though one would not like to disparage the merits of the performance, the wonder seems to be pretty simple. Trollope had been to Harrow and Winchester, and the headmaster of one had become a dean, and the headmaster of the other a bishop. He afterwards spent two years riding through English country, and a visit, during this period, to Salisbury close, had suggested the first Barchester novel. It is not wonderful that, after such experience, he should have been equal to the costume of archdeacons; and, apart from their costumes, archdeacons are not essentially different, I fancy, from bishops or headmasters, or from the average adult male of the upper classes. Archdeacon Grantly is certainly an excellent and life-like person; an honourable, narrow-minded English gentleman with just the necessary tinge of ecclesiastical dignity. Still, if our hypothetical descendants asked us, Were English archdeacons like that? we should be a little puzzled. If Miss Yonge could be called as a witness to character, she would certainly demonstrate. Archdeacons, she would say, in her time, high-church archdeacons at least, were generally saints. They could be spiritual guides; they had listened to Newman or been misled by *Essays and Reviews*; but had, at least, been interested in the religious movements of the day. Trollope's archdeacon is as indifferent to all such matters as were the much-reviled dignitaries of an older generation. He is supposed to do his official duties, and he carefully says, "Good Heavens!" where a layman would use another phrase; but he never gives the slightest indication of having any religious views whatever beyond a dislike to dissenters. He has a landed estate, and is as zealous as any squire to keep up the breed of foxes, and he threatens to disinherit his son for making an unworldly marriage as if he were the great Barchester magnate—the Duke of Omnium himself.

I do not presume to inquire how far such a man represents the prevalent type more accurately than the more ethereal divine of pious lady novelists. The Trollope theory of the archdeacons might be held to confirm Matthew Arnold's description of the Church as an "appendage of the barbarian"; and the philosophical historian might infer that in the nineteenth century the normal country farmer was a very slightly modified squire. Perhaps Trollope's view may be a useful corrective to the study of the ordinary lives in which the saintliness of respectable clergymen tends to be a little over-emphasised; still, it omits or attenuates one element—the religious, namely—which must have had some importance in the character of contemporary divines. And what can we say for the young women who charmed his readers so thoroughly? Vulgar satire in those days was denouncing the "girl of the period"—the young lady who was chafing against established conventions of all kinds. The young women of Barchester seem to have been entirely innocent of such extravagance. Trollope's heroines are as domestic as Clarissa Harlowe. They haven't a thought beyond housekeeping or making a respectable marriage. We could hardly expect such delineations of the fair feminine qualities as could be given by feminine novelists alone. We could not ask him for a Jane Eyre or still less for a Maggie Tulliver. But were the average girls of forty years back made of such very solid flesh and blood with so small an allowance of the romantic? His are so good-natured, sensible, and commonplace that he has the greatest difficulty in preventing them from at once marrying their lovers. He has to make them excessively punctilious on some point of their little code of propriety. One is loved by a lord, whose mother objects to a *mésalliance*; another is of doubtful legitimacy, and a third is the daughter of an excellent man whose character is for a moment under a cloud. They have to hold out till their lovers and their lovers' families have got over such scruples, or the cause has been removed. The most popular of all was Miss Lily Dale, whom Trollope himself unkindly describes as "somewhat of a French prig." She will not marry the man whom she loves because she has been cruelly jilted by a thorough snob, and makes it a point of honour not to accept consolation or admit that she can love twice. Readers, it seems, fell in love with her, and used to write to Trollope entreating him to reconcile her to making her lover happy. Posterity, I think, will make a mistake if it infers that English girls were generally of this type; but it must admit though with a certain wonder that the type commended itself to a sturdy, sensible Briton of the period, as the very ideal of Womanhood, and delighted a large circle of readers.

The prosaic person, it must remember, has a faculty for ignoring all the elements of life and character which are not prosaic, and if Trollope's picture is accurate it is not exhaustive. The weakness thus indicated is significant. Trollope made it a first principle to keep rigorously to the realities of life. He inferred that nothing strange or improbable should ever be admitted. That is not the way to be life-like. Life, as we all find out, is full of the strange and improbable. Every character has its idiosyncrasies: its points of divergence from the ordinary. If the average man whose qualities are just at the mean between the extremes, who is half-way between genius and idiot, villain and saint, must be allowed to exist, it may be doubted whether he is not, on the whole, more exceptional than the so-called exceptions. Trollope inclines to make everybody an average specimen, and in his desire to avoid exaggeration inevitably exaggerates the commonplaceness of life. He is afraid of admitting any one into his world who will startle us by exhibiting any strength of character. His lovers, for example, have to win the heroine by showing superiority to the worldly scruples of their relations. The archdeacon's son proposes to marry a beautiful and specially-virtuous and clever girl, although her father had been accused of stealing. He endangers his prospects of inheriting an estate, but he had, in any case, enough to live upon. Surely some men would be up to such heroism, even though the girl herself hesitates to accept the sacrifice. But, to make things probable, we are carefully told that the hero has great difficulty in rising to the occasion; he has to be screwed up to the effort by the advice of a sensible lady; and even her encouragement would scarcely carry the point, had not the accusation been disproved. In this, and other cases, the heroes have all the vigour taken out of them, that they may not shock us by diverging from the most commonplace standard. When a hero does something energetic, gives a thrashing, for example, to the man who has jilted a girl, we are carefully informed that he does it in a blundering and unsatisfactory way.

By the excision of all that is energetic, or eccentric, or impulsive, or romantic, you do not really become more lifelike; you only limit yourself to the common and uninteresting. That misconception inspires Trollope's work and accounts, I suspect, for the decline of our interest. An artist who systematically excludes all lurid colours or strong lights, shows a dingy, whitey-brown universe, and is not more true to nature. Barsetshire surely had its heroes and its villains, its tragedy and its farce, as well as its archdeacons and young ladies bound hand and foot by the narrowest rules of contemporary propriety. Yet, after all, Trollope's desire to be faithful had its good result in spite of this misconception. There are, in the first place, a good many commonplace people in the world; and, moreover, there were certain types into which he could throw himself with real vigour. He can appreciate energy when it does not take a strain of too obvious romance. His best novel, he thinks, and his readers must agree with him, was the *Last Chronicle of Barset*. The poor parson, Mr. Crawley, is at once the most lifelike and (in his sense) the most improbable of his characters. He is the embodiment of Trollope's own "doggedness." One fancies that Trollope's memory of his sufferings under the "three hundred tyrants" of his school-days, and of his father's flounderings in money matters, entered into his sympathy with his hero. Anyhow, the man with his strange wrong-headed conscientiousness, his honourable independence, blended with bitter resentment against the more successful; his strong domestic affections, which yet make him a despot in his family, is a real triumph of which more ambitious novelists might be proud. Such men, he might have observed, though exceptional, are far more real than the average persons with whom he is generally content. Another triumph, of which he speaks with justifiable complacency, is the famous Mrs. Proudie. He knew, he declares, "all the little shades of her character." She was bigoted, bullying and vulgar, but really conscientious, no hypocrite, and at last dies in bitter regret for the consequences of her misrule. He killed her because he heard two clergymen in the Athæneum complaining of her too frequent reappearances. But he thoroughly enjoyed her, and continued, as he declares, to "live much in company with her ghost." I should guess, though I cannot speak from a wide personal observation of the class, that no British bishop was ever so thoroughly henpecked as Dr. Proudie. The case was at any rate exceptional, and yet, or therefore, is thoroughly lifelike. Mrs. Proudie, that is, is one genuine type, albeit a very rare one, of the Englishwoman of the period, and Trollope draws her vigorously, because her qualities are only an excessive development of very commonplace failings. In such cases

Trollope can deal with his characters vigorously and freely, and we do not feel that their vitality has been lowered from a mistaken desire to avoid a strain upon our powers of belief. He can really understand people on a certain plane of intelligence; pompous officials at public offices, and dull members of Parliament, and here and there such disreputable persons as he ventures to sketch, as, for example, the shrewd contractor in *Dr. Thorne*, who is ruined by his love of gin, are solid and undeniable realities. We see the world as it was, only in a dark mirror which is incapable of reflecting the fairer shades of thought and custom.

Hawthorne's appreciation of Trollope's strain was perhaps due in part to his conviction that John Bull was a huge mass of solid flesh incapable of entering the more ethereal regions of subtle fancy of which he was himself a native. Trollope was to him a John Bull convicting himself out of his own mouth, and yet a good fellow in his place. When our posterity sits in judgment, it will discover, I hope, that the conventional John Bull is only an embodiment of one set of the national qualities, and by no means an exhaustive portrait of the original. But taking Trollope to represent the point of view from which there is a certain truthfulness in the picture—and no novelist can really do more than give one set of impressions—posterity may after all consider his novels as a very instructive document. Perhaps, though it would be idle to prophesy confidently, one remark will be suggested. The middle of the nineteenth century—our descendants may possibly say—was really a time in which a great intellectual, political, and social revolution was beginning to make itself perceptible. The vast changes now (that is, in the twenty-first century) so familiar to everybody could then have been foretold by any intelligent observer. And yet in this ancient novelist we see the society of the time, the squires and parsons and officials, and the women whom they courted, entirely unconscious of any approaching convulsions; imagining that their little social arrangements were to endure for ever; that their social conventions were the only ones conceivable; and, on the whole, numbers occupied in carrying on business in a humdrum way and sweetening life by flirtation with healthy and pretty young women without two ideas in their heads. Then they will look back to the early days of Queen Victoria as a delightful time, when it was possible to take things quietly, and a good, sound, sensible optimism was the prevalent state of mind. How far the estimate would be true is another question; but Trollope, as representing such an epoch, will supply a soothing if rather mild stimulant for the imagination, and it will be admitted that if he was not among the highest intellects of his benighted time, he was as sturdy, wholesome, and kindly a human being as could be desired.

GAMALIEL BRADFORD, JR.
From "Anthony Trollope"
Atlantic, March 1902, pp. 426–31

It is pleasant to see signs of a Trollope revival, and we may well hope that readers who are a little tired of cloak and sword romance will be glad to seek variety in the pages of *Doctor Thorne* and the *Barchester Chronicles*. Perhaps no writer represents more perfectly than Trollope the great development of social and domestic tendencies in the English novel of the middle and third quarter of the last century. A man of real genius, he yet had not genius enough to stand out from and above his time; and for that very reason he portrays it more fully, just as Ben Jonson brings us nearer to the Elizabethan Age than does Shakespeare.

Trollope was essentially a realist: by which I do not mean that he had any elaborate theory as to his art, but simply that he described common life as common people see it. Realism is genius in the expression of the commonplace. Imagine a beef-eating, fox-hunting, Gaul-hating Englishman, red-cheeked, arrogant, stuffed full of prejudice, loathing a radical, idolizing a bishop and a lord, and worshiping British liberty,—imagine such a one with the exceptional gift of depicting himself and many another like him to the very life, and you have the author of *Orley Farm* and *Phineas Finn*.

It would be desirable to reprint Trollope's *Autobiography* with the novels, as no novelist has left us a more entertaining and instructive account of himself and his objects and methods of work. No character in his stories stands out more distinctly before us than the awkward, unfortunate, neglected boy, who tripped and stumbled through an imperfect education and a premature manhood, a burden and annoyance to his friends, an object of disgust and dissatisfaction to himself. Nor does any novel present a happier ending to the imagination of the sympathetic reader than that pleasant picture of a way found out of difficulties, of success achieved by honest industry, of self-respecting middle-class virtue rewarded with unlimited whist, wine, cigars, and fox-hunting. It is enough to turn the ambition of every poor boy in the direction of authorship.

What is especially delightful in Trollope's confessions is the utter absence of shame. Other artists—some others—do their pot-boiling in private, and proclaim publicly their scorn of pecuniary gain, their adoration of art for art's sake. Trollope writes for money, and is proud of getting it. He speaks of "that high-flown doctrine of the contempt of money, which I have never admired." If he can make a work of perfect art, well and good; but perfect or imperfect, it must sell. He gives an elaborate table—doubtless to many young authors the most interesting portion of the book—containing a full, dated list of all his writings and the sums received for each of them up to the year 1879, amounting to three hundred and fifty thousand dollars.

Nor did Trollope believe that genius must be pampered, humored, taken at its propitious times and seasons. In the nineteenth century everything should be manufactured mechanically, books as well as shoes. "I had long since convinced myself that in such work as mine the great merit consisted in acknowledging myself to be bound by rules of labor similar to those which an artisan or a mechanic is forced to obey. A shoemaker, when he has finished one pair of shoes, does not sit down and contemplate his work in idle satisfaction: 'There is my pair of shoes finished at last! What a pair of shoes it is!' The shoemaker who so indulged himself would be without wages half his time. It is the same with a professional writer of books. . . . Having thought much of all this, and having made up my mind that I could be really happy only when I was at work, I had now quite accustomed myself to begin a second pair so soon as the first was out of my hands."

All the details of this cobbling process are complacently revealed to us. So many words an hour,—"to write with my watch before me, and to require from myself two hundred and fifty words every quarter of an hour. I have found that the two hundred and fifty words were forthcoming as regularly as my watch went,"—so many hours a day, so many novels a year! Carlyle required absolute silence and leisure for production: the hand-organ over the way tormented him to fury. But this characteristic author of the nineteenth century is indifferent to time and place. "I made for myself, therefore, a little tablet,

and found, after a few days' exercise, that I could write as quickly in a railway carriage as I could at my desk." But these bits of insight into the method of production will mean more to us when we come to look more closely into the product itself.

Trollope's novels deal almost entirely with the author's own time; no mediæval history, bravos, swordplay, moonlight romance. His people are common people; that is, they are human beings like other human beings before they are anything else. It is this constant detection of ordinary human nature under the disguises of wealth and aristocracy which misleads Mr. Saintsbury into calling Trollope a painter of middle-class life. His painting of middle-class life is good, much better than his painting of low life; but certainly his best work is on the upper classes,—dukes and duchesses, earls and barons, bishops and Cabinet ministers, or, more briefly, ladies and gentlemen. Only somehow, under his quiet but penetrating insight, all these high personages, without becoming in the least vulgar or unnatural, [1] seem to drop their titles and tinsel and appear just as middling as the middlest of us. This, too, without any of those constant depreciatory remarks which so abound in Thackeray and constitute a sort of back-handed snobbishness. Trollope's great ones are simply and naturally men and women,—nothing more.

So far as plot goes, in the stricter sense of the word, Trollope confesses that he is weak, and few will be found to differ from him. Sir Walter Besant's entertaining pamphlet containing a recipe for producing novels—Besant novels—has no application here. The elaborate machinery of scenarii, with every motive and every climax carefully fitted into place before one line is written, does not at all suit our easy-going improvisator. "There are usually some hours of agonizing doubt, almost of despair,—so, at least, it has been with me. And then, with nothing settled in my brain as to the final development of events, with no capability of settling anything, but with a most distinct conception of some character or characters, I have rushed at the work as a rider rushes at a fence which he does not see." And speaking of that arch-plotter of plotters, Wilkie Collins, he says: "When I sit down to write a novel, I do not at all know and I do not very much care how it is to end. Wilkie Collins seems so to construct his that he not only, before writing, plans everything on, down to the minutest detail, from the beginning to the end; but then plots it all back again to see that there is no piece of necessary dovetailing which does not dovetail with absolute accuracy. . . . Such work gives me no pleasure. I am, however, quite prepared to admit that the want of pleasure comes from fault of my intellect."

Yet, although the dramatic continuity of Trollope's stories is seldom complete, we constantly come across those intensely effective and striking scenes which are perhaps the best thing in a good novel, which we pause to read twice over, which cling in the memory and keep returning to us, yet are always fresh and delightful when we come to them again. Mr. Slope's slap in the face and his fierce fight with Mrs. Proudie for the domination of the Bishop, the pitched battle between Mrs. Proudie and Mrs. Grantly, the delicious scene between Lady Lufton and Lucy Roberts, and the somewhat similar one between the Archdeacon and Grace Crawley, Johnny Eames and the bull, Lord Chiltern riding Dandolo, Madame Max and the Duchess over the jewels, Phineas' acquittal,—these are but a tithe of what lovers of Trollope will take joy in recalling.

The life of such scenes comes from the ever present and admirably sustained interest of character, and this interest gives to Trollope's novels a unity which is wanting in their plots. One can never insist too much on the immense superiority of English literature in general over all others on this point of character. Richness and fullness of human life is what distinguishes the drama of Shakespeare from that of Sophocles, of Calderon, of Racine, of Dumas fils. An excellence of the same kind, unusual in French writers, but far inferior not only to Shakespeare's, but to Jonson's or Fletcher's or Massinger's, gives Molière his great reputation. So in the novel, French fiction may surpass English in skill of construction, in finished elegance of style, in grace and charm. It never approaches it in fertility, variety, and strength of character production. One has only to compare Dumas with Scott, George Sand with George Eliot, to feel the force of this. Balzac, like Molière, is great because he is an exception; but, like Molière, he accomplishes with titanic effort what Shakespeare, Fielding, Miss Austen, Thackeray, and Dickens do with divine ease and unerring instinct. With a great price bought he this freedom, but they were born free.

Without placing Trollope on a level with these greatest masters, it is easy to see that with him also character is a strong point. He always recognizes this himself, and in his *Autobiography* he has some admirable observations on the subject in connection with the sensational in novels. Speaking of *The Bride of Lammermoor*, of *Esmond*, of *Jane Eyre*, he says: "These stories charm us, not simply because they are tragic, but because we feel that men and women with flesh and blood, creatures with whom we can sympathize, are struggling amid their woes. It all lies in that. No novel is anything, for the purposes either of comedy or tragedy, unless the reader can sympathize with the characters whose names he finds upon the pages. . . . Truth let there be, truth of description, truth of character, human truth as to men and women. If there be such truth, I do not know that a novel can be too sensational."

From the very fact of pitching his characters so largely on a middle note, of choosing them and keeping them always in the common light of every day, Trollope gives peculiarly the impression of having lived with them and of making us live with them. He often goes into very diffuse analyses of the thoughts and actions of his heroes and heroines; yet in so doing he does not seem to sap their vitality as do Thackeray and George Eliot. The reason of this is that he does not appear to be explaining, but speculating. He does not say, "I made this machine, and I can tell you just how it goes." He talks to you as a friend would talk about another friend in a desultory, twilight chat before a smouldering fire. His characters seem to exist entirely independent of their author, and to work out their own natures with no volition or even control from him. This is doubtless one of the advantages of his rapid and instinctive method of working.

This common naturalness of Trollope's characters, this feeling that we have lived with them and known them, is much intensified by their constant reappearance in different stories. Of course, many other authors have held their characters along from one book to another; but neither Dumas nor Balzac nor Mr. Howells has done it to the same extent as Trollope. He speaks somewhere of his lack of memory; but surely a memory approaching instinct was needed to carry a company of people through thirty-two volumes, [2] with long intervals of time both in the subjects and in the composition, and to keep constantly a distinct grasp not only of general traits of character, but of eyes and hair, of gait and gesture. In this vast and loose sequence of events and circumstances slips and inaccuracies doubtless occur, but their rarity is wonderful.

In such a crowd of characters we can hardly single out many for special consideration. Mr. Saintsbury, who has written of Trollope with sympathy and appreciation, speaks of Mr. Crawley as almost the only one of his personages who stands out with real originality and permanent significance, and Trollope himself has an unusual affection for that eccentric gentleman; but Mr. Crawley is too exceptional, too near the limits of sanity, for the deepest human interest. How inferior he is to the Archdeacon, the admirable Archdeacon, at once perfect (artistically perfect) man and perfect English clergyman! How we love him, with his conventional dignity, his conventional religion, his bustling meddlesomeness, his tyrannous impertinence, his sturdy British common sense, his never failing ejaculation, "Good Heavens!"—how we love him! And in a far different fashion how we love Mr. Harding, one of the tenderest, simplest, most touching figures in fiction, whose gentle memory brings the tears to one's eyes! How we should delight, unobserved, to watch him in one of the stalls of his beloved cathedral choir, turning over the pages of his own church music, gently and absently playing seraphic airs on an imaginary violoncello!

> Heard melodies are sweet, but those unheard
> Are sweeter.

Mr. Harding, perhaps the most striking of all Trollope's creations, because so totally unlike Trollope himself, whereas the Archdeacon is clearly the very image of the author of his being.

Then the women. Mrs. Proudie,—we all detest her. Yet we have a sneaking fondness for her, too. There is one of the marks of large humanness in Trollope: he brings out something not wholly hateful in the worst character he touches. The masters of human life in literature, Shakespeare and Scott, have the same trait. And Lady Glencora,—how well we know her, and who does not feel her fascination! Trollope's own observations on her show how far a true artist's judgment may be below his genius: "She has, or has been intended to have, beneath the thin stratum of her follies a basis of good principle, which enabled her to live down the original wrong that was done to her, and taught her to endeavor to do her duty in the position to which she was called." And this is Lady Glen,—the sprightly, the mobile, the petulant, the willful, the bewitching Lady Glen! It would be instructive if we had the original skeletons of Rosalind and Die Vernon to range and ticket on the same shelf with this inert anatomy.

Nor is it only in what dramatic slang would call "character parts" that Trollope succeeds. In the still more difficult task of giving individual life to heroes and heroines he shows himself equally skillful. Phineas Finn, for example, is intended to be and is a very ordinary person; yet an indescribable and indefinable something of lovableness pervades his character everywhere, so that one cannot choose but love him. As for Trollope's girls,—Eleanor Harding, Mary Thorne, Lucy Roberts, Lily Dale, Grace Crawley, Violet Effingham, Isabel Boncassen, and the rest,—they are charming, and at the same time they are remarkably distinct: each keeps her individuality in the midst of the general fascination.

The style in which Trollope writes about all these personages is what might be expected from the author's method of working,—loose, free, easily followed. After all, perhaps this is the best style for story-telling, when a man has the gift of it. The curious felicity of Flaubert and Stevenson is a precious thing; but one never escapes the sense that it is born of painful effort, and one feels a little guilty not to enjoy it with a certain effort, also. The De Goncourts speak somewhere of the struggle with which an author tears forth a beautiful page from his very vitals. Trollope never tore any pages from his vitals; he had no vitals, literarily speaking. Easy, rapid, graceful improvisation, at the rate of a thousand words an hour, as aforesaid, was good enough for him—and for most of his readers. Gautier said that the production of copy was a natural function with George Sand. So it was with Trollope: he wrote as easily as he breathed,—or hunted,—yet his style is full of individuality. It has neither dignity nor power nor remarkable precision; but it has a peculiar, homely, personal flavor, as of a man loosely noting his natural thought, writing in old clothes, with a pipe in his mouth and a glass of old wine beside him. The very tricks of it—that most marked one, which Mr. Saintsbury has noted, of repeating and emphasizing words—are characteristic of the man, and one gets attached to them as to him.

As for observation, Trollope had little, so far as the external world is concerned; but his moral insight is close and keen on the somewhat superficial plane to which he was limited by nature. "That which enables the avaricious and unjust to pass scathless through the world is not the ignorance of the world as to their sins, but the indifference of the world as to whether they be sinful or no." "The little sacrifices of society are all made by women, as are also the great sacrifices of life. A man who is good for anything is always ready for his duty, and so is a good woman for her sacrifice." "Men are cowards before women till they become tyrants." "Why is it that girls so constantly do this? So frequently ask men who have loved them to be present at their marriages with other men? There is no triumph in it; it is done in sheer kindness and affection. 'You can't marry me yourself,' the lady seems to say, 'but the next greatest blessing I can offer you, you shall have: you shall see me married to somebody else.' I fully appreciate the intention, but in all honesty I doubt the eligibility of the proffered entertainment."

The last quotation shows the sort of good-natured satire which keeps one smiling through a great part of Trollope's work. Mr. Howells, in his otherwise most appreciative criticism, charges Trollope with a lack of humor. To most of Trollope's admirers it seems that his novels are full of humor; not indeed overcharged and farcical, like Dickens's, always restrained within the limits of nature, but true humor nevertheless.

I have said nothing as yet, however, of that which constitutes the greatest claim of Trollope's novels to permanence; that is, their picture of contemporary English life. Even where plot and character are weakest there is always something of vitality and truth, and so of interest in the background and surroundings; but when we come to the Barchester and parliamentary series, the richness and accuracy of detail is wonderful. Every syllable that deals with Barchester has the accent of truth. I have already referred to Archdeacon Grantly, who is so clerical and so English as well as so human; but all his surroundings, the bishops and the deans and canons, and the wives of these dignitaries, and their very children, and all that they say and do, bring the quaint, quiet air of the cathedral town about us. Surely future ages will turn to Trollope more than to any other author for a true and vivid picture of this life, when it shall have wholly passed away.

Notes

1. In spite of some odd lapses of grammar and occasionally of manners, which make it seem as if Trollope himself had not always lived with dukes and bishops.

2. It may interest some of Trollope's admirers to have a complete list of the long series of connected novels which includes most of his best work. The six chronicles of Barset come first, as follows: *The Warden, Barchester Towers, Doctor Thorne, Framley Parsonage, The Small House at Allington, The Last Chronicle of Barset.* These are followed by the parliamentary novels, the connection between them being maintained through Mr. Palliser and some others: *Can You Forgive Her?, Phineas Finn, The Eustace Diamonds, Phineas Redux, The Prime Minister, The Duke's Children.*

EMILY DICKINSON

EMILY DICKINSON

1830–1886

Emily Dickinson was born on December 10, 1830, in Amherst, Massachusetts, the second of three children. She was particularly close to her younger sister Lavinia, who lived at home her entire life, as well as to her older brother Austin, who married a friend of hers and lived next door to the Dickinson home. Emily Dickinson was descended from a long line of Puritan leaders, including her grandfather, who helped found Amherst College, and her father Edward, who served as the college's treasurer. A prominent lawyer, Edward Dickinson served as a state judge and later as a U.S. Congressman from 1853 to 1855.

Emily attended the Amherst Academy from 1834 to 1847. She then spent a year at the Mount Holyoke Female Seminary under the guidance of Mary Lyon; however, poor health forced her to end her formal education in 1848. Thereafter, she spent much of her time at home reading and writing poetry, a habit she had begun as a young girl. Much of her early poetry was influenced by Emerson's writings, although her poetry generally exhibits a superior control of both rhyme and meter. As a young woman, Dickinson also was influenced by the poetry of Emily Brontë.

Throughout Dickinson's life several men exerted important influences on both her poetry and her personal life. Benjamin F. Newton, a young law clerk in her father's office, encouraged her to continue writing. After his sudden death, Dickinson traveled to Washington, D.C., with her father and sister. On their way south they stopped in Philadelphia, where they heard the Rev. Charles Wadsworth preach. Dickinson soon began corresponding with him and she later referred to him as her "dearest earthly friend." In 1862 Wadsworth decided to travel to San Francisco as a missionary, a move which deeply hurt Dickinson.

In April 1862 Dickinson sent four of her poems to Thomas Wentworth Higginson, a writer for the *Atlantic*. He was impressed with their originality and served as Dickinson's quasi-literary agent for the rest of her life. Disappointed by her two failed romances, Dickinson began to devote more and more time to writing. In 1864 she traveled to Cambridge, Massachusetts, to receive treatment for an eye disorder. After returning to Amherst in 1865 she never again left the village, and after 1870 she never ventured beyond the confines of her home and its gardens. During her later years she always dressed in white and was regarded by the people of Amherst as an eccentric spinster.

During her lifetime only six of her poems were published. All appeared anonymously and without her consent, and most were heavily edited. By the time of her death on May 15, 1886, she had written almost 2000 short lyrics, many of which were bound in small handsewn books that she had begun preparing in 1858. Although her sister was determined to publish Emily's poems, family squabbles as well as the chaotic state of her manuscripts resulted in the delayed and haphazard publication of Dickinson's work. Three separate editions of her poetry appeared during the 1890s, but it was not until 1955, with the publication of a three-volume scholarly edition (ed. Thomas H. Johnson), that all of Dickinson's poems were collected. Many of the earlier editions attempted to standardize her unorthodox punctuation and alter some of her unusual constructions; however, with the 1955 edition her poetry finally appeared much as it was originally written.

Although she received only modest critical attention during the late nineteenth and early twentieth centuries, Dickinson's reputation has grown steadily since the 1920s. Amy Lowell, as a leader of the Imagists, was among the first major poets to recognize Dickinson's contributions to American letters. Today Dickinson stands at the forefront of America's nineteenth-century poets.

Personal

In a recent letter from Boston, published in *Book News*, Nathan Haskell Dole gave an interesting summary of a paper by Mrs. Mabel Loomis Todd, on the late Emily Dickinson and her poems.

"Mrs. Todd," said Mr. Dole, "was one of the comparatively few who were admitted to anything like intimacy with the weird recluse of Amherst. Her friendship began in this way: Mrs. Todd, wishing to send Miss Dickinson a little gift, painted a panel with the pale Indian pipe. It happened that this delicate flower was a particular passion with the poetess, and the gift went straight to her heart. This incident explains the appropriate employment of the flower as a decoration of the cover of the first volume of her poems. Indeed the drawing was made from the very panel which always stood in Miss Dickinson's room.

"Mrs. Todd exploded the popular notion that Miss Dickinson was always a recluse. When her father was in Congress she spent several winters in Washington, and mingled in gay society, which she enjoyed, though still feeling that she had no real part in it. It was only in the last years of her life that she lived in her own home, somewhat like a dear ghost, seen but scarcely tangible, dwelling among her favorite flowers and in the shadows. She had once played the piano in a most individual manner, but this practice she gave up while still retaining her love for music. She delighted to have her friends sing or play to her at twilight. She herself would not come into the music room, but sat outside in the entry, and rewarded the performer, not with praise, nor even with speech, but with some dainty refreshment of cream or cake or with a higher guerdon of a slip of paper with a poem written on the spot during the music.

"Mrs. Todd never, in all the years of her acquaintance with her, had a face-to-face conversation about commonplace, mundane affairs. She dressed always in white, but such was her dislike to being 'fitted,' that her sister was obliged to act as her model. In spite of the white dresses, she was neither morbid nor an invalid, but possessed of a keen sense of humor, which sometimes betrayed itself in grotesque plays upon words, and always in the queerest, quaintest turns of expression. Her letters are full of daring originalities, which, if they were not so evidently the coruscations of her individuality, would be affectations. She was always doing odd, undreamed-of things. Once, when her father desired her presence at church, she stoutly refused. A conflict of wills ensued, such as is possible only in an old New England 'orthodox' family. In the end Mr. Dickinson went to church alone. When the family returned home Emily was nowhere to be found. She did not appear at dinner. At last, toward the close of the day, she was discovered sitting in the cellar bulkhead, calmly reading a book, and her only remark was that she had not cared to discuss the question of going to church, and so had retired underground.

"It happened that once in her service of laying the table she put at her father's place a plate that had a bad nick in it. This annoyed the old gentleman very much, and he rather sternly forbade her ever again to let him see that plate. But perverse fate brought it about that twice in succession again the offending plate, with the old nick in it, fell to Mr. Dickinson's share, who was very indignant. It did not happen again, for after that last dinner Emily disappeared, and was found back of the barn under a big tree with a hammer and a stone, between which she was reducing the plate into the most infinitesimal fragments, and she remarked that now she hoped she should remember not to put it on the table again."—UNSIGNED, "Emily Dickinson's Personality," *Book Buyer*, May 1892, pp. 157–58

Works

POETRY

The verses of Emily Dickinson belong emphatically to what Emerson long since called "the Poetry of the Portfolio,"—something produced absolutely without the thought of publication, and solely by way of expression of the writer's own mind. Such verse must inevitably forfeit whatever advantage lies in the discipline of public criticism and the enforced conformity to accepted ways. On the other hand, it may often gain something through the habit of freedom and the unconventional utterance of daring thoughts. In the case of the present author, there was absolutely no choice in the matter; she must write thus, or not at all. A recluse by temperament and habit, literally spending years without setting her foot beyond the doorstep, and many more years during which her walks were strictly limited to her father's grounds, she habitually concealed her mind, like her person, from all but a very few friends; and it was with great difficulty that she was persuaded to print, during her lifetime, three or four poems. Yet she wrote verses in great abundance; and though curiously indifferent to all conventional rules, had yet a rigorous literary standard of her own, and often altered a word many times to suit an ear which had its own tenacious fastidiousness.

Miss Dickinson was born in Amherst, Mass., Dec. 10, 1830, and died there May 15, 1886. Her father, Hon. Edward Dickinson, was the leading lawyer of Amherst, and was treasurer of the well-known college there situated. It was his custom once a year to hold a large reception at his house, attended by all the families connected with the institution and by the leading people of the town. On these occasions his daughter Emily emerged from her wonted retirement and did her part as gracious hostess; nor would any one have known from her manner, I have been told, that this was not a daily occurrence. The annual occasion once past, she withdrew again into her seclusion, and except for a very few friends was as invisible to the world as if she had dwelt in a nunnery. For myself, although I had corresponded with her for many years, I saw her but twice face to face, and brought away the impression of something as unique and remote as Undine or Mignon or Thekla.

This selection from her poems is published to meet the desire of her personal friends, and especially of her surviving sister. It is believed that the thoughtful reader will find in these pages a quality more suggestive of the poetry of William Blake than of anything to be elsewhere found,—flashes of wholly original and profound insight into nature and life; words and phrases exhibiting an extraordinary vividness of descriptive and imaginative power, yet often set in a seemingly whimsical or even rugged frame. They are here published as they were written, with very few and superficial changes; although it is fair to say that the titles have been assigned, almost invariably, by the editors. In many cases these verses will seem to the reader like poetry torn up by the roots, with rain and dew and earth still clinging to them, giving a freshness and a fragrance not otherwise to be conveyed. In other cases, as in the few poems of shipwreck or of mental conflict, we can only wonder at the gift of vivid imagination by which this recluse woman can delineate, by a few touches, the very crises of physical or mental conflict. And sometimes again we catch glimpses of a lyric strain, sustained perhaps but for a line or two at a time, and making the reader regret its sudden cessation. But the main quality of these poems is that of extraordinary grasp and insight, uttered with an uneven vigor sometimes exasperating, seemingly wayward, but really unsought and inevitable. After all, when a thought takes one's breath away, a lesson on grammar seems an impertinence. As Ruskin wrote in his earlier and better days, "No weight nor mass nor beauty of execution can outweigh one grain or fragment of thought." —THOMAS WENTWORTH HIGGINSON, "Preface" to *Poems by Emily Dickinson*, eds. Mabel Loomis Todd, T. W. Higginson, 1890, pp. iii–vi

She resolutely refused to publish her verses, showing them only to a very few friends. As a consequence, she had almost no criticism, and was absolutely untrammelled; so that the verses are sometimes almost formless, while at other times they show great capacity for delicate and sweet melody, suggesting the chance strains of an Æolian harp. But in compass of thought, grasp of feeling, and vigor of epithet, they are simply extraordinary, and strike notes, very often, like those of some deep-toned organ. Take, for instance, this, which fully sustains the Blake-like quality suggested by the editors in their preface (p. 119):

> I died for beauty, but was scarce
> Adjusted in the tomb,
> When one who died for truth was lain
> In an adjoining room.
>
> He questioned softly why I failed?
> 'For beauty,' I replied.
> 'And I for truth,—the two are one;
> We brethren are,' he said.
>
> And so, as kinsmen met a night,

We talked between the rooms,
Until the moss had reached our lips
And covered up our names.

The extraordinary terseness and vigor of that weird conclusion
runs through all the poems; in this case it so grasps the ear that
you hardly notice the defect in the rhyme. Little cared she for
that, provided she uttered her thought. Yet at times she
reached with the same sudden grasp a completeness of utterance that was nothing less than lyric—as in the two verses on
the opposite page to the above (p. 118):

A train went through a burial gate;
    A bird broke forth and sang,
And trilled, and quivered, and shook his throat
    Till all the churchyard rang;

And then adjusted his little notes
    And bowed and sang again,
Doubtless he thought it meet of him
    To say good-bye to men.

With all its inequalities and even oddities on its face, there
is power enough on many a page of this little book to set up
whole volumes of average poetry; and the public will inevitably
demand to know more of the thoughts and mental processes of
Emily Dickinson.—UNSIGNED, "Recent Poetry," *Nation,*
Nov. 27, 1890, p. 423

⟨Higginson⟩ notes "the quality suggestive of the poetry of
William Blake" in her, but he leaves us the chance to say that
it is a Blake who had read Emerson who had read Blake. The
fantasy is as often Blakian as the philosophy is Emersonian; but
after feeling this again and again, one is ready to declare that
the utterance of this most singular and authentic spirit would
have been the same if there had never been an Emerson or a
Blake in the world. She sometimes suggests Heine as much as
either of these; all three in fact are spiritually present in some
of the pieces; yet it is hardly probable that she had read Heine,
or if she had, would not have abhorred him.

Here is something that seems compact of both Emerson
and Blake, with a touch of Heine too:

I taste a liquor never brewed,
    From tankards scooped in pearl;
Not all the vats upon the Rhine
    Yield such an alcohol!

Inebriate of air am I,
    And debauchee of dew,
Reeling, through endless summer days,
    From inns of molten blue.

When landlords turn the drunken bee
    Out of the foxglove's door,
When butterflies renounce their drams,
    I shall but drink the more!

Till seraphs swing their snowy hats,
    And saints to windows run,
To see the little tippler
    Leaning against the sun!

But we believe it is only seeming; we believe these things
are as wholly her own as this:

The bustle in a house
    The morning after death
Is solemnest of industries
    Enacted upon earth,—

The sweeping up the heart,
    And putting love away
We shall not want to use again
    Until eternity.

Such things could have come only from a woman's heart
to which the experiences in a New England town have brought
more knowledge of death than of life. Terribly unsparing many
of these strange poems are, but true as the grave and certain as
mortality. The associations of house-keeping in the following
poem have a force that drags us almost into the presence of the
poor, cold, quiet thing:

TROUBLED ABOUT MANY THINGS

How many times these low feet staggered,
    Only the soldered mouth can tell;
Try! can you stir the awful rivet?
    Try! can you lift the hasps of steel?

Stroke the cool forehead, hot so often,
    Lift, if you can, the listless hair;
Handle the adamantine fingers
    Never a thimble more shall wear.

Buzz the dull flies on the chamber window;
    Brave shines the sun through the freckled pane;
Fearless the cobweb swings from the ceiling—
    Indolent housewife, in daisies lain!

Then in this, which has no name—how could any phrase
nominate its weird witchery aright?—there is the flight of an
eerie fancy that leaves all experience behind:

I died for beauty, but was scarce
    Adjusted in the tomb,
When one who died for truth was lain
    In an adjoining room.

He questioned softly why I failed.
    "For beauty," I replied.
"And I for truth,—the two are one;
    We brethren are," he said.

And so, as kinsmen met a night,
    We talked between the rooms,
Until the moss had reached our lips,
    And covered up our names.

All that Puritan longing for sincerity, for veracious conduct, which in some good New England women's natures is
almost a hysterical shriek, makes its exultant grim assertion in
these lines:

REAL

I like a look of agony,
    Because I know it's true;
Men do not sham convulsion,
    Nor simulate a throe.

The eyes glaze once, and that is death,
    Impossible to feign
The beads upon the forehead
    By homely anguish strung.

These mortuary pieces have a fascination above any others
in the book; but in the stanzas below there is a still, solemn,
rapt movement of the thought and music together that is of
exquisite charm:

New feet within my garden go,
    New fingers stir the sod;
A troubadour upon the elm
    Betrays the solitude.

New children play upon the green,
    New weary sleep below;
And still the pensive spring returns,
    And still the punctual snow!

This is a song that sings itself; and this is another such, but
thrilling with the music of a different passion:

SUSPENSE

Elysium is as far as to
The very nearest room,
If in that room a friend await
Felicity or doom.
What fortitude the soul contains,
That it can so endure
The accent of a coming foot,
The opening of a door!

The last poem is from the group which the editors have named "Love"; the other groups from which we have been quoting are "Nature," and "Time and Eternity"; but the love poems are of the same piercingly introspective cast as those differently named. The same force of imagination is in them; in them, as in the rest, touch often becomes clutch. In them love walks on heights he seldom treads, and it is the heart of full womanhood that speaks in the words of this nun-like New England life.

Few of the poems in the book are long, but none of the short, quick impulses of intense feeling or poignant thought can be called fragments. They are each a compassed whole, a sharply finished point, and there is evidence, circumstantial and direct, that the author spared no pains in the perfect expression of her ideals. Nothing, for example, could be added that would say more than she has said in four lines:

Presentiment is that long shadow on the lawn
Indicative that suns go down;
The notice to the startled grass
That darkness is about to pass.

Occasionally, the outside of the poem, so to speak, is left so rough, so rude, that the art seems to have faltered. But there is apparent to reflection the fact that the artist meant just this harsh exterior to remain, and that no grace of smoothness could have imparted her intention as it does. It is the soul of an abrupt, exalted New England woman that speaks in such brokenness. The range of all the poems is of the loftiest; and sometimes there is a kind of swelling lift, an almost boastful rise of feeling, which is really the spring of faith in them:

I never saw a moor,
I never saw the sea;
Yet know I how the heather looks,
And what a wave must be.

I never spoke with God,
Nor visited in heaven;
Yet certain am I of the spot
As if the chart were given.

There is a noble tenderness, too, in some of the pieces; a quaintness that does not discord with the highest solemnity:

I shall know why, when time is over,
And I have ceased to wonder why;
Christ will explain each separate anguish
In the fair school-room of the sky.

He will tell me what Peter promised,
And I, for wonder at his woe,
I shall forget the drop of anguish
That scalds me now, that scalds me now.

The companionship of human nature with inanimate nature is very close in certain of the poems; and we have never known the invisible and intangible ties binding all creation in one, so nearly touched as in them.—WILLIAM DEAN HOWELLS, "Editor's Study," *Harper's New Monthly Magazine*, Jan. 1891, pp. 319–20

In the poems ranged under the heading "Love," Miss Dickinson struck a note more intimate and personal, but not so welcome. Here, if anywhere—and in writing so individual as this, and so little meant to reach strange eyes, one looks instinctively to find it here—the clue to her proud seclusion may be sought. Now and then one's hand is almost on it. The jar in her music is now inward, and not, as elsewhere, simply a matter of rhyme and rhythm. It recurs again and again, faint, strange, remote, like a phrase half-remembered from some angelic melody, but beaten back and made dissonant by perverse limits when it would rise to its true altitude. It sounds, haughty and full, in these lines which close a poem on the soul's exclusiveness:

I've known her from an ample nation
Choose one;
Then close the valves of her attention
Like stone.

It degrades to a natural level the assurance of immortality, often so wonderfully expressed and so proudly felt; and in the poem called "In Vain" it ranges the God, the Christ, the heaven that she believes in and pays homage to, as, after all, but accessories, necessary indeed, but ancillary, to merely human love—the love of man and woman at its natural best. The note is false. It strikes into the true melody from below, and makes a discord, but one strangely powerful in seductive charm. What the real theme is, one may learn who studies it in Mr. Coventry Patmore's poems; more especially in the volume called "The Unknown Eros."—UNSIGNED, "Talk about New Books," *Catholic World*, Jan. 1891, pp. 603–4

The poems of Miss Emily Dickinson (who has hitherto been known to Englishmen chiefly if not only by some very injudicious praise of the kind usual with Mr. Howells) are posthumously published, and from the short preface written by her sympathetic and friendly editor we learn some interesting facts of her life. She appears never to have travelled, or, indeed, left the house of her father in Amherst, Mass., where she led the life of an absolute recluse, and only appeared in society at a yearly reception given by her father to his friends. We are told that she wrote verses abundantly, but "absolutely without the thought of publication, and solely by way of expression of the writer's own mind." The editor prepares us for the want of form and polish in her poems, but expects us to regard them as "poetry torn up from the roots, with rain and dew and earth still clinging to them, giving a freshness and a fragrance not otherwise to be conveyed." A merit is here implied in their very imperfections as producing the effect of poetry drawn from an absolutely natural unconventional source. We very much doubt, however, whether this conclusion may be fairly adduced from the uneducated and illiterate character of some of these verses, although we fully recognize in them the unmistakable touch of a true poet. In these days considerable mastery over form in poetry is not uncommon, but in our minor poets it is rare indeed to find much original thought, or a strongly marked individuality. For this reason it is, perhaps, difficult not to overvalue these qualities, when we find them, as in Miss Dickinson, separated from any merits in form. We continually see the thoughts of prose put into verse, but, while some of the poems in the present volume can scarcely be described as in verse at all, they almost all contain a genuinely poetical thought, or image, or feeling. Miss Dickinson's chief characteristics are, first, a faculty for seizing the impression or feelings of the moment, and fixing them with rare force and accuracy; secondly, a vividness of imagery, which impresses the reader as thoroughly unconventional, and shows considerable imaginative power. The following quotation is a fair specimen of some of the most striking poems in the book:—

Exultation is the going
Of an inland soul to sea—
Past the houses, past the headlands,
Into deep eternity!

Bred as we, among the mountains,
Can the sailor understand
The divine intoxication
Of the first league out from land?

The editor suggests a comparison between the poems of this writer and those of William Blake; but, beyond the fact that they are both quite indifferent to the technical rules of art, the comparison is not very far-reaching. Miss Dickinson possesses little of that lyrical faculty to which Blake owes his reputation; but, on the other hand, she is gifted with a far saner mind. Her poems, however, may be said to be distinctively American in their peculiarities, and occasionally call to mind the verses of Emerson. The editor with his unfailing sympathy tells us that, "though curiously indifferent to all conventional rules," she yet had "a vigorous literary standard of her own, and often altered a word many times to suit an ear which had its own tenacious fastidiousness." Some of the poems, however, seem destitute of any metre whatever, the lines do not scan, the rhymes are arbitrarily thrown in or left out, in accordance with no fixed system, and grammar, and even good taste are sometimes only conspicuous by their absence. But in some of her roughest poems there is still an idea which forces the reader to attend to its meaning, and impresses him, in spite of the irritation he may feel at the form. Take, for instance, the little poem on "The Mystery of Pain":—

Pain has an element of blank;
It cannot recollect
When it began, or if there were
A day when it was not.
It has no future but itself,
Its infinite realms contain
Its past, enlightened to perceive
New periods of pain.

These poems for the most part are of a purely reflective character; but a few, such as the two on shipwreck, show considerable descriptive and emotional power. Moreover, though never perfectly finished or satisfactory in form, some of them are conceived in a lyrical way, and are not without music. Take this verse, for instance:—

Night after night her purple traffic
Strews the landing with opal bales;
Merchantmen poise upon horizons,
Dip, and vanish with fairy sails.

In many of the poems there is a deep underlying sense of the mystery of existence, a yearning to set the soul free, and to know the "why" of things. Death is a subject constantly harped upon, either from the point of view of the dying, or of those who watch the departure of others to that "undiscovered country, from whose bourn no traveller returns." The writer dwells on the final pomp and ceremony which attends the poor as well as the rich when they leave this world; the equality of death; the sense that the finite ended is the infinite begun; the agonizing and absorbing watchfulness over life that is ebbing, and then the sudden stillness, the "awful leisure," that succeeds when the end has come and the watchers can do no more. There is much that is very striking in these poems, they reveal great depth of feeling, and the tone of them, though melancholy, is not morbid. In some there is a kind of exultation and a concentrated force of expression which is really remarkable:—

At last to be identified!
At last, the lamps upon thy side,
The rest of life to see!
Past midnight, past the morning star!
Past sunrise! Ah! what leagues there are
Between our feet and day!

The little volume contains much to exercise the satire and scorn of critics. The sublime in Miss Dickinson's poems comes sometimes dangerously near to the ridiculous; but any fair-minded reader will, nevertheless, acknowledge that there is something in her poems which cannot be found in the mechanical productions of mere verse-writers, and that the editor is not far wrong when he says that her poetry contains "flashes of wholly original and profound insight into nature and life, words and phrases exhibiting an extraordinary vividness of descriptive and imaginative power, yet often set in a seemingly whimsical, or even rugged, frame."—UNSIGNED, "A Poet and Some Others," *Saturday Review*, Sept. 5, 1891, p. 279

The English critic who said of Miss Emily Dickinson that she might have become a fifth-rate poet "if she had only mastered the rudiments of grammar and gone into metrical training for about fifteen years,"—the rather candid English critic who said this somewhat overstated his case. He had, however, a fairly good case. If Miss Dickinson had undergone the austere curriculum indicated, she would, I am sure, have become an admirable lyric poet of the second magnitude. In the first volume of her poetical chaos is a little poem which needs only slight revision in the initial stanza in order to make it worthy of ranking with some of the odd swallow flights in Heine's lyrical *intermezzo*. I have ventured to desecrate this stanza by tossing a rhyme into it, as the other stanzas happened to rhyme, and here print the lyric, hoping the reader will not accuse me of overvaluing it:—

I taste a liquor never brewed
In vats upon the Rhine;
No tankard ever held a draught
Of alcohol like mine.

Inebriate of air am I,
And debauchee of dew,
Reeling, through endless summer days,
From inns of molten blue.

When landlords turn the drunken bee
Out of the Foxglove's door,
When butterflies renounce their drams,
I shall but drink the more!

Till seraphs swing their snowy caps
And saints to windows run,
To see the little tippler
Leaning against the sun!

Certainly those inns of molten blue, and that disreputable honey-gatherer who got himself turned out-of-doors at the sign of the Foxglove, are very taking matters. I know of more important things that interest me less. There are three or four bits in this kind in Miss Dickinson's book; but for the most part the ideas totter and toddle, not having learned to walk. In spite of this, several of the quatrains are curiously touching, they have such a pathetic air of yearning to be poems.

It is plain that Miss Dickinson possessed an extremely unconventional and grotesque fancy. She was deeply tinged by the mysticism of Blake, and strongly influenced by the mannerism of Emerson. The very way she tied her bonnet-strings, preparatory to one of her nunlike walks in her claustral garden, must have been Emersonian. She had much fancy of a queer sort, but only, as it appears to me, intermittent flashes of imagination. I fail to detect in her work any of that profound thought which her editor professes to discover in it. The phenomenal insight, I am inclined to believe, exists only in his partiality; for whenever a woman poet is in question Mr. Higginson always put on his rose-colored spectacles. This is being chivalrous; but the invariable result is not clear vision. That Miss Dickinson's whimsical memoranda have a certain something which, for want of a more precise name, we term *quality* is not to be denied except by the unconvertible heathen who are not worth conversion. But the incoherence and formlessness of her—I don't know how to designate them— versicles are fatal. Sydney Smith, or some other humorist, mentions a person whose bump of veneration was so inadequately developed as to permit him to damn the equator if he wanted to. This certainly established a precedent for independence; but an eccentric, dreamy, half-educated recluse in an out-of-the-way New England village (or anywhere else) cannot with impunity set at defiance the laws of gravitation and grammar. In his charming preface to Miss Dickinson's collection, Mr. Higginson insidiously remarks: "After all, when a thought takes one's breath away, a lesson on grammar seems an impertinence." But an ungrammatical thought does not, as a general thing, take one's breath away, except in a sense the reverse of flattering. Touching this matter of mere technique Mr. Ruskin has a word to say (it appears that he said it "in his earlier and better days"), and Mr. Higginson quotes it: "No weight, nor mass, nor beauty of execution can outweigh one grain or fragment of thought." This is a proposition to which one would cordially subscribe, if it were not so intemperately stated. A suggestive commentary on Mr. Ruskin's impressive dictum is furnished by the fact that Mr. Ruskin has lately published a volume of the most tedious verse that has been printed in this century. The substance of it is weighty enough, but the workmanship lacks just that touch which distinguishes the artist from the bungler,—the touch which Mr. Ruskin seems not to have much regarded either in his later or "in his earlier and better days."

If Miss Dickinson's *disjecta membra* are poems, then Shakespeare's prolonged imposition should be exposed without further loss of time, and Lord Tennyson ought to be advised of the error of his ways before it is too late. But I do not hold the situation to be so desperate. Miss Dickinson's versicles have a queerness and a quaintness that have stirred a momentary curiosity in emotional bosoms. Oblivion lingers in the immediate neighborhood.—THOMAS BAILEY ALDRICH, "In Re Emily Dickinson," *Atlantic,* Jan. 1892, pp. 143–44

In your issue of Dec. 19 an evidently competent reviewer refers to the first volume of Miss Dickinson's poems, issued a year ago, as a 'volume of curiously formless poems,' and suggests that the fact of the issuance of several editions proves 'that a great many persons care little for the form of expression in poetry so long as the thoughts expressed are startling, eccentric and new.' In the same review the critic says of the two volumes taken together that 'their absolute formlessness keeps them almost outside the pale of poetry.' The thought here seems to be that real poetry must have perfection of technique, must have metrical and grammatical finish: the poems of Emily Dickinson do not have such finish; hence these verses are almost out of the pale of poetry. The major premise here set down has not been attacked of late. The minor one is not so easily disposed of. For Miss Dickinson's poems may be formless, or they may be worded to so fine and subtle a device that they seem formless, just as the spectrum of a far-off star

may seem blankness until examined with a lens of especial power. I wish to examine one poem of Miss Dickinson's, taken almost at random, and search for the fine lines of the spectrum. For such example I take this poem:—

> I died for beauty, but was scarce
>   Adjusted in the tomb,
> When one who died for truth was lain
>   In an adjoining room.
> He questioned, softly, why I failed?
>   For beauty; I replied.
> And I for truth,—the two are one;
>   We brethren are; he said.
>
> And so as kinsmen met a night,
>   We talked between the rooms,
>   Until the moss had reached our lips,
> And covered up our names.

Now the notion here is the notion of the unity of truth and beauty. If harmony with the thought is to prevail in the verse we should expect a closely parallel structure with a figure in dual accent—i.e., based upon two factors. Such a figure we get:—

> I died´ for beauty´, but was scarce
>   Adjusted´ in the tomb´,
> When one who died´ for truth´ was lain
>   In an adjoin´ing room´.

Two pairs of lines, each with two accents, the similar words being matched in pairs—*'justed´ : joining´, died´ : died´, tomb´ : room´. Beauty´* and *truth´* do not perfectly match, of course, because not yet proved to be one in nature. These exact correspondences would produce mechanical regularity and overprove the proposition by overemphasizing the innate notion of harmony, if care were not taken. So care is taken to contrast the positions of the members of the separate pairs. That is, in the first line, the slurred words *but was scarce* are at the end, while in the corresponding line the slurred words *when one who* are at the beginning. Similarly, the slurred words *in the* in the second line are contrasted in position with the slurred words *in an* in the fourth line.

In the second stanza we have a more perfectly parallel figure, in accord with the development of the notion of harmony between truth and beauty.

> He questioned´, softly´, why´ I failed´?
>   For beauty´; I replied´.
> And I´—for truth´—the two´ are one´,
>   We brethren´ are; he said´.

Almost a formal balancing, but with a suggestion of relief; as, for example, in the harmonic echo of *he questioned´,* in the opening line, with *We brethren´,* in the closing line, suggesting a recurrence of the first verse motive.

In the last verse comes the deeper verity that though truth and beauty are one spiritually, they can never be at one in this world. So at the close the pattern changes and together with the hint of the attainment of perfect harmony we have a reversion both in form and tone. It is a suggestion of the death reversion which springs the thought to a harmony more subtle and remote.

> And so as kinsmen´ met a night´,
>   We talked´ between the rooms´,
>   Until the moss´ had reached our lips´
> And covered´ up our names´.

The rhyme changes to alliteration which is beginning-rhyme instead of end-rhyme—*night : names.* That is, our earthly names are lost in the endless night of death; ourselves, at one with each other, at one with truth and beauty, entered into the endless day of beauty and of truth.

I submit that such art as this may be subtle and mediæval, but it is not formlessness.—FRANCIS H. STODDARD, "Technique in Emily Dickinson's Poems," *Critic*, Jan. 9, 1892, pp. 24–25

I have seen Emily Dickinson's poems, and enjoy their queer gleaming and shadowy incoherences. It does not seem as if her mind could have been fairly balanced. But her love of nature redeems many faults.—LUCY LARCOM, Letter to Miss Forbes (March 14, 1893), cited in Daniel Dulany Addison, *Lucy Larcom: Life, Letters, and Diary*, 1894, p. 285

The intellectual activity of Emily Dickinson was so great that a large and characteristic choice is still possible among her literary material, and this third volume of her verses is put forth in response to the repeated wish of the admirers of her peculiar genius.

Much of Emily Dickinson's prose was rhythmic,—even rhymed, though frequently not set apart in lines. Also many verses, written as such, were sent to friends in letters; these were published in 1894, in the volumes of her *Letters*. It has not been necessary, however, to include them in this Series, and all have been omitted, except three or four exceptionally strong ones, as "A Book," and "With Flowers."

There is internal evidence that many of the poems were simply spontaneous flashes of insight, apparently unrelated to outward circumstance. Others, however, had an obvious personal origin; for example, the verses "I had a Guinea golden," which seem to have been sent to some friend travelling in Europe, as a dainty reminder of letter-writing delinquencies. The surroundings in which any of Emily Dickinson's verses are known to have been written usually serve to explain them clearly; but in general the present volume is full of thoughts needing no interpretation to those who apprehend this scintillating spirit.—MABEL LOOMIS TODD, "Preface" to *Poems by Emily Dickinson*, 1896, pp. vii–viii

The curious fame of this author is something unique in literature, being wholly posthumous and achieved without puffing or special effort, and, indeed, quite contrary to the expectation of both editors and publishers. No volumes of American poetry, not even the most popular of Longfellow's, have had so wide or so steady a sale. On the other hand, the books met with nothing but vehement hostility and derision on the part of leading English critics, and the sale of the first volume, when reprinted there, did not justify the issue of a second. The sole expressed objection to them, in the English mind, lay in their defects or irregularities of manner; and yet these were not nearly so defiant as those exhibited by Whitman, who has always been more unequivocally accepted in England than at home. There is, however, ample evidence that to a minority, at least, of English readers, Emily Dickinson is very dear. Some consideration is also due to the peculiarly American quality of the landscape, the birds, the flowers, she delineates. What does an Englishman know of the bobolink, the whippoorwill, the Baltimore oriole, even of the American robin or blue jay? These have hardly been recognized as legitimate stock-properties in poetry, either on the part of the London press or that portion of the American which calls itself "cosmopolitan." To use them is still regarded, as when Emerson and Lowell were censured for their use, "a foolish affectation of the familiar." Why not stick to the conventional skylark and nightingale? Yet, as a matter of fact, if we may again draw upon Don Quixote's discourse to the poet,

it is better that a Spaniard should write as a Spaniard and a Dutchman as a Dutchman. If Emily Dickinson wishes to say, in her description of a spirit, "'Tis whiter than an Indian pipe" (p. 156), let her say it, although no person born out of her own land may ever have seen that wondrous ghost of a flower (*Monotropa uniflora*, or Indian pipe) which appears on the cover of her volumes, but unhappily in a blaze of gilding that makes it meaningless. Perhaps, in the end, the poet who is truest to his own country may best reach all others. An eminent American librarian, lately visiting England, made it a practice to inquire in the country bookstores what American poet was most in demand with their customers, and was amazed at the discovery that it was usually Whittier.

It is needless to say that Miss Dickinson's poetry achieves its success, in spite of all its flagrant literary faults, by what Ruskin describes as "the perfection and precision of the instantaneous line." She is to be tested, not by her attitude, but by her shot. Does she hit the mark? As a rule she does. Is it a question what a book represents to a human being? This is her answer—only eight lines, but they tell the story (p. 29):

A BOOK

There is no frigate like a book
    To take us leagues away,
Nor any coursers like a page
    Of prancing poetry.
This traverse may the poorest take
    Without oppress of toll;
How frugal is the chariot
    That bears a human soul!

Again, how many a heart has been vaguely touched in some old and neglected country cemetery by the thought so tersely uttered here (p. 157):

THE MONUMENT

She laid her docile crescent down,
    And this mechanic stone
Still states, to dates that have forgot,
    The news that she is gone.

So constant to its stolid trust,
    The shaft that never knew,
It shames the constancy that fled
    Before its emblem flew.

The "docile crescent" may be supposed to imply that the life commemorated was immature, and ended while yet expanding.

It is known that Miss Dickinson very rarely gave a title to her poems, and it is to be presumed that in this volume, as in the others, these are supplied by the editor. The fourfold division, "Life," "Love," "Nature," "Time and Eternity," is that preserved in the earlier volumes, and the tolerably equal distribution of the poems into the four departments suggests that this strange, secluded life, seemingly wayward, had in reality a method and balance of its own. It is noticeable, also, that in a few of the poems (as on pp. 79, 200) there is an unexampled regularity of form, beyond anything to be found in the earlier volumes, and perhaps hinting at a growing tendency in her mind. This "Song," for instance (p. 79), surprises the reader, trained to the Dickinsonian muse, with an almost startling commonplaceness of melody. It was apparently sent with a flower.—THOMAS WENTWORTH HIGGINSON, "Recent Poetry," *Nation*, Oct. 8, 1896, p. 275

From another Amherst woman, Emily Dickinson, an elfish recluse in her father's house and garden, have been wafted to the world a few showers of sibylline leaves more curious than anything else in our minor poetry. In demure and dashing strokes her letters vividly paint that typical New England household, the father "pure and terrible," who "never played," the mother who did not "care for thought," but, as life went on, "achieved in sweetness what she lost in strength," the brother and sister, the pets and flowers, and Irish Maggie "warm and wild and mighty." Safely cloistered in this environment, the shy little poet loved no words so well as *gallant* and *martial* and posed as roguish rebel against the traditional solemnities of Puritanism.—KATHARINE LEE BATES, *American Literature*, 1897, pp. 178–79

A rarer vein is that of Emily Dickinson, whose condensed little poems on nature and life startle and stab by their erratic originality of thought and phrase.—WALTER C. BRONSON, *A Short History of American Literature*, 1900, p. 285

Emily Dickinson is, in her jerky transcendentalism and strained style, too faithful a disciple of Emerson, but much of her work has real merit.—JOHN CHURTON COLLINS, "The Poetry and Poets of America," *Studies in Poetry and Criticism*, 1905, p. 75

One must study Emily Dickinson not merely mainly, but almost wholly, through her verse; the outward facts of her life were the fewest and, in a way, the least characteristic. The daughter of a professor at Amherst College, she was born on the 12th of December, 1830. Like Jane Austen, she never married. Her fifty-six years were passed with a few friends; her intimates were the sunsets and breezes, her companions the birds and her thoughts. She died in the May of 1886; a recluse by habit and temperament, often for months at a time not venturing beyond the hedge of the garden set on the fringe of that academic town; a hermit, a thinker, a poetess.

If there be those who question her right to the last of these words they cannot, surely, have read her all-too-scanty poetry; and none may justly hesitate to grant her title to the second. A hermit she obviously was, but not of the sort who come to look upon themselves as the meanest of God's creatures. Colonel Higginson once said: "Emily looked through Nature up to Nature's God with a very Emersonian self-possession." This was distinctly the fact; she was none of those who could use of themselves the word "worm"; she thought of her Father *as* a father, and wrote of Him as if she were not merely His clear-eyed equal, but, as well, His most loving friend.

> I never saw a moor,
> I never saw the sea,
> Yet know I how the heather looks
> And what a wave must be.
>
> I never spoke with God,
> Nor visited in Heaven,
> Yet certain am I of the spot,
> As if the chart were given.

These few lines are as indicative of Emily Dickinson as anything she ever wrote. There lies her honest, certain religion, as well as her intuitive knowledge of Mother Nature in whatever garb she chose to wear. There also, to the ear trained in verse criticism, is her ever-recurring disregard for the accepted rules of rhyme and scansion, but even with this before one's eyes comes back Ruskin's saying: "No weight, nor mass, nor beauty of execution can outweigh one grain or fragment of thought." When a person can offer us genuine thought, gives it to us so simply and spontaneously as almost to take away the breath, then talk of metre and grammar seems impertinent. Emily herself says as much:

> The pedigree of honey
> Does not concern the bee.

> A clover any time to him,
> Is aristocracy!

Thought is what one finds from top to bottom of every page in the three slim volumes of Emily Dickinson's verse, posthumously published.

That her work was given to the world of type after her death, deprived her of the help which would have come from honest public criticism, and perhaps for this very reason she so ignored extrinsic form. She always felt, however (and always wrote with that feeling uppermost), an absolute, untrammelled freedom; it shows not only in the outward form of her work, but as well in the unconventional, daring thought which lay behind. Not a sheet of those found in her desk after her death a quarter of a century ago, bore evidence of having been written with an idea of publication; each is an expression of sincerity itself.

To give point to this comment, as to others, one may best quote from her work. "Constant" will, for instance, give a just glimpse of the poet's far remove from the outward and visible in rhyme and metre, as it will show how real were her inward and spiritual graces of love.

> Alter? When the hills do.
> Falter? When the sun
> Question if his glory
> Be the perfect one.
> Surfeit? When the daffodil
> Doth of the dew;
> Even as herself, O Friend!
> I will of you.

Here and there among the few critics who have commented upon Miss Dickinson's work, is one who speaks of her "consistent note of complaint." Such a strain is beyond question occasionally to be heard, but the adjective used must be objected to; the poetess voiced her differings with this world not often enough for them to be fairly spoken of as characteristic. Rather are her most marked characteristics her power of natural description by mere suggestion and her almost prophetic insight into life, whether of nature or of man. Nature she surely knew in all her forms; without her diadem, as well as in her gala dress. She fairly felt the sap of March run through her veins, and none perceived more quickly than she the change in the year which came as the first timid leaf hurried through the altered air.—WARWICK JAMES PRICE, "Three Forgotten Poetesses," *Forum*, March 1912, pp. 361–63

LETTERS

That passionate, tender spirit which was content to expend its great wealth upon a few chosen friends and a more catholic circle of inanimate loves of the woods, fields and gardens, is reflected in all its narrow beauty in the *Letters of Emily Dickinson*. Ethereal in life, just as her poems are, these Letters must, in a certain way, be a disappointment to those who were expecting to find in them a tangible solution of her many mysteries. The young girl who had said, "It makes me shiver to hear a great many people talk—they take all the clothes off their souls," would not be likely to reveal to another her own inner life. Most of her letters are strangely impersonal, coming from a recluse whose solitude must largely have been spent in introspection; and yet, while they contain so little of self, they contain still less of the affairs of the great world outside of her home. Indeed, had not one of her Amherst friends been killed in the war, no reader would have learned from her that the rebellion had been raging three years. "*My* business is love," she writes with very truth. "I found a bird this morning, down—down on a little bush at the foot of the garden. And wherefore sing, I said, since nobody *hears?* One sob in the throat, one flutter of bosom—'My business is to *sing*'—and away she rose! How do I know but cherubim, once themselves as patient, listened and applauded her unnoticed hymn?" Why, it might be asked, with the same answer as applicable to her, was she constantly writing verses, jotting down evanescent flashes of thought on margins of newspapers, backs of envelopes or other scraps of paper, tucking the songs secretly away, to be discovered only after her death? Many of the verses which formed parts of letters, having been published in the collection of her poems, have been omitted here, with loss both to the poems and the letters, we believe.

This soulful woman, with her stern self-repression, often suggesting her English namesake, Emily Brontë, possessed, like her, an intensity of love for Nature in her larger aspects as well as her lowliest individual forms, which sometimes seemed to constitute for these two ardent souls the whole world. The events of the day, with Emily Dickinson, were the blooming of a violet, the screeching of some bluejays, or the purpling of the lovely hills about her home in the evening twilight.

How intensely she loved her few friends can only be imagined after reading these impassioned letters written to Dr. and Mrs. Holland, Mr. and Mrs. Samuel Bowles, her brother Austin, Mrs. Gordon L. Ford and a few others, breathing out lyrical projectiles, in the midst of her prose stanzas, when the thought seemed best suited to verse. In spite of her seclusion, it would often seem that she was longing for poetic appreciation and sympathy—a longing which if felt was suppressed, with many another ungratified desire. Although an undercurrent of sadness thus flows through her life, there nevertheless ripples along quite merrily a sparkling humor, original, as everything she said was sure to be, and quite incompatible with one's preconceived ideas of this spirituelle recluse. "Mrs. —— gets bigger and rolls down to church like a reverend marble," she writes in one of those charmingly natural, spontaneous letters to her young cousins, which perhaps, more than any others, reveal most of that elusive personality—her real self. If these volumes were to be read simply for the disclosure of her inner life, too sacredly enshrined for even these friends of her lonely soul to gaze upon, they would be a disappointment indeed. Happily, the letters are, for the most part, so refreshingly original and quaint, that while they do dimly shadow forth the isolated individuality of a most interesting woman, they can and will be enjoyed for themselves alone.—UN-SIGNED, "Emily Dickinson's Letters," *Book Buyer*, Nov. 1894, pp. 485–86

These letters begin in reasonable conformity to the principles of the polite letter-writer. By degrees, date, address, formal structure drop off or are developed away. At all events, the last of the periods into which the editor divides the letters holds only notes, whose structure reminds the reader of sheet-lightning when they are most connected, of nothing in literature when they are disconnected. These letters cannot fail to arouse sharp differences of opinion, but also they cannot fail to arouse interest. They are an important contribution to our collection of human documents. Valued at their lowest as literature, they are suggestive studies in applied Lombroso. At their best, they are brilliant expressions of an unusual and original personality.

They extend from 1845 to the author's death in 1886, and the labor involved in arranging them, mainly from internal evidence, has been simply enormous. It has been a task, too, calling for exceptional powers of interpretation and sympathy.

Mrs. Todd's preface suggests the two lines of interest likely to be felt in the letters: they deepen the impression made by Miss Dickinson's poems, and they afford material for the study of an extraordinary style. The style of a recluse is as definite and legitimate an object of investigation as the conditions that make the writer seclude herself; and these letters, in their early stage, show the usual human tendency to commonplaceness. Miss Dickinson defines genius as the ignition of the affections, and the definition seems likely in her case to have been true. Certainly the preternatural compression and point of her literary expression appears to be the revenge exacted by an over-sensitive temperament for its failure to maintain the ordinary social relations.

The contents of the letters show the writer a less sprite-like, more human, being than she seemed in the poems. There is less of the dæmonic love in her affections, more of the familiar attachment to horse and house, kith and kin. Her enjoyments, too, sometimes fall short of the elevated ecstasy of a metaphysical sunset or of the consolations of death. But her easy acceptance of the terms of life becomes more and more impossible as the letters go on. The pathos of her recurring, short-lived revivals of the effort to live life whole instead of by spasms is extreme. One cannot help wishing that the writer's sense of humor had been more persistently indulged, or, perhaps, less persistently translated into paradox. The epigram and paradox of the later periods are excellent of their kind, and were doubtless a relief to the writer; but we cannot help profanely wondering what would have been the effect on the author's genius if she had reduced the nervous tension now and then by indulging in a genuine bout of gossip. Her attitude is depressingly superior. She does not abuse her neighbors enough to love them temperately. Her life grows more and more interior, until it reminds the reader of Plato's cave dweller who saw life only as it shadowed itself in the mouth of the den. Her family affections and her friendships are passionately strong, her hold on life slight and shifting. The contemporary life of her country, for example, does not interest her except as a source of disturbance to her own emotional condition, or to the wider self that she found in certain aspects of family, neighborhood, and town. The civil war was apparently unthinkable, and so unspeakable to her. Its record is the slightest possible in her pages, but the reserve is formidable. Things had a tendency to become unthinkable to her. She had little practical skill in what a clever writer calls "the art of taking hold by the small end."

What name will be given to experience of this sort, what estimate made of its expression, is an interesting question. A still more interesting question is what ought to be the name and estimate. Opinion will probably swing between the conviction that these letters are a precious legacy of genius for which we have to thank the scrupulous industry of Mrs. Todd and the generosity of Miss Lavinia Dickinson, and the equally strong feeling that they are the abnormal expression of a woman abnormal to the point of disease, and that their publication by a friend and a sister is not the least abnormal thing about them.—UNSIGNED, "Emily Dickinson's Letters," *Nation*, Dec. 13, 1894, p. 446

In publishing the letters of that remarkable woman Emily Dickinson, Mrs. Todd has not merely performed a labor of love, but has given to American literature a unique book. To review Miss Dickinson's letters is like reviewing her poetry: the critic instantly sees that here is something of unquestionable power that may not be labeled off-hand with any of the well-worn formulas that fit most books. In the conventional sense of the word, artist is not the term that one thinks of applying to Miss Dickinson. She had the Emersonic habit of trying to express her meaning poignantly and letting the rest go. This trait becomes a confused and irritating abruptness in writers whose meaning is of little worth; in writers of genius it is the startling abruptness of the seer. Men of the one class are ignorant of the value of art, and men of the other class deem their unrestrained utterance more precious than artistic success. But having something to say, and saying it in the way that most perfectly expresses the speaker's personality—this is after all the supreme, though not the only, element of art. Beyond any doubt, to Miss Dickinson must be ascribed this cardinal literary virtue. Spontaneity—the birth-right gift of the lyric poet and of woman—was hers also. Poetic spontaneity means not merely the desire to speak, but the need to speak. Miss Dickinson's reluctance to publish (it need only be recalled that her two volumes of poetry are posthumous) and her constant literary activity confirm, if confirmation be needed, her possession of the poetic instinct, which seeks utterance for the sake of utterance, because silence is impossible. "And when," she says, "a sudden light on orchards, or a new fashion in the wind troubled my attention, I felt a palsy, here, the verses just relieve." Herein is the note of every line that she penned—sincerity. Her letters, not a few of which are poems in everything but the conventional typographical arrangement in verses, help to make evident this vital characteristic of her poetry. And they bring to our knowledge the woman as well as the poet.—UNSIGNED, "Letters of Emily Dickinson," *Critic*, Feb. 16, 1895, p. 119

Not quite able to avail herself of the wider scope which the New England revolt was disclosing to her, and incapable of satisfaction with the creeds and moods in which she had been brought up, Emily Dickinson retired into herself, and found solace and serenity in her vivid apprehensions of the truth, and the manifestations of that truth in Nature, which became to her a symbol easily read and transparent to the meaning which it contained. Her correspondence is replete with a gay and delicate humor; the recluse was full of wit and of gentle happiness with her friends. Perhaps she did not take herself and her abandonment of the world with too much seriousness; probably she saw something of its humorous aspect, and would gladly enough have had the strength to share the generous life outside; the effort, doubtless, was too great, and the sympathetic appreciation not sufficiently vigorous and insistent. The letters are free from that strain of morbidness which we sometimes find in her poems, especially in those dealing with the subject of death and its dark accompaniments. Here we have such exquisite passages as this:

> The bed on which he came was enclosed in a large casket, shut entirely, and covered from head to foot with the sweetest flowers. He went to sleep from the village church. Crowds came to tell him good night, choirs sang to him, pastors told how brave he was—early-soldier heart. And the family lowered their heads, as the reeds the wind shakes.

As the introspective habit grew upon her, every incident of a life simple and unvarying in the extreme became touched with an illumination that her thoughts and mood poured forth. "A letter," she says, "always feels to me like immortality, because it is the mind alone without corporeal friend."

⟨. . .⟩ The extent of her correspondence, and the character of much of it, indicate how deeply she felt the need and how warmly she would have welcomed the possibility of closer relations with her fellows. The nun and the saint make a figure

delicate and unique; but the poet with something real to say to mankind deserves our larger appreciation.—LOUIS J. BLOCK, "A New England Nun," *Dial*, March 1, 1895, pp. 146–47

THOMAS WENTWORTH HIGGINSON
From "Emily Dickinson's Letters"
Atlantic, October 1891, pp. 444–53

Few events in American literary history have been more curious than the sudden rise of Emily Dickinson into a posthumous fame only more accentuated by the utterly recluse character of her life and by her aversion to even a literary publicity. The lines which form a prelude to the published volume of her poems are the only ones that have yet come to light indicating even a temporary desire to come in contact with the great world of readers; she seems to have had no reference, in all the rest, to anything but her own thought and a few friends. But for her only sister, it is very doubtful if her poems would ever have been printed at all; and when published, they were launched quietly and without any expectation of a wide audience; yet the outcome of it is that six editions of the volume have been sold within six months, a suddenness of success almost without a parallel in American literature.

One result of this glare of publicity has been a constant and earnest demand by her readers for further information in regard to her; and I have decided with much reluctance to give some extracts from her early correspondence with one whom she always persisted in regarding—with very little ground for it—as a literary counselor and confidant.

It seems to be the opinion of those who have examined her accessible correspondence most widely, that no other letters bring us quite so intimately near to the peculiar quality and aroma of her nature; and it has been urged upon me very strongly that her readers have the right to know something more of this gifted and most interesting woman.

On April 16, 1862, I took from the post office in Worcester, Mass., where I was then living, the following letter:—

> MR. HIGGINSON,—Are you too deeply occupied to say if my verse is alive?
>
> The mind is so near itself it cannot see distinctly, and I have none to ask.
>
> Should you think it breathed, and had you the leisure to tell me, I should feel quick gratitude.
>
> If I make the mistake, that you dared to tell me would give me sincerer honor toward you.
>
> I inclose my name, asking you, if you please, sir, to tell me what is true?
>
> That you will not betray me it is needless to ask, since honor is its own pawn.

The letter was postmarked "Amherst," and it was in a handwriting so peculiar that it seemed as if the writer might have taken her first lessons by studying the famous fossil bird-tracks in the museum of that college town. Yet it was not in the slightest degree illiterate, but cultivated, quaint, and wholly unique. Of punctuation there was little; she used chiefly dashes, and it has been thought better, in printing these letters, as with her poems, to give them the benefit in this respect of the ordinary usages; and so with her habit as to capitalization, as the printers call it, in which she followed the Old English and present German method of thus distinguishing every noun substantive. But the most curious thing about the letter was the total absence of a signature. It proved, however, that she had written her name on a card, and put it under the shelter of a smaller envelope inclosed in the larger; and even this name was written—as if the shy writer wished to recede as far as possible from view—in pencil, not in ink. The name was Emily Dickinson. Inclosed with the letter were four poems, two of which have been already printed,—"Safe in their alabaster chambers" and "I'll tell you how the sun rose," together with the two that here follow. The first comprises in its eight lines a truth so searching that it seems a condensed summary of the whole experience of a long life:—

> We play at paste
> Till qualified for pearl;
> Then drop the paste
> And deem ourself a fool.
>
> The shapes, though, were similar
> And our new hands
> Learned gem-tactics,
> Practicing sands.

Then came one which I have always classed among the most exquisite of her productions, with a singular felicity of phrase and an aerial lift that bears the ear upward with the bee it traces:—

> The nearest dream recedes unrealized.
> The heaven we chase,
> Like the June bee
> Before the schoolboy,
> Invites the race,
> Stoops to an easy clover,
> Dips—evades—teases—deploys—
> Then to the royal clouds
> Lifts his light pinnace,
> Heedless of the boy
> Staring, bewildered, at the mocking sky.
> Homesick for steadfast honey,—
> Ah! the bee flies not
> Which brews that rare variety.

The impression of a wholly new and original poetic genius was as distinct on my mind at the first reading of these four poems as it is now, after thirty years of further knowledge; and with it came the problem never yet solved, what place ought to be assigned in literature to what is so remarkable, yet so elusive of criticism. The bee himself did not evade the schoolboy more than she evaded me; and even at this day I still stand somewhat bewildered, like the boy. ⟨. . .⟩

At last, after many postponements, on August 16, 1870, I found myself face to face with my hitherto unseen correspondent. It was at her father's house, one of those large, square, brick mansions so familiar in our older New England towns, surrounded by trees and blossoming shrubs without, and within exquisitely neat, cool, spacious, and fragrant with flowers. After a little delay, I heard an extremely faint and pattering footstep like that of a child, in the hall, and in glided, almost noiselessly, a plain, shy little person, the face without a single good feature, but with eyes, as she herself said, "like the sherry the guest leaves in the glass," and with smooth bands of reddish chestnut hair. She had a quaint and nun-like look, as if she might be a German canoness of some religious order, whose prescribed garb was white piqué, with a blue net worsted shawl. She came toward me with two day-lilies, which she put in a childlike way into my hand, saying softly, under her breath, "These are my introduction," and adding, also, under her breath, in childlike fashion, "Forgive me if I am frightened; I never see strangers, and hardly know what I say." But soon she began to talk, and thenceforward continued almost con-

stantly; pausing sometimes to beg that I would talk instead, but readily recommencing when I evaded. There was not a trace of affectation in all this; she seemed to speak absolutely for her own relief, and wholly without watching its effect on her hearer. Led on by me, she told much about her early life, in which her father was always the chief figure,—evidently a man of the old type, *la vieille roche* of Puritanism—a man who, as she said, read on Sunday "lonely and rigorous books;" and who had from childhood inspired her with such awe, that she never learned to tell time by the clock till she was fifteen, simply because he had tried to explain it to her when she was a little child, and she had been afraid to tell him that she did not understand, and also afraid to ask any one else lest he should hear of it. Yet she had never heard him speak a harsh word, and it needed only a glance at his photograph to see how truly the Puritan tradition was preserved in him. He did not wish his children, when little, to read anything but the Bible; and when, one day, her brother brought her home Longfellow's *Kavanagh*, he put it secretly under the pianoforte cover, made signs to her, and they both afterwards read it. It may have been before this, however, that a student of her father's was amazed to find that she and her brother had never heard of Lydia Maria Child, then much read, and he brought *Letters from New York*, and hid it in the great bush of old-fashioned tree-box beside the front door. After the first book she thought in ecstasy, "This, then, is a book, and there are more of them." But she did not find so many as she expected, for she afterwards said to me, "When I lost the use of my eyes, it was a comfort to think that there were so few real books that I could easily find one to read me all of them." Afterwards, when she regained her eyes, she read Shakespeare, and thought to herself, "Why is any other book needed?"

HAMILTON AÏDÉ
"Poems by Emily Dickenson"
Nineteenth Century, April 1892, pp. 703–6

An American lady, who nearly missed being the most distinguished poetess her country has yet produced, died in middle age some six years ago. In life she was but little known, and rarely even seen. This aloofness, tinged with eccentricity, and possibly attributable to some early sorrow, characterises all she wrote. Her scattered verse has only been published since her death; and such fame as Emily Dickenson has achieved as yet is, therefore, posthumous. She avoided publicity in any form; and this indifference to recognition, I take it, accounts for the imperfection of her verse. I cannot subscribe to the idea that her audacious violation of rhyme, her careless obscurity were wilful. I rather incline to the belief that, writing for herself alone, so long as she committed the thought that burned within her to paper, with some assonance which pleased her ear—or even, in some cases, without it—she was satisfied. She would not have been satisfied that these thoughts, clearly the cries wrung from a passionate, suffering soul, should have been given to the world without further polish. Yet we cannot regret the publication of this little volume. The world is richer by some exquisite lines, some beautiful couplets; only in one or two instances by a poem which is complete and perfect. But in all, the possession of Imagination—that rarest gift—is conspicuous: Imagination, and a strong individuality, akin to that of no other writer, though at moments there is something that recalls Blake, and, at others, Emily Brontë. The following is a vivid example of her strong conception. One can almost fancy that the writer had before her eyes some grand allegorical design by G. Watts when she sat down, and wrote at white heat:—

THE CHARIOT

Because I could not stop for Death,
  He kindly stopped for me;
The carriage held but just ourselves,
  And Immortality.

We slowly drove, he knew no haste,
  And I had put away
My labor, and my leisure, too,
  For his civility.

We passed the school where children played,
  Their lessons scarcely done;
We passed the fields of gazing grain:
  We passed the setting sun.

We paused before a house that seemed
  A swelling of the ground;
The roof was scarcely visible,
  The cornice but a mound.

Since then 'tis centuries; but each
  Feels shorter than the day
I first surmised the horses' heads
  Were toward eternity.

Those five stanzas, though I suppose they cannot be called perfect, inasmuch as the rhymes in the second and fifth must be judged incorrect, have a quality which is rare in poetry of any period. Miss Dickenson's gift of *seeing*, now as in an Apocalyptic vision, now as in a dream of fairyland, is unique among minor minstrels. Her range, it is true, is limited: as though the solitary soul only looked outwardly on certain phases of nature, inwardly on certain insoluble problems of life. But in such exquisite poems as the following—exquisite, in spite of its provoking imperfection—one sees how Imagination with her could descend from its lofty pedestal and pipe and frisk away among the meadows to a fanciful tune of its own.

THE GRASS

The grass so little has to do—
  A sphere of simple green,
With only butterflies to brood,
  And bees to entertain,

And stir all day to pretty tunes
  The breezes fetch along,
And hold the sunshine in its lap,
  And bow to everything;

And thread the dews all night, like pearls,
  And make itself so fine,—
A duchess were too common
  For such a noticing.

And even when it dies, to pass
  In odours so divine,
As lowly spices gone to sleep,
  Or amulets of pine.

And then to dwell in sov'reign barns,
  And dream the days away,—
The grass so little has to do,
  I wish I were the hay!

The blemishes in these stanzas are obvious; and the third one seems to me entirely bad; but one pardons a great deal for the sake of the second (in spite of its careless neglect of rhyme), and the last, which contains two exquisite lines. A common singer would have *seen* no further than the cutting down of the grass, 'which to-day is and to-morrow is cast into the oven.'

Akin to this, but deeper in feeling, is the nearly perfect little song numbered ix. in the collection labelled 'Love.'

I
Have you got a brook in your little heart,
  Where bashful flowers blow,
And blushing birds go down to drink,
  And shadows tremble so?
II
And nobody knows, so still it flows,
  That any brook is there;
And yet your little draught of life
  Is daily drunken there.
III
Then look out for the little brook in March,
  When the rivers overflow,
And the snows come hurrying from the hills,
  And the bridges often go.
IV
And later, in August it may be,
  When the meadows parching lie,
Beware, lest this little brook of life,
  Some burning noon go dry!

Many of the poems, as a whole, are poor, but in nearly all occurs some original thought struck out in a finely-turned line. In one, which expresses the intense longing to know how a beloved and absent one died, she asks

And was he confident until
  Ill fluttered out in everlasting well?

and she concludes her tender, anxious catechism thus:

Was he afraid or tranquil?
  Might he know
How conscious consciousness could grow,
Till love that was, and love too blest to be
Meet,—and the junction be Eternity?

I could quote many more passages showing the pearls that are strung on pack-thread, alongside common beads, throughout these curious poems. But space will only allow me to transcribe two couplets, which are complete in themselves, and which, as the cry of a suffering soul, not bereft of faith, and struggling for resignation, seem to me wonderfully pathetic, in their passionate, child-like simplicity.

I shall know why, when time is over,
  And I have ceased to wonder why;
Christ will explain each separate anguish,
  In the fair schoolroom of the sky.

He will tell me what Peter promised,
  And I, for wonder at his woe,
I shall forget the drop of anguish
  That scalds me now, that scalds me now.

In the short preface which tells how Miss Dickenson spent years without setting her foot beyond the doorstep of her father's house, Mrs. T. W. Higgenson says: 'In many cases these verses will seem to the reader like poetry torn up by the roots, with rain and dew and earth still clinging to them, giving a freshness and fragrance not otherwise to be conveyed.' That is a very apt image. And yet the last thing that could be said of this volume is that it is 'of the earth, earthy.'

MABEL LOOMIS TODD
"Introduction"
Letters of Emily Dickinson
1894

The lovers of Emily Dickinson's poems have been so eager for her prose that her sister has asked me to prepare these volumes of her letters.

Emily Dickinson's verses, often but the reflection of a passing mood, do not always completely represent herself,—rarely, indeed, showing the dainty humor, the frolicsome gayety, which continually bubbled over in her daily life. The sombre and even weird outlook upon this world and the next, characteristic of many of the poems, was by no means a prevailing condition of mind; for, while fully apprehending all the tragic elements in life, enthusiasm and bright joyousness were yet her normal qualities, and stimulating moral heights her native dwelling-place. All this may be glimpsed in her letters, no less full of charm, it is believed, to the general reader, than to Emily Dickinson's personal friends. As she kept no journal, the letters are the more interesting because they contain all the prose which she is known to have written.

It was with something almost like dread that I approached the task of arranging these letters, lest the deep revelations of a peculiarly shy inner life might so pervade them that in true loyalty to their writer none could be publicly used. But with few exceptions they have been read and prepared with entire relief from that feeling, and with unshrinking pleasure; the sanctities were not invaded. Emily kept her little reserves, and bared her soul but seldom, even in intimate correspondence. It was not so much that she was always on spiritual guard, as that she sported with her varying moods, and tested them upon her friends with apparent delight in the effect, as airy and playful as it was half unconscious.

So large is the number of letters to each of several correspondents, that it has seemed best to place these sets in separate chapters. The continuity is perhaps more perfectly preserved in this way than by the usual method of mere chronological succession; especially as, in a life singularly uneventful, no marked periods of travel or achievement serve otherwise to classify them. On this plan a certain order has been possible, too; the opening letters in each chapter are always later than the first of the preceding, although the last letters of one reach a date beyond the beginning of the next. The less remarkable writing, of course, fills the first chapters; but even this shows her love of study, of Nature, and a devotion to home almost as intense as in strange Emily Brontë.

Nothing is perhaps more marked than the change of style between the diffuseness of girlhood and the brilliant sententiousness of late middle life, often startlingly unexpected. And yet suggestions of future picturesque and epigrammatic power occasionally flash through the long, youthful correspondence. Lowell once wrote of the first letters of Carlyle, "The man . . . is all there in the earliest of his writing that we have (potentially there, in character wholly there)." It is chiefly for these "potential" promises that Emily Dickinson's girlish letters are included, all the variations in the evolution of a style hardly having less interest for the student of human nature than of literature. Village life, even in a college town, was very democratic in the early days when the first of these letters were written, and they suggest a refreshing atmosphere of homely simplicity.

Unusual difficulties have been encountered in arranging the letters with definite reference to years, as none but the very earliest were dated. The change in handwriting, of which specimens are given in facsimile, was no less noticeable than Emily Dickinson's development in literary style; and this alone has been a general guide. The thoughtfulness of a few correspondents in recording the time of the letters' reception has been a further and most welcome assistance; while occasionally the kind of postage-stamp and the postmark helped to indicate when they were written, although generally the envelopes had not been preserved. But the larger part have been placed by searching out the dates of contemporaneous incidents mentioned,—for instance, numerous births, marriages, and deaths; any epoch in the life of a friend was an event to Emily Dickinson, always noticed by a bit of flashing verse, or a graceful, if mystically expressed, note of comfort or congratulation. If errors are found in assignment to the proper time, it will not be from lack of having interrogated all available sources of information.

In more recent years, dashes instead of punctuation and capitals for all important words, together with the quaint handwriting, give to the actual manuscript an individual fascination quite irresistible. But the coldness of print destroys that elusive charm, so that dashes and capitals have been restored to their conventional use.

In her later years, Emily Dickinson rarely addressed the envelopes: it seemed as if her sensitive nature shrank from the publicity which even her handwriting would undergo, in the observation of indifferent eyes. Various expedients were resorted to,—obliging friends frequently performed this office for her; sometimes a printed newspaper label was pasted upon the envelope; but the actual strokes of her own pencil were, so far as possible, reserved exclusively for friendly eyes.

Emily Dickinson's great disinclination for an exposition of the theology current during her girlhood is matter for small wonder. While her fathers were men of recognized originality and force, they did not question the religious teaching of the time; they were leaders in town and church, even strict and uncompromising in their piety. Reverence for accepted ways and forms, merely as such, seems entirely to have been left out of Emily's constitution. To her, God was not a far-away and dreary Power to be daily addressed,—the great "Eclipse" of which she wrote,—but He was near and familiar and pervasive. Her garden was full of His brightness and glory; the birds sang and the sky glowed because of Him. To shut herself out of the sunshine in a church, dark, chilly, restricted, was rather to shut herself away from Him; almost pathetically she wrote, "I believe the love of God may be taught not to seem like bears."

In essence, no real irreverence mars her poems or her letters. Of malice aforethought,—an intentional irreverence,—she is never once guilty. The old interpretation of the biblical estimate of life was cause to her for gentle, wide-eyed astonishment. No one knew better the phrases which had become cant, and which seemed always to misrepresent the Father Whom she knew with personal directness and without necessity for human intervention. It was a theologically misconceived idea of a "jealous God," for which she had a profound contempt; and the fact that those ideas were still held by the stricter New England people of her day made not the slightest difference in her expression of disapproval. Fearless and daring, she had biblical quotation at her finger-tips; and even if she sometimes used it in a way which might shock a conventionalist, she had in her heart too profound an adoration for the great, ever-living, and present Father to hold a shadow of real irreverence toward Him, so peculiarly near. No soul in which dwelt not a very noble and actual love and respect for the essentials could have written as she did of real triumph, of truth, of aspiration.

> We never know how high we are,
>   Till we are called to rise;
> And then, if we are true to plan,
>   Our statures touch the skies.
>
> The heroism we recite
>   Would be a daily thing
> Did not ourselves the cubits warp,
>   For fear to be a king.

Must not one who wrote that have had her ever-open shrine, her reverenced tribunal?

The whims and pretences of society, its forms and unrealities, seemed to her thin and unworthy. Conventionalities, while they amused, exasperated her also; and the little poem beginning,

> The show is not the show,
> But they that go,

expresses in large measure her attitude toward society, when she lived in the midst of it. Real life, on the other hand, seemed vast and inexpressibly solemn. Petty trivialities had no part in her constitution, and she came to despise them more and more,—so much, indeed, that with her increasing shyness, she gradually gave up all journeys, and finally retired completely from even the simple life of a New England college town.

As has been said of Emily Brontë, "To this natural isolation of spirit we are in a great measure indebted for that passionate love of Nature which gives such a vivid reality and exquisite simplicity to her descriptions." Emily Dickinson's letters, almost as much as the poems, exhibit her elf-like intimacy with Nature. She sees and apprehends the great mother's processes, and shares the rapture of all created things under the wide sky. The letters speak of flowers, of pines and autumnal colors; but no natural sight or sound or incident seems to have escaped her delicate apprehension.

Bird songs, crickets, frost, and winter winds, even the toad and snake, mushrooms and bats, have an indescribable charm for her, which she in turn brings to us. March, "that month of proclamation," was especially dear; and among her still unpublished verses is a characteristic greeting to the windy month. In all its aspects "Nature became the unique charm and consolation of her life, and as such she has written of it."

Warm thanks are due the friends who have generously lent letters for reproduction. That they were friends of Emily Dickinson, and willing to share her words with the larger outside circle, waiting and appreciative, entitles them to the gratitude, not merely of the Editor, but of all who make up the world that Emily "never saw," but to which, nevertheless, she sent a "message."

JAMES FULLARTON MUIRHEAD
From "Some Literary Straws"
The Land of Contrasts:
A Briton's View of His American Kin
1898, pp. 178–86

My next example of the American in literature is, I think, to the full as national a type as Mr. Howells, though her Americanism is shown rather in subjective character than in objective theme. Miss Emily Dickinson is still a name so unfamiliar to English readers that I may be pardoned a few lines of biographical explanation. She was born in 1830, the daughter of the leading lawyer of Amherst, a small and quiet town of New England, delightfully situated on a hill, looking out over the undulating woods of the Connecticut valley. It is a little larger than the English Marlborough, and like it owes its distinctive tone to the presence of an important educational institute, Amherst College being one of the best-known and worthiest of the smaller American colleges. In this quiet little spot Miss Dickinson spent the whole of her life, and even to its limited society she was almost as invisible as a cloistered nun except for her appearances at an annual reception given by her father to the dignitaries of the town and college. There was no definite reason either in her physical or mental health for this life of extraordinary seclusion; it seems to have been simply the natural outcome of a singularly introspective temperament. She rarely showed or spoke of her poems to any but one or two intimate friends; only three or four were published during her lifetime; and it was with considerable surprise that her relatives found, on her death in 1886, a large mass of poetical remains, finished and unfinished. A considerable selection from them has been published in three little volumes, edited with tender appreciation by two of her friends, Mrs. Mabel Loomis Todd and Col. T. W. Higginson.

Her poems are all in lyrical form—if the word form may be applied to her utter disregard of all metrical conventions. Her lines are rugged and her expressions wayward to an extraordinary degree, but "her verses all show a strange cadence of inner rhythmical music," and the "thought-rhymes" which she often substitutes for the more regular assonances appeal "to an unrecognised sense more elusive than hearing" (Mrs. Todd). In this curious divergence from established rules of verse Miss Dickinson may be likened to Walt Whitman, whom she differs from in every other particular, and notably in her pithiness as opposed to his diffuseness; but with her we feel in the strongest way that her mode is natural and unsought, utterly free from affectation, posing, or self-consciousness.

Colonel Higginson rightly finds her nearest analogue in William Blake; but this "nearest" is far from identity. While tenderly feminine in her sympathy for suffering, her love of nature, her loyalty to her friends, she is in expression the most unfeminine of poets. The usual feminine impulsiveness and full expression of emotion is replaced in her by an extraordinary condensation of phrase and feeling. In her letters we find the eternal womanly in her yearning love for her friends, her brooding anxiety and sympathy for the few lives closely intertwined with her own. In her poems, however, one is rather impressed with the deep well of poetic insight and feeling from which she draws, but never unreservedly. In spite of frequent strange exaggeration of phrase one is always conscious of a fund of reserve force. The subjects of her poems are few, but the piercing delicacy and depth of vision with which she turned from death and eternity to nature and to love make us feel the presence of that rare thing, genius. Hers is a wonderful instance of the way in which genius can dispense with experience; she sees more by pure intuition than others distil from the serried facts of an eventful life. Perhaps, in one of her own phrases, she is "too intrinsic for renown," but she has appealed strongly to a surprisingly large band of readers in the United States, and it seems to me will always hold her audience. Those who admit Miss Dickinson's talent, but deny it to be poetry, may be referred to Thoreau's saying that no definition of poetry can be given which the true poet will not somewhere sometime brush aside. It is a new departure, and the writer in the *Nation* (Oct. 10, 1895) is probably right when he says: "So marked a new departure rarely leads to further growth. Neither Whitman nor Miss Dickinson ever stepped beyond the circle they first drew." ⟨. . .⟩

Her interest in all the familiar sights and sounds of a village garden is evident through all her verses. Her illustrations are not recondite, literary, or conventional; she finds them at her own door. The robin, the buttercup, the maple, furnish what she needs. The bee, in particular, seems to have had a peculiar fascination for her, and hums through all her poems. She had even a kindly word for that "neglected son of genius," the spider. Her love of children is equally evident, and no one has ever better caught the spirit of

SATURDAY AFTERNOON

From all the jails the boys and girls
    Ecstatically leap,
Beloved, only afternoon
    That prison doesn't keep.

They storm the earth and stun the air,
    A mob of solid bliss.
Alas! that frowns could lie in wait
    For such a foe as this!

The bold extravagance of her diction (which is not, however, *mere* extravagance) and her ultra-American familiarity with the forces of nature may be illustrated by such stanzas as:

What if the poles should frisk about
    And stand upon their heads!
I hope I'm ready for the worst,
    Whatever prank betides.

If I could see you in a year,
    I'd wind the months in balls,
And put them each in separate drawers
    Until their time befalls.

If certain, when this life was out,
    That yours and mine should be,
I'd toss it yonder like a rind,
    And taste eternity.

For her the lightnings "skip like mice," the thunder "crumbles like a stuff." What a critic has called her "Emersonian self-possession" towards God may be seen in the little poem on the last page of her first volume, where she addresses the Deity as "burglar, banker, father." There is, however, no flippancy in this, no conscious irreverence; Miss Dickinson is not "orthodox," but she is genuinely spiritual and religious. Inspired by its truly American and "*actuel*" freedom, her muse does not fear to sing of such modern and mechanical phenomena as the railway train, which she loves to see "lap the miles and lick the valleys up," while she is fascinated by the contrast between its prodigious force and the way in which it stops, "docile and omnipotent, at its own stable door." But even she can hardly bring the smoking locomotive into such pathetic relations with nature as the "little brig," whose "white foot tripped, then dropped from sight," leaving "the ocean's heart too smooth, too blue, to break for you."

Her poems on death and the beyond, on time and eternity, are full of her peculiar note. Death is the "one dignity" that "delays for all;" the meanest brow is so ennobled by the majesty of death that "almost a powdered footman might dare to touch it now," and yet no beggar would accept "the *éclat* of death, had he the power to spurn." "The quiet nonchalance of death" is a resting-place which has no terrors for her; death "abashed" her no more than "the porter of her father's lodge." Death's chariot also holds Immortality. The

setting sail for "deep eternity" brings a "divine intoxication" such as the "inland soul" feels on its "first league out from land." Though she "never spoke with God, nor visited in heaven," she is "as certain of the spot as if the chart were given." "In heaven somehow, it will be even, some new equation given." "Christ will explain each separate anguish in the fair schoolroom of the sky."

A death-blow is a life-blow to some
Who, till they died, did not alive become;
Who, had they lived, had died, but when
They died, vitality begun.

The reader who has had the patience to accompany me through these pages devoted to Miss Dickinson will surely own, whether in scoff or praise, the essentially American nature of her muse. Her defects are easily paralleled in the annals of English literature; but only in the liberal atmosphere of the New World, comparatively unshadowed by trammels of authority and standards of taste, could they have co-existed with so much of the highest quality.

MARTHA HALE SHACKFORD
From "The Poetry of Emily Dickinson"
Atlantic, January 1913, pp. 93–97

There is no doubt that critics are justified in complaining that her work is often cryptic in thought and unmelodious in expression. Almost all her poems are written in short measures, in which the effect of curt brevity is increased by her verbal penuriousness. Compression and epigrammatical ambush are her aids; she proceeds, without preparation or apology, by sudden, sharp zigzags. What intelligence a reader has must be exercised in the poetic game of hare-and-hounds, where ellipses, inversions, and unexpected climaxes mislead those who pursue sweet reasonableness. Nothing, for instance, could seem less poetical than this masterpiece of unspeakable sounds and chaotic rhymes:—

COCOON

Drab habitation of whom?
Tabernacle or tomb,
Or dome of worm,
Or porch of gnome,
Or some elf's catacomb.

If all her poems were of this sort there would be nothing more to say; but such poems are exceptions. Because we happen to possess full records of her varying poetic moods, published, not with the purpose of selecting her most artistic work, but with the intention of revealing very significant human documents, we are not justified in singling out a few bizarre poems and subjecting these to skeptical scrutiny. The poems taken in their entirety are a surprising and impressive revelation of poetic attitude and of poetic method in registering spiritual experiences. To the general reader many of the poems seem uninspired, imperfect, crude, while to the student of the psychology of literary art they offer most stimulating material for examination, because they enable one to penetrate into poetic origins, into radical, creative energy. However, it is not with the body of her collected poems but with the selected, representative work that the general reader is concerned. Assuredly we do not judge an artist by his worst, but by his best, productions; we endeavor to find the highest level of his power and thus to discover the typical significance of his work.

To gratify the æsthetic sense was never Emily Dickinson's

desire; she despised the poppy and mandragora of felicitous phrases which lull the spirit to apathy and emphasize art for art's sake. Poetry to her was the expression of vital meanings, the transfer of passionate feeling and of deep conviction. Her work is essentially lyric; it lacks the slow, retreating harmonies of epic measures, it does not seek to present leisurely details of any sort; its purpose is to objectify the swiftly-passing moments and to give them poignant expression.

Lyric melody finds many forms in her work. Her repressed and austere verses, inexpansive as they are, have persistent appeal. Slow, serene movement gives enduring beauty to these elegiac stanzas:—

Let down the bars, O Death!
The tired flocks come in
Whose bleating ceases to repeat,
Whose wandering is done.

Thine is the stillest night,
Thine the securest fold;
Too near thou art for seeking thee,
Too tender to be told.

The opposite trait of buoyant alertness is illustrated in the cadences of the often-quoted lines on the hummingbird:—

A route of evanescence
With a revolving wheel;
A resonance of emerald,
A rush of cochineal.

Between these two margins come many wistful, pleading, or triumphant notes. The essential qualities of her music are simplicity and quivering responsiveness to emotional moods. Idea and expression are so indissolubly fused in her work that no analysis of her style and manner can be attempted without realizing that every one of her phrases, her changing rhythms, is a direct reflection of her personality. The objective medium is entirely conformable to the inner life, a life of peculiarly dynamic force which agitates, arouses, spurs the reader.

The secret of Emily Dickinson's wayward power seems to lie in three special characteristics, the first of which is her intensity of spiritual experience. Hers is the record of a soul endowed with unceasing activity in a world not material, but one where concrete facts are the cherished revelation of divine significances. Inquisitive always, alert to the inner truths of life, impatient of the brief destinies of convention, she isolated herself from the petty demands of social amenity. A sort of tireless, probing energy of mental action absorbed her, yet there is little speculation of a purely philosophical sort in her poetry. Her stubborn beliefs, learned in childhood, persisted to the end,—her conviction that life is beauty, that love explains grief, and that immortality endures. The quality of her writing is profoundly stirring, because it betrays, not the intellectual pioneer, but the acutely observant woman, whose capacity for feeling was profound. The still, small voice of tragic revelation one hears in these compressed lines:—

PARTING

My life closed twice before its close;
It yet remains to see
If Immortality unveil
A third event to me.

So huge, so hopeless to conceive,
As these that twice befell.
Parting is all we know of heaven,
And all we need of hell.

For sheer, grim, unrelieved expression of emotional truth there are few passages which can surpass the personal experience revealed in the following poem:—

Pain has an element of blank;
It cannot recollect
When it began, or if there were
A day when it was not
It has no future but itself,
Its infinite realms contain
Its past, enlightened to perceive
New periods of pain.

Her absorption in the world of feeling found some relief in associations with nature; yet although she loved nature and wrote many nature lyrics, her interpretations are always more or less swayed by her own state of being. The colors, the fragrances, the forms of the material world, meant to her a divine symbolism; but the spectacle of nature had in her eyes a more fugitive glory, a lesser consolation, than it had for Wordsworth and other true lovers of the earth.

Brilliant and beautiful transcripts of bird-life and of flower-life appear among her poems, although there is in some cases a childish fancifulness that disappoints the reader. Among the touches of unforgettable vividness there are:—

These are the days when skies put on
The old, old sophistries of June,—
A blue and gold mistake;

and

Nature rarer uses yellow
Than another hue;
Leaves she all of that for sunsets,—
Prodigal of blue,

Spending scarlet like a woman,
Yellow she affords
Only scantly and selectly,
Like a lover's words.

Never has any poet described the haunting magic of autumnal days with such fine perception of beauty as marks the opening stanzas of 'My Cricket':—

Farther in summer than the birds,
Pathetic from the grass,
A minor nation celebrates
Its unobtrusive mass.

No ordinance is seen,
So gradual the grace,
A pensive custom it becomes,
Enlarging loneliness.

Most effective, however, are those poems where she describes not mere external beauty, but, rather, the effect of nature upon a sensitive observer:—

There's a certain slant of light,
On winter afternoons,
That oppresses, like the weight
Of cathedral tunes.

Heavenly hurt it gives us;
We can find no scar,
But internal difference
Where the meanings are.

None may teach it anything,
'Tis the seal, despair,—
An imperial affliction
Sent us of the air.

When it comes, the landscape listens,
Shadows hold their breath;
When it goes, 't is like the distance
On the look of death.

It is essentially in the world of spiritual forces that her depth of poetic originality is shown. Others may describe nature, but few can describe life as she does. Human nature, the experiences of the world of souls, was her special study, to which she brought, in addition to that quality of intensity, a second characteristic,—keen sensitiveness to irony and paradox. Nearly all her perceptions are tinged with penetrating sense of the contrasts in human vicissitude. Controlled, alert, expectant, aware of the perpetual compromise between clay and spirit, she accepted the inscrutable truths of life in a fashion which reveals how humor and pathos contend in her. It is this which gives her style those sudden turns and that startling imagery. Humor is not, perhaps, a characteristic associated with pure lyric poetry, and yet Emily Dickinson's transcendental humor is one of the deep sources of her supremacy. Both in thought and in expression she gains her piercing quality, her undeniable spiritual thrust, by this gift, stimulating, mystifying, but forever inspiring her readers to a profound conception of high destinies.

The most apparent instances of this keen, shrewd delight in challenging convention, in the effort to establish, through contrast, reconcilement of the earthly and the eternal, are to be found in her imagery. Although her similes and metaphors may be devoid of languid æsthetic elegance, they are quivering to express living ideas, and so they come surprisingly close to what we are fond of calling the commonplace. She reverses the usual, she hitches her star to a wagon, transfixing homely daily phrases for poetic purposes. Such an audacity has seldom invaded poetry with a desire to tell immortal truths through the medium of a deep sentiment for old habitual things. It is true that we permit this liberty to the greatest poets, Shakespeare, Keats, Wordsworth, and some others; but in America our poets have been sharply charged not to offend in this respect. Here tradition still animates many critics in the belief that real poetry must have exalted phraseology.

The poem already quoted, 'Let down the bars, O Death!' has its own rustic vividness of association. Even more homely is the domestic suggestion wherewith the poet sets forth an eternally, profoundly significant fact:—

> The trying on the utmost,
> The morning it is new,
> Is terribler than wearing it
> A whole existence through.

Surely such a commonplace comparison gives startling vividness to the innate idea. ⟨. . .⟩

She took delight in piquing the curiosity, and often her love of mysterious challenging symbolism led her to the borderland of obscurity. No other of her poems has, perhaps, such a union of playfulness and of terrible comment upon the thwarted aspirations of a suffering soul as has this:—

> I asked no other thing,
> No other was denied.
> I offered Being for it;
> The mighty merchant smiled.
>
> Brazil? He twirled a button,
> Without a glance my way:
> 'But, madam, is there nothing else
> That we can show to-day?'

Since life seemed, to her, seldom to move along wholly simple and direct ways, she delighted to accentuate the fact that out of apparent contradictions and discords are wrought the subtlest harmonies:—

> To learn the transport by the pain,
> As blind men learn the sun;

and

> Sufficient troth that we shall rise—
> Deposed, at length, the grave—
> To that new marriage, justified
> Through Calvaries of Love;

and

> The lightning that preceded it
> Struck no one but myself,
> But I would not exchange the bolt
> For all the rest of life.

The expectation of finding in her work some quick, perverse, illuminating comment upon eternal truths certainly keeps a reader's interest from flagging, but passionate intensity and fine irony do not fully explain Emily Dickinson's significance. There is a third characteristic trait, a dauntless courage in accepting life. Existence, to her, was a momentous experience, and she let no promises of a future life deter her from feeling the throbs of this one. No false comfort released her from dismay at present anguish. An energy of pain and joy swept her soul, but did not leave any residue of bitterness or of sharp innuendo against the ways of the Almighty. Grief was a faith, not a disaster. She made no effort to smother the recollections of old companionship by that species of spiritual death to which so many people consent. Her creed was expressed in these stanzas:—

> They say that 'time assuages,'—
> Time never did assuage;
> An actual suffering strengthens,
> As sinews do, with age.
>
> Time is a test of trouble,
> But not a remedy.
> If such it prove, it proves too
> There was no malady.

The willingness to look with clear directness at the spectacle of life is observable everywhere in her work. Passionate fortitude was hers, and this is the greatest contribution her poetry makes to the reading world. It is not expressed precisely in single poems, but rather is present in all, as key and interpretation of her meditative scrutiny. Without elaborate philosophy, yet with irresistible ways of expression, Emily Dickinson's poems have true lyric appeal, because they make abstractions, such as love, hope, loneliness, death, and immortality, seem near and intimate and faithful. She looked at existence with a vision so exalted and secure that the reader is long dominated by that very excess of spiritual conviction. A poet in the deeper mystic qualities of feeling rather than in the external merit of precise rhymes and flawless art, Emily Dickinson's place is among those whose gifts are

> Too intrinsic for renown.

MATTHEW ARNOLD

MATTHEW ARNOLD

1822–1888

Matthew Arnold was born in Laleham, Surrey, on December 24, 1822, the son of the Rev. Thomas Arnold, later headmaster of Rugby. Matthew Arnold was educated at Rugby, and in 1841 entered Balliol College, Oxford, where he formed a close friendship with the poet Arthur Hugh Clough. In 1843 he was awarded the Newdigate Prize for his poem "Cromwell," and in the following year he received his degree from Oxford. During 1845 Arnold taught briefly at Rugby, then became a fellow of Oriel College, Oxford. He traveled in France and Switzerland during 1846, and in 1847 became private secretary to the Marquis of Lansdowne, Lord President of the Privy Council and head of the Committee of Council on Education. In 1851 Arnold was appointed one of Her Majesty's Inspectors of Schools, a position he held for thirty-five years, eventually rising to the rank of Chief Inspector. From 1851 onwards Arnold, as an inspector, spent much time traveling throughout England and also in Europe, observing the social conditions that prompted his later critical works. Also in 1851 Arnold married Frances Lucy Wightman, a judge's daughter, by whom he had six children.

Arnold's first volume of poetry, *The Strayed Reveller and Other Poems*, was published in 1849. This collection contained such poems as "The Forsaken Merman," "The Sick King in Bokhara," and a number of sonnets written at Balliol, including "Shakespeare." It was followed by *Empedocles on Etna and Other Poems* (1852), which contains "Tristan and Iseult," and "Yes! in the sea of life enisled," and *Poems* (1853), consisting of selections from earlier volumes, with the addition of some new verses, including "Sohrab and Rustum," "The Scholar-Gypsy," "Memorial Verses to Wordsworth" (who had been a close personal friend), and "Stanzas in Memory of the Author of *Obermann*." In 1859 and again in 1865 Arnold visited Europe in order to study the educational systems there; these investigations resulted in a series of books, including *The Popular Education of France* (1861), *A French Eton* (1864), and *Schools and Universities on the Continent* (1868).

In 1865, after returning from his second European trip, Arnold published *Essays in Criticism*, a volume that almost immediately established him as one of the foremost critics in England. In 1867 he left his position at Oxford, where he had been a professor of poetry since 1857, and in that same year published *On the Study of Celtic Languages* and *New Poems*, a collection that included "Thyrsis," "Heine's Grave," and "Rugby Chapel." Arnold's essay *Culture and Anarchy* appeared in 1869, and was followed by such other works as *Friendship's Garland* (1871) and *Literature and Dogma* (1873). In 1883 Arnold visited America, where he gave a series of lectures, gathered in *Discourses in America* (1885). Arnold declined a re-nomination for Oxford Professorship in 1885, and in 1886 resigned his inspectorship. He died of heart failure on April 15, 1888. Shortly after his death the *Essays in Criticism: Second Series* (1888) was published.

Arnold's diverse activities as a poet and as literary, educational, and social critic made him one of the most widely read authors of his day. Later writers who were influenced by him include T. S. Eliot, F. R. Leavis, Raymond Williams, and Max Weber. Among recent editions of Arnold's writing special mention may be made of the *Complete Prose Works* (1960–77), edited by R. H. Super, *Poetical Works* (1950), edited by C. B. Tinker and H. F. Lowry, and *Poems* (1965), edited by Kenneth Allott.

Personal

I thank you much for your letter, as well as for all your care of and kindness to my boys during the holidays. You must let me know what they have cost you in point of actual expense, for I believe that you have advanced money to them, and I am sure that they could not be kept for nothing, judging from the actual state of their appetites. I agree with all that you say of them. Matt does not know what it is to work because he so little knows what it is to think. But I am hopeful about him more than I was: his amiableness of temper seems very great, and some of his faults appear to me less; and he is so loving to me that it ought to make me not only hopeful, but very patient and long-suffering towards him. Besides, I think that he is not so idle as he was, and that there is a better prospect of his beginning to read in earnest. Alas! that we should have to talk of prospect only, and of no performance as yet which deserves the name of 'earnest reading.' Tom also gives me grounds of

hope, though it is true that he also has not much fondness for work. I think that Rugby is good for them; I am sure that it does not weaken their affection for me, which might perhaps have been feared. Edward is in the Fifth Form, Willy all alive in the Lower Fifth.—THOMAS ARNOLD, Letter to William Charles Lake (Aug. 17, 1840), cited in Katharine Lake, *Memorials of William Charles Lake*, 1901, p. 161

It is observable that Matthew Arnold, the eldest son, and the author of the volume of poems to which you allude, inherits his mother's defect. Striking and prepossessing in appearance, his manner displeases from its seeming foppery. I own it caused me at first to regard him with regretful surprise; the shade of Dr. Arnold seemed to me to frown on his young representative. I was told, however, that 'Mr. Arnold improved upon acquaintance.' So it was: ere long a real modesty appeared under his assumed conceit, and some genuine intellectual aspirations, as well as high educational acquirements, displaced superficial affectations. I was given to understand that his theological opinions were very vague and unsettled, and indeed he betrayed as much in the course of conversation. Most unfortunate for him, doubtless, has been the untimely loss of his father.—CHARLOTTE BRONTË, Letter to James Taylor (Jan. 15, 1851)

Matthew Arnold has just come in, and we have had a talk. I thought at first he looked a little as if he did not approve of my pitching into him, but then he said very nicely that he had seen a speech of mine, which he liked very much. I told him Shairp was here and wished to see him. "Ah!" he said, "Shairp and you must diverge a good deal." I told him Shairp was not so narrow as he used to be. "Ah!" he said again, "he has so much feeling. He moves hither and thither under the impulse of his enthusiasm." Arnold's manner is very ha-ha; but I have no doubt he is a very good fellow.—JOHN TULLOCH, Letter (1874), cited in Margaret Oliphant, A *Memoir of the Life of John Tulloch*, 1889, p. 287

Mr. Arnold has been to the college, and has given his lecture on Emerson. The audience was made up of three hundred students, and three hundred guests from town. Never was a man listened to with so much attention. Whether he is right in his judgment or not, he held his audience by his manly way, his kindly dissection, and his graceful English. Socially, he charmed us all. He chatted with every one, he smiled on all. He said he was sorry to leave the college, and that he felt he must come to America again. We have not had such an awakening for years. It was like a new volume of old English poetry.—MARIA MITCHELL, *Journal* (Jan. 9, 1884), *Life, Letters, and Journals of Maria Mitchell*, ed. Phebe Mitchell Kendall, 1896, pp. 195–96

> Thou, that didst bear my Name, and deck it so
> That—coming thus behind—hardly I know
> If I shall hold it worthily, and be
> Meet to be mentioned in one Age with thee—
> Take, Brother! to the Land, where no strifes are,
> This praise thou wilt not need! Before the Star
> Is kindled for thee, let my funeral torch
> Light thee, dear Namesake! to th' Elysian Porch!
> Dead Poet! let a poet of thy House
> Lay, unreproved, these bay-leaves on thy brow,
> We, that seemed only friends, were lovers: Now
> Death knows it! and Love knows! and I! and Thou!
> —SIR EDWIN ARNOLD, "To Matthew Arnold,"
> *Pall Mall Gazette*, April 15, 1888

General

⟨The⟩ evangelizing prepossession of Arnold's mind must be recognized in order to understand alike his attitude of superiority, his stiffly didactic method, and his success in attracting converts in whom the seed proved barren. The first impression that his entire work makes is one of limitation; so strict is this limitation, and it profits him so much, that it seems the element in which he had his being. On a close survey, the fewness of his ideas is most surprising, though the fact is somewhat cloaked by the lucidity of his thought, its logical vigor, and the manner of its presentation. He takes a text, either some formula of his own or some adopted phrase that he has made his own, and from that he starts out only to return to it again and again with ceaseless iteration. In his illustrations, for example, when he has pilloried some poor gentleman, otherwise unknown, for the astounded and amused contemplation of the Anglican monocle, he cannot let him alone. So too when, with the journalist's knack for nicknames, he divides

all England into three parts, he cannot forget the rhetorical exploit. He never lets the points he has made fall into oblivion; and hence his work in general, as a critic, is skeletonized to the memory in watchwords, formulas, and nicknames, which, taken altogether, make up only a small number of ideas.

His scale, likewise, is meager. His essay is apt to be a book review or a plea merely; it is without that free allusiveness and undeveloped suggestion which indicate a full mind and give to such brief pieces of writing the sense of overflow. He takes no large subject as a whole, but either a small one or else some phases of the larger one; and he exhausts all that he touches. He seems to have no more to say. It is probable that his acquaintance with literature was incommensurate with his reputation or apparent scope as a writer. As he has fewer ideas than any other author of his time of the same rank, so he discloses less knowledge of his own or foreign literatures. His occupations forbade wide acquisition; he husbanded his time, and economized also by giving the best direction to his private studies; and he accomplished much; but he could not master the field as any man whose profession was literature might easily do. Consequently, in comparison with Coleridge or Lowell, his critical work seems dry and bare, with neither the fluency nor the richness of a master.—GEORGE EDWARD WOODBERRY, "Matthew Arnold" (1890), *Literary Essays*, 1920, pp. 75–76

On the last day of October 1891 a bust of Matthew Arnold was unveiled in Westminster Abbey by his friend and contemporary Lord Coleridge. Lord Coleridge on that occasion delivered an address in which, by way of conveying to his audience a clear conception of what Matthew Arnold was, he explained to them with great particularity what Matthew Arnold was not. 'Thackeray' said he 'may have written more pungent social satire, Tennyson may be a greater poet, John Morley may be a greater critical biographer, Cardinal Newman may have a more splendid style, Lightfoot or Ellicott or Jowett may be greater ecclesiastical scholars and have done more for the interpretation of St Paul.' Here the list ends: I cannot imagine why; for it appears to me that if I were once started I could go on like that for ever. Mr Chevallier may be a more accomplished vocalist, Mr Gladstone may be an older Parliamentary hand, Mr Stoddart may have made higher scores against the Australians, the Lord Chief Justice may have sentenced a greater number of criminals to penal servitude—where is one to stop? all these personages have as much business here as that great biographer Mr John Morley. And as for the superb constellation of divines,—Lightfoot and Ellicott and Jowett,—what I want to know is, where is Archdeacon Farrar? But if, after all, Lord Coleridge's account of what Arnold was not, leaves it still a trifle vague what Arnold was, let me take you to the *Daily Chronicle* of April 17, 1888. I copied down its remarks that same day; and ever since, I carry them about with me wherever I go as a sort of intellectual sal-volatile. Whenever I am in any ways afflicted or distressed in mind, body or estate, I take out this extract and read it; and then, like the poet Longfellow when he gazed on the planet Mars, I am strong again. The following are the salient characteristics of Matthew Arnold's poetry—'His muse mounted upward with bright thoughts, as the skylark shakes dewdrops from its wing as it carols at "Heaven's Gate," or, like a mountain brooklet carrying many a wild flower on its wavelets, his melody flowed cheerily on. Sometimes too his music rises like that of the mysterious ocean casting up pearls as it rolls.'

Now at last I hope you have a clear conception of the real Matthew Arnold: now you will be able to recognise his poetry when you come across it; and no doubt you will easily distinguish between his three poetical manners,—that in which he shakes the dewdrops from his wing, that in which he carries wildflowers on his wavelets, and that in which he casts up pearls as he rolls. I declare, I can liken such writing to nothing but the orgies in which the evil genii may be supposed to have indulged when they heard of the death of Solomon. The great critic of our land and time is dead, and the uncritical spirit of the English nation proceeds to execute this dance of freedom over his grave. He spent a lifetime trying to teach his countrymen how to use their minds, and the breath is hardly out of his body before the sow that was washed returns with majestic determination to her wallowing in the mire.

I can find no better words in which to speak of the loss of Arnold than those which were used by Gerard Hamilton at the death of Johnson. 'He has made a chasm which not only nothing can fill up, but which nothing has a tendency to fill up. Johnson is dead. Let us go the next best: there is nobody; no man can be said to put you in mind of Johnson.' I will not compare Arnold with the mob of gentlemen who produce criticism ('quales ego vel Chorinus'), such woful stuff as I or Lord Coleridge write: I will compare him with the best. He leaves us behind him to whom we cannot refuse the name of critic; but then we need to find some other name for him and to call him more than a critic, as John the Baptist was called more than a prophet. I go to Mr Leslie Stephen, and I am always instructed, though I may not be charmed. I go to Mr Walter Pater, and I am always charmed, though I may not be instructed. But Arnold was not merely instructive or charming nor both together: he was what it seems to me no one else is: he was illuminating.—A. E. HOUSMAN (c. 1891), *Selected Prose*, ed. John Carter, 1961, pp. 196–98

He always asserted himself to be a good Liberal. So in truth he was. A better Liberal than many a one whose claim to that title it would be thought absurd to dispute. He did not indeed care very much about some of the articles of the Liberal creed as now professed. He had taken a great dislike to the Deceased Wife's Sister Bill. He wished the Church and the State to continue to recognise each other. He had not that jealousy of State interference in England which used to be (it is so no longer) a note of political Liberalism. He sympathised with Italian national aspirations because he thought it wrong to expect a country with such a past as Italy to cast in her lot with Austria. He did not sympathise with Irish national aspirations because he thought Ireland ought to be willing to admit that she was relatively to England an inferior and less interesting country, and therefore one which had no moral claim for national institutions. He may have been right or wrong on these points without affecting his claim to be considered a Liberal. Liberalism is not a creed, but a frame of mind. Mr. Arnold's frame of mind was Liberal. No living man is more deeply permeated with the grand doctrine of Equality than was he. He wished to see his countrymen and countrywomen all equal: Jack as good as his master, and Jack's master as good as Jack; and neither taking claptrap. He had a hearty un-English dislike of anomalies and absurdities. He fully appreciated the French Revolution and was consequently a Democrat. He was not a democrat from irresistible impulse, or from love of mischief, or from hatred of priests, or like the average British workman from a not unnatural desire to get something on account of his share of the family inheritance—but all roads lead to Rome, and Mr. Arnold was a democrat from a sober and partly sorrowful conviction that no other form of government was possible. He was an Educationalist, and Education is

the true Leveller. His almost passionate cry for better middle-class education arose from his annoyance at the exclusion of large numbers of this great class from the best education the country afforded. It was a ticklish job telling this great, wealthy, middle class—which according to the newspapers had made England what she is and what everybody else wishes to be—that it was, from an educational point of view, beneath contempt. 'I hear with surprise,' said Sir Thomas Bazley at Manchester, 'that the education of our great middle class requires improvement.' But Mr. Arnold had courage. Indeed he carried one kind of courage to an heroic pitch. I mean the courage of repeating yourself over and over again. It is a sound forensic maxim: Tell a judge twice whatever you want him to hear. Tell a special jury thrice, and a common jury half-a-dozen times the view of a case you wish them to entertain. Mr. Arnold treated the middle class as a common jury and hammered away at them remorselessly and with the most unblushing iteration. They groaned under him, they snorted, and they sniffed—but they listened, and, what was more to the purpose, their children listened, and with filial frankness told their heavy sires that Mr. Arnold was quite right, and that their lives were dull, and hideous, and arid, even as he described them as being. Mr. Arnold's work as a School Inspector gave him great opportunities of going about amongst all classes of the people. Though not exactly apostolic in manner or method, he had something to say both to and of everybody. The aristocracy were polite and had ways he admired, but they were impotent of ideas and had a dangerous tendency to become studiously frivolous. Consequently the Future did not belong to them. Get ideas and study gravity, was the substance of his discourse to the Barbarians, as, with that trick of his of miscalling God's creatures, he had the effrontery to dub our adorable nobility. But it was the middle class upon whom fell the full weight of his discourse. His sermons to them would fill a volume. Their great need was culture, which he declared to be *a study of perfection*, the sentiment for beauty and sweetness, the sentiment against hideousness and rawness. The middle class, he protested, needed to know all the best things that have been said and done in the world since it began, and to be thereby lifted out of their holes and corners, private academies and chapels in side streets, above their tenth-rate books and miserable preferences, into the main stream of national existence. The lower orders he judged to be a mere rabble, and thought it was as yet impossible to predict whether or not they would hereafter display any aptitude for Ideas, or passion for Perfection. But in the meantime he bade them learn to cohere, and to read and write, and above all he conjured them not to imitate the middle classes.—AUGUSTINE BIRRELL, "Matthew Arnold," *Res Judicatae*, 1892, pp. 185–89

There is always ⟨. . .⟩ a relative element in Arnold's judgments, and he is always, and above all things, a teacher. I do not mean to insist upon his profession as an Inspector of Schools. That was what we may call an accident, and one to be regretted. Arnold felt much of his work as an inspector to be irksome, because he was conscious that thousands could do it practically as well as he, while the necessity of doing it made impossible work of which no one else was capable. He resolutely faced the necessity, and with a cool sense worthy of Scott himself, pronounced that the grind of official work was preferable to dependence on the pen. And when the work was not mere drudgery, he showed that he had inherited from his father a genuine interest in education, in the ordinary sense of the word—the education given in schools and colleges. He had the state of elementary and intermediate schools very much at heart; and when, as in his inquiries into education in France and Germany, he was entrusted with work which really demanded great powers and high attainments, he threw himself into it with vigour and enthusiasm.

In calling Arnold a teacher, however, I use the word in a much wider sense. It is worth while to remember that one of the greatest masters of English style constantly asks himself what is the practical effect of his writings, and continues to write on unpopular subjects because of his conviction that our duty is to acquire what we lack, not to laud and magnify what we have. Hence his constant inculcation of the need of clear ideas, his persistent ridicule of Philistinism and of the "dissidence of dissent," his deep sense of the futility of "calling our darkness light." Hence, too, he goes on "saying imperturbably what he thinks, and making a good many people uncomfortable." He is throughout trying to educate his country.—HUGH WALKER, *Academy*, Dec. 21, 1895, p. 538

A careful reading of his essays amply warrants the statement that he did not contemplate absolute abstention from action even as a temporary expedient. What he deprecated was *ill-advised* action, based on an incomplete and misleading conception of circumstances and relations. No doubt he would have included under this head a very large proportion of the philanthropic action, individual and organized, of his time,—too large a proportion, if you will. But such a mere mistaking of degree, if mistake there was, does not bring him into conflict with progress, and is of little importance. It certainly bore a less ratio to his *quantum* of correct judgment than the mistakes of the average British or American social reformer and philanthropist to his instances of wise action. With penetrating insight, he was painfully aware that an immense amount of earnest and well-intended effort was at best missing its aim, and in many cases doing positive harm, because of the lack of "a free play of ideas" upon the subject in question. Such a free play of ideas he considered it his mission to promote. And we may say that his aim was everywhere this, as well as to say that it was everywhere social. But when we approach it from this side it is easy to see that his work does not necessarily pass from the domain of living importance with the age that produced it. The habit of ill-considered action, growing out of the failure to bring a free play of ideas to bear, is as old as human history and bids fair to remain among us for many generations yet to come. And while it does remain, there will always be occasion for effort to deprecate over-hasty action, and to stimulate thought, in all lines of social progress. Hebraism in its own home produced a literature of conduct which the world has never yet passed by, and never will pass by until some other nation puts a better in its place. Hellenism likewise bore fruit for which the world is sure to have use until it is surpassed in its own kind. Arnold saw that the highest type of human development must effect a fitting synthesis of the two (not of course excluding the possibility of the development of still other traits, which neither Hebrews nor Hellenes brought into prominence), and he gave to English letters an extended series of brilliant essays in that direction. He did not think to revolutionize society at once,—though he was no pessimist, as many who have not read him, and are hardly prepared to understand him if they should, would have us believe. ⟨. . .⟩ What he wanted was to set up a process of "osmosis" of the best traits of Hebraism and Hellenism through the separating membrane of British prejudice and indifference, and by this means he trusted to accelerate the rise from the culture-level of the majority to that of the remnant. No one would have been less pleased than he to be told that his work was on a level with that of the Greeks

and Hebrews, for he would readily have recognized such a statement as clumsy and insincere flattery; but he was a good judge of effective English expression, and he doubtless expected his books to live and carry on his mission until superseded by another who should say substantially the same things in a manner still more attractive and effective. That has not yet been done, and perhaps one will not give unpardonable offense to the literary guild of the present day by suggesting that there is no immediate prospect of its being done. And yet no thoughtful friend of Arnold need feel any satisfaction that this is so, for he himself was so single-minded in pursuit of his end that he would have hailed gladly an eclipse of that sort. ⟨. . .⟩

As some of our older bards have gradually fallen into the position of "poets of the poets," so Arnold, if we mistake not, will become more and more the reformer of reformers. With the earnest desire for the good of his fellow-men which is characteristic of all sincere reformers, he had also the mental poise, the control of the emotions, and the logical temper, which the reform spirit is too apt to lack. And the multiplied cases of well-intended effort that failed because of that lack must gradually drive intelligent philanthropic endeavor toward the path which he has pointed out. One can hardly conceive of his writings becoming popular in the usual sense of that term. The scores of thousands of working-men who have devoured the pages of *Looking Backward* during the past decade, as if it were a divine revelation, will live and die with no knowledge of Arnold; but here and there there will be one of a thousand among them, with keener power of discernment, who will loosen with disgust his hold upon the air-castles of Bellamy and drop to the solid ground of the apostle of *culture*;—not, of course, the mawkish product which the enemies of Arnold have persistently attributed to him under that name, but the culture of which all classes may partake at the price of using such opportunities for self-improvement as are open to their efforts. And the philanthropist who can persuade men of thought to give Arnold a careful reading will do much more to put the ground in condition for a fruitful harvest than he who begins with an attempt to get Arnold himself out of the way. —W. H. JOHNSON, "The 'Passing' of Matthew Arnold," *Dial*, Nov. 16, 1899, pp. 352–53

Matthew Arnold, like every other great man, especially in that great transition age in which he lived, brought one or two really great and personal contributions. The most obvious, if the most superficial of these, and in a way the most entertaining, lay in the fact that he invented, if ever man did, an entirely new and original mode of controversy. He discovered the vast and militant power of a quite inexhaustible mildness. The Radical and Anglomaniac disputants against whom he was pitted were men of the trenchant school of Macaulay, accustomed to give hard blows and to be on the lookout for them. They were entirely bewildered when they found that they were fronted by a mysteriously meek person, and that the more often and more resoundingly they smote him over the head the meeker and meeker he became. If they had caught out an ordinary Whig or Tory controversialist in some apparent vagueness or inconsistency the man would have justified himself and hit out, showing that it was his enemy who was the fool and not he. Matthew Arnold merely said mournfully, "Now that my triumphant enemy, in his clear way, has shown that I am unfit for speculative pursuits, what remains to me but to fall back on picking up the truth here and there, in which he, with all his superiority," and so on; every arrow they shot at him he wore meekly as a decoration, but he sat in the same spot and continued his humble and respectful monologue.

Only toward the end of it did half his opponents realise that he was laughing at them; when they did, the discovery was infinitely more paralysing and disarming than a storm of successful repartees. It was easier to feel superior in face of the ringing dexterity of Macaulay, or the haughty rhetoric of Ruskin, than of that limpid but unfathomable irony. It is true that more than one of the great men of that period owed their intellectual domination to a quality greatly lacking in the clever people of to-day—this great quality of patience. Both Newman and Gladstone were great controversialists precisely because they were not, in the modern sense, debaters. They did not appear solely anxious to answer some one else; they did not jump up like the modern parliamentarian, with their mouths full of fiery epigrams; they were positive, not negative; they unfolded themselves slowly and calmly as in a soliloquy. Amid all the talk there has been about the speech and spirit of Gladstone, it has scarcely been noticed sufficiently that those distant and stately openings, those rolling clauses, those ample and leisurely parentheses, were really valuable and had their great public effect because they conveyed a certain air of confidence and self-knowledge, of being untouched; of being clear of thought and certain of victory. Men like Mr. Chamberlain and Sir William Harcourt are entirely admirable in the use of the retort; but every retort is the cry of a man hit. It is true, as I have said, that both Newman and Gladstone had this dangerous patience, this menacing air of leisure. But they had it only as a prelude which lent instantaneousness and a dramatic violence to the great moment when they turned on their opponents. But Matthew Arnold never turned on his opponents; he was a philosophic worm who never turned, but bored on to its goal. His controversial books are among the most humorous and entertaining books that can be read in the world, but from one end of them to the other there is scarcely a sentence which can be called in the popular sense "a score," scarcely a sentence that a reporter would mark with "cheers and laughter." He had gone into the depths of criticism and found there a very ultimate and awful kind of power, the power of non-resistance. It reveals a truth of which advantage has seldom been taken, that the most powerful and independent being on earth might be a really consistent Quaker. Passive resistance is far more maddening than active resistance, as anyone knows who has ever tried to open a drawer that was jammed tight. This power, which would lie in an enemy who really refused to put himself in the wrong, is really what I have called it, a very dangerous power. It might be used more wickedly than the sword of a soldier or the halter of an evil law. Nor can it be said that Matthew Arnold always used it well. Sincere as he was, he was sometimes positively unscrupulous in his politeness. He answered his enemies in a spirit which can only be described as a kind of malicious Christianity.

If this meandering and maddening urbanity was the chief example of Matthew Arnold's peculiar power and distinction in its external form, the essence of his internal originality, of his internal message and philosophy is, of course, by no means so easy to summarise. His splendid ideal of a great central school of wisdom and beauty, disdaining provincialisms, however large and noisy, resisting second-rate innovations, however fascinating and fashionable, was a great conception, and one to which he was loyal in a bold and logical degree. There is something sublime in that concentration upon the standards of mind and not of matter which could in one untroubled sentence dismiss America as a suburb. Unquestionably he laid his finger on the typical English defect when he objected to the authority of Deborah Butler and Newman Weeks being spoken of as if it were equivalent to the authority of Plato and St. Paul.

Only the other day I saw in a paper called *The Agnostic Journal*, so called because it knows everything about everything, an exclamation expressing the honourable thought of how noble a thing is human nature, which ran on, "To what heights can it rise in a Shakespeare, a Burns and an Ingersoll!" I was so violently amused that I felt inclined to rush away and whisper it into Matthew Arnold's tomb at the Abbey, that we might enjoy it together. But Arnold's insistence on the necessity of discriminating between an established reputation and a private preference had its dangers both for him and for others. He fell sometimes into that mean and diabolical heresy which declares that we should insist on the best of everything. There were times when he came at last to prefer criticism to admiration; to dwell far less on the excellence of Dante than on any defects he could find in Burns or Macaulay. He was sometimes affected by criticism in the same way that charitable people are affected by joining the Charity Organisation Society; through worshipping literary success he came to see nothing but failure, just as an impulse of Christian philanthropy ends so often under the other auspices in utter distrust of human nature. He held in some degree the mistaken idea that the best is the enemy of the good. It is not true that admiring a farthing rushlight leads us to despise the sun; if we once really admired a farthing rushlight we should admire the great conflagration of a million rushlights a million times more. It is not true that enjoying a detective story leads us to think lightly of Milton; if once we really respected another man for his ability to keep a secret from us, we should respect infinitely more another man for his ability to unfold to us an overpowering pageant of heaven and earth. Arnold's real case lay rather in the matter of the grounds and reason of admiration. It is not wrong to admire Newman Weeks: the question is, what do we admire him for? We are quite right to admire Ingersoll for being an honest man, or for being an erect animal on two legs, or for being the image of God in whom he didn't believe, but not for being comparable to Shakespeare, since that he was not. Everything in the world, including *The Daily Telegraph* or a cabbage, has a right to be admired, but not in a literary sense. It was Arnold's misfortune, but hardly his fault, if he sometimes, in insisting on the necessity of a reason and measure in literary enjoyment, lost sight of the vast and uproarious and noble enjoyment which can be obtained from everything that is not literary. He was a great critic and a wise and fearless man, waging an eternal and implacable war against frivolity, the frivolity which is to be found in the fashionable, the equally maddening frivolity which is to be found in the moral and religious. Under all his badinage he was, even in the age of Carlyle and Ruskin, perhaps the most serious man alive.—G. K. CHESTERTON, "Matthew Arnold," *Bookman* (New York), Oct. 1902, pp. 118–20

Works

POETRY

Containing as it did poems of merit so high as these, it may seem strange that this volume ⟨*The Strayed Reveller and Other Poems*⟩ should not have received a more ready recognition, for there is no excellence which the writer of the passages which we have quoted could hereafter attain, the promise of which would not be at once perceived in them. But the public are apt to judge of books of poetry by the rule of mechanism, and try them not by their strongest parts but by their weakest; and in the present instance (to mention nothing else) the stress of weight in the title which was given to the collection was laid upon what was by no means adequate to bearing it. Whatever be the merits of the *Strayed Reveller* as poetry, it is certainly not a poem in the sense which English people generally attach to the word, looking as they do not only for imaginative composition but for verse;—and as certainly if the following passage had been printed merely as prose, in a book which professed to be nothing else, no one would have suspected that it was composed of an agglutination of lines.

> The gods are happy; they turn on all sides their
> shining eyes, and see below them earth and men.
> They see Tiresias sitting staff in hand on the warm
> grassy Asopus bank, his robe drawn over his old,
> sightless head, revolving inly the doom of Thebes.
> They see the Centaurs in the upper glens of Pelion,
> on the streams where the red-berried ashes fringe the
> clear brown shallow pools; with streaming flanks and
> heads reared proudly, snuffing the mountain wind.
> They see the Scythian on the wide steppe, unharnes-
> sing his wheeled house at noon; he tethers his beast
> down and makes his meal, mare's milk and bread
> baked on the embers; all around the boundless
> waving grass plains stretch, thick starred with saffron
> and the yellow hollyhock and flag-leaved isis flowers.

No one will deny that this is fine imaginative painting, and as such poetical,—but it is the poetry of well written, elegant prose. Instead of the recurring sounds, whether of rhyme or similarly weighted syllables, which constitute the outward form of what we call verse, we have the careless grace of uneven, undulating sentences, flowing on with a rhythmic cadence indeed, but free from all constraint of metre or exactitude of form. It may be difficult, perhaps it is impossible, to fix the measure of license which a poet may allow himself in such matters, but it is at least certain that the greatest poets are those who have allowed themselves the fewest of such liberties: in art as in morals, and as in everything which man undertakes, true greatness is the most ready to recognize and most willing to obey those simple outward laws which have been sanctioned by the experience of mankind, and we suspect the originality which cannot move except on novel paths.—JAMES ANTHONY FROUDE, "Arnold's Poems" (1854), *Essays in Literature and History*, 1906, pp. 4–5

And now, before taking leave of these poems ⟨*Poems: First Series*⟩, we must advert to one thing which strikes us as their prevailing fault. We read them separately, and see many separate excellencies; but there is no one predominant interest to give life to the whole. High gifts, beautiful poems you do see; but one thing you miss—the one pervading poet's heart, that throb of feeling which is the true inspiration, the life of life to all true poetry, without which all artistic gifts are of little worth. Where this is present you cannot but feel its presence, not by self-revelations of the poet's own feelings, but by the living personality and interest which it breathes through whatever it touches. If you associate much with a man of strong character and deep heart, you cannot but feel what kind of man he is. So you cannot read poems which come from a strong poetic soul without their thrilling to your own. But when you have read these poems, and read with admiration, you are still at a loss to know what the author most lays to heart—what kind of country he has lived in—what scenery is dear to him—what part of past or present history he cares for—in what range of human feeling and action he is peculiarly at home. Certain characteristics they do contain—admiration for Greek Art and a uniformly artistic style; but these are not enough to stamp individuality on the poems. The two earlier volumes, it must be allowed, were pervaded by a strong sense of man's nothing-

ness in presence of the great powers of nature—that effort and sorrow are alike vain—that our warm hopes and fears, faiths and aspirations, are crushed like moths beneath the omnipotence of deaf adamantine laws. But such a view of life can give birth to nothing great and noble in character, nor anything high or permanent in poetry. This last volume has much less of that blank dejection and fatalistic apathy which were the main tones of the former ones; and though it has hereby lost in unity of purpose, we gladly welcome the change. In some of the newer poems we seem to catch strains which may prelude a higher music, but they have not yet attained compass enough to set the tone of the book. They may grow to this—we trust they may. Meanwhile we cannot but remind Mr. Arnold that there is a difference between poetic gifts and the poet's heart. That he possesses the former no candid judge can doubt; of the existence of the latter in him he has as yet given less evidence. But it is the beat of this poetic pulse that gives unity of impression and undying interest to the works of the noblest poets. At the outset we noticed the difference between what we called the natural and the artistic poets; those chiefly remarkable for what they say; these for the manner in which they say it. And although in the great poet-kings the two qualities meet and combine, they are not the less in other men distinct and in danger of falling asunder. Where the nature is strong, and the heart full, the poet is apt to rely entirely on this, and to care little for the form to which he entrusts his thoughts. Where the sense of artistic beauty and power of expression predominate, their owner, intent on these, is ever ready to divorce himself from the warmth of life and human interests. This is Mr. Arnold's danger. If we are to judge from these poems, his interest in the poetic art would seem to be stronger than his interest in life, or in those living powers which move the souls of men, and are the fountains of real poetry and of all genuine art. Indeed it is only in proportion as it expresses these that any art is truly valuable. Before he again gives anything to the world, we hope that he will take honest counsel with himself, ask himself the simple question:—What is there which he cares about, for its own sake,—apart from its poetic capabilities, what side of human life, what aspects of nature, what of thought or passion is there, in which he is more at home, about which he feels more intensely than common men do? When he has found this, let him forget the ancient masters and all theories of poetry, and stick to his subject resolutely with his whole heart. For, after all that has been said about it, the soul alone is the true inspirer. Let him be true to this, and seek no other inspiration. And when he has found a self-prompted subject, let him turn on it his full strength of poetic gift and power of expression. These will manifest themselves all the more fully when employed on something which has a real base in human interests, and his future productions will awake a deeper response in other breasts when he speaks from out of the fulness of his own.

Criticism steps beyond its province when it prescribes limits to the poet, or attempts to dictate what his subject should be, or chains him down to the present. All ages, past, present, and future, are alike open to him. Which he is to choose his own instinct must decide. But some are more promising, because they have a deeper hold on men's minds than others. Therefore we cannot but doubt whether Mr. Arnold, or any man, will succeed in really interesting his countrymen by merely disinterring and reconstructing, however skilfully, the old Greek legends. And we are quite sure, that if he is ever to take permanent possession of men's thoughts it must be in the strength of some better, healthier spirit than the blank dejection of his early poems. Mr. Arnold must learn, if he has indeed to learn, that whatever are the faults or needs of our own time, the heart has not yet died out of it; that if he thinks it bad, it is the duty of poets, and all thoughtful men, to do their part to mend it, not by weak-hearted lamentations, but by appealing to men's energies, their hopes, their moral aspirations. Let him be quite sure that these are still alive, if he can but arouse them, and that if he cannot the fault lies elsewhere than in his age. To arouse, to strengthen, to purify whatever is good in the men of his own and after times, this is the work which the true poet does. A noble work, if any is, and it takes a noble unworldly nature rightly to fulfil it.

"To console the afflicted, to add sunshine to daylight, by making the happy happier, to teach the young and gracious of every age to see, to think, and feel, and therefore to become more active and securely virtuous, this is their office, which I trust they will perform long after we (that is, all that is mortal of us) are mouldered in our graves." It was thus that Wordsworth looked forward to the destiny of his own poems at the very time when all the world were combining to scorn them. This calm and invincible confidence was supported, not more by the consciousness of innate power than by the feeling that his poetry had left conventional taste behind it, and struck home into the essential harmony of things. For Mr. Arnold we can have no better wish than that his future efforts may be guided by as true and elevated a purpose, and win for him, according to his measure, as worthy a success.—J. C. SHAIRP, "Poems by Matthew Arnold," *North British Review*, Aug. 1854, pp. 502–4

The name of Matthew Arnold on a volume of Poems is a sufficient recommendation to the notice of all those who are careful to supply themselves with poetry of a new vintage, so we need not regret, except on our own account, that we have made rather a late acquaintance with his Second Series of Poems, published last quarter. If we had written of these poems after reading them only once, we should have given them a tepid kind of praise, but after reading them again and again, we have become their partizan, and are tempted to be intolerant of those who will not admit their beauty. Our first impression from a poem of Mr. Arnold's—and with some persons this is the sole impression—generally is, that it is rather tame and prosaic. The thought is always refined and unhackneyed, sometimes new and sublime, but he seems not to have found the winged word which carries the thought at once to the mind of the reader; his poems do not come to us like original melodies, which are beautiful facts that one never thinks of altering any more than a pine-tree or a river; we are haunted by the feeling that he might have said the same thing much better. But when, simply for the sake of converse with a nature so gifted and cultivated as Mr. Arnold's, we linger over a poem which contains some deep and fresh thought, we begin to perceive poetic beauties—felicities of expression and description, which are too quiet and subdued to be seized at the first glance. You must become familiar with his poems before you can appreciate them as poetry, just as in the early spring you must come very near to the woods before you can discern the delicate glossy or downy buds which distinguish their April from their winter clothing. He never attains the wonderful word-music of Tennyson, which lives with you like an Adelaide of Beethoven, or a *Preghiera* of Rossini; but his combinations and phrases are never common, they are fresh from the fountain, and call the reader's mind into new activity. Mr. Arnold's grand defect is want of rhythm—we mean of that rhythm which is music to an English ear. His imitations of the classical metres can no more win a place in our lasting national

poetry than orange and olive-trees can flourish in our common English gardens; and his persistence in these imitations is, we think, a proof that he lacks that fine sense of word-music, that direct inspiration of song, as distinguished from speech, which is the crowning gift of the poet.—GEORGE ELIOT, *Westminster Review*, July 1855, pp. 297–98

I have not tried to "place" Mr. Arnold—to give him his rank among modern English poets. Class-lists of that sort are impertinences. Mr. Arnold has not Mr. Tennyson's quantity of poetic force, nor his unsurpassed music of diction, nor his variety of topic. Neither does he possess the fluency and sonorous emphasis of Mr. Swinburne. But to some readers his poems come more closely home than those of his contemporaries. His calm, his reserve, his stately numbers, sustain, and charm, and comfort.—ANDREW LANG, "Matthew Arnold," *Century Magazine*, April 1882, pp. 863–64

Mr. Arnold is not of the stuff of which heroes or martyrs are made, neither is there in his poetry the inspiration which makes a man die for a cause. But heroes and martyrs tarry not to reason, neither do they wait for the inspiration of poetry as stimulus to action; the world's crises evoke them, their lives are the response, and give material for epics to the singers of revolutions, through whose voice the many "out of weakness are made strong." The heroes and martyrs see the vision, and have faith in its accomplishment; the many, purblind and without capacity to nurture lofty ideals, desirous only to "call their lands after their own names," need most the incitement to rise above sordid aims into a larger, purer air which verse like Matthew Arnold's exhales.

The abiding qualities which render that verse so wholesome an influence in these times, and in all times of unquiet and practicalness, are its clearness, absolute freedom from sophisms, its frank, fearless attitude towards problems the recognition of whose insolubleness is no excuse for paralysis in thought or action; its nutritive suggestiveness, its pure emotion, without taint, "its joy within its calm," its healthiness in counselling introspection based upon faith in the sanity and essential goodness, and capacity for yet greater goodness, of humanity. Its philosophy lies in this—

> Yearn to the greatness of Nature,
>   Rally the good in the depths of thyself.

—EDWARD CLODD, "Matthew Arnold's Poetry," *Gentleman's Magazine*, March 1886, p. 359

> Within that wood where thine own scholar strays,
>   O! Poet, thou art passed, and at its bound
>   Hollow and sere we cry, yet win no sound
> But the dark muttering of the forest maze
> We may not tread, nor pierce with any gaze;
>   And hardly love dare whisper thou hast found
>   That restful moonlit slope of pastoral ground
> Set in dark dingles of the songful ways.
>
> Gone! They have called our shepherd from the hill,
>   Passed is the sunny sadness of his song,
>   That song which sang of sight and yet was brave
>   To lay the ghosts of seeing, subtly strong
>   To wean from tears and from the troughs to save;
> And who shall teach us now that he is still!

—RICHARD LE GALLIENNE, "Matthew Arnold" (1888), *English Poems*, 1892, p. 113

If one were to write out of mere personal preference, and praise most that which best fits one's private moods, I suppose I should place Mr. Matthew Arnold at the head of contemporary English poets. Reason and reflection, discussion and critical judgment, tell one that he is not quite there.

Mr. Arnold had not the many melodies of the Laureate, nor his versatile mastery, nor his magic, nor his copiousness. He had not the microscopic glance of Mr. Browning, nor his rude grasp of facts, which tears the life out of them as the Aztec priest plucked the very heart from the victim. We know all that, but yet Mr. Arnold's poetry has our love; his lines murmur in our memory through all the stress and accidents of life. 'The Scholar Gipsy,' 'Obermann,' *Switzerland*, the melancholy majesty of the close of 'Sohrab and Rustum,' the tenderness of those elegiacs on two kindred graves beneath the Himalayas and by the Midland Sea; the surge and thunder of 'Dover Beach,' with its 'melancholy, long-withdrawing roar'; these can only cease to whisper to us and console us in that latest hour when life herself ceases to 'moan round with many voices.'

My friends tell me that Mr. Arnold is too doubting, and too didactic, that he protests too much, and considers too curiously, that his best poems are, at most, 'a chain of highly valuable thoughts.' It may be so; but he carries us back to 'wet, bird-haunted English lawns'; like him 'we know what white and purple fritillaries the grassy harvest of the river yields,' with him we try to practise resignation, and to give ourselves over to that spirit

> Whose purpose is not missed,
> While life endures, while things subsist.

Mr. Arnold's poetry is to me, in brief, what Wordsworth's was to his generation. He has not that inspired greatness of Wordsworth, when nature does for him what his '*lutin*' did for Corneille, 'takes the pen from his hand and writes for him.' But he has none of the creeping prose which, to my poor mind, invades even 'Tintern Abbey.' He is, as Mr. Swinburne says, 'The surest-footed' of our poets. He can give a natural and lovely life even to the wildest of ancient imaginings, as to 'these bright and aged snakes, that once were Cadmus and Harmonia.'

Bacon speaks of the legends of the earlier and ruder world coming to us 'breathed softly through the flutes of the Grecians.' But even the Grecian flute, as in the lay of the strife of Apollo and Marsyas, comes more tunably in the echo of Mr. Arnold's song, that beautiful song in *Empedocles on Etna*, which has the perfection of sculpture and the charm of the purest colour. It is full of the silver light of dawn among the hills, of the music of the loch's dark, slow waves among the reeds, of the scent of the heather, and the wet tresses of the birch.—ANDREW LANG, "Introductory: Of Modern English Poetry," *Letters on Literature*, 1889, pp. 11–14

In every page of Arnold the poet there is something to return upon and to admire. There are faults, and these of a kind this present age is ill-disposed to condone. The rhymes are sometimes poor; the movement of the verse is sometimes uncertain and sometimes slow; the rhythms are obviously simple always; now and then the intention and effect are cold even to austerity, are bald to uncomeliness. But then, how many of the rarer qualities of art and inspiration are represented here, and here alone in modern work! There is little of that delight in material for material's sake which is held to be essential to the composition of a great artist; there is none of that rapture of sound and motion and none of that efflorescence of expression which are deemed inseparable from the endowment of the true singer. For any of those excesses in technical accomplishment, those ecstasies in the use of words, those effects of sound which are so rich and strange as to impress the hearer with something of their author's own emotion of creation—for any, indeed, of the characteristic attributes of modern poetry—you shall turn to him in vain. In matters of form this poet is no romantic but

a classic to the marrow. He adores his Shakespeare, but he will none of his Shakespeare's fashions. For him the essentials are dignity of thought and sentiment and distinction of manner and utterance. It is no aim of his to talk for talking's sake, to express what is but half felt and half understood, to embody vague emotions and nebulous fancies in language no amount of richness can redeem from the reproach of being nebulous and vague. In his scheme of art there is no place for excess, however magnificent and Shakespearean—for exuberance, however overpowering and Hugoesque. Human and interesting in themselves, the ideas apparelled in his verse are completely apprehended; natural in themselves, the experiences he pictures are intimately felt and thoroughly perceived. They have been resolved into their elements by the operation of an almost Sophoclean faculty of selection, and the effect of their presentation is akin to that of a gallery of Greek marbles.

Other poets say anything—say everything that is in them. Browning lived to realise the myth of the Inexhaustible Bottle; Mr. William Morris is nothing if not fluent and copious; Mr. Swinburne has a facility that would seem impossible if it were not a living fact; even the Laureate is sometimes prodigal of unimportant details, of touches insignificant and superfluous, of words for words' sake, of cadences that have no reason of being save themselves. Matthew Arnold alone says only what is worth saying. In other words, he selects: from his matter whatever is impertinent is eliminated and only what is vital is permitted to remain. Sometimes he goes a little astray, and his application of the principle on which Sophocles and Homer wrought results in failure. But in these instances it will always be found, I think, that the effect is due not to the principle nor the poet's application of it but to the poet himself, who has exceeded his commission, and attempted more than is in him to accomplish. The case is rare with Arnold, one of whose qualities—and by no means the least Hellenic of them—was a fine consciousness of his limitations. But that he failed, and failed considerably, it were idle to deny. There is *Merope* to bear witness to the fact; and of *Merope* what is there to say? Evidently it is an imitation Greek play: an essay, that is, in a form which ceased long since to have any active life, so that the attempt to revive it—to create a soul under the ribs of very musty death—is a blunder alike in sentiment and in art. As evidently Arnold is no dramatist. *Empedocles*, the *Strayed Reveller*, even the 'Forsaken Merman,' all these are expressions of purely personal feeling—are so many metamorphoses of Arnold. In *Merope* there is no such basis of reality. The poet was never on a level with his argument. He knew little or nothing of his characters—of Merope or Æpytus or Polyphontes, of Arcas or Laias or even the Messenger; at every step the ground is seen shifting under his feet; he is comparatively void of matter, and his application of the famous principle is labour lost. He is winnowing the wind; he is washing not gold but water.—W. E. HENLEY, "Matthew Arnold," *Views and Reviews*, 1890, pp. 83–86

Arnold's poems are of two kinds: there are the narrative poems, whether dramatic or otherwise; and the lyrical, emotional, or meditative poems. Now, it is observable that Arnold is at his best in poems neither long nor short: in poems equal in length to the average Hebrew psalm, the average Greek ode. No doubt there are exceptions: "Sohrab and Rustum" among the longer poems, "Requiescat" among the shorter, are nearly faultless. But, for the most part, it is in such poems as "Thyrsis," "A Summer Night," "Stanzas from the Grande Chartreuse," that we find the true Arnold; not in "Balder Dead," "Progress," "Revolutions." In other words, Arnold, to use his own phrase, had not "the architectonics of poetry, the faculty which presides at the evolution of works like the *Agamemnon* or *Lear*." Nor was he in the literal sense a singer, such as was Heine or Catullus. Rather, his quality was meditative; he accepted, at least in practice, Wordsworth's definition of poetry, that it is "emotion remembered in tranquillity." But it may be objected that Arnold is genial, exultant, even rapturous; that he wrote nothing in the least like *The Excursion*. That is true; but let us consider a little more curiously. Arnold was fond of national distinctions, qualities of race and temperament. Were one to distinguish Arnold's own qualities, the conclusion might be of this kind. From the Greek culture, he took a delight in the beauty of life and of fine imagination; from the Hebrew genius, a sense of reverence and meditation; from the French, a certain grace and lucidity of spirit; from the German, a steady seriousness of mind. By descent he was, in part, a Celt: that gave him a "natural magic" of emotion and of soul; while from his English origin, he took that daring common sense which enabled him to hold in harmony these various qualities. Trained in those chosen places of beauty and high tradition, Winchester and Oxford, with all the strength of his father's influence at Rugby, he was always attached to the English ideal: to the ideals of Milton and of Burke. A scholar, a man of the world, a government official, his affections were not narrow, not provincial; but they were not cosmopolitan, not unsettled. His heart was at home in the quiet dignity and peace of an English life, among the great books of antiquity, and the great thoughts of "all time and all existence." Hence came his limitations; not from prejudice, nor from ignorance, but from a scrupulous precision and delicacy of taste. No one loved France more than he; no one abhorred more than he "the great goddess Aselgeia." He reverenced the German seriousness, depth, moderation of life and thought; he disliked and ridiculed pedantry, awkwardness, want of humour and of grace. In all his criticisms, the same balance between excess and deficiency appears: he was a true Aristotelian. And so, when it is said that Arnold was not a poet of profound philosophy, not a thinker of consistency, or not a man whom we can classify at all, the only answer is a *distinguo*. It was Arnold's work to find beauty and truth in life, to apprehend the meaning and moral worth of things, to discriminate the trivial from the grave, and to show how the serene and ardent life is better than the mean and restless. His poetry, then, is not didactic; but meditative, in the classical sense, it is. Lord Coleridge—in those papers which make us regret that he has "to law given up what was made for mankind"—is of opinion that Arnold's meditative poems are not destined to live, "not from any defect of their own, but from the inherent mortality of their subjects." Yet, surely these poems are more than records of a transitory emotion, the phase and habit of an age. Such a description would apply to Clough; his mournful, homesick, desultory poems are indeed touched with decay, because they are composed without care, in no wide spirit of contemplation; reading them we do not think of "Sophocles by the Aegaean," nor of the *lacrimae rerum*. But Arnold's thoughts and emotions are profoundly human; we cannot say of them, that only an Oxford man, under such and such influences, at such and such a time, could have felt them in youth and expressed them in after life. True, their immediate tone is that of one "touched by the Zeit Geist" in the latter end of the nineteenth century; but their fundamental character is common to all times. For Arnold is human; and what is humanism but the belief

> that nothing which has ever interested living men and women can wholly lose its vitality: no language they have spoken, no oracle beside which they have

hushed their voices, no dream which has once been entertained by actual human minds, nothing about which they have ever been passionate, or expended time and zeal?

Arnold, if this be so, was himself a true humanist, and no true humanist will ever forget him. No doubt the *Christian Year* or the *Essay on Man* have lost their charm and their significance; but we read the one as the memorial of a great phase of sentiment, and the other for its brilliant setting of a very tarnished theory. Much more will Arnold live in these grave and lovely poems, which have so little in them of merely transient feeling. Whatever be the future estimate of Arnold's poems, there is no doubt of their singular charm now. They possess the secret of great verse, its power of haunting the memory, and of profoundly satisfying it. Sad as are some of them, their melancholy is true to nature, and leaves us calm; rejoicing as are others, they never soar out of sight, away from life. But they give a view of nature and of life as contemplated by a mind of great sympathy and insight, acquainted with the choice spirits of ancient civility, and with the living emotions of our own age. No hymn to Dolores can so touch us as the lines "To Marguerite": the feverish, antiquarian rhetoric of the one may thrill the nerves and leave us tired; the pure beauty and the austere passion of the other appeals to every faculty in us, and leaves a sense of the beauty of human sorrow. Paradoxical as it may sound, there is something very hieratic about Arnold; his apprehension of the beauty of holiness, his love for what is clear and lofty in the pleasures of thought, his constant service of meditation.

> Ah, les Voix, montez donc, mourantes que vous êtes,
> Sentences, mots en voix, metaphores mal faites,
> Toute la rhétorique en fuite des péchés,
> Ah, les Voix, montez donc, mourantes que vous êtes!"

Arnold would not have liked M. Verlaine's poetry; but those lines express much of Arnold's mind. The false worship of words, the conventional acceptance of phrases, all the spurious wisdom in the world, he fought against, and conquered much of it; and there is no one left to take his place in the struggle against vulgarity and imposture. No voice like his to sing as he sang of calm and peace among the turbulent sounds of modern life.—LIONEL JOHNSON, *Academy*, Jan. 10, 1891, pp. 31–32

CRITICISM

If we examine carefully the earlier prose essays of Mr. Arnold, we shall find that his method of assailing English Philistinism was by a sudden, a violent change of the point of view in his way of looking at things specially repugnant to the English mind. In his dissertations on "The Function of Criticism at the Present Time," and "The Literary Influence of Academies," he opened a lively campaign at everything insular and provincial in English habits of thought, and he showed no toleration for what he considered the brag and bluster of English political and literary conceit. He was necessarily one-sided; but he made narrowness an agent to promote comprehensiveness. Desiring to get the English mind "out of its ruts," he urged English thinkers to include in their confident generalizations a number of facts and ideas which they had hitherto excluded; and these neglected facts and ideas he exaggerated out of their true relations, in order to force them on public attention. He lacked ⟨. . .⟩ the kindling, magnetic power which springs from original energy of nature; but he possessed, in a striking degree, the minor quality of suggestiveness. He had light in abundance, though he was wanting in the heat which ordinarily accompanies light. His suggestiveness made him command the attention of many thinkers who, like Emerson, believe that the best benefit we receive from other minds is not so much instruction as "provocation."

In his essay on the "Function of Criticism," Mr. Arnold takes the ground that the critic, earnest to acquire the best that is thought and known in the world, and to see all things as they really are, should avoid direct contact with practical life, and decline to apply his advanced ideas to existing facts. Reformers naturally resented the principle thus confidently announced, because they knew, by experience, that it was impossible to prevent ideas from coming into conflict with current abuses in church and state. Thus M. Renan said, in substance, to the Emperor Napoleon the Third: "Allow us thinkers and scholars to think and investigate freely, and communicate the results of our thinking and research to the few other scholars who care for the things of the mind, and we will not interfere with our impertinent objections to anything you may do with the uneducated and prejudiced millions of France. We do not address them at all." Well, the eventual result was Renan's *Life of Jesus*, which became such an element of disturbance in the whole Imperial system of government, that any alcove in a large public library might be packed full of books and pamphlets which this truly incendiary volume called forth from all classes of the French population, clerical and political. Mr. Arnold, as an Englishman, could not expect to rival M. Renan in creating a similar outburst of the public mind by such a volume as *St. Paul and Protestantism*, or *Literature and Dogma*; but everything that could be done by the audacities of theological thinking, aimed directly at the cherished tenets of all English churches and sects that pretended to orthodoxy, was done by Mr. Arnold in these two heretical books. He fondly thought, like Renan, that he could keep at a distance from the smoke and dust of a combat that his own writings tended to provoke. Such men may flatter themselves that they are addressing thinkers alone, when they are really rousing mobs. One is reminded of the intelligent contraband who, during our civil war, entertained an audience in Dedham, Massachusetts, with an account of a furious conflict of Federals and Rebels on the banks of the Potomac. "But," asked a critical auditor of his flaming narrative, "where were you when the battle was raging?" "Oh! I was back among the baggage." "But how far were you from the bullets and the cannon-balls?" "Well," was the instant reply, "not so far as Dedham!" Probably the critic was a thoughtful abolitionist, who, discontented with the avowed objects of the war, concluded to stay at home until Emancipation was proclaimed; but he doubtless was soon swept into the crowd of volunteers, conscripts, colonels, and brigadier-generals that reënforced the army of the Potomac. He had, like Renan and Arnold, intended to judge dispassionately of battles from a discreet and distant point of view, but was whirled into the midst of the contest by a fate he could not withstand.

The prose of Mr. Arnold, when he is in his best mood, almost realizes his ideal of what he calls the Attic style, having its "warm glow, blithe movement, and soft pliancy of life." Take such an essay as that on "Religious Sentiment," and it seems, as we read, that it cannot be improved. In some of his theological and political discussions his style, it must be confessed, loses much of its charm. It is important, however, to discriminate between listening to Mr. Arnold and reading him. It is well known that some of the ablest Englishmen scandal-

ously neglect the elementary rules of elocution. In the United States almost every person, from the farmer who speaks in a town meeting to the accomplished orator who addresses the Senate of the country, considers that the second part of his sentence should be as audible as the first. As far as we have heard eminent English speakers who have addressed American audiences, we have been surprised at the difference between the effect produced by what they speak and the effect produced by what they write. In Mr. Arnold's case, we remember a singular illustration of this general fact. One of his masterpieces of compact criticism is certainly his lecture on Heine. An accomplished professor of literature in one of our best colleges heard it delivered at Oxford, and came home fully impressed with the belief that Mr. Arnold was an overrated man. When published, as an article in a magazine, it attracted the notice of Mr. Emerson, who was vehement in its praise, and asked every person he met why there were no such critics in America. Even Carlyle heard of it, and had to read it. He was, of course, enraged, for he was accused of mistaking the main current of German literature after Goethe. "Have you heard," he growled to an American friend, "of poor Matt Arnold? What creature do you think he has selected as the writer who has continued, since Goethe, the main current of German literature? Why, it is that PIG, Heine!"—EDWIN P. WHIPPLE, "Matthew Arnold," *North American Review*, May 1884, pp. 439–42

He has opinions and the courage of them; he has assurance and he has charm; he writes with an engaging clearness. It is very possible to disagree with him; but it is difficult indeed to resist his many graces of manner, and decline to be entertained and even interested by the variety and quality of his matter. He was described as 'the most un-English of Britons,' the most cosmopolitan of islanders; and you feel as you read him that in truth his mind was French. He took pattern by Goethe, and was impressed by Leopardi; he was judiciously classic, but his romanticism was neither hidebound nor inhuman; he apprehended Heine and Marcus Aurelius, Spinoza and Sainte-Beuve, Joubert and Maurice de Guérin, Wordsworth and Pascal, Rachel and Sarah Bernhardt, Burke and Arthur Clough, Eliza Cook and Homer; he was an authority on education, poetry, civilisation, the *Song of Roland*, the love-letters of Keats, the Genius of Bottles, the significance of *eutrapelos* and *eutrapelia*. In fact, we have every reason to be proud of him. For the present is a noisy and affected age; it is given overmuch to clamorous devotion and extravagant repudiation; there is an element of swagger in all its words and ways; it has a distressing and immoral turn for publicity. Matthew Arnold's function was to protest against its fashions by his own intellectual practice, and now and then to take it to task and to call it to order. He was not particularly original, but he had in an eminent degree the formative capacity, the genius of shaping and developing, which is a chief quality of the French mind and which is not so common among us English as our kindest critics would have us believe. He would take a handful of golden sentences—things wisely thought and finely said by persons having authority—and spin them into an exquisite prelection; so that his work with all the finish of art retains a something of the freshness of those elemental truths on which it was his humour to dilate. He was, that is to say, an artist in ethics as in speech, in culture as in ambition. 'Il est donné,' says Sainte-Beuve, 'de nos jours, à un bien petit nombre, même parmi les plus délicats et ceux qui les apprécient le mieux, de recueillir, d'ordonner sa vie selon ses admirations et selon ses goûts, avec suite, avec noblesse.' That is true enough;

but Arnold was one of the few, and might 'se vanter d'être resté fidèle à soi-même, à son premier et à son plus beau passé.' He was always a man of culture in the good sense of the word; he had many interests in life and art, and his interests were sound and liberal; he was a good critic of both morals and measures, both of society and of literature, because he was commonly at the pains of understanding his matter before he began to speak about it. It is therefore not surprising that the part he played was one of considerable importance or that his influence was healthy in the main. He was neither prophet nor pedagogue but a critic pure and simple. Too well read to be violent, too nice in his discernment to be led astray beyond recovery in any quest after strange gods, he told the age its faults and suggested such remedies as the study of great men's work had suggested to him. If his effect was little that was not his fault. He returned to the charge with imperturbable good temper, and repeated his remarks—which are often exasperating in effect—with a mixture of mischievousness and charm, of superciliousness and sagacity, and a serene dexterity of phrase, unique in modern letters.— W. E. HENLEY, "Matthew Arnold," *Views and Reviews*, 1890, pp. 88–91

The real value of Mr Arnold as a critic—apart from his indirect merit of providing much delightful English prose shot with wit and humour, and enclosing endless sweetmeats if not solids of sense—consisted chiefly in the comparative novelty of the style of literary appreciation which he adopted, and in the stimulus which he accordingly gave to literary study. Since Hazlitt, we had been deficient in critics who put appreciation before codification; and Hazlitt himself was notoriously untrustworthy through caprice. The following of Sainte-Beuve saved Mr Arnold from both errors to some extent, but to some extent only. Though well read, he was not extremely learned; and though acute, he was the very reverse of judicial. He had fortunately been brought up on classical literature, to which he pinned his faith; and it is impossible that anyone with this advantage should be a literary heretic of the worst description. But he constantly committed the fault of Shylock in regard to his classics. What was not in the classical bond, what "was not so expressed," could not be good, could not at least be of the best. Now I will yield to no man in my respect for the classics; and I do not think that, at least as far as the Greeks are concerned, anyone will ever do better the things that they did. But it is absurd to suppose or maintain that the canon of literary perfections was closed when the Muses left Philemon's house.

Mr Arnold, then, as a critic seemed to me at first, and has always seemed to me, flawed with those very faults of freak and crotchet against which he was never tired of protesting, and, though a very useful alternative, stimulant, and check, not a good model, and a still worse oracle. I should say of him, and I think I have always recked my own rede from 1865 to the present day in this respect, "Admire, enjoy, and be thankful for Mr Arnold as a critic; but be careful about imitating him, and never obey him without examination."—GEORGE SAINTSBURY, "Matthew Arnold," *Corrected Impressions*, 1895

About Matthew Arnold as critic of literature it is needless to enlarge, for the simple reason that we have all long ago agreed that he has no superior, indeed no rival. His judgments on our poets have passed into current opinion, and have ceased to be discussed or questioned. It is, perhaps, a grave loss to English literature that Arnold was not able, or perhaps never strove, to devote his whole life to the interpretation of our best poetry and prose, with the same systematic, laborious, concentrated energy which has placed Sainte-Beuve at the head of French critics. With his absorbing professional duties, his far from austere aloofness from the whirlpool of society, his guerilla warfare with journalism, Radicals, theologians, and all devotees of Dagon, it was not fated that Arnold could vie with the vast learning and Herculean industry of Sainte-Beuve. Neither as theologian, philosopher, or publicist, was Arnold at all adequately equipped by genius or by education for the office of supreme arbiter which he so airily, and perhaps so humorously, assumed to fill. And as poet, it is doubtful whether, with his Aurelian temperament and treacherous ear, he could ever have reached a much higher rank. But as critic of literature, his exquisite taste, his serene sense of equity, and that genial magnanimity which prompted him to give just value for every redeeming quality of those whom he loved the least—this made him a consummate critic of style. Though he has not left us an exhaustive review of our literature, as Sainte-Beuve has done for France, he has given us a group of short, lucid, suggestive canons of judgment, which serve as landmarks to an entire generation of critics.

The function of criticism—though not so high and mighty as Arnold proclaimed it with superb assurance—is not so futile an art as the sixty-two minor poets and the 11,000 minor novelists are now wont to think it. Arnold committed one of the few extravagances of his whole life when he told us that poetry was the criticism of life, that the function of criticism was to see all things as they really are in themselves—the very thing Kant told us we could never do. On the other hand, too much of what is now called criticism is the improvised chatter of a raw lad, portentously ignorant of the matter in hand. It is not the 'indolent reviewer' that we now suffer under, but the 'lightning reviewer,' the young man in a hurry with a Kodak, who finally disposes of a new work on the day of its publication. One of them naïvely complained the other morning of having to cut the pages, as if we ever suspected that he cut the pages of more than the preface and table of contents.

Criticism, according to Arnold's practice, if not according to his theory, had as its duty to lay down decisive canons of cultured judgment, to sift the sound from the vicious, and to maintain the purity of language and of style. To do all this in any masterly degree requires most copious knowledge, an almost encyclopædic training in literature, a natural genius for form and tone, and above all a temper of judicial balance. Johnson in the last century, Hallam, and possibly Southey, in this century, had some such gift: Macaulay and Carlyle had not; for they wanted genius for form and judicial balance. Now Arnold had this gift in supreme degree, in a degree superior to Johnson or to Hallam. He made far fewer mistakes than they did. He made very few mistakes. The touchstone of the great critic is to make very few mistakes, and never to be carried off his balance by any pet aversion or pet affection of his own, not to be biassed so much as a hair's breadth by any salient merit or any irritating defect, and always to keep an eye well open to the true proportion of any single book in the great world of men and of affairs and in the mighty realm of general literature.

For this reason we have so very few great critics, for the combination of vast knowledge, keen taste, and serene judgment is rare. It is thus so hard for any young person, for women, to become great in criticism: the young lack the wide experience; women lack the cool judicial temper. It is common enough to find those who are very sensitive to some rare charm, very acute to detect a subtle quality, or justly severe on some seductive failure. The rare power is to be able to apply to a complicated set of qualities the nicely adjusted compensations, to place a work, an author, in the right rank, and to do this for all orders of merit, with a sure, constant, unfailing touch—and without any real or conspicuous mistake.

This is what Arnold did, at any rate for our later poetry. He taught us to do it for ourselves, by using the instruments he brought to bear. He did much to kill a great deal of flashy writing, and much vulgarity of mind that once had a curious vogue. I am myself accused of being *laudator temporis acti*, and an American newspaper was pleased to speak of me as 'this hopeless old man'; but I am never weary of saying, that at no epoch of our literature has the bulk of minor poetry been so graceful, so refined, so pure; the English language in daily use has never been written in so sound a form by so many writers; and the current taste in prose and verse has never been so just. And this is not a little owing to the criticism of Arnold, and to the ascendency which his judgment exerted over his time.

To estimate that lucidity and magnanimity of judgment he possessed, we should note how entirely open-minded he was to the defects of those whom he most loved, and to the merits of those whom he chiefly condemned. His ideal in poetry is essentially Wordsworthian, yet how sternly and how honestly he marks the *longueurs* of Wordsworth, his flatness, his mass of inferior work. Arnold's ideal of poetry was essentially alien to Byron, whose vulgar, slipshod, rhetorical manner he detested, whilst he recognised Byron's Titanic power: 'our *soul* had felt him like the thunder's roll.' Arnold saw all the blunders made by Dryden, by Johnson, by Macaulay, by Coleridge, by Carlyle—but how heartily he can seize their real merits! Though drawn by all his thoughts and tastes towards such writers as Sénancour, Amiel, Joubert, Heine, the Guérins, he does not affect to forget the limitations of their influence, and the idiosyncrasy of their genius. In these days, when we are constantly assured that the function of criticism is to seize on some subtle and yet undetected quality that happens to have charmed you, and to wonder, in Delphic oracles, if Milton or Shelley ever quite touched that mystic circle, how refreshing it is to find Arnold always cool, always judicial—telling us even that Shakespeare has let drop some random stuff, and calmly reminding us that he had not 'the sureness of a perfect style,' as Milton had. Let us take together Arnold's summing up of all the qualities of Wordsworth, Byron, Keats, Shelley, and we shall see with what a just but loving hand he distributes the alternate meed of praise and blame. *Amant alterna Camœnæ.* But of all the Muses, she of criticism loves most the alternate modulation of *soprano* and *basso*.

Not that Arnold was invariably right, or that all his judgments are unassailable. His canons were always right; but it is not in mortals to apply them unerringly to men and to things. He seems somewhat inclined to undervalue Tennyson, of whom he speaks so little. He has not said enough for Shelley, perhaps not enough for Spenser, nor can we find that he loved with the true ardour the glorious romances of Walter Scott. But this is no place, nor can I pretend to be the man, to criticise our critic. For my own part, I accept his decisions in the main for all English poetry, and on general questions of style. Accept them, that is, so far as it is in human nature to accept such high matters;—'errors excepted,' *exceptis excipiendis.* The important point on which his judgment is the most likely to be doubted or reversed by the supreme court of the twentieth century, lies in the relative places he has assigned to Wordsworth and to Shelley. He was by nature akin to Wordsworth, alien to Shelley; and the 'personal equation' may have told in this case. For my own part, I feel grateful to Arnold for asserting so well the dæmonic power of Byron, and so justly distinguishing the poet in his hour of inspiration from the peer in his career of affectation and vice. Arnold's piece on

the 'Study of Poetry,' written as an introduction to the collected *English Poets*, should be preserved in our literature as the *norma*, or *canon* of right opinion about poetry, as we preserve the standard coins in the Pyx, or the standard yard measure in the old Jewel-house at Westminster.—FREDERIC HARRISON, "Matthew Arnold," *Nineteenth Century*, March 1896, pp. 441–43

THEOLOGY

This great aim ⟨. . .⟩ is what Mr. Arnold proposes to himself,— to provide a new religion of the Bible for the people, which shall dispense with the assumption of anything as to God which is not verifiable. Whether the account he gives of the state of mind of the people, or the masses, is an altogether accurate one, is, I think, open to question. I do not know why they should be represented as "rude and hard reasoners." To judge by the style of the writings which circulate most readily amongst them, and of the addresses made to them by those whom they most like to hear, it might, I fear, be said with truth that they are liable to be influenced by claptrap arguments and by appeals to their feelings, rather than by scientific reasoning. Here and there you may find, no doubt, amongst the working classes a man who has imbibed something of the scientific thought of the day, because there is nothing to hinder an intelligent and inquiring mind in any class from obtaining access to books, and receiving the cultivation which the reading of books will supply. It may be admitted also that the current language of scientific men,—as, for example, that certitude is produced by verification,—is in favour with a somewhat larger number. But it is surely not characteristic of "the masses," as compared with the classes above them, that they are influenced by strict reasoning more than by emotion. It would be strange if it were. It does not follow that because a man has hard hands, he therefore has a hard head. To ascribe hard reasoning to the masses, appears to me to be much the same thing as it would be to ascribe it to women or to boys. Logical "hits" are attractive to all whose minds have been less instructed and less exercised; but no one knows better than Mr. Arnold what a difference there is between an enjoyment of logical form and the patient demand for verification. It is a help towards the understanding of what "the masses" are now, to call to mind what schoolboys were before the modern period,—say thirty years ago. In those days, if the boys of a public school had been told that they might do as they pleased on Sundays,—they might either rise in good time and go to church and read good books, or lie in bed, make a feast, and wander about the country,—I am afraid the good ones would have been in a small minority. And I believe that with the bulk of the common people there is not much more deliberation in their neglect of religion than there would have been in the case of the schoolboys. It is unquestionable, however, that religion is greatly neglected by the common people; and it is true also, that in all classes, in proportion to the spread of the modern sceptical spirit, there is a disposition to demand new and satisfying proofs of what they are called upon to believe. There is abundant reason why Mr. Arnold should try to do what he can for the Bible and for religion; and if there are only a few working men who are qualified to follow him, those few, and many more in the classes above them, will follow him with the keenest interest. They may even become his disciples; but, to do so, they must come out from every existing school; for there is no sect which will not find some especially cherished persuasion repudiated and ridiculed by Mr. Arnold. —J. LLEWELYN DAVIES, "Mr. Arnold's New Religion," *Contemporary Review*, May 1873, pp. 845–46

Surely the truth is, that Mr. Arnold's Neo-Christianity is essentially a religion for the cultivated and comfortable, for those who are removed from the grosser temptations, who have learnt by experience that the exercise of the virtues under these conditions on the whole increases the sum of their comfort, and who feel that that touch of emotion which elevates morality into religion will give the finishing refinement to their happiness. They can find that emotion nearly anywhere,—in Buddhism, in Pantheism, in Positivism, in almost any "ism"; but whenever they have to look about for it, as Mr. Arnold has had to do in his own case, and now recommends them to do; whenever they have to invent their religion instead of its forcing itself upon them, they may depend upon it that it is an *article de luxe* suitable only for consumption by them and their like, and no more fit to serve those who need religion for their support in poverty, in sickness, and under deadly temptations, than whipped cream is fit to stay the stomach of a hungry man.

It may be answered that meats which have lost their nutritious properties are equally unfit for that purpose; and this, no doubt, is the melancholy truth. What new foods mankind may discover for the sustentation of their moral natures time alone can show, and to time also it must be left to discover whether man, as some of his admirers assure us, has reached that etherealized condition in which he can dispense with food altogether,—has so completely organized morality that he needs no religion to support it. But be that as it may, I find it impossible to believe that Neo-Christianity can be its destined support in the future, or that the draperies which Mr. Arnold has disposed in such graceful folds about the form of the old religion could ever do more than enable her becomingly to breathe her last.—H. D. TRAILL, "Neo-Christianity and Mr. Matthew Arnold," *Contemporary Review*, April 1884, pp. 575–76

In insisting on the striking, I might almost say the dismaying, contrast between the great Oxford leader ⟨John Henry Newman⟩, whose whole mind has been occupied with theological convictions from his earliest years of Oxford life to the present day, and the Oxford leader who has avowed himself unable to see even a slender probability that God is a being who thinks and loves, I said that I hoped to do something to attenuate the paradox before I had done. This is probably the right place to say a few words on the subject, for undoubtedly it is the assumption running through Mr. Arnold's theoretical writings, that no belief is trustworthy which has not what he calls the verification of experience to sustain it, to which we owe his repudiation of all theology. Undoubtedly, the twenty years or so by which he is Cardinal Newman's junior made an extraordinary difference in the intellectual atmosphere of Oxford, and of the English world of letters outside Oxford, during the time at which a thoughtful man's mind matures. Mr. Arnold was not too late at Oxford to feel the spell of Dr. Newman, but his mind was hardly one to feel the whole force of that spell, belonging as his mind does, I think, rather to the Stoical than to the religious school—the school which magnifies self-dependence, and regards serene calm, not passionate worship, as the highest type of the moral life. And he was at Oxford too late, I think, for the full experience of the limits within which alone the scientific conception of life can be said to be true. A little later, men came to see that scientific methods are really quite inapplicable to the sphere of moral truth—that the scientific assumption that whatever is true can be verified, is, in the sense of the word "verification" which science applies, a very serious blunder, and that such verification as we can get of moral truth is of a very different,

though I will not scruple to say a no less satisfactory, kind, from that which we expect to get of scientific truth. Mr. Arnold seems to me to have imbibed the prejudices of the scientific season of blossom, when the uniformity of nature first became a kind of gospel, when the *Vestiges of Creation* was the book in vogue, when Emerson's and Carlyle's imaginative scepticism first took hold of cultivated Englishmen, and Mr. Froude published the sceptical tales by which his name was first known amongst us. Mr. Arnold betrays the immovable prejudices by which his intellectual life is overridden in a hundred forms; for example, by the persistency with which he remarks that the objection to miracles is that they do not happen, the one criticism which I venture to say no one who had taken pains to study evidence in the best accredited individual cases, not only in ancient but in modern times, would choose to repeat. And again, he betrays it by the pertinacity with which he assumes that you can verify the secret of self-renunciation, the secret of Jesus, in the same sense in which you can verify the law of gravitation, one of the most astounding and I think false assumptions of our day. I make bold to say that no one ever verified the secret of self-renunciation yet, or ever even wished to verify it, who had not assumed the moral obligation it involves, before even attempting a verification; while with the law of gravitation it is quite different: we believe it solely because it has been verified, or, in the case of the discoverer, because evidence was before him that it might very probably be verified. But though Mr. Arnold's mind is of the Stoical rather than the religious type, and though certain premature scientific assumptions, which were in vogue before the limits of the region in which the uniformity of nature has been verified, had been at all carefully defined, run through all his theoretical writings, it is nevertheless true that his whole intellectual strength has been devoted to sustaining, I cannot say the cause of religion—for I do not think his constant cry for more emotion in dealing with morality has been answered—but the cause of good, the cause of noble conduct, and in exalting the elation of duty, the rapture of righteousness. Allow for his prepossessions—his strangely obstinate prepossessions—and he remains still a figure on which we can look with admiration. We must remember that, with all the scorn which Matthew Arnold pours on the trust we place in God's love, he still holds to the conviction that the tendency to righteousness is a power on which we may rely even with *rapture*. Israel, he says, took "his religion in rapture, because he found for it an evidence irresistible. But his own words are the best: 'Thou, O Eternal, art the thing that I *long* for, thou art my hope, even from my youth; through thee have I been *holden up* ever since I was born; there is nothing *sweeter* than to take heed unto the commandments of the Eternal. The Eternal is my strength; my heart has trusted in Him, and I am *helped*; therefore my heart *danceth for joy*, and in my song I will *praise* him.'" (*Literature and Dogma*, p. 319.) And Mr. Arnold justifies that language, though it seems to me clear that with his views he could never have been the first to use it. Still, do not let us forget that he does justify it, that the great Oxonian of the third quarter of this century, though he is separated wide as the poles from Cardinal Newman in faith, yet uses even the most exalted language of the Hebrew seers with all the exultation which even Cardinal Newman could evince for it. I think it is hardly possible to think of such an attitude of mind as the attitude of a common agnostic. The truth is, that his deep poetical idealism saves Mr. Arnold from the depressing and flattening influences of his theoretical views. The poet of modern thought and modern tendencies cannot be, even though he strives to be, a mere agnostic. The insurrection of the agnosticism of the day against faith is no doubt one of its leading features; but the failure of that insurrection to overpower us, the potent resistance it encounters in all our hearts, is a still more remarkable feature. Matthew Arnold reflects both of these characteristics, though the former perhaps more powerfully than the latter.—RICHARD HOLT HUTTON, "Newman and Arnold: II. Matthew Arnold," *Contemporary Review*, April 1886, pp. 526–28

HENRY SIDGWICK
"The Prophet of Culture"

Macmillan's Magazine, August 1867, pp. 271–80

The movement against anonymous writing, in which this journal some years ago took a part, has received, I think, an undeniable accession of strength from the development (then unexpected) of Mr. Matthew Arnold. Some persons who sympathised on the whole with that movement yet felt that the case was balanced, and that if it succeeded we should have sacrificed something that we could not sacrifice without regret. One felt the evils that "irresponsible reviewers" were continually inflicting on the progress of thought and society: and yet one felt that, in form and expression, anonymous writing tended to be good writing. The buoyant confidence of youth was invigorated and yet sobered by having to sustain the *prestige* of a well-earned reputation; while the practised weapon of age, relieved from the restraints of responsibility, was wielded with almost the elasticity of youth. It was thought we should miss the freedom, the boldness, the reckless vivacity with which one talented writer after another had discharged his missiles from behind the common shield of a coterie of unknown extent, or at least half veiled by a pseudonym. It was thought that periodical literature would gain in carefulness, in earnestness, in sincerity, in real moral influence: but that possibly it might become just a trifle dull. We did not foresee that the dashing insolences of "we-dom" that we should lose would be more than compensated by the delicate impertinences of egotism that we should gain. We did not imagine the new and exquisite literary enjoyment that would be created when a man of genius and ripe thought, perhaps even elevated by a position of academic dignity, should deliver profound truths and subtle observations with all the dogmatic authority and self-confidence of a prophet: at the same time titillating the public by something like the airs and graces, the playful affectations of a favourite comedian. We did not, in short, foresee a Matthew Arnold: and I think it must be allowed that our apprehensions have been much removed, and our cause much strengthened, by this new phenomenon.

I have called Mr. Arnold the prophet of culture: I will not call him an "elegant Jeremiah," because he seems to have been a little annoyed (he who is never annoyed) by that phrase of the *Daily Telegraph*. "Jeremiah!" he exclaims, "the very Hebrew prophet whose style I admire the least." I confess I thought the phrase tolerably felicitous for a Philistine, from whom one would not expect any very subtle discrimination of the differentiæ of prophets. Nor can I quite determine which Hebrew prophet Mr. Arnold does most resemble. But it is certainly hard to compare him to Jeremiah, for Jeremiah is our type of the lugubrious; whereas there is nothing more striking than the imperturbable cheerfulness with which Mr. Arnold seems to sustain himself on the fragment of culture that is left him, amid the deluge of Philistinism that he sees submerging our age and country. A prophet however, I gather, Mr. Arnold does not object to be called; as such I wish to consider and

weigh him; and thus I am led to examine the lecture with which he has closed his connexion with Oxford,—the most full, distinct, and complete of the various utterances in which he has set forth the Gospel of Culture.

As it will clearly appear in the course of this article, how highly I admire Mr. Arnold as a writer, I may say at once, without reserve or qualification, that this utterance has disappointed me very much. It is not even so good in style as former essays; it has more of the mannerism of repeating his own phrases, which, though very effective up to a certain point, may be carried too far. But this is a small point: and Mr. Arnold's style, when most faulty, is very charming. My complaint is, that though there is much in it beautifully and subtly said, and many fine glimpses of great truths, it is, as a whole, ambitious, vague, and perverse. It seems to me over-ambitious, because it treats of the most profound and difficult problems of individual and social life with an airy dogmatism that ignores their depth and difficulty. And though dogmatic, Mr. Arnold is yet vague; because when he employs indefinite terms he does not attempt to limit their indefiniteness, but rather avails himself of it. Thus he speaks of the relation of culture and religion, and sums it up by saying, that the idea of culture is destined to "transform and govern" the idea of religion. Now I do not wish to be pedantic; and I think that we may discuss culture and religion, and feel that we are talking about the same social and intellectual facts, without attempting any rigorous definition of our terms. But there is one indefiniteness that ought to be avoided. When we speak of culture and religion in common conversation, we sometimes refer to an ideal state of things and sometimes to an actual. But if we are appraising, weighing, as it were, these two, one with the other, it is necessary to know whether it is the ideal or the actual that we are weighing. When I say ideal, I do not mean something that is not realized at all by individuals at present, but something not realized sufficiently to be much called to mind by the term denoting the general social fact. I think it clear that Mr. Arnold, when he speaks of culture, is speaking sometimes of an ideal, sometimes of an actual culture, and does not always know which. He describes it in one page as "a study of perfection, moving by the force, not merely or primarily of the scientific passion for pure knowledge, but of the moral and social passion for doing good." A study of this vast aim, moving with the impetus of this double passion, is something that does, I hope, exist among us, but to a limited extent: it is hardly that which has got itself stamped and recognised as culture. And Mr. Arnold afterwards admits as much. For we might have thought, from the words I have quoted, that we had in culture, thus possessed by the passion of doing good, a mighty social power, continually tending to make "reason and the will of God prevail." But we find that this power only acts in fine weather. "It needs times of faith and ardour to flourish in." Exactly; it is not itself a spring and source of faith and ardour. Culture "believes" in making reason and the will of God prevail, and will even "endeavour" to make them prevail, but it must be under very favourable circumstances. This is rather a languid form of the passion of doing good; and we feel that we have passed from the ideal culture, towards which Mr. Arnold aspires, to the actual culture in which he lives and moves.

Mr. Arnold afterwards explains to us a little further how much of the passion for doing good culture involves, and how it involves it. "Men are all members of one great whole, and the sympathy which is in human nature will not allow one member to be indifferent to the rest, or to have a perfect welfare independent of the rest. . . . The individual is obliged, under pain of being stunted and enfeebled in his own development if he disobeys, to carry others along with him in his march towards perfection." These phrases are true of culture as we know it. In using them Mr. Arnold assumes implicitly what, perhaps, should have been expressly avowed—that the study of perfection, as it forms itself in members of the human race, is naturally and primarily a study of the individual's perfection, and only incidentally and secondarily a study of the general perfection of humanity. It is so incidentally and secondarily for the two reasons Mr. Arnold gives, one internal, and the other external: first, because it finds sympathy as one element of the human nature that it desires harmoniously to develop; and secondly, because the development of one individual is bound up by the laws of the universe with the development of at least some other individuals. Still the root of culture, when examined ethically, is found to be a refined eudæmonism: in it the social impulse springs out of and re-enters into the self-regarding, which remains predominant. That is, I think, the way in which the love of culture is generally developed: an exquisite pleasure is experienced in refined states of thought and feeling, and a desire for this pleasure is generated, which may amount to a passion, and lead to the utmost intellectual and moral effort. Mr. Arnold may, perhaps, urge (and I would allow it true in certain cases) that the direct impulse towards perfection, whether realized in a man's self or in the world around, may inspire and impassion some minds, without any consideration of the enjoyment connected with it. In any case, it must be admitted that the impulse toward perfection in a man of culture is not practically limited to himself, but tends to expand in infinitely increasing circles. It is the wish of culture, taking ever wider and wider sweeps, to carry the whole race, the whole universe, harmoniously towards perfection.

And, if it were possible that all men, under all circumstances, should feel what some men, in some fortunate spheres, may truly feel—that there is no conflict, no antagonism, between the full development of the individual and the progress of the world—I should be loth to hint at any jar or discord in this harmonious movement. But this paradisaical state of culture is rare. We dwell in it a little space, and then it vanishes into the ideal. Life shows us the conflict and the discord: on one side are the claims of harmonious self-development, on the other the cries of struggling humanity: we have hitherto let our sympathies expand along with our other refined instincts, but now they threaten to sweep us into regions from which those refined instincts shrink. Not that harmonious self-development calls on us to *crush* our sympathies; it asks only that they should be a little repressed, a little kept under: we may become (as Mr. Arnold delicately words it) philanthropists "tempered by renunciation." There is much useful and important work to be done, which may be done harmoniously: still we cannot honestly say that this seems to us the most useful, the most important work, or what in the interests of the world is most pressingly entreated and demanded. This latter, if done at all, must be done as self-sacrifice, not as self-development. And so we are brought face to face with the most momentous and profound problem of ethics.

It is at this point, I think, that the relation of culture and religion is clearly tested and defined. Culture (if I have understood and analysed it rightly) inevitably takes one course. It recognises with a sigh the limits of self-development, and its first enthusiasm becomes "tempered by renunciation." Religion, of which the essence is self-sacrifice, inevitably takes the other course. We see this daily realized in practice: we see those we know and love, we see the *élite* of humanity in history and

literature, coming to this question, and after a struggle answering it: going, if they are strong clear souls, some one way and some the other; if they are irresolute, vacillating and "moving in a strange diagonal" between the two. It is because he ignores this antagonism, which seems to me so clear and undeniable if stated without the needless and perilous exaggerations which preachers have used about it, that I have called Mr. Arnold perverse. A philosopher ⟨Hegel⟩ with whom he is more familiar than I am speaks, I think, of "the reconciliation of antagonisms" as the essential feature of the most important steps in the progress of humanity. I seem to see profound truth in this conception, and perhaps Mr. Arnold has intended to realize it. But, in order to reconcile antagonisms, it is needful to probe them to the bottom; whereas Mr. Arnold skims over them with a lightly-won tranquillity that irritates instead of soothing.

Of course we are all continually trying to reconcile this and other antagonisms, and many persuade themselves that they have found a reconciliation. The religious man tells himself that in obeying the instinct of self-sacrifice he has chosen true culture, and the man of culture tells himself that by seeking self-development he is really taking the best course to "make reason and the will of God prevail." But I do not think either is quite convinced. I think each dimly feels that it is necessary for the world that the other line of life should be chosen by some, and each and all look forward with yearning to a time when circumstances shall have become kinder and more pliable to our desires, and when the complex impulses of humanity that we share shall have been chastened and purified into something more easy to harmonize. And sometimes the human race seems to the eye of enthusiasm so very near this consummation: it seems that if just a few simple things were done it would reach it. But these simple things prove mountains of difficulty; and the end is far off. I remember saying to a friend once—a man of deep culture—that his was a "fair-weather theory of life." He answered with much earnestness, "We mean it to be fair weather henceforth." And I hope the skies are growing clearer every century; but meanwhile there is much storm and darkness yet, and we want—the world wants—all the self-sacrifice that religion can stimulate. Culture diffuses "sweetness and light;" I do not undervalue these blessings: but religion gives fire and strength, and the world wants fire and strength even more than sweetness and light. Mr. Arnold feels this when he says that culture must "borrow a devout energy" from religion; but devout energy, as Dr. Newman somewhere says, is not to be borrowed. At the same time, I trust that the ideal of culture and the ideal of religion will continually approach one another: that culture will keep developing its sympathy, and gain in fire and strength; that religion will teach that unnecessary self-sacrifice is folly, and that whatever tends to make life harsh and gloomy cometh of evil. And if we may allow that the progress of culture is clearly in this direction, surely we may say the same of religion. Indeed the exegetic artifices by which the Hellenic view of life is introduced and allowed a place in Christian preaching would sometimes be almost ludicrous, if they were not touching, and if they were not, on the whole, such a sign of hopeful progress; of progress not as yet, perhaps, very great or very satisfactory, but still very distinct. I wish Mr. Arnold had recognised this. I do not think he would then have said that culture would transform and absorb religion, any more than religion transform and absorb culture. To me the ultimate and ideal relation of culture and religion is imaged like the union of the golden and silver sides of the famous shield—each leading to the same "orbed perfection" of actions and results, but shining with a diverse splendour in the light of its different principle.

Into the difficulties of this question I have barely entered;

but I hope I have shown the inadequacy of Mr. Arnold's treatment of it. I think we shall be more persuaded of this inadequacy when we have considered how he conceives of actual religion in the various forms in which it exists among us. He has but one distinct thing to say of them,—that they subdue the obvious faults of our animality. They form a sort of spiritual police: that is all. He says nothing of the emotional side of religion; of the infinite and infinitely varied vent which it gives, in its various forms, for the deepest fountains of feeling. He says nothing of its intellectual side: of the indefinite but inevitable questions about the world and human destiny into which the eternal metaphysical problems form themselves in minds of rudimentary development; questions needing confident answers, nay, imperatively demanding, it seems, from age to age, different answers: of the actual facts of psychological experience, so strangely mixed up with and expressed in the mere conventional "jargon" of religion (which he characterizes with appropriate contempt)—how the moral growth of men and nations, while profoundly influenced and controlled by the formulæ of traditional religions, is yet obedient to laws of its own, and in its turn reacts upon and modifies these formulæ: of all this Mr. Arnold does not give a hint. He may say that he is not treating of religions, but of culture. But it may be replied that he is treating of the relation of culture to religions; and that a man ought not to touch cursorily upon such a question, much less to dogmatize placidly upon it, without showing us that he has mastered the elements of the problem.

I may, perhaps, illustrate my meaning by referring to another essayist—one of the very few whom I consider superior to Mr. Arnold—one who is as strongly attached to culture as Mr. Arnold himself, and perhaps more passionately,—M. Renan. It will be seen that I am not going to quote a partisan. From "my countryman's" judgment of our Protestant organizations I appeal boldly to a Frenchman and an infidel. Let any one turn to M. Renan's delicate, tender, sympathetic studies of religious phenomena—I do not refer to the *Vie de Jésus,* but to a much superior work, the *Essais d'histoire religieuse,*—he will feel, I think, how coarse, shallow, unappreciative, is Mr. Arnold's summing up, "they conquer the more obvious faults of our animality." To take one special point. When Mr. Arnold is harping on the "dissidence of Dissent," I recall the little phrase which M. Renan throws at the magnificent fabric of Bosuet's attack upon Protestantism. "En France," he says, "on ne comprend pas qu'on se divise pour si peu de chose." M. Renan knows that ever since the reviving intellect of Europe was turned upon theology, religious dissidence and variation has meant religious life and force. Mr. Arnold, of course, can find texts inculcating unity: how should unity not be included in the ideal of a religion claiming to be universal? But Mr. Arnold, as a cultivated man, has read the New Testament records with the light of German erudition, and knows how much unity was attained by the Church in its fresh and fervent youth. Still, unity is a part of the ideal even of the religion that came not to send peace, but a sword: let us be grateful to any one who keeps that in view, who keeps reminding us of that. But it may be done without sneers. Mr. Arnold might know (if he would only study them a little more closely and tenderly) the passionate longing for unity that may be cherished within small dissident organizations. I am not defending them. I am not saying a word for separatism against multitudinism. But those who feel that worship ought to be the true expression of the convictions on which it is based, and out of which it grows, and that in the present fragmentary state of truth it is supremely difficult to reconcile unity of worship with sincerity of conviction; those who know that the struggle to realize in combination the ideals of truth and peace in many minds reaches the pitch of agony; will hardly think that Mr. Arnold's taunt is the less cruel because it is pointed with a text.

I wish it to be distinctly understood that it is as judged by his own rules and principles that I venture to condemn Mr. Arnold's treatment of our actual religions. He has said that culture in its most limited phase is curiosity, and I quite sympathise in his effort to vindicate for this word the more exalted meaning that the French give to it. Even of the ideal culture he considers curiosity (if I understand him rightly) to be the most essential, though not the noblest, element. Well, then, I complain that in regard to some of the most important elements of social life he has so little curiosity; and therefore so thin and superficial an appreciation of them. I do not mean that every cultivated man ought to have formed for himself a theory of religion. "Non omnia possumus omnes," and a man must, to some extent, select the subjects that suit his special faculties. But every man of deep culture ought to have a conception of the importance and intricacy of the religious problem, a sense of the kind and amount of study that is required for it, a tact to discriminate worthy and unworthy treatment of it, an instinct which, if he has to touch on it, will guide him round the lacunæ of apprehension that the limits of his nature and leisure have rendered inevitable. Now this cultivated tact, sense, instinct (Mr. Arnold could express my meaning for me much more felicitously than I can for myself) he seems to me altogether to want on this topic. He seems to me (if so humble a simile may be pardoned) to judge of religious organizations as a dog judges of human beings, chiefly by the scent. One admires in either case the exquisite development of the organ, but feels that the use of it for this particular object implies a curious, an almost ludicrous, limitation of sympathy. When these popular religions are brought before Mr. Arnold, he is content to detect their strong odours of Philistinism and vulgarity; he will not stoop down and look into them; he is not sufficiently interested in their dynamical importance; he does not care to penetrate the secret of their fire and strength, and learn the sources and effects of these; much less does he consider how sweetness and light may be added without any loss of fire and strength.

This limitation of view in Mr. Arnold seems to me the more extraordinary, when I compare it with the fervent language he uses with respect to what is called, *par excellence,* the Oxford movement. He even half associates himself with the movement—or rather he half associates the movement with himself.

It was directed, he rightly says, against "Liberalism as Dr. Newman saw it." What was this? "It was," he explains, "the great middle class Liberalism, which had for the cardinal points of its belief the Reform Bill of 1832 and local self-government in politics; in the social sphere free trade, unrestricted competition, and the making of large industrial fortunes; in the religious sphere the dissidence of Dissent and the Protestantism of the Protestant religion." Liberalism to Dr. Newman may have meant something of all this; but what (as I infer from the *Apology*) it more especially meant to him was a much more intelligent force than all these, which Mr. Arnold omits; and *pour cause*; for it was precisely that view of the functions of religion and its place in the social organism in which Mr. Arnold seems at least complacently to acquiesce. Liberalism, Dr. Newman thought (and it seems to me true of one phase or side of Liberalism), wished to extend just the languid patronage to religion that Mr. Arnold does. What priesthoods were good for in the eyes of Liberalism were the functions, as I have said, of spiritual police; and that is all Mr. Arnold thinks they are good for at present; and even in the future (unless I misunderstand him), if we want more, he would have us come to culture. But Dr. Newman knew that even the existing religions, far as they fell below his ideal, were good for much more than this; this view of them seemed to him not only shallow and untrue, but perilous, deadly, soul-destroying; and inasmuch as it commended itself to intellectual men, and was an intelligent force, he fought against it, not, I think, with much sweetness or light, but with a blind, eager, glowing asperity which, tempered always by humility and candour, was and is very impressive. Dr. Newman fought for a point of view which it required culture to appreciate, and therefore he fought in some sense with culture; but he did not fight for culture, and to conceive him combating side by side with Mr. Matthew Arnold is almost comical.

I think, then, that without saying more about religion, Mr. Arnold might have said truer things about it; and I think also that without saying less about culture—we have a strong need of all he can say to recommend it—he might have shown that he was alive to one or two of its besetting faults. And some notice of these might have strengthened his case; for he might have shown that the faults of culture really arise from lack of culture; and that more culture, deeper and truer culture, removes them. I have ventured to hint this in speaking of Mr. Arnold's tone about religion. What I dislike in it seems to me, when examined, to be exactly what he calls Philistinism; just as when he commences his last lecture before a great university by referring to his petty literary squabbles, he seems to me guilty of what he calls "provincialism."—And so, again, the attitude that culture often assumes towards enthusiasm in general seems to spring from narrowness, from imperfection of culture. The fostering care of culture, and a soft application of sweetness and light, might do so much for enthusiasm—enthusiasm does so much want it. Enthusiasm is often a turbid issue of smoke and sparks. Culture might refine this to a steady glow. It is melancholy when, instead, it takes to pouring cold water on it. The worst result is not the natural hissing and sputtering that ensues, though that cannot be pleasing to culture or to anything else, but the waste of power that is the inevitable consequence.

It is wrong to exaggerate the antagonism between enthusiasm and culture; because, in the first place, culture has an enthusiasm of its own, by virtue of which indeed, as Mr. Arnold contemplates, it is presently to transcend and absorb religion. But at present this enthusiasm, so far from being adequate to this, is hardly sufficient—is often insufficient—to prevent culture degenerating into dilettantism. In the second place, culture has an appreciation of enthusiasm (with the source of which it has nothing to do), when that enthusiasm is beautiful and picturesque, or thrilling and sublime, as it often is. But the enthusiasm must be very picturesque, very sublime; upon some completed excellence of form culture will rigorously insist. May it not be that culture is short-sighted and pedantic in the rigour of these demands, and thus really defeats its own ends, just as it is often liable to do by purely artistic pedantry and conventionality? If it had larger and healthier sympathies, it might see beauty in the stage of becoming (if I may use a German phrase), in much rough and violent work at which it now shudders. In pure art culture is always erring on the side of antiquity—much more in its sympathy with the actual life of men and society. In some of the most beautiful lines he has written, Owen Meredith expresses a truth that deserves to be set in beautiful language:

> I know that all acted time
> By that which succeeds it is ever received
> As calmer, completer, and more sublime,
> Only because it is finished; because
> We only behold the thing it achieved,
> We behold not the thing that it was.
> For while it stands whole and immutable
> In the marble of memory, how can we tell
> What the men that have hewn at the block may have
>   been?
> Their passion is merged in its passionlessness;
> Their strife in its stillness closed for ever;
> Their change upon change in its changelessness;
> In its final achievement their feverish endeavour.

Passion, strife, feverish endeavour—surely in the midst of these have been produced not only the rough blocks with which the common world builds, but the jewels with which culture is adorned. Culture the other day thought Mr. Garrison a very prosy and uninteresting person, and did not see why so much fuss should be made about him; but I should not be surprised if in a hundred years or so he were found to be poetical and picturesque.

And I will go farther, and plead for interests duller and vulgarer than any fanaticism.

If any culture really has what Mr. Arnold in his finest mood calls its noblest element, the passion for propagating itself, for making itself prevail, then let it learn "to call nothing common or unclean." It can only propagate itself by shedding the light of its sympathy liberally; by learning to love common people and common things, to feel common interests. Make people feel that their own poor life is ever so little beautiful and poetical; then they will begin to turn and seek after the treasures of beauty and poetry outside and above it. Pictorial culture is a little vexed at the success of Mr. Frith's pictures, at the thousands of pounds he gets, and the thousands of people that crowd to see them. Now I do not myself admire Mr. Frith's pictures; but I think he diffuses culture more than some of his acid critics, and I should like to think that he got twice as many pounds and spectators. If any one of these grows eagerly fond of a picture of Mr. Frith's, then, it seems to me, the infinite path of culture is open to him; I do not see why he should not go on till he can conscientiously praise the works of Pietro Perugino. But leaving Mr. Frith (and other painters and novelists that might be ranked with him), let us consider a much greater man, Macaulay. Culture has turned up its nose a little at our latest English classic, and would, I think, have done so more, but that it is touched and awed by his wonderful devotion to literature. But Macaulay, though he loved literature, loved also common people and common things, and therefore he can make the common people who live among common things love literature. How Philistinish it is of him to be stirred to eloquence by the thought of "the opulent and enlightened states of Italy, the vast and magnificent cities, the ports, the arsenals, the villas, the museums, the libraries, the marts filled with every article of comfort and luxury, the factories swarming with artizans, the Apennines covered with rich cultivation up to their very summits, the Po wafting the harvest of Lombardy to the granaries of Venice, and carrying back the silks of Bengal and the furs of Siberia to the palaces of Milan." But the Philistine's heart is opened by these images; through his heart a way is found to his taste; he learns how delightful a melodious current of stirring words may be; and then, when Macaulay asks him to mourn for "the wit and the learning and the genius" of Florence, he does not refuse faintly to mourn; and so Philistinism and culture kiss each other.

Again, when our greatest living poet "dips into the future," what does he see?

> The heavens fill with commerce, argosies of magic
>   sails,
> Pilots of the purple twilight, dropping down with
>   costly bales.

Why, it might be the vision of a young general merchant. I doubt whether anything similar could be found in a French or German poet (I might except Victor Hugo to prove the rule): he would not feel the image poetical, and perhaps if he did, would not dare to say so. The Germans have in their way immense honesty and breadth of sympathy, and I like them for it. I like to be made to sympathize with their middle-class enthusiasm for domestic life and bread-and-butter. Let us be bold, and make them sympathize with our middle-class affection for commerce and bustle.

Ah, I wish I could believe that Mr. Arnold was describing the ideal and not the actual, when he dwells on the educational, the missionary, function of culture, and says that its greatest passion is for making sweetness and light prevail. For I think we might soon be agreed as to how they may be made to prevail. Religions have been propagated by the sword: but culture cannot be propagated by the sword, nor by the pen sharpened and wielded like an offensive weapon. Culture, like all spiritual gifts, can only be propagated by enthusiasm: and by enthusiasm that has got rid of asperity, that has become sympathetic; that has got rid of Pharisaism, and become humble. I suppose Mr. Arnold would hardly deny that in the attitude in which he shows himself, contemplating the wealthy Philistine through his eyeglass, he has at least a superficial resemblance to a Pharisee. Let us not be too hard on Pharisaism of any kind. It is better that religion should be self-asserting than that it should be crushed and stifled by rampant worldliness; and where the worship of wealth is predominant it is perhaps a necessary antagonism that intellect should be self-asserting. But I cannot see that intellectual Pharisaism is any less injurious to true culture than religious Pharisaism to true worship; and when a poet keeps congratulating himself that he is not a Philistine, and pointing out (even exaggerating) all the differences between himself and a Philistine, I ask myself, Where is the sweetness of culture. For the moment it seems to have turned sour.

Perhaps what is most disappointing in our culture is its want of appreciation of the "sap of progress," the creative and active element of things. We all remember the profound epigram of Agassiz, that the world in dealing with a new truth passes through three stages: it first says that it is not true, then that it is contrary to religion, and finally, that we knew it before. Culture is raised above the first two stages, but it is apt to disport itself complacently in the third. "Culture," we are told, "is always assigning to the system-maker and his system a smaller share in the bent of human destiny than their friends like." Quite so: a most useful function: but culture does this with so much zest that it is continually overdoing it. The system-maker may be compared to a man who sees that mankind want a house built. He erects a scaffolding with much unassisted labour, and begins to build. The scaffolding is often unnecessarily large and clumsy, and the system-maker is apt to keep it up much longer than it is needed. Culture looks at the unsightly structure with contempt, and from time to time kicks over some useless piece of timber. The house however gets built, is seen to be serviceable, and culture is soon found benevolently diffusing sweetness and light through the apartments. For culture perceives the need of houses; and is even

ready to say in its royal way, "Let suitable mansions be prepared; only without this eternal hammering, these obtrusive stones and timber." We must not forget, however, that construction and destruction are treated with equal impartiality. When a miserable fanatic has knocked down some social abuse with much peril of life and limb, culture is good enough to point out to him that he need not have taken so much trouble: culture had seen the thing was falling; it would soon have fallen of its own accord; the crash has been unpleasant, and raised a good deal of disagreeable dust.

All this criticism of action is very valuable; but it is usually given in excess, just because, I think, culture is a little sore in conscience, is uncomfortably eager to excuse its own evident incapacity for action. Culture is always hinting at a convenient season, that rarely seems to arrive. It is always suggesting one decisive blow that is to be gracefully given; but it is so difficult to strike quite harmoniously, and without some derangement of attitude. Hence an instinctive, and, I think, irrational, discouragement of the action upon which less cultivated people are meanwhile spending themselves. For what does action, social action, really mean? It means losing oneself in a mass of disagreeable, hard, mechanical details, and trying to influence many dull or careless or bigoted people for the sake of ends that were at first of doubtful brilliancy, and are continually being dimmed and dwarfed by the clouds of conflict. Is this the kind of thing to which human nature is desperately prone, and into which it is continually rushing with perilous avidity? Mr. Arnold may say that he does not discourage action, but only asks for delay, in order that we may act with sufficient knowledge. This is the eternal excuse of indolence—insufficient knowledge: still, taken cautiously, the warning is valuable, and we may thank Mr. Arnold for it: we cannot be too much stimulated to study the laws of the social phenomena that we wish to modify, in order that "reason the card" may be as complete and accurate as possible. But we remember that we have heard all this before at much length from a very different sort of prophet. It has been preached to us by a school small, but energetic (energetic to a degree that causes Mr. Arnold to scream "Jacobinism!"): and the preaching has been not in the name of culture, but in the name of religion and self-sacrifice.

I do not ask much sympathy for the people of action from the people of culture: I will show by an example how much. Paley somewhere, in one of his optimistic expositions of the comfortableness of things, remarks, that if he is ever inclined to grumble at his taxes, when he gets his newspaper he feels repaid; he feels that he could not lay out the money better than in purchasing the spectacle of all this varied life and bustle. There are more taxes now, but there are more and bigger newspapers: let us hope that Paley would still consider the account balanced. Now, might not Mr. Arnold imbibe a little of this pleasant spirit? As it is, no one who is doing anything can feel that Mr. Arnold hearing of it is the least bit more content to pay his taxes—that is, unless he is doing it in some supremely graceful and harmonious way.

One cannot think on this subject without recalling the great man who recommended to philosophy a position very similar to that now claimed for culture. I wish to give Mr. Arnold the full benefit of his resemblance to Plato. But when we look closer at the two positions, the dissimilarity comes out: they have a very different effect on our feelings and imagination; and I confess I feel more sympathy with the melancholy philosopher looking out with hopeless placidity "from beneath the shelter of some wall" on the storms and dust-clouds of blind and selfish conflict, than with a cheerful modern liberal, tempered by renouncement, shuddering aloof from the rank exhalations of vulgar enthusiasm, and holding up the pouncet-box of culture betwixt the wind and his nobility.

To prolong this fault-finding would be neither pleasant nor profitable. But perhaps many who love culture much—and respect the enthusiasm of those who love it more—may be sorry when it is brought into antagonism with things that are more dear to them even than culture. I think Mr. Arnold wishes for the reconciliation of antagonisms: I think that in many respects, with his subtle eloquence, his breadth of view, and above all his admirable temper, he is excellently fitted to reconcile antagonisms; and therefore I am vexed when I find him, in an access of dilettante humour, doing not a little to exasperate and exacerbate them, and dropping from the prophet of an ideal culture into a more or less prejudiced advocate of the actual.

ALGERNON CHARLES SWINBURNE
From "Matthew Arnold's New Poems" (1867)
Essays and Studies
1875, pp. 152–83

As with all poets of his rank, so with Mr. Arnold, the technical beauty of his work is one with the spiritual; art, a poet's art above all others, cannot succeed in this and fail in that. Success or achievement of an exalted kind on the spiritual side ensures and enforces a like executive achievement or success; if the handiwork be flawed, there must also have been some distortion or defect of spirit, a shortcoming or a misdirection of spiritual supply. There is no such thing as a dumb poet or a handless painter. The essence of an artist is that he should be articulate. It is the mere impudence of weakness to arrogate the name of poet or painter with no other claim than a susceptible and impressible sense of outward or inward beauty, producing an impotent desire to paint or sing. The poets that are made by nature are not many; and whatever 'vision' an aspirant may possess, he has not the 'faculty divine' if he cannot use his vision to any poetic purpose. There is no cant more pernicious to such as these, more wearisome to all other men, than that which asserts the reverse. It is a drug which weakens the feeble and intoxicates the drunken; which makes those swagger who have not learnt to walk, and teach who have not been taught to learn. Such talk as this of Wordsworth's is the poison of poor souls like David Gray's.[1] Men listen, and depart with the belief that they have this faculty or this vision which alone, they are told, makes the poet; and once imbued with that belief, soon pass or slide from the inarticulate to the articulate stage of debility and disease. Aspiration foiled and impotent is a piteous thing enough, but friends and teachers of this sort make it ridiculous as well. A man can no more win a place among poets by dreaming of it or lusting after it than he can win by dream or desire a woman's beauty or a king's command; and those encourage him to fill his belly with the east wind who feign to accept the will for the deed, and treat inarticulate or inadequate pretenders as actual associates in art. The Muses can bear children and Apollo can give crowns to those only who are able to win the crown and beget the child; but in the school of theoretic sentiment it is apparently believed that this can be done by wishing.

Small things suffice to give immediate proof or disproof of the requisite power. In music or in painting all men admit this for a truth; it is not less certain in poetry. There is nothing in either of the poets I speak of more distinctive and significant than the excellence of their best sonnets. These are almost equally noble in style; though the few highest of Wordsworth's remain out of reach of emulation, not out of sight of worship. Less adorable and sublime, not less admirable and durable, Mr. Arnold's hold their own in the same world of poetry with these. All in this new volume are full of beauty, sound and sweet fruits of thought and speech that have ripened and brought forth together; the poetry of religious thought when most pure and most large has borne no fairer than that one on the drawing in the Catacombs of the Good Shepherd bearing the young, not of a sheep, but of a goat; or that other on the survival of grace and spirit when the body of belief lies dead; but all, I repeat, have a singular charm and clearness. I have used this word already more than once or twice; it comes nearest of all I can find to the thing I desire to express; that natural light of mind, that power of reception and reflection of things or thoughts, which I most admire in so much of Mr. Arnold's work. I mean by it much more than mere facility or transparency; more than brilliance, more than ease or excellence of style. It is a quality begotten by instinct upon culture; one which all artists of equal rank possess in equal measure.

There are in the English language three elegiac poems so great that they eclipse and efface all the elegiac poetry we know; all of Italian, all of Greek. It is only because the latest born is yet new to us that it can seem strange or rash to say so. The 'Thyrsis' of Mr. Arnold makes a third with 'Lycidas' and *Adonais*. It is not so easy as those may think who think by rote and praise by prescription to strike the balance between them. The first however remains first, and must remain; its five opening lines are to me the most musical in all known realms of verse; there is nothing like them; and it is more various, more simple, more large and sublime than the others; lovelier and fuller it cannot be.

> The leader is fairest,
> But all are divine.

The least pathetic of the three is *Adonais*, which indeed is hardly pathetic at all; it is passionate, subtle, splendid; but 'Thyrsis,' like 'Lycidas,' has a quiet and tender undertone which gives it something of sacred. Shelley brings fire from heaven, but these bring also 'the meed of some melodious tear.' There is a grace ineffable, a sweet sound and sweet savour of things past, in the old beautiful use of the language of shepherds, of flocks and pipes: the spirit is none the less sad and sincere because the body of the poem has put on this dear familiar raiment of romance; because the crude and naked sorrow is veiled and chastened with soft shadows and sounds of a 'land that is very far off'; because the verse remembers and retains a perfume and an echo of Grecian flutes and flowers,

> Renews the golden world, and holds through all
> The holy laws of homely pastoral,
> Where flowers and founts, and nymphs and semi-
> gods,
> And all the Graces find their old abodes.

Here, as in 'The Scholar Gipsy,' the beauty, the delicacy and affluence of colour, the fragrance and the freedom as of wide wings of winds in summer over meadow and moor, the freshness and expansion of the light and the lucid air, the spring and the stream as of flowing and welling water, enlarge and exalt the pleasure and power of the whole poem. Such English-coloured verse no poet has written since Shakespeare, who chooses his field-flowers and hedgerow blossoms with the same sure and loving hand, binds them in as simple and sweet an order. All others, from Milton downward to Shelley and onward from him, have gathered them singly or have mixed them with foreign buds and alien bloom. No poem in any language can be more perfect as a model of style, unsurpassable certainly, it may be unattainable. Any couplet, any line proves it. No countryman of ours since Keats died has made or has found words fall into such faultless folds and forms of harmonious line. He is the most efficient, the surest-footed poet of our time, the most to be relied on; what he does he is the safest to do well; more than any other he unites personality and perfection; others are personal and imperfect, perfect and impersonal; with them you must sometimes choose between inharmonious freedom and harmonious bondage. Above all, he knows what as a poet he should do, and simply does that; the manner of his good work is never more or less than right; his verse comes clean and full out of the mould, cast at a single jet; placed beside much other verse of the time, it shows like a sculptor's work by an enameller's. With all their wealth and warmth of flowers and lights, these two twin poems are solid and pure as granite or as gold. Their sweet sufficiency of music, so full and calm, buoys and bears up throughout the imperial vessel of thought. Their sadness is not chill or sterile, but as the sorrow of summer pausing with laden hands on the middle height of the year, the watershed that divides the feeding fountains of autumn and of spring; a grave and fruitful sadness, the triumphant melancholy of full-blown flowers and souls full-grown. The stanzas from the sixth to the fourteenth of 'Thyrsis,' and again from the sixteenth to the twentieth, are if possible the most lovely in either poem; the deepest in tone and amplest in colour; the choiceness and sweetness of single lines and phrases most exquisite and frequent.

> O easy access to the hearer's grace,
> When Dorian shepherds sang to Proserpine !
>   For she herself had trod Sicilian fields,
> She knew the Dorian water's gush divine,
>   She knew each lily white which Enna yields,
>   Each rose with blushing face;
> She loved the Dorian pipe, the Dorian strain.
>   But, ah! of our poor Thames she never heard!
>   Her foot the Cumnor cowslips never stirred;
>   And we should tease her with our plaint in vain.

She has learnt to know them now, the river and the river-meadows, and access is as easy for an English as a Dorian prayer to the most gentle of all worshipped gods. It is a triumphal and memorial poem, a landmark in the high places of verse to which future travellers studious of the fruits and features of the land may turn and look up and see what English hands could rear.

This is probably the highest point of Mr. Arnold's poetry, though for myself I cannot wholly resign the old preference of things before familiar; of one poem in especial, good alike for children and men, 'The Forsaken Merman'; which has in it the pathos of natural things, the tune of the passion we fancy in the note of crying birds or winds weeping, shrill and sweet and estranged from us; the swift and winged wail of something lost midway between man's life and the life of things soulless, the wail overheard and caught up by the fitful northern fancy, filling with glad and sad spirits the untravelled ways of nature; the clear cry of a creature astray in the world, wild and gentle and mournful, heard in the sighing of weary waters before dawn under a low wind, in the rustle and whistle and whisper of leaves or grasses, in the long light breaths of twilight air heaving all the heather on the hills, in the coming and going of the sorrowful strong seas that bring delight and death, in the tender touch and recoil of the ripple from the sand; all the fanciful pitiful beauty of dreams and legends born in grey windy lands on shores and hillsides whose life is quiet and wild.

No man's hand has pressed from the bells and buds of the moors and downs by cape or channel of the north a sweeter honey than this. The song is a piece of the sea-wind, a stray breath of the air and bloom of the bays and hills: its mixture of mortal sorrow with the strange wild sense of a life that is not after mortal law—the childlike moan after lost love mingling with the pure outer note of a song not human—the look in it as of bright bewildered eyes with tears not theirs and alien wonder in the watch of them—the tender, marvellous, simple beauty of the poem, its charm as of a sound or a flower of the sea—set it and save it apart from all others in a niche of the memory. This has all the inexplicable inevitable sweetness of a child's or a bird's in its note; 'Thyrsis' has all the accomplished and adult beauty of a male poem. In the volume which it crowns there is certainly no new jewel of equal water. 'Palladium' is a fresh sample of the noble purity and clearness which we find always and always praise in his reflective poetry; its cool aërial colour like that of a quiet sky between full sunset and full moonrise, made ready for the muster of the stars, swept clean of cloud and flame, and laved with limpid unruffled air from western green to eastern grey; a sky the cenotaph of unburied sunlight, the mould of moonlight unborn. 'A Southern Night' is steeped in later air, as gentle and more shining; the stanzas on the Grande Chartreuse are stamped with the impression of a solemn charm, and so the new verses on Obermann,[2] the new verses on Marguerite, strange to read for those who remember reading the first at the time when all the loves we read of assume a form and ascend a throne in our thoughts, the old and the new side by side, so that now this poem comes under our eyes like a new love-song of Petrarca to Laura or Coleridge to Geneviève. It is fine and high in tone, but not such as the famous verses, cited and admired even by critics sparing of their priceless praise, beginning

> Yes, in this sea of life enisled—.

These in their profound and passionate calm strike deeper and sound fuller than any other of the plaintive dejected songs of Switzerland. 'Dover Beach' marks another high point in the volume; it has a grand choral cadence as of steady surges, regular in resonance, not fitful or gusty but antiphonal and reverberate. But nothing of new verse here clings closer to the mind than the overture of that majestic fragment from the chorus of a *Dejaneira*.

> O frivolous mind of man,
> Light ignorance, and hurrying, unsure thoughts,
> Though man bewails you not,
> How I bewail you!

We must hope to have more of the tragedy in time; that must be a noble statue which could match this massive fragment. The story of Merope, though dramatic enough in detail, is upon the whole more of a narrative romance than a tragic subject; in Mr. Arnold's poem the deepest note is that struck by the tyrant Polyphontes, whose austere and patient figure is carved with Sophoclean skill of hand. It is a poem which Milton might have praised, an august work, of steady aim and severe success; but this of Dejaneira has in it a loftier promise and a larger chance. Higher matter of tragedy there can be none; none more intense and impressive, none fuller of keen and profound interest, none simpler and statelier; none where the weight and gravity, the sweetness and shapeliness of pure thought, could be better or closelier allied with the warmth and width of common tenderness and passion. We must all hope that the poet will keep to this clear air of the ancient heights, more natural and wholesome for the spirit than the lowlands of depression and dubiety where he has set before now a too frequent foot. This alone I find profitless and painful in his work; this occasional habit of harking back and loitering in mind among the sepulchres. Nothing is to be made by an artist out of scepticism, half-hearted or double-hearted doubts or creeds; nothing out of mere dejection and misty mental weather. Tempest or calm you may put to use, but hardly a flat fog. In not a few of his former poems, in some reprinted here, there is a sensible and stagnant influence of moist vapour from those marshes of the mind where weaker souls paddle and plunge and disappear. Above these levels the sunnier fields and fresher uplands lie wide and warm; and there the lord of the land should sit at peace among his good things. If a spirit by nature clear and high, a harmonious and a shining soul, does ever feel itself 'immured in the hot prison of the present,' its fit work is not to hug but break its chain; and only by its own will or weakness can it remain ill at ease in a thick and difficult air. Of such poetry I would say what Joubert, as cited by Mr. Arnold, says of all coarse and violent literature: it may be produced in any amount of supply to any excess of effect, but it is no proper matter of pure art, and 'the soul says all the while, You hurt me.' Deep-reaching doubt and 'large discourse' are poetical; so is faith, so are sorrow and joy; but so are not the small troubles of spirits that nibble and quibble about beliefs living or dead; so are not those sickly moods which are warmed and weakened by feeding on the sullen drugs of dejection; and the savour of this disease and its medicines is enough to deaden the fresh air of poetry. Nothing which leaves us depressed is a true work of art. We must have light though it be lightning, and air though it be storm.

Where the thought goes wrong, the verse follows after it. In Mr. Arnold's second book there was more of weak or barren matter, and more therefore of feeble or faulty metre. Rhyme is the native condition of lyric verse in English; a rhymeless lyric is a maimed thing, and halts and stammers in the delivery of its message. There are some few in the language as good as rare; but the habit of rule is bad. The fragments of his *Antigone* and *Dejaneira* no reader can wish other than they are; and the chorus for example in *Merope* which tells of Arcas and Callisto is a model of noble form and colour; but it does not fasten at once upon the memory like a song of Callicles, or like 'The Merman,' or like any such other. To throw away the natural grace of rhyme from a modern song is a wilful abdication of half the power and half the charm of verse. It is hard to realise and hopeless to reproduce the musical force of classic metres so recondite and exquisite as the choral parts of a Greek play. Even Milton could not; though with his godlike instinct and his godlike might of hand he made a kind of strange and enormous harmony by intermixture of assonance and rhyme with irregular blank verse, as in that last Titanic chorus of Samson which utters over the fallen Philistines the trumpet-blast and thunder of its triumph. But Milton, it may be said, even if he knew them, did not obey the laws of the choral scheme, and so forfeited the legitimate condition of its music. Who then has observed those laws and obtained that success which he did not? I scarcely think that Mr. Arnold has; and if ever man was qualified for the work it is he only. I have never seen other attempts at rhymeless choral metre which were not mere amorphous abortions of misshapen prose, halting on helpless broken limbs and feet. A poet of Mr. Arnold's high station cannot of course but write in verse, and in good verse as far as the kind will allow; but that is not far enough to attain the ultimate goal, to fill up the final measure of delight. We lose something of the glory and the joy of poetry, of which he has no reason and no right to defraud us. It is in no wise a question of scholarship, or in the presence of a scholar I should be silent;

as it is, I must say how inexplicable it seems to me that Mr. Arnold, of all men, should be a patron of English hexameters. His own I have tried in vain to reduce by scansion into any metrical feet at all; they look like nothing on earth, and sound like anapæsts broken up and driven wrong; neither by ear nor by finger can I bring them to any reckoning. I am sure of one thing, that some of them begin with a pure and absolute anapæst; and how a hexameter can do this it passes my power to conceive. And at best what ugly bastards of verse are these self-styled hexameters! how human tongues or hands could utter or could write them except by way of burlesque improvisation I could never imagine, and never shall. Once only, to be candid—and I will for once show all possible loyalty and reverence to past authority—once only, as far as I know, in Dr. Hawtrey's delicate and fluent verse, has the riddle been resolved; the verses are faultless, are English, are hexametric; but that is simply a graceful interlude of pastime, a well-played stroke in a game of skill played with language. Such as pass elsewhere for English hexameters I do hope and suppose impossible to Eton. Mr. Clough's I will not presume to be serious attempts or studies in any manner of metre; they are admirable studies in graduated prose, full of fine sound and effect. Even Mr. Kingsley's 'Andromeda,' the one good poem extant in that pernicious metre, for all its spirit and splendour, for all the grace and glory and exultation of its rushing and ringing words, has not made possible the impossible thing. Nothing but loose rhymeless anapæsts can be made of the language in that way; and we hardly want these, having infinite command and resource of metre without them, and rhyme thrown in to turn the overweighted scale. I am unwilling to set my face against any doctrine or practice of a poet such as Mr. Arnold, but on this matter of metre I was moved to deliver my soul.

This is not the only example in his writings of some quality which seems to me intrusive and incoherent with his full general accuracy and clearness. These points of view and heads of theory which in my eyes seem out of perspective do indeed cohere each with the other; but hardly with his own high practice and bright intuition of the best thing. His alliance is so precious against the mailed and gowned array of the Philistines, that the least defection, the least error of movement, imperils more than his own position; a whole regiment may be misled into ruin by the general, while the heat and burden of the day lie before us yet. No man has done so much to exalt and to correct men's view of the higher criticism and its office. Wherever therefore in things great or small he outruns or falls short of the immediate goal of a just judgment, the instant aim of a pure argument, it is worth while to take note of the slippery or oblique reasoning, or at least to sift and strain it, on the chance that here may be some error. 'The light of the body is the eye'; he is the eye of English criticism; and if ever for some passing purblind minute the light that is in that body be darkness, how great indeed is that darkness! Dark however he properly never is, but I think at times oblique or drowsy. He has smitten the Janus of Philistine worship on one face; under the other, if he has not himself burnt a pinch or two of adulterate incense, he has encouraged or allowed others to burn. At the portal by which English devotees press thickest into the temple of Dagon he has stood firm as in a breach, and done good service; but he has left unguarded other points of entrance. All that is said in his essays on the religious tradition and the religious idea, as opposed to Philistine demolition or to Philistine edification, I accept and admire as truth, excellent if not absolute, and suggestive if not final; but from his own vantage ground of meditation and idea I start my objection to this inference and that. Protestantism, conservative and destructive, is the form in which the enemy has appeared to him; such in his eyes has been the banner, such the watchword under which they serve. All Philistia for him is resumed in the English Philistine; who may probably be the most noisome example in the world, but is assuredly not the only one. I do not say that marriage dissoluble only in an English divorce court is a lovely thing or a venerable; I do say that marriage indissoluble except by Papal action is not. It is irrelevant and unfair for a soldier of light to ally himself with Philistine against Philistine. From the ideal point of meditation to which he would recall us, where the pure justice and the naked beauty of thought are alone held sacred, I cannot 'find the marriage theory of Catholicism refreshing and elevating' merely because the Protestant theory, which 'neither makes divorce impossible nor makes it decent,' has assumed in English law-courts a gross and hideous incarnation. What is anomalous, what is unjust, cannot surely be beautiful to purged eyes looking from 'the ideal sphere.' Of course the idea of a lifelong union has its beauty and significance; so has the idea of liberty and sincerity of action. Faith is good, and freedom is good; the office of the idea is to give free play and full justice to both. The Philistines on either side would fain draw sharper and harder the lines of demarcation and division; the thinkers on neither side would fain not reject but reconcile.

Again, it is doubtless the best and most direct service that a critic can do his countrymen to strip and smite their especial errors, to point out and fence off their peculiar pitfalls; and this Mr. Arnold has done for his English not once or twice only. I doubt if he has ever assailed or advised them without due cause: in one point above all he has done them most loyal and liberal service; he has striven to purge them of the pestilence of provincial thought and tradition, of blind theory and brute opinion, of all that hereditary policy of prejudice which substitutes self-esteem for self-culture, self-worship for self-knowledge; which clogs and encrusts all powers and all motions of the mind with a hard husk of mechanical conceit. And here, heaven knows, in his dull dumb way the Briton stands ahead of all men, towers above all men in stolid and sublime solitude, a massive, stupid, inarticulate god and priest in one; his mute and majestic autolatry is a deeper and more radical religion than the self-love of other nations, the more vocal vanities of France or America. In the stone walls and iron girders of this faith our champion has done what a man may to make a breach; and the weapon was well chosen, the brand of provinciality, wherewith to stamp and mark that side of the double-faced head of Dagon which looks towards us with English features. But, to use his own term, there are two notes of provinciality perceptible, one or other, in most criticism of foreign things; error in praise and error in dispraise. He could have prescribed for the soul-sick British Philistine, 'sick of self-love,' no better method of cure than study and culture of the French spirit, of its flexible intelligence and critical ambition, its many-sided faith in perfection, in possible excellence and ideal growth outward and upward, and the single-hearted love of all these which goes hand in hand with that faith. Faith in light and motion is what England has not and France has; often a blind, erring, heretical faith, often perverse and fanatical, a faith which kills its prophets and stones its proto-martyrs; but in art as in politics, in literature as in ethics, an active and a living faith. To show this to English eyes and impress upon English ears its truth and its importance is to do a good work; but to pass from general doctrine to example and detail is hard and unsafe for a foreign preacher. Those who deserve gratitude at our hands deserve also candour; and I must

in candour say that Mr. Arnold is not a sure guide over French ground. He does not know quite how the land lies: he turns down this declivity or stops short by that well-head, where a native guide would hardly bid one halt. With a large and fine appreciation of the beauties and capacities of the national character, with a justice and strength of insight into these which compared with an average English judgment are wonderful and admirable, he has not the eyes and the nerves of one to the manner born, the sudden and sensitive intuition of an innate instinct: he thinks right, but he feels wrong; some men are right without being reasonable, he is reasonable without being right. He sets up a rational argument to prove why France should be, and why she is, weak in poetry and strong in prose; a very keen and clear argument, only the facts are all against it. Of classic verse Mr. Arnold is so much more competent to speak than I am that I dare not press the debateable question of choric metre; but of French verse I must have leave to say that he is not competent to speak. His touch has in it no pulse or play of French blood; his fine ear is deaf on that side. It would clearly be impossible to show him, to make him feel, the silent horror and wonder with which other ears receive such utterances from him as from the common Briton we expect and accept with all composure. Whether it be 'the German paste in his composition' which so far thickens and deadens his subtle sense of song, I cannot say; but I can say that in that case it would be well for him to get quit of it. The cadence and impulse of harmonies in French verse are of course unlike those in English verse or Italian, and the laws which are their outgrowth are unlike too; but the one is not more sure and satisfying than the other: only there must be the right hands to play and the right ears to hear. Mr. Arnold says that a Frenchman born with the faculty or instinct of poetry finds in prose a fuller and easier expression than in verse. As justly might a French critic say this of an Englishman. In either case, the man who is a poet or nothing must be judged by his power of writing verse. If he can neither do that well nor do any other work, whatever his charm of aspiration and sentiment and sincerity may be, he slips into the second rank as surely if French as if English. Imagine that Frenchman's tone of mind, or his tone of ear, who should proclaim the inadequacy of a language which has sufficed for all the great lyric poets of France, all the copious and glorious roll from François Villon and Charles of Orleans to Victor Hugo and Théophile Gautier, but is now convicted of inaptitude to render in full the sentiments of a Maurice de Guérin! The English poet is here hopelessly at sea without oar or rudder, haven or guiding-star. He cannot even be trusted to speak of the academic poets, easier though they are of access and apprehension even to the run of Englishmen. The thin, narrow, shallow, but very real melodies of Racine are as inaudible to him as the mightier symphonies of the great school; this perhaps, as he says, is natural in a foreigner. But no such excuse will serve for the confusion of judgment which places on a level the very best man of his kind, Pope, and Boileau, the very worst. Perhaps their respective Odes on St. Cecilia's Day and the Siege of Namur may be allowed to pair off as the shamefullest two lyrical poems in the world; but compare for a moment their general work, their didactic and satirical verse! the comparison is an insult too absurd to affect the Englishman. He is the finest, Boileau the dullest craftsman of their age and school.

It is singular and significant that Mr. Arnold, himself established and acknowledged as a poet standing in the first rank among his own people, has chosen for special praise and patronage men who have tried their hands at his work and failed, men who have fallen back baffled from the cliff-side he has climbed. Again I cite the evidence of his French critic; who naturally feels that he has paid the French but a poor compliment in praising as their best men those who fall short of their own aim and his achievement: 'Il y a quelque chose de louche, de suspect, dans les louanges que prodigue aux poëtes manqués un poëte réussi. Or, parmi tous les nôtres c'est à M. Sainte-Beuve, poëte manqué dont le temps a fait un critique réussi, que le poëte anglais adresse son hommage respectueux. Il a eu mille fois raison d'étudier, d'apprécier, de louer cet illustre écrivain; il n'a peut-être pas eu tort de le suivre les yeux fermés lorsqu'il s'envole à tire d'ailes dans les nuages du paradoxe, de le croire sur parole quand il affirme qu'on peut être grand poëte tout en échouant dans le champ poétique: pour moi, je préfère, soit dit en passant, les peintres qui sachent peindre, les médecins qui sachent guérir, les poëtes qui font des vers. Passons-lui ces spécialités; ce n'est pas une raison d'affirmer qu'il ne saurait être en France de meilleurs poëtes que ces prosateurs, de plus forts travailleurs que ces lutteurs étiques, que ces génies tronqués. Quand on dénonce chez autrui les jugements saugrenus, les bêtises réciproques de l'esprit insulaire et provincial, il faudrait se garder par exemple de ranger au niveau des grands poëtes les talents délicats, de prendre pour des Keats les Maurice de Guérin, pauvres belles âmes étiolées, douces et frêles petites fleurs effeuillées en pleine éclosion. Ces roses pâles, ces pousses maladives, ont bien leur charme et leur parfum, valent bien la peine qu'on les arrose et les recueille; mais on ne tresse point avec celles-là les grandes couronnes poétiques.'

The gentle pupil of Lamennais is to Mr. Arnold what the lesser celandine was to Wordsworth: he has unearthed a new favourite, and must have some three or four who will love his little flower. It were churlish and foolish to refuse; the small petals are fresh and dewy, the slim stem bends and sways with a sylvan grace. But it is something too much to hold up a bit of pilewort as the rose of Sharon; it provokes one to deny the poor blossom a place among flowers at all: it is indecorous and ludicrous. 'The Centaur' is really so fine and graceful a little study, there are really such delicate and distinctive touches of expression and feeling, such traces of a bright clear sense of beauty and charm and meaning in nature, that it was but just, when the man was well dead and could get no good of it and no harm, to praise him without grudging and pick up his leavings as a windfall. A place in the cabinet of M. Sainte-Beuve was no more than his desert. But the place which Mr. Arnold assigns him is reserved for men far other than this tender dreamer: five minutes of their life outweigh five centuries of such lives as his; one breath of the common air of their spirit would burn up the little tremulous soul as with fire. No tender Semele, but the queen of heaven alone, can face and enjoy the lightning of heaven. Of the contact of mortal and immortal, ashes are the only fruits. In Keats there was something of the spirit and breath of the world, of the divine life of things; in Guérin there was hardly a soft breathless pulse of fluttering sympathy; here was the *anima mundi*, made flesh once more in the body of a divine interpreter such as all great poets must be after their kind; there was the *animula vagula, blandula*, of a tentative, sensitive, impressible nature; full of little native pieties and sincere little sensibilities, amiable and laudable enough. But the demigods of our kind are not cast in such clay as that. M. Sainte-Beuve knew better than Mr. Arnold what was the rank and what the kindred of their foster-child when he called him a latter-day Lakist. If we must needs find him kinsmen among English poets, he may take his stand as a subordinate in the school of Gray[3] or the household

of Cowper. With them he had some good things in common; his letters, if less worth reading than the best of theirs, have the same frank delicacy and gentle play of personal sentiment applied to the landscape or the hearthside, and couched sometimes in choice and excellent words. But Keats, of all men born the ablest to hold his own with nature, and translate her gods into verbal incarnation; Keats, who was at once the lyrist and the lyre of that nature, the priest and the altar of those gods; more than all other poets receptive and passive of her influences and forces, and more than all other poets able and active to turn them all to a divine use, to transfigure them without transformation, to attune all colours and attemper all harmonies; whose power upon these things, whose gift of transfusion and expression, places him apart from all in his sovereign command of nature, able to do for nature what in his own day Shelley could not achieve nor Wordsworth attempt; above all Greece and all Italy and all England in his own line and field of work; to push forward as a competitor with him in that especial field of work where all the giants and all the gods of art would fail to stand against him for an hour, a man who in his own craft could not use the tools that lay ready to his hand—who was nothing (it seems) if not a poet, and could not as much as prove himself a poet by writing passable verse at all; this is a madness of mistake explicable and excusable only as the error of a foreign and provincial judgment. Any stanza of 'Thyrsis,' any fragment of 'Callicles,' would outweigh in point of 'natural magic' all Guérin's work, even were his thoughts clothed in the beauty of verse instead of the prettiness of prose; to weigh against it the entire work of Keats, or any such single poem as the 'Ode to Psyche' or that 'On a Grecian Urn'— poems which for perfect apprehension and execution of all attainable in their own sphere would weigh down all the world of poetry—is inexpressibly impossible. ⟨. . .⟩

Again, Mr. Arnold has a fond faith in the French Academy and in the *Revue des Deux Mondes* which is nothing short of pathetic; he seems actually to take them at their own valuation. The too outspoken critic before cited ventures to express in ribald phrase his wonder that such a pair of 'hoarse and haggard old temptresses' (*vieilles tentatrices hâves et rauques*) should play the part of Delilah to the scourger of Philistines. Not, as he adds, that he would impugn the venerable maiden reputation of their hoary hairs; but such as they are, 'ces étranges séductrices ont failli couper de leurs ciseaux émoussés les cheveux au Samson anglais. Déjà son engouement a manqué l'aveugler. Aux yeux de M. Arnold, l'amour a refait à l'Académie une virginité; il est tout prêt à épouser sa Marion, à prôner ses quelques appas émérites, à faire courber toutes les têtes anglaises devant cette Dulcinée à quarante. Il est l'amant fougueux du bon sens, l'apôtre échauffé de la froide raison, l'avocat furibond du goût sain.' This is not a fair or clear judgment; it is indigested and violent and deformed in expression; but it shows as in a cracked and blurred mirror the reflection thrown upon other minds by Mr. Arnold's act of homage in the outer courts of the Philistine temple: for thither he has unwittingly turned, and there has bent his knee, as no Frenchman could have done who was not a Philistine born and baptized and branded to the bone with the signet of the sons of Dagon. We may grant that the real office of an Academy should be—what the nominal office of this Academy is—culture and perfection of intelligence, elevation of the general standard of work, the average of mind and taste and sense which precludes absurdity or aberration and ensures something of care and conscience among the craftsmen of literature. Greater work an ideal Academy could hardly undertake, for greater work would require the vivid and personal advent of genius; and that, I presume, it could hardly undertake to supply. But has the actual Academy done this? Whom has it controlled, whom has it impelled, who but for such influence would either have gone wrong or failed to go right? whom at least among men really memorable and precious? Has it constantly done homage to the best? has it constantly rejected or rebuked the worst? Is it to the Academy that we owe the sound judgment, taste, temperance of the French prose classics whom Mr. Arnold eloquently extols? Did not the great Richelieu, its founder, set in motion the still virgin machinery of his engine against the greater Corneille? What was Molière in its eyes? and what was not Boileau? Where now are its great men, in an age for France so fruitful of literary greatness? Does it include one of high and fine genius besides Mérimée? and do the rest of the sacred forty respect in him the official antiquary or the faultless writer on whose dawn Goethe looked out and prophesied overmuch? There are names indeed still greater on its roll, but you do not see appended to them the academic title. Once for all, waiving its mere theories and reserving its mere pretensions, let us inquire if in effect it now does, if it ever has done, if it ever will do, any real and good service whatever to pure literature? The advice which Mr. Arnold gives by implication to his English audience while preaching on the text of academies is precious and necessary in itself, if the mass of English literature now current or floating is ever to be in any measure elevated or purified; but the selection of text is merely fantastic, the process of deduction vicious and baseless. This double impression was made on me by the lecture when I heard it delivered at Oxford; I have read it since more than once, and the impression is strengthened and deepened. It is possible to start from some incongruous or ignorant assumption and yet proceed to speak words of truth and soberness; the sermon may be useful and noble though the text be strained and misapplied. For the *Revue des Deux Mondes* I have as earnest a respect as Mr. Arnold; so far from regarding it with the eyes of irreverence and ribaldry, as an old lady of pleasure, a Delilah of dangerously gay repute, the ideas of pleasure or gaiety are the last I should associate with a name so justly venerated, a fame so sound and round and solid. Rather would I regard it, as the author of *Mademoiselle de Maupin* used to regard virtue in the days which found him unambitious of academic eminence, with such eyes as turn towards a fond and watchful grandmother. It is dangerous to ruffle the robe of that dowager. But I cannot regard her bosom as a safe pillow for the yet unshorn head of a Nazarite champion. Too many of the uncircumcised Philistines lie in wait for him slumbering in the lap of M. Buloz. Are there not giants among them, and the sons of the old giant, all of them children of uncircumcision? and the least of these has twice the thews and seven times the wits of the heavy-headed, horny-eyed English Philistine. Some of them there are that sleep with their father Goliath, and some abide to this day; and the acts of them past and present, and all that they did, and their might, are they not written in the books of the *Revue des Deux Mondes?* There is M. Gustave Planche, the staff of whose spear was so very like a weaver's beam; there is M. Armand de Pontmartin, a man of great moral stature, having on every hand six fingers to fight with, if haply he may give the flesh of poets to the fowls of the air and to the beasts of the field; there is M. Louis Etienne, who lately laid lance in rest against me unoffending in championship of the upper powers. Since the time of Goliath it has been a holy habit and tradition with the Philistines to curse 'by their gods'—which indeed seems the chief utility of those divine beings.

The comparative culture and relative urbanity of respon-

sible criticism—qualities due to no prescription of academic authority, but in part to natural sense and self-respect, in part to the code of habitual honour which rather impels than compels a man to avow his words and his works—these qualities, which preserve from mere contempt even the Philistines of French literature when we turn from them to their English fellow-soldiers, have I suspect blinded Mr. Arnold to the real colours under which they also serve. As yet however they have not made a prey of him; Delilah has merely woven the seven locks of the champion's head with the web and fastened it with the pin; he has but to awake out of his sleep and go away with the pin of the beam and with the web. But next time he goes to Gaza and sees there the Academy he must beware of going in unto that siren, or in the morning he may find the gates too heavy to carry off. We may trust indeed never to find him there eyeless at the mill with slaves; but it is no good sign that he should ever be blind of this eye or deaf of that ear—blind to infirmities on this side, or deaf to harmonies on that. I write not as a disciple of the dishevelled school, 'romantique à tous crins'; all such false and foolish catchwords as the names of classic and romantic I repudiate as senseless, and revere form or harmony as the high one law of all art. It is because, both as poet and critic, Mr. Arnold has done the service he has in the front rank of an army which finds among us few enough of able recruits, that I grudge in him the least appearance of praise or dispraise unworthy of his rank and office. Otherwise he would be as welcome for me as another Englishman to deny the power and variety, the supple sweetness and the superb resources of French verse in its depths and heights of song; as welcome to ignore the higher and enhance the minor merits of a foreign literature; to mistake for the causes the effects of these minor merits, which in their turn become (as in this case of the Academy) causes of grave error and defect, weakening where they should strengthen the hands and eyes they have in training. But in a child and champion of the light the least obliquity or obscurity of vision is to be noted as dangerous. If to any one these seem things of minor moment, to a poet such as he is they cannot; to him they must be more serious than to another. We owe him too much to keep silence here, though we might allow as harmless such graceful errors of pastime or paradox as the faith in Oxford which will not allow that she has ever 'given herself to the Philistines'; the beauty of the valley of Sorek has surely blinded him to the nation and nature of the Gazites and Ascalonites who have dwelt there now and again as surely as have many of their betters. Both here and in the Academy there may be a profession, a tradition of culture, of sweetness, urbanity, loyalty to the light; but where, we may too often have had to ask, are the things themselves? By their fruits ye shall know them; and what are these? In them both, if not of them, there may be good men and great; have such been always their leaders? or were ever such their types?

> Not here, O Apollo!
>   Are haunts meet for thee;
> But where Helicon breaks down
>   In cliff to the sea.

There, and not in the academies or the market-places of the Philistines, for peace or war; there, where all airs are full of the breath and all fields of the feet of the gods; where the sea-wind that first waved the wet hair of Venus moves now only the ripples that remember her rising limbs; where the Muses are, and their mother. There is his place, who in such a place long since found Circe feasting and heard Apollo play; there, below the upper glens and wellsprings of the Centaurs, above the scooped sea-shelves and flushing sands of the Sirens. Whatever now he say or do, he has been and will remain to us a lover and a giver of light; unwittingly, by impulse, for pure love of it; and such lead further and lighten otherwise than they know. All conscious help or guidance serves us less than unconscious leadership. In his best words there is often a craft and a charm; but in his best work there is always rest, and air, and a high relief; it satisfies, enlarges, refreshes with its cool full breath and serenity. On some men's nerves the temperature strikes somewhat cold; there are lungs that cannot breathe but in the air of a hothouse or a hospital. There is not much indeed of heat or flame in the Vestal or lunar light that shines from this hearth; but it does not burn down. His poetry is a pure temple, a white flower of marble, unfretted without by intricate and grotesque traceries, unvexed within by fumes of shaken censers or intoning of hoarse choristers; large and clear and cool, with many chapels in it and outer courts, full of quiet and of music. In the plainest air played here there is a sound of sincerity and skill; as in one little *Requiescat*, which without show of beauty or any thought or fancy leaves long upon the ear an impressure of simple, of earnest, of weary melody, wound up into a sense of rest. We do not always want to bathe our spirit in overflowing waters or flaming fires of imagination; pathos and passion and aspiration and desire are not the only springs we seek for song. Sorrows and joys of thought or sense meet us here in white raiment and wearing maiden crowns. In each court or chapel there is a fresh fragrance of early mountain flowers which bring with them the wind and the sun and a sense of space and growth, all of them born in high places, washed and waved by upper airs and rains. Into each alike there falls on us as we turn a conscience of calm beauty, of cool and noble repose, of majestic work under melodious and lofty laws; we feel and accept the quiet sovereignties of happy harmony and loyal form, whose service for the artist is perfect freedom: it is good for us to be here. Nor are all these either of modern structure or of Greek; here is an Asiatic court, a Scandinavian there. And everywhere is the one ruling and royal quality of classic work, an assured and equal excellence of touch. Whether for Balder dead and the weeping gods in Asgard, or for the thought-sick heart-sore king of a weary land far east, blinded and vexed in spirit with the piteous pains and wrongs of other men, the same good care and wise charm of right words are used to give speed of wing and sureness of foot to the ministering verse. The stormy northern world of water and air and iron and snow, the mystic oppression of eastern light and cruel colour in fiery continents and cities full of sickness and splendour and troubled tyrannies, alike yield up to him their spirit and their secret, to be rendered again in just and full expression. These are the trophies of his work and the gifts of his hand; through these and such as these things, his high and distinct seat is assured to him among English poets.

Notes

1. This was a poor young Scotchman who may be remembered as having sought and found help and patronage at the hands first of Mr. Dobell and afterwards of Lord Houghton. In some of his sonnets there are touches of sweet and sincere emotion; but the most remarkable points in his poor little book, and those which should be most memorable to other small poets of his kind (if at least the race of them were capable of profiting by any such lesson), are first the direct and seemingly unconscious transference of some of the best known lines or phrases from such obscure authors as Shakespeare and Wordsworth into the somewhat narrow and barren field of his own verse, and secondly the incredible candour of expression given in his correspondence to such flatulent ambition and such hysterical self-esteem as the author of 'Balder' must have

regarded, I should think, with a sorrowful sense of amusement. I may add that the poor boy's name was here cited with no desire to confer upon it any undeserved notoriety for better or for worse, and assuredly with no unkindlier feeling than pity for his poor little memory, but simply as conveying the most apt and the most flagrant as well as the most recent instance I happened to remember of the piteous and grievous harm done by false teaching and groundless encouragement to spirits not strong enough to know their own weakness. It was a kindly but uncritical reference in Mr. Arnold's kindly but uncritical essay on Maurice de Guérin—an essay of which I have said a few words further on—that upon this occasion for once recalled the name to my mind, and supplied me with the illustration required.

2. Among these the stanzas on the advent of Christianity, of 'the Mother with the Child,' and their enduring life while only faith in them endured, recall the like passage, more thoughtful and fruitful still, in that wise and noble poem, Mr. W. B. Scott's 'Year of the World'; a poem to whose great qualities and affluent beauties of letter and of spirit the requisite and certain justice of time remains hitherto a debt unpaid. Its author must divide with Mr. Arnold the palm of intellectual or philosophic poetry, the highest achieved in England since Wordsworth, and in many things of moment higher than his.

3. I am here reminded to ask in passing how Mr. Arnold, who says of Gray that he never used the popular metre of his century, came to forget his admirable fragment of a didactic poem in the ten-syllable couplet; and tempted, while on this ground, to appeal against the judgment which ranks him as a poet above Collins, the man of all his age, it seems to me, who had most in him of the pure and high and durable spirit of poetry. The overture of his 'Ode to Liberty' is worthy of Coleridge or Shelley; Gray's best ode by its side is somewhat hard and thin.

HENRY JAMES
"Matthew Arnold" (1884)
Literary Reviews and Essays, ed. Albert Mordell
1957, pp. 341–53

It seems perhaps hardly fair that while Matthew Arnold is in America and exposed to the extremity of public attention in that country, a native of the United States should take up the tale in an English magazine and let him feel the force of American observation from the rear as well as from the front. But, on the other hand, what better occasion could there be for a transatlantic admirer of the distinguished critic to speak his mind, without considering too much the place or the vehicle, than this interesting moment of Mr. Arnold's visit to the great country of the Philistines? I know nothing, as I write these lines, of the fruits of this excursion; we have heard little, as yet, of Mr. Arnold's impressions of the United States, or of the impression made upon their inhabitants by Mr. Arnold. But I would much rather not wait for information on these points: the elements of the subject are already sufficiently rich, and I prefer to make my few remarks in independence of such knowledge. A personal acquaintance with American life may have offered to the author of *Culture and Anarchy* a confirmation strong of his worst preconceptions; it may, on the other hand, have been attended with all sorts of pleasant surprises. In either event it will have been a satisfaction to one of his American readers (at least) to put on record a sentiment unaffected by the amount of material he may have gathered on transatlantic shores for the most successful satirical work of these last years. Nothing could be more delightful than the news that Mr. Arnold has been gratified by what he has seen in the western world; but I am not sure that it would not be even more welcome to know that he has been disappointed—for such disappointments, even in a mind so little irritable as his, are inspiring, and any record he should make of them would have a high value.

Neither of these consequences, however, would alter the fact that to an American in England, and indeed to any stranger, the author of the *Essays in Criticism*, of *Friendship's Garland*, of *Culture and Anarchy*, of the verses on Heine's grave, and of innumerable other delightful pages, speaks more directly than any other contemporary English writer, says more of these things which make him the visitor's intellectual companion, becomes in a singular way nearer and dearer. It is for this reason that it is always in order for such a visitor to join in a commemoration of the charming critic. He discharges an office so valuable, a function so delicate, he interprets, explains, illuminates so many of the obscure problems presented by English life to the gaze of the alien; he woos and wins to comprehension, to sympathy, to admiration, this imperfectly initiated, this often slightly bewildered observer; he meets him half way, he appears to understand his feelings, he conducts him to a point of view as gracefully as a master of ceremonies would conduct him to a chair. It is being met half way that the German, the Frenchman, the American appreciates so highly, when he approaches the great spectacle of English life; it is one of the greatest luxuries the foreign inquirer can enjoy. To such a mind as his, projected from a distance, out of a set of circumstances so different, the striking, the discouraging, I may even say the exasperating thing in this revelation, is the unconsciousness of the people concerned in it, their serenity, their indifference, their tacit assumption that their form of life is the normal one. This may very well be, of course, but the stranger wants a proof of some kind. (The English, in foreign lands, I may say in parenthesis, receive a similar impression; but the English are not irritated—not irritable—like the transplanted foreigner.) This unconsciousness makes a huge blank surface, a mighty national wall, against which the perceptive, the critical effort of the presumptuous stranger wastes itself, until, after a little, he espies in the measureless spaces, a little aperture, a window which is suddenly thrown open, and at which a friendly and intelligent face is presented, the harbinger of a voice of greeting. With this agreeable apparition he communes—the voice is delightful, it has a hundred tones and modulations; and as he stands there the great dead screen seems to vibrate and grow transparent. In other words it is the fact that Mr. Arnold is, of all his countrymen, the most conscious of the national idiosyncrasies that endears him to the soul of the stranger. I may be doing him a poor service among his own people in saying this, I may be sacrificing him too much to my theory of the foreigner and his longing for sympathy. A man may very well not thank you for letting it be known that you have found him detached from the ranks of his compatriots. It would perhaps be discreet on the part of the Frenchman or the American not to say too loudly that to his sense Matthew Arnold is, among the English writers of our day, the least of a matter-of-course Englishman—the pair of eyes to which the English world rounds itself most naturally as a fact among many facts. This, however, is after all unnecessary; for what is so agreeable in his composition is that he is *en fin de compte* (as the foreigner might say) English of the English. Few writers have given such proof of this; few writers have had such opportunity to do so; for few writers have English affairs, the English character, the future, the development, the happiness, of England, been matters of such constant and explicit concern. It is not in the United States that Mr. Arnold will have struck people as not being a devoted child of the mother-country. He has assimilated

certain continental ways of looking at things, his style has a kind of European accent, but he is full of English piety and English good-humour (in addition to an urbanity still more personal), and his spirit, in a word, is anchored in the deeps of the English past.

He is both a poet and a critic, but it is perhaps, primarily, because he is a representative of the critical spirit—apart from the accident of his having practised upon the maternal breast, as it were—that the sojourner, the spectator, has a kindness for the author of so many happy formulas, the propagator of so many capital instances. He, too, is necessarily critical, whatever his ultimate conclusion of reconciliation, and he takes courage and confidence from the sight of this brilliant writer, who knowing English life so much better than he can ever hope to do, is yet struck with so many of the same peculiarities, and makes so many of the same reflections. It is not the success of the critical effort at large that is most striking to-day to the attentive outsider; it is not the flexibility of English taste, the sureness of English judgment, the faculty of reproducing in their integrity the impressions made by works of art and literature, that most fixes the attention of those who look to see what the English mind is about. It may appear odd that an American should make this remark, proceeding as he does from a country in which high discernment in such matters has as yet only made a beginning. Superior criticism, in the United States, is at present not written; it is, like a great many superior things, only spoken; therefore I know not why a native of that country should take note of the desuetude of this sort of accomplishment in England, unless it be that in England he naturally expects great things. He is struck with the immense number of reviews that are published, with the number of vehicles for publicity, for discussion. But with the lightness of the English touch in handling literary and artistic questions he is not so much struck, nor with a corresponding interest in the manner, the meaning, the quality, of an artistic effort: corrupted (I should add) as he perhaps may be by communications still more foreign than those he has enjoyed on the other side of the Atlantic, and a good deal more forcible. For I am afraid that what I am coming to in saying that Matthew Arnold, as an English writer, is dear to the soul of the outsider, is the fact, (not equally visible, doubtless, to all judges) that he reminds the particular outsider who writes these lines (and who feels at moments that he has so little claim to the title), just the least bit of the great Sainte-Beuve. Many people do not care for Sainte-Beuve; they hold that his method was unscientific, his temper treacherous, his style tiresome, and that his subjects were too often uninteresting. But those who do care for him care for him deeply, and cultivate the belief, and the hope, that they shall never weary of him; so that as it is obviously only my limited personal sentiment that (with this little play of talk about the outsider in general) I venture to express, I may confess that the measure of my enjoyment of a critic is the degree to which he resembles Sainte-Beuve. This resemblance exists in Matthew Arnold, with many disparities and differences; not only does he always speak of the author of *Causeries* with esteem and admiration, but he strikes the lover of Sainte-Beuve as having really taken lessons from him, as possessing a part of his great quality—closeness of contact to his subject. I do not in the least mean by this that Mr. Arnold is an imitator, that he is a reflection, pale or intense, of another genius. He has a genius, a quality, all his own, and he has in some respects a largeness of horizon which Sainte-Beuve never reached. The horizon of Sainte-Beuve was French, and we know what infinite blue distances the French see there; but that of Matthew Arnold, as I have hinted, is European, more than

European, inasmuch as it includes America. It ought to be enough for an American that Sainte-Beuve had no ideas at all about America; whereas Mr. Arnold has a great many, which he is engaged at the moment at which I write, in collating with the reality. Nevertheless, Sainte-Beuve, too, on his side, had his larger movement; he had of course his larger activity, which indeed it will appear to many that Mr. Arnold might have emulated if it had not been for a certain amount of misdirected effort. There is one side on which many readers will never altogether do justice to Matthew Arnold, the side on which we see him as the author of *St. Paul and Protestantism*, and even of many portions of *Literature and Dogma*. They will never cease to regret that he should have spent so much time and ingenuity in discussing the differences—several of which, after all, are so special, so arbitrary—between Dissenters and Anglicans, should not rather have given these earnest hours to the interpretation of literature. There is something dry and dusty in the atmosphere of such discussions, which accords ill with the fresh tone of the man of letters, the artist. It must be added that in Mr. Arnold's case they are connected with something very important, his interest in religious ideas, his constant, characteristic sense of the reality of religion.

The union of this element with the other parts of his mind, his love of literature, of perfect expression, his interest in life at large, constitutes perhaps the originality of his character as a critic, and it certainly (to my sense) gives him that seriousness in which he has occasionally been asserted to be wanting. Nothing can exceed the taste, the temperance, with which he handles religious questions, and at the same time nothing can exceed the impression he gives of really caring for them. To his mind the religious life of humanity is the most important thing in the spectacle humanity offers us, and he holds a due perception of this fact is (in connection with other lights) the measure of the acuteness of a critic, the wisdom of a poet. He says in his essay on Marcus Aurelius an admirable thing—"The paramount virtue of religion is that it has *lighted up* morality;" and such a phrase as that shows the extent to which he feels what he speaks of. To say that this feeling, taken in combination with his love of letters, of beauty, of all liberal things, constitutes an originality is not going too far, for the religious sentiment does not always render the service of opening the mind to human life at large. Ernest Renan, in France, is, as every one knows, the great and brilliant representative of such a union; he has treated religion as he might have treated one of the fine arts. Of him it may even be said, that though he has never spoken of it but as the sovereign thing in life, yet there is in him, as an interpreter of the conscience of man, a certain dandyism, a slight fatuity, of worldly culture, of which Mr. Arnold too has been accused, but from which (with the smaller assurance of an Englishman in such matters) he is much more exempt. Mr. Arnold touches M. Renan on one side, as he touches Sainte-Beuve on the other (I make this double *rapprochement* because he has been spoken of more than once as the most Gallicised of English writers); and if he has gone less into the details of literature than the one, he has gone more than the other into the application of religion to questions of life. He has applied it to the current problems of English society. He has endeavoured to light up with it, to use his own phrase, some of the duskiest and most colourless of these. He has cultivated urbanity almost as successfully as M. Renan, and he has cultivated reality rather more. As I have spoken of the reader who has been a stranger in England feeling that Mr. Arnold meets him half way, and yet of our author being at bottom English of the English, I may add here, in confirmation of this, that his theological pertinacity, as one

may call it, his constant implication of the nearness of religion, his use of the Scriptures, his love of biblical phraseology, are all so many deeply English notes. He has all the taste for theology which characterises our race when our race is left to its own devices; he evidently has read an immense number of sermons. He is impregnated with the associations of Protestantism, saturated with the Bible, and though he has little love for the Puritans, no Puritan of them all was ever more ready on all occasions with a text either from the Old Testament or from the New. The appreciative stranger (whom I go on imagining) has to remind himself of the force of these associations of Protestantism in order to explain Mr. Arnold's fondness for certain quotations which doubtless need the fragrance that experience and memory may happen to give them to reveal their full charm. Nothing could be more English, more Anglican, for instance, than our author's enjoyment of sundry phrases of Bishop Wilson—phrases which to the uninitiated eye are often a little pale. This does not take from the fact that Mr. Arnold has a real genius for quotation. His pages are full, not only of his own good things, but of those of every one else. More than any critic of the day he gives, from point to point, an example of what he means. The felicity of his illustrations is extreme; even if he sometimes makes them go a little further than they would and sees in them a little more than is visible to the average reader. Of course, in his frequent reference to the Bible, what is free and happy and personal to himself is the use he makes of it.

If it were the purpose of these few pages to give in the smallest degree a history of Mr. Arnold's literary career, I ought promptly to have spoken of his Poems—I ought to enumerate his works in their order. It was by his Poems that I first knew and admired him, and many such readers—early or late admirers—will have kept them in a very safe corner of memory. As a poet, Matthew Arnold is really singular; he takes his place among the most fortunate writers of our day who have expressed themselves in verse, but his place is somewhat apart. He has an imagination of his own, but he is less complete, less inevitable, as he says in his essay on Wordsworth that that poet said of Goethe, than the others. His form at moments is less rich than it might be, and the Wordsworthian example may perhaps be accused here and there of having sterilized him. But this limited, just a little precarious, character of his inspiration adds to his value for people who like the quality of rareness in their pleasures, like sometimes to perceive just a little the effort of the poet, like to hear him take breath. It reminds them of the awkwardness of line which we see in certain charming painters of early schools (not that Mr. Arnold is early!) and which seems a condition of their grace and a sign of their freshness. Splendour, music, passion, breadth of movement and rhythm we find in him in no great abundance; what we do find is high distinction of feeling (to use his own word), a temperance, a kind of modesty of expression, which is at the same time an artistic resource—the complexion of his work; and a remarkable faculty for touching the chords which connect our feelings with the things that others have done and spoken. In other words, though there is in Mr. Arnold's poems a constant reference to nature, or to Wordsworth, which is almost the same thing, there is even a more implicit reference to civilisation, literature, and the intellectual experience of man. He is the poet of the man of culture, that accomplished being whom he long ago held up for our consideration. Above all he is the poet of his age, of the moment in which we live, of our "modernity," as the new school of criticism in France gives us perhaps license to say. When he speaks of the past, it is with the knowledge which only our own time has of it. With its cultivated simplicity, its aversion to cheap ornament, its slight abuse of meagreness for distinction's sake, his verse has a kind of minor magic and always goes to the point—the particular ache, or regret, or conjecture, to which poetry is supposed to address itself. It rests the mind, after a good deal of the other poetical work of the day—it rests the mind, and I think I may add that it nourishes it.

It was, as every one remembers, in the essay on "The Function of Criticism at the Present Time," and that on "The Literary Influence of Academies," that, in 1864, Mr. Arnold first appeared in the character in which since then he has won so much fame, and which he may really be said to have invented; that of the *general* critic, the commentator of English life, the observer and expostulator, the pleader with the Dissenters, the genial satirist. His manner, since this light, sweet prelude, has acquired much amplitude and confidence; but the suggestiveness, the delightful temper were there from the first. Those who have been enjoying Mr. Arnold these twenty years will remember how fresh and desirable his voice sounded at that moment; if since then the freshness has faded a little we must bear in mind that it is through him and through him only that we have grown familiar with certain ideas and terms which now form part of the common stock of allusion. When he began his critical career there were various things that needed immensely to be said and that no one appeared sufficiently detached, sufficiently independent and impartial to say. Mr. Arnold attempted to say them, and succeeded—so far as the saying goes—in a manner that left nothing to be desired. There is, of course, another measure of success in regard to such an attempt—the question of how far the critic has had an influence, produced an effect—how far he has acted upon the life, the feelings, the conduct of his audience. The effect of Mr. Arnold's writings is of course difficult to gauge; but it seems evident that the thoughts and judgments of Englishmen about a good many matters have been quickened and coloured by them. All criticism is better, lighter, more sympathetic, more informed, in consequence of certain things he has said. He has perceived and felt so many shy, disinterested truths that belonged to the office, to the limited specialty, of no one else; he has made them his care, made them his province and responsibility. This flattering unction Mr. Arnold may, I think, lay to his soul—that with all his lightness of form, with a certain jauntiness and irresponsibility of which he has been accused—as if he affected a candour and simplicity almost more than human—he has added to the interest of life, to the charm of knowledge, for a great many of those plain people among whom he so gracefully counts himself. As we know, in the number of the expressive phrases to which he has given circulation, none has had a wider currency than his application of Swift's phrase about sweetness and light. Assuredly it may be said that that note has reverberated, that it has done something—in the realm of discussion—towards making civility the fashion and facilitating the exchange of ideas. They appear to have become more accessible—they bristle rather less with mutual suspicion. Above all, the atmosphere has gained in clearness in the great middle region in which Philistinism is supposed to abide. Our author has hung it about—the grey confusion—with a multitude of little coloured lanterns, which not only have a charming, a really festive effect, but which also help the earnest explorer to find his way. It was in the volume entitled *Culture and Anarchy*, published in 1869, and perhaps his most ingenious and suggestive production, that he offered his most celebrated definitions, and exposed himself most to the penalties which the general critic is foredoomed to encounter. In some of his later books he has called down the

displeasure of the Dissenters, but in the extremely witty volume to which I allude he made it a matter of honour with society at large to retaliate. But it has been Mr. Arnold's good fortune from the first that he has been fed and stimulated by criticism; his antagonist, in the phrase that he is fond of quoting from Burke, has ever been his helper. Rejoinder and refutation have always furnished him with texts and examples and offered a spring-board, as it were, to his polemical agility. He has had the further advantage, that though in his considerate, bantering way a disputant, having constantly to defend himself, as is inevitable for a man who frequently attacks, he has never lost his good humour, never shown a touch of the *odium theologicum*, nor ceased to play fair. This incorrigible fondness for his joke doubtless has had something to do with the reproach sometimes made him that he is not serious, that he does not really care for the causes for which he pleads, that he is a talker, an artist even, a charming humorist, but not a philosopher, nor a reformer, nor a teacher. He has been charged with having no practical advice to offer. To these allegations he would perhaps plead guilty, for he has never pretended to have a body of doctrine nor to approach the public with an infallible nostrum. He has been the plain man that we have alluded to, he has been only a skirmisher and a suggester. It is certain that a good many fallacies and prejudices are limping about with one of his light darts still sticking to them. For myself, when I have heard it remarked that he is not practical, the answer has seemed to be that there is surely nothing more practical than to combine that degree of wit with that degree of good feeling, and that degree of reason with both of them. It is quite enough to the point to be one of the two or three best English prose-writers of one's day. There is nothing more practical, in short, than, if one praises culture and desires to forward it, to speak in the tone and with the spirit and impartiality of culture. The Dissenters, I believe, hold that Mr. Arnold has not been impartial, accuse him of misrepresenting them, of making the absurd proposal that they shall come over to the Church merely because from the church-window, as it were, their chapels and conventicles interfere with the view. I do not pretend to judge this matter, or even to have followed closely enough to give an account of them the windings of that controversial episode, of which the atmosphere, it must be confessed, has at moments been more darkened than brightened with Biblical references and which occupies the middle years of the author's literary career. It is closed, and well closed, and Mr. Arnold has returned to literature and to studies which lie outside the controversial shadow. It is sufficient that, inveterate satirist as he is, it is impossible to read a page of him without feeling that his satire is liberal and human. The much abused name of culture rings rather false in our ears, and the fear of seeming priggish checks it as it rises to our lips. The name matters little, however, for the idea is excellent, and the thing is still better. I shall not go so far as to say of Mr. Arnold that he invented it; but he made it more definite than it had been before—he vivified and lighted it up. We like today to see principles and convictions embodied in persons, represented by a certain literary or political face. There are so many abroad, all appealing to us and pressing towards us, that these salient incarnations help us to discriminate and save us much confusion. It is Mr. Arnold, therefore, that we think of when we figure to ourselves the best knowledge of what is being done in the world, the best appreciation of literature and life. It is in America especially that he will have had the responsibility of appearing as the cultivated man—it is in this capacity that he will have been attentively listened to. The curiosity with regard to culture is extreme in that country; if there is in some quarters a considerable uncertainty as to what it may consist of, there is everywhere a great wish to get hold of it, at least on trial. I will not say that Mr. Arnold's tact has absolutely never failed him. There is a certain want of it, for instance (the instance is small), in his quoting, in *Culture and Anarchy*, M. Renan's opinion on the tone of life in America, in support of his own contention that Philistinism was predominant there. This is a kind of authority that (in such a case) almost discredits the argument—M. Renan being constitutionally, and as it were officially, incapable of figuring to himself the aspect of society in the United States. In like manner Mr. Arnold may now and then have appeared to satisfy himself with a definition not quite perfect, as when he is content to describe poetry by saying that it is a criticism of life. That surely expresses but a portion of what poetry contains—it leaves unsaid much of the essence of the matter. Literature in general is a criticism of life—prose is a criticism of life. But poetry is a criticism of life in conditions so peculiar that they are the sign by which we know poetry. Lastly, I may venture to say that our author strikes me as having, especially in his later writings, pushed to an excess some of the idiosyncracies of his delightful style—his fondness for repetition, for ringing the changes on his text, his formula—a tendency in consequence of which his expression becomes at moments slightly wordy and fatiguing. This tendency, to give an example, is visible, I think, in the essay which serves as an introduction to Mr. Ward's collection of the English poets, and in that on Wordsworth, contained in the volume of Mr. Arnold's own selections from him. The defect, however, I should add, is nothing but an exaggeration of one of the author's best qualities—his ardent love of clearness, his patient persuasiveness. These are minor blemishes, and I allude to them mainly, I confess, because I fear I may have appeared to praise too grossly. Yet I have wished to praise, to express the high appreciation of all those who in England and America have in any degree attempted to care for literature. They owe Matthew Arnold a debt of gratitude for his admirable example, for having placed the standard of successful expression, of literary feeling and good manners, so high. They never tire of him—they read him again and again. They think the wit and humour of *Friendship's Garland* the most delicate possible, the luminosity of *Culture and Anarchy* almost dazzling, the eloquence of such a paper as the article on Lord Falkland in the *Mixed Essays* irresistible. They find him, in a word, more than any one else, the happily-proportioned, the truly distinguished man of letters. When there is a question of his efficacy, his influence, it seems to me enough to ask one's self what we should have done without him, to think how much we should have missed him, and how he has salted and seasoned our public conversation. In his absence the whole tone of discussion would have seemed more stupid, more literal. Without his irony to play over its surface, to clip it here and there of its occasional fustiness, the life of our Anglo-Saxon race would present a much greater appearance of insensibility.

SIR LESLIE STEPHEN
"Matthew Arnold" (1893)[1]
Studies of a Biographer
1899, Volume 2, pp. 76–122

When your Principal asked me to select a topic for a lecture, I replied, in a moment of weakness, that I would speak of Matthew Arnold. The choice was partly

suggested by an observation made on a recent visit to the United States. It struck me that Arnold's merits were even more fully recognised there than in his own country; though I hope that here, too, they do not lack appreciation. American opinion is probably not infallible. Still, fame on the other side of the Atlantic establishes a certain presumption of excellence. It proves that a man's influence was not created by, and may sometimes indicate that it has been partly obscured by, our local prejudices. At any rate, the observation suggested some thoughts, which, it occurred to me, might be worth submitting to an English audience. Well, I have been ever since repenting my decision. The reasons against my enterprise are indeed so strong that I am now almost afraid to mention them. In the first place, I knew Arnold personally, though I cannot boast of having known him so intimately as to be provided with reminiscences. At one of my meetings with him, indeed, I do remember a remark which was made, and which struck me at the moment as singularly happy. Unfortunately, it was a remark made by me and not by him. Nothing, therefore, should induce me to report it, although, if you attend to what I am about to say, you will perhaps hear it, and, I hope, recognise it by this description. But, though our acquaintance was not so close as I could have wished, it left me with a singularly strong impression of Arnold's personal charm. Though some objects of my worship were to him mere wooden idols; though I once satisfactorily confuted him in an article, now happily forgotten by myself and everybody else; though I was once even his Editor, and forced in that capacity to decline certain articles, on grounds, of course, quite apart from literary merit; yet he was always not only courteous but cordial, and, I may almost say, affectionate in manner. He had that obvious sweetness of nature, which it is impossible not to recognise and not to love. Though in controversy he took and gave many shrewd blows, he always received them with a courtesy, indicative not of mere policy or literary tact, but of dislike to inflicting pain and of incapacity for hating any tolerably decent antagonist in flesh and blood. He was on excellent terms with the classes whose foibles he ridiculed most unsparingly, and even his own foibles were attractive. He had his vanity; but vanity is a quality to which moralists have never done justice. As distinguished from conceit, from a sullen conviction of your own superiority, it often implies a craving for sympathy and a confidence in the sincerity of your fellows, which is in the main, as his certainly was, an amiable and attractive characteristic. If it just savoured of intellectual coxcombry, it was redeemed by a simplicity and social amenity which showed that his nature had resisted the ossifying process which makes most of us commonplace and prosaic in later life. Now, I dislike criticism of men whose personal acquaintance I have valued. 'I love Robertson,' said Johnson, 'and I won't talk of his books.' I feel the same, in a rather different sense, about Arnold. It is difficult to reconcile the claims of honest criticism and personal esteem. But, besides this, I have a difficulty to which I must refer at the risk of giving an impression of mock-modesty. I feel, that is, the great difficulty of speaking to purpose of a man whose intellectual type was so different from my own. Had Arnold been called upon to pronounce judgment upon me, he must, however reluctantly, have set me down as a Philistine. It is a word which I dislike; but I cannot deny that, in his phraseology, it would be indisputably appropriate. Arnold was a typical Oxford man in the days when Oxford was stirred by the 'movement' of which it is supposed to be proper to speak respectfully. I was taught in my childhood to regard 'Puseyism' and 'Tractarianism' with a vague shuddering horror; and, as I grew older, I am afraid that the horror only became milder as it was mixed with something too like contempt. The young leader whose opinions I assimilated in college days belonged to a different and more prosaic school. They scorned sentimentalism and æsthetic revivals, and, if they took any interest in speculative matters, read John Stuart Mill, and were sound Utilitarians and orthodox Political Economists. A hard-headed senior wrangler is in his own conceit a superior being to a flighty double first-class man. But perhaps his solid conviction that he was in the right path made him rather unfitted to judge of the sister University. He thought her impulsive, ill-balanced, too easily hurried into the pursuit of all kinds of theological, philosophical, and literary chimeras; and therefore was unjust to her substantial merits and even to the intellectual impulse which, with all its vagaries, was yet better than stagnation. After all, I am probably only trying to hint at the fundamental difference between the poetic and the prosaic mind. We—for I may perhaps assume that some of you belong, like me, to the prosaic faction—feel, when dealing with such a man as Arnold, at a loss. He has intuitions where we have only calculations; he can strike out vivid pictures where we try laboriously to construct diagrams; he shows at once a type where our rough statistical and analytical tables fail to reveal more than a few tangible facts; he perceives the spirit and finer essence of an idea where it seems to slip through our coarser fingers, leaving only a residuum of sophistical paradox. In the long-run, the prosaic weigher and measurer has one advantage: he is generally in the right as far as he goes. His tests may be coarser, but they are more decisive and less dependent upon his own fancies; but, when he tries to understand his rival, to explain how at a bound the intuitive perception has reached conclusions after which he can only hobble on limping feet, he is apt to make a bungle of it: to despise the power in which he is so deficient: and probably to suggest unreasonable doubts as to its reality and value.

Here is, I feel, my real weakness in speaking of Arnold; for I may certainly say at once that Arnold, whatever else he was, was a genuine poet. I do not dispute the general opinion of the day that there were only two poets of the first rank in his generation. Arnold must, on the whole, take a lower place than Tennyson and Browning. But, though I cannot avoid falling into the method of comparison, I do not accept with satisfaction the apparently implied doctrine that poets can be satisfactorily arranged in order of merit. We cannot give so many marks for style and so many for pathos or descriptive power. It is best to look at each poet by himself. We need only distinguish between the sham and the genuine article; and my own method of distinguishing is a simple one. I believe in poetry which learns itself by heart. There are poems which dominate and haunt one; which, once admitted, sting and cling to one; the tune of which comes up and runs in one's head at odd moments; and which suddenly revive, after years of forgetfulness, as vigorous and lively as ever. Such poetry, as Wordsworth told Arnold, has the characteristic of being 'inevitable,'—a phrase which has become something of a nuisance, but cannot be always avoided. You feel that the thing had to be said just as it was said; and that, once so said, nothing said by anybody else will just hit the same mark. Of course, this test, being personal, is not conclusive. I remember, I am ashamed to say it, some poetry which I know to be trash, merely, I suppose, because it jingles pleasantly; and I forget a great deal which I know to be good because I can perceive that it dominates other people; but then I do my best to keep my tastes on such occasions to myself. Now, Matthew Arnold's poetry has, in an eminent degree, the quality—if not of inevitable-

ness—of adhesiveness. I don't know whether my experience is peculiar; but I have never got out of my head, since I read it, the little poem about the Neckan, who sings his plaintive song on the Baltic headlands, or the charming verses—the last, I fancy, which he wrote—about the dachshund Geist, whose grave at Cobham should be a goal for all poetic pilgrims. In certain of his more laboured poems, I am conscious rather that I ought to admire than that I do admire. To my brutal mind, the recollection of the classical models is a source of annoyance, as suggesting that the scholar is in danger of suppressing the man. But there are other poems which I love, if not because of, at any rate in spite of, the classical propensities which they reveal. 'Sohrab and Rustum' is to me among the most delightful of modern poems, though in it Arnold indulges, perhaps more than enough, in the long-tailed Homeric metaphor, which drags in upon principle all the points on which the thing compared does not resemble the object. I can always read 'Tristram and Iseult,' and the 'Church of Brou' and *Empedocles on Etna*; and know that they leave behind them a sense of sweetness and delicacy and exquisite feeling, if they do not present those vivid phrases into which the very greatest men—the Dantes or Shakespeares—can infuse their very life-blood. In his *Essays upon Celtic Literature*—perhaps the most delightful of his books—Arnold says that English poetry derived three things mainly from Celtic sources: its turn for style, its turn for melancholy, and its turn for natural magic. The distinction is indicated with admirable fineness; and my perceptions are not quite fine enough to follow it. Keats, Arnold is able to perceive, is looking at nature like a Greek when he asks

> What little town by river or sea-shore
> Or mountain-built with peaceful citadel,
> Is emptied of its folk, this pious morn?

but becomes Celtic when he speaks of

> Magic casements, opening on the foam
> Of perilous seas, in faery lands forlorn!

Possibly: but I am shy of endeavouring to discriminate these exquisite essences, and I will not attempt to say whether it is the power of style or of magic, whether it is the presence of a Greek or a Celtic mode of looking at nature, that charms us in what is perhaps Arnold's masterpiece, the 'Scholar Gipsy.' Whether the exquisite concluding stanzas, for example, be an instance of the Greek or of the Celtic element, I know not; but I am quite sure that they are delightful. At his best Arnold reaches a felicity of style in which Tennyson alone, of all our modern poets, if Tennyson himself, was his superior. The comparison, much as I dislike comparisons, may suggest at least the question why Arnold's popularity is still, as I think it is, below his deserts. One answer is obvious. I cannot doubt that Arnold fully appreciated the greatest of contemporary artists. But certain references to Tennyson in his essays are significant. Arnold incidentally quotes Tennyson's 'great, broad-shouldered, genial Englishman,' by way of illustrating his favourite proposition that this broad-shouldered personage was a 'barbarian,' and conspicuous for insensibility to ideas. He refers with a certain scorn to the self-complacency implied in the phrase about freedom broadening slowly down from precedent to precedent. Though Arnold does not criticise the poetry, he evidently felt—what, to say the truth, I think must be admitted—that Tennyson interpreted the average—shall I say, the Philistine or the commonplace English sentiment?—a little too faithfully; but it may be inferred—though Arnold does not draw the inference—that the extraordinary popularity of Tennyson was partly owing to the fact that he could express what occurred to everybody in language that could be approached by nobody. Arnold, on the contrary, is, in all his poems, writing for the cultivated, and even for a small class of cultivated people. The ideas which he expresses are not only such as do not commend themselves, but sometimes such as are rather annoying, to the average reader. The sentiments peculiar to a narrow, however refined, class are obviously so far less favourable to poetical treatment. Arnold seems to admit this in his occasional employment of that rhymeless metre which corresponds to the borderland between prose and poetry. A characteristic piece is that upon 'Heine's Grave.' We all remember the description of England, the 'Weary Titan,' who with deaf

> Ears, and labour-dimm'd eyes,
> Regarding neither to right
> Nor left, goes passively by,
> Staggering on to her goal, etc.

and a phrase which tells us how the spirit of the world, beholding men's absurdity, let a sardonic smile

> For one short moment, wander o'er his lips.
> *That smile was Heine!*

That, of course, is rather epigram than poetry. It matters, indeed, very little whether we call it by one name or another, so long as we allow it to be effective. But writing of this kind, call it poetry or prose, or a hybrid genus, in which the critic shows through the poet, is not likely to suit the popular mind. It presupposes a whole set of reflections which are the property of a special class. And the same may be said of the particular mood which is specially characteristic of Arnold. In the 'Scholar Gipsy' he laments 'the strange disease of modern life,'

> With its sick hurry, its divided aims;

speaks of us 'light half-believers of our casual creeds'; tells how the wisest of us takes dejectedly 'his seat upon the intellectual throne,' and lays bare his sad experience of wretched days, and 'all his hourly varied anodynes'; while we, who are not the wisest, can only pine, wish that the long, unhappy dream would end, and keep as our only friend 'sad patience, too near neighbour to despair.' This note jars upon some people, who prefer, perhaps, the mild resignation of the 'Christian Year.' I fail of sympathy for the opposite reason. I cannot affect to share Arnold's discomfort. I have never been able—doubtless it is a defect—to sympathise with the Obermanns and Amiels whom Arnold admired; excellent but surely effeminate persons, who taste of the fruit of the Tree of Knowledge, and finding the taste bitter, go on making wry faces over it all their lives; and, admitting with one party that the old creeds are doomed, assert with the other that all beauty must die with them. The universe is open to a great many criticisms; there is plenty of cause for tears and for melancholy; and great poets in all ages have, because they were great poets, given utterance to the sorrows of their race. But I don't feel disposed to grumble at the abundance of interesting topics or the advance of scientific knowledge, because some inconveniences result from both. I say all this simply as explaining why the vulgar—including myself—fail to appreciate these musical moans over spilt milk, which represent rather a particular eddy in an intellectual revolution than the deeper and more permanent emotions of human nature. But I do not mean to depreciate Arnold's power; only to suggest reasons for the want of a wider recognition. The 'Scholar Gipsy,' for example, expresses in certain passages sentiment which I must call morbid, but for all that, even for me, it remains one of the most exquisite poems in the language.

This leads me to another point. In his essay upon Joubert

(*Essays in Criticism*, p. 249), Arnold spoke of literature as a 'criticism of life.' Elsewhere (Introduction to Mr. H. Ward's *Collection of Poems*) he gave the same account of poetry. But to poetry, he says in the same breath, we shall have to turn for consolation, and it will replace much of 'what now passes with us for religion and philosophy.' If so, he obviously cannot mean that poetry and criticism are really the same thing. The phrase 'criticism of life' gave great offence, and was much ridiculed by some writers, who were apparently unable to distinguish between an epigram and a philosophical dogma. To them, indeed, Arnold's whole position was naturally abhorrent. For it is not uncommon now to hear denunciations of all attempts to connect art with morality and philosophy. It is wicked, we are told, for a poet, or a novelist, or a painter, to take any moral consideration into account; and therefore to talk of poetry as destined to do for us much that philosophy and religion used to do is, of course, manifestly absurd. I will not argue the point at length, being content to observe that the cry seems to me oddly superfluous. Of all the dangers to which modern novelists, for example, are exposed, that against which they are least required to guard is the danger of being too philosophical. They really may feel at their ease; nor do I think that they need feel much alarmed as to the risk of being too moral. Meanwhile, it is my belief that nobody is the better in any department of life or literature for being a fool or a brute: and least of all in poetry. I cannot think that a man is disqualified for poetry either by thinking more deeply than others or by having a keener perception of (I hope I may join the two words) moral beauty. A perception of what it is that makes a hero or saint is, I fancy, as necessary to a great literary artist as a perception of what it is that constitutes physical beauty to a painter. The whole doctrine, in short, seems to me to be a misstatement of the very undeniable and very ancient truth that it is a poet's business to present types, for example, and not to give bare psychological theory: not that he is the worse for being even a deep philosopher or a subtle logician; on the contrary, he is so far the better; but that he is the worse if he gives the abstract reasoning instead of incarnating his thought in concrete imagery. And so, when Arnold called poetry a criticism of life, he only meant to express what seems to me to be an undeniable truth. The Elgin marbles might, in his sense, be called a criticism of the physique of the sight-seers. To contrast their perfect forms and unapproachable grace with the knock-kneed, spindle-shanked, narrow-chested, round-shouldered product of London slums who passes before them, is to criticise the poor creature's defects of structure in the most effective way. In a similar sense, when a poet or a novelist presents us with a type, when Addison gives us a Roger de Coverley, or Goldsmith a Vicar of Wakefield, or Scott a Dandie Dinmont, or Thackeray a Colonel Newcome, or Dickens a Mr. Creakle (I chose this example of Dickens only because Arnold made use of it himself), they present us with ideal portraits which set off—more effectively than any deliberate analysis—the actual human beings known to us, who more or less represent similar classes. In his essay upon the 'Function of Criticism,' Arnold explained his lofty conception of the art, and showed why, in his sense of the word, it should be the main aim of all modern literature. 'Criticism,' he said, 'is the disinterested endeavour to learn and propagate the best that is known or thought in the world.' The difference between poetry and criticism is that one gives us the ideal and the other explains to us how it differs from the real. What is latent in the poet is made explicit in the critic. Arnold, himself, even when he turned to criticism, was primarily a poet. His judgments show greater skill in seizing characteristic aspects than in giving a logical analysis or a convincing proof. He goes by intuition, not by roundabout logical approaches. No recent English critic, I think, has approached him in the art of giving delicate portraits of literary leaders; he has spoken, for example, precisely the right word about Byron and Wordsworth. Many of us, who cannot rival him, may gain from Arnold's writings a higher conception of what will be our true function if we could discharge it. He did, I think, more than any man to impress upon his countrymen that the critic should not be a mere combatant in a series of faction fights, puffing friends, and saying to an enemy, 'This will never do.' The weak side, however, of the poetical criticism is its tendency to be 'subjective,' that is, to reflect too strongly the personal prejudices of the author. It must virtually consist in giving the impression made upon the critic; and, however delicate his perception and wide his sympathy, he will be scarcely human if his judgments are not affected by his personal equation. No one could be more alive to the danger than Arnold, and his most characteristic teaching turns upon the mode of avoiding it. There are times, no doubt, when he relies too confidently upon the fineness of his perception, and then obviously has a slight spasm of diffidence. I have noticed how, in his *Essays on Celtic Literature*, he uses the true poetical or intuitive method: he recognises the precise point at which Shakespeare or Keats passes from the Greek to the Celtic note; he trusts to the fineness of his ear, like a musician who can detect the slightest discord. And we feel perhaps that a man who can decide, for example, an ethnological question by such means, who can by simple inspiration determine which are the Celtic and which are the Teutonic and which are the Norman elements in English character, is going a little beyond his tether. Arnold obviously feels so too. In the same book he speaks most respectfully of the opposite or prosaic method. Zeuss, the great Celtic scholar, is praised because he uses a scientific test to determine the age of documents. This test is that in Welsh and Irish the letters p and t gradually changed into b or d (as if the Celts had caught a cold in their head); that *map* became *mab*, and *coet, coed*. This, says Arnold, is a verifiable and scientific test. When Arnold is himself trying to distinguish the Celtic element in Englishmen, he starts by remarking that a Frenchman would speak of German *bêtise*, but of English *gaucherie*: the German is *balourd*, and the Englishman *empêtré*; and the German *niais*, while the Englishman is *mélancolique*. We can hardly say that the difference of meaning between *balourd* and *empêtré* is as clear as the difference of sound between t and d: and Arnold is, perhaps, too much inclined to trust to his intuitions, as if they were equivalent to scientific and measurable statements. The same tendency shows itself in his curious delight in discovering catch-words, and repeating them sometimes to weariness. He uses such phrases as 'sweetness and light' with a certain air of laying down a genuine scientific distinction, as clear-cut and unequivocal as a chemist's analysis. He feels that he has thoroughly analysed English characteristics when he has classified his countrymen as 'Philistines, Barbarians, and the Populace.' To fix a certain aspect of things by an appropriate phrase is the process which corresponded with him to a scientific analysis. But may not this method merely lead to the substitution of one set of prejudices for another; the prejudices, say, of the fastidious don for the prejudices of the coarser tradesman? The Frenchman who calls the Englishman *empêtré* may be as narrow-minded as the Englishman who calls the Frenchman a frog-eater. Certainly, Arnold would reply. What we need is to make a stream of fresh thought play freely about our stock 'notions and habits.'[2] We have to get out of an unfruitful and mechanical routine. Or, as

he puts it in another way, his one qualification for teaching his countrymen is, he says, his belief in the 'primary needfulness of seeing things as they really are, and of the greater importance of ideas than of the machinery which exists for them.'[3] That is, we want, above all things, to get rid of prejudices in general, not of any special prejudice; to have our opinions constructed out of pure, impartial, unbiassed thought, free from all baser alloy of mephitic vapours. The mere self-willed assertion of our own fancies can never lift us to the higher point of view which would reveal our narrowness and ignorance. Hence the vast importance of 'culture': the one thing needful; which, again, in another view, is equivalent to a frank submission of ourselves to the Zeitgeist. The Zeitgeist, indeed, is an entity not quite easy to define. But it at least supposes that genuine philosophy and scientific thought is a reality; that there is a real difference between the scholar and the charlatan; that criticism in a wide sense has achieved some permanent and definite results; and that, although many antiquated prejudices still survive and dominate us, especially in England, and constitute the whole mental furniture of the Philistine, they are doomed to decay, and those who hold by them doomed to perish with them. To recognise, therefore, the deep, underlying currents of thought, to get outside of the narrow limits of the popular prejudice, to steep our minds in the best thought of the past, and to be open to the really great thoughts of the present, is the one salvation for the race and for reasonable men. The English people, he often said,[4] had entered the prison of Puritanism, and had the key turned upon their spirit for two centuries. To give them the key and to exhort them to use it was his great aim. Heine had called himself a 'brave soldier in the war of the liberation of humanity,' and Arnold took service in the same army. Only—and this was the doctrine upon which he laid emphasis—to fight effectually we must recognise the true leaders, those who really spoke with authority, and who were the true advanced guard in the march to the land of promise. Your individualist would only take off the fetters so as to allow a free fight among the prisoners. The prophet of culture alone can enable us to get free from the prison-house itself. His strong sense of the mischief of literary anarchy appeared in his once famous essay upon the French Academy. Though he guarded himself against recommending an English institution, he was fascinated by the charm of an acknowledged tribunal of good taste, an outward and visible symbol of right reason, of a body which, by its moral authority, should restrain men from those excesses and faults of taste into which even the greatest Englishmen are apt to fall, and which should keep distinctly before our minds the conviction that we only obtain worthy intellectual liberty when we recognise the necessity of subordination to the highest minds. To imbibe the teaching of the Zeitgeist, to know what is the true living thought of the age and who are its great men, is to accept a higher rule, and not merely (as he put it) to exchange the errors of Miall for the errors of Mill: to become a vulgar Freethinker instead of a vulgar Dissenter.

The doctrine of culture is, of course, in some sense the common property of all cultivated men. Carlyle, like Arnold, wished for an exit from Houndsditch and a relinquishment of Hebrew old clothes. But Arnold detested Carlyle's Puritanism, and was alienated by his sulphurous and volcanic explosiveness. Mill hated the tyranny of the majority, and, of course, rejected the Puritan theology. But Mill was a Benthamite, and Benthamism was the natural doctrine of the Philistine. Mill's theories would lead, though in spite of himself, to that consummation which Arnold most dreaded—the general dominion of the Commonplace: to the definitive imposition upon the world of the code of the Philistine. To define Arnold's point of view, we should have, I think, to consider what in our modern slang is called his environment. Any one who reads the life of his father will see how profound was the influence upon the son. 'Somewhere, surely, afar,' as he says in the lines in Rugby Chapel,

> In the sounding labour-house vast
> Of being, is practised that strength,
> Zealous, beneficent, firm!

Some of the force, may one say, had passed into the younger man, though he had lost something of the austere strength, and had gained much in delicacy, and certainly in a sense of humour curiously absent in the elder, as it is, I think, in most good men. Dr. Arnold shared the forebodings common at the period of the Reform Bill. The old dogged Conservatism of the George III. and Eldon type was doomed. But who was to profit by the victory? The Radicals, led by Bentham and James Mill? That meant confiscation and disestablishment in practice; and in theory, materialism or atheism. This was the 'liberalism' denounced and dreaded by Newman.[5] But then, to Dr. Arnold, the Oxford Movement itself meant a revival of superstition and sacerdotalism. He held that there was a truer liberalism than Benthamism, a liberalism of which Coleridge expounded and suggested the philosophy: a doctrine which could reanimate the old creeds by exposing them to the light, and bring them into harmony with the best modern thought. The Church, neither plundered nor enslaved by superstition, might be lifted to a higher intellectual level, and become once more the great national organ of spiritual influence and development. Matthew Arnold always held to this aspiration. He hoped that the Church might open its doors to all dissenters—not only to Protestants, but even in course of time to Roman Catholics.[6] He hated disestablishment, and even in the case of the Church of Ireland, condemned a measure which, though it removed an injustice, removed it at the cost of an alliance with the narrow dissenting prejudices. But the views of the young man were also modified by the fascination of the Newman school. Of Oxford he could never speak without enthusiasm, if he could not quite refrain from a touch of irony. 'Adorable dreamer!' he exclaims,[7] 'whose heart has been so romantic! who hast given thyself prodigally, given thyself to sides and to heroes not mine, only not to the Philistines! Home of lost causes and forsaken beliefs, and unpopular names and impossible loyalties!' Oxford, as he says elsewhere,[8] had taught the truth that 'beauty and sweetness are essential characters of a complete human perfection.' Bad philosophies, another critic (I think Professor Flint) has said, when they die, go to Oxford. Arnold admitted the badness of the philosophies, but the beauty and sweetness, he would have added, are immortal. The effect, therefore, upon him was not to diminish his loyalty to philosophy; no one more hated all obscurantism: his belief in 'culture,' in the great achievements of scholarship, of science, of historical criticism, was part of his nature. He was not the man to propose to put back the hand of the dial, or to repel the intellectual ocean with the mop of an orthodox Mrs. Partington. But his keen appreciation of the beauty of the old ideals governed his thought. He even held[9] that the Christianity of the future would be Catholicism, though Catholicism 'purged' and 'opening itself to the light,' 'conscious of its own poetry, freed from its sacerdotal despotism, and freed from its pseudo-scientific apparatus of superannuated dogma.' Meanwhile, his classical training and his delight in the clearness and symmetry of the great French writers affected his taste. He has told us how his youthful enthusiasm took him at one time to Paris, to spend two months

in seeing Rachel's performances[10] on the French stage, and at another, to visit George Sand in her country retirement. And then came the experience of his official career which made him familiar with the educational systems of France and Germany, and with the chaotic set of institutions which represented an educational system in England. The master-thought, he says,[11] by which his politics were governed was the thought of the 'bad civilisation of the English middle-class.' This was, in fact, the really serious aim to which his whole literary activity in later life converged. Condemned to live and work among the middle-class, while imbued with the ideas in which they were most defective, loving, as he did, the beauty and freshness of Oxford, the logical clearness and belief in ideas of France, the devotion to scientific truth and philosophical thoroughness in Germany, the sight of the dogged British Philistine became to him a perpetual grievance. The middle-class, as he said in one of his favourite formulæ,[12] has a 'defective type of religion, a narrow range of intellect and knowledge, a stinted sense of beauty, and a low type of manners.' Accordingly, the function which he took for himself was to be a thorn in the side of the Philistine: to pierce the animal's thick hide with taunts, delicate but barbed; to invent nicknames which might reveal to the creature his own absurdity; to fasten upon expressions characteristic of the blatant arrogance and complacent ineffable self-conceit of the vulgar John Bull, and repeat them till even Bull might be induced to blush. Somebody's unlucky statement that the English was the best breed in the world; the motto about the 'dissidence of dissent and the Protestantism of the Protestant religion'; the notice of Wragg—the woman who was taken up for child-murder; the assertion of *The Saturday Review* that we were the most logical people in the world; the roarings of the 'young lions of *The Daily Telegraph*,' and their like, which covered our impotence in European wars; the truss-manufactory which ornamented the finest site in Europe: upon these and other texts he harped—perhaps with a little too much repetition—in the hope of bringing to us some sense of our defects. I must confess that, as a good Philistine, I often felt, and hope I profited by the feeling, that he had pierced me to the quick, and I submitted to his castigations as I have had to submit to the probings of a dentist—I knew they were for my good. And I often wished, I must also confess, that I too had a little sweetness and light that I might be able to say such nasty things of my enemies. We who were young radicals in the days when Arminius von Thunder-Ten Tronckh was writing to *The Pall Mall Gazette*, tried to retort by calling him a mere dandy, a kid-gloved Oxford coxcomb, who was thinking that revolutions could be made with rosewater. I can see now that we did not do justice to the real seriousness of his purpose. You do not, we said sometimes, propose any practical measure. He replied fairly enough that it was not his business, nor the business of philosophers and poets generally, to mix in actual politics and draft Acts of Parliament. They had to modify ideas. He might have added that in his own sphere, he had made very practical criticisms upon our educational system; and had, for example, pointed out the defects of English secondary education with a clearness which is only now beginning to have some recognition from practical politicians. But it was no doubt his conviction that his countrymen required less a change of machinery than an intellectual change. What is indispensable, he said,[13] is that we should not only *do* to Ireland something different, but that we should *be* something different. A writer, however great a thinker and artist, who deliberately proposes to change the character of his countrymen, is undoubtedly undertaking a superhuman task. If Philistinism be really part of our character we shall be Philistines to the end, let our Carlyles and Newmans or Mills and Arnolds preach never so wisely and never so frequently. And yet their preaching is not the less useful: more useful, perhaps, than that of the politicians who boast of keeping to the practical and confine their energies to promoting such measures as are likely to catch votes at the next election. 'To see things as they really are': that, he said, was his great aim; and it is clearly a good one. And what is the great obstacle to seeing things as they really are? The great obstacle is, I take it, that we are ourselves part of the things to be seen; and that there is an ancient and proverbial difficulty about seeing ourselves. When certain prejudices have become parts of our mental furniture, when our primary data and our methods of reasoning imply a set of local narrow assumptions, the task of getting outside them is almost the task of getting outside of our own skins. Our pigtails, as the poet observes, persist in hanging behind us in spite of all our circumgyrations. The greatness of a thinker is measured by the width of his intellectual horizon, or by the height to which he can rise above the plane of ordinary thought. Arnold's free play of thought implies the process by which he hoped to achieve liberation for himself. Be yourself cultured, and your eyes will be opened to the ugliness of the Philistines. To be cultured, widen your intellectual horizon, and steep yourself in the best thought of all ages and all civilised men. If Arnold trusted a little too much to the æsthetic perceptions thus generated, he succeeded, I think, in reaching a position from which he both discerned and portrayed most clearly some palpable blots. Such a service is a great one, whatever the accuracy of the judgment. It is good to breathe a new atmosphere if only for a space. I have more respect than he had for the masculine common-sense of Macaulay—the great apostle, as Arnold called him, of the Philistines—but, after Macaulay's unhesitating utterances of the old Whig creed, which to him was an ultimate and infallible gospel, Arnold's utterances lift us at once to a higher point of view. When one attempts, under Arnold's guidance, to assign to the Whig his proper place in European history, and to see how far he is from fully representing the ultimate verdict of philosophy, whatever our political creed—and mine is very different from Arnold's—he really helps us to cure the mind's eye of the cataract of dogged prejudice, of whose very existence we were unconscious.

His position was, no doubt, one which we may call unpractical. He was a democrat in one sense: for aristocracy was unfavourable to ideas, and the Zeitgeist has condemned the system. Inequality, as he said in a remarkable essay,[14] 'materialises our upper classes, vulgarises our middle classes, brutalises our lower classes.' He speaks as one shocked, not less in his moral than in his æsthetic capacity, by the 'hardly human horror, the abjection and uncivilisedness' of the populace in Glasgow and the East of London. He held that the French Revolution, by promoting equality, had raised the lower classes of France to a marked superiority in civilisation above the corresponding class in England. Democracy, he admitted, might get too much of its own way in England. The remedy was to be sought in a stronger action of the central power. We have not, he complains, the notion, so familiar on the Continent and to antiquity, of the State; and the English hatred of all authority has tended to make us drift towards mere anarchy.[15] When Fawcett preached self-help, Arnold held that to exhort to self-help in England was to carry coals to Newcastle. It was the parrot-like repetition of old formulæ that made our liberalism barren. Our danger was all the other way, the danger of exaggerating the blessings of self-will and self-assertion.[16] I do not quote Arnold's view to show that he was

right, or to claim foresight for his predictions. I doubt, for example, whether any one would say now that we hear too much of self-help, or that there is no danger on the opposite side, or whether Arnold himself would have been attracted by State Socialism. He was, indeed, deliberately in the habit of giving one side of a question without caring to add even the corrections of which he himself approved. That is natural in a man who wishes to stimulate thought, rather than to preach any definite practical conclusion. I only urge that there was a real and very rare merit in such a position taken by a man of so much insight. The effort to see English life and society and thought, as a German professor or a French politician might see it, to get outside of the prejudices which are part of ourselves, is itself a most useful experience. And when such criticism is carried on with a singular fulness of perception, with pungent flashes of sarcasm, but with a power of speaking truths as undeniable as they are unpleasant, and yet with so much true urbanity—in spite of certain little defects, when he seems to be rather forcing himself to be humorous, and becomes liable to an accusation of flippancy—in such a case, I say that we owe the deepest gratitude to our critic. His criticism is anything but final, but it is to be taken into account by every man who believes in the importance of really civilising the coming world. How the huge, all-devouring monster which we call Democracy is to be dealt with: how he is to be coaxed or lectured or preached into taking as large a dose as possible of culture, of respect for true science and genuine thought, is really one of the most pressing of problems. Some look on with despair, doubting only by whatever particular process we shall be crushed into a dead level of monotonous mediocrity. I do not suppose that Arnold or any one else could give any solution of the great problems; what he could do, and did, I think, more effectually than any one, was to wake us out of our dull complacency—to help to break through the stolid crust, whatever seeds may be sown by other hands. Perhaps this explains why he is read in America, where the Philistine is a very conspicuous phenomenon and the ugly side of middle-class mediocrity is even more prominent than here.

I have reserved to the last, in order that I may pass lightly, the point which to Arnold himself doubtless appeared to be the most important part of his teaching—I mean, of course, the criticism of religion, to which he devoted his last writings. In his last books, Arnold preached a doctrine which will hardly find many followers. He seemed even to be taking pains to get into a position scarcely intelligible to people who take things practically. He poses, one may say, as a literary critic; he disavows all logical system, and declares almost ostentatiously that he is no metaphysician; but his apparent conclusion is, not that he is incompetent to speak of philosophy, but that philosophy is mere pedantry, so far as it is not poetry in disguise. The organ by which we are to discover religious truth does not employ the prosaic method of examining evidence, nor the logical method of *à priori* reasoning; but that free play of thought which is our guide in letters: the judgment, as he says, which insensibly forms itself in a fair mind, familiar with the best thoughts of the world. The prophet is inspired by the Zeitgeist, and judges by a cultivated instinct, not by systematic argument. The rather airy mode of treating great problems which emerges is often bewildering to the ordinary mind. The orthodox may revolt against the easy confidence with which the Zeitgeist puts aside 'miracles' and the supernatural,—not as disproved, but as obviously not worth the trouble of disproving. The agnostic is amazed to find that Arnold, while treating all theological dogma as exploded rubbish, expatiates upon the supreme value of the sublimated essence of theology. God,

Arnold tells us, is not a term of science, but a term of poetry and eloquence—a term 'thrown out' at a not fully grasped object of consciousness—a literary term, in short—with various indefinite meanings for different people. [17] The 'magnified and non-natural man' of whom theologians speak is to be superseded by the 'stream of tendency' or the 'not ourselves which makes for righteousness'; and, in expressing his contempt for the vulgar conceptions, he perhaps sometimes forgot his usual good taste, as in the famous reference to the three Lords Shaftesbury. Such phrases might be taken for the scoffing which he condemned in others. I glanced the other day at a satirical novel, in which the writer asks whether an old Irishwoman is to say, instead of 'God bless you,' 'the stream of tendency bless you.' I then opened the preface to Arnold's *God and the Bible* and found him making a similar criticism upon Mr. Herbert Spencer. Nobody, he observes, would say, 'The unknowable is our refuge and strength, a very present help in trouble.'

Arnold's answer to his critic would, in fact, have been that he never proposed that the old Irishwoman should give up her form of expression. He professed to be simply explaining her real meaning. He apparently thought, as I have said, that a modified form of Catholicism would be the religion of the future; the modification amounting to this, that it would only profess to be poetry instead of science, and giving symbols 'thrown out' at truth, not dogmas with the validity of theorems in geometry. He argued not only that the Hebrew religion itself is to be taken by us in the poetical sense, but that by the prophets themselves it was never understood differently. So the text which says that 'Man must be born of a spirit' means only that man must be born of an influence; and, moreover, never meant anything more. This was the original sense of the first utterance, which was only twisted into pseudo-science by later dogmatists. It follows that orthodox theology is an 'immense misunderstanding of the Bible'—a misunderstanding because it takes poetry for prose. By clearing away the accretions we see that the Bible is to be read throughout in this sense; and therefore that, to restore its true value, we are not to throw it aside, but to take it as the original authors meant us to take it.

The weakness of the poetic or imaginative treatment is the tendency to confound a judgment of beauty with a judgment of fact. A creed is so charming or so morally stimulating that it must be true. Arnold did not accept this way of putting it. He had too genuine a respect for the daylight of the understanding, too much hearty loyalty to the Zeitgeist and scientific thought to accept a principle which would lead to simple reaction and recrudescence of superstition. He unequivocally accepts the results obtained by German critics, heavy-eyed and pedantic as they may sometimes be, for he believes with all his heart in thorough, unflinching, scholar-like research. He will not shut his eyes or mistake mere æsthetic pleasure for logical conviction. But, he argues, the essence of the creed is precisely its moral beauty; the power with which it expresses certain ethical truths—its grasp of the doctrine (to quote his favourite, though I cannot think very fortunate, formula) that conduct is three-fourths of life, that it is the essence of the religion, or rather, is itself the religion; and that the whole framework of historical fact and ecclesiastical dogma is unimportant. We read Homer, he says, [18] for our enjoyment, and to turn the book to our benefit. We should read the Bible in the same way. The truth of the Greek or Hebrew mythology and history is irrelevant. The true lights of the Christian Church, he says, [19] are not Augustine and Luther or Bossuet, but à Kempis and Tauler and St. Francis of Sales; not, that is, the legislators or reformers or systematisers of dogma, but the mystics and

pietists and men who have uttered the religious sentiment in the most perfect form. It is characteristic that in his book upon St. Paul, while dwelling enthusiastically upon the apostle's ethical teaching, he says nothing of the work which to St. Paul himself, as to most historians, must surely have seemed important, the freeing of Christian doctrine from fetters of Judaism; and treats the theological reasons by which St. Paul justified his position as mere surplusage or concessions to contemporary prejudice.

The problem here suggested is a very wide one. We may agree that the true value of a religion is in its ethical force. We may admit that the moral ideas embodied in its teaching are the only part which is valuable when we cease to believe in the history or the dogma; and that they still preserve a very high value. We may still be edified by Homer or by Æschylus, or by Socrates and Epictetus, though we accept not a word of their statements of fact or philosophy. But can the essence of a religion be thus preserved intact when its dogma and its historical assertions are denied? Could St. Paul have spread the Church of the Gentiles without the help of the theories which Arnold regarded as accretions? Would the beautiful spirit of the mystics have conquered the world as well as touched the hearts of a few hermits without the rigid framework of dogmas in which they were set and the great ecclesiastical organisation for which a definite dogmatic system was required? We may love the mystical writers, but, without the organisers of Churches and creeds, can we believe that they would ever have made a church for the world? To set forth a great moral ideal is undoubtedly an enormous service. But the prosaic mind will ask, Is it enough to present us with ideals? Do we not also require statements of fact? It is all very well to say be good, and to say this and that is the real meaning of goodness; but to make men good, you have also got to tell them why they should be good, and to create a system of discipline and dogma for effectually stimulating their love of goodness.

I do not presume to discuss such a point here. I confine myself to saying that Arnold's solution of the difficulty not only shows admirable candour and courage, but may seem to correspond to the most probable goal of the modern evolution of thought. It often gives a singular impression to compare the apologists of orthodoxy in the present day with their predecessors of a past generation. The old divine used to prove the historical assertions of his creed by evidence and to demonstrate its dogmas by reasoning. He tried, at least, to 'confute' cavillers by argument. The modern apologist entirely changes the system. He admits that the evidence is inadequate, and that the dogmas, as formerly understood, were really false and repulsive. He accepts positions once supposed to be essentially sceptical. And yet, all the same, he ends by concluding that it does not matter. The sceptic was in the right; but in spite of this, believers are somehow justified. That strikes some people as dishonest, and the best excuse is that it is an approximation to Arnold's position. Agree fully and frankly that the value of a creed is not to be tested by its historical and philosophical validity; that it really belongs to the sphere of poetry and provides symbols for the emotions, not truths for the understanding; that, therefore, all the argumentation about 'evidences' and so forth is the application of a totally inappropriate test; and you certainly reach an intelligible position. It is moreover one to which the modern mind, with its growing indifference to the old controversies, its apparently unaltered, if not growing, conviction that some religion is necessary, combined with the conviction that one set of dogmas is about as good as another, may seem to be approximating. The Churches would escape a good many difficulties, and apologists a good deal of trouble, in connecting their premises with their conclusions, if they could boldly follow Arnold and say that they do not appeal to the reason but to the imagination. Leave out the awkward words 'I believe'; or substitute, 'I feign for purposes of edification,' and all would go right. Unity must be sought, not by the triumph of one set of dogmas, all equally absolute, but by giving up dogma, or treating it as essentially poetry, and admitting that to take it as a prosaic statement of fact always is and always has been a blunder. It is true that the prosaic person has a difficulty in accepting this position. He will not admit that a religion is good for anything when it abandons its ancient claims to give genuine knowledge as well as providing modes of utterance of our sentiments. The questions which arise are those which upon Arnold's method seem to be passed over. It is his indifference to them which gives sometimes the very erroneous impression of a want of seriousness. Arnold was undeniably and profoundly in earnest, though he seems scarcely to have realised the degree in which, to ordinary minds, he seemed to be offering not stones, but mere vapour when asked for bread. He felt that he was occupied with the most serious of problems, and he saw at least some of the conditions of successful treatment. On all sides his loyalty to culture (the word has been a little spoilt of late), his genuine and hearty appreciation of scholarship and scientific thought, his longing to set himself in the great current of intellectual progress, are always attractive, and are the more marked because of his appreciation (his excessive appreciation, may I say?) of the 'sweetness,' if not the light, of the Oxford Movement. If, indeed, his appreciation was excessive, I am conscious, I hope, of the value of the doctrine which led him. We ought, he says,[20] to have an 'infinite tenderness' for the popular science of religion. It is 'the spontaneous work of nature, the travail of the human mind, to adapt to its grasp and employment great ideas of which it feels the attraction.' I feel the truth of this teaching more, I fear, than I have acted upon it. I belong, as I have said, to the prosaic class of mankind. We ought to catch at least something of Arnold's spirit, so far as to admit, at least, that the great problem is to reconcile unflinching loyalty to truth with tenderness 'infinite,' if possible, for the errors which are but a grasping after truth. If Arnold combined the two tendencies in a fashion of his own, he set a most valuable example, even to those who cannot think his method successful. He said of a great contemporary that he was always beating the bush without starting the hare. I am under the impression that Arnold, if he started the hare, did not quite catch it. But beating the bushes is an essential preliminary. He stirred and agitated many brains which could not be reached by sober argument or by coarser invective, and he applied good wholesome irritants to our stolid self-satisfaction. When one remarks how little is left of most philosophers in the way of positive result, and yet remembers gratefully the service they have done in the way of stimulus to thought, one may feel grateful to a man who, while renouncing all claims to be a philosopher, did more than most philosophers to rouse us to new perception of our needs and was one of the most effective agents in breaking up old crusts of prejudice.

Putting on a mask, sometimes of levity, sometimes of mere literary dandyism, with an irony which sometimes is a little too elaborate, but which often expresses the keenest intelligence trying to pass itself off as simplicity, he was a skirmisher, but a skirmisher who did more than most heavily-armed warriors, against the vast oppressive reign of stupidity and prejudice. He made the old dragon Philistinism (to use his phrase) wince at times, and showed the ugliness and clumsiness of the creature; and after all he did it in a spirit as of one who recognised the monster was after all a most kindly monster at bottom. He may be enlisted in useful service if you can only apply the goad successfully, and made effective, in his ponderous way, like the Carthaginian elephants, if only you can mount his neck and goad him in the right direction. No single arm is sufficient for such a task; the dragon shakes himself and goes to sleep again in a stertorous and rather less complacent fashion, let us hope; and we feel that the struggle will too probably endure till we have ceased to be personally interested.

I cannot, indeed, get it out of my head that we slow-footed and prosaic persons sometimes make our ground surer; and that, for example, poor Bishop Colenso, whom Arnold ridiculed as the typical Philistine critic, did some good service with his prosaic arithmetic. There are cases in which the four rules are better than the finest critical insight. But there is room for poets as well as for arithmeticians; and Arnold, as at once poet and critic, has the special gift—if I may trust my own experience—of making one feel silly and tasteless when one has uttered a narrow-minded, crude, or ungenerous sentiment; and I dip into his writings to receive a shock, unpleasant at times, but excellent in its effects as an intellectual tonic.

Notes

1. A lecture delivered at the Owens College, Manchester, 13th November 1893.
2. *Culture and Anarchy* (1893), p. 121.
3. *St. Paul and Protestantism* (1870), p. 70.
4. *Essays on Criticism*, p. 70.
5. *Culture and Anarchy*, p. 23.
6. *St. Paul and Protestantism*.
7. *Essays on Criticism*, p. xvii.
8. *Culture and Anarchy*, p. 23.
9. *Mixed Essays*, p. 121.
10. *Irish Essays*, p. 151.
11. Ibid., p. 17.
12. *Mixed Essays*, p. 167.
13. Preface to *Irish Essays*.
14. *Irish Essays*, p. 91.
15. *Culture and Anarchy*, p. 36.
16. *Irish Essays*, p. 96.
17. *Literature and Dogma*, p. 12.
18. *God and the Bible*, p. 99.
19. *Literature and Dogma*, p. 290.
20. *Literature and Dogma*, p. 303.

ROBERT BROWNING

ROBERT BROWNING

1812–1889

Robert Browning was born in London on May 7, 1812. The son of a clerk in the Bank of England, he was largely educated at home. In 1828 he enrolled at London University but withdrew during his second term. Browning's first published poem, *Pauline: A Fragment of a Confession*, appeared anonymously in 1833, attracting little attention. During 1834 he traveled in Russia, and in 1835 he published *Paracelsus*, a dramatic poem in blank verse, which was very well received. The success of this poem led to several important friendships, notably with the critic John Forster and the actor William Charles Macready. In 1837 Browning's play *Strafford* was produced at Covent Garden, with Macready playing the principal part.

In 1838 Browning made his first trip to Italy; his impressions there inspired his narrative poem *Sordello* (1840). The critical reception of this poem was extremely hostile and marked the beginning of a decline in his reputation, from which he did not recover for many years. Between 1841 and 1846 Browning published, under the general title *Bells and Pomegranates*, a series of plays and verse collections, consisting of *Pippa Passes* (1841), *King Victor and King Charles* (1842), *Dramatic Lyrics* (1842), *The Return of the Druses* (1843), *A Blot in the 'Scutcheon* (1843), *Colombe's Birthday* (1844), *Dramatic Romances and Lyrics* (1845), and, in one volume, *Luria* and *A Soul's Tragedy* (1846).

In September 1846 Browning married Elizabeth Barrett, with whom he had been corresponding since January 1845, when he first read and admired her poetry. In November 1846 the Brownings moved to Italy, where they remained, principally in Florence and Rome, until Elizabeth's death in 1861. They had one child, Robert Wiedemann Barrett Browning ("Pen," 1849–1913). In 1850 Browning published his poem *Christmas-Eve and Easter Day*, followed in 1855 by the verse collection *Men and Women*. After returning to England in 1861 he published *Dramatis Personae* (1864), a verse collection, and *The Ring and the Book* (1868–69), a long poem that brought about the restoration of his reputation. During the remaining twenty years of his life, which he spent partly in London and partly in the countryside or abroad, Browning published numerous poems and verse collections, including *Balaustion's Adventure* (1871), *Prince Hohenstiel-Schwangau* (1871), *Fifine at the Fair* (1872), *Red Cotton Night-Cap Country* (1873), *Aristophanes' Apology* (1875), *The Inn Album* (1875), *Pacchiarotto with Other Poems* (1876), *La Saisiaz* and *The Two Poets of Croisic* (1878), *Dramatic Idyls* (1879), *Dramatic Idyls: Second Series* (1880), *Jocoseria* (1883), *Ferishtah's Fancies* (1884), and *Parleyings with Certain People of Importance in Their Day* (1887). Browning's last volume of poems, *Asolando*, was published on December 12, 1889, the day of his death. The standard edition of his *Poetical Works* is being edited by Ian Jack and Margaret Smith (1983–   ). Many editions of his letters have been published.

Personal

Mr. Browning was very popular with the whole party; his simple and enthusiastic manner engaged attention and won opinions from all present; he looks and speaks more like a youthful poet than any man I ever saw.—WILLIAM CHARLES MACREADY, *Diary*, Dec. 31, 1835

Browning's conversation is like the poetry of Chaucer, or like his own, simplified and made transparent. His countenance is so full of vigor, freshness, and refined power, that it seems impossible to think that he can ever grow old. His poetry is subtle, passionate and profound; but he himself is simple, natural, and playful. He has the repose of a man who has lived much in the open air; with no nervous uneasiness and no unhealthy self-consciousness.—GEORGE STILLMAN HILLARD, *Six Months in Italy*, 1853, p. 114

⟨. . .⟩ Mr. Browning introduced himself to me,—a younger man than I expected to see, handsome, with brown hair. He is very simple and agreeable in manner, gently impulsive, talking as if his heart were uppermost. He spoke of his pleasure in meeting me, and his appreciation of my books; and—which has not often happened to me—mentioned that *The Blithedale Romance* was the one he admired most. I wonder why. I hope I showed as much pleasure at his praise as he did at mine; for I was glad to see how pleasantly it moved him.—NATHANIEL HAWTHORNE, *The English Note-Books*, July 13, 1856

I thought I was getting too old to make new friends. But I believe that I have made one—Mr. Browning, the poet, who has been staying with me during the last few days. It is impossible to speak without enthusiasm of his open, generous nature and his great ability and knowledge. I had no idea that there was a perfectly sensible poet in the world, entirely free from vanity, jealousy, or any other littleness, and thinking no more of himself than if he were an ordinary man. His great energy is very remarkable, and his determination to make the most of the remainder of life.—BENJAMIN JOWETT, Letter (June 12, 1865), cited in Evelyn Abbott, Lewis Campbell, *The Life and Letters of Benjamin Jowett*, 1897, Vol. 1, pp. 400–401

TO MY GOOD FRIEND
ROBERT BROWNING,
WHOSE GENIUS AND GENIALITY
WILL BEST APPRECIATE WHAT MAY BE BEST,
AND MAKE MOST ALLOWANCE FOR WHAT MAY BE WORST,
THIS VOLUME
IS AFFECTIONATELY DEDICATED.
—ALFRED, LORD TENNYSON, Dedication to *Tiresias and Other Poems*, 1885

Of course, in the recollections of an Englishman living during those years in Florence, Robert Browning must necessarily stand out in high relief, and in the foremost line. But very obviously this is neither the time nor the place, nor is my dose of presumption sufficient for any attempt at a delineation of the man. To speak of the poet, since I write for Englishmen, would be very superfluous. It may be readily imagined that the "tag-rag and bob-tail" of the men who mainly constituted that very pleasant but not very intellectual society, were not likely to be such as Mr. Browning would readily make intimates of. And I think I see in memory's magic glass that the men used to be rather afraid of him. Not that I ever saw him rough or uncourteous with the most exasperating fool that ever rubbed a man's nervous system the wrong way; but there was a quiet, lurking smile which, supported by very few words, used to seem to have the singular property of making the utterers of platitudes and the mistakers of *non-sequiturs* for *sequiturs*, uncomfortably aware of the nature of their words within a very few minutes after they had uttered them. I may say, however, that I believe that in any dispute on any sort of subject between any two men in the place, if it had been proposed to submit the matter in dispute for adjudication to Mr. Browning, the proposal would have been jumped at with a greater readiness of *consensus* than in the case of any other man there.—THOMAS ADOLPHUS TROLLOPE, *What I Remember*, 1888

The poet was then about thirty-five. His figure was not large, but compact, erect, and active; the face smooth, the hair dark; the aspect that of active intelligence, and of a man of the world. He was in no way eccentric, either in manner or appearance. He talked freely, with great vivacity, and delightfully, rising and walking about the room as his talk sparkled on.—GEORGE WILLIAM CURTIS, "Editor's Easy Chair," *Harper's New Monthly Magazine*, March 1890, p. 637

He spent, we have seen, most of his years in London; and this seems fit. There, where man and his problems and ways touched and interested him. He was a man with men, mixing with the life of his fellows; friendly and manly, taking his part in conversation frankly, and in fit circles an able and interesting talker. In a certain way he was a man of the world, measuring men and their affairs at their due value in the world, yet independent and unworldly at the heart of him. Observant, practical, common-sensible, but with a core of passion and ideality. His nature was, in fact, richly passioned, on a ground of strong intellect, with manly control and even reserve of emotion. But in his love for his mother and for his wife, and in the disturbance of feeling roused by the deaths of these, or by whatever touched the memory of the latter, we see the depth and force, we feel the fire and tenderness of his mind. His strong sensibility to music is another test of his emotional quality. He had, owing to this, a marked tenacity and constancy of affection. He had a keen memory for suffering and a certain shrinking from it. He was thus an optimist by temper and habit, forced by bias and energy of the brain, and by dramatic observation and sympathy, to weigh his optimism, yet inclined to make the best of things. He was not on the surface sympathetic, and never sentimental. His centre was not in the emotions any more than it was in the sphere of facts. With the core of passion went a power of "abstraction," a life of thought and imagination. He was, we may say, very real and down upon the earth, but aware, too, and all the time, of the "world unseen," that world of principles, laws, ideals, souls, which seems shadowy and remote to many, but is life of life to the true and sure discerner.—JAMES FOTHERINGHAM, *Studies of the Mind and Art of Robert Browning*, 1898, pp. 42–43

Robert Browning, for all his original genius and fine culture in literature, painting, and music, had less of the eccentric in him than almost any famous man of his time. A man of the world to his finger tips, who knew every one, went everywhere, and had seen everything, he might pass as a social lion, but not as a poet, or a genius. His animal spirits, his bonhommie, his curious versatility and experience, made him the autocrat of the London dinner table, of which he was never the tyrant—or the bore. Dear old Browning! how we all loved him; how we listened to his anecdotes; how we enjoyed his improvised "epitaphs in country churchyards," till we broke into shouts of laughter as we detected the amusing forgery. At home in the smoking room of a club, in a lady's literary tea-party, in a drawing-room concert, or in a river picnic, he might have passed for a retired diplomat, but for his buoyancy of mind and brilliancy of talk. His heart was as warm, his moral judgment as sound as his genius was original.—FREDERIC HARRISON, "Personal Reminiscences," *George Washington and Other American Addresses*, 1901, p. 207

At Cortina I met and first knew Browning, who, with his sister Sariana, our old and dear friend, came to stay at the inn where we were. I am not much inclined to reckon intellectual greatness as a personal charm, for experience has shown me that the relation is very remote; but Browning always impressed me—and then and after I saw a good deal of him—as one of the healthiest and most robust minds I have ever known, sound to the core, and with an almost unlimited intellectual vitality and an individuality which nothing could infringe on, but which a singular sensitiveness towards others prevented from ever wounding even the most morbid sensibility; a strong man armed in the completest defensive armor, but with no aggressive quality. His was a nature of utter sincerity, and what had seemed to me, reading his poetry before knowing him, to be more or less an affectation of obscurity, a cultivation of the cryptic sense, I found to be the pure expression of his individuality. He made short cuts to the heart of his theme, perhaps more unconscious than uncaring that his line of approach could not be followed by his general readers, as a mathematician leaves a large hiatus in his demonstration, seeing the result the less experienced must work out step by step.—WILLIAM JAMES STILLMAN, *The Autobiography of a Journalist*, 1901, Vol. 2, p. 627

General

⟨. . .⟩ from Browning some "Pomegranate," which, if cut deep
   down the middle,
Shows a heart within blood-tinctured, of a veined humanity.
      —ELIZABETH BARRETT BROWNING, *Lady Geraldine's Courtship*, 1844, Stanza 41

There is delight in singing, though none hear
Beside the singer; and there is delight
In praising, though the praiser sit alone
And see the prais'd far off him, far above.
Shakspeare is not *our* poet, but the world's,
Therefore on him no speech; and short for thee,
Browning! Since Chaucer was alive and hale,
No man hath walk'd along our roads with step
So active, so inquiring eye, or tongue
So varied in discourse. But warmer climes
Give brighter plumage, stronger wing; the breeze
Of Alpine heights thou playest with, borne on
Beyond Sorrento and Amalfi, where
The Siren waits thee, singing song for song.
      —WALTER SAVAGE LANDOR, "To Robert Browning," 1845

His writings have, till lately, been clouded by obscurities, his riches having seemed to accumulate beyond his mastery of them. So beautiful are the picture gleams, so full of meaning the little thoughts that are always twisting their parasites over his main purpose, that we hardly can bear to wish them away, even when we know their excess to be a defect. They seem, each and all, too good to be lopped away, and we cannot wonder the mind from which they grew was at a loss which to reject. Yet, a higher mastery in the poetic art must give him skill and resolution to reject them. Then, all true life being condensed into the main growth, instead of being so much scattered in tendrils, off-shoots and flower-bunches, the effect would be more grand and simple; nor should we be any loser as to the spirit; it would all be there, only more concentrated as to the form, more full, if less subtle, in its emanations. The tendency to variety and delicacy, rather than to a grasp of the subject and concentration of interest, are not so obvious in Browning's minor works as in *Paracelsus*, and in his tragedy of *Strafford*.—MARGARET FULLER, "Browning's Poems" (1846), *Art, Literature, and the Drama*, 1860, p. 209

To read poems is often a substitute for thought: fine-sounding conventional phrases and the sing-song of verse demand no co-operation in the reader; they glide over his mind with the agreeable unmeaningness of 'the compliments of the season', or a speaker's exordium on 'feelings too deep for expression'. But let him expect no such drowsy passivity in reading Browning. Here he will find no conventionality, no melodious commonplace, but freshness, originality, sometimes eccentricity of expression; no didactic laying-out of a subject, but dramatic indication, which requires the reader to trace by his own mental activity the underground stream of thought that jets out in elliptical and pithy verse. To read Browning he must exert himself, but he will exert himself to some purpose. If he finds the meaning difficult of access, it is always worth his effort—if he has to dive deep, 'he rises with his pearl'. Indeed, in Browning's best poems he makes us feel that what we took for obscurity in him was superficiality in ourselves. We are far from meaning that all his obscurity is like the obscurity of the stars, dependent simply on the feebleness of men's vision. On the contrary, our admiration for his genius only makes us feel the more acutely that its inspirations are too often straitened by the garb of whimsical mannerism with which he clothes them. This mannerism is even irritating sometimes, and should at least be kept under restraint in *printed* poems, where the writer is not merely indulging his own vein, but is avowedly appealing to the mind of his reader.

Turning from the ordinary literature of the day to such a writer as Browning, is like turning from Flotow's music, made up of well-pieced shreds and patches, to the distinct individuality of Chopin's Studies or Schubert's Songs. Here, at least, is a man who has something of his own to tell us, and who can tell it impressively, if not with faultless art. There is nothing sickly or dreamy in him: he has a clear eye, a vigorous grasp, and courage to utter what he sees and handles. His robust energy is informed by a subtle, penetrating spirit, and this blending of opposite qualities gives his mind a rough piquancy that reminds one of a russet apple. His keen glance pierces into all the secrets of human character, but, being as thoroughly alive to the outward as to the inward, he reveals those secrets, not by a process of dissection, but by dramatic painting. We fancy his own description of a poet applies to himself:

> He stood and watched the cobbler at his trade,
> The man who slices lemons into drink,
> The coffee-roaster's brazier, and the boys

> That volunteer to help him at the winch.
> He glanced o'er books on stalls with half an eye,
> And fly-leaf ballads on the vendor's string,
> And broad-edge hold-print posters by the wall
> *He took such cognizance of men and things,*
> *If any beat a horse, you felt he saw,*
> *If any cursed a woman, he took note;*
> *Yet stared at nobody,—they stared at him,*
> *And found, less to their pleasure than surprise,*
> *He seemed to know them and expect as much.*

Browning has no soothing strains, no chants, no lullabys; he rarely gives voice to our melancholy, still less to our gaiety; he sets our thoughts at work rather than our emotions. But though eminently a thinker, he is as far as possible from prosaic; his mode of presentation is always concrete, artistic, and, where it is most felicitous, dramatic.—GEORGE ELIOT, *Westminster Review*, Jan. 1856, pp. 290–91

⟨. . .⟩ Robert Browning is unerring in every sentence he writes of the Middle Ages; always vital, right, and profound; so that in the matter of art, ⟨. . .⟩ there is hardly a principle connected with the mediæval temper, that he has not struck upon in those seemingly careless and too rugged rhymes of his. There is a curious instance, by the way, in a short poem ⟨"The Bishop Orders His Tomb in St. Praxed's Church"⟩ referring to this very subject of tomb and image sculpture; and illustrating just one of those phases of local human character which, though belonging to Shakespere's own age, he never noticed, because it was specially Italian and un-English ⟨. . .⟩

I know no other piece of modern English, prose or poetry, in which there is so much told, as in these lines, of the Renaissance spirit,—its worldliness, inconsistency, pride, hypocrisy, ignorance of itself, love of art, of luxury, and of good Latin. It is nearly all that I said of the central Renaissance in thirty pages of the *Stones of Venice* put into as many lines, Browning's being also the antecedent work. The worst of it is that this kind of concentrated writing needs so much *solution* before the reader can fairly get the good of it, that people's patience fails them, and they give the thing up as insoluble; though, truly, it ought to be to the current of common thought like Saladin's talisman, dipped in clear water, not soluble altogether, but making the element medicinal.—JOHN RUSKIN, *Modern Painters*, 1856, Pt. 5, Ch. 20

Robert Browning, a really great thinker, a true and splendid genius, though his vigorous and restless talents often overpower and run away with his genius so that some of his creations are left but half redeemed from chaos, has this simplicity in abundant measure. In the best poems of his last two works, *Men and Women* and *Dramatis Personæ*, its light burns so clear and steadfast through the hurrying clouds of his language (Tennyson's style is the polished reflector of a lamp) that one can only wonder that people in general have not yet recognised it. I cannot recommend a finer study of a man possessed by the spirit of which I am writing than the sketch of Lazarus in Browning's "Epistle of Karshish, an Arab Physician."—JAMES THOMSON ("B.V."), "The Poems of William Blake" (1864), *Biographical and Critical Studies*, 1896, pp. 266–67

I have been thinking of you so much for the last two or three days, while the first volume of Browning's *Poem* has been on my table, and I have been trying in vain to read it, and yet the *Athenaeum* tells me it is wonderfully fine. And so sometimes I am drawn to write to you (with only one eye, the other scorched by reading with a paraffin lamp these several winters), and, whether you care for my letter or not, you won't care to answer; and yet I want to know what you yourself think of this poem; you, who are the one man able to judge of it, and magnanimous enough to think me capable of seeing what is fine in it. I never could read Browning. If Browning only gave a few pence for the book he drew from, what will posterity give for his version of it, if posterity ever find it on a stall? If Shakespeare, Milton, Dryden, Pope and Tennyson survive, what *could* their readers make out of this Browning a hundred years hence? Anything so utterly unlike the *Ring* too which he considers he has wrought out of the old gold—this shapeless thing. "You are unjust, Fitz"—that is what you will say or think, I fancy.—EDWARD FITZGERALD, Letter to Alfred, Lord Tennyson (April 1869)

I have called him the most original and the most unequal of living poets; he continually descends to a prosaic level, but at times is elevated to the Laureate's highest flights. Without realizing the proper functions of art, he nevertheless sympathizes with the joyous liberty of its devotees; his life may be conventional, but he never forgets the Latin Quarter, and often celebrates that freedom in love and song which is the soul of Béranger's

> Dans un grenier qu'on est bien à vingt ans.

Then, too, what working man of letters does not thank him when he says,—

> But you are of the trade, my Puccio!
> You have the fellow-craftsman's sympathy.
> There's none knows like a fellow of the craft
> The all unestimated sum of pains
> That go to a success the world can see.

He is an eclectic, and will not be restricted in his themes; on the other hand, he gives us too gross a mixture of poetry, fact, and metaphysics, appearing to have no sense of composite harmony, but to revel in arabesque strangeness and confusion. He has a barbaric sense of color and lack of form. Striving against the trammels of verse, he really is far less a master of expression than others who make less resistance. We read in *Pippa Passes:* "If there should arise a new painter, will it not be in some such way by a poet, now, or a musician (spirits who have conceived and perfected an Ideal through some other channel), transferring it to this, and escaping our conventional roads by pure ignorance of them?" This is the Pre-Raphaelite idea, and, so far, good; but Browning's fault is that, if he has "conceived," he certainly has made no effort to "perfect" an Ideal.

And here I wish to say,—and this is something which, soon or late, every thoughtful poet must discover,—that the structural exigencies of art, if one adapts his genius to them, have a beneficent reaction upon the artist's original design. By some friendly law they help the work to higher excellence, suggesting unthought-of touches, and refracting, so to speak, the single beam of light in rays of varied and delightful beauty.

The brakes which art applies to the poet's movement not only regulate, but strengthen its progress. Their absence is painfully evinced by the mass of Browning's unread verse. Works like *Sordello* and *Fifine*, however intellectual, seem, like the removal of the Malvern Hills, a melancholy waste of human power. When some romance like the last-named comes from his pen,—an addition in volume, not in quality, to what he has done before,—I feel a sadness like that engendered among hundreds of gloomy folios in some black-letter alcove: books, forever closed, over which the mighty monks of old wore out their lives, debating minute points of casuistic theology, though now the very memory of their discussions has passed away. Would that Browning might take

to heart his own words, addressed, in "Transcendentalism," to a brother-poet:—

> Song's our art:
> Whereas you please to speak these naked thoughts
> Instead of draping them in sights and sounds.
> —True thoughts, good thoughts, thoughts fit to
> treasure up!
> But why such long prolusion and display,
> Such turning and adjustment of the harp?
> . . .
> But here's your fault; grown men want thought, you
> think;
> Thought's what they mean by verse, and seek in
> verse:
> Boys seek for images and melody,
> Men must have reason,—so you aim at men.
> Quite otherwise!

Incidentally we have noted the distinction between the drama of Browning and that of the absolute kind, observing that his characters reflect his own mental traits, and that their action and emotion are of small moment compared with the speculations to which he makes them all give voice. Still, he has dramatic insight, and a minute power of reading other men's hearts. His moral sentiment has a potent and subtile quality:—through his early poems he really founded a school, and had imitators, and, although of his later method there are none, the younger poets whom he has most affected very naturally began work by carrying his philosophy to a startling yet perfectly logical extreme.

Much of his poetry is either very great or very poor. It has been compared to Wagner's music, and entitled the "poetry of the future"; but if this be just, then we must revise our conception of what poetry really is. The doubter incurs the contemptuous enmity of two classes of the dramatist's admirers: first, of the metaphysical, who disregard considerations of passion, melody, and form; secondly, of those who are sensitive to their master's failings, but, in view of his greatness, make it a point of honor to defend them. That greatness lies in his originality; his error, arising from perverseness or congenital defect, is the violation of natural and beautiful laws. This renders his longer poems of less worth than his lyrical studies, while, through avoidance of it, productions, differing as widely as *The Eve of St. Agnes* and *In Memoriam*, will outlive *The Ring and the Book*. In writing of Arnold I cited his own quotation of Goethe's distinction between the dilettanti, who affect genius and despise art, and those who respect their calling though not gifted with high creative power. Browning escapes the limitations of the latter class, but incurs the reproach visited upon the former; and by his contempt of beauty, or inability to surely express it, fails of that union of art and spiritual power which always characterizes a poet entirely great.—EDMUND CLARENCE STEDMAN, *Victorian Poets*, 1875, pp. 338–41

The charge of obscurity is perhaps of all charges the likeliest to impair the fame or to imperil the success of a rising or an established poet. It is as often misapplied by hasty or ignorant criticism as any other on the roll of accusations; and was never misapplied more persistently and perversely than to an eminent writer of our own time. The difficulty found by many in certain of Mr. Browning's works arises from a quality the very reverse of that which produces obscurity properly so called. Obscurity is the natural product of turbid forces and confused ideas; of a feeble and clouded or of a vigorous but unfixed and chaotic intellect. 〈. . .〉 Now if there is any great quality more perceptible than another in Mr. Browning's intellect it is his decisive and incisive faculty of thought, his sureness and intensity of perception, his rapid and trenchant resolution of aim. To charge him with obscurity is about as accurate as to call Lynceus purblind or complain of the sluggish action of the telegraphic wire. He is something too much the reverse of obscure; he is too brilliant and subtle for the ready reader of a ready writer to follow with any certainty the track of an intelligence which moves with such incessant rapidity, or even to realize with what spider-like swiftness and sagacity his building spirit leaps and lightens to and fro and backward and forward as it lives along the animated line of its labour, springs from thread to thread and darts from centre to circumference of the glittering and quivering web of living thought woven from the inexhaustible stores of his perception and kindled from the inexhaustible fire of his imagination. He never thinks but at full speed; and the rate of his thought is to that of another man's as the speed of a railway to that of a waggon or the speed of a telegraph to that of a railway. It is hopeless to enjoy the charm or to apprehend the gist of his writings except with a mind thoroughly alert, an attention awake at all points, a spirit open and ready to be kindled by the contact of the writer's. To do justice to any book which deserves any other sort of justice than that of the fire or the waste-paper basket, it is necessary to read it in the fit frame of mind; and the proper mood in which to study for the first time a book of Mr. Browning's is the freshest, clearest, most active mood of the mind in its brightest and keenest hours of work. Read at such a time, and not "with half-shut eyes falling asleep in a half-dream," it will be found (in Chapman's phrase) "pervial" enough to any but a sluggish or a sandblind eye; but at no time and in no mood will a really obscure writer be found other than obscure. The difference between the two is the difference between smoke and lightning; and it is far more difficult to pitch the tone of your thought in harmony with that of a foggy thinker, than with that of one whose thought is electric in its motion.—ALGERNON CHARLES SWINBURNE, *George Chapman: A Critical Essay*, 1875, pp. 15–18

It was a wonderful event to me,—my first acquaintance with his poetry.—Mr. Macready put *Paracelsus* into my hand, when I was staying at his house; and I read a canto before going to bed. For the first time in my life, I passed a whole night without sleeping a wink. The unbounded expectation I formed from that poem was sadly disappointed when *Sordello* came out. I was so wholly unable to understand it that I supposed myself ill. But in conversation no speaker could be more absolutely clear and purpose-like. He was full of good sense and fine feeling, amidst occasional irritability; full also of fun and harmless satire; with some little affectations which were as droll as any thing he said. A real genius was Robert Browning, assuredly; and how good a man, how wise and morally strong, is proved by the successful issue of the perilous experiment of the marriage of two poets.—HARRIET MARTINEAU, *Autobiography*, ed. Maria Weston Chapman, 1877, Vol. 1, pp. 314–15

Mr. Browning ⟨. . .⟩ delights in perplexed problems of character and life—in studying the effects of strange contrasting forces of passion coming into play under peculiar and distracting conditions. All that lies beneath the surface; all that is out of the common track of emotion; all that is possible, that is poetically conceivable, but that the outer air and the daily walks of life never see, this is what specially attracts Mr. Browning. ⟨. . .⟩ No poet ⟨. . .⟩ certainly can be more often wanting in grace of form and delight of soft sound than Mr. Browning. There are many passages and even many poems of

Browning which show that the poet could be melodious if he would; but he seems sometimes as if he took a positive delight in perplexing the reader's ear with harsh, untuneful sounds. Mr. Browning commonly allows the study of the purely psychological to absorb too much of his moods and of his genius. It has a fascination for him which he is seemingly unable to resist. He makes of his poems too often mere searchings into strange deeps of human character and human error. He seldom abandons himself altogether to the inspiration of the poet; he hardly ever deserves the definition of the minstrel given in Goethe's ballad who "sings but as the song-bird sings." Moreover, Mr. Browning has an almost morbid taste for the grotesque; he is not unfrequently a sort of poetic Callot. It has to be added that Mr. Browning is seldom easy to understand, and that there are times when he is only to be understood at the expense of as much thought and study as one might give to a controverted passage in an ancient author. This is a defect of art, and a very serious defect. The more devoted of Mr. Browning's admirers will tell us, no doubt, that the poet is not bound to supply us with brains as well as poetry, and that if we cannot understand what he says it is the fault simply of our stupidity. But an ordinary man who finds that he can understand Shakspeare and Milton, Dryden and Wordsworth, Byron and Keats without any trouble, may surely be excused if he does not set down his difficulty about some of Browning's poems wholly to the account of his own dulness. It may well be doubted whether there is any idea so subtle that if the poet can actually realize it in his own mind clearly for himself, the English language will not be found capable of expressing it with sufficient clearness. The language has been made to do this for the most refined reasonings of philosophical schools, for transcendentalists and utilitarians, for psychologists and metaphysicians. No intelligent person feels any difficulty in understanding what Mill, or Herbert Spencer, or Huxley means; and it can hardly be said that the ideas Mr. Browning desires to convey to his readers are more difficult of exposition than some of those which the authors we name have contrived to set out with a white light of clearness all round them. The plain truth is that Mr. Browning is a great poet, in spite of some of the worst defects that ever stood between a poet and popularity. He is a great poet by virtue of his commanding genius, his fearless imagination, his penetrating pathos. He strikes an iron harp-string. In certain of his moods his poetry is like that of the terrible lyre in the weird old Scottish ballad, the lyre that was made of the murdered maiden's breastbone, and which told its fearful story in tones "that would melt a heart of stone." In strength and depth of passion and pathos, in wild humor, in emotion of every kind, Mr. Browning is much superior to Mr. Tennyson.—JUSTIN MCCARTHY, A *History of Our Own Times*, 1879–80, Ch. 29

There is no poet of our time more original, be that originality good or bad, than Browning. ⟨. . .⟩ There is no poetry on which opinions are so much divided, none so at variance with preconceived ideas, none, therefore, which it is so difficult fairly to appreciate. There is no poet of our time so uneven, none so voluminous, none so obscure. There is no poet, then, who so much needs an interpreter. ⟨. . .⟩

His poetry, then, is for Browning, but a form of activity, a means of realizing his own individuality. He is not an Eglamour; his poetry is not the end of his existence; he does not submit to his art, nor sacrifice his perfection as a man to the perfection of his work. Like Goethe, he writes not so much to produce a great work,—to please others, as to afford play to his own individuality. Necessarily, then, as he points out in

Sordello, his work is imperfect. He has himself rather than his reader in view. He is seeking to give complete and accurate expression to what is within him, rather than to give beauty and artistic completeness to his work. Accordingly, the incongruous and non-essential from the artistic point of view, he does not prune away; these are needful for the true and complete expression of his own mind.—WILLIAM JOHN ALEXANDER, *An Introduction to the Poetry of Robert Browning*, 1889, pp. 2, 210

There are many who make it a kind of religion to regard Mr. Browning as the greatest of living English poets. In him, too, one is thankful for a veritably great poet; but can we believe that impartial posterity will rate him with the Laureate, or that so large a proportion of his work will endure? The charm of an enigma now attracts students who feel proud of being able to understand what others find obscure. But this attraction must inevitably become a stumbling-block.

Why Mr. Browning is obscure is a long question; probably the answer is that he often cannot help himself. His darkest poems may be made out by a person of average intelligence who will read them as hard as, for example, he would find it necessary to read the *Logic* of Hegel. There is a story of two clever girls who set out to peruse *Sordello*, and corresponded with each other about their progress, 'Somebody is dead in *Sordello*,' one of them wrote to her friend. 'I don't quite know *who* it is, but it must make things a little clearer in the long run.' Alas! a copious use of the guillotine would scarcely clear the stage of *Sordello*. It is hardly to be hoped that *Sordello*, or *Red Cotton Night Cap Country*, or *Fifine*, will continue to be struggled with by posterity. But the mass of *Men and Women*, that unexampled gallery of portraits of the inmost hearts and secret minds of priests, prigs, princes, girls, lovers, poets, painters, must survive immortally, while civilisation and literature last, while men care to know what is in men.

No perversity of humour, no voluntary or involuntary harshness of style, can destroy the merit of these poems, which have nothing like them in the letters of the past, and must remain without successful imitators in the future. They will last all the better for a certain manliness of religious faith—something sturdy and assured—not moved by winds of doctrine, not paltering with doubts, which is certainly one of Mr. Browning's attractions in this fickle and shifting generation. He cannot be forgotten while, as he says,

> A sunset touch,
> A chorus ending of Euripides,

reminds men that they are creatures of immortality, and move 'a thousand hopes and fears.'—ANDREW LANG, "Introductory: Of Modern English Poetry," *Letters on Literature*, 1889, pp. 8–11

The truth is that, from a fortunate fusion of several races and characters, we find united in Browning the poet's sensuous love of all earthly beauty, keen ear for rhythm and turn of speech, pregnant eloquence and high range of thought and image, run through by a steel fibre of unflinching probity and courage, high mystic and religious tendencies, philosophic insight, plastic and perceptive gifts, and virile stability. But he is necessarily, by this very fusion, a poet of a unique growth. It is waste of time to compare or associate him with other poets, English or not—to draw parallels as to style or cast of thought; and, though you may parody, you can never imitate him. It has taken the English people nearly half-a-century to make up their minds about him in any large numbers; and even now a great majority of his admirers seek philosophy where they

might easily find live men and women. To Browning, from the minutest detail of gesture or habit to the most thrilling psychological crisis, all humanity has been welcome material; while in actual poetic construction the manner of a phrase or even a grotesque rhyme have, when needful, been as carefully studied in producing and finishing a mental portrait or scene as have his most resonant and majestic passages of poetic eloquence.—JOHN T. NETTLESHIP, "Robert Browning," *Academy*, Dec. 21, 1889, p. 406

> The clearest eyes in all the world they read
>   With sense more keen and spirit of sight more true
>   Than burns and thrills in sunrise, when the dew
> Flames, and absorbs the glory round it shed,
> As they the light of ages quick and dead,
>   Closed now, forsake us: yet the shaft that slew
>   Can slay not one of all the works we knew,
> Nor death discrown that many-laurelled head.
> The works of words whose life seems lightning wrought,
> And moulded of unconquerable thought,
>   And quickened with imperishable flame,
> Stand fast and shine and smile, assured that nought
>   May fade of all their myriad-moulded fame,
>   Nor England's memory clasp not Browning's name.
>   —ALGERNON CHARLES SWINBURNE, "A Sequence
>   of Sonnets on the Death of Robert Browning:
>   I," *Fortnightly Review*, Jan. 1890, p. 1

> Gone from us! that strong singer of late days—
> Sweet singer should be strong—who, tarrying here,
> Chose still rough music for his themes austere,
> Hard-headed, aye but tender-hearted lays,
> Carefully careless, garden half, half maze.
> His thoughts he sang, deep thoughts to thinkers dear,
> Now flashing under gleam of smile or tear,
> Now veiled in language like a breezy haze
> Chance-pierced by sunbeams from the lake it covers.
> He sang man's ways—not heights of sage or saint,
> Not highways broad, not haunts endeared to lovers;
> He sang life's byways, sang its angles quaint,
> Its Runic lore inscribed on stave or stone;
> Song's short-hand strain,—its key oft his alone.
>   —AUBREY DE VERE, "Robert Browning," *Macmillan's Magazine*, Feb. 1890, p. 258

No poet ever had more perfect opportunity to study woman's character in its sweetest and noblest aspects than Mr. Browning, and nowhere does this great artist show more consummate power, or more delicate intuition, than in his portraiture of women. Independently of all mere conventional claim on our sympathy, relying by no means exclusively upon slender forms, taper fingers, ruby lips, or the like, Mr. Browning's women step out of shadowland into the atmosphere of breathing humanity. They have their adorable perfections and imperfections; they are feminine to the very core. Each word-painting of physical beauty has its spiritual counterpart in characters whose every outward trait bespeaks a corresponding moral quality.—ANNIE E. IRELAND, "Browning's Types of Womanhood," *The Woman's World*, 1890

Browning is animated by a robust optimism, turning fearless somersaults upon the brink of the abyss.—JOHN ADDINGTON SYMONDS, "A Comparison of Elizabethan with Victorian Poetry," *Essays Speculative and Suggestive*, 1890, Vol. 2, p. 246

Emerson's obscurity comes, I think, from want of coherently systematic thought. Browning's, on the other hand, as some recent critic has eagerly maintained, is only an "alleged obscurity." What he meant he always knew. The trouble is that, like Shakspere now and then, he generally meant so much and took so few words to say it in, that the ordinary reader, familiar with the simple diffuseness of contemporary style, does not pause over each word long enough to appreciate its full significance. What reading I have done in Browning inclines me to believe this opinion pretty well based. He had an inexhaustible fancy, too, for arranging his words in such order as no other human being would have thought of. Generally, I fancy, Browning could have told you what he meant by almost any passage, and what relation that passage bore to the composition of which it formed a part; but it is not often that you can open a volume of Browning and explain, without a great deal of study, what the meaning of any whole page is.—BARRETT WENDELL, *English Composition*, 1891, p. 208

Gilbert: Nowadays we have so few mysteries left to us that we cannot afford to part with one of them. The members of the Browning Society, like the theologians of the Broad Church Party, or the authors of Mr. Walter Scott's Great Writers Series, seem to me to spend their time in trying to explain their divinity away. Where one had hoped that Browning was a mystic they have sought to show that he was simply inarticulate. Where one had fancied that he had something to conceal, they have proved that he had but little to reveal. But I speak merely of his incoherent work. Taken as a whole the man was great. He did not belong to the Olympians, and had all the incompleteness of the Titan. He did not survey, and it was but rarely that he could sing. His work is marred by struggle, violence and effort, and he passed not from emotion to form, but from thought to chaos. Still, he was great. He has been called a thinker, and was certainly a man who was always thinking, and always thinking aloud; but it was not thought that fascinated him, but rather the processes by which thought moves. It was the machine he loved, not what the machine makes. The method by which the fool arrives at his folly was as dear to him as the ultimate wisdom of the wise. So much, indeed, did the subtle mechanism of mind fascinate him that he despised language, or looked upon it as an incomplete instrument of expression. Rhyme, that exquisite echo which in the Muse's hollow hill creates and answers its own voice; rhyme, which in the hands of the real artist becomes not merely a material element of metrical beauty, but a spiritual element of thought and passion also, waking a new mood, it may be, or stirring a fresh train of ideas, or opening by mere sweetness and suggestion of sound some golden door at which the Imagination itself had knocked in vain; rhyme, which can turn man's utterance to the speech of gods; rhyme, the one chord we have added to the Greek lyre, became in Robert Browning's hands a grotesque, misshapen thing, which at times made him masquerade in poetry as a low comedian, and ride Pegasus too often with his tongue in his cheek. There are moments when he wounds us by monstrous music. Nay, if he can only get his music by breaking the strings of his lute, he breaks them, and they snap in discord, and no Athenian tettix, making melody from tremulous wings, lights on the ivory horn to make the movement perfect, or the interval less harsh. Yet, he was great: and though he turned language into ignoble clay, he made from it men and women that live. He is the most Shakespearian creature since Shakespeare. If Shakespeare could sing with myriad lips, Browning could stammer through a thousand mouths. Even now, as I am speaking, and speaking not against him but for him, there glides through the room the pageant of his persons. There, creeps Fra Lippo Lippi with his

cheeks still burning from some girl's hot kiss. There, stands dread Saul with the lordly male-sapphires gleaming in his turban. Mildred Tresham is there, and the Spanish monk, yellow with hatred, and Blougram, and Ben Ezra, and the Bishop of St. Praxed's. The spawn of Setebos gibbers in the corner, and Sebald, hearing Pippa pass by, looks on Ottima's haggard face, and loathes her and his own sin, and himself. Pale as the white satin of his doublet, the melancholy king watches with dreamy treacherous eyes too loyal Strafford pass forth to his doom, and Andrea shudders as he hears the cousins whistle in the garden, and bids his perfect wife go down. Yes, Browning was great. And as what will he be remembered? As a poet? Ah, not as a poet! He will be remembered as a writer of fiction, as the most supreme writer of fiction, it may be, that we have ever had. His sense of dramatic situation was unrivalled, and, if he could not answer his own problems, he could at least put problems forth, and what more should an artist do? Considered from the point of view of a creator of character he ranks next to him who made Hamlet. Had he been articulate, he might have sat beside him. The only man who can touch the hem of his garment is George Meredith. Meredith is a prose Browning, and so is Browning. He used poetry as a medium for writing in prose.—OSCAR WILDE, *The Critic as Artist*, 1891

Browning's style may be compared to a Swiss pasture, where the green meadows which form the foreground of a sublime landscape are yet cumbered with awkward blocks and boulders—things not without a certain rough dignity of their own, but essentially out of place.—ARTHUR CHRISTOPHER BENSON, "The Poetry of Edmund Gosse" (1894), *Essays*, 1896, p. 298

Critical estimate of Browning's poetry was for years hampered by, and cannot even yet be said to have been quite cleared from, the violent prepossessions of public opinion respecting him. For more than a generation, in the ordinary sense, he was more or less passionately admired by a few devotees, stupidly or blindly ignored by the public in general, and persistently sneered at, lectured, or simply disliked by the majority of academically educated critics. The sharp revulsion of his later years has been noticed; and it amounted almost to this, that while dislike to him in those who had intelligently, if somewhat narrowly, disapproved of his ways was not much affected, a Browning *cultus*, almost as blind as the former pooh-poohing or ignoring, set in, and extended from a considerable circle of ardent worshippers to the public at large. A "Browning Society" was founded in 1881, and received from the poet a kind of countenance which would certainly not have been extended to it by most English men of letters. During his later years handbooks solemnly addressed to neophytes in Browningism, as if the cult were a formal science or art, appeared with some frequency; and there has been even a bulky *Browning Dictionary*, which not only expounds the more recondite (and, it is fair to say, tolerably frequent) allusions of the master, but provides for his disciples something to make up for the ordinary classical and other dictionaries with which, it seemed to be presumed, their previous education would have made them little conversant.

This not very wise adulation in its turn not unnaturally excited a sort of irritation and dislike, to a certain extent renewing the old prejudice in a new form. To those who could discard extraneous considerations and take Browning simply as he was, he must, from a period which only very old men can now remember, have always appeared a very great, though also a very far from perfect poet. His imperfections were always on the surface, though perhaps they were not always confined to it;

and only uncritical partisanship could at any time have denied them, while some of them became noticeably worse in the period of rapid composition or publication from 1870 to 1885. A large license of unconventionality, and even of defiance of convention, may be claimed by, and should be allowed to, persons of genius such as Mr. Browning undoubtedly possessed. But it can hardly be denied that he, like his older contemporary Carlyle, whose example may not have been without influence upon him, did set at naught not merely the traditions, but the sound norms and rules of English phrase to a rather unnecessary extent. A beginning of deliberate provocation and challenge, passing into an after-period of more or less involuntary persistence in an exaggeration of the mannerisms at first more or less deliberately adopted, is apt to be shown by persons who set themselves in this way to innovate; and it was shown by Mr. Browning. It is impossible for any intelligent admirer to maintain, except as a paradox, that his strange modulations, his cacophonies of rhythm and rhyme, his occasional adoption of the foreshortened language of the telegraph or the comic stage, and many other peculiarities of his, were not things which a more perfect art would have either absorbed and transformed, or at least have indulged in with far less luxuriance. Nor does it seem much more reasonable for anybody to contend that his fashion of soul-dissection at a hand-gallop, in drama, in monologue, in lay sermon, was not largely, even grossly, abused. Sometimes the thing was not worth doing at all—there are at least half a dozen of the books between *The Ring and the Book* and *Asolando* from the whole of which a judicious lover of poetry would not care to save more than the bulk of the smallest of them should they be menaced with entire destruction. Even in the best of these what is good could generally, if not always, have been put at the length of the shorter *Men and Women* with no loss, nay, with great advantage. The obscurity so much talked of was to some extent from the very first, and to the last continued to be, in varying degrees, an excuse, or at least an occasion, for putting at great length thought that was not always so far from commonplace as it looked into expression which was very often not so much original as unkempt. "Less matter with more art" was the demand which might have been made of Mr. Browning from first to last, and with increasing instance as he became more popular.

But though no competent lover of poetry can ever have denied the truth and cogency of these objections, the admission of them can never, in any competent lover of poetry, have obscured or prevented an admiration of Browning none the less intense because not wholly unreserved. Even his longer poems, in which his faults were most apparent, possessed an individuality of the first order, combined the intellectual with no small part of the sensual attraction of poetry after a fashion not otherwise paralleled in England since Dryden, and provided an extraordinary body of poetical exercise and amusement. The pathos, the power, at times the humour, of the singular soul-studies which he was so fond of projecting with little accessory of background upon his canvas, could not be denied, and have not often been excelled. If he was not exactly what is commonly called orthodox in religion, and if his philosophy was of a distinctly vague order, he was always "on the side of the angels" in theology, in metaphysics, in ethics; and his politics, if exceedingly indistinct and unpractical, were always noble and generous. Further, though he seems to have been utterly destitute of the slightest gift of dramatic construction, he had no mean share of a much rarer gift, that of dramatic character; and in a century of descriptions of nature his, if not the most exquisite, have a freedom and truth, a

largeness of outline combined with felicity of colour, not elsewhere to be discovered.

But it is as a lyric poet that Browning ranks highest; and in this highest class it is impossible to refuse him all but the highest rank, in some few cases the very highest. He understood love pretty thoroughly; and when a lyric poet understands love thoroughly there is little doubt of his position. But he understood many other things as well, and could give strange and delightful voice to them. Even his lyrics, still more his short non-lyrical poems, admirable as they often are, and closely as they group with the lyrics proper, are not untouched by his inseparable defect. He cannot be prevented from inserting now and then in the midst of exquisite passages more or fewer of his quirks and cranks of thought and phrase, of his vernacularity or his euphuism, of his outrageous rhymes (which, however, are seldom or never absolutely bad), of those fantastic tricks of his in general which remind one of nothing so much as of dashing a bladder with rattling peas in the reader's face just at the height of the passion or the argument.

Yet the beauty, the charm, the variety, the vigour of these short poems are as wonderful as the number of them. He never lost the secret of them to his latest years. The delicious lines "Never the time and the place, And the loved one all together" are late; and there are half a dozen pieces in *Asolando*, latest of all, which exhibit to the full the almost bewildering beauty of combined sound, thought, and sight, the clash of castanets and the thrill of flutes, the glow of flower and sunset, the subtle appeal for sympathy in feeling or assent in judgment. The song snatches in *Pippa Passes*, "Through the Metidja," "The Lost Leader," "In a Gondola," "Earth's Immortalities," "Mesmerism," "Women and Roses," "Love among the Ruins," "A Toccata of Galuppi's," "Prospice," "Rabbi Ben Ezra," "Porphyria's Lover," "After," with scores of others, and the "Last Ride Together," the poet's most perfect thing, at the head of the list, are such poems as a very few—Shakespeare, Shelley, Burns, Coleridge—may surpass now and then in pure lyrical perfection, as Tennyson may excel in dreamy ecstasy, as some seventeenth century songsters may outgo in quaint and perfect fineness of touch, but such as are nowhere to be surpassed or equalled for a certain volume and variety of appeal, for fulness of life and thought, of action and passion.
—GEORGE SAINTSBURY, *A History of Nineteenth Century Literature*, 1896, pp. 272–76

Robert Browning is far too near us to enable even the most far-seeing to lay out his kingdom by metes and bounds. Besides, who ever dare tether the spirit of poesy? It bloweth where it lists. In old days one was sometimes asked, 'But who reads Browning?' It was always easy to reply, 'More people than are dreamed of in your philosophy.' But that particular foolish question, at all events, is no longer asked. The obscure author of the undoubtedly obscure *Sordello*, who came from nobody knew where, and wrote a poem about nobody knew what; who was vouched for by none of the great schools and universities, of which Englishmen are wont to make much; who courted no critic and sought no man's society; slowly, very slowly, won his audience, made his way, earned his fame without puffs preliminary in the newspapers, or any other of the now well-worn expedients of attracting attention to that lamentable object one's self. ⟨. . .⟩

Is it any wonder we love Browning? With him life is full of great things—of love and beauty and joy. His poems, particularly of that period which ends in *The Ring and the Book*, are all aglow with the colour of life, its many-hued interests. Hence, while we are reading him, we find it easy to share his strenuous hope, his firm faith, particularly his undying faith in immortality. It is the poverty of our lives that renders it hard to believe in immortality.—AUGUSTINE BIRRELL, "Robert Browning" (1897), *Essays and Addresses*, 1901, pp. 185–94

I began to read the two poets ⟨Tennyson and Browning⟩ at about the same period, 1841, when I was not quite eighteen, and long before the collected poems of either had been brought together. I then read them both constantly and knew by heart most of those of Tennyson, in particular, before I was twenty years old. To my amazement I now find that I can read these last but little; the charm of the versification remains, but they seem to yield me nothing new; whereas the earlier poems of Browning, *Paracelsus, Sordello, Bells and Pomegranates*—to which last I was among the original subscribers—appear just as rich a mine as ever; I read them over and over, never quite reaching the end of them. In case I were going to prison and could have but one book, I should think it a calamity to have Tennyson offered me instead of Browning, simply because Browning has proved himself to possess, for me at least, so much more staying power.—THOMAS WENTWORTH HIGGINSON, "The Biography of Browning's Fame," *The Boston Browning Society Papers*, 1897, p. 5

Browning is the most hotly disputed of all indisputable poets. Such a critic as Mr. Henley will not hear of his being a poet at all; neither would such a critic as Mr. Coventry Patmore. The reason of both was the same: Browning's extreme disregard of recognised poetic form and conventions. He would, even in the midst of his most poetical poems, introduce passages of unquestionable rhymed prose; he could never proceed for long without exhibiting flagrant roughness and unmetricalness in metre. Consequently, such critics said that he lacked the most primary requisite of a singer—he could not sing. In our opinion, there are two distinct things to be separated in metre—ruggedness and roughness. ⟨. . .⟩ Shakespeare, in his greatest blank verse, that of his latest period, is rugged in the very nature of his harmonies. They roll with the grandeur of mountain boulders, only to be understood by a large and masculine ear. It is not so with Browning. There are in him no harmonies moving on so colossal a scale, that the individual frictions play only the part of the frictions in a male, as compared with a female voice. It is not ruggedness; it is veritable roughness, like the roughness of a harsh male voice. We must allow, therefore, that he lacks something of the quality of a singer. Yet it sometimes happens that a singer with a rough voice commands attention in despite of its roughness. And so, we think, it is with Browning. Donne is another example. Criticism has come round to the recognition of Donne, in spite of the roughest utterance ever employed by a poet of like gifts. Upon this precedent we rest our recognition of Browning as a poet. He went out of his way to be rough, apparently for roughness' sake, and without any large scale of harmonies to justify it. But his intrinsic qualities, far more than in the case of Donne, make him a poet in the teeth of this defect of execution: such is our opinion. Fineness of manner has often carried off smallness of matter. And, though to a rarer extent, we think that fineness of matter may sometimes carry off defect of manner.—FRANCIS THOMPSON, "Academy Portraits: XXVI. Robert Browning," *Academy*, May 8, 1897, p. 499

It has been objected against Browning's claim to greatness that he did but little to reflect the aims and aspirations of his own countrymen, that he was very little moved by the stream of events, and that his historical value is affected by his lack of immediate value to his time. It is true, indeed, that Browning was at no time a "topical" poet; and much of his long unpopularity was, no doubt, due to his disinclination to come down into the market-place, with his singing robes about him, and make great ballads of the day to the chorus of the crowd. But there is a higher part even than that of a national poet; and Browning is, in a very real sense, the poet, not of England alone, but of the world. His attitude to men and life was never distraught by petty interests of blood or party: the one claim upon him was the claim of humanity. He was a man, and nothing that pertained to man was foreign to himself. What will be his final place in the long array of English poetry it is still impossible to say. It took long for him to come into his own, and even then many outside developments helped him. We think ourselves to-day far wiser than our grandparents: we fancy, perhaps, that, if *Pauline* had come to one of us fresh from the press, we should have hailed it forthwith as a work of coming genius. All this may be, and yet the last word will always remain to be said. Time brings in, not only revenges, but redresses; and it is probable that Robert Browning is not even yet appreciated as he will be by our children's children. But even now we know him for much that he is,—the subtlest, strongest master of human aspiration, save only Shakespeare, that has ever dignified the English language with poetry; a man who felt for men with all the intensity of a great, unselfish heart; a genius crowned with one guerdon which genius cannot always boast,—a pure and noble life. Standing in the twilight shades of the whispering Abbey, in that sacred corner full of haunting melodies and immortal yearnings, we may gladly feel that, however long and weary was the neglect of him, he is now, at last, gathered to his peers.

> Lofty designs must close in like effects:
>   Loftily lying,
> Leave him,—still loftier than the world suspects,
>   Living and dying.

—ARTHUR WAUGH, *Robert Browning*, 1899, pp. 150–52

Works

PARACELSUS

This poem is what few modern publications either are, or affect to be; it is a work. It is the result of thought, skill, and toil. Defects and irregularities there may be, but they are those of a building which the architect has erected for posterity, and not the capricious anomalies of the wattled pleasure house, which has served its turn when the summer-day's amusement is over, and may be blown about by the next breeze, or washed away by the next torrent, to be replaced by another as fantastic and as transient.—W. J. FOX, *Monthly Repository*, Nov. 1835, p. 716

Some questions may be raised as to points in the execution of Mr Browning's poem, but there can be none as to the high poetic power displayed in it. There are, as it appears to us, some marks of haste in the composition, and we should have been better pleased with the absence both of the statement in the preface, that the poem had not been imagined six months before its publication, and of any ground for making such a statement; for we cannot doubt that the same genius which, in the space of time mentioned, produced the work as it now appears, would not have spent six months longer in brooding over its conceptions and their first rapid embodiment, without making the finished whole something still finer than it is. —LEIGH HUNT, *London Journal*, Nov. 21, 1835, p. 405

⟨*Paracelsus*⟩ opens a deeper vein of thought, of feeling, and of passion, than any poet has attempted for years. Without the slightest hesitation we name Mr. Robert Browning at once with Shelley, Coleridge, Wordsworth. He has entitled himself to a place among the acknowledged poets of the age. This opinion will possibly startle many persons; but it is most sincere. It is no practice of ours to think nothing of an author because all the world have not pronounced in his favour, any more than we would care to offer him our sympathy and concern on the score of the world's indifference. A man of genius, we have already intimated, needs neither the one nor the other. He who is conscious of great powers can satisfy himself by their unwearied exercise alone. His day will come. He need never be afraid that truth and nature will wear out, or that Time will not eventually claim for its own all that is the handywork of Nature. Mr. Browning is a man of genius, he has in himself all the elements of a great poet, philosophical as well as dramatic,—

> The youngest he
> That sits in shadow of Apollo's tree

—but he sits there, and with as much right to his place as the greatest of the men that are around him have to theirs. For the reception that his book has met with he was doubtless already well prepared,—as well for the wondering ignorance that has scouted it, as for the condescending patronage which has sought to bring it forward, as one brings forward a bashful child to make a doubtful display of its wit and learning. "We hope the best; put a good face on the matter; but are sadly afraid the thing cannot answer." We tell Mr. Browning, on the other hand, what we do not think *he* needs to be told, that the thing WILL answer. He has written a book that will live—he has scattered the seeds of much thought among his countrymen— he has communicated an impulse and increased activity to reason and inquiry, as well as a pure and high delight to every cultivated mind;—and this in the little and scantily-noticed volume of *Paracelsus!*—JOHN FORSTER, "Evidences of a New Genius for Dramatic Poetry," *New Monthly Magazine*, March 1836, pp. 289–90

Paracelsus is evidently the work of a young poet of premature powers—of one who sought to project his imagination beyond the bounds of his future, as well as present, experience, and whose intellect had resolved to master all the results thus obtained. We say the powers were premature, simply because such a design could only be conceived by the most vigorous energies of a spirit just issuing forth with "blazing wings," too full of strength and too far of sight to believe in the ordinary laws and boundaries of mortality. It is the effort of a mind that wilfully forgets, and resolves to set aside its corporeal conditions. Even its possible failure is airily alluded to at the outset, and treated in the same way, not merely as no sort of reason for hesitating to make the attempt to gain "forbidden knowledge," but as a result which is solely referable to the Cause of its own aspirations and impulses. ⟨. . .⟩

A Promethean character pervades the poem throughout; in the main design, as well as the varied aspirations and struggles to attain knowledge, and power, and happiness for mankind. But at the same time there is an intense craving after the forbidden secrets of creation, and eternity, and power, which place *Paracelsus* in the same class as *Faust*, and in close affinity with all those works, the object of which is an attempt to penetrate the mysteries of existence—the infinity within us and without us. Need it be said, that the result is in all the same?—and the baffled magic—the sublime occult—the impassioned poetry—all display the same ashes which were once wings. The form, the mode, the impetus and course of thought

and emotion, admit, however, of certain varieties, and *Paracelsus* is an original work. Its aim is of the highest kind; in full accord and harmony with the spirit of the age; and we admit that it has been accomplished, in so far as such a design can well be: for since the object of all such abstractions as *Paracelsus* must necessarily fail, individually and practically, the true end obtained is that of refining and elevating others, by the contemplation of such efforts, and giving a sort of polarity to the vague impulses of mankind towards the lofty and the beneficent. It also endeavours to sound the depths of existence for hidden treasures of being.—R. H. HORNE, "Robert Browning and J. W. Marston," *A New Spirit of the Age*, 1844, pp. 280–82

My journey brought me thro' Basel, where Paracelsus (not Mr. Browning's) (the historical P. was a complete charlatan, seldom sober, clever and cunning, living on the appetite of his contemporaneous public for the philosopher's stone and the universal medicine; castrated as a child by the jaws of a pig, all his life a vagabond, who at last died drunk in his single shirt at Salzburg:) where P. burnt Galen's works openly as professor of the university, beginning the medical reform so, as Luther did that in religion by his public conflagration of the bull launched against him.—THOMAS LOVELL BEDDOES, Letter to Thomas Forbes Kendall (Nov. 13, 1844)

⟨. . .⟩ Paracelsus lives, and will continue to live, not so much through the subtlety of its metaphysical speculations, and through certain scattered passages of the narrative, which are instinct with the highest kind of imaginative beauty, nor even through the rich and haunting music of the superb song, "Over the sea our galleys went;" but because in it the youth of twenty-three discovered his own distinctive and surpassing gift,—the divination of individual human character as an organic whole. Nobody had known for several hundred years, nor cared particularly to know, what manner of man Paracelsus was. The callow youth at Camberwell resuscitated and evoked him out of the past; not without patient research, to be sure, yet still by a species of magic. The dry and laborious investigations of later students have all gone to confirm the main truth to historic fact of what then seemed the creation of an audacious fancy.

Paracelsus, in the nature of things, could never have won more than a success of esteem; but incidentally it brought its author the acquaintance of Wordsworth, Carlyle, Talfourd, Horne, and Landor, and fairly launched him among men of letters.—HARRIET WATERS PRESTON, "Robert and Elizabeth Browning," *Atlantic*, June 1899, p. 814

STRAFFORD

Read *Strafford* in the evening, which I fear is too historical; it is the policy of the man, and its consequence upon him, not the heart, temper, feelings, that work on this policy, which Browning has portrayed—and how admirably.—WILLIAM CHARLES MACREADY, *Diary*, March 19, 1837

In the general phraseology of the play,—even in the manner in which the rough old Puritans address each other,—there is a sort of affected, fondling tone, which perfectly disconcerts us. As for poor Lady Carlisle, seeing that she is desperately in love with Strafford from the beginning of the play, we can perhaps excuse his calling her 'girl', and 'Lucy', in every line; but really we do not think there was any thing in the character of the lady to justify him in supposing that Denzil Hollis would have taken the liberty of addressing her as 'girl' too.

All these, we must once more repeat it, are, chiefly,

defects of taste. They are peculiarities belonging to that which (by the leave of Mr Landor) we must still take the liberty of calling, for want of a better name, the 'Cockney school' of dramatic authorship. And we have not been thus severe in our observations on the bad taste and affectation with which this play abounds, from any malice of criticism. But the author is a young man, and this essay exhibits powers which we can ill afford to see thrown away in the pursuit of false reputation. Had it been otherwise, we should not have taken the trouble to examine his claims to the distinction which he has earned. His defects are fostered by a corrupt taste in theatrical matters; and those defects in turn, meeting with applause instead of correction, tend to increase and perpetuate the evil. For the rest, his success is a proof that his work affords striking situations and dramatic interest. He has developed his matter with breadth and simplicity of purpose, instead of breaking it up into highly-wrought details and insulated scenes; and this is the first great requisite in order to produce effect on miscellaneous readers and spectators. Even his style, of which we have thought it our duty to present a few singular specimens, is, on other occasions, wanting neither in power nor richness. When he lays aside affectation, and condescends to employ continuous dramatic dialogue, there is an energy about him not unworthy of the scenes and epochs which he has chosen to represent.—HERMAN MERIVALE, "Browning's *Strafford*; A Tragedy," *Edinburgh Review*, July 1837, pp. 147–48

Is there a more potential moment in the life of England than that which poises, in even scales, the struggle between the king's prerogative and the people's will? Is there another man than Strafford who so perfectly incarnates the fated issue of that portentous clash of the old with the new? It is this moment that Browning selects for the opening of his first stage-play; it is this man he makes its protagonist.

The subject he chose has been called difficult. Its great difficulty consists, I think, in the peculiarly modern quality of its motive, and in the fact that an original path for it had to be struck out. Fate steers the action of the Greek tragedies through the personal adventures of the heroes of famous houses. Revenge, reconciliation, pride, ambition, passion, dominate the later European drama, or that punctilio of "honour" which Spanish playwrights introduced and which has been cunningly appropriated by France no less in the romantic drama of Victor Hugo than in the classic drama of Corneille. What road in common have such plays of family or personal interest with the play whose attempt must be to show personal interests and abilities in the vague grasp of an impersonal and unrecognised—until then an almost unexistent—power? ⟨. . .⟩

Strafford rests under this adverse cloud of pre-conceived opinion as to the capabilities of art. Yet, in the light which Browning's genius has shed upon these "possibilities of future evil," I believe a new fact in the development of dramatic craft may be descried which promises to show that they are not necessarily undramatic.—CHARLOTTE PORTER, "Dramatic Motive in Browning's *Strafford*" (1893), *The Boston Browning Society Papers*, 1897, pp. 190–91

A BLOT IN THE 'SCUTCHEON

Browning's play has thrown me into a perfect passion of sorrow. To say that there is anything in its subject save what is lovely, true, deeply affecting, full of the best emotion, the most earnest feeling, and the most true and tender source of interest, is to say that there is no light in the sun, and no heat in blood. It is full of genius, natural and great thoughts, profound, and yet simple and beautiful in its vigour. I know nothing that is so

affecting, nothing in any book I have ever read, as Mildred's recurrence to that "I was so young—I had no mother." I know no love like it, no passion like it, no moulding of a splendid thing after its conception, like it. And I swear it is a tragedy that MUST be played; and must be played, moreover, by Macready. There are some things I would have changed if I could (they are very slight, mostly broken lines); and I assuredly would have the old servant *begin his tale upon the scene*; and be taken by the throat, or drawn upon, by his master, in its commencement. But the tragedy I never shall forget, or less vividly remember than I do now. And if you tell Browning that I have seen it, tell him that I believe from my soul there is no man living (and not many dead) who could produce such a work.—CHARLES DICKENS, Letter to John Forster (Nov. 25, 1842)

Mr Browning—a writer whose career we watch with great interest, because we believe him to be a man of genius and a true poet—is the author of a tragedy in three acts, produced at this theatre, on Saturday last, and entitled A *Blot on the 'Scutcheon*. In performance it was successful: a result which it had been hardly safe to predict of a work of so much rare beauty, and of such decisive originality.

These are qualities that seldom, at first starting, make their way in the world, more especially the world theatrical. And we are not sanguine of the chances of continued patronage to the *Blot in the 'Scutcheon*. People are already finding out, we see, that there is a great deal that is equivocal in its sentiment, a vast quantity of mere artifice in its situations, and in its general composition not much to 'touch humanity.' We do not pretend to know what should touch humanity, beyond that which touches our own hearts, but we would give little for the feelings of the man who could read this tragedy without a deep emotion. It is very sad; painfully and perhaps needlessly so; but it is unutterably tender, passionate, and true. It is not copied from this or that existing notion; it is not moulded on this or the other of the old authors; it is the growth of the writer's heart, and has the distinct truth, the animated pathos, the freshness and unexaggerated strength, which spring in that soil alone.—JOHN FORSTER, *Examiner*, Feb. 18, 1843, p. 101

As a rule, Mr Macready always read the new plays. But owing, I suppose, to some press of business, the task was intrusted on this occasion to the head prompter,—a clever man in his way, but wholly unfitted to bring out, or even to understand, Mr Browning's meaning. Consequently, the delicate subtle lines were twisted, perverted, and sometimes even made ridiculous in his hands. My "cruel father" was a warm admirer of the poet. He sat writhing and indignant, and tried by gentle asides to make me see the real meaning of the verse. But somehow the mischief proved irreparable, for a few of the actors during the rehearsals chose to continue to misunderstand the text, and never took the interest in the play which they must have done had Mr Macready read it,—for he had great power as a reader. I always thought it was chiefly because of this *contretemps* that a play, so thoroughly dramatic, failed, despite its painful story, to make the great success which was justly its due.—HELENA FAUCIT MARTIN, "On Some of Shakespeare's Female Characters: III. Desdemona," *Blackwood's Edinburgh Magazine*, March 1881, p. 326

We are so carried along by the fervor and fire and passion which he puts into his production that we pay no heed to its failure to fulfill the first conditions of dramatic propriety. But a play as a literary product must stand, not upon the excellence of detailed scenes, but upon its perfection as an artistic whole; not upon the beauty of its poetry, but upon its adequate representation of life. The necessities of the drama at times exact, or at least permit, an occasional neglect of probability in the conduct of the characters; but they certainly do not require a persistent defiance of it, as is exhibited throughout this tragedy, which is in no sense a picture of any life that was ever lived. We are in a world of unreal beings, powerfully portrayed; for the situations are exciting, and the pathos of the piece is harrowing. But the action constantly lies out of the realm of the reality it purports to represent, and therefore out of the realm of the highest art.—THOMAS R. LOUNSBURY, "A Philistine View," *Atlantic*, Dec. 1899, p. 773

MEN AND WOMEN

What a magnificent series is *Men and Women!* Of course you have it half by heart ere this. The comparative stagnation, even among those I see, and complete torpor elsewhere, which greet this my Elixir of Life, are awful signs of the times to me—'and I must hold my peace!'—for it isn't fair to Browning (besides, indeed, being too much trouble) to bicker and flicker about it. I fancy we shall agree pretty well on favourites, though one's mind has no right to be quite made up so soon on such a subject. For my own part, I don't reckon I've read them at all yet, as I only got them the day before leaving town, and couldn't possibly read them then,—the best proof to you how hard at work I was for once—so heard them read by William; since then read them on the journey again, and some a third time at intervals; but they'll bear lots of squeezing yet. My prime favourites hitherto (without the book by me) are 'Childe Roland', *Bishop Blougram*, 'Karshish', 'The Contemporary', 'Lippo Lippi', 'Cleon', and 'Popularity'; about the other lyrical ones I can't quite speak yet, and their names don't stick in my head; but I'm afraid 'The Heretic's Tragedy' rather gave me the gripes at first, though I've tried since to think it didn't on finding *The Athenæum* similarly affected.—DANTE GABRIEL ROSSETTI, Letter to William Allingham (Nov. 25, 1855)

Elizabeth has been reading Browning's poem (*Men and Women*), and she tells me it is great. I have only dipped into it, here and there, but it is not exactly comfortable reading. It seemed to me like a galvanic battery in full play—its spasmodic utterances and intense passion make me feel as if I had been taking a bath among electric eels. But I have not read enough to criticise.—JOHN GREENLEAF WHITTIER, Letter to Lucy Larcom (1855), cited in Samuel T. Pickard, *Life and Letters of John Greenleaf Whittier*, 1895, Vol. 1, p. 370

Only very few of his *Men and Women* is it possible to make out: indeed, we fear that the Andrea and the Bishop Blougram are about the only intelligible sketches, to our poor apprehension, in the volumes; but there is a pleasant glimmer of the author himself through the rent and tortured fabric of his poetry, which commends him to a kindly judgment; and, unlike those brothers of his who use the dramatic form with an entire contravention of its principles, this writer of rugged verses has a dramatic gift, the power of contrasting character, and expressing its distinctions.—MARGARET OLIPHANT, "Modern Light Literature—Poetry," *Blackwood's Edinburgh Magazine*, Feb. 1856, p. 137

The book by which Mr. Browning was best known was the two green volumes of *Men and Women*. In these, I still think, is the heart of his genius beating most strenuously and with an immortal vitality. Perhaps this, for its compass, is the collection of poetry the most various and rich of modern English times, almost of any English times. But just as Mr. Fitzgerald cared little for what Lord Tennyson wrote after 1842, so I have

never been able to feel quite the same enthusiasm for Mr. Browning's work after *Men and Women.*—ANDREW LANG, "Adventures among Books," *Scribner's Magazine*, Nov. 1891, p. 652

THE RING AND THE BOOK

P.P.S.—How do you like the *Ring and the Book?* It is full of wonderful work, but it seems to me that whereas other poets are the more liable to get incoherent the more fanciful their starting-point happens to be, the thing that makes Browning drunk is to give him a dram of prosaic reality, and unluckily this time the 'gum tickler' is less like pure Cognac than Seven Dials Gin. Whether the consequent evolutions will be bearable to their proposed extent without the intervening walls of the station-house to tone down their exuberance may be dubious. This *entre nous.*—DANTE GABRIEL ROSSETTI, Letter to William Allingham (Dec. 23, 1868)

It is certain that by whatever other deficiencies it may be marked the *Ring and the Book* is blameless for the most characteristic of all the shortcomings of contemporary verse, a grievous sterility of thought. And why? Because sterility of thought is the blight struck into the minds of men by timorous and halt-footed scepticism, by a half-hearted dread of what chill thing the truth might prove itself, by unmanly reluctance or moral incapacity to carry the faculty of poetic vision over the whole field; and because Mr. Browning's intelligence, on the other hand, is masculine and courageous, moving cheerfully on the solid earth of an articulate and defined conviction, and careful not to omit realities from the conception of the great drama, merely for being unsightly to the too fastidious eye, or jarring in the ear, or too bitterly perplexing to faith or understanding. It is this resolute feeling after and grip of fact which is at the root of his distinguishing fruitfulness of thought, and it is exuberance of thought, spontaneous, well-marked, and sapid, that keeps him out of poetical preaching, on the one hand, and mere making of music, on the other. Regret as we may the fantastic rudeness and unscrupulous barbarisms into which Mr. Browning's art too often falls, and find what fault we may with his method, let us ever remember how much he has to say, and how effectively he communicates the shock of new thought which was first imparted to him by the vivid conception of a large and far-reaching story. The value of the thought, indeed, is not to be measured by poetic tests; but still the thought has poetic value, too, for it is this which has stirred in the writer that keen yet impersonal interest in the actors of his story and in its situations which is one of the most certain notes of true dramatic feeling, and which therefore gives the most unfailing stimulus to the interest of the appreciative reader.—JOHN MORLEY, "On *The Ring and the Book*," *Fortnightly Review*, March 1869, pp. 341–42

At last, the *opus magnum* of our generation lies before the world—the 'ring is rounded'; and we are left in doubt which to admire most, the supremely precious gold of the material or the wondrous beauty of the workmanship. The fascination of the work is still so strong upon us, our eyes are still so spell-bound by the immortal features of Pompilia (which shine through the troubled mists of the story with almost insufferable beauty), that we feel it difficult to write calmly and without exaggeration; yet we must record at once our conviction, not merely that *The Ring and the Book* is beyond all parallel the supremest poetical achievement of our time, but that it is the most precious and profound spiritual treasure that England has produced since the days of Shakspeare. Its intellectual greatness is as nothing compared with its trancendent spiritual teaching.

Day after day it grows into the soul of the reader, until all the outlines of thought are brightened and every mystery of the world becomes more and more softened into human emotion. Once and for ever must critics dismiss the old stale charge that Browning is a mere intellectual giant, difficult of comprehension, hard of assimilation. This great book *is* difficult of comprehension, *is* hard of assimilation; not because it is obscure—every fibre of the thought is clear as day; not because it is intellectual,—and it is intellectual in the highest sense,—but because the capacity to comprehend such a book must be spiritual; because, although a child's brain might grasp the general features of the picture, only a purified nature could absorb and feel its profoundest meanings. The man who tosses it aside because it is 'difficult' is simply adopting a subterfuge to hide his moral littleness, not his mental incapacity. It would be unsafe to predict anything concerning a production so many-sided; but we quite believe that its true public lies outside the literary circle, that men of inferior capacity will grow by the aid of it, and that feeble women, once fairly initiated into the mystery, will cling to it as a succour passing all succour save that which is purely religious.

We should be grossly exaggerating if we were to aver that Mr. Browning is likely to take equal rank with the supreme genius of the world; only a gallery of pictures like the Shaksperean group could enable him to do that; and, moreover, his very position as an educated modern must necessarily limit his field of workmanship. What we wish to convey is, that Mr. Browning exhibits—to a great extent in all his writings, but particularly in this great work—a wealth of nature and a perfection of spiritual insight which we have been accustomed to find in the pages of Shakspeare, and in those pages only. His fantastic intellectual feats, his verbosity, his power of quaint versification, are quite other matters. The one great and patent fact is, that, with a faculty in our own time at least unparalleled, he manages to create beings of thoroughly human fibre; he is just without judgment, without preoccupation, to every being so created; and he succeeds, without a single didactic note, in stirring the soul of the spectator with the concentrated emotion and spiritual exaltation which heighten the soul's stature in the finest moments of life itself.—Robert Buchanan, *Athenaeum*, March 20, 1869, p. 399

I read some, not much, of *The Ring and the Book*, but as the tale was not edifying and one of our people, who had been reviewing it, said that further on it was coarser, I did not see, without a particular object, sufficient reason for going on with it. So far as I read I was greatly struck with the skill in which he displayed the facts from different points of view: this is masterly, and to do it through three volumes more shews a great body of genius. I remember a good case of 'the impotent collection of particulars' of which you speak in the description of the market place at Florence where he found the book of the trial: it is a pointless photograph of still life, such as I remember in Balzac, minute upholstery description; only that in Balzac, who besides is writing prose, all tells and is given with a reserve and simplicity of style which Browning has not got. Indeed I hold with the oldfashioned criticism that Browning is not really a poet, that he has all the gifts but the one needful and the pearls without the string; rather one should say raw nuggets and rough diamonds. I suppose him to resemble Ben Jonson, only that Ben Jonson has more real poetry.—Gerard Manley Hopkins, Letter to R. W. Dixon (Oct. 12, 1881)

The dramatic monologue repeats itself in the finest poems of the *Men and Women*, and *Dramatis Personæ*; and Mr. Browning's constructive power thus remains, as it were, dif-

fused, till it culminates again in *The Ring and the Book*: at once his greatest constructive achievement, and the triumph of the monologue form. From this time onwards, the monologue will be his prevailing mode of expression, but each will often form an independent work. *The Ring and the Book* is thus our next object of interest.

Mr. Browning was strolling one day through a square in Florence, the Piazza San Lorenzo, which is a standing market for old clothes, old furniture, and old curiosities of every kind, when a parchment-covered book attracted his eye, from amidst the artistic or nondescript rubbish of one of the stalls. It was the record of a murder which had taken place in Rome. ⟨. . .⟩

The book proved, on examination, to contain the whole history of the case, as carried on in writing, after the fashion of those days: pleadings and counter-pleadings, the depositions of defendants and witnesses; manuscript letters announcing the execution of the murderer; and the "instrument of the Definitive Sentence" which established the perfect innocence of the murdered wife: these various documents having been collected and bound together by some person interested in the trial, possibly the very Cencini, friend of the Franceschini family, to whom the manuscript letters are addressed. Mr. Browning bought the whole for the value of eightpence, and it became the raw material of what appeared four years later as *The Ring and the Book*.—Alexandra Orr, *A Handbook to the Works of Robert Browning*, 1885, pp. 75–76

I think I may class the *Ring and the Book* among ⟨my literary passions⟩, though I have never been otherwise a devotee of Browning. But I was still newly home from Italy, or away from home, when that poem appeared, and whether or not it was because it took me so with the old enchantment of that land, I gave my heart promptly to it. Of course, there are terrible *longueurs* in it, and you do get tired of the same story told over and over from the different points of view, and yet it is such a great story, and unfolded with such a magnificent breadth and noble fulness, that one who blames it lightly blames himself heavily. There are certain books of it—"Caponsacchi's story," "Pompilia's story," and "Count Guido's story"—that I think ought to rank with the greatest poetry ever written, and that have a direct, dramatic expression of the fact and character, which is without rival. There is a noble and lofty pathos in the close of Caponsacchi's statement, an artless and manly break from his self-control throughout, that seems to me the last possible effect in its kind; and Pompilia's story holds all of womanhood in it, the purity, the passion, the tenderness, the helplessness. But if I begin to praise this or any of the things I have liked, I do not know when I should stop. Yes, as I think it over, the *Ring and the Book* appears to me one of the great few poems whose splendor can never suffer lasting eclipse, however it may have presently fallen into abeyance. If it had impossibly come down to us from some elder time, or had not been so perfectly modern in its recognition of feeling and motives ignored by the less conscious poetry of the past, it might be ranked with the great epics.—William Dean Howells, "Certain Preferences and Experiences," *My Literary Passions*, 1895

THE INN ALBUM

This is a decidedly irritating and displeasing performance. It is growing more difficult every year for Mr. Browning's old friends to fight his battles for him, and many of them will feel that on this occasion the cause is really too hopeless, and the great poet must himself be answerable for his indiscretions. Nothing that Mr. Browning writes, of course, can be vapid; if this were possible, it would be a much simpler affair. If it were a case of a writer "running thin," as the phrase is, there would be no need for criticism; there would be nothing in the way of matter to criticise, and old readers would have no heart to reproach. But it may be said of Mr. Browning that he runs thick rather than thin, and he need claim none of the tenderness granted to those who have used themselves up in the service of their admirers. He is robust and vigorous; more so now, even, than heretofore, and he is more prolific than in the earlier part of his career. But his wantonness, his wilfulness, his crudity, his inexplicable want of secondary thought, as we may call it, of the stage of reflection that follows upon the first outburst of the idea, and smooths, shapes, and adjusts it— all this alloy of his great genius is more sensible now than ever. *The Inn Album* reads like a series of rough notes for a poem— of hasty hieroglyphics and symbols, decipherable only to the author himself. A great poem might perhaps have been made of it, but assuredly it is not a great poem, nor any poem whatsoever. It is hard to say very coherently what it is. Up to a certain point, like everything of Mr. Browning's, it is highly dramatic and vivid, and beyond that point, like all its companions, it is as little dramatic as possible. It is not narrative, for there is not a line of comprehensible, consecutive statement in the two hundred and eleven pages of the volume. It is not lyrical, for there is not a phrase which in any degree does the office of the poetry that comes lawfully into the world—chants itself, images itself, or lingers in the memory. "That bard's a Browning; he neglects the form!" one of the characters exclaims with irresponsible frankness. That Mr. Browning knows he "neglects the form," and does not particularly care, does not very much help matters; it only deepens the reader's sense of the graceless and thankless and altogether unavailable character of the poem. And when we say unavailable, we make the only reproach which is worth addressing to a writer of Mr. Browning's intellectual power. A poem with so many presumptions in its favor as such an authorship carries with it is a thing to make some intellectual use of, to care for, to remember, to return to, to linger over, to become intimate with. But we can as little imagine a reader (who has not the misfortune to be a reviewer) addressing himself more than once to the perusal of *The Inn Album*, as we can fancy cultivating for conversational purposes the society of a person afflicted with a grievous impediment of speech. ⟨. . .⟩

The whole picture indefinably appeals to the imagination. There is something very curious about it and even rather arbitrary, and the reader wonders how it came, in the poet's mind, to take exactly that shape. It is very much as if he had worked backwards, had seen his dénouement first, as a mere picture—the two corpses in the inn-parlor, and the young man and his cousin confronted above them—and then had traced back the possible motives and sources. In looking for these Mr. Browning has of course encountered a vast number of deep discriminations and powerful touches of portraiture. He deals with human character as a chemist with his acids and alkalies, and while he mixes his colored fluids in a way that surprises the profane, knows perfectly well what he is about. But there is too apt to be in his style that hiss and sputter and evil aroma which characterize the proceedings of the laboratory. The idea, with Mr. Browning, always tumbles out into the world in some grotesque hind-foremost manner; it is like an unruly horse backing out of his stall, and stamping and plunging as he comes. His thought knows no simple stage—at the very moment of its birth it is a terribly complicated affair. We frankly confess, at the risk of being accused of deplorable levity of mind, that we have found this want of clearness of

explanation, of continuity, of at least superficial verisimilitude, of the smooth, the easy, the agreeable, quite fatal to our enjoyment of *The Inn Album*. It is all too argumentative, too curious and recondite. The people talk too much in long set speeches, at a moment's notice, and the anomaly so common in Browning, that the talk of the women is even more rugged and insoluble than that of the men, is here greatly exaggerated. We are reading neither prose nor poetry; it is too real for the ideal, and too ideal for the real. The author of *The Inn Album* is not a writer to whom we care to pay trivial compliments, and it is not a trivial complaint to say that his book is only barely comprehensible. Of a successful dramatic poem one ought to be able to say more.—HENRY JAMES, "Browning's *Inn Album*," *Nation*, Jan. 20, 1876, p. 49

After reading such poetry as this, in which the passionate expression is but just touched by the defect we have been noticing, we have little cause to fear that a mannerism, which must help to shorten the fame of Mr. Browning's later poems, has become inevitable to him. Everyone must hope that he will yet produce works not defaced by it. And happily no one can doubt that he has still in him rich stores of poetic energy, and of an energy which is in ceaseless activity in the most diverse directions.

But the imperfection of form is not the only thing which will, we believe, make productions like the *Inn Album* short-lived. Form and matter alike, the poem is pitched at a low level; and not even Mr. Browning's genius is sufficient to dignify a story which contains the elements of so little real pathos, and so painfully little beauty. With all its power, we are not refreshed, nor awed, nor uplifted by the *Inn Album*; it has no form to charm us, little brightness to relieve its gloom, and, except for the dramatic touches we have tried to indicate, the human nature it shows us is too mean, or too commonplace, or too repellent, to excite more than the pleasure of following a psychological revelation.—A. C. BRADLEY, "Mr. Browning's *Inn Album*," *Macmillan's Magazine*, Feb. 1876, p. 354

WALTER BAGEHOT
From "Wordsworth, Tennyson, and Browning;
or, Pure, Ornate, and Grotesque Art
in English Poetry" (1864)
Collected Works, ed. Norman St. John-Stevas
1965, Volume 2, pp. 352–61

There is, however, a third kind of art which differs from these ⟨ornate art and pure art⟩ on the point in which they most resemble one another. Ornate art and pure art have this in common, that they paint the types of literature in as good perfection as they can. Ornate art, indeed, uses undue disguises and unreal enhancements; it does not confine itself to the best types; on the contrary it is its office to make the best of imperfect types and lame approximations; but ornate art, as much as pure art, catches its subject in the best light it can, takes the most developed aspect of it which it can find, and throws upon it the most congruous colours it can use. But grotesque art does just the contrary. It takes the type, so to say, *in difficulties*. It gives a representation of it in its minimum development, amid the circumstances least favourable to it, just while it is struggling with obstacles, just where it is encumbered with incongruities. It deals, to use the language of science, not with normal types but with abnormal specimens; to use the language of old philosophy, not with what nature is striving to be, but with what by some lapse she has happened to become.

This art works by contrast. It enables you to see, it makes you see, the perfect type by painting the opposite deviation. It shows you what ought to be by what ought not to be; when complete, it reminds you of the perfect image by showing you the distorted and imperfect image. Of this art we possess in the present generation one prolific master. Mr. Browning is an artist working by incongruity. Possibly hardly one of his most considerable efforts can be found which is not great because of its odd mixture. He puts together things which no one else would have put together, and produces on our minds a result which no one else would have produced, or tried to produce. His admirers may not like all we may have to say of him. But in our way we too are among his admirers. No one ever read him without seeing not only his great ability but his great *mind*. He not only possesses superficial useable talents, but the strong something, the inner secret something, which uses them and controls them; he is great, not in mere accomplishments, but in himself. He has applied a hard strong intellect to real life; he has applied the same intellect to the problems of his age. He has striven to know what *is*: he has endeavoured not to be cheated by counterfeits, not to be infatuated with illusions. His heart is in what he says. He has battered his brain against his creed till he believes it. He has accomplishments too, the more effective because they are mixed. He is at once a student of mysticism and a citizen of the world. He brings to the club sofa distinct visions of old creeds, intense images of strange thoughts: he takes to the bookish student tidings of wild Bohemia, and little traces of the *demi-monde*. He puts down what is good for the naughty and what is naughty for the good. Over women his easier writings exercise that imperious power which belongs to the writings of a great man of the world upon such matters. He knows women, and therefore they wish to know him. If we blame many of Browning's efforts, it is in the interest of art, and not from a wish to hurt or degrade him.

If we wanted to illustrate the nature of grotesque art by an exaggerated instance, we should have selected a poem which the chance of late publication brings us in this new volume. Mr. Browning has undertaken to describe what may be called *mind in difficulties*—mind set to make out the universe under the worst and hardest circumstances. He takes 'Caliban,' not perhaps exactly Shakespeare's Caliban, but an analogous and worse creature; a strong thinking power, but a nasty creature— a gross animal, uncontrolled and unelevated by any feeling of religion or duty. The delineation of him will show that Mr. Browning does not wish to take undue advantage of his readers by a choice of nice subjects.

> 'Will sprawl, now that the heat of day is best,
> Flat on his belly in the pit's much mire,
> With elbows wide, fists clenched to prop his chin.
> And, while he kicks both feet in the cool slush,
> And feels about his spine small eft-things course,
> Run in and out each arm, and make him laugh;
> And while above his head a pompion-plant,
> Coating the cave-top as a brow its eye,
> Creeps down to touch and tickle hair and beard,
> And now a flower drops with a bee inside,
> And now a fruit to snap at, catch and crunch,—

This pleasant creature proceeds to give his idea of the origin of the universe, and it is as follows. Caliban speaks in the third person, and is of opinion that the maker of the universe took to making it on account of his personal discomfort:—

> Setebos, Setebos, and Setebos!
> 'Thinketh, He dwelleth i' the cold o' the moon.

> 'Thinketh He made it, with the sun to match,
> But not the stars; the stars came otherwise;
> Only made clouds, winds, meteors, such as that;
> Also this isle, what lives and grows thereon,
> And snaky sea which rounds and ends the same.
> 'Thinketh, it came of being ill at ease:
> He hated that He cannot change His cold,
> Nor cure its ache. 'Hath spied an icy fish
> That longed to 'scape the rock-stream where she
>   lived,
> And thaw herself within the lukewarm brine
> O' the lazy sea her stream thrusts far amid,
> A crystal spike 'twixt two warm walls of wave;
> Only she ever sickened, found repulse
> At the other kind of water, not her life,
> (Green-dense and dim-delicious, bred o' the sun)
> Flounced back from bliss she was not born to
>   breathe,
> And in her old bounds buried her despair,
> Hating and loving warmth alike: so He.
> 'Thinketh, He made thereat the sun, this isle,
> Trees and the fowls here, beast and creeping thing.
> Yon otter, sleek-wet, black, lithe as a leech;
> Yon auk, one fire-eye, in a ball of foam,
> That floats and feeds; a certain badger brown
> He hath watched hunt with that slant white-wedge
>   eye
> By moonlight; and the pie with the long tongue
> That pricks deep into oakwarts for a worm,
> And says a plain word when she finds her prize,
> But will not eat the ants; the ants themselves
> That build a wall of seeds and settled stalks
> About their hole—He made all these and more,
> Made all we see, and us, in spite: how else?

It may seem perhaps to most readers that these lines are very difficult, and that they are unpleasant. And so they are. We quote them to illustrate, not the *success* of grotesque art, but the *nature* of grotesque art. It shows the end at which this species of art aims, and if it fails it is from over-boldness in the choice of a subject by the artist, or from the defects of its execution. A thinking faculty more in difficulties—a great type—an inquisitive, searching intellect under more disagreeable conditions, with worse helps, more likely to find falsehood, less likely to find truth, can scarcely be imagined. Nor is the mere description of the thought at all bad: on the contrary, if we closely examine it, it is very clever. Hardly anyone could have amassed so many ideas at once nasty and suitable. But scarcely any readers—any casual readers—who are not of the sect of Mr. Browning's admirers will be able to examine it enough to appreciate it. From a defect, partly of subject, and partly of style, many of Mr. Browning's works make a demand upon the reader's zeal and sense of duty to which the nature of most readers is unequal. They have on the turf the convenient expression 'staying power': some horses can hold on and others cannot. But hardly any reader not of especial and peculiar nature can hold on through such composition. There is not enough of 'staying power' in human nature. One of his greatest admirers once owned to us that he seldom or never began a new poem without looking on in advance, and foreseeing with caution what length of intellectual adventure he was about to commence. Whoever will work hard at such poems will find much mind in them: they are a sort of quarry of ideas, but whoever goes there will find these ideas in such a jagged, ugly, useless shape that he can hardly bear them.

We are not judging Mr. Browning simply from a hasty recent production. All poets are liable to misconceptions, and if such a piece as 'Caliban upon Setebos' were an isolated error, a venial and particular exception, we should have given it no prominence. We have put it forward because it just elucidates both our subject and the characteristics of Mr. Browning. But many other of his best known pieces do so almost equally ⟨. . .⟩

It is very natural that a poet whose wishes incline, or whose genius conducts him, to a grotesque art, should be attracted towards mediæval subjects. There is no age whose legends are so full of grotesque subjects, and no age where real life was so fit to suggest them. Then, more than at any other time, good principles have been under great hardships. The vestiges of ancient civilisation, the germs of modern civilisation, the little remains of what had been, the small beginnings of what is, were buried under a cumbrous mass of barbarism and cruelty. Good elements hidden in horrid accompaniments are the special theme of grotesque art, and these mediæval life and legends afford more copiously than could have been furnished before Christianity gave its new elements of good, or since modern civilisation has removed some few at least of the old elements of destruction. A *buried* life like the spiritual mediæval was Mr. Browning's natural element, and he was right to be attracted by it. His mistake has been, that he has not made it pleasant; that he has forced his art to topics on which no one could charm, or on which he, at any rate, could not; that on these occasions and in these poems he has failed in fascinating men and women of sane taste.

We say 'sane' because there is a most formidable and estimable *insane* taste. The will has great though indirect power over the taste, just as it has over the belief. There are some horrid beliefs from which human nature revolts, from which at first it shrinks, to which, at first, no effort can force it. But if we fix the mind upon them they have a power over us just because of their natural offensiveness. They are like the sight of human blood: experienced soldiers tell us that at first men are sickened by the smell and newness of blood almost to death and fainting, but that as soon as they harden their hearts and stiffen their minds, as soon as they *will* bear it, then comes an appetite for slaughter, a tendency to gloat on carnage, to love blood, at least for the moment, with a deep, eager love. It is a principle that if we put down a healthy instinctive aversion, nature avenges herself by creating an unhealthy insane attraction. For this reason, the most earnest truth-seeking men fall into the worst delusions; they will not let their mind alone; they force it towards some ugly thing, which a crotchet of argument, a conceit of intellect recommends, and nature punishes their disregard of her warning by subjection to the ugly one, by belief in it. Just so, the most industrious critics get the most admiration. They think it unjust to rest in their instinctive natural horror: they overcome it, and angry nature gives them over to ugly poems and marries them to detestable stanzas.

Mr. Browning possibly, and some of the worst of Mr. Browning's admirers certainly, will say that these grotesque objects exist in real life, and therefore they ought to be, at least may be, described in art. But though pleasure is not the end of poetry, pleasing is a condition of poetry. An exceptional monstrosity of horrid ugliness cannot be made pleasing, except it be made to suggest—to recall—the perfection, the beauty, from which it is a deviation. Perhaps in extreme cases no art is equal to this; but then such self-imposed problems should not be worked by the artist; these out-of-the-way and detestable subjects should be let alone by him. It is rather characteristic of Mr. Browning to neglect this rule. He is the most of a realist, and the least of an idealist, of any poet we know. He evidently sympathises with some part at least of Bishop Blougram's apology. Anyhow this world exists. 'There *is* good wine—there

are pretty women—there *are* comfortable benefices—there *is* money, and it is pleasant to spend it. Accept the creed of your age and you get these, reject that creed and you lose them. And for what do you lose them? For a fancy creed of your own, which no one else will accept, which hardly anyone will call a "creed," which most people will consider a sort of unbelief.' Again, Mr. Browning evidently loves what we may call the realism, the grotesque realism, of Orthodox Christianity. Many parts of it in which great divines have felt keen difficulties are quite pleasant to him. He must *see* his religion, he must have an 'object-lesson' in believing. He must have a creed that will *take*, which wins and holds the miscellaneous world, which stout men will heed, which nice women will adore. The spare moments of solitary religion—the 'obstinate questionings,' the 'high instincts,' the 'first affections,' the 'shadowy recollections,'

> Which, be they what they may,
> Are yet the fountain light of all our day,
> Are yet a master light of all our seeing;

the great but vague faith—the unutterable tenets—seem to him worthless, visionary; they are not enough 'immersed in matter;' they move about 'in worlds not realised.' We wish he could be tried like the prophet once; he would have found God in the earthquake and the storm; he would have deciphered from them a bracing and a rough religion: he would have known that crude men and ignorant women felt them too, and he would accordingly have trusted them; but he would have distrusted and disregarded the 'still small voice;' he would have said it was 'fancy'—a thing you thought you heard to-day, but were not sure you had heard to-morrow: he would call it a nice illusion, an immaterial prettiness; he would ask triumphantly, 'How are you to get the mass of men to heed this little thing?' he would have persevered and insisted, '*My wife* does not hear it.'

But although a suspicion of beauty, and a taste for ugly reality, have led Mr. Browning to exaggerate the functions, and to caricature the nature of grotesque art, we own, or rather, we maintain, that he has given many excellent specimens of that art within its proper boundaries and limits. Take an example, his picture of what we may call the *bourgeois* nature in *difficulties*; in the utmost difficulty, in contact with magic and the supernatural. He has made of it something homely, comic, true; reminding us of what *bourgeois* nature really is. By showing us the type under abnormal conditions, he reminds us of the type under its best and most satisfactory conditions.

EDWARD DOWDEN
From "Mr. Browning's *Sordello*"
Fraser's Magazine, October 1867, pp. 518–22

Here is a singular fact: Mr. Browning is declared by his contemporaries to be a distinguished poet, a true artist, a profound and original thinker; and when we ask, 'What of his most laborious undertaking?' the answer is (the answer of his ablest critic), 'We do not at all doubt that Mr. Browning understands his own drift clearly enough,' but 'probably no man or woman except the author ever yet understood it;' and 'We suspect that if it be true, as his dedication appears to indicate, that there is really one mortal who to his own satisfaction has understood Mr. Browning in *Sordello*, it would be found on crossexamination of that one, that (like Hegel's sole philosophical confidant) even he has *mis*understood him.'

So wrote an admirable critic in the *National Review*. And what says Mr. Browning himself? That the poem is one which the many may not like, but which the few must; that he imagined it with so clear a power of vision, and so faithfully declared what he saw, that no material change can be made in it without injury; and that though the faults of expression are numerous, they are such as 'with care for a man or book' may be surmounted.[1] The truth on the critic's side—not a very productive truth—has perhaps received adequate consideration in the last twenty-seven years; we may now perhaps with a good conscience try to see the truth on the author's side, which may happen to be more productive.

One word on the obscurity of *Sordello*. It arises not so much from peculiarities of style, and the involved structure of occasional sentences (too much has been said on this; as a rule the style of *Sordello* is vigorously straightforward), as from the unrelaxing demand which is made throughout upon the intellectual and imaginative energy and alertness of the reader. This constant demand exhausts the power of attention in a short time, and the mind is unable to sustain its watchfulness and sureness of action, so that if we read much at a sitting we often find the first few pages clear and admirable, while the last three or four over which the eye passes before we close the book leave us bewildered and jaded; and we say, '*Sordello* is so dreadfully obscure.' The truth is, Mr. Browning has given too much in his couple of hundred pages; there is not a line of the poem which is not as full of matter as a line can be; so that if the ten syllables sometimes seem to start and give way under the strain, we need not wonder. We come to no places in *Sordello* where we can rest and dream or look up at the sky. Ideas, emotions, images, analyses, descriptions, still come crowding on. There is too much of everything; we cannot see the wood for the trees. Towards the end of the third book Mr. Browning interrupts the story that he may 'pause and breathe.' That is an apt expression; but Mr. Browning seems unable to slacken the motion of his mind, and during this breathing-space heart and brain, perceptive and reflective powers, are almost more busily at work than ever.

Before proceeding to trace in detail the story of *Sordello*, including what the author has called 'the incidents in the development of a soul,' it will be right to indicate the place of *Sordello* amongst the poems of Mr. Browning, and to make clear its purport as a whole. *Sordello* is a companion poem of *Paracelsus* (five years after the publication of which it appeared), and no one can possess himself of the ideas of Mr. Browning without a study of the two. 'Je sens en moi l'infini,' exclaimed Napoleon one day, with his hand upon his breast. 'Je sens en moi l'infini' is the germ-idea of these poems. An account of Mr. Browning as a thinker would be an insufficient account of his genius, for he is also an artist. But more than almost any other poet he is an intellectual artist, and especially in *Paracelsus* and *Sordello* he worked—worked too much, perhaps—under the guidance of ideas, abstract views of character, or the translation into intellectual theorems of the instincts of the heart (an 'analyst' Mr. Browning calls himself in *Sordello*), too little perhaps through a pure sympathy with life in some of its individual, concrete forms. If any artist may be said to embody in his work a clearly defined system of thought, this may be said of Mr. Browning; a system, however, which is not manufactured by logic, but the vital growth of his whole nature in an intellectual direction. Man here on earth, according to the central and controlling thought of Mr. Browning, man here in a state of preparation for other lives, and surrounded by wondrous spiritual influences, is too great for the sphere that contains him, while at the same time he can

exist only by submitting for the present to the conditions it imposes; never without fatal loss becoming content with such submission, or regarding those conditions as final. Our nature here is unfinished, imperfect; but its glory, its peculiarity—that which makes us men, not God and not brutes—lies in this very character of imperfection, giving scope as it does for indefinite growth and progress. This progress is at the present time commonly thought of as progress of the race; Mr. Browning does not forget this (witness the concluding pages of *Paracelsus*), but he dwells chiefly upon the progress of the individual. Now a man may commit either of two irretrievable errors: he may renounce (through temptations of sense and other causes, but most frequently through supineness of heart, or brain, or hand, or else through prudential motives) his future, his spiritual, his infinite life and its concerns. That is one error. Or he may try to force those concerns, and corresponding states of thought, feeling, and endeavour into the present material life, the life of limitation and of inadequate and imperfect resources. That is the other. He may deny his higher nature, which is ever yearning upward to God through all high forms of human thought, emotion, and action (Mr. Browning loves to insist on this point); he may weary of failure, which is his glory (as generating a higher tendency), and fall back upon a limited and improgressive perfection; or else he may spurn at the conditions of existence, and endeavour to realise in this life what is work for eternity. To deny heaven and the infinite life—that is one extreme; to deny earth and the finite life—that is the other. If we are content with the limited and perishable joys, and gifts and faculties of the world, we see not God and never shall see him. If, on the contrary, we aim at accomplishing under all the restrictions of this life the work of eternity—if we desire absolute knowledge or none at all, infinite love or no love, a boundless exercise of our will, the manifestation of our total power, or no exercise of our will—then we shall either destroy ourselves, dash ourselves to pieces against the walls of time and space, or else, seeing that our objects are unattainable, sink into a state of hopeless enervation. But between these two extremes lies a middle course, and in it will be found the true life of man. He must not rest content with earth and the gifts of earth; he must not aim at 'thrusting in time eternity's concern;' but he must perpetually grasp at things which are just within, or almost without his reach, and, having attained them, find that they are unsatisfying; so that by an endless series of aspirations and endeavours, which generate new aspirations and new endeavours, he may be sent on to God and Christ and heaven.

These ideas lead us to the central point, from which we can perceive the peculiarity and origin of Mr. Browning's feeling with regard to nature, art, religion, love, beauty, knowledge. Around them we observe, as we read through his works, one poem after another falling into position, each bringing in addition something of its own.

Is it of external nature that Mr. Browning speaks? The preciousness of external nature lies in its being but the manifest power and love of God to which our heart springs as fire. In that *Easter Dream* of the last judgment what is the doom of God upon the condemned soul? It is to take all that the soul desires; and since the soul of the lost man loved the world, the world with its beauty, and wonder, and delight, but never yearned upward to God, who dwelt in them, the decree is pronounced:

> Thou art shut
> Out of the heaven of spirit; glut
> Thy sense upon the world.

And no condemnation could have been more awful; for nature has betrayed and ruined us if we rest in it,—betrayed and ruined us unless it sends us onward unsatisfied to God.

And what are Mr. Browning's chief doctrines on the subject of art? No one has so profoundly exposed the worldliness of the connoisseur or virtuoso, who, feeling none of the unsatisfied aspirations of the artist, rests in the visible products of art, and looks for nothing beyond them. 'The Bishop Orders His Tomb at St. Praxed's,' will recur to the mind of the reader. The true glory of art is that in its creation there arise desires and aspirations which can never be satisfied on earth; but which generate new aspirations and new desires, by which the spirit mounts to God himself. The artist who can realise his ideal has missed the true gain of art. In *Pippa Passes* the regeneration of Jules the sculptor's art turns on his foreseeing in the very perfection he had attained to an ultimate failure. And Andrea del Sarto being weighed is found wanting, precisely because he is 'the faultless painter:'

> A man's reach should exceed his grasp,
> Or what's a heaven for? All is silver-grey,
> Placid and perfect with my art—the worse!

But Andrea with a copy of one of Raphael's paintings before him can imagine his contemporary

> Reaching, that heaven might so replenish him,
> Above and through his art—for it gives way;
> That arm is wrongly put—and these again—
> A fault to pardon in the drawing's lines.

The true artist is ever sent through and beyond his art to God. Tears start into the eyes of Abt Vogler, who has been extemporising on his musical instrument, because now in the silence he feels the beauty of that palace of music which he reared, and which is gone never to be recalled. There is in the silence a sense of loss, vacancy, and failure. But the failure generates a higher aspiration, and the musician reaches upward to God:

> Therefore to whom turn I but to Thee, the ineffable
>   Name?
> Builder and maker, thou, of houses not made with
>   hands.
> What, have fear of change from thee who art ever the
>   same?
> Doubt that thy power can fill the heart that thy power
>   expands?

Honour to the early Christian painters who rejected a limited perfection such as that of Greek art, the subject of which was finite, and which taught men to submit, and who dared to be faulty; faulty, because the subject of their art was full of infinite hopes and fears, and because they would lead men to aspire. [2] Is it love of which Mr. Browning speaks? No passion so much as love can

> Make time break,
> And let us pent-up creatures through
> Into eternity our due. [3]

But the means which love can command on earth are always incommensurate to its nature and its desires. Yet in apparent failure there may be gain, not loss. Let the reader turn to those companion poems—poems of subtle meaning—*Love in a Life*, and, *Life in a Love*. In each poem love is represented as pursuing its object without ever attaining it. This is a real failure, says Mr. Browning, when love is dependent on a life, and controlled by a life's limitations. But in its own nature, love is infinite; and if we could but *live in love*, life would partake of the infinity and eternity of the passion or essence with which it would be consubstantial; the object of desire

could never be attained, but it would be for ever pursued, and apparent failure would but urge on to the real success, to everlasting aspiration and endeavour. Once more: does Mr. Browning speak of knowledge? Its gleams were meant to 'sting with hunger for full light.' Its goal is God himself. Its most precious part is that which is least positive; those momentary intuitions of things which eye hath not seen, nor ear heard— 'fallings from us, vanishings.' [4] Even the revelation of God in Christianity left room for doubts and guesses; because growth is the law of man's nature, and perfect knowledge would have stayed his growth; [5] while, at the same time, its assurances of a boundless life beyond the grave saved Christianity from the failure of heathenism, which could not extinguish man's longings for a higher than material or worldly perfection, but was unable to utilise them, or suggest how they could be changed from restlessness and self-conflict to a sustaining hope. [6] The reader may complete the impression now produced by a thoughtful reading of a poem in which these ideas of Mr. Browning find perhaps their noblest expression,—'Rabbi Ben Ezra.'

So far Mr. Browning's system of thought has been illustrated chiefly by his shorter poems. But to the same central ideas belong *Paracelsus* (published 1835), *Sordello* (1840), and *Easter Day* (1850). In each we read 'a soul's tragedy.' Paracelsus aspires to absolute knowledge, and to power based on such knowledge, the attainment of which is forbidden by the conditions of our existence. In the same poem, a second phase of the same error—that of refusing for the present to submit to the terms of life—is represented in Aprile, who would '*love* infinitely and be loved;' the boundlessness of his desires produces a disdain of such attainments and accomplishments as are possible on this earth; his ideal being beyond possibility of realisation, he rejects all the means of life since they are proved inadequate to his aspirations, and rejects the results of life because they are limited and imperfect; he cannot stoop from his sublime isolation in a world of dreams to task himself for the good of his fellows, and he sinks into a state of hopeless enervation. Paracelsus is the victim of the temptations of an aspiring *intellect*; Aprile, of the temptations of a yearning, passionate *heart*. Mr. Browning decided to complete our view of this side of the subject by showing the failure of an attempt to manifest the infinite scope, and realise the infinite energy of *will*, the inability of a great nature to deploy all its magnificent resources, and by compelling men in some way or other to acknowledge that nature as their master, to gain a full sense of its existence. With this purpose he wrote *Sordello*.

Notes

1. 'My own faults of expression were many; but with care for a man or book such would be surmounted, and without it what avails the faultlessness of either? I blame nobody, least of all myself, who did my best then and since; for I lately gave time and pains to turn my work into what the many might, instead of what the few must like; but after all I imagined another thing at first, and therefore leave it as I find it.'—*Dedication of Sordello to J. Milsand of Dijon*. M. Milsand's article on Mr. Browning's poetry which appeared many years ago in the *Revue des Deux Mondes*, may still be read with advantage.
2. *Old Pictures in Florence*.
3. *Dîs Aliter Visum, or Le Byron de nos jours*.
4. *Easter Day*, xxvii., xxviii.
5. *A Death in the Desert*.
6. *Cleon*.

ALFRED AUSTIN
From "The Poetry of the Period"
Temple Bar, June 1869, pp. 320–33

Whether Mr. Browning keeps a Commonplace Book, we have no means of knowing; but we have every means of knowing that he thinks in prose, for the prose thoughts are there before us, gratuitously turned by some arbitrary whim, which we confess completely puzzles us, into metre. Mr. Browning is, as we have said, a profound thinker, and nearly all his thoughts have the quality of depth. Now, probably all thoughts to which this quality of depth can be ascribed, arrive at the portals of the brain in this prose—their natural vesture; whilst, on the contrary, lofty thoughts, their antitheses, usually enter it in the subtle garb of music. Here we have a clear difference in kind; prose thoughts, so to speak, from below—poetical thoughts, so to speak, from above. If we suppose a permeable plane dividing these two regions of thought, we can easily understand how there comes to be what we may call a sliding scale of poets, and a sliding scale of philosophical thinkers; some of the latter, to whom the faculty of philosophising cannot be denied, being rather shallow—some of the former, whose claims to poetical status cannot fairly be questioned, not being very soaring; and we can further understand how the natural denizens of one sphere may ever and anon cross the permeable plane, invade the other sphere, and seem to belong to it in the sense in which foreigners belong to a country they are constantly visiting. But for all that there ever remains a substantial difference between the two spheres and between their respective native inhabitants, between the country of poetry and the country of prose, between poetical power and instinct and philosophical power and proclivity. Accordingly, where a man talks the language of the sphere to which he properly belongs—in other words, when a philosophical thinker publishes his thoughts in prose, or a poetical thinker addresses us in verse—our task is comparatively simple. All we have got to do is to decide whether the former be profound or shallow, and whether the latter have a lofty or a lagging pinion. It is when a man affects to talk the language of the sphere to which he does not essentially belong, that he deceives some people, and puzzles us all. This is precisely what Mr. Browning has done. Hence most people scarcely know what to make of this poetico-philosophical hybrid, this claimant to the great inheritance of bardic fame, whose hands are the hands of Esau, but whose voice is the voice of Jacob. Several, whose eyes, like those of Isaac, are dim, and who therefore cannot see, admit the claim—hesitatingly, it is true, again like Isaac—of the hands, and accept him as a poet. But it is the true resonant voice, not the made-up delusive hand, which is the test of the singer; and to those whose sight is not dim, Mr. Browning is not a poet at all—save in the sense that all cultivated men and women of sensitive feelings are poets—but a deep thinker, a profound philosopher, a keen analyser, and a biting wit. With this key to what to most persons is a riddle—for, despite the importunate attempts of certain critics who, as we have already said, having placed Mr. Tennyson on a poetical pedestal considerably too high for him, are now beginning to waver in their extravagant creed, and are disposed to put him on one a trifle lower, placing Mr. Browning there instead, the general public has not yet become quite reconciled to the operation—we think we shall be able to rid them of their perplexities. At any rate, we will keep applying it as we go along.

Let us revert to *Paracelsus* and take our start from it, as Mr. Browning himself did. His lyrical pieces apart—of which

something anon—and the humoristic faculty which has since developed itself in him, Mr. Browning in *Paracelsus* is what Mr. Browning is in all the many so-called poetical works he has since given to the world. He is Mr. Browning, naturally not yet grown to his full size; not yet quite so deep, shrewd, obscure, fantastical, unmusical; but with the exceptions we have just made, what manner and matter of mental man he is may there be satisfactorily scrutinised. He is at his never-abandoned natural task of thinking deep thoughts in prose, and his artificial trick of turning them into verse. He is, as he imagines, working like a dramatist, just as he has since imagined himself to be working as a dramatist in such pieces as *Bishop Blougram's Apology*, "Caliban on Setebos," &c. Indeed, he has let us into the secret of his method in *Sordello*, written very shortly after *Paracelsus*, in the following lines; which we quote, though at the risk perhaps of most of our readers declaring that they have not the faintest notion as to what they mean:

> How I rose,
> And how you have advanced! since evermore
> Yourselves effect what I was fain before
> Effect, what I supplied yourselves suggest,
> What I leave bare yourselves can now invest.
> How we attain to talk as brothers talk,
> In half-words, call things by half-names, no balk
> From discontinuing old aids. To-day
> Takes in account the work of Yesterday:
> Has not the world a Past now, its adept
> New aids? A single touch more may enhance,
> A touch less turn to insignificance,
> Those structures' symmetry the Past has strewed
> The world with, once so bare. Leave the mere rude
> Explicit details! 'tis but brother's speech
> We need, speech where an accent's change gives each
> The other's soul—no speech to understand
> By former audience: need was then to expand,
> Expatiate—hardly were we brothers! true—
> Nor I lament my small remove from you,
> Nor reconstruct what stands already. Ends
> Accomplished turn to means: my art intends
> New structure from the ancient.

It must not be supposed that we quote this passage with approbation. Not only do we think it not poetry, but we think it detestable gibberish, even if we look at it as prose. Had Mr. Browning been writing bonâ-fide prose, he would have put it very differently and much more intelligibly; but talking, to revert to our metaphor, in a foreign language over which he has not obtained due mastery, he is shockingly unintelligible, or at least painfully difficult to understand. By dint of great trouble we have arrived at understanding the above passage, and will endeavour briefly to explain its meaning. Our readers have no doubt heard the vulgar proverb, "A nod is as good as a wink to a blind horse." Mr. Browning wishes to intimate that a nod or a wink is really and seriously as good to an intelligent man of the nineteenth century as formal speech. Shakespeare and such unfortunate individuals, having had to deal with an inferior set of people, were compelled to use "rude explicit details." Mr. Browning's "art intending new structure from the ancient," has only to "talk in half-words, call things by half-names," and if they do not understand him, the fault is theirs of course, not his. They are not his brothers. In this same *Sordello*, from which we are quoting, over each page stands a prose heading, which is a continuation of the foregoing one. Over the passage from which we have made the above extract, the following headings occur: "He asserts the poet's rank and right, Basing these on their proper ground, Recognizing true dignity in service, Whether successively that of Epoist, *Dramatist or, so to call him, analyst,* Who turns in due course synthesist."

Now the last two headings are of great importance, just as is the passage in verse below them which we have quoted, because, however false may be their matter, and however deplorable their manner, they contain Mr. Browning's own estimate of his office, and his own account of his method. As such, they are invaluable to us. Just one more brief confession on his part will complete for us the idea, as understood by himself, of his functions as a poet. In the Dedication of *Sordello* to Mr. Milsand, written in 1863, or twenty-three years after it was first published, Mr. Browning writes: "The historical decoration was purposely of no more importance than a background requires; and my stress lay on the incidents in the development of a soul: *little else is worth study. I, at least, always thought so.*" Thus Mr. Browning's office, according to his own account, is that of an analyst who turns in due course synthesist and develops a soul by half-words; or, as we should put it, it is to get inside an imaginary or historical personage, and evolve him for the benefit of the intelligent public by nods and winks. This is how his "new art intends new structure from the ancient."

We hope our readers understand us; for, if they do not, they will certainly never understand Mr. Browning, and it is highly desirable that they should understand so much of him as the foregoing, both in order to be able to measure him as he asks to be measured, and to appreciate our account of him, which a very little reflection shows to be in perfect harmony with, and indeed substantially the same as, his own account of himself. What is his own account of himself? An analyst who turns in due course synthesist, whose subject matter is souls, and whose method of communication with the outer world is half-words arranged in metre. What is our account of him? A subtle, profound, conscious psychologist, who scientifically gets inside souls, and, having scrutinised their thoughts and motives in a prose and methodical fashion, then makes them give the result, as if they had been scrutinising themselves, in verse. This latter operation Mr. Browning evidently imagines is synthesis. There never was a more ludicrous mistake. It is, in reality, nothing more than the analysis completed and stated, and is no more synthesis than a lecture by Professor Huxley on the *vertebrata* is an animal. Mr. Browning labours under the greatest possible delusion when he imagines that he ever "turns in due course synthesist." That is precisely what he never does. He remains a mere analyst to the end of the chapter, pottering about among the brains and entrails of the souls he has dissected, and utterly unable to do anything with them, except to call attention to the component parts he has skilfully laid bare with his knife. It would be wonderful if he could do anything more; just as wonderful as it would be if the anatomical professor could put together again the poor carcass of the dog he has reduced to so many inanimate members. He can galvanise them, it is true, for a moment, into simulating life. So can Mr. Browning. But that is the range of the synthesis of both of them. If Mr. Browning wants to know of a dramatist who is a real synthesist, we can easily tell him of one. His name is Shakespeare. But, then, Shakespeare was, luckily, not so great in analysis as Mr. Browning. Speaking properly, Shakespeare never analyses at all in our presence, and probably never did so even in the presence of his own consciousness, any more than millions of men who speak grammatically analyse the construction of their sentences before they utter them. Every real drama—indeed every real work of plastic (as opposed

to mere technic) art—is an organism, a growth, a vitality, just as much as is a bird, a tree, or a mammal. Not only is it true that a poet is born, not made, but it is equally true that his poem is born, not made. [1] In his brain, heart, soul, whatever we like to call it—in his being would be, perhaps, the best word—exists the seed or germ of a poem or of many poems; and all that external conditions, sights, sounds, experiences, can do for this seed or germ is to foster or to check it. But the thing itself, the real living, poetic protoplasm, is not to be had or got *ab extra.* Going about seizing upon objects and submitting them to analysis, even though synthesis be then superadded, will by no means produce poetry, or any work of plastic art—using the word art properly, as opposed to craft. Otherwise a chemist, who finds out what a particular kind of gunpowder is made of, and then makes it, would be a poet. For to him is peculiarly applicable Mr. Browning's definition of "dramatist"—terrible dramatist indeed! "or, so to speak, analyst, who turns in due course synthesist." But we assure Mr. Browning there is an impassable difference between dramas and detonating powder, and also between the processes by which they are to be produced. We freely grant—indeed, we more than grant, we insist—that Mr. Browning, whatever may be said against his synthetical powers (and, as we have seen, even if he had them to perfection, he would not necessarily be a poet), is great as an analyst. But the analysed goose of the fable laid no more golden eggs; and analysed souls are just as little likely ever again to speak golden words. It is not the province of the poet to perform any such operation. It is the province of such men as Hartley, James Mill, and Professor Bain, and admirably do they perform their work. But we have not got any poems from them, nor is it likely that from the only living one of the illustrious trio we ever shall. Having a distinct comprehension of their office and its limits, they have accordingly kept within the sphere—the sphere of deep prose thoughts as opposed to that of lofty poetical thoughts, of which we have spoken—to which their talents and task naturally belonged. Hence their labours have been of inestimable service to the world. But Mr. Browning has perversely flitted from one sphere to the other, insisted on making himself at home where he is a perfect stranger, uttered profound thoughts in would-be poetic idiom, an idiom foreign to them and to him, and involved them accordingly in such abominable jargon that, when he and his affected admirers have passed away, they will be utterly lost to the world—for they *will* be a loss, on account of their depth—and buried in permanent oblivion. Should he possibly be remembered at all, it will be because posterity, condensing this our judgment, will inscribe on his grave the words of Martial:

> Carmina . . . scribis et Apolline nullo
> Laudari debes.

Anglicè:

> You kept on twanging at your lyre,
> Though no Apollo did inspire.

So much for Mr. Browning's *novum organum,* or new method of making poetry. Having considered the subject-matter of his work, and the process by which he labours on it, we have now only to examine the form in which he presents it, when finished, to the public gaze. In other words, having scrutinised his matter and method, we have now to look at his manner, or, to speak still more plainly, his expression—those "half-words," as he has himself called them, whereby he communicates with intelligent readers. Now, why does Mr. Browning communicate his thoughts in this fashion of half-words? The answer is exceedingly simple. Because, if he communicated them in full ones—i.e. explicitly and clearly—though still in verse, their prose nature would be seen at a glance by everybody; and everybody, the simplest person as well as the most pedantic, could not fail to perceive that the author was whimsically and gratuitously measuring them out into certain lengths, instead of unaffectedly not caring how many metrical feet there were in them, or whether they formed feet at all. For there is no difficulty in putting anything into verse, as may be seen in the versified rules of the "Gradus ad Parnassum," or in the advertisements of Mr. Moses, the cheap outfitter. It would require very little ingenuity to turn "Euclid" into metre, and, for anything we know, it may already have been done. But, as in these instances the primary object is to be understood, the reader sees at once that he is not reading, or supposed to be reading, poetry, but only metre, so employed for mnemonic or for catchpenny purposes. In Mr. Browning's case the unsophisticated reader really does not know what it is he is reading. It is printed in arbitrary lengths, and therefore looks as if it cannot well be prose; yet it does not, as a rule, read like verse, and in nearly all cases its meaning is obscure, and in none very obvious. It if were, Mr. Browning would be found out without more ado. We do not mean to say that he consciously deceives his readers; he deceives his readers and himself too. He is the real M. Jourdain, who has been writing prose all his life without knowing it; very bad prose, it is true, as half-words arranged in lengths necessarily must be, but prose all the same. It would be idle to quote instances of this, for his works are one long almost uninterrupted instance of it. You may open any one of his volumes at any page you like for proof of the assertion. Surely the two passages we have already quoted from him, though for a totally different purpose, will suffice as instances. If

> Since evermore
> Yourselves effect what I was fain before
> Effect, what I supplied yourselves suggest,
> What I leave bare yourselves can now invest

does not strike everybody as very bad prose, consisting of half-words arranged in lengths, we own ourselves completely beaten, or at least baffled, in our demonstration. And what is true of these passages is true of Mr. Browning's compositions *passim*. For poetic thought has its natural utterance or expression, just as everything else has, and you cannot make it express itself differently save by travestying it. To put the case as extremely as possible, yet without travelling one hair's breadth beyond the limits of the strictest truth, a living tree expresses itself in foliage not more necessarily than does poetic thought express itself in a certain and inevitable kind and form of diction. But what is the diction of poetry? Is it half-words arranged in lengths? Is it obscure diction of any sort? Is the diction of poetry anything but diction that is at once clear—*that*, it shares with other diction—lofty, and musical? Who are the clearest and most musical poets? Unquestionably the great poets. Whose blank verse is fit to be mentioned, even for mere sound, after Shakespeare's? Only Milton's; and his, *longo intervallo*. Mr. Tennyson's, smooth as it is, is the poorest stuff compared with the blank verse of Shakespeare or Milton. It is melodious enough, no doubt (just as Moore, in rhyme, is the perfection of melody); but where is its harmony—where are the infinite harmonies in it? They are wanting. For melody is not the only thing in music. All the wonderful combinations that come of an innate familiarity with the use of fugue and counterpoint make something very different from mere melody. Shakespeare and Milton betray this innate familiarity in blank verse; Spenser and Byron betray it in rhyme; and so, whilst they are the greatest of our poets in other respects, they

are, when one once knows what music really means and is, the most musical. Similarly they are the most clear. Poor Mr. Browning is both muddy and unmusical to the last degree. In fact, his style may fairly be described as the very incarnation of discordant obscurity. Is it wonderful? He has no voice, and yet he wants to sing. He is not a poet, and yet he would fain write poetry. We have no right to be surprised if he is inarticulate, and if we get only half-words cut into lengths. The wonder would be if we got anything else. In reading Mr. Browning, we are perpetually reminded of those lines in Mr. Bailey's *Festus*:

> The dress of words,
> Like to the Roman girl's enticing garb,
> Should let the play of limb be seen through it.
> . . . *A mist of words,*
> *Like halos round the moon, though they enlarge*
> *The seeming size of thoughts, make the light less.* [2]

But, it will be urged, there is occasionally something else in Mr. Browning, which, if not poetry, is at least something very like poetry. Exactly: there is. But when? When Mr. Browning ceases to be Mr. Browning proper, when his *differentia* disappears, and he is no longer Mr. Browning "the dramatist, or, so to call him, analyst," but Mr. Browning the man pure and simple. It will be remembered that we have already incidentally said that Mr. Browning is not a poet save in the sense that all cultivated men and women of sensitive feelings are poets; and we made the statement deliberately and with the intention of reverting to it here. It would therefore be strange indeed if in the course of thirty-five years' obstinate practice of writing verse Mr. Browning had not once or twice deviated into penning something that resembled poetry, and was so much on the borderland of poetry or even across it that it ought to bear that name. Be it so. All that we are arguing for is that Mr. Browning is not specifically a poet, but is specifically something quite different. The poetic temperament and intellect are not the *proprium* of Mr. Browning, but only the *accidens*. But let us see what is the highest result, when the latter has, so to speak, the upper hand, or the command of him.

> Oh! to be in England
> Now that April's there;
> And whosoever wakes in England
> Sees, some morning, unaware,
> That the lowest boughs and the brush-wood sheaf
> Round the elm-tree bole are in tiny leaf,
> While the chaffinch sings on the orchard bough
> In England—now!
>   (*Lyrics.*)
> Love like mine must have return,
> I thought: no river starts but to some sea.
>   (*A Soul's Tragedy.*)

Is this poetry? If it is, it is of a very commonplace sort, rather above than below average Magazine verse, and we could produce many examples of it from Mr. Browning if we had space, inasmuch as he perpetually, indeed invariably, lapses into commonplace when he allows himself to think, on the poetic side, naturally. Often, as though conscious that what poetic utterance he has in common with ordinary cultivated men and women of sensitive feelings is of this complexion, he will not allow himself to think naturally, but strains at being original whilst still wanting to remain poetical. Then the result is lamentable; is, in fact, spasmodic. For instance:

> Earth is a wintry clod:
> But spring-wind, like a dancing psaltress, passes
> Over its breast to waken it.
>   (*Paracelsus.*)

    The sprinkled isles,
Lily on lily, that o'erlace the sea,
And laugh their pride when the light wave lisps,
'Greece.'

          (Cleon.)

     One wave,
 Feeling the foot of Him upon its neck,
Gaped as a snake does, lolled out its large tongue,
And licked the whole labour flat.

       (Dramatis Personæ.)

Is it better in May? I ask you. You've summer all at
  once;
In a day he leaps complete with a few strong April
  suns!
'Mid the sharp short emerald wheat, scarce risen
  three fingers well,
The wild tulip, at end of its tube, blows out its great
  red bell,
Like a thin clear bubble of blood, for the children to
  pick and sell.

    (Up at a Villa—Down in the City.)

These are pure spasms; specimens of the mental action of a man who is striving earnestly to be an original poet, and who for the life of him cannot be—since no striving will make a man such, any more than it will give him wings. Mr. John Stuart Mill has in one of his admirable *Dissertations and Discussions* made the unfortunate remark that probably any man of good abilities might by determination and persistence end by becoming as great a poet as Wordsworth—he himself thinking very highly of Wordsworth as a poet. In any philosophical question we should differ from Mr. Mill with great diffidence; but we have not a moment's hesitation in saying that such an assertion, save as applied to—say—one-half of Wordsworth's compositions, which, as we have already remarked, are perhaps not poetry at all, but only verse, must be described, despite the reverence we feel for Mr. Mill, as fundamentally erroneous. Accepted, however, to the limited extent we have prescribed to it, the assertion is true enough, and it is singularly applicable to Mr. Browning. Any ordinarily cultivated person of sensitive feelings who could write verse might have written the first two commonplace passages we have just quoted from Mr. Browning, and, being resolved to be original, might have strained himself till he concocted the last four. The former are examples of such natural versified speech as might be attained by almost anybody. The latter are instances of that artificial, acquired, laborious, *foreign* speech which is necessarily fallen into by people who are clumsily translating complex thoughts into an alien tongue. As for such pieces as "Marching Along," and "How They Brought the Good News from Ghent," they cannot be classed, at the very highest estimate, save with Macaulay's *Lays of Rome*, to which surely no impartial person can doubt they are very inferior—and yet no one talks or thinks of Macaulay as specifically a poet—and ought more fairly to be classed with the Cavalier Songs of Mr. Walter Thornbury, whom no one has ever dreamt of alluding to save as a very spirited versifier.

Thus, as far as we have inquired, we find Mr. Browning, in his attempted *rôle* of poet, to be doing three things, and generally the first of them. Either playing the part of analyst, getting inside souls, and developing them to the reader by half-words, which is not writing poetry at all; or writing simple intelligible verse, which, if it is to be considered poetry, must honestly be described as commonplace poetry, both easy and by no means infrequent of production; or, in dread and dislike of being commonplace, writing what has so happily been

termed spasmodic poetry, poetry that comes of violent straining after effect, and which ought, on no account, to be written by anybody, since it sins against that eternal truth, so well put in the same passage in *Festus* from which we have already quoted:

      Simplicity
 Is nature's first step, and the last of art.

Which quotation we may supplement, for the benefit of Mr. Browning and his admirers, by another from a still higher authority, and in itself still more suggestive and instructive:

     This is an art
 Which doth mend nature, change it rather, but
 The art itself is nature.

       (Winter's Tale, iv. 3.)

That is just the art which Mr. Browning has not got.

But how about "Andrea del Sarto," "Fra Lippo Lippi," "A Death in the Desert," "Caliban on Setebos," and *Bishop Blougram's Apology?* What have we to say about these? This much. That, with the exception of "Caliban on Setebos"—which, on account of its rendering certain prevailing modes of thought on theological questions, has been very much over-estimated—they are productions betraying the possession of peculiar imagination, of mordant wit of almost the highest kind, of a delicious sense of humour, and, in "Andrea del Sarto," of deep tenderness. But neither tenderness, nor humour, nor wit, nor even imagination, nor indeed all these together, will constitute a man a poet. Laplace, Bacon,[3] Copernicus, Newton, Mr. Darwin, all have immense imagination; and we might, of course, extend the list indefinitely. We think we have allowed it to be seen that we regard Mr. Browning's intellectual powers as very considerable indeed. *Bishop Blougram's Apology* is an astonishing production, which we invariably read almost throughout with unflagging zest. But it is not poetry. There is not a line of poetry in it from first to last, and we confess we prefer it to all Mr. Browning's compositions. Suppose he had never written anything else, would it have occurred to anybody that he was a poet, or even aspiring to be a poet? In order still further to illustrate our meaning, suppose Mr. Tennyson had never written anything but "The Northern Farmer"—a piece we chuckle over with inexpressible delight—again, would it have occurred to anybody that Mr. Tennyson was a poet, or was pretending to be such? Of course not; no more than it would have occurred to his contemporaries to have regarded Cowper as a poet if he had never written anything but *John Gilpin*, whose pre-eminent success positively annoyed its author? So with *Bishop Blougram's Apology*, and all of Mr. Browning's compositions, or passages in his compositions, which are *ejusdem generis* with it. They are witty, wise, shrewd, deep, true, wonderful—anything or everything but poetry. It is the greatest, though apparently the commonest, mistake in the world to suppose that the quality of verse, provided the thoughts it expresses are excellent thoughts, involves for those thoughts and their expression the quality of poetry. This has been Mr. Browning's ignis fatuus through life; and the absurd chase it has led him he in turn has led those who have not found out what it is he has all along been following. In a word, Mr. Browning's so-called Muse is a *lusus naturæ*, a sport, to use gardeners' language; but certain sapient critics have been exulting over it, as though it were a new and finer specimen of the old true poetic stock. Moreover, Mr. Browning's undoubted faculty of depth has bewitched and bewrayed them. Despite their protestations of being perfectly content with Mr. Tennyson as the great poet who justifies the period, they are not content with him. They have all along more or less consciously felt what we insisted on in our article last month—his want of loftiness. Now, in Mr.

Browning they have found something that unquestionably is not in Mr. Tennyson, and they have begun to fancy that that something may possibly supply Mr. Tennyson's shortcomings. That comes of not having thought the matter out with regard to either of these authors.[4] They know Mr. Tennyson wants something or other: they know Mr. Browning has something or other. But from lack of patient reflection and investigation they fail to perceive for themselves that what Mr. Tennyson wants is height, and what Mr. Browning has is depth. This once clearly perceived, it is obvious that the latter characteristic cannot mend the imperfection of the former characteristic. You might just as well try to make a mountain higher by excavating round it, or make swallows fly more soaringly by yourself descending a coal-pit. We have already very explicitly given our estimate of Mr. Tennyson as a poet; and though it is such as thousands of men who have fancied themselves beloved of the Muses would have given anything to have honestly formed of them, it is far removed from that in which his more ardent admirers at times affect to indulge. One thing, however, is certain. They need be in no fear lest Mr. Tennyson should be displaced by any critic in his sound senses to make way for Mr. Browning. When men desire to behold the flight of an eagle, and cannot get it, they do not usually regard the tramp of an elephant as a substitute.

We therefore beg of the general public to return to the bent of its own original judgment, and, unbewildered by those who would fain be its guides, to treat Mr. Browning's *Poetical Works* as it treated *Paracelsus*, &c., on its first appearance—as though they were non-existent. We know it has now much to contend against. When the academy and the drawing room, when pedantry and folly, combine to set a fashion, it requires more self-confidence than the meek public commonly possesses to laugh the silly innovation down. To Mr. Tennyson's credit be it spoken, he has never gone looking for fame. The ground we tread on is delicate; and we will, therefore, only add that we should have been better pleased if the author, who is now so ridiculously obtruded as his rival, had imitated him in that particular. Small London literary coteries, and large fashionable London salons, cannot crown a man with the bays of Apollo. They may stick their trumpery tinsel wreaths upon him, but these will last no longer than the locks they encircle. They may confer notoriety, but fame is not in their gift. All they can bestow is as transitory as themselves. Let the sane general public, therefore, we say, take heart, and bluntly forswear Mr. Browning and all his works. It is bad enough that there should be people, pretending to authority among us, who call a man a great poet when, though unquestionably a poet, he has no marks of greatness about him. But that is a venial error, and a trifling misfortune, compared to what would be the misery of living in an age which gibbetted itself beforehand for the pity of posterity, by deliberately calling a man a poet who—however remarkable his mental attributes and powers—is not specifically a poet at all. We hope we shall be spared this humiliation. At any rate, we must protest against being supposed willingly to participate in it.

P.S.—It will be observed that we have abstained from all mention of *The Ring and the Book*. Our readers must not, however, suppose that the foregoing paper was written before that work appeared. Not at all. But *The Ring and the Book* throws no new light on the subject; and what we have said of Mr. Browning's aim, method, and manner, whilst examining his other compositions, holds equally good of his latest, wonderful but unpoetical, production. We have refrained from scrutinising it, only because conscientious criticism of art, like art itself, is long, and Magazine articles are short.

Notes

1. Hence the difficulty of defining poetry, just as there exists the well-known difficulty of defining life. But just as despite the latter difficulty we can always say in any particular instance what is *not* life, so despite the former one we can say in any particular instance what is not poetry.

2. Could we allow, which we cannot, that Mr. Browning is to be classed among poets, instead of among a totally different order of intellects, Mr. Bailey is the poet with whom we should be compelled to compare him; and were the comparison possible, it would certainly have to be pronounced that the author of *Festus* is, poetically speaking, immeasurably the superior of the author of *Paracelsus, Sordello*, &c., with which the former has occasionally many points in common. Mr. Bailey is unquestionably a poet. How is it he has for years persisted in silence? Is the following passage in *Festus* the explanation?—

    Student.   Say, did thy friend
          Write aught beside the work thou tell'st of?
    Festus.   Nothing.
          After that, like to the burning peak, he fell
          Into himself, and was missing ever after.

3. A brief extract from Mr. Bain upon the nature of Bacon's genius will throw some light on this subject. "Although Bacon's imagery," says that profound and accurate writer, "sometimes rises to poetry, this is not its usual character; his was not a poetic sense of Nature, but a broad general susceptibility, partaking more of the natural historian than of the poet, by which all the objects coming before his view or presented to his imagination took a deep hold, and, by the help of his intense attraction of similarity, were recalled on the slightest similitude. Many great writers in English literature have had this strong susceptibility to the sensible world at large without a special poetic sense, while some have had the poetic sense superadded. These last are our greatest poets." This is nearly as good an account of Mr. Browning's "sense of Nature" as it is of Bacon's.

4. To illustrate the lax nonsense that is written on this subject, take the following propositions from the *Spectator*. "Mr. Browning would perhaps make a great dramatist," using the word dramatist in the sense of writer for the stage. The critic who hazards such an assertion can either know nothing really of Mr. Browning or nothing of the very elements of dramatic representation. Again: "Though not the widest, the most powerful, or the freest, we hold Tennyson the deepest, by far (Clough perhaps excepted, above whom, of course, in almost all other respects he must rank), of all English poets after Shakespeare, and superior to Byron in every characteristic of a poet, except one of the greater characteristics, fire." The only epithet that properly describes this sentence, which mainly consists of a series of clashing indefinite adjectives, is muddle-speeched. The writer, who signs himself "Ed. Spectator," obviously does not even know what he himself thinks on the subject. In other words, he has never thought the matter out. Why will the *Spectator* persist in always serving up its thoughts *raw*?

ARTHUR GALTON
From "Mr. Browning"
Urbana Scripta
1885, pp. 59–76

Mr. Browning is not so much an artist as an anatomist. The greatest poets are like sculptors: they show us a lovely work of art, whose growth we do not think of, and can hardly guess at. But Mr. Browning is like a man of science, who builds up an antediluvian monster, bone by bone. He differs only from the geologist in that his constructions are not bodies only, but bodies with minds; Mr. Browning can construct a mind, as the geologist does a skeleton. And this simile gives us the clue to all his poetry; he is a mental anatomist. His power and his skill, in his own peculiar province, are undeniable; and among his English contemporaries unequalled. Though, in spite of his unrivalled power of describing character, we cannot call him a great dramatist; that is, if we mean by dramas, complete plays: because Mr. Browning's anatomical instincts, the minuteness of his dissection of individual characters, spoil his plays as wholes. His dramas, like most of his lyrics, are revelations of individual minds; and his searching power of showing single characters prevents him from completing his plays; he is a subtle dramatic poet, then, but not a great dramatist.

So that we may describe the bulk of his work, by calling it mental anatomy; and in this art of his, Mr. Browning is a most skilful master. His reading must be large, and the grasp of his mind much larger; and his mind is certainly both keen and strong. While he has an amazing power of realizing the spirit of other days; so that his pictures of bygone ages are living and forcible. His characters are taken from many sources, Eastern and Western, modern, mediæval and classical, but undoubtedly his firmest, truest drawing has been of people of the Italian Renascence: and from this source, his masterpieces are types of ecclesiastical life.

The greatest of his works, as a whole, is *The Ring and the Book*, in which is told the story of a Roman trial for murder, in the seventeenth century. Mr. Browning shows us the most intimate feelings and motives of the murderer, the victim, the judges, the advocates on either side; the arguments of partisans, the prejudices of the people; all these are expressed with a master-hand. Such pictures of the workings of many minds, from different standpoints, and on so large a scale, are marvellous for their subtlety and force. The work is more than a narrative, but we cannot call it either a drama or an epic, though it inclines to be both, with a leaning towards the epic. Still, it is chiefly a series of wonderful sketches of character; and we are always, in Mr. Browning's work, driven back to our definition; he is a master of mental anatomy.

But while doing homage to Mr. Browning's greatness, we must not be blind to his faults, and they are many and serious. His thought is too often abrupt and jerky, so much so, that at times it is difficult to follow. This difficulty is caused by his obscurity rather than his depth, for generally when most deep, where his thought is greatest, he is singularly clear.

His words match his thoughts, and are too often rugged and uncouth; though this again is only because he chooses to be odd, for his expression, when he likes, can be transparently limpid. Since this is so, he must bear the penalty; the workmanship of many of his poems is frightful. Poetry should teach us, but should always minister to pleasure and to beauty; and there are times when Mr. Browning affords neither. A poet's work should be like a sculptor's, he should chisel his marble into forms of beauty. Mr. Browning has marble—marble most precious—but it is only rough-hewn from the quarry; or, to make a better comparison, he has gold to give us, jewels of the finest gold, but it is formless and unrefined, as it is encumbered still with minerals and dross. It is given to few readers to remove these, few have the patience, and fewer the skill; so that Mr. Browning's disciples are few. While his thought is so keen, and so deep, that of those who reach it, a part only can grasp it. His greatness may make us overlook, but not forgive, his want of workmanship; even the power of his style in some of his poetry makes it harder for us to pardon his carelessness in the rest.

Many of his lines are so magnificent in their energy, their rhythm, their alliteration, that we cannot possibly suppose Mr. Browning has not the fulness of the poetical gift, if he likes to

make use of it. Genius, it is true, is beyond rules; greatness must be unfettered; we cannot confine the sea in bottles, or, with all due deference to Mr. Ruskin, the clouds either; nor can we measure the mountains with compasses. We do not judge Shakespeare by foolish rules of grammar and pedantry; and we are quite willing to allow Mr. Browning an almost equal freedom of defiance; though there are certain bounds which are not pedantic, but are true in the nature of things. Art cannot be violated and remain artistic. Poetry which has not beauty may have force, or keenness, or coarseness, or weakness, but it cannot be artistic if it is not beautiful. Now, form is a quality about which there are many discussions, and these are not always wise or moderate. Form may even be insisted on too much, or striven for too much; but still, good form is an excellence in poetry. It is an essential to the best poetry; and if a writer has not cultivated form, it cannot be true criticism to say he is the greater for his neglect, or that his work will not bear refinement. Surely it is his business to make it bear refinement, or if it will not, to utter it in prose. The strength of a great artist must be hidden, veiled by his beauty, as Raphael's strength is hidden. We should not call him a greater painter if he were coarser in his work, all his other qualities remaining the same; neither should we say Mr. Browning is not less great because he has not given his work the last touches of finish. His admirers cannot, in much of his work, call him beautiful; the wildest of them cannot, in much of his work, call him musical; so that two important qualities of good poetry are not found always in his. It is undoubtedly far better to have thought like Mr. Browning's, than the most exquisite wording if it is empty of meaning; and it takes a greater man to give us such thought. But when we concede this to the enthusiasts of the Browning Society, we should remind ourselves that those poets whom the world considers the greatest are conspicuous for their form, for their splendid workmanship. All their mental powers might remain, but had they expressed their minds less well, we should certainly not rank them so high as artists. Style, then, is not a mere luxury; it is an essential of classical poetry; and since the poets who are classics would have suffered, had their style been less excellent, we may conclude that no poet, not even the greatest, can afford to despise style; so that we cannot allow even Mr. Browning to despise style. His greatness is undoubted, his poetry, we may even say, is wonderful; but we must always hold that it would be greater and more splendid had its utterance been more beautiful.

Two qualities, then, of good poetry, beauty and music, are frequently absent from Mr. Browning's; but two others are always present, power and insight. When a third is found in his work, clearness, Mr. Browning is a forcible wielder of words. To compare him with other poets would be almost idle, even if comparison were our purpose; he is so unlike any of them, that we are stopped on the threshold by his peculiar manner. Even to compare his characters with those of other poets is not easy, they are treated so differently. We know Shakespeare's characters even better than we know Mr. Browning's, but Shakespeare's are never dissected.

Mr. Browning shows us his men and women as a watchmaker shows the wheels of a clock, with all its springs and machinery laid bare. His characters are very real or they would not bear the process and live; and his people are very living. And they are worth knowing, even when we know them through and through. ⟨. . .⟩

Mr. Browning's enemies are not those who are willing to pay every due homage to his enormous greatness, but a reasonable homage. They are those who will praise him for that in which he is not great; or who set up new ideals of poetry to suit their fancies, and the eccentricities of their poet. But, in spite of his feeble enemies, the defenders of a meaningless form; in spite of his false friends, who admire him wrongly; Mr. Browning's fame must grow. His work is so real, so solid, and so great, that those who have once learnt to know it, will like it more and more. They will forget its shortcomings when they think of its strength and solidity. And his poetry wears well, it stands the test of time and use. Though acknowledging all this, we cannot overlook its serious faults; and we must not forget that, perhaps, to us, its faults are less serious than they will be to future readers. If any age had been represented to us, in poetry like Mr. Browning's, we might think it was serious and searching in its aims, and that it meant well: but we should not have a high idea of its sense of art and beauty. So that Mr. Browning must suffer, because he has violated the principles of perfect art.

Misshapen monsters have their uses: they bring out the beauty of the perfect type. Earthquakes, volcanoes, and thunderings, have their uses: they clear the air, and show us the power which underlies the calm beauty of nature. And Mr. Browning's workmanship is like a monster: it shows us how beautiful the true types are. His spirit, too, has the uses of a storm: it shows us the power which should underlie a poet's beauty, if his words are not to be mere tinkling cymbals. Let us hope that like other storms he will clear the air, that he will help to drive away the clinging mists of luxuriant but senseless words which threaten to enfold us.

If disgust at his ruggedness leads our writers to study more those deathless masters of perfect verse, whose great thoughts are enshrined in forms of faultless art, and expressed in tones of godlike music, he will be a great literary benefactor. But this work is more likely to be done by their followers, than by one whose poetry shows too little of their touch; though we must always remember how largely it is dowered with some of their other and their highest gifts.

HENRY JAMES
"Browning in Westminster Abbey"
Speaker, January 4, 1890, pp. 10–12

The lovers of a great poet are the people in the world who are most to be forgiven for an imaginative way of thinking of him, for they have before them, in his genius and work, an irresistible example of the application of that method to a thousand subjects. Certainly, therefore, there are many confirmed admirers of Robert Browning to whom it will not have failed to occur that the consignment of his ashes to the great temple of fame of the English race was exactly one of those occasions in which his own analytic spirit would have rejoiced, and his irrepressible faculty for looking at human events in all sorts of oblique lights have found a signal opportunity. If he had been taken with it as a subject, if it had moved him to the confused and comprehensive utterance of which he was master, we can immediately guess at some of the sparks he would have scraped from it, guess how splendidly, in the case, the pictorial sense would have intertwined itself with the metaphysical. For such an occasion would have lacked, for the author of *The Ring and the Book*, none of the complexity and convertibility that were dear to him. Passion and ingenuity, irony and solemnity, the impressive and the unexpected, would each have forced their way through; in a word, the author would have been sure to take the special, circumstantial view (the inveterate mark of all his speculation)

even of so foregone a conclusion as that England should pay her greatest honour to one of her greatest poets. At any rate, as they stood in the Abbey on Tuesday last, those of his admirers and mourners who were disposed to profit by his warrant for inquiring curiously, may well have let their fancy range, with its muffled step, in the direction which *his* fancy would probably not have shrunk from following, even perhaps to the dim corners where humour and the whimsical lurk. Only, we hasten to add, it would have taken Robert Browning himself to render the multifold impression.

One part of it on such an occasion is, of course, irresistible the sense that these honours are the greatest that a generous nation has to confer, and that the emotion that accompanies them is one of the high moments of a nation's life. The attitude of the public, of the multitude, at such hours, is a great expansion, a great openness to ideas of aspiration and achievement; the pride of possession and of bestowal, especially in the case of a career so complete as Mr. Browning's, is so present as to make regret a minor matter. We possess a great man most when we begin to look at him through the glass plate of death; and it is a simple truth, though containing an apparent contradiction, that the Abbey never strikes us so benignantly as when we have a valued voice to commit to silence there. For the silence is articulate after all, and in worthy instances the preservation great. It is the other side of the question that would pull most the strings of irresponsible reflection—all those conceivable postulates and hypotheses of the poetic and satiric mind to which we owe the picture of how the Bishop ordered his tomb in St. Praxed's. Macaulay's "temple of silence and reconciliation"—and none the less perhaps because he himself is now a presence there— strikes one, as one stands in it, not only as a place but as a society, a sort of corporate company; so thick, under its high arches, its dim transepts and chapels, is the population of its historic names and figures. They are a company in possession, with a high standard of distinction, of immortality, as it were; for there is something serenely inexpugnable even in the position of the interlopers. As they look out, in the rich dusk, from the cold eyes of statues and the careful identity of tablets, they seem, with their converging faces, to scrutinise decorously the claims of each new recumbent glory, to ask each other how he is to be judged as an accession. How difficult to banish the idea that Robert Browning would have enjoyed prefiguring and disintegrating the mystifications, the reservations, even perhaps the slight buzz of scandal in the Poets' Corner, to which his own obsequies might give rise! Would not his great relish, in so characteristic an interview with his crucible, have been his perception of the bewildering modernness, to much of the society, of the new candidate for a niche? That is the interest and the fascination, from what may be termed the inside point of view, of Mr. Browning's having received, in this direction of becoming a classic, the only official assistance that is ever conferred upon English writers.

It is as classics, on one ground and another—some members of it perhaps on that of not being anything else—that the numerous assembly in the Abbey holds together, and it is as a tremendous and incomparable modern that the author of *Men and Women* takes his place in it. He introduces to his predecessors a kind of contemporary individualism which, surely, for many a year, they had not been reminded of with any such force. The tradition of the poetic character as something high, detached and simple, which may be assumed to have prevailed among them for a good while, is one that Browning has broken at every turn; so that we can imagine his new associates to stand about him, till they have got used to him, with rather a sense of failing measures. A good many oddities and a good many great writers have been entombed in the Abbey; but none of the odd ones have been so great and none of the great ones so odd. There are plenty of poets whose right to the title may be contested, but there is no poetic head of equal power—crowned and re-crowned by almost importunate hands—from which so many people would withhold the distinctive wreath. All this will give the marble phantoms at the base of the great pillars and the definite personalities of the honorary slabs something to puzzle out until, by the quick operation of time, the mere fact of his lying there among the classified and protected makes even Robert Browning lose a portion of the bristling surface of his actuality.

For the rest, judging from the outside and with his contemporaries, we of the public can only feel that his very modernness—by which we mean the all-touching, all-trying spirit of his work, permeated with accumulations and playing with knowledge—achieves a kind of conquest, or at least of extension, of the rigid pale. We cannot enter here upon any account of either that or any other element of his genius, though surely no literary figure of our day is a more challenging one to attempt to paint. The very imperfections of this original are fascinating, for they never present themselves as weaknesses—they are boldnesses and overgrowths, rich roughnesses and humours—and the patient critic need not despair of digging to the primary soil from which so many disparities and contradictions spring. He may finally even put his finger on some explanation of the great mystery, the imperfect conquest of the poetic form by a genius in which the poetic passion had such volume and range. He may successfully say how it was that a poet without a lyre—for that is practically Browning's deficiency: he had the scroll, but not often the sounding-strings—was nevertheless, in his best hours, wonderfully rich in the magic of his art, a magnificent master of poetic emotion. He will justify, on behalf of a multitude of devotees, the great position assigned to a writer of verse of which the nature or the fortune has been (in proportion to its value and quantity) to be treated rarely as quotable. He will do all this and a great deal more beside; but we need not wait for it to feel that something of our latest sympathies, our latest and most restless selves, passed the other day into the high part—the show part, to speak vulgarly—of our literature. To speak of Mr. Browning only as he was in the last twenty years of his life, how quick such an imagination as his would have been to recognise all the latent or mystical suitabilities that, in the last resort, might link to the great Valhalla by the Thames a figure that had become so conspicuously a figure of London! He had grown to be intimately and inveterately of the London world; he was so familiar and recurrent, so responsive to all its solicitations, that, given the noble evocations that he stands for to-day, he would have been missed from the congregation of worthies whose memorials are the special pride of the Londoner. Just as his great sign, to those who knew him, was that he was a force of health, of temperament, of tone, so what he takes into the Abbey is an immense expression of life—of life rendered with large liberty and free experiment, with an unrespecting intellectual eagerness to put himself in other people's place, to participate in complications and consequences—a restlessness of psychological research that might well alarm any pale company for their formal orthodoxies.

But the illustrious whom he rejoins may be reassured, as they will not fail to discover; in so far as they are representative, it will clear itself up that, in spite of a surface unsuggestive of marble and a reckless individualism of form, he is quite as representative as any of them. For the great value of Browning is that at bottom, in all the deep spiritual and human essentials, he is unmistakably in the great tradition—is, with all his Italianisms and cosmopolitanisms, all his victimisation by societies organised to talk about him, a magnificent example of the best and least dilettantish English spirit. That constitutes indeed the main chance for his eventual critic, who will have to solve the refreshing problem of how, if subtleties are not what the English spirit most delights in, the author of, for instance, *Any Wife to Any Husband* made them his perpetual pasture and yet remained typically of his race. He was indeed a wonderful mixture of the universal and the alembicated. But he played with the curious and the special, they never submerged him, and it was a sign of his robustness that he could play to the end. His voice sounds loudest, and also clearest, for the things that, as a race, we like best—the fascination of faith, the acceptance of life, the respect of its mysteries, the endurance of its charges, the vitality of the will, the validity of character, the beauty of action, the seriousness, above all, of the great human passion. If Browning had spoken for us in no other way he ought to have been made sure of, tamed and chained as a classic, on account of the extraordinary beauty of his treatment of the special relation between man and woman. It is a complete and splendid picture of the matter, which somehow places it, at the same time, in the region of conduct and responsibility. But when we talk of Robert Browning's speaking "for" us, we go to the end of our privilege, we say all. With a sense of security, perhaps a certain complacency, we leave our complicated modern conscience, and even our heterogeneous modern vocabulary, in his charge among the illustrious. There will possibly be moments in which these things will seem to us to have widened the allowance, to have made the high abode more comfortable for some of those who are yet to enter it.

GEORGE EDWARD WOODBERRY
"On Browning's Death"
Studies in Letters and Life
1890, pp. 276–96

The death of Browning brings one stage nearer the too plainly approaching end of a literary age which will long be full of curious interest to the student of the moods of the mind of man. Time has linked his name with that of Tennyson, and the conjunction gives to England another of those double stars of genius in which her years are rich, and by which the spirit of an age has a twofold expression. The old opposition, the polarity of mind, by virtue of which the Platonist differs from the Aristotelian, the artist from the thinker, Shakespeare from Jonson, shows its efficacy here, too, in the last modern age, and divides the poets and their admirers by innate preferences. It is needful to remember this contrast, though not to insist upon it unduly, in order to approach the work of Browning rightly, to be just to those who idolize him without offense to those who are repelled by him. The analysis of his powers, the charting of his life and work, are not difficult; but the value of his real achievement is more uncertain. Interest centres entirely in his poetry, for his career has been without notable incident, and is told when it is said that he has lived the life of a scholar and man of letters in England and Italy amid the social culture of his time. For the world, his career is the succession of books he has put forth, and this is as he would have it; publicity beyond this he did not seek, but refused with violence and acrimony.

In his earliest poem, youthful in its self-portraiture, its literary touch, and its fragmentary plan, the one striking quality is the flow of language. Here was a writer who would never lack for words; fluent, as if inexhaustible, the merely verbal element in *Pauline* shows no struggle with the medium of the poet's art. This gift of facility was, as is usual, first to show itself. In *Paracelsus* the second primary quality of Browning was equally conspicuous,—the power of reasoning in verse. These two traits have for a poet as much weakness as strength, and they lie at the source of Browning's defects as a master of poetic art. His facility allowed him to be diffuse in language, and his reasoning habit led him often to be diffuse in matter. In *Sordello* the two produced a monstrosity, both in construction and expression, not to be rivaled in literature. Picturesque detail, intellectual interest, moral meaning, struggle in vain in that tale to make themselves felt and discerned through the tangle of words and the labyrinth of act and reflection. But already in these poems Browning had shown, to himself, if not to the world, that he had come to certain conclusions, to a conception of human life and a decision as to the use of his art in regard to it, which were to give him substantial power. He defined it by his absorption in *Paracelsus* with the broad ideas of infinite power and infinite love, which in his last poem still maintain their place in his system as the highest solvents of experience and speculation; and in *Sordello* he stated the end of art, which he continued to seek, in his maxim that little else is worth study except the "history of a soul." His entire poetic work, broadly speaking, is the illustration of this short sentence. Such prepossessions with the spiritual meaning of life as these poems show made sure the predominance in his work of the higher interests of man; and he won his audience finally by this fact, that he had something to say that was ethical and religious. The development, however, of both the theory and practice of his mind had to be realized in far more definite and striking forms than the earlier poems before the attention of the world could be secured.

It would seem natural that a man with such convictions as Browning acknowledged, should be preëminently an idealist, and that his point of weakness should prove to be the tendency to metaphysical and vague matter not easily putting on poetical form. But he was, in fact, a realist,—one who is primarily concerned with things, and uses the method of observation. His sense for actual fact is always keen. In that poem of *Paracelsus*, which is a discussion in the air if ever a poem was, it is significant to find him emphasizing the circumstance that he had taken very few liberties with his subject, and bringing books to show evidence of historical fidelity. But, little of the dramatic spirit as there is in *Paracelsus*, there was much in Browning when it should come to be released, and it belongs to the dramatist to be interested in the facts of life, the flesh and blood reality, in which he may or may not (according to his greatness) find a soul. Browning was thus a realist, and he chose habitually the objective method of art—but to set forth "the history of a soul." Had he been an idealist, his subject would have been "the history of *the* soul;" his method might or might not have been different. This change of the particle is a slight one, but it involves that polarity of mind which sets Browning opposite to Tennyson. He deals with individuals, takes in imagination their point of view, assumes for the time being their circumstances and emotions; and one who does this in our time, with a preoccupation with the soul in the individual, cannot escape from one overpowering impression, repeated from every side of the modern age,—the impression, namely, of the relativity of human life.

This is the lesson which is spread over Browning's pages,

with line on line and precept on precept. By it he comes into harmony with the very spirit of the century on its intellectual side, and represents it. The "history of a soul" differs very greatly according to circumstance, native impulses, the needs of life at different stages of growth, the balance of faculties and desires in it, the temperament of its historical period, the access to it of art or music or thought, and in a thousand ways; and Browning devotes himself oftentimes to the exposition of all this web of circumstance, in order that we may see the soul as it was under its conditions, instead of leaping to a conclusion by a hard-and-fast morality based upon the similarity of the soul in all men. The task happily falls in with his fine gift of reasoning, and increases by practice the suppleness and subtlety of this faculty of his. One might say, indeed, without close computation, that the larger part of his entire poetic work is occupied with such reasoning upon psychological cases, in the manner of a lawyer who educes a client's justification from the details of his temptation. Many of the longer poems are only instances of special pleading, and have all the faults that belong to that form of thought. *The Ring and the Book* is such an interminable argument, marvelous for intellectual resource, for skill in dialectic, for plausibility. *Bishop Blougram, Mr. Sludge, Prince Hohenstiel-Schwangau*, and others, readily occur to mind as being in the same way "apologies;" and in these one feels that, while it is well to know what the prisoner urges on his own behalf, it is the shabby, the cowardly, the criminal, the base, the detestable, that is masking under a too well-woven cloak of words, and that the special pleader is pursuing his game at the risk of a higher honesty than consists in the mere understanding of the mechanism of motive and act. Yet this catholicity, which seems to have for its motto, "Who understands all, forgives all," is a natural consequence in a mind so impressed with the doctrine of the relativity of human life as was Browning's. The tendency of the doctrine is to efface moral judgment, and to substitute for it intellectual comprehension; and usually this results in a practical fatalism, acquiesced in if not actively held. Here, too, Browning's mental temperament has another point of contact with the general spirit of the age, and allows him to take up into his genius the humanitarian instinct so powerful in his contemporaries. For the perception of the excuses for men's action in those of low or morbid or deformed development liberalizes the mind, and the finding of the spark of soul in such individuals does mean to the Christian the finding of that immortal part which equalizes all in an equal destiny, however the difference may look between men while the process of life is going on. Browning came very early to this conviction, that in all men, however weak or grossly set this spark may be, it is to be sought for. In this he is consistently philanthropic and democratic, Christian in spirit and practice, comprehensive in tolerance, large in charity, intellectually (but not emotionally) sympathetic. It is perhaps unnecessary to add that his love of righteousness is not so striking a trait.

But what in all this view of life is most original in Browning is something that possibly perplexes even his devoted admirers. Life, he says, no matter what it may be in its accidents of time, or place, or action, is the stuff to make the soul of. In the humblest as the noblest, in Caliban as in Prospero, the life vouchsafed is the means (adequate, he seems to say, in all cases) of which the soul makes use to grow in. He thus avoids the deadening conclusions to which his doctrine of relativity might lead, by asserting the equal and identical opportunity in all to develop the soul. He unites with this the original theory—at least one that he has made his own—that whatever the soul seeks it should seek with all its might; and, pushing to the extreme, he urges that if a man sin, let him sin to the uttermost of his desire. This is the moral of the typical poem of this class, "The Statue and the Bust," and he means more by this than that the intention, sinning in thought, is equivalent to sinning in act,—he means that a man should have his will. No doubt this is directly in accord with the great value he places on strength of character, vitality in life, on resolution, courage, and the braving of consequences. But the ignoring of the immense value of restraint as an element in character is complete; and in the case of many whose choice is slowly and doubtfully made in those younger years when the desire for life in its fullness of experience is strongest, and the wisdom of knowledge of life in its effects is weakest, the advice to obey impulse at all costs, to throw doubt and authority to the winds, and "live my life and have my day," is of dubious utility. Over and over again in Browning's poetry one meets with this insistence on the value of moments of high excitement, of intense living, of full experience of pleasure, even though such moments be of the essence of evil and fruitful in all dark consequences. It is probable that a deep optimism underlies all this; that Browning believed that the soul does not perish in its wrong-doing, but that through this experience, too, as through good, it develops finally its immortal nature, and that, as in his view the life of the soul is in its energy of action, the man must act even evil if he is to grow at all. Optimism, certainly, of the most thorough-going kind this is; but Browning is so consistent an optimist in other parts of his philosophy that this defense may be made for him on a point where the common thought and deepest conviction of the race, in its noblest thinkers and purest artists, are opposed to him, refusing to believe that the doing of evil is to be urged in the interest of true manliness.

The discussion of Browning's attitude towards life in the actual world of men has led away from the direct consideration of the work in which he embodied his convictions. The important portion of it came in middle life, when he obtained mastery of the form of poetic art known as the dramatic monologue. A realist, if he be a poet, must resort to the drama. It was inevitable in Browning's case. Yet the drama, as a form, offered as much unfitness for Browning's genius as it did fitness. The drama requires energy, it is true, and interest in men as individuals; and these Browning had. It also requires concentration, economy of material, and constructive power; and these were difficult to Browning. He did not succeed in his attempts to write drama in its perfect form. He could make fragments of intense power in passion; he could reveal a single character at one critical moment of its career; he could sum up a life history in a long soliloquy; but he could not do more than this and keep the same level of performance. Why he failed is a curious question, and will doubtless be critically debated with a plentiful lack of results. His growth in dramatic faculty, in apprehension of the salient points of character and grasp in presenting them, in perception of the value of situation and power to use it to the full, can readily be traced; but there comes a point where the growth stops. Superior as his mature work is to that of his youth in all these qualities, it falls short of that perfect and complex design and that informing life which mark the developed dramatist. In the monologues he deals with incidents in a life, with moods of a personality, with the consciousness which a man has of his own character at the end of his career; but he seizes these singly, and at one moment. His characters do not develop before the eye; he does not catch the soul in the very act; he does not present life so much as the results of life. He frequently works by the method of retrospect, he tells the story, but does not enact it. In all these he displays

the governing motive of his art, which is to reveal the soul; but if the soul reveals itself in his verses, it is commonly by confession, not presentation. He has, in fact, that malady of thought which interferes with the dramatist's control of his hand; he is thinking *about* his characters, and only indirectly *in* them, and he is most anxious to convey his reflections upon the psychical phenomenon which he is attending to. In other words, he is, primarily, a moralist; he reasons, and he is fluent in words and fertile in thoughts, and so he loses the object itself, becomes indirect, full of afterthought and parenthesis, and impairs the dramatic effect. These traits may be observed, in different degrees, in many of the poems, even in the best. In the dramas themselves the lack of constructive power is absolute. *Pippa Passes* is only a succession of dramatic fragments artificially bound together, and in the others the lack of body and interdependent life between the parts is patent to all. In "A Balcony," certainly one of his finest wrought poems, is only an incident. He is at his best when his field is most narrow—in such a poem as "The Laboratory."

There is a compensation for these deficiencies of power in that the preference of his mind for a single passion or mood or crisis at its main moment opens to him the plain and unobstructed way to lyrical expression. His dramatic feeling of the passion and the situation supplies an intensity which finds its natural course in lyrical exaltation. It may well be thought, if it were deemed necessary to decide upon the best in Browning's work, that his genius is most nobly manifest in those lyrics and romances which he called dramatic. The scale rises from his argumentative and moralizing verse, however employed, through those monologues which obey the necessity for greater concentration as the dramatic element enters into them, up to those most powerful and direct poems in which the intensity of feeling enforces a lyrical movement and lift; and akin to these last are the songs of love or heroism into which the dramatic element does not enter. Indeed, Browning's lyrical gift was more perfect than his dramatic gift; he knew the secret of a music which has witchery in it independent of what the words may say, and when his hand fell on that chord, he mastered the heart with real poetic charm. It was seldom, however, that this happy moment came to him, ennobling his language and giving wing to his emotion; and, such poems being rare, it remains true that the best of his work is to be sought in those pieces, comprehending more of life, where his dramatic power takes on a lyrical measure. Such work became more infrequent as years went on, and he declined again into that earlier style of wordy ratiocination, of tedious pleading as of a lawsuit, of mere intellectuality as of the old hair-splitting schoolmen, though he retained the strength and definiteness of mind which mere growth had brought to him, and he occasionally produced a poem which was only less good than the best of his middle age. The translations from the Greek with which he employed his age stand in a different class from his original poems, and were a fortunate resort for his vigorous but now feebly creative mind. At the end he still applied himself to the interpretation of individual lives, but in choosing them he was attracted even more uniformly by something exceptional, often grotesque, in them, and hence they are more curious and less instructive than the earlier work of the same kind.

The mass of Browning's writings which has been glanced at as the expression of the reasoning, the dramatic, or the lyrical impulse in his genius has attracted attention as wide as the English language, and it has been intimated that this success has been won in some degree on other than poetic grounds. It is fair to say, in view of the facts, that many who have felt his appeal to them have found a teacher rather than a poet. Two points in which he reflects his age have been mentioned, but there is a third point which has perhaps been more efficacious than his sense of the relativity of human life or his conviction of the worth of every human soul: he adds to these cardinal doctrines a firm and loudly asseverated religious belief. It is the more noteworthy because his reasoning faculty might in his time have led him almost anywhere rather than to the supreme validity of truth arrived at by intuition. This makes his character the more interesting, for the rationalizing mind which submits itself to intuitive faith exactly parallels in Browning the realist with a predominating interest in the soul. There is no true contradiction in this, no inconsistency; but the combination is unusual. It is natural that, in a time of decreasing authority in formal religion, a poet in Browning's position should wield an immense attraction, and owe something, as Carlyle did, to the wish of his audience to be reassured in their religious faith. Browning had begun with that resolution of the universe into infinite power and infinite love of which something has already been said, and he continued to teach that through nature we arrive at the conception of omnipotence, and through the soul at the conception of love, and he apparently finds the act of faith in the belief that infinite power will finally be discerned as the instrument and expression of infinite love. This is pure optimism; and in accordance with it he preaches his gospel, which is that each soul should grow to its utmost in power and in love, and in the face of difficulties—of mysteries in experience or thought—should repose with entire trust on the doctrine that God has ordered life beneficently, and that we who live should wait with patience, even in the wreck of our own or others' lives, for the disclosure hereafter which shall reconcile to our eyes and hearts the jar with justice and goodness of all that has gone before. This is a system simple enough and complete enough to live by, if it be truly accepted. It is probable, however, that Browning wins less by these doctrines, which are old and commonplace, than by the vigor with which he dogmatizes upon them; the certainty with which he speaks of such high matters; the fervor, and sometimes the eloquence, with which, touching on the deepest and most secret chords of the heart's desire, he strikes out the notes of courage, of hope and vision, and of the foretasted triumph. The energy of his own faith carries others along with it; the manliness of his own soul infects others with its cheer and its delight in the struggle of spiritual life on earth; and all this the more because he is learned in the wisdom of the Rabbis, is conversant with modern life and knowledge in all its range, is gifted with intellectual genius, and yet displays a faith the more robust because it is not cloistered, the more credible because it is not professional.

The character of Browning's genius, his individual traits, the general substance of his thought, do not admit of material misconception. It is when the question is raised upon the permanent value of his work that the opportunity for wide divergence arises. That there are dreary wastes in it cannot be gainsaid. Much is now unreadable that was excused in a contemporary book; much never was readable at all; and of the remainder how much will the next age in its turn cast aside? Its serious claim to our attention on ethical, religious, or intellectual grounds may be admitted, without pledging the twentieth century, which will have its own special phases of thought, and thinkers to illustrate them. Browning must live, as the other immortals do, by the poetry in him. It is true he has enlarged the field of poetry by annexing the experience that belongs to the artist and the musician, and has made some of

his finest and most original poems out of such motives; and his wide knowledge has served him in other ways, though it has stiffened many a page with pedantry and antiquarianism. It is true that there is a grotesque quality in some of his work, but his humor in this kind is really a pretense; no one laughs at it; it arouses only an amazed wonder, like the stone masks of some mediæval church. In all that he derived from learning and scholarship there is the alloy of mortality; in all his moralizing and special pleading and superfine reasoning there enters the chance that the world may lose interest in his treatment of the subject; in all, except where he sings from the heart itself or pictures life directly and without comment save of the briefest, there is some opportunity for time to breed decay. The faith he preached was the poetical complement of Carlyle's prose, and proceeded from much the same grounds and by the same steps: believe in God, and act like a man—that was the substance of it. But Carlyle himself already grows old and harsh. The class of mind to which Browning belongs depends on its matter for its life; unless he has transformed it into poetry, time will deal hardly with it.

To come to the question which cannot be honestly set aside, although it is no longer profitable to discuss it, Browning has not cared for that poetic form which bestows perennial charm, or else he was incapable of it. He fails in beauty, in concentration of interest, in economy of language, in selection of the best from the common treasure of experience. In those works where he has been most indifferent, as in the *Red Cotton Night-Cap Country*, he, has been merely whimsical and dull; in those works where the genius he possessed is most felt, as in "Saul," "A Toccata of Galuppi's," "Rabbi Ben Ezra," "The Flight of the Duchess," "The Bishop Orders His Tomb in St. Praxed's Church," "Hervé Riel," "Cavalier Tunes," "Time's Revenges," and many more, he achieves beauty or nobility or fitness of phrase such as only a poet is capable of. It is in these last pieces and their like that his fame lies for the future. It was his lot to be strong as the thinker, the moralist with "the accomplishment of verse," the scholar interested to rebuild the past of experience, the teacher with an explicit dogma to enforce in an intellectual form with examples from life, the anatomist of human passions, instincts, and impulses in all their gamut, the commentator on his own age; he was weak as the artist, and indulged, often unnecessarily and by choice, in the repulsive form—in the awkward, the obscure, the ugly. He belongs with Jonson, with Dryden, with the heirs of the masculine intellect, the men of power not unvisited by grace, but in whom mind is predominant. Upon the work of such poets time hesitates, conscious of their mental greatness, but also of their imperfect art, their heterogeneous matter; at last the good is sifted from that whence worth has departed.

GEORGE SANTAYANA
From "The Poetry of Barbarism:
III. Robert Browning"
Interpretations of Poetry and Religion
1900, pp. 188–214

If we would do justice to Browning's work as a human document, and at the same time perceive its relation to the rational ideals of the imagination and to that poetry which passes into religion, we must keep, as in the case of Whitman, two things in mind. One is the genuineness of the achievement, the sterling quality of the vision and inspiration; these are their own justification when we approach them from below and regard them as manifesting a more direct or impassioned grasp of experience than is given to mildly blatant, convention-ridden minds. The other thing to remember is the short distance to which this comprehension is carried, its failure to approach any finality, or to achieve a recognition even of the traditional ideals of poetry and religion.

In the case of Walt Whitman such a failure will be generally felt; it is obvious that both his music and his philosophy are those of a barbarian, nay, almost of a savage. Accordingly there is need of dwelling rather on the veracity and simple dignity of his thought and art, on their expression of an order of ideas latent in all better experience. But in the case of Browning it is the success that is obvious to most people. Apart from a certain superficial grotesqueness to which we are soon accustomed, he easily arouses and engages the reader by the pithiness of his phrase, the volume of his passion, the vigour of his moral judgment, the liveliness of his historical fancy. It is obvious that we are in the presence of a great writer, of a great imaginative force, of a master in the expression of emotion. What is perhaps not so obvious, but no less true, is that we are in the presence of a barbaric genius, of a truncated imagination, of a thought and an art inchoate and ill-digested, of a volcanic eruption that tosses itself quite blindly and ineffectually into the sky.

The points of comparison by which this becomes clear are perhaps not in every one's mind, although they are merely the elements of traditional culture, æsthetic and moral. Yet even without reference to ultimate ideals, one may notice in Browning many superficial signs of that deepest of all failures, the failure in rationality and the indifference to perfection. Such a sign is the turgid style, weighty without nobility, pointed without naturalness or precision. Another sign is the "realism" of the personages, who, quite like men and women in actual life, are always displaying traits of character and never attaining character as a whole. Other hints might be found in the structure of the poems, where the dramatic substance does not achieve a dramatic form; in the metaphysical discussion, with its confused prolixity and absence of result; in the moral ideal, where all energies figure without their ultimate purposes; in the religion, which breaks off the expression of this life in the middle, and finds in that suspense an argument for immortality. In all this, and much more that might be recalled, a person coming to Browning with the habits of a cultivated mind might see evidence of some profound incapacity in the poet; but more careful reflection is necessary to understand the nature of this incapacity, its cause, and the peculiar accent which its presence gives to those ideas and impulses which Browning stimulates in us.

There is the more reason for developing this criticism (which might seem needlessly hostile and which time and posterity will doubtless make in their own quiet and decisive fashion) in that Browning did not keep within the sphere of drama and analysis, where he was strong, but allowed his own temperament and opinions to vitiate his representation of life, so that he sometimes turned the expression of a violent passion into the last word of what he thought a religion. He had a didactic vein, a habit of judging the spectacle he evoked and of loading the passions he depicted with his visible sympathy or scorn.

Now a chief support of Browning's popularity is that he is, for many, an initiator into the deeper mysteries of passion, a means of escaping from the moral poverty of their own lives and of feeling the rhythm and compulsion of the general striving. He figures, therefore, distinctly as a prophet, as a bearer of glad tidings, and it is easy for those who hail him as such to imagine that, knowing the labour of life so well, he must know something also of its fruits, and that in giving us the feeling of existence, he is also giving us its meaning. There is serious danger that a mind gathering from his pages the raw materials of truth, the unthreshed harvest of reality, may take him for a philosopher, for a rationalizer of what he describes. Awakening may be mistaken for enlightenment, and the galvanizing of torpid sensations and impulses for wisdom.

Against such fatuity reason should raise her voice. The vital and historic forces that produce illusions of this sort in large groups of men are indeed beyond the control of criticism. The ideas of passion are more vivid than those of memory, until they become memories in turn. They must be allowed to fight out their desperate battle against the laws of Nature and reason. But it is worth while in the meantime, for the sake of the truth and of a just philosophy, to meet the varying though perpetual charlatanism of the world with a steady protest. As soon as Browning is proposed to us as a leader, as soon as we are asked to be not the occasional patrons of his art, but the pupils of his philosophy, we have a right to express the radical dissatisfaction which we must feel, if we are rational, with his whole attitude and temper of mind.

The great dramatists have seldom dealt with perfectly virtuous characters. The great poets have seldom represented mythologies that would bear scientific criticism. But by an instinct which constituted their greatness they have cast these mixed materials furnished by life into forms congenial to the specific principles of their art, and by this transformation they have made acceptable in the æsthetic sphere things that in the sphere of reality were evil or imperfect: in a word, their works have been beautiful as works of art. Or, if their genius exceeded that of the technical poet and rose to prophetic intuition, they have known how to create ideal characters, not possessed, perhaps, of every virtue accidentally needed in this world, but possessed of what is ideally better, of internal greatness and perfection. They have also known how to select and reconstruct their mythology so as to make it a true interpretation of moral life. When we read the maxims of Iago, Falstaff, or Hamlet, we are delighted if the thought strikes us as true, but we are not less delighted if it strikes us as false. These characters are not presented to us in order to enlarge our capacities of passion nor in order to justify themselves as processes of redemption; they are there, clothed in poetry and imbedded in plot, to entertain us with their imaginable feelings and their interesting errors. The poet, without being especially a philosopher, stands by virtue of his superlative genius on the plane of universal reason, far above the passionate experience which he overlooks and on which he reflects; and he raises us for the moment to his own level, to send us back again, if not better endowed for practical life, at least not unacquainted with speculation.

With Browning the case is essentially different. When his heroes are blinded by passion and warped by circumstance, as they almost always are, he does not describe the fact from the vantage-ground of the intellect and invite us to look at it from that point of view. On the contrary, his art is all self-expression or satire. For the most part his hero, like Whitman's, is himself; not appearing, as in the case of the American bard, *in puris naturalibus*, but masked in all sorts of historical and romantic finery. Sometimes, however, the personage, like Guido in *The Ring and the Book* or the "frustrate ghosts" of other poems, is merely a Marsyas, shown flayed and quivering to the greater glory of the poet's ideal Apollo. The impulsive utterances and the crudities of most of the speakers are passionately adopted by the poet as his own. He thus perverts what might have been a triumph of imagination into a failure of reason.

This circumstance has much to do with the fact that Browning, in spite of his extraordinary gift for expressing emotion, has hardly produced works purely and unconditionally delightful. They not only portray passion, which is interesting, but they betray it, which is odious. His art was still in the service of the will. He had not attained, in studying the beauty of things, that detachment of the phenomenon, that love of the form for its own sake, which is the secret of contemplative satisfaction. Therefore, the lamentable accidents of his personality and opinions, in themselves no worse than those of other mortals, passed into his art. He did not seek to elude them: he had no free speculative faculty to dominate them by. Or, to put the same thing differently, he was too much in earnest in his fictions, he threw himself too unreservedly into his creations. His imagination, like the imagination we have in dreams, was merely a vent for personal preoccupations. His art was inspired by purposes less simple and universal than the ends of imagination itself. His play of mind consequently could not be free or pure. The creative impulse could not reach its goal or manifest in any notable degree its own organic ideal.

We may illustrate these assertions by considering Browning's treatment of the passion of love, a passion to which he gives great prominence and in which he finds the highest significance.

Love is depicted by Browning with truth, with vehemence, and with the constant conviction that it is the supreme thing in life. The great variety of occasions in which it appears in his pages and the different degrees of elaboration it receives, leave it always of the same quality—the quality of passion. It never sinks into sensuality; in spite of its frequent extreme crudeness, it is always, in Browning's hands, a passion of the imagination, it is always love. On the other hand it never rises into contemplation: mingled as it may be with friendship, with religion, or with various forms of natural tenderness, it always remains a passion; it always remains a personal impulse, a hypnotization, with another person for its object or its cause. Kept within these limits it is represented, in a series of powerful sketches, which are for most readers the gems of the Browning gallery, as the last word of experience, the highest phase of human life.

> The woman yonder, there's no use in life
> But just to obtain her! Heap earth's woes in one
> And bear them—make a pile of all earth's joys
> And spurn them, as they help or help not this;
> Only, obtain her!
> When I do come, she will speak not, she will stand,
>   Either hand
> On my shoulder, give her eyes the first embrace Of
>   my face,
> Ere we rush, ere we extinguish sight and speech
>   Each on each. . . .
> O heart, O blood that freezes, blood that burns!
>   Earth's returns
> For whole centuries of folly, noise, and sin—Shut
>   them in—
> With their triumphs and their follies and the rest.
>   Love is best.

In the piece called "In a Gondola" the lady says to her lover:—

> Heart to heart
> And lips to lips! Yet once more, ere we part,
> Clasp me and make me thine, as mine thou art.

And he, after being surprised and stabbed in her arms, replies:—

> It was ordained to be so, sweet!—and best
> Comes now, beneath thine eyes, upon thy breast:
> Still kiss me! Care not for the cowards; care
> Only to put aside thy beauteous hair
> My blood will hurt! The Three I do not scorn
> To death, because they never lived, but I
> Have lived indeed, and so—(yet one more kiss)—
>   can die.

We are not allowed to regard these expressions as the cries of souls blinded by the agony of passion and lust. Browning unmistakably adopts them as expressing his own highest intuitions. He so much admires the strength of this weakness that he does not admit that it is a weakness at all. It is with the strut of self-satisfaction, with the sensation, almost, of muscular Christianity, that he boasts of it through the mouth of one of his heroes, who is explaining to his mistress the motive of his faithful services as a minister of the queen:—

> She thinks there was more cause
> In love of power, high fame, pure loyalty?
> Perhaps she fancies men wear out their lives
> Chasing such shades. . . .
> I worked because I want you with my soul.

Readers of the fifth chapter of this volume ("Platonic Love in Some Italian Poets") need not be reminded here of the contrast which this method of understanding love offers to that adopted by the real masters of passion and imagination. They began with that crude emotion with which Browning ends; they lived it down, they exalted it by thought, they extracted the pure gold of it in a long purgation of discipline and suffering. The fierce paroxysm which for him is heaven, was for them the proof that heaven cannot be found on earth, that the value of experience is not in experience itself but in the ideals which it reveals. The intense, voluminous emotion, the sudden, overwhelming self-surrender in which he rests was for them the starting-point of a life of rational worship, of an austere and impersonal religion, by which the fire of love, kindled for a moment by the sight of some creature, was put, as it were, into a censer, to burn incense before every image of the Highest Good. Thus love ceased to be a passion and became the energy of contemplation: it diffused over the universe, natural and ideal, that light of tenderness and that faculty of worship which the passion of love often is first to quicken in a man's breast.

Of this art, recommended by Plato and practised in the Christian Church by all adepts of the spiritual life, Browning knew absolutely nothing. About the object of love he had no misgivings. What could the object be except somebody or other? The important thing was to love intensely and to love often. He remained in the phenomenal sphere: he was a lover of experience; the ideal did not exist for him. No conception could be farther from his thought than the essential conception of any rational philosophy, namely, that feeling is to be treated as raw material for thought, and that the destiny of emotion is to pass into objects which shall contain all its value while losing all its formlessness. This transformation of sense and emotion into objects agreeable to the intellect, into clear ideas and beautiful things, is the natural work of reason; when it has been accomplished very imperfectly, or not at all, we have a barbarous mind, a mind full of chaotic sensations, objectless passions, and undigested ideas. Such a mind Browning's was, to a degree remarkable in one with so rich a heritage of civilization.

The nineteenth century, as we have already said, has nourished the hope of abolishing the past as a force while it studies it as an object; and Browning, with his fondness for a historical stage setting and for the gossip of history, rebelled equally against the Pagan and the Christian discipline. The *Soul* which he trusted in was the barbarous soul, the "Spontaneous Me" of his half-brother Whitman. It was a restless personal impulse, conscious of obscure depths within itself which it fancied to be infinite, and of a certain vague sympathy with wind and cloud and with the universal mutation. It was the soul that might have animated Attila and Alaric when they came down into Italy, a soul not incurious of the tawdriness and corruption of the strange civilization it beheld, but incapable of understanding its original spirit; a soul maintaining in the presence of that noble, unappreciated ruin all its own lordliness and energy, and all its native vulgarity.

Browning, who had not had the education traditional in his own country, used to say that Italy had been his university. But it was a school for which he was ill prepared, and he did not sit under its best teachers. For the superficial ferment, the worldly passions, and the crimes of the Italian Renaissance he had a keen interest and intelligence. But Italy has been always a civilized country, and beneath the trappings and suits of civilization which at that particular time it flaunted so gayly, it preserved a civilized heart to which Browning's insight could never penetrate. There subsisted in the best minds a trained imagination and a cogent ideal of virtue. Italy had a religion, and that religion permeated all its life, and was the background without which even its secular art and secular passions would not be truly intelligible. The most commanding and representative, the deepest and most appealing of Italian natures are permeated with this religious inspiration. A Saint Francis, a Dante, a Michael Angelo, breathe hardly anything else. Yet for Browning these men and what they represented may be said not to have existed. He saw, he studied, and he painted a decapitated Italy. His vision could not mount so high as her head.

One of the elements of that higher tradition which Browning was not prepared to imbibe was the idealization of love. The passion he represents is lava hot from the crater, in no way moulded, smelted, or refined. He had no thought of subjugating impulses into the harmony of reason. He did not master life, but was mastered by it. Accordingly the love he describes has no wings; it issues in nothing. His lovers "extinguish sight and speech, each on each"; sense, as he says elsewhere, drowning soul. The man in the gondola may well boast that he can die; it is the only thing he can properly do. Death is the only solution of a love that is tied to its individual object and inseparable from the alloy of passion and illusion within itself. Browning's hero, because he has loved intensely, says that he has lived; he would be right, if the significance of life were to be measured by the intensity of the feeling it contained, and if intelligence were not the highest form of vitality. But had that hero known how to love better and had he had enough spirit to dominate his love, he might perhaps have been able to carry away the better part of it and to say that he could not die; for one half of himself and of his love would have been dead already and the other half would have been eternal, having fed—

On death, that feeds on men;
And death once dead, there's no more dying then.

The irrationality of the passions which Browning glorifies, making them the crown of life, is so gross that at times he cannot help perceiving it.

How perplexed
Grows belief! Well, this cold clay clod
Was man's heart:
Crumble it, and what comes next? Is it God?

Yes, he will tell us. These passions and follies, however desperate in themselves and however vain for the individual, are excellent as parts of the dispensation of Providence:—

Be hate that fruit or love that fruit,
It forwards the general deed of man,
And each of the many helps to recruit
The life of the race by a general plan,
Each living his own to boot.

If we doubt, then, the value of our own experience, even perhaps of our experience of love, we may appeal to the interdependence of goods and evils in the world to assure ourselves that, in view of its consequences elsewhere, this experience was great and important after all. We need not stop to consider this supposed solution, which bristles with contradictions; it would not satisfy Browning himself, if he did not back it up with something more to his purpose, something nearer to warm and transitive feeling. The compensation for our defeats, the answer to our doubts, is not to be found merely in a proof of the essential necessity and perfection of the universe; that would be cold comfort, especially to so uncontemplative a mind. No: that answer, and compensation are to come very soon and very vividly to every private bosom. There is another life, a series of other lives, for this to happen in. Death will come, and—

I shall thereupon
Take rest, ere I be gone
Once more on my adventure brave and new,
Fearless and unperplexed,
When I wage battle next,
What weapons to select, what armour to endue

For sudden the worst turns the best to the brave,
The black minute's at end,
And the element's rage, the fiend-voices that rave
Shall dwindle, shall blend,
Shall change, shall become first a peace out of pain,
Then a light, then thy breast,
O thou soul of my soul! I shall clasp thee again
And with God be the rest!

Into this conception of continued life Browning has put, as a collection of further passages might easily show, all the items furnished by fancy or tradition which at the moment satisfied his imagination—new adventures, reunion with friends, and even, after a severe strain and for a short while, a little peace and quiet. The gist of the matter is that we are to live indefinitely, that all our faults can be turned to good, all our unfinished business settled, and that therefore there is time for anything we like in this world and for all we need in the other. It is in spirit the direct opposite of the philosophic maxim of regarding the end, of taking care to leave a finished life and a perfect character behind us. It is the opposite, also, of the religious *memento mori*, of the warning that the time is short before we go to our account. According to Browning, there is no account: we have an infinite credit. With an unconscious and characteristic mixture of heathen instinct with Christian doctrine, he thinks of the other world as heaven, but of the life to be led there as of the life of Nature.

Aristotle observes that we do not think the business of life worthy of the gods, to whom we can only attribute contemplation; if Browning had had the idea of perfecting and rationalizing this life rather than of continuing it indefinitely, he would have followed Aristotle and the Church in this matter. But he had no idea of anything eternal; and so he gave, as he would probably have said, a filling to the empty Christian immortality by making every man busy in it about many things. And to the irrational man, to the boy, it is no unpleasant idea to have an infinite number of days to live through, an infinite number of dinners to eat, with an infinity of fresh fights and new love-affairs, and no end of last rides together.

But it is a mere euphemism to call this perpetual vagrancy a development of the soul. A development means the unfolding of a definite nature, the gradual manifestation of a known idea. A series of phases, like the successive leaps of a water-fall, is no development. And Browning has no idea of an intelligible good which the phases of life might approach and with reference to which they might constitute a progress. His notion is simply that the game of life, the exhilaration of action, is inexhaustible. You may set up your tenpins again after you have bowled them over, and you may keep up the sport for ever. The point is to bring them down as often as possible with a master-stroke and a big bang. That will tend to invigorate in you that self-confidence which in this system passes for faith. But it is unmeaning to call such an exercise heaven, or to talk of being "with God" in such a life, in any sense in which we are not with God already and under all circumstances. Our destiny would rather be, as Browning himself expresses it in a phrase which Atilla or Alaric might have composed, "bound dizzily to the wheel of change to slake the thirst of God."

Such an optimism and such a doctrine of immortality can give no justification to experience which it does not already have in its detached parts. Indeed, those dogmas are not the basis of Browning's attitude, not conditions of his satisfaction in living, but rather overflowings of that satisfaction. The present life is presumably a fair average of the whole series of "adventures brave and new" which fall to each man's share; were it not found delightful in itself, there would be no motive for imagining and asserting that it is reproduced *in infinitum*. So too if we did not think that the evil in experience is actually utilized and visibly swallowed up in its good effects, we should hardly venture to think that God could have regarded as a good something which has evil for its condition and which is for that reason profoundly sad and equivocal. But Browning's philosophy of life and habit of imagination do not require the support of any metaphysical theory. His temperament is perfectly self-sufficient and primary; what doctrines he has are suggested by it and are too loose to give it more than a hesitant expression; they are quite powerless to give it any justification which it might lack on its face.

It is the temperament, then, that speaks; we may brush aside as unsubstantial, and even as distorting, the web of arguments and theories which it has spun out of itself. And what does the temperament say? That life is an adventure, not a discipline; that the exercise of energy is the absolute good, irrespective of motives or of consequences. These are the maxims of a frank barbarism; nothing could express better the lust of life, the dogged unwillingness to learn from experience, the contempt for rationality, the carelessness about perfection, the admiration for mere force, in which barbarism always betrays itself. The vague religion which seeks to justify this attitude is really only another outburst of the same irrational impulse.

In Browning this religion takes the name of Christianity, and identifies itself with one or two Christian ideas arbitrarily selected; but at heart it has far more affinity to the worship of Thor or of Odin than to the religion of the Cross. The zest of life becomes a cosmic emotion; we lump the whole together and cry, "Hurrah for the Universe!" A faith which is thus a pure matter of lustiness and inebriation rises and falls, attracts or repels, with the ebb and flow of the mood from which it springs. It is invincible because unseizable; it is as safe from refutation as it is rebellious to embodiment. But it cannot enlighten or correct the passions on which it feeds. Like a servile priest, it flatters them in the name of Heaven. It cloaks irrationality in sanctimony; and its admiration for every bluff folly, being thus justified by a theory, becomes a positive fanaticism, eager to defend any wayward impulse.

Such barbarism of temper and thought could hardly, in a man of Browning's independence and spontaneity, be without its counterpart in his art. When a man's personal religion is passive, as Shakespeare's seems to have been, and is adopted without question or particular interest from the society around him, we may not observe any analogy between it and the free creations of that man's mind. Not so when the religion is created afresh by the private imagination; it is then merely one among many personal works of art, and will naturally bear a family likeness to the others. The same individual temperament, with its limitations and its bias, will appear in the art which has appeared in the religion. And such is the case with Browning. His limitations as a poet are the counterpart of his limitations as a moralist and theologian; only in the poet they are not so regrettable. Philosophy and religion are nothing if not ultimate; it is their business to deal with general principles and final aims. Now it is in the conception of things fundamental and ultimate that Browning is weak; he is strong in the conception of things immediate. The pulse of the emotion, the bobbing up of the thought, the streaming of the reverie—these he can note down with picturesque force or imagine with admirable fecundity.

Yet the limits of such excellence are narrow, for no man can safely go far without the guidance of reason. His long poems have no structure—for that name cannot be given to the singular mechanical division of *The Ring and the Book*. Even his short poems have no completeness, no limpidity. They are little torsos made broken so as to stimulate the reader to the restoration of their missing legs and arms. What is admirable in them is pregnancy of phrase, vividness of passion and sentiment, heaped-up scraps of observation, occasional flashes of light, occasional beauties of versification,—all like

> the quick sharp scratch
> And blue spurt of a lighted match.

There is never anything largely composed in the spirit of pure beauty, nothing devotedly finished, nothing simple and truly just. The poet's mind cannot reach equilibrium; at best he oscillates between opposed extravagances; his final word is still a *boutade*, still an explosion. He has no sustained nobility of style. He affects with the reader a confidential and vulgar manner, so as to be more sincere and to feel more at home. Even in the poems where the effort at impersonality is most successful, the dramatic disguise is usually thrown off in a preface, epilogue or parenthesis. The author likes to remind us of himself by some confidential wink or genial poke in the ribs, by some little interlarded sneer. We get in these tricks of manner a taste of that essential vulgarity, that indifference to purity and distinction, which is latent but pervasive in all the products of this mind. The same disdain of perfection which appears in his ethics appears here in his verse, and impairs its beauty by allowing it to remain too often obscure, affected, and grotesque.

Such a correspondence is natural: for the same powers of

conception and expression are needed in fiction, which, if turned to reflection, would produce a good philosophy. Reason is necessary to the perception of high beauty. Discipline is indispensable to art. Work from which these qualities are absent must be barbaric; it can have no ideal form and must appeal to us only through the sensuousness and profusion of its materials. We are invited by it to lapse into a miscellaneous appreciativeness, into a subservience to every detached impression. And yet, if we would only reflect even on these disordered beauties, we should see that the principle by which they delight us is a principle by which an ideal, an image of perfection, is inevitably evoked. We can have no pleasure or pain, nor any preference whatsoever, without implicitly setting up a standard of excellence, an ideal of what would satisfy us there. To make these implicit ideals explicit, to catch their hint, to work out their theme, and express clearly to ourselves and to the world what they are demanding in the place of the actual—that is the labour of reason and the task of genius. The two cannot be divided. Clarification of ideas and disentanglement of values are as essential to æsthetic activity as to intelligence. A failure of reason is a failure of art and taste.

The limits of Browning's art, like the limits of Whitman's, can therefore be understood by considering his mental habit. Both poets had powerful imaginations, but the type of their imaginations was low. In Whitman imagination was limited to marshalling sensations in single file; the embroideries he made around that central line were simple and insignificant. His energy was concentrated on that somewhat animal form of contemplation, of which, for the rest, he was a great, perhaps an unequalled master. Browning rose above that level; with him sensation is usually in the background; he is not particularly a poet of the senses or of ocular vision. His favourite subject-matter is rather the stream of thought and feeling in the mind; he is the poet of soliloquy. Nature and life as they really are, rather than as they may appear to the ignorant and passionate participant in them, lie beyond his range. Even in his best dramas, like *A Blot in the 'Scutcheon* or *Colombe's Birthday*, the interest remains in the experience of the several persons as they explain it to us. The same is the case in *The Ring and the Book*, the conception of which, in twelve monstrous soliloquies, is a striking evidence of the poet's predilection for this form.

The method is, to penetrate by sympathy rather than to portray by intelligence. The most authoritative insight is not the poet's or the spectator's, aroused and enlightened by the spectacle, but the various heroes' own, in their moment of intensest passion. We therefore miss the tragic relief and exaltation, and come away instead with the uncomfortable feeling that an obstinate folly is apparently the most glorious and choiceworthy thing in the world. This is evidently the poet's own illusion, and those who do not happen to share it must feel that if life were really as irrational as he thinks it, it would be not only profoundly discouraging, which it often is, but profoundly disgusting, which it surely is not; for at least it reveals the ideal which it fails to attain.

This ideal Browning never disentangles. For him the crude experience is the only end, the endless struggle the only ideal, and the perturbed *Soul* the only organon of truth. The arrest of his intelligence at this point, before it has envisaged any rational object, explains the arrest of his dramatic art at soliloquy. His immersion in the forms of self-consciousness prevents him from dramatizing the real relations of men and their thinkings to one another, to Nature, and to destiny. For in order to do so he would have had to view his characters from above (as Cervantes did, for instance), and to see them not merely as they appeared to themselves, but as they appear to reason. This higher attitude, however, was not only beyond Browning's scope, it was positively contrary to his inspiration. Had he reached it, he would no longer have seen the universe through the *Soul*, but through the intellect, and he would not have been able to cry, "How the world is made for each one of us!" On the contrary, the *Soul* would have figured only in its true conditions, in all its ignorance and dependence, and also in its essential teachableness, a point against which Browning's barbaric wilfulness particularly rebelled. Rooted in his persuasion that the soul is essentially omnipotent and that to live hard can never be to live wrong, he remained fascinated by the march and method of self-consciousness, and never allowed himself to be weaned from that romantic fatuity by the energy of rational imagination, which prompts us not to regard our ideas as mere filling of a dream, but rather to build on them the conception of permanent objects and overruling principles, such as Nature, society, and the other ideals of reason. A full-grown imagination deals with these things, which do not obey the laws of psychological progression, and cannot be described by the methods of soliloquy.

We thus see that Browning's sphere, though more subtle and complex than Whitman's, was still elementary. It lay far below the spheres of social and historical reality in which Shakespeare moved; far below the comprehensive and cosmic sphere of every great epic poet. Browning did not even reach the intellectual plane of such contemporary poets as Tennyson and Matthew Arnold, who, whatever may be thought of their powers, did not study consciousness for itself, but for the sake of its meaning and of the objects which it revealed. The best things that come into a man's consciousness are the things that take him out of it—the rational things that are independent of his personal perception and of his personal existence. These he approaches with his reason, and they, in the same measure, endow him with their immortality. But precisely these things—the objects of science and of the constructive imagination—Browning always saw askance, in the outskirts of his field of vision, for his eye was fixed and riveted on the soliloquizing Soul. And this Soul being, to his apprehension, irrational, did not give itself over to those permanent objects which might otherwise have occupied it, but ruminated on its own accidental emotions, on its love-affairs, and on its hopes of going on so ruminating for ever.

The pathology of the human mind—for the normal, too, is pathological when it is not referred to the ideal—the pathology of the human mind is a very interesting subject, demanding great gifts and great ingenuity in its treatment. Browning ministers to this interest, and possesses this ingenuity and these gifts. More than any other poet he keeps a kind of speculation alive in the now large body of sentimental, eager-minded people, who no longer can find in a definite religion a form and language for their imaginative life. That this service is greatly appreciated speaks well for the ineradicable tendency in man to study himself and his destiny. We do not deny the achievement when we point out its nature and limitations. It does not cease to be something because it is taken to be more than it is.

G. K. CHESTERTON
From *Robert Browning*
1903, pp. 177–202

The great fault of most of the appreciation of Browning lies in the fact that it conceives the moral and artistic value of his work to lie in what is called "the message of Browning," or "the teaching of Browning," or, in other words, in the mere opinions of Browning. Now Browning had opinions, just as he had a dress-suit or a vote for Parliament. He did not hesitate to express these opinions any more than he would have hesitated to fire off a gun, or open an umbrella, if he had possessed those articles, and realised their value. For example, he had, as his students and eulogists have constantly stated, certain definite opinions about the spiritual function of love, or the intellectual basis of Christianity. Those opinions were very striking and very solid, as everything was which came out of Browning's mind. His two great theories of the universe may be expressed in two comparatively parallel phrases. The first was what may be called the hope which lies in the imperfection of man. The characteristic poem of "Old Pictures in Florence" expresses very quaintly and beautifully the idea that some hope may always be based on deficiency itself; in other words, that in so far as man is a one-legged or a one-eyed creature, there is something about his appearance which indicates that he should have another leg and another eye. The poem suggests admirably that such a sense of incompleteness may easily be a great advance upon a sense of completeness, that the part may easily and obviously be greater than the whole. And from this Browning draws, as he is fully justified in drawing, a definite hope for immortality and the larger scale of life. For nothing is more certain than that though this world is the only world that we have known, or of which we could even dream, the fact does remain that we have named it "a strange world." In other words, we have certainly felt that this world did not explain itself, that something in its complete and patent picture has been omitted. And Browning was right in saying that in a cosmos where incompleteness implies completeness, life implies immortality. This then was the first of the doctrines or opinions of Browning: the hope that lies in the imperfection of man. The second of the great Browning doctrines requires some audacity to express. It can only be properly stated as the hope that lies in the imperfection of God. That is to say, that Browning held that sorrow and self-denial, if they were the burdens of man, were also his privileges. He held that these stubborn sorrows and obscure valours might, to use a yet more strange expression, have provoked the envy of the Almighty. If man has self-sacrifice and God has none, then man has in the Universe a secret and blasphemous superiority. And this tremendous story of a Divine jealousy Browning reads into the story of the Crucifixion. If the Creator had not been crucified He would not have been as great as thousands of wretched fanatics among His own creatures. It is needless to insist upon this point; any one who wishes to read it splendidly expressed need only be referred to "Saul." But these are emphatically the two main doctrines or opinions of Browning which I have ventured to characterise roughly as the hope in the imperfection of man, and more boldly as the hope in the imperfection of God. They are great thoughts, thoughts written by a great man, and they raise noble and beautiful doubts on behalf of faith which the human spirit will never answer or exhaust. But about them in connection with Browning there nevertheless remains something to be added.

Browning was, as most of his upholders and all his opponents say, an optimist. His theory, that man's sense of his own imperfection implies a design of perfection, is a very good argument for optimism. His theory that man's knowledge of and desire for self-sacrifice implies God's knowledge of and desire for self-sacrifice is another very good argument for optimism. But any one will make the deepest and blackest and most incurable mistake about Browning who imagines that his optimism was founded on any arguments for optimism. Because he had a strong intellect, because he had a strong power of conviction, he conceived and developed and asserted these doctrines of the incompleteness of Man and the sacrifice of Omnipotence. But these doctrines were the symptoms of his optimism, they were not its origin. It is surely obvious that no one can be argued into optimism since no one can be argued into happiness. Browning's optimism was not founded on opinions which were the work of Browning, but on life which was the work of God. One of Browning's most celebrated biographers has said that something of Browning's theology must be put down to his possession of a good digestion. The remark was, of course, like all remarks touching the tragic subject of digestion, intended to be funny and to convey some kind of doubt or diminution touching the value of Browning's faith. But if we examine the matter with somewhat greater care we shall see that it is indeed a thorough compliment to that faith. Nobody, strictly speaking, is happier on account of his digestion. He is happy because he is so constituted as to forget all about it. Nobody really is convulsed with delight at the thought of the ingenious machinery which he possesses inside him; the thing which delights him is simply the full possession of his own human body. I cannot in the least understand why a good digestion—that is, a good body—should not be held to be as mystic a benefit as a sunset or the first flower of spring. But there is about digestion this peculiarity throwing a great light on human pessimism, that it is one of the many things which we never speak of as existing until they go wrong. We should think it ridiculous to speak of a man as suffering from his boots if we meant that he had really no boots. But we do speak of a man suffering from digestion when we mean that he suffers from a lack of digestion. In the same way we speak of a man suffering from nerves when we mean that his nerves are more inefficient than any one else's nerves. If any one wishes to see how grossly language can degenerate, he need only compare the old optimistic use of the word nervous, which we employ in speaking of a nervous grip, with the new pessimistic use of the word, which we employ in speaking of a nervous manner. And as digestion is a good thing which sometimes goes wrong, as nerves are good things which sometimes go wrong, so existence itself in the eyes of Browning and all the great optimists is a good thing which sometimes goes wrong. He held himself as free to draw his inspiration from the gift of good health as from the gift of learning or the gift of fellowship. But he held that such gifts were in life innumerable and varied, and that every man, or at least almost every man, possessed some window looking out on this essential excellence of things.

Browning's optimism then, since we must continue to use this somewhat inadequate word, was a result of experience—experience which is for some mysterious reason generally understood in the sense of sad or disillusioning experience. An old gentleman rebuking a little boy for eating apples in a tree is in the common conception the type of experience. If he really wished to be a type of experience he would climb up the tree himself and proceed to experience the apples. Browning's faith was founded upon joyful experience, not in the sense that he selected his joyful experiences and ignored his painful ones, but in the sense that his joyful experiences selected themselves and stood out in his memory by virtue of their own extraordinary intensity of colour. He did not use experience in that mean and pompous sense in which it is used by the worldling advanced in years. He rather used it in that healthier and more joyful sense in which it is used at revivalist meetings. In the Salvation Army a man's experiences mean his experiences of the mercy of God, and to Browning the meaning was much the same. But the revivalists' confessions deal mostly with experiences of prayer and praise; Browning's dealt pre-eminently with what may be called his own subject, the experiences of love.

And this quality of Browning's optimism, the quality of detail, is also a very typical quality. Browning's optimism is of that ultimate and unshakeable order that is founded upon the absolute sight, and sound, and smell, and handling of things. If a man had gone up to Browning and asked him with all the solemnity of the eccentric, "Do you think life is worth living?" it is interesting to conjecture what his answer might have been. If he had been for the moment under the influence of the orthodox rationalistic deism of the theologian he would have said, "Existence is justified by its manifest design, its manifest adaptation of means to ends," or, in other words, "Existence is justified by its completeness." If, on the other hand, he had been influenced by his own serious intellectual theories he would have said, "Existence is justified by its air of growth and doubtfulness," or, in other words, "Existence is justified by its incompleteness." But if he had not been influenced in his answer either by the accepted opinions, or by his own opinions, but had simply answered the question "Is life worth living?" with the real, vital answer that awaited it in his own soul, he would have said as likely as not, "Crimson toadstools in Hampshire." Some plain, glowing picture of this sort left on his mind would be his real verdict on what the universe had meant to him. To his traditions hope was traced to order, to his speculations hope was traced to disorder. But to Browning himself hope was traced to something like red toadstools. His mysticism was not of that idle and wordy type which believes that a flower is symbolical of life; it was rather of that deep and eternal type which believes that life, a mere abstraction, is symbolical of a flower. With him the great concrete experiences which God made always come first; his own deductions and speculations about them always second. And in this point we find the real peculiar inspiration of his very original poems.

One of the very few critics who seem to have got near to the actual secret of Browning's optimism is Mr. Santayana in his most interesting book *Interpretations of Poetry and Religion*. He, in contradistinction to the vast mass of Browning's admirers, had discovered what was the real root virtue of Browning's poetry; and the curious thing is, that having discovered that root virtue, he thinks it is a vice. He describes the poetry of Browning most truly as the poetry of barbarism, by which he means the poetry which utters the primeval and indivisible emotions. "For the barbarian is the man who regards his passions as their own excuse for being, who does not domesticate them either by understanding their cause, or by conceiving their ideal goal." Whether this be or be not a good definition of the barbarian, it is an excellent and perfect definition of the poet. It might, perhaps, be suggested that barbarians, as a matter of fact, are generally highly traditional and respectable persons who would not put a feather wrong in their head-gear, and who generally have very few feelings and think very little about those they have. It is when we have grown to a greater and more civilised stature that we begin to realise and put to ourselves intellectually the great feelings that sleep in the depths of us. Thus it is that the literature of our day

has steadily advanced towards a passionate simplicity, and we become more primeval as the world grows older, until Whitman writes huge and chaotic psalms to express the sensations of a schoolboy out fishing, and Maeterlinck embodies in symbolic dramas the feelings of a child in the dark.

Thus, Mr. Santayana is, perhaps, the most valuable of all the Browning critics. He has gone out of his way to endeavour to realise what it is that repels him in Browning, and he has discovered the fault which none of Browning's opponents have discovered. And in this he has discovered the merit which none of Browning's admirers have discovered. Whether the quality be a good or a bad quality, Mr. Santayana is perfectly right. The whole of Browning's poetry does rest upon primitive feeling; and the only comment to be added is that so does the whole of every one else's poetry. Poetry deals entirely with those great eternal and mainly forgotten wishes which are the ultimate despots of existence. Poetry presents things as they are to our emotions, not as they are to any theory, however plausible, or any argument, however conclusive. If love is in truth a glorious vision, poetry will say that it is a glorious vision, and no philosophers will persuade poetry to say that it is the exaggeration of the instinct of sex. If bereavement is a bitter and continually aching thing, poetry will say that it is so, and no philosophers will persuade poetry to say that it is an evolutionary stage of great biological value. And here comes in the whole value and object of poetry, that it is perpetually challenging all systems with the test of a terrible sincerity. The practical value of poetry is that it is realistic upon a point upon which nothing else can be realistic, the point of the actual desires of man. Ethics is the science of actions, but poetry is the science of motives. Some actions are ugly, and therefore some parts of ethics are ugly. But all motives are beautiful, or present themselves for the moment as beautiful, and therefore all poetry is beautiful. If poetry deals with the basest matter, with the shedding of blood for gold, it ought to suggest the gold as well as the blood. Only poetry can realise motives, because motives are all pictures of happiness. And the supreme and most practical value of poetry is this, that in poetry, as in music, a note is struck which expresses beyond the power of rational statement a condition of mind, and all actions arise from a condition of mind. Prose can only use a large and clumsy notation; it can only say that a man is miserable, or that a man is happy; it is forced to ignore that there are a million diverse kinds of misery and a million diverse kinds of happiness. Poetry alone, with the first throb of its metre, can tell us whether the depression is the kind of depression that drives a man to suicide, or the kind of depression that drives him to the Tivoli. Poetry can tell us whether the happiness is the happiness that sends a man to a restaurant, or the much richer and fuller happiness that sends him to church.

Now the supreme value of Browning as an optimist lies in this that we have been examining, that beyond all his conclusions, and deeper than all his arguments, he was passionately interested in and in love with existence. If the heavens had fallen, and all the waters of the earth run with blood, he would still have been interested in existence, if possible a little more so. He is a great poet of human joy for precisely the reason of which Mr. Santayana complains: that his happiness is primal, and beyond the reach of philosophy. He is something far more convincing, far more comforting, far more religiously significant than an optimist: he is a happy man.

This happiness he finds, as every man must find happiness, in his own way. He does not find the great part of his joy in those matters in which most poets find felicity. He finds much of it in those matters in which most poets find ugliness and vulgarity. He is to a considerable extent the poet of towns. "Do you care for nature much?" a friend of his asked him. "Yes, a great deal," he said, "but for human beings a great deal more." Nature, with its splendid and soothing sanity, has the power of convincing most poets of the essential worthiness of things. There are few poets who, if they escaped from the rowdiest waggonette of trippers, could not be quieted again and exalted by dropping into a small wayside field. The speciality of Browning is rather that he would have been quieted and exalted by the waggonette.

To Browning, probably the beginning and end of all optimism was to be found in the faces in the street. To him they were all the masks of a deity, the heads of a hundred-headed Indian god of nature. Each one of them looked towards some quarter of the heavens, not looked upon by any other eyes. Each one of them wore some expression, some blend of eternal joy and eternal sorrow, not to be found in any other countenance. The sense of the absolute sanctity of human difference was the deepest of all his senses. He was hungrily interested in all human things, but it would have been quite impossible to have said of him that he loved humanity. He did not love humanity but men. His sense of the difference between one man and another would have made the thought of melting them into a lump called humanity simply loathsome and prosaic. It would have been to him like playing four hundred beautiful airs at once. The mixture would not combine all, it would lose all. Browning believed that to every man that ever lived upon this earth had been given a definite and peculiar confidence of God. Each one of us was engaged on secret service; each one of us had a peculiar message; each one of us was the founder of a religion. Of that religion our thoughts, our faces, our bodies, our hats, our boots, our tastes, our virtues, and even our vices, were more or less fragmentary and inadequate expressions.

In the delightful memoirs of that very remarkable man Sir Charles Gavan Duffy, there is an extremely significant and interesting anecdote about Browning, the point of which appears to have attracted very little attention. Duffy was dining with Browning and John Forster, and happened to make some chance allusion to his own adherence to the Roman Catholic faith, when Forster remarked, half jestingly, that he did not suppose that Browning would like him any the better for that. Browning would seem to have opened his eyes with some astonishment. He immediately asked why Forster should suppose him hostile to the Roman Church. Forster and Duffy replied almost simultaneously, by referring to *Bishop Blougram's Apology*, which had just appeared, and asking whether the portrait of the sophistical and self-indulgent priest had not been intended for a satire on Cardinal Wiseman. "Certainly," replied Browning cheerfully, "I intended it for Cardinal Wiseman, but I don't consider it a satire, there is nothing hostile about it." This is the real truth which lies at the heart of what may be called the great sophistical monologues which Browning wrote in later years. They are not satires or attacks upon their subjects, they are not even harsh and unfeeling exposures of them. They are defences; they say or are intended to say the best that can be said for the persons with whom they deal. But very few people in this world would care to listen to the real defence of their own characters. The real defence, the defence which belongs to the Day of Judgment, would make such damaging admissions, would clear away so many artificial virtues, would tell such tragedies of weakness and failure, that a man would sooner be misunderstood and censured by the world than exposed to that awful and merciless eulogy. One of the most practically difficult matters which

arise from the code of manners and the conventions of life, is that we cannot properly justify a human being, because that justification would involve the admission of things which may not conventionally be admitted. We might explain and make human and respectable, for example, the conduct of some old fighting politician, who, for the good of his party and his country, acceded to measures of which he disapproved; but we cannot, because we are not allowed to admit that he ever acceded to measures of which he disapproved. We might touch the life of many dissolute public men with pathos, and a kind of defeated courage, by telling the truth about the history of their sins. But we should throw the world into an uproar if we hinted that they had any. Thus the decencies of civilisation do not merely make it impossible to revile a man, they make it impossible to praise him.

Browning, in such poems as *Bishop Blougram's Apology*, breaks this first mask of goodness in order to break the second mask of evil, and gets to the real goodness at last; he dethrones a saint in order to humanise a scoundrel. This is one typical side of the real optimism of Browning. And there is indeed little danger that such optimism will become weak and sentimental and popular, the refuge of every idler, the excuse of every ne'er-do-weel. There is little danger that men will desire to excuse their souls before God by presenting themselves before men as such snobs as Bishop Blougram, or such dastards as Sludge the Medium. There is no pessimism, however stern, that is so stern as this optimism, it is as merciless as the mercy of God.

It is true that in this, as in almost everything else connected with Browning's character, the matter cannot be altogether exhausted by such a generalisation as the above. Browning's was a simple character, and therefore very difficult to understand, since it was impulsive, unconscious, and kept no reckoning of its moods. Probably in a great many cases, the original impulse which led Browning to plan a soliloquy was a kind of anger mixed with curiosity; possibly the first charcoal sketch of Blougram was a caricature of a priest. Browning, as we have said, had prejudices, and had a capacity for anger, and two of his angriest prejudices were against a certain kind of worldly clericalism, and against almost every kind of spiritualism. But as he worked upon the portraits at least, a new spirit began to possess him, and he enjoyed every spirited and just defence the men could make of themselves, like triumphant blows in a battle, and towards the end would come the full revelation, and Browning would stand up in the man's skin and testify to the man's ideals. However this may be, it is worth while to notice one very curious error that has arisen in connection with one of the most famous of these monologues.

When Robert Browning was engaged in that somewhat obscure quarrel with the spiritualist Home, it is generally and correctly stated that he gained a great number of the impressions which he afterwards embodied in *Mr. Sludge the Medium*. The statement so often made, particularly in the spiritualist accounts of the matter, that Browning himself is the original of the interlocutor and exposer of Sludge, is of course merely an example of that reckless reading from which no one has suffered more than Browning despite his students and societies. The man to whom Sludge addresses his confession is a Mr. Hiram H. Horsfall, an American, a patron of spiritualists, and, as it is more than once suggested, something of a fool. Nor is there the smallest reason to suppose that Sludge considered as an individual bears any particular resemblance to Home considered as an individual. But without doubt *Mr. Sludge the Medium* is a general statement of the view of spiritualism at which Browning had arrived from his acquaintance with Home and Home's circle. And about that view of spiritualism there is something rather peculiar to notice. The poem, appearing as it did at the time when the intellectual public had just become conscious of the existence of spiritualism, attracted a great deal of attention, and aroused a great deal of controversy. The spiritualists called down thunder upon the head of the poet, whom they depicted as a vulgar and ribald lampooner who had not only committed the profanity of sneering at the mysteries of a higher state of life, but the more unpardonable profanity of sneering at the convictions of his own wife. The sceptics, on the other hand, hailed the poem with delight as a blasting exposure of spiritualism, and congratulated the poet on making himself the champion of the sane and scientific view of magic. Which of these two parties was right about the question of attacking the reality of spiritualism it is neither easy nor necessary to discuss. For the simple truth, which neither of the two parties and none of the students of Browning seem to have noticed, is that *Mr. Sludge the Medium* is not an attack upon spiritualism. It would be a great deal nearer the truth, though not entirely the truth, to call it a justification of spiritualism. The whole essence of Browning's method is involved in this matter, and the whole essence of Browning's method is so vitally misunderstood that to say that *Mr. Sludge the Medium* is something like a defence of spiritualism will bear on the face of it the appearance of the most empty and perverse of paradoxes. But so, when we have comprehended Browning's spirit, the fact will be found to be.

The general idea is that Browning must have intended *Sludge* for an attack on spiritual phenomena, because the medium in that poem is made a vulgar and contemptible mountebank, because his cheats are quite openly confessed, and he himself put into every ignominious situation, detected, exposed, throttled, horsewhipped, and forgiven. To regard this deduction as sound is to misunderstand Browning at the very start of every poem that he ever wrote. There is nothing that the man loved more, nothing that deserves more emphatically to be called a speciality of Browning, than the utterance of large and noble truths by the lips of mean and grotesque human beings. In his poetry praise and wisdom were perfected not only out of the mouths of babes and sucklings, but out of the mouths of swindlers and snobs. Now what, as a matter of fact, is the outline and development of the poem of *Sludge?* The climax of the poem, considered as a work of art, is so fine that it is quite extraordinary that any one should have missed the point of it, since it is the whole point of the monologue. Sludge the Medium has been caught out in a piece of unquestionable trickery, a piece of trickery for which there is no conceivable explanation or palliation which will leave his moral character intact. He is therefore seized with a sudden resolution, partly angry, partly frightened, and partly humorous, to become absolutely frank, and to tell the whole truth about himself for the first time not only to his dupe, but to himself. He excuses himself for the earlier stages of the trickster's life by a survey of the border-land between truth and fiction, not by any means a piece of sophistry or cynicism, but a perfectly fair statement of an ethical difficulty which does exist. There are some people who think that it must be immoral to admit that there are any doubtful cases of morality, as if a man should refrain from discussing the precise boundary at the upper end of the Isthmus of Panama, for fear the inquiry should shake his belief in the existence of North America. People of this kind quite consistently think Sludge to be merely a scoundrel talking nonsense. It may be remembered that they thought the same thing of Newman. It is actually supposed, apparently in the current use of words, that casuistry is the name of a crime; it does not

appear to occur to people that casuistry is a science, and about as much a crime as botany. This tendency to casuistry in Browning's monologues has done much towards establishing for him that reputation for pure intellectualism which has done him so much harm. But casuistry in this sense is not a cold and analytical thing, but a very warm and sympathetic thing. To know what combinations of excuse might justify a man in manslaughter or bigamy, is not to have a callous indifference to virtue; it is rather to have so ardent an admiration for virtue as to seek it in the remotest desert and the darkest incognito.

This is emphatically the case with the question of truth and falsehood raised in *Sludge the Medium.* To say that it is sometimes difficult to tell at what point the romancer turns into the liar is not to state a cynicism, but a perfectly honest piece of human observation. To think that such a view involves the negation of honesty is like thinking that red is green, because the two fade into each other in the colours of the rainbow. It is really difficult to decide when we come to the extreme edge of veracity, when and when not it is permissible to create an illusion. A standing example, for instance, is the case of the fairy-tales. We think a father entirely pure and benevolent when he tells his children that a beanstalk grew up into heaven, and a pumpkin turned into a coach. We should consider that he lapsed from purity and benevolence if he told his children that in walking home that evening he had seen a beanstalk grow halfway up the church, or a pumpkin grow as large as a wheelbarrow. Again, few people would object to that general privilege whereby it is permitted to a person in narrating even a true anecdote to work up the climax by any exaggerative touches which really tend to bring it out. The reason of this is that the telling of the anecdote has become, like the telling of the fairy-tale, almost a distinct artistic creation; to offer to tell a story is in ordinary society like offering to recite or play the violin. No one denies that a fixed and genuine moral rule could be drawn up for these cases, but no one surely need be ashamed to admit that such a rule is not entirely easy to draw up. And when a man like Sludge traces much of his moral downfall to the indistinctness of the boundary and the possibility of beginning with a natural extravagance and ending with a gross abuse, it certainly is not possible to deny his right to be heard.

We must recur, however, to the question of the main development of the Sludge self-analysis. He begins, as we have said, by urging a general excuse by the fact that in the heat of social life, in the course of telling tales in the intoxicating presence of sympathisers and believers, he has slid into falsehood almost before he is aware of it. So far as this goes, there is truth in his plea. Sludge might indeed find himself unexpectedly justified if we had only an exact record of how true were the tales told about Conservatives in an exclusive circle of Radicals, or the stories told about Radicals in a circle of indignant Conservatives. But after this general excuse, Sludge goes on to a perfectly cheerful and unfeeling admission of fraud: this principal feeling towards his victims is by his own confession a certain unfathomable contempt for people who are so easily taken in. He professes to know how to lay the foundations for every species of personal acquaintanceship, and how to remedy the slight and trivial slips of making Plato write Greek in naughts and crosses.

> As I fear, sir, he sometimes used to do
> Before I found the useful book that knows.

It would be difficult to imagine any figure more indecently confessional, more entirely devoid of not only any of the restraints of conscience, but of any of the restraints even of a wholesome personal conceit, than Sludge the Medium. He confesses not only fraud, but things which are to the natural man more difficult to confess even than fraud—effeminacy, futility, physical cowardice. And then, when the last of his loathsome secrets has been told, when he has nothing left either to gain or to conceal, then he rises up into a perfect bankrupt sublimity and makes the great avowal which is the whole pivot and meaning of the poem. He says in effect: "Now that my interest in deceit is utterly gone, now that I have admitted, to my own final infamy, the frauds that I have practised, now that I stand before you in a patent and open villainy which has something of the disinterestedness and independence of the innocent, now I tell you with the full and impartial authority of a lost soul that I believe that there is something in spiritualism. In the course of a thousand conspiracies, by the labour of a thousand lies, I have discovered that there is really something in this matter that neither I nor any other man understands. I am a thief, an adventurer, a deceiver of mankind, but I am not a disbeliever in spiritualism. I have seen too much for that." This is the confession of faith of Mr. Sludge the Medium. It would be difficult to imagine a confession of faith framed and presented in a more impressive manner. Sludge is a witness to his faith as the old martyrs were witnesses to their faith, but even more impressively. They testified to their religion even after they had lost their liberty, and their eyesight, and their right hands. Sludge testifies to his religion even after he has lost his dignity and his honour.

It may be repeated that it is truly extraordinary that any one should have failed to notice that this avowal on behalf of spiritualism is the pivot of the poem. The avowal itself is not only expressed clearly, but prepared and delivered with admirable rhetorical force:—

> Now for it, then! Will you believe me, though?
> You've heard what I confess: I don't unsay
> A single word: I cheated when I could,
> Rapped with my toe-joints, set sham hands at work,
> Wrote down names weak in sympathetic ink.
> Rubbed odic lights with ends of phosphor-match,
> And all the rest; believe that: believe this,
> By the same token, though it seem to set
> The crooked straight again, unsay the said,
> Stick up what I've knocked down; I can't help that,
> It's truth! I somehow vomit truth to-day.
> This trade of mine—I don't know, can't be sure
> But there was something in it, tricks and all!

It is strange to call a poem with so clear and fine a climax an attack on spiritualism. To miss that climax is like missing the last sentence in a good anecdote, or putting the last act of *Othello* into the middle of the play. Either the whole poem of *Sludge the Medium* means nothing at all, and is only a lampoon upon a cad, of which the matter is almost as contemptible as the subject, or it means this—that some real experiences of the unseen lie even at the heart of hypocrisy, and that even the spiritualist is at root spiritual.

One curious theory which is common to most Browning critics is that Sludge must be intended for a pure and conscious impostor, because after his confession, and on the personal withdrawal of Mr. Horsfall, he bursts out into horrible curses against that gentleman and cynical boasts of his future triumphs in a similar line of business. Surely this is to have a very feeble notion either of nature or art. A man driven absolutely into a corner might humiliate himself, and gain a certain sensation almost of luxury in that humiliation, in pouring out all his imprisoned thoughts and obscure victories. For let it never be forgotten that a hypocrite is a very unhappy man; he

is a man who has devoted himself to a most delicate and arduous intellectual art in which he may achieve masterpieces which he must keep secret, fight thrilling battles, and win hair's-breadth victories for which he cannot have a whisper of praise. A really accomplished impostor is the most wretched of geniuses; he is a Napoleon on a desert island. A man might surely, therefore, when he was certain that his credit was gone, take a certain pleasure in revealing the tricks of his unique trade, and gaining not indeed credit, but at least a kind of glory. And in the course of this self-revelation he would come at last upon that part of himself which exists in every man—that part which does believe in, and value, and worship something. This he would fling in his hearer's face with even greater pride, and take a delight in giving a kind of testimony to his religion which no man had ever given before—the testimony of a martyr who could not hope to be a saint. But surely all this sudden tempest of candour in the man would not mean that he would burst into tears and become an exemplary ratepayer, like a villain in the worst parts of Dickens. The moment the danger was withdrawn, the sense of having given himself away, of having betrayed the secret of his infamous freemasonry, would add an indescribable violence and foulness to his reaction of rage. A man in such a case would do exactly as Sludge does. He would declare his own shame, declare the truth of his creed, and then, when he realised what he had done, say something like this:—

> R-r-r, you brute-beast and blackguard! Cowardly
>   scamp!
> I only wish I dared burn down the house
> And spoil your sniggering!

and so on, and so on.

He would react like this; it is one of the most artistic strokes in Browning. But it does not prove that he was a hypocrite about spiritualism, or that he was speaking more truthfully in the second outburst than in the first. Whence came this extraordinary theory that a man is always speaking most truly when he is speaking most coarsely? The truth about oneself is a very difficult thing to express, and coarse speaking will seldom do it.

When we have grasped this point about *Sludge the Medium*, we have grasped the key to the whole series of Browning's casuistical monologues—*Bishop Blougram's Apology*, *Prince Hohenstiel-Schwangau*, *Fra Lippo Lippi*, *Fifine at the Fair*, *Aristophanes' Apology*, and several of the monologues in *The Ring and the Book*. They are all, without exception, dominated by this one conception of a certain reality tangled almost inextricably with unrealities in a man's mind, and the peculiar fascination which resides in the thought that the greatest lies about a man, and the greatest truths about him, may be found side by side in the same eloquent and sustained utterance.

> For Blougram, he believed, say, half he spoke.

Or, to put the matter in another way, the general idea of these poems is, that a man cannot help telling some truth even when he sets out to tell lies. If a man comes to tell us that he has discovered perpetual motion, or been swallowed by the sea-serpent, there will yet be some point in the story where he will tell us about himself almost all that we require to know.

If any one wishes to test the truth, or to see the best examples of this general idea in Browning's monologues, he may be recommended to notice one peculiarity of these poems which is rather striking. As a whole, these apologies are written in a particularly burly and even brutal English. Browning's love of what is called the ugly is nowhere else so fully and extravagantly indulged. This, like a great many other things for which Browning as an artist is blamed, is perfectly appropriate to the theme. A vain, ill-mannered, and untrustworthy egotist, defending his own sordid doings with his own cheap and weather-beaten philosophy, is very likely to express himself best in a language flexible and pungent, but indelicate and without dignity. But the peculiarity of these loose and almost slangy soliloquies is that every now and then in them there occur bursts of pure poetry which are like a burst of birds singing. Browning does not hesitate to put some of the most perfect lines that he or anyone else have ever written in the English language into the mouths of such slaves as Sludge and Guido Franceschini. Take, for the sake of example, *Bishop Blougram's Apology*. The poem is one of the most grotesque in the poet's works. It is intentionally redolent of the solemn materialism and patrician grossness of a grand dinner-party *à deux*. It has many touches of an almost wild bathos, such as the young man who bears the impossible name of Gigadibs. The Bishop, in pursuing his worldly argument for conformity, points out with truth that a condition of doubt is a condition that cuts both ways, and that if we cannot be sure of the religious theory of life, neither can we be sure of the material theory of life, and that in turn is capable of becoming an uncertainty continually shaken by a tormenting suggestion. We cannot establish ourselves on rationalism, and make it bear fruit to us. Faith itself is capable of becoming the darkest and most revolutionary of doubts. Then comes the passage:—

> Just when we are safest, there's a sunset-touch,
> A fancy from a flower-bell, some one's death,
> A chorus ending from Euripides,—
> And that's enough for fifty hopes and fears
> As old and new at once as Nature's self,
> To rap and knock and enter in our soul,
> Take hands and dance there, a fantastic ring,
> Round the ancient idol, on his base again,—
> The grand Perhaps!

Nobler diction and a nobler meaning could not have been put into the mouth of Pompilia, or Rabbi Ben Ezra. It is in reality put into the mouth of a vulgar, fashionable priest, justifying his own cowardice over the comfortable wine and the cigars.

Along with this tendency to poetry among Browning's knaves, must be reckoned another characteristic, their uniform tendency to theism. These loose and mean characters speak of many things feverishly and vaguely; of one thing they always speak with confidence and composure, their relation to God. It may seem strange at first sight that those who have outlived the indulgence, and not only of every law, but of every reasonable anarchy, should still rely so simply upon the indulgence of divine perfection. Thus Sludge is certain that his life of lies and conjuring tricks has been conducted in a deep and subtle obedience to the message really conveyed by the conditions created by God. Thus Bishop Blougram is certain that his life of panic-stricken and tottering compromise has been really justified as the only method that could unite him with God. Thus Prince Hohenstiel-Schwangau is certain that every dodge in his thin string of political dodges has been the true means of realising what he believes to be the will of God. Every one of these meagre swindlers, while admitting a failure in all things relative, claims an awful alliance with the Absolute. To many it will at first sight appear a dangerous doctrine indeed. But, in truth, it is a most solid and noble and salutary doctrine, far less dangerous than its opposite. Every one on this earth should believe, amid whatever madness or moral failure, that his life and temperament have some object on the earth. Every one on the earth should believe that he has something to give to the world which cannot otherwise be given. Every one should, for the good of men and the saving of his own soul, believe that it is possible, even if we are the enemies of the human race, to be the friends of God. The evil wrought by this mystical pride, great as it often is, is like a straw to the evil wrought by a materialistic self-abandonment. The crimes of the devil who thinks himself of immeasurable value are as nothing to the crimes of the devil who thinks himself of no value. With Browning's knaves we have always this eternal interest, that they are real somewhere, and may at any moment begin to speak poetry. We are talking to a peevish and garrulous sneak; we are watching the play of his paltry features, his evasive eyes, and babbling lips. And suddenly the face begins to change and harden, the eyes glare like the eyes of a mask, the whole face of clay becomes a common mouthpiece, and the voice that comes forth is the voice of God, uttering His everlasting soliloquy.

Herman Melville

HERMAN MELVILLE

1819–1891

Herman Melville was born in New York City on August 1, 1819. He attended the New-York Male High School (1825–30), and in 1830 enrolled at the Albany Academy but withdrew after his father's death in 1832. Melville worked at various jobs between 1832 and 1838, and in 1839 joined the crew of a packet sailing to Liverpool. After his return to New York he taught briefly, and then in 1841 shipped on a whaler for the South Seas. In 1842 he jumped ship in the Marquesas Islands, and then, after several months among supposedly cannibalistic natives, escaped by joining the crew of an Australian whaler. After a brief confinement at Tahiti as an accused mutineer, Melville spent several months in Maui and Honolulu, then enlisted in the United States Navy and sailed for home. After serving briefly in Boston, he was discharged in the fall of 1844.

After returning to Lansingburgh, New York, where his family had moved in 1838, Melville began writing a fictionalized travel account based on his adventures, *Typee; or, A Peep at Polynesian Life* (1846). This book, Melville's most popular during his lifetime, was followed by a sequel, *Omoo: A Narrative of Adventures in the South Seas* (1847), which was also well received. His next book, *Mardi and a Voyage Thither* (1849), was not a success. From then on Melville's writing was increasingly ignored, and it was not until the 1920s that critics began to praise his later works, many of which were belatedly hailed as masterpieces.

Having married Elizabeth Shaw, the daughter of the chief justice of Massachusetts, in 1847, and with, eventually, four children to support, Melville continued to write prolifically, despite the poor reception of much of his work. His realistic sea stories, *Redburn: His First Voyage* and *White-Jacket; or, The World in a Man-of-War*, appeared in 1849 and 1850 respectively, and were followed by *Moby-Dick; or, The Whale* (1851), a heavily symbolic work partly inspired by his recent friendship with Hawthorne. Melville published *Pierre; or, The Ambiguities* in 1852, and between 1853 and 1856 wrote anonymous magazine stories for *Putnam's Monthly* and *Harper's New Monthly Magazine*; these stories, among them "Bartleby the Scrivener" and "Benito Cereno," were later collected and published as the *Piazza Tales* (1856). Melville's historical novel *Israel Potter: His Fifty Years of Exile* appeared in 1855.

In order to recover from a physical breakdown, Melville traveled in Europe and Palestine in 1856–57. His last novel, the satirical *Confidence Man* (1857), was published shortly before his return to New York. After a series of unsuccessful lecture tours (1857–60), Melville in 1866 became a district inspector of customs for New York harbor, a position he retained until his resignation in 1885. His collection of bitter, disillusioned Civil War poems, *Battle-Pieces and Aspects of the War*, appeared in 1866, and was followed in 1876 by his narrative poem *Clarel*, which reflected his experiences in the Holy Land. *John Marr and Other Sailors* (1888), a collection of miscellaneous pieces, and the verse collection *Timoleon* (1891), were the two last works published during Melville's lifetime; both were privately printed and issued in limited editions. Melville died on September 28, 1891, leaving his novel *Billy Budd, Foretopman* in manuscript; it was not published until 1924. Since that time various editions of his works have appeared, including *The Writings of Herman Melville*, eds. Harrison Hayford et al. (1968–   ), and *Letters*, eds. Merrell R. Davis and William H. Gilman (1960).

General

It is upon the far-off deep South Seas,
The island Nukuheva, its degrees
In vain,—I may not reckon, but the bold
Adventurous Melville there by chance was rolled,
And for four months in its delights did dwell,
And of this Island writ what I may tell.
So far away, it is a Paradise
To my unfolded, stationary eyes,
Around it white the heavy billows beat,
Within its vales profoundest cataracts meet,
Drawn from the breasts of the high purple mountains,
And to those Islanders perpetual fountains.
　　　—WILLIAM ELLERY CHANNING, "The Island Nukuheva," 1847

I met Melville the other day, and liked him so much that I have asked him to spend a few days with me before leaving these parts.—NATHANIEL HAWTHORNE, Letter to Horatio Bridge (Aug. 7, 1850), cited in Horatio Bridge, *Personal Recollections of Nathaniel Hawthorne*, 1893, p. 123

Our friend Melville's books begin to accumulate. His literary family increases rapidly. He had already a happy and smiling progeny around him, but lo! at the appointed time another child of his brain, with the accustomed signs of the family, claims our attention and regard. We bid the book a hearty welcome. We assure the "happy father" that his "labors of love" are no "love's labor lost."

We confess an admiration for Mr. Melville's books, which, perhaps, spoils us for mere criticism. There are few writers, living or dead, who describe the sea and its adjuncts with such true art, such graphic power, and with such powerfully resulting interest. *Typee, Omoo, Redburn, Mardi*, and *White Jacket*, are equal to anything in the language. They are things of their own. They are results of the youthful experience on the ocean of a man who is at once philosopher, painter, and poet. This is not, perhaps, a very unusual mental combination, but it is not usual to find such a combination "before the mast." So far Mr. Melville's early experiences, though perhaps none of the pleasantest to himself, are infinitely valuable to the world. We say *valuable* with a full knowledge of the terms used; and, not to enter into details, which will be fresh in the memory of most of Mr. Melville's readers, it is sufficient to say that the humanities of the world have been quickened by his works. Who can forget the missionary *exposé*—the practical good sense which pleads for "Poor Jack," or the unsparing but just severity of his delineations of naval abuses, and that crowning disgrace to our navy— flogging? Taken as matters of art these books are amongst the largest and the freshest contributions of original thought and observation which have been presented in many years. Take the majority of modern writers, and it will be admitted that however much they may elaborate and rearrange the stock of ideas pre-existant, there is little added to this "common fund." Philosophers bark at each other—poets sing stereotyped phrases—John Miltons re-appear in innumerable *Pollock's Courses of Time*—novelists and romances stick to the same overdone incidents, careless of the memories of defunct Scotts and Radcliffs, and it is only now and then when genius, by some lucky chance of youth, ploughs deeper into the soil of humanity and nature, that fresher experience—perhaps at the cost of much individual pain and sorrow—are obtained; and the results are books, such as those of Herman Melville and Charles Dickens. Books which are living pictures, at once of the practical truth, and the ideal amendment: books which mark epochs in literature and art.

It is, however, not with Mr. Melville generally as a writer that we have now to deal, but with *Moby Dick, or the Whale*, in particular; and at first let us not forget to say that in "taking titles" no man is more felicitous than our author. Sufficiently dreamy to excite one's curiosity, sufficiently explicit to indicate some main and peculiar feature. *Moby Dick* is perhaps a creation of the brain—*The Whale* a result of experience; and the whole title a fine polished result of both. A title may be a truth or a lie. It may be clap-trap, or true art. A bad book may have a good title, but you will seldom find a good book with an inappropriate name.

Moby Dick, or the Whale, is all whale. Leviathan is here in full amplitude. Not one of your museum affairs, but the real, living whale, a bona-fide, warm-blooded creature, ransacking the waters from pole to pole. His enormous bulk, his terribly destructive energies, his habits, his food, are all before us. Nay, even his lighter moods are exhibited. We are permitted to see the whale as a lover, a husband, and the head of a family. So to speak, we are made guests at his fire-side; we set our mental legs beneath his mahogany, and become members of his interesting social circle. No book in the world brings together so much whale. We have his history, natural and social, living and dead. But Leviathan's natural history, though undoubtedly valuable to science, is but a part of the book. It is in the personal adventures of his captors, their toils, and, alas! not unfrequently their wounds and martyrdom, that our highest interest is excited. This mingling of human adventure with new, startling, and striking objects and pursuits, constitute one of the chief charms of Mr. Melville's books. His present work is a drama of intense interest. A whale, *Moby Dick*—a dim, gigantic, unconquerable, but terribly destructive being is one of the persons of the drama. We admit a disposition to be critical on this character. We had doubts as to his admissibility as an actor into dramatic action, and so it

would seem had our author, but his chapter, "The Affidavit," disarms us; all improbability or incongruity disappears, and *Moby Dick* becomes a living fact, simply doubtful at first, because he was so new an idea, one of those beings whose whole life, like the Palladius or the Sea-serpent, is a romance, and whose memoirs unvarnished are of themselves a fortune to the first analist or his publisher.

Moby Dick, or the Whale, is a "many-sided" book. Mingled with much curious information respecting whales and whaling there is a fine vein of sermonizing, a good deal of keen satire, much humor, and that too of the finest order, and a story of peculiar interest. As a romance its characters are so new and unusual that we doubt not it will excite the ire of critics. It is not tame enough to pass this ordeal safely. Think of a monomaniac whaling captain, who, mutilated on a former voyage by a particular whale, well known for its peculiar bulk, shape, and color—seeks, at the risk of his life and the lives of his crew, to capture and slay this terror of the seas! It is on this idea that the romance hinges. The usual staple of novelists is entirely wanting. We have neither flinty-hearted fathers, designing villains, dark caverns, men in armor, nor anxious lovers. There is not in the book any individual, who, at a certain hour, *"might have been seen"* ascending hills or descending valleys, as is usual. The thing is entirely new, fresh, often startling, and highly dramatic, and with those even, who, oblivious of other fine matters, scattered with profusest hand, read for the sake of the story, must be exceedingly successful. ⟨. . .⟩ we must conclude by strongly recommending *Moby Dick, or the Whale*, to all who can appreciate a work of exceeding power, beauty, and genius.—WILLIAM T. POR-TER (?), "Moby Dick, or the Whale," *Spirit of the Times*, Dec. 6, 1851

Mr. Melville does not improve with time. His later books are a decided falling off, and his last scarcely deserves naming; this however we scarce believe to be an indication of exhaustion. Keats says beautifully in his preface to *Endymion*, that "The imagination of a boy is healthy, and the mature imagination of a man is healthy, but there is a space of life between, in which the soul is in a ferment, the character undecided, the way of life uncertain, the ambition thick-sighted."

Just at present we believe the author of *Pierre* to be in this state of ferment. *Typee*, his first book, was healthy; *Omoo* nearly so; after that came *Mardi*, with its excusable wildness; then came *Moby Dick*, and *Pierre* with its inexcusable insanity. We trust that these rhapsodies will end the interregnum of nonsense to which Keats refers, as forming a portion of every man's life; and that Mr. Melville will write less at random and more at leisure, than of late.—FITZ-JAMES O'BRIEN, "Our Young Authors—Melville," *Putnam's Monthly*, Feb. 1853, p. 163

Whoever has read the writings of Melville must I think feel disposed to consider *Moby Dick* as his finest work. It is indeed all about the sea, whilst *Typee* and *Omoo*, are chiefly famous for their lovely descriptions of the South Sea Islands, and of the wild and curious inhabitants of those coral strands; but though the action of the story is altogether on shipboard, the narrative is not in the least degree nautical in the sense that Cooper's and Marryat's novels are. The thread that strings a wonderful set of fancies and incidents together, is that of a whaler, whose master, Captain Ahab, having lost his leg by the teeth of a monstrous white whale, to which the name of Moby Dick has been given, vows to sail in pursuit of his enemy. The narrator embarks in the ship that is called the *Pequod*, which he describes as having an "old-fashioned, claw-footed look about her."

She was apparelled like any barbaric Ethiopic Emperor, his neck heavy with pendants of polished ivory. She was a thing of trophies. A cannibal of a craft, tricking herself forth in the chased bones of her enemies. All round her unpanelled, open bulwarks were garnished like one continuous jaw, with the long sharp teeth of the sperm-whale, inserted there for pins to fasten her old hempen thews and tendons to. Those thews ran not through base blocks of land wood, but deftly travelled over sheaves of ivory. Scorning a turnstile wheel at her reverend helm she sported there a tiller; and that tiller was in one mass, curiously carved from the long narrow jaw of her hereditary foe. The helmsman, who steered by that tiller in a tempest, felt like the Tartar when he holds back his fiery steed by clutching its jaw. A noble craft, but somehow a most melancholy! All noble things are touched with that.

Melville takes this vessel, fills her full of strange men, and starts her on her insane quest, that he may have the ocean under and around him to muse upon, as though he were in a spacious burial-ground, with the alternations of sunlight and moonlight and deep starless darkness to set his thoughts to. *Moby Dick* is not a sea-story—one could not read it as such—it is a medley of noble impassioned thoughts born of the deep, pervaded by a grotesque human interest, owing to the contrast it suggests between the rough realities of the cabin and the forecastle, and the phantasms of men conversing in rich poetry, and strangely moving and acting in that dim weather-worn Nantucket whaler. There is a chapter where the sailors are represented as gathered together on the forecastle; and what is made to pass among them, and the sayings which are put into their mouths, might truly be thought to have come down to us from some giant mind of the Shakspearean era. As we read, we do not need to be told that seamen don't talk as those men do; probabilities are not thought of in this story. It is like a drawing by William Blake, if you please; or, better yet, it is of the *Ancient Mariner* pattern, madly fantastic in places, full of extraordinary thoughts, yet gloriously coherent—the work of a hand which, if the desire for such a thing had ever been, would have given a sailor's distinctness to the portrait of the solemn and strange Miltonic fancy of a ship built in the eclipse and rigged with curses dark. In *Typee*, and *Omoo*, and *Redburn*, he takes other ground, and writes—always with the finest fancy—in a straight-headed way. I am concerned with him only as a seafarer. In *Redburn* he tells a sailor's yarn, and the dream-like figures of the crew of the *Pequod* make place for Liverpool and Yankee seamen, who chew tobacco and use bad language. His account of the sufferings of the emigrants in this book leaves a deep impression upon the mind. His accuracy is unimpeachable here, for the horrors he relates were as well known thirty and forty years ago as those of the middle passages were in times earlier still. In *Omoo*, again, he gives us a good deal of the sea, and presumably relates his own experiences on board a whaler. He seems proud of his calling, for in *Moby Dick* he says:—

And as for me, if by any possibility there be any as yet undiscovered prime thing in me; if I shall ever deserve any real repute in that small but high-hushed world which I might not be unreasonably ambitious of; if hereafter I shall do anything that, upon the whole, a man might rather have done than left undone; if at my death my executors, or more properly my creditors, find any precious MSS. in my desk, then here I prospectively ascribe all the honour and the glory to whaling; for a whale-ship was my Yale College and my Harvard.

He returns to the whaleman in *Omoo*, and in his barque, the *Little Jule*, charms the nautical reader with the faithfulness of his portraiture, and the humour and the poetry he puts into it. There is some remarkable character-drawing in this book: notably John Jermin, the mate of the *Little Jule*, and Doctor Long Ghost, the nickname given by the sailors to a man who shipped as a physician, and was rated as a gentleman and lived in the cabin, until both the captain and he falling drunk, he drove home his views on politics by knocking the skipper down, after which he went to live forward. He is as quaint, striking, and original a personage as may be found in English fiction, and we find him in the dingy and leaky forecastle of the *Little Jule*, where he is surrounded by coarse and worn whalemen in Scotch caps and ragged clothes quoting Virgil, talking of Hobbes, "besides repeating poetry by the canto, especially *Hudibras*." Yet his portrait does not match that of John Jermin, the mate, whom, spite of his love of rum and homely method of reasoning with a man by means of a handspike, one gets to heartily like and to follow about with laughter as, intoxicated, he chases the sun all over the deck at noon with an old quadrant at his eye, or tumbles into the forecastle after a seaman who has enraged him by contemptuous remarks. —W. CLARK RUSSELL, "Sea-Stories," *Contemporary Review*, Sept. 1884, pp. 356–58

Meantime my sun-like music-maker,
  Shines solitary and apart;
Meantime the brave sword-carrying Quaker
  Broods in the peace of his great heart,—
While Melville, sea-compelling man,
Before whose wand Leviathan
Rose hoary white upon the Deep,
With awful sounds that stirred its sleep,
Melville, whose magic drew Typee,
Radiant as Venus, from the sea,
Sits all forgotten or ignored,
While haberdashers are adored!
He, ignorant of the drapers' trade,
  Indifferent to the art of dress,
Pictured the glorious South-sea maid
  Almost in mother nakedness—
Without a hat, or boot, or stocking,
A want of dress to most so shocking,
With just one chemisette to dress her
She *lives*,—and still shall live, God bless her!
Long as the sea rolls deep and blue,
  While heaven repeats the thunder of it,
Long as the White Whale ploughs it through,
The shape my sea-magician drew
  Shall still endure, or I'm no prophet!
  —ROBERT BUCHANAN, "Socrates in Camden, with a Look Round," *Academy*, Aug. 15, 1885, p. 103

At this period English and American literature (of course including poetry and prose fiction) were beginning to feel the scientific and economic influence of the age,—an age which on its superficial side was searching for facts rather than dreams or fancies. ⟨. . . A⟩ response was made by Herman Melville in his brisk and stirring tales of the sea or sketches of travel, in which fact and fancy were mingled by the nervously impatient author, in the proportion desired by his immediate public. Melville's own adventures had been those of a modern Captain

John Smith in the Pacific islands and waters; so that the *pars magna fui* of his lively books gave them the needed fillip of personality, and duly magnified their elements of wonder. That brilliant power of delineation which, in Melville's conversation, so charmed his warm friends the Hawthornes, is apparently not heightened in his books, but would seem to be rather diminished by the exigencies of writing. But the personal narrative or fiction of *Typee, Omoo,* and *Moby Dick,* with their adventurous rapidity of description of Pacific seas, ships, savages and whales, represented the restless facility which has always been an American trait, and which occasionally develops into some enduring literary success.—CHARLES F. RICHARDSON, *American Literature, 1607–1885,* 1887, Vol. 2, pp. 403–4

Herman Melville, after astonishing the public with a rapid succession of original novels, the scene of which was placed in the islands of the Pacific, suddenly dropped his pen, as if in disgust of his vocation.—EDWIN P. WHIPPLE, "American Literature" (1886), *American Literature and Other Papers,* 1887, p. 125

I shall have a fine book of travels, I feel sure; and will tell you more of the South Seas after very few months than any other writer has done—except Herman Melville perhaps, who is a howling cheese.—ROBERT LOUIS STEVENSON, Letter to Charles Baxter (Sept. 6, 1888)

There has died and been buried in this city, during the current week, at an advanced age, a man who is so little known, even by name, to the generation now in the vigor of life that only one newspaper contained an obituary account of him, and this was but of three or four lines. Yet forty years ago the appearance of a new book by Herman Melville was esteemed a literary event, not only throughout his own country, but so far as the English-speaking race extended. To the ponderous and quarterly British reviews of that time, the author of *Typee* was about the most interesting of literary Americans, and men who made few exceptions to the British rule of not reading an American book not only made Melville one of them, but paid him the further compliment of discussing him as an unquestionable literary force. Yet when a visiting British writer a few years ago inquired at a gathering in New-York of distinctly literary Americans what had become of Herman Melville, not only was there not one among them who was able to tell him, but there was scarcely one among them who had ever heard of the man concerning whom he inquired, albeit that man was then living within a half mile of the place of the conversation. Years ago the books by which Melville's reputation had been made had long been out of print and out of demand. The latest book, now about a quarter of a century old, *Battle Pieces and Aspects of the War,* fell flat, and he has died an absolutely forgotten man.

In its kind this speedy oblivion by which a once famous man so long survived his fame is almost unique, and it is not easily explicable. Of course, there are writings that attain a great vogue and then fall entirely out of regard or notice. But this is almost always because either the interest of the subject matter is temporary, and the writings are in the nature of journalism, or else the workmanship to which they owe their temporary success is itself the produce or the product of a passing fashion. This was not the case with Herman Melville. Whoever, arrested for a moment by the tidings of the author's death, turns back now to the books that were so much read and so much talked about forty years ago has no difficulty in determining why they were then read and talked about. His

difficulty will be rather to discover why they are read and talked about no longer. The total eclipse now of what was then a literary luminary seems like a wanton caprice of fame. At all events, it conveys a moral that is both bitter and wholesome to the popular novelists of our own day.

Melville was a born romancer. One cannot account for the success of his early romances by saying that in the Great South Sea he had found and worked a new field for romance, since evidently it was not his experience in the South Sea that had led him to romance, but the irresistible attraction that romance had over him that led him to the South Sea. He was able not only to feel but to interpret that charm, as it never had been interpreted before, as it never has been interpreted since. It was the romance and the mystery of the great ocean and its groups of islands that made so alluring to his own generation the series of fantastic tales in which these things were celebrated. *Typee* and *Omoo* and *Mardi* remain for readers of English the poetic interpretation of the Polynesian Islands and their surrounding seas. Melville's pictorial power was very great, and it came, as such power always comes, from his feeling more intensely than others the charm that he is able to present more vividly than others. It is this power which gave these romances the hold upon readers which it is surprising that they have so completely lost. It is almost as visible in those of his books that are not professed romances, but purport to be accounts of authentic experiences—in *White Jacket,* the story of life before the mast in an American man-of-war; in *Moby Dick,* the story of a whaling voyage. The imagination that kindles at a touch is as plainly shown in these as in the novels, and few readers who have read it are likely to forget Melville's poetizing of the prosaic process of trying out blubber in his description of the old whaler wallowing through the dark and "burning a corpse." Nevertheless, the South Pacific is the field that he mainly made his own, and that he made his own, as those who remember his books will acknowledge, beyond rivalry. That this was a very considerable literary achievement there can be no question. For some months a contemporaneous writer, of whom nobody will dispute that he is a romancer and a literary artist, has been working in the same field, but it cannot seriously be pretended that Mr. Stevenson has taken from Herman Melville the laureateship of the Great South Sea. In fact, the readers of Stevenson abandon as quite unreadable what he has written from that quarter.—UNSIGNED, *New York Times,* Oct. 2, 1891, p. 4

There was a wealth of imagination in the mind of Mr. Melville, but it was an untrained imagination, and a world of the stuff out of which poetry is made, but no poetry, which is creation and not chaos. He saw like a poet, felt like a poet, thought like a poet, but he never attained any proficiency in verse, which was not among his natural gifts. His vocabulary was large, fluent, eloquent, but it was excessive, inaccurate and unliterary. He wrote too easily, and at too great length, his pen sometimes running away with him, and from his readers. There were strange, dark, mysterious elements in his nature, as there were in Hawthorne's, but he never learned to control them, as Hawthorne did from the beginning, and never turned their possibilities into actualities.—RICHARD HENRY STODDARD, *Critic,* Nov. 14, 1891, p. 272

With this renaissance of the South Seas, it was inevitable that there should come a demand for the republication of *Typee* and *Omoo,*—those wonderful "real romances" in which the inspired usher, who passed his time between keeping school at Green Bush, N.Y., and sailing among the islands, told the world how he had lived under the shadow of the bread-fruit trees, a life which, as far as sensuous delight and physical beauty were concerned, could only be compared to that of ancient Hellas. There, in vales lovelier than Tempe, and by waters brighter than those of the Ægean, he had seen the flower-crowned and flower-girdled Mænads weave the meshes of their rhythmic dance; had sat at feasts with youths whose forms might have inspired Lysippus and Praxiteles; had watched in amazement and delight the torches gleaming through the palm-groves, while the votaries of mysteries, like those of Demeter or Dionysus, performed their solemn rites and meet oblations; and yet, in spite of all, had yearned with a passionate yearning for the pleasant fields of New England and the wholesome prose of modern life,—the incomparable charities of hearth and home.

Though Melville has not the literary power of Mr. Stevenson, the description in *Typee* of the life he led among a cannibal tribe in the Marquesas islands has a charm beyond the charm of *The Wrecker*, the *Island Nights*, or those studies of the Marquesas which Mr. Stevenson contributed to the earlier numbers of *Black and White*. *Typee* is the "document" *par excellence* of savage life, and a document written by one who knew how to write as well as to look. We have said that Mr. Melville does not write as well as Mr. Stevenson, but this does not mean that he is not a literary artist. Mr. Melville is no mean master of prose, and had his judgment been equal to his feeling for form, he might have ranked high in English literature on the ground of style alone. Unfortunately, he was apt to let the last great master of style he had been reading run away with him. For example, in *Moby Dick*—one of the best and most thrilling sea-stories ever written—Mr. Melville has "hitched to his car" the fantastic Pegasus of Sir Thomas Browne. With every circumstance of subject favourable, it would be madness to imitate the author of *Urne Burial*. When his style is made the vehicle for describing the hunting of sperm-whales in the Pacific, the result cannot but be disastrous. Yet so great an artist is Mr. Melville and so strong are the fascinations of his story, that we defy any reader of sense to close this epic of whaling without the exclamation,—"With all its faults I would not have it other than it is." Discovering a right line in obliquity and by an act of supreme genius forcing his steed to run a pace for which he was not bred, Mr. Melville contrives, in spite of Sir Thomas Browne, to write a book which is not only enchanting as a romance, but a genuine piece of literature. No one who has read the chapter on "Nantucket" and its seafarers, and has learned how at nightfall the Nantucketer, like "the landless gull that at sunset folds her wings and is rocked to sleep between billows," "furls his sails and lays him to his rest, while under his very pillow rush herds of walruses and whales," will have the heart to cavil at Melville's style. In *White Jacket*—a marvellous description of life on a man-of-war—we see yet another deflection given to Mr. Melville's style, and with still worse results. He had apparently been reading Carlyle before he wrote it; and Carlylisms, mixed with the dregs of the *Religio Medici*, every now and then crop up to annoy the reader. In spite, however, of this heavy burden, *White Jacket* is excellent reading, and full of the glory of the sea and the spirit of the Viking. And here we may mention a very pleasant thing about Mr. Melville's books. They show throughout a strong feeling of brotherhood with the English. The sea has made him feel the oneness of the English kin, and he speaks of Nelson and the old Admirals like a lover or a child. Though Mr. Melville wrote at a time when English insolence and pig-headedness, and Yankee bumptiousness, made a good deal of ill-blood between the two peoples, he at heart feels that, on the sea at least, it is the English kin against the world.—JOHN ST. LOE STRACHEY, "Herman Melville," *Spectator*, June 24, 1893, pp. 858–59

Fortune, which seemed not long since to have deserted Herman Melville as completely as ⟨William Gilmore⟩ Simms, has at last smiled again upon the former since a generation fond of narratives full of not too improbable adventure and of tropical glow has accepted, with at least fair complacency, the republication of books that won the warm commendation of Robert Louis Stevenson. The author of *Typee* was born in New York, and ultimately died there, after a long period of seclusion. He had no special incentive save his own love of adventure to desert farming at an early age and go to sea as a cabin-boy. He then tried teaching, but shipped again in 1841, this time on a whaler bound for the South Seas. The cruelty of his captain caused him—with a companion, the Toby of *Typee*—to desert the ship as she lay in a harbour in the Marquesas. Then followed the adventures so interestingly told in *Typee*, which was published in 1846, soon after Melville's return to civilization. His book was very successful in both England and America, although some persons refused to give credence to it or to *Oomoo*, which immediately followed it. Marriage and literary success then transformed the adventurer into a fairly prolific man of letters. But as early as 1848 the quasi-speculative, chaotic romance entitled *Mardi* gave premonition of aberration and of the eventual frustration of a promising career. Melville's greatest achievement still awaited him, however, for after two other fair books of adventure he published, in 1851, his masterpiece, *Moby Dick, or the White Whale*. If it were not for its inordinate length, its frequently inartistic heaping up of details, and its obvious imitation of Carlylean tricks of style and construction, this narrative of tremendous power and wide knowledge might be perhaps pronounced the greatest sea story in literature. The breath of the sea is in it and much of the passion and charm of the most venturous of all the venturous callings plied upon the deep. It is a cool reader that does not become almost as eager as the terrible Captain Ahab in his demoniacal pursuit of Moby Dick, the invincible whale, a creation of the imagination not unworthy of a great poet. In this uneven, but on the whole genuine, work of genius, Melville probably overtasked himself. He published several other books while, like his friend Hawthorne, attending to his duties in the custom-house, but nothing comparable to his earlier works. One, *Israel Potter*, deserved Hawthorne's praise because of its spirited portraits of Franklin and Paul Jones, but no revival of their author's fame will justify the republication of these productions of his decline.—WILLIAM P. TRENT, A *History of American Literature*, 1903, pp. 389–91

Years ago I looked into *Typee* and *Omoo*, but as I didn't find there what I am looking for when I open a book I did go no further. Lately I had in my hand *Moby Dick*. It struck me as a rather strained rhapsody with whaling for a subject and not a single sincere line in the 3 vols of it.—JOSEPH CONRAD, Letter to Humphrey Milford (Jan. 15, 1907)

Works

TYPEE

It records the adventures of a young American who ran away from a whale ship at the Marquesas, and spent some months as the guest, or captive, of a native tribe, of which scarcely anything had been hitherto known to the civilized world.—The book is lightly but vigorously written; and we are acquainted with no work that gives a freer and more effective picture of barbarian life, in that unadulterated state of which there are now so few specimens remaining. The gentleness of disposition that seems akin to the delicious climate, is shown in contrast with traits of savage fierceness;—on one page, we read of manners and modes of life that indicate a whole system of innocence and peace; and on the next, we catch a glimpse of a smoked human head, and the half-picked skeleton of what had been (in a culinary sense) a *well-dressed* man. The author's descriptions of the native girls are voluptuously colored, yet not more so than the exigencies of the subject appear to require. He has that freedom of view—it would be too harsh to call it laxity of principle—which renders him tolerant of codes or morals that may be little in accordance with our own; a spirit proper enough to a young and adventurous sailor, and which makes his book the more wholesome to our staid landsmen. The narrative is skillfully managed, and in a literary point of view, the execution of the work is worthy of the novelty and interest of its subject.—NATHANIEL HAWTHORNE, *Salem Advertiser*, March 25, 1846

In the evening we finished the first volume of *Typee*, a curious and interesting book with glowing descriptions of life in the Marquesas.—HENRY WADSWORTH LONGFELLOW, *Journal* (July 29, 1846), cited in Samuel Longfellow, *Life of Henry Wadsworth Longfellow*, 1891, Vol. 2, p. 52

⟨. . .⟩ for my part, I am heartily sick of *Typee*.—JAMES RUSSELL LOWELL, Letter to Sydney H. Gay (Sept. 1848)

I read *Typee* at one sitting, and had, of course, no doubt of its success; but the better to assure it, I advised the diplomatic brother to take a copy to London, and have it issued there simultaneously with its publication in New York. I felt sure that the reviewers of the English press would make its American success, and I was not at all sure that the process could be reversed. It was accordingly brought out by Mr. Murray, in London, as *Life in the Marquesas*, and Harper Brothers in New York, and made at once a brilliant reputation for the author. It was one of the few instances of the first work of an unknown literary adventurer making for him a very desirable reputation. I met Herman Melville often, after I had read *Typee* before and after its publication. He was a simple-hearted, enthusiastic man of genius, who wrote with the consciousness of an impelling force, and with great power and beauty.—THOMAS LOW NICHOLS, *Forty Years of American Life, 1821–1861*, 1864, Ch. 25

Cooper outgoes all American competitors in extravagant fabrications of salt-water adventure. Herman Melville's South Sea stories are more direct and convincing, his *Typee*, especially, having the realistic shudder of an author who barely escaped a dishing up for cannibals.—KATHARINE LEE BATES, *American Literature*, 1897, p. 276

"Taipi" the chart spelled it, and spelled it correctly, but I prefer "Typee," and I shall always spell it "Typee." When I was a little boy, I read a book spelled in that manner—Herman Melville's *Typee*; and many long hours I dreamed over its pages. Nor was it all dreaming. I resolved there and then, mightily, come what would, that when I had gained strength and years, I, too, would voyage to Typee. For the wonder of the world was penetrating to my tiny consciousness—the wonder that was to lead me to many lands, and that leads and never palls. The years passed, but Typee was not forgotten.—JACK LONDON, "Typee" (1910), *The Cruise of the Snark*, 1911, pp. 154–55

MOBY-DICK

The present volume is a "Whaliad," or the Epic of that veritable old leviathan, who "esteemeth iron as straw, and laughs at the spear, the dart, and the habergeon," no one being able to "fill his skin with a barbed iron, or his head with fish-hooks." Mr. Melville gives us not only the romance of his history, but a great mass of instruction on the character and habits of his whole race, with complete details of the wily stratagems of their pursuers.

The interest of the work pivots on a certain Captain Ahab, whose enmity to Moby-Dick, the name of the whale-demon, has been aggravated to monomania. In one rencounter with this terror of the seas, he suffers a signal defeat; loses a leg in the contest; gets a fire in his brain; returns home a man with one idea; feels that he has a mission; that he is predestined to defy his enemy to mortal strife; devotes himself to the fulfillment of his destiny; with the persistence and cunning of insanity gets possession of another vessel; ships a weird, supernatural crew of which Ishmael, the narrator of the story, is a prominent member; and after a "wild huntsman's chase" through unknown seas, is the only one who remains to tell the destruction of the ship and the doomed Captain Ahab by the victorious, indomitable Moby-Dick.

The narrative is constructed in Herman Melville's best manner. It combines the various features which form the chief attractions of his style, and is commendably free from the faults which we have before had occasion to specify in this powerful writer. The intensity of the plot is happily relieved by minute descriptions of the most homely processes of the whale fishery. We have occasional touches of the subtle mysticism, which is carried to such an inconvenient excess in Mardi, but it is here mixed up with so many tangible and odorous realities, that we always safely alight from the excursion through mid-air upon the solid deck of the whaler. We are recalled to this world by the fumes of "oil and blubber," and are made to think more of the contents of barrels than of allegories. The work is also full of episodes, descriptive of strange and original phases of character. One of them is given in the commencement of the volume, showing how "misery makes a man acquainted with strange bedfellows."

⟨. . .⟩ We part with the adventurous philosophical Ishmael, truly thankful that the whale did not get his head, for which we are indebted for this wildly imaginative and truly thrilling story. We think it the best production which has yet come from that seething brain, and in spite of its lawless flights, which put all regular criticism at defiance, it gives us a higher opinion of the author's originality and power than even the favorite and fragrant first-fruits of his genius, the never-to-be-forgotten *Typee*.—HORACE GREELEY, *New York Daily Tribune*, Nov. 22, 1851

A new work by Herman Melville, entitled *Moby Dick; or, The Whale*, has just been issued by Harper and Brothers, which, in point of richness and variety of incident, originality of conception, and splendor of description, surpasses any of the former productions of this highly successful author. *Moby Dick* is the name of an old White Whale; half fish and half devil; the terror of the Nantucket cruisers; the scourge of distant oceans; leading an invulnerable, charmed life; the subject of many grim and ghostly traditions. This huge sea monster has a conflict with one Captain Ahab; the veteran Nantucket salt comes off second best; not only loses a leg in the affray, but receives a twist in the brain; becomes the victim of a deep, cunning monomania; believes himself predestined to take a bloody revenge on his fearful enemy; pursues him with fierce demoniac energy of purpose; and at last perishes in the dreadful fight, just as he deems that he has reached the goal of his frantic passion. On this slight framework, the author has constructed a romance, a tragedy, and a natural history, not without numerous gratuitous suggestions on psychology, ethics, and theology. Beneath the whole story, the subtle, imaginative reader may perhaps find a pregnant allegory, intended to illustrate the mystery of human life. Certain it is that the rapid, pointed hints which are often thrown out, with the keenness and velocity of a harpoon, penetrate deep into the heart of things, showing that the genius of the author for moral analysis is scarcely surpassed by his wizard power of description.

In the course of the narrative the habits of the whale are fully and ably described. Frequent graphic and instructive sketches of the fishery, of sea-life in a whaling vessel, and of the manners and customs of strange nations are interspersed with excellent artistic effect among the thrilling scenes of the story. The various processes of procuring oil are explained with the minute, painstaking fidelity of a statistical record, contrasting strangely with the weird, phantom-like character of the plot, and of some of the leading personages, who present a no less unearthly appearance than the witches in *Macbeth*. These sudden and decided transitions form a striking feature of the volume. Difficult of management, in the highest degree, they are wrought with consummate skill. To a less gifted author, they would inevitably have proved fatal. He has not only deftly avoided their dangers, but made them an element of great power. They constantly pique the attention of the reader, keeping curiosity alive, and presenting the combined charm of surprise and alternation.

The introductory chapters of the volume, containing sketches of life in the great marts of Whalingdom, New Bedford and Nantucket, are pervaded with a fine vein of comic humor, and reveal a succession of portraitures, in which the lineaments of nature shine forth, through a good deal of perverse, intentional exaggeration. To many readers, these will prove the most interesting portions of the work. Nothing can be better than the description of the owners of the vessel, Captain Peleg and Captain Bildad, whose acquaintance we make before the commencement of the voyage. The character of Captain Ahab also opens upon us with wonderful power. He exercises a wild, bewildering fascination by his dark and mysterious nature, which is not at all diminished when we obtain a clearer insight into his strange history. Indeed, all the members of the ship's company, the three mates, Starbuck, Stubbs, and Flash, the wild, savage Gayheader, the case-hardened old blacksmith, to say nothing of the pearl of a New Zealand harpooner, the bosom friend of the narrator—all stand before us in the strongest individual relief, presenting a unique picture gallery, which every artist must despair of rivaling.

The plot becomes more intense and tragic, as it approaches toward the denouement. The malicious old Moby Dick, after long cruisings in pursuit of him, is at length discovered. He comes up to the battle, like an army with banners. He seems inspired with the same fierce, inveterate cunning with which Captain Ahab has followed the traces of his mortal foe. The fight is described in letters of blood. It is easy to foresee which will be the victor in such a contest. We need not say that the ill-omened ship is broken in fragments by the wrath of the weltering fiend. Captain Ahab becomes the prey of his intended victim. The crew perish. One alone escapes to tell the tale. Moby Dick disappears unscathed, and for aught we know, is the same "delicate monster," whose power in destroying another ship is just announced from

Panama.—GEORGE RIPLEY (?), "Literary Notices," *Harper's New Monthly Magazine*, Dec. 1852, p. 137

PIERRE

This work is generally considered a failure. The cause of its ill-success is certainly not to be sought in its lack of power. None of Melville's novels equals the present in force and subtlety of thinking and unity of purpose. Many of the scenes are wrought out with great splendor and vigor, and a capacity is evinced of holding with a firm grasp, and describing with a masterly distinctness, some of the most evanescent phenomena of morbid emotions. But the spirit pervading the whole book is intolerably unhealthy, and the most friendly reader is obliged at the end to protest against such a provoking perversion of talent and waste of power. The author has attempted seemingly to combine in it the peculiarities of Poe and Hawthorne, and has succeeded in producing nothing but a powerfully unpleasant caricature of morbid thought and passion. Pierre, we take it, is crazy, and the merit of the book is in clearly presenting the psychology of his madness; but the details of such a mental malady as that which afflicts Pierre are almost as disgusting as those of physical disease itself.—UNSIGNED, "Review of New Books," *Graham's Magazine*, Oct. 1852, p. 445

This volume is a would-be utterance of 'Young Yankee' sentimentalism:—but beyond that its writer may be a subject of the States, we can discern nothing either American or original in its pages. It reads like an "upsetting" into English of the first novel of a very whimsical and lackadaisical young student at

the U—
niversity of Gottingen.

It is one of the most diffuse doses of transcendentalism offered for a long time to the public. When he sat down to compose it, the author evidently had not determined what he was going to write about. Its plot is amongst the inexplicable "ambiguities" of the book,—the style is a prolonged succession of spasms,—and the characters are a marrowless tribe of phantoms, flitting through dense clouds of transcendental mysticism. "Be sure," said Pope to a young author, "when you have written any passage that you think particularly fine—*to erase it*." If this precept were applied to *Pierre; or, the Ambiguities*,—its present form would shrink into almost as many pages as there are now chapters. German literature with its depths and shallows is too keenly appreciated in this country for readers to endure Germanism at second hand. We take up novels to be amused—not bewildered,—in search of pleasure for the mind—not in pursuit of cloudy metaphysics; and it is no refreshment after the daily toils and troubles of life, for a reader to be soused into a torrent rhapsody uttered in defiance of taste and sense. ⟨. . .⟩

That many readers will not follow "the moody way" of Pierre, is in our apprehension not amongst the "ambiguities" of the age. The present chaotic performance has nothing American about it, except that it reminds us of a prairie in print,—wanting the flowers and freshness of the savannahs, but almost equally puzzling to find a way through it.—UNSIGNED, "New Novels," *Athenaeum*, Nov. 20, 1852, pp. 1265–66

⟨. . .⟩ his only novel or romance, whichever it be, was also the most impossible of all his books, and really a terrible example of the enormities which a man of genius may perpetrate when working in a direction unsuited to him. I refer, of course, to *Pierre, or the Ambiguities*.—JULIAN HAWTHORNE, "The American Element in Fiction," *North American Review*, Aug. 1886, p. 175

EVERT A. DUYCKINCK
From "Melville's *Moby Dick; or, The Whale*"

Literary World, November 15, 1851, p. 381;
November 22, 1851, pp. 403–4

Every reader throughout the United States has probably perused in the newspapers the account of a recent incident in the whale fishery which would stagger the mind by its extent of the marvellous, were it not paralleled by a well known case—that of the Essex of Nantucket, still authenticated by living witnesses. It appears from a narrative published in the *Panama Herald* (an American newspaper in that region, itself one of the wonders of the age!), taken down from the lips of the captain of the vessel, John S. Deblois, that the ship Ann Alexander, of New Bedford, having left that port in June of last year with the usual vicissitudes of Cape Horn service, losing a New Hampshire man overboard in a storm at that point, had entered upon her Pacific hunting-grounds, and in the recent month of August was coursing within a few degrees of the Equator—a well known haunt of the whale. On the 20th of that month, nine in the morning, fish were discovered; two boats were lowered in pursuit, and by mid-day a particular sperm whale was struck and fast to the line. The first mate commanded the boat, thus far successful, and the Captain himself the other. After running some time, in the words of the narrative, the whale turned upon the boat to which he was attached, and rushing at it with tremendous violence, lifted open its enormous jaws, and taking the boat in, actually crushed it to fragments as small as a common-sized chair. Captain Deblois struck for the spot, and rescued the nine members of the boat's crew—a feat, we presume, which could only be accomplished among men hardy, resolute, and full of vitality as whalemen, strung at the moment by excitement to almost superhuman energy and superiority to the elements. The Captain, with his double boat's crew, proceeded to the ship, some six miles off. There the waist-boat was fitted out, the men divided, and both parties went again in pursuit of the whale, the mate again taking the lead. The whale perceived the coming renewal of the attack, made for the boat, crushed it with his jaw, the men again throwing themselves into the deep. The Captain once more rescuing them, was himself pursued by the whale, which passed the boat with distended jaw; but they reached the ship in safety. A boat was sent for the oars of the broken vessels floating on the water, which were secured. Sail was set on the ship, and it was determined to proceed after the whale. He was overtaken, and a lance thrown into his head! The ship passed on, when it was immediately discovered that the whale was in pursuit. The ship manœuvred out of his way. *After he had fairly passed they kept off to overtake and attack him again.* The whale settled down deep below the surface. It was then near sundown. Capt. Deblois, continues the account, was at this time standing on the knight-heads on the larboard bow, with shaft in hand, ready to strike the monster a deadly blow should he appear, the ship moving about five knots, when looking over the side of the ship he discerned the whale rushing towards her at the rate of fifteen knots. In an instant the monster struck the ship with tremendous violence, shaking her from stem to stern. She quivered under the violence of the shock as if she had struck upon a rock. Captain Deblois descending to the forecastle, discovered that *the whale had struck the ship about two feet from the keel, abreast the foremast, knocking a great hole entirely through her bottom.* The ship was sinking rapidly. All hands were ordered into the boats, the captain leaving the deck last, throwing himself into the sea, and swimming to his comrades. That night was passed in the boats, with but twelve quarts of water saved, and no provisions for twenty-two men. In the morning the ship still lay on her beam-ends. Not a man would board her to cut away the masts, right the vessel, and procure provisions—fearing her sinking instantly—except the captain, who undertook the work with a single hatchet, and succeeded in getting the ship nearly on her keel. Nothing could be procured by cutting through the decks but some vinegar and a small quantity of wet bread, with which they abandoned the dangerous vessel. At the close of the next day they hailed the ship Nantucket of Nantucket, and were welcomed by its Captain, Gibbs, with the utmost hospitality. They were landed at Paita, where an authenticated protest of this extraordinary series of occurrences was made before the United States Consul.

By a singular coincidence this extreme adventure is, even to very many of the details, the catastrophe of Mr. Melville's new book, which is a natural-historical, philosophical, romantic account of the person, habits, manners, ideas of the great sperm whale; of his haunts and of his belongings; of his associations with the world of the deep, and of the not less remarkable individuals and combinations of individuals who hunt him on the oceans. Nothing like it has ever before been written of the whale; for no man who has at once seen so much of the actual conflict, and weighed so carefully all that has been recorded on the subject, with equal powers of perception and reflection, has attempted to write at all on it—the labors of Scoresby covering a different and inferior branch of the history. To the popular mind this book of Herman Melville, touching the Leviathan of the deep, is as much of a discovery in Natural History as was the revelation of America by Christopher Columbus in geography. Let any one read this book with the attention which it deserves, and then converse with the best informed of his friends and acquaintances who have not seen it, and he will notice the extent and variety of treatment; while scientific men must admit the original observation and speculation.

Such an infuriated, resolute sperm whale as pursued and destroyed the Ann Alexander is the hero, Moby Dick, of Mr. Melville's book. The vengeance with which he is hunted, which with Capt. Deblois was the incident of a single, though most memorable day, is the leading passion and idea of Captain Ahab of the Pequod for years, and throughout the seas of the world. Incidentally with this melo-dramatic action and spiritual development of the character of Ahab, is included a full, minute, thorough investigation, and description of the whale and its fishery. Such is a short-hand account of this bulky and multifarious volume.

It opens, after a dedication to Nathaniel Hawthorne, with a preliminary flourish in the style of Carlyle and the *Doctor* of etymology, followed by a hundred or so of extracts of "Old Burton," passages of a quaint and pithy character from Job and King Alfred to Miriam Coffin; in lieu of the old style of Scott, Cooper, and others, of distributing such flourishes about the heads of chapters. Here they are all in a lump, like the grace over the Franklin barrel of pork, and may be taken as a kind of bitters, a whet and fillip to the imagination, exciting it to the curious, ludicrous, sublime traits and contemplations which are to follow.

It is some time after opening with Chapter I. before we get fairly afloat, but the time is very satisfactorily occupied with some very strange, romantic, and, withal, highly humorous adventures at New Bedford and Nantucket. A scene at the Spouter Inn, of the former town, a night in bed with a Pacific

Islander, and a mid-ocean adventure subsequently with a Frenchman over some dead whales in the Pacific, treat the reader to a laugh worthy of Smollet. ⟨. . .⟩

A difficulty in the estimate of this, in common with one or two other of Mr. Melville's books, occurs from the double character under which they present themselves. In one light they are romantic fictions, in another statements of absolute fact. When to this is added that the romance is made a vehicle of opinion and satire through a more or less opaque allegorical veil, as particularly in the latter half of *Mardi*, and to some extent in this present volume, the critical difficulty is considerably thickened. It becomes quite impossible to submit such books to a distinct classification as fact, fiction, or essay. Something of a parallel may be found in Jean Paul's German tales, with an admixture of Southey's *Doctor*. Under these combined influences of personal observation, actual fidelity to local truthfulness in description, a taste for reading and sentiment, a fondness for fanciful analogies, near and remote, a rash daring in speculation, reckless at times of taste and propriety, again refined and eloquent, this volume of *Moby Dick* may be pronounced a most remarkable sea-dish—an intellectual chowder of romance, philosophy, natural history, fine writing, good feeling, bad sayings—but over which, in spite of all uncertainties, and in spite of the author himself, predominates his keen perceptive faculties, exhibited in vivid narration.

There are evidently two if not three books in *Moby Dick* rolled into one. Book No. 1. we could describe as a thorough exhaustive account admirably given of the great Sperm Whale. The information is minute, brilliantly illustrated, as it should be—the whale himself so generously illuminating the midnight page on which his memoirs are written—has its level passages, its humorous touches, its quaint suggestion, its incident usually picturesque and occasionally sublime. All this is given in the most delightful manner in *The Whale*. Book No. 2 is the romance of Captain Ahab, Queequeg, Tashtego, Pip & Co., who are more or less spiritual personages talking and acting differently from the general business run of the conversation on the decks of whalers. They are for the most part very serious people, and seem to be concerned a great deal about the problem of the universe. They are striking characters withal, of the romantic spiritual cast of the German drama; realities of some kinds at bottom, but veiled in all sorts of poetical incidents and expressions. As a bit of German melodrama, with Captain Ahab for the Faust of the quarter-deck, and Queequeg with the crew, for Walpurgis night revellers in the forecastle, it has its strong points, though here the limits as to space and treatment of the stage would improve it. *Moby Dick* in this view becomes a sort of fishy moralist, a leviathan metaphysician, a folio Ductor Dubitantium, in fact, in the fresh water illustration of Mrs. Malaprop, "an allegory on the banks of the Nile." After pursuing him in this melancholic company over a few hundred squares of latitude and longitude, we begin to have some faint idea of the association of whaling and lamentation, and why blubber is popularly synonymous with tears.

The intense Captain Ahab is too long drawn out; something more of *him* might, we think, be left to the reader's imagination. The value of this kind of writing can only be through the personal consciousness of the reader, what he brings to the book; and all this is sufficiently evoked by a dramatic trait or suggestion. If we had as much of Hamlet or Macbeth as Mr. Melville gives us of Ahab, we should be tired even of their sublime company. Yet Captain Ahab is a striking conception, firmly planted on the wild deck of the Pequod—a dark disturbed soul arraying itself with every ingenuity of material resources for a conflict at once natural and supernatural in his eye, with the most dangerous extant physical monster of the earth, embodying, in strongly drawn lines of mental association, the vaster moral evil of the world. The pursuit of the White Whale thus interweaves with the literal perils of the fishery—a problem of fate and destiny—to the tragic solution of which Ahab hurries on, amidst the wild stage scenery of the ocean. To this end the motley crew, the air, the sky, the sea, its inhabitants are idealized throughout. It is a noble and praiseworthy conception; and though our sympathies may not always accord with the train of thought, we would caution the reader against a light or hasty condemnation of this part of the work.

Book III., appropriating perhaps a fourth of the volume, is a vein of moralizing, half essay, half rhapsody, in which much refinement and subtlety, and no little poetical feeling, are mingled with quaint conceit and extravagant daring speculation. This is to be taken as in some sense dramatic; the narrator throughout among the personages of the Pequod being one Ishmael, whose wit may be allowed to be against everything on land, as his hand is against everything at sea. This piratical running down of creeds and opinions, the conceited indifferentism of Emerson, or the run-a-muck style of Carlyle is, we will not say dangerous in such cases, for there are various forces at work to meet more powerful onslaught, but it is out of place and uncomfortable. We do not like to see what, under any view, must be to the world the most sacred associations of life violated and defaced.

We call for fair play in this matter. Here is Ishmael, telling the story of this volume, going down on his knees with a cannibal to a piece of wood, in the second story fireplace of a New-Bedford tavern, in the spirit of amiable and transcendent charity, which may be all very well in its way; but why dislodge from heaven, with contumely, "long-pampered Gabriel, Michael and Raphael." Surely Ishmael, who is a scholar, might have spoken respectfully of the Archangel Gabriel, out of consideration, if not for the Bible (which might be asking too much of the school), at least for one John Milton, who wrote *Paradise Lost*.

Nor is it fair to inveigh against the terrors of priestcraft, which, skilful though it may be in making up its woes, at least seeks to provide a remedy for the evils of the world, and attribute the existence of conscience to "hereditary dyspepsias, nurtured by Ramadans"—and at the same time go about petrifying us with imaginary horrors, and all sorts of gloomy suggestions, all the world through. It is a curious fact that there are no more bilious people in the world, more completely filled with megrims and head shakings, than some of these very people who are constantly inveighing against the religious melancholy of priestcraft.

So much for the consistency of Ishmael—who, if it is the author's object to exhibit the painful contradictions of this self-dependent, self-torturing agency of a mind driven hither and thither as a flame in a whirlwind, is, in a degree, a successful embodiment of opinions, without securing from us, however, much admiration for the result.

With this we make an end of what we have been reluctantly compelled to object to this volume. With far greater pleasure, we acknowledge the acuteness of observation, the freshness of perception, with which the author brings home to us from the deep, "things unattempted yet in prose or rhyme," the weird influences of his ocean scenes, the salient imagination which connects them with the past and distant, the world of books and the life of experience—certain prevalent traits of manly sentiment. These are strong powers with which Mr. Melville wrestles in this book. It would be a great glory to subdue them to the highest uses of fiction. It is still a great honor, among the crowd of successful mediocrities which throng our publishers' counters, and know nothing of divine impulses, to be in the company of these nobler spirits on any terms.

UNSIGNED

From *"Pierre; or, The Ambiguities"*

Literary World, August 21, 1852, pp. 118–20

The purpose of Mr. Melville's story, though vaguely hinted, rather than directly stated, seems to be to illustrate the possible antagonism of a sense of duty, conceived in the heat and impetuosity of youth, to all the recognised laws of social morality; and to exhibit a conflict between the virtues. The hero of the tale is Pierre, a fiery youth full of love and ardor. He is the last of the Glendennings, a family that can boldly face the memory of at least two generations back without blushing, which is a pretty fair title to an American nobility. He is an only son, the pride of his mother and his house, and the expectant heir of its wide domains. A warm affection unites Mrs. Glendenning, an aristocratic dame, and Pierre, and the heart of the proud woman is all content in the responsive love of her son. A certain Lucy Tartan, with all the requisite claims for a novelist's beauty, wins the affection of and in due course of time is betrothed to Pierre. All appears smooth and prosperous to a future of happiness, when a mysterious darkeyed, dark-haired damsel, Isabel, proves herself to the satisfaction of Pierre, though on testimony that would not pass current in any court of law, to be his sister, the natural child of his father. Here is a sad blot upon the memory of a Glendenning, a living testimony of the sin of one who had been embalmed in the heart of Pierre, as pure and without reproach. Pierre, tortured with this damning fact that pollutes his filial ideal of a virtuous parent, conceives and rightly, that he has two duties to perform: to screen his dead father's memory and give to a living sister her due, a brother's affection. Pierre impetuously decides that the only way of reconciling these two duties is by the expedient of a pretended marriage with Isabel, and thus shield the memory of his father while he protects and unites himself in brotherly affection with his sister.

Mark the tragical result. The proud mother's proudest hopes are blasted by this supposed marriage; she drives Pierre from her house, disinherits him and dies a maniac. Pierre, an outcast, seeks in the company of his sister, his pretended wife, a refuge with his cousin, a rich denizen of the city, is totally ignored by him and repelled from his door. He is compelled to seek his livelihood with his pen. While he is thus engaged, struggling with poverty and misery, Lucy Tartan, who has survived the first shock from the agony of Pierre's abandonment and supposed marriage, unable to live without Pierre and instinctively justifying his infidelity on a principle, by no means clear to the reader, of abstract faith to her former lover, resolves to live with him, and joins the household of Pierre and Isabel. Lucy is followed to Pierre's dwelling by her brother and Pierre's cousin, who has succeeded Pierre as a suitor of Lucy. They attempt to force Lucy away, but she is rescued by Pierre with the aid of his fellow lodgers. Vengeance is sworn by the brother and cousin. An insulting letter is written to Pierre, denouncing him as a seducer and liar. To add to the agony of Pierre he receives at the same time a letter from his publishers,

rejecting his novel. Pierre is outrageous, and arming himself with two pistols, seeks out his cousin, finds him, is struck by him, and in return shoots his cousin doubly dead with the two pistols. He is thrown into prison. He is sought out there by Isabel and Lucy. Lucy learning for the first time, from an agonizing cry of "brother" from Isabel, that she was Pierre's sister and not his wife, swoons away and dies. While Isabel and Pierre, conjointly help themselves in a fraternal way, to a draught of poison that Isabel has concealed upon her person, and they also die—*felo de se*. Nor is this the end of the casualty, the full list of the dead and wounded, for the surviving Tartan family must be necessarily plunged in irretrievable agony, leading to the probable result of some broken and various wounded hearts, on account of the death and supposed dishonor of Lucy.

Mr. Melville may have constructed his story upon some new theory of art to a knowledge of which we have not yet transcended; he evidently has not constructed it according to the established principles of the only theory accepted by us until assured of a better, of one more true and natural than truth and nature themselves, which are the germinal principles of all true art.

The pivot of the story is the pretended marriage of Pierre with his sister, in order to conceal her illegitimacy and protect his father's memory. Pierre, to carry out his purpose, abandons mother, home, his betrothed, all the advantages of his high social position, wealth and its appointments of ease and luxury and respect, and invites poverty, misery, infamy, and death. Apart from the very obvious way of gaining the same object at an infinitely smaller cost, is it natural that a loving youth should cast away the affection of his mother and his betrothed and the attachment of home to hide a dim stain upon his father's memory and to enjoy the love of an equivocal sister? Pierre not only acts thus absurdly, but pretends to act from a sense of duty. He is battling for Truth and Right, and the first thing he does in behalf of Truth is to proclaim to the whole world a falsehood, and the next thing he does is to commit in behalf of Right, a half a dozen most foul wrongs. The combined power of New England transcendentalism and Spanish Jesuitical casuistry could not have more completely befogged nature and truth, than this confounded Pierre has done. It is needless to test minutely the truth and nature of each character. In a word, Pierre is a psychological curiosity, a moral and intellectual phenomenon; Isabel, a lusus naturæ; Lucy, an incomprehensible woman; and the rest not of the earth nor, we may venture to state, of heaven. The object of the author, perhaps, has been, not to delineate life and character as they are or may possibly be, but as they are not and cannot be. We must receive the book, then, as an eccentricity of the imagination.

The most immoral *moral* of the story, if it has any moral at all, seems to be the impracticability of virtue; a leering demoniacal spectre of an idea seems to be speering at us through the dim obscure of this dark book, and mocking us with this dismal falsehood. Mr. Melville's chapter on "Chronometricals and Horologicals," if it has any meaning at all, simply means that virtue and religion are only for gods and not to be attempted by man. But ordinary novel readers will never unkennel this loathsome suggestion. The stagnant pool at the bottom of which it lies, is not too deep for their penetration, but too muddy, foul, and corrupt. If truth is hid in a well, falsehood lies in a quagmire.

We cannot pass without remark, the supersensuousness with which the holy relations of the family are described. Mother and son, brother and sister are sacred facts not to be disturbed by any sacrilegious speculations. Mrs. Glendenning and Pierre, mother and son, call each other brother and sister, and are described with all the coquetry of a lover and mistress. And again, in what we have termed the supersensuousness of description, the horrors of an incestuous relation between Pierre and Isabel seem to be vaguely hinted at.

In commenting upon the vagueness of the book, the uncertainty of its aim, the indefiniteness of its characters, and want of distinctness in its pictures, we are perhaps only proclaiming ourselves as the discoverers of a literary mare's nest; this vagueness, as the title of the *Ambiguities* seems to indicate, having been possibly intended by the author, and the work meant as a problem of impossible solution, to set critics and readers a woolgathering. It is alone intelligible as an unintelligibility. ⟨. . .⟩

All the male characters of the book have a certain robust, animal force and untamed energy, which carry them through their melodramatic parts—no slight duty—with an effect sure to bring down the applause of the excitable and impulsive. Mr. Melville can think clearly, and write with distinctness and force—in a style of simplicity and purity. Why, then, does he allow his mind to run riot amid remote analogies, where the chain of association is invisible to mortal minds? Why does he give us incoherencies of thought, in infelicities of language? Such incoherency as this:—"Love is both Creator's and Saviour's gospel to mankind; a volume bound in rose-leaves, clasped with violets, and by the beaks of humming birds, printed with peach-juice on the leaves of lilies. Endless is the account of love. Time and space cannot contain Love's story. All things that are sweet to see, or taste, or feel, or hear, all these things were made by Love, and none other things were made by Love. Love made not the Arctic zones, but Love is ever reclaiming them. Say, are not the fierce things of this earth daily, hourly going out? Where are now your wolves of Britain? Where in Virginia now find you the panther and the pard? Oh, Love is busy everywhere. Everywhere Love hath Moravian missionaries. No propagandist like to Love. The south wind wooes the barbarous north; on many a distant shore the gentler west wind persuades the arid east. All this earth is Love's affianced; vainly the demon Principle howls to stay the banns." Such infelicities of expression, such unknown words as these, to wit: "human*ness*," "heroic*ness*," "patriarchal*ness*," "descended*ness*," "flushful*ness*," "amaranth*iness*," "instantaneous*ness*," "leapingly acknowledging," "fateful frame of mind," "protecting*ness*," "young*ness*," "infantile*ness*," "visible*ness*," *et id genus omne!*

The author of *Pierre; or, the Ambiguities*; the writer of a mystic romance, in which are conjured up unreal nightmare-conceptions, a confused phantasmagoria of distorted fancies and conceits, ghostly abstractions and fitful shadows, is certainly but a spectre of the substantial author of *Omoo* and *Typee*, the jovial and hearty narrator of the traveller's tale of incident and adventure. By what *diablerie*, hocus-pocus, or thimble-rigging, "now you see him and now you don't" process, the transformation has been effected, we are not skilled in necromancy to detect. Nor, if it be a true psychological development, are we sufficiently advanced in transcendentalism to lift ourselves skywards and see clearly the coming light with our heads above the clouds. If this novel indicates a chaotic state of authorship,—and we can distinguish fragmentary elements of beauty—out of which is to rise a future temple of order, grace, and proportion, in which the genius of Mr. Melville is to enshrine itself, we will be happy to worship there; but let its foundation be firmly based on *terra firma*, or, if in the heavens, let us not trust our common sense to the flight of

any waxen pinion. We would rejoice to meet Mr. Melville again in the hale company of sturdy sailors, men of flesh and blood, and, strengthened by the wholesome air of the outside world, whether it be land-breeze or sea-breeze, listen to his narrative of a traveller's tale, in which he has few equals in power and felicity.

UNSIGNED
From *"Pierre, or The Ambiguities"*
American Whig Review, November 1852, pp. 446–54

A bad book! Affected in dialect, unnatural in conception, repulsive in plot, and inartistic in construction. Such is Mr. Melville's worst and latest work.

Some reputations seem to be born of accident. There are common-place men who on some fine day light, unknown to themselves, upon a popular idea, and suddenly rise on the strength of it into public favor. They stride the bubble for a little while, but at last its prismatic hues begin to fade; men see that the object of their applause has after all but an unsubstantial basis, and when at length the frail foundation bursts, they fall back into their original obscurity, unheeded and unlamented. Mr. Melville has experienced some such success. A few years back, he gave to the world a story of romantic adventure; this was untrue in its painting, coarse in its coloring, and often tedious and prolix in its descriptive passages. But there was a certain air of rude romance about it, that captivated the general public. It depicted scenes in a strange land, and dealt with all the interests that circle around men whose lives are passed in peril. Nor were appeals to the grosser instincts of humanity wanting. Naked women were scattered profusely through the pages, and the author seemed to feel that in a city where the ballet was admired, *Typee* would be successful.[1] Mr. Melville thought he had hit the key-note to fame. His book was reprinted in all directions, and people talked about it, as much from the singularity of its title as from any intrinsic merit it possessed.

This was encouraging, and Mr. Melville evidently thought so, for he immediately issued a series of books in the same strain. *Omoo, Mardi, White-Jacket, Redburn,* followed one another in quick succession; and the foolish critics, too blind to perceive that the books derived their chief interest from the fact of the scenes being laid in countries little known, and that the author had no other stock in trade beyond tropical scenery and eccentric sailors, applauded to the very echo. This indiscriminating praise produced its usual effect. Mr. Melville fancied himself a genius, and the result of this sad mistake has been—*Pierre.*

As a general rule, sea-stories are very effective, and to those versed in nautical lore, very easy writing. The majority of the reading public are landsmen, and the events of an ocean-life come to them recommended by the charm of novelty. They cannot detect the blunders, and incongruity passes with them for originality. The author can make his vessel and his characters perform the most impossible feats, and who, except the favored few that themselves traverse the sea professionally, will be one bit the wiser? The scope for events is also limited, and this very limitation renders the task of writing a sea-tale more simple. A storm, a wreck, a chase and a battle, a mutiny, desertions, and going into and leaving port, with perhaps a fire at sea, form the principal "properties" of a salt-water artist. Considerable descriptive powers are, we admit, necessary to the management of these materials. The storm must be wild, the battle fierce, and the fire terrible; but these, after all, are broad outlines, and require little delicacy of handling to fill them in. Sometimes, as in the *Pilot*, one finds a veil of pathetic tenderness and grace flung over the characters, but as a general rule in nautical fictions, the wit is coarse, the pathos clumsy, and the most striking characters are invariably unnatural.

It is when a writer comes to deal with the varied interests of a more extended life; when his hand must touch in harmonious succession the numberless chords of domestic sorrows, duties and affections, and draw from each the proper vibration; when he has to range among the ever-changing relations of every-day humanity, and set each phase of being down in its correct lineaments; it is then he discovers that something more is necessary for the task than a mere arrangement of strong words in certain forms,—or the trick of painting nature, until, like a ranting actress, she pleases certain tastes according as she deviates from truth.

Mr. Melville's previous stories, all seaborn as they were, went down the public throat because they were prettily gilt with novelty. There are crowds of people who will run after a new pill, and swallow it with avidity, because it is new, and has a long Greek name. It may be made of bread, or it may be made of poison; the novelty of the affair renders all considerations of its composition quite immaterial. They learn the name, eat the bolus, and pay the doctor. We have a shrewd suspicion that the uncouth and mysterious syllables with which Mr. Melville baptized his books had much to do with their success. Like Doctor Dulcamara, he gave his wares an exciting title, and trusted to Providence for the rest. The enchantment worked. The mystic cabala of *"Omoo, by the author of Typee,"* was enough in itself to turn any common novel-reader's brain, and the books went off as well as a collection of magic rings would in Germany, or the latest batch of *Agnus Deis* in an Italian village. People had little opportunity of judging of their truth. Remote scenes and savage actors gave a fine opportunity for high coloring and exaggerated outline, of which Mr. Melville was not slow to avail himself, and hence Fayaway is as unreal as the scenery with which she is surrounded.

We do not blame Mr. Melville for these deviations from truth. It is not much matter if South Sea savages are painted like the heroes of a penny theatre, and disport themselves amid pasteboard groves, and lakes of canvas. We can afford Mr. Melville full license to do what he likes with "Omoo" and its inhabitants; it is only when he presumes to thrust his tragic *Fantoccini* upon us, as representatives of our own race, that we feel compelled to turn our critical Ægis upon him, and freeze him into silence.

Pierre aims at something beyond the mere records of adventure contained in *Mardi* and *Omoo*. The author, doubtless puffed up by the very false applause which some critics chose to bestow upon him, took for granted that he was a genius, and made up his mind to write a fine book; and he has succeeded in writing a fine book with a vengeance. Our experience of literature is necessarily large, but we unhesitatingly state, that from the period when the Minerva press was in fashion, up to the present time, we never met with so turgid, pretentious, and useless a book as *Pierre*. It is always an unpleasant and apparently invidious statement for a critic to make, that he can find nothing worthy of praise in a work under consideration; but in the case of *Pierre* we feel bound to add to the assertion the sweeping conclusion, that there we find every thing to condemn. If a repulsive, unnatural and indecent plot, a style disfigured by every paltry affectation of the worst German school, and ideas perfectly unparalleled for earnest

absurdity, are deserving of condemnation, we think that our already expressed sentence upon *Pierre* will meet with the approval of every body who has sufficient strength of mind to read it through.

Mr. Pierre Glendinning, the hero of the book, and intended by the author to be an object of our mournful admiration, supports in the course of the story the arduous characters of a disobedient son, a dishonest lover, an incestuous brother, a cold-blooded murderer, and an unrepentant suicide. This *repertoire* is agreeably relieved by his playing the part of a madman whenever he is not engaged in doing any thing worse.

This agreeable young gentleman is the only son of a widow lady of large fortune, who coquets in her old age with suitors about the same age as Pierre. And to render the matter still more interesting, Pierre by mutual consent sinks the son, and deports himself by word and look towards his mother as a lover; while she, charming coquette of fifty that she is, readily imitates this delightful *abandon*. The early character of Mr. P. Glendinning, as traced by our author, is exceedingly fine; we will, however, spare it to our readers, merely stating on Mr. Melville's authority, that in him might be observed "the polished steel of the gentleman, girded with Religion's silken sash;" which sash, his great-grandfather had somehow or other taught him, "should, in the last bitter trial, furnish its wearer with glory's shroud." Setting aside the little incompatibility of religion having any thing to do, even in sashes, with martial glory, we cannot help thinking that the mere mention of making a shroud out of so scanty an article as a sash, is quite sufficient to scandalize any respectable undertaker.

Well, this be-sashed young gentleman, who lives alone with his mother at the family place of Saddle Meadows, is engaged formally to a very flighty young lady named Lucy Tartan. If there is any thing to which we object particularly in this young couple, it is the painful habit they have contracted of *tutoyer*-ing each other through whole pages of insane rhapsody. We cannot believe that the indiscriminate use of "thee" and "thou" makes the nonsense with which it is generally connected one atom more readable. On the contrary, it has a most unpleasant effect, for it deprives the mad passages in which it occurs of the only recommendation that can palliate insanity, that is, simplicity.

Notwithstanding Mr. P. Glendinning's being already supplied with a mother and a mistress, he is pursued by indefinite longings for a sister. His reason for this imperious craving is rather a pugnacious one, and almost inclines us to believe that the young gentleman must have had some Celtic blood in his veins. If he had but a sister, he alleges he would be happy, because "it must be a glorious thing to engage in a mortal quarrel on a sweet sister's behalf!" This, it must be confessed, is a strange fancy, but we suppose it is to be accounted for by the fact of Saddle Meadows being rather a dull place, and Mr. Pierre believing that a little fighting was the best thing in the world for the blues.

By a chain of the most natural circumstances in the world—we mean in Mr. Melville's books—this sister is most unexpectedly supplied. In fact, though the author says nothing about it, we are inclined to think that he imported her direct from a lunatic asylum for the occasion. She proves to be an illegitimate daughter of Pierre's father, and judging from her own story, as well as we could understand it, appears to have been dry-nursed by an old family guitar; an allegory almost as fine as that of Romulus and Remus. If we suppose this paternal instrument to have been out of tune at the time that it assumed the responsibility of the little Isabel, that young lady's singular turn of mind is at once accounted for; but if we go a little farther, and suppose the worthy instrument to have been cracked, we explain still more satisfactorily the origin of her very erratic conduct.

"Sister Isabel," being an illegitimate Glendinning, is of course inadmissible to the refined atmosphere breathed by the aristocratic Mrs. Glendinning, who has rather strong ideas upon such subjects. Accordingly, Pierre, who is afraid to mention to his mother the discovery he has made, and moved to compassion by the forlorn state of the young lady, who lives with her faithful guitar in a charming cottage on the edge of a beautiful lake, takes compassion on her desolate condition, and determines to devote his life to her. He therefore conceives the sublime idea of obviating all difficulties—for difficulties there must have been, or Mr. Melville would not say so, though we confess that we have not been so fortunate as to discover them—by presenting her to the world as his wife! The reasons alleged by this virtuous hero are detailed at some length by Mr. Melville, as if he knew that he could not apologize too much for presenting such a picture to the world. Firstly, Pierre wishes to conceal the fact of Isabel's being the offspring of his father's sin, and thereby protect his parent's reputation. Secondly, he is actuated by a desire not to disturb his mother's mind by any disclosure which would destroy the sacredness of her deceased husband's memory; and lastly, he entertains towards this weird sister feelings which Mr. Melville endeavors to gloss over with a veil of purity, but which even in their best phase can never be any thing but repulsive to a well constituted mind.

Now, in this matter Mr. Melville has done a very serious thing, a thing which not even unsoundness of intellect could excuse. He might have been mad to the very pinnacle of insanity; he might have torn our poor language into tatters, and made from the shreds a harlequin suit in which to play his tricks; he might have piled up word upon word, and adjective upon adjective, until he had built a pyramid of nonsense, which should last to the admiration of all men; he might have done all this and a great deal more, and we should not have complained. But when he dares to outrage every principle of virtue; when he strikes with an impious, though, happily, weak hand, at the very foundations of society, we feel it our duty to tear off the veil with which he has thought to soften the hideous features of the idea, and warn the public against the reception of such atrocious doctrines. If Mr. Melville had reflected at all—and certainly we find in him but few traces of reflection—when he was writing this book, his better sense would perhaps have informed him that there are certain ideas so repulsive to the general mind that they themselves are not alone kept out of sight, but, by a fit ordination of society, every thing that might be supposed to even collaterally suggest them is carefully shrouded in a decorous darkness. Nor has any man the right, in his morbid craving after originality, to strip these horrors of their decent mystery. But the subject which Mr. Melville has taken upon himself to handle is one of no ordinary depravity; and however he may endeavor to gloss the idea over with a platonic polish, no matter how energetically he strives to wrap the mystery in a cloud of high-sounding but meaningless words, the main conception remains still unaltered in all its moral deformity. We trust that we have said enough on this topic. It is a subject that we would gladly not have been obliged to approach, and which we are exceedingly grieved that any gentleman pretending to the rank of a man of letters should have chosen to embody in a book. Nor can we avoid a feeling of surprise, that professedly moral and apparently respectable publishers like the Messrs. Harper should have ever consented

to issue from their establishment any book containing such glaring abominations as *Pierre*.

But to return to the development of this chaotic volume. Mr. P. Glendinning, actuated by this virtuous love for his sister, informs his proud mother that he is married. She, knowing not the true relationship that binds them together, spurns her unworthy son from her house for having degraded the family name so far by making a *mésalliance*; and the worthy young gentleman, after having nearly killed Miss Lucy Tartan, his betrothed, with the same intelligence, and left his mother in a fit of indignation which has every chance of becoming a fit of apoplexy, sets out with—we really do not know what to call her, for Mr. Melville has so intwined and confused the wife with the sister, and the sister with the wife, that we positively cannot tell one from the other; so we may as well compromise the matter by calling her simply Isabel. He sets out then with Isabel, in a perfect enthusiasm of virtue, for the city, having first apprised a fashionable cousin of his, one Mr. Glendinning Stanly, that he was on his way, and requesting him to prepare his house for his reception. This fashionable cousin, however, takes very little trouble about the matter; and accordingly, when Pierre and Isabel arrive accompanied by a young lady of loose morals named Delly, they find no house or welcome. A series of incidents here follow, which are hardly worth reciting. They consist of Pierre's quarrel with Stanly, a scene in a police station, a row with a cabman, and ending by Pierre's taking rooms in some out-of-the-way place, inhabited by a colony of poor authors, who bear the general denomination of Apostles. Just in this part of the book it comes out suddenly that Pierre is an author, a fact not even once hinted at in the preceding pages. Now the reader is informed, with very little circumlocution, and as if he ought to have known all about it long ago, that Mr. P. Glendinning is the author of a sonnet called the "Tropical Summer," which it seems has called forth the encomiums of the literati, and induced certain proprietors of certain papers to persecute him for his portrait. All this is told in a manner that proves it very clearly to be nothing more than an afterthought of Mr. Melville's, and not contemplated in the original plan of the book, that is, if it ever had a plan. It is dragged in merely for the purpose of making Pierre a literary man, when the author had just brought him to such a stage that he did not know what else to do with him.

Of course, under such circumstances, Mr. P. Glendinning, having the responsibility upon his back of Mrs.—Miss Isabel, his wife-sister, (as Mr. Melville himself would express it,) and the young lady of loose morals, and having no money wherewith to support them, can do nothing better than make his living by writing. Accordingly he writes away in his garret; and we cannot help thinking here, that if he wrote at all in the same style that he speaks, his MSS. must have been excessively original and amusing. Here in this poor place he starves his time away in company with Isabel and the young lady of loose morals. Meanwhile he hears of his mother's death, her bequest of all the property to his cousin Stanly, and the betrothal of that gentleman to his late mistress, Lucy Tartan. This intelligence, however, is soon followed by a remarkable event. Miss Lucy Tartan, true to her old habits of flightiness, conceives the resolution of coming to live with Pierre and Isabel, whom she believes to be his wife. Accordingly, she arrives at the haunt of the Apostles, and takes up her abode with her old lover, very much to the disgust of Madam Isabel, who acts much more like a jealous wife than a sister. In this comfortable state they all live together until Mr. Glendinning Stanly and Miss Lucy Tartan's brother arrive at Pierre's domicile to reclaim the fugitive. She refuses to go, however, and Mr. Pierre thrusts them out of the house. Immediately after he receives two notes: one from a bookseller, for whom he was writing a work, informing him that he is a swindler; the other from Messrs. Stanly and Tartan, putting him in possession of the fact that he is a liar and a scoundrel—all of which conclusions the reader arrives at long before this epoch.

Mr. P. Glendinning on reading these notes immediately proceeds to stand on them. This operation is minutely described by our author, and is evidently considered by him as a very effective piece of business. Putting a note under each heel of his boots, appears to be with Mr. P. Glendinning the very climax of vengeance. Having stood for a sufficiently long time upon the epistles, he proceeds to enter an Apostle's room, and burglariously abstract from thence a pair of pistols, which he loads with the unpleasant letters. Then marching into the street, he meets with, and is cowhided by, Mr. Stanly, and in consequence thereof shoots that individual with two distinct pistols. One would have been meagre, but two bullet-holes make the thing dramatic.

Mr. P. Glendinning now makes his appearance in prison; a place that, if fitness were any recommendation, he ought to have been in long ago. Here he raves about as usual in compound words and uncompounded ideas, until Lucy and Isabel enter, when there is a terrific amount of dying, and the usual vial of poison makes its appearance. How many persons give up the ghost in the last chapter of this exciting work, we are really unable to decide. But we have a dim consciousness that every body dies, save and except the young lady of loose morals.

Previous to entering more closely upon the singular merits of this book, we have endeavored, we fear but feebly, to give the reader some idea of the ground-work on which Mr. Melville has strung his farrago of words. If we have succeeded, so much the better, for our readers will perhaps appreciate more fully our approaching remarks. If we have not, it matters but little, for the reader will have lost nothing that is worth a regret.

We have already dismissed the immorality of Mr. Melville's book, which is as horrible in its tendency as Shelley's *Cenci*, without a ray of the eloquent genius that lights up the deformity of that terrible play; but we have yet another and less repulsive treat in store for the reader. Mr. Melville's style of writing in this book is probably the most extraordinary thing that an American press ever beheld. It is precisely what a raving lunatic who had read Jean Paul Richter *in a translation* might be supposed to spout under the influence of a particularly moonlight night. Word piled upon word, and syllable heaped upon syllable, until the tongue grows as bewildered as the mind, and both refuse to perform their offices from sheer inability to grasp the magnitude of the absurdities. Who would have believed that in the present day a man would write the following, and another be found to publish it?

> Now Pierre began to see mysteries interpierced with mysteries, and mysteries eluding mysteries; and began to seem to see the mere imaginariness of the so supposed solidest principle of human association. Fate had done this for them. Fate had separated brother and sister, till to each other they somehow seemed so not at all.—Page 193.

There, public! there's a style for you! There, Mr. Hawthorne, you who rely so much upon the quiet force of your language, read that and profit by it! And you, Mr. Longfellow, who love the Germans, and who in *Hyperion* have given us a sample of an ornate and poetical style, pray read it

too, and tell us if it is a wise thing to bind 495 pages of such stuff together, and palm it off upon the public as a book! But here is a string of assertions that we think are not to be surpassed; it is positively refreshing to read them:

> Of old Greek times, before man's brain went into doting bondage, and bleached and beaten in Baconian fulling mills, his four limbs lost their barbaric tan and beauty; when the round world was fresh, and rosy, and spicy as a new-plucked apple; all's wilted now! In those bold times, the great dead were not, turkey-like, dished in trenchers, and set down all garnished in the ground to glut the damned Cyclop like a cannibal; but nobly envious Life cheated the glutton worm, and gloriously burned the corpse; so that the spirit uppointed, and visibly forked to heaven!—Page 269.

We pause here. And when our readers have sufficiently recovered their senses to listen, we will remark that until now we were quite unaware that it was the modern practice to bury people in cover dishes or soup tureens, after having garnished them with parsley. Mr. Melville however asserts it, so it *must* be correct. Neither do we see what the Cyclop has to do with the funereal ceremonies alluded to. A church-yard is the last place in which we should think of looking for Polyphemus.

It is rather a curious study, that of analyzing a man's style. By a little careful examination and comparison, we are always able to hunt out the lurking secret of a writer's diction. We can discover Bulwer's trick of culminating periods, and Dickens's dodge of impossible similes and startling adjectives. A perfectly plain and pure style is the only one which we cannot properly analyze. Its elements are so equally combined that no one preponderates over the other, and we are not able to discover the exact boundary line that separates the art of the author from the nature of the man. But who writes such a style now-a-days? We feel convinced that echo will *not* answer, "Mr. Melville."

The author of *Omoo* has his own peculiarities. The English language he seems to think is capable of improvement, but his scheme for accomplishing this end is rather a singular one. Carlyle's compound words and Milton's latinic ones sink into insignificance before Mr. Melville's extraordinary concoctions. The gentleman, however, appears to be governed by a very distinct principle in his eccentricities of composition, and errs systematically. The essence of this great eureka, this philological reform, consists in "est" and "ness," added to every word to which they have no earthly right to belong. Feeling it to be our duty to give currency to every new discovery at all likely to benefit the world or literature, we present a few of Mr. Melville's word-combinations, in the hope that our rising authors will profit by the lesson, and thereby increase the richness and intelligibility of their style:

Flushfulness,	page	7	Solidest,	page	193
Patriarchalness,	page	12	Uncapitulatable	page	229
Humanness,	page	16	Ladylikeness,	page	235
Heroicness,	page	do.	Electricalness,	page	206
Perfectest,	page	41	Ardentest,	page	193
Imaginariness,	page	193	Unsystemizable	page	191
Insolubleness,	page	188	Youngness,	page	190
Recallable,	page	186	Unemigrating,	page	470
Entangledly,	page	262	Unrunagate,	page	do.
Intermarryingly,	page	151	Undoffable,	page	do.
Magnifiedly,	page	472			

After such a list, what shall we say? Shall we leave Mr. Melville to the tender mercies of the Purists, or shall we execute vengeance upon him ourselves? We would gladly pursue the latter course if we only knew how to accomplish it. As to destroying or abusing the book, we cannot make it appear worse than it is; and if we continue our remarks upon it, it is simply because we have a duty to perform by every improper work, which we have no right to leave unfinished. We shall, then, instead of turning executioners, simply assume the post of monitors, and warn all our little authors who are just now learning to imitate the last celebrity, to avoid Mr. Melville and his book, as they would some loathsome and infectious distemper.

Perhaps one of the most remarkable features in *Pierre*, is the boldness of the metaphors with which it is so thickly studded. Mr. Melville's imagination stops at nothing, and clears a six-barred simile or a twenty-word antithesis with equal dexterity and daring. It is no light obstacle that will bring him up in his headlong course, and he scoffs alike at the boundaries of common sense and the limits of poetical propriety. We have just caught an image which will serve our purpose, and transfix it, butterfly-like, on our critical pin, for the admiration of scientific etymologists. It is a fine specimen, and quite perfect of its kind. Fortunately for the world, however, the species is very rare:

An infixing stillness now thrust a long rivet through the night, and fast nailed it to that side of the world!—Page 219.

This is a grand and simple metaphor. To realize it thoroughly, all we have to do is to imagine some Titanic upholsterer armed with a gigantic nail, and hammer to match, hanging one hemisphere with black crape.

His description of a lady's forehead is equally grand and incomprehensible. He says, "The vivid buckler of her brow seemed as a magnetic plate." Trephining is rather an uncommon operation, but we fancy that this lady's head must have undergone some such treatment, in order to warrant her forehead being likened to a "vivid buckler."

Mr. Melville, among other improvements, has favored us with a new substantive of his own invention. We are very grateful to him for this little attention, but our thankfulness would be rendered still more willingly if he had appended a little note explaining the meaning of this—no doubt very forcible—word. At page 242 we find the following sentence: "Thy *instantaneousness* hath killed her." On a first reading of this we hurriedly came to the conclusion that "instantaneousness" must be either some very old or some very new weapon of destruction. We judged simply from the fatal results attributed to it in the sentence. Can it be possible, thought we to ourselves, that the reign of the sanguinary Colt is over? that revolvers are gone out of fashion and "instantaneousnesses" come in? What can these new weapons be like? Have they six barrels, or are they worked by steam? In the midst of these perplexities we were still further bewildered by coming suddenly upon this passage, at page 248:

The strange, imperious *instantaneousness in* him.

Here in an instant was our whole theory upset. The hieroglyph on the Rosetta stone was not more puzzling than this noun of Mr. Melville's. It was evident from the context in the last sentence that it could not be a weapon of destruction, so we immediately formed a conception that it must be some newly discovered magnetic power, which resided *in* the man, but could be used with fatal effect if necessary. Upon this hypothesis we were proceeding to build another theory, far more magnificent than our first, when we lit upon a *third* sentence that sent to the winds all previous speculations. It ran as follows:

That *instantaneousness* now impelled him.—Page 252.

Eureka! we shouted, we have it. Success has crowned our toil, and the enigma is for ever solved. "Instantaneousness" is a new motive power! We leave our readers to brood over this discovery.

Mr. Melville's lingual improvements do not stop here. He discards all commonplace words, and substitutes much better ones of his own in their stead. He would not for the world call the travelling from one place to another "a journey"—*that* would be far too common. In Mr. Melville's refined diction it becomes "a displacement." Every thing that is dim is with him "nebulous." Hence we have nebulous stories, nebulous landscapes, nebulous meanings, and though last, not least, Mr. Melville himself has given us a very nebulous book!

His descriptive passages are very vivid. The following "night piece" is somewhat after the manner of Callot:

The obscurely open window, which ever and anon was still softly illuminated by the mild heat-lightning and ground lightning, that wove their wonderfulness without, in the unsearchable air of that *ebonly warm* and most noiseless summer night.—Page 203.

In the same page, a little further on, we find that

The casement was suddenly and *wovenly* illumined.

This is no doubt fine to those that understand, but, strange as the confession may appear, we are foolhardy enough to acknowledge that we have not the remotest conception of what it all means. We cannot, by any mental process hitherto discovered, induce our reasoning faculties to accept "ebonly warm" and "wovenly illuminated" as conveying any tangible idea. The first two words we do not recognize as belonging to any known language, and we have a shrewd suspicion that the idea—if the author intended any—is quite as undiscoverable.

Again, he hits off a lady's eyes after the following fashion. It may be poetical, but we cannot call it complimentary:

Her dry burning eyes of long-fringed fire.— Page 202.

This young lady must have been the original performer of the "lightning glance" and the "look of flashing scorn," once used so freely by a certain class of novel-writers.

At page 60 we find the following singular expression:

It was no wonder that Pierre should flush a bit, and *stammer in his attitudes* a little.

It was an old-fashioned idea that the disease of stammering was usually confined to the organs of speech. In modern times, however, it seems to embrace a wider sphere; and we shall, no doubt, soon hear of "stuttering legs" and "a man with a hesitation in his arm." Nor do we see why the converse should not be adopted, or why a man should not have a "club tongue," or "bunions upon his conversation!"

We have been so far particular in pointing out Mr. Melville's faults. We have attached a certain degree of importance to each of them, from the fact that we are obliged to look upon him in the light of an experienced author, and cannot allow him that boyish license which we are always ready to grant to tyros who lose themselves for the first time amid the bewildering paths of literature. Mr. Melville has written good books, and tasted largely of success, and he ought to have known better. ⟨. . .⟩

We have dwelt long enough upon these *Ambiguities*. We fear that if we were to continue much longer, we should become ambiguous ourselves. We have, we think, said sufficient to show our readers that Mr. Melville is a man wholly unfitted for the task of writing wholesome fictions; that he possesses none of the faculties necessary for such work; that his fancy is diseased, his morality vitiated, his style nonsensical and ungrammatical, and his characters as far removed from our sympathies as they are from nature.

Let him continue, then, if he must write, his pleasant sea and island tales. We will be always happy to hear Mr. Melville discourse about savages, but we must protest against any more Absurdities, misnamed *Ambiguities*.

Notes

1. Mr. Cornelius Mathews was, we believe, the first to designate this prurient taste under the happy and specific head of "the ballet-feeling."

"SIR NATHANIEL"
"American Authorship: IV. Herman Melville"
New Monthly Magazine, July 1853, pp. 300–308

The Muses, it was once alleged by Christopher North, have but scantly patronised sea-faring verse: they have neglected ship-building, and deserted the dockyards,—though in Homer's days they kept a private yacht, of which he was captain. "But their attempts to reestablish anything like a club, these two thousand years or so, have miserably failed; and they have never quite recovered their nerves since the loss of poor Falconer, and their disappointment at the ingratitude shown to Dibdin." And Sir Kit adds, that though they do indeed now and then talk of the "deep blue sea," and occasionally, perhaps, skim over it like sea-plovers, yet they avoid the quarter-deck and all its discipline, and decline the dedication of the cat-o'-nine-tails, in spite of their number.

By them, nevertheless, must have been inspired—in fitful and irregular afflatus—some of the prose-poetry of Herman Melville's sea-romances. Ocean breezes blow from his tales of Atlantic and Pacific cruises. Instead of landsman's grey goose quill, he seems to have plucked a quill from skimming curlew, or to have snatched it, a fearful joy, from hovering albatross, if not from the wings of the wind itself. The superstition of life on the waves has no abler interpreter, unequal and undisciplined as he is—that superstition almost inevitably engendered among men who live, as it has been said, "under a solemn sense of eternal danger, one inch only of plank (often worm-eaten) between themselves and the grave; and who see for ever one wilderness of waters."[1] His intimacy with the sights and sounds of that wilderness, almost entitles him to the reversion of the mystic "blue cloak" of Keats's submarine greybeard, in which

every ocean form
Was woven with a black distinctness; storm,
And calm, and whispering, and hideous roar
Were emblem'd in the woof; with every shape
That skims, or dives, or sleeps 'twixt cape and cape.[2]

A landsman, somewhere observes Mr. Tuckerman, can have no conception of the fondness a ship may inspire, before he listens, on a moonlight night, amid the lonely sea, to the details of her build and workings, unfolded by a complacent tar. Moonlight and midseas are much, and a complacent tar is something; but we "calculate" a landsman *can* get some conception of the true-blue enthusiasm in question, and even become slightly inoculated with it in his own *terra firma* person, under the tuition of a Herman Melville. This graphic

narrator assures us, and there needs no additional witness to make the assurance doubly sure, that his sea adventures have often served, when spun as a yarn, not only to relieve the weariness of many a night-watch, but to excite the warmest sympathies of his shipmates. Not that we vouch for the fact of his having experienced the adventures in literal truth, or even of being the pet of the fo'castle as yarn-spinner extraordinary. But we do recognise in him and in his narratives (the earlier ones, at least) a "capital" fund of even untold "interest," and so richly veined a nugget of the *ben trovato* as to "take the shine out of" many a golden *vero*. Readers there are, who, having been enchanted by a perusal of *Typee* and *Omoo*, have turned again and rent the author, when they heard a surmise, or an assertion, that his tales were more or less imagination. Others there are, and we are of them, whose enjoyment of the history was little affected by a suspicion of the kind during perusal (which few can evade), or an affirmation of it afterwards. "And if a little more romantic than truth may warrant, it will be no harm," is Miles Coverdale's morality, when projecting a chronicle of life at Blithedale. Miles *a raison*.

Life in the Marquesas Islands!—how attractive the theme in capable hands! And here it was treated by a man "out of the ordinary," who had contrived, as Tennyson sings,

To burst all links of habit—there to wander far away,
On from island unto island at the gateways of the day.
Larger constellations burning, mellow moons and happy skies,
Breadths of tropic shade and palms in cluster, knots of Paradise,—
Droops the heavy-blossom'd bower, hangs the heavy-fruited tree—
Summer isles of Eden lying in dark-purple spheres of sea.

"The Marquesas! what strange visions of outlandish things," exclaims *Tommo* himself, "does the very name spirit up! Lovely houris—cannibal banquets—groves of cocoa-nuts—coral reefs—tattooed chiefs, and bamboo temples; sunny valleys planted with bread-fruit trees—carved canoes dancing on the flashing blue waters—savage woodlands guarded by horrible idols—heathenish rites and human sacrifices." And then the zest with which Tommo and Toby, having deserted the ship, plunge into the midst of these oddly-assorted charms—cutting themselves a path through cane-brakes—living day by day on a stinted tablespoonful of "a hash of soaked bread and bits of tobacco"—shivering the livelong night under drenching rain—traversing a fearful series of dark chasms, separated by sharp-crested perpendicular ridges—leaping from precipice above to palm-tree below—and then their entrance into the Typee valley, and introduction to King Mehevi, and initiation into Typee manners, and willy-nilly experience of Typee hospitality. Memorable is the portrait-gallery of the natives: Mehevi, towering with royal dignity above his faithful commons; Marnoo, that all-influential Polynesian Apollo, whose tattooing was the best specimen of the Fine Arts in that region, and whose eloquence wielded at will that fierce anthropophagic *demos*; Marheyo, paternal and warm-hearted old savage, a time-stricken giant—and his wife, Tinor, genuine busybody, most notable and exacting of housewives, but no termagant or shrew for all that; and their admirable son, Kory-Kory—his face tattooed with such a host of pictured birds and fishes, that he resembled a pictorial musuem of natural history, or an illuminated copy of Goldsmith's *Animated Nature*—and whose devotion to the stranger no time could wither nor custom stale. And poor

Fayaway, olive-cheeked nymph, with sweet blue eyes of placid yet unfathomable depth, a child of nature with easy unstudied graces, breathing from infancy an atmosphere of perpetual summer—whom, deserted by the roving Tommo, we are led to compare (to *his* prejudice) with Frederika forsaken by Goethe—an episode in the many-sided Baron's life which we have not yet come to regard so tolerantly as Mr. Carlyle.

Omoo, the Rover, keeps up the spirit of *Typee* in a new form. Nothing can be livelier than the sketches of ship and ship's company. "Brave *Little Jule,* plump *Little Jule,*" a very witch at sailing, despite her crazy rigging and rotten bulwarks—blow high, blow low, always ready for the breeze, and making you forget her patched sails and blistered hull when she was dashing the waves from her prow, and prancing, and pawing the sea—flying before the wind—rolling now and then, to be sure, but in very playfulness—with spars erect, looking right up into the wind's eye, the pride of her crew; albeit they had their misgivings that this playful craft, like some vivacious old mortal all at once sinking into a decline, might, some dark night, spring a leak, and carry them all to the bottom. The Captain, or "Miss Guy,"—essentially a cockney, and no more meant for the sea than a hairdresser. The bluff mate, John Jermin, with his squinting eye, and rakishly-twisted nose, and grey ringleted bullet head, and generally pugnacious looks, but with a heart as big as a bullock—obstreperous in his cups, and always for having a fight, but loved as a brother by the very men he flogged, for his irresistibly good-natured way of knocking them down. The ship's carpenter, "Chips," ironically styled "Beauty" on strict *lucus à non lucendo* principles—as ugly in temper as in visage. Bungs, the cooper, a man after a bar-keeper's own heart; who, when he felt, as he said, "just about right," was characterised by a free lurch in his gait, a queer way of hitching up his waistbands, and looking unnecessarily steady at you when speaking. Bembo, the harpooner, a dark, moody savage—none of your effeminate barbarians, but a shaggy-browed, glaring-eyed, crisp-haired fellow, under whose swart, tattooed skin the muscles worked like steel rods. Rope Yarn, or Ropey, the poor distraught land-lubber—a forlorn, stunted, hook-visaged creature, erst a journeyman baker in Holborn, with a soft and underdone heart, whom a kind word made a fool of. And, best of all, Doctor Long Ghost, a six-feet tower of bones, who quotes Virgil, talks of Hobbes of Malmesbury, and repeats poetry by the canto, especially *Hudibras;* and who sings mellow old songs, in a voice so round and racy, the real juice of sound; and who has seen the world from so many angles, the acute of civilisation and the obtuse of savagedom; and who is as inventive as he is incurable in the matter of practical jokes—all effervescent with animal spirits and tricksy good-humour. Of the Tahiti folks, Captain Bob is an amusing personage, a corpulent giant, of three-alderman-power in gormandising feats, and so are Po-po and his family, and the irreverently-ridiculed court of Queen Pomare. It is uncomfortable to be assured in the preface, that "in every statement connected with missionary operations, a strict adherence to facts has, of course, been scrupulously observed"—and the satirist's rather flippant air in treating this subject makes his protestation not unnecessary, that "nothing but an earnest desire for truth and good has led him to touch upon it at all." Nevertheless, there is mournful emphasis in these revelations of *mickonaree* progress—and too much reason to accept the tenor of his remarks as correct, and to bewail the inapplicability to modern missionaries in general, of Wordsworth's lines—

Rich conquest waits them:—the tempestuous sea
Of Ignorance, that ran so rough and high

These good men humble by a few bare words,
And calm with awe of God's divinity.

For does not even so unexceptionable a pillar of orthodoxy as Sir Archibald Alison, express doubt as to the promise of Missions, in relation to any but European ethnology? affirming, indeed,[3] that had Christianity been adapted to man in his rude and primeval state, it would have been revealed at an earlier period, and would have appeared in the age of Moses, not in that of Cæsar:—a dogmatic assertion, by the way, highly characteristic of the somewhat peremptory baronet, and not very harmonious, either in letter or spirit, with the broad text on which worldwide missionary enterprise is founded, and for which Sir Archibald must surely have an *ethnic* gloss of his own private interpretation: Πορευθέντες μαθητεύσατε πάντα τὰ ἔθνη.

But to Mr. Melville. And in a new, and not improved aspect. *Exit* Omoo; *enter* Mardi. And the cry is, *Heu! quantum mutatus ab illo—*

Alas, how changed from him,
This vein of Ercles, and this soul of whim—

changed enough to threaten an *exeunt omnes* of his quondam admirers. The first part of *Mardi* is worthy of its antecedents; but too soon we are hurried whither we would not, and subjected to the caprices, *velut ægri somnia,* of one who, of malice aforethought,

Delphinum silvis appingit, fluctibus aprum—

the last clause signifying that he *bores* us with his "sea of troubles," and provokes us to take arms against, and (if possible) by opposing, end them. Yet do some prefer his new shade of marine blue, and exult in this his "sea-change into something rich and strange." And the author of *Nile Notes* defines *Mardi,* as a whole, to be unrhymed poetry, rhythmical and measured—the swell of its sentences having a low, lapping cadence, like the dip of the sun-stilled, Pacific waves,—and sometimes the grave music of Bacon's Essays! Thou wert right, O Howadji, to add, "Who but an American could have written them." Alas, Cis-Atlantic criticism compared them to Foote's "What, no soap? So he died, and she very imprudently married the barber,"—with the wedding concomitants of the Picninnies and Great Panjandrum and gunpowder-heeled terpsichorics—Foote being, moreover, preferred to Melville, on the score of superiority in sense, diversion, and brevity. Nevertheless, subsequent productions have proved the author of *Mardi* to plume himself on his craze, and love to have it so. And what will he do in the end thereof?

In tone and taste *Redburn* was an improvement upon *Mardi,* but was as deficient as the latter was overfraught with romance and adventure. Whether fiction or fact, this narrative of the first voyage of Wellingborough Redburn,[4] a New York merchant's son, as sailor-boy in a merchant-vessel, is even prosy, bald, and eventless; and would be dull beyond redemption, as a story, were not the author gifted with a scrutinising gaze, and a habit of taking notes as well as "prenting" them, which ensures his readers against absolute common-place. It is true, he more than once plunges into episodic extravaganzas—such as the gambling-house frenzy of Harry Bolton—but these are, in effect, the dullest of all his moods; and tend to produce, what surely they are inspired by, blue devils. Nor is he over chary of introducing the repulsive,—notwithstanding his disclaimer, "Such is the fastidiousness of some readers, that, many times, they must lose the most striking incidents in a narrative like mine:"[5] for not only some, but most readers, are too fastidious to enjoy such scenes as that of the starving, dying mother and children in a Liverpool cellar, and that of the dead mariner, from whose lips darted out, when the light touched them, "threads of greenish fire, like a forked tongue," till the cadaverous face was "crawled over by a swarm of worm-like flames"—a hideous picture, as deserving of a letter of remonstrance on æsthetic grounds, as Mr. Dickens' spontaneous combustion case (Krook) on physical.[6] Apart from these exceptions, the experiences of Redburn during his "first voyage" are singularly free from excitement, and even incident. We have one or two "marine views" happily done, though not in the artist's *very* happiest style. The picture of a wreck may be referred to—that of a dismantled, water-logged schooner, that had been drifting about for weeks; her bulwarks all but gone—the bare stanchions, or posts, left standing here and there, splitting in two the waves which broke clear over the deck—her open main-hatchway yawning into view every time she rolled in the trough of the sea, and submerged again, with a rushing, gurgling sound of many waters; the relic of a jacket nailed atop of the broken mainmast, for a signal; and, sad, stern sight—most strange and most unnatural—"three dark, green, grassy objects," lashed, and leaning over sideways against the taffrail—slowly swaying with every roll, but otherwise motionless! There is a spirited sketch, too, of the sailor-boy's first ascent to "loose the mainskysail"—not daring to look down, but keeping his eyes glued to the shrouds—panting and breathing hard before he is half-way up—reaching the "Jacob's ladder," and at last, to his own amazement, finding himself hanging on the skysail yard, holding on might and main to the mast, and curling his feet round the rigging, as if they were another pair of hands; thence gazing at length, mute and awe-stricken, on the dark midnight sea beneath, which looks like a great, black gulf, hemmed in all round by beetling black cliffs—the ship below, seeming like a long narrow plank in the water—the boy above, seeming in utter loneliness to tread the swart night clouds, and every second expecting to find himself falling—falling—falling, as he used to feel when the nightmare was on him. Redburn managed his first ascent deftly, and describes it admirably. Sir Nathaniel, indeed, never has been sedentary διὰ νυκτός on a main skysail; but he is pretty sure, from these presents, that Mr. Melville *has.* Equally sure, in his own case, is Sir N., that *had* he attained that giddy eminence, not only should he have expected to find himself falling—falling—falling, but would have found himself, or been found, fallen: which Redburn was *not.* Gallant boy—clear-headed, light-hearted, fast-handed, nimble-footed!—he deserved to reach the top of the tree, and, having reached, to enjoy the sweet peril, like blossom that hangs on the bough: and that in time he did come to enjoy it we find from his record of the wild delirium there is about it—the fine rushing of the blood about the heart—the glad thrilling and throbbing of the whole system, to find yourself tossed up at every pitch into the clouds of a stormy sky, and hovering like a judgment angel between heaven and earth; both hands free, with one foot in the rigging, and one somewhere behind you in the air.

The crew, again, are sketched by a true draughtsman—though one misses the breadth and finish of his corresponding descriptions in *Omoo.* There is Captain Riga, all soft-sawder ashore, all vinegar and mustard at sea—a gay Lothario of all inexperienced, sea-going youths, from the capital or the country—who condoles and sympathises with them in dock, but whom they will not know again when he gets out of sight of land, and mounts his cast-off clothes, and adjusts his character to the shabbiness of his coat, and holds the perplexed lads a little better than his boots, and will no more think of addressing them than of invoking wooden Donald, the figure-head at the ship's bows. There is Jackson—a meagre, consumptive, overbearing bully—

squinting, broken-nosed, rheumatic—the weakest body and strongest will on board—"one glance of whose squinting eye was as good as a knock-down, for it was the most subtle, deep, infernal-looking eye ever lodged in a human head," and must have once belonged to a wolf, or starved tiger,—no oculist could ever "turn out a glass eye half so cold, and snaky, and deadly"—fit symbol of a man who, "though he could not read a word, was spontaneously an atheist," and who, during the long night-watches, would enter into arguments to prove that there was nothing to be believed, or loved, or worth living for, but everything to be hated, in the wide world: in short, "a Cain afloat; branded on his yellow brow with some inscrutable curse; and going about corrupting and searing every heart that beat near him." There is Jack Blunt, the "Irish Cockney," with his round face like a walrus, and his stumpy figure like a porpoise standing on end—full of dreams and marine romance—singing songs about susceptible mermaids—and holding fast a comfortable creed that all sailors are saved, having plenty of squalls here below, but fair weather aloft. There is Larry, the whaleman, or "blubber-boiler," ever extolling the delights of the free and easy Indian Ocean, and deprecating civilised life, or, as he styles it, "snivelisation," which has "spiled him complete, when he might have been a great man in Madagasky." There is Dutch Max, stolid and seemingly respectable, but a systematic bi-(if not poly-)gamist. And there is the black cook, serious, metaphysical, "and given to talk about original sin"—sitting all Sunday morning over his boiling pots, and reading grease-spotted good books; yet tempted to use some bad language occasionally, when the sea dashes into his stove, of cold, wet, stormy mornings. And, to conclude, there is the steward, a dandy mulatto, yclept Lavender; formerly a barber in West-Broadway, and still redolent of Cologne water and relics of his stock-in-trade there—a sentimental darky, fond of reading *Charlotte Temple,* and carrying a lock of frizzled hair in his waistcoat pocket, which he volunteers to show you, with his handkerchief to his eyes. Mr. Melville is perfectly *au fait* in nautical characterisation of this kind, and as thoroughly vapid when essaying revelations of English aristocratic life, and rhapsodies about Italian organ-boys, whose broken English resembles a mixture of "the potent wine of Oporto with some delicious syrup," and who discourse transcendentally and ravishingly about their mission, and impel the author to affirm that a Jew's-harp hath power to awaken all the fairies in our soul, and make them dance there, "as on a moonlit sward of violets;" and that there is no humblest thing with music in it, not a fife, not a negro-fiddle, that is not to be reverenced[7] as much as the grandest organ that ever rolled its flood-tide of harmony down a cathedral nave! What will Mr. Melville think of our taste, when we own to a delight in the cathedral organ, but also to an incurable irreverence towards street-organ, vagrant fiddle, and perambulatory fife?—against which we have a habit of shutting the window, and retiring to a back room. That we are *moved* by their concord of sweet sounds, we allow; but it is to a wish that *they* would "move on," and sometimes to a mental invocation of the police. Whence, possibly, Mr. Melville will infer, on Shakspearian authority, that we are meet only for

Treasons, stratagems, and spoils;

and will demand, *quoad* our critical taste,

Let no such man be trusted.

Next came *White Jacket; or, the World in a Man-of-War.* The hero's *soubriquet* is derived from his—shirt, or "white duck frock," his only wrap-rascal—a garment patched with old socks and old trouser-legs, bedarned and bequilted till stiff as King James's cotton-stuffed and dagger-proof doublet—provided, moreover with a great variety of pockets, pantries, clothes-presses, and cupboards, and "several unseen recesses behind the arras,"—insomuch, exclaims the proud, glad owner, "that my jacket, like an old castle, was full of winding stairs, and mysterious closets, crypts, and cabinets; and like a confidential writingdesk, abounded in snug little out-of-the-way lairs and hiding-places, for the storage of valuables." The adventures of the adventurous proprietor of this encyclopædic toga, this cheap magazine of a coat, are detailed with that eager vivacity, and sometimes that unlicensed extravagance, which are characteristic of the scribe. Some of the sea-pictures are worthy of his highest mood—when a fine imagination over-rides and represses the chaos of a wanton fancy. Give him to describe a storm on the wide waters—the gallant ship labouring for life and against hope—the gigantic masts snapping almost under the strain of the top-sails—the ship's bell dismally tolling, and this at murk midnight—the rampant billows curling their crests in triumph—the gale flattening the mariners against the rigging as they toil upwards, while a hurricane of slanting sleet and hail pelts them in savage wrath: and he will thrill us quiet landsmen who dwell at home at ease.

For so successful a trader in "marine stores" as Mr. Melville, *The Whale* seemed a speculation every way big with promise. From such a master of his harpoon might have been expected a prodigious hit. There was about blubber and spermaceti something unctuously suggestive, with him for whaleman. And his three volumes entitled *The Whale* un-doubtedly contain much vigorous description, much wild power, many striking details. But the effect is distressingly marred throughout by an extravagant treatment of the subject. The style is maniacal—mad as a March hare—mowing, gibbering, screaming, like an incurable Bedlamite, reckless of keeper or strait-waistcoat. Now it vaults on stilts, and performs *Bombastes Furioso* with contortions of figure, and straining strides, and swashbuckler fustian, far beyond *Pistol* in that Ancient's happiest mood. Now it is seized with spasms, acute and convulsive enough to excite bewilderment in all beholders. When he pleases, Mr. Melville can be so lucid, straightfor-ward, hearty, and unaffected, and displays so unmistakable a shrewdness, and satirical sense of the ridiculous, that it is hard to suppose that *he* can have indited the rhodomontade to which we allude. Surely the man is a Doppelganger—a dual number incarnate (singular though he be, in and out of all con-science):—surely he is two single gentlemen rolled into one, but retaining their respective idiosyncrasies—the one sensible, sagacious, observant, graphic, and producing admirable mat-ter—the other maundering, drivelling, subject to paroxysms, cramps, and total collapse, and penning exceeding many pages of unaccountable "bosh." So that in tackling every new chapter, one is disposed to question it beforehand, "Under which king, Bezonian?"—the sane or the insane; the constitu-tional and legitimate, or the absolute and usurping? Writing of Leviathan, he exclaims, "Unconsciously my chirography ex-pands into placard capitals. Give me a condor's quill! Give me Vesuvius' crater for an inkstand! Friends, hold my arms!" Oh that his friends had obeyed that summons! They might have saved society from a huge dose of hyperbolical slang, maudlin sentimentalism, and tragi-comic bubble and squeak.

His Yankeeisms are plentiful as blackberries. "I am tormented," quoth he, "with an everlasting itch for things remote." Remote, too frequently, from good taste, good manners, and good sense. We need not pause at such expres-sions as "looking a sort of diabolically funny;"—"beefsteaks done rare;"—"a speechlessly quick chaotic bundling of a man into eternity;"—"bidding adieu to circumspect life, to exist

only in a delirious throb." But why wax fast and furious in a thousand such paragraphs as these:—"In landlessness alone resides the highest truth, indefinite as the Almighty. . . . Take heart, take heart, O Bulkington! Bear thee grimly, demi-god! Up from the spray of thy ocean-perishing—straight up, leaps thy apotheosis!"—"Thou [*scil.* Spirit of Equality] great God! who didst not refuse to the swart convict, Bunyan, the pale, poetic pearl; Thou who didst clothe with doubly hammered leaves of finest gold the stumped and paupered arm of old Cervantes; Thou who didst pick up Andrew Jackson from the pebbles; who didst hurl him upon a war-horse; who didst thunder him higher than a throne!"—"If such a furious trope may stand, his [Capt. Ahab's] special lunacy stormed his general sanity, and carried it, and turned all its concentrated cannon upon its own mad mark. . . . then it was, that his torn body and gashed soul bled into one another; and so interfusing made him mad."—"And the miser-merman, Wisdom, re-vealed [to a diving negro] his hoarded heaps; and among the joyous, heartless, ever-juvenile eternities, Pip saw the multi-tudinous, God-omnipresent, coral insects, that out of the firmament of waters heaved the colossal orbs. He saw God's foot upon the treadle of the loom, and spoke it; and therefore his shipmates called him mad."

The story itself is a strange, wild, furibund thing—about Captain Ahab's vow of revenge against one Moby Dick. And who is Moby Dick? A fellow of a whale, who has made free with the captain's leg; so that the captain now stumps on ivory, and goes circumnavigating the globe in quest of the old offender, and raves by the hour in a lingo borrowed from Rabelais, Carlyle, Emerson, newspapers transcendental and transatlantic, and the magnificent proems of our Christmas pantomimes. Captain Ahab is introduced with prodigious efforts at preparation; and there is really no lack of rude power and character about his presentment—spoiled, however, by the Cambyses' vein in which he dissipates his vigour. His portrait is striking—looking "like a man cut away from the stake, when the fire has overrunningly wasted all the limbs without consuming them, or taking away one particle from their compacted aged robustness"—a man with a brow gaunt and ribbed, like the black sand beach after some stormy tide has been gnawing it, without being able to drag the firm thing from its place. Ever since his fell encounter with Moby Dick, this impassioned veteran has cherished a wild vindictiveness against the whale, frantically identifying with him not only all his bodily woes, but all his feelings of exasperation—so that the White Whale swims before him "as the monomaniac incarnation of all those malicious agencies which some deep men feel eating in them, till they are left living on with half a heart and half a lung." The amiable cannibal Queequeg occasions some stirring and some humorous scenes, and is probably the most reasonable and cultivated creature of the ship's company. Starbuck and Stubb are both tiresome, in different ways. The book is rich with facts connected with the natural history of the whale, and the whole art and process of whaling; and with spirited descriptions of that process, which betray an intense straining at effect. The climax of the three days' chase after Moby Dick is highly wrought and sternly exciting—but the catastrophe, in its whirl of waters and fancies, resembles one of Turner's later nebulous transgres-sions in gamboge.

Speaking of the passengers on board Redburn's ship *Highlander*, Mr. Melville significantly and curtly observes, "As for the ladies, I have nothing to say concerning them; for ladies are like creeds; if you cannot speak well of them, say nothing." He will pardon us for including in this somewhat arbitrary classification of forms of beauty and forms of faith, his own, last, and worst production, *Pierre; or, the Ambiguities*.

O author of *Typee* and *Omoo*, we admire so cordially the proven capacity of your pen, that we entreat you to doff the "non-natural sense" of your late lucubrations—to put off your worser self—and to do your better, real self, that justice which its "potentiality" deserves.

Notes

1. Thomas De Quincey.
2. *Endymion*, Book III.
3. See Alison's *History of Europe* (New Series), vol. i., p. 74.
4. The hero himself is a sort of amalgam of Perceval Keene and Peter Simple—the keenness strangely antedating the simplicity.
5. *Redburn* vol. ii., ch. 27.
6. See G. H. Lewes' Two Letters.
7. No parallel passage is that fine saying of Sir Thomas Browne in *Religio Medici*, ii., 9.

HENRY S. SALT
"Marquesan Melville"
Gentleman's Magazine, March 1892, pp. 248–57

Has America a literature? I am inclined to think it a grave mistake to argue seriously with those afflicted persons who periodically exercise themselves over this idlest of academic questions. It is wiser to meet them with a practical counter-thrust, and pointedly inquire, for example, whether they are familiar with the writings of Herman Melville. Whereupon, confusion will in most cases ensue, and you will go on to suggest that to criticise *Hamlet*, with the prince's part omitted, would be no whit more fatuous than to demonstrate the non-existence of an American literature, while taking no account of its true intellectual giants. When it was announced, a few months ago, that "Mr. Herman Melville, the author," had just died in New York at the age of seventy-two, the news excited but little interest on this side of the Atlantic; yet, forty years ago, his name was familiar to English, as to American readers, and there is little or no exaggeration in Robert Buchanan's remark, that he is "the one great imaginative writer fit to stand shoulder to shoulder with Whitman on that continent."

It was in 1846 that Melville fairly took the world by storm with his *Typee: the Narrative of a four months' residence in the Marquesas Islands*, the first of a brilliant series of volumes of adventure, in which reality was so deftly encircled with a halo of romance that readers were at once captivated by the force and freshness of the style and puzzled as to the personality of the author. Who and what was this mysterious sojourner in the far islands of the Pacific—this "Marquesan Melville," as a writer in *Blackwood* denominated him? Speculation was rife, and not unaccompanied by suspicion; for there were some critics who not only questioned the veracity of Herman Melville's "Narratives," but declared his very name to be fictitious. "Separately," remarked one sagacious reviewer, "the names are not uncommon; we can urge no valid reason against their juncture; yet in this instance they fall suspiciously on our ear."

Herman Melville, however, was far from being a mythical personage, though in his early life, as in his later, he seems to have instinctively shrunk from any other publicity than that which was brought him by his books. He was a genuine child of nature, a sort of nautical George Borrow, on whom the irresistible sea-passion had descended in his boyhood, and won

him away from the ordinary routine of respectable civilised life, until, to quote his own words, to travel had become a necessity of his existence, "a way of driving off the spleen and regulating the circulation." The son of a cultured American merchant, of Scotch extraction, he had early imbibed from his father's anecdotes a romantic attachment to the sea. "Of winter evenings," he says, "by the well-remembered sea-coal fires in old Greenwich Street, New York, he used to tell my brother and me of the monstrous waves at sea, mountain-high, and of the masts bending like twigs." At the age of eighteen, his father having died in bankruptcy, he found himself unexpectedly face to face with poverty and disappointment, and was forced to embark as a common seaman in a merchant vessel bound to Liverpool, a voyage of disillusionment and bitter experience, of which he has left us what is apparently an authentic record in one of his early volumes. [1]

Returned from this expedition, he essayed for a time to gain a quiet livelihood as a teacher. But destiny and his natural genius had willed it otherwise; it was no academic lecture-room, but the deck of a whale-ship, that was to be "his Yale College and his Harvard." "Oh, give me again the rover's life," he exclaims, "the joy, the thrill, the whirl! Let me feel thee again, old sea! Let me leap into thy saddle once more! I am sick of these *terra firma* toils and cares, sick of the dust and reek of towns. Let me snuff thee up, sea-breeze, and whinny in thy spray!" So in 1841 the child of nature was again aboard, and off to the Pacific on a whaler; and it was the adventures that befell him, during this absence of nearly four years' duration, that subsequently furnished the material for the chief series of his volumes. In *Typee* he related the story of his romantic captivity among a tribe of noble savages in the Marquesas; in *Omoo* we have his further wanderings in the Society and Sandwich Islands; in *White Jacket*, his return voyage as a common sailor in a man-of-war. *Mardi*, on the other hand, is a phantasy, in which the imaginative element, having slipped from the control of the narrative, runs riot in the wildest and most extravagant luxuriance.

Typee must be regarded as, on the whole, the most charming of Melville's writings, and the one which may most surely count on lasting popularity; it is certainly the master-piece of his earlier period, during which the artistic sense was still predominant over those transcendental tendencies which characterised his later volumes. Coming at a time when men's minds were filled with a vague, undefined interest in the wonders of the Pacific, and when the French annexation of Tahiti, of which Melville was an eyewitness, had drawn universal attention to that quarter of the globe, it gained an instantaneous and wide-spread success, both in America and England, and was quickly translated into several European tongues. Alike in the calm beauty of its descriptive passages, and in the intense vividness of its character-sketches, it was, and is, and must ever be, a most powerful and fascinating work. Indeed, I think I speak within the mark in saying that nothing better of its kind is to be found in English literature, so firm and clear is it in outline, yet so dreamily suggestive in the dim mystic atmosphere which pervades it. Here is a passage from one of the early chapters, itself as rhythmical as the rhythmical drifting of the whaler *Dolly* under the trade-winds of the Pacific:

> The sky presented a clear expanse of the most
> delicate blue, except along the skirts of the horizon,
> where you might see a thin drapery of pale clouds
> which never varied their form or colour. The long,
> measured, dirge-like swell of the Pacific came rolling
> along with its surface broken by little tiny waves,

sparkling in the sunshine. Every now and then a shoal of flying fish, scared from the water under the bows, would leap into the air, and fall the next moment like a shower of silver into the sea. Then you would see the superb albicore, with his glittering sides, sailing aloft, and, often describing an arc in his descent, disappear on the surface of the water. Far off, the lofty jet of the whale might be seen, and nearer at hand the prowling shark, that villainous foot-pad of the seas, would come skulking along, and at a wary distance regard us with his evil eye. At times some shapeless monster of the deep, floating on the surface, would, as we approached, sink slowly into the blue waters, and fade away from the sight. But the most impressive feature of the scene was the almost unbroken silence that reigned over sky and water. Scarcely a sound could be heard but the occasional breathing of the grampus and the rippling at the cutwater.

And Typee itself, the scene of Melville's detention, when he and a companion sailor had deserted from the whale-ship— what a fairyland of tropical valleys, and crystal streams, and groves of cocoa-palms and bread-fruit trees, is here magically depicted for us! How life-like the portraiture of the innocent, placid, happy islanders, who, albeit cannibals at times, were yet far superior to civilised nations in many of the best qualities by which civilisation is supposed to be distinguished! And Fayaway—surely never was Indian maiden so glorified by poet or romancer[2] as is the gentle, beautiful, faithful Fayaway in Melville's marvellous tale! The strongest and tenderest pictures that George Borrow has drawn for us of his friendly relations with the wandering gipsy-folk by roadside or dingle are not more strong and tender than Melville's reminiscences of this "peep at Polynesian life." As Borrow possessed the secret of winning the confidence of the gipsies, so Melville, by the same talisman of utter simplicity and naturalness, was able to fraternise in perfect good fellowship with the so-called savages of the Pacific.

It is, furthermore, significant that Melville's familiarity with these "noble savages" was productive of a feeling the very opposite of contempt; he bears repeated and explicit testimony to the enviable healthfulness and happiness of the uncivilised society in which he sojourned so long. "The continual happiness," he says, "which, so far as I was able to judge, appeared to prevail in the valley, sprung principally from that all-pervading sensation which Rousseau has told us he at one time experienced, the mere buoyant sense of a healthful, physical existence. And indeed, in this particular, the Typees had ample reason to felicitate themselves, for sickness was almost unknown. During the whole period of my stay, I saw but one invalid among them; and on their smooth, clear skins you observed no blemish or mark of disease." Still more emphatic is his tribute to their moral qualities. "Civilisation does not engross all the virtues of humanity: she has not even her full share of them. . . . If truth and justice, and the better principles of our nature, cannot exist unless enforced by the statute-book, how are we to account for the social condition of the Typees? So pure and upright were they in all the relations of life, that entering their valley, as I did, under the most erroneous impressions of their character, I was soon led to exclaim in amazement: Are these the ferocious savages, the blood-thirsty cannibals, of whom I have heard such frightful tales! . . . I will frankly declare that after passing a few weeks in this valley of the Marquesas, I formed a higher estimate of human nature than I had ever before entertained. But, alas!

since then I have been one of the crew of a man-of-war, and the pent-up wickedness of five hundred men has nearly overturned all my previous theories."

But here it may be asked by later, as by earlier readers, "Was Melville's narrative a true one? Is his testimony on these subjects a testimony of any scientific value?" The answer to this question, despite the suspicion of the critics, is a decided affirmative. Not only is Melville's account of Typee in close agreement with that of earlier voyagers, as, for example, Captain Porter's *Journal of a Cruise to the Pacific Ocean*, published in 1822, but it has been expressly corroborated by later adventurers. "I cannot resist," wrote an American naval officer,[3] "paying the faint tribute of my own individual admiration to Mr. Melville. Apart from the innate beauty and charming tone of his narratives, the delineations of island life and scenery, from my own personal observation, are most correctly and faithfully drawn." Another witness, who has recently been cited, was the Rev. Titus Coan, of the Hawaiian Islands, who "had personally visited the Marquesas group, found the Typee valley, and verified in every detail the romantic descriptions of the gentle but man-devouring island-ers."[4]

After the publication of *Typee*, Melville married the daughter of Chief Justice Shaw, to whom the book was dedicated, and made his home, from 1850 to 1863, in an old spacious farmhouse at Pittsfield, Massachusetts, commanding picturesque views of Greylock and the other Berkshire mountains. He was here a neighbour of Nathaniel Hawthorne, who was then living at Lenox, and there are records of many friendly intimacies between the two authors, whose intellects were in many ways akin. We read in the Hawthorne diaries of "Mr. Omoo's visits," and how he came accompanied by "his great dog," and how he held transcendental conversations with Hawthorne "about time and eternity, things of this world and of the next, and books, and publishers, and all possible and impossible matters, that lasted pretty deep into the night." It is during this residence at Pittsfield, the adventurous struggles of his early life being now concluded, that we note the commencement of the second, the transcendental period of Melville's literary career. It has been truly said of him that "he had all the metaphysical tendencies which belong so eminently to the American mind;" and it is interesting to observe in this, as in other cases, the conjunction of the practical with the metaphysical temperament. "The chief characteristic of Herman Melville's writings"—so I have elsewhere remarked[5]—"is this attempted union of the practical with the ideal. Commencing with a basis of solid fact, he loves to build up a fantastic structure, which is finally lost in the cloudland of metaphysical speculation."

As *Typee* is the best production of the earlier and simpler phase of Melville's authorship, so undoubtedly is *The Whale* (or *Moby Dick*, as it is sometimes styled) the crown and glory of the later phase; less shapely and artistic than *Typee*, it far surpasses it in immensity of scope and triumphant energy of execution.[6] It is in *The Whale* that we see Melville casting to the winds all conventional restrictions, and rioting in the prodigality of his imaginative vigour. It is in *The Whale* that we find the fullest recognition of that magical influence of the sea—the "image of the ungraspable phantom of life"—which from first to last was the most vital inspiration of his restless and indomitable genius. ("The ocean," he finely wrote in a later volume, "brims with natural griefs and tragedies; and into that watery immensity of terror man's private grief is lost like a drop.") Ostensibly nothing more than a wild story of a strange voyage of vengeance, a "quenchless feud" between a fierce old sea-captain and a particular white sperm-whale of renowned strength and audacity, the book, which abounds with real facts concerning the details of the whale-fishery, has a mystic esoteric significance which lifts it into a wholly different category. In the character of Captain Ahab, who "looked like a man cut away from the stake when the fire has overrunningly wasted all the limbs without consuming them," we see a lurid personification of the self-destructive spirit of Hatred and Revenge, while Moby Dick, the white whale, "swam before him as the monomaniac incarnation of all those malicious agencies which some deep men feel eating in them." To quote detached passages from a work of such ambitious conception and colossal proportions would be worse than useless; I must therefore content myself with saying that *The Whale*, faulty as it is in many respects, owing to the turgid mannerisms of Melville's transcendental mood, is nevertheless the supreme production of a master mind—let no one presume to pass judgment on American literature unless he has read, and re-read, and wonderingly pondered, the three mighty volumes of *The Whale*.

The increasing transcendentalism of Melville's later thought was accompanied and reflected by a corresponding complexity of language, the limpid simplicity so remarkable in *Typee*, and *Omoo*, and *White Jacket* being now succeeded by a habit of gorgeous and fantastic word-painting, which, though brilliantly effective at its best, degenerated, at its worst, into mere bombast and rhetoric, a process which had already been discernible in the concluding portions of *Mardi*, while in *Pierre* (or *The Ambiguities*, as it was appropriately designated) it reached the fatal climax of its development. This unfortunate book, published in 1852, was to a great extent the ruin of its author's reputation; for the critics not unfairly protested against the perversity of "a man born to create, who resolves to anatomise; a man born to see, who insists upon speculating." Of *The Confidence Man* (1857), and Melville's later books in general, it is not necessary to speak; though it is noticeable that in his narrative of *Israel Potter* (1855), and one or two of the short stories in *The Piazza Tales* (1856), he partly recovered his old firmness of touch and delicacy of workmanship.

For, in spite of all the obscurities and mannerisms which confessedly deform his later writings, it remains true that *naturalness* is, on the whole, Melville's prime characteristic, both in the tone and in the style of his productions. His narratives are as racy and vigorous as those of Defoe or Smollett or Marryat; his character-sketches are such as only a man of keen observation, and as keen a sense of humour, could have realised and depicted. His seamen and his sea-captains all, his savages ashore or aboard, from the noble unsophisticated Mehevi in *Typee* to the semi-civilised comical Queequeg in *The Whale*, are admirably vivid and impressive, and the reader who shall once have made their acquaintance will thenceforward in no wise be persuaded that they are not real and living personages. Moreover, there is a large-souled humanity in Melville—the direct outcome of his generous, emotional, yet uniformly sane temperament—which differentiates him entirely from the mere artist or *littérateur*. "I stand for the heart," he writes, in one of his letters to Nathaniel Hawthorne, a statement fully substantiated by the many humane sentiments that find expression in his pages, whether on the subject of modern warfare, or negro slavery, or the barbarities of naval discipline, or the cruel treatment of the harmless "savages" of the Pacific by the more savage apostles of "civilisation." For the rest of it, Melville appears as a frank, simple believer in common human nature, and so little a respecter of persons that his democracy was described by Hawthorne as "ruthless."

"With no son of man," says Melville, "do I stand upon any etiquette or ceremony, except the Christian ones of charity and honesty. . . . A thief in jail is as honourable a personage as General George Washington."

It may be surmised that this uncompromising attitude was scarcely calculated to win the favour of society. A friend who visited Melville at Pittsfield described him as an Ishmael who was "apparently considered by the good people of Pittsfield as little better than a cannibal or a beach-comber." "In vain," he says,[7] "I sought to hear of Typee and those Paradise islands; he preferred to pour forth his philosophy and his theories of life. The shade of Aristotle arose like a cold mist between myself and Fayaway. But what a talk it was! Melville is transformed from a Marquesan to a gipsy student, the gipsy element still remaining strong in him. And this contradiction gives him the air of one who has suffered from opposition, both literary and social."

There is no doubt that Melville's characteristic reticence on personal matters, together with his increasing love of retirement, was in large measure the cause of his otherwise unaccountable loss of literary fame; for even the well-merited failure of such books as *Pierre* and *The Confidence Man* would be in itself insufficient to explain the neglect of his genuine masterpieces. It is true that for a few years he was induced to lecture, in various parts of the States, on the subject of his voyages to the South Seas; but, as a rule, he could not, or would not, cultivate the indispensable art of keeping his name before the public. The man who could win the affections of a cannibal community in the Pacific was less at home in the intricacies of self-advertisement and "business." "Dollars damn me," he remarks in one of his letters. "When I feel most moved to write, that is banned—it will not pay. Yet, altogether, write the *other* way I cannot. So the product is a final hash, and all my books are botches." That he felt keenly mortified at the ill success of *Pierre*, is beyond question. When, on the occasion of a tour in Europe, in 1856, he visited Hawthorne at the Liverpool consulate, he told his friend that "the spirit of adventure had gone out of him." He is described by Hawthorne as looking "a little paler, perhaps, and a little sadder, and with his characteristic gravity and reserve of manner. . . . He has suffered from too constant literary occupations, pursued without much success latterly; and his writings, for a long while past, have indicated a morbid state of mind."

In 1863, Melville found it necessary, for the better education of his children, to leave his home at Pittsfield, and to take up his quarters at New York, where for many years he held an inspectorship in the custom-house. His life became now altogether one of quietude and retirement; content to let the noisy world go by, he made no attempt to recover the fame which had once been his, and to which he still possessed an inalienable title. During these years, however, he published two volumes of poetry; *Battle Pieces*, which deals mainly with incidents of the civil war, and *Clarel, a Pilgrimage in the Holy Land*, described by Melville himself, in a letter to an English correspondent, as "a metrical affair, a pilgrimage or what not, of several thousand lines, eminently adapted for unpopularity." More interesting than these is a little story, *John Marr and Other Sailors*, issued in 1888, and limited to twenty-five copies—a limitation which affords a pathetic and significant comment on the acumen of a "reading public" which had allowed itself to become almost entirely oblivious of the author of *Typee* and *The Whale*! We need not doubt, however, that Melville found ample compensation for this neglect in that assurance of ultimate and lasting recognition which is seldom denied to men of genius. "His tall, stalwart figure," says Mr. Stedman, [8] "until recently could be seen almost daily, tramping through the Fort George district or Central Park; his roving inclination leading him to obtain as much out-door life as possible. His evenings were spent at home, with his books, his pictures, and his family, and usually with them alone."

His love of literature was fully sustained to the end. I have before me a most interesting batch of letters, dated between 1884 and 1888, addressed by him to Mr. James Billson, of Leicester, and mostly dealing with the poems of James Thomson ("B.V."), of which he was a great admirer. Some of these comments and appreciations are in Melville's best style. "*Sunday up the River,*" he writes, "contrasting with the *City of Dreadful Night,* is like a Cuban humming-bird, beautiful in faery tints, flying against the tropic thundercloud. Your friend was a sterling poet, if ever one sang. As to pessimism, although neither pessimist nor optimist myself, nevertheless I relish it in the verse, if for nothing else than as a counterpoise to the exorbitant hopefulness, juvenile and shallow, that makes such a muster in these days—at least in some quarters."

"Exorbitant hopefulness" could indeed have been hardly otherwise than distasteful to one who, like his own *John Marr* (a retired sailor whose fate it was to live on a "frontier-prairie," among an unresponsive inland people who cared nothing for the sea), had so long experienced the solitude of disappointed genius. But it is impossible to believe that this undeserved neglect can be permanent. The opinion of those competent judges who are students of Melville's works is so clear and emphatic in his favour, [9] that it is not too much to say that to read his books is generally to appreciate them; nor is it only those who have what is called an "educated taste" who are thus impressed, for I have been told of instances in which English working-men became his hearty admirers. It is satisfactory to know that a new edition of his best books is forthcoming, both in America and England, and that the public will thus have an opportunity, I will not say of repairing a wrong done to a distinguished writer, for, as I have already shown, the decay of his fame was partly due to circumstances of his own making, but at least of rehabilitating and confirming its earlier and truer judgment. Herman Melville will then resume his honourable place in American literature (for, to end as I began, I hold that the existence of an American literature is a fact and not a supposition), as the prose-poet of the Pacific—

> the sea-compelling man,
> Before whose wand Leviathan
> Rose hoary-white upon the deep,
> With awful sounds that stirred its sleep;
> Melville, whose magic drew Typee,
> Radiant as Venus, from the sea. [10]

Notes

1. *Redburn, His First Voyage: Being the Sailor-boy Confessions and Reminiscences of the Son of a Gentleman in the Merchant Service,* 1849.
2. Unless it be Paquita, in Joaquin Miller's *Life among the Modocs.*
3. Lieut. Wise, in *Los Gringos,* a volume of travels published in 1849.
4. For this and other particulars I am indebted to the courtesy of Mr. Arthur Stedman of New York, the friend and literary executor of Herman Melville.
5. *Art Review,* November 1889.
6. *The Whale* was dedicated to Hawthorne, and is referred to in his *Wonder-Book.* "On the hither side of Pittsfield sits Herman Melville, shaping out the gigantic conception of his 'White Whale,' while the gigantic shadow of Greylock looms upon him from his study window."

7. Dr. Titus Coan's letter, quoted in the *New York World's* obituary notice of Melville.
8. *New York Tribune,* October 1, 1891.
9. I may instance Mr. William Morris, Mr. Theodore Watts, Mr. R. L. Stevenson, Mr. Robert Buchanan, and Mr. W. Clark Russell.
10. Robert Buchanan's *Socrates in Camden.*

ARCHIBALD MacMECHAN
From "The Best Sea Story Ever Written"
Queen's Quarterly, October 1899, pp. 120–30

Anyone who undertakes to reverse some judgment in history or criticism, or to set the public right regarding some neglected man or work, becomes at once an object of suspicion. Nine times out of ten he is called a literary snob for his pains, or a prig who presumes to teach his betters, or a "phrase-monger," or a "young Osric," or something equally soul-subduing. Besides, the burden of proof lies heavy upon him. He preaches to a sleeping congregation. The good public has returned its verdict upon the case, and is slow to review the evidence in favour of the accused, or, having done so, to confess itself in the wrong. Still, difficult as the work of rehabilitation always is, there are cheering instances of its complete success; notably, the rescue of the Elizabethan dramatists by Lamb and Hazlitt and Leigh Hunt. Nor in such a matter is the will always free. As Heine says, ideas take possession of us and force us into the arena, there to fight for them. There is also the possibility of triumph to steel the raw recruit against all dangers. Though the world at large may not care, the judicious few may be glad of new light, and may feel satisfaction in seeing even tardy justice meted out to real merit. In my poor opinion much less than justice has been done to an American writer, whose achievement is so considerable that it is hard to account for the neglect into which he has fallen.

This writer is Herman Melville, who died in New York in the autumn of 1891, aged eighty-three. That his death excited little attention is in consonance with the popular apathy towards him and his work. The civil war marks a dividing line in his literary production as well as in his life. His best work belongs to the *ante-bellum* days, and is cut off in taste and sympathy from the distinctive literary fashions of the present time. To find how complete neglect is, one has only to put question to the most cultivated and patriotic Americans north or south, east or west, even professed specialists in the nativist literature, and it will be long before the Melville enthusiast meets either sympathy or understanding. The present writer made his first acquaintance with *Moby Dick* in the dim, dusty Mechanics' Institute Library (opened once a week by the old doctor) of an obscure Canadian village, nearly twenty years ago; and since that time he has seen only one copy of the book exposed for sale, and met only one person (and that not an American) who had read it. Though Kingsley has a good word for Melville, the only place where real appreciation of him is to be found of recent years is in one of Mr. Clark Russell's dedications. There occurs the phrase which gives this paper its title. Whoever takes the trouble to read this unique and original book will concede that Mr. Russell knows whereof he affirms.

Melville is a man of one book, and this fact accounts possibly for much of his unpopularity. The marked inferiority of his work after the war, as well as changes in literary fashion, would drag the rest down with it. Nor are his earliest works, embodying personal experience like *Redburn* and *White*

Jacket, quite worthy of the pen which wrote *Moby Dick*. *Omoo* and *Typee* are little more than sketches, legitimately idealized, of his own adventures in the Marquesas. They are notable works in that they are the first to reveal to civilized people the charm of life in the islands of the Pacific, the charm which is so potent in *Vailima Letters* and *The Beach of Falesà*. Again, the boundless archipelagos of Oceanica furnish the scenes of *Mardi*, his curious political satire. This contains a prophecy of the war, and a fine example of obsolete oratory in the speech of the great chief Alanno from Hio-Hio. The prologue in a whale-ship and the voyage in an open boat are, perhaps, the most interesting parts. None of his books are without distinct and peculiar excellences, but nearly all have some fatal fault. Melville's seems a case of arrested literary development. The power and promise of power in his best work are almost unbounded; but he either did not care to follow them up or he had worked out all his rifts of ore. The last years of his life he spent as a recluse.

His life fitted him to write his one book. The representative of a good old Scottish name, his portrait shows distinctively Scottish traits. The head is the sort that goes naturally with a tall, powerful figure. The forehead is broad and square; the hair is abundant; the full beard masks the mouth and chin; the general aspect is of great but disciplined strength. The eyes are level and determined; they have speculation in them. Nor does his work belie his blood. It shows the natural bent of the Scot towards metaphysics; and this thoughtfulness is one pervading quality of Melville's books. In the second place, his family had been so long established in the country (his grandfather was a member of the "Boston tea-party") that he secured the benefits of education and inherited culture: and this enlightenment was indispensable in enabling him to perceive the literary "values" of the strange men, strange scenes and strange events amongst which he was thrown. And then, he had the love of adventure which drove him forth to gather his material at the ends of the earth. He made two voyages; first as a green hand of eighteen in one of the old clipper packets to Liverpool and back; and next, as a young man of twenty-three, in a whaler. The latter was sufficiently adventurous. Wearying of sea-life, he deserted on one of the Marquesas Islands, and came near being killed and eaten by cannibal natives who kept him prisoner for four months. At last he escaped, and worked his way home on a U.S. man-o'-war. This adventure lasted four years and he went no more to sea.

After his marriage, he lived at Pittsfield for thirteen years, in close intimacy with Hawthorne, to whom he dedicated his chief work. My copy shows that it was written as early as 1851, but the title page is dated exactly twenty years later. It shows as its three chief elements this Scottish thoughtfulness, the love of literature and the love of adventure.

When Mr. Clark Russell singles out *Moby Dick* for such high praise as he bestows upon it, we think at once of other sea-stories,—his own, Marryatt's, Smollet's perhaps, and such books as Dana's *Two Years before the Mast*. But the last is a plain record of fact; in Smollet's tales, sea-life is only part of one great round of adventure; in Mr. Russell's mercantile marine, there is generally the romantic interest of the way of a man with a maid; and in Marryatt's the rise of a naval officer through various ranks plus a love-story or plenty of fun, fighting and prize-money. From all these advantages Melville not only cuts himself off, but seems to heap all sorts of obstacles in his self appointed path. Great are the prejudices to be overcome; but he triumphs over all. Whalers are commonly regarded as a sort of sea-scavengers. He convinces you that their business is poetic; and that they are finest fellows afloat.

He dispenses with a love-story altogether; there is hardly a flutter of petticoat from chapter first to last. The book is not a record of fact; but of fact idealized, which supplies the frame for a terrible duel to the death between a mad whaling-captain and a miraculous white sperm whale. It is not a love-story but a story of undying hate.

In no other tale is one so completely detached from the land, even from the very suggestion of land. Though Nantucket and New Bedford must be mentioned, only their nautical aspects are touched on; they are but the steps of the saddle-block from which the mariner vaults upon the back of his sea-horse. The strange ship "Pequod" is the theatre of all the strange adventures. For ever off soundings, she shows but as a central speck in a wide circle of blue or stormy sea; and yet a speck crammed full of human passions, the world itself in little. Comparison brings out only more strongly the unique character of the book. Whaling is the most peculiar business done by man upon the deep waters. A war-ship is but a mobile fort or battery; a merchantman is but a floating shop or warehouse: fishing is devoid of any but the ordinary perils of navigation; but sperm-whaling, according to Melville, is the most exciting and dangerous kind of big game hunting. One part of the author's triumph consists in having made the complicated operations of this strange pursuit perfectly familiar to the reader; and that not in any dull, pedantic fashion, but touched with the imagination, the humor, the fancy, the reflection of a poet. His intimate knowledge of his subject and his intense interest in it make the whaler's life in all its details not only comprehensible but fascinating.

A bare outline of the story, though it cannot suggest its peculiar charm, may arouse a desire to know more about it. The book takes its name from a monstrous, invincible, sperm whale of diabolical strength and malice. In an encounter with this leviathan, Ahab, the captain of a Nantucket whaler, has had his leg torn off. The long illness which ensues drives him mad; and his one thought upon recovery is vengeance upon the creature that has mutilated him. He gets command of the "Pequod," concealing his purpose with the cunning of insanity until the fitting moment comes: then he swears the whole crew into his fatal vendetta. From this point on, the mad captain bears down all opposition, imposes his own iron will upon the ship's company, and affects them with like heat, until they are as one keen weapon fitted to his hand and to his purpose. In spite of all difficulties, in spite of all signs and portents and warnings, human and divine, he drives on to certain destruction. Everything conduces to one end, a three day's battle with the monster, which staves and sinks the ship, like the ill-fated "Essex."

For a tale of such length, *Moby Dick* is undoubtedly well constructed. Possibly the "Town-Ho's Story," interesting as it is, somewhat checks the progress of the plot; but by the time the reader reaches this point, he is infected with the leisurely, trade-wind, whaling atmosphere, and has no desire to proceed faster than at the "Pequod's" own cruising rate. Possibly the book might be shortened by excision, but when one looks over the chapters it is hard to decide which to sacrifice. The interest begins with the quaint words of the opening sentence: "Call me Ishmael"; and never slackens for at least a hundred pages. Ishmael's reasons for going to sea, his sudden friendship with Queequeg, the Fijian harpooneer, Father Mapple's sermon on Jonah, in the seamen's bethel, Queequeg's rescue of the country bumpkin on the way to Nantucket, Queequeg's Ramadan, the description of the ship "Pequod" and her two owners, Elijah's warning, getting under way and dropping the pilot, make up an introduction of great variety and picturesqueness. The second part deals with all the particulars of the various operations in whaling from manning the mast-heads and lowering the boats to trying out the blubber and cleaning up the ship, when all the oil is barrelled. In this part Ahab, who has been invisible in the retirement of his cabin, comes on deck and in various scenes different sides of his vehement, iron-willed, yet pathetic nature, are made intelligible. Here also is much learning to be found, and here, if anywhere, the story dawdles. The last part deals with the fatal three days' chase, the death of Ahab, and the escape of the White Whale.

One striking peculiarity of the book is its Americanism— a word which needs definition. The theme and style are peculiar to this country. Nowhere but in America could such a theme have been treated in such a style. Whaling is peculiarly an American industry; and of all whale-men, the Nantucketers were the keenest, the most daring, and the most successful. Now, though there are still whalers to be found in the New Bedford slips, and interesting as it is to clamber about them and hear the unconscious confirmation of all Melville's details from the lips of some old harpooneer or boat-header, the industry is almost extinct. The discovery of petroleum did for it. Perhaps Melville went to sea for no other purpose than to construct the monument of whaling in this unique book. Not in his subject alone, but in his style is Melville distinctly American. It is large in idea, expansive; it has an Elizabethan force and freshness and swing, and is, perhaps, more rich in figures than any style but Emerson's. It has the picturesque-ness of the new world, and, above all, a free-flowing humour, which is the distinct *cachet* of American literature. No one would contend that it is a perfect style; some mannerisms become tedious, like the constant moral turn, and the curiously coined adverbs placed before the verb. Occasionally there is more than a hint of bombast, as indeed might be expected; but, upon the whole, it is an extraordinary style, rich, clear, vivid, original. It shows reading and is full of thought and allusion; but its chief charm is its freedom from all scholastic rules and conventions. Melville is a Walt Whitman of prose.

Like Browning he has a dialect of his own. The poet of *The Ring and the Book* translates the different emotions and thoughts and possible words of pope, jurist, murderer, victim, into one level uniform Browningese; reduces them to a common denominator, in a way of speaking, and Melville gives us not the actual words of American whalemen, but what they would say under the imagined conditions, translated into one consistent, though various Melvillesque manner of speech. The life he deals with belongs already to the legendary past, and he has us completely at his mercy. He is completely successful in creating his "atmosphere." Granted the condi-tions, the men and their words, emotions and actions, are all consistent. ⟨. . .⟩

The humour has the usual tinge of Northern melancholy, and sometimes a touch of Rabelais. The exhortations of Stubb to his boat's crew, on different occasions, or such chapters as "Queen Mab," "The Cassock," "Leg and Arm," "Stubb's Supper," are good examples of his peculiar style.

But, after all, his chief excellence is bringing to the landsman the very salt of the sea breeze, while to one who has long known the ocean, he is as one praising to the lover the chiefest beauties of the Beloved. The magic of the ship and the mystery of the sea are put into words that form pictures for the dullest eyes. The chapter, "The Spirit Spout," contains these two aquarelles of the moonlit sea and the speeding ship side by side:

It was while gliding through these latter waters that one serene and moonlight night, when all the waves rolled by like scrolls of silver; and by their soft, suffusing seethings made all things made what seemed a silvery silence, not a solitude; on such a silent night a silvery jet was seen far in advance of the white bubbles at the bow. Lit up by the moon it looked celestial; seemed some plumed and glittering god uprising from the sea. . . .

Walking the deck, with quick, side-lunging strides, Ahab commanded the t'gallant sails and royals to be set, and every stunsail spread. The best man in the ship must take the helm. Then, with every mast-head manned, the piled-up craft rolled down before the wind. The strange, upheaving, lifting tendency of the taffrail breeze filling the hollows of so many sails made the buoyant, hovering deck to feel like air beneath the feet.

In the chapter called "The Needle," ship and sea and sky are blended in one unforgettable whole:

Next morning the not-yet-subsided sea rolled in long, slow billows of mighty bulk, and striving in the "Pequod's" gurgling track, pushed her on like giants' palms outspread. The strong, unstaggering breeze abounded so, that sky and air seemed vast outbellying sails; the whole world boomed before the wind. Muffled in the full morning light, the invisible sun was only known by the spread intensity of his place; where his bayonet rays moved on in stacks. Emblazonings, as of crowned Babylonian kings and queens, reigned over everything. The sea was a crucible of molten gold, that bubblingly leaps with light and heat.

It would be hard to find five consecutive sentences anywhere containing such pictures and such vivid, pregnant, bold imagery: but this book is made up of such things.

The hero of the book is, after all, not Captain Ahab, but his triumphant antagonist, the mystic white monster of the sea, and it is only fitting that he should come for a moment at least into the saga. A complete scientific memoir of the Sperm Whale as known to man might be quarried from this book, for Melville has described the creature from his birth to his death, and even burial in the oil casks and the ocean. He has described him living, dead and anatomized. ⟨. . .⟩

This book is at once the epic and the encyclopaedia of whaling. It is a monument to the honour of an extinct race of daring seamen; but it is a monument overgrown with the lichen of neglect. Those who will care to scrape away the moss may be few, but they will have their reward. To the class of gentleman-adventurer, to those who love both books and free life under the wide and open sky, it must always appeal. Melville takes rank with Borrow, and Jefferies, and Thoreau, and Sir Richard Burton; and his place in this brotherhood of notables is not the lowest. Those who feel the salt in their blood that draws them time and again out of the city to the wharves and the ships, almost without their knowledge or their will; those who feel the irresistible lure of the spring, away from the cramped and noisy town, up the long road to the peaceful companionship of the awaking earth and the untainted sky; all those—and they are many—will find in Melville's great book an ever fresh and constant charm.

ALFRED, LORD TENNYSON

ALFRED, LORD TENNYSON

1809–1892

Alfred Tennyson, first baron Tennyson, was born in Somersby, Tennyshire, on August 6, 1809. He attended the Louth Grammar School between 1815 and 1820, and was subsequently educated at home by his father, the Rev. George Clayton Tennyson. In 1827 Alfred and his brother Charles published *Poems by Two Brothers*. Later that same year Alfred entered Trinity College, Cambridge, where he formed a friendship with Arthur Henry Hallam and became a member of the exclusive intellectual society "The Apostles." In 1829 Tennyson was awarded the Chancellor's Gold Medal for his poem *Timbuctoo*, and in the following year he published *Poems, Chiefly Lyrical* (1830), containing "Mariana."

In 1831, following his father's death, Tennyson left school without taking a degree. In December 1832 he published a further volume, *Poems* (dated 1833), which included "The Two Voices," "Œnone," "The Lotos-Eaters," and "A Dream of Fair Women." Tennyson's friend Arthur Henry Hallam died in Vienna in September 1833, and as a tribute to him Tennyson shortly afterwards began to compose *In Memoriam*, first published anonymously in 1850. In 1837 Tennyson moved from Somersby to High Beech, Epping, and in the following year he became engaged to Emily Sellwood; the engagement was, however, broken off in 1840, and they were not married until 1850. They had two children, Hallam and Lionel.

In 1842 Tennyson published another collection of *Poems*. Volume I included revised selections from the collections of 1830 and 1832, while Volume II comprised new work, including "Morte d'Arthur," "Locksley Hall," "Ulysses," and "St. Simeon Stylites." In 1845 Tennyson was awarded a civil list pension of £200 a year, which he received for the rest of his life. His narrative poem *The Princess* appeared in 1847, and in 1850 he was chosen to succeed Wordsworth as Poet Laureate. The *Ode on the Death of the Duke of Wellington* appeared in 1852, and was followed in 1854 by "The Charge of the Light Brigade." Also in 1854 Tennyson settled in Farringford on the Isle of Wight, where he entertained many celebrities and was visited by numerous admirers.

In 1855 Tennyson published *Maud and Other Poems*, followed in 1859 by the first four *Idylls of the King*; *Enoch Arden* appeared in 1864. In 1868 Tennyson began building a second residence, Aldworth, near Haslemere, Surrey. In 1869 he published *The Holy Grail and Other Poems* (December 1869; dated 1870), and in 1872 *Gareth and Lynette*, intended as part of the *Idylls of the King*. *Queen Mary*, Tennyson's first play, was published in 1875, and followed by other dramas, including *Harold* (1876), *The Cup* (1884), *The Falcon* (1884), and *Becket* (1884). *Ballads and Other Poems*, containing "The Voyage of Maeldune," "Rizpah," and "The Revenge," appeared in 1880. In 1883 Tennyson accepted the baronetcy he had refused in 1865, 1873, and 1874, and in 1884 he was seated in the House of Lords. *Balin and Balan*, the last of the *Idylls of the King*, although written in 1872–74, was first published in 1885, when *Tiresias and Other Poems* also appeared. In 1886 Tennyson's son Lionel died at sea. After suffering a severe illness during 1888, Tennyson in 1889 published *Demeter and Other Poems*. His play *The Foresters* appeared early in 1892, and on October 6 of that year Tennyson died at home in Surrey. *The Death of Œnone, Akbar's Dream, and Other Poems* appeared posthumously in 1892, and in 1897 Tennyson's son Hallam published a two-volume memoir.

Personal

Mrs. Clarke, Miss James, the Messrs. M——; and Alfred Tennyson dined with us. I am always a little disappointed with the exterior of our poet when I look at him, in spite of his eyes, which are very fine; but his head and face, striking and dignified as they are, are almost too ponderous and massive for beauty in so young a man; and every now and then there is a slightly sarcastic expression about his mouth that almost frightens me, in spite of his shy manner and habitual silence. But, after all, it is delightful to see and be with any one that one admires and loves for what he has done, as I do him.
—FRANCES ANN KEMBLE, *Journal* (March 16, 1832), *Record of a Girlhood*, 1878, Vol. 3, p. 209

Long have I known thee as thou art in song,
And long enjoy'd the perfume that exhales
From thy pure soul, and odour sweet entails
And permanence, on thoughts that float along

The stream of life, to join the passive throng
Of shades and echoes that are memory's being.
Hearing we hear not, and we see not seeing,
If passion, fancy, faith move not among
The never-present moments of reflection.
Long have I view'd thee in the crystal sphere
Of verse, that, like the beryl, makes appear
Visions of hope, begot of recollection.
Knowing thee now, a real earth-treading man,
Not less I love thee, and no more I can.
—HARTLEY COLERIDGE, "To Alfred Tennyson,"
1835

Three of the autographs, which I send you to-day, are first-rate. A Yankee would almost give a dollar apiece for them. Entire characteristic letters from Pickwick, Lytton Bulwer, and Alfred Tennyson; the last the greatest genius of the three, though the vulgar public have not as yet recognised him for such. Get his poems if you can, and read the 'Ulysses,' 'Dora,' the 'Vision of

Sin,' and you will find that we do not overrate him. Besides he is a very handsome man, and a noble-hearted one, with something of the gipsy in his appearance, which, for me, is perfectly charming. Babbie never saw him, unfortunately, or perhaps I should say fortunately, for she must have fallen in love with him on the spot, unless she be made absolutely of ice; and then men of genius have never anything to keep wives upon!—JANE WELSH CARLYLE, Letter to Helen Welsh (March 1843), *Letters and Memorials of Jane Welsh Carlyle*, ed. James Anthony Froude, 1883, Vol. 1, pp. 191–92

Alfred is one of the few British or Foreign Figures (a not increasing Number, I think!) who are and remain beautiful to me;—a true human soul, or some authentic approximation thereto, to whom your own soul can say, Brother!—However, I doubt he will not come; he often skips me, in these brief visits to Town; skips everybody indeed; being a man solitary and sad, as certain men are, dwelling in an element of gloom,—carrying a bit of Chaos about him, in short, which he is manufacturing into Cosmos!

   Alfred is the son of a Lincolnshire Gentleman Farmer, I think; indeed you see in his verses that he is a native of "moated granges," and green fat pastures, not of mountains and their torrents and storms. He had his breeding at Cambridge, as if for the Law, or Church; being master of a small annuity on his Father's decease, he preferred clubbing with his Mother and some Sisters, to live unpromoted and write Poems. In this way he lives still, now here now there; the family always within reach of London, never in it; he himself making rare and brief visits, lodging in some old comrade's rooms. I think he must be under forty, not much under it. One of the finest looking men in the world. A great shock of rough dusty-dark hair; bright-laughing hazel eyes; massive aquiline face, most massive yet most delicate, of sallow brown complexion, almost Indian-looking; clothes cynically loose, free-and-easy;—smokes infinite tobacco. His voice is musical metallic,—fit for loud laughter and piercing wail, and all that may lie between; speech and speculation free and plenteous: I do not meet, in these late decades, such company over a pipe!—We shall see what he will grow to. He is often unwell; very chaotic,—his way is thro' Chaos and the Bottomless and Pathless; not handy for making out many miles upon.—THOMAS CARLYLE, Letter to Ralph Waldo Emerson (Aug. 5, 1844)

I saw Tennyson, first, at the house of Coventry Patmore, where we dined together. His friend Brookfield was also of the party. I was contented with him, at once. He is tall, scholastic-looking, no dandy,—but a great deal of plain strength about him, &, though cultivated, quite unaffected.—Quiet sluggish sense & strength, refined, as all English are,—and good humoured. The print of his head in Horne's book is too rounded & handsome. There is in him an air of general superiority, that is very satisfactory. He lives very much with his college set, Spedding, Brookfield, Hallam, Rice, & the rest and has the air of one who is accustomed to be petted and indulged by those he lives with, like George Bradford. Take away Hawthorne's bashfulness, & let him talk easily & fast, & you would have a pretty good Tennyson. He had just come home from Ireland, where he had seen much vapouring of the Irish youth against England, & described a scene in some tavern, I think, where a hot young man was flourishing a drawn sword, & swearing that he would drive it to the hilt into the flesh & blood of Englishmen. Tennyson was disgusted, &, going up to the young man, took out his penknife, & offered it to him. "I am an Englishman," he said, "and there is my penknife, and, you know, you will not so much as stick that

into me." The youth was disconcerted, & said, "he knew he was not an Englishman." "Yes, but I am." Hereupon the companions of the youth interfered, & apologized for him, he had been in drink, & was excited, &c.—RALPH WALDO EMERSON, *Journal*, 1848

> I entreat you, Alfred Tennyson,
> Come and share my haunch of venison.
> I have too a bin of claret,
> Good, but better when you share it.
> Tho 'tis only a small bin,
> There's a stock of it within,
> And as sure as I'm a rhymer,
> Half a butt of Rudesheimer.
> Come; among the sons of men is one
> Welcomer than Alfred Tennyson?
> —WALTER SAVAGE LANDOR, Untitled poem, 1853

Left Ambleside by the 9.15 coach for Coniston, where I arrived a little before 12. Put up at the hotel and walked over to call at Tent Lodge, to ask leave to take the children's pictures. I asked for Mrs. Tennyson, as I had seen her before, and was shown into the drawing room. After I had waited some little time the door opened, and a strange shaggy-looking man entered: his hair, moustache and beard looked wild and neglected: these very much hid the character of the face. He was dressed in a loosely fitting morning coat, common grey flannel waist-coat and trousers, and a carelessly tied black silk neckerchief. His hair is black: I think the eyes too; they are keen and restless—nose acquiline—forehead high and broad—both face and head are fine and manly. His manner was kind and friendly from the first: there is a dry lurking humour in his style of talking.

   I was disappointed to find that they were going away tomorrow morning; however they will be back by Friday night, so I think I may yet manage the photographs. They will not return to Tent Lodge, but to the Marshalls. Mr. Tennyson took me over there to ask leave to take the pictures on their premises, which was readily granted by Mrs. Marshall, Mr. Marshall being from home. We stayed luncheon there and met a son of Mrs. Marshall's, about sixteen years old; a daughter, Julia, about eleven, and the son's tutor. The little girl has a very striking, animated face, not unlike Katie Murdoch. ⟨. . .⟩

   After luncheon Mr. Tennyson returned to the lodge, and I took a walk through Coniston, having first brought my books of photographs to Mrs. Marshall to be looked at.

   At six I went by invitation to dine at Tent Lodge, and spent a most delightful evening. I saw the little boys for a short time; I had met them in a donkey cart near Coniston during my walk. Mrs. Marshall sent over the books in the course of the evening, and Mr. and Mrs. Tennyson admired some of them so much that I have strong hopes of ultimately getting a sitting from the poet, though I have not yet ventured to ask for it.

   Some of the photographs called out a good deal of fun on Mr. Tennyson's part. The picture of Skeffington in a fishing costume, he said, had the expression, (stroking down his beard as he spoke) 'Well! I've come down here to catch trout, and if I don't catch a trout this season, the great business of my life will be gone'; and his half-length portrait 'By Jupiter! all my labour gone for nothing, and not one single trout!' The first portrait of Mr. Webster was interpreted 'Now, sir, I am ready to argue the question with you on any point—What is the particular subject you would like to discuss, predestination or what?' And the second 'Well, it may be so, or it may not: there are differences of opinion'.

   He remarked on the similarity of the monkey's skull to the human, that a young monkey's skull is quite human in shape and gradually alters—the analogy being borne out by the human skull being at first more like the statues of the gods, and gradually degenerating into human—and then, turning to Mrs. Tennyson, 'There, that's the second original remark I've made this evening!'

We talked a good deal of Ruskin, whom he seemed to have a profound contempt for as a critic, though he allowed him to be a most eloquent writer. He said that Ruskin had written to him, asking to make his acquaintance, that he had answered it in a friendly spirit, and that Ruskin had then sent him an impertinent letter, of which he had taken no notice, nor of any letter received from him since.

He threw out several hints of his wish to learn photography, but seems to be deterred by a dread of the amount of patience required. I left at what I believed to be a little after nine, but which to my horror I found to be after eleven, having had a most interesting and delightful evening. The hotel was shut up for the night, and I had to wait and ring a long while at the door.

Dies mirabilis!—LEWIS CARROLL, *Diary*, Sept. 22, 1857

Tennyson is the most picturesque figure, without affectation, that I ever saw; of middle size, rather slouching, dressed entirely in black, and with nothing white about him except the collar of his shirt, which, methought, might have been whiter the day before. He had on a black wide-awake hat, with round crown and wide, irregular brim, beneath which came down his long black hair, looking terribly tangled; he had a long pointed beard, too, a little browner than the hair, and not so abundant as to encumber any of the expression of his face. His frock coat was buttoned up across the breast, though the afternoon was warm. His face was very dark, and not exactly a smooth face, but worn, and expressing great sensitiveness, though not at that moment the pain and sorrow that is seen in his bust. His eyes were black; but I know little of them, as they did not rest on me, nor on anything but the pictures. He seemed as if he did not see the crowd, nor think of them, but as if he defended himself from them by ignoring them altogether; nor did anybody but myself cast a glance at him. ⟨. . .⟩

Knowing how much my wife would delight to see him, I went in search of her, and found her and the rest of us under the music gallery; and we all, Fanny and Rosebud included, went back to the saloon of the Old Masters. So rapid was his glance at the pictures, that in the little interval Tennyson had got half-way along the other side of the saloon, and, as it happened, an acquaintance had met him—an elderly gentleman and lady—and he was talking to them as we approached. I heard his voice,—a bass voice, but not of a resounding depth,—a voice rather broken, as it were, and ragged about the edges, but pleasant to the ear. His manner, while conversing with these people, was not in the least that of an awkward man, unaccustomed to society; but he shook hands and parted with them, evidently, as soon as he conveniently could, and shuffled away quicker than before. He betrayed his shy and secluded habits more in this than in anything else that I observed; though, indeed, in his whole presence I was indescribably sensible of a morbid painfulness in him,—a something not to be meddled with. Very soon he left the saloon, shuffling along the floor with short, irregular steps,—a very queer gait, as if he were walking in slippers too loose for him. I had observed that he seemed to turn his feet slightly inward, after the fashion of Indians.

I should be glad to smoke a cigar with him. Mr. Ireland says that, having heard he was to be at the Exhibition, and not finding him there, he conjectured that he must have gone into the Botanical Garden to smoke; and, sure enough, he found him there. He told me an anecdote about Tennyson while on a visit to Paris. He had a friend with him who could not speak very good French, any more than the poet himself. They were sitting at the fireside in the parlor of the hotel; and the friend proposed a walk about the city, and finally departed, leaving Tennyson at the fireside, and telling the waiter 'ne souffrez pas le faire sortir.' By and by Tennyson also rose to go out; but the waiter opposed him with might and main, and called another waiter to his assistance; and when Tennyson's friend returned, he found him really almost fit for a straitjacket. He might well enough pass for a madman at any time, there being a wildness in his aspect which doubtless might readily pass from quietude to frenzy. He is exceedingly nervous.—NATHANIEL HAW-THORNE (1857), cited in Julian Hawthorne, *Nathaniel Hawthorne and His Wife*, 1884, Vol. 2, pp. 143–46

After luncheon saw the great Poet *Tennyson* in dearest Albert's room for nearly an hour;—and most interesting it was. He is grown very old—his eyesight much impaired *and he is very shaky on his legs.* But he was very kind. Asked him to sit down. He talked of the many friends he had lost and what it would be if he did not feel and know that there was another World, where there would be no partings; and then he spoke with horror of the unbelievers and philosophers who would make you believe there was *no* other world, no Immortality—who tried to explain *all* away in a miserable manner. We agreed that were such a thing possible, God, who is Love, would be far more cruel than any human being. He quoted some well-known lines from Goethe whom he so much admires. Spoke of the poor Lily of Hanover so kindly—asked after my grandchildren. He spoke of Ireland with abhorrence and the wickedness in ill using poor Animals. 'I am afraid I think the world is darkened, I daresay it will brighten again.'

I told him what a comfort *In Memoriam* had again been to me which pleased him; but he said I could not believe the number of shameful letters of abuse he had received about it. Incredible! When I took leave of him, I thanked him for his kindness and said I needed it, for I had gone through so much—and he said you are so alone on the 'terrible height, it is Terrible. I've only a year or two to live but I'll be happy to do anything for you I can. Send for me whenever you like.' I thanked him warmly.—QUEEN VICTORIA, *Journal*, Aug. 7, 1883

O you that dwell 'mid farm and fold,
    Yet keep so quick undulled a heart,
I send you here that book of gold,
    So loved so long;
The fairest art,
    The sweetest English song.
And often in the far-off town,
    When summer sits with open door,
I'll dream I see you set it down
    Beside the churn,
Whose round shall slacken more and more,
    Till you forget to turn.
And I shall smile that you forget,
    And Dad will scold—but never mind!
Butter is good, but better yet,
    Think such as we,
To leave the farm and fold behind,
    And follow such as he.
    —RICHARD LE GALLIENNE, "'Tennyson' at the Farm," *English Poems*, 1892, p. 102

General

These poems ⟨*Poems, Chiefly Lyrical*⟩ are anything but heavy; anything but stiff and pedantic, except in one particular, which shall be noticed before we conclude; anything but cold and logical. They are graceful, very graceful; they are animated, touching, and impassioned. And they are so, precisely because they are philosophical; because they are not made up of metrical cant and conventional phraseology; because there is sincerity where the author writes from experience, and accuracy whether he writes from experience or observation; and he only writes from experience or observation, because he has felt and thought, and learned to analyze thought and feeling; because his own mind is rich in poetical associations, and he has wisely been content with its riches; and because, in his composition, he has not sought to construct an elaborate and artificial harmony, but only to pour forth his thoughts in those expressive and simple melodies whose meaning, truth, and power, are the soonest recognized and the longest felt.—W. J. Fox, "Tennyson's Poems," *Westminster Review*, Jan. 1831, p. 214

Mr. Tennyson belongs decidedly to the class we have already described as Poets of Sensation. He sees all the forms of nature with the "eruditus oculus," and his ear has a fairy fineness. There is a strange earnestness in his worship of beauty which throws a charm over his impassioned song, more easily felt than described, and not to be escaped by those who have once felt it. We think he has more definitiveness and roundness of general conception than the late Mr. Keats, and is much more free from blemishes of diction and hasty capriccios of fancy. He has also this advantage over that poet and his friend Shelley, that he comes before the public unconnected with any political party or peculiar system of opinions. Nevertheless, true to the theory we have stated, we believe his participation in their characteristic excellencies is sufficient to secure him a share of their unpopularity. The volume of *Poems, Chiefly Lyrical*, does not contain above 154 pages; but it shows us much more of the character of its parent mind, than many books we have known of much larger compass, and more boastful pretensions. The features of original genius are clearly and strongly marked. The author imitates nobody; we recognise the spirit of his age, but not the individual form of this or that writer. His thoughts bear no more resemblance to Byron or Scott, Shelley or Coleridge, than to Homer or Calderon, Firdúsí or Calidasa. We have remarked five distinctive excellencies of his own manner. First his luxuriance of imagination, and at the same time, his control over it. Secondly, his power of embodying himself in ideal characters, or rather moods of character, with such extreme accuracy of adjustment, that the circumstances of the narration seem to have a natural correspondence with the predominant feeling, and, as it were, to be evolved from it by assimilative force. Thirdly, his vivid, picturesque delineation of objects, and the peculiar skill with which he holds all of them *fused*, to borrow a metaphor from science, in a medium of strong emotion. Fourthly, the variety of his lyrical measures, and exquisite modulation of harmonious words and cadences to the swell and fall of the feelings expressed. Fifthly, the elevated habits of thought, implied in these compositions, and imparting a mellow soberness of tone, more impressive to our minds, than if the author had drawn up a set of opinions in verse, and sought to instruct the understanding rather than to communicate the love of beauty to the heart.—ARTHUR HENRY HALLAM, "Extract from a Review of Tennyson's Poems" (1831), *Remains in Verse and Prose*, 1863, pp. 304–5

Mr. Tennyson's admirers say he excels wondrously in personating mermen and mermaids, fairies, *et id genus omne*, inhabiting sea-caves and forest glades, "in still or stormy weather," the "gay creatures of the element," be that element air, earth, fire, or water, so that the denizens thereof be but of "imagination all compact." We beg of you to hear, for a few sentences, the quack in the Westminster. "Our author has the secret of the transmigration of the soul. He can cast his own spirit into any living thing, real or imaginary. Scarcely Vishnu himself becomes incarnate more easily, frequently, or perfectly. And there is singular refinement, as well as solid truth, in his impersonations, whether they be of inferior creatures, or of such elemental beings as sirens, as mermen, and mermaidens. He does not merely assume their external shapes, and exhibit his own mind masquerading. He takes their senses, feelings, nerves, and brain, along with their names and local habitations; still it is himself in them, modified but not absorbed by their peculiar constitution and mode of being. In the 'Merman,' one seems to feel the principle of thought injected by a strong volition into the cranium of the finny worthy, and coming under all the influences, as thinking principles do, of the physical organization to which it is for the time allied: for a moment the identification is complete; and then a consciousness of contrast springs up between the reports of external objects brought to the mind by the senses, and those which it has been accustomed to receive, and this consciousness gives to the description a most poetical colouring." We could quote another couple of critics—but as the force of nature could no farther go, and as to make one fool she joined the other two, we keep to the Westminster. It is a perfect specimen of the super-hyperbolical ultra-extravagance of outrageous Cockney eulogistic foolishness, with which not even a quantity of common sense less than nothing has been suffered, for an indivisible moment of time, to mingle; the purest mere matter of moonshine ever mouthed by an idiot-lunatic, slavering in the palsied dotage of the extremest superannuation ever inflicted on a being, long ago, perhaps, in some slight respects and low degrees human, but now sensibly and audibly reduced below the level of the Pongos. "Coming under all the influences, as thinking principles do, of the physical organization to which it is for the time allied!" There is a bit of Cockney materialism for you! "The principle of thought injected by a strong volition into the cranium of the finny worthy!" Written like the Son of a Syringe. O the speculative sumph! 'Tis thus that dishonest Cockneys would fain pass off in their own vile slang, and for their own viler meaning, murdered and dismembered, the divine Homeric philosophy of the Isle of Circe. Was not Jupiter still Jove— aye, every inch the thunderous king of heaven, whose throne was Olympus—while to languishing Leda the godhead seemed a Swan? In the eyes of a grazier, who saw but Smithfield, he would have been but a bull in the Rape of Europa. Why, were the Cockney critic's principle of thought injected by a strong volition into the skull of a donkey—has he vanity to imagine, for a moment, that he would be a more consummate ass than he now brays? Or if into that of the Great Glasgow Gander, that his quackery would be more matchless still? O no, no, no! He would merely be "assuming their external shapes;" but his asinine and anserine natural endowments would all remain unchanged—a greater goose than he now is, depend upon it, he could not be, were he for a tedious lifetime to keep waddling his way through this weary world on web-feet, and with uplifted wings and outstretched neck, hissing the long-red-round-cloaked beggar off the common; a superior ass he might in no ways prove, though untethered in the lane where gipsy gang had encraal'd, he were left free to roam round the canvass walls, eminent among all the "animals that chew the thistle."—JOHN WILSON, "Tennyson's Poems," *Blackwood's Edinburgh Magazine*, May 1832, pp. 728–29

I have not read through all Mr. Tennyson's poems, which have been sent to me; but I think there are some things of a good deal of beauty in what I have seen. The misfortune is, that he has begun to write verses without very well understanding what metre is. Even if you write in a known and approved metre, the odds are, if you are not a metrist yourself, that you will not write harmonious verses; but to deal in new metres without considering what metre means and requires, is preposterous. What I would, with many wishes for success, prescribe to Tennyson,—indeed without it he can never be a poet in act,— is to write for the next two or three years in none but one or two well-known and strictly defined metres, such as the heroic couplet, the octave stanza, or the octosyllabic measure of the "Allegro" and "Penseroso." He would, probably, thus get imbued with a sensation, if not a sense, of metre without knowing it, just as Eton boys get to write such good Latin verses by conning Ovid and Tibullus. As it is, I can scarcely scan his verses.—SAMUEL TAYLOR COLERIDGE, *Table Talk*, April 24, 1833

I have just been reading the new poems of Tennyson. Much has he thought, much suffered, since the first ecstasy of so fine an organization clothed all the world with rosy light. He has not suffered himself to become a mere intellectual voluptuary, nor the songster of fancy and passion, but has earnestly revolved the problems of life, and his conclusions are calmly noble. In these later verses is a still, deep sweetness; how different from the intoxicating, sensuous melody of his earlier cadence! I have loved him much this time, and taken him to heart as a brother. One of his themes has long been my favorite,—the last expedition of Ulysses,—and his, like mine, is the Ulysses of the *Odyssey*, with his deep romance of wisdom, and not the worldling of the *Iliad*. How finely marked his slight description of himself and of Telemachus. In "Dora," "Locksley Hall," the "Two Voices," "Morte D'Arthur," I find my own life, much of it, written truly out.—MARGARET FULLER, *Journal* (Aug. 1842), *Memoirs*, 1852, Vol. 2, p. 66

Tennyson is more simply the songster than any poet of our time. With him the delight of musical expression is first, the thought second. It was well observed by one of our companions, that he has described just what we should suppose to be his method of composition in this verse from "The Miller's Daughter."

> A love-song I had somewhere read,
> An echo from a measured strain,
>   Beat time to nothing in my head
>   From some odd corner of the brain.
> It haunted me, the morning long,
>   With weary sameness in the rhymes,
> *The phantom of a silent song,*
>   *That went and came a thousand times.*

So large a proportion of even the good poetry of our time is either over-ethical or over-passionate, and the stock poetry is so deeply tainted with a sentimental egotism, that this, whose chief merits lay in its melody and picturesque power, was most refreshing. What a relief, after sermonizing and wailing had dulled the sense with such a weight of cold abstraction, to be soothed by this ivory lute!

Not that he wanted nobleness and individuality in his thoughts, or a due sense of the poet's vocation; but he won us to truths, not forced them upon us; as we listened, the cope

> Of the self-attained futurity
> Was cloven with the million stars which tremble
> O'er the deep mind of dauntless infamy.

And he seemed worthy thus to address his friend,

> Weak truth a-leaning on her crutch,
> Wan, wasted truth in her utmost need,
> Thy kingly intellect shall feed,
> Until she be an athlete bold.

Unless thus sustained, the luxurious sweetness of his verse must have wearied. Yet it was not of aim or meaning we thought most, but of his exquisite sense for sounds and melodies, as marked by himself in the description of Cleopatra.

> Her warbling voice, a lyre of widest range,
> Touched by all passion, did fall down and glance
> From tone to tone, and glided through all change
> Of liveliest utterance.

Or in the fine passage in the "Vision of Sin," where

> Then the music touched the gates and died;
> Rose again from where it seemed to fail,
> Stormed in orbs of song, a growing gale; &c.

Or where the Talking Oak composes its serenade for the pretty Alice;—but indeed his descriptions of melody are almost as abundant as his melodies, though the central music of the poet's mind is, he says, as that of the

>   fountain
>   Like sheet lightning,
>   Ever brightening
> With a low melodious thunder;
> All day and all night it is ever drawn
> From the brain of the purple mountain
> Which stands in the distance yonder:
> It springs on a level of bowery lawn,
> And the mountain draws it from heaven above,
> And it sings a song of undying love.

Next to his music, his delicate, various, gorgeous music, stands his power of picturesque representation. And his, unlike those of most poets, are eye-pictures, not mind-pictures. And yet there is no hard or tame fidelity, but a simplicity and ease at representation (which is quite another thing from reproduction) rarely to be paralleled. How, in the "Palace of Art," for instance, they are unrolled slowly and gracefully, as if painted one after another on the same canvass. The touch is calm and masterly, though the result is looked at with a sweet, self-pleasing eye. Who can forget such as this, and of such there are many, painted with as few strokes and with as complete a success?

> A still salt pool, locked in with bars of sand;
>   Left on the shore; that hears all night
> The plunging seas draw backward from the land
>   Their moon-led waters white.

Tennyson delights in a garden. Its groups, and walks, and mingled bloom intoxicate him, and us through him. So high is his organization, and so powerfully stimulated by color and perfume, that it heightens all our senses too, and the rose is glorious, not from detecting its ideal beauty, but from a perfection of hue and scent, we never felt before. All the earlier poems are flower-like, and this tendency is so strong in him, that a friend observed, he could not keep up the character of the tree in his Oak of Summer Chase, but made it talk like an "enormous flower." The song,

A spirit haunts the year's last hours,

is not to be surpassed for its picture of the autumnal garden.
—RALPH WALDO EMERSON, *Dial*, April 1843

Of all the successors of Shelley, he possesses the most sureness of insight. He has a subtle mind, of keen, passionless vision. His poetry is characterized by intellectual intensity as distinguished from the intensity of feeling. He watches his consciousness with a cautious and minute attention, to fix, and condense, and shape into form, the vague and mystical shadows of thought and feeling which glide and flit across it. He listens to catch the lowest whisperings of the soul. His imagination broods over the spiritual and mystical elements of his being with the most concentrated power. His eye rests firmly on an object until it changes from film into form. Some of his poems are forced into artistical shape by the most patient and painful intellectual processes. His utmost strength is employed on those mysterious facts of consciousness which form the staple of the dreams and reveries of others. His mind winds through the mystical labyrinths of thought and feeling, with every power awake, in action, and wrought up to the highest pitch of intensity. The most acute analysis is followed, step by step, by a suggestive imagination, which converts refined abstractions into pictures, or makes them audible to the soul through the most cunning combinations of sound. Everything that is done is the result of labor. There is hardly a stanza in his writings but was introduced to serve some particular purpose, and could not be omitted without injury to the general effect. Everything has meaning. Every idea was won in a fair conflict with darkness, or dissonance, or gloom. The simplicity, the barrenness of ornament, in some of his lines, are as much the result of contrivance as his most splendid images. With what labor, for instance, with what attentive watching of consciousness, must the following stanza have been wrought into shape:—

> All those sharp fancies, by down-lapsing thought
> Streamed onward, lost their edges, and did creep,
> Rolled on each other, rounded, smoothed and brought
> Into the gulfs of sleep.

This intense intellectual action is displayed in his delineations of nature and individual character, as well as in his subjective gropings into the refinements of his consciousness. In describing scenery, his microscopic eye and marvellously delicate ear are exercised to the utmost in detecting the minutest relations and most evanescent melodies of the objects before him, in order that his representation shall include everything which is important to their full perception. His pictures of English rural scenery, among the finest in the language, give the inner spirit as well as the outward form of the objects, and represent them, also, in their relation to the mind which is gazing on them. But nothing is spontaneous; the whole is wrought out elaborately by patient skill. The picture in his mind is spread out before his detecting and dissecting intellect, to be transferred to words only when it can be done with the most refined exactness, both as regards color, and form, and melody. He takes into calculation the nature of his subject, and decides whether it shall be definitely expressed in images, or indefinitely through tone, or whether both modes shall be combined. His object is expression, in its true sense; to reproduce in other minds the imagination or feeling which lies in his own; and he adopts the method which seems best calculated to effect it. He never will trust himself to the impulses of passion, even in describing passion. All emotion, whether turbulent or evanescent, is passed through his intel-

lect, and curiously scanned. To write furiously would to him appear as ridiculous, and as certainly productive of confusion, as to paint furiously, or carve furiously. We only appreciate his art when we consider that many of his finest conceptions and most sculptural images originally appeared in his consciousness as formless and mysterious emotions, having seemingly no symbols in nature or thought.

If our position is correct, then most certainly nothing can be more incorrect than to call any poem of Tennyson's unmeaning. Such a charge simply implies a lack in the critic's mind, not in the poet's. The latter always *means* something in everything he writes; and the form in which it is embodied is chosen with the most careful deliberation. It seems to us that the purely intellectual element in Tennyson's poetry has been overlooked, owing perhaps to the fragility of some of his figures, and the dreaminess of outline apparent in others. Many think him to be a mere rhapsodist, fertile in nothing but a kind of melodious empiricism. No opinion is more contradicted by the fact. There are few authors who will bear the probe of analysis better.

The poetry of Tennyson is, moreover, replete with magnificent pictures, flushed with the finest hues of language, and speaking to the eye and the mind with the vividness of reality. We not only see the object, but feel the associations connected with it. His language is penetrated with imagination; and the felicity of his epithets, especially, leaves nothing to desire. "Godiva" combines simplicity of feeling with a subtle intensity of imagination, which remind us half of Chaucer and half of Shelley. Like the generality of Tennyson's poems, though short, it contains elements of interest capable of being expanded into a much larger space. But the poem which probably displays to the best advantage his variety of power is "The Gardener's Daughter." It is flushed throughout with the most ethereal imagination, though the incidents and emotions come home to the common heart, and there is little appearance of elaboration in the style. It is bathed in beauty—perfect as a whole, and finished in the nicest details with consummate art. There is a seeming copiousness of expression with a real condensation; and the most minute threads of thought and feeling,—so refined as to be overlooked in a careless perusal, yet all having relation to the general effect,—are woven into the texture of the style with the most admirable felicity. "Locksley Hall," "Ænone," "The May Queen," "Ulysses," "The Lotos-Eaters," "The Lady of Shalott," "Mariana," "Dora," "The Two Voices," "The Dream of Fair Women," "The Palace of Art," all different, all representing a peculiar phase of nature or character, are still all characterized by the cunning workmanship of a master of expression, giving the most complete form to the objects which his keen vision perceives. The melody of verse, which distinguishes all, ranging from the deepest organ tones to that

> Music which gentlier on the spirit lies
> Than tired eyelids upon tired eyes,

is also of remarkable beauty, and wins and winds its way to the very fountains of thought and feeling.—EDWIN P. WHIPPLE, "English Poets of the Nineteenth Century" (1845), *Essays and Reviews*, 1850, Vol. 1, pp. 339–42

We do not expect that he will ever produce any great work; his mind is unequal to a long flight; he is master of one or two instruments, and his power over them is perfect; his orchestra is not, however, full enough to bring out that mighty volume of sound which sleeps in the Epic and the Drama. His last production, *The Princess, a Medley*, has been a great disappointment to his friends, as it convinces them he is unequal to a sustained undertaking. We do not see why they should be surprised or grieved at the failure; this is not an age for long narratives, it is essentially the "age of emphasis," every production now must be intensed. Men will not sit to be lectured or read asleep; they want to be aroused, excited and kept awake. They do not look for instruction, they demand power and sensation!—delight is their object, not quiescence or tranquillity. Soothing syrups are past: electrical flashes are in vogue. —THOMAS POWELL, "Alfred Tennyson," *The Living Authors of England*, 1849, p. 48

⟨. . .⟩ in perfect sincerity I regard him as the noblest poet that ever lived ⟨. . .⟩ I call him, and *think* him the noblest of poets— *not* because the impressions he produces are, at *all* times, the most profound—*not* because the poetical excitement which he induces is, at *all* times, the most intense—but because it *is*, at all times, the most ethereal—in other words, the most elevating and the most pure.—EDGAR ALLAN POE, "The Poetic Principle" (1850), *Essays and Reviews*, ed. G. R. Thompson, 1984, p. 92

In Memoriam, Maud, "The Miller's Daughter," and such like will always be my own pet rhymes, yet I am quite prepared to admit this to be as good as any, for its own peculiar audience. Treasures of wisdom there are in it, and word-painting such as never was yet for concentration, nevertheless it seems to me that so great power ought not to be spent on visions of things past but on the living present. For one hearer capable of feeling the depth of this poem I believe ten would feel a depth quite as great if the stream flowed through things nearer the hearer. And merely in the facts of modern life, not drawing-room formal life, but the far away and quite unknown growth of souls in and through any form of misery or servitude, there is an infinity of what men should be told, and what none but a poet can tell. I cannot but think that the intense masterful and unerring transcript of an actuality, and the relation of a story of any real human life as a poet would watch and analyze it, would make all men feel more or less what poetry was, as they felt what Life and Fate were in their instant workings.

This seems to me the true task of the modern poet. And I think I have seen faces, and heard voices by road and street side, which claimed or conferred as much as ever the loveliest or saddest of Camelot. As I watch them, the feeling continually weighs upon me, day by day, more and more, that not the grief of the world but the loss of it is the wonder of it. I see creatures so full of all power and beauty, with none to understand or teach or save them. The making in them of miracles and all cast away, for ever lost as far as we can trace. And no "in memoriam." —JOHN RUSKIN, Letter to Alfred, Lord Tennyson (1860), cited in Hallam Tennyson, *Alfred Lord Tennyson: A Memoir*, 1897, Vol. 1, pp. 453–54

Tennyson is a most distinguished and charming poet; but the very essential characteristic of his poetry is, it seems to me, an extreme subtlety and curious elaborateness of thought, an extreme subtlety and curious elaborateness of expression. In the best and most characteristic productions of his genius, these characteristics are most prominent. They are marked characteristics, as we have seen, of the Elizabethan poets; they are marked, though not the essential, characteristics of Shakspeare himself. Under the influences of the nineteenth century, under wholly new conditions of thought and culture, they manifest themselves in Mr. Tennyson's poetry in a wholly new way. But they are still there. The essential bent of his poetry is towards such expressions as—

Now lies the Earth all Danaë to the stars;

O'er the sun's bright eye

Drew the vast eyelid of an inky cloud;
When the cairned mountain was a shadow, sunned
The world to peace again;
The fresh young captains flashed their glittering teeth,
The huge bush-bearded barons heaved and blew;
He bared the knotted column of his throat,
The massive square of his heroic breast,
And arms on which the standing muscle sloped
As slopes a wild brook o'er a little stone,
Running too vehemently to break upon it.

And this way of speaking is the least *plain*, the most *un-Homeric*, which can possibly be conceived. Homer presents his thought to you just as it wells from the source of his mind: Mr. Tennyson carefully distils his thought before he will part with it. Hence comes, in the expression of the thought, a heightened and elaborate air. In Homer's poetry it is all natural thoughts in natural words; in Mr. Tennyson's poetry it is all distilled thoughts in distilled words. Exactly this heightening and elaboration may be observed in Mr. Spedding's

While the steeds *mouthed their corn aloof*,

(an expression which might have been Mr. Tennyson's) on which I have already commented; and to one who is penetrated with a sense of the real simplicity of Homer, this subtle sophistication of the thought is, I think, very perceptible even in such lines as these,—

And drunk delight of battle with my peers,
Far on the ringing plains of windy Troy,—

which I have seen quoted as perfectly Homeric. Perfect simplicity can be obtained only by a genius of which perfect simplicity is an essential characteristic.—MATTHEW ARNOLD, *On Translating Homer: Last Words*, 1862

Yes, Tennyson is a greatly successful, but he is not a great poet. The next age will surely reverse the verdict of this. He is sugar sweet, pretty-pretty, full of womanly talk and feminine stuff. Lilian, Dora, Clara, Emmeline—you can count up thirty such pretty names, but you cannot count any great poem of the Laureate's. Shelley has his "Ode to the Skylark," Keats his to the Grecian Urn, Coleridge his Geneviéve," his weird *Ancient Mariner*, Wordsworth that touching, yea, aching sublimity on the "Intimations of Immortality"—where is there one thing of Tennyson which can approach that? He has kept himself aloof from men; he has polished his poems till all are ripe and rotten; he has no fire and no fault; he has never lifted one to Heaven nor plunged us to the lower depths. He has no creed, no faith, no depth. When another poet would bare his heart he talks of his pulses:

My *pulses*—therefore beat again
For other friends that once I met;
Nor can it suit me to forget
The mighty hopes that make us men.

What a grand line is that last, and what a feeble beast crawls on its belly before it! Can we forgive a poet "suiting to forget" Heaven, Hell, Christ and His Death upon the Cross, His agony and bloody sweat?—Heavens, that a Christian poet should be found lisping out *that*!

No, he is no great poet. Mr. Tennyson has been very discreet, and a very good Court poet,—for a manufactured article really none better; but he is like the lady who did not want to "look frightful when dead," and so put on the paint and the fucus, and he will take no deep hold of the world. What did sweet Will Shakespeare do? Did he not say that he had

gored mine own thoughts;
Sold cheap what is most dear,
And made myself a motley to the view.

Did he not give us blood and passion with his poetry? But what says Tennyson: "Nor can it suit me to forget" that I am admired by all young ladies, and am a Laureate. Further he adds,

I count it crime
To mourn for any overmuch.

And posterity will count it folly to place a half-hearted and polished rhymster amongst her shining great ones who were fellows with poverty and disrespect in this life, and who learnt in suffering that they might teach in song.—J. HAIN FRISWELL, "Mr. Alfred Tennyson," *Modern Men of Letters Honestly Criticised*, 1870, pp. 155–56

The great task of an artist is to find subjects which suit his talent. Tennyson has not always succeeded in this. His long poem, *In Memoriam*, written in praise and memory of a friend who died young, is cold, monotonous, and often too prettily arranged. He goes into mourning; but, like a correct gentleman, with brand-new gloves, wipes away his tears with a cambric handkerchief, and displays throughout the religious service, which ends the ceremony, all the compunction of a respectful and well-trained layman. He was to find his subjects elsewhere. To be poetically happy is the object of a dilettante-artist. For this many things are necessary. First of all, that the place, the events, and the characters shall not exist. Realities are coarse, and always, in some sense, ugly; at least they are heavy; we do not treat them at our pleasure, they oppress the fancy; at bottom there is nothing truly sweet and beautiful in our life but our dreams. We are ill at ease whilst we remain glued to earth, hobbling along on our two feet, which drag us wretchedly here and there in the place which impounds us. We need to live in another world, to hover in the wide-air kingdom, to build palaces in the clouds, to see them rise and crumble, to follow in a hazy distance the whims of their moving architecture, and the turns of their golden volutes. In this fantastic world, again, all must be pleasant and beautiful, the heart and senses must enjoy it, objects must be smiling or picturesque, sentiments delicate or lofty; no crudity, incongruity, brutality, savageness must come to sully with its excess the modulated harmony of this ideal perfection. This leads the poet to the legends of chivalry. Here is the fantastic world, splendid to the sight, noble and specially pure, in which love, war, adventures, generosity, courtesy, all spectacles and all virtues which suit the instincts of our European races, are assembled, to furnish them with the epic which they love, and the model which suits them.—HIPPOLYTE TAINE, *History of English Literature*, tr. H. Van Laun, 1871, Bk. 5, Ch. 6

Poet! I come to touch thy lance with mine;
Not as a knight, who on the listed field
Of tourney touched his adversary's shield
In token of defiance, but in sign
Of homage to the mastery, which is thine,
In English song; nor will I keep concealed,
And voiceless as a rivulet frost-congealed,
My admiration for thy verse divine.
Not of the howling dervishes of song,
Who craze the brain with their delirious dance,
Art thou, O sweet historian of the heart!
Therefore to thee the laurel-leaves belong,
To thee our love and our allegiance,
For thy allegiance to the poet's art.
—HENRY WADSWORTH LONGFELLOW, "Wapen-

take: To Alfred Tennyson," A *Book of Sonnets*, 1873

The course of progressive politics (democracy) is so certain and resistless, not only in America but in Europe, that we can well afford the warning calls, threats, checks, neutralizings, in imaginative literature, or any department, of such deep-sounding and high-soaring voices as Carlyle's and Tennyson's. Nay, the blindness, excesses, of the prevalent tendency—the dangers of the urgent trends of our times—in my opinion, need such voices almost more than any. I should, too, call it a signal instance of democratic humanity's luck that it has such enemies to contend with—so candid, so fervid, so heroic. But why do I say enemies? Upon the whole is not Tennyson—and was not Carlyle (like an honest and stern physician)—the true friend of our age?

Let me assume to pass verdict, or perhaps momentary judgment, for the United States on this poet—a remov'd and distant position giving some advantages over a nigh one. What is Tennyson's service to his race, times, and especially to America? First, I should say—or at least not forget—his personal character. He is not to be mention'd as a rugged, evolutionary, aboriginal force—but (and a great lesson is in it) he has been consistent throughout with the native, healthy, patriotic spinal element and promptings of himself. His moral line is local and conventional, but it is vital and genuine. He reflects the upper-crust of his time, its pale cast of thought—even its *ennui*. Then the simile of my friend John Burroughs is entirely true, 'his glove is a glove of silk, but the hand is a hand of iron.' He shows how one can be a royal laureate, quite elegant and 'aristocratic,' and a little queer and affected, and at the same time perfectly manly and natural. As to his non-democracy, it fits him well, and I like him the better for it. I guess we all like to have (I am sure I do) some one who presents those sides of a thought, or possibility, different from our own—different and yet with a sort of home-likeness—a tartness and contradiction offsetting the theory as we view it, and construed from tastes and proclivities not at all his own.

To me, Tennyson shows more than any poet I know (perhaps has been a warning to me) how much there is in finest verbalism. There is such a latent charm in mere words, cunning collocations, and in the voice ringing them, which he has caught and brought out, beyond all others—as in the line,

And hollow, hollow, hollow, all delight,

in 'The Passing of Arthur,' and evidenced in 'The Lady of Shalott,' 'The Deserted House,' and many other pieces. Among the best (I often linger over them again and again) are 'Lucretius,' 'The Lotos Eaters,' and 'The Northern Farmer.' His mannerism is great, but it is a noble and welcome mannerism. His very best work, to me, is contain'd in the books of *The Idyls of the King*, and all that has grown out of them. Though indeed we could spare nothing of Tennyson, however small or however peculiar—not 'Break, Break,' nor 'Flower in the Crannied Wall,' nor the old, eternally-told passion of 'Edward Gray:'

Love may come and love may go,
And fly like a bird from tree to tree.
But I will love no more, no more
Till Ellen Adair come back to me.

Yes, Alfred Tennyson's is a superb character, and will help give illustriousness, through the long roll of time, to our Nineteenth Century. In its bunch of orbic names, shining like a constellation of stars, his will be one of the brightest. His very faults, doubts, swervings, doublings upon himself, have been typical of our age. We are like the voyagers of a ship, casting off for new seas, distant shores. We would still dwell in the old suffocating and dead haunts, remembering and magnifying their pleasant experiences only, and more than once impell'd to jump ashore before it is too late, and stay where our fathers stay'd, and live as they lived.

May-be I am non-literary and non-decorous (let me at least be human, and pay part of my debt) in this word about Tennyson. I want him to realize that here is a great and ardent Nation that absorbs his songs, and has a respect and affection for him personally, as almost for no other foreigner. I want this word to go to the old man at Farringford as conveying no more than the simple truth; and that truth (a little Christmas gift) no slight one either. I have written impromptu, and shall let it all go at that. The readers of more than fifty millions of people in the New World not only owe to him some of their most agreeable and harmless and healthy hours, but he has enter'd into the formative influences of character here, not only in the Atlantic cities, but inland and far West, out in Missouri, in Kansas, and away in Oregon, in farmer's house and miner's cabin.

Best thanks, anyhow, to Alfred Tennyson—thanks and appreciation in America's name.—WALT WHITMAN, "A Word about Tennyson" (1887), *Prose Works*, ed. Floyd Stovall, 1964, Vol. 2, pp. 570–72

Let us attempt to get rid of every bias and, thinking as dispassionately as we can, we still seem to read the name of Tennyson in the golden book of English poetry. I cannot think that he will ever fall to a lower place, or be among those whom only curious students pore over, like Gower, Drayton, Donne, and the rest. Lovers of poetry will always read him as they will read Wordsworth, Keats, Milton, Coleridge, and Chaucer. Look his defects in the face, throw them into the balance, and how they disappear before his merits! He is the last and youngest of the mighty race, born, as it were, out of due time, late, and into a feebler generation.

Let it be admitted that the gold is not without alloy, that he has a touch of voluntary affectation, of obscurity, even an occasional perversity, a mannerism, a set of favourite epithets ('windy' and 'happy'). There is a momentary echo of Donne, of Crashaw, nay, in his earliest pieces, even a touch of Leigh Hunt. You detect it in pieces like 'Lilian' and 'Eleanore,' and the others of that kind and of that date.

Let it be admitted that *In Memoriam* has certain lapses in all that meed of melodious tears; that there are trivialities which might deserve (here is an example) 'to line a box,' or to curl some maiden's locks, that there are weaknesses of thought, that the poet now speaks of himself as a linnet, singing 'because it must,' now dares to approach questions insoluble, and again declines their solution. What is all this but the changeful mood of grief? The singing linnet, like the bird in the old English heathen apologue, dashes its light wings painfully against the walls of the chamber into which it has flown out of the blind night that shall again receive it.

I do not care to dwell on the imperfections in that immortal strain of sympathy and consolation, that enchanted book of consecrated regrets. It is an easier if not more grateful task to note a certain peevish egotism of tone in the heroes of 'Locksley Hall,' of *Maud*, of 'Lady Clara Vere de Vere.' 'You can't think how poor a figure you make when you tell that story, sir,' said Dr. Johnson to some unlucky gentleman whose 'figure' must certainly have been more respectable than that which is cut by these whining and peevish lovers of Maud and Cousin Amy.

Let it be admitted, too, that King Arthur, of the *Idyls*, is like an Albert in blank verse, an Albert cursed with a Guinevere for a wife, and a Lancelot for friend. The *Idyls*, with all their beauties, are full of a Victorian respectability, and love of talking with Vivien about what is not so respectable. One wishes, at times, that the 'Morte d'Arthur' had remained a lonely and flawless fragment, as noble as Homer, as polished as Sophocles. But then we must have missed, with many other admirable things, the 'Last Battle in the West.'

People who come after us will be more impressed than we are by the Laureate's versatility. He has touched so many strings, from 'Will Waterproof's Monologue,' so far above Praed, to the agony of 'Rizpah,' the invincible energy of 'Ulysses,' the languor and the fairy music of the 'Lotus Eaters,' the grace as of a Greek epigram which inspires the lines to Catullus and to Virgil. He is with Milton for learning, with Keats for magic and vision, with Virgil for graceful recasting of ancient golden lines, and even in the latest volume of his long life, 'we may tell from the straw,' as Homer says, 'what the grain has been.'—ANDREW LANG, "Introductory: Of Modern English Poetry," *Letters on Literature*, 1889, pp. 4–8

If, then, we might take Tennyson as an example of the result of the action of democracy upon literature, we might indeed congratulate ourselves. But a moment's reflection shows that to do so is to put the cart before the horse. The wide appreciation of such delicate and penetrating poetry is, indeed, an example of the influence of literature on democracy, but hardly of democracy on literature. We may examine the series of Tennyson's volumes with care, and scarcely discover a copy of verses in which he can be detected as directly urged to expression by the popular taste. This prime favourite of the educated masses never courted the public, nor strove to serve it. He wrote to please himself, to win the applause of the "little clan," and each round of salvos from the world outside seemed to startle him in his obstinate retirement. If it grew easier and easier for him to consent to please the masses, it was because he familiarised them more and more with his peculiar accent. He led literary taste, he did not dream of following it.—EDMUND GOSSE, "The Influence of Democracy" (1891), *Questions at Issue*, 1893, p. 40

The land whose loveliness in verse of thine
    Shows lovelier yet than prank'd on Nature's page
    Shall prove *thy* poet in some future age,
    Sing thee—*her* poet—not in measured line
Or metric stave, but music more benign;
    Shall point to British Galahads who wage
    Battle on wrong; to British maids who gage,
    Like Agnes, heart and hope to love divine.
Worn men like thy Ulysses, scorning fear,
    Shall tempt strange seas beneath an alien star;
    Old men from honored homes and faces dear
Summoned by death to realms unknown and far
    Thy "Silent Voices" from on high shall hear;
    With happier auspice cross the "Harbour Bar."
        —AUBREY DE VERE, "To Alfred Tennyson,"
        Century Magazine, May 1893, p. 37

The gifts by which Tennyson has won, and will keep, his place among the great poets of England are pre-eminently those of an artist. His genius for vivid and musical expression was joined to severe self-restraint, and to a patience which allowed nothing to go forth from him until it had been refined to the utmost perfection that he was capable of giving to it. And his 'law of pure and flawless workmanship' (as Matthew Arnold defines the artistic quality in poetry) embraced far more than language: the same instinct controlled his composition in the larger sense;

it is seen in the symmetry of each work as a whole, in the due subordination of detail, in the distribution of light and shade, in the happy and discreet use of ornament. His versatility is not less remarkable: no English poet has left masterpieces in so many different kinds of verse. On another side the spiritual subtlety of the artist is seen in the power of finding words for dim and fugitive traits of consciousness; as the artist's vision, at once minute and imaginative, is seen in his pictures of nature. By this varied and consummate excellence Tennyson ranks with the great artists of all time.

This is the dominant aspect of his poetry. But there is another which presents itself as soon as we take the historical point of view, and inquire into the nature of his influence upon his age. Tennyson was not primarily, like Wordsworth, a philosophical thinker, who felt called upon to be a teacher. But from the middle of the century onwards he was the accepted poet, in respect to thought on religion and on many social questions, of that large public which might be described as the world of cultivated and moderately liberal orthodoxy. Multitudes of these readers were imperfectly capable of appreciating him as an artist: have not some of them been discussing who is 'the Pilot' in 'Crossing the Bar'? But at any rate they heard a voice which they could generally understand; they felt that it was beautiful and noble; and they loved it because it soothed and elevated them. They cherished a poet who placed the centre of religion in a simple reliance on the divine love; who taught that, through all struggles and perplexities, the time was being guided towards some final good; who saw the results of science not as dangers but as reinforcements to faith; who welcomed material progress and industrial vigour, but always sought to maintain the best traditions of English history and character. Now, this popular element in Tennyson's fame—as it may be called relatively to those elements which sprang from a full appreciation of his art—was not due to any conscious self-adaptation on his part to prevailing currents of thought and feeling. It arose from the peculiar relation of his genius to the period in which he grew up to manhood. His early youth was in England a day of bright dreams and confident auguries; for democracy and steam, all things were to be possible. Then came the reaction; doubts and difficulties thickened; questions started up in every field, bringing with them unrest, discouragement, or even despair. At such a season the poet who is pre-eminently an artist has a twofold opportunity; by creating beauty he can comfort the weary; but a yet higher task is to exercise, through his art, an ennobling and harmonizing influence on those more strenuous yet half-desponding spirits who bear the stress of the transition, while new and crude energies are threatening an abrupt breach with the past. It is a great work to do for a people, to win the popular ear at such a time for counsels of reverence and chivalry; to make them feel that these things are beautiful, and are bonds of the national life, while the forces that tend to disintegration are also tending to make the people sordid and cynical. This is the work that Sophocles, in his later years, did for Athens, and this is what Tennyson did for the England of his prime.—R. C. JEBB, "Alfred, Lord Tennyson," *The English Poets*, ed. Thomas Humphry Ward (1880), 1894, Vol. 4, pp. 755–57

⟨. . .⟩ if the whole of English poetry is not to-day unmitigatedly pre-Raphaelite, it is due merely to the fortunate accident that, contemporaneously with the pre-Raphaelites, so sound a poet as Tennyson has lived and worked. The official honours bestowed on him as Poet Laureate, his unexampled success among readers, pointed him out to a part at least of the petty strugglers and aspirants as worthy of imitation, and so it comes

about that among the chorus of the lily-bearing mystics there are also heard other street-singers who follow the poet of the *Idylls of the King.*—MAX NORDAU, *Degeneration*, 1895, p. 99

⟨. . .⟩ I do not think that any one can ever have had and maintained a greater admiration for the author of "The Lotos-Eaters" than I have. This admiration was born early, but it was not born full grown. I am so old a Tennysonian that though I can only vaguely remember talk about *Maud* at the time of its first appearance, I can remember the *Idylls* themselves fresh from the press. I was, however, a little young then to appreciate Tennyson, and it must have been a year or two later that I began to be fanatical on the subject. Yet there must have been a little method in that youthful madness,—some criticism in that craze. A great many years afterwards I came across the declaration of Edward FitzGerald, one of the poet's oldest and fastest friends, to the effect that everything he had written after 1842 was a falling off. That, of course, was a crotchet. FitzGerald, like all men of original but not very productive genius who live much alone, was a crotcheteer to the *n*th. But it has a certain root of truth in it; and as I read it I remembered what my own feelings had been on reading *Enoch Arden*, the first volume that came out after I had enrolled myself in the sacred band. It was just at the end of my freshman's year; and I bought a copy of the book (for which there had been some waiting, and a tremendous rush) on my way home from the prize-giving of my old school. To tell the truth, I was a little disappointed. For *Enoch Arden* itself, as a whole, I have never cared, despite the one splendid passage describing the waiting in the island; nor for "Aylmer's Field"; nor for divers other things. "The Voyage" was of the very best, and "In the Valley at Cauterets," and one or two other things. "Boadicea" was an interesting experiment. But on the whole one was inclined to say, Where is "The Lotos-Eaters"? Where is the "Dream of Fair Women"? Where is "The Palace of Art"?

Perhaps they were nowhere; perhaps only in the very best of the *Ballads* of 1880, and once or twice later, did the poet ever touch the highest points of his first fine raptures. But he never failed, even to his death day, to show that he was the author of these raptures, and that he could still go very near, if not absolutely up to them, when he chose. It has, however, been a constant critical amusement of mine to try to find out if possible whether this impression was a mere fallacy of youth, and if so how far. And some of the results of the inquiry which has been going on more or less ever since I turned through the Marble Arch into Hyde Park, and took *Enoch Arden* out of my pocket on that summer day, may not improperly form the subject of this and another of these papers. For the inevitable post-mortem depreciation has set in in reference to this great poet already, and it may not be uninteresting to others to see how it strikes a contemporary who had prepared himself for it.

⟨. . .⟩ We have all heard of the strange objections which even Coleridge, who might have been thought most likely of all living men to appreciate Tennyson, made (though he did not fail wholly in his appreciation) to the new poet's manner. I knew a much lesser but even more curious and far more recent instance myself. A boy of eighteen or nineteen, altogether average except that he had, I think, some Eurasian strain in him, neither a dunce nor a genius and decidedly fond of reading, once took out of a library the *Poems*,—THE *Poems*, that is to say, the volume containing everything before the *Idylls* except *Maud*, *The Princess*, and *In Memoriam*. After a day or so he returned it, saying sadly to the librarian that "he could not read it. It was just like prose." Had he been Dr Johnson he would probably have said that "the rhymes were harsh and the numbers unpleasing," just as the Doctor did of "Lycidas."

To us, of course, on the other hand, the whole or the greatest charm of Tennyson comes from the fact that he affects us in exactly the opposite way. But I think there is a certain excuse for the laughers of 1830, for Coleridge, and for my Eurasian schoolfellow. I am sure at least that I myself read Tennyson and liked him (for I always liked him) for several years before his peculiar and divine virtue dawned upon me. It has never set or paled since, and I am as sure as I can be that if I were to live to be a Struldbrug (which Heaven forbid) one of the very last things of the kind that I should forget or lose my relish for would be this. But comparatively few people, I think, have ever fully recognised how extremely original this virtue of his is. The word "great" is most irritatingly misused about poets; and we have quite recently found some persons saying that "Tennyson is as great as Shakespeare," and other people going into fits of wrath, or smiling surprise with calm disdain, at the saying. If what the former mean to say and what the latter deny is that Tennyson has a supreme and peculiar poetic charm, then I am with the former and against the latter. He has: and from the very fact of his having it he will not necessarily be appreciated at once, and may miss appreciation altogether with some people.—GEORGE SAINTSBURY, "Tennyson," *Corrected Impressions*, 1895

It was merely the accident of his hour, the call of his age, which made Tennyson a philosophic poet. He was naturally not only a pure lover of beauty, but a pure lover of beauty in a much more peculiar and distinguished sense even than a man like Keats, or a man like Robert Bridges. He gave us scenes of Nature that cannot easily be surpassed, but he chose them like a landscape painter rather than like a religious poet. Above all, he exhibited his abstract love of the beautiful in one most personal and characteristic fact. He was never so successful or so triumphant as when he was describing not Nature, but art. He could describe a statue as Shelley could describe a cloud. He was at his very best in describing buildings, in their blending of aspiration and exactitude. He found to perfection the harmony between the rhythmic recurrences of poetry and the rhythmic recurrences of architecture. His description, for example, of the Palace of Art is a thing entirely victorious and unique. The whole edifice, as described, rises as lightly as a lyric, it is full of the surge of the hunger for beauty; and yet a man might almost build upon the description as upon the plans of an architect or the instructions of a speculative builder. Such a lover of beauty was Tennyson, a lover of beauty most especially where it is most to be found, in the works of man. He loved beauty in its completeness, as we find it in art, not in its more glorious incompleteness as we find it in Nature. There is, perhaps, more loveliness in Nature than in art, but there are not so many lovely things. The loveliness is broken to pieces and scattered; the almond tree in blossom will have a mob of nameless insects at its root, and the most perfect cell in the great forest-house is likely enough to smell like a sewer. Tennyson loved beauty more in its collected form in art, poetry and sculpture; like his own Lady of Shalott, it was his office to look rather at the mirror than at the object. He was an artist, as it were, at two removes: he was a splendid imitator of the splendid imitations. It is true that his natural history was exquisitely exact, but natural history and natural religion are things that can be, under certain circumstances, more unnatural than anything in the world. In reading Tennyson's natural descriptions we never seem to be in physical contact with the earth. We learn nothing of the coarse good-temper and rank

energy of life. We see the whole scene accurately, but we see it through glass. In Tennyson's works we see Nature indeed, and hear Nature, but we do not smell it.

But this poet of beauty and a certain magnificent idleness lived at a time when all men had to wrestle and decide. It is not easy for any person who lives in our time, when the dust has settled and the spiritual perspective has been restored, to realise what the entrance of the idea of evolution meant for the men of those days. To us it is a discovery of another link in a chain which, however far we follow it, still stretches back into a divine mystery. To many of the men of that time it would appear from their writings that it was the heart-breaking and desolating discovery of the end and origin of the chain. To them had happened the most black and hopeless catastrophe conceivable to human nature; they had found a logical explanation of all things. To them it seemed that an ape had suddenly risen to gigantic stature and destroyed the seven heavens. It is difficult, no doubt, for us in somewhat subtler days to understand how anybody could suppose that the origin of species had anything to do with the origin of being. To us appears that to tell a man who asks who made his mind that evolution made it, is like telling a man who asks who rolled a cab-wheel over his leg that revolution rolled it. To state the process is scarcely to state the agent. But the position of those who regarded the opening of the *Descent of Man* as the opening of one of the seals of the last days is a great deal sounder than people have generally allowed. It has been constantly supposed that they were angry with Darwinism because it appeared to do something or other to the Book of Genesis; but this was a pretext or a fancy. They fundamentally rebelled against Darwinism, not because they had a fear that it would affect Scripture, but because they had a fear, not altogether unreasonable or ill-founded, that it would affect morality. Man had been engaged, through innumerable ages, in a struggle with sin. The evil within him was as strong as he could cope with—it was as powerful as a cannonade and as enchanting as a song. But in this struggle he had always had Nature on his side. He might be polluted and agonised, but the flowers were innocent and the hills were strong. All the armoury of life, the spears of the pine wood and the batteries of the lightning went into battle beside him. Tennyson lived in the hour when, to all mortal appearance, the whole of the physical world deserted to the devil. The universe, governed by violence and death, left man to fight alone, with a handful of myths and memories. Men had now to wander in polluted fields and lift up their eyes to abominable hills. They had to arm themselves against the cruelty of flowers and the crimes of the grass. The first honour, surely, is to those who did not faint in the face of that confounding cosmic betrayal; to those who sought and found a new vantage ground for the army of Virtue. Of these was Tennyson, and it is surely the more to his honour, since he was the idle lover of beauty who has been portrayed. He felt that the time called him to be an interpreter. Perhaps he might even have been something more of a poet if he had not sought to be something more than a poet. He might have written a more perfect Arthurian epic if his heart had been as much buried in prehistoric sepulchres as the heart of Mr. W. B. Yeats. He might have made more of such poems as "The Golden Year" if his mind had been as clean of metaphysics and as full of a poetic rusticity as the mind of William Morris. He might have been a greater poet if he had been less a man of his dubious and rambling age. But there are some things that are greater than greatness; there are some things that no man with blood in his body would sell for the throne of Dante, and one of them is to fire the feeblest shot in a war that really awaits decision, or carry the meanest musket in an army that is really marching by. Tennyson may even have forfeited immortality; but he and the men of his age were more than immortal; they were alive.

Tennyson had not a special talent for being a philosophic poet, but he had a special vocation for being a philosophic poet. This may seem a contradiction, but it is only because all the Latin or Greek words we use tend endlessly to lose their meaning. A vocation is supposed to mean merely a taste or faculty, just as economy is held to mean merely the act of saving. Economy means the management of a house or community. If a man starves his best horse, or causes his best workman to strike for more pay, he is not merely unwise, he is uneconomical. So it is with a vocation. If this country were suddenly invaded by some huge alien and conquering population, we should all be called to become soldiers. We should not think in that time that we were sacrificing our unfinished work on Cattle-Feeding or our hobby of fretwork, our brilliant career at the bar, or our taste for painting in water-colours. We should all have a call to arms. We should, however, by no means agree that we all had a vocation for arms. Yet a vocation is only the Latin for a call.

In a celebrated passage in *Maud*, Tennyson praised the moral effects of war, and declared that some great conflict might call out the greatness even of the pacific swindlers and sweaters whom he saw around him in the commercial age. He dreamed, he said, that if

> . . . The battle-bolt sang from the three-decker out
>   on the foam,
> Many a smooth-faced, snub-nosed rogue would leap
>   from his counter or till,
> And strike, were it but with his cheating yard-wand,
>   home.

Tennyson lived in the time of a conflict more crucial and frightful than any European struggle, the conflict between the apparent artificiality of morals and the apparent immorality of science. A ship more symbolic and menacing than any foreign three-decker hove in sight in that time—the great, gory pirate-ship of Nature, challenging all the civilisations of the world. And his supreme honour is this, that he behaved like his own imaginary snub-nosed rogue. His honour is that in that hour he despised the flowers and embroideries of Keats as the counter-jumper might despise his tapes and cottons. He was by nature a hedonistic and pastoral poet, but he leapt from his poetic counter and till and struck, were it but with his gimcrack mandolin, home.

Tennyson's influence on poetry may, for a time, be modified. This is the fate of every man who throws himself into his own age, catches the echo of its temporary phrases, is kept busy in battling with its temporary delusions. There are many men whom history has for a time forgotten to whom it owes more than it could count. But if Tennyson is extinguished, it will be with the most glorious extinction. There are two ways in which a man may vanish—through being thoroughly conquered or through being thoroughly the Conqueror. In the main the great Broad Church philosophy which Tennyson uttered has been adopted by every one. This will make against his fame. For a man may vanish as Chaos vanished in the face of creation, or he may vanish as God vanished in filling all things with that created life.—G. K. CHESTERTON, "Two Great Victorian Poets: I. Tennyson," *Bookman* (New York), Oct. 1902, pp. 349–51

Works

THE PRINCESS

Fields came out in the afternoon, and brought me an English copy of Tennyson's new poem, *The Princess*. F. read it in the evening. Strange enough! a university of women! A gentle satire, in the easiest and most flowing blank verse, with two delicious unrhymed songs, and many exquisite passages. I went to bed after it, with delightful music ringing in my ears; yet half disappointed in the poem, though not knowing why. There is a discordant note somewhere.—HENRY WADSWORTH LONG-FELLOW, *Journal* (Feb. 7, 1848), cited in Samuel Longfellow, *Life of Henry Wadsworth Longfellow*, 1891, Vol. 2, p. 109

I had the misfortune to be deeply intoxicated yesterday—with Tennyson's new poem, *The Princess*, which I shall bring to thee when I return home. I dare not keep it with me. For the future, for a long time at least, I dare not read Tennyson. His poetry would be the death of mine, and, indeed, a *pervadence* of his spirit would ruin me for the great purposes of life. His intense perception of beauty haunts me for days, and I cannot drive it from me.—BAYARD TAYLOR, Letter to Mary Agnew (Feb. 13, 1848), *Life and Letters of Bayard Taylor*, eds. Marie Hansen-Taylor, Horace E. Scudder, 1884, Vol. 1, p. 119

I had a note from Alfred three months ago. He was then in London: but is now in Ireland, I think, adding to his new poem, the *Princess*. Have you seen it? I am considered a great heretic for abusing it; it seems to me a wretched waste of power at a time of life when a man ought to be doing his best; and I almost feel hopeless about Alfred now. I mean, about his doing what he was born to do.—EDWARD FITZGERALD, Letter to Frederick Tennyson (May 4, 1848)

IN MEMORIAM

I am thoroughly tired of Oxford, and hope I shall feel jollier again when we sit together on your tower and smoke a weed; but no *In Memoriam*, rather something about airy, fairy Lilians and other sweet creatures without a soul. However, I do not mean to say that Tennyson's last poems are not very beautiful, yet I do not like those open graves of sorrow and despair, and wish our poets would imitate the good Christian fashion of covering them with flowers, or a stone with a short inscription on it.—MAX MÜLLER, Letter to F. Palgrave (June 18, 1850), *Life and Letters of Max Müller*, ed. Georgina Max Müller, 1902, Vol. 1, p. 116

I have just received your kind present of *In Memoriam*; many thanks. What a treasure it will be, if I can but think of it and feel about it as you do, and as Mr. T—— does! You said, "the finest strain since Shakespeare;" and afterwards that you and Mr. T—— agreed that it set the author above all modern poets, save only W. W. and S. T. C.—SARA COLERIDGE, Letter to Aubrey De Vere (Aug. 6, 1850), *Memoir and Letters of Sara Coleridge*, ed. Edith Coleridge, 1873, Vol. 2, p. 287

I agree with Mr. Kenyon and Lady Palgrave, who are not mere *friend*-critics, that *In Memoriam* is a highly interesting volume, and worthy to be compared with the poems of Petrarch. I think it like his poems, both in the general scheme, and the execution of particular pieces. The pervading, though not universal, fault, as you, I think, say too, is quaintness and violence, instead of force, in short, want of truth, which is at the bottom of all affectation, an endeavour to be something more, and higher, and better, than the aspirant really and properly is. The Heaven of poetry is not to be taken by these means. It is like the Elysium, described to Laodamia, whatever is valuable in that way flows forth spontaneously like the products of nature, silently and without struggle or noise. How smoothly do all the finest strains of poetry flow on! the noblest passages in the *Paradise Lost*, and in Mr. Wordsworth's and my father's finest poems! The mind stumbles not over a single word or image.—SARA COLERIDGE, Letter to Edward Quillinan (Aug. 15, 1850), *Memoir and Letters of Sara Coleridge*, ed. Edith Coleridge, 1873, Vol. 2, pp. 292–93

I have read Tennyson's *In Memoriam*, or rather part of it; I closed the book when I had got about halfway. It is beautiful; it is mournful; it is monotonous. Many of the feelings expressed bear, in their utterance, the stamp of truth; yet, if Arthur Hallam had been somewhat nearer Alfred Tennyson—his brother instead of his friend—I should have distrusted this rhymed, and measured, and printed monument of grief. What change the lapse of years may work I do not know; but it seems to me that bitter sorrow, while recent, does not flow out in verse.—CHARLOTTE BRONTË, Letter to Elizabeth Gaskell (Aug. 27, 1850)

I know not how to express what I have felt. My first sentiment was surprise, for, though I now find that you had mentioned the intention to my daughter, Julia, she had never told me of the poems. I do not speak as another would to praise and admire: few of them indeed I have as yet been capable of reading, the grief they express is too much akin to that they revive. It is better than any monument which could be raised to the memory of my beloved son, it is a more lively and enduring testimony to his great virtues and talents that the world should know the friendship which existed between you, that posterity should associate his name with that of Alfred Tennyson.—HENRY HALLAM, Letter to Alfred, Lord Tennyson (1850), cited in Hallam Tennyson, *Alfred Lord Tennyson: A Memoir*, 1897, Vol. 1, p. 327

In Memoriam is a poem of triumph, but of triumph overcast. The pall of gloom that broods heavily above the soul at the beginning is indeed soon broken by far, sad regions of light. Towards the end the sun itself streams forth, illumining the sorrow to beauty; but it is an English sunlight, white, not golden, still filtered through a veil of pensive mists.

It is difficult to conceive a poem wider and more subtle in rendering the possible sufferings of a soul shaken free from all convention by the shock of pain. Problems of the mind, the conduct, and the heart blend and break, one against the other, with the pathetic inconsistency, the alternations of fervor and stupor, of sorrowful life itself. In the Prelude, Cantos 1–28, the forces, stunned by sorrow, gather themselves together for conflict. In the first Cycle, Cantos 28–78, sometimes called the Cycle of the Past, are concentrated the most poignant problems of thought; in the second, the Cycle of the Present, Cantos 78–104, are faced the problems of the life of feeling and action which the soul, on earth, cannot escape; while in the Cycle of the Future, Cantos 104–119, the outlook is mainly towards an ideal social order, and the humanity to be. The concluding poems give the summary and interpretation, in the light of faith won at last, of the great problem. From the very beginning, the personal grief is taken up into a larger sorrow. The problem that confronts the poet is to find a witness to eternal life in the presence of that vast witness to perpetual death seemingly given by nature and our human fears. The great question is viewed, now from the side of emotion, now from that of thought, and at times the shore of assurance seems far away. In the fluctuating motion that tosses the bitter foam of doubt over most dear and sacred desires, one firm fact alone

remains, giving to the poem the necessary coherence of structure. It is the constancy of human love on earth, to which from the beginning the poet desperately and blindly clings. Before the end of the great soul-epic, this constancy, gathering to itself all of thought and feeling that can minister to faith, becomes to him the calm revealer of a love beyond the grave.

In Memoriam, taken as a whole, has a tone profoundly Christian, it advances towards a triumphant and Christian end. Yet, if we regard not conclusion but method, we find the poem in essence skeptical. Its agnosticism lies intellectually though not spiritually as deep as its Christianity, its very faith is of the agnostic type. For this faith is held by effort of the will, not by demonstration of reason. From the first awakening of volition when the fumes of sorrow roll away, to the final apostrophe:—

> O Living Will that shalt endure
> When all that seems shall suffer shock,

choice, not conviction, determines creed. There is much meditation suffused with thoughtful argument, but the arguments do but circle around the central problem, disposing of minor difficulties but never touching its gloomy heart. Next to the will, feeling is the great champion of faith. The heart in wrath gives to the cruel suggestions of reason the reiterated answer: "I have felt." They are lame hands of faith indeed that the poet stretches out. The final triumph won is that of simple trust: trust adequate to console and even to nerve to conduct, not adequate to create even the illusion of knowledge. Reason, Tennyson emphasizes again and again with calm and sad assurance, can never attain to truth. We must "faintly trust the larger hope," "believing where we cannot prove;" and as this sad phrase confronts us in the Prologue, we find it once more at the very end, where once more we are bidden to trust "with faith that comes *of self-control*" "the truths that never can be proved" on earth.

The intellectual problems are indeed hardly met, much less answered; and yet, before the end, reason in a sense is satisfied. The movement of the poem is close to that of experience, far from that of pure thought, and hence comes its very vitality and power. Facts of nature and of the soul come to the poet whose love is clasping grief with desperate instinct, as mocking, hideous, serene denials of the spiritual truth for which he longs. Tortured, but touchingly sincere, the soul again and again faces and voices with unflinching completeness the message of despair: it then turns away, exhausted by the very intensity of thought-sorrow, and sinks for rest into the healing and normal sorrow of the heart. Long after, when much new experience has been entered, when the spirit has been strengthened by courageous endurance and the conquest of practical solutions, the same face will recur: and behold! it is no longer dark with insidious denial, but the radiant witness to faith. In the mystery of sub-consciousness, the great change has been wrought.

Thus, for instance, the first hint of wider thought that comes to the dazed spirit is the terrible conception of nature as a great phantom, hollow and unsubstantial, the mere mocking image of man. The conception is languidly dropped; for at first the pathetic hints at thought of the bruised spirit are lame and broken, and it is long before they have strength to gather themselves into consecutive sequence. But far later, in the triumphant conclusion, the idea reappears, and how different is its aspect! Once it forced the soul into the very solitude of death: now it is the joyous witness of perfect idealism. The world is shadow indeed, but the shadow of immortal spirit. The solid lands may melt like mists, like clouds may shape themselves and go: the poet knows that they exist as symbol only of eternal love.—VIDA D. SCUDDER, *The Life of the Spirit in the Modern English Poets*, 1895, pp. 284–88

MAUD

The general characteristic ⟨of Tennyson's poetry⟩ is, that the passion there shown in operation is a purifying, strengthening, sustaining power; that it allies itself with conscience and reason, and braces instead of debilitating the will. The small poem called 'Fatima' is the only instance in which Mr. Tennyson has expended his powers in portraying any love that incapacitates for the common duties of life, unless the two 'Marianas' be regarded in this light, which would be a perverse misconception of their main purpose. In 'Locksley Hall' the ghost of a murdered love is fairly laid, and the man comes out of his conflict the stronger and the clearer for his experience. Nothing that can with any propriety be called morbid or unhealthy belongs to any of the great love poems in the collection; and surely the view of the relation of the sexes in the *Princess* is as sound a basis for a noble life as was ever propounded. It would be singular if, with such antecedents, Mr. Tennyson should, in the maturity of his intellect and experience, have descended to exhibit the influence of love upon a weak and worthless character, and have chosen for that purpose a melodramatic story of suicide, murder, and madness, dished up for popular applause with vehement invective on the vices of the English nation, and claptrap appeals to the war-feeling of the day. This, however, is what we are asked to believe of Mr. Tennyson's latest production, *Maud*, by the loudest professional critics of the journals and magazines. The critics give us some gauge of their opinion by tracing Mr. Tennyson's gradual degradation through the *Princess*, lower still in *In Memoriam*, to its climax of weakness and absurdity in *Maud*; and it is but justice to say that these opinions are not now for the first time put forth on the provocation of the last-named poem, but appear to be the deliberate convictions of the writers. We believe that both the *Princess* and *In Memoriam* are in their sixth edition, which, apart from private experience, necessarily limited, of the impression the works have produced, leads to the conclusion that these writers do not in this case fairly represent the opinion of the English public. Whether they represent it any better in respect to *Maud* remains to be seen. Meanwhile it is well not to be frightened out of the enjoyment of fine poetry, and out of the instruction to be gained from a great poet's views of life, as exhibited dramatically in the destiny of a particular sort of character subjected to a particular set of influences, by such epithets as 'morbid,' 'hysterical,' 'spasmodic,' which may mean one thing or another, according to the sense, discrimination, and sympathy of the man who applies them.

There is little question as to the artistic merits of *Maud*. It is only the aim of the poet that has been assailed; his execution is generally admitted to be successful. It may be at once conceded that the writer of the fragments of a life which tell the story of *Maud*, is not in a comfortable state of mind when he begins his record; and that if a gentleman were to utter such sentiments at a board of railway directors, or at a marriage breakfast, he might not improperly be called hysterical. Like the hero of 'Locksley Hall,' his view of the life around him, of the world in which his lot is cast, has been coloured by a grievous personal calamity; and the character of the man is originally one in which the sensibilities are keen and delicate, the speculative element strong, the practical judgment unsteady, the will and active energies comparatively feeble. A Shelley or a Keats may stand for example of his type; not perfect men, certainly, but scarcely so contemptible as not to possess

both dramatic interest and some claim to human sympathy. Chatterton, a much lower type than either, has been thought a subject of psychological and moral interest, in spite or in consequence of the vulgar, petulant, weak melodrama of his life and death. You see, God makes these morbid, hysterical, spasmodic individuals occasionally, and they have various fates; some die without a sign; others try the world, and dash themselves dead against its bars; some few utter their passionate desires, their weak complaints, their ecstastic raptures in snatches of song that make the world delirious with delight,—and somehow, for their sake the class becomes interesting, and we are at times inclined to measure the spiritual capacity of an age by its treatment of these weak souls,—by the fact, whether the general constitution of society cherishes such souls into divine lovers and singers of the beautiful, or lashes and starves and changes them into moping idiots and howling madmen. The autobiographer of *Maud* belongs to this class by temperament, as anyone may understand from the turn of his angry thoughts to those social evils which must and ought to excite indignation and scorn in gentle and loving natures that are at the same time inspired with generous and lofty ideas; from the speculative enigmas he torments himself with at the prevalence of rapine and pain in creation, at the insignificance of man in a boundless universe, subject to iron laws; from the penetrating tenderness, the rich fancy, the childlike *naïveté* of his love for the young girl who saves him from himself and his dark dreams. There lies in such a character, from the beginning, the capacity for weakness and misery, for crime and madness. That capacity is inseparable from keen sensibility, powerful emotions, and active imagination; and if events happen which paralyze the will already feeble, turn the flow of feeling into a stream of bitterness, and present to the imagination a world of wrong and suffering, the capacity fulfils itself according to the force and direction of the events. In *Maud* the tendency meets with events that carry it on through these stages; and the question is whether any one of these events is impossible or improbable, whether English society is misrepresented when it is made capable of furnishing the unwholesome nutriment for such a character. ⟨. . .⟩

The fact is, that Mr. Tennyson, without abandoning his lyric forms, has in *Maud* written a tragedy—a work, that is, which demands to be judged, not by the intrinsic goodness and beauty of the actions and emotions depicted, but by their relation to character; that character, again, being not only an interesting study in itself and moving our sympathy, but being related dynamically to the society of the time which serves as the background of the picture, and thus displaying the characteristics of the society by showing its influence, under particular circumstances, upon the character selected. Mr. Tennyson's critics have for the most part read the poem as if its purpose were to hold up an example for our imitation, and have condemned it because, viewed in this light, it offers nothing but a nature of over-excitable sensibilities, first rendered moody by misfortune, then driven mad by its own crime, and finally recovered to a weak exultation in a noble enterprise it has not the manliness to share. But no one feels that Shakspeare is immoral in making Othello kill himself; no one attributes the cynicism of Mephistopheles to Goethe. —GEORGE BRIMLEY, "Tennyson's Poems" (1855), *Essays*, ed. George William Clark, 1868, pp. 75–84

Maud ⟨. . .⟩ with its strength and weakness, has divided public opinion more than any other of the author's works. I think that his judicious students will not demur to my opinion that it is quite below his other sustained productions; rather, that it is not sustained at all, but, while replete with beauties, weak and uneven as a whole,—and that this is due to the poet's having gone outside his own nature, and to his surrender of the joy of art, in an effort to produce something that should at once catch the favor of the multitude. *Maud* is scanty in theme, thin in treatment, poor in thought; but has musical episodes, with much fine scenery and diction. It is a greater medley than *The Princess*, shifting from vague speculations to passionate outbreaks, and glorying in one famous and beautiful nocturne,— but all intermixed with cheap satire, and conspicuous for affectations unworthy of the poet. The pity of it was that this production appeared when Tennyson suddenly had become fashionable, in England and America, through his accession to the laureate's honors, and for this reason, as well as for its theme and eccentric qualities, had a wider reading than his previous works: not only among the masses, to whom the other volumes had been sealed books, but among thoughtful people, who now first made the poet's acquaintance and received *Maud* as the foremost example of his style. First impressions are lasting, and to this day Tennyson is deemed, by many of the latter class, an apostle of tinsel and affectation. In our own country especially, his popular reputation began with *Maud*,— a work which, for lack of constructive beauty, is the opposite of his other narrative poems.—EDMUND CLARENCE STEDMAN, "Alfred Tennyson," *Victorian Poets*, 1875, pp. 173–74

IDYLLS OF THE KING

The Duke of Argyll called, and left me the sheets of a forthcoming poem of Tennyson. I like it extremely—notwithstanding some faults, extremely. The parting of Lancelot and Guinivere, her penitence, and Arthur's farewell, are all very affecting. I cried over some passages; but I am now ἀρτίδακρυς, as Medea says.—THOMAS BABINGTON MACAULAY, *Journal* (July 11, 1859), cited in G. Otto Trevelyan, *The Life and Letters of Lord Macaulay*, 1876, Vol. 2, p. 398

We have no doubt that Mr. Tennyson has carefully considered how far his subject is capable of fulfilling the conditions of an epic structure. The history of Arthur is not an epic as it stands, but neither was the Cyclic song, of which the greatest of all epics, the *Iliad*, handles a part. The poem of Ariosto is scarcely an epic, nor is that of Bojardo; but is not this because each is too promiscuous and crowded in its brilliant phantasmagoria to conform to the severe laws of that lofty and inexorable class of poem? Though the Arthurian romance be no epic, it does not follow that no epic can be made from out of it. It is grounded in certain leading characters, men and women, conceived upon models of extraordinary grandeur; and as the Laureate has evidently grasped the genuine law which makes man and not the acts of man the base of epic song, we should not be surprised were he hereafter to realise the great achievement towards which he seems to be feeling his way. There is a moral unity and a living relationship between the four poems before us, and the first effort of 1842 as a fifth, which, though some considerable part of their contents would necessarily rank as episode, establishes the first and most essential condition of their cohesion. The achievement of Vivien bears directly on the state of Arthur by withdrawing his chief councillor—the brain, as Lancelot was the right arm, of his court; the love of Elaine is directly associated with the final catastrophe of the passion of Lancelot for Guinevere. Enid lies somewhat further off the path, nor is it for profane feet to intrude into the sanctuary, for reviewers to advise poets in these high matters; but while we presume nothing, we do not despair of seeing Mr. Tennyson achieve on the basis he has chosen the structure of a full-formed epic.—W. E. GLADSTONE, "Tennyson's Poems—*Idylls of the King*," *Quarterly Review*, Oct. 1859, pp. 479–80

Will you forgive me if I intrude on your leisure with a request which I have thought some little time of making, viz. that you would be good enough to write your name in the accompanying volume of your *Idylls of the King*? You would thus add a peculiar interest to the book, containing those beautiful songs, from the perusal of which I derived the greatest enjoyment. They quite rekindle the feeling with which the legends of King Arthur must have inspired the chivalry of old, whilst the graceful form in which they are presented blends those feelings with the softer tone of our present age.—PRINCE ALBERT, Letter to Alfred, Lord Tennyson (May 17, 1860)

We read, at first, Tennyson's *Idyls*, with profound recognition of the finely elaborated execution, and also of the inward perfection of *vacancy*,—and, to say truth, with considerable impatience at being treated so very like infants, tho the lollipops were so superlative.—THOMAS CARLYLE, Letter to Ralph Waldo Emerson (Jan. 27, 1867)

There are very fine childish things in Tennyson's poem and fine manly things, too, as it seems to me, but I conceive the theory to be wrong. I have the same feeling (I am not wholly sure of its justice) that I have when I see these modern-mediæval pictures. I am defrauded; I do not see reality, but a masquerade. The costumes are all that is genuine, and the people inside them are shams—which, I take it, is just the reverse of what ought to be. One special criticism I should make on Tennyson's new *Idyls*, and that is that the similes are so often dragged in by the hair. They seem to be taken (*à la* Tom Moore) from note-books, and not suggested by the quickened sense of association in the glow of composition. Sometimes it almost seems as if the verses were made for the similes, instead of being the cresting of a wave that heightens as it rolls. This is analogous to the costume objection and springs perhaps from the same cause—the making of poetry with malice prepense. However, I am not going to forget the lovely things that Tennyson has written, and I think they give him rather hard measure now. However, it is the natural recoil of a too rapid fame. Wordsworth had the true kind—an unpopularity that roused and stimulated while he was strong enough to despise it, and honor, obedience, troops of friends, when the grasshopper would have been a burthen to the drooping shoulders. Tennyson, to be sure, has been childishly petulant; but what have these whipper-snappers, who cry "Go up, baldhead," done that can be named with some things of his? He has been the greatest artist in words we have had since Gray—and remember how Gray holds his own with little fuel, but real fire. He had the secret of the inconsumable oil, and so, I fancy, has Tennyson.—JAMES RUSSELL LOWELL, Letter to Charles Eliot Norton (Dec. 4, 1872)

The real and radical flaw in the splendid structure of the *Idylls* is not to be found either in the antiquity of the fabulous groundwork or in the modern touches which certainly were not needed, and if needed would not have been adequate, to redeem any worthy recast of so noble an original from the charge of nothingness. The fallacy which obtrudes itself throughout, the false note which incessantly jars on the mind's ear, results from the incongruity of materials which are radically incapable of combination or coherence. Between the various Arthurs of different national legends there is little more in common than the name. It is essentially impossible to construct a human figure by the process of selection from the incompatible types of irreconcilable ideals. All that the utmost ingenuity of eclecticism can do has been demonstrated by Lord Tennyson in his elaborate endeavour after the perfection of this process; and the result is to impress upon us a complete and irreversible conviction of its absolute hopelessness. Had a poet determined to realize the Horatian ideal of artistic monstrosity, he could hardly have set about it more ingeniously than by copying one feature from the Mabinogion and the next from the Morte d'Arthur. So far from giving us 'Geoffrey's' type or 'Mallory's' type, he can hardly be said to have given us a recognizable likeness of Prince Albert; who, if neither a wholly gigantic nor altogether a divine personage, was at least, one would imagine, a human figure. But the spectre of his laureate's own ideal knight, neither Welsh nor French, but a compound of 'Guallia and Gaul, soul-curer and body-curer,' sir priest and sir knight, Mallory and Geoffrey, old style and middle style and new style, makes the reader bethink himself what might or might not be the result if some poet of similar aim and aspiration were to handle the tale of Troy, for instance, as Lord Tennyson has handled the Arthurian romance. The half godlike Achilles of Homer is one in name and nothing else with the all brutish Achilles of Shakespeare; the romantic Arthur of the various volumes condensed by Mallory into his English compilation—incoherent itself and incongruous in its earlier parts, but so nobly consistent, so profoundly harmonious in its close—has hardly more in common with the half impalpable hero of British myth or tradition. And I cannot but think that no very promising task would be undertaken by a poet who should set before himself the design of harmonizing in one fancy portrait, of reconciling in one typic figure, the features of Achilles as they appear in the Iliad with the features of Achilles as they appear in *Troilus and Cressida.*—ALGERNON CHARLES SWINBURNE, "Tennyson and Musset" (1881), *Miscellanies*, 1886, pp. 249–51

DRAMA

I cannot trust myself to say how greatly I admire the play (*Queen Mary*). Beyond the immediate effect, you'll have hit a more fatal blow than a thousand pamphleteers and controversialists; besides this you have reclaimed one more section of English History from the wilderness and given it a form in which it will be fixed for ever. No one since Shakespeare has done that. When we were beginning to think that we were to have no more from you, you have given us the greatest of all your works. Once more I thank you for having written this book with all my heart.—JAMES ANTHONY FROUDE, Letter to Alfred, Lord Tennyson (May 7, 1875), cited in Hallam Tennyson, *Alfred Lord Tennyson: A Memoir*, 1897, Vol. 2, pp. 180–81

Tennyson, the dramatist, labours under the serious disadvantage that he has always to enter the lists against Tennyson the lyrist, Tennyson the elegist, Tennyson the idyllist. He is his own most formidable rival, and perhaps in this fact lies the explanation of that respectful coldness which on the whole has marked the reception of his dramas by both the critics and the public. Then, too—though no one could think of saying that Lord Tennyson had been positively infelicitous in his selection of dramatic subjects—there has yet always been some barrier to complete surrender of one's sympathies to his theme. In *Queen Mary* one could hardly help feeling that the poet, obeying a noble impulse of justice towards the wearer of that ensanguined name, had unduly gone outside himself, by imaginative abnegation of his own prepossessions, to invest her with a pathos too tender for her deserts. In *Harold*, again, the

conflicting issues provided a great theme for a poetic-historic study, but impaired the simplicity and singleness of interest which are desirable in a dramatic poem. We have the Norman in us as well as the Saxon. "Saxon and Norman and Dane are we," and more besides; and it is impossible for us to swear undivided spiritual allegiance to the Saxon protagonist. *Becket*, the most ambitious of the plays, and in parts the most splendid and powerful, was embarrassed by too great opulence of material. The struggle of crown and crosier was itself a subject quite large enough for a single play. An enamoured king, an embowered mistress, and a jealous queen, were also in themselves a large subject. And the two interests stood rather apart, over against each other; the effect being variety at the cost of continuity. In all these cases, however, great poetry was achieved in the face of all opposition on the part of refractory history; but the makers of history seem to have been culpably indifferent to form, and negligent as to grouping, and even a master like the Laureate is to some extent their slave. Is it because Lord Tennyson has at times been disposed to chafe against the inflexibility of events, that he has now chosen a theme in which he can evade the dull despotism of the annalist, and reign as supreme in Sherwood as Shakspere in the forest of Arden?

A spiritual or material conflict has in every case formed the basis for the subject-matter of Lord Tennyson's dramas. The struggle (as fought out in England) between Rome and Geneva; between invading Norman and invaded Saxon; between the Church and the English monarchy—these have in turn engaged his dramatic imagination. In his latest production the theme is the contest between arbitrary and misused power, as embodied in the person of Prince John, and the spirit of justice and freedom, as represented by the people and their champion the outlawed Earl of Huntingdon. If Lord Tennyson should see fit to make yet another incursion upon the domain of drama, it is conceivable, and perhaps probable, that he will again look for his material in the incidents of some great conflict or controversy in which opposing principles have incarnated themselves in human agents. Mere dynastic feuds, like those of York and Lancaster, involving no strife of ideas, no oppugnancy of principles, do not seem to attract the author of *Becket* and *Queen Mary*. And, besides, Shakspere has left little to be gleaned in that field. But the great strife of King and Parliament still awaits its great dramatist; and one can scarcely help believing that if the Laureate were to found a play upon the more essentially human as distinguished from the purely political aspects of that struggle, the result might be the most memorable English drama of modern times. Possibly the subject would afford scant opportunity for those lyrical features which are so delightful a characteristic of his plays. But the same defect might have been supposed inherent in the subject-matter of the Laureate's first drama; yet *Queen Mary* contains some of the loveliest of his incidental snatches of song. His sympathy with the aristocratic idea is deep, but his sympathy with popular causes, when such causes are identical with the spirit of justice and the legitimate aspirations of a free-born people, is no less deep; and I can think of no other English poet who has had anything like his natural qualifications and equipment for such a work. To say that Tennyson's genius is worthy of such a subject would be almost an impertinence; but it is, perhaps, permissible to observe that the subject is worthy of Tennyson's genius. On the one hand, there is the immense impersonal pathos of dissolving forces, the tragedy of fading sentiments and perishing ideas; on the other hand, the stirring spectacle of a people for the first time fully confident in itself and the validity of its cause; added to which, the innumerable picturesque personalities of the scene offer an extraordinary range of dramatic material.—WILLIAM WATSON, *Academy*, April 9, 1892, p. 341

When we come down to later years the principal change visible in Tennyson's work is the development of the dramatic element. The dramas proper have been the most neglected of all sections of his work; but 'the dramatic element' is by no means confined to them. They are rather just the final result of a process which had been long going on. Tennyson, as we have already seen, gradually put more and more thought into his verse. In doing so he felt the need of a closer grip of reality, and he found, as other poets have found too, that the dramatic mode of conception brought him closest to the real. This is all the more remarkable because nothing could well be more foreign to the dramatic spirit than his early work. His youthful character sketches are not in the least dramatic. Neither is there much trace of humour, a quality without which true dramatic conception is impossible. The change begins to show itself about the middle of the century. In 'The Grandmother' and 'The Northern Farmer' we have genuine dramatic sketches of character. The poet does not regard them from his own point of view, he speaks from theirs. 'The Northern Farmer' is moreover rich in humour. Tennyson never surpassed this creation, but he multiplied similar sketches. All his poems in dialect are of a like kind. They are in dialect not from mere caprice, but because the characters could only be painted to the life by using their own speech. Other pieces, not in dialect, like 'Sir John Oldcastle' and 'Columbus,' are likewise dramatic in their nature. Less prominent, but not less genuine, is the dramatic element in the patriotic ballads, such as 'The Revenge.' The greater part of the work of Tennyson's last twenty years is, in fact, of this nature, and herein we detect the principal cause of the change of which all must be sensible in that work as compared with the work of his youth. The old smoothness and melody are in great part gone, but a number of pieces prove that Tennyson retained the skill though he did not always choose to exercise it. It is the early style with which his name is still associated, and probably the majority of his readers have never been quite reconciled to the change. But while we may legitimately mourn for what time took away, we ought to rejoice over what it added, rather than left. If there is less melody there is more strength; if the delightful dreamy languor of 'The Lotos-Eaters' is gone, we have the vivid truth of 'The Northern Farmer' and 'The Northern Cobbler,' and the tragic pathos of 'Rizpah'; if the romantic sentiment of 'Locksley Hall' is lost, something more valuable has taken its place in the criticism of life in 'Locksley Hall Sixty Years After.'

Tennyson's dramas then, surprising as they were when they first appeared, are merely the legitimate and almost the inevitable outcome of his course of development. Inevitable he seems to have felt them, for he persevered in the face of censure or half-hearted approval, perhaps it should be said, in the face of failure. A deep-rooted scepticism of his dramatic powers has stood in the way of a fair appreciation. The fame of his earlier poetry has cast a shadow over these later fruits of his genius; and the question, 'Is Saul also among the prophets?' was hardly asked with greater surprise than the question whether Tennyson could possibly be a dramatist. And, in truth, at sixty-six he had still to learn the rudiments of his business. *Queen Mary* (1875) is a failure. It is not a great poem, and still less is it a great drama. The stage is overcrowded with *dramatis personæ* who jostle each other and hide one another's features. *Harold* (1877) showed a marked advance; but *Becket*

(1885) was the triumph which justified all the other experiments. It is a truly great drama, and, though not yet recognised as such, will probably rank finally among the greatest of Tennyson's works. The characters are firmly and clearly delineated. Becket and Henry, closely akin in some of their natural gifts, are different in circumstances and develop into very different men. Rosamond and Eleanor are widely contrasted types of female character, the former a little commonplace, the latter a subtle conception excellently worked out. All the materials out of which the play is built are great. No finer theme could be found than the mediæval conflict between Church and State; and Tennyson has seized it in the true dramatic way, as concentrated in the single soul of Becket, torn between his duty to the Church and his duty to the King, whose Chancellor and trusted friend he had been and to whom he owed his promotion.—HUGH WALKER, *The Age of Tennyson*, 1897, pp. 224–27

GEORGE GILFILLAN
"Alfred Tennyson" (1847)
A Second Gallery of Literary Portraits
1850, pp. 214–31

The subject of the following sketch seems a signal example of the intimate relation which sometimes exists between original genius, and a shrinking, sensitive, and morbid nature. We see in all his writings the struggle of a strong intellect to "turn and wind the fiery Pegasus" of a most capricious, volatile, and dream-driven imagination. Tennyson is a curious combination of impulse, strength, and delicacy approaching to weakness. Could we conceive, not an Eolian harp, but a grand piano, played on by the swift fingers of the blast, it would give us some image of the sweet, subtle, tender, powerful, and changeful movements of his verse, in which are wedded artificial elegance, artistic skill, and wild, impetuous impulse. It is the voice and lute of Ariel; but heard not in a solitary and enchanted island, but in a modern drawing-room, with beautiful women bending round, and moss-roses breathing, in their faint fragrance, through the half-opened windows. Here, indeed, lies the paradox of our author's genius. He is haunted, on the one hand, by images of ideal and colossal grandeur, coming upon him from the isle of the Syrens, the caves of the Kraken, the heights of Ida, the solemn cycles of Cathay, the riches of the Arabian heaven; but, on the other hand, his fancy loves, better than is manly or beseeming, the tricksy elegancies of artificial life—the "white sofas" of his study—the trim walks of his garden—the luxuries of female dress—and all the tiny comforts and beauties which nestle round an English parlour. From the sublime to the snug, and *vice versa*, is with him but a single step. This moment toying on the carpet with his cat, he is the next soaring with a roc over the valley of diamonds. We may liken him to the sea-shell which, sitting complacently and undistinguished amid the commonplace ornaments of the mantelpiece, has only to be lifted to give forth from its smooth ear the far-rugged boom of the ocean breakers. In this union of feminine feebleness and imaginative strength, he much resembles John Keats, who at one time could hew out the vast figure of the dethroned Saturn, "quiet as a stone," with the force of a Michael Angelo, and, again, with all the gusto of a milliner, describe the undressing of his heroine in the *Eve of St. Agnes*. Indeed, although we have ascribed, and we think justly, original genius to Tennyson, there is much in his mind, too, of the imitative and the composite. He adds the occasional langour, the luxury of descriptive beauty, the feminine tone, the tender melancholy, the grand aspirations, perpetually checked and chilled by the access of morbid weakness, and the mannerisms of style which distinguish Keats, to much of the simplicity and the philosophic tone of Wordsworth, the peculiar rhythm and obscurity of Coleridge, and a portion of the quaintness and allegorising tendency which were common with the Donnes, Withers, and Quarleses, of the seventeenth century. What is peculiar to himself is a certain carol, light in air and tone, but profound in burden. Hence his little lyrics—such as "Oriana," "Mariana at the Moated Grange," the "Talking Oak," the "May Queen"—are among his most original and striking productions. They tell tales of deep tragedy, or they convey lessons of wide significance, or they paint vivid and complete pictures, in a few lively touches, and by a few airy words, as if caught in dropping from the sky. By sobs of sound, by half-hints of meaning, by light, hurrying strokes on the ruddy chords of the heart, by a ringing of changes on certain words and phrases, he sways us as if with the united powers of music and poetry. Our readers will, in illustration of this, remember his nameless little song, beginning

> Break, break, break,
> On thy cold grey crags, O sea!

which is a mood of his own mind, faithfully rendered into sweet and simple verse. It is in composition no more complicated or elaborate than a house built by a child, but melts you, as that house would, were you to see it after the dear infant's death. But than this he has higher moods, and nobler, though still imperfect aspirations. In his "Two Voices," he approaches the question of all ages—Whence evil? And if he, no more than other speculators, unties, he casts a soft and mellow light around this Gordian knot. This poem is no fancy piece, but manifestly a transcript from his own personal experience. He has sunk into one of those melancholy moods incident to his order of mind, and has become "aweary of the sun," and of all the sun shines upon—especially of his own miserable idiosyncrasy. There slides in at that dark hour a still small voice: how different from that which thrilled on Elijah's ear in the caves of Horeb! It is the voice of that awful lady whom De Quincey calls *Mater tenebrarum*, our lady of darkness. It hints at suicide as the only remedy for human woes.

> Thou are so full of misery,
> Were it not better not to be?

And then there follows an eager and uneasy interlocution between the "dark and barren voice," and the soul of the writer, half spurning and half holding parley with its suggestions. Seldom, truly, since the speech by which Despair in Spenser enforces the same sad argument, did misanthropy breathe a more withering blight over humanity and human hopes; seldom did unfortunate by a shorter and readier road reach the conclusion, "there is one remedy for all," than in the utterance of this voice. Death in it looks lovely; nay, the one lovely thing in the universe. Again and again the poet is ready to yield to the desire of his own heart, thus seconded by the mystic voice, and, in the words of one who often listened to the same accents, to "lie down like a tired child, and weep away this life of care." But again and again the better element of his nature resists the temptation, and beats back the melancholy voice. At length, raising himself from his lethargy, he rises, looks forth—it is the Sabbath morn, and, as he sees the peaceful multitudes moving on to the house of God, and as, like the Anciente Mariner, he "blesses them unaware,"

straightway the spell is broken, the "dull and bitter voice is gone," and, hark!

> A second voice is at his ear,
> A little whisper, silver-clear,

and it gives him a hidden and humble hope, which spreads a quiet heaven within his soul. Now he can go forth into the fields, and

> Wonder at the bounteous hours,
> The slow result of winter showers,
> *You scarce can see the grass for flowers.*

All nature calls upon him to rejoice, and to the eye of his heart, at least, the riddle is read. Nay, we put it to every heart if this do not, more than many elaborate argumentations, touch the core of the difficulty. "Look up," said Leigh Hunt to Carlyle, when he had been taking the darker side of the question, and they had both come out under the brilliance of a starry night—"look up, and find your answer there!" And although the reply failed to convince the party addressed, who, looking aloft at the sparkling azure, after a deep pause, rejoined, with a sigh, and in tones we can well imagine, so melancholy and far withdrawn, "Oh! it's a sad sight;" yet, apart from the divine discoveries, it was the true and only answer. The beauty, whether of Tennyson's fields—where we "scarce can see the grass for flowers"—or of Leigh Hunt's skies, "whose unwithered countenance is young as on creation's day," and where we find an infinite answer to our petty cavils—is enough to soothe, if not to satisfy, to teach us the perfect patience of expectancy, if not the full assurance of faith.

Tennyson, in some of his poems as well as this, reveals in himself a current of thought tending towards very deep and dark subjects. This springs partly from the metaphysical bias of his intellect, and partly from the morbid emotions of his heart. And yet he seems generally to toy and trifle with such tremendous themes—to touch them lightly and hurriedly, as one might hot iron—at once eager and reluctant to intermeddle with them. Nevertheless, there is a perilous stuff about his heart, and upon his verse lies a "melancholy compounded of many simples." He is not the poet of hope, or of action, or of passion, but of sentiment, of pensive and prying curiosity, or of simple stationary wonder, in view of the great sights and mysteries of Nature and man. He has never thrown himself amid the heats and hubbub of society, but remained alone, musing with a quiet but observant eye upon the tempestuous pageant which is sweeping past him, and concerning himself little with the political or religious controversies of his age. There are, too, in some of his writings, mild and subdued vestiges of a wounded spirit, of a heart that has been disappointed, of an ambition that has been repressed, of an intellect that has wrestled with doubt, difficulty, and disease.

In "Locksley Hall," for instance, he tells a tale of unfortunate passion with a gusto and depth of feeling, which (unless we misconstrue the mark of the branding-iron) betray more than a fictitious interest in the theme. It is a poem breathing the spirit of, and not much inferior to, Byron's "Dream," in all but that clear concentration of misery which bends over it like a bare and burning heaven over a bare and burning desert. "Locksley Hall," again, is turbid and obscure in language, wild and distracted in feeling. The wind is down, but the sea still runs high. You see in it the passion pawing like a lion who has newly missed his prey, not fixed as yet in a marble form of still and hopeless disappointment. The lover, after a season of absence, returns to the scene of his early education and hapless love, where of old he

Wander'd, nourishing a youth sublime
With the fairy tales of science, and the long result of
time.

A feeling, cognate with, and yet more imperious than those of his high aspirations, springs up in his mind. It arises in spring like the crest of a singing-bird. It is the feeling of love for Amy his cousin, sole daughter of her father's house and heart. The feeling is mutual, and the current of their true love flows smoothly on, till interrupted by the interference of relatives. Thus far he remembers calmly; but here recollection strikes the fierce chord of disappointment, and he bursts impetuously forth—

O, my cousin, shallow-hearted. O, my Amy, mine
no more.
O, the dreary, dreary moorland. O, the barren,
barren shore.

Darting then one hasty and almost vindictive glance down her future history, he predicts that she shall lower to the level of the clown she has wedded, and that he will use his victim a little better than his dog or his horse. Nay, she will become

Old and formal, suited to her petty part;
With her little hoard of maxims, preaching down a
daughter's heart.

But himself, alas! what is to become of him? Live he must—suicide is too base an outlet from existence for his brave spirit. But what to do with this bitter boon of being? There follow some wild and half-insane stanzas expressive of the ambitions and uncertainties of his soul. It is the Cyclops mad with blindness, and groping at the sides of his cave. He will hate and despise all women, or, at least, all British maidens. He will return to the orient land, whose "larger constellations" saw a father die. He will, in his despair, take some savage woman who shall rear his dusky race. But no—the despair is momentary—he may not mate with a squalid savage; he will rather revive old intellectual ambitions, and renew old aspirations, for he feels within him that the "crescent promise of his spirit has not set." It is resolved—but, ere he goes, let every ray of remaining love and misery go forth in one last accusing, avenging look at the scene of his disappointment and the centre of his wo.

Howsoever these things be, a long farewell to
Locksley Hall.
Now, for me, the woods may wither; now, for me,
the roof-tree fall,
Comes a vapour from the margin, blackening over
heath and holt;
Cramming all the blast before it, in its breast a
thunderbolt.
Let it fall on Locksley Hall, with rain, or hail, or fire,
or snow,
For a mighty wind arises, roaring seaward, and I go.

And thus the ballad closes, leaving, however, with us the inevitable impression that the unfortunate lover is not done with Locksley Hall nor its bitter memories—that Doubting Castle is not down, nor giant Despair dead—that the calls of the curlews around it will still resound in his ears, and the pale face of its Amy, still unutterably beloved, will come back upon his dreams—that the iron has entered into his soul—and that his life and his misery are henceforth commensurate and the same.

Among the more remarkable of Tennyson's poems, besides those already mentioned, are "The Poet," "Dora," "Recollections of the Arabian Nights," "Œnone," "The Lotos Eaters," "Ulysses," "Godiva," and "The Vision of Sin." "The Poet" was written when the author was young, and when the

high ideal of his heart was just dawning upon his mind. It is needless to say that his view of the powers and influences of poetry is different with what prevails with many in our era. Poetry is, with him, no glittering foil to be wielded gaily on gala days. It is, or ought to be, a sharp two-edged sword. It is not a baton in the hand of coarse authority—it is a magic rod. It is not a morning flush in the sky of youth, that shall fade in the sun of science—it is a consuming and imperishable fire. It is not a mere amusement for young love-sick men and women—it is as serious as death, and longer than life. It is tuned philosophy—winged science—fact on fire—"truth springing from earth"—high thought voluntarily moving harmonious numbers. His "Poet" is "dowered with the hate of hate, the scorn of scorn, the love of love," and his words "shake the world."

The author, when he wrote "The Poet," was fresh from school, and from Shelley, his early idol. Ere writing "Dora" he had become conversant with the severer charms of Wordsworth; and that poem contains in it not one figure or flower—is bare, literal, and pathetic as the book of Ruth. Its poetry is that which lies in all natural life, which, like a deep quiet pool, has only to be disturbed in the slightest degree to send up in dance those bells and bubbles which give it instantly ideal beauty and interest, and suddenly the pool becomes a poem!

His "Recollections of the Arabian Nights" is a poem of that species which connects itself perpetually, in feeling and memory, with the original work, whose quintessence it collects. It speaks out the sentiments of millions of thankful hearts. We feel in it what a noble thing was the Arabian mind—like the Arabian soil, "all the Sun's"—like the Arabian climate, fervid, golden—like the Arabian horse, light, elegant, ethereal, swift as the wind. "O, for the golden prime of good Haroun Alras-chid!" O, for one look—though it were the last—of that Persian maid, whom the poet has painted in words vivid as colours, palpable almost as sense. Talk of enchantment! The *Thousand-and-One Nights* is one enchantment—more powerful than the lamp of Aladdin, or the "Open Sesame" of Ali Baba. The author, were he *one*—not many—is a magician—a geni—greater than Scott, than Cervantes, equal to Shakspere himself. What poetry, passion, pathos, beauty of sentiment, elegance of costume, ingenuity of contrivance, wit, humour, farce, interest, variety, tact in transition, sunniness of spirit, dream-like wealth of imagination, incidental but precious light cast upon customs, manners, history, religion—everything, in short, that can amuse or amaze, instruct or delight, the human spirit! Like the *Pilgrim's Progress*—devoured by boys, it is a devout study for bearded men.

Tennyson has expressed, especially, the moonlight voluptuousness of tone and spirit which breathes around those delicious productions, as well as the lavish magnificence of dress and decoration, of furniture and architecture, which were worthy of the witch element, the sunny climate, and the early enchanted era, where and when they were written. But we doubt if he mates adequately with that more potent and terrible magic which haunts their higher regions, as in the sublime picture of the Prince's daughter fighting with the Enchanter in mid air, or in the mysterious grandeur which follows all the adventures of Aboulfaouris. With this, too, indeed, he must have sympathy; for it is evident that he abundantly fulfils Coleridge's test of a genuine lover of the *Arabian Nights*. 'Do you admire," said the author of *Kubla Khan* to Hazlitt, "the *Thousand-and-One Nights*?" "No," was the answer. "That's because you *don't dream*." But surely, since the "noticeable man, with large grey eyes," awoke in death from his long life-dream, no poet has arisen of whom the word were more true than of Tennyson, whether in reproach or commendation, asleep or awake—"Behold this dreamer cometh."

In "Œnone," we find him up on the heights of Ida, with the large foot-prints of gods and goddesses still upon its sward, and the citadel and town of Troy, as yet unfallen, as yet unassailed, visible from its summit. Here the poet sees a vision of his own—a vision which, recorded in verse, forms a high third with Wordsworth's "Laodamia" and Keats's *Hyperion*, in the classical style. Less austere and magnificent than the poem of Keats, which seems not so much a torso of earthly art as a splinter fallen from some other exploded world—less chaste, polished, and spiritual, than "Laodamia," that Elgin marble set in Elysian light, it surpasses both in picturesque distinctness and pathetic power. The story is essentially that of "Locksley Hall," but the scene is not the flat and sandy moorland of Lincolnshire, but the green gorges and lawns of Ida. The deceived lover is Œnone, daughter of a river god. She has been deceived by Paris, and her plaint is the poem. Melancholy her song, as that of a disappointed woman—melodious, as that of an aggrieved goddess. It is to Ida, her mother mountain, that she breathes her sorrow. She tells her of her lover's matchless beauty—of her yielding up her heart to him—of the deities descending to receive the golden apple from his hands—of his deciding it to Venus, upon the promise of the "fairest and most loving wife in Greece"—of his abandonment of Œnone, and of her despair. Again and again, in her agony, she cries for Death; but the grim shadow, too busy in hewing down the happy, will not turn aside at her miserable bidding. Her despair at last becomes fury; her tears begin to burn; she will arise; she will leave her dreadful solitude—

> I will rise, and go
> Down into Troy, and, ere the stars come forth,
> Talk with the wild Cassandra; for she says
> A fire dances before her, and a sound
> Rings ever in her ears of armed men.
> What this may be I know not; but I know
> That, wheresoe'er I am, by night and day
> All earth and air seems only burning fire.

And fancy follows Œnone to Ilium, and sees the two beautiful broken-hearted maidens meeting, like two melancholy flames, upon one funeral pile, mingling their hot tears, exchanging their sad stories, and joining, in desperate exultation, at the prospect of the ruin which is already darkening, like a tempest, round the towers and temples of Troy. It is pleasant to find from such productions that, after all, the poetry of Greece is not dead—that the oaks of Delphos and Dodona have not shed all their oracular leaves—that the lightnings in Jove's hand are still warm—and the snows of Olympus are yet clear and bright, shining over the waste of years—that Mercury's feet are winged still—and still is Apollo's hair unshorn—that the mythology of Homer, long dead to belief, is still alive to the airy purposes of poetry—that, though the "dreadful infant's hand" hath smitten down the gods upon the capitol, it has left them the freedom of the Parnassian Hill; and that a Wordsworth, or a Tennyson, may even now, by inclining the ear of imagination, hear the river god plunging in Scamander—Œnone wailing upon Ida—Old Triton blowing his wreathed horn; for never was a truth more certain than that "a thing of beauty is a joy for ever."

We had intended to say something of his "Lotos-Eaters," but are afraid to break in upon its charmed rest—to disturb its sleepy spell—to venture on that land "in which it seemed always afternoon"—or to stir its melancholy, mildeyed inhabitants. We will pass it by, treading so softly that the "blind mole

may not hear a footfall." We must beware of slumbering, and we could hardly but be dull on the enchanted ground.

While the "Lotos-Eaters" breathes the very spirit of luxurious repose, and seems, to apply his own words, a perfect poem in "perfect rest," "Ulysses" is the incarnation of restlessness and insatiable activity. Sick of Ithaca, Argus, Telemachus, and (*sub rosa*) of Penelope too, the old, much-enduring Mariner King, is again panting for untried dangers and undiscovered lands.

> My purpose holds,
> To sail beyond the sunset, and the baths
> Of all the western stars, until I die.

Tennyson, with his fine artistic instinct, saw that the idea of Ulysses at rest was an incongruous thought, and has chosen rather to picture him journeying ever onwards toward infinity or death—

> It may be that the gulphs will wash us down—
> It may be, we shall reach the happy isles,
> And see the great Achilles, whom we knew.

And with breathless interest, and a feeling approaching the sublime, we watch the grey-headed monarch stepping, with his few aged followers, into the bark, which is to be their home till death, and stretching away toward eternity; and every heart and imagination cry out after him—"Go, and return no more."

"Godiva" is an old story newly told—a delicate business delicately handled—the final and illuminated version of an ancient and world-famous tradition. Its beauty is, that, like its heroine, it is "clothed on with chastity." It represses the imagination as gently and effectually as her naked virtue did the eye. We hold our breath, and shut every window of our fancy, till the great ride be over. And in this trial and triumph of female resolution and virtue, the poet would have us believe that Nature herself sympathised—that the light was bashful, and the sun ashamed, and the wind hushed, till the sublime pilgrimage was past—and that, when it ended, a sigh of satisfaction, wide as the circle of earth and heaven, proclaimed Godiva's victory.

The "Vision of Sin" strikes, we think, upon a stronger, though darker, chord than any of his other poems. There are in it impenetrable obscurities, but, like jet black ornaments, some may think them dearer for their darkness. You cannot, says Hazlitt, make "an allegory go on all fours." A vision must be hazy—a ghost should surely be a shadow. Enough, if there be a meaning in the mystery, an oracle speaking through the gloom. The dream is that of a youth, who is seen riding to the gate of a palace, from which

> Came a child of sin,
> And took him by the curls and led him in.

He is lost straightway in mad and wicked revel, tempestuously yet musically described. Meanwhile, unheeded by the revellers, a "vapour, (*the mist of darkness!*) heavy, hueless, formless, cold," is floating slowly on toward the palace. At length it touches the gate, and the dream changes, and such a change!

> I saw
> A grey and gap-toothed man, as lean as Death,
> Who slowly rode across a wither'd heath,
> And lighted at a ruined inn.

And, lighted there, he utters his bitter and blasted feelings in lines, reminding us, from their fierce irony, their misanthropy, their thrice-drugged despair, of Swift's "Legion Club;" and—as in that wicked, wondrous poem—a light sparkle of contemptuous levity glimmers with a ghastly sheen over the putrid pool of malice and misery below, and cannot all disguise the workings of that remorse which is not repentance. At length this sad evil utterance dies away in the throat of the expiring sinner, and behind his consummated ruin there arises a "mystic mountain range," along which voices are heard lamenting, or seeking to explain the causes of his ruin. One says—

> Behold, it was a crime
> Of sense, avenged by sense, that wove with time.

Another—

> The crime of sense became
> The crime of malice, and is equal blame.

A third—

> He had not wholly quenched his power—
> A little grain of conscience made him sour.

And thus at length, in a darkness visible of mystery and grandeur, the "Vision of Sin" closes:—

> At last I heard a voice upon the slope
> Cry to the summit, Is there any hope?
> To which an answer peal'd from that high land,
> But in a tongue no man could understand;
> And on the glimmering limit, far withdrawn,
> God made himself an *awful rose of dawn*.

A reply there is; but whether in the affirmative or negative we do not know. A revelation there is; but whether it be an interference in behalf of the sinner, or a display, in ruddy light, of God's righteousness in his punishment, is left in deep uncertainty. Tennyson, like Addison in his "Vision of Mirza," ventures not to withdraw the veil from the left side of the eternal ocean. He leaves the curtain to be the painting. He permits the imagination of the reader to figure, if it dare, shapes of beauty, or forms of fiery wrath, upon the "awful rose of dawn," as upon a vast back-ground. It is his only to start the thrilling suggestion.

After all, we have considerable misgivings about placing Tennyson—for what he has hitherto done—among our great poets. We cheerfully accord him great powers; but he is, as yet, guiltless of great achievements. His genius is bold, but is waylaid at almost every step by the timidity and weakness of his temperament. His utterance is not proportionate to his vision. He sometimes reminds us of a dumb man with important tidings within, but only able to express them by gestures, starts, sobs, and tears. His works are loopholes, not windows, through which intense glimpses come and go, but no broad, clear, and rounded prospect is commanded. As a thinker, he often seems like one who should perversely pause a hundred feet from the summit of a lofty hill, and refuse to ascend higher. "Up! the breezes call thee—the clouds marshal thy way—the glorious prospect waits thee, as a bride for her husband—angels or gods may meet thee on the top—it may be thy Mountain of Transfiguration." But, no; the pensive or wilful poet chooses to remain below.

Nevertheless, the eye of genius is flashing in Tennyson's head, and his ear is unstopped, whether to the harmonies of nature, or to the still sad music of humanity. We care not much in which of the tracks he has already cut out he may choose to walk; but we would prefer if he were persuaded more frequently to see visions and dream dreams—like his "Vision of Sin"—imbued with high purpose, and forming the Modern Metamorphoses of truth. We have no hope that he will ever be, in the low sense, a popular poet, or that to him the task is allotted of extracting music from the railway train, or of setting in song the "fairy tales of science"—the great astronomical or geological discoveries of the age. Nor is he likely ever to write anything which, like the poems of Burns, or Campbell, can go directly to the heart of the entire nation. For no "Song of the Shirt" even, need we look from him. But the imaginativeness of his nature, the deep vein of his moral sentiment, the bias given to his mind by his early reading, the airy charm of his versification, and the seclusion in which he lives, like a flower in its own peculiar jar, all seem to prepare him for becoming a great spiritual dreamer, who might write not only "Recollections of the Arabian Nights," but Arabian Nights themselves, equally graceful in costume, but impressed with a deeper sentiment, chastened into severer taste, and warmed with a holier flame. Success to such pregnant slumbers! soft be the pillow as that of his own "Sleeping Beauty;" may every syrup of strength and sweetness drop upon his eyelids, and may his dreams be such as to banish sleep from many an eye, and to people the hearts of millions with beauty!

On the whole, perhaps Tennyson is less a prophet than an artist. And this alone would serve better to reconcile us to his silence, should it turn out that his poetic career is over. The loss of even the finest artist may be supplied—that of a prophet, who has been cut off in the midst of his mission, or whose words some envious influence or circumstance has snatched from his lips, is irreparable. In the one case, it is but a painter's pencil that is broken; in the other it is a magic rod shivered. Still, even as an artist, Tennyson has not yet done himself full justice, nor built up any structure so shapely, complete, and living, as may perpetuate his name.[1]

Alfred Tennyson is the son of an English clergyman in Lincolnshire. He is of a retiring disposition, and seldom, though sometimes, emerges from his retirement into the literary coteries of London. And yet welcome is he ever among them—with his eager physiognomy, his dark hair and eyes, and his small, black tobacco pipe. Some years ago, we met a brother of his in Dumfries, who bore, we were told, a marked, though miniature resemblance to him, a beautiful painter and an expert versifier, after the style of Alfred.

The particulars of his literary career are familiar to most. His first production was a small volume of poems, published in 1831. Praised in the *Westminster* elaborately, and extravagantly eulogised in the *Englishman's Magazine* (a periodical conducted by William Kennedy, but long since defunct, and which, according to some malicious persons, died of this same article)—it was sadly mangled by less generous critics. *Blackwood's Magazine* doled it out some severely-sifted praise; and the author, in his next volume, rhymed back his ingratitude in the well-known lines to "Rusty, musty, fusty, crusty Christopher," whose blame he forgave, but whose praise he could not. Meanwhile, he was quietly forming a small but zealous cohort of admirers; and some of his poems, such as "Mariana," &c., were universally read and appreciated. His second production was less successful, and deserved to be less successful, than the first. It was stuffed with wilful impertinencies and affectations. His critics told him he wrote ill, and he answered them by writing worse. His third exhibited a very different spirit. It consisted of a selection from his two former volumes, and a number of additional pieces—the principal of which we have already analysed. In his selection, he winnows his former works with a very salutary severity; but what has he done with that delectable strain of the "Syrens?" We think he has acted well in stabling and shutting up his "Krakens" in their dim, ocean managers; but we are not so willing to part with that beautiful sisterhood, and hope to see them again at no distant day, standing in their lovely isle, and singing—

> Come hither, come hither, and be our lords,
>   For merry brides are we.
> We will kiss sweet kisses and speak sweet words.

> . . .

Ye will not find so happy a shore,
Weary mariners all the world o'er.
Oh fly, oh fly no more.

Notes

1. His "Princess," published since the above, is a medley of success, failure, and half-success—not even an attempt towards a whole.

CHARLES KINGSLEY
"Tennyson" (1850)
Literary and General Essays
1880, pp. 103–24

Critics cannot in general be too punctilious in their respect for an incognito. If an author intended us to know his name, he would put it on his title-page. If he does not choose to do that, we have no more right to pry into his secret than we have to discuss his family affairs or open his letters. But every rule has its exceptional cases; and the book which stands first upon our list ⟨In Memoriam⟩ is surely such. All the world, somehow or other, knows the author. His name has been mentioned unhesitatingly by several reviews already, whether from private information, or from the certainty which every well-read person must feel that there is but one man in England possessed at once of poetic talent and artistic experience sufficient for so noble a creation. We hope, therefore, that we shall not be considered impertinent if we ignore an incognito which all England has ignored before us, and attribute *In Memoriam* to the pen of the author of *The Princess*.

Such a course will probably be the more useful one to our readers; for this last work of our only living great poet seems to us at once the culmination of all his efforts and the key to many difficulties in his former writings. Heaven forbid that we should say that it completes the circle of his powers. On the contrary, it gives us hope of broader effort in new fields of thought and forms of art. But it brings the development of his Muse and of his Creed to a positive and definite point. It enables us to claim one who has been hitherto regarded as belonging to a merely speculative and peirastic school as the willing and deliberate champion of vital christianity, and of an orthodoxy the more sincere because it has worked upward through the abyss of doubt; the more mighty for good because it justifies and consecrates the æsthetics and the philosophy of the present age. We are sure, moreover, that the author, whatever right reasons he may have had for concealing his own name, would have no quarrel against us for alluding to it, were he aware of the idolatry with which every utterance of his is regarded by the cultivated young men of our day, especially at the universities, and of the infinite service of which this *In Memoriam* may be to them, if they are taught by it that their superiors are not ashamed of faith, and that they will rise instead of falling, fulfil instead of denying the cravings of their hearts and intellects, if they will pass upwards with their teacher from the vague though noble expectations of "Locksley Hall," to the assured and everlasting facts of the proem to *In Memoriam*—in our eyes the noblest christian poem which England has produced for two centuries.

To explain our meaning, it will be necessary, perhaps, to go back to Mr. Tennyson's earlier writings, of which he is said to be somewhat ashamed now—a fastidiousness with which we will not quarrel; for it should be the rule of the poet, forgetting those things which are behind, to press on to those things

which are before, and "to count not himself to have apprehended but—" no, we will not finish the quotation; let the readers of *In Memoriam* finish it for themselves, and see how, after all, the poet, if he would reach perfection, must be found by Him who found St. Paul of old. In the meantime, as a true poet must necessarily be in advance of his age, Mr. Tennyson's earlier poems, rather than these latter ones, coincide with the tastes and speculations of the young men of this day. And in proportion, we believe, as they thoroughly appreciate the distinctive peculiarities of those poems, will they be able to follow the author of them on his upward path.

Some of our readers, we would fain hope, remember as an era in their lives the first day on which they read those earlier poems; how, fifteen years ago, Mariana in the Moated Grange, "The Dying Swan," "The Lady of Shalott," came to them as revelations. They seemed to themselves to have found at last a poet who promised not only to combine the cunning melody of Moore, the rich fulness of Keats, and the simplicity of Wordsworth, but one who was introducing a method of observing nature different from that of all the three and yet succeeding in everything which they had attempted, often in vain. Both Keats and Moore had an eye for the beauty which lay in trivial and daily objects. But in both of them there was a want of deep religious reverence, which kept Moore playing gracefully upon the surface of phenomena without ever daring to dive into their laws or inner meaning; and made poor Keats fancy that he was rather to render nature poetical by bespangling her with florid ornament, than simply to confess that she was already, by the grace of God, far beyond the need of his paint and gilding. Even Wordsworth himself had not full faith in the great dicta which he laid down in his famous Introductory Essay. Deep as was his conviction that nature bore upon her simplest forms the finger-mark of God, he did not always dare simply to describe her as she was, and leave her to reveal her own mystery. We do not say this in depreciation of one who stands now far above human praise or blame. The wonder is, not that Wordsworth rose no higher, but that, considering the level on which his taste was formed, he had power to rise to the height above his age which he did attain. He did a mighty work. He has left the marks of his teaching upon every poet who has written verses worth reading for the last twenty years. The idea by which he conquered was, as Coleridge well sets forth, the very one which, in its practical results on his own poetry, procured him loud and deserved ridicule. This, which will be the root idea of the whole poetry of this generation, was the dignity of nature in all her manifestations, and not merely in those which may happen to suit the fastidiousness or Manichæism of any particular age. He may have been at times fanatical on his idea, and have misused it, till it became self-contradictory, because he could not see the correlative truths which should have limited it. But it is by fanatics, by men of one great thought, that great works are done; and it is good for the time that a man arose in it of fearless honesty enough to write *Peter Bell* and the "Idiot Boy," to shake all the old methods of nature-painting to their roots, and set every man seriously to ask himself what he meant, or whether he meant anything real, reverent, or honest, when he talked about "poetic diction," or "the beauties of nature." And after all, like all fanatics, Wordsworth was better than his own creed. As Coleridge thoroughly shows in the second volume of the *Biographia Literaria*, and as may be seen nowhere more strikingly than in his grand posthumous work, his noblest poems and noblest stanzas are those in which his true poetic genius, unconsciously to himself, sets at naught his own pseudo-naturalist dogmas.

Now Mr. Tennyson, while fully adopting Wordsworth's principle from the very first, seemed by instinctive taste to have escaped the snares which had proved too subtle both for Keats and Wordsworth. Doubtless there are slight *niaiseries*, after the manner of both those poets, in the first editions of his earlier poems. He seems, like most other great artists, to have first tried imitations of various styles which already existed, before he learnt the art of incorporating them into his own, and learning from all his predecessors, without losing his own individual peculiarities. But there are descriptive passages in them also which neither Keats nor Wordsworth could have written, combining the honest sensuous observation which is common to them both, with a self-restrained simplicity which Keats did not live long enough to attain, and a stately and accurate melody, an earnest songfulness (to coin a word) which Wordsworth seldom attained, and from his inaccurate and uncertain ear, still seldomer preserved without the occurrence of a jar or a rattle, a false quantity, a false rapture, or a bathos. And above all, or rather beneath all—for we suspect that this has been throughout the very secret of Mr. Tennyson's power—there was a hush and a reverent awe, a sense of the mystery, the infinitude, the awfulness, as well as of the mere beauty of wayside things, which invested these poems as wholes with a peculiar richness, depth, and majesty of tone, beside which both Keats's and Wordsworth's methods of handling pastoral subjects looked like the colouring of Julio Romano or Watteau by the side of Correggio or Titian.

This deep simple faith in the divineness of Nature as she appears, which, in our eyes, is Mr. Tennyson's differentia, is really the natural accompaniment of a quality at first sight its very opposite, and for which he is often blamed by a prosaic world; namely, his subjective and transcendental mysticism. It is the mystic, after all, who will describe Nature most simply, because he sees most in her; because he is most ready to believe that she will reveal to others the same message which she has revealed to him. Men like Behmen, Novalis, and Fourier, who can soar into the inner cloud-world of man's spirit, even though they lose their way there, dazzled by excess of wonder—men who, like Wordsworth, can give utterance to such subtle anthropologic wisdom as the "Ode on the Intimations of Immortality," will for that very reason most humbly and patiently "consider the lilies of the field, how they grow." And even so it is just because Mr. Tennyson is, far more than Wordsworth, mystical, and what an ignorant and money-getting generation, idolatrous of mere sensuous activity, calls "dreamy," that he has become the greatest naturalistic poet which England has seen for several centuries. The same faculty which enabled him to draw such subtle subjective pictures of womanhood as Adeline, Isabel, and Eleanor, enabled him to see, and therefore simply to describe, in one of the most distinctive and successful of his earlier poems, how

The creeping mosses and clambering weeds,
    And the willow branches hoar and dank,
And the wavy swell of the soughing reeds,
    And the wave-worn horns of the echoing bank,
    And the silvery marish flowers that throng
    The desolate creeks and pools among,
Were flooded over with eddying song.

No doubt there are in the earlier poems exceptions to this style—attempts to adorn nature, and dazzle with a barbaric splendour akin to that of Keats—as, for instance, in the "Recollections of the Arabian Nights." But how cold and gaudy, in spite of individual beauties, is that poem by the side of either of the Marianas, and especially of the one in which

the scenery is drawn, simply and faithfully, from those counties which the world considers the quintessence of the prosaic—the English fens.

Upon the middle of the night
    Waking she heard the night-fowl crow;
The cock sang out an hour ere light:
    From the dark fen the oxen's low
Came to her: without hope of change,
    In sleep she seemed to walk forlorn,
    Till cold winds woke the gray-eyed morn
About the lonely moated grange.

. . .

About a stone-cast from the wall
    A sluice with blackened waters slept,
And o'er it many, round and small,
    The cluster'd marish-mosses crept.
Hard by a poplar shook alway,
    All silver-green with gnarled bark,
    For leagues no other tree did mark
The level waste, the rounding gray,

Throughout all these exquisite lines occurs but one instance of what the vulgar call "poetic diction." All is simple description, in short and Saxon words, and yet who can deny the effect to be perfect—superior to any similar passage in Wordsworth? And why? Because the passage quoted, and indeed the whole poem, is perfect in what artists call tone—tone in the metre and in the sound of the words, as well as in the images and the feelings expressed. The weariness, the dreariness, the dark mysterious waste, exist alike within and without, in the slow monotonous pace of the metre and the words, as well as in the boundless fen, and the heart of her who, "without hope of change, in sleep did seem to walk forlorn."

The same faith in Nature, the same instinctive correctness in melody, springing from that correct insight into Nature, ran through the poems inspired by medieval legends. The very spirit of the old ballad writers, with their combinations of mysticism and objectivity, their freedom from any self-conscious attempt at reflective epithets or figures, runs through them all. We are never jarred in them, as we are in all the attempts at ballad-writing and ballad-restoring before Mr. Tennyson's time, by discordant touches of the reflective in thought, the picturesque in Nature, or the theatric in action. To illustrate our meaning, readers may remember the ballad of "Fair Emmeline," in Bishop Percy's *Reliques*. The bishop confesses, if we mistake not, to have patched one end of the ballad. He need not have informed us of that fact, while such lines as these following meet our eyes:

The Baron turned aside,
And wiped away the rising tears
He proudly strove to hide.

No old ballad writer would have used such a complicated concetto. Another, and even a worse instance is to be found in the difference between the old and new versions of the grand ballad of "Glasgerion." In the original, we hear how the elfin harper could

Harp fish out of the water,
    And water out of a stone,
And milk out of a maiden's breast
    That bairn had never none.

For which some benighted "restorer" substitutes—

Oh, there was magic in his touch,
    And sorcery in his string!

No doubt there was. But while the new poetaster informs

you of the abstract notion, the ancient poet gives you the concrete fact; as Mr. Tennyson has done with wonderful art in his exquisite "St. Agnes," where the saint's subjective mysticism appears only as embodied in objective pictures:

> Break up the heavens, oh Lord! and far
>   Through all yon starlight keen
> Draw me, thy bride, a glittering star,
>   In raiment white and clean.

Sir Walter Scott's ballads fail just on the same point. Even Campbell cannot avoid an occasional false note of sentiment. In Mr. Tennyson alone, as we think, the spirit of the Middle Age is perfectly reflected; its delight, not in the "sublime and picturesque," but in the green leaves and spring flowers for their own sake—the spirit of Chaucer and of the "Robin Hood Garland"—the naturalism which revels as much in the hedgerow and garden as in Alps, and cataracts, and Italian skies, and the other strong stimulants to the faculty of admiration which the palled taste of an unhealthy age, from Keats and Byron down to Browning, has rushed abroad to seek. It is enough for Mr. Tennyson's truly English spirit to see how

> On either side the river lie
> Long fields of barley and of rye,
> That clothe the wold and meet the sky;
> And through the field the road runs by
>   To many-tower'd Camelot.

Or how

> In the stormy east wind straining,
> The pale yellow woods were waning,
> The broad stream in his banks complaining,
> Heavily the low sky raining
>   Over tower'd Camelot.

Give him but such scenery as that which he can see in every parish in England, and he will find it a fit scene for an ideal myth, subtler than a casuist's questionings, deep as the deepest heart of woman.

But in this earlier volume the poet has not yet arrived at the art of combining his new speculations on man with his new mode of viewing Nature. His objective pieces are too exclusively objective, his subjective too exclusively subjective; and where he deals with natural imagery in these latter, he is too apt, as in "Eleanore," to fall back upon the old and received method of poetic diction, though he never indulges in a commonplace or a stock epithet. But in the interval between 1830 and 1842 the needful interfusion of the two elements has taken place. And in "Locksley Hall" and the "Two Voices" we find the new doubts and questions of the time embodied naturally and organically, in his own method of simple natural expression. For instance, from the Search for Truth in the "Two Voices"—

> Cry, faint not, climb: the summits lope
> Beyond the furthest flights of hope,
> Wrapt in dense cloud from base to cope.
>
> Sometimes a little corner shines
> As over rainy mist inclines
> A gleaming crag with belts of pines.
>
> "I will go forward," sayest thou;
> "I shall not fail to find her now.
> Look up, the fold is on her brow."

Or again, in "Locksley Hall," the poem which, as we think deservedly, has had most influence on the minds of the young men of our day:

> Eager-hearted as a boy when first he leaves his
>   father's field,
> And at night along the dusky highway near and

> nearer drawn,
> Sees in heaven the light of London flaring like a
>   dreary dawn;
> And his spirit leaps within him to be gone before him
>   then,
> Underneath the light he looks at, in among the
>   throngs of men;
> Men, my brothers, men the workers, ever reaping
>   something new;
> That which they have done but earnest of the things
>   which they shall do:

and all the grand prophetic passage following, which is said, we know not how truly, to have won for the poet the respect of that great statesman whose loss all good men deplore.

In saying that "Locksley Hall" has deservedly had so great an influence over the minds of the young, we shall, we are afraid, have offended some who are accustomed to consider that poem as Werterian and unhealthy. But, in reality, the spirit of the poem is simply anti-Werterian. It is man rising out of sickness into health—not conquered by Werterism, but conquering his selfish sorrow, and the moral and intellectual paralysis which it produces, by faith and hope—faith in the progress of science and civilisation, hope in the final triumph of good. Doubtless, that is not the highest deliverance—not a permanent deliverance at all. Faith in God and hope in Christ alone can deliver a man once and for all from Werterism, or any other moral disease; that truth was reserved for "In Memoriam:" but as far as "Locksley Hall" goes, it is a step forward—a whole moral æon beyond Byron and Shelley; and a step, too, in the right direction, just because it is a step forward—because the path of deliverance is, as "Locksley Hall" sets forth, not backwards towards a fancied paradise of childhood—not backward to grope after an unconsciousness which is now impossible, an implicit faith which would be unworthy of the man, but forward on the road on which God has been leading him, carrying upward with him the aspirations of childhood, and the bitter experience of youth, to help the organised and trustful labour of manhood. There are, in fact, only two deliverances from Werterism possible in the nineteenth century; one is into Popery, and the other is—

> Forward, forward, let us range;
> Let the peoples spin for ever down the ringing
>   grooves of change;
> Through the shadow of the world we sweep into the
>   younger day:
> Better fifty years of Europe than a cycle of Cathay.

But such a combination of powers as Mr. Tennyson's naturally develop themselves into a high idyllic faculty; for it is the very essence of the idyl to set forth the poetry which lies in the simpler manifestations of Man and Nature; yet not explicitly, by a reflective moralising on them, as almost all our idyllists—Cowper, Gray, Crabbe, and Wordsworth—have been in the habit of doing, but implicitly, by investing them all with a rich and delightful tone of colouring, perfect grace of manner, perfect melody of rhythm, which, like a gorgeous summer atmosphere, shall glorify without altering the most trivial and homely sights. And it is this very power, as exhibited in the "Lord of Burleigh," "Audley Court," and the "Gardener's Daughter," which has made Mr. Tennyson, not merely the only English rival of Theocritus and Bion, but, in our opinion, as much their superior as modern England is superior to ancient Greece.

Yet in *The Princess*, perhaps, Mr. Tennyson rises higher still. The idyllic manner alternates with the satiric, the pathetic, even the sublime, by such imperceptible gradations, and continual delicate variations of key, that the harmonious medley of his style becomes the fit outward expression of the bizarre and yet harmonious fairyland in which his fancy ranges. In this work, too, Mr. Tennyson shows himself more than ever the poet of the day. In it more than ever the old is interpenetrated with the new—the domestic and scientific with the ideal and sentimental. He dares, in every page, to make use of modern words and notions, from which the mingled clumsiness and archaism of his compeers shrinks, as unpoetical. Though, as we just said, his stage is an ideal fairyland, yet he has reached the ideal by the only true method—by bringing the Middle Age forward to the Present one, and not by ignoring the Present to fall back on a cold and galvanised Medievalism; and thus he makes his "Medley" a mirror of the nineteenth century, possessed of its own new art and science, its own new temptations and aspirations, and yet grounded on, and continually striving to reproduce, the forms and experiences of all past time. The idea, too, of *The Princess* is an essentially modern one. In every age women have been tempted, by the possession of superior beauty, intellect, or strength of will, to deny their own womanhood, and attempt to stand alone as men, whether on the ground of political intrigue, ascetic saintship, or philosophic pride. Cleopatra and St. Hedwiga, Madame de Staël and the Princess, are merely different manifestations of the same self-willed and proud longing of woman to unsex herself, and realise, single and self-sustained, some distorted and partial notion of her own as to what the "angelic life" should be. Cleopatra acted out the pagan ideal of an angel; St. Hedwiga, the medieval one; Madame de Staël hers, with the peculiar notions of her time as to what "spirituel" might mean; and in *The Princess* Mr. Tennyson has embodied the ideal of that nobler, wider, purer, yet equally fallacious, because equally unnatural, analogue, which we may meet too often up and down England now. He shows us the woman, when she takes her stand on the false masculine ground of intellect, working out her own moral punishment, by destroying in herself the tender heart of flesh: not even her vast purposes of philanthropy can preserve her, for they are built up, not on the womanhood which God has given her, but on her own self-will; they change, they fall, they become inconsistent, even as she does herself, till, at last, she loses all feminine sensibility; scornfully and stupidly she rejects and misunderstands the heart of man; and then falling from pride to sternness, from sternness to sheer inhumanity, she punishes sisterly love as a crime, robs the mother of her child, and becomes all but a vengeful fury, with all the peculiar faults of woman, and none of the peculiar excellences of man.

The poem being, as its title imports, a medley of jest and earnest, allows a metrical licence, of which we are often tempted to wish that its author had not availed himself; yet the most unmetrical and apparently careless passages flow with a grace, a lightness, a colloquial ease and frolic, which perhaps only heighten the effect of the serious parts, and serve as a foil to set off the unrivalled finish and melody of these latter. In these come out all Mr. Tennyson's instinctive choice of tone, his mastery of language, which always fits the right word to the right thing, and that word always the simplest one, and the perfect ear for melody which makes it superfluous to set to music poetry which, read by the veriest schoolboy, makes music of itself. The poem, we are glad to say, is so well known that it seems unnecessary to quote from it; yet there are here and there gems of sound and expression of which, however well our readers may know them, we cannot forbear reminding them again. For instance, the end of the idyl in book vii.

beginning "Come down, O maid" (the whole of which is perhaps one of the most perfect fruits of the poet's genius):

> Myriads of rivulets hurrying through the lawn,
> The moan of doves in immemorial elms,
> And murmuring of innumerable bees.

Who, after three such lines, will talk of English as a harsh and clumsy language, and seek in the effeminate and monotonous Italian for expressive melody of sound? Who cannot hear in them the rapid rippling of the water, the stately calmness of the wood-dove's note, and, in the repetition of short syllables and soft liquids in the last line, the

> Murmuring of innumerable bees?

Or again, what combination of richness with simplicity in such a passage as this:

> Breathe upon my brows;
> In that fine air I tremble, all the past
> Melts mist-like into this bright hour, and this
> I scarce believe, and all the rich to come
> Reels, as the golden Autumn woodland reels
> Athwart the smoke of burning leaves.

How Mr. Tennyson can have attained the prodigal fulness of thought and imagery which distinguishes this poem, and especially the last canto, without his style ever becoming overloaded, seldom even confused, is perhaps one of the greatest marvels of the whole production. The songs themselves, which have been inserted between the cantos in the last edition of the book, seem, perfect as they are, wasted and smothered among the surrounding fertility; till we discover that they stand there, not merely for the sake of their intrinsic beauty, but serve to call back the reader's mind, at every pause in the tale of the Princess's folly, to that very healthy ideal of womanhood which she has spurned.

At the end of the first canto, fresh from the description of the female college, with its professoresses, and hostleresses, and other utopian monsters, we turn the page, and—

> As through the land at eve we went,
> And pluck'd the ripen'd ears.
> We fell out, my wife and I,
> And kissed again with tears:
> And blessings on the falling-out
> That all the more endears,
> When we fall out with those we love,
> And kiss again with tears!
> For when we came where lies the child
> We lost in other years,
> There above the little grave,
> We kissed again with tears.

Between the next two cantos intervenes the well-known cradle-song, perhaps the best of all; and at the next interval is the equally well-known bugle-song, the idea of which is that of twin-labour and twin-fame, in a pair of lovers:

> Our echoes roll from soul to soul,
> And grow for ever and for ever.

In the next, the memory of wife and child inspirits the soldier in the field; in the next, the sight of the fallen hero's child opens the sluices of his widow's tears; and in the last, and perhaps the most beautiful of all, the poet has succeeded, in the new edition, in superadding a new form of emotion to a canto in which he seemed to have exhausted every resource of pathos which his subject allowed; and prepares us for the triumph of that art by which he makes us, after all, love the heroine whom he at first taught us to hate and despise, till we see that the naughtiness is after all one that must be kissed and not whipped out of her, and look on smiling while she repents, with Prince Harry of old, "not in sackcloth and ashes, but in new silk and old sack:"

> Ask me no more: the moon may draw the sea;
>   The cloud may stoop from Heaven and take the
>   shape,
>   With fold to fold, of mountain or of cape;
> But, O too fond, when have I answered thee?
>   Ask me no more.
>
> Ask me no more: what answer should I give?
>   I love not hollow cheek or faded eye:
>   Yet, O my friend, I will not have thee die!
> Ask me no more, lest I should bid thee live;
>   Ask me no more.
>
> Ask me no more: thy fate and mine are seal'd:
>   I strove against the stream and all in vain:
>   Let the great river take me to the main:
> No more, dear love, for at a touch I yield;
>   Ask me no more.

We now come to *In Memoriam*; a collection of poems on a vast variety of subjects, but all united, as their name implies, to the memory of a departed friend. We know not whether to envy more—the poet the object of his admiration, or that object the monument which has been consecrated to his nobleness. For in this latest and highest volume, written at various intervals during a long series of years, all the poet's peculiar excellences, with all that he has acquired from others, seem to have been fused down into a perfect unity, and brought to bear on his subject with that care and finish which only a labour of love can inspire. We only now know the whole man, all his art, all his insight, all his faculty of discerning the *più nell' uno*, and the *uno nell' più*. As he says himself:

> My love has talked with rocks and trees,
>   He finds on misty mountain-ground,
>   His own vast shadow glory-crowned;
> He sees himself in all he sees.

Everything reminds him of the dead. Every joy or sorrow of man, every aspect of nature, from

> The forest crack'd, the waters curl'd,
>   The cattle huddled on the lea.
>
> The thousand waves of wheat
> That ripple round the lonely grange.

In every place where in old days they had met and conversed; in every dark wrestling of the spirit with the doubts and fears of manhood, throughout the whole outward universe of Nature, and the whole inward universe of spirit, the soul of his dead friend broods—at first a memory shrouded in blank despair, then a living presence, a ministering spirit, answering doubts, calming fears, stirring up noble aspirations, utter humility, leading the poet upward, step by step, to faith, and peace, and hope. Not that there runs throughout the book a conscious or organic method. The poems seem often merely to be united by the identity of their metre, so exquisitely chosen, that while the major rhyme in the second and third lines of each stanza gives the solidity and self-restraint required by such deep themes, the mournful minor rhyme of each first and fourth line always leads the ear to expect something beyond, and enables the poet's thoughts to wander sadly on, from stanza to stanza and poem to poem, in an endless chain of

> Linkèd sweetness long drawn out.

There are records of risings and fallings again, of alternate cloud and sunshine, throughout the book; earnest and passionate, yet never bitter; humble, yet never abject; with a depth and vehemence of affection "passing the love of woman," yet

without a taint of sentimentality; self-restrained and dignified, without ever narrowing into artificial coldness; altogether rivalling the sonnets of Shakespeare; and all knit together into one spiritual unity by the proem at the opening of the volume—in our eyes, the noblest English Christian poem which several centuries have seen.

We shall not quote the very poems which we should most wish to sink into men's hearts. Let each man find for himself those which suit him best, and meditate on them in silence. They are fit only to be read solemnly in our purest and most thoughtful moods, in the solitude of our chamber, or by the side of those we love, with thanks to the great heart who has taken courage to bestow on us the record of his own friendship, doubt, and triumph.

It has been often asked why Mr. Tennyson's great and varied powers had never been concentrated on one immortal work. The epic, the lyric, the idyllic faculties, perhaps the dramatic also, seemed to be all there, and yet all sundered, scattered about in small fragmentary poems. "In Memoriam," as we think, explains the paradox. Mr. Tennyson had been employed on higher, more truly divine, and yet more truly human work than either epos or drama. Within the unseen and alone truly Real world which underlies and explains this mere time-shadow, which men miscall the Real, he had been going down into the depths, and ascending into the heights, led, like Dante of old, by the guiding of a mighty spirit. And in this volume, the record of seventeen years, we have the result of those spiritual experiences in a form calculated, as we believe, to be a priceless benefit to many an earnest seeker in this generation, and perhaps to stir up some who are priding themselves on a cold dilettantism and barren epicurism, into something like a living faith and hope. Blessed and delightful it is to find, that even in these new ages the creeds which so many fancy to be at their last gasp, are still the final and highest succour, not merely of the peasant and the outcast, but of the subtle artist and the daring speculator. Blessed it is to find the most cunning poet of our day able to combine the complicated rhythm and melody of modern times with the old truths which gave heart to martyrs at the stake; and to see in the science and the history of the nineteenth century new and living fulfilments of the words which we learnt at our mother's knee. Blessed, thrice blessed, to find that hero-worship is not yet passed away; that the heart of man still beats young and fresh; that the old tales of David and Jonathan, Damon and Pythias, Socrates and Alcibiades, Shakespeare and his nameless friend, of "love passing the love of woman," ennobled by its own humility, deeper than death, and mightier than the grave, can still blossom out, if it be but in one heart here and there, to show men still how, sooner or later, "he that loveth knoweth God, for God is love."

WALTER BAGEHOT
From "Tennyson's *Idylls*" (1859)
Collected Works, ed. Norman St. John-Stevas
1965, Volume 2, pp. 179–207

It is a hardship on quarterly reviewers that good books should be published at the beginning of a quarter. Before the next number of the Review appears, they are scarely new books at all. Everything which need be, or ought to be, perhaps everything which can be said, has been said. Doubtless the best remarks are forestalled. Yet what is to be done? A critical journal, which hopes to influence the taste of its time, must not omit to notice any remarkable books. When they are so attractive as the *Idylls of the King*, what critic can neglect a chance of reviewing them? Although, therefore, the last poem of Mr. Tennyson has already been some time before the public, and much has already been written about it, we must devote a few words to the delineation of its peculiarities.

The *Idylls of the King* is, we think, more popular with the general public than with Mr. Tennyson's straiter disciples. It is the characteristic—in some cases it is the calamity—of every great and peculiar poet, to create for himself a school of readers. Wordsworth did so during the first twenty years of the century. For the whole of that time, and perhaps for some years longer, his works could scarcely be said to belong to general English literature: the multitude did not read them. Some of the acutest of those who gave away reputation in those days laughed at them. But a secret worship was all the while forming itself; a sect accumulated. If you read the reviews of that time, you will find that the Wordsworthians were considered a kind of Quakers in literature, that rejected finery, disliked ornate art, and preferred a 'thee and thou' simplicity in poetry. Some of the defects of Wordsworth's poems may be in part traced to the narrowing influence of this species of readers. Even the greatest artist thinks sometimes of his peculiar public. The more solitary his life is, the more he broods on it. The more rejected he is by the multitude, the more he thinks of his few disciples. It is scarcely conceivable that such a habit should not narrow the mind and straiten the sympathies. The class of persons who are the first to take up a very peculiar writer, are themselves commonly somewhat peculiar. 'I am not sure of missionaries,' said some one; 'but I detest converts.' The first believers in anything are rarely good critics of it. The first enthusiasts for a great poet are heedless in their faith; a fault in their idol is like a fault in themselves: they have to defend him in discussion, and in consequence they come to admire the most those parts of his poems which are attacked most frequently: they have a logical theory in defence of them, and are attached to the instances that show its ingenuity and that exemplify its nature: in short, they admire, not what is best in the great writer, but what is most characteristic of him; they incite him to display his eccentricities and to develop his peculiarities. 'Beware of thy friends,' says the oriental proverb; 'for affection is but the flattery of the soul.' Many of Wordsworth's best poems would have been better if he had been more on his guard against the misleading influence of a sectarian sympathy. A few years ago Mr. Tennyson was in a rather similar position. We should not like to specify the date of his ratified acceptance by the public at large; but it is indisputable that at one time he was not so accepted. Everybody admires Tennyson now; but to admire him fifteen years or so ago, was to be a 'Tennysonian.' We know what the *Quarterly* said of his first volume, and the feeling there indicated lingered a long time in many quarters. He has now vanquished it; but an observant eye may still detect in literary, and still more in semi-literary society, several differences in taste and in feeling between the few disciples of the early school and the numerous race of new admirers.

Perhaps the first Tennysonians were not among the wisest of men,—at least they were not taken from the class which is apt to be the wisest. The early poetry of Mr. Tennyson—and the same may be said of nearly all the poetry of Shelley and Keats—labours under the defect that it is written, almost professedly, for young people—especially young men—of rather heated imaginations. All poetry, or almost all poetry, finds its way more easily to the brains of young men, who are

at once intellectual and excitable, than to those of men of any other kind. Persons engaged in life have rarely leisure for imaginative enjoyment: the briefs, the sums, the politics intervene. Slowly, even in the case of young men, does the influence of a new poet enter into the mind; you hear the snatch of a stanza here; you see an extract in a periodical; you get the book and read it; you are pleased with it, but you do not know whether the feeling will last. It is the habitual pleasure that such works give which alone is the exact criterion of their excellence. But what number of occupied men read new poetry habitually? What number of them really surrender their minds to the long task of gradually conceiving new forms of imagery, to the even more delicate task of detecting the healthiness or unhealthiness of unfamiliar states of feeling? Almost all poetry, in consequence, is addressed more to young men than to others. But the early poetry of Tennyson, and of the other poets we have named, is addressed to that class even more peculiarly. In the greatest poets, in Shakespeare and in Homer, there is a great deal besides poetry. There are broad descriptions of character, dramatic scenes, eloquence, argument, a deep knowledge of manly and busy life. These interest readers who are no longer young; they refer to the world in which almost all of us have to act; they reflect with the strong light of genius the scenes of life in which the mass of men live and move. By the aid of these extraneous elements, the poetry of these great writers reaches and impresses those who would never be attracted by it in itself, or take the pains to understand it if it had been presented to them alone. Shelley and Keats, on the other hand, have presented their poetry to the world in its pure essence; they have not added—we scarcely know whether they would have been able to add—the more worldly and terrestrial elements; probably their range in the use of these would have been but limited; at any rate, they have not tried—parts of Shelley's *Cenci* perhaps excepted—to use them; they have been content to rely on imaginatively expressed sentiment, and sentiment-exciting imagery; in short, on that which in its more subtle sense we call poetry, exclusively and wholly. In consequence, their works have had a great influence on young men; they retain a hold on many mature men only because they are associated with their youth; they delineate

> Such sights as youthful poets dream
> On summer eves by haunted stream:

and young men, who were not poets, have eagerly read them, have fondly learned them, and have long remembered them.—A good deal of this description applies to the writings of Tennyson,—some years ago we should have said that almost the whole of it was applicable to him. His audience formerly consisted entirely of young men of cultivated tastes and susceptible imaginations; and it was so because his poetry contained most of the elements which are suitable to such persons in a country like England, and an age such as this is. But whatever be the cause,—whether or not our analysis of the ingredients in Mr. Tennyson's poetry which attracted young men of this kind be correct or otherwise,—the fact that it did so attract them, and that it attracted but few others with great force, is very certain. His public was limited and peculiar; it was almost as much so as Wordsworth's was at an earlier time.

When Mr. Tennyson published *Maud*, we feared that the influence of this class of admirers was deteriorating his powers. The subject was calculated to call out the unhealthier sort of youthful imaginations; and his treatment of it, so far from lessening the danger, seemed studiously selected to increase it. The hero of *Maud* is a young man who lives very much out of the world, who has no definite duties or intelligible occupations, who hates society because he is bound by no social ties and is conscious of no social courage. This young gentleman sees a young lady who is rich, and whose father has an unpleasant association with his own father, who was a bankrupt. He has all manner of feelings about the young lady, and she is partial to him; but there is a difficulty about their interviews. As he is poor and she is wealthy, they do not meet in common society; and a stolen visit in her garden ends, if we understand the matter, in his killing her brother. After this he leads a wandering life, and expresses his sentiments. Such a story is evidently very likely to bring into prominence the exaggerated feelings and distorted notions which we call unhealthy. The feelings of a young man who has nothing to do, and tries to do nothing; who is very poor, and regrets that he is not very rich; who is in love, and cannot speak to the lady he loves; who knows he cannot marry her, but notwithstanding wanders vaguely about her,—are sure to be unhealthy. Solitude, social mortification, wounded feeling, are the strongest sources of mental malaria; and all of these are here crowded together, and are conceived to act at once. Such a representation, therefore, if it was to be true, must be partially tinctured with unhealthiness. This was inevitable; and it was inevitable, too, that this taint should be rather agreeable than otherwise to many of the poet's warmest admirers. The Tennysonians, as we have said, were young men; and youth is the season of semi-diseased feeling. Keats, who knew much about such matters, remarked this. 'The imagination,' he said, 'of a man is healthy, and the imagination of a boy is healthy; but between' there is an uncertain time, when the fancy is restless, the principles are unfixed, the sentiments waver, and the highest feelings have not acquired consistency Upon young men in such a frame of mind a delineation like that of the hero of *Maud*, adorned, as it was, with rare fragments of beautiful imagery, and abiding snatches of the sweetest music, could not but be attractive, and could not but be dangerous. It seemed to be the realised ideal of their hopes, of their hearts, of themselves; it half consecrated their characteristic defects, it confirmed their hope that their eccentricities were excellencies. Such a danger could not be avoided; but Mr. Tennyson, so far from trying to shun it, seemed intentionally to choose to aggravate it. He seemed to sympathise with the feverish railings, the moody nonsense, the very entangled philosophy, which he put into the mouth of his hero. There were some odd invectives against peace, against industry, against making your livelihood, which seemed by no means to be dramatic exhibitions of represented character, but, on the contrary, confidential expositions of the poet's own belief. He not only depicted the natural sentiments of an inactive, inexperienced, and neglected young man, but seemed to agree with them. He sympathised with moody longings; he was not severe on melancholy vanity; he rather encouraged a general disaffection to the universe. He appeared not only to have written, but to have accepted the 'Gospel according to the Unappreciated.' The most charitable reader could scarcely help fancying, that in describing an irritable confusion of fancy and a diseased moodiness of feeling, the poet for the time imbibed a certain taint of those defects.

The *Idylls of the King* suggest to us a peculiar doubt. Was not Mr. Tennyson, after all, laughing at his admirers? *Did* he believe in *Maud*, though he seemed to say he did? We do not know; but at all events we have now a poem not only of a different, but of the very opposite kind. Every line of it is defined with the delicate grace of a very composed genius; shows the trace of a very mature judgment; will bear the scrutiny of the most choice and detective taste. The feelings are

natural, the thoughts such as people in life have or might have. The situations, though in a certain sense unnatural, have, we believe, a peculiar artistic propriety. There is a completeness in the whole.

> For when the Roman left us, and their law
> Relax'd its hold upon us, and the ways
> Were fill'd with rapine, here and there a deed
> Of prowess done redress'd a random wrong.
> But I was first of all the kings who drew
> The knighthood-errant of this realm and all
> The realms together under me, their Head,
> In that fair Order of my Table Round,
> A glorious company, the flower of men,
> To serve as model for the mighty world,
> And be the fair beginning of a time.

The general public will like this, but scarcely the youthful admirers of broken art and incomplete beauties who accepted *Maud* with great delight. The world we know is opposed to earnest enthusiasts and fond disciples, and Mr. Tennyson has sided with the world. ⟨. . .⟩

Mr. Tennyson has in the *Idylls* used these elements of the chivalric legend with instinctive felicity and dexterity. The tale of Prince Geraint, as the first Idyll might be called, is, in its main incidents, as pure a tale of chivalry as could be conceived. His love of Enid at first sight; his single combat with her cousin, who keeps her out of her inheritance; the general plentifulness of banditti, and his conquests over them,—are all features belonging essentially to that kind of story. It would be needless criticism to show that the poet has made a great deal of them, that the narrative is very clear and very flowing, that the choice of the events is very skilful; every reader must have perceived these excellencies.

It is more necessary to point out what the careful art of the poet disguises—that he has avoided the greatest danger of such a theme. The danger of a topic abounding in romantic and extraordinary events is, that its treatment may have a sort of glare. The first miracle we meet petrifies us, the next only astonishes, the third tires, and a fourth bores. The perpetual stimulus of such events as those which we have shown to be particularly characteristic of the chivalric legend would become wearisomely tedious, if a relieving element were not introduced in order to prevent it. Mr. Tennyson has found us such an element. He has managed to introduce to us, incidentally and without effort, many pictures of the quieter parts of human nature. He has fully availed himself of the license which his subject gives him. He never goes into any detail of life, which cannot be made attractive, which may have disenchanting associations, which may touch with a prosaic breath the accomplished exquisiteness of his art. But no mistaken hesitation, none of the over-caution which a less practised artist would have felt, has restrained him from using to the utmost the entire range of that part of life which he can make attractive. We have spoken of the first Idyll, as in its story one of the most purely chivalric of the four. Yet even in this there are several relieving elements. There is scarcely anything to be imagined of higher excellence in this kind than the character of Yniol and his wife. Yniol is an old lord who has lost his property, whose followers have deserted him, and who lives in poverty at an old castle upon sufferance. He thus describes how his nephew ejected him, and what are the feelings with which he contemplates his life:

> 'And since the proud man often is the mean,
> He sow'd a slander in the common ear,
> Affirming that his father left him gold,
> And in my charge, which was not render'd to him;

Bribed with large promises the men who served
About my person, the more easily
Because my means were somewhat broken into
Thro' open doors and hospitality;
Raised my own town against me in the night
Before my Enid's birthday, sack'd my house;
From mine own earldom foully ousted me;
Built that new fort to overawe my friends,
For truly there are those who love me yet;
And keeps me in this ruinous castle here,
Where doubtless he would put me soon to death,
But that his pride too much despises me:
And I myself sometimes despise myself;
For I have let men be, and have their way;
Am much too gentle, have not used my power:
Nor know I whether I be very base
Or very manful, whether very wise
Or very foolish; only this I know,
That whatsoever evil happen to me,
I seem to suffer nothing heart or limb,
But can endure it all most patiently.'

The quiet contemplative character, which suffers so many calamities in rude times, and which is often so puzzled to find out why it has experienced them, is a most suitable shading element to relieve the mind from always admiring great knights who strike hard, who throw immense lances, and who can kill anyone they wish. The feminine reflections—if such they can be called—of Yniol's wife, on the changes of her fortune, are equally appropriate, and quite as true to nature:

'For I myself unwillingly have worn
My faded suit, as you, my child, have yours,
And howsoever patient, Yniol his.
Ah, dear, he took me from a goodly house,
With store of rich apparel, sumptuous fare,
And page, and maid, and squire, and seneschal,
And pastime both of hawk and hound, and all
That appertains to noble maintenance.
Yea, and he brought me to a goodly house;
But since our fortune swerved from sun to shade,
And all thro' that young traitor, cruel need
Constrain'd us, but a better time has come;
So clothe yourself in this, that better fits
Our mended fortunes and a Prince's bride:
For tho' ye won the prize of fairest fair,
And tho' I heard him call you fairest fair,
Let never maiden think, however fair,
She is not fairer in new clothes than old.'

The whole story of the dress, of which this is a part, is a very delicate instance of relieving and softening skill; but we have no room to make any more remarks upon it.

Mr. Tennyson has, however, introduced another element into the description of the chivalric state of society, which, though in some sense it relieves it, does not so well harmonise with it. As we have observed, he avails himself of the peculiar manner—the sudden manner—of falling in love, characteristic of that society. In the first Idyll, Geraint falls in love with Enid on the first evening of their acquaintance; he proposes for her at once, fights a tournament, and is accepted the next morning. In the third Idyll we have the reverse history: a young lady named Elaine falls in love at once with the great Sir Lancelot; but as he does not like her as well as the Queen, she is not accepted. These are love affairs very characteristic of a state of society when women were seen but rarely, and even when seen were but little spoken to; but side by side with them in the Idyll there are other scenes indicative of a great familiarity between them and men, full of intellectual friction

between the two, showing on both sides the nice and critical knowledge of our civilised world. It seems hardly fair that a writer should insist on the good side of both species of life; upon being permitted to use the sudden love which arises from not knowing women, and the love-tinged intercourse of thought and fancy which is the result of knowing them, together and at once. The nature of the story seems to have led Mr. Tennyson into this complication. The reign of Arthur, as is well known, was believed to have been for many years clouded, and at length terminated, by the unlawful affection of his Queen Guinevere for Sir Lancelot, the greatest and most renowned of his courtiers. This is evidently a very delicate topic for art to handle. King Arthur and Sir Lancelot are both to be made interesting: the Queen, of

imperial-moulded form,
And beauty such as never woman wore,

is to be made interesting likewise. A great deal of intellectual detail is necessary for this end; many slight touches of delicate insight must conduce to it; a hundred pencillings of nice art must be accumulated to effect it. If the subject was to be treated for modern readers, some additions to the bareness of old romance and legend were indispensable; and even a critic could hardly object to them. But Mr. Tennyson has gone further. There being a Queen at court who was not immaculate, he has thought it proper that there should be ladies about her who are no better. 'Vivien,' the young lady who gives her name to the second Idyll, is more fitted for the court of Louis Quinze than for that of the saintly king of chivalry. ⟨. . .⟩

There is undoubtedly much that is not modern in Merlin's character, or rather in his occupation, for he is a faint kind of being; but the enchanter who has a charm of 'woven paces and of waving hands,' and who has read lines of lore which no other person can read, does not belong to the drawing-room. His pursuits, at any rate, do not. ⟨. . .⟩

But however removed from us Merlin's character may be, that of Vivien in its essence rather belongs to an over-civilised and satirical, than to an uncultivated and romantic time. It rather mars our enjoyment of the new book of chivalry, to have a character so discordant with its idea placed in such prominence, and drawn out in such development.

A similar charge cannot, however, be justly brought against the main story of the poem. The contrast of character between King Arthur and Sir Lancelot is one of those which exists in some degree in all ages, but which the exciting circumstances of an unsettled time necessarily tend to bring out and exaggerate. In our last Number we had occasion, in writing on another subject, to draw out at some length the delineation of the two kinds of *goodness* which have long been contrasted, and always seem likely to be contrasted, in the world,—the ascetic and the sensuous. The characteristic of the latter is to be sensitive to everything in this world, tempted by every stimulus, exposed to every passion; the characteristic of the former is to be repelled from the ordinary pleasures of the world, to be above them, to feel a warning instinct against them. In the course of life the fate of the ascetic character is to be absorbed in a somewhat chill ideal; that of the sensuous character is to purchase a fascinating richness of earthly experience by a serious number of grave errors. We had some difficulty formerly in illustrating the distinction between the two characters at once clearly and expressively, but we should have had no such difficulty if Mr. Tennyson had published his new poem a little earlier. The character of Arthur, absorbed in the ideal conception of a chivalrous monarchy, is the very type of the highest abstract or ascetic character; that of Lancelot, the great knight of many exploits and full-lipped enjoyment, whom Guinevere prefers, is the type of the sensuous and sensitive. ⟨. . .⟩

There can be no doubt that Mr. Tennyson has judged wisely in telling the story of Arthur and Guinevere in a series of tales rather than in a single connected epic. The peculiar and painful nature of that story requires, in a singular degree, the continual use of relieving elements; and yet it is of the first importance that no one of these elements should assume an undue prominence, or be more interesting than the story itself. If other interesting characters had been introduced into the main plot of a continuous poem, the latter effect would have been nearly inevitable. The imagination cannot rest with satisfaction either on Guinevere's relation to Arthur or on her relation to Lancelot. In each there is a disagreeable and disenchanting something. If a competing interest had been introduced into the central plot, it could hardly fail to be intrinsically pleasanter, and might have distracted the attention intended from the chosen theme. The form which the poet has adopted—that of a set of stories, with continual allusion to a latent thread—prevents this result, and also gives the requisite shading to the painful subject. There is a continued succession of relieving interests; but there is none which can compete with the central one, or be compared with it.

We have said enough of the merits of this poem to entitle us to say what ought to be said against it. We have not, indeed, a long list of defects to set forth. On the contrary, we think we perceive only one of real importance; and it is very probable that many critics will think us quite wrong as to that one. It appears to us that the *Idylls* are defective in dramatic power. Madame de Staël said that Coleridge was admirable in monologue, but quite incapable of dialogue. Something analogous may perhaps be said of Mr. Tennyson. His imagination seems to fix itself on a particular person in a particular situation; and he pours out, with ease and abundance, with delicacy and exactness, all which is suitable to that person in that situation. This was so with 'Ulysses' in former years; it is so in his 'Grandmother's Apology', published the other day. Unnumbered instances of it may be found in the *Idylls*. But the power of writing a soliloquy is very different from that of writing a conversation; so different, indeed, that the person who is most likely to wish to write one, is most likely not to wish to write the other. Dialogue requires a very changing imagination, ready to move with ease from the mental position of one mind to the mental position of another, quick with the various language suited to either. Soliloquy—prolonged soliloquy, at any rate—requires a very steady imagination, steadily accumulating, slowly realising the exact position of a single person. The glancing mind will tend to one sort of composition; the meditative, solitary, and heavy mind to the other. All Mr. Tennyson's poems show more of the latter tendency than of the first. His genius gives the notion of a slow depositing instinct; day by day, as the hours pass, the delicate sand falls into beautiful forms—in stillness, in peace, in brooding. You fancy Shakespeare writing quick, the hasty dialogue of the parties passing quickly through his brain: we have no such idea of our great contemporary poet. He keeps his verses in his head: a meditative and scrupulous Muse is prayed to

> Let him write his random lines
> Ere they be half forgotten,
> Nor add or alter many times
> Till all be ripe and rotten.

The lightly-flowing dialogue is not so written. The lightly-moving imagination which is necessary to its composition gallops quicker, has a more varied tread, alters its point of view more frequently. If we look into the various dialogues of these *Idylls*, we shall not only observe that the tendency to monologue is great, and is greatest at the most striking points and telling situations, but also be struck with what is nearly the same phenomenon in another form—the remarkable similarity of the conversational powers of all the various personages. It is not only that a peculiar kind of language, a sort of a dialect of sentimental chivalry, pervades the whole,—this is quite in keeping with the design, and is perhaps essential to the perfect effect of such a book; but the similarity seems to go deeper: each dramatic personage is fully endowed with the expressive capacities of Mr. Tennyson's imagination; each one has them all, and consequently they are all on a level; no one has a superiority. No fact can more exactly and instructively define the precise difference between a genuine dramatic expression and the superficially analogous, but really different, art of delineative soliloquy. In the latter, it is right that the state of feeling to be expressed should be expressed with all the poet's power: we are representing the man's notion of himself; we take the liberty to say for him what he could never say; we translate into similes and phrases the half thoughts and floating feelings which he never could for a moment have expressed in that way, or probably in any other way. But in the genuine drama we are delineating a scene with more than one actor, and we are to state an imaginary dialogue. The mode in which people express themselves is an essential fact of that dialogue. The degree in which people can express themselves is one of the most dramatic parts of their characters; it is therefore contrary to all the principles of art to give to each character the same command, especially if it be a singular command over very imaginative language. The state of the supposed speaker's mind is no doubt brought out by that mode more effectually than by any other; but the effect of the scene—of the speaking mind which can delineate itself, and of the dumb mind which cannot—is altogether impaired, for the striking contrast is destroyed.

The only other defect with which the *Idylls* are, we think, to be charged, is not so much a positive defect in the poetry itself, as rather a negative deficiency in it when compared with other poems of Mr. Tennyson's that we have known for many years. A certain subtlety seems to pervade some of the latter; and it is in part ascribable to the subtlety of thought, and is greatly heightened by a peculiar subtlety of expression. There are lines in some of the older poems for which perhaps every one has

> A pleasurable feeling of blind love.

We know what they express: they *do* express it to us: they dwell in our memories; they haunt us with their echo. Yet, if we try to analyse them, their charm is gone. Is the meaning expressed? Did Mr. Tennyson really mean this?—is there not this ambiguity? Might he not have intended something else? We can conceive a foreign critic, thoroughly acquainted with our language for almost all other purposes, to be quite incapable of seeing the merit of some of the more characteristic of these poems, from a want of those early floating and mysterious associations with language, in the instinctive and delicate use of which that charm consists. We have known literal-minded English persons, who preferred the plainer phraseology—the 'commin print,' as Lisbeth would have called it—of every-day rhymers. And, in some sense, their preference was correct. All that they could perceive was more perfect in the entirely valueless rhyme than in the entirely invaluable. The logical structure is better; it would construe better into other words, or into a foreign language: and this the literal critics perceive. The hovering air of power and beauty which the words really have, they do not perceive. If you were to suggest the existence they would smile. We believe that of this subtle sort of beauty, there is less in the *Idylls* than in Mr. Tennyson's earlier poetry. Perhaps they have not been in our hands long enough for us to judge. These super-logical beauties, if we may so say, are those which require the longest time to perceive, and the most perfect familiarity to appreciate. Still we do think so. We think there are few passages, considering the length of the poems, which will have years hence that inexplicable and magical power over our minds which some of Mr. Tennyson's old lines have. Perhaps the subject may have something to do with it. The sentiments in these poems are simpler than his sentiments used to be; they are not 'clothed in white samite, mystic, wonderful.' The thoughts are broader and plainer. The old mystic grace of language may, therefore, not have been so much used, only because it was no longer so much needed.

Every poem of Mr. Tennyson's must suggest the inquiry, what is the place which he occupies in the series of our poets? This poem must do so most of all; because, as we have explained, it removes some of the doubts which his warmest admirers formerly felt as to the limits of the range of his genius. It shows that he has the skill to adapt, the instinctive taste and self-restraint to preserve a continued interest of considerable length. Architectonic power the long-worded critics used to say he had not; but we have now discovered that he has it. The puzzling question returns, Where is Mr. Tennyson to be placed in the rank of our poets? We know that he has genius; but is that genius great or small, when compared with others like it?

It is most natural to compare him with Keats and Shelley. The kind of readers he addresses is, as we observed, the same: a sort of intellectual sentiment pervades his works as well as theirs: the superficial resemblances of the works of all the three are many. But, on the other hand, Mr. Tennyson is deficient in the most marked peculiarity which Shelley and Keats have in common. Both of these poets are singularly gifted with a sustained faculty of lyrical expression. They seem hurried into song; and, what is more, kept there when they have been hurried there. Shelley's *Skylark* is the most familiar example of this. A rather young musician was once asked, what was Jenny Lind's charm in singing. 'Oh,' he replied, 'she went up so high, and staid up high so long.' There is something of this sustainment at a great height in all Shelley's lyrics. His strains are profuse. He is ever soaring; and whilst soaring, ever singing. Keats, it is true, did not ascend to so extreme an elevation. He did not belong to the upper air. He had no abstract labour, no haunting speculations, no attenuated thoughts. He was the poet of the obvious beauty of the world. His genius was of the earth—of the autumn earth—rich and mellow; and it was lavish. He did not carry his art high or deep; he neither enlightens our eyes much, nor expands our ears much; but pleases our fancies with a prolonged strain of simple rich melody. He does not pause, or stay, or hesitate. His genius is continuous; the flow of it is as obvious at the best moments as the excellence, and at inferior moments is more so. Mr. Tennyson, on the other hand, has no tendencies of this kind. He broods, as we have said. There are undoubtedly several beautiful songs in his writings,—several in which the sentiment cleaves to the words, and cannot even in our memories be divorced from them. But their beauty is not continuous. A few lines fasten upon us with an imperious and evermastering charm; but the whole composition, as a whole, has not much value. The run of it, as far as it has a run, expresses nothing.

The genius of Mr. Tennyson is delineative; it muses and meditates; it describes moods, feelings, and objects of imagination; but it does not rush on to pour out passion, or express overwhelming emotion.

In the special lyrical impulse, therefore, we think it indisputable that Mr. Tennyson is inferior both to Keats and to Shelley. To Shelley he is moreover evidently inferior in general intensity of mind. This intense power of conception is, indeed, the most striking of all Shelley's peculiarities. There is something nervously exciting about his way of writing, even on simple subjects. He takes them up so vividly into his brain that they seem to make it quiver, and that of a sensitive reader at times quivers in sympathy. The subjects are no doubt often abstract; too abstract, perhaps, occasionally for art. But that only makes the result more singular. That an excitable mind should be stimulated by the strong interest of the facts of the world, by the phenomena of life, by the expectation of death, is what we should expect. It is intelligible to our understanding, and in obvious accordance with our experience. But that this extreme excitement should be caused in the poet's mind very often, and in the reader's mind sometimes, by the abstractions of singular tenuity, is what few would expect. So, however, it is. The mind of Shelley seems always to work in a kind of pure rare ether, clearer, sharper, more eager than the ordinary air. The reader feels that he is on a kind of mountainous elevation, and perhaps he feels vivified by it: at times almost all persons do so, but at times also they are chilled at its cold, and half-frightened at the lifelessness and singularity. It is characteristic of Shelley that he was obliged to abandon one of his favourite speculations, 'dizzy from thrilling horror.' Of all this abstract intensity Mr. Tennyson has not a particle. He is never very eager about anything, and he is certainly not over-anxious about phantoms and abstractions. In some respects this deficiency may not have injured his writings: it has rather contributed to his popularity. The English mind, which, like its great philosophers, likes to work upon 'stuff,' is more pleased with genial chivalric pictures than with chiselled phantoms and intense lyrics. Still, a critic who appreciates Shelley at all, will probably feel that he has a degree of inner power, of telling mental efficiency, which Mr. Tennyson does not equal. Horrible as the *Cenci* must ever be, it shows an eager and firmer grasp of mind—a greater tension of the imagination—than the *Idylls*.

Over Keats, however, Mr. Tennyson may perhaps claim a general superiority. We are, indeed, making a comparison which is scarcely fair; Keats died when he was still very young. His genius was immature; and his education, except the superficial musing education he gave himself, was very imperfect. Mr. Tennyson has lived till his genius is fully ripe, and he has gathered in the fruits of his century. No one can read his poems without feeling this: some of his readers have probably felt it painfully. Twenty years ago, when there was an idea in the high places of criticism that he was a silly and affected writer, many ignorant persons thought they were showing their knowledge in laughing at a language which nevertheless was both most emphatic and most accurate. The amount of thought which is held in solution,—if we may be pardoned so scientific a metaphor,—in Mr. Tennyson's poetry, is very great. If you come to his poems a hundred times, it is very probable that you will even to the end find there some new allusion, some recondite trace of high-bred thought, which you had not seen before. His reflections are often not new; he would not advance for himself perhaps, his just admirers, we are sure, would not claim for him, the fame of an absolutely original thinker. But he indicates the possession of a kind of faculty which in an age of intellect and cultivation is just as important, possibly is even more important, than the power of first-hand discovery. He is a first-rate *realiser*; and realisation is a test of truth. Out of the infinite thoughts, discoveries, and speculations which are scattered, more or less perfectly, through society, certain minds have a knack of taking up and making their own that which is true, and healthy, and valuable; and they reject the rest. It is often not by a very strict analysis or explicit logical statement that such minds arrive at their conclusions. They are continually thinking the subjects in question over: they have the details of them in their minds: they have a floating picture of endless particulars about them in their imaginations. In consequence, by musing over a true doctrine, they see that it is true: it fits their picture, adapts itself to it, forms at once a framework for it. On the contrary, they find that a false tenet does not suit the facts which they have in their minds: they muse over it, find out its unsuitability, and think no more of it. The belief of these remarkably sane and remarkably meditative persons about the facts to which they devote their own understandings is one of the best criteria of truth in this world. It is the discriminating winnow of civilisation, which receives the real corn of the true discoverer, and leaves the vexing chaff of the more pompous science to be forgotten and pass away. This kind of meditative tact and slow selective judgment Mr. Tennyson possesses in a very great measure; and there is nothing of which Keats was so entirely destitute. It does not, perhaps, occur to you while reading him that he is deficient in it. It belongs to an order of merit completely out of his way. It is the reflective gift of a mature man: Keats's best gifts are those of an impulsive, original, and refined boy. But if we compare—as in some degree we cannot help doing—the indications of general mind which are scattered through the three writers, we shall think, perhaps, that in these Mr. Tennyson excels Keats, even remembering the latter's early death, and, in consequence, giving him all fair credit for the possibilities of subsequent development; just as we found before that the intellectual balance seemed, when similarly adjusted, to incline against Mr. Tennyson, and in favour of Shelley.

Some one has said that Tennyson was a drawing-room Wordsworth. There is no deep felicity or instruction in the phrase, but it has some superficial appropriateness. Wordsworth's works have no claim to be in the drawing-room: they have the hill-side and the library, and those places are enough for them. Wordsworth, as we know, dealt with two subjects, and with two subjects only,—the simple elemental passions, 'the pangs by which the generations are prepared,' and in which they live and breathe and move; and secondly, the spiritual conception of nature, which implies that the universe is, in its beauties and its changes, but the expression of an inherent and animating spirit. Neither of these subjects suits the drawing-room. The simple passions are there carefully covered over; nature is out-of-doors. Mr. Tennyson, however, has given some accounts of the more refined and secondary passions in Wordsworth's intense manner; and if he does not give the exact sketches of external nature, or preach any gospel concerning it, he gives us a mental reflex of it, and a Lotus-eater's view of what it ought to be, and what it is rather a shame on the whole that it is not, which are not inadmissible in a luxurious drawing-room. A little of the spirit of Wordsworth, thus modified, may be traced in Mr. Tennyson; and perhaps this is the only marked trace of a recent writer that can be found in his writings. If we were to be asked as before, whether Mr. Wordsworth or Mr. Tennyson were the superior in general imaginative power, we think we should say that the

latter was the superior, but that Wordsworth had achieved a greater task than he has as yet achieved, with inferior powers. The mind of Wordsworth was singularly narrow; his range peculiarly limited; the object he proposed to himself unusually distinct. He has given to us a complete embodiment of the two classes of subjects which he has treated of: perhaps it would be impossible to imagine one of them—the peculiar aspect of outward nature which we mentioned—to be better delineated; certainly as yet, we apprehend, it is not delineated nearly so well any where else. Although we should be inclined to believe that Mr. Tennyson's works indicate greater powers, we do not think that they evince so much concentrated efficiency, that they leave any single result upon the mind which is at once so high and so definite.

If we were asked, as we shall be asked, why we think Mr. Tennyson to have greater powers than Wordsworth, we would venture to allege two reasons. In the first place, Mr. Tennyson has a power of making fun. No one can claim that, of all powers, for Wordsworth, it is certain: no human being more entirely destitute of humour is perhaps discoverable anywhere in literature, or possibly even in society. Not a tinge of it seems ever to have influenced him. He had, through life, the narrow sincerity of the special missionary; but he had not, what is all but incompatible with it, the restraining tact of the man of the world, which teaches that all things and all gospels are only now and then in season; that it is absurd always to be teaching a single doctrine; that it is not wise to fatigue oneself by trying to interest others in that which it is perfectly certain they will not be interested in. The world of 'cakes and ale,' indisputably, is not that of Wordsworth. There are quite sufficient indications that Mr. Tennyson appreciates it. Secondly, it may be said that, far more completely than Wordsworth, and far more completely than any other recent poet, Mr. Tennyson has conceived in his mind, and his delineated in his works, a general picture of human life. He certainly does not give us the whole of it, there is a considerable portion which he scarcely touches; but an acute eye can observe that he sees more than he says; and even judging exclusively and rigidly from what is said, the amount of life which Mr. Tennyson has delineated, even in these *Idylls* only, far surpasses in extent and range that which Wordsworth has described. Wordsworth's range is so narrow, and the extent of life and thought which these *Idylls* go over, slight as is their seeming structure, is so great, that perhaps no one will question this conclusion. Some may, however, deny its sufficiency; they may suggest that it does not prove our conclusion. In Shelley's case, it may be said that we allowed a certain defined intensity to have a higher imaginative value than a more diffused fertility and a less concentrated art; why is not Wordsworth entitled to share the benefit of this doctrine also? The plea is very specious, but we are not inclined to think that it is sound. Shelley has shown in a single direction, or in a few directions, an immense general power of imagination and mind. We may not pause to prove this: it is in the nature of allusive criticism to be dogmatic; we must appeal to the memory of our readers. On the other hand, we think, by a certain doggedness of nature, by high resolution, and even, in a certain sense, by an extreme limitation of mind, Wordsworth, with far less of imagination, was able in special directions to execute most admirable works. But the power displayed is, in a great degree, that of character rather than of imagination. He put all his mind into a single task, and he did it. Wordsworth's best works are the saved-up excellencies of a rather barren nature; those of Shelley are the rapid productions of a very fertile one. When we are speaking of mere intellectual and imaginative power, we run, therefore, no risk of contradiction in ranking Mr. Tennyson at a higher place than Wordsworth, notwithstanding that we have adjudged him to be inferior in the same quality to Shelley.

Perhaps we can, after this discussion, fix, at least approximately and incompletely, Mr. Tennyson's position in the hierarchy of our poets. We think that the poets of this century of whom we have been speaking,—and Coleridge may be added to the number,—may be, in a certain sense, classed together as the intellectualised poets. We do not, of course, mean that there ever was a great poet who was destitute of great intellect, or who did not show that intellect distinctly in his poems. But the poets of whom we speak show that intellect in a further and special sense. We are all conscious of the difference between talking to an educated man and to an uneducated. The difference by no means is, that the educated man talks better; that he either says better things, or says them in a more vigorous way. Possibly uneducated persons, as a rule, talk more expressively, and send whatever meaning they have farther into the hearer's mind; perhaps their meaning on the subjects which they have in common with educated men, is not very much inferior. Still there is a subtle charm about the conversation of the educated which that of other persons has not. That charm consists in the constant presence and constant trace of a cultivated intellect. The words are used with a certain distinct precision; a distinguishing tact of intellect is indicated by that which is said; a discriminating felicity is shown in the mode in which it is said. The charm of cultivated expression is like the charm of a cultivated manner; it is easy and yet cautious, natural and yet improved, ready and yet restrained. The fascination of a cultivated intellect in literature is the same. It is more easy to describe its absence, perhaps, than its presence. The style of Shakespeare, for example, wants entirely this peculiar charm. He had the manifold experience, the cheerful practicality, the easy felicity of the uneducated man; but he had not the measured abundance, the self-restraining fertility, which the very highest writer may be conceived to have. There is no subtle discretion in his words: there is the nice tact of native instinct; there is not the less necessary, but yet attractive, precision of an earnest and anxious education. Perhaps it will be admitted that the writers we have mentioned—Shelley, Coleridge, Keats, Wordsworth, and Tennyson—may all be called, as far as our own literature is concerned, in a peculiar sense the intellectualised poets. Milton indeed would, in positive knowledge, be superior to any of them, and to many of them put together, but he is an exceptional poet in English literature, to be classed apart, and seldom to be spoken of in contrast or comparison with any other; and even he, from a want of natural subtlety of mind, does not perhaps show us, in the midst of his amazing knowledge, the most acute and discriminating intellectuality. But if we except Milton, these poets may almost certainly be classed apart: and if they are to be so, we have indicated the place which Mr. Tennyson holds in this class in relation to all of them save Coleridge. A real estimate of the latter is not to be expected of us at the end of an article, and as a parenthesis in the estimate of another poet. He will long be a problem to the critics, and a puzzle to the psychologists. But, so far as the general powers of mind shown in his poems are concerned,— and this is the only aspect of his genius which we are at present considering,—we need have no hesitation in saying that they are much inferior to those shown in the poems of our greatest contemporary poet. Their great excellence is, in truth, almost confined to their singular power in the expression of one single idea. Both *Christabel* and the *Ancient Mariner* are substantially developments of the same conception; they delineate almost exclusively the power which the supernatural has, when it is thrust among the detail of the natural. This idea is worked out with astonishing completeness; but it is left to stand alone. There are no characters, no picture of life at large, no extraordinary thoughts, to be found in these poems; their metre and their strangeness are their charm. After what has been said, we need not prove at large that such an exclusive concentration upon such an idea proves that these poems are inferior, or rather indicate inferior imaginative genius to that of Tennyson. The range of the art is infinitely less; and the peculiar idea, which is naturally impressive, and in comparison with others easy to develop, hardly affords scope for the clear exhibition of a very creative genius, even if there were not other circumstances which would lead us to doubt whether Coleridge, rich and various as were his mental gifts, was possessed of that one. On the whole, we may pause in the tedium of our comparative dissertation. We may conclude, that in the series of our intellectualised poets Mr. Tennyson is to be ranked as inferior in the general power of the poetic imagination to Shelley, and to Shelley only;—and if this be true, the establishment of it is a contribution to criticism quite sufficient for a single article.

EDWARD DOWDEN
From "Mr Tennyson and Mr Browning" (1867)
Studies in Literature
1878, pp. 195–211

Let us start in our study,—a partial study made from a single point of view,—with what may be an assumption for the present, but an assumption which will lead to its own verification. Let us start by saying that Mr Tennyson has a strong sense of the dignity and efficiency of *law*,—of *law* understood in its widest meaning. Energy nobly controlled, an ordered activity delight his imagination. Violence, extravagance, immoderate force, the swerving from appointed ends, revolt,—these are with Mr Tennyson the supreme manifestations of evil.

Under what aspect is the relation of the world and man to God represented in the poems of Mr Tennyson? Surely,—it will be said,—one who feels so strongly the presence of law in the physical world, and who recognises so fully the struggle in the moral nature of man between impulse and duty, assigning to conscience a paramount authority, has the materials from which arises naturally a vivid feeling of what is called the personal relation of God to his creatures. A little reflection will show that this is not so. It is quite possible to admit in one's thoughts and feelings the existence of a physical order of the material world, and a moral order of the spiritual world, and yet to enter slightly into those intimate relations of the affections with a Divine Being which present him in the tenderest way as a Father,—as a highest Friend. Fichte, the sublime idealist, was withheld from seeing God by no obtruding veil of a material universe. Fichte, if any man ever did, recognised the moral order of the world. But Fichte—living indeed the blessed life in God,—yet annihilated for thought his own personality and that of God, in the infinity of this moral order. No: it is not law but will that reveals will; it is not our strength but our weakness that cries out for the invisible Helper and Divine Comrade; it is not our obedience but our aspiration, our joy, our anguish; it is the passion of self-surrender, the grief that makes desolate, the solitary rapture which demands a partaker of its excess, the high delight which must save itself from as deep dejection by a passing over into gratitude.

Accordingly, although we find the idea of God entering largely into the poems of Mr Tennyson, there is little recognition of special contact of the soul with the Divine Being in any supernatural ways of quiet or of ecstasy. There is, on the contrary, a disposition to rest in the orderly manifestation of God, as the supreme Law-giver, and even to identify him with his presentation of himself, in the physical and moral order of the universe. And if this precludes all spiritual rapture, that "glorious folly, that heavenly madness, wherein true wisdom is acquired,"[1] it preserves the mind from despair or any deep dejection; unless, indeed, the faith in this order itself give way, when in the universal chaos, no will capable of bringing restoration being present, a confusion of mind, a moral obscurity greater than any other, must arise.

Wordsworth in some of his solitary trances of thought really entered into the frame of mind which the mystic knows as union or as ecstacy, when thought expires in enjoyment, when the mind is blessedness and love, when "the waters of grace have risen up to the neck of the soul, so that it can neither advance nor retreat." With Mr Tennyson the mystic is always the visionary, who suffers from an over-excitable fancy. The nobler aspects of the mystical religious spirit, are unrepresented in his poetry. St Simeon upon his pillar is chiefly of interest, as affording an opportunity for studying the phenomena of morbid theopathetic emotion. We find nowhere among the persons of his imagination a Teresa, uniting as she did in so eminent a degree an administrative genius, a genius for action with the genius of exalted piety. The feeble Confessor beholds visions; but Harold strikes ringing blows upon the helms of his country's enemies. Harold is no virgin, no confessor, no seer, no saint, but a loyal, plain, strong-thewed, truth-loving son of England, who can cherish a woman, and rule a people, and mightily wield a battle-axe. In the Idylls when the Grail passes before the assembled knights, where is the king? He is absent, actively resisting evil, harrying the bandits' den; and as he returns, it is with alarm that he perceives the ominous tokens left by the sacred thing:—

> Lo there! the roofs
> Of our great hall are rolled in thunder smoke!
> Pray heaven, they be not smitten by the bolt.

The Grail is a sign to maim the great order which Arthur has reared. The mystical glories which the knights pursue are "wandering fires." If Galahad beheld the vision, it was because Galahad was already unmeet for earth, worthy to be a king, not in this sad yet noble city of men, but in some far-off spiritual city.

> And spake I not too truly, O my knights?
> Was I too dark a prophet when I said
> To those who went upon the Holy Quest,
> That most of them would follow wandering fires,
> Lost in the quagmire?—lost to me and gone,
> And left me gazing at a barren board,
> And a lean Order—scarce return'd a tithe—
> And out of those to whom the vision came
> My greatest hardly will believe he saw;
> Another hath beheld it afar off,
> And leaving human wrongs to right themselves,
> Cares but to pass into the silent life.
> And one hath had the vision face to face,
> And now his chair desires him here in vain,
> However they may crown him otherwhere.

The Round Table is dissolved, the work of Arthur is brought to an end, because two passions have overthrown the order of the realm, which it has been the task of the loyal, steadfast and wise king to create,—first, the sensual passion of Lancelot and Guinevere; secondly, the spiritual passion hardly less fatal, which leaped forth when the disastrous quest was avowed. Only that above all order of human institution, a higher order abides, we might well suppose that chaos must come again; but it is not so:—

> The old order changeth giving place to new,
> And God fulfils himself in many ways.

Thus, as has been already remarked, Mr Tennyson's sense of a beneficent unfolding in our life of a divine purpose, lifts him through and over the common dejections of men. With his own friend, it is as with his ideal king; he will not mourn for any overmuch. The fame which he predicted to his friend is quenched by an early death; but he will not despair:—

> The fame is quench'd that I foresaw,
> The head hath missed an earthly wreath;
> I curse not nature, no, nor death;
> For nothing is that errs from law.

Even the thought of the foul corruption of the grave becomes supportable, when it is conceived as a part of the change which permits the spirit to have its portion in the self-evolving process of the higher life:—

> Eternal process moving on,
> From state to state the spirit walks;
> And these are but the shatter'd stalks,
> Or ruin'd chrysalis of one.

It is only when the doubt of a beneficent order of the world cannot be put away—it is only when nature (as discovered by the investigations of geology), seems ruthless alike to the individual and the species, "red in tooth and claw with ravine," it is only then that the voice of the mourner grows wild, and it appears to him that his grief has lost its sanctity and wrongs the quiet of the dead.

Mr Tennyson finds law present throughout all nature, but there is no part of nature in which he dwells with so much satisfaction upon its presence as in human society. No one so largely as Mr Tennyson, has represented in art the new thoughts and feelings, which form the impassioned side of the modern conception of progress. His imagination is for ever haunted by "the vision of the world, and all the wonder that would be." But the hopes and aspirations of Mr Tennyson are not those of the radical or movement character. He is in all his poems conservative as well as liberal. It may be worth while to illustrate the feeling of Shelley, in contrast with that of Mr Tennyson, with reference to this idea of progress. In the year 1819 Shelley believed that England had touched almost the lowest point of social and political degradation:

> An old, mad, blind, despised, and dying king,—
> Princes, the dregs of their dull race, who flow
> Through public scorn, mud from a muddy spring,—
> Rulers, who neither see, nor feel, nor know,
> But leech-like to their fainting country cling,
> Till they drop, blind in blood, without a blow,—
> A people starv'd and stabb'd in the untilled field,—
> An army which liberticide and prey
> Make as a two-edged sword to all who wield,—
> Golden and sanguine laws which tempt and slay,—
> Religion Christless, Godless,—a book sealed,
> A Senate—time's worst statute unrepealed.—

Such laws, such rulers, such a people Shelley found in his England of half a century since. Did he therefore despair, or if he hoped was the object of his hope some better life of man in some distant future? No: all these things

> Are graves, from which a glorious Phantom may
> Burst, to illumine our tempestuous day.

The regeneration of society, as conceived by Shelley, was to appear suddenly, splendidly shining with the freshness and glory of a dream; as the result of some bright, brief national struggle; as the consequence of the apparition of some pure being, at once a poet and a prophet, before whose voice huge tyrannies and cruel hypocrisies must needs go down, as piled-up clouds go down ruined and rent before a swift, pure wind; in some way or another which involves a catastrophe, rather than according to the constantly operating processes of nature.

Now Mr Tennyson's conception of progress, which he has drawn from his moral and intellectual environment, and which accords with his own moral temper, is widely different. No idea perhaps occupies a place in his poems so central as that of the progress of the race. This it is which lifts out of his idle dejection and selfish dreaming the speaker in "Locksley Hall;"

> Not in vain the distance beacons. Forward, forward
>   let us range,
> Let the great world spin for ever down the ringing
>   grooves of change.

This it is which suggests an apology for the fantasies of "The Day-Dream." This it is which arms the tempted with a weapon of defence, and the tempter with a deadlier weapon of attack in "The Two Voices." This it is of which Leonard writes, and at which old James girds in "The Golden Year." This it is which gives a broad basis of meditative thought to the Idyll that tells of the passing of Arthur, and renders it something more than a glorious fable. This it is which is the sweetness of "The Poet's Song," making the wild swan pause, and the lark drop from heaven to earth. This it is which forms the closing prophecy of *The Princess*, the full confession of the poet's faith. This it is which is heard in the final chords of the *In Memoriam*, changing the music from a minor to a major key. And the same doctrine is taught from the opposite side in "The Vision of Sin," in which the most grievous disaster which comes upon the base and sensual heart is represented as hopelessness with reference to the purpose and the progress of the life of man:

> Fill the can and fill the cup,
>   All the windy ways of men
> Are but dust that rises up
> And is lightly laid again. [2]

But in all these poems throughout which the idea of progress is so variously expressed, and brought into relation with moods of mind so diverse, the progress of mankind is uniformly represented as the evolution and self-realisation of a law; it is represented as taking place gradually and slowly, and its consummation is placed in a remote future. We "hear the roll of the ages;" the "increasing purpose" runs through centuries; it is "with the process of the suns" that the thoughts of men are widened. It is when our sleep should have been prolonged through many decades and quinquenniads that we might wake to reap the flower and quintessence of change:

> For we are Ancients of the earth,
>   And in the morning of the times.

It is because millenniums will not bring the advance of knowledge near its term that the tempted soul in "The Two Voices" feels how wretched a thing it must be to watch the increase of intellectual light during the poor thirty or forty years of a life-time. It is "in long years" that the sexes shall attain to the fulness of their mighty growth, until at last, man and woman

> Upon the skirts of Time
> Sit side by side, full-summ'd in all their powers,

Dispensing harvest, sowing the To-be,

. . .

> Then comes the statelier Eden back to man:
> Then reign the world's great bridals, chaste and calm;
> Then springs the crowning race of humankind.
> May these things be!

And the highest augury telling of this "crowning race" is drawn from those who already having moved upward through the lower phases of being become precursors and pledges of the gracious children of the future:

> For all we thought and loved and did,
>   And hoped, and suffer'd, is but seed
> Of what in them is flower and fruit;
>
> Whereof the man, that with me trod
>   This planet, was a noble type
>   Appearing ere the times were ripe,
> That friend of mine who lives in God,
>
> That God, which ever lives and loves,
>   One God, one law, one element,
>   And one far-off divine event,
> To which the whole creation moves.

The great hall which Merlin built for Arthur, is girded by four zones of symbolic sculpture; in the lowest zone, beasts are slaying men; in the second, men are slaying beasts;

> And on the third are warriors, perfect men,
>   And on the fourth are men with growing wings.

To work out the beast is the effort of long ages; to attain to be "a perfect man" is for those who shall follow us afar off; to soar with wings is for the crowning race of the remotest future.

Apart from the growth of the individual that golden age to which the poet looks forward, the coming of which he sees shine in the distance, is characterized, as he imagines it, chiefly by a great development of knowledge, especially of scientific knowledge; this first; and, secondly, by the universal presence of political order and freedom, national and international, secured by a vast and glorious federation. It is quite of a piece with Mr Tennyson's feeling for law, that his imagination should be much impressed by the successes of science, and that its promises should correspond with his hopes. The crowning race will be a company

> Of those that, eye to eye, shall look
>   On knowledge; under whose command
>   Is Earth and Earth's, and in their hand
> Is Nature like an open book.

Were we to sleep the hundred years, our joy would be to wake

> On science grown to more,
>   On secrets of the brain, the stars.

It is the promises and achievements of science which restore sanity to the distraught lover of "Locksley Hall." In *The Princess* the sport half-science of galvanic batteries, model steam-engines, clock-work steamers and fire-balloons, suggest the thought of a future of adult knowledge:

> This fine old world of ours is but a child
>   Yet in the go-cart. Patience! Give it time
>   To learn its limbs: there is a hand that guides.

But Mr Tennyson's dream of the future is not more haunted by visionary discoveries and revelations of science than by the phantoms of great political organizations. That will be a time

> When the war-drum throbs no longer, and the battle
>   flags are furl'd
> In the Parliament of men, the Federation of the
>   world.

A time in which

> Phantoms of other forms of rule,
> New Majesties of mighty states

will appear, made real at length; a time in which the years will bring to being

> The vast Republics that may grow,
> The Federations and the Powers;
> Titanic forces taking birth.

These days and works of the crowning race are, however, far beyond our grasp; and the knowledge of this, with the faith that the progress of mankind is the expression of a slowly, self-revealing law, puts a check upon certain of our hopes and strivings. He who is possessed by this faith will look for no speedy regeneration of men in the social or political sphere, and can but imperfectly sympathise with those enthusiastic hearts whose expectations, nourished by their ardours and desires, are eager and would forestall futurity. Mr Tennyson's justness of mind in a measure forsakes him, when he has to speak of political movements into which passion in its uncalculating form has entered as a main motive power. Yet passion of this type is the right and appropriate power for the uses of certain times and seasons. It is by ventures of faith in politics that mountains are removed. The Tory member's elder son estimates the political movements of France in an insular spirit which, it may be surmised, has in it something of Mr Tennyson's own feeling:—

> Whiff! there comes a sudden heat,
> The gravest citizen seems to lose his head,
> The king is scared, the soldier will not fight,
> The little boys begin to shoot and stab.

Yet to France more than to England the enslaved nations have turned their faces when they have striven to rend their bonds. It is hardly from Mr Tennyson that we shall learn how a heroic failure may be worth as much to the world as a distinguished success. It is another poet who has written thus:—

> When liberty goes out of a place it is not the first to
>   go, nor the second or third to go,
> It waits for all the rest to go—it is the last.
> When there are no more memories of heroes and
>   martyrs,
> And when all life, and all the souls of men and
>   women are discharged from any part of the
>   earth,
> Then only shall liberty, or the idea of liberty, be
>   discharged from that part of the earth,
> And the infidel come into full possession.

Mr Tennyson's ideal for every country is England, and that is a blunder in politics:

> A land of settled government,
> A land of just and old renown,
> Where Freedom slowly broadens down
> From precedent to precedent.

That is an admirable verse; but it is nobler to make than to follow precedents; and great emotions, passionate thought, audacities of virtue quickly create a history and tradition of precedents in the lives alike of individuals and of nations. Mr Tennyson loves freedom, but she must assume an English costume before he can recognize her; the freedom which he loves is

> That sober freedom out of which there springs
> Our loyal passion to our temperate kings.

She is

> Freedom in her royal seat
> Of England, not the schoolboy heat—
> The blind hysterics of the Celt.

He cannot squander a well-balanced British sympathy on hearts that love not wisely but too well:—

> Love thou thy land with love far brought
> From out the storied Past, and used
> Within the Present, but transfused
> Through future time by power of thought.

What Mr Tennyson has written will indeed lead persons of a certain type of character in their true direction; for those of a different type it will for ever remain futile and false. "Reason," Vauvenargues has said, "deceives us more often than does nature." "If passion advises more boldly than reflection, it is because passion gives greater power to carry out its advice." "To do great things, one must live as if one could never die." England can celebrate a golden wedding with Freedom, and gather children about her knees; let there be a full and deep rejoicing. But why forbid the more unmeasured joy of the lover of Freedom who has dreamed of her and has fought for her, and who now is glad because he has once seen her, and may die for her?

Mr Tennyson's political doctrine is in entire agreement with his ideal of human character. As the exemplar of all nations is that one in which highest wisdom is united with complete self-government, so the ideal man is he whose life is led to sovereign power by self-knowledge resulting in self-control, and self-control growing perfect in self-reverence. The golden fruit which Herè prays for, promising power, which Aphrodite prays for, promising pleasure, belongs of right to Pallas alone, who promises no other sovereignty, no other joy than those that come by the freedom of perfect service,—

> To live by law,
> Acting the law we live by without fear.

Mr Tennyson has had occasion to write two remarkable poetical *éloges*—one on the late Prince Consort, the other on the great Duke. In both, the characters are drawn with fine discrimination, but in both, the crowning virtue of the dead is declared to have been the virtue of obedience, that of self-subjugation to the law of duty. In both the same lesson is taught, that he who toils along the upward path of painful right-doing

> Shall find the toppling crags of Duty scaled
> Are close upon the shining table-lands
> To which our God Himself is moon and sun.

Even Love "takes part against himself" to be at one with Duty, who is "loved of Love." Through strenuous self-mastery, through the strong holding of passion in its leash, Enoch Arden attains the sad happiness of strong heroic souls. But it is not only as fortitude and endurance that Mr Tennyson conceives the virtue of noble obedience; it flames up into a chivalric ardour in the passionate loyalty of the Six Hundred riders at Balaclava; and Cranmer redeems his life from the dishonour of fear, of faltering and of treason, by the last gallantry of a soldierlike obedience to the death:

> He pass'd out smiling, and he walk'd upright;
> His eye was like a soldier's, whom the general
> He looks to, and he leans on as his God,
> Hath rated for some backwardness, and bidd'n him
> Charge one against a thousand, and the man
> Hurls his soil'd life against the pikes and dies.

Self-reverence, self-knowledge, self-control, the recognition of a divine order and of one's own place in that order, faithful adhesion to the law of one's highest life,—these are the elements from which is formed the ideal human character. What is the central point in the ethical import of the Arthurian story as told by Mr Tennyson? It is the assertion that the highest

type of manhood is set forth in the poet's ideal king, and that
the worthiest work of man is work such as his. And what is
Arthur? The blameless monarch, who "reverenced his conscience as a king;" unseduced from his appointed path by the
temptations of sense or the wandering fires of religious mysticism; throughout the most passionate scene of the poem
"sublime in self-repression":—

> I wanted warmth and colour, which I found
> In Lancelot,—now I see thee what thou art,
> Thou art the highest, and most human too,
> Not Lancelot, not another.

Arthur's task has been to drive back the heathen, to quell
disorder and violence, to bind the wills of his knights to
righteousness in a perfect law of liberty. It is true that Arthur's
task is left half done. While he rides forth to silence the riot of
the Red Knight and his ruffian band, in his own court are held
those "lawless jousts," and Tristram sings in the ears of that
small, sad cynic, Dagonet, his licentious song:—

> Free love—free field—we love but while we may.

And thus were it not that a divine order overrules our efforts,
our successes, and our failures, we must needs believe that the
realm is once more reeling back into the beast.

Disorder of thoughts, of feelings and of will is, with Mr
Tennyson, the evil of evils, the pain of pains. The Princess
would transcend, through the temptation of a false ideal, her
true sphere of womanhood; even this noblest form of disobe-
dience to law entails loss and sorrow; she is happy only when
she resumes her worthier place through the wisdom of love. In
"Lucretius" the man who had so highly striven for light and
calm, for "the sober majesties of settled, sweet Epicurean life,"
is swept by a fierce tempest in his blood back into chaos; there
is but one way of deliverance, but one way of entering again
under the reign of law,—to surrender his being once more to
Nature, that she may anew dash together the atoms which
make him man, in order that as flower, or beast, or fish, or
bird, or man, they may again move through her cycles; and so
Lucretius roughly wooes the passionless bride, Tranquillity.
And may we not sum up the substance of Mr Tennyson's
personal confessions in "In Memoriam," by saying that they
are the record of the growth through sorrow of the firmer mind,
which becomes one with law at length apparent through the
chaos of sorrow; which counts it crime "to mourn for any
overmuch;" which turns its burden into gain, and for which
those truths that never can be proved, and that had been lost in
the first wild shock of grief, are regained by "faith that comes of
self-control."

Notes

1. S. Teresa, *Life*, ch. xvi.
2. So in the *In Memoriam* when the "light is low" and the heart is sick,
   Time appears not as a wise master-builder, but as a "maniac,
   scattering dust."

SIR LESLIE STEPHEN
"Life of Tennyson"
Studies of a Biographer
1899, Volume 2, pp. 196–240

Every one, I presume, has read the deeply interesting
volumes in which Lord Tennyson has paid most appropriate homage to the memory of his father; and the life has
probably suggested to most of us some comments upon the
familiar poetry. A remark reported by Tennyson's old friend,
Jowett, is a useful warning against overambitious attempts in
that direction. 'There was,' said Tennyson, 'one intellectual
process in the world of which he could not even entertain an
apprehension—that was' (the process which created) 'the plays
of Shakespeare.' If Tennyson could not imagine the
Shakespearean intellect, it is impossible for people who are not
poets even to guess at the Tennysonian. The most obvious of
his merits is the most tantalising to a would-be explainer. It is
especially difficult, as he observes, and as other people have
observed before him, to be 'at once commonplace and poetical'; to find the one incomparable and magical phrase for the
thought which has been trying to get itself uttered for centuries.
There are interesting accounts in these volumes of the way in
which some of Tennyson's most perfect passages sprang from
accidental phrases, 'rolled about' in his mind; but phrases may
roll about in some minds for a very long time to very little
purpose. Leave a phrase to simmer in your memory; brood over
it, let it crystallize into form in your mind, and the feat will be
done. It will, that is, if your mind is Tennysonian; but there is
the mystery. One trivial example comes home to the Alpine
traveller. He has seen and tried for years to tell how he is
impressed by his beloved scenery, and annoyed by his own
bungling whenever he has tried to get beyond arithmetical
statements of hard geographical facts. And then Tennyson,
who was never in his life more than 7000 feet above the sea,
just glances at the Monte Rosa from the cathedral at Milan,
and in a four-line stanza gives the whole spirit of the scene to
perfection. It does not seem fair, but if justice supposes an
equal distribution of abilities, the world is not remarkable for
fairness. Tennyson's superlative skill in this art is too conspicuous and too universally acknowledged to justify more than a
passing recognition of an undeniable truth. And, perhaps,
criticism of really great and familiar poetry should be mainly
reserved for the select few who may without arrogance claim to
be more or less of the same spiritual order. One may, however,
say something upon various points suggested by this biography,
and especially as to the audience which first listened to the new
poetical revelation.

I will begin with a few words as to my own experience in
regard to that matter. Tennyson had already made his mark
when I was a schoolboy; and when I was at college all youths
who professed a literary turn knew the earlier poems by heart.
Ebullient Byronism was a thing of the past. There was no
longer any need for the missionary zeal which had taken
Cambridge men of an earlier generation to propagate the
worship of Shelley at Oxford. 'Chatter' about that luminary
was already becoming commonplace; a mere repetition of
accepted poetical orthodoxy. Admiration of Browning, though
it was distinctly beginning, implied a certain claim to esoteric
appreciation. But Tennyson's fame was established, and yet
had not lost the full bloom of novelty. It was delightful to catch
a young man coming up from the country and indoctrinate
him by spouting 'Locksley Hall' and the 'Lotus Eaters.' *In
Memoriam* had just appeared when I was a freshman—
Tennyson became Poet Laureate in my first term—and *Maud*
came out the year after I had graduated. Any one who cares to
know by contemporary evidence how Tennyson's poetry affected the young men of that period may turn to the essays of
George Brimley, a man of fine taste, who died prematurely,
and who, as librarian of Trinity, gave utterance to the correct
sentiment of Tennyson's old college. Tennyson, he declares, is
doing for us of the nineteenth century what Shakespeare and
Chaucer did for the England of their own days. Brimley spoke
for the civilised part of University society: Tennyson's friends,

Thompson (afterwards master) and W. G. Clark, the editor of Shakespeare, were conspicuous in that exalted region; and the younger generation all accepted the Tennysonian faith as that becoming enlightened persons. I only followed my companions when I tacitly assumed that 'poet' was a phrase equivalent to 'Tennyson.' The enthusiasm no doubt was partly obligatory; to repudiate it would have been to write oneself down an ass; but it was also warm and spontaneous. For that one owes a debt of gratitude to the poet not easily to be estimated. It is a blessing to share an enthusiasm, and I hope, rather than believe, that modern undergraduates have some equally wholesome stimulus of the kind. I do not think that we of the older generation have changed our estimate of Tennyson's merits, even though our 'enthusiasm' may have subsided into a more temperate warmth of approval. I mean, however, our estimate of the old poems. One could love them without putting the later works on the same level. Some readers were sensible of a considerable difficulty in that matter. The first series of *Idylls of the King* appeared in 1859. This volume at once extended Tennyson's popularity beyond all previous limits. Ten thousand copies were sold in the first week; hundreds went off monthly; Tennyson made such a success in the merely bookselling sense as to rival Scott, Macaulay, and Dickens. The success, too, was as marked if judged by some higher tests. Thackeray wrote in 'a rapture of gratitude' to acknowledge the greatest delight that had ever come to him since he was a young man. The Duke of Argyll reported that even Macaulay had been conquered, and predicted, truly enough, that many would appreciate the new poems who had failed to appreciate the old. Mr. Gladstone welcomed the *Idylls* in the *Quarterly*, and Jowett wrote as enthusiastically as Thackeray. These judgments, too, are still repeated, and Mr. Stopford Brooke's recent volume upon Tennyson contains a long commentary, which, if more discriminative, is still cordially reverential. I have conscientiously tried to enlighten myself by studying it, but even a knowledge that one ought to be enthusiastic is a different thing from enthusiasm. Not to recognise the wonderful literary skill and the exceeding beauty of many passages would, of course, imply more stupidity than any one would willingly admit; but I am afraid that from the publication of the *Idylls* I had to admit that I was not quite of the inner circle of true worshippers. I am glad to shelter myself to some extent behind higher authorities. Edward FitzGerald confessed when the *Holy Grail* appeared (in 1870) that he was inclined to prefer the old 'Lady of Shalott' method of dealing with the Round Table to the elaborated epic poem. He supposed that a bit must be wanting in the map of his brain, but anyhow, while feeling 'how pure, noble, and holy' the work was, he passed on to where the old Lincolnshire farmer drew tears to his eyes. He got back to 'substantial rough-spun nature,' and felt that the 'old brute' was 'a more pathetic phenomenon' than the Knights of the Round Table. This is only, as he explains, one of 'old Fitz's crotchets' (and it may be said incidentally that FitzGerald's letters, crotchety or not, are among the best things in these volumes). Mr. Ruskin, on the appearance of the first *Idylls*, puts virtually the same point in more formal language. He thinks that 'the true task of the modern poet' should be to 'give the intense, masterful, and unerring transcript of an actuality.' He is not sure, he confesses, that he does not 'feel the art and finish in these poems a little more than he likes to feel it.' Upon this Lord Tennyson makes an interesting remark. The *Idylls*, he tells us, were not carefully elaborated. '"Guinevere" and "Elaine" were each written in a few weeks, and hardly corrected at all.' The poet, of course, had been long brooding over them; and many phrases had come to him from accidental suggestions, and

gone through a slow incubation; but the actual execution was rapid. This, however, does not quite meet the criticism. It is not a question, I fancy, of the elaboration of the language, but of the vividness and spontaneity of the thought to be elaborated. The art becomes obvious, because Tennyson seems not so much to be inspired by an overmastering idea as to be looking about for appropriate images to express certain ethical and religious sentiments. He has obviously seen the Northern farmer with his own eyes; he has only contrived his knights, who never seem to me to be clothed in real flesh and blood. Jowett remarks that the 'allegory in the distance greatly strengthens, also elevates, the meaning of the poem.' To me, I humbly confess, 'allegory,' rightly or wrongly, means nuisance. The 'meaning' which it sticks on to a poem is precisely what the poem cannot properly 'mean.' The old 'Morte d'Arthur,' as it appeared with the charming old setting, was one of the poems which we all knew by heart. One of the charms was surely that the behaviour of the persons was delightfully illogical and absurd. Rather, perhaps, it took one to the world in which true logic demands illogical behaviour. Things take place there according to a law of their own, which is the more attractive just because it is preposterous and apparently arbitrary. When Sir Bedivere throws Excalibur into the lake, the whole proceeding is, as indeed Sir Bedivere very properly perceives and points out, contrary to all commonsense. His reluctance gives us warning that we have got into the world governed by phantastic laws. Throwing a sword into a lake does not, within ordinary experience, produce a barge occupied by three queens with crowns of gold; just as shooting an albatross does not, as a rule, produce a dead calm and death of a ship's crew by thirst. But though things of dreamland follow laws of their own, even dreamland has laws, and they ought to be observed when once you get there. The 'Ancient Mariner' was ridden by a nightmare, and all things happened to him according to the genuine laws of the nightmare world. Arthur's Round Table was a dream of the mediæval imagination, and the historian of its adventures should frankly put himself in the corresponding attitude of mind. It lends itself admirably to represent the ideals which were in the minds of the dreamer, and therefore unconsciously determined the constitution of the imaginary world. But when the personages, instead of obeying the laws of their own world, are converted into allegory, they lose their dream reality without gaining the reality of ordinary life. The arbitrariness especially ceases to be delightful when we suspect that the real creatures of the fancy have become the puppets of a judicious moralist. The question, What is the meaning? throws one's mind out of gear. When Sir Bedivere made his second appearance somebody asked Tennyson whether the three queens were not Faith, Hope, and Charity. The poet replied that they were, and that they were not. They might be the Virtues or they might be the Three Graces. There was, he said, an 'allegorical, or perhaps rather a parabolic, drift,' in the poem; but he added there was not a single fact or incident in the *Idylls* which might not be explained without any mystery or allegory whatever. This explanation may be very satisfactory to some readers, and if they are satisfied, their state is the more gracious; but I humbly confess that so soon as genuine inhabitants of Fairyland can be interpreted as three virtues or three graces, they cease to fascinate me. In the *Holy Grail* the mystical purpose is most distinctly avowed. We are told to learn what it means by studying the visions of Sir Percival, and his 'subsequent fall and nineteenth century temptations.' The result of my study is that the visions are turned into waking shams, and leave a residuum of edifying sermon. The intrusion of the nineteenth century is simply disenchantment. If I want to be moral, I should get much more instruction out of *Mme. Bovary* or some other 'masterful transcript of actuality' than out of Tristram and Iseult, and if I want to be romantic, the likeness of King Arthur to the Prince Consort takes all the vigour out of the prehistoric personage. The Prince Consort, no doubt, deserved Tennyson's profound respect; but when we find him masquerading among the Knights of the Round Table, his admirable propriety of behaviour looks painfully like insipidity and incapacity for his position.

This line of criticism is, of course, very obvious; and, I admit, may be simply a proof of the critic's unsuitability. I desire simply to state the historical fact that the publication of the *Idylls* marks the point at which some disciples were sensible of a partial refrigeration of their zeal. The old Tennysonian power was not extinct; many of the poems up to the last had all the old exquisite charm, and the older poetry never lost it. But from this time a certain class of admirers—perhaps the duller class—felt that they dwelt in the outer court, and that they could not enter the inmost shrine with befitting reverence. There was not, I must add, in my case at least, any objection to the combination, as it is called, of philosophy with poetry. 'Your poetry,' as Jowett said to Tennyson, 'has an element of philosophy more to be considered than any regular philosophy in England.' 'It is,' he adds, 'almost too much impregnated with philosophy,' although this again 'will be to some minds its greatest charm.' Tennyson himself was amused by discovering that he had been talking Hegelianism without knowing it. The fact is, I take it, that poetry in a mind of great general power, not only may be, but cannot help being, philosophy. Philosophy itself, it may be plausibly urged, is in reality nothing but poetry expressed by the cumbrous methods of dialectical formulæ. It labours painfully to put together ostensible reasons for the truth of the conceptions of life and the world which are directly presented in the poetic imagery. Tennyson's philosophy would have been present, though not consciously indicated, if he had simply recast the Arthurian legends in the spirit of the original creators. Nor will I argue that dislike to allegory is anything better than a prosaic prejudice, or, perhaps, an application of some pretentious æsthetic canon. Perhaps, indeed, the allegorical form was not so much the stumbling-block as the philosophical or ethical system itself which was meant to be adumbrated. Or rather, for that, I think, is the true account, we who fell off disliked a philosophy which required to be insinuated through an allegorical clothing. We were going through an intellectual crisis; and if we exaggerated its importance, Tennyson at least, as many other utterances prove, and as his memoirs show most convincingly, was equally impressed by the greatness of the issues. But for that reason, we (I repeat that by 'we' I only mean the wicked) wanted something more downright and dogmatic. A religious philosophy which hides itself behind mythical figures and vague personifications of abstract qualities; which can only be shadowed forth and insinuated through a rehabilitated romance, seemed inadequate and even effeminate. We fancied that if it ventured into broad daylight it would turn out to be mere commonplace disguised or made of moonshine and flimsy sentimentalisms. Or, possibly, we were not distinctly aware that there really was any mystical meaning at all, and simply felt that when such vital questions were being raised, we could not be really interested in this dim poetic land of unsubstantial shadows. When, a little later, we began to know what Omar Khàyyàm had said some eight centuries before, we felt the power of a direct and intensely powerful utterance of one mode of treating the eternal problem.

All this, it may be replied, is to explain that a certain class of young men were partially alienated from Tennyson's poetry because they did not like his philosophy; which is a proof that they were æsthetically dull and philosophically grovelling. I will not dispute the inference; I think, indeed, that there is much to be said for it; and as I have admitted my tendencies that way, I am obviously disqualified from speaking as an impartial judge. I only wish to urge, by way of extenuation at any rate, that we were still accessible to other Tennysonian influences, and, indeed, to poems in which his doctrine finds a more direct utterance. I love *In Memoriam*, and should be sorry if I were forced to admit that I could not understand the true secret of its extraordinary beauty. Professor Sidgwick contributes to this volume a most interesting account of its influence upon him. For certain reasons, I could not adopt all that he says, and my intellectual dissent from Tennyson begins, I may say, at an earlier stage; but I decline to admit that I am for that reason incapable of feeling the emotional power. Therefore, without attempting to argue the æsthetical canons, I return to the purely historical question suggested by these volumes. Froude, in a letter to the author, says that in his estimate, Tennyson stands 'far away, by the side of Shakespeare, above all other English poets, with this relative superiority even to Shakespeare, that he speaks the thoughts and speaks to the perplexities and misgivings of his own age.' Froude adds characteristically that Tennyson came before the world had become inflated 'with the vanity of progress, and there was still an atmosphere in which such a soul could grow. There will be no such others for many a long age.' It is rash, I think, to prophesy about 'long ages,' but Froude is at any rate a good witness as to the facts. Froude had known better than most people the doubts and perplexities by which Tennyson's contemporaries were distracted; and though Froude's own view remains rather a mystery, the impression made upon a man so alive to many sides of modern thought is no small proof of Tennyson's power. Now the memoirs ought to show us how Tennyson was prepared for the office of prophet. It has become common, as Mr. Palgrave remarks in his reminiscences, to treat of a poet as though he were 'evolved by a natural law'; and he gives an amusing instance in Taine's *à priori* speculations as to the evolution of Tennyson. Tennyson, as Taine suggested in a conversation, must have been brought up in luxury, and 'surrounded with things of costly beauty.' Mr. Palgrave was able to upset this theory, so far as concerned Tennyson's personal history. There is, of course, one absolute limit to any such speculation. No human being can presume to guess what are the conditions which determine the innate qualities of a man of genius. No one can say why such a plant, or a whole family of such plants, should have suddenly sprung up in a Lincolnshire vicarage, or why, a few years after, a similar phenomenon should have presented itself at Haworth. One can only ask how far the genius was influenced by its 'environment'? In both cases it might seem at first sight to be most unfavourable. The Brontës had an even less congenial atmosphere in Yorkshire than the Tennysons among the rough farmers of Lincolnshire. And yet in both cases there is this much similarity in the result, that, as the Brontës became even fanatical admirers of the cross-grained, hard-fisted York-shireman, Tennyson acquired at least a keen imaginative sympathy with the race of 'Northern farmers.' It would be as easy as absurd to deduce from these instances a general theory about the advantage of a bracing atmosphere for sensitive plants. In the case of Tennyson it must be admitted that the scantiness of details in the earlier parts of the memoir is rather tantalising. When Tennyson had become famous, materials of course became abundant, and Lord Tennyson tells us that he has had to make selections from forty thousand letters. For the early years, in which the mind and character were being formed, he had had little beyond a few recollections of his parents' talk. One would gladly know more of the crusty old grandfather who disinherited his eldest son; and of the stalwart son himself, six feet two in height, famous for social geniality and yet given to fits of despondency, and capable of being something of a tyrant in his family. His soul, we are told, was 'daily racked by bitter fancies, and tossed about by stormy troubles.' He had strange adventures in Russia and on the Continent. From the age of eleven the son had this father for his sole instructor, and must have profited, and also, one guesses, have suffered from the 'dominating force' of the paternal intellect. Then there is only a glimpse of the charming aunt, who would 'weep for hours' over the infinite goodness of God. He had damned most of her friends, and 'picked out for eternal salvation,' her who was 'no better than her neighbours.' One would like again to know more even of the cook, who declared that if you 'raäked out hell with a smaäll tooth coämb' you wouldn't find the likes of her master and mistress. Was this characteristic of the cook or of her employers? It might conceivably be interpreted as confirming a later statement that Tennyson's mother, being an angel, was undiscoverable in the lower regions, and she appears to have been in fact a most charming old lady, with a strong sense of humour. There are hints enough here for a hypothetical biography, with any number of remarks about 'heredity' and 'environment.' All that can be safely said is that Tennyson was obviously a born poet, writing verses of unmistakable promise at the age of fourteen and fifteen; even getting, at the age of seventeen, £20 from a singularly discriminative country bookseller for the volume (written with his brother); and accumulating at least the materials for other poems, including the 'Ode to Memory,' which, we are told, he considered to be one of the best among his 'very early and peculiarly concentrated Nature poems.' Personally, I have always been grateful to it for one of those life-giving touches which went far to reveal or justify for me the charm of fen scenery. Whatever the influences, Tennyson came up to Cambridge as a poet, and even, it seems, as a man already set aside for poetry. At Cambridge, at any rate, he was contented to stand aside from the ordinary competitions. Like other men of poetical genius, he felt little respect for the regular studies of the place; and melodiously complained that the authorities 'taught us nothing, feeding not the heart.' The heart, indeed, cannot be fed upon Newton's *Principia*. There might, I think, be some reply to the charge of 'lethargy' made against the University of that time: the place was really waking up under the influence (among others) of Julius Hare and Thirlwall and Whewell; but, undoubtedly, the influence of his own contemporaries was the really important matter for Tennyson. There may be, in many ways, better official teaching now; but the existing generation must be congratulated if it includes any large admixture of young men so keenly interested in intellectual pursuits as were Tennyson's special circle. The Union had just ceased to be thrilled by the eloquence of Charles Austin and Macaulay and Praed, and their rivals who supplied recruits to the 'philosophical Radicals,' and sought glory in the Reform Bill agitation. Charles Buller, the most beloved by his friends the Radicals, left college soon after Tennyson came up; Maurice, who had already founded the 'apostles,' with Sterling, the most attractive of men, represented the other school of Liberalism, which regarded Coleridge as its oracle. Among Tennyson's intimates and warm friends in later life were such men as Spedding, and

Monckton Milnes, and Trench, and many others keenly interested, at least, in the literature of to-day. Edward FitzGerald, though a contemporary, was not as yet known to Tennyson; but Lord Houghton seems to have been fully justified in saying that the Cambridge of those days could boast a body of young men such as had been rarely surpassed in promise. Chief among them, in Tennyson's opinion, and in that of many good judges, was Arthur Hallam. Whatever might be the dreariness of the lecture-room, a young man of genius could have no reason to complain that his lot was cast in barren places. Tennyson in later years always looked back with affection to those 'dawn-golden times'; and, indeed, his memory inspired phrases too familiar for more than a passing allusion. To students of the might-have-been, it might be tempting to ask what would have happened if Tennyson had gone to Oxford and come under the influence of Newman and Hurrell Froude. The Dean of Westminster tells us how, when he first met Tennyson among his intimates, in 1841–2, he was startled by their indifference to the Tractarian Controversy, and to the questions which interested the disciples of Arnold. Would an Oxford-bred Tennyson have written another *Christian Year*, or achieved that poem which Clough never succeeded in writing?

Anyhow, the retrospective view of Tennyson's college life might suggest some melancholy reflections. Death cut short some promising careers; some, though they did good work, failed to make a public mark: they have left an impression upon their personal friends, but an impression of which even the tradition will expire in the next generation; and others, perhaps for want of some quality of mind or character, eventually dropped behind the real leaders of the time, and compounded with the commonplace world. Why did not Tennyson fall to the rear? Such a catastrophe must at one time have seemed not improbable to an outside observer. His friends, indeed, seem to have fully recognised his abilities. He was, briefly, one of the 'mighty of the earth,' said Blakesley. 'He was,' says Fanny Kemble, whose brother John was a college friend, 'the great hero of the day.' His tall, powerful figure, his 'Shakespearian' head, finely poised, 'crowned with dark, wavy hair,' made him look the character of the 'coming poet' as well as could be desired by a painter. The striking point about him, then as afterwards, was the 'union of strength with refinement.' And yet one imagines that the college dons, the 'lion-like' Whewell, for example, also conspicuous for physical as well as intellectual prowess, must have shaken their heads when Tennyson not only declined to enter the Senate House competitions, but apparently decided to become a mere looker-on at life, and passed years in a quiet Bohemian company; smoking pipes at intervals with Carlyle and joining friends at the Cock; but mainly vegetating in the country with no very obvious prospects, and apparently surrendering his mind a little too unreservedly to a 'wise passiveness,' though he might be slowly secreting a few exquisite poems.

That, no doubt, represents one aspect of Tennyson. Mr. Lecky remarks that 'nature evidently intended him for the life of the quietest and most secluded of country gentlemen, for a life spent among books and flowers and a few intimate friends,' sheltered from all outside shocks. And at the period to which the recollection refers (late in the 'sixties) this was an obvious, though, as Mr. Lecky of course recognises, very far indeed from an exhaustive, judgment. The house at Farringford, the Mecca of many future generations of Tennysonians, looks as if it had been secreted, like the shell of a mollusc, by the nature of the occupant. The sweet English scenery, which no one ever painted so well, and the sea, which he loved like a true

Englishman, show themselves through the belt of wood, calculated to keep the profane vulgar at a distance. It seemed a providential *habitat* for a man so very open to even petty irritations. 'A flea will annoy me,' as he said to Tyndall; 'a fleabite will spread a square inch over the surface of my skin. . . . I *am* thin-skinned, and I take no pains to hide it.' And, indeed, though the fact is fully admitted, it is perhaps less conspicuous in these volumes than it was to casual observers. They were apt to carry away the impression that Tennyson must spend an unreasonably large part of his time in fretting over the wounds made by trumpery critics. The absolute simplicity of the man, indeed, which was equally obvious, suggested pity instead of contempt for what must be regarded as an infirmity. No poet since Pope was so sensitive to the assaults of Grub Street; though happily he was altogether incapable of condescending to Pope's miserable methods of retort. It is, however, easy to understand the view which commended itself to Taine. His theory was that Tennyson was a kind of refined epicurean; a man lapping himself in British comfort against all disagreeable sights and painful truths; averting his eyes as much as possible from harsh contrasts and harrowing doubts; and enveloped in a panoply made from the soothing creeds of political and religious opportunists, with only just enough of the light of reason filtered through a screen of tradition to pass for being at once liberal and respectable. Though Taine had to give up his theory as to Tennyson's personal environment, he still draws a picture of English country life as seen from the railway—its well-ordered parks and neat country houses embowered in well-ordered gardens—and contrasts it with the stimulating, though rough realities of Parisian life, among which his favourite De Musset penetrated the true secret of life. Taine naturally prefers De Musset, and his criticism, though it is obviously from a partial outsider, hits off one view which cannot be overlooked. Matthew Arnold, as I have observed elsewhere, introduces the 'great, broad-shouldered genial Englishman' of the 'Princess' as a type of British 'Philistinism,' and intimates his opinion that the creator is too much in sympathy with the type.

It is equally true that no lover of Tennyson's poetry could admit Taine's scornful account of the *In Memoriam* as the mourning of a correct gentleman, wiping away his tears with a cambric pocket-handkerchief. I can subscribe, on the contrary, without hesitation, to the commonplace British opinion that no poet has ever shown such depths of tenderness or such skill in interweaving the most delicate painting of nature with the utterance of profound emotion. And this brings us back to the biographical problem. Over twenty years intervened between Tennyson's departure from Cambridge and the settlement in Farringford. Here again, through no fault of Lord Tennyson, we feel the want of a few more documents. No doubt a reader may be content with what is expressed or can be inferred from the poetry. Yet the matter-of-fact personal history, if it could have been told, would surely have had a deep interest. In the first place, one would like to know, if a purely prosaic person, something about the bare pounds, shillings, and pence. Tennyson, as we discover from a remark of Carlyle's, inherited a 'small annuity on his father's decease' (1831), and chose to 'club with his mother and sisters,' and so to 'live unpromoted and write poems.' This may be all very well for a bachelor; and we are glad to discover that from 1850 his copyrights were producing five hundred pounds a year, which, considering the small bulk of his publications, shows that he was doing remarkably well for a poet. In 1845, however, he had still been in need of a pension; and the smallness of his income was of serious importance. He had met his future wife in 1836; he had

become engaged to her apparently in 1837, and felt the need of making a livelihood. It was from the vagueness of his expectations in that direction that the correspondence between him and Miss Sellwood was forbidden in 1840, and they apparently did not meet again for ten years. Meanwhile all his independent property was lost about 1844, together with part of his brothers' and sisters', in an unfortunate speculation, and distress caused 'real hardship,' and even an attack of illness. He must, therefore, have gone through a period of trial, affecting not only his pocket, but his hopes of domestic happiness, of which one would have liked to know a little more. That he took his troubles bravely, whatever they may have been, is proved by his literary history. Whatever else he did, he never condescended to lower his aims or the perfection of his workmanship. He allowed his poetry to ripen in his mind, as though he had been in possession of Taine's hypothetical luxuries; and, it would seem, he kept his feelings, whatever they may have been, to himself. His extreme sensibility led him to seek for the utmost possible perfection; not to court immediate popularity. The years of comparative nonrecognition must have been trying, and the relative slightness of the personal record of these twenty years is the more regrettable. Fuller materials, had they been accessible, must have brought out more distinctly the real strength which lay beneath the morbidly sensitive outside. His 'sensitiveness,' as Mr. Lecky observes, 'seemed to me,' as it did to others, curiously out of harmony with 'his large, powerful frame.' Whether there is any real incompatibility between athletic vigour and delicacy of nervous organisation is a problem which I must leave to physiologists. Another instance of the same combination may be found, for example, in Hawthorne; and, I dare say, in plenty of other instances. Generally speaking, we are inclined, with whatever reason, to anticipate from an athletic giant more of the rollicking vigour of a Christopher North than of the exquisite workmanship which makes 'jewels five words long'— the power, as Johnson put it, of hewing a colossus from a rock, not of carving figures on cherry-stones. Tennyson, no doubt, though this side of his character is a little in the background, could have taken his part in one of the jovial 'Noctes,' if he had been sure that no reporters were present. But the massive physical framework seems to be indicated by a certain slowness which might pass into indolence. Your giant may be sensitive, but he carries too much ballast to be easily stirred to utterance. He is contemplative or dreamy rather than impetuous and excitable. If Shelley had put on more flesh, he might have been equally poetical, but he would not have indulged in the boyish explosions which imply an excessive mobility of the nervous system. Byron's extraordinary alternations between corpulence and thinness induced by starvation appear to be clearly connected both with his power and his weakness, and might be considered at length in the essay which ought to be written upon the relation between fat and poetry. But I must not be led into such a digression here. One sees in Tennyson's portraits the deep, dreamy eyes under the noble brow, and recognises the man predestined to be a thoughtful spectator of the battle of life, rather than an active participator in the superficial contests.

And here, of course, we have the obvious remarks about the spirit of his generation. Young men were ceasing to feel the revolutionary inspiration, though they were still accessible to the utterances of the departing period. When Byron died in 1824, Carlyle exclaimed that the news came upon his heart 'like a mass of lead'; he felt a 'painful twinge,' as if he had lost a brother. Tennyson, then only fourteen, felt the same news to be an 'awful calamity,' and rushed out-of-doors to write upon the sandstone, 'Byron is dead.' But Byronism soon followed Byron. Shelley was unknown to Tennyson, till his college days at least, and the successor, though, of course, admiring his predecessor's marvellous powers, admitted that Shelley was 'after too much in the clouds' for him. Keats, on the other hand, he declared, 'would have been among the very greatest of us if he had lived. There is something of the innermost soul of the poet in everything he ever wrote.' 'Wordsworth's very best,' he said, 'is the best in its way that has been sent out by the moderns,' and one is glad to hear that he was once able to express to Wordsworth himself his deep sense of the 'obligation which all Englishmen owed to him.' From various scattered remarks it is clear that Tennyson, like other poets, could be an admirable critic of his brethren; but these sayings are interesting as indicating his own tendencies in early days. How much he actually owed to Keats and Wordsworth must be uncertain. Probably he would have been much the same had he never read a line of either. But one may say that he wished to utter teaching congenial to Wordsworth's in language as perfect as that of Keats's most finished workmanship. The famous hypothetical addition to Wordsworth's poems,

A Mister Wilkinson, a Clergyman,

the authorship of which was claimed both by Tennyson and FitzGerald, indicates the weakness which was naturally avoided by one who could equally appreciate Keats. Like Keats's, at any rate, Tennyson's poetry shows the dying-out of the old fervour which had stimulated Wordsworth's first efforts, made Coleridge and Southey 'pantisocratists,' and inspired Byron and Shelley during the days of the Holy Alliance. The movements of 1830, both in Europe and England, roused some of Tennyson's circle, such as Sterling and Kemble; but, as far as one can infer from the indications, both Tennyson and Arthur Hallam looked at least doubtfully upon the Reform agitation in England. The Tennysons, indeed, set the bells ringing to the horror of the parson at Somersby when the Bill was passed; but Hallam thought that William IV., when he met the 'first assembly of delegates from a sovereign people' (that is, the first Reformed Parliament), would perhaps be the last King of England; and even Tennyson, a little later, hopes against hope that there are still true hearts in old England 'that will never brook the sight of Baal in the Sanctuary, and St. Simon' (the leader of the famous sect) 'in the Church of Christ.' The St. Simonians show what an 'immense mass of evil' is in existence, and are 'a focus which gathers all its rays.' The Reform Bill was not to be a descent of Niagara, but a passage over the rapids into a superficially quiet reach. A judicious friend gives another view. Sterling, he says, had been misled, like Shelley, by the desire to abolish unjust institutions, but had afterwards perceived that the right method was to 'implant a principle with which selfishness cannot coexist.' Reformers would complain that they must wait for a long time if they have first to extirpate selfishness. With this we may associate a criticism of Spedding upon the early poems, which showed, he thought, over indulgence 'in the luxuries of the senses, a profusion of splendours, harmonies, perfumes, gorgeous apparels, luscious meats and drinks,' and so forth, which rather 'pall upon the sense,' and make the outward obscure the inner world. The remark falls in with Taine's criticism. Such a Tennyson might be too easily reconciled to the creature-comforts of the upper classes in England and become a mere dreaming Sybarite. His own view of the situation is apparently given in the 'Palace of Art.' It was a comment, as we are told, upon a remark made to him at college by Trench: 'Tennyson, we cannot live in art.' The poem itself is so marvellous a collection of those felicities of description in which Tennyson is unapproachable, that perhaps it rather raises the question why the architect of the palace should not have stayed there quietly and worshipped 'art for art' for the rest of his days. The conversion comes rather abruptly, but, at least, shows how much Tennyson's mind was occupied with the problem of how the artist is to be also the moralist. I certainly do not quarrel with his solution, which in some sense worked itself out in *In Memoriam*. The moral crisis through which he passed is indicated by the 'Two Voices' or 'Thoughts of a Suicide' (that is, of somebody who decided not to commit suicide), written contemporaneously with the first poems of *In Memoriam*, under a 'cloud of overwhelming sorrow.' All joy, he said, was 'blotted out' of his life and he 'longed for death.' He continued, however, to write, and his writing does not suggest unbroken gloom. He was finally, it would seem, restored to full mental health by the love which was to be the blessing of later years. If we may not call it morbid, it is at least abnormal that the loss of a college friend should cause not only immoderate agony, but such prolonged depression. Arthur Hallam may have deserved all that was said of him, though for us he can only be, like Sterling, a symbol of the virtue of friendship, a type canonised by genius, but, like some other saints, a little wanting in individuality. We cannot define the merits which prompted eulogies in some ways unparalleled in our literature. Lycidas, as Tennyson and others have said, is a test of poetical sensibility. I deny parenthetically that there can be any universal test in such matters, but the meaning is no doubt that it is a test of the appreciation of such poetical merits as are independent of the pathos of the theme. It is a test, that is, precisely because the beauty of the poetry does not imply any very keen sensibility about the person ostensibly commemorated. Milton could be noble and melodious, though one does not suppose that he lost his appetite for breakfast for a single day after hearing of King's death. The sincerity of Tennyson's grief, on the contrary, is implied in every section. He was, we are told, profoundly impressed by Shakespeare's sonnets when he was writing *In Memoriam*, and we can understand why at the time he then thought them even greater than the plays. The intense passion of some of the sonnets ('no longer mourn for me when I am dead,' for example) equals or surpasses in its way anything in *In Memoriam*. But, whatever the solution of their mystery, they do not convince me that Shakespeare was at any time disqualified by his emotions from attending to the interests of the Globe Theatre. As an embodiment of the purest passion of friendship, the *In Memoriam* is, I take it, unapproachable; and, in spite of any reservations upon other points, that must be, to some minds, the great source of Tennyson's power over his readers. Mr. Palgrave ends his reminiscences of Tennyson by saying that forty-three years of friendship made him recognise 'lovableness' as the 'dominant note' of his friend's character. That, I think, is also the impression, and certainly there cannot be a better one, which is made by the whole of this biography. Tennyson had his weaknesses, which can be divined where filial reverence properly refrains from an articulate statement or a distinct insistence upon them. Nor, as I shall say directly, can I admit without reservations some other claims to our allegiance. But the unsurpassed sweetness and tenderness of character is evident in every chapter. It is impossible to read the book without learning to love the man better. It is needless to speak of the beauty of the domestic life; needless, at any rate, to express more than the sense of satisfaction that, for once, a poet, of abnormally sensitive character even for a poet, was surrounded by an atmosphere of unbroken harmony for so many years. If he lost Hallam, he always preserved the friendship of Carlyle (tempered by an occasional growl); of the inimitable FitzGerald, never less delightful because he could never affect insincere admiration; of the wise and placid Spedding, the 'Pope,' as Tennyson called him, of the young men at Trinity; of Maurice, revered by all who knew him for saintliness of character if not for lucidity of intellect; of the cordial and generous Kingsley, and of Mr. Aubrey de Vere, and others who still live and cherish his memory. If he was over-sensitive to 'fleabites' of petty criticism, the irritation never embittered him; no ungenerous and 'nasty' remark about his contemporaries seems to mar the impression of real dignity of character. He thought a good deal about himself: most people do; but any little vanity he shows is perfectly innocent and consistent with substantial simplicity and modesty. His foibles added a certain piquancy to the sentiment of his friends: it is pleasant to feel that you are petting a tender and childlike nature as well as simply sitting at a great man's feet. Undoubtedly a man might be equally lovable and yet unable to write a line which would not have set Tennyson's teeth on edge. But even Tennyson's astonishing sensibility to the 'music of words,' and his power of compressing into a stanza the quintessence of sentiments or perceptions which other men might dilute into volumes, would have been thrown away without this singular sweetness of character. When I read 'Tears, Idle Tears,' I feel that a man might be forgiven even by a stern moralist for devoting a lifetime to stringing together a few melodious phrases as a perpetual utterance of our better moods. Gray did something of the kind; but Tennyson, though not a voluminous poet, has probably left an unsurpassed number of phrases which will live in the memory both of gentle and simple—the most punctilious 'æsthete' and the reader whose ignorance, better than knowledge, allows him to be charmed without knowing or asking why.

If these volumes contain what we had all more or less divined, they call attention to a claim which may provoke more discussion. Jowett, as we see, regarded Tennyson as a teacher of philosophy. Maurice dedicated his most characteristic volume to Tennyson as to one who has been a great spiritual teacher; and Dr. Martineau, giving an account of the meeting at the 'Metaphysical Society,' speaks of Maurice's fellowship of thought with 'the truest *vates* of his age.' It becomes an outsider to treat these and other weighty testimonies with all respect. And yet the insistence upon this aspect of Tennyson's work strikes one perhaps as a little excessive. There is, of course, no question as to the depth of Tennyson's interest in theological questions. The frequent recurrence of this claim, however, tends, I think, to give an impression that the famous line ought to have been 'A Mr. Tennyson, a clergyman,' and to put a little too much out of sight the fact that he was not always in the pulpit. He could yield himself, it is obvious, to perfectly unsophisticated enjoyment of sensuous impressions; he could talk very effectively and very humorously as a simple man of letters, or even, if we may say so without offence, as a man of this world capable of hearty contempt for clerical as well as other cants and hypocrisies. I have more than once had a similar surprise in reading biographies of men whom I have seen in the flesh; and the explanation is not far to seek. Fuller tells us somewhere of the bishop who used to go down to the cellar with his old friend and chaplain, where they could throw their canonicals aside, pledge each other in a good glass of wine, and refresh their souls in a jolly conversation. No doubt they showed on such occasions a side which did not get into official biographies. Tennyson certainly could doff his 'canonicals'; but, however this may be, it suggests another point which demands some delicacy of handling. Professor

Sidgwick thinks that *In Memoriam* expresses with admirable clearness a true philosophical judgment of certain tendencies of modern speculation. I cannot discuss that problem on which Professor Sidgwick speaks with authority as well as sympathy. In any case the poetical merit of a work does not depend upon its philosophical orthodoxy. The orthodox, whoever they may be, can be terribly vapid and the heretics much more inspiring. A man would be a very narrow-minded critic who was unable to admire any of the great men from Lucretius to Dante who have embodied the most radically opposite conceptions of the world. But we must draw a line, as Tennyson is reported to have said, between such poets as Keats, Byron, and Shelley, and the 'great sage poets,' at once thinkers and artists, such as Æschylus, Shakespeare, 'Dante, and Goethe.' Can we think of Tennyson himself as belonging to the highest class? Did he not only accept the right view, whatever that may be, but express it forcibly and majestically as one of the small class which represents poetry thoroughly transfused with philosophy? I at least cannot see my way to such a conclusion; and the mere comparison seems to me to suggest the real limitations to Tennyson's art. I will only notice what is suggested by many passages in these volumes. Carlyle, we are told, was first attracted to Tennyson by the 'Ulysses.' He quotes in his first letter to Tennyson the noble passage:—

> It may be that the gulfs will wash us down:
> It may be we shall touch the Happy Isles,
> And see the great Achilles, whom we knew.

'These lines,' he says, 'do not make me weep, but there is in me what would fill whole lachrymatories as I read.'[1] Afterwards Carlyle appears to have suggested that Tennyson was wasting his time by scribbling verses. Carlyle, late in life, would occasionally quote the 'Ulysses' by way of contrast with Tennyson's later performances. The old poem, he thought, had the true heroic ring; and Tennyson himself, it may be remarked, says that it was written soon after Hallam's death, and gave his feelings about fighting the battle of life perhaps more simply than anything in *In Memoriam*. Carlyle's criticism came to this, that Tennyson had declined into a comparatively sentimental and effeminate line of writing, mere 'æstheticisms' instead of inspiring a courageous spirit of confronting the spiritual crisis. The *Idylls of the King* could not be the epic of the future, but at best a melodious version of conventional and superficial solutions of the eternal problem. King Arthur had (in Carlylese) too much of the 'gigman' to be a great leader of modern men. The average critic, as we are frequently reminded in these volumes, complained that Tennyson was 'morbid.' *Maud*, in particular, gave that offence in spite of irresistible beauties. Tennyson himself argued that the critics confounded the author with his creature. The hero of *Maud* was only a dramatic personage; he was a 'morbid poetic soul,' and the poem was to be taken as 'a little *Hamlet*.' The original *Hamlet* would itself be now criticised, he thought, as 'morbid.' Mr. Gladstone, who first took the poem to represent the worship of Jingo, recanted on further consideration, and discovered that Tennyson had only approved of 'lawful war'—which makes a great difference. *Maud*, I must say in passing, fell in, at any rate, too easily with the curious delusion of the time (embodied also in Kingsley's *Two Years Ago*) that the Crimean War implied the moral regeneration of the country. Necessary or absurd, I don't think that the war can now be credited with that effect. *Maud*, I fancy, will be remembered for the surpassing beauty of the love lyrics, and not from any lively interest in a hero who is not only morbid, but silly. Hamlet may have been morbid—an interview with one's father's ghost is rather upsetting—but at least he was not contemptible. However, we will not for a moment identify the gentleman in *Maud* with Tennyson. Another poem, 'Despair,' provoked, we are told, bitter criticism, 'because the public did not recognise it as a dramatic monologue.' It is, I think—as I believe the most ardent Tennysonians admit—a distinctly inferior specimen of his art; but it expresses something not purely dramatic. Tennyson himself remarked that he would commit suicide if he thought there was no 'future life'; and his hero acts upon that principle. He is equally shocked by the 'horrible know-nothing books,' and by a view of hell such as commended itself to Tennyson's aunt; and the suggestion is natural that the reasonable course for a man equally horrified by both opinions is to put an end to himself. It would not be fair to lay any stress upon an admitted shortcoming, and the 'dramatic monologue' argument may be taken for what it is worth. But this, too, is, I think, clear. When Tennyson is presented to us as giving the true solution of the doubts which beset our time, we should have some positive as well as negative testimony to his merits. We cannot, it is true, expect a full solution. A gentleman is reported to have asked him whether the existence of evil was not the great difficulty. Tennyson certainly could not be expected to throw much light upon Job's difficulties, and seems to have judiciously diverted the conversation by referring to the 'charge of the heavy brigade.' No poet, and indeed no philosopher, can be asked to solve the eternal problems off-hand. What we do see, is that Tennyson, like many noble and deep thinkers, was terribly perplexed by the alternatives apparently offered: by his aversion on one side to certain orthodox dogmas, and by his dread and hatred of some tendencies which claim at least to be scientific. His ideal hero was the man who faced doubts boldly and attained clear convictions of one kind or other. On the other hand, he is always haunted by the fear of depriving your sister of her 'happy views' (a woefully feeble phrase, by the way, for Tennyson), and praises a philosopher for keeping his doubts to himself. The resulting attitude of mind may not be morbid: certainly it may fairly be called pathetic, and even those who do not sympathise with his doctrine will do well to feel for his distress. It may teach them, at least, what is in any case worth knowing: why their teaching is so repulsive to many tender and delicate minds. But I confess to share Carlyle's regret for the loss of the old heroic tone of the 'Ulysses.' Noble poetry, let us admit, may express either faith or scepticism: a conviction that we know or that we can never know; it may be openly pessimistic, or expressive of an enthusiastic faith in the future; but Tennyson, even in the *In Memoriam*, always seems to me to be like a man clinging to a spar left floating after a shipwreck, knowing that it will not support him, and yet never able to make up his mind to strike out and take his chance of sinking or swimming. That may be infinitely affecting, but it is not the attitude of the poet who can give a war-cry to his followers, or of the philosopher who really dares to 'face the spectres of the mind.' He can lay them for the moment; but they are always in the background, and suggest, too often, rather a querulous protest against an ever-recurring annoyance than any such mental victory as issues in a coherent and settled conviction on either side. I merely wish to indicate an impression, and will not attempt to indicate the similar attitude in regard to the great social and political movements. I cannot, though my inability may be owing to my own spiritual blindness, place him among the 'great sage poets,' but I have wished to intimate that such as I am are not therefore disqualified from appreciating his poetry in another capacity: as a document indicating the effect of modern movements of

thought upon a mind of extraordinary delicacy and a nature of admirable sweetness; but, far more, as a perfect utterance of emotions which are all equally beautiful in themselves whatever the 'philosophy' with which they are associated. The life, I believe, will help to strengthen that impression, though I have only attempted to notice some of the more obvious remarks which it may suggest.

Notes

1. I remember to have heard Carlyle in his old age speak with equal enthusiasm of this poem.

LEWIS E. GATES
"Nature in Tennyson's Poetry"
Studies and Appreciations
1900, pp. 77–91

One of the most important effects of the Romantic movement was the closeness of the relation it established between nature and the human soul. The intense and oftentimes eccentric emotions that tended to throw the Romantic poet out of sympathy with his fellow men and with conventional life became the solvent of the rigid forms of the material universe. The poet's fervid mood proved the very fire necessary to fuse nature once and for all with emotion, to make it coalesce with thought and the inner life of man, and to unite matter and spirit more subtly and intimately than ever before. The Romantic poets subdued nature to spirit; they interpreted nature in terms of human feeling; they sent their imaginations out along countless lines of subtle association, drew all nature into sympathy with their intense experiences, and converted all the facts and forms of nature into "the passion-wingèd ministers of thought." Nature was no longer to stand apart from man as a system of half-hostile forces, or a mass of dry facts, meaningless except for science: it was not to be as for Pope and the Deists merely a great machine of infinitely ingenious construction, set running once and for all by the great Mechanician and for ever after grinding out effects unerringly and inevitably. For many Romantic poets—notably for Wordsworth, Coleridge, and Shelley—nature was a direct emanation from the one great spiritual force which manifests itself also in the myriad individuals that make up the human race. The countless ideas and feelings that float through the mind of man and the countless shapes and aspects of the world of nature were alike the utterance of one great imaginative Artist, who expressed through these two sets of symbols his thoughts of beauty and truth. Hence the poet who seeks a proper image to stand for his thought has simply to let his imagination guide him through the beautiful forms of nature till he finds a fitting symbol; his thoughts are God's thoughts, and have been already uttered in some fixed shape of beauty, or through some changing aspect, of the outside world. This is really the postulate on which Wordsworth's and Coleridge's theory of imagination depends; imagination, they urge leads to objective truth, while fancy only plays prettily with images; imagination discerns essential analogies between mind and matter, and brings once more into at least transient unity the world of spirit and the world of nature.

Tennyson's poetry carries on with fine loyalty and in some ways with increased effectiveness the Romantic tradition in the treatment of nature. Not that he accepts or expresses extreme transcendental conceptions of the relation of nature to man and of nature and man to God. The scientific spirit is continually imposing its check upon him and compelling him to recognize, at least transiently, the literal meaning of the facts of nature as interpreted by the analytic, positive mind of his day and generation. Yet the Romantic mood of intimacy with nature survives in Tennyson, not simply undiscouraged by the revelations of science, but even quickened and intensified in its delicate susceptibility. He has done more than perhaps any other single poet of this century to spiritualize nature in the sense of making it subservient to the needs of the human soul and of forcing it to become symbolical of human moods and passions. He has done even more than Wordsworth to give a new meaning to nature; for whereas Wordsworth worked continually in the interests of a few simple moods with which many men nowadays cannot fully sympathize, Tennyson has had at his service an exquisitely graduated temperament, varying through an almost limitless range of complex moods, nearly every one of which may be shared by a sensitive reader.

From the outset Tennyson's poetry was noteworthy for its powerful and suggestive use of landscape. "Mariana" in his first volume, and "Mariana in the South," "Fatima," and "Œnone" in his second volume were experiments after effects not before attempted in English literature. These poems are not studies of different "ways of love," or merely portraits of different types of women; they are immensely imaginative studies of irresistible and all-dominating moods, each of which is symbolized through the figure of a woman portrayed against a sympathetic background of nature. They are studies of landscape as landscape is seen through an atmosphere determined by feeling. Each poem owes its power to the congruity of its details, to the imaginative unity that pervades it and subdues every minutest circumstance of colour and light and shade and motion till they all breathe out one inevitable chord of feeling. The blinding light and the stifling heat of the landscapes in "Mariana in the South" seem the very exhalation of defeated passion; in the other "Mariana," the details of the "lonely moated grange," from the "blackest moss" of the flower-plots to the "glooming flats" and "dark fens," all image "Mariana's" deadly languor and desolation. The poem is a study in black of a passion of melancholy as the other poem is a study in flame-colours of a passion of consuming tenderness and devotion.

Of course, there are not many of the poems that have such absolute imaginative unity. But there is a second group where noticeably similar effects are gained by somewhat similar methods; this group contains most of the other poems that are called by the names of women,—"Lilian," "Isabel," "Madeline," "Eleänore," "Adeline," and "Margaret." Each poem portrays a temperament in terms of look, gesture, bearing, complexion, and form; each is the interpretation of a woman's soul as it reveals itself by means of subtle material symbols. The power of each poem is due to the poet's intuitive appreciation of the value of material facts as the expression of thought and feeling. Two of the poems, "Adeline" and "Margaret," beside portraying typical women, have a symbolical value; the "twin-sisters" symbolize the Romantic spirit as it shows itself now in the fanciful interpretation of nature, and now in the deeply imaginative interpretation of the passionate life of past generations. The less human of the sisters, "shadowy, dreaming Adeline," weaves into bright and tender myths all she sees in the outside world; she dreams childlike dreams over butterflies, bluebells, and "lilies at dawn," and finds all nature instinct with half-fantastic life. Margaret is the type of the Romantic spirit in its more serious moods and its "more human" sympathies; of its passion for "dainty sorrow" and of its

ardent reveries over the great deeds and glorious tragedies of history.

> What can it matter, Margaret,
>   What songs below the waning stars
> The lion-heart, Plantagenet,
>   Sang looking thro' his prison bars?
>   Exquisite Margaret, who can tell
> The last wild thought of Chatelet,
> Just ere the falling axe did part
> The burning brain from the true heart,
>   Even in her sight he loved so well.

Thoughts and images like these are the "feast of sorrow" from which the pale lady of Romance is loath to part. The mood that is suggested is much like that of Keats's more sombre odes; it has much in common with the mood of those verses which in the "Ode to a Nightingale" describe Ruth "amid the alien corn." Both passages send the imagination travelling back along the dark ways of history to the intense passionate experience of an isolated soul; both depend for their effectiveness on the curious modern mood that finds a special charm in the uncertain lights and shades, the mysterious chiaroscuro of the past.

The other poems of this group probably have no symbolical meaning; but they are quite as remarkable for their portrayal of temperament through bodily signs. And the interesting point to be noted with reference to all these poems is that they form one more illustration of the far-reaching sensitiveness to harmonies between matter and spirit which is perhaps in the last analysis the deepest source of Tennyson's power.

Besides the poems of the two general groups already considered, there are, of course, many others in Tennyson's earliest volumes which contain atmospheric landscapes of remarkable beauty and suggestiveness. In the "Ode to Memory" there occurs a series of landscapes which are called up out of the poet's boyhood; and they all have the dewy splendour, the freshness, the brilliancy of the impressions of youth; there rests on all of them the light of early morning. The "Lotos-Eaters" portrays a series of scenes from the land where "it seemed always afternoon"; the poem is a study in yellow and gold and orange; the landscapes are seen through a dreamy mellow haze and in the light of a westering sun; and not one of them could be conceived of as occurring in the "Ode to Memory." Nor could the following landscape be found by any possibility in the "Lotos-Eaters":—

> Pour round my ears the livelong bleat
> Of the thick-fleeced sheep from wattled folds,
>   Upon the ridged wolds,
> When the first matin-song hath waken'd loud
> Over the dark dewy earth forlorn,
> What time the amber morn
> Forth gushes from beneath a low-hung cloud.

There breathe through these lines the sense of mystery and the awe and yet the hope and the keen delight that are stirred in the heart of an impressionable boy by the sights and sounds of dawn. The Lotos-Eaters knew no such nature as this.

Nor is it only in Tennyson's early or short poems that this atmospheric treatment of landscape is to be found. His later long narrative poems are full of equally good illustrations of his power to re-create nature in terms of a dominating mood. The action of these poems goes on in the midst of natural scenery which is perpetually varying in tone and colour, and light and shade, in sympathy with the mood of the moment. In *Maud*, this suffusion of nature with passion is especially noticeable; and the hysterics and bad psychology of that poem are made endurable by the beauty of such imaginative sketches as the following:—

> I heard no sound where I stood
> But the rivulet on from the lawn
> Running down to my own dark wood;
> Or the voice of the long sea-wave as it swell'd
> Now and then in the dim-gray dawn;
> But I look'd, and round, all round the house I beheld
> The death-white curtain drawn;
> Felt a horror over me creep,
> Prickle my skin and catch my breath,
> Knew that the death-white curtain meant but sleep,
> Yet I shudder'd and thought like a fool of the sleep of
>   death.

This should be compared with Wordsworth's "Strange fits of passion have I known"; the mood is substantially the same; but Tennyson's lines are far finer in phrasing, more suggestive in imagery, and more thoroughly atmospheric.

In *Enoch Arden*, too, there are many passages where, with like intensity and imaginative power, nature is subdued to the passion of the moment. What could be finer from this point of view or more inappropriate from the point of view of Enoch's psychology than the famous lines describing Enoch's sense of isolation on the desert island?—

> No sail from day to day, but every day
> The sunrise broken into scarlet shafts
> Among the palms and ferns and precipices;
> The blaze upon the waters to the east;
> The blaze upon his island overhead;
> The blaze upon the waters to the west;
> Then the great stars that globed themselves in
>   Heaven,
> The hollower-bellowing ocean, and again
> The scarlet shafts of sunrise—but no sail.

In order to bring out more unmistakably the peculiar transformation to which in such descriptions as these nature submits in passing through Tennyson's temperament, it may be well to quote two or three of his simpler descriptions of natural scenery where he merely portrays frankly and delicately some clearly visualized aspect or object of the outside world. Descriptions of this sort also abound, and are wrought out with an exquisite fineness of detail that does not preclude breadth of treatment, and with marvellous felicity of phrase. The first of the following passages is from "Margaret" and the second from *Maud*:—

> The sun is just about to set,
> The arching limes are tall and shady,
> And faint, rainy lights are seen,
> Moving in the leavy beech.

> I was walking a mile,
> More than a mile from the shore,
> The sun look'd out with a smile
> Betwixt the cloud and the moor,
> And riding at set of day
> Over the dark moor land,
> Rapidly riding far away,
> She waved to me with her hand.
> There were two at her side,
> Something flash'd in the sun,
> Down by the hill I saw them ride,
> In a moment they were gone.

The lines from "Margaret" show as loving and faithful a study of nature as Wordsworth's, and as great delicacy of phrase in recording unusual or little noticed aspects of the outside world. The passage from *Maud* is a masterpiece of description; the landscape is sketched, in its broad features, with bold, free strokes, and the figures are flashed upon the reader's imagination by a gleam of light and a motion. In both these passages the treatment is sincere and simple; nature is shown under a white light, with no modifying or harmonizing atmosphere. But description of this kind, though attractive enough in its way and bearing witness to the perfection of Tennyson's technique, lacks the specific charm and peculiar power of Romantic description; it is not imaginative in the distinctively Romantic meaning of the term; it does not, to use Lamb's words, "draw all things to one." In the passages earlier considered, the unifying and harmonizing power of imagination pervades every line, phrase, and word, and makes them all eloquent of a single thought and mood. This action of imagination is compared by Wordsworth in a famous passage of the last book of the *Prelude*, to the light of the moon as this light is seen, from the summit of a lofty hill, falling on a widespread landscape, and blending all the infinitely various details into a single harmonious impression of splendour and power.

Such Romantic imagination in dealing with nature Tennyson possessed in a high degree; and indeed, from one point of view, he may be said simply to have carried on to richer conclusions the work which the Romanticists began. As has already been suggested, he has probably been more influential than even Wordsworth, in conveying widely and permanently into the English temperament a delicate and swiftly responsive sensitiveness to the emotional suggestiveness of nature. Wordsworth was, in large measure, preoccupied with the moral meaning of the external world; to quote his own words, he sought "to exhibit the most ordinary appearances of the material universe under moral relations." Tennyson subdues nature still further and makes it eloquent of all our moods and passions. Wordsworth's moods are comparatively limited in variety and in subtlety; their very grandeur and their lofty elevation, when Wordsworth is at his best, prevent great refinement or great subtlety of feeling. His temperament is too simple, and his nature has too great mass, to admit of complex combinations of feelings or of quick and ravishing changes. "Admiration, love, and awe," these are the moods Wordsworth most insists on; and in the service of these cogent but comparatively simple feelings he is fondest of interpreting the great world of nature. Tennyson's moods, on the other hand, run through a very wide range and shade into each other through an infinite series of gradations. He plays on an instrument of far greater delicacy of adjustment and of much greater variety of tone-colour. He was heir to all the rich emotional life of the Romantic poets, and received by way of artistic inheritance a temperament already sensitive to a thousand influences that would have left the men of an earlier century unmoved; and to these inherited aptitudes for feeling subtly and richly were added all the half-tones and minor gradations of feeling that the intense spiritual and intellectual life of the post-Romantic period tended to develop. With this exquisitely sensitive temperament, he looked on the outside world and found everywhere correspondences between his moods and the aspects of nature. To catch and interpret, in all its range and subtlety and evanescent beauty, this emotional suggestiveness of nature was Tennyson's task, just as Wordsworth's task was to catch and register its moral and spiritual suggestiveness. Tennyson's poetry, then, may be regarded as in a very special sense, a continuation of the Wordsworthian tradition, and as carrying still further that subdual of nature to the needs of man's spirit that Wordsworth wrought at so faithfully.

The variety and the subtlety of Tennyson's moods are most noticeable when we turn from his treatment of landscape to his use of natural sights and sounds as symbols. It is, of course, only by the use of these symbols that he could hope to suggest the thousand and one changes of mood he tried to portray. These evanescent moods have no names; there are no conventional signs that the poet can use to place them before his readers; hence for each mood he must find some natural equivalent—some symbol that shall stand in its place, and, by touching secret springs in our minds and hearts, evoke the subtle complex of feeling he aims to suggest. These equivalents and symbols Tennyson finds chiefly in nature; and his use of them is the last means to be noted by which he brings about a closer union between matter and spirit.

This symbolical use of nature, together with its effect in giving a spiritual meaning to the world of the senses, is well illustrated in the lyric, "Tears, idle tears." The mood that the thought of the past calls up is highly complex—a resultant of many strangely blending elements; and the poet uses a series of sensuous images, a series of natural sights and sounds, to suggest the elementary feelings that enter into this mood. The "freshness" of delight with which the past is for a moment restored, the infinite "sadness" with which its irrevocableness forces itself once more on the thought, the "strangeness" of the far-away dim regions of memory,—these are the notes of feeling that go to make up the whole rich chord of the mood; and each has as its symbol, to call it into being, an image from nature:—

> Fresh as the first beam glittering on a sail,
> That brings our friends up from the under-world,
> Sad as the last which reddens over one
> That sinks with all we love below the verge;
> So sad, so fresh, the days that are no more.
>
> Ah, sad and strange as in dark summer dawns
> The earliest pipe of half-awaken'd birds
> To dying ears, when unto dying eyes
> The casement slowly grows a glimmering square;
> So sad, so strange, the days that are no more.

Each of the images in these verses is a symbol charged with feeling. And not only does the series of symbols serve to suggest at the moment of reading the precise mood of the poet, but always thereafter a reddening sail at sunset and the song of birds at dawn mean something more to us than they meant before Tennyson used them as symbols. Nature has taken on a whole new range of spiritual associations.

There are later poets who have surpassed Tennyson in variety and complexity of mood and in suggestiveness and subtlety of symbolic phrasing. In both these respects Dante Gabriel Rossetti was probably Tennyson's superior. But his superiority was gained at great cost. Nature, in his poetry, is broken up into a mere collection of symbolic sights and sounds; we miss the breadth of treatment and the fine open-air quality of Tennyson's work; there is often a sense of artificiality, of exaggeration, almost of violence done to nature to force her into the service of the poet's moods. Moreover, the variety and the subtlety of Rossetti's moods are gained at a like cost. Delight in moods became with Rossetti moodiness, and the study of moods reached the point of morbid introspection: subjectivity became a disease.

Tennyson, then, resembles the Romantic poets in his lack of sympathy with real life. He lived in a dream-world rather than in the world of real men and real women; and it is this dream-world, with its iridescence of beauty and its simplified and intensified characters, that he portrays for us in his poetry, save where he shows us the distorted pictures of life to be found in the minds of men half-mad with disappointed passion. His impatience of conventional life, his lack of interest in concrete character, and his intense subjectivity mark him out as akin to the Romantic poets, and as not having passed so decisively beyond the Romantic point of view and the Romantic mood as Browning, for example, passed beyond them. He was like the Romantic poets, too, in the fact that it was to nature that he turned to find escape from the crude actualities of everyday life; and it is probably through his share in the great Romantic work of spiritualizing nature that he will be most enduringly influential.

WALT WHITMAN

WALT WHITMAN

1819–1892

Walter Whitman, Jr., was born in West Hills, Long Island, on May 31, 1819. He attended public school in Brooklyn (1825–30), leaving prematurely; he then worked as an office boy (1830–31), a printer (1835–36), a schoolteacher (1836–41), and a contributor to and editor of various periodicals and magazines, including the *Long Islander* (1836–37), the *Aurora* (1842), the *Tatler* (1842), the *Statesman* (1843), the *New York Democrat* (1844), the *New York Mirror* (1844), and the Brooklyn *Daily Eagle* (1846–48). In 1848 Whitman left (or was fired from) the *Eagle*; he went to New Orleans, where he edited the *Crescent*, before returning to Brooklyn later that year. After editing the Brooklyn *Freeman* (1848–49) Whitman probably worked as a carpenter and bookseller between 1850 and 1854.

In 1855, at the age of thirty-six, Whitman published the first edition of his most famous book, *Leaves of Grass*. This edition consisted of twelve poems, including *Song of Myself* (then titled *Walt Whitman, an American*). Whitman sent the volume to Emerson, who responded with enormous enthusiasm, calling it "the most extraordinary piece of wit and wisdom that America has yet contributed." A second edition, adding twenty-one poems, appeared in 1856, and a third, adding 122, appeared in 1860. Six further editions appeared over Whitman's lifetime, the result of a continuous process of revision and expansion.

In 1857 Whitman began editing the Brooklyn *Times*. After leaving the *Times* in 1859, Whitman worked during the Civil War as a clerk in the office of the army paymaster in Washington and as a volunteer in military hospitals (1863–64). During 1865 he worked briefly as a clerk in the Department of the Interior before being fired when Secretary Harlan read *Leaves of Grass* and condemned it as pornographic. Also in 1865 Whitman published a collection of Civil War poems, *Drum-Taps*, followed in 1866 by the *Sequel to Drum-Taps*, containing his elegy on Lincoln, "When lilacs last in the dooryard bloom'd." Whitman, who had been largely disregarded in the United States, began around this time to develop a reputation in England, where his poetry was championed by William Michael Rossetti, Swinburne, and Anne Gilchrist.

In 1873 Whitman suffered a paralyzing stroke and moved from Washington to Camden, New Jersey, to live with his brother George. "Prayer of Columbus," the most despairing of Whitman's late poems, appeared in 1874, and was followed in 1875 by the prose work *Memoranda during the War*. During 1875 Whitman recovered partially from his paralysis, but his remaining years were nonetheless marked by a decline in creative powers. In 1888, the year he published *November Boughs*, Whitman suffered another stroke. He contracted pneumonia in December 1891 and died on March 26, 1892. His prose, poetry, diaries, and correspondence have been published under the general editorship of Gay Wilson Allen and Sculley Bradley (1961–80).

Personal

Walt the Satyr, the Bacchus, the very God Pan, and here as we found, or as I did, to my admiring surprise, bodily, boldly, standing before us—the complement your Modern Pantheon to be sure. We met with him for two hours, and much to our delight.—A. BRONSON ALCOTT, *Diary*, Nov. 10, 1856

We passed the remainder of the day roaming, or "loafing," on Staten Island, where we had shade, and many miles of a beautiful beach. Whilst we bathed, I was impressed by a certain grandeur about the man, and remembered the picture of Bacchus on the wall of his room. I then perceived that the sun had put a red mask on his face and neck, and that his body was a ruddy blonde, pure and noble, his form being at the same time remarkable for fine curves and for that grace of movement which is the flower of shapely and well-knit bones. His head was oviform in every way; his hair, which was strongly mixed with grey, was cut close to his head, and, with his beard, was in strange contrast to the almost infantine fulness and serenity of his face. This serenity, however, came from the quiet light blue eyes, and above these there were three or four deep horizontal furrows, which life had ploughed. The first glow of any kind that I saw about him, was when he entered the water, which he fairly hugged with a lover's enthusiasm. But when he was talking about that which deeply interested him, his voice, always gentle and clear, became slow, and his eyelids had a tendency to decline over his eyes. It was impossible not to feel at every moment the *reality* of every word and movement of the man, and also the surprising delicacy of one who was even freer with his pen than modest Montaigne.

After making an appointment to meet Walt again during the week, when we would saunter through the streets of New York, I went off to find myself almost sleepless with thinking of this new acquaintance. He had so magnetised me, so charged me, as it were, with somewhat indefinable, that for the time the only wise course of life seemed to be to put on a blue shirt and a blouse, and loafe about Manahatta and Paumanok—"loafe, and invite my soul," to use my new friend's phrase. I found time hanging heavily on my hands, and the sights of the brilliant city tame, whilst waiting for the next meeting, and wondered if he would seem such a grand fellow when I saw him again.—MONCURE D. CONWAY, "Walt Whitman," *Fortnightly Review*, Oct. 15, 1866, pp. 544–45

Here is Walt Whitman—a man who has lived a brave, simple, clean, grand, manly life, irradiated with all good works and offices to his country and his fellow-men—intellectual service to the doctrines of liberty and democracy, personal service to slaves, prisoners, the erring, the sick, the outcast, the poor, the wounded and dying soldiers of the land. He has written a book, welcomed, as you know, by noble scholars on both sides of the Atlantic; and this, for ten years, has made every squirt and scoundrel on the press fancy he had a right to insult him. Witness the recent editorial in the Chicago *Republican.* Witness the newspapers and literary journals since 1856, spotted with squibs, pasquinades, sneers, lampoons, ferocious abuse, libels. The lying jabber of the boys, drunkards and libidinous persons privileged to control many of the public prints, has passed as evidence of his character; the ridiculous opinions of callow brains, the refraction of filthy hearts, have been received as true interpretations of his volume. All this is notorious. You know it, I suppose, as well as I. And finally after the years of defamation, calumny, private affronts, public contumely, my pamphlet refers to—after the social isolation, the poverty, the adversity which an evil reputation thus manufactured for a man and following him into every detail of his life, must involve—Mr. James Harlan, Secretary of the Interior, lifting the charge of autorial obscenity into the most signal consequence, puts on the top-stone of outrage by expelling him from office with this brand upon his name. The press spreads the injury. It was telegraphed from Washington to the Eastern and Western papers. It was made the subject of insulting paragraphs in some journals and of extended and actional abuse in others. Now all this, too, you seem to consider of little or no importance. You think ten years of injurious calumny crowned with this conspicuous outrage, offers no "fit occasion for such an apotheosis of the victim." —WILLIAM DOUGLAS O'CONNOR, *"The Good Gray Poet:* Supplement" (1866), *In Re Walt Whitman,* eds. Horace L. Traubel, Richard Maurice Bucke, Thomas B. Harned, 1893, p. 154

When I shook hands with him there, at the door of his little house in Camden, I scarcely realised the great privilege that had been given to me—that of seeing face to face the wisest and noblest, the most truly great, of all modern literary men. I hope yet, if I am spared, to look upon him again, for well I know that the earth holds no such another nature. Nor do I write this with the wild hero-worship of a boy, but as the calm, deliberate judgment of a man who is far beyond all literary predilections or passions. In Walt Whitman I see more than a mere maker of poems, I see a personality worthy to rank even above that of Socrates, akin even, though lower and far distant, to that of Him who is considered, and rightly, the first of men. I know that if that Other were here, his reception in New England might be very much the same. I know, too, that in some day not so remote, humanity will wonder that men could dwell side by side with this colossus, and not realise his proportions. We have other poets, but we have no other divine poet. We have a beautiful singer in Tennyson, and some day it will be among Tennyson's highest honours that he was once named kindly and appreciatively by Whitman. When I think of that gray head, gently bowing before the contempt of the literary class in America, when I think that Boston crowns Emerson and turns aside from the spirit potent enough to create a hundred Emersons and leave strength sufficient for the making of the whole Bostonian cosmogony, from Lowell upwards, I for a moment lose patience with a mighty nation; but only for a moment: the voice of my gentle master sounds in my ear, and I am reminded that if he is great and good, it is because he represents the greatness and goodness of a free and noble people. He would not be Walt Whitman, if he did not love his contemporaries more, not less, for the ingratitude and

misconception of the Scribes and Pharisees who have outlawed him. Praise, and fame, and money are of course indifferent to him. He has spoken his message, he has lived his life, and is content. But it is we that honour and love him who are not content, while the gospel of man-millinery is preached in every magazine and every newspaper, and every literary money-changer and poetaster has a stone to throw at the patient old prophet of modern Democracy.—ROBERT BUCHANAN, *A Look round Literature,* 1887, pp. 345–46

Here health we pledge you in one draught of song,
Caught in this rhymer's cup from earth's delight,
Where English fields are green the whole year long,
The wine of might,
That the new-come Spring distils, most sweet and strong,
In the viewless air's alembic, wrought too fine for sight.

Good health! we pledge, that care may lightly sleep,
And pain of age be gone for this one day,
As of this loving cup you take, and, drinking deep,
Grow glad at heart straightway
To feel once more the kindly heat of the sun
Creative in you, as when in youth it shone,
And pulsing brainward with the rhythmic wealth
Of all the summer whose high minstrelsy
Shall soon crown field and tree,
And call back age to youth again, and pain to perfect health.
          —ERNEST RHYS, "To Walt Whitman on His
          Seventieth Birthday" (1889), *A London Rose
          and Other Rhymes,* 1894, p. 84

          Good-bye, Walt!
Good-bye, from all you loved of earth—
Rock, tree, dumb creature, man and woman—
          To you, their comrade human.
          The last assault
Ends now; and now in some great world has birth
A minstrel, whose strong soul finds broader wings,
          More brave imaginings.
Stars crown the hilltop where your dust shall lie,
          Even as we say good-bye,
          Good-bye, old Walt!
          —EDMUND CLARENCE STEDMAN, "W. W." 1892

Serene, vast head, with silver cloud of hair,
Lined on the purple dusk of death
A stern medallion, velvet set—
Old Norseman throned, not chained upon thy chair:
Thy grasp of hand, thy hearty breath
Of welcome thrills me yet
     As when I faced thee there.

Loving my plain as thou thy sea,
Facing the east as thou the west,
I bring a handful of grass to thee,
The prairie grasses I know the best—
Type of the wealth and width of the plain,
Strong of the strength of the wind and sleet,
Fragrant with sunlight and cool with rain—
I bring it, and lay it low at thy feet,
     Here by the eastern sea.
          —HAMLIN GARLAND, "Walt Whitman," *In Re
          Walt Whitman,* eds. Horace L. Traubel,
          Richard Maurice Bucke, Thomas B. Harned,
          1893, p. 328

General

That Walt Whitman, of whom I wrote to you, is the most interesting fact to me at present. I have just read his second edition (which he gave me), and it has done me more good than any reading for a long time. Perhaps I remember best the poem of *Walt Whitman, an American,* and the "Sun-Down Poem." There are two or three pieces in the book which are disagreeable, to say the least; simply sensual. He does not celebrate love at all. It is as if the beasts spoke. I think that men have not been ashamed of themselves without reason. No doubt there have always been dens where such deeds were unblushingly recited, and it is no merit to compete with their inhabitants. But even on this side he has spoken more truth than any American or modern that I know. I have found his poem exhilarating, encouraging. As for its sensuality,—and it may turn out to be less sensual than it appears,—I do not so much wish that those parts were not written, as that men and women were so pure that they could read them without harm, that is, without understanding them. One woman told me that no woman could read it,—as if a man could read what a woman could not. Of course Walt Whitman can communicate to us no experience, and if we are shocked, whose experience is it that we are reminded of?

On the whole, it sounds to me very brave and American, after whatever deductions. I do not believe that all the sermons, so called, that have been preached in this land put together are equal to it for preaching.

We ought to rejoice greatly in him. He occasionally suggests something a little more than human. You can't confound him with the other inhabitants of Brooklyn or New York. How they must shudder when they read him! He is awfully good.

To be sure I sometimes feel a little imposed on. By his heartiness and broad generalities he puts me into a liberal frame of mind prepared to see wonders,—as it were, sets me upon a hill or in the midst of a plain,—stirs me well up, and then—throws in a thousand of brick. Though rude, and sometimes ineffectual, it is a great primitive poem,—an alarum or trumpet-note ringing through the American camp. Wonderfully like the Orientals, too, considering that when I asked him if he had read them, he answered, "No: tell me about them."

I did not get far in conversation with him,—two more being present,—and among the few things which I chanced to say, I remember that one was, in answer to him as representing America, that I did not think much of America or of politics, and so on, which may have been somewhat of a damper to him.

Since I have seen him, I find that I am not disturbed by any brag or egoism in his book. He may turn out the least of a braggart of all, having a better right to be confident.

He is a great fellow.—HENRY DAVID THOREAU, Letter to Harrison Blake (Dec. 7, 1856)

⟨. . .⟩ Mr. Whitman prides himself especially on the substance—the life—of his poetry. It may be rough, it may be grim, it may be clumsy—such we take to be the author's argument—but it is sincere, it is sublime, it appeals to the soul of man, it is the voice of a people. He tells us ⟨. . .⟩ that the words of his book are nothing. To our perception they are everything, and very little at that. A great deal of verse that is nothing but words has, during the war, been sympathetically sighed over and cut out of newspaper corners, because it has possessed a certain simple melody. But Mr. Whitman's verse, we are confident, would have failed even of this triumph, for the simple reason that no triumph, however small, is won but through the exercise of art, and that this volume is an offense against art. It is not enough to be grim and rough and careless; common sense is also necessary, for it is by common sense that we are judged. There exists in even the commonest minds, in

literary matters, a certain precise instinct of conservatism, which is very shrewd in detecting wanton eccentricities. To this instinct Mr. Whitman's attitude seems monstrous. It is monstrous because it pretends to persuade the soul while it slights the intellect; because it pretends to gratify the feelings while it outrages the taste. The point is that it does this *on theory,* wilfully, consciously, arrogantly. It is the little nursery game of "open your mouth and shut your eyes." Our hearts are often touched through a compromise with the artistic sense, but never in direct violation of it. Mr. Whitman sits down at the outset and counts out the intelligence. This were indeed a wise precaution on his part if the intelligence were only submissive! But when she is deliberately insulted, she takes her revenge by simply standing erect and open-eyed. This is assuredly the best she can do.—HENRY JAMES, "Mr. Walt Whitman," *Nation,* Nov. 16, 1865, p. 626

That glorious man Whitman will one day be known as one of the greatest sons of Earth, a few steps below Shakspeare on the throne of immortality. What a tearing-away of the obscuring veil of use & wont from the visage of man & of life!

⟨. . .⟩ The sort of thing that people object to in Whitman's writings is not so easily surmised until one sees them. It mt. be expressed thus—that he puts into print physical matters with the same bluntness & directness almost as that with wh. they present themselves to the eye & mind, or are half-worded in the thought. From one point of view this is even blameless: but from another, the modern reader's point of view, it is quite intolerable.—WILLIAM MICHAEL ROSSETTI, Letter to Anne Gilchrist (June 23, 1869)

I think it was very manly and kind of you to put the whole of Walt Whitman's poems into my hands; and that I have no other friend who would have judged them and me so wisely and generously.

I had not dreamed that words could cease to be words, and become electric streams like these. I do assure you that, strong as I am, I feel sometimes as if I had not bodily strength to read many of these poems. In the series headed *Calamus,* for instance, in some of the *Songs of Parting,* the "Voice out of the Sea," the poem beginning "Tears, Tears," etc., there is such a weight of emotion, such a tension of the heart, that mine refuses to beat under it—stands quite still—and I am obliged to lay the book down for a while. Or again, in the piece called *Walt Whitman,* and one or two others of that type, I am as one hurried through stormy seas, over high mountains, dazed with sunlight, stunned with a crowd and tumult of faces and voices, till I am breathless, bewildered, half dead. Then come parts and whole poems in which there is such calm wisdom and strength of thought, such a cheerful breadth of sunshine, that the soul bathes in them renewed and strengthened. Living impulses flow out of these that make me exult in life, yet look longingly towards "the superb vistas of Death." Those who admire this poem, and don't care for that, and talk of formlessness, absence of meter, etc., are quite as far from any genuine recognition of Walt Whitman as his bitter detractors.—ANNE GILCHRIST, Letter to William Michael Rossetti (July 11, 1869), *In Re Walt Whitman,* eds. Horace L. Traubel, Richard Maurice Bucke, Thomas B. Harned, 1893, pp. 42–43

If I ever saw anything in print that deserved to be characterized as atrociously bad, it is the poetry of Walt Whitman; and the three critics of repute, Dr. Dowden, Mr. W. Rossetti, and Mr. Buchanan, who have praised his performances, appear to me to be playing off on the public a well-intentioned, probably good-humoured, but really cruel hoax. ⟨. . .⟩

The *Leaves of Grass*, under which designation Whitman includes all his poems, are unlike anything else that has passed among men as poetry. They are neither in rhyme nor in any measure known as blank verse; and they are emitted in spurts or gushes of unequal length, which can only by courtesy be called lines. Neither in form nor in substance are they poetry; they are inflated, wordy, foolish prose; and it is only because he and his eulogists call them poems, and because I do not care to dispute about words, that I give them the name. Whitman's admirers maintain that their originality is their superlative merit. I undertake to show that it is a mere knack, a "trick of singularity," which sound critics ought to expose and denounce, not to commend.

The secret of Whitman's surprising newness—the principle of his conjuring trick—is on the surface. It can be indicated by the single word, extravagance. In all cases he virtually, or consciously, puts the question, What is the most extravagant thing which it is here in my power to say? What is there so paradoxical, so hyperbolical, so nonsensical, so indecent, so insane, that no man ever said it before, that no other man would say it now, and that therefore it may be reckoned on to create a sensation? ⟨. . .⟩

Whitman's writings abound with reproductions of the thoughts of other men, spoiled by obtuseness or exaggeration. He can in no case give the finely correct application of a principle, or indicate the reserves and exceptions whose appreciation distinguishes the thinker from the dogmatist: intense black and glaring white are his only colours. The mysterious shadings of good into evil and evil into good, the strange minglings of pain with pleasure and of pleasure with pain, in the web of human affairs, have furnished a theme for musing to the deepest minds of our species. But problems that were felt to be insoluble by Shakespeare and Goethe have no difficulty for this bard of the West. Extravagant optimism and extravagant pessimism, both wrong and shallow, conduct him to "the entire denial of evil" (the words are Professor Dowden's), to the assertion that "there is no imperfection in the present and can be none in the future," and to the vociferous announcement that success and failure are pretty much the same.

⟨. . .⟩ If here and there we have tints of healthful beauty, and tones of right and manly feeling, they but suffice to prove that he can write sanely and sufferably when he pleases, that his monstrosities and solecisms are sheer affectation, that he is not mad, but only counterfeits madness. He is in no sense a superlatively able man, and it was beyond his powers to make for himself a legitimate poetical reputation. No man of high capacity could be so tumid and tautological as he—could talk, for instance, of the "fluid wet" of the sea; or speak of the aroma of his armpits, or make the crass and vile mistake of bringing into light what nature veils, and confounding liberty with dissolute anarchy. The poet of democracy he is not; but his books may serve to buoy, for the democracy of America, those shallows and sunken rocks on which, if it is cast, it must inevitably, amid the hootings of mankind, be wrecked. Always, unless he chooses to contradict himself for the sake of paradox, his political doctrine is the consecration of mutinous independence and rabid egotism and impudent conceit. In his ideal city "the men and women think lightly of the laws." His advice is to resist much and to obey little. This is the political philosophy of Bedlam, unchained in these ages chiefly through the influence of Rousseau, which has blasted the hopes of freedom wherever it has had the chance, and which must be chained up again with ineffable contempt if the self-government of nations is to mean anything else than the death and putrescence of civilization. Incapable of true poetical

originality, Whitman had the cleverness to invent a literary trick, and the shrewdness to stick to it. As a Yankee phenomenon, to be good-humouredly laughed at, and to receive that moderate pecuniary remuneration which nature allows to vivacious quacks, he would have been in his place; but when influential critics introduce him to the English public as a great poet, the thing becomes too serious for a joke. While reading Whitman, in the recollection of what had been said of him by those gentlemen, I realized with bitter painfulness how deadly is the peril that our literature may pass into conditions of horrible disease, the raging flame of fever taking the place of natural heat, the ravings of delirium superseding the enthusiasm of poetical imagination, the distortions of tetanic spasm caricaturing the movements, dance-like and music-measured, of harmonious strength. Therefore I suspended more congenial work to pen this little counterblast to literary extravagance and affectation.—PETER BAYNE, "Walt Whitman's Poems," *Contemporary Review*, Dec. 1875, pp. 49–51, 68–69

Whitman says that they who most loudly praise him are those who understand him least. I, perhaps, will not come under the censure, though I do under the description; for I confess that I do not understand this man. The logical sense of the words, the appositeness and accuracy of the images, one can indeed apprehend and enjoy; but there is an undertone of meaning in Whitman which can never be fully comprehended. This, doubtless, is true of all first-rate poetry; but it must be applied in a special sense to the writings of a man who is not only a poet but a mystic—a man who thoroughly enjoys this world, yet looks confidently to one diviner still beyond; who professes a passionate attachment to his friends, yet says that he has other friends, not to be seen with the eye, closer and nearer and dearer to him than these. The hardening, vulgarising influences of life have not hardened and vulgarised the spiritual sensibilities of this poet, who looks at this world with the wondering freshness of a child, and to the world beyond with the gaze of a seer. He has what Wordsworth lost, and in his old age comes trailing clouds of glory—shadows cast backward from a sphere which we have left, thrown forward from a sphere to which we are approaching.

He is the noblest literary product of modern times, and his influence is invigorating and refining beyond expression.—ARTHUR CLIVE, "Walt Whitman, the Poet of Joy," *Gentleman's Magazine*, Dec. 1875, p. 716

We are rather vexed, now it is too late, that I did not carry out a sort of incipient intention to expunge a motto from Walt Whitman which I inserted in Book IV ⟨of *Daniel Deronda*⟩. Of course the whole is irrevocable by this time, but I should have otherwise thought it worth while to have a new page, not because the motto itself is objectionable to me—it was one of the finer things which had clung to me from among his writings—but because, since I quote so few poets, my selection of a motto from Walt Whitman might be taken as the sign of a special admiration which I am very far from feeling.—GEORGE ELIOT, Letter to John Blackwood (April 18, 1876)

The real American poet is Walt Whitman—a man enormously greater than Longfellow or any other of his poetic compatriots.—WILLIAM MICHAEL ROSSETTI, "Henry Wadsworth Longfellow," *Lives of Famous Poets*, 1878, p. 391

These are quite glorious things you have sent me. Who *is* Walt (Walter?) Whitman, and is much of him like this?—JOHN RUSKIN, Letter to William Harrison Riley (1879), *In Re Walt Whitman*, eds. Horace L. Traubel, Richard Maurice Bucke, Thomas B. Harned, 1893, p. 352

⟨. . .⟩ I may as well say what I should not otherwise have said, that I always knew in my heart Walt Whitman's mind to be more like my own than any other man's living. As he is a very great scoundrel this is not a pleasant confession. And this also makes me the more desirous to read him and the more determined that I will not. ⟨. . .⟩ His 'savage' style has advantages, and he has chosen it; he says so. But you cannot eat your cake and keep it: he eats his offhand, I keep mine. It makes a very great difference. Neither do I deny all resemblance. In particular I noticed in 'Spirit that formed this scene' a preference for the alexandrine. I have the same preference: I came to it by degrees, I did not take it from him.—GERARD MANLEY HOPKINS, Letter to Robert Bridges (Oct. 18, 1882)

He is perhaps of all writers the most repellent to the reader who glances at him superficially. In the first place he is indecent, and that too not accidentally but on principle. Whatever may be thought of his morality, and that I hold to be essentially sound and healthy, it cannot be denied that in one section of his work, and occasionally throughout the poems and prose, he outrages every ordinary rule of decency. There is nothing impure in this kind of exposure; it has indeed the direct antithesis to prurient suggestion, and the intention of it is unquestionably honest, but from an artistic point of view it is the gravest of faults, it is essentially and irredeemably ugly and repulsive. We are most of us agreed that there is and ought to be a region of reticence, and into this region the writer has rushed himself and drags us unwillingly after him. He stands convicted of ἀπειροκαλία, if of nothing worse. Akin to this first instance of defect in artistic perception is a second—his use, namely, of words which are either not English or essentially vulgar; and to this must be added a not unfrequent neglect of syntax, which, together with looseness in the application of some words, makes him at times vague or unintelligible. Occasionally there occur words or expressions which, though not ordinarily found in literature, have a native force which justifies them; but generally it is the case that for the French word or for the vulgarism savouring either of the gutter on the one hand or of the Yankee penny a liner on the other might be substituted a good English word equally expressive. But here also we too probably have before us a fault of wilfulness, for we know that he will not allow the language of English literature to be large enough for the poets of America, but expects accessions to it from Tennessee and California. If, however, he has in his choice of words sought that simplicity which (to quote his own words) is 'the art of art, the glory of expression, and the sunshine of the light of letters,' he has certainly not seldom failed to attain it, and it was hardly to be attained by pouring out indiscriminately into his pages the words which ran naturally off his pen. The 'art of sinking' is illustrated in his juxtaposition of the most incongruous things, and this especially in his well-known catalogues, which, though sometimes picturesque and interesting, are generally only absurd and dull. The fact that they are introduced on principle is not to be admitted as an excuse for their inartistic and formless character, any more than a similar excuse is to be allowed for offences against decency. From many of these faults a sense of humour would have protected him; and this also might have preserved him from some of that violently feeble exaggeration with which he speaks especially of his own countrymen and their institutions, and from the parade with which he sometimes announces truisms, as if they had been just now for the first time discovered by himself. His defence on the general charge is finely given in a poem now published for the first time, written in Platte Cañon, Colorado.

Spirit that formed this scene,
These tumbled rock-piles grim and red,
These reckless heaven-ambitious peaks,
These gorges, turbulent-clear streams, this naked freshness,
These formless wild arrays . . .
Was't charged against my chants they had forgotten art? . . .
But thou that revelest here, spirit that formed this scene,
They have remembered thee.

But the grandeur of nature is not always to be attained by heaping together uncouth masses. We complain not so much that the work lacks polish, as that the writer has not been preserved by his own native genius from ugly excrescences.

These artistic defects and his general disregard of form make many of his works repulsive, and do not allow us to accept any one as faultless. But they are mostly such as expurgation could remove, and therefore are not vital. The characteristic which cannot be got rid of, and yet repels, is his intense egotism and self-assertion. His longest, and in some respects most important, work—a poem of twelve or fourteen hundred lines, with which the original *Leaves of Grass* opened—has or had his own name as the title and his own personality as the subject; and this self-assertion of the individual is perhaps the prevailing characteristic of Whitman's work, that which makes it in fact representative in some degree of the spirit of the age; and the egotism, after all, is not so much personal as typical. The poet is a Kosmos, and contains within himself all unity and all diversity. What he claims for himself he thereby claims for others on the same terms. 'Underneath all, to me is myself, to you yourself.' We feel when the poet proclaims himself 'an acme of things accomplished,' for whose birth all the forces of the universe have been a preparation, he is speaking less for himself individually than for humanity, the humanity of his own day and of future days. The egotism becomes more offensive when it is obviously personal and indicates himself as the Michael Angelo of literature; and that, it must be admitted, is not unseldom, though here too he claims to be speaking less for himself than for the future race of democratic poets. To these charges it may be added that, notwithstanding his boasted freedom from the trammels of conventionality, he is in his more ordinary work a mannerist of the most vulgar kind. 'Oh! to realise space!' 'Have you reckoned a thousand acres much?' 'Has any one supposed it lucky to be born? I hasten to inform him or her that it is just as lucky to die.' 'I have said that the soul is not more than the body, and I have said that the body is not more than the soul.' 'I swear I think there is nothing but immortality, that the exquisite scheme is for it, and the nebulous float is for it, and the cohering is for it!' If these are not all exact quotations, every one will recognise them as genuine types. No style lends itself more readily to parody and burlesque. But when he is at his best the mannerism is in a great measure shaken off. ⟨. . .⟩

If we were asked for justification of the high estimate of this poet, which has been implied, if not expressed, in what has been hitherto said, the answer would be perhaps first, that he has a power of passionate expression, of strong and simple utterance of the deepest tones of grief, which is almost or altogether without its counterpart in the world. Not often has he exerted his power, but often enough to let us understand that he possesses it, and to stamp him as a poet inferior to few, if any, of our time in strength of native genius, however he may fall behind many in artistic perception.—G. C. MACAULAY, "Walt Whitman," *Nineteenth Century*, Dec. 1882, pp. 905–9

Here let me first carefully disclaim and condemn all that flippant and sneering tone which dominates so many discussions of Whitman. While I differ from him utterly as to every principle of artistic procedure; while he seems to me the most stupendously mistaken man in all history as to what constitutes true democracy, and the true advance of art and man; while I am immeasurably shocked at the sweeping invasions of those reserves which depend on the very personality I have so much insisted upon, and which the whole consensus of the ages has considered more and more sacred with every year of growth in delicacy; yet, after all these prodigious allowances, I owe some keen delights to a certain combination of bigness and naïvety which make some of Whitman's passages so strong and taking, and indeed, on the one occasion when Whitman has abandoned his theory of formlessness and written in form he has made "My Captain, O My Captain" surely one of the most tender and beautiful poems in any language. ⟨. . .⟩

In examining ⟨Whitman's doctrine⟩, a circumstance occurs to me at the outset which throws a strange but effective light upon the whole argument. It seems curious to reflect that the two poets who have most avowedly written for the people, who have claimed most distinctively to represent and embody the thought of the people, and to be bone of the people's bone and flesh of the people's flesh, are precisely the two who have most signally failed of all popular acceptance and who have most exclusively found audience at the other extreme of culture. These are Wordsworth and Whitman. We all know how strenuously and faithfully Wordsworth believed that in using the simplest words and treating the lowliest themes, he was bringing poetry back near to the popular heart; yet Wordsworth's greatest admirer is Mr. Matthew Arnold, the apostle of culture, the farthest remove from anything that could be called popular: and in point of fact it is probable that many a peasant who would feel his blood stir in hearing "A man's a man for a' that," would grin and guffaw if you should read him Wordsworth's "Lambs" and *Peter Bells*.

And a precisely similar fate has met Whitman. Professing to be a mudsill and glorying in it, chanting democracy and shirt-sleeves and equal rights, declaring that he is nothing if not one of the people, nevertheless the people, the democracy, will yet have nothing to do with him, and it is safe to say that his sole audience has lain among such representatives of the highest culture as Emerson and the English *illuminated*.

The truth is, that if closely examined, Whitman, instead of being a true democrat, is simply the most incorrigible of aristocrats masquing in a peasant's costume, and his poetry, instead of being the natural outcome of a fresh young democracy, is a product which would be impossible except in a highly civilized society.—SIDNEY LANIER, *The English Novel*, 1883, pp. 45–47

Let me round off with an opinion or two, the result of my thirteen years' acquaintance. ⟨. . .⟩ Both Walt Whitman's book and personal character need to be studied a long time and in the mass, and are not to be gauged by custom. I never knew a man who—for all he takes an absorbing interest in politics, literature, and what is called 'the world'—seems to be so poised on himself alone. Dr. Drinkard, the Washington physician who attended him in his paralysis, wrote to the Philadelphia doctor into whose hands the case passed, saying among other things: 'In his bodily organism, and in his constitution, tastes and habits, Whitman is the most *natural* man I have ever met.' The primary foundation of the poet's character, at the same time, is certainly spiritual. Helen Price, who knew him for fifteen years, pronounces him (in Dr. Bucke's book) the most

essentially religious person she ever knew. On this foundation has been built up, layer by layer, the rich, diversified, concrete experience of his life, from its earliest years. Then his aim and ideal have not been the technical literary ones. His strong individuality, wilfulness, audacity, with his scorn of convention and rote, have unquestionably carried him far outside the regular metes and bounds. No wonder there are some who refuse to consider his *Leaves* as 'literature.' It is perhaps only because he was brought up a printer, and worked during his early years as newspaper and magazine writer, that he has put his expression in typographical form, and made a regular book of it, with lines, leaves and binding.—GEORGE SELWYN, "Walt Whitman at Camden," *Critic*, Feb. 28, 1885, p. 98

In absolute ability he is about equal to Taylor, Stoddard, Stedman, or Aldrich; but by minimizing the spiritual and the artistic, and magnifying the physical and the crudely spontaneous, he has attracted an attention among critics in America, England, and the Continental nations greater, for the moment, than that bestowed upon any contemporary singer of his nation, and fairly rivalling the international adulation of his exact opposite, Poe. To him the ideal is little and the immediately actual is much; love is merely a taurine or passerine passion; and to-day is a thing more important than all the past. His courage is unquestionable; his vigor is abounding; and therefore, by the very paradox of his extravagant demands, he has impressed some and interested more, and has induced a limited but affectionate and exceedingly vociferous coterie to attempt, for his sake, to revise the entire canon of the world's art. Many famous authors have bestowed upon him high praise—sometimes revoked or ignored in the calmer years of advancing life; and though unread by the masses whose spokesman and prophet he claims to be, and without special influence or increasing potency, he has been for a generation one of the most conspicuous of his country's authors.—CHARLES F. RICHARDSON, *American Literature, 1607–1885*, 1887, Vol. 2, p. 269

⟨. . .⟩ Walt Whitman, who originally burst upon the literary world as "one of the roughs," and whose "barbaric yawp" was considered by a particular class of English critics as the first original note which had been struck in American poetry, and as good as an Indian war-whoop. Wordsworth speaks of Chatterton as "the marvellous boy;" Walt Whitman, in his first *Leaves of Grass*, might have been styled the marvellous "b'hoy." Walt protested against all convention, even all forms of conventional verse; he seemed to start up from the ground, an earth-born son of the soil, and put to all cultivated people the startling question, "What do you think of Me?" They generally thought highly of him as an original. Nothing is more acceptable to minds jaded with reading works of culture than the sudden appearance of a strong, rough book, expressing the habits, ideas, and ideals of the uncultivated; but, unfortunately, Whitman declined to listen to the suggestion that his daring disregard of convention should have one exception, and that he must modify his frank expression of the relations of the sexes. The author refused, and the completed edition of the *Leaves of Grass* fell dead from the press. Since that period he has undergone new experiences; his latest books are not open to objections urged against his earliest; but still the *Leaves of Grass*, if thoroughly cleaned, would even now be considered his ablest and most original work. But when the first astonishment subsides of such an innovation as Walt Whitman's, the innovator pays the penalty of undue admiration by unjust neglect.—EDWIN P. WHIPPLE, "American Literature" (1886), *American Literature and Other Papers*, 1887, pp. 112–14

Could there be a greater, and apparently more dismal, paradox than the sight of the seer of democracy sitting serene under the total neglect of the democracy? If anything could bely the faith of the *Democratic Vistas*, if anything could make one think the loud energetic civilisation of America nothing but a gigantic imposture, it is the spectacle of the only great living American poet dependent in his old age upon the sympathy—and at one moment almost upon the maintenance—of foreign friends. And yet he keeps his faith in the faithless people unshaken, for it is not at the mercy of personal neglect or personal discomfort; and, if he is right in his robust belief, surely the solution of the paradox lies in the meaning of that much-abused word the "people." The "people" in whom his confidence burns so unquenchably are not the rich people, not the millions of wire-pullers and place-hunters, not the spurious *élite* of culture, but the mass of the people, who know little of Whitman and his books, or of any books, who labour obscurely, manfully, and restlessly, who represent the vast sum-total of energy comparable to the energies of nature herself—the mass of the people whose force and fertility are independent of all possible vicissitudes in institutions.

Mr. Ellis's account of this great poet is probably the best that has been supplied by anyone except the poet himself. There is but one departure from sobriety—a sufficiently startling one—in almost his first words. "Whitman," he says, "has been placed while yet alive by the side of the world's greatest teachers, beside Jesus and Socrates." Who said this is not stated; but it would be small honour to be canonised by a person who could perpetrate such a comparison. This is the sole extravagance in the whole essay; but it is not the only thing that will arouse resentment in the orthodox breast. The large number of persons who are blinded to Whitman's genius by the incidental nakedness of his writing would do well to ponder Mr. Ellis's most apposite contrast in this particular of Whitman with Swift. Swift regarded men and women not only as beasts, but as lower than other beasts, on account of the grotesque hypocrisy which leads them to muffle up their beasthood under decorous names; and this mask his dire indignation and misapplied sincerity impelled him ruthlessly to strip off. There is all the legacy of mediaeval body-hatred in the portrait of the Yahoo; and Swift is a Christian *manqué*. Whitman is a pagan, and takes his nudity as sanely as he does everything else. Neither writer is likely to hurt any healthy and grown person; it is the thin and eager minds, the erotic mystics, who really have the "seminal principle in their brains," not these burly and virile spirits. Where many of Whitman's poems fall short is, in one word, in *Art*. That is a sufficiently fatal shortcoming, and one which avenges itself speedily by the extinction of the peccant work. Whitman's capacity for inspiration, for prophecy, and for hope if very far ahead of his literary sense; he wrestles with difficulties of expression and construction, and constantly succumbs before them. Now and then he conquers; and an immortal flower of verse is born like

> Warble me now for joy of lilac-time,

or like "Captain! my Captain!" Some, therefore, of the poetry, or rhythmic prose, which contains certain of Whitman's farthest-reaching thought, is artistically faulty; and Mr. Ellis, as befits his somewhat doctrinal purpose, puts aside the question of Whitman's poetic accomplishment, and is engrossed rather with inquiring what creed he can extract from him.—OLIVER ELTON, *Academy*, April 5, 1890, p. 231

Yes, Walt Whitman has appeared. He has his place upon the stage. The drama is not ended. His voice is still heard. He is the Poet of Democracy—of all people. He is the poet of the body and soul. He has sounded the note of Individuality. He has given the pass-word primeval. He is the Poet of Humanity—of Intellectual Hospitality. He has voiced the aspirations of America—and, above all, he is the poet of Love and Death.—ROBERT G. INGERSOLL, "Liberty in Literature" (1890), *In Re Walt Whitman*, eds. Horace L. Traubel, Richard Maurice Bucke, Thomas B. Harned, 1893, p. 281

Whitman offers enormous difficulties to the critic who wishes to deal fairly with him. The grotesqueness of his language and the uncouth structure of his sentences render it almost impossible to do justice to the breadth of his thought and the sublimity of his imagination. He ought to be taken in large draughts, to be lived with in long solitudes. His peculiar mode of utterance suffers cruelly by quotation. Yet it is needful to extract his very words, in order to escape from the vagueness of a summary.

The inscription placed upon the forefront of *Leaves of Grass* contains this phrase: "I speak the word of the modern, the word EN-MASSE." What this word means for Whitman is expressed at large throughout his writings. We might throw light upon it from the following passage:

> I speak the pass-word primeval—I give the sign of
>   democracy;
> By God! I will accept nothing which all cannot have
>   their counterpart of on the same terms.

Thus Democracy implies the absolute equality of heritage possessed by every man and woman in the good and evil of this life. It also involves the conception that there is nothing beautiful or noble which may not be discovered in the simplest human being. As regards physical structure:

> Whoever you are! how superb and how divine is your
>   body, or any part of it.

As regards emotion and passions which throb and pulsate in the individual:

> Wherever the human heart beats with terrible throes
>   out of its ribs.

"Whoever" and "wherever" are the emphatic words in these quotations. The human body in itself is august; the heart has tragedy implicit in its life-beats. It does not signify *whose* body, or *whose* heart. Here, there, and everywhere, the seeing eye finds majesty, the sentient intelligence detects the stuff of drama.

The same principle is applied to the whole sphere of nature. Miracles need not be sought in special occurrences, in phenomena which startle us out of our ordinary way of regarding the universe:

> To me, every hour of the light and dark is a miracle,
> Every inch of space is a miracle,
> Every square yard of the surface of the earth is spread
>   with the same,
> Every cubic foot of the interior swarms with the
>   same;
> Every spear of grass—the frames, limbs, organs of
>   men and women, and all that concern them,
> All these to me are unspeakable miracles.

At this point science shakes hands with the democratic ideal. We are not forced to gaze upon the starry heavens, or to shudder at islands overwhelmed by volcanic throes, in order to spy out the marvellous. Wonders are always present in the material world, as in the spiritual:

> A morning-glory at my window satisfies me more
>   than the metaphysics of books.

The heroic lies within our reach, if we but stretch a finger forth to touch it:

> Lads ahold of fire-engines and hook-and-ladder ropes
>   no less to me than the Gods of the antique wars;
> Minding their voices peal through the crash of
>   destruction,
> Their brawny limbs passing safe over charred laths—
>   their white foreheads whole and unhurt out of
>   the flames.

Whitman expels miracles from the region of mysticism, only to find a deeper mysticism in the world of which he forms a part, and miracles in commonplace occurrences. He dethrones the gods of old pantheons, because he sees God everywhere around him. He discrowns the heroes of myth and romance; but greets their like again among his living comrades. What is near to his side, beneath his feet, upon the trees around him, in the men and women he consorts with, bears comparison with things far off and rarities imagined.—JOHN ADDINGTON SYMONDS, "Democratic Art," *Essays Speculative and Suggestive*, 1890, Vol. 2, pp. 47–50

When beginning his self-imposed task, Whitman appears to have been staggered by the vastness of his own conceptions. The view was so extensive, the distance was so great, the sights that could be seen, and the tendencies that were unseen, so overwhelming, that the poet was intoxicated by the vision. He lacked, too, discrimination and art. He had absorbed divine influences from past thinkers, but he had no sense of the laws of style, or, indeed, the sense that there were any laws. Hence, the sometimes—one might be induced to say, the frequent—formless lines, and the attempts to produce effects which no great artist would have employed. The poet was unable, through lack of literary culture, to clothe his novel and often glowing conceptions in any ideal poetic form. Rather he flings his ideas at us in a heap, leaving it to us to arrange them in order in our own minds. His results, therefore, fail to satisfy many not unsympathetic readers. And yet of these results Mr. Havelock Ellis has truly said that "they have at times something of the divine felicity, unforeseen and incalculable, of Nature; yet always, according to a rough but convenient distinction, it is the poetry of energy rather than the poetry of art. When Whitman speaks prose, the language of science, he is frequently incoherent, emotional, unbalanced, with no very just and precise sense of the meaning or words, or the structure of reasoned language."

But it may be fairly argued whether, when he began to write, Whitman did not gain immensely from this imperfect artistic form. He in some sense carried on the tradition of English literature in some of its most virile representatives; which, as has been well said by one of our greatest critics, is a literature of power, as contrasted with the French literature of intelligence. And, further, Whitman the more faithfully expressed the life of his own nation, the very character of his own continent. America had scarcely arrived, has hardly arrived yet, at any consciousness of her true life. She is the land of beginnings and tendencies, her very physical aspect is shaggy and unshorn. She is like a vast edifice, only half finished, with the scaffolding up, and the litter of masonry all round. An American lady is said to have asked a gardener in one of the beautiful Oxford quadrangles, how a lawn could be brought to such a condition of perfection as the emerald turf she saw before her. The reply was, "If you roll and water it regularly for about three centuries you will get such results as you see here." America, with her brief history, rush of immigrants, and dominating materialism, has not been able to reach the artistic repose, the placid beauty to which we are accustomed in Western Europe. Had Whitman lived in an atmosphere of such repose; had he been brought up on European culture, he could only at best have added to the kind of work which Longfellow and Irving did so well. In that case he could not have been the voice of this great, rough, virile America, with its "powerful uneducated persons," of whom the cultivated Bostonian authors knew no more than they did of the working-classes of Europe. The very value of Whitman, then, is that he is a genuine American bard. In the conditions of his life and work must be found the justification of his method. His writings contain the promise and potency of future greatness; and he makes no claim for them beyond that they are the first rough draft of a great American literature.—WILLIAM CLARKE, *Walt Whitman*, 1892, pp. 50–52

The persistence of prejudice is illustrated by various phases of Walt Whitman's reputation at home and abroad. In spite of the appreciative sympathy of fellow-poets who feel the wide swing of his imagination and the force of its literary expression, in spite of the tardy acknowledgments of critics who have gradually learned to find power and melody in some of his rugged verse, it cannot be said that the venerable bard is widely honored in his own country. Songs which celebrate the toils and pleasures of the masses have thus far found small audience among the common people of the nation, being read chiefly by the cultivated few. Aristocratic rhymesters, weavers of triolets and madrigals, have reached a greater number of humble homes than this prophet of democracy, and the toilers of the land care more for jingles than for the barbaric majesty of his irregular measures. The poet of the people is neglected by the people, while the works of scholarly singers like Longfellow and Bryant find a place in every farmer's library.

Humanity does not enjoy the scientific method of reasoning from facts to theories, preferring unphilosophically to adjust the facts to its preconceived ideas. In this country we are proud of the swift conquests of civilization, and too willing to forget the free simplicity and uncouth heroism of pioneer times. We boast of our borrowed culture and keep our truly great achievements in the background. We look forward to a powerful future and too often obliterate the memory of a valiant past, allowing details to slip unrecorded into oblivion which might serve as the foundation of epics as majestic as Homer's. Reason about it as we will, Americans have an instinctive feeling that the formative period of the national character should be out of sight and out of mind as soon as possible, so that our virgin republic may at once take a place of assured wisdom among the gray and hardened dames of the old world, decked like them with the splendid trophies of twenty centuries of civilization.

Walt Whitman tries to arrest this ill-directed current of false vanity, to reveal to the nation her true glory of physical and moral prowess, to unveil a superb figure of strong and courageous youth playing a new part in the world with all of youth's tameless energy and daring. He finds her achievements beautiful and heroic, worthy to be celebrated and immortalized by art, and feels that the adornments of culture and civilization must be gradually wrought out from her own consciousness, not imitated from outworn models or adopted ready-made. Thus he strives to discard from his singing all the incidents of American life which are not indigenous to American soil, bringing himself closely in contact with the primeval elements of nature and man.

> Long I roamed the woods of the North—long I
>   watched Niagara pouring;

> I travelled the prairies over, and slept on their
> breast—I crossed the Nevadas, I crossed the
> plateaus;
> I ascended the towering rocks along the Pacific, I
> sailed out to sea;
> I sailed through the storm, I was refreshed by the
> storm.

Then from the majesty of ocean and plain to the higher
majesty of cities:—

> What, to pavements and homesteads here—what
> were those storms of the mountains and sea?
> What, to passions I witness around me to-day, was
> the sea risen?

The glory of cataracts and thunders, of crowds and wars, appeals to him for utterance, and with the scrupulous loyalty of a true poet he does his utmost to answer the call. Whether his answer is adequate or not, we must honor his fidelity. The spirit of modern criticism becomes too finical, too much a command that the aspirant should fling away ambition, should be content with pleasant little valleys, and avoid the unexplored heights where precipices and avalanches threaten to destroy. This spirit is a blight upon all high endeavor, and he who resists it and travels upward, even though he fall exhausted by the wayside, achieves a nobler success than a thousand petty triumphs could have brought him.

It is too soon for the world to decide how far this barbaric poet has fulfilled his mission. At present the mass of his countrymen brush aside his writings with a gesture of contempt, finding there what they most wish to forget—a faithful reflection of the rudeness, the unsettled vastness, the formlessness of an epoch out of which much of our country has hardly yet emerged. But theirs is not the final verdict; their desire to be credited with all the decorative embellishments which older states enjoy may yield when ours shall have won these ornaments and learned to regret the old unadorned strength and simplicity. Races which have passed their youth appreciate these vigorous qualities, which put them once more in touch with primitive nature, with the morning, with the wisdom of children, which is, after all, the serenest wisdom. Thus in England Walt Whitman's singing has thus far been more effectual than at home. There his work humors the prepossessions of the people, who find in him the incarnation of young democracy. To minds puzzled by the formality of other American poets, by Longfellow's academic precision, Whittier's use of time-worn measures, and Poe's love of rich orchestral effects of rhythm, Whitman's scorn of prosodical rules and of the accepted limitations of artistic decorum brings the revelation of something new in the brown old world. They greet him as a poet fresh from the wilds of which, to their persistent ignorance, both Americas are still made up. To them his songs seem as free and trackless as his native prairies, revealing once more the austerity and joyousness of primeval nature, so different from their elaborate civilization. It is possible that the next century of our own national life may find the same relief in his open-air honesty and moral ruggedness. It may turn to him to gain ideal comprehension of the forces which peopled this continent and redeemed its wastes from barrenness. His poetry is unruly and formless, but so were the times it mirrors—no harmony of fulfilment, but a chaos of forces struggling and toiling together for the evolution of a great nation. He sweeps the continent and gathers up all he finds, good, bad and indifferent, serenely conscious that to omniscience all is good, that to omnipotence all is important. The result is not art, perhaps; for art chooses and combines, gives form and life and color to nature's elements of truth. Art realizes the limitations of our finite humanity, appreciates our poverty of time for the multitudinous objects of thought, and indulgently omits all that is trivial and inessential from her epitome of truth. What does not emphasize she discards; to her fine judgment an hundred details serve but to weaken the force of one. Thus Walt Whitman may never be called an artist. What he finds he gives us with all the exact faithfulness of an inventory. In the mass of his discoveries there is much that is precious, many a treasure of rare and noble beauty; but its beauty is that of rich quartz, of uncut jewels, rather than that of the coin and the cameo. He offers us a collection of specimens from the splendid laboratory of nature. It will scarcely be strange if the future guards them in cabinets instead of circulating them far and wide among the people.—HARRIET MONROE, "A Word about Walt Whitman," *Critic*, April 16, 1892, p. 231

Whatever Walt Whitman's subject matter, whether he is ostensibly speaking of himself, of some other individual, of the animals, of something impersonal, he is always speaking really of himself—of himself treated as the typical man, and so treated not so much as being better than others but as seeing more clearly the divinity that is in every human being:

> I celebrate myself, and sing myself,
> And what I assume you shall assume.

The man himself, the whole man, body and soul, including his relations to the material world about him and the practical and social life of his time, is faithfully mirrored in his book. The outward and inward experiences of a long life are vividly and truthfully briefed; nothing is omitted, the most trivial and the most vital equally finding place. The whole is done in a manner far removed from the usual direct autobiographic prose; in a manner, indeed, quite unusual, special, poetic and indirect. The result is such that future ages will know this man as perhaps no human being heretofore has been ever known either to his cotemporaries or successors. The exposition of the person involving equally that of his environment gives us incidentally a photograph of America, 1850–90. The breathing man, Walt Whitman, in his surroundings, as he lived, is so faithfully reproduced, and with such vitality, that all must admit the justice of his final dictum:

> This is no book,
> Who touches this touches a man.

The reader who should peruse *Leaves of Grass* as he would an ordinary book, for the thoughts which the words immediately express, and should rest there, would be like a child who, having learned the alphabet, should consider his education complete. The thoughts, feelings, images, emotions which lie directly behind the words constitute merely the façade of the temple, the introduction to the real object to be presented. That object, as has been said, is an embodiment of its author, Walt Whitman. This being the case, the value of the book will depend largely upon the sort of man he proves to be.—RICHARD MAURICE BUCKE, "The Man Walt Whitman," *In Re Walt Whitman*, eds. Horace L. Traubel, Richard Maurice Bucke, Thomas B. Harned, 1893, p. 59

In this same period, however, there is a single figure who seems steadily and constantly to face not what is now past, but what is now present or to come. Though his right to respect is questioned oftenest of all, we cannot fairly pass Walt Whitman without mention. He lacks, of course, to a grotesque degree, artistic form; but that very lack is characteristic. Artistic form, as we have seen, is often the final stamp that marks human expression as a thing of the past. Whitman remarkably illustrates this principle: he lacks form chiefly because he is stammeringly overpowered by his bewildering vision of what he believes to be the future. He is uncouth, inarticulate, whatever you please that is least orthodox; yet, after all, he can make you feel for the moment how even the ferry-boats plying from New York to Brooklyn are fragments of God's eternities. Those of us who love the past are far from sharing his confidence in the future. Surely, however, that is no reason for denying the miracle that he has wrought by idealizing the East River. The man who has done this is the only one who points out the stuff of which perhaps the new American literature of the future may in time be made, who foreruns perhaps a spirit that may inspire that literature, if it grow at last into an organic form of its own, with a meaning not to be sought in other worlds than this western world of ours.—BARRETT WENDELL, "American Literature," *Stelligeri and Other Essays concerning America*, 1893, pp. 142–43

Walt Whitman's figure is surely one of the most commanding in American literature, yet its full stature will never be realized by the cultivated public at large, so long as the fanatical devotees of the poet's memory continue to lavish their extravagant encomiums upon his faults and his virtues alike. —WILLIAM MORTON PAYNE, "Whitmaniana," *Dial*, Dec. 16, 1893, p. 390

I remember how he leaned back in his chair, and reached out his great hand to me, as if he were going to give it me for good and all. He had a fine head, with a cloud of Jovian hair upon it, and a branching beard and mustache, and gentle eyes that looked most kindly into mine, and seemed to wish the liking which I instantly gave him, though we hardly passed a word, and our acquaintance was summed up in that glance and the grasp of his mighty fist upon my hand. I doubt if he had any notion who or what I was beyond the fact that I was a young poet of some sort, but he may possibly have remembered seeing my name printed after some very Heinesque verses in the Press. I did not meet him again for twenty years, and then I had only a moment with him when he was reading the proofs of his poems in Boston. Some years later I saw him for the last time, one day after his lecture on Lincoln, in that city, when he came down from the platform to speak with some handshaking friends who gathered about him. Then and always he gave me the sense of a sweet and true soul, and I felt in him a spiritual dignity which I will not try to reconcile with his printing in the forefront of his book a passage from a private letter of Emerson's, though I believe he would not have seen such a thing as most other men would, or thought ill of it in another. The spiritual purity which I felt in him no less than the dignity is something that I will no more try to reconcile with what denies it in his page; but such things we may well leave to the adjustment of finer balances than we have at hand. I will make sure only of the greatest benignity in the presence of the man. The apostle of the rough, the uncouth, was the gentlest person; his barbaric yawp, translated into the terms of social encounter, was an address of singular quiet, delivered in a voice of winning and endearing friendliness.

As to his work itself, I supposed that I do not think it so valuable in effect as in intention. He was a liberating force, a very "imperial anarch" in literature; but liberty is never anything but a means, and what Whitman achieved was a means and not an end, in what must be called his verse. I like his prose, if there is a difference, much better; there he is of a genial and comforting quality, very rich and cordial, such as I felt him to be when I met him in person. His verse seems to me not poetry, but the materials of poetry, like one's emotions; yet I would not misprize it, and I am glad to own that I have had moments of great pleasure in it. Some French critic quoted in the Saturday Press (I cannot think of his name) said the best thing of him when he said that he made you a partner of the enterprise, for that is precisely what he does, and that is what alienates and what endears in him, as you like or dislike the partnership. It is still something neighborly, brotherly, fatherly, and so I felt him to be when the benign old man looked on me and spoke to me.—WILLIAM DEAN HOWELLS, "First Impressions of Literary New York," *Harper's New Monthly Magazine*, June 1895, p. 65

⟨. . .⟩ one of the deities to whom the degenerate and hysterical of both hemispheres have for some time been raising altars. Lombroso ranks him expressly among 'mad geniuses.' Mad Whitman was without doubt. But a genius? That would be difficult to prove. He was a vagabond, a reprobate rake, and his poems contain outbursts of erotomania so artlessly shameless that their parallel in literature could hardly be found with the author's name attached. For his fame he has to thank just those bestially sensual pieces which first drew to him the attention of all the pruriency of America. He is morally insane, and incapable of distinguishing between good and evil, virtue and crime. 'This is the deepest theory of susceptibility,' he says in one place, 'without preference or exclusion; the negro with the woolly head, the bandit of the highroad, the invalid, the ignorant—none are denied.' And in another place he explains he 'loves the murderer and the thief, the pious and good, with equal love.' An American driveller, W. D. O'Connor, has called him on this account 'The good gray Poet.' We know, however, that this 'goodness,' which is in reality moral obtuseness and morbid sentimentality, frequently accompanies degeneration, and appears even in the cruellest assassins, for example, in Ravachol. ⟨. . .⟩

In his patriotic poems he is a sycophant of the corrupt American vote-buying, official-bribing, power-abusing, dollar-democracy, and a cringer to the most arrogant Yankee conceit. His war poems—the much renowned *Drum Taps*—are chiefly remarkable for swaggering bombast and stilted patter.

His purely lyrical pieces, with their ecstatic 'Oh!' and 'Ah!' with their soft phrases about flowers, meadows, spring and sunshine, recall the most arid, sugary and effeminate passages of our old Gessner, now happily buried and forgotten.

As a man, Walt Whitman offers a surprising resemblance to Paul Verlaine, with whom he shared all the stigmata of degeneration, the vicissitudes of his career, and, curiously enough, even the rheumatic ankylosis. As a poet, he has thrown off the closed strophe as too difficult, measure and rhyme as too oppressive, and has given vent to his emotional fugitive ideation in hysterical exclamations, to which the definition of 'prose gone mad' is infinitely better suited than it is to the pedantic, honest hexameters of Klopstock. Unconsciously, he seemed to have used the parallelism of the Psalms, and Jeremiah's eruptive style, as models of form. We had in the last century the *Paramythien* of Herder, and the insufferable 'poetical prose' of Gessner already mentioned. Our healthy taste soon led us to recognise the inartistic, retrogressive character of this lack of form, and that error in taste has found no imitator among us for a century. In Whitman, however, his hysterical admirers commend this *réchauffé* of a superannuated literary fashion as something to come; and admire, as an invention of genius, what is only an incapacity for methodical work. Nevertheless, it is interesting to point out that two persons so dissimilar as Richard Wagner and Walt Whitman have, in different spheres, under the pressure of the same motives, arrived at the same goal—the former at 'infinite melody,' which is no longer melody; the latter at verses which are no longer verses, both in consequence of their incapacity to submit their capriciously vacillating thoughts to the yoke of those rules which in 'infinite' melody, as in lyric verse, govern by measure and rhyme.—MAX NORDAU, *Degeneration*, 1895, pp. 230–32

Speaking of monuments reminds one that there is more talk about a monument to Walt Whitman, "the good, gray poet." Just why the adjective good is always applied to Whitman it is difficult to discover, probably because people who could not understand him at all took it for granted that he meant well. If ever there was a poet who had no literary ethics at all beyond those of nature, it was he. He was neither good nor bad, any more than are the animals he continually admired and envied. He was a poet without an exclusive sense of the poetic, a man without the finer discriminations, enjoying everything with the unreasoning enthusiasm of a boy. He was the poet of the dung hill as well as of the mountains, which is admirable in theory but excruciating in verse. In the same paragraph he informs you that, "The pure contralto sings in the organ loft," and that "The malformed limbs are tied to the table, what is removed drop horribly into a pail." No branch of surgery is poetic, and that hopelessly prosaic word "pail" would kill a whole volume of sonnets. Whitman's poems are reckless rhapsodies over creation in general, sometimes sublime, sometimes ridiculous. He declares that the ocean with its "imperious waves, commanding" is beautiful, and that the fly-specks on the walls are also beautiful. Such catholic taste may go in science, but in poetry their results are sad. The poet's task is usually to select the poetic. Whitman never bothers to do that, he takes everything in the universe from fly-specks to the fixed stars. His *Leaves of Grass* is a sort of dictionary of the English language, and in it is the name of everything in creation set down with great reverence but without any particular connection.

But however ridiculous Whitman may be there is a primitive elemental force about him. He is so full of hardiness and of the joy of life. He looks at all nature in the delighted, admiring way in which the old Greeks and the primitive poets did. He exults so in the red blood in his body and the strength in his arms. He has such a passion for the warmth and dignity of all that is natural. He has no code but to be natural, a code that this complex world has so long outgrown. He is sensual, not after the manner of Swinburne and Gautier, who are always seeking for perverted and bizarre effects on the senses, but in the frank fashion of the old barbarians who ate and slept and married and smacked their lips over the mead horn. He is rigidly limited to the physical, things that quicken his pulses, please his eyes or delight his nostrils. There is an element of poetry in all this, but it is by no means the highest. If a joyous elephant should break forth into song, his lay would probably be very much like Whitman's famous *Song of Myself*. It would have just about as much delicacy and deftness and discrimination. He says: "I think I could turn and live with the animals. They are so placid and self-contained, I stand and look at them long and long. They do not sweat and whine about their condition. They do not lie awake in the dark and weep for their sins. They do not make me sick discussing their duty to God. Not one is dissatisfied nor not one is demented with the mania of many things. Not one kneels to another nor to his kind that lived thousands of years ago. Not one is respectable or unhappy, over the whole earth." And that is not irony on nature, he means just that, life meant no more to him. He

accepted the world just as it is and glorified it, the seemly and unseemly, the good and the bad. He had no conception of a difference in people or in things. All men had bodies and were alike to him, one about as good as another. To live was to fulfil all natural laws and impulses. To be comfortable was to be happy. To be happy was the ultimatum. He did not realize the existence of a conscience or a responsibility. He had no more thought of good or evil than the folks in Kipling's *Jungle Book*.

And yet there is an undeniable charm about this optimistic vagabond who is made so happy by the warm sunshine and the smell of spring fields. A sort of good fellowship and whole-heartedness in every line he wrote. His veneration for things physical and material, for all that is in water or air or land, is so real that as you read him you think for the moment that you would rather like to live so if you could. For the time you half believe that a sound body and a strong arm are the greatest things in the world. Perhaps no book shows so much as *Leaves of Grass* that keen senses do not make a poet. When you read it you realize how spirited a thing poetry really is and how great a part spiritual perceptions play in apparently sensuous verse, if only to select the beautiful from the gross.—WILLA CATHER, "Whitman" (1896), *The Kingdom of Art*, ed. Bernice Slote, 1966, pp. 351–53

Walt Whitman was unable or unwilling to master the art of writing, and consequently his works, though abounding in lines and phrases of the highest excellence in form as well as in substance, are so uneven and unfinished that he cannot be called a great writer, and can hardly be expected to endure. But he was a man of great democratic ideas. He is the only author yet produced, in his country or in any other, who has perceived what democracy really means, and who has appreciated the beauty and the heroism which are found in the daily lives of the common people.—HENRY CHILDS MERWIN, "Men and Letters," *Atlantic*, May 1897, p. 719

Speaking of Walt Whitman, he ⟨Tennyson⟩ said to me, "Walt neglects form altogether, but there is a fine spirit breathing through his writings. Some of them are quite unreadable from nakedness of expression." HALLAM TENNYSON, *Alfred Lord Tennyson: A Memoir*, 1897, Vol. 2, p. 424

It is a curious phase of Whitman's greatness—this intense personal following. There has been nothing like it in the history of letters. Johnson had only one Boswell. No man, apparently, could come near Whitman without being swayed from his own orbit. John Burroughs appears to be almost the only man who, knowing him very well, is able to stand up straight after it. The rest—some of them more and some of them less—have lost their sense of proportion. They have fallen into an embarrassing habit of referring to Whitman and Jesus of Nazareth in the same breath. (Implication in favor of Whitman.) We are willing that the Whitman buttons should be irradiated. It is harmless enough; but when we are obliged to see the buttons eclipse the person of Whitman, and the person of Whitman eclipse the personality, we are roused to mild resentment. It is, of course, a matter of some public interest to know how many times a day Mr. Whitman washed his hands, but we confess to a much larger curiosity as to the attitude of Walt Whitman the man towards comradship and life. Even the reiterated statement of his "cheerfulness" can hardly be said to be exhaustive.

A friend of mine, a man-of-letters, is wont to say that he "only hopes to live long enough to see that Whitman bubble burst." Anyone can recall more than one contemporary critic who will charge across a whole field in pursuit of any ragtag of

Whitman that flutters in sight. Even the journals take sides. It would not be difficult to draw up two lists headed "Whitman-ite" and "Anti-Whitmanite," and assign to one or the other almost every critical journal of the day. The situation is not to be solved by a sneer. One can only observe respectfully and ponder. There is something a little uncanny about the intense seriousness of the two sides. If the Whitmanites lay themselves open to ridicule by their assertive self-effacement, the Anti-Whitmanites come dangerously near the grotesque in their scathing contempt for this inoffensive man who only wished to "loafe and invite his soul."

"I am not a Comtist nor a Buddhist nor a Whitmanite," a friend writes me. Is the shade of ridicule towards the last class a figment of the fancy? A Whitmanite, it is to be feared, no matter how dignified his bearing, is never taken quite seriously. Perhaps it is the "ite," the remnant of the prejudice that hovers in the minds of men over the Hittites, Kenites, Perizzites, Jebusites. Perhaps it is phonetic. While Whitman lived he was never, in spite of the well-intentioned efforts of his friends, a ridiculous figure. The robustness and breeziness of the man put sentimentality where it belonged, and turned childish adulation into decent praise. Even the charity that his admirers brought upon him he accepted with sturdy good humor—and opened a bank-account. But now that Whitman is dead, all this is changed. Now that the head is gone, the decapitated body waves wild members, and calls it eulogy. First there was *In Re*, a volume that some of us who admire Whitman's genius cannot even yet open without qualms; and then *Whitman the Man*, and then *The Pete Letters*, and now, worse and most persistent of all, this Whitman journal. Is it any wonder that Whitman had the foresight to enter protest:

> I call the world to distrust the accounts of my friends,
>   but listen to my enemies, as I myself do.
> I charge you forever reject those who would expound
>   me, for I cannot expound myself.
> I charge that there be no theory or school founded
>   out of me,
> I charge you to leave all free, as I have left all free.

—Jennette Barbour Perry, "Whitmania," *Critic*, Feb. 26, 1898, pp. 137–38

Whitman can never be classed, as Spinoza was by Schleiermacher, among "God-intoxicated" men; but he was early inebriated with two potent draughts—himself and his country:—

> One's self I sing, a simple separate person,
> Yet utter the word Democratic, the word, En Masse.

With these words his collected poems open, and to these he has always been true. They have brought with them a certain access of power, and they have also implied weakness; on the personal side leading to pruriency and on the national side to rant. For some reason or other our sexual nature is so ordained that it is very hard for a person to dwell much upon it, even for noble and generous purposes, without developing a tendency to morbidness; the lives of philanthropists and reformers have sometimes shown this; and when one insists on this part of our nature for purposes of self-glorification, the peril is greater. Whitman did not escape the danger; it is something that he outgrew it; and it is possible that if let entirely alone, which could hardly be expected, he might have dropped *Children of Adam*, and some of the more nauseous passages in other effusions, from his published works. One thing which has always accentuated the seeming grossness of the sensual side of his poems has been the entire absence of that personal and ideal side of passion which alone can elevate and dignify it.

Probably no poet of equal pretensions was ever so entirely wanting in the sentiment of individual love for woman; not only has he given us no love-poem, in the ordinary use of that term, but it is as difficult to conceive of his writing one as of his chanting a serenade beneath the window of his mistress. His love is the blunt, undisguised attraction of sex to sex; and whether this appetite is directed towards a goddess or a streetwalker, a Queensbury or a handmaid, is to him absolutely unimportant. This not only separates him from the poets of thoroughly ideal emotion, like Poe, but from those, like Rossetti, whose passion, though it may incarnate itself in the body, has its sources in the soul.

As time went on, this less pleasing aspect became soft-ened; his antagonisms were disarmed by applauses; although this recognition sometimes took a form so extreme and adula-tory that it obstructed his path to that simple and unconscious life which he always preached but could not quite be said to practice. No one can be said to lead a noble life who writes puffs of himself and offers them to editors, or who borrows money of men as poor as himself and fails to repay it. Yet his career purified itself, as many careers do, in the alembic of years, and up to the time of his death (March 26, 1892) he gained constantly both in friends and in readers. Intellectually speaking, all critics now admit that he shows in an eminent degree that form of the ideal faculty which Emerson conceded to Margaret Fuller—he has "lyric glimpses." Rarely construct-ing anything, he is yet singularly gifted in phrases, in single cadences, in casual wayward strains as from an Æolian harp. It constantly happens that the titles or catch-words of his poems are better than the poems themselves; as we sometimes hear it said in praise of a clergyman that he has beautiful texts. "Proud Music of the Storm," "When lilacs last in the door-yard bloomed," and others, will readily occur to memory. Often, on the other hand, they are inflated, as "Chanting the Square Deific," or affected and feeble, as "Eidolons." One of the most curiously un-American traits in a poet professedly so national is his way of interlarding foreign, and especially French, words to a degree that recalls the fashionable novels of the last genera-tion, and gives an incongruous effect comparable only to Theodore Parker's description of an African chief seen by some one at Sierra Leone,—"With the exception of a dress-coat, his Majesty was as naked as a pestle." In the opening lines, already quoted from one of his collected volumes (ed. 1881), Whitman defines "the word Democratic, the word En Masse;" and everywhere French phrases present themselves. The vast sub-limity of night on the prairies only suggests to him "how plenteous! how spiritual! how *résumé*," whatever that may mean; he talks of "*Mélange* mine own, the seen and the unseen;" writes poems "with reference to *ensemble*;" says "the future of the States I *harbinge* glad and sublime;" and else-where, "I blow through my *embouchures* my loudest and gayest for them." He is "the extolled of *amies*,"—meaning apparently mistresses; and says that neither youth pertains to him, "nor *delicatesse*." Phrases like these might be multiplied indefinitely, and when he says, "No dainty *dolce affettuoso* I," he seems vainly to disclaim being exactly what he is. He cannot even introduce himself to the audience without borrowing a foreign word,—"I, Walt Whitman, one of the roughs, a kosmos,"—and really stands in this respect on a plane not much higher than that of those young girls at boarding-school who commit French phrases to memory in order to use them in conversation and give a fancied tone of good society.

But after all, the offense, which is a trivial affectation in a young girl, has a deeper foundation in a man who begins his literary career at thirty-seven. The essential fault of Whitman's poetry was well pointed out by a man of more heroic nature and higher genius, Lanier, who defined him as a dandy. Of all our poets, he is really the least simple, the most meretricious; and this is the reason why the honest consciousness of the classes which he most celebrates,—the drover, the teamster, the soldier,—has never been reached by his songs. He talks of labor as one who has never really labored; his *Drum-Taps* proceed from one who has never personally responded to the tap of the drum. This is his fatal and insurmountable defect; and it is because his own countrymen instinctively recognize this, and foreigners do not, that his following has always been larger abroad than at home. But it is also true that he has, in a fragmentary and disappointing way, some of the very highest ingredients of a poet's nature: a keen eye, a ready sympathy, a strong touch, a vivid but not shaping imagination. In his cyclopædia of epithets, in his accumulated directory of details, in his sandy wastes of iteration, there are many scattered particles of gold—never sifted out by him, not always abundant enough to pay for the sifting, yet unmistakable gold. He has something of the turgid wealth, the self-conscious and mouthing amplitude of Victor Hugo, and much of his broad, vague, indolent desire for the welfare of the whole human race; but he has none of Hugo's structural power, his dramatic or melodramatic instinct, and his occasionally terse and brilliant condensation. It is not likely that he will ever have that place in the future which is claimed for him by his English admirers or even by the more cautious indorsement of Mr. Stedman; for, setting aside all other grounds of criticism, he has phrase, but not form—and without form there is no immortality. —Thomas Wentworth Higginson, "Whitman," *Contemporaries*, 1899, pp. 79–84

To many intellectual and cultured readers this latest prophet of brotherhood will seem a mere unintelligible babbler, because of the form of his verse, so alien to all the traditions of poetry. We can conceive the admirers of Pope's balanced couplets, or the lovers of Tennyson's mellifluous lines, turning up their noses at these shaggy and amorphous verses. Yet, for the passionate ardours with which he has fired so many readers, for his heroic strength, his creative impulse, his noble hopes, much may be forgiven to this herald of a new epoch. When such men as Tennyson, Ruskin, and Carlyle could find in him a kindred soul, his position cannot so easily be sneered away. For, in truth, his poems have the smack of life, of action, of hope; they were never written in a mock twilight by some peevish scribbler, whose verses are a penance to read, and their existence a slander upon human nature. They may, it is conceivable, disappoint those who think of poetry as mere candied sugar,

> sweeter than the lids of Juno's eyes
> Or Cytherea's breath.

Yet to those who love the sunlight and the breeze, and who cherish the hopes that make us manful, they will always be beloved and turned to as a source of inspiration and of strength.—J. A. MacCulloch, "Walt Whitman: The Poet of Brotherhood," *Westminster Review*, Nov. 1899, pp. 563–64

He seems to be as much the victim of jargon as of cant. His catalogues, his trailing lines, his blundering foreign locutions are as little spontaneous, as little appropriate to his purposes and subjects, as any mannerisms known to the student of pedantic epochs. They are scarcely signs of decadence, as we have seen, nor are they to be set down as mere affectations. They are far more probably effects of an inborn want of art, of a combination of overearnestness and underculture. It is worth

noting, however, that they seem to produce on some readers a sort of hypnotic effect, and that during the latter half of Whitman's career he appeared to slough them off to a fair extent. For this reason a beginner in Whitman might almost be advised to read *Leaves of Grass* backward. However this may be, it is surely a mistake to suppose that Whitman is throughout his work the cataloguer in jargon that so jostles the poet of "Starting from Paumanok" and "I Sing the Body Electric." As for his free rhythm, it must suffice to say that this too has its hypnotic effects, and that it is on the whole satisfactory to many cultivated ears. Whitman loved music, and there is music in his best verse, which, if not precisely metrical, is not altogether lawless. That the compositions couched in it are entitled to the name of poems seems obvious, not merely on account of their emotional and imaginative power when the poet is at his best, but also because they do not often suggest the rhythm of prose. At least it is apparent to the student of Whitman's prose that its rhythmical qualities are different from those of his hypothetical verse.—William P. Trent, *A History of American Literature*, 1903, pp. 493–94

Works

LEAVES OF GRASS

I am not blind to the worth of the wonderful gift of *Leaves of Grass*. I find it the most extraordinary piece of wit & wisdom that America has yet contributed. I am very happy in reading it, as great power makes us happy. It meets the demand I am always making of what seemed the sterile & stingy Nature, as if too much handiwork or too much lymph in the temperament were making our western wits fat & mean.

I give you joy of your free & brave thought. I have great joy in it. I find incomparable things said incomparably well, as they must be. I find the courage of *treatment*, which so delights us, & which large perception only can inspire.

I greet you at the beginning of a great career, which yet must have had a long foreground somewhere, for such a start. I rubbed my eyes a little to see if this sunbeam were no illusion; but the solid sense of the book is a sober certainty. It has the best merits, namely, of fortifying & encouraging.

I did not know until I, last night, saw the book advertised in a newspaper, that I could trust the name as real & available for a Post-office. I wish to see my benefactor, & have felt much like striking my tasks, & visiting New York to pay you my respects.—Ralph Waldo Emerson, Letter to Walt Whitman (July 21, 1855)

His *Leaves of Grass* are doubtless intended as an illustration of the natural poet. They are certainly original in their external form, have been shaped on no pre-existent model out of the author's own brain. Indeed, his independence often becomes coarse and defiant. His language is too frequently reckless and indecent though this appears to arise from a naive unconsciousness rather than from an impure mind. His words might have passed between Adam and Eve in Paradise, before the want of fig-leaves brought no shame; but they are quite out of place amid the decorum of modern society, and will justly prevent his volume from free circulation in scrupulous circles. With these glaring faults, the *Leaves of Grass* are not destitute of peculiar poetic merits, which will awaken an interest in the lovers of literary curiosities. They are full of bold, stirring thoughts—with occasional passages of effective description, betraying a genuine intimacy with Nature and a keen appreciation of beauty—often presenting a rare felicity of diction, but so disfigured with eccentric fancies as to prevent a consecutive perusal without offense, though no impartial reader can fail to be impressed with the vigor and quaint beauty of isolated portions.—CHARLES A. DANA, *New York Tribune*, July 23, 1855, p. 3

To give judgment on real poems, one needs an account of the poet himself. Very devilish to some, and very divine to some, will appear the poet of these new poems, the *Leaves of Grass*; an attempt, as they are, of a naive, masculine, affectionate, contemplative, sensual, imperious person, to cast into literature not only his own grit and arrogance, but his own flesh and form, undraped, regardless of models, regardless of modesty or law, and ignorant or slightly scornful, as at first appears, of all except his own presence and experience, and all outside the fiercely loved land of his birth and the birth of his parents, and their parents for several generations before him. Politeness this man has none, and regulation he has none. A rude child of the people!—no imitation—no foreigner—but a growth and idiom of America. No discontented—a careless slouch, enjoying today. No dilettante democrat—a man who is part-and-part with the commonalty, and with immediate life—loves the streets—loves the docks—loves the free rasping talk of men—likes to be called by his given name, and nobody at all need Mr. him—can laugh with laughers—likes the ungenteel ways of laborers—is not prejudiced one mite against the Irish—talks readily with them—talks readily with niggers—does not make a stand on being a gentleman, nor on learning or manners—eats cheap fare, likes the strong flavored coffee of the coffee-stands in the market, at sunrise—likes a supper of oysters fresh from the oyster-smack—likes to make one at the crowded table among sailors and workpeople—would leave a select soirée of elegant people any time to go with tumultuous men, roughs, receive their caresses and welcome, listen to their noise, oaths, smut, fluency, laughter, repartee—and can preserve his presence perfectly among these, and the like of these. The effects he produces in his poems are no effects of artists or the arts, but effects of the original eye or arm, or the actual atmosphere, or tree, or bird. You may feel the unconscious teaching of a fine brute, but will never feel the artificial teaching of a fine writer or speaker.

Other poets celebrate great events, personages, romances, wars, loves, passions, the victories and power of their country, or some real or imagined incident—and polish their work, and come to the conclusions, and satisfy the reader. This poet celebrates natural propensities in himself; and that is the way he celebrates all. He comes to no conclusions, and does not satisfy the reader. He certainly leaves him what the serpent left the woman and the man, the taste of the Paradisaic tree of the knowledge of good and evil, never to be erased again.

What good is it to argue about egotism? There can be no two thoughts on Walt Whitman's egotism. That is avowedly what he steps out of the crowd and turns and faces them for. Mark, critics! Otherwise is not used for you the key that leads to the use of the other keys to this well-enveloped man. His whole work, his life, manners, friendships, writings, all have among their leading purposes an evident purpose to stamp a new type of character, namely his own, and indelibly fix it and publish it, not for a model but an illustration, for the present and future of American letters and American young men, for the South the same as the North, and for the Pacific and Mississippi country, and Wisconsin and Texas and Kansas and Canada and Havana and Nicaragua, just as much as New York and Boston. Whatever is needed toward this achievement he puts his hand to, and lets imputations take their time to die.

First be yourself what you would show in your poem—

such seems to be this man's example and inferred rebuke to the schools of poets. He makes no allusions to books or writers; their spirits do not seem to have touched him; he has not a word to say for or against them, or their theories or ways. He never offers others; what he continually offers is the man whom our Brooklynites know so well. Of pure American breed, large and lusty—age thirty-six years (1855)—never once using medicine—never dressed in black, always dressed freely and clean in strong clothes—neck open, shirt-collar flat and broad, countenance tawny transparent red, beard well-mottled with white, hair like hay after it has been mowed in the field and lies tossed and streaked—his physiology corroborating a rugged phrenology—a person singularly beloved and looked toward, especially by young men and the illiterate—one who has firm attachments there, and associates there—one who does not associate with literary people—a man never called upon to make speeches at public dinners—never on platforms amid the crowds of clergymen, or professors, or aldermen, or congressmen—rather down in the bay with pilots in their pilot-boat—or off on a cruise with fishers in a fishing-smack—or riding on a Broadway omnibus, side by side with the driver—or with a band of loungers over the open grounds of the country—fond of New York and Brooklyn—fond of the life of the great ferries—one whom, if you should meet, you need not expect to meet an extraordinary person—one in whom you will see the singularity which consists in no singularity—whose contact is no dazzle or fascination, nor requires any deference, but has the easy fascination of what is homely and accustomed—as of something you knew before, and was waiting for—there you have Walt Whitman, the begetter of a new offspring out of literature, taking with easy nonchalance the chances of its present reception, and, through all misunderstandings and distrusts, the chances of its future reception.—WALT WHITMAN, *Brooklyn Daily Times*, Sept. 29, 1855

How I loathe *Wishi-washi*,—of course without reading it. I have not been so happy in loathing anything for a long while—except, I think, *Leaves of Grass*, by that Orson of yours. I should like just to have the writing of a valentine to him in one of the reviews.—DANTE GABRIEL ROSSETTI, Letter to William Allingham (April 1856)

I've read *Leaves of Grass*, and found it rather pleasant, but little new or original; the portrait the best thing. Of course, to call it poetry, in any sense, would be mere abuse of language. In poetry there is a special freedom, which, however, is *not* lawlessness and incoherence.—WILLIAM ALLINGHAM, Letter to Dante Gabriel Rossetti (April 10, 1857)

I read through the three volumes on Sunday: and upon a sober comparison I think Walt Whitman's *Leaves of Grass* worth at least a million of *Among My Books* and *Atalanta in Calydon*. In the two latter I could not find anything which has not been much better said before: but *Leaves of Grass* was a real refreshment to me—like rude salt spray in your face—in spite of its enormous fundamental error that a thing is good because it is natural, and in spite of the world-wide difference between my own conceptions of art and its author's.—SIDNEY LANIER, Letter to Bayard Taylor (Feb. 3, 1878)

Every sincere and capable writer puts himself into his books, impressing even quotations and translations with his personality, but *Leaves of Grass* contains more than this. It is a unique autobiography. Many persons have written down the story of their lives, so far as, in their old age, they could recollect it. Looking back upon their career as a whole, they necessarily give to the record the impress of their later judgment. Usually such works are filled with incidents, though, here and there,—notably in the case of John Stuart Mill—they present a photograph of the mind. Walt Whitman did not wait until his later years to begin his autobiography. Life seemed a wondrous experience to him, worth putting on record while it was passing. He jotted down what he saw and heard and felt, while the events were still fresh and alive and in instant relation to himself. In *Leaves of Grass* Whitman has bodied forth a biography of the human soul; of his own ostensibly, of all souls really, for the experience of the individual is simply the experience of the race in miniature. *Leaves of Grass* is a record of the soul's voyage through life; a gathering of experience, of joy and sorrow, of feeling, emotion and thought. This gives to the book its power and charm, and also, in some aspects and to some persons, makes it repellent.—WALTER LEWIN, *"Leaves of Grass," Murray's Magazine*, Sept. 1887, pp. 327–28

No great poem or other literary or artistic work of any scope, old or new, can be essentially consider'd without weighing first the age, politics (or want of politics) and aim, visible forms, unseen soul, and current times, out of the midst of which it rises and is formulated: as the Biblic canticles and their days and spirit—as the Homeric, or Dante's utterance, or Shakspere's, or the old Scotch or Irish ballads, or Ossian, or Omar Khayyam. So I have conceiv'd and launch'd, and work'd for years at, my *Leaves of Grass*—personal emanations only at best, but with specialty of emergence and background—the ripening of the nineteenth century, the thought and fact and radiation of individuality, of America, the Secession war, and showing the democratic conditions supplanting everything that insults them or impedes their aggregate way. Doubtless my poems illustrate (one of novel thousands to come for a long period) those conditions; but 'democratic art' will have to wait long before it is satisfactorily formulated and defined—if it ever is.—WALT WHITMAN, "An Old Man's Rejoinder" (1890), *Good-Bye My Fancy*, 1891

So bold and so varied are the eccentricities displayed in *Leaves of Grass* that one scarcely knows where to begin. What first strikes the superficial reader—and few readers have the courage to be anything more!—is the strange dithyrambic style of the so-called poems. A short line, or series of short lines, with no suspicion of meter, is suddenly followed by a long jumble of rough, jagged words, thrown higgledy-piggledy together, utterly without rhyme and often without reason. One of these enormities of verse will sometimes stretch, with its prolix enumerations and repetitions, to the length of a good-sized paragraph.

The portentous appearance sadly puzzled the reviewers, and, at first reading, one is surely apt to conclude that the author was mad as a March hare. At best it reminds one of the English translation of the Hindu epics, or an awkwardly rendered passage from the song of the Hebrew prophets. For these broken, passionate utterances, like the war poetry of Brihtnoth and the old Anglo-Saxon battle-ax swingers, did have strength and fire, whatever be their limitations considered as literature.

But the strange property of these wordy outpourings is that they actually begin to have a charm when one has fallen into some sympathy with Whitman. The very ruggedness and candid disclaiming of all title to esthetic beauty contain a certain fascination.

As to rhythm, it is not to be found at all until one has read conscientiously and painfully; then, with the composite effect of several pages in the mind, a sort of deep, weird rhythm does shape itself, how or whence one cannot tell. Mr. Stedman

avers that these dithyrambs were carefully evolved according to some regular plan—which we take the liberty of doubting—and that Whitman's idea was to catch the deep underlying melodies of nature,—the break of the sea-surges, the rush of the winds, the cries of animals.—C. D. LANIER, "Walt Whitman," *Chautauquan*, June 1902, p. 310

GEORGE SAINTSBURY
Academy, October 10, 1874, pp. 398–400

Several years have now passed since Walt Whitman's poetical works and claims were first brought before the notice of Englishmen of letters, yet it is more than doubtful whether, even among this class, there is any clear and decided view of his merits to be found prevailing. His poems have suffered the usual fate of such abnormal productions; it has been considered that admiration of them must be a kind of voluntary eccentricity, a gratuitous flourish in the face of respectability and orthodoxy. And it cannot be denied that he has not altogether escaped that worst of all calamities to a literary man, the admiration of the incompetent. It is true that he has been praised, with discrimination as well as with emphasis, by Mr. Swinburne; but unfortunately Mr. Swinburne's praise is mainly a passport to the favour of those who would be likely to appreciate Whitman without any passport at all. The testimony of his other panegyrists has been not a little weakened: in some by supposed national or political prejudices; in others, as already mentioned, by notorious literary incompetence.

It is very much to be hoped that the publication of this new edition of the *Leaves of Grass* may be the occasion of a deeper and wider study of the American poet, a study which may be carried on purely as a matter of literature, and not with any lurking intention to illustrate preconceived ideas as to the merits or demerits of Walt Whitman's principles, practice, or mode of expression.

The volume now before us is very different in outward appearance from the edition of fourteen years ago, which has so long caught the eye by its dissimilarity to its brother occupants of the bookshelf. The old cloth boards, deeply and mystically stamped with strange emblems, have given way to an outer coat of sober and decent green suitable to any modern English poem. Thick paper and bold type have yielded to the exigencies of increased matter. The very titles of some of the poems have made concessions to conventionality. *Enfants d'Adam* have transplanted themselves into plain English; "Proto-Leaf" has disappeared from the contents; and "A Boston Ballad the 78th year T. S.," which used to excite vague and uncomfortable chronological uncertainties, has become, to the great solace of the reader, "A Boston Ballad, 1854." Altogether the book might seem to a too-fanciful critic to have abandoned, at least in externals, its former air of youthful and exuberant provocation, and to demand, more soberly if not less confidently, the maturer consideration of the student of letters.

But it is still as ever far more easy to argue for or against the book than to convey a clear account of it to persons not acquainted with it. Although the contents are divided and subdivided by the headings which the author has prefixed, yet these headings convey but little idea of what comes under them, sometimes indeed have very little reference to it. Nor is the connection of the different divisions of the work and their interdependence more obvious. It may be easy to explain the meaning of *Children of Adam*, of "Passage to India," and some others; but what shall we make of *Calamus*, or of *Leaves of*

Grass itself? For the answers we must refer the reader to the book that it may give its own reply.

Moreover, the poet has in this edition availed himself of the incorporation of *Drum-taps* and other recently published matter, to dispose the whole contents of the volume in a new order, and to make many additions, alterations, and transpositions in individual poems. These changes are for the most part, as it appears to us, decided improvements, and the whole work possesses at present a unity and a completeness which are no small advantage. There are few poets who require to be studied as a whole so much as Walt Whitman—quotations and even tolerably extensive selections will not do—and it is a great gain to be directed by the author himself as to the order in which he would have us conduct the study.

It is not difficult to point out the central thesis of Walt Whitman's poetical gospel. It is briefly this: the necessity of the establishment of a universal republic, or rather brotherhood of men. And to this is closely joined another, or rather a series of others, indicating the type of man of which this universal republic is to consist, or perhaps which it is to produce. The poet's language in treating the former of these two positions is not entirely uniform; sometimes he speaks as of a federation of nations, sometimes as if mankind at large were to gravitate towards the United States, and to find in them the desired Utopia. But the constitution of the United States, at least that constitution as it ought to be, is always and uniformly represented as a sufficient and the only sufficient political means of attaining this Utopia, nay, as having to some extent already presented Utopia as a fact. Moreover, passing to the second point, the ideal man is imaged as the ideal Yankee, understanding that word of course as it is understood in America, not in Europe. He is to be a rather magnificent animal, almost entirely uncultured (this is not an unfair representation, although there are to be found certain vague panegyrics on art, and especially on music), possessing a perfect *physique*, well nourished and clothed, affectionate towards his kind, and above all things firmly resolved to admit no superior. As is the ideal man, so is the ideal woman to be. Now it may be admitted frankly and at once, that this is neither the creed nor the man likely to prove attractive to many persons east of the Atlantic. If it be said that the creed is a vague creed, and the man a detestable man, there will be very little answer attempted. Many wonderful things will doubtless happen "when," as the poet says, "through these States walk a hundred millions of superb persons;" but it must be allowed that there is small prospect of any such procession. One is inclined for very many sound reasons, and after discarding all prejudices, to opine that whatever salvation may await the world may possibly come from quarters other than from America. Fortunately, however, admiration for a creed is easily separable from admiration for the utterance and expression of that creed, and Walt Whitman as a poet is not difficult to disengage from Walt Whitman as an evangelist and politician. The keyword of all his ideas and of all his writings is universality. His Utopia is one which shall be open to everybody; his ideal of man and woman one which shall be attainable by everybody; his favourite scenes, ideas, subjects, those which everybody, at least to some extent, can enjoy and appreciate. He cares not that by this limitation he may exclude thoughts and feelings, at any rate phases of thought and feeling, infinitely choicer and higher than any which he admits. To express this striving after universality he has recourse to methods both unusual and (to most readers) unwelcome. The extraordinary jumbles and strings of names, places, employments, which deface his pages, and which have encouraged the profane to liken them to auctioneers' catalogues or indexes of encyclopædias, have no other object than to express this universal sympathy, reaching to the highest and penetrating to the lowest forms of life. The exclusion of culture, philosophy, manners, is owing also to this desire to admit nothing but what is open to every human being of ordinary faculty and opportunities. Moreover it is to this that we may fairly trace the prominence in Whitman's writings of the sexual passion, a prominence which has given rise, and probably will yet give rise, to much unphilosophical hubbub. This passion, as the poet has no doubt observed, is almost the only one which is peculiar to man as man, the presence of which denotes virility if not humanity, the absence of which is a sign of abnormal temperament. Hence he elevates it to almost the principal place, and treats of it in a manner somewhat shocking to those who are accustomed to speak of such subjects (we owe the word to Southey) *enfarinhadamente*. As a matter of fact, however, the treatment, though outspoken, is eminently "clean," to use the poet's own word; there is not a vestige of prurient thought, not a syllable of prurient language. Yet it would be a great mistake to suppose that sexual passion occupies the chief place in Whitman's estimation. There is according to him something above it, something which in any ecstasies he fails not to realize, something which seems more intimately connected in his mind with the welfare of mankind, and the promotion of his ideal republic. This is what he calls "robust American love." He is never tired of repeating "I am the poet of comrades"—Socrates himself seems renascent in this apostle of friendship. In the ears of a world (at least on this side the Atlantic) incredulous of such things, he reiterates the expressions of Plato to Aster, of Socrates respecting Charmides, and in this respect fully justifies (making allowance for altered manners) Mr. Symonds' assertion of his essentially Greek character, an assertion which most students of Whitman will heartily endorse. But we must again repeat that it is not so much in the matter as in the manner of his Evangel that the strength of Whitman lies. It is impossible not to notice his exquisite descriptive faculty, and his singular felicity in its use. Forced as he is, both by natural inclination and in the carrying out of his main idea, to take note of "the actual earth's equalities," he has literally filled his pages with the song of birds, the hushed murmur of waves, the quiet and multiform life of the forest and the meadow. And in these descriptions he succeeds in doing what is most difficult, in giving us the actual scene or circumstance as it impressed him, and not merely the impression itself. This is what none but the greatest poets have ever save by accident done, and what Whitman does constantly and with a sure hand. "You shall," he says at the beginning of his book:

> You shall no longer take things at second or third
> hand, nor look through the eyes of the dead, nor
> feed on the spectres in books:
> You shall not look through my eyes either, nor take
> things from me:
> You shall listen to all sides and filter them from
> yourself.

But affluent as his descriptions are, there are two subjects on which he is especially eloquent, which seem indeed to intoxicate and inspire him the moment he approaches them. These are Death and the sea. In the latter respect he is not, indeed, peculiar, but accords with all poets of all times, and especially of this time. But in his connection of the two ideas (for the one always seems to suggest the other to him), and in his special devotion to Death, he is more singular. The combined influence of the two has produced what is certainly the most perfect specimen of his work, the "Word out of the Sea" (in this edition it has, we are sorry to see, lost its special title, and become the first merely of *Sea-Shore Memories*). Unfortunately it is indivisible, and its length precludes the possibility of quotation. But there is another poem almost equally beautiful, which forms part of "President Lincoln's Burial Hymn," and for this space may perhaps be found:—

DEATH-CAROL

Come, lovely and soothing Death,
Undulate round the world serenely arriving, arriving,
In the day, in the night, to all, to each,
Sooner or later, delicate Death.

Prais'd be the fathomless universe,
For life and joy, and for objects and knowledge curious;
And for love, sweet love. But praise! praise! praise!
For the sure-enwinding arms of cool-enfolding Death.

Dark Mother, always gliding near, with soft feet,
Have none chanted for thee a chant of fullest welcome?
Then I chant it for thee—I glorify thee above all;
I bring thee a song that when thou must indeed come, come unfalteringly.

Approach, strong Deliveress!
When it is so—when thou hast taken them, I joyously sing the dead,
Lost in the loving, floating ocean of thee,
Laved in the flood of thy bliss, O Death.

From me to thee glad serenades,
Dances for thee I propose, saluting thee—adornments and feastings for thee;
And the sights of the open landscape and the high spread sky are fitting,
And life and the fields and the huge and thoughtful night.

The night, in silence under many a star;
The ocean-shore, and the husky whispering wave whose voice I know;
And the soul turning to thee, O vast and well-veiled death,
And the body gratefully nestling close to thee.

Over the tree-tops I float thee a song!
Over the rising and sinking waves—over the myriad fields and the prairies wide;
Over the dense-packed cities all and the teeming wharves and ways,
I float this carol with joy, with joy to thee, O Death!

It is easy enough to connect this cultus of Death, and the pantheism which necessarily accompanies it, with the main articles of Whitman's creed. Death is viewed as the one event of great solemnity and importance which is common to all—the one inevitable, yet not commonplace incident in every life, however commonplace; and, further, it must not be overlooked that Death is pre-eminently valuable in such a system as this, in the capacity of reconciler, ready to accommodate all difficulties, to sweep away all rubbish. The cheeriest of optimists with the lowest of standards cannot pretend to assert or expect that everyone will live the ideal life—but Death pays all scores and obliterates all mistakes.

There remains, however, still to be considered a point not least in importance—the vehicle which Whitman has chosen for the conveyance of these thoughts. He employs, as most people know who know anything at all about him, neither rhyme nor even regular metre; the exceptions to this rule

occurring among his more recent poems are few and insignificant. A page of his work has little or no look of poetry about it; it is not, indeed, printed continuously, but it consists of versicles, often less in extent than a line, sometimes extending to many lines. Only after reading these for some time does it become apparent that, though rhyme and metre have been abandoned, rhythm has not; and, moreover, that certain figures and tricks of language occur which are generally considered more appropriate to poetry than to prose. The total effect produced is dissimilar to that of any of the various attempts which have been made to evade the shackles of metre and rhyme, while retaining the other advantages of poetical form and diction. Whitman's style differs very much from that of such efforts as Baudelaire's *Petits Poèmes en prose*, for from these all rhythm, diction, and so forth not strictly appropriate to prose is conscientiously excluded. It is more like the polymeters of the poet's namesake Walt in Richter's *Flegeljahre*, except that these latter being limited to the expression of a single thought are not divided into separate limbs or verses. Perhaps the likeness which is presented to the mind most strongly, is that which exists between our author and the verse divisions of the English Bible, especially in the poetical books, and it is not unlikely that the latter did actually exercise some influence in moulding the poet's work. It is hard to give a fair specimen of it in the way of quotation—that already given is not representative, being too avowedly lyrical—and the rhythm is as a rule too varying, complex, and subtle to be readily seized except from a comparison of many instances. Perhaps, however, the following stanza from *Children of Adam* may convey some idea of it:—

I have perceived that to be with those I like is enough;
To stop in company with the rest at evening is enough;
To be surrounded by beautiful, curious, breathing, laughing flesh is enough;
To pass among them, or touch any one, or rest my arm ever so lightly round his or her neck for a moment—what is this then?
I do not ask any more delight—I swim in it as in a sea.
There is something in staying close to men and women, and looking on them, and in the contact and odour of them, that pleases the soul well;
All things please the soul—but these please the soul well.

It will be observed that the rhythm is many-centred, that it takes fresh departures as it goes on. The poet uses freely alliteration, chiasmus, antithesis, and especially the retention of the same word or words to begin and end successive lines, but none of these so freely as to render it characteristic. The result, though perhaps uncouth at first sight and hearing, is a medium of expression by no means wanting in excellence, and certainly well adapted for Whitman's purposes. Strange as it appears to a reader familiarised with the exquisite versification of modern England or France, it is by no means in disagreeable contrast therewith, being at least in its earlier forms (for in some of the later poems reminiscences of the English heroic, of Longfellow's hexameters, and even of Poe's stanzas occur) singularly fresh, light, and vigorous. Nor should the language pass unmentioned—for though of course somewhat Transatlantic in construction and vocabulary, it is not offensively American. The chief blemish in the eyes of the sensitive critic is an ugly trick of using foreign words, such as "Libertad" for liberty, "*habitan* of the Alleghanies," "to become *élève* of mine," "with reference to *ensemble*," and so forth; but even this does not occur very frequently. Few books abound more in "jewels five words long;" it is hardly possible to open a page without lighting upon some happy and memorable conceit, expression, thought, such as this of the grass:

> It is the handkerchief of the Lord;
> A scented gift and remembrance designedly dropt,
> Bearing the owner's name someway in the corners,
>   that we may see and remark, and say Whose?

Or this of children's love to a father:

> They did not love him by allowance, they loved him
>   with personal love.

Or again of the grass:

> And now it seems to me the beautiful uncut hair of
>   graves.

Such in matter and in manner are Walt Whitman's *Leaves of Grass*, and there only remains to be added one recommendation to their study. The book, aggressive and vainglorious as it seems, is in reality remarkably free from vituperativeness of tone. Hardly to some "eunuchs, consumptive and genteel persons" is strong language used, and after all it rests with every reader whether he chooses to class himself with these. Amid all the ecstatic praise of America there is no abuse of England; amid all the excitement of the poems on the War there is little personal abuse of the Secessionists. No Englishman, no one indeed, whether American or Englishman, need be deterred from reading this book, a book the most unquestionable in originality, if not the most unquestioned in excellence, that the United States have yet sent us.

EDMUND CLARENCE STEDMAN
From "Walt Whitman"
Scribner's Monthly, November 1880, pp. 54–63
III

Here we may as well consider a trait of Mr. Whitman's early work that most of all has brought it under censure. I refer to the blunt and open manner in which the consummate processes of nature, the acts of procreation and reproduction, with all that appertain to them, are made the theme or illustration of various poems, notably of those with the title *Children of Adam*. Landor says of a poet that, "on the remark of a learned man that irregularity is no indication of genius, he began to lose ground rapidly, when on a sudden he cried out in the Haymarket, 'There is no God.' It was then rumored more generally and more gravely that he had something in him. . . . 'Say what you will,' once whispered a friend of mine, 'there are things in him strong as poison, and original as sin.'" But those who looked upon Whitman's sexuality as a shrewd advertisement, justly might be advised to let him reap the full benefit of it, since, if he had no more sincere basis, it would receive the earlier judgment—and ere long be "outlawed of art." This has not been its fate, and therefore it must have had something of conviction to sustain it. Nevertheless, it made the public distrustful of this poet, and did much to confine his volumes to the libraries of the select few. Prurient modesty often is a sign that people are conscious of personal defects; but Whitman's physical excursions are of a kind which even Thoreau, refreshed as he was by the new poet, found it hard to keep pace with. The fault was not that he discussed matters which others timidly evade, but that he did not do it in a clean way,—that he was too anatomical and malodorous withal; furthermore,

that in this department he showed excessive interest, and applied its imagery to other departments, as if with a special purpose to lug it in. His pictures sometimes were so realistic, his speech so free, as to excite the hue and cry of indecent exposure; the display of things natural, indeed, but which we think it unnatural to exhibit on the highway, or in the sitting-room, or anywhere except their wonted places of consignment.

On the poet's side it is urged that the ground of this exposure was, that thus only could his reform be consistent; that it was necessary to celebrate the body with special unction, since, with respect to the physical basis of life, our social weakness and hypocrisy are most extreme. Not only should the generative functions be proclaimed, but, also,—to show that "there is in nature nothing mean or base,"—the side of our life which is hidden, because it is of the earth, earthy, should be plainly recognized in these poems; and thus, out of rankness and coarseness, a new virility be bred, an impotent and squeamish race at last be made whole.

Entering upon this field of dispute, what I have to say—in declaring that Whitman mistakes the aim of the radical artist or poet—is perhaps different from the criticism to which he has been subjected. Let us test him solely by his own rules. Doing this, we presuppose his honesty of purpose, otherwise his objectionable phrases and imagery would be outlawed, not only of art but of criticism. Assume, then, first, that they were composed as a fearless avowal of the instincts and conditions which pertain to him in common with the race which he typifies; secondly, that he deems such a presentation essential to his revolt against the artifice of current life and sentiment, and makes it in loyal *reliance upon the excellence, the truth of nature.* To judge him in conformity with these ideas lessens our estimate of his genius. Genius is greatly consistent when most audacious. Its instinct will not violate nature's logic, even by chance, and it is something like obtuseness that does so upon a theory.

In Mr. Whitman's sight, that alone is to be condemned which is against nature, yet, in his mode of allegiance, he violates her canons. For, if there is nothing in her which is mean or base, there is much that is ugly and disagreeable. If not so in itself (and on the question of absolute beauty I accept his own ruling, "that whatever tastes sweet to the most perfect person, that is finally right"), if not ugly in itself, it seems so to the conscious spirit of our intelligence. Even Mother Earth takes note of this, and resolves, or disguises and beautifies, what is repulsive upon her surface. It is well said that an artist shows inferiority by placing the true, the beautiful, or the good above its associates. Nature is strong and rank, but not externally so. She, too, has her sweet and sacred sophistries, and the delight of Art is to heighten her beguilement, and, far from making her ranker than she is, to portray what she might be in ideal combinations. Nature, I say, covers her slime, her muck, her ruins, with garments that to us are beautiful. She conceals the skeleton, the frame-work, the intestinal thick of life, and makes fair the outside of things. Her servitors swiftly hide or transform the fermenting, the excrementitious, and the higher animals possess her instinct. Whitman fails to perceive that she respects certain decencies, that what we call decency is grounded in her law. An artist should not elect to paint the part of her to which Churchill rashly avowed that Hogarth's pencil was devoted. There is a book—"*L'Affaire Clémenceau*"—in which a Frenchman's regard for the lamp of beauty, and his indifference to that of goodness, are curiously illustrated. But Dumas points out, in the rebuke given by a sculptor to a pupil who mistakenly elevates the arm of his first model, a beautiful girl, that the Underside of things should be avoided in art,—since Nature, not meaning it to be shown, often deprives it of beauty. Finally, Mr. Whitman sins against his mistress in questioning the instinct we derive from her, one which of all is most elevating to poetry, and which is the basis of sensations that lead childhood on, that fill youth with rapture, impress with longing all human kind, and make up, impalpable as they are, half the preciousness of life. He draws away the final veil. It is not squeamishness that leaves something to the imagination, that hints at guerdons still unknown. The law of suggestion, of half-concealment, determines the choicest effects, and is the surest road to truth. Grecian as Mr. Whitman may be, the Greeks better understood this matter, as scores of illustrations, like that of the attitude of the Hermaphroditus in the Louvre, show. A poet violates nature's charm of feeling in robbing love, and even intrigue, of their esoteric quality. No human appetites need be pruriently ignored, but coarsely analyzed they fall below humanity. He even takes away the sweetness and pleasantness of stolen waters and secret bread. *Furto cuncta magis bella.* Recalling the term "over-soul," the reader insensibly accuses our poet of an over-bodiness. The mock-modesty and effeminacy of our falser tendencies in art should be chastised, but he misses the true corrective. Delicacy is not impotence, nor rankness the sure mark of virility. The model workman is both fine and strong. Where Mr. Whitman sees nothing but the law of procreation, poetry dwells upon the union of souls, devotion unto death, joys greater for their privacy, things of more worth because whispered between the twilights. It is absolutely true that the design of sexuality is the propagation of species. But the delight of lovers who now inherit the earth is no less a natural right, and those children often are the finest that were begot without thought of offspring. There are other lights in which a dear one may be regarded than as the future mother of men, and these—with their present hour of joy—are unjustly subordinated in the *Leaves of Grass.* Marked as the failure of this pseudo-naturalism has been hitherto, even thus will it continue,—so long as savages have instincts of modesty,—so long as we draw and dream of the forms and faces, not the internal substance and mechanism, of those we hold most dear,—so long as the ivy trails over the ruin, the southern jessamine covers the blasted pine, the moss hides the festering swamp,—so long as our spirits seek the spirit of all things; and thus long shall art and poesy, while calling every truth of science to their aid, rely on something else than the processes of science for the attainment of their exquisite results.

From the tenor of Mr. Whitman's later works, I sometimes have thought him half-inclined to see in what respect his effort toward a perfect naturalism was misdirected. In any case, there would be no inconsistency in a further modification of his early pieces,—in the rejection of certain passages and words, which, by the law of strangeness, are more conspicuous than ten times their amount of common phraseology, and grow upon the reader until they seem to pervade the whole volume. The examples of Lucretius, Rabelais, and other masters, who wrote in other ages and conditions, and for their own purposes, have little analogy. It well may be that our poet has more claim to a wide reading in England than here, since his English editor, without asking consent, omitted entirely every poem "which could with tolerable fairness be deemed offensive." Without going so far, and with no falseness to himself, Mr. Whitman might re-edit his home-editions in such wise that they would not be counted wholly among those books which are meat for strong men, but would have a chance among those greater books that are the treasures of the simple and the learned, the young and the old.

IV

The entire body of his work has a sign-metrical by which it is recognized—a peculiar and uncompromising style, conveyed in a still more peculiar unrhymed verse, irregular, yet capable of impressive rhythmical and lyrical effects.

The faults of his method, glaring enough in ruder passages, are quite his own; its merits often are original, but in his chosen form there is little original and new. It is an old fashion, always selected for dithyrambic oracular outpourings,—that of the Hebrew lyrists and prophets, and their inspired English translators,—of the Gaelic minstrels,—of various Oriental and Shemitic peoples,—of many barbarous dark-skinned tribes,—and in recent times put to use by Blake, in the *Prophetic Visions,* and by other and weaker men. There are symptoms in Whitman's earlier poems, and definite proof in the later, that his studies have included Blake,—between whose traits and his own there is a superficial, not a genuine, likeness. Not as an invention, then, but as a striking and persistent renaissance, the form that has become his trademark, and his extreme claims for it, should have fair consideration. An honest effort to enlarge the poet's equipment, too long unaided, by something rich and strange, deserves praise, even though a failure; for there are failures worthier than triumphs. Our chanter can bear with dignity the provincial laughter of those to whom all is distasteful that is uncommon, and regard it as no unfavorable omen. From us the very strangeness of his chant shall gain for it a welcome, and the chance to benefit us as it may. Thereby we may escape the error pointed out by Mr. Benjamin, who says that people in approaching a work, instead of learning from it, try to estimate it from their preconceived notions. Hence, original artists at first endure neglect, because they express their own discoveries in nature of what others have not yet seen,—a truth well to bear in mind whenever a singer arrives with a new method.

Probably the method under review has had a candid hearing in more quarters than the author himself is aware of. If some men of independent thought and feeling have failed to accept his claims and his estimate of the claims of others, it possibly has not been through exclusiveness or malice, but upon their own impression of what has value in song.

Mr. Whitman never has swerved from his primal indictment of the wonted forms, rhymed and unrhymed, dependent upon accentual, balanced and stanzaic effects of sound and shape,—and until recently has expressed his disdain not only of our poets who care for them, but of form itself. So far as this cry was raised against the technique of poetry, I not merely think it absurd, but that when he first made it he had not clearly thought out his own problem. Technique, *of some kind,* is an essential, though it is equally true that it cannot atone for poverty of thought and imagination. I hope to show that he never was more mistaken than when he supposed he was throwing off form and technique. But first it may be said that no "form" ever has sprung to life, and been handed from poet to poet, that was not engendered by instinct and natural law, and each will be accepted in a sound generalization. Whitman avers that the time has come to break down the barriers between prose and verse, and that only thus can the American bard utter anything commensurate with the liberty and splendor of his themes. Now, the mark of a poet is that he is at ease everywhere,—that nothing can hamper his gifts, his exultant freedom. He is a master of expression. There are certain points—note this—where expression takes on rhythm, and certain other points where it ceases to be rhythmical,—places where prose becomes poetical, and where verse grows prosaic; and throughout Whitman's productions these points are more frequent and unmistakable than in the work of any other writer of our time. However bald or formal a poet's own method, it is useless for him to decry forms that recognize the pulses of time and accent, and the linked sweetness of harmonic sound. Some may be tinkling, others majestic, but each is suited to its purpose, and has a spell to charm alike the philosopher and the child that knows not why. The human sense acknowledges them; they are the earliest utterance of divers peoples, and in their later excellence still hold their sway. Goethe discussed all this with Eckermann, and rightly said there were "great and mysterious agencies" in the various poetic forms. He even added that if a sort of poetic prose should be introduced, it would only show that the distinction between prose and poetry had been lost sight of completely. Rhyme, the most conventional feature of ballad verse, has its due place, and will keep it; it is an artifice, but a natural artifice, and pleases accordingly. Milton gave reasons for discarding it when he perfected an unrhymed measure for the stateliest English poem; but what an instrument rhyme was in his hands that made the sonnets and minor poems! How it has sustained the whole carnival of our heroic and lyric song, from the sweet pipings of Lodge and Chapman and Shakspere, to the undertones of Swinburne and Poe. There are endless combinations yet in the gamut. The report is that Mr. Whitman's prejudice is specially strong against our noblest unrhymed form, "blank-verse." Its variety and freedom, within a range of accents, breaks, cæsural effects,—its rolling organ-harmonies,—he appreciates not at all. Rhythmical as his own verse often can be, our future poets scarcely will discard blank-verse in its behalf—not if they shall recall *The Tempest*, "Hail, Holy Light," "Tintern Abbey," *Hyperion*, the *Hellenics*, *Ulysses*, and *Thanatopsis*. Mr. Parke Godwin, in a recent private letter, terms it "the grandest and most flexible of English measures," and adds, with quick enthusiasm: "Oh, what a glory there is in it, when we think of what Shakspere, Milton, Wordsworth and Landor made of it, to say nothing of Tennyson and Bryant!" I doubt not that new handlings of this measure will produce new results, unsurpassed in any tongue. It is quite as fit as Mr. Whitman's own, if he knows the use of it, for "the expression of American democracy and manhood." Seeing how dull and prolix he often becomes, it may be that even for him his measure has been too facile, and that the curb of a more regular unrhymed form would have spared us many tedious curvetings and grewsome downfalls.

Strenuous as he may be in his belief that the old methods will be useless to poets of the future, I am sure that he has learned the value of technique through his long practice. He well knows that whatever claims to be the poetry of the future speedily will be forgotten in the past, unless consonant with the laws of expression in the language to which it belongs; that verse composed upon a theory, if too artificial in its contempt of art, may be taken up for a while, but, as a false fashion, anon will pass away. Not that his verse is of this class; but it justly has been declared that, in writing with a purpose to introduce a new mode or revolutionize thought, and not because an irresistible impulse seizes him, a poet is so much the less a poet. Our question, then, involves the spontaneity of his work, and the results attained by him.

His present theory, like most theories which have reason, seems to be derived from experience: he has learned to discern the good and bad in his work, and has arrived at a rationale of it. He sees that he has been feeling after the irregular, various

harmonies of nature, the anthem of the winds, the roll of the surges, the countless laughter of the ocean waves. He tries to catch this "under-melody and rhythm." Here is an artistic motive, distinguishing his chainless dithyrambs from ordinary verse, somewhat as the new German music is distinguished from folk-melody, and from the products of an early, especially the Italian, school. Here is not only reason, but a theoretical advance to a grade of art demanding extreme resources, because it affords the widest range of combination and effect.

But this comprehension of his own aim is an afterthought, the result of long groping. The genesis of the early *Leaves* was in motives less artistic and penetrating. Finding that he could not think and work to advantage in the current mode, he concluded that the mode itself was at fault; especially, that the poet of a young, gigantic nation, the prophet of a new era, should have a new vehicle of song. Without looking farther, he spewed out the old forms, and avowed his contempt for American poets who use them. His off-hand course does not bring us to the conclusion of the whole matter. So far as the crudeness of the *juventus mundi* is assumed by him, it must be temporal and passing, like the work of some painters, who, for the sake of startling effects, use ephemeral pigments. A poet does not, perforce, restore the lost foundations of his art by copying the manner natural to an aboriginal time and people. He is merely exchanging masters, and certainly is not founding a new school. Only as he discovers the inherent tendencies of song does he belong to the future. Still, it is plain that Whitman found a style suited to his purposes, and was fortunate both as a poet and a diplomatist. He was sure to attract notice, and to seem original, by so pronounced a method. Quoth the monk to Gargantua, "A mass, a matin, or vesper, well rung, is half said." It was suited to him as a poet, because he has that somewhat wandering sense of form, and of melody, which often makes one's conceptions seem the more glorious to himself, as if invested with a halo or blended with concurrent sound, and prevents him from lessening or enlarging them by the decisive master-hand, or at once perfecting them by sure control.

A man who finds that his gloves cripple him does right in drawing them off. At first, Whitman certainly meant to escape all technique. But genius, in spite of itself, makes works that stand the test of scientific laws. And thus he now sees that he was groping toward a broader technique. Unrhymed verse, the easiest to write, is the hardest to excel in, and no measure for a bardling. And Mr. Whitman never more nearly displayed the feeling of a true artist than when he expressed a doubt as to his present handling of his own verse, but hoped that, in breaking loose from ultramarine forms, he had sounded, at least, the key for a new pæan. I have referred to his gradual advances in the finish of his song. Whether he has revived a form which others will carry to a still higher excellence, is doubtful. Blank-verse, limitless in its capacities, forces a poet to stand without disguise, and reveals all his defects. Whitman's verse, it is true, does not subject him to so severe a test. He can so twist and turn himself, and run and jump, that we are puzzled to inspect him at all, or make out his contour. Yet the few who have ventured to follow him have produced little that has not seemed like parody, or unpleasantly grotesque. It may be that his mode is suited to himself alone, and not to the future poets of These States,—that the next original genius will have to sing "as Martin Luther sang," and the glorious army of poetic worthies. I suspect that the old forms, in endless combinations, will return as long as new poets arise with the old abiding sense of time and sound.

The greatest poet is many-sided, and will hold himself

slavishly to no one thing for the sake of difference. He is a poet, too, in spite of measure and material, while, as to manner, the style is the man. Genius does not need a special language; it newly uses whatever tongue it finds. Thought, fire, passion, will overtop everything,—will show, like the limbs of Teverino, through the clothes of a prince or a beggar. A cheap and common instrument, odious in foolish hands, becomes the slave of music under the touch of a master. I attach less importance, therefore, to Mr. Whitman's experiment in verse than he and his critics have, and inquire of his mannerism simply how far it represents the man. To show how little there is in itself, we only have to think of Tupper; to see how rich it may be, when the utterance of genius, listen to Whitman's teacher, William Blake. It does not prove much, but still is interesting, to note that the pieces whose quality never fails with any class of hearers—of which "My Captain" is an example—are those in which our poet has approached most nearly, and in a lyrical, melodious manner, to the ordinary forms.

He is far more original in his style proper than in his metrical inventions. His diction, on its good behavior, is copious and strong, full of surprises, utilizing the brave, homely words of the people, and assigning new duties to common verbs and nouns. He has a use of his own for Spanish and French catch-words, picked up, it may be, on his trip to Louisiana or in Mexican war times. Among all this is much slang that now has lived its life, and is not understood by a new generation with a slang of its own. This does not offend so much as the mouthing verbiage, the "ostent evanescent" phrases, wherein he seems profoundest to himself, and really is at his worst. The titles of his books and poems are varied and sonorous. Those of the latter often are taken from the opening lines, and are key-notes. What can be fresher than *Leaves of Grass* and *Calamus*? What richer than "The Mystic Trumpeter," "O Star of France!" "Proud Music of the Storm," or simpler than *Drum-Taps*, "The Wound-Dresser," "The Ox-Tamer"? or more characteristic than "Give me the Splendid Silent Sun," "Mannahatta," "As a Strong Bird on Pinions Free," "Joy, Shipmate, Joy"? Some are obscure and grandiose—"Eidolons," "Chanting the Square Deific," but usually his titles arrest the eye and haunt the ear; it is an artist that invents them, and the best pieces have the finest names. He has the art of "saying things"; his epithets, also, are racier than those of other poets; there *is* something of the Greek in Whitman, and his lovers call him Homeric, but to me he shall be our old American Hesiod, teaching us works and days.

V

His surest hold, then, is as an American poet, gifted with language, feeling, imagination, and inspired by a determined purpose. Some estimate, as I have said, may be made of his excellence and short-comings, without waiting for that national absorption which he himself declares to be the test.

As an assimilating poet of nature he has positive genius, and seems to me to present his strongest claims. Who else, in fact, has so true a hand or eye for the details, the sweep and color, of American landscape? Like others, he confronts those superb physical aspects of the New World which have controlled our poetry and painting, and deferred the growth of a figure-school, but in this conflict with nature he is not overcome; if not the master, he is the joyous brother-in-arms. He has heard the message of the pushing, wind-swept sea, along Paumanok's shore; he knows the yellow, waning moon and the rising stars,—the sunset, with its cloud-bar of gold above the horizon,—the birds that sing by night or day, bush and brier, and every shining or swooning flower, the peaks, the prairie, the mighty, conscious river, the dear common grass that children fetch with full hands. Little escapes him, not even "the mossy scabs of the worm fence, and heap'd stones, mullen and poke-weed"; but his details are massed, blended,—the wind saturates and the light of the American skies transfigures them. Not that to me, recalling the penetrative glance of Emerson, the wood and way-side craft that Lowell carried lightly as a sprig of fir, and recalling other things of others, does Whitman seem our "only" poet of nature; but that here he is on his own ground, and with no man his leader.

Furthermore, his intimacy with nature is always subjective,—she furnishes the background for his self-portraiture and his images of men. None so apt as he to observe the panorama of life, to see the human figure,—the hay-maker, wagoner, boatman, soldier, woman and babe and maiden, and brown, lusty boy,—to hear not only "the bravuras of birds, bustle of growing wheat, gossip of flames, clack of sticks cooking my meals," but also "the sound I love, the sound of the human voice." His town and country scenes, in peace or in war, are idyllic. Above the *genre*, for utter want of sympathy, he can only name and designate—he does not depict. A single sketch, done in some original way, often makes a poem; such is that reminiscence (in rhyme) of the old Southern negress, "Ethiopia Saluting the Colors," and such the touching conceit of Old Ireland—no fair and green-robed Hibernia of the harp, but an ancient, sorrowful mother, white-haired, lean and tattered, seated on the ground, mourning for her children. He tells her that they are not dead, but risen again, with rosy and new blood, in another country. This is admirable, I say, and the true way to escape tradition; this is imaginative,—and there is imagination, too, in his apostrophe to "The Man-of-War-Bird" (carried beyond discretion by this highest mood, he finds it hard to avoid blank-verse):

> Thou who hast slept all night upon the storm,
> Waking renewed on thy prodigious pinions!
>
> . . .
>
> Thou, born to match the gale (thou art all wings)!
> To cope with heaven and earth and sea and hurri-
>   cane;
> Thou ship of air that never furl'st thy sails,
> Days, even weeks, untried and onward, through
>   spaces—realms gyrating.
> At dark that look'st on Senegal, at morn, America;
> That sport'st amid the lightning-flash and thunder-
>   cloud!
> In these—in thy experiences—hadst thou my soul,
> What joys! What joys were thine!

Imagination is the essential thing; without it poetry is as sounding brass or a tinkling cymbal. Whitman shows it in his sudden and novel imagery, and in the subjective rapture of verse like this, but quite as often his vision is crowded and inconsistent. The editor of a New York magazine writes to me: "In so far as imagination is thinking through types (*eidullia*), Whitman has no equal," adding that he does not use the term as if applied to Coleridge, but as limited to the use of types, and that "in this sense it is really more applicable to a master of science than to a poet. In the poet the type is lodged in his own heart, and when the occasion comes . . . he is mastered by it, and he must sing. In Whitman the type is not so much in his heart as in his thought. . . . While he is moved by thought, often grand and elementary, he does not give the intellectual satisfaction warranted by the thought, but a moving panorama of objects. He not only puts aside his 'singing robes,' but his 'thinking-cap,' and resorts to the stereopticon." How acute, how true! There is, however, a peculiar quality in these long catalogues of types,—such as those in the "Song of the Broad-Axe" and "Salut au Monde," or, more poetically treated, in "Longings for Home." The poet appeals to our synthetic vision. Look through a window; you see not only the framed landscape, but each tree and stone and living thing. His page must be seized with the eye, as a journalist reads a column at a glance, until successive "types" and pages blend in the mind like the diverse colors of a swift-turning wheel. Whitman's most inartistic fault is that he overdoes this method, as if usually unable to compose in any other way.

The tenderness of a strong and robust nature is a winning feature of his song. There is no love-making, no yearning for some idol of the heart. In the lack of so refining a contrast to his realism, we have gentle thoughts of children, images of grand old men, and of women clothed with sanctity and years. This tenderness, a kind of natural piety, marks also his poems relating to the oppressed, the suffering, the wounded and dying soldiers. It is the soul of the pathetic, melodious threne for Lincoln, and of the epilogue—"My Captain!" These pieces remind us that he has gained some command of his own music, and in the matter of tone has displayed strength from the first. In revising his early poems he has improved their effect as a whole. It must be owned that his wheat often is more welcome for the chaff in which it is scattered; there is none of the persistent luxury which compels much of Swinburne's unstinted wealth to go unreckoned. Finally, let us note that Whitman, long ago, was not unread in the few great books of the world, nor inapt to digest their wisdom. He was among the first to perceive the grandeur of the scientific truths which are to give impulse to a new and loftier poetic imagination. Those are significant passages in the poem *Walt Whitman*, written by one who had read the xxxviiith chapter of Job, and beginning, "Long I was hugg'd close—long and long."

The *Leaves of Grass*, in thought and method, avowedly are a protest against a hackney breed of singers, singing the same old song. More poets than one are born in each generation, yet Whitman has derided his compeers, scouted the sincerity of their passion, and has borne on his mouth Heine's sneer at the eunuchs singing of love. In two things he fairly did take the initiative, and might, like a wise advocate, rest his case upon them. He essayed, without reserve or sophistry, the full presentment of the natural man. He devoted his song to the future of his own country, accepting and outvying the loudest peak-and-prairie brag, and pledging These States to work out a perfect democracy and the salvation of the world. Striking words and venturesome deeds, for which he must have full credit. But in our studies of the ideal and its votaries, the failings of the latter cannot be lightly passed over. There is an inconsistency, despite the gloss, between his fearful arraignment, going beyond Carlyle's, of the outgrowth of our democracy, thus far, and his promise for the future. In his prose, he sees neither physical nor moral health among us: all is disease, impotency, fraud, decline. In his verse, the average American is lauded as no type ever was before. These matters renew questions which, to say the least, are still open. Are the lines of caste less sharply divided every year, or are the high growing higher, and the low lower, under our democracy? Is not the social law of more import than the form of government, and has not the quality of race much to do with both? Does Americanism in speech and literature depend upon the form and letter, or upon the spirit? Can the spirit of literature do much more than express the national spirit as far as it has gone, and has it not, in fact, varied with the atmosphere? Is a nation changed by literature, or the latter by the former, in

times when journalism so swiftly represents the thought and fashion of each day? As to distinctions in form and spirit between the Old-World literature and our own, I have always looked for this to enlarge with time. But with the recent increase of travel and communication, each side of the Atlantic now more than ever seems to affect the other. Our "native flavor" still is distinct in proportion to the youth of a section, and inversely to the development. It is an intellectual narrowness that fails to meditate upon these things.

Thus we come to a defect in Mr. Whitman's theories, reasoning and general attitude. He professes universality, absolute sympathy, breadth in morals, thought, workmanship,—exemption from prejudice and formalism. Under all the high poetic excellences which I carefully have pointed out, I half suspect that his faults lie in the region where, to use his own word, he is most complacent: in brief, that a certain *narrowness* holds him within well-defined bounds. In many ways he does not conform to his creed. Others have faith in the future of America, with her arts and letters, yet hesitate to lay down rules for her adoption. These must come of themselves, or not at all. Again, in this poet's specification of the objects of his sympathy, the members of every class, the lofty and the lowly, are duly named; yet there always is an implication that the employer is inferior to the employed,—that the man of training, the civilizee, is less manly than the rough, the pioneer. He suspects those who, by chance or ability, rise above the crowd. What attention he does pay them is felt to be in the nature of patronage, and insufferable. Other things being equal, a scholar is as good as an ignoramus, a rich man as a poor man, a civilizee as a boor. Great champions of democracy—poets like Byron, Shelley, Landor, Swinburne, Hugo—often have come from the ranks of long descent. It would be easy to cite verses from Whitman that apparently refute this statement of his feeling, but the spirit of his whole work confirms it. Meanwhile, though various editions of his poems have found a sale, he is little read by our common people, who know him so well, and of whose democracy he is the self-avowed herald. In numberless homes of working-men—and all Americans are workers—the books of other poets are treasured. Some mental grip and culture are required, of course, to get hold of the poetry of the future. But Whittier, in this land, is a truer type of the people's poet,—the word "people" here meaning a vast body of freemen, having a common-school education, homes, an honest living, and a general comprehension far above that of the masses in Europe. These folks have an instinct that Whittier, for example, has seized his day with as much alertness and self-devotion as this other bard of Quaker lineage, and has sung songs "fit for the New World" as he found it. Whitman is more truly the voice and product of the culture of which he bids us beware. At least, he utters the cry of culture for escape from over-culture, from the weariness, the finical precision, of its own satiety. His warmest admirers are of several classes: those who have carried the art of verse to super-refined limits, and seeing nothing farther in that direction, break up the mold for a change; those radical enthusiasts who, like myself, are interested in whatever hopes to bring us more speedily to the golden year; lastly, those who, radically inclined, do not think closely, and make no distinction between his strength and weakness. Thus he is, in a sense, the poet of the over-refined and the doctrinaires. Such men, too, as Thoreau and Burroughs have a welcome that scarcely would have been given them in an earlier time. From the discord and artifice of our social life we go with them to the woods, learn to name the birds, note the beauty of form and flower, and love these healthy comrades who know each spring that bubbles beneath the lichened crag and trailing hemlock. Theocritus learns his notes upon the mountain, but sings in courts of Alexandria and Syracuse. Whitman, through propagandists who care for his teachings from metaphysical and personal causes, and compose their own ideals of the man, may yet reach the people, in spite of the fact that lasting works usually have pleased all classes in their own time.

Reflecting upon his metrical theory, we also find narrowness instead of breadth. I have shown that the bent of a liberal artist may lead him to adopt a special form, but not to reject all others; he will see the uses of each, demanding only that it shall be good in its kind. Swinburne, with his cordial liking for Whitman, is too acute to overlook his formalism. Some of his eulogists, those whom I greatly respect, fail in their special analysis. One of them rightly says that Shakspere's sonnets are artificial, and that three lines which he selects from *Measure for Measure* are of a higher grade of verse. But these are the reverse of "unmeasured" lines,—they are in Shakspere's free and artistic, yet most measured, vein. Here comes in the distinction between art and artifice; the blank-verse is conceived in the broad spirit of the former, the finish and pedantry of the sonnet make it an artificial form. A master enjoys the task of making its artifice artistic, but does not employ it exclusively. Whitman's irregular, manneristic chant is *at the other extreme of artificiality*, and equally monotonous. A poet can use it with feeling and majesty; but to use it invariably, to laud it as the one mode of future expression, to decry all others, is formalism of a pronounced kind. I have intimated that Whitman has carefully studied and improved it. Even Mr. Burroughs does him injustice in admitting that he is not a poet and artist in the current acceptation of those terms, and another writer simply is just in declaring that when he undertakes to give us poetry he can do it. True, the long prose sentences thrown within his ruder pieces resemble nothing so much as the comic recitativos in the buffo-songs of the concert-cellars. This is not art, nor wisdom, but sensationalism. There is narrowness in his failure to recast and modify these and other depressing portions of various poems, and it is sheer Philistinism for one to coddle all the weaknesses of his experimental period, because they have been a product of himself.

One effect of the constant reading of his poetry is that, like the use of certain refections, it mars our taste for the proper enjoyment of other kinds. Not, of course, because it is wholly superior, since the subtlest landscape by Corot or Rousseau might be utterly put to nought by a melodramatic neighbor, full of positive color and extravagance. Nor is it always, either, to our bard's advantage that he should be read with other poets. Consider Wordsworth's exquisite lyric upon the education which Nature gives the child whom to herself she takes, and of whom she declares:

> The stars of midnight shall be dear
> To her; and she shall lean her ear
> In many a secret place,
> Where rivulets dance their wayward round,
> And beauty born of murmuring sound
> Shall pass into her face.

It happens that Whitman has a poem on the same theme, describing the process of growth by sympathy and absorption, which thus begins and ends:

> There was a child went forth every day;
> And the first object he look'd upon, that object he became;
> And that object became part of him for the day, or a

certain part of the day, or for many years, or stretching cycles of years.

. . .

> The horizon's edge, the flying sea-crow, the fragrance of salt-marsh and shore-mud;
> These became part of that child who went forth every day, and who now goes, and will always go forth every day.

Plainly there are some comparative advantages in Wordsworth's treatment of this idea. It would be just as easy to reverse this showing by quoting other passages from each poet: the purpose of my digression is to declare that by means of comparative criticism any poet may be judged unfairly, and without regard to his general claims.

So far as Mr. Whitman's formalism is natural to him, no matter how eccentric, we must bear with it; whenever it partakes of affectation, it is not to be desired. The charge of attitudinizing, so often brought against his writings and personal career, may be the result of a popular impression that the border-line is indistinct between his self-assertion as a type of Man, and the ordinary self-esteem and self-advancement displayed by men of common mold. Pretensions have this advantage, that they challenge analysis, and make a vast noise even as we are forced to examine them. In the early preface to the *Leaves* there is a passage modeled, in my opinion, upon the style of Emerson, concerning simplicity,—with which I heartily agree, having constantly insisted upon the test of simplicity in my discussion of the English poets. Yet this quality is the last to be discerned in many portions of the *Leaves of Grass*. In its stead we often find boldness, and the "pride that apes humility,"—until the reader is tempted to quote from the "Poet of Feudalism" those words of Cornwall upon the roughness which brought good Kent to the stocks. Our bard's self-assertion, when the expression of his real manhood, is bracing, is an element of poetic strength. When it even seems to be "posing," it is a weakness, or a shrewdness, and 'tis a weakness in a poet to be unduly shrewd. Of course a distinction must be carefully made between the fine extravagance of genius, the joy in its own conceptions, and self-conscious vanity or affectation,—between, also, occasional weaknesses of the great, of men like Browning, and like the greatest of living masters, Hugo, and the afflatus of small men, who only thus far succeed in copying them. And it would be unjust to reckon Whitman among the latter class.

Doubtless his intolerant strictures upon the poets of his own land and time have made them hesitate to venture upon the first advances in brotherhood, or to intrude on him with their recognition of his birthright. As late as his latest edition, his opinion of their uselessness has been expressed in withering terms. It may be that this is merely consistent, an absolute corollary of his new propositions. There is no consistency, however, in a complaint of the silence in which they have submitted to his judgments. They listen to epithets which Heine spared Platen and his clique, and surely Heine would have disdained to permit a cry to go up in his behalf concerning a want of recognition and encouragement from the luckless victims of his irony. There is ground enough for his scorn of the time-serving, unsubstantial quality of much of our literature. But I should not be writing this series of papers, did I not well know that there are other poets than himself who hear the roll of the ages, who look before and after, above and below. The culture which he deprecates may have done them an ill turn in lessening their worldly tact. I am aware that Mr. Whitman's poems are the drama of his own life and passions. His subjectivity is so great that he not only absorbs all others into himself, but insists upon being absorbed by whomsoever he addresses. In his conception of the world's equality, the singer himself appears as the one Messianic personage, the answerer and sustainer, the universal solvent,—in all these respects holding even "Him that was crucified" to be not one whit his superior. It is his kiss, his consolation, that all must receive,—whoever you are, these are given especially to you. But men are egotists, and not all tolerant of one man's selfhood; they do not always deem the affinities elective. Whitman's personality is too strong and individual to be universal, and even to him it is not given to be all things to all men.

ROBERT LOUIS STEVENSON
From "Walt Whitman"
Familiar Studies of Men and Books
1882, pp. 104–12

Of late years the name of Walt Whitman has been a good deal bandied about in books and magazines. It has become familiar both in good and ill repute. His works have been largely bespattered with praise by his admirers, and cruelly mauled and mangled by irreverent enemies. Now, whether his poetry is good or bad as poetry, is a matter that may admit of a difference of opinion without alienating those who differ. We could not keep the peace with a man who should put forward claims to taste and yet depreciate the choruses in *Samson Agonistes*; but, I think, we may shake hands with one who sees no more in Walt Whitman's volume, from a literary point of view, than a farrago of incompetent essays in a wrong direction. That may not be at all our own opinion. We may think that, when a work contains many unforgettable phrases, it cannot be altogether devoid of literary merit. We may even see passages of a high poetry here and there among its eccentric contents. But when all is said, Walt Whitman is neither a Milton nor a Shakespeare; to appreciate his works is not a condition necessary to salvation; and I would not disinherit a son upon the question, nor even think much the worse of a critic, for I should always have an idea what he meant.

What Whitman has to say is another affair from how he says it. It is not possible to acquit any one of defective intelligence, or else stiff prejudice, who is not interested by Whitman's matter and the spirit it represents. Not as a poet, but as what we must call (for lack of a more exact expression) a prophet, he occupies a curious and prominent position. Whether he may greatly influence the future or not, he is a notable symptom of the present. As a sign of the times, it would be hard to find his parallel. I should hazard a large wager, for instance, that he was not unacquainted with the works of Herbert Spencer; and yet where, in all the history books, shall we lay our hands on two more incongruous contemporaries? Mr. Spencer so decorous—I had almost said, so dandy—in dissent; and Whitman, like a large shaggy dog, just unchained, scouring the beaches of the world and baying at the moon. And when was an echo more curiously like a satire, than when Mr. Spencer found his Synthetic Philosophy reverberated from the other shores of the Atlantic in the "barbaric yawp" of Whitman?

Whitman, it cannot be too soon explained, writes up to a system. He was a theorizer about society before he was a poet. He first perceived something wanting, and then sat down squarely to supply the want. The reader, running over his works, will find that he takes nearly as much pleasure in

critically expounding his theory of poetry as in making poems. This is as far as it can be from the case of the spontaneous village minstrel dear to elegy, who has no theory whatever, although sometimes he may have fully as much poetry as Whitman. The whole of Whitman's work is deliberate and preconceived. A man born into a society comparatively new, full of conflicting elements and interests, could not fail, if he had any thoughts at all, to reflect upon the tendencies around him. He saw much good and evil on all sides, not yet settled down into some more or less unjust compromise as in older nations, but still in the act of settlement. And he could not but wonder what it would turn out; whether the compromise would be very just or very much the reverse, and give great or little scope for healthy human energies. From idle wonder to active speculation is but a step; and he seems to have been early struck with the inefficacy of literature and its extreme unsuitability to the conditions. What he calls "Feudal Literature" could have little living action on the tumult of American democracy; what he calls the "Literature of Wo," meaning the whole tribe of Werther and Byron, could have no action for good in any time or place. Both propositions, if art had none but a direct moral influence, would be true enough; and as this seems to be Whitman's view, they were true enough for him. He conceived the idea of a Literature which was to inhere in the life of the present; which was to be, first, human, and next, American; which was to be brave and cheerful as per contract; to give culture in a popular and poetical presentment; and, in so doing, catch and stereotype some democratic ideal of humanity which should be equally natural to all grades of wealth and education, and suited, in one of his favorite phrases, to "the average man." To the formation of some such literature as this his poems are to be regarded as so many contributions, one sometimes explaining, sometimes superseding, the other: and the whole together not so much a finished work as a body of suggestive hints. He does not profess to have built the castle, but he pretends he has traced the lines of the foundation. He has not made the poetry, but he flatters himself he has done something toward making the poets.

His notion of the poetic function is ambitious, and coincides roughly with what Schopenhauer has laid down as the province of the metaphysician. The poet is to gather together for men, and set in order, the materials of their existence. He is "The Answerer;" he is to find some way of speaking about life that shall satisfy, if only for the moment, man's enduring astonishment at his own position. And besides having an answer ready, it is he who shall provoke the question. He must shake people out of their indifference, and force them to make some election in this world, instead of sliding dully forward in a dream. Life is a business we are all apt to mismanage; either living recklessly from day to day, or suffering ourselves to be gulled out of our moments by the inanities of custom. We should despise a man who gave as little activity and forethought to the conduct of any other business. But in this, which is the one thing of all others, since it contains them all, we cannot see the forest for the trees. One brief impression obliterates another. There is something stupefying in the recurrence of unimportant things. And it is only on rare provocations that we can rise to take an outlook beyond daily concerns, and comprehend the narrow limits and great possibilities of our existence. It is the duty of the poet to induce such moments of clear sight. He is the declared enemy of all living by reflex action, of all that is done betwixt sleep and waking, of all the pleasureless pleasurings and imaginary duties in which we coin away our hearts and fritter invaluable years. He has to electrify his readers into an instant unflagging activity, founded on a wide and eager observation of the world, and make them direct their ways by a superior prudence, which has little or nothing in common with the maxims of the copy-book. That many of us lead such lives as they would heartily disown after two hours' serious reflection on the subject is, I am afraid, a true, and, I am sure, a very galling thought. The Enchanted Ground of dead-alive respectability is next, upon the map, to the Beulah of considerate virtue. But there they all slumber and take their rest in the middle of God's beautiful and wonderful universe; the drowsy heads have nodded together in the same position since first their fathers fell asleep; and not even the sound of the last trumpet can wake them to a single active thought. The poet has a hard task before him to stir up such fellows to a sense of their own and other people's principles in life.

And it happens that literature is, in some ways, but an indifferent means to such an end. Language is but a poor bull's-eye lantern wherewith to show off the vast cathedral of the world; and yet a particular thing once said in words is so definite and memorable, that it makes us forget the absence of the many which remain unexpressed; like a bright window in a distant view, which dazzles and confuses our sight of its surroundings. There are not words enough in all Shakespeare to express the merest fraction of a man's experience in an hour. The speed of the eyesight and the hearing, and the continual industry of the mind, produce, in ten minutes, what it would require a laborious volume to shadow forth by comparisons and roundabout approaches. If verbal logic were sufficient, life would be as plain sailing as a piece of Euclid. But, as a matter of fact, we make a travesty of the simplest process of thought when we put it into words; for the words are all colored and forsworn, apply inaccurately, and bring with them, from former uses, ideas of praise and blame that have nothing to do with the question in hand. So we must always see to it nearly, that we judge by the realities of life and not by the partial terms that represent them in man's speech; and at times of choice, we must leave words upon one side, and act upon those brute convictions, unexpressed and perhaps inexpressible, which cannot be flourished in an argument, but which are truly the sum and fruit of our experience. Words are for communication, not for judgment. This is what every thoughtful man knows for himself, for only fools and silly schoolmasters push definitions over far into the domain of conduct; and the majority of women, not learned in these scholastic refinements, live all-of-a-piece and unconsciously, as a tree grows, without caring to put a name upon their acts or motives. Hence, a new difficulty for Whitman's scrupulous and argumentative poet; he must do more than waken up the sleepers to his words; he must persuade them to look over the book and at life with their own eyes.

This side of truth is very present to Whitman; it is this that he means when he tells us that "To glance with an eye confounds the learning of all times." But he is not unready. He is never weary of descanting on the undebatable conviction that is forced upon our minds by the presence of other men, of animals, or of inanimate things. To glance with an eye, were it only at a chair or a park railing, is by far a more persuasive process, and brings us to a far more exact conclusion, than to read the works of all the logicians extant. If both, by a large allowance, may be said to end in certainty, the certainty in the one case transcends the other to an incalculable degree. If people see a lion, they run away; if they only apprehend a deduction, they keep wandering around in an experimental humor. Now, how is the poet to convince like nature, and not like books? Is there no actual piece of nature that he can show

the man to his face, as he might show him a tree if they were walking together? Yes, there is one: the man's own thoughts. In fact, if the poet is to speak efficaciously, he must say what is already in his hearer's mind. That, alone, the hearer will believe; that, alone, he will be able to apply intelligently to the facts of life. Any conviction, even if it be a whole system or a whole religion, must pass into the condition of commonplace, or postulate, before it becomes fully operative. Strange excursions and high-flying theories may interest, but they cannot rule behavior. Our faith is not the highest truth that we perceive, but the highest that we have been able to assimilate into the very texture and method of our thinking. It is not, therefore, by flashing before a man's eyes the weapons of dialectic; it is not by induction, deduction, or construction; it is not by forcing him on from one stage of reasoning to another, that the man will be effectually renewed. He cannot be made to believe anything; but he can be made to see that he has always believed it. And this is the practical canon. It is when the reader cries, "Oh, I know!" and is, perhaps, half irritated to see how nearly the author has forestalled his own thoughts, that he is on the way to what is called in theology a Saving Faith.

Here we have the key to Whitman's attitude. To give a certain unity of ideal to the average population of America—to gather their activities about some conception of humanity that shall be central and normal, if only for the moment—the poet must portray that population as it is. Like human law, human poetry is simply declaratory. If any ideal is possible, it must be already in the thoughts of the people; and, by the same reason, in the thoughts of the poet, who is one of them. And hence Whitman's own formula: "The poet is individual—he is complete in himself: the others are as good as he; only he sees it, and they do not." To show them how good they are, the poet must study his fellow-countrymen and himself somewhat like a traveller on the hunt for his book of travels. There is a sense, of course, in which all true books are books of travel; and all genuine poets must run their risk of being charged with the traveller's exaggeration; for to whom are such books more surprising than to those whose own life is faithfully and smartly pictured? But this danger is all upon one side; and you may judiciously flatter the portrait without any likelihood of the sitter's disowning it for a faithful likeness. And so Whitman has reasoned: that by drawing at first hand from himself and his neighbors, accepting without shame the inconsistencies and brutalities that go to make up man, and yet treating the whole in a high, magnanimous spirit, he would make sure of belief, and at the same time encourage people forward by the means of praise.

WALKER KENNEDY
From "Walt Whitman"

North American Review, June 1884, pp. 593–601

What is the *raison d'être* of *Leaves of Grass*? Has the author ever stated in intelligible English the purpose of his book? Is its aim moral, political, scientific, æsthetic? Is it written in the interest of democracy, or of the intellectual classes? Very likely its author would claim that its purpose is collective. Has it inspired any one with greater love for humanity; has it caused the torch of patriotism in the hand of any individual to burn the brighter; has it lifted a single soul from its despair; has it brought sunshine to any heart; has it given new hopes; has it sweetened religion; has it encouraged science; has it given new wings to the imagination; has it led the intellect into new paths of light and knowledge; has it cleared up any of our doubts or thrown the slightest ray of helpful light upon our questionings? If it has done none of these things, the reason of its being is not apparent.

But, some of Mr. Whitman's admirers say, it is written from a democratic stand-point. If this is the case, the people ought to be able to understand it; but the ordinary man would regard *Leaves of Grass* as the production of a maniac. Only the "gifted few" can discover any sense in *Leaves of Grass*; and what particular message they get from it is past the comprehension of one of the ungifted many. The work, of course, is defective in its literary form. Even its author admits that. Moreover, it has the faults of bad grammar, incomplete sentences, misuse of words, and incoherence of ideas. There is about as much consecutiveness in the *Song of Myself* as there is in a dream originating in too much shrimp salad for supper. A transcript of the dream would be as valuable as the *Song of Myself*.

Mr. Whitman says that "the volumes were intended to be most decided, serious, *bona fide* expressions of an identical individual personality—egotism if you choose, for I shall not quarrel about the word." In this connection, Mr. Whitman quotes a saying of Carlyle's, that "there is no grand poem in the world but is at bottom a biography—the life of a man." It is noticeable here that Carlyle does not say an autobiography. Mr. Whitman is mistaken. The "ego" is usually voted a nuisance in fiction and works of imagination. And it is just as well for us to continue setting down as a vain and disagreeable fellow the man who speaks always of himself as if he were the universe. Egotism hardly does justice to Mr. Whitman's condition. It should be termed the delirium of self-conceit.

The *Song of Myself* is probably a fair sample of Walt Whitman's style and purposes, and there is no injustice in judging him by it. If the critic or the laborious reader were to devote himself to this "poem," what would he find in it? I will attempt a partial summary of it. He begins by saying "I celebrate myself and sing myself." After celebrating and singing himself, he continues: "I loafe, and invite my soul." We may define him then to be a sort of loafer-poet. Having shown that he is not too much of a loafer to be a poet, and *vice versa*, he continues: "I harbor for good or bad. I permit to speak at every hazard nature without check, with original energy." In other words, he erases the words restraint, modesty, and shame from his vocabulary, and drops the distinction between decency and indecency. He would confound all our previous conceptions of good and evil; and, if his theory were carried out, where would be maidenly modesty and youthful delicacy? He might as well contend that everybody should forswear clothes and strut about *in puris naturalibus*. The poet begins his pilgrimage in houses full of fragrance; then he goes out in the air to the bank by the wood and becomes undisguised and naked. "I am mad," he says, "for the air to come in contact with me." This is the language of the lunatic asylum rather than of poetry. Then follows an enumeration of abstract and concrete things, about which he predicates nothing. It reminds one of the negro's story of the storm that blew down the house but left the roof standing. The poet fails to provide an adequate support for his words, but leaves them suspended in mid-air. After he has made mincemeat of these barbaric phrases, he says: "Stop this day and night with me, and you shall possess the origin of all poems." In the phantasmagoria that follows, if the reader can discover the origin of anything, he is entitled to it. Whitman continues:

> There was never any more inception than there is now,
> Nor any more youth or age than there is now;
> And will never be any more perfection than there is now,
> Nor any more heaven or hell than there is now.

This is the climax of nonsense, and carries one back to the alleged philosophers who claimed that motion was an impossibility, and pain a myth. What becomes of evolution, progress, civilization? There could be no more depressing belief than this, for it means nothing but universal death. Fortunately, it is disproved by science, by history, and by religion. After winging his way through another space of inky obscurity, the poet says: "The unseen is proved by the seen, till that becomes unseen and receives proof in its turn." Now what does this mean? He starts out with the seen, which needs no proof, and establishes from it the unseen. So far, it is clear; but now the seen becomes unseen, and receives proof in turn. Proof of what? That it is unseen. The necessity for proving the unseen is not apparent. If the poet intends to convey the idea that there is an invisible order of things, an unseen universe, why does he not say so? And if he did, it is not a matter of proof or demonstration, but of hope and conjecture. His dictum is mere verbal jugglery.

The poet then exalts his body, and this physical delirium runs all through the song at intervals; but there is no new and divine message here. The doctors tell us that the body is not vile, nor any of its parts; and when a genuine poet called it the temple of God, he said all that was necessary to say concerning it. Whitman "believes in the flesh and the appetites," meaning libidinous desire. In this respect he is not unlike the libertine. Indeed, this *Song of Myself* is the chant of the *roué*. Resuming, he enumerates the people around him, the events happening about him, the battles, the feelings, anything and everything that chances to run in his mind, and concerning them all he says:

> These come to me days and nights, and go from me again,
> But they are not the Me myself.

Has this passage any meaning? Whitman says he is not a battle, or a fever, or a dress, or a dinner, or a compliment. Neither is he a pancake, a turnip, or a sardine. If he means that his soul stands apart from and uncontrolled by matter, why does he not say so? If he means the contrary, why not say so? If he means that he is a mere isolated spectator of human events, is it not easy enough for him to make his meaning clear to the average intellect?

Then he announces to his soul that he believes in it, and goes on to chant: "Loafe with me on the grass, loose the stop from your throat," etc. Naturally, one would infer that he was still addressing his soul. If so, he becomes ridiculous; for he gives the soul a throat and a voice. When we read farther we find he is addressing someone else, but whom we cannot divine. He says:

> I mind how once we lay, such a transparent summer morning, etc.

The matter that follows is too vulgar for quotation. The passage is simply nauseating and devoid of sense.

The next incident is a child's bringing him a handful of grass, and asking him what it is. Of course, he does not know, but he proceeds to make up a wild "yawp" about it, nevertheless; and he drifts next to the subject of death, and says it is as lucky to die as to be born, and he knows it. For one, I don't believe he knows anything of the kind. He says:

I am not an earth, nor an adjunct of an earth;
I am the mate and companion of people, all just as
Immortal and fathomless as myself;
(They do not know how immortal, but I know).

Nor is he a comet, a meteor, or a ring of Saturn. "They do not know how immortal they are, but I know," is evidently regarded by him as a valuable bit of confidence. The plebeian mind, however, will wonder how there can be degrees of immortality. We could just as well ask how long a man would live if he lived forever.

Now follows another jungle of people and things, which he says are for him; but he omits to say why they are "for him," and what he intends doing with them. Let us catalogue them in regular order: Male and female, boys, those that love women, the proud man, the sweetheart, the old maid, mothers, mothers of mothers, lips, eyes, children, the baby, the youngster, the red-faced girl, the suicide, the corpse, the blab of the pave, tires of carts, sluff of boot-soles, talk of promenaders, omnibus, driver, sleighs, clank of horses, jokes, snowballs, hurrahs, the mob's fury, flap of litter, a sick man, meeting of enemies, oaths, blows, a fall, crowd, policeman, stones, groans, exclamations, speech, arrests, slights, assignations, rejections, etc. The writer gives us here a bare enumeration of living beings, inanimate objects, abstractions, that have no bearing on each other, obey no sequence, and teach no lesson. An inroad into Mitchell's geography would be far more significant and useful. As a description of a street scene it is lame, hueless, and unnatural.

The bard's next transition is to the country; but he fails to give us any connecting links to show whence he went, why he went, or whither he went, though he does not fail to tell us what he did when he got there. He did exactly what one would expect him to do, after one has read the *Song of Myself* up to this point. Instead of acting as a rational man, he "jumps from the cross-beams of the wagon, seizes the clover and timothy, and rolls head over heels and tangles his hair full of wisps." This kind of individual would jump out of a third-story window, instead of contenting himself with viewing the prospect through it. He is next hunting out in the wilds; then he is at sea; then at a clambake; then at the marriage of a trapper and an Indian girl. A runaway slave comes to his house and sits next to him at his table. This episode fixes his attention for a moment, and his mind wanders again, and he sees twenty-eight young men bathing by the shore—

Twenty-eight young men, and all so friendly:
Twenty-eight years of womanly life, and all so
lonesome.

In the next paragraph the poet says:

She owns the fine house by the rise of the bank;
She hides, handsome and richly drest, aft the blinds
of the window.
Which of the young men does she like the best?
Ah, the homeliest of them is beautiful to her.
Where are you off to, lady? for I see you;
You splash in the water there, yet stay stock still in
your room.
Dancing and laughing along the beach came the
twenty-ninth bather;
The rest did not see her, but she saw them and loved
them.
The beards of the young men glistened with wet, it
ran from their long hair:
Little streams pass'd all over their bodies.
An unseen hand also pass'd over their bodies;
It descended tremblingly from their temples and ribs.

Who they are, what they have to do with the poem, how they could lead twenty-eight years of "womanly" life, what difference it makes whether they were so friendly and so lonesome or not, how they could be so lonesome if there were twenty-eight of them, and how they could be so friendly if they were all lonesome, are a few of the riddles suggesting themselves to the mind of the unbeliever in reading this passage. It has been suggested to me that the paragraph is intended as a picture of twenty-eight women who are lonesome because deprived of the society of twenty-eight men who are accustomed to associate together to the neglect of the women; but the phrase "twenty-eight years of womanly life" is hardly synonymous with "twenty-eight women." And who is this mysterious "she," and what is she doing? Is she engaged in the unmaidenly act of watching the men bathe? If there is any suggestiveness here except the suggestiveness of an unclean mind, it is not apparent.

By this time the reader is in a positive whirl; but the poet continues to exhibit his wax-works, and introduces the butcherboy, the blacksmith, and possibly the baker and the candlestick maker. He next sees a negro driving a dray, and from him he goes by the usual degrees to the wild gander leading his flock. A little further on, "the pure contralto sings in the organ loft," and "the carpenter dresses his plank." Another convulsion seizes the writer at this juncture, and he gives us a catalogue of all sorts of people and professions. He jumps from a steam-boat to a ball, from one of the seasons to one of the States. At one time he is in Missouri, and at another in a street-car. There is no telling where he will alight next.

It would not be profitable to carry the analysis further. It is evident that the *Song of Myself* leads nowhither, and that it is the unsystematic, unpruned expression of a very peculiar mind. A few more quotations may be pardoned, as showing to what extremes language can go. For instance, this abrupt paragraph:

Who goes there? hankering, gross, mystical, nude;
How is it I extract strength from the beef I eat?

It is, of course, impossible for the reader to say who goes there. Possibly he doesn't care. As for the second question, that may be respectfully referred to the physiologist, who can answer it to any man's satisfaction. One fails to see what the bard is hankering after, and why he is nude. The connection between his being mystical and his eating beef is also a mystery, from which he has not lifted the veil. Again he says:

I do not snivel that snivel the world over,
That months are vacuums, and the ground but
wallow and filth.

In one place he says, "I know that I am deathless," and in another declares himself a materialist. He speaks of the sea as the "howler and scooper of storms." He finds the scent of the armpits "aroma finer than prayer." These quotations might be strung out endlessly, but they would afford merely cumulative proof of the rankest kind of rebellion against common sense. It is not to be denied that at times the reader detects the gleam of the diamond in this mass of rubbish. The poet has evidently thought and read of many things, but his comments convey a hint of indigestion. When one finishes reading the *Song of Myself*, it is impossible for him to give a rational review of what it is, and what it is intended to teach. It is a failure, because the writer has neglected that very art which he professes to despise. The word "art," which is as wide in its significance as the heavens, has often been degraded by careless thinkers into a synonym of form, when it is in reality the execution of truth. Thought is never valuable unless it is clear and comprehensible. An obscure thought is hueless, tasteless, and devoid of nourishment. If Mr. Whitman's thinking is obscure, it is not worth the preserving. On the other hand, his thoughts may be true and clear, but he may lack fitting expression, just as a man may have a perfect conception of harmony and have no voice for song. It is in giving adequate, tangible expression to clean, valuable thinking, that the writer or poet justifies himself. He should have something to tell, and he should tell it. Unless he can do so, he has no business posing as a poet. Shakespeare found the English language and the established modes of composition spacious enough for his transcendent genius. Cicero, Virgil, and Horace were not trammeled by the polished completeness of Latin. Dante could express all his thoughts in artistic Italian, while Goethe and Schiller never thought of rebelling against the rules of German grammar and the accepted modes of composition. The man who has a story to build will never fail for want of verbal tools; if he falters, it will be because he knows not how to use them. If he has a message to deliver, wings are convenient; but he must know how to fly with them. We have a right to insist that a definite subject or story shall be selected, and that it shall be developed artistically, and in such a way as to be grasped. When Wagner, the musical revolutionist, set about the consummation of his theories, every musician understood perfectly what his theories were, though many angrily doubted and denied that music could respond to the call he made upon it. In all his labor there were system, consecutiveness, and art; otherwise, he would have failed. Has Mr. Whitman enunciated an intelligible theory? He speaks vaguely about poetry being written under the influence of our democratic institutions. Well and good. Now, Dame Columbia may insist on free thought and free speech; but she is not maudlin, nor incoherent. Her head is clear, her mien self-reliant, her actions brisk and animated, her perception acute, and her imagination warm and glowing. There is nothing confused or aimless about her. A literature in accord with democracy would partake of these attributes. If Mr. Whitman desires an original American literature, his plea is praiseworthy. The material for a literature that will do honor to the English tongue is to be found in this country, and the mine is now being worked. I feel no hesitation in saying that the spirit of Mr. Whitman's poetry is the contrary of the democratic spirit, because it is deficient in clearness, in consistency, in art, and in common sense. At first blush there may seem to be a kinship of liberty; but the liberty of democracy is the highest evolutionary step in the struggle for the rights of man, while the liberty of Walt Whitman's poetry is license of thought and anarchy of expression. Most people take pride in conquering the thoughts which he takes a riotous glee in giving vent to.

The thinking man of to-day finds himself beset with incrowding problems, and the mission of literature should be to relieve him from the depressing sense of the infinities. In no way can cheer be flashed into his darkened, perplexed mind except by preserving as a holy thing his faith in the unseen and spiritual, by keeping a line perpetually drawn between the just and the unjust, by placing what is good aloft in conspicuous splendor and sending evil to the gloomy shadows below; by preserving the ideals of purity and "sweetness and light"; by fixing virtue on a lasting pedestal and dethroning vice from its seat in the hearts of men. The man who obscures these valuable results of moral teaching, who leaves a doubt in the mind as to whether good is preferable to evil, who exalts the flesh—that incubus upon the loftiest dreams of purity—and calls the soul the body, can hardly be considered as bringing

with him a message that we are bound either to receive or to respect.

ALGERNON CHARLES SWINBURNE
"Whitmania"
Fortnightly Review, August 1887, pp. 170–76

The remarkable American rhapsodist who has inoculated a certain number of English readers and writers with the singular form of ethical and æsthetic rabies for which his name supplies the proper medical term of definition is usually regarded by others than Whitmaniacs as simply a blatant quack—a vehement and emphatic dunce, of incomparable vanity and volubility, inconceivable pretentions, and incompetence. That such is by no means altogether my own view I need scarcely take the trouble to protest. Walt Whitman has written some pages to which I have before now given praise enough to exonerate me, I should presume, from any charge of prejudice or prepossession against a writer whose claims to occasional notice and occasional respect no man can be less desirous to dispute than I am. Nor should I have thought it necessary to comment on the symptoms of a disorder which happily is not likely to become epidemic in an island or on a continent not utterly barren of poetry, had the sufferers not given such painfully singular signs of inability to realize a condition only too obvious to the compassionate bystander. While the preachers or the proselytes of the gospel according to Whitman were content to admit that he was either no poet at all, or the only poet who had ever been born into this world— that those who accepted him were bound to reject all others as nullities—they had at least the merit of irrefragable logic; they could claim at least the credit of indisputable consistency. But when other gods or godlings are accepted as participants in the divine nature; when his temple is transformed into a pantheon, and a place assigned his godhead a little beneath Shakespeare, a little above Dante, or cheek by jowl with Homer; when Isaiah and Æschylus, for anything we know, may be admitted to a greater or lesser share in his incommunicable and indivisible supremacy—then, indeed, it is high time to enter a strenuous and (if it be possible) a serious protest. The first apostles alone were the depositaries of the pure and perfect evangel: these later and comparatively heterodox disciples have adulterated and debased the genuine metal of absolute, coherent, unalloyed and unqualifed nonsense.

To the better qualities discernible in the voluminous and incoherent effusions of Walt Whitman it should not be difficult for any reader not unduly exasperated by the rabid idiocy of the Whitmaniacs to do full and ample justice: for these qualities are no less simple and obvious than laudable and valuable. A just enthusiasm, a genuine passion of patriotic and imaginative sympathy, a sincere though limited and distorted love of nature, an eager and earnest faith in freedom and in loyalty—in the loyalty that can only be born of liberty; a really manful and a nobly rational tone of mind with regard to the crowning questions of duty and of death; these excellent qualities of emotion and reflection find here and there a not inadequate expression in a style of rhetoric not always flatulent or inharmonious. Originality of matter or of manner, of structure or of thought, it would be equally difficult for any reader not endowed with a quite exceptional gift of ignorance or of hebetude to discover in any part of Mr. Whitman's political or ethical or physical or proverbial philosophy. But he has said wise and noble things upon such simple and eternal subjects as life and death, pity and enmity, friendship and fighting; and even the intensely conventional nature of its elaborate and artificial simplicity should not be allowed, by a magnanimous and candid reader, too absolutely to eclipse the genuine energy and the occasional beauty of his feverish and convulsive style of writing.

All this may be cordially conceded by the lovers of good work in any kind, however imperfect, incomposite, and infirm; and more than this the present writer at any rate most assuredly never intended to convey by any tribute of sympathy or admiration which may have earned for him the wholly unmerited honour of an imaginary enlistment in the noble army of Whitmaniacs. He has therefore no palinode to chant, no recantation to intone; for if it seems and is unreasonable to attribute a capacity of thought to one who has never given any sign of thinking, a faculty of song to one who has never shown ability to sing, it must be remembered, on the other hand, that such qualities of energetic emotion and sonorous expression as distinguish the happier moments and the more sincere inspirations of such writers as Whitman or as Byron have always, in common parlance, been allowed to pass muster and do duty for the faculty of thinking or the capacity of singing. Such an use of common terms is doubtless inaccurate and inexact, if judged by the "just but severe law" of logical definition or of mathematical precision: but such abuse or misuse of plain words is generally understood as conveying no more than a conventional import such as may be expressed by the terms with which we subscribe an ordinary letter, or by the formula through which we decline an untimely visit. Assuredly I never have meant to imply what most assuredly I never have said—that I regarded Mr. Whitman as a poet or a thinker in the proper sense; the sense in which the one term is applicable to Coleridge or to Shelley, the other to Bacon or to Mill. Whoever may have abdicated his natural right, as a being not born without a sense of music or a sense of reason, to protest against the judgment which discerns in *Childe Harold* or in *Drum-Taps* a masterpiece of imagination and expression, of intelligence or of song, I never have abdicated mine. The highest literary quality discoverable in either book is rhetoric: and very excellent rhetoric in either case it sometimes is; what it is at other times I see no present necessity to say. But Whitmaniacs and Byronites have yet to learn that if rhetoric were poetry John Bright would be a poet at least equal to John Milton, Demosthenes to Sophocles, and Cicero to Catullus. Poetry may be something more—I certainly am not concerned to deny it—than an art or a science; but not because it is not, stricly speaking, a science or an art. There is a science of verse as surely as there is a science of mathematics: there is an art of expression by metre as certainly as there is an art of representation by painting. To some poets the understanding of this science, the mastery of this art, would seem to come by a natural instinct which needs nothing but practice for its development, its application, and its perfection: others by patient and conscientious study of their own abilities attain a no less unmistakable and a scarcely less admirable success. But the man of genius and the dullard who cannot write good verse are equally out of the running. "Did you ask dulcet rhymes from me?" inquires Mr. Whitman of some extraordinary if not imaginary interlocutor; and proceeds, with some not ineffective energy of expression, to explain that "I lull nobody—and you will never understand me." No, my dear good sir—or camerado, if that be the more courteous and conventional address (a modest reader might deferentially reply): not in the wildest visions of a distempered slumber could I ever have dreamed of doing anything of the kind. Nor do we ask them

even from such other and inferior scribes or bards as the humble Homer, the modest Milton, or the obsolete and narrow-minded Shakespeare—poets of sickly feudality, of hidebound classicism, of effete and barbarous incompetence. But metre, rhythm, cadence not merely appreciable but definable and reducible to rule and measurement, though we do not expect from you, we demand from all who claim, we discern in the works of all who have achieved, any place among poets of any class whatsoever. The question whether your work is in any sense poetry has no more to do with dulcet rhymes than with the differential calculus. The question is whether you have any more right to call yourself a poet, or to be called a poet by any man who knows verse from prose, or black from white, or speech from silence, or his right hand from his left, than to call yourself or to be called, on the strength of your published writings, a mathematician, a logician, a painter, a political economist, a sculptor, a dynamiter, an old parliamentary hand, a civil engineer, a dealer in marine stores, an amphimacer, a triptych, a rhomboid, or a rectangular parallelogram. "Vois-tu bien, tu es baron comme ma pantoufle!" said old Gillenormand—the creature of one who was indeed a creator or a poet: and the humblest of critics who knows any one thing from any one other thing has a right to say to the man who offers as poetry what the exuberant incontinence of a Whitman presents for our acceptance—"Tu es poète comme mon—soulier."

But the student has other and better evidence than any merely negative indication of impotence in the case of the American as in the case of the British despiser and disclaimer of so pitiful a profession or ambition as that of a versifier. Mr. Carlyle and Mr. Whitman have both been good enough to try their hands at lyric verse: and the ear which has once absorbed their dulcet rhymes will never need to be reminded of the reason for their contemptuous abhorrence of a diversion so contemptible as the art of Coleridge and Shelley.

>   Out of eternity
>   This new day is born:
>   Into eternity
>   This day shall return.

Such were the flute-notes of Diogenes Devilsdung: comparable by those who would verify the value of his estimate with any stanza of Shelley's "To a Skylark." And here is a sample of the dulcet rhymes which a most tragic occasion succeeded in evoking from the orotund oratist of Manhattan.

>   The port is near, the bells I hear, the people all
>   exulting,
>   *While follow eyes the steady keel*, the vessel grim and
>   daring;
>   . . .
>   For you bouquets and ribbon'd wreaths—for you the
>   shores a-crowding; *(sic)*
>   For you they call, the surging mass, their eager faces
>   turning.

Ἰοὺ ἰού, ὣ ὣ κακά. Upon the whole, I prefer Burns—or Hogg—to Carlyle, and Dibdin—or Catnach—to Whitman. A pedantic writer of poems distilled from other poems (which, as the immortal author of the imperishable *Leaves of Grass* is well aware, must "pass away")—a Wordsworth, for example, or a Tennyson—would hardly have made "eyes" follow the verb they must be supposed to govern. Nor would a poor creature whose ear was yet unattuned to the cadence of "chants democratic" have permitted his Pegasus so remarkable a capriole as to result in the rhythmic reverberation of such rhymes as these. When a boy who remains unable after many efforts to cross the Asses' Bridge expresses his opinion that Euclid was a beastly old fool, his obviously impartial verdict is generally received by his elders with exactly the same amount of respectful attention as is accorded by any competent reader to the equally valuable and judicial deliverances of Messrs. Whitman, Emerson, and Carlyle on the subject of poetry—that is, of lyrical or creative literature. The first critic of our time—perhaps the largest-minded and surest-sighted of any age—has pointed out, in an essay on poetry which should not be too long left buried in the columns of the *Encyclopædia Britannica*, the exhaustive accuracy of the Greek terms which define every claimant to the laurel as either a singer or a maker. There is no third term, as there is no third class. If then it appears that Mr. Walt Whitman has about as much gift of song as his precursors and apparent models in rhythmic structure and style, Mr. James Macpherson and Mr. Martin Tupper, his capacity for creation is the only thing that remains for us to consider. And on that score we find him, beyond all question, rather like the later than like the earlier of his masters. Macpherson could at least evoke shadows: Mr. Tupper and Mr. Whitman can only accumulate words. As to his originality in the matter of free speaking, it need only be observed that no remarkable mental gift is requisite to qualify man or woman for membership of a sect mentioned by Dr. Johnson—the Adamites, who believed in the virtue of public nudity. If those worthies claimed the right to bid their children run about the streets stark naked, the magistrate, observed Johnson, "would have a right to flog them into their doublets;" a right no plainer than the right of common sense and sound criticism to flog the Whitmaniacs into their strait-waistcoats; or, were there any female members of such a sect, into their strait-petticoats. If nothing that concerns the physical organism of men or of women is common or unclean or improper for literary manipulation, it may be maintained, by others than the disciples of a contemporary French novelist who has amply proved the sincerity of his own opinion to that effect, that it is not beyond the province of literature to describe with realistic exuberance of detail the functions of digestion or indigestion in all its processes—the objects and the results of an aperient or an emetic medicine. Into "the troughs of Zolaism," as Lord Tennyson calls them (a phrase which bears rather unduly hard on the quadrupedal pig), I am happy to believe that Mr. Whitman has never dipped a passing nose: he is a writer of something occasionally like English, and a man of something occasionally like genius. But in his treatment of topics usually regarded as no less unfit for public exposition and literary illustration than those which have obtained notoriety for the would-be bastard of Balzac—the Davenant of the (French) prose Shakespeare, he has contrived to make "the way of a man with a maid" (Proverbs xxx. 19) almost as loathsomely ludicrous and almost as ludicrously loathsome—I speak merely of the æsthetic or literary aspect of his effusions—as the Swiftian or Zolaesque enthusiasm of bestiality which insists on handling what "goeth into the belly, and is cast out into the draught" (St. Mark xv. 17). The Zolas and the Whitmen, to whom nothing, absolutely and literally nothing, is unclean or common, have an obvious and incalculable advantage over the unconverted who have never enjoyed the privilege of a vision like St. Peter's, and received the benefit of a supernatural prohibition to call anything common or unclean. They cannot possibly be exposed, and they cannot possibly be put to shame: for that best of all imaginable reasons which makes it proverbially difficult to "take the breeks off a Highlander."

It would really seem as though, in literary and other matters, the very plainness and certitude of a principle made it doubly necessary for those who maintain it to enforce and reinforce it over and over again; as though, the more obvious it were, the more it needed indication and demonstration, assertion and reassertion. There is no more important, no more radical and fundamental truth of criticism than this: that, in poetry perhaps above all other arts, the method of treatment, the manner of touch, the tone of expression, is the first and last thing to be considered. There is no subject which may not be treated with success (I do not say there are no subjects which on other than artistic grounds it may not be as well to avoid, it may not be better to pass by) if the poet, by instinct or by training, knows exactly how to handle it aright, to present it without danger of just or rational offence. For evidence of this truth we need look no further than the pastorals of Virgil and Theocritus. But under the dirty clumsy paws of a harper whose plectrum is a muck-rake any tune will become a chaos of discords, though the motive of the tune should be the first principle of nature—the passion of man for woman or the passion of woman for man. And the unhealthily demonstrative and obtrusive animalism of the Whitmaniad is as unnatural, as incompatible with the wholesome instincts of human passion, as even the filthy and inhuman asceticism of SS. Macarius and Simeon Stylites. If anything can justify the serious and deliberate display of merely physical emotion in literature or in art, it must be one of two things: intense depth of feeling expressed with inspired perfection of simplicity, with divine sublimity of fascination, as by Sappho; or transcendant supremacy of actual and irresistible beauty in such revelation of naked nature as was possible to Titian. But Mr. Whitman's Eve is a drunken apple-woman, indecently sprawling in the slush and garbage of the gutter amid the rotten refuse of her overturned fruit-stall: but Mr. Whitman's Venus is a Hottentot wench under the influence of cantharides and adulterated rum. Cotytto herself would repudiate the ministration of such priestesses as these.

But what then, if anything, is it that a rational creature who has studied and understood the work of any poet, great or small, from Homer down to Moschus, from Lucretius down to Martial, from Dante down to Metastasio, from Villon down to Voltaire, from Shakespeare down to Byron, can find to applaud, to approve, or to condone in the work of Mr. Whitman? To this very reasonable and inevitable question the answer is not far to seek. I have myself repeatedly pointed out—it may be (I have often been told so) with too unqualified sympathy and too uncritical enthusiasm—the qualities which give a certain touch of greatness to his work, the sources of inspiration which infuse into its chaotic jargon some passing or seeming notes of cosmic beauty, and diversify with something of occasional harmony the strident and barren discord of its jarring and erring atoms. His sympathies, I repeat, are usually generous, his views of life are occasionally just, and his views of death are invariably noble. In other words, he generally means well, having a good stock on hand of honest emotion; he sometimes sees well, having a natural sensibility to such aspects of nature as appeal to an eye rather quick than penetrating; he seldom writes well, being cabined, cribbed, confined, bound in, to the limits of a thoroughly unnatural, imitative, histrionic and affected style. But there is a thrilling and fiery force in his finest bursts of gusty rhetoric which makes us wonder whether with a little more sense and a good deal more cultivation he might not have made a noticeable orator. As a poet, no amount of improvement that self-knowledge and self-culture might have brought to bear upon such exceptionally raw material could ever have raised him higher than a station to which his homely and manly patriotism would be the best claim that could be preferred for him; a seat beside such writers as Ebenezer Elliot—or possibly a little higher, on such an elevation as might be occupied by a poet whom careful training had reared and matured into a rather inferior kind of Southey. But to fit himself for such promotion he would have in the first place to resign all claim to the laurels of Gotham, with which the critical sages of that famous borough have bedecked his unbashful brows; he would have to recognise that he is no more, in the proper sense of the word, a poet, than Communalists or Dissolutionists are, in any sense of the word, Republicans; that he has exactly as much claim to a place beside Dante as any Vermersch or Vermorel or other verminous and murderous muckworm of the Parisian Commune to a place beside Mazzini: in other words, that the informing principle of his work is not so much the negation as the contradiction of the creative principle of poetry. And this it is not to be expected that such a man should bring himself to believe, as long as he hears himself proclaimed the inheritor of a seat assigned a hundred years ago by the fantastic adulation of more or less distinguished literary eccentrics to a person of the name of Jephson—whose triumphs as a tragic poet made his admirers tremble for Shakespeare.

PAULINE W. ROOSE
From "A Child-Poet: Walt Whitman"

Gentleman's Magazine, May 1892, pp. 473–80

His imagination being of a character at once wild and practical, he exhibits the most fantastic notions in a matter-of-fact manner, as if they were nothing out of the way. With a child's spirit of wilful self-deception he tries to beguile himself into the belief that the birds in his favourite haunts sing and fly about for his especial benefit, and repays such of them as have mainly contributed to his comfort with the dedication of a part of one of his books; nor them only, but likewise a whole array of trees and insects, amid whose motley crew the mosquitoes are honoured by particular mention. Nor is he by any means sure but that those queer allies of his will somehow get wind of the compliment. In a sublimer mood he has fancied the ocean and the daylight, the mountain and the forest, putting their spirit in judgment on our writings.

Independently of all witchcraft and fairy lore, he can create for himself the very miracles and transformations of which the little ones are always dreaming. The old woodland kings, in his belief, hold great thoughts, which they drop down upon him as he passes beneath them. There was a small boy who once prayed that God would make the trees walk. This very conceit was almost realised by the vivid fancy of Walt Whitman, who, in a "sort of dream-trance," as he calls it, beheld his favourite trees "step out and promenade up, down, and around, very curiously—with a whisper from one, leaning down as he passed me: 'We do all this on the present occasion, exceptionally, just for you.'" That they could do it if they chose seems indeed to be his deliberate opinion.

Children are notably devoid of humour, and in Whitman that quality is conspicuous by its absence. Who, however, better than children—or than Whitman—can appeal to the humour of others? There is something touching in the unconsciousness with which he lays himself open to the sneers of whoever may be willing to avail himself of the opportunity. His sense of fun, of which he has his full share, never interferes with the most preposterous statements on his own part, even while he allows no oddity of life nor any ludicrous effect of

nature to escape him. Of what has been called the *cockneyism* of the nineteenth century not a trace is to be found in him, nor of the modern smartness and indifference. He cannot content himself with superficial views any more than childhood can be put off with the flippant answers which grown-up persons of a certain calibre amuse themselves by returning to its earnest questionings. Life to him is not a speculation nor a "bon-mot." He does not profess to know what it is, "except that it is grand, and that it is happiness"; also (and this above all), that it is never ending, and that death will make no very appreciable difference in it.

"I have dreamed," he says, with one of those sudden startling glimpses which he is in the habit of flashing, not only backward upon the past but onward into the future, "that we are not to be changed so much, nor the law of us changed."

Amid what to others might seem the most appalling, most annihilating discoveries in science, he moves familiarly as in his old paternal homestead, and finds in them the wholesomest nutriment for his dreams of universal joy and immortality. For it is not in his relations to earth alone that he maintains his trustful attitude. A child of the universe, he can not only look with unflinching gaze at the sun in its noon-day splendour, but he loves also to blend himself with the shadows, to creep into the very heart of midnight, that he may come upon the "budding morrow" there, and discover it to others. For of the child no less than of the philosopher it is a distinctive attribute to be everywhere at home. With his unbiassed spiritual vision he can discern, through all the perplexities of life, that "divine clue and unseen thread which holds the whole congeries of things, all history and time, and all events, however trivial, however momentous, like a leashed dog in the hand of the hunter." The "ultimate perfecton" toward which all, according to his judgment, are tending, links everything, from the lowest to the highest, together in one unbroken chain:

> All, all for immortality,
> Love like the light silently wrapping all,
> Nature's amelioration blessing all. . . .

"Is it a dream?" he pauses in his rapt soliloquy to ask:

> Nay, but the lack of it the dream,
> And failing it life's lore and wealth a dream,
> And all the world a dream.

His thoughts, like those of the old philosophers (or *philosophs*, as, with his peculiar partiality for the suggestion of something foreign in a word, he calls them), flit from present to past and back again with sympathetic quickness. Many a passage, indeed, from Marcus Aurelius in particular, in its unadorned enumeration of things passing under his notice, its unexpected rapid turns of observation and keen appreciation of effect, might have been penned—all but the moral—by Walt Whitman. The poet of to-day, in very much the manner of the Imperial philosopher of old, is given to reflect how all those who have gone before, who have "feasted and married, and were sick and chaffered, and fought, and flattered, and plotted, and grumbled . . . are dead; and all the idle people who are doing the same thing now are doomed to die." Only Whitman cannot reconcile himself, as did the Emperor of old, to the thought of man's nothingness; that oblivion is to swallow up all him and his:

> O, I know that those men and women were not for
>   nothing, any more than we are for nothing. . . .
> I believe of all those men and women that filled the
>   unnamed lands, everyone exists this hour here
>   or elsewhere, invisible to us.

He will not believe that seventy years, "nor that seventy

millions of years" (with a child's love of large impressions), is the span of human life. He is too sure of his own identity to be afraid of ever losing it. Nor in his eyes do the most fleeting, the most insignificant of things appear ephemeral and worthless. The music of humanity is by no means still and sad to him; there is no lost chord in its harmonies. Past, present, and to-come are blent in one bright, invigorating strain of trust and promise. His is the optimism of a child, as different from the shallow, unreal hopes with which some are able to content themselves as the void Nirvana is from Paradise. He clings to present possessions, and would have nothing but the merest accidents of evil done away with, if even them; for Whitman has all the defects of his quality, amongst which inconsistency is by no means least. Emerson's doctrine that what is excellent is permanent does not suffice for him. Opinions differ as to what is excellent. Things which to some may not come within that definition belong, with others, to their hopes of heaven.

Now and then, with something of that vague, unspeakable reluctance peculiar almost to childhood, he will entertain the possibility of his being deceived. Amid his sense of what is real, the misgiving lest after all it should prove unreal will dart through his mind, as through that of the representative child of his poem. Nay, a dark suspicion will occasionally overtake him, "that maybe identity beyond the grave is a beautiful fable only"—as when, in the midst of some gay scene, the thought occurs to him of a ship going down at sea, of women sinking "while the passionless wet flows on"; and he ponders within himself: "Are those women indeed gone?"

> Are souls drown'd and destroy'd so?
> Is only matter triumphant?

But again and again he returns victorious answer:

> Did you think life was so well provided for, and Death, the purport of all Life, is not well provided for?
> I do not doubt that wrecks at sea, no matter what the horrors of them, no matter whose wife, child, husband, father, lover, has gone down, are provided for, to the minutest points.

How inspiriting in their juvenile positiveness, in these days of doubt and pessimism, are his hearty assurances of immortality, in which not man alone, but all nature, what we deem the inanimate as well as the animate, is included:

> I swear I think now that everything without exception has an eternal soul!
> The trees have, rooted in the ground! the weeds of the sea have! the animals!

And in this he goes no further than Charles Lamb, who, loving houses as Walt Whitman loves trees, hazards the wild and beautiful surmise that "as men, when they die, do not die all, so of their extinguished habitations there may be a hope—a germ to be revivified."

Whitman's belief, however, is no vague theory reserved for imaginative moods. He subjects it to the most crucial tests. In the midst of the conflicting emotions roused in him by the news of the death of Carlyle, whose personality had powerfully impressed him, "and now that he has gone hence," he asks, "can it be that Thomas Carlyle, soon to chemically dissolve in ashes and by winds, remains an identity still? In ways, perhaps, eluding all the statements, lore, and speculations of ten thousand years—eluding all possible statements to mortal sense—does he yet exist, a definite, vital being, a spirit, an individual. . . . I have no doubt of it." When depressed, he tells us, by some specially sad event or tearing problem, he waits till he can go out under the stars at midnight to consider

it, to be soothed and spiritualised, and to receive an answer to his soul. It was to this means of tranquillity he had resorted on the present occasion, and this was the answer he received concerning the author of *Sartor Resartus.*

There is something so touching in this consideration of the death of one lonely old man by another, in a different hemisphere, younger, but in the evening of his day, and appearing feebler and more helpless in every glimpse we have of him, that the momentary departure from our point of view in referring to it may be pardoned. [1]

For all Whitman's love of life, for all the joy of existence with which he overflows, the themes he loves best, according to his own statement, are "night, sleep, death, and the stars." Death's gloomier aspects he ignores as completely as the child of Wordsworth's poem, not, however, in the spirit of thoughtless childhood, by denying its reality, but by adopting it into his life. "Chanter of pains and joys, uniter of here and hereafter," his object is to bridge the way from life to death. As different from the Emperor Adrian's melancholy foreboding as the gay anticipation of a young sailor setting out on his first voyage, the spirit of adventure strong upon him, differs from the troubled outlook of some anxious mariner, is his brief lyrical address to his soul on parting:

> Joy, shipmate, joy!
>   (Pleas'd to my soul at death I cry)
> Our life is closed, our life begins,
> The long, long anchorage we leave,
> The ship is clear at last, she leaps!
> She swiftly courses from the shore,
> Joy, shipmate, joy!

Life may be full of suffering and contradictions, but "sane and sacred death" will make amends for all. It is the answer to every question; the fall of the young hero in battle, the unsatisfied love, the disappointed life—all sorrows, wants, and imperfections will be accounted for by this.

As if aware, by some subtle undefined instinct, of the child-element in himself, he traces back the full-flowing stream of his poetry to its first source in his awakened child's heart. In soft hushed strains, like the whispers rapt and awestruck of a child just wakened from some dream of heaven, he tells us how it was a wild bird moaning for its mate (and whose wistful ignorant lament he interprets with such exquisite insight that it seems he has taken its spirit into his own) which roused the fire, the "unknown want" within him, when a boy, with bare feet, the wind wafting his hair, he wandered down to the shore by night and listened, with childish intuitive sympathy, to the lone singer calling on his love; till, revisiting the scene,

> A man, yet by these tears a little boy again,

he confronted the dark problem of earthly griefs and partings.

> O give me the clue (it lurks in the night here somewhere)!
> O if I am to have so much, let me have more!

rose his yearning cry toward heaven. And from the wet sands, the calm unhurrying sea, the stars, the winds, came the answer whispering through the night, reiterated with strong reverberation:

> Death, death, death, death, death.

Once again he became the peaceful child he was before the nameless longing had been roused, though with the added assurance of one who has wrestled with an angel and prevailed; and it is henceforth in the spirit of confiding happy childhood that he goes through life:

My own songs awaked from that hour,
And with them the key, the word up from the waves,
The word of the sweetest song and all songs,
That strong and delicious word which, creeping to
    my feet . . . the sea whisper'd me.

In accordance with this faith the dead to Whitman are living, "Haply the only living, only real." Item for item, body as well as soul, they have eluded burial and passed to fitting spheres. He walks often when in solitude as if accompanied by his departed, and scatters flowers to them on his way, not so much in kind remembrance as for present token of affection.

        As if a phantom caress'd me,

he bursts forth, in one of those rare abrupt little Heine-like effusions of his which suggest so much in a line or two.

I thought I was not alone walking here by the shore;
But the one I thought was with me . . .
As I lean and look through the glimmering light, that
    one has utterly disappear'd,
And those appear that are hateful to me and mock
    me:

the unexpected turn of the last line being, however, singularly out of keeping with his usual utterances, for to Walt Whitman in his normal mood no one is hateful. Like the little child of the story, he loves everyone. "I am in love with you, and with all my fellows upon the earth," is from first to last the burden of his poems.

Whitman alludes somewhere to "the great charity of the earth." Of the same kind is his own. Subjected to the alchemy of his close loving sympathy, his respectful consideration, the vilest things seem to emerge purified and fit for noble uses. Nothing is too abandoned in its baseness but he will shed some shadow of healing, some light of comfort on it. To him the dirtiest puddle reflects the beauty of the skies. We have heard of a child who wept on being told that a flower she admired was nothing but a weed. To Whitman there are no weeds in the world. With the child's simple eye to nature he takes them all for plants of precious growth, bearing each one of them, buried deep, perhaps, within its calyx, the seed of perfection. And in this he is not like the child, that his trust can be destroyed by the first rude unthinking hand. With authority, as if he spoke for God, he gives his imperious verdict on behalf of what the world despises and pronounces it also to be good. He rejects nothing, he despises nothing: "Good or bad, I never question you, I love all—I do not condemn anything." For the poet, as in one of his softly rounded, tenderly suggestive phrases he asserts, "judges not as the judge judges, but as the sun falling round a helpless thing;" or else, as in this case, like the young child who has no standard but its own clinging nature to measure people by. To his pure, spiritualised vision "objects gross and the unseen soul are one." No head to him but wears its "nimbus of gold-coloured light." He takes everyone, the meanest and most worthless, by the hand, and whispers to him or her that he understands and loves what none others have understood or loved; that the true being, soul and body (he will never separate them), stands revealed in its glory and perfection to him, unhidden by the most repulsive exterior; that at the worst, though premature death should have already fallen, the means will be provided that it may "pick its way."

"Maybe I am non-literary and non-decorous," Whitman says of himself on some special occasion. Maybe he is. But literature and decorum are not the highest things. What might shock and disgust if it came from any one else only startles us with its note of strangeness from him. His coarseness is as the coarseness of the earth, which, with "disdainful innocence,"

takes all for clean. Or rather, to maintain our point of view, he is a "vulgar child" indeed, but after the fashion of the youngster to whose harmless improprieties Sterne, in justification of his own deliberate offences, drew its mother's attention—not after that of the sentimentalist himself. The "chaste indecency of childhood" is not so hard to forgive.

As we study him his utterances take on power and beauty. His character seems to gather cohesion and to expand; so that whereas, in our first perusal of him, when we came across some passage of exquisite beauty or on some announcement of matured wisdom, we were startled almost as if a very child amid its careless babblings had uttered words of inspiration, we end by acknowledging in him both the giant and the child, a man

        full-statured in magnificence.

Notes

1. Since this was written Walt Whitman has passed away.

JOHN ADDINGTON SYMONDS
From *Walt Whitman: A Study*
1893, pp. 67–76

The section of Whitman's works which deals with adhesiveness, or the love of comrades, is fully as important, and in some ways more difficult to deal with, than his *Children of Adam*. He gave it the title *Calamus*, from the root of a water-rush, adopted by him as the symbol of this love. [1] Here the element of spirituality in passion, of romantic feeling, and of deep enduring sentiment, which was almost conspicuous by its absence from the section on sexual love, emerges into vivid prominence, and lends peculiar warmth of poetry to the artistic treatment. We had to expect so much from the poem quoted by me at the commencement of this disquisition. There Whitman described the love of man for woman as "fast-anchor'd, eternal"; the thought of the bride, the wife, as "more resistless than I can tell." But for the love of man for man he finds quite a different class of descriptive phrases: "separate, disembodied, another born, ethereal, the last athletic reality, my consolation." He hints that we have left the realm of sex and sense, and have ascended into a different and rarer atmosphere, where passion, though it has not lost its strength, is clarified. "Largior hic æther, et campos lumine vestit purpureo."

This emphatic treatment of an emotion which is usually talked about under the vague and formal term of friendship, gives peculiar importance to *Calamus*. No man in the modern world has expressed so strong a conviction that "manly attachment," "athletic love," "the high towering love of comrades," is a main factor in human life, a virtue upon which society will have to lay its firm foundations, and a passion equal in permanence, superior in spirituality, to the sexual affection. Whitman regards this emotion not only as the "consolation" of the individual, but also as a new and hitherto unapprehended force for stimulating national vitality.

There is no softness or sweetness in his treatment of this theme. His tone is sustained throughout at a high pitch of virile enthusiasm, which, at the same time, vibrates with acutest feeling, thrills with an undercurrent of the tenderest sensibility. Not only the sublimest thoughts and aspirations, but also the shyest, most shame-faced, yearnings are reserved for this love. At one time he exclaims:

O I think it is not for life that I am chanting here my
    chant of lovers—I think it must be for Death,

For how calm, how solemn it grows, to ascend to the
    atmosphere of lovers,
Death or life I am then indifferent—my soul declines
    to prefer,
I am not sure but the high soul of lovers welcomes
    death most;
Indeed, O Death, I think now these leaves mean
    precisely the same as you mean;
Grow up taller, sweet leaves, that I may see! Grow up
    out of my breast!
Spring away from the concealed heart there!
Do not fold yourselves so, in your pink-tinged roots,
    timid leaves!
Do not remain down there so ashamed, herbage of
    my breast!

The leaves are Whitman's emotions and the poems they
engender; the root from which they spring is "manly attachment," "athletic love," symbolised for him in the blushing root
of the pond-calamus which he plucked one day and chose to be
the emblem of the love of lovers:

O here I last saw him that tenderly loves me—and
    returns again, never to separate from me,
And this, O this shall henceforth be the token of
    comrades—this Calamus-root shall,
Interchange it, youths, with each other! Let none
    render it back!

At another time, in minor key, he writes as follows:

O you when I often and silently come where you are,
    that I may be with you;
As I walk by your side, or sit near, or remain in the
    same room with you,
Little you know the subtle, electric fire that for your
    sake is playing within me.

These extracts were necessary, because there is some
misapprehension abroad regarding the precise nature of what
Whitman meant by *Calamus*. His method of treatment has, to
a certain extent, exposed him to misconstruction. Still, as his
friend and commentator, Mr. Burroughs, puts it: "The sentiment is primitive, athletic, taking form in all manner of large
and homely out-of-door images, and springs, as any one may
see, directly from the heart and experience of the poet." The
language has a passionate glow, a warmth of devotion, beyond
anything to which the world is used in the celebration of
friendship. At the same time the false note of insincerity or
sensuousness is never heard. The melody is in the Dorian
mood—recalling to our minds that fellowship in arms which
flourished among the Dorian tribes, and formed the chivalry of
pre-historic Hellas.

In the preface to the 1880 edition of *Leaves of Grass* and
Two Rivulets, Whitman gives his own explanation of
Calamus, and of the feelings which inspired that section of his
work.

> Something more may be added—for, while I
> am about it, I would make a full confession. I also
> sent out *Leaves of Grass* to arouse and set flowing in
> men's and women's hearts, young and old, endless
> streams of living, pulsating love and friendship,
> directly from them to myself, now and ever. To this
> terrible, irrepressible yearning (surely more or less
> down underneath in most human souls), this never-
> satisfied appetite for sympathy and this boundless
> offering of sympathy, this universal democratic com-
> radeship, this old, eternal, yet ever-new interchange
> of adhesiveness, so fitly emblematic of America, I
> have given in that book, undisguisedly, declaredly,

the openest expression. Besides, important as they
are in my purpose as emotional expressions for
humanity, the special meaning of the *Calamus*,
cluster of *Leaves of Grass* (and more or less running
through the book and cropping out in *Drum Taps*),
mainly resides in its political significance. In my
opinion, it is by a fervent accepted development of
comradeship, the beautiful and sane affection of
man for man, latent in all the young fellows, north
and south, east and west—it is by this, I say, and by
what goes directly and indirectly along with it, that
the United States of the future (I cannot too often
repeat) are to be the most effectually welded together,
intercalated, annealed into a living union.

This being so, Whitman never suggests that comradeship
may occasion the development of physical desire. On the other
hand, he does not in set terms condemn desires, or warn his
disciples against their perils. There is indeed a distinctly
sensuous side to his conception of adhesiveness. To a Western
Boy he says:

If you be not silently selected by lovers, and do not
    silently select lovers,
Of what use is it that you seek to become elect of
    mine?

Like Plato, in the *Phædrus*, Whitman describes an enthusiastic type of masculine emotion, leaving its private details to
the moral sense and special inclination of the individuals
concerned.

The poet himself appears to be not wholly unconscious
that there are dangers and difficulties involved in the highly-
pitched emotions he is praising. The whole tenor of two
carefully-toned compositions, entitled "Whoever you are,
Holding me now in hand," and "Trickle, Drops," suggest an
underlying sense of spiritual conflict. The following poem,
again, is sufficiently significant and typical to call for literal
transcription:

Earth, my likeness!
Though you look so impassive, ample and spheric
    there,
I now suspect that is not all;
I now suspect there is something fierce in you,
    eligible to burst forth;
For an athlete is enamoured of me—and I of him,
But toward him there is something fierce and terrible
    in me, eligible to burst forth,
I dare not tell it in word—not even in these songs.

The reality of Whitman's feeling, the intense delight
which he derives from the personal presence and physical
contact of a beloved man, find luminous expression in "A
Glimpse," "Recorders ages hence," "When I heard at the
Close of Day," "I saw in Louisiana a Live-Oak growing,"
"Long I thought that Knowledge alone would suffice me,"[2] "O
Tan-faced Prairie-Boy," and "Vigil Strange I kept on the Field
one Night."[3]

It is clear then that, in his treatment of comradeship, or
the impassioned love of man for man, Whitman has struck a
keynote, to the emotional intensity of which the modern world
is unaccustomed. It therefore becomes of much importance to
discover the poet-prophet's *Stimmung*—his radical instinct
with regard to the moral quality of the feeling he encourages.
Studying his works by their own light, and by the light of their
author's character, interpreting each part by reference to the
whole and in the spirit of the whole, an impartial critic will, I
think, be drawn to the conclusion that what he calls the
"adhesiveness" of comradeship is meant to have no interblend-

ing with the "amativeness" of sexual love. Personally, it is undeniable that Whitman possessed a specially keen sense of the fine restraint and continence, the cleanliness and chastity, that are inseparable from the perfectly virile and physically complete nature of healthy manhood. Still we have the right to predicate the same ground-qualities in the early Dorians, those founders of the martial institution of Greek love; and yet it is notorious to students of Greek civilisation that the lofty sentiment of their masculine chivalry was intertwined with much that is repulsive to modern sentiment.

Whitman does not appear to have taken some of the phenomena of contemporary morals into due account, although he must have been aware of them. Else he would have foreseen that, human nature being what it is, we cannot expect to eliminate all sensual alloy from emotions raised to a high pitch of passionate intensity, and that permanent elements within the midst of our society will imperil the absolute purity of the ideal he attempts to establish. It is obvious that those unenviable mortals who are the inheritors of sexual anomalies, will recognise their own emotion in Whitman's "superb friendship, exalté, previously unknown," which "waits, and has been always waiting, latent in all men," the "something fierce in me, eligible to burst forth," "ethereal comradeship," "the last athletic reality." Had I not the strongest proof in Whitman's private correspondence with myself that he repudiated any such deductions from his *Calamus*, I admit that I should have regarded them as justified; and I am not certain whether his own feelings upon this delicate topic may not have altered since the time when *Calamus* was first composed.

Notes

1. Its botanical name is Acorus Calamus. We call it "sweet-rush" or "sweet sedge."
2. Not included in the *Complete Poems and Prose*. It will be found in *Leaves of Grass*, Boston, 1860–61.
3. The two last are from *Drum-Taps*.

JOHN BURROUGHS
From "His Ruling Ideas and Aims"
Whitman: A Study
1896, pp. 73–80

I

Let me here summarize some of the ideas and principles in which *Leaves of Grass* has its root, and from which it starts. A collection of poems in the usual sense, a variety of themes artistically treated and appealing to our æsthetic perceptibilities alone, it is not. It has, strictly speaking, but one theme,—personality, the personality of the poet himself. To exploit this is always the main purpose, and, in doing so, to make the book both directly and indirectly a large, impassioned utterance upon all the main problems of life and of nationality. It is primitive, like the early literature of a race or people, in that its spirit and purpose are essentially religious. It is like the primitive literatures also in its prophetic cry and in its bardic simplicity and homeliness, and unlike them in its faith and joy and its unconquerable optimism.

It has been not inaptly called the bible of democracy. Its biblical features are obvious enough with the darker negative traits left out. It is Israel with science and the modern added.

Whitman was swayed by a few great passions,—the passion for country, the passion for comrades, the cosmic passion, etc. His first concern seems always to have been for his country. He has touched no theme, named no man, not related in some way to America. The thought of it possessed him as thoroughly as the thought of Israel possessed the old Hebrew prophets. Indeed, it is the same passion, and flames up with the same vitality and power,—the same passion for race and nativity enlightened by science and suffused with the modern humanitarian spirit. Israel was exclusive and cruel. Democracy, as exemplified in Walt Whitman, is compassionate and all-inclusive:—

> My spirit has passed in compassion and determination around the whole earth,
> I have looked for equals and lovers, and found them ready for me in all lands;
> I think some divine rapport has equalized me with them.
> O vapors! I think I have risen with you, and moved away to distant continents, and fallen down there, for reasons,
> I think I have blown with you, O winds,
> O waters, I have fingered every shore with you.

II

The work springs from the modern democratic conception of society,—of absolute social equality.

It embodies the modern scientific conception of the universe, as distinguished from the old theological conception,—namely, that creation is good and sound in all its parts.

It embodies a conception of evil as a part of the good, of death as the friend and not the enemy of life.

It places comradeship, manly attachment, above sex love, and indicates it as the cement of future states and republics.

It makes the woman the equal of the man, his mate and not his toy.

It treats sexuality as a matter too vital and important to be ignored or trifled with, much less perverted or denied. A full and normal sexuality,—upon this the race stands. We pervert, we deny, we corrupt sex at our peril. Its perversions and abnormalities are to be remedied by a frank and fervent recognition of it, almost a new priapism.

It springs from a conception of poetry quite different from the current conception. It aims at the poetry of things rather than of words, and works by suggestion and indirection rather than by elaboration.

It aims to project into literature a conception of the new democratic man,—a type larger, more copious, more candid, more religious, than we have been used to. It finds its ideals, not among scholars or in the parlor or counting-houses, but among workers, doers, farmers, mechanics, the heroes of land and sea.

Hence the atmosphere which it breathes and effuses is that of real things, real men and women. It has not the perfume of the distilled and concentrated, but the all but impalpable odor of the open air, the shore, the wood, the hilltop. It aims, not to be a book, but to be a man.

Its purpose is to stimulate and arouse, rather than to soothe and satisfy. It addresses the character, the intuitions, the ego, more than the intellect or the purely æsthetic faculties. Its end is not taste, but growth in the manly virtues and powers.

Its religion shows no trace of theology, or the conventional pietism.

It aspires to a candor and a directness like that of Nature herself.

It aims to let Nature speak without check, with original energy. The only checks are those which health and wholeness demand.

Its standards are those of the natural universal.

Its method is egocentric. The poet never goes out of himself, but draws everything into himself and makes it all serve to illustrate his personality.

Its form is not what is called artistic. Its suggestion is to be found in organic nature, in trees, clouds, and in the vital and flowing currents.

In its composition the author was doubtless greatly influenced by the opera and the great singers, and the music of the great composers. He would let himself go in the same manner and seek his effects through multitude and the quality of the living voice.

Finally, *Leaves of Grass* is an utterance out of the depths of primordial, aboriginal human nature. It embodies and exploits a character not rendered anæmic by civilization, but preserving a sweet and sane savagery, indebted to culture only as a means to escape culture, reaching back always, through books, art, civilization, to fresh, unsophisticated nature, and drawing his strength from thence.

Another of the ideas that master Whitman and rule him is the idea of identity,—that you are you and I am I, and that we are henceforth secure whatever comes or goes. He revels in this idea; it is fruitful with him; it begets in him the ego-enthusiasm, and is at the bottom of his unshakable faith in immortality. It leavens all his work. It cannot be too often said that the book is not merely a collection of pretty poems, themes elaborated and followed out at long removes from the personality of the poet, but a series of *sorties* into the world of materials, the American world, piercing through the ostensible shows of things to the interior meanings, and illustrating in a free and large way the genesis and growth of a man, his free use of the world about him, appropriating it to himself, seeking his spiritual identity through its various objects and experiences, and giving in many direct and indirect ways the meaning and satisfaction of life. There is much in it that is not poetical in the popular sense, much that is neutral and negative, and yet is an integral part of the whole, as is the case in the world we inhabit. If it offends, it is in a wholesome way, like objects in the open air.

III

Whitman rarely celebrates exceptional characters. He loves the common humanity, and finds his ideals among the masses. It is not difficult to reconcile his attraction toward the average man, towards workingmen and "powerful, uneducated persons," with the ideal of a high excellence, because he finally rests only upon the most elevated and heroic personal qualities,—elevated but well grounded in the common and universal.

The types upon which he dwells the most fondly are of the common people. ⟨. . .⟩ All the *motifs* of his work are the near, the vital, the universal; nothing curious, or subtle, or far-fetched. His working ideas are democracy, equality, personality, nativity, health, sexuality, comradeship, self-esteem, the purity of the body, the equality of the sexes, etc. Out of them his work radiates. They are the eyes with which it sees, the ears with which it hears, the feet upon which it goes. The poems are less like a statement, an argument, an elucidation, and more like a look, a gesture, a tone of voice.

"The word I myself put primarily for the description of them as they stand at last," says the author, "is the word Suggestiveness."

Leaves of Grass requires a large perspective; you must not get your face too near the book. You must bring to it a magnanimity of spirit,—a charity and faith equal to its own.

Looked at too closely, it often seems incoherent and meaningless; draw off a little and let the figure come out. The book is from first to last a most determined attempt, on the part of a large, reflective, loving, magnetic, rather primitive, thoroughly imaginative personality, to descend upon the materialism of the nineteenth century, and especially upon a new democratic nation now in full career upon this continent, with such poetic fervor and enthusiasm as to lift and fill it with the deepest meanings of the spirit and disclose the order of universal nature. The poet has taken shelter behind no precedent, or criticism, or partiality whatever, but has squarely and lovingly faced the oceanic amplitude and movement of the life of his times and land, and fused them in his fervid humanity, and imbued them with deepest poetic meanings. One of the most striking features of the book is the adequacy and composure, even joyousness and elation, of the poet in the presence of the huge materialism and prosaic conditions of our democratic era. He spreads himself over it all, he accepts and absorbs it all, he rejects no part; and his quality, his individuality, shines through it all, as the sun through vapors. The least line, or fragment of a line, is redolent of Walt Whitman. It is never so much the theme treated as it is the man exploited and illustrated. Walt Whitman does not write poems, strictly speaking,—does not take a bit of nature or life or character and chisel and carve it into a beautiful image or object, or polish and elaborate a thought, embodying it in pleasing tropes and pictures. His purpose is rather to show a towering, loving, composite personality moving amid all sorts of materials, taking them up but for a moment, disclosing new meanings and suggestions in them, passing on, bestowing himself upon whoever or whatever will accept him, tossing hints and clues right and left, provoking and stimulating the thought and imagination of his reader, but finishing nothing for him, leaving much to be desired, much to be completed by him in his turn.

GEORGE SANTAYANA
From "The Poetry of Barbarism:
II. Walt Whitman"
Interpretations of Poetry and Religion
1900, pp. 177–87

The works of Walt Whitman offer an extreme illustration of this phase of genius ⟨barbarism⟩, both by their form and by their substance. It was the singularity of his literary form—the challenge it threw to the conventions of verse and of language—that first gave Whitman notoriety: but this notoriety has become fame, because those incapacities and solecisms which glare at us from his pages are only the obverse of a profound inspiration and of a genuine courage. Even the idiosyncrasies of his style have a side which is not mere perversity or affectation; the order of his words, the procession of his images, reproduce the method of a rich, spontaneous, absolutely lazy fancy. In most poets such a natural order is modified by various governing motives—the thought, the metrical form, the echo of other poems in the memory. By Walt Whitman these conventional influences are resolutely banished. We find the swarms of men and objects rendered as they might strike the retina in a sort of waking dream. It is the most sincere possible confession of the lowest—I mean the most primitive—type of perception. All ancient poets are sophisticated in comparison and give proof of longer intellectual and moral training. Walt Whitman has gone back to the innocent style of Adam, when the animals filed before him one by one and he called each of them by its name.

In fact, the influences to which Walt Whitman was subject were as favourable as possible to the imaginary experiment of beginning the world over again. Liberalism and transcendentalism both harboured some illusions on that score; and they were in the air which our poet breathed. Moreover he breathed this air in America, where the newness of the material environment made it easier to ignore the fatal antiquity of human nature. When he afterward became aware that there was or had been a world with a history, he studied that world with curiosity and spoke of it not without a certain shrewdness. But he still regarded it as a foreign world and imagined, as not a few Americans have done, that his own world was a fresh creation, not amenable to the same laws as the old. The difference in the conditions blinded him, in his merely sensuous apprehension, to the identity of the principles.

His parents were farmers in central Long Island and his early years were spent in that district. The family seems to have been not too prosperous and somewhat nomadic; Whitman himself drifted through boyhood without much guidance. We find him now at school, now helping the labourers at the farms, now wandering along the beaches of Long Island, finally at Brooklyn working in an apparently desultory way as a printer and sometimes as a writer for a local newspaper. He must have read or heard something, at this early period, of the English classics; his style often betrays the deep effect made upon him by the grandiloquence of the Bible, of Shakespeare, and of Milton. But his chief interest, if we may trust his account, was already in his own sensations. The aspects of Nature, the forms and habits of animals, the sights of cities, the movement and talk of common people, were his constant delight. His mind was flooded with these images, keenly felt and afterward to be vividly rendered with bold strokes of realism and imagination.

Many poets have had this faculty to seize the elementary aspects of things, but none has had it so exclusively; with Whitman the surface is absolutely all and the underlying structure is without interest and almost without existence. He had had no education and his natural delight in imbibing sensations had not been trained to the uses of practical or theoretical intelligence. He basked in the sunshine of perception and wallowed in the stream of his own sensibility, as later at Camden in the shallows of his favourite brook. Even during the civil war, when he heard the drum-taps so clearly, he could only gaze at the picturesque and terrible aspects of the struggle, and linger among the wounded day after day with a canine devotion; he could not be aroused either to clear thought or to positive action. So also in his poems; a multiplicity of images pass before him and he yields himself to each in turn with absolute passivity. The world has no inside; it is a phantasmagoria of continuous visions, vivid, impressive, but monotonous and hard to distinguish in memory, like the waves of the sea or the decorations of some barbarous temple, sublime only by the infinite aggregation of parts.

This abundance of detail without organization, this wealth of perception without intelligence and of imagination without taste, makes the singularity of Whitman's genius. Full of sympathy and receptivity, with a wonderful gift of graphic characterization and an occasional rare grandeur of diction, he fills us with a sense of the individuality and the universality of what he describes—it is a drop in itself yet a drop in the ocean. The absence of any principle of selection or of a sustained style enables him to render aspects of things and of emotion which

would have eluded a trained writer. He is, therefore, interesting even where he is grotesque or perverse. He has accomplished, by the sacrifice of almost every other good quality, something never so well done before. He has approached common life without bringing in his mind any higher standard by which to criticise it; he has seen it, not in contrast with an ideal, but as the expression of forces more indeterminate and elementary than itself; and the vulgar, in this cosmic setting, has appeared to him sublime.

There is clearly some analogy between a mass of images without structure and the notion of an absolute democracy. Whitman, inclined by his genius and habits to see life without relief or organization, believed that his inclination in this respect corresponded with the spirit of his age and country, and that Nature and society, at least in the United States, were constituted after the fashion of his own mind. Being the poet of the average man, he wished all men to be specimens of that average, and being the poet of a fluid Nature, he believed that Nature was or should be a formless flux. This personal bias of Whitman's was further encouraged by the actual absence of distinction in his immediate environment. Surrounded by ugly things and common people, he felt himself happy, ecstatic, overflowing with a kind of patriarchal love. He accordingly came to think that there was a spirit of the New World which he embodied, and which was in complete opposition to that of the Old, and that a literature upon novel principles was needed to express and strengthen this American spirit.

Democracy was not to be merely a constitutional device for the better government of given nations, not merely a movement for the material improvement of the lot of the poorer classes. It was to be a social and a moral democracy and to involve an actual equality among all men. Whatever kept them apart and made it impossible for them to be messmates together was to be discarded. The literature of democracy was to ignore all extraordinary gifts of genius or virtue, all distinction drawn even from great passions or romantic adventures. In Whitman's works, in which this new literature is foreshadowed, there is accordingly not a single character nor a single story. His only hero is Myself, the "single separate person," endowed with the primary impulses, with health, and with sensitiveness to the elementary aspects of Nature. The perfect man of the future, the prolific begetter of other perfect men, is to work with his hands, chanting the poems of some future Walt, some ideally democratic bard. Women are to have as nearly as possible the same character as men: the emphasis is to pass from family life and local ties to the friendship of comrades and the general brotherhood of man. Men are to be vigorous, comfortable, sentimental, and irresponsible.

This dream is, of course, unrealized and unrealizable, in America as elsewhere. Undeniably there are in America many suggestions of such a society and such a national character. But the growing complexity and fixity of institutions necessarily tends to obscure these traits of a primitive and crude democracy. What Whitman seized upon as the promise of the future was in reality the survival of the past. He sings the song of pioneers, but it is in the nature of the pioneer that the greater his success the quicker must be his transformation into something different. When Whitman made the initial and amorphous phase of society his ideal, he became the prophet of a lost cause. That cause was lost, not merely when wealth and intelligence began to take shape in the American Commonwealth, but it was lost at the very foundation of the world, when those laws of evolution were established which Whitman, like Rousseau, failed to understand. If we may trust Mr. Herbert Spencer, these laws involve a passage from the homogeneous to the heterogeneous, and a constant progress at once in differentiation and in organization—all, in a word, that Whitman systematically deprecated or ignored. He is surely not the spokesman of the tendencies of his country, although he describes some aspects of its past and present condition: nor does he appeal to those whom he describes, but rather to the *dilettanti* he despises. He is regarded as representative chiefly by foreigners, who look for some grotesque expression of the genius of so young and prodigious a people.

Whitman, it is true, loved and comprehended men; but this love and comprehension had the same limits as his love and comprehension of Nature. He observed truly and responded to his observation with genuine and pervasive emotion. A great gregariousness, an innocent tolerance of moral weakness, a genuine admiration for bodily health and strength, made him bubble over with affection for the generic human creature. Incapable of an ideal passion, he was full of the milk of human kindness. Yet, for all his acquaintance with the ways and thoughts of the common man of his choice, he did not truly understand him. For to understand people is to go much deeper than they go themselves; to penetrate to their characters and disentangle their inmost ideals. Whitman's insight into man did not go beyond a sensuous sympathy; it consisted in a vicarious satisfaction in their pleasures, and an instinctive love of their persons. It never approached a scientific or imaginative knowledge of their hearts.

Therefore Whitman failed radically in his dearest ambition: he can never be a poet of the people. For the people, like the early races whose poetry was ideal, are natural believers in perfection. They have no doubts about the absolute desirability of wealth and learning and power, none about the worth of pure goodness and pure love. Their chosen poets, if they have any, will be always those who have known how to paint these ideals in lively even if in gaudy colours. Nothing is farther from the common people than the corrupt desire to be primitive. They instinctively look toward a more exalted life, which they imagine to be full of distinction and pleasure, and the idea of that brighter existence fills them with hope or with envy or with humble admiration.

If the people are ever won over to hostility to such ideals, it is only because they are cheated by demagogues who tell them that if all the flowers of civilization were destroyed its fruits would become more abundant. A greater share of happiness, people think, would fall to their lot could they destroy everything beyond their own possible possessions. But they are made thus envious and ignoble only by a deception: what they really desire is an ideal good for themselves which they are told they may secure by depriving others of their preëminence. Their hope is always to enjoy perfect satisfaction

themselves; and therefore a poet who loves the picturesque aspects of labour and vagrancy will hardly be the poet of the poor. He may have described their figure and occupation, in neither of which they are much interested; he will not have read their souls. They will prefer to him any sentimental story-teller, any sensational dramatist, any moralizing poet; for they are hero-worshippers by temperament, and are too wise or too unfortunate to be much enamoured of themselves or of the conditions of their existence.

Fortunately, the political theory that makes Whitman's principle of literary prophecy and criticism does not always inspire his chants, nor is it presented, even in his prose works, quite bare and unadorned. In *Democratic Vistas* we find it clothed with something of the same poetic passion and lighted up with the same flashes of intuition which we admire in the poems. Even there the temperament is finer than the ideas and the poet wiser than the thinker. His ultimate appeal is really to something more primitive and general than any social aspirations, to something more elementary than an ideal of any kind. He speaks to those minds and to those moods in which sensuality is touched with mysticism. When the intellect is in abeyance, when we would "turn and live with the animals, they are so placid and self-contained," when we are weary of conscience and of ambition, and would yield ourselves for a while to the dream of sense, Walt Whitman is a welcome companion. The images he arouses in us, fresh, full of light and health and of a kind of frankness and beauty, are prized all the more at such a time because they are not choice, but drawn perhaps from a hideous and sordid environment. For this circumstance makes them a better means of escape from convention and from that fatigue and despair which lurk not far beneath the surface of conventional life. In casting off with self-assurance and a sense of fresh vitality the distinctions of tradition and reason a man may feel, as he sinks back comfortably to a lower level of sense and instinct, that he is returning to Nature or escaping into the infinite. Mysticism makes us proud and happy to renounce the work of intelligence, both in thought and in life, and persuades us that we become divine by remaining imperfectly human. Walt Whitman gives a new expression to this ancient and multiform tendency. He feels his own cosmic justification and he would lend the sanction of his inspiration to all loafers and holiday-makers. He would be the congenial patron of farmers and factory hands in their crude pleasures and pieties, as Pan was the patron of the shepherds of Arcadia: for he is sure that in spite of his hairiness and animality, the gods will acknowledge him as one of themselves and smile upon him from the serenity of Olympus.

WALTER PATER

WALTER PATER

1839–1894

Walter Horatio Pater was born in Shadwell, East London, on August 4, 1839. Both of his parents died while he was quite young, his father in 1844, his mother in 1854. He was educated at King's School, Canterbury (1853–58), and at Queen's College, Oxford (1858–62). In 1864 he was elected a Fellow of Brasenose College, Oxford, where he taught classics; he maintained this position for the rest of his life. Pater's first publication was an article on Coleridge in the *Westminster Review* in 1866, but he first became widely known after the appearance in 1873 of *Studies in the History of the Renaissance*, which included critical essays on Winckelmann, Boticelli, and Da Vinci's "Mona Lisa."

Pater's first published work of fiction, "The Child in the House," appeared in *Macmillan's Magazine* in 1878. In 1885 he published his only completed novel, *Marius the Epicurean*. Shortly after the appearance of this book Pater moved to London, in order to escape the hostility and suspicion his somewhat morbid and decadent literary sensibility had aroused at Oxford. In London he formed friendships with Swinburne, Dante Gabriel Rossetti, the Humphry Wards, and the Mark Pattisons, and lived in a style much influenced by the aesthetics and ideals of Pre-Raphaelitism. In 1887 Pater published *Imaginary Portraits*, followed in 1889 by a widely celebrated critical work, *Appreciations: With an Essay on Style*. "Emerald Uthwart" (1892) and "Apollo in Picardy" (1893) were two short historical romances, the former appearing first in the *New Review*, the latter in *Harper's New Monthly Magazine*. In 1893 Pater published *Plato and Platonism*, a collection of lectures that finally secured him the academic recognition he had sought during the whole of his career. Shortly after its appearance Pater returned to Oxford, where he died on July 30, 1894.

Following his death several of Pater's works were brought out for the first time in book form, including *Greek Studies* (1895); *Gaston de Latour* (1896), an unfinished novel intended as a sequel to *Marius*; and *Essays from* The Guardian (1901). Pater's works remained widely popular until World War I, and he was a great influence on such *fin-de-siècle* writers as Oscar Wilde, George Moore, Arthur Symons, and W. B. Yeats. Since 1914, however, he has largely fallen out of critical favor.

General

The freshness of the light, its secrecy,
Spices, or honey from sweet-smelling bower,
The harmony of time, love's trembling hour
Struck on thee weith a new felicity.
Standing, a child, by a red hawthorn-tree,
Its perishing, small petals' flame had power
To fill with masses of soft, ruddy flower
A certain roadside in thy memory:
And haply when the tragic clouds of night
Were slowly wrapping round thee, in the cold
Of which men always die, a sense renewed
Of the things sweet to touch and breath and sight,
That thou didst touch and breathe and see of old
Stole on thee with the warmth of gratitude.
—MICHAEL FIELD, "Walter Pater," *Academy*,
Aug. 11, 1894, p. 102

When Pater was first seized with an ambition to write, the individuals of his own age with whom he came into competition were mainly poets. Those were the early days of Gabriel and Christina Rossetti, of Morris, of Swinburne; and most of the still younger men made their first steps in the field of verse, however far they might afterwards diverge from it. Pater, in this nest of singing-birds, resolved to be in prose no less painstaking, no less elaborate, no less bound by rule and art than the poets were. He is to be distinguished from those who had so much to say that their speech was forced out of them in a torrent, nor less from those whose instinct led them to bubble forth in periods of a natural artless grace. If we take these symbols of a mountain-stream or of a fountain for other prose-writers who have won the ear of the public with little

effort, then for Pater the appropriate image seems the artesian well, to reach the contents of which, strata of impermeable clay must be laboriously bored. It was not that there was any lack of material there, nor any doubt about the form it must take when it emerged, but that it was so miraculously deep down and hard to reach. I have known writers of every degree, but never one to whom the act of composition was such a travail and an agony as it was to Pater.

In his earlier years the labour of lifting the sentences was so terrific that any one with less fortitude would have entirely abandoned the effort. I recollect the writing of the opening chapters of *Marius*, and the stress that attended it—the intolerable languor and fatigue, the fevers and the cold fits, the grey hours of lassitude and insomnia, the toil as at a deep petroleum well when the oil refuses to flow. With practice, this terrific effort grew less. A year or two ago I was reminding him of those old times of storm and stress, and he replied, "Ah! it is much easier now. If I live long enough, no doubt I shall learn quite to like writing." The public saw the result of the labour in the smooth solidity of the result, and could suppose, from the very elaboration, that great pains had been taken. How much pains, very few indeed can have guessed!

It may be of interest to record the manner in which this most self-conscious and artistic of prose-writers proceeded. First of all, another pretty fable must be knocked on the head. It has been said, and repeated, that Pater composed his best sentences without any relation to a context, and wrote them down on little squares of paper, ready to stick them in at appropriate and effective places. This is nonsense; it is quite true that he used such squares of paper, but it was for a very different purpose. He read with a box of these squares beside him, jotting down on each, very roughly, anything in his author which struck his fancy, either giving an entire quotation, or indicating a reference, or noting a disposition. He did not begin, I think, any serious critical work without surrounding himself by dozens of these little loose notes. When they were not direct references or citations, they were of the nature of a *memoria technica*. Here is an example:

"Something about the gloomy Byzantine archit., belfries, solemn night come in about the birds attracted by the Towers."

Here is another:

"? did he suppose predestination to have taken place, only *after* the Fall?"

These papers would be placed about him, like the pieces of a puzzle, and when the right moment came the proper square would serve as a monitor or as a guide.

Having prepared his box of little squares, he would begin the labour of actual composition, and so conscious was he of the modifications and additions which would supervene that he always wrote on ruled paper, leaving each alternate line blank. Mr. Austin Dobson reminds me that Goldsmith did the same. On this broad canvas of alternate lines, then, Pater would slowly begin to draw his composition, the cartoon of what would in time be a finished essay. In the first draft the phrase would be a bald one; in the blank alternate line he would at leisure insert fresh descriptive or parenthetical clauses, other adjectives, more exquisitely related adverbs, until the space was filled. It might then be supposed that the MS. was complete. Far from it! Cancelling sheet by sheet, Pater then began to copy out the whole—as before, on alternate lines of copy-book pages; this revise was treated in the same way—corrected, enlarged, interleaved, as it were, with minuter shades of feeling and more elaborate apparatus of parenthesis.

No wonder that certain disadvantages were attendant upon the excessive finish of such a style. It is not possible to work in this way, with a cold hammer, and yet to avoid a certain deadness and slipperiness of surface. Pater's periods, in attaining their long-drawn harmony and fulness, were apt to lose vigour. Their polish did not quite make up for their languor, for the faintness and softness which attended their slow manipulation. Verse will bear an almost endless labour of the file; prose, as the freer and more spontaneous form, is less happy in subjection to it. "What long sentences Plato writes!" Pater says in his *Platonism*, and no doubt Plato might return the compliment. The sentences of the Oxford critic are often too long, and they are sometimes broken-backed with having had to bear too heavy a burden of allusion and illustration. His style, however, was his peculiarity. It had beautiful qualities, if we have to confess that it had the faults of those qualities. It was highly individual; it cannot be said that he owed it to any other writer, or that at any period of his thirty years of literary labour he faltered or swerved from his own path. He was to a high degree self-centred. Pater did not study his contemporaries; a year or two ago, he told me that he had read scarcely a chapter of Mr. Stevenson and not a line of Mr. Kipling. "I feel, from what I hear about them," he said, "that they are strong; they might lead me out of my path. I want to go on writing in my own way, good or bad. I should be afraid to read Kipling, lest he should come between me and my page next time I sat down to write." It was the excess of a very native and genuine modesty. He, too, was strong, had he but known it, strong enough to have resisted the magnets of contemporary style. Perhaps his own writing might have grown a little simpler and a little more supple if he had had the fortitude to come down and fight among his fellows.—EDMUND GOSSE, "Walter Pater" (1894), *Critical Kit-Kats*, 1896, pp. 261–65

I return with much appreciation the vivid pages on Pater. They fill up substantially the void of one's ignorance of his personal history, and they are of a manner graceful and luminous; though I should perhaps have relished a little more insistence on—a little more of an inside view of—the nature of his mind itself. Much as they tell, however, how curiously negative and faintly-grey he, after all telling, remains! I think he has had—will have had—the most exquisite literary fortune: i.e. to have taken it out all, wholly, exclusively, with the pen (the style, the genius) and absolutely not at all with the person. He is the mask without the face, and there isn't in his total superficies a tiny point of vantage for the newspaper to flap its wings on. You have been lively about him—but about whom *wouldn't* you be lively? I think you'd be lively about *me!*—Well, faint, pale, embarrassed, exquisite Pater! He reminds me, in the disturbed midnight of our actual literature, of one of those lucent matchboxes which you place, on going to bed, near the candle, to show you, in the darkness, where you can strike a light: he shines in the uneasy gloom—vaguely, and has a phosphorescence, not a flame. But I quite agree with you that he is not of the little day—but of the longer time.—HENRY JAMES, Letter to Edmund Gosse (Dec. 13, 1894)

Mr. Pater's work (which perhaps requires, for the complete comprehension and appreciation of its nature, either some personal acquaintance with its author, or more biographical detail than has yet been given to the public) has two characteristics which usually, if not always, impart distinction. It was full of personal note without any personal intrusion, and it was also full of a certain note of the time. Further, it was capable of being regarded from at least three rather different points of view: as containing an ethical theory, as giving a certain appreciation of literature, and as literature itself, marked by qualities of style rather than of matter. From the ethical side we need not here consider it at any length; it is perhaps sufficient to say that it usually illustrated, and sometimes inculcated directly, a sort of intellectual Hedonism—a neo-Cyrenaicism, as its author preferred to call it, in treatments half-critical, half-expository—which was, scarcely with more accuracy than kindness, called by some literary Paganism. Its critical as distinguished from its ethical note was, as distinctly and now not at all contentiously, Hedonist—that is to say, it recommended and exemplified what may be called the intellectual *degustation* of styles, periods, and literary manners, with the object of extracting from them the greatest possible amount of intelligent enjoyment. It was objected by some that the periods and examples which seemed most to Mr. Pater's taste—the late and curious classical time which exhibits, so to speak, reflections of Oriental and anticipations of mediæval sentiment and thought, the Renaissance, the remoter and more mystical exercitations of the modern Romantic movement—all had in them something morbid.

It is not necessary to take sides on either of these questions here, though it may be fairly said that Mr. Pater's views were, if not entirely shared, yet understood, and the expression of them admired, by persons who certainly have no sympathy with Paganism or with morbidity. But what is less contentious, and fortunately more germane, is the peculiarity, and, according to some tastes at least, the excellence of his style. This style, which is shown at its best in the *Renaissance* studies and in *Marius the Epicurean*, with some passages of *Appreciations* (for in *Imaginary Portraits* it is extremely unequal, and sometimes even slipshod), has no pretension to please or to be praised if the judge is wedded either to an exceedingly simple and natural style, or to one which, though ornate, observes the traditions of English prose as fashioned between 1660 and 1800. But for those who do not "rule out" Corinthian or even Composite from their list of orders of rhetorical architecture, Mr. Pater's style at its best had from the first an extreme attraction, and has not lost it in nearly a quarter of a century's acquaintance.

In one point indeed Mr. Pater may challenge the respect of even the severest critics who do not allow their dislike in other matters to obscure their vision in this. No writer since the revolutionary movement in English prose at the beginning of this century, not even Landor, has paid such extraordinary and successful attention to the architecture of the sentence. As against the snipsnap shortness of some writers, the lawless length of others, and the formlessness of a third class, his best sentences are arranged with an almost mathematical precision of clause-building, while their rhythm, though musical, is rarely poetic. Yet it must be acknowledged that this elaborate construction never became a perfectly learnt art with him; and that his sentences in his later work were sometimes apt to waver and wander. Still, on the whole, Mr. Pater, as an exponent in prose of the tendencies of which in verse Rossetti and Mr. Swinburne have been the chief masters, deserves a rank which it is impossible for any careful and impartial critic to ignore or to refuse. Few writers are fortunate in their imitators, and he has been especially unfortunate. His theories sometimes, his style often, have been the victims of a following not seldom silly, and not very seldom disgusting. But it would be unjust to charge this on the author himself. In himself, though owing a little, and not always happily, to Matthew Arnold and more to Newman, he is an extremely careful and on the whole a distinctly original producer of literature, who has chosen to make literature itself the main subject of his production, and has enforced views distinct in kind in a manner still more distinct. It is possible that Oxford men may be sometimes disposed to undervalue Mr. Pater, and sometimes to overvalue him, for the exact reason that he has not merely conveyed to outsiders much of the special flavour and *ethos* of Oxford teaching for some generations past, but has perhaps over-flavoured it with essences of his own. But from the expressions of the more intelligent among such outsiders it may be not obscurely gathered that he has partially effected the convey-ance—which, if in a more aristocratic age capable of being regarded as sacrilege, is in a democratic one perhaps a public service. And, apart from these disputable points, he is, as must be once more said, a remarkable, a very remarkable writer as such.

The least contentious, and, to the classical scholar at any rate, not the least satisfactory documents of his powers may perhaps be found in the masterly paraphrases of "Cupid and Psyche," of the *Pervigilium Veneris*, and of Lucian's *Hermotimus* to be found in *Marius the Epicurean*. But it has seemed better and fairer, in the present selection, to take things more purely original. The passages given below have been chosen with a view to exhibit Mr. Pater, not so much at his most florid, as at the perfection of the peculiar mood of ornate literary quietism—of delicate appreciation of shades of thought and vision—of which he was, as it seems to the present writer, the great exponent, and which he would probably not have disclaimed. The defect of this mood, in substance as in expression, is its extreme one-sidedness, and its consequent liability to topple over into the positively unhealthy and deformed. But if we take things at their best, it is worthy, not indeed of an unqualified, but of a decided admiration. —GEORGE SAINTSBURY, "Walter H. Pater," *English Prose*, ed. Henry Craik, 1896, Vol. 5, pp. 747–50

The spiritual evolution of the late Walter Pater—with whose name I am proud to conclude my second, as with it I began my first book on Renaissance matters—had been significantly similar to that of his own Marius. He began as an æsthete, and ended as a moralist. By faithful and self-restraining cultivation of the sense of harmony, he appears to have risen from the perception of visible beauty to the knowledge of beauty of the spiritual kind, both being expressions of the same perfect fittingness to an ever more intense and various and congruous life.

Such an evolution, which is, in the highest meaning, an æsthetic phenomenon in itself, required a wonderful spiritual endowment and an unflinchingly discriminating habit. For Walter Pater started by being above all a writer, and an æsthete in the very narrow sense of twenty years ago: an æsthete of the school of Mr. Swinburne's *Essays*, and of the type still common on the Continent. The cultivation of sensations, vivid sensations, no matter whether healthful or unhealthful, which that school commended, was, after all, but a theoretic and probably unconscious disguise for the cultivation of something to be said in a new way, which is the danger of all persons who regard literature as an end, and not as a means, feeling in order that they may write, instead of writing because they feel. And of this Mr. Pater's first and famous book was a very clear proof. Exquisite in technical quality, in rare percep-tion and subtle suggestion, it left, like all similar books, a sense of caducity and barrenness, due to the intuition of all sane persons that only an active synthesis of preferences and repulsions, what we imply in the terms *character* and *moral*, can have real importance in life, affinity with life—be, in short, vital; and that the yielding to, nay, the seeking for, variety and poignancy of experience, must result in a crum-bling away of all such possible unity and efficiency of living. But even as we find in the earliest works of a painter, despite the predominance of his master's style, indications already of what will expand into a totally different personality, so even in this earliest book, examined retrospectively, it is easy to find the characteristic germs of what will develop, extrude all foreign admixture, knit together congruous qualities, and give us presently the highly personal synthesis of *Marius* and the *Studies on Plato*.

These characteristic germs may be defined, I think, as the recurrence of impressions and images connected with physical sanity and daintiness; of aspiration after orderliness, congruity, and one might almost say *hierarchy*; moreover, a certain exclusiveness, which is not the contempt of the craftsman for the *bourgeois*, but the aversion of the priest for the profane uninitiated. Some day, perhaps, a more scientific study of æsthetic phenomena will explain the connection which we all feel between physical sanity and purity and the moral qualities called by the same names; but even nowadays it might have been prophesied that the man who harped upon the clearness and livingness of water, upon the delicate bracingness of air, who experienced so passionate a preference for the whole gamut, the whole palette, of spring, of temperate climates and of youth and childhood; a person who felt existence in the terms of its delicate vigour and its restorative austerity, was bound to become, like Plato, a teacher of self-discipline and self-harmony. Indeed, who can tell whether the teachings of Mr. Pater's maturity—the insistence on scrupulously disci-plined activity, on cleanness and clearness of thought and feeling, on the harmony attainable only through moderation, the intensity attainable only through effort—who can tell whether this abstract part of his doctrine would affect, as it does, all kindred spirits if the mood had not been prepared by some of those descriptions of visible scenes—the spring morning above the Catacombs, the Valley of Sparta, the paternal house of Marius, and that temple of Æsculapius with its shining rhythmical waters—which attune our whole being, like the music of the Lady in *Comus*, to modes of *sober certainty of waking bliss?*

This inborn affinity for refined wholesomeness made Mr. Pater the natural exponent of the highest æsthetic doctrine—the search for harmony throughout all orders of existence. It gave the nucleus of what was his soul's synthesis, his system (as Emerson puts it) of rejection and acceptance. Supreme craftsman as he was, it protected him from the craftsman's delusion—rife under the inappropriate name of "art for art's sake" in these uninstinctive, over-dextrous days—that subtle treatment can dignify all subjects equally, and that expression, irrespective of the foregoing *impression* in the artist and the subsequent *impression* in the audience, is the aim of art. Standing as he did, as all the greatest artists and thinkers (and he was both) do, in a definite, inevitable relation to the universe—the equation between himself and it—he was utterly unable to turn his powers of perception and expression to idle and irresponsible exercises; and his conception of art, being the outcome of his whole personal mode of existence, was inevitably one of art, not for art's sake, but of art for the sake of life—art as one of the harmonious functions of existence.

Harmonious, and in a sense harmonising. For, as I have said, he rose from the conception of physical health and congruity to the conception of health and congruity in matters of the spirit; the very thirst for healthiness, which means congruity, and congruity which implies health, forming the vital and ever-expanding connection between the two orders of phenomena. Two orders, did I say? Surely to the intuition of this artist and thinker, the fundamental unity—the unity between man's relations with external nature, with his own thoughts and with others' feelings—stood revealed as the secret of the highest æsthetics.

This which we guess at as the completion of Walter Pater's message, alas! must remain for ever a matter of surmise. The completion, the rounding of his doctrine, can take place only in the grateful appreciation of his readers. We have been left with unfinished systems, fragmentary, sometimes enigmatic, utterances. Let us meditate their wisdom and vibrate with their beauty; and, in the words of the prayer of Socrates to the Nymphs and to Pan, ask for beauty in the inward soul, and congruity between the inner and the outer man; and reflect in such manner the gifts of great art and of great thought in our soul's depths. For art and thought arise from life; and to life, as principle of harmony, they must return.—VERNON LEE (Violet Paget), *Renaissance Fancies and Studies*, 1896, pp. 255–60

There has been, perhaps, no more luminous example of the faculty of sharing the experience of a past age, of entering into the thought and feeling of a vanished race, than the peculiar divination and rehabilitation of certain extinct phases of emotion and thought which one finds in the pages of Walter Pater. In those pages there are, it is true, occasional lapses from a perfectly sound method; there is at times a loss of simplicity, a cloying sweetness in the style of this accomplished writer. These are, however, the perils of a very sensitive temperament, an intense feeling for beauty, and a certain seclusion from the affairs of life. That which characterises Mr. Pater at all times is his power of putting himself amid conditions that are not only extinct, but obscure and elusive; of winding himself back, as it were, into the primitive Greek consciousness and recovering for the moment the world as the Greeks saw, or, rather, felt it.

It is an easy matter to mass the facts about any given period, it is a very different and a very difficult matter to set those facts in vital relations to each other, to see them in true perspective. And the difficulties are immensely increased when the period is not only remote, but deficient in definite registry of thought and feeling; when the record of what it believed and felt does not exist by itself, but must be deciphered from those works of art in which is preserved the final form of thought and feeling, and in which are gathered and merged a great mass of ideas and emotions.—HAMILTON WRIGHT MABIE, *Books and Culture*, 1896, pp. 100–102

Some day a biography of Pater will be written, and we shall learn what he was like when a child: I should like to know if he played games. If he did it was not from impulse, but because he thought it would be indecorous to refuse. It is easy to imagine Pater remembering that he was a child and therefore should play at games, though games wearied him not a little. I can imagine Pater's childhood—an extraordinary childhood! He must have suffered, and felt from the first that he was different from other children, and no doubt he began to practise writing in his teens. It would be interesting to know what his early writings were like, but it is doubtful if we shall ever see these writings. His instinct was never to show himself to the world except in a carefully considered attitude and light; he destroyed, no doubt, all traces of his intellectual development, and if he overlooked any papers his sisters have destroyed them. They understood their brother. A mystery is more interesting than an explanation, and why should we not leave *The Renaissance* a mystery? The more so because Pater is the only example in literature of a man coming before the public in the perfect accomplishment of his genius: Turgenieff—it seems impossible to escape talking of him—wrote well from the first, but *The Tales of a Sportsman*, though perfect, are slight—they are but Tanagra figures; the later stories are—it has been said—the most beautiful things since antiquity; but *The Renaissance* is a May morning: we know it as morning because there is some incomparable haze on the water. Who shall say that Pater's genius is not complete in *The Renaissance?* But who shall say that his genius is not as ripe in *The Renaissance* as it is in the *Imaginary Portraits?* It were better to say that his genius was over-ripe in *Marius* and the *Imaginary Portraits*. *The Renaissance* is the younger book; it is the Maytime, a morning of sunshine and haze, when in the words of an old Irish poet "the talk of the rushes is come," whereas *Imaginary Portraits* is like the end of a long July afternoon before the year has begun to decline. An extraordinary exaltation is in the air; the swallows are flying high, high as our thoughts; and we are aware that we participate in the vast harmony reaching from the beetle in the grass to the pale moon. Last week was spent reading this book—a happy week, lying almost at length in an armchair, rousing a little from time to time, as from delight too intense to be borne, happy, however, in the knowledge that the dream lay always within reach—a happy, melodious dream, full of faint colour and dim perfume, flowing on page after page. But last week's reading was not my first reading of this book. The very copy of the book that I read last week I had seen before, and had tried to read it, but it had seemed to me somewhat faint, too luscious to my taste, and it had been put aside. But last week I was moved by the first few lines, my whole nature responded, and there began a soft interior purring at the prospect of coming happiness; yet the book had once been put aside as a thing that I did not believe to be quite intended for me.

We shall never escape from the mistake of thinking that a

book is bad or useless because it does not satisfy the need of the moment; that mistake is inherent in us—we are but the need of the moment, and our need is changing; new ideas are always ripening in us, and the book we put aside last year is the book that we read eagerly this year; we are always becoming our books. Could we remember this, life would be more decorous, for it is certainly an indecorous thing to open Pater's *Imaginary Portraits* and say, "This book will never be mine." Mood follows mood, and whosoever keeps the book by him shall read it some day in the right mood, and then his enjoyment will be a unique one; he will experience a delight not to be found anywhere else, in literature, in painting or in sculpture; nor will his enjoyment be the enjoyment that he experiences in music, though it will be more akin to that enjoyment than to any other. While he reads this book it will seem to him that he is listening to music, for the book breathes a natural music, the music one hears in Maytime when—to quote the same old Irish poet again—"the harp of the forest sounds music." Methinks Pater desired the ear more than any other sense. Has he not said, in an incomparable passage, that the tendency of all arts is to aspire to music, to tend to become—would that I could remember the exact words! they are to be found in the first book he wrote, *The Renaissance*—I think the words are that the tendency of all the arts is to aspire to the condition of music?

But, however sure we may be that there is nothing in Pater of more permanent value than *The Renaissance*, we must admit that if the condition of music be accepted as the literary ideal towards which he aspired, he realised it more completely in the *Imaginary Portraits* than in the *Renaissance*, perhaps than in *Marius*. In no art, perhaps, is the gift of construction as necessary as it is in music. Some books are remembered for a single passage—for a phrase; a musical phrase is more dependent on the general context than a literary phrase. A musical phrase is like a beautiful ornament in architecture, a beautiful piece of carving; the conditions of music are architectural conditions, and beauty of detail is of little value unless it be inherent in the scheme. The structure of music comes before detail; and the weariness that overtakes us in music begins when the musical structure vacillates or wanders. Without doubt the structure of music is more apparent to musicians than the structure of a literary article is to a man of letters, because musicians know more about their art than men of letters know about theirs. Let us put the expert aside and consider how an elaborate piece of music is heard by the ordinary ear. We have a distinct recollection of how the prelude to *Tristan* affected us the first time we heard it: it seemed to us as if masses of iridescent colour were passing before our eyes with here and there a trace of design quickly absorbed, lost like a forest path amid profuse undergrowths. What I am working towards is this, that the structure of Pater's *Imaginary Portraits* was for a long time as unanalysable, to me at least, and now it does not seem exaggeration to say that the construction of the prelude to *Tristan* can be more readily picked out than the structure of Pater's portraits. The prose of any one of these portraits, excepting perhaps "The Prince of Court Painters," bewilders the professional reader: it seems to him to be thrown together like the essay of a schoolboy; it seems to him to wander as casually as a lost dog; the theme lingers, it is lost, and then it appears farther on, only to be dropped again. But in the end all the floating colours become one, and we are thrilled by an extraordinary, undefinable harmony, obeying laws profound as Nature's and hidden from us as profoundly. This is the impression that Pater's prose produces; but all art yields to patient analysis—if it did not, it

would not be art; and if the critic be patient and acute, he will discern sooner or later the structure which underlies these shifting harmonies: he will discover that an essay by Pater can be resolved into three parts, just like an article in the *Daily Telegraph*—the statement, the argument in favour of it, and the conclusion—for Pater knew how to write his prose separately, and to put it together was his secret. Every essay must have been written in twenty or thirty paragraphs, and these paragraphs were put together afterwards like a puzzle, with here and there a few connecting words written in. We must first be able to compose according to measurement, like the article in the *Daily Telegraph*, and, as we make progress in art, we are able to overshadow, to overlay the primary structure, to hide every joining, to write as it were without transition, and to do this without ever losing the basic lines on which every work of art is built. The trouble that Pater took to raise his prose, to the condition of music must have been extraordinary; months must have been spent upon a single article; and it was in this way that he achieved in literature the floating, unrealisable beauty which exists in music, and perhaps only in music heard for the first or the second time.

Pater's biographer will have to apply to his sisters, who may remember something of his manner of working; but it may be doubted if we shall ever know much more than Pater has chosen to let us know himself. There may be something to be told about his life at Oxford. Wherever he was, his life must have been the same—it must have moved along the same simple lines. I am sure he wore the same mask there as in London; he was kind and courteous always, but revealing himself to no one. We know he was a scholar—he was a Fellow of Brasenose College—but there was no trace of the scholar in his conversation, nor is there any in his writings. He was probably compelled towards scholarship as a means of obtaining an income which would allow him to devote his life to literature; for he cannot have taken much pleasure in his studies; his Greek studies may have interested him a little more than the others. I suppose we may trace Plato's influence in Pater's style, but no—there is nothing of Plato in his style. One speaks of Plato for want of something to say, because one must try to trace Pater's writing back to some model. There is cause for everything, therefore Pater's style must have come from somewhere, and if we had his early writings we might be able to trace it back. But Pater has destroyed these; I say he destroyed them, meaning that they are unpublished, and it is perhaps the absence of these papers that makes Pater's style so original, the most original in literature. If it be difficult to trace the underlying structure in his essays, it is impossible to trace his literary style. It reminds us, it is true, of many things—of the countries he is describing, France, Holland and Germany, not only the aspects of these countries, but their mental attitudes. The style varies, but it is always the same style. In the portrait of Duke Carl of Rosenmold the style overflows, as the old ducal palace overflows with furniture. Here, more than elsewhere, the sentences turn into unexpected passages and courts; here and there modern turns of speech are placed so naturally that they charm us by their strangeness, just as a modern picture might hanging amid the architecture of a German ducal palace. Pater's style, more than any other style, springs from his manner of thinking. He wished to exhibit a mind full of wistful uncertainties, a mind that slowly unwinds like soft silk, with many a pause, and with hesitation and some fear, and this is why he wrote each sentence on a separate piece of paper. His only known aphorism is that it were well to read the dictionary in order to learn what words to avoid; and when Arthur Symonds pointed out a sentence he could not understand, a long intricate sentence of ten lines or more, Pater examined it, comma by comma, a puzzled look upon his face all the while; at last he said, "I see that the printer has omitted a dash."—GEORGE MOORE, "Avowals: VI. Walter Pater," *Pall Mall Magazine*, Aug. 1904, pp. 528–31

For myself, I never have had, and never could have, the slightest hesitation in recommending (though I always feel it rather impertinent to "recommend") the study of such a writer and such a thinker to everyone who possesses sense and wit. One may sometimes disagree with him, and more often think that his view wants expanding and varying. But in literature (I do not pretend to speak of other kinds of art with technical knowledge) I know no one who supplies at once so much stimulus, and so much practical help, with such a range of illustrative enjoyment into the bargain. And apart from literature—in almost the widest ranges of thought and life—I can see no reason why his method should not be applied with an infinite gain of satisfaction to the soul as well as to the senses; and with no necessary—with no even probable—prospect of disaster, except in cases where disaster was antecedently all but certain.—GEORGE SAINTSBURY, "Walter Pater" (1906), *Prefaces and Essays*, 1933, pp. 359–60

It is more than fifteen years since Walter Pater died, and his more famous books have been before the world for a quarter of a century. If it is still too soon to determine his exact place in English letters, there can be no doubt that that place is a permanent and a high one. He is already a classic, ranking not among the greater kings of literature, but among the sovereigns of small and exclusive territories, like De Quincey and Peacock and Landor. The popular school with which he seemed to have affinities has long since disappeared. The aestheticism which flourished in the early "eighties" is as *démodé* as the Della-Cruscans. The world has gone after other gods, and in judging Walter Pater we are not hampered by the illegitimate developments with which a school is always apt to credit a master. We can take him wholly on his merits as a sincere scholar and thinker, who had much to say to his generation, and who strove to say it, not in the easy phrases of popular rhetoric, but in a style of a rigorous and classic perfection. It is one of the ironies of literary history that work so laborious, so laden with thought, so morally serious and sincere, should have been adopted as the gospel of a school of facile impressionists. Mr. Rose in *The New Republic* is a good caricature of certain Paterians, but he has no sort of resemblance to their master. Pater was never foolish, never flippant, never petty. In all his work there is the evidence of a strong and penetrating intellect. So far from deifying sensations, it was the intellectual element in them, the discipline of their evaluation, which interested him. He combined, indeed, two qualities which are generally dissociated,—an intense love of the concrete, and a passion for some principle which would link natural beauty to the life of the human soul.

The starting-point of his intellectual development was probably a revolt from easy metaphysics. He got his Fellowship at Oxford on his work in philosophy, and he was well read in the classics of speculation; but he never seems to have had any of the passion for unification which we associate with the philosopher. Among the many imaginary portraits which he has drawn, only one—that of Sebastian van Storck—is a metaphysician, and he is the most tragically fated of Pater's types, and obviously the least sympathetic to its author. In the "seventies" the revolt against the narrow ratiocination of Mill and Mansel was driving the better minds to Hegel and German metaphysics. Pater was sensitive to this influence, as he was to all others, but

something in him reacted against it. Like Nietzsche in a later day, he protested against a unification which made life a featureless plain. He became the apostle of the concrete, the individual. He insisted upon a value in the sensation which the thinkers who merely regarded it as the raw material of a concept would not grant it. It is necessary to be very clear as to this attitude. He did not revive any crude version of the old Cyrenaicism; he laid down no metaphysical theory; he merely insisted upon a greater reverence, a fuller analysis, a more dignified destiny, for the content of sensation, the phenomena of our everyday life. He wished to rationalise it, but without depleting it, an aim which he shared with Hegel, and, indeed, with all metaphysicians worthy of the name. But for Pater the interest was always less rectitude of thought than rectitude of conduct. He was a humanist, and therefore a moralist. Nowadays we are inclined—not without justice perhaps—to put the moralist outside philosophy proper. His point of view is embarrassing in the quest for truth. Most modern heresies take their origin in his plea that man wants a rule of conduct rather than the reason of things. So, leaving the narrow and thorny path of metaphysics, Pater sought for a principle which would, as they say in the schools, "maximise" life. With his intense love of beauty in art and Nature, his temperament responding like a sensitised plate to the *nuances* of atmosphere and memory, he strove to give men a key to the rich datum of life. But he never lost sight of his own metaphysics. The beauty of Nature and art was impregnated with spirit. Every detail of a picture, every line of a statue, every delicacy of a spring morning was alive with a vast and spiritual significance. The truly spiritual were they whose souls were like a transparency, in which the wonders of the sensuous world could be reflected through a fine medium. Hence he created the "diaphanous" type—for, like Plato, he always thought in types—the soul which is aloof from the bustle of action, which does not create or construct, but which reflects and transmits the subtleties of beauty which would otherwise be lost to men.

The true ritualist is wholly passive, and the earlier Pater was an austere ritualist. He was like some community of mystics, waiting with hushed breath on the blowing of the Spirit. Marius, the greatest of his creations, is a harp played on by every wind. Few more searching and beautiful histories of the progress of a soul have been written than the study of this Falkland of the Roman Empire. He dies on the eve of finding salvation in the Church; but, remember, he does not find it. He is too diaphanous; creeds and emotions are too adequately appreciated by him to remain; they flit through his soul and find no resistance. But as the years went on Pater's mind turned to something harder and less passive. Instead of the unconscious discrimination between good and evil of a delicately poised soul, he groped after active principles of selection. There is always a discipline in ritualism, but it is a prison discipline; one endures because one has no other choice. But the *ascēsis* which Plato taught, and Pater began to emphasise, is the discipline of free men. The soul is master of itself, and will shape the world to its will. Sensations, the sensuous world, are still vital things, but the mind is not subject to them; it uses and adapts them. In his last work, *Plato and Platonism*, it is permissible, we think, to see a real change of attitude. The chapter on "Lacedaemon" would not have been written by the writer of the postscript to *The Renaissance*. The discipline of the ritualist was changing to the discipline of the thinker. He has not lost his grip upon the infinite and various beauty of the world; but he is ready to subdue it consciously to spirit, to select and recreate and remodel. The soul is no longer a mirror, but a fire.

Some such spiritual development we may with justice, using the books as our evidence, attribute to Walter Pater. He has left no autobiography and no materials for a biography, so we are driven to read the history of his soul in his writings. And when all is said, what a performance these ten volumes constitute! Where else in English letters are we to find so much subtlety of thought and feeling embodied in so adequate a medium? It may be that later generations will care little for our old controversies of the spirit. Some new master may supersede all our conundrums with some profounder organon. But by the happy law of things style cannot be superseded, and Pater will be read for the unique blandishments of his style. In this matter he has been vastly overpraised, and vastly underrated, and in both cases on the wrong grounds. His is not a model of English prose. It is far too cumbrous, too recondite, too unworkable. The exact meaning is hammered out laboriously; it does not spring up fresh and unexpected like a spring flower. There is always the air of heavy thought and effort about the sentences. It is not, therefore, a true working weapon, like Milton's tremendous periods, or Burke's golden flow of eloquence, or Ruskin's transmuted poetry. Still less is it a model, like Huxley's or Newman's prose, which the humble man may strive after because it is English in its simplest and most central form. Pater wrote great sentences, sometimes great paragraphs, but he rarely wrote a great page. The vital force ran low in his style. For one thing, in the successful search for the right word he forgot sometimes to look for the right cadence, and there are many passages where there is not a word wrong, but yet the sentence does not please. Nevertheless, languid, overstrained, and overstudied as he often is, there are many moments when he attains the purest melody. From the too famous postscript to *The Renaissance* and the description of Monna Lisa, through a dozen passages in *Marius* and the *Imaginary Portraits*, to the grave dignity of some of the *Greek Studies* and of *Plato and Platonism*, he has left us a treasury of prose which will endure. No man perhaps can come so near giving our rugged prose language the exquisite and intangible effect of music. He is a *petite chapelle* in style, like Lamb, and Borrow, and Stevenson, but it is a *chapelle* whose walls are well founded and whose worshippers will not decrease.—JOHN BUCHAN, "Walter Pater," *Spectator*, June 25, 1910, pp. 1075–76

Works

THE RENAISSANCE

The great distinction of this book is that its author has been completely conscious of what he wished to achieve, and has succeeded in the elaboration of a style perfectly suited to his matter and the temper of his mind. He has studied his prose as carefully as poets study their verses, and has treated criticism as though it were the art of music. Yet he is no mere rhetorician. The penetrative force and subtlety of his intellect are everywhere apparent. There is scarcely a superfluous word or a hasty phrase in the whole volume. Each paragraph, each sentence is saturated with thought; not with that kind of thought which Novalis described as a "dead feeling, a wan, weak life," but with the very substance of the feeling which only becomes thought in order that it may receive expression in words. To do justice to such a style either by quotation or by description is difficult. Yet the following sentences may be extracted as containing in brief something of the peculiar flavour which gives value to the book:—"A certain strangeness, something of the blossoming of the aloe, is, indeed, an element in all true works of art; that they shall excite or surprise us is indispensable" (p. 62). "No one ever expressed more truly than Michel Angelo the notion of inspired sleep, of faces charged with dreams" (p. 59). "The spiritualist is satisfied in seeing the sensuous elements escape from his conceptions; his interest grows, as the dyed garment bleaches in the keener air" (p. 195). "I suppose nothing brings the real air of a Tuscan town so vividly to mind as those pieces of pale blue and white porcelain, by which he is best known, like fragments of the milky sky itself fallen into the cool streets and breaking into the darkened churches" (p. 53). So consummate is Mr. Pater's style that we are surprised to find that he should ever have allowed himself to repeat the same phrase (pp. 64, 66, "but only blank ranges of rock and dim vegetable forms as blank as they"). In like manner he is so patient and perfect in his study of picturesque details that we are almost in spite of ourselves forced to challenge the veracity of his images. For the most part, he will be found as accurate as he is subtle. Yet when he speaks (p. 30) of "that map or system of the world held as a great target or shield in the hands of the grey-headed father of all things, in one of the earlier frescoes of the Campo Santo at Pisa," he has forgotten that the point of this old picture lies in the fact that it is *not* the creative Demeurgus, but Christ, in the prime of manhood, who supports the disc of the universe, with its concentric rings of created beings. Such minute criticism, however, is mere cavilling.

The unity of the book, which is made up for the most part of essays collected from periodicals and polished by their author, consists in this, that each article treats of some phase of the Renaissance through a representative character or work of art. Two are devoted to French literature, and Mr. Pater is particularly happy in his exposition of the theory that the renaissance of modern Europe originated in France. The truth of this theory, which may easily be exaggerated, is that the renaissance was not a sudden and violent explosion of the fifteenth century, but that in all the countries of Europe which possessed the elements of culture—in southern Spain, in Provence, in Frederick the Second's Sicily, in the Paris of Abélard, in the Florence of Boccaccio, and in the Lombardy of the Paterini heretics—the qualities of renaissance striving after liberty were discernible within the middle age itself. Of Mr. Pater's two French studies, that on Du Bellay, in whom he sees "the subtle and delicate sweetness which belong to a refined and comely decadence," is perhaps the more interesting. Like Théophile Gautier and like Baudelaire, Mr. Pater has a sympathetic feeling for the beauty of autumn and decay. He is not even insensible to "what may be called the fascination of corruption." This, which is a very genuine note of his æsthetic temperament, leads him at times, I think, to make mistakes of criticism. A notable instance of this is to be found in his interpretation of Botticelli's Madonnas. They are all painted after one fixed type of beauty—Botticelli, like all true artists, having selected and assimilated for himself from the multitudes of forms just that which represented his peculiar ideal. Mr. Pater imagines that in that sad, languid, sleepy, pallid woman, Botticelli sought to depict one who, "though she holds in her hands the 'Desire of all nations,' is one of those who are neither for God nor for his enemies". . . . one to whom the visit of Gabriel brought an "intolerable honour." I cannot do justice to the eloquence and grace with which this theory is worked out in the essay on Sandro Botticelli. But I must suggest that it ascribes to the painter a far greater amount of sceptical self-consciousness than he was at all likely to have possessed. However we may explain Botticelli's preference for that melancholy type of beauty, we must remember that Lippo Lippi, his master, and Filippino Lippi, his fellow-student, present us with two other varieties of the same type, markedly different, it is true, in sentiment from Botticelli's, but yet like enough to justify the belief that the type itself was the note of a specific school, and not the deliberate invention of an antagonist of the most cherished Catholic tradition. It is far more consistent with Florentine feeling to suppose that in his Madonna's melancholy Botticelli tried to delineate her premonition of the coming sword, and not her weariness in being the mother of the sinless Saviour. A criticism of Michel Angelo, which is marked by the same subtlety and originality, may be questioned in like manner as somewhat over-refined. In the essay on Luca Della Robbia, Mr. Pater defines with much delicacy what are the different methods by which great sculptors have spiritualized their several kinds of work. Passing to Michel Angelo, and noticing the incompleteness of much that he has left, he says: "Well! that incompleteness is Michel Angelo's equivalent for colour in sculpture; it is his way of etherealizing pure form, relieving its hard realism, communicating to it breath, pulsation, the effect of life." This is extremely ingenious, and subjectively it is, perhaps, true: *we* gain by the suggestive ruggedness of much of Michel Angelo's work—in which it seems as if a soul were escaping from the stone. But did Michel Angelo really calculate this effect? That is what is more than doubtful. When he had the time, the will, the opportunity, he finished with the utmost polish. His "Moses" and his "Night"—the latter of which he illustrated by one of his most splendid poems—are smoothed and rounded and completed in their slightest curves. And to this perfection of finish his work was always approximating. That it often fell short may be explained simply by the facts of his life and the strange qualities of his temperament.

In the essay on "The Poetry of Michel Angelo" Mr. Pater shows the truest sympathy for what has generally been overlooked in this stern master—his sweetness. The analysis of the nature of that sweetness is one of the triumphs of Mr. Pater's criticism. Leonardo da Vinci attracts him less as an artist merely than as a personality of deep and splendid fascination. Pico della Mirandola again receives a separate study, in which we are made to feel with an intensity peculiar to Mr. Pater's style, the charm, as of some melody, which clung about him. The longest essay in the book is on Winckelmann, which, besides containing a very interesting sketch of the man, is full of good criticism of the Greek in contrast with the modern spirit. What is said on p. 195 about the way in which Winckelmann was privileged to approach Greek art is perfect. As the book begins with a preface which sets forth the author's theory of criticism, so it ends with a conclusion in which he expresses his theory of life. Between the cradle and the grave we have but a short breathing space. How are we to use it best by "getting as many pulsations as possible into the given time?" Mr. Pater's answer is that Art is after all the most satisfactory pursuit: "Of this wisdom, the poetic passion, the desire of beauty, the love of art for art's sake has most; for art comes to you professing frankly to give nothing but the highest quality to your moments as they pass, and simply for those moments' sake."—JOHN ADDINGTON SYMONDS, "Art and Archaeology," *Academy*, March 15, 1873, pp. 104–5

I agreed very warmly with the remarks made by your contributor this month on Mr. Pater's book, which seems to me quite poisonous in its false principles of criticism and false conceptions of life.—GEORGE ELIOT, Letter to John Blackwood (Nov. 5, 1873)

MARIUS THE EPICUREAN

It is open to doubt if it has been Mr. Pater's intention to offer an apology for the higher Epicureanism: possibly he has merely endeavoured to trace the development of a cultured mind in a period that bears no slight resemblance to our own—development from belief in a venerable inherited creed to the adoption of a strictly worldly philosophy, a philosophy of how to make the most of life, the latter yielding in turn to spiritual weariness and even hopelessness; relieved, perchance, not by vision of any ultimate individual good, but by a somewhat broader view of the future of humanity than had formerly been entertained. On the other hand, there are, at any rate, some pages here and there in these two volumes which unmistakably express the personal opinions of the author, and these, conjointly with portions of Mr. Pater's other published writings, constitute sufficient basis for the assumption that he does, indeed, recognize the teaching of Epicurus as—in its quintessential doctrine—not unworthy, even in these days of manifold *isms*, of serious consideration as a practical philosophy of life. Of course, no one can be better aware that this teaching in its entirety is antagonistic to the attachment of wide culture; but as this antagonism is more the result of the ancient philosopher's own idiosyncrasy than the logical outcome of his philosophy of sensation as the means of knowledge and of self-satisfaction as the end of life, Mr. Pater may well be willing to join hands with him so far.

If, however, it has been his intention to demonstrate the futility of either Epicurean or Stoic philosophy, and to show that Christianity is alone in any sense really responsive to man's deepest aspirations, then he has been only very partially successful. Indubitably he has in *Marius* skilfully, and without precipitation, disclosed the lees that abide in the bottom of the cup that contains the mellow wine of the wisdom of Epicurus; but at most he only vaguely suggests that in its place, if we care to partake thereof, there is a draught of more vivifying essence, of more estimable flavour—yet of the permanency of whose subtle regenerative quality he can say, as he knows, nothing.

In a word, the mental history of Marius the Epicurean will hardly help any one in the same plight as was Marius himself after all his years of careful introspection, anxious thought, and vague expectancy. There is no real transition, on the part of the latter, from refined and in some points greatly modified Epicureanism to Christianity; nor, even if he had not, with strange irony of circumstance, perished so untimely, is it in the least degree likely that he would ever have become an actual convert to the new faith. He would have found it impossible to reconcile two teachings so really antagonistic—or, rather, so really distinct—as that of the pagan philosopher and that of the new God. His first conversion took place when, still a youth undisturbed in his reverence for and belief in the ancient religion of Rome, he hearkened with keenly receptive ears to the lessons of the young priest of the Temple of Æsculapius; as for a second conversion, does it ever really take place, or even seem as if it might have taken place if death had not intervened?

In impassioned contemplation, Mr. Pater says in that essay on Wordsworth already referred to, lies the true moral significance of art and poetry. But the passion must arise out of intensity of insight and be no mere mystical emotion; with this writer, as with the Marius of whom he tells, there is a keen appreciation "of the poetic beauty of mere clearness of mind—the actually æsthetic charm of a cold austerity of thought; as if the kinship of that to the clearness of physical light were something more than a figure of speech."

There is no living writer who excels Mr. Pater in grace of style. He does not indulge in passages of sustained eloquence, but every word he writes is calculated to be the best word in that place, to have its full signification brought out. Here and there, of course, there are passages of exceptional beauty; but fine as these are, Mr. Pater's special faculty for verbal expression is more noticeable in his occasional use of certain words which in his mouth, so to speak, act like a charm. While he is the most rhythmical of English prosewriters, his is the music of the viola rather than of the violin.

It is no joyous evangel that Mr. Pater proclaims in these two volumes, albeit it clearly infers the possibility of many joyous experiences. Everything that is is evanescent. The darkness beyond is still darkness for us; hence it is that these joys, these exhilarating flashes of insight and moments of vivid pleasurable emotion, are enhanced, "like the glow of summer itself," by the thought of their brevity. Consciously or unconsciously, there is in all that he has written a strain of that partly sad, partly genuinely contentful resignation of the great Aurelius which found fullest expression in these words:—

Sayest thou, "I have not played five acts." True! but in human life three acts only make sometimes a complete play. That is the composer's business, not thine. Retire with a good will; for that too hath, perchance, a good will which dismisseth thee from thy part.
—WILLIAM SHARP, *Athenaeum*, Feb. 28, 1885, pp. 272–73

Marius I have not read. I suppose I must. But I shrink from approaching Pater's style, which has a peculiarly disagreeable effect upon my nerves—like the presence of a civet cat. Still, I believe I must read it.—JOHN ADDINGTON SYMONDS, Letter to Henry Sidgwick (April 5, 1885)

Mr. Pater, it will be observed, still speaks of morals as it were in terms of aesthetics. His hero advances, or partially advances, from the aesthetic to the ethical standpoint, not because of any "conventional first principles" on which morals may depend for their sanction, but because of the enriched experience, the "quickened sympathies" which are to be gained from the advance. Practically, the same motive power is at work in the second stage as in the first. But as the sphere of its operation enlarges, it tends to coalesce and join hands with other powers, starting from very different bases. The worship of beauty, carried far enough, tends to transform itself into a passion moral in essence and in aim. "For the variety of men's possible reflections on their experience, as of that experience itself, is not really as great as it seems. All the highest spirits, from whatever contrasted points they may have started, will yet be found to entertain in their moral consciousness, as actually realised, much the same kind of company."

One feels as though one were reading another "Palace of Art" with a difference! Here, in Mr. Pater's system, the soul ceases to live solitary in the midst of a dainty world of its own choice, not because it is overtaken by any crushing conviction of sin and ruin in so doing, but because it learns to recognise that such a worship of beauty defeats its own ends, that by opening the windows of its palace to the outside light and air, and placing the life within under the common human law, it really increases its own chances of beautiful impressions, of "exquisite moments." To put it in the language of the present book, "Marius saw that he would be but an inconsistent Cyrenaic—mistaken in his estimate of values, of loss and gain, and untrue to the well-considered economy of life which he had brought to Rome with him—that some drops of the great cup would fall to the ground"—if he did not make the concession of a "voluntary curtailment of liberty" to the ancient and wonderful order actually in possession of the world, if he did not

purchase by a willing self-control, participation in that rich store of crystallised feeling represented by the world's moral beliefs.

Still, although the fundamental argument is really the same as that on which Mr. Pater based a general view of life twelve years ago, the practical advance in position shown by the present book is considerable. "That theory, or idea, or system," said the writer of the *Studies*, in 1873, "which requires of us the sacrifice of any part of experience in consideration of some interest into which we cannot enter, or some abstract morality we have not identified with ourselves, or what is only conventional, has no real claim upon us." Now the legitimacy and necessity of some such sacrifice is admitted; for evidently the one mental process, in spite of the indirectness of its presentation, is but a continuation of the other. *Marius* carries on the train of reflection begun by the *Studies*, and the upshot of the whole so far is a utilitarian or Epicurean theory of morals. For, stripped of its poetical dress, the ethical argument of *Marius* is essentially utilitarian. After protesting against the curtailment of experience in favour of "some abstract morality we have not identified with ourselves," Mr. Pater now presents obedience to this same morality as desirable, not because of any absolute virtue or authority inherent in it, but because practically obedience is a source of pleasure and quickened faculty to the individual.—MRS. HUMPHRY WARD, "*Marius the Epicurean*," *Macmillan's Magazine*, May 1885, pp. 136–37

The Book Beautiful. *Marius the Epicurean* is pre-eminently that for many of us. Perhaps no book since *Sartor Resartus* has been read with such a sense of awakening, and indeed it may be said that it has, in some needed measure, modified the influence of *Sartor*, with its sublime factory gospel of work. For the imperative 'Do!' of Carlyle it substitutes the gentle pleading 'Be!' 'Be ye perfect!' The culture of the individual in a well-ordered unity, body, soul, and spirit: that is its message. But not a selfish culture. 'He must satisfy, with a kind of sacred equity, he must be very cautious not to be wanting to the claims of others, in their joys and calamities.' That was one of the earliest axioms Marius took with him on his progress from the primitive religion of his fathers, through Epicureanism, to that final mood of his mind in which the careful justice of such an axiom was being deepened by the warmer sentiment of a Christian pity. What that mood quite was we are left a little in doubt—as how else could it be in regard to a complex being such as Marius? His experience of life had been too various, too humanising, for him to become the bondsman of any mere dogma; though in the formulæ of Christianity, the earlier, unmonastic Christianity, he had, perhaps, come nearest to finding the formulæ which most expressed his own gentle individuality—if formula must be!

Some people will have nothing of Mr. Pater. One has heard them say that he is all manner and no matter. A strange doctrine, for certainly it seemed to some of us, when first we read *Marius* with glowing heart, that it was full indeed of burning matters. It seemed that no 'spiritual pastor' had so harmonised the claims of body and soul, so wondrously captured for us those fine elusive moods of which we are hardly aware till we recognise them in another; and that no one had written more movingly of friendship, of goodness, of beauty, or of death—great matters as we thought. It is true that Mr. Pater's manner is occasionally a little too priestlike in its extreme, its maiden-like fastidiousness. But even so, such fastidiousness comes but of his sincerity towards his meaning. It is instructive to remember what he writes of Flavian: 'His dilettantism, his assiduous preoccupation with what might seem but the details of mere form or manner, was, after all, bent upon the function of bringing to the surface, sincerely, and in their integrity, certain strong personal intuitions, certain visions or apprehensions of things as being, with important results, in this way rather than that.'—RICHARD LE GALLIENNE, "Walter Pater: *Marius the Epicurean*" (1892), *Retrospective Reviews*, 1896, Vol. 1, pp. 174–75

APPRECIATIONS

When I first had the privilege—and I count it a very high one—of meeting Mr. Walter Pater, he said to me, smiling, "Why do you always write poetry? Why do you not write prose? Prose is so much more difficult."

It was during my undergraduate days at Oxford; days of lyrical ardour and of studious sonnet-writing; days when one loved the exquisite intricacy and musical repetitions of the ballade, and the villanelle with its linked long-drawn echoes and its curious completeness; days when one solemnly sought to discover the proper temper in which a triolet should be written; delightful days, in which, I am glad to say, there was far more rhyme than reason.

I may frankly confess now that at the time I did not quite comprehend what Mr. Pater really meant; and it was not till I had carefully studied his beautiful and suggestive essays on the Renaissance that I fully realised what a wonderful self-conscious art the art of English prose-writing really is, or may be made to be. Carlyle's stormy rhetoric, Ruskin's winged and passionate eloquence, had seemed to me to spring from enthusiasm rather than from art. I do not think I knew then that even prophets correct their proofs. As for Jacobean prose, I thought it too exuberant; and Queen Anne prose appeared to me terribly bald, and irritatingly rational. But Mr. Pater's essays became to me "the golden book of spirit and sense, the holy writ of beauty." They are still this to me. It is possible, of course, that I may exaggerate about them. I certainly hope that I do; for where there is no exaggeration there is no love, and where there is no love there is no understanding. It is only about things that do not interest one, that one can give a really unbiassed opinion; and this is no doubt the reason why an unbiassed opinion is always valueless.

But I must not allow this brief notice of Mr. Pater's new volume to degenerate into an autobiography. I remember being told in America that whenever Margaret Fuller wrote an essay upon Emerson the printers had always to send out to borrow some additional capital "I's," and I feel it right to accept this transatlantic warning.

Appreciations, in the fine Latin sense of the word, is the title given by Mr. Pater to his book, which is an exquisite collection of exquisite essays, of delicately wrought works of art—some of them being almost Greek in their purity of outline and perfection of form, others mediaeval in their strangeness of colour and passionate suggestion, and all of them absolutely modern, in the true meaning of the term modernity. For he to whom the present is the only thing that is present, knows nothing of the age in which he lives. To realise the nineteenth century one must realise every century that has preceded it, and that has contributed to its making. To know anything about oneself, one must know all about others. There must be no mood with which one cannot sympathise, no dead mode of life that one cannot make alive. The legacies of heredity may make us alter our views of moral responsibility, but they cannot but intensify our sense of the value of Criticism; for the true critic is he who bears within himself the dreams and ideas and feelings of myriad generations, and to

whom no form of thought is alien, no emotional impulse obscure.

Perhaps the most interesting, and certainly the least successful, of the essays contained in the present volume is that on "Style." It is the most interesting because it is the work of one who speaks with the high authority that comes from the noble realisation of things nobly conceived. It is the least successful, because the subject is too abstract. A true artist like Mr. Pater is most felicitous when he deals with the concrete, whose very limitations give him finer freedom, while they necessitate more intense vision. And yet what a high ideal is contained in these few pages! How good it is for us, in these days of popular education and facile journalism, to be reminded of the real scholarship that is essential to the perfect writer, who, "being a true lover of words for their own sake, a minute and constant observer of their physiognomy," will avoid what is mere rhetoric, or ostentatious ornament, or negligent misuse of terms, or ineffective surplusage, and will be known by his tact of omission, by his skilful economy of means, by his selection and self-restraint, and perhaps above all by that conscious artistic structure which is the expression of mind in style. I think I have been wrong in saying that the subject is too abstract. In Mr. Pater's hands it becomes very real to us indeed, and he shows us how, behind the perfection of a man's style, must lie the passion of a man's soul.

As one passes to the rest of the volume, one finds essays on Wordsworth and on Coleridge, on Charles Lamb and on Sir Thomas Browne, on some of Shakespeare's plays and on the English kings that Shakespeare fashioned, on Dante Rossetti, and on William Morris. As that on Wordsworth seems to be Mr. Pater's last work, so that on the singer of the *Defence of Guenevere* is certainly his earliest, or almost his earliest, and it is interesting to mark the change that has taken place in his style. This change is, perhaps, at first sight not very apparent. In 1868 we find Mr. Pater writing with the same exquisite care for words, with the same studied music, with the same temper, and something of the same mode of treatment. But, as he goes on, the architecture of the style becomes richer and more complex, the epithet more precise and intellectual. Occasionally one may be inclined to think that there is, here and there, a sentence which is somewhat long, and possibly, if one may venture to say so, a little heavy and cumbersome in movement. But if this be so, it comes from those side-issues suddenly suggested by the idea in its progress, and really revealing the idea more perfectly; or from those felicitous after-thoughts that give a fuller completeness to the central scheme, and yet convey something of the charm of chance; or from a desire to suggest the secondary shades of meaning with all their accumulating effect, and to avoid, it may be, the violence and harshness of too definite and exclusive an opinion. For in matters of art, at any rate, thought is inevitably coloured by emotion, and so is fluid rather than fixed, and, recognising its dependence upon moods and upon the passion of fine moments, will not accept the rigidity of a scientific formula or a theological dogma. The critical pleasure, too, that we receive from tracing, through what may seem the intricacies of a sentence, the working of the constructive intelligence, must not be overlooked. As soon as we have realised the design, everything appears clear and simple. After a time, these long sentences of Mr. Pater's come to have the charm of an elaborate piece of music, and the unity of such music also. ⟨. . .⟩

Finally, one cannot help noticing the delicate instinct that has gone to fashion the brief epilogue that ends this delightful volume. The difference between the classical and romantic spirits in art has often, and with much over-emphasis, been discussed. But with what a light sure touch does Mr. Pater write of it! How subtle and certain are his distinctions! If imaginative prose be really the special art of this century, Mr. Pater must rank amongst our century's most characteristic artists. In certain things he stands almost alone. The age has produced wonderful prose styles, turbid with individualism, and violent with excess of rhetoric. But in Mr. Pater, as in Cardinal Newman, we find the union of personality with perfection. He has no rival in his own sphere, and he has escaped disciples. And this, not because he has not been imitated, but because in art so fine as his there is something that, in its essence, is inimitable.—OSCAR WILDE, "Mr. Pater's Last Volume," *Speaker*, March 22, 1890

JOHN MORLEY
From "Mr. Pater's Essays"

Fortnightly Review, April 1873, pp. 471–77

Mr. Pater's studies in the history of the Renaissance and the essay on Winckelmann which he has appropriately enough attached to them, constitute the most remarkable example of this younger movement towards a fresh and inner criticism, and they are in themselves a singular and interesting addition to literature. The subjects are of the very kind in which we need instruction and guidance, and there is a moral in the very choice of them. From the point of view of form and literary composition they are striking in the highest degree. They introduce to English readers a new and distinguished master in the great and difficult art of writing prose. Their style is marked by a flavour at once full and exquisite, by a quality that mixes richness with delicacy, and a firm coherency with infinite subtlety. The peril that besets a second-rate writer who handles a style of this kind lies in the direction of effeminate and flaccid mannerism, and the peril is especially great when he is dealing with æsthetic subjects; they tempt to an expansion of feeling, for the expression of which no prose can ever become a proper medium. Mr. Pater escapes the danger, first by virtue of his artistic sense which reveals to him the limits of prose and gives him spontaneous respect for them, keeping him well away from all bastard dithyramb, and secondly by virtue of a strain of clear, vigorous, and ordered thought, which underlies and compacts his analysis of sensuous impressions. Hence his essays, while abounding in passages of an exquisite and finished loveliness that recall the completeness of perfected verse, are saved by a marked gravity and reserve from any taint of the sin of random poetical expatiation and lyric effusion. Mr. Pater's style is far too singular in its excellence not to contain the germs of possible excess in some later day. All excellent style does so; if it is of a large and noble eloquence, like Burke's or Bossuet's, it holds the seeds of turgidity; if it is racy and generously imaginative, it may easily degenerate into vulgarity or weedy rankness or the grotesque; if it is of a severe and chastened elevation, it is apt to fall over, and substitute ætherialised phrase for real and robust ideas. And so subtlety and love of minor tones may lead a writer who is not in constant and rigorous discipline, into affectation and a certain mawkishness. Meantime we trust to Mr. Pater's intellectual firmness, to his literary conscience and scrupulosity, and above all to his reserve. This fine reserve, besides the negative merit of suppressing misplaced effusion, has a positive effect of its own, an effect of subtle and penetrating suggestiveness that but for the sobriety and balance of the general colour would leave one with half weird, unsatisfied, unreal impressions. Thus at the close of the beautiful piece on Joachim Du Bellay, after giving us the song which is the writer's title to commemoration, Mr. Pater justly says that nearly all the pleasure of it "is in the surprise at the happy and dexterous way in which a thing slight in itself is handled," and then concludes generally: "One seems to hear the measured falling of the fans with a child's pleasure on coming across the incident for the first time in one of those great barns of Du Bellay's own country, La Beauce, the granary of France. A sudden light transfigures a trivial thing, a weather-vane, a wind-mill, a winnowing flail, the dirt in the barn-door; a moment,—and the thing has vanished, because it was pure effect; but it leaves a relish behind it, a longing that the accident may happen again." This brief sentence is the happiest summary of criticism, leaving the reader with the key, and leaving him, too, with a desire to use it and explore what further may be locked up in verse or picture. This is the manner of Mr. Pater's criticism throughout. The same passage illustrates another of its qualities. It is concrete and positive, not metaphysical; a record or suggestion of impressions, not an analysis of their ultimate composition, nor an abstract search for the law of their effects. "The more you come to understand what imaginative colouring really is, that *all colour is no mere delightful quality of outward things, but a spirit upon them by which they become expressive to the spirit*, the better you will like this peculiar quality of colour" (p. 48). How full at once of suggestion, and of explanation, yet without that parade of speculative and technical apparatus, which has made most art criticism, especially among ourselves, so little nourishing, so little real or life-like. "What is important," as Mr. Pater says in words that define his own method and position, "is not that the critic should possess a correct abstract definition of beauty, but a certain kind of temperament, the power of being deeply moved by the presence of beautiful objects. He will remember that beauty exists in many forms. And often," he continues, "it will require great nicety to disengage this virtue from the commoner elements with which it may be found in combination." It is probably this keen susceptibility to minute suggestions that underlies the writer's care for the lesser stars in the great firmament, his love for bits of work other than the gigantic or sublime, the attraction to him of hints of beauty and faintly marked traces of exquisite peculiarity, rather than the noon-day splendour of master works. We can suppose that the simplicity of some Gregorian chant would please him better than a great Beethoven symphony, and that the church at Gernerode or St. Cunibert's at Cologne would give him more heartfelt delight than the glories of the great Cölner Dom itself. After all anybody may be stirred by the sublime or the superb. We can well afford to welcome to literature one of the less common spirits, gifted with a sense for the dinner beauties, and to whom the more distant tones are audible and harmonious. Such gifts are extraordinarily welcome to our own literature, which rich as it is in magnificent as in sweet and homely productions, is anything but rich in work marked by subtlety of æsthetic vision. If Mr. Pater continues to remember that it is exactly in the region of a man's gifts where he most needs caution and self-discipline, lest the fatal flaw of excess turn his strength into his weakness, we may expect from him delight and instruction of the rarest kind.

In one or two places there is perhaps to be noticed a tinge of obscurity, or at least of doubtfulness of meaning, the result of a refining of thought into excess of tenuity. It is so difficult a thing rigorously to put aside as taken for granted all commonplace impression and obvious phrase, and only to seize what is the inner virtue of the matter, without going beyond the sight and grasp of plainer men. We have one man of genius who is as great a master of subtle insight into character, as Mr. Pater is of analysis of beautiful impressions; Mr. Meredith, like Mr. Pater, is not always easy to follow, and for the same reason. After all the plain men are at least as much in fault as those who touch them with perplexity. This fault, however, in Mr. Pater's case, if it is really there, and not merely a fancy of my own, is only to be found in the essay on Winckelmann, which is the earliest of the compositions in the volume; and so we may suppose that it is a fault of which the writer has already cured himself. We may, perhaps, also venture to notice the occasional appearance of a very minor defect, which is far too common in all contemporary writing and conversation, but which jars more than usually in so considerable a stylist as Mr. Pater; I mean the use of German and French phrases, like *intimité, Allgemeinheit, Heiterkeit,* and the rest. It seems just now to be peculiarly the duty of a writer who respects his own language, and has the honourable aspiration of maintaining its purity, strength, and comprehensiveness, carefully to resist every temptation to introduce a single foreign word into his prose upon any pretext whatever. Even quotations from foreign writers ought, as I presume to think, to be given in English, and not in French, German, Greek, Italian, excepting of course quotations in verse, and of these the good prose writer is naturally most sparing in any language.

Concreteness, prevented from running to unprofitable amplitude of description alike by the reserve of the writer's style, and by the subtlety of the only impressions which he thinks worth recording, is connected with a prime characteristic of Mr. Pater's work, its constant association of art with the actual moods and purposes of men in life. He redeems beautiful production in all its kinds from the arid bondage of their technicalities, and unfolds its significance in relation to human culture and the perplexities of human destiny. This is to make art veritably fruitful, and criticism too. His criticism is endowed with strength and substance by the abundance of intellectual ideas which have come to him from the union of careful cultivation with an original individuality, and these intellectual ideas are grouped in an unsystematic way round a distinct theory of life and its purport, which thus in the manner we pointed out at first gives colour and meaning to all that Mr. Pater has to say about the special objects of his study. This theory is worth attention. The exponent of it sees only the fluid elements in life, only its brevity and the inevitable abyss that lies at the end of our path. "We have an interval and then our place knows us no more. Some spend their interval in listlessness, some in high passions, the wisest in art and song. For our one chance is in expanding that interval, in getting as many pulsations as possible into the given time. High passions give one this quickened sense of life, ecstasy and sorrow of love, political or religious enthusiasm, or 'the enthusiasm of humanity.' Only, be sure that it does yield you this fruit of a quickened multiplied consciousness. Of this wisdom, the poetic passion, the desire of beauty, the love of art for art's sake has most; for art comes to you professing frankly to give nothing but the highest quality to your moments as they pass and simply for those moments' sake" (p. 212). Of course this neither is, nor is meant to be, a complete scheme for wise living and wise dying. The Hedonist, and this is what Mr. Pater must be called by those who like to affix labels, holds just the same maxims with reference to the bulk of human conduct, the homespun substance of our days, as are held by other people in their senses. He knows perfectly well that the commonplace virtues of honesty, industry, punctuality, and the like, are the condi-

tions of material prosperity, and moral integrity. Here he stands on the same ground as the rest of the world. He takes all that for granted, with or without regret that these limitations should be imposed by inexorable circumstance upon the capacity of human nature for fine delight in the passing moments. He has no design of interfering with the minor or major morals of the world, but only of dealing with what we may perhaps call the accentuating portion of life. In the majority of their daily actions a Catholic, a Protestant, a Positivist, are indistinguishable from one another; just as they are indistinguishable in the clothes they wear. It is the accentuating parts of conduct and belief that reveal their differences, and this is obviously of the most extreme importance,—less in its effect upon commonplace external morality which can take care of itself on independent grounds, than in its influence over the spiritual drift of the believer's life. It is what remains for a man seriously to do or feel, over and above earning his living and respecting the laws. What is to give significance and worth to his life, after complying with the conditions essential to its maintenance and outward order? A great many people in all times, perhaps the most, give a practical answer to the question by ignoring it, and living unaccented lives of dulness or frivolity. A great many others find an answer in devotion to divine mysteries, which round the purpose of their lives and light the weariness of mechanical days. The writer of the essays before us answers it as we have seen, and there is now a numerous sect among cultivated people who accept his answer and act upon it. So far as we know, there never was seen before in this country so distinct an attempt to bring the æsthetical element closely and vividly round daily life. It has an exaggerated side. Dutch farmhouses are systematically swept by brokers, that the vulgarity of ormolu may be replaced by delft, and nankin, and magic bits of oriental blue and white. There is an orthodoxy in wall-papers, and you may commit the unpardonable sin in discordant window-curtains. Members of the sect are as solicitous about the right in tables and the correct in legs of chairs, as members of another sect are careful about the cut of chasuble or dalmatica. Bric-a-brac rises to the level of religions, and the whirligig of time is bringing us back to fetishism and the worship of little domestic gods, not seldom bleak and uncouth.

In all this, notwithstanding its exaggeration, there is something to be glad of. It is the excess of a reaction, in itself very wholesome, against the vulgar luxury of commonplace decoration, and implies a certain appreciation of the permanent principles of beautiful ornament. But there is something deeper than this underneath, at least in the minds of the vigorous leaders of the movement, and in such men as Mr. Pater, just as there was something deeper than the puerilities of the fussier and sillier sort of ritualists in the mind of Mr. Ward or Dr. Newman. Indeed, this more recent pagan movement is one more wave of the great current of reactionary force which the Oxford movement first released. It is infinitely less powerful, among other reasons because it only appeals to persons with some culture, but it is equally a protest against the mechanical and graceless formalism of the modern era, equally an attempt to find a substitute for a narrow popular creed in a return upon the older manifestations of the human spirit, and equally a craving for the infusion of something harmonious and beautiful about the bare lines of daily living. Since the first powerful attempt to revive a gracious spirituality in the country by a renovation of sacramentalism, science has come. The Newmanite generation in Oxford was followed by a generation who were formed on Mr. Mill's *Logic* and Grote's *Greece.* The æsthetic spirits were no longer able to find rest in a system associated with theology. Then Mr. Ruskin came, and the Præ-Raphaelite painters, and Mr. Swinburne, and Mr. Morris, and now lastly a critic like Mr. Pater, all with faces averted from theology, most of them indeed blessed with a simple and happy unconsciousness of the very existence of the conventional gods. Many of them are as indifferent to the conventional aims and phrases of politics and philanthropy as they are to things called heavenly. Mr. Ruskin indeed, as we all know, has plunged chivalrously into the difficult career of the social reconstructor, but hardly with a success that any man can call considerable. And Mr. Swinburne, like that most powerful of all French poets whom he calls master, has always shown a generous ardour in the greater human causes. But here is Mr. Pater courageously saying that the love of art for art's sake has most of the true wisdom that makes life full. The fact that such a saying is possible in the mouth of an able and shrewd-witted man of wide culture and knowledge, and that a serious writer should thus raise æsthetic interest to the throne lately filled by religion, only shows how void the old theologies have become.

And if such a doctrine fails of their inspiring earnestness and gravity, at the same time it escapes their cramping narrowness. It is pregnant with intellectual play and expansion, and it is this intellectual play and expansion that we require, before the social changes craved by so many can fully ripen. It is assuredly good for us to possess such a school. There is no reason to be afraid of their taking too firm a hold, or occupying too much ground, to the detriment of energetic social action in the country. We have suffered more from the excessive absorption of national interest in theological strife and the futilities of political faction, than we are at all likely to suffer from the devotion of a few men of special impulses to the subjects where those impulses will tell with most effect. The prodigious block of our philistinism needs to have wedges driven in at many points, and even then they will be all too few. Sincere and disinterested work by competent hands upon exactly such subjects as Mr. Pater has chosen, real yet detached from the clamour of to-day, is one of the first among the many fertilising agents that the time demands. To excite people's interests in numerous fields, to persuade them of the worth of other activity than material and political activity, is to make life more various, and to give the many different aptitudes of men an ampler chance of finding themselves.

Politics and the acquisition of wealth do not constitute the only peril to the growth of culture in England. The specialism of physical science threatens dangers of a new kind. On this side too we need protection for other than scientific manifes-tations of intellectual activity and fruitfulness. Only on condi-tion of this spacious and manifold energizing in diverse directions, can we hope in our time for that directly effective social action which some of us think calculated to give a higher quality to the moments as they pass than art and song, just because it is not "simply for those moments' sake." For after all, the Heraclitean word which Mr. Pater has expounded with such singular attractiveness both of phrase and sentiment only represents one aspect of the great world. If all is very fluid, yet in another way how stable it all is. Our globe is whirling through space like a speck of dust borne on a mighty wind, yet to us it is solid and fixed. And so with our lives and all that compasses them. Seen in reference to the long æons, they are as sparks that glow for an indivisible moment of time, and then sink into darkness, but for ourselves the months are threads which we may work into a stout and durable web.

ARTHUR SYMONS
"Walter Pater" (1896)
Studies in Prose and Verse
1904, pp. 63–76

Walter Pater was a man in whom fineness and subtlety of emotion were united with an exact and profound scholarship; in whom a personality singularly unconventional, and singularly full of charm, found for its expression an absolutely personal and an absolutely novel style, which was the most carefully and curiously beautiful of all English styles. The man and his style, to those who knew him, were identical; for, as his style was unlike that of other men, concentrated upon a kind of perfection which, for the most part, they could not even distinguish, so his inner life was peculiarly his own, centred within a circle beyond which he refused to wander; his mind, to quote some words of his own, "keeping as a solitary prisoner its own dream of a world." And he was the most lovable of men; to those who rightly apprehended him, the most fascinating; the most generous and helpful of private friends, and in literature a living counsel of perfection, whose removal seems to leave modern English prose without a contemporary standard of values.

"For it is with the delicacies of fine literature especially, its gradations of expression, its fine judgment, its pure sense of words, of vocabulary—things, alas! dying out in the English literature of the present, together with the appreciation of them in our literature of the past—that his literary mission is chiefly concerned." These words, applied by Pater to Charles Lamb, might reasonably enough have been applied to himself; espe-cially in that earlier part of his work, which remains to me, as I doubt not it remains to many others, the most entirely delightful. As a critic, he selected for analysis only those types of artistic character in which delicacy, an exquisite fineness, is the principal attraction; or if, as with Michelangelo, he was drawn towards some more rugged personality, some more massive, less finished art, it was not so much from sympathy with these more obvious qualities of ruggedness and strength, but because he had divined the sweetness lying at the heart of the strength: "ex forti dulcedo." Leonardo da Vinci, Joachim Du Bellay, Coleridge, Botticelli: we find always something a little exotic, or subtle, or sought out, a certain rarity, which it requires an effort to disengage, and which appeals for its perfect appreciation to a public within the public; those fine students of what is fine in art, who take their artistic pleasures con-sciously, deliberately, critically, with the learned love of the amateur.

And not as a critic only, judging others, but in his own person as a writer, both of critical and of imaginative work, Pater showed his preoccupation with the "delicacies of fine literature." His prose was from the first conscious, and it was from the first perfect. That earliest book of his, *Studies in the History of the Renaissance*, as it was then called, entirely individual, the revelation of a rare and special temperament, though it was, had many affinities with the poetic and pictorial art of Rossetti, Swinburne, and Burne-Jones, and seems, on its appearance in 1873, to have been taken as the manifesto of the so-called "æsthetic" school. And, indeed, it may well be compared, as artistic prose, with the poetry of Rossetti; as fine, as careful, as new a thing as that, and with something of the same exotic odour about it: a savour in this case of French soil, a Watteau grace and delicacy. Here was criticism as a fine art, written in prose which the reader lingered over as over poetry;

modulated prose which made the splendour of Ruskin seem gaudy, the neatness of Matthew Arnold a mincing neatness, and the brass sound strident in the orchestra of Carlyle.

That book of *Studies in the Renaissance*, even with the rest of Pater to choose from, seems to me sometimes to be the most beautiful book of prose in our literature. Nothing in it is left to inspiration; but it is all inspired. Here is a writer who, like Baudelaire, would better nature; and in this goldsmith's work of his prose he too has "rêvé le miracle d'une prose poétique, musicale sans rhythme et sans rime." An almost oppressive quiet, a quiet which seems to exhale an atmosphere heavy with the odour of tropical flowers, broods over these pages; a subdued light shadows them. The most felicitous touches come we know not whence, "a breath, a flame in the doorway, a feather in the wind"; here are the simplest words, but they take colour from each other by the cunning accident of their placing in the sentence, "the subtle spiritual fire kindling from word to word."

In this book prose seemed to have conquered a new province; and further, along this direction, prose could not go. Twelve years later, when *Marius the Epicurean* appeared, it was in a less coloured manner of writing that the "sensations and ideas" of that reticent, wise, and human soul were given to the world. Here and there, perhaps, the goldsmith, adding more value, as he thought, for every trace of gold that he removed, might seem to have scraped a little too assiduously. But the style of *Marius*, in its more arduous self-repression, has a graver note, and brings with it a severer kind of beauty. Writers who have paid particular attention to style have often been accused of caring little *what* they say, knowing how beautifully they can say anything. The accusation has generally been unjust: as if any fine beauty could be but skin-deep! The merit which, more than any other, distinguishes Pater's prose, though it is not the merit most on the surface, is the attention to, the perfection of, the ensemble. Under the soft and musical phrases an inexorable logic hides itself, sometimes only too well. Link is added silently, but faultlessly, to link; the argument marches, carrying you with it, while you fancy you are only listening to the music with which it keeps step. Take an essay to pieces, and you will find that it is constructed with mathematical precision; every piece can be taken out and replaced in order. I do not know any contemporary writer who observes the logical requirements so scrupulously, who conducts an argument so steadily from deliberate point to point towards a determined goal. And here, in *Marius*, though the story is indeed but a sequence of scenes, woven around a sequence of moods, there is a scarcely less rigorous care for the ensemble, as that had been intended, the story being properly speaking no story, but the philosophy of a soul. And thus it is mainly by a kind of very individual atmosphere, mental and physical, that the sense of unity is conveyed. It is a book to read slowly, to meditate over; more than any of Pater's books, it is a personal confession and the scheme of a doctrine.

In this book, and in the *Imaginary Portraits* of three years later, which seems to me to show his imaginative and artistic faculties at their point of most perfect fusion, Pater has not endeavoured to create characters in whom the flesh and blood should seem to be that of life itself; he had not the energy of creation, and he was content with a more shadowy life than theirs for the children of his dreams. What he has done is to give a concrete form to abstract ideas; to represent certain types of character, to trace certain developments, in the picturesque form of narrative; to which, indeed, the term portrait is very happily applied; for the method is that of a very patient and elaborate brushwork, in which the touches that go to form the

likeness are so fine that it is difficult to see quite their individual value, until, the end being reached, the whole picture starts out before you. Each, with perhaps one exception, is the study of a soul, or rather of a consciousness; such a study as might be made by simply looking within, and projecting now this now that side of oneself on an exterior plane. I do not mean to say that I attribute to Pater himself the philosophical theories of Sebastian van Storck, or the artistic ideals of Duke Carl of Rosenmold. I mean that the attitude of mind, the outlook, in the most general sense, is always limited and directed in a certain way, giving one always the picture of a delicate, subtle, aspiring, unsatisfied personality, open to all impressions, living chiefly by sensations, little anxious to reap any of the rich harvest of its intangible but keenly possessed gains; a personality withdrawn from action, which it despises or dreads, solitary with its ideals, in the circle of its "exquisite moments," in the Palace of Art, where it is never quite at rest. It is somewhat such a soul, I have thought, as that which Browning has traced in *Sordello*; indeed, when reading for the first time *Marius the Epicurean*, I was struck by a certain resemblance between the record of the sensations and ideas of Marius of White-Nights and that of the sensations and events of Sordello of Goito.

The style of the *Imaginary Portraits* is the ripest, the most varied and flawless, their art the most assured and masterly, of any of Pater's books: it was the book that he himself preferred in his work, thinking it, to use his own phrase, more "natural" than any other. And of the four portraits the most wonderful seems to me the poem, for it is really a poem, named "Denys l'Auxerrois." For once, it is not the study of a soul, but of a myth; a transposition (in which one hardly knows whether to admire most the learning, the ingenuity, or the subtle imagination) of that strangest myth of the Greeks, the "Pagan after-thought" of Dionysus Zagreus, into the conditions of mediæval life. Here is prose so coloured, so modulated, as to have captured, along with almost every sort of poetic richness, and in a rhythm which is essentially the rhythm of prose, even the suggestiveness of poetry, that most volatile and unseizable property, of which prose has so rarely been able to possess itself. The style of "Denys l'Auxerrois" has a subdued heat, a veiled richness of colour, which contrasts curiously with the silver-grey coolness of "A Prince of Court Painters," the chill, more leaden gray of "Sebastian van Storck," though it has a certain affinity, perhaps, with the more variously-tinted canvas of "Duke Carl of Rosenmold." Watteau, Sebastian, Carl: unsatisfied seekers, all of them, this after an artistic ideal of impossible perfection, that after a chill and barren ideal of philosophical thinking and living, that other after yet another ideal, unattainable to him in his period, of life "im Ganzen, Guten, Schönen," a beautiful and effective culture. The story of each, like that of *Marius*, is a vague tragedy, ending abruptly, after so many uncertainties, and always with some subtly ironic effect in the accident of its conclusion. The mirror is held up to Watteau while he struggles desperately or hesitatingly forward, snatching from art one after another of her reticent secrets; then, with a stroke, it is broken, and this artist in immortal things sinks out of sight, into a narrow grave of red earth. The mirror is held up to Sebastian as he moves deliberately, coldly, onward in the midst of a warm life which has so little attraction for him, freeing himself one by one from all obstructions to a clear philosophic equilibrium; and the mirror is broken, with a like suddenness, and the seeker disappears from our sight, to find, perhaps, what he had sought. It is held up to Duke Carl, the seeker after the satisfying things of art and experience, the dilettante in material and spiritual enjoyment, the experimenter on life; and again it is broken, with an almost terrifying shock, just as he has come to a certain rash crisis: is it a step upward or downward? a step, certainly, towards the concrete, towards a possible material felicity.

We see Pater as an imaginative writer, pure and simple, only in these two books, *Marius* and the *Imaginary Portraits*, in the unfinished romance of *Gaston de Latour* (in which detail had already begun to obscure the outlines of the central figure), and in those *Imaginary Portraits* reprinted in various volumes, but originally intended to form a second series under that title: "Hippolytus Veiled," "Apollo in Picardy," "Emerald Uthwart"; and that early first chapter of an unwritten story of modern English life, "The Child in the House." For the rest, he was content to be a critic: a critic of poetry and painting in the *Studies in the Renaissance* and the *Appreciations*, of sculpture and the arts of life in the *Greek Studies*, of philosophy in the volume on *Plato and Platonism*. But he was a critic as no one else ever was a critic. He had made a fine art of criticism. His criticism, abounding in the close and strenuous qualities of really earnest judgment, grappling with his subject as if there were nothing to do but that, the "fine writing" in it being largely mere conscientiousness in providing a subtle and delicate thought with words as subtle and delicate, was, in effect, written with as scrupulous a care, with as much artistic finish, as much artistic purpose, as any imaginative work whatever; being indeed, in a sense in which, perhaps, no other critical work is, imaginative work itself.

"The æsthetic critic," we are told in the preface to the *Studies in the Renaissance*, "regards all the objects with which he has to do, all works of art, and the fairer forms of nature and human life, as powers or forces producing pleasurable sensations, each of a more or less peculiar and unique kind. This influence he feels, and wishes to explain, analysing it, and reducing it to its elements. To him, the picture, the landscape, the engaging personality in life or in a book, *La Gioconda*, the hills of Carrara, Pico of Mirandola, are valuable for their virtues, as we say in speaking of a herb, a wine, a gem; for the property each has of affecting one with a special, a unique, impression of pleasure." To this statement of what was always the aim of Pater in criticism, I would add, from the later essay on Wordsworth, a further statement, applying it, as he there does, to the criticism of literature. "What special sense," he asks, "does Wordsworth exercise, and what instincts does he satisfy? What are the subjects which in him excite the imaginative faculty? What are the qualities in things and persons which he values, the impression and sense of which he can convey to others, in an extraordinary way?" How far is this ideal from that old theory, not yet extinct, which has been briefly stated, thus, by Edgar Poe: "While the critic is *permitted* to play, at times, the part of the mere commentator—while he is *allowed*, by way of merely *interesting* his readers, to put in the fairest light the merits of his author—his *legitimate* task is still, in pointing out and analysing defects, and showing how the work might have been improved, to aid the cause of letters, without undue heed of the individual literary men." And Poe goes on to protest, energetically, against the more merciful (and how infinitely more fruitful!) principles of Goethe, who held that what it concerns us to know about a work or a writer are the merits, not the defects, of the writer and the work. Pater certainly carried this theory to its furthest possible limits, and may almost be said never, except by implication, to condemn anything. But then the force of this implication testifies to a fastidiousness infinitely greater than that of the most destructive of the destructive critics. Is it necessary to *say* that one dislikes a thing? It need but be ignored; and Pater ignored whatever did

not come up to his very exacting standard, finding quite enough to write about in that small residue which remained over.

Nor did he merely ignore what was imperfect, he took the further step, the taking of which was what made him a creative artist in criticism. "It was thus," we are told of Gaston de Latour, in one of the chapters of the unfinished romance, "it was thus Gaston understood the poetry of Ronsard, *generously expanding it to the full measure of its intention*." That is precisely what Pater does in his criticisms, in which criticism is a divining-rod over hidden springs. He has a unique faculty of seeing, through every imperfection, the perfect work, the work as the artist saw it, as he strove to make it, as he failed, in his measure, quite adequately to achieve it. He goes straight to what is fundamental, to the root of the matter, leaving all the rest out of the question. The essay on Wordsworth is perhaps the best example of this, for it has fallen to the lot of Wordsworth to suffer more than most at the hands of interpreters. Here, at last, is a critic who can see in him "a poet somewhat bolder and more passionate than might at first be supposed, but not too bold for true poetical taste; an unimpassioned writer, you might sometimes fancy, yet thinking the chief aim, in life and art alike, to be a certain deep emotion"; one whose "words are themselves thought and feeling"; "a master, an expert, in the art of impassioned contemplation." Reading such essays as these, it is difficult not to feel that if Lamb and Wordsworth, if Shakespeare, if Sir Thomas Browne, could but come to life again for the pleasure of reading them, that pleasure would be the sensation: "Here is some one who understands just what I meant to do, what was almost too deep in me for expression, and would have, I knew, to be divined; that something, scarcely expressed in any of my words, without which no word I ever wrote would have been written."

Turning from the criticisms of literature to the studies in painting, we see precisely the same qualities, but not, I think, precisely the same results. In a sentence of the essay on "The School of Giorgione," which is perhaps the most nicely balanced of all his essays on painting, he defines, with great precision: "In its primary aspect, a great picture has no more definite message for us than an accidental play of sunlight and shadow for a moment on the floor: is itself in truth a space of such fallen light, caught as the colours are caught in an Eastern carpet, but refined upon, and dealt with more subtly and exquisitely than by nature itself." But for the most part it was not in this spirit that he wrote of pictures. His criticism of pictures is indeed creative, in a fuller sense than his criticism of books; and, in the necessity of things, dealing with an art which, as he admitted, has, in its primary aspect, no more definite message for us than the sunlight on the floor, he not merely divined, but also added, out of the most sympathetic knowledge, certainly. It is one thing to interpret the meaning of a book; quite another to interpret the meaning of a picture. Take, for instance, the essay on Botticelli. That was the first sympathetic study which had appeared in English of a painter at that time but little known; and it contains some of Pater's most exquisite writing. All that he writes, of those Madonnas "who are neither for Jehovah nor for his enemies," of that sense in the painter of "the wistfulness of exiles," represents, certainly, the impression made upon his own mind by these pictures, and, as such, has an interpretative value, apart from its beauty as a piece of writing. But it is after all a speculation before a canvas, a literary fantasy; a possible interpretation, if you will, of one mood in the painter, a single side of his intention; it is not a criticism, inevitable as that criticism of Wordsworth's art, of the art of Botticelli.

This once understood, we must admit that Pater did more than any one of our time to bring about a more intimate sympathy with some of the subtler aspects of art; that his influence did much to rescue us from the dangerous moralities, the uncritical enthusiasms and prejudices, of Ruskin; that of no other art-critic it could be said that his taste was flawless. In some of the *Greek Studies* in the essays on "The Beginnings of Greek Sculpture," and the rest, he has made sculpture a living, intimate thing; and, with no addition of his fancy, but in a minute, learned, intuitive piecing together of little fact by little fact, has shown its growth, its relation to life, its meaning in art. I find much of the same quality in his studies in Greek myths: that coloured, yet so scrupulous "Study of Dionysus," the patient disentanglings of the myth of Demeter and Persephone. And, in what is the latest work, practically, that we have from his hand, the lectures on *Plato and Platonism*, we see a like scrupulous and discriminating judgment brought to bear, as upon an artistic problem, upon the problems of Greek ethics, Greek philosophy.

"Philosophy itself indeed, as he conceives it," Pater tells us, speaking of Plato (he might be speaking of himself), "is but the systematic appreciation of a kind of music in the very nature of things." And philosophy, as he conceives it, is a living, dramatic thing, among personalities, and the strife of temperaments; a doctrine being seen as a vivid fragment of some very human mind, not a dry matter of words and disembodied reason. "In the discussion even of abstract truth," he reminds us, "it is not so much what he thinks as the person who is thinking, that after all really tells." Thus, the student's duty, in reading Plato, "is not to take his side in a controversy, to adopt or refute Plato's opinions, to modify, or make apology for what may seem erratic or impossible in him; still less, to furnish himself with arguments on behalf of some theory or conviction of his own. His duty is rather to follow intelligently, but with strict indifference, the mental process there, as he might witness a game of skill; better still, as in reading *Hamlet* or *The Divine Comedy*, so in reading *The Republic*, to watch, for its dramatic interest, the spectacle of a powerful, of a sovereign intellect, translating itself, amid a complex group of conditions which can never in the nature of things occur again, at once pliant and resistant to them, into a great literary monument." It is thus that Pater studies his subject, with an extraordinary patience and precision; a patience with ideas, not, at first sight, so clear or so interesting as he induces them to become; a precision of thinking, on his part, in which no licence is ever permitted to the fantastic side-issues of things. Here again we have criticism which, in its divination, its arrangement, its building up of many materials into a living organism, is itself creation, becomes imaginative work itself.

We may seem to be far now, but are not in reality so far as it may seem, from those "delicacies of fine literature," with which I began by showing Pater to be so greatly concerned. And, in considering the development by which a writer who had begun with the *Studies in the Renaissance* ended with *Plato and Platonism*, we must remember, as Mr. Gosse has so acutely pointed out in his valuable study of Pater's personal characteristics, that, after all, it was a philosophy which attracted him before either literature or art, and that his first published essay was an essay on Coleridge, in which Coleridge the metaphysician, and not Coleridge the poet, was the interesting person to him. In his return to an early, and one might think, in a certain sense, immature interest, it need not surprise us to find a development, which I cannot but consider as technically something of a return to a primitive lengthiness and involution, towards a style which came to lose many of the

rarer qualities of its perfect achievement. I remember that when he once said to me that the *Imaginary Portraits* seemed to him the best written of his books, he qualified that very just appreciation by adding: "It seems to me the most *natural*." I think he was even then beginning to forget that it was not natural to him to be natural. There are many kinds of beauty in the world, and of these what is called natural beauty is but one. Pater's temperament was at once shy and complex, languid and ascetic, sensuous and spiritual. He did not permit life to come to him without a certain ceremony; he was on his guard against the abrupt indiscretion of events; and if his whole life was a service of art, he arranged his life so that, as far as possible, it might be served by that very dedication. With this conscious ordering of things, it became a last sophistication to aim at an effect in style which should bring the touch of unpremeditation, which we seem to find in nature, into a faultlessly combined arrangement of art. The lectures on Plato, really spoken, show traces of their actual delivery in certain new, vocal effects, which had begun already to interest him as matters of style; and which we may find, more finely, here and there in *Gaston de Latour*. Perhaps all this was but a pausing-place in a progress. That it would not have been the final stage, we may be sure. But it is idle to speculate what further development awaited, at its own leisure, so incalculable a life.

EDWARD DOWDEN
"Walter Pater" (1902)
Essays Modern and Elizabethan
1910, pp. 1–25

Let us imagine to ourselves a boy born some ten years before the middle of the last century, of a family originally Dutch, a family with the home-loving, reserved temper of the Dutch, and that slow-moving mind of Holland which attaches itself so closely, so intimately to things real and concrete, not tempted away from its beloved interiors and limited prospects by any glories of mountain heights or wide-spreading and radiant horizons; a family settled for long in the low-lying, slow-moving Olney of Buckinghamshire—Cowper's Olney, which we see in the delicate vignettes of *The Task*, and in the delightful letters, skilled in making so much out of so little, of the half-playful, half-pathetic correspondent of John Newton and Lady Hesketh. Dutch, but of mingled strains in matters of religion, the sons, we are told, always, until the tradition was broken in the case of Walter Pater, brought up as Roman Catholics, the daughters as members of the Anglican communion. Walter Pater's father had moved to the neighbourhood of London, and it was at Enfield, where Lamb, about whom the critic has written with penetrating sympathy, Lamb and his sister Mary, had lately dwelt, that Pater spent his boyhood. "Not precocious," writes his friend of later years, Mr. Gosse, "he was always meditative and serious." Yes, we cannot think of him at any time as other than serious; withdrawn from the boisterous sports of boyhood; fed through little things by the sentiment of home—that sentiment which was nourished in Marius at White Nights by the duteous observances of the religion of Numa; in Gaston at the Château of Deux-Manoirs with its immemorial associations and its traditional Catholic pieties; in Emerald Uthwart at Chase Lodge, with its perfumes of sweet peas, the neighbouring fields so green and velvety, and the church where the ancient buried Uthwarts slept, that home to which Emerald came back to die, a broken man; in Florian

Deleal by "the old house," its old staircase, its old furniture, its shadowy angles, its swallow's nest below the sill, its brown and golden wall-flowers, its pear tree in springtime, and the scent of lime-flowers floating in at the open window.

And with this nesting sense of home there comes to the boy from neighbouring London, from rumours of the outer world, from the face of some sad wayfarer on the road, an apprehension of the sorrow of the world, and the tears in mortal things, which disturbs him and must mingle henceforth with all his thoughts and dreams. He is recognised as "the clever one in the family," but it is not a vivacious cleverness, not a conscientious power of intellect, rather a shy, brooding faculty, slow to break its sheath, and expand into a blossom, a faculty of gradual and exact receptiveness, and one of which the eye is the special organ. This, indeed, is a central fact to remember. If Pater is a seeker for truth, he must seek for it with the eye, and with the imagination penetrating its way through things visible; or if truth comes to him in any other way, he must project the truth into colour and form, since otherwise it remains for him cold, loveless, and a tyranny of the intellect, like that which oppressed and almost crushed out of existence his Sebastian van Storck. We may turn elsewhere to read of "the conduct of the understanding." We learn much from Pater concerning the conduct of the eye. Whatever his religion may hereafter be, it cannot be that of Puritanism, which makes a breach between the visible and the invisible. It cannot be reached by purely intellectual processes; it cannot be embodied in a creed of dogmatic abstractions. The blessing which he may perhaps obtain can hardly be that of those who see not and yet have believed. The evidential value of a face made bright by some inner joy will count with him for more than any syllogism however correct in its premises and conclusions. A life made visibly gracious and comely will testify to him of some hidden truth more decisively than any supernatural witnessing known only by report. If he is impressed by any creed it will be by virtue of its living epistles, known and read of all men. He will be occupied during his whole life with a study not of ideas apart from their concrete embodiment, not of things concrete apart from their inward significance, but with a study of expression—expression as seen in the countenance of external nature, expression in Greek statue, mediæval cathedral, Renaissance altar-piece, expression in the ritual of various religions, and in the visible bearing of various types of manhood, in various exponents of tradition, of thought, and of faith.

His creed may partake somewhat of that natural or human catholicism of Wordsworth's poetry, which reveals the soul in things of sense, which is indeed, as Pater regards it, a kind of finer, spiritual sensuousness. But why stop where Wordsworth stopped in his earlier days? Why content ourselves with expression as seen in the face of hillside and cloud and stream, and the acts and words of simple men, through whom certain primitive elementary passions play? Why not also seek to discover the spirit in sense in its more complex and subtler incarnations—in the arts and crafts, in the shaping of a vase, the lines and colours of a tapestry, the carving of a capital, the movements of a celebrant in the rites of religion, in a relief of Della Robbia, in a Venus of Botticelli, in the mysterious Gioconda of Lionardo? Setting aside the mere dross of circumstances in human life, why not vivify all amidst which we live and move by translating sense into spirit, and spirit into sense, thus rendering opaque things luminous, so that if no pure white light of truth can reach us, at least each step we tread may be impregnated with the stains and dyes of those coloured morsels of glass, so deftly arranged, through which such light as we are able to endure has its access to our eyes?

If such thoughts as these lay in Pater's mind during early youth they lay unfolded and dormant. But we can hardly doubt that in the account of Emerald Uthwart's schooldays he is interpreting with full-grown and self-conscious imagination his experiences as a schoolboy at Canterbury, where the cathedral was the presiding element of the *genius loci*: "If at home there had been nothing great, here, to boyish sense, one seems diminished to nothing at all, amid the grand waves, wave upon wave, of patiently wrought stone; the daring height, the daring severity, of the innumerable long, upward ruled lines, rigidly bent just at last in one place into the reserved grace of the perfect Gothic arch." Happy Emerald Uthwart in those early days, and happy Walter Pater with such noble, though as yet half-conscious, discipline in the conduct of the eye! If Pater thought of a profession, the military profession of his imagined Emerald would have been the last to commend itself to his feelings. His father was a physician, but science had no call for the son's intellect, and we can hardly imagine him as an enthusiastic student in the school of anatomy. He felt the attractions of the life and work of an English clergyman, and when a little boy, Mr. Gosse tells us, he had seen the benign face of Keble during a visit to Hursley, and had welcomed Keble's paternal counsel and encouragement. Had Pater lived some years longer it is quite possible that his early dream might have been realised, but Oxford, as things were, dissolved the dream of Canterbury.

Two influences stood over against each other in the Oxford of Pater's undergraduate days. There was the High Church movement, with which the name of the University has been associated. The spell of Newman's personal charm and the echoes of his voice in the pulpit of St. Mary's were not yet forgotten. The High Church movement had made the face of religion more outwardly attractive to such a spirit as Pater's; there had been a revival, half serious, half dilettante, of ecclesiastical art. But the High Church movement was essentially dogmatic; the body of dogma had to some extent hardened into system, and Pater's mind was always prone to regard systems of thought—philosophical or theological—as works of art, to be examined and interpreted by the historical imagination; from which, when interpreted aright, something might be retained, perhaps, in a transposed form, but which could not be accepted and made one's own *en bloc*. On the other hand there was a stirring critical movement, opening new avenues for thought and imagination, promising a great enfranchisement of the intellect, and claiming possession of the future. Jowett was a nearer presence now at Oxford than Newman, and Pater had already come under the influence of German thinkers and had discovered in Goethe—greatest of critics—a master of the mind. Art, to which he had found access through the *Modern Painters* of an illustrious Oxford graduate, had passed beyond the bounds of the ecclesiastical revival, and, following a course like that of the mediæval drama, was rapidly secularising itself. We see the process at work in the firm of which William Morris was the directing manager, at first so much occupied with church decoration, and by-and-by extending its operations to the domestic interiors of the wealthier lay-folk of England. Pater's dream of occupying an Anglo-Catholic pulpit re-shaped itself into the dream of becoming an Unitarian minister, and by degrees it became evident that the only pulpit which he could occupy was that of the Essayist, who explores for truth, and ends his research not without a sense of insecurity in his own conclusions, or rather who concludes without a conclusion, and is content to be faithful through manifold suggestions.

We can imagine that with a somewhat different composition of the forces within him Pater's career might have borne some resemblance to that of Henri Amiel, "in wandering mazes lost." But the disputants in Amiel's nature were more numerous and could not be brought to a conciliation. One of them was for ever reaching out toward the indefinite, which Amiel called the infinite, and the Maya of the Genevan Buddhist threw him back in the end upon a world of *ennui*. Pater was saved by a certain "intellectual astringency," by a passion for the concrete, and by the fact that he lived much in and through the eye. He had perhaps learnt from Goethe that true expansion lies in limitation, and he never appreciated as highly as did Amiel the poetry of fog. His boyish faith, such as it was, had lapsed away. How was he to face life and make the best of it? Something at least could be gained by truth to himself, by utter integrity, by living, and that intensely, in his best self and in the highest moments of his best self, by detaching from his intellectual force, as he says of Winckelmann, all flaccid interests. If there was in him any tendency to mystic passion and religious reverie this was checked, as with his own Marius, by a certain virility of intellect, by a feeling of the poetic beauty of mere clearness of mind. Is nothing permanent? Are all things melting under our feet? Well, if it be so, we cannot alter the fact. But we need not therefore spend our few moments of life in listlessness. If all is passing away, let the knowledge of this be a stimulus toward intenser activity, let it excite within us the thirst for a full and perfect experience.

And remember that Pater's special gift, his unique power, lay in the eye and in the imagination using the eye as its organ. He could not disdain the things of sense, for there is a spirit in sense, and mind communes with mind through colour and through form. He notes in Marcus Aurelius, the pattern of Stoical morality, who would stand above and apart from the world of the senses, not, after all, an attainment of the highest humanity, but a mediocrity, though a mediocrity for once really golden. He writes of Pascal with adequate knowledge and with deep sympathy, but he qualifies his admiration for the great friend of Jansenism by observing that Pascal had little sense of the beauty even of holiness. In Pascal's "sombre, trenchant, precipitous philosophy," and his perverse asceticism, Pater finds evidence of a diseased spirit, a morbid tension like that of insomnia. Sebastian van Storck, with the warm life of a rich Dutch interior around him, and all the play of light and colour in Dutch art to enrich his eye, turns away to seek some glacial Northwest passage to the lifeless, colourless Absolute. Spinoza appears to Pater not as a God-intoxicated man, but as climbing to the barren pinnacle of egoistic intellect. Such, at all events, could not possibly be his own way. There is something of the true widsom of humility in modestly remembering that we are not pure intelligence, pure soul, and in accepting the aid of the senses. How reassuring Marius finds it to be, after assisting at a long debate about rival criteria of truth, "to fall back upon direct sensation, to limit one's aspiration after knowledge to that." To live intensely in the moment, "to burn with a gemlike flame," to maintain an ecstasy, is to live well, with the gain, at least for a moment, of wisdom and of joy. "America is here and now—here or nowhere," as Wilhelm Meister, and, after him, Marius the Epicurean discovered.

There is no hint in Pater's first volume of the fortifying thought which afterwards came to him, that some vast logic of change, some law or rhythm of evolution may underlie all that is transitory, all the pulsations of passing moments, and may bind them together in some hidden harmony. Looking back on the period of what he calls a new Cyrenaicism, he saw a most

depressing theory coming in contact, in his own case as in that of Marius, with a happy temperament—happy though subject to moods of deep depression, and he saw that by virtue of this happy temperament he had converted his loss into a certain gain. Assuredly he never regarded that view of life which is expressed in the *Conclusion to Studies in the History of the Renaissance* as mere hedonism, as a mere abandonment to the lust of the eye, the lust of the flesh, and the pride of life. No: looking back, he perceived that his aim was not pleasure, but fulness and vividness of life, a perfection of being, an intense and, as far as may be, a complete experience; that this was not to be attained without a discipline, involving some severity; that it demanded a strenuous effort; that here, too, the loins must be girt and the lamp lit; that for success in his endeavour he needed before all else true insight, and that insight will not come by any easy way, or, as we say, by a royal road; that on the contrary it must be sought by a culture, which may be, and ought to be, joyous, but which certainly must be strict. The precept, "Be perfect in regard to what is here and now," is one which may be interpreted, as he conceived it, into lofty meanings. A conduct of the intellect in accordance with this precept, in its rejection of many things which bring with them facile pleasures, may in a certain sense be called a form of asceticism. The eye itself must be purified from all grossness and dulness. "Such a manner of life," writes Pater of the new Cyrenaicism of his Marius, "might itself even come to seem a kind of religion. . . . The true 'æsthetic culture' would be realisable as a new form of the 'contemplative life,' founding its claim on the essential 'blessedness' of 'vision'—the vision of perfect men and things." At the lowest it is an impassioned ideal life.

Such is Pater's own *apologia pro vita sua*—that is, for life during his earlier years of authorship—as given in *Marius the Epicurean*. But the best apologia is, indeed, the outcome of that life, the volume of *Studies in the History of the Renaissance*, and later essays, which are essentially one with these in kind. The richness of colour and delicacy of carving in some of Pater's work have concealed from many readers its intellectual severity, its strictness of design, its essential veracity. A statue that is chryselephantine may be supposed to be less intellectual than the same statue if it were worked in marble; yet more of sheer brainwork perhaps is required for the design which has to calculate effects of colour. There are passages in Pater's writing which may be called, if you like, decorative, but the decoration is never incoherent ornament of *papier maché* laid on from without; it is, on the contrary, a genuine outgrowth of structure, always bringing into relief the central idea.

This central idea he arrives at only through the process of a steadfast and strenuous receptiveness, which has in it something of the nature of fortitude. Occasionally he gives it an express definition, naming it, not perhaps quite happily, the *formula* of the artist or author who is the subject of his study. Thus, the formula of Raphael's genius, if we must have one, is this: "The transformation of meek scholarship into genius—triumphant power of genius." The essay on Raphael is accordingly the record of a series of educations, from which at last emerge works showing a synoptic intellectual power, and large theoretic conceptions, but these are seen to act in perfect unison with the pictorial imagination and a magic power of the hand. The formula, to turn from pictorial art to literature, of Prosper Mérimée, who met the disillusion of the post-Revolution period by irony, is this: "The enthusiastic amateur of rude, crude, naked force in men and women wherever it could be found; himself carrying ever, as a mask, the conventional attire of the modern world—carrying it with an infinite contemptuous grace, as if that too were an all-sufficient end in itself." Nothing could be more triumphantly exact and complete than Pater's brief formula of Mérimée. But perhaps his method is nowhere more convincingly shown than in the companion studies of two French churches, Notre Dame of Amiens, pre-eminently the church of a city, of a commune, and the Madeleine of Vézelay, which is typically the church of a monastery. Here the critic does not for a moment lose himself in details; in each case he holds, as it were, the key of the situation; he has grasped the central idea of each structure; and then with the aid of something like creative imagination, he assists the idea—the vital germ—to expand itself and grow before us into leaf and tendril and blossom.

In such studies as these we perceive that the eye is itself an intellectual power, or at least the organ and instrument of such a power. And this imaginative criticism is in truth constructive. But the creative work of imagination rises from a basis of adequate knowledge and exact perception. To see precisely what a thing is—what, before all else, it is to *me*; to feel with entire accuracy its unique quality; to find the absolutely right word in which to express the perception and the feeling—this indeed taxes the athletics of the mind. Sometimes, while still essentially a critic, Pater's power of construction and reconstruction takes the form of a highly intellectual fantasy. Thus "A Study of Dionysus" reads like a fantasia suggested by the life of the vine and the "spirit of sense" in the grape; yet the fantasia is in truth the tracing out, by a learned sympathy, of strange or beautiful sequences of feeling or imagination in the Greek mind. In "Denys l'Auxerrois" and "Apollo in Picardy," which should be placed side by side as companion pieces, the fancy takes a freer range. They may be described as transpositions of the classical into the romantic. Apollo—now for mediæval contemporaries bearing the ill-omened name Apollyon—appears in a monkish frock and wears the tonsure; yet he remains a true Apollo, but of the Middle Age, and, in a passage of singular romance, even does to death the mediæval Hyacinthus. Denys, that strange flaxen and flowery creature, the organ-builder of Auxerre, has all the mystic power and ecstatic range of Dionysus. Are these two elder brothers of Goethe's Euphorion, earlier-born children of Faust and Helena?

Even these fantasies are not without an intellectual basis. For Pater recognises in classical art and classical literature a considerable element of romance—strangeness allied with beauty; and to re-fashion the myths of Dionysus and even of Apollo in the romantic spirit is an experiment in which there is more than mere fantasy. Very justly and admirably he protests in writing of Greek sculpture against a too intellectual or abstract view of classical art. Here also were colour and warmth and strange ventures of imaginative faith, and fears and hopes and ecstasies, which we are apt to forget in the motionless shadow or pallid light of our cold museums. Living himself at a time, as we say, of "transition," when new and old ideas were in conflict, and little interested in any form of action except that of thought and feeling, he came to take a special interest in the contention and also in the conciliation of rival ideas. Hence the period of the Renaissance—from the auroral Renaissance within the Middle Age to the days of Ronsard and Montaigne, with its new refinements of mediævalism—seen, for example, in the poetry of the *Pleiad*—its revival in an altered form of the classical temper, and the invasions of what may be summed up under the name of "the modern spirit"—had a peculiar attraction for him. His Gaston de Latour, as far as he is known to us through what is unhappily a fragment, seems almost created for no other purpose than to be a subject for the play of contending influences. The old pieties of the Middle Age survive within him, leaving a deep and abiding deposit in his spirit; but he is caught by the new grace and delicate magic of Ronsard's verse, of Ronsard's personality; he is exposed to all the enriching, and yet perhaps disintegrating forces of Montaigne's undulant philosophy—the philosophy of the relative; and he is prepared to be lifted—lifted, shall we say, or lowered?—from his state of suspended judgment by the ardent genius of that new knight of the Holy Ghost, Giordano Bruno, with his glowing exposition of the Lower Pantheism.

His Marius, again, cannot rest in the religion of Numa, which was the presiding influence of his boyhood. His Cyrenaicism is confronted by the doctrine of the Stoics—sad, grey, depressing, though presented with all possible amiability in the person of Marcus Aurelius. And in the Christian house of Cecilia, and among the shadowy catacombs of Rome, his eyes are touched by the radiance of a newer light, which thrills him with the sense of an unapprehended joy, a heroic—perhaps a divine—hope. In the eighteenth century Pater's Watteau, creating a new and delicate charm for the society of his own day, is yet ill at ease, half detached from that society, and even—saddening experience!—half detached from his own art, for he dreams, unlike his age, of a better world than the actual one; and by an anachronism which is hardly pardonable (for it confuses the chronology of eighteenth-century moods of mind) the faithful and tender diarist of Valenciennes, whose more than sisterly interest in young Antoine has left us this Watteau myth, becomes acquainted—and through Antoine himself—with the Manon Lescaut of many years later, in which the ardent passion of the period of Rousseau is anticipated. And, again, in that other myth of the eighteenth century, Duke Carl of Rosenmold—myth of a half-rococo Apollo—the old stiff mediævalism of German courts and the elegant *fadeurs* of French pseudo-classicism are exhibited in relation to a throng of fresher influences—the classical revival of which Winckelmann was the apostle, the revival of the Middle Age as a new and living force, the artistic patriotism which Lessing preached, the "return to nature" of which a little later the young Goethe—he, a true Apollo—was the herald, and that enfranchisement of passion and desire, which, now when Rousseau is somewhere in the world, brooding, kindling, about to burst into flame, seems no anachronism.

I cannot entirely go along with that enthusiastic admirer who declared—surely not without a smile of ironic intelligence—that the trumpet of doom ought to have sounded when the last page of *Studies in the History of the Renaissance* was completed. Several copies of the golden book in its first edition, containing the famous Conclusion, would probably have perished in the general conflagration; and Pater was averse to noise. But a memorable volume it is, and one which testifies to the virtue of a happy temperament even when in the presence of a depressing philosophy. Too much attention has been centred on that Conclusion; it has been taken by many persons as if it were Pater's ultimate confession of faith, whereas, in truth, the Conclusion was a prologue. Pater's early years had made a home for his spirit among Christian pieties and the old moralities. When Florian Deleal, quitting for the first time the house of his childhood, runs back to fetch the forgotten pet bird, and sees the warm familiar rooms "lying so pale, with a look of meekness in their denudation," a clinging to the cherished home comes over him. And had Pater in his haughty philosophy of manhood in like manner dismantled and desecrated the little white room of his early faith? The very question seemed to carry with it something of remorse; but Pater's integrity of mind, his intellectual virility, could not permit itself to melt in sentiment. In the essay on Aucassin and Nicolette, he had spoken of the rebellious antinomian spirit connected with the outbreak of the reason and imagination, with the assertion of the liberty of heart, in the Middle Age. "The perfection of culture," he knew, "is not rebellion, but peace;" yet on the way to that end, he thought, there is room for a noble antinomianism. Now, like his own Marius, he began to think that in such antinomianism there might be a taint, he began to question whether it might not be possible somehow to adjust his new intellectual scheme of things to the old morality. His culture had brought with it a certain sense of isolation, like that of a spectator detached from the movement of life and the great community of men. His Cyrenaic theory was one in keeping with the proud individualism of youth. From the Stoic Fronto his Marius hears of an august community, to which each of us may perchance belong, "humanity, an universal order, the great polity, its aristocracy of elect spirits, the mastery of their example over their successors." But where are these elect spirits? Where is this comely order? The Cyrenaic lover of beauty begins to feel that his conception of beauty has been too narrow, too exclusive; not positively unsound perhaps, for it enjoined the practice of an ideal temperance, and included a seriousness of spirit almost religious, so that, as Marius reflects, "the saint and the Cyrenaic lover of beauty would at least understand each other better than either would understand the mere man of the world." His pursuit of perfection was surely not in itself illegitimate, but by its exclusiveness of a more complete ideal of perfection it might almost partake of the nature of a heresy. Without rejecting his own scheme of life, might it not be possible to adjust it to the old morality as a part to a whole? Viewed even from a purely egoistic standpoint had not such attainments as were his—and the attainments were unquestionably precious—been secured at a great sacrifice? Was it a true economy to forfeit perhaps a greater gain for the less? The Stoical ideal, which casts scorn upon the body, and that visible beauty in things which for Marius was indeed a portion of truth, as well as beauty, he must needs reject. But might there not be a divination of something real, an imperfect vision of a veritable possibility in the Stoical conception of an ordered society of men, a Celestial City, *Uranopolis, Callipolis?* And what if the belief of Marcus Aurelius in the presence of a divine companion, a secret Providence behind the veil, contained some elevating truth? What if the isolated seeker for a narrow perfection could attach himself to some venerable system of sentiment and ideas, and so "let in a great tide of experience, and make, as it were, with a single step, a great experience of his own; with a great consequent increase to his own mind, of colour, variety, and relief, in the spectacle of men and things"?

There are two passages of rare spiritual beauty in *Marius the Epicurean:* one is that which tells of Marius wandering forth with such thoughts as these—keeping all these things in his heart—to one of his favourite spots in the Alban or the Sabine hills; the other is the description of the sacred memorial celebration in the Christian house of Cecilia. After a night of perfect sleep Marius awakes in the morning sunlight, with almost the joyful waking of childhood. As he rides toward the hills his mood is, like the season's, one of flawless serenity; a sense of gratitude—gratitude to what?—fills his heart, and must overflow; he leans, as it were, toward that eternal, invisible Companion of whom the Stoic philosopher and emperor spoke. Might he not, he reflects, throw in the election of his will, though never faltering from the truth, on the side of his best thought, his best feeling, and perhaps receive in due

course the justification, the confirmation of this venture of faith? What if the eternal companion were really by his side? What if his own spirit were but a moment, a pulse, in some great stream of spiritual energy? What if this fair material universe were but a creation, a projection into sense of the perpetual mind? What if the new city, let down from heaven, were also a reality included in the process of that divine intelligence? Less through any sequence of argument than by a discovery of the spirit in sense, or rather of the imaginative reason, Marius seems to live and move in the presence of the Great Ideal, the Eternal Reason, nay, the Father of men. A larger conception assuredly of the reasonable Ideal than that of his Cyrenaic days has dawned for him, every trace or note of which it shall henceforth be his business to gather up. *Paratum cor meum, Deus! paratum cor meum!*

It is a criticism of little insight which represents Marius as subordinating truth to any form of ease or comfort or spiritual self-indulgence; an erroneous criticism which represents him as only extending a refined hedonism so as to include within it new pleasures of the moral sense or the religious temper. For Marius had never made pleasure his aim and end; his aim and end had been always perfection, but now he perceives that his ideal of perfection had been incomplete and inadequate. He discovers the larger truth, and the lesser falls into its due place. His experiences among the Sabine hills, which remind one of certain passages in Wordsworth's *Excursion,* may have little evidential value for any other mind than his own; even for himself they could hardly recur in like manner ever again. But that such phenomena—however we may interpret their significance—are real cannot be doubted by any disinterested student of human nature. What came to Marius was not a train of argument, but what we may call a revelation; it came as the last and culminating development, under favouring external conditions, of many obscure processes of thought and feeling. The seed had thrust up its stalk, which then had struggled through the soil; and at last sunlight touches the folded blossom, which opens to become a flower of light.

Marius had already seen in Cornelius the exemplar of a new knighthood, which he can but imperfectly understand. Entirely virile, Cornelius is yet governed by some strange hidden rule which obliges him to turn away from many things that are commonly regarded as the rights of manhood; he has a blitheness, which seems precisely the reverse of the temper of the Emperor, and yet some veiled severity underlies, perhaps supports, this blitheness. And in the gathering at Cecilia's house, where the company—and among them, children—are singing, Marius recognises the same glad expansion of a joyful soul, "in people upon whom some all-subduing experience had wrought heroically." A grave discretion; an intelligent seriousness about life; an exquisite courtesy; all chaste affections of the family, and these under the most natural conditions; a temperate beauty; all are here; the human body, which had been degraded by Pagan voluptuousness and dishonoured by Stoic asceticism, is here reverenced as something sacred, or as something sanctified; and death itself is made beautiful through a new hope. Charity here is not painfully calculated, but joyous and chivalrous in its devotion; peaceful labour is rehabilitated and illumined with some new light. A higher ideal than Marius had ever known before—higher and gladder—is operative here, ideal of woman, of the family, of industry, including all of life and death. And its effects are visible, addressing themselves even to the organ of sight, which with Marius is the special avenue for truth; so that he has only to read backward from effects to causes in order to be assured that some truth of higher import and finer efficacy than any previously known to him must be working among the forces which have created this new beauty. What if this be the company of elect souls dreamed of by the rhetorician Fronto? And with the tenderest charity in this company of men and women a heroic fortitude—the fortitude of the martyrs, like those of Lyons—is united. What if here be Uranopolis, Callipolis, the City let down from heaven? For Marius in the house of Cecilia the argument is irrefragable—rather the experience is convincing. Possibly in the light of a more extended survey of history new doubts and questions may arise; but these were days of purity and of love, the days of the minor peace of the church.

Yet even in the end Marius is brought only to his Pisgah—the mount of vision. He does not actually set foot within the promised land. Even that act of surrender, by which Cornelius is delivered and Marius goes to his death, is less an act of divine self-sacrifice than the result of an impulse, half careless, half generous, of comradeship. His spirit—*anima naturaliter Christiana*—departs less in assured hope than with the humble consolation of memory—*tristem neminem fecit*; he had at least not added any pang to the total sum of the world's pain.

And although the creator of Marius had arrived, by ways very different from those of Pascal, at some of Pascal's conclusions, and had expressed these with decisiveness in a review of Amiel's *Journal*, we cannot but remember that essentially his mind belonged to the same order as the mind of Montaigne rather than to the order of the mind of Pascal. We can imagine Pater, had he lived longer, asking himself, as part of that endless dialogue with self which constituted his life, whether the deepest community with his fellows could not be attained by a profound individuality without attaching himself to institutions. Whether, for example, the fact of holding a fellowship at Brasenose, or the fact of knowing Greek well, bound him the more intimately to the society of Greek scholars. We can imagine him questioning whether other truths might not be added to those truths which made radiant the faces in Cecilia's house. Whether even those same truths might not, in a later age, be capable of, might not even require, a different conception, and a largely altered expression.

While in the ways indicated in *Marius the Epicurean* Pater was departing from that doctrine of the perpetual flux—with ideals of conduct corresponding to that doctrine—or was at least subordinating this to a larger, really a more liberal view of things, his mind was also tending, and now partly under the influence of Plato, away from the brilliantly-coloured versatile, centrifugal Ionian temper of his earlier days toward the simpler, graver, more strictly ordered, more athletic Dorian spirit.

Plato and Platonism, in noticing which I shall sometimes use Pater's own words, is distinguished less by colour than by a pervasive light. The demand on a reader's attention is great, but the demand is not so much from sentence to sentence as from chapter to chapter. If we may speak of the evolution or development of a theme by literary art, such evolution in this book is perhaps its highest merit. No attempt is made to fix a dogmatic creed, or to piece together an artificial unity of tessellated opinions. Philosophies are viewed very much as works of art, and the historical method is adopted, which endeavours to determine the conditions that render each philosophy, each work of art, and especially this particular work of art, the Platonic philosophy, possible. And there is something of autobiography, for those who can discern it, below the surface of the successive discussions of ideas, which yet are often seemingly remote from modern thought.

The doctrine of the Many, of the perpetual flux of things, which was so consonant to the mobile Ionian temper, is set over against the doctrine of the One, for which all that is phenomenal becomes null, and the sole reality is pure Being, colourless, formless, impalpable. It was Plato's work to break up the formless unity of the philosophy of the One into something multiple, and yet not transitory—the starry Platonic ideas, Justice, Temperance, Beauty, and their kindred luminaries of the intellectual heaven. Platonism in one sense is a witness for the unseen, the transcendental. Yet, austere as he sometimes appears, who can doubt that Plato's austerity, his temperance is attained only by the control of a richly sensuous nature? Before all else he was a lover; and now that he had come to love invisible things more than visible, the invisible things must be made, as it were, visible persons, capable of engaging his affections. The paradox is true that he had a sort of sensuous love of the unseen. And in setting forth his thoughts he is not a dogmatist but essentially an essayist—a questioning explorer for truth, who refines and idealises the manner of his master Socrates, and who, without the oscillating philosophy of Montaigne, anticipates something of Montaigne's method as a seeker for the knowledge of things.

At this point in Pater's long essay, a delightful turn is given to his treatment of the subject by that remarkable and characteristic chapter in which he attempts to revive for the eye, as well as for the mind, the life of old Lacedæmon—Lacedæmon, the highest concrete embodiment of that Dorian temper of Greece, that Dorian temper of which his own ideal Republic would have been a yet more complete development. Those conservative Lacedæmonians, "the people of memory pre-eminently," are made to live and move before us by creative imagination working among the records, too scanty, of historical research. There in hollow Laconia, a land of organised slavery under central military authority, the genius of conservatism was enthroned. The old bore sway; the young were under strict, but not unjoyous discipline. Every one, at every moment, must strive to be at his best, with all superfluities pruned away. "It was a type of the Dorian purpose in life—a sternness, like sea-water infused into wine, overtaking a matter naturally rich, at the moment when fulness may lose its savour and expression." There in clear air, on the bank of a mountain torrent, stands Lacedæmon; by no means a "growing" place, rather a solemn, ancient mountain village, with its sheltering plane trees, and its playing-fields for youthful athletes, all under discipline, who when robed might almost have seemed a company of young monks. A city not without many venerable and beautiful buildings, civic and religious, in a grave hieratic order of architecture, while its private abodes were simple and even rude. The whole of life is evidently conceived as matter of attention, patience, fidelity to detail, like that of good soldiers or musicians. The Helots, who pursue their trades and crafts from generation to generation in a kind of guild, may be indulged in some illiberal pleasures of abundant food and sleep; but it is the mark of aristocracy to endure hardness. And from these half-military, half-monastic modes of life are born the most beautiful of all people in Greece, in the world. Everywhere one is conscious of reserved power, and the beauty of strength restrained—a male beauty, far remote from feminine tenderness. Silent these men can be, or, if need arise, can speak to the point, and with brevity. With them to read is almost a superfluity, for whatever is essential has become a part of memory, and is made actual in habit; but such culture in fact has the power to develop a vigorous imagination. Their muscle has in it a high moral stimulus; their dance is not mere form, but full of subject; they dance a theme, and that with absolute correctness, a dance full of delight, yet with something of the character of a liturgical service, something of a military inspection. And these half-monastic people are also—as monks may be—a very cheerful people, devoted to a religion of sanity, worshippers of Apollo, sanest of the national gods; strong in manly comradeship, of which those youthful demi-gods, the Dioscuri, are the patrons. Why all this strenuous task-work day after day? An intelligent young Spartan might reply, "To the end that I myself may be a perfect work of art."

It is this Dorian spirit which inspires the Republic of Plato. He would, if possible, arrest the disintegration of Athenian society, or at least protest against the principle of flamboyancy in things and thoughts—protest against the fluxional, centrifugal, Ionian element in the Hellenic character. He conceives the State as one of those disciplined Spartan dancers, or as a well-known athlete; he desires not that it shall be gay, or rich, or populous, but that it shall be strong, an organic unity, entirely self-harmonious, each individual occupying his exact place in the system; and the State being thus harmoniously strong, it will also be of extreme æsthetic beauty—the beauty of a unity or harmony enforced on highly disparate elements, unity as of an army or an order of monks, unity as of liturgical music.

It could hardly happen that Pater's last word in this long study should be on any other subject than art. It is no false fragment of traditional Platonism which insists on the close connection between the æsthetic qualities of things and the formation of moral character; on the building of character through the eye and ear. And this ethical influence of art resides even more in the form—its concision, simplicity, rhythm—than in the matter. In the ideal Republic the simplification of human nature is the chief affair; therefore art must be simple and even austere. The community will be fervently æsthetic, but withal fervent renunciants as well, and, in the true sense of the word *ascetic*, will be fervently ascetic. "The proper art of the Perfect City is in fact the art of discipline." In art, in its narrower meaning, in literature, what the writer of the Republic would most desire is that quality which solicits an effort from the reader or spectator, "who is promised a great expressiveness on the part of the writer, the artist, if he for his part will bring with him a great attentiveness." Temperance superinduced on a nature originally rich and impassioned—this is the supreme beauty of the Dorian art. Plato's own prose is, indeed, a practical illustration of the value of intellectual astringency. He is before all else a lover, and infinite patience, quite as much as fire, is the mood of all true lovers. It is, indeed, this infinite patience of a lover which in large measure gives to Pater's own studies of art and literature their peculiar value. The bee, that has gone down the long neck of a blossom, is not more patient in collecting his drop of honey.

RICHARD LE GALLIENNE
"On Re-reading Walter Pater"

North American Review, February 1912, pp. 214–24

It is with no small satisfaction, and with a sense of reassurance of which one may, in moods of misgiving, have felt the need during two decades of the Literature of Noise, that one sees a writer so pre-eminently a master of the Literature of Meditation coming, for all the captains and the shouting, so surely into his own. The acceptance of Walter Pater is not merely widening all the time, but it is more and more becoming an acceptance such as he himself would have

most valued, an acceptance in accordance with the full significance of his work rather than a one-sided appreciation of some of its Corinthian characteristics. The Doric qualities of his work are becoming recognized also, and he is being read, as he has always been read by his true disciples—so not inappropriately to name those who have come under his graver spell—not merely as a *prosateur* of purple patches, or a sophist of honeyed counsels tragically easy to misapply, but as an artist of the interpretative imagination of rare insight and magic, a writer of deep humanity as well as esthetic beauty, and the teacher of a way of life at once ennobling and exquisite. It is no longer possible to parody him—after the fashion of Mr. Mallock's brilliancy in *The New Republic*—as a writer of "all manner and no matter," nor is it possible any longer to confuse his philosophy with those gospels of unrestrained libertinism which have taken in vain the name of Epicurus. His highly wrought, sensitively colored, and musically expressive style is seen to be what it is because of its truth to a matter profound and delicate and intensely meditated and such faults as it has come rather of too much matter than too little; while his teaching, far from being that of a facile "Epicureanism," is seen, properly understood, to involve something like the austerity of a fastidious Puritanism, and to result in a jealous asceticism of the senses rather than in their indulgence. "Slight as was the burden of positive moral obligation with which he had entered Rome," he writes of Marius, as on his first evening in Rome the murmur comes to him of "the lively, reckless call to 'play,' from the sons and daughters of foolishness," "it was to no wasteful and vagrant affections, such as these, that his Epicureanism had committed him." Such warnings against misunderstanding Pater is careful to place, at, so to say, all the cross-roads in his books, so scrupulously concerned is he lest any reader should take the wrong turning. Few writers, indeed, manifest so constant a consideration for, and, in minor matters, such a sensitive courtesy toward, their readers, while in matters of conscience Pater seems to feel for them an actual pastoral responsibility. His well-known withdrawal of the "Conclusion" to *The Renaissance* from its second edition, from a fear that "it might possibly mislead some of those young men into whose hands it might fall," is but one of many examples of his solicitude; and surely such as have gone astray after such painstaking guidance have but their own natures to blame. As he justly says, again of Marius, "in the reception of metaphysical *formulæ*, all depends, as regards their actual and ulterior result, on the pre-existent qualities of that soil of human nature into which they fall—the company they find already present there, on their admission into the house of thought."

That Pater's philosophy could ever have been misunderstood is not to be entertained with patience by any one who has read him with even ordinary attention; that it may have been misapplied, in spite of all his care, is, of course, possible; but if a writer is to be called to account for all the misapplications, or distortions, of his philosophy, writing may as well come to an end. Yet, inconceivable as it may sound, a critic very properly held in popular esteem recently gave it as his opinion that the teaching of Walter Pater was responsible for the tragic career of the author of *The Picture of Dorian Gray*. Certainly that remarkable man was an "epicurean"—but one, to quote Meredith, "whom Epicurus would have scourged out of his garden"; and the statement made by the critic in question that *The Renaissance* is the book referred to in *The Picture of Dorian Gray* as having had a sinister influence over its hero is so easily disposed of by a reference to that romance itself that it is hard to understand its ever having been made. Here is the passage describing the demoralizing book in question:

> His eye fell on the yellow book that Lord Henry had sent him. . . . It was the strangest book he had ever read. It seemed to him that in exquisite raiment, and to the delicate sound of flutes, the sins of the world were passing in dumb show before him. Things that he had dimly dreamed of were suddenly made real to him. Things of which he had never dreamed were gradually revealed.
>
> It was a novel without a plot, and with only one character, being, indeed, simply a psychological study of a certain young Parisian who spent his life trying to realize in the nineteenth century all the passions and modes of thought that belonged to every century except his own, and to sum up, as it were, in himself the various moods through which the world-spirit had ever passed, loving for their mere artificiality those renunciations that men have un-wisely called virtue, as much as those natural rebel-lions that wise men still call sin. The style in which it was written was that curious jeweled style, vivid and obscure at once, full of *argot* and of archaisms, of technical expressions and of elaborate paraphrases, that characterizes the work of some of the finest artists of the French school of *Décadents*. There were in it metaphors as monstrous as orchids, and as evil in color. The life of the senses was described in the terms of mystical philosophy. One hardly knew at times whether one was reading the spiritual ecstasies of some medieval saint or the morbid confessions of a modern sinner. It was a poisonous book. The heavy odor of incense seemed to cling about its pages and to trouble the brain. The mere cadence of the sen-tences, the subtle monotony of their music, so full as it was of complex refrains and movements elaborately repeated, produced in the mind of the lad, as he passed from chapter to chapter, a form of reverie, a malady of dreaming, that made him unconscious of the falling day and the creeping shadows. . . .
>
> For years Dorian Gray could not free himself from the memory of this book. Or perhaps it would be more accurate to say that he never sought to free himself from it. He procured from Paris no less than five large paper copies of the first edition, and had them bound in different colors, so that they might suit his various moods and the changing fancies of a nature over which he seemed, at times, to have almost entirely lost control.

The book thus characterized is obviously by a French writer—I have good reason for thinking that it was À *Rebours* by Huysmans—and how any responsible reader can have imagined that Walter Pater's The Renaissance answers to this description passes all understanding. A critic guilty of so patent a misstatement must either never have read *The Picture of Dorian Gray*, or never have read *The Renaissance*. On the other hand, if on other more reliable evidence it can be found that Oscar Wilde was one of those "young men" misled by Pater's book, for whose spiritual safety Pater, as we have seen, was so solicitous, one can only remind oneself again of the phrase quoted above in regard to "that soil of human nature" into which a writer casts his seed. If that which was sown a lily comes up a toadstool, there is evidently something wrong with the soil.

Let us briefly recall what this apparently so "dangerous" philosophy of Pater's is, and we cannot do better than examine

it in its most concentrated and famous utterance, this oft-quoted passage from that once-suppressed "Conclusion" to *The Renaissance*:

> Not the fruit of experience, but experience itself, is the end. A counted number of pulses only is given to us of a variegated dramatic life. How may we see in them all that there is to be seen in them by the finest senses? How shall we pass most swiftly from point to point, and be present always at the focus where the greatest number of vital forces unite in their purest energy? To burn always with this hard, gem-like flame, to maintain this ecstasy, is success in life. . . . While all melts under our feet, we may well grasp at any exquisite passion, or any contribution to knowledge that seems by a lifted horizon to set the spirit free for a moment, or any stirring of the senses, strange dyes, strange colors, and curious odors, or work of the artist's hands, or the face of one's friend. . . . With this sense of the splendor of our experience and of its awful brevity, gathering all we are into one desperate effort to see and touch, we shall hardly have time to make theories about the things we see and touch. . . . Well! we are all *condamnés*, as Victor Hugo says: we are all under sentence of death, but with a sort of indefinite reprieve—*les hommes sont tous condamnés à mort avec des sursis indéfinis*: we have an interval, and then our place knows us no more. Some spend this interval in listlessness, some in high passions, the wisest, at least among 'the children of this world,' in art and song. For our one chance lies in expanding that interval, in getting as many pulsations as possible into the given time. Great passions may give us this quickened sense of life, ecstasy and sorrow of love, the various forms of enthusiastic activity, dis-interested or otherwise, which come naturally to many of us. Only be sure it is passion—that it does yield you this fruit of a quickened, multiplied con-sciousness. Of such wisdom, the poetic passion, the desire of beauty, the love of art for its own sake, has most. For art comes to you proposing frankly to give nothing but the highest quality to your moments as they pass, and simply for those moments' sake.

Now, if it be true that the application, or rather the misapplication, of this philosophy led Oscar Wilde to Reading Gaol, it is none the less true that another application of it led Marius to something like Christian martyrdom, and Walter Pater himself along an ever loftier and serener path of spiritual vision.

Nothing short of wilful misconstruction can make of the counsel thus offered, with so priestly a concern that the writer's exact meaning be brought home to his reader, other than an inspiration toward a noble employment of that mysterious opportunity we call life. For those of us, perhaps more than a few, who have no assurance of the leisure of an eternity for idleness or experiment, this expansion and elevation of the doctrine of the moment, carrying a merely sensual and trivial moral in the Horatian maxim of *carpe diem*, is once thrillingly charged with exhilaration and sounding a solemn and yet seductive challenge to us to make the most indeed, but also to make the best, of our little day. To make the most, and to make the best, of life! Those who misinterpret or misapply Pater forget his constant insistence on the second half of that precept. We are to get "as many pulsations as possible into the given time," but we are to be very careful that our use of those pulsations shall be the finest. Whether or not it is "simply for those moments' sake," our attempt must be to give *"the highest quality,"* remember, to those "moments as they pass." And who can fail to remark the fastidious care with which Pater selects various typical interests which he deems most worthy of dignifying the moment? The senses are, indeed, of natural right, to have their part; but those interests on which the accent of Pater's pleading most persuasively falls are not so much the "strange dyes, strange colors, and curious odors," but rather "the face of one's friend," ending his subtly musical sentence with a characteristic shock of simplicity, almost incongruity— or "some mood of passion or insight or intellectual excitement," or "any contribution to knowledge that seems by a lifted horizon to set the spirit free for a moment." There is surely a great gulf fixed between this lofty preoccupation with great human emotions and high spiritual and intellectual excitements, and a vulgar gospel of "eat, drink, for to-morrow we die," whether or not both counsels start out from a realization of "the awful brevity" of our mortal day. That realization may prompt certain natures to unbridled sensuality. Doomed to perish as the beasts, they choose, it would seem with no marked reluctance, to live the life of the beast, a life apparently not without its satisfactions. But it is as stupid as it is infamous to pretend that such natures as these find any warrant for their tragic libertinism in Walter Pater. They may, indeed, have found esthetic pleasure in the reading of his prose, but the truth of which that prose is but the beautiful garment has passed them by. For such it can hardly be claimed that they have translated into action the aspiration of this tenderly religious passage:

> Given the hardest terms, supposing our days are indeed but a shadow, even so we may well adorn and beautify, in scrupulous self-respect, our souls and whatever our souls touch upon—these wonderful bodies, these material dwelling-places through which the shadows pass together for a while, the very raiment we wear, our very pastimes, and the intercourse of society.

Here in this passage from *Marius* we find, to use Pater's own words once more, "the spectacle of one of the happiest temperaments coming, so to speak, to an understanding with the most depressing of theories." That theory, of course, was the doctrine of the perpetual flux of things as taught by Aristippus of Cyrene, making a man of the world's practical application of the old Heraclitean formula, his influence depending on this, "that in him an abstract doctrine, originally somewhat acrid, had fallen upon a rich and genial nature, well fitted to transform it into a theory of practice of considerable stimulative power toward a fair life." Such, too, was Pater's nature, and such his practical usefulness as what one might call a philosophical artist. Meredith, Emerson, Browning, and even Carlyle were artists so far related to him and each other in that each of them wrought a certain optimism, or, at all events, a courageous and even blithe working theory of life and conduct, out of the unrelenting facts of existence unflinchingly faced, rather than ecclesiastically smoothed over—the facts of death and pain and struggle, and even the cruel mystery that surrounds with darkness and terror our mortal lot. Each one of them deliberately faced the worst, and with each, after his own nature, the worst returned to laughter. The force of all these men was in their artistic or poetic embodiment of philosophical conceptions, but had they not been artists and poets their philosophical conceptions would have made but little way. And it is time to recall, what critics preoccupied with his "message" leave unduly in the background, that Pater was an artist of remarkable power and fascination, a maker of beautiful

things, which, whatever their philosophical content, have for our spirits the refreshment and edification which all beauty mysteriously brings us, merely because it is beauty. *Marius the Epicurean* is a great and wonderful book, not merely on account of its teaching, but because it is simply one of the most *beautiful* books, perhaps the most beautiful book, written in English. It is beautiful in many ways. It is beautiful, first of all, in the uniquely personal quality of its prose, prose which is at once austere and sensuous, simple at once and elaborate, scientifically exact and yet mystically suggestive, cool and hushed as sanctuary marble, sweet-smelling as sanctuary incense; prose that has at once the qualities of painting and of music, rich in firmly visualized pictures, yet moving to subtle, half-submerged rhythms, and expressive with every delicate accent and cadence; prose highly wrought, and yet singularly surprising one at times with, so to say, sudden innocencies, artless and instinctive beneath all its sedulous art. It is no longer necessary, as I hinted above, to fight the battle of this prose. Whether it appeal to one or not, no critic worth attention any longer disparages it as mere ornate and perfumed verbiage, the elaborate mannerism of a writer hiding the poverty of his thought beneath a pretentious raiment of decorated expression. It is understood to be the organic utterance of one with a vision of the world all his own striving through words, as he best can, to make that vision visible to others as nearly as possible as he himself sees it. Pater himself has expounded his theory and practice of prose, doubtless with a side-thought of self-justification, in various places up and down his writings, notably in his pregnant essay on "Style," and perhaps even more persuasively in the chapter called "Euphuism" in *Marius*. In this last he thus goes to the root of the matter:

> That preoccupation of the *dilettante* with what might seem mere details of form, after all, did but serve the purpose of bringing to the surface, sincerely and in their integrity, certain strong personal intuitions, a certain vision or apprehension of things as really being, with important results, thus, rather than thus—intuitions which the artistic or literary faculty was called upon to follow, with the exactness of wax or clay, clothing the model within.

This striving to express the truth that is in him has resulted in a beauty of prose which for individual quality must be ranked with the prose of such masters as De Quincey and Lamb, and, to make a not irrelevant comparison, above the very fine prose of his contemporary Stevenson, by virtue of its greater personal sincerity.

There is neither space here, nor need, to illustrate this opinion by quotation, though it may not be amiss, the musical and decorative qualities of Pater's prose having been so generally dwelt upon, to remind the reader of the magical simplicities by which it is no less frequently characterized. Some of his quietest, simplest phrases have a wonderful evocative power: "the long reign of these quiet Antonines," for example; "the thunder which had sounded all day among the hills"; "far into the night, when heavy rain-drops had driven the last lingerers home"; "Flavian was no more. The little marble chest with its dust and tears lay cold among the faded flowers." What could be simpler than these brief sentences, yet how peculiarly suggestive they are; what immediate pictures they make! And this magical simplicity is particularly successful in his descriptive passages, notably of natural effects, effects caught with an instinctively selected touch or two, an expressive detail, a gray or colored word. How lightly sketched, and yet how clearly realized in the imagination, is the ancestral countryhouse of

Marius's boyhood, "White-Nights," "that exquisite fragment of a once large and sumptuous villa"—"Two centuries of the play of the sea-wind were in the velvet of the mosses which lay along its inaccessible ledges and angles." Take again this picture:

> The cottagers still lingered at their doors for a few minutes as the shadows grew larger, and went to rest early; though there was still a glow along the road through the shorn corn-fields, and the birds were still awake about the crumbling gray heights of an old temple.

And again this picture of a wayside inn:

> The room in which he sat down to supper, unlike the ordinary Roman inns at that day, was trim and sweet. The firelight danced cheerfully upon the polished three-wicked *lucernæ* burning cleanly with the best oil, upon the whitewashed walls, and the bunches of scarlet carnations set in glass goblets. The white wine of the place put before him, of the true color and flavor of the grape, and with a ring of delicate foam as it mounted in the cup, had a reviving edge or freshness he had found in no other wine.

Those who judge of Pater's writing by a few purple passages such as the famous rhapsody on the "Mona Lisa," conceiving it as always thus heavy with narcotic perfume, know but one side of him, and miss his gift for conveying freshness, his constant happiness in light and air and particularly running water, "green fields—or children's faces." His lovely chapter on the temple of Æsculapius seems to be made entirely of morning light, bubbling springs, and pure mountain air; and the religious influence of these lustral elements is his constant theme. For him they have a natural sacramental value, and it is through them and such other influences that Pater seeks for his hero the sanctification of the senses and the evolution of the spirit. In his preoccupation with them, and all things lovely to the eye and to the intelligence, it is that the secret lies of the singular purity of atmosphere which pervades his *Marius*, an atmosphere which might be termed the soul-beauty of the book, as distinct from its, so to say, body-beauty as beautiful prose.

Considering *Marius* as a story, a work of imagination, one finds the same evocative method used in the telling of it, and in the portrayal of character, as Pater employs in its descriptive passages. Owing to certain violent, cinematographic methods of story-telling and character-drawing to which we have become accustomed, it is too often assumed that stories cannot be told or characters drawn in any other way. Actually, of course, as many an old masterpiece admonishes us, there is no one canon in this matter, but, on the contrary, no limit to the variety of method and manner a creative artist is at liberty to employ in his imaginative treatment of human life. All one asks is that the work should live, the characters and scenes appear real to us, and the story be told. And Pater's *Marius* entirely satisfies this demand for those to whom such a pilgrimage of the soul will alone appeal. It is a real story, no mere German scholar's attempt to animate the dry bones of his erudition; and the personages and the scenes do actually live for us, as by some delicate magic of hint and suggestion: and, though at first they may seem shadowy, they have a curious way of persisting, and, as it were, growing more and more alive in our memories. The figure of Marcus Aurelius, for example, though so delicately sketched, is a masterpiece of historical portraiture, as the pictures of Roman life, done with so little, seem to me far more convincing than the like of over-elaborated pictures of antiquity, so choked with learned detail of Flaubert and of Gautier—Mr. Swinburne's famous praise of whose *Mademoiselle de Maupin* applies with far greater fitness to Pater's masterpiece; for, if ever a book deserved to be described as

> The golden book of spirit and sense,
> The holy writ of beauty,

it is *Marius the Epicurean*.

It has been natural to dwell so long on this "golden book," because Pater's various gifts are concentrated in it, to make what is, of course, his masterpiece; though some one or other of these gifts is to be found employed with greater mastery in other of his writings, notably that delicate dramatic gift of embodying in a symbolic story certain subtle states of mind and refinements of temperament which reaches its perfection in *Imaginary Portraits*, to which the later "Apollo in Picardy" and "Hippolytus Veiled" properly belong. It is only necessary to recall the exquisitely austere "Sebastian van Storck" and the strangely contrasting Dionysiac "Denys L'Auxerrois" to justify one's claim for Pater as a creative artist of a rare kind, with a singular and fascinating power of incarnating a philosophic formula, a formula no less dry than Spinoza's, or a mood of the human spirit, in living, breathing types and persuasive tragic fables.

This genius for creative interpretation is the soul and significance of all his criticism. It gives their value to the studies of *The Renaissance*, but perhaps its finest flower is to be found in the later *Greek Studies*. To Flavian, Pater had said in *Marius*, "old mythology seemed as full of untried, unexpressed motives and interest as human life itself," and with what marvelous skill and evocative application of learning, he himself later developed sundry of those "untried, unexpressed motives," as in his studies of the myths of Dionysus—"The spirit of fire and dew, alive and leaping in a thousand vines"—and Demeter and Persephone—"the peculiar creation of country people of a high impressibility, dreaming over their work in spring or autumn, half consciously touched by a sense of its sacredness, and a sort of mystery about it"—no reader of Pater needs to be told. This same creative interpretation gives a like value to his studies of Plato; and so by virtue of this gift, active throughout the ten volumes which constitute his collected work, Pater proved himself to be of the company of the great humanists.

Along with all the other constituents of his work, its sacerdotalism, its subtle reverie, its sensuous color and perfume, its marmoreal austerity, its honeyed music, its frequent preoccupation with the haunted recesses of thought, there goes an endearing homeliness and simplicity, a deep human tenderness, a gentle friendliness, a something childlike. He has written of her, "the presence that rose thus so strangely beside the waters," to whom all experience had been "but as the sound of lyres and flutes," and he has written of "The Child in the House." Among all "the strange dyes, strange colors, and curious odors, and work of the artist's hand," one never misses "the face of one's friend"; and, in all its wanderings, the soul never strays far from the white temples of the gods and the sound of running water.

It is by virtue of this combination of humanity, edification, and esthetic delight that Walter Pater is unique among the great teachers and artists of our time.

Robert Louis Stevenson

ROBERT LOUIS STEVENSON

1850–1894

Robert Louis (originally Lewis) Balfour Stevenson was born in Edinburgh on November 13, 1850, the son of an engineer. In 1867 he entered Edinburgh University, with the intention of following his father's profession; by 1871, however, his poor health compelled him to abandon engineering and take up the study of law. From that point on much of Stevenson's life was spent in traveling in order to gain relief from the chronic bronchial condition that had plagued him since early childhood. In 1875 he was admitted to the Scottish bar, but by then he had already decided to become a writer.

In 1878 Stevenson, who had already published a number of pieces in various periodicals, brought out his travel book *An Inland Voyage*, which described a tour by canoe taken in Belgium and France in 1876. This was followed by *Deacon Brodie* (1880), the first of several undistinguished plays written in collaboration with his friend William Ernest Henley, the others being *Beau Austin* (1884), *Admiral Guinea* (1884), and *Macaire* (1885). *Travels with a Donkey in the Cévennes* appeared in 1879, the year in which Stevenson went to America in pursuit of Fanny Osbourne, whom he married in 1880.

In 1881 Stevenson published *Virginibus Puerisque*, a collection of short stories, essays, and travel pieces that had mostly been published previously in periodicals. This was followed by *Familiar Studies of Men and Books* (1882) and *The New Arabian Nights* (1882), an episodic novel. In 1883 Stevenson published *The Silverado Squatters*, which recorded a stay at Calistoga, and also brought out his first full-length piece of fiction, the adventure novel *Treasure Island*, which made him famous. This was followed by such works as *A Child's Garden of Verses* (1885); *Dr. Jekyll and Mr. Hyde* (1886), a novel that increased Stevenson's popularity; *Kidnapped* (1886), another popular novel; and *Underwoods* (1887), a volume of poetry.

In 1888 Stevenson sailed to the South Seas with his family in search of better health. In 1889 he purchased an estate in Vailima, Samoa, where he settled permanently in 1890. During the few remaining years of his life Stevenson published his novels *The Wrong Box* (1889), written with his stepson Lloyd Osbourne, and *The Master of Ballantrae* (1889), and also a short-story collection, *Island Nights' Entertainments* (1893), which contains his famous story "The Beach of Falesá." In 1893 Fanny suffered a nervous breakdown. Despite this Stevenson brought out one more novel, *The Ebb-Tide*, written with Lloyd Osbourne, before dying from a brain hemorrhage on December 3, 1894. At the time of his death Stevenson was at work on yet another novel, *Weir of Hermiston*, published as a fragment in 1896. A *Life* by Graham Balfour appeared in 1901, and there have been several editions of his collected letters, including *Vailima Letters* (to Sidney Colvin, 1895) and *Selected Letters*, ed. Sidney Colvin (2 vols., 1899; 4 vols., 1911).

Personal

Thin-legged, thin-chested, slight unspeakably,
Neat-footed and weak-fingered: in his face—
Lean, large-boned, curved of beak, and touched with race,
Bold-lipped, rich-tinted, mutable as the sea,
The brown eyes radiant with vivacity—
There shines a brilliant and romantic grace,
A spirit intense and rare, with trace on trace
Of passion and impudence and energy.
Valiant in velvet, light in ragged luck,
Most vain, most generous, sternly critical,
Buffoon and poet, lover and sensualist:
A deal of Ariel, just a streak of Puck,
Much Antony, of Hamlet most of all,
And something of the Shorter-Catechist.
    —W. E. HENLEY, "Apparition," *In Hospital*,
      1888, p. 41

Her hands about her brows are pressed,
  She goes upon her knees to pray,
Her head is bowed upon her breast,
  And oh, she's sairly failed the day!

Her breast is old, it will not rise,
  Her tearless sobs in anguish choke,
God put His finger on her eyes,
  And then it was her tears that spoke.

"I've ha'en o' brawer sons a flow,
  My Walter mair renown could win,
And he that followed at the plough,
  But Louis was my Benjamin!

"Ye sons wha do your little best,
  Ye writing Scots, put by the pen,
He's deid, the ane abune the rest,
  I winna look at write again!

"It's sune the leave their childhood drap,
  I've ill to ken them, gaen sae grey,
But aye he climbed intil my lap,
  Or pu'd my coats to mak me play.

"He egged me on wi' mirth and prank,
  We hangit gowans on a string,
We made the doakens walk the plank,
  We mairit snails withoot the ring.

"'I'm auld,' I pant, 'sic ploys to mak,
  To games your mither shouldna stoup.'
'You're gey an' auld,' he cries me back,
  'That's for I like to gar you loup!'

"O' thae bit ploys he made sic books,
  A' mithers cam to watch us playing;
I feigned no to heed their looks,
  But fine I kent what they was saying!

"At times I lent him for a game
   To north and south and east and west,
But no for lang, he sune cam hame,
   For here it was he played the best.

"And when he had to cross the sea,
   He wouldna lat his een grow dim,
He bravely dree'd his weird for me,
   I tried to do the same for him.

"Ahint his face his pain was sair,
   Ahint hers grat his waefu' mither;
We kent that we should meet nae mair,
   The ane saw easy thro' the ither.

"For lang I've watched wi' trem'ling lip,
   But Louis ne'er sin syne I've seen,
The greedy island keepit its grip,
   The cauldriff oceans rolled atween.

"He's deid, the ane abune the rest,
   Oh, wae, the mither left alane!
He's deid, the ane I loo'ed the best,
   Oh, mayna I hae back my nain!"

Her breast is old, it will not rise,
   Her tearless sobs in anguish choke,
God put His finger on her eyes,
   It was her tears alone that spoke.

Now out the lights went stime by stime,
   The towns crept closer round the kirk,
Now all the firths were smoored in rime,
   Lost winds went wailing thro' the mirk.

A star that shot across the night
   Struck fire on Pala's mourning head,
And left for aye a steadfast light,
   By which the mother guards her dead.

"The lad was mine!" Erect she stands,
   No more by vain regrets oppress't,
Once more her eyes are clear; her hands
   Are proudly crossed upon her breast.
     —J. M. BARRIE, "Scotland's Lament," *McClure's
     Magazine*, Feb. 1895, pp. 286–88

It is impossible to deal, however lightly, with the personal qualities of Robert Louis Stevenson without dwelling on the extreme beauty of his character. In looking back over the twenty years in which I knew him, I feel that, since he was eminently human, I ought to recall his faults, but I protest that I can remember none. Perhaps the nearest approach to a fault was a certain want of discretion, always founded on a wish to make people understand each other, but not exactly according to wisdom. I recollect that he once embroiled me for a moment with John Addington Symonds in a manner altogether blood-thirsty and ridiculous, so that we both fell upon him and rended him. This little weakness is really the blackest crime I can lay to his charge. And on the other side, what courage, what love, what an indomitable spirit, what a melting pity! He had none of the sordid errors of the little man who writes—no sick ambition, no envy of others, no exaggeration of the value of this ephemeral trick of scribbling. He was eager to help his fellows, ready to take a second place, with great difficulty offended, by the least show of repentance perfectly appeased.

Quite early in his career he adjusted himself to the inevitable sense of physical failure. He threw away from him all the useless impediments: he sat loosely in the saddle of life. Many men who get such a warning as he got take up something to lean against; according to their education or temperament, they support their maimed existence on religion, or on cynical indifference, or on some mania of the collector or the *dilettante*. Stevenson did none of these things. He determined to make the sanest and most genial use of so much of life as was left him. As any one who reads his books can see, he had a deep strain of natural religion; but he kept it to himself; he made no hysterical or ostentatious use of it.

Looking back at the past, one recalls a trait that had its significance, though one missed its meaning then. He was careful, as I have hardly known any other man to be, not to allow himself to be burdened by the weight of material things. It was quite a jest with us that he never acquired any possessions. In the midst of those who produced books, pictures, prints, bric-à-brac, none of these things ever stuck to Stevenson. There are some deep-sea creatures, the early part of whose life is spent dancing through the waters; at length some sucker or tentacle touches a rock, adheres, pulls down more tentacles, until the creature is caught there, stationary for the remainder of its existence. So it happens to men, and Stevenson's friends, one after another, caught the ground with a house, a fixed employment, a "stake in life;" he alone kept dancing in the free element, unattached. I remember his saying to me that if ever he had a garden he should like it to be empty, just a space to walk and talk in, with no flowers to need a gardener nor fine lawns that had to be mown. Just a fragment of the bare world to move in, that was all Stevenson asked for. And we who gathered possessions around us—a little library of rare books, a little gallery of drawings or bronzes—he mocked us with his goblin laughter; it was only so much more luggage to carry on the march, he said, so much more to strain the arms and bend the back.

Stevenson thought, as we all must think, that literature is a delightful profession, a primrose path. I remember his once saying so to me, and then he turned, with the brimming look in his lustrous eyes and the tremulous smile on his lips, and added, "But it is not all primroses, some of it is brambly, and most of it uphill." He knew—no one better—how the hill catches the breath and how the brambles tear the face and hands; but he pushed strenuously, serenely on, searching for new paths, struggling to get up into the light and air.

One reason why it was difficult to be certain that Stevenson had reached his utmost in any direction was what I will call, for want of a better phrase, the *energetic modesty* of his nature. He was never satisfied with himself, yet never cast down. There are two dangers that beset the artist—the one is being pleased with what he has done, and the other being dejected with it. Stevenson, more than any other man whom I have known, steered the middle course. He never conceived that he had achieved a great success, but he never lost hope that by taking pains he might yet do so. Twelve years ago, when he was beginning to write that curious and fascinating book, *Prince Otto*, he wrote to me describing the mood in which one should go about one's work—golden words, which I have never forgotten. "One should strain," he said, "and then play, strain again, and play again. The strain is for us, it educates; the play is for the reader, and pleases. In moments of effort one learns to do the easy things that people like."

He learned that which he desired, and he gained more than he hoped for. He became the most exquisite English writer of his generation; yet those who lived close to him are apt to think less of this than of the fact that he was the most unselfish and the most lovable of human beings.—EDMUND GOSSE, "Robert Louis Stevenson" (1895), *Critical Kit-Kats*, 1896, pp. 299–302

Mr. Stevenson possessed more than any man I ever met, the power of making other men fall in love with him. I mean that he excited a passionate admiration and affection, so much so that I verily believe some men were jealous of other men's place in his liking. I have met a stranger who, having become acquainted with him, spoke of him with a touching fondness and pride, his fancy reposing, as it seemed, in a fond contemplation of so much genius and charm. What was so taking in him? and how is one to analyze that dazzling surface of pleasantry, that changeful shining humor, wit, wisdom, recklessness; beneath which beat the most kind and tolerant of hearts?

People were fond of him, and people were proud of him: his achievements, as it were, sensibly raised their pleasure in the world, and, to them, became parts of themselves. They warmed their hands at that centre of light and heat. It is not every success which has these beneficent results. We see the successful sneered at, decried, insulted, even when success is deserved. Very little of all this, hardly aught of all this, I think, came in Mr. Stevenson's way. After the beginning (when the praises of his earliest admirers were irritating to dull scribes) he found the critics fairly kind, I believe, and often enthusiastic. He was so much his own severest critic, that he probably paid little heed to professional reviewers. In addition to his *Rathillet*, and what other MSS. he destroyed, he once, in the Highlands, long ago, lost a portmanteau with a batch of his writings. Alas, that he should have lost or burned anything! "King's chaff," says our country proverb, "is better than other folk's corn."

I have remembered very little, or very little that I can write, here and now; and about our last meeting, when he was so near death, in appearance, and so full of courage—how can I speak? His courage was a strong rock, not to be taken or subdued. When unable to utter a single word, his pencilled remarks to his attendants were pithy and extremely characteristic. This courage and spiritual vitality made one hope that he would, if he desired it, live as long as Voltaire, that reed among oaks. There were, of course, in so rare a combination of characteristics, some which were not equally to the liking of all. He was highly original in costume, but, as his photographs are familiar, the point does not need elucidation. Life was a drama to him, and he delighted, like his own British admirals, to do things with a certain air. He observed himself, I used to think, as he observed others, and "saw himself" in every part he played. There was nothing of the *cabotin* in this self-consciousness; it was the unextinguished childish passion for "playing at things" which remained with him. I have a theory that *all* children possess genius, and that it dies out in the generality of mortals, abiding with people whose genius the world is forced to recognize. Mr. Stevenson illustrates, and perhaps partly suggested, this private philosophy of mine. —ANDREW LANG, "Recollections of Robert Louis Stevenson," *North American Review*, Feb. 1895, pp. 191–93

These to his Memory. May the Age arriving
　　As ours recall
That bravest heart, that gay and gallant striving,
　　That laurelled pall!

Blithe and rare spirit! We who later linger
　　By bleaker seas,
Sigh for the touch of the Magician's finger,—
　　His golden keys!
　　　　—AUSTIN DOBSON, "R. L. S.: In Memoriam"
　　　　(1901), *Poetical Works*, 1923, p. 398

It has often been asked what gave Mr. Stevenson his standing in Samoa; what it was that made this English man of letters such a power in the land of his adoption. It must be remembered that to the Samoan mind he was inordinately rich, and many of them believe in the bottom of their hearts that the story of the bottle-imp was no fiction, but a tangible fact. Mr. Stevenson was a resident, a considerable land-owner, a man like themselves, with taro-swamps, banana plantations, and a Samoan *ainga* or family. He was no official with a hired house, here to-day with specious good-will on his lips, and empty promises, but off to-morrow in the mail steamer to that vague region called "papalagi" or "the white country." He knew Samoan etiquette, and was familiar with the baser as well as the better side of the native character; he was cautiously generous after the fashion of the country, and neither excited covetousness by undue prodigality nor failed to respond in a befitting way for favors received. Moreover, he was a consistent partisan of Mataafa, the ill-fated rebel king, a man of high and noble character, who though beaten and crushed by the government forces was nevertheless looked up to and covertly admired by all Samoa. The divinity that doth hedge a king, even a defeated and fallen one, cast a glamour over his close friend, Mr. Stevenson. And when the British man-of-war brought the unfortunate ex-king to Apia with many of his chiefs, it was Mr. Stevenson that first boarded the ship with sympathy and assistance; it was Mr. Stevenson that lighted the great ovens and brought down his men weighted with food-baskets when all were afraid and stood aloof; it was Mr. Stevenson that attended to the political prisoners in the noisome jail after they had been flogged through the streets and foully mishandled under the very guns of the men-of-war; it was Mr. Stevenson that brought and paid the doctor, that had the stinking prison cleansed, that fed the starving wretches from his own pocket until the officials were shamed and terrified into action. These things made a deep impression at the time, and will never be altogether forgotten. No wonder the government chiefs said to one another: "Behold, this is indeed a friend; would our white officials have done the same had the day gone against us?" And the expression, "Once Tusitala's friend, always Tusitala's friend," went about the countryside like a proverb.—ISOBEL STRONG, LLOYD OSBOURNE, *Memories of Vailima*, 1902, pp. 151–54

General

A friend recommended me if I met with them to read L. Stevenson's stories, the *New Arabian Nights* and others since. I read a story by him in *Longman's*, I think, and a paper by him on Romance. His doctrine, if I apprehend him, is something like this. The essence of Romance is incident and that only, the type of pure Romance the *Arabian Nights*: those stories have no moral, no character-drawing, they turn altogether on interesting incident. The incidents must of course have a connection, but it need be nothing more than that they happen to the same person, are aggravations and so on. As history consists essentially of events likely or unlikely, consequences of causes chronicled before or what may be called chance, just retributions or nothing of the sort, so Romance, which is fictitious history, consists of event, of incident. His own stories are written on this principle; they are very good and he has all the gifts a writer of fiction should have, including those he holds unessential, as characterisation, and at first you notice no more than an ordinary well told story, but on looking back in the light of this doctrine you see that the persons illustrate the incident or strain of incidents, the plot, *the story*, not the story and incidents the persons. There was a tale of his called 'Treasure of Fourvières' or something like that; it is the story of an old treasure found, lost, and found again. The finding of the treasure acts of course and rather for the worse upon the finder,

a retired French doctor, and his wife; the loss cures them; you wait and see the effect of the refinding; but not at all, the story abruptly ends—because its hero was, so to say, this triplet of incidents. His own remarks on the strength and weakness of the Waverleys are excellent. But I have been giving my own version of the doctrine (which is, I think, clearly true) rather than his for I do not remember well enough what he says.
—GERARD MANLEY HOPKINS, Letter to R. W. Dixon (Aug. 15, 1883)

His earliest writings, descriptive and critical, are astonishingly mature; yet it seems to me that an increasing seriousness, a deepening tenderness, can be traced in the sequence of his works. At first he gloried in his mere strength, he took the athlete's delight in achieving feats of invention and expression. He has told us how imitative was the training to which he subjected himself in boyhood; and he is still, in his first books of travel, criticisms and stories, "playing the sedulous ape," as he phrased it—imitating very eclectically and originally, but still imitating. It is noteworthy that in the Edinburgh Edition of the *Travels with a Donkey* (how good that he lived to enjoy the homage implied in the instant success of this edition!) we no longer find the italicised proper names, which gave a pretty but somewhat mechanical touch of quaintness to the original copies. He never wrote anything more consummate in their kind than the *New Arabian Nights*; yet one is glad to think that these exercises in blood-curdling humour came at the beginning of his career as a story-teller, and the Dutch scenes of *Catriona* near the close. In *Treasure Island*, masterpiece though it be, he is still imitating, parodying, pouring his genius into a ready-made form. In *Kidnapped* he breaks away, half unwittingly perhaps, from the boy's-book convention. *The Master of Ballantrae* is an independent, self-sufficing romance, no more imitative than *The Bride of Lammermoor* or *Esmond*; and *Catriona*, imperfect though it be in structure, carries the boy's book projected in *Kidnapped* into the higher region of serious character-study and exquisite emotion. Not even Catriona—that pearl of maidenhood, whom Viola and Perdita would hail as their very sister—not even Catriona has succeeded in dissipating the illusion that Robert Louis Stevenson could not draw a woman. This very day I have seen the dreary old stereotype rearing its undiminished head in more quarters than one. And Catriona does not stand alone. She has on one hand the Princess Seraphina, on the other the woman who loved the Master of Ballantrae, and became his brother's wife. Nay more—even a half share in Beau Austin's Dorothy Musgrave should be enough to acquit a man of incompetence in the matter of female character-drawing.
—WILLIAM ARCHER, "In Memoriam: R. L. S.," *New Review*, Jan. 1895, p. 94

To-day is not the moment—we have not the time, and it would require a literary capacity to which I make no pretence—to-day is not the opportunity to enter into any review of the works of Stevenson. But there are two or three points to which, as an outside reader, I must call your attention before I sit down. The first is the style of the man himself—it was a tool carefully finished and prepared by himself in order the better to work out the business to which his genius led him. I daresay many of you may think that style is a light, accidental art of inspiration which comes easily to a gifted writer. But what does Stevenson say himself? "Whenever a book or a passage particularly pleased me, in which a thing was said or an effect rendered with propriety, in which there was either some conspicuous force or some happy distinction in the style, I must sit down at once and set myself to ape that quality. I was unsuccessful, and

I knew it, and tried again, and was again unsuccessful, and always unsuccessful. But at least in these vain bouts I got some practice in rhythm, in harmony, in construction, and the co-ordination of parts. I have thus played the sedulous ape to Hazlitt, to Lamb, to Wordsworth, to Sir Thomas Browne, to Defoe, to Hawthorne, to Montaigne, to Baudelaire, and Oberman." And to these he adds afterwards, in a later passage, Ruskin, Browning, Morris, Keats, Swinburne, Chaucer, Webster, Congreve, and Thackeray; and he sums it all up by saying, "*that*, like it or not, is the way to write." If a dullard were to pursue that practice which Stevenson enjoins, he would be at the end of it be probably only as at the beginning, a "sedulous ape." But with Stevenson there was the genius to mould what he had acquired by this painful practice. Mr. Fox said of Mr. Pitt that he himself (Mr. Fox) had always a command of words, but that Mr. Pitt had always a command of the right words, and that is the quality which strikes us in the style of Stevenson. I do not know whether his method was easy or laborious. I strongly suspect it may have been laborious, but, whichever it was, he never was satisfied with any word which did not fully embody the idea that he had in his mind, and therefore you have in his style something suggestive, something musical, something pregnant, a splendid vehicle for whatever he had to say.

He was not satisfied with style; he infused into his style a spirit which, for want of a better word, I can only call a spirit of irony of the most exquisite kind. He, as you know, adopted a style of diction which reminds us sometimes more of Addison's *Spectator* or Steele's *Tatler* than of the easier and more emotional language of these later days. But as he put into these dignified sentences this spirit which, for want of a better word, I must call irony, he relieved what otherwise might have been heavy. Now, I think you will all recognise what I mean when I speak of this spirit of irony. You will find it in, I think, every page of his works. I do not mean that of the savage and gruesome parable which has added a household word to the English language, and which is called *Dr. Jekyll and Mr. Hyde*, but I will take one instance from one of the works of his highest imagination, *The New Arabian Nights*. He takes Rudolf out of *The Mysteries of Paris*, and puts him down in London as a plump and respectable Prince of Bohemia, bent on adventure, but comfortably situated, hovering always between the sublime and the ridiculous, till the author at last makes up his mind for the ridiculous and settles him down in a cigar divan. But no one can read the account of Florizel, Prince of Bohemia, without recognising the essential quality of irony which makes Stevenson's style so potent. In some of his books he develops an even more bitter power of the same kind. In *The Dynamiter* you will find that in a form sometimes which by neither Swift nor Thackeray could be excelled. The picture of the scheming dynamiter, full of the high impulse of his mission, and constantly baffled by the cruel fate of circumstances in his efforts for an exhaustive explosion, is perhaps one of the most powerful instances of sardonic treatment to be met with in the whole history of English literature.—LORD ROSEBERY, "Robert Louis Stevenson" (1896), *Miscellanies Literary and Historical*, 1921, Vol. 2, pp. 24–26

If the critics of this century were ready to agree with Sir Philip Sidney, Ben Jonson, and their contemporaries, in the opinion that verse is "an ornament and no cause to poetry," and that a poet may consequently write in prose, it would be easy to find in the word "poetry" a comprehensive description of all Stevenson's work. Alike in his essays and romances, in his critical judgments and his records of fact, what he touches is transfigured by the light of his imagination, and expressed in periods as carefully modelled as the periods of blank verse. He has not one set of themes for his verse and another for his prose, his poems are often echoes of what he has rendered elsewhere by the instrument of his dearer choice and study. But it would be unfair to so great an artist in prose to confuse the issue even for a moment. For it was a true instinct that led Stevenson through the arduous course of training that he gave himself in the schools of Sir Thomas Browne and Montaigne, Bunyan and Defoe, on the way to his own style. The subjects that appealed to him, the handling that was his natural gift, alike are ill-suited to the severity of verse. He is a traveller and no architect; the Latins, in calling prose *sermo pedestris*, described by anticipation the chief merits of the happiest master of vagabond discourse in all the nineteenth century. And hence those critics are ill-advised who separate his essays and his romances to give preference to the former. The fireside talker, who said wise and gay things concerning love and marriage, art and death, to a select and delighted company at the inn, came thither for a night's lodging with no intention of residence. Romance, or what is happening round the next turn of the road, and beyond the next bend of the river, was the lodestar of his life. Now and again he would describe the scenes he passed through, sometimes he would beguile the way with reflections and aphorisms gathered by the roadside or caught out of the air; but for the most part the accidents of travel served him by suggesting the unknown history of the past and the untried possibilities of the future. Experience, which was a law of limitation to Fielding, was to Stevenson an incessantly renewed provocation to dreaming. A short story like "The Pavilion on the Links" serves to show how his fancy worked on the suggestions caught from the sand-dunes and the sea, with perhaps a stray figure passing in the dusk. What is best in his romances and essays they catch from each other; the romances are convincing by virtue of their sheer hold on the ultimate conditions of human life, the essays deal in no abstract fashion with high themes of policy and philosophy, but flash their light upon common objects at an angle that reveals the glitter in the quartz.

The constant quantity in all Stevenson's writing is himself. A complete life of him might be compiled from his works; the skeleton itinerary of his wanderings, with names and dates, might easily be clothed with the living tissue of sensations and impressions that is furnished by his books. Yet he is the least obtrusive of egotists, and his heroic endeavours to escape from himself in the creation of character achieve some veritable successes. Alan Breck Stewart is perhaps the finest Highlander in English literature—he is at any rate second to none. David Balfour, Captain Nares, Jim Pinkerton, and some half-dozen others, are breathing human beings, created by sympathy and never really deformed by the humours of the comic spirit. The rival heroines of Stevenson's longest work may safely challenge comparison with any of Scott's goddesses. Indeed it is not in his firmer grasp of character that Scott's superiority as a romancer is made manifest, but rather in his frank unquestioning acceptance of the fundamental facts of life, its loves and hates, its joys and sorrows. Axioms are as necessary in romance as in mathematics, and Stevenson might perhaps have raised his structure of romance higher had he been less addicted to digging at the foundations. His attitude towards the business and desire of grown men had always something of the child's open-eyed wonder; he was to the last a stranger on the earth. His view of human things is as clear as it is fresh, but he stands aloof from them, and his sympathies are not to be tamed by the affections. He knew this touch of chilliness in himself, as he

knew most things that can be discovered by introspection, and he shunned the introduction of women in his earlier stories. Although he learned from Scott how to make pirates seem execrably wicked without the minute reproduction of ruffianly talk, he would not have dared to follow Scott to the blunt extremity of terror by letting his heroines fall into the hands of a drunken pirate crew. Such a crisis could never bear the curious consideration which Stevenson, in the very vein of Hamlet, would have given it. The broad gust and generous prejudices of his great forerunners are no part of his faculty; he is unwilling to owe the greatness of his effects to the strength of a universal passion rather than to his own exquisite and subtle treatment of it.

Hence it is that style, which is the intrusion of the artist's individuality upon lifeless matter and impersonal truth, is the beginning and end of his writing. Commonplace morality and conventional expression are impossible to him, his questing avidity could never be harnessed in the shafts of everyday purpose. In an age of journalism, of barren repetition and fruitless expatiation, it is high praise to give even to a great prose-writer to say of him that he never proses. This praise is due to Stevenson; his chisel, which rang in the workshops of many masters, was always wielded under the direction of a marvellously quick eye, by a hand that gathered strength and confidence every year. He has left no slovenly work, none that has not an inimitable distinction, and the charm of expression that belongs only to a rare spirit. If the question be raised of his eventual place in the great hierarchy of English writers, it is enough to say that the tribunal that shall try his claims is not yet in session when the time comes he will be summoned to the bar, not with the array of contemporaries whose names a foolish public linked to his, but with the chief prose-writers of the century, few of whom can face the trial with less to extenuate and less to conceal.—WALTER RALEIGH, "Robert Louis Stevenson," *English Prose*, ed. Henry Craik, 1896, Vol. 5, pp. 761–64

If we can lay our finger on the reason of Stevenson's—I will not say failure, but inadequate success—as a playwright, perhaps it may help us to understand the still more inadequate success of greater men.

And here let me follow the example of that agreeable essayist, Euclid, and formulate my theorem in advance—or, in other words, indicate the point towards which I hope to lead you. We shall find, I think, that Stevenson, with all his genius, failed to realize that the art of drama is not stationary, but progressive. By this I do not mean that it is always improving; what I do mean is that its conditions are always changing, and that every dramatist whose ambition it is to produce live plays is absolutely bound to study carefully, and I may even add respectfully—at any rate not contemptuously—the conditions that hold good for his own age and generation. This Stevenson did not—would not—do. We shall find, I think, that in all his plays he was deliberately imitating outworn models, and doing it, too, in a sportive, half-disdainful spirit, as who should say, "The stage is a realm of absurdities—come, let us be cleverly absurd!" In that spirit, success never was and never will be attained. I do not mean to imply, of course, that this was the spirit in which the other great writers I have mentioned—Shelley, Browning, Tennyson, and the rest—approached their work as dramatists. But I do suggest that they one and all, like Stevenson, set themselves to imitate outworn models, instead of discovering for themselves, and if necessary ennobling, the style of drama really adapted to the dramatist's one great end—that of showing the age and body of the time his form and pressure. The difference is that while Stevenson imitated the transpontine plays of the early nineteenth century, most of the other writers I have named imitated the Elizabethan dramatists. The difference is not essential to my point—the error lies in the mere fact of imitation. One of the great rules—perhaps the only universal rule—of the drama is that you cannot pour new wine into old skins.—ARTHUR WING PINERO, "Robert Louis Stevenson: The Dramatist," *Critic*, April 1903, p. 342

The fact is, that the whole mass of Stevenson's spiritual and intellectual virtues have been partly frustrated by one additional virtue—that of artistic dexterity. If he had chalked up his great message on a wall, like Walt Whitman, in large and straggling letters, it would have startled men like a blasphemy. But he wrote his light-headed paradoxes in so flowing a copy-book hand that everyone supposed they must be copy-book sentiments. He suffered from his versatility, not, as is loosely said, by not doing every department well enough, but by doing every department too well. As a child, cockney, pirate, or Puritan, his disguises were so good that most people could not see the same man under all. It is an unjust fact that if a man can play the fiddle, give legal opinions, and black boots just tolerably, he is called an Admirable Crichton, but if he does all three thoroughly well, he is apt to be regarded, in the several departments, as a common fiddler, a common lawyer, and a common boot-black. This is what has happened in the case of Stevenson. If *Dr Jekyll, The Master of Ballantrae, The Child's Garden of Verses*, and *Across the Plains* had been each of them one shade less perfectly done than they were, everyone would have seen that they were all parts of the same message; but by succeeding in the proverbial miracle of being in five places at once, he has naturally convinced others that he was five different people. But the real message of Stevenson was as simple as that of Mahomet, as moral as that of Dante, as confident as that of Whitman, and as practical as that of James Watt.

The conception which unites the whole varied work of Stevenson was that romance, or the vision of the possibilities of things, was far more important than mere occurrences: that one was the soul of our life, the other the body, and that the soul was the precious thing. The germ of all his stories lies in the idea that every landscape or scrap of scenery has a soul: and that soul is a story. Standing before a stunted orchard with a broken stone wall, we may know as a mere fact that no one has been through it but an elderly female cook. But everything exists in the human soul: that orchard grows in our own brain, and there it is the shrine and theatre of some strange chance between a girl and a ragged poet and a mad farmer. Stevenson stands for the conception that ideas are the real incidents: that our fancies are our adventures. To think of a cow with wings is essentially to have met one. And this is the reason for his wide diversities of narrative: he had to make one story as rich as a ruby sunset, another as grey as a hoary monolith: for the story was the soul, or rather the meaning, of the bodily vision. It is quite inappropriate to judge 'The Teller of Tales' (as the Samoans called him) by the particular novels he wrote, as one would judge Mr George Moore by *Esther Waters*. These novels were only the two or three of his soul's adventures that he happened to tell. But he died with a thousand stories in his heart.—G. K. CHESTERTON, "Stevenson" (1901), *Five Types*, 1910, pp. 39–43

Works

DR. JEKYLL AND MR. HYDE

I doubt whether anyone has the right so to scrutinise "the abysmal deeps of personality." You see I have been reading *Dr.*

Jekyll. At least I think he ought to bring more of distinct belief in the resources of human nature, more faith, more sympathy with our frailty, into the matter than you have done. The art is burning and intense. The *Peau de chagrin* disappears, and Poe's work is water. Also one discerns at once that this is an allegory of all twy-natured souls who yield consciously to evil. Most of us are on the brink of educating a Mr. Hyde at some epoch of our being. But the scientific cast of the allegory will only act as an incentive to moral self-murder with those who perceive the allegory's profundity. Louis, how had you the "ilia dura, ferro et ære triplici duriora," to write Dr. Jekyll? I know now what was meant when you were called a sprite.

You see I am trembling under the magician's wand of your fancy, and rebelling against it with the scorn of a soul that hates to be contaminated with the mere picture of victorious evil. Our only chance seems to me to be to maintain, against all appearances, that evil can never and in no way be victorious.

I would that you would tell me whether you only used your terrible *motif* as a good ground-work for a ghastly tale, or whether you meant it to have a moral purpose. But I suppose you won't tell me.

I seem to have lost you so utterly that I can afford to fling truth of the crudest in your face. And yet I love you and think of you daily, and have Dew Smith's portrait of you in front of me.

The suicide end of Dr. Jekyll is too commonplace. Dr. Jekyll ought to have given Mr. Hyde up to justice. This would have vindicated the sense of human dignity which is so horribly outraged in your book.—JOHN ADDINGTON SYMONDS, Letter to Robert Louis Stevenson (March 1, 1886), cited in Horatio N. Brown, *John Addington Symonds: A Biography*, 1895, Vol. 2, pp. 256–57

What piece of prose fiction is less likely to be forgotten? To begin with, the central idea, strange as it is, at once comes home to everybody. The double personality, which the very habit of a dream-land existence must have forced in upon Mr. Stevenson, corresponds with facts of which we are all obscurely conscious. It heightens immensely the interest of a book thus to carry an allegory on the very face of it, provided that the allegory does not interfere with the illusion, but speaks the moral with the poignancy of life itself. Further, this is the only case where Mr. Stevenson, working by himself, has used a mystery; and most skilfully it is used in the opening chapters to stimulate curiosity. The book falls into three parts. First, the mystery, which is set out with wonder that rises from the mere question of an onlooker about this uncanny person Hyde, to the agonised inquiry of Jekyll's friend, who knows all but the answer to the riddle, when he batters at Jekyll's locked door, and is answered by the voice of Hyde. Then follows the explanation; and remark the skill with which a medical man is made the witness of the change. He recounts the phenomena with a practised accuracy which would have been unnatural, say, in Utterson. In the third part, when the mystery has been solved, nothing but consummate art could have saved the interest from collapsing. But Jekyll's own written statement gives the crowning emotion when it recites the drama that passed in the study behind the locked door; the appalling conflict between the two personages in the same outwardly changing breast. Other writers have approached the same idea. Gautier, for instance, has a curious story of a gentleman who gets translated into another man's body to court the other's wife; but Mr. Stevenson has everything to gain by the comparison. Remember the passage where Jekyll wakes for the first time to find that he has in sleep become Hyde, and the look of Hyde's hairy hand on the sheet.—STEPHEN GWYNN, "Mr. Robert Louis Stevenson," *Fortnightly Review*, Dec. 1894, p. 787

Let us take the strange case of R. L. Stevenson, and especially his *Jekyll and Hyde*, which, in some ways, is his most characteristic and most effective book. Now I suppose that instructed opinion (granting its existence) was about equally divided as to the class in which this most skilful and striking story was to be placed. Many, I have no doubt, gave it a very high place in the ranks of imaginative literature, or (as we should now say) in the ranks of literature; while many other judges set it down as an extremely clever piece of sensationalism, and nothing more. Well, I think both these opinions are wrong; and I should be inclined to say that *Jekyll and Hyde* just scrapes by the skin of its teeth, as it were, into the shelves of literature, and no more. On the surface it would seem to be merely sensationalism; I expect that when you read it you did so with breathless absorption, hurrying over the pages in your eagerness to find out the secret, and this secret once discovered I imagine that *Jekyll and Hyde* retired to your shelf—and stays there, rather dusty. You have never opened it again? Exactly. I *have* read it for a second time, and I was astonished to find how it had, if I may say so, evaporated. At the first reading one was enthralled by mere curiosity, but when once this curiosity had been satisfied, what remained? If I may speak from my own experience, simply a rather languid admiration of the ingenuity of the plot with its construction, combined with a slight feeling of impatience, such as one might experience if one were asked to solve a puzzle for the second time. You see that the secret once disclosed all the steps which lead to the disclosure become, *ipso facto*, insignificant, or rather they become nothing at all, since their only significance and their only existence lay in the secret, and when the secret has ceased to be a secret, the signs and cyphers of it fall also into the world of nonentity. You may be amazed, and perplexed, and entranced by a cryptogram, while you are solving it, but the solution once attained, your cryptogram is either nothing or perilously near to nothingness.

Well, all this points, doesn't it? towards mere sensationalism, very cleverly done. But, as I said, I think *Jekyll and Hyde* just scrapes over the border-line and takes its place, very low down, among books that are literature. And I base my verdict solely on the Idea, on the conception that lies, buried rather deeply, beneath the plot. The plot, in itself, strikes me as mechanical—this actual physical transformation, produced by a drug, linked certainly with a theory of ethical change, but not linked at all with the really mysterious, the really psychical— all this affects me, I say, as ingenious mechanism and nothing more; while I have shown how the construction is ingenious artifice, and the style is affected by the same plague of laboured ingenuity. Throughout it is a thoroughly conscious style, and in literature all the highest things are unconsciously, or at least subconsciously produced. It has music, but it has no under-music, and there are no phrases in it that seem veils of dreams, echoes of the "inexpressive song." It is on the conception, then, alone, that I justify my inclusion of *Jekyll* amongst works of art; for it seems to me that, lurking behind the plot, we divine the presence of an idea, of an inspiration. "Man is not truly one, but truly two," or, perhaps, a polity with many inhabitants, Dr. Jekyll writes in his confession, and I think that I see here a trace that Stevenson had received a vision of the mystery of human nature, compounded of the dust and of the stars, of a dim vast city, splendid and ruinous as drowned Atlantis deep beneath the waves, of a haunted quire where a flickering light burns before the Veil. This, I believe, was the vision that came to the artist, but the admirable artificer seized hold of it at once and made it all his own, omitting what he did not understand, translating roughly from the unknown tongue, materialising, coarsening, hardening. Don't you see how thoroughly *physical* the actual plot is? and if one escapes for a moment from the atmosphere of the laboratory it is only to be confronted by the most obvious vein of moral allegory; and from this latter light *Jekyll and Hyde* seems almost the vivid metaphor of a clever preacher. You mustn't imagine, you know, that I condemn the powder business as bad in itself, for (let us revert for a moment to philosophy) man is a sacrament, soul manifested under the form of body, and art has to deal with each and both and to show their interaction and interdependence. The most perfect form of literature is, no doubt, lyrical poetry, which is, one might say, almost pure idea, art with scarcely an alloy of artifice, expressed in magic words, in the voice of music. In a word, a perfect lyric, such as Keat's "Belle Dame sans Mercy" is *almost* pure soul, a spirit with the luminous body of melody. But (in our age, at all events) a prose romance must put on a grosser and more material envelope than this, it must have incident, corporeity, relation to material things, and all these will occupy a considerable part of the whole. To a certain extent, then, the idea must be materialised, but still it must always shine through the fleshly vestment; the body must never be mere body but always the body of the spirit, existing to conceal and yet to manifest the spirit; and here it seems to me that Stevenson's story breaks down. The transformation of Jekyll into Hyde is solely material as you read it, without artistic significance; it is simply an astounding incident, and not an outward sign of an inward mystery. As for the possible allegory I have too much respect for Stevenson as an artificer to think that he would regard this element as anything but a very grave defect. Allegory, as Poe so well observed, is always a literary vice, and we are only able to enjoy *The Pilgrim's Progress* by forgetting that the allegory exists. Yes, that seems to me the *vitium* of *Jekyll and Hyde*: the conception has been badly realised, and by badly I do not mean clumsily, because from the logical, literal standpoint the plot and the construction are marvels of cleverness; but I mean inartistically: ecstasy, which as we have settled is the synonym of art, gave birth to the idea, but immediately abandoned it to artifice, and to artifice only, instead of presiding over and inspiring every further step in plot, in construction and in style.—ARTHUR MACHEN, *Hieroglyphics: A Note upon Ecstasy in Literature* (1902), 1923, pp. 70–74

THE MASTER OF BALLANTRAE

So unanimous have been the journals of culture in their praise of Mr. Stevenson's genius, especially as manifested in his new book—and so perturbed is the public mind by the oracular utterances regarding the great store future generations will set upon it, and the high place it will one day take among English classics—that I am almost constrained to apologise for the unseemliness of a perverse taste which refuses to accept even as excellent that which others are agreed to praise as sublime. My difficulty is certainly not inconsiderable; a man, not to say a critic, may very well write himself down an ass before he well knows where he is; and yet it seems sure when one considers it that all cannot be right with a book of adventure in which no very decided story is told. Of course I am aware that it is ridiculous for me to decry a book that the *Spectator*, the *Saturday Review*, the whole of Bedford Park, and all the aesthetics of Clapham and Peckham Rye have in oecumenical council decided is to live for ever. For plea of my condemnation of a work already canonized and enthroned amongst the Immortals, I will again suggest to its many erudite admirers that it is, perhaps, after all only a story of adventure with the story left out. In making this suggestion, I feel like the child in Hans Andersen's tale of the lying weavers who persuaded the King and his court that they were supplying them with garments of magical lightness when they had only persuaded them to walk about naked. When the child said: 'No father, the King and his court are walking about naked,' everybody recognised the truth and the weavers were stoned out of the town.

As naked of story as the King and his court were of clothes, *The Master of Ballantrae* seems in my eyes. No doubt diligent searching would reveal the workings of the plot—diligent searching will discover the departure and arrival of a train in *Bradshaw*—but it does not strike me as being any part of my critical duty to follow up the various zigzag lights which flickered across the pages. Suffice it to say for the condemnation of the book, that the story—if there is a story—is involved in many disjointed narratives. The author fails to set forth his scheme as he did in *Treasure Island*, as Defoe did in *Robinson Crusoe*, as did, indeed, every writer who has written a book of adventures that has outlasted a generation. I have read all but the last thirty or forty pages—these the very strictest sense of critical duty could not induce me to toil through—without receiving one distinct impression concerning either the Master of Ballantrae, his sons, the steward, Mr. MacKellar, their aims, or their achievements. Never does Mr. Stevenson grasp his story and do his will of it. His claim upon it is that of a white, languid hand, dreamily laid, and fitfully attempting to detain a gallant who would escape; ineffectively the hand is laid on the lappet and on the sleeve. The hand is long and delicate, somewhat epicene; and fingers are long and weak; the skin is pallid and relieved by the brilliancy of numerous rings.

Some three or four scenes, however, fix themselves upon my mind. I remember the pirate vessel and its captain, and this captain Mr. Stevenson has characterised very skilfully, but merely from the outside. It is a clever 'make-up': just such a one as a clever actor would invent; and the life on board is also excellently well invented. But nowhere any breadth of design, nor are we held under spell of any imaginative impulse, creative or descriptive. We float on a painted ocean in a painted boat, among a little wretchedness of cardboard and tinsel. The thing is a toy—a pretty daintily conceived toy, equivalent in artistic value to a Savoy opera or a view of Bedford Park on a fine day. Indeed, I utterly fail to see in what this portion of the book is better than similar scenes described again and again by Captain Marryat. A memory of *Percival Keene* rises, and if I remember rightly the blunter narrative is, in all those qualities through which the tooth of time cuts slowest, superior to the dilettantism before me.

As soon as we are quit of the pirate vessel the story is taken up by another person, and we drift into a mist of vapidities, we wade through dry deserts of barren artificialities, until at last we fall in with an oasis in the shape of a duel between two brothers. And upon my word the scene is very nicely done. Yes; it is very nice in the modern and in the original sense of the word. So nice is it, so beguiling is the art that there are times when it seems that Mr. Stevenson is rising to the situation, and is really investing his subject with some passion and dignity. But hardly has the impression entered the mind than it is destroyed by some more than usually irritating trick of phrase. Again the story becomes a doll, and the author a doll-

maker; an eyelash is added, and a touch of carmine is laid on the corner of the lips.

The duel done with, we drift again into vain seas of speech where windless sails of narrative hang helpless and death-like, and vague shapes, impersonal as unimagined hosts, people the gloom; and through the sepulchral weariness, the self-conscious style sounds like a fog horn. Suddenly, when the soul of hope is well nigh dead within us, comes another incident; whence it comes and to what scheme of life it belongs I know not, but it is a rift in the darkness.

Mr. Stevenson tells how some people took a path by night, which led through a wood and 'debouched' upon the high road. He describes with admirable picturesqueness the departure of a carriage, how it descended into the vale, mounted the succeeding hill, and stopped on the summit, and one of the travellers took out one of the lamps and waved it for a farewell sign. This third incident was the last that arrested my attention. But dulness is not a provable quantity; what one finds dull, another may declare to be bright and entertaining; bad writing is more demonstrable, and to the task of making good this accusation, I will now apply myself.

We know from Euclid that before even the simplest proposition can be proved, it is necessary to presuppose the acceptance of certain truths, self-evident, because the human mind cannot think them otherwise than as they are stated. Now I submit that the statement that two straight lines cannot enclose a space, is not more self-evident than that the first excellence of a writer is the power to press in a paragraph that which might be easily expanded in a column. As corollary to the axiom, I will add that matter and form cannot exist independently of each other. To deny this is equivalent to saying that something may be created out of nothing. If this premiss be granted, I ask how is it possible to admire the following passage:—

> Not that I ever lost the love I bore my master. But, for one thing, he had the less use for my society. For another, I could not but compare the case of Mr. Alexander with that of Miss Katharine; for whom my lord had never found the least attention. And, for a third, I was wounded by the change he discovered to his wife, which struck me in the nature of an infidelity. I could but admire, besides, the constancy and kindness she displayed. Perhaps her sentiment to my lord, as it had been founded from the first in pity, was that rather of a mother than a wife; perhaps it pleased her—if I may say so—to behold her two children so happy in each other; the more as one had suffered so unjustly in the past. But for all that, and though I could never trace in her one spark of jealousy, she must fall back for society on poor neglected Miss Katharine; and I, on my part, came to pass my spare hours more and more with the mother and daughter. It would be easy to make too much of this diversion, for it was a pleasant family, as families go; still the thing existed; whether my lord knew it or not, I am in doubt. I do not think he did; he was bound up so entirely in his son; but the rest of us knew it, and in a manner suffered from the knowledge.

This seems to me as bad a page of English as I ever read; but let my opinion be waived, it is well-known that I am no judge of nice and delicate things. I will ask, however, Mr. Andrew Lang, the entire Savile Club, all the aesthetes of Clapham, and even those living in the farthest limits of Peckham Rye, to put their hands over their heart and say if the quoted page is not lacking in those qualities which go to make a good page of prose—clearness of vision and strength of outline. I challenge all these judges to say that it is not, if I may be permitted to make a bull, miniature painting on a large scale—a maudlin design, stippled with a camel-hair brush on a sheet of ivory a yard and a half square. Anything more limp and insipid I cannot imagine. But if the quoted passage can be described as being vigorously and excellently drawn, then the book will most assuredly become an English classic, for it would be easy to point to a vast number of pages that differ in nowise from it.—GEORGE MOORE, *Hawk*, Nov. 5, 1889, pp. 489–90

The Master of Ballantrae ⟨. . .⟩ aims high, and falls very little short of the point aimed at. It may, perhaps, be less graphic than *Kidnapped*, and lack the continuous stir of *Treasure Island*, but it is broader in its scope, and freer in its handling than either of its predecessors. It contains one carefully elaborated and delicately-drawn female figure in Alison Graeme, whose whole character, in its strength and in its perversity, is admirably natural and original. The male characters, too, are a stronger group than he has ever before brought together. Besides the central Mephistophelean figure of the master, there is his no less formidable brother Harry, both drawn with extraordinary vigour and intensity. Then on a smaller scale, but almost equally good, are the sprightly Chevalier Burke and the admirable old lord. How clearly we are made to see him when the news of his son's death is carried to him in the night. "He, too, sat up in bed; very aged and bloodless he looked; and whereas he had a certain largeness of appearance when dressed for daylight, he now seemed frail and little, and his face (the wig being laid aside) not bigger than a child's." The minor characters are all good, from the pragmatical Mackellar, and the faithful Secundra Dass, down to the objectionable, piratical gentleman who burns sulphur, and shrieks "Hell! hell!" in his cabin. We do not seem to see the *Sarah* and her crew quite as plainly as we did the old *Walrus*, nor is there a Long John upon her ship's books. The whole story centres, however, round the diabolical master, and it is upon his cold, methodical, black-hearted villainy that it must chiefly depend for its effect. A more utterly ruthless scoundrel has never been depicted. Here is one episode which gives his character in a nutshell, and is at the same time a very good example of Stevenson's terse and startling manner of producing an effect. They are escaping, three of them, *arcades omnes*, across an American swamp with some treasure. The common seaman of the party, who is somewhat *de trop*, blunders into a dangerous bog.

> Presently we saw him sink a little down, draw up his feet and sink again; and so, twice. Then he turned his face to us, pretty white.
> "Lend a hand," said he; "I am in a bad place."
> "I don't know about that," says Ballantrae, standing still.
> Dutton burst out into the most violent oaths, sinking a little lower as he did so, so that the mud was nearly up to his waist, and plucking a pistol from his belt—
> "Help me," he cries, "or die and be damned to you!"
> "Nay," says Ballantrae, "I did but jest. I am coming." And he set down his own packet and Dutton's, which he was then carrying. "Do not venture near until we see if you are needed," said he to me, and went forward alone to where the man was bogged. He was quiet now, though he still held the pistol, and the marks of terror on his countenance were very moving to behold.
> "For the Lord's sake," said he, "look sharp!"
> Ballantrae was now got close up.
> "Keep still," says he, and seemed to consider; and then, "Reach out both your hands."
> Dutton laid down his pistol, and so watery was the top surface that it went clear out of sight; with an oath he stooped to snatch it, and as he did so Ballantrae leaned forth and stabbed him between the shoulders. Up went his hands over his head—I know not whether with the pain, or to ward himself—and the next moment he doubled forward in the mud.
> Ballantrae was already over the ankles, but he plucked himself out and came back to me where I stood with my knees smiting one another.
> "The devil take you, Francis!" says he. "I believe you are a half-hearted fellow, after all."

That is a truly Stevensonian scene, and one that haunts the reader like some grisly nightmare. Associate this horrid deed with a gentleman of polished address, striking features, elegant dress, and immense personal courage and energy, and you have one of the most effective and thorough-going villains in fiction—A. CONAN DOYLE, "Mr. Stevenson's Methods in Fiction," *National Review*, Jan. 1890, pp. 653–54

HENRY JAMES
"Robert Louis Stevenson"

Century Magazine, April 1888, pp. 869–79

I

If there be a writer of our language, at the present moment, who has the effect of making us forget the extinction of the pleasant fashion of the literary portrait, it is certainly the bright particular genius whose name is written at the head of these remarks. Mr. Stevenson fairly challenges portraiture, as we pass him on the highway of literature (if that be the road, rather than some wandering, sun-checkered by lane that he may be said to follow), just as the possible model, in local attire, challenges the painter who wanders through the streets of a foreign town looking for subjects. He gives us new ground to wonder why the effort to fix a face and figure, to seize a literary character and transfer it to the canvas of the critic, should have fallen into such discredit among us and have given way to the mere multiplication of little private judgment-seats, where the scales and the judicial wig, both of them considerably awry and not rendered more august by the company of a vicious-looking switch, have taken the place, as the symbols of office, of the kindly, disinterested palette and brush. It has become the fashion to be effective at the expense of the sitter, to make some little point, or inflict some little dig, with a heated party air, rather than to catch a talent in the face, follow its line, and put a finger on its essence; so that the exquisite art of criticism, smothered in grossness, finds itself turned into a question of 'sides.' The critic industriously keeps his score, but it is seldom to be hoped that the author, criminal though he may be, will be apprehended by justice through the handbills given out in the case; for it is of the essence of a happy description that it shall have been preceded by a happy observation and a free curiosity; and desuetude, as we say, has overtaken these amiable, uninvidious faculties, which have not the advantage of organs and chairs.

I hasten to add that it is not the purpose of these few pages to restore their lustre, or to bring back the more penetrating vision of which we lament the disappearance. No individual can bring it back, for the light that we look at things by is, after all, made by all of us. It is sufficient to note, in passing, that if Mr. Stevenson had presented himself in an age or in a country of portraiture, the painters would certainly each have had a turn at him. The easels and benches would have bristled, the circle would have been close, and quick, from the canvas to the sitter, the rising and falling of heads. It has happened to all of us to have gone into a studio, a studio of pupils, and seen the thick cluster of bent backs and the conscious model in the midst. It has happened to us to be struck, or not to be struck, with the beauty or the symmetry of this personage, and to have made some remark which, whether expressing admiration or disappointment, has elicited from one of the attentive workers the exclamation, 'Character—character is what he has!' These words may be applied to Mr. Robert Louis Stevenson: in the language of that art which depends most on observation, character—character is what he has. He is essentially a model, in the sense of a sitter; I do not mean, of course, in the sense of a pattern or a guiding light. And if the figures who have a life in literature may also be divided into two great classes, we may add that he is conspicuously one of the draped; he would never, if I may be allowed the expression, pose for the nude. There are writers who present themselves before the critic with just the amount of drapery that is necessary for decency, but Mr. Stevenson is not one of these; he makes his appearance in an amplitude of costume. His costume is part of the character of which I just now spoke; it never occurs to us to ask how he would look without it. Before all things he is a writer with a style—a model with a complexity of curious and picturesque garments. It is by the cut and the colour of this rich and becoming frippery—I use the term endearingly, as a painter might—that he arrests the eye and solicits the brush.

That is, frankly, half the charm he has for us, that he wears a dress and wears it with courage, with a certain cock of the hat and tinkle of the supererogatory sword; or, in other words, that he is curious of expression, and regards the literary form not simply as a code of signals, but as the keyboard of a piano and as so much plastic material. He has that vice deplored by Mr. Herbert Spencer, a manner—a manner for a manner's sake, it may sometimes doubtless be said. He is as different as possible from the sort of writer who regards words as numbers and a page as the mere addition of them; much more, to carry out our image, the dictionary stands for him as a wardrobe, and a proposition as a button for his coat. Mr. William Archer, in an article so gracefully and ingeniously turned that the writer may almost be accused of imitating even while he deprecates, speaks of him as a votary of 'lightness of touch' at any cost, and remarks that 'he is not only philosophically content, but deliberately resolved, that his readers shall look first to his manner and only in the second place to his matter.' I shall not attempt to gainsay this; I cite it rather, for the present, because it carries out my own sense. Mr. Stevenson delights in a style, and his own has nothing accidental or diffident; it is eminently conscious of its responsibilities and meets them with a kind of gallantry—as if language were a pretty woman and a person who proposes to handle it had, of necessity, to be something of a Don Juan. This element of the gallant is a noticeable part of his nature, and it is rather odd that, at the same time, a striking feature of that nature should be an absence of care for things feminine. His books are for the most part books without women, and it is not women who fall most in love with them. But Mr. Stevenson does not need, as we may say, a petticoat to inflame him; a happy collocation of words will serve the purpose, or a

singular image, or the bright eye of a passing conceit, and he will carry off a pretty paradox without so much as a scuffle. The tone of letters is in him—the tone of letters as distinct from that of philosophy or of those industries whose uses are supposed to be immediate. Many readers, no doubt, consider that he carries it too far; they manifest an impatience for some glimpse of his moral message. They may be heard to ask what it is he proposes to deduce, to prove, to establish, with such a variety of paces and graces.

The main thing that he establishes, to my own perception, is that it is a delight to read him and that he renews this delight by a constant variety of experiment. Of this anon, however; and meanwhile it may be noted as a curious characteristic of current fashions that the writer whose effort is perceptibly that of the artist is very apt to find himself thrown on the defensive. A work of literature is a form, but the author who betrays a consciousness of the responsibilities involved in this circumstance not rarely perceives himself to be regarded as an uncanny personage. The usual judgment is that he may be artistic, but that he must not be too much so; that way, apparently, lies something worse than madness. This queer superstition has so successfully imposed itself that the mere fact of having been indifferent to such a danger constitutes in itself an originality. How few they are in number and how soon we could name them, the writers of English prose, at the present moment, the quality of whose prose is personal, expressive, renewed at each attempt! The state of things that would have been expected to be the rule has become the exception, and an exception for which, most of the time, an apology appears to be thought necessary. A mill that grinds with regularity and with a certain commercial fineness—that is the image suggested by the manner of a good many of the fraternity. They turn out an article for which there is a demand, they keep a shop for a speciality, and the business is carried on in accordance with a useful, well-tested prescription. It is just because he has no speciality that Mr. Stevenson is an individual, and because his curiosity is the only receipt by which he produces. Each of his books is an independent effort—a window opened to a different view. *Dr. Jekyll and Mr. Hyde* is as dissimilar as possible from *Treasure Island*; *Virginibus Puerisque* has nothing in common with *The New Arabian Nights*, and I should never have supposed *A Child's Garden of Verses* to be from the hand of the author of *Prince Otto*.

Though Mr. Stevenson cares greatly for his phrase, as every writer should who respects himself and his art, it takes no very attentive reading of his volumes to show that it is not what he cares for most, and that he regards an expressive style only, after all, as a means. It seems to me the fault of Mr. Archer's interesting paper that it suggests too much that the author of these volumes considers the art of expression as an end—a game of words. He finds that Mr. Stevenson is not serious, that he neglects a whole side of life, that he has no perception, and no consciousness, of suffering; that he speaks as a happy but heartless pagan, living only in his senses (which the critic admits to be exquisitely fine), and that, in a world full of heaviness, he is not sufficiently aware of the philosophic limitations of mere technical skill. (In sketching these aberrations Mr. Archer himself, by the way, displays anything but ponderosity of hand.) He is not the first reader, and he will not be the last, who shall have been irritated by Mr. Stevenson's jauntiness. That jauntiness is an essential part of his genius; but, to my sense, it ceases to be irritating—it indeed becomes positively touching, and constitutes an appeal to sympathy and even to tenderness—when once one has perceived what lies beneath the dancing-tune to which he mostly moves. Much as he cares for his phrase he cares more for life, and for a certain transcendently lovable part of it. He feels, as it seems to us, and that is not given to every one; this constitutes a philosophy which Mr. Archer fails to read between his lines—the respectable, desirable moral which many a reader doubtless finds that he neglects to point. He does not feel everything equally, by any manner of means; but his feelings are always his reasons; he regards them, whatever they may be, as sufficiently honourable, does not disguise them in other names or colours, and looks at whatever he meets in the brilliant candle-light that they shed. As in his extreme artistic vivacity he seems really disposed to try everything, he has tried once, by way of a change, to be inhuman, and there is a hard glitter about *Prince Otto* which seems to indicate that in this case, too, he has succeeded, as he has done in most of the feats that he has attempted. But *Prince Otto* is even less like his other productions than his other productions are like each other.

The part of life that he cares for most is youth, and the direct expression of the love of youth is the beginning and the end of his message. His appreciation of this delightful period amounts to a passion; and a passion, in the age in which we live, strikes us, on the whole, as a sufficient philosophy. It ought to satisfy Mr. Archer, and there are writers graver than Mr. Stevenson on whose behalf no such moral motive can be alleged. Mingled with his almost equal love of a literary surface it represents a real originality. This combination is the key-note of Mr. Stevenson's faculty and the explanation of his perversities. The feelings of one's teens, and even of an earlier period (for the delights of crawling, and almost of the rattle, are embodied in A *Child's Garden of Verses*), and the feeling for happy turns—these, in the last analysis (and his sense of a happy turn is of the subtlest), are the corresponding halves of his character. If *Prince Otto* and *Dr. Jekyll* left me a clearer field for the assertion, I should say that everything he has written is a direct apology for boyhood; or rather (for it must be confessed that Mr. Stevenson's tone is seldom apologetic) a direct rhapsody on the age of little jackets. Even members of the very numerous class who have held their breath over *Treasure Island* may shrug their shoulders at this account of the author's religion; but it is none the less a great pleasure—the highest reward of observation—to put one's hand on a rare illustration, and Mr. Stevenson is certainly rare. What makes him so is the singular maturity of the expression that he has given to young sentiments; he judges them, measures them, sees them from the outside, as well as entertains them. He describes credulity with all the resources of experience, and represents a crude stage with infinite ripeness. In a word, he is an artist accomplished even to sophistication, whose constant theme is the unsophisticated. Sometimes, as in *Kidnapped*, the art is so ripe that it lifts even the subject into the general air; the execution is so serious that the idea (the idea of a boy's romantic adventures) becomes a matter of universal relations. What he prizes most in the boy's ideal is the imaginative side of it, the capacity for successful make-believe. The general freshness in which this is a part of the gloss seems to him the divinest thing in life; considerably more divine, for instance, than the passion usually regarded as the supremely tender one. The idea of making believe appeals to him much more than the idea of making love. That delightful little book of rhymes, the *Child's Garden*, commemorates, from beginning to end, the picturing, personifying, dramatizing faculty of infancy, the view of life from the level of the nursery-fender. The volume is a wonder, for the extraordinary vividness with which it reproduces early impressions; a child might have written it if a child could see childhood from the outside, for it

would seem that only a child is really near enough to the nursery-floor. And what is peculiar to Mr. Stevenson is that it is his own childhood he appears to delight in, and not the personal presence of little darlings. Oddly enough, there is no strong implication that he is fond of babies; he doesn't speak as a parent, or an uncle, or an educator—he speaks as a contemporary absorbed in his own game. That game is almost always a vision of dangers and triumphs; and if emotion, with him, infallibly resolves itself into memory, so memory is an evocation of throbs and thrills and suspense. He has given to the world the romance of boyhood, as others have produced that of the peerage, the police, and the medical profession.

This amounts to saying that what he is most curious of in life is heroism—personal gallantry, if need be, with a manner, or a banner—though he is also abundantly capable of enjoying it when it is artless. The delightful exploits of Jim Hawkins, in *Treasure Island*, are unaffectedly performed; but none the less 'the finest action is the better for a piece of purple,' as the author remarks in the paper on 'The English Admirals,' in *Virginibus Puerisque*—a paper of which the moral is, largely, that 'we learn to desire a grand air in our heroes; and such a knowledge of the human stage as shall make them put the dots on their own i's and leave us in no suspense as to when they mean to be heroic.' The love of brave words as well as brave deeds—which is simply Mr. Stevenson's essential love of style—is recorded in this little paper with a charming, slightly sophistical ingenuity. 'They served their guns merrily, when it came to fighting, and they had the readiest ear for a bold, honourable sentiment of any class of men the world ever produced.' The author goes on to say that most men of high destinies have even high-sounding names. Alan Breck, in *Kidnapped*, is a wonderful picture of the union of courage and swagger; the little Jacobite adventurer, a figure worthy of Scott at his best, and representing the highest point that Mr. Stevenson's talent has reached, shows us that a marked taste for tawdry finery—tarnished and tattered, some of it, indeed, by ticklish occasions—is quite compatible with a perfectly high mettle. Alan Breck is, at bottom, a study of the love of glory, carried out with extreme psychological truth. When the love of glory is of an inferior order, the reputation is cultivated rather than the opportunity; but when it is a pure passion, the opportunity is cultivated for the sake of the reputation. Mr. Stevenson's kindness for adventurers extends even to the humblest of all, the mountebank and the strolling player, or even the peddler whom he declares that in his foreign travels he is habitually taken for, as we see in the whimsical apology for vagabonds which winds up *An Inland Voyage*. The hungry conjurer, the gymnast whose *maillot* is loose, have something of the glamour of the hero, inasmuch as they, too, pay with their person.

> To be even one of the outskirters of art leaves a fine stamp on a man's countenance. . . . That is the kind of thing that reconciles me to life; a ragged, tippling, incompetent old rogue, with the manners of a gentleman and the vanity of an artist, to keep up his self-respect!

What reconciles Mr. Stevenson to life is the idea that in the first place it offers the widest field that we know of for odd doings, and that in the second these odd doings are the best of pegs to hang a sketch in three lines or a paradox in three pages.

As it is not odd, but extremely usual, to marry, he deprecates that course in *Virginibus Puerisque*, the collection of short essays which is most a record of his opinions—that is, largely, of his likes and dislikes. It all comes back to his sympathy with the juvenile, and that feeling about life which leads him to regard women as so many superfluous girls in a boy's game. They are almost wholly absent from his pages (the main exception is *Prince Otto*, though there is a Clara apiece in *The Rajah's Diamond* and *The Pavilion on the Links*), for they don't like ships and pistols and fights; they encumber the decks and require separate apartments; and, almost worst of all, have not the highest literary standard. Why should a person marry, when he might be swinging a cutlass or looking for a buried treasure? Why should he go to the altar when he might be polishing his prose? It is one of those curious, and, to my sense, fascinating inconsistencies that we encounter in Mr. Stevenson's mind that, though he takes such an interest in the childish life, he takes no interest in the fireside. He has an indulgent glance for it in the verses of the *Garden*, but to his view the normal child is the child who absents himself from the family-circle, in fact when he can, in imagination when he cannot, in the disguise of a buccaneer. Girls don't do this, and women are only grown-up girls, unless it be the delightful maiden, fit daughter of an imperial race, whom he commemorates in *An Inland Voyage*.

> A girl at school in France began to describe one of our regiments on parade to her French schoolmates; and as she went on, she told me the recollection grew so vivid, she became so proud to be the countrywoman of such soldiers, and so sorry to be in another country, that her voice failed her, and she burst into tears. I have never forgotten that girl, and I think she very nearly deserves a statue. To call her a young lady, with all its niminy associations, would be to offer her an insult. She may rest assured of one thing, although she never should marry a heroic general, never see any great or immediate result of her life, she will not have lived in vain for her native land.

There is something of that in Mr. Stevenson. When he begins to describe a British regiment on parade (or something of that sort) he, too, almost breaks down for emotion, which is why I have been careful to traverse the insinuation that he is primarily a chiseller of prose. If things had gone differently with him (I must permit myself this allusion to his personal situation, and I shall venture to follow it with two or three others), he might have been an historian of famous campaigns—a great painter of battle-pieces. Of course, however, in this capacity it would not have done for him to break down for emotion.

Although he remarks that marriage 'is a field of battle, and not a bed of roses,' he points out repeatedly that it is a terrible renunciation, and somehow, in strictness, incompatible even with honour—the sort of roving, trumpeting honour that appeals most to his sympathy. After that step

> there are no more by-path meadows where you may innocently linger, but the road lies long and straight and dusty to the grave. . . . You may think you had a conscience and believed in God; but what is a conscience to a wife? . . . To marry is to domesticate the Recording Angel. Once you are married, there is nothing left for you, not even suicide, but to be good. . . . How, then, in such an atmosphere of compromise, to keep honour bright and abstain from base capitulations? . . . The proper qualities of each sex are, indeed, eternally surprising to the other. Between the Latin and the Teuton races there are similar divergences, not to be bridged by the most liberal sympathy. . . . It is better to face the fact and

know, when you marry, that you take into your life a creature of equal if unlike frailties; whose weak human heart beats no more tunefully than yours.

If there is a grimness in that, it is as near as Mr. Stevenson ever comes to being grim, and we have only to turn the page to find the corrective—something delicately genial, at least, if not very much less sad:

> 'The blind bow-boy' who smiles upon us from the end of terraces in old Dutch gardens laughingly hurls his bird-bolts among a fleeting generation. But for as fast as ever he shoots, the game dissolves and disappears into eternity from under his falling arrows; this one is gone ere he is struck; the other has but time to make one gesture and give one passionate cry; and they are all the things of a moment.

That is an admission that though it is soon over, the great sentimental surrender is inevitable. And there is geniality too, still over the page (in regard to quite another matter), geniality, at least, for the profession of letters, in the declaration that there is

> one thing you can never make Philistine natures understand; one thing which yet lies on the surface, remains as unseizable to their wits as a high flight of metaphysics—namely, that the business of life is mainly carried on by the difficult art of literature, and according to a man's proficiency in that art shall be the freedom and fullness of his intercourse with other men.

Yet it is difficult not to believe that the ideal in which our author's spirit might most gratefully have rested would have been the character of the paterfamilias, when the eye falls on such a charming piece of observation as these lines about children, in the admirable paper on 'Child's Play':

> If it were not for this perpetual imitation, we should be tempted to fancy they despised us outright, or only considered us in the light of creatures brutally strong and brutally silly, among whom they condescended to dwell in obedience, like a philosopher at a barbarous court.

II

We know very little about a talent till we know where it grew up, and it would halt terribly at the start any account of the author of *Kidnapped* which should omit to insist promptly that he is a Scot of the Scots. Two facts, to my perception, go a great way to explain his composition, the first of which is that his boyhood was passed in the shadow of Edinburgh Castle, and the second, that he came of a family that had set up great lights on the coast. His grandfather, his uncle, were famous constructors of light-houses, and the name of the race is associated above all with the beautiful and beneficent tower of Skerryvore. We may exaggerate the way in which, in an imaginative youth, the sense of the 'story' of things would feed upon the impressions of Edinburgh—though I suspect it would be difficult really to do so. The streets are so full of history and poetry, of picture and song, of associations springing from strong passions and strange characters, that for my own part I find myself thinking of an urchin going and coming there as I used to think—wonderingly, enviously—of the small boys who figured as supernumeraries, pages, or imps in showy scenes at the theatre; the place seems the background, the complicated 'set' of a drama, and the children the mysterious little beings who are made free of the magic world. How must it not have beckoned on the imagination to pass and repass, on the way to school, under the Castle rock, conscious acutely, yet familiarly, of the gray citadel on the summit, lighted up with the tartans and bagpipes of Highland regiments! Mr. Stevenson's mind, from an early age, was furnished with the concrete Highlander, who must have had much of the effect that we nowadays call decorative. I encountered somewhere a fanciful paper of our author's in which there is a reflection of half-holiday afternoons and, unless my own fancy plays me a trick, of lights red, in the winter dusk, in the high-placed windows of the Old Town—a delightful rhapsody on the penny sheets of figures for the puppet-shows of infancy, in life-like position, and awaiting the impatient yet careful scissors. 'If landscapes were sold,' he says in *Travels with a Donkey*, 'like the sheets of characters of my boyhood, one penny plain and twopence coloured, I should go the length of twopence every day of my life.'

Indeed, the colour of Scotland has entered into him altogether, and though, oddly enough, he has written but little about his native country, his happiest work shows, I think, that she has the best of his ability. *Kidnapped* (whose inadequate title I may deplore in passing) breathes in every line the feeling of moor and loch, and is the finest of his longer stories; and 'Thrawn Janet,' a masterpiece in thirteen pages (lately republished in the volume of *The Merry Men*), is, among the shorter ones, the strongest in execution. The latter consists of a gruesome anecdote of the supernatural, related in the Scotch dialect; and the genuineness which this medium—at the sight of which, in general, the face of the reader grows long—wears in Mr. Stevenson's hands is a proof of how living the question of form always is to him, and what a variety of answers he has for it. It never would have occurred to us that the style of *Travels with a Donkey*, or *Virginibus Puerisque*, and the idiom of the parish of Balweary could be a conception of the same mind. If it is a good fortune for a genius to have had such a country as Scotland for its primary stuff, this is doubly the case when there has been a certain process of detachment, of extreme secularization. Mr. Stevenson has been emancipated—he is, as we may say, a Scotchman of the world. None other, I think, could have drawn with such a mixture of sympathetic and ironical observation the character of the canny young Lowlander David Balfour, a good boy but an exasperating. *Treasure Island, The New Arabian Nights, Prince Otto, Dr. Jekyll and Mr. Hyde*, are not very directly founded on observation; but that quality comes in with extreme fineness as soon as the subject is Scotch.

I have been wondering whether there is something more than this that our author's pages would tell us about him, or whether that particular something is in the mind of an admirer, because he happens to have had other lights upon it. It has been possible for so acute a critic as Mr. William Archer to read pure high spirits and the gospel of the young man rejoicing in his strength and his matutinal cold bath between the lines of Mr. Stevenson's prose. And it is a fact that the note of a morbid sensibility is so absent from his pages, they contain so little reference to infirmity and suffering, that we feel a trick has really been played upon us on discovering by accident the actual state of the case with the writer who has indulged in the most enthusiastic allusion to the joy of existence. We must permit ourselves another mention of his personal situation, for it adds immensely to the interest of volumes through which there draws so strong a current of life to know that they are not only the work of an invalid, but have largely been written in bed, in dreary 'health resorts,' in the intervals of sharp attacks. There is almost nothing in them to lead us to guess this; the direct evidence, indeed, is almost all contained in the limited compass of *The Silverado Squatters*. In such a case, however,

it is the indirect that is the most eloquent, and I know not where to look for that, unless in the paper called 'Ordered South' and its companion 'Æs Triplex,' in *Virginibus Puerisque*. It is impossible to read 'Ordered South' attentively without feeling that it is personal; the reflections it contains are from experience, not from fancy. The places and climates to which the invalid is carried to recover or to die are mainly beautiful, but

> In his heart of hearts he has to confess that they are not beautiful for him. . . . He is like an enthusiast leading about with him a stolid, indifferent tourist. There is some one by who is out of sympathy with the scene, and is not moved up to the measure of the occasion; and that some one is himself. . . . He seems to himself to touch things with muffled hands and to see through a veil. . . . Many a white town that sits far out on the promontory, many a comely fold of wood on the mountain-side, beckons and allures his imagination day after day, and is yet as inaccessible to his feet as the clefts and gorges of the clouds. The sense of distance grows upon him wonderfully; and after some feverish efforts and the fretful uneasiness of the first few days he falls contentedly in with the restrictions of his weakness. . . . He feels, if he is to be thus tenderly weaned from the passion of life, thus gradually inducted into the slumber of death, that when at last the end comes it will come quietly and fitly. . . . He will pray for Medea: when she comes, let her rejuvenate or slay.

The second of the short essays I have mentioned has a taste of mortality only because the purpose of it is to insist that the only sane behaviour is to leave death and the accidents that lead to it out of our calculations. Life 'is a honeymoon with us all through, and none of the longest. Small blame to us if we give our whole hearts to this glowing bride of ours'; the person who does so 'makes a very different acquaintance with the world, keeps all his pulses going true and fast, and gathers impetus as he runs, until, if he be running towards anything better than wildfire, he may shoot up and become a constellation in the end.' Nothing can be more deplorable than to 'forgo all the issues of living in a parlour with a regulated temperature.' Mr. Stevenson adds that as for those whom the gods love dying young, a man dies too young at whatever age he parts with life. The testimony of 'Æs Triplex' to the author's own disabilities is, after all, very indirect; it consists mainly in the general protest not so much against the fact of extinction as against the theory of it. The reader only asks himself why the hero of *Travels with a Donkey*, the historian of Alan Breck, should think of these things. His appreciation of the active side of life has such a note of its own that we are surprised to find that it proceeds in a considerable measure from an intimate acquaintance with the passive. It seems too anomalous that the writer who has most cherished the idea of a certain free exposure should also be the one who has been reduced most to looking for it within, and that the figures of adventurers who, at least in our literature of to-day, are the most vivid, should be the most vicarious. The truth is, of course, that, as the *Travels with a Donkey* and *An Inland Voyage* abundantly show, the author has a fund of reminiscences. He did not spend his younger years 'in a parlour with a regulated temperature.' A reader who happens to be aware of how much it has been his later fate to do so may be excused for finding an added source of interest—something, indeed, deeply and constantly touching—in this association of peculiarly restrictive conditions with the vision of high spirits and romantic accidents of a kind of honourably picturesque career. Mr. Stevenson is, however, distinctly, in spite of his occasional practice of the gruesome, a frank optimist, an observer who not only loves life, but does not shrink from the responsibility of recommending it. There is a systematic brightness in him which testifies to this and which is, after all, but one of the innumerable ingenuities of patience. What is remarkable in his case is that his productions should constitute an exquisite expression, a sort of whimsical gospel, of enjoyment. The only difference between *An Inland Voyage*, or *Travels with a Donkey* and *The New Arabian Nights*, or *Treasure Island*, or *Kidnapped*, is, that in the later books the enjoyment is reflective,—though it simulates spontaneity with singular art,—whereas in the first two it is natural and, as it were, historical.

These little histories—the first volumes, if I mistake not, that introduced Mr. Stevenson to lovers of good writing—abound in charming illustrations of his disposition to look at the world as a not exactly refined, but glorified, pacified Bohemia. They narrate the quest of personal adventure—on one occasion in a canoe on the Sambre and the Oise, and on another at a donkey's tail over the hills and valleys of the Cévennes. I well remember that when I read them, in their novelty, upward of ten years ago, I seemed to see the author, unknown as yet to fame, jump before my eyes into a style. His steps in literature presumably had not been many; yet he had mastered his form—it had in these cases, perhaps, more substance than his matter—and a singular air of literary experience. It partly, though not completely, explains the phenomenon, that he had already been able to write the exquisite little story of 'Will of the Mill,' published previously to *An Inland Voyage*, and now republished in the volume of *The Merry Men*; for in 'Will of the Mill' there is something exceedingly rare, poetical, and unexpected, with that most fascinating quality a work of imagination can have, a dash of alternative mystery as to its meaning, an air—the air of life itself—of half inviting, half defying, you to interpret. This brief but finished composition stood in the same relation to the usual 'magazine story' that a glass of Johannisberg occupies to a draught of table d'hôte *vin ordinaire*.

> One evening, he asked the miller where the river went. . . . 'It goes out into the lowlands, and waters the great corn country, and runs through a sight of fine cities (so they say) where kings live all alone in great palaces, with a sentry walking up and down before the door. And it goes under bridges with stone men upon them, looking down and smiling so curious at the water, and living folks leaning their elbows on the wall and looking over too. And then it goes on and on, and down through marshes and sands, until at last it falls into the sea, where the ships are that bring parrots and tobacco from the Indies.'

It is impossible not to open one's eyes at such a paragraph as that, especially if one has taken a common texture for granted. Will of the Mill spends his life in the valley through which the river runs, and through which, year after year, post-chaises and wagons, and pedestrians, and once an army, 'horse and foot, cannon and tumbrel, drum and standard,' take their way, in spite of the dreams he has once had of seeing the mysterious world, and it is not till death comes that he goes on his travels. He ends by keeping an inn, where he converses with many more initiated spirits, and though he is an amiable man, he dies a bachelor, having broken off, with more plainness than he would have used had he been less untravelled—of course he remains sadly provincial—his engagement

to the parson's daughter. The story is in the happiest key, and suggests all kinds of things, but what does it in particular represent? The advantage of waiting, perhaps—the valuable truth, that, one by one, we tide over our impatiences. There are sagacious people who hold that if one doesn't answer a letter it ends by answering itself. So the sub-title of Mr. Stevenson's tale might be 'The Beauty of Procrastination.' If you don't indulge your curiosities your slackness itself makes at last a kind of rich element, and it comes to very much the same thing in the end. When it came to the point, poor Will had not even the curiosity to marry; and the author leaves us in stimulating doubt as to whether he judges him too selfish or only too philosophic.

I find myself speaking of Mr. Stevenson's last volume (at the moment I write) before I have spoken, in any detail, of its predecessors, which I must let pass as a sign that I lack space for a full enumeration. I may mention two more of his productions as completing the list of those that have a personal reference. *The Silverado Squatters* describes a picnicking episode, undertaken on grounds of health, on a mountain-top in California; but this free sketch, which contains a hundred humorous touches, and in the figure of Irvine Lovelands one of Mr. Stevenson's most veracious portraits, is perhaps less vivid, as it is certainly less painful, than those other pages in which, some years ago, he commemorated the twelvemonth he spent in America—the history of a journey from New York to San Francisco in an emigrant-train, performed as the sequel to a voyage across the Atlantic in the same severe conditions. He has never made his points better than in that half-humorous, half-tragical recital, nor given a more striking instance of his talent for reproducing the feeling of queer situations and contacts. It is much to be regretted that this little masterpiece has not been brought to light a second time, as also that he has not given the world—as I believe he came very near doing—his observations in the steerage of an Atlantic liner. If, as I say, our author has a taste for the impressions of Bohemia, he has been very consistent and has not shrunk from going far afield in search of them. And as I have already been indiscreet, I may add that if it has been his fate to be converted in fact from the sardonic view of matrimony, this occurred under an influence which should have the particular sympathy of American readers. He went to California for his wife; and Mrs. Stevenson, as appears moreover by the title-page of the work, has had a hand—evidently a light and practised one—in *The Dynamiter*, the second series, characterized by a rich extravagance, of *The New Arabian Nights*. *The Silverado Squatters* is the history of a honeymoon—prosperous, it would seem, putting Irvine Lovelands aside, save for the death of dog Chuchu 'in his teens, after a life so shadowed and troubled, continually shaken with alarms, and the tear of elegant sentiment permanently in his eye.'

Mr. Stevenson has a theory of composition in regard to the novel, on which he is to be congratulated, as any positive and genuine conviction of this kind is vivifying so long as it is not narrow. The breath of the novelist's being is his liberty; and the incomparable virtue of the form he uses is that it lends itself to views innumerable and diverse, to every variety of illustration. There is certainly no other mould of so large a capacity. The doctrine of M. Zola himself, so meagre if literally taken, is fruitful, inasmuch as in practice he romantically departs from it. Mr. Stevenson does not need to depart, his individual taste being as much to pursue the romantic as his principle is to defend it. Fortunately, in England to-day, it is not much attacked. The triumphs that are to be won in the portrayal of the strange, the improbable, the heroic, especially as these things shine from afar in the credulous eye of youth, are his strongest, most constant incentive. On one happy occasion, in relating the history of *Dr. Jekyll*, he has seen them as they present themselves to a maturer vision. *Dr. Jekyll* is not a 'boys' book,' nor yet is *Prince Otto*; the latter, however, is not, like the former, an experiment in mystification—it is, I think, more than anything else, an experiment in style, conceived one summer's day, when the author had given the reins to his high appreciation of Mr. George Meredith. It is perhaps the most literary of his works, but it is not the most natural. It is one of those coquetries, as we may call them for want of a better word, which may be observed in Mr. Stevenson's activity—a kind of artful inconsequence. It is easy to believe that if his strength permitted him to be a more abundant writer he would still more frequently play this eminently literary trick—that of dodging off in a new direction—upon those who might have fancied they knew all about him. I made the reflection, in speaking of 'Will of the Mill,' that there is a kind of anticipatory malice in the subject of that fine story; as if the writer had intended to say to his reader, 'You will never guess, from the unction with which I describe the life of a man who never stirred five miles from home, that I am destined to make my greatest hits in treating of the rovers of the deep.' Even here, however, the author's characteristic irony would have come in; for—the rare chances of life being what he most keeps his eye on—the uncommon belongs as much to the way the inquiring Will sticks to his door-sill as to the incident, say, of John Silver and his men, when they are dragging Jim Hawkins to his doom, hearing, in the still woods of Treasure Island, the strange hoot of the Maroon.

The novelist who leaves the extraordinary out of his account is liable to awkward confrontations, as we are compelled to reflect in this age of newspapers and of universal publicity. The next report of the next divorce case—to give an instance—shall offer us a picture of astounding combinations of circumstance and behaviour, and the annals of any energetic race are rich in curious anecdote and startling example. That interesting compilation, *Vicissitudes of Families*, is but a superficial record of strange accidents; the family—taken, of course, in the long piece—is, as a general thing, a catalogue of odd specimens and strong situations, and we must remember that the most singular products are those which are not exhibited. Mr. Stevenson leaves so wide a margin for the wonderful—it impinges with easy assurance upon the text—that he escapes the danger of being brought up by cases he has not allowed for. When he allows for Mr. Hyde he allows for everything; and one feels, moreover, that even if he did not wave so gallantly the flag of the imaginary and contend that the improbable is what has most character, he would still insist that we ought to make believe. He would say we ought to make believe that the extraordinary is the best part of life, even if it were not, and to do so because the finest feelings—suspense, daring, decision, passion, curiosity, gallantry, eloquence, friendship—are involved in it, and it is of infinite importance that the tradition of these precious things should not perish. He would prefer, in a word, any day in the week, Alexandre Dumas to Honoré de Balzac; and it is, indeed, my impression that he prefers the author of *The Three Musketeers* to any novelist except Mr. George Meredith. I should go so far as to suspect that his ideal of the delightful work of fiction would be the adventures of Monte Cristo related by the author of *Richard Feverel*. There is some magnanimity in his esteem for Alexandre Dumas, inasmuch as in *Kidnapped* he has put into a fable worthy of that inventor a fineness of grain with which Dumas never had anything to

do. He makes us say, Let the tradition live, by all means, since it was delightful; but at the same time he is the cause of our perceiving afresh that a tradition is kept alive only by something being added to it. In this particular case—in *Dr. Jekyll* and *Kidnapped*—Mr. Stevenson has added psychology.

The New Arabian Nights offers us, as the title indicates, the wonderful in the frankest, most delectable form. Partly extravagant, and partly very specious, they are the result of a very happy idea, that of placing a series of adventures which are pure adventures in the setting of contemporary English life, and relating them in the placidly ingenious tone of Scheherezade. This device is carried to perfection in *The Dynamiter*, where the manner takes on more of a kind of high-flown serenity in proportion as the incidents are more 'steep.' In this line 'The Suicide Club' is Mr. Stevenson's greatest success; and the first two pages of it, not to mention others, live in the memory. For reasons which I am conscious of not being able to represent as sufficient, I find something ineffaceably impressive—something really haunting—in the incident of Prince Florizel and Colonel Geraldine, who, one evening in March, are 'driven by a sharp fall of sleet into an Oyster Bar in the immediate neighbourhood of Leicester Square,' and there have occasion to observe the entrance of a young man followed by a couple of commissionaires, each of whom carries a large dish of cream-tarts under a cover—a young man who 'pressed these confections on every one's acceptance with exaggerated courtesy.' There is no effort at a picture here, but the imagination makes one of the lighted interior, the London sleet outside, the company that we guess, given the locality, and the strange politeness of the young man, leading on to circumstances stranger still. This is what may be called putting one in the mood for a story. But Mr. Stevenson's most brilliant stroke of that kind is the opening episode of *Treasure Island*—the arrival of the brown old seaman, with a sabre cut, at the 'Admiral Benbow,' and the advent, not long after, of the blind sailor, with a green shade over his eyes, who comes tapping down the road, in quest of him, with his stick. *Treasure Island* is a 'boy's book,' in the sense that it embodies a boy's vision of the extraordinary; but it is unique in this, and calculated to fascinate the weary mind of experience, that what we see in it is not only the ideal fable, but, as part and parcel of that, as it were, the young reader himself and his state of mind: we seem to read it over his shoulder, with an arm around his neck. It is all as perfect as a well-played boy's game, and nothing can exceed the spirit and skill, the humour and the open air feeling, with which the whole thing is kept at the critical pitch. It is not only a record of queer chances, but a study of young feelings; there is a moral side in it, and the figures are not puppets with vague faces. If Jim Hawkins illustrates successful daring, he does so with a delightful, rosy goodboyishness, and a conscious, modest liability to error. His luck is tremendous, but it doesn't make him proud; and his manner is refreshingly provincial and human. So is that, even more, of the admirable John Silver, one of the most picturesque, and, indeed, in every way, most genially presented, villains in the whole literature of romance. He has a singularly distinct and expressive countenance, which, of course, turns out to be a grimacing mask. Never was a mask more knowingly, vividly painted. *Treasure Island* will surely become—it must already have become, and will remain—in its way a classic; thanks to this indescribable mixture of the prodigious and the human, of surprising coincidences and familiar feelings. The language in which Mr. Stevenson has chosen to tell his story is an admirable vehicle for these feelings; with its humorous braveries and quaintnesses, its echoes of old ballads and yarns, it touches all kinds of sympathetic chords.

Is *Dr. Jekyll and Mr. Hyde* a work of high philosophic intention, or simply the most ingenious and irresponsible of fictions? It has the stamp of a really imaginative production, that we may take it in different ways, but I suppose it would be called the most serious of the author's tales. It deals with the relation of the baser parts of man to his nobler—of the capacity for evil that exists in the most generous natures, and it expresses these things in a fable which is a wonderfully happy invention. The subject is endlessly interesting, and rich in all sorts of provocation, and Mr. Stevenson is to be congratulated on having touched the core of it. I may do him injustice, but it is, however, here, not the profundity of the idea which strikes me so much as the art of the presentation—the extremely success-ful form. There is a genuine feeling for the perpetual moral question, a fresh sense of the difficulty of being good and the brutishness of being bad, but what there is above all is a singular ability in holding the interest. I confess that that, to my sense, is the most edifying thing in the short, rapid, concentrated story, which is really a masterpiece of concision. There is something almost impertinent in the way, as I have noticed, in which Mr. Stevenson achieves his best effects without the aid of the ladies, and *Dr. Jekyll* is a capital example of his heartless independence. It is usually supposed that a truly poignant impression cannot be made without them, but in the drama of Mr. Hyde's fatal ascendency they remain altogether in the wing. It is very obvious—I do not say it cynically—that they must have played an important part in his development. The gruesome tone of the tale is, no doubt, deepened by their absence; it is like the late afternoon light of a foggy winter Sunday, when even inanimate objects have a kind of wicked look. I remember few situations in the pages of mystifying fiction more to the purpose than the episode of Mr. Utterson's going to Dr. Jekyll's to confer with the butler, when the doctor is locked up in his laboratory and the old servant, whose sagacity has hitherto encountered successfully the problems of the sideboard and the pantry, confesses that this time he is utterly baffled. The way the two men, at the door of the laboratory, discuss the identity of the mysterious personage inside, who has revealed himself in two or three inhuman glimpses to Poole, has those touches of which irresistible shudders are made. The butler's theory is that his master has been murdered, and that the murderer is in the room, personating him with a sort of clumsy diabolism. 'Well, when that masked thing like a monkey jumped from among the chemicals and whipped into the cabinet, it went down my spine like ice.' That is the effect upon the reader of most of the story. I say of most rather than all, because the ice rather melts in the sequel, and I have some difficulty in accepting the business of the powders, which seems to me too explicit and explanatory. The powders constitute the machinery of the transformation, and it will probably have struck many readers that this uncanny process would be more conceivable (so far as one may speak of the conceivable in such a case), if the author had not made it so definite.

I have left Mr. Stevenson's best book to the last, as it is also the last he has given, at the present speaking, to the public—the tales comprising *The Merry Men* having already appeared; but I find that, on the way, I have anticipated some of the remarks that I had intended to make about it. That which is most to the point is that there are parts of it so fine as to suggest that the author's talent has taken a fresh start, various as have been the impulses in which it had already indulged, and serious the impediments among which it is condemned to

exert itself. There would have been a kind of perverse humility in his keeping up the fiction that a production so literary as *Kidnapped* is addressed to immature minds; and though it was originally given to the world, I believe, in a 'boy's paper,' the story embraces every occasion that it meets to satisfy the higher criticism. It has two weak spots, which need simply to be mentioned. The cruel and miserly uncle, in the first chapters, is rather in the tone of superseded tradition, and the tricks he plays upon his ingenuous nephew are a little like those of country conjurors; in these pages we feel that Mr. Stevenson is thinking too much of what a 'boy's paper' is expected to contain. Then the history stops without ending, as it were; but I think I may add that this accident speaks for itself. Mr. Stevenson has often to lay down his pen for reasons that have nothing to do with the failure of inspiration, and the last page of David Balfour's adventures is an honourable plea for indulgence. The remaining five-sixths of the book deserve to stand by *Henry Esmond*, as a fictive autobiography in archaic form. The author's sense of the English idiom of the last century, and still more of the Scotch, have enabled him to give a gallant companion to Thackeray's *tour de force*. The life, the humour, the colour of the central portions of *Kidnapped* have a singular pictorial virtue; these passages read like a series of inspired footnotes on some historic page. The charm of the most romantic episode in the world—though perhaps it would be hard to say why it is the most romantic, when it was intermingled with so much stupidity—is over the whole business, and the forlorn hope of the Stuarts is revived for us without evoking satiety. There could be no better instance of the author's talent for seeing the actual in the marvellous, and reducing the extravagant to plausible detail, than the descrip-tion of Alan Breck's defence in the cabin of the ship, and the really magnificent chapters of 'The Flight in the Heather.' Mr. Stevenson has, in a high degree (and doubtless for good reasons of his own), what may be called the imagination of physical states, and this has enabled him to arrive at a wonderfully exact notation of the miseries of his panting Lowland hero, dragged for days and nights over hill and dale, through bog and thicket, without meat or drink or rest, at the tail of an Homeric Highlander. The great superiority of the book resides, to my mind, however, in the fact that it puts two characters on their feet in an admirably upright way. I have paid my tribute to Alan Breck, and I can only repeat that he is a masterpiece. It is interesting to observe that, though the man is extravagant, the author's touch exaggerates nothing; it is, throughout, of the most truthful, genial, ironical kind, full of penetration, but with none of the grossness of moralizing satire. The figure is a genuine study, and nothing can be more charming than the way Mr. Stevenson both sees through it and admires it. Shall I say that he sees through David Balfour? This would be, perhaps, to underestimate the density of that medium. Beau-tiful, at any rate, is the expression which this unfortunate though circumspect youth gives to those qualities which combine to excite our respect and our objurgations in the Scottish character. Such a scene as the episode of the quarrel of the two men on the mountain-side is a real stroke of genius, and has the very logic and rhythm of life—a quarrel which we feel to be inevitable, though it is about nothing, or almost nothing, and which springs from exasperated nerves and the simple shock of temperaments. The author's vision of it has a profundity which goes deeper, I think, than *Dr. Jekyll*. I know of few better examples of the way genius has ever a surprise in its pockets—keeps an ace, as it were, up its sleeve. And in this case it endears itself to us by making us reflect that such a passage as the one I speak of is in fact a signal proof of what the novel can do at its best and what nothing else can do so well. In the presence of this sort of success we perceive its immense value. It is capable of a rare transparency—it can illustrate human affairs in cases so delicate and complicated that any other vehicle would be clumsy. To those who love the art that Mr. Stevenson practises he will appear, in pointing this incidental moral, not only to have won a particular triumph, but to have given a delightful pledge.

J. M. BARRIE
From "Robert Louis Stevenson"
An Edinburgh Eleven
1889, pp. 118–28

Mr. Stevenson is not to be labelled novelist. He wanders the byways of literature without any fixed address. Too much of a truant to be classified with the other boys, he is only a writer of fiction in the sense that he was once an Edinburgh University student because now and again he looked in at his classes when he happened to be that way. A literary man without a fixed occupation amazes Mr. Henry James, a master in the school of fiction which tells, in three volumes, how Hiram K. Wilding trod on the skirt of Alice M. Sparkins without anything's coming of it. Mr. James analyzes Mr. Stevenson with immense cleverness, but without summing up. That *Dr. Jekyll and Mr. Hyde* should be by the author of *Treasure Island*, *Virginibus Puerisque* by the author of *The New Arabian Nights*, *A Child's Garden of Verses* by the author of *Prince Otto*, are to him the three degrees of comparison of wonder, though for my own part I marvel more that the author of *Daisy Miller* should be Mr. Stevenson's eulogist. One conceives Mr. James a boy in velveteens looking fearfully at Stevenson playing at pirates.

There is nothing in Mr. Stevenson's sometimes writing essays, sometimes romances, and anon poems to mark him versatile beyond other authors. One dreads his continuing to do so, with so many books at his back, lest it means weakness rather than strength. He experiments too long; he is still a boy wondering what he is going to be. With Cowley's candor he tells us that he wants to write something by which he may be forever known. His attempts in this direction have been in the nature of trying different ways, and he always starts off whistling. Having gone so far without losing himself, he turns back to try another road. Does his heart fail him, despite his jaunty bearing, or is it because there is no hurry? Though all his books are obviously by the same hand, no living writer has come so near fame from so many different sides. Where is the man among us who could write another *Virginibus Puerisque*, the most delightful volume for the hammock ever sung in prose? The poems are as exquisite as they are artificial. *Jekyll and Hyde* is the greatest triumph extant in Christmas literature of the morbid kind. The donkey on the Cévennes (how Mr. Stevenson belabored him!) only stands second to the *Inland Voyage*. *Kidnapped* is the outstanding boy's book of its generation. *The Black Arrow* alone, to my thinking, is second class. We shall all be doleful if a marksman who can pepper his target with inners does not reach the bull's-eye. But it is quite time the great work was begun. The sun sinks while the climber walks round his mountain, looking for the best way up.

Hard necessity has kept some great writers from doing their best work, but Mr. Stevenson is at last so firmly established that if he continues to be versatile it will only be from choice. He has attained a popularity such as is, as a rule, only accorded to classic authors or to charlatans. For this he has America to thank rather than Britain, for the Americans buy his books, the only honor a writer's admirers are slow to pay him. Mr. Stevenson's reputation in the United States is creditable to that country, which has given him a position here in which only a few saw him when he left. Unfortunately, with popularity has come publicity. All day the reporters sit on his garden wall.

No man has written in a finer spirit of the profession of letters than Mr. Stevenson, but this gossip vulgarizes it. The adulation of the American public and of a little band of clever literary dandies in London, great in criticism, of whom he has become the darling, has made Mr. Stevenson complacent, and he always tended perhaps to be a thought too fond of his velvet coat. There is danger in the delight with which his every scrap is now received. A few years ago, when he was his own severest and sanest critic, he stopped the publication of a book after it was in proof—a brave act. He has lost this courage, or he would have rewritten *The Black Arrow*. There is deterioration in the essays he has been contributing to an American magazine, graceful and suggestive though they are. The most charming of living stylists, Mr. Stevenson is self-conscious in all his books now and again, but hitherto it has been the self-consciousness of an artist with severe critics at his shoulder. It has become self-satisfaction. The critics have put a giant's robe on him, and he has not flung it off. He dismisses *Tom Jones* with a simper. Personally Thackeray "scarce appeals to us as the ideal gentleman; if there were nothing else [what else is there?], perpetual nosing after snobbery at least suggests the snob." From Mr. Stevenson one would not have expected the revival of this silly charge, which makes a cabbage of every man who writes about cabbages. I shall say no more of these ill-considered papers, though the sneers at Fielding call for indignant remonstrance, beyond expressing a hope that they lie buried between magazine covers. Mr. Stevenson has reached the critical point in his career, and one would like to see him back at Bournemouth, writing within high walls. We want that big book; we think he is capable of it, and so we cannot afford to let him drift into the seaweed. About the writer with whom his name is so often absurdly linked we feel differently. It is as foolish to rail at Mr. Rider Haggard's complacency as it would be to blame Christopher Sly for so quickly believing that he was born a lord.

The key-note of all Mr. Stevenson's writings is his indifference, so far as his books are concerned, to the affairs of life and death on which their minds are chiefly set. Whether man has an immortal soul interests him as an artist not a whit: what is to come of man troubles him as little as where man came from. He is a warm, genial writer, yet this is so strange as to seem inhuman. His philosophy is that we are but as the light-hearted birds. This is our moment of being; let us play the intoxicating game of life beautifully, artistically, before we fall dead from the tree. We all know it is only in his books that Mr. Stevenson can live this life. The cry is to arms; spears glisten in the sun; see the brave bark riding joyously on the waves, the black flag, the dash of red color twisting round a mountainside. Alas! the drummer lies on a couch beating his drum. It is a pathetic picture, less true to fact now, one rejoices to know, than it was recently. A common theory is that Mr. Stevenson dreams an ideal life to escape from his own sufferings. This sentimental plea suits very well. The noticeable thing, however, is that the grotesque, the uncanny, holds his soul; his brain will only follow a colored clew. The result is that he is chiefly picturesque, and, to those who want more than art for art's sake, never satisfying. Fascinating as his verses are, artless in the perfection of art, they take no reader a step forward. The children of whom he sings so sweetly are cherubs without souls. It is not in poetry that Mr. Stevenson will give the great book to the world, nor will it, I think, be in the form of essays. Of late he has done nothing quite so fine as *Virginibus Puerisque*, though most of his essays are gardens in which grow few weeds. Quaint in matter as in treatment, they are the best strictly literary essays of the day, and their mixture of tenderness with humor suggests Charles Lamb. Some think Mr. Stevenson's essays equal to Lamb's, or greater. To that I say, no. The name of Lamb will for many a year bring proud tears to English eyes. Here was a man, weak like the rest of us, who kept his sorrows to himself. Life to him was not among the trees. He had loved and lost. Grief laid a heavy hand on his brave brow. Dark were his nights; horrid shadows in the house; sudden terrors; the heart stops beating waiting for a footstep. At that door comes Tragedy, knocking at all hours. Was Lamb dismayed? The tragedy of his life was not drear to him. It was wound round those who were dearest to him; it let him know that life has a glory even at its saddest, that humor and pathos clasp hands, that loved ones are drawn nearer, and the soul strengthened in the presence of anguish, pain, and death. When Lamb sat down to write, he did not pull down his blind on all that is greatest, if most awful, in human life. He was gentle, kindly; but he did not play at pretending that there is no cemetery round the corner. In Mr. Stevenson's exquisite essays one looks in vain for the great heart that palpitates through the pages of Charles Lamb.

The great work, if we are not to be disappointed, will be fiction. Mr. Stevenson is said to feel this himself, and, as I understand, *Harry Shovel* will be his biggest bid for fame. It is to be, broadly speaking, a nineteenth-century *Peregrine Pickle*, dashed with Meredith, and this in the teeth of many admirers who maintain that the best of the author is Scottish. Mr. Stevenson, however, knows what he is about. Critics have said enthusiastically—for it is difficult to write of Mr. Stevenson without enthusiasm—that Alan Breck is as good as anything in Scott. Alan Breck is certainly a masterpiece, quite worthy of the greatest of all story-tellers, who, nevertheless, it should be remembered, created these rich side characters by the score, another before dinnertime. English critics have taken Alan to their hearts, and appreciate him thoroughly; the reason, no doubt, being that he is the character whom England acknowledges as the Scottish type. The Highlands, which are Scotland to the same extent as Northumberland is England, present such a character to this day, but no deep knowledge of Mr. Stevenson's native country was required to reproduce him. An artistic Englishman or American could have done it. Scottish religion, I think, Mr. Stevenson has never understood, except as the outsider misunderstands it. He thinks it hard because there are no colored windows. "The color of Scotland has entered into him altogether," says Mr. James, who, we gather, conceives in Edinburgh Castle a place where tartans glisten in the sun, while rocks re-echo bagpipes. Mr. James is right in a way. It is the tartan, the claymore, the cry that the heather is on fire, that are Scotland to Mr. Stevenson. But the Scotland of our day is not a country rich in color; a sombre gray prevails. Thus, though Mr. Stevenson's best romance is Scottish, that is only, I think, because of his extraordinary aptitude for the picturesque. Give him any period in any country that is romantic, and he will soon steep himself in the kind of knowledge he can best turn to account. Adventures suit him best, the ladies being left behind; and so long as he is in fettle it matters little whether the scene be Scotland or Spain. The

great thing is that he should now give to one ambitious book the time in which he has hitherto written half a dozen small ones. He will have to take existence a little more seriously—to weave broadcloth instead of lace.

ANDREW LANG
"Mr. Stevenson's Works"
Essays in Little
1891, pp. 24–35

Perhaps the first quality in Mr. Stevenson's works, now so many and so various, which strikes a reader, is the buoyancy, the survival of the child in him. He has told the world often, in prose and verse, how vivid are his memories of his own infancy. This retention of childish recollections he shares, no doubt, with other people of genius: for example, with George Sand, whose legend of her own infancy is much more entertaining, and perhaps will endure longer, than her novels. Her youth, like Scott's and like Mr. Stevenson's, was passed all in fantasy: in playing at being some one else, in the invention of imaginary characters, who were living to her, in the fabrication of endless unwritten romances. Many persons, who do not astonish the world by their genius, have lived thus in their earliest youth. But, at a given moment, the fancy dies out of them: this often befalls imaginative boys in their first year at school. "Many are called, few chosen"; but it may be said with probable truth, that there has never been a man of genius in letters, whose boyhood was not thus fantastic, "an isle of dreams." We know how Scott and De Quincey inhabited airy castles; and Gillies tells us, though Lockhart does not, that Scott, in manhood, was occasionally so lost in thought, that he knew not where he was nor what he was doing.

The peculiarity of Mr. Stevenson is not only to have been a fantastic child, and to retain, in maturity, that fantasy ripened into imagination: he has also kept up the habit of dramatising everything, of playing, half consciously, many parts, of making the world "an unsubstantial fairy place." This turn of mind it is that causes his work occasionally to seem somewhat freakish. Thus, in the fogs and horrors of London, he plays at being an Arabian tale-teller, and his *New Arabian Nights* are a new kind of romanticism—Oriental, freakish, like the work of a changeling. Indeed, this curious genius, springing from a family of Scottish engineers, resembles nothing so much as one of the fairy children, whom the ladies of Queen Proserpina's court used to leave in the cradles of Border keeps or of peasants' cottages. Of the Scot he has little but the power of touching us with a sense of the supernatural, and a decided habit of moralising; for no Scot of genius has been more austere with Robert Burns. On the other hand, one element of Mr. Stevenson's ethical disquisitions is derived from his dramatic habit. His optimism, his gay courage, his habit of accepting the world as very well worth living in and looking at, persuaded one of his critics that he was a hard-hearted young athlete of iron frame. Now, of the athlete he has nothing but his love of the open air: it is the eternal child that drives him to seek adventures and to sojourn among beach-combers and savages. Thus, an admiring but far from optimistic critic may doubt whether Mr. Stevenson's content with the world is not "only his fun," as Lamb said of Coleridge's preaching; whether he is but playing at being the happy warrior in life; whether he is not acting that part, himself to himself. At least, it is a part fortunately conceived and admirably sustained: a difficult part too, whereas that of the pessimist is as easy as whining.

Mr. Stevenson's work has been very much written about, as it has engaged and delighted readers of every age, station, and character. Boys, of course, have been specially addressed in the books of adventure, children in *A Child's Garden of Verse*, young men and maidens in *Virginibus Puerisque*,—all ages in all the curiously varied series of volumes. *Kidnapped* was one of the last books which the late Lord Iddesleigh read; and I trust there is no harm in mentioning the pleasure which Mr. Matthew Arnold took in the same story. Critics of every sort have been kind to Mr. Stevenson, in spite of the fact that the few who first became acquainted with his genius praised it with all the warmth of which they were masters. Thus he has become a kind of classic in his own day, for an undisputed reputation makes a classic while it lasts. But was ever so much fame won by writings which might be called scrappy and desultory by the *advocatus diaboli?* It is a most miscellaneous literary baggage that Mr. Stevenson carries. First, a few magazine articles; then two little books of sentimental journeyings, which convince the reader that Mr. Stevenson is as good company to himself as his books are to others. Then came a volume or two of essays, literary and social, on books and life. By this time there could be no doubt that Mr. Stevenson had a style of his own, modelled to some extent on the essayists of the last century, but with touches of Thackeray; with original breaks and turns, with a delicate freakishness, in short, and a determined love of saying things as the newspapers do not say them. All this work undoubtedly smelt a trifle of the lamp, and was therefore dear to some and an offence to others. For my part, I had delighted in the essays, from the first that appeared in *Macmillan's Magazine*, shortly after the Franco-German war. In this little study, "Ordered South," Mr. Stevenson was employing himself in extracting all the melancholy pleasure which the Riviera can give to a wearied body and a mind resisting the clouds of early malady.

> Alas, the worn and broken board,
>   How can it bear the painter's dye!
> The harp of strained and tuneless chord,
>   How to the minstrel's skill reply!
> To aching eyes each landscape lowers,
>   To feverish pulse each gale blows chill,
> And Araby's or Eden's bowers
> Were barren as this moorland hill,—

wrote Scott, in an hour of malady and depression. But this was not the spirit of "Ordered South": the younger soul rose against the tyranny of the body; and that familiar glamour which, in illness, robs Tintoretto of his glow, did not spoil the midland sea to Mr. Stevenson. His gallant and cheery stoicism were already with him; and so perfect, if a trifle overstudied, was his style, that one already foresaw a new and charming essayist.

But none of those early works, nor the delightful book on Edinburgh, prophesied of the story teller. Mr. Stevenson's first published tales, the *New Arabian Nights*, originally appeared in a quaintly edited weekly paper, which nobody read, or nobody but the writers in its columns. They welcomed the strange romances with rejoicings: but perhaps there was only one of them who foresaw that Mr. Stevenson's *forte* was to be fiction, not essay writing; that he was to appeal with success to the large public, and not to the tiny circle who surround the essayist. It did not seem likely that our incalculable public would make themselves at home in those fantastic purlieus which Mr. Stevenson's fancy discovered near the Strand. The impossible Young Man with the Cream Tarts, the ghastly revels of the Suicide Club, the Oriental caprices of the

Hansom Cabs—who could foresee that the public would taste them! It is true that Mr. Stevenson's imagination made the President of the Club, and the cowardly member, Mr. Malthus, as real as they were terrible. His romance always goes hand in hand with reality; and Mr. Malthus is as much an actual man of skin and bone, as Silas Lapham is a man of flesh and blood. The world saw this, and applauded the *Noctes of Prince Floristan*, in a fairy London.

Yet, excellent and unique as these things were, Mr. Stevenson had not yet "found himself." It would be more true to say that he had only discovered outlying skirts of his dominions. Has he ever hit on the road to the capital yet? and will he ever enter it laurelled, and in triumph? That is precisely what one may doubt, not as without hope. He is always making discoveries in his realm; it is less certain that he will enter its chief city in state. His next work was rather in the nature of annexation and invasion than a settling of his own realms. "Prince Otto" is not, to my mind, a ruler in his proper soil. The provinces of George Sand and of Mr. George Meredith have been taken captive. *Prince Otto* is fantastic indeed, but neither the fantasy nor the style is quite Mr. Stevenson's. There are excellent passages, and the Scotch soldier of fortune is welcome, and the ladies abound in subtlety and wit. But the book, at least to myself, seems an extremely elaborate and skilful *pastiche*. I cannot believe in the persons: I vaguely smell a moral allegory (as in "Will of the Mill"). I do not clearly understand what it is all about. The scene is fairyland; but it is not the fairyland of Perrault. The ladies are beautiful and witty; but they are escaped from a novel of Mr. Meredith's, and have no business here. The book is no more Mr. Stevenson's than *The Tale of Two Cities* was Mr. Dickens's.

It was probably by way of mere diversion and child's play that Mr. Stevenson began *Treasure Island*. He is an amateur of boyish pleasures of masterpieces at a penny plain and twopence coloured. Probably he had looked at the stories of adventure in penny papers which only boys read, and he determined sportively to compete with their unknown authors. *Treasure Island* came out in such a periodical, with the emphatic woodcuts which adorn them. It is said that the puerile public was not greatly stirred. A story is a story, and they rather preferred the regular purveyors. The very faint archaism of the style may have alienated them. But, when *Treasure Island* appeared as a real book, then every one who had a smack of youth left was a boy again for some happy hours. Mr. Stevenson had entered into another province of his realm: the king had come to his own again.

They say the seamanship is inaccurate; I care no more than I do for the year 30. They say too many people are killed. They all died in fair fight, except a victim of John Silver's. The conclusion is a little too like part of Poe's most celebrated tale, but nobody has bellowed "Plagiarist!" Some people may not look over a fence: Mr. Stevenson, if he liked, might steal a horse,—the animal in this case is only a skeleton. A very sober student might add that the hero is impossibly clever; but, then, the hero is a boy, and this is a boy's book. For the rest, the characters live. Only genius could have invented John Silver, that terribly smooth-spoken mariner. Nothing but genius could have drawn that simple yokel on the island, with his craving for cheese as a Christian dainty. The blustering Billy Bones is a little masterpiece: the blind Pew, with his tapping stick (there are three such blind tappers in Mr. Stevenson's books), strikes terror into the boldest. Then, the treasure is thoroughly satisfactory in kind, and there is plenty of it. The landscape, as in the feverish, fog-smothered flat, is gallantly painted. And there are no interfering petticoats in the story.

As for the *Black Arrow*, I confess to sharing the disabilities of the "Critic on the Hearth," to whom it is dedicated. *Kidnapped* is less a story than a fragment; but it is a noble fragment. Setting aside the wicked old uncle, who in his later behaviour is of the house of Ralph Nickleby, *Kidnapped* is all excellent—perhaps Mr. Stevenson's masterpiece. Perhaps, too, only a Scotchman knows how good it is, and only a Lowland Scot knows how admirable a character is the dour, brave, conceited David Balfour. It is like being in Scotland again to come on "the green drive-road running wide through the heather," where David "took his last look of Kirk Essendean, the trees about the manse, and the big rowans in the kirkyard, where his father and mother lay." Perfectly Scotch, too, is the mouldering, empty house of the Miser, with the stamped leather on the walls. And the Miser is as good as a Scotch Trapbois, till he becomes homicidal, and then one fails to recognise him unless he is a little mad, like that other frantic uncle in *The Merry Men*. The scenes on the ship, with the boy who is murdered, are better—I think more real—than the scenes of piratical life in *The Master of Ballantrae*. The fight in the Round House, even if it were exaggerated, would be redeemed by the "Song of the Sword of Alan." As to Alan Breck himself, with his valour and vanity, his good heart, his good conceit of himself, his fantastic loyalty, he is absolutely worthy of the hand that drew Callum Bey and the Dougal creature. It is just possible that we see, in *Kidnapped*, more signs of determined labour, more evidence of touches and retouches, than in *Rob Roy*. In nothing else which it attempts is it inferior; in mastery of landscape, as in the scene of the lonely rock in a dry and thirsty land, it is unsurpassed. If there are signs of laboured handling on Alan, there are none in the sketches of Cluny and of Rob Roy's son, the piper. What a generous artist is Alan! "Robin Oig," he said, when it was done, "ye are a great piper. I am not fit to blow in the same kingdom with you. Body of me! ye have mair music in your sporran than I have in my head."

Kidnapped, we said, is a fragment. It ends anywhere, or nowhere, as if the pen had dropped from a weary hand. Thus, and for other reasons, one cannot pretend to set what is not really a whole against such a rounded whole as *Rob Roy*, or against *The Legend of Montrose*. Again, *Kidnapped* is a novel without a woman in it: not here is Di Vernon, not here is Helen McGregor. David Balfour is the pragmatic Lowlander; he does not bear comparison, excellent as he is, with Baillie Nicol Jarvie, the humorous Lowlander: he does not live in the memory like the immortal Baillie. It is as a series of scenes and sketches that *Kidnapped* is unmatched among Mr. Stevenson's works.

In *The Master of Ballantrae* Mr. Stevenson makes a gallant effort to enter what I have ventured to call the capital of his kingdom. He does introduce a woman, and confronts the problems of love as well as of fraternal hatred. The "Master" is studied, is polished *ad unguem*; it is a whole in itself, it is a remarkably daring attempt to write the tragedy, as, in *Waverley*, Scott wrote the romance, of Scotland about the time of the Forty-Five. With such a predecessor and rival, Mr. Stevenson wisely leaves the pomps and battles of the Forty-Five, its chivalry and gallantry, alone. He shows us the seamy side: the intrigues, domestic and political; the needy Irish adventurer with the Prince, a person whom Scott had not studied. The book, if completely successful, would be Mr. Stevenson's *Bride of Lammermoor*. To be frank, I do not think it completely successful—a victory all along the line. The obvious weak point is Secundra Dass, that Indian of unknown nationality; for surely his name marks him as no Hindoo. The

Master could not have brought him, shivering like Jos Sedley's black servant, to Scotland. As in America, this alien would have found it "too dam cold." My power of belief (which verges on credulity) is staggered by the ghastly attempt to reanimate the buried Master. Here, at least to my taste, the freakish changeling has got the better of Mr. Stevenson, and has brought in an element out of keeping with the steady lurid tragedy of fraternal hatred. For all the rest, it were a hard judge that had anything but praise. The brilliant blackguardism of the Master; his touch of sentiment as he leaves Durisdeer for the last time, with a sad old song on his lips; his fascination; his ruthlessness; his irony;—all are perfect. It is not very easy to understand the Chevalier Bourke, that Barry Lyndon, with no head and with a good heart, that creature of a bewildered kindly conscience; but it is easy to like him. How admirable is his undeflected belief in and affection for the Master! How excellent and how Irish he is, when he buffoons himself out of his perils with the pirates! The scenes are brilliant and living, as when the Master throws the guinea through the Hall window, or as in the darkling duel in the garden. It needed an austere artistic conscience to make Henry, the younger brother, so unlovable with all his excellence, and to keep the lady so true, yet so much in shadow. This is the best woman among Mr. Stevenson's few women; but even she is almost always reserved, veiled as it were.

The old Lord, again, is a portrait as lifelike as Scott could have drawn, and more delicately touched than Scott would have cared to draw it: a French companion picture to the Baron Bradwardine. The whole piece reads as if Mr. Stevenson had engaged in a struggle with himself as he wrote. The sky is never blue, the sun never shines: we weary for a "westland wind." There is something "thrawn," as the Scotch say, about the story; there is often a touch of this sinister kind in the author's work. The language is extraordinarily artful, as in the mad lord's words, "I have felt the hilt dirl on his breast-bone." And yet, one is hardly thrilled as one expects to be, when, as Mackellar says, "the week-old corpse looked me for a moment in the face."

Probably none of Mr. Stevenson's many books has made his name so familiar as *Dr. Jekyll and Mr. Hyde*. I read it first in manuscript, alone, at night; and, when the Butler and Mr. Urmson came to the Doctor's door, I confess that I threw it down, and went hastily to bed. It is the most gruesome of all his writings, and so perfect that one can complain only of the slightly too obvious moral; and, again, that really Mr. Hyde was more of a gentleman than the unctuous Dr. Jekyll, with his "bedside manner."

So here, not to speak of some admirable short stories like "Thrawn Janet," is a brief catalogue—little more—of Mr. Stevenson's literary baggage. It is all good, though variously good; yet the wise world asks for the masterpiece. It is said that Mr. Stevenson has not ventured on the delicate and dangerous ground of the novel, because he has not written a modern love story. But who has? There are love affairs in Dickens, but do we remember or care for them? Is it the love affairs that we remember in Scott? Thackeray may touch us with Clive's and Jack Belsize's misfortunes, with Esmond's melancholy passion, and amuse us with Pen in so many toils, and interest us in the little heroine of the "Shabby Genteel Story." But it is not by virtue of those episodes that Thackeray is so great. Love stories are best done by women, as in "Mr. Gilfil's Love Story"; and, perhaps, in an ordinary way, by writers like Trollope. One may defy critics to name a great English author in fiction whose chief and distinguishing merit is in his pictures of the passion of Love. Still, they all give Love his due stroke in the battle, and perhaps Mr. Stevenson will do so some day. But I confess that, if he ever excels himself, I do not expect it to be in a love story.

Possibly it may be in a play. If he again attempt the drama, he has this in his favour, that he will not deal in supernumeraries. In his tales his minor characters are as carefully drawn as his chief personages. Consider, for example, the minister, Henderland, the man who is so fond of snuff, in *Kidnapped*, and, in the *Master of Ballantrae*, Sir William Johnson, the English Governor. They are the work of a mind as attentive to details, as ready to subordinate or obliterate details which are unessential. Thus Mr. Stevenson's writings breathe equally of work in the study and of inspiration from adventure in the open air, and thus he wins every vote, and pleases every class of reader.

ARTHUR SYMONS
"Robert Louis Stevenson" (1894)
Studies in Prose and Verse
1904, pp. 77–82

The death of Robert Louis Stevenson deprived English literature of the most charming and sympathetic writer of the present day. He was a fastidious craftsman, caring, we might almost say pre-eminently, for style; yet he was popular. He was most widely known as the writer of boys' books of adventure; yet he was the favourite reading of those who care only for the most literary aspects of literature. Within a few days after the news of his death reached England, English newspapers vied with each other in comparing him with Montaigne, with Lamb, with Scott, with Defoe; and he has been not merely compared, but preferred. Uncritical praise is the most unfriendly service a man can render to his friend; but here, where so much praise is due, may one not try to examine a little closely just what those qualities are which call for praise, and just what measure of praise they seem to call for?

Stevenson somewhere describes certain of his own essays as being "but the readings of a literary vagrant." And, in truth, he was always that, a literary vagrant; it is the secret of much of his charm, and of much of his weakness. He wandered, a literary vagrant, over the world, across life, and across literature, an adventurous figure, with all the irresponsible and irresistible charm of the vagabond. To read him is to be for ever setting out on a fresh journey, along a white, beckoning road, on a blithe spring morning. Anything may happen, or nothing; the air is full of the gaiety of possible chances. And in this exhilaration of the blood, unreasoning, unreasonable, as it is, all the philosophies merge themselves into those two narrow lines which the *Child's Garden of Verses* piously encloses for us:

> The world is so full of a number of things,
> I am sure we should all be as happy as kings.

It is the holiday mood of life that Stevenson expresses, and no one has ever expressed it with a happier abandonment to the charm of natural things. In its exquisite exaggeration, it is the optimism of the invalid, due to his painful consciousness that health, and the delights of health, are what really matter in life. Most of those who have written captivatingly of the open air, of what are called natural, healthy things, have been invalids: Thoreau, Richard Jefferies, Stevenson. The strong man has leisure to occupy his thoughts with other things; he can indulge in abstract thinking without a twinge of the brain,

can pursue the moral issues of conduct impersonally; he is not condemned to the bare elements of existence. And, in his calm acceptance of the privileges of ordinary health, he finds no place for that lyric rapture of thanksgiving which a bright day, a restful night, wakens in the invalid. The actual fever and languor in the blood: that counts for something in Stevenson's work, and lies at the root of some of its fascination.

His art, in all those essays and extravagant tales into which he put his real self, is a romantic art, alike in the essay on "Walking Tours" and in the "Story of the Young Man with the Cream Tarts." Stevenson was passionately interested in people; but there was something a trifle elvish and uncanny about him, as of a bewitched being who was not actually human, had not actually a human soul, and whose keen interest in the fortunes of his fellows was really a vivid curiosity, from one not quite of the same nature as those about him. He saw life as the most absorbing, the most amusing, game; or, as a masquerade, in which he liked to glance behind a mask, now and again, on the winding and coloured way he made for himself through the midst of the pageant. It was only in his latest period that he came to think about truth to human nature; and even then it was with the picturesqueness of character, with its adaptability to the humorous freaks of incident, that he was chiefly concerned.

He was never really himself except when he was in some fantastic disguise. From "The Pavilion on the Links" to *Dr Jekyll and Mr Hyde*, he played with men and women as a child plays with a kaleidoscope; using them freakishly, wantonly, as colours, sometimes as symbols. In some wonderful, artificial way, like a wizard who raises, not living men from the dead, but the shadows of men who had once died, he calls up certain terrifying, but not ungracious, phantoms, who frisk it among the mere beings of flesh and blood, bringing with them the strangest "airs from heaven or blasts from hell." No; in the phrase of Beddoes, Stevenson was "tired of being merely human." Thus there are no women in his books, no lovers; only the lure of hidden treasures and the passion of adventure. It was for the accidents and curiosities of life that he cared, for life as a strange picture, for its fortunate confusions, its whimsical distresses, its unlikely strokes of luck, its cruelties, sometimes, and the touch of madness that comes into it at moments. For reality, for the endeavour to see things as they are, to represent them as they are, he had an impatient disregard. These matters did not interest him.

But it is by style, largely, we are told, that Stevenson is to live, and the names of Lamb and of Montaigne are called up on equal terms. Style, with Stevenson, was certainly a constant preoccupation, and he has told us how, as a lad, he trained himself in the use of language; how, in his significant phrase, he "lived with words"; by "playing the sedulous ape to Hazlitt, to Lamb, to Wordsworth, to Sir Thomas Browne, to Defoe, to Hawthorne, to Montaigne, to Baudelaire, and to Obermann." He was resolved from the first to reject the ready-made in language, to combine words for himself, as if no one had ever used them before; and, with labour and luck, he formed for his use a singularly engaging manner of writing, full of charm, freshness, and flexibility, and with a certain human warmth in the words. But it is impossible to consider style in the abstract without taking into account also what it expresses; for true style is not the dress, but the very flesh, of the informing thought. Stevenson's tendency, like that of his admirers, was rather to the forgetfulness of this plain and sometimes uncongenial fact. But, in comparing him with the great names of literature, we cannot but feel all the difference, and all the meaning of the difference, between a great intellect and a bright intelligence.

The lofty and familiar homeliness of Montaigne, the subtle and tragic humour of Lamb, are both on a far higher plane than the gentle and attractive and whimsical confidences of Stevenson. And, underlying what may seem trifling in both, there is a large intellectual force, a breadth of wisdom, which makes these two charming writers not merely charming, but great. Stevenson remains charming; his personality, individual and exquisite as it was, had not the strength and depth of greatness. And, such as it was, it gave itself to us completely; there was no sense, as there is with the really great writers, of reserve power, of infinite riches to draw upon. Quite by himself in a certain seductiveness of manner, he ranks, really, with Borrow and Thoreau, with the men of secondary order in literature, who appeal to us with more instinctive fascination than the very greatest; as a certain wayward and gipsy grace in a woman thrills to the blood, often enough, more intimately and immediately than the august perfection of classic beauty. He is one of those writers who speak to us on easy terms, with whom we may exchange affections. We cannot lose our heart to Shakespeare, to Balzac; nay, even to Montaigne, because of the height and depth, the ardour and dignity, of the wisdom in his "smiling" pages (to use Stevenson's own word). But George Borrow makes every one who comes under his charm a little unfit for civilisation, a little discontented with drawing-rooms; Thoreau leads his willing victim into the ardent austerity of the woods; and Stevenson awakens something of the eternal romance in the bosom even of the conventional. It is a surprising, a marvellous thing to have done; and to afford such delights, to call forth such responsive emotions, is a boon that we accept with warmer rejoicing than many more solid gifts. But to be wine and song to us for a festive evening is, after all, not the highest form of service or the noblest ministration of joy. It is needful to discriminate in these generous and perilous enthusiasms, as it is in judging fairly of the character of a friend. Let us love our friend, with all his shortcomings; let him be the more lovable for them, if chance wills it; but it is better to be aware of the truth, before we proceed to act with affectionate disregard of it. Stevenson captivates the heart: that is why he is in such danger of being wronged by indiscriminate eulogy. Let us do him justice: he would have wished only for justice. It is a dishonour to the dead if we strive to honour their memory with anything less absolute than truth.

SIR LESLIE STEPHEN
"Robert Louis Stevenson"
Studies of a Biographer
1902, Volume 4, pp. 206–46

Nearly thirty years have passed since Stevenson began to attract a circle of appreciative readers. From the first it was clear that the literary appreciation coincided with a personal attraction. As his fame extended, the admiration of readers remotest in the flesh had a tinge of friendship, while the inner circle could not distinguish between their enthusiastic affection for the man and their cordial enjoyment of his genius. So far as the biographer is concerned, the identity of the two sentiments is a clear gain. Affection, though not a sufficient, is an almost necessary qualification for a good biography. It may be doubted, however, whether a man's friends are his best critics. The keen eye of the candid outsider has detected a tacit conspiracy in this case. The circle of friends looks unpleasantly like a clique, trying to gain a reflex glory

from the fame of its hero, or to make a boast of its superior insight. The connection, it is true, has other dangers. The tie may be broken, and the rupture, it appears, cancels all obligations to reticence. No one can then lay on the lash like the old friend who knows the weak places and has, or fancies that he has, an injury to resent. But even fidelity to old ties is not necessarily blinding. No one can read Mr. Colvin's notes upon his friend's letters without admitting that his friendship has sharpened his insight. To him belongs the credit of having been the first, outside the home circle, to recognise Stevenson's genius and to give encouragement when encouragement was most needed. The keen interest enabled him to interpret both the personal and the artistic characteristics of his friend with a clearness which satisfies us of the essential fidelity of the portrait. If we differ from the valuation which he puts upon certain qualities, he gives essential help to perceiving them. We often learn more from the partisan than from the candid historian; and in criticism, as well as in history, candour may be an alias for insensibility.

It was to Mr. Colvin that I owe what is perhaps my chief claim to such respect as readers of a periodical may concede to an editor. Through his good offices, Stevenson became one of my contributors, and I may be allowed to boast that, in his case at least, I did not nip rising genius in the bud—the feat which, according to some young authors, represents the main desire of the editorial mind. Fate, however, withheld from me the privilege of forming such an intimacy as could materially bias my opinions; and so far I have a negative qualification for answering the question which so many people are eager to put: what, namely, will posterity think about Stevenson? I am content to leave the point to posterity; but in trying to sum up my own impressions, corrected by the judgment of his closer friends and critics, I may contribute to the discussion of the previous question: what is the species, not what is the degree, of praise which he will receive? Friendly criticism is apt to fail in this direction. Enthusiasts fancy that to define a man's proper sphere is to limit his merits; they assume that other sects are necessarily hostile, and that they must remove another bust from Poets' Corner in order to make room for doing honour to their favourite. Such controversies lead to impossible problems and attempts to find a common measure for disparate qualities. We may surely by this time agree that Tennyson and Browning excelled in different lines without asking which line was absolutely best. That will always be a matter of individual taste.

Whatever Stevenson was, he was, I think, a man of genius. I do not mean to bring him under any strict definition. My own conception of genius has been formed by an induction from the very few cases which I have been fortunate enough to observe. I may try to describe one characteristic by perverting the language of one of those instances. The late W. K. Clifford, who had the most unmistakable stamp of genius, held that the universe was composed of 'mindstuff.' I don't know how that may be, but a man has genius, I should say, when he seems to be made of nothing but 'mindstuff.' We of coarser make have a certain infusion of mind; but it is terribly cramped and held down by matter. What we call 'thinking' is often a mechanical process carried on by dead formulæ. We work out results as a phonograph repeats the sound when you insert the diaphragm already impressed with the pattern. The mental processes in the man of genius are still vital instead of being automatic. He has, as Carlyle is fond of repeating about Mirabeau, 'swallowed all formulas,' or rather, he is not the slave but the master of those useful intellectual tools. It is this pervading vitality which has marked such geniuses as I have known, though it assumes very various forms. A proposition of

Euclid, such as 'coaches' hammer into the head of a dunce to be reproduced by rote, developed instantly, when inserted into Clifford's brain, into whole systems of geometry. Genius of a different type was shown by the historian J. R. Green. You pointed out a bit of old wall, or a slope of down, and it immediately opened to him a vista of past ages, illustrating bygone social states and the growth of nations. So Stevenson heard an anecdote and it became at once the nucleus of a story, and he was on the spot a hero of romance plunging into a whole series of thrilling adventures. Connected with this, I suppose, is the invincible boyishness so often noticed as a characteristic of genius. The mind which retains its freshness can sympathise with the child to whom the world is still a novelty. Both Clifford and Green were conspicuous for this possession of the prerogative of genius, and showed it both in being boyish themselves and in their intense sympathy with children. Clifford was never happier than in a child's party, and Green sought relief from the dreariness of a clergyman's life at the East-end by associating with the children of the district. Stevenson's boyishness was not only conspicuous, but was the very mainspring of his best work. That quality cannot be shown in a mathematical dissertation or an historical narrative, but it is invaluable for a writer of romances. The singular vivacity of Stevenson's early memories is shown by Mr. Balfour's account of his infancy as it was sufficiently revealed in the delightful *Child's Garden*. It is amusing to note that Stevenson could not even imagine that other men should be without this experience. You are indulging in 'wilful paradox,' he replied to Mr. Henry James. 'If a man have never been' (Mr. James alleged that he had not been) 'on a quest for hidden treasure, it can be demonstrated that he has never been a child.' His scheme of life, as he puts it in a charming letter to Mr. Monkhouse, was to be alternately a pirate and a leader of irregular cavalry 'devastating whole valleys.' Some of us, I fear, have never been pirates; and if we were anything, were perhaps already preaching infantile sermons. In any case, the castle-building propensity is often so weak as not even to leave a trace in memory. Stevenson's most obvious peculiarity was that it only strengthened with life, and, which is rarer, always retained some of the childish colouring.

A common test—for it is surely not the essence—of genius is the proverbial capacity for taking pains. Stevenson again illustrates the meaning of the remark. Nothing is easier, says a recent German philosopher, than to give a receipt for making yourself a good novelist. Write a hundred drafts, none of them above two pages long: let each be so expressed that every word is necessary: practise putting anecdotes into the most pregnant and effective shapes; and after ten years devoted to these and various subsidiary studies, you will have completed your apprenticeship. Few novelists, I suppose, carry out this scheme to the letter; but Stevenson might have approved the spirit of the advice. Nobody would adopt it unless he had the passion for the art, which is a presumption of genius, and, without genius, the labour would be wasted. That, indeed, raises one of those points which are so delightful to discuss because they admit of no precise solution. When people ask whether 'form' or 'content,' style or matter, be the most important, it is like asking whether order or progress should be the aim of a statesman, or whether strength or activity be most needed for an athlete. Both are essential, and neither excellence will supersede necessity for the other. If you have nothing to say, there is no manner of saying it well; and if not well said, your something is as good as nothing. For Stevenson, the question of style was the most pressing. His mind was already, as it continued to be, swarming with any number of

projects; he was always acting 'some fragment from his dream of human life'; the storehouse of his imagination was full to overflowing, and the question was not what to say but how to say it. Moreover, a singular delicacy of organisation gave him a love of words for their own sake; the mere sound of 'Jehovah Tsidkenu' gave him a thrill (it does not thrill me!); he was sensitive from childhood to assonance and alliteration, and in his later essay upon the 'technical elements of style' shows how a sentence in the *Areopagitica* involves a cunning use of the letters P V F. Language, in short, had to him a music independently of its meaning. That, no doubt, is one element of literary effect, though without a fine ear it would be hopeless to decide what pleases; and the finest ear cannot really explain what are the conditions of pleasing. This precocious sensitiveness developed into a clear appreciation of various qualities of style. Like other young men, he began by imitating; taking for models such curiously different writers as Hazlitt, Sir Thomas Browne, Defoe, Hawthorne, Montaigne, Beaudelaire, and Ruskin. In the ordinary cases imitation implies that the model is taken as a master. Milton probably meant, in youth, to be a second Spenser. But the variety of Stevenson's models implies an absence of strict discipleship. He was trying to discover the secret which gave distinction to any particular style; and without adopting the manner would know how to apply it on occasion for any desired effect. How impressionable he was is curiously shown by his statement towards the end of his life, that he would not read Livy for fear of the effect upon his style. He had long before acquired a style of his own so distinctive that such a danger would strike no one else. I will not dwell upon its merits. They have been set forth, far better than I could hope to do, in Professor Raleigh's admirable study. He is a critic who shares the perceptiveness of his author. I will only note one point. A 'stylist' sometimes becomes a mannerist; he acquires tricks of speech which intrude themselves inappropriately. Stevenson's general freedom from this fault implies that hatred to the commonplace formula of which I have spoken. His words are always alive. He came to insist chiefly upon the importance of condensation. 'There is but one art,' he says, 'the art to omit'; or, as Pope puts it, perhaps more accurately, 'the last and greatest art' is 'the art to blot.' That is a corollary from the theory of the right word. A writer is an 'amateur,' says Stevenson, 'who says in two sentences what can be said in one.' The artist puts his whole meaning into one perfectly accurate line, while a feebler hand tries to correct one error by superposing another, and ends by making a blur of the whole.

Stevenson, by whatever means, acquired not only a delicate style, but a style of his own. If it sometimes reminds one of models, it does not suggest that he is speaking in a feigned voice. I think, indeed, that this precocious preoccupation with style suggests the excess of self-consciousness which was his most obvious weakness; a daintiness which does not allow us to forget the presence of the artist. But Stevenson did not yield to other temptations which beset the lover of exquisite form. He was no 'æsthete' in the sense which conveys a reproach. He did not sympathise with the doctrine that an artist should wrap up himself in luxurious hedonism and cultivate indifference to active life. He was too much of a boy. A true boy cannot be 'æsthetic.' He had 'day-dreams,' but they were of piracy; tacit aspirations towards stirring adventure and active heroism. His dreams were of a future waking. Stevenson's energies had to take the form of writing; and though he talks about his 'art' a little more solemnly than one would wish, he betrays a certain hesitation as to its claims. In a late essay, he suggests that a man who has failed in literature should take to some 'more manly way of life.' To 'live by pleasure,' he declares, 'is not a high calling'; and he illustrates the proposition by speaking of such a life (not quite seriously) as a kind of intellectual prostitution. He laments his disqualification for active duties. 'I think *David Balfour* a nice little book,' he says, 'and very artistic and just the thing to occupy the leisure of a busy life; but for the top flower of a man's life it seems to be inadequate. . . . I could have wished to be otherwise busy in this world. I ought to have been able to build lighthouses and write *David Balfours* too.' This may be considered as the legitimate outcome of the boyish mood. It might have indicated a budding Nelson instead of a budding writer of romance. One result was the curious misunderstanding set forth in the interesting letters to Mr. William Archer. Mr. Archer had pleased him by an early appreciation; but had—as Stevenson complains—taken him for a 'rosy-gilled æsthetico-æsthete'; whereas he was really at this time 'a rickety and cloistered spectre.' To Mr. Archer, Stevenson's optimism had seemed to indicate superabundant health, and a want of familiarity with sorrow and sickness. A rheumatic fever, it was suggested, would try his philosophy. Mr. Archer's hypothesis (if fairly reported) was of course the reverse of the fact. Stevenson's whole career was a heroic struggle against disease, and it is needless to add that his sympathy with other sufferers was such as became an exquisitely sensitive nature. Neither would he admit that he overlooked the enormous mass of evil in the world. His view is characteristic. His own position as an invalid, with 'the circle of impotence closing very slowly but quite steadily round him,' makes him indignant with the affectation of the rich and strong 'bleating about their sorrows and the burthen of life.' In a world so full of evil 'one dank and dispirited word' is harmful, and it is the business of art to present gay and bright pictures which may send the reader on his way rejoicing. Then, ingeniously turning the tables, he argues that Mr. Archer's acceptance of pessimism shows him to be a happy man, 'raging at the misery of others.' Had his critic tried for himself 'what unhappiness was like,' he would have found how much compensation it contains. He admits the correctness of one of Mr. Archer's remarks, that he has 'a voluntary aversion from the painful sides of life.' On the voyage to the leper settlement at Molokai he speaks of the Zola view of the human animal; and upon reaching the place sees 'sights that cannot be told and hears stories that cannot be repeated.' M. Zola would have managed perhaps to tell and repeat. Stevenson is sickened by the spectacle but 'touched to the heart by the sight of lovely and effective virtues in the helpless.' The background of the loathsome is there; but he would rather dwell upon the moral beauty relieved against it.

Stevenson might certainly claim that his optimism did not imply want of experience or want of sympathy. And, indeed, one is inclined to ask why the question should be raised at all. A man must be a very determined pessimist if he thinks it wrong for an artist to express moods of cheerfulness or the simple joy of eventful living. We may surely be allowed to be sometimes in high spirits. It would require some courage to infer from *Treasure Island* that the author held any philosophy. Stevenson, of course, was not a philosopher in such a sense as would have entitled him to succeed to the chair of Sir William Hamilton at Edinburgh. Yet it is true that he had some very strong and very characteristic convictions upon the questions in which philosophy touches the conduct of life. The early difficulties, the abandonment of the regular professional careers, the revolt against the yoke of the lesser catechism, the sentence to a life of invalidism enforced much reflection, some results of which are embodied in various essays. A curious indication of the progress of thought is given in his account of

the 'books which influenced him.' It is a strangely miscellaneous list. He begins with Shakespeare, Dumas, and Bunyan; then comes Montaigne, always a favourite; next, 'in order of time,' the Gospel according to St. Matthew; and then Walt Whitman. By an odd transition (as he observes elsewhere) Walt Whitman's influence blends with that of Mr. Herbert Spencer. 'I should be much of a hound,' he says, 'if I lost my gratitude to Herbert Spencer.' Next comes Lewes's *Life of Goethe*—though there is no one whom he 'less admires than Goethe.' Martial, Marcus Aurelius, Wordsworth, and Mr. George Meredith's *Egoist* follow, and he notes that an essay of Hazlitt 'on the spirit of obligation' formed a 'turning-point in his life.' One would have been glad of a comment upon the last, for the essay is one in which Hazlitt shows his most cynical side, and explains how frequently envy and selfishness are concealed under a pretence of conferring obligations. Stevenson, perhaps, took it as he took Mr. Meredith's novel, for an ethical lecture, revealing the Protean forms of egoism more or less common to us all.

Stevenson clearly was not one of the young gentlemen who get up a subject systematically. He read as chance and curiosity dictated. A new author did not help him to fill up gaps in a theory, but became a personal friend, throwing out pregnant hints and suggesting rapid glances from various points of view into different aspects of life. Each writer in turn carried on a lively and suggestive conversation with him; but he cares little for putting their remarks into the framework of an abstract theory. He does not profess to form any judgment of Mr. Spencer's system; he is content to find him 'bracing, manly, and honest.' He feels the ethical stimulant. He is attracted by all writers whose words have the ring of genuine first-hand conviction; who reveal their own souls—with a good many defects, it may be, but at least bring one into contact with a bit of real unsophisticated human nature. He can forgive Walt Whitman's want of form, and rejoice in the 'barbaric yawp' which utterly rejects and denounces effete conventionalism. What he hates above all is the Pharisee. 'Respectability,' he says in *Lay Morals*, is 'the deadliest gag and wet blanket that can be laid on man.' He is, that is to say, a Bohemian; but he is a Bohemian who is tempered for good, or (as some critics would say) for bad, by morality and the lesser catechism. He sympathises with Whitman's combination of egoism and altruism. 'Morality has been ceremoniously extruded at the door (by Whitman) only to be brought in again by the window.' So Stevenson's Bohemianism only modifies without obliterating his moral prejudices. Scotsman as he was to the verge of fanaticism, he refused to shut his eyes to the coarser elements in the national idol. The *Lay Morals* is specially concerned with the danger of debasing the moral currency. In spirit the Christian principles are absolutely right; but as soon as they are converted into an outward law, the spirit tends to be superseded by the letter, and the hypocrite finds a convenient shelter under the formula which has parted company from the true purpose. An interesting bit of autobiography is made to illustrate the point. 'Thou shalt not steal,' he says, is a good rule; but what is stealing? Something is to be said for the communist theory that property is theft. While his father was supporting him at the University, where he was surrounded by fellow students whose lives were cramped by poverty, he considered that his allowance could be excusable only when regarded as a loan advanced by mankind. He lived as sparingly as he could, grudged himself all but necessaries, and hoped that in time he might repay the debt by his services.

No very definite conclusion was to emerge from such speculation. Stevenson was to become a novelist, not a writer of systematic treatises upon ethics or sociology. The impulses, however, survived in various forms. They are shown, for example, in the striking essay called 'Pulvis et Umbra.' It is his answer to the pessimistic view of men considered as merely multiplying and struggling units. Everywhere we find that man has yet aspirations and imperfect virtues. 'Of all earth's meteors,' he says, 'here, at least, is the most strange and consoling; that this ennobled lemur, this hair-crowned bubble of the dust, this inheritor of a few years and sorrows, should yet deny himself his rare delights and add to his frequent pains and live for an ideal, however misconceived.' This view implies his sympathy with the publican as against the Pharisee. We should cherish whatever aspirations may exist, even in the pot-house or the brothel, instead of simply enforcing conformity to the law. We should like the outcast because he is, after all, the really virtuous person. To teach a man blindly to obey public opinion is to 'discredit in his eyes the one authoritative voice of his own soul. He may be a docile citizen; he will never be a man.' The sanctity of the individual in this sense explains, perhaps, what was the teaching in which Walt Whitman and Mr. Herbert Spencer seemed to him to coincide.

The 'philosophy' is the man. It is the development of the old boyish sentiment. Disease and trouble might do their worst; the career of the 'pirate,' or even more creditable forms of the adventurous, might be impracticable; but at least he could meet life gallantly, find inexhaustible interest even in trifling occupations when thrown upon his back by ill-health, and cheer himself against temptations to pessimistic melancholy by sympathy with every human being who showed a touch of the heroic spirit. His essay upon the old 'Admirals' is characteristic. His heart goes out to Nelson, with his 'peerage or Westminster Abbey,' and even more to the four marines of the 'Wager,' abandoned of necessity to a certain death, but who yet, as they watched their comrades pulling away, gave three cheers and cried, 'God bless the King!' In 'Æs Triplex' he gives the same moral with a closer application to himself:

It is best [he says] to begin your folio; even if the doctor does not give you a year, even if he hesitates about a month, make one brave push, see what can be finished in a week. . . . All who have meant good work with their whole heart have done good work, although they may die before they have the time to sign it . . . Life goes down with a better grace foaming in full tide over a precipice, than miserably struggling to an end in sandy deltas.

That, he explains, is the true meaning of the saying about those whom the gods love. At whatever age death may come, the man who dies so dies young.

This gallant spirit, combined with extraordinarily quick and vivid sympathy, gives, I think, a main secret of the charm which endeared Stevenson both to friends and readers. His writings showed anything but the insensibility to human sorrows of the jovial, full-blooded athlete. It must be admitted, however, that if he did not ignore the darker side of things, he disliked dwelling upon it or admitting the necessity of surrender to melancholy, or even to incorporating sad thoughts in your general view of life. In some of his early work, especially in 'Ordered South,' his first published essay, and in 'Will o' the Mill,' a different note of sentiment is sounded. The invalid ordered south is inclined to console himself by reflecting that he is 'one too many in the world.' This, says Stevenson in a later note, is a 'very youthful view.' As prolonged life brings more interests, the thought that we cannot play out our part becomes more, not less, painful. To some of us, I fear, every year that we live only emphasises our insignificance. To Stevenson such resignation savoured of cowardice. 'Will o' the Mill' is certainly one of his most finished and exquisite pieces of work. He told Mr. Balfour that it was written as an 'experiment.' His own favourite doctrine was that 'acts may be forgiven, but not even God can forgive the hanger back.' 'Will o' the Mill' was written 'to see what could be said in support of the opposite theory.' The essay suggests the influence of Hawthorne and shows a similar skill in symbolising a certain mood. It implies, no doubt, a capacity for so far assuming the mood as to make it harmonious or self-consistent; but I cannot perceive that it makes it attractive. Translated into vulgar realism, Will would be a stout innkeeper, who will not risk solid comfort by marrying the girl whom he likes. He hardly loves her. He prefers to help his guests to empty his cellar. Will lives in so vague a region that we do not detest him as we should in real life; but, after all, the story affects me less as an apology than as a satire. If that be really all that can be said for the prudential view of life, it is surely as contemptible as Stevenson thought the corresponding practice. He has a little grudge against Matthew Arnold, whose general merits he acknowledges, for having introduced him to Obermann, for in Obermann he finds only 'inhumanity.' The contrast is shown, as Professor Raleigh points out, by Arnold's poem on the 'Grande Chartreuse' and Stevenson's 'Our Lady of the Snows.' Arnold is tempted for the time to seek peace among the recluses, though he cannot share their belief. Stevenson treats them to a sharp remonstrance. He prefers to be 'up and doing.' He warns them that the Lord takes delight in deeds, and approves those who—

Still with laughter, song and shout,
Spin the great wheel of earth about.

'Perhaps,' he concludes,

Our cheerful general on high
With careless look may pass you by.

If I had to accept either estimate as complete, I should agree with Stevenson. Yet Stevenson's attitude shows his limitations. The sentiment which makes men ascetic monks; the conviction of the corruption of mankind; of the futility of all worldly pleasures; the renunciation of the active duties of life; and the resolute trampling upon the flesh as the deadly enemy of the spirit, may strike us as cowardly and immoral, or at best representing Milton's 'fugitive and cloistered virtue.' Still it is a mood which has been so conspicuous in many periods that it is clearly desirable to recognise whatever appeal it contained to the deeper instincts of humanity. Matthew Arnold recurred fondly but provisionally to the peacefulness and harmony of the old order of conception, though he was as convinced as any one that it rested on a decayed foundation. The enlightenment of the species is, of course, desirable, and may lead ultimately to a more satisfactory solution; but for the moment its destructive and materialising tendencies justify a tender treatment of the survival of the old ideal. Stevenson was no bigot, and could most cordially admire the Catholic spirit as embodied in the heroism of a Father Damien. But when it took this form of simple renunciation it did not appeal to him. In fact, it corresponds to the kind of pessimism which was radically uncongenial. Life, for him, is, or can be made, essentially bright and full of interest. He agrees with Mr. Herbert Spencer that it is a duty to be happy; and to be happy not by crushing your instincts but by finding employment for them. Confined to his bed and sentenced to silence, he could still preserve his old boyishness; even his childish amusements. 'We grown people,' he says in an essay, 'can tell ourselves a story, give and take strokes till the bucklers ring, ride far and fast, marry, fall, and die; all the while sitting quietly by the fire or lying prone in bed'—whereas a child must have a toy sword or fight with a bit of furniture. Indeed, he was not above toys in later days. He spent a large part of one winter, as Mr. Balfour tells us, building with toy bricks; and, beginning to join in a schoolboy's amusement of tin soldiers, developed an elaborate 'war game' which occupied many hours at Davos. We can understand why Symonds called him 'sprite.' The amazing vitality which kept him going under the most depressing influences was combined with the 'sprite's' capricious, and, to most adults, unintelligible modes of spending superfluous energy. Whatever he took up, serious or trifling, novel writing, childish toys, or even, for a time, political agitation, he threw his whole soul into it as if it were the sole object of existence. He impressed one at first sight as a man whose nerves were always in a state of over-tension. Baxter says that Cromwell was a man 'of such a vivacity, hilarity, and alacrity as another man hath when he hath drunken a cup too much.'[1] Stevenson—not very like Cromwell in other respects—seemed to find excitement a necessity of existence. He speaks to a correspondent of the timidity of youth. 'I was,' he says, 'a particularly brave boy'—ready to plunge into rash adventures, but 'in fear of that strange blind machinery in which I stood. I fear life still,' he adds, and 'that terror for an adventurer like myself is one of the chief joys of living.' Terror keeps one wide awake and highly strung. Inextinguishable playfulness, with extraordinary quickness of sympathy; an impulsiveness which means accessibility to every generous and heroic nature; and a brave heart in a feeble body, ought to be, as they are, most fascinating qualities. But it is true that they imply a limitation. So versatile a nature, glancing off at every contact, absorbed for the moment by every impulse, has not much time for listening to the 'Cherub Contemplation.' Stevenson turns from 'the painful aspects of life,' not from the cowardice which refuses to look evils in the face, but from the courage which manages to treat them as a counter-irritant. His 'view of life,' he says, 'is essentially the comic and the romantically comic.' He loves, as he explains, the comedy 'which keeps the beauty and touches the terrors of life'; which tells its story 'not with the one eye of pity but with the two of pity and mirth.' We should arrange our little drama so that, without ignoring the tragic element, the net outcome may be a state of mind in which the terror becomes, as danger became to Nelson, a source of joyous excitement.

What I have so far said has more direct application to the essayist than to the novelist; and to most readers, I suppose, the novelist is the more interesting of the two. As an essayist, however, Stevenson becomes an unconscious critic of the stories. The essays define the point of view adopted by the story-teller. One quality is common to all his writings. The irrepressible youthfulness must be remembered, to do justice to the essays. We must not ask for deep thought employed upon long experience; or expect to be impressed, as we are impressed in reading Bacon, by aphorisms in which the wisdom of a lifetime seems to be concentrated. We admire the quick feeling, the dexterity and nimbleness of intellect. The thought of 'Crabbed Age and Youth' is obvious enough, but the performance reminds us of Robin Oig in *Kidnapped*. Robin repeated the air played by Alan Breck, but 'with such ingenuity and sentiment, with so odd a fancy and so quick a knack in the grace-notes that I was amazed to hear him.' Stevenson's 'grace-notes' give fresh charm to the old theme. The critical essays, again, may not imply a very wide knowledge of literature or familiarity with orthodox standards of judgment. They more than atone for any such defects by the freshness and the genuine ring of youthful enthusiasm. I am hopelessly unable, for example, to appreciate Walt Whitman. Stevenson himself only regretted that he had qualified his enthusiasm by noticing too pointedly some of his author's shortcomings. The shortcomings still stick in my throat; but if I cannot catch the enthusiasm, my dulness is so far enlightened that I can partly understand why Whitman fascinated Stevenson and other good judges. That, at least, is so much clear gain. To read Stevenson's criticisms is like revisiting a familiar country with a young traveller who sees it for the first time. He probably makes some remarks that we have heard before; but he is capable of such a thrill of surprise as Keats received from Chapman's *Homer*.

The 'love of youth,' says Mr. Henry James in an admirable essay, 'is the beginning and end of Stevenson's message.' Mr. James was writing before Stevenson's last publications, and was thinking specially, perhaps, of *Treasure Island*. Now to me, I confess, for I fear that it is a confession, *Treasure Island* is the one story which I can admire without the least qualification or reserve. The aim may not be the highest, but it is attained with the most thorough success. It may be described as a 'message' in the sense that it appeals to the boyish element. Stevenson has described the fit of inspiration in which he wrote it. He had a schoolboy for audience; his father became a schoolboy to collaborate; and when published it made schoolboys of Gladstone and of the editor of the 'cynical' *Saturday Review*. We believe in it as we believe in *Robinson Crusoe*. My only trouble is that I have always thought that, had I been in command of the *Hispaniola*, I should have adopted a different line of defence against the conspirators. My plan would have spoilt the story, but I regret the error as I regret certain real blunders which were supposed to have changed the course of history. I have always wondered that, after such a proof of his powers of fascination, Stevenson should only have achieved full recognition by *Dr. Jekyll and Mr. Hyde*. That book, we are told, was also written in a fit of inspiration, suggested by dreaming a 'fine bogey tale.' The public liked it because it became an allegory—a circumstance, I fear, which does not attract me. But considered as a 'bogey tale,' able to revive the old thrill of delicious horror in one who does not care for psychical research, it has the same power of carrying one away by its imaginative intensity. These masterpieces in their own way suggest one remark. Mr. Balfour points out that Stevenson did an enormous quantity of work, considering not only his ill-health, but the fact that he often worked very slowly, that he destroyed many sketches, and that he rewrote some articles as often as seven or eight times. Thanks to his 'dire industry,' as he said himself, he had 'done more with smaller gifts' (one must excuse the modest formula), 'than almost any man of letters in the world.' This restless energy, however, did not mean persistent labour upon one task; but a constant alternation of tasks. When inspiration failed him for one book, he took up another, and waited for the fit to return. One result is that there is often a want of continuity, when his stories do not, as in *Treasure Island*, represent a single uninterrupted effort. *Kidnapped*, for example, is made up of two different stories, and *The Wrecker* is a curious example of piecing together heterogeneous fragments. Moreover, a good deal of the work is the product of a feebler exercise of the fancy intercalated between the general fits of inspiration. The undeniably successful books, where he has thrown himself thoroughly into the spirit of the story, stand out among a good deal of very inferior merit. I will confine myself to speaking of the four Scottish novels which appear to be accepted as his best achievements, and to endeavouring to point out what was the proper sphere of his genius.

They represent a development of the *Treasure Island* method. He began *Kidnapped* as another book for boys, and the later stories may be classed for some purposes with the Waverley series. Stevenson was fond of discussing the classification of novels. He contrasts the 'novel of adventure,' the novel of character, and the dramatic novel. Properly speaking, this is not a classification of radically different species, but an indication of the different sources of interest upon which a novelist may draw. 'Adventure' need not exclude 'character.' A perfect novel might accept, with a change of name, Mr. Meredith's title *The Ordeal of Richard Feverel*. The facts are interesting, because they show character in the crucible; and the character displays itself most forcibly by the resulting action. A complete fusion, however, is no doubt rare, and requires consummate art. *Treasure Island*, of course, is a pure novel of adventure. It satisfies what he somewhere describes as the criterion of a good 'romance.' The writer and his readers throw themselves into the events, enjoy the thrilling excitement, and do not bother themselves with questions of psychology. *Treasure Island*, indeed, contains Silver, who, to my mind, is his most successful hero. But Silver incarnates the spirit in which the book is to be read; the state of mind in which we accept genial good humour as a complete apology for cold-blooded murder. Piracy is for the time to be merely one side of the game; and in a serious picture of human life, which of course is out of that sphere, we should have required a further attempt to reconcile us to the psychological monstrosity. In the later stories we assume that the adventurers are to be themselves interesting as well as the adventure. Still, the story is to hold the front place. We may come to be attracted to the problems of character presented by the author, but the development of the story must never for a moment be sacrificed to expositions of the sentiments. We must not expect from Stevenson such reflections as Thackeray indulges upon the 'Vanity of Vanities' or a revelation, such as George Eliot gives in *The Mill on the Floss*, of the inner life of the heroine. Either method may be right for its own purpose; and I mean so far only to define, not to criticise, Stevenson's purpose. Not only is it possible to tell a story in Stevenson's manner, 'cutting off the flesh off the bones' of his stories, as he says, and yet to reveal the characters; but critics who object to all intrusions of the author as commentator hold this to be the most legitimate and effective method of revelation. Here, however, the limitation means something more than a difference of method. I do not think, to speak frankly, that any novelist of power comparable to his has created so few living and attractive characters. Mr. Sidney Colvin confesses to having been for a time blinded to the imaginative force of *The Ebb Tide* by his dislike to the three wretched heroes. One is deservedly shot, and the two others, credited with some redeeming points, lose whatever interest they possessed when they accept conversion to avoid death from a missionary's revolver. However vivid the scenery, I cannot follow the fate of such wretches with a pretence of sympathy. There is a similar drawback about *The Master of Ballantrae*. The younger brother, who is blackmailed by the utterly reprobate Master, ought surely to be interesting instead of being simply sullen and dogged. In the later adventures, we are invited to forgive him on the ground that his brain has been affected; but the impression upon me is that he is sacrificed throughout to the interests of the story. He is cramped in character because a man of any real strength would have broken the meshes upon which the adventure depends. The curious exclusion of women is natural in the purely boyish stories, since to a boy woman is simply an incumbrance upon reasonable modes of life. When in

'Catriona' Stevenson introduces a love-story, it is still unsatisfactory because David Balfour is so much of the undeveloped animal, that his passion is clumsy, and his charm for the girl unintelligible. I cannot feel, to say the truth, that in any of these stories I am really living among human beings with whom, apart from their adventures, I can feel any very lively affection or antipathy. Mr. Balfour praises Stevenson for his sparing use of the pathetic. That is to apologise for a weakness on the ground that it is not the opposite weakness. It is quite true that an excessive use of pathos is offensive, but it is equally true that a power of appealing to our sympathies by genuine pathos is a mark of the highest power in fiction. The novelist has to make us feel that it is a necessity, not a mere luxury; that he is forced to weep, not weeping to exhibit his sensibility; but to omit it altogether is to abnegate one of his chief functions. That Stevenson's feelings, far from being cold, were abnormally keen, can be doubted by no one; but his view of fiction keeps him out of the regions in which pathos is appropriate. Any way, I feel that there is a whole range of sentiment familiar to other writers which Stevenson rarely enters or even touches.

The character to which I am generally referred as a masterpiece is that of Alan Breck. Mr. Henry James speaks of that excellent Highlander as a psychological triumph, and regards him as a study of the passion for glory. Mr. James speaks with authority; and I will admit that he is a very skilful combination of the hero and the braggart—qualities which are sometimes combined, as they were to some degree in Nelson and Wolfe. Somehow, perhaps because I am not a Gael, I can never feel that he is fully alive. He suggests to me the artist's study, not the man who appeals to us because his creator has really thrown himself unreservedly into the part. When I compare him, for example, with Dugald Dalgetty (I must venture a comparison for once) he seems to illustrate the difference between skilful construction and genial intuition. He may suggest one other point. Scott was for Stevenson the 'King of the Romanticists.' Romance, as understood by Scott, meant among other things the attempt to revive a picture of old social conditions. He was interested, in his own phraseology, in the contrast between ancient and modern manners, and his favourite periods are those in which the feudal ideals came into conflict with the more modern commercial state. This interest often interferes with his art as a storyteller. The hero of Waverley, for example, is a mere walking letter of introduction to Fergus MacIvor, the type of a chief of a clan modified by modern civilisation. The story halts in order to give us a full portrait of the state of things in which a semi-barbarous order was confronted with the opposing forces. Scott, in fact, began from a profound interest in the social phenomena (to use a big word) around him. He was full of the legends, the relics of the old customs and ways of thought, but was also a lawyer and a keen politician. His story-telling often represents a subordinate aim. Stevenson just reverses the process. He started as an 'artist,' abnormally sensitive to the qualities of style and literary effect to which Scott was audaciously indifferent. His first interest is in any scene or story which will fit in with his artistic purposes. Life swarmed with themes for romance, as rivers are made to supply canals. The attitude is illustrated by his incursions into politics. He was stirred to wrath by Mr. Gladstone's desertion (as he thought it) of Gordon, and could not afterwards write a letter to the guilty statesman because he would have had to sign himself 'Your fellow-criminal in the sight of God.' He was roused by the boycotting of the Curtin family to such a degree that he could scarcely be withheld from settling on their farm to share their dangers and stir his countrymen to a sense of shame. His righteous indignation in the case of Father Damien, and the zeal with which he threw himself into the Samoan troubles, are equally in character. The small scale of the Samoan business made it a personal question. He came to the conclusion, however, that politics meant 'the darkest, most foolish, and most random of human employments,' and, though he had an aversion to Gladstone, had no definite political creed. Political strife, that is, only touched him when some individual case appealed to the chivalrous sentiment. In the same way the story of the clans interests him by its artistic capabilities. The flight of Alan Breck gave an opportunity, seized with admirable skill, for a narrative of exciting adventure; and he takes full advantage of picturesque figures in the history of his time. But one peculiarity is significant. The adventure turns upon a murder which, according to him, was not committed, though certainly not disapproved, by Alan Breck. Now, complicity in murder, or, let us say, homicide, is a circumstance of some importance. Before landlord-shooting is regarded as a venial or a commendable practice, we ought to be placed at the right point of view to appreciate it. We cannot take it as easily as Mr. Silver took piracy. We should see enough of the evictions or of the social state of the clansmen to direct our sympathies. No doubt if Stevenson had insisted upon such things, he would have written a different book. He would have had to digress from the adventures and to introduce characters irrelevant in that sense, who might have been types of the classes of a semi-civilised society. Perhaps the pure story of adventure is a better thing. I only say that it involves the omission of a great many aspects of life which have been the main preoccupation of novelists of a different class. Stevenson once told Mr. Balfour that a novelist might devise a plot and find characters to suit, or he might reverse the process; or finally, he might take a certain atmosphere and get 'both persons and actions to express it.' He wrote *The Merry Men* as embodying the sentiment caused by a sight of a Scottish island. That, indeed, is an explanation of some of his most skilful pieces of work, and the South Seas as well as his beloved country gave materials for such 'impressionist' pictures. But besides the atmosphere of scenery, there is what may be called the social atmosphere. To reproduce the social atmosphere of a past epoch is the aim—generally missed—of the historical novelist; but it is the prerogative of the more thoughtful novelist to set before you, in concrete types, not only personal character but the moral and intellectual idiosyncrasies of the epoch, whether remote or contemporary. The novelist is not to lecture; but the great novels give the very age and body of the time 'its form and feature.' I will give no instances because they would be superfluous and also because they would suggest a comparison which I would rather exclude as misleading. That is the element which is absent from Stevenson's work.

The affection which Stevenson inspires needs no justification. The man's extraordinary gallantry, his tenderheartedness, the chivalrous interest so easily roused by any touch of heroism, the generosity shown in his hearty appreciation of possible rivals, are beyond praise. His rapid glances at many aspects of life show real insight and singular delicacy, a sensibility of moral instinct, and the thought is expressed or gently indicated with the most admirable literary tact. The praise of versatility again is justified by the variety of themes which he has touched, always with vivacity and often with a masterly handling within certain limits. When panegyrics, dwelling upon these topics, have been most unreservedly accepted, it is a mistake to claim incompatible merits. The 'Bohemian'—taking Stevenson's version of the character—the man who looks from the outside upon the ordinary humdrum citizen, may be a very fascinating personage; but he really lacks something. Delighted with the exceptional and the picturesque, he has less insight into the more ordinary and, after all, most important springs of action. The excitable temperament, trying to stir every moment of life with some thrill of vivid feeling, and dreaming adventures to fill up every interstice of active occupation, is hardly compatible with much reflection. The writer, whose writing is the outcome of long experience, who has brooded long and patiently over the problems of life, who has tried to understand the character of his fellows and to form tenable ideals for himself, may not have accepted any systematic philosophy; but he represents the impression made by life upon a thoughtful mind, and has formed some sort of coherent and often professedly interesting judgment upon its merits. He is sometimes a bore, it is true; but sometimes, too, we have experience which is ripe without being mouldy. The rapid, vivid 'Sprite,' the natural Bohemian impinging upon society at a dozen different parts, turning from the painful aspects of life, and from the first considering life as intended to suggest romance rather than romance as reflecting life, could not possibly secrete that kind of wisdom. He had a charm of his own, and I do not inquire whether it was better or worse; I only think that we do him injustice when we claim merits belonging to a different order. His admirers hold that *Weir of Hermiston* would have shown profounder insight founded upon longer experience. I will not argue the point. That it contains one very powerful scene is undeniable. That it shows power of rivalling on their own ground the great novelists who have moved in a higher sphere is not plain to me. At any rate, the claim seems to be a tacit admission of the absence of certain qualities from the previous work. 'He might have,' implies 'he did not.' But I have said enough to indicate what I take to be the right method of appreciating Stevenson without making untenable claims.

Notes

1. A similar remark was made about Ninon de l'Enclos. They make a queer trio.

JOHN RUSKIN

JOHN RUSKIN

1819–1900

John Ruskin was born in London on February 8, 1819, the son of a rich wine merchant. He was largely educated at home, and traveled frequently with his parents in Britain and on the Continent. He attended Christ Church, Oxford, between 1837 and 1841, and in 1840, on his twenty-first birthday, began receiving an allowance of £200 a year; upon his father's death in 1864 he became independently wealthy.

Having already contributed poems, stories, critical essays, and nature studies to a variety of periodicals, and having also studied drawing, Ruskin in 1843 anonymously published the first volume of his critical work *Modern Painters*, to which a second volume was added in 1846, a third and fourth in 1856, and a fifth in 1860. In 1848 Ruskin married Euphemia Gray, who divorced him in 1854 on the grounds of impotence and soon afterwards married the painter John Everett Millais. During the years of his marriage to "Effie" Ruskin published two works on architecture, *The Seven Lamps of Architecture* (1849) and *The Stones of Venice* (3 vols., 1851–53); his fairy tale *The King of the Golden River* (1850), originally written for "Effie" in 1841; and his pamphlet *Pre-Raphaelitism* (1851), in which he defended Millais and William Holman Hunt.

In 1853 Ruskin delivered his first public lectures, published the next year as *Lectures on Architecture and Painting*. He taught at the Working Men's College in London during 1854, and in 1855 began an annual series of *Notes on the Royal Academy* (1855–59, 1875), in which he championed the Pre-Raphaelites. *The Political Economy of Art* and *The Two Paths*, published in 1857 and 1859 respectively, were collections of lectures that signaled an increasing interest in socioeconomic questions. The attack on established economic theory that was sketchily developed in these lectures did not assume definite form until 1860, when Ruskin published in *Cornhill Magazine* four essays on political economy, appearing in book form as *"Unto This Last"* in 1862. In place of a capitalist society based on competition and self-interest, Ruskin postulated a return to an age of heroic feudalism dominated by Christian social values.

This utopian vision was developed over the years in a series of books that made Ruskin a widely known and influential social philosopher. These books, mostly based on lectures, include *Sesame and Lilies* (1865), on education; *The Ethics of the Dust* (1866), on crystallography and other subjects; *The Crown of Wild Olive* (1866), also on education; *Time and Tide* (1867), a series of letters on economics addressed to a workman; *The Queen of the Air* (1869), on Greek myth; and a series of volumes collecting lectures delivered at Oxford, where Ruskin became Slade Professor of Fine Art in 1869, including *Aratra Pentelici* (1872), *The Eagle's Nest* (1872), *Love's Meinie* (1873), and *Ariadne Florentina* (1873–76). In 1871 Ruskin inaugurated monthly "Letters to the Workmen and Labourers of Great Britain," collectively titled *Fors Clavigera*, which he continued with interruptions until 1884. In 1878 he founded a utopian society, the Guild of St. George.

Ruskin resigned his professorship in 1879 after many senior members of the university expressed their distaste for certain of his opinions. In 1881 he suffered the first attack of the mental instability that was to incapacitate him in later life; this instability was characterized in part by an obsession with Rose La Touche, a much younger woman to whom he had unsuccessfully proposed marriage before her death in 1875. Ruskin was reappointed Slade Professor at Oxford in 1883 but resigned again in 1885, having given even more offense than before. In 1885 he published the first volume of his never-completed autobiography, *Praeterita* (2 vols., 1885–89). Ruskin made a last tour of the Continent in 1888, and from 1889 until the end of his life, his mental condition having deteriorated completely, he lived at Brantwood, where he was under the care of Joan and Arthur Severn. Ruskin died on January 20, 1900.

Personal

You constantly hear a great many people saying I am very bad, and perhaps you have been yourself disposed lately to think me very good. I am neither the one nor the other. I am very self-indulgent, very proud, very obstinate, and *very* resentful; on the other side, I am very upright—nearly as just as I suppose it is possible for man to be in this world—exceedingly fond of making people happy, and devotedly reverent to all true mental or moral power. I never betrayed a trust—never wilfully did an unkind thing—and never, in little or large matters, depreciated another that I might raise myself. I believe I once had affections as warm as most people; but partly from evil chance, and partly from foolish misplacing of them, they have got tumbled down and broken to pieces. It is a very great, in the long-run the greatest, misfortune of my life that, on the whole, my relations, cousins and so forth, are persons with whom I can have no sympathy, and that circumstances have always somehow or another kept me out of the way of the people of whom I could have made friends. So that I have no friendships, and no loves.

Now you know the best and worst of me; and you may rely upon it it is the truth. If you hear people say I am utterly hard and cold, depend upon it it is untrue. Though I have no friendships and no loves, I cannot read the epitaph of the Spartans at Thermopylæ with a steady voice to the end; and there is an old glove in one of my drawers that has lain there these eighteen years, which is worth something to me yet. If, on the other hand, you ever feel disposed to think me particularly good, you will be just as wrong as most people are on the other side. My pleasures are in seeing, thinking, reading, and making people happy (if I can, consistently with my own comfort). And I *take* these pleasures. And I suppose, if my pleasures were in smoking, betting, dicing, and giving pain, I should take *those* pleasures. It seems to me that one man is made one way, and one another—the measure of effort and self-denial can never be known, except by each conscience to itself. Mine is small enough.

But, besides taking pleasure thus where I happen to find it, I have a theory of life which it seems to me impossible as a rational being to be altogether without—namely, that we are all sent into the world to be of such use to each other as we can, and also that my particular use is likely to be in the things that I know something about—that is to say, in matters connected with painting.—JOHN RUSKIN, Letter to Dante Gabriel Rossetti (c. April 1855), *Ruskin: Rossetti: Preraphaelitism*, ed. William Michael Rossetti, 1899, pp. 71–73

On Sunday night I dined with Monckton Milnes, and met all the advanced liberals in religion and politics ⟨. . .⟩ Froude ⟨. . .⟩ was there, and Browning, and Ruskin; the latter and I had some talk, but I should never like him.—MATTHEW ARNOLD, Letter to His Mother (June 16, 1863)

As I recall my first welcome, I recall too the face and figure of the man who tendered it. But it was the manner that first attracted and arrested attention. In no other man have I seen sweetness, gentleness, genial frankness, and sympathetic cordiality so perfectly allied with virility and activity of mind. His look inspired confidence, just as his hand-grip awoke friendship—a magic quality, it has often been remarked, that he shares in equal degree with his political *bête noire*, Mr. Gladstone. His smile is sweet and tender, and his whole bearing instinct with kindness, courtesy, and good fellowship. But it is his eyes that pin you—bright, clear, frank blue eyes that look you through and through, and make you wonder—eyes so pure and truthful that they seem to disarm at once all disingenuousness, but keenly intelligent, notwithstanding, and full of fun; the eyes, in short, that the novelists tell us "dance" upon occasion. Their strong blue—of the intensity of an Italian sky—for all that in these latest years they are to be seen through the screen of the bushy, overhanging eyebrows, is echoed in the satin stock-tie, of the same hue which he has worn for half a century or more.

There he stands, erect though bent; for the chronic stoop, the result of a feeble spine in early manhood, hardly prevents him from holding himself upright, though it has reduced his height from that of a tall to that of a medium-sized man, and set his head well down between his shoulders. More often than not he wears a dark blue frockcoat, and trousers and double-breasted waistcoat of good homespun tweed, woven by his own St. George's Guild—a manufacture which has taken firm root in England among the village industries, but which has not exactly flooded the market, because the quality is (to the trade) so exasperatingly good that the linens and cloths will not wear out. But although through the slightness of his build his weight is reduced to little if any more than ten stone of humanity, such is the brilliancy of his conversation—or, on occasion, may be, the polite significance of his "brilliant flashes of silence"—that nothing remains in the memory of his friends but a commanding, magnetic personality whose merry smile

and sympathetic gaze have removed all sense of size or of comparative diminutiveness.

Thus he is when he is the host: his ample iron-gray locks, long and silky, combed back, but falling rebelliously about his temples; and his beard, well-trimmed for a time after he began to grow it in 1881, but now long and partriarchal, dropping within his waistcoat, or; when he is in bed, picturesquely flowing down the dressing-gown in a stately sweep. It was that beard, by the way, which he admits, with his charmingly confessed tenderness about his appearance, he thought made him look "the least bit nice;" but which, he declared, made him "come out like an ourang-outang" in his photographs. And nothing could be more vivacious than his conversation, partly through his enormous range of information and experience, partly through his command of language and expression, and partly, too, through his keen and rapid intelligence and striking originality of thought; so that I have often noticed how impossible it is to tell—unless he chose to let you know—whether he was giving you his first hasty impression of the subject under discussion, or whether that was his firm opinion, formed long ago, and petrified by time. His sentences—need I say?—are fluent in the highest degree, but saved from being mellifluous by a certain Carlylean ruggedness or occasional archaism, which together form that delightful compound known by the world as Ruskinese. A slight intonation in the voice, an inability to pronounce the letter "r" otherwise than as a guttural, strike one at first as strongly individual; but the sensation is soon lost in listening to the words, which in point of choice and handling—especially in respect to the humor that Ruskin has a strange genius for twisting out of them—and in point of range of vocabulary, excite the surprise and admiration of the listener, and puzzle him to determine by what he is most dazzled, the words, or the ideas which they clothe. But touch upon a tender subject, and you will find the Ruskin militant flare out at once, just as it did in his younger years when he turned upon the yapping critics at his heels, and emptied upon them the vials of his wrath and scathing invective, which have few, if any, parallels in the language. —M. H. SPIELMANN, "John Ruskin at Home," *McClure's Magazine*, March 1894, pp. 316–17

We had been expecting his release from the frail 'body of this death' any time in the past three or four years. The Master whose fire and fervour and restless energy of brain and tireless hand had done the work of three men for St. George and Merrie England, had been all this while sitting at Brantwood, as it were, with folded hands, waiting, with calm serenity, for his angel friend. And very kindly and with tenderness of approach had Death at last come.

A little touch of feverish cold, a retiring to his bed for a single day, and then a sinking into that "golden slumber" spoken of in the song whose music last fell upon his willing ears; and then his eyes, with their memory of St. Gothard as Turner saw it, still undimmed, closed, and he went beyond the pass that is so cold, and sometimes so full of storm and pain, into the land of life and peace and endless spring.

Almost it would seem as if the heavens built their gates of gold and opened doors of glory for his bright spirit's welcoming. The day had been a day of cloud and storm. The hills, purple black, had stood in gloom above a leaden lake, when, on Friday, January 19, 1900, the call came. Ruskin sank to rest, and sudden radiance seemed showered out of heaven. A great light lay upon the water-flood, cloud-bastions of fire reared themselves above the hills, and such splendour fell on Coniston and Wetherlam and the russet crags of Tilberthwaite and Yewdale that the shepherd stared and the yeoman wondered, and the mourners took it for a sign. On Saturday, the 20th of January, within a few weeks of fulfilling the eighty-first year—for John Ruskin was born on the 8th of February, 1819—the laborious life of art criticism, of thought for the helping of the world, of high ideals, of noble philosophy, of impassioned utterance, of continual benevolence, was laid down without a sigh.—H. D. RAWNSLEY, *Ruskin and the English Lakes*, 1901, pp. 189–90

⟨. . .⟩ apart from questions of art, he always remains to me one of the largest and noblest of all the men I have known, liberal and generous beyond limit, with a fineness of sympathy in certain directions and delicacy of organization quite womanly. Nothing could shake my admiration for his moral character or abate my reverence for him as a humanist. That art should have been anything more than a side interest with him, and that he should have thrown the whole energy of his most energetic nature into the reforming of it, was a misfortune to him and to the world, but especially to me.—WILLIAM JAMES STILLMAN, *The Autobiography of a Journalist*, 1901, Vol. 1, p. 320

General

I don't know whether you look out for Ruskin's books whenever they appear. His little book on the *Political Economy of Art* contains some magnificent passages, mixed up with stupendous specimens of arrogant absurdity on some economical points. But I venerate him as one of the great Teachers of the day his absurdities on practical points do no harm, but the grand doctrines of truth and sincerity in art, and the nobleness and solemnity of our human life, which he teaches with the inspiration of a Hebrew prophet, must be stirring up young minds in a promising way. Mr. Lewes has been enjoying a week's holiday at Vernon Hill, and was very pleased to find Alice Helps the eldest daughter there, a girl of seventeen, become an enthusiastic student of painting under Ruskin, and stoutly battling against the falsity that paints what the painter does not see. The two last volumes of *Modern Painters* contain, I think, some of the finest writing of this age. He is strongly akin to the sublimest part of Wordsworth, whom, by the bye, we are reading now with fresh admiration for his beauties and tolerance for his faults.—GEORGE ELIOT, Letter to Sara Sophia Hennell (Jan. 17, 1858)

May I get Ruskin's late volumes of *Modern Painters* from Mr Langford? I have got the *Life of Turner*, but I believe the last of these volumes is much occupied with that strange, shabby divinity. I suppose it does not much matter in choosing a god what sort of creature it is you choose, as persistent worship seems always to gain a certain amount of credit for the object of it.—MARGARET OLIPHANT, Letter to William Blackwood (Nov. 4, 1861), *Autobiography and Letters*, ed. Mrs. Harry Coghill, 1899, p. 180

His faults are not many, but we may mention them. He preaches a kind of Communism, which, although practised by the Apostles and early Christians, was in no way commanded, and which nowhere, except in Utopian Cloud Land, could exist beneficially. He believes too much in worldly prosperity *for the mass*, while he rightly tells us how miserably evil it is to almost all individuals. He talks very proudly and cruelly of those who, like us, have "dared to insolently preach contentment to a man with thirty shillings a-week;" and he is hasty in his denunciations of follies which arise from education, from a long peace and prosperity, and from the cowardice of our preachers and our writers for many years, and from the selfishness of the ministries of all parties, who have given all the honours and rewards to rich men, and have therefore made riches the only incentive. But Ruskin has a very noble heart, and one that is very tender, too; is most nobly eloquent, and will be listened to; he sympathises with poverty and ignorance, but is tempestuously moved at vice and folly, forgetting that they are the saddest phases of poverty and ignorance. He raises up a warning voice at a time when change has come upon us, and tells us to go back to the old times of earnestness, of trade guilds, of honour, obedience, reverence; of industry and work in each man; "every youth in the State, from the King's son downwards, should learn to do something finely and thoroughly,"—not forward to mere wallowing in wealth, and corrupting, selfish ease. And Ruskin must be listened to; or else, so surely as we allow thousands to starve in ignorance and want, to fester in slothful ease, to plot and plan selfish murders, to die starving and helpless while we are full of meat and wine, to go on in the wretched ignorant way we allow our lowest classes to do, we shall pass away as Persia and Greece and Rome have passed away, with more guilt to ourselves and less excuse. "Take unto yourselves heed," says Joshua, "that ye love the Lord your God; else if ye do in any wise go back, know for a certainty that the Lord your God will no more drive out any of these nations before you; but they shall be snares and traps unto you, and scourges in your sides, and thorns in your eyes, until ye perish from off this good land which the Lord your God hath given you." These, simply, are the ethics of John Ruskin, even the ethics of the Bible. Let us be just, and fear not; let us follow this great teacher; but alas! how can we be just, when out of one thousand children in Manchester, barely four hundred can read, and the rest are ignorant, and know not good from evil?—J. HAIN FRISWELL, "The Ethics of Ruskin," *Modern Men of Letters Honestly Criticised*, 1870, pp. 115–16

⟨. . .⟩ quite alone stands Ruskin, whose writing is art, and whose art is unworthy his writing. To him and his example do we owe the outrage of proffered assistance from the unscientific—the meddling of the immodest—the intrusion of the garrulous. Art, that for ages has hewn its own history in marble, and written its own comments on canvas, shall it suddenly stand still, and stammer, and wait for wisdom from the passer-by?—for guidance from the hand that holds neither brush nor chisel? Out upon the shallow conceit! What greater sarcasm can Mr. Ruskin pass upon himself than that he preaches to young men what he cannot perform! Why, unsatisfied with his own conscious power, should he choose to become the type of incompetence by talking for forty years of what he has never done!

Let him resign his present professorship, to fill the chair of Ethics at the university. As master of English literature, he has a right to his laurels, while, as the populariser of pictures he remains the Peter Parley of painting.—JAMES MCNEILL WHISTLER (1878), *The Gentle Art of Making Enemies*, 1890, pp. 33–34

It is inevitable that any one who now undertakes to form a candid opinion of what comes from Mr. Ruskin's pen should approach the subject in a spirit quite different from what Mr. Ruskin would think fair or right. When he began to write, notwithstanding the hostility with which he met, he had certain advantages on his side in the condition of criticism itself which were sure in the long run to tell in his favor. It was an epoch when, for a variety of reasons, the literary faculty as such counted for more than it does now; and Mr. Ruskin has always possessed what some of his imitators would call a very precious literary faculty. The early part of this century was distinguished by the appearance on the scene of a number of men gifted with a marked facility and power of expression, the nature of whose influence upon their contemporaries we now find it often difficult to understand. To take but two examples, Carlyle and Emerson: both exerted in their prime an influence which bears no comparison with any moral literary force that we can now discover in any quarter, and yet it is impossible for us to conceive of their exerting the same influence now, were they to begin their work over again, upon anybody. We do not speak of Emerson's poetry nor of Carlyle's historical pictures—for these alone are to be judged by purely literary standards—but of the didactic writing by which they gained and fixed public attention. Why was it that their teaching so aroused and moved their contemporaries, while it so often leaves us cold and puzzled? It must have been in some measure because with the public of their day the possession of the power of expression carried a much greater *auctoritas* with it, apart from the value of the matter expressed, than it would now. The progress of positive methods of thought has in the last fifty years done a great deal to produce a change. When Mr. Ruskin began to write, the mere fact that he could write vigorous and impressive and poetic English would have been of itself almost enough to equip him as an art critic; and if he subsequently fell into the mistake of supposing that he was by the same fact qualified to instruct the public in military science, railroads, strikes, wages, arbitration, cooperation, or anything else that happened to attract his attention for the moment, his experience of the public gave him a sort of right to assume that it would continue to listen.

Of course his equipment as an art critic consisted of a great deal more than his literary faculty, and he did so much for the development of sound artistic taste in England that the world owes him a profound debt of gratitude; but so far as his public was concerned, they were from the moment he had secured their ear completely under the influence of his power of expression, and they followed him blindly wherever he led, regardless of logical consequences. This has produced, too, upon him the same effect that it has had upon many other reformers. In the first instance meeting with violent opposition, and having after a stout struggle succeeded in silencing his enemies and obtaining a following of disciples, he seems to have come to the conclusion that opposition is a kind of test of truth, and that his holding unpopular opinions on any subject is a proof that they are probably correct. ⟨. . .⟩

Mr. Ruskin has unquestionably greatly weakened his influence even as an art-critic by his extraordinary excursions during the last ten or fifteen years into non-æsthetic fields. Nobody who feels the force and beauty and moral elevation of much of his writing can help regretting that the fatal gift of expression should have misled him into attempting to deal with subjects with which he is totally unfamiliar.—ARTHUR GEORGE SEDGWICK, "Ruskin's *Arrows of the Chace*," *Nation*, Sept. 15, 1881, pp. 220–21

To speak in a few words of the manifold lessons on art, and life, and national polity which Mr Ruskin has given to his countrymen may appear less becoming than to be silent; but in truth the cardinal doctrine which runs through all his teaching can be stated in a line. It is that men—men and not the works of men, men and not materials, or machines, or gold, or even pictures, or statues, or public buildings—should be the prime objects of our care, and reverence, and love. Hence it is that, as a writer on art, he necessarily becomes a moralist, since he must needs inquire from what human faculties does this work

of art arise, and to what human faculties does it appeal? Hence it is that in the decline of architecture or painting he reads the degradation of national character. Hence it is that the life of the workman appears to him to be of higher importance than the quantity of work which he turns out. Hence it is that he has opposed himself to the orthodox political economy, with a sense that man, and the life and soul of man, cannot be legitimately set aside while we consider apart from these the laws of wealth or of so-called utility. No other truth can be quite so important for our own age, or for any age, as the truth preached so unceasingly and so impressively by Mr Ruskin. —EDWARD DOWDEN, "Victorian Literature," *Transcripts and Studies*, 1888, p. 233

As a teacher ⟨. . .⟩ Mr. Ruskin is to be accepted with reservations. Persons who regard him as an oracle are likely to derive more harm than benefit, not only by reason of the surrender they make of their own self-reliance and judgment, but because, under guidance so erratic, they are pretty sure to "fall into bewilderment." Critical discernment is, as I have said, peculiarly neccessary in this case. When it is exercised, good may, or rather must, come. Mr. Ruskin as a master is a mistake. Mr. Ruskin as a man of noble instinct, of deep wisdom and deeper insight, whose words have the force, not of laws, but of valuable suggestions, becomes a good "friend and aider of those who would live in the spirit." His very weaknesses—his fussiness, fickleness, and vanity—when they take their right relation, give a certain grace to the service he renders. No longer an autocratic leader, often stumbling and misleading, but a friend and brother, greater than ourselves, his words, taken for what they are worth, are often found to be worth very much. We need not admire his random talk about "eggs of vermin, embryos of apes, and other idols of genesis enthroned in Mr. Darwin's or Mr. Huxley's shrines," or fall into raptures over his disquisitions on goose-pie, or deny that he is insolent when he speaks of John Stuart Mill and Herbert Spencer as "geese."—WALTER LEWIN, *Academy*, Feb. 21, 1891, p. 177

Has all Mr. Ruskin's criticism of life ⟨. . .⟩ really failed, as he frequently says it has, to influence the action of his age? He says men read and praise his books, but do not obey them; women do him homage, but do not join his Society of St. George. That is true; and if nothing will satisfy him but such visible obedience and such adhesion to his personally conducted Society, he may well go to his grave broken-hearted. Society will never be changed by being filtered through private institutions: it must modify its own; and that can never be done save slowly, and will never be done wisely and consciously save on a wide knowledge and a comprehensive plan. But such plan and knowledge necessarily exclude the sway of egoism; and the teacher who cherishes the poor ambition to rule over a society of disciples who call him master, rather than the pure ambition of seeing men increasingly able to be their own masters, so as to make feudal masterhood as impossible as it is barbarous— such a teacher is doomed to end in bitterness, unless his ideal narrows with his powers. He has lost what vestige of rational significance lay under the theistic formula of resignation to the will of God. For him there can be no comfort save in the realisation of his own will; and the will of the egoist is, in the terms of the case, as narrow as his own life. Doubtless every reformer is so, primarily, because it is essential to his peace of mind to see things go in a certain direction. But let him beware how he makes his predilection narrower than the possibilities; or how he sets his heart on more than the necessary conditions of forward movement. Let him carefully think out these and strive for them, and let him cheerfully leave the rest to the unmeasured instinct and aspiration of mankind. So will he best have his part in them. To aspire to play Confucius for Europe, and to fix an eternal order in the light of certain ancient and dead orders, is to sink philanthropy in egoism; and he who would not see Europe ape Cathay, must rejoice that his fellows refuse to be hypnotised by their prophets.

Now, it lies on the face of all Ruskin's work, that in him an intense egoism is the condition of his eloquence and energy. At times, certainly, it seems to disappear, in homage to some one of his masters, Carlyle or another; but even then he identifies his prejudice with theirs, and never does he long abide in the attitude of impersonal concern for simple truth. In all his polemic, even at its best and justest, is visible his normal inability to conceive, or even suspect, how any life or opinion can be right or good which clashes with his tastes and convictions. He lays down binding principles for the regulation of all life in terms of his sentiments for the time being. Professing at times a transcendental reverence for women, he lays down the lines on which they are to live and think, and this in the very act of denouncing the masculine notion that men ought to think for women. Men must not, but Mr. Ruskin may. And the law laid down varies according as Mr. Ruskin happens last to have been stimulated. One day it is that women are to govern the house: "The woman's power is for rule, . . . and her intellect is not for invention or creation, but for sweet ordering, arrangement, and decision." Another day, things are different. "You fancy, perhaps, as you have been told so often, that a wife's rule should only be over her husband's house, not over his mind. Ah, no! the true rule is just the reverse of that; a true wife, in her husband's house, is his servant; it is in his heart that she is queen." Mind here appears to be identical with heart. But in the other book we had been told this: "Speaking broadly, a man ought to know any language or science he learns, thoroughly—while a woman ought to know the same language, or science, only in so far as may enable her to sympathise in her husband's pleasures, and in those of his best friends." Then follows some sophistry about the difference between limited knowledge and superficial knowledge: the woman is to know "with exquisite accuracy so far as she reaches," which means, I suppose, that she is to know the Greek alphabet, or the conjugations, with exquisite accuracy, in order to sympathise with her husband's views on corrupt passages in Æschylus; and to know a botany primer with exquisite accuracy, in order to share in discussions on the relations of fossil flora. To these sentimental follies the answer lies ready in Mill: it is a gross presumption on the part of any man, nay, on the part of any woman, to lay down what is forever to be done, and what not to be done, by all women. Who are you, forsooth, that the human race is to live by your directions? And if your directions, moreover, are admittedly always changing, who can be sure that any one of them is ever right for anybody?

Ruskin is, so far as my reading goes, the most self-contradictory writer who ever lived. He stultifies himself as vehemently as Carlyle, and for the same fundamental reason, that he is just a talking temperament; but he meddles with far more matters than Carlyle did, and dogmatises proportionally. In his art criticism he has a first principle for every day of the year and every hour of the day: pictures and practices are for ever being praised or blamed under general laws set up for that occasion only. At one time he will denounce as unworthy all writing for money: at another he will present as model lives those of Shakspere and Scott, who systematically wrote to make money. In the earlier *Lectures on Art* he lays it down that the

highest subject for the artist is the human face and figure: in a later lecture he pooh-poohs figure-painting as being within the reach of anybody, and sets up landscape as the really difficult and noble work. But he contradicts himself in the same book and sometimes in the same chapter, sometimes in the same page.

One result of his temper is that his criticism of individuals are often outrageously unjust. He forbids Harriet Martineau's books to the pupils who surrender to him their docile judgments, "not because she is an infidel"—he admits Voltaire freely because "his voice is mighty among the ages"—"but because she is a vulgar and foolish one." Yet he goes on to admit that some of her writing in *Deerbrook* is entirely admirable; and he proceeds thus to excuse his abuse:—

> I use the word vulgar here in its first(!) sense of egoism, not of selfishness, but of not seeing one's own relations to the universe. Miss Martineau plans a book, afterwards popular, and goes to breakfast, "not knowing what a great thing had been done." So Mr. Buckle dying, thinks only—he shall not finish *his* book. Not at all whether God will ever make up *His.*

The memory of Harriet Martineau, who, whatever might be his natural exultations over her successes, was one of the sanest of writers in her self-estimate, will survive such an attack, from a man whose notions of his "own relation to the universe" have reached heights of extravagance seldom attained in black-on-white. But the attack on Buckle calls for a warmer reprobation. Had I read it without knowing its author, without knowing it was made by a mouthpiece of passionate caprice, I should have been disposed to call it the most meanly ungenerous impeachment I ever saw in secular literature. And the most malignant of priests, one would think, would have scrupled so to handle the pathetic cry of the dying scholar who left his work undone.

It all comes of lack of patience and lack of care for consistency, which two lacks are correlative to the prophetic temper of overweening self-confidence and the self-worship which poses as Theism. The worst of it all is that the genius seems to be correlative with the unwisdom; that the man has his eloquence and his dazzling flashes of insight on condition of a prophetic fury which will not stay to reconsider; that the command of language rests on an over-balance of that faculty, which keeps him chronically at the mercy of verbal allurements, leading him into those etymological mysticisms over which Arnold shrugged his shoulders; and that the burning moral earnestness is bound up with the primitive habit of theosophy which he acquired at his mother's knee, so keeping him to the last a possessed Scripturalist, turning to the old Hebrew literature, genuine and forged, for principles of present conduct, as Cromwell's pikemen did. With such an all-round lack of security for good judgment, no child of impulse can miss giving men occasional stones for bread and occasional poison for medicine. At times Ruskin seems to have triumphed over the darker human passions, and to have attained to hating war and judicial murder; but anon he warms with the old evil fires, and presents you with an execrable homily on the nobleness of true war as a means of deciding which is the best man—save the mark!—which has "the strongest arm and the steadiest heart," as if these meant the best heart or the wisest head; and again you will have pæans to the hangman that might have made Carlyle feel his occupation gone.—JOHN M. ROBERTSON, "John Ruskin," *Modern Humanists*, 1891, pp. 206–10

Ruskin is one of the most turbid and fallacious minds, and one of the most powerful masters of style, of the present century. To the service of the most wildly eccentric thoughts he brings the acerbity of a bigot and the deep sentiment of Morel's 'emotionalists.' His mental temperament is that of the first Spanish Grand Inquisitors. He is a Torquemada of æsthetics. He would liefest burn alive the critic who disagrees with him, or the dull Philistine who passes by works of art without a feeling of devout awe. Since, however, stakes do not stand within his reach, he can at least rave and rage in word, and annihilate the heretic figuratively by abuse and cursing. To his ungovernable irascibility he unites a great knowledge of all the minutiæ in the history of art. If he writes of the shapes of clouds he reproduces the clouds in seventy or eighty existing pictures, scattered amongst all the collections of Europe. And be it noted that he did this in the forties, when photographs of the masterpieces of art, which render the comparative study of them to-day so convenient, were yet unknown. This heaping up of fact, this toilsome erudition, made him conqueror of the English intellect, and explains the powerful influence which he obtained over artistic sentiment and the theoretic views concerning the beautiful of the Anglo-Saxon world. The clear positivism of the Englishman demands exact data, measures, and figures. Supplied with these he is content, and does not criticise starting-points. The Englishman accepts a fit of delirium if it appears with footnotes, and is conquered by an absurdity if it is accompanied by diagrams. Milton's description of hell and its inhabitants is as detailed and conscientious as that of a land-surveyor or a natural philosopher, and Bunyan depicts the *Pilgrim's Progress* to the mystical kingdom of Redemption in the method of the most graphic writer of travels—a Captain Cook or a Burton. Ruskin has in the highest conceivable degree this English peculiarity of exactness applied to the nonsensical, and of its measuring and counting applied to fevered visions.—MAX NORDAU, *Degeneration*, 1895, pp. 77–78

The sources of Mr Ruskin's peculiarities, both in merit and defect, appear to me to have lain as usual in his nature, and to have been developed as usual by his education. This latter (as in the case of that other eccentric Camberwell man, Mr Browning) was of a home-keeping and haphazard kind, very different from the usual up-bringing of well-to-do middle-class youth in England. It is true that Mr Ruskin, unlike Mr Browning, went to a University, though, like him, he went to no school; and his comparative chastity of form may be partly ascribed to this frequentation of the Muses. But Christ Church, which does not like to be called a "college" at all, is even now probably the college of both Universities in which the University and, strictly speaking, collegiate influences are weakest; while for a gentleman-commoner in Mr Ruskin's time they were weaker still. The shaping, moulding, training influence of the ordinary English liberal education has been abused as well as lauded, and I suppose that it may to a certain extent and in certain cases act as a cramp and a restraint; but it certainly acts in a far greater number as a beneficial discipline. Discipline is what Mr Ruskin has always lacked; as well in methods of expression as in the serene self-confidence which has enabled him to deliver himself on any and every subject, without any suspicion that he is talking ill-informed nonsense. Discipline Oxford did not give, had indeed no full opportunity of giving, to Mr Ruskin; but she gave him, there can be no doubt, additional inspiration. She nourished in him that passion for architecture which no single city in the United Kingdom is so richly dowered with the means of exciting and

gratifying; and she, no doubt, also strengthened in him the general Romantic tendency of which he is so characteristic an exponent.

For the other part of the matter it has long ago seemed to me—I do not know that I have seen it noticed or suggested by anybody else—that the central peculiarity of Mr Ruskin is a singular and almost unparalleled union of two main characteristics, one of which is usually thought of as specially French, the other as specially English. The first is an irresistible and all-pervading tendency to generalise,—to bring things under what, at any rate, seems a law, to erect schemes, and deduce, and connect. The other is the unconquerably ethical tone of all his speculations. To follow out the ramifications of this strangely crossed nature of his would take a very great deal of space, and would partake more of the style of abstract criticism than would perhaps be suitable to this book and plan. But one or two applications and corollaries of what has just been said may be indicated.

Thus it may be pointed out that Mr Ruskin's extraordinary insensibility to the ludicrous hangs on to both the un-English and the English sides of his intellectual temperament. His mania for generalising blinds him to the absurd on the one side, as we constantly find it doing in Continental thinkers; his insatiable appetite for moral applications, and his firm belief in his moral mission blind him, as we find these things do often in Britons. When Mr Ruskin says that a square leaf on any tree would be ugly, being a violation of the law of growth in trees, we feel at once that we are in the company of an intellectual kinsman of the learned persons whom Molière satirised. He deprecates expenditure on plate and jewels (while admitting that "noble art may occasionally exist in these") because they are matters of ostentation, a temptation to the dishonest, and so on,—a moral paralogism which would be almost impossible to any one not of British blood.

But I must leave this key to Mr Ruskin in the hands of the ingenious reader, who will find it do a great deal of unlocking. A man with an ardent sense of duty combined with an ardent desire to do good; eager to throw everything into the form of a general law, but eager also to give that general law, directly or indirectly, mystically or simply, an ethical bearing and interpretation; extremely fond of throwing his discourse into an apparently argumentative form, but probably more prone than any man of equal talents who has lived during this century to logical fallacies and illicit processes of every kind,—grasp the man as this, and the works will cease to be a puzzle or an irritation, because the reason of them will at once be plain.

And it would be a very great pity, indeed, if the Book of Ruskin were to remain to any one merely a closed book, as irritation or as puzzle. For, if these curious volumes are taken with a due amount of rational salt, they cannot fail to enlarge and exercise the tastes and powers of the reader; while, if read simply for enjoyment, they will be found to contain the very finest prose (without exception and beyond comparison) which has been written in English during the last half of the nineteenth century. The great merit of this prose is that it is never, as most of the ornate prose styles of a more recent day are, affected and unnatural. Great pains have been spent on the writing of English prose during the last twenty years—greater, I think, than had been taken for several generations. But the result has almost always had (to my taste at least) something too much of the lamp—a too constant reminder that here the gentleman did take great pains, that he turned the sentence this way and that to convey an air of distinction, that he picked his words so as to give them, if not quite a new meaning and collocation, at any rate a collocation and meaning as different as possible from that which they had usually had. One thinks far too often of the story of Paul de Saint-Victor (a real artist, too) scattering single words about a paper, and then filling in and writing up to them. Our latter-day prose of this kind is sometimes eloquent, but it is rarely elegant; it is sometimes splendid, but it is seldom or never at ease; it is often quaint and rare in embellishment, but it is seldom or never unconscious of its dress.

Now, Mr Ruskin's purple patches—despite a rather too great tendency to run not merely into definitely rhythmical, but into definitely metrical forms—are never laboured, they never suggest effort, strain, or trick. He warms to them naturally, he turns them out without taking his coat off. They are to be found, it is true, mainly, though by no means wholly, in his earlier books. The practice of alternately chatting and scolding, to which he unfortunately betook himself some five-and-twenty years ago, is not favourable to the production of fine English, unless the writer can rise to the level of a real *sæva indignatio*. This Mr Ruskin can seldom do; and, as has been already noted, his weaknesses never betray themselves so much as when he is talking of what he does not like.

But in his early days of enthusiasm he was often magnificent—no lesser word will do. It was some time before I could bring myself (well knowing what the comparative result would be) to compare the second of the two recent volumes of selections, which cover his whole work, with the early and now precious volume which was published in 1861, and which was perforce confined to the greater and earlier books—the *Modern Painters*, the *Stones of Venice*, the *Seven Lamps*, the *Lectures on Architecture and Painting*, and a very few others. In this older volume you will, no doubt, find the crochet and the waywardness, the paralogism and the undue preaching, not, as he once put it, of "the connection between art and human passion" (which is perfectly true and important), but of that between art and its influence on the life of the artist (which is chiefly not to the point). But you will also find far more frequently than later—indeed, in this volume on almost every page—a phrasing so admirable, a selection of imagery so fertile and felicitous as to compel admiration, even if the matter, instead of being almost always noble (if not always quite sane), were purely wrong-headed or purely unimportant. For more than forty years artists in flamboyant prose have been writing after and after the famous description of the Falls of Schaffhausen in *Modern Painters*. Mr Swinburne, in his *Blake*, once very nearly, if not quite, equalled it; all the rest are nowhere. The *Stones of Venice* is crammed with similar passages; in fact, it is *the* book of descriptive prose in English, and all others toil after it in vain.

For happier expressions of crotchety fancy, where shall we look than in the rather numerous passages where Mr Ruskin sets forth his favourite craze that bright colours are virtuous, dark and neutral tints wicked? The thing is false, it is almost silly; but it is so charmingly put that you chuckle at once with keen pleasure and mild scorn. Also, the man can observe, which is the most uncommon of all gifts. The fault of our modern impressionists lies in just this—that the artist seems to think he must empty out of his representation everything but the mere individual impression itself, so that he does not really give what he sees, or what anybody sees, but what is or might be seen with an arbitrary subtraction of allowance for the seer's presumed idiosyncrasy. This is as bad as the most slavish convention or the most exaggerated personal crotchet. Now, Mr Ruskin certainly does not minimise the personal element; yet he can, when he chooses, keep it to its lowest terms.

But I am outrunning my limits. To sum up the impression

side of the matter,—when I was young, Mr Ruskin's crotchets used to irritate me more than they ought; they now irritate me hardly at all, and only bore me a little. But I think I like his beauties more than ever; and I am disposed to think, also, that he has brought more folk to art than he has ever bitten with his own heresies about it.—GEORGE SAINTSBURY, "Mr Ruskin," *Corrected Impressions*, 1895

If the student rejects for the moment, as of secondary or even tertiary importance, all that Mr. Ruskin has written for the last forty years, and confines his attention to those solid achievements, the first three volumes of *Modern Painters*, the *Stones of Venice*, and the *Seven Lamps of Architecture*, he will find himself in presence of a virtuoso whose dexterity in the mechanical part of prose style has never been exceeded. The methods which he adopted almost in childhood—he was a finished writer by 1837—were composite; he began by mingling with the romantic freshness of Scott qualities derived from the poets and the painters, "vialfuls, as it were, of Wordsworth's reverence, Shelley's sensitiveness, Turner's accuracy." Later on, to these he added technical elements, combining with the music of the English Bible the reckless richness of the seventeenth-century divines perhaps, but most certainly and fatally the eccentric force of Carlyle. If, however, this olla-podrida of divergent mannerisms goes to make up the style of Ruskin, that style itself is one of the most definite and characteristic possible.

What it was which Mr. Ruskin gave to the world under the pomp and procession of his effulgent style, it is, perhaps, too early yet for us to realise. But it is plain that he was the greatest phenomenal teacher of the age; that, dowered with unsurpassed delicacy and swiftness of observation, and with a mind singularly unfettered by convention, the book of the physical world lay open before him as it had lain before no previous poet or painter, and that he could not cease from the ecstasy of sharing with the public his wonder and his joy in its revelations. It will, perhaps, ultimately be discovered that his elaborate, but often whimsical and sometimes even incoherent disquisitions on art resolve themselves into this—the rapture of a man who sees, on clouds alike and on canvases, in a flower or in a missal, visions of illuminating beauty, which he has the unparalleled accomplishment of being able instantly and effectively to translate into words.

The happy life being that in which illusion is most prevalent, and Mr. Ruskin's enthusiasm having fired more minds to the instinctive quest of beauty than that of any other man who ever lived, we are guilty of no exaggeration if we hail him as one of the first of benefactors. Yet his intellectual nature was from the start imperfect, his sympathies always violent and paradoxical; there were whole areas of life from which he was excluded; and nothing but the splendour and fulness of his golden trumpets concealed the fact that some important instruments were lacking to his orchestra. It is as a purely descriptive writer that he has always been seen at his best, and here he is distinguished from exotic rivals—at home he has had none—by the vivid moral excitement that dances, an incessant sheet-lightning, over the background of each gorgeous passage. In this effect of the metaphysical temperament, Mr. Ruskin is sharply differentiated from Continental masters of description and art initiation—from Fromentin, for instance, with whom he may be instructively contrasted.—EDMUND GOSSE, *A Short History of Modern English Literature*, 1897, pp. 356–58

As to the lack of form in Mr. Ruskin's style, there is likely to be far more dispute. Let it be said at once that his style has countless felicities. At times it carries one away with it. You forget any notions you may have about the essential character-istics of prose, or recall them only to feel yourself a pedant. It is when he is speaking of nature especially that this is true, as I have implied—when "the waves of everlasting green roll silently into their long inlets under the shadows of the pines." You doubt if Wordsworth's poetry has surpassed such expres-sion of the power of nature over the emotions. And there is a great deal of it in Ruskin. But its first effect past, the old notions about prose recur, as they do after reading Jeremy Taylor or Elizabethan prose. You feel there is something lacking, some element tending to repose, to sanity. Such a force as is applied by the reserve of poetic form, reducing to calmer movement and severer outline the tumultuous cadences in which Mr. Ruskin's emotional genius riots, would be of advantage, perhaps, even in such a splendid passage as that whose closing lines I have quoted. Even outbursts of impassioned eloquence, when they merely or mainly express emotion, gain in elevation and permanent charm through the element of artistic restraint. But there is no room for doubt that the positive need of this is illustrated by the mass of Mr. Ruskin's rhapsodical writing. His exuberance is very often absolutely savage and meaningless. It is pure feeling exhaled in the worst possible taste. Take, among a multitude of examples, the once admired passage describing the piazza and church of St. Mark. It is perfectly unscrupulous in its rhetorical devices, and thoroughly puerile in its cheap tropicality. Mr. Ruskin would infallibly and correctly describe such a passage in another writer as "cockney." It is because his great defect is excess of emotion, and because emotion in one way or another is nearly his only source of strength, and because poetical form is almost sure to counteract excess, that English literature has perhaps lost from Mr. Ruskin's exclusive devotion to prose. To the preponderance of his emotional over his intellectual side, at all events, are justly attributable the two great defects which imperil his position as an English classic, namely, the lack of substance in his matter and the lack of form in his style.—W. C. BROWNELL, "John Ruskin," *Scribner's Magazine*, April 1900, pp. 505–6

At the bottom of what Mr. Ruskin did was the main trouble of teaching not art, but Mr. Ruskin; a perfectly fair thing, as a practical teaching, if Mr. Ruskin had been a practical artist. For then he would have been checked continually by the natural development of his pupil in some one method, which would have had to take its place in the world, as one of many methods; for studying carefully one method in our art, so as to prevail in it, is sure to connect with some other method.

But also there was with him, and there still is with many minds like his, a certainty that everything can be divided into wrong and right, and that the processes of the Last Judgment can always be applied by us finite beings.

Besides this instinct or tendency of fallen man, the mistake has perhaps an honorable origin in a confusion of ideas; as far as I can remember Mr. Ruskin's confused statements, some notion that the end of art was truth.

Through the many beautiful and absurd inquiries, state-ments, and declarations of Mr. Ruskin, it is possible to see a thread of influence; an impression produced upon a mind incapable of supposing itself in error,—a mind thoroughly respectable and middle-class,—the impression, perhaps, of his first teaching in art or in drawing; the teaching of the drawing-master, say of Harding of the Drawing Books, or any others. There is perpetually recurrent the notion that there is one excellent manner, in reality the very best, of drawing a tree or anything else with exterior touches, motions or twists of hand that may succeed in characterizing the said species of

tree, and make it evident as that kind of a tree to the person whose mind it is intended to influence, for his good we must suppose. And anything that cannot explain what will reach the mind of that person for whom the tree is supposed to be drawn, at first for one's drawing-teacher, then for one's family, then for the public or acquaintances, is wrong and vaguely criminal. Drawing or art received as a school lesson is continued as a lesson in his mind; it is to be used as a means of obtaining something; in his own mind,—a delicate and refined mind, though middle-class,—a means of obtaining good for others by instructing them in tree-trunks or in noble views. But in lower minds trained in exactly the same way, and believing in the same way, it is merely to so draw as to affect the public desire for trees, and thus get money or influence of some kind, by never doing the unexpected, the difficult to apprehend. All through what Mr. Ruskin has written or done he has dragged this chain of early error, an error quite legitimate at one time, born in the boy, who has to be told something and to be taught somehow or other, and with whose childish mind people often agree and reason in a childish manner, trusting that later he will see more clearly, and forget the explanation given to appease him.

This error Mr. Ruskin has ennobled as he has lived longer and seen more of greater things; he has asked of art to teach us as science does, and to uplift us as does religion or morality.

This error is, perhaps, the more general error at the foundation of Mr. Ruskin's thoughts and actions. It is what the French would call the *"thought behind the head," "la pensée de derrière la tête."* That is to say that there is a general turn that directs the action of men, which is too far back in their training, in their circumstances, in their heredity, to allow them to see themselves thinking; to go through that "exami-nation of conscience" which the religious person, anxious to be pure minded, has learned to apply to himself so as to clear his intentions. That is to say to test his sincerity. Even truth, if we can risk so large a statement, that is to say a truth or some truths, can be used insincerely. It is difficult to disentangle the lines of error in Mr. Ruskin's thoughts. The anxiety to hit hard, to assert himself and his views was so great that he has never been able, as I can remember, to state anything however true or valuable or noble, without some singular disturbing error. I say singular and disturbing because contrariwise to himself, I do not believe in the doctrine just quoted from his lectures that it is possible for us, even in art, to be perfect. No popes, no councils of the Church, have ever assumed the possible perfection of man,—in fact, I am troubled with having to deal with a foundation of moving sand, the foundation of Mr. Ruskin's proposition.

Art, the art of representation by images, of which he spoke and wrote, has not truth for its object any more than beauty, except in so far as truth and beauty, if we can isolate these by any chemistry of the mind, give us pleasure. What is sad, what is terrible, what is astonishing, what is commonplace, even what is ugly, are a part of the means used by art, which deals with *emotions*; and, therefore, art also uses grace, elegance, dignity for similar purposes.

And least of all can art teach, if by teaching we mean the orderly statement of facts for our improvement. If it teaches for our improvement, that is only incidental. It may teach us to see better because in art the eye is employed to discern certain things and to represent them, in so far as they belong to the unity of the work, but no further. To go beyond that and to prove or explain a matter of sight, by painting, let us say, or by sculpture, would be to destroy the artistic balance which resides in a relation of perfection, and not in the absolute perfection asked by Mr. Ruskin, which belongs, we suppose, to God alone. Incidentally, also, moral truths can be derived from plastic art as from any travel in the minds of men, and most especially in those cases when there has been no plotted attempt to teach, so that the mind and body, together affected by the work of art, are caught and addressed unawares. To give this moral impression, art has only lines and shapes and colors. In a rough way, it gives us the kind of impression that we get from the human face, which carries with it various impressions determining our judgment, our affection, our sense of physical pleasure, but about which we cannot reason absolutely unless we can suppose that, like God alone, we hold the entire soul and body of man in our hands. Hence art is a complement of science as it is also to a certain extent its opposite.

Moreover, to consider more largely the general views of Mr. Ruskin they are based on applications of ideas which he himself has, perhaps more than any one, condemned. They are in the modern shape not so far from the ideas of that *late Renaissance* which he hated. That was a moment in the history of art when as with Mr. Ruskin, teachers of art began to think that they could obtain every virtue and every quality in their work, by certain rules which would encourage certain things and eliminate a great many things. Thereby again, they limited what they meant to be comprehensive and their rules are not so far from what the direct pupils of Mr. Ruskin obtained in direct antagonism.

Man is quite as important as mountains and clouds, in the story of humanity, and the expression of his sentiment or feeling or appreciation of any kind, through art, is as surely a function of nature as the cataract or the snowflake. That Mr. Ruskin has invariably forgotten.

The absurdity of asking the artist to represent historical truth as if he had been a bystander, to ask that his representation of Moses, Elijah, David and Deborah, Gideon and Isaiah should be so correct that we know as we stand before them that such was absolutely the way they looked, destroys itself as being beyond the power of man. Even a collection of photographs of a man and a phonographic copy of his speech may be a collection of misapprehensions of his usual look and speech, and even they are influenced by the circumstances under which they were taken,—the kind of mind that chose those circumstances.

Mr. Ruskin admired rightly, I think, many of the earlier painters in their telling of stories; and in this we should certainly agree, even though they were extremely incorrect as to accuracies of history. Their real value is that these, more especially than later ones, were done by the entire man. They are not the results of analogies and investigations and cross-questionings, and historic doubts and higher criticisms and balance of theology and of sociology, as the later work which Mr. Ruskin's instinct disliked, but which his theory recommended. For in many ways, when he himself put aside his thinking and his investigations and whatever he was proud of, like the most of us, he was able to see straight in the work of art.—JOHN LA FARGE, "Ruskin, Art and Truth," *International Monthly*, Vol. 2 (1900), pp. 513–17

———

H. H. LANCASTER
From "The Writings of John Ruskin"
North British Review, February 1862, pp. 3–36

In England art has been unfortunate in its literature. Till Mr Ruskin wrote, most of our criticism was technical and external, dreary and unprofitable. The real principle whereby a picture should be judged—i.e., the quantity and quality of thought which it expresses—was rarely recognised. There were a few exceptions to this prevailing barrenness. Conspicuous among these, is a charming little book, now too seldom seen, called the *Picture Galleries of England*, by Hazlitt. Even there we may remark some defects,—arising perhaps from a limited range of observation, as, for instance, his insufficient estimate of Holbein; but, on the whole, there is more of the soul of criticism in these few pages than in any other work we know of, prior to the publication of *Modern Painters*. Not less admirable are two essays by Charles Lamb, on 'The Productions of Modern Art,' and 'The Genius and Character of Hogarth.' In Wilkie's letters there is the same strain of thinking; nor, when true art criticism is spoken of, should some old papers in *Frazer's Magazine* be forgotten, which bore the now well-known signature of Michael Angelo Titmarsh. What good can be said of the academicians' lectures—of Barry and the fluent Opie, with their worship of the Caracci—or of the fanciful Fuseli? It may be our own fault, but neither do we find ourselves much instructed by Sir Joshua Reynolds, either in his lectures, or in his special criticisms on the great pictures of the Continent. He is always sound, so far as he goes; he is generous and hearty in his estimates, seeing the best of everything; but, partly from his own habit of mind, partly because our modern analysis was a stranger to his age, he seems to have rested at the outward form—never to have penetrated to the soul of art. Later critics—too proud to learn of Ruskin—have not much improved matters. Kugler is declamatory, and restlessly inquisitive after hidden meanings; Waagen is hard, unenthusiastic, and technical.

Much may be said both for and against technicalities. It were mere folly to denounce them altogether; but after all their main value consists in this, that they conduce to brevity. They are a sort of formulæ; and, like all formulæ, can only be understood by the initiated. Therefore their use should be confined to occasions when the initiated alone are addressed; in all writing intended for the unprofessional public, they should be carefully avoided. Their place can easily be supplied by two or three additional words of plain English; and prolixity is better than obscurity. We may be uncharitable, but we suspect that the inveterate use of them arises from a desire to seem learned. Now we have the less patience with this folly, because art has suffered from it severely. People have been led to believe that in order, not to judge of a picture, but even to understand the principles by which a picture should be judged, it is necessary to 'get up' a whole vocabulary of hard words. Accordingly the public have turned away from the matter altogether, and have surrendered themselves up to guides too often unworthy. Since the days of Goldsmith, the art critic has been a good deal of a humbug: his trick, of course, being 'to say the painter might have done better had he done his best, and to praise the works of Pietro Perugino.' To this day, why are popular notices of pictures in our best papers expressed in a mysterious jargon? It is not so with their literary articles. In them ideas are conveyed in plain English; it is not thought necessary to obscure the meaning by hard grammatical terms. The public understand what is said, and are instructed by it.

Hence they are able to form literary judgments for themselves, and they have confidence in these judgments. But the public has little confidence in its judgments with regard to pictures. And, indeed, the less it has the better; because its judgments are formed upon no principle, and are utterly worthless. But what is the reason of this? Not, surely, that a picture is harder to understand than a book. No; but the reason is rather this, that the public have never been taught to comprehend painting, because for years and years almost all criticism on pictures has been so expressed as to be quite unintelligible. To understand pictures is not easy; to criticise them worthily, is very hard; but neither difficulty is simplified by all ideas regarding them being communicated in an unknown tongue. The first great excellence which we admire in Mr Ruskin, is his freedom from all this wretched affectation. He has written the most profound art criticism in the English language; and he has so written it, that any man of ordinary education can readily discern his meaning. This has not arisen from ignorance; on the contrary, here, as elsewhere, simplicity has flowed from knowledge. It certainly seems rather odd to notice, as a special merit in an author, the fact that he knows his subject. But the truth is, that with regard to this particular subject, such merit is by no means very common. It has been possessed by very few of the writers who are so fond of darkening what counsel they have by the use of long words. And, indeed, on any subject, knowledge such as Mr Ruskin's is rare. We may dispute the soundness of his judgments; but we cannot dispute the extent and the accuracy of his knowledge. He has seen, we believe, every great picture in Europe, and he has studied each one with as much minuteness as if he had never seen any other. And at the same time, with an avoidance of pedantry which deserves high praise, he has confined his minuter criticism, so far as was possible, to well-known pictures—more particulary to works in the Dulwich and National Galleries. His readers are, therefore, the better able to comprehend him, while at the same time they reap the benefit of his more extended experience. It is hardly necessary to say that such experience has not been gained without hard and constant labour. Writers who labour to depreciate Mr Ruskin should pause with reverence, if they have any reverence in them, before such a passage as the following:—

> The winter was spent mainly in trying to get at the mind of Titian; not a light winter's task; of which the issue, being in many ways very unexpected to me (the reader will find it partly told towards the close of this volume), necessitated my going in the spring to Berlin, to see Titian's portrait of Lavinia there, and to Dresden to see the Tribute Money, the elder Lavinia, and girl in white, with the flag fan. Another portrait, at Dresden, of a lady in a dress of rose and gold, by me unheard of before, and one of an admiral, at Munich, had like to have kept me in Germany all summer.—*Modern Painters*, vol. v., Preface, p. viii.

Surely such a simple, unaffected picture of conscientious work must command our respect. The reward has been that, on art, Mr Ruskin never speaks without authority. It is lamentable to think how many opinions he has expressed on other subjects, to the formation of which he has devoted no similar toil. ⟨. . .⟩

Yet Mr Ruskin's writing has faults, and serious ones. When we first noticed *Modern Painters*, we remarked 'a tendency to overdo, a certain redundance, an accumulation of words and images;' and we expressed a fear that these faults might go further. We are sorry to say that this fear proves to have been well founded. These faults have grown upon Mr Ruskin, and that to a very painful degree. The Highland scene which we quoted above is to be found in the fifth volume of *Modern Painters*; but, with few exceptions, all the finest specimens of his writing are to be gathered from his earlier works. Latterly, his redundancy has become tedious; the disproportion of his style to his subjects almost ludicrous. Formerly, his eloquence was called forth only by the wonders of art, or the stupendous effects of nature; now, it is poured forth profusely and indiscriminately on all things. He writes of every subject in the same grandiose strain. No one can read his rhapsodies at the beginning of the fifth volume, about the 'slow-fingered, constant-hearted lichens,' the 'sacrifices, gloriously sustained, of poor dying sprays,' and 'the gentle law of respect observed by the leaves of the aspen,' without a strong feeling of the grotesque coming over him. They are far worse than even Wordsworth's overpraised lines:

> To me the meanest flower that blows can give
> Thoughts that do often lie too deep for tears.

We refrain from quoting them, for it is no pleasure to laugh at a man like Mr Ruskin. But all this is very mischievous. There is more harm in it than any mere blemish in literary art. It is untrue. No man can live through the world concerning himself up to this pitch about lichens, and buds, and 'dying sprays.' He would become totally unfit for better duties if he did. Such exaggeration can only lead to unreality; and it leads Mr Ruskin into unreality many and many a time. His style gallops off with him into the merest verbiage and incoherence. Magnificent as is the language in the chapter 'On the Two Boyhoods,' it is very much sound and fury, signifying vastly little. Even in the description of Venice, at the beginning, the ideas are completely obscured by the glory of the words. Like Tarpeia, they are crushed beneath the weight of ornament. The ear is filled with sound; but no picture is presented to the mind. If the reader will contrast this passage with some of the descriptions in the earlier volumes,—as, for instance, with that of the Campagna, quoted above,—he will not fail, we think, to perceive the wide distinction between powerful representation and vague fine writing. And when we come to the following description of the world of Turner's boyhood, Cimmerian darkness falls upon us at least, utterly:—

> A goodly landscape this, for the lad to paint, and under a goodly light. Wide enough the light was, and clear; no more Salvator's lurid chasm on jagged horizon, nor Durer's spotted rest of sunny gleam on hedgerow and field; but light over all the world. Full shone now its awful globe, one pallid charnel-house,—a ball strewn bright with human ashes, glaring in poised sway beneath the sun, all blinding-white with death from pole to pole,—death, not of myriads of poor bodies only, but of will, and mercy, and conscience; death, not once inflicted on the flesh, but daily fastening on the spirit; death, not silent or patient, waiting his appointed hour, but voiceful, venomous; death with the taunting word, and burning grasp, and infixed sting.—*Modern Painters*, vol. v., p. 301.

Deep thinking and beautiful expression may, of course, be found even in volume v.; for when did Mr Ruskin write a whole volume without thinking deeply, and expressing his thoughts beautifully? But, for the most part, the thought is shallow and exaggerated, and the style detestable. We could select passage after passage, harsh and uncouth, in which Carlyle has been feebly echoed. Nay, a hint seems occasionally to have been borrowed from Alexander Dumas or Mrs Marsh; and short, ungainly sentences stand abruptly dotted over the page, trying to look emphatic. The whole thing is like an inflated and incoherent sermon. Such spasmodic writing, with the affected titles of the chapters, will, of course, be admired by the uneducated and the ignorant, but is quite unworthy of Mr Ruskin. In short, this unlucky volume reminds us of nothing so much as those Annuals, or 'Gift-Books,' in which beautiful engravings are accompanied, and made ridiculous, by the verses of Ladies of Quality.

We have hitherto been considering only Mr Ruskin's qualifications as an art critic. So far as we have gone, these have appeared of the highest order. But defects not a few have been urged against him; and foremost among all the charges has ever been the charge of dogmatism. Now, at this particular time, we would readily forgive dogmatism much greater than that of Mr Ruskin. In all branches of English literature, really sound criticism—a conscientious endeavour to see things as they really are—is exceedingly rare. With regard to art, it is almost unknown; and the absurdity is, that the public seems to suppose that it has no application there. Nothing is more common than remarks of this sort: 'It may or may not be a good picture, but I like it.' Nor do people appear to be aware that, when they indulge in such observations, they are making great fools of themselves. On the contrary, they really believe that there is no room for judgment as to pictures, but that they are to be liked or disliked according to the dictates of mere caprice. Hence, for example, we have Frederika Bremer declaring Raphael's Madonnas 'soulless and lifeless' compared with the large Murillo in the Louvre; and, still worse, Mrs H. Beecher Stowe disparaging the Sistine Madonna. As if such opinions proved anything at all, except the ignorance and bad taste of those who entertain them. The vanity of Mrs Stowe would, of course, think even her ignorance capable of enlightening the world on anything or everything; but Miss Bremer would never probably have said anything about this subject, had she not been led away by the prevailing idea that the world is bound to accept 'likings' or 'dislikings' as intelligent art criticism. It would be much better were it generally admitted that pictures form no exception to the rule, that people should only talk of what they understand; that a man like Mr Ruskin has some principle of judgment according to which he can pronounce a picture to be good or bad; and that, when a man says he 'likes' a bad picture, he makes himself as ridiculous as if he were to confess a preference of *Festus* to *Paradise Lost*. In the present state of matters, 'there is something grateful in any *positive* opinion, as even weeds are useful that grow on a bank of sand.' But Mr Ruskin's opinions are more than merely positive. They are the results of knowledge; they are based on principle; and, therefore, we may well excuse the vehemence with which they are occasionally expressed. For there is a truth of the ideal which the imagination can be taught to reach; but if that truth is altogether lost sight of, art may indeed afford some sensuous pleasure, but all usefulness, all nobleness is gone. On the other hand, Mr Ruskin cannot be defended in his trick of imputing motives. There he has no knowledge to guide—no principles on which to rest. Instances abound in all his works. What right, for example, has he to say that, because Rembrandt has painted his wife and himself supping on a peacock and champagne, such was the painter's ideal of happiness? Still worse is it to denounce Rubens as 'without any clearly perceptible traces of a soul;' and nothing can excuse the awful language used of Salvator (*Modern Painters*, vol. v., pp. 241–2). Condemn paintings as may be fit; but to speak of one's fellowmen as 'lost spirits' and 'fallen souls,' is perfectly appalling. What a contrast to all this is presented by the gentleness and generous appreciation of Sir Joshua Reynolds' criticism!

How much truer, for example, as well as kinder, is the feeling of Hazlitt: 'It is a consolation to us to meet with a fine Salvator. His is one of the great names in art; and it is among our sources of regret that we cannot always admire his works as we would do, from our respect to his reputation and our love of the man. Poor Salvator! he was unhappy in his life-time; and it vexes us to think that we cannot make him amends by fancying him so great a painter as some others, whose fame was not their only inheritance.'

Again, many exult mightily over Mr Ruskin's inconsistency. One ingenious critic is very wroth because he complains, in his odd way, that '*Modern Painters* have not a proper sense of the value of Dirt; cottage children never appear but in freshly got-up caps and aprons, and white-handed beggars excite compassion in unexceptionable rags:' while elsewhere he blames Murillo for elaborately painting the dirt on little boys' feet. So, too, no man is more severe than Mr Ruskin on violations of the laws of nature for the sake of effect; and yet, when on the canvas of Tintoret an angel wrapt in light casts a shadow before over the objects of his wrath, Mr Ruskin forgives the license, nay, pronounces it 'beautiful in its application.' In a similar spirit, he denounces the Pitti Magdalen as disgusting; and then again tells us that in that very picture Titian teaches a true and lofty lesson, having dared to 'doubt a romantic fable, and reject the narrowness of sentimental faith.' Such instances might be easily multiplied. But they are not vital inconsistencies. Who, that has ever been irritated by the offensive cleanliness of painters like Herring, will refuse to acknowledge the value of dirt? and who but an uncandid critic can fail to see that what Mr Ruskin condemns in Murillo, is not that he has painted dirt, but that he has painted it obtrusively and unnecessarily? Who, again, will hesitate to admit that a profound genius may, for some great imaginative purpose, indulge in a license which to meaner men must be denied? Still less can we give up Mr Ruskin as inconsistent in any evil sense, because his views as to particular artists have not been always the same. It does not, to our thinking, impair the value of his teaching, that in youth he admired, as he now thinks, too keenly, the power and sweep of Rubens[1]—that the reaction from this led him at one time to reverence too exclusively the holy feeling of the early religious painters—that advancing years, and extended study, have taught him to comprehend the nobility of Venetian art. Such changes are not inconsistencies of opinion; they are growth of thought. They are not oscillations, but progressions. But it cannot be denied that Mr Ruskin makes these changes—in themselves slight—assume proportions of serious magnitude by the manner in which he expresses them. This is another of the mischiefs which are to be ascribed to his inflated style. Why should he have called the Pitti Magdalen 'disgusting?' or why, because he admires the Venetians more than he once did, should he now assail Rubens in language utterly unbecoming? Any conscientious critic, who will take the trouble carefully to compare and candidly to reconcile Mr Ruskin's statements, will be surprised to find how what at first sight seemed glaring inconsistencies, finally disappear. He will be hardly less surprised to find how often the appearance of inconsistency took its rise solely in vehemence of expression. Would that Mr Ruskin would apply to his own style that word which he tells us should be 'relieved out in deep letters of pure gold over the doors of every school of art'—the word Moderation.

Able critics have based this same accusation on deeper grounds. Mr Ruskin, they say, is not only inconsistent in his judgment of pictures, and in his estimates of schools of art. That might be forgiven. But an abiding fault is, that his principles are absolutely contradictory. A writer in the *Revue des Deux Mondes* for August declares that, to any ordinary reader, *Modern Painters* will prove an insoluble enigma. In one page, the author is a realist of the School of Comte; in the next, he is an idealist, who might have learned from the lips of Plato. He attempts to reconcile these two extremes, and, in the attempt, falls into utter and irreconcilable confusion. Now, on the real point here at issue, it is the critic who is in fault. He maintains that the only truth possible in art is a 'truth of sentiment,'—meaning, we presume, that the motive of every picture is to be the chance feeling or emotion of the artist—bearing, however, no relation to the reality of nature. Mr Ruskin maintains that the truth of art is a truth of the imagination; and that part of that truth consists in the manner in which the imagination of the artist has regarded reality in its working. On the one hand, the imagination must be conscious of its own ideality, or it becomes madness; on the other, it must seek its materials from reality, or it becomes grotesque and meaningless. Thus, the highest motives of pictures must be combined with the strictest adherence to nature: any revelations of the unseen and eternal, within the power of art, can only be made when what is seen and known is faithfully represented. And thus, too, the lofty sphere which Mr Ruskin claims for art, the lofty functions which he assigns to artists, are to be reconciled with his repeated injunctions to study actual facts—with what the French critic calls his realism.

Yet here, too, Mr Ruskin has himself erred, and erred grievously. In working out a theory so subtle, there was need for the greatest precision both of thought and expression. Unfortunately, the Graduate of Oxford is not much given to either. Especially is he deficient in the power of consecutive reasoning. He is very fond of rebuking others for being illogical; and writes of himself, with no apparent consciousness of doing anything odd: 'Any error into which I may fall will not be an illogical deduction: I may mistake the meaning of a symbol, or the angle of a rock-cleavage, but not draw an inconsequent conclusion.' It's the old story—'Wad some friend the giftie gie us,' etc. For it so happens that there never was a writer more destitute of the capacity for logical thinking than Mr Ruskin. Assertion is his only wear. In all his lectures this is obvious, but in none more than in his lectures on the Economy of Art. And this natural inability is increased by his faults of style. His redundancy of language effectually prevents him from carrying on clearly any line of argument. His faults of temper also aggravate this evil. Instead of cooly refuting an opposite view, he conjures up an opposing controversialist, and rushes off into sarcasm, into reproach, into fierce denunciation. He has, besides, a most unpleasant way of attempting to discuss a point, by asking a series of questions—a device probably intended to impart liveliness, but which, to our mind, only imparts obscurity. Thus, in vol. iii., ch. 10, he starts an inquiry as to the use of pictures compared with real landscape. No inquiry could be more interesting or more instructive, if clear and precise. But it is disfigured with questions, and abrupt transitions, and polemical episodes, till the reader comes to the end, wearied, perplexed, and indignant.

Worst of all is, that a want of arrangement and connection marks *Modern Painters* as a whole. To this Mr Ruskin would, of course, reply, that the book has grown to its present size unexpectedly; that at first it was intended merely as a defence of Turner—as a reply to ignorant critics who failed to honour the great painter duly. But though we may admit this defence to be a good defence, it does not remove the blemish. The disproportion of the various parts is indeed accounted for, and that in a very natural way; but it still remains a blot on the completed work. In spite of it, the book will live; more than that: in spite of it, the book will mark an era in the history of art; but it is a drawback, and a grave one. It prevents these volumes from being, what they ought, and easily might have been, the development of a perfect philosophy of art criticism. We would not willingly descend to minute criticism on such a matter. But the whole of vol. ii. is an excrescence. Every line of it, excepting possibly the four chapters on the Imagination, should have been worked up with other portions of the book. It is embarrassing to the most patient student, to have principles thus separated from their application. Almost the same may be said of vol. iii. It is, in many respects, the most interesting and beautiful of all, but it does not cohere with the plan (if there ever was any plan) of the work. In vol. i., the ideas which are to be received from art were classified into ideas of Power, Imitation, Truth, Beauty, and Relation. Now ideas of Imitation are never treated of at all; ideas of Power are never treated of fully; ideas of Truth and Beauty are fully worked out; and we hear nothing of ideas of Relation, which involve 'the noblest subjects of Art,' till we come to the middle of vol. v., and are bewildered by those chapters with the wonderful titles which foolish people think very fine, but which no man of sense can read with patience.

This want of a sense of proportion is especially prejudicial to Mr Ruskin as a critic of architecture. For architecture, beyond any other art, is concerned with ideas of symmetry and of relation—of subordination of the parts to the whole. No man can be a great architect—no man can be a great critic of architecture—in whose mind the feeling of proportion is not a commanding idea. In Mr Ruskin's mind this feeling does not exist. He fails to keep the main purpose constantly before him; he runs off into disproportionate elaboration of details. Criticism like his leads to a style of architecture rich, and in a certain sense beautiful; but in which adaptation and completeness are both wanting. Buildings in this style—as, for instance, the New Museum at Oxford—are so elaborated in every particular, that the meaning and purpose of the whole is altogether obscured. The ornament is indeed all vital ornament; but it is so studied that it becomes disproportionate, and throws the main object out of view.

We have already noticed Mr Ruskin's prejudices, and occasional injustice. His omissions affect us with not less surprise. Of course the answer to this is, to repeat that the book was not a treatise on painting, but a pamphlet in defence of Turner. But whatever may have been the original intention, *Modern Painters* has now grown to a size which entitles us to expect that there should be few serious omissions. It is impossible not to regret Mr Ruskin's comparative silence on the Spanish school, and his entire neglect of the early Flemish painters. Nor is the list of notable English painters exhausted. Wilkie, though not strictly a landscape painter, surely deserved some notice; and still more unaccountable is the treatment of Linnell. That truly English painter is only mentioned twice—once in an appendix, and once in a foot-note. All who remember the beautiful Linnells in the Manchester Exhibition—especially the 'Landing of Ulysses'—will wonder at this, and regret it. Mr Ruskin's remarks on Linnell would have been most interesting and most instructive.

With all its faults and shortcomings, *Modern Painters* has done more for art than any one book in the English language. Mr Ruskin began to write filled with noble aims. He was resolved on vindicating the fame of a great artist; and, as the best means of so doing, on expounding to the world the true glory of art. That glory he taught us to find not in mere dexterity and tricks of skill; but in reverently approaching the perfection of nature, and in declaring the external beauty of the universe. For immediate effect he did not hope; yet he cherished the expectation that 'conviction would follow in due time.' His last volume breathes bitter disappointment: 'Once I could speak joyfully about beautiful things, thinking to be understood; now I cannot any more, for it seems to me that no one regards them.' We confess to a very different estimate of Mr Ruskin's labours. To the painter he has given deep and true rules for the interpretation of nature: the public he has taught to judge of art by rational and intelligible standards. Much of Mr Ruskin's advice to the painter has, of course, been given before. He has before been told that his first business is to learn to paint, though the invariable connection between the highest artistic merit and the greatest expressional power has never been so distinctly enforced as in Appendix 15 to vol. i. of *The Stones of Venice*. He has before been told of the duty of finish; but never was the duty so strictly inculcated as in the second and third volumes of *Modern Painters*:—'No truly great man can be named in the arts, but it was that of one who finished to his utmost.' But the originality of Mr Ruskin's criticism lies in this, that he insists on judging pictures by the amount of thought which they exhibit and convey: 'He is the greatest artist who has embodied, in the sum of his works, the greatest number of the greatest ideas.' The perfect landscape, for example, is that which brings before the eye of the spectator some scene of nature, and at the same time guides his imagination to those thoughts and feelings which such a scene is calculated to excite. To accomplish this, there is requisite truth of imitation, and worthiness in the thing imitated. In treating this latter point, Mr Ruskin has fallen foul of the Dutch and Flemish schools, and has excited much foolish indignation thereby. ⟨. . .⟩

No one can, we think, adequately estimate either Mr Ruskin or his writings, who does not keep constantly in mind this his law or test whereby to judge of pictures, i.e., the thoughts which they convey and suggest. It proves his honesty, it explains his inconsistencies, it accounts for the enmity he has excited. It proves his honesty, because no man who was otherwise would have ventured to work out a theory so difficult and so dangerous. In this respect the constitution of Mr Ruskin's mind is a great puzzle. He is, on occasion, sophistical beyond measure in thought and argument; he is never, we really believe, other than honest in his aims. He shows this by the courage with which he faces the real difficulties of every question which he discusses. Here in painting, for example, he has not shrouded himself in technicalities, or contented himself with external criticism. On the contrary, he can boast with truth that 'every principle which I have stated is traced to some vital and spiritual fact.' So, too, in architecture, his point of judgment is a comparison of the influences of the various schools on the minds of the workman—a position which leads him into endless trouble; and even his papers on Political Economy in the *Cornhill* possess this merit, that they at least attempt to solve the apparent contradiction between the selfish maxims of the science and the higher feelings of human nature. His earnest wish for truth forces him to encounter these subtle themes; but his courage makes him unconscious of paradox, and his illogical habits of mind lead him into the wildest regions of sophism and self-contradiction. Thus, in the present case, the endeavour to work out his law or test of painting is the true cause of the seeming inconsistency of his judgments. When things so very doubtful as thought or feeling are the grounds of judgment, the judgments can scarcely be uniform. It is so hard to trace them on any stedfast principle, to mark with certainty their presence or their absence. So

much, too, depends on ourselves. In some instances, we may supply them when they were wanting; in other instances, they may abound and yet be undiscerned by us. And this difficulty is increased by the fact, that many painters never painted with this test present to their minds. Not a few even of the great names in art never troubled themselves about it. And it is not easy, where all other excellence is found, to detect and condemn the absence of feeling. Let no one doubt but that it is the true test of excellence, in painting as in all other art; but it is not the less a test most difficult to apply. Charles Lamb, as we before observed, was one of the few former critics who penetrated to the heart and sentiment of a picture. We have already alluded to his two essays: in the same spirit are the following lines on a portrait by Titian, which had succeeded a more worthy portrait by Leonardo:—

> Who art thou, fair one, who usurp'st the place
> Of Blanch, the lady of the matchless grace?
> Come, fair and pretty, tell to me,
> Who, in thy life-time, thou might'st be.
> Thou pretty art and fair,
> But with the Lady Blanch thou never must compare.
> No need for Blanch her history to tell;
> Whoever saw her face, they there did read it well.
> But when I look on thee, I only know
> There lived a pretty maid some hundred years ago.

Let us not, however, be misunderstood. We do not mean to say, and Mr Ruskin never meant to say, that painting, viewed merely as an art, has no excellence peculiarly its own. Undoubtedly it has such an excellence: the goodness or the badness of the vehicle of our thought is a matter of no slight moment. But we do mean to say that this excellence is an excellence of expression—of language only. In its highest development, it is almost always combined with excellence of the thought expressed or spoken. But when it falls short of this, it is foolishness and emptiness. It may be beautiful exceedingly—it may be rich in gorgeous colouring, and lovely with all the loveliness of effective light and shadow; but if 'the little bright drop from the soul' be absent, it is not the highest art. To take poetry once more as an illustration: it cannot be denied that rhythm, and music, and felicity of expression are charms of no common power. But, like mere personal beauty, such charms are faint and fleeting, unless they come from the heart and go to the heart. No poetry dwells in the mind which possesses external perfection only. On the other hand, when the heart is caught by the feeling of the poem, howsoever simple the words may be, as in Scott's 'Proud Maisie,' the charm endures for ever. Compare, too, on this point, portrait-painting and photography. The photographist catches only the external appearance of a single moment. The portrait painter, if he be equal to his art, must accomplish far more. He must reach to the character and real essence of the man, and make that appear in the outward similitude; even although that appearance may be rare, though he himself may have never seen it worn. He must not paint a face merely; he must represent a human being. As in Leonardo's portrait, there must be 'no need for Blanch her history to tell.' So, too, the landscape painter may paint a scene on which, in all its details, his visible eye has never gazed; but which the inner eye of the imagination has revealed to him as true to the reality of nature. Sculpture, the most ideal of all the arts, affords yet another illustration. The sculptor must speak with faltering lips, and with a half-utterance which we often fail to hear. There is less beauty and perfectness in his language as such, than in the language of any other art. It is apt to be obscure, may be quite meaningless, and when it is so, possessing no loveliness in itself at all. Exquisite may be the proportions of the marble; but if the soul is wanting, the rest is a small matter. Kenyon's bust of Donatello possessed, to those who caught its meaning, a far deeper attraction than the Faun of Praxiteles. When truth and thought do speak clearly through the imperfect medium, they come to our imagination with a power and an appealing unrivalled by the other arts. Sculpture attains an ideality altogether its own when it achieves its highest triumphs—when even in the ὀμμάτων ἀχηνίαις nature and life shine visible, though love may stray unsatisfied. The same holds good with music. The 'concord of sweet sounds' is not enough—something more should charm than melody pleasant to the ear. All music, worthy of the name, bears the impress of the feelings which inspired the composer; and thus it is that the works of the great masters—especially, for example, Beethoven—impart a pleasure, far higher and purer than can be derived from any gratification of an outward sense. In short, the great painter, to quote Reynolds—not generally a profound or analytical critic—must labour to express an 'idea subsisting only in the mind: the sight never beheld it, nor has the hand expressed it; it is an idea residing in the breast of the artist, which he is always labouring to impart, and which he dies at last without imparting.'

We have said that this high standard of criticism insisted on by Mr Ruskin accounts for much of the enmity which has been excited against him. The reason of this is perfectly obvious. If power of thought and vigour of imagination are required to make an artist, artists will be few. Now it is a melancholy fact that there are more second-rate painters than second-rate anything else in the world, except, perhaps, second-rate wines. Whole hosts of worthy men, doubtless perfectly well adapted to the ordinary pursuits of trade, are encouraged by Art Unions to cover canvas with inane combinations of bad colouring which they call pictures, and are in consequence deluded into the belief that they are men of genius, and that Charles V., were he now alive, would think it an honour to pick up their palette-brush, as he did the brush of Titian. In the productions of these men there are no traces of thought, because they are incapable of thinking; and they are, not unnaturally, impatient of a canon of criticism which exposes their deficiencies. Mr Ruskin has done no better service than the exposure of such foolish pretension. 'The gems alone of thought and fancy,' says Mill, 'are worth setting with the finished and elaborate workmanship of verse; and even of them, only those whose effect is heightened by it.' Dr Arnold used to say there was no waste of time so great as that of reading second-rate poetry, and disapproved even of schoolboys being drilled over Tibullus and Propertius. What is true of poetry is not less true of painting. Second-rate painters do no good to the world, and do much harm to themselves. The specimens of hopeless mediocrity which are yearly multiplied on the walls of our Exhibitions are a melancholy spectacle. They afford no amusement, neither can they elevate the mind or improve the taste. They are but examples of energies which surely might have been good for some purpose, utterly wasted—devoted to a pursuit which can never reward them, save by ministering to a foolish vanity. If a man be not really a true genius, he had better never seek to rise above scene-painting.

Mr Ruskin's writings have done more for us than give us conclusions and estimates; they have fulfilled the true end of criticism in this, that they have taught us to think rightly on artistic subjects. Nor should we forget to mention, what Mr Ruskin himself would regard their chiefest glory, that they have taught us to value and understand the greatest of English painters. It was Bayle, we think, who said of Scaliger, that 'his

learning and talents were too great for a good commentator; the one making him discover in authors more hidden sense than they possessed, the other leading him to perceive a thousand allusions which had never been designed.' The remark, though paradoxical, has much truth, and is eminently applicable to Ruskin on Turner. On the other hand, no one has any love for art who does not read in pictures or statues far more than is actually expressed. They must be looked on with the eye of faith, as well as with the faculty of appreciation. In proportion to the grandeur and the beauty of the conception of the artist, must be the self-surrender of the gazer, must be his readiness to bring all his sensibility and imagination to complete and perfect the idea which the imperfection of the painter's language can but dimly shadow forth. The best artists are the most suggestive; and he is a bold critic who will venture to limit the suggestiveness of Turner. To measure his genius is like attempting to measure the genius of Shakspeare. Hallam, with his usual calm, clear criticism, says of our great dramatist, that 'no man ever had at once so much strength and so much variety of imagination.' The same words may be applied to our great painter. His artist-life seems to us marked by three stages of progress. The first stage is when he is a patient and humble student of other artists and of nature,—his 'noble and puissant' imagination is 'mewing its mighty youth.' This early time is marked, especially in his water-colours, by sweetness, solemnity, and peace. Then came the second stage—the period of his middle life, when his genius had attained bold independence—the days of his golden prime, when we see him 'soaring with supreme dominion through the azure depths of air,' when he realized the infinity of space—the days of the Bay of Baiæ and of the Old Temeraire, of the horrors of his shipwrecks, and of the glowing beauty of the sunny fields of France and the mountain glories of Switzerland. And at last came to him, as to all men, the inevitable decay, when this great light went down in wild and wasted splendour. Mr Ruskin will of course think us very common-place; but we really do not see how this is explained by saying that Turner 'died without hope' (whatever that may mean); or that England, 'the Iron-hearted,' killed him, as she had killed Byron and Keats. Whatever may be thought of the treatment these poets received from their country, there can, we think, be little doubt of this, that the genius of no man was ever more appreciated in his life-time, or more tangibly rewarded, than the genius of Turner, except perhaps the genius of Scott—whom, to be sure, Mr Ruskin includes in his dolorous list of great men who have died heart-broken by the cruel neglect of their country. We believe the cause to have been merely the decay of his physical powers. And even in these works of the time of decay there is the old glory, though obscured. But in the works of the fulness of his strength there is a boundless prodigality of thought, which distinguishes them from all other pictures. You never get to the end of them. As you look, one thing after another comes out and reveals itself, just as in nature; and one idea after another is awakened in the mind, exactly in the same way as when we look on some surpassing landscape. It is idle criticism to limit the suggestiveness of the works of a man of genius by his own conscious meaning. For is it not true that the highest genius is, like prophecy, in a great measure unconscious of itself? People go about repeating the cuckoo-cry, 'Oh, Turner himself said that Mr Ruskin saw things in his pictures he had never meant.' And why not? That very power of vision is itself genius; and why should Mr Ruskin be hindered from its use, or from teaching us to understand it? When we look on Turner's scenes of beauty, bathed in sunshine—his glittering lagunes of Venice, foaming English seas, and fairy sunsets,—why should we be forced to restrict our thoughts to what was actually before the mind of the painter? No one supposes that Shakspeare wrote with a full and adequate conception of his meaning; and Shakspeare is not more indisputably the first of dramatists than Turner is the first of landscape painters.

What now remains of our task is less pleasant; for we have to speak of Mr Ruskin as a writer on other matters than upon art, and it is impossible to do this without fault-finding. He tells us, with a sort of self-gratulation, that his work is broken by digressions respecting social questions, which had for him 'an interest tenfold greater than the work he had been forced into undertaking.' He digresses not only into social questions; but into questions of metaphysics, of literature, and of politics, unfortunately for his reputation. It is not too much to say, that in handling these matters Mr Ruskin has succeeded in giving his enemies an easy triumph, and causing sorrow and shame to his sincere admirers. He is seldom right except by chance; and that chance is very rare. Here all his faults as a writer become painfully apparent. For his dogmatism is now the dogmatism of ignorance; his inconsistencies are the inconsistencies of ca-price; his intolerance is the intolerance of arrogance. Few things, perhaps, test better the value of a man's opinion on any subject than his familiarity with its details. Mr Ruskin is never impatient of the minutest point in art or nature; in all other things accuracy is held of no account. Thus, he writes on political economy, and lectures on the economy of art; and yet he tells us that he never read any work on economical science save Adam Smith, and for the reason, that all the rest go too deeply into details.[2] Nor is this the worst. His language regarding some of the great names in art, though sometimes bad enough, was always justifiable by some show of reason; but nothing can excuse the gratuitous impertinence of the follow-ing sneer at the fame of Newton:—'I hear of a wonderful solution of nettles, or other unlovely herb, which is green when shallow, red when deep. Perhaps some day, as the motion of the heavenly bodies by the help of an apple, their light by the help of a nettle, may be explained to mankind' (*Modern Painters*, v. 110). Of metaphysics—that is, of everybody's metaphysics but his own—he seems to think as lightly as he does of science. His own metaphysics, as ex-plained in vol. ii., are a sort of Aristotle and water. The value of his literary judgments may be estimated by what he tells us of his literary instructors. In the third appendix to the third volume he tells us he owes most to Wordsworth, Carlyle, and Helps. Mr Helps is a very painstaking writer, and sometimes shows considerable ingenuity in making ordinary ideas appear imposing; but really his name in this society does remind us of the fly in amber. But as Mr Ruskin advances, or, as we venture to think, deteriorates, Mr Helps changes his position. He becomes himself the leading spirit. In a note to page 288 of the fifth volume, we find:—'I had hoped, before concluding this book, to have given it a higher value by extracts from the works which have chiefly helped or guided me, especially from the writings of Helps, Lowell, and the Rev. A. J. Scott. But if I were to begin making such extracts, I find that I should not know, either in justice or affection, how to end.' But though Carlyle is discarded, traces of Carlylcism linger long. Even in the fifth volume we have many passages which look like intentional caricatures of that author's faults. The following has numerous parallels:—'The public remonstrated loudly in the cause of Python: he had been so yellow, quiet, and pleasant a creature; what meant these azure-shafted arrows, this sudden glare into darkness, this Iris message;—Thaumantian—miracle-working; scattering our slumber down in Cocytus?' Mr Ruskin may take our word for it, the British public never

remonstrated, on this or any other subject, in such very unintelligible language.

We cannot wonder at any literary eccentricities on the part of a man who has made for himself such gods. Sir Walter Scott is perhaps the only author whom Mr Ruskin fairly estimates. But this arises, we suspect, only from Scott's love of nature. That it is not based upon any principle of literary judgment, is shown conclusively by his instancing, as rival specimens of the perfect play of the imagination, Ariel, Titania, and the White Lady of Avenel (*Modern Painters*, iii. 98)—that vulgar and most unspiritual spirit, admitted by Scott himself to have been a hopeless failure. The same capricious taste prefers Cary's Dante to our own Milton (*Stones of Venice*, ii. 264); and quotes to us, as 'rivalless' in pathos and tenderness of heart, such characters as Virginia and Fleur de Marie (*Modern Painters*, iii. 302). As to *Paul and Virginia*, we will only quote Carlyle's 'What a world of prurient corruption lies visible in that super-sublime of modesty!' But, as for the other, it is with astonishment that we see Mr Ruskin selecting for praise any character in the *Mysteries of Paris*,—a book beside which the broad indecencies of Paul de Kock seem virtuous. Nor are Mr Ruskin's inconsistencies on litarary points less extraordinary than his capricious judgments. In one place he condemns Keats as 'sickly;' and in another he says that he has 'come to such a pass of admiration for him, that he dare not read him.' In his third volume of *Modern Painters* he tells us that Shakspeare's view of Fate 'closely resembled that of the ancients;' and in his fifth, he draws an elaborate contrast between the two—developing the astounding theory, that Shakspeare's tragedy is but the sport of Fortune ending in darkness and final death; while, 'at the close of a Greek tragedy, there are far-off sounds of a divine triumph, and a glory as of resurrection.' So, too, we are told in vol. v. of *Modern Painters* that the Homeric temper is 'tender, and practical, and cheer-ful;' and but a few pages farther on, we read of 'the deep horror which vexed the soul of Æschylus or Homer.' Indeed, on all questions of ancient literature, Mr Ruskin exhibits his faults as a writer in painful prominence. He is for ever dogmatizing about Greek and the Greeks, while it is perfectly obvious that he knows little or nothing either of their nature or their language. His telling us to conceive of the Greek mind, by taking as its type 'a good, conscientious, but illiterate, Scotch Presbyterian Border farmer of a century or two back,' is one of the most ludicrous things in literature. He gives Homer as the best representative of the Greek nature; which is precisely what Homer is not, and from the scope of his genius could not possibly have been. He never even alludes to Thucydides or Sophocles, the two most purely classical of all Greek authors. He admires Plato, without understanding him; and when he mentions Aristotle, it is to pass upon him the preposterous criticism, that he is 'forced, false, confused; and has given rise to inaccurate habits of thought, and forced love of systematiz-ing' (*Stones of Venice*, ii. 3, 19). Throughout the fifth volume—especially towards the close of it—he interprets the old Greek mythology into subtle meanings, after the fashion of the later Greek schools—a fashion all sound criticism has long ago rejected. The theory which would explain the early mythology of Greece by making it symbolical of moral or philosophical truths, is as absurd as the theory which would ascribe it to the inventive genius of Homer and Hesiod. The mythopœic age was neither conscious nor artificial. Mythology in its origin was altogether material, connected with place, derived from language and from the impressions of external nature. To invest it, in its beginnings, with a conscious moral teaching, is to falsify its real character, and destroy all its value as the strangest phenomenon in the history of the human mind. 〈. . .〉

Mr Ruskin's historical and political opinions are not less singular. Venice is, beyond all others, the country of his love. 'Deep-hearted, majestic, terrible as the sea—the men of Venice moved in sway of pomp and war; pure as her pillars of alabaster stood her mothers and maidens; from foot to brow all noble, walked her knights.' Such are his grandiloquent words. The plain fact is, that from the first foundation of the state down to her later days, when she deserted the allies whose succour she had implored, and made a shameful peace with the Turks even after the great victory of Lepanto, the history of Venice is the unvarying record of a policy of ungenerous self-seeking. Sparta, the Venice of the ancient world, grasping, and jealous, and treacherous as she was, could yet boast the glory of Thermopylæ, and was rich in the virtues of Brasidas and Kallicratides. But the Queen of the Adriatic, through twelve hundred years of prosperity and power, can point to not one heroic name—has left the memory of not one noble action. A haughty and implacable oligarchy oppressed the people, murdered their best Doges, and performed their proudest exploit when they sacked the sacred Capitol which all Christendom was leagued together to defend. A nation with such a history fell unregretted. No heart pitied, no hand was raised to succour, when Venice was cast from her high estate by the Confederates of Cambray. And it is very characteristic of Mr Ruskin, that, as he reverences the old government of that

Den of drunkards with the blood of princes,

so he sympathizes with her oppressors now. His deliberate verdict on the Austrian government in Italy is, that he 'never heard a single definite ground of complaint against it—never saw any instance of oppression, but several of much kindness and consideration' (*Stones of Venice*, iii. Book iii.). Nor is this to be wondered at; for he never seems to regard the wishes of the people—to allow them freedom of thought, or independence of life. His whole theory of government is that of minute and constant supervision—the people drilled and trained into education[3] certainly, but, above all, into unhesitating and unintelligent obedience. Freedom of action, and the strength of character, the patriotism, the loyalty, and the thousand civic virtues which freedom of action fosters, find no place in his system. And in perfect keeping with all this, is his selfish aristocratic way of regarding the people, if any real equality is claimed for them. He will gladly concede them favours—and favours far beyond their wishes or their power to use; yet he will not accord them their rights. He regards them as a Roman senator of the best type would have regarded them, with toleration, even with indulgence; if so only they will be quiet and obey, not seeking for power, not intruding on the tasteful enjoyments of their superiors. Even the beauties of nature must be reserved for the educated appreciation of the few, uninjured by the noisy presence of the uncultivated many. Thus he bewails the bridges over the Fall of Schaffhausen, and round the Clarens shore of the Lake of Geneva, because they 'have destroyed the power of two pieces of scenery of which nothing can ever supply the place, in appeal to the higher ranks of European mind;' and, in the same spirit, he lauds Wordsworth's poetical crusades against railways, as a noble attempt to defend a district from 'the offence and foulness of mercenary uses.' Now in all this we can see nothing but selfishness. To make railways from large towns into the regions of lake and mountain, seems to us the very reverse of 'a mercenary use' of nature. Rather is nature thereby enabled to accomplish fully the best use possible to her—that of refreshing

and elevating the mass of mankind. Men and women are not to remain throughout life pent up in lanes and alleys, sighing vainly for 'the meadow's sweet breath,' in order that artists and poets may gaze on nature's beauties undisfigured by railway bridges. And in the endeavour to veil the selfish cruelty of such a position, these men of taste abuse the lanes and alleys, and the manufactures which create them. But they begin at the wrong end. They cry out for impossibilities; and lament the state of the country because their own pleasures cannot be preserved. All their eloquent comparisons between cottages covered with woodbine, and five-storied mills,[4] will never do away with the latter. They can't abolish the lanes and the alleys; and, therefore, the best thing they can do is to provide the best means of escaping from them. It is no true philanthropy to demand for the working classes conditions of happiness which are impossible, while we deny them those conditions of happiness which are within our power. It is at once the most rational and the kindest course to accept things which we cannot prevent, and at the same time to welcome any remedy; and, among others, to build railway bridges over all the waterfalls and round lakes in the universe, if so the people of our towns are enabled 'to stand sometimes upon grass or heath.' We freely confess that we have more pleasure in the idea of an excursion-train, full of Manchester working men and women hurrying to refresh their life of labour with a glimpse of Windermere, than in the idea of a dozen Wordsworths reciting their own poetry in the selfish solitude of unapproachable hills.

But neither in this nor in any other cheerful view of our present condition does Mr Ruskin concur. His heart is filled with gloom, and with disgust at the times in which he lives. Catholic emancipation is probably the reason; but whatever be the reason, the fact is certain, that the state of England is deplorable. Lord Macaulay tells us that Burke once compared George Grenville 'to the evil spirit whom Ovid described looking down on the stately temples and wealthy haven of Athens, and scarce able to refrain from weeping because she could find nothing at which to weep.' Much of this sort is the temper of Mr Ruskin. His baseless discontent has grown upon him gradually. His tone has become gloomier with every succeeding volume of his works, until at last it has come to this, that England is 'with her right hand casting away the souls of men, and with her left the gifts of God' (*Modern Painters*, v. 354). What this may mean we cannot guess; but mills seem to be dimly hinted at, when we are told that it may be well that 'every kind of sordid, foul, or venomous work, which in other countries men dreaded or disdained, it should become England's duty to do,—becoming thus the offscourer of the earth, and taking the hyena instead of the lion upon her shield' (*Modern Painters*, v. 331). And Carlyle, of course, is imitated in sneers at our 'Houses of Talk.' Finally, inquiring readers, coming at last on a passage like the following, according to their various tempers, sink into sulky despair, or break out into vehement indignation:—

> In each city and country of past time, the master-minds had to declare the chief worship which lay at the nation's heart; to define it; adorn it; show the range and authority of it. Thus in Athens, we have the Triumph of Pallas; and in Venice the Assumption of the Virgin; here, in England, is our great spiritual fact for ever interpreted to us—the Assumption of the Dragon. No St George any more to be heard of; no more dragon-slaying possible: this child, born on St George's Day, can only make manifest the dragon, not slay him, sea-serpent as he

is; whom the English Andromeda, not fearing, takes for her lord. The fairy English Queen once thought to command the waves, but it is the sea-dragon now who commands her valleys; of old the Angel of the Sea ministered to them, but now the Serpent of the Sea; where once flowed their clear springs now spreads the black Cocytus pool; and the fair blooming of the Hesperid meadows fades into ashes beneath the Nereid's Guard. Yes, Albert of Nuremberg; the time has at last come. Another nation has risen in the strength of its black anger; and another hand has portrayed the spirit of its toil. Crowned with fire, and with the wings of the bat.—*Modern Painters*, vol. v., p. 318.

We confess to have no patience or tolerance at all for nonsense like this. For such a style of writing Mr Ruskin deserves far more severe condemnation than for all his literary vagaries. These, at the worst, could do no great harm; but vague denunciations like the above, may be productive of much mischief. If any man sees aught that is out of joint in the times in which he lives, it is his duty to state it clearly and plainly, so that no one can misunderstand him. He may not be able to suggest the remedy, but he must be able to point out the fault. Unless he can do this, he had best be silent. Unexplained grumbling is but the indulgence of a luxury long ago described by Charles Lamb: 'There is a pleasure (we sing not to the profane) far beyond the reach of all the world counts joy—a deep, enduring satisfaction in the depths, where the superficial seek it not, of discontent. . . . To grow bigger every moment in your own conceit, and the world to lessen; to deify yourself at the expense of your species; to judge the world,—this is the acme and supreme point of your mystery—these are the true pleasures of sulkiness.' A taste for these pleasures is growing on Mr Ruskin; and, what is worse, he tries to communicate the same taste to his readers. Against this we beg to enter our most decided protest. If a man will enjoy these pleasures, let him do so with regard to trifles. He is not entitled to them at the expense of his country—of the whole state of the society in which he lives. We always come back to the decisive point—Tell us distinctly what is wrong, Mr Carlyle or Mr Ruskin, and we will try to mend it. But when you abuse us as hastening to perdition, and as throwing away the bounty of God, and can specify no deeper ground of offence than building bridges over waterfalls, then we reject you as false teachers and false censors alike, and return to our common-place but satisfactory belief in the general happiness and advancement of the present generation.

But it is not with these objections—heartily as we entertain them—that we would close this article. We must recur to a leading characteristic of Mr Ruskin's writings which gives to them their purest beauty and their deepest truth: we mean the profound religious feeling which pervades them all. He tells us in the *Seven Lamps*, that he has been blamed for this; if so, the blame was most unwise. More, perhaps, than any other quality of his mind, this seriousness of thought has made him the great art critic that he is. For all true art is but a reflex of religion; as Cousin has it, 'a presentation of moral beauty by physical.' In speaking of the great things of sacred art, Mr Ruskin never fails to refer to the greater and holier realities of which that art is but the feeble copy; in depicting the solemnities of nature, he never fails to lead us to those eternal truths with which certain aspects of nature are for ever associated. He cannot look on the flaming wings of the angels of Angelico, without rising in thought to the heavenly hosts above; when he reveals to us the 'mountain glory,' his mind sweeps on to the special holiness of the mountains on which the Lawgiver and the High Priest of Israel

were taken to their God, and the yet more profound sanctity of the mountain on which the divinity of our Lord was proclaimed from heaven. The greatest of sacred writers, not excepting Jeremy Taylor himself, have written nothing more deeply splendid than the close of the fourth volume of *Modern Painters*, where we read of the mysteries which were accomplished on Mount Abarim, and Mount Hor, and on the Mount of Transfiguration. It is in such high arguments that Mr Ruskin's style achieves its greatest triumphs. His descriptive powers, are always wonderful; his sarcasm is always powerful; but when themes which demand a sustained exaltation of style inspire him, then he manifests his perfect strength. At such times we have no pomp of verbiage wasted on leaves and lichens; we have the whole force of the English language, wielded as few men have ever wielded it before, devoted to subjects far transcending its utmost powers of utterance. Then Mr Ruskin's language throws into the shade the most splendid declamations of Burke—makes even the prose of Milton appear tame—rises into 'a sevenfold chorus of hallelujahs and harping symphonies.' We quote one of such passages; not, perhaps, the very finest, but the one best adapted to our limits:—

This, I believe, is the ordinance of the firmament; and it seems to me that in the midst of the material nearness of these heavens God means us to acknowledge His own immediate presence as visiting, judging, and blessing us. 'The earth shook, the heavens also dropped, at the presence of God.' 'He doth set His bow in the cloud,' and thus renews, in the sound of every drooping swathe of rain, His promises of everlasting love. 'In them hath He set a *tabernacle* for the sun;' whose burning ball, which without the firmament would be seen but as an intolerable and scorching circle in the blackness of vacuity, is by that firmament surrounded with gorgeous service, and tempered by mediatorial ministries; by the firmament of clouds the golden pavement is spread for his chariot-wheels at morning; by the firmament of clouds the temple is built for his presence to fill with light at noon; by the firmament of clouds the purple veil is closed at evening round the sanctuary of his rest; by the mists of the firmament his implacable light is divided, and its separated fierceness appeased into the soft blue that fills the depth of distance with its bloom, and the flush with which the mountains burn as they drink the overflowing of the dayspring. And in this tabernacling of the unendurable sun with men, through the shadows of the firmament, God would seem to set forth the stooping of His own majesty to men, upon the *throne* of the firmament. As the Creator of all the worlds, and the Inhabiter of eternity, we cannot behold Him; but, as the Judge of the earth and the Preserver of men, those heavens are indeed His dwelling-place. 'Swear not, neither by heaven, for it is God's throne; nor by the earth, for it is His footstool.' And all those passings to and fro of fruitful shower and grateful shade, and all those visions of silver palaces built about the horizon, and voices of moaning winds and threatening thunders, and glories of coloured robe and cloven ray, are but to deepen in our hearts the acceptance, and distinctness, and dearness of the simple words, 'Our Father, which art in heaven.'—*Modern Painters*, vol. iv., p. 89.

With the majestic music of these words sounding in our ears, and the exaltedness of these thoughts dwelling in our hearts, let us conclude. Now, at the last, we would willingly forget all fault-finding, and take leave of Mr Ruskin with feelings only of admiration and gratitude. The greatest art critic that has ever written, he has done more than afford us pleasure—he has opened up to us new worlds of emotion. Often, as we gaze on the perfection of landscape, we may fail, even after Mr Ruskin's teaching, to think of the Maker of it all—to look into the unfathomable eyes of the Sistine Madonna may not be religion; yet it cannot be but that we are so raised, for the time at least, above the thoughts and cares of common life. Great art, he tells us, may be defined as the 'art of dreaming.' If so, then the sleep in which such dreams may come is better than most of our waking. Mr Ruskin has shown us what visions high of beauty, and goodness, and truth, can bless the sleep of genius. More than this, he will lead every docile reader to the portals at least of that happy dreamland, where he can catch a glimpse of the far-off glory; where all the poetry of his nature will be stirred within him; where he can forget, for a while, disappointment, and sorrow, and cruel separation; where his unrest can be quieted, his vague longings for the moment satisfied; and whence he can return, comforted and strengthened, to the light and the labour of the day.

Notes

1. If Mr Ruskin would be restored to this his youthful, and, as we think, well-founded admiration, he should read a hearty and powerful estimate of the great Fleming in a 'Roundabout Journey,' in the first volume of the *Cornhill Magazine*.
2. *Lectures on the Economy of Art*.
3. And what an education! In addition to reading, writing, etc., every child should be taught 'the first principles of natural history, physiology, and medicine; also to sing perfectly, so far as it has any capacity, and to draw any definite form accurately, to any scale.' —*Modern Painters*, v. 333, note.
4. See the *Two Paths*.

STOPFORD A. BROOKE
From "Ruskin's Lectures on Art"
Macmillan's Magazine, October 1870, pp. 423–34

There are few men of our time who have been more largely praised or more bitterly attacked than Mr. Ruskin. There are none who have deserved more praise or more resolutely challenged attack. He has been so lavish in his approbation of certain artists and schools of art, that he has raised against them a cloud of opponents. He has been so unsparing in blame of certain others, so curiously inventive in terms of reproach, so audacious in his tilting against received opinions, and so felicitous sometimes in his hits, that he has forced into combination against him a number of determined foes. Of all men he should be the last to object to criticism, for his own sword seldom seeks the scabbard. And on the whole, though he professes with a certain archness a desire for peace, nothing gives him so much pleasure, or brings out his intellect so well, as war, when it is on a subject with which he is acquainted. He will run on, giving birth to paradox after paradox in an apparently gloomy manner, choosing for very wilfulness the obscurity of the Pythoness, as long as his listeners sit rapt and receptive at his feet. But the moment one of them, seeing that the paradoxes are becoming intolerable, starts up and meets them with a blunt contradiction, and declares war, Mr. Ruskin becomes radiant with good humour, his intellect becomes incisive, and he rushes to the fight with joy. Nothing is worse for him than worship; and if he had had less of it, he would

have done the State more service. Half of his morbid and hopeless writing comes directly of this—that he has not been of late sufficiently excited by respectful opposition to feel happy.

It may be said that he has had plenty of opposition of late, but it is not the sort which makes a man draw his sword with pride. Since he has devoted himself to economical and political subjects, the criticism he has met has been a criticism of laughter from his enemies and of dismay from his friends. It has been felt impossible to go seriously into battle against him, for his army of opinions are such stuff as dreams are made of, and their little life is rounded with a sleep. Throw upon them a clear light and they disperse—

> The earth hath bubbles, as the water has,
> And these are of them. Whither have they vanished?

We cannot say with Macbeth, "Would they had stayed;" but when we look back on the extraordinary series of proposals for regenerating the country, and remember the criminal classes set to draw canal boats under the lash, and the poor dressed all in one sad-coloured costume, and other things of this character, we may follow with Banquo's words,

> Were such things here as we do speak about?
> Or have we eaten on the insane root
> Which takes the reason prisoner?

In this way he has brought upon himself the loss of the impulse he derives from respectful and vigorous war. He has left the Delectable mountains where he fed his sheep, and gone back to the valley of the shadow of death. There, impressed with the withered image of Carlylism, which having surrendered hope sits now like giant Pope shaking its hands at the pilgrims of the world, and unable to do more than mutter curses at Liberalism, and invoke the help of the aristocracy to sanctify and redeem the people: enthralled by this phantom of a past glory, he has found it almost impossible to go on drawing, with the peace necessary for an artist, the tombs of Verona, or to note down the fleeting loveliness of a sunset cloud. While the poor were perishing for want of fresh water and decent houses, he seemed to himself, we conjecture, to be like Nero, fiddling while Rome was burning. So he abandoned his own sphere— in which, whatever may be his faults, he was supreme by genius—to follow, *haud passibus æquis*, in the track of our Jeremiah, whose style is open to the same charge which Mr. Arnold makes so pathetically against the Jewish prophet. But the prophetic cry does not suit the gentler temper of Mr. Ruskin. With all his efforts we are thankful to say that he cannot arrive at making the uncouth noise which Carlyle made, and the uncouthness of which gave what he said more than half its force. He is too tender-hearted to curse heartily, and he cannot bear, like his prototype, to pour forth torrents of blame without proposing remedies for evils. But the remedies Ruskin has proposed are unpractical at this time and in this country, owing to his ignorance of the state of the poor. No man is less fitted to understand their true position. He is too sensitive to beauty, to cleanliness, to quietude, not to exaggerate the apparent misery of a life passed in the midst of ugliness, dirt, and noise. He thinks all the poor feel these things nearly as much as he does, and he cannot conceive, as we see from these lectures, that they should endure to live. We should suppose that he has never lived among them, nor seen how things among them are seasoned by custom. Those who have gone from room to room in the courts which Ruskin thinks so unendurable, know that there is, on the whole, as much happiness among them as there is among the upper classes; that there is more self-sacrifice, more of the peace of hard work, more good humour, more faithfulness to others in misfortune, more every-day righteousness. Their chief evils are drunkenness, which has only lately vanished from among the upper classes; the torrent of alms which has been poured upon them, and which has drowned their independence and postponed their learning the lesson of prudence as opposed to their reckless extravagance. Their main wants are a really active sanitary board, directed by gentlemen in the cities and provinces, who will see that the common work is done with common honesty; and education, especially education in physical science. The commonest training in the first principles of physiology and chemistry, given accurately, will soon produce that state of active anger at their condition, and determination to have it rectified, which no State interference can give them, and which State interference sends to sleep. True, Ruskin advocates this kind of education, and has advocated it well; but he has done it as part of an elaborate system of direction by the State and by the upper classes,—direction which would be as evil to its victims as Romish direction is to the moral force of its patients. No nation has ever been saved by foreign help: the poor can never be saved by the action of the rich, only by their native exertion, and everything that Ruskin says on the subject, in these Lectures and elsewhere, is open to this most grave objection, that it takes away from the people the education which is gained by personal mistakes and personal conquest of mistakes.

Owing to these two things then,—ignorance of the real state of the poor, and the vicious idea of interference from above with the poor,—the remedies which Ruskin proposes are unpractical. At the same time many of his hints, divorced from their principles, are valuable, and we cannot doubt the earnestness and charity with which he speaks, nor refrain from loving him, though we disagree with him. But with the want of practical knowledge has come exaggeration, and with exaggeration disproportioned remedies; and the world, listening to the recital of woes rendered unreal by the violence of the denunciations, and still more unreal by the proposals for their abolition, has lent its ear to Mr. Ruskin for a transient hour, and smiled and gone on its way, and he, having expended so much force for nought, and meeting no real opposition, has slid into melancholy, and from thence into despair.

Moreover, the treatment of such subjects at all, at least their direct treatment, was a great mistake on his part, the error of mistaking his calling. He has been given great powers, as great as those bestowed on any man in this century. He has read the book of nature with unwearied diligence and conscientious observation. He is in every sense a student. But he is far more, in that he is a man of genius; for he can not only see rightly (see the outline beneath the fulfilment), but he can express with passion which is sufficiently tempered to be intense, and with copiousness sufficiently charged with fact to be interesting, that which he has seen in the natural world. It is not too much to say that for many of us whose deepest pleasure is in the beauty of the world, he has tripled our power of pleasure. And it has been done, not as the Poet does it by developing intensity of feeling, but by appealing to feeling through the revelation of fact, and by the exquisite delight which we feel he takes in the discovery and the beauty of the fact, and by the charm of the vehicle through which he tells his story. Nobody before him took the trouble to tell us what mountains were like, for the descriptions of the geologist bear the same relation to the actual mountains that the detail of the skeleton bears to the living man. Nobody before him made the aspect of the sky, morning, noon, and evening, familiar as a household word, nor led us to look on clouds and all their beauty as as much objects of daily observation and delight as

the ways of our children or the face of those we love. No one before him took us by the brooks of water and upon the sea, and made every ripple of the one and every waveform of the other a recognized pleasure. Wordsworth gave us much help, but he taught us to feel more than to observe and understand. But Ruskin has taught us to observe and understand, not as the scientific man does for the ends of science, but for the ends of *delight* received from the perception of truth, and no more faithful and splendid work has ever been done. One would say that this observer of the vaster aspects of nature for the end of Art, would be likely to fail in seeing the loveliness of the infinitely little, of the "beetle panoplied in gems and gold," of the "daisy's shadow on the naked stone," of the opening of a sheaf of buds, of the fairy wilderness of an inch or two of meadow. But neither here has he failed, and the reader of Mr. Ruskin's books may lie on his face in a field for half an hour, or watch the water of a stream eddying round a mossy trunk, and not only feel unremitting pleasure in what he sees, as Keats or Wordsworth would make him feel, but know why he feels his pleasure, add to his stock of artistic fact, and gain additional power of knowing beauty. All our hours of recreation have been blessed through him.

The same delicate sensitiveness to beauty combined with acute critical perception of minuter points of excellence has been applied by him to poetry. Since Coleridge we have had no finer work done on the Poets. It is a pity that his criticisms on Dante, Shakespeare, Scott, Wordsworth, Keats, and others, are not collected out of his volumes and published separately. [1] A book of this kind would be of infinitely more value than the useless *Selections from Ruskin*; a book which irritates one, even more than selections usually do, and has given an entirely false impression of his work to that luckless personage, the general reader.

The work which he has done on Pictures has been equally good of the same kind. He was perfectly capable of explaining their technical excellence, but he did not choose to write for artists, and we are glad that he laid this sort of work aside. For, however good it might be for special students, it gave no help to the public, and only led certain would-be connoisseurs to prate about morbidezza and chiar'oscuro, and bold handling and a hundred other things, which in their mouths were little better than cant. We have been delivered by Mr. Ruskin from the technicalities of ignorant persons. He has led us more than all others to look for the conception of a picture, and to study the way in which the artist carried out that conception. He has taught us to compare it with the facts of nature which we are capable of observing, and to judge it partly from the artist's reverence for truth. We can now, having a certain method, enjoy the thing done with a great deal of delight, without knowing how it is done. Of course the enjoyment is not so great as his who can not only appreciate the ideas but also the mode of work; but it is something, and the smattering we had before of artistic phrase was worth nothing. Those who have time and inclination can go further, but the many who cannot, have now a real pleasure; they can give a reason why they like a picture instead of talking nonsense. Of course the dilettante Pharisees are angry, but that only increases the general thankfulness of the public.

Mr. Ruskin has not only shown us how to go to work. He has a rare power of seeing into the central thought of a picture, and his wide knowledge of the aspects of nature enables him to pronounce upon truth of representation. He has performed this labour notably on Turner and Tintoret. Turner's phrase, that "he sees meanings in my pictures which I did not mean," is the exact truth; and Shakespeare would no doubt have said the same had he read Schlegel. He has revealed the genius of Turner to the world by comparing Turner with Nature; and those who have spent hour after hour in the enchanted rooms of the Ducal Palace, or wandered day after day through the sombre galleries of the Scuola San Rocco, know what he has done for Tintoret. It has been said that the world appreciated Turner before Ruskin spoke. A few persons and the artists did (no one ever imagined that the artists did not heartily acknowledge his genius), but artists have not the gift of speech, nor, with an exception or two, such as Eastlake, the faculty of criticism, and we have only found out at last from their biographies what they thought. It is absurd to quote their isolated sayings as a proof that the public understood and valued Turner before Ruskin wrote. Artists say that they pointed out Tintoret to Ruskin, but why did not they point him out to the world? The public wish to be taught, and the artists are silent. We expect it is that they have not much to say. They know what is good; so does Mr. Ruskin. But he takes the trouble to tell us what is good and why it is good, and we owe no gratitude to the artists and a very great deal to him.

Now to do all this, to read Nature, Poetry and Painting for us, and to continue doing it, was Ruskin's peculiar work, and the greater part of it was most nobly done. We ask, with sorrow, why he abandoned it? We have suffered no greater grief than when he left it and took up other labours, for which he was eminently unfitted, and the effect of which was to spoil his powers for his especial business. Sanitary reform, political economy, the dressing of England, manufactories, crime, poverty! *que diable allait-il faire dans cette galère?* A man must have iron nerves and little acute sense of beauty, to play his part in that battle-field, and the result on Ruskin has been like that which would follow on sending a poet like Shelley into one of the war hospitals. He ceases to be able to write poetry and he kills the patients.

This is one of the great mistakes which are scarcely ever remedied, and we trace its results in every one of these Lectures, which are weakened by the forced introduction of irrelevant matter, and by the hopeless tone which much musing on miserable subjects has brought into his temper and his style. We trace the latter in the very first page, where he says that it "has chanced to him of late to be so little acquainted either with pride or hope that he can scarcely recover so much as he now needs of the one for strength, and of the other for foresight." We appeal to him to throw by altogether the peculiar class of subjects of which we speak, and to believe that when God has given him so plainly a particular work to do, it is his first duty to stick to that work, and to put aside everything which interferes with it. Hope will return when he does his proper labour, and the noble pride of the workman in his toil will give him strength when a crowd of importunate duties outside his sphere are sternly shut out, and he concentrates himself on the one great duty of his life—the unveiling to men Truth and Beauty in Art and in Nature.

We trace this despondent tone, and the consequent false view of the world, still more pathetically in a passage in the "Catalogue of Examples," where he describes himself as walking in his garden early in the morning to hear the nightingale sing, and sees "the sunlight falling on the grass through thickets of the standard peach, and of plum and pear in their first showers of fresh silver looking more like much broken and far-tossed spray of fountains than trees," and hears the roar of the railroads sounding in the distance, "like the surf of a strong sea," and thinks that "of all the myriads imprisoned by the English Minotaur of lust for wealth, and condemned to live, if it is to be called life, in the labyrinth of black walls and

loathsome passages between them, which now fills the valley of the Thames—not one could hear, this day, any happy bird sing or look upon any quiet space of the pure grass that is good for seed." It is so strongly expressed and so prettily ended, and has so much of fact to bear it out, that one at first is inclined to believe it all. But it is very far from the whole truth. Every year sees more grass in London, and more trees; the parks are more crowded with children and working men and roughs, who with all their rudeness respect the flowers and enjoy the meadow; the song of the thrush is not quite gone from the gardens of Kensington and Victoria Park; in spring and summer time, owing to the very railways which Ruskin seems anxious to abolish, thousands pour out of London every week to Epping and Richmond and Hampton and the Downs, and even drink the sea-breeze at Margate and Brighton. Our poor see far more of the country and of lovely places than they did in the past times which we glorify so foolishly; and bad as London is, it is better now that we have proved that we can actually stamp out the cholera, than it was in the days when the Black Death strode unopposed through its streets, and reaped a harvest in its filthy lanes and reeking cottages, which it could not reap at the present time, when the whole nation is ten times cleaner.

It is a picture by Cima of Conegliano, which he introduces to the students with this burst of sorrow, and he bids them look upon it when they would be in the right temper for work. "It will seem to speak to you if you look long: and say again, and yet again, Ἴδε ὁ αἴρων. His own Alps are in the distance, and he shall teach us how to paint their wild flowers, and how to think of them." Professor Ruskin seems to infer from the whole of this passage, and from others in the Lectures, that when these delicate and beautiful pictures were painted by Bellini, Cima, and others, there was more enjoyment of the country and of lovely things by the poor, (as if our love of landscape was not ten times more wide-spread than that of the Venetians!) and that the poor were better off, and lived a cleanlier and healthier life, and had better dwellings than they now possess in London. Neither Bellini nor Conegliano, we imagine, troubled themselves as much about the poor as even a vestryman of St. Pancras, and if we take the city of Venice, to whose school Cima belonged, the facts which speak of dirt, disease, and ill living, are appalling. In 1392 the Doge Morosini died of a great plague which swept away 19,000 souls. Not quite a century afterwards, in 1476, the Pest came again, and in 1484 it was again raging with unremitting fury. In 1556 plague and famine again devastated the city. Checked for a time, it broke out again with desolating violence in 1576; and in 1630 the great church of S. M. della Salute, which guards the entrance of the Grand Canal, was built by the vows of the Senate to beseech the prayers of the Virgin to avert another awful destruction from the people. We know now pretty well, by our own sad experience, what these visitations mean. They mean that the curse of darkness and low living, and vile dwellings, and pestilential crowding was as deep over the sun-girt city where Cima of Conegliano worked, as it ever has been in England, as it is not now in England. None of the other Italian cities were much better off, though plague was naturally worse in Venice, from its closer connection with the East, from its vast population, and from its want of fresh-water and drainage.

This curious inability of seeing facts, when he is entangled with matters irrelevant to his proper work, has spoiled some of Professor Ruskin's past labour, and diminishes the influence of these Lectures. In another man it would be culpable negligence. In his case, he is partly blinded by his crowning mistake, to which we have alluded, and partly swept away by his theory. But men should not be blinded, and should not be swept away, and Ruskin's work suffers in consequence. For by and by (and this is frequently the case) he is sure to see the other side of his theory and to dwell on that with equal force. Both statements are set over one against each other, but in different portions of his works; and the world of readers naturally declares that he has contradicted himself. He denies this, saying that he has stated both sides of the truth; but stating both these sides separately and with equal vehemence, without having balanced them, he runs into exaggeration in both, and, instead of distinctly defining one truth, rushes into two mistakes. The result is that those who admire and revere his teaching, as we ourselves most sincerely do, are greatly troubled at times to defend him and to understand him. They are wearied by the efforts they have to make to set aside what is due to impetuosity, and to find by a laborious comparison of passages what the truth really is which he desires to tell.

We hoped, for example, that in the lecture on "The Relation of Art to Morality" he would have laid down plainly what he meant on this vext subject. But we are bound to say that he has done so in a confused manner. His first phrase is, "You must have the right moral State or you cannot have the Art." He does not say you must have certain moral qualities in an artist or a nation, or you cannot have noble art:—he makes the immense requirement of a *right moral state*, which is either too vague a definition, or means that the whole state of any artist's moral character must be right or he will not produce good work. Everybody at once denies this, and brings examples to disprove it. Ruskin says that those who have misapprehended the matter have done so because they did not know who the great painters were, such as those "who breathed empyreal air, sons of the morning, under the woods of Assisi, and the crags of Cadore." Well, let us take him of Cadore. The life of Titian is not the life of a man in a right moral state, in our usual sense of the words; nor does it agree with Ruskin's sketch of a moral life, in which he includes "any actual though unconscious violation of even the least law to which obedience is essential for the glory of life and the pleasing of its giver." Titian lived the life of a noble natural character, but his morals were entirely unrestrained by any considerations belonging to high morality. He was the friend of Aretino, and that speaks volumes for his moral standard. Tintoret, a much higher moral character, despised Aretino. Titian dined with that vile person with the vilest of women. It does not say much for his reverence that he had no objection to chant the Magnificat over a dish of savoury partridges. He lived freely, he spent his money freely, he drank freely, though wisely. Nor was the society of his city in a right moral state. It had not sunk down into the faded baseness of Venice before the French Revolution. It had still a reverence for truth, and honour, and generosity, but these were combined with an audacious immorality of the body, with fiery jealousies, with the most headlong following of passions. A good deal of this is confessed by Professor Ruskin, but his confession only proves that his original phrase is far too large for his meaning. What he does mean, if we take the illustrations which follow as explanations, is this, that whatever is good in an artist's work springs from some corresponding element of good in his character, as, for example, truth of representation from love of truth. But this only predicates the existence in him of some moral qualities, not that he is in a right moral state, which means that the whole of his character is moral. With these moral qualities may exist immoral qualities, such as sensuality, and the evil influence of that will also be seen in his work. Stated thus,

Ruskin only means that a man's character is accurately reflected in his art, and this, with respect to the *ideas* of his work, we are by no means disposed to deny, seeing it may be called a truism.

But in other places, in scattered phrases, he seems to speak directly from the large statement, and to assume that it is true in its entirety, though he has modified it again and again. This is the element of confusion in the lecture, and it is at times extremely provoking.

⟨. . .⟩ We have spoken with openness of the faults which we find in Professor Ruskin's work, and it has been difficult to assume the critic: for our own gratitude to him has been and is so deep, and we are so persuaded of the influence for good which he has had on England, that blame had to become as great a duty as praise before we could express it. And even in the midst of our blame, we felt the blessing of contact with a person of a strong individuality, the pleasure of meeting in the middle of a number of writers cut out after the same pattern, with one who cuts out his own pattern and alters it year by year. His theories may, many of them, be absurd, but we may well put up with the absurdity of some for the sake of the excellence of others, more especially for the sake of the careful work which hangs on to them and can be considered apart from them. We should be dismayed to lose the most original man in England. It is quite an infinite refreshment to come across a person who can gravely propose to banish from England all manufactories which require the use of fire, who has the quiet audacity to contradict himself in the face of all the reviewers, and who spins his web of fancies and thoughts without caring a straw what the world thinks of them. The good which a man of so marked an originality does to us all is great, if it is provoking; and we had rather possess him with his errors than a hundred steady-going writers who can give solemn reasons for all they say. The intellectual excitement which he awakens, the delight and anger which he kindles in opposite characters, and the way in which his words create a stir of debate, marks the man of genius whose mistakes are often as good as other persons' victories, and who from this very quality of individuality, united to the personal attractiveness of his simple and sympathetic humanity, is calculated to be of great and lasting good to Oxford.

We have read many lectures on Art Subjects, many books on Art Criticism. They have their merits, merits which Mr. Ruskin's work does not possess. They are formal, easily understood, carefully arranged; all scattered thought, or impetuous fancy, or wild theory is banished from their pages. We walk through a cultivated garden, the beds are trimly laid down, the paths are neat and straight, the grass is closely shaven, the trees are trees of culture, the very limes on the edge are kept in order, and walls surround it on all sides. At last, on the very outskirts of the garden, beyond the bounding wall, and looked down upon by a row of pert hollyhocks who have in the course of many seasons arrived at the power of producing double flowers in an artistic manner, we catch a glimpse of a wild bit of grassy land, full of grey boulders and some noble trees growing as they like it, and below a brook chattering pleasantly over the stones. Every flower of the field blooms here and runs in and out among the rocks and roots after its own sweet will. The woodbine, the wild rose sprays, the ivy and moss, play the maddest and prettiest pranks by the brook-side. The sky is blue above, with a world of drifting clouds, and the ground below is a mystery of light and colour. It is true there are burnt spaces of grass here and there, and clusters of weeds, and now and then a decayed tree stem; but for all that, when we see the pleasant place, we do not think twice about it, we forget our garden, we leap the wall—and we live far more than half of our art life with the books of Ruskin.

Notes

1. We do not mean to say that we agree with all Mr. Ruskin's views on Poetry. On the contrary, we often disagree with him, entirely so, for example, when he represents Keats as morbid and sad—a man of the healthiest nature and of the most happy temperament, till disease laid its hand upon his splendid but undeveloped powers.

FREDERIC HARRISON
From "Past and Present" (1876)[1]
The Choice of Books and Other Literary Pieces
1886, pp. 121–35

You encourage me to attempt some answer to the sentence pronounced on me by *Fors* in June; but I am loth to seem impatient under the rebuke of Fate, or to raise an unduteous hand against you. I cannot forget how much I owe you, and how much our age has owed you; and what we owe to those who have taught us is a debt that we never can repay, a claim that never grows stale. There are so few whose lips have been touched as it were with sacred fire, having eyes that see behind the veil, and whose ears can hear the voices to which the rest are deaf; and when the utterances of such do seem to us to wander—I will almost say to mislead—it is better to keep silence even from good words. Yet when I find you publishing to the world things about those whom I honour, very contrary as I think to the fact, I will ask you to consider your judgment again. You can yet stir men of the finer fibre, and your words from time to time make us all pause and think, as men pause when violet flashes of lightning glance across the sky. Genius, like nobility, has its duties. But to me all blackening of the human race, all outbursts against the generation and its hopes are profoundly painful, born, I should say, of unnatural self-musing and self-torture, sad as those fulminous imprecations on mankind, when Lear bows his head to the storm.

I will try what I can say in mitigation of sentence pronounced by *Fors* on the world in general; an allocution addressed not only *orbi et urbi*, but *contra orbem et urbem*, but I cannot be sure that I always understand it. *Fors* seems to come down from an empyrean of her own and hold converse in an airy form of speech, which we on earth have much ado to follow—a language glancing from grave to gay, in which (as you remind me) I only stammer; so that I have nothing for it but to answer the diapason of her poetry in the flat monotone of prose.

To turn *Fors* into prose, as Mr. Bohn's translators turn Homer and Æschylus, you reprove me for believing with Auguste Comte that the human race is worthy of our regard, that it is growing wiser, stronger, and nobler. You say, on the contrary, that mankind is now very crazy and utterly vile; that beauty, nobility, and truth are all but gone out of the world, though they did flourish once in a date undetermined. You find proof of this in wild roses, in lines from the older poets, and some newspaper cuttings. Those who speak of evolution have nothing to do with ancient times or old forms of beauty, with nature or things poetic at all; for we are chiefly occupied (you say) with frogs and lice, with clamouring for women's rights, and the noisy apotheosis of liberty and machinery. It is the mark of our tribe to mangle our mother tongue with uncouth terms, and in general we are an unpleasant Gradgrind sort of people; and you finally invoke me to answer you, tracing

my birth to a species of slug whom you take to be founder eponymous of our numerous but respectable clan.[2] And in public and in private you call on me to break a lance with you as I am a true man; though mine, as you see, is little better than a reed, and your own is like a weaver's beam.

You begin by asking me "if I think you as handsome as the Elgin Theseus." Well, I must admit that when I saw you last you had not yet developed the thews of the demigod; but still, to take you all round, body, mind, and soul, I do think you a nobler specimen of man than the wrestler who sat to Pheidias. Your argument, I suppose, done into gasteropodic prose, is simply that the human kind have utterly gone backward since the statue was carved. Are you sure of that if you think of man as a whole? Pheidias, if I remember, was the acknowledged lover of Pantarces the athlete; and over the inner history of Greek art we have to draw the veil which it tore so rudely from the unblushing Phryne. Whilst the Parthenon was rising, millions of slaves rotted in the mines, and the idlers who lived upon their labour knew neither home, nor wife, nor work, nor duty, in any sense that is worth counting. One of the grandest of Greek statues recalls to us the city where the entire male population was massacred in cold blood by the fellow-citizens of Pheidias, who besides treated their great sculptor with wanton ingratitude. Indeed, when I remember Aristophanes, and think of Cleon, Alcibiades, ostracism, and another very "peculiar institution," I must say that the radiant medal of Athene has a truly sinister obverse. Theseus was of old my ideal in art, and many a holiday have I spent as a boy, yet under the roof of the paternal zoophyte, in wondering at his immortal calm. But would you say that an athletic form is the whole duty of man, or art the end of life? And, besides, could you not find youths at Oxford to win the parsley from Pantarces himself; and do you think a man in the fleet at Salamis could swim, like Matthew Webb, from England to France? A civilised man can roll over a savage; is bigger, stronger, and lives longer; can bear twice as much, and do twice as much. Men nowadays cannot get into the puny armour of ancient days; and, if a pampered aristocracy in an age of slavery, by giving their whole lives to care of their skins, did reach a special type of beauty, the race as a whole has a higher physical standard. So that, if you are not so handsome as Theseus, and Hamlet is not to be compared to Hercules, you and Hamlet have something to set against the want of muscle, and you may console yourself by thinking that there are more fine men and women in Europe to-day than there were two thousand years ago.

For further proof of the degeneracy of man you quote Virgil's picture of Camilla in arms, and you beg me to contrast it with the tale of a farcical prizefight in New York between two dancing girls, so that I shall see and acknowledge the downfall of modern womanhood. But why compare Camilla with an American mime? I suppose there were mimes at Rome in Virgil's day? Indeed, just at the time these clarion-ringing lines about Camilla appeared, a dear friend of the poet wrote some verses beginning, *Ambubaiarum collegia, pharmacopolœ,* showing an altogether different type of womanhood and manhood in that polished society for which Camilla was imagined. I love my Virgil, and am dumb with awe before the Theseus; but neither Athens nor Rome gives me quite the type of the virtuous life. And frankly I cannot say that Camilla is the finest ideal of woman. A modern poet has drawn for us finer; Cordelia, and Imogen, Desdemona, Ophelia, and the rest; or to come to our own age, there is the homely but true story of Jeannie Deans. Are you thinking of women famous in war? Well, Jeanne d'Arc is a far greater heroine than Camilla, though she lived some twenty centuries later. And as you beg me to compare the ideals of ages, I will ask you to compare the ancient vision of the warrior maid with the modern reality of Florence Nightingale.

Your bit about roses perplexes me. When I said that the flowers of our gardens had been gathered from all parts of the earth, and were greatly changed by man's care, I thought I was saying something familiar to any gardener, and entirely true in fact. And you swear that the flowers and the plants have never been developed at all, that man has never improved one of them (for you can't get a good pippin as you used when a boy), and that all we can do by nature is to leave her alone. Do you mean that the varieties in a modern garden grow wild at Coniston, and that you find pippins amidst the heather? Or do you mean that the gardens and cornfields, the orchards, and the watermeadows of these latter days are deteriorations from the primitive face of nature, and all bear the mark of the beast—man? Tell us the exact point of wildness to which you wish man and the earth to return. Will clothes, wheaten flour, and ploughshares be suffered in the golden age, or will St. George appear amidst moor and brushwood in the garb of Theseus adorned with woad?

I am sorry to be told that, when once we speak of evolution, we may never more meddle with roses; but are warned to keep close to our frogs and our lice. I certainly thought that the theory of evolution was a good deal occupied with the habits of plants. And there is a bit of fortuitous logic in which I require some help. When I said that flowers under man's *cultivation* change greatly from their *wild* forms, I was rebuked by *Fors*, who reminds me that the *wild* rose of Etruscan art is the *wild* rose of your hills today. But is the old wild rose the same as the cultivated rose of our time? Can *Fors* pick *Devoniensis* growing wild on the moors, or do you find it in the British Museum? I agree with your love for the wild rose, and I trust evolution will never extinguish either that or other wild things. But Adam and Eve tended theirs; and if it be wicked to work at our gardens, it is no proof of the degeneracy of man, for it is a form of offence as old as original sin—of which peradventure it was either cause or effect.

And I was a little hurt to be told so peremptorily never again to allude to traceries. Why, all that I did was to make two friends in talk at Oxford speak of some flowers near the gray traceries of Magdalen. And for this rather feeble bit of local colour I am rebuked by *Fors*, "in the name of common sense and common modesty," for "chattering about" traceries. I am only, you say, making a jackdaw of myself, for I don't know a good one from a bad one, and couldn't design a tracery for my life. Now, did I ever presume that I could, for I am neither architect, professor, nor critic? It does happen that I have had a special foible for Gothic churches in my molluscous way for some thirty years, and have crawled, as a gasteropod best may, over many an one, from porch to belfry, and in and out the wavy foliage of the capitals, and round the irridescent mysteries of the rose windows, and so through all the *Seven Lamps*—

Vagliami il lungo studio e il grande amore,
Che m'han fatto cercar lo tuo volume;

but as to *knowing* anything about it that you would call *knowing*, spare me! Newton might as well ask a schoolboy, stammering out his Asses Bridge, why he was "chattering about" mathematics.

You mean (for your lightest play has a meaning, as all play should have) that the Holothurian and Pedicular tribe to which I have the honour to belong are incapable of a feeling for Gothic art or mediæval life. I will not undertake to answer for the rest of the Echinodermata, but so far as concerns Comte,

I suppose no one ever held in such deep honour the genius of the Middle Age at its best, its religion, its chivalry, its poetry, and its art, going to it indeed for the type and ideal of man's spiritual force. As to Gothic architecture, I should like to quote you what he says: "That the ideas and feelings of man's moral nature have never found so perfect expression in form as they found in the noble cathedrals of Catholicism;" and no right mind, he says, "can ever look on them without an exquisite sense of emotion, born of deep sympathy with the spirit that then inspired society." This was said long before the bubble of our Gothic mania, as a bit of history not of art, and before a famous "Graduate" had passed his "Little-go." I do wish that besides punning on Comte's name you would look at his books, at least before making game of him; and I think you would see that he had pierced as truly as you have, and long before you, into the spiritual meaning of mediæval art, including, by the way, its music, a most important branch of art, about which I think you have been silent. So if I and my fellows are Goths about Gothic architecture, it is no fault of Comte's, but must come from the original sin of the "mere slimy mass of helpless blackness" that we are, our protozoic infirmity of the flesh.

You next take me to task for using the mere word "Humanity," as uncouth English, and you say with a whack of your cane that my terms are as muddled as my head. It was needless to tell me that you know something of organic English whilst I do not, for that is certainly true; and I feel that to reason with you about language is to argue with the master of forty legions. But are you sure that you see what we try to express by "Humanity?" You say that "an aggregate of men is a mob." Surely not always; for an aggregate of men may be a regiment or an army, which is not a mob, or indeed a tribe or a family. Where men work and live together gregariously, in a disciplined and organic way, they are not a mob, as I suppose your own St. George's company is not to be a mob. And if we think of the human race all working together in an organic way, as will be the case if you ever convert the entire world to become "companions of St. George," we should get near our notion of Humanity. We do not mean simply the human race now extant; but the past and the present members who have made it, and those to come who will inherit its tasks—just as by England we mean our nation, its history, and its future. We call all this Humanity, and though I acknowledge your mastery of organic English, I doubt if you can find a simpler word for this complex notion. Even as a piece of philology, it is surely as good as "Deity," which I see you use.

I thirst as you do for that "well of English undefiled," which you have done much to keep fresh and limpid; but the passion for the stalwart speech of Sir Philip Sidney may grow into affectation; and there is visible in our day that most simpering of all tongues, a sort of archaic Euphuism; so that many a man who has to say "some people are fools," Osricises his remark thus, "There be who are as the wild ass." Human wants cannot always be cribbed within the range of lyric poetry and the native woodnotes of art. Science and organisation must have their vocabulary, to which we shall have to screw our mouths, though it makes us as wry as the wrenching of teeth. The manly course when we need a hard word and cannot find a better, is to bring it out without wincing till it becomes quite natural. "Ganglion" is not pretty, but can you express its meaning in less than a sentence? "Sociology," they tell us, is a barbarous term; but the pedants have never supplied us with a better; and as to objecting to use the words which mankind make current, you might as well decline to endure the west wind, on the ground that you like it south. I could not justify to a purist in grammar the word "locomotive." But I use the word and the thing without a pish; for I have no time to travel as you do by the road, or to be always saying, "The pieces of steel put together into a frame which run along on iron rails." Nor do I think it mends matters to invent some Biblical trope, and call it "The Pale Horse." I admit that the "precession of the equinoxes" does not go kindly in a sonnet; but if we wish to know something of the law, we can hardly express it in old Saxon or old English. It would be to quarrel with our bread and butter like children, if we refused to eat till we had renamed our bits of daily food. I see that in St. George's schools you have begun to invent new titles for the flowers. But how far do you intend to carry the process? Do you mean to have fresh words for the old ones—truth, modesty, sense, and obedience; and is science to be taught in an *abracadabra*, and religion in a bran-new *fi-fo-fum*? But in this case St. George's company will end like the Tower of Babel; for I assure you that there is one thing which genius itself cannot invent, and that is a language. The Anarchists of '93 tried hard to rename many things, but it never occurred to them to revolutionise the French speech. After all, the first proof of social discipline and manly obedience is to use the language to which we are born as the air in which we live; for it is very certain that no one of us can make either for himself. You see that you cannot mark my place in the animal kingdom without using such a queer term as "Holothurian."

This is not a trifle, this impatience of scientific words, merely because they are long and will not come well into a stanza. It is only a form for impatience of science—that is, of knowledge. Here are you, and many a man of high poetic sensibility, crying pish at the word "evolution," and hotly denouncing the thing it expresses, because you cannot find it in the Bible or in Shakespeare. You say, and you say it with complete truth, that you know much more than I do of organic Nature and her processes. Well, can you describe for a mammal that process of unfolding from the ovum to birth, without using the words "evolution," "differentiation," or some equally complex synonym? The truth is, that you really forswear "evolution" and all its works, because you find it difficult to square with the poetic and prophetic scheme of life. And thousands, and they are some of the brightest and some of the devoutest natures, nurse themselves into a noble defiance of solid knowledge, on the ground that, because it is solid, it is necessarily hard and dry. And you, and some others I could name, are ready with ample encouragement to ignorance, sometimes it may be with a pathetic kind of Hebrew melody, and sometimes with racy Rabelaisian fun. But *Sartor Resartus* having been edited once for all can never be renewed; and attempts to imitate it are as hopeless as those of a man whom I saw the other day artistically "restoring" a thirteenth-century statue. Leave the inimitable torso in its vast pathos, rugged with the winds and the storm of heaven.

You undertake to say that those who believe in evolution do not study men and women, but frogs and lice; and your warning perchance will inspire a groan round many a decorated tea-table, and in many an early-pointed sermon. But can you say, with your hand on the book, that the advocates of evolution do *not* study men and women? Do you tell the jury that this is true of Comte? Have you read his theory of history? Do you know what he says about religion, family, government, education? How much of his "Polity" is given to frogs and lice, and how much to men and women? Do you deny that ninety out of every hundred pages speak directly of men and women? And yet you tell him to keep to his worshipful Batrachianity, his divine Pedicularity. And you name therewith Mr. Herbert

Spencer, Mr. John Stuart Mill; have neither of them ever spoken of men and women, but are both absorbed with reptiles and parasites? You tell the court that Mr. Spencer and Mr. Mill are occupied mostly with frogs and lice; and you tell your pupils of St. George's new schools that if we wish to know about *geese*, we must go to these writers. And by way of a lesson in the manner of Sidney, you speak to them of a lady whom you describe as "Cobbe." Oh, the pity o't! The light of the Seven Lamps is dim, and the music of the choir where they burned comes from afar to us like sweet bells jangled, harsh, and out of tune.

I take shame to myself, that I can note this with anything but a smile, or that I can be drawn into telling you plainly how little I like it; for all that you press me to tell you something. But what you write is not, and cannot be, the mere wind moaning in the branches. The soul and the eye which have sent a spark through every fibre of this whole generation of Englishmen can never be of no account; and the memory of some memorable teaching still lives in its echoes. Men of science and of the new learning, secure in their logic and academic approval, are but too ready to make light of the Jeremiahs who cry woe! woe! in the streets in the name of tradition and poetry and religion. And the rich and the powerful hear of one complaining of the age of steam, as they would hear of a beggar whining out an old song. But there are some, who are not learned, and not powerful, who do listen and are touched and moved to the core by it—and who have hearts and passions and brains also, that thrill with the finer spiritual motions and forces. These you have often led; these men and women, these poets, priests, artists, these mothers, wives, and daughters you speak for; and all the while science and progress wonder to find a vast silent weight against them, and they are sore that they do not advance. And the strange part of it is that science and progress do not altogether deserve to advance without a halt in that grand triumphant car with patent axles and automatic steam apparatus, which seems to the twin powers the perfection of reason and mechanism. You, and the greater and lesser prophets of the older faith of Israel, are truly so far right, that science without religion *is* materialist, immoral, inhuman; modern life *is* in many ways chaotic and brutal; industry *is* often cruel; and progress *is* something of a scramble.

And for this very reason it is so urgent that those who, like you, have a heart for the pathos of human nature, and the soul to make even the callous hear its cry, should do nothing to increase the chaos. Human life without knowledge is blind; and you mock at knowledge, or, at least, at the systematic knowledge of disciplined philosophy. The laws of physical and organic nature can only be summed by patient combination of the labour of ages; and you tell us, with the fervour of Peter the Hermit, that we shall find them all in the Bible and a bank of wild flowers. Religion can be nothing unless it be true; and you tell us that truth must all be discovered anew in St. George's schools. So that the only bond of society, a reasonable use of tradition, is to you a more worthless old rag than it is to the wildest communist.

Notes

1. A letter to Professor Ruskin in reply to one addressed to the Writer by Mr. Ruskin, published in *Fors Clavigera* for June 1876.
2. As I understand the words, "Human Son of Holothurian Harries."

SIR LESLIE STEPHEN
"John Ruskin" (1900)
Studies of a Biographer
1902, Volume 3, pp. 83–118

Ruskin's death, as we all agreed, deprived us of the one man of letters who had a right to burial in Westminster Abbey. We may rejoice that his representatives preferred Coniston. The quiet churchyard in a still unpolluted country was certainly more appropriate for him than the 'central roar' of what he somewhere calls 'loathsome London.' But the general consent marks the fact that Ruskin had come to be recognised as a compeer of the greatest writers of the age. By many he is also revered as one who did more than almost any contemporary to rouse the sluggish British mind from its habitual slumber. His career, indeed, suggests many regrets. His later writings are too often a cry of despair and vexation of spirit. The world is out of joint, and all his efforts to set it right have failed. To those who cannot quite agree that we are all driving post-haste to the devil, the pessimism may seem to indicate the want of intellectual balance which did much to waste surpassing abilities. But if his vagaries are sometimes provoking, at any rate they are always interesting. Though my intellectual idols in old days were of a different school, I was never so dull as to be indifferent to the curious fascination of his books. I have been refreshing my memory of them lately, and if I cannot profess myself an ardent disciple, I have at least read with renewed or increased admiration of his literary power. One excellence is conspicuous at first sight. The cardinal virtue of a good style is that every sentence should be alive to its fingers' ends. There should be no cumbrous verbiage: no barren commonplace to fill the interstices of thought: and no mannerism simulating emotion by fictitious emphasis. Ruskin has that virtue in the highest degree. We are everywhere in contact with a real human being, feeling intensely, thinking keenly, and, even when rhetorical, writing, not to exhibit his style or his eloquence, but because his heart burns within him. In his later moods, indeed, Ruskin held that he had been at first too much given to the ornate: he had been seduced by his admiration for Hooker to indulge in elaborate long-winded sentences: and he certainly had a weakness for very deliberate 'purple patches.' That was a venial fault as a young man, and was sufficiently punished by misdirected admiration. People, as he complained, would take him for a coiner of fine phrases, instead of a real philosopher and a serious critic of art. *Modern Painters*, as even an artistic ignoramus could see, was something much more than rhetoric. It was an intellectual feat which becomes more surprising the more one thinks of it. The first volume, we remember, was not only written when he was twenty-three, but when he had had, in some respects, a singularly narrow education. Ruskin, we may note, was at Oxford during the most exciting period of the 'movement.' His ablest contemporaries were all going through the Newman fever. Ruskin seems never to have been aware that such a person as Newman existed. He amused himself with geology and botany, and seems to have been as blind as became the son of a sound Evangelical wine-merchant to the very existence of any spiritual ferment. That might seem to prove that he cared nothing for intellectual speculations. Yet within a year or two he was writing a book of which it may be said that no work produced by an English author of the same period of life has ever done so much to set people thinking in a fresh direction. The generous desire to do justice to Turner, which prompted

the book, led, I suppose, to the most triumphant vindication of the kind ever published. In any case, the argument was so forcibly put as to fall like a charge of dynamite into the camp of the somnolent critics of the day. The book, whatever its errors, is, I fancy, the only one in the language which treats to any purpose what is called æsthetics. It is amusing to notice what difficulty the young critic has in finding any previous authorities to confute. He goes back to Locke's essay, and Burke on the *Sublime and Beautiful*, and Alison on *Taste*, and the papers by Reynolds in Johnson's *Idler*, which have also, as he remarks, the high sanction of their editor. In truth, English speculation on such matters was nearly a blank. Untrammelled by any solemn professors of æsthetics, Ruskin could be all the fresher; and perhaps the better able to impress readers who were neither philosophical nor æsthetic. People who shared the indifference to art of those dark ages (I can answer for one) were suddenly fascinated, and found to their amazement that they knew a book about pictures almost by heart. They did not foresee the day in which a comfortable indifference to artistic matters, instead of being normal and respectable, would be pitiable and almost criminal. Ruskin, no doubt, gave the first impulse to the change.

His popular reputation was partly due to the passages which a severe taste can only just approve. Yet the worst one can say of such famous bits of rhetoric as the comparison of Claude's skies with Turner's is that they approach Shelley's finest imagery too nearly for prose. The rhetoric rests, in any case, upon some remarkable qualities. His defence of Turner is mainly an exposition of Turner's truthfulness to nature, and shows that his eulogist is qualified to judge of his fidelity. Ruskin has watched sky and sea and mountains so closely, that he is revolted by the old conventional portraits and demonstrates his point with extraordinary fulness of knowledge. He surpasses the average critic in that respect as a scientific specialist surpasses a mere popular observer. Ruskin, indeed, took himself to have a specially scientific mind. So far as aptitude for science means power of observation, the claim, I imagine, was perfectly justified. He came in later years to detest science 'in the lump,' and to speak of leaders of science with unfortunate arrogance. But his power of seeing the phenomena vividly was as remarkable as his power, not always shared by scientific writers, of making description interesting. I owe him a personal debt. Many people had tried their hands upon Alpine descriptions since Saussure; but Ruskin's chapters seemed to have the freshness of a new revelation. The fourth volume of *Modern Painters* infected me and other early members of the Alpine Club with an enthusiasm for which, I hope, we are still grateful. Our prophet indeed ridiculed his disciples for treating Mont Blanc as a greased pole. We might well forgive our satirist,[1] for he had revealed a new pleasure, which we might mix with ingredients which he did not fully appreciate. The power of giving interest and fascination even to dry geological details was no doubt due to the singular fervour of his nature-worship. One pardons a lover for some excess of interest even in the accessories of his mistress's charms. How Ruskin's passion for nature was developed by his surroundings may be learnt from many of his most interesting reminiscences. But the surroundings worked upon innate predispositions which must have been almost unique. He speaks in *Modern Painters* of his 'intense joy, mingled with awe,' when his nurse took him to Friar's Crag on Derwentwater. It was 'comparable only to the joy of being near a noble and kind mistress'—and equally inexplicable. Long afterwards he tells us how, as a boy, he would pass entire days rambling on 'Cumberland hillsides or staring at the lines of surf on a low sand,' and traces his whole power of judging in art to the habit thus acquired. In this quality, and in this alone, he was, he thinks, remarkable as a child. Most children have a certain taste for ponds and rocks, as offering romantic chances of dirt and danger, and as the habitat of things catchable, and partly, if they are imaginative, as probable haunts of pirates and Robinson Crusoes. Those are surely rare who, as Ruskin tells us of himself, found a 'strange delight' in getting a 'land-line cutting against the sky.' Wordsworth was another recorded instance, and Ruskin himself compares this early passion to that which prompted the famous ode. Heaven lies about us in our infancy, if we happen to be Wordsworths or Ruskins, and till he had grown to manhood its indulgence gave him a pleasure infinitely greater than he had since found in anything. This enthusiasm, however psychologists may explain it, not only gave charm to Ruskin's early writings, but gave the substance of the æsthetic doctrine to which, as he observes rather ruefully, people would pay no attention. He set out with the intention of systematically expounding a theory of the beautiful. Unfortunately, he had one infirmity fatal to such an attempt. He was incapable of arranging his thoughts in orderly symmetrical pigeon-holes: his mind was essentially discursive: he could see things more vividly than any one, and could argue acutely and ingeniously; but he had never the patience to consider how his thoughts should be co-ordinated and wrought into consistent unity. The *Modern Painters*, we know, could never be really completed at all, because he was attracted by all manner of irrelevant and collateral issues. In later years his incapacity for consecutive writing becomes bewildering. You can never tell in reading a lecture whether the next paragraph will take you to questions of religion or art or social evils or autobiography. In a letter to Carlyle in 1855 he humorously declares that he is reading German metaphysics, poetry, political economy, cookery, music, geology, dress, agriculture, horticulture, and navigation all at once, which, as he observes, 'takes time.' No human intellect, one might add, performing such rapid flights from topic to topic, could ever get any of them fairly worked out. A letter from an unnamed friend, which he published in the *Fors Clavigera*, suggests a partial explanation. 'You can,' said this frank critic, 'see an individual concrete fact better than any man of the generation; but an invisible fact, an abstraction, . . . you have, I fancy, been as incapable of seeing as of seeing through a stone wall.' With necessary deductions from the judgment of a candid friend there is, I fancy, much truth in this. Ruskin was too much absorbed in the individual and concrete to be a good system-monger. Intellectually, he resembles a short-sighted man to whom every detail is so abnormally vivid in turn that he forgets the whole. He has to make his theories—if theories he must have—not by patient induction, but by flashes of intuition. His theory of the beautiful simply formulates his own childish instincts. Wordsworth had seen, we know, in his own early feelings a proof of the soul's pre-existence 'with God, who is our home.' So Ruskin, though he somewhere calls this fanciful, regards the sense of beauty as a revelation—as something like the inner light of mystics. All natural beauty, he says, is 'typical of the divine attributes'; and he tries to show in detail how the sense of beauty corresponds to a perception of Infinity, Order, Symmetry, Unity, and so forth, and how the external world is thus a divinely appointed system of symbols, dimly recognised even in childhood. This theory, no doubt, is as good as others. Like others, indeed, which present themselves as a direct inspiration of the prophet, it may fail to convince opponents; and the elaboration into a symmetrical system must not be taken too seriously. Ruskin quaintly

remarks how hard he found it to prevent his *Seven Lamps of Architecture* from becoming eight or nine upon his hands. No doubt his first follower, if he had found one, would have redistributed his symbols, and interpreted various objects to mean entirely different truths. It should be taken, as we take Wordsworth's ode, not as a prosaic argument, but as an imaginative way of expressing his own sentiments. If disputable as a general theory, it shows what the love of nature meant for Ruskin. To him it seemed to be a part of religion; and a description is for him not a mere catalogue of forms and colours and sensations, but a divine language to be interpreted by the 'high instincts' (if I may quote the inevitable ode again) before which our mortal nature trembles like a guilty thing surprised. To read the true meaning of these outward and visible signs is the function of what he calls the 'theoretic faculty'; and, parenthetically, I may add that his theory, good or bad in itself, leads him to very interesting literary criticisms. I do not know whether the chapters in which he discusses the 'theoretic' faculty or imagination will pass muster with later psychologists better than his theory of the beautiful with professors of æsthetics. But I never read anything which seemed to me to do more than these chapters to make clear the true characteristics of good poetry. Ruskin's critical judgments are certainly not always right; no critic can always judge rightly, unless at the cost of being thoroughly commonplace, and Ruskin is often wayward and sometimes extravagant. But his sense of what was excellent was so keen and genuine, and he could often analyse his impressions so subtly, that I have seemed to myself (perhaps it was an illusion) to have really learnt something from his remarks.

Ruskin's theory suggested many difficulties—which, indeed, is the chief use of a theory. Contemporary critics condemned him and his clients, the Pre-Raphaelites, as 'realists.' He was taken to hold, that is, that the merit of a work of art was measurable entirely by the quantity of 'truth' which it contained. I fancy that the employment of the word 'truth,' when what is really meant is 'likeness,' leads to as many fallacies as any known misuse of language. It seems, in particular, to make a moral duty of what is a simple question of artistic method. In the *Modern Painters* he is constantly struggling against this interpretation, though he never gets the point quite clear. There is a difficulty in carrying out the theory consistently. The painter, it seems, is to give the facts pure and simple, but then it is just because the facts signify ideas. The greater the realism, though it may sound paradoxical, the greater the idealism. If, indeed, the 'love of nature'—the intense joy and awe which Ruskin and Wordsworth felt in their early days—be interpreted to mean that the natural scenery which Turner painted is symbolic of divine truths, the closer the imitation the fuller will be the revelation. But when Ruskin is showing the marvellous accuracy of Turner's perceptions, he seems to become simply scientific or prosaic. Turner's merit is explained to be that he instinctively grasped the laws of mountain structure and saw what later geologists tried to explain. It is only by a kind of after-thought that the scenery is made to be somehow edifying and symbolic. There is a greater difficulty behind. After all, is the 'love of nature' so clearly a religious or moral sentiment? In a chapter of *Modern Painters* upon the 'Moral of Landscape,' Ruskin tries, with great ingenuity, to show that the passion is at any rate congenial to the highest moral feelings. Yet he betrays some doubt. With Byron, the 'love of nature'—if we are to take his word for it— was a corollary of his misanthropy. He loved the deep and dark blue ocean precisely because it has a pleasant way of sending man shivering and howling to his gods. Is not that the logical view? To love rock and stream precisely for their wildness surely means that you dislike the garden and the field which are useful to human beings. The love of nature, as interpreted by Rousseau and his followers, meant, in fact, a condemnation of civilised man, not misanthropy, indeed, but a conviction of the thorough corruption of men as they are—whatever we may hope for men as they are to be.

When, in the *Modern Painters*, Ruskin tried to extend his theory from the beauty of inanimate nature to the beauty of organised beings, he felt this difficulty. Some animals, and many men, are undoubtedly ugly. If they are symbolic of anything, it is of something the very opposite of divine—of sensuality, greed, and cruelty. In the language of his Evangelical days, Ruskin regards this as a result of the 'Adamite fall.' As the love of nature is essentially a part of religion, he naturally comes to a theory which identifies the 'aesthetic' with the moral or religious instinct, and scandalised many people who did not wish their love of art to be trammelled by any crotchets of morality. The change from the Ruskin of the *Modern Painters* to the Ruskin of the later days is, of course, marked by the development of this feeling. The vileness of man, instead of the beauties of nature, becomes his chief preoccupation. In the early volumes he is not only enthusiastic, but seems to count upon the enthusiasm of his readers. He is exultingly smiting the Philistine hip and thigh with a certain complacency; and the good time is coming in which Turner and the Pre-Raphaelites will be duly honoured. The fervid rhetoric is the natural language of one who is leading a band of followers to the promised land. Something gradually changed; not his character, but his habitual tone of feeling. In his natural temper, he tells us, he had most sympathy with Marmontel;[2] in his 'enforced and accidental temper,' with Swift. If any one asks how Swift was soured, there is no want of sufficient explanation. We cannot say of Ruskin that he ever became 'soured': the genial and generous qualities which suggest the comparison to Marmontel were always there; but, certainly, his 'enforced and accidental temper' became only too like Swift's. The modern Englishman was, for him, painfully like the Yahoo. A man hardly becomes a pessimist out of simple logic, and Ruskin had personal sorrows and sufferings, and an exquisitely sensitive and affectionate nature. The intellectual change was, perhaps, rather effect than cause, but it was, at any rate, characteristic. He was distracted from the *Modern Painters* by the keen interest in architecture which produced the *Stones of Venice* and the *Seven Lamps*. The study gave prominence to a new point of view. In his early work he might pass for a believer in progress. The 'love of nature' is, in some sense, a product of the last century or two; and the modern painters of whom he wrote, with Turner at their head, were, he thought, incomparably superior to Claude or Salvator. But in architecture, he saw decay instead of progress. The ancient buildings, whose glory he set forth, were being recklessly destroyed or 'restored,' and the art of building itself was a thing of the past. Great architecture presupposes continuous traditions and a certain social harmony. The mediæval cathedrals were the product of a spontaneous instinct, in which each man took his part as naturally as the bee in the honeycomb, and thought as little of his separate interests. We have lost the power because society has been disintegrated; instead of a common ideal, we have a dozen conflicting fashions, and depend upon self-seeking architects, and greedy contractors and demoralised workmen. Whatever may be the true way of stating the relation between art and morals, there is a close connection between good art and sound social conditions. If a people become selfish and brutalised, no national art, at least, can flourish. Far be it from me to attempt an accurate statement; but I cannot doubt that Ruskin's vehement assertions were at least approximations to a most important truth. He was thus in face of a dilemma. Delicate and refined natures, indeed, might shut themselves up in a Tennysonian 'palace of art,' and cultivate ideals as remote as possible from the prosaic ugliness of the modern world. Ruskin's sympathies and moral feelings were too strong. Even in his early writings, he objected to use the word 'æsthetic' because it suggested the effeminate taste which 'ministers to morbid sensibilities.' Like William Morris, on the same grounds, he held that art as a social product could only be renewed by regenerating society itself. That was a tolerably large enterprise, into which he threw himself with, perhaps, more energy than reflection; but which led, at least, to the utterance of some very pungent and much-needed truths.

About 1860 he began his warfare against the creed of the modern world, which for him was represented by the Political Economists. He was taken to be a dangerous heretic. Readers were so much outraged that Thackeray had to stop 'Unto this Last' in the *Cornhill*, and Froude to decline 'Munera Pulveris' for *Fraser*. The strength of the popular prejudice surprises later readers. For some years we have been flouting the old Political Economists with a scorn as unqualified as the respect with which they were formerly greeted. Ruskin, indeed, had precedents enough for identifying political economy with the degrading and materialising tendencies of modern society. The doctrine had been denounced from its very birth by Conservatives, Socialists, and Radicals of many types as heartily as Ruskin could wish. He declared himself to be an interpreter of Carlyle, to whom, as he said, he owed more than to any one, and who had spoken the whole truth about the matter in *Past and Present*. No one could acknowledge an intellectual debt more loyally and heartily, and Carlyle's philosophy in general, as well as his special denunciations of the 'dismal science,' had clearly a potent influence upon his disciple. The Christian Socialists, too, with whom Ruskin associated, were protesting against the old orthodox doctrine in the same spirit—to say nothing of other critics who arose within the ranks of the Economists themselves. There was nothing new in the simple fact of a revolt. Carlyle, however, to the ordinary Briton, passed for an eccentric old Diogenes—a railer at things in general, or perhaps a humorist whose misanthropy was half affectation. The Christian Socialist might be treated as amiable and excellent crotchet-mongers, whose philanthropy wanted common-sense. And undoubtedly there was a vulgar version of Political Economy, which used the orthodox phrases ignorantly and blatantly enough, preached an absolute and selfish 'individualism,' and discovered that every scheme of social reform was somehow condemned by inexorable scientific law. Ruskin, therefore, resolved, he tells us, to come to close quarters with pseudo-science; and to make it the 'central work of his life to write an exhaustive treatise upon Political Economy.' He began, apparently, by reading Ricardo and Mill and such other authorities with attention; though with a strong impression that they would turn out to be humbugs. One result was that he attributed to some of his opponents, to J. S. Mill in particular, a complicity with a vulgar version of their doctrines which they altogether repudiated. He should have recognised that Mill could speak as emphatically as himself of the injustice of the actual social order; and sympathised quite as much with the Socialist aspiration, if not with the Socialist solution. There was, undoubtedly, a radical antagonism of principle; but Ruskin was too passionately eager to distinguish between the stupid and selfish opponents, and men whose ability and genuine zeal he ought to have appreciated.[3]

Ruskin struck some sharp blows. The craftsmen still believed implicitly in their Diana of the Ephesians. Carlyle's huge growls had passed over men's heads like distant thunder, too vague to be effective. Ruskin meant to be the lightning, striking distinct and tangible points. He had, as he had showed in his other works, a singular power of putting nasty questions, of hitting weak points, exposing loose and wordy phrases, and generally making himself disagreeable to self-complacent phrasemongers. He succeeded in irritating, if not in convincing. For the time the respectable world shut its ears and kept him out of correct periodicals. Naturally, he has now the credit which comes to the earlier mouthpieces of a rising sentiment. I cannot believe, indeed, that those 'arrows of the chace'—to adopt his title for his occasional letters—really advanced economics. He could make special points, but not construct a mere scientific theory. His moral sense was in too great a hurry to step in. He could not look at the facts quietly before fulminating his spiritual censures. When, for example, he convinced himself that usury was wicked, he jumped—most generously but most impatiently—to rash and, as I think, absurd conclusions. To tell him that his theory would be fatal to the whole structure of modern industry might convince him that it must be true, for modern industry is one mass of corruption. To me, I confess, his doctrine seems to show that one's conscience may be a dangerous guide unless it condescends to be enlightened by patient and impartial inquiry. We cannot honour too cordially Ruskin's sensibility to social evils, and the vehement hatred of baseness and brutality which inspired his headlong assault. But one result of his errors was that they gave some apparent excuse to the infinitely commoner fault of cultivating indifference.

Ruskin's righteous indignation took, it must be admitted, some very queer forms. 'I will put up with this state of things not an hour longer,' he says in the first letter of the *Fors Clavigera*. The singular series which followed must always be one of the curiosities of literature. No man of genius, in the first place, ever treated his public with such unceremonious frankness. One is often inclined to accept his own view that his style had improved by increased directness and sacrifice of rhetorical ornament. On the other hand, the incapacity for keeping to any line of thought has reached its highest point. The twenty-fifth letter begins, *à propos* to nothing, with a famous receipt for a 'Yorkshire Goosepie,' a Brobdingnagian pie, which engulfs also a turkey, ducks, woodcocks, a hare, and any quantity of spices and butter. He proceeds at once to a description of the British penny, diverges into heraldry, and ends by an account of Edward III.'s fight with the French at Calais. Amazed correspondents, he tells us, inquired into the meaning of this pie, and his answer, though it manages to introduce an assault upon Darwinism, hardly clears the point. One can hardly doubt that the discursiveness and eccentricity were indicative of a morbid irritability of brain which was to cloud his intellect, and which is the best apology for certain utterances which offended his readers. When a correspondent complained of his speaking of Mill and Mr. Herbert Spencer as 'geese,' he replied that he said so simply because he 'knew a goose when he saw one.' Other phrases show a rudeness strange in one who in personal intercourse was the most courteous of men. When, indeed, he has said something specially sharp, he generally proceeds to insist upon the extreme care and moderation of his language. 'Whatever is set down for you in *Fors*,' he says, 'is assuredly true, inevitable, trustworthy to the uttermost, however strange.' He quaintly admits in a note that

he may make a mistake or two upon merely 'accessory points.' Such extravagancies, and there are plenty of them, shocked the critic of well-regulated mind. Matthew Arnold, if I remember rightly, refers to some of them as instances of British crudity. We may forgive them if we take them as due to a physical cause. No doubt, however, he had a tendency to such escapades: he took a pleasure, as he admits somewhere, in a 'freakish' exaggeration of his natural humour. Carlyle used often to qualify his extravagant remarks by a huge guffaw, which implied that he was only half serious; and Ruskin's sharp sayings were entitled to the same allowance. He is partly soothing himself by equivalents for a good 'mouth-filling' oath, and partly amusing himself by the neatness with which he can hit a weak point.

The *Fors*, however, shows feeling deep and genuine enough. It fully explains his enforced resemblance to Swift. He is as vehement, if neither so coarse nor so pithy. 'I perceive,' he says, 'that I live in the midst of a nation of thieves and murderers; that everybody around me is trying to rob everybody else, and that, not bravely and strongly, but in the most cowardly and loathsome way of lying trade; that "Englishman" is now merely another word for blackleg and swindler; and English honour and courtesy changed to the sneaking and the smiles of a whipped pedlar, an inarticulate Autolycus, with a steam hurdy-gurdy instead of a voice.' He only hopes to 'pluck up some drowned honour by the locks out of this festering mass of scum of the earth and miserable coagulation of frog-spawn soaked in ditch-water.' He follows an equally bitter passage elsewhere by observing that his words are 'temperate and accurate—except in short-coming of blame.' Our great teachers, he tells us, even Carlyle and Emerson, accept too easily the comforting belief that right will speedily become might. That is not the ordinary view of Carlyle, who was gloomy enough for most of us. Ruskin, in passages like the above, seems to be trying to surpass his master. We are worse, he assures us, than Eccelin of Padua, who slew two thousand innocent persons to maintain his power, whereas we lately slew in cold blood five hundred thousand persons by slow starvation—that is, as he explains, did not prevent a famine is Orissa. The cases are not strictly parallel. In spite of such feats of logic, Ruskin's bitter utterances constantly made you wince. His attacks on modern society might be caricatures, but clearly there were very ugly things to caricature. Whether he bewailed the invasion of country solitudes by railways and suburban villas, or the mean and narrow life of the dwellers in villas, or went further and produced hideous stories of gross brutality in the slums of London or Manchester, he had an unpleasant plausibility. If you tried to reply that such things were not unprecedented, you felt that the line of defence was rather mean, and that even if Ruskin was over-angry you had no business to be too cool. When I read *Fors* I used always to fancy that I could confute him, and yet to feel uncomfortable that he might be more in the right than was pleasant. The evils which had stung so fine a nature to such wrath must at least be grievous.

How much Ruskin did to awaken people to a sense of social diseases, or how far his diagnosis was correct, is another question. I am only considering the literary aspect. Ruskin is now often compared to his master, and although attempts to compare great writers, and especially to place them in order of merit, are generally vexatious, the relation between the master and his disciple may suggest certain points. In the twenty-five years which preceded Ruskin's assault upon the Economists, Carlyle had been, one may say, the leader of the intellectual opposition. He denounced the prevailing tendencies, one outcome of which was in his dialect the 'pig philosophy' of Utilitarians and Materialists. His disciples were few, and even those who shared his antipathies were often shocked by his rugged idiosyncrasies and what seemed to be his deliberate mannerisms. Yet, considered as a prophet, it seems to me that Carlyle had a far more potent influence upon the more thoughtful young men of the time than Ruskin ever possessed. He might be grotesque and extravagant, but his influence embodied a more vigorous and coherent philosophy. He had the uncompromising thoroughness of the Puritan, and in this respect was a quaint contrast to his disciple. Carlyle, as a descendant of John Knox, approved of the famous sentiment, 'May the devil fly away with the fine arts!' He sympathised with Cromwell's view of the right method of dealing with cathedrals, and would have been ready enough to smash painted windows and deface the images of saints. Ruskin, who drew his early religious impression from an enfeebled version of Puritanism, was alienated from it precisely by this iconoclastic tendency. Though he never followed Newman, he came to admire mediæval art so warmly that he has some difficulty in explaining why, at a later period, he did not become a Catholic. There was a point of contact, no doubt, in the hatred of the 'pig philosophy' (the word does not represent my own prejudices) and Ruskin's conviction of the desirable subordination of art to morality. Ruskin saw, as he tells us, that art had decayed as much in Catholic as in Protestant countries, and fell back upon a religious creed, vague enough except as expressing antipathy to scientific materialism. But his version is curiously modified in the process of engrafting the love of the beautiful upon Carlyle's sterner philosophy.

The arrogance of Ruskin's language was partly adopted from Carlyle, and, indeed, is one of the awkward consequences of being an inspired prophet. It is implied in your very position that your opponents are without an essential mental faculty. You do not condescend to argue, but have a direct vision of truth not perceptible to the blind. Carlyle's famous conversion left him facing the 'Everlasting No' of Atheism in a humour of 'indignation and grim fire-eyed defiance.' But he held equally that we must disengage ourselves from the old creeds and legends which were once the embodiment, but had now become mere obstructions to the religious spirit. We must 'clear our minds from cant,' and 'cant' included a great deal that was dear to weaker brethren. Ruskin, without positively dissenting, represents a different sentiment. He really loved the old symbols which to Carlyle appeared to be outworn rags of 'Houndsditch.' It is characteristic that while professing his debt to Carlyle, he associates him (of all people) with George Herbert, the Anglican divine. He was affected, at times, not only by the sweetness of sentiment of Herbert's poetry, but by the ingenuity in finding everywhere symbols of religious truth. The method becomes characteristic; as external nature is a divine symbolism, the old religious art, and all great poetry and philosophy, Shakespeare and Dante and Homer and the Book of Genesis, are a kind of mystic adumbration of esoteric truths. The *Tempest* is an allegory; the labyrinths of Crete and the legend of the Sirens contain profound wisdom. Though he did not read German, he was impressed by the second part of *Faust*, just because it is intolerably allegorical, and has a bearing upon the theory of usury. Quaintly enough, he complains that the greatest men have found it necessary to wrap up their truths in enigmas soluble only by the wise; and declares that even the parables in the New Testament are 'necessarily misleading' to the profane. When a man interprets books or, as sometimes happens, history by his fancy instead of his understanding, he becomes simply absurd to plain

common-sense, unless one gives him credit for not being quite in earnest. But if considered merely as products of graceful fancy, investing tender feeling or sharp satire with the charm of poetical ingenuity, his discourses sometimes make admirable literature. The very titles of his books, the *Sesame and Lilies* and *Love's Meinie*, and so forth, are promises that his moralising shall be transfigured into the most poetical forms. I do not know that the promise is always kept: the fancies become too palpably arbitrary, and aggravate the strange discursiveness. But the little book which seems to be his most popular, the *Sesame and Lilies*, deserved its success. His style, I think, was at its best. He can still be as eloquent as of old, though less ornate; and, though the argument wanders a little, he manages to give a regular and concentrated expression of his real convictions. The last section in that volume, 'The Mystery of Life and Its Arts,' is, to my mind, the most perfect of his essays. Perhaps I am a little prejudiced by its confession, franker than usual, of the melancholy conviction that, after all, life is a mystery: and no solution really satisfactory. It is a good bit of pessimism, especially if you omit the moral at the end.

To most admirers, however, this would hardly be a recommendation. Rather they were drawn to Ruskin because, in spite of the gloomy views which he shared with Carlyle, he did not give the same impression of 'grim fire-eyed despair.' Carlyle, we used to say, though he could denounce the world, could suggest no remedy. Ruskin, hardly more hopeful in fact, was yet always suggesting a possible regeneration. Wisdom is to be found, though it is strangely hidden away; and the Marmontel side of him comes out in his pictures of a conceivable Utopia. There is something pathetic in the kind of helpless and yet enthusiastic way in which he expounds the scheme of the 'St. George's Company.' He protests that he only undertakes such a task against his will; he would infinitely rather plunge into his favourite studies; he is forced to try to reform the world because the sight of all the wrongs and miseries is a torment to his spirit, and because he can find no one else to share his views or take up the burthen. He showed that he was in earnest by lavish generosity, and managed, at least, to start a museum. He seems to have made an oversight characteristic of nearly all founders of such societies. He began, as they all begin, by acquiring a piece of freehold land. He arranged, which also seems to be a fascinating amusement, for the currency which his followers were to use when they were established. The difficulty which he never really contemplated was the rather serious one, how the society was to be kept in order. His tenants are to adopt the laws of 'Florence in the fourteenth century'—with some modifications. Above all things, they are to renounce altogether the modern heresies about liberty. Implicit obedience to the 'Master' is to be a first principle. They are to make a curious profession of faith embodying this promise, and they are to keep their vows. They will prosper, he says, because they will all be strictly honest, and their word, therefore, implicitly accepted in all transactions. If the founder of a new society could be sure that all his followers would be perfectly good and absolutely obedient, he would, no doubt, have surmounted the great initial difficulty. He is more likely, it is to be feared, to collect a mixed crowd of fanatics and humbugs, ready to dispute his authority or sponge upon his benevolence. But that is the criticism of cold common-sense, which would be inappropriate. The Utopia served to set forth Ruskin's view of the existing social evils and contrast them with an ideal of a purer and sweeter life. He contrasts a sketch of peasant life from Marmontel with the gangs of rowdy labourers who, it appears, cultivate Californian fields with the help of the latest machinery; or takes an idyllic story from Gotthelf, the

Swiss novelist—unknown, I must confess, to me; or recalls the wholesome Tyrolese peasant whom he has heard singing 'like a robin' in the still uncorrupted mountain-guarded districts. It is the old story of the men of nature contrasted with corruption and luxury. He seems, for a moment, to be in the most congenial surroundings at Assisi, copying Giotto's dream of the marriage of St. Francis to the Lady Poverty. He admits that he does not quite like the look of St. Francis' camel's-hair coat, and doubts whether the Saint's vow of poverty was the right thing. Perhaps, however, a Ruskin in an earlier period might have really founded an order, instead of fondly imagining one; and, perhaps too, it would have illustrated once more the tendency of impossible ideals to stimulate a reaction to corruption. If I were capable of composing 'imaginary conversations,' I should try one between St. Francis and some sound political economist, Malthus for example, and contrast the idealist who scorns all compromise, and proposes to change men into angels off-hand, and the solid matter-of-fact reasoner who perceives—perhaps too clearly—that we shall not develop wings just yet. Both classes, I take it, are useful, but there can be no doubt which is most beloved. With all Ruskin's waywardness and dogmatism, and hopeless collisions with common-sense, he attracts people who lean to the ideal side— little as he could himself hope to fight victoriously against the great brutal forces of the world. It is tolerably clear that machinery will be made and coal-mines worked, and even that men will take interest for money, for some time to come. But we may hope that steam-engines are not really in deadly antagonism to all virtue and purity and simplicity of life; and that the leaven of Ruskin's teaching may further the desirable reconciliation.

Such problems are beyond me. The real charm of Ruskin will perhaps be most perceptible to the future reader in a region less disturbed by controversy. Ruskin's distaste for the actual world led him often to look fondly to the days of his infancy, when there were still honest merchants and unpolluted fields even at Dulwich, and some people—especially his father and mother—who could lead simple lives of reasonable happiness. People, I observe, have lately acquired a habit of insisting upon the extraordinary stupidity and selfishness of the last generation. They are good enough sometimes to make allowances for poor people born before the Reform Bill, on the ground that it is unfair for the historian to apply to a rude age the loftier standards of modern life. It is pleasant for the elderly to be reminded that some of their fathers and mothers were really worthy people, though Ruskin's estimate cannot be taken as unbiassed. To say the truth, one has a kind of suspicion that the objects of his reverence would not have appeared to us quite as they do to him. That does not prevent the *Præterita* from being one of the most charming examples of the most charming kind of literature. No autobiographer surpasses him in freshness and fulness of memory, nor in the power of giving interest to the apparently commonplace. There is an even remarkable absence of striking incident, but somehow or other the story fascinates, and, in the last resort, no doubt on account of the unconscious revelation of character. One point is the way in which a singular originality of mind manages to work out a channel for itself, though hedged in by the prejudices of a sufficiently narrow-minded class and an almost overstrained deference to his elders and his spiritual guides. But it is enough to say here that the book should be acceptable even to those to whom his social and artistic dogmas have ceased to have much significance.

Notes

1. I will venture to add a reminiscence. Ruskin was induced by his friend, St. John Tyrwhitt, to attend a dinner of the Alpine Club about 1868. He declined to speak, and at first looked upon us, I think, as rather questionable characters; but he rapidly thawed and became not only courteous, but cordially appreciative of our motives. I think that he called us 'fine young men'! At any rate he joined the Club and was a member for many years, although, of course, he could still speak very frankly of our frailties.
2. So Mill tells us in his *Autobiography* that a passage in Marmontel's Memoirs gave him the first help in rousing him from his youthful fit of melancholy.
3. See *Time and Tide*, p. 167, for an assault upon Mill's 'wilful equivocations.' Ruskin's wrath prevented him from seeing that Mill, as was shown by his approval of 'land nationalisation,' was attacking 'landlordism' as sincerely as his critic.

OSCAR WILDE

OSCAR WILDE

1854–1900

Oscar Fingal O'Flahertie Wills Wilde was born in Dublin on October 16, 1854, the son of Dr. William (later Sir William) Wilde, a surgeon, and Jane Francesca Elgee, well known under the pen-name "Speranza." Wilde studied classics with great success at Trinity College, Dublin (1871–74), and then at Magdalen College, Oxford (1874–78), where in 1878 he won the Newdigate Prize for his poem *Ravenna*. In 1881 Wilde published *Poems*, a volume that was successful enough to lead to a lecture tour in the United States during 1882. In all his public appearances Wilde, who proclaimed himself a disciple of Pater, displayed a flamboyant aestheticism that did much to increase his notoriety.

Wilde returned to America in 1883 in order to attend an unsuccessful New York production of his play *Vera*, written the year before. In 1884, after moving to London, he married Constance Lloyd, although shortly afterwards he began to assert his repressed homosexuality. *The Happy Prince and Other Tales*, a volume of fairy tales written for his two sons, appeared in 1888, and was followed by his only novel, *The Picture of Dorian Gray*, which appeared in *Lippincott's Magazine* in 1890 and in book form in 1891. Also in 1891 Wilde's play *The Duchess of Padua* was produced in New York under another title and anonymously, without much success. Wilde's essay "The Soul of Man under Socialism," a plea for artistic freedom, appeared in 1891, as did *Intentions*, containing the critical dialogues "The Decay of Lying" and "The Critic as Artist"; *Lord Arthur Savile's Crime and Other Stories*; and another collection of fairy tales, *The House of Pomegranates*.

Wilde first found theatrical success with his play *Lady Windermere's Fan* (1893), which combined social observation with a witty, epigrammatic style. This formula was pursued successfully in the plays that followed, including *A Woman of No Importance* (1894), *An Ideal Husband* (1899), and *The Importance of Being Earnest* (1899). *Salomé*, published in French in 1893, was translated into English by Lord Alfred Douglas in 1894 and performed in Paris by Sarah Bernhardt in 1896, after being denied a license in England. Lord Alfred, whom Wilde had first met in 1891, was Wilde's homosexual lover, a relationship that so disturbed the Marquess of Queensberry, Lord Alfred's father, that he publicly insulted Wilde on several occasions beginning in 1894. This prompted Wilde to bring a charge of criminal libel against Lord Queensberry, but the suit misfired and Wilde himself was imprisoned for homosexual offenses in 1895. In prison, where he remained for two years, Wilde wrote a letter to Lord Alfred that was partially published in 1905 as *De Profundis*; it contained his own justification for his conduct. After his release in 1897 Wilde went to France, where he published *The Ballad of Reading Gaol* (1898), inspired by his prison experiences. In exile he adopted the name Sebastian Melmoth, taken from Charles Robert Maturin's Gothic romance *Melmoth the Wanderer*. Wilde died in Paris on November 30, 1900. His *Collected Works* were edited by Robert Ross (12 vols., 1909). His *Letters*, edited by Rupert Hart-Davis, appeared in 1962; a supplementary volume was published in 1985.

Personal

Mr. Wilde laid himself out to play a certain *rôle*, and when he attitudinised he did it sufficiently well to make it pay, and to induce the world to take him seriously. When he was interviewed by newspaper correspondents his remarks made what is professionally known as "good copy," because he usually said something that startled a serious world by its audacity. When, after crossing the Atlantic, he responded to an inquiry on the subject by expressing his disappointment with the "mighty ocean," persons of a superior type, who expect poetic rhapsodies on such an occasion, in accordance with precedent, were naturally shocked.

He set conventionality at defiance in other respects, and in his lectures expressed some revolutionary sentiments with reference to modern costume, from an art point of view. He had a good word to say for knee-breeches and silk stockings, but spoke disrespectfully of coats and trousers, and more in sorrow than in anger of the chimney-pot hat, which he did not regard as "the thing of beauty" referred to by the poet as "a joy for ever." He even had the hardihood to insinuate that the nineteenth-century Englishman in his "Sunday best" was not,

from a spectacular point of view, comparable to the ancient Greek in his temple get-up. As neither the fashionable tailors nor Mrs. Grundy could endorse anything so heterodox, it need hardly be said that he made but few converts to his views on costume, and we go on "just in the old sweet way" in the matter of outward apparel. The freedom with which he enunciated extreme opinions, such as these, induced the polite world, or, as we prefer to term them nowadays, the "smart people," who are always on the look-out for something piquant, to flock to his lectures in order to listen to the next dreadful thing he would say; and this must have been very much in consonance with Mr. Wilde's expectations and desires.—THOMAS F. PLOWMAN, "The Aesthetes: The Story of a Nineteenth-Century Cult," *Pall Mall Magazine*, Jan. 1895, pp. 41–42

To the many Wilde was an unspeakable person, but to the few he was an accomplished scholar and gentleman, suffering from one of the most terrible and loathsome forms of insanity, which two years of prison life increased rather than diminished. I met him in Paris a few weeks after he finally left England, and his appearance was burnt in on my memory. A tall, stalwart figure, with a face scored with suffering and a mistaken life. The gray, wearied eyes, the mocking curves of the mobile mouth, reminded me of Charles Reade's description of Thomas of Sarranza at the time that he sat in the Fisherman's Seat—'a *gentilhomme blasé*, a high-bred and highly-cultivated gentleman who had done, and said, and seen, and known everything, and whose body was nearly worn out.'

Wilde was then living in the Rue des Beaux Arts, under the name of Sebastian Melmoth. He invited me to lunch, and we had déjeuner at a little restaurant on the Boulevard St. Michel, where for over two hours he talked with the same delightful insouciance which had characterized him in his best days. Wilde detested coarse language or coarse conduct, and I remember him moving his chair away from the vicinity of some students who, with their Mimis and Marcelles, were talking in a strain that would have made Rabelais blush. He talked lightly about his trial, but his face lighted up with savage indignation when he spoke of his prison treatment. Of one prison official he said: 'He had the eyes of a ferret, the body of an ape, and the soul of a rat.' The chaplains he characterized as 'the silliest of God's silly sheep,' and gave an instance of the kind of reading they select for the prisoners under their charge. A man had been sentenced to seven years' imprisonment, six months of which was to be endured in solitary confinement. The book served out to him by the chaplain at —— Prison was 'Sermons Delivered at —— Prison to Prisoners under Sentence of Death.' I had had the advantage of reading *The Ballad of Reading Gaol* in manuscript some days before I met the author, and I asked him whether he intended to write further in the same vein.

'Do not ask me about it!' Wilde said with a sigh. 'It is the cry of Marsyas, not the song of Apollo. I have probed the depths of most of the experiences of life, and I have come to the conclusion that we are meant to suffer. There are moments when life takes you, like a tiger, by the throat, and it was when I was in the depths of suffering that I wrote my poem. The man's face will haunt me till I die.'

The conversation drifted on to Aubrey Beardsley, who was then on the point of becoming a Catholic.

'I never guessed,' said Wilde, 'when I invented Aubrey Beardsley, that there was an atom of aught but pagan feeling in him.'

I happened to mention something that Herr Max Nordau had told me the day before on the subject of 'The Degenerates,' and on Nordau's firm belief that all men of genius were mad.

'I quite agree with Dr. Nordau's assertion that all men of genius are insane,' said Wilde, 'but Dr. Nordau forgets that all sane people are idiots.'

He leaned back in his chair, lit a cigarette, and gazed reflectively at the beautiful scarab ring on his finger. 'I shall start working again, and trust to the generosity of the English people to judge it on its merits, and apart from their Philistine prejudices against myself. I do not acknowledge that I have ever been wrong . . . only society is stronger than I. Should the English people refuse my work, then I shall cross to America, a great country which has always treated me kindly. I have always been drawn towards America, not only because it has produced a very great poet—its only one—in Walt Whitman, but because the American people are capable of the highest things in art, literature, and life.'

'Do you not care for Longfellow, then?'

'Longfellow is a great poet only for those who never read poetry. But America is great because it is the only country in the world where slang is borrowed from the highest literature.

I remember some years ago, when I was travelling out West, I was passing by a store when a cowboy galloped past. The man with me said: "Last night that fellow painted the town red." It was a fine phrase, and familiar. Where had I heard it? I could not remember, but the same afternoon, when I was taken to see the public buildings—the only ones in this place were the gaols and cemeteries—I was shown a condemned cell where a prisoner, who had been sentenced to death, was calmly smoking a cigarette and reading *The Divine Comedy* of Dante in the original. Then I saw that Dante had invented the phrase "painting the town red." Do you remember the scene where Dante, led by Virgil, comes to the cavernous depths of the place swept by a mighty wind, where are confined those who have been the prey of their passions? Two pale faces arise from the mist—the faces of Francesca da Rimini and her lover. "Who art thou?" cries Dante in alarm, and Francesca replies sadly: "We are those who painted the world red with our sin." It is only a great country which can turn the greatest literature into colloquial phrases.' ⟨. . .⟩

The end of his meteoric career is too sad to be dealt with here. Suffice it to say that, if his terrible mania made him sin in the eyes of the world, he suffered no less terribly. Apart from this side of his character, he had a rare delicacy in the things of this world, and his remark that Zola was a writer of immoral books, to which my 'Mawworm' critic objected, was made in all sincerity. Those who really knew him made due allowance on his behalf, ignoring the maniac who had fallen under the ban of English displeasure, and recking only of the rare artist, the accomplished scholar, the greatest sonneteer in the world of poetry since the days of Rossetti and John Keats, and the kindly gentleman whose heart was a mine of generosity and good-nature. May his soul rest in peace and his sins be forgiven him!—CHRIS HEALY, *Confessions of a Journalist*, 1904, pp. 131–38

Yesterday I saw ⟨Robert⟩ Ross, Oscar Wilde's friend, who was with him in his last hours. I was curious to know about these and he told me everything. Ross is a good honest fellow as far as I can judge, and stood by Oscar when all had abandoned him. He used to go to him in prison, being admitted on an excuse of legal business, for Ross managed some of Mrs. Wilde's affairs while her husband was shut up. He told me Oscar was very hardly treated during his first year, as he was a man of prodigious appetite and required more food than the prison allowance gave him, also he suffered from an outbreak of old symptoms and was treated as a malingerer when he complained of it. Ross's representation got attention paid to these things, and in the last eight months of his imprisonment, Wilde had books and writing materials in abundance and so was able to write his *De Profundis*. I asked him how much of this poem was sincere. He said, 'As much as possible in a man of Oscar's artificial temperament. While he was writing he was probably sincere, but his "style" was always in his mind. It was difficult to be sure about him. Sometimes when I called he was hysterical, at other times laughing. When Oscar came out of prison he had the idea of becoming a Catholic, and he consulted me about it, for you know I am a Catholic. I did not believe in his sincerity and told him if he really meant it, to go to a priest, and I discouraged him from anything hasty in the matter. As a fact, he had forgotten all about it in a week, only from time to time he used to chaff me as one standing in the way of his salvation. I would willingly have helped him if I had thought him in earnest, but I did not fancy religion being made ridiculous by him. I used to say that if it came to his dying I would bring a priest to him, not before. I am not at all a moral man, but I had my feeling on this point and so the matter remained between us. After he had been nearly a year out of prison he took altogether to drink, and the last two years of his life were sad to witness. I was at Rome when I heard that he was dying and returned at once to Paris and found him in the last stage of meningitis. It is a terrible disease for the bystanders, though they say the sufferer himself is unconscious. He had only a short time to live, and I remembered my promise and got a priest to come to him. I asked him if he would consent to see him, and he held up his hand, for he could not speak. When the priest, an Englishman, Cuthbert Dunn, came to him he asked him whether he wished to be received and put the usual questions, and again Oscar held up his hand, but he was in no condition to make a confession nor could he say a word. On this sign, however, Dunn allowing him the benefit of the doubt, gave him conditional baptism, and afterwards extreme unction but not communion. He was never able to speak and we do not know whether he was altogether conscious. I did this for the sake of my own conscience and the promise I had made.' Wilde's wife died a year after he left prison. She would have gone to see him at Paris but he had already taken to drink, and Ross did not encourage her to do so. Ross made £800 by the *De Profundis*. He had intended to pay off Oscar's Paris debts with £400 of it and devote the rest to the use of the boys, but just as he was going to do this the whole sum was claimed by the bankruptcy court and the affair is not yet settled.—WILFRED SCAWEN BLUNT, *My Diaries* (entry for Nov. 16, 1905), 1920, Vol. 2, pp. 125–26

Wilde himself I met only in his later years. I remember being at a garden party of the Bishop of London, and hearing behind me a conversation so indelicate that I could not resist turning around. Oscar Wilde, very fat, with the remainder of young handsomeness—even of young beauty—was talking to a lady. It would be more precise to say that the lady was talking to Wilde, for it was certainly she who supplied the indelicacies in their conversation, for as I knew Wilde he had a singularly cleanly tongue.

But I found him exceedingly difficult to talk to, and I only once remember hearing him utter one of his brilliancies. This was at a private view of the New Gallery. Some one asked Wilde if he were not going to the soirée of the O. P. Club. Wilde, who at that time had embroiled himself with that organization, replied: "No. Why, I should be like a poor lion in a den of savage Daniels."

I saw him once or twice afterwards in Paris, where he was, I think, rather shamefully treated by the younger denizens of Montmartre and of the Quartier Latin. I remember him as, indeed, a tragic figure, seated at a table in a little cabaret, lachrymosely drunk, and being tormented by an abominable gang of young students of the four arts.

Wilde possessed a walking-stick with an ivory head, to which he attached much affection—and, indeed, in his then miserable poverty it was an object of considerable intrinsic value. Prowling about the same cabaret was one of those miserable wrecks of humanity, a harmless, parasitic imbecile, called Bibi Latouche. The young students were engaged in persuading poor Wilde that this imbecile was a dangerous malefactor. Bibi was supposed to have taken a fancy to Wilde's walking-stick, and the young men persuaded the poet that if he did not surrender this treasure he would be murdered on his way home through the lonely streets. Wilde cried and protested.

I do not know that I acted any heroic part in the matter. I was so disgusted that I went straight out of the café,

permanently cured of any taste for Bohemianism that I may ever have possessed. Indeed, I have never since been able to see a student, with his blue béret, his floating cloak, his floating tie, and his youthful beard, without a feeling of aversion.

One of Wilde's French intimates of that date assured me, and repeated with the utmost earnestness and many asseverations, that he was sure Wilde only sinned *par pure snobisme*, and in order to touch the Philistine on the raw. Of this I am pretty well satisfied, just as I am certain that such a trial as that of Wilde was a lamentable error of public policy on the part of the police. He should have been given his warning, and have been allowed to escape across the Channel. That any earthly good could come of the trial, no one, I think, would be so rash as to advance. I did not like Wilde, his works seemed to me derivative and of no importance, his humour thin and mechanical, and I am lost in amazement at the fact that in Germany and to some extent in France, Wilde should be considered a writer of enormous worth. Nevertheless, I cannot help thinking that his fate was infinitely more bitter than anything he could have deserved. As a scholar he was worthy of the greatest respect. His conversation, though it did not appeal to me, gave, as I can well believe, immense pleasure to innumerable persons; so did his plays, so did his verse. Into his extravagances he was pushed by the quality of his admirers, who demanded always more and more follies; when they had pushed him to his fall, they very shamefully deserted this notable man.

On the afternoon when the sentence against Wilde had been pronounced, I met Dr. Garnett on the steps of the British Museum. He said gravely: "This is the death-blow to English poetry." I looked at him in amazement, and he continued: "The only poets we have are the Pre-Raphaelites, and this will cast so much odium upon them that the habit of reading poetry will die out in England."

I was so astonished that I laughed out loud. I had hardly imagined that Wilde could be called a Pre-Raphaelite at all. Indeed, it was only because of the confusion that existed between Pre-Raphaelism and Æstheticism that the name ever became attached to this group of poets. Pre-Raphaelism as it existed in the 'forties and 'fifties was a sort of Realism inspired by high moral purpose.

Æstheticism, which originated with Burne-Jones and Morris, was a movement that concerned itself with idealizing anything that was mediæval. It may be symbolized by the words, "long necks and pomegranates." Wilde carried this ideal one stage further. He desired to live upon the smell of a lily. I do not know that he ever did, but I know that he was in the habit of sending to young ladies whom he admired a single lily flower, carefully packed in cotton-wool. And the cry from the austere realism of my grandfather's picture of *Work*, or Holman Hunt's *Saviour in the Temple*, was so far that I may well be pardoned for not recognizing Wilde at all under the mantle of a *soi-disant* Pre-Raphaelite.—FORD MADOX FORD, *Ancient Lights and Certain New Reflections*, 1911, pp. 150–53

Presently came Oscar, and growing accustomed to the darkness one could see how like he was to the photographs of him which were all about the room, full-face, half-face, three-quarter face; full-length, half-length, three-quarter length; head only; in a fur coat; in a college gown; in ordinary clothes. He came and stood under the limelight so to speak, in the centre of the room. There was some sort of divan or ottoman there on which Miss Fortescue and he sat for a while in conversation. The shaded light had been arranged so as to fall upon them.

With him had come in the girl who was afterwards to have the irreparable misfortune to be his wife, poor picturesque pretty Constance Lloyd, dressed all in brown, a long brown cloak, a wide brown velvet hat with a plume. How charming it is in one's memory now that feminine fashions have reached the nadir of hideousness. She was a delicate charming creature, little fitted to endure the terrible fate that was to be hers. At the time, doubtless many people thought her fate enviable.

One was brought up to Oscar and introduced. Then and always I found him pleasant, kind and interested. My impression of his looks was of an immense fat face, somewhat pendulous cheeks, and a shock of dark hair, a little like the poet Bunthorne perhaps—a little also like Marat or Robespierre. I found nothing in him of the witty impertinence other people record him. I remember that Hannah Lynch's introduction to him was in this way. Lady Wilde said: "This is Miss Hannah Lynch, Oscar: a young Irish genius." Oscar: "Are not young Irish geniuses as plentiful as blackberries?"—KATHARINE TYNAN, *Twenty-five Years: Reminiscences*, 1913, pp. 149–50

General

That sovereign of insufferables, Oscar Wilde, has ensued with his opulence of twaddle and his penury of sense. He has mounted his hind legs and blown crass vapidities through the bowel of his neck, to the capital edification of circumjacent fools and foolesses, fooling with their foolers. He has tossed off the top of his head and uttered himself in copious overflows of ghastly bosh. The ineffable dunce has nothing to say and says it—says it with a liberal embellishment of bad delivery, embroidering it with reasonless vulgarities of attitude, gesture and attire. There was never an impostor so hateful, a blockhead so stupid, a crank so variously and offensively daft. Therefore is the she fool enamored of the feel of his tongue in her ear to tickle her understanding.

The limpid and spiritless vacuity of this intellectual jellyfish is in ludicrous contrast with the rude but robust mental activities that he came to quicken and inspire. Not only has he no thoughts, but no thinker. His lecture is mere verbal ditch-water—meaningless, trite and without coherence. It lacks even the nastiness that exalts and refines his verse. Moreover, it is obviously his own; he had not even the energy and independence to steal it. And so, with a knowledge that would equip an idiot to dispute with a cast-iron dog, an eloquence to qualify him for the duties of caller on a hog-ranch and an imagination adequate to the conception of a tom-cat, when fired by contemplation of a fiddle-string, this consummate and star-like youth, missing everywhere his heaven-appointed functions and offices, wanders about, posing as a statue of himself, and, like the sun-smitten image of Memnon, emitting meaningless murmurs in the blaze of women's eyes. He makes me tired.

And this gawky gowk has the divine effrontery to link his name with those of Swinburne, Rossetti and Morris—this dunghill he-hen would fly with eagles. He dares to set his tongue to the honored name of Keats. He is the leader, quoth'a, of a *renaissance* in art, this man who cannot draw—of a revival in letters, this man who cannot write! This littlest and looniest of a brotherhood of simpletons, whom the wicked wits of London, haling him dazed from his obscurity, have crowned and crucified as King of the Cranks, has accepted the distinction in stupid good faith and our foolish people take him at his word. Mr. Wilde is pinnacled upon a dazzling eminence but the earth still trembles to the dull thunder of the kicks that set him up.—AMBROSE BIERCE, "Prattle," *Wasp*, March 31, 1882

We have the irresponsible Irishman in life, and would gladly get rid of him. We have him now in literature and in the things of the mind, and are compelled perforce to see that there is a good deal to be said for him. The men I described to you the other day under the heading, "A Reckless Century," thought they might drink, dice, and shoot each other to their hearts' content, if they did but do it gaily and gallantly, and here now is Mr. Oscar Wilde, who does not care what strange opinions he defends or what time-honoured virtue he makes laughter of, provided he does it cleverly. Many were injured by the escapades of the rakes and duellists, but no man is likely to be the worse for Mr. Wilde's shower of paradox. We are not likely to poison any one because he writes with appreciation of Wainwright—art critic and poisoner—nor have I heard that there has been any increased mortality among deans because the good young hero of his last book tries to blow up one with an infernal machine; but upon the other hand we are likely enough to gain something of brightness and refinement from the deft and witty pages in which he sets forth these matters.

"Beer, bible, and the seven deadly virtues have made England what she is," wrote Mr. Wilde once; and a part of the Nemesis that has fallen upon her is a complete inability to understand anything he says. We should not find him so unintelligible—for much about him is Irish of the Irish. I see in his life and works an extravagant Celtic crusade against Anglo-Saxon stupidity. "I labour under a perpetual fear of not being misunderstood," he wrote, a short time since, and from behind this barrier of misunderstanding he peppers John Bull with his pea-shooter of wit, content to know there are some few who laugh with him. There is scarcely an eminent man in London who has not one of those little peas sticking somewhere about him. "Providence and Mr. Walter Besant have exhausted the obvious," he wrote once, to the deep indignation of Mr. Walter Besant; and of a certain notorious and clever, but coldblooded Socialist, he said, "he has no enemies, but is intensely disliked by all his friends." Gradually people have begun to notice what a very great number of those little peas are lying about, and from this reckoning has sprung up a great respect for so deft a shooter, for John Bull, though he does not understand wit, respects everything that he can count up and number and prove to have bulk. He now sees beyond question that the witty sayings of this man whom he has so long despised are as plenty as the wood blocks in the pavement of Cheapside. As a last resource he has raised the cry that his tormentor is most insincere, and Mr. Wilde replies in various ways that it is quite an error to suppose that a thing is true because John Bull sincerely believes it. Upon the other hand, if he did not believe it, it might have some chance of being true. This controversy is carried on upon the part of John by the newspapers; therefore, those who only read them have as low an opinion of Mr. Wilde as those who read books have a high one. *Dorian Grey* with all its faults of method, is a wonderful book. *The Happy Prince* is a volume of as pretty fairy tales as our generation has seen; and *Intentions* hides within its immense paradox some of the most subtle literary criticism we are likely to see for many a long day.—W. B. YEATS, "Oscar Wilde's Last Book" (1891), *Uncollected Prose*, ed. John P. Frayne, 1970, Vol. 1, pp. 203–4

When the *Ballad of Reading Gaol* was published, it seemed to some people that such a return to, or so startling a first acquaintance with, real things, was precisely what was most required to bring into relation, both with life and art, an extraordinary talent, so little in relation with matters of common experience, so fantastically alone in a region of intellectual abstractions. In this poem, where a style formed on other lines seems startled at finding itself used for such new purposes, we see a great spectacular intellect, to which, at last, pity and terror have come in their own person, and no longer as puppets in a play. In its sight, human life has always been something acted on the stage; a comedy in which it is the wise man's part to sit aside and laugh, but in which he may also disdainfully take part, as in a carnival, under any mask. The unbiassed, scornful intellect, to which humanity has never been a burden, comes now to be unable to sit aside and laugh, and it has worn and looked behind so many masks that there is nothing left desirable in illusion. Having seen, as the artist sees, further than morality, but with so partial an eyesight as to have overlooked it on the way, it has come at length to discover morality in the only way left possible, for itself. And, like most of those who, having "thought themselves weary," have made the adventure of putting thought into action, it has had to discover it sorrowfully, at its own incalculable expense. And now, having become so newly acquainted with what is pitiful, and what seems most unjust, in the arrangement of human affairs, it has gone, not unnaturally, to an extreme, and taken, on the one hand, humanitarianism, on the other realism, at more than their just valuation, in matters of art. It is that odd instinct of the intellect, the necessity of carrying things to their furthest point of development, to be more logical than either life or art, two very wayward and illogical things, in which conclusions do not always follow from premises.

Well, and nothing followed, after this turning-point, as it seemed, in a career. "Whatever actually occurs is spoiled for art," Oscar Wilde has said. One hoped, but he had known at least himself, from the beginning. Nothing followed. Wit remained, to the very end, the least personal form of speech, and thus the kindest refuge for one who had never loved facts in themselves. "I am dying beyond my means" was the last word of his which was repeated to me.

His intellect was dramatic, and the whole man was not so much a personality as an attitude. Without being a sage, he maintained the attitude of a sage; without being a poet, he maintained the attitude of a poet; without being an artist, he maintained the attitude of an artist. And it was precisely in his attitudes that he was most sincere. They represented his intentions; they stood for the better, unrealised part of himself. Thus his attitude, towards life and towards art, was untouched by his conduct; his perfectly just and essentially dignified assertion of the artist's place in the world of thought and the place of beauty in the material world being in nowise invalidated by his own failure to create pure beauty or to become a quite honest artist. A talent so vividly at work as to be almost genius was incessantly urging him into action, mental action. Just as the appropriate word always came to his lips, so the appropriate attitude always found him ready to step into it, as into his own shadow. His mind was eminently reasonable, and if you look closely into his wit, you will find that it has always a basis of logic, though it may indeed most probably be supported by its apex at the instant in which he presents it to you. Of the purely poetical quality he had almost nothing; his style, even in prose, becomes insincere, a bewildering echo of Pater or of some French writer, whenever he tries to write beautifully. Such imagination as he had was like the flickering of light along an electric wire, struck by friction out of something direct and hard, and, after all, only on the surface.

"But then it is only the Philistine," he has said, in his essay on Wainewright, "who seeks to estimate a personality by the vulgar test of production. This young dandy sought to be somebody rather than to do something. He recognised that Life itself is an art, and has its modes of style no less than the arts that seek to express it." "Art never expresses anything but itself," he has said, in another essay in the same book, so aptly called *Intentions*; and that "principle of his new æsthetics" does but complete his view of the function of life. Art and life are to be two things, absolutely apart, each a thing made to a pattern, not a natural, or, as he would take it to be, an accidental, growth. It is the old principle of art for art's sake, pushed to its furthest limits, where every truth sways over into falsehood. He tells us that "the highest art rejects the burden of the human spirit, and gains more from a new medium or a fresh material than she does from any enthusiasm for art, or from any lofty passion, or from any fresh awakening of the human consciousness." But he forgets that he is only discussing technique, and that faultless technique, though art cannot exist without it, is not art.

And so with regard to life. Realising as he did that it is possible to be very watchfully cognisant of the "quality of our moments as they pass," and to shape them after one's own ideal much more continuously and consciously than most people have ever thought of trying to do, he made for himself many souls, souls of intricate pattern and elaborate colour, webbed into infinite tiny cells, each the home of a strange perfume, perhaps a poison. Every soul had its own secret, and was secluded from the soul which had gone before it or was to come after it. And this showman of souls was not always aware that he was juggling with real things, for to him they were no more than the coloured glass balls which the juggler keeps in the air, catching them one after another. For the most part the souls were content to be playthings; now and again they took a malicious revenge, and became so real that even the juggler was aware of it. But when they became too real he had to go on throwing them into the air and catching them, even though the skill of the game had lost its interest for him. But as he never lost his self-possession, his audience, the world, did not see the difference.

Among these souls there was one after the fashion of Flaubert, another after the fashion of Pater, others that had known Baudelaire, and Huysmans, and De Quincey, and Swinburne. Each was taken up, used, and dropped, as in a kind of persistent illustration of "the truth of masks." "A truth in art is that whose contradictory is also true." Well, it was with no sense of contradiction that the critic of beautiful things found himself appealing frankly to the public in a series of the wittiest plays that have been seen on the modern stage. It was another attitude, that was all; something external, done for its own sake, "expressing nothing but itself," and expressing, as it happened by accident, precisely what he himself was best able to express.

It may be, perhaps, now that the man is dead, that those who admired him too much or too little will do him a little justice. He was himself systematically unjust, and was never anxious to be understood too precisely, or to be weighed in very level balances. But he will be remembered, if not as an artist in English literature, at all events in the traditions of our time, as the supreme artist in intellectual attitudes.—ARTHUR SYMONS, "An Artist in Attitudes: Oscar Wilde" (1901), *Studies in Prose and Verse*, 1904, pp. 124–28

There was a coincidence last week in London. An exhibition of Whistler's paintings was opened, and a book by Oscar Wilde was published; and all the critics are writing, and the gossips gossiping, very glibly, about the greatness of Whistler, and about the greatness of Oscar Wilde. Whistler during the 'seventies and 'eighties, and Oscar Wilde during the 'eighties and early 'nineties, cut very prominent figures in London; and both were by the critics and the gossips regarded merely as clever *farceurs*. Both, apart from their prominence, were doing serious work; but neither was taken at all seriously. Neither was thanked. Whistler got a farthing damages, Oscar Wilde two years' hard labour. None of the critics or gossips took exception to either verdict. Time has rolled on. Both men are dead. A subtly apocalyptic thing, for critics and gossips (especially in England), is the tomb; and praises are by envious humanity sung the more easily when there is no chance that they will gratify the subjects of them. And so, very glibly, very blandly, we are all magnifying the two men whom we so lately belittled. M. Rodin was brought over to open the Whistler exhibition. Perhaps the nation will now commission him to do a statue of Oscar Wilde. *Il ne manque que ça.*

Some of the critics, wishing to reconcile present enthusiasm with past indifference, or with past obloquy, have been suggesting that *De Profundis* is quite unlike any previous work of Oscar Wilde—a quite sudden and unrelated phenomenon. Oscar Wilde, according to them, was gloriously transformed by incarceration. Their theory comprises two fallacies. The first fallacy is that Oscar Wilde had been mainly remarkable for his wit. In point of fact, wit was the least important of his gifts. Primarily, he was a poet, with a life-long passion for beauty; and a philosopher, with a life-long passion for thought. His wit, and his humour (which was of an even finer quality than his wit), sprang from a very solid basis of seriousness, as all good wit or humour must. They were not essential to his genius; and, had they happened not to have been there at all, possibly his genius would, even while he himself was flourishing, have been recognised in England, where wisdom's passport is dulness, and gaiety of manner damns. The right way of depreciating Oscar Wilde would have been to say that, beautiful and profound though his ideas were, he never was a real person in contact with realities. He created his poetry, created his philosophy: neither sprang from his own soul, or from his own experience. His ideas were for the sake of ideas, his emotions for the sake of emotions. This, I take it, is just what Mr. Robert Ross means, when, in his admirable introduction to *De Profundis*, he speaks of Oscar Wilde as a man of "highly intellectual and artificial nature." Herein, too, I find the key to an old mystery; why Oscar Wilde, so saliently original a man, was so much influenced by the work of other writers; and why he, than who none was more fertile in invention, did sometimes stoop to plagiarism. If an idea was beautiful or profound, he cared not what it was, nor whether it was his or another's. In *De Profundis* was he, at length, expressing something that he really and truly felt? Is the book indeed a heart-cry? It is pronounced so by the aforesaid critics. There we have the second fallacy.

I think no discerning reader can but regard the book as essentially the artistic essay of an artist. Nothing seemed more likely than that Oscar Wilde, smitten down from his rosy-clouded pinnacle, and dragged through the mire, and cast among the flints, would be *diablement changé en route*. Yet lo! he was unchanged. He was still precisely himself. He was still playing with ideas, playing with emotions. "There is only one thing left for me now," he writes, "absolute humility." And about humility he writes many beautiful and true things. And, doubtless, while he wrote them, he had the sensation of humility. Humble he was not. Emotion was not seeking outlet: emotion came through its own expression. The artist spoke,

and the man obeyed. The attitude was struck, and the heart pulsated to it. Perhaps a Cardinal Archbishop, when he kneels to wash the feet of the beggars, is filled with humility, and revels in the experience. Such was Oscar Wilde's humility. It was the luxurious complement of pride. In *De Profundis*, for the most part, he is frankly proud—proud with the natural pride of a man so richly endowed as he, and arrogant with all his old peculiar arrogance. Even "from the depths" he condescended. Nor merely to mankind was he condescending. He enjoyed the greater luxury of condescending to himself. Sometimes the condescension was from his present self to his old self; sometimes from his old self to his present self. Referring to the death of his mother, "I, once a lord of language," he says, "have no words in which to express my anguish and my shame." Straightway, he proceeds to revel in the survival of that lordship, and refutes in a fine passage his own dramatic plea of impotence. "She and my father had bequeathed to me a name they had made noble and honoured. . . . I had disgraced that name eternally. I had made it a low byword among low people. I had dragged it through the very mire. I had given it to brutes that they might make it brutal, and to fools that they might turn it into folly. What I suffered then, and still suffer, is not for pen to write or paper to record." Yet pen wrote it, and paper recorded it, even so. And sorrow was turned to joy by the "lord of language."

"A lord of language." Certainly that was no idle boast. Fine as are the ideas and emotions in *De Profundis*, it is the actual writing—the mastery of prose—that most delights me. Except Ruskin in his prime, no modern writer has achieved through prose the limpid and lyrical effects that were achieved by Oscar Wilde. One does not seem to be reading a written thing. The words sing. There is nothing of that formality, that hard and cunning precision, which marks so much of the prose that we admire, and rightly admire. The meaning is artificial, but the expression is always magically natural and beautiful. The simple words seem to grow together like wild flowers. In his use of rhyme and metre, Oscar Wilde was academic—never at all decadent, by the way, as one critic has suggested. But the prose of *Intentions*, and of his plays, and of his fairy-stories, was perfect in its lively and unstudied grace. It is a joy to find in this last prose of his the old power, all unmarred by the physical and mental torments that he had suffered.

Oscar Wilde was immutable. The fineness of the book as a personal document is in the revelation of a character so strong that no force of circumstance could change it, or even modify it. In prison Oscar Wilde was still himself—still with the same artistry in words, still with the same detachment from life. We see him here as the spectator of his own tragedy. His tragedy was great. It is one of the tragedies that will live always in romantic history. And the protagonist had an artist's joy in it. Be sure that in the dock of the Old Bailey, in his cell at Reading, on "the centre platform of Clapham Junction," where he stood "in convict dress, and handcuffed, for the world to look at," even while he suffered he was consoled by the realisation of his sufferings and of the magnitude of his tragedy. Looking joyously forward to his release, "I hope," he says, "to be able to recreate my creative faculty." It is a grim loss to our literature that the creative faculty, which prison-life had not yet extinguished in him, did not long survive his liberation. But, broken as he was thereafter, and powerless, and aimless, the invincible artist in him must have had pleasure in contemplation of himself draining the last bitter dregs of the cup that Fate had thrust on him.
—MAX BEERBOHM, "'A Lord of Language,'" *Vanity Fair*, March 2, 1905, p. 309

Wilde's best work was unquestionably, I think, done for the stage, and here it may be conceded he struck out a path of his own. He had the sense of the theatre, a genuine instinct for those moments in the conflict of character to which the proper resources of the theatre can grant both added force and added refinement. It is not an uncommon assumption, especially among writers of fiction, that the drama by comparison is an art of coarse fibre, incapable, by reason of its limitations, of presenting the more intimate realities of character, or the more delicate shades of feeling. The truth is that each art has its own force, its own refinement, and cannot borrow them of another. What is perfectly achieved in one form remains incomparable, and for that very reason cannot in its completed form be appropriated by an art that has other triumphs and is subject to other laws and conditions. And it is here that the novelist so often breaks down in attempting to employ his own special methods in the service of the stage. Wilde made no such blunder. By constant study as well as by natural gift he knew well the arena in which he was working when he chose the vehicle of the drama. His wit has perhaps been over-praised; his epigrams so loudly acclaimed at the time bear the taint of modishness that seems to render them already old-fashioned. But his grip of the more serious situations in life, and his ability to exhibit and interpret them by means genuinely inherent in the resources at the disposal of the dramatist, are left beyond dispute.—J. COMYNS CARR, *Some Victorian Poets*, 1908, pp. 213–14

The fact is, Wilde despised the theatre. He was a born dramatist in the sense that he was naturally equipped with certain very valuable gifts for writing for the stage. But he was not a dramatist from conviction in the sense that Ibsen was or that Mr. Shaw is. Ibsen wrote plays, not because play-writing seemed a particularly promising or remunerative calling in the Norway of his day. It did not. He wrote plays because the dramatic form irresistibly attracted him. Mr. Shaw writes plays because he believes in the stage as an influence, as the most powerful and the most far-reaching of pulpits. Wilde's attitude towards the theatre was utterly different from either of these. He wrote plays frankly for the market and because play-writing was lucrative. Of course, he put a certain amount of himself into them. No artist can help doing that. But no artist of Wilde's power and originality ever did it less. His plays were frankly manufactured to meet a demand and to earn money. There is, of course, no reason why an artist should not work for money. Indeed, all artists do so more or less. They have to live like their neighbours. Unhappily, Wilde wanted a great deal of money, and he wanted it quickly. He loved luxury, and luxury cannot be had for nothing. And if an artist wants a large income and wants it at once, he generally has to condescend a good deal to get it. Wilde condescended. He looked around him at the kind of stuff which other playwrights were making money by, examined it with contemptuous acumen, saw how it was done—and went and did likewise. The only one of his plays which seems to me to be written with conviction, because he had something to express and because the dramatic form seemed to him the right one in which to express it, is *Salomé*—and *Salomé* was not written for the theatre. When Wilde wrote it he had no idea of its ever being acted. But when Madame Bernhardt one day asked him in jest why he had never written her a play, he replied, equally in jest, "I have," and sent her *Salomé*. She read it, and, as we know, would have produced it in London if the Censor of Plays had not intervened. But when Wilde wrote it, it was not with a view to its ever being performed, and so his genius had free scope. He was writing to please himself, not to please a manager, and

the result is that *Salomé* is his best play. *The Importance of Being Earnest* is written with conviction, in a sense. That is to say, it is the expression of the author's own temperament and his attitude towards life, not an insincere re-statement of conventional theatrical ideas. But *The Importance of Being Earnest* is only a joke, though an amazingly brilliant one, and Wilde seems to have looked upon it with the same amused contempt with which he looked on its predecessors. Perhaps he did not realise how good it was. At least he treated it with scant respect, for the original script was in four acts, and these were boiled down into three and the loose ends joined up in perfunctory fashion for purposes of representation. I wonder whether there is any copy of that four-act version still in existence, by the way? It is just possible that a copy is to be found at the Lord Chamberlain's office, for it may have been submitted for license in its original form. If so, I hope Mr. Ross will obtain permission to copy it with a view to its publication. If the deleted act is half as delightful as the three that survive, every playgoer will long to read it. But that a man of Wilde's theatrical skill and experience should have written a play which required this drastic "cutting"—or should have allowed it to be so cut if it did not require it—is an eloquent proof of his contempt for play-writing as an art.

Yes, Wilde despised the drama, and the drama avenged itself. With his gifts for dialogue and characterisation, his very remarkable "sense of the theatre," he might have been a great dramatist if he had been willing to take his art seriously. But he was not willing. The result was that in the age of Ibsen and of Hauptmann, of Strindberg and Brieux, he was content to construct like Sardou and think like Dumas *fils*. Had there been a National Theatre in this country in his day, or any theatre of dignity and influence to which a dramatist might look to produce plays for their artistic value, not solely for their value to the box office, Wilde might, I believe, have done really fine work for it. But there was not. And Wilde loved glitter and success. It would not have amused him to write "uncommercial" masterpieces to be produced for half a dozen *matinées* at a Boxers' Hall. His ambition—if he can be said to have had any "ambition" at all where the theatre was concerned—did not lie in that direction. So he took the stage as he found it, and wrote "pot-boilers." It is not the least of the crimes of the English theatre of the end of the nineteenth century that it could find nothing to do with a fine talent such as Wilde's save to degrade and waste it.—ST. JOHN HANKIN, "The Collected Plays of Oscar Wilde," *Fortnightly Review*, May 1908, pp. 801–2

The publication in twelve volumes by Messrs. Methuen of the complete works of Oscar Wilde marks, in a striking way, the complete literary rehabilitation which this author has achieved. When one considers that at the time of Oscar Wilde's downfall the whole of his copyrights could have been purchased for about £100, one cannot help entertaining grave suspicions as to the value of criticism in England. It must be remembered that the contempt with which Mr. Wilde's work was greeted by the general mass of contemporary criticism was not confined to the period after his condemnation. A reference to the files of the newspapers containing the criticisms of his plays as they came out would reveal the fact that almost without any exception they were received with mockery, ridicule, and rudeness.

It is intensely amusing to read the comments in the daily papers at the present juncture on the same subject. Oscar Wilde is referred to, as a matter of course, as a great genius and a great wit, and takes his place, in the eyes of those who write these articles, if not with Shakespeare, at any rate with the other highest exponents of English dramatic art. This, of course, is as it should be, but we wonder what the gentlemen who write these glowing accounts of Mr. Wilde's genius were doing at the time when these works of genius were being poured out, and why it should have been necessary for him in order to obtain recognition to undergo the processes of disgrace and death. With the exception of the *Ballad of Reading Gaol* and *De Profundis* every work of Oscar Wilde's was written before his downfall. If these works are brilliant works of genius now, they were so before, and the failure of contemporary criticism to appreciate this fact is a lasting slur upon the intelligence of the country.

If any one wishes to see a fair sample of the sort of criticism that used to be meted out to Oscar Wilde, let him turn to the dramatic criticism in *Truth* which appeared on the production of *Lady Windermere's Fan*. The article was, we believe, written by the late unlamented Clement Scott, and at this time of day, of course, Clement Scott's dramatic criticism is not taken seriously; but at the time it was taken quite seriously, and it is astounding to think that such a criticism should have passed absolutely unresented by anybody of importance, with the obvious exception of Oscar Wilde himself. Nowadays if a critic were to write such an article about a playwright of anything approaching the status of Oscar Wilde he would be refused admission to every theatre in London.

This state of affairs must give pause to those good people who have decided that the late W. E. Henley was a "great editor" and a "great critic." If Henley had been anything approaching either of these two things he would have seen and appreciated the value of Oscar Wilde; and if we refer to any of the much-lauded and much-regretted reviews or journals which were conducted by Henley, we find that so far from appreciating Oscar Wilde it was he who led the attack against him, an attack which was conducted with the utmost malevolence and violence, and which was, moreover, distinguished by a brainlessness which is almost incredible in a man who, like Henley (overrated as he is), was not without great talents of his own. That Henley was a great poet or a great writer of prose we have never believed, and the recent publication of his collected works by Messrs. Nutt does not give us any reason to alter our opinion.

The subject of the first great attack made by Henley on Oscar Wilde was *The Picture of Dorian Gray*. Henley affected to think this was an immoral work, and denounced it as such. Now, anybody who having read *Dorian Gray* can honestly maintain that it is not one of the greatest moral books ever written, is an ass. It is, briefly, the story of a man who destroys his own conscience. The visible symbol of that conscience takes the form of a picture, the presentment of perfect youth and perfect beauty, which bears on its changing surface the burden of the sins of its prototype. It is one of the greatest and most terrible moral lessons that an unworthy world has had the privilege of receiving at the hands of a great writer.

It is characteristic of what we may call the "Henleyean School" of criticism to confuse the life of a man with his art. It would be idle to deny that Oscar Wilde was an immoral man (as idle as it would be to contend that Henley was a moral one); but it is a remarkable thing that while Oscar Wilde's life was immoral his art was always moral. At the time when the attack by Henley was made there was a confused idea going about London that Oscar Wilde was a wicked man, and this was quite enough for Henley and the group of second-rate intelligences which clustered round him to jump to the conclusion that anything he wrote must also necessarily be wicked.

The crowning meanness of which Henley was guilty with

regard to Oscar Wilde was his signed review of the *Ballad of Reading Gaol*. Henley was always an envious man; his attack on the memory of Stevenson is sufficient to show that; but he certainly surpassed himself when he wrote that disgraceful article. Surely a man possessing the smallest nobility of soul would have refrained at that juncture from attacking an old enemy—if, indeed, Wilde could properly be called an enemy of Henley's. Henley chose to make an unprovoked attack upon Wilde, from whom, as a matter of fact, he had received many benefits and kindnesses, but Wilde never retaliated in an ungenerous way, although his enormous intellectual superiority would have rendered it an easy task for him to pulverise Henley. It was always Wilde's way to take adverse criticism contemptuously, and, to the last, he never spoke of Henley with anything but good humour, albeit with some deserved disdain. The slow revenge of time has in this particular case bestirred itself to some purpose, and if we cannot say with justice "Who now reads Henley?" we can at any rate state very positively that for every reader that he has, Oscar Wilde has twenty. The reason is not far to seek. Wilde, putting aside his moral delinquencies, which have as much and as little to do with his works as the colour of his hair, was a great artist, a man who passionately loved his art. He was so great an artist that, in spite of himself, he was always on the side of the angels. We believe that the greatest art is always on the side of the angels, to doubt it would be to doubt the existence of God, and all the Henleys and all the Bernard Shaws that the world could produce would not make us change our opinion. It was all very well for Wilde to play with life, as he did exquisitely, and to preach the philosophy of pleasure, and plucking the passing hour; but the moment he sat down to write he became different. He saw things as they really were; he knew the falsity and the deadliness of his own creed; he knew that "the end of these things is Death;" and he wrote in his own inimitable way the words of Wisdom and Life. Like all great men, he had his disciples, and a great many of them (more than a fair share) turned out to be Iscariots; but it is his glory that he founded no school, no silly gang of catchword repeaters; he created no "journalistic tradition," and he was not referred to by ridiculous bumpkins occupying subordinate positions in the offices of third-rate Jewish publishing-houses as "dear old Wilde." Those who knew and loved him as a man and as a writer were men who had their own individualities and were neither his shadows nor his imitators. If they achieved any greatness they did it because they had greatness in them, and not because they aped "the master." Henley has his school of "Henley's young men," of whom we do not hear much nowadays. Wilde has his school of young men in those who copy what was least admirable in him, but from a literary point of view he has no school. He stands alone, a phenomenon in literature. From the purely literary point of view he was unquestionably the greatest figure of the nineteenth century. We unhesitatingly say that his influence on the literature of Europe has been greater than that of any man since Byron died, and, unlike Byron's, it has been all for good. The evil that he did, inasmuch as he did a tithe of the things imputed to him, was interred with his bones, the good (how much the greater part of this great man!) lives after him and will live for ever.—LORD ALFRED DOUGLAS, "The Genius of Oscar Wilde," *Academy*, July 11, 1908, p. 35

The time has certainly come when this extraordinary man, Oscar Wilde, may be considered merely as a man of letters. He sometimes pretended that art was more important than morality, but that was mere play-acting. Morality or immorality was more important than art to him and everyone else. But the very cloud of tragedy that rested on his career makes it easier to treat him as a mere artist now. His was a complete life, in that awful sense in which your life and mine are incomplete; since we have not yet paid for our sins. In that sense one might call it a perfect life, as one speaks of a perfect equation; it cancels out. On the one hand we have the healthy horror of the evil; on the other the healthy horror of the punishment. We have it all the more because both sin and punishment were highly civilized; that is, nameless and secret. Some have said that Wilde was sacrificed; let it be enough for us to insist on the literal meaning of the word. Any ox that is really sacrificed is made sacred.

But the very fact that monstrous wrong and monstrous revenge cancel each other, actually does leave this individual artist in that very airy detachment which he professed to desire. We can really consider him solely as a man of letters.

About Oscar Wilde, as about other wits, Disraeli or Bernard Shaw, men wage a war of words, some calling him a great artist and others a mere charlatan. But this controversy misses the really extraordinary thing about Wilde: the thing that appears rather in the plays than the poems. He was a great artist. He also was really a charlatan. I mean by a charlatan one sufficiently dignified to despise the tricks that he employs. A vulgar demagogue is not a charlatan; he is as coarse as his crowd. He may be lying in every word, but he is sincere in his style. Style (as Wilde might have said) is only another name for spirit. Again, a man like Mr. Bernard Shaw is not a charlatan. I can understand people thinking his remarks hurried or shallow or senselessly perverse, or blasphemous, or merely narrow. But I cannot understand anyone failing to feel that Mr. Shaw is being as suggestive as he can, is giving his brightest and boldest speculations to the rabble, is offering something which he honestly thinks valuable. Now Wilde often uttered remarks which he must have known to be literally valueless. Shaw may be high or low, but he never talks down to the audience. Wilde did talk down, sometimes very far down.

Wilde and his school professed to stand as solitary artistic souls apart from the public. They professed to scorn the middle class, and declared that the artist must not work for the bourgeois. The truth is that no artist so really great ever worked so much for the bourgeois as Oscar Wilde. No man, so capable of thinking about truth and beauty, ever thought so constantly about his own effect on the middle classes. He studied them with exquisite attention, and knew exactly how to shock and how to please them. Mr. Shaw often gets above them in seraphic indignation, and often below them in sterile and materialistic explanations. He disgusts them with new truths or he bores them with old truths; but they are always living truths to Bernard Shaw. Wilde knew how to say the precise thing which, whether true or false, is irresistible. As, for example, "I can resist everything but temptation."

But he sometimes sank lower. One might go through his swift and sparkling plays with a red and blue pencil marking two kinds of epigrams; the real epigram which he wrote to please his own wild intellect, and the sham epigram which he wrote to thrill the very tamest part of our tame civilization. This is what I mean by saying that he was strictly a charlatan—among other things. He descended below himself to be on top of others. He became purposely stupider than Oscar Wilde that he might seem cleverer than the nearest curate. He lowered himself to superiority; he stooped to conquer.

One might easily take examples of the phrase meant to lightly touch the truth and the phrase meant only to bluff the bourgeoisie. For instance, in *A Woman of No Importance*, he makes his chief philosopher say that all thought is immoral,

being essentially destructive; "Nothing survives being thought of." That is nonsense, but nonsense of the nobler sort; there is an idea in it. It is, like most professedly modern ideas, a death-dealing idea not a life-giving one; but it is an idea. There is truly a sense in which all definition is deletion. Turn a few pages of the same play and you will find somebody asking, "What is an immoral woman?" The philosopher answers, "The kind of woman a man never gets tired of." Now that is not nonsense, but rather rubbish. It is without value of any sort or kind. It is not symbolically true; it is not fantastically true; it is not true at all.

Anyone with the mildest knowledge of the world knows that nobody can be such a consuming bore as a certain kind of immoral woman. That vice never tires men, might be a tenable and entertaining lie; that the individual instrument of vice never tires them is not, even as a lie, tenable enough to be entertaining. Here the great wit was playing the cheap dandy to the incredibly innocent; as much as if he had put on paper cuffs and collars. He is simply shocking a tame curate; and he must be rather a specially tame curate even to be shocked. This irritating duplication of real brilliancy with snobbish bluff runs through all his three comedies. "Life is much too important to be taken seriously"; that is the true humorist. "A well-tied tie is the first serious step in life"; that is the charlatan. "Man can believe the impossible, but man can never believe the improbable"; that is said by a fine philosopher. "Nothing is so fatal to a personality as the keeping of promises, unless it be telling the truth"; that is said by a tired quack. "A man can be happy with any woman so long as he does not love her"; that is wild truth. "Good intentions are invariably ungrammatical"; that is tame trash.

But while he had a strain of humbug in him, which there is not in the demagogues of wit like Bernard Shaw, he had, in his own strange way, a much deeper and more spiritual nature than they. Queerly enough, it was the very multitude of his falsities that prevented him from being entirely false. Like a many-coloured humming top, he was at once a bewilderment and a balance. He was so fond of being many-sided that among his sides he even admitted the right side. He loved so much to multiply his souls that he had amongst them one soul at least that was saved. He desired all beautiful things—even God.

His frightful fallacy was that he would not see that there is reason in everything, even in religion and morality. Universality is a contradiction in terms. You cannot be everything if you are anything. If you wish to be white all over, you must austerely resist the temptation to have green spots or yellow stripes. If you wish to be good all over, you must resist the spots of sin or the stripes of servitude. It may be great fun to be many-sided; but however many sides one has there cannot be one of them which is complete and rounded innocence. A polygon can have an infinite number of sides; but no one of its sides can be a circle.—G. K. CHESTERTON, "Oscar Wilde" (1909), *A Handful of Authors*, ed. Dorothy Collins, 1953, pp. 143–46

This is not the place to examine the strange problem of the life of Oscar Wilde, nor to determine to what extent heredity and the epileptic tendency of his nervous system can excuse that which has been imputed to him. Whether he was innocent or guilty of the charges brought against him, he undoubtedly was a scapegoat. His greater crime was that he had caused a scandal in England, and it is well known that the English authorities did everything possible to persuade him to flee before they issued an order for his arrest. An employee of the Ministry of Internal Affairs stated during the trial that, in London alone, there are more than 20,000 persons under police surveillance, but they remain footloose until they provoke a scandal. Wilde's letters to his friends were read in court, and their author was denounced as a degenerate obsessed by exotic perversions: 'Time wars against you; it is jealous of your lilies and your roses', 'I love to see you wandering through violet-filled valleys, with you honey-coloured hair gleaming'. But the truth is that Wilde, far from being a perverted monster who sprang in some inexplicable way from the civilization of modern England, is the logical and inescapable product of the Anglo-Saxon college and university system, with its secrecy and restrictions.

Wilde's condemnation by the English people arose from many complex causes; but it was not the simple reaction of a pure conscience. Anyone who scrutinizes the graffiti, the loose drawings, the lewd gestures of those people will hesitate to believe them pure at heart. Anyone who follows closely the life and language of men, whether in soldiers' barracks or in the great commercial houses, will hesitate to believe that all those who threw stones at Wilde were themselves spotless. In fact, everyone feels uncomfortable in speaking to others about this subject, afraid that his listener may know more about it than he does. Oscar Wilde's own defence in the *Scots Observer* should remain valid in the judgment of an objective critic. Everyone, he wrote, sees his own sin in Dorian Gray (Wilde's best known novel). What Dorian Gray's sin was no one says and no one knows. Anyone who recognizes it has committed it.

Here we touch the pulse of Wilde's art—sin. He deceived himself into believing that he was the bearer of good news of neo-paganism to an enslaved people. His own distinctive qualities, the qualities, perhaps, of his race—keenness, generosity, and a sexless intellect—he placed at the service of a theory of beauty which, according to him, was to bring back the Golden Age and the joy of the world's youth. But if some truth adheres to his subjective interpretations of Aristotle, to his restless thought that proceeds by sophisms rather than syllogisms, to his assimilations of natures as foreign to his as the delinquent is to the humble, at its very base is the truth inherent in the soul of Catholicism: that man cannot reach the divine heart except through that sense of separation and loss called sin.

In his last book, *De Profundis*, he kneels before a gnostic Christ, resurrected from the apocryphal pages of *The House of Pomegranates*, and then his true soul, trembling, timid, and saddened, shines through the mantle of Heliogabalus. His fantastic legend, his opera—a polyphonic variation on the rapport of art and nature, but at the same time a revelation of his own psyche—his brilliant books sparkling with epigrams (which made him, in the view of some people, the most penetrating speaker of the past century), these are now divided booty.

A verse from the book of Job is cut on his tombstone in the impoverished cemetery at Bagneux. It praises his facility, 'eloquium suum',—the great legendary mantle which is now divided booty. Perhaps the future will also carve there another verse, less proud but more pious:

> Partiti sunt sibi vestimenta mea et super
> vestem meam miserunt sortis.
> —James Joyce, "Oscar Wilde: The Poet of
> *Salomé*" (1909), *Critical Writings*, eds. Ells-
> worth Mason, Richard Ellmann, 1959, pp.
> 203–5

At bottom and in essence, Wilde is a master in the art of selection. He is eminently successful in giving the most diverting character to our moments as they pass. His art is the apotheosis of the moment. What may not be said, he once asked, for the moment and the "moment's monument"? Art itself, he averred, is "really a form of exaggeration, and selection, which is the very spirit of art, is nothing more than an intensified mode of over-emphasis." Wilde was a painter, a Neo-Impressionist. From the palette of his observation, which bore all the radiant shades and colors of his temperament, he selected and laid upon the canvas many brilliant yet distinct points of color. Seen in the proper light and from the just distance, the canvas takes on the appearance of a complete picture—quaint, unique, marvellous. It is only by taking precisely Wilde's point of view that the spectator is enabled to synthesize the isolated brilliant points into a harmonious whole. Oscar Wilde is a Pointilliste.

There is no room for doubt that Oscar Wilde was, as Nordau classed him, a pervert and a degenerate. And yet his case warrants distrust of the dictum that an artist's work and life are fundamentally indissociable. Wilde was a man, not only of multiple personality, but of manifest and disparate achievement. The style is not always the man; and the history of art and literature reveals not a few geniuses whose private life could not justly be cited in condemnation of their pictures, their poetry, or their prose. If Wilde's life were to be cited as the sole criterion of his works, then must they forever remain *res tacenda* in the republic of letters. It is indubitable that Wilde, with his frequently avowed doctrine of irresponsible individualism and Pagan insistence upon the untrammelled expansion of the Ego, gave suicidal counsel to the younger generation. He based his apostolate upon the paradox; and as he himself asserts, the paradox is always dangerous. In his search for the elusive, the evanescent, the imaginative, he found certain exquisite truths; but they were only very partial and obscure truths, embedded in a mass of charmingly phrased, yet damnably perverse, falsehood. Much of his verse—flagrant output of what Robert Buchanan maliciously crystallized in the damning phrase, "The Fleshly School of Poetry"—is a faithful reflex of his personality and feeling, with its morbid and sensuous daydreams, its vain regrets for "barren gain and bitter loss," its unhealthy and myopic vision, its obsession with the wanton and the *macabre*. And yet, in spite not only of these things but also of the persistent reminder of alien influences, certain of his poems are lit with the divine spark and fitfully flame out with startling and disturbing lustre.

As an artist in words, as *prosateur*, Wilde was possessed of real gifts. The social ease of his paradoxes, the opulence of his imaginative style, the union of simplicity and beauty of phraseology with vague and sometimes almost meaningless gradations and shades of thought, his insight into the real meaning of art, his understanding of the "thing as in itself it really is," and his rapt glimpses of art's holy of holies—all these things, at times and at intervals, were his. His faculty of imitation was caricature refined and sublimated to an infinite degree; and, with less real comprehension of the *arcana* of art, Wilde might have been the author of a transcendent *Borrowed Plumes*. And if he himself did not actually and literally masquerade in the literary garments of other men, certainly he possessed that rare faculty, now almost a lost art, of creeping into another's personality, temporarily shedding the husk of self, and looking out upon the world with new and alien eyes. There lies, it would seem, the secret of his genius—the faculty of creative and imaginative interpretation in its ultimate refinement. He was ever the critic as artist, never the creator in the fine frenzy of creation. It has been said of him that he knew everything; but in the last analysis his supreme fault, both as man and artist, was his arrogance and his overweening sense of superiority. Breaks down in Wilde's case—as does many another truism—the maxim: *Tout comprendre c'est tout pardonner.*

"To be free," wrote a celebrity, "one must not conform." Wilde secured a certain sort of freedom in the drama through his refusal to conform to the laws of dramatic art. He claimed the privileges without shouldering the responsibilities of the dramatist. He imported the methods of the *causerie* into the domain of the drama, and turned the theatre into a house of mirth. Whether or no his destination was the palace of truth, certain it is that he always stopped at the half-way house. Art was the dominant note of his literary life; but it was the art of conversation, not the art of drama. His comedies, as dramas, were cheap sacrifices to the god of success. He made many delightful, many pertinent and impertinent observations upon English life, and upon life in general; but they had no special relation to the dramatic theme he happened for the moment to have in mind. His plays neither enlarge the mental horizon nor dilate the heart. Wilde was too self-centred an egoist ever to come into any real or vital relation with life. It was his primal distinction as artist to be consumed with a passionate love of art. It was his primal deficiency as artist to have no genuine sympathy with humanity. And although he imaged life with clearness, grace, and distinction, certain it is that he never saw life steadily, nor ever saw it whole.

Wilde called one of his plays *The Importance of Being Earnest.* In his inverted way, he aimed at teaching the world the importance of being frivolous. Only from this standpoint is it possible to appreciate, in any real sense, Wilde the comic dramatist. Wilde is the arch enemy of boredom and ennui; we can always enjoy him in his *beau rôle* as a purveyor of amusement and a killer of time. But we are warned by his own confession against taking Wilde, as dramatist, too seriously. "The plays are not great," he once confessed to André Gide. "I think nothing of them—but if you only knew how amusing they are!" And the author of "The Decay of Lying" added: "Most of them are the results of bets"!—ARCHIBALD HENDERSON, *Interpreters of Life and the Modern Spirit,* 1911, pp. 99–103

Works

THE PICTURE OF DORIAN GRAY

There is always something of an excellent talker about the writing of Mr. Oscar Wilde; and in his hands, as happens so rarely with those who practise it, the form of dialogue is justified by its being really alive. His genial, laughter-loving sense of life and its enjoyable intercourse, goes far to obviate any crudity there may be in the paradox, with which, as with the bright and shining truth which often underlies it, Mr. Wilde, startling his "countrymen," carries on, more perhaps than any other writer, the brilliant critical work of Matthew Arnold. "The Decay of Lying," for instance, is all but unique in its half-humorous, yet wholly convinced, presentment of certain valuable truths of criticism. Conversational ease, the fluidity of life, felicitous expression, are qualities which have a natural alliance to the successful writing of fiction; and side by side with Mr. Wilde's *Intentions* (so he entitles his critical efforts) comes a novel, certainly original, and affording the reader a fair opportunity of comparing his practise as a creative artist with many a precept he has enounced as critic concerning it.

A wholesome dislike of the common-place, rightly or wrongly identified by him with the *bourgeois,* with our middle-class—its habits and tastes—leads him to protest emphatically

against so-called "realism" in art; life, as he argues, with much plausibility, as a matter of fact, when it is really awake, following art—the fashion an effective artist sets; while art, on the other hand, influential and effective art, has never taken its cue from actual life. In *Dorian Gray* he is true certainly, on the whole, to the æsthetic philosophy of his *Intentions;* yet not infallibly, even on this point: there is a certain amount of the intrusion of real life and its sordid aspects—the low theatre, the pleasures and griefs, the faces of some very unrefined people, managed, of course, cleverly enough. The interlude of Jim Vane, his half-sullen but wholly faithful care for his sister's honour, is as good as perhaps anything of the kind, marked by a homely but real pathos, sufficiently proving a versatility in the writer's talent, which should make his books popular. Clever always, this book, however, seems to set forth anything but a homely philosophy of life for the middle-class—a kind of dainty Epicurean theory, rather—yet fails, to some degree, in this; and one can see why. A true Epicureanism aims at a complete though harmonious development of man's entire organism. To lose the moral sense therefore, for instance, the sense of sin and righteousness, as Mr. Wilde's heroes are bent on doing as speedily, as completely as they can, is to lose, or lower, organisation, to become less complex, to pass from a higher to a lower degree of development. As a story, however, a partly supernatural story, it is first-rate in artistic management; those Epicurean niceties only adding to the decorative colour of its central figure, like so many exotic flowers, like the charming scenery and the perpetual, epigrammatic, surprising, yet so natural, conversations, like an atmosphere all about it. All that pleasant accessory detail, taken straight from culture, the intellectual and social interests, the conventionalities, of the moment, have, in fact, after all, the effect of the better sort of realism, throwing into relief the adroitly-devised supernatural element after the manner of Poe, but with a grace he never reached, which supersedes that earlier didactic purpose, and makes the quite sufficing interest of an excellent story. ⟨. . .⟩

Dorian himself, though certainly a quite unsuccessful experiment in Epicureanism, in life as a fine art, is (till his inward spoiling takes visible effect suddenly, and in a moment, at the end of his story) a beautiful creation. But his story is also a vivid, though carefully considered, exposure of the corruption of a soul, with a very plain moral, pushed home, to the effect that vice and crime make people coarse and ugly. General readers, nevertheless, will probably care less for this moral, less for the fine, varied, largely appreciative culture of the writer, in evidence from page to page, than for the story itself, with its adroitly managed supernatural incidents, its almost equally wonderful applications of natural science; impossible, surely, in fact, but plausible enough in fiction. Its interest turns on that very old theme, old because based on some inherent experience or fancy of the human brain, of a double life: of Döppelgänger—not of two *persons,* in this case, but of the man and his portrait; the latter of which, as we hinted above, changes, decays, is spoiled, while the former, through a long course of corruption, remains, to the outward eye, unchanged, still in all the beauty of a seemingly immaculate youth—"the devil's bargain." But it would be a pity to spoil the reader's enjoyment by further detail. We need only emphasise, once more, the skill, the real subtlety of art, the ease and fluidity withal of one telling a story by word of mouth, with which the consciousness of the supernatural is introduced into, and maintained amid, the elaborately conventional, sophisticated, disabused world Mr. Wilde depicts so cleverly, so mercilessly. The special fascination of the piece is, of course, just there—at that point of contrast. Mr. Wilde's work may fairly claim to go with that of Edgar Poe, and with some good French work of the same kind, done, probably, in more or less conscious imitation of it.—WALTER PATER, "A Novel by Mr. Wilde" (1891), *Sketches and Reviews*, 1919, pp. 126–33

INTENTIONS

Mr. Wilde, in speaking of the methods open to the critic, well says that Mr. Pater's narrative is, of course, only criticism in disguise: his figures are but personifications of certain moods of mind, in which he is for the time interested, and which he desires to express. Now I have been wondering whether one should not, similarly, regard Mr. Wilde essentially as a humorist who has taken art-criticism for his medium, just as Carlyle was a humorist in the odd disguise of a prophet. Certainly, I am inclined to think that much of his intricate tracery of thought and elaborate jewel-work of expression is simply built up to make a casket for one or two clever homeless paradoxes. "The fact of a man being a poisoner is nothing against his prose." Mr. Wilde somehow struck that out, and saw that it was deserving of a better fate than to remain a waif of traditional epigram; so he went to work on Lamb's strange friend, Thomas Griffiths Wainewright, one of the subtlest art-critics and poisoners of his time, unearthed his curious history, made selections from his criticism, and then set his own epigram, diamond-wise, in the midst of a biographical essay. Various readers solemnly add to their historical knowledge, discuss the strange character of the man, study his criticism; but Mr. Wilde sits and watches his epigram sparkling far within. About Wainewright he cares far less than the reader, about his own epigram—far more.

Of course this is not the whole truth about these *Intentions*; the whole truth is a many-coloured thing about a personality so complex as that of the author of *Dorian Gray*. But it is the dominant tendency among many others hardly less powerful. Mr. Wilde's worship of beauty is proverbial, it has made a latter-day myth of him before his time; and yet, at least in these essays, his gift of comic perception is above it, and, rightly viewed, all his "flute-toned" periods are written in the service of the comic muse. Where he is not of malice aforethought humorous, where he seems to be arguing with serious face enough, is it not simply that he may smile behind his mask at the astonishment, not to say terror, of a public he has from the first so delighted in shocking? He loves to hear it call him "dangerous," as some men delight to be called "roué."

There will be many who will, as the phrase is, take him seriously; but let me assure them that Mr. Wilde is not of the number. It all depends what one means by the phrase; for I, for one, take Mr. Wilde very seriously as a creator of work which gives me much and various new pleasure: he is so absolutely alive at every point, so intensely practical—if people could only see it—and therefore so refreshingly unsentimental; he is wittier than is quite fair in a man of his nationality, and he often writes prose that one loves to say over for mere pleasure of ear—his own literary touchstone. The artistic temperament should delight in him, for the serious in the pursuit of literary pleasure he is as serious as every new joy must be; it is only in the domain of thought where it is rather funny to see him taken with such open mouth. Not that Mr. Wilde is not a thinker, and a very subtle one too; but it is rather, so to say, as a damascener of thought, than a forger of it, that he is to be regarded. ⟨. . .⟩

It belongs to Mr. Wilde's paradoxical method that he should continually play on the convertibility of terms. Thus, the whole contention of his essays on criticism is that criticism and creation are essentially one and the same, or, at least, that they necessarily dovetail one into the other; and yet towards the end of this essay we find Gilbert saying "it is certain that the subject-matter at the disposal of creation is always diminishing, while the subject-matter of criticism increases daily." Here we have the two terms crystallised once more to their hard and fast everyday meaning, while all through they have been used as convertible. This is apt to bewilder. As a rule, however, Mr. Wilde gains his effects by adhering to the concrete signification of words. This reduces some of his contentions to a mere question of terms. One often feels: Now, if that word were but changed for another, for which it really stands, there would be nothing further to say. But that, of course, would not do for Mr. Wilde, nor, indeed, for us, to whom, presumably, subject is nought and treatment is all. Occasionally, by this means, it follows that Mr. Wilde seems to beg the question; as, for instance, in his remarks on morality in art. When he says, "All art is immoral," he is using the word in its narrow relative sense; he does not mean by it the same as those who use it seriously against certain schools and forms of art: though they say "immoral" they mean "unspiritual," and that is the meaning many people will attach to the word in Mr. Wilde's phrase. They will thus be quite unnecessarily shocked by a mere quibble of words, and their real position is left unassailed; the real question at issue being whether or not there is certain art which is dangerous to the spirit, of which one should feel as Mr. Pater says in *Marius*: "This is what I may not look at." If life be really a struggle between higher and lower, if art is anything more than a form of sensuous indulgence, this is a question to be answered. Mr. Wilde does not leave us quite clear as to his side in the matter, though he seems to lay over-much stress on the sensuous side of art, a side which is, after all, external and impossible without an informing, formative soul. He echoes, too, Gautier's tirades against "virtue," and Mr. Swinburne's

> What ailed us, oh gods, to desert you
> For the creeds that refuse and restrain?

and says hard things of chastity and self-sacrifice—really a very "young" and quite illogical position in an age which has accepted evolution. He quotes M. Renan to the effect that "Nature cares little about chastity"; but does that prove anything save that Nature is always behind the age, as Mr. Wilde tells us in another place? Surely it is by such ideals, of which, once seen, the beauty haunts him through all his sinnings, that man evolves at all, striving and failing and striving, till slowly what was once the ideal becomes the instinct.

But I am not recking my own rede, and am in danger of growing quite "heated," as they say of politicians, while Mr. Wilde is doubtless smiling in his sleeve.

Let us leave contention and enjoy. I have referred to two or three of the interesting qualities in these papers. They are so absolutely alive. Every sentence is full of brain. There is no padding, no vagueness, all is "thought out," as the painters say. One has that safe, untroubled feeling in reading that Matthew Arnold's calm dissecting method gives us—though, needless to say, the austerity of the *Essays in Criticism* is a very different thing from this luxuriously coloured prose: however difficult the thesis, we leave it to the writer with perfect confidence that he will speedily make all clear. Mr. Wilde has, indeed, a rare power of keeping his eye steadily "on the object." It is doubtless, too, a part of his perversity that while, as we have seen, he will, when it suits him, adhere rigidly to the fixed signification of words, he can at other times exercise a quite remarkable power of reducing them to their elements, of remorselessly forcing them to say what they really mean. "You must not be frightened by words," said Gilbert to his young neophyte; and certainly, if you set such words as "unpractical," "dangerous," or "dreamer" on to Mr. Wilde they will come in for the same summary dissection that befel the lion which attacked the strong man in Holy Writ.—RICHARD LE GALLI-ENNE, *Academy*, July 4, 1891, pp. 7–8

Ever since the first printers with misguided zeal dipped an innocent world in ink, those books have been truly popular which reflected faithfully and enthusiastically the foibles and delusions of the hour. This is what is called "keeping abreast with the spirit of the times," and we have only to look around us at present to see the principle at work. With an arid and dreary realism chilling us to the heart, and sad-voiced novelists entreating us at every turn to try to cultivate religious doubts, fiction has ceased to be a medium of delight. Even nihilism, which is the only form of relief that true earnestness permits, is capable of being overstrained, and some narrowly conservative people are beginning to ask themselves already whether this new development of "murder as a fine art" has not been sufficiently encouraged. Out of the midst of the gloom, out of the confusion and depression of conflicting forms of serious-ness, rises from London a voice, clear, languid, musical, shaken with laughter, and speaking in strange sweet tones of art and beauty, and of that finer criticism which is one with art and beauty, and claims them forever as its own. The voice comes from Mr. Oscar Wilde, and few there are who listen to him, partly because his philosophy is alien to our prevalent modes of thought, and partly because of the perverse and paradoxical fashion in which he delights to give it utterance. People are more impressed by the way a thing is said than by the thing itself. A grave arrogance of demeanor, a solemn and self-assertive method of reiterating an opinion until it grows weighty with words, are weapons more convincing than any subtlety of argument. "As I have before expressed to the still reverberating discontent of two continents," this is the mode in which the public loves to have a statement offered to its ears, that it may gape, and wonder, and acquiesce.

Now, nothing can be further from such admirable solidity than Mr. Wilde's flashing sword-play, than the glee with which he makes out a case against himself, and then proceeds valiantly into battle. There are but four essays in his recent volume, rather vaguely called *Intentions*, and of these four only two have real and permanent value. "The Truth of Masks" is a somewhat trivial paper, inserted apparently to help fill up the book, and "Pen, Pencil, and Poison" is visibly lacking in sincerity. The author plays with his subject very much as his subject, "kind, light-hearted Wainewright," played with crime, and in both cases there is a subtle and discordant element of vulgarity. It is not given to our eminently respectable age to reproduce that sumptuous and horror-laden atmosphere which lends an artistic glamor to the poisonous court of the Medicis. This "study in green" contains, however, some brilliant passages, and at least one sentence—"The domestic virtues are not the true basis of art, though they may serve as an excellent advertisement for second-rate artists"—that must make Mr. George Moore pale with envy when he reflects that he missed saying it, where it belongs, in his clever, truthful, ill-natured paper on "Mummer-Worship."

The significance and the charm of Mr. Wilde's book are centred in its opening chapter, "The Decay of Lying," re-printed from *The Nineteenth Century*, and in the long two-part essay entitled "The Critic as Artist," which embodies some of his most thoughtful, serious, and scholarly work. My own

ineffable content rests with "The Decay of Lying," because under its transparent mask of cynicism, its wit, its satire, its languid mocking humor, lies clearly outlined a great truth that is slipping fast away from us,—the absolute independence of art—art nourished by imagination and revealing beauty. This is the hand that gilds the grayness of the world; this is the voice that sings in flute tones through the silence of the ages. To degrade this shining vision into a handmaid of nature, to maintain that she should give us photographic pictures of an unlovely life, is a heresy that arouses in Mr. Wilde an amused scorn which takes the place of anger. "Art," he says, "never expresses anything but itself. It has an independent life, just as Thought has, and develops purely on its own lines. It is not necessarily realistic in an age of realism, nor spiritual in an age of faith. So far from being the creation of its time, it is usually in direct opposition to it, and the only history that it preserves for us is the history of its own progress." That we should understand this, it is necessary to understand also the "beauti-ful untrue things" which exist only in the world of fancy; the things that are lies, and yet that help us to endure the truth. Mr. Wilde repudiates distinctly and almost energetically all lying with an object, all sordid trifling with a graceful gift. The lies of newspapers yield him no pleasure; the lies of politicians are ostentatiously unconvincing; the lies of lawyers are "briefed by the prosaic." He reviews the world of fiction with a swift and caustic touch; he lingers among the poets; he muses raptur-ously over those choice historic masterpieces, from Herodotus to Carlyle, where "facts are either kept in their proper subor-dinate position, or else entirely excluded on the general ground of dulness." He laments with charming frankness the serious virtues of his age. "Many a young man," he says, "starts in life with a natural gift for exaggeration which, if nurtured in congenial and sympathetic surroundings, or by the imitation of the best models, might grow into something really great and wonderful. But, as a rule, he comes to nothing. He either falls into careless habits of accuracy, or takes to frequenting the society of the aged and the well-informed. Both things are equally fatal to his imagination, and in a short time he develops a morbid and unhealthy faculty of truth-telling, begins to verify all statements made in his presence, has no hesitation in contradicting people who are much younger than himself, and often ends by writing novels that are so like life that no one can possibly believe in their probability." Surely this paragraph has but one peer in the world of letters, and that is the immortal sentence wherein De Quincey traces the murderer's gradual downfall to incivility and procrastination.

"The Critic as Artist" affords Mr. Wilde less scope for his humor and more for his erudition, which, perhaps, is some-what lavishly displayed. Here he pleads for the creative powers of criticism, for its fine restraints, its imposed self-culture, and he couches his plea in words as rich as music. Now and then, it is true, he seems driven by the whips of our modern Furies to the verge of things which are not his to handle—problems, social and spiritual, to which he holds no key. When this occurs, we can only wait with drooping heads and what patience we can muster until he is pleased to return to his theme; or until he remembers, laughing, how fatal is the habit of imparting opinions, and what a terrible ordeal it is to sit at table with the man who has spent his life in educating others rather than himself. "For the development of the race depends on the development of the individual, and where self-culture has ceased to be the ideal, the intellectual standard is instantly lowered, and often ultimately lost." I like to fancy the ghost of the late rector of Lincoln, of him who said that an appreciation of Milton was the reward of consummate scholarship, listening in the Elysian Fields, and nodding his assent to this much-neglected view of a much-disputed question. Everybody is now so busy teaching that nobody has any time to learn. We are growing rich in lectures, but poor in scholars, and the triumph of mediocrity is at hand. Mr. Wilde can hardly hope to become popular by proposing real study to people burning to impart their ignorance; but the criticism that develops in the mind a more subtle quality of apprehension and discernment is the criticism that creates the intellectual atmosphere of the age.—AGNES REPPLIER, "The Best Book of the Year," *North American Review*, Jan. 1892, pp. 97–100

SALOMÉ

That mouthpiece of Philistinism, the daily press, surpassed itself in the stern and indignant condemnation of the book which it had not read and the play which it had not seen; never before it declared had such an outrage on decency and good taste been committed, never had a more infamous plot against morality and the Bible been nipped in the bud. For it *was* nipped in the bud, the censor had refused to license its production, England was saved from lasting disgrace. The daily press positively swelled with pride, it metaphorically slapped its chest and thanked God it was an Englishman. It is hard to understand the attitude taken up by the anonymous scribblers who propounded these pompous absurdities. Why it should be taken for granted that because a writer takes his subject from a sublime and splendid literature, he should necessarily treat it in a contemptible manner, is a mystery it is hard to solve. Apparently it never occurred to these enlightened beings that the very sublimity and grandeur of such a subject would be a sufficient guarantee that the artist had put his very best work into it, and had done his utmost to exalt his treatment to the high level his subject demanded. To a man who takes for the scene of a vulgar farce, the back drawing-room of a house in Bloomsbury, and who brings on to the stage a swindling stockbroker or a rag-and-bone merchant, they are ready to listen with delighted attention, to laugh at his coarse jokes and revel in his cockney dialogue; good healthy English fun they call it. But a man who actually takes for the scene of a tragedy the gorgeous background of a Roman Tetrarch's court, and who brings on to the stage a real prophet out of the Bible, and all in French too! 'No, it is too much,' they say, 'we don't want to hear anything more about it, it is an outrage and an infamy.' O Happy England, land of healthy sentiment, roast beef and Bible, long may you have such men to keep guard over your morals, to point out to you the true path, and to guide your feet into the way of cant! 〈. . .〉

One thing strikes one very forcibly in the treatment, the musical form of it. Again and again it seems to one that in reading one is *listening*; listening, not to the author, not to the direct unfolding of a plot, but to the tones of different instruments, suggesting, suggesting, always indirectly, till one feels that by shutting one's eyes one can best catch the suggestion. The author's personality nowhere shews itself.

The French is as much Mr. Wilde's own as is the psychological motive of the play, it is perfect in scholarship, but it takes a form new in French literature. It is a daring experiment and a complete success. The language is rich and coloured, but never precious, and shows a command of expression so full and varied that the ascetically artistic restraint of certain passages stands out in strong relief. Such a passage is the one quoted above: the conversation of the soldiers on the terrace; in which by-the-bye certain intelligent critics have discovered a resemblance to Ollendorf, and with extraordinary

shallowness and lack of artistic sensibility have waxed facetious over. O wonderful men!

Artistically speaking the play would gain nothing by performance, to my mind it would lose much. To be appreciated it must be abstracted, and to be abstracted it must be read. Let it, 'not to the sensual ear but more endeared, pipe to the spirit ditties of no tone.'

It only remains to say that the treatment of St. John the Baptist is perfectly refined and reverend.

I suppose the play is unhealthy, morbid, unwholesome, and un-English, ça va sans dire. It is certainly un-English, because it is written in French, and therefore unwholesome to the average Englishman, who can't digest French. It is probably morbid and unhealthy, for there is no representation of quiet domestic life, nobody slaps anybody else on the back all through the play, and there is not a single reference to roast beef from one end of the dialogue to the other, and though it is true that there is a reference to Christianity, there are no muscular Christians. Anyone, therefore, who suffers from that most apalling and widespread of diseases which takes the form of a morbid desire for health had better avoid and flee from *Salomé*, or they will surely get a shock that it will take months of the daily papers and Charles Kingsley's novels to counteract. But the less violently and aggressively healthy, those who are healthy to live and do not live to be healthy, will find in Mr. Oscar Wilde's tragedy the beauty of a perfect work of art, a joy for ever, ambrosia to feed their souls with honey of sweet-bitter thoughts.—LORD ALFRED DOUGLAS, *Spirit Lamp*, May 1893, pp. 21–27

Mr. Oscar Wilde never troubles one with taking himself too seriously, and the history of *Salomé* is Oscar Wilde all over. It was written in French and produced in Paris. Desirous then of favoring his own countrymen, Mr. Wilde made preparation to present it in London. In this worthy attempt, however, he was hindered—so the papers told us—by some official folly which enraged him so much that he was even strongly tempted to stop being an Englishman, in favor of that less imbecile people across the Channel. But not wishing to keep his anger forever, Mr. Wilde finally allowed his noble friend Lord Alfred Bruce Douglas to do the play into English. It was then "pictured," as the phrase is, by Mr. Aubrey Beardsley, and is now ready for the delight of a somewhat indifferent world.

Such an extraordinary conjunction of affections is ominous. But, strangely enough, there are some things in *Salomé* that are good. It is impossible to read it without feeling curiously moved and stirred. The careless talk of the loungers on the terrace, the soldiers and the Cappadocian, is good; the squabbling of the Jews, the Pharisee, the Sadducee, the Nazarene, is good. So, also, is Herod,—indeed the character of Herod is quite the best conceived thing in the play, as his description of his treasure is the best written. The play may well have been very effective on the stage, for there is a constant feeling of movement, of life, and it is certainly worth reading now that it is published.

With all this, however, the play is wholly ephemeral. Its action is trivial and its dialogue affected. Its ideas, and its language too, are extravagances, without much more foundation than the extravagances of Mr. Hamlin Garland. But while in Mr. Garland we have the prophet of Literature as Life, we have in Mr. Wilde the follower of Literature as Art. Mr. Garland is a "veritist," and prefers the fresh novelties of nature. But Mr. Wilde seeks beauty, in art and art's most latent subtleties. He contrives expressions and conceptions of the most curious and self-conscious refinement, of the strangest and most ultra-precious distinction. As ever, he scorns the ordinary, the every-day, the generally pleasing, and is unremitting to attain the romantic beauty, the strange, the wonderful, the remote, the reward of no art but the most devoted, the delight of no taste but the most distinguished.

As such, his work lends itself eminently to the illustration of Mr. Aubrey Beardsley. Mr. Aubrey Beardsley receives a good many hard words nowadays,—and certainly his pictures are strange things, more affected than Oscar Wilde himself, and more remote from obvious apprehension. What one is first inclined to criticise in Mr. Beardsley is his lack of originality. His pictures remind us of almost every phase of art that has ever existed; or, at any rate, of every phase which had ever a tinge of the grotesque or the trivial in its character. From the bald priestly pictures mingled among Egyptian hieroglyphics, down to the graceful frivolities of Willette of the Red Windmill, Mr. Beardsley seems to have laid everything under contribution. His work seems by turns one thing and then another— Japanese, Gothic, Preraphaelite, what you will. So it seems at first. But the great excellence is that, however Protean, Mr. Aubrey Beardsley, like Satan in *Paradise Lost*, is always himself, even in the midst of his disguises. Just what is his own quality, is hard to say; but there can be little doubt that it exists, and it would be worth somebody's while to determine it in the shifting dazzle of his influences,—to fix it for an instant for us, to get its true character and flavor unadulterated. But whatever be his quality, it is eminently in keeping with the work of Mr. Oscar Wilde.—EDWARD E. HALE, JR., "Signs of Life in Literature," *Dial*, July 1, 1894, pp. 12–13

A WOMAN OF NO IMPORTANCE
AN IDEAL HUSBAND

There is no such thing as "absolute pitch" in criticism; the intervals are everything. In other words, the critic is bound to deal in odious comparisons; it is one of the painful necessities of his calling. He must clearly indicate the plane, so to speak, on which, in his judgment, any given work of art is to be taken; and the value of his terms, whether of praise or blame, must then be estimated in relation to that plane. Well, the one essential fact about Mr Oscar Wilde's dramatic work is that it must be taken on the very highest plane of modern English drama, and furthermore, that it stands alone on that plane. In intellectual calibre, artistic competence—ay, and in dramatic instinct to boot—Mr Wilde has no rival among his fellow-workers for the stage. He is a thinker and a writer; they are more or less able, thoughtful, original playwrights. This statement may seem needlessly emphatic, and even offensive; but it is necessary that it should be made if we are to preserve any sense of proportion in criticism. I am far from exalting either *Lady Windermere's Fan* or *A Woman of No Importance* to the rank of a masterpiece; but while we carp at this point and cavil at that, it behoves us to remember and to avow that we are dealing with works of an altogether higher order than others which we may very likely have praised with much less reserve.

Pray do not suppose that I am merely dazzled by Mr Wilde's pyrotechnic wit. That is one of the defects of his qualities, and a defect, I am sure, that he will one day conquer, when he begins to take himself seriously as a dramatic artist. At present, he approaches his calling as cynically as Mr George R. Sims; only it is for the higher intellects, and not the lower, among the play-going public, that Mr Wilde shows his polite contempt. He regards prose drama (so he has somewhere stated) as the lowest of the arts; and acting on this principle— the falsity of which he will discover as soon as a truly inspiring

subject occurs to him—he amuses himself by lying on his back and blowing soap-bubbles for half an evening, and then pretending, during the other half, to interest himself in some story of the simple affections such as audiences, he knows, regard as dramatic. Most of the soap bubbles are exceedingly pretty, and he throws them off with astonishing ease and rapidity—

> One *mot* doth tread upon another's heels,
> So fast they follow—

but it becomes fatiguing, in the long run, to have the whole air a-shimmer, as it were, with iridescent films. Mr Wilde will one day be more sparing in the quantity and more fastidious as to the quality of his wit, and will cease to act up to Lord Illingworth's motto that "nothing succeeds like excess." It is not his wit, then, and still less his knack of paradox-twisting, that makes me claim for him a place apart among living English dramatists. It is the keenness of his intellect, the individuality of his point of view, the excellence of his verbal style, and, above all, the genuinely dramatic quality of his inspirations. I do not hesitate to call the scene between Lord Illingworth and Mrs Arbuthnot at the end of the second act of this play the most virile and intelligent—yes, I mean it, the most intelligent—piece of English dramatic writing of our day. It is the work of a man who knows life, and knows how to transfer it to the stage. There is no situation-hunting, no posturing. The interest of the scene arises from emotion based upon thought, thought thrilled with emotion. There is nothing conventional in it, nothing insincere. In a word, it is a piece of adult art. True, it is by far the best scene in the play, the only one in which Mr Wilde does perfect justice to his talent. But there are many details of similar, though perhaps not equal, value scattered throughout. How fine and simple in its invention, for instance, is the scene in which the mother tells her son the story of Lord Illingworth's treachery, only to hear him defend the libertine on the ground that no "nice girl" would have let herself be entrapped! This exquisite touch of ironic pathos is worth half a hundred "thrilling tableaux," like that which follows almost immediately upon it.

For it is not to be denied that in his effort to be human— I would say "to be popular," did I not fear some subtle and terrible vengeance on the part of the outraged author—Mr Wilde has become more than a little conventional. How different is the "He is your father!" tableau at the end of Act III from the strong and simple conclusion of Act II—how different, and how inferior! It would be a just retribution if Mr Wilde were presently to be confronted with this tableau, in all the horrors of chromolithography, on every hoarding in London, with the legend, "Stay, Gerald! He is your father!" in crinkly letters in the corner. Then, indeed, would expatriation—or worse—be the only resource of his conscience-stricken soul. His choice would lie between Paris and prussic acid. The conventional element seems to me to come in with the character of Mrs Arbuthnot. Why does Mr Wilde make her such a terribly emphatic personage? Do ladies in her (certainly undesirable) position brood so incessantly upon their misfortune? I have no positive evidence to go upon, but I see no reason why Mrs Arbuthnot should not take a more common-sense view of the situation. That she should resent Lord Illingworth's conduct I quite understand, and I applaud the natural and dignified revenge she takes in declining to marry him. But why all this agony? Why all this hatred? Why can "no anodyne give her sleep, no poppies forgetfulness"? With all respect for Mrs Arbuthnot, this is mere empty phrase-making. I am sure she has slept very well, say, six nights out of the seven, during these twenty years; or, if not, she has suffered from a stubborn determination to be unhappy, for which Lord Illingworth can scarcely be blamed. After all, what material has she out of which to spin twenty years of unceasing misery? She is—somehow or other—in easy circumstances; she has a model son to satisfy both her affections and her vanity; it does not even appear that she is subjected to any social slights or annoyances. A good many women have led fairly contented lives under far more trying conditions. Perhaps Mr Wilde would have us believe that she suffers from mild religious mania—that it is the gnawing thought of her unpardonable "sin" that nor poppy nor mandragora can soothe. But she herself admits that she does not repent the "sin" that has given her a son to love. Well then, what is all this melodrama about? Does not Mrs Arbuthnot sacrifice our interest, if not our sympathy, by her determination "in obstinate condolement to persever"? May we not pardonably weary a little (to adapt Lord Illingworth's saying) of "the Unreasonable eternally lamenting the Unalterable"? Mrs Arbuthnot is simply a woman who has been through a very painful experience, who has suffered a crushing disappointment in the revelation of the unworthiness of the man she loved, but for whom life, after all, has turned out not so very intolerably. That is the rational view of her situation; and she herself might quite well take that view without the sacrifice of one scene or speech of any real value. The masterly scene at the end of the second act would remain practically intact, and so would the scene between mother and son in the third act; for the complacent cruelty of Gerald's commentary on her story could not but cause a bitter pang to any mother. It is only in the fourth act that any really important alteration would be necessary, and there it could only be for the better. The young man's crude sense of the need for some immediate and heroic action is admirably conceived, and entirely right; but how much better, how much truer, how much newer, would the scene be if the mother met his Quixotism with sad, half-smiling dignity and wisdom, instead of with passionate outcries of unreasoning horror! There is a total lack of irony, or, in other words, of commonsense, in this portion of the play. Heroics respond to heroics, until we feel inclined to beg both mother and son (and daughter-in-law, too, for that matter) to come down from their stilts and look at things a little rationally. Even Mr Wilde's writing suffers. We are treated to such noble phrases as "I am not worthy or of her or of you," and it would surprise no one if Master Gerald were to drop into blank verse in a friendly way. How much more telling, too, would the scene between Mrs Arbuthnot and Lord Illingworth become if she took the situation more ironically and less tragically, if she answered the man of the world in the tone of a woman of the world! How much more complete, for one thing, would be his humiliation! As it is, the vehemence of her hatred can only minister to his vanity. From the point of view of vanity, to be hated for twenty years is just as good as to be loved. It is indifference that stings. It was all very well, in the second act, for Mrs Arbuthnot to be vehement in her protest against the father's annexation of the son; in the fourth act, when that danger is past, a tone of calm superiority would be ten times as effective. In short, the play would have been a much more accomplished work of art if the character of Mrs Arbuthnot had been pitched in another key. And I am not without a suspicion that Mr Wilde's original design was something like what I have indicated. The last word spoken, "A man of no importance" (which was doubtless the first word conceived) seems to belong to the woman I imagine rather than to the one who actually speaks it. I think, too, that the concluding situation would be more effective if some more

definite indication of the unspeakable cad who lurks beneath Lord Illingworth's polished surface were vouchsafed us earlier in the play. True, his conduct towards the fair American was sufficiently objectionable; but I fear I, for my part, did not quite seriously believe in it, taking it rather as a mere *ficelle*, and not a very ingenious one, leading up to the startling picture-poster at the end of the third act.—WILLIAM ARCHER, "A *Woman of No Importance*" (1893), *The Theatrical "World" of 1893*, 1894, pp. 105–12

Mr Oscar Wilde's new play at the Haymarket ⟨*An Ideal Husband*⟩ is a dangerous subject, because he has the property of making his critics dull. They laugh angrily at his epigrams, like a child who is coaxed into being amused in the very act of setting up a yell of rage and agony. They protest that the trick is obvious, and that such epigrams can be turned out by the score by any one lightminded enough to condescend to such frivolity. As far as I can ascertain, I am the only person in London who cannot sit down and write an Oscar Wilde play at will. The fact that his plays, though apparently lucrative, remain unique under these circumstances, says much for the self-denial of our scribes. In a certain sense Mr Wilde is to me our only thorough playwright. He plays with everything: with wit, with philosophy, with drama, with actors and audience, with the whole theatre. Such a feat scandalizes the Englishman, who can no more play with wit and philosophy than he can with a football or a cricket bat. He works at both, and has the consolation, if he cannot make people laugh, of being the best cricketer and footballer in the world. Now it is the mark of the artist that he will not work. Just as people with social ambitions will practise the meanest economies in order to live expensively; so the artist will starve his way through incredible toil and discouragement sooner than go and earn a week's honest wages. Mr Wilde, an arch-artist, is so colossally lazy that he trifles even with the work by which an artist escapes work. He distils the very quintessence, and gets as product plays which are so unapproachably playful that they are the delight of every playgoer with twopenn'orth of brains. The English critic, always protesting that the drama should not be didactic, and yet always complaining if the dramatist does not find sermons in stones and good in everything, will be conscious of a subtle and pervading levity in *An Ideal Husband*. All the literary dignity of the play, all the imperturbable good sense and good manners with which Mr Wilde makes his wit pleasant to his comparatively stupid audience, cannot quite overcome the fact that Ireland is of all countries the most foreign to England, and that to the Irishman (and Mr Wilde is almost as acutely Irish an Irishman as the Iron Duke of Wellington) there is nothing in the world quite so exquisitely comic as an Englishman's seriousness. It becomes tragic, perhaps, when the Englishman acts on it; but that occurs too seldom to be taken into account, a fact which intensifies the humor of the situation, the total result being the Englishman utterly unconscious of his real self, Mr Wilde keenly observant of it and playing on the self-unconsciousness with irresistible humor, and finally, of course, the Englishman annoyed with himself for being amused at his own expense, and for being unable to convict Mr Wilde of what seems an obvious misunderstanding of human nature. He is shocked, too, at the danger to the foundations of society when seriousness is publicly laughed at. And to complete the oddity of the situation, Mr Wilde, touching what he himself reverences, is absolutely the most sentimental dramatist of the day.

It is useless to describe a play which has no thesis: which is, in the purest integrity, a play and nothing less. The six worst epigrams are mere alms handed with a kind smile to the average suburban playgoer; the three best remain secrets between Mr Wilde and a few choice spirits. The modern note is struck in Sir Robert Chiltern's assertion of the individuality and courage of his wrongdoing as against the mechanical idealism of his stupidly good wife, and in his bitter criticism of a love that is only the reward of merit. It is from the philosophy on which this scene is based that the most pregnant epigrams in the play have been condensed. Indeed, this is the only philosophy that ever has produced epigrams. In contriving the stage expedients by which the action of the piece is kept going, Mr Wilde has been once or twice a little too careless of stage illusion: for example, why on earth should Mrs Cheveley, hiding in Lord Goring's room, knock down a chair? That is my sole criticism.—GEORGE BERNARD SHAW, "Two New Plays" (1895), *Works*, 1930–38, Vol. 23, pp. 9–11

THE IMPORTANCE OF BEING EARNEST

A dead man's voice has been heard again, and as we listened to it the artist himself once more stood before us. Forgotten was the history of the man, forgotten the past. The hands of the clock had moved for seven years, but the situation remained unchanged. Oscar Wilde has come to life again, and on the night of December 2, when literary and social London foregathered at the reproduction of *The Importance of Being Earnest*, there was celebrated a feast of absolution, and, to a certain extent, of rehabilitation. In the midst of our intellectual joy there sounded but two discordant notes—the one of anger, the other of sadness. It made some of us angry to read on the programme *"The Importance of Being Earnest*, by the author of *Lady Windermere's Fan,"* whereby was indicated that, though it was good to use the artist's work, his name was not sufficiently honourable to be given out to the public. I know full well that the publisher has erred in this direction, as well as the manager, but there is no excuse for either. The note of sadness was that so great a mind as Oscar Wilde's had prematurely come to a standstill; that matters independent of art had bereft us of the most brilliant wit of the period, and that subsequent events, instead of leading to regeneration, brought a broken career to an untimely termination.

In 1895, when *The Importance of Being Earnest* saw the light at the St. James's Theatre, it was voted a perfect farce, and, but for the catastrophe, it would have been played for centuries of evenings. I recall this not merely as a chronological fact, but more particularly in order to emphasise the exceeding cleverness of the play, since the duality of its fibre escaped most of the critics, and certainly the majority of the public. The practised eye discovered at once that the first and second acts and the third act were not of the same mould. They made the impression of wines of different vintages served in the same glasses. Those two acts—perfect, not only as farce, but as comedy, too, for they reflect the manners of the period, and are richly underlaid with humorous current—were written in days when the poet basked in the hot sun of popularity, when his every saying darted like an arrow through the land, when the whole of the English speaking world echoed sallies which, though they were not always Oscar Wilde's, were as *ben trovato* as if they had been his. The third act was—I know it authoritatively—composed under stress of circumstances, when the web was tightening round the man, and menaces of exposure must have rendered his gaiety forced, like that of a being condemned to the stocks. Under pressure a lofty mind often does excellent work, and it is undeniable that in the third act of *The Importance of Being Earnest* there is more cleverness than in one round dozen English comedies *en bloc*. There are

epigrams in it for the paternity of which some people would give a few years of their lives, and as a solution to a tangle well-nigh inextricable it is by no means unhappy. Yet it is not of the same quality as those other two acts, in which the real, the probable, and the impossible form a *ménage à trois* of rare felicity. And as we listen to the play, what strikes us most of all is not so much the utterances of a mind which could not fail to be brilliant, but the prospect that this comedy—for I prefer to call it a comedy—will enjoy a kind of perennial youth somewhat akin to Congreve's work or that of Sheridan. It is a bold thing to say, I know, but if there is exaggeration, let it pass, for the sake of the argument that when the artist's working powers were shut off he had not yet thoroughly felt his feet, but was only just beginning to plough his furrow in a new field. *The Importance of Being Earnest* ranks high, not only on account of its gaiety—a gaiety which in many produces the smile of intimate understanding, and in the less *blasé* guffaws straight from a happy mood—but because it satirises vividly, pointedly, yet not unkindly, the mannerisms and foibles of a society which is constantly before the public eye. I need not dive into details, for the plot is, or ought to be, known to every lover of the Theatre. And I do not quote epigrams, for it is but a poor glory to feather one's own cap with another man's cleverness. Anon, when the play is revived at the St. James Theatre, when the book of an author whose name one need no longer express with bated breath, is sold by the thousand, there will be ample opportunity to refresh one's memory, and spend a joyful hour with *The Importance of Being Earnest*.—J. T. GREIN, *"The Importance of Being Earnest"* (1901), *Dramatic Criticism*, 1902, Vol. 3, pp. 264–66

The Importance of Being Earnest has been revived by Mr Alexander at the St James's Theatre, and is as fresh and as irresistible as ever. It is vain to speculate what kind of work Oscar Wilde would have done had the impulse for play-writing survived in him. It is certain that a man of such variegated genius, and a man so inquisitive of art-forms, would not, as some critics seem to think he would, have continued to turn out plays in the manner of *The Importance of Being Earnest*. This, his last play, is not the goal at which he would have rested. But, of the plays that he wrote specifically for production in London theatres, it is the finest, the most inalienably his own. In *Lady Windermere's Fan* and *A Woman of No Importance* and *An Ideal Husband*, you are aware of the mechanism—aware of Sardou. In all of them there is, of course, plenty of humanity, and of intellectual force, as well as of wit and humour; and these qualities are the more apparent for the very reason that they are never fused with the dramatic scheme, which was a thing alien and ready-made. The Sardou manner is out-of-date; and so those three plays do, in a degree, date. It is certain that Oscar Wilde would later have found for serious comedy a form of his own, and would have written serious comedies as perdurable as his one great farce.

In *The Importance of Being Earnest* there is a perfect fusion of manner and form. It would be truer to say that the form is swallowed up in the manner. For you must note that not even in this play had Oscar Wilde invented a form of his own. On the contrary, the bare scenario is of the tritest fashion in the farce-writing of the period. Jack pretends to his niece, as an excuse for going to London, that he has a wicked brother whom he has to look after. Algernon, as an excuse for seeing the niece, impersonates the wicked brother. Jack, as he is going to marry and has no further need of a brother, arrives with the news of the brother's death; and so forth. Just this sort of thing had served as the staple for innumerable farces in the 'sixties and 'seventies and 'eighties—and would still be serving so if farce had not now been practically snuffed out by musical comedy. This very ordinary clod the magician picked up, turning it over in his hands—and presto! a dazzling prism for us.

How was the trick done? It is the tedious duty of the critic to ask such questions, and to mar what has been mere delight by trying to answer them. Part of the play's fun, doubtless, is in the unerring sense of beauty that informs the actual writing of it. The absurdity of the situation is made doubly absurd by the contrasted grace and dignity of everyone's utterance. The play abounds, too, in perfectly chiselled apothegms—witticisms unrelated to action or character, but so good in themselves as to have the quality of dramatic surprise. There are perhaps, in the course of the play, a dozen of those merely verbal inversions which Oscar Wilde invented, and which in his day the critics solemnly believed—or at any rate solemnly declared—to be his only claim to the title of wit. And of these inversions perhaps half-a-dozen have not much point. But, for the rest, the wit is of the finest order. 'What between the duties expected of one during one's lifetime, and the duties exacted after one's death, land has ceased to be either a profit or a pleasure. It gives one a position, and prevents one from keeping it up. That's all that can be said about land.' One cannot help wishing it were all that 'the Dukes' had had to say recently. It is a perfect presentation of the case which they have presented so lengthily and so maladroitly. And it is only a random sample of the wit that is scattered throughout *The Importance of Being Earnest*. But, of course, what keeps the play so amazingly fresh is not the inlaid wit, but the humour, the ever-fanciful and inventive humour, irradiating every scene. Out of a really funny situation Oscar Wilde would get dramatically the last drop of fun, and then would get as much fun again out of the correlative notions aroused in him by that situation. When he had to deal with a situation which, dealt with by any ordinary dramatist, would be merely diagrammatic, with no real fun at all in it, always his extraneous humour and power of fantastic improvisation came triumphantly to the rescue. Imagine the final scenes of this play treated by an ordinary dramatist! How tedious, what a signal for our departure from the theatre, would be the clearing-up of the mystery of Jack Worthing's parentage, of the baby in the handbag, the manuscript in the perambulator! But the humour of the writing saves the situation, makes it glorious. Lady Bracknell's recital of the facts to the trembling Miss Prism—'Through the elaborate investigations of the Metropolitan police, the perambulator was discovered at midnight, standing by itself in a remote corner of Bayswater. It contained the manuscript of a three-volume novel of more than usually revolting sentimentality'—and Miss Prism's subsequent recognition of the hand-bag by 'the injury it received through the upsetting of a Gower Street omnibus in younger and happier days' and by 'the stain on the lining caused by the explosion of a temperance beverage, an incident that occurred at Leamington'—these and a score of other extraneous touches keep us laughing whole-heartedly until the actual fall of the curtain.—MAX BEERBOHM, "A Classic Farce" (1909), *Last Theatres*, ed. Rupert Hart-Davis, 1970, pp. 508–11

DE PROFUNDIS

This is an unfailingly and now and then poignantly interesting work; it contains some beautiful prose, some confessions that cannot leave the reader unmoved and may even touch him a little with shame at his own fortunate rectitude; and a passage of theological conjecture that is most engaging in its ingenuity and of a very delicate texture. The book contains all this and more, and yet while realizing the terrible conditions under which it was written, and possessed by every wish to understand the author and feel with him in the utter wreck of his career, it is impossible, except very occasionally, to look upon his testament as more than a literary feat. Not so, we find ourselves saying, are souls laid bare. This is not sorrow, but its dexterously constructed counterfeit.

Yet when we ask ourselves in what other way we would have had Oscar Wilde's cry from the depths we are unable to reply; for the bitter truth is that he was probably unable to cry from the depths at all; perhaps, paradoxical as it may sound, was unable really to be in the depths. For this book might be held to fortify the conviction that there is an armour of egotism which no arrow of fate can pierce. How Wilde felt in the watches of the night in that squalid cell we can only conjecture; this book gives little clue. In this book he is as much as ever the bland and plausible artist in phrase, except that for the most part he is advocating a new creed of humility in place of earlier gospels. Even in prison, even at the end of everything he most valued, his artifice was too much for him; his poses were too insistent—had become too much a part of the man—to be abandoned. If the heart of a broken man shows at all in this book, it must be looked for between the lines. It is not in them.

That a man who had travelled by Wilde's courses to Wilde's end should write, in prison, an analysis of his temperament, and a history of his ruin, coming therein to such conclusions as are here set forth, and during his task should pen no word that bore the mark of sincerity unadorned, is in its way a considerable feat. But it vitiates the book; or rather takes the book from the category of genuine emotion and places it among the *tours de force*. But it enables us now to know absolutely—what we had perhaps before guessed—that Oscar Wilde, however he may have begun life, grew to be incapable of deliberately telling the truth about himself or anything else. Being a man of genius, he often stumbled on it; but he could not say, "I will be truthful," and be truthful; he lost that power. We doubt if he was truthful even to himself towards the end. ⟨. . .⟩

Wilde speaks in this little book of his artistic creed, his teaching, his philosophy of life; but it is very doubtful if he had ever really formulated one and made any sustained effort to understand it and conform to it. For his genius lay in lawlessness. He was essentially lawless, and his work is of value only when the author has forgotten that he is the exponent of a system. Every writer has somewhere an intimate personal gift which distinguishes him from every other writer—although it is often so minute as to escape detection. Wilde's particular and precise gift was lawless irresponsibility—humorous inconsistency is perhaps as good a description of it. If all his work could be spread out like an extinct river bed in the Klondike, a tiny thread of gold would be seen to break out here and there fitfully and freakishly within it. That vein of gold would represent those moments in Wilde's literary career when he forgot who he was and what he thought he stood for and allowed his native self to frolic and turn somersaults amid verities and conventions. Essentially an improviser and of hand-to-mouth intellect, he allowed himself to believe himself a constructive philosopher; essentially a mocker he was weak enough to affect to be a high priest of reverence. The result is that, although he essayed almost every variety of literary expression, in none except sheer irresponsibility did he come near perfection. We have always considered *The Importance of Being Earnest* his high-water mark of completed achievement; and we should associate with it those passages in his other writings where the same mood has play. Of Wilde's other work it is conceivable that industrious disciples might have produced it with more or less—perhaps sufficient—success. In any case it does not really matter. The failure of Wilde's life and the failure of his work have the same root; he could not resist temptation. We would not say that as a writer he was tempted in the same degree as a pleasure-loving man; his artistic conscience was made of better stuff than his civic conscience; but he was tempted often, and he always fell. His real destiny was to be an improviser, an inconsistent but often inspired commentator, a deviser of paradoxes, an exponent of the unfamiliar side of things; instead, he thought himself a leader of men, a prophet, a great writer of prose, a serious dramatic poet. By nature a witty and irresponsible Irishman, he grew to believe himself a responsible neo-Hellene. Born to be a lawless wit he was often something very like a pedant. Had he possessed a sense of humour he might have been saved—another illustration of the total independence of humour and wit. ⟨. . .⟩

What, then, is the value of *De Profundis?* Its value is this—that it is an example of the triumph of the literary temperament over the most disadvantageous conditions; it is further documentary evidence as to one of the most artificial natures produced by the nineteenth century in England; and here and there it makes a sweet and reasonable contribution to the gospel of humanity.—E. V. Lucas, *Times Literary Supplement*, Feb. 24, 1905, pp. 64–65

To Heine it seemed an unintelligible caprice in Shakespeare to have been born an Englishman. But Shakespeare, after all, has in him much that is English, and much that the English can genuinely admire. It is otherwise with some of our men of genius—with William Blake, for example, with Shelley, and, later, with Oscar Wilde. Of them we could make nothing, except martyrs. Blake, it is true, we ignored, as a lunatic; but Shelley we excommunicated; and Oscar Wilde we slowly murdered in prison. Why? What does it mean? Who is wrong? Is it we or they? It is time we asked ourselves these questions, and tried to answer them candidly, without sentimentality and without illusion.

The trouble between these men and us is, that they are artists and we are not. By which I do not mean that they were members of what has now become a "respectable" profession, "in the ordinary sense of that extraordinary word." I mean that they had, by nature, a certain attitude towards life, one which, of all attitudes, it is hardest for us, who are English, to understand. I will not attempt to describe it; I will let the artist speak for himself.

> . . . By the inevitable law of self-perfection, the poet must sing, and the sculptor think in bronze, and the painter make the world a mirror for his moods, as surely and as certainly as the hawthorn must blossom in spring, and the corn turn to gold at harvest-time, and the moon in her ordered wanderings change from shield to sickle, and from sickle to shield.

The artist is the man who lives by impulse, as we like to believe that Nature does. He is an individualist, though he has perhaps never heard of individualism. He develops himself, though perhaps he does not believe in self-development. By instinct, rather than conviction, he neglects conventions, rules, and forecasts. Above all, he ignores morality. "Morality does not help me. I am a born antinomian. I am one of those who are made for exceptions, not for laws." "I see that there is nothing wrong in what one does." But then, on the other hand: "I see that there is something wrong in what one becomes." To become the right thing, that is, the thing his impulses drive him to be, that is the artist's aim, or rather his instinct.

Whatever happens to him he will accept, so only he can grow by it. And, among other things, he will accept sin, even though he repent of it. The *De Profundis*, in essence, is a confession of repentance; but the repentance involves no regret.

> I don't regret for a single moment having lived for pleasure. I did it to the full, as one should do everything that one does. There was no pleasure I did not experience. I threw the pearl of my soul into a cup of wine. I went down the primrose path to the sound of flutes. I lived on honey-comb. But to have continued the same life would have been wrong, because it would have been limiting. I had to pass on. The other half of the garden had its secrets for me also.

Such an attitude, by its mere existence, is a challenge to every law and every convention of society. The artist may or may not break these laws and conventions; that depends upon the character of his impulses. But he is a standing menace to them; he will always break them if he wants to. And it is this that society cannot forgive. Is society right or wrong?

Society represents morality; from which it does not follow that it represents virtue. Morality means rule, calculation, subordination, self-suppression. Every impulse it arrests with the questions: Whither do you tend? What are your consequences? Are you safe? Shan't I be sorry afterwards? Won't society suffer by my act? And morality is right to ask these questions. The pity is, that it should answer them so badly. Its answer is embodied in the whole fabric of our laws and conventions. And this fabric we are not simply wrong in declining to set aside, on the plea of some sudden cry of somebody's inmost self. Yet the cry is none the less imperative, none the less legitimate. The tragedy lies in the conflict between the soul and the soul's dead products. But in this conflict all the right is not on either side. The artist sins, and society sins; but society is the stronger, and the artist is crushed. The artist sins, because impulses are not necessarily good, either in themselves or in what they lead to. He has to sin if he is to grow, and, in proportion as he is a great artist, he turns to account his sin and its punishment. Society sins, because it has no impulses but only rules; and its rules at best are mere makeshifts. Society is at once the cause and the effect of Philistinism; for "he is the Philistine who upholds and aids the heavy, cumbrous, blind, mechanical forces of society, and who does not recognise dynamic force when he meets it, either in a man or a movement."

Thus it is that both the artist and society are always right and always wrong. The artist is the deliverer, and the only possible deliverer. But mankind can only be redeemed by crucifying its redeemer; and there is a sense in which the redeemer deserves to be crucified.

It follows from this, that the artist's life must be a tragedy. But tragedy, in a world like this, is not necessarily to be regretted. So, at least, it is deliberately affirmed by this latest of our victims. This pagan, this lover of beauty and joy, this subtlest, finest, and not least profound intelligence of our age, is suddenly blasted from the blue, hurled into a pit of infamy, shut out from the colour and light he loved as few have loved them, condemned to the most lingering of deaths, and a death, as it proved, not only of body, but of mind. And what has he to say about it? Only that he would not choose to have missed it; that suffering has crowned his life; and that the fact of suffering is itself a proof of love.

> It seems to me that love of some kind is the only possible explanation of the extraordinary amount of suffering that there is in the world. I cannot conceive

of any other explanation. I am convinced that there is no other, and that if the world has indeed, as I have said, been built of sorrow, it has been built by the hands of love, because in no other way could the soul of man, for whom the world was made, reach the full stature of its perfection. Pleasure for the beautiful body, but pain for the beautiful soul.

Never has the Christian religion been more triumphantly vindicated than by this pagan whom Christians have abhorred.

But, even though it be true that there are cases where suffering may redeem, that does not excuse those who inflict the suffering. On this point, too, let us endeavour to "clear our minds of cant." Let it be admitted that there are matters in which the conduct of Oscar Wilde was such as every society, even the most enlightened and humane, would legitimately and reasonably condemn. Every society has a duty to protect the immature. Every society has a duty, and one more extensive than any society has ever yet admitted, to control sexual relations in the interest of the children to be born of them. But everything beyond that is a question of private morals and taste. Now the private morals and taste of our society are not such that it has a right to throw the first stone at any man. And our law, on the matter in question, is a mere survival of barbarism, supported, not by reason, but by sheer prejudice. It rests on no knowledge, no principle, no common sense; it rests on our instinct to persecute what we cannot understand. Oscar Wilde may have sinned, not only, as he admits, against himself, but against society. But who shall measure the moral gulf by which he is removed from the crowd of fallen women and sensual men who mobbed him at the gates of the court, who jeered at him on the platform of the railway station, and pointed at this man of genius, no word of whose message they could comprehend, the index of their gross and prurient scorn? It is of such elements, among others, that the society that condemns the artist is composed. Is the account clear between him and them?

And there is another point. Let us ignore the iniquities of opinion and of the law. Let us suppose that Oscar Wilde was as great a criminal as he was judged to be by all the basest and some of the finer elements of our society. Even so, was it right or, let us say, was it wise, to treat him as we did? This is a question which touches our whole system of punishment, and affects the case, not only of this isolated man of genius, but of hundreds and thousands of dumb and obscure offenders. —G. Lowes Dickinson, *Independent Review*, April 1905, pp. 375–77

ROBERT H. SHERARD
From *Oscar Wilde: The Story of an Unhappy Friendship*
1905, pp. 183–94

The day of the trial dawned as a day of relief to all of us in Oakley Street, but to none more so than to my unhappy friend. It had never entered my mind to be present at the Old Bailey, where he was to be exposed to such humiliations. We breakfasted together, and afterwards one of the men who had found his bail came to escort him to surrender. This man was bright and cheerful. "I have a nice carriage to drive there in," he said, "and I have retained a nice room near the Old Bailey, to which he can retire during the intervals."

I remember saying, "You would have done much better to retain a nice room for him on the Calle del Sol in Madrid." I

never hoped for a moment that the trial would be otherwise than fatal to him.

I have no recollection of the impressions of those days, save that they were days of shifting hopes and fears. The town was placarded with his name; and one night, alluding to this, I said, "Well, you have got your name before the public at last." He laughed and said, "Nobody can pretend now not to have heard of it."

I did not read the papers, and all I knew of the progress of the trial was what I gathered from the announcements on the posters and what little was said in Oakley Street when the accused returned home. But there was nothing to encourage me, and what I dreaded most was the effect he would produce when placed in person in the witness-box. I feared his bent for flippancy and paradox would dispose the jury against him; but what disturbed me most was, that he was obviously in no state of health to defend himself effectively. His nerve was all gone, and I feared that his physical collapse would be construed as a sign of the consciousness of guilt. He himself dreaded this ordeal. "I shall break down," he said, the evening before. "I know that I shall break down." I understood, however, from those that were present, that he acquitted himself with courage and dignity.

There was one evening when everybody was glad, and when I was pointed at as a prophet of evil and a foolish counsellor. It was the evening of the day on which the judge had contemptuously pitchforked back on to the dungheap, from which it had exuded, a certain part of the Evidence.

On the eve of the fatal last day, however, everybody seemed resigned for the worst. He was very fine, and I admired him greatly. His old serenity had come back to him. His face was calm; all traces of nervousness had gone; there was a manliness in his bearing which years of self-indulgence had masked till then. He spent his last evening in arranging for his mother's needs in the event of a forced separation, and disposed of the few trinkets of which he had not been plundered, as souvenirs to his friends. He retired early, taking leave of those assembled in turn. I put my arms round his neck and embraced him, and I said, "God bless you, Oscar," for I thought that I should never see him again. Apart from my conduct, which was prompted by my great sorrow and a weakness of nerve which bordered on hysteria, that farewell-taking was not lacking in dignity. And the cruelty of it was, that but for the charge against him, his attitude that night in the face of imminent danger would have authorised his friends to proclaim the man a hero.

I had thought that I should never see him again. But as that dreadful Saturday dragged on, the impulse grew stronger and stronger within me to go to him, so as to be with him at the end. In the afternoon then, meeting Ernest Dowson, I asked him to accompany me to the Old Bailey. We drove there, and as we alighted in front of the court-house, a shout arose from the rabble that thronged the street, "Here are some more aristocrats! Here are some more of them!"

I said to Dowson, as we passed through the doorway which leads into the little yard between the court-house and Newgate, "That shout explains that much of the popular execration of our friend proceeds from class hatred. He represents the aristocrat, poor fellow, to them, and they are exulting in the downfall of an aristocrat."

We found a few friends in the passage from which judge and barristers by one staircase, and witnesses by another, reach the court-room, and I heard that after a deadly summing-up the jury had retired. There could be no hope of a favourable verdict. I was fully prepared for this news, but none the less it came as a shock. A friend diverted my thoughts by pointing to something on the other side of the yard—a something that was seated on a bench,—a multiple something that was giggling and chatting and smoking cigarettes. It was The Evidence. After awhile, a friend came out of the Court and told me that if I cared to come in, there was a place for me. I entered, and found the room by no means as crowded as I had expected, and amongst those present very few faces that I recognised. My friend was sitting in the dock, covering a sheet of paper with innumerable Deltas. I saluted him, but he only acknowledged my greeting with the faintest inclination of the head. I sat down on the bench behind the counsel for the Crown, and next to a barrister who was a friend of mine. He whispered to me that all chance was gone. Still, the jury were a long time in discussion, and each minute strengthened hope. After a long while we heard a bell, an usher came bustling in, and a great silence fell upon the buzzing Court. It was the silence of a beast of prey which, to seize its victim, opens a yawning mouth, and perforce suspends its roar. But it was a false alarm. The jury had sent a question to the judge.

"That means an acquittal," said the Treasury counsel.

"No, no, no," said Sir Edward, shaking his head.

"Thus do they compliment each other," I whispered to my neighbour. The Treasury counsel overheard my whisper, and turned round, with a mighty face suffused with joviality. It was like a sudden sun in a very evil mist, and it quite cheered me to see that my friend's adversary was such a pleasant gentleman. And still the minutes went by. "There may be another disagreement," said my friend. But whilst he yet spoke the die had been cast.

I noticed that the judge's hand shook as in a palsy as he arranged his papers on the desk. As to the jury, a glance at their faces was sufficient. Six questions had been put to them, and "Guilty" was the answer to each. Such was the foreman's enthusiasm of conviction, that to the question "Is that the verdict of you all?" he answered with another "Guilty,"—a piece of overweight—a bonus to public opinion. I had laid my head down on my arms at the first "Guilty" and groaned, and each fresh condemnation, like a lash on my back, drew from me an exclamation of pain.

I could not look at my friend. Amongst all those eyes turned on him in that moment, he should not notice mine. But I looked at him when the judge was passing sentence, and the face is one I shall never forget. It was flushed purple, the eyes protruded, and over all was an expression of extreme horror. When the judge had finished speaking, and whilst a whirr of satisfaction buzzed through the Court, Wilde, who had recovered himself, said, "And I? May I say nothing, my lord?" But the judge made no answer—only an impatient sign with his hand to the warders. I jumped up, to do what or say what I cannot fancy, but was pulled down by my friend the barrister. "You'll do no good," he said, "and you'll be sent to Holloway."

Warders touched my poor friend on the shoulder. He shuddered and gave one wild look round the Court. Then he turned and lumbered forward to the head of the stairs which led to the bottomless pit. He was swept down and disappeared.

As I staggered down the steps to leave the court-house, I dimly heard the cries of exultation which those crowding down with me were uttering. But this fiendish joy in the ruin of a life was to be impressed upon me still more vividly. For when the verdict and the sentence on 'the aristocrat' reached the rabble in Old Bailey, men and women joined hands and danced an ungainly farandole, where ragged petticoats and yawning boots flung up the London mud in *feu de joie*, and the hideous faces

were distorted with savage triumph. I stood and watched this dance of death for a few minutes, regretting that Veretschagin was not by my side; and whilst I was standing there, I saw The Evidence, still laughing and smoking cigarettes, being driven off in cabs. And I said to Dowson, "This is a trial in which, out of nine people incriminated, eight have been admitted to act as Queen's Evidence." Then we walked on—I as in a dream.

That evening I went to see Daudet. He said, "This is a fine country. I admire a country where justice is administered as it is here, as is shown by to-day's verdict and sentence."

I said nothing, for there was nothing to say, and there was nothing to do but to bend under the inevitable. I dined with the Daudets and a Lord Somebody that night, and the dinner was a luxurious one. But every mouthful I took had a strange savour, for I was thinking of what poor Wilde might at that moment be scooping out of a greasy pannikin with a wooden spoon, and the thought flavoured all the sauces of that dinner.

I know little of his prison life, for I never spoke to him on the subject after his release, and what I do know is from hearsay only, but it appears that that first evening in Wandsworth Gaol was to him one of terrible suffering—indeed, that he revolted when he was told to enter a filthy bath in which other prisoners had preceded him. But his experiences cannot have been worse than I pictured them.

Daudet was very kind to me all the evening; and when I was leaving, he invited me to come early on the morrow, so that we might have a long time at our book; "For," he said, "it is in work only that you will find consolation."

"Ah, yes," I answered; "but when the mainspring is broken and one can work no longer—"

It was on the following day, I think, that I said to him, "I want to write a story, *maître*, which I shall call "The Misanthrope by Philanthropy,"—the story of a man who becomes a hermit because he has a tender and a susceptible heart, and wishes to escape the certain suffering which would fall to his lot, if he lived in the world, and formed attachments and grew fond of friends."

HUGH WALKER
"The Birth of a Soul:
(Oscar Wilde: The Closing Phase)"

Hibbert Journal, January 1905, pp. 756–68

Forty years ago Robert Browning declared that, besides "the incidents in the development of a soul," there was little that was worth study; and all his poetry proves that he not only said it with his lips but believed it in his heart. If he was right, how supereminent must be the interest of an incident, or a group of incidents, the effect of which is so great that it is best described, not as the development of a soul, but as its re-birth! Such is the supreme interest which belongs to the two books, *De Profundis* and *A Ballad of Reading Gaol*, written by Oscar Wilde after the awful overthrow of his disgrace, condemnation and imprisonment. Whoever compares these books with any of Wilde's earlier writings, whether in prose or in verse, must surely be driven to the conclusion that their author was the child of a second birth in a sense far deeper than that which is usually attached to the glibly-repeated phrases of traditional theology. He may even be led to question the propriety of speaking about the "ruin" of Wilde, though Wilde applies the word to himself. "I must," he says, "say to myself that I ruined myself, and that nobody great or small can be ruined except by his own hand." Yet the question suggested by the two books above named is whether the apparent ruin was not in reality salvation; and whether, in the eye of infinite wisdom, the whole process of sin, and degradation, and suffering, might not be just the process most to be desired for such a man as Wilde. His condemnation smirched Wilde for ever with the "bar sinister" of the prison, made his name a name of reproach, and himself an outcast from society; but it led to the production of two works which, in their moral depth and permanent significance, dwarf all he had before written, all that he gave promise of writing. The tree is known by its fruit. Could such a tree have borne such fruit unless it had been watered by the bloody sweat of those appalling sufferings? Would anything but the utter disgrace and infamy of the sentence have wrung from Wilde the indispensable bloody sweat? But if the sufferings were necessary, then the sins from which they sprang were necessary too; and in that case it would seem that we must modify the ordinary conception of the nature of sin and suffering. Carlyle in a noble figure reminds us that the rose is none the less a rose although it springs from a dungheap. The metaphor is flung at that realism which belittles the higher elements of humanity because they are inseparably associated with the animal part. We accept it as a fine expression of the truth; but we probably shrink from asking ourselves what may be the components of that heap from which the rose draws its life. Neither, fortunately, is there the least necessity of descending to details; but *De Profundis* irresistibly impels us to ask the question whether there is any form of evil which is absolutely, irredeemably and immutably evil. We are accustomed to think of certain forms of evil as being capable of transformation into good. The suffering which is brought upon us by the action of others, or that which is due to our own inadvertent transgression, may be matter for thanksgiving. The baser passions are, we know, no more identical with the family affections, which are the glory of humanity, than is the festering corruption at the roots identical with the beautiful flower. Both have undergone a transformation "into something rich and strange." But dare we apply this same conception to the sins which we are conscious of committing against our own higher nature, which we feel have degraded us? Is there any moral alchemy which can alter the character of lying, and slander, and covetousness, and the thousand forms of impurity? This is the question which *De Profundis* forces us to raise. Wilde was neither the first to ask it nor the first to answer it; but probably no one else has so vividly illustrated the answer by his own life and work.

We need not lift the curtain from Wilde's history farther than he has lifted it himself in *De Profundis*. There he tells us, sufficiently for the purpose, what he was before his life was cleft in twain by the closing of the prison doors behind him. "The gods had given me almost everything," he says. "But I let myself be lured into long spells of senseless and sensual ease. I amused myself with being a *flâneur*, a dandy, a man of fashion. I surrounded myself with the smaller and the meaner minds. I became the spendthrift of my own genius, and to waste an eternal youth gave me a curious joy. Tired of being on the heights, I deliberately went to the depths in the search for new sensation." . . . "It was always springtime once in my heart. My temperament was akin to joy. I filled my life to the very brim with pleasure, as one might fill a cup to the very brim with wine." Nor must it be supposed that Wilde ever, even doing his imprisonment, turned his back completely upon his old life, or wholly renounced the principles which governed it. The new conception which filled his mind in prison was that they were, not so much false, as partial and one-sided. "I don't," he says, "regret for a single moment having lived for pleasure. I did it to the full, as one should do everything that one does. There was no pleasure I did not experience. I threw the pearl of my soul into a cup of wine. I went down the primrose path to the sound of flutes. I lived on honeycomb. But to have continued the same life would have been wrong, because it would have been limiting. I had to pass on."

The mistake, then, in Wilde's opinion, was, not in living for pleasure, but in living for that *alone*. He had been unfaithful to his own resolution, "to eat of the fruit of all the trees in the garden of the world": he had confined himself to those which grew on "the sunlit side of the garden." Richly endowed with genius, and with that charm which does not always accompany genius, even in his youth the apostle of a school, master of epigram and paradox, "the glass of fashion," he could say with truth that the gods had given him almost everything; and his friends might well think that he had but to go on with the same almost god-like ease, in order to make his life one triumphal procession. Yet they were certainly wrong. Wilde stood in a false relation to life. The elegancies would have palled, the pleasures would have cloyed, one ray of nature's sun would have revealed the theatrical falsity of the light. Artistically, even,—the one thing which Wilde cared for—he would have become intolerable. The phrase-monger speedily wears himself out, the man who is always in a pose ends by becoming ridiculous. When he spoke condescendingly of the Atlantic Ocean, Wilde revealed to the discerning the goal towards which he was travelling. He had to learn something which was yet concealed from him.

Wilde learnt the indispensable lesson not voluntarily, but by the sternest of necessities. He had been told the truth, but he refused to believe it. "My mother," he says, "who knew life as a whole, used often to quote to me Goethe's lines, written by Carlyle in a book he had given her years ago, and translated by him, I fancy, also:—

> Who never ate his bread in sorrow,
>   Who never spent the midnight hours
> Weeping and waiting for the morrow,—
>   He knows you not, ye heavenly powers."

Wilde "absolutely declined to accept or admit the enormous truth hidden" in these lines. He "could not understand it." That his eyes might be opened, he had to pass within the prison doors,—to stand at Clapham Junction, manacled, in a garb of shame, the loadstone of all eyes as if he were some cynosure of the nether pit,—to think the dreadful thoughts of "the man who had to swing," and to realise the horror of the doom with a vividness far beyond the reach of the criminal's own mind. What such experiences must have meant to a bundle of nerves like Wilde, even his own words can but very imperfectly tell: no one else can attempt to tell it at all. Not often have such experiences been narrated by the man to whom they have come; where, except in these books, are they to be found narrated by such a "lord of language" as Wilde? No words can exaggerate, few minds can comprehend, the intensity of the mental sufferings of such a man in such a position. *De Profundis* and the *Ballad of Reading Gaol* show, as perhaps no other books have ever shown, the immensity of the difference which may divide punishments nominally the same. They illustrate in a startling fashion the crudity of human justice. And yet perhaps their effect upon Wilde may be the best vindication of its methods. The stolid criminal would certainly not have suffered as Wilde did; but neither would he have found Wilde's redemption.

It is the revelation of the effect of such a discipline of sin and punishment and suffering that gives Wilde's last two books their unique value; and it is herein too that we find their deepest agreement. In more ways than one *De Profundis* is widely different from the *Ballad of Reading Gaol.* The fact that the former is in prose and the latter in verse is not important; for in conception both are poetical and tragic. But the spirit is different, as the circumstances of composition were different. *De Profundis*, written in prison, is more submissive. It does indeed condemn the system of punishment: "The prison style is absolutely and entirely wrong." But Wilde adds that "the spirit of the Christ who is not in the churches, may make it, if not right, at least possible to be borne without too much bitterness of heart." *Reading Gaol*, written after the prisoner's release, indicates a reaction. The picture of the warders "strutting up and down," keeping "their herd of brutes," and of their mockery of "the swollen purple throat," is full charged with bitterness; and it is doubtful whether anyone would infer from the ballad that sense of obligation to the prison officials, or at least to the Governor, which Wilde expresses in the letter prefixed to *De Profundis*. The reader perceives that, notwithstanding his condemnation of the prison system, the author of the ballad was profoundly indebted to that system; but he does not perceive that the poet himself was conscious of the debt. The chief purpose of *De Profundis*, on the other hand, is to proclaim it. Society is wrong in its treatment of the offender, the prison system is wrong,—yet in spite of the wrong there comes to him, through the treatment and through the system, the boon of a deeper and a larger life.

In some ways, therefore, the *Ballad of Reading Gaol* seems to show that Wilde was reverting towards something less alien from his former self than were his thoughts in prison; and on that account it may be held to justify the suspicion that the change in his character was less complete and profound than it would be judged from *De Profundis* to be. In at least one respect, however, and that the most vital, the *Ballad* shows continued progress along the same line. It is the most sincere of all Wilde's writings. *De Profundis* is incomparably more sincere than any of his earlier works; but the greatest flaw in it is the suggestion conveyed by some passages that perhaps after all the writer is only posing. That this is so is no matter for wonder; it would be marvellous, rather, if even such a tremendous catastrophe as his had all at once revolutionised the inborn disposition or the acquired character of the man. Wilde had breathed the breath of artifice and affectation; and even the prison could not all at once sweep it away and replace it with an atmosphere of simple truth and sincerity. But in the ballad every line bears its own guarantee of sincerity. The thoughts which the author expresses or suggests may be wrong; but it is impossible to doubt that they are the thoughts of a man deeply in earnest. Here, then, *De Profundis* is inferior; yet not so inferior as to be tainted in its essence. As the *Ballad of Reading Gaol* carries a guarantee in its tone, so does *De Profundis* in its substance. The thoughts in it are beyond, immeasurably beyond, Wilde's former range; the reader is forced to believe in their sincerity, because he feels certain that they would never have occurred to such a man by the mere exercise of imagination. He had to die to society, and almost to himself, in order that he might live again with alien powers and with thoughts hitherto inconceivable by him. It is significant that he believed his central conception to have been expressed only once before, and even then to have been misunderstood; yet he must have read it in one of the great poets of his own day. He read it; but only the prison experience gave him the key to its meaning.

To expect in Wilde an ordinary reformation, even as the result of such an experience, would be to misunderstand the man; and he leaves us in no doubt about the futility of such an expectation. "I need not tell you," he says, "that to me reformations in morals are as meaningless and vulgar as Reformations in theology. But while to propose to be a better man is a piece of unscientific cant, to have become a deeper man is the privilege of those who have suffered. And such I think I have become." Such, indeed, he had become. The worshipper of beauty who had turned away from sorrow and suffering of all kinds as modes of imperfection, now declares that pain is the indispensable condition of the highest beauty of all. He who had said that there was "enough suffering in one narrow London lane to show that God did not love man," now writes: "It seems to me that love of some kind is the only possible explanation of the extraordinary amount of suffering that there is in the world. I cannot conceive of any other explanation. I am convinced that there is no other, and that if the world has indeed, as I have said, been built of sorrow, it has been built by the hands of love, because in no other way could the soul of man, for whom the world was made, reach the full stature of its perfection. Pleasure for the beautiful body, but pain for the beautiful soul."

Part of Wilde's doctrine is, as has been already said, commonly accepted; and he himself was, in the earlier part of his life, exceptional in denying it. Theologians would have no difficulty in accepting Wilde's words in the passage quoted above: they would consider them admirably orthodox. They have taught the moral value of suffering, and their recognition of it is the most vital difference between their ethical teaching and that of the Greek philosophers. It is likewise the most vital difference between the teaching of Christianity and that of Judaism: "prosperity," says Bacon, "is the blessing of the Old Testament; adversity is the blessing of the New." But while they have taught this, theologians have, at the same time, drawn the broadest of lines between suffering and sin. They conceive of the former as something which is, somehow, necessary for the moral good of humanity, though they cannot understand it. "Clergymen," says Wilde, "and people who use phrases without wisdom sometimes talk of suffering as a mystery. It is really a revelation." But while they regard suffering as, though mysterious, necessary, and in some uncomprehended way right, towards sin their attitude is altogether negative. It would be right to court suffering for a good cause; but many have taught that to commit the most venial sin, were it even to secure the most transcendent good, would be to deserve damnation. And probably many more, who are unable to banish all sense of proportion in face of the word "sin," would feel themselves holier men if they only could do so. To them sin is evil, absolute and immitigable. The ecclesiastical conception of saintship rests almost wholly on the conviction that it is a higher thing to have committed no sin than, in achieving great results, to have gathered also the spots and stains of a world where evil is plentifully mingled with good. The view is negative rather than positive; innocence is set above a life of strenuous but not immaculate virtue.

Now, it is important to notice that Wilde recognises no such absolute distinction between, on the one hand, a form of evil called sin, which is always and incurably evil, and which has to be simply blotted out by a special act of divine grace; and, on the other hand, forms of evil called pain and suffering, which are even essential to the highest good. Not only so, but he justifies his own view by a reference to the teaching of Christ. "The world had always loved the saint as being the nearest possible approach to the perfection of God. Christ, through some divine instinct in him, seems to have always loved the sinner as being the nearest possible approach to the perfection of man. His primary desire was not to reform people, any more than his primary desire was to relieve suffering. To turn an interesting thief into a tedious honest man was not his aim. . . . In a manner not yet understood of the world, he regarded sin and suffering as being in themselves beautiful holy things and modes of perfection."

There is a suggestion of phrase-making in the sentence about the interesting thief and the tedious honest man. There can be no doubt that Christ did aim at turning the thief, although he might be interesting, into an honest man, even if in the process he became tedious; and Wilde must have been perfectly well aware of the fact. The sentence is one of the lingering traces of insincerity which mar the book. But the main thought expressed was deeply and seriously felt. Wilde had indeed come to regard "sin and suffering as being . . . . beautiful holy things and modes of perfection"; and he believed that Christ so regarded them.

"It seems a very dangerous idea," he goes on. "It is—all great ideas are dangerous. That it was Christ's creed admits of no doubt. That it is the true creed I do not doubt myself.

"Of course the sinner must repent. But why? Simply because otherwise he would be unable to realise what he had done. The moment of repentance is the moment of initiation. More than that: it is the means by which one alters one's past. The Greeks thought that impossible. They often say in their Gnomic aphorisms, 'Even the Gods cannot alter the past.' Christ showed that the commonest sinner could do it, that it was the one thing he could do. Christ, had he been asked, would have said—I feel quite certain about it—that the moment the prodigal son fell on his knees and wept, he made his having wasted his substance on harlots, his swine-herding and hungering for the husks they ate, beautiful and holy moments in his life. It is difficult for most people to grasp the idea. I daresay one has to go to prison to understand it. If so, it may be worth while going to prison."

It should be noticed that there is in the former of these passages an apparent oversight of expression. Wilde speaks of Christ as having regarded "sin and suffering as being *in themselves* beautiful and holy things." When he comes to illustrate, what he says is that when the prodigal son fell on his knees and wept, he made his sins beautiful and holy moments in his life. The difference is important: the sins are no longer beautiful and holy *in themselves*, but in their results. The repentant prodigal is a better man—or, if Wilde prefers it, a deeper man—than many just men which need no repentance; but his sins alone, without the repentance, would not make him better or deeper.

These paragraphs are the core of *De Profundis*. Out of the depths to which he had sunk, or from the heights towards which he was rising, Wilde proclaimed this startling gospel, that sin and suffering are beautiful holy things and modes of perfection. That is what one of the most appalling of all imaginable experiences had taught him. He appears to have believed that this doctrine was original with him, or rather that it was original with Christ, and that he was the first who had taken it from the teaching of Christ. He was not altogether right: it was not absolutely necessary—for all men, though probably it was for him—to go to prison in order to learn it. The doctrine is closely akin to that of Hegel, who likewise taught that good is evolved out of evil; and though Wilde, who tells us that metaphysics interested him very little and morality not at all, may well have neglected the philosopher, it is more strange that he had not detected the same teaching in the verse of Browning. One of the most frequently recurrent thoughts in Browning's poetry is that of the necessity of evil to progress. It

runs through his work from beginning to end, appearing at least as early as *Sordello*, and finding perhaps its clearest and fullest expression in the last volume he ever published. It is the whole meaning of the poem *Rephan*, where the sentence pronounced upon the aspiring soul is, "Thou art past Rephan, thy place be Earth." And Browning as well as Wilde refuses to take shelter behind the distinction between suffering and sin. Both are necessary. The soul must be "by hate taught love." The Earth to which the growing spirit is sent is earth with all her innumerable forms of evil:—

> Diseased in the body, sick in soul,
> Pinched poverty, satiate wealth,—your whole
> Array of despairs.

Doubtless Wilde read Browning at a time when such teaching was wholly alien from his mind, and for that reason missed the poet's meaning. He is less original than he believed himself to be; but he is even more interesting than he knew. For in one respect he is unique. He not only taught this doctrine, but he affords in his own person the most striking illustration of it. To him it came, not from books, but fresh stamped with the impress of truth from the mint of experience. From him it passes to the reader, not a mere theory, but a life. There, on the one hand, is Oscar Wilde, *flâneur* and dandy, treading the primrose path to the sound of flutes, sporting upon the surface of life, beautiful as a floating bubble played upon by the sunlight, and almost as evanescent,—here, on the other, is a new Oscar Wilde, branded with infamy, worn with suffering, but forced by that very infamy and suffering to work down towards the depths, where he finds and makes his own, as no one else had ever done, the thought of the greatest European philosopher and the most philosophic English poet of the nineteenth century. By that achievement he has probably made his fame permanent; and he has certainly made it impossible for any contemporary to ignore him.

A catastrophe more utter and apparently irretrievable than Wilde's can hardly be conceived. His very fame made it the more hopeless. Other prisoners might retire into obscurity, they could easily hide themselves from the few who knew them. But for him the whole earth was "shrivelled to a handsbreadth," and he must wear the brand of infamy in the face of day. It was just from the completeness of the ruin, in the worldly sense, that the new soul took its birth. With penetrating insight Wilde perceived that he must not attempt to deny his imprisonment, or to pretend that such an incident had never occurred in his life. Not only would the pretence in his case have been hopeless, but it would have been a blunder even if he could have succeeded in deceiving men. "I want," he says, "to get to the point when I shall be able to say quite simply, and without affectation, that the two great turning-points in my life were when my father sent me to Oxford, and when society sent me to prison." . . . "To deny one's own experiences is to put a lie into the lips of one's own life. It is no less than a denial of the soul."

It is pathetic to observe this pleasure-loving spirit bent by an iron necessity to a fate as hard as the worst which mediæval asceticism ever contrived for itself. But the justification of the suffering comes from the extraordinary change which it produced. "Most people," says he, "are other people. Their thoughts are someone else's opinions, their lives a mimicry, their passions a quotation." It is profoundly true; and, though to the end he did not suspect the fact, it is true of Wilde himself till the period of his imprisonment. He was, indeed, the leader of a fashion; but the fashion itself was an unconscious plagiarism from a highly artificial society. Until his terrible disaster

Wilde had never been forced to dive into the depths of his own spirit; he had delighted to play on the surface. By compulsion he learnt wisdom.

The change worked in Wilde is so enormous that it may fairly be described as the birth of a soul. The new soul was begotten by sin and born of agony. Its life was short; and there is sad reason to fear that even before the close Wilde had slid far back towards the gulf from which he had emerged. Probably he had by his early career too completely sapped and undermined his own character to be capable of standing firm upon the height which he had gained. Yet even so the change was sufficient reward for the throes of birth; it was worth while to have trodden even such a wine-press of the wrath of God. The prodigal had fallen on his knees and wept, his soul had had one glimpse of the immortal sea, he had stood for a moment upon the peak in Darien; and however long had been his life, however stained with errors, weaknesses and vices, it must have been influenced by that transmuting experience. It had changed Wilde's whole view of life; and though he might have sinned deeply against himself, he could never have forgotten the "revelation" of suffering.

The most momentous question suggested by the amazing result is: Could the reformation have been brought about at a cheaper price? Could the new soul have been born of any other parentage? Would anything but that terrible suffering have given the apostle of æstheticism the depth and the earnestness necessary to conceive the *Ballad of Reading Gaol* and *De Profundis*? If not, for him it may have been worth while, not only to go to prison, but even to sin as deeply as he did. The idea may be, as he says, a dangerous one; but what if it be true? Have all the churches, in nineteen centuries, thrown such light upon the problem of evil as is shed by these two books in contrast with their author's earlier writings?

WILFRID M. LEADMAN
"The Literary Position of Oscar Wilde"
Westminster Review, August 1906, pp. 201–8

Maeterlinck has shown us in one of his admirable essays how impossible and how absurd it is to attempt to reconcile human affairs with the idea of an intelligent external justice impartially and invariably meting out good for good and evil for evil. All injustice springs originally from man himself or from what we are pleased to call Nature. The intelligence of Nature is purely mechanical; she has smiles and frowns for both moral and immoral alike, without regard to character or conduct. The "justice" or "injustice" of man is purely arbitrary, hence its seeming inexplicability. In no sense, perhaps, is the cruelty and caprice of human justice shown more painfully than in the history of literature. Here and there, scattered over the globe, we find lonely and unrecognised geniuses whose messages have faded and remain forgotten because no one has been found to appreciate or to understand them. And too often the fault lay, not in the message or its deliverer, but in the world. On the other hand we find writers (not always so deserving) concerning whose high position the world has spoken decisively. She has placed them on lofty pedestals. And those whom she chooses for this honour are usually the writers who have made a successful appeal to some strong force in human nature. They count their followers by millions; for they have a straightforward message for plain minds. True, in distant years their names may fade for ever to make room for other names bearing similar messages, but,

whatever their ultimate fate be, they have at least the satisfaction of present glory and the supreme consolation of being understood by their fellows. In the contemplation of these darlings of public opinion we feel no pain; but, when we turn to the victims of that same public opinion, we cannot but feel angered at the grotesque caprice of human justice. Among the writers so rejected by the world there are some whom she has spurned simply because she has not troubled to understand them. Prominent among this mournful group is Oscar Wilde. Around that hapless man controversy incessantly played in the past and apparently will continue to play in the future. His whole literary work (plays, poems, essays, and fiction) in vain cried out for just criticism—prejudice, misconception, and a strained sense of respectability refused it. His few admirers were dubbed a senseless clique dazzled by the showy glitter of his language. Wilde was always considered a mere "poseur." Fault was found with all his writings. It was said that his prose was disfigured by incongruous ornament; his poetry was a feeble echo of Keats and Swinburne. His wonderful essays—especially "The Decay of Lying" and "The Soul of Man"—were admired only for their peculiar brilliance; their inherent depths of philosophy was overlooked. His plays were deemed conventional in construction and overloaded with spurious wit. Great and undue stress was invariably laid on the man's eccentricities; in the public eye Wilde was only a witty fellow yearning for celebrity and capable of performing weird literary antics to attain that object. He is indeed a tragic figure. Laughed at in his youth, misunderstood in his maturity, spurned in his closing years, accused of plagiarism, blamed for his love of posture, constantly charged with artificiality, an object of unceasing attack from pulpit and press—in a word, roundly abused all his life—Wilde would seem to have small chance, in this country, at any rate, of literary fame. Long before the catastrophe of 1895 he had an extraordinary amount of prejudice against him. His downfall was the crowning condemnation. After that it looked as though he were indeed doomed to an eternal outer darkness. And yet, leaving the question of his conduct on one side, his sole fault was simply his unswerving fidelity to his own intellectual bias. He could not write about ordinary things in an ordinary way. He could not present the British public with its favourite dish of love and sport. He was incapable of moulding his maxims on traditional conceptions of virtue and vice. It was, perhaps, inevitable that the uneducated British public should turn its back on one who at almost every opportunity flaunted in its face the most unusual doctrines. For it must be confessed, Oscar Wilde enunciated doctrines utterly alien to the ingrained Puritanism and athleticism of English people. The man who runs counter to national traditions and prejudices is bound to provoke bitter hostility. The man who, in this country, places art before muscle or sets the individual will above the conventional law, seems sure sooner or later to come to grief. Yet, in spite of his unpopularity, Wilde was never discouraged. Borne up by his own motto, "To be great is to be misunderstood," he moved steadily forward, and made his mark. True his influence was limited to the very few, but it existed and will expand further in the time to come. The unconventional will always thank him for his unflinching advocacy of things unconventional. The artist will remember him because he was one of the courageous few who helped to remove English theories of art from the tyranny of rigid tradition to the freedom of unfettered originality. He may have been rash, he may have been inclined to pose, his writings may show traces of plagiarism—an innocent sort of plagiarism that is almost a transformation—but there was always a thoroughness' about his work which certainly deserved fairer consideration. To the average English mind his doctrines could only suggest the bizarre and the unnatural; but that was because the English mind had not yet learnt to appreciate an oblique point of view. Not that Wilde's outlook was always unusual. On the contrary, some of his short stories—especially "The Happy Prince," "The Star-Child," and "The Model Millionaire"—though necessarily tinted with his peculiar colouring, would satisfy the most exacting moralist by their tone of "poetic justice." If Wilde occasionally trampled on cherished national convictions or sometimes thrust strangely-hued flowers amongst our soberer blossoms, it was not from love of opposition; it was rather because he had to drift whither his fantastic and exuberant intellect listed.

Wilde's descent into the abyss seemed at the time to be the death-blow to what little influence he had already gained. The hasty verdict of a rather superficial morality said then that his influence must have been essentially unhealthy. From that time to the publication of *De Profundis* it was even deemed a breach of manners to allude to Wilde in any way. However, that interesting posthumous book has been the cause of a partial change of the public attitude. We are once more allowed to discuss Wilde's book without hearing a shocked "hush," or being suspected of loose views on moral matters. Whatever one's opinion may be as to the genuineness of the repentance shown in *De Profundis*, one may at any rate be deeply thankful for what it has undoubtedly done toward the rehabilitation of its author. He is no longer under a ban. He may eventually receive a high place in English literature. After all, his admitted writings cannot fairly be deemed unhealthy. Those who see "an undercurrent of nasty suggestion" in some of his literary productions must surely be so obsessed by their knowledge of his unfortunate behaviour as to lose all power of disconnecting two absolutely independent things, namely, his art and his private life. The ludicrous charges of immorality brought against that book of painted words and lordly language, *Dorian Gray*, fall to the ground at once when it is known that the book was written solely for money. As Mr. Sherard says in his *Life of Oscar Wilde*, no author would risk the financial success of a book by filling it with immoral teachings. The marvel to me is that Wilde managed to produce such a transcendent work of art under the pressure of such a prosaic stimulus.

In the past, before his downfall, Wilde's works were only read carefully by a select few. Others, it is true, granted a certain momentary admiration to his prose, but it was the sort of admiration involuntarily and temporarily evoked by gorgeous fireworks rather than the lasting admiration felt for a permanent object of art. Now, if justice is to be done to any author's work the impersonal attitude is imperative. The intellectual reader must sink his personal predilections, he must not keep asking himself whether he agree with this or that sentiment expressed by an author. It is not very hard to do. There are minds which dislike stories packed with scenes of love, but such minds need not on that account be debarred from appreciating the almost faultless love-scenes in *Richard Feverel*. Of course, when the reader is by nature in perfect accord with the writer's sentiments, the enjoyment will be fuller and more satisfactory than when his appreciation be acquired, but in both cases the object of the writer's genius will have been attained. In the case of Wilde's works there is a real necessity for impartiality of standpoint, because only the few are by nature and inclination in tune with his work. The majority must learn to put themselves into tune. Two difficulties—broadly speaking—hamper anything like a general and intelligent recognition of Wilde's genius. The first is

undoubtedly the moral obliquity or seeming moral obliquity revealed by the criminal trial of 1895. The second is the lack of effort or ability to understand Oscar Wilde's trend of thought. Would that the former might be for ever forgotten! After all, his writings are of vastly more importance to posterity than his private conduct. The stolid Englishman, however, finds it hard to differentiate between a man's private character and his books. Certain unfortunate impressions received in 1895 cloud his honest judgment in the matter of Wilde's position in literature. Now this is not the place to discuss the pathological aspect of Oscar Wilde's conduct, but I may be permitted to say that his restitution—to be permanent—must depend on a fuller knowledge of an obscure branch of morbid pathology.

This at present, for obvious reasons, is impossible. No doubt *De Profundis* with its confession of humility and its partial admission of error will impress many minds favourably, but the more matter of fact minds care little whether that book be entirely sincere or merely a huge pose intended to transform public opinion. What they do care about is a *locus standi* based on sound scientific grounds. Once such a basis be generally accepted, perhaps the worst obstacle to the recognition of Wilde will have been taken away. Let it be admitted that Wilde erred greatly; then charity reminds us that there is such a thing as forgiveness of sin. Let it be granted that pathological research will explain and even excuse much of his conduct; common-sense will then bid us banish our rigid prudery and consign once and for all to oblivion what really has absolutely nothing to do with our unchecked contemplation of a great artist.

The other obstacle to an unbiassed conception of this writer's productions is not so easily defined as that just discussed, for the latter sprang into existence at a definite time, whilst this one had existed ever since Wilde published his first book of poems. From the beginning Wilde's ideas were diametrically opposed to all our eminently respectable British traditions of art. The reading world failed to grasp his meaning. And that was mainly due to what one may call our national inability to understand a creed whose keynote was the worship of beauty. We are, above all, a stolid race, in no way over-attracted by beauty; we certainly love personal cleanliness and comfort, but it is a cleanliness derived from cold water rather than from warm, and a comfort obtained from blankets and brick rather than from silks and marble. We cannot see the use of any one's making a fuss of a beautiful thing simply because of its beauty. Such a proceeding savours to us of lunacy or idolatry. And when Wilde, in 1881, burst upon our sober minds with his first book of poems—saturated as it was with a lavish reckless admiration of beauty—we felt that here indeed was a strange apostle teaching a still stranger cult. Coming, as this book did, on the heels of Wilde's æsthetic campaign—after all, but as pardonable youthful extravagance, and, as, Mr. Sherard points out, completely cured by that American tour, which taught a needed practical lesson—there was, perhaps, some reason for its hostile reception. "Here is a man," said the critics, "who values all glittering evanescence of a coloured bubble above morality itself." This sweeping opinion represented the belief of many critics at that time, and, unfortunately for Wilde, later events seemed confirmatory. In one sense possibly Wilde did set beauty above morality, but it was above the conventional conception of morality—that is something arbitrary and too often uncharitable—*not* above goodness. In any case, one must not base one's conception of Wilde's attitude towards morality on anything which he has written. Some men do, indeed, project their own personalities into their books, in spite of Wilde's splendid dictum: "To reveal art and to conceal the artist is the true aim of art. The artist can express everything." But one may be confident that the author of *Dorian Gray* has been guilty of no such literary soul-dissecting. An intimate friend of his—a man, perhaps, more fitted to speak authoritatively on this subject than any other man living—told me that Wilde only revealed *one* aspect of his own character in his books, and that not the most attractive aspect.

Read in the clear light of intelligent criticism, the first book of poems teaches only one thing, namely, that here is an author almost unique in his whole-hearted worship of form and colour, a worship, too, that is not casual, capricious, and superficial, but serious, terribly serious, and thoroughly healthy. Of course, all this was horribly unpractical, and most Englishmen, with their innate dislike of "hollow beauty," shrugged their shoulders. Wilde, in his first as in his later efforts, wrote only for minds attuned to his. Others must take the right attitude or else pass on elsewhere.

Wilde has plainly this to his credit that he never tried to win the public, never debased the art of literature by pandering to any popular movement. Of that exquisite set of allegories *The House of Pomegranates* he finely said (in answer to some mystified critics) that "it was intended neither for the British child nor for the British public." Indeed, some think that much, if not all, of his work was the accidental, irresponsible, yet irresistible overflow of an ever creative intellect, and not literature written with any definite purpose. On this question, however, it is better to keep an open mind.

Wilde had an inherent horror of the commonplace, and this seems to have led him occasionally into a rather strained effort after a rather petty kind of originality. Of course his numerous enemies laid hold of that habit and made it the foundation of a great deal of silly abuse. Frivolous, frothy remarks put into the mouths of some of Wilde's characters were solemnly quoted as part of Wilde's creed. Witty repartees deliberately torn from their proper context in his plays were seriously construed as Wilde's own gospel. The words of few men have undergone such distortion and misinterpretation as have those of this genius. One can only be thankful that now at any rate there are signs of the advent of Truth, there are signs of a strong fresh breeze sweeping away those murky mists and grotesque masks that have so long hidden the real Wilde. It is at last dawning on men's minds that his writings are not so much external ornament concealing a blank void, and that his wit is often wisdom, only occasionally nonsense. Some critics say that Wilde's art may be very entertaining and very clever, but that (with the exception of *De Profundis*) it leads us nowhere. But is that, even if true, a sound objection to his work? For some people, at any rate, it is refreshing to step aside from the hustle and bustle of literary missionaries and to enjoy a healthy rest with an author who does not burden his readers with any tedious lesson. As a matter of fact, whether Wilde had any fixed aim or not, his work most certainly points—and points clearly—to a definite goal. I think that there are those who will say that they have been led by this author to very fruitful regions. If some people feel that Wilde only takes them a giddy dance over tracts of glittering but useless beauty, there are others who feel that his restless flights helped them to realise the wonder of much that previously seemed common and graceless. What, pray, are many of Wilde's short stories, such as the "Young King" and "The Happy Prince," but artistically embroidered pleas for social reform? Who can read *Dorian Gray* intelligently without hearing the deep bass note of doom at first faint, but gradually growing louder and louder amid the brilliant cascade of frivolous treble notes till it drowns them in the final crash of just punishment for error? Can any one fail to note the stern moral lesson of *Salomé*? Who can study his other plays carefully without learning the superb philosophy of human life that runs through them like a silver thread amid a many-hued skein? And who can help observing the high aspirations which lift so much of his verse out of the sphere of mere decorated rhyme? The truth is, Wilde's work bristles with moral advice, but—partly owing to his own oft-repeated condemnation of stories with a moral, and partly owing to the innate obtuseness of most of his readers—it is constantly overlooked.

In the early nineties Wilde's position was almost unique; he was looked upon as a literary phenomenon defying satisfactory solution. His art bewildered, amazed, repelled; if a few here hailed him as worthy to rank with intellectual giants, a multitude there said his art was unreal, frothy, and sometimes dangerous. He was a kaleidoscope puzzle even to his own friends. This is shown by the impressions of him recorded by various personal friends; they all seemed to see a different man: none of their presentations agree. Still, Wilde kept on his way gyrating giddily onward. His art must sooner or later bear fruit and find its home; such ability could not be destined to be wasted. Then, just as he seemed on the point of grasping honour and glory, there came in his career that fatal crisis, the one bright spot in which was, perhaps, that it saved him from worse things. Prison life steadied him. It helped him to take a fuller, broader view of life, to recognise how incomplete had been his former life when it confined itself to the enjoyment of this world's splendour and refused to acknowledge or share in the world's sorrow. In the quiet of his cell he could write the pleading, passionate prose afterwards given us as *De Profundis*. This book has struck the public imagination. And to me, of all the puzzling problems connected with the unfortunate Oscar Wilde, none is so inexplicable as this. A book, the keynote of which is an abject almost grovelling humility, has captivated the hearts of a people whose chief characteristics are sturdiness and independence of character. It may seem a dreadful statement, but if I were asked to name any book by Wilde that was not quite healthy in tone, I should promptly mention *De Profundis*. At the same time, I should hasten to add that the unhealthy part of the book was the unavoidable outcome of the author's terrible position. The crushed must needs be very humble.

But, apart from that one demoralising note of excessive humility, *De Profundis* is a splendid progression of noble thoughts leading in very truth from the dank gutter to the gleaming stars. The price paid for its evolution by the author was awful, but, as a writer said recently in the *Hibbert Journal*, it may have been absolutely necessary. Both this book and *A Ballad of Reading Gaol* fill the gaps left in Oscar Wilde's earlier work—gaps which might have remained empty but for his downfall. Neither of these books is, perhaps, any real advance (from a purely literary point of view) on his former work. But because they are both serious, both more in accordance with the tastes of the "man in the street," they have effected a considerable change in the public attitude. It would be safe to say that Wilde's literary position was never less insecure than at the present time. The favourable reception awarded to his last two books has opened the door to a more sensible and fairer examination of all his books. And that is all we admirers of Wilde's genius demand. The rest—the eventual granting to Wilde of a niche in the temple of English literature—will follow in due course. Some of his work already smacks of "the day before yesterday," it is true; but much of it is imperishable, capable of standing the test of ages. Much of it represents some of the finest prose-poetry in our language. Oscar Wilde was our *one* English artist in words.

At length a turning-point has been reached. Oscar Wilde is once more on trial, but it is a trial whose result can involve no disgrace, but which may—surely will—bring him a radiant wreath of fame. It will last long, for there is a strong array of witnesses on either side, and there is much up-hill work for his advocates. The scarlet flame of his disgrace still throws a lurid light on all his literary works, but it has begun to grow paler and smaller, and ere long it may become extinct, and in its place will dazzle forth the jewelled light of his undying intellect, teaching our descendants about the eternity of beauty and joy, but bidding them never forget the temporary reign of pain and sorrow, beseeching them to sweep away the tainted refuse that hides the crystal purity below, asking them for justice. And will not these requests be granted? On the Continent, in America, the great awakening has begun; there, the genius has triumphed over the convict, the sinner has been lost in the artist. Must it be said, then, by a later generation that Britain alone never forgave the strange errors of one of her brightest thinkers, but was content to let foreign hands raise him and his from the mire? Surely no; surely we are not so rich in intellectual wealth that we can afford to pass *any* of our artists by "on the other side."

Anyhow, when the haze of Time has finally covered all trace of the human frailties of Oscar Wilde, his genius, now slowly forcing its way upward through many a clogging obstacle, will rise resplendent and glorious before the eyes of an understanding posterity.

LEWIS PIAGET SHANKS
"Oscar Wilde's Place in Literature"
Dial, April 16, 1910, pp. 261–63

After a decade of noisy oblivion, the writings of Oscar Wilde have received the recognition of a definitive edition, worthy as to form and complete in contents. No longer need we contend with the pornographic stock-broker at the book-auction, or shake our heads over the excessive prices of items listed in the catalogues under the dreadful caption of *Oscariana*. However, no one but the collector will complain that Wilde is no longer a rarity. Now at last we can fight in the light: we may "adopt an attitude," to use a phrase of Wilde's own, toward a definitely presented literary talent; and even the apologists who plead that Villon was a rascal and Shakespeare a poacher, may judge whether or not we shall forget that the "apostle of the English Renaissance" was an improper person.

Will Wilde survive? The answer lies in these substantial volumes; the evidence is all in, though it may be over-early to discuss it. What strikes one first is the range of the writings: there are plays, novels, poems, essays, art-criticism, book-reviews, and autobiography; nothing is lacking but history and the "miscellaneous divinity" of the old-book stores! Wilde preferred making history to writing it (we are still trying to forget the lily!); and if he worshipped Pater's style, he did not care in the least for patristic literature. Here, therefore, we must content ourselves with the Pre-Raphaelite lyrics, filled with æsthetic religiosity as the poems of Dante Gabriel Rossetti: charming decorative pieces surely, but insincere in spirit as most of our modern cathedral glass. Mediæval feeling, after all, can hardly be reproduced in a copy of a copy.

Rossetti is but one of Wilde's literary models; every great poet of the Victorian age finds a second immortality in his verses. They pass before us in "The Garden of Eros"—Keats, Shelley, Swinburne, Morris, and the poet-painter himself. But

if we add to these self-confessed mentors most of the other great English poets, and to these Homer and the Greeks, and Dante, and a few of the lyrists of France, we shall get a better idea of the range of his reading and the strength of his memory. No academic ear is needed to detect this; echo follows echo as in a musical comedy. "The true artist is known," said Wilde in one of his reviews, "by the use he makes of what he annexes; and he annexes everything." So our poet modestly lived up to his maxim, aware that in literature at least there is no Monroe Doctrine. Had not Molière said, before him, "Je prends mon bien où je le trouve"? Like Molière, we are all plagiarists—though hardly, perhaps, with such an excuse; and some Elysian day, when all but the scholars have ceased to read the classics, judicious plagiarism may become a literary virtue, supported by a socialistic culture and justified by the pedagogic theories of Rousseau.

So perhaps might Wilde have justified his imitations. But his plagiarism was of the old-fashioned sturdier sort, like Shakespeare's or Molière's. He copied from other poets, hoping, as all plagiarists hope, that in the course of time others might copy him. He copied himself, to show that he was not unworthy of the compliment. Did not Homer repeat his adjectives, his similes? So in these books the best refuses to be hidden, and telling epithets, aphorisms, and puns reappear like comets in the cosmic life. Over a score of the epigrams in *A Woman of No Importance* are taken from *Dorian Gray*. Like the bird in Browning's verses, Wilde

> Sings each song twice over,
> Lest you should think he never could recapture
> The first fine careless rapture.

One cannot see how much of the early verse can survive. We soon tire of hydromel, and a Keats devoid of genius becomes the most dreadful of literary diets. Alas for Wilde! he feasted too long on ambrosia, and drank too deeply of his "poppy-seeded wine." To read his verse at all is cloying, and to read much of it is like a literary debauch. The best things are the Sonnets, in which the imagery is definitely limited by the form: there at least the reader is sure of one thought for every fourteen lines. Next to these come, not the "Pagan" verses, far too morbidly romantic to be Greek, but the pastel-like pictures inspired by Gautier, some of which have all the delicate impressionism of *Emaux et camées*. What could be better in its way than this:

La Fuite de la Lune

> To outer senses there is peace,
>   A dreamy peace on either hand,
>   Deep silence in the shadowy land,
> Deep silence where the shadows cease.
>
> Save for a cry that echoes shrill
>   From some lone bird disconsolate;
>   A corncrake calling to its mate;
> The answer from the misty hill.
>
> And suddenly the moon withdraws
>   Her sickle from the lightening skies,
>   And to her sombre cavern flies,
> Wrapped in a veil of yellow gauze.

No minor poet in England ever attained a more thorough mastery of technique than Wilde: we see it in the sonnets, as nearly perfect in construction as the study of Milton could make them; we see it pushed to the extreme of *l'art pour l'art* in that bit of Byzantine mosaic, *The Sphinx*. Yet of these early poems none are to be found in the anthologies save "Ave Imperatrix," which alone catches a breath of national feeling in an adequate chord. Most of them, to be sure, are esoteric;

when we read them we wonder what is the matter, but when we have read them we conclude that there isn't any. Never did Wilde conform more closely to his maxim, "Youth is rarely original."

The Ballad of Reading Gaol was written fifteen years later. We all remember how it was received; we remember—alas!—how it was compared to *The Ancient Mariner.* Such judgments show the evils of literary journalism: they indicate that the critic has had no time to read Coleridge since his college days. *Reading Gaol* has more limp-leather editions to its credit in the department stores,—but where in Wilde's ballad do we find anything like the conception, the imaginative power, and the classic simplicity of *The Ancient Mariner,* whose every sentence is as full of meaning as the etcher's line? *Reading Gaol* does recall Coleridge, as "Charmides" recalls something of Keats; but the first poem is too brutal, the second too delicately indelicate, to carry out the comparison invited by occasional imitative lines. No realism, however, poignant, can match the serene imaginative reality of the earlier poem; we want no paradoxes in the ballad, we want no ballad so artistic as to be artificial. And, after all, Wilde never forgets that the important thing in his poem is the manner.

The tyranny of technique is Wilde's real prison-wall. If art is not able to effect itself—*ars est celare artem*—better to write without regard for style than use the diction of "The Decay of Lying." Such prose makes one think that it is possible for an artist to be too articulate. "The world was created," said Stéphane Mallarmé, "in order to lead up to a fine book." For Wilde, apparently, the cosmic processes led up to the paradox. "Pen, Pencil, and Poison" was built around an epigram, and "The Model Millionaire" was written for the sake of a pun. "Paradoxy is my doxy" is the basis of his artistic creed; and the principle of his method is simple contrariety. For example:

> After the death of her third husband her hair turned quite gold from grief.
> We live in an age that reads too much to be wise, and thinks too much to be beautiful.

What could be simpler than the *modus operandi?* Yet each of these phrases occurs three times in the volumes before us, with many another gem of rare and recurrent wit. Surely Wilde knew that the best of paradoxes will scarce bear repetition, and that the wittiest of epigrams loses its flavor when it becomes a refrain.

The least affected of Wilde's prose is to be found in the journalistic criticism which fills a volume and a half of the collected works; book-reviews of purely ephemeral interest, yet written with sprightly grace and wit, and full of literary judgments which will be turned against their author—when our would-be doctors fall upon the difference between Wilde's preaching and his practice! And to reward their labors, they will find some charming "purple patches"; the best of these were afterwards worked into the pages of *Intentions.* Wilde might have become a critic of importance, had it been given him to outgrow his paradoxes and to chasten his style. He had a nice appreciation of all the arts, and a sense of the melodic possibilities of language that puts his best work beside that of Pater; and, unlike Pater, he never falls from music to mosaic. Truly, *Intentions* is a delightful book,—but how far below Pater, if we consider it as a collection of essays! How far below Landor in its management of the dialogue form! Wilde's adversary is always the man of straw; there is none of the play of personality, the contrast of opposite standpoints, that we find in such books as Mallock's *New Republic.* Wilde could not project himself into the intellectual life of another.

This is the fault of all his work. The very types in his plays, excepting those that call for a mere surface characterization, are at heart merely dramatic phases of the moods or poses of their author. He gives them emotions, but not minds or characters; he makes them real by their repartee. They are puppets animated by puns; they bedazzle our judgment with a pyrotechnic shower of epigrams. We are carried away by it all, but we are left nothing which we can carry away. The æsthetic "katharsis" of his dramatic theories is lost sight of; we must purge our souls with paradoxes, and in improper situations make them clean. After all, the characters of these plays are not characters, for all they have the tone of good society. They are sometimes society men and women, but more often only marionettes with manners.

Marionettes, too, are the men and women of *Dorian Gray.* Lord Henry Wotton, brilliant, autobiographic, the monocled Mephisto of an ineffectual Faust, may alone be said to live, and at times the reader finds him more lively than alive. Dorian simply doesn't exist; he has sold his conscience for an eternal youth,—and what man can exist without a conscience? Sybil Vane is a shadow, and the painter Hallward the shadow of a shade. He is never so living as when he is slain, and his corpse sits sprawling in the dreadful attic. Only a few of the minor characters, sketched in, like the unctuous Jew of the theatre, with broad realistic touches, may be said to live even as properties. No, *Dorian Gray* is a good subject spoiled. One can imagine how Flaubert would have told the story, how Balzac would have filled it with fiery-colored life. Yet some have compared this novel to *La Peau de chagrin!*

The shorter stories need not detain us; they are less real than the fairy-tales. We turn with pleasure to *The Happy Prince* and *The House of Pomegranates,*—for the luxuriance that cloys in the poems becomes delightful when submitted to the partial restraint of a poetic prose. No one, of course, would go to Oscar Wilde for the trenchant simplicity of the German folk-tale. His are merely artistic apologues, touching life with the light satire of the drawing-room. One forgets their author, excepting when he is sticking pins into his puppets to create an artistic pathos; only then do we rebel. However, Wilde did not take his heroes seriously, nor need we. Let us be thankful that he does not, that he drags in no pompous moral, for without it these fables have all the honesty of the frankly artificial, and in their very slightness of texture lies the secret of their charm.

The case is the same with the plays. The best of the comedies have a sort of frivolous unity; they are often terribly affected, but they never affect a moral. Sincerity makes Wilde inconsistent with his art; he becomes impossible when he assumes a purpose, and intolerable when he has a paradox to prove. Could anything be worse than the essay on Socialism? But no problems spoil his plays, and when we find that the least serious of them is incomparably the best, the inference is easy. He felt too much the charm of his material; he found it easier to play with constructions than to construct a play. As a follower of *l'art pour l'art,* a purpose would spoil him, and he admitted sincerity only in his attitude toward æsthetics. Yet the value of a fundamental seriousness is nowhere more apparent than in the superiority of his art-lectures to such work as "Pen, Pencil, and Poison."

The final necessity of subduing style and spirit in a deeper unity is shown in *De Profundis.* Reading Gaol, and not Oxford, gave us the final development of Wilde's prose. It is said that prisons make men liars; but it was none the less a prison that made *De Profundis* sincere. Here first his art attains its final unity,—a unity of spirit and form which puts certain pages of his confession almost beyond criticism. All of his early work, in comparison, seems little more than a promise; for here alone he attains the simplicity of great art.

When we add to this its value as a "document," we cannot doubt that *De Profundis* will survive. It is a pity that this is all we can be sure of. But *The Ballad of Reading Gaol* contains too much alloy; if it becomes a classic our classics will have lived. The art-criticism, the æsthetic "philosophy," will be stolen and rewritten, as it was originally stolen and rewritten by Wilde. The life of the plays is limited by the life of their paradoxes, as we can see from the puns in Shakespeare; and even the fairy tales need more human nature to keep them alive. Wilde's place in literature, in so far as he concerns us, is that of a precursor: he prepared the way for Shaw's paradoxes, and the success of Chesterton is to be laid at his door. He revealed to us a certain kind of wit, but he has made some of our critics tremendously trifling. Everything considered, Wilde's literary executors would have done better to give us a selection from his works—a careful selection, with all the cheapest epigrams expunged. Not even a reviewer can read a dozen volumes of this sort with impunity!

ARTHUR RANSOME
From "Afterthought"
Oscar Wilde: A Critical Study
1912, pp. 220–34

There is a word, often applied to Wilde in his lifetime, that has, since his death, been used to justify a careless neglect of his work. That word is "pose." In all such popular characterizations there is hidden a distorted morsel of truth. Such a morsel of truth is hidden here. We need not examine the dull envy of brilliance, the envy felt by timid persons of a man who dared to display the hopes and the intentions that were making holiday within him, the envy that used that word as a reproach, and sought to veil the fact that it was a confession. But we shall do well to discover what it was beside that envy that made the word applicable to Wilde.

Wilde "posed" as an æsthete. He was an æsthete. He "posed" as brilliant. He was brilliant. He "posed" as cultured. He was cultured. The quality in him to which that word was applied was not pretence, though that was willingly suggested, but display. Wilde let people see, as soon as he could, and in any way that was possible, who and what he was or wished to be. No bushel hid his lamp. He arranged it where it could best be seen, and beat drums before it to summon the spectators. He had every quality of a charlatan, except one: the inability to keep his promises. Wilde promised nothing that he could not perform. But, because he promised so loudly, he earned the scorn of those whom charlatans do not outwit. He has even met with the scorn of charlatans, who cannot understand why he made so much noise when he really could do what he promised.

The noise and the display that were inseparable from any stage of Wilde's career, and were not without an indirect echo and repetition in his books, were partly due to the self-consciousness that was among his most valuable assets. He knew himself, and he knew his worth, and, conscious of an intellectual pre-eminence over most of his fellows, assumed its recognition, and was in a hurry to bring the facts level with his assumption. He had, more than most men, a dramatic conception of himself. "There is a fatality," says the painter of Dorian Gray, "about all physical and intellectual distinction,

the sort of fatality that seems to dog the faltering steps of kings. It is better not to be different from one's fellows." Wilde was always profoundly conscious of his own "physical and intellectual distinction," not with the almost scornful consciousness of Poe, but with a deprecating pride and a sense of what was due to it from himself and from others. Wilde's "pose"—call it what you will—is easily adopted by talent since Wilde created it with genius. Its origin was a sense of the possession of genius, of being distinct from the rest of the world. Poe emphasized this distinction by looking at people from a distance. Wilde emphasized it by charming them, with a kind of desperate generosity. He knew that he had largesse to scatter, and not till the end of his life did he begin to feel that he had wasted it, that in him a vivid personality had passed through the world and was not leaving behind it a worthy memorial. This was not the common regret at having been unable to accomplish things. It was a regret at leaving insufficient proof of a power of accomplishment that he did not doubt, but had never exerted to the uttermost. In thinking of the virtuosity of Wilde's manner, a thing not at all common in English literature, we must remember the consciousness of power that wrapped his days in a bright light, served him sometimes as a mantle of invisibility, and made him loved and hated with equal vehemence. His tasks were always too easy for him. He never strained for achievement, and nothing requires more generosity to forgive than success without effort.

This consciousness of his power excused in him an extravagance that in a lesser man would have been laughable. He would have it recognized at all costs, for confirmation's sake. He needed admiration at once, from the world, from England, from London, from any small company in which he happened to be. The same desires whose gratification earned him the epithet "poseur," made him expend in conversation energies that would have multiplied many times the volume if not the value of his writings. He pawned much of himself to the moment, and was never able to redeem it.

He leaves three things behind him, a legend, his conversation, and his works. The legend will be that of a beautiful boy, so gifted that all things were possible to him, so brilliant that in middle age men still thought him young, stepping through imaginary fields of lilies and poisonous irises, and finding the flowers turned suddenly to dung, and his feet caught in a quagmire not only poisonous but ugly. It will include the less intimate horror of a further punishment, an imprisonment without the glamour of murder, as with Wainewright, or that of burglary, as with Deacon Brodie, but a hideous publication to the world of the sordid transformation of those imagined flowers. The lives of Villon and of a few saints can alone show such swift passage from opulence to wretchedness, from ease to danger, from the world to a cell. We are not here concerned to blame or palliate the deeds that made this catastrophe possible, but only to remark that to Wilde himself, in comparison with the life of his intellect, they probably seemed infinitely unimportant and insignificant. The life of the thinker is in thought, of the artist in art. He feels it almost unfair that mere actions should be forced into a position where they have power over his destiny. As time goes on, the legend will, no doubt, be modified. It is too dramatic to be easily forgotten.

In earlier chapters I have spoken of the conversational quality of Wilde's prose, but not, so far, of his conversation, which, to some of those who knew him best, seemed more valuable than the echo of it in his books. It varied at different periods and in different companies. More than one writer has described it, and the descriptions do not agree. With an audience that he thought stupid he was startling, said extravagant things and asked impossible questions. With another, he would trace an idea through history, filling out the facts he needed for his argument with bright pageants of colour, like the paragraphs of *Intentions*. At one dinner-table he discoursed; at another he told stories. Wilde "ne causait pas; il contait," says M. Gide. He spoke in parables, and, as he was an artist, men made more of the parables than of their meanings. An idea of this fairy-tale talk may be gathered from his *Poems in Prose*. These things, among the most wonderful that Wilde wrote, are said to be less beautiful in their elaborate form than as he told them over the dinner-table, suggested by the talk that passed. They are certainly a little heavy with gold and precious stones. They are wistful, like princesses in fairy-tales who look out on the world from under their crowns, when other children toss their hair in the wind. But we may well fail to imagine the conversation in which such anecdotes could have a part, not as excrescences but one in texture with the rest. No other English talker has talked in this style, and the Queen Scheherazada did not surpass it when she talked to save her life. Beside Lamb's stuttered jests, Hazlitt's incisions, Coleridge's billowy eloquence, Wilde's tapestried speech must be set among the regrettable things of which time has carelessly deprived us. I have heard it said that Wilde talked for effect. The peacock spreads his tail in burning blue and gold against the emerald lawn, and as Whistler made a room of it, so Wilde made conversation. He talked less to say than to make, and his manner is suggested by his own description of the talk of Lord Henry Wotton in *The Picture of Dorian Gray*:—

"He played with the idea, and grew wilful; tossed it into the air and transformed it; let it escape and recaptured it; made it iridescent with fancy, and winged it with paradox. The praise of folly, as he went on, soared into a philosophy, and Philosophy herself became young, and catching the mad music of Pleasure, wearing, one might fancy, her wine-stained robe and wreath of ivy, danced like a Bacchante over the hills of life, and mocked the slow Silenus for being sober. Facts fled before her like frightened forest things. Her white feet trod the huge press at which wise Omar sits, till the seething grape-juice rose round her bare limbs in waves of purple bubbles, or crawled in red foam over the vat's black, dripping, sloping sides. It was an extraordinary improvisation."

Wilde improvised like that. A metaphor would suddenly grow more important in his eyes than the idea that had called it into being. The idea would vanish in the picture; the picture would elaborate itself and become story, and then, dissolving like a pattern in a kaleidoscope, turn to idea again, and allow him to continue on his way. Wilde talked tapestries, as he wrote them. He saw his conversation, and made other men see it. They thought him a magician. ⟨. . .⟩

Wilde provides us with the rare spectacle of a man most of whose powers are those of a spectator, a connoisseur, a man for whom pictures are painted and books written, the perfect collaborator for whom the artist hopes in his heart; the spectacle of such a man, delighting in the delicacies of life no less than in those of art, and yet able to turn the pleasures of the dilettante and the amateur into the motives of the artist. In some ages, when talk has been more highly valued than in ours, he would have been ready to let his criticism die in the air: he would have been content that all who knew him should

credit him with the power of doing wonderful things if he chose, and with the preference of touching with the tips of his fingers the baked and painted figurine over the modelling of it in cold and sticky clay. Such credit is not to be had in our time, and he had to take the clay in his fingers and prove his mastery. Besides, he had not the money that would have let him live at ease among blue china, books wonderfully bound, and men and women as strange as the moods it would have pleased him to induce. If he had been rich, I think it possible that he would have been a des Esseintes or a Dorian Gray, and left nothing but a legend and a poem or two, and a few curiosities of luxury to find their way into the sale-rooms.

Wilde preserved, even in those of his writings that cost him most dearly, a feeling of recreation. His books are those of a wonderfully gifted and accomplished man who is an author only in his moments of leisure. Only one comparison is possible, and that is with Horace Walpole; but Wilde's was infinitely the richer intellect. Walpole is weighted by his distinction. Wilde wears his like a flower. Walpole is without breadth, or depth, and equals only as a gossip Wilde's enchanting freedom as a juggler with ideas. Wilde was indolent and knew it. Indolence was, perhaps, the only sin that stared him in the face as he lay dying, for it was the only one that he had committed with a bad conscience. It had lessened his achievement, and left its marks on what he had done. Even in his best work he is sometimes ready to secure an effect too easily. "Meredith is a prose Browning, and so is Browning," may be regarded as an example of such effects. Much of his work fails; much of it has faded, but *Intentions*, *The Sphinx*, *The Ballad of Reading Gaol*, *Salomé*, *The Importance of Being Earnest*, one or two of the fairy tales, and *De Profundis*, are surely enough with which to challenge the attention of posterity.

These things were the toys of a critical spirit, of a critic as artist, of a critic who took up first one and then another form of art, and played with it almost idly, one and then another form of thought, and gave it wings for the pleasure of seeing it in the light; of a man of action with the eyes of a child; of a man of contemplation curious of all the secrets of life, not only of those that serve an end; of a virtuoso with a distaste for the obvious and a delight in disguising subtlety behind a mask of the very obvious that he disliked. His love for the delicate and the rare brought him into the power of things that are vulgar and coarse. His attempt to weave his life as a tapestry clothed him in a soiled and unbeautiful reality. Even this he was able to subdue. *Nihil tetigit quod non ornavit*. He touched nothing that he did not decorate. He touched nothing that he did not turn into a decoration.

I do not care to prophesy which in particular of these decorations, of these friezes and tapestries of vision and thought, will enjoy that prolongation of life, insignificant in the eternal progress of time, which, for us, seems immortality. Art is, perhaps, our only method of putting off death's victory, but what does it matter to us if the books that feed the intellectual life of our generation are stones to the next and manna to the generation after that? Of this, at least, we may be sure: whether remembered or no, the works that move us now will have an echo that cannot be denied them, unheard but still disturbing, or, perhaps, carefully listened for and picked out, among the myriad roaring of posterity along the furthest and least imaginable corridors of time.

STEPHEN CRANE

STEPHEN CRANE

1871–1900

Stephen Crane was born in Newark, New Jersey, on November 1, 1871, the fourteenth and last child of the Rev. Dr. Jonathan Townley Crane. He attended Lafayette College (1890) and Syracuse University (1891), both of which he left without taking a degree, and then went to New York where he worked, without much success, as a journalist. In 1893 Crane brought out his first novel, *Maggie: A Girl of the Streets*, printed privately at his own expense. This was followed by *The Red Badge of Courage* (1895), a novel of the American Civil War that was widely hailed as a masterpiece of psychological realism. In 1896 Crane began working as a war reporter in Cuba, where he met Cora Taylor, who became his common-law wife. In 1897 he traveled to Greece to report on the Turkish war, then went to England, where he developed a close friendship with Joseph Conrad, to whom his work is often compared.

Crane returned to the United States in 1898, during the Spanish-American War. He volunteered for military service but was rejected because of signs of tuberculosis. Instead, he became a war correspondent and sent home some of the war's best dispatches from the front, before his increasing illness forced him to return to New York late in 1898. During Christmas week of 1899 Crane suffered a massive tubercular hemorrhage; Cora Taylor then took him to Baden-Baden in a desperate attempt to restore his health. Crane died on June 5, 1900, almost immediately after his arrival in Germany.

During his lifetime Crane also published two collections of free verse, *The Black Riders* (1895) and *War Is Kind* (1899), the short-story collections *The Open Boat and Other Tales of Adventures* (1890) and *Whilomville Stories* (1900), and two unsuccessful novels, *The Third Violet* (1896) and *Active Service* (1899). Crane's *Letters* were published in 1960, in an edition prepared by R. W. Stallman and Lillian Gilkes. An edition of his *Works* has been prepared by Fredson Bowers (10 vols., 1969–75).

General

You will look in vain through the pages of the *Trade Circular* for any record of a story of New York life entitled *Maggie: A Girl of the Streets*, which was published three or four years ago in this city. At the moment of going to press the timorous publishers withdrew their imprint from the book, which was sold, in paper covers, for fifty cents. There seems to be considerable difficulty now in securing copies, but the fact that there is no publisher's name to the book, and that the author appears under the *nom de plume* of "Johnston Smith," may have something to do with its apparent disappearance. The copy which came into the writer's possession was addressed to the Rev. Thomas Dixon a few months ago, before the author went West on a journalistic trip to Nebraska, and has these words written across the cover: "It is inevitable that this book will greatly shock you, but continue, pray, with great courage to the end, for it tries to show that environment is a tremendous thing in this world, and often shapes lives regardlessly. If one could prove that theory, one would make room in Heaven for all sorts of souls (notably an occasional street girl) who are not confidently expected to be there by many excellent people." The author of this story and the writer of these words is Stephen Crane, whose *Lines* (he does not call them poems) have just been published by Copeland and Day, and are certain to make a sensation.

Stephen Crane is not yet twenty-four years old, but competent critics aver that his command of the English language is such as to raise the highest hopes for his future career. The impression he makes on his literary co-workers is that he is a young man of almost unlimited resource. The realism of his *Maggie*—a story that might have taken a greater hold on the public than even *Chimmie Fadden*, had the publishers been less timid—is of that daring and terrible

directness which in its iconoclasm is the very characteristic of rugged undisciplined strength in a youth of genius. We hear the echo of this mood in number XLV. of his *Lines*:

> Tradition, thou art for suckling children,
> Thou art the enlivening milk for babes;
> But no meat for men is in thee.
> Then——
> But, alas, we all are babes.

Mr. Crane started to write for the press when only sixteen, and he has been at newspaper work ever since. He has done very little outside of journalism; some of his stories have been contributed to the *Cosmopolitan*, and a story entitled *The Red Badge of Courage*; which relates the adventures of a recruit under fire for the first time during the Civil War, was one of the most successful serials which the Bachelor Syndicate have handled in a long time. This serial has now been set up in book form, and will be published in the summer by Messrs. Appleton and Company, who think very highly of his work. Among other manuscripts which are now in the publishers' hands is one entitled *A Woman without Weapons*. It is a story of New York Life, like *Maggie*, but its scenes are laid on the borderland of the slums, and not down in the Devil's Row and Rum Alley. When Mr. Hamlin Garland read *Maggie* and reviewed it in the *Arena* on its appearance, he sought out the intrepid young author and introduced him to Mr. W. D. Howells, who in turn extended his kindness to young Crane, and made him acquainted with several of his *confrères* who were likely to encourage his literary aspirations. For over a year Mr. Crane has been on the staff of the Bachelor Syndicate, and he is now in Mexico "writing up" that country for them.

Mr. Crane is a New Yorker, and both his father and mother are dead. All the stanzas in the little volume which has just been published were written in a sudden fit of inspiration, in less than three days, and were polished and finished and sent off within a fortnight. The cover design of *The Black Riders* was drawn by Mr. F. C. Gordon, whose work on the beautiful holiday edition of Tennyson's *Becket*, published last Christmas, met with signal approbation. A review of *The Black Riders* appears in "Some Recent Volumes of Verse" on another page. What Hamlin Garland said of the author a few years ago may be now repeated with a more certain assurance of fulfilment: "With such a technique already in command, with life mainly before him, Stephen Crane is to be henceforth reckoned with."—HARRY THURSTON PECK, "Stephen Crane," *Bookman* (New York), May 1895, pp. 229–30

But *my* great excitement was reading your stories. Garnett's right. "A Man and Some Others" is immense. I can't spin a long yarn about it but I admire it without reserve. It is an amazing bit of biography. I am envious of you—horribly. Confound you—you fill the blamed landscape—you—by all the devils—fill the sea-scape. The boat thing is immensely interesting. I don't use the word in its common sense. It is fundamentally interesting to me. Your temperament makes old things new and new things amazing. I want to swear at you, to bless you—perhaps to shoot you—but I prefer to be your friend.

    You are an everlasting surprise to one. You shock—and the next moment you give the perfect artistic satisfaction. Your method is fascinating. You are a complete impressionist. The illusions of life come out of your hand without a flaw. It is not life—which nobody wants—it is art—art for which everyone—the abject and the great—hanker—mostly without knowing it.—JOSEPH CONRAD, Letter to Stephen Crane (Dec. 1, 1897)

I had Crane here last Sunday. We talked and smoked half the night. He is strangely hopeless about himself. I like him. The two stories are excellent. Of course, "A Man and Some Others" is the best of the two but the boat thing interested me more. His eye is very individual and his expression satisfies me artistically. He certainly is *the* impressionist and his temperament is curiously unique. His thought is concise, connected, never very deep—yet often startling. He is *the only* impressionist and *only* an impressionist. Why is he not immensely popular? With his strength, with his rapidity of action, with that amazing faculty of vision—why is he not? He has outline, he has colour, he has movement, with that he ought to go very far. But—will he? I sometimes think he won't. It is not an opinion—it is a feeling. I could not explain why he disappoints me—why my enthusiasm withers as soon as I close the book. While one reads, of course he is not to be questioned. He is the master of his reader to the very last line—then—apparently for no reason at all—he seems to let go his hold. It is as if he had gripped you with greased fingers. His grip is strong but while you feel the pressure on your flesh you slip out from his hand—much to your own surprise. This is my stupid impression and I give it to you in confidence. It just occurs to me that it is perhaps my own self that is slippery. I don't know. You would know. No matter.—JOSEPH CONRAD, Letter to Edward Garnett (Dec. 5, 1897)

Mr. Stephen Crane grows, and this is no small thing to say of a writer who sprang full-armed on the public with his first book. When it transpired that *The Red Badge of Courage* was the work of a mere boy, that it was the result of intuition, not experience, one felt misgivings whether the experience when it came would not blur the visions which came unsought into the crystal mirror of Mr. Crane's imagination. His new volume, *The Open Boat*, based in regard to the story which gives its

name to the collection on Mr. Crane's escape from the steamer *Commodore*, conclusively dispels this anxiety. Mr. Crane has never done anything finer than this truly wonderful picture of four men battling for their lives in a cockleshell off the coast of Florida. How finely it begins: "None of them knew the colour of the sky. Their eyes glanced level, and were fastened upon the waves that swept toward them. These waves were of the hue of slate, save for the tops, which were of foaming white, and all of the men knew the colours of the sea." Here at once we are confronted with a device—borrowed, perhaps, from Mae-terlinck—which Mr. Crane employs with great effect in this and other sketches,—the device of iteration. In the dialogue it emphasises the dreary monotony of the long agony; in the descriptive passages it is like the *ritornello* of a song; but in both the effect is entirely artistic. Very touching, again, is the way Mr. Crane illustrates the "subtle brotherhood" established between the four comrades by the stress of a common peril, and the drowning of the poor "oiler" when within an acre of rescue brings the recital to a harrowing conclusion. Here, again, we are tempted to quote the last words, so characteristic of Mr. Crane's method, of this enthralling narrative: "The welcome of the land for the men from the sea was warm and generous, but a still and dripping shape was carried slowly up the beach, and the land's welcome for it could only be the different and sinister hospitality of the grave. When it came night, the white waves paced to and fro in the moonlight, and the wind brought the sound of the great sea's voice to the men on shore, and they felt that they could then be interpreters." That drives home the point we endeavoured to make at the outset. Mr. Crane is no longer a clairvoyant, he is an interpreter as well. In "A Man, and Some Others" we have a wonderfully vivid account of a night attack by Mexican "greasers" on the camp of a "sheep-herder" and a chance comrade,—both Americans. Here is a "nocturne" in Mr. Crane's most striking manner:—

> Long, smouldering clouds spread in the western sky, and to the east silver mists lay on the purple gloom of the wilderness. Finally, when the great moon climbed the heavens and cast its ghastly radiance on the bushes, it made a new and more brilliant crimson of the camp fire, where the flames capered merrily through its mesquit branches, filling the silence with the fire chorus, an ancient melody which surely bears a message of the inconsequence of individual tragedy,—a message that is in the boom of the sea, the sliver of the wind through the grass-blades, the silken clash of hemlock boughs. No figures moved in the rosy space of the camp, and the search of the moonbeams failed to disclose a living thing in the bushes. There was no owl-faced clock to chant the weariness of the long silence which brooded upon the plain. The dew gave the darkness under the mesquit a velvet quality that made air seem nearer to water, and no eye could have seen through it the black things that moved like monster lizards toward the camp.

We have no space left to dwell in detail on the humour of the strange home-coming of the town-marshal of Yellow Sky and his newly wedded wife, on the thrilling night-escape on horseback of an American traveller from a den of Mexican cutthroats, or on the splendid portrait of the filibustering Captain Flanagan, whose expedition, for reasons which Mr. Crane so vividly sets forth, never became historic. We hope, however, that we have said enough to induce the curious reader to make acquaintance with the most striking and irresistible of all the younger American writers.—UNSIGNED, "Recent Short Stories," *Spectator*, July 23, 1898, pp. 120–21

What Mr. Crane has got to do is very simple: he must not mix reporting with his writing. To other artists the word must often be passed: rest, work at your art, live more; but Mr. Crane has no need of cultivating his technique, no need of resting, no need of searching wide for experiences. In his art he is unique. Its certainty, its justness, it peculiar perfection of power arrived at its birth, or at least at that precise moment in its life when other artists—and great artists too—were preparing themselves for the long and difficult conquest of their art. I cannot remember a parallel case in the literary history of fiction. Maupassant, Meredith, Mr. James, Mr. Howells, Tolstoi, all were learning their expression at the age where Mr. Crane had achieved his, achieved it triumphantly. Mr. Crane has no need to learn anything. His technique is absolutely his own, and by its innate laws of being has arrived at a perfect fulness of power. What he has not got he has no power of acquiring. He has no need to acquire it. To say to Mr. Crane, "You are too much anything, or too little anything; you need concentration, or depth, subtlety, or restraint," would be absurd; his art is always just in itself, rhythmical, self-poising as is the art of a perfect dancer. There are no false steps, no excesses. And, of course, his art is strictly limited. We would define him by saying he is the perfect artist and interpreter of the surfaces of life. And that explains why he so swiftly attained his peculiar power, what is the realm his art commands, and where his limitations come in.

Take *George's Mother*, for example—a tale which I believe he wrote at the ridiculous age of twenty-one. In *method* it is a masterpiece. It is a story dealing simply with the relations between an old woman and her son, who live together in a New York tenement block. An ordinary artist would seek to dive into the mind of the old woman, to follow its workings hidden under the deceitful appearances of things, under the pressure of her surroundings. A great artist would so recreate her life that its griefs and joys became significant of the griefs and joys of all motherhood on earth. But Mr. Crane does neither. He simply reproduces the surfaces of the individual life in so marvellous a way that the manner in which the old woman washes up the crockery, for example, gives us her. To dive into the hidden life is, of course, for the artist a great temptation and a great danger—the values of the picture speedily get wrong, and the artist, seeking to interpret life, departs from the truth of nature. The rare thing about Mr. Crane's art is that he keeps closer to the surface than any living writer, and, like the great portrait-painters, to a great extent makes the surface betray the depths. But, of course, the written word in the hands of the greatest artist often deals directly with the depths, plunges us into the rich depths of consciousness that cannot be more than hinted at by the surface; and it is precisely here that Mr. Crane's natural limitation must come in. At the supreme height of art the great masters so plough up the depths of life that the astonished spectator loses sight of the individual life altogether, and has the entrancing sense that all life is really one and the same thing, and is there manifesting itself before him. He feels that, for example, when he watches Dusé at her best, or when he stands before Da Vinci's "La Joconda" in the Louvre and is absorbed by it. I do not think that Mr. Crane is ever great in the sense of so fusing all the riches of the consciousness into a whole, that the reader is struck dumb as by an inevitable revelation; but he is undoubtedly such an interpreter of the significant surface of things that in a few swift strokes he gives us an amazing insight into what

the individual life is. And he does it all straight from the surface; a few oaths, a genius for slang, an exquisite and unique faculty of exposing an individual scene by an odd simile, a power of interpreting a face or an action, a keen realising of the primitive emotions—that is Mr. Crane's talent. In "The Bride Comes to Yellow Sky," for example, the art is simply immense. There is a page and a half of conversation at the end of this short story of seventeen pages which, as a dialogue revealing the whole inside of the situation, is a lesson to any artist living. And the last line of this story, by the gift peculiar to the author of using some odd simile which cunningly condenses the feeling of the situation, defies analysis altogether. Foolish people may call Mr. Crane a reporter of genius; but nothing could be more untrue. He is thrown away as a picturesque reporter: a secondary style of art, of which, let us say, Mr. G. W. Steevens is, perhaps, the ablest exponent to-day, and which is the heavy clay of Mr. Kipling's talent. Mr. Crane's technique is far superior to Mr. Kipling's, but he does not experiment ambitiously in various styles and develop in new directions, as Mr. Kipling has done. I do not think that Mr. Crane will or can develop further. Again, I do not think that he has the building faculty, or that he will ever do better in constructing a perfect whole out of many parts than he has arrived at in *The Red Badge of Courage*. That book was a series of episodic scenes, all melting naturally into one another and forming a just whole; but it was not constructed, in any sense of the word. And, further, Mr. Crane does not show any faculty of taking his characters and revealing in them deep mysterious worlds of human nature, of developing fresh riches in them acting under the pressure of circumstance. His imaginative analysis of his own nature on a battlefield is, of course, the one exception. And similarly the great artist's arrangement of complex effects, striking contrasts, exquisite grouping of devices, is lacking in him. His art does not include the necessity for complex arrangements; his sure instinct tells him never to quit the passing moment of life, to hold fast by simple situations, to reproduce the episodic, fragmentary nature of life in such artistic sequence that it stands in place of the architectural masses and co-ordinated structures of the great artists. He is the chief impressionist of this age, as Sterne was the great impressionist, in a different manner, of his age. If he fails in anything he undertakes, it will be through abandoning the style he has invented. He may, perhaps, fail by and by, through using up the picturesque phases of the environment that nurtured him, as Swinburne came to a stop directly he had rung the changes a certain number of times on the fresh rhythms and phrases he created. But that time is not yet, and every artist of a special unique faculty has that prospect before him. Mr. Crane's talent is unique; nobody can question that. America may well be proud of him, for he has just that perfect mastery of form which artists of the Latin races often produce, but the Teutonic and Anglo-Saxon races very rarely. And undoubtedly of the young school of American artists Mr. Crane is the genius—the others have their talents.—EDWARD GARNETT, "Mr. Stephen Crane: An Appreciation," *Academy*, Dec. 17, 1898, pp. 483–84

The physical slightness, if I may so suggest one characteristic of Crane's vibrant achievement, reflected the delicacy of energies that could be put forth only in nervous spurts, in impulses vivid and keen, but wanting in breadth and bulk of effect. Curiously enough, on the other hand, this very lyrical spirit, whose freedom was its life, was the absolute slave of reality. It was interesting to hear him defend what he had written, in obedience to his experience of things, against any change in the interest of convention. "No," he would contend, in behalf of the profanities of his people, "that is the way they *talk*. I have thought of that, and whether I ought to leave such things out, but if I do I am not giving the thing as I *know* it." He felt the constraint of those semi-savage natures, such as he depicted in *Maggie*, and *George's Mother*, and was forced through the fealty of his own nature to report them as they spoke no less than as they looked. When it came to *The Red Badge of Courage*, where he took leave of these simple æsthetics, and lost himself in a whirl of wild guesses at the fact from the ground of insufficient witness, he made the failure which formed the break between his first and his second manner, though it was what the public counted a success, with every reason to do so from the report of the sales.

The true Stephen Crane was the Stephen Crane of the earlier books, the earliest book; for *Maggie* remains the best thing he did. All he did was lyrical, but this was the aspect and accent as well as the spirit of the tragically squalid life he sang, while *The Red Badge of Courage*, and the other things that followed it, were the throes of an art failing with material to which it could not render an absolute devotion from an absolute knowledge. He sang, but his voice erred up and down the scale, with occasional flashes of brilliant melody, which could not redeem the errors. New York was essentially his inspiration, the New York of suffering and baffled and beaten life, of inarticulate or blasphemous life; and away from it he was not at home, with any theme, or any sort of character. It was the pity of his fate that he must quit New York, first as a theme, and then as a habitat; for he rested nowhere else, and wrought with nothing else as with the lurid depths which he gave proof of knowing better than any one else. Every one is limited, and perhaps no one is more limited than another; only, the direction of the limitation is different in each. Perhaps George Douglas, if he had lived, would still have done nothing greater than *The House with the Green Shutters*, and might have failed in the proportion of a larger range as Stephen Crane did. I am not going to say that either of these extraordinary talents was of narrower bound than Frank Norris; such measures are not of the map. But I am still less going to say that they were of finer quality because their achievement seems more poignant, through the sort of physical concentration which it has. Just as a whole unhappy world agonizes in the little space their stories circumscribe, so what is sharpest and subtlest in that anguish finds its like in the epical breadths of Norris's fiction.—WILLIAM DEAN HOWELLS, "Frank Norris," *North American Review*, Dec. 1902, pp. 770–71

Works

MAGGIE: A GIRL OF THE STREETS

I think that what strikes me most in the story of *Maggie* is that quality of fatal necessity which dominates Greek tragedy. From the conditions it all had to be, and there were the conditions. I felt this in Mr. Hardy's *Jude*, where the principle seems to become conscious in the writer; but there is apparently no consciousness of any such motive in the author of *Maggie*. Another effect is that of an ideal of artistic beauty which is as present in the working out of this poor girl's squalid romance as in any classic fable. This will be foolishness, I know, to the many foolish people who cannot discriminate between the material and the treatment in art, and think that beauty is inseparable from daintiness and prettiness, but I do not speak to them. I appeal rather to such as feel themselves akin with every kind of human creature, and find neither high nor low when it is a question of inevitable suffering, or of a soul struggling vainly with an inexorable fate.

My rhetoric scarcely suggests the simple terms the author uses to produce the effect which I am trying to repeat again. They are simple, but always most graphic, especially when it comes to the personalities of the story; the girl herself, with her bewildered wish to be right and good, with her distorted perspective, her clinging and generous affections, her hopeless environments; the horrible old drunken mother, a cyclone of violence and volcano of vulgarity; the mean and selfish lover, dandy, rowdy, with his gross ideals and ambitions; her brother, an Ishmaelite from the cradle, who with his warlike instincts beaten back into cunning, is what the b'hoy of former times has become in òur more strenuously policed days. He is, indeed, a wonderful figure in a group which betrays no faltering in the artist's hand. He, with his dull hates, his warped good-will, his cowed ferocity, is almost as fine artistically as Maggie, but he could not have been so hard to do, for all the pathos of her fate is rendered without one maudlin touch. So is that of the simple-minded and devoted and tedious old woman who is George's mother in the book of that name. This is scarcely a study at all, while Maggie is really and fully so. It is the study of a situation merely; a poor inadequate woman, of a commonplace religiosity, whose son goes to the bad. The wonder of it is the courage which deals with persons so absolutely average, and the art which graces them with the beauty of the author's compassion for everything that errs and suffers. Without this feeling the effects of his mastery would be impossible, and if it went further, or put itself into the pitying phrases, it would annul the effects. But it never does this; it is notable how in all respects the author keeps himself well in hand. He is quite honest with his reader. He never shows his characters or his situations in any sort of sentimental glamour; if you will be moved by the sadness of common fates you will feel his intention; but he does not flatter his portraits of people on conditions to take your fancy.—WILLIAM DEAN HOWELLS, "An Appreciation," *Maggie: A Girl of the Streets*, 1896

THE RED BADGE OF COURAGE

The Red Badge of Courage is a book that has been getting a good deal of belated praise within the past few weeks, but we cannot admit that much of it is deserved. There is almost no story to Mr. Crane's production, but merely an account, in roughshod descriptive style, of the thoughts and feelings of a young soldier during his first days of active fighting. The author constructs for his central character a psychological history that is plausible, but hardly convincing. We do not know, nor does the writer, that it is what actually does go on in the mind of a man who is passing through his baptism of fire. It may be retorted that we do not know any the more that Count Tolstoi is giving us the real thing in his war-stories, or "Stendhal" in the *Chartreuse de Parme*, but the descriptions in these books at least seem inevitable while we are reading them, and Mr. Crane's descriptions do not.—WILLIAM MORTON PAYNE, "Recent Fiction," *Dial*, Feb. 1, 1896, p. 80

Must we come to judge of books only by what the newspapers have said of them, and must we abandon all the old standards of criticism? Can a book and an author, utterly without merit, be puffed into success by entirely undeserved praise, even if that praise come from English periodicals?

One must ask these questions after he has been seduced into reading a book recently reprinted in this country entitled *The Red Badge of Courage, an Episode of the American Civil War*. The chorus of praise in the English papers has been very extravagant, but it is noticeable that so far, at least, the American papers have said very little about the merits or demerits of the book itself. They simply allude to the noise made over it abroad, and therefore treat its author as a coming factor in our literature. Even *The Dial*'s very acute and usually very discerning critic of contemporary fiction (Mr. Payne) treats the book and the author (in your issue of Feb. 1) in very much this way—that is, as a book and an author to be reckoned with, not because of any good which he himself finds in them, but because they have been so much talked about.

The book has very recently been reprinted in America, and would seem to be an American book, on an American theme, and by an American author, yet originally issued in England. If it is really an American production one must suppose it to have been promptly and properly rejected by any American publishers to whom it may have been submitted, and afterward more naturally taken up by an English publisher.

It is only too well known that English writers have had a very low opinion of American soldiers, and have always, as a rule, assumed to ridicule them. ⟨. . .⟩

Under such circumstances we cannot doubt that *The Red Badge of Courage* would be just such a book as the English would grow enthusiastic over, and we cannot wonder that the redoubtable *Saturday Review* greeted it with the highest encomiums, and declared it the actual experiences of a veteran of our War, when it was really the vain imaginings of a young man born long since that war, a piece of intended realism based entirely on unreality. The book is a vicious satire upon American soldiers and American armies. The hero of the book (if such he can be called—"the youth" the author styles him) is an ignorant and stupid country lad, who, without a spark of patriotic feeling, or even of soldierly ambition, has enlisted in the army from no definite motive that the reader can discover, unless it be because other boys are doing so; and the whole book, in which there is absolutely no story, is occupied with giving what are supposed to be his emotions and his actions in the first two days of battle. His poor weak intellect, if indeed he has any, seems to be at once and entirely overthrown by the din and movement of the field, and he acts throughout like a madman. Under the influence of mere excitement, for he does not even appear to be frightened, he first rushes madly to the rear in a crazy panic, and afterward plunges forward to the rescue of the colors under exactly the same influences. In neither case has reason or any intelligent motive any influence on his action. He is throughout an idiot or a maniac, and betrays no trace of the reasoning being. No thrill of patriotic devotion to cause or country ever moves his breast, and not even an emotion of manly courage. Even a wound which he finally gets comes from a comrade who strikes him on the head with his musket to get rid of him; and this is the only *Red Badge of Courage* (!) which we discover in the book. A number of other characters come in to fill out the two hundred and thirty-three pages of the book,—such as "the loud soldier," "the tall soldier," "the tattered soldier," etc., but not one of them betrays any more sense, self-possession, or courage than does "the youth." On the field all is chaos and confusion. "The young lieutenant," "the mounted officer," even "the general," are all utterly demented beings, raving and talking alike in an unintelligible and hitherto unheard-of jargon, rushing about in a very delirium of madness. No intelligent orders are given; no intelligent movements are made. There is no evidence of drill, none of discipline. There is a constant, senseless, and profane babbling going on, such as one could hear nowhere but in a madhouse. Nowhere are seen the quiet, manly, self-respecting, and patriotic men, influenced by the highest sense of duty, who in reality fought our battles.

It can be said most confidently that no soldier who fought in our recent War ever saw any approach to the battle scenes in this book—but what wonder? We are told that it is the work of a young man of twenty-three or twenty-four years of age, and so of course must be a mere work of diseased imagination. And yet it constantly strains after so-called realism. The result is a mere riot of words. ⟨. . .⟩

It is extraordinary that even a prejudiced animus could have led English writers to lavish extravagant praise on such a book; it is still more extraordinary that an attempt should be made to foist it upon the long-suffering American public, and to push it into popularity here. Respect for our own people should have prevented its issue in this country.

There may have been a moderate number of men in our service who felt and acted in battle like those in this book; but of such deserters were made. They did not stay when they could get away: why should they? The army was no healthy place for them, and they had no reason to stay; there was no moral motive. After they had deserted, however, they remained "loud soldiers," energetic, and blatant,—and they are possibly now enjoying good pensions. It must have been some of these fellows who got the ear of Mr. Crane and told him how they felt and acted in battle.—A. C. McClurg, "The Red Badge of Hysteria," *Dial*, April 16, 1896, pp. 227–28

It is with a certain hesitation that we write you to correct the author of a somewhat bitter letter published in your journal for April 16, for we recognize the signature as that of a gallant soldier, as well as a student of literature. But as the author of that letter labors under several misapprehensions, we think that he will be glad to learn the facts.

The Red Badge of Courage was read and accepted by us in December, 1894, and, in book form, it was first published in this country in October, 1895. Although the book was copyrighted in England at the same time, it was not formally published there for two months. Meantime the American journals had reviewed it and had begun an almost universal chorus of eulogy. October 19, 1895, the *New York Times* devoted a column and a half to a strong review of "this remarkable book." On October 13, the *Philadelphia Press* compared Mr. Crane and Bret Harte, not to the disadvantage of the former. On October 26, the *New York Mail and Express*, in one of several notices, said, "The author has more than talent—there is genius in the book." On October 26, the *Boston Transcript*, in speaking of "this tremendous grasping of the glory and carnage of war," added at the close of a long and enthusiastic review, "The book forces upon the reader the conviction of what fighting really means." Other favorable reviews appeared in October issues of the following American newspapers: *New York Herald, Brooklyn Eagle, Cleveland World, St. Paul Pioneer Press, Boston Daily Advertiser, New York World, St. Paul Globe, New York Commercial Advertiser, Kansas City Journal, Chicago Evening Post, Boston Courier, Cleveland Plain Dealer, Boston Beacon, Hartford Times, Sioux City Times, New Haven Leader,* and *Minneapolis Journal,* and to these names, taken almost at random, we might add many others. These journals reviewed *The Red Badge* favorably in October, and others, including weeklies like *The Critic* and *The Outlook,* followed in November with emphatic recognition of the strength and high talent shown in the book.

It was not until the end of November, two months after publication here, that the first reviews appeared in England. By that time American reviewers from Maine to California had "greeted" the book with the highest "encomiums." The English "encomiums" became specially marked in late December, January, and February.

We state these facts in view of your correspondent's remarks that "So far, at least, the American papers have said very little about the merits or demerits of the book," and, "The book has very recently been reprinted in America," and, "Respect for our own people should have prevented its issue in this country." "Our country" was the first to recognize Mr. Crane's genius, and our people have read his book so eagerly that it continues to be the most popular work of fiction in the market, and it has been the one most talked of and written about since October last.

A glance at the back of the *Red Badge* title-page would have shown that the book could not have been "first published" in England and "reprinted" here, while the literary departments of journals throughout our country, and the opinions of American men of letters like Mr. Howells and Mr. Hamlin Garland, have proved, happily, that Americans are ready to recognize American talent, and that, *pare* your correspondent, a prophet is not without honor even in his own country.

As to other points, against the opinion of the gallant veteran who criticizes the book might be put the opinions of other veterans who have found only words of praise.
—D. APPLETON & COMPANY, "*The Red Badge of Courage*: A Correction," *Dial*, May 1, 1896, p. 263

The trend of the whole work—to prove the absence of such a thing as a gentleman in the union army—may be justly expected to arouse the resentment of the class of whom "A. C. McC." is such a striking and honorable example. If this work is realism, it is realism run mad, rioting in all that is revolting to man's best instincts, and utterly false to nature and to life.
—J. L. ONDERDONK, "A Red Badge of Bad English," *Dial*, May 1, 1896, p. 263

Mr. Stephen Crane's story, *The Red Badge of Courage*, has received higher praise than it is usual to bestow, with sincerity, upon the work of a living writer. It certainly sounds extravagant to say (as has been said) that his work is "inspired," and that, if he has not himself experienced the sensations of a soldier in the heat of battle, his achievement in writing the story is "a miracle." Yet the story is so remarkable that one may be pardoned for saying almost anything about it while the flush of its reading is still upon one. Two things in this tale strike most persons very forcibly: the high pitch at which it is sustained throughout a good-sized volume, and the multiplicity of detail with which it is heaped and rounded up.

In a conversation, recently, Mr. Crane said that he began the tale as a pot-boiler, intending to make a short story for a newspaper; that he selected a battle as his subject as affording plenty of "color" and range for the imagination, although he had, of course, never been in a battle in his life. But as he went on, the story grew under his hand, and he determined to put the best work into it of which he was capable. "I don't believe in inspiration," said he. "I am one of those who believe that an enthusiasm of concentration in hard work is what a writer must depend on to bring him to the end he has in view." And he went on to say that he had kept this story in hand for nearly a year, polishing and bettering it. Perhaps this is the most amazing thing about a thoroughly amazing book. If he had said he wrote it in three days (as he wrote the *Black Riders*) one might understand such a *tour de force*. But to be able to keep the *Red Badge* in his desk and do days' work upon it—to assume at will the frame of mind which would seem necessary to set down such a memorandum of a whirlwind—this is astonishing, indeed. The story is like a picture by Verestchagin

in its seemingly commonplace sward of homely words through which one suddenly sees the pale faces of dead men tumbled headlong into twisted and horrifying shapes. The reader of the story is caught up into the chariot, and forgets any mechanical flaws in the English in the excitement of being present at such a dance of death.

⟨. . .⟩ Somebody said, quite gravely, the other day, that he believed the soul of some great soldier—not a general, but a fighter in the ranks—had gone into Stephen Crane at his birth, and that the *Red Badge* came from his mind as spontaneously as the galley-slave's tale was told by the pale-faced London lad in Kipling's "'Greatest Story in the World.'" Should this ingenious theory be true, Mr. Crane will never write any good stories except of battles; but it is pretty safe to assume that the writer of the *Red Badge* is not a man of one story; he is bound to write many more which shall brighten the shining reputation he has already gained. And yet, this theory of reincarnation is a fascinating one, for it would explain how Mr. Crane, who "has never been in battle in his life," has been able to write down descriptions in such a guise of seer's authority as to compel the reader to accept his statements without thought of question.—UNSIGNED, "The Rambler," *Book Buyer*, April 1896, pp. 140–41

We read of an ethical motive as "a yellow light thrown upon the color of his ambitions"; in the army a soldier is part of "a vast blue demonstration"; we read of "liquid stillness" and "red rage," a "black procession" of oaths, the "red sickness of battle," and so on, and so on. The attempt in the book from which these expressions are taken is to make every page blaze with color, in order to affect the mind through the eye. It is all very interesting. Every page is painted, perhaps I should say saturated, with this intensity of color. Undeniably the reader is strongly affected by it—though the effect is weakened in time. The natural eye cannot stand a constant glare of brilliant light, and the mind soon wearies of the quality that has come to be called "intensity" in literature. Great literature is always calm, and produces its effects by less apparent effort. This is of course a truism, but at the same time the reader does love warmth and color and the occasional show of vivid pictures on the printed page.

The story to which I have referred is in many respects a remarkable one. It is the description of the feeling and experience of a raw soldier lad in a couple of days of battle, and it has gained foreign approval as one of the most real pictures of war ever made, one that could only have been drawn from personal experience. I believe, in fact, that it is purely the work of imagination, and it might not have been written but for Tolstoi's *Sevastopol*. And yet it is quite original in its manner. I have been curious to hear what the "Realists" would say about it. The conversations are plainly vernacular, and there is no attempt to idealize the persons of the vivid drama. There is a studied commonplaceness about the talk and the characters, which seems nature itself. But I have talked with many soldiers of what they actually saw and felt in great battles, and I never got from any of them such a literary appreciation of a battle as this, nothing, in fact, half so interesting. I would not dare to say, from internal evidence, that this young soldier was "not in it," but any man who could see these pictures, have these sensations, and go through this mental and moral struggle in such circumstances ought not to be food for powder. He is needed in the New York drama. I do not wish to be misunderstood. I liked the book very much. I was carried along by its intensity, and felt at the end as if I had experienced a most exciting and melodramic dream, which I could not shake off when waking. I do not know how much of this effect was due to the scheme of color. It is almost a poem—quite, except in form. It is real, in a way. But what worried me was the thought of the verdict of the Realists. Would they not call it lurid realism?—CHARLES DUDLEY WARNER, "Editor's Study," *Harper's New Monthly Magazine*, May 1896, p. 962

The Red Badge of Courage: an Episode of the American War is a remarkable book, and has been received by English reviewers with an unanimity of praise which we are in no wise desirous that its author—a young man, as it is understood—should have been deprived of. But we believe that Mr. Stephen Crane, the author in question, has received his good marks not exactly on right grounds. His episode has been praised as a novel; we are inclined to praise it chiefly as an interesting and painful essay in pathology. The substance and "thesis" of the book, as the serious theatrical reviewers might say, consists in a presentation of the effects of physical danger, in the thousand forms which danger wears in modern warfare, upon the human nervous system. Nor is this all; the nervous system on which Mr. Crane chooses to illustrate his prelection is not a normal organism but an abnormal one,—morbid, hypersensitive, and over-conscious. Mr. Crane notes the effect upon his patient of each day and hour and minute of pained experience with a precision which would do credit to Mr. Lauder Brunton or a brother specialist. We are inclined to believe that his notes are the exact production by an extraordinary memory of moments that have been lived; yet it is believed that Mr. Crane has seen nothing of actual fighting. As an achievement in imagination, in the art of placing one's self in the situation of another—of an exceptional other in exceptional surroundings—Mr. Crane's document can hardly be praised too much. It convinces; one feels that not otherwise than as he describes did such a man fall wounded and another lie in the grasp of corruption. But when we are asked to say that a specialised record of morbid introspection and an exact description of physical horrors is good art we demur; there *is* art in *The Red Badge of Courage*—an infelicitous title by the way—but the general effect which it leaves behind it is not artistic.

But it is time to cease generalising. The scene, to come to detail, is laid in the American Civil War, and the hero is one Harry Fleming, who is spoken of invariably as "The Youth." We may note here an adroitness of Mr. Crane's. A narrative told in the first person must have been a limited affair. The author desires primarily to show us the nervous system under fire. But "The Youth," left to tell his story, could have given us only his own blurred impression of the terrible background of war which Mr. Crane, in the interest of the truth, as he conceives it, desires to present to us. Accordingly, "The Youth's" impressions are given in the third person, and he is presented to us *totus, teres, atque rotundus*, and against the lurid background of his adventures. It is a tactful arrangement. "The Youth" then enlisted in a Northern regiment, and has been some months a soldier when we are introduced to him. He has never met the enemy, and is weary of the tedium which has succeeded the first excitement of leaving home with his regiment. He has had time to fall back on his nerves, and the problem has begun to front him: will he or will he not run away?—

A sufficient time before he would have allowed the problem to kick its heels at the outer portals of his mind, but now he felt compelled to give serious attention to it. A little panic-fear grew in his mind. As his imagination went forward to a fight, he saw hideous possibilities. He contemplated the lurking menaces of the future and failed in an effort to see himself standing stoutly in the midst of them. He recalled his visions of broken-bladed glory, but in the shadow of the impending tumult he suspected them to be impossible pictures.

At last he finds himself face to face with danger, and Mr. Crane's descriptions of approaching conflict are wonderfully right and picturesque:—

The sun spread disclosing rays, and one by one, regiments burst into view like armed men first born of the earth. The youth perceived that the time had come. He was about to be measured. For a moment he felt in the face of his great trial like a babe, and the flesh over his heart seemed very thin. He seized time to look after him calculatingly. But he instantly saw that it would be impossible for him to escape from the regiment. It enclosed him. And there were iron laws of tradition and law on four sides. He was in a moving box.

The recorded sensations which follow in the youth's mind are far too many and too minute to pursue. But there are conspicuous moments which may be given as examples of many. The youth, it should be said, did run away at first, his regiment, it must be understood, retiring in disorder:—

He wondered what they would remark when later he appeared in camp. His mind heard howls of derision. Their density would not enable them to understand his sharper point of view. He began to pity himself acutely. He was ill-used. He was trodden beneath the feet of an iron injustice. He had proceeded with wisdom and from the most righteous motives under Heaven's blue, only to be frustrated by hateful circumstances.

In this key of self-pity and self-defence he stumbled on a dead man:—

He was being looked at by a dead man, who was seated with his back against a column-like tree. The eyes, staring at the youth, had changed to the dull hue to be seen on the side of a dead fish. The mouth was open. Its red had changed to an appalling yellow. Over the grey skin ran little ants. One was *trundling some sort of a bundle along the upper lip.*

Presently he came on a line of wounded men, the description of whom is the best thing in the book. This encounter was his salvation. He got back with them to the body of the regiment, and the sight of his comrades, notably the heroic death of one of them, made a beginning of the end in his egoism. After a series of endeavours to play the man he succeeded, was the first in a rush by the men of his regiment, and won his way not to glory but to self-respect:—

He found that he could look back upon the brass and bombast of his earlier gospels and see them truly. He was gleeful when he discovered that he now despised them. With this distinction came a store of assurance. He felt a quiet manhood, non-assertive, but of sturdy and strong blood. He knew that he would no more quail before his guides wherever they should point. He had to touch the great death to find that, after all, it was but the great death. He was a man.

A story like this is a mosaic. It is impossible to illustrate its effect by fragments. Tolstoi and another author, whose war stories are too little known, though it seems probable that Mr. Crane knows them—Mr. Ambrose Bierce to wit—have given us the aspect of war as war is seen by ordinary men; and Tolstoi, of course, with the epic touch of a great literary artist. But as a bundle of impressions received by a temperament especially sensitive, *The Red Badge of Courage* is a remarkable performance, and we believe without example—UNSIGNED, *"The Red Badge of Courage," Spectator,* June 27, 1896, p. 924

UNSIGNED
From "The Latest Fiction"

New York Times, October 19, 1895, p. 3

Stephen Crane is very young—not yet twenty-five, it is said—and this picture he presents of war ⟨*The Red Badge of Courage*⟩ is therefore a purely imaginative work. The very best thing that can be said about it, though, is that it strikes the reader as a statement of facts by a veteran. The purpose of the book is to set forth the experiences of a volunteer soldier in his first battle. The poetical idea of the hero and the coward in war was long since abandoned by well-informed writers. A recent autobiographical account of actual experiences in our civil war bears testimony that every soldier is frightened at the moment of entering battle, and his fright increases rather than diminishes as he grows old in service and more familiar with the dangers he has to encounter. It is true, also, that once in battle all men are much alike. They fight like beasts. Cowards and skulkers are the exception, and cowardice is often the result of some sudden physical disability.

The young private soldier who is the central personage in this remarkable work was a farm boy in one of the Middle States, probably Ohio, though certain peculiarities of the dialect in which Mr. Crane chooses to clothe the speech of all his persons, belong also to Western Pennsylvania and the Hoosier country. Except for those few expressions, such as "Watch out" for "Look out," the talk is a very fair phonetic equivalent for the common speech in parts of this State and Connecticut. The boy does not enlist at the beginning of the war, but his duty to go to the front weighs upon him day and night. He is the only son of his mother, and she is a widow and a typical American woman of the old New-England stock, who ever conceals her emotions, and seems to possess no imaginative faculty whatever. She is peeling potatoes when her boy, in his new blue clothes, says "Goodbye," and the exhortation she then delivers is perfectly practical and devoid of all sentiment. There is a black-eyed girl, nameless in the story, who looks after the youth as he trudges down the road, but when he looks back pretends to be gazing at the sky.

In other words, the early environment of Mr. Crane's hero is absolutely typical, differing in no particular from that of tens of thousands of young men who went to the front in the interval between the Sumter episode and the fall of Richmond. But as to his temperament and the quality of his mind, we cannot speak so positively. He is certainly of a more emotional type than any one of his comrades. His aspirations, perhaps, are no higher than theirs, his mental capacity no larger, his will, certainly, no stronger. But there is a touch of poetry in his nature which most men lack.

Probably Mr. Crane has put some of his own mental traits into the composition of his otherwise commonplace hero. Therefore, it is not possible to accept this graphic study of his mind under the stress of new and frightful experiences as an exact picture of the mental states of every green soldier under his first fire. All its complexities are surely not typical.

Yet it is as a picture which seems to be extraordinarily true, free from any suspicion of ideality, defying every accepted

tradition of martial glory, that the book commends itself to the reader. The majesty, the pomp and circumstance of glorious war, Mr. Crane rejects altogether. War, as he depicts it, is a mean, nasty, horrible thing; its seeming glories are the results of accident or that blind courage when driven to bay and fighting for life that the meanest animal would show as strongly as man. For it must be remembered that the point of view is consistently that of the humblest soldier in the ranks, who never knows where he is going or what is expected of him until the order comes, who never comprehends the whole scheme, but only his small share of it, who is frequently put forward as an intentional sacrifice, but yet it is a sentient human being, who is bound to have his own opinions founded on the scanty knowledge he possesses, his own hopes and fears and doubts and prejudices.

Private Henry Fleming goes to war a hot-headed young patriot with his mind brimful of crude ideas of glory and a settled conviction that his capacity for heroism is quite out of the common. Weary months of drill in camp reduce him seemingly to the proper machinelike condition. He learns many things, among them that the glories of war have been greatly exaggerated in books, that the enemy is not composed chiefly of bragging cowards, that victory is rare and dear, and that the lot of a private soldier is very hard. On the eve of his first battle he has about abandoned all hope of ever getting a chance to distinguish himself. Yet when the hour comes it brings depression instead of exhilaration. He communes with himself, and fears that he is a coward.

The battle Mr. Crane describes is one of those long and bloody conflicts of our civil war that we now freely admit were badly mismanaged through lack of good generalship, which had no particular result except the destruction of human life, and were claimed as prodigious victories by both sides. The green regiment is part of a brigade which is in the centre at first, and for a long while it has nothing to do. Then it has to stand on the edge of a piece of woods and receive the enemy's fire, and return it. This is a short and sharp proceeding, and while it lasts Private Henry Fleming acquits himself creditably. When the enemy's fire stops, he feels himself a hero and feels also that he has done the greatest day's work of his life. The nervous tension has been awful, the revulsion of feeling is correspondingly great. When the enemy's fire is resumed, a few minutes later, he is entirely unprepared. Panic seizes him, he drops his musket and runs for his life.

All that day he is a skulker in the rear of a great battle. His emotions, his mental vagaries, his experiences with the dead and dying, and the terrible nervous ordeal he undergoes are depicted by Mr. Crane with a degree of vividness and original power almost unique in our fiction. The night of the first day finds him back in the camp of his own regiment, lauded by his surviving comrades as a wounded hero. His scalp was cut by a blow of a musket by a retreating soldier, whose flight he tried to stop, for no reason, and he has tied his handkerchief over the wound. He is physically exhausted and his conscience troubles him sorely.

In the next day's conflict he remains with his regiment. His nervous excitement has increased, but he is no longer so greatly shocked by the spectacle of the dead and dying. He has lost all control of his tongue, and he jabbers oaths incessantly. When his regiment is called upon to repel an advance of the enemy, he excels all his comrades in the ferocious rapidity of his fire. He is again extolled as a hero, but scarcely comprehends the praise. His regiment, esteemed by the division officers, apparently with good reason, as nearly worthless is selected to make a charge which is intended merely to check a contemplated attack of the enemy on the left until reinforcements can be forwarded to that point. It is not expected that any member of the regiment will return alive, and some rude remarks of a staff officer to this effect reach the ears of the men and transform them into demons, but very impotent and purposeless demons. The order is only half carried out. A file of soldiers in gray, behind a rail fence, keeps the blue fellows at bay. They stand like lost sheep, and scarcely return the fire which is destroying them. Yet, on their retreat, they combat bravely enough with a small Confederate body which tries to cut them off. Returning to their own lines, they are received with derision, while their Colonel is roundly abused by his superior. The charge has been a failure, yet it has transformed Private Henry Fleming. He has saved the colors, and he has sounded his own depths. He feels that he will never run away again.

> At last his eyes seem to open to some new ways. He found that he could look back upon the brass and bombast of his earlier gospels and see them truly. He was gleeful when he discovered that he now despised them. With this conviction came a store of assurance. He felt a quiet manhood, non-assertive, but of sturdy and strong blood. He knew that he would no more quail before his guides wherever they should point. He had been in touch with the great death, and found that after all, it was but the great death. He was a man.

The book is written in terse and vigorous sentences, but not without some unpleasant affectations of style which the author would do well to correct. His natural talent is so strong that it is a pity its expression should be marred by petty tricks. When he begins a sentence with "too," for instance, he makes a sensitive reader squirm. But he is certainly a young man of remarkable promise.

GEORGE WYNDHAM
From "A Remarkable Book"
New Review, January 1896, pp. 32–40

Mr. Stephen Crane, the author of *The Red Badge of Courage* (London: Heinemann), is a great artist, with something new to say, and consequently, with a new way of saying it. His theme, indeed, is an old one, but old themes re-handled anew in the light of novel experience, are the stuff out of which masterpieces are made, and in *The Red Badge of Courage* Mr. Crane has surely contrived a masterpiece. He writes of war—the ominous and alluring possibility for every man, since the heir of all the ages has won and must keep his inheritance by secular combat. The conditions of the age-long contention have changed and will change, but its certainty is coeval with progress: so long as there are things worth fighting for fighting will last, and the fashion of fighting will change under the reciprocal stresses of rival inventions. Hence its double interest of abiding necessity and ceaseless variation. Of all these variations the most marked has followed, within the memory of most of us, upon the adoption of long-range weapons of precision, and continues to develop, under our eyes, with the development of rapidity in firing. And yet, with the exception of Zola's *La Débâcle*, no considerable attempt has been made to pourtray war under its new conditions. The old stories are less trustworthy than ever as guides to the experiences which a man may expect in battle and to the emotions which those experiences are likely to arouse. No doubt the prime factors in the personal problem—the chances of death and mutilation—continue to be about the same. In these respects it matters little whether you are pierced by a bullet at two thousand yards or stabbed at hands' play with a dagger. We know that the most appalling death-rolls of recent campaigns have been more than equalled in ancient warfare; and, apart from history, it is clear that, unless one side runs away, neither can win save by the infliction of decisive losses. But although these personal risks continue to be essentially the same, the picturesque and emotional aspects of war are completely altered by every change in the shape and circumstance of imminent death. And these are the fit materials for literature—the things which even dull men remember with the undying imagination of poets, but which, for lack of the writer's art, they cannot communicate. The sights flashed indelibly on the retina of the eye; the sounds that after long silences suddenly cypher; the stenches that sicken in after-life at any chance allusion to decay; or, stirred by these, the storms of passions that force yells of defiance out of inarticulate clowns; the winds of fear that sweep by night along prostrate ranks, with the acceleration of trains and the noise as of a whole town waking from nightmare with stertorous, indrawn gasps—these colossal facts of the senses and the soul are the only colours in which the very image of war can be painted. Mr. Crane has composed his palette with these colours, and has painted a picture that challenges comparison with the most vivid scenes of Tolstoï's *La Guerre et la Paix* or of Zola's *La Débâcle*. This is unstinted praise, but I feel bound to give it after reading the book twice and comparing it with Zola's *Sédan* and Tolstoï's account of Rostow's squadron for the first time under fire. Indeed, I think that Mr. Crane's picture of war is more complete than Tolstoï's, more true than Zola's. Rostow's sensations are conveyed by Tolstoï with touches more subtle than any to be found even in his *Sébastopol*, but they make but a brief passage in a long book, much else of which is devoted to the theory that Napoleon and his marshals were mere waifs on a tide of humanity or to the analysis of divers characters exposed to civilian experiences. Zola, on the other hand, compiles an accurate catalogue of almost all that is terrible and nauseating in war; but it is his own catalogue of facts made in cold blood, and not the procession of flashing images shot through the senses into one brain and fluctuating there with its rhythm of exaltation and fatigue. *La Débâcle* gives the whole truth, the truth of science, as it is observed by a shrewd intellect, but not the truth of experience as it is felt in fragments magnified or diminished in accordance with the patient's mood. The terrible things in war are not always terrible; the nauseating things do not always sicken. On the contrary, it is even these which sometimes lift the soul to heights from which they become invisible. And, again, at other times, it is the little miseries of most ignoble insignificance which fret through the last fibres of endurance.

Mr. Crane, for his distinction, has hit on a new device, or at least on one which has never been used before with such consistency and effect. In order to show the features of modern war, he takes a subject—a youth with a peculiar temperament, capable of exaltation and yet morbidly sensitive. Then he traces the successive impressions made on such a temperament, from minute to minute, during two days of heavy fighting. He stages the drama of war, so to speak, within the mind of one man, and then admits you as to a theatre. You may, if you please, object that this youth is unlike most other young men who serve in the ranks, and that the same events would have impressed the average man differently; but you are convinced that this man's soul is truly drawn, and that the impressions made in it are faithfully rendered. The youth's temperament is merely the medium which the artist has chosen: that it is exceptionally plastic makes but for the deeper incision of his work. It follows from Mr. Crane's method that he creates by his art even such a first-hand report of war as we seek in vain among the journals and letters of soldiers. But the book is not written in the form of an autobiography: the author narrates. He is therefore at liberty to give scenery and action, down to the slightest gestures and outward signs of inward elation or suffering, and he does this with the vigour and terseness of a master. Had he put his descriptions of scenery and his atmospheric effects, or his reports of overheard conversations, into the mouth of his youth, their very excellence would have belied all likelihood. Yet in all his descriptions and all his reports he confines himself only to such things as that youth heard and saw, and, of these, only to such as influenced his emotions. By this compromise he combines the strength and truth of a monodrama with the directness and colour of the best narrative prose. The monodrama suffices for the lyrical emotion of Tennyson's *Maud*; but in Browning's *Martin Relf* you feel the constraint of a form which in his *Ring and the Book* entails repetition often intolerable.

Mr. Crane discovers his youth, Henry Fleming, in a phase of disillusion. It is some monotonous months since boyish "visions of broken-bladed glory" impelled him to enlist in the Northern Army towards the middle of the American war. That impulse is admirably given:—"One night as he lay in bed, the winds had carried to him the clangouring of the church bells, as some enthusiast jerked the rope frantically to tell the twisted news of a great battle. This voice of the people rejoicing in the night had made him shiver in a prolonged ecstasy of excitement. Later he had gone down to his mother's room, and had spoken thus: 'Ma, I'm going to enlist.' 'Henry, don't you be a fool,' his mother had replied. She had then covered her face with the quilt. There was an end to the matter for that night." But the next morning he enlists. He is impatient of the homely injunctions given him in place of the heroic speech he expects in accordance with a tawdry convention, and so departs, with a "vague feeling of relief." But, looking back from the gate, he sees his mother "kneeling among the potato parings. Her brown face upraised and stained with tears, her spare form quivering." Since then the army has done "little but sit still and try to keep warm" till he has "grown to regard himself merely as a part of a vast blue demonstration." In the sick langour of this waiting, he begins to suspect his courage and lies awake by night through hours of morbid introspection. He tries "to prove to himself mathematically that he would not run from a battle"; he constantly leads the conversation round to the problem of courage in order to gauge the confidence of his messmates.

> "How do you know you won't run when the time comes?" asked the youth. "Run?" said the loud one, "run?—of course not!" He laughed. "Well," continued the youth, "lots of good-a-'nough men have thought they was going to do great things before the fight, but when the time come they skedaddled." "Oh, that's all true, I s'pose," replied the other, "but I'm not going to skedaddle. The man that bets on my running will lose his money, that's all." He nodded confidently.

The youth is a "mental outcast" among his comrades, "wrestling with his personal problem," and sweating as he listens to the muttered scoring of a card game, his eyes fixed on the "red, shivering reflection of a fire." Every day they drill; every night they watch the red campfires of the enemy on the far shore of a river, eating their hearts out. At last they march:—"In the gloom before the break of the day their uniforms glowed a deep purple blue. From across the river the red eyes were still peering. In the eastern sky there was a yellow patch, like a rug laid for the feet of the coming sun; and against it, black and pattern-like, loomed the gigantic figure of the colonel on a gigantic horse." The book is full of such vivid impressions, half of sense and half of imagination:—The columns as they marched "were like two serpents crawling from the cavern of night." But the march, which, in his boyish imagination, should have led forthwith into melodramatic action is but the precursor of other marches. After days of weariness and nights of discomfort, at last, as in life, without preface, and in a lull of the mind's anxiety, the long-dreaded and long-expected is suddenly and smoothly in process of accomplishment:—"One grey morning he was kicked on the leg by the tall soldier, and then, before he was entirely awake, he found himself running down a wood road in the midst of men who were panting with the first effects of speed. His canteen banged rhythmically upon his thigh, and his haversack bobbed softly. His musket bounced a trifle from his shoulder at each stride and made his cap feel uncertain upon his head." From this moment, reached on the thirtieth page, the drama races through another hundred and sixty pages to the end of the book, and to read those pages is in itself an experience of breathless, lambent, detonating life. So brilliant and detached are the images evoked that, like illuminated bodies actually seen, they leave their fever-bright phantasms floating before the brain. You may shut the book, but you still see the battle-flags "jerked about madly in the smoke," or sinking with "dying gestures of despair," the men "dropping here and there like bundles"; the captain shot dead with "an astonished and sorrowful look as if he thought some friend had done him an ill-turn"; and the litter of corpses, "twisted in fantastic contortions," as if "they had fallen from some great height, dumped out upon the ground from the sky." The book is full of sensuous impressions that leap out from the picture: of gestures, attitudes, grimaces, that flash into portentous definition, like faces from the climbing clouds of nightmare. It leaves the imagination bounded with a "dense wall of smoke, furiously slit and slashed by the knife-like fire from the rifles." It leaves, in short, such indelible traces as are left by the actual experience of war. The picture shows grisly shadows and vermilion splashes, but, as in the vast drama it reflects so truly, these features, though insistent, are small in size, and are lost in the immensity of the theatre. The tranquil forest stands around; the "fairy-blue of the sky" is over it all. And, as in the actual experience of war, the impressions which these startling features inflict, though acute, are localised and not too deep: are as it were mere pin-pricks, or, at worst, clean cuts from a lancet in a body thrilled with currents of physical excitement and sopped with anæsthetics of emotion. Here is the author's description of a forlorn hope:—

> As the regiment swung from its position out into a cleared space the woods and thickets before it awakened. Yellow flames leaped toward it from many directions. The line swung straight for a moment. Then the right wing swung forward; it in turn was surpassed by the left. Afterward the centre careered to the front until the regiment was a wedge-shaped mass. . . . the men, pitching forward insanely, had burst into cheerings, mob-like and barbaric, but tuned in strange keys that can arouse the dullard and the stoic. . . . There was the delirium that encounters despair and death, and is heedless and blind to

odds. . . . Presently the straining pace ate up the energies of the men. As if by agreement, the leaders began to slacken their speed. The volleys directed against them had a seeming wind-like effect. The regiment snorted and blew. Among some stolid trees it began to falter and hesitate. . . . The youth had a vague belief that he had run miles, and he thought, in a way, that he was now in some new and unknown land. . . .

The charge withers away, and the lieutenant, the youth, and his friend run forward to rally the regiment.

> In front of the colours three men began to bawl, "Come on! Come On!" They danced and gyrated like tortured savages. The flag, obedient to these appeals, bended its glittering form and swept toward them. The men wavered in indecision for a moment, and then with a long wailful cry the dilapidated regiment surged forward and began its new journey. Over the field went the scurrying mass. It was a handful of men splattered into the faces of the enemy. Toward it instantly sprang the yellow tongues. A vast quantity of blue smoke hung before them. A mighty banging made ears valueless. The youth ran like a madman to reach the woods before a bullet could discover him. He ducked his head low, like a football player. In his haste his eyes almost closed, and the scene was a wild blur. Pulsating saliva stood at the corner of his mouth. Within him, as he hurled forward, was born a love, a despairing fondness for this flag that was near him. It was a creation of beauty and invulnerability. It was a goddess radiant, that bended its form with an imperious gesture to him. It was a woman, red and white, hating and loving, that called him with the voice of his hopes. Because no harm could come to it he endowed it with power. He kept near, as if it could be a saver of lives, and an imploring cry went from his mind.

This passage directly challenges comparison with Zola's scene, in which the lieutenant and the old tradition, of an invincible Frenchman over-running the world "between his bottle and his girl," expire together among the morsels of a bullet-eaten flag. Mr. Crane has probably read *La Débâcle*, and wittingly threw down his glove. One can only say that he is justified of his courage.

Mr. Crane's method, when dealing with things seen and heard, is akin to Zola's: he omits nothing and extenuates nothing, save the actual blasphemy and obscenity of a soldier's oaths. These he indicates, sufficiently for any purpose of art, by brief allusions to their vigour and variety. Even Zola has rarely surpassed the appalling realism of Jim Conklin's death in Chapter X. Indeed, there is little to criticise in Mr. Crane's observation, except an undue subordination of the shrill cry of bullets to the sharp crashing of rifles. He omits the long chromatic whine defining its invisible arc in the air, and the fretful snatch a few feet from the listener's head. In addition to this gift of observation, Mr. Crane has at command the imaginative phrase. The firing follows a retreat as with "yellings of eager metallic hounds"; the men at their mechanic loading and firing are like "fiends jigging heavily in the smoke" in a lull before the attack "there passed slowly the intense moments that precede the tempest"; then, after single shots, "the battle roar settled to a rolling thunder, which was a single long explosion." And, as I have said, when Mr. Crane deals with things felt he gives a truer report than Zola. He postulates his hero's temperament—a day-dreamer given over to morbid

self-analysis who enlists, not from any deep-seated belief in the holiness of fighting for his country, but in hasty pursuit of a vanishing ambition. This choice enables Mr. Crane to double his picturesque advantage with an ethical advantage equally great. Not only is his youth, like the sufferer in "*The Fall of the House of Usher*," super-sensitive to every pin-prick of sensation, he is also a delicate meter of emotion and fancy. In such a nature the waves of feeling take exaggerated curves, and hallucination haunts the brain. Thus, when awaiting the first attack, his mind is thronged with vivid images of a circus he had seen as a boy: it is there in definite detail, even as the Apothecary's shop usurps Romeo's mind at the crisis of his fate. And thus also, like Herodotus' Aristodemus, he vacillates between cowardice and heroism. Nothing could well be more subtle than his self-deception and that sudden enlightenment which leads him to "throw aside his mental pamphlets on the philosophy of the retreated and rules for the guidance of the damned." His soul is of that kind which, "sick with self-love," can only be saved "so as by fire"; and it is saved when the battle-bond of brotherhood is born within it, and is found plainly of deeper import than the cause for which he and his comrades fight, even as that cause is loftier than his personal ambition. By his choice of a hero Mr. Crane displays in the same work a pageant of the senses and a tragedy of the soul.

But he does not obtrude his moral. The "tall soldier" and the lieutenant are brave and content throughout, the one by custom as a veteran, the other by constitution as a hero. But the two boys, the youth and his friend, "the loud soldier," are at first querulous braggarts, but at the last they are transmuted by danger until either might truly say:

> We have proved we have hearts in a cause, we are
>   noble still,
> And myself have awaked, as it seems, to the better
>   mind;
> It is better to fight for the good than to rail at the ill;
> I have felt with my native land, I am one with my
>   kind,
> I embrace the purpose of God, and the doom
>   assigned.

Let no man cast a stone of contempt at these two lads during their earlier weakness until he has fully gauged the jarring discordance of battle. To be jostled on a platform when you have lost your luggage and missed your train on an errand of vital importance gives a truer pre-taste of war than any field-day; yet many a well-disciplined man will denounce the universe upon slighter provocation. It is enough that these two were boys and that they became men.

Yet must it be said that this youth's emotional experience was singular. In a battle there are a few physical cowards, abjects born with defective circulations, who literally turn blue at the approach of danger, and a few on whom danger acts like the keen, rare atmosphere of snow-clad peaks. But between these extremes come many to whom danger is as strong wine, with the multitude which gladly accepts the "iron laws of tradition" and finds welcome support in "a moving box." To this youth, as the cool dawn of his first day's fighting changed by infinitesimal gradations to a feverish noon, the whole evolution pointed to "a trap"; but I have seen another youth under like circumstances toss a pumpkin into the air and spit it on his sword. To this youth the very landscape was filled with "the stealthy approach of death." You are convinced by the author's art that it was so to this man. But to others, as the clamour increases, it is as if the serenity of the morning had taken refuge in their brains. This man "stumbles over the stones as he runs breathlessly forward"; another realises for the first time how right it is to be adroit even in running. The movement of his body becomes an art, which is not self-conscious, since its whole intention is to impress others within the limits of a modest decorum. We know that both love and courage teach this mastery over the details of living. You can tell from the way one woman, out of all the myriads, walks down Piccadilly, that she is at last aware of love. And you can tell from the way a man enters a surgery or runs toward a firing-line that he, too, realises how wholly the justification of any one life lies in its perfect adjustment to others. The woman in love, the man in battle, may each say, for their moment, with the artist, "I was made perfect too." They also are of the few to whom "God whispers in the ear."

But had Mr. Crane taken an average man he would have written an ordinary story, whereas he has written one which is certain to last. It is glorious to see his youth discover courage in the bed-rock of primeval antagonism after the collapse of his tinsel bravado; it is something higher to see him raise upon that rock the temple of resignation. Mr. Crane, as an artist, achieves by his singleness of purpose a truer and completer picture of war than either Tolstoï, bent also upon proving the insignificance of heroes, or Zola, bent also upon prophesying the regeneration of France. That is much; but it is more that his work of art, when completed, chimes with the universal experience of mankind; that his heroes find in their extreme danger, if not confidence in their leaders and conviction in their cause, at least the conviction that most men do what they can or, at most, what they must. We have few good accounts of battles—many of shipwrecks; and we know that, just as the storm rises, so does the commonplace captain show as a god, and the hysterical passenger as a cheerful heroine.

It is but a further step to recognise all life for a battle and this earth for a vessel lost in space. We may then infer that virtues easy in moments of distress may be useful also in everyday experience.

HAROLD FREDERIC
"Stephen Crane's Triumph"
New York Times, January 26, 1896, p. 22

Who in London knows about Stephen Crane? The question is one of genuine interest here. It happens, annoyingly enough, that the one publishing person who might throw some light on the answer is for the moment absent from town. Other sources yield only the meagre information that the name is believed to be a real, and not an assumed, one, and that its owner is understood to be a very young man, indeed. That he is an American, or, at least, learned to read and write in America, is obvious enough. The mere presence in his vocabulary of the verb "loan" would settle that, if the proof were not otherwise blazoned on every page of his extraordinary book. For this mysteriously unknown youth has really written an extraordinary book.

The Red Badge of Courage appeared a couple of months ago, unheralded and unnoticed, in a series which, under the distinctive label of *Pioneer*, is popularly supposed to present fiction more or less after the order of *The Green Carnation*, which was also of that lot. The first one who mentioned in my hearing that this *Red Badge* was well worth reading happened to be a person whose literary admirations serve me generally as warnings what to avoid, and I remembered the title languidly from the standpoint of self-protection. A little later others began to speak of it. All at once, every bookish person had it at his tongue's end. It was clearly a book to read, and I read it. Even as I did so, reviews burst forth in a dozen different quarters, hailing it as extraordinary. Some were naturally more excited and voluble than others, but all the critics showed, and continue to show, their sense of being in the presence of something not like other things. George Wyndham, M.P., has already written of it in *The New Review* as "a remarkable book." Other magazine editors have articles about it in preparation, and it is evident that for the next few months it is to be more talked about than anything else in current literature. It seems almost equally certain that it will be kept alive, as one of the deathless books which must be read by everybody who desires to be, or to seem, a connoisseur of modern fiction.

If there were in existence any books of a similar character, one could start confidently by saying that it was the best of its kind. But it has no fellows. It is a book outside of all classification. So unlike anything else it is, that the temptation rises to deny that it is a book at all. When one searches for comparisons, they can only be found by culling out selected portions from the trunks of masterpieces, and considering these detached fragments, one by one, with reference to the *Red Badge*, which is itself a fragment, and yet is complete. Thus one lifts the best battle pictures from Tolstoi's great *War and Peace* from Balzac's *Chouans*, from Hugo's *Les Miserables*, and the forest fight in 93, from Prosper Mérimée's assault of the redoubt, from Zola's *La Débacle*, and *Attack on the Mill*, (it is strange enough that equivalents in the literature of our own language do not suggest themselves,) and studies them side by side with this tremendously effective battle painting by the unknown youngster. Positively they are cold and ineffectual beside it. The praise may sound exaggerated, but really it is inadequate. These renowned battle descriptions of the big men are made to seem all wrong. The *Red Badge* impels the feeling that the actual truth about a battle has never been guessed before.

In construction, the book is as original as in its unique grasp of a new grouping of old materials. All the historic and prescribed machinery of the romance is thrust aside. One barely knows the name of the hero; it is only dimly sketched in that he was a farm boy and had a mother when he enlisted. These facts recur to him once or twice; they play no larger part in the reader's mind. Only two other characters are mentioned by name—Jim Conklin and Wilson; more often even they are spoken of as the tall soldier and the loud soldier. Not a word is expended on telling where they come from, or who they are. They pass across the picture, or shift from one posture to another in its moving composition, with the impersonality of one's chance fellow-passengers in a railroad car. There is a lieutenant who swears new oaths all the while, another officer with a red beard, and two or three still vaguer figures, revealed here and there through the smoke. We do not know, or seek to know, their names, or anything about them except what, staring through the eyes of Henry Fleming, we are permitted to see. The regiment itself, the refugees from other regiments in the crowded flight, and the enemy on the other side of the fence, are differentiated only as they wear blue or gray. We never get their color out of our mind's eye. This exhausts the dramatis personae of the book, and yet it is more vehemently alive and heaving with dramatic human action than any other book of our time. The people are all strangers to us, but the sight of them stirs the profoundest emotions of interest in our breasts. What they do appeals as vividly to our consciousness as if we had known them all our life.

The central idea of the book is of less importance than the magnificent graft of externals upon it. We begin with the young raw recruit, hearing that at last his regiment is going to see some fighting, and brooding over the problem of his own behavior under fire. We follow his perturbed meditations through thirty pages, which cover a week or so of this menace of action. Then suddenly, with one gray morning, the ordeal breaks abruptly over the youngster's head. We go with him, so close that he is never out of sight, for two terrible crowded days, and then the book is at an end. This cross-section of his experience is made a part of our own. We see with his eyes, think with his mind, quail or thrill with his nerves. He strives to argue himself into the conventional soldier's bravery; he runs ingloriously away; he excuses, defends, and abhors himself in turn; he tremblingly yields to the sinister fascination of creeping near the battle; he basely allows his comrades to ascribe to heroism the wound he received in the frenzied "sauve qui peut" of the fight; he gets at last the fire of combat in his veins, and blindly rushing in, deports himself with such hardy and temeraious valor that even the Colonel notes him, and admits that he is a "jim-hickey." These sequent processes, observed with relentless minutiae, are so powerfully and speakingly portrayed that they seem the veritable actions of our own minds. To produce this effect is a notable triumph, but is commonplace by comparison with the other triumph of making us realize what Henry saw and heard as well as what he felt. The value of the former feat has the limitation of the individual. No two people are absolutely alike; any other young farm boy would have passed through the trial with something different somewhere. Where Henry fluttered, he might have been obtuse; neither the early panic nor the later irrational ferocity would necessarily have been just the same. But the picture of the trial itself seems to me never to have been painted as well before.

Oddly enough *The Saturday Review* and some other of the commentators take it for granted that the writer of the *Red Badge* must have seen real warfare. "The extremely vivid touches of detail convince us," says *The Review*, "that he has had personal experience of the scenes he depicts. Certainly, if his book were altogether a work of imagination, unbased on personal experience, his realism would be nothing short of a miracle." This may strike the reader who has not thought much about it as reasonable, but I believe it to be wholly fallacious. Some years ago I had before me the task of writing some battle chapters in a book I was at work upon. The novel naturally led up to the climax of a battle, and I was excusably anxious that when I finally got to this battle, I should be as fit to handle it as it was possible to make myself. A very considerable literature existed about the actual struggle, which was the Revolutionary battle of Oriskany, fought only a few miles from where I was born. This literature was in part the narratives of survivors of the fight, in part imaginative accounts based on these by later writers. I found to my surprise that the people who were really in the fight gave one much less of an idea of a desperate forest combat than did those who pictured it in fancy. Of course, here it might be that the veterans were inferior in powers of narration to the professional writer. Then I extended the text to writers themselves. I compared the best accounts of Franco-German battles, written for the London newspapers by trained correspondents of distinction who were on the spot, with the choicest imaginative work of novelists, some of them mentioned above, who had never seen a gun fired in anger. There was literally no comparison between the two. The line between journalism and literature obtruded itself steadily. Nor were cases lacking in which some of these war correspondents had in other departments of work showed themselves capable of true literature. I have the instance of

David Christie Murray in mind. He saw some of the stiffest fighting that was done in his time, and that, too, at an early stage of his career, but he never tried to put a great battle chapter into one of his subsequent novels, and if he had I don't believe it would have been great.

Our own writers of the elder generation illustrate this same truth. Gen. Lew Wallace, Judge Tourgée, Dr. Weir Mitchell, and numbers of others saw tremendous struggles on the battlefield, but to put the reality into type baffles them. The four huge volumes of The Century's *Battles and Leaders of the Civil War* are written almost exclusively by men who took an active part in the war, and many of them were in addition men of high education and considerable literary talent, but there is not a really moving story of a fight in the whole work. When Warren Lee Goss began his *Personal Recollections of a Private*, his study of the enlistment, the early marching and drilling, and the new experiences of camp life was so piquant and fresh that I grew quite excited in anticipation. But when he came to the fighting, he fell flat. The same may be said, with more reservations, about the first parts of Judge Tourgée's more recent *Story of a Thousand*. It seems as if the actual sight of a battle has some dynamic quality in it which overwhelms and crushes the literary faculty in the observer. At best, he gives us a conventional account of what happened; but on analysis you find that this is not what he really saw, but what all his reading has taught him that he must have seen. In the same way battle painters depict horses in motion, not as they actually move, but as it has been agreed by numberless generations of draughtsmen to say that they move. At last, along comes a Muybridge, with his instantaneous camera, and shows that the real motion is entirely different.

It is this effect of a photographic revelation which startles and fascinates one in *The Red Badge of Courage*. The product is breathlessly interesting, but still more so is the suggestion behind it that a novel force has been disclosed, which may do all sorts of other remarkable things. Prophecy is known of old as a tricky and thankless hag, but all the same I cannot close my ears to her hint that a young man who can write such a first book as that will make us all sit up in good time.

H. D. TRAILL
From "The New Realism"
Fortnightly Review, January 1897, pp. 63–66

In a day when the spurious is everywhere supposed to be successfully disguised and sufficiently recommended to the public by merely being described as new, it need not surprise us to find our attention solicited by a New Realism, of which the two most obvious things to be said are that it is unreal with the falsity of the half truth, and as old as the habit of exaggeration. One of the latest professors of this doubtful form of art, is the very young American writer, Mr. Stephen Crane, who first attracted notice in this country by a novel entitled *The Red Badge of Courage*. Whether that work was or was not described by its admirers as an achievement in realism, I am not aware. As a matter of fact, and as the antecedents, and indeed the age, of the writer showed, it was not a record of actual observation. Mr. Crane had evidently been an industrious investigator and collator of the emotional experiences of soldiers, and had evolved from them a picture of the mental state of a recruit going into action. It was artistically done and obtained a not undeserved success; but no method, of course, could be less realistic, in the sense on which the professors of the New

Realism insist, than the process which resulted in this elaborate study of the emotions of the battlefield from the pen of a young man who has never himself smelt powder.

Since then, however, Mr. Crane has given us two small volumes, which are presumably realistic or nothing. If circumstances have prevented the author from writing about soldiers in action "with his eye on the object," there are no such obstacles to his studying the Bowery and "Bowery boys" from the life; we may take it, therefore, that *Maggie* and *George's Mother* are the products of such study. According to Mr. Howell's effusive "Appreciation," which prefaces it, *Maggie* is a remarkable story having "that quality of fatal necessity which dominates Greek tragedy." Let us see then what this Sophoclean work is like.

The story of *Maggie* opens with a fight between the boys of Rum Alley and those of Devil's Row. Jimmie, the heroine's brother, is a boy of Rum Alley, aged nine, and when the curtain draws up he is the centre of a circle of urchins who are pelting him with stones. "Howls of wrath went up from them. On their small convulsed faces shone the grins of true assassins. As they charged they threw stones and cursed in shrill chorus. . . . Jimmie's coat had been torn to shreds in a scuffle, and his hat was gone. He had bruises on twenty parts of his body, and blood was dripping from a cut in his head. His wan features looked like those of a tiny insane demon. . . . The little boys ran to and fro hurling stones and swearing in barbaric trebles. . . . A stone had smashed in Jimmie's mouth. Blood was bubbling over his chin and down upon his ragged shirt. Tears made furrows on his dirt-stained cheeks. His thin legs had begun to tremble and turn weak, causing his small body to reel. His roaring curses of the first part of the fight had changed to a blasphemous chatter. In the yells of the whirling mob of Devil's Row children there were notes of joy like songs of triumphant savagery. The little boys seemed to leer gloatingly at the blood on the other child's face."

A lad of sixteen, afterwards destined to play an important part in the story, then approaches. He smites one of the Devil's Row children on the back of the head, and the little boy falls to the ground and gives a tremendous howl. A reinforcement of the Rum Alley children then arrives, and there is a momentary pause in the fight, during which Jimmie becomes involved in a quarrel with Blue Billie, one of his own side.

> They struck at each other, clinched, and rolled over on the cobblestones.
> "Smash 'im, Jimmie, kick d' face off 'im," yelled Pete, in tones of delight.
> The small combatants pounded and kicked, scratched and tore. They began to weep, and their curses struggled in their throats with sobs. The other little boys clasped their hands and wriggled their legs in excitement. They formed a bobbing circle round the pair.

At this juncture Jimmie's father arrives on the scene and endeavours to separate the combatants with a view of "belting" his son. To this end he begins to kick into the chaotic mass on the ground. "The boy Billie felt a heavy boot strike his head. He made a furious effort and disentangled himself from Jimmie. He tottered away. Jimmie arose painfully from the ground and confronting his father began to curse him." His parent kicked him. "Come home now," he cried, "an' stop yer jawin' or I'll lam the everlasting head off yer." Upon this they go home, the boy swearing "luridly," for he "felt that it was a degradation for one who aimed to be some vague kind of a soldier or a man of blood, with a sort of sublime licence, to be taken home by a father."

That is the first chapter much condensed. In the original there are eight pages of it. Is it art? If so, is the making of mud-pies an artistic occupation, and are the neglected brats who are to be found rolling in the gutters of every great city unconscious artists?

In the next chapter Jimmie pummels his little sister, and his mother quarrels with and rates her husband till she drives him to the public-house, remaining at home to get drunk herself. In the third chapter, Jimmie, who has stopped out to avoid an outbreak of her intoxicated fury, steals home again late at night, listens outside the door to a fight going on within between his father and mother, and at last creeps in with his little sister to find both parents prostrate on the floor in a drunken stupor and to huddle in a corner until daybreak, cowering with terror lest they should awaken. For when you are a "realist's" little boy, you have to be very handy and adaptable and do exactly what that realist requires of you: so that, though you may have been defying and cursing your father at one moment, like the daring little imp you have been described as being, you may at the next moment, and for the purpose of another sort of painful picture, have to behave like a cowed and broken-spirited child of a totally different type.

These opening scenes take up about one-fifth of the short book, and those that follow are like unto them. There is a little less fighting, but a good deal more drinking. Jimmie becomes a truck driver, and fights constantly with other drivers, but the fights are not described at length. His father dies, probably of drink, and his mother takes to drinking harder than ever. Maggie is seduced and deserted by Pete, the youth who appeared on the scene during the opening fight and hits one of the infant fighters on the back of the head. Jimmie resents the proceedings of the Bowery Lovelace as a breach of good manners, and, going with a friend to the tavern where Pete acts as "bar-tender," the two set upon him and there ensues a fight, in the course of which the lips of the combatants "curl back and stretch tightly over the gums in ghoul-like grins." It lasts for four pages, and is brought to a close by the intervention of the police, and the escape of Jimmie "with his face drenched in blood." How this story continues, how Maggie falls lower and lower and finally dies, and how after her death her gin-sodden mother is passionately entreated to forgive her, and at last graciously consents to do so—all this may be read in Mr. Crane's pages, and shall not here be summarised from them. Is it necessary to do so? Or to give a *précis* of the companion volume, *George's Mother*, the story of a "little old woman" actually of sober and industrious habits, and of her actually not vicious though weak son, of whose backslidings she dies? Need I give specimen extracts from it? I hope not—I think not. The extracts which have been already given are perfectly fair samples of Mr. Crane's work. Anyone who likes to take it from the writer of this article, that to read these two little books through would be to wade through some three hundred and thirty pages of substantially the same stuff as the above extracts, will do Mr. Crane no injustice. So I will pass from him to a Realist of considerably larger calibre.

For Mr. Arthur Morrison, author of *Tales of Mean Streets* and *A Child of the Jago*, undoubtedly carries heavier guns than Mr. Crane. To begin with, he can tell a story, while Mr. Crane can only string together a series of loosely cohering incidents. Many of his characters are vividly and vigorously drawn, while the American writer puts us off for the most part with sketches and shadowy outlines. Mr. Morrison's ruffians and their ruffianism are better discriminated, and though there is plenty of fighting and drinking and general brutality in his last and strongest work—one of the faction fights in which, indeed, is related at quite inordinate length—he understands that the description of these things alone will not suffice to make a satisfactory story even about blackguards, and he has outgrown that touching *naïveté* displayed in the younger realist's obvious belief in the perpetual freshness and charm of mere squalor. He perceives that merely to follow his characters, as Mr. Crane does his, from the drinking-bar to the low music-hall and thence home again, day after day, with interludes of brawling and "bashing" and other like recreations, becomes, after a hundred pages or so, a little monotonous, and that the life of the criminal in his constant struggle with the law, and in perpetual danger from its officers, possesses at least the element of "sport," and presents features of variety and interest which that of the mere sot and tavern-brawler cannot possibly offer. Above all, Mr. Morrison wields a certain command of pathos, a power in which Mr. Crane is not only deficient, but of which he does not even appear to know the meaning; and were it not for a certain strange and, in truth, paradoxical defect, of which more hereafter, in his method of employing it, he would at times be capable of moving his readers very powerfully indeed. In a word, the English writer differs from the American by all the difference which divides the trained craftsman from the crude amateur, and deserves to that extent more serious and detailed criticism.

STEPHEN GWYNN
From "Novels of American Life"
Edinburgh Review, April 1898, pp. 411–14

Mr. Crane merits consideration precisely as a stylist. He made his mark, by universal acclamation, three or four years back, with the *Red Badge of Courage*, written when he was twenty-one. This book is an elaborate study of the psychological experiences undergone by a recruit. It has value not as a record, but as a *tour de force* of the imagination, for Mr. Crane had never seen war; so it is not surprising that many soldiers dissent from his theory of the emotions of combat. According to Mr. Crane, everything passes in a red haze; men advance or retreat as if in a lurid dream; they are something quite different from their everyday selves. A very clever man, who has seen no lack of fighting, Colonel Baden-Powell, comments in a record of South African war upon this theory, read by him somewhere out in the veldt. Man, upon his view, goes into action very much as he goes into a game of football; he is simply more alert, more high-strung, more completely alive, though, in consequence of the tension, subject to fits of blind fury. It must, however, be said that Mr. Crane in his story does not generalise; he takes a single type and individual emotions. Still we have the misfortune not to find credible the processes by which the recruit is coward one day and hero the next; as a psychological document his book appears to us valueless. But there is no doubt that certain impressions of war detach themselves strongly in his work; the blind actions of men, moved by masses, they know not where or why; their total ignorance of whatever lies beyond eyeshot or earshot, the uncertainty as to whether the various movements spell victory or defeat. And certain scenes—the rush across an open against a wood set thick with riflemen, or the sudden coming upon a corpse in a thicket—present themselves to the senses as vividly as in life. That is, of course, Mr. Crane's object, to stimulate sense-perceptions by the use of words. The thing done is very clever, but is it agreeable? He wants, in the first place, to get an impression of confused masses of men weltering through a forest amid a deafening noise; and words are heaped on words to render this, till one feels as if one had been beaten about the head with epithets. Every device is used to quicken the jaded faculty of image-making; words are violently flung together in fanciful collocations and outlandish metaphors; you read of red shouts and green smells, flags 'shaking with laughter,' and cannon talking to each other, 'slightly casual, unexcited in their challenges and warnings.' Men speak, not language, but half-articulate yelps, barely recognisable in their distorted spelling for words. One reads, one thinks how clever it is, and one puts away the book with a sense of relief, feeling as if one had been seeing a curious gymnastic contortion or feat of strength. It is so evident that here is a man straining every nerve to get a certain result, not so much trying to make his readers see as trying to force his own imagination into seeing. Here, for instance, is a picture from *The Little Regiment*, Mr. Crane's volume of short studies of war—a better book than *The Red Badge*, to our thinking:—

> In one mystic changing of the fog as if the fingers of spirits were drawing aside these draperies, a small group of the grey skirmishers, silent, statuesque, were suddenly disclosed to Dan and those about him. So vivid and near were they that there was something uncanny in the revelation. There might have been a second of mutual wonder. Then each rifle in the group was at the shoulder. As Dan's glance flashed along the barrel of his weapon, the figure of a man suddenly loomed as if the musket had been a telescope. The short black beard, the slouch hat, the pose of the man as he sighted to shoot, made a quick picture in Dan's mind. The same moment, it would seem, he pulled his own trigger, and the man, smitten, lurched forward, while his exploding rifle made a slanting crimson streak in the air, and the slouch hat fell before the body. The billows of the fog, governed by singular impulses, rolled in between.
>
> "You got that feller sure enough," said a comrade to Dan. Dan looked at him absent-mindedly.

If a man were in a fight, would he be thinking of shapes and colours like this? Does a man in a football match have similar impressions? Dan, be it observed, is a veteran; the recruit may have naturally such a confusion of ideas as would be in the mind of a young foreigner put into a side of Rugby football and told to play without knowing the rules. Mr. Crane's description of war does not convince like Mr. Kipling's, in so far as it describes the emotions; it shows entirely false beside what we should take for the touchstone in these matters—Sir Charles Napier's account of his experiences at Corunna. In so far as it aims at rendering external impressions of sight, it seems to us radically bad art, because it tries to do with words what should be done with lines and colours. It may be confidently said that no one unacquainted with the methods of modern impressionist art on canvas will see the pictures that Mr. Crane is trying to convey; and those who are acquainted with them will see that he sees the thing not directly, but, as it were, translated into paint.

Mr. Crane is too young to have written a good novel, and *The Third Violet*, his only attempt at the ordinary story of familiar life, is simply amazing in its futility. But he has written a short study of New York slums which may compare with Mr. Arthur Morrison's Jago sketches and Mr. Maugham's *Liza of Lambeth*. *Maggie* appears with a prefatory commendation from Mr. Howells. We have no objection to stories of slum life; Mr. R. H. Davies's *Gallegher* is a wonderful and attractive picture of the New York street-arab. But *Maggie* does not seem to us to justify its existence. Given a drunken father, a drunken mother, and their children, a pretty girl and a boy, stunted but as brave as a weasel; this is very likely how the lives will shape themselves. Tragic pathos there certainly is in the girl's devotion to her swaggering lover, a fighting bartender, who deserts her without the shadow of compunction. But it seems as if one needed more than this to repay one for wading through such a mass of revolting details—street fights of little boys, fights of grown men in bars, scenes in dirty beer saloons, and everywhere the dialect of the Bowery, which, as Mr. Crane writes it, is the most hideous representation of human speech that we have ever met with. One may read a book like this as a tract, to keep one alive to the misery existent somewhere in the world; but we can conceive no other motive for reading it. As a work of art we disbelieve in it. Take Mr. Maugham's *Liza*, a work equally unsparing and in some ways more revolting; here you have at least credible human beings, with natural affections. In Mr. Crane's book Maggie's passion for Pete is the one trace of human coherence; there is no other tie between any two of the characters. It is an impression; that is to say, a study made to emphasise certain traits; and an impression of sheer brutality. The admiration for work of this sort savours of the latest modern cant, which preaches that to see things artistically you must see them disagreeably. Mr. Crane has seen a piece of life in a hard superficial way, and rendered it in the spirit of a caricaturist. That is the true formula for producing what, in the cant of the day, is called uncompromising realism.

Mr. Crane, however, stands by himself, and we trust that with advancing maturity he may slough this crude and violent mannerism, alien to all the old traditions of delicacy and reserve whether in style or subject. He has too much talent to be wasted in a wild-goose chase after the ideal of gentlemen in France who write sonnets describing the colours of different vowels. For the present he alone among the writers we have dealt with affords us no human document; his folk in the Bowery have neither country nor class; all he offers is a distorted psychology of combat and an exaggerated theory of style. Yet it is of the essence of talent to go wrong at first and to run into mannerisms.

WILLA CATHER
"When I Knew Stephen Crane"
Library, June 23, 1900

It was, I think, in the spring of '95, that a slender, narrow-chested fellow in a shabby grey suit, with a soft felt hat pulled low over his eyes, sauntered into the office of the managing editor of the *Nebraska State Journal* and introduced himself as Stephen Crane. He stated that he was going to Mexico to do some work for the Bacheller Syndicate and get rid of his cough, and that he would be stopping in Lincoln for a few days. Later he explained that he was out of money and would be compelled to wait until he got a check from the East before he went further. I was a Junior at the Nebraska State University at the time, and was doing some work for the *State Journal* in my leisure time, and I happened to be in the managing editor's room when Mr. Crane introduced himself. I was just off the range: I knew a little Greek and something about cattle and a good horse when I saw one, and beyond horses and cattle I considered nothing of vital importance except good stories and the people who wrote them. This was

the first man of letters I had ever met in the flesh, and when the young man announced who he was, I dropped into a chair behind the editor's desk where I could stare at him without being too much in evidence.

Only a very youthful enthusiasm and a large propensity for hero worship could have found anything impressive in the young man who stood before the managing editor's desk. He was thin to emaciation, his face was gaunt and unshaven, a thin dark moustache straggled on his upper lip, his black hair grew low on his forehead and was shaggy and unkempt. His grey clothes were much the worse for wear and fitted him so badly it seemed unlikely he had ever been measured for them. He wore a flannel shirt and a slovenly apology for a necktie, and his shoes were dusty and worn gray about the toes and were badly run over at the heel. I had seen many a tramp printer come up the *Journal* stairs to hunt a job, but never one who presented such a disreputable appearance as this story-maker man. He wore gloves which seemed rather a contradiction to the general slovenliness of his attire, but when he took them off to search his pockets for his credentials, I noticed that his hands were singularly fine; long, white, and delicately shaped, with thin, nervous fingers. I have seen pictures of Aubrey Beardsley's hands that recalled Crane's very vividly.

At that time Crane was but twenty-four, and almost an unknown man. Hamlin Garland had seen some of his work and believed in him, and introduced him to Mr. Howells, who recommended him to the Bacheller Syndicate. *The Red Badge of Courage* had been published in the *State Journal* that winter along with a lot of other syndicate matter, and the grammatical construction of the story was so faulty that the managing editor had several times called on me to edit the copy. In this way I had read it very carefully, and through the careless sentence-structure I saw the wonder of that remarkable performance. But the grammar certainly was bad. I remember one of the reporters who had corrected the phrase "it don't" for the tenth time remarked savagely, "If I couldn't write better English than this, I'd quit."

Crane spent several days in the town, living from hand to mouth and waiting for his money. I think he borrowed a small amount from the managing editor. He lounged about the office most of the time, and I frequently encountered him going in and out of the cheap restaurants on Tenth Street. When he was at the office he talked a good deal in a wandering, absent-minded fashion, and his conversation was uniformly frivolous. If he could not evade a serious question by a joke, he bolted. I cut my classes to lie in wait for him, confident that in some unwary moment I could trap him into serious conversation, that if one burned incense long enough and ardently enough, the oracle would not be dumb. I was Maupassant mad at that time, a malady particularly unattractive in a Junior, and I made a frantic effort to get an expression of opinion from him on *Le Bonheur*. "Oh, you're Moping, are you?" he remarked with a sarcastic grin, and went on reading a little volume of Poe that he carried in his pocket. At another time I cornered him in the Funny Man's room and succeeded in getting a little out of him. We were taught literature by an exceedingly analytical method at the University, and we probably distorted the method, and I was busy trying to find the least common multiple of *Hamlet* and greatest common divisor of *Macbeth*, and I began asking him whether stories were constructed by cabalistic formulae. At length he sighed wearily and shook his drooping shoulders, remarking:

"Where did you get all that rot? Yarns aren't done by mathematics. You can't do it by rule any more than you can dance by rule. You have to have the itch of the thing in your fingers, and if you haven't,—well, you're damned lucky, and you'll live long and prosper, that's all."—And with that he yawned and went down the hall.

Crane was moody most of the time; his health was bad and he seemed profoundly discouraged. Even his jokes were exceedingly drastic. He went about with the tense, preoccupied, self-centered air of a man who is brooding over some impending disaster, and I conjectured vainly as to what it might be. Though he was seemingly entirely idle during the few days I knew him, his manner indicated that he was in the throes of work that told terribly on his nerves. His eyes I remember as the finest I have ever seen, large and dark and full of lustre and changing lights, but with a profound melancholy always lurking deep in them. They were eyes that seemed to be burning themselves out.

As he sat at the desk with his shoulders drooping forward, his head low, and his long, white fingers drumming on the sheets of copy paper, he was as nervous as a race horse fretting to be on the track. Always, as he came and went about the halls, he seemed like a man preparing for a sudden departure. Now that he is dead it occurs to me that all his life was a preparation for sudden departure. I remember once when he was writing a letter he stopped and asked me about the spelling of a word, saying carelessly, "I haven't time to learn to spell." Then, glancing down at his attire, he added with an absent-minded smile, "I haven't time to dress either; it takes an awful slice out of a fellow's life."

He said he was poor, and he certainly looked it, but four years later when he was in Cuba, drawing the largest salary ever paid a newspaper correspondent, he clung to this same untidy manner of dress, and his ragged overalls and buttonless shirt were eyesores to the immaculate Mr. Davis, in his spotless linen and neat khaki uniform, with his Gibson chin always freshly shaven. When I first heard of his serious illness, his old throat trouble aggravated into consumption by his reckless exposure in Cuba, I recalled a passage from Maeterlinck's essay, "The Pre-Destined," on those doomed to early death: "As children, life seems nearer to them than to other children. They appear to know nothing, and yet there is in their eyes so profound a certainty that we feel they must know all.—In all haste, but wisely and with minute care do they prepare themselves to live, and this very haste is a sign upon which mothers can scarce bring themselves to look." I remembered, too, the man's melancholy and his tenseness, his burning eyes, and his way of slurring over the less important things, as one whose time is short.

I have heard other people say how difficult it was to induce Crane to talk seriously about his work, and I suspect that he was particularly averse to discussions with literary men of wider education and better equipment than himself, yet he seemed to feel that this fuller culture was not for him. Perhaps the unreasoning instinct which lies deep in the roots of our lives, and which guides us all, told him that he had not time enough to acquire it.

Men will sometimes reveal themselves to children, or to people whom they think never to see again, more completely than they ever do to their confreres. From the wise we hold back alike our folly and our wisdom, and for the recipients of our deeper confidences we seldom select our equals. The soul has no message for the friends with whom we dine every week. It is silenced by custom and convention, and we play only in the shallows. It selects its listeners willfully, and seemingly delights to waste its best upon the chance wayfarer who meets us in the highway at a fated hour. There are moments too, when the tides run high or very low, when self-revelation is necessary to every man, if it be only to his valet or his gardener. At such a moment, I was with Mr. Crane.

The hoped for revelation came unexpectedly enough. It was on the last night he spent in Lincoln. I had come back from the theatre and was in the *Journal* office writing a notice of the play. It was eleven o'clock when Crane came in. He had expected his money to arrive on the night mail and it had not done so, and he was out of sorts and deeply despondent. He sat down on the ledge of the open window that faced on the street, and when I had finished my notice I went over and took a chair beside him. Quite without invitation on my part, Crane began to talk, began to curse his trade from the first throb of creative desire in a boy to the finished work of the master. The night was oppresively warm; one of those dry winds that are the curse of that country was blowing up from Kansas. The white, western moonlight threw sharp, blue shadows below us. The streets were silent at that hour, and we could hear the gurgle of the fountain in the Post Office square across the street, and the twang of banjos from the lower veranda of the Hotel Lincoln, where the colored waiters were serenading the guests. The drop lights in the office were dull under their green shades, and the telegraph sounder clicked faintly in the next room. In all his long tirade, Crane never raised his voice; he spoke slowly and monotonously and even calmly, but I have never known so bitter a heart in any man as he revealed to me that night. It was an arraignment of the wages of life, an invocation to the ministers of hate.

Incidentally he told me the sum he had received for *The Red Badge of Courage*, which I think was something like ninety dollars, and he repeated some lines from *The Black Riders*, which was then in preparation. He gave me to understand that he led a double literary life; writing in the first place the matter that pleased himself, and doing it very slowly; in the second place, any sort of stuff that would sell. And he remarked that his poor was just as bad as it could possibly be. He realized he said, that his limitations were absolutely impassable. "What I can't do, I can't do at all, and I can't acquire it. I only hold one trump."

He had no settled plans at all. He was going to Mexico wholly uncertain of being able to do any successful work there, and he seemed to feel very insecure about the financial end of his venture. The thing that most interested me was what he said about his slow method of composition. He declared that there was little money in story-writing at best, and practically none in it for him, because of the time it took him to work up his detail. Other men, he said, could sit down and write up an experience while the physical effect of it, so to speak, was still upon them, and yesterday's impressions made to-day's "copy". But when he came in from the streets to write up what he had seen there, his faculties were benumbed, and he sat twirling his pencil and hunting for words like a schoolboy.

I mentioned *The Red Badge of Courage*, which was written in nine days, and he replied that, though the writing took very little time, he had been unconsciously working the detail of the story out through most of his boyhood. His ancestors had been soldiers, and he had been imagining war stories ever since he was out of knickerbockers, and in writing his first war story he had simply gone over his imaginary campaigns and selected his favorite imaginary experiences. He declared that his imagination was hide-bound; it was there, but it pulled hard. After he got a notion for a story, months passed before he could get any sort of personal contract with it, or feel any potency to handle it. "The detail of a thing has to filter through my blood, and then it comes out like a native product, but it takes forever," he remarked. I distinctly remember the illustration, for it rather took hold of me.

I have often been astonished since to hear Crane spoken of as "the reporter in fiction," for the reportorial faculty of superficial reception and quick transference was what he conspicuously lacked. His first newspaper account of his shipwreck on the filibuster *Commodore* off the Florida coast was as lifeless as the "copy" of a police court reporter. It was many months afterwards that the literary product of his terrible experience appeared in that marvellous sea story "The Open Boat," unsurpassed in its vividness and constructive perfection.

At the close of our long conversation that night, when the copy boy came in to take me home, I suggested to Crane that in ten years he would probably laugh at all his temporary discomfort. Again his body took on that strenuous tension and he clenched his hands, saying, "I can't wait ten years, I haven't time."

The ten years are not up yet, and he has done his work and gathered his reward and gone. Was ever so much experience and achievement crowded into so short a space of time? A great man dead at twenty-nine! That would have puzzled the ancients. Edward Garnett wrote of him in *The Academy* of December 17, 1899: "I cannot remember a parallel in the literary history of fiction. Maupassant, Meredith, Henry James, Mr. Howells and Tolstoy, were all learning their expression at an age where Crane had achieved his and achieved it triumphantly." He had the precocity of those doomed to die in youth. I am convinced that when I met him he had a vague premonition of the shortness of his working day, and in the heart of the man there was that which said, "That thou doest, do quickly."

At twenty-one this son of an obscure New Jersey rector, with but a scant reading knowledge of French and no training had rivaled in technique the foremost craftsmen of the Latin races. In the six years since I met him, a stranded reporter, he stood in the firing line during two wars, knew hairbreadth escapes on land and sea, and established himself as the first writer of his time in the picturing of episodic, fragmentary life. His friends have charged him with fickleness, but he was a man who was in the preoccupation of haste. He went from country to country, from man to man, absorbing all that was in them for him. He had no time to look backward. He had no leisure for *camaraderie*. He drank life to the lees, but at the banquet table where other men took their ease and jested over their wine, he stood a dark and silent figure, sombre as Poe himself, not wishing to be understood; and he took his portion in haste, with his loins girded, and his shoes on his feet, and his staff in his hand, like one who must depart quickly.

HAMLIN GARLAND
"Stephen Crane: A Soldier of Fortune"
Saturday Evening Post, July 28, 1900

The death of Stephen Crane, far away in the mountains of Bavaria, seems to me at this moment a very sorrowful thing. He should have continued to be one of our most distinctive literary workers for many years to come. And yet I cannot say I am surprised. His was not the physical organization that runs to old age. He was old at twenty.

It happened that I knew Crane when he was a boy and have had some years exceptional opportunities for studying him. In the summer of 1888 or 1889 I was lecturing for a seaside assembly at Avon, New Jersey. The report of my first lecture (on "The Local Novelists," by the way) was exceedingly well done in the *Tribune,* and I asked for the name of the

reporter. "He is a mere boy," was the reply of Mr. Albert, the manager of the assembly, "and his name is Stephen Crane."

Crane came to see me the following evening, and turned out to be a reticent young fellow, with a big German pipe in his mouth. He was small, sallow and inclined to stoop, but sinewy and athletic for all that—for we fell to talk of sports, and he consented to practice baseball pitching with me. I considered him at this time a very good reporter, and a capital catcher of curved balls—no more, and I said goodby to him two weeks later with no expectation of ever seeing him again.

In the summer of '91, if I do not mistake, I was visiting Mr. and Mrs. Albert at their school in New York City, when a curious book came to me by mail. It was a small yellow-covered volume, hardly more than a pamphlet, without a publisher's imprint. The author's name was Johnston Smith. The story was called *Maggie, a Girl of the Streets,* and the first paragraph described the battle of some street urchins with so much insight and with such unusual and vivid use of English that I became very much excited about it. Next day I mailed the book to Mr. Howells, in order that he might share the discovery with me. The author had the genius which makes an old world new.

On that very afternoon Crane called upon me and confessed that he had written the book and had not been able to get any one to publish it. Even the firm of printers that put it together refused to place their imprint upon it. He said that the bulk of the edition remained unsold, and that he had sent the book to a number of critics and also to several ministers. On the cover of each copy (as on mine) was written, in diagonal lines, these words or their substance in Crane's beautiful script: "The reader of this story must inevitably be shocked, but let him persist, and in the end he will find this story to be moral." I cannot remember exactly the quaint terms of this admonition, but these words give the idea.

I said to him: "I hardly dare tell you how good that story is. I have sent it to Mr. Howells as a 'find.' Go and see him when he has read it. I am sure he will like it."

He then told me that he had been discharged from the staff of the *Tribune.* He seemed to be greatly encouraged by our conversation, and when he went away I talked with his friends about the book, which appealed to me with great power. I have it still. This desperate attempt of a young author to get a hearing is amusing to an outsider, but it was serious business with Crane then.

I did not see him again until the autumn of 1892, when I went to New York to spend the winter. He wrote occasionally, saying, "Things go pretty slow with me, but I manage to live."

My brother Franklin was in Mr. Herne's Shore Acres Company in those days, and as they were playing an all-season engagement at Daly's theater we decided to take a little flat and camp together for the winter. Our flat was on One Hundred and Fifth street, and there Crane visited us two or three times a week. He was always hungry and a little gloomy when he came, but my brother made a point of having an extra chop or steak ready for a visitor and Crane often chirped like a bird when he had finished dinner. We often smiled over it then, but it is a pleasure to us now to think we were able to cheer him when he needed it most.

He was living at this time with a group of artists—"Indians," he called them—in the old studio building on East Twenty-third street. I never called to see him there, but he often set forth their doings with grim humor. Most of them slept on the floor and painted on towels, according to his report. Sometimes they ate, but they all smoked most villainous tobacco, for Crane smelled so powerfully of their "smoketalks" that he filled our rooms with the odor. His fingers were yellow with cigarette reek, and he looked like a man badly nourished.

This crowd of artists, according to his story, spent their days in sleep and their nights in "pow-wows" around a big table where they beat and clamored and assaulted each other under a canopy of tobacco smoke. They hated the world. They were infuriated with all hanging committees and art editors, and each man believed religiously in his own genius. Linson was one of those Crane mentioned, and Vosburgh and Green. Together they covenanted to go out some bleak day and slay all the editors and art critics of the city.

Crane at this time wore a light check suit and over it a long gray ulster which had seen much service. His habitual expression was a grim sort of smile. One day he appeared in my study with his outside pockets bulging with two rolls of manuscript. As he entered he turned ostentatiously to put down his hat, and so managed to convey to my mind an impression that he was concealing something. His manner was embarrassed, as if he had come to do a thing and was sorry about it.

"Come now, out with it," I said. "What is the roll I see in your pocket?"

With a sheepish look he took out a fat roll of legal cap paper and handed it to me with a careless, boyish gesture.

"There's another," I insisted, and he still more abruptly delivered himself of another but smaller parcel.

I unrolled the first package, and found it to be a sheaf of poems. I can see the initial poem now, exactly as it was then written, without a blot or erasure—almost without punctuation—in blue ink. It was beautifully legible and clean of outline.

It was the poem which begins thus:

"God fashioned the ship of the world carefully."

I read this with delight and amazement. I rushed through the others, some thirty in all, with growing wonder. I could not believe they were the work of the pale, reticent boy moving restlessly about the room.

"Have you any more?" I asked.

"I've got five or six all in a little row up here," he quaintly replied, pointing to his temple. "That's the way they come—in little rows, all made up, ready to be put down on paper."

"When did you write these?"

"Oh! I've been writing five or six every day. I wrote nine yesterday. I wanted to write some more last night, but those 'Indians' wouldn't let me do it. They howled over the other verses so loud they nearly cracked my ears. You see, we all live in a box together, and I've no place to write, except in the general squabble. They think my lines are funny. They make a circus of me." All this with a note of exaggeration, of course.

"Never you mind," I replied; "don't you do a thing till you put all these verses down on paper."

"I've got to eat," he said, and his smile was not pleasant.

"Well, let's consider. Can't we get some work for you to do? Some of these press syndicate men have just been after me to do short stories for them. Can't you do something there?"

"I'll try," he said, without much resolution. "I don't seem to be the kind of writer they want. The newspapers can't see me at all."

"Well, now, let's see what can be done. I'll give you a letter to Mr. Flower, of the *Arena*, and one to Mr. Howells. And I want to take these poems to Mr. Howells to-morrow; I'm sure he'll help you. He's kind to all who struggle."

Later in the meal I said: "Why don't you go down and do a study of this midnight bread distribution which the papers are making so much of? Mr. Howells suggested it to me, but it isn't my field. It is yours. You could do it beyond anybody."

"I might do that," he said; "it interests me."

"Come to-morrow to luncheon," I said, as he went away visibly happier. "Perhaps I'll have something to report."

I must confess I took the lines seriously. If they were direct output of this unaccountable boy, then America had produced another genius, singular as Poe. I went with them at once to Mr. Howells, whose wide reading I knew and relied upon. He read them with great interest, and immediately said:

"They do not seem to relate directly to the work of any other writer. They seem to be the work of a singularly creative mind. Of course they reflect the author's reading and sympathies, but they are not imitations."

When Crane came next day he brought the first part of a war story which was at that time without a name. The first page of this was as original as the verses, and it passed at once to the description of a great battle. Such mastery of details of war was sufficiently startling in a youth of twenty-one who had never smelled any more carnage than a firecracker holds, but the seeing was so keen, the phrases so graphic, so fresh, so newly coined, that I dared not express to the boy's face my admiration. I asked him to leave the story with me. I said:

"Did you do any more 'lines'?"

He looked away bashfully.

"Only six."

"Let me see them."

As he handed them to me he said: "Got three more waiting in line. I could do one now."

"Sit down and try," I said, glad of his offer, for I could not relate the man to his work.

He took a seat and began to write steadily, composedly, without hesitation or blot or interlineation, and so produced in my presence one of his most powerful verses. It flowed from his pen as smooth as oil.

The next day I asked for the other half of the novel. "We must get it published at once," I said. "It is a wonderful study. A mysterious product for you to have in hand. Where is the other part?"

He looked very much embarrassed. "It's in 'hock,'" he said.

"To whom?"

"To the typewriter."

We all laughed, but it was serious business to him. He could see the humor of the situation, but there was a bitter rebellion in his voice.

"How much is it 'hung up' for?"

"Fifteen dollars."

I looked at my brother. "I guess we can spare that, don't you think?"

So Crane went away joyously and brought the last half of *The Red Badge of Courage*, still unnamed at the time. He told us that the coming of that story was just as mysterious as in the case of the verses, and I can believe it. It literally came of its own accord like sap flowing from a tree.

I gave him such words of encouragement as I could. "Your future is secure. A man who can write *The Red Badge of Courage* can not be forever a lodger in a bare studio."

He replied: "That may be, but if I had some money to buy a new suit of clothes I'd feel my grip tighten on the future."

"You'll laugh at all this—we all go through it," said I.

"It's ridiculous, but it doesn't make me laugh," he said, soberly.

My predictions of his immediate success did not come true. *The Red Badge of Courage* and *Maggie* were put through the Syndicate with very slight success. They left Crane almost as poor as before.

In one of his letters, in April, he wrote: "I have not been up to see you because of various strange conditions—notably my toes coming through one shoe, and I have not been going out into society as much as I might. I mail you last Sunday's *Press*. I've moved now—live in a flat. People can come to see me now. They come in shoals, and say I am a great writer. Counting five that are sold, four that are unsold and six that are mapped out, I have fifteen short stories in my head and out of it. They'll make a book. The *Press* people pied some of *Maggie*, as you will note."

I saw little of him during '93 and '94, but a letter written in May, '94, revealed his condition:

"I have not written you because there has been little to tell of late. I am plodding along on the *Press* in a quiet and effective way. We now eat with charming regularity at least two times a day. I am content and am now writing another novel which is a bird. . . . I am getting lots of free advertising. Everything is coming along nicely now. I have got the poetic spout so that I can turn it on and off. I wrote a Decoration Day thing for the *Press* which aroused them to enthusiasm. They said in about a minute, though, that I was firing over the heads of the soldiers."

His allusion to free advertising means that the critics were wrangling over *The Black Riders* and *Maggie*. But the public was not interested. I had given him a letter to a Syndicate Press Company, and with them he had left the manuscript of his war novel. In a letter written in November, 1894, he makes sad mention of his lack of success:

"My Dear Friend: So much of my row with the world has to be silence and endurance that sometimes I wear the appearance of having forgotten my best friends, those to whom I am indebted for everything. As a matter of fact, I have just crawled out of the fifty-third ditch into which I have been cast, and now I feel that I can write you a letter which will not make you ill.——put me in one of the ditches. He kept *The Red Badge* six months until I was near mad. Oh, yes—he was going to use it but—Finally I took it to B. They use it in January in a shortened form. I have just completed a New York book that leaves *Maggie* at the post. It is my best thing. Since you are not here I am going to see if Mr. Howells will not read it. I am still working for the *Press*."

At this point his affairs took a sudden turn, and he was made the figure I had hoped to see him two years before. The English critics spoke in highest praise of *The Red Badge*, and the book became the critical bone of contention between military objectors and literary enthusiasts here at home, and Crane became the talk of the day. He was accepted as a very remarkable literary man of genius.

He was too brilliant, too fickle, too erratic to last. Men cannot go on doing stories like *The Red Badge of Courage*. The danger with such highly individual work lies in this—the words which astonish, the phrases which excite wonder and admiration, come eventually to seem like tricks. They lose force with repetition, and come at last to be absolutely distasteful. *The Red Badge of Courage* was marvelous, but manifestly Crane could not go on doing such work. If he wrote in conventional phrase, his power lessened. If he continued to write in his own phrases he came under the charge of repeating himself.

It seems now that he was destined from the first to be a sort of present-day Poe. His was a singular and daring soul, as irresponsible as the wind. He was a man to be called a genius, for we call that power genius which we do not easily under-

stand or measure. I have never known a man whose source of power was so unaccounted for.

The fact of the matter seems to be this. Crane's mind was more largely subconscious in its workings than that of most men. He did not understand his own mental processes or resources. When he put pen to paper he found marvelous words, images, sentences, pictures already to be drawn off and fixed upon paper. His pen was "a spout," as he says. The farther he got from his own field, his own inborn tendency, the weaker he became. Such a man cannot afford to enter the white-hot public thoroughfare, for his genius is of the lonely and the solitary shadow-land.

H. G. WELLS
From "Stephen Crane: From an English Standpoint"
North American Review, August 1900, pp. 233–42

The untimely death at thirty of Stephen Crane robs English literature of an interesting and significant figure, and the little world of those who write, of a stout friend and a pleasant comrade. For a year and more he had been ailing. The bitter hardships of his Cuban expedition had set its mark upon mind and body alike, and the slow darkling of the shadow upon him must have been evident to all who were not blinded by their confidence in what he was yet to do. Altogether, I knew Crane for less than a year, and I saw him for the last time hardly more than seven weeks ago. He was then in a hotel at Dover, lying still and comfortably wrapped about, before an open window and the calm and spacious sea. If you would figure him as I saw him, you must think of him as a face of a type very typically American, long and spare, with very straight hair and straight features and long, quiet hands and hollow eyes, moving slowly, smiling and speaking slowly, with that deliberate New Jersey manner he had, and lapsing from speech again into a quiet contemplation of his ancient enemy. For it was the sea that had taken his strength, the same sea that now shone, level waters beyond level waters, with here and there a minute, shining ship, warm and tranquil beneath the tranquil evening sky. Yet I felt scarcely a suspicion then that this was a last meeting. One might have seen it all, perhaps. He was thin and gaunt and wasted, too weak for more than a remembered jest and a greeting and good wishes. It did not seem to me in any way credible that he would reach his refuge in the Black Forest only to die at the journey's end. It will be a long time yet before I can fully realize that he is no longer a contemporary of mine; that the last I saw of him was, indeed, final and complete.

Though my personal acquaintance with Crane was so soon truncated, I have followed his work for all the four years it has been known in England. I have always been proud, and now I am glad, that, however obscurely, I also was in the first chorus of welcome that met his coming. It is, perhaps, no great distinction for me; he was abundantly praised; but, at least, I was early and willing to praise him when I was wont to be youthfully jealous of my praises. His success in England began with *The Red Badge of Courage*, which did, indeed, more completely than any other book has done for many years, take the reading public by storm. Its freshness of method, its vigor of imagination, its force of color and its essential freedom from many traditions that dominate this side of the Atlantic, came—in spite of the previous shock of Mr. Kipling—with a positive effect of impact. It was a new thing, in a new school. When one looked for sources, one thought at once of Tolstoi; but, though it was clear that Tolstoi had exerted a powerful influence upon the conception, if not the actual writing, of the book, there still remained something entirely original and novel. To a certain extent, of course, that was the new man as an individual; but, to at least an equal extent, it was the new man as a typical young American, free at last, as no generation of Americans have been free before, of any regard for English criticism, comment or tradition, and applying to literary work the conception and theories of the cosmopolitan studio with a quite American directness and vigor. For the great influence of the studio on Crane cannot be ignored; in the persistent selection of the essential elements of an impression, in the ruthless exclusion of mere information, in the direct vigor with which the selected points are made, there is Whistler even more than there is Tolstoi in *The Red Badge of Courage*. And witness this, taken almost haphazard:

> At nightfall the column broke into regimental pieces, and the fragments went into the fields to camp. Tents sprang up like strange plants. Camp fires, like red, peculiar blossoms, dotted the night. . . . From this little distance the many fires, with the black forms of men passing to and fro before the crimson rays, made weird and satanic effects.

And here again; consider the daring departure from all academic requirements, in this void countenance:

> A warm and strong hand clasped the youth's languid fingers for an instant, and then he heard a cheerful and audacious whistling as the man strode away. As he who had so befriended him was thus passing out of his life, it suddenly occurred to the youth that he had not once seen his face.

I do not propose to add anything here to the mass of criticism upon this remarkable book. Like everything else which has been abundantly praised, it has occasionally been praised "all wrong;" and I suppose that it must have been said hundreds of times that this book is a subjective study of the typical soldier in war. But Mr. George Wyndham, himself a soldier of experience, has pointed out in an admirable preface to a re-issue of this and other of Crane's war studies, that the hero of the *Red Badge* is, and is intended to be, altogether a more sensitive and imaginative person than the ordinary man. He is the idealist, the dreamer of boastful things brought suddenly to the test of danger and swift occasions and the presence of death. To this theme Crane returned several times, and particularly in a story called "Death and the Child" that was written after the Greek war. That story is considered by very many of Crane's admirers as absolutely his best. I have carefully re-read it in deference to opinions I am bound to respect, but I still find it inferior to the earlier work. The generalized application is, to my taste, a little too evidently underlined; there is just that touch of insistence that prevails so painfully at times in Victor Hugo's work, as of a writer not sure of his reader, not happy in his reader and seeking to drive his implication (of which also he is not quite sure) home. The child is not a natural child; there is no happy touch to make it personally alive; it is THE CHILD, something unfalteringly big; a large, pink, generalized thing, I cannot help but see it, after the fashion of a Vatican cherub. The fugitive runs panting to where, all innocent of the battle about it, it plays; and he falls down breathless to be asked, "Are you a man?" One sees the intention clearly enough; but in the later story it seems to me there is a new ingredient that is absent from the earlier stories, an ingredient imposed on Crane's natural genius from without—a concession to the demands of a criticism it had been wiser, if less modest, in him to disregard—criticism that

missed this quality of generalization and demanded it, even though it had to be artificially and deliberately introduced.

Following hard upon the appearance of *The Red Badge of Courage* in England came reprints of two books, *Maggie* and *George's Mother*, that had already appeared in America six years earlier. Their reception gave Crane his first taste of the peculiarities of the new public he had come upon. These stories seem to me in no way inferior to the *Red Badge*; and at times there are passages, the lament of Maggie's mother at the end of *Maggie*, for example, that it would be hard to beat by any passage from the later book. But on all hands came discouragement or tepid praise. The fact of it is, there had been almost an orgie of praise—for England, that is; and ideas and adjectives and phrases were exhausted. To write further long reviews on works displaying the same qualities as had been already amply discussed in the notices of the *Red Badge* would be difficult and laborious; while to admit an equal excellence and deny an equal prominence would be absurd. But to treat these stories as early work, to find them immature, dismiss them and proceed to fresher topics, was obvious and convenient. So it was, I uncharitably imagine, that these two tales have been overshadowed and are still comparatively unknown. Yet, they are absolutely essential to a just understanding of Crane. In these stories, and in these alone, he achieved tenderness and a compulsion of sympathy for other than vehement emotions, qualities that the readers of *The Third Violet* and *On Active Service*, his later love stories, might well imagine beyond his reach.

And upon the appearance of these books in England came what, in my present mood, I cannot but consider as the great blunder and misfortune of Crane's life. It is a trait of the public we writers serve, that to please it is to run the gravest risk of never writing again. Through a hundred channels and with a hundred varieties of seduction and compulsion, the public seeks to induce its favorite to do something else—to act, to lecture, to travel, to jump down volcanoes or perform in music halls, to do anything, rather than to possess his soul in peace and to pursue the work he was meant to do. Indeed, this modern public is as violently experimental with its writers as a little child with a kitten. It is animated, above all things, by an insatiable desire to plunge its victim into novel surroundings, and watch how he feels. And since Crane had demonstrated, beyond all cavil, that he could sit at home and, with nothing but his wonderful brain and his wonderful induction from recorded things, build up the truest and most convincing picture of war; since he was a fastidious and careful worker, intensely subjective in his mental habit; since he was a man of fragile physique and of that unreasonable courage that will wreck the strongest physique; and since, moreover, he was habitually a bad traveller, losing trains and luggage and missing connections even in the orderly circumstances of peace, it was clearly the most reasonable thing in the world to propose, it was received with the applause of two hemispheres as a most right and proper thing, that he should go as a war correspondent, first to Greece and then to Cuba. Thereby, and for nothing but disappointment and bitterness, he utterly wrecked his health. He came into comparison with men as entirely his masters in this work as he was the master of all men in his own; and I read even in the most punctual of his obituary notices the admission of his journalistic failure. I have read, too, that he brought back nothing from these expeditions. But, indeed, even not counting his death, he brought back much. On his way home from Cuba he was wrecked, and he wrote the story of the nights and days that followed the sinking of the ship with a simplicity and vigor that even he cannot rival elsewhere.

"The Open Boat" is to my mind, beyond all question, the

crown of all his work. It has all the stark power of the earlier stories, with a new element of restraint; the color is as full and strong as ever, fuller and stronger, indeed; but those chromatic splashes that at times deafen and confuse in *The Red Badge*, those images that astonish rather than enlighten, are disciplined and controlled. "That and 'Flanagan'," he told me, with a philosophical laugh, "was all I got out of Cuba." I cannot say whether they were worth the price, but I am convinced that these two things are as immortal as any work of any living man. ⟨. . .⟩

"The Open Boat" gives its title to a volume containing, in addition to that and "Flanagan," certain short pieces. One of these others, at least, is also to my mind a perfect thing, "The Wise Men." It tells of the race between two bar-tenders in the city of Mexico, and I cannot imagine how it could possibly have been better told. And in this volume, too, is that other masterpiece—the one I deny—"Death and the Child."

Now I do not know how Crane took the reception of this book, for he was not the man to babble of his wrongs; but I cannot conceive how it could have been anything but a grave disappointment to him. To use the silly phrase of the literary shopman, "the vogue of the short story" was already over; rubbish, pure rubbish, provided only it was lengthy, had resumed its former precedence again in the reviews, in the publishers' advertisements and on the library and book-sellers' counters. The book was taken as a trivial by-product, its author was exhorted to abandon this production of "brilliant fragments"—anything less than fifty thousand words is a fragment to the writer of literary columns—and to make that "sustained effort," that architectural undertaking, that alone impresses the commercial mind. Of course, the man who can call "The Open Boat" a brilliant fragment would reproach Rodin for not completing the edifice his brilliant fragments of statuary are presumably intended to adorn, and would sigh, with the late Mr. Ruskin for the day when Mr. Whistler would "finish" his pictures. Moreover, he was strongly advised—just as they have advised Mr. Kipling—to embark upon a novel. And from other quarters, where a finer wisdom might have been displayed, he learned that the things he had written were not "short stories" at all; they were "sketches" perhaps, "anecdotes"—just as they call Mr. Kipling's short stories "anecdotes;" and it was insinuated that for him also the true, the ineffable "short story" was beyond his reach. I think it is indisputable that the quality of this reception, which a more self-satisfied or less sensitive man than Crane might have ignored, did react very unfavorably upon his work. They put him out of conceit with these brief intense efforts in which his peculiar strength was displayed.

It was probably such influence that led him to write *The Third Violet*. I do not know certainly, but I imagine, that the book was to be a demonstration, and it is not a successful demonstration, that Crane could write a charming love story. It is the very simple affair of an art student and a summer boarder, with the more superficial incidents of their petty encounters set forth in a forcible, objective manner that is curiously hard and unsympathetic. The characters act, and on reflection one admits they act, *true*, but the play of their emotions goes on behind the curtain of the style, and all the enrichments of imaginative appeal that make love beautiful are omitted. Yet, though the story as a whole fails to satisfy, there are many isolated portions of altogether happy effectiveness, a certain ride behind an ox cart, for example. Much more surely is *On Active Service* an effort, and in places a painful effort, to fit his peculiar gift to the uncongenial conditions of popular acceptance. It is the least capable and least satisfactory of all Crane's work.

While these later books were appearing, and right up to his last fatal illness, Crane continued to produce fresh war pictures that show little or no falling off in vigor of imagination and handling; and, in addition, he was experimenting with verse. In that little stone-blue volume, *War Is Kind*, and in the earlier *Black Riders*, the reader will find a series of acute and vivid impressions and many of the finer qualities of Crane's descriptive prose, but he will not find any novel delights of melody or cadence or any fresh aspects of Crane's personality. There remain some children's stories to be published and an unfinished romance. With that the tale of his published work ends, and the career of one of the most brilliant, most significant and most distinctively American of all English writers comes to its unanticipated *finis*.

It would be absurd, here and now, to attempt to apportion any relativity of importance to Crane, to say that he was greater than A. or less important than B. That class-list business is, indeed, best left forever to the newspaper plebiscite and the library statistician; among artists, whose sole, just claim to recognition and whose sole title to immortality must necessarily be the possession of unique qualities, that is to say, of unclassifiable factors, these gradations are absurd. Suffice it that, even before his death, Crane's right to be counted in the hierarchy of those who have made a permanent addition to the great and growing fabric of English letters was not only assured, but conceded. To define his position in time, however, and in relation to periods and modes of writing will be a more reasonable undertaking; and it seems to me that, when at last the true proportions can be seen, Crane will be found to occupy a position singularly cardinal. He was a New Englander of Puritan lineage, and the son of a long tradition of literature. There had been many Cranes who wrote before him. He has shown me a shelf of books, for the most part the pious and theological works of various antecedent Stephen Cranes. He had been at some pains to gather together these alien products of his kin. For the most part they seemed little, insignificant books, and one opened them to read the beaten *clichés*, the battered outworn phrases, of a movement that has ebbed. Their very size and binding suggested a dying impulse, that very same impulse that in its prime had carried the magnificence of Milton's imagery and the pomp and splendors of Milton's prose. In Crane that impulse was altogether dead. He began stark—I find all through this brief notice I have been repeating that in a dozen disguises, "freedom from tradition," "absolute directness" and the like—as though he came into the world of letters without ever a predecessor. In style, in method and in all that is distinctively *not* found in his books, he is sharply defined, the expression in literary art of certain enormous repudiations. Was ever a man before who wrote of battles so abundantly as he has done, and never had a word, never a word from first to last, of the purpose and justification of the war? And of the God of Battles, no more than the battered name; "Hully Gee!"—the lingering trace of the Deity! And of the sensuousness and tenderness of love, so much as one can find in *The Third Violet*! Any richness of allusion, any melody or balance of phrase, the half quotation that refracts and softens and enriches the statement, the momentary digression that opens like a window upon beautiful or distant things, are not merely absent, but obviously and sedulously avoided. It is as if the racial thought and tradition had been razed from his mind and its site ploughed and salted. He is more than himself in this; he is the first expression of the opening mind of a new period, or, at least, the early emphatic phase of a new initiative—beginning, as a growing mind must needs begin, with the record of impressions, a record of a vigor and intensity beyond all precedent.

ADDITIONAL READING

WILLIAM MAKEPEACE THACKERAY

Brown, John. "Thackeray's Literary Career." In *Spare Hours: Second Series*. Boston: Houghton Mifflin, 1861, pp. 239–323.

Brownell, W. C. "William Makepeace Thackeray." *Scribner's Magazine* 25 (1899): 236–49.

Hotten, John Camden. *Thackeray: The Humourist and the Man of Letters*. London: J. C. Hotten, 1864.

Jack, Adolphus Alfred. *Thackeray: A Study*. London: Macmillan, 1895.

Johnson, Charles Plumptree. *The Early Writings of William Makepeace Thackeray*. London: Elliot Stock, 1888.

Matthews, Brander. "On a Novel of Thackeray's." In *The Historical Novel and Other Essays* (1897). New York: Scribner's, 1901, pp. 149–62.

Merivale, Herman, and Frank T. Marzials. *Life of W. M. Thackeray*. London: Walter Scott, 1891.

Nadal, E. S. "Thackeray's Relation to English Society." In *Essays at Home and Elsewhere*. London: Macmillan, 1882.

Rideing, William Henry. *Thackeray's London: His Haunts and the Scenes of His Novels*. Boston: Cupples, Upsham, 1885.

Stephen, Sir Leslie. "The Writings of W. M. Thackeray." In *The Works of William Makepeace Thackeray*. London: Smith, Elder, 1878–79, Volumes 24, pp. 315–78.

Stoddard, Richard Henry. *Anecdote Biographies of Thackeray and Dickens*. New York: Scribner, Armstrong, 1874.

Trollope, Anthony. *Thackeray*. London: Macmillan, 1879.

NATHANIEL HAWTHORNE

Bradfield, Thomas. "The Romances of Nathaniel Hawthorne." *Westminster Review* 142 (1894): 203–14.

Conway, Moncure D. *Life of Nathaniel Hawthorne*. London: Walter Scott, 1890.

Courtney, W. L. "Hawthorne's Romances." *Fortnightly Review* 46 (1886): 511–22.

Curtis, George William. "Hawthorne" (1854) and "The Works of Nathaniel Hawthorne" (1864). In *Literary and Social Essays*. New York: Harper & Brothers, 1894, pp. 33–60, 63–93.

Curtis, Jessie Kingsley. "The Marble Faun." *Andover Review* 18 (1892): 139–45.

Fields, James T. "Hawthorne." In *Yesterdays with Authors*. Boston: J. R. Osgood, 1871, pp. 41–124.

Griswold, Rufus W. "Nathaniel Hawthorne." *International Magazine* 3 (1851): 156–60.

Holden, George H. "Hawthorne among His Friends." *Harper's New Monthly Magazine* 63 (1881): 260–67.

Lathrop, Rose Hawthorne. *Memories of Hawthorne*. Boston: Houghton Mifflin, 1897.

More, Paul Elmer. "The Solitude of Nathaniel Hawthorne." *Atlantic* 88 (1901): 588–99.

Schuyler, Eugene. "The Italy of Hawthorne" (1889). In *Italian Influences*. New York: Scribner's, 1901, pp. 308–22.

Smith, George Barnett. "Nathaniel Hawthorne." In *Poets and Novelists*. London: Smith, Elder, 1875, pp. 151–206.

Smyth, Albert H. "Hawthorne's *Marble Faun*." *Chatauquan* 30 (1900): 522–26.

Tuckerman, Henry T. "The Prose-Poet: Nathaniel Hawthorne." In *Mental Portraits*. London: Richard Bentley, 1853, pp. 250–70.

Whipple, Edwin P. "Nathaniel Hawthorne." *Atlantic* 5 (1860): 614–22.

CHARLES DICKENS

Austin, Alfred. "Charles Dickens." *Temple Bar* 29 (1870): 554–62.

Canning, Albert S. G. *Philosophy of Charles Dickens*. London: Smith, Elder, 1880.

Davey, Samuel. "Charles Dickens." In *Darwin, Carlyle, and Dickens, with Other Essays*. London: James Clark, 1876, pp. 121–56.

Dickens, Charles, Jr. "Glimpses of Charles Dickens." *North American Review* 160 (1895): 525–37.

Dolby, George. *Charles Dickens as I Knew Him*. London: T. Fisher Unwin, 1885.

Horne, Richard Henry. "Charles Dickens." In *A New Spirit of the Age*. London: Smith, Elder, 1844, pp. 9–52.

Hughes, James L. *Dickens as an Educator*. London: Edward Arnold, 1900.

Irving, Walter. *Charles Dickens*. London: Simpkin, Marshall, 1874.

Jones, Charles H. *A Short Life of Charles Dickens*. New York: Appleton, 1880.

Kent, Charles. *Charles Dickens as a Reader*. London: Chapman & Hall, 1872.

Kitton, Frederic G. *Charles Dickens: His Life, Writings, and Personality*. London: T. C. & E. C. Jack, 1902.

Lang, Andrew. "Charles Dickens." *Fortnightly Review* 70 (1898): 944–60.

Mackenzie, R. Shelton. *Life of Charles Dickens*. Philadelphia: T. B. Peterson, 1870.

Marzials, Frank T. *Life of Charles Dickens*. London: Walter Scott, 1887.

Trollope, Anthony. "Charles Dickens." *Saint Paul's Magazine* 6 (1870): 370–75.

GEORGE ELIOT

Blinde, Mathilde. *George Eliot*. Boston: Roberts Brothers, 1883.

Brown, John Crombie. *The Ethics of George Eliot's Works*. Edinburgh: William Blackwood & Sons, 1879.

Browning, Oscar. "The Art of George Eliot." *Fortnightly Review* 49 (1888): 538–53.

Call, W. M. W. "George Eliot." *Westminster Review* 116 (1881): 154–98.

Cleveland, Rose Elizabeth. "George Eliot's Poetry." In *George Eliot's Poetry and Other Studies*. New York: Funk & Wagnalls, 1885, pp. 9–23.

Dowden, Edward. "George Eliot." In *Studies in Literature*. London: C. Kegan Paul, 1878, pp. 240–310.

Hutton, Richard Holt. "George Eliot." In *Essays, Theological and Literary*. London: Macmillan, 1871, Volume 2, pp. 294–367.

Lancaster, Henry H. "George Eliot's Works" (1866). In *Essays and Reviews*. Edinburgh: Edmonston & Douglas, 1876, pp. 351–98.

Mallock, W. H. "Impression of *Theophrastus Such*." *Edinburgh Review* 150 (1879): 557–86.

Perry, S. S. "George Eliot's *Middlemarch*." *North American Review* 116 (1873): 432–40.

Scherer, Edmond. *"Daniel Deronda"* (1877). In *Essays on English Literature.* Tr. George Saintsbury. New York: Scribner's, 1891, pp. 51–69.

Simcox, Edith. "George Eliot." *Nineteenth Century* 9 (1881): 778–801.

Skelton, John. "Poetry and George Eliot." *Fraser's Magazine* 78 (1868): 468–79.

Thomson, Clara. *George Eliot.* London: C. Kegan Paul, 1901.

Whipple, Edwin P. *"Daniel Deronda." North American Review* 124 (1877): 31–52.

Woolson, Abba Goold. *George Eliot and Her Heroines: A Study.* New York: Harper & Brothers, 1886.

THOMAS CARLYLE

Arnold, A. S. *The Story of Thomas Carlyle.* London: Ward & Downey, 1888.

Davey, Samuel. "The Writings of Thomas Carlyle." In *Darwin, Carlyle, and Dickens, with Other Essays.* London: James Clarke, 1876, pp. 45–90.

Duffy, Charles Gavan. *Conversations with Carlyle.* London: Sampson Low, 1892.

Garnett, Richard. *Life of Thomas Carlyle.* London: Walter Scott, 1887.

Guernsey, Alfred H. *Thomas Carlyle: His Life, His Books, His Theories.* New York: Appleton, 1879.

Hood, E. P. *Thomas Carlyle: Philosophic Thinker, Theologian, Historian and Poet.* London: James Clarke, 1875.

Larkin, Henry. *Carlyle and the Open Secret of His Life.* London: Kegan Paul, Trench, 1886.

Lecky, W. E. H. "Carlyle's Message to His Age." *Contemporary Review* 40 (1891): 521–28.

Lilly, W. S. *Four English Humourists of the Nineteenth Century.* London: John Murray, 1895.

Macpherson, Hector C. *Thomas Carlyle.* Edinburgh: Oliphant, Anderson & Ferrier, 1896.

Masson, David. *Carlyle Personally and in His Writings.* London: Macmillan, 1885.

Morley, John. "Carlyle." *Fortnightly Review* 14 (1870): 1–22.

Shepherd, Richard Herne. *Memoirs of the Life and Writings of Thomas Carlyle.* London: W. H. Allen, 1881. 2 vols.

Symington, Andrew J. *Some Personal Reminiscences of Carlyle.* Paisley: Alexander Gardner, 1886.

Wilson, David. *Mr. Froude and Carlyle.* London: William Heinemann, 1898.

RALPH WALDO EMERSON

Albee, John. *Remembrances of Emerson.* New York: Robert G. Cooke, 1901.

Alcott, A. Bronson. *Ralph Waldo Emerson: An Estimate of His Character and Genius in Prose and Verse.* Boston: A. Williams, 1882.

Cabot, James Eliot. *A Memoir of Ralph Waldo Emerson.* Boston: Houghton Mifflin, 1887. 2 vols.

Chapman, John Jay. "Emerson." In *Emerson and Other Essays.* New York: Scribner's, 1898, pp. 3–108.

Conway, Moncure Daniel. *Emerson at Home and Abroad.* Boston: J. R. Osgood, 1882.

Cooke, G. W. *Ralph Waldo Emerson: His Life, Writings, and Philosophy.* Boston: J. R. Osgood, 1881.

Dana, William F. *The Optimism of Ralph Waldo Emerson.* Boston: Cupples, Upham, 1886.

Emerson, Edward Waldo. *Emerson in Concord.* Boston: Houghton Mifflin, 1889.

Guernsey, Alfred H. *Ralph Waldo Emerson: Philosopher and Poet.* New York: Appleton, 1881.

Holmes, Oliver Wendell. *Ralph Waldo Emerson.* Boston: Houghton Mifflin, 1884.

Ireland, Alexander. *Ralph Waldo Emerson.* London: Simpkin, Marshall, 1882.

Morley, John. *Ralph Waldo Emerson: An Essay.* New York: Macmillan, 1884.

Sanborn, Benjamin Franklin, ed. *The Genius and Character of Emerson.* Boston: J. R. Osgood, 1885.

Thayer, William R. *The Influence of Emerson.* Boston: Cupples, Upham, 1886.

Woodbury, Charles H. *Talks with Ralph Waldo Emerson.* New York: Baker & Taylor, 1890.

HENRY WADSWORTH LONGFELLOW

Austin, George Lowell. *Henry Wadsworth Longfellow: His Life, His Works, His Friendships.* Boston: Lee & Shepard, 1883.

Henry Wadsworth Longfellow: Seventy-fifth Birthday. Proceedings of the Maine Historical Society. Portland, ME: Hoyt, Fogg & Donham, 1882.

Higginson, Thomas Wentworth. *Henry Wadsworth Longfellow.* Boston: Houghton Mifflin, 1902.

Kennedy, W. Sloane, ed. *Henry W. Longfellow.* Cambridge, MA: King, 1882.

Lang, Andrew. "Longfellow." In *Letters on Literature.* London: Longmans, 1889, pp. 41–54.

Lawton, William Cranston. *The New England Poets.* New York: Macmillan, 1898, pp. 105–54.

Macchetta, Blanche Roosevelt. *The Home Life of Henry W. Longfellow.* New York: G. W. Carleton, 1882.

More, Paul Elmer. "The Centenary of Longfellow." In *Shelburne Essays: Fifth Series.* Boston: Houghton Mifflin, 1908, pp. 132–57.

Saunders, Frederick. "Henry Wadsworth Longfellow." In *Character Studies.* New York: T. Whittaker, 1894.

Stoddard, Richard Henry, ed. *Henry Wadsworth Longfellow: A Medley in Prose and Verse.* New York: G. W. Harlan, 1882.

Underwood, Francis H. *Henry Wadsworth Longfellow: A Biographical Sketch.* Boston: J. R. Osgood, 1882.

ANTHONY TROLLOPE

Dallas, E. S. *London Times,* 23 May 1859, p. 12.

Gwynn, Stephen. "Anthony Trollope." *Macmillan's Magazine* 81 (1900): 217–26.

Harrison, Frederic. "Anthony Trollope's Place in Literature." *Forum* 19 (1895): 324–37.

Lyons, Anne K. *Anthony Trollope: An Annotated Bibliography of Periodical Works by and about Him in the United States and Great Britain to 1900.* Greenwood, FL: Penkevill Publishing Co., 1985.

MacLeod, Donald. "Anthony Trollope." *Good Words* 25 (1884): 248–52.

Morley, John, and Mary Ward. "Anthony Trollope." *Macmillan's Magazine* 49 (1883): 47–56.

Peck, Harry Thurston. "Anthony Trollope." *Bookman* (New York) 13 (1901): 114–25.

Shand, Alexander I. "The Literary Life of Anthony Trollope." *Edinburgh Review* 159 (1884): 186–212.

Street, G. S. "Anthony Trollope." *Cornhill Magazine* 83 (1901): 349–55.

Tuckerman, Bayard. "Anthony Trollope." *Princeton Review* 59 (July 1883): 17–28.

Whitehurst, E. C. "Anthony Trollope." *Westminster Review* 121 (1884): 83–115.

Unsigned. "Mr. Trollope's Novels." *National Review* 7 (1858): 416–35.

EMILY DICKINSON

Buckingham, Willis J. *Emily Dickinson: An Annotated Bibliography*. Bloomington: Indiana University Press, 1970.

Hampson, Alfred Leete. *Emily Dickinson: A Bibliography*. Northampton, MA: Hampshire Bookshop, 1930.

Hughes, Rupert. "The Ideas of Emily Dickinson." *Godey's Lady's Book* 133 (1896): 541–43.

Kelley, William Valentine. "Emily Dickinson: The Hermit Thrush of Amherst." In *Down the Road and Other Essays of Nature, Life, Literature, and Religion*. New York: Eaton & Mains, 1911, pp. 214–83.

Lubbers, Klaus. *Emily Dickinson: The Critical Revolution*. Ann Arbor: University of Michigan Press, 1968.

Price, Warwick James. "The Poetry of Emily Dickinson." *Yale Literary Magazine* 59 (1893): 25–27.

Unsigned. *Emily Dickinson: A Bibliography*. Amherst, MA: Jones Library, 1930.

MATTHEW ARNOLD

Brownell, W. C. "Matthew Arnold." *Scribner's Magazine* 30 (1901): 105–20.

Fitch, Sir Joshua. *Thomas and Matthew Arnold and Their Influence on English Education*. New York: Scribner's, 1897.

Galton, Arthur. *Two Essays upon Matthew Arnold with Some of His Letters to the Author*. London: Elkin Mathews, 1897.

Gates, Lewis E. "Matthew Arnold." In *Three Studies in Literature*. London: Macmillan, 1899.

Lewisohn, Ludwig. "A Study of Matthew Arnold." *Sewanee Review* 9 (1901): 442–56; 10 (1902): 143–59, 302–19.

Lund, T. W. M. *Matthew Arnold: The Message and Meaning of a Life*. London: Simpkin, Marshall, 1888.

Morley, John. "Matthew Arnold." *Nineteenth Century* 26 (1895): 1041–55.

Newman, F. W. "Literature and Dogma." *Fraser's Magazine* 8 (1873): 114–34.

Oakeshott, B. N. "Matthew Arnold as a Political and Social Critic." *Westminster Review* 149 (1898): 161–76.

Paul, Herbert W. *Matthew Arnold*. New York: Macmillan, 1903.

Roosevelt, Theodore. "Some Recent Criticism of America." *Murray's Magazine* 5 (1888): 299–310.

Russell, G. W. E. *Matthew Arnold*. London: Hodder & Stoughton, 1904.

Saintsbury, George. *Matthew Arnold*. Edinburgh: William Blackwood, 1899.

Tovey, Duncan C. "Arnold's *Essays in Criticism: Second Series*." In *Reviews and Essays in English Literature*. London: George Bell, 1897, pp. 71–87.

ROBERT BROWNING

Berdoe, Edward, ed. *Browning Studies*. London: George Allen, 1895.

Birrell, Augustine. "On the Alleged Obscurity of Mr. Browning's Poetry." In *Obiter Dicta*. London: E. Stock, 1884, pp. 55–95.

Cary, Elisabeth Luther. *Browning Poet and Man: A Survey*. New York: Putnam's, 1899.

Gosse, Edmund. "The Early Writings of Robert Browning." *Century Magazine* 23 (1881): 189–200.

Little, Marion. *Essays on Robert Browning*. London: Swan Sonnenschein, 1899.

Lowell, James Russell. "Browning's Plays and Poems." *North American Review* 66 (1848): 357–400.

Orr, Alexandra. *Life and Letters of Robert Browning*. London: Smith, Elder, 1891.

Pigou, Arthur Cecil. *Robert Browning as a Religious Teacher*. London: C. J. Clay & Sons, 1901.

Scudder, Vida D. "Browning as a Humourist." In *The Life of the Spirit in the Modern English Poets*. Boston: Houghton Mifflin, 1895, pp. 208–36.

Sharp, William. *Life of Robert Browning*. London: Walter Scott, 1890.

Skelton, John. "Robert Browning." *Fraser's Magazine* 67 (1863): 240–56.

Symons, Arthur. *An Introduction to the Study of Browning*. London: Cassell, 1886.

Vincent, Leon H. *A Few Words on Robert Browning*. Philadelphia: Arnold, 1890.

Walters, Frank. *Studies of Some of Robert Browning's Poems*. London: Sunday School Association, 1893.

Weiss, John. "Browning." *Massachusetts Quarterly Review* 4 (1850): 347–85.

HERMAN MELVILLE

Coan, Titus Munson. "Herman Melville." *Literary World* (Boston) 22 (1891): 492–93.

Hetherington, Hugh W. *Melville's Reviewers: British and American 1846–1891*. Chapel Hill: University of North Carolina Press, 1961.

Higgins, Brian. *Herman Melville: An Annotated Bibliography: 1846–1930*. Boston: G. K. Hall, 1979.

O'Brien, Fitz-James. "Our Authors and Authorship: Melville and Curtis." *Putnam's Monthly* 9 (1857): 384–93.

Parker, Hershel. *The Recognition of Herman Melville: Selected Criticism since 1846*. Ann Arbor: University of Michigan Press, 1967.

Peck, G. W. "Omoo." *American Review* 6 (1847): 36–46.

Salt, Henry S. "Herman Melville." *Scottish Art Review* 2 (1889): 186–90.

Stedman, Arthur. "Melville of Marquesas." *Review of Reviews* 4 (1891): 428–30.

Unsigned. "Herman Melville's *Whale*." *Spectator*, 25 October 1851, pp. 1026–27.

———. "A Trio of American Sailor-Authors." *Dublin University Magazine* 47 (1856): 47–57.

ALFRED, LORD TENNYSON

Bradley, A. C. *A Commentary on Tennyson's In Memoriam*. London: Macmillan, 1901.

Brooke, Stopford A. *Tennyson: His Art and Relation to Modern Life*. London: Isbister, 1894.

Cary, Elizabeth L. *Tennyson: His Homes, His Friends and His Work*. New York: Putnam's, 1898.

Collins, John Churton. *Illustrations of Tennyson*. London: Chatto & Windus, 1891.

Dixon, William Macneile. *A Primer of Tennyson*. London: Methuen, 1896.

Genung, John F. *Tennyson's In Memoriam: Its Purpose and Its Structure*. Boston: Houghton Mifflin, 1896.

Jennings, Henry J. *Lord Tennyson: A Biographical Sketch*. London: Chatto & Windus, 1892.

Jones, Richard. *The Growth of the Idylls of the King*. Philadelphia: Lippincott, 1895.

King, John M. *A Critical Study of In Memoriam*. Toronto: G. N. Morang, 1898.

Lang, Andrew. *Alfred Tennyson*. Edinburgh: William Blackwood & Sons, 1901.

Luce, Morton. *Tennyson*. London: J. M. Dent, 1901.

Lyall, Sir Alfred. *Tennyson*. London: Macmillan, 1902.

Rawnsley, H. D. *Memories of the Tennysons*. Glasgow: James MacLehose & Sons, 1900.

Sneath, E. Hershey. *The Mind of Tennyson*. New York: Scribner's, 1900.

Tanish, Edward Campbell. *A Study of the Works of Alfred Tennyson*. London: Chapman & Hall, 1868.

Wace, Walter E. *Alfred Tennyson: His Life and Works*. Edinburgh: MacNiven & Wallace, 1881.

Walters, J. Cuming. *Tennyson: Poet, Philosopher, Idealist*. London: Kegan Paul, Trench, Trübner, 1893.

Waugh, Arthur. *Alfred, Lord Tennyson: A Study of His Life and Work*. New York: Macmillan, 1896.

WALT WHITMAN

Boughton, Willis. "Walt Whitman." *Arena* 6 (1892): 471–80.

Chapman, John Jay. "Walt Whitman." In *Emerson and Other Essays*. New York: Scribner's, 1898, pp. 111–28.

Curtis, William O'Leary. "Whitman's Defects and Beauties." *Month* 71 (1891): 527–36.

Garrison, William H. "Walt Whitman." *Lippincott's Magazine* 49 (1892): 623–26.

Gay, William. *Walt Whitman: His Relation to Science and Philosophy*. Melbourne: Mason, Firth & M'Cutcheon, 1895.

Giantvalley, Scott. *Walt Whitman 1838–1939: A Reference Guide*. Boston: G. K. Hall, 1981.

Gilchrist, Grace. "Chats with Walt Whitman." *Temple Bar* 113 (1898): 200–212.

Gosse, Edmund. "A Note on Walt Whitman." *New Review* 10 (1894): 447–57.

Kennedy, William Sloane. *Reminiscences of Walt Whitman*. London: Alexander Gardner, 1896.

Perry, Nora. "A Few Words about Walt Whitman." *Appleton's Journal* 15 (1876): 531–33.

Robertson, John. *Walt Whitman Poet and Democrat*. Edinburgh: William Brown, 1884.

Savage, M. J. "The Religion of Walt Whitman's Poems." *Arena* 10 (1894): 433–52.

Valentine, Edward A. Uffington. "The Poet of Manhood." *Conservative Review* 1 (1899): 140–46.

WALTER PATER

Addleshaw, Stanley. "Walter Pater." *Gentleman's Magazine* 282 (1897): 227–51.

Benson, A. C. *Walter Pater*. London: Macmillan, 1906.

Bowen, Edwin W. "Walter Pater." *Sewanee Review* 15 (1907): 271–84.

Bradford, Gamaliel, Jr. "Walter Pater." *Andover Review* 10 (1888): 141–55.

Cecil, Algernon. "Walter Pater." In *Six Oxford Thinkers*. London: John Murray, 1909, pp. 214–51.

Gosse, Edmund. "Mr. Walter Pater on Platonism." *New Review* 8 (1893): 419–29.

Greenslet, Ferris. *Walter Pater*. New York: McClure, Phillips, 1903.

Jacobus, Russell P. "The Blessedness of Egoism: Maurice Barrès and Walter Pater." *Fortnightly Review* 65 (1896): 40–57, 384–96.

Johnson, Lionel. "The Work of Mr. Pater." *Fortnightly Review* 62 (1894): 352–67.

Lang, Andrew. "Mr. Pater's *Greek Studies*." *Illustrated London News*, 9 March 1895, p. 299.

Ransome, Arthur. "Walter Pater." In *Portraits and Speculations*. London: Macmillan, 1913, pp. 131–59.

Sharp, William. "Some Personal Reminiscences of Walter Pater." *Atlantic* 74 (1894): 801–14.

Wright, Thomas. *The Life of Walter Pater*. New York: Putnam's, 1907. 2 vols.

ROBERT LOUIS STEVENSON

Armour, Margaret. *The Home Life and Early Haunts of Robert Louis Stevenson*. Edinburgh: W. H. White, 1895.

Baildon, H. Bellyse. *Robert Louis Stevenson: A Life Study in Criticism*. London: Chatto & Windus, 1901.

Bailey, J. C. "Stevenson's Letters." *Fortnightly Review* 73 (1900): 91–103.

Balfour, Graham. *The Life of Robert Louis Stevenson*. New York: Scribner's, 1901. 2 vols.

Black, Margaret Moyes. *Robert Louis Stevenson*. Edinburgh: Oliphant, Anderson, & Ferrier, 1898.

Burton, Richard. "Robert Louis Stevenson." In *Literary Likings*. Boston: Copeland & Day, 1898, pp. 3–34.

Cornford, L. Cope. *Robert Louis Stevenson*. Edinburgh: William Blackwood & Sons, 1899.

Fraser, Marie. *In Stevenson's Samoa*. London: Smith, Elder, 1895.

Genung, John Franklin. *Stevenson's Attitude to Life*. New York: Thomas Y. Crowell, 1901.

Gosse, Edmund. "Mr. R. L. Stevenson as a Poet." In *Questions at Issue*. London: Heinemann, 1893, pp. 237–54.

Henley, W. E. "'R. L. S.'" *Pall Mall Magazine* 25 (1901): 505–14.

Kirk, Sophia. "Robert Louis Stevenson." *Atlantic* 60 (1887): 747–55.

MacCulluch, J. A. "R. L. Stevenson: Characteristics." *Westminster Review* 149 (1898): 631–47.

Muirhead, J. H. "Robert Louis Stevenson's Philosophy of Life." In *Philosophy and Life and Other Essays*. London: S. Sonnenschein, 1902, pp. 37–57.

Nicoll, W. Robertson, and G. K. Chesterton. *Robert Louis Stevenson*. London: Hodder & Stoughton, 1902.

Raleigh, Walter. *Robert Louis Stevenson*. London: Edward Arnold, 1895.

Sharp, William. "In Stevenson's Country." *Harper's Monthly Magazine* 105 (1902): 497–504.

Wallace, William. "The Life and Limitations of Stevenson." *Scottish Review* 35 (1900): 13–35.

JOHN RUSKIN

Collingwood, W. C. *Ruskin's Relics*. New York: Thomas Y. Crowell, 1904.

———. *The Life of John Ruskin*. Boston: Houghton Mifflin, 1902.

Cook, Edward T. *Studies in Ruskin*. London: George Allen, 1890.

Downes, R. P. *John Ruskin: A Study*. London: A. W. Hall, 1890.

Fitzgerald, Percy. "Mr. Ruskin, Artist and Publisher." *Gentleman's Magazine* 268 (1890): 126–47.

Harrison, Frederic. *John Ruskin*. London: Macmillan, 1902.

Hobson, J. A. "Ruskin and Democracy." *Contemporary Review* 81 (1902): 103–12.

Kaufmann, M. "Mr. Ruskin as a Practical Teacher." *Scottish Review* 24 (1894): 21–44.

Longfellow, William P. P. "John Ruskin." *Forum* 29 (1900): 298–312.

Mather, J. Marshall. *Life and Teaching of John Ruskin.* Manchester: Tubbs, Brook & Chrystal, 1883.

Maynell, Alice. *John Ruskin.* Edinburgh: William Blackwood & Sons, 1900.

Ritchie, Anne Thackeray. "John Ruskin: An Essay." *Harper's New Monthly Magazine* 80 (1889–90): 578–603.

Sizeranne, Robert de la. "Is Ruskin out of Date?" *Magazine of Art* 24 (1900): 258–65.

Stephen, Sir Leslie. "Mr. Ruskin's Recent Writings." *Fraser's Magazine* 89 (1874): 688–701.

Stillman, W. J. "John Ruskin." *Century Magazine* 35 (1888): 357–66.

Stimson, F. J. "Ruskin as a Political Economist." *Quarterly Journal of Economics* 2 (1888): 414–42.

Waldstein, Charles. "The Work of John Ruskin." *Harper's New Monthly Magazine* 76 (1888–89): 382–418.

OSCAR WILDE

Birnstingl, H. J. "An Essay on Oscar Wilde." *Westminster Review* 174 (1910): 514–28.

Brémont, Anna, Comtesse de. *Oscar Wilde and His Mother.* London: Everett, 1911.

Esdaile, Arundell. "The New Hellenism." *Fortnightly Review* 94 (1910): 706–22.

Gide, André. *Oscar Wilde.* Tr. Bernard Frechman. New York: Philosophical Library, 1949.

Howe, P. P. "Oscar Wilde." In *Dramatic Portraits.* London: Martin Secker, 1913, pp. 83–114.

Ingleby, Leonard Criswell. *Oscar Wilde.* London: T. Werner Laurie, 1907.

Jackson, Holbrook. "Oscar Wilde: The Last Phase." In *The Eighteen Nineties.* London: Grant Richards, 1913, pp. 86–108.

Kenilworth, Walter Winston. A *Study of Oscar Wilde.* New York: R. F. Fenno, 1912.

Kennedy, J. M. "Oscar Wilde." In *English Literature 1880–1905.* Boston: Small, Maynard, 1913, pp. 59–97.

Newman, Ernest. "Oscar Wilde: A Literary Appreciation." *Free Review,* 1 June 1895, pp. 193–206.

Pollard, Percival. *Their Day in Court.* New York: Neale Publishing Co., 1909, pp. 340–73.

Sherard, Robert Harborough. *The Life of Oscar Wilde.* New York: Mitchell Kennerley, 1907.

Symons, Arthur. *Athenaeum,* 16 May 1908, pp. 598–600.

Vickery, Willis. *Oscar Wilde: A Sketch.* Cedar Rapids, IA: Torch Press, 1906.

Woodbridge, Homer E. "Oscar Wilde as a Poet." *Poet-Lore* 19 (1908): 439–57.

STEPHEN CRANE

Banks, Nancy. "The Novels of Two Journalists." *Bookman* (New York) 2 (1895): 217–20.

Bierce, Ambrose. *San Francisco Examiner,* 26 July 1896.

Harriman, Karl Edwin. "A Romantic Idealist: Mr. Stephen Crane." *Literary Review* (Boston) 4 (1900): 85–87.

Higginson, Thomas Wentworth. Review of *The Red Badge of Courage. Philistine* 3 (1896): 33–38.

Norris, Frank. "The Green Stone of Unrest, by St——n Cr—e." *San Francisco Wave,* 24 December 1897.

Penn, Jonathan. "A Little Study of Stephen Crane." *Lotus* 2 (1896): 208–11.

Sedgwick, A. C. *Nation,* 2 July 1896, p. 15.

Stallman, R. W. *Stephen Crane: A Critical Bibliography.* Ames: Iowa State University Press, 1972.

Stolper, J. R. *Stephen Crane: A List of His Writings and Articles about Him.* Newark: Stephen Crane Association, 1930.

Williams, Ames W., and Vincent Starrett. *Stephen Crane: A Bibliography.* Glendale, CA: John Valentine, 1948.